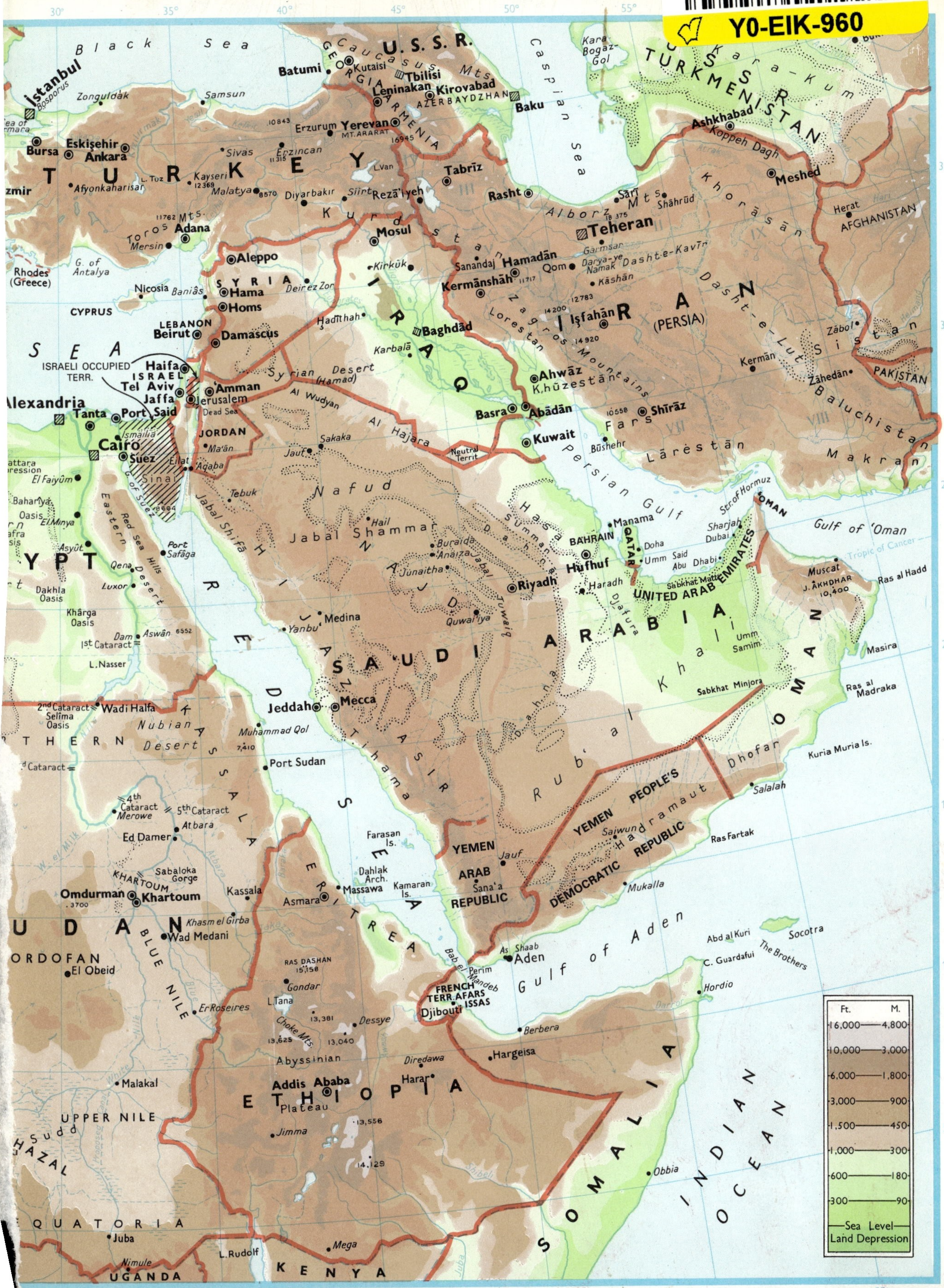

Scale 1:19 m. 1 inch to 300 miles approx.

THE MIDDLE EAST AND NORTH AFRICA
1973-1974

A survey and directory of Afghanistan, Algeria, Bahrain, Cyprus, Egypt, Iran, Iraq, Israel, Jordan, Kuwait, Lebanon, Libya, Morocco, Oman, Qatar, Saudi Arabia, Spanish North Africa, Sudan, Syria, Tunisia, Turkey, United Arab Emirates, Yemen Arab Republic and Yemen People's Democratic Republic.

For Reference

Not to be taken from this room

THE MIDDLE EAST AND NORTH AFRICA

1973-74

TWENTIETH EDITION

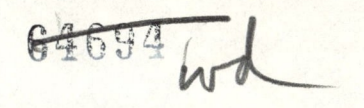

EUROPA PUBLICATIONS LIMITED
18 BEDFORD SQUARE LONDON WC1B 3JN

St. Thomas Aquinas College Library
Sparkill, N. Y. 10976

Previous Editions:

1948	1950	1953
1955	1957	1958
1959	1961	1962
1963	1964	1965
1966	1967	1968
1969	1970	1971
	1972	

© EUROPA PUBLICATIONS LIMITED 1973

ISBN 0 900 36260 X

Library of Congress Catalog Card Number 48-3250

AUSTRALIA AND NEW ZEALAND
James Bennett (Collaroy) Pty. Ltd., Collaroy, N.S.W., Australia

INDIA
UBS Publishers' Distributors Pvt. Ltd., P.O.B. 1882, 5 Ansari Road, Daryaganj, Delhi 6

JAPAN
Maruzen Co. Ltd., 6 Tori-Nichome, Nihonbashi, Tokyo 103

Printed and bound in England by
STAPLES PRINTERS LIMITED
at The Stanhope Press, Rochester, Kent.

Foreword

THE two topics which have dominated the Middle Eastern scene over the past year have been the continued confrontation between the Arabs and Israel and the ever-growing importance of Middle Eastern oil in the world economy. At the time of going to press the prospect of a lasting peace between Israel and the Arabs appeared to be no nearer, but any developments in this direction have been recorded both in Michael Adams' account of the Arab-Israeli confrontation, and in the individual histories of the various countries.

Michael Field has dealt at some length with oil developments in the Middle East, giving details of the various participation agreements secured by the oil-producing countries with the various oil companies. Professor W. B. Fisher has contributed an essay on the past year in the Middle East in which he examines oil developments and considers some of the political aspects.

Once again we would like to thank the numerous individuals and organizations who have sent us both revised and new information for inclusion in this edition of THE MIDDLE EAST AND NORTH AFRICA. Without their assistance the book could not have become a recognized authority on the region.

August 1973

Acknowledgements

We express our thanks for much help and information kindly supplied by many Foreign Ministries and National Statistical Offices and by the following embassies and other bodies.

Afghan Embassy, London
Algerian Embassy, London
Arab League
Arab Report and Record
Bahrain Embassy, London
British Embassy, Kuwait
Central Treaty Organization
Cyprus High Commission, London
French Embassy, London
Imperial Iranian Embassy, London
Institute of Petroleum Information Service, London
Iraq Interests Section of the Afghan Embassy
Israel Embassy, London
Jordan Embassy, London
Kuwait Embassy, London
Kuwait Oil Company
Lebanese Embassy, London
Lebanese Embassy (Syrian Interests), London
Libyan Embassy, London
Michael Rice Group Middle East

Middle East Economic Digest
National Bank of Egypt, Cairo
Moroccan Embassy, London
Oman Embassy, London
Organization of African Unity
Organization of Petroleum Exporting Countries (OPEC)
Private Information Center on Eastern Arabia
Regional Co-operation for Development
Saudi Arabian Embassy, London
Spanish Embassy, London
Sudanese Embassy, London
Tunisian Embassy, London
Turkish Embassy, London
United Nations Information Centre, London
United Nations Relief and Works Agency for Palestine Refugees in the Near East
Embassy of the Yemen Arab Republic
Embassy of the Yemen People's Democratic Republic

We are also very grateful to Youssef Azmeh, Michael Emslie, Chris Glynn, Mrs. M. Jibb and Trevor Taylor for their assistance in revising the articles on individual countries. We also acknowledge with thanks the co-operation of the International Institute for Strategic Studies, 18 Adam Street, London, WC2N 6AL, in permitting us to use data on defence manpower and finance from *The Military Balance 1972–1973*.

Contents

	Page
Late Information	x
Abbreviations	xi
Transcription of Arabic Names	xiv

	Page
Calendar of Events	xv
The Year in the Middle East *W. B. Fisher*	xxi

PART ONE

General Survey

THE MIDDLE EAST AND NORTH AFRICA: AN INTRODUCTION *W. B. Fisher*	3
THE RELIGIONS OF THE MIDDLE EAST AND NORTH AFRICA	25
Islam *R. B. Serjeant*	25
Christianity	31
Judaism	32
THE ARAB-ISRAELI CONFRONTATION 1967–73 *Michael Adams*	34
THE JERUSALEM ISSUE *Michael Adams*	44
DOCUMENTS ON PALESTINE	46
PALESTINE ORGANIZATIONS	60
OIL IN THE MIDDLE EAST AND NORTH AFRICA *Michael Field*	63
Teheran Agreement	72
Oil Statistics	75
Oil Groups in the Gulf	78
THE SUEZ CANAL	82

PART TWO

Regional Organizations

	Page		Page
UNITED NATIONS IN THE MIDDLE EAST AND NORTH AFRICA	87	INTERNATIONAL DEVELOPMENT ASSOCIATION (IDA)	95
MEMBERS, CONTRIBUTIONS, YEAR OF ADMISSION	87	INTERNATIONAL FINANCE CORPORATION (IFC)	96
PERMANENT MISSIONS TO THE UNITED NATIONS	88	OTHER UN ORGANIZATIONS	96
		THE ARAB LEAGUE	98
UNITED NATIONS TRUCE SUPERVISION ORGANIZATION (UNTSO)	88	CENTRAL TREATY ORGANIZATION (CENTO)	108
UNITED NATIONS RELIEF AND WORKS AGENCY FOR PALESTINE REFUGEES IN THE NEAR EAST (UNRWA)	89	THE EUROPEAN ECONOMIC COMMUNITY AND THE MIDDLE EAST AND NORTH AFRICA	112
		FEDERATION OF ARAB REPUBLICS	117
UNITED NATIONS MIDDLE EAST MISSION (UNMEM)	91	ISLAMIC CONFERENCE	120
		THE MAGHREB PERMANENT CONSULTATIVE COMMITTEE	121
UNITED NATIONS PEACE-KEEPING FORCE IN CYPRUS (UNFICYP)	92	ORGANIZATION OF ARAB PETROLEUM EXPORTING COUNTRIES	124
ECONOMIC COMMISSION FOR AFRICA (ECA)	92	ORGANIZATION OF THE PETROLEUM EXPORTING COUNTRIES (OPEC)	125
UNITED NATIONS DEVELOPMENT PROGRAMME (UNDP)	94		
		REGIONAL CO-OPERATION FOR DEVELOPMENT (RCD)	129
INTERNATIONAL BANK FOR RECONSTRUCTION AND DEVELOPMENT (IBRD-WORLD BANK)	95	OTHER REGIONAL ORGANIZATIONS	134

CONTENTS

PART THREE
Country Surveys

AFGHANISTAN
	Page
Physical and Social Geography *W. B. Fisher*	141
History *M. C. Gillett*	144
Economy *Arthur Paul*	150
Statistics	156
Directory	164
Bibliography	170

ALGERIA
Physical and Social Geography	171
History	173
Economy	184
Statistics	191
Directory	195
Bibliography	203

BAHRAIN
Geography	205
History	205
Economy	205
Statistics	207
Directory	209
Bibliography	212

CYPRUS
Physical and Social Geography *W. B. Fisher*	213
History	213
Economy	220
Statistics	222
Directory	229
Bibliography	238

EGYPT
Physical and Social Geography *W. B. Fisher*	239
History	242
Economy	259
Statistics	267
Directory	273
Bibliography	287

IRAN
Physical and Social Geography *W. B. Fisher*	289
History	291
Economy	299
Statistics	303
Directory	308
Bibliography	321

IRAQ
	Page
Physical and Social Geography *W. B. Fisher*	323
History	325
Economy	338
Statistics	345
Directory	351
Bibliography	359

ISRAEL
Physical and Social Geography *W. B. Fisher*	361
History *Tom Little*	363
Economy	370
Statistics	376
Directory	383
Bibliography	402

JORDAN
Physical and Social Geography *W. B. Fisher*	405
History	406
Economy	412
Statistics	416
Directory	421
Bibliography	428

KUWAIT
Physical and Social Geography	429
History	429
Economy	431
Statistics	436
Directory	440
Bibliography	447

LEBANON
Physical and Social Geography *W. B. Fisher*	449
History	450
Economy	459
Statistics	463
Directory	467
Bibliography	478

LIBYA
Physical and Social Geography *W. B. Fisher*	479
History	480
Economy	488
Statistics	493
Directory	496
Bibliography	502

viii

CONTENTS

	Page
MOROCCO	
Physical and Social Geography *D. R. Harris*	503
History	504
Economy	511
Statistics	517
Directory	522
Bibliography	531
OMAN	
Geography	533
History	533
Economy	534
Statistics	535
Bibliography	537
QATAR	
Geography	539
History	539
Economy	539
Statistics	541
Directory	543
SAUDI ARABIA	
Physical and Social Geography of the Arabian Peninsula	545
History	546
Economy	551
Statistics	555
Directory	560
Bibliography	566
SPANISH NORTH AFRICA	
Spanish Sahara	567
Ceuta and Melilla	570
THE SUDAN	
Physical and Social Geography *L. Berry*	573
History *Muddathir Abdel Rahim*	574
Economy *Ali Ahmed Suliman*	583
Statistics	590
Directory	597
Bibliography	605
SYRIA	
Physical and Social Geography *W. B. Fisher*	607
History	608
Economy *Youssef Azmeh*	615
Statistics	620
Directory	625
Bibliography	632

	Page
TUNISIA	
Physical and Social Geography *D. R. Harris*	633
History	634
Economy	642
Statistics	650
Directory	655
Bibliography	660
TURKEY	
Physical and Social Geography *W. B. Fisher*	661
History	662
Economy	674
Statistics	680
Directory	688
Bibliography	706
UNITED ARAB EMIRATES	
Geography	709
History	709
Economy	711
Statistics	712
Directory	714
Bibliography	718
YEMEN ARAB REPUBLIC	
Physical and Social Geography	719
History	719
Economy *M. Jibb*	722
Statistics	725
Directory	728
Bibliography	730
YEMEN PEOPLE'S DEMOCRATIC REPUBLIC	
Physical and Social Geography *W. B. Fisher*	731
History	732
Economy *M. Jibb*	739
Statistics	741
Directory	745
Bibliography	748

PART FOUR
Other Reference Material

WHO'S WHO IN THE MIDDLE EAST AND NORTH AFRICA	751
CALENDARS, TIME RECKONING AND WEIGHTS AND MEASURES	857
BIBLIOGRAPHIES	860
RESEARCH INSTITUTES	867

Maps

	Page
Sketch of structural elements	5
Rainfall: North Africa	8
Rainfall: Middle East	9
Natural Vegetation	16
The expansion of Israel	57
Oil fields, loading terminals and pipelines in the Gulf	64
CENTO: road and rail developments	109

LATE INFORMATION

Afghanistan

CABINET
(formed July 28th, 1973)

Head of State, Prime Minister, Minister of National Defence and Minister of Foreign Affairs: MOHAMMAD DAUD.
Deputy Prime Minister: Dr. MOHAMMAD HASSAN SHARK.
Minister of Justice: Dr. ABDUL MAJID.
Minister of Finance: SAID ABDUL ALA.
Minister of the Interior: FAIZ MASOUD.
Minister of Education: Dr. NEMATULLAH PAZHWAK.
Minister for the Security of the Frontiers: Eng. PACHA GUL.
Minister of Mines and Industries: Dr. ABDUL KAYOUM WARDAK.
Minister of Communications: Eng. ABDUL HAMID MOHTAT.
Minister of Public Health: Prof. Dr. NAZAR MOHAMMAD SKANDAR.
Minister of Information: Prof. Dr. ABDUL RAHIM NAWIN.
Minister of Agriculture: GHULAM JAILANI BAKHTARI.
Minister of Planning: (to be appointed).
Minister of Commerce: (to be appointed).

Jordan

CABINET CHANGES
(August 21st, 1973)

Minister of Culture and Information: MARWAN DUNIN.
Minister of Cabinet Affairs: TOUKAN AL-HINDAWI.
Minister of Court Affairs: BAHUDDINE TOUKAN.

Abbreviations

A	..	Ambassador
AAHO	..	Afro-Asian Housing Organization
AAPSO	..	Afro-Asian People's Solidarity Organization
Acad.	..	Academy
accred.	..	accredited
AD	..	Algerian Dinars
A.D.C.	..	Aide-de-camp
Admin.	..	Administrative; Administration; Administrator
Admin.-Gen.	..	Administrator-General
ADMA	..	Abu Dhabi Marine Areas
ADOCO	..	Abu Dhabi Oil Company
ADPC	..	Abu Dhabi Petroleum Company
AfDB	..	African Development Bank
Afs.	..	Afghanis
AIWO	..	Agudath Israel World Organization
ALF	..	Arab Liberation Front
ALN	..	Armée de Libération Nationale (National Liberation Army of Algeria)
Amb.	..	Ambassador
AMINOIL	..	American Independent Oil Company
AMOSEAS	..	American Overseas Petroleum Ltd.
AOC	..	Arabian Oil Company
AOF	..	Afrique Occidentale Française (French West Africa)
API	..	American Petroleum Institute
approx.	..	approximately
apptd.	..	appointed
A.R.	..	Arab Republic
Aramco	..	Arabian-American Oil Company
A.R.E.	..	Arab Republic of Egypt
ARGAS	..	Arabian Geophysical Survey Company
ASFEC	..	Regional Centre for Functional Literacy in Rural Areas for the Arab States
Ass.	..	Assembly
Asscn.	..	Association
Assoc.	..	Associate
Asst.	..	Assistant
ATAS	..	Anatolian Refinery Company
ATUC	..	African Trade Union Confederation
AUA	..	Austrian Airlines
AUXERAP	..	Société Auxiliaire de la Régie du Pétrole
Ave.	..	Avenue
b.	..	born
B.A.	..	Bachelor of Arts
BAPCO	..	The Bahrain Petroleum Company Ltd.
bbl(s).	..	barrel(s)
BD	..	Bahrain Dinars
Bd.	..	Board
Bde.	..	Brigade
BEA	..	British European Airways Corporation
B.Lit(t).	..	Bachelor of Letters
Blvd.	..	Boulevard
BOAC	..	British Overseas Airways Corporation
B.P.	..	Boîte Postale (Post Office Box)
BP	..	British Petroleum
BPC	..	Basrah Petroleum Company
br(s).	..	branch(es)
B.Sc.	..	Bachelor of Science
B.S.T.	..	British Standard Time
BUSHCO	..	Bushire Petroleum Company
CA	..	Chargé d'Affaires
CAFRAD	..	Centre Africain de Formation et de Recherches Administratives pour le Développement
CAMEL	..	Compagnie Algérienne du Methane Liquid
cap.	..	capital
Capt.	..	Captain
CARE	..	Co-operative for American Relief Everywhere
CENTO	..	Central Treaty Organization
CEP	..	Compagnie d'Exploration Pétrolière
CEPT	..	Conférence Européenne des Administrations des Postes et des Télécommunications
CFP	..	Compagnie Française des Pétroles
Chair.	..	Chairman
Cie.	..	Compagnie (Company)
c.i.f.	..	cost, insurance, freight
C.-in-C.	..	Commander-in-Chief
Co.	..	Company
Comm.	..	Commission
Commdr.	..	Commander
Commdt.	..	Commandant
Commr.	..	Commissioner
Conf.	..	Conference
Contrib.	..	Contributor; Contribution
COPE	..	Compagnie Orientale des Pétroles
COPEFA	..	Compagnie des Pétroles France-Afrique
Corpn.	..	Corporation
CPA	..	Compagnie des Pétroles d'Algérie
CREPS	..	Compagnie de Recherches et d'Exploration de Pétrole du Sahara
CRNA	..	National Council of the Algerian Revolution
CRUA	..	Revolutionary Council for Unity and Action (now FLN)
ČSA	..	Československé Aerolinie
Cttee.	..	Committee
Del.	..	Delegate; Delegation
Dem.	..	Democratic
dep.	..	deposits
Dept.	..	Department
Devt.	..	Development
Dir.	..	Director
Div.	..	Division
DPA	..	Deutsche Presse-Agentur
Dr.	..	Doctor
DUP	..	Democratic Unionist Party (Sudan)
d.w.	..	dead weight
ECOSOC	..	Economic and Social Council (UN)
Ed.	..	Educated
Edn.	..	Edition
Educ.	..	Education
EEC	..	European Economic Community
EFTA	..	European Free Trade Association
EOKA	..	National Organization of the Struggle for Freedom of Cyprus
ERAP	..	Entreprise des Recherches et d'Activités Pétrolières
est.	..	estimate(d)
excl.	..	excluded; excluding
Exec.	..	Executive
Extra.	..	Extraordinary
f.	..	founded
FAO	..	Food and Agriculture Organization
FCM	..	Federation of Muslim Councillors
Fed.	..	Federation; Federal
FFS	..	Socialist Forces Front
FIDES	..	Fonds d'Investissement pour le Développement Economique et Sociale de la France d'Outre-Mer

ABBREVIATIONS

FLN	..	Front de Libération Nationale (National Liberation Front)
FLOSY	..	Front for the Liberation of Occupied South Yemen
fmr...	..	former
f.o.b.	..	free on board
ft. ..	..	feet; foot
gal. ..	..	gallons
GDA	..	Gas Distribution Administration
G.D.P.	..	Gross Domestic Product
Gen. Man.	..	General Manager
GFCM	..	General Fisheries Council for the Mediterranean
G.H.Q.	..	General Headquarters
G.M.T.	..	Greenwich Mean Time
G.N.P.	..	Gross National Product
G.O.C.-in-C.	..	General Officer Commanding-in-Chief
Gov.	..	Governor
Govt.	..	Government
GPRA	..	Gouvernement Provisoire de la République Algérienne (Provisional Government of the Republic of Algeria)
GUPCO	..	Gulf of Suez Petroleum Company
ha. ..	..	hectares
H.E.	..	His Eminence; His Excellency
H.I.M.	..	His Imperial Majesty
Hist.	..	Historical
H.M.	..	His (or Her) Majesty
Hon.	..	Honourable; Honorary
HOPECO	..	Hormuz Petroleum Company
H.Q.	..	Headquarters
IAEA	..	International Atomic Energy Authority
IATA	..	International Air Transport Association
IBRD	..	International Bank for Reconstruction and Development
ICAO	..	International Civil Aviation Organization
ICATU	..	International Conference of Arab Trade Unions
ICFTU—AFRO	..	International Confederation of Free Trade Unions—African Regional Organization
ICOO	..	Iraqi Company for Oil Operations
IDA	..	International Development Association
IFC ..	..	International Finance Corporation
ILO ..	..	International Labour Organization
IMF	..	International Monetary Fund
IMINOCO	..	Iranian Marine International Oil Company
Inc. ..	..	Incorporated
incl...	..	included; including
Ind...	..	Independent
Insp.	..	Inspector
Inst.	..	Institute; Institution
Int. ..	..	International
INOC	..	Iraq National Oil Company
IOP..	..	Iranian Oil Participants
IPAC	..	Iran-Pan American Oil Company
IPC ..	..	Iraq Petroleum Company
IPO ..	..	Iranian Plan Organization
IRCAN	..	Iran Canada Oil Company
IROPCO	..	Iranian Offshore Petroleum Company
ITU ..	..	International Telecommunications Union
JAL	..	Japan Airlines
JAT	..	Jugoslovenski Aerotransport
kg. ..	..	kilogram
kl. ..	..	kilolitre
KLM	..	Koninklijke Luchtvaart Maatschappij NV
km. ..	..	kilometres
KNPC	..	Kuwait National Petroleum Company
KOC	..	Kuwait Oil Company
KSPC	..	Kuwait Spanish Petroleum Company
kWh.	..	kilowatt
L ..	..	Legation
LAPCO	..	Lavan Petroleum Company
lb. ..	..	pounds (weight)
LINOCO	..	Libyan National Oil Corporation
LL.B.	..	Bachelor of Laws
LN ..	..	League of Nations
LOT	..	Polskie Linie Lotnicze
Ltd...	..	Limited
M ..	..	Minister
m. ..	..	million
M.A.	..	Master of Arts
Maj.	..	Major
Maj.-Gen.	..	Major-General
Malev	..	Magyar Légyar Légiköz-lekedési Vállalat
Man.	..	Manager; Managing
M.B.E.	..	Member of the (Order of the) British Empire
M.D.	..	Doctor of Medicine
MEA	..	Middle Eastern Airlines Airliban
Mem(s).	..	Member(s)
MEOC	..	Middle East Oil Company
Mgr.	..	Monseigneur; Monsignor
Mil. ..	..	Military
Min.	..	Minister; Ministry
MNA	..	Mouvement Nationale Algérienne (Algerian National Movement)
M.P.	..	Member of Parliament
MPC	..	Mosul Petroleum Company
MRP	..	Mouvement Républicain Populaire
M.Sc.	..	Master of Science
MSS.	..	Manuscripts
MTA	..	Mineral Research and Exploration Institute of Turkey
MTLD	..	Mouvement au Triomphe des Libertés Démocratiques (Movement for the Triumph of Democratic Liberties in Algeria)
n.a. ..	..	not available
Nat.	..	National
NATO	..	North Atlantic Treaty Organization
NDRC	..	National Defence Research Council
NECCCRW	..	Near East Christian Council Committee for Refugee Work
n.e.s.	..	not elsewhere specified
n.i.e.	..	not included elsewhere
NIOC	..	National Iranian Oil Company
NLF	..	National Liberation Front (People's Democratic Republic of Yemen)
no. ..	..	number
NUP	..	National Unionist Party (Sudan)
N.Y.	..	New York (City)
OAS	..	Secret Army Organization (Algeria)
OAU	..	Organization for African Unity
O.B.E.	..	Officer of the (Order of the) British Empire
OCAM	..	Organisation Commune Africaine, Malgache et Mauricienne
OCRA	..	Clandestine Organization of the Algerian Revolution
OECD	..	Organisation for Economic Co-operation and Development
ORP	..	Organisation de la Résistance Populaire (Organization of Popular Resistance in Algeria)

ABBREVIATIONS

OPEC	..	Organization of Petroleum Exporting Countries
Parl.	..	Parliament; Parliamentary
PDFLP	..	Popular Democratic Front for the Liberation of Palestine
PDO	..	Petroleum Development Oman
PDP	..	People's Democratic Party (Sudan)
PDR	..	People's Democratic Republic
PEGUPCO	..	Persian Gulf Petroleum Company
Perm.	..	Permanent
Perm. Del.	..	Permanent Delegate
Perm. Rep	..	Permanent Representative
PFLOAG	..	Popular Front for the Liberation of the Occupied Arabian Gulf
PFLP	..	Popular Front for the Liberation of Palestine
Ph.D.	..	Doctor of Philosophy
PIA	..	Pakistan International Airlines
PLA	..	Palestine Liberation Army
PLO	..	Palestine Liberation Organization
P.O.B.	..	Post Office Box
Pres.	..	President
Prof.	..	Professor
Prop.	..	Proprietor
PSD	..	Parti Socialiste Destourien (Tunisia)
PPA	..	Parti des Peuples Algériennes (Party of the Algerian People)
P.R.	..	People's Republic
p.u.	..	paid up
Publ(s).	..	Publication(s)
QPC	..	Qatar Petroleum Company
R.A.F.	..	Royal Air Force
RCC	..	Revolutionary Command Council (Libya)
RCD	..	Regional Co-operation for Development
Rd.	..	Road
RDA	..	Rassemblement Démocratique Africain
reg.	..	registered
Rep.	..	Representative; Represented
resgnd.	..	resigned
retd.	..	retired
R.P.	..	Révérend Père (Reverend Father)
RPP	..	Republican People's Party
Rt. Hon.	..	Right Honourable
Rt. Rev.	..	Right Reverend
SAS	..	Scandinavian Airlines System
SCAP	..	Supreme Command Allied Powers
SDF	..	Sudan Defence Force
Sec.	..	Secretary
Sec.-Gen.	..	Secretary-General
SEHR	..	Société d'Exploitation des Hydrocarbons de Hassi—R'Mel
SIRIP	..	Société Irano-Italienne des Pétroles
SNPA	..	Société Nationale des Pétroles d'Aquitaine
SNREPAL	..	Société Nationale de Recherche et d'Exploitation des Pétroles en Algérie
Soc.	..	Society; Société
SOFIRAN	..	Société Française des Pétroles d'Iran
SONATRACH		Société Nationale pour la Recherche, la Production, la Transformation et la Commercialisation des Hydrocarbures
SOPEG	..	Société Pétrolière de Gérance
Sq.	..	Square
St.	..	Street
TAL	..	Trans-Alpine Line
Tapline	..	Trans-Arabian Pipeline Company
TAROM	..	Transporturile Aeriene Române
THY	..	Türk Hava Yollari
TMA	..	Trans Mediterranean Airways
TPAO	..	Turkish Petroleum Corporation
trans.	..	translated; translation
TRAPES	..	Société de Transport de Pétrole de l'Est Saharien
TRAPSA	..	Compagnie de Transport par Pipe-line au Sahara
TWA	..	Trans World Airlines
U.A.E.	..	United Arab Emirates
U.A.R.	..	United Arab Republic
UBAF	..	Union des Banques Arabes et Françaises
UDMA	..	Union Démocratique du Manifeste Algérienne (Democratic Union of the Algerian Manifesto)
UGTA	..	Union Générale des Travailleurs Algériens (Algerian General Workers Union)
U.K.	..	United Kingdom
UN	..	United Nations
UNDP	..	United Nations Development Programme
UNEA	..	Union National des Etudiants Algériennes (National Union of Algerian Students)
UNESCO	..	United Nations Educational, Scientific and Cultural Organization
UNFICYP	..	United Nations Peace-Keeping Force in Cyprus
UNFP	..	Union National des Forces Populaires (National Union of Popular Forces in Morocco)
UNICEF	..	United Nations International Children's Emergency Fund
Univ.	..	University
UNMEM	..	United Nations Middle East Mission
UNRWA	..	United Nations Relief and Works Agency for Palestine Refugees in the Near East
UNTSO	..	United Nations Truce Supervision Organization
UPAF	..	Union Postale Africaine (African Postal Union)
U.P.	..	University Press
UPI	..	United Press International
U.S.A. (U.S.)	..	United States of America (United States)
USIS	..	United States Information Services
U.S.S.R.	..	Union of Soviet Socialist Republics
UTA	..	Union de Transports Aériens
vols.	..	volumes
VSO	..	Voluntary Service Overseas Limited
WEPCO	..	Western Desert Petroleum Company
WFTU	..	World Federation of Trade Unions
WHO	..	World Health Organization

TRANSCRIPTION OF ARABIC NAMES

The Arabic language is used over a vast area. Though the written language and the script are standard throughout the Middle East, the spoken language and also the pronunciation of the written signs show wide variation from place to place. This is reflected, and even exaggerated, in the different transcriptions in use in different countries. The same words, names and even letters will be pronounced differently by an Egyptian, a Lebanese, or an Iraqi—they will be heard and transcribed differently by an Englishman, a Frenchman, or an Italian. There are several more or less scientific systems of transliteration in use, sponsored by learned societies and Middle Eastern governments, most of them requiring diacritical marks to indicate Arabic letters for which there are no Latin equivalents.

Arabic names occurring in the historical and geographical sections of this book have been rendered in the system most commonly used by British and American Orientalists, but with the omission of the diacritical signs. For the convenience of the reader, these are explained and annotated below. The system used is a transliteration—i.e. it is based on the writing, which is standard throughout the Arab world, and not on the pronunciation, which varies from place to place. In a few cases consistency has been sacrificed in order to avoid replacing a familiar and accepted form by another which, though more accurate, would be unrecognisable.

Consonants:

d   represents two Arabic letters. The second, or emphatic *d*, is transliterated *ḍ*. It may also be represented, for some dialects, by *dh* and by *z*, e.g. Qāḍī, qadhi, qazi.

dh   in literary Arabic and some dialects pronounced like English *th* in *this*. In many dialects pronounced *z* or *d*.

gh   A strongly guttural *g*—sometimes written *g*, e.g. Baghdād, Bagdad.

h   represents two Arabic letters. The second, more guttural *h*, is transliterated *ḥ*, e.g. Husain, Husein.

j   as English *j* in *John*, also represented by *dj* and *g*. In Egypt this letter is pronounced as a hard *g*, and may be thus transcribed (with *u* before *e* and *i*), e.g. Najib, Nadjib, Nagib, Naguib, Neguib.

kh   as *ch* in Scottish *loch*, also sometimes represented by *ch* and *h*, e.g. Khalīl, Chalil, Halil.

q   A guttural *k*, pronounced farther back in the throat. Also transcribed *ḳ*, *k*, and, for some dialects, *g*, e.g. Waqf, Wakf, Wakf, Wagf.

s   represents two Arabic letters. The second, emphatic *s*, is transliterated *ṣ*. It may also be represented by *ç*, e.g. Sālih, Saleh, Çaleh.

t   represents two Arabic letters. The second, emphatic *t*, is transliterated *ṭ*.

th   in literary Arabic and some dialects pronounced as English *th* in *through*. In many dialects pronounced *t* or *s*, e.g. Thābit, Tabit, Sabit.

w   as in English, but often represented by *ou* or *v*, e.g. Wādī, Vadi, Oued.

z   represents two Arabic letters. The second, or emphatic *z*, is transliterated *ẓ*. It may also be represented, for some dialects, by *dh* or *d*, e.g. Hāfiz, Hafidh, Hafid.

'   A glottal stop, as in Cockney *'li'l bo'ls'*. May also represent the sound transliterated ʻ, a deep guttural with no English equivalent.

Vowels

The Arabic script only indicates three short vowels, three long vowels, and two diphthongs, as follows:

a   as in English *hat*, and often rendered *e*, e.g. balad, beled, emir, amir; with emphatics or gutturals usually pronounced as *u* in *but*, e.g. Khalīfa, Baghdād.

i   as in English *bit*. Sometimes rendered *e*, e.g. jihād, jehād.

u   as in English *good*. Often pronounced and written *o*, e.g. Muhammad, Mohammad.

In some Arabic dialects, particularly those of North Africa, unaccented short vowels are often omitted altogether, and long vowels shortened, e.g. Oued for Wādī, bled for balad, etc.

ā   Long *a*, variously pronounced as in *sand*, *dart* and *hall*.

ī   As *ee* in *feet*. In early books often rendered *ee*.

ū   As *oo* in *boot*. The French transcription *ou* is often met in English books, e.g. Mahmūd, Mahmood, Mahmoud.

ai   Pronounced in classical Arabic as English *i* in *hide*, in colloquial Arabic as *a* in *take*. Variously transcribed as *ai, ay, ei, ey* and *ê*, e.g. sheikh, shaikh, shaykh, etc.

aw   Pronounced in classical Arabic as English *ow* in *town*, in colloquial Arabic as in *grow*. Variously rendered *aw, ew, au, ô, av, ev*, e.g. Tawfīq, Taufiq, Tevfik, etc.

TURKISH ORTHOGRAPHY AND PRONUNCIATION

Turkish has been written in Roman characters since 1928. The following pronunciations are invariable:

c   hard *j*, as in *majority, jam*.

ç   *ch*, as in *church*.

g   hard *g*, as in *go, big*.

ğ   not voiced, or pronounced *y*; Ereğli is pronounced *erayly*.

ı   short vowel, as the second vowel of '*centre*', or French '*le*'.

i   *i* sound of *Iran, bitter* (NOT as in *bite, might*).

o   *o*, as in *hot, boss*.

ö   *i* sound of '*birth*', or French '*oeuvre*'.

u   as in *do, too*, German '*um*'.

ü   as in *burette*, German '*Hütte*'.

xiv

CALENDAR OF EVENTS

1971

JANUARY
14 New agreement between Jordanian Government and Palestinian guerrillas after continuing fighting between the two sides.
29 Flow of oil in Tapline resumed after Syria allowed repairs to be made.

FEBRUARY
14 New five-year agreement between 23 international oil companies and Abu Dhabi, Iran, Iraq, Kuwait, Qatar and Saudi Arabia.
24 Algerian Government nationalizes CFP and Elf-ERAP, the two French companies.

MARCH
4 Royal decree extended term of Jordanian House of Representatives for two years.
7 President Sadat announced cease-fire with Israel not to be renewed again.
12 General Assad elected President of Syria for seven years.
    Army threatened to take over in Turkey; Demirel resigned; Erim formed new government.
28 Bahi Ladgham, chairman of committee supervising Jordanian agreements, accused Jordanian Government of violating them.
    President Gaddafi called for King Hussein's overthrow.

APRIL
2 Agreement in Tripoli between international oil companies and Libyan Government, acting for Algeria, Iraq and Saudi Arabia as well; posted price for Libyan crude raised 90c.
3 New government in Syria formed under Maj.-Gen. Abdal Rahman Khlefawi.
    Mahmoud Ayyoubi appointed Vice-President of Syria.
13-14 Meeting of heads of state of Libya, Sudan, Syria and U.A.R. in Cairo and Benghazi.
17 Announcement of plan to federate Libya, Syria and U.A.R.; Sudan's membership of federation postponed.

MAY
2 U.A.R.'s Vice-President, Ali Sabry, dismissed.
1-8 U.S. Secretary of State, William Rogers, visited Saudi Arabia, Jordan, Lebanon, U.A.R. and Israel to discuss plans for reopening Canal.
13 More Ministers in U.A.R. dismissed after planning coup.
17 Etemadi Government resigned in Afghanistan.
18 "Black Panthers" demonstrated in Jerusalem against discrimination against Jews of oriental origin.
27 Fifteen-year treaty of friendship between U.A.R. and U.S.S.R.

JUNE
2-9 President Makarios of Cyprus in Moscow.
3 Palestinian guerrillas, including Fatah, call for overthrow of Hussein.
11 President Gaddafi announced Arab Socialist Union to be formed as Libya's only party.
13-16 Jordanian army attacked Palestinian guerrilla positions in Jordan; Iraq and Syria closed their borders with Jordan; Algeria suspended relations; King Hussein said guerrilla problem now "solved".
30 Agreement reached between Algerian Government and CFP on compensation for nationalization, on tax reference price, etc.

CALENDAR OF EVENTS

JULY

10 Unsuccessful attempt by section of army to overthrow King Hassan of Morocco; many people killed; thirteen officers executed; full powers granted to Gen. Oufkir.
18 Six of seven Trucial States agreed to federate before British withdrew from Gulf at end of year; Ras al Khaimah elected to become independent.
19 Negotiations began between Algerian Government and Elf-ERAP.
19-21 Unsuccessful attempt at communist take-over in Sudan; 13 leading communists later executed for their part in it.
26 New Afghan cabinet under Abdul Zahir took office.

AUGUST

2 U.S.S.R. and other Warsaw pact states condemn Sudan's "reign of terror".
4 Malta's Prime Minister, Mr. Mintoff, visited Tripoli; Libya promised aid.
11-13 Jordan-Syria border clashes.
12 Syria broke off diplomatic relations with Jordan.
15 Bahrain became independent.
30 Gen. Grivas disappeared from his home in Athens; thought to have returned to Cyprus.

SEPTEMBER

2 United Arab Republic became Arab Republic of Egypt.
4 Ahmad Mestiri dismissed as Interior Minister in Tunisia.
7 Formation of Jordanian National Union, Jordan's only legal political organization, announced; renamed Arab National Union on March 16th, 1945.
17 Marrakesh trial of 193 UNFP supporters ended in Morocco; 5 sentenced to death, 4 in their absence.
28 Wasfi Tal, Jordanian Prime Minister, assassinated in Cairo by members of the Black September Organization.

OCTOBER

10-13 President Sadat visited Moscow.
12-19 Celebrations in Persepolis of 2,500th anniversary of foundation of Persian monarchy.
14 President Bourguiba named Hedi Nouira as his successor as Head of State of Tunisia.

NOVEMBER

29 Sheikh of Sharjah agreed to share island of Abu Musa with Iran.
30 Iran occupied the Greater and Lesser Tumbs, expelling Arab inhabitants.
    Iraq broke off relations with Iran in retaliation, and began to expel 60,000 Iranians resident in Iraq.

DECEMBER

1 Britain's treaties with Trucial States terminated.
2 United Arab Emirates formed as independent state without membership of Ras al Khaimah.
7 Libya nationalized BP and withdrew deposits from British banks.
14 Libya expelled from Sterling Area.
15 Final agreement between Algerian Government and Elf-ERAP.
    Attempt to assassinate Jordanian ambassador in London.
16 Attempt to blow up Jordanian ambassador to Switzerland.

1972

JANUARY

13 President Sadat said that plan for action against Israel by end of 1971 dropped because of Indo-Pakistan war.

xvi

CALENDAR OF EVENTS

JANUARY—*continued*

25 Student riots in Cairo; Sadat met leaders and said decision to go to war against Israel already taken.

29 Sheikh Khalid, Ruler of Sharjah, killed by rebels; rebels captured and Sheikh Sultan, Khalid's younger brother, took over as Ruler.

FEBRUARY

2-4 President Sadat visited Moscow.

9 Greek Government alleged that President Makarios had imported large quantities of Czechoslovak arms for use against Gen. Grivas.

10 Ras al Khaimah joined United Arab Emirates.

17 King Hassan of Morocco announced new constitution.

22 Bloodless coup in Qatar deposed Sheikh Khalifa; his cousin Sheikh Ahmad took over.

24-28 Israeli attack on Lebanon.

29 Trial of 1,082 army officers and cadets for their part in attempted coup of July 1971 against King Hassan of Morocco ended; all but 75 acquitted.
Third conference of Islamic foreign ministers opened in Jeddah.

MARCH

1 Constitutional referendum in Morocco showed 98.75 per cent in favour.

2 Three bishops of Orthodox Church of Cyprus called for resignation of President Makarios.

7 Syrian National Progressive Front of five parties, including Baath and the Communists, formed.

15 King Hussein announced plan for United Arab Kingdom.

27 Three NATO technicians kidnapped by the Turkish Peoples' Liberation Army and later found dead.
Addis Ababa agreement between Sudan Government and Southern Sudanese rebels ratified.

APRIL

9 Iraq signed 15-year friendship treaty with U.S.S.R.

17 Professor Nihat Erim's government resigned in Turkey.

27-29 President Sadat visited Moscow.

MAY

5 Omani air force attacked Yemen P.D.R. border positions.

8 Black September Organization hijacked Sabena plane to Lydda and held passengers hostage until Israeli commandos rescued them.

10-14 Marshal Grechko, Soviet Defence Minister, visited Damascus.

22 Ferit Melen forms new government in Turkey.

27 Saeb Salam, the outgoing Prime Minister, forms new government in Lebanon.

30 Massacre at Lod airport by three Japanese gunmen belonging to PFLP.

JUNE

1 Iraq nationalized Iraq Petroleum Company.
Syria nationalized all oil installations.

11 President Gaddafi of Libya said he was supplying arms and money to the Irish Republican Army in Northen Ireland.

13 OAU Summit in Rabat.

16 New Council of Ministers in Cyprus: only three ministers retain posts.

21-23 Israeli attacks on Lebanon; 36 civilians and 30 guerrillas killed; 80 civilians and 50 guerrillas wounded; five Syrian army officers kidnapped.

CALENDAR OF EVENTS

JULY

16 New Libyan cabinet formed; Maj. Jalloud Prime Minister; only two members are officers; President Gaddafi's position as Chairman of the Revolutionary Command Council and Minister of Defence later confirmed.

17 Soviet advisers begin to leave Egypt at President Sadat's request; by August 8th all advisers had withdrawn except some instructors, mainly on the SAM-3 ground-to-air missiles.

25 Renewal of diplomatic links between Sudan and U.S.A. announced.

27 U.S.A. announced interests section to be opened in Iraq in September.

AUGUST

1 Sudan and Iraq resumed diplomatic relations, broken off after July 1971 coup attempt.

2 Egypt and Libya announce agreement on union by September 1st, 1973.

3 French sources said Mirage deliveries to Libya to continue until merger takes more concrete form.

Yemen P.D.R. nationalized residential and commercial housing; each family allowed to retain one dwelling.

8 Sudanese People's Council of 207 members announced.

16 National unity law in Egypt imposed greater restrictions on political opposition and expression.

Fighter planes of Moroccan air force failed to shoot down King Hassan's plane or to kill him in later raids on airport and royal palace in Rabat.

17 Announcement of the suicide of Gen. Oufkir, the Moroccan Defence Minister and Chief of Staff.

19 King Hassan took personal control of the Moroccan armed forces.

SEPTEMBER

5 Eleven Israeli athletes murdered by Arab terrorists at Munich Olympic Games.

8 Dr. Mohamed Hassan el-Zayyat became Egyptian Foreign Minister.
Heavy airstrikes by Israeli Air Force on guerrilla bases in Lebanon and Syria.

19-20 Letter bomb killed Israeli diplomat in London; 17 other letter bombs addressed to Israelis discovered in other parts of the world.

26 Serious fighting broke out on border of Yemen A.R. and Yemen P.D.R.

30 Libyan oil participation agreement signed with Italian State Co. (ENI).

OCTOBER

4-12 Arab League mediation mission in Aden and Sana'a secured ceasefire between Yemen A.R. and Yemen P.D.R.

5 Agreement reached between Abu Dhabi, Iraq, Kuwait, Qatar and Saudi Arabia on the one hand, and representatives of various oil companies on the other hand, on eventual 51 per cent participation of the producing countries in the various concessions.

15 Israeli Air Force attacked guerrilla targets in Lebanon and Syria.

21-28 Delegations from Yemen A.R. and Yemen P.D.R. met in Cairo for peace talks and agreed on eventual unification of the two countries.

NOVEMBER

7 Eleven men condemned to death in Morocco for complicity in attack on King Hassan in August.

9 Air battle between Israeli and Syrian planes over the Golan Heights.

15 Attempt to overthrow King Hussein of Jordan by Maj. Rafeh Hindawi was thwarted in Amman.

19 New cabinet formed in Morocco under Ahmed Osman as Prime Minister.

CALENDAR OF EVENTS

NOVEMBER—*continued*

28 President Iriani of Yemen A.R. and President Rubbayi of Yemen P.D.R. signed an agreement for eventual unification of their two countries in the presence of Col. Gaddafi, in Tripoli, Libya.

DECEMBER

6 Association agreement between EEC and Cyprus signed.
8 UN General Assembly adopted resolution on Middle East calling for speedy implementation of Security Council resolution 242 of 1967.
Clash between Lebanese regular troops and Palestinian Arab guerrillas in S. Lebanon.
18 Five-year preferential trade agreement signed by EEC and Egypt.
24 New government formed in Syria under Mahmoud Ayoubi.
28-29 Israeli Embassy in Bangkok occupied by 4 armed members of Palestine Black September Organization.

1973

JANUARY

31 New draft Constitution approved by People's Council in Syria.

FEBRUARY

8 President Makarios re-elected unopposed for a third five-year term as President of Cyprus.
13 Abu Daoud and other Palestinian guerrillas arrested for subversive activities in Jordan.
16 Rauf Denktash elected Vice-President of Cyprus in succession to Dr. Fazil Kutchuk.
21 Libyan airliner shot down by Israeli fighters over Sinai desert. 108 passengers killed.
Israeli commandos conducted raid into Lebanon against Palestinian Arab guerrilla training bases.

MARCH

1 Arab guerrillas killed U.S. Ambassador and Belgian Chargé d'Affaires after raiding reception at Saudi Arabian Embassy in Khartoum. Sudan subsequently banned Palestinian Arab organizations.
8 Bishops of Kitium, Paphos and Kyrenia announced that they will unfrock Archbishop Makarios in view of his refusal to relinquish Presidency of Cyprus.
25-26 General elections in Syria. National Progressive Front won big victories.
26 President Anwar Sadat of Egypt assumed office of Prime Minister and formed new government. Sadat also became Military Governor of Egypt.

APRIL

6 Senator Fahri Korutürk elected President of Turkey in succession to Cevdet Sunay.
9 Arab guerrillas made unsuccessful attempts to kill Israeli Ambassador in Nicosia.
10 Israeli shock troops in civilian dress killed three Palestinian Arab guerrilla leaders in Beirut.
Professor Ephraim Katzir (Katchalski), an internationally known scientist, elected President of Israel.
12 New government formed in Turkey under Naim Talu.
15 Col. Gaddafi launched "cultural revolution" in Libya, condemning foreign ideologies and promoting society based on Islamic principles.

MAY

8 New permanent constitution in Sudan came into force and new government is formed.
17 Lebanese authorities and Palestinian guerrillas reached agreement on terms under which guerrillas would remain in Lebanon. Heavy fighting between the guerrillas and the Lebanese army had preceded the settlement.

xix

CALENDAR OF EVENTS

MAY—*continued*

20 U.A.E. dirham introduced in United Arab Emirates, replacing Bahrain dinar in Abu Dhabi and Qatar/Dubai riyal in Dubai and other Emirates.

24 Iran and the Consortium signed agreement in Teheran whereby National Iranian Oil Co. took over operations in Consortium area while in return the Western oil companies were granted a 20-year supply of crude oil as privileged buyers.

26 Zaid Rifai succeeded Ahmed Louzi (who resigned for health reasons) as Prime Minister of Jordan.

JUNE

2 OPEC reached new oil-price agreement in Geneva with Western oil companies, giving 11.9 per cent aggregate price increase to compensate producing countries for losses resulting from dollar devaluation of February 1973.

14 Dr. Amin Hafez resigned as Prime Minister of Lebanon.

30 Lieut.-Gen. Hamad Shehab, the Iraqi Defence Minister, was killed as a result of an unsuccessful plot to seize power in Iraq by Col. Nazem Kazzar, the Director of Public Security.

JULY

5 First stage of Euphrates Dam inaugurated in Syria by President Assad.

8 Takieddine Solh formed a 22-man Cabinet in the Lebanon.

15 A synod of the Eastern Orthodox Churches in the Middle East deposed and unfrocked the three Bishops who had previously tried to have President Makarios of Cyprus unfrocked (*see* March 1973).

17 Mohammad Daud Khan seized power in Afghanistan while King Mohammad Zahir Shah (Daud's cousin and brother-in-law) was in Italy for health reasons, and declared that a Republic would be set up.

18 Several thousand Libyans set off from Libya to march to Cairo demanding recognition of full union between Libya and Egypt. The marchers were turned back before reaching Cairo.

28 12-member Cabinet, with President Daud as Prime Minister and Minister of Defence and Foreign Affairs, set up in Afghanistan.

AUGUST

16 Libya announced that the independent members of the Oasis group of oil companies had agreed to its 51 per cent nationalization demands.

24 King Mohammad Zahir Shah of Afghanistan announced that he had abdicated.

The Year in the Middle East—June 1972-73

W. B. Fisher

Two major issues stand out in Middle Eastern affairs: relations between the Arabs and Israel, and the greatly enhanced economic, political and social effects of petroleum exploitation. The first of these topics is dealt with at length elsewhere in this volume and so will not be examined at length here—though it is impossible to avoid some references; whilst the second forms a basic *leitmotiv* that recurs through and through all discussions of contemporary activities in the Middle East. Apart from its obvious and enormous importance for Middle Eastern countries themselves, oil exploitation in the region is now a most significant element in what can be described as the growing world energy crisis. Exploitation of petroleum sets as it were the frame and scale for development: it provides very clearly "the limit of the possible". Without it, as in the Yemen and Jordan, economic poverty and political impotence prevail; for major producers, totally new and undreamed-of vistas of influence, power and wealth are now opening.

The period mid-1972 to mid-1973 could, from some points of view, rank as a major turning-point or stage in Middle Eastern affairs. For the first time, there was frank appraisal and some analysis of a situation that had gradually been taking shape over several decades. This situation is, in short, realization that about 60 per cent of the world's proved reserves of oil lie in the Middle East; together with a world demand for oil that is increasing at an accelerating pace; and only limited prospects in the short term of substantial alternative energy supplies becoming available to meet a world energy demand that is expected to multiply by eight by the end of the century. The oil-producing states of the Middle East broke through last year to a realization that, as regards supply of petroleum they henceforward held a dominant position, and they appreciated for the first time that they could actually summon entrepreneurs and consumer organizations to hear and accept in effect whatever terms the producer countries offered. Thus the Shah of Iran could say in March 1973 that the oil companies "had totally surrendered" to becoming "mere customers"; and entire local possession of oil concessions and operations is now adumbrated for the near future. All this stems from clear awareness that, given the cut-back in world coal production and the inability of nuclear power to substitute (at least in the short run), oil has become indisputably the prime world fuel.

When, 15 or so years ago, suggestions were made that the U.S.A. would eventually become an importer, and even possibly a net importer of oil, these were received with incredulity and some derision. This year has seen how a local triumph of environmental conservationists in the U.S.A. in securing postponement of construction of pipelines that would allow major exploitation of the Arctic "north-slope" oilfields was promptly followed by closure of petrol stations (up to 1,000 according to some authorities) and the temporary rationing of petrol and fuel-oil in certain parts of the country. Whether direct cause and effect, or whether dramatic propaganda only, the fact remains that the near unthinkable has happened: there are now discernible limits to petroleum consumption in the U.S.A. Parallel with this, the BBC in London put out at peak time a major TV series providing assessment of the world energy situation, and the effect of the series on the ordinary public was, for a short time at least, quite marked. What had hitherto been remote, or restricted to academic discussion, or blandly swept under the carpet, is now shown to have extreme relevance to everyday life.

Within Middle Eastern countries, the effects of petroleum exploitation may be traced in several ways. For some countries it is a matter of maximizing the discovery and development of new resources, wherever these may be. In the same vein, but at a later stage, some other countries are concerned to develop superior—larger, more efficient or more numerous—infrastructures to handle production: more pipelines, terminals, plant, refineries and communications systems. But a few governments have taken deliberate decisions to cut back production, or at least threaten this, with the aims partly of conserving supplies in a world situation where money values are steadily declining—oil sold in ten years' time may be much more valuable in real terms—or, equally, of avoiding over-rapid internal expansion now at the expense of difficulties later. There is now also the possibility of linking sales of oil to foreign consumers with direct political and economic aims—in short, using oil as a direct bargaining weapon, thus making the Persian Gulf as geopolitically important now as the Suez Canal ever was. Another major aspect is the new awareness of enhanced financial strength that can permit diversification into outside economic activities in other countries. For some time, wealthy oil states have been investing assets, thought to amount for the four leading Gulf provinces alone to $8 to 9 billion, and possibly to a total of over $100 billion within ten years, into a widening spectrum of business, financial and industrial activities. Iran holds 23 per cent of the capital of SASOL (South African Synthetic Oil); there is an increasing flow of Arab capital into Japanese enterprises; and Saudi Arabia has recently proposed arrangements that would give her a privileged position in the American domestic market for oil and natural gas. As well, there is a funding of economic enterprises of a general kind through normal shareholding, in for example, domestic municipal loans in Spain and Britain, and loans for development, particularly in the Arab world. "Compensatory" or "special" payments have also been made to Arab countries affected by the Arab-Israeli war, and the closure of the Suez Canal. At the same

THE YEAR IN THE MIDDLE EAST—JUNE 1972-73

time, oil wealth is a two-edged political weapon, and the vulnerability of installations (especially pipelines and storage tanks) has induced dissident Arab groups to sabotage these as a means of putting pressure on local governments; Tapline was cut in January near the Iraqi border with Saudi Arabia, and storage tanks at Zahrani (Lebanon) were attacked in April.

Significant new discoveries of oil made in the twelve-month period to June 1973 were in Oman (July); a "huge" strike around Abu Musa island (October: exploitation to be shared by Iran and Abu Dhabi); at Dehloran in southern Iran (December); on the Egyptian coast of the Gulf of Suez (January); and in Saudi Arabia east of Riyadh (February). A natural gas deposit was reported at Dardara Island off the Red Sea coast of the Sudan—this is the first windfall of its kind for the Sudan, which hitherto has been singularly unfortunate in the matter of oil and gas. New refineries came into operation at Abu Dhabi, Alexandria (Egypt), Aliaga (Turkey) and Gabès (Tunisia), while Iran announced a programme of building a new refinery every two years in the future, and major export plans for the large gas field located round Kharg islands.

As regards concessions, the period opened with increasing pressures by Iraq on the foreign Iraq Petroleum Co., which was finally declared to be nationalized in March 1973. Iraq desired that Syria and Lebanon, through which IPC pipelines passed to the Mediterranean, would undertake parallel action. Syria needed relatively little urging, but an Iraqi ban on Lebanese imports was necessary before Lebanon too announced a state takeover of IPC installations. Iraqi claims had been strongly supported by the Eighth Arab Petroleum Congress which opened in Algiers in May 1972, and the Congress later gave the oil companies two months' time limit to accept major participation in the concessions. In October it was announced that the principle of participation up to 51 per cent of equity by 1981 had been accepted by the oil companies and would be the subject of detailed individual negotiations by country. By the beginning of 1973 (January in the case of Saudi Arabia) it had been agreed that in effect the oil companies would be taken over by the early 1980s. Libya was not a direct party to this, but played a somewhat lone hand based on partial nationalization at once with up to 100 per cent ownership; and Iran (which had not observed a boycott of the west during the 1967 war with Israel) also conducted somewhat separate negotiations—with, however, broadly the same result: takeover.

In February, devaluation of the American dollar led to further demands on the grounds that, because of a price basis involving the dollar, producer states had lost 11.1 per cent of revenues. After some months of discussion, during which the threat of sanctions within a sellers' market proved irresistible, agreement was arrived at in June 1973 by which "posted" crude oil prices were increased by 11.9 per cent. Arrangements were also agreed for closer revision of the international monetary situation (which affects posted prices) and the agreement will hold, it was hoped at least on one side, until 1975. However, later in June 1973 Kuwait announced that it wished to re-negotiate.

The effects of the new prices are to raise the Middle Eastern governmental share (in U.S. $ per barrel) from between $1.41 minimum quality and $2.27 maximum in January 1973 to $1.57 and $2.54 respectively. Overall, this means that payments during 1973 will be of the following order: to Saudi Arabia $4,250 million, Iran $3,600 million, Libya $2,200 million, Kuwait $1,800 million, and Iraq $1,200 million. Should these sums appear inordinately large, it is useful to preserve a perspective. From the retail sale of a refined gallon of petrol in a Western filling station the Middle Eastern producer government will still only get 8 to 10 per cent as direct royalty, the rest going as governmental taxes imposed by the "consumer" government, and for costs of production, transport and distribution.

Output of petroleum reportedly declined in Iraq, Oman, Kuwait and Libya. For the first two countries, decline was not at all welcome, and efforts are in hand to reverse it; but for the last two it was a matter of choice, reflecting careful appraisal of the factors mentioned above. Saudi Arabia, on the contrary, secure in the fact that known reserves have risen from 84.4 billion barrels in 1968 to 93 billion at the end of 1972 (despite an increased daily average production of 2.8 million barrels in 1968 to 5.7 million in 1972), has increased production by 25 to 30 per cent over the twelve-month period. This formidable position as third world producer and leading world exporter underlay the statement in June 1973 that Arab countries "will deny oil to our enemies". Point had been also given to this when, on May 15th, Algeria, Iraq, Libya and Kuwait suspended oil pumping for a token period in order to demonstrate the potential of oil as a direct economic and political weapon.

Relationships within the Middle East

The year was notable for a number of distinct changes in relationships between various countries. Détente, where conditions had been strained, broke in, as did also the opposite. Most dramatic of these changes was the announcement in August that Egypt and Libya were to unite in September 1973, thus creating a new political unit with a population of c. 37 million, a G.N.P. of $8,500 million and an area of 2.8 million square km.—the largest territory of Africa, with Cairo as its capital. Received with perhaps rather less enthusiasm than could have been expected, it appeared that the main impetus came from Libya. Syria later declared intention of adhering in principle to "this federation", no precise date being given. As well, after a period of coolness with the Sudan, due to Sudanese resumption of diplomatic relations with the U.S.A., and the banning of Libyan aircraft on their way to help President Amin in Uganda, Egyptian-Sudanese relations at least improved, and a Sudanese army contingent returned to the Suez Canal Israeli front. Libyan-Iraqi cordiality, strained for a time by Iraq's increasingly closer

THE YEAR IN THE MIDDLE EAST—JUNE 1972-73

contacts with the U.S.S.R., also improved during this period.

Action by Jordan against Palestinian guerrillas in 1971 had led Syria to close her frontier with Jordan, but the frontier was re-opened, and the new accord underlined (or underwritten) by grants to both countries of £10 million sterling from Saudi Arabia with the stated aim of supporting confrontation with Israel. In this vein, June 1973 saw suggestions that a substantial Kuwait loan might be available if the Syrian-Lebanese frontier were re-opened too. Another *rapprochement* was between Iraq and Turkey, with agreements over trade and routeing of pipelines.

On the debit side, sporadic guerrilla activity increased on the borders of North and South Yemen, with some Saudi Arabian interest and support for the North; and fighting on the frontiers of South Yemen and Oman increased rather than declined. Maintenance of troops to contain this dissident activity, which is also actively encouraging subversion in other Gulf states, is partly supported by Maoists from outside the region and could be costing the state of Oman up to half its revenues from oil. Farther east, friction between tribesmen of Fujairah and Sharjah in June 1972, resulting in 22 killed, led some observers to suggest that this reflected the unequal distribution of oil wealth in the United Arab Emirates. Border incidents occurred during March between Iraq and Kuwait, where a state of emergency was declared; but in the following month the Iraqi troops withdrew. Other disturbed areas were along the Iraqi-Iranian frontier, where Kurds were partly involved, and in Afghanistan, where the border with Pakistan was sealed for several weeks.

In the wider context, there have been a few significant positive moves towards a broader unity, sometimes fairly local, sometimes not. Partial and limited steps to financial and economic unity have been taken by various Gulf states; and an idea recently canvassed from Kuwait with Saudi Arabian interest could have considerable world-wide implications—the formation of an Arab reserve currency: a pan-Arab dinar backed by gold in which oil royalties might be deposited. Of perhaps more immediate concern is the idea of a Mediterranean Free Trade zone, which has made some progress. Talks between the EEC and countries bordering the Mediterranean also took place, and despite some U.S. reservations, agreements were reached between the EEC and all Mediterranean countries with the sole exeptions of Albania, Libya and Syria. Jordan, Kuwait and the Sudan were also involved.

External Relations

The chief development here during the period was the decision of Egypt on July 18th, 1972, to "terminate the functions" of the Soviet military advisers in Egypt. The reason officially given was the unwillingness of the U.S.S.R. to supply offensive weapons, hence impeding Egypt's potential in the struggle with Israel; but it became clear by September that there was more than just a military aspect involved. Replacement of a pro-Soviet Foreign Minister by Mr. Al Zayyat indicated a major shift of policy towards greater links with the West; and Russian technicians both military and civil withdrew without incident. Meantime, diplomatic relations had been resumed with West Germany, and a new cordiality appeared as regards Britain, part of this certainly as regards West Germany being related to participation in the proposed Suez-Alexandria oil pipeline and possible irrigation development in the Qattara Depression. If, however, marked cordiality prevailed in the eastern portion of the Egyptian-Libyan federation, the same was hardly true of the western partner. Statements by President Gaddafi that he was supplying arms and money to "Irish revolutionaries" appeared to be substantiated soon after by the capture by Eire authorities of a German boat running in arms said to be from Libya. During the year President Gaddafi took an uncompromising stand over the importance of Arabic as a world language, and the obligation to accept literally Koranic precepts as the mainsprings of everyday life. This was in some ways a refreshing ingenuousness, but it also led to incidents when foreign passports not in Arabic were refused, and travellers denied entry. As well, the President announced that "popular committees" of workers and students would take over much responsibility for running businesses, some bureaucracies, and the universities. Libya also demonstrated support of the rebels against King Hassan of Morocco, and for the Muslim General Amin of Uganda by despatching troops by air—a matter that, as we have seen, caused difficulties with the Sudanese government. Libya, however, gained world sympathy over the shooting down by Israelis of a Libyan airliner in February 1973. Sale of petroleum from the nationalized BP field to Communist Europe, and alignment with Malta partly to counter British influence there precluded closer relations with Britain and also with the U.S.A., whose oil interests are closely affected too. Cyprus had a recrudescence of civil trouble due to the activities of Colonel Grivas, who, supported by a few Cypriot bishops, campaigned violently for union with Greece. On the other hand, considerable improvement of external relations was apparent in Algeria. Agreements were made with West Germany, now Algeria's largest customer for oil, with France over supply of oil to the new industrial complex at Fos (Marseille), with Britain over a major tourist scheme, and with the U.S.A. over oil and gas—this will shortly make Algeria one of the U.S.A.'s principal suppliers.

Russian pull-back in Egypt was partially at least balanced by closer relations with Iran, Turkey, Iraq, Syria and South Yemen, chiefly in the economic sphere through assistance in specific development projects. In October 1972 a comprehensive economic treaty was signed between the U.S.S.R. and Iran envisaging trade expansion by a factor of ten, and involving assistance to Iran over industrialization. Syria and Iraq also received arms supplies. This last underlines another fundamental matter in Middle Eastern political relationships: the willingness of Soviet Russia and the U.S.A. to supply arms and

THE YEAR IN THE MIDDLE EAST—JUNE 1972-73

political support to protagonists in the Arab-Israeli war. At its best, this is no more than a policy of balance; but at its worst it is patronage of satellites of the sort that prevailed before 1914 and between the Wars. This is why in May 1973 a group of observers of Middle Eastern affairs in Europe addressed an open letter to President Nixon, as the more accessible statesman, suggesting an end to "American discrimination in favour of Israel in the provision of military and financial aid" as the only apparent way to break the trend towards escalation of military support from both sides. So long as there are protegé states in the Middle East, each supported militarily and politically by major power blocks, prospects for détente remain poor.

The Economy

In the agricultural sector, conditions have been varied. Turkey recorded no growth in agriculture, but her neighbour, Syria had an excellent cereal crop (a record for wheat) and good cotton yields—this latter accounts normally for about a third of total exports. Conditions were also generally favourable in northern Iran, where a large agricultural extension started in Azerbaijan, and in Libya and Tunisia, where major irrigation barrages are under construction. Conditions, however, were poor in Afghanistan, Jordan, south-east Iran and the Sudan due to drought, though in 1973 conditions seemed to be improving. Unseasonable frosts caused some damage in the interior of Saudi Arabia.

Tourism is playing an increasingly significant role in many national economies, particularly those of Mediterranean countries, though Iran also plans to spend $200 million over the next five years in developing tourism on the Caspian and Persian Gulf coasts. Internal unrest has hampered what could have been useful improvements in Cyprus, but despite some guerrilla activity, the Lebanese experienced a tourist boom after two years of set-back. Morocco and especially Tunis forged ahead.

Industrialization proceeds apace in those countries fortunate enough to have oil money. Some heavier types of activity (mineral smelting and steelworking) are developing on a modest scale, but main emphasis is on production of consumer goods and some import substitutes, particularly in lighter engineering products and vehicles. Chemicals, especially petrochemicals, are increasingly important, and textile working has expanded during the year. Countries like Morocco and Tunisia, which have a fairly limited resource-base, are attempting to develop light industry: Morocco's Five Year Plan, 1973-78, gives especial weight to labour-intensive industries; and Saudi Arabia, hardly as yet an industrialized state, announced that it saw its main future in industrialization.

For some countries, last year added up to unprecedented boom conditions. Iran claims the current fastest growth of any country in the world (14.3 per cent at constant prices). As a result, her new Plan (1973-78) could look forward to unbroken expansion with, however, a greater balance as between agriculture and commerce on the one hand, and her two major performers, mineral exploitation and industry. Syria also had excellent conditions. Here, good harvests, liberalization of government regulations and currency restrictions, and useful income from cotton, phosphate and oil exports produced a 30 per cent increase in general revenue, with prospects of further growth. Saudi Arabian oil reserves give the country the greatest potential for growth of all Middle Eastern countries. Iran and Egypt have more actual development, and larger internal markets due to larger population numbers, but once the financial strength of Saudi Arabia can be fully deployed, greatest development potential will inevitably lie with this last country. Infrastructure is still lacking, given the large size of the country and scantiness of population, but this was wisely given high priority in the current Development Plan. As we have seen, events over the last year allow a totally new perspective regarding oil revenues, and there has already been a distinct response. "Industrialization", declared the Minister for Petroleum and Mineral Resources, Sheikh Yamani, "will offer the best way of avoiding inflation and broadening the economy".

How far the military confrontation of the Arabs and Israelis has stimulated the economies of Middle Eastern countries is a matter of conjecture. It must be borne in mind that so long as arms and support loans are available from outside, the true cost of warfare does not fall on the antagonists themselves, and the military demands for goods and services can actually stimulate development. Rapid growth in wealth has allowed re-alignment of economic perspectives, with the Suez Canal little more than an antique relegated to the past. Conditions in the Middle East often appear brittle or poised on razor edge, but can show surprising durability, and the last twelve months have demonstrated this to a remarkable extent. If peace seems no nearer, and violence and injustice still prevail, the Middle East shows a considerable capacity to live with these and cocoon them.

One minor, but perhaps happier note in conclusion. For the first time an international conference was held at Beirut during May, to consider the growing problem of pollution in the Mediterranean, which, if unchecked, could turn the whole area into a sterile waste and ruin the beaches upon which, through tourism, so much of the non-oil wealth of the Middle East is going to depend. Though positive steps were rather faltering and hardly numerous, at least there was agreement on the scope of the problems involved, and on the need to co-operate in finding solutions.

PART ONE

General Survey

The Middle East and North Africa: An Introduction

W. B. Fisher

Definition of the Area

The term, "Middle East and North Africa" is a cumbersome, and, possibly to some, even a misleading description. Besides already embracing part of northern Africa, "Middle East" has the further objection of meaning different things to different people. Some would apply it to areas much farther east, and not to Africa at all—which is geographically more logical—but then Libya and Egypt would no longer be in the "Middle East", a nonsense for some others. Perhaps only when we come to consider alternatives do the merits, such as they are, of our present title begin to emerge. "Muslim World" is too extensive in that it could reach as far as Pakistan, Malaysia and Indonesia; whilst reference to "Arab" only would exclude Turkey, Iran, Cyprus (80 per cent Greek) and, logically to one way of thinking, the Berber areas of Tunisia, Algeria and Morocco.

We can trace popular use of "Middle East" back to the Second World War. It developed in a casual, almost haphazard, manner following the territorial expansion of a unified military command that was originally based on countries lying east of the Suez Canal. In this way, the British and American publics grew accustomed to the association of Jerusalem, Damascus, Cairo and then Benghazi and even Tripoli with the collective description "Middle East"; and, in the writer's view, the expression has come to have a validity based on popular usage which it is now difficult to challenge. There are, however, numerous geographers and historians who are unwilling to abandon the older concept of southern Asia as divisible into a Near, Middle and Far East; and in 1946 the Royal Geographical Society protested against the British Government's continued official usage of "Middle East" to indicate Palestine, Egypt and countries further west. If we talk of a Middle East, the logical argument runs, there is also implied a Near East; and in fact this term was once in great vogue, as referring to the territories along the seaboard of the eastern Mediterranean. It was, moreover, a useful collective geographical description for the lands of the former Ottoman Empire.

However, usage of "Middle East" in the present volume may be justified on several grounds. (*a*) Few definitions of a Near East ever agreed—some authors extended it eastwards to include Afghanistan, others terminated it at the coastal ranges of Syria and Palestine; and some included Egypt, whilst others did not. (*b*) "Near East" is convenient to apply, in an historical sense only, to the now defunct Ottoman Empire. (*c*) Nowadays, for the English-speaking public at least, the term "Middle East" would have no validity if applied, in a strictly logical sense, to Afghanistan, Pakistan and India. (*d*) The term can be taken as denoting a single geographical area in which occur broadly similar features of physical environment and ways of life.

We thus arrive at the definition of the Middle East as given on the title-page of earlier editions of this volume—the highland countries of Turkey and Iran; Cyprus; the Arab-speaking states of the eastern Mediterranean seaboard; Israel; the Arabian peninsula; the valley of the Tigris-Euphrates (chiefly but not entirely comprising Iraq), the Nile Valley (Egypt, and also Sudan); and Libya. This, in no sense an ideal or unassailable solution, has at least considerable sanction in popular usage and technical utility. Subsequently, the addition of chapters on north-western Africa and on Afghanistan has extended the range of the present volume beyond many but by no means all of the numerous definitions of the "Middle East" which have been proposed. North-western Africa (Tunisia, Algeria and Morocco) spoken of by Arab geographers as "Jeziret al Maghreb" ("island of the west", or "setting sun"), or usually nowadays just "Maghreb" ("west"), surrounded as it is to the south by deserts and on its remaining sides by sea, may be looked on in many ways as linked to the Middle East both by environment and culture, whilst retaining something of the separateness indicated by the term "island".

Physical Background

STRUCTURE

Geologically speaking, the entire area can be regarded as deriving from two distinct provinces. The south consists largely of continental massifs (increasingly spoken of today as "plates") that would appear once to have been joined in one large mass, known as Gondwanaland. To the north of this mass there has been throughout most geological time a trough or geosyncline. This, a zone of crustal weakness and adjustment, has often (as now, partly) been occupied by deep seas of varying extent, and alternate periods of quiescence and disturbance have occurred here. During quiescent phases, material eroded from the neighbouring continental masses accumulated in the oceanic deeps of the geosyncline; then periods of contraction occurred, heaving up marine sediments in enormous flexures or fold-structures to produce mountain chains. Sometimes the flexures were relatively simple, like hogs' backs; in other instances they were much more intense, giving rise to tightly packed, highly distorted folds, with extremes where shearing and total deformation of the structures

THE MIDDLE EAST AND NORTH AFRICA—(Physical Background)

produced an overthrust ("nappe") rather than a recognizable fold.

From various parts of the geosyncline has emerged a great series of fold-mountain chains that are traceable from Western Europe and North-West Africa as far as Northern India. This is the so-called "Alpine" or Tertiary fold system, since it is the latest in geological time of three major mountain-building periods. The Pyrenees and Sierra Nevada of Spain, the Alps, Appennines, and Carpathians in Europe, and the massive Atlas Mountains of Africa are all part of this system. Further east many of the mountain chains of Asia Minor, the Caucasus, the Zagros and Elburz Ranges of Iran, and the complex of ridges that form the Afghan Pamir are all part of this "Alpine" system—geologically young in age, and relatively uneroded.

This is by no means the whole story. Besides the actual fold ranges, simple and complex, there are often embedded between them portions of older, more resistant structures. Some of these are remnants of the first two mountain building phases: Palaeozoic (or Caledonian) and Mesozoic (Hercynian), the latter now being found extensively in central Europe. Parts of these remnant structures, certainly of Hercynian age and possibly also Caledonian, are found in western Morocco, the central Atlas, Asia Minor, the interior of Iran, and western Afghanistan. One cannot trace any simple pattern in the arrangement of the folds, which may occur in straight parallel ranks, or sinuous arcs and garlands that may alter trend abruptly.

North Africa is a good example of the complexity of conditions. Generally speaking, the entire highland zone consists of a series of parallel-fold mountain chains of Tertiary age running east-west or north-east/south-west, and separated by tablelands or narrow trough-like valleys. In the extreme west, however, areas of Palaeozoic and Mesozoic remnant structures are prominent. The whole mountain system is higher and wider in the west (Morocco) and diminishes considerably in width towards the east (Tunisia), as well as declining in height. Much discussion centres on how far the Tertiary Atlas fold structures can be regarded as continuations of the fold mountains of southern Spain and Italy: whether there is in fact an almost continuous ring of folds enclosing the entire western Mediterranean basin, and breached only by the Straits of Gibraltar and the narrows between Tunis, Sicily and Italy.

Somewhat different conditions obtain in Asia Minor, where much larger interior plateaux, often eroded into sumps or basins, are surrounded by Tertiary fold ranges. Of this kind are the Taurus and Anti-Taurus Ranges of the south, and the coastal ranges of the north, which continue into the Caucasus and Iranian mountains. Within Iran the interior basins (composed in part of Hercynian nuclei) are even more developed, so that, with minor variations, the whole country can be regarded as saucer-shaped, a rim of Tertiary fold mountains very clearly framing and defining a series of interior basins—which are hardly plains, since most are above 2,000 ft. in altitude.

Further east still, in Afghanistan, the Tertiary folds again develop into enormous dominating ridges that bunch together eastwards and northwards to form a formidable, though relatively narrow, mountain complex that presents a major barrier between central and southern Asia. The first portion of it is the Pamir "knot"—a "swag" or bunch of mountain ranges enclosing tenuous and restricted valleys. Intervening blocks or interior plateaux, present in the west on a small scale, disappear entirely towards the east, with topography passing unbroken into the main Himalaya.

The southern geological province of the Middle East contrasts markedly with that of the north as just described. It consists essentially of the platform (or basement) of extremely ancient rocks, some amongst the oldest known in the world (Precambrian and Archaean). These—chiefly granites, schists and quartzites—most likely once made up the enormous Gondwana continent, which included much of Australia, southern India, Arabia, most of Africa, and parts of South America. Whilst generally rigid and resistant to the pressures that rucked up the sediments of the geosyncline, this ancient mass was from time to time, especially on its northern fringe, overrun by shallow seas, which deposited thin, often horizontal layers of limestones and sandstones. In addition, wind- and water-eroded silts and sands from the surface became consolidated in similar thin, level strata. Thus the basement area of the south, whilst generally flat and fairly uniform in character, is not wholly so, since much of its surface is covered by these deposits, which erode differentially, the harder bands standing out as ridges and the less resistant as vales. The whole aspect of this southern basement/platform is one of a vast open plateau diversified here and there by small-scale hill-systems and shallow valleys. Much is occupied by sand deposits in the form of major dunes or as irregular shifting masses—the "sand-seas" of the Sahara and inner Arabia.

One major feature of considerable importance—part, in fact, of a world-wide process—is the drift apart of the two major platforms of Arabia and Africa, which once, as noted, formed a single larger continent. Extensive fissuring (faulting) in the area of the Red Sea and Gulf of Aden led to the separation of Arabia from northern Africa and the tilting of the entire block of Arabia, uplifting the west (Red Sea coast) and downwarping the east (Persian/Arabian Gulf). At first, the foundering of the Red Sea trough was thought to represent a simple rifting process—the downletting of a segment between two parallel sets of faults. Latest research suggests, however, that the situation is somewhat more involved. Once crustal weakness developed through fissuring and rifting, the sea floor of the Red Sea began to "spread", due to the rise of deep-seated strata from the lower parts of the earth's crust. In this way, Arabia and Africa were forced apart, a process that may well still be continuing. The zone of fissuring and faulting continues southwards into the Great Rift Valley of East Africa, and northwards on a diminishing scale through the Jordan valley, the Lebanon and western Syria as far as southern Turkey.

4

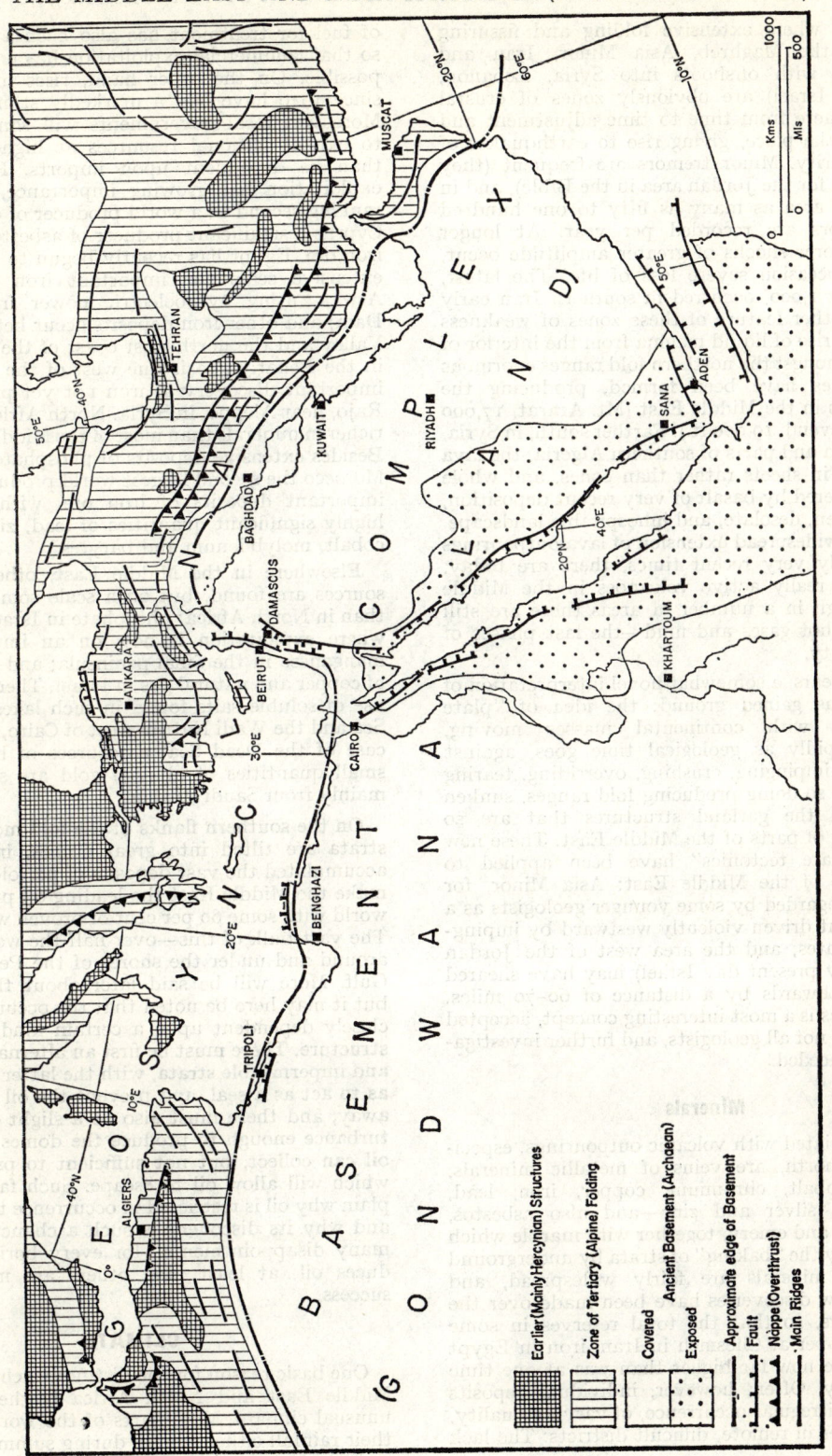

THE MIDDLE EAST AND NORTH AFRICA—(PHYSICAL BACKGROUND)

Sketch of structural elements.

THE MIDDLE EAST AND NORTH AFRICA—(Physical Background)

The areas where extensive folding and fissuring occur (e.g. the Maghreb, Asia Minor, Iran and Afghanistan, with offshoots into Syria, Lebanon, Jordan and Israel) are obviously zones of crustal weakness, where from time to time adjustment and movement take place, giving rise to earthquakes of varying severity. Minor tremors are frequent (they are described for the Jordan area in the Bible), and in the Istanbul area as many as fifty to one hundred minor tremors are recorded per year. At longer intervals severer shocks of greater amplitude occur, causing on occasion severe loss of life. The latest, killing nearly 1,000, occurred in southern Iran early in 1972. Another feature of these zones of weakness has been the rise of liquid magma from the interior of the earth. Amongst the northern fold ranges enormous volcanic cones have been formed, producing the highest peaks in the Middle East (Mt. Ararat, 17,000 ft., Mt. Demavend, 19,000 ft.). Farther south, in Syria, Jordan, Libya and parts of southern Algeria, the lava has emerged in sheets rather than cones, and whole areas are covered by basalt of very recent deposition, giving a barren, desolate, and inhospitable landscape. Despite this widespread extension of lava outpourings in geologically very recent times, there are today, however, no really active volcanoes in the Middle East, although in a number of areas there are still emissions of hot gases and mud—the last phases of igneous activity.

In recent years, a somewhat novel interpretation of conditions has gained ground: the idea of "plate movements", with continental masses moving, relatively rapidly as geological time goes, against one another: impinging, crushing, overriding, tearing apart, and in so doing producing fold ranges, sunken troughs, and the garland structures that are so characteristic of parts of the Middle East. These new ideas of "plate tectonics" have been applied to several areas of the Middle East: Asia Minor, for example, is regarded by some younger geologists as a plate fragment driven violently westward by impinging larger plates; and the area west of the Jordan River (mainly present day Israel) may have sheared laterally southwards by a distance of 60–70 miles. Plate tectonics is a most interesting concept, accepted by many, but not all geologists, and further investigation may be needed.

Minerals

Often associated with volcanic outpourings, especially in the north, are veins of metallic minerals, antimony, cobalt, chromium, copper, iron, lead, molybdenum, silver and zinc—and also asbestos, barytes, coal, and emery, together with marble which is produced by the "baking" of strata by underground heat. These minerals are fairly widespread, and important new discoveries have been made over the last few years, so that the total reserves in some instances (copper at Chesmeh in Iran, iron in Egypt and Syria) are now far higher than was at one time thought likely. Often, however, individual deposits tend to be of irregular occurrence, of varying quality, and sometimes in remote, difficult districts. The lack of fuel for treatment has also been a disadvantage, so that commercial exploitation has not always been possible. On the other hand, rises in world prices since 1940 have had a markedly stimulating effect. Moreover, local governments will sometimes prefer to exploit national resources at higher cost rather than be dependent upon imports. Hence mineral exploitation has growing importance, with Turkey ranking second as a world producer of chromium and Cyprus a significant producer of asbestos, copper and iron ore. Egypt has recently begun to develop on an extensive scale the important iron deposits near Aswan, using hydroelectric power from the High Dam; and other iron deposits occur between the Nile Valley and the north-west coast of the Red Sea, and in the Behariya oasis due west of the Nile. Another important discovery of iron not yet producing is at Rajo, near Aleppo, in Syria. North Africa is distinctly richer in minerals than most of the Middle East proper. Besides extensive deposits of phosphate (which make Morocco the second largest world producer), there are important deposits of iron ore, with smaller, but highly significant quantities of lead, zinc, antimony, cobalt, molybdenum and barytes.

Elsewhere in the Middle East, other mineral resources are found, but on a scale somewhat smaller than in North Africa: phosphate in Israel and Jordan, where exploitation is now on an important scale; manganese in the Sinai peninsula; and small deposits of copper and natural gas in Israel. There is increasing use of soluble salts found in such lakes as the Dead Sea and the Wadi Natrun west of Cairo, chiefly (in the case of the Dead Sea) as sources of bromine. Very small quantities of alluvial gold are still produced, mainly from Saudi Arabia.

On the southern flanks of the fold mountains, rock strata are tilted into great domes, in which have accumulated the vast deposits of petroleum that now make the Middle East the leading oil province in the world with some 60 per cent of proven world reserves. The vast bulk of this—over half the world's oil—lies around and under the shores of the Persian/Arabian Gulf. More will be said later about these deposits, but it may here be noted that the occurrence of oil is closely dependent upon a certain kind of geological structure. There must be first an alternation of porous and impermeable strata, with the latter uppermost so as to act as a seal, and prevent the oil from running away; and there must also be a slight degree of disturbance enough to produce the domes in which the oil can collect, but not sufficient to produce cracks which will allow oil to escape. Such factors can explain why oil is restricted in occurrence to a few zones, and why its discovery is such a chancy affair, with many disappointments—for every boring that produces oil, at least nine others are made without success.

CLIMATE

One basic reason for the distinctive character of the Middle East and North Africa is the special and unusual climate. Most parts of the world experience their rainfall either mostly during summer (the warm season) or distributed throughout the year. Only in a very few areas is there a maximum in winter (the cold season). This is the so-called "Mediterranean" climate, giving a long intensely hot summer, and a relatively mild, rainy winter, with occasional cold spells. The distinction does not seem very important, but it "conditions" plant life to a remarkable degree, and thus also agriculture and general ways of life. Native plants "rest" in the hot season, not in the cold one, which is the opposite to what happens in cooler temperate climates. Some indigenous plants, such as cereals, mature quickly in order to complete a rapid growth cycle before the onset of hot weather; others, chiefly bulbs, flower in spring or autumn; whilst some, such as the citrus, bear fruit in winter. All this has a marked effect on agricultural routines and general living habits. One obvious result is the summer "siesta", which involves breaking the day into two rest periods, with a very early morning start, and continuance of work well into the evening.

Weather conditions are dominated by the long, hot and dry summer, which then quickly gives way to a relatively rainy winter that is mild near the coast but can be surprisingly cold inland. Autumn is warm and sunny, and spring changeable and liable to cold spells —both are short, merely intermediate, seasons. Because of the absence of cloud during summer (away from the coast there can be days without any cloud whatever) the sun beats down uninterruptedly, and the temperatures reached are far higher than those at the Equator. Day maxima of 100° to 115° F. are usual, and a figure of over 125° F. is known. Parts of the interior of Arabia, Algeria, Libya and Iran may experience the highest temperatures occurring in the world.

In winter, though frost is uncommon actually at sea level, the land interior can be cold, especially at higher altitudes. Snow can fall as far south as central Morocco and Algeria, Aswan, the Yemen A.R. and southern Iran, whilst the presence of high mountains has the effect of intensifying winter cold. The plateaux of Turkey and Iran in particular, and to a slightly lesser degree of the Atlas region, experience severe winters, with several months of frost, and up to 120 days of snow cover—a reminder of their geographical position adjacent respectively to Russia and to Spain, which is surprisingly cold in winter. Considerable seasonal change is thus the keynote of Middle Eastern climate, with 40° to 50° F. of temperature range between one part of the year and another (cf. the 26° F. range in London). Wide changes of temperature as between day and night are also characteristic of the interior, but not close to the coast.

The second characteristic of Middle Eastern climate is the scantiness and irregularity of rainfall (*see* pages 8 and 9). Much of the entire region has less than 10 ins. (250 mm.) annually, and this deficiency is intensified by the highly sporadic and irregular nature of the actual fall—for instance, in 1972 Kuwait and parts of the Gulf coast had unprecedented floods that washed away parked cars, whilst the Yemen A.R. in the opposite corner of the Arabian peninsula was just ending seven years of drought. As much as three to four inches have been known to fall in a single day; there can be heavy rain in one locality and none a few kilometres away; and years may go by in some places without any substantial fall. On the other hand, there are a few regions where special circumstances produce annual totals of 30-40 ins. (750-1000 mm.). These are usually upland areas close to large seas— northern Israel and Jordan, the Lebanon and western Syria, south and west Turkey, the north of Iran close to the Caspian Sea, and the higher parts of the North African mountain zones, in Morocco and as far east as northern Tunisia. The extreme south and east of Arabia can, as it were, be "brushed" by the monsoonal current from the Indian Ocean, and thus have a local summer rainfall: parts of the interior of the Yemen A.R., the Yemen P.D.R. and Oman are influenced in this way.

Normally, the winter rains begin in October, with a series of storms (the "Former Rains" of the Bible). Heaviest rain falls during January in the west, and February or March in the east. Towards the end of April there may be a final onset of rain (the "Latter Rains"), and then from June to September no rain whatever falls in the south, and only very small amounts in the north.

Two other phenomena may be mentioned: the occurrence from time to time of hot, and sometimes dust- or sand-laden, winds from desert areas, and the prevalence of high atmospheric humidity near the coasts. The sand winds—known as *Khamsins*, *Simooms* (Iran) *Chehili* (Morocco) or *Ghibli* (Libya)— are unpleasant visitations that can last up to 48 hours, and their main effect, apart from personal inconvenience and mental irritation among humans, is to wither growing crops on a large scale. High humidity, especially in summer, makes living conditions difficult in such areas as the Persian/Arabian Gulf, the Red Sea, and parts of the Lebanon and Asia Minor, so that the wealthier sections of the community try to pass this season in hill stations. Though, as we have seen, the summer is almost rainless, humidity in coastal areas may be highest at the hottest time of the year. One other effect is the intense evaporation from water surfaces, due not only to the high temperatures, but also to the windiness of much of the region, again more pronounced in summer.

The effects of climate are now increasingly mitigated by modern technology. Irrigation and, in a few places, large-scale distillation of sea water allows crops to be grown throughout the summer and new towns to develop. Temperature and humidity difficulties can be reduced by air conditioning, which is spreading rapidly, at least among the better-off classes. Public demand for electricity is now at a peak in summer because of air-conditioning.

Social Geography

The lands of the Middle East occupy a unique geographical position as lying between and linking the three continents of the Old World. We may there-

[*continued on p.* 10

THE MIDDLE EAST AND NORTH AFRICA—(Physical Background)

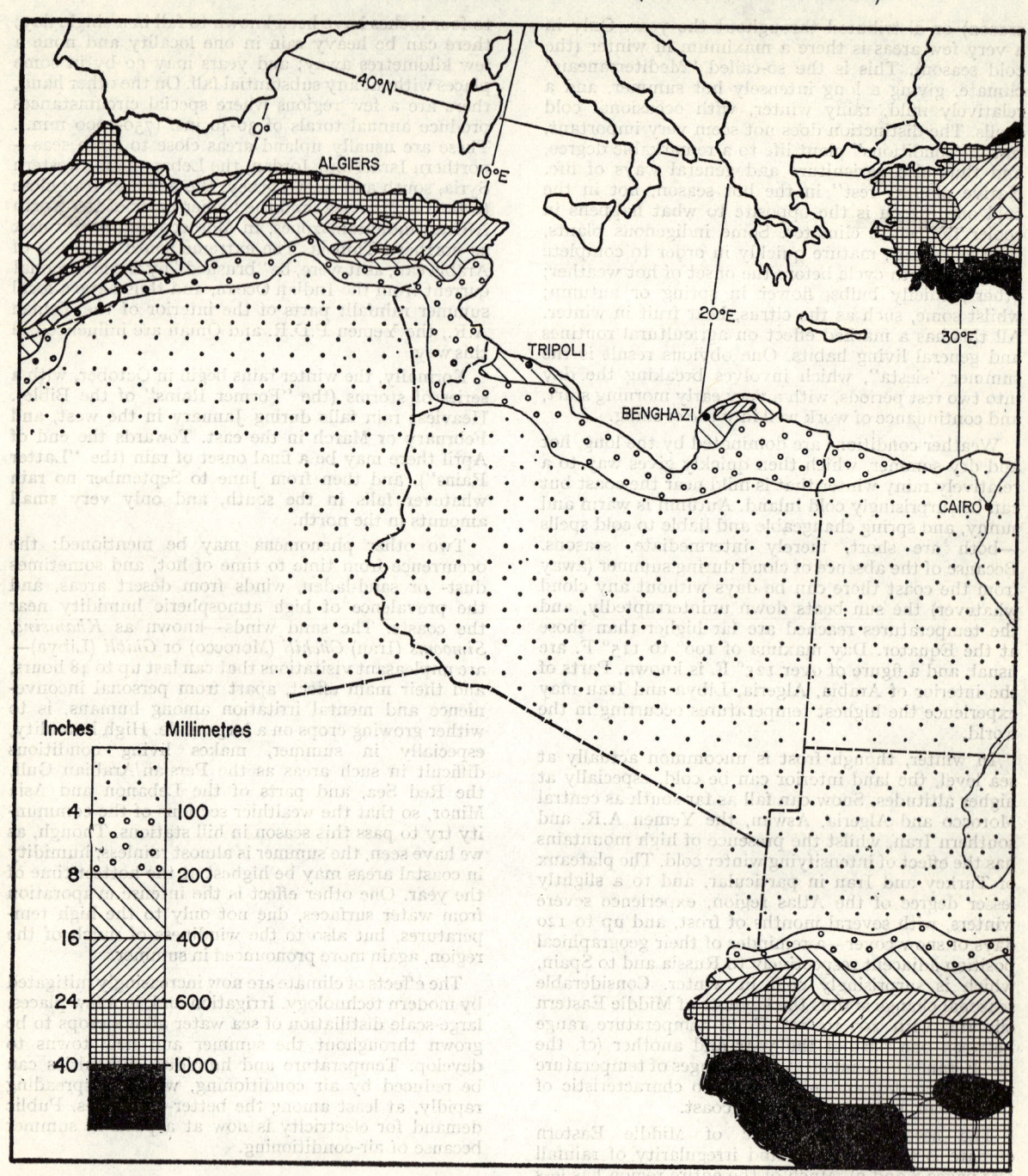

Rainfall: North Africa.

THE MIDDLE EAST AND NORTH AFRICA—(Physical Background)

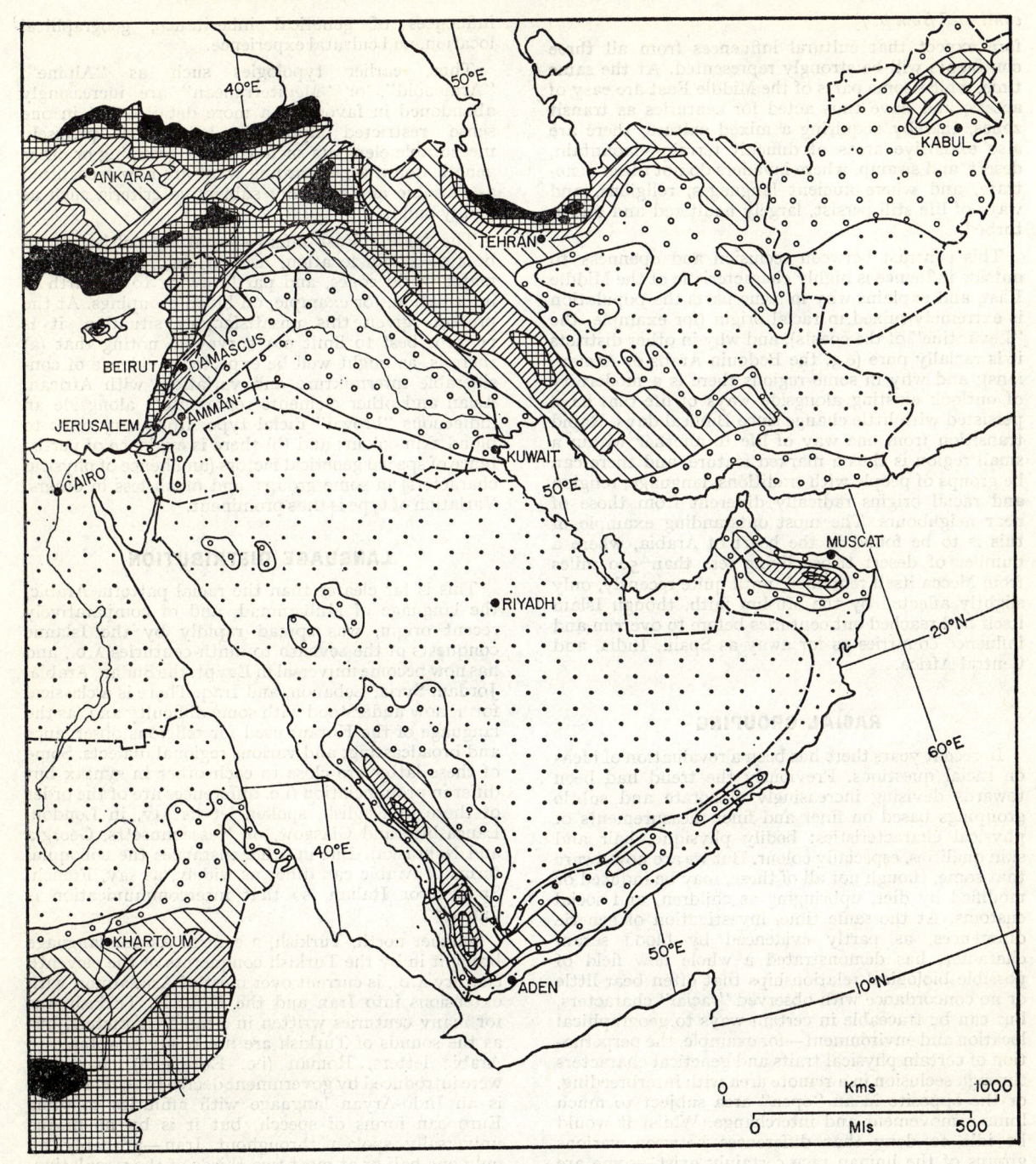

Rainfall: Middle East.

continued from p. 7]

fore expect that cultural influences from all three continents will be strongly represented. At the same time, whilst some parts of the Middle East are easy of access, and have thus acted for centuries as transit zones, thereby acquiring a mixed culture, there are also extensive areas of difficult terrain—mountain, desert, and swamp, where invaders do not often penetrate, and where ancient languages, religions, and ways of life still persist, largely unaltered and undisturbed.

This contrast between seclusion and openness to outside influence is highly characteristic of the Middle East, and explains why in some parts the population is extremely mixed in racial origin (for example, the "Levantine" of the coasts), and why in other districts it is racially pure (e.g. the Bedouin Arabs or Armenians); and why in some regions there is a modernity of outlook existing alongside ways of life that have persisted with little change since Biblical days. Rapid transition from one way of life to another within a small region is thus a marked feature, and there can be groups of people with traditions, language, religion and racial origins radically different from those of near neighbours. The most outstanding example of this is to be found in the heart of Arabia, where a number of desert tribes living less than 500 miles from Mecca itself remained, until quite recently, only slightly affected by the Muslim faith, though Islam itself had reached out centuries before to overrun and influence countries as far away as Spain, India, and Central Africa.

RACIAL GROUPING

In recent years there has been a revaluation of ideas on racial questions. Previously the trend had been towards devising increasingly elaborate and subtle groupings based on finer and finer measurements of physical characteristics: bodily physique, hair and skin qualities, especially colour. But we are now aware that some, though not all of these, may be induced or modified by diet, upbringing as children, and social customs. At the same time, investigation of genetic differences, as partly evidenced by blood serum character, has demonstrated a whole new field of possible biological relationships that often bear little or no concordance with observed "racial" characters, but can be traceable in certain ways to geographical location and environment—for example, the perpetuation of certain physical traits and genetical characters through seclusion in a remote area with interbreeding, or the opposite in an "open" area subject to much human movement and interchange. Whilst it would be idle to deny that differences between various groups of the human race certainly exist—some are darker- or lighter-skinned, or with slight physical and anatomical differences—it would appear far less possible than was once thought to devise meaningful categories of racial groupings. Some authorities now speak only of a very few distinctive groups: "caucasoid" or white, "brown", "yellow" etc., and then distinguish minor variations as arising from the influences of genetical inheritance, geographical location, and cultural experience.

Thus, earlier typologies such as "Alpine", "Armenoid", or "Mediterranean" are increasingly abandoned in favour of a more detailed but in one sense restricted approach based on precisely measurable elements such as blood grouping or other genetic qualities, discarding what are now recognized as variable and partially subjective criteria such as bodily build.

The Middle East offers special difficulties partly because of its location, as just described, between major world zones, and partly owing to a dearth of information, for example, on blood groupings. At the present, given this unsatisfactory situation, it is perhaps best to limit our survey to noting that (a) there is, as might well be expected, evidence of considerable intermixture and variation, with African, Asian and other elements represented, alongside an indigenous "brown" racial type, from very dark to blond skin colour; and (b) there is evidence of persistence of special genetical factors (and hence of physical characters) in some groups, and much less in others. Variation of type is thus prominent.

LANGUAGE DISTRIBUTION

This is far clearer than the racial pattern. Arabic, the language of Muhammad, and of comparatively recent origin, was spread rapidly by the Islamic conquests of the seventh to ninth centuries A.D., and has now become universal in Egypt, the Sudan, Arabia, Jordan, Syria, Lebanon, and Iraq. There is a classical form, now understood with some difficulty and (as the language of the Koran) used for religious observance and broadcasting; and various regional dialects. Some of these latter are close to each other in syntax but differ in pronunciation (i.e. differences are of the order of those in English, spoken let us say, in London, Lancashire and Glasgow, or Massachusetts, Georgia and Nebraska). But in other instances the colloquial forms of Arabic can differ as widely, as say, French, Spanish or Italian, so that intercommunication is difficult.

Farther north, Turkish, a central Asiatic language brought in by the Turkish conquerors of the eleventh century A.D., is current over most of Asia Minor, with extensions into Iran and the U.S.S.R. Turkish was for many centuries written in Arabic characters, but as the sounds of Turkish are not easily adaptable to Arabic letters, Roman (i.e. European) characters were introduced by government decree in 1928. Persian is an Indo-Aryan language with affinities to some European forms of speech, but it is by no means universally spoken throughout Iran—probably by only one-half or at most two-thirds of the population. It is written in Arabic script. A variation known as Dari Persian is spoken in Afghanistan, as is the Pashtu language. The hill country from Asia Minor as far east as the Indian frontier is a mosaic of different dialects spoken by various tribal groups. Some of these dialects are remnants of ancient forms of speech that were once more widely current; some are of fairly recent origin; whilst some show relationships to languages of central and eastern Asia. Aramaic, the language of Palestine at the time of Christ, now persists in a modern and altered form only in a few villages near Damascus and Mosul; Kurdish has a fairly wide extension in the hills from central Turkey as far as south-west Iran; and Armenian, owing to the persecution and dispersal of Armenians from their homeland, is spoken in many large towns. Greek is the chief language of Cyprus. In Israel, Hebrew and Arabic are the two official languages, the former predominating. Berber is dominant in parts of the hill country and adjacent areas of Morocco, Algeria and Tunisia, with a few offshoots into Libya. Prior to invasion by the Arabs in the tenth and eleventh centuries, Berber was the major language in what is now Tripolitania, but it survives today in only a few towns—Aujila, Zuara and Garian.

Language and Educational Problems

Variation of language, as between written and spoken forms of the same dialect and as between families of languages, presents a serious problem at the present time, and is an important factor in the isolation and retarded economic level of several Middle Eastern states. In education, the problem is more complicated, because for a long time practically all modern scientific and technological works were written in English, French, German or Russian, with higher teaching often in the hands of foreigners. To the complication of having several indigenous languages within one country was thus added the difficulty of having higher instruction carried on by foreigners in their own tongue. Thus school and university teaching was frequently enmeshed in the toils of language, and timetables heavily weighted towards language teaching, as an essential preliminary to any other work. Because of the lack of contact, and the smallness of the potential market, which rarely make translation of serious works into Arabic, Turkish or Persian a commercial proposition, only a minority of standard texts from Europe or America could, until very recently, be read in the native languages of the Middle East. This has been a considerable, but not recognized, factor in the cultural and educational separation which has for long existed between the Middle East and other countries. Within the last few years certain governments, notably those of Egypt, Iran and Turkey, have tackled the problem, by sponsoring translation; and UNESCO has also been active in this connection. Another significant change is that with the expansion of general education, there is a greater flow of Middle Easterners abroad, and many of these have now returned as teachers, technicians and officials. In addition, locally trained Arabic-speaking personnel, chiefly Egyptian, but also Palestinian and Syrian Arab, have tended to take up appointments in less developed Arab countries. Thus there is distinctly more general instruction in Arabic as compared with, say, twenty years ago. Nationalist feeling in itself, and the reduced openings for expatriates also foster this tendency. Some universities still use English as the main medium of instruction, but opinion is divided as to whether this should continue. To some observers it appears that fuller use of Arabic will allow more effective teaching; to others, that it will reduce the reading of textbooks (a number of which are available only in a foreign language) and limit yet further the possibility of employing expatriate staff.

NOMADS

With much of the Middle East arid or semi-arid, animal rearing plays an important part in the life of the region, with numerous migratory tribes moving regularly in search of fresh pasture. Though the actual numbers of people who live as pastoral nomads are relatively small and now declining, their way of life is of great significance, and contrasts sharply with that of the townspeople and peasant cultivators. The impact of desert life and ideas upon neighbouring peoples has from time to time been immense, through invasion and destruction, but also in more positive, ways often leading to cultural progress, particularly in the fields of religion and abstract thought. The Old Testament deals continually with the theme of desert against town; and we may also recall the words of T. E. Lawrence that the edge of the desert is littered with the relics of religions and ideas developed from the interaction of nomadic and sedentary ways of life. Many of these movements have perished, but a few have gained strength enough to affect the whole world.

The unit among nomads is the tribe—a group that ensures a certain advantage in numbers, yet is small enough to exist within the limits set by a hard environment. Tribal discipline is strong, and direction is in the hands of a leader whose right to rule is based partly on hereditary descent, and partly on personal merit. This system of rule may to some extent explain the general importance of leaders and persons, rather than principles and party doctrines, in the general political life of the present-day Middle East.

The mobility of the nomads, their predilection for raiding and skirmishing, and their scanty material possessions for long made them difficult subjects for any national government that attempted to impose its rule. An unusually vigorous head of state, such as Reza Shah in Iran, could from time to time successfully break or limit the power of the tribes; but a better policy (followed by the Ottomans, and by several present-day governments) has been to let the nomads go their way, with a minimum of interference. This was the situation until very recently, but the exploitation of oil has been a powerful solvent of ancient custom. Thus many former nomads have found sedentary occupations within oilfields, or in towns, or as semi-settled cultivators using irrigation water paid for or supplied largely by oil revenues. Now, nomadism and tribalism are in rapid decline, and it is the stated policy of certain governments to encourage sedentarization. Nevertheless, something like 7 per cent of the peoples of the area are still predominantly nomadic: about 2–2.5 million in the Sahara, located within Morocco, Algeria, Tunisia and Libya; about 1.5 million in Arabia and in Turkey; under 1 million in Iran; 300,000 in Syria and about the same in Iraq; 30-40,000 in Egypt; 15,000 in Israel; and an uncertain number in the Sudan, some of whom move to escape seasonal floods.

One important feature in the sedentarization of nomads has been land-reform schemes by which plots of agricultural land, sometimes even with houses, have been made over to former pastoral nomads, e.g. in parts of the Nile valley, northern Syria and in north-east Iran; for such schemes to be successful, education in cultivation methods, and the provision of facilities and agricultural credit schemes are essentials.

RELIGIOUS DIVERSITY

Religious divisions are still strong, though now declining, within the Middle East; and for many persons religious and sectarian fidelity even replaces nationality, so that it is frequently possible, on asking an Arab to what country he belongs, to receive the answer, "I am a follower of Islam". A remarkable feature of the area, possibly connected with its geographical function as a meeting-place of peoples and ideas, is that three great religions of the modern world —Judaism, Christianity and Islam—have arisen within its limits; and that others, notably Zoroastrianism (now confined almost entirely to the Parsees of Bombay), Manichaeism, and Mithraism (of great influence in the later Roman Empire) should also be associated with the Middle East. The most recent example is the rise of Baha'i.

Judaism

All three of the modern religions have various branches or sects. Little need be mentioned concerning Judaism, except to note that one of the main social problems of the State of Israel is to absorb Jewish immigrants of widely differing backgrounds and religious traditions. Because of the dispersals of Jews in various continents, there have developed Hebrews of Oriental and African affinities, besides the two European groups of northern (Ashkenazim) and southern (Sephardim) Jews. Since the establishment of the State of Israel divergence of view as to the part religion should play in everyday life, and its general relationship with politics have proved intractable questions in the Israel Parliament, and have led to several Cabinet crises. Because of greater levels of immigration and a generally higher birthrate Israelis of "Oriental" descent now outnumber those of "European" origin.

Christianity

Christianity in the Middle East is even more widely divided. Geographical separation and the development of regional feeling during and after the end of the Roman Empire resulted in the rise of many cults that varied greatly in dogma, ritual and opinion; and despite the efforts of the early Fathers of Christianity, it proved impossible to reconcile all conflicting views, and maintain the unity of Christian peoples. There arose the Greek (or Orthodox) Church; the Roman Catholic Church (called the Latin Church in the Middle East); the Nestorians, who were once widespread from Mesopotamia and Asia Minor as far as India and China; the Armenians (or Gregorians); Copts; Abyssinians; Jacobites (or Syrian followers of Jacob Baradeus); and the Maronites (adherents of St. John Maroun). All of these sects came in time to possess complete autonomy, but following the rise of Islam in the seventh century A.D. the fortunes of many of them declined. Numbers of Armenians, Copts, Greeks, Jacobites, Nestorians and others (and the entire Maronite Church) were driven to accept aid from Rome, but at the price of recognizing the Pope as their titular Head. Thus we have what are termed the Uniate Churches—Armenian, Coptic, Nestorian Catholics, etc.—which further reduced the strength of the older autonomous groups, most of which managed to continue, though no longer of great importance. At present, therefore, we have more than twenty separate Christian sects, some powerful and world wide, others purely local in allegiance. The appearance of Protestant missionaries in the nineteenth century and after has added further to the religious bodies represented, although the number of converts is small.

Islam

Division in Islam began on the death of Muhammad. As the prophet designated no successor, most followers agreed that leadership of Islam could pass from any individual to another, according to merit and circumstance. This group came to be known as the *Sunni*, or Orthodox, and numbers about 90 per cent of all Muslims. A minority supported the claims of the next male relative of Muhammad, and these Muslims took the name of *Shi'a*, or Party. Shi'a adherents are strongest in Iran and the Yemen Arab Republic; in southern Iraq, where they form a large minority of the inhabitants; and as minorities in Syria, the Lebanon, and Turkey. Many sub-sects of the Shi'a are known, representing different forms of belief; and one such group was for a time a warlike military order, with much power in Syria and Iran. Its head was finally forced to take refuge in India, where his direct descendant is today the Aga Khan. Groups of his followers still remain in Iran and Syria. Many Muslims believe that there will one day arise a Mahdi (Messiah) who will conquer the world for Islam, and this circumstance has led to the appearance at various times of leaders who have claimed to be the long-awaited incarnation—for example, the Mahdi in the Sudan in the late nineteenth century.

The revival during the present century of Wahhabi power may briefly be noticed. The Wahhabis, by reason of their dislike of ostentation in religious observance, and their desire to revive the earlier, simpler tenets of the Faith, have been termed the Puritans of Islam. Under the vigorous and skilled leadership of their late head, King Ibn Saud of Arabia, they rose from obscurity as a desert people to control of most of the Arabian peninsula, and hence domination of the holy cities of Mecca and Medina. One factor in the present Arab disunity is the division on general religious grounds between the Wahhabis, who tend to despise the Muslims of Egypt, Jordan and Syria as lax in observance, and as backsliders in the

Faith, and who are in turn criticized as primitive reactionaries. There have also been acute personal differences involving King Ibn Saud, who in conquering Mecca displaced the former ruler, Sharif Husain, a direct descendant of the Prophet. A descendant of the former Sharif rules in Jordan (as also until 1958 in Iraq), hence something of the animosity displayed between Saudi Arabia and its northern neighbours owed its origin to personal feuds.

Political Complications

There are other questions of a general political nature that stem from religious differences within the Middle East. The willingness of outside nations to support various religious groups in their struggle against each other has from time to time led to large-scale intervention. France has championed the cause of the Latin and Uniate Churches, basing many of her claims to influence and territory within Syria and the Lebanon on her long connection with the Uniates, who form the largest single sect in the latter country.

Russia, under Tsarist and Soviet rule alike, has maintained a link with the Orthodox Church, and from time to time Russian bishops visit Jerusalem, where the larger part of Christian shrines are owned by the Orthodox Church. Within the last few years Russia has strongly supported, by means of legal and diplomatic action, Orthodox claims to ownership of property and privileges; and whatever the position within the U.S.S.R., Soviet policy is firmly directed to maintaining the rights and position of the Orthodox Christians within the Middle East. Because of its territorial ownership within Old Jerusalem, Russia could in some respects make a good case for trusteeship of the Christian Holy Places. Britain, rather curiously, has at times supported Muslim groups—sometimes orthodox, sometimes dissident. American interest, though of long standing (as much as a century in one or two localities) has generally been much less direct, but over the last ten to fifteen years has greatly expanded. There are now within the Middle East a number of American educational institutions of great influence and standing (for example, the American University of Beirut and the American Colleges of Istanbul). Most of these were founded as Protestant missionary activities, but have since developed into secular institutions covering a wide range of subjects.

One final effect of religious differences may be noted. With the possibilities of appeal to outside assistance, and the internal vigorousness of religious feeling, it has happened that a political *modus vivendi* can be achieved only by a distribution of offices and appointments among the interested religious sects. Thus the Maronites of the Lebanon have in practice the right of nominating the President of the Republic, and a close public eye is kept on the relative number of Muslim and Christian appointments; whilst in Iraq Sunni Muslims, at least until 1958, had a major influence in Cabinet policy, though the majority of the population is Shi'a in adherence.

It is, however, necessary to state that the pattern of religious life in the Middle East is at the present time rapidly altering. Among many, there is a decline of religious belief, with the growth of a secular and materialist outlook in its place—a phenomenon also prominent in contemporary Europe. Also it is true to say that an opposite tendency prevails in certain groups. Religious brotherhoods of an extremist character, dedicated to subversion and fanaticism have come into prominence over the last few years, and a number of these—the *Ikhwan* of Egypt, *Fidaiyai* of Iran, and *Tijaniya* of Turkey—exert growing political influence. At the same time, however, the traditionally close relationship of religion and politics is tending slowly to change in character, with secular nationalism becoming more and more a feature.

CITY LIFE IN THE MIDDLE EAST

From very early times, long before Plato commended the city-state as an ideal form of political organization, town life has exercised a predominant influence in lands of the Mediterranean; and this predominance, amounting to a marked disproportion, has been particularly characteristic of the Middle East. Here, towns stand out as islands of relative wealth, culture and progress in a poor and backward countryside; and it is significant that the two centres that dispute the title of the oldest, continuously inhabited site in the world are Damascus and Aleppo, whilst the oldest undoubted port is Byblos (modern Jbeil, 20 miles north of Beirut), which from its trade in papyrus gave us the word Bible.

There have been several contributing factors in the precocious growth of Middle Eastern cities. Firstly, because of a wide variety in geographical environment —rich oasis or coastal plain, mountain, desert, steppe and forest—there soon arose a diversity of economic production, and hence a need for exchange and market centres. Then too, with frequent warfare and invasion, defence became a necessity, and strong points on mounds or peaks, commanding corridors, defiles and river passages soon developed and gathered around them a township. Examples of former simple tribal strongholds that have evolved into great cities are Aleppo, Ankara, Jerusalem, Mosul and Tabriz, the third city of Iran. Another feature of the Middle East is the number of "planted" towns—sites deliberately planned or designated to be important. Of this nature is Teheran, which before it was chosen as a new capital by the Qajar rulers in 1788 had few functions other than that of a wintering spot for pastoral nomads. Amman was largely uninhabited for several centuries previous to 1880, though the site (Philadelphia) had held importance in Roman times; and there are other towns whose origins can be clearly traced to planned development in early Arab, Roman or Classical Greek times. Alexander the Great, and especially his successors, fostered many new towns and extended others.

The City in Conquest

It is a feature of Middle Eastern history that, time and time again, small but energetic groups of people seized power, and for a limited period ruled a large territory. The Hyksos Kings of Egypt, the Medes, Assyrians, Macedonian Greeks, Romans, Arabs, and Ottomans can all be cited as examples; and for each conqueror there soon arose the acute problem of maintaining a hold on defeated but numerically superior subject races, and of spreading the language, religion and traditions of the minority ruling group.

Most conquerors found that it was usually easier to dominate the cities, partly for the reason that military operations could be undertaken with more success against the inhabitants of a closely packed town, rather than against the nomads or peasants of trackless steppes, deserts, or mountains; partly because the towns with their trade could easily be taxed to support military rule; and partly because the population of the cities, polyglot in origin and in touch with outside conditions, could be more often induced to accept a new idea, a new language, or even a new religion. It is no accident that the great evangelical religions of the modern world should have extended from towns—that men first called themselves Christians in Antioch, or that Muhammad could feel that his cause had succeeded when Mecca and Medina acknowledged his rule, or that Jewish ritual should include the phrase "Next year in Jerusalem". We also have the curious position that the towns of the Middle East may often be strikingly different in wealth, in outlook and even in language and religion, as compared with the immediately surrounding countryside. The most famous example may be cited from the New Testament, as when the inscription on the Cross of Christ indicated the presence of a Latin-speaking ruling class, a Greek-speaking town and professional class, and an Aramaic-speaking peasantry. Such contrasts are apparent even today, though, of course, involving different languages.

Economic and Political Dominance

Another feature of Middle Eastern cities is their economic dominance, amounting almost to a stranglehold, in the life of each country. Town merchants are in touch with world markets and can control or "corner" the produce of the rural areas in their own district, for which, owing to the difficulties of transport, they are the only outlet. The strength of the merchants is indicated by the fact that in many Middle Eastern countries there is relatively little, or even in a few instances no, direct taxation, most governmental revenue being raised by indirect imposts.

We also find that in many cities there is an important community of wealthy absentee landlords. Unlike that of Europe, the Middle Eastern countryside offers few amenities—rather is it a stronghold of poverty, discomfort and disease. Hence landowners tend to remain most of the time in the towns, and visit their estates only rarely, sometimes merely to collect the rents, for which, occasionally, an armed guard may be necessary. The same can be said of religious communities, Christian and Muslim, many of which possess landed estates, or which actually control the exploitation of land by tenant farmers. In either case, there is a general flow of money, derived from the country, but spent in the towns, and this provides a living not only for the wealthy, but for artisans, domestic servants, and shopkeepers.

Another feature of town life in the Middle East until recently was the absence, or relatively slight development, of traditions of civic government and responsibility. There was little to parallel the growth of the burgher class that became so prominent in parts of Europe, and hence less of a corporate pride and pattern of local, as distinct from provincial or national, interest in problems of rule. The situation is changing markedly in some localities; but the absence of a bourgeois outlook (in its best sense) is still a feature.

Lastly, it is interesting to observe that towns have long tended to dominate Middle Eastern political life. The lure of greater wealth attracts the energetic, dissatisfied, and sometimes turbulent elements from the countryside. Many such immigrants, together with the occupants of city slums who become periodically unemployed because of trade slumps, and also a third element, inexperienced secondary school and university students, form a very dangerous combination—the Middle Eastern city mob. Mob violence, awakened at first over a political matter, sometimes assumes a religious complexion directed against minorities and foreigners, and among the demonstrators are often groups with few political or religious convictions, but whose aim is to spread disorder so that shops can be broken open and looted. Most Middle Eastern shops in the cities carry iron shutters that can cover the whole of the shop-front at the slightest sign of trouble. A restless, underfed proletariat, excited by political and religious issues, and inflamed by student agitators, can be very menacing in close, narrow streets. Even politicians themselves may ultimately go in fear of the tide of disorder that they themselves have had a hand in provoking. Over and over again in Middle Eastern affairs, demonstrators in the streets have swayed or brought about a total change of government; and, as in 1951 (Egypt), 1956 (the Lebanon), 1958 (Iraq), 1960 (Turkey) and 1963 (Iraq, Syria and Jordan), the dilemma of Pontius Pilate—how far to give way to turbulence in the streets—arises in an acute form at unhappily frequent intervals. The swift explosion of anti-American and anti-British feeling, expressed through mob violence in centres as far apart as Kuwait, Benghazi and Tunis, was a feature of June 1967.

Urban Growth

A further considerable problem now arises from the exceedingly rapid physical growth of a few urban centres. Cairo, with a population now over four million, is not only the capital of Egypt but the largest town of the Mediterranean area and by far the largest city in Africa. "Greater" Teheran is now over two million in population, and Baghdad with its suburbs is approaching that figure. Beirut and Casablanca with their suburbs are near or beyond the one million mark. Algiers has about one million; about one-quarter of the country's population live in Tunis. This rapid and accelerating growth—placed at six to ten per cent per annum for many large towns—is leading to a concentration of economic power, political influence, and social prestige which poses acute problems of two kinds. Besides the difficulties of providing adequate amenities and methods of administration—the demand for electricity in Beirut is doubling at present every five years, and the traffic problems are monumental—there is also a retrogression of provincial life, with stagnation in more distant parts. The problems associated with the "drift to London" in Britain are repeated in another form in parts of the Middle East.

Economic Geography

By far the greater part of the land surface in the Middle East is either mountain, desert, or swamp, and cultivated areas are extremely small in extent, covering no more than 5 to $7\frac{1}{2}$ per cent of the total area. Nevertheless, agriculture is the main occupation of a large majority of the inhabitants; and a further proportion of the people is employed in processing the products of agriculture, as cotton and tobacco packers, fruit driers, or canners of fruit, vegetables, and olive oil. It is obvious therefore, that the remaining activities in the Middle East are of relatively restricted extent. Pastoral nomadism is found in many districts, as the only possible way of life in an arid or mountainous environment; but few people are involved, and the nomads live mainly a self-sufficient existence, so that their contribution to general economic activity is greatly limited. Despite the fact that a substantial majority of Middle East populations live by agriculture or pastoralism, the total contribution of these two activities to Gross National Product is often well under 50 per cent.

AGRICULTURE
Cereals

The chief food crops grown in the Middle East are wheat, barley and rye in the north, and millet, maize and rice in the south. Wheat, the chief crop of Turkey, Syria, the Lebanon, Jordan, Israel, Algeria and Tunisia, is of the hard variety, planted in autumn, and harvested in late spring or early summer. The use of Mexican strains of high-yielding wheat has spread over the past few years, with good, sometimes dramatic, results. Barley is more important than wheat in Libya, Iraq, Morocco and parts of Iran, since it is hardier and more resistant to insects. Rye (with some oats) is restricted to the colder and hillier parts of Turkey and Iran, whilst rice though much prized as a luxury, and also for its very high yield per unit of farm land, needs much heat and abundant water, and is grown only in a few specially fertile and favoured localities—Lower Egypt, southern Iraq, the valleys of southern Turkey, and a few parts of North Africa, especially Morocco. In some countries, because of its demands on irrigation water, and its tendency to spread malaria (owing to the flooded ground), the cultivation of rice is limited by law. Maize is the chief cereal in Egypt, and its cultivation is also being greatly extended in Israel. Farther south, towards Arabia and the Sudan, millets of various species become of increasing importance.

Cotton and Tobacco

In addition to these food crops, which, except for barley, are mostly of indifferent quality and are grown for home consumption only, there is increasing emphasis on cash crops, as communications develop and an export market can be found. Some of the finest cotton in the world is grown in Egypt, where about 20 per cent of the agricultural land is given over to its production, and four-fifths of the total exports are in the form of raw cotton. The same crop is also a chief export of the Sudan. Elsewhere, quality is much lower, but cultivation is spreading, especially in the Seyhan plain of southern Turkey around Adana, in the Aleppo and Jezireh districts of Syria, and in parts of Iran.

Production of tobacco, introduced into the Middle East during the sixteenth century, is considerable, mainly in the Black Sea and Aegean coastlands of Turkey, and in Cyprus. Pure Turkish tobacco is no longer in favour among British and American smokers, but most "Virginian" cigarette and pipe tobaccos contain a small admixture of Turkish leaf; and Central Europe still prefers the unmixed Turkish variety. Many Arab farmers grow small quantities for their own use, but here quality is generally low, except in the district of Latakia, from which there is some export.

Fruit

The Middle East has an extremely wide variety of fruit. Vines are found both wild and cultivated, and besides their use in Turkey and Cyprus for currants and sultanas, much local wine is made, the best probably coming from Cyprus, the Lebanon and Israel. North Africa is especially favourable for wine-growing, which immigrants from France did much to foster. As a result, quantities of *vin ordinaire* are sold abroad, to France especially, where the local product had to some extent been superseded by the cheaper Algerian wine, until pressure from domestic growers forced the government to reduce imports. The U.S.S.R. has recently become a large-scale importer.

Citrus fruits are of increasing importance along the north-eastern Mediterranean coast, whilst apricots, figs, peaches and plums are widespread. Olives form a very important part of Middle Eastern diet, since animal fats are scarce, and the poorer fraction of the oil also serves as a domestic illuminant and for soap-making. Other products of some importance are hazel nuts, liquorice, and dates.

Dates are a principal article of food in the arid areas of the south—Arabia, southern Iran, and parts of the Sudan. In addition, there is export on a large scale from the Basra district of southern Iraq, which produces 80 per cent of the world's supply. Nearness to the sea, allowing cheap transport by water, gives Basra a considerable advantage over its competitors in North Africa—though it must also be stated that Algerian dates, and especially those from Biskra, are superior in quality to those from Iraq. Mention must also be made of bananas, citrus fruit and apples, the importance of which has greatly increased in the last few years following expansion of export markets, and demands from the oilfields. In contrast to the "soft"

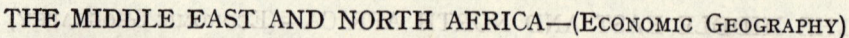

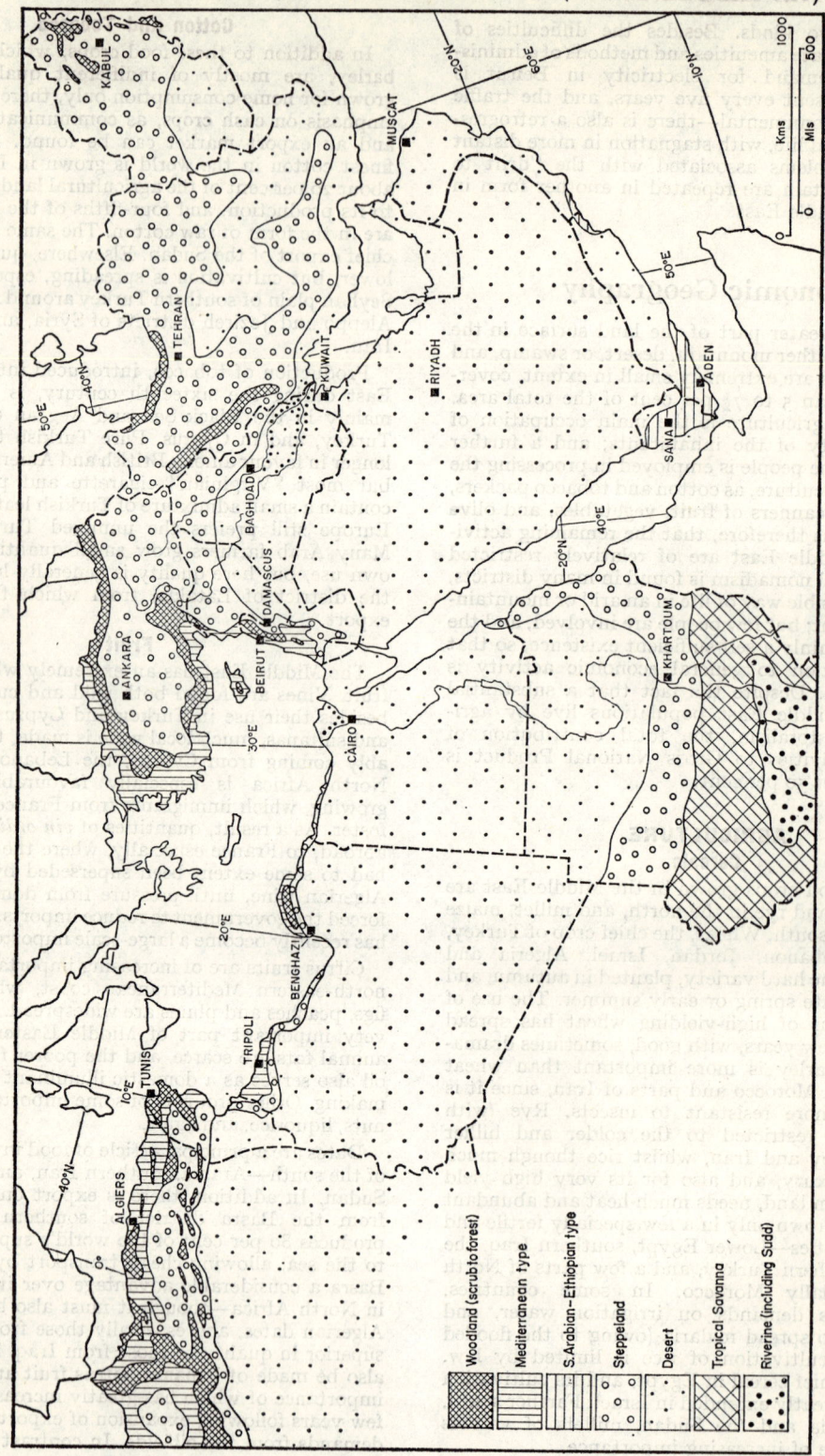

THE MIDDLE EAST AND NORTH AFRICA—(ECONOMIC GEOGRAPHY)

Natural vegetation.

Woodland (scrub to forest)
Mediterranean type
S. Arabian – Ethiopian type
Steppeland
Desert
Tropical Savanna
Riverine (including Sudd)

fruits already discussed, the three latter types of fruit can be more easily transported without damage, and are also less likely to be carriers of human disease. A feature of the last few years also has been considerable development of market gardening (fruit and vegetables) near larger towns.

Narcotics

Finally, reference may be made to the cultivation of narcotics—opium and hashish—the first of which is the source of morphine and heroin; and also of qat, which has a very local market. There is a legal and strictly controlled world trade in morphine, and about one-half of the legal supplies come from Turkey; but in addition, quantities above the legal maximum are grown illicitly in the Lebanon, Syria, and Iran, since prices are very high, and supervision lax. There is consequently much temptation in the way of a poor peasant farmer to grow a few plants for sale to the illicit buyer. Qat is grown only on the hill slopes of south-west Arabia, in the Yemen A.R. and near Aden, and when chewed induces a feeling of euphoria. It can only be used fresh, so for long its consumption was closely limited to the environs of where it could be grown. But now, air transport has allowed wider markets, reaching as far as East Africa, and cultivation has increased. Opinion is divided as to the dangers of qat—some hold that it can be regarded as no more than a harmless addiction, whilst others believe it to be a dangerous drug. At one time the Government of Aden prohibited its production and sale.

YIELDS AND LEVELS OF PRODUCTION

In general, though with some conspicuous exceptions, the level of production, and quality of crops are low. It has been reckoned that the Middle Eastern farmer is only one-eighth to one-quarter as efficient a producer as his counterparts in Western Europe or the U.S.A.; and many parts of the Middle East, despite an overwhelming emphasis on cultivation and self-subsistence, are among the poorest fed in the world.

The reasons for this low level of agricultural productivity are complex. In the first place, there are the obvious handicaps of heat and aridity, together with the resulting effects of this climatic régime upon soil character. Many Middle Eastern soils are lacking in humus; and another difficulty is that when watered copiously by artificial means (e.g. by irrigation) certain soils that would appear to be capable of bearing heavy crops can turn saline and sterile. This is at present a problem in the Nile Delta, where heavy irrigation is tending to induce soil salinity; and a number of large irrigation schemes, notably round Konya in Anatolia, and along the Karun River of south-west Iran, have failed to achieve success for the same reason. In 1949 it was estimated that for the whole of Iraq some 60 per cent of all irrigated land had become salinated to a certain degree; and that about 1 per cent of area is abandoned each year. Relatively little would appear to have been done to alter this general situation; though the development of the Wadi Tharthar drainage scheme could have some effect when it is fully in operation. The Tigris and Euphrates carry double the quantity of salts near their mouth as compared with upstream above Baghdad. The best remedy is to have extensive underground drains in the fields, to prevent accumulation of excess water. This is, however, expensive and adds greatly to the overall cost of irrigation schemes.

Another limiting factor is the unusually high soil temperature during summer—of the order of 130° to 180° F., which has the effect of destroying organic material within the soil itself, and of preventing the efficient use of fertilizers. There is a fundamental problem, as yet not solved, of maintaining soil fertility by artificial means, because the techniques successful in wetter and colder parts of the world do not always answer in the Middle East.

Pests and Diseases

One other source of agricultural loss occurs in the pests and diseases that affect both plants and man. As much as 60 per cent of a year's crops may be destroyed by locusts, which breed in the deserts of Arabia, Africa and Somalia, and move as swarms into cultivated areas. In Iraq and Iran the much smaller *sunna* fly causes periodic devastation—one reason for the emphasis on barley growing is that it ripens faster, and hence can be harvested before the arrival of the *sunna* insect in late summer. Scale diseases, rusts, and mildew are other handicaps. An encouraging feature is the expansion of activity on an international scale directed towards locust control. Faced with growing annual losses, Middle Eastern governments are now co-operating not only with neighbours but also with such organizations as FAO and UNESCO in preventive measures.

Equally severe, if not actually more damaging, are the diseases of man himself. In Egypt, rates of incidence of serious maladies were not long ago up to 70-75 per cent of the whole population, and there are still a few areas in districts of Iraq, Turkey, the Sudan and the Yemen A.R. where malaria affects over half the population. Plague was endemic, whilst Turkey, owing to its colder winter climate, has long been a stronghold of tuberculosis. Eye diseases, chiefly trachoma, are rife, and in some areas produce blindness in up to 20 per cent of the population. Smallpox, typhoid and venereal diseases are still prevalent, and from time to time there are outbreaks of cholera, sometimes minimized or "played down" by local governments. The Sudan has a particularly poor level of public health, especially in the south, where diseases are not only endemic but spread easily from tropical Africa. The riverine areas of Egypt and Iraq are particularly notorious for parasitic infections—ankylostomiasis, bilharzia and hookworm—which, most unfortunately, tend to spread with the expansion of irrigation. Dysentery (usually of a relatively mild form) is an almost ubiquitous feature, especially affecting newcomers. Despite this depressing list, it is also true to say that very considerable changes have been brought about in many areas by better public health measures—control of insect and animal disease vectors, provision of cleaner drinking water, and improved medical care. In a few regions (e.g.

Kuwait) hospital services are among the best in the world. Thus incidence of many diseases, especially in towns, has shown a marked drop over the past decade.

The high incidence of disease has been, and still partly remains, an important contributing factor in the low level of agricultural efficiency, since it reduces the peasant's physical capacity for sustained work, and also dulls his mental faculties, thus making it more difficult to introduce better methods and new ideas. Many Middle Easterners possess the minimum of physical strength that will just suffice to carry them through a moderate day's routine, and there arises a vicious circle—the peasant is diseased and cannot work hard; his yield is therefore precarious, and he is hence the victim of frequent malnutrition, which makes him the more susceptible to disease. Malaria alone has been cited as a principal cause of backwardness in many areas of the Middle East at present; and it would also appear that the decay of the once brilliant Arab civilization can be attributed in part to the spread of the disease.

It must, however, be noted that successful measures have been taken in most, though not all, areas to reduce or eradicate the malarial mosquito, and conspicuous, though uneven, improvements in public health have resulted. Twenty years ago, mosquito nets were always provided in the better hotels of most cities; now they are hardly to be seen.

Land Tenure

Yet more factors in agricultural backwardness are the methods of land holding and forms of tenancy. Full ownership, with the possibility of applying long-term methods of improvement, is not frequent among Middle Eastern farmers. Instead, there are various forms of share-cropping or tribal ownership, which collectively tend to perpetuate old, wasteful methods, to emphasize conservatism in outlook, and to make it extremely difficult for an individual to introduce any innovation. Holdings are often small and scattered, so that modern ploughs, tractors, or reaping machinery cannot easily be introduced; and owing to extremely high rents and dues, amounting in some instances to 65 per cent of the total yield of the holding, the peasant farmer is entirely lacking in capital for improvements, and remains dependent on his landlord for seed and even implements. Land-reform schemes now in progress in several countries, notably Iran, Iraq, Syria and Egypt, are altering this picture, but they do not affect all areas. When they do become more widespread there is a risk that production will decline initially, owing to the lack of capital and knowledge of new techniques of the new owners.

A further feature of Middle Eastern farming has been the existence of numerous absentee landlords, who invest money in land purely as a safe outlet for surplus capital, and have no real interest in farming itself. Such owners live mainly in the towns, and delegate control of their agricultural estates to overseers, being satisfied if the same level of production is maintained from one year to another. Such owners are not often willing to sink capital in new methods or machines, but are content to perpetuate existing methods. Because of the lack of outlet for investment in most Middle Eastern countries—movable property may be stolen, paper securities may be repudiated, and foreign currency, particularly the franc, lira, and pound sterling have depreciated—real property represents a fairly safe long-term investment that cannot easily depreciate.

In recent years, many Middle Eastern governments have made attempts to improve the position by redistribution of holdings, and enactments limiting the total area of land held by one individual. This has had some good effect, but in some cases the laws have been loosely applied, or even remained a dead-letter; and ways of ignoring or circumventing them have further reduced their efficiency. Extensive handing over of Crown land to peasant ownership in Iran, followed by the redistribution to peasant ownership on a national scale of all large estates, and the organization of Liberation Province in Egypt, mainly from expropriated and irrigated land, are outstanding but by no means the only large-scale examples of reallocation of big estates, which has also been energetically pursued in Iraq. In Iran, the process has been so fully pursued as to invite the description "White Revolution".

It is also necessary to state that despite all the handicaps noted above considerable progress has been achieved in certain areas of the Middle East. In parts of the Nile Valley, yields per acre of one or two crops are among the highest in the world; and in Israel a remarkable development of mixed farming, based on cereals, vegetables and animal husbandry, has transformed conditions in many areas. Much the same could be said of parts of Cyprus, Syria and Lebanon. The influence of French and Italian settlers in North Africa and Libya respectively was to demonstrate what might be done to improve yields and methods. Iran and Turkey, too, have experienced considerable agricultural development in certain directions over the last twenty to thirty years. Such ameliorations stand, however, in sharp contrast to conditions elsewhere in the Middle East.

INDUSTRIAL ACTIVITIES

In medieval times Middle Eastern industrial products had a high reputation. Steelwork, silverware, pottery, leather, and above all, textiles (from Damascus and Mosul, giving the words damask and muslin) found their way into many parts of Europe. At the present time, however, the scale of Middle Eastern industries is small; lack of fuel (particularly of coal and hydro-electric power), scarcity of mineral ores and some other raw materials, and the poverty of local markets being severe limiting factors. There is only one coalfield of any great importance—this is in north-west Turkey, at Ereğli (Heraclea), and production is only 4–5 million tons per annum; whilst very much smaller amounts are produced from fields in the region of Teheran.

In recent years a significant degree of industrial development has, however, taken place in Egypt, Turkey, Israel and Iran, with some industry on a smaller scale in Iraq, the Lebanon and Syria. Some industrial activity, on a smaller scale, and related chiefly to production of building materials, processing of agricultural produce, or the limited treatment of mineral ores for export, has developed in North Africa. Textiles—chiefly cotton, but also silk, wool and mohair—are important, together with the transformation of agricultural products (sugar, tobacco, fruit processing and distilling) and the making of cement and bricks, for which there is a considerable local demand.

A further feature has been the growth of light consumer industries. Acute shortages during the Second World War impelled many Middle Eastern governments to try to develop local manufactures, even where local conditions were not outstandingly favourable; and over the last fifteen years there has been a marked growth of new power stations, factories and mills (detailed instances of which can be found in the economic surveys of the individual countries). Heavy capital goods such as machinery and vehicles are still imported on a large scale, though there are now assembly plants for motors and electrical machinery in Turkey, Iran, Israel and Egypt, with plans for similar plants, e.g. in the Lebanon, Syria and Iraq. Since 1960, however, there have been the beginnings of local manufacture of motors (in Egypt, Iran and Israel) and other machinery. Industrial expansion is marked in Egypt, Israel, Turkey, the Lebanon and Iran, and especially in the first two; and the last few years have seen the start of petro-chemical industries in Egypt, Israel, Kuwait and Iraq, based on local supplies of oil. In many places, however, restricted size of the potential market, and competition of foreign produced goods (it is cheaper to import Indian cement, for instance, in parts of the Oman Gulf) inhibit industrial development on a large scale.

PETROLEUM RESOURCES

The general geological factors involved in the occurrence of petroleum have already been touched on; but it remains to add that there are a number of features special to the Middle East. Exploration has been retarded by the presence of what may be described as misleading surface structures—in some places, the possibility of finding oil was at first entirely discounted (as in Saudi Arabia); whilst in others, leakages of oil to the surface have given rise to optimism that has not always been justified. Moreover, the oilfields are often of extraordinarily large size, and the oil is held under considerable pressure, so that very few wells need be sunk to tap a large area, and the crude oil often rises of itself without much pumping—factors that allow an unusually low cost of production. The open nature of the country, as compared with the jungle of the East Indies, and the mangrove swamps of Venezuela, has been another favourable circumstance. Hence the cost of production of Middle Eastern oil is distinctly lower than that of oil from the U.S.A., the Caribbean, and from South-east Asia, both in terms of actual production costs and in terms of capital investment. As the selling price of most oil is based on American costs, this disparity in costs has meant a higher rate of profit on Middle East oil for the exploiting companies. (Petroleum development is dealt with in more detail in a later chapter).

One important factor in oilfield development has been the utility of pipelines. Broadly speaking, as compared with sea transport via the Cape, or, before 1967, the Suez Canal, a pipeline can move oil more cheaply from the Persian Gulf to the Mediterranean, and hence countries through which pipelines pass have been able to exact substantial royalties and other payments. Increasing demands of this nature (together with political troubles) have led to suggestions of developing alternative routes (e.g. through Turkey), events since 1956 having demonstrated the vulnerability of European consumers dependent on a single pipeline route. Use of larger tankers has, however, diminished the margin of profitability in using pipelines, and in 1972 the Iraq Petroleum Co. stated that it had become commercially cheaper to exploit fields closer to the Persian Gulf and export via the Cape, rather than move oil from the northern fields by pipeline to the Mediterranean.

Present-Day Problems

In the context of a rapid survey, it is possible to do no more than hint at a few acute issues which exert a profound influence on current trends in the Middle East. These issues may be summarized as population pressure, the question of finding a reasonably equitable basis for the distribution of wealth between social classes, political leadership, and the cultural crisis within Islam.

POPULATION PRESSURE

The population problem arises as the result of a high birth-rate, together with a fairly high death-rate which is now in some parts declining rapidly, as the result of improvements in public health. There is, in consequence, an increasing number of survivors, producing a population growth of the order of 3 per cent annually in Turkey, and 2.7 per cent in Egypt (cf. 0.3 per cent in England and Wales). Between 1900 and 1970 the population of Turkey grew from approximately 9 million to 36 million, producing an annual increase now of just under one million. Even an increase of 2 per cent per annum in population can, if unchecked, lead to a doubling of numbers in less than forty years. So long as food supplies can be increased at a commensurate rate, either by farming within the country, or by an expansion of industry and commerce that can pay for imported food, the position is without danger; but it is in fact difficult to maintain a continuous improvement in agriculture and industry of 2 per cent per annum, particularly under Middle Eastern conditions. Hence, there are signs of severe pressure of numbers on resources—in a few parts of the Nile Valley there are now over 6,000 persons per square mile living by agriculture—with a resulting decline in standards of living. As regards Turkey, FAO has said that the situation calls for a "truly heroic" agricultural programme, and that "many farm animals are so seriously underfed that it is surprising they stay alive". Another economist suggests that the production of foodstuffs has actually fallen within Egypt during the last thirty years, despite a growth in population numbers. Under such conditions it is not difficult to suggest a possible relationship between the current demographic situation of an underemployed, underfed but increasing proletariat, and the disturbed political conditions of many parts of the Middle East.

EXTREMES OF WEALTH

A second group of problems arises from the social inequality that is a feature of many Middle Eastern countries. There is the large mass of the poor, and a small number of wealthy families, with few of a "middle" class. At present it is fair to say that the gap between the groups is widening rather than closing, as the standard of living of the poor remains the same, or even falls, and that of the rich rises rapidly, owing to profits from high world prices in cotton, tobacco, and, above all, in petroleum. Equally significantly, the appearance of western luxuries—large automobiles, radios, refrigerators, furs, and luxury hotels—tends to increase the visible gap between rich and poor. Until 1918, an Arab who lived ostentatiously risked the vigorous attentions of the Ottoman tax-collector; today, the wealthy Arab is himself often closely connected with the government, and can manipulate its fiscal policy closely to his advantage. We have noted that the larger proportion of the revenues of Middle Eastern states is usually derived from indirect taxation of necessities such as food and clothing—a system that bears heaviest on the poorer classes.

AUTHORITARIAN RULE

A third problem concerns the political organization in certain Middle East states. By temperament and experience, many Middle Easterners incline to personal and authoritarian forms of rule. Nomadic and pastoral ways of life tend to throw up individuals of much prestige and personal leadership; and even in religion —as indicated by the importance of prophetic revelation in Islam and Christianity—there is a tendency to respect the man equally with, if not more than, the principle. In consequence the idea of parliamentary democracy, introduced after 1920 partly in deference to the Western European views, has had a limited and uncertain extension. The average man has tended to be impatient of rule by general consent, as expressed through Western democratic methods, preferring to follow a single individual of superior appeal and ability. Where such a figure has not been forthcoming, there has been acquiescence in rule by a caucus or oligarchy. In this situation, the importance of armed services is very great. As the final repository of physical power—only artillery, tanks, and aircraft can really control a large dissident mob—the army leaders especially come often to be the final arbiters in a struggle for power. Moreover, as something of a meritocracy in which able officers can most easily rise from humble origins to positions of power, the armed forces in the Middle East have often come to a centre of evolved middle-class, or even radical, opinion essentially different from the bourgeois attitude of the merchant groups.

Saudi Arabia and the Gulf states are ruled by absolute monarchs. For the twenty years preceding 1940 Turkey and Iran were ruled by despots. In more recent times, there has been a partial rejection of democracy on the Western pattern in countries where parliaments existed, and the last few years have seen a tendency towards a recrudescence of personal rule, the outstanding instances being in Egypt and Iraq. Parliamentary government seemed fairly strongly developed in Turkey until about 1955, but later events have suggested a return to the now normal pattern within the Middle East. A few years ago, it was perhaps widely felt that, eventually, monarchy would be largely displaced by a rising tide of republicanism, as actually has happened in Egypt, Iraq and Libya. But latterly, partly due to increased oil revenues, monarchs have shown considerable leadership and resilience, whilst republicanism is rather less successful.

MODERNIZING ISLAM

The widest problem of all concerns the cultural crisis within modern Islam. Until the end of the Middle Ages, Islamic culture was vigorous, and in many respects more advanced than that of Europe. Islamic thought greatly influenced the West, with a parallel superiority, or at least equality, in the political sphere. Since that time, however, there has been a considerable decline in power and intellectual strength: large-scale political penetration and domination from Europe began in the nineteenth century, and for several centuries material standards of life have no longer approximated to those of the West. There has, as a result, been much speculation in the Arab world upon the reasons for this decline. Three broad points of view can be discerned. There are those who see no good prospect in a continuance of Islamic traditions, and so wish to follow new ways of life— either Christian and western, or, less clearly, new materialistic doctrines, one ultimate expression of which may be Communism. At the opposite extreme are those who suggest a return to a stricter form of Islam; and this policy is followed at the present time to a varying extent in Saudi Arabia and Algeria. Then there is a third group of intermediates, whose position is perhaps the most difficult of all, since they wish to combine modernity with a maintenance of internal traditions. How far exactly can one go in this respect? And too often an attempt at combining widely diverse elements leads to superficiality, a rejection of fundamentals and a real understanding of neither aspect. We therefore have the phenomenon of the 'angry young Arab'—given more and more to rejection of existing ways and now actively critical of the failure of leadership over Palestine, and of inequalities in and lack of opportunity for economic advancement. He has an increasing sense of frustration which becomes more and more vocal with the spread of literacy. A further development, reflecting the special position of the Middle East between East and West, is the emergence of a specifically "Arab" socialism: neither Soviet nor Maoist communism, according to some Arab intellectuals, and certainly not "western" socialism, but reflecting the special social traditions of Islam.

Summing Up

Having made a cursory survey of Middle Eastern lands and their resources, it is now possible to attempt a summary of conclusions. We may recall once again what was said concerning the geographical position of the Middle East as the land connexion between three continents; from this situation has arisen its main role in the world—as an intermediary between the nations of Europe, Asia, and Africa, both in the economic and cultural spheres. Sometimes this historic function has been discharged purely, so to speak, as an agent or middleman, without any indigenous contribution—as when, for example, silk, sugar, citrus fruit, paper, gunpowder, and the compass were introduced from Further Asia into Europe. At other times, a technique or an idea has been received or developed in the Middle East, expanded there into a great movement, and transmitted elsewhere. One may cite, for example, the system of garden irrigation brought by the Arabs to Spain, which is still a highly productive element in Spanish agriculture, or the religions of Christianity and Islam, or the scientific ideas of the Greeks and Hindus, which were preserved throughout the Dark Ages of Europe and later made available to the West through the works of Muslim commentators.

With the discovery of the sea route to India in the fifteenth century, the importance of the Middle East as a transit area greatly declined, but since the opening of the Suez Canal, and the growth of air communications, the situation has once more altered. We are at present witnessing a return to the ancient position in a modern guise, with air and sea routes largely contributing to a revival of prosperity. It is no accident that Beirut should have been chosen as one of the fuelling stages for the first all-jet air liner service from Britain to South Africa, or that Cairo should be served by so many international air-lines. Because of its central geographical position, a climate that is in the main exceptionally favourable for air navigation, and its level open topography (at least, in the south) the Middle East has become a nodal centre of air traffic. In a broader sense still, there has been a major shift of political influence in the world. For several centuries power and wealth were largely concentrated in north-western Europe, but since 1900 the rise of America and Russia, the independence of India, the revival of China, and the dependence of Europe on foodstuffs imported from Australasia and Africa have brought about an expansion of global relationships. The Middle East, situated at the cross-roads of the world, has begun to profit once more from its central position. Now that the region contains more than half the proven world reserves of oil, the situation has changed further, even though the Suez Canal, were it to be reopened, is unlikely to capture all of its former traffic.

A question that has been anxiously debated in the West during 1973 is how far the Middle East, because of its reserves of increasingly valuable oil, will come to play a much greater financial role in world economic affairs, with resulting political effects.

One feature due in large part to geography is its potential as a tourist centre. It is probable that currently north-west Europe is experiencing a small climatic oscillation towards cooler, rainier summers; hence with "guaranteed" sunshine, excellent beaches, and considerable archaeological and human interest, certain parts of the Middle East have been able to develop a growing tourist attraction. New hotels, amenities and sports stadia are under construction; and given stable political conditions, this activity could well develop much further in the next few years, not merely for one season, but through a large proportion of the whole year.

POLITICAL OUTLINE

Similarly, there have been shifts in political fortune since the First World War. In 1916 the allocation of almost the entire Middle East as spheres of influence for European powers—Britain, France, Russia, Italy and Greece—had been agreed on. Treaties were actually in existence envisaging a territorial division which would have left only a fraction of Asia Minor under autonomous local rule.

From that apparent high water mark of Western influence, there has been a considerable decline; but the interest of external powers in the Middle East continues, fostered by the petroleum resources and strategic geographical location of the area.

At the same time there has been a parallel rise in nationalist feeling, helped on partly by differences among interested European powers and the skill with which these were exploited by Middle Eastern governments, and partly by the growth of internal wealth in the states themselves. This process became particularly vigorous after 1940, when from being a small marginal producer of in the main low-quality commodities, the Middle East became an important world supplier of petroleum, cotton, tobacco, wool and cereals.

The main element in the present-day politics of the Middle East is the existence of the state of Israel. To most Arabs, the creation first of a National Home for Jews and later of a Jewish State was a clear demonstration of hostility toward the Arab world on the part of Britain, France and the U.S.A.—a view which the events of 1956, and then of 1967, seemed only to confirm. As the Arabs see it, Western patronage of Zionism was a Machiavellian device to disrupt the Arab Middle East; and there can be no real friendship or understanding with the West until support for Zionism is disavowed. Moreover, uncertain of their own strength, Arab governments have increasingly turned to the U.S.S.R. for support against Zionism and its patrons. At times too it has been possible to take advantage of American divergence in policy from that of Britain and/or France (e.g. over oil concessions, Algeria, Cyprus and Suez). Moreover, the Middle East may offer a counterpoise to the forces balanced within the other southern extremity of Asia—in Viet-Nam especially. Thus the present situation in many ways resembles that of the pre-1914 Balkans, with a number of small and antagonistic states manoeuvering between independence and "protection" from a great power in the background. But the Balkans never possessed more than half the world's oil.

ECONOMIC TRENDS

In the economic sphere, it is more difficult to present a clearly defined picture. There is the unique asset of petroleum, which has already transformed ways of life in areas where it is exploited, and brought unexpected wealth to port terminals such as Abadan, Bahrain, Tripoli (Lebanon), Baniyas, Sidon, Kuwait and Benghazi. A striking inequality has consequently developed between various countries. Those actually producing oil have substantial extra wealth, and can embark on schemes of improvement, with at some time the possibility of a relatively unfettered foreign policy. Next in order come the non-producers with locational advantages—pipelines, good harbours or oil refineries. These countries can profit in a minor way from petroleum exploitation, but a ceiling is set by the cost of alternative transport. If too much is demanded by way of transit dues, the oil traffic could be re-routed either via Suez (when the Canal is open), the Cape of Good Hope, or even by alternative pipeline routes, such as that from Eilat on the Gulf of Aqaba to Haifa, or from Iran to the Mediterranean via Turkey, or the proposed one from Suez to Alexandria.

The relationships of foreign exploiting companies have undergone much change since the 1920s, when approximately only 16 per cent of oil revenue was paid over to native governments, and companies had almost extra-territorial legal and fiscal rights. One problem remains—the corroding effect upon native society (especially at highest levels) of sudden and easy wealth.

As regards agriculture and industry, the position is less satisfactory. Though there are certainly richly endowed spots (especially parts of the Nile Valley), the Middle East is on the whole a poor area, condemned by aridity and scantiness of resources to a marginal place as a producer. Nevertheless, the last twenty years have seen highly significant increases, particularly in Egypt, Iran and Turkey, which are now undoubtedly in numbers and wealth the leading states of the Middle East.

Turkey

Though an agricultural country, Turkey in 1920 imported almost one-half of her foodstuffs: most of the few public utilities were foreign-owned; and modern industry could hardly be said to exist. Following several phases of development (the last of which from 1947 onwards amounting almost to an agricultural revolution) Turkey is almost self-sufficient in food, and in favourable years since 1950 has even exported wheat. Foreign ownership has been very greatly reduced, and a variety of light industry created. At first much of this activity was state-sponsored and owned, but since 1950 there has been a partial denationalization of industry.

Egypt

Progress in Egypt has also been considerable. The careful use of river barrage systems has made the lower Nile valley one of the most productive agricultural areas in the world, with highest unit yields in maize and sugar, and highest quality in cotton. Intensity and quality of farming are unrivalled elsewhere in the Middle East, though there are ominous signs that future progress will be difficult—almost all the Nile water is now in use, and more and more fertilizers must be imported. Also, war periods greatly stimulated the growth of local industry, which, until the 1952 revolution, had always been on a capitalist, *laissez faire*, basis. Textiles are most important, but the increased wealth of the upper and middle classes has provided a market for light consumer goods that is now largely supplied within the country. An outstandingly important development is the full implementation of the Aswan High Dam project which, besides adding one-third to the present total of cultivated land in Egypt, provides electric power for heavy and light industry on a very considerable scale, at prices comparable with those of Europe.

Israel

Israel had certain advantages when it began the desperate task of attempting to support relatively large numbers in a poor environment at high standards of life. There were the energy and skill of its European-trained population; an overriding determination to make a success from unpromising beginnings, much machinery imported from Europe (Hitler allowed refugees from Nazi Germany to take plant, but not capital), and financial support from outside, chiefly the U.S.A. The country is not richly endowed—though mineral deposits (oil, natural gas, copper and phosphates) on a relatively small scale have recently been discovered—and transport is difficult. Moreover, most of the south is arid, and good agricultural land is everywhere severely restricted. A further handicap has been the determination to maintain European rather than Arab levels of wages—a matter in which powerful trade unions are involved. The advances achieved both in agriculture and industry have been very great but some restriction of consumption of food and clothing is still necessary, and there is a severe adverse balance of trade with exports amounting to only one-half or in some recent years, one-quarter of imports. In consequence, despite stringent controls, and great efforts to expand production, loans from abroad are still vital to the Israel economy, and unemployment on a moderate scale had come to be a problem before the 1967 War. Since then, however, the Israeli economy has enjoyed a sustained boom.

THE MIDDLE EAST AND NORTH AFRICA—(SUMMING UP)

Iran

Iran has a long tradition of craft industry, especially in wool; and there are varied mineral deposits, including coal. With the exception of petroleum, however, these deposits are scattered, small in amount, often of low grade. Within the last few years, however, there has been a considerable degree of industrial growth in Teheran city, which now has an industrial quarter that produces a wide range of consumer goods and building materials, especially bricks. The construction of a gas-grid from Gach Saran to Shiraz, and then farther north, is a further impetus to development, and a large steel-making plant is now being built at Isfahan. Overall, Iran now claims a 10 per cent annual growth rate.

Iraq

Until recently there was hardly any industry of any kind in Iraq, in distinct contrast to many of its neighbours. But since 1945 oil revenues have been allocated to a national Development Board, which has fostered the development of communications and agriculture, and begun to plan some industrial activity. Now, in addition to the processing of agricultural products, there is some textile manufacturing (chiefly cotton and rayon), a little light engineering, and a small chemical industry. Plans are in hand to expand these, especially the last. Agriculture is less developed than in Egypt, owing in part to the difficult nature of the two rivers, which have been more difficult to control and develop for irrigation. Since 1954, however, with the completion of Wadi Tharthar and other flood control and irrigation projects, the situation has changed, and large areas of good land which have hitherto remained unused can now be developed.

Syria, Lebanon, Jordan

At one time, Syria was the most industrialized province of the Ottoman Empire, with Aleppo second only to Constantinople in size. Loss of markets since 1918 has hampered but not destroyed the textile and metal manufactures of Aleppo and Damascus, and there are a small number of other industrial activities. Agriculturally, Syria has developed greatly since 1945. The irrigated "Fertile Crescent" has been expanded, and parts of the Euphrates valley brought back into cultivation for the first time in many centuries. Syria is self-sufficient in cereals, and exports these, together with raw cotton, to her less well-placed neighbours, the Lebanon and Jordan. The cotton is used both in the Middle East and in central Europe and Japan. The building of a dam across the Euphrates at Tabqa east of Aleppo (begun 1968 with German interests involved) will, when completed in 1973/4, greatly assist Syrian development.

The Lebanon, like Israel, has severe natural handicaps. The rugged nature of the hills, which occupy most of the country, and aridity in the east greatly limit cultivation, and there are no mineral resources. Dependent on the import of foodstuffs, the country nevertheless has a considerable transit traffic, with the intelligence, adaptability and highly developed commercial sense of its people as the chief assets of the country. There is an international trade in gold, and Beirut (with four universities) has become a major cultural centre for the entire Middle East. Tourism could also become much more important.

Jordan, with almost no sea outlet, is in a very different situation. Most of the country is either arid or covered by bare sheets of lava—the only cultivable areas are west of the Jordan (Israeli-occupied since June 1967), in the Judaean uplands, and around Amman. Nomadic pastoralism is the only possible activity over much of the country—though the exploitation of substantial phosphate deposits provides a further source of occupation. An artificial territorial unit, with very few resources, Jordan is hardly viable, and has depended on outside subsidies, at present provided by Britain, the U.S.A. and, for varying periods since 1967, by Saudi Arabia, Kuwait and Libya.

Libya

A somewhat similar situation obtained in Libya until very recently where, despite the imposing size of territory, cultivated land is restricted to certain districts near or along the coast, together with a few inland oasis settlements. Now, discoveries of oil on a large scale are rapidly transforming the situation, and there is marked growth, especially in towns such as Benghazi and Tripoli.

Arabia

The Arabian peninsula is, so to speak, a stage beyond Libya. Before 1940 the territory was possibly the poorest in all the Middle East—only scattered oases with a largely nomadic population. Now the economic situation has been completely transformed; Saudi Arabia and Kuwait are, with Iran, the largest oil producers in the area by a considerable margin, and some of the small sheikhdoms along the Persian Gulf are also becoming major contributors. The immense oil revenues have financed lavish public works and welfare programmes, but the ease with which all imports needed for the small population can be paid for has reduced the incentive to develop the peninsula's other resources.

Cyprus

Cyprus though small, had (at least until the Emergency) a very good agricultural system (over 55 per cent of the total area is used—a figure far higher than in any other Middle Eastern country), and there are small but useful deposits of iron, copper and asbestos. Given stable internal conditions, Cyprus could be one of the most prosperous parts of the Middle East.

The Maghreb

Lastly, North Africa is still suffering from the effects of colonial rule. The efforts of prolonged and bitter warfare, the withdrawal of French "colons"

THE MIDDLE EAST AND NORTH AFRICA—(Summing Up)

who contributed in predominant measure to the more highly developed economic activities, and the resulting disequilibrium in an economy that until independence was strongly integrated with that of France—all these will take time to dissipate. Whilst over and above, there is the desperate need to provide for the rapidly growing numbers of inhabitants, with the concomitant problem of greater imbalance between urban and rural areas—a declining countryside, resulting in a fall-off in agricultural production, and congestion at declining levels of subsistence in the larger towns.

The most hopeful element is the presence of substantial mineral resources. Oil and gas could be used in part directly as fuel for industry; and revenues from exports might be directed to an expansion both of home manufacturing and improved agricultural techniques. Hydro-electricity is another possible source of energy, and this could foster *inter alia* more methodical exploitation and treatment of metallic mineral resources. At long term, the problem is also one of transferring the liability of an underemployed and growing population into the economic asset of a large pool of labour and consumer demand.

The Religions of the Middle East and North Africa

Islam
R. B. Serjeant

Islam is a major world religion and the faith predominating throughout the Middle East (with the exception of Lebanon the population of which is approximately half Muslim and half Christian) and North Africa. There are substantial Christian minorities in some countries and communities of oriental Jews and other faiths, for centuries integrated with the Muslim majority. Islam is not only a highly developed religious system but an established and distinctive culture embracing every aspect of human activity from theology, philosophy, literature to the visual arts and even man's routine daily conduct. Its characteristic intellectual manifestation therefore is in the field of Islamic law, the *Shari'ah*. Though in origin a Semitic Arabian faith, Islam was also the inheritor of the legacy of classical Greek and Roman civilization and, in its major phase of intellectual, social and cultural development after its emergence from its Arabian womb, it was affected by Christian, Jewish and Persian civilization. In turn, Greek scientific and philosophical writings—direct translations into Arabic or forming a principal element in the books of Arab scholars began to enter medieval Europe in Latin renderings about the early 12th century from the brilliant intellectual circles of Islamic Spain, and formed a potent factor in the little Renaissance of western Europe.

Islamic civilization had, by about the 18th century, clearly lost its initiative to the ascendant West and has not since regained it.

HISTORY

The founder of the religion of Islam was the Prophet Muhammad b. 'Abdullah, born about A.D. 570, a member of the noble house of Hashim, belonging to the 'Abd Manaf clan, itself a part of the Quraish tribal confederation of Mecca. 'Abd Manaf may be described as semi-priestly since they had the privilege of certain functions during the annual pilgrimage to the Meccan Ka'bah, a cube-shaped temple set in the sacred enclave (*haram*). Quraish controlled this enclave which was maintained inviolate from war or killing, and they had established a pre-eminence and loose hegemony even over many Arabian tribes which they had induced to enter a trading alliance extending over the main Arabian land routes, north and south, east and west. With the powerful Quraish leaders in Mecca, temple guardians, chiefs, merchant adventurers, Muhammad clashed, when, aged about 40, he began to proclaim the worship of the one God, Allah, as against their multiplicity of gods. These Quraish leaders were contemptuous of his mission.

While his uncle Abu Talib, head of the house of Hashim, lived, he protected Muhammad from physical harm, but after his death Muhammad sought protection from tribes outside Mecca—they would not accept him even when he asked only to remain quietly without preaching—Thaqif of Taif drove him roughly away. Ultimately pilgrims of the Aws and Khazraj tribes of Yathrib (Medina), some 200 miles north of Mecca, agreed to protect him there, undertaking to associate no other god with Allah and accepting certain moral stipulations. Muhammad left Mecca with his Companion Abu Bakr in the year 622—this is the year of the *hijrah* or hegira.

Arriving in Yathrib, Muhammad formed a federation or community (*ummah*) of Aws and Khazraj, known as the "Supporters" (*Ansar*), followed by their Jewish client tribes, and the "Emigrants" (*Muhajirun*), his refugee Quraish adherents, with himself as the ultimate arbiter of the *ummah* as a whole, though there remained a local opposition covertly antagonistic to him, the Munafiqun, rendered as "Hypocrites". Two internal issues had now to be fought by Muhammad—the enforcement of his position as theocratic head of the federation, and the acquisition of revenue to maintain his position; externally he took an aggressive attitude to the Meccan Quraish.

In Yathrib his disposal of the Jewish tribes who made common cause with the "Hypocrites" improved his financial position. The Meccan Quraish he overcame more by skilful political manoeuvre than through the occasional armed clashes with them, and in year 8 he entered Mecca without fighting. Previously he had declared Yathrib a sacred enclave (*haram*), renaming it Medina, the City (of the Prophet)—the two cities known as al-Haraman have become the holy land of Islam. Muhammad was conciliatory to his defeated Quraish kinsmen, and after his success against Taif, south of Mecca, deputations came from the Arabian tribes to make terms with the new Prophet—the heritor of the influence of the Meccan Quraish.

Early Islam

The two main tenets of Islam are embodied in the formula of the creed, "There is no god but Allah and Muhammad is the Apostle of God." Unitarianism (*tawhid*), as opposed to polytheism (*shirk*) or making partners with God, is Islam's basic principle, coupled with Muhammad's authority conferred on him by God. Muhammad made little change to the ancient Arabian religion—he abolished idolatry but confirmed the pilgrimage to the Ka'bah; the Koran, the sacred Book in Arabic revealed to Muhammad for his people, lays down certain social and moral rules. Among these are the condemnation of usury or interest (*riba*) on loans and prohibition of wine (*khamr*)—both ordinances have always been difficult to enforce. On the whole the little change involved seems to have made it easy for Arabia to accept Islam. While there is incontrovertible evidence of Muhammad's contact with Judaism, and even with Christianity, and the Koran contains versions of narrative known to the sacred books of these faiths, yet these are used to point purely Arabian morals. The limited social law laid down by the Koran is supplemented by a body of law and precept derived from the *Hadith* or Tradition of Muhammad's practice (*Sunnah*) at Medina, and welded into the Islamic system, mainly in its second and third centuries.

Subsequent History

Immediately after Muhammad's death in 632, Abu Bakr delegated by him to lead the prayer during his last indisposition became his successor or Caliph. Some Medinan Supporters had attempted a breakaway from Quraish overlordship but Abu Bakr adroitly persuaded them to accept himself to follow Muhammad. But office in Arabia, generally speaking, is hereditary within a family group, though elective within that group, and Abu Bakr's action had taken no account of the claims of 'Ali, the Prophet's cousin and son-in-law—the house of Hashim to which Muhammad and 'Ali belonged was plainly aggrieved that a member of a minor Quraish clan should have snatched supreme power. Muhammad's Arabian coalition also showed tendencies to dissolve, the tribes particularly objecting to paying taxes to Medina, but Abu Bakr's firm line held it together. The expansionist thrusts beyond Arabia during his Caliphate, continued under his successor 'Umar and part of the reign of the third Caliph 'Uthman, diverted tribal energies to profitable warfare in Mesopotamia, Palestine-Syria, Egypt and Persia. Muslim armies were eventually to conquer North Africa, much of Spain, parts of France, and even besiege Rome, while in the east they later penetrated to Central Asia and India.

During 'Uthman's tenure of office the tide of conquest temporarily slackened and the turbulent tribes, now settled in southern Iraq and Egypt, began to dispute the Caliph's disposal of booty and revenue, maintaining that he unduly favoured members of his own house. A delegation of tribal malcontents from Egypt murdered 'Uthman in the holy city of Medina, and in the resultant confusion 'Ali, Muhammad's cousin was elected Caliph with the support of the tribesmen responsible for murdering 'Uthman. This raised grave constitutional problems for the young Muslim state, and is regarded as the origin of the greatest schism in Islam.

If Legitimist arguments were the sole consideration 'Ali's claims to succession seem the best, but he had previously lost it to 'Uthman—whose father belonged to the Umaiyah clan which had opposed Muhammad, but whose mother was of Hashim. 'Uthman naturally appointed Umaiyah men loyal to him to commands in the Empire, notably Mu'awiyah as governor of Syria—the son of that very Abu Sufyan who headed Quraish opposition to Muhammad at Mecca—though later reconciled to him. Mu'awiyah demanded 'Uthman's murderers be brought to justice in accordance with the law, but 'Ali, unable to cope with the murderers, his supporters, was driven by events to take up arms against Mu'awiyah. When they clashed at Siffin in Syria 'Ali was forced, against his better judgement to submit to the arbitration of the Koran and Sunnah, thus automatically losing the position of supreme arbiter, inherited by the Caliphs from Muhammad. Though history is silent as to what the arbiters actually judged it was most likely as to whether 'Ali had broken the law established by Muhammad, and that he was held to have sheltered unprovoked murderers. The arbiters deposed him from the Caliphial office though the historians allege trickery entered into their action.

'Ali shortly after was murdered by one of a group of his former supporters which had come out against the arbitration it had first urged upon him. This group, the Khawarij, is commonly held to be the forerunner of the Ibadis of Oman and elsewhere. Mu'awiyah became Caliph and founder of the Umaiyad dynasty with its capital at Damascus. The ambitions of the Hashim house were not however allayed, and when Umaiyad troops slew 'Ali's son Husain at Karbala' in south Iraq they created the greatest Shi'ah martyr.

The house of Hashim also included the descendants of 'Abbas the Prophet's uncle, a relative, in Arabian eyes, as close as 'Ali to him, but 'Abbas had opposed Muhammad till late in the day. The 'Abbasids made common cause with the 'Ali-id Shi'ah against the Umaiyads, but were evidently abler in the political field. In the Umaiyad empire the Arabian tribes formed a kind of military élite but were constantly at factious war with one another. The Hashimites rode to power on the back of a rebellion against the Umaiyads which broke out in Khurasan in east Persia, but it was the 'Abbasid branch of Hashim which assumed the Caliphate and ruled from the capital they founded at Baghdad.

The 'Abbasid Caliphate endured up to the destruction of Baghdad in 1258 by the devastating Mongol invaders of the eastern empire, but the Caliphs had long been mere puppets in the hands of Turkish and other mercenaries, and the unwieldy empire had fragmented into independent states which rose and fell though they mostly conceded nominal allegiance to the 'Abbasid Caliphs.

The Mongol Ilkhanid sovereigns, now turned Muslim, were in turn displaced by the conquests of Tamerlane at the end of the 14th century. In fact the Islamic empire had largely been taken over by Turkic soldiery. The Mameluke or Slave rulers of medieval Egypt who followed the Aiyubid (Kurdish) dynasty of Saladin were mainly Turks or Circassians. It was they who checked the Mongol advance at 'Ain Jalut in Palestine (1260). The Ottoman Turks captured Constantinople in 1453, and took Egypt from the Mamelukes in 1516, following this up by occupying the Hejaz where the Ashraf, descendants of the Prophet, ruled in Mecca and Medina, first under Mameluke then Turkish suzerainty. In 1533 the Turks took Baghdad and Iraq became part of the Ottoman Empire. The Ottoman Sultans assumed the title of Caliph—though in Islamic constitutional theory it is not easy to justify this. The Ottoman Caliphs endured till the Caliphate was abolished by Mustafa Kamal in 1924. The Turks have always been characterized by their adherence to Sunni orthodoxy.

THE RELIGIONS OF THE MIDDLE EAST AND NORTH AFRICA

Throughout history the 'Ali-ids have constantly asserted their right to be the Imams or leaders of the Muslim community—this in the religious and political senses, since Islam is fundamentally theocratic. The Shi'ah or followers of 'Ali and his descendants were in constant rebellion against the 'Abbasids and came to form a distinct schismatic group of Legitimist sects—at one time the Fatimid Shi'ah rulers of Egypt were near to conquering the main part of the Islamic world. The main Shi'ah sects today are the Ithna-'asharis, the Isma'ilis, and the near-orthodox Zaidis of the Yemen. The Safavids who conquered Persia at the beginning of the 16th century brought it finally into the Shi'ah fold. Sunni Hashimite dynasties flourish today in Jordan and Morocco as they did till fairly recently in Iraq and Libya, and the Shi'ah Zaidi ruler of Yemen was only displaced in 1962. The main difference between Sunnis and Shi'ah is over the Imamate i.e. the temporal and spiritual leader of Islam, for whereas Sunnis while they respect the Prophet's house, do not consider the Imam *must* be a member of it—the Shi'ah insist on an Imam of the descendants of 'Ali and Fatimah his wife, the Prophet's daughter.

It has been too readily assumed that, during the later Middle Ages and long Turkish domination, the Islamic Middle East was completely stagnant. The shift in economic patterns after the New World was discovered, and the Cape route to India, coupled with widening Western intellectual horizons and the development of science and technology did push European culture far ahead of the Muslim Middle East. It was confronted by a vigorous and hostile Christianity intent on proselytising in its very homelands. Muslims had to face the challenge of the ideas and attitudes of Christian missionaries. Muslim thinkers like Muhammad 'Abduh (1849–1905) of Egypt and his school asserted that Islam had become heavily overlaid with false notions—hence its decline; like earlier reformers they were convinced that present difficulties could be solved by reversion to and (idealized) pure primitive Islam. Sometimes, in effect, this meant re-interpreting religious literature to suit attitudes and ideas of modern times—as for instance when they saw the virtual prohibition of polygamy in the restrictions which hedge it about. Since the earlier modern days political leaders like Mustafa Kamal of Turkey have often taken drastic measures, secularizing the state itself even up to the sensitive field of education, and accusing the more conservative forms of Islam of blocking progress. Today the Islamic Middle East has régimes ranging from the strong supporters of traditional Islam—like Sa'udi Arabia and Libya—to the anti-religious Marxist group controlling Aden.

ISLAMIC LAW

Orthodox Sunni Islam finds its main expression in *Shari'ah* law which it regards with great veneration. The Sunnis have crystallized into four "schools" (*madhhab*) or "rites", all of which are recognized as valid. Though in practice the adherents of one school can sometimes be at loggerheads with another, in modern times it is claimed that the law of any one of the rites can be applied to a case. The schools, named after their founders, are the Hanbali, regarded as the strictest, with adherents mainly in Sa'udi Arabia, the Shafi'is, the widest in extent with adherents in Egypt, Syria-Palestine, Egypt, South Arabia, and the Far East, the moderate Hanafi school which was the official rite of the Ottoman Turkish empire and to which most Muslims in the Indian sub-continent belong, and the Malikis of the North African states, Nigeria, and the Sudan. The Shi'ite sects have developed their own law, and give prominence to *ijtihad*, the forming of independent judgement, whereas the Sunnis are more bound by *taqlid* or following ancient models. However as the law of Sunnis, the moderate Shi'ah, and the Ibadis is basically derived from the same sources the differences are generally more of emphasis than principle.

Civil Courts. In the modern states of the Islamic world there exists, side by side with the *Shari'ah* court (judging cases on personal status, marriage, divorce, etc.), the secular court which has a wide jurisdiction (based on Western codes of law) in civil and criminal matters. This court is competent to give judgment irrespective of the creed or race of the defendant.

Islamic Law as Applying to Minorities. In cases of minorities (Christian or Jewish) residing as a community in Muslim countries, spiritual councils are established where judgment is passed according to the law of the community, in matters concerning personal status, by the recognised head of that community.

Tribal Courts. In steppe and mountain areas of countries where a proportion of the population is still tribal, tribal courts administer law and justice in accordance with ancient custom and tribal procedure.

Awqaf. In Muslim countries the law of Awqaf is the law applied to religious and charitable endowments, trusts and settlements. This important Islamic institution, found in all Eastern countries, is administered by the *Shari'ah* courts. Awqaf, or endowments, are pious bequests made by Muslims for the upkeep of religious institutions, public benefits, etc.

SUFIS

As in other religions, many Muslims find their emotional needs are not satisfied by observing a code of law and morals alone, and turn to mysticism. From early times Islamic mystics existed, known as Sufis, allegedly from their wearing a woollen garment. They seek complete identification with the Supreme Being and annihilation of the self—the existence of which latter they call polytheism (*shirk*). The learned doctors of Islam often think ill of the Sufis, and indeed rogues and wandering mendicants found Sufism a convenient means of livelihood. Certain Sufi groups allowed themselves dispensations and as stimulants even used hashish and opium which are not sanctioned by the Islamic moral code. The Sufis became organized in what are loosely called brotherhoods (*tariqah*), and have to a large extent been incorporated into the structure of orthodox Islamic society. Some *tariqahs* induce ecstatic states by their performance of the *dhikr*, meaning, literally, the mentioning (of Allah). Today there is much disapproval of the more extravagant manifestations of the Sufis and in some places these have been banned entirely.

The completely Islamic state as the theorists envisage it, run in conformity with the rules of the *Shari'ah* has probably never been achieved, and people's practice is often at variance with some or other requirements of *Shari'ah*. The imprint of Islam is nevertheless unmistakably evident on every country in this volume.

BELIEF AND PRACTICE

"Islam" means the act of submitting or resigning oneself to God, and a Muslim is one who resigns or submits himself to God. Muslims disapprove of the term "Muhammadan" for the faith of Islam, since they worship Allah, and Muhammad is only the Apostle of Allah whose duty it was to convey revelation, though he is regarded as the "Best of Mankind". He is the Seal (*Khatam*) of the Prophets, i.e. the ultimate Prophet in a long series in which both Moses and Jesus figure. They are revered, but, like Muhammad the Prophet, they are not worshipped.

Nearly all Muslims agree on acceptance of six articles of the faith of Islam: (i) Belief in God; (ii) in His angels; (iii) in His revealed books; (iv) in His Apostles; (v) in the Resurrection and Day of Judgement; and (vi) in His predestination of good and evil.

Faith includes works, and certain practices are obligatory on the believing Muslim. These are five in number:

1. The recital of the creed (*Shahadah*)—"There is no god but God (Allah) and Muhammad is the Apostle of God." This formula is embodied in the call to prayer made by the muezzin (announcer) from the minaret of the mosque before each of the five daily prayers.

2. The performance of the Prayer (*Salat*) at the five appointed canonical times—in the early dawn before the sun has risen above the horizon, in the early afternoon when the sun has begun to decline, later when the sun is about midway in its course towards setting, immediately after sunset, in the evening between the disappearance of the red glow in the west and bedtime. In prayer Muslims face towards the Ka'bah in Mecca. They unroll prayer mats and pray in a mosque (place of prostration), at home, or wherever they may be, bowing and prostrating themselves before God and reciting set verses in Arabic from the Koran. On Fridays it is obligatory for men to attend congregational Prayer in the central mosque of the quarter in which one lives—women do not normally attend. On this occasion formal prayers are preceded by a sermon.

3. The payment of the legal alms (*Zakat*). In early times this contribution was collected by officials of the Islamic state, and devoted to the relief of the poor, debtors, aid to travellers and other charitable and state purposes. Nowadays the fulfilment of this religious obligation is left to the conscience of the individual believer.

4. The thirty days of the fast in the month of Ramadan, the ninth month in the lunar year. As the lunar calendar is shorter by 11 days than the solar calendar Ramadan moves from the hottest to the coldest seasons of the solar year. It is observed as a fast from dawn to sunset each day by all adults in normal health, during which time no food or drink may be taken. The sick, pregnant women, travellers and children are exempt; some states exempt students, soldiers and factory workers. The fast ends with one of the two major Muslim festivals, 'Id al-Fitr.

5. The pilgrimage (*Hajj*) to Mecca. Every Muslim is obliged, circumstances permitting, to perform this at least once in his lifetime, and when accomplished he may assume the title, *Hajji*. About a million pilgrims go each year to Mecca, but the holy cities of Mecca and Medina are prohibited to non-Muslims.

Before entering the sacred area around Mecca by the seventh day of Dhu 'l-Hijjah, the twelfth month of the Muslim year, pilgrims must don the *ihram*, consisting of two unseamed lengths of white cloth, indicating that they are entering a state of consecration and casting off what is ritually impure. The pilgrims circumambulate the Ka'bah seven times, endeavouring to kiss the sacred Black Stone. Later they run seven times between the near-by twin hills of Safa and Marwa, thus recalling Hagar's desperate search for water for her child Ishmael (from whom the Arabs claim descent). On the eighth day of the month the pilgrims leave the city for Mina, a small town six miles to the east. Then before sunrise of the next day all make for the plain below Mount 'Arafat some twelve miles east of Mecca where they pass the day in prayers and recitation until sunset. This point is the climax of the pilgrimage when the whole gathering returns, first to Muzdalifah where it spends the night, then to Mina where pilgrims stone the devil represented by three heaps of stones (*jamrah*). The devil is said to have appeared to Abraham here and to have been driven away by Abraham throwing stones at him. This day, the 10th of Dhu 'l-Hijjah is 'Id al-Adha, the Feast of the Sacrifices, and the pilgrims sacrifice an animal, usually a sheep, and have their heads shaved by one of the barbers at Mina. They return to Mecca that evening.

The Holy War (*Jihad*) against the infidel was the means whereby Arab Muslim rule made its immense expansion in the first centuries of Islam, but despite pressures to do so it has never been elevated to form a sixth Pillar of Islam. Today many theologians interpret *jihad* in a less literal sense as the combatting of evil.

The Koran (*Qur'an*, "recital", "reading") is for Muslims the very Word of God. The Koran consists of 114 chapters (*surah*) of uneven length, the longest coming first after the brief opening chapter called *al-Fatihah*. (The Koran is about as long as the New Testament). *Al-Fatihah* (The Opener) commences with the words, "*Bismillahi 'l-Rahmani 'l-Rahim*, In the name of God, the Compassionate, the Merciful",

THE RELIGIONS OF THE MIDDLE EAST AND NORTH AFRICA

and forms part of the ritual five prayers (*salat*). Other special verses and chapters are also used on a variety of occasions, and of course Muslim children are taught to recite by heart a portion of the Koran or, preferably, the whole of it. The Koran has been the subject of vast written commentaries, but translation into other languages is not much approved by Muslims, though inter-linear translations (a line of Koran underneath which is a line of translation) are used, and a number of modern translations into English exists. The earlier (Meccan) chapters of the Koran speak of the unity of God and his wonders, of the Day of Judgement and Paradise, while the Medinan chapters tend to be occupied more with social legislation for marriage, divorce, personal and communal behaviour. The definitive redaction of the Koran was ordered by the Caliph 'Uthman (644–56).

HOLY PLACES

Mecca: Hijaz province of Sa'udi Arabia. Mecca is centred around the Ka'bah, the most venerated building in Islam, traditionally held to have been founded by Abraham, recognized by Islam also as a Prophet. It stands in the centre of the vast courtyard of the Great Mosque and has the form of a cube; its construction is of local grey stone and its walls are draped with a black curtain embroidered with a strip of writing containing Koran verses. In the eastern corner is set the famous Black Stone. The enlarging of the Great Mosque commenced under the second Caliph 'Umar. Both the Ka'bah and Great Mosque have undergone many renovations, notably recently since 1952. Mecca is the centre of the annual pilgrimage from all Muslim countries.

Medina (*The City*, i.e. of the Prophet): Hijaz province of Sa'udi Arabia. Medina, formerly called Yathrib, was created a sacred enclave (*haram*) by Muhammad who died there in the year 11 of the *hijrah* and was buried in the Mosque of the Prophet. Close to his tomb are those of Abu Bakr and 'Umar and a little further away that of his daughter Fatimah. Frequently damaged, restored and enlarged, the mosque building was extensively renovated by the Sa'udi Government in 1955.

Jerusalem (Arabic *al-Quds* or *Bait al-Maqdis*, *The Hallowed/Consecrated*): Jordan (currently annexed by Israel). Jerusalem is Islam's next most holy city after al-Haraman (Mecca and Medina), not only because it is associated with so many pre-Islamic prophets, but because Muhammad himself is popularly held to have made the "Night Journey" there. Jerusalem contains the magnificent Islamic shrine, the Dome of the Rock (688–91), built by the Caliph 'Abd al-Malik, and the famous al-Masjid al-Aqsa recently severely damaged by arson.

Hebron (Habrun): Israel-occupied Jordan. The Mosque of Abraham, called al-Khalil, the "Friend of God" is built over the tomb of Abraham, the Cave of Machpelah; it also contains the tombs of Sarah, Isaac, Rebecca, Jacob, and Leah. The shrine is revered by Muslims and Jews, and is also important to Christians.

Qairawan: Tunisia. The city is regarded as a holy place for Muslims, seven pilgrimages to the Great Mosque of Sidi 'Uqbah b. Nafi' (an early Muslim general who founded Qairawan as a base for the Muslim invaders of North Africa) being considered equivalent of one pilgrimage to Mecca.

Muley Idris: Morocco. The shrine at the burial-place of the founder of the Idrisid dynasty in the year 687, at Walili.

* * *

Every Middle Eastern country has a multitude of shrines and saints' tombs held in veneration, except Wahhabi states which consider saint cults to be polytheism (*shirk*). In Turkey, however, the policy of secularization led to Aya Sofya Mosque (St. Sophia) being turned into a museum.

The following shrines are associated with the Shi'ah or Legitimist sects of Islam.

Mashhad (Meshed): Iran. The city is famous for the shrine of Imam 'Ali al-Rida/Riza, the eighth Imam of the Ithnaashari group, which attracts some hundred thousand pilgrims each year. The shrine is surrounded by many buildings with religious or historical associations.

Qum: Iran. A Shi'ah centre, it is venerated as having the tomb of Fatimah the sister of Imam al-Rida/Riza and hundreds of saints and kings including Imams 'Ali b. Ja'far and Ibrahim, Shah Safi and Shah 'Abbas II.

Najaf: Iraq. Mashhad 'Ali, reputed to be constructed over the place where 'Ali b. Abi Talib, the cousin and son-in-law of Muhammad is buried, is a most venerated Shi'ah shrine drawing many pilgrims.

Karbala': Iraq. The shrine of Husain b. 'Ali where, at Mashhad Husain, he was slain with most of his family, is today more venerated by the Shi'ah than the Mashhad 'Ali. 'Ashura Day (10th Muharram) when Husain was killed is commemorated by passion plays (*ta'ziyah*) and religious processions when the drama of his death is re-enacted with extravagant expressions of emotion.

Baghdad: Iraq. The Kazimain/Kadhimain Mosque is a celebrated Shi'ah shrine containing the tomb of Musa al-Kazim/Kadhim, the 7th Imam of the Ithna'asharis.

RELIGIOUS GROUPINGS

Sunnis

The great majority, probably over 80 per cent of Muslims, is Sunni, followers of the *Sunnah*, i.e. the way, course, rule or manner of conduct of the Prophet Muhammad; they are generally called "Orthodox". The Sunnis recognize the first four Caliphs (Abu Bakr, 'Umar, 'Uthman, 'Ali) as Rashidun, i.e. following the right course. They base their *Sunnah* upon the Koran and "Six Books" of Traditions, and

29

are organized in four Orthodox schools or rites (*madhhab*), all of equal standing within the Orthodox fold. Many Muslims today prefer to avoid identification with any single school.

Wahhabis

The adherents of "Wahhabism" strongly disapprove of this title by which they are known outside their own group, for they call themselves Muwahhidun or Unitarians. In fact they belong to the strict Hanbali school following its noted exponent, the 13th/14th century Syrian reformer Ibn Taimiyah. The founder of "Wahhabism", Muhammad b. 'Abd al-Wahhab of Arabian Najd (1703–87), sought to return to the pristine purity of early Islam freed from all accretions and what he regarded as innovations contrary to its true spirit, such as saint worship, lax sexual practices, and superstition. His doctrine was accepted by the chief Muhammad b. Sa'ud of Dar'iyah (near al-Riyadh). Ibn Sa'ud and his son 'Abd al-'Aziz—who proved a capable general—conquered much of Arabia. Medina fell in 1804 and Mecca in 1806 to Sa'ud son of 'Abd al-'Aziz, but after his death in 1814 the Wahhabis were gradually broken by the armies of the Pasha of Egypt, Muhammad 'Ali acting nominally on behalf of the Ottoman Sultan of Turkey. After varying fortunes in the 19th century the Wahhabis emerged as an Arabian power in the opening years of the 20th century. By the close of 1925 they held the Holy Cities and Jeddah and are today the strongest power in the Arabian Peninsula. Though Wahhabism remains the strictest of the Orthodox groups, Sa'udi Arabia has made some accommodation to modern times.

The Tariqahs or Religious Orders

In many Middle Eastern countries the Religious Orders (*Tariqahs*) have important political cum religious roles in society. There are the widely spread Qadiriyah who with the Tijaniyah are found in North Africa, the Khatmiyah in the Sudan, the Rifa'iyah in Egypt and Syria to pick out a few at random. The West has no organizations exactly equivalent to these Sufi orders into which an individual has to be initiated, and in which, by dint of ascetic excercises and study he may attain degrees of mystical enlightenment—this can also bring moral influence over his fellow men. The Orders may be Sunni or Shi'ah; some few Orders are even so unconventional as to be hardly Islamic at all. It was the Orthodox reformist Sanusi Order that has played the most significant role in our time. The Grand Sanusi, Muhammad b. 'Ali, born at Mustaghanem in Algeria of a Sharif family, founded the first *zawiyah* or lodge of the Sanusis in 1837. The Sanusi *Tariqah* is distinguished for its exacting standards of personal morality. The Sanusis set up a network of lodges in Cyrenaica (Libya) and put up strong resistance to Italian colonization. The Grand Sanusi was recognized as King Idris of Libya in 1951, but lost his throne at the military revolt led by Colonel Gaddafi in 1969.

Shi'ah

The Legitimist Shi'ah pay allegiance to 'Ali as mentioned above. 'Ali's posterity which must number at least hundreds of thousands, scattered all over the Muslim world, are customarily called Sharifs if they trace descent to his son al-Hasan, and Saiyids if descended from al-Husain, but while the Sharifs and Saiyids, the religious aristocracy of Islam, traditionally are accorded certain privileges in Islamic society, not all are Shi'ah, many being Sunnis. By the 9th century many strange sects and even pagan beliefs had become associated with the original Shi'ah or Party of 'Ali, but these extremist sects called *ghulat* have mostly vanished except a few, often practising a sort of quietism or dissimulation (*taqiyah*) for fear of persecution. All Shi'ah accord 'Ali an exalted position, the extreme (and heretical) Shi'ah at one time according him a sort of divinity even. Shi'ite Islam does not in the main differ on fundamental issues from the Sunni Orthodox since they draw from the same ultimate sources, but Shi'ah *mujtahids* have, certainly in theory, greater freedom to alter the application of law since they are regarded as spokesmen of the Hidden Imam.

The Ithna'asharis (Twelvers)

The largest Shi'ah school or rite is the Ithna'ashariyah or Twelvers, acknowledging twelve Imams. From 1502 Shi'ism became the established school in Iran under the Safavid ruler Sultan Shah Isma'il who claimed descent from Musa al-Kazim (see below). There are also Ithna'ashariyah in southern Iraq, al-Hasa, Bahrain and the Indian sub-continent.

The last Shi'ah Imam, Muhammad al-Mahdi disappeared in 878, but the Ithna'asharis believe he is still alive and will re-appear in the last days before the Day of Judgement as the Mahdi (Guided One)—a sort of Messiah—who will rule personally by divine right.

The twelve Imams recognized by the Twelver, Ithna'ashari Shi'ah are:

(1) 'Ali b. Abi Talib, cousin and son-in-law of the Prophet Muhammad.
(2) Al-Hasan, son of 'Ali.
(3) Al-Husain, second son of 'Ali.
(4) 'Ali Zain al-'Abidin, son of Husain.
(5) Muhammad al-Baqir, son of 'Ali Zain al-'Abidin.
(6) Ja'far al-Sadiq, son of Muhammad al-Baqir.
(7) Musa al-Kazim, son of Ja'far al-Sadiq.
(8) 'Ali al-Rida, son of Musa al-Kazim.
(9) Muhammad al-Taqi, son of 'Ali al-Rida.
(10) 'Ali al-Naqi, son of Muhammad al-Taqi.
(11) Al-Hasan al-Zaki, son of 'Ali al-Naqi, al-'Askari.
(12) Muhammad al-Mahdi, son of al-Hasan b. 'Ali, al-'Askari, known as al-Hujjah, the Proof.

Isma'ilis

This group of the Shi'ah does not recognize Musa al-Kazim as seventh Imam, but holds that the last Imam visible on earth was Isma'il, the other son of Ja'far al-Sadiq. For this reason they are also called the Sab'iyah or Seveners. There is however much

THE RELIGIONS OF THE MIDDLE EAST AND NORTH AFRICA

disagreement among the Seveners as to whether they recognized Isma'il himself as seventh Imam, or one of his several sons, and the Fatimids of Egypt (10th–12th centuries) in fact recognized a son of Isma'il's son Muhammad. Schismatic off-shoots from the Fatimid-Isma'ili group are the Druzes, the Musta'lians first settled in the Yemen but now with their main centre in Bombay—where the Daudi section is known as Bohoras, and the Nizari Isma'ilis of whom the Aga Khan is the spiritual head. The sect has a secret literature embodying its esoteric philosophy. Small groups of Isma'ilis are to be found in north-west Syria, Iran, Afghanistan, East Africa and Zanzibar, and larger numbers in India and Pakistan.

'Alawis (Nusairis)

The 'Alawis believe Muhammad was a mere forerunner of 'Ali and that the latter was an incarnation of Allah. This Shi'i extremist sect established in the ninth century has also adopted practices of both Christian and pagan origin. Most of its members today live in north-west Syria.

Druze

The Druzes are heretics, an off-shoot of the Fatimid Isma'ilis (see above), established in Lebanon and Syria. Their name (Duruz) derives from al-Darazi, a missionary of Persian origin who brought about the conversion of these Syrian mountaineers to the belief of the divine origin of the Fatimid Caliph al-Hakim. The origins of this sect and its subsequent expansion are still obscure. Hamzah b. 'Ali, a Persian contemporary of al-Darazi is the author of several of the religious treatises of the Druze. This community acknowledges one God and believes that he has on many occasions become incarnate in man. His last appearance was in the person of the Fatimid Caliph al-Hakim (disappeared 1020). The Druze have played a distinctive role in the political and social life of their country and are renowned for their independence of character.

Zaidis

The Zaidis are a liberal and moderate sect of the Shi'ah close enough to the Sunnis to call themselves the "Fifth School" (al-madhhab al-khamis). Their name is derived from a grandson of al-Husain b. 'Ali called Zaid b. 'Ali whom they recognize as fifth Imam. They reject religious dissimulation (taqiyah) and are extremely warlike. Zaidism is the dominant school of Islam in the Yemen Arab Republic, but Shafi'is form roughly half the population.

Ibadis

The Ibadis are commonly held to have their origins in the Khawarij who disassociated themselves from 'Ali b. Abi Talib when he accepted arbitration in his quarrel with Mu'awiyah, but this is open to question. They broke off early from the main stream of Islam and are usually regarded as heretics though with little justification. Groups of the sect, which has often suffered persecution, are found in Oman where Ibadism is the state religion, Zanzibar, Libya and Algeria, mainly in the Mzab.

Christianity

DEVELOPMENT IN THE MIDDLE EAST

Christianity was adopted as the official religion of the Roman empire in A.D. 313, and the Christian Church came to be based on the four leading cities, Rome, Constantinople (capital from A.D. 330), Alexandria and Antioch. From the divergent development of the four ecclesiastical provinces there soon emerged four separate churches: the Roman Catholic or Latin Church (from Rome), the Greek Orthodox Church (from Constantinople), the Syrian or Jacobite Church (from Antioch) and the Coptic Church (from Alexandria).

Later divisions resulted in the emergence of the Armenian (Gregorian) Church, which was founded in the fourth century, and the Nestorian Church, which grew up in the fifth century in Syria, Mesopotamia and Iran, following the teaching of Nestorius of Cilicia (d. 431). From the seventh century on followers of St. Maron began to establish themselves in northern Lebanon, laying the foundations of the Maronite Church.

Subsequently the Uniate Churches were brought into existence by the renunciation by formerly independent churches of doctrines regarded as heretical by the Roman Church and by the acknowledgement of Papal supremacy. These churches—the Armenian Catholic, the Chaldean (Nestorian) Catholic, Greek Catholic, the Coptic Catholic, the Syrian Catholic and the Maronite Church did, however, retain their Oriental customs and rites. The independent churches continued in existence alongside the Uniate Churches with the exception of the Maronites, all of whom reverted to Rome.

HOLY PLACES

Bethlehem: Israeli-occupied Jordan. The traditional birthplace of Jesus is enclosed in the Basilica of the Nativity, revered also by Muslims. Christmas is celebrated here by the Roman and Eastern Rite Churches on December 25th, by the Greek Orthodox, Coptic and Syrian Orthodox Churches on January 6th and 7th, by the Ethiopian Church on January 8th, and by the Armenian Church on January 19th. The tomb of Rachel, important to the three faiths, is just outside the town.

Jerusalem: Jordan (but annexed by Israel). The most holy city of Christianity has been a centre for pilgrims since the Middle Ages. It is the seat of the patriarchates of the Roman, Greek Orthodox and Armenian Churches, who share the custodianship of the Church of the Holy Sepulchre and who each own land and buildings in the neighbouring area.

The Church of the Holy Sepulchre stands on the hill of Golgotha in the higher north-western part of the Old City. In the central chamber of the church is the Byzantine Rotunda built by twelfth century crusaders, which shelters the small shrine on the traditional site of the tomb. Here the different patriarchates exercise their rights in turn. Close by is the Rock of Calvary, revered as the site of the Crucifixion.

Most pilgrims devoutly follow the Way of the Cross leading from the Roman Praetorium through several streets of the Old City to the Holy Sepulchre. Franciscan monks, commemorating the journey to the Crucifixion, follow the course of this traditional route each Friday; on Good Friday this procession marks a climax of the Easter celebrations of the Roman Church.

Outside the Old City stands the Mount of Olives, the scene of Jesus' Ascension. At the foot of its hill is the Garden of Gethsemane which is associated with the vigil on the eve of the Crucifixion. The Cenaculum or traditional room of the Last Supper is situated on Mount Zion in Israel.

Nazareth: Israel. This town, closely associated with the childhood of Jesus, has been a Christian centre since the fourth century A.D. The huge, domed Church of the Annunciation has recently been built on the site of numerous earlier churches to protect the underground Grotto of the Annunciation. Nearby the Church of St. Joseph marks the traditional site of Joseph's workshop.

Galilee: Israel. Many places by this lake are associated with the life of Jesus: Cana, scene of the miracle of water and wine, which is celebrated by an annual pilgrimage on the second Sunday after Epiphany; the Mount of Beatitudes; Tabgha, scene of the multiplication of the loaves and fish; and Capurneum, scene of the healing of the Centurion's servant.

Mount Tabor: Israel. The traditional site of the Transfiguration, which has drawn pilgrims since the fourth century, is commemorated by a Franciscan Monastery and a Greek Basilica, where the annual Festival of the Transfiguration is held.

Jericho: Israeli-occupied Jordan. The scene of the baptism of Jesus; nearby is the Greek Monastery of St. John the Baptist.

Nablus (*Samaria*): Israeli-occupied Jordan. This old town contains Jacob's Well, associated with Jesus, and the Tomb of Joseph.

Qubaibah (*Emmaus*): Israeli-occupied Jordan. It was near this town that two of the Disciples encountered Jesus after the Resurrection.

'Azariyyah (*Bethany*): Israeli-occupied Jordan. A town frequented by Jesus, the home of Mary and Martha, and the scene of the Raising of Lazarus.

Mount Carmel: Haifa, Israel. The Cave of Elijah draws many pilgrims, including Muslims and Druzes, who celebrate the Feast of Mar Elias on July 20th.

Ein Kerem: Israel. Traditional birthplace of John the Baptist, to whom a Franciscan church is dedicated; nearby is the Church of the Visitation.

Ephesus: Turkey. The city, formerly a great centre of pagan worship, where Paul founded the first of the seven Asian Churches. The recently restored Basilica, built by Justinian, is dedicated to John the Evangelist, who legend claims died here; a fourth century church on Aladag Mountain commemorating Mary's last years spent here now draws an annual pilgrimage in August.

Judaism

There are two main Jewish communities, the Ashkenazim and the Sephardim, the former from east, central and northern Europe, the latter from Spain, the Balkans, the Middle East and North Africa. The majority of immigrants into Israel were from the Ashkenazim, and their influence predominates there, though the Hebrew language follows Sephardim usage. There is no doctrinal difference between the two communities, but they observe distinct rituals.

HOLY PLACES

Wailing Wall: Jerusalem. This last remnant of the western part of the wall surrounding the courtyard of Herod's Temple, finally destroyed by the Romans in A.D. 70, is visited by devout Jews, particularly on the Fast Day of the 9th of Av, to grieve the destruction of the First and Second Temples which had once stood on the same site.

Mount Zion: Israel. A hill south-west of the Old City of Jerusalem, venerated particularly for the tomb of David, acknowledged by Muslims as abi Dawud (The Jebuzite hill on which David founded his Holy City is now known as Mount Ophel, and is in Jordan, just to the east of the modern Mount Zion). Not far from the foot of the hill are the rock-cut tombs of the family of King Herod.

Cave of Machpelah: Hebron, Israeli-occupied Jordan. The grotto, over which was built a mosque, contains the tombs of Abraham and Sarah, Isaac and Rebecca, Jacob and Leah.

Bethlehem: Israeli-occupied Jordan. The traditional tomb of Rachel is in a small shrine outside the town, venerated also by Muslims and Christians.

Mount Carmel: Israel. The mountain is associated with Elijah, whose Cave in Haifa draws many pilgrims. (*See* Christianity section).

Safad: Israel. Centre of the medieval Cabbalist movement, this city contains several synagogues from the sixteenth century associated with these scholars, and many important tombs, notably that of Rabbi Isaac Louria.

Meiron: Israel. The town contains the tombs of Shimon bar Yohai, reputed founder in the second century of the medieval Cabbalist movement, and his son Eleazer. A yearly Hassidic pilgrimage is held to the tomb to celebrate Lag Ba'Omer with a night of traditional singing and dancing in which Muslims also participate.

Tiberias: Israel. An ancient city containing the tombs of Moses Maimonides and Rabbi Meir Baal Harness. Famous as an historical centre of Cabbalist scholarship, it is with Jerusalem, Safad and Hebron, one of the four sacred cities of Judaism, and once accommodated a university and the Sandhedrin.

THE RELIGIONS OF THE MIDDLE EAST AND NORTH AFRICA

Other Communities

ZOROASTRIANS

Zoroastrianism developed from the teaching of Zoroaster, or Zarathustra, who lived in Iran some time between 700 and 550 B.C. Later adopted as the official religion of the Persian empire, Zoroastrianism remained predominant in Iran until the rise of Islam. Many adherents were forced by persecution to emigrate, and the main centre of the faith is now Bombay, where they are known as Parsees. Technically a monotheistic faith, Zoroastrianism retained some elements of polytheism. It later became associated with fire-worship.

Yazd: Iran. This city was the ancient centre of the Zoroastrian religion, and was later used as a retreat during the Arab conquest. It contains five fire temples and still remains a centre for this faith, of which some 35,000 adherents live in Iran.

BAHA'IS

Baha'ism made its appearance in Persia during the middle of the nineteenth century. It was founded by Baha'ullah, who, after a revelation in Baghdad in 1863, declared himself to be the "Promised One". A member of the Persian nobility he devoted his life to preaching against the corruption endemic in Persian society and as a result spent many years in exile; he died at Acre in Palestine in 1892. The Sect was administered by his descendants until 1957; the 56 national branches now elect the present governing body, the Universal House of Justice.

Baha'ism claims complete independence from all other faiths. Its followers believe that the basic principles of the great religions of the world are in complete harmony and that their aims and functions are complementary. Other tenets include belief in the brotherhood of man, the abolition of racial and colour discrimination, the equality of the sexes, progress towards world government and the use of an international language, monogamy, chastity and the encouragement of family life. There is no Baha'i priesthood, and asceticism and monasticism are discouraged. Most of the Middle Eastern adherents of the faith live in Iran or Israel.

Haifa: Israel. Shrine of the Bab and gardens, world centre of the Baha'i faith. Pilgrims visit this centre, and one in Acre where Baha'ullah was imprisoned, on the anniversaries of the birth and death of Bab and Baha'ullah.

SAMARITANS

Mount Gerazim: Jordan. The mountain is sacred to this small sect, who celebrate Passover here. The Samaritan High Priest lives at Nablus.

The Arab-Israeli Confrontation 1967-73

Michael Adams

Introduction

Israel's decisive victory over the Arab states in the war of June 1967 raised hopes that at last it would be possible to reach a definitive settlement of the Arab-Israeli conflict. These hopes were swiftly dashed and instead it became apparent that the conflict had merely been complicated by the occupation of further Arab territory, the displacement of more refugees and the aggravation of the sense of grievance felt by the Palestinians. Neither party to the dispute showed any disposition to accept a solution based on compromise and it was left to the world community, acting sometimes through the machinery of the United Nations and sometimes on the basis of proposals initiated by individual powers or groups of powers, to take up the running in pursuit of a negotiated settlement.

During the five years that followed the June war there were five main attempts from outside the area to provide an acceptable basis for agreement between the parties in the Middle East. The first of these was made at the United Nations in the autumn of 1967 when the Security Council, after anxious debate, adopted a unanimous resolution dealing with all the points at issue between Israel and her Arab neighbours. As a result of this resolution (No. 242 of November 22nd, 1967) a Swedish diplomat, Dr. Gunnar Jarring, was appointed as the Special Representative of the Secretary-General of the United Nations, with the task of establishing contact with the conflicting parties and helping them to reach agreement. The fact that the resolution was supported by all the major powers gave it a strength which enabled it to survive as the basis for a potential settlement; but, despite the patient efforts of Dr. Jarring, the varied interpretations placed upon the resolution prevented its implementation. Five years later the resolution still stood and Dr. Jarring had not renounced his mission, although the mission was in abeyance and agreement between the disputants seemed further away than ever.

The second initiative was taken early in 1969 at the suggestion of the French Government, in the conviction that Dr. Jarring would be unable to make any progress until the major powers agreed on a single interpretation of the Security Council resolution. Accordingly, Four-Power talks were started in New York between the representatives at the UN of the United States, the Soviet Union, Britain and France and these were later superseded by bilateral talks between the United States and the Soviet Union. The stumbling-block continued to be the interpretation of the clause in resolution 242 which provided for Israeli withdrawal "from territories occupied" in the conflict of June 1967 and by the end of the year it was clear that the two super-powers had failed to reach agreement.

The American Secretary of State, Mr. William Rogers, then took the third initiative, putting forward in December 1969 a series of proposals which came to be known as the "Rogers Plan". The plan left the details of a settlement to be negotiated between the interested parties, but made it clear that the American Government envisaged only minor rectifications in the pre-June 1967 borders between Israel and her Arab neighbours and favoured granting to the Palestinians the right so often promised in UN resolutions to choose between returning to Palestine or receiving compensation for their lost properties.

The Rogers proposals were badly received by all parties and although they continued to be discussed throughout 1970 the United States Government finally abandoned them in favour of a less ambitious plan to achieve a partial settlement between Israel and Egypt. Aimed at achieving the reopening of the Suez Canal in exchange for a limited withdrawal by the Israelis, this fourth initiative again failed and was replaced towards the end of 1971 by a fifth, coming this time from the Organization for African Unity. A committee of ten African Heads of State was formed and in November 1971 a delegation of four African leaders visited Israel and Egypt to put forward proposals which included the reactivation of Dr. Jarring's mission, the reopening of the Suez Canal, an Israeli withdrawal and international guarantees for secure borders and the freedom of navigation. Once again there was no result and the fifth anniversary of the June War was reached with Dr. Jarring's mission still in suspense and with a settlement no nearer than it had been on the day of his appointment in 1967.

New factors in the Middle East

While the international community was trying to grapple with the problem of devising a settlement of the conflict in the Middle East, a number of developments took place in the area itself which significantly affected the attitudes and the prospects of the main contestants.

DEATH OF PRESIDENT NASSER

By far the most important of these was the death of President Nasser in September 1970. Even the catastrophe of the June War had not substantially lessened Nasser's authority in the Arab world; within Egypt itself, it had certainly confirmed and in a sense even strengthened it. For all Egyptians and for most Arabs, Nasser represented now not only a leader without rivals, but also their only hope of recovery from a desperate and humiliating situation. Moreover, at the moment of his death, besides being the only figure commanding sufficient authority to carry through a settlement of the Arab-Israeli conflict—if the opportunity should present itself—

THE ARAB-ISRAELI CONFRONTATION 1967-73

Nasser was the only man who might have been able to resolve the internal conflicts which divided the Arab world, and especially the tragic confrontation between the Palestinian resistance movement and the Government of King Hussein in Jordan. He died, indeed, almost in the act of negotiating an agreement which was to provide a *modus vivendi* between the Jordan army and the guerrillas. Once Nasser's commanding influence was removed, the agreement soon collapsed and the reconciliation which might just have been maintained while he was alive gave way to renewed bitterness and conflict.

President Nasser's death made even more remote the prospect of a peaceful settlement with Israel. Although the succession of Anwar Sadat to the presidency was confirmed without opposition, it was inevitable that there should be a loss of confidence in the Egyptian leadership and likely that there would be some competition for influence within its ranks, arising out of the kind of rivalry that had previously been restrained by Nasser's unchallenged authority. In May 1971 a number of prominent Egyptians were arrested, including the Vice-President, the Minister of the Interior and the Minister of War, and charged with conspiracy against the régime. Apart from its other implications, this evidence of disagreement in the highest reaches of the Egyptian political structure made it still harder for the régime to consider making substantive concessions to Israel. Coming as it did at a time when the new president had already shown an unexpected degree of flexibility in response to a fresh initiative from Dr. Jarring, the internal dispute played a part in forcing President Sadat back towards a position of no compromise.

FEDERATION OF ARAB REPUBLICS

An important factor in promoting what seems to have been a movement of revolt against President Sadat's policies was the decision to establish a form of federal union between Egypt, Libya and Syria. An agreement had been signed at Benghazi on April 18th, 1971, and it was when the question of ratifying the agreement came up at a meeting of the Central Committee of the Arab Socialist Union in Cairo that the opposition manifested itself. Once the leaders of the opposition had been removed and placed under arrest, the agreement was ratified and the federation came into existence, with a direct bearing on the question of a political settlement with Israel. While President Nasser was alive, he had made it plain that he would be prepared to negotiate such a settlement, provided the Israelis agreed to withdraw and to accept a just solution for the problem of the Palestinian refugees. During the first six months of his rule, President Sadat had shown himself willing to follow and extend the same policy, even at some political risk to his own position. But the creation of a federal union, in which Egypt linked her fortunes to those of Libya and Syria—neither of which accepted the Security Council's resolution, while both gave active support to the Palestinian guerrillas—made it easy for the Israelis to claim that Egypt was not sincere in her pursuit of a political settlement and that she would indeed be prevented from accepting one by her new and more bellicose federal partners.

The establishment of the Federation of Arab Republics, as the federal union was called, thus affected Egypt's position vis-à-vis Israel in two ways. On the face of it, it represented a consolidation of the Arab front against the common enemy, offering Egypt in particular the reassurance of Libya's great economic resources. On the other hand, it complicated the search for a political settlement by limiting Cairo's freedom of movement in the field of external affairs.

NEW REGIMES IN LIBYA AND SUDAN

For a year or so after the war of 1967, the Arab world lay stunned by the extent of the disaster. Until the end of 1968, while feverish discussion and self-criticism went on in every Arab country, the régimes which had suffered defeat or shared in it vicariously in 1967 survived without apparent difficulty. In 1969 the façade began to crumble.

In May of that year a military régime under Colonel Jaafar Nemery established itself in the Sudan in place of the civilian government which had itself overthrown the earlier military régime of General Abboud. Since 1969, the Sudan has veered between an inclination to join with its neighbours to the north in the movement of pan-Arabism and the necessity of setting its own house in order first. When the Federation of Arab Republics was projected, it appeared likely that the Sudan would be one of its founder-members; in the event, the prospect of achieving a settlement of the long-standing rebellion in the southern Sudan persuaded Colonel Nemery to give precedence to this vital internal problem. Agreement was reached with the southern rebels at the beginning of 1972 and it seems probable that for the immediate future the government in Khartoum will be too preoccupied with consolidating Sudanese internal unity to take any further steps on the road to wider Arab unity.

The emergence, three months after the revolution in the Sudan, of a radical régime in Libya had more important implications, both for the future of the pan-Arab movement and for the Arab confrontation with Israel. Ten years earlier it would have been difficult to imagine that Libya, with its tiny population, its fledgling oil industry and its conservative monarchical régime, could influence to any significant degree the balance of forces between the Arabs and Israel. The overthrow of the monarchy in September 1969 and the establishment in its place of a Revolutionary Command Council under the leadership of Colonel Muammar Gaddafi, a fervent admirer of President Nasser, radically altered the picture. Three years later, with oil revenues running at the rate of some $1,500 million a year, Libya's revolutionary régime presented a factor of incalculable weight, not only in the immediate sense of its potential contribution to the Arab effort against Israel, but also on account of the political influence its enormous oil reserves must give it as the Western world becomes steadily more dependent for its oil supplies on the Middle East.

THE PALESTINIAN RESISTANCE MOVEMENT

At first sight, the overwhelming defeat of the Arab armies in 1967 put Israel's security beyond doubt. But it also gave a tremendous stimulus to the growth of a Palestinian guerrilla movement, which was to experience a bewildering fluctuation in its fortunes during the next five years.

The Palestine Liberation Organization (PLO), which had been established with the official support of the Arab states in 1964 but had never been much more than a symbol of Palestinian hopes, was now galvanized into activity. Besides organizing its own guerrilla group, it prepared a Palestine Congress which met in January and again in July 1968 to adopt a formal platform for the Palestinian resistance movement.

The limelight was captured, however, by one of the individual guerrilla groups theoretically linked under the organizational umbrella of the PLO. This was Al Fatah, the Palestine Movement of National Liberation, which had been founded several years before the June war but which again was spurred into active life by the failure of the Arab regular armies in 1967. At a time when Arab morale was particularly low, it derived great encouragement and a perhaps disproportionate amount of prestige from an incident early in 1968, when units of the Israeli army moved across the River Jordan to attack the village of Al Karameh and suffered heavy casualties at the hands of the guerrillas acting in concert with Jordan Government forces. A year later the leader of Al Fatah, Yasser Arafat, was elected Chairman of the executive committee of the PLO and for a time the name of Al Fatah became almost synonymous with the Palestine resistance movement.

Its activities were, however, limited both by the effective counter-measures taken by the Israelis, which prevented the guerrilla movement from establishing an effective underground organization in the occupied territories, and by internal dissensions within the movement itself. A smaller group, the Popular Front for the Liberation of Palestine, which had grown out of the pre-war Arab Nationalist Movement, replied by extending its attacks to Israeli aircraft and a series of such attacks provoked a violent Israeli reprisal raid on Beirut airport at the end of 1968. The policy of hijacking aircraft was denounced by Al Fatah and helped to widen the divisions within the guerrilla movement. It also rendered more acute the dilemma of the Jordan Government, which was subjected to frequent reprisal raids by Israeli air and land forces and which was unable to control the activities of the guerrillas. The tensions which this provoked within Jordan led to repeated clashes between the guerrillas and the forces of the Jordan Government until, after a multiple hijack operation by the Popular Front in September 1970, King Hussein ordered his army to crush the guerrillas and heavy fighting took place in the streets of Amman.

This marked the beginning of the end for the resistance movement in Jordan, where it was seriously weakened in the fighting of September 1970 and finally suppressed during the following twelve months. The surviving units were forced to transfer their bases to Syria or the Lebanon, where the scope for operations against Israel was much more limited and where again they found themselves increasingly in conflict with the local governments. Early in 1972 an extensive Israeli reprisal raid into south Lebanon led to an attempt to reassert the authority of the Lebanese army in the area adjoining the Israeli border, and these efforts were redoubled after a brutal attack on Lydda airport by Japanese gunmen acting on behalf of a splinter group of the Popular Front at the end of May.

As a result of these incidents it appeared at the time of the fifth anniversary of the June war that the resistance movement had been frustrated in its primary objectives and would henceforth be confined to isolated terrorist attacks which, however temporarily damaging to Israel, were more likely to harden Israeli attitudes than to induce a mood of conciliation. Such incidents served to remind world opinion of the continuing sense of Palestinian grievance, but at the cost of almost unanimous denunciation of the methods employed. In the absence of any movement towards a political settlement in the Middle East, the likelihood remained that such incidents would be renewed, with an increased disregard for would opinion (since the world had done nothing to remove the grievance) and with still less discrimination in the choice of targets.

RELATIONS BETWEEN EGYPT AND THE SOVIET UNION

After the defeat of 1967 the Soviet Union had rebuilt Egypt's military strength and during the succeeding years Arab dependence on Soviet aid had become total. It came as a surprise therefore when President Sadat, in July 1972, ordered the withdrawal from Egypt of the Soviet advisers who had been integrated into the Egyptian defence system. This move, with its momentous implications for the balance of power in the Mediterranean, reflected Arab disillusionment over the refusal of the Russians to provide the means of liberating the occupied territories. It also weakened the argument that American support for Israel was justified by the need to prevent communist infiltration in the eastern Mediterranean, especially in view of the close alliance between Egypt and the strongly anti-communist régime of President Gaddafi in Libya.

The course of events after June 1967

The war came to an end on June 10th, 1967, when the Governments of Syria and Israel followed those of Egypt and Jordan in accepting the Security Council's call for a ceasefire. Immediately a series of international consultations began with the aim of bringing to a final conclusion the nineteen year old conflict between Israel and her Arab neighbours.

Once the ceasefire was in operation, the Security Council's next step was to pass a resolution (No. 237, of 14th June, 1967), calling on Israel to facilitate the return of the new refugees who had fled (and were still fleeing) from the areas occupied by Israel during the war. The resolution also called on Israel to ensure the safety, welfare and security of the inhabitants of the "Occupied Areas".

President Johnson, who had announced on the outbreak of the war the United States' neutrality and support for the territorial integrity of all states in the Middle East, invited Mr. Kosygin, who was attending the United Nations session, to meet him to discuss "five great principles for peace". These were: the right of every state to exist in security; justice for the refugees; the right of free navigation in international waterways; the dangers of an arms race; and the need to recognize the political independence and territorial integrity of all states in the area. The two leaders met at the "Glasboro Summit" from June 23rd to 25th and agreed on the urgency of the need for action; but the dividing line which was to bedevil all efforts to achieve a settlement began to appear. The Russians, who had started to replace the arms lost by Egypt during the war, insisted that an Israeli withdrawal must be the preliminary to negotiations. The Americans upheld the right of the Israelis to maintain their occupation of Arab territory until the Arabs should recognize Israel and agree to negotiate directly with her.

An emergency meeting of the UN General Assembly reiterated on July 4th, the Security Council's call for the return of the refugees and on the same day it declared "invalid" the Israeli decision to annex the Arab sector of Jerusalem; but the Assembly failed to produce an agreed resolution on the basis for a settlement. A plan put forward later in the month by President Tito of Yugoslavia, calling for an Israeli withdrawal to the pre-war frontiers and a guarantee of those frontiers by the international community, was rejected by Israel on the ground that to recreate the pre-war situation would endanger that country's security.

The deadlock became total when an Arab summit conference, held in Khartoum between August 29th and September 3rd, 1967, confirmed earlier decisions not to negotiate directly with Israel, not to accord her recognition and not to sign a peace treaty. The Israeli Government, for its part, announced its refusal to undertake any but direct negotiations; if no such negotiations developed, Israeli forces would maintain their occupation of the Arab territories conquered during the war.

RESOLUTION 242

It was against this background that the UN Security Council met in the autumn of 1967 to consider the situation. A number of draft resolutions were submitted but failed to gain approval, either because (in the eyes of the supporters of the Arabs) they condoned the acquisition or occupation of territory by military force, or because (in the eyes of the supporters of Israel) they contained no adequate guarantee for Israel's security.

Finally, on November 22nd, 1967, the Security Council unanimously adopted a resolution put forward by the British delegate, Lord Caradon, and supported by the United States on the ground that it was entirely consistent with the five principles stated by President Johnson. The resolution, which was to remain the basis of all subsequent peace initiatives during the next five years, emphasized in its preamble "the inadmissibility of the acquisition of territory by war and the need to work for a just and lasting peace in which every state in the area can live in security". It then stated that such a peace should involve the withdrawal of Israeli armed forces "from territories occupied in the recent conflict" and the termination of the state of belligerency, with acknowledgment of the right of every state in the area to live in peace "within secure and recognized boundaries, free from threats or acts of force". The resolution affirmed the necessity to guarantee freedom of navigation through international waterways, to achieve a just settlement of the refugee problem and to guarantee the territorial integrity and political independence of every state in the area. Finally, the resolution requested the Secretary-General to appoint a Special Representative who would make contact with the parties in the Middle East and "assist efforts to achieve a peaceful and accepted settlement" on the basis of the provisions of the resolution.

This, the famous Resolution 242 of November 1967, precariously bridged the gap between the Arab and Israeli positions, which were also the positions adopted by their super-power supporters, the Soviet Union and the United States. By emphasizing the inadmissibility of the acquisition of territory by war, the resolution satisfied the demand of the Arabs and the Russians for an Israeli withdrawal. By being less than categorical about the extent of that withdrawal, it became acceptable to the Israelis and the Americans. All the subsequent arguments which developed centred around the question of whether the Israelis, in return for a definitive peace treaty, would have the right to retain parts of the Arab territories occupied during the war.

PALESTINIAN RESISTANCE

Even before these arguments developed, and during the interval of nearly six months which elapsed between the ceasefire and the adoption of the Security Council's resolution, events on the ground had hardened the positions of both sides. In the immediate aftermath of the fighting, despite the Israeli Prime Minister's declaration on the eve of the war that Israel had no intention of annexing "even one foot of Arab territory", the Israeli Knesset had legislated the "reunification" of Jerusalem,* which amounted in fact to the annexation of the Arab sector of the city. The Israelis had also destroyed a number of Arab villages, notably the three villages of Imwas, Beit Nuba and Yalu in the Latrun area, and had expelled their inhabitants. These actions, which

---

* For a discussion of the Jerusalem issue, *see* p. 44.

appeared to confirm Arab accusations of Israeli expansionism, greatly encouraged the rise of a Palestinian resistance movement, already stimulated by the failure of the Arab governments and the humiliation which that failure had brought on the Arab world. When the Israelis began, as early as September 1967, to establish Jewish settlements in the occupied territories,* at a time when the stream of Arab refugees set in motion by the June war was still flowing eastward at the rate of several hundred a day, support for the resistance movement became widespread in the Arab world. It was strengthened when the Israelis, after agreeing in response to United Nations resolutions to allow the return of these new refugees, arbitrarily closed the border again after only 14,000 had been allowed to re-enter Palestine, out of 150,000 who had filed applications with the Red Cross to do so.

The situation, then, was deteriorating even before Dr. Gunnar Jarring, whom the Secretary-General had appointed as his Special Representative in accordance with Resolution 242, went to the Middle East to undertake his mission at the end of 1967. During the first half of 1968 there were increasingly frequent breaches of the ceasefire along the Suez Canal (which remained blocked to traffic), while Palestinian guerrilla raids led to heavy Israeli reprisal actions in the Jordan valley. After the first anniversary of the June war, and while Dr. Jarring was patiently pursuing his contacts with both sides, the trend towards violence accelerated. In July 1968 guerrillas of the Popular Front for the Liberation of Palestine carried out the first hijack operation in the Middle East, diverting an Israeli airliner to Algiers. President Nasser in the same month warned that another explosion in the area was inevitable if a stalemate which left Israel in occupation of territory belonging to three of its neighbours was allowed to continue indefinitely. In the course of artillery duels across the Canal the towns of Suez and Ismailia were virtually destroyed by the Israelis and their populations had to be evacuated into the interior of Egypt.

PHANTOMS FOR ISRAEL

The governments of Egypt and Jordan had accepted Resolution 242, while Syria rejected it. Israel, while not rejecting the resolution, said it could not be a substitute for specific agreements between the parties. When the UN General Assembly met in the autumn of 1968, Israel put forward a nine-point plan for a Middle East settlement which made no mention of withdrawal, speaking instead of "a boundary settlement compatible with the security of Israel and the honour of the Arab states". This produced no response from the Arab governments, which were shocked when President Johnson at the height of the American election campaign, announced that the United States was considering the sale of Phantom aircraft to Israel. A month later Richard Nixon was elected as President Johnson's successor and sent Governor William Scranton on a fact-finding mission to the Middle East. Mr. Scranton was reported as saying that the United States should adopt "a more even-handed policy in the Middle East", but the sale of fifty Phantoms to Israel was confirmed at the end of December and marked an important stage in the escalation of the arms race in the Middle East.

The day after the sale of Phantoms was announced, Israeli parachutists raided Beirut airport, in reprisal for an Arab guerrilla attack on an Israeli airliner in Athens, and destroyed thirteen aircraft. This incident, which for the first time directly involved the Lebanon in the Arab-Israeli confrontation, brought about renewed diplomatic activity to arrest the worsening situation. After the Security Council had unanimously condemned Israel for the Beirut raid, the Soviet Government took up an earlier French proposal that there should be Four-Power talks between the Soviet Union, the United States, Britain and France to obtain agreement between the major powers over the implementation of Resolution 242.

FOUR-POWER TALKS

Dr. Jarring withdrew from the scene while the "Big Four" tried to reconcile the conflicting interpretations of the Security Council resolution. At first the prospects seemed encouraging, with President Nixon eager to register an initial success in the field of foreign affairs and with general agreement that the drift to war in the Middle East threatened the peace of the world. At the beginning of February 1969, President Nasser declared his willingness to enter into direct negotiations once Israeli forces had withdrawn from Arab territory. Mr. Eshkol, the Prime Minister of Israel, stated his readiness to meet President Nasser and declared that Israel was prepared to be flexible about all the occupied territories except Jerusalem and the Golan Heights (captured from Syria in 1967). But as the year wore on, spasmodic fighting continued along both the Suez Canal and the Jordan fronts, until in July 1969 President Nasser publicly gave up hope of a peaceful settlement, forecasting that a long "war of attrition" would be necessary to dislodge Israel from the occupied territories. A month later a severe fire at Al Aqsa mosque in the Old City of Jerusalem, for which an Australian immigrant to Israel was later blamed, caused a further dangerous increase in tension.

THE ROGERS PLAN

The Four-Power talks were suspended while Soviet and American representatives engaged in bilateral contacts. There was a moment of optimism when it appeared likely that a formula had been found for "Rhodes-style" negotiations (on the pattern of the talks conducted in Rhodes which led to the armistice agreements between Israel and the Arab states in 1949), but the optimism faded when an Israeli suggestion that this would amount to direct negotiations led the Arabs to reject the formula. Instead the American Secretary of State, Mr. William Rogers, produced on December 9th, 1969, a set of proposals which came to be known as the Rogers Plan. The

---

* By June 1973, forty-six such settlements had been established in the occupied areas of the West Bank, the Gaza Strip, the Golan Heights and Sinai.

proposals represented an attempt to steer a middle course between the Arab view, that the Security Council resolution should be implemented *in toto* and did not call for negotiation, and the Israeli preference for direct negotiations which would decide where the new borders should be drawn. The most important aspect of the plan was that it made clear the American view that there should only be minor rectifications of the pre-June 1967 boundaries. This ensured Israeli hostility to the plan, since despite the insistence of the Israeli Foreign Minister, Abba Eban, that "everything is negotiable", it had now become clear that his cabinet colleagues were deeply divided on this crucial question.

President Nasser, impatient with what he saw as the hypocritical attitude of the American Government, also rejected the plan, which in any case was presently swept aside by a serious renewal of hostilities in January 1970, when the Israelis initiated a series of deep penetration bombing raids (using the new American Phantom aircraft) on targets inside Egypt. General Dayan announced at the beginning of February that the Israeli bombing attacks had three aims: to force the Egyptians (who had been sustaining heavy casualties along the Canal front) to respect the ceasefire, to prevent Egyptian preparations for a new war and to weaken the Egyptian régime. In practice, the raids (which caused heavy civilian casualties) had three results: they strengthened Egyptian support for President Nasser; they damaged Israel's image in the outside world; and they drew the Russians into providing further assistance to Egypt. In March 1970 the first reports appeared of the installation in Egypt of Soviet SAM-3 anti-aircraft missiles in the vicinity of Cairo, Alexandria and key targets in the Nile delta, while the number of Soviet military advisers in Egypt rose to an estimated 6,000.

International concern over these developments paved the way for a renewal of diplomatic efforts. In April 1970 the American Assistant Secretary of State, Joseph Sisco, visited the Middle East to explain the objectives of the Rogers Plan. Israeli requests for more Phantoms were not granted and it appeared that the immediate American objectives were to obtain a renewal of the ceasefire and to extract from the Israeli Government an undertaking to withdraw from the greater part of the occupied territories as part of an overall peace settlement. President Nasser, in a speech on May 1st said that "despite Phantoms and napalm" he was keeping the door open to the American initiative. The Israelis made no public commitment on withdrawal, but their response in private was sufficiently encouraging for Mr. Rogers to relaunch his proposals, with the backing of the four major powers. After a variety of bilateral contacts between the various parties, President Nasser announced in a speech on July 23rd, 1970, Egypt's acceptance of the American proposal for a renewal of the ceasefire, followed by negotiations through Dr. Jarring for the implementation of Resolution 242. A week later, the Israeli Government, after receiving assurances on the future supply of arms from the United States, also agreed to the American proposal, with the proviso that Israel would never return to the pre-war boundaries and that none of its troops would be withdrawn from the ceasefire lines until a binding peace agreement had been signed. Even so, the price of Israel's qualified acceptance of the Rogers proposals was a cabinet crisis which resulted in the resignation from Mrs. Golda Meir's cabinet of the right-wing Gahal party led by Mr. Menachem Begin.

The renewed ceasefire along the Suez Canal front came into operation on the night of August 7th/8th, with a duration of ninety days, during which the two sides were to engage in indirect negotiations under the auspices of Dr. Jarring. Two fresh developments, however, frustrated the movement towards an overall settlement. After a single meeting with Dr. Jarring in New York, the Israeli representative was recalled to Jerusalem and the Israeli Government protested that the ceasefire had been violated by the movement of Soviet missiles behind the Egyptian lines. The confused American reaction suggested that there had been a genuine misunderstanding about the conditions agreed to, but the negotiations in New York had not been renewed when a serious crisis in Jordan distracted the attention of all the parties concerned.

KING HUSSEIN AND THE PALESTINE GUERRILLAS

On September 6th, 1970, Palestine guerrillas of the Popular Front for the Liberation of Palestine hijacked two airliners and flew them to a desert airfield in Jordan. A third airliner was taken to Cairo and destroyed on the airfield there. Three days later a fourth aircraft was hijacked and joined the two in the desert near Zerqa, where the guerrillas, after releasing a number of passengers, held some three hundred others as hostages, demanding in exchange for them the release of a substantial number of Palestinians held prisoner in Israel.

This episode, which marked the high point of guerrilla activity, proved also the last straw as far as the Government of Jordan was concerned. During the previous two years, as the strength of the guerrilla movement increased, the Jordan Government had faced a dilemma. If it allowed the guerrillas freedom of movement in Jordan, it invited retaliation from Israel—and the retaliation had been heavy, in the form of ground and air raids which had depopulated the East Bank of the Jordan river and caused severe casualties in Irbid, Salt and other towns and villages of east Jordan. If the Government tried to control or suppress the activities of the guerrillas, it faced the possibility of civil war in Jordan.

The relationship between the Government and the guerrillas was linked to the question of a political settlement with Israel. The Palestine resistance movement, whose declared objective was the reconstitution in Palestine of a democratic state open to Jews and Arabs alike, opposed the idea of a political settlement with Israel, since this would involve the recognition and the perpetuation of a Zionist state. King Hussein had followed the lead of President Nasser in accepting the Rogers Plan and was thus committed to the principle of a political settlement involving the recognition of Israel. So long as a political settlement was not in prospect, it had been possible for the King and the guerrillas to pursue their diverse objectives without coming into open conflict, but as soon as such a settlement became a serious possibility the uneasy coexistence between them was threatened. On several previous occasions in 1969 and 1970 the Jordan Government and the guerrillas had come close to a confrontation and after the renewal of the ceasefire in August 1970 and the acceptance by the Jordan Government of the Rogers Plan, a clash became inevitable.

The multiple hijack operation by the PFLP, which explicitly challenged the authority of the Jordan Government, provided the spark and on September 16th King Hussein appointed a military government in Jordan which next day set about the liquidation of the resistance movement. After ten days of heavy fighting in Amman, mediation efforts by other Arab governments, and in particular by President Nasser, brought about a truce, which was signed in Cairo on September 27th, 1970. On the following day President Nasser suffered a heart attack and died almost immediately.

As far as a settlement between Israel and the Arabs was concerned, it looked as though the position so painstakingly established in August had been undermined. The ceasefire along the Suez Canal endured, though precariously; but the negotiations through Dr. Jarring were not renewed and until President Nasser's successor had had time to consolidate his position, it seemed unlikely that they would be. Jordan was faced with the task of overcoming the effects of an inconclusive civil war and only Israel, which had achieved its objective of a renewal of the ceasefire, had any reason to feel satisfied with the turn of events. Miraculously, all of the hostages held in Amman throughout the fighting were released unharmed (indeed, they praised their captors for the care they had taken to protect them), although the three airliners were blown up by the guerrillas.

PRESIDENT SADAT AND THE CEASEFIRE

There was both surprise and relief, therefore, when the new President of Egypt, Anwar Sadat, established himself without opposition and showed himself willing to take up the search for a settlement where it had been left by his predecessor. He agreed to renew the ceasefire for a further 90 days and, after intensive consultations between Israeli and American leaders and the extension to Israel of American credits worth $500 million, Israel agreed to return to the Jarring talks. Preliminary discussions took place in New York and in January 1971 Dr. Jarring visited Israel and Egypt, where both sides restated their positions to him on all the points at issue. When the ceasefire agreement was again coming to an end, on February 5th, 1971, President Sadat once more agreed to renew it, this time for 30 days, adding the proposal that Israel should begin to withdraw its forces from the east bank of the canal, in which case Egypt would be able to clear the canal for navigation. This was to constitute the first stage in the implementation of Resolution 242; but, as things turned out, this new suggestion was to provide the pretext for delaying further movement towards an overall settlement.

On February 8th Dr. Jarring wrote to the Governments of Israel and Egypt, expressing his optimism about the desire of both parties for a settlement and inviting each of them to give firm commitments which would resolve the central deadlock. Israel, Dr. Jarring suggested, should agree on certain stated conditions (providing guarantees for security and freedom of navigation) to withdraw to the international boundary between Egypt and the Palestine of the British Mandate. Egypt should give a parallel undertaking to conclude a peace agreement explicitly ending the state of belligerency and recognizing Israel's right to exist in peace and security. In other words, both parties were asked formally to accept the principal obligations laid on them by Resolution 242.

The Egyptian reply gave the undertaking called for by Dr. Jarring, provided that Israel did the same and agreed to withdraw its forces to the international border. The Israeli reply stated firmly that, while Israel would be prepared to withdraw its forces to "secure, recognized and agreed boundaries to be established in the peace agreement", it would in no circumstances withdraw to the pre-June 1967 lines.

This official confirmation of Israel's insistence on territorial expansion as part of a peace settlement embarrassed the American Government, which had first withheld and then granted military and economic assistance to Israel, in the attempt to persuade the Israeli Government to accept only "minor rectifications" of the armistice lines. The Americans made one further attempt when Mr. Rogers, at a press conference on March 16th, 1971, urged the Israelis to accept international guarantees in place of territorial gains, adding that security did not "necessarily require additions of territory" and that in the American view "the 1967 boundary should be the boundary between Israel and Egypt".

PROPOSAL FOR A "PARTIAL SETTLEMENT"

When this too met with an Israeli refusal, the American Government took up instead President Sadat's suggestion of an Israeli withdrawal for some distance in Sinai to allow the reopening of the Suez Canal. But the opportunity had been lost and the new proposal for a partial settlement quickly became bogged down in arguments over the extent of the Israeli withdrawal and the question of whether it should be seen as the first step in a complete withdrawal or not. The arguments dragged on through most of 1971 until the proposal was finally dropped by the Americans on November 22nd—the fourth anniversary of the passage of Resolution 242.

Before this a new initiative had been launched, this time by the Organization for African Unity, which on June 22nd, 1971, had come out in support of Dr. Jarring's mission and had adopted a strong resolution calling for an Israeli withdrawal and the full implementation of Resolution 242. A committee of ten African Heads of State was formed to undertake a peace mission and in November 1971 four members of this committee visited the Middle East for discussions with the contending parties. They submitted to President Sadat and Mrs. Meir proposals based closely on the provisions of Resolution 242 and appeared for a time to have some hopes of narrowing the gap between the two sides. In the growing mood of frustration and disillusionment which had by now gripped the Arab world, and with the Israelis confident that, with an election less than a year away in the United States, they could count on American benevolence, such hopes seemed over-optimistic and before the end of the year the OAU initiative had quietly foundered.

In December the UN General Assembly, in a resolution reaffirming the "inadmissibility of the acquisition of territory by war" and calling for an Israeli withdrawal, also urged Israel to "respond favourably" to the proposals made by Dr. Jarring in February. Only seven states voted against the resolution (Israel and six Latin American states) and it was noted that the United States, which in the past had always voted in support of Israel on territorial questions, abstained, reflecting the American view that Israel should withdraw from all but insubstantial portions of the occupied territories. However, no action followed and the year ended with President Sadat in a dangerously weakened position. He had taken considerable risks in going so far in pursuit of a political settlement and had promised the Egyptian people that 1971 would be the "year of decision". He blamed the lack of progress on American "political manoeuvring", and when the American Government ushered in the new—election—year by promising Israel a further 42 Phantom and 90 Sky-hawk aircraft, there was little likelihood that a fresh American suggestion of indirect talks between Israeli and Egyptian representatives in New York would come to anything

In February 1972 the Israelis launched a large-scale incursion into the Lebanon, stating that its aim was the elimination of guerrilla bases near Israel's northern border. When there was a revival of guerrilla action in May and June, in the form of another hijacking and an attack by Japanese gunmen (acting for the PFLP) on Lydda airport, there was speculation about further Israeli action against the Lebanon (where the PFLP had established its headquarters after being driven out of Jordan). In June a further Israeli raid on the Lebanon was condemned by the Security Council after more than 70 civilians had been killed or wounded by what the Israeli Deputy Prime Minister described as an "error".

Before this, in March 1972, King Hussein had announced a plan for the reorganization of his kingdom along federal lines, with the Palestinians on the West Bank enjoying autonomy. The plan was conditional on an Israeli withdrawal and so had no immediate significance. It was nevertheless denounced on all sides, by the Palestinian resistance organizations, by the other Arab governments (Egypt went so far as to break off relations with Jordan on account of it) and by Israel, whose Prime Minister vied with the Arab leaders in the strength of her criticisms.

When the storm had abated, there were signs in Israel, in the occupied territories and in the rest of the Arab world that on second thoughts many people were prepared to take a less jaundiced view of the King's proposals.

An unexpected development followed when President Sadat, in July 1972, called for the withdrawal from Egypt of the large contingent of Soviet advisers engaged on the reorganization of Egypt's defence system. This surprise move, which gravely damaged Egypt's defensive capability—to say nothing of its capacity ever to develop the power to launch an attack against the forces of Israel—was interpreted as a final appeal to the American Government to bring pressure to bear on Israel to accept a settlement involving an Israeli withdrawal from Sinai. If this was its intention, the move was ill-timed, since the approach of the Presidential election made it virtually certain that no American politician would advocate a course of action so unwelcome to Zionist opinion in the United States. There was in fact no American response to President Sadat's gesture before the election in November; nor, after it, apart from generalized statements about the need for a new initiative to restore peace in the Middle East, was there any sign of a reappraisal of American policy towards the area. Even the painful conclusion of the war in Viet-Nam, which followed early in the new year and which had been widely envisaged as the precursor to an attempt to reach a similar settlement in the Middle East, brought no fresh move from Washington.

In Europe, however, partly out of a feeling that an important opportunity was being allowed to slip and partly as a reflection of a sense of disillusionment with American leadership, a reappraisal of Middle Eastern policy was taking place. In preparation for Britain's entry into the European Community (which took place on January 1st, 1973) an attempt was being made to concert a European approach to important questions of foreign policy. The attempt found expression in the voting at the end of the annual Middle East debate in the General Assembly of the United Nations when, with the single exception of Denmark, all the members of the Community followed the lead of Britain and France in voting for a resolution strongly critical of Israel. (The United States again abstained.) (*See* Documents on Palestine, p. 58.)

TERROR AND COUNTER-TERROR IN THE MIDDLE EAST

The cease-fire along the Suez Canal was maintained, but along the northern borders of Israel and Israeli-held territory there was a renewal of violence in the second half of 1972, accompanied by a mounting series of terrorist attacks by both Israelis and Palestinians in various parts of the world. In July and August 1972, a number of Palestinian leaders were killed or seriously injured by explosive devices sent to them in Beirut. In September, during the Olympic

Games in Munich, Palestinian guerrillas captured a number of Israeli athletes and held them hostage in an attempt to obtain the release of Palestinians held captive in Israel. The attempt failed when West German police, after promising the Palestinians safe conduct out of Germany, opened fire on them at Munich airport, whereupon the guerrillas killed the hostages and were themselves either killed or captured. (The three Palestinians who survived were later released when a West German airliner was hijacked and flown, with the guerrillas on board, to Libya.)

The Munich attack was followed by heavy Israeli ground and air raids into the Lebanon, which the Israeli Government held responsible for the activities of guerrillas whose bases (since their expulsion from Jordan in 1970 and 1971) were in the refugee camps of the Lebanon and in Beirut. The fact that many civilians were killed in these raids, among them women and children in the refugee camps, provoked a confused international response and a growing sense of alarm as the unsettled conflict in the Middle East sparked violence in countries far from the conflict itself. Letter bombs were posted to Israeli representatives in various countries—an attaché at the Israeli Embassy in London was killed by one in September—and after the Israeli Prime Minister, Mrs. Meir, had announced that "we have no alternative but to strike at the terrorist organizations wherever we can locate them", representatives of the Palestine Liberation Organization were attacked by gunmen or with explosive devices in Rome, Stockholm, Paris and Nicosia.

For a brief period at the beginning of 1973 it looked as though an effort would be made to take the conflict out of the hands of the terrorists and return it to the political arena. In rapid succession Mr. Hafez Ismail (President Sadat's political adviser), King Hussein of Jordan and Mrs. Meir visited Washington for talks with President Nixon. But the frail hopes aroused by this diplomatic activity were dashed when, in February 1973, a heavy Israeli attack on guerrilla installations in a refugee camp in North Lebanon was followed immediately by the shooting down by Israeli fighters of a Libyan airliner whose French captain had strayed over occupied Sinai in a sandstorm. The two incidents caused the death of 150 people—almost all of them civilians—within twenty-four hours and provoked an unprecedented wave of criticism of the Israelis on the eve of Mrs. Meir's arrival in Washington. Before she left, however, Palestinian guerrillas had diverted international indignation onto themselves by attacking the Saudi Arabian Embassy in Khartoum, where they held hostage and eventually murdered the American Ambassador and two other diplomats, one American and the other Belgian. A month later, following an abortive Palestinian attack on the Israeli Embassy in Nicosia, Israeli commandos mounted a carefully planned and ruthlessly executed attack in Beirut, penetrating into a residential district in the heart of the Lebanese capital and killing, among a number of other people, three leading members of the PLO.

CRISIS IN LEBANON

The Israeli raid provoked a serious crisis in the Lebanon, where fighting broke out between Palestinian guerrillas and Lebanese Government forces. The agreement signed in Cairo between representatives of the PLO and the Lebanese Government in 1969, which had regulated relations between the two sides ever since, was called in question and for a time it looked as though the Lebanese Government might follow the example of King Hussein of Jordan and try to suppress guerrilla activity in the Lebanon altogether. However, the Lebanese instinct for compromise asserted itself and a fresh agreement was reached in May 1973 which imposed further restrictions on guerrilla activity. Heavy casualties had been caused during the fighting, in which the Lebanese Government had ordered airstrikes against guerrilla positions in the refugee camps on the outskirts of Beirut, and the resulting bitterness on both sides inevitably threw doubt on the durability of the new agreement.

On May 7th, 1973, the twenty-fifth anniversary of the creation of the State of Israel was celebrated with a massive military parade in Jerusalem. The parade symbolized Israel's commanding military position but was widely criticized, both inside and outside Israel, as an indication of the Israeli Government's refusal to consider any compromise formula which might lead to peace with the Arabs. Public opinion polls in Israel, as well as the pronouncements of leading figures in the Israeli political and military establishment, indicated a significant hardening of Israeli attitudes over the crucial question of withdrawal from the territories occupied in 1967.

ENERGY CRISIS

A new factor which affected international attitudes towards the Arab-Israeli conflict began to make itself felt during the first half of 1973. This was the prospect of a serious energy crisis arising out of the rapidly increasing demand for oil products in Europe, the United States and Japan. In the United States in particular, the realization that industrial expansion in the following decade was likely to become much more dependent on imports of oil and natural gas from Middle Eastern producing countries caused serious concern at a time when America's support for Israel made the United States a particular target for criticism throughout the Arab world.

SUMMARY

Six years after the war of June 1967, the Arab-Israeli conflict appeared to be further than ever from solution. The Israelis, whose military supremacy had if anything increased, remained in control of all the territories they had occupied in 1967 and had established in these territories some 46 civilian and paramilitary settlements. The Arab Governments remained disunited and, while they refused to envisage a peace settlement which did not provide for the return of all the occupied territories, they lacked the means (both

THE ARAB-ISRAELI CONFRONTATION 1967-73

political and military) to bring about such a settlement. The Palestinian resistance movement was at its lowest ebb since the June war and its continued existence as an independent movement rested on the fragile basis of the agreement reached with the Lebanese Government in May 1973. The United Nations found all its efforts to devise a settlement frustrated by Israel's refusal to relinquish its 1967 conquests and the refusal of the Arab states to envisage a settlement on any other terms. A dangerous mood of frustration enveloped the Middle East and for the outside world the anxiety over a possible renewal of the conflict was compounded by apprehensions about the maintenance of vital oil supplies. More than ever, the key to the situation rested in the hands of the United States, which found itself isolated in support of Israel and yet faced with the prospect of becoming increasingly dependent on Arab oil. The Watergate scandal in Washington appeared to make it even less likely than before that the Americans would take the lead in proposing any fresh initiative which might break the deadlock in the Middle East. The isolation of the United States was emphasized during the debate in the Security Council in the summer of 1973. After prolonged discussion, the Council considered a resolution put forward by eight non-aligned members which was strongly critical of Israel's continued occupation of Arab territory. The U.S.A. found it necessary to use its veto to prevent the passage of the resolution, which obtained the affirmative votes of all the other Council members except China, which abstained.

The Jerusalem Issue

Michael Adams

The Arab sector of Jerusalem, including the old walled city, was captured during the June War by Israeli forces, which went on to occupy all the Jordanian territory lying west of the River Jordan. Theoretically, there was no difference in status between Jerusalem and the rest of the West Bank; both were occupied territory. In practice, the Israelis immediately removed the walls and barriers dividing the western (Israeli) and eastern (Arab) sectors of the city and at the end of June 1967 the Knesset passed legislation incorporating the Arab sector into a reunited Jerusalem under Israeli sovereignty. At the same time the boundaries of the municipal area of Jerusalem were greatly extended, reaching to near Bethlehem in the south and incorporating Kalandia airport (close to Ramallah) in the north.

Juridically speaking, the status of Jerusalem was already complicated. The plan for the partition of Palestine adopted by the General Assembly of the United Nations in 1947 had envisaged separate Arab and Jewish states, with the city and environs of Jerusalem constituting an international enclave. In the war of 1948, Israeli and Jordanian forces had fought for possession of Jerusalem and the armistice of April 1949 had left each in control of part of the divided city. The international community had never recognized this *de facto* arrangement, which endured for 18 years until the June War of 1967.

Faced with Israel's effective annexation of the Arab sector, the General Assembly on July 4th, 1967, ruled, by 99 votes to none, that the annexation was invalid and called on Israel not to take any measures to alter the status of the city. Ten days later the Assembly adopted a second resolution "reiterating" the earlier one and "deploring" Israel's failure to implement it.

Before the first of these resolutions was passed, the Israeli authorities had embarked on a series of structural alterations and demolitions in the Old City of Jerusalem, which aroused strong Arab protests and whose continuation was to lead to considerable international controversy. In clearing the area in front of the Western (Wailing) Wall, they expropriated 50 Arab families at very short notice and demolished their houses, while in the Jewish Quarter they dispossessed a further 200 Arab families. In all, and before the end of June 1967, some 4,000 Arabs in Jerusalem had lost their homes. In some cases, but not all, they were provided with alternative accommodation.

In November 1967 the UN Security Council passed its unanimous resolution number 242 setting out the basis for an overall settlement between Israel and its Arab neighbours. The resolution spoke of "withdrawal of Israeli armed forces from territories occupied in the recent conflict", but made no specific mention of Jerusalem, where the anxiety of the Arab population was increased by the growing signs of Israel's intention to exclude the city from the scope of any eventual negotiations. In January 1968 the Israeli authorities expropriated more than 800 acres of land in the Arab sector and announced plans for the construction of the housing estates on the slopes of Mount Scopus, overlooking the Old City. A joint protest signed by fifty leading members of the Muslim and Jewish communities in Jerusalem had no result, beyond provoking the expulsion by the Israelis of the Mayor of Arab Jerusalem, but in May 1968, after the Israelis had held (in defiance of a unanimous resolution by the Security Council) a military parade in Jerusalem to commemorate the foundation of the State of Israel, the Security Council passed its first resolution dealing specifically with the Jerusalem issue.

The resolution (No. 252 of May 21st, 1968) deplored Israel's failure to comply with the two General Assembly resolutions of July 4th and 14th, 1967, confirmed that any measures taken by Israel to alter the status of Jerusalem were invalid and called on Israel to rescind all such measures and to refrain from similar action in the future. The effect was only to increase the haste with which the Israelis set about changing the face of the city. Bulldozers had been at work on Mount Scopus since February and soon the first of the new housing estates began to take shape beside the Nablus Road leading northwards out of Jerusalem. In the absence of any progress towards a peace settlement, it became clear that the Israeli Government intended to forestall, by establishing a physical presence in the Arab sector of Jerusalem, any future attempt to challenge their sovereignty over the whole of the municipal area.

Meeting again to consider the question in July 1969, the Security Council adopted, this time by a unanimous vote (in the previous year the United States had abstained from voting on the Jerusalem resolution), an even stronger resolution (No. 267 of July 3rd, 1969). Reaffirming its earlier stand and deploring "the failure of Israel to show any regard" for the previous resolutions both of the General Assembly and of the Security Council, the Council "censured in the strongest terms" all measures taken by Israel to change the status of Jerusalem, confirmed that all such measures were "invalid" and again called on Israel to desist from taking any further action of the same kind. The Israelis formally rejected the resolution and the Israeli Minister of Information stated in Jerusalem that it could not influence the "facts" which had been intentionally created by Israel "after due consideration of the political danger involved".

The situation in Jerusalem itself was further aggravated in August 1969 by a disastrous fire in Al Aqsa mosque, which at first sight appeared to confirm the fears of the Arabs for the safety of the Muslim and Christian shrines in the Old City. Israeli investigations showed that the fire had been caused by a deranged Australian religious fanatic and the Australian was later brought to trial; but from that moment the concern of Muslim communities throughout the world reinforced the Arab sense of grievance at the loss of the Holy city.

In the following year Christian concern also began to make itself felt, especially after the publication of an Israeli "master plan" for the future of Jerusalem. This plan envisaged the doubling of the Jewish population of the city by 1980 and an eventual total population of 900,000. An international conference of town planners, convoked by the Israeli municipal authorities at the end of 1970 to consider the plan, was almost unanimous in condemning its aesthetic implications. Early in 1971 a dispute also developed between the United Nations and the Israeli Government over the intention, announced in the master plan, to build another housing estate in the neighbourhood of Government House, the headquarters in Jerusalem of the United Nations. In March 1971 articles in the official Vatican newspaper *L'Osservatore Romano* and in the English Catholic weekly *The Tablet* revealed the strength of Catholic feeling over developments in the Holy City, and these feelings were strengthened when it became known that in the same month the Israelis had destroyed an Arab village on the hill of Nebi Samwil, north-west of Jerusalem, in preparation for the building on Arab land of yet another housing estate for immigrant Jews.

Israeli opinion was divided over the future of Jerusalem. Only a small minority of Israelis were in favour of relinquishing Israeli sovereignty over the Arab sector of the city, if negotiations for an overall settlement of the Arab-Israeli conflict should ever materialize. In the absence of any sign of such negotiations, the issue remained a hypothetical one and the Israeli Government made no secret of its determination to establish a hold on Jerusalem which would prove unbreakable. A further resolution by the Security Council (No. 298 of September 25th, 1971—see Documents on Palestine, p. 58) was rejected as brusquely as the previous ones and even the provision in the resolution that the Secretary-General, "using such instrumentalities as he may choose", should report to the Council within 60 days on the implementation of the resolution, failed to achieve any result since the Secretary-General had to report at the end of that period that he had been unable to execute his mission, for lack of co-operation from the Israeli authorities.

On purely aesthetic grounds, however, many Israelis were disturbed by the physical changes overtaking Jerusalem. Within five years of the June War of 1967 the construction of large housing estates had transformed the appearance of Mount Scopus, where the Old City (and the whole of the Arab sector) was dominated by a row of apartment blocks breaking the historic skyline. There were acute disagreements between the Mayor of Jerusalem and the Ministers of Housing and of Tourism over some of the implications of this building programme, but continuing uncertainty over the prospects for a political settlement with the Arabs gave encouragement to the "activists" in Israel, and the creation of "facts" continued, in Jerusalem as in the rest of the occupied territories, throughout 1972 and 1973.

Documents on Palestine

DECLARATION OF FIRST WORLD ZIONIST CONGRESS

The Congress, convened in Basle by Dr. Theodor Herzl in August 1897, adopted the following programme:*

The aim of Zionism is to create for the Jewish people a home in Palestine secured by public law.

The Congress contemplates the following means to the attainment of this end:

1. The promotion on suitable lines, of the settlement of Palestine by Jewish agriculturists, artisans and tradesmen.

2. The organization and binding together of the whole of Jewry by means of appropriate institutions, local and general, in accordance with the laws of each country.

3. The strengthening of Jewish sentiment and national consciousness.

4. Preparatory steps towards obtaining government consent as are necessary, for the attainment of the aim of Zionism.

McMAHON CORRESPONDENCE†

Ten letters passed between Sir Henry McMahon, British High Commissioner in Cairo, and Sherif Husain of Mecca from July 1915 to March 1916. Husain offered Arab help in the war against the Turks if Britain would support the principle of an independent Arab state. The most important letter is that of October 24th, 1915, from McMahon to Husain:

... I regret that you should have received from my last letter the impression that I regarded the question of limits and boundaries with coldness and hesitation; such was not the case, but it appeared to me that the time had not yet come when that question could be discussed in a conclusive manner.

I have realized, however, from your last letter that you regard this question as one of vital and urgent importance. I have, therefore, lost no time in informing the Government of Great Britain of the contents of your letter, and it is with great pleasure that I communicate to you on their behalf the following statement, which I am confident you will receive with satisfaction:

The two districts of Mersina and Alexandretta and portions of Syria lying to the west of the districts of Damascus, Homs, Hama and Aleppo cannot be said to be purely Arab, and should be excluded from the limits demanded.

With the above modification, and without prejudice to our existing treaties with Arab chiefs, we accept those limits.

As for those regions lying within those frontiers wherein Great Britain is free to act without detriment to the interests of her ally, France, I am empowered in the name of the Government of Great Britain to give the following assurances and make the following reply to your letter:

(1) Subject to the above modifications, Great Britain is prepared to recognize and support the independence of the Arabs in all the regions within the limits demanded by the Sherif of Mecca.

(2) Great Britain will guarantee the Holy Places against all external aggression and will recognize their inviolability.

(3) When the situation admits, Great Britain will give to the Arabs her advice and will assist them to establish what may appear to be the most suitable forms of government in those various territories.

(4) On the other hand, it is understood that the Arabs have decided to seek the advice and guidance of Great Britain only, and that such European advisers and officials as may be required for the formation of a sound form of administration will be British.

(5) With regard to the *vilayets* of Bagdad and Basra, the Arabs will recognize that the established position and interests of Great Britain necessitate special administrative arrangements in order to secure these territories from foreign aggression, to promote the welfare of the local populations and to safeguard our mutual economic interests.

I am convinced that this declaration will assure you beyond all possible doubt of the sympathy of Great Britain towards the aspirations of her friends the Arabs and will result in a firm and lasting alliance, the immediate results of which will be the expulsion of the Turks from the Arab countries and the freeing of the Arab peoples from the Turkish yoke, which for so many years has pressed heavily upon them. . . .

ANGLO-FRANCO-RUSSIAN AGREEMENT (SYKES—PICOT AGREEMENT)

April-May 1916

The allocation of portions of the Ottoman empire by the three powers was decided between them in an exchange of diplomatic notes. The Anglo-French agreement‡ dealing with Arab territories became known to Sherif Husain only after publication by the new Bolshevik government of Russia in 1917:

1. That France and Great Britain are prepared to recognize and protect an independent Arab State or a Confederation of Arab States in the areas (A) and (B)

---

* Text supplied by courtesy of Josef Fraenkel.
† British White Paper, Cmd. 5957, 1939.

‡ E. L. Woodward and Rohan Butler (Eds.), *Documents on British Foreign Policy 1919–1939*. First Series, Vol. IV, 1919. London, H.M.S.O., 1952.

46

marked on the annexed map, under the suzerainty of an Arab Chief. That in area (A) France, and in area (B) Great Britain shall have priority of right of enterprises and local loans. France in area (A) and Great Britain in area (B) shall alone supply foreign advisers or officials on the request of the Arab State or the Confederation of Arab States.

2. France in the Blue area and Great Britain in the Red area shall be at liberty to establish direct or indirect administration or control as they may desire or as they may deem fit to establish after agreement with the Arab State or Confederation of Arab States.

3. In the Brown area there shall be established an international administration of which the form will be decided upon after consultation with Russia, and after subsequent agreement with the other Allies and the representatives of the Sherif of Mecca.

4. That Great Britain be accorded
   (*a*) The ports of Haifa and Acre;
   (*b*) Guarantee of a given supply of water from the Tigris and the Euphrates in area (A) for area (B).

His Majesty's Government, on their part, undertake that they will at no time enter into negotiations for the cession of Cyprus to any third Power without the previous consent of the French Government.

5. Alexandretta shall be a free port as regards the trade of the British Empire and there shall be no discrimination in treatment with regard to port dues or the extension of special privileges affecting British shipping and commerce; there shall be freedom of transit for British goods through Alexandretta and over railways through the Blue area, whether such goods are going to or coming from the Red area, area (A) or area (B); and there shall be no differentiation in treatment, direct or indirect, at the expense of British goods on any railway or of British goods and shipping in any port serving the areas in question.

Haifa shall be a free port as regards the trade of France, her colonies and protectorates, and there shall be no differentiation in treatment or privilege with regard to port dues against French shipping and commerce. There shall be freedom of transit through Haifa and over British railways through the Brown area, whether such goods are coming from or going to the Blue area, area (A) or area (B), and there shall be no differentiation in treatment, direct or indirect, at the expense of French goods on any railway or of French goods and shipping in any port serving the areas in question.

6. In area (A), the Baghdad Railway shall not be extended southwards beyond Mosul, and in area (B), it shall not be extended northwards beyond Samarra, until a railway connecting Baghdad with Aleppo along the basin of the Euphrates will have been completed, and then only with the concurrence of the two Governments.

7. Great Britain shall have the right to build, administer and be the sole owner of the railway connecting Haifa with area (B). She shall have, in addition, the right in perpetuity and at all times of carrying troops on that line. It is understood by both Governments that this railway is intended to facilitate communication between Baghdad and Haifa, and it is further understood that, in the event of technical difficulties and expenditure incurred in the maintenance of this line in the Brown area rendering the execution of the project impracticable, the French Government will be prepared to consider plans for enabling the line in question to traverse the polygon formed by Banias-Umm Qais-Salkhad-Tall 'Osda-Mismieh before reaching area (B).

8. For a period of twenty years, the Turkish customs tariff shall remain in force throughout the Blue and Red areas as well as in areas (A) and (B), and no increase in the rates of duties and no alteration of *ad valorem* duties into specific duties shall be made without the consent of the two Powers.

There shall be no internal customs barriers between any of the areas mentioned above. The customs duties to be levied on goods destined for the interior shall be collected at the ports of entry and remitted to the Administration of the area of destination.

9. It is understood that the French Government will at no time initiate any negotiations for the cession of their rights and will not cede their prospective rights in the Blue area to any third Power other than the Arab State or Confederation of Arab States, without the previous consent of His Majesty's Government who, on their part, give the French Government a similar undertaking in respect of the Red area.

10. The British and French Governments shall agree to abstain from acquiring and to withold their consent to a third Power acquiring territorial possessions in the Arabian Peninsula; nor shall they consent to the construction by a third Power of a naval base in the islands on the eastern seaboard of the Red Sea. This, however, will not prevent such rectification of the Aden boundary as might be found necessary in view of the recent Turkish attack.

11. The negotiations with the Arabs concerning the frontiers of the Arab State or Confederation of Arab States shall be pursued through the same channel as heretofore in the name of the two Powers.

12. It is understood, moreover, that measures for controlling the importation of arms into the Arab territory will be considered by the two Governments.

BALFOUR DECLARATION
November 2nd, 1917

Balfour was British Foreign Secretary, Rothschild the British Zionist leader.

Dear Lord Rothschild,

I have much pleasure in conveying to you on behalf of His Majesty's Government the following declaration of sympathy with Jewish Zionist aspirations, which has been submitted to and approved by the Cabinet.

"His Majesty's Government view with favour the establishment in Palestine of a national home for the Jewish people, and will use their best endeavours to facilitate the achievement of this object, it being clearly understood that nothing shall be done which may prejudice the civil and religious rights of existing non-Jewish communities in Palestine, or the rights and political status enjoyed by Jews in any other country."

I should be grateful if you would bring this declaration to the knowledge of the Zionist Federation.

Yours sincerely,
Arthur James Balfour.

HOGARTH MESSAGE*
January 4th, 1918

The following is the text of a message which Commander D. G. Hogarth, C.M.G., R.N.V.R., of the Arab Bureau in Cairo, was instructed on January 4th, 1918, to deliver to King Husain of the Hejaz at Jeddah:

1. The *Entente* Powers are determined that the Arab race shall be given full opportunity of once again forming a nation in the world. This can only be achieved by the Arabs themselves uniting, and Great Britain and her Allies will pursue a policy with this ultimate unity in view.

2. So far as Palestine is concerned, we are determined that no people shall be subject to another, but—
   (a) In view of the fact that there are in Palestine shrines, Wakfs and Holy places, sacred in some cases to Moslems alone, to Jews alone, to Christians alone, and in others to two or all three, and inasmuch as these places are of interest to vast masses of people outside Palestine and Arabia, there must be a special régime to deal with these places approved of by the world.
   (b) As regards the Mosque of Omar, it shall be considered as a Moslem concern alone, and shall not be subjected directly or indirectly to any non-Moslem authority.

3. Since the Jewish opinion of the world is in favour of a return of Jews to Palestine, and inasmuch as this opinion must remain a constant factor, and, further, as His Majesty's Government view with favour the realization of this aspiration, His Majesty's Government are determined that in so far as is compatible with the freedom of the existing population, both economic and political, no obstacle should be put in the way of the realization of this ideal.

In this connection the friendship of world Jewry to the Arab cause is equivalent to support in all States where Jews have political influence. The leaders of the movement are determined to bring about the success of Zionism by friendship and co-operation with the Arabs, and such an offer is not one to be lightly thrown aside.

ANGLO-FRENCH DECLARATION†
November 7th, 1918

The object aimed at by France and Great Britain in prosecuting in the East the war let loose by the ambition of Germany is the complete and definite emancipation of the peoples so long oppressed by the Turks and the establishment of national Governments and Administrations deriving their authority from the initiative and free choice of the indigenous populations.

In order to carry out these intentions France and Great Britain are at one in encouraging and assisting the establishments of indigenous Governments and Administrations in Syria and Mesopotamia, now liberated by the Allies, and in the territories the liberation of which they are engaged in securing and recognizing these as soon as they are actually established.

Far from wishing to impose on the populations of these regions any particular institutions they are only concerned to ensure by their support and by adequate assistance the regular working of Governments and Administrations freely chosen by the populations themselves. To secure impartial and equal justice for all, to facilitate the economic development of the country by inspiring and encouraging local initiative, to favour the diffusion of education, to put an end to dissensions that have too long been taken advantage of by Turkish policy, such is the policy which the two Allied Governments uphold in the liberated territories.

RECOMMENDATIONS OF THE KING—CRANE COMMISSION‡
August 28th, 1919

The Commission was set up by President Wilson of the U.S.A. to determine which power should receive the Mandate for Palestine. The following are extracts from their recommendations on Syria:

1. We recommend, as most important of all, and in strict harmony with our Instructions, that whatever foreign administration (whether of one or more Powers) is brought into Syria, should come in, not at all as a colonising Power in the old sense of that term, but as a Mandatory under the League of Nations with the clear consciousness that 'the well-being and development', of the Syrian people form for it a 'sacred trust'.

2. We recommend, in the second place, that the unity of Syria be preserved, in accordance with the earnest petition of the great majority of the people of Syria.

3. We recommend, in the third place, that Syria be placed under one mandatory Power, as the natural way to secure real and efficient unity.

4. We recommend, in the fourth place, that Amir Faisal be made the head of the new united Syrian State.

5. We recommend, in the fifth place, serious modification of the extreme Zionist programme for Palestine of unlimited immigration of Jews, looking finally to making Palestine distinctly a Jewish State.

---

* British White Paper, Cmd. 5964, 1939.

† Report of a Committee set up to consider Certain Correspondence between Sir Henry McMahon and the Sherif of Mecca in 1915 and 1916, March 16th, 1939 (British White Paper, Cmd. 5974).

‡ U.S. Department of State. *Papers Relating to the Foreign Relations of the Untied States. The Paris Peace Conference 1919.* Vol. XII. Washington, 1947.

(1) The Commissioners began their study of Zionism with minds predisposed in its favor, but the actual facts in Palestine, coupled with the force of the general principles proclaimed by the Allies and accepted by the Syrians have driven them to the recommendation here made.

(2) The Commission was abundantly supplied with literature on the Zionist program by the Zionist Commission to Palestine; heard in conferences much concerning the Zionist colonies and their claims; and personally saw something of what had been accomplished. They found much to approve in the aspirations and plans of the Zionists, and had warm appreciation for the devotion of many of the colonists, and for their success, by modern methods in overcoming great, natural obstacles.

(3) The Commission recognised also that definite encouragement had been given to the Zionists by the Allies in Mr. Balfour's often-quoted statement, in its approval by other representatives of the Allies. If, however, the strict terms of the Balfour Statement are adhered to—favoring 'the establishment in Palestine of a national home for the Jewish people', 'it being clearly understood that nothing shall be done which may prejudice the civil and religious rights of existing non-Jewish communities in Palestine'—it can hardly be doubted that the extreme Zionist program must be greatly modified. For 'a national home for the Jewish people' is not equivalent to making Palestine into a Jewish State; nor can the erection of such a Jewish State be accomplished without the gravest trespass upon the 'civil and religious rights of existing non-Jewish communities in Palestine'. The fact came out repeatedly in the Commission's conference with Jewish representatives, that the Zionists looked forward to a practically complete dispossession of the present non-Jewish inhabitants of Palestine, by various forms of purchase.

In his address of July 4th, 1918, President Wilson laid down the following principle as one of the four great 'ends for which the associated peoples of the world were fighting': 'The settlement of every question, whether of territory, of sovereignty, of economic arrangement, or of political relationship upon the basis of the free acceptance of that settlement by the people immediately concerned, and not upon the basis of the material interest or advantage of any other nation or people which may desire a different settlement for the sake of its own exterior influence or mastery.' If that principle is to rule, and so the wishes of Palestine's population are to be decisive as to what is to be done with Palestine, then it is to be remembered that the non-Jewish population of Palestine—nearly nine-tenths of the whole—are emphatically against the entire Zionist program. The tables show that there was no one thing upon which the population of Palestine were more agreed than upon this. To subject a people so minded to unlimited Jewish immigration, and to steady financial and social pressure to surrender the land, would be a gross violation of the principle just quoted, and of the people's rights, though it kept within the forms of law.

It is to be noted also that the feeling against the Zionist program is not confined to Palestine, but shared very generally by the people throughout Syria, as our conferences clearly showed. More than 72 per cent—1,350 in all—of all the petitions in the whole of Syria were directed against the Zionist program. Only two requests—those for a united Syria and for independence—had a larger support. This general feeling was duly voiced by the General Syrian Congress in the seventh, eighth and tenth resolutions of their statement.

The Peace Conference should not shut its eyes to the fact that the anti-Zionist feeling in Palestine and Syria is intense and not lightly to be flouted. No British officer, consulted by the Commissioners, believed that the Zionist program could be carried out except by force of arms. The officers generally thought that a force of not less than 50,000 soldiers would be required even to initiate the program. That of itself is evidence of a strong sense of the injustice of the Zionist program, on the part of the non-Jewish populations of Palestine and Syria. Decisions requiring armies to carry out are sometimes necessary, but they are surely not gratuitously to be taken in the interests of serious injustice. For the initial claim, often submitted by Zionist representatives, that they have a 'right' to Palestine, based on an occupation of 2,000 years ago, can hardly be seriously considered.

There is a further consideration that cannot justly be ignored, if the world is to look forward to Palestine becoming a definitely Jewish State, however gradually that may take place. That consideration grows out of the fact that Palestine is the Holy Land for Jews, Christians, and Moslems alike. Millions of Christians and Moslems all over the world are quite as much concerned as the Jews with conditions in Palestine, especially with those conditions which touch upon religious feelings and rights. The relations in these matters in Palestine are most delicate and difficult. With the best possible intentions, it may be doubted whether the Jews could possibly seem to either Christians or Moslems proper guardians of the holy places, or custodians of the Holy Land as a whole.

The reason is this: The places which are most sacred to Christians—those having to do with Jesus—and which are also sacred to Moslems, are not only not sacred to Jews, but abhorrent to them. It is simply impossible, under those circumstances, for Moslems and Christians to feel satisfied to have these places in Jewish hands, or under the custody of Jews. There are still other places about which Moslems must have the same feeling. In fact, from this point of view, the Moslems, just because the sacred places of all three religions are sacred to them, have made very naturally much more satisfactory custodians of the holy places than the Jews could be. It must be believed that the precise meaning in this respect of the complete Jewish occupation of Palestine has not been fully sensed by those who urge the extreme Zionist program. For it would intensify, with a certainty like fate, the anti-Jewish feeling both in Palestine and in all other portions of the world which look to Palestine as the Holy Land.

In view of all these considerations, and with a deep sense of sympathy for the Jewish cause, the Commissioners feel bound to recommend that only a greatly reduced Zionist program be attempted by the Peace Conference, and even that, only very gradually initiated. This would have to mean that Jewish immigration should be definitely limited, and that the project for making Palestine distinctly a Jewish commonwealth should be given up.

There would then be no reason why Palestine could not be included in a united Syrian State, just as other portions of the country, the holy places being cared for by an international and inter-religious commission, somewhat as at present, under the oversight and approval of the Mandatory and of the League of Nations. The Jews, of course, would have representation upon this commission.

ARTICLE 22 OF THE COVENANT OF THE LEAGUE OF NATIONS

1. To those colonies and territories which as a consequence of the late War have ceased to be under the sovereignty of the States which formerly governed them and which are inhabited by peoples not yet able to stand by themselves under the strenuous conditions of the modern world, there should be applied the principle that the well-being and development of such peoples form a sacred trust of civilization and that securities for the performance of this trust should be embodied in this Covenant.

2. The best method of giving practical effect to this principle is that the tutelage of such peoples should be entrusted to advanced nations who by reason of their resources, their experience or their geographical position can best undertake this responsibility, and who are willing to accept it, and that this tutelage should be exercised by them as Mandatories on behalf of the League.

3. The character of the Mandate must differ according to the stage of the development of the people, the geographical situation of the territory, its economic conditions and other similar circumstances.

4. Certain communities formerly belonging to the Turkish Empire have reached a stage of development where their existence as independent nations can be provisionally recognized subject to the rendering of administrative advice and assistance by a Mandatory until such time as they are able to stand alone. The wishes of these communities must be a principal consideration in the selection of the Mandatory.

7. In every case of Mandate, the Mandatory shall render to the Council an annual report in reference to the territory committed to its charge.

8. The degree of authority, control, or administration to be exercised by the Mandatory shall, if not previously agreed upon by the Members of the League, be explicitly defined in each case by the Council.

9. A permanent Commission shall be constituted to receive and examine the annual reports of the Mandatories and to advise the Council on all matters relating to the observance of the Mandates.

MANDATE FOR PALESTINE*

July 24th, 1922

The Council of the League of Nations:

Whereas the Principal Allied Powers have agreed, for the purpose of giving effect to the provisions of Article 22 of the Covenant of the League of Nations to entrust to a Mandatory selected by the said Powers the administration of the territory of Palestine, which formerly belonged to the Turkish Empire, within such boundaries as may be fixed by them; and

Whereas the Principal Allied Powers have also agreed that the Mandatory should be responsible for putting into effect the declaration originally made on November 2nd, 1917, by the Government of His Britannic Majesty, and adopted by the said Powers, in favour of the establishment in Palestine of a National Home for the Jewish people, it being clearly understood that nothing should be done which might prejudice the civil and religious rights of existing non-Jewish communities in Palestine, or the rights and political status enjoyed by Jews in any other country; and

Whereas recognition has thereby been given to the historical connection of the Jewish people with Palestine and to the grounds for reconstituting their National Home in that country; and

Whereas the Principal Allied Powers have selected His Britannic Majesty as the Mandatory for Palestine; and

Whereas the Mandate in respect of Palestine has been formulated in the following terms and submitted to the Council of the League for approval; and

Whereas His Britannic Majesty has accepted the Mandate in respect of Palestine and undertaken to exercise it on behalf of the League of Nations in conformity with the following provisions; and

Whereas by the afore-mentioned Article 22 (paragraph 8), it is provided that the degree of authority, control or administration to be exercised by the Mandatory, not having been previously agreed upon by the Members of the League, shall be explicitly defined by the Council of the League of Nations;

Confirming the said Mandate, defines its terms as follows:

ARTICLE 1. The Mandatory shall have full powers of legislation and of administration, save as they may be limited by the terms of this Mandate.

ARTICLE 2. The Mandatory shall be responsible for placing the country under such political, administrative and economic conditions as will secure the establishment of the Jewish National Home, as laid down in the preamble, and the development of self-governing institutions, and also for safeguarding the civil and religious rights of all the inhabitants of Palestine, irrespective of race and religion.

ARTICLE 3. The Mandatory shall, so far as circumstances permit, encourage local autonomy.

---

* British White Paper, Cmd. 1785.

ARTICLE 4. An appropriate Jewish Agency shall be recognized as a public body for the purpose of advising and co-operating with the Administration of Palestine in such economic, social and other matters as may affect the establishment of the Jewish National Home and the interests of the Jewish population in Palestine, and, subject always to the control of the Administration, to assist and take part in the development of the country.

The Zionist organization, so long as its organization and constitution are in the opinion of the Mandatory appropriate, shall be recognized as such agency. It shall take steps in consultation with His Britannic Majesty's Government to secure the co-operation of all Jews who are willing to assist in the establishment of the Jewish National Home.

ARTICLE 5. The Mandatory shall be responsible for seeing that no Palestine territory shall be ceded or leased to, or in any way placed under the control of, the Government of any foreign Power.

ARTICLE 6. The Administration of Palestine, while ensuring that the rights and position of other sections of the population are not prejudiced, shall facilitate Jewish immigration under suitable conditions and shall encourage, in co-operation with the Jewish Agency referred to in Article 4, close settlement by Jews on the land, including State lands and waste lands not required for public purposes.

ARTICLE 7. The Administration of Palestine shall be responsible for enacting a nationality law. There shall be included in this law provisions framed so as to facilitate the acquisition of Palestinian citizenship by Jews who take up their permanent residence in Palestine.

ARTICLE 13. All responsibility in connection with the Holy Places and religious buildings or sites in Palestine, including that of preserving existing rights and of securing free access to the Holy Places, religious buildings and sites and the free exercise of worship, while ensuring the requirements of public order and decorum, is assumed by the Mandatory, who shall be responsible solely to the League of Nations in all matters connected herewith, provided that nothing in this Article shall prevent the Mandatory from entering into such arrangements as he may deem reasonable with the Administration for the purpose of carrying the provisions of this Article into effect; and provided also that nothing in this Mandate shall be construed as conferring upon the Mandatory authority to interfere with the fabric of the management of purely Moslem sacred shrines, the immunities of which are guaranteed.

ARTICLE 14. A special Commission shall be appointed by the Mandatory to study, define and determine the rights and claims in connection with the Holy Places and the rights and claims relating to the different religious communities in Palestine. The method of nomination, the composition and the functions of this Commission shall be submitted to the Council of the League for its approval, and the Commission shall not be appointed or enter upon its functions without the approval of the Council.

ARTICLE 28. In the event of the termination of the Mandate hereby conferred upon the Mandatory, the Council of the League of Nations shall make such arrangements as may be deemed necessary for safeguarding in perpetuity, under guarantee of the League, the rights secured by Articles 13 and 14, and shall use its influence for securing, under the guarantee of the League, that the Government of Palestine will fully honour the financial obligations legitimately incurred by the Administration of Palestine during the period of the Mandate, including the rights of public servants to pensions or gratuities.

CHURCHILL MEMORANDUM*
June 3rd, 1922

The Secretary of State for the Colonies has given renewed consideration to the existing political situation in Palestine, with a very earnest desire to arrive at a settlement of the outstanding questions which have given rise to uncertainty and unrest among certain sections of the population. After consultation with the High Commissioner for Palestine the following statement has been drawn up. It summarizes the essential parts of the correspondence that has already taken place between the Secretary of State and a Delegation from the Moslem Christian Society of Palestine, which has been for some time in England, and it states the further conclusions which have since been reached.

The tension which has prevailed from time to time in Palestine is mainly due to apprehensions, which are entertained both by sections of the Arab and by sections of the Jewish population. These apprehensions, so far as the Arabs are concerned, are partly based upon exaggerated interpretations of the meaning of the Declaration favouring the establishment of a Jewish National Home in Palestine, made on behalf of His Majesty's Government on November 2nd, 1917. Unauthorized statements have been made to the effect that the purpose in view is to create a wholly Jewish Palestine. Phrases have been used such as that Palestine is to become "as Jewish as England is English." His Majesty's Government regard any such expectation as impracticable and have no such aim in view. Nor have they at any time contemplated, as appears to be feared by the Arab Delegation, the disappearance or the subordination of the Arabic population, language or culture in Palestine. They would draw attention to the fact that the terms of the Declaration referred to do not contemplate that Palestine as a whole should be converted into a Jewish National Home, but that such a Home should be founded *in Palestine*. In this connection it has been observed with satisfaction that at the meeting of the Zionist Congress, the supreme governing body of the Zionist Organization, held at Carlsbad in September 1921, a resolution was passed expressing as the official statement of Zionist aims "the determination of the Jewish people to live with the Arab people on terms

---

* Palestine, Correspondence with the Palestine Arab Delegation and the Zionist Organization (British White Paper, Cmd. 1700), pp. 17–21.

of unity and mutual respect, and together with them to make the common home into a flourishing community, the upbuilding of which may assure to each of its peoples an undisturbed national development."

It is also necessary to point out that the Zionist Commission in Palestine, now termed the Palestine Zionist Executive, has not desired to possess, and does not possess, any share in the general administration of the country. Nor does the special position assigned to the Zionist Organization in Article IV of the Draft Mandate for Palestine imply any such functions. That special position relates to the measures to be taken in Palestine affecting the Jewish population, and contemplates that the Organization may assist in the general development of the country, but does not entitle it to share in any degree in its Government.

Further, it is contemplated that the status of all citizens of Palestine in the eyes of the law shall be Palestinian, and it has never been intended that they, or any section of them, should possess any other juridical status.

So far as the Jewish population of Palestine are concerned, it appears that some among them are apprehensive that His Majesty's Government may depart from the policy embodied in the Declaration of 1917. It is necessary, therefore, once more to affirm that these fears are unfounded, and that that Declaration, re-affirmed by the Conference of the Principal Allied Powers at San Remo and again in the Treaty of Sèvres, is not susceptible of change.

During the last two or three generations the Jews have recreated in Palestine a community, now numbering 80,000, of whom about one-fourth are farmers or workers upon the land. This community has its own political organs; and elected assembly for the direction of its domestic concerns; elected councils in the towns; and an organization for the control of its schools. It has its elected Chief Rabbinate and Rabbinical Council for the direction of its religious affairs. Its business is conducted in Hebrew as a vernacular language, and a Hebrew Press serves its needs. It has its distinctive intellectual life and displays considerable economic activity. This community, then, with its town and country population, its political, religious and social organizations, its own language, its own customs, its own life, has in fact "national" characteristics. When it is asked what is meant by the development of the Jewish National Home in Palestine, it may be answered that it is not the imposition of a Jewish nationality upon the inhabitants of Palestine as a whole, but the further development of the existing Jewish community, with the assistance of Jews in other parts of the world, in order that it may become a centre in which the Jewish people as a whole may take, on grounds of religion and race, an interest and a pride. But in order that this community should have the best prospect of free development and provide a full opportunity for the Jewish people to display its capacities, it is essential that it should know that it is in Palestine as of right and not on sufferance. That is the reason why it is necessary that the existence of a Jewish National Home in Palestine should be internationally guaranteed, and that it should be formally recognized to rest upon ancient historic connection.

This, then, is the interpretation which His Majesty's Government place upon the Declaration of 1917, and, so understood, the Secretary of State is of opinion that it does not contain or imply anything which need cause either alarm to the Arab population of Palestine or disappointment to the Jews.

For the fulfilment of this policy it is necessary that the Jewish community in Palestine should be able to increase its numbers by immigration. This immigration cannot be so great in volume as to exceed whatever may be the economic capacity of the country at the time to absorb new arrivals. It is essential to ensure that the immigrants should not be a burden upon the people of Palestine as a whole, and that they should not deprive any section of the present population of their employment. Hitherto the immigration has fulfilled these conditions. The number of immigrants since the British occupation has been about 25,000. . . .

REPORT OF PALESTINE ROYAL COMMISSION PEEL COMMISSION*

July 1937

The Commission under Lord Peel was appointed in 1936. The following are extracts from recommendations made in Ch. XXII:

Having reached the conclusion that there is no possibility of solving the Palestine problem under the existing Mandate (or even under a scheme of cantonization), the Commission recommend the termination of the present Mandate on the basis of Partition and put forward a definite scheme which they consider to be practicable, honourable and just. The scheme is as follows:

The Mandate for Palestine should terminate and be replaced by a Treaty System in accordance with the precedent set in Iraq and Syria.

Under Treaties to be negotiated by the Mandatory with the Government of Transjordan and representatives of the Arabs of Palestine on the one hand, and with the Zionist Organization on the other, it would be declared that two sovereign independent States would shortly be established—(1) an Arab State consisting of Transjordan united with that part of Palestine allotted to the Arabs, (2) a Jewish State consisting of that part of Palestine allotted to the Jews. The Mandatory would undertake to support any requests for admission to the League of Nations made by the Governments of the Arab and Jewish States. The Treaties would include strict guarantees for the protection of minorities. Military Conventions would be attached to the Treaties.

A new Mandate should be instituted to execute the trust of maintaining the sanctity of Jerusalem and Bethlehem and ensuring free and safe access to them

---

* *Palestine Royal Commission: Report*, 1937 (British Blue Book, Cmd. 5479).

for all the world. An enclave should be demarcated to which this Mandate should apply, extending from a point north of Jerusalem to a point south of Bethlehem, and access to the sea should be provided by a corridor extending from Jerusalem to Jaffa. The policy of the Balfour Declaration would not apply to the Mandated Area.

The Jewish State should pay a subvention to the Arab State. A Finance Commission should be appointed to advise as to its amount and as to the division of the public debt of Palestine and other financial questions.

In view of the backwardness of Transjordan, Parliament should be asked to make a grant of £2,000,000 to the Arab State.

WHITE PAPER*
May 1939

The main recommendations are extracted below:

10. ... His Majesty's Government make the following declaration of their intentions regarding the future government of Palestine:

(i) The objective of His Majesty's Government is the establishment within ten years of an independent Palestine State in such treaty relations with the United Kingdom as will provide satisfactorily for the commercial and strategic requirements of both countries in the future. This proposal for the establishment of the independent State would involve consultation with the Council of the League of Nations with a view to the termination of the Mandate.

(ii) The independent State should be one in which Arabs and Jews share in government in such a way as to ensure that the essential interests of each community are safeguarded.

(iii) The establishment of the independent State will be preceded by a transitional period throughout which His Majesty's Government will retain responsibility for the government of the country. During the transitional period the people of Palestine will be given an increasing part in the government of their country. Both sections of the population will have an opportunity to participate in the machinery of government, and the process will be carried on whether or not they both avail themselves of it.

(iv) As soon as peace and order have been sufficiently restored in Palestine steps will be taken to carry out this policy of giving the people of Palestine an increasing part in the government of their country, the objective being to place Palestinians in charge of all the Departments of Government, with the assistance of British advisers and subject to the control of the High Commissioner. With this object in view His Majesty's Government will be prepared immediately to arrange that Palestinians shall be placed in charge of certain Departments, with British advisers. The Palestinian heads of Departments will sit on the Executive Council, which advises the High Commissioner. Arab and Jewish representatives will be invited to serve as heads of Departments approximately in proportion to their respective populations. The number of Palestinians in charge of Departments will be increased as circumstances permit until all heads of Departments are Palestinians, exercising the administrative and advisory functions which are at present performed by British officials. When that stage is reached consideration will be given to the question of converting the Executive Council into a Council of Ministers with a consequential change in the status and functions of the Palestinian heads of Departments.

(v) His Majesty's Government make no proposals at this stage regarding the establishment of an elective legislature. Nevertheless they would regard this as an appropriate constitutional development, and, should public opinion in Palestine hereafter show itself in favour of such a development, they will be prepared, provided that local conditions permit, to establish the necessary machinery.

(vi) At the end of five years from the restoration of peace and order, an appropriate body representative of the people of Palestine and of His Majesty's Government will be set up to review the working of the constitutional arrangements during the transitional period and to consider and make recommendations regarding the Constitution of the independent Palestine State.

(vii) His Majesty's Government will require to be satisfied that in the treaty contemplated by sub-paragraph (i) or in the Constitution contemplated by sub-paragraph (vi) adequate provision has been made for:

(a) the security of, and freedom of access to, the Holy Places, and the protection of the interests and property of the various religious bodies;

(b) the protection of the different communities in Palestine in accordance with the obligations of His Majesty's Government to both Arabs and Jews and for the special position in Palestine of the Jewish National Home;

(c) such requirements to meet the strategic situation as may be regarded as necessary by His Majesty's Government in the light of the circumstances then existing.

His Majesty's Government will also require to be satisfied that the interests of certain foreign countries in Palestine, for the preservation of which they are at present responsible, are adequately safeguarded.

(viii) His Majesty's Government will do everything in their power to create conditions which will enable the independent Palestine State to come into being within ten years. If, at the end of ten years, it appears to His Majesty's Government that, contrary to their hope, circumstances require the postponement of the establishment of the independent State, they will consult with representatives

---
* British White Paper, Cmd. 6019.

of the people of Palestine, the Council of the League of Nations and the neighbouring Arab States before deciding on such a postponement. If His Majesty's Government come to the conclusion that postponement is unavoidable, they will invite the co-operation of these parties in framing plans for the future with a view to achieving the desired objective at the earliest possible date.

11. During the transitional period steps will be taken to increase the powers and responsibilities of municipal corporations and local councils.

14. ... they believe that they will be acting consistently with their Mandatory obligations to both Arabs and Jews, and in the manner best calculated to serve the interests of the whole people of Palestine by adopting the following proposals regarding immigration:

(i) Jewish immigration during the next five years will be at a rate which, if economic absorptive capacity permits, will bring the Jewish population up to approximately one-third of the total population of the country. Taking into account the expected natural increase of the Arab and Jewish populations, and the number of illegal Jewish immigrants now in the country, this would allow of the admission, as from the beginning of April this year, of some 75,000 immigrants over the next five years. These immigrants would, subject to the criterion of economic absorptive capacity, be admitted as follows:

(a) For each of the next five years a quota of 10,000 Jewish immigrants will be allowed, on the understanding that a shortage in any one year may be added to the quotas for subsequent years, within the five-year period, if economic absorptive capacity permits.

(b) In addition, as a contribution towards the solution of the Jewish refugee problem, 25,000 refugees will be admitted as soon as the High Commissioner is satisfied that adequate provision for their maintenance is ensured, special consideration being given to refugee children and dependants.

(ii) The existing machinery for ascertaining economic absorptive capacity will be retained, and the High Commissioner will have the ultimate responsibility for deciding the limits of economic capacity. Before each periodic decision is taken, Jewish and Arab representatives will be consulted.

(iii) After the period of five years no further Jewish immigration will be permitted unless the Arabs of Palestine are prepared to acquiesce in it.

(iv) His Majesty's Government are determined to check illegal immigration, and further preventive measures are being adopted. The numbers of any Jewish illegal immigrants who, despite these measures, may succeed in coming into the country and cannot be deported will be deducted from the yearly quotas.

15. His Majesty's Government are satisfied that, when the immigration over five years which is now contemplated has taken place, they will not be justified in facilitating, nor will they be under any obligation to facilitate, the further development of the Jewish National Home by immigration regardless of the wishes of the Arab population.

16. The Administration of Palestine is required, under Article 6 of the Mandate, "while ensuring that the rights and position of other sections of the population are not prejudiced," to encourage "close settlement by Jews on the land," and no restriction has been imposed hitherto on the transfer of land from Arabs to Jews. The Reports of several expert Commissions have indicated that, owing to the natural growth of the Arab population and the steady sale in recent years of Arab land to Jews, there is now in certain areas no room for further transfers of Arab land, whilst in some other areas such transfers of land must be restricted if Arab cultivators are to maintain their existing standard of life and a considerable landless Arab population is not soon to be created. In these circumstances, the High Commissioner will be given general powers to prohibit and regulate transfers of land. These powers will date from the publication of this statement of Policy and the High Commissioner will retain them throughout the transitional period.

17. The policy of the Government will be directed towards the development of the land and the improvement, where possible, of methods of cultivation. In the light of such development it will be open to the High Commissioner, should he be satisfied that the "rights and position" of the Arab population will be duly preserved, to review and modify any orders passed relating to the prohibition or restriction of the transfer of land.

BILTMORE PROGRAMME*
May 11th, 1942

The following programme was approved by a Zionist Conference held in the Biltmore Hotel, New York City:

1. American Zionists assembled in this Extraordinary Conference reaffirm their unequivocal devotion to the cause of democratic freedom and international justice to which the people of the United States, allied with the other United Nations, have dedicated themselves, and give expression to their faith in the ultimate victory of humanity and justice over lawlessness and brute force.

2. This Conference offers a message of hope and encouragement to their fellow Jews in the Ghettos and concentration camps of Hitler-dominated Europe and prays that their hour of liberation may not be far distant.

3. The Conference sends its warmest greetings to the Jewish Agency Executive in Jerusalem, to the Va'ad Leumi, and to the whole Yishuv in Palestine, and expresses its profound admiration for their steadfastness and achievements in the face of peril

---

* Text supplied by courtesy of Josef Fraenkel.

and great difficulties. The Jewish men and women in field and factory, and the thousands of Jewish soldiers of Palestine in the Near East who have acquitted themselves with honour and distinction in Greece, Ethiopia, Syria, Libya and on other battlefields, have shown themselves worthy of their people and ready to assume the rights and responsibilities of nationhood.

4. In our generation, and in particular in the course of the past twenty years, the Jewish people have awakened and transformed their ancient homeland; from 50,000 at the end of the last war their numbers have increased to more than 500,000. They have made the waste places to bear fruit and the desert to blossom. Their pioneering achievements in agriculture and in industry, embodying new patterns of cooperative endeavour, have written a notable page in the history of colonization.

5. In the new values thus created, their Arab neighbours in Palestine have shared. The Jewish people in its own work of national redemption welcomes the economic, agricultural and national development of the Arab peoples and states. The Conference reaffirms the stand previously adopted at Congresses of the World Zionist Organization, expressing the readiness and the desire of the Jewish people for full cooperation with their Arab neighbours.

6. The Conference calls for the fulfilment of the original purpose of the Balfour Declaration and the Mandate which *"recognizing the historical connexion of the Jewish people with Palestine"* was to afford them the opportunity, as stated by President Wilson, to found there a Jewish Commonwealth.

The Conference affirms its unalterable rejection of the White Paper of May 1939 and denies its moral or legal validity. The White Paper seeks to limit, and in fact to nullify Jewish rights to immigration and settlement in Palestine, and, as stated by Mr. Winston Churchill in the House of Commons in May 1939, constitutes "a breach and repudiation of the Balfour Declaration". The policy of the White Paper is cruel and indefensible in its denial of sanctuary to Jews fleeing from Nazi persecution; and at a time when Palestine has become a focal point in the war front of the United Nations, and Palestine Jewry must provide all available manpower for farm and factory and camp, it is in direct conflict with the interests of the allied war effort.

7. In the struggle against the forces of aggression and tyranny, of which Jews were the earliest victims, and which now menace the Jewish National Home, recognition must be given to the right of the Jews of Palestine to play their full part in the war effort and in the defence of their country, through a Jewish military force fighting under its own flag and under the high command of the United Nations.

8. The Conference declares that the new world order that will follow victory cannot be established on foundations of peace, justice and equality, unless the problem of Jewish homelessness is finally solved.

The Conference urges that the gates of Palestine be opened; that the Jewish Agency be vested with control of immigration into Palestine and with the necessary authority for upbuilding the country, including the development of its unoccupied and uncultivated lands; and that Palestine be established as a Jewish Commonwealth integrated in the structure of the new democratic world.

Then and only then will the age old wrong to the Jewish people be righted.

UN GENERAL ASSEMBLY RESOLUTION ON THE FUTURE GOVERNMENT OF PALESTINE (PARTITION RESOLUTION)

November 29th, 1947

The General Assembly,

Having met in special session at the request of the mandatory Power to constitute and instruct a special committee to prepare for the consideration of the question of the future government of Palestine at the second regular session;

Having constituted a Special Committee and instructed it to investigate all questions and issues relevant to the problem of Palestine, and to prepare proposals for the solution of the problem, and

Having received and examined the report of the Special Committee (document A/364) including a number of unanimous recommendations and a plan of partition with economic union approved by the majority of the Special Committee,

Considers that the present situation in Palestine is one which is likely to impair the general welfare and friendly relations among nations;

Takes note of the declaration by the mandatory Power that it plans to complete its evacuation of Palestine by August 1st, 1948;

Recommends to the United Kingdom, as the mandatory Power for Palestine, and to all other Members of the United Nations the adoption and implementation, with regard to the future government of Palestine, of the Plan of Partition with Economic Union set out below;

Requests that

(a) The Security Council take the necessary measures as provided for in the plan for its implementation;

(b) The Security Council consider, if circumstances during the transitional period require such consideration, whether the situation in Palestine constitutes a threat to the peace. If it decides that such a threat exists, and in order to maintain international peace and security, the Security Council should supplement the authorization of the General Assembly by taking measures, under Articles 39 and 41 of the Charter, to empower the United Nations Commission, as provided in this resolution, to exercise in Palestine the functions which are assigned to it by this resolution;

(c) The Security Council determine as a threat to the peace, breach of the peace or act of aggression, in accordance with Article 39 of the Charter, any attempt to alter by force the settlement envisaged by this resolution;

(d) The Trusteeship Council be informed of the responsibilities envisaged for it in this plan;

Calls upon the inhabitants of Palestine to take such steps as may be necessary on their part to put this plan into effect;

Appeals to all Governments and all peoples to refrain from taking any action which might hamper or delay the carrying out of these recommendations, and

Authorizes the Secretary-General to reimburse travel and subsistence expenses of the members of the Commission referred to in Part 1, Section B, paragraph 1 below, on such basis and in such form as he may determine most appropriate in the circumstances, and to provide the Commission with the necessary staff to assist in carrying out the functions assigned to the Commission by the General Assembly.

Official Records of the second session of the General Assembly, Resolutions, p. 131.

UN GENERAL ASSEMBLY RESOLUTION 194 (III)

December 11th, 1948

The resolution's terms have been reaffirmed every year since 1948.

11. ... the refugees wishing to return to their homes and live at peace with their neighbours should be permitted to do so at the earliest practicable date, and that compensation should be paid for the property of those choosing not to return and for the loss of or damage to property which, under principles of international law or in equity, should be made good by the Governments or authorities responsible;

Official Records of the third session of the General Assembly, Part 1, Resolutions, p. 21.

UN GENERAL ASSEMBLY RESOLUTION ON THE INTERNATIONALIZATION OF JERUSALEM

December 9th, 1949

The General Assembly,

Having regard to its resolution 181 (II) of November 29th, 1947 and 194 (III) of December 11th, 1948,

Having studied the reports of the United Nations Conciliation Commission for Palestine set up under the latter resolution,

I. *Decides*

In relation to Jerusalem,

Believing that the principles underlying its previous resolutions concerning this matter, and in particular its resolution of November 29th, 1947, represent a just and equitable settlement of the question,

1. To restate, therefore, its intention that Jerusalem should be placed under a permanent international regime, which should envisage appropriate guarantees for the protection of the Holy Places, both within and outside Jerusalem, and to confirm specifically the following provisions of General Assembly resolution 181 (II): (1) The City of Jerusalem shall be established as a *corpus separatum* under a special international regime and shall be administered by the United Nations; (2) The Trusteeship Council shall be designated to discharge the responsibilities of the Administering Authority . . .; and (3) The City of Jerusalem shall include the present municipality of Jerusalem plus the surrounding villages and towns, the most eastern of which shall be Abu Dis; the most southern, Bethlehem; the most western, Ein Karim (including also the built-up area of Motsa); and the most northern, Shu'fat, as indicated on the attached sketchmap; [*map not reproduced: Ed.*]

2. To request for this purpose that the Trusteeship Council at its next session, whether special or regular, complete the preparation of the Statute of Jerusalem, omitting the now inapplicable provisions, such as Articles 32 and 39, and, without prejudice to the fundamental principles of the international regime for Jerusalem set forth in General Assembly resolution 181 (II) introducing therein amendments in the direction of its greater democratization, approve the Statute, and proceed immediately with its implementation. The Trusteeship Council shall not allow any actions taken by any interested Government or Governments to divert it from adopting and implementing the Statute of Jerusalem;

II. *Calls upon* the States concerned to make formal undertakings, at an early date and in the light of their obligations as Members of the United Nations, that they will approach these matters with good will and be guided by the terms of the present resolution.

Official Records of the fourth session of the General Assembly, Resolutions, p. 25.

TEXT OF UN SECURITY COUNCIL RESOLUTION NOVEMBER 22nd, 1967

The Security Council,

Expressing its continued concern with the grave situation in the Middle East,

Emphasizing the inadmissibility of the acquisition of territory by war and the need to work for a just and lasting peace in which every state in the area can live in security,

Emphasizing further that all Member States in their acceptance of the Charter of the United Nations have undertaken a commitment to act in accordance with Article 2 of the Charter

1. *Affirms* that the fulfilment of Charter principles requires the establishment of a just and lasting peace in the Middle East which should include the application of both the following principles:

(i) Withdrawal of Israel armed forces from territories occupied in the recent conflict;

DOCUMENTS ON PALESTINE

TERRITORIES OCCUPIED IN 1948, 1949 AND 1967

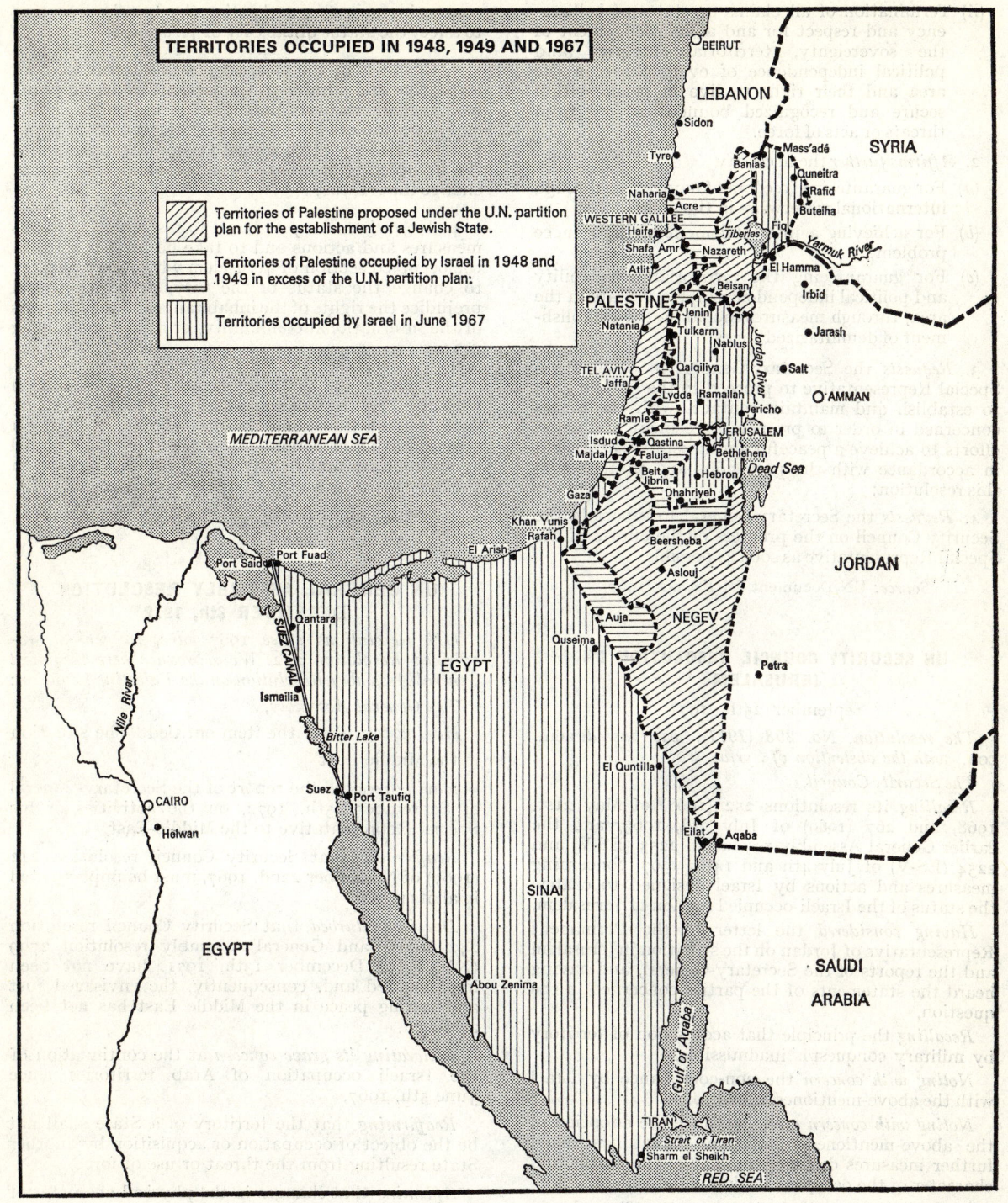

- Territories of Palestine proposed under the U.N. partition plan for the establishment of a Jewish State.
- Territories of Palestine occupied by Israel in 1948 and 1949 in excess of the U.N. partition plan.
- Territories occupied by Israel in June 1967.

The expansion of Israel.

(ii) Termination of all claims or states of belligerency and respect for and acknowledgement of the sovereignty, territorial integrity and political independence of every State in the area and their right to live in peace within secure and recognized boundaries free from threats or acts of force.

2. *Affirms further* the necessity

(a) For guaranteeing freedom of navigation through international waterways in the area;

(b) For achieving a just settlement of the refugee problem;

(c) For guaranteeing the territorial inviolability and political independence of every State in the area, through measures including the establishment of demilitarized zones;

3. *Requests* the Secretary-General to designate a Special Representative to proceed to the Middle East to establish and maintain contacts with the States concerned in order to promote agreement and assist efforts to achieve a peaceful and accepted settlement in accordance with the provisions and principles in this resolution;

4. *Requests* the Secretary-General to report to the Security Council on the progress of the efforts of the Special Representative as soon as possible.

Source: UN Document S/RES/242 (1967).

UN SECURITY COUNCIL RESOLUTION ON JERUSALEM

September 25th, 1971

The resolution, No. 298 (1971), was passed nem. con., *with the abstention of Syria.*

The Security Council,

Recalling its resolutions 252 (1968) of May 21st, 1968, and 267 (1969) of July 3rd, 1969, and the earlier General Assembly resolution 2253 (ES-V) and 2254 (ES-V) of July 4th and 14th, 1967, concerning measures and actions by Israel designed to change the status of the Israeli-occupied section of Jerusalem,

Having considered the letter of the Permanent Representative of Jordan on the situation in Jerusalem and the reports of the Secretary-General, and having heard the statements of the parties concerned in the question,

Recalling the principle that acquisition of territory by military conquest is inadmissible,

Noting with concern the non-compliance by Israel with the above-mentioned resolutions,

Noting with concern also that since the adoption of the above-mentioned resolutions Israel has taken further measures designed to change the status and character of the occupied section of Jerusalem.

1. *Reaffirms* its resolutions 252 (1968) and 267 (1969);

2. *Deplores* the failure of Israel to respect the previous resolutions adopted by the United Nations concerning measures and actions by Israel purporting to affect the status of the City of Jerusalem;

3. *Confirms* in the clearest possible terms that all legislative and administrative actions taken by Israel to change the status of the City of Jerusalem, including expropriation of land and properties, transfer of populations and legislation aimed at the incorporation of the occupied section, are totally invalid and cannot change that status;

4. *Urgently calls upon* Israel to rescind all previous measures and actions and to take no further steps in the occupied section of Jerusalem which may purport to change the status of the City, or which would prejudice the rights of the inhabitants and the interests of the international community, or a just and lasting peace;

5. *Requests* the Secretary-General, in consultation with the President of the Security Council and using such instrumentalities as he may choose, including a representative or a mission, to report to the Council as appropriate and in any event within 60 days on the implementation of the present resolution.

Source: UN Document S/RES/298 (1971).

UN GENERAL ASSEMBLY RESOLUTION DECEMBER 8th, 1972

UN Resolutions since 1967 have, in general, reaffirmed Resolution 242. We reproduce here the latest General Assembly Resolution on the Palestine situation:

The General Assembly,

Having considered the item entitled "The situation in the Middle East",

Having received the report of the Secretary-General of September 15th, 1972, on the activities of his Special Representative to the Middle East,

Reaffirming that Security Council resolution 242 (1967) of November 22nd, 1967, must be implemented in all its parts,

Deeply perturbed that Security Council resolution 242 (1967) and General Assembly resolution 2799 (XXVI) of December 13th, 1971, have not been implemented and, consequently, the envisaged just and lasting peace in the Middle East has not been achieved,

Reiterating its grave concern at the continuation of the Israeli occupation of Arab territories since June 5th, 1967,

Reaffirming that the territory of a State shall not be the object of occupation or acquisition by another State resulting from the threat or use of force,

Affirming that changes in the physical character or demographic composition of occupied territories are contrary to the purposes and principles of the Charter of the United Nations, as well as to the provisions of the relevant applicable international conventions,

Convinced that the grave situation prevailing in the Middle East constitutes a serious threat to international peace and security,

Reaffirming the responsibility of the United Nations to restore peace and security in the Middle East in the immediate future,

1. *Reaffirms* its resolution 2799 (XXVI);

2. *Deplores* the non-compliance by Israel with General Assembly resolution 2799 (XXVI), which in particular called upon Israel to respond favourably to the peace initiative of the Special Representative of the Secretary-General to the Middle East;

3. *Expresses its full support* for the efforts of the Secretary-General and his Special Representative;

4. *Declares once more* that the acquisition of territories by force is inadmissible and that, consequently, territories thus occupied must be restored;

5. *Reaffirms* that the establishment of a just and lasting peace in the Middle East should include the application of both the following principles:
   (a) Withdrawal of Israeli armed forces from territories occupied in the recent conflict;
   (b) Termination of all claims or states of belligerency and respect for and acknowledgement of the sovereignty, territorial integrity and political independence of every State in the area and its right to live in peace within secure and recognized boundaries free from threats or acts of force;

6. *Invites* Israel to declare publicly its adherence to the principle of non-annexation of territories through the use of force;

7. *Declares* that changes carried out by Israel in the occupied Arab territories in contravention of the Geneva Convention of 1949 are null and void, and calls upon Israel to rescind forthwith all such measures and to desist from all policies and practices affecting the physical character or demographic composition of the occupied Arab territories;

8. *Calls upon* all States not to recognize any such changes and measures carried out by Israel in the occupied Arab territories and invites them to avoid actions, including actions in the field of aid, that could constitute recognition of that occupation;

9. *Recognizes* that respect for the rights of the Palestinians is an indispensable element in the establishment of a just and lasting peace in the Middle East;

10. *Requests* the Security Council, in consultation with the Secretary-General and his Special Representative, to take all appropriate steps with a view to the full and speedy implementation of Security Council resolution 242 (1967), taking into account all the relevant resolutions and documents of the United Nations in this connexion;

11. *Requests* the Secretary-General to report to the Security Council and the General Assembly on the progress made by him and his Special Representative in the implementation of Security Council resolution 242 (1967) and of the present resolution;

12. *Decides* to transmit the present resolution to the Security Council for its appropriate action and requests the Council to keep the General Assembly informed.

Source: UN Document A/RES/2949 (XXVII).

Palestine Organizations

Palestine Liberation Organization (PLO)

The Palestine Liberation Organization was founded in 1964 at the first Arab Summit Meeting, and the Palestine Liberation Army was established in the same year. The supreme organ of the PLO is the Palestine National Assembly (see below), while the Palestine Executive Committee, consisting of 9 members and a Treasurer, deals with the day to day business. Fatah (the Palestine National Liberation Movement) joined the Palestine National Assembly in 1968, and all the guerrilla organizations joined the Assembly in 1969. The Palestine Executive Committee controls the following seven departments, and a member of the Executive Committee is at the head of each department:

(i) People's Liberation Army.
(ii) Cultural and Educational (includes Palestine Research Centre).
(iii) Political and International Relations.
(iv) Palestine National Fund.
(v) Social Affairs (includes Palestine Red Crescent).
(vi) Occupied Territories.
(vii) Popular Organizations (Trade Unions, Students, Workers, Women, etc.).

The PLO has offices and representatives in every Arab country as well as in non-Arab states such as U.S.A., China, Yugoslavia, Switzerland and Britain.

Chairman: 1964-67 Ahmed Shukairi.
1967-68 Yahya Hammouda.
1968- Yasser Arafat.

Main Regional Offices:
Beirut: Dir. SHAFFIQ HOUT.
Damascus: Dir. MAHMOUD KHALIDI.
Kuwait: Dir. ALI YASSIM.
Cairo: Dir. JAMAL SOURANI.
Algiers: AHMED WAFI.
Tripoli: SULEIMAN SHURAFA.

PALESTINE NATIONAL ASSEMBLY

It has 115 members and meets once a year in Cairo. As well as the guerrilla organizations, the other PLO bodies, trade and student unions, etc. are represented. Of the 115 members, 60 represent guerrilla organizations, of which 40 represent Fatah.
Chairman: KHALED FAHOUM.

EXECUTIVE COMMITTEE

This is elected by the Palestine National Assembly and is responsible for the running of the PLO in between meetings of the Council.
Chairman: YASSER ARAFAT.

PALESTINE LIBERATION ARMY (PLA)
Commander-in-Chief: YASSER ARAFAT.
Chief-of-Staff: MUSBAH BUDAIRI.

PALESTINE NATIONAL FUND

The fund is financed by a contribution of 5 per cent from the income of every Palestinian and also aid from Arab and friendly countries.
Chairman: Dr. YUSEF SAYEGH.
Director: DARWICHE ABYAD.

PALESTINE PLANNING BOARD
Director: Dr. NABIL SHAATH.

PALESTINE RESEARCH CENTRE
Director: Dr. ANIS SAYEGH.

CENTRAL COMMITTEE OF THE PALESTINE RESISTANCE MOVEMENT

It was created early in 1970 and represents all the guerrilla groups. The most important guerrilla organizations are:

Fatah (The Palestine National Liberation Movement): leader YASSER ARAFAT.

Popular Front for the Liberation of Palestine (PFLP): leaders GEORGE HABASH and Dr. WADIE HADDAD.

Saiqa (Vanguard of the Popular Liberation War): Syrian-backed; leader ZUHEIR MUHSEN.

Popular Democratic Front for the Liberation of Palestine (PDFLP): leader NAIF HAWATMEH.

Arab Liberation Front (ALF): Iraq-backed; leader ABDUL WAHHAB KAYYAL.

PALESTINE ORGANIZATIONS

THE PALESTINIAN NATIONAL CHARTER

(Palestine Liberation Organization)*

1. Palestine is the homeland of the Palestinian Arab people; it is an indivisible part of the Arab homeland, and the Palestinian people are an integral part of the Arab nation.

2. Palestine, with the boundaries it had during the British mandate, is an indivisible territorial unit.

3. The Palestinian Arab people possess the legal right to their homeland and have the right to determine their destiny after achieving the liberation of their country in accordance with their wishes and entirely of their own accord and will.

4. The Palestinian identity is a genuine, essential and inherent characteristic; it is transmitted from parents to children. The Zionist occupation and the dispersal of the Palestinian Arab people, through the disasters which befell them, do not make them lose their Palestinian identity and their membership of the Palestinian community, nor do they negate them.

5. The Palestinians are those Arab nationals who, until 1947, normally resided in Palestine regardless of whether they were evicted from it or have stayed there. Anyone born, after that date, of a Palestinian father—whether inside Palestine or outside it—is also a Palestinian.

6. The Jews who had normally resided in Palestine until the beginning of the Zionist invasion will be considered Palestinians.

7. That there is a Palestinian community and that it has material, spiritual and historical connection with Palestine are indisputable facts. It is a national duty to bring up individual Palestinians in an Arab revolutionary manner. All means of information and education must be adopted in order to acquaint the Palestinian with his country in the most profound manner, both spiritual and material, that is possible. He must be prepared for the armed struggle and ready to sacrifice his wealth and his life in order to win back his homeland and bring about its liberation.

8. The phase in their history, through which the Palestinian people are now living, is that of national struggle for the liberation of Palestine. Thus the conflicts among the Palestinian national forces are secondary, and should be ended for the sake of the basic conflict that exists between the forces of Zionism and of imperialism on the one hand, and the Palestinian Arab people on the other. On this basis the Palestinian masses, regardless of whether they are residing in the national homeland or in diaspora, constitute—both their organizations and the individuals—one national front working for the retrieval of Palestine and its liberation through armed struggle.

9. Armed struggle is the only way to liberate Palestine. Thus it is the overall strategy, not merely a tactical phase. The Palestinian Arab people assert their absolute determination and firm resolution to continue their armed struggle and to work for an armed popular revolution for the liberation of their country and their return to it. They also assert their right to normal life in Palestine and to exercise their right to self-determination and sovereignty over it.

10. Commando action constitutes the nucleus of the Palestinian popular liberation war. This requires its escalation, comprehensiveness and the mobilization of all the Palestinian popular and educational efforts and their organization and involvement in the armed Palestinian revolution. It also requires the achieving of unity for the national struggle among the different groupings of the Palestinian people, and between the Palestinian people and the Arab masses so as to secure the continuation of the revolution, its escalation and victory.

11. The Palestinians will have three mottoes: national unity, national mobilization and liberation.

12. The Palestinian people believe in Arab unity. In order to contribute their share towards the attainment of that objective, however, they must, at the present stage of their struggle, safeguard their Palestinian identity and develop their consciousness of that identity, and oppose any plan that may dissolve or impair it.

13. Arab unity and the liberation of Palestine are two complementary objectives, the attainment of either of which facilitates the attainment of the other. Thus, Arab unity leads to the liberation of Palestine; the liberation of Palestine leads to Arab unity; and work towards the realization of one objective proceeds side by side with work towards the realization of the other.

14. The destiny of the Arab nation, and indeed Arab existence itself, depends upon the destiny of the Palestine cause. From this interdependence springs the Arab nation's pursuit of, and striving for, the liberation of Palestine. The people of Palestine play the role of the vanguard in the realization of this sacred national goal.

15. The liberation of Palestine, from an Arab viewpoint, is a national duty and it attempts to repel the Zionist and imperialist aggression against the Arab homeland, and aims at the elimination of Zionism in Palestine. Absolute responsibility for this falls upon the Arab nation—peoples and governments—with the Arab people of Palestine in the vanguard. Accordingly the Arab nation must mobilize all its military, human, moral and spiritual capabilities to participate actively with the Palestinian people in the liberation of Palestine. It must, particularly in the phase of the armed Palestinian revolution, offer and furnish the Palestinian people with all possible help, and material and human support, and make available to them the means and opportunities that will enable them to continue to carry out their leading role in the armed revolution, until they liberate their homeland.

16. The liberation of Palestine, from a spiritual point of view, will provide the Holy Land with an atmosphere of safety and tranquillity, which in turn will safeguard the country's religious sanctuaries and guarantee freedom of worship and of visit to all, without discrimination of race, color, language, or

---

* Decisions of the National Congress of the Palestine Liberation Organization held in Cairo July 1st–17th, 1968.

religion. Accordingly, the people of Palestine look to all spiritual forces in the world for support.

17. The liberation of Palestine, from a human point of view, will restore to the Palestinian individual his dignity, pride and freedom. Accordingly the Palestinian Arab people look forward to the support of all those who believe in the dignity of man and his freedom in the world.

18. The liberation of Palestine, from an international point of view, is a defensive action necessitated by the demands of self-defence. Accordingly, the Palestinian people, desirous as they are of the friendship of all people, look to freedom-loving, justice-loving and peace-loving states for support in order to restore their legitimate rights in Palestine, to re-establish peace and security in the country, and to enable its people to exercise national sovereignty and freedom.

19. The partition of Palestine in 1947 and the establishment of the state of Israel are entirely illegal, regardless of the passage of time, because they were contrary to the will of the Palestinian people and to their natural right in their homeland, and inconsistent with the principles embodied in the Charter of the United Nations, particularly the right to self-determination.

20. The Balfour Declaration, the mandate for Palestine and everything that has been based upon them, are deemed null and void. Claims of historical or religious ties of Jews with Palestine are incompatible with the facts of history and the true conception of what constitutes statehood. Judaism, being a religion, is not an independent nationality. Nor do Jews constitute a single nation with an identity of its own; they are citizens of the states to which they belong.

21. The Palestinian Arab people, expressing themselves by the armed Palestinian revolution, reject all solutions which are substitutes for the total liberation of Palestine and reject all proposals aiming at the liquidation of the Palestinian problem, or its internationalization.

22. Zionism is a political movement organically associated with international imperialism and antagonistic to all action for liberation and to progressive movements in the world. It is racist and fanatic in its nature, aggressive, expansionist and colonial in its aims, and fascist in its methods. Israel is the instrument of the Zionist movement, and a geographical base for world imperialism placed strategically in the midst of the Arab homeland to combat the hopes of the Arab nation for liberation, unity and progress. Israel is a constant source of threat *vis-à-vis* peace in the Middle East and the whole world. Since the liberation of Palestine will destroy the Zionist and imperialist presence and will contribute to the establishment of peace in the Middle East, the Palestinian people look for the support of all the progressive and peaceful forces and urge them all, irrespective of their affiliations and beliefs, to offer the Palestinian people all aid and support in their just struggle for the liberation of their homeland.

23. The demands of security and peace, as well as the demands of right and justice, require all states to consider Zionism an illegitimate movement, to outlaw its existence, and to ban its operations, in order that friendly relations among peoples may be preserved, and the loyalty of citizens to their respective homelands safeguarded.

24. The Palestinian people believe in the principles of justice, freedom, sovereignty, self-determination, human dignity, and in the right of all peoples to exercise them.

25. For the realization of the goals of this Charter and its principles, the Palestine Liberation Organization will perform its role in the liberation of Palestine in accordance with the Constitution of this Organization.

26. The Palestine Liberation Organization, representative of the Palestinian revolutionary forces, is responsible for the Palestinian Arab people's movement in its struggle—to retrieve its homeland, liberate and return to it and exercise the right to self-determination in it—in all military, political and financial fields and also for whatever may be required by the Palestine case on the inter-Arab and international levels.

27. The Palestine Liberation Organization shall cooperate with all Arab states, each according to its potentialities; and will adopt a neutral policy among them in the light of the requirements of the war of liberation; and on this basis it shall not interfere in the internal affairs of any Arab state.

28. The Palestinian Arab people assert the genuineness and independence of their national revolution and reject all forms of intervention, trusteeship and subordination.

29. The Palestinian people possess the fundamental and genuine legal right to liberate and retrieve their homeland. The Palestinian people determine their attitude towards all states and forces on the basis of the stands they adopt *vis-à-vis* the Palestinian case and the extent of the support they offer to the Palestinian revolution to fulfill the aims of the Palestinian people.

30. Fighters and carriers of arms in the war of liberation are the nucleus of the popular army which will be the protective force for the gains of the Palestinian Arab people.

31. The Organization shall have a flag, an oath of allegiance and an anthem. All this shall be decided upon in accordance with a special regulation.

32. Regulations, which shall be known as the Constitution of the Palestine Liberation Organization, shall be annexed to this Charter. It shall lay down the manner in which the Organization, and its organs and institutions, shall be constituted; the respective competence of each; and the requirements of its obligations under the Charter.

33. This Charter shall not be amended save by (vote of) a majority of two-thirds of the total membership of the National Congress of the Palestine Liberation Organization (taken) at a special session convened for that purpose.

Oil in the Middle East and North Africa*

Michael Field

INTRODUCTION

The twelve months from June 1st, 1972, when the Iraq Petroleum Company was nationalized, to June 1st, 1973, when the Organization of Petroleum Exporting Countries negotiated a new price agreement in Geneva, have seen spectacular changes throughout the Middle Eastern and world oil industries.

Saudi Arabia, Kuwait, Abu Dhabi and Qatar have gained a 25 per cent stake in the world's largest concessions, Iran has taken over its oil industry entirely, and Iraq has reached a final settlement with IPC. At the same time America, with surprising suddenness, has become aware of an "energy crisis", which will force it to import up to 15 million barrels of oil a day† by the mid-1980s—as much as all western Europe's consumption in 1972. And the Arabs and Iran in their turn have realized that this will involve their pushing production from 1,077 million tons in 1972 up to 2,500 million tons in 1983, and receiving cumulative revenues over the next decade in the region of $400 billion.

These developments have removed two cornerstones of the world oil business. First the U.S.A. has ceased to be self sufficient, and its oil industry can no longer be regarded as entirely separate from the rest of the world—known in the oil industry as FWONA (Free World Outside North America). And secondly the conventional concessions system has been turned into a series of partnerships. So there has appeared a new buyer—the U.S.A., and new sellers—the Middle Eastern National oil companies, which may either sell their crude "at arms length" from their loading terminals, or go "downstream" entering the tankering, refining and distribution business.

In mid-1973 the oil industry had little idea of what would emerge from this situation, and there were still a number of changes pending—in Iraq, where the state had yet to take a share in its remaining concessionaire the Basrah Petroleum Company; in Libya, where the Government was considering a 100 per cent take-over; and in Algeria, where the national company, Sonatrach, having established control of its industry in 1971, was beginning to invite western companies back on its own terms.

Accordingly none of the parties concerned—producers, western companies and consumer governments—had evolved any detailed long term national or corporate policies. No clear patterns of supply between the new national producers and individual markets had appeared, and there was little sign of a re-establishment of equilibrium in the strength and bargaining power of consumer and producer.

Under stable conditions in the oil industry the production of a country or field is normally allocated to a market/refinery/buyer months or years in advance, but in early 1973 there was an unusually large amount of Middle Eastern crude planned for the next few years which had not been found a market. The oil industry has traditionally made its profits "at the margin", and unless it can rely on a projection of the volume, type and origin of its crude supplies and some stability of price, it cannot plan projects—like refineries—whose economics are liable to be radically upset by a minor reduction of input or a price change of even a few cents a barrel.

In spite of this state of flux there were already a few indications on the part of some consumer governments—though less so on the part of companies, both western and middle eastern—of what their future policies might be. The Europeans and British, whose energy supplies are under somewhat less pressure than those of other major consumers, remained fairly silent, but in April President Nixon delivered his long awaited but rather limited energy message to Congress —announcing: (1) A new quota system under which existing holders of crude import licences could import their 1973 allocations without paying "fees". Crude imported in excess of these allocations would be subject to a fee rising from 10.5 cents a barrel during April-November 1973 to 21 cents a barrel by the end of 1974. In 1974 90 per cent of the levels imported in 1973 would be exempt from fees, to be cut back to 20 per cent by 1979 and abolished altogether in 1980. In order to encourage refinery construction imported products would be liable to higher fees rising in 1974 to 63 cents a barrel. (2) Offshore federal acreage leased annually would be trebled. (3) A request to Congress to lift price controls on new natural gas wells. (4) A request to Congress to create a new department of Energy and Natural Resources.

Japan, with virtually no indigenous energy supplies and correspondingly less room for manoeuvre than any other major consumer, has already begun building up a series of high price direct crude purchases from national companies. In February 1973 the big tanker concern Japan Line signed a ten year 100 million ton contract with Abu Dhabi. At a price of up to 25 cents a barrel over the sum at which the state's western operating partners would "buy back" the crude, this disposed of virtually all the Abu Dhabi National Oil Company's spare production for the next three years. Japan has always been a major market for Abu Dhabi's low sulphur crude, and the increasing pollution consciousness of the Japanese has recently given this state's oil an added attraction. It is also for pollution reasons—as well as adding to their competitiveness as buyers—that the Japanese have agreed to participate in a number of export refineries and

---

* For detailed information on the oil industries of individual countries, *see* the economic surveys and directory sections on oil in each country chapter.

† 1 metric ton = 7.3 barrels. 1 barrel = 35 gallons. To convert barrels a day to tons a year multiply by 49.2.

OIL IN THE MIDDLE EAST AND NORTH AFRICA—(INTRODUCTION)

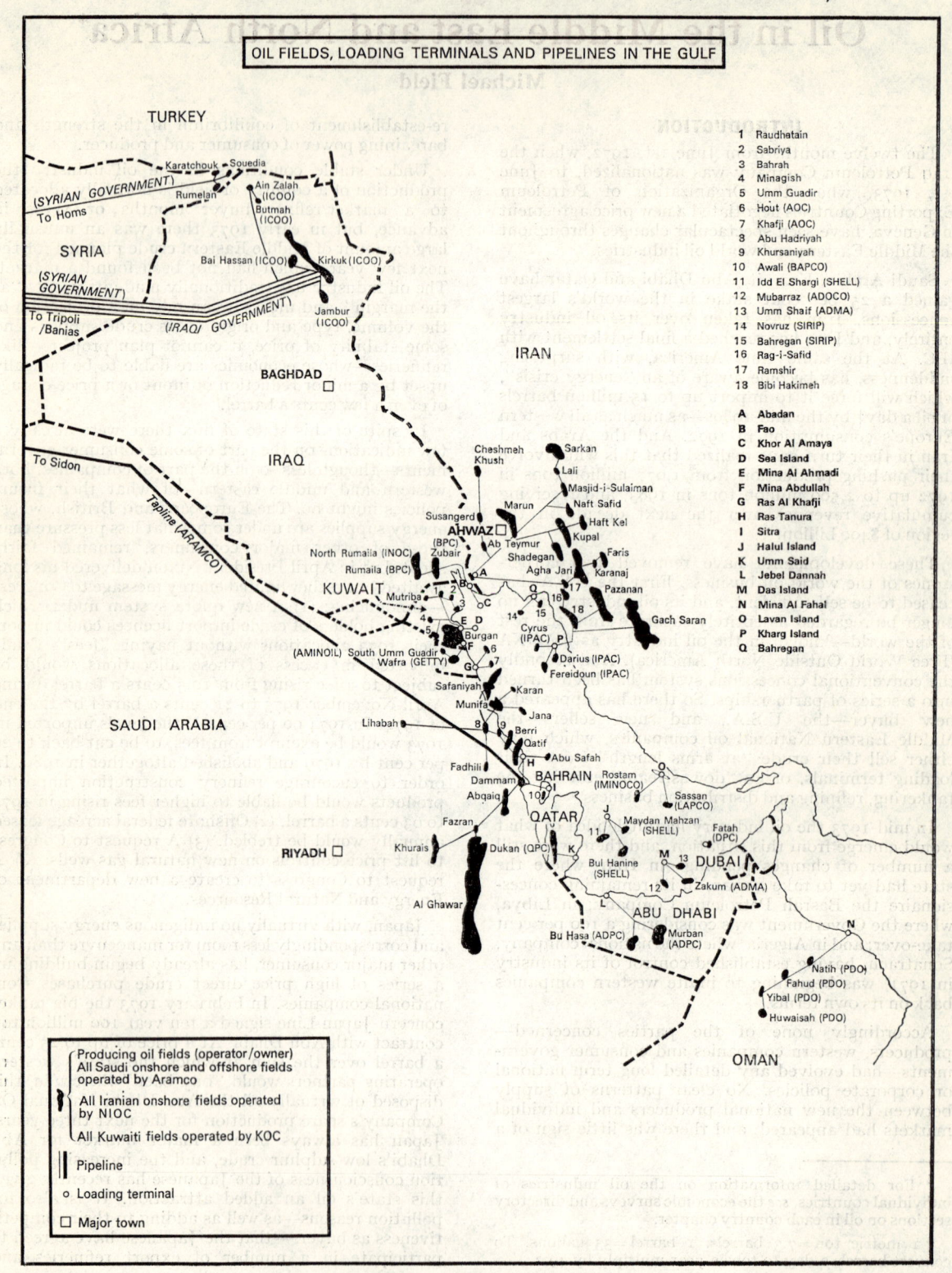

OIL FIELDS, LOADING TERMINALS AND PIPELINES IN THE GULF

1. Raudhatain
2. Sabriya
3. Bahrah
4. Minagish
5. Umm Guadir
6. Hout (AOC)
7. Khafji (AOC)
8. Abu Hadriyah
9. Khursaniyah
10. Awali (BAPCO)
11. Idd El Shargi (SHELL)
12. Mubarraz (ADOCO)
13. Umm Shaif (ADMA)
14. Novruz (SIRIP)
15. Bahregan (SIRIP)
16. Rag-i-Safid
17. Ramshir
18. Bibi Hakimeh

A. Abadan
B. Fao
C. Khor Al Amaya
D. Sea Island
E. Mina Al Ahmadi
F. Mina Abdullah
G. Ras Al Khafji
H. Ras Tanura
I. Sitra
J. Halul Island
K. Umm Said
L. Jebel Dannah
M. Das Island
N. Mina Al Fahal
O. Kharg Island
P. Lavan Island
Q. Bahregan

Legend:
- Producing oil fields (operator/owner). All Saudi onshore and offshore fields operated by Aramco
- All Iranian onshore fields operated by NIOC
- All Kuwaiti fields operated by KOC
- Pipeline
- ○ Loading terminal
- □ Major town

64

petrochemical plants in producing states. (The Americans, as shown by the Nixon message, are less anxious to be supplied from foreign refineries because of security considerations.)

Although it is difficult to forecast more than six years ahead—which is the normal lead time for a new plant or oil field to come on stream—it seems that, with the exception of Britain, the west is facing at least ten years of increasing dependence on Middle Eastern oil. Apart from Nigeria, there is little spare production capacity outside the Middle East, while in the Western Hemisphere, except Canada, output in all the established producers is either stagnant or declining. The U.S.S.R. has vast landlocked reserves east of the Urals at Tyumen, but it seems that it lacks the capital, and possibly the expertise to develop them very quickly, and although the Russians are seeking American and Japanese help, their oil is unlikely to make more than a small contribution to American imports.

The Middle East's dominance will probably begin to come to an end around the mid-1980s, when at roughly the same time Arab and Iranian production will be reaching its maximum limits, and the price of oil in the U.S.A. will be around the $5 a barrel mark. At about this point non-conventional oil sources—like the Athabasca tar sands in northern Alberta and some shale deposits—will start to become economic, and although the process will be gradual, starting in the mid-west before the east and west coasts, America will begin to become self-sufficient in energy again. The rest of the world will probably stay dependent on conventional crude for somewhat longer, and for ten years from the mid-1980s to mid-1990s there may be a considerable difference between the energy sources of the western and eastern hemispheres.

Meanwhile the Middle East is well able to support a big increase in production. The Gulf countries contain some 54 per cent of the world's proven reserves, and as most of these states have not been particularly extensively explored, reserve estimates are constantly being revised upwards. In December 1971 Saudi Arabia announced a new field, al Mazalij, which may be as big as Saudi's al Ghawar (itself containing more oil than the whole of the U.S.A. plus Alaska), but because the field has not yet been properly appraised, it is not included in the current proven reserve estimates. Iraq is even less well explored—it was this that led to Baghdad's original expropriations from IPC (see Concessions below)—and it is thought that the country may contain reserves second only to Saudi Arabia. In Kuwait there is probably no more oil to be found onshore, but offshore there is an area known as the Golden Triangle, where Shell's drilling has been held up by a boundary dispute with Iran and Saudi Arabia.

With Iraq still geologically and politically an unknown quantity, the bulk of the increased western demand is likely to fall on three states. By 1983 Saudi Arabia may be producing over 20 million barrels per day (over twice as much as the U.S.A. ever produced), Iran 8 million barrels per day, and Abu Dhabi 4/5 million barrels per day. Some indication of the future can already be seen in the output of these states in 1972—their production rose by 18 per cent to 11.8 million barrels per day, their share of world output from 20 per cent to 22.5 per cent, and their revenues by 29 per cent to $5,755 million. Libya and Algeria may play a smaller role in supplying very light low sulphur crudes, but here relatively small reserves and the attitude of the Government in Tripoli are unlikely to encourage any massive increases. Elsewhere Kuwait has proven reserves as large as those in Iran, but the lack of any immediate prospect of their increasing means that production will probably not be allowed above the Government's present 3 million barrels per day limit. In Qatar only one field—Dukan—has been found onshore, and while prospects offshore are more encouraging, production is never likely to rise above 1 million barrels per day.

Although the price rises of 1971-73 have removed much of the competitive edge from Middle Eastern crude, in terms of cost it is still by far the cheapest oil in the world. Investment per barrel a day of production capacity averages $100 onshore in the Gulf, against $600 in Nigeria, and $2,000/2,500 off the Scottish mainland. Production costs are likewise low—in the Gulf they range from 6 cents in Kuwait to 35 cents offshore Dubai, which compares very well with some of the more recent finds in the U.S.A. where costs may be in the $3 range. Middle Eastern wells are extremely productive. In Iran in 1971 the average well produced 16,000 barrels per day, against an average of 19 barrels per day in the U.S.A. (These figures exaggerate the situation slightly because in 1971 many U.S. wells were allocated an "allowable" production of less than 100 per cent of their capacity, and of the 500,000 odd wells in operation a large number were "stripper wells" in dying fields producing less than 30 barrels per day.)

CONCESSIONS

Until the end of 1972 the bulk of the Middle East's and North Africa's output was still produced under the traditional concession arrangements. The first of these, granted by the Persian Government to the British prospector D'Arcy in 1901 served as an archetype for all later concessions—covering such matters as: the granting of rights for research, extraction, export and sale of petroleum; the exclusive right to build pipelines, immunity from taxes and customs dues, and the payment of royalties.

In the 1920s and 1930s following the success of drilling in Iran in 1908, and the Anglo-Iranian Oil Company (later BP) bringing the oil on stream, the other "majors"—Exxon (Esso), Standard of California (Chevron), Texaco, Gulf, Mobil, Shell and Compagnie Française des Pétroles—CFP (Total)—moved in and obtained concessions in Iraq, Bahrain, Saudi Arabia, Kuwait and Qatar. But with the growing sophistication of the local population as production got under way after the Second World War, the concessions began to come under attack. Apart from the fact that their financial terms were not over-generous to the host governments, the producer states found various other features objectionable on nationalist grounds.

OIL IN THE MIDDLE EAST AND NORTH AFRICA—(PARTNERSHIPS, SERVICE CONTRACTS)

The main complaints were that the concessionaires had appropriated to themselves a quasi-colonial authority, their concession areas were too large and their duration too long, and they were run almost entirely by foreign nationals.

The terms of Iran's concession were revised in 1933, but the first major change in the Arab World occurred in 1950/51 after the Venezuelans—who have always been ahead of Middle Eastern states in innovations in company/government relations—sent a delegation to the Gulf to explain the advantages of the 50-50 profit split they had legislated into being in 1948. Under the new system, introduced in Saudi Arabia at the end of 1950 and in Iraq and Kuwait a few months later, the concessionaire company's "profits"—arrived at by deducting the production cost per barrel from the posted or tax reference price—were divided equally between the company and the government.

In three countries the change in concession terms did not proceed so amicably. In 1938 Mexico and in 1951 Iran nationalized their concessionaires. Both countries encountered extreme difficulties in selling their oil, and although Mexico was later helped by the circumstances of World War II, Iran was finally obliged to compromise in 1953. The Government signed an agreement with an international consortium, Iranian Oil Participants, composed of all the major companies, granting a lease incorporating the 50-50 profit split, which was in almost all but name a new concession. In the third country, Iraq, a dispute blew up in the late 1950s over the fact that the Iraq Petroleum Company and its sisters the Basrah Petroleum Company and the Mosul Petroleum Company, had only developed a very minor part of their 160,000 square mile concession. Combined with disagreements over the group's accounting procedures, which had a bearing on Government revenues, the dispute led to Law 80 of 1961 expropriating over 99½ per cent of the group's concession area.

The rifts in Mexico, Iran and Iraq more or less marked the end of the concession granting era. Although new concessions have been signed since in Abu Dhabi, Qatar, Dubai, Oman and Libya, they have been far less all-embracing than the original Gulf concessions, and have not given the whole state to a single group. Nor has it necessarily been the majors who have got the best acreage. In Libya for instance there are now twelve producing groups—and the companies who found most oil in their concessions, Occidental (VIP/Oxy), Conoco (Jet), Amerada and Marathon, were U.S. independents who broke into the European market in the early 1960s and caused the price cutting war which continued until the end of the decade.

PARTNERSHIPS

Towards the end of the 1950s a new formula of company/government relationship emerged as producing states began to replace traditional concession arrangements on new acreage with the more favourable partnerships. It was found that the American independents and the state owned European companies were prepared to bear greater burdens of exploration and development (exploitation) costs, pay large cash bonuses, and take greater risks in order to break into the Middle Eastern oil business. The first to sign a partnership was AGIP, a subsidiary of the Italian state company ENI, when it formed the Société Irano-Italienne des Pétroles (SIRIP) with the National Iranian Oil Company (NIOC) in 1957. Under the terms of the agreement the Italian company bore the whole exploration cost—only to be repaid 50 per cent if oil was actually found (which it was). Half the oil produced is owned by NIOC and sold by AGIP on the Iranians' behalf, and half belongs to the Italian company and is taxed at the normal 50-50 rate—giving the Government in effect a 75-25 profit split, together with valuable experience.

One year after the formation of SIRIP the Iranians substantially improved their terms in a new partnership with Amoco (a subsidiary of Standard of Indiana) creating IPAC—the Iran Pan-American Oil Company. NIOC was paid a bonus of $25 million and given a guarantee that the American company would spend $82 million on exploration over twelve years and share any unused money with NIOC if oil was struck earlier.

The major companies disliked the new arrangements and were quick to point out their disadvantages, but in 1964 Shell, which was then and still is running by far the biggest production deficit of the majors, gave in, and with NIOC formed DOPCO, the Dashtestan Offshore Petroleum Company. A year later NIOC concluded five more partnerships making eight in all, but only four—SIRIP, IPAC, IMINOCO (including AGIP, an Indian company and Phillips), and LAPCO (including four American independents) have struck oil, and the rest have relinquished their acreage. In 1971 Iran signed three new partnerships—with Amerada Hess, a Japanese group, and Mobil (another major running a production deficit).

Iran's example has been followed in differing forms by Saudi Arabia, Kuwait, Libya and Egypt—whose oil industry is composed entirely of partnerships, and while in some cases the relationship between state company and foreign partner has been somewhat uneasy, the arrangement has been fairly successful. Although partnerships have now been partially superceded by more radical new arrangements, the system is still popular—particularly in the form of carried interest used on new acreage in Abu Dhabi, Qatar, Saudi Arabia and Norway—where the state will take a 50 per cent participation when oil is discovered.

SERVICE CONTRACTS

In 1966 a much more revolutionary concept, service contracts, was introduced, and as with partnerships it was again Iran which led the way when NIOC signed a deal with a French group called SOFIRAN. More recently Iran has also contracted a multi-national European group, AREPI, and the American Conoco, while the Iraq National Oil Company (INOC) has signed a contract with the French state concern ERAP, which after a promising discovery at Buzurgan is likely to be productive, and Venezuela has announced that in future it will conclude nothing but contract arrangements.

Like foreign partners contractors pay the cost of exploration in full, but if oil is struck they are refunded completely, and the host national company similarly provides exploitation investment. The national company is the sole owner of all oil produced—as it is also of all facilities built during the course of operations. In Iran's case, which is fairly representative of contracts generally, the contractor acts as a broker for NIOC on a commission of 2 per cent of the realized price, and is paid by the guaranteed purchase of between 35 and 45 per cent of production at cost price plus 2 per cent. Fifty per cent of the difference between this sum and the realized price is payable as income tax. There has been some dispute over the true advantages of contracts for the producers—with estimates of government profits varying from 91.5 to 45 per cent.

OPEC AND PRICE NEGOTIATIONS
Formation and role of OPEC

The development of partnerships took place through the individual producer governments acting on their own accord, but the general dissatisfaction with the terms of the traditional concessions, led in 1960 to the creation of a body aimed at co-ordinating the policies of all large exporters—the Organization of Petroleum Exporting Countries. The immediate cause of OPEC's appearance was a successive lowering of posted prices by the companies, culminating in 1959 and 1960 in two reductions totalling 28 cents. At the Arab Petroleum Congress in Cairo in 1959—to which Iran and Venezuela had been invited as observers—it was agreed that the exporters should set up a joint organization, and after the second round of price cuts they met in Baghdad in September 1960 and formed OPEC.

The Organization's original members were Iran, Venezuela, Saudi Arabia, Kuwait and Iraq, but since then other countries have been admitted. These are Qatar in 1961, Libya and Indonesia in 1962, Abu Dhabi in 1967, Algeria in 1969, Nigeria in 1971, and Trinidad in 1972—though as of mid-1973 Trinidad's membership had still not been ratified by Iraq. In future the Organization may admit Ecuador, subject to its fulfilling various conditions, and Malaysia has said it would like to join, although its present production of around 5 million tons is well below what is generally regarded as the OPEC minimum—about one per cent of the world total.

OPEC is now in an exceedingly strong position. In 1972 it accounted for just over 51 per cent of world output and about 85 per cent of world oil exports; and it is the major companies particularly who are especially vulnerable to OPEC action. Their dependence for crude on Organization members varies from 98 per cent in the case of BP to 68 per cent for Texaco.

OPEC's original aims were quite varied—it had plans for setting up a Petroleum Court, unifying its members' Petroleum Laws, and organizing a system of production programming—an idea strongly supported by Venezuela, but turned down by the Arabs and Iran who in the 1960s were as interested in securing maximum output in competition with each other, as increasing the unit cost per barrel. But as it has turned out OPEC has become almost entirely a negotiating forum of producers versus companies. This is partly because the rapid rotation of its staff has precluded the development of a corporate character; and more importantly because the individual members, while eager to unite in OPEC when facing the companies, are much less anxious to see the Organization evolve any sort of supra-national authority which might bring pressure to bear on their own oil policies.

Royalty Expensing

In its early years the majors ignored OPEC, and up to the end of 1970 its only achievements, apart from preventing a further erosion of prices, and backing Libya in its decision to levy taxes on posted rather than realized prices in December 1965, were two agreements on royalty expensing in 1964 and 1968, together with a compromise on marketing allowances which the companies had previously been able to deduct from their taxable income before dividing their profits.

Although the producers' revenues had always nominally been made up of royalties of $12\frac{1}{2}$ per cent of the posted price—as payment for the oil itself, and income tax—representing a tax on the profits from the sale of this oil, payments made under the heading of royalties were totally deducted from income tax, and OPEC claimed might just as well never have existed. The OPEC states, referring to the situation in the U.S.A., where the royalty payer was only entitled to deduct the royalty from his gross income when computing his tax liability, wanted royalties in their own countries also treated as an expense—and in 1964 and 1968 this is what was agreed.

Under the new system the companies deducted both their production cost and the $12\frac{1}{2}$ per cent royalty from the posted price, then split the remainder 50–50, and then added the royalty onto the governments' share. As compensation it was agreed that for a time the companies would be granted diminishing discounts off the posted price in respect of royalty expensing, plus further diminishing discounts in respect of gravity differential (crudes of different specific gravities or degrees API have different prices—and in this case discounts were given off the postings of lighter crudes normally regarded as of higher quality.) Both these discounts, together with the remains of the marketing allowance were eliminated in the Teheran Agreement of February 1971—shortly before they were due to expire anyway.

Teheran Agreement

It was ten years after OPEC's foundation before the Organization was able to fulfill its main aim of the restoration (and increase) of crude oil prices. In 1970 a combination of circumstances—mainly the unexpectedly rapid increase in European demand, the closure of Tapline by a Syrian bulldozer, and enforced production cutbacks used as a lever for higher prices on the vulnerable independents in Libya, depriving the companies of part of their short haul Mediterranean crude—sent freight rates from the Gulf soaring to record levels, and for the first time in a decade created a very tight supply situation.

The Libyans were demanding higher prices— following the example of Algeria earlier in the year— and led by Texaco the companies operating there gave in one by one to a substantial rise in posted prices, and an increase in tax rates in the hope of having their production restored. Although in theory these changes were made only to bring Libyan short haul prices into line with those in the Gulf, the Gulf members of OPEC immediately demanded better prices themselves, and the companies promptly surrendered by agreeing to pay a higher tax rate of 55 per cent. Venezuela characteristically wasted no time in discussions and raised its tax rate by legislation to 60 per cent.

Then in December 1970 at OPEC's 21st Conference in Caracas the Organization decided that the Gulf countries should press for a round of posted price increases. In Teheran during January and February a company delegation led by BP met representatives of Iran, Iraq and Saudi Arabia, negotiating on behalf of all the Gulf producers, and on February 14th, 1971, one day before the OPEC deadline, signed an agreement which gave the producers a 33 cents rise in posted prices, plus provision for prices to be raised by 5 cents in respect of escalation (rising demand for oil) and by 2.5 per cent in respect of inflation on June 1st, 1971, and by the same amount on January 1st, 1973, 1974 and 1975. In return the companies were guaranteed that there would be no further claims until after December 31st, 1975, no more "leapfrogging" if the Mediterranean producers concluded better terms, and no embargoes.

Tripoli Agreement

Later, in March, negotiations were resumed in Libya, and on April 2nd in Tripoli a much more expensive and complex agreement was reached— giving Libya a straight 55 per cent tax rate and 90 cents on the posted price (incorporating a 13 cents element of freight differential which would be reduced as freight rates from the Gulf fell, a 10 cents low sulphur content premium, and a Suez Canal allowance —to be removed on the canal's reopening—of 12 cents). In addition 5 cents escalation, 2 cents low sulphur premium, and 2.5 per cent inflation increments were to be added annually. Later negotiations secured similar terms for the Iraqi and Saudi crude arriving at Mediterranean terminals through the IPC pipe and Tapline.

First Geneva Agreement

It was hoped that the Teheran, Tripoli and Baghdad Agreements would give complete price stability for five years. But in August 1971 President Nixon's economic measures leading eventually to the devaluation of the dollar produced further OPEC claims for compensation—though on this occasion in a notably moderate tone. The claim was settled on January 20th, 1972 when the companies agreed in Geneva to an immediate 8.49 per cent rise in posted prices in the Gulf; and later, in May, after rather tougher negotiations the same was agreed for Libya.

Second Geneva Agreement

In February 1973 the dollar was devalued a second time by 10 per cent, and under the terms of the Geneva Agreement posted prices were duly adjusted upwards by 5.8 per cent on April 1st. The OPEC states were disappointed by the time the adjustment mechanism took to operate, and by the small size of their compensation, and a committee composed of the oil ministers of Libya, Iraq and Kuwait was instructed to begin negotiations with the companies. The mainly radical composition of the delegation made negotiations considerably harder than in early 1972, and after three abortive rounds in Cairo, Vienna and Tripoli, the talks nearly broke down completely, until an OPEC conference was called in Vienna and the moderating influence of Iran and Saudi Arabia was brought to bear. Iranian and Saudi delegates then joined the negotiations, and on June 1st a second dollar compensation agreement was signed in Geneva. The producers obtained an 11.9 per cent increase in posted prices (which included the 5.8 per cent rise in April, plus compensation for the further slide in the dollar's parity during May). It was agreed that prices would in future be adjusted monthly according to a weighted average movement of eleven major currencies against the dollar.

As of June 2nd, 1973 therefore the tax calculations in force (until January 1st, 1974 or such time as the new dollar adjustment mechanism is used) for a representative barrel of light Gulf crude, in this 34° Arabian Light ex Ras Tanura, are as follows: From the posted price of $2.890 Aramco will deduct its production cost—$0.11, and a royalty of 12½ per cent —$0.361. The remaining $2.419, representing the company's profits, is then taxed at 55 per cent, giving Saudi Arabia $1.330. Aramco then adds the royalty onto the Government take, giving Saudi Arabia a total revenue of $1.691.

PARTICIPATION AND THE END OF CONCESSIONS

Although the price negotiations have attracted a lot of attention, the companies have always been able to pass on their extra tax burdens to the consumer, and none of the agreements have altered the structure of the industry or the role of the different parties involved. But in addition to restoring price levels, OPEC has always felt as a matter of principle that its members should have control of the oil industry in their own states, and this claim was given formal voice in the Declaratory Statement of Petroleum Policy issued after the 16th Conference in June 1968. The idea was summed up by one of OPEC's Secretary Generals, Nadim Pachachi: "Over the last twenty years circumstances have changed, and nowhere do Governments accept the role of a sleeping partner. They want a direct role in the management and exploitation of oil resources so as to gain know-how, and develop national expertise in the production and marketing of crude oil." Unlike the price negotiations though, the movement towards participation in local operations has not generally gone forward under the direct auspices of OPEC, but rather by individual states or groups of states acting, alone with the blessing of other Organization members.

Algeria

The first Middle Eastern state to gain control over its oil industry was Algeria, where the price negotiations of 1970–71 broke down completely. Algeria had always been in a rather different position from the other producers since the Franco-Algerian agreement of 1965, and the nationalization in 1967 of its American concessionaires and Shell, which had left its oil industry an exclusively Franco-Algerian business. Hopes of a mutually satisfactory relationship on the basis of the 1965 agreement were not fulfilled, and under the terms of this agreement, in 1969 Algeria opened negotiations with the French companies CFP and ERAP. The talks were inconclusive, and in July 1970 Algeria increased its posted prices unilaterally by 77 cents a barrel. Then after further fruitless discussions it took 51 per cent of all French companies operating in the country on February 24th, 1971, which led to the French sponsoring a highly effective boycott.

On June 30th CFP settled its differences with the Government—Algeria agreeing to pay $60 million compensation while CFP paid $40 million back payments and accepted a posted price of $3.60. In December a further agreement was signed with ERAP. The French company handed over the remaining 49 per cent of its local operations, and claims for compensation and back payments were cancelled out against each other. ERAP agreed to buy 7 million tons of oil a year for a fixed price of $2.70 a barrel.

The Gulf States and Saudi Arabia

The Algerians' negotiations with the French were not yet settled when OPEC's 24th Conference in Vienna in July 1971 announced that its members were going to open formal talks with the companies on "Participation". It soon became apparent that Libya and Nigeria would negotiate separately, and that Iran was also a somewhat special case because it officially had no concession, while Venezuela and Indonesia, having gained different degrees of control over their industries already, were not affected at all. So following the first Geneva Agreement, when talks opened in Riyadh between the Saudi Oil Minister, Shaikh Ahmed Zaki Yamani, and the Aramco partners, the only countries concerned were Saudi Arabia itself, Kuwait, Iraq, Abu Dhabi, and Qatar. In March the concessionaires of all these states agreed in principle to hand over 20 per cent of their companies to their host governments, but two months later IPC was nationalized, and the later stages of the talks, held in San Francisco, Beirut, London and New York, were in effect concerned only with the Gulf states and Saudi Arabia.

In view of their revolutionary nature the talks were allowed to proceed slowly throughout the summer, with the main issues of contention being the formula on which compensation should be paid by governments for their stake in the concessionaire companies, and the price at which the companies would buy back the crude produced by the governments' share in operations, if the national companies were unable to market this production.

Towards the end of the discussions a difference of interest arose between the Aramco partners—Exxon, Socal, Texaco and Mobil—whose concession had vast potential to make up any production that was lost to the Saudi Government, and BP, Gulf, Shell and CFP, whose concessions in Kuwait and Qatar were either subject to a production freeze or had little scope for a rise in output. The disagreement centred on the timetable by which the producers' initial stake would rise to 51 per cent, with the BP group requesting a longer period for them to be able to adjust their supply arrangements. In the end the two groups and Shaikh Yamani compromised—giving the producers a larger initial stake of 25 per cent but a longer share-holding "escalation" timetable—and on October 5th the General Agreement on Participation was announced in New York. By mid-1973 the Agreement had been signed by all states concerned, but the Kuwait National Assembly had still to ratify its accord with KOC.

Under the General Agreement, which came into force on January 1st, 1973, compensation was fixed on a formula of "updated book value"—which involved Saudi Arabia paying Aramco $500 million, Kuwait paying KOC $150 million, Abu Dhabi paying $162 million (half to ADMA and half to ADPC), and Qatar paying $71 million ($28 million to QPC and $43 million to Shell). Payment was to be made either within thirty days of January 1st in a lump sum, or in three instalments—of 30 per cent at the beginning of 1973, 35 per cent in 1974 and 35 per cent in 1975.

The earliest date for majority participation was agreed as January 1st, 1982, with the initial 25 per cent shareholding rising by 5 per cent in 1978, 1979, 1980 and 1981, and by 6 per cent in 1982. This schedule is not binding on the producer states, they may either take longer to reach 51 per cent, or not obtain a controlling interest at all—but four years notice is required of a producer's intention to raise its shareholding to 30 per cent, and one year's notice for subsequent increments.

Buy-back arrangements were more complicated, with buy-back oil divided into two categories—"bridging crude" and "phase-in" crude. The bridging crude is to "bridge" the western companies/operating partners over their current supply commitments, and for the first three years the producer government is obliged to sell back to the companies diminishing amounts of its production share—75 per cent in 1973, 50 per cent in 1974 and 25 per cent in 1975. The buy-back bridging crude price formula is based on the Quarter Way Price (QWP—between the Tax Paid Cost—TPC—and the posting) plus a certain number of cents a barrel depending on the crude in question. As of June 2nd, 1973 the formula for Arabian Light works as follows: On a posted price of $2.890, the TPC = income tax $1.330 + royalty $0.361 + production cost $0.110=$1.801. The QWP is therefore $2.073, plus $0.190 as the extra cents applied to Arabian Light = $2.263 as the bridging crude buy-back price.

Phase-in crude is the part of its production share which the producer government may oblige the companies to buy if it feels unable to sell this oil itself. The maximum percentages of the governments' 25 per cent share which may be passed back as phase-in crude rise as bridging crude is phased out and then gradually decline as follows: 1973 15%, 1974 30%, 1975 50%, 1976 70%, 1977 65%, 1978 60%, 1979 50%, 1980 40%, 1981 30%, 1982 10%. Each time a government increases its participation an additional phase-in schedule will start for percentages of the new crude acquired: 90, 80, 75, 70, 65, 60, 50, 40, 30, 10 per cent. The price formula applied to phase-in crude is TPC plus a certain number of cents a barrel depending on the crude in question. For Arabian Light as of June 2nd, 1973, the formula is TPC = $1.801 + $0.350 = $2.151 as the phase-in crude buy-back price.

The producers are not obliged under the General Agreement to sell any phase-in crude back to their operating partners, but all signatories have decided to sell back the maximum amount for the first four years, which will involve them selling on their own only 10 per cent of their 25 per cent production share in 1973, 20 per cent in 1974, 25 per cent in 1975, and 30 per cent in 1976.

For the purpose of planning future output and investment in production capacity, each year the state company and the Western operating partners will table their requirements for the next three years. If any party tables a requirement in excess of its entitlement (according to its percentage shareholding) the excess will be known as "forward avails", and it will be sold to that party at a contract price agreed in annual Implementing Agreements.

Iraq

In the spring of 1972, at about the time that the Western companies agreed to participation in principle, a new dispute developed in Iraq when IPC cut the throughput of its pipeline from Kirkuk to the Mediterranean terminals of Tripoli (Lebanon) and Banias. The company explained that in a period of low Gulf/Europe freight rates the extremely high prices negotiated for all Mediterranean crudes in 1971 made it uneconomic for its owners to run the pipe at more than half capacity. The Iraqi Government claimed that the cut-back was politically motivated, and presented IPC with alternatives: either the company was to restore Kirkuk production to normal levels and hand the extra production over to the Government, or it was to surrender the field entirely and concentrate production on BPC's acreage in the south.

The conflict was further exacerbated by IPC's threats of legal action to prevent the sale of INOC's crude from North Rumaila (in expropriated BPC acreage) which had come on stream that April, combined with a number of old issues including an Iraqi claim for royalty back payments dating from 1964 and 1968 which IPC had refused to pay until it received the compensation it was claiming for the acreage expropriated in 1961. On May 31st IPC presented its answers to the Iraqi ultimatum. These did not satisfy the Government, and on the following day IPC was nationalized. The affiliates BPC and MPC were not immediately affected.

In mid-July negotiations got underway with Nadim Pachachi, then Secretary General of OPEC, and M. Jean Duroc-Danner of CFP acting as mediators. IPC promptly announced that it would not pursue legal action against buyers of Kirkuk crude while mediation efforts were in progress, and the Iraqis were then able to sell substantial amounts of oil—including a deal in February 1973 under which CFP agreed to take 23.75 per cent of Kirkuk's output (equivalent to the company's former stake in IPC) over ten years.

On February 28th an agreement between IPC and the Iraqi Government was finally reached. IPC accepted the expropriations of Law 80 in 1961 and the nationalization of the Kirkuk producing area, and at the same time handed over MPC and paid Iraq £141 million of outstanding royalty back payments. In return it was to receive 15 million tons of oil in two batches in 1973 and 1974, and was given some assurance of the long term security of its investment and growth of output from BPC's southern fields, where it agreed to more than double production from 31.5 million tons in 1972 to 80 million tons by 1976. Negotiations between BPC and the Iraqi Government on 25 per cent participation began in Baghdad on March 1st.

Iran

Although it was fairly clear before the Iraqi crisis that the Iranians were not very interested in the Saudi Arabian participation programme (because the Consortium's lease was due to expire in 1979 anyway) it was not until June 24th, 1972 that the Shah formally confirmed that he was working towards an entirely different type of arrangement. He announced at a press conference in London that Iran was negotiating with the Consortium an agreement which would extend its lease while giving NIOC large amounts of cheap crude to sell on its own. This new policy caused considerable stir at an OPEC Conference in Vienna two days later, but during the autumn the Iranians remained silent while they examined the terms of the participation agreement obtained by the other Gulf states.

By the beginning of 1973 it was apparent that the Iranians were seeking a somewhat more radical agreement than that which they had originally proposed. On January 23rd the Shah gave the Consortium an ultimatum—under no circumstances would Iran extend its lease, and the companies could either continue under existing arrangements until 1979 and then become ordinary arms-length buyers, or negotiate an entirely new "agency" agreement immediately.

The Consortium opted for the latter plan, and on May 24th a contract was signed in Teheran under which NIOC formally took over operations in the Consortium area, agreeing to provide all investment capital for expansion, while the Consortium was to set up a new operating company, Iranian Oil Services, which would act as production contractor for NIOC. In return the western companies were granted a 20 year supply of crude as privileged buyers, which they would take in proportion to their shareholding in the Consortium. As production had already been scheduled to increase to 8 million barrels per day by 1978, the companies were able to calculate their offtake to within about 200,000 barrels per day over the next 20 years. NIOC kept a share of crude, thought to be about 20 per cent of total production, for its own arms-length sales or downstream operations.

Libya

It was only a matter of weeks after OPEC's 24th Conference in July 1971, and the formal announcement of the participation demand, that Libya let it be known that it would be interested in nothing less than an immediate 50 or 51 per cent participation, and would pursue its negotiations on its own. But although in December 1971 Libya nationalized BP's local interests for purely political reasons (as retaliation for Britain allowing Iran to take over the Abu Musa and Tumbs islands in the Gulf), the Government in Tripoli made no real moves towards participation throughout 1972—preferring to watch the progress of Shaikh Ahmed Zaki Yamani's talks and events in Iraq and Iran.

In January 1973 Libya began negotiations on its usual company by company basis with its biggest operator, Oasis (Conoco/Amerada/Marathon/Shell), and then on 30 April presented it with an ultimatum that it should agree to the principle of a 100 per cent take over, and compensation at net book value (lower than the updated book value formula adopted in the New York agreement). This demand was subsequently presented to the second and third largest operators—Occidental and Amoseas (Socal and Texaco), but the companies found the Libyan demands totally unacceptable. The majors were particularly concerned that any concessions to the Libyans would jeopardize the agreements in Iran and the Gulf, while the independents, with virtually no other producing interests in the Middle East, were afraid of driving the Libyans into some action like nationalization or a cut in supplies which for them would bring disaster. The talks were broken off on May 24th after the Libyans had refused to accept an offer of majority participation.

NATIONAL OIL COMPANIES AND DOWNSTREAM OPERATIONS

While Shaikh Ahmed Zaki Yamani was negotiating the later stages of the participation agreement in New York he surprised the oil industry by a dramatic statement on September 30th, 1972 at the Middle East Institute's annual conference in Washington, D.C., when he suggested that in return for Saudi's crude being given preferential access to the U.S. market, the Saudi state company, Petromin, would make heavy downstream investments in the U.S.A. His statement and the participation agreement a week later focused attention on the previously fairly insignificant national oil companies, and during the next few months there were a number of other dramatic statements by the Shah, and by Prince Saud, a son of King Faisal who worked his way up from the bottom of the Ministry of Petroleum to become Yamani's deputy.

But, although contracts were signed for the sale of considerable quantities of participation crude by all the producers concerned, by mid-1973 the Saudis had still not announced any definite plans for downstream operations outside Arabia itself, where Petromin already has a number of wholly owned or joint venture operations in geophysical surveying, drilling, offshore engineering, coastal tankering, refining, lubricants production (with Mobil), sulphuric acid production, and fertilizers.

Of the other Middle Eastern national companies, five—including the new concerns set up in Libya, Abu Dhabi and Qatar—were showing no immediate signs of interest in external investment. The Kuwait National Petroleum Company has already entered some highly unprofitable ventures. Chief among these is its very modern hydrogen process Shuaiba refinery, which has been afflicted by a series of technical troubles and was rendered uneconomic by the closure of the Suez Canal just before it came on stream in 1968. Other unsuccessful investments were a distribution operation in Denmark—which was to be supplied by Shuaiba—and a share in Rhodesia's Umtali refinery which was closed by sanctions in 1965. The privately owned Kuwait Oil Tankers Company has been more profitable in recent years—and has six vessels, three of 210,000 d.w.t., with another 324,000 tonner being built in Spain.

The Iraq National Oil Company, which does not have the same investment funds to draw on as Kuwait and Saudi Arabia, is confining itself to managing exploration and production in its own territory, though it is receiving seven 35,000 ton tankers from Spain to carry crude from North Rumaila.

By far the most sophisticated of the Middle Eastern national companies are Sonatrach and NIOC. Sonatrach has already placed orders for liquified natural gas carriers to supply the huge contracts it has concluded with El Paso and Eascogas in the U.S.A., and it has four export liquifaction plants either completed or under construction in its own territory. But in oil its main activity (apart from arms-length sales) has been directed internally, where it has formed a number of joint ventures covering all sections of the industry which may later provide a basis for foreign expansion with its established partners.

NIOC is by far the oldest and most experienced on the national companies, and it has already made downstream investments on a substantial scale. The company has shares in refineries in South Africa and Madras, both supplied by Iranian partnership crude, and agreements to participate in further refineries near Athens and in the Philippines. It also has a fertilizer plant in Madras, schemes for marketing joint ventures in Austria and Yugoslavia, and two blocks with BP in the North Sea—numbers 15/13 and 3/29. In July 1973 the Shah announced in Washington that NIOC was to take a 50 per cent share in the New York state operations of the large American independent Ashland Oil—involving a refinery, a petrochemical plant in Buffalo and 180 service stations together with transport and related facilities.

Although NIOC's ventures are the only cases of Middle Eastern/Western company partnerships outside a producing state signed up to mid-1973, the scope for Middle Eastern concerns investing in the oil business worldwide is considerable. The 1972 edition of the Chase Manhattan Bank's survey of "The Capital Investments of the World Petroleum Industry" estimated requirements over the 1973–88 period at one trillion (million million) dollars, and it did not see how, on its current rate of return, the western industry could possibly generate this capital internally or raise it on the market.

Teheran Agreement between Gulf States and Oil Companies

Abu Dhabi, Iran, Iraq, Kuwait, Qatar and Saudi Arabia (the said six States being hereinafter known as "the Gulf States" insofar as their exports from the Gulf are concerned) and the 13 Companies and their affiliates (hereinafter known as "the Companies"), to establish security of supply and stability in financial arrangements agree:

1. The existing arrangements between each of the Gulf States and each of the Companies to which this Agreement is an overall amendment, will continue to be valid in accordance with their terms.

2. The following provisions constitute a settlement of the terms relating to government take and other financial obligations of the Companies operating in the Gulf States as to the subject matters referred to in OPEC Resolutions and as regards oil exported from the Gulf, for a period from 15th February, 1971 through 31st December, 1975. These provisions shall be binding on both the Gulf States and the Companies for the said period.

3. These provisions are:

    (a) **No Leapfrogging.** During this Agreement no Gulf State will seek any increase in government take or other financial obligation, as a result of:

    (1) The application of different terms in:
        (i) any Gulf State as a Mediterranean exporter; or
        (ii) any Mediterranean producer; or
        (iii) any producer from any other area; or
    (2) The breach of contract through unilaterial action by any Government in the Gulf; or
    (3) The elimination of existing disparities in the Gulf under paragraph (c) (2) (iv) or any settlement under paragraph (c) (3) THIRDLY; or
    (4) The application of different terms to any future agreement in any country bordering on the Gulf.

    (b) **No Embargo:** The requirements of the six Member Countries of OPEC bordering the Gulf under OPEC Resolutions XXI.120 and XXII.131 are satisfied by the terms of this Agreement. During the period of this Agreement the Gulf States shall not take any action in the Gulf to support any OPEC member which may demand either any increase in government take above the terms now agreed, or any increase in government take or any other matter not covered by Resolution XXI.120.

    (c) **Financial Terms to Meet OPEC Resolution XXI.120, Paragraph 1:**

    (1) Total tax rates on income shall be stabilized in accordance with existing arrangements, except that insofar as present tax laws provide for total rates lower than 55 per cent, the Companies concerned will submit to an amendment to the relevant income tax laws raising the total rates to 55 per cent.

    (2) In satisfaction of the several claims arising out of paragraphs 2 and 3 of OPEC Resolution XXI.120.

    (i) Each of the Companies shall uniformly increase as from the effective date its crude posted prices at the Gulf terminals of the Gulf States by 33 cents per barrel.

    (ii) (aa) Each of the Companies shall make further upward adjustments to its crude posted prices to the nearest tenth* of a cent per barrel by increasing on 1st June 1971 each of such posted prices by an amount equal

---

* For each decimal fraction of a cent of 0.05 cents or above the amount is to be increased to the next higher whole 0.1 cent. For each decimal fraction of a cent below 0.05 cents the amount is decreased by this fraction

OIL IN THE MIDDLE EAST AND NORTH AFRICA—(TEHERAN AGREEMENT)

              to 2½% of such posted price on the day following the effective date. On 1st January of each of the years 1973 through 1975 a further increase to the nearest tenth of a cent shall be made in each such posted price equivalent to 2½% of the posted price prevailing on 31st December of the preceding year.

  (ii) (bb) Each of the Companies shall increase its crude posted prices on 1st June, 1971 by 5 cents per barrel and by a further increase of 5 cents per barrel on 1st January in each of the years 1973-75.

  (ii) (cc) Each of the Companies shall further increase its crude posted prices as from the effective date by 2 cents per barrel which, together with paragraphs 3(d) is in satisfaction of claims related to freight disparities.

  (iii) The increases included in (ii) above shall be in satisfaction of claims in respect of freight, escalation and of inflation under both OPEC Resolution XXI.120 and OPEC Resolution XXI.122, and also in satisfaction of certain other economic considerations raised by the Gulf States.

  (iv) Each of the Gulf States having an existing claim under negotiation based on posted price disparity has discussed and resolved such claim with the Companies exporting the crude grade concerned as follows: In the case of Iranian Heavy, Saudi Arab Medium and Kuwait, the posted prices shall each be increased by the Companies concerned by one cent with effect from the effective date. In the case of Basrah after the adjustment provided for in (3) FIRSTLY the posted price will be $1.805 for 35° API.

(3) OPEC 120 Paragraph 4:

Firstly: For crude oil API gravity 30.0° to 39.9° with effect from the effective date each posted price shall be further increased by the Companies by ½ cent per barrel for each degree such crude is less than API° 40. A table showing the resulting increases before taking into account the settlement of disparities under (c) (2) (iv) is attached (Annexe 2) and forms part of this Agreement.

Secondly: Posted prices shall apply to shipments falling within the range of .0 to .09 degrees of any full degree of API gravity and shall be subject to a gravity differential on the basis of 0.15 cents per barrel for each full 0.1 degree API.

Thirdly: In the case of crudes under 30° API the Governments and Companies shall agree on a basis for adjusting the posted price. However, if no such agreement is reached the same principles applied in firstly and secondly above shall apply.

The existing per cent allowance, the gravity allowance and the ½ cent per barrel marketing allowance shall be eliminated as from the effective date of this Agreement.

(d) If Libya is receiving a premium for short haul crude which premium is to fluctuate according to freight conditions in accordance with a freight formula and if in respect of any period the premium applied by any major oil company which has produced in Libya and the Gulf States exceeds for any reason the lowest level permitted by such formula for such period the Gulf States shall be entitled to additional payments as set out in Annexe 3.

4. "Affiliate" shall mean in relation to any Company, any company which is wholly or partly owned directly or indirectly by that Company.

5. Each of the Gulf States accepts that the Companies' undertakings hereunder constitute a fair appropriate and final settlement between each of them, and those of the Companies operating within their respective jurisdictions, of all matters related to the applicable bases of taxation and the levels of posted prices up to the effective date.

6. The effective date of this Agreement shall be 15th February, 1971.

Done this 14th Day of February, 1971 at Teheran, Iran.

OIL IN THE MIDDLE EAST AND NORTH AFRICA—(Teheran Agreement)

ANNEXE 3
SHORT HAUL FREIGHT

The following provisions shall apply with respect to the implementation of paragraph 3(d) of the Agreement to which this Annexe 3 is attached.

(1) Any major oil company concerned shall pay to each Gulf State (as a supplemental payment) that proportion of a "balancing amount" as such Company's crude production exported from Gulf terminals (including Arabia/Bahrein pipeline) in such Gulf State bear to the total of such Company's crude exports in such period from all Gulf States in the Gulf.

(2) The "balancing amount" will be equal to the monetary amount by which the Company's payments to Libya for the period exceed the monetary amount which the Company would have paid to Libya for the period if it had effected the full reduction of premium permitted by its agreement with Libya or if it had effected a reduction in premium equal to 21½ cents/B which is agreed with the Gulf States to be the short haul premium whichever reduction is smaller.

(3) "Major Oil Company" for the above purpose means any of Esso, Texaco, Socal, Gulf, Mobil, BP, Shell and CFP.

(4) Illustrative examples of the implementation of the terms of this annexe are shown in Exhibit A, attached.

EXHIBIT A
ILLUSTRATIVE EXAMPLE OF "BALANCING AMOUNT"

Cents/BBL

Shorthaul Premium agreed with the Gulf States	21.5	21.5	21.5	21.5
Libyan "Premium" for illustrative purposes:	18.0	21.5	24.0	30.0

Lesser of Under-Reduction of Libyan Freight Premium or 21½ cents B:

1. Libyan Premium should be reduced by 25% but is not	4.5	5.375	6.0	7.5
2. Libyan Premium should be reduced by 50% but is not	9.0	10.75	12.0	15.0
3. Libyan Premium should be reduced by 100% but is not	18.0	21.5	21.5	21.5
4. Libyan Premium should be reduced by 100% but was only reduced to 50%.	9.0	10.75	12.0	15.0
5. Libyan Premium should be reduced by 100% but was only reduced by 25%	13.5	16.125	18.0	21.5

To obtain balancing amount:

(a) Multiply figure given under 1-5 by the total Libyan tax rate on income plus (100 per cent minus such rate) applied to the royalty, all as applicable to the producer concerned

(b) Multiply resultant dollar/B figure in (a) by the barrels of the major company's crude production exported from Libya

Oil Statistics

(compiled by Michael Field)

CRUDE OIL PRODUCTION
(million metric tons)

	1938	1970	1971	1972	1971–72 % CHANGE
Iran	10.4	191.7	227.0	251.9	10.9
Saudi Arabia	0.1	176.9	223.4	285.5	27.8
Kuwait	—	137.4	147.1	151.2	2.8
Iraq	4.4	76.6	83.5	71.6	−14.3
Abu Dhabi	—	33.3	44.9	50.6	12.6
Partitioned Zone	—	26.7	28.3	29.2	3.4
Qatar	—	17.3	20.5	23.2	12.9
Libya	—	159.2	133.1	106.7	−19.8
Algeria	—	47.3	36.5	52.0	42.5
Egypt	0.2	20.9*	21.0*	15.9*	−24.3
Oman	—	17.2	14.4	14.2	−1.5
Syria	—	4.4	6.5	6.4	−1.6
Dubai	—	4.3	6.5	7.7	11.8
Tunisia	—	4.1	4.2	4.0	−4.8
Bahrain	1.1	3.8	3.8	3.5	−7.9
Turkey	—	3.5	3.5	3.4	−3.1
Israel	—	0.08	0.07	0.07	—
Morocco	—	0.05	0.02	0.03	50.0
M.E. TOTAL	16.2	924.5	996.4	1,077.3	8.1
M.E. % WORLD TOTAL	7.7	39.6	40.4	41.3	0.9
Venezuela	28.1	193.2	187.7	170.8	−9.0
Nigeria	—	53.4	74.7	88.8	18.9
Indonesia	7.4	42.1	44.1	51.9	17.7
U.S.A.	170.7	533.6	530.0	532.2	0.4
U.S.S.R.	37.7	353.3	372.0	394.0	5.9
Canada	0.9	63.7	76.6	89.1	16.3
Mexico	5.5	25.0	23.9	24.5	2.6
Argentina	2.4	20.5	22.1	22.5	1.9
Trinidad	2.4	7.3	6.7	7.7	14.3
WORLD TOTAL	280.5	2,336.2	2,475.9†	2,609.6†	5.4

* Includes output of Sinai now Israeli-occupied.
† Includes North Sea: 300,000 tons in 1971, 1.8 million tons in 1972 (500 per cent increase).

OIL IN THE MIDDLE EAST AND NORTH AFRICA—(Oil Statistics)

PROVEN RESERVES*
(million tons)

	End 1972	% World		End 1972	% World
Saudi Arabia	19,700	21.5	Venezuela	1,880	2.0
Kuwait	8,890	10.0	Nigeria	2,060	2.3
Iran	8,900	10.0	Indonesia	1,370	1.5
Iraq	4,900	5.3	U.S.A.	4,970	5.5
Partitioned Zone	2,200	2.4	Soviet Area	13,420	14.7
Abu Dhabi	2,840	3.1	Canada	1,570	1.7
Qatar	960	1.0	Argentina	670	0.7
			Mexico	380	0.4
Libya	4,160	4.6	Trinidad and Tobago	270	0.2
Algeria	3,100	3.4	U.K. North Sea	680	0.7
			Norway North Sea	280	0.2
Syria	990	1.1			
Oman	680	0.7	World Total	91,000	+7% over 1971
Egypt	710	0.8			
Dubai	270	0.2			
Bahrain	50	0.01			
M.E. Total	58,350	64.1			

* Reserve figures are subject to wide margins of error, and there are considerable differences between sources—including oil companies and governments. In general Middle Eastern reserves are consistently being revised upwards. The Iranians have announced that their reserves may be as big as 13,000 million tons; recent discoveries in Saudi Arabia may prove reserves of well over 20,000 million tons, and it is thought that the relatively unexplored Iraq could have resources second only to Saudi Arabia.

GOVERNMENT OIL REVENUES
(million U.S. dollars)

	1963	1964	1965	1966	1967	1968	1969	1970	1971	1972*
Iran	398	470	522	593	737	817	938	1,093	1,870	2,400
Saudi Arabia	502	561	655	777	852	966	1,008	1,200	2,160	2,779
Kuwait	557	655	671	707	718	766	812	895	1,395	1,549
Iraq	325	353	375	394	361	476	484	521	840	780
Abu Dhabi	6	12	33	100	105	153	191	233	431	575
Qatar	60	66	69	92	102	110	115	122	198	244
Libya	109	197	371	476	631	952	1,132	1,295	1,766	1,560
Algeria	n.a.	n.a.	102	145	200	262	299	325	320	870

* Estimated.

OIL IN THE MIDDLE EAST AND NORTH AFRICA—(Oil Statistics)
REFINERY CAPACITY AND OWNERSHIP
(million tons/year)

State	Refinery	Capacity	State Total	Ownership
Iran	Abadan	20.6		National Iranian Oil Co.
	Masjid-i-Sulaiman	3.5		NIOC
	Teheran	4.25		NIOC
	Alborz	0.5		NIOC
	Kermanshah	0.1		NIOC
	Naft-i-Shah	0.35	29.3	NIOC
Iraq	Daurah	3.75		Government Oil Refineries Admin.
	Alwand	0.6		GORA
	Muftiyah	0.2		GORA
	Qaiarah	0.1		GORA
	Basra	3.4		GORA
	K3	2.75	10.8	GORA
Kuwait	Mina al Ahmadi	14.5		KOC
	Mina Abdullah	6.5		AMINOIL
	Shuaiba	6.5	27.5	KNPC
Partitioned Zone	Mina Saud	2.25		Getty
	Ras al Khafji	1.5	3.75	AOC
Saudi Arabia	Ras Tanura	20.0		ARAMCO
	Jeddah	0.6	20.6	PETROMIN
Bahrain	Sitra	12.3	12.3	BAPCO
Qatar	Umm Said	0.03	0.03	QPC
Yemen, P.D.R.	Aden	8.3	8.3	BP
Lebanon	Tripoli	1.75		Government
	Sidon	1.25	3.0	MEDRECO
Jordan	Zerqa	0.8	0.8	Government
Syria	Homs	2.95	2.95	Government
Egypt	Suez*	4.0		Nasr Oil Fields
	Suez*	3.2		Government
	Alexandria	3.0	10.2	SERCOP
Libya	Mersa Brega	0.45		Exxon
	Hofra Amal	0.2		Mobil
	Dahra	0.12		Oasis
	C Structure	0.02	0.79	Government
Algeria	Maison Carree	2.1		Raffineries d'Algérie
	Hassi Massoud	0.16	2.26	CRAN

* Destroyed in 1967.

77

OIL IN THE MIDDLE EAST AND NORTH AFRICA—(OIL GROUPS IN THE GULF)

Oil Groups Producing and Exploring in the Gulf

Iran

NATIONAL IRANIAN OIL COMPANY (NIOC)

Operations in the Agreement Area: As from May 1973 the state owned National Iranian Oil Company took over the management and development of all fields formerly run by Iranian Oil Participants (the Consortium). Under a twenty year agreement the Consortium became an operating contractor and privileged buyer of Iranian crude. The new contracting company, replacing the Consortium's previous operator, the Iranian Oil Exploration and Producing Company, is Iranian Oil Services, owned by the Consortium partners:

OWNERSHIP:
British Petroleum	40%
Royal Dutch/Shell	14%
Exxon	7%
Standard Oil of California	7%
Texaco	7%
Gulf	7%
Mobil	7%
Compagnie Française des Pétroles (CFP)	6%
Iricon Agency	5%
Atlantic Richfield (Arco)	4/12%
Reynolds	2/12%
Charter Company	2/12%
Getty	2/12%
Continental	1/12%
Standard Oil of Ohio	1/12%

Operations at Naft-i-Shah: NIOC operating on its own has developed a field at Naft-i-Shah on the border between Iraq and the province of Kermanshah.

SOCIÉTÉ IRANO-ITALIENNE DES PÉTROLES (SIRIP)

PARTNERSHIP: Twenty-five years from the start of sales. Three areas totalling 8,839 sq. miles: offshore the northern Gulf, east-central Zagros, and Gulf of Oman coast. Oil is now being produced.

OWNERSHIP:
National Iranian Oil Company (NIOC)	50%
AGIP Mineraria	50%

IRAN PAN-AMERICAN OIL COMPANY (IPAC)

PARTNERSHIP: Twenty-five years from the date when the first 629,000 barrels of oil have been produced. Two areas totalling 6,176 sq. miles, offshore north and south of SIRIP's block. Oil is being produced.

OWNERSHIP:
NIOC	50%
Amoco	50%

IRANIAN MARINE INTERNATIONAL OIL COMPANY (IMINOCO)

PARTNERSHIP: Twenty-five years from the start of production. Area of 7,960 sq. km. on four offshore locations in the Gulf Oil is now being produced.

OWNERSHIP:
NIOC	50%
AGIP	16⅔%
Phillips	16⅔%
Hydrocarbons India	16⅔%

LAVAN PETROLEUM COMPANY (LAPCO)

PARTNERSHIP: Twenty-five years from the start of production. Area of 8,500 sq. km. in three offshore areas. Oil is now being produced.

OWNERSHIP:
NIOC	50%
Atlantic Richfield (Arco)	12½%
Sun	12½%
Murphy	12½%
Union Oil of California	12½%

IRAN PETROLEUM DEVELOPMENT COMPANY (INPECO)

PARTNERSHIP: Twenty years from 1971, extendable by two five-year periods. Area of 8,000 sq. km. in Lurestan. Exploration is now in progress.

OWNERSHIP:
NIOC	50%
Japanese Consortium	50%

(Teijin, Mitsui, North Sumatra Oil Development, Mitsubishi Shoji).

BUSHIRE PETROLEUM COMPANY (BUSHCO)

PARTNERSHIP: Twenty-five years from 1971 extendable by two five-year periods. Area of 3,100 sq. km. offshore near the port of Bushire. Exploration is in progress.

OWNERSHIP:
NIOC	50%
Amerada Hess	50%

HORMUZ PETROLEUM COMPANY (HOPECO)

PARTNERSHIP: Twenty-five years from 1971 extendable by two five-year periods. Area of 3,500 sq. km. offshore near the Straits of Hormuz. Exploration is in progress.

OWNERSHIP:
NIOC	50%
Mobil	50%

SOCIÉTÉ FRANÇAISE DES PÉTROLES D'IRAN (SOFIRAN)

SERVICE CONTRACT: Signed in 1966 for 10,800 sq. km. onshore and offshore. The French company as contractor will manage exploration and production and act as sales agent for NIOC. Exploration is in progress.

OWNERSHIP OF CONTRACTOR:
Entreprise de Recherches et d'Activités Pétroliers (ERAP)	80%
Aquitaine	20%

AREPI

SERVICE CONTRACT: Signed in 1969 for 27,260 sq. km. onshore. ERAP will act as managing agent on behalf of the European group, and as exploration contractor and sales agent for NIOC. Exploration is now in progress.

OWNERSHIP OF CONTRACTOR:
ERAP (French)	35%
AGIP (Italian)	25%
Petrofina (Belgian)	20%
Hispanoil (Spanish)	15%
Oesterreichische Mineraloelverwaltung (OMV)	5%

CONOCO

SERVICE CONTRACT: Signed in 1969 for onshore acreage north of the Hormuz Straits. Exploration is in progress.

OWNERSHIP OF CONTRACTOR:
Continental (Conoco)	100%

OIL IN THE MIDDLE EAST AND NORTH AFRICA—(OIL GROUPS IN THE GULF)

Iraq

IRAQ NATIONAL OIL COMPANY (INOC)

Production and Exploration Operations: The state-owned Iraq National Oil Company runs two production operations—the small Khanaqin field near the Iranian border, and the North Rumaila field in the south of the country which came on stream in April 1972. INOC also manages the marketing of North Rumaila crude. With the assistance of Russian and Hungarian drilling companies INOC is appraising a number of other promising finds.

IRAQI COMPANY FOR OIL OPERATIONS (ICOO)

Kirkuk Production: The state-owned Iraqi Company for Oil Operations was formed in June 1972 to take over the production operations of the nationalized Iraq Petroleum Company (same ownership as Basrah Petroleum Company below). ICOO manages production from the Kirkuk, Bai Hassan, and Jambur fields on former IPC acreage, and from Ain Zalah and Butmah on former acreage of the Mosul Petroleum Company (dissolved by the IPC group early in 1973). Marketing is managed by INOC.

ENTREPRISE DES RECHERCHES ET D'ACTIVITÉS PÉTROLIERS (ERAP)

SERVICE CONTRACT: Signed between the Iraq National Oil Company (INOC) and ERAP, under which the French group acts as contractor to the national company. Area of 10,800 sq. km. onshore and offshore. Oil has been discovered but has not yet been brought on stream.

OWNERSHIP OF CONTRACTOR:
ERAP 100%

BASRAH PETROLEUM COMPANY (BPC)

CONCESSION: Seventy-five years from 1938, expires 2013. Now confined to producing areas west of Basra since expropriation measures of 1961. The Iraqi Government is likely to take a share in BPC as a result of the 1972 Participation agreement reached between the other Arab producers in the Gulf and their former concessionaires.

OWNERSHIP:
British Petroleum 23¾%
Royal Dutch/Shell 23¾%
Compagnie Française des Pétroles . . 23¾%
Near East Development Corporation . 23¾%
   Exxon 50%
   Mobil 50%
Participations and Explorations Corpn.
  (Gulbenkian) 5%

Kuwait

KUWAIT OIL COMPANY (KOC)

PARTNERSHIP: Originally a Gulf/BP concession of seventy-five years from 1934, extended in 1951 to expire in 2026. Covered all of Kuwait including territorial waters to a six mile limit, though areas totalling 11,414 sq. km. were relinquished in 1962, 1967 and 1971. In 1973, as a result of the Participation agreement of October 1972, the Kuwaiti Government took a 25% share of KOC with an option to raise its shareholding by 5% in 1979, 1980, 1981 and 1982, and by 6% in 1983—giving a majority interest of 51%. As of June 1st, 1973 the agreement had been signed by the Government, but not yet ratified by the National Assembly.

OWNERSHIP:
British Petroleum 37½%
Gulf 37½%
Kuwait Government 25%

KUWAIT SHELL PETROLEUM DEVELOPMENT

CONCESSION: Forty-five years from 1961. Area of 1,500 sq. miles offshore. Drilling began on promising acreage in 1962, and was abandoned in the following year as a result of a still unresolved boundary dispute.

OWNERSHIP:
Royal Dutch/Shell 100%

KUWAIT SPANISH PETROLEUM COMPANY (KSPC)

PARTNERSHIP: Thirty-five years with the option of a five-year extension. Area of 9,000 sq. km. on relinquished KOC acreage. Although drilling has revealed shows of oil, commercial production has not been justified.

OWNERSHIP:
Kuwait National Petroleum Company (KNPC)
  (60% Government, 40% Public) . . 51%
Hispanoil 49%

Partitioned Zone

AMERICAN INDEPENDENT OIL COMPANY (AMINOIL)

CONCESSION: Sixty years from 1948, expires 2008. All of Kuwait's half of the Partitioned Zone including territorial waters and islands. Oil is now being produced.

OWNERSHIP:
R. J. Reynolds Industries . . . 100%

GETTY OIL COMPANY

CONCESSION: Sixty years from 1949, expires 2009. All of Saudi Arabia's half of the Partitioned Zone including territorial waters and islands. Oil is being produced.

OWNERSHIP:
Getty 100%

ARABIAN OIL COMPANY (AOC)

PARTNERSHIP: All areas offshore the Partitioned Zone outside the six-mile limit. Oil is being produced.

OWNERSHIP:
Japan Petroleum Trading Company . . 80%
Kuwaiti Government 10%
Saudi Government 10%

Saudi Arabia

ARABIAN AMERICAN OIL COMPANY (ARAMCO)

PARTNERSHIP: Originally two concession areas of sixty-six years from 1933 and sixty-six years from 1939, expiring in 1999 and 2005. Covering most of Eastern Province and other areas. In 1973, as a result of the October 1972 Participation Agreement, the Saudi Arabian state company Petromin took a shareholding on the terms described for KOC above.

OWNERSHIP:
Exxon 22½%
Standard Oil of California . . . 22½%
Texaco 22½%
Mobil 7½%
Petromin 25%

79

OIL IN THE MIDDLE EAST AND NORTH AFRICA—(OIL GROUPS IN THE GULF)

TENNECO
PARTNERSHIP: Signed in 1965 for 26,000 sq. km. in three areas onshore and offshore along the Red Sea coast. Gas has already been struck in the northern Red Sea, and exploration is continuing.
OWNERSHIP:
Petromin 10%
Tenneco 90%

Bahrain

BAHRAIN PETROLEUM COMPANY (BAPCO)
CONCESSION: Ninety-five years from 1929, expires 2024. All onshore areas, territorial waters and islands. Parts of this acreage have been relinquished. Oil is being produced from one field at Awali which is now running dry.
OWNERSHIP:
Caltex (Standard of California & Texaco 50-50) . 100%

SUPERIOR OIL COMPANY BAHRAIN
CONCESSION: Granted in 1970 for 1,307 sq. miles offshore in areas relinquished by BAPCO. Exploration is in progress.
OWNERSHIP:
Superior 100%

Qatar

QATAR PETROLEUM COMPANY (QPC)
PARTNERSHIP: Originally a concession of seventy-five years from 1935, expiring in 2010. Onshore the Qatar peninsula excluding large areas relinquished in the north and east. In 1973, as a result of the Participation agreement, the Qatar Government took a stake on the terms described for KOC above.
OWNERSHIP:
British Petroleum . . . . . . $17\frac{13}{16}$%
Royal Dutch/Shell . . . . . . $17\frac{13}{16}$%
CFP . . . . $17\frac{13}{16}$%
Near East Development Corpn. (Exxon & Mobil 50–50) . . . . $17\frac{13}{16}$%
Participations and Explorations Corpn. (Gulbenkian) . . . . $3\frac{3}{4}$%
Qatar Government 25%

SHELL QATAR
PARTNERSHIP: Originally a concession of seventy-five years from 1952 expiring in 2027. Offshore north east of the Qatar peninsula. In 1973 as a result of the Participation agreement the Qatar Government took a stake on the terms described for KOC above.
OWNERSHIP:
Royal Dutch/Shell 75%
Qatar Government 25%

QATAR OIL COMPANY
CONCESSION: Thirty-five years from 1969, expires 2004. Area of 15,800 sq. km. offshore south-east of the Qatar peninsula. Exploration is in progress, and if oil is found in commercial quantities the Qatar Government has the option to take a fifty per cent stake.
OWNERSHIP:
Qatar Oil Company (Japan) . . . 100%
(Fuji, Kansai, Tokyo Electric Power, Kansai Electric Power.)

Qatar/Abu Dhabi

AL BUNDUQ COMPANY
CONCESSION: Granted in 1970 to develop the offshore al Bunduq field on the median line between Qatar and Abu Dhabi. Any future revenues will be divided equally between Abu Dhabi and Qatar. Appraisal wells are being drilled.
OWNERSHIP:
British Petroleum . . . . . . $33\frac{1}{3}$%
Compagnie Française des Pétroles . . . $33\frac{1}{3}$%
Japanese group (ADOCO, QPC, North Slope Oil, Alaska Oil) . . . . $33\frac{1}{3}$%

Abu Dhabi

ABU DHABI PETROLEUM COMPANY (ADPC)
PARTNERSHIP: Originally a concession of seventy-five years from 1939, expiring in 2014. Includes onshore acreage and a three mile belt of territorial waters around the coast and islands, minus areas relinquished. In 1973, as a result of the Participation agreement, the Abu Dhabi Government took a stake on the terms described for KOC above.
OWNERSHIP:
British Petroleum . . . . . . $17\frac{13}{16}$%
Royal Dutch/Shell . . . . . . $17\frac{13}{16}$%
CFP . . . . $17\frac{13}{16}$%
Near East Development Corpn. (Exxon & Mobil 50–50) . . . . $17\frac{13}{16}$%
Participations and Explorations Corpn. (Gulbenkian) . . . . $3\frac{3}{4}$%
Abu Dhabi Government 25%

ABU DHABI MARINE AREAS (ADMA)
PARTNERSHIP: Originally a concession held by BP (two-thirds) and CFP (one-third) running from 1953 to 2018, and covering areas of the continental shelf beyond the three-mile limit. In December 1972 BP sold part of its stake to a large group of Japanese industrial companies (OPC), and in 1973, as a result of the Participation agreement the state-owned Abu Dhabi National Oil Company took a stake on the terms described for KOC above.
OWNERSHIP:
British Petroleum . . . . . . $27\frac{1}{2}$%
CFP 25%
Overseas Petroleum Corporation (OPC) . . $22\frac{1}{2}$%
Abu Dhabi National Oil Company . . . 25%

ABU DHABI OIL COMPANY (ADOCO)
PARTNERSHIP: Originally a concession with a government participation option of forty-five years from 1967 to 2011, covering two offshore areas relinquished by ADMA totalling 4,416 sq. km. In May 1975 the company's first field, Mubarraz, was brought on stream, and the Abu Dhabi National Oil Company announced that it was exercising its option to take a 50 per cent stake.
OWNERSHIP:
Abu Dhabi National Oil Company . . . 50%
Maruzen . . . . $16\frac{2}{3}$%
Daikyo . . . . $16\frac{2}{3}$%
Nippon Mining . . . . $16\frac{2}{3}$%

ABU AL BU-KOOSH GROUP
CONCESSION: Hived off from ADMA in December 1972 to operate a small portion of LAPCO's Iranian field, Sassan, which extends into Abu Dhabi waters, where it is known as Abu al Bu-Koosh. The Abu Dhabi National Oil Company has reserved the right to 25% participation when production begins in June 1974.

THE MIDDLE EAST AND NORTH AFRICA—(OIL GROUPS IN THE GULF)

OWNERSHIP:
CFP	51%
New England Petroleum	24½%
Sunningdale	24½%

MIDDLE EAST OIL COMPANY (MEOC)
CONCESSION: Granted in 1966. Two areas relinquished by ADPC onshore totalling 15,566 sq. km. Exploration is in progress.
OWNERSHIP:
Mitsubishi	100%

PHILLIPS/AGIP/AMINOIL
CONCESSION: Granted in 1965. Three areas relinquished by ADPC onshore totalling 9,000 sq. km. Exploration is in progress.
OWNERSHIP:
Phillips	41 2/3%
AGIP	41 2/3%
Aminoil (R. J. Reynolds)	16 2/3%

AMERADA GROUP
CONCESSION: Two offshore blocks relinquished by ADMA totalling 3,150 sq. km. Exploration is in progress.
OWNERSHIP:
Amerada Hess	31½%
Pan Ocean	31½%
Bow Valley Industries	20%
Wington Enterprises	17%

Dubai
DUBAI MARINE AREAS
CONCESSION: Sixty years from 1952, expires 2012. Continental shelf area beyond the three mile limit. The ownership of the concession, originally held by BP and CFP, has changed several times. Oil is on stream from the Fatah field.
OWNERSHIP:
Continental	30%
Texaco	10%
CFP	25%
Hispanoil	25%
Sun	5%
Wintershall	5%

Sharjah
BUTTES GROUP
CONCESSION: All Gulf coast offshore areas including islands and territorial waters awarded in 1969. A commercial discovery has been made east of the island of Abu Musa in an area disputed with Umm al Qaiwain's concessionaire Occidental.
OWNERSHIP:
Buttes	37½%
Ashland	25%
Skelly	25%
Kerr-McGee	12½%

Ras Al Khaimah
UNION OIL OF CALIFORNIA
CONCESSION: Onshore and offshore areas on the Gulf coast. A very deep gas strike was made in December 1971, but the discovery has not proved commercial.
OWNERSHIP:
Union Oil of California	80%
Southern Natural Gas	20%

Ajman and Umm Al Qaiwain
OCCIDENTAL
CONCESSION: Offshore concession. Exploration has been held up by a dispute with Sharjah's concessionaire, Buttes, over acreage near the island of Abu Musa.
OWNERSHIP:
Occidental	100%

Oman
PETROLEUM DEVELOPMENT OMAN (PDO)
CONCESSION: Seventy-five years from 1937, expires 2012. Onshore concession originally covering northern provinces, now including Dhofar. Oil is being produced.
OWNERSHIP:
Royal Dutch/Shell	85%
Compagnie Française des Pétroles	10%
Participations and Explorations Corpn. (Gulbenkian)	5%

The Suez Canal

The Suez Canal joins the Mediterranean and Red Seas between Port Said and Suez, in Egypt. It has been closed since the war of June 1967, and now forms the demarcation line between Egypt and the Israeli-occupied Sinai peninsula. Super tankers are now too large to use the old canal and an Italian plan for a new larger Suez Canal west of the existing one, to be built by an international consortium, was announced in April 1973. The Egyptian Government has denied any knowledge of the plan.

ORGANIZATION

Suez Canal Authority (*Hay'at Canal Al-Suess*): Ismailia, Egypt; Chair. and Man. Dir. Eng. M. A. MASHOUR. The Suez Canal Authority manages the Canal on behalf of the Government of Egypt.

PRINCIPAL FACTS

Length: 107 miles including approach fairways.
Maximum Depth: 50 ft.
Maximum Width: 660 ft.
Minimum Width: 600 ft.
Transit Time: Average transit time was fifteen hours.

CHRONOLOGY

1854 Ferdinand de Lesseps granted building concession.
1859 Excavation began.
1869 Canal opened.
1875 Ismail Pasha of Egypt sold his shares in the French Suez Canal Company (44% of total to the British Government for nearly £4m.).
1888 Convention of Constantinople declared Canal open to vessels of all nations.
1956 President Nasser of Egypt nationalized Canal. Canal closed (October) following invasion of Egypt.
1957 Canal re-opened under the control of the Egyptian Suez Canal Authority (April).
1959 World Bank lend Authority U.S.$56.5m.
1961 UN surcharge of 3% on transit dues, levied in 1958 to pay for clearing the Canal, was lifted (March).
1964 Loan of £E9.8m. granted by Kuwait Fund for Arab Development for dredging and widening operations.
      Permissible draught increased to 38 ft.
1965 Transit rates increased 1%, July.
1966 Transit rates increased 1%, July.
1967 Canal closed (June) during war with Israel.

IMPROVEMENT SCHEMES

In the years following the opening of the Canal the depth of the channel was 26.2 ft. (8 m.) and its breadth at the bottom 72.2 ft. (22 m.), with a wet cross-sectional area of 3,272 sq. ft. (304 sq. m.). The average gross tonnage of transiting vessels was then 1,700 tons and the highest authorized draught was 24.6 ft. (7.5 m.). Navigation speed was 6.21 miles (10 km.) per hour.

NASSER PROJECT

Seven programmes of improvement were executed between 1876 and 1954. The eighth programme had started before nationalization, was modified thereafter to achieve better results and is now called the Nasser Project. Under this scheme the Canal was widened and deepened to take large tankers. New navigational aids and dockyard facilities were built and tug and salvage services improved. A new railroad bridge was completed crossing the Canal at km. 68,150 from Port Said. A Research Centre has been founded at Ismailia.

Under the first stage, finished in 1961, the Canal was widened and deepened to take vessels of 37 ft. draught. Under the second stage, finished in 1964, the Canal was widened and deepened to take vessels of 38 ft. draught. The installation of two salvage stations and a system of direct radio between vessels and the traffic control station at Ismailia were finished during 1962.

THE SUEZ CANAL
STATISTICS

SUEZ CANAL TRAFFIC

Year	Ships Number	Ships Net Tonnage ('000 tons)	Merchandise Northbound ('000 tons)	Merchandise Southbound ('000 tons)	Number of Passengers	Total Transit Receipts (E £'000)
1957 Apr./Dec.	10,958	89,911	67,219	14,104	188,361	24,514
1958	17,842	154,479	114,430	24,943	342,404	42,157
1959	17,731	163,386	121,749	26,505	326,446	44,536
1960	18,734	185,322	139,630	29,253	366,562	50,408
1961	18,148	187,059	139,599	32,795	322,842	51,088
1962	18,518	197,837	151,190	31,207	269,685	53,958
1963	19,146	210,498	159,482	34,050	297,955	71,294
1964	19,943	227,991	172,463	38,518	269,569	77,697
1965	20,289	246,817	183,441	42,001	291,085	85,792
1966	21,250	274,250	194,168	47,725	299,557	95,187

NORTHBOUND GOODS TRAFFIC
('000 tons)

	1964	1965	1966
Crude petroleum	132,685	143,664	154,092
Petroleum products	11,976	11,422	12,626
Ores and Metals	6,745	7,116	6,490
Cereals	2,601	2,665	1,787
Oil Seeds	1,587	1,367	1,588
Textile fibres	1,918	1,861	1,838
Rubber	1,289	1,417	1,387
Oil seed cake	1,559	1,436	1,484
Sugar	1,270	1,287	1,338
Fruits	850	973	941
Wood	980	949	891
Tea	430	455	397
Others	8,573	8,829	9,309
Total	172,463	183,441	194,168

SOUTHBOUND GOODS TRAFFIC
('000 tons)

	1964	1965	1966
Crude petroleum	2,255	2,140	2,893
Petroleum products	3,881	5,768	6,060
Fabricated metals	5,096	4,727	5,015
Fertilizers	3,897	5,168	6,748
Cereals	8,190	8,042	9,738
Cement	1,760	1,215	1,407
Machinery and parts	1,421	1,506	1,464
Chemical products	974	1,040	1,017
Wood-pulp and paper	764	681	675
Sugar	1,122	1,695	1,231
Salt	606	544	412
Lubricating oils	579	493	577
Ores and Metals	n.a.	404	925
Others	7,973	8,578	9,563
Total	38,518	42,001	47,725

DISTRIBUTION OF NORTHBOUND CRUDE OIL 1966
('000 tons)

Country of Origin	To Europe	To American Countries	To Africa	To Others
Kuwait	56,624	1,881	160	24
Saudi Arabia	33,052	1,819	392	53
Iran	28,535	5,168	415	125
Abu Dhabi	9,210	185	—	—
Iraq	6,781	823	—	—
Qatar	5,730	—	—	—
U.A.R.	1,148	211	59	—
Indonesia	225	—	—	—
Bahrain	188	—	—	—
Others	1,240	44	—	—
Total	142,733	10,131	1,026	202

THE SUEZ CANAL

FLAG DISTRIBUTION OF NET TONNAGE
('000 tons)

	1965 Tankers	1965 All Vessels	1966 Tankers	1966 All Vessels
United Kingdom	26,881	41,494	31,301	45,580
Liberia	46,126	48,390	53,260	56,455
Norway	33,852	37,450	40,282	43,840
France	13,255	16,082	13,730	16,517
Italy	10,712	14,368	11,394	15,231
Greece	7,879	12,673	6,930	12,554
Netherlands	6,104	9,685	5,457	9,106
Germany	4,069	8,136	3,825	7,904
U.S.A.	2,168	6,998	1,816	6,686
Sweden	5,674	6,862	6,992	8,196
Panama	6,332	7,358	6,530	7,755
U.S.S.R.	4,327	8,619	5,335	10,156
Denmark	4,668	5,881	5,325	6,775
Japan	1,383	2,945	4,104	5,896
Others	9,765	19,876	9,851	21,599
Total	183,195	246,817	206,132	274,250

CARGO BY DESTINATION AND ORIGIN

NORTH OF CANAL
('000 tons)

	1964	1965	1966
North and West Europe and U.K.	100,589	99,387	98,887
Baltic Sea	4,828	4,119	4,584
North Mediterranean	53,110	66,637	78,034
East and South Mediterranean	4,624	4,308	4,084
West and South Mediterrranean	4,423	4,332	4,464
Black Sea	11,176	12,604	13,848
America	21,649	22,595	26,234
Other	10,582	11,460	11,758
Total	210,981	225,442	241,893

SOUTH OF CANAL
('000 tons)

	1964	1965	1966
Red Sea	8,124	7,132	6,523
East Africa and Aden	5,835	6,107	6,295
India, Pakistan, Burma and Ceylon	23,400	24,722	26,263
Persian Gulf	139,191	151,184	163,105
South-East Asia	7,144	7,566	8,583
Far East	14,742	16,230	19,532
Australia	5,792	5,963	5,292
Other	6,753	6,538	6,300
Total	210,981	225,442	241,893

PART TWO

Regional Organizations

PART TWO

Regional Organizations

United Nations in the Middle East and North Africa

(% contribution to UN Budget for 1973)

MEMBERS, CONTRIBUTIONS, YEAR OF ADMISSION

Country	%	Year	Country	%	Year
Afghanistan	0.04	1946	Morocco	0.09	1956
Algeria	0.09	1962	Oman	0.04	1971
Bahrain	0.04	1971	Qatar	0.04	1971
Cyprus	0.04	1960	Saudi Arabia	0.07	1945
Egypt	0.18	1945	Sudan	0.04	1956
Iran	0.22	1945	Syria	0.04	1945
Iraq	0.07	1945	Tunisia	0.04	1956
Israel	0.20	1949	Turkey	0.35	1945
Jordan	0.04	1955	United Arab Emirates	0.04	1971
Kuwait	0.08	1963	Yemen (Arab Republic)	0.04	1947
Lebanon	0.05	1945	Yemen (People's Democratic Republic)	0.04	1967
Libya	0.07	1955			

MEMBERSHIP OF THE UNITED NATIONS AND RELATED AGENCIES IN THE MIDDLE EAST AND NORTH AFRICA

	UN	IAEA	ILO	FAO	UNESCO	WHO	IBRD	IFC	IDA	IMF	ICAO	UPU[1]	ITU[2]	WMO	IMCO	GATT[3]	UNCTAD
Afghanistan	x	x	x	x	x	x	x	x	x	x	x	x	x	x			x
Algeria	x	x	x	x	x	x	x		x	x	x	x	x	x	x		x
Bahrain	x			x	x	x	x			x	x						x
Cyprus	x	x	x	x	x	x	x	x	x	x	x	x	x	x	x	x	x
Egypt	x	x	x	x	x	x	x	x	x	x	x	x	x	x	x	x	x
Iran	x	x	x	x	x	x	x	x	x	x	x	x	x	x	x		x
Iraq	x	x	x	x	x	x	x	x	x	x	x	x	x	x			x
Israel	x	x	x	x	x	x	x	x	x	x	x	x	x	x	x		x
Jordan	x	x	x	x	x	x	x	x	x	x	x	x	x	x	x	x	x
Kuwait	x	x	x	x	x	x	x	x	x	x	x	x	x	x	x		x
Lebanon	x	x	x	x	x	x	x	x	x	x	x	x	x	x	x		x
Libya	x	x	x	x	x	x	x		x	x	x	x	x	x	x		x
Morocco	x	x	x	x	x	x	x	x	x	x	x	x	x	x	x	x	x
Oman	x				x	x	x			x	x	x	x				x
Qatar	x			x	x	x	x			x	x	x	x				x
Saudi Arabia	x	x		x	x	x	x	x	x	x	x	x	x	x			x
Sudan	x		x	x	x	x	x	x	x	x	x	x	x	x			x
Syria	x	x	x	x	x	x	x	x	x	x	x	x	x	x	x		x
Tunisia	x	x	x	x	x	x	x	x	x	x	x	x	x	x	x		x
Turkey	x	x	x	x	x	x	x	x	x	x	x	x	x	x	x	x	x
United Arab Emirates	x		x		x	x	x			x	x	x	x				x
Yemen Arab Republic	x		x	x	x	x	x		x	x	x	x	x				x
Yemen, People's Democratic Republic	x		x	x	x	x	x		x	x	x	x	x				x

[1] The Spanish Province in Africa is also a member of UPU.

[2] The Spanish Province in Africa is also a member of ITU.

[3] The following countries have special forms of relationship with GATT: *Acceded provisionally:* Tunisia; *applying GATT de facto pending final decisions as to their future commercial policy:* Algeria, Bahrain, Qatar, People's Democratic Republic of Yemen.

UNITED NATIONS IN THE MIDDLE EAST AND NORTH AFRICA

PERMANENT MISSIONS TO THE UNITED NATIONS
(with Permanent Representatives)

Afghanistan: 866 United Nations Plaza, 4th Floor, New York, N.Y. 10017; Abdur-Rahman Pazhwak.

Algeria: 750 Third Ave., 14th Floor, New York, N.Y. 10017; Abdellatif Rahal.

Bahrain: 605 Third Ave., Room 1616, New York, N.Y. 10016; Dr. Salman Mohamed Al Saffar.

Cyprus: 820 Second Ave., 12th Floor, New York, N.Y. 10017; Zenon Rossides.

Egypt: 36 East 67th St., New York, N.Y. 10021; Dr. Ahmed Esmat Abdel Meguid.

Iran: 777 Third Ave., 26th Floor, New York, N.Y. 10017; Fereydoun Hoveyda.

Iraq: 14 East 79th St., New York, N.Y. 10021; Abdul Karim Al-Shaikhly.

Israel: 800 Second Ave., New York, N.Y. 10017; Yosef Tekoah.

Jordan: 866 United Nations Plaza, Room 550–552, New York, N.Y. 10017; Sherif Abdul Hamid Sharaf.

Kuwait: 235 East 42nd St., 27th Floor, New York, N.Y. 10017; Abdalla Yaccoub Bishara.

Lebanon: 866 United Nations Plaza, Room 533–535, New York, N.Y. 10017; Edouard Ghorra.

Libya: 866 United Nations Plaza, New York, N.Y. 10017; Kamel Hassan Maghur.

Morocco: 757 Third Ave., 23rd Floor, New York, N.Y. 10017; Mehdi Mrani Zentar.

Oman: 605 Third Ave., Room 3304, New York, N.Y. 10016; Faisal Bin Ali Al-Said.

Qatar: 845 Third Ave., 20th Floor, New York, N.Y. 10022; Jasim Yousif Jamal.

Saudi Arabia: 6 East 43rd St., 26th Floor, New York, N.Y. 10017; (vacant).

Sudan: 757 Third Ave., 12th Floor, New York, N.Y. 10017; Rahmatalla Abdulla.

Syria: 150 East 58th St., Room 1500, New York, N.Y. 10022; Haissam Kelani.

Tunisia: 40 East 71st St., New York, N.Y. 10021; Rachid Driss.

Turkey: 866 United Nations Plaza, Suite 525, New York, N.Y. 10017; Osman Olcay.

United Arab Emirates: 866 Second Ave., New York, N.Y. 10017; Dr. Ali Humaidan.

Yemen (Arab Republic): 211 East 43rd St., 19th Floor, New York, N.Y. 10017; Dr. Mohamed Said Al-Attar.

Yemen (People's Democratic Republic): 211 East 43rd St., Room 903, New York, N.Y. 10017; (vacant).

U.N. INFORMATION CENTRES

Afghanistan: Shah Mahmoud Ghazi Watt, Kabul; P.O. Box 5.

Algeria: 19 Avenue Claude Debussy, Algiers; P.O. Box 803.

Egypt: Sh. Osiris, Tagher Building, Garden City, Cairo; P.O.B. 262 (also covers Saudi Arabia and Yemen).

Iran: Off. Takhte Jamshid, 12 Kh. Bandar Pahlavi, Teheran; P.O.B. 1555.

Iraq: House 167/1 Abu Nouwas St., Bataween, Baghdad; P.O.B. 2398, Alwiyah.

Lebanon: P.O.B. 4656, Apt. No. 1, Fakhoury Building, Ardati St., Manara Section, Beirut (also covers Jordan, Kuwait and Syria).

Morocco: "Casier ONU", Angle ave. Urbain Blanc et rue de Nîmes, Rabat.

Sudan: House No. 9, Block 6.5.D.E., Nejumi St., Khartoum; P.O.B. 1992.

Tunisia: 61 Boulevard Bab Benat, Tunis; P.O.B. 863 (also covers Libya).

UNITED NATIONS TRUCE SUPERVISION ORGANIZATION—UNTSO

Government House, Jerusalem

Set up to observe and maintain the ceasefire ordered by the Security Council in July 1948 and to assist the parties to the 1949 Armistice Agreements between Egypt, Jordan, Lebanon and Syria on the one hand and Israel on the other in the supervision of the application of those Agreements.

Following the June 1967 war and pursuant to Security Council resolutions of June 1967, United Nations military observers were deployed along the Israeli and Syrian Forward Defended Localities (FDLs) in the Golan Heights and on each side of the Suez Canal. In April 1972, under a Security Council consensus, UNTSO observation operations were extended to southern Lebanon.

As of May 1973, the staff of UNTSO, headed by a Chief of Staff, consists of United Nations advisory and administrative staff (about 200 international civilian staff and 140 local personnel) and 221 military observers provided by the following 16 member states: Argentine, Australia, Austria, Belgium, Canada, Chile, Denmark, Finland, France, Ireland, Italy, the Netherlands, New Zealand, Norway, Sweden and the United States. Since 1968 two aircraft with aircrew have been provided by the Swiss Government.

Chief of Staff: Maj.-Gen. E. Siilasvuo (Finland).

UNITED NATIONS IN THE MIDDLE EAST AND NORTH AFRICA

UNITED NATIONS RELIEF AND WORKS AGENCY FOR PALESTINE REFUGEES IN THE NEAR EAST—UNRWA

Museitbeh Quarter, Beirut, Lebanon

Founded in 1950 to provide relief, health, education and welfare services for needy Palestine refugees in the Near East.

REGIONAL OFFICES

Gaza Strip: UNRWA Field Office, P.O.B. 61, Gaza.
East Jordan: UNRWA Field Office, P.O.B. 484, Amman.
West Bank: UNRWA Field Office, P.O.B. 19149, Jerusalem.
Lebanon: UNRWA Field Office, P.O.B. 947, Beirut.
Syria: UNRWA Field Office, 19 Salah Eddin el Ayoubi St., Abou Rummaneh, Damascus.
Egypt: UNRWA Liaison Office, 2 Dar el Shifa, Garden City, P.O.B. 277, Cairo.
Europe: UNRWA Liaison Office, Palais des Nations, Geneva 10.
United States: UNRWA Liaison Office, United Nations, New York.

ORGANIZATION

Commissioner-General: Sir JOHN S. RENNIE, G.C.M.G., O.B.E. (U.K.).

Deputy Commissioner-General: C. WILLIAM KONTOS (U.S.A.).

UNRWA is a subsidiary organ of the United Nations General Assembly, and began operations in May 1950; it has a mandate currently extending to June 30th, 1975, and employs an international staff of 114 and some 14,558 local staff, mainly Palestine refugees. The Commissioner-General is assisted by an Advisory Commission consisting of representatives of the governments of:

Belgium	Jordan	Turkey
Egypt	Lebanon	United Kingdom
France	Syria	U.S.A.
Japan		

STATISTICS

REFUGEES REGISTERED WITH UNRWA
(as at April 1st, 1973)

Country or Field	In Camps	Not in Camps	Total
East Jordan	178,127	384,864	562,991[1]
West Bank	71,821	210,358	282,179
Gaza	199,876	128,202	328,078
Lebanon	105,255	81,393	186,648
Syria	46,877	125,514	172,391[2]
TOTAL	601,956	930,331	1,532,287

[1] Includes 242,060 refugees displaced in 1967.
[2] Includes 19,578 refugees displaced in 1967.

DISPLACED PERSONS
(other than UNRWA-registered Palestine refugees)
WITHIN AND FROM THE UNRWA AREAS OF OPERATIONS SINCE JUNE 1967[1]

In East Jordan	234,502[2]
In Syria	125,000
In Egypt	21,485

[1] These figures are government estimates and include the natural increase.
[2] Including 206,087 persons to whom UNRWA distributes rations subject to reimbursement by the Jordan Government.

ACTIVITIES

Since 1950, UNRWA has fed and provided medical services for the needy among a registered refugee population which now numbers around 1,532,000, including 602,000 in refugee camps. It has served 300,000,000 meals to young children and distributed about 31,000 tons of clothing. A simple but effective community health service has been built up with technical guidance from WHO and there has never been a major epidemic among the refugees in UNRWA's care. An education system has been developed with technical advice and guidance from UNESCO and there are 260,107 children in 542 elementary and preparatory schools operated by UNRWA. UNRWA also operates eight vocational centres (capacity: 4,358 trainees) for training young refugee men and women as teachers or in a variety of industrial and semi-professional skills, with the result that UNRWA has become one of the most important channels for this type of technical assistance in the Middle East.

UNITED NATIONS IN THE MIDDLE EAST AND NORTH AFRICA

THE REFUGEES

For UNRWA's purposes, a *bona fide* Palestine refugee is one whose normal residence was in Palestine for a minimum of two years before the 1948 conflict and who, as a result of the hostilities, lost his home and means of livelihood. To be eligible for assistance, a refugee must reside in one of the "host" countries in which UNRWA operates, and be in need. Children and grandchildren who fulfil certain criteria are also eligible for UNRWA assistance. By April 1st, 1973, there were 1,532,287 persons registered with UNRWA, not all of whom were eligible for assistance.

THE EFFECTS OF THE 1967 HOSTILITIES

After the renewal of Arab-Israeli hostilities in the Middle East in June 1967, hundreds of thousands of people fled from the fighting and Israeli-occupied areas. UNRWA was additionally empowered by a UN General Assembly resolution to provide "humanitarian assistance, as far as practicable, on an emergency basis and as a temporary measure" for those persons other than Palestine refugees who were newly displaced and in urgent need. In practice, UNRWA has lacked the funds to aid the other displaced persons and the main burden of supporting them has fallen on the Arab governments concerned. In agreement with the Israeli government, UNRWA has continued to provide assistance for registered refugees living in the Israeli-occupied territories of the West Bank and the Gaza Strip.

NUMBER OF REFUGEE PUPILS RECEIVING EDUCATION IN UNRWA/UNESCO SCHOOLS
(as at January 31st, 1973)

Field	Number of Schools	Pupils in Elementary Classes Boys	Girls	Total	Pupils in Preparatory Classes Boys	Girls	Total	Total Number of Pupils
East Jordan	168	38,781	35,954	74,735	11,417	8,402	19,819	94,554
West Bank	87	11,782	12,573	24,355	3,599	2,994	6,593	30,948
Gaza	117	26,145	22,334	48,479	7,671	7,368	15,039	63,518
Lebanon	76	15,346	13,458	28,804	4,239	3,412	7,651	36,455
Syria	94	13,740	11,739	25,479	5,225	3,928	9,153	34,632
Total	542	105,794	96,058	201,852	32,151	26,104	58,255	260,107

Additionally in the 1972–73 school year an estimated number of 63,000 refugee children received education in government schools and an estimated 9,900 in private schools in the host countries, partly with grants paid by UNRWA.

FINANCE

BUDGET

UNRWA's budget for 1973 is $61,325,000.

In recent years about 95½ per cent of the total income has been contributed by governments, the remainder being provided by voluntary agencies, business corporations and private sources.

UNRWA's average expenditure per refugee per year is about $41, or 11 cents per day.

FINANCIAL DIFFICULTIES

Due to the re-alignment of currencies in early 1973 and the continuous rise in costs within and outside the Middle East, UNRWA's estimated expenditure in 1973 has risen to $61,325,000 and the estimated income is $57,225,000 leaving a prospective deficit for the year of $4.1 million. If additional income is not forthcoming, the Commissioner-General will be forced to consider the possibility of reductions in the Agency's programmes.

The Working Group for the Financing of UNRWA, which was established by the United Nations General Assembly in December 1970 to assist in finding solutions to the Agency's financial problem, has been alerted to this serious situation.

The essence of the financial problem is the need to provide class-rooms and teachers for a growing school population, and rising unit costs due to inflation, set against an income which has been increasing less rapidly.

UNITED NATIONS IN THE MIDDLE EAST AND NORTH AFRICA

ESTIMATED EXPENDITURE, 1973
(as at June 6th, 1973)

	Estimated Expenditure (U.S. $'000)	Percentage (Approx.)
Relief Services:		
Basic Rations	15,224	—
Supplementary Feeding	3,169	—
Shelter	412	—
Special Hardship Assistance	510	—
Share of Common Costs*	4,302	—
Total Relief Services	23,617	38
Health Services:		
Medical Services	4,557	—
Environmental Sanitation	1,907	—
Share of Common Costs*	1,372	—
Total Health Services	7,836	13
Education Services:		
General Education	21,467	—
Vocational and Professional Training	4,482	—
Share of Common Costs*	3,396	—
Total Education Services	29,345	48
Other Costs:		
Costs due to local disturbances	27	—
Adjustment of Provision for Staff Separation due to devaluation of U.S. dollar	500	—
Total Other Costs	527	1
Grand Total	61,325	100

* Common costs include all operations involving supply and transport services, other internal services and general administration. The above summary table sets out the allocation of common costs to each of the Agency's operational programmes.

UNITED NATIONS MIDDLE EAST MISSION—UNMEM

P.O.B. 2324, Nicosia, Cyprus

Established by the UN Security Council in November 1967* to form and maintain contact with the States concerned in the 1967 Arab-Israeli conflict, in order to assist efforts to achieve a peaceful and acceptable settlement in the area.

ORGANIZATION

Secretary-General's Special Representative: Gunnar V. Jarring (Sweden).

* For text of resolution *see* p. 56.

UNITED NATIONS IN THE MIDDLE EAST AND NORTH AFRICA

UNITED NATIONS PEACE-KEEPING FORCE IN CYPRUS—UNFICYP

P.O.B. 1642, Nicosia, Cyprus

Set up in March 1964 by Security Council Resolution, for a three-month period, subsequently extended to December 1973 by 23 successive Resolutions. The purpose of the Force is to keep the peace between the Greek and Turkish communities pending a resolution of outstanding issues between them.

Commander: Maj.-Gen. D. PREM CHAND (India).

Special Representative of the Secretary-General: BIBIANO F. OSORIO-TAFALL (Mexico).

COMPOSITION OF FORCE
(May 26th, 1973)

	Military	Police
Australia	—	37
Austria	339*	54
Canada	580	—
Denmark	295	40
Finland	287	—
Ireland	142	—
Sweden	286	40
United Kingdom	1,044	—
TOTAL	2,973	171

* Including 54 in medical unit.

FINANCE
Provisional estimate of cost for the period from March 1964 to June 15th, 1973 was $158.1 million.

ECONOMIC COMMISSION FOR AFRICA—ECA

Africa Hall, Addis Ababa, Ethiopia
Telephone: 447200.

Initiates and takes part in measures for facilitating Africa's economic development. Member countries must be independent, be members of the UN and within the geographical scope of the African continent and the islands bordering it. ECA was founded in 1958 by a resolution of ECOSOC as the fourth UN regional economic commission.

MEMBERS

Algeria	Gabon	Malawi	Somalia
Botswana	The Gambia	Mali	South Africa*
Burundi	Ghana	Mauritania	Sudan
Cameroon	Guinea	Mauritius	Swaziland
Central African Republic	Ivory Coast	Morocco	Tanzania
Chad	Kenya	Niger	Togo
Congo (Brazzaville)	Lesotho	Nigeria	Tunisia
Dahomey	Liberia	Rwanda	Uganda
Egypt	Libya	Senegal	Upper Volta
Equatorial Guinea	Madagascar	Sierra Leone	Zaire
Ethiopia			Zambia

* Suspended by ECOSOC since 1963.

ASSOCIATE MEMBERS

(a) Non-Self-Governing Territories situated within the geographical scope of the Commission.

(b) Powers other than Portugal responsible for the international relations of those territories (France, Spain and the United Kingdom).

Associate Members may take part in the Commission's activities but may not vote.

UNITED NATIONS IN THE MIDDLE EAST AND NORTH AFRICA

ORGANIZATION

COMMISSION

Executive Secretary: ROBERT K. A. GARDINER (Ghana).

The Commission has held eleven sessions since its inception:

1958	December	Addis Ababa
1960	January	Addis Ababa
1961	February	Tangier
1962	February	Addis Ababa
1963	February	Léopoldville
1964	February	Addis Ababa
1965	February	Nairobi
1967	February	Lagos
1969	February	Addis Ababa
1971	February	Tunis
1973	February	Accra

Sub-Regional Offices: Lusaka, Niamey, Tangier, Kinshasa.

ACTIVITIES

Objectives. The work of the Commission is determined by decisions of its plenary sessions. The Commission is charged with the responsibility of promoting and facilitating concerted action for the economic and social development of Africa; to maintain and strengthen the economic relations of African countries, both among themselves and with other countries of the world; to undertake or sponsor investigations, research and studies of economic and technological problems and developments; to collect, evaluate and disseminate economic, technological and statistical information; and to assist in the formulation and development of co-ordinated policies in promoting economic and technological development in the region.

Institutional Machinery. As a result of recommendations made at ECA's ninth session the following institutional machinery was set up:

(a) *Conference of Ministers* which is vested with full powers to consider matters of general policy and the priorities to be assigned to the programme and other activities of the Commission. It reviews programme implementation and examines and approves the proposed programme of work, and considers reports submitted to it by the Executive Committee and the Technical Committee of Experts. The Conference of Ministers holds its meetings every two years. The second meeting was held in Accra in February 1973.

(b) *Technical Committee of Experts* which meets once a year. It is composed of senior officials of member states concerned with economic affairs, and it examines studies prepared by the ECA Secretariat and assists in the formulation of the work programme aimed at ensuring co-operation between the Secretariat and member governments. It held its fourth meeting in Addis Ababa in September 1972.

(c) *Executive Committee* which is composed of representatives of 16 members states and which assists the Executive Secretary in the implementation of the resolutions and the work programme of the Commission, and provides links between the Secretariat, member states and the sub-regions. The Executive Committee meets at least twice a year. It held its ninth meeting in Addis Ababa in June 1973.

WHO maintains a liaison office at ECA; in co-operation with ITU, work has begun on a pan-African telecommunications system. ECA also runs a Joint Agricultural Division in conjunction with FAO. Plans are under way for the setting up of a joint ECA/UNIDO Division during 1973.

Co-operation between ECA and the Organization of African Unity started with the signing of a UN/OAU agreement by the Secretary-General of the United Nations, U Thant, and the Secretary-General of the OAU, Diallo Telli, on November 15th, 1965. The seventh ECA/OAU Joint Meeting on Trade and Development was held in Geneva in August 1972. During 1973 the following joint meetings have taken place: the OAU/ADB/ECA Meeting of the Group of Experts in Preparation for the African Ministerial Conference on Trade, Development and Monetary Problems (February); the OAU/ADB/ECA Meetings of Specialized Committees (March); and the OAU/ADB/ECA African Ministerial Conference on Trade, Development and Monetary Problems (May). Meetings scheduled for the latter half of 1973 are: the AGC/OAU/ECA Groundnuts/Oilseeds Meeting (July); the eighth ECA/OAU Joint Meeting on Trade and Development (August); and the second session of the UNIDO/OAU/ECA Conference of Ministers of Industry.

PUBLICATIONS

Economic Bulletin for Africa (twice yearly).
The Statistical Newsletter (quarterly).
Foreign Trade Newsletter (quarterly).
Agricultural Economics Bulletin (twice yearly).
Social Welfare Services in Africa (thrice yearly).
Natural Resources, Newsletter (quarterly).
Foreign Trade Statistics for Africa, Series A: Direction of Trade (quarterly).
Foreign Trade Statistics for Africa, Series B: Trade by Commodity (thrice yearly).
African Target (quarterly).
Planning Newsletter (quarterly).
Statistical and Economic Information Bulletin for Africa.
Social Work Training Newsletter (quarterly).
Training Information Notice (quarterly).
African Population Newsletter (quarterly).
Rural Development (quarterly).
Statistical Yearbook.
Survey of Economic Conditions in Africa (annual).
Population Newsletter (quarterly).

AFRICAN INSTITUTE FOR ECONOMIC DEVELOPMENT AND PLANNING
Dakar, Senegal

An autonomous organ of the ECA opened in 1963 with Special Fund assistance to train senior African officials in techniques of development planning and to serve as a clearing house and documentation centre on all African development questions.

Director: SAMIR AMIN (Egypt).

UNITED NATIONS IN THE MIDDLE EAST AND NORTH AFRICA

UNITED NATIONS DEVELOPMENT PROGRAMME—UNDP

United Nations, New York, U.S.A.

Established in 1965 to replace the Expanded Programme of Technical Assistance and the UN Special Fund.

Aden: Resident Rep. of UNDP in the Democratic People's Republic of Yemen, P.O.B. 1188, Tawahi, Aden, Yemen P.D.R.

Algiers: Resident Rep. of UNDP in Algeria, B.P. 803 B.P., Algiers, Algeria.

Amman: Resident Rep. of UNDP in Jordan, P.O.B. 565, Amman, Jordan.

Ankara: Resident Rep. of UNDP in Turkey, P.K. 407, Ankara, Turkey.

Baghdad: Resident Rep. of UNDP in Iraq, P.O.B. 2048, Alwiyah Post Office, Baghdad, Iraq.

Beirut: Resident Rep. of UNDP in Lebanon, P.O.B. 3216, Beirut, Lebanon.

Cairo: Resident Rep. of UNDP in Egypt, P.O.B. 982, Cairo, Egypt.

Damascus: Resident Rep. of UNDP in the Syrian Arab Republic, P.O.B. 2317, Damascus, Syria.

Jerusalem: Resident Rep. of UNDP in Israel, 39 Jabotinsky St., Komemiut (Talbieh), Jerusalem, Israel.

Kabul: Resident Rep. of UNDP in Afghanistan, P.O.B. 5, Kabul, Afghanistan.

Khartoum: Resident Rep. of UNDP in the Sudan, P.O.B. 913, Khartoum, Sudan.

Kuwait: Resident Rep. of UNDP in Kuwait, P.O.B. 2993, Kuwait.

Nicosia: Resident Rep. of UNDP in Cyprus, P.O.B. 3521, Nicosia, Cyprus.

Rabat: Resident Rep. of UNDP in Morocco, Casier ONU, Rabat-Chellah, Rabat, Morocco.

Riyadh: Resident Rep. of UNDP in Saudi Arabia and the Gulf Area, P.O.B. 558, Riyadh, Saudi Arabia.

Sana'a: Resident Rep. of UNDP in the Yemen Arab Republic, P.O.B. 551, Sana'a, Yemen Arab Republic.

Teheran: Resident Rep. of UNDP in Iran, P.O.B. 1555, Teheran, Iran.

Tripoli: Resident Rep. of UNDP in Libya, P.O.B. 358, Tripoli, Libya.

Tunis: Resident Rep. of UNDP in Tunisia, B.P. 863, Tunis, Tunisia.

SELECTED NATIONAL PROJECTS CURRENTLY ASSISTED BY THE UNDP IN THE MIDDLE EAST AND NORTH AFRICA, AND EXECUTING AGENCIES

Afghanistan: Allocation of $2,135,000 for highway maintenance programme (IBRD).

Algeria: Allocation of $1,739,300 for National Water Supply Authority (WHO).

Cyprus: Allocation of $1,050,000 for Hotel and Catering Institute, Nicosia (ILO).

Egypt: Allocation of $1,087,300 for Meteorological Institute for Research and Training, Cairo (Phase II) (WMO).

Iran: Allocation of $965,200 for Institute of Standards and Industrial Research, Karaj (UNIDO).

Iraq: Allocation of $1,506,900 for pilot project in soil reclamation and irrigated farming development in Greater Mussayib area (Phase II) (FAO).

Israel: Allocation of $607,220 for research and training in environmental control of growth of high-value crops (FAO).

Jordan: Allocation of $897,100 for the Jordan Housing Corporation (UN).

Kuwait: Allocation of $671,700 for Shuwaikh Industrial Training Centre (ILO).

Lebanon: Allocation of $1,179,200 for teacher-training in mathematics and science, Beirut (UNESCO).

Morocco: Allocation of $1,080,200 for mineral survey in the Anti-Atlas (UN).

Qatar: Allocation of $530,900 for vocational training scheme (ILO).

Saudi Arabia: Allocation of $1,111,300 for Telecommunications and Broadcasting Training Centre, Jeddah (ITU).

Sudan: Allocation of $929,500 for savanna development (FAO).

Syria: Allocation of $1,225,800 for dairying in Ghouta region (FAO).

Tunisia: Allocation of $955,700 for preservation of historic sites and monuments in Tunis-Carthage region (UNESCO).

Turkey: Allocation of $1,164,000 for geothermal energy survey of Western Anatolia (UN).

Yemen Arab Republic: Allocation of $1,551,400 for food and nutrition programme (FAO).

Yemen, PDR: Allocation of $1,651,600 for soil and water utilization and conservation in the Wadi Tuban watershed area (FAO).

Regional projects are also in progress, among them:

Technical Studies of the Trans-Saharan road: Allocation of $2,003,000.

UNITED NATIONS IN THE MIDDLE EAST AND NORTH AFRICA

INTERNATIONAL BANK FOR RECONSTRUCTION AND DEVELOPMENT—IBRD (WORLD BANK)

1818 H Street, N.W., Washington, D.C. 20433, U.S.A.

Aims to assist the economic development of member nations by making loans, in cases where private capital is not available on reasonable terms, to finance productive investments. Loans are made either direct to governments, or to private enterprise with the guarantee of their governments.

Regional Vice-President, Europe, Middle East and North Africa Department: MUNIR P. BENJENK.

LOANS TO MIDDLE EASTERN AND NORTH AFRICAN COUNTRIES (U.S. $'000)

Total Loans (1947–June 1972)

Country	Amount
Algeria	80,500
Cyprus	57,700
Egypt	56,500
Iran	743,700
Iraq	76,200
Israel	184,500
Lebanon	27,000
Morocco	227,300
Sudan	134,000
Tunisia	149,350
Turkey	378,400
TOTAL	2,115,150

(July 1971–June 1972)

Country	Purpose	Amount
Cyprus	Development Finance and Electric Power	12,000
Iran	Port, Oil Pipelines, Development Finance, Agricultural Credit	125,000
Iraq	Telecommunications, Education	40,400
Israel	Highways	30,000
Morocco	Development Finance, Agricultural Credit	39,000
Tunisia	Tourism, Agricultural Credit, Development Finance, Power	41,000
Turkey	Industry, Water Supply	137,000

INTERNATIONAL DEVELOPMENT ASSOCIATION—IDA

1818 H Street, N.W., Washington, D.C. 20433, U.S.A.

The International Development Association began operations in November 1960. Affiliated to the World Bank, IDA advances capital on more flexible terms to developing countries.

Regional Vice-President, Europe, Middle East and North Africa Development: MUNIR P. BENJENK.

DEVELOPMENT CREDITS TO MIDDLE EASTERN AND NORTH AFRICAN COUNTRIES (U.S. $'000)

Total Credits (1960–June 1972)

Country	Amount
Afghanistan	18,500
Egypt	56,000
Jordan	22,900
Morocco	36,800
Sudan	32,800
Syria	22,300
Tunisia	62,800
Turkey	148,500
Yemen Arab Republic	7,700
Yemen, P.D.R.	1,600
TOTAL	409,900

(July 1971–June 1972)

Country	Purpose	Amount
Egypt	Railways	30,000
Jordan	Education	5,400
Morocco	Agricultural Credit, Education	18,500
Sudan	Agriculture	11,250
Syria	Highways	13,800
Tunisia	Agricultural Credit, Fisheries, Tourism	15,000
Turkey	Irrigation, Livestock, Urban Studies	36,300
Yemen Arab Republic	Highways	7,700

UNITED NATIONS IN THE MIDDLE EAST AND NORTH AFRICA

INTERNATIONAL FINANCE CORPORATION—IFC

1818 H Street, N.W., Washington, D.C. 20433, U.S.A.

Founded in 1956 as an affiliate of the World Bank to encourage the growth of productive private enterprise in its less-developed member countries.

Director of Investments, Africa and Middle East: CHERIF HASSAN.

IFC OPERATIONAL INVESTMENTS IN MIDDLE EASTERN AND NORTH AFRICAN COUNTRIES
(up to June 30th, 1972)
(U.S.$)

COUNTRY	TYPE OF BUSINESS	FISCAL YEAR	AMOUNT*
Iran	Ceramic Tiles	1959	300,000
	Steel Products	1969	3,874,361
	Textiles	1971	4,500,000
Lebanon	Pulp and Paper	1972	14,200,000
	Textiles	1971	930,000
	Ceramic Tiles	1971	1,200,000
Morocco	Development Financing	1963	1,495,775
	Food Processing and Canning	1966	1,388,486
Sudan	Textiles	1964, 1972	2,211,795
Tunisia	Fertilizers	1963	3,500,000
	Development Financing	1966, 1970	1,208,231
	Tourism Financing	1969	9,986,582
Turkey	Development Financing	1964, 1967, 1969, 1972	2,096,996
	Textiles	1966, 1969, 1971, 1972	4,566,865
	Pulp, Paper and Paper Products	1970, 1971	3,168,889
	Glass and Glass Products	1970	11,583,330
	Aluminium Sheets and Foil	1970	8,371,429

* Includes standby and underwriting commitments

OTHER UN ORGANIZATIONS AND RELATED AGENCIES

ECONOMIC AND SOCIAL COUNCIL—ECOSOC
New York, N.Y. 10017, U.S.A.

UN Economic and Social Office in Beirut: P.O.B. 4656, Beirut, Lebanon.

UNITED NATIONS CHILDREN FUND—UNICEF
New York, N.Y. 10017, U.S.A.

Office of the Director for the Eastern Mediterranean: Director for the Eastern Mediterranean, UNICEF, P.O.B. 5902, Beirut, Lebanon (covers Cyprus, Israel, Jordan, Lebanon, Saudi Arabia and Syria).

Office of the Director for Europe and North Africa: Director, European Office, UNICEF, Palais des Nations, CH-1211 Geneva 10, Switzerland.

FOOD AND AGRICULTURE ORGANIZATION—FAO
Rome, Italy

FAO Regional Office for the Near East: FAO Regional Rep., P.O.B. 2223, Cairo, Egypt.

FAO Regional Office for Africa: FAO Regional Rep. P.O.B. 1628, Accra, Ghana.

Regional Councils and Commissions

Commission for Controlling the Desert Locust in the Near East: c/o UNDP Resident Representative, P.O.B. 3216, Beirut, Lebanon; f. 1965 to carry out all possible measures to control plagues of the desert locust within the Middle East and to reduce crop damage. Mems.: 9 states.

Commission on Wheat and Barley Improvement and Production in the Near East: to strengthen national programmes on wheat and barley improvement through advice on breeding procedures, seed muliplication and distribution, training, supply of outstanding sources of germ plasma, etc.

FAO Commission on Horticultural Production in the Near East and North Africa: c/o FAO Regional Office for the Near East, P.O.B. 2223, Cairo, Egypt; f. 1966 to promote international collaboration in the study of technical problems and the establishment of a balanced programme of horticultural research at an interregional level. Mems.: 21 states.

Chair. D. ALLOUM; Sec. Y. SALAH.

UNITED NATIONS IN THE MIDDLE EAST AND NORTH AFRICA

General Fisheries Council for the Mediterranean—(GFCM): Viale delle Terme di Caracalla, Rome, Italy; f. 1952 to formulate oceanographical and technical aspects of developing and utilizing aquatic resources, to encourage and co-ordinate research in the fishing and allied industries, to assemble and publish information, and to recommend the standardization of scientific equipment, techniques and nomenclature. Mems.: 18 governments.

Chair. A. Z. BEN MUSTAPHA. Publs. *Session Reports* (biennially), *GFCM Circulars* (irregularly), *Studies and Reviews* (irregularly).

Near East Commission on Agricultural Planning: f. 1963 to review and exchange information and experience on agricultural plans and planning, and to make recommendations to members on means of improving their agricultural plans. Mems.: 17 states.

Near East Commission on Agricultural Statistics: f. 1962 to review the state of food and agricultural statistics in the region and advise member countries on the development and standardization of agricultural statistics. Mems.: 20 states.

Near East Forestry Commission: c/o FAO Regional Office for the Near East, P.O.B. 2223, Cairo, Egypt; f. 1955 to review the political, economic and technical problems relating to forests and forest products in the Region. Mems.: 19 countries.

Chair. Dr. M. H. DJAZIREI; Sec. K. HAMAD.

Near East Plant Protection Commission: c/o FAO Regional Office for the Near East, P.O.B. 2223, Cairo, Egypt; f. 1963 to advise member countries on matters relating to the protection of plant resources in the region. Mems.: 15 states.

Near East Region Animal Production and Health Commission: c/o FAO Regional Office for the Near East, P.O.B. 2223, Cairo, Egypt; f. 1966 to provide a means of initiating and promoting agricultural development with special reference to the field of animal production and health. Mems.: FAO member nations in the Near East region.

Chair. Dr. SULTAN HAIDAR; Sec. Dr. D. E. FAULKNER.

Regional Commission on Land and Water Use in the Near East: c/o FAO Regional Office for the Near East, P.O.B. 2223, Cairo, Egypt; f. 1967 to study land and water use in the region and the problems concerning the development of land and water resources. Mems.: 16 states.

Chair. H. A. ELTOBJY.

Regional Project on the Improvement and Production of Field Food Crops in the Near East and North Africa: c/o FAO Regional Office for the Near East, P.O.B. 2223, Cairo, Egypt; f. 1971 (replacing the Technical Committee on Cereal Improvement and Production in the Near East); aims to increase overall crop production in the region through research, co-operative investigations and other forms of international action. Mems: 22 states.

WORLD HEALTH ORGANIZATION—WHO
Geneva, Switzerland

WHO Regional Office for the Eastern Mediterranean: The Director, P.O.B. 1517, Alexandria, Egypt.

WHO Regional Office for Africa: The Director, P.O. Box 6, Brazzaville, People's Republic of Congo.

INTERNATIONAL CIVIL AVIATION ORGANIZATION—ICAO
Montreal, Canada

ICAO Regional Office for the Middle East and Eastern Africa: 16 Hassan Sabri, Zamalek, Cairo, Egypt.

ICAO Regional Office for Africa: P.O.B. 2356, 15 boulevard de la République, Dakar, Senegal.

INTERNATIONAL LABOUR ORGANIZATION—ILO
Geneva, Switzerland

ILO Regional Office for Africa: P.O.B. 2788, Addis Ababa, Ethiopia.

ILO Regional Office for the Middle East and Europe: CH-1211 Geneva 22, Switzerland.

ILO Area Office in Algiers: B.P. 226, Algiers, Algeria.

ILO Area Office in Beirut: B.P. 4656, Beirut, Lebanon.

ILO Area Office in Cairo: 9 Sharia Willcocks, Zamalek, Cairo, Egypt.

ILO Area Office in Istanbul: Gümüşsuyu Caddesi 96, Ayazpaşa, Istanbul, Turkey.

Country Representative in Kuwait: P.O.B. 20275 Safat, Kuwait, Kuwait.

Representative in Teheran: P.O.B. 1555, Teheran, Iran.

UNITED NATIONS EDUCATIONAL, SCIENTIFIC AND CULTURAL ORGANIZATION—UNESCO
Paris, France

Africa Division.   **Arab States Division.**

The Arab League

Midan Al Tahrir, Cairo, Egypt

The League of Arab States is a voluntary association of sovereign Arab states designed to strengthen the close ties linking them and to co-ordinate their policies and activities and direct them towards the common good of all the Arab countries.

MEMBERS

Algeria	Lebanon	Sudan
Bahrain	Libya	Syria
Egypt	Morocco	Tunisia
Iraq	Oman	United Arab Emirates
Jordan	Qatar	Yemen Arab Republic
Kuwait	Saudi Arabia	Yemen People's Democratic Republic

ORGANIZATION

THE COUNCIL

The supreme organ of the Arab League. Meets in March and September. Consists of representatives of the eighteen member states, each of which has one vote, and a representative for Palestine.

PERMANENT COMMITTEES

There are ten Permanent Committees for Political, Cultural, Economical, Social, Military, Legal Affairs, Information, Health, Communications and Arab Human Rights.

SECRETARIAT

Secretary-General: MAHMOUD RIAD (Egypt).

Assistant Secretaries-General: Dr. S. NOFAL (Egypt), AHMED EL-SAIED HAMAD (Sudan), ASSAAD EL ASSAAD (Lebanon), SELIM EL YAFI (Syria).

Military Assistant Secretary: Gen. SA'AD EL DIN EL SHAZLY (Egypt).

Economic Assistant Secretary: AHMED EL SAIED HAMAD (Sudan).

The Secretariat has departments of Economic, Political, Legal, Cultural, Social and Labour affairs, and for Petroleum, Finance, Palestine, Health, Press and Information, Secretariat, Communications, and Protocol.

ECONOMIC COUNCIL

Established in 1950; first meeting 1953; composed of the Ministers of Economic Affairs or their representatives.

COUNCIL OF ARAB ECONOMIC UNITY

In June 1957 the Economic Council approved a Convention for Economic Unity; the Economic Unity Agreement has been signed by Jordan (1962), Syria (1962), U.A.R. (1962), Kuwait (1962), Morocco (1962), Iraq (1963), Yemen (1963) and Sudan (1968). It has been ratified by Kuwait (1962), U.A.R. (1963), Syria (1964), Iraq (1964), Jordan (1964), Yemen (1967) and Sudan (1969). After ratification by five members a *Council of Arab Economic Unity* was set up in June 1964: the aims of the Arab Economic Unity Agreement include removal of internal tariffs, establishing common external tariffs, freedom of movement of labour and capital, and adoption of common economic policies; Sec.-Gen. Dr. ABDEL AAL AL SAKBAN (*see below:* text of Arab Economic Unity Agreement, and further details).

In August 1964 U.A.R., Iraq, Kuwait, Syria and Jordan ratified a resolution establishing the *Common Market of Arab States*, to operate from January 1st, 1965. Kuwait's National Assembly voted against implementation of the agreement in July 1965. A further common market agreement between Iraq, Syria and the U.A.R. came into force on January 1st, 1971.

SPECIALIZED AGENCY

Arab Educational, Cultural and Scientific Organization: Cairo; proposed by Charter of Arab Cultural Unity, Baghdad 1964; aims to promote the ideals of Arab Cultural Unity (*see below*) and particularly to establish specialized institutes propagating Arab ideals and preparing research workers specializing in Arab civilization.

Director-General: Dr. ABDEL-AZIZ EL SAYED IBRAHIM.

An Arab League Permanent Delegation has been established at UNESCO, and may act on behalf of Arab states not having delegates at UNESCO.

Each member state submits an annual report on progress in education, cultural matters, and science.

First session of General Conference was held in Cairo, July-August 1970.

The Organization includes:

Arab Regional Literacy Organization: Cairo.

Institute of Arab Research and Studies: Cairo.

Institute of Arabic Manuscripts.

Permanent Bureau for Co-ordination of Arabization in the Arab World: Rabat.

Museum of Arab Culture: Cairo.

Arab States Industrial Development Centre: f. 1968; began operating 1970.

OTHER BODIES

Joint Defence Council: Established in 1950 to implement joint defence; consists of the Foreign Ministers and Defence Ministers, or their representatives.

THE ARAB LEAGUE

Permanent Military Commission: Established 1950; composed of representatives of army General Staffs; main purpose: to draw up plans of joint defence for submission to the Joint Defence Council.

Regional Broadcasting Union of the Arab Countries: 23 Kasr el Nile St., Cairo. Mems.: 16 Arab radio and TV stations and four foreign associates; Sec.-Gen. SALEH ABDEL KADER. Publs. *Arab Broadcasts* (monthly), *ASBU Review* (quarterly), *Broadcast Reports* (monthly).

Federation of Arab News Agencies: Beirut; f. 1965; this Federation will work on the establishment of an Arab Central News Agency.

Arab Financial Institution for Economic Development: A resolution was passed in 1957 to establish an Arab Development Bank; Egypt, Yemen, Saudi Arabia, Jordan, Lebanon, Libya, Iraq and Kuwait signed the resolution; capital £20 million in gold; Kuwait has declared she will contribute a further £E 5 million.

Arab Postal Union: 28 Adly Street, Cairo, Egypt; f. 1954; Aims: to establish more strict postal relations between the Arab countries than those laid down by the Universal Postal Union, to pursue the development and modernization of postal services in member countries; Dir. Dr. ANOUAR BAKIR. Publs. *Bulletin* (monthly), *Review* (quarterly), *News* (annual) and occasional studies.

Arab Telecommunications Union: 83 Ramses Street, Cairo, Egypt; f. 1958; to co-ordinate and develop telecommunications between member countries; to exchange technical aid and encourge research. Mems.: Arab League countries; Pres. MAHMOUD MUHAMMAD RIAD.

Arab Labour Organization: 7 Midan El Misaha, Cairo; established in 1965 for co-operation between member states in labour problems; unification of labour legislation and general conditions of work wherever possible; research; technical assistance; social insurance; training, etc.; Gen. Dir. Dr. TAYEB LAHDIRI.

Arab Board for the Diversion of the Jordan River: Cairo; f. 1964 to co-ordinate engineering aspects of diverting the headwaters of the River Jordan, to deprive Israel of water; main projects include the Mukhaiba Dam on the River Yarmuk (Jordan), to be linked by tunnel to the East Ghor Irrigation Scheme, and to serve as a storage dam for water diverted from rivers farther north (Litani, Hasbani, Wazzani and Banias); the activities of the Board have been interrupted by the Arab-Israeli hostilities.

Arab Unified Military Command: Cairo; f. 1964 to co-ordinate military policies for the liberation of Palestine.

Arab Organization for Standardization and Metrology (ASMO): 11 Mohamed Marashly St., Zamalek, P.O.B. 690, Cairo, Egypt; f. 1968 to assist in the establishment of national standardization and metrology bodies in the Arab States, co-ordinate and unify specifications and standards; to unify technical terms and symbols, methods of testing, analysis, measurements, calibration and quality control systems; and to co-ordinate Arab activities in these areas with corresponding international efforts. Mems.: Algeria, Egypt, Iraq, Jordan, Kuwait, Lebanon, Libya, Morocco, Saudi Arabia, Sudan, Syria. Sec.-Gen. Dr. MAHMOUD MOHAMAD SALAMA (Egypt). Publs. *Annual Report* (in French and English), *Standardization and Metrology* (in Arabic), reports, recommendations and information pamphlets.

Civil Aviation Council of Arab States: 10 El Nil St., Cairo; f. 1967 to control and co-ordinate the technical aspects of aviation between member countries.

Arab Air Carriers' Organization (AACO): 707 South Bloc, Starco Bldg., Rue Omar Daouk, Lebanon; f. 1965 to co-ordinate and promote co-operation in the activities of Arab airline companies; Pres. (1973-74) ABDUL KADER GUIBANI/ Sec.-Gen. SALIM A. SALAAM.

Arab Union of Automobile Clubs and Tourist Societies: 8 Kasr El Nil St., Cairo; f. 1965.

Arab Engineering Union: 81 Ramses St., Cairo; co-operates with the Arab League in matters concerning the engineering profession; holds a conference on scientific engineering studies every two years.

Arab Cities Organization: P.O.B. 4954, Kuwait; f. 1967; deals with the scientific, cultural and social aspects of town development, planning, administration, etc.; holds conferences every two years—last Conference Tunis, summer 1971; the main Arab Town Councils are members; 44 were represented at the First Conference in Beirut; Dir. TALEB AL-TAHER.

Arab Organization for Administrative Sciences: 8 Salaheldin St., Cairo; f. 1969 to develop administrative sciences and improve administrative machinery and financial affairs related to administration; Pres. Dr. HASSAN TEWFIK.

Administrative Tribunal of the Arab League: Cairo; f. 1964; began operations 1966.

SPECIAL BUREAUX

Bureau for Boycotting Israel, Damascus; Director-General MUHAMMAD MAHGOUB.

Pan-Arab Organization for Social Defence: Arab League Bldg., Midan Al Tahrir, Cairo; Sec.-Gen. Dr. ABDEL-WAHHAB EL-ASCHMAOUI. The Organization comprises the three bureaux below.

The International Arab Bureau for Narcotics: Cairo; Dir.-Gen. Gen. AHMAD AMEN ALHADIQAH (Egypt).

The International Arab Bureau for the Prevention of Crime: Baghdad; Dir.-Gen. AMER AL-MUKHTAR (Iraq).

The International Arab Bureau of Criminal Police: Damascus; Dir.-Gen. Col. ASHEK ALDEIRY (Syria).

Information Offices: New York (with branches at Washington, Chicago, San Francisco, Dallas), Geneva, Bonn, Rio de Janeiro, London, New Delhi, Rome, Ottawa, Buenos Aires, Tokyo, Paris, Dakar and Nairobi. Offices are planned in Addis Ababa, Ankara, Lagos, Copenhagen and Madrid.

THE ARAB LEAGUE

BUDGET

CONTRIBUTIONS (%)
(1972)

Egypt	14.00	Sudan		3.80
Kuwait	14.00	Tunisia		3.00
Saudi Arabia	11.50	Lebanon		2.50
Libya	11.00	Syria		2.50
Iraq	10.00	Jordan		1.30
Morocco	6.40	Bahrain		1.00
Algeria	6.00	Oman		1.00
United Arab Emirates	6.00	Yemen A.R.		1.00
		Yemen P.D.R.		1.00
Qatar	4.00			
			Total	**100.00**

EXPENDITURE 1972–73

	£E	$
General Secretariat	442,590	1,271,398
Information System	156,753	2,615,241
Industrial Development Centre	233,648	496,869
Pan-Arab Organization for Social Defence against Crime	17,582	75,462
Total	**850,573**	**4,458,970**

RECORD OF EVENTS

1945 Pact of the Arab League signed, March.

1946 Cultural Treaty signed.

1950 Joint Defence and Economic Co-operation Treaty.

1952 Agreements on extradition, writs and letters of request, nationality of Arabs outside their country of origin.

1953 Formation of Arab Telecommunications and Radio Communications Union.
Agreements for facilitating trade between Arab countries.
Founding of Institute of Advanced Arab Studies, Cairo.
Convention on the privileges and immunities of the League.
First Conference of Arab Education Ministers, Cairo, December.

1954 Formation of Arab Postal Union.
Nationality Agreement.

1956 Agreement on the adoption of a Common Tariff Nomenclature. Establishment of the Arab Potassium Company.

1957 Agreement on the creation of Arab Financial Institution for Economic Development, June.
Cultural Agreement with UNESCO signed, November.

1958 Co-operation Agreement between the Arab League and the International Labour Organisation.

1959 First Arab Oil Congress, Cairo, April.

1960 Inauguration of new Arab League HQ at Midan Al Tahrir, Cairo, March.
Second Arab Petroleum Congress, Beirut, October.
Co-operation Agreement between the Arab League and the Food and Agriculture Organization of the UN.

1961 Agreement to establish a Universal Arab Airline.

1961 Third Arab Petroleum Congress, Alexandria.
Kuwait joins League.
Arab League force sent to Kuwait.
Syrian Arab Republic rejoins League as independent member.
Agreement on the establishment of the Arab Organization for Administrative Sciences.
Agreement with WHO on exchange of medical information, May.

1962 Agreement to establish economic unity (see sections on Council of Arab Economic Unity and on Arab Economic Unity Agreement).
Council Meeting at Shtoura, Lebanon in August, to hear Syrian complaints against the U.A.R.
U.A.R. announced intention of leaving Arab League.
Council Meeting re-convened at Cairo in September to reappoint Secretary-General. Boycotted by U.A.R.

1963 Arab League decides to withdraw troops from Kuwait, leaving only token force, January–February.
U.A.R. resumes active membership of League, March.
Agreement to establish an Arab Navigation Company, December.
Agreement on establishment of an Arab Organization on Social Defence against Crime.
Fourth Arab Petroleum Congress, Beirut, November.

1964 Cairo conference of Arab leaders on the exploitation by Israel of the Jordan waters, January.
Second Conference of Arab Education Ministers, Baghdad, February.
First session of the Council of Arab Information Ministers, Cairo, March.

THE ARAB LEAGUE

1964   Arab Common Market approved by Arab Economic Unity Council, August.

Second meeting on Jordan waters, September.

First Conference of Arab Ministers of Communications, Beirut, November.

1965   Arab Common Market established, January.

Emergency meeting on German recognition of Israel, March.

Fifth Arab Petroleum Congress, Cairo, March.

Second session of the Council of Arab Information Ministers, Amman, April.

Third Meeting on Jordan waters, May. Tunisia absent.

Casablanca Conference of Arab leaders, September. Tunisia absent.

Establishment of Arab Air Carriers' Organization. Agreement on Arab Co-operation for the Peaceful Uses of Atomic Energy.

Establishment of Arab Union of Automobile Clubs and Tourist Societies, October.

1966   Third Session of the Council of Arab Information Ministers, Damascus, February.

Cairo Conference of Arab leaders, March. Tunisia absent.

Cairo Conference of Arab leaders, June.

Cairo Conference of Arab Foreign Ministers, September. Tunisia absent.

First session of Arab League Administrative Court, September.

1967   Fourth session of the Council of Arab Information Officers, February.

Sixth Arab Petroleum Congress, Baghdad, March. Meeting of Arab Foreign Ministers, Kuwait, June, Cairo meeting of Heads of State of Algeria, Iraq, Sudan, Syria, U.A.R., July.

Meeting of Arab Foreign Ministers, Khartoum, August. Topics discussed included Arab oil embargo against U.S.A. and U.K., and preparations for a meeting of Arab leaders.

Conference of Arab leaders in Khartoum, August. It was decided to resume oil supplies to the West. Syria absent.

Extraordinary Session of the Council of Arab Information Ministers, Bizerta, September.

Meeting of Arab Economic Ministers, Algiers, November.

Meeting of Arab Foreign Ministers, Cairo, December.

Establishment of Civil Aviation Council for Arab States.

Agreement to establish an Arab Tanker Company, December.

1968   First Conference of Arab Tourist Ministers, Cairo, February.

Third Conference of Arab Education Ministers, Kuwait, February.

1968   Meeting of Arab Foreign Ministers, Cairo, September. Tunisia absent.

Establishment of an Arab Fund for Economic and Social Development.

1969   Permanent Council of Co-operation Experts established to promote co-operative movement in Arab States, January.

First Session of the Arab States Broadcasting Union (ASBU), Khartoum, February.

Fifth session of the Council of Arab Information Ministers, Cairo, February.

Emergency meeting of Foreign Ministers, Cairo, August. Planned response to the Al Aqsa mosque fire and called for an Islamic Summit Conference to be held in September.

Meeting of Joint Defence Council, November. Discussed acceleration of military mobilization against Israel.

Summit Meeting held in Rabat, December. Heads of State unable to agree on the question of member states' commitments to a joint military contingency plan.

Establishment of the Industrial Development Centre for the Arab States.

First Conference of Arab Health Ministers, Cairo.

1970   Sixth session of the Council of Arab Information Ministers, Cairo, January.

Establishment of the Arab Organization for Agricultural Development.

Establishment of the Arab Educational, Cultural and Scientific Organization.

Seventh Arab Petroleum Congress, Kuwait, March.

1971   Seventh session of the Council of Arab Information Ministers, Cairo, February.

First Conference for Arab Social Affairs Ministers, Cairo, March.

Council of Arab Economic Unity Meeting, Cairo, May and August.

Conference on Arab Place Names, Beirut, August.

Bahrain, Qatar and Oman admitted to Arab League, September.

Meeting of Foreign Ministers, Cairo, November, to consider diplomatic confrontation with Israel.

Arab League Defence Council meets, Cairo, November.

1972   Second Arab Regional Literacy Conference, January.

Eighth Ordinary Session of the Arab Information Ministers Council, February.

Emergency Meeting of Arab Labour Ministers, April.

First Arab Traffic Conference, May.

Mahmoud Riad succeeds Abdel Khalek Hassouna as Secretary-General, June.

Meeting of Foreign Ministers, Cairo, September.

THE ARAB LEAGUE

1972 cont.	Conference on Arab Women and National Development, Cairo, September.	1973	Twenty-third session of the Arab Permanent Information Committee, Cairo, February.

1972 cont.
Conference on Arab Women and National Development, Cairo, September.

Meeting of the Arab Agricultural Development Organization, Khartoum, October.

Fourteenth Regional Conference on the Combat of Tuberculosis, Cairo, November.

Thirty-third Arab Conference on the boycott of Israel, Cairo, November.

Sixth Arab Conference for Administrative Sciences, Cairo, December.

Eighteenth Session of the Arab Economic Council, Cairo, December.

1973
Twenty-third session of the Arab Permanent Information Committee, Cairo, February.

Ninth session the Arab Information Ministers, Cairo, February.

Second session of the Conference on Arab Women, Cairo, February.

Second Conference of the Arab Labour Organization, Cairo, March.

Treaty for Technical Co-operation between the Afro-Asian Rural Reconstruction Organization (AARRO) and the Arab League signed, May.

Sudan joined Pan-Arab Shipping Company, May.

PUBLICATIONS

Daily and fortnightly *Bulletin* (Arabic and English).
New York Office: *Arab World* (monthly), and *News and Views*.
Geneva Office: *Le Monde Arabe* (monthly), and *Nouvelles du Monde Arabe* (weekly).
Buenos Aires Office: *Arabia Review* (monthly).
Paris Office: *Actualités Arabes* (fortnightly).

Rio de Janeiro Office: *Oriente Arabe* (monthly).
Rome Office: *Rassegna del Mondo Arabo* (monthly).
London Office: *The Arab* (monthly).
New Delhi Office: *Al Arab* (monthly).
Bonn Office: *Arabische Korrespondenz* (fortnightly).
Ottawa Office: *Spotlight on the Arab World* (fortnightly); *The Arab Case* (monthly).

THE PACT OF THE LEAGUE OF ARAB STATES

(March 22nd, 1945)

Article 1

The League of Arab States is composed of the independent Arab States which have signed this Pact.

Any independent Arab state has the right to become a member of the League. If it desires to do so, it shall submit a request which will be deposited with the Permanent Secretariat-General and submitted to the Council at the first meeting held after submission of the request.

Article 2

The League has as its purpose the strengthening of the relations between the member states; the co-ordination of their policies in order to achieve co-operation between them and to safeguard their independence and sovereignty; and a general concern with the affairs and interests of the Arab countries. It has also as its purpose the close co-operation of the member states, with due regard to the organization and circumstances of each state, on the following matters:

(a) Economic and financial affairs, including commercial relations, customs, currency, and questions of agriculture and industry.
(b) Communications: this includes railways, roads, aviation, navigation, telegraphs and posts.
(c) Cultural affairs.
(d) Nationality, passports, visas, execution of judgments, and extradition of criminals.
(e) Social affairs.
(f) Health problems.

Article 3

The League shall possess a Council composed of the representatives of the member states of the League; each state shall have a single vote, irrespective of the number of its representatives.

It shall be the task of the Council to achieve the realization of the objectives of the League and to supervise the execution of agreements which the member states have concluded on the questions enumerated in the preceding article, or on any other questions.

It likewise shall be the Council's task to decide upon the means by which the League is to co-operate with the international bodies to be created in the future in order to guarantee security and peace and regulate economic and social relations.

Article 4

For each of the questions listed in Article 2 there shall be set up a special committee in which the member states of the League shall be represented. These committees shall be charged with the task of laying down the principles and extent of co-operation. Such principles shall be formulated as draft agreements, to be presented to the Council for examination preparatory to their submission to the aforesaid states.

Representatives of the other Arab countries may take part in the work of the aforesaid committees. The Council shall determine the conditions under which these representatives may be permitted to participate and the rules governing such representation.

Article 5

Any resort to force in order to resolve disputes arising between two or more member states of the League is prohibited. If there should arise among them a difference which does not concern a state's independence, sovereignty, or territorial integrity, and if the parties to the dispute have recourse to the Council for the settlement of this difference, the decision of the Council shall then be enforceable and obligatory.

In such a case, the states between whom the difference has arisen shall not participate in the deliberations and decisions of the Council.

The Council shall mediate in all differences which threaten to lead to war between two member states, or a member state and a third state, with a view to bringing about their reconciliation.

Decisions of arbitration and mediation shall be taken by majority vote.

Article 6

In case of agression or threat of aggression by one state against a member state, the state which has been attacked or threatened with aggression may demand the immediate convocation of the Council.

The Council shall by unanimous decision determine the measures necessary to repulse the aggression. If the aggressor is a member state, his vote shall not be counted in determining unanimity.

If, as a result of the attack, the government of the State attacked finds itself unable to communicate with the Council, that state's representative in the Council shall have the right to request the convocation of the Council for the purpose indicated in the foregoing paragraph. In the event that this representative is unable to communicate with the Council, any member state of the League shall have the right to request the convocation of the Council.

Article 7

Unanimous decisions of the Council shall be binding upon all member states of the League; majority decisions shall be binding only upon those states which have accepted them.

In either case the decisions of the Council shall be enforced in each member state according to its respective basic laws.

Article 8

Each member state shall respect the systems of government established in the other member states and regard them as exclusive concerns of those states. Each shall pledge to abstain from any action calculated to change established systems of government.

Article 9

States of the League which desire to establish closer co-operation and stronger bonds than are provided by this Pact may conclude agreements to that end.

Treaties and agreements already concluded or to be concluded in the future between a member state and another state shall not be binding or restrictive upon other members.

Article 10

The permanent seat of the League of Arab States is established in Cairo. The Council may, however, assemble at any other place it may designate.

Article 11

The Council of the League shall convene in ordinary session twice a year, in March and in September. It shall convene in extraordinary session upon the request of two member states of the League whenever the need arises.

Article 12

The League shall have a permanent Secretariat-General which shall consist of a Secretary-General, Assistant Secretaries, and an appropriate number of officials.

The Council of the League shall appoint the Secretary-General by a majority of two-thirds of the states of the League. The Secretary-General, with the approval of the Council shall appoint the Assistant Secretaries and the principal officials of the League.

The Council of the League shall establish an administrative regulation for the functions of the Secretariat-General and matters relating to the Staff.

The Secretary-General shall have the rank of Ambassador and the Assistant Secretaries that of Ministers Plenipotentiary.

The first Secretary-General of the League is named in an Annex to this Pact.

Article 13

The Secretary-General shall prepare the draft of the budget of the League and shall submit it to the Council for approval before the beginning of each fiscal year.

The Council shall fix the share of the expenses to be borne by each state of the League. This share may be reconsidered if necessary.

Article 14

The members of the Council of the League as well as the members of the committees and the officials who are to be designated in the administrative regulation shall enjoy diplomatic privileges and immunity when engaged in the exercise of their functions.

The building occupied by the organs of the League shall be inviolable.

Article 15

The first meeting of the Council shall be convened at the invitation of the head of the Egyptian Government. Thereafter it shall be convened at the invitation of the Secretary-General.

The representatives of the member states of the League shall alternately assume the presidency of the Council at each of its ordinary sessions.

Article 16

Except in cases specifically indicated in this Pact, a majority vote of the Council shall be sufficient to make enforceable decisions on the following matters:

(a) Matters relating to personnel.
(b) Adoption of the budget of the League.
(c) Establishment of the administrative regulations for the Council, the Committees, and the Secretariat-General.
(d) Decisions to adjourn the sessions.

Article 17

Each member state of the League shall deposit with the Secretariat-General one copy of every treaty or agreement concluded or to be concluded in the future between itself and another member state of the League or a third state.

Article 18

If a member state contemplates withdrawal from the League, it shall inform the Council of its intention one year before such withdrawal is to go into effect.

The Council of the League may consider any state which fails to fulfil its obligations under this Pact as having become separated from the League, this to go into effect upon a unanimous decision of the states, not counting the state concerned.

Article 19

This Pact may be amended with the consent of two-thirds of the states belonging to the League, especially in order to make firmer and stronger ties between the member states, to create an Arab Tribunal of Arbitration, and to regulate the relations of the League with any international bodies to be created in the future to guarantee security and peace.

Final action on an amendment cannot be taken prior to the session following the session in which the motion was initiated.

If a state does not accept such an amendment it may withdraw at such time as the amendment goes into effect, without being bound by the provisions of the preceding article.

Article 20

This Pact and its Annexes shall be ratified according to the basic laws in force among the High Contracting Parties.

The instruments of ratification shall be deposited with the Secretariat-General of the Council and the Pact shall become operative as regards each ratifying state fifteen days after the Secretary-General has received the instruments of ratification from four states.

This Pact has been drawn up in Cairo in the Arabic language on this 8th day of Rabi' II, thirteen hundred and sixty-four (March 22nd, 1945), in one copy which shall be deposited in the safe keeping of the Secretariat-General.

An identical copy shall be delivered to each state of the League.

Annex Regarding Palestine

Since the termination of the last great war the rule of the Ottoman Empire over the Arab countries, among them Palestine, which had become detached from that Empire, has come to an end. She has come to be autonomous, not subordinate to any other state.

The Treaty of Lausanne proclaimed that her future was to be settled by the parties concerned.

However, even though she was as yet unable to control her own affairs, the Covenant of the League (of Nations) in 1919 made provision for a regime based upon recognition of her independence.

Her international existence and independence in the legal sense cannot, therefore, be questioned, any more than could the independence of the other Arab countries.

Although the outward manifestations of this independence have remained obscured for reasons beyond her control, this should not be allowed to interfere with her participation in the work of the Council of the League.

The states signatory to the Pact of the Arab League are therefore of the opinion that, considering the special circumstances of Palestine and until that Country can effectively exercise its independence, the Council of the League should take charge of the selection of an Arab representative from Palestine to take part in its work.

Annex Regarding Co-operation with Countries which are not Members of the Council of the League

Whereas the member states of the League will have to deal in the Council as well as in the committees with matters which will benefit and affect the Arab world at large;

And whereas the Council has to take into account the aspirations of the Arab countries which are not members of the Council and has to work toward their realization;

Now therefore, it particularly behoves the states signatory to the Pact of the Arab League to enjoin the Council of the League, when considering the admission of those countries to participation in the committees referred to in the Pact, that it should do its utmost to co-operate with them, and furthermore, that it should spare no effort to learn their needs and understand their aspirations and hopes; and that it should work thenceforth for their best interests and the safeguarding of their future with all the political means at its disposal.

SUMMARY OF CHARTER OF ARAB CULTURAL UNITY

The Charter of Arab Cultural Unity supersedes the Cultural Treaty of 1945.
It was drawn up in Baghdad on February 29th, 1964.

PREAMBLE

Concerning the common basis of the cultural and intellectual heritage of the Arab States and the value of co-operation in education, culture and science to the insurance of Arab human rights and the building and advancement of human civilization.

Article 1. The aims of education in bringing up a generation in Arab ideals.

Article 2. Agreement between Member States for co-operation and exchange of personnel, organization of conferences and co-ordination of activities in educational and technical matters.

Article 3. Agreement to develop and merge the Cultural Department, Institutes of Arabic Manuscripts and the Institute of Higher Arabic Studies to be included in framework of Arab League and to be called The Arab Educational, Cultural and Scientific Organization.

Article 4. On standardization of education methods and qualifications, teacher training and administration of educational institutes.

Article 5. On co-ordination in higher education; aim to establish a federation of Arab Universities.

Article 6. On co-operation in the endeavour to make primary education compulsory and improve secondary education.

Article 7. On exchange of specializations.

Article 8. On the endeavour to bring up the younger generation adherent to religious principles.

Article 9. On promoting the education of women.

Article 10. Arabic to be the common language of instruction wherever possible.

Article 11. On the endeavour to spread knowledge of all aspects of the Arab countries among member states.

Article 12. On the production of a "master book" as main reference book for education in Arab history, etc.

Article 13. On the spiritual, national, professional and scientific basis for the education of teachers.

THE ARAB LEAGUE

Article 14. On the establishment of a teachers' association.

Article 15. On revival, safeguarding and dissemination of Islamic Arab culture, language and script.

Article 16. On translation of ancient and foreign books, and encouragement of intellectual production.

Article 17. On the unification of scientific and civilization terms to assist Arabization.

Article 18. On the establishment of a council for Academics.

Article 19. On the endeavour to improve relations between public libraries, museums and art galleries, and on archaeological co-operation.

Article 20. On co-operation in the arts and mass media.

Article 21. On co-operation to issue special literary, scientific and artistic copyright laws for Arab League Countries.

Article 22. On the establishment of a publication registration centre in each country; bibliographical information to be sent to the Arab Educational, Cultural and Scientific Organization.

Article 23. On regulations governing the exchange of professors, teachers and experts.

Article 24. On the interchange of pupils and students and interim agreements on the equality of certificates pending implementation of Article 4.

Article 25. On general co-operation.

Article 26. On encouraging travel for cultural, scouting, and sporting purposes in the Arab countries.

Article 27. On bringing closer together and unifying where possible separate legislative trends; and on introducing comparative legal studies of Arab countries in schools and universities.

Article 28. On co-operation in the co-ordinating of efforts internationally and especially with UNESCO.

Articles 29–32. On procedures for ratification, membership of non-Arab League countries, and method of withdrawal.

ARAB ECONOMIC UNITY AGREEMENT

The Economic Unity Agreement between the member states of the Arab League was drawn up in Cairo on June 6th, 1962, and subsequently came into effect on April 30th, 1964. The Agreement was signed in 1962 by Jordan, Kuwait, Morocco, Syria and U.A.R., in 1963 by Iraq and Yemen, and in 1968 by Sudan. It has been ratified by Kuwait (1962), U.A.R. (1963), Iraq, Jordan and Syria (1964), Yemen (1967) and Sudan (1969). The Unity Council held its first meeting in Cairo on June 3rd, 1964.

The Agreement is summarized below.

OBJECTS

Preamble

The Governments of the member-states of the Arab League, desirous of organizing between them and unifying their relations on bases accommodating to the natural and historical ties between them, and for the purpose of creating the best conditions for the growth of their economy, for promoting their riches, and for ensuring the prosperity of their peoples, have agreed on creating a complete unity between them, to be achieved gradually with the maximum possible speed ensuring the transition to the desired situation without causing harm to their essential interests.

Article 1

The main objective of the Agreement is to attain complete Arab Economic Unity. The Arab State will thus have a unified, integrated, proportionate Arab economy guided by one single economic policy for all the component parts. The member-states and their nationals are guaranteed equality in the following:

(1) Freedom of movement of persons and capital.

(2) Freedom of exchange of domestic and foreign goods and products.

(3) Freedom of residence, work, employment, and exercise of economic activities.

(4) Freedom of transport and transit and of using means of transport, ports and civil airports.

(5) Rights of ownership, of making one's will, and of inheritance.

METHODS

Article 2

The Arab states are required to work for accomplishing the following:

(1) The Arab states should be made one customs zone subject to a single administration. Customs tariffs, legislations, and regulations applied in these states should be standardized. This is to be achieved by gradual abolition of customs duties between the Arab states for ensuring the exchange of Arab-made goods and the eventual removal of duties altogether. In addition customs duties should be adjusted between the Arab states so as to arrive at standard rates in respect of the outside world. In this way, the Arab states would be converted into one market where both home-produced and imported goods could move without being subject to any duties other than those imposed in respect of the outside world.

(2) The Arab states should work for standardizing their import-export policies and all relevant regulations. It is a prerequisite for the creation of one Arab market to have import-export policies and regulations unified and co-ordinated.

(3) Standardizing transport and transit systems. As

the means of transport will enjoy freedom of movement between all parts of the Arab homeland, they should necessarily become subject to standard regulations.

(4) Trade agreements and payments agreements with outside countries are to be concluded collectively by the Arab states. The creation of one Arab market makes it necessary to have such agreements concluded jointly. Relations with the outside world will be unified.

(5) Policies related to agriculture, industry and internal trade should be co-ordinated. Economic legislation should be standardized in a manner ensuring equal terms to all nationals of the contracting countries in respect of work in agriculture, industry, or any other calling. The co-ordination of these policies and legislations is an inevitable sequence to the creation of the United Arab Market where Arab nationals are to be guaranteed the right of taking up any profession or any economic activity anywhere in the Arab world.

(6) Steps should be taken to co-ordinate labour and social legislation. In so far as Arab workers are to enjoy the freedom of working anywhere they please in the Arab homeland, it is necessary to make them all subject to one labour law and to the same social security rules.

(7) (a) Steps should be taken to co-ordinate legislation concerning government and municipal taxes and duties and all other taxes pertaining to agriculture, industry, trade, real estate, and investments in a manner ensuring equal opportunities.

(b) Measures should be taken to prevent the duplication of taxes and duties levied on the nationals of the contracting countries.

(8) The monetary and fiscal policies and all relevant regulations of the contracting countries should be co-ordinated before the standardization of currency.

(9) Standardizing the methods of the classification of statistics.

(10) All necessary measures should be taken to ensure the attainment of the goals specified in Articles 1 and 2 of the Agreement.

It is however possible to by-pass the principle of standardization in respect to certain circumstances and certain countries—this being made with the approval of the Arab Economic Unity Council.

ORGANIZATION

Articles 3–10

Article 3 provides for the establishment of a body with the name of "The Arab Economic Unity Council". This Council will have its centre in Cairo and will be composed of a full member from each of the contracting parties. Decisions are taken by a two-thirds majority. Each state has one vote.

The Council has been vested with all necessary powers for implementing the rules of the Agreement and its protocols, for running the subsidiary committees and establishments and for appointing members of staff and experts.

Branching from the Unity Council are a number of permanent and provisional committees.

The permanent committees are:

(1) The Customs Committee, whose task will be to handle customs technical and administrative affairs and transit affairs.

(2) The Monetary and Financial Committee. This Committee will undertake the handling of affairs pertaining to monetary matters, banking taxes, duties and other financial affairs. Two Sub-Committees have been formed:

(a) Sub-Committee on Financial and Taxation Affairs;

(b) Sub-Committee on Monetary Affairs.

(3) The Economic Committee. It will be the duty of this Committee to handle matters pertaining to agriculture, industry, trade, transport, communications, labour and social affairs. Five Sub-Committees have been formed:

(a) Agricultural Growth Sub-Committee; (b) Industrial Co-ordination and Mineral Wealth Development Sub-Committee; (c) Planning and Trade Co-ordination Sub-Committee; (d) Planning and Transport and Communications Co-ordination Sub-Committee; (e) Social Affairs Sub-Committee.

The Council and its subsidiaries enjoy financial and administrative autonomy. The Council will have a special budget to which the member-states will subscribe at the rate of their subscriptions to the budget of the Secretariat-General of the Arab League. The Council has been entrusted with the tasks of formulating regulations and legislations aiming at the creation of a unified Arab customs zone and at co-ordinating foreign trade policy. The conclusion of trade agreements and of payments agreements has been made subject to the approval of the Council. The Council is also entrusted with the task of co-ordinating economic growth, laying down programmes for the attainment of common economic development plans, co-ordinating policies for agriculture, industry and external trade, working out transport and transit regulations and unification of regulations on labour and social security, and harmonizing financial and monetary policies with the purpose of standardizing currency. It will also formulate all other legislation necessary for the achievement of the purposes of the Agreement.

IMPLEMENTATION

Articles 11–20, Protocols

The implementation of the Agreement is to take place in successive stages and in the shortest possible time. The Council has been required to draw up a practical plan for the stages of implementation and to define the legislative, administrative and technical measures necessary for each stage taking into consideration the appendix concerning the necessary steps for the realization of Arab Economic Unity, which is attached to the Agreement and constitutes an integral part of it. Article 15 stipulates that any two or more of the contracting parties have the right to conclude agreements for economic unity wider than that provided for under the Agreement.

The Council shall exercise its powers in accordance with resolutions which it will pass, which will be executed by the member-states in accordance with their constitutional rules.

The Governments of the contracting parties have pledged not to promulgate any laws, regulations or administrative decisions of a nature which might conflict with the Agreement or its Protocols. However, the contracting parties have been given the freedom, under the Agreement's

First Protocol, to conclude bilateral economic agreements, for extraordinary political or defensive purposes, with outside parties, provided that such bilateral agreements contain nothing prejudicial to the objectives of this Agreement.

The Agreement's Second Protocol places limitations on the powers of the Arab Economic Unity Council. In the course of an initial period not exceeding five years (but which can be renewed for up to ten years) the Council is required to study the necessary steps for co-ordinating the economic, financial and social policies and for the attainment of the following objectives:

(*a*) The freedom of the movement of persons and the freedom of work, employment, residence, ownership, making one's will, and inheritance.

(*b*) Giving unrestricted and unqualified freedom to the movement of transit goods without any restrictions in respect of the type or nationality or the means of transport.

(*c*) Facilitating the exchange of Arab goods and Arab products.

(*d*) The freedom of exercising economic activities—it should be understood that this should cause no harm to the interests of some of the contracting parties at this stage.

(*e*) The freedom of using ports and civil airports in a manner guaranteeing activation and development.

At its first session held in Cairo from June 3rd–6th, 1964, the Economic Unity Council decided to interpret the time periods suggested in the Second Protocol in such a manner as to speed up the accomplishment of the various phases. Thus the Council considered the five-year period proposed as a maximum limit for the completion of the necessary studies. The Council also resolved to benefit from the rule established in Article 4 of the Protocol, which provided for the following:

"Two parties or more can, if they so desire, agree on ending the introductory stage or any other stage, and move directly to comprehensive economic unity."

The Council has therefore begun by studying the practical steps to be taken for the achievement of economic unity. It was decided that the Arab Common Market project should be accomplished as quickly as possible. A Technical Committee was assigned with the study of the subject, and its detailed report was debated and approved by the Council at its second meeting on August 7th, 1964.

The resolution passed at that meeting called for exempting from customs duties all agricultural and animal products as well as natural resources and industrial goods exchanged between the members of the Arab Market. This exemption will be either complete or gradual. It was also resolved that, in the case of gradual exemption, the rate should be ten per cent in respect of industrial goods and twenty per cent for agricultural products, to be effective from the beginning of 1965.

The Arab Common Market came into operation on January 1st, 1965, with U.A.R., Iraq, Syria, Jordan and Kuwait as members. However, the Kuwait National Assembly voted against ratification of the Agreement in July 1965. The four remaining members of the Council met again in Amman in November 1965.

In mid-1966 the Economic Unity Council adopted a resolution calling for the creation of an *Arab Payments Union*. The purpose of the projected Union is to reduce or eliminate non-tariff restrictions, imposed by national governments for balance of payments reasons.

In May 1968 at a meeting of the Economic Unity Council it was agreed that free movement of industrial products between member states should be achieved by 1971, and tariffs on agricultural products were to be completely abolished during 1969.

Central Treaty Organization—CENTO

Old Grand National Assembly Building, Ankara, Turkey

The Central Treaty Organization aims to provide mutual security and defence for member countries and seeks the peaceful economic development of the region through co-operative effort. CENTO replaced the Baghdad Pact Organization after the withdrawal of Iraq in March 1959.

MEMBERS

Iran   Pakistan   Turkey   United Kingdom

The United States is a member of the Organization's Military, Economic, and Counter-Subversion Committees, and signed bilateral agreements of military and economic co-operation with Iran, Pakistan and Turkey in Ankara in March 1959.

ORGANIZATION

THE COUNCIL

Ministerial Level: Meets normally once each year in rotation at CENTO country capitals. Attended by Foreign Ministers or senior Cabinet Ministers.

Deputies Level: Meets in Ankara under the Chairmanship of the Secretary-General. Attended by Ambassadors resident in Ankara, and a senior representative from the Turkish Ministry of Foreign Affairs. The United States is represented at the Council meetings, both at Ministerial and Deputy level, by an observer who participates fully in the discussions.

Committees of the Council: (1) Military Committee, (2) Counter-Subversion Committee, (3) Liaison Committee, (4) Economic Committee.

SECRETARIAT

Eski Büyük Millet Meclisi Binası, Ankara, Turkey.

Secretary-General: H.E. NASSIR ASSAR (Iran). The Secretariat is divided into four divisions: Political and Administration, Economic, Public Relations, and Security.

PERMANENT MILITARY DEPUTIES GROUP

The Military Committee is represented in Ankara by the Permanent Military Deputies Group comprising five senior officers of the rank of Lieutenant-General or its equivalent. The Group advises the Military Committee on the current military problems in the area and provides direction to the Combined Military Planning Staff.

COMBINED MILITARY PLANNING STAFF

Chief of Staff: Maj.-Gen. JOSEPH MCDONOUGH (United States); has international staff of officers from three services of the five member nations of the Military Committee.

CENTRAL TREATY ORGANIZATION

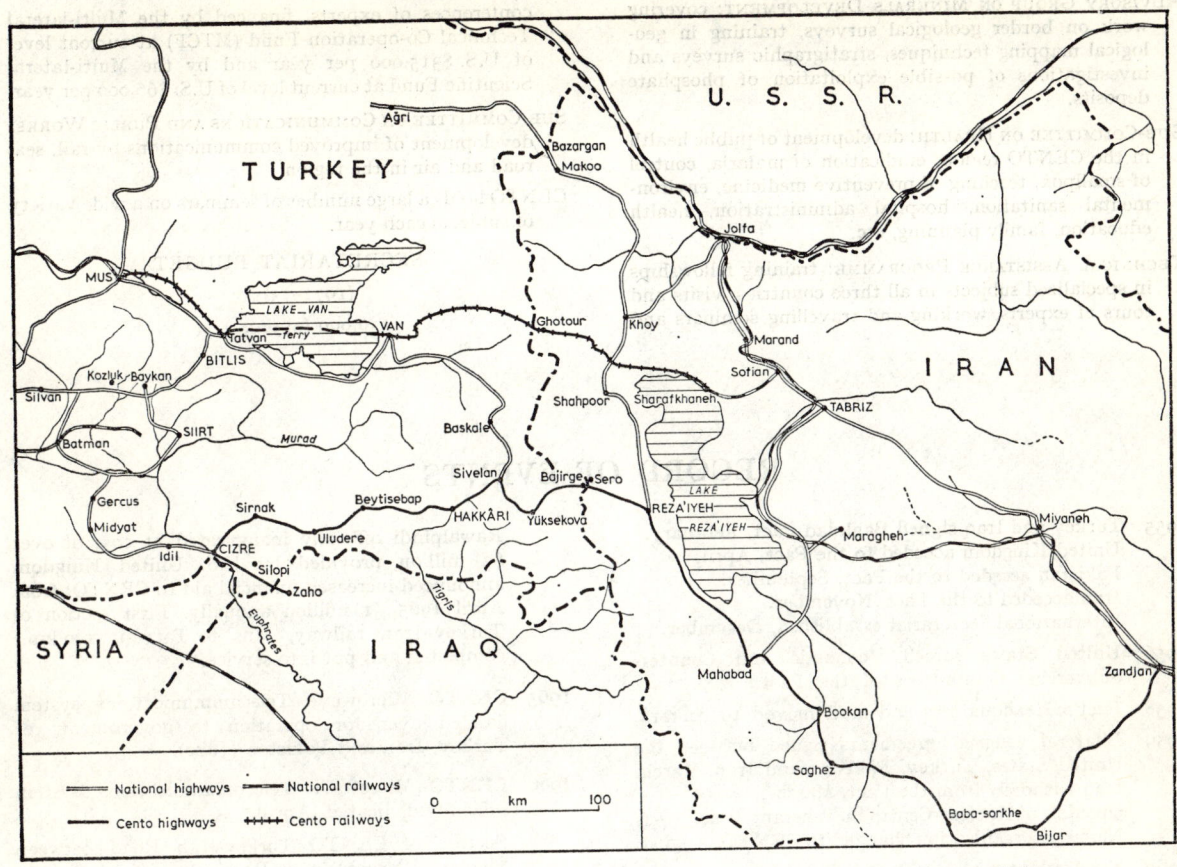

Map shows projected Turkey – Iran road and rail developments. For progress to date see below.

ECONOMIC DEVELOPMENT PROGRAMME

Pakistan–Iran road link joining Karachi, Kunnar, Khuzdar, Quetta, Baratagzai, Zahedan, and Kerman, partly constructed, partly under construction.

Turkey–Iran road, Cizre–Hakkari–Bağlişi–Serow–Rezaiyeh partly constructed, partly under construction.

Iran road link joining Ivoghloo–Rezaiyeh–Saqquez–Divandareh–Bijar–Zanjan under construction.

Turkey–Iran rail link (including a ferry across Lake Van) joining Muş, Tatvan, Van, Qatur and Tabriz completed in 1971.

Development of the ports of Trabzon and Iskenderun; Trabzon project completed in 1963. Iskenderun project completed in 1972.

CENTO Airway; U.S.A. and the United Kingdom have contributed considerable amounts towards improved navigational and other aids for regional air traffic.

High-frequency radio telecommunication links between London and key regional stations, i.e. Istanbul, Ankara, Teheran and Karachi. First stage completed in 1964; in full operation 1968.

Ankara–Teheran–Karachi microwave links project, involving 88 relay stations and 13 air navigation stations, opened 1965, completed 1966. Teheran Control Centre opened 1969.

ECONOMIC ORGANIZATIONS REPORTING TO THE ECONOMIC COMMITTEE

SUB-COMMITTEE ON AGRICULTURE: increased production, development policy, banking and credit, forestry, pest control, land classification and soil survey, irrigation systems, improved annual breeding and control of virus and parasitic diseases of livestock.

COUNCIL FOR SCIENTIFIC EDUCATION AND RESEARCH: development of science and technology and the peaceful uses of atomic energy; undertakes research in all three countries of the region.

CENTRAL TREATY ORGANIZATION

Advisory Group on Minerals Development: covering work on border geological surveys, training in geological mapping techniques, stratigraphic surveys and investigations of possible exploitation of phosphate deposits.

Sub-Committee on Health: development of public health in the CENTO region, eradication of malaria, control of smallpox, teaching of preventive medicine, environmental sanitation, hospital administration, health education, family planning, etc.

Technical Assistance Programme: training fellowships in specialized subjects in all three countries, visits and tours of experts, working and travelling seminars and conferences of experts, financed by the Multi-lateral Technical Co-operation Fund (MTCF) at current level of U.S. $315,000 per year and by the Multi-lateral Scientific Fund at current level of U.S. $66,000 per year.

Sub-Committee on Communications and Public Works: development of improved communications by rail, sea, road and air in the region.

CENTO holds a large number of seminars on a wide variety of subjects each year.

SECRETARIAT BUDGET
(1972–73)

£330,000 (approx.)

RECORD OF EVENTS

1955 Turkey and Iraq signed Baghdad Pact, February.
United Kingdom acceded to the Pact, April.
Pakistan acceded to the Pact, September.
Iran acceded to the Pact, November.
International Secretariat established, December.

1956 United States joined Economic and Counter-Subversion Committees of the Pact.

1958 Pact's Headquarters and staff moved to Ankara.

1959 Bilateral defence agreements signed between the United States, Turkey, Pakistan and Iran, March.
Iraq withdrew from the Pact, March.
Opening of Nuclear Centre in Teheran, June.
Name of Organisation changed to CENTO, August.

1960 Establishment of new Permanent Military Deputies Group in Ankara, January.
Development Loan Fund agreed to loan $6 million to Turkey to help build Turkey-Iran Railway.

1961 First stage of High-Frequency Telecommunication link opened between London, Istanbul, Ankara and Teheran, June.
Contract for $16,490,000 awarded by U.S. Government to build microwave telecommunications system.

1962 Visit to CENTO Headquarters of Vice-President of the United States, Mr. Lyndon Johnson, August.
Visit to CENTO Headquarters of His Imperial Majesty the Shahanshah of Iran, October.

1963 CENTO project for the development of the Turkish port of Trabzon completed, aided by a grant of £180,000 from the United Kingdom.

1964 United States Development Loan Fund agreed to loan over $18 million to meet foreign exchange requirements for completion of CENTO Turkey-Iran railway. CENTO Permanent Military Telecommunication System linking Ankara, Teheran and Rawalpindi officially inaugurated at cost of over $2 million provided by U.S. United Kingdom announced increased financial aid to CENTO: from April 1965 £1 million annually. First section of Turkey–Iran railway, Muş to Tatvan (100 km.) completed and put into service.

1965 CENTO Microwave Telecommunications system handed over for operation to governments of Turkey, Iran and Pakistan (June).

1966 CENTO Microwave Telecommunications System officially dedicated (April).
Section of CENTO Turkey-Iran Road between Sivelan (Turkey) and Rezaiyeh (Iran) officially dedicated (June).

1969 Decision to set up an Industrial Development Wing within the CENTO Secretariat (May).

1970 17th Session of the Council of Ministers held in Washington (May).

1971 18th Session of the Council of Ministers held in Ankara (April-May).
Turkey-Iran railway link officially opened in September (*see also Economic Development Programme*).

1972 19th Session of the Council of Ministers held in London (June).
U.S.-CENTO Scientific Fund inaugurated (July).
U.S. Government transferred the responsibility for administering U.S.-sponsored seminars, conferences, etc. to the CENTO Secretariat (July).

1973 20th Session of the Council of Ministers held in Teheran (June).

CENTRAL TREATY ORGANIZATION

PACT OF THE CENTRAL TREATY ORGANIZATION

(February 24th, 1955)

Article 1

Consistent with Article 51 of the United Nations Charter the High Contracting Parties will co-operate for their security and defence. Such measures as they agree to take to give effect to this co-operation may form the subject of special agreement with each other.

Article 2

In order to ensure the realization and effect application of the co-operation provided for in Article 1 above, the competent authorities of the High Contracting Parties will determine the measures to be taken as soon as the present Pact enters into force. These measures will become operative as soon as they have been approved by the Governments of the High Contracting Parties.

Article 3

The High Contracting Parties undertake to refrain from any interference whatsoever in each other's internal affairs. They will settle any dispute between themselves in a peaceful way in accordance with the United Nations Charter.

Article 4

The High Contracting Parties declare that the dispositions of the present Pact are not in contradiction with any of the international obligations contracted by either of them with any third state or states. They do not derogate from, and cannot be interpreted as derogating from, the said international obligations. The High Contracting Parties undertake not to enter into any international obligation incompatible with the present Pact.

Article 5

This Pact shall be open for accession to any member state of the Arab League or any other state actively concerned with the security and peace in this region which is fully recognized by both of the High Contracting Parties. Accession shall come into force from the date of which the instrument of accession of the state concerned is deposited with the Ministry of Foreign Affairs of Iraq.

Any acceding State Party to the present Pact, may conclude special agreements, in accordance with Article 1, with one or more states Parties to the present Pact. The competent authority of any acceding State may determine measures in accordance with Article 2. These measures will become operative as soon as they have been approved by the Governments of the Parties concerned.

Article 6

A Permanent Council at Ministerial level will be set up to function within the framework of the purposes of this Pact when at least four Powers become parties to the Pact.

The Council will draw up its own rules of procedure.

Article 7

This Pact remains in force for a period of five years renewable for other five-year periods. Any Contracting Party may withdraw from the Pact by notifying the other parties in writing of its desire to do so, six months before the expiration of any of the above mentioned periods, in which case the Pact remains valid for the other Parties.

Article 8

This Pact shall be ratified by the Contracting Parties and ratifications shall be exchanged at Ankara as soon as possible. Thereafter it shall come into force from the date of the exchange of ratifications.

The European Economic Community and the Middle East and North Africa

THE MEDITERRANEAN POLICY OF THE EUROPEAN COMMUNITY

In June 1972 the Council of Ministers of the European Community asked the Commission to draw up proposals for a "global" or overall approach in all the Community's relations with Mediterranean countries. The Commission drew up these proposals at the end of September, and they have since been under discussion in the Council.

Broadly, the Commission proposed that the European Community should follow up and amplify the trade relations that had been created with Mediterranean countries (*see* below), and that a start should be made on a consistent programme of aid and co-operation in the region.

Under the Commission's proposals, new agreements would be negotiated removing all obstacles to free trade between the Community and each Mediterranean country. Industrial goods should move freely—except for certain sensitive goods—between the Community and the more developed countries by July 1st, 1977. Less advanced countries would take a longer period. Agricultural products, being sensitive ones for both the Community and the Mediterranean countries, should be freed gradually, the concessions varying according to the product in question.

The Council of Ministers, acting upon the Commission's proposals, affirmed their determination to work out a mandate for negotiations with, in the first instance, six Mediterranean countries before July 1st, 1973. These six were Spain, Israel, Algeria, Morocco and Tunisia—with whom trade, technical co-operation, and aid relations were to be negotiated—and Malta, in relation to whom the Ministers wished to define a mandate for talks on technical and financial co-operation. In June 1973 the Council of Ministers had made substantial progress on negotiating positions with Spain, Israel, Algeria, Morocco and Tunisia. Agreement had been reached on a system of ceilings for imports of refined petroleum products from these countries, on measures relating to migrant workers from the Maghreb countries and on concessions for some agricultural imports from the five countries, including wines, fresh and processed fruit and vegetables, sherry, citrus fruit and beef.

If suitable terms can be found, similar relations are contemplated with Malta, Cyprus, Turkey, Egypt and Lebanon, and, although they are in a different category as far as the Community is concerned, with Portugal and Yugoslavia.

EXISTING EEC AGREEMENTS WITH MEDITERRANEAN COUNTRIES

The agreements in existence or being negotiated between the EEC and countries in the Middle East and North Africa fall into two categories: preferential and non-preferential agreements.

I. PREFERENTIAL AGREEMENTS

These are either associated agreements under the terms of Article 238 of the Treaty of Rome or agreements under the terms of Article 113 of the Treaty.

A. Agreements concluded under Article 238 of the Treaty

Country	Duration	Date of Coming into Force	Date of Expiry	Opening of Negotiations
Turkey	unlimited	1.12.64		
Tunisia	5 years	1.9.69	31.8.74	Not later than 31.8.72
Morocco	5 years	1.9.69	31.8.74	Not later than 31.8.72
Algeria		negotiations in progress		
Cyprus	9½ years	1.6.73	30.11.82	

THE MIDDLE EAST AND NORTH AFRICA—(THE EEC)

B. Agreements concluded under Article 113 of the Treaty

There are preferential agreements between the Community and Israel, Egypt and Lebanon. The content of these agreements is the same as that laid down for the first phases of the agreements concluded with Tunisia and Morocco. The movement of goods is subject to rules of origin and conditional on cetificates of origin.

Country	Duration	Date of Coming into Force	Date of Expiry	Date of Opening Negotiations
Israel	5 years	1.10.70	30.9.75	1.4.73
Egypt	5 years	1.1.73	31.12.77	1.7.76
Lebanon	5 years	1.1.73	31.12.77	1.7.76

SUMMARIES OF AGREEMENTS*

TURKEY

Signature: Ankara, September 12th, 1963.

Date of coming into force: December 1st, 1964.

Type: Association Agreement concluded by the Community and the Member States.

Legal basis: Article 238.

Duration: Unlimited.

Object: The phased establishment of a customs union between Turkey and the EEC, with the long-term possibility of full Turkish membership of the Community.

A customs union will be established in three phases. These are:

(a) *Preparatory phase.* It was provided that Turkey would strengthen its economy with help from the Community during this phase so as to achieve a level of development adequate for assuming the obligations involved in the transitional and final phases. Thus, Turkey received help from the EEC in the form of loans of 175 million units of account over a five-year period under the first financial protocol. Preferential tariff quotas were granted for four agricultural products accounting for 40 per cent of Turkey's exports to the EEC: unmanufactured tobacco, dried raisins, dried figs and nuts.

(b) *Transitional phase,* in force January 1st, 1973 after all Member States and Turkey had ratified the Additional Protocol to the Ankara Agreement (signed on November 23rd, 1970). This protocol laid down the detailed arrangements for implementing the transitional period. A new Financial Protocol has also been signed. An Interim Agreement, signed on July 27th, 1971, brought into force on September 1st, 1971, the commercial provisions of the Additional Protocol before the completion of the ratification procedures.

The Additional Protocol provides for the gradual establishment of a customs union during the course of a transitional phase of 12 to 22 years, depending on the product. Turkish industrial exports enjoy immediate duty and quota free entry to the EEC, except for petroleum products and three textile products. The EEC will grant Turkey concessions on 90 per cent of its agricultural exports to the EEC. Turkey will dismantle its tariffs on EEC imports over a 12-year period, but for a list of products accounting for 45 per cent of its imports from the EEC the period will be 22 years.

As for agriculture, the Association Council will lay down the provisions necessary to achieve the free movement of agricultural products between the Community and Turkey at the end of a 22-year period and will also adopt procedures for implementing the provisions relating to freedom of establishment, freedom to provide services, transport and approximation of economic policies.

Financial help to be granted under the Financial Protocol amounts to 195 million units of account over a period of five-and-a-half years. The European Investment Bank may supplement this with loans amounting to 25 million units of account from its own resources.

(c) *Final phase.* The transitional stage will be followed by a final situation in which the customs union will develop towards full economic union with the EEC through intensified co-ordination of economic policies. Article 28 of the agreement provides for the possibility of accession to the Community in due course.

The Association Council, with equal Community and Turkish representation, is responsible for examining progress under the agreement, and during the transitional stage is able to take decisions regarding concerted action not provided for in the agreement which may appear necessary for the attainment of the association's objectives, both parties being required to implement such decisions. The Joint Parliamentary Committee, consisting of 15 members of the European Parliament and 15 members of the Turkish parliament, is responsible for facilitating contact and co-operation between the two parliaments.

---

* All the agreements described on these pages have been supplemented by protocols making adjustments occasioned by the accession to the European Community of Denmark, Ireland and the United Kingdom.

THE MIDDLE EAST AND NORTH AFRICA—(THE EEC)

TUNISIA AND MOROCCO

Signature: Tunis, March 28th, 1969; Rabat, March 31st, 1969.
Date of coming into force: September 1st, 1969.
Date of expiry: September 1st, 1974.
Date for the opening of further negotiations: not later than September 1st, 1972.
Type: Association Agreement concluded by the Community on the basis of Article 238.
Object: The Tunis and Rabat Agreements are at present restricted to trade. The movement of goods is subject to control over origin.

These "partial association" agreements grant duty and quota free entry to the EEC for Moroccan and Tunisian industrial products (with the exception of a few sensitive products) and *ad hoc* reductions (100 per cent, 80 per cent and 50 per cent) on a variety of agricultural products accounting for 35 per cent of Morocco's exports to the Community and about 70 per cent of Tunisia's.

In return Morocco and Tunisia grant the Community a number of tariff and quota concessions.

Although these are purely commercial agreements they are regarded as constituting an important step towards the negotiation of agreements which will associate Morocco and Tunisia more fully with the Community.

Following talks with the delegations of the Moroccan and Tunisian governments the Commission of the European Communities recommended in November 1972 that the Council of Ministers should authorize negotiations with a view to wider-ranging agreements (*see* Algeria below).

The operation of each agreement is supervised by an Association Council comprising members of the Moroccan Government or the Tunisian Government and members of the EEC Council and Commission.

ISRAEL

Signature: June 29th, 1970.
Date of coming into force: October 1st, 1970.
Duration: limited.
Date of expiry: September 30th, 1975.
Date of opening of further negotiations: April 1st, 1974.
Type: Preferential trade agreement.
Legal basis: Article 113.
Object: The aim of the agreement is to promote trade between the two parties and provide for the possibility of a new agreement on a wider basis when the gradual elimination of obstacles to the bulk of trade can be continued.

This agreement involves a 50 per cent reduction (phased over 4 years) in CCT duties on industrial products (with the exception of a few sensitive ones), and, in the agricultural sector, 30 to 40 per cent reductions for staple Israeli exports (including citrus fruits, grapefruit and pimentos).

On Israel's part, the agreement provides for phased tariff reductions of 30, 25, 15 and 10 per cent on over half of the EEC industrial and agricultural products liable to import duty and for the consolidation of liberalisation. If Israel subsequently imposes a duty on goods which now enter freely, the EEC will automatically receive a 15 per cent preference over other suppliers.

The agreement is managed by a joint committee of Israeli and EEC representatives.

ALGERIA

Exploratory talks between the Community and Algeria on the possibility of concluding a preferential agreement took place in March 1970. As a result of Algerian reluctance to negotiate a first-stage, purely commercial agreement, similar to those in force with Morocco and Tunisia, in March 1972 the Council agreed to opening negotiations with Algeria on an overall agreement, involving not only preferential trading relations, but economic and financial co-operation as well.

The broad commercial contents of the agreement to be negotiated have been defined. Algerian industrial projects would benefit from intra-Community treatment, except for petroleum products. Limited concessions would apply to processed farm products. The EEC would operate the same system as the one already in force for Morocco and Tunisia concerning fishery products, olive oil, durum wheat, preserved fruit and vegetables and citrus fruit. For wine, a 60 per cent tariff reduction is proposed, subject to reference-price conditions and a prohibition on blending. In the commercial sphere, Algeria's interests lie mainly in the pursuit of a solution to the problem of disposal of its wines. Algeria wants a multi-national agreement assuring its disposal of minimum quantities on the Community markets.

The EEC asks for certain tariff preferences and for the consolidation of preferences, as well as for the binding of liberalisation measures and certain guaranteed quotas. The EEC will also demand a non-discrimination clause, as in the agreements negotiated with Egypt and Lebanon. Measures for economic and financial co-operation will be introduced in the framework of Community policy for development co-operation.

Under the agreements in force with Morocco and Tunisia re-negotiations began in the latter months of 1972. The Council of Ministers has informed Tunisia and Morocco that it is prepared to begin re-negotiations with a view to an overall agreement at the same time as negotiations begin with Algeria. The Council wishes the agreements with the Maghreb countries to be concluded simultaneously and, if possible, before the expiry of the agreements with Morocco and Tunisia in August 1974.

CYPRUS

Signature: Brussels, December 19th, 1972.
Date of Coming into force: June 1st, 1973.
Type: Association Agreement concluded by the European Community on the basis of Article 238.
Object: the phased establishment of a customs union between the Community and Cyprus.

The first phase of negotiations with a view to reaching an agreement with Cyprus began in January 1972.

The agreement is aimed at the removal of nearly all barriers to trade between Cyprus and the Community, and is scheduled to be achieved in two phases over a period of nine and a half years. The first stage runs until mid-1977.

Details of the second stage are to be worked out in negotiations to be begun eighteen months before the end of the first stage.

Under the agreement the Community makes an immediate 70 per cent tariff cut in the industrial sector, except for petroleum products, and agrees to a 40 per cent preference for Cypriot citrus fruit and a 100 per cent preference for carob beans.

Cyprus reduces its tariffs by 15 per cent immediately, by 25 per cent at the beginning of the third year and by 35 per cent at the beginning of the fifth year. Some Cypriot products will continue to enjoy protection, to help certain sectors of the economy that are not sufficiently competitive and also to maintain privileges of a fiscal character.

An additional protocol to the agreement provides that Cyprus, as a Commonwealth country, remains entitled to some of its existing trade preferences in the British and Irish markets, particularly with regard to its sherry exports.

LEBANON AND EGYPT

Signature: Brussels, December 18th, 1972.

Date of coming into force: January 1st, 1973.

Type: Preferential trade agreement concluded on the basis of Article 113.

Object: To promote increased trade between the European Community and Egypt and Lebanon, and thereby to contribute to the development of international commerce.

Initial negotiations with a view to concluding five-year preferential agreements between the Community and Lebanon and Egypt began in September 1970. For a fairly long period, however, negotiations remained interrupted over the inclusion of a non-discrimination clause: the EEC was unable to accept discrimination against its companies because of their trade with Israel—which has special links with the Community—whereas the two Arab countries were not willing explicitly to give up the principle of a boycott. However, in April 1972 a pragmatic compromise solution satisfying both EEC and Arab governments was found and a non-discrimination clause has been successfully negotiated.

Under the two agreements 45 per cent of Egypt's industrial products and 58 per cent of Lebanon's benefit from tariff concessions. In both cases the reduction in tariffs amounts to 55 per cent, 45 per cent being taken off on the coming into force of the agreements, while the further 10 per cent is to be deducted on January 1st, 1974.

For certain products, such as vehicles and aluminium products, the concessions are less, ranging from 35 to 41 per cent. Other products for which there exist agreed quotas—cotton fabrics and petroleum products in the case of Egypt, and cotton fabrics alone in the case of Lebanon—come into the same category.

Other products, still, are not covered by the agreement. In the case of Egypt, these include veneers, wood laminates and certain textile products. In the case of Lebanon they include veneers, wood laminates, textile products and petroleum products. Agricultural produce already regulated by the Common Agricultural Policy of the European Community is also outside the scope of the agreements.

In the agricultural sector, cuts are to be made in customs duties or import levies for citrus fruits, onions and garlic cloves, and, additionally, in the case of Egypt, rice, and, in the case of Lebanon, crude olive oil.

In return, Egypt grants concessions on machinery, electrical equipment, organic and inorganic chemical products and certain agricultural produce. Lebanon grants concessions on these products and also on certain textile products.

THE MIDDLE EAST AND NORTH AFRICA—(The EEC)

II. NON-PREFERENTIAL AGREEMENTS

(1) Iran: a trade agreement, signed on October 14th, 1963, came into force on January 1st, 1964.

(2) Lebanon: the Community's first trade and technical co-operation agreement, signed on May 21st, 1965, came into force on July 1st, 1968.

IRAN

A limited 3-year renewable trade agreement between the EEC and Iran—the Community's first purely commercial agreement on the basis of Articles 111 and 114 of the Treaty of Rome—came into force on January 1st, 1964. It has been renewed on an annual basis and expires next in November 1973. The agreement provided for limited reductions in the common customs tariff for imports of carpets, dried grapes, dried apricots and caviar as well as for a non-discriminatory tariff quota for dried grapes. This agreement was amended in 1967 to provide further limited concessions for Iran.

The Community has been examining possibilities for developing relations with Iran further, both by enlarging trade links and by eventually extending its contractual obligations to technical, economic and financial co-operation. Since Iran's manufactured exports to the Community already benefit from the system of "generalised preferences", it seems than at improvement in relations between the Community and Iran must focus on oil and natural gas and on financial and technical co-operation.

LEBANON

The 3-year renewable trade and technical co-operation agreement between the Community and the Member States on the one hand, and Lebanon on the other, was signed on May 21st, 1965, and came into force on July 1st, 1968. Following its expiry in June 1971, the agreement has been renewed twice for a one-year period.

This is a "mixed" agreement in that some of the points in the agreement regarding technical co-operation are under the jurisdiction of the individual Member States.

With regard to trade, the agreement provides that the two parties shall grant each "most-favoured-nation" treatment, under certain conditions: the "most-favoured-nation" clause does not, for example, include the special advantages granted by Lebanon to Arab League states nor to advantages granted by either party with a view to establishing a free trade area or a customs union.

Under the agreement, which is notable chiefly for its technical assistance provisions, Member States shall coordinate the action they take as regards technical co-operation with Lebanon. This technical co-operation includes:

(a) sending experts, specialists or teachers to public bodies or research or teaching institutions in Lebanon;

(b) the technical training of Lebanese subjects at public bodies, educational institutions, industrial, agricultural, commercial or banking concerns in the Member States of the Community;

(c) the preparation of studies and enquiries into making the most of the resources of Lebanon;

(d) if need be, supplying technical equipment to research on teaching institutions in Lebanon.

A mixed group on technical co-operation was set up and this body is responsible for examining Lebanese applications for technical assistance and for supervising the execution of approved schemes. By May 1972 the technical provisions had been given no real content, although Lebanon recently put forward suggestions on restarting technical co-operation. Technical co-operation is subject to joint agreements reached through a bilateral procedure between each of the Member States and Lebanon, bearing in mind the conclusions arrived at by the mixed group.

A new preferential type of trade agreement has been negotiated between the Community and Lebanon (*see* above), and co-exists with the present agreement.

Federation of Arab Republics

The establishment of the Federation of Arab Republics was approved by the electorates of Egypt, Libya and Syria in referenda on September 1st, 1971. Of the total electorate in all three countries, 98.1 per cent voted in favour of the Federation.

PRESIDENTIAL COUNCIL

ANWAR SADAT (Egypt) (Chair.), Col. MUAMMAR AL GADDAFI (Libya), Lt.-Gen. HAFEZ ASSAD (Syria).

FEDERAL MINISTERIAL COUNCIL
(formed December 24th, 1971)

Chairman, Federal Ministerial Council: AHMED EL KHATIB (Syria).

Speaker, Federal National Assembly: Dr. KHAIRY AL SOUGHAYAR (Libya).

Secretary-General, Presidential Council: MOHAMED AHMED (Egypt).

Minister of State, Chairman, Council of Scientific Research Affairs: SALAH HEDAYAT (Egypt).

Minister of State, Chairman, Council of Economic and Planning Affairs: SAMY SOUFAN (Syria).

Minister of State, Chairman, Council of Transportation and Communication Affairs: Eng. ALI EL SAYYED (Egypt).

Minister of State, Chairman, Council of Foreign Affairs: Dr. MOHAMED FATHALLAH EL KHATIB (Egypt).

Minister of State, Chairman, Council of Service Affairs: MOHAMED EL KHAWAGA (Egypt).

Minister of State, Chairman, Council of Information Affairs: ABDEL KADER GHUKAH (Libya).

Minister of State, Chairman, Council of Educational and Cultural Affairs: Dr. ALI FAHMY KHSHIM (Libya).

FEDERAL NATIONAL ASSEMBLY

Twenty members elected from each Republic by its People's Assembly. The Federal Assembly has a four-year term, with two ordinary sessions a year, and met for the first time in March 1972.

EXTRACTS FROM THE DECLARATION ON THE SETTING UP OF THE FEDERATION

(Signed by the three Presidents, Benghazi, April 17th, 1971)

"In a bid to link the three Revolutions in the United Arab Republic, in the Libyan Arab Republic and in the Syrian Arab Republic—for their linking responds to a public demand and is a necessity for struggle which gives the struggle of the Arab people new dimensions and potentialities, thus confirming the historical inevitability of the victory of the Arab Revolution;

confirming the resolutions of the Tripoli Charter states and strengthening integration and association between them and safeguarding the march of the Arab struggle, the banner of which was raised by the immortal leader, Gamal Abdel Nasser, the three Presidents' signing of this declaration stems from the unshaken belief in the necessity for the setting up of a nation which pools Arab forces and potentialities and the belief that this nation will be, by the virtue of the ability of our peoples and the potentialities of the three states, a solid base for the Arab struggle and one of the important tributaries of the international movements, and the natural and practical reply to all the imperialist and Zionist plots engineered against our Arab nation in an attempt to strike at its human and historical civilisation and reduce it to backwardness and dependence".

The three Presidents, having agreed to set up the Federation of Arab Republics, set out the principles on which the federal structure would be established as follows:

First: The State should serve as the nucleus for polarizing the pro-unity Arab struggle and, consequently, serve as the nucleus for total Arab unity.

Second: That it should serve as the means for the Arab people to achieve their goal of establishing a unified Arab socialist society.

Third: That this State serve as the basic instrument of the Arab nation in the battle of liberation.

On the basis of these points, the three Presidents unanimously agreed to the following:

That the liberation of the occupied Arab territories is the one objective towards which all potential should be committed; that there will be no negotiations or reconciliation with Israel; that not one inch of Arab land is to be given up; that there will be no doing away with the Palestinian question or compromise over it.

The three Heads of State emphasize that the Democratic Republic of the Sudan and its militant Arab people, who participated under the leadership of brother President Gaafar Mohamed Nemery and his brother members of the Revolutionary Command Council, earnestly and effectively, in promoting work within the context of the Tripoli Charter, will remain active in the struggle for achieving union. The Sudan will remain closely linked to the Federation of Arab Republics till it joins it.

The three Presidents, setting as their goal that the Federation of Arab Republics should answer all the needs of our people, achieve their hopes and their national aims, stress that the strengthening of the Federation and its objective values and principles, demands from the leading forces in the three Republics, the formation of a political front among them. This front should adhere to a charter of national work, with the ultimate aim of realizing

FEDERATION OF ARAB REPUBLICS

interaction and solidarity among the peoples of the Federation and to deepen the foundations of democracy and its values.

This front will also co-ordinate their efforts towards a common political goal, methods of political work in the three Republics, and create a suitable atmosphere in which the new Arab Movement can flourish.

The action taken to lose no time in implementing this Federation is but a successful move to attain a transitional objective on the road to comprehensive Arab unity. For this purpose, it (the Federation) will keep its doors open to any liberated Arab State that believes in Arab unity and works to establish a faithful Socialist Arab society.

Through the help of God, and looking forward to the future with the confidence of those who have faith in God, and in corroboration of all these meanings, agreement has been reached between the three Heads of State to consider the attached statutes attached to this announcement. The statutes will serve as a basis for the set up of the Federation of Arab Republics, and the formation of a three-man committee to work out a draft constitution within the framework of these statutes. The draft constitution shall be ratified in each Republic.

It has also been decided to put forward the statutes of the Federation of Arab Republics to the people by holding a referendum in each Republic on one and the same date.

BASIC STATUTES

1. The Arab people in each of the United Arab Republic, the Arab Republic of Libya and the Arab Republic of Syria, have approved, on the basis of free choice and equal rights, the proclamation of a Federal State entitled the Federation of Arab Republics.

2. The goal of the proclamation of the Federation of Arab Republics is to work towards the realization of a total Arab unity, to protect the Arab nation, defend the independence and structure of the Arab socialist society, work towards the liberation of the occupied territories, strengthen the Arab national liberation movement, as well as other liberation movements all over the world.

3. The people in the Federation of Arab Republics are part of the Arab nation.

4. The Federation of Arab Republics has one flag, one emblem, one anthem and one capital.

5. The system of rule in the Federation of Arab Republics is socialist democratic.

6. This Federation shall be open to all the other Arab countries which have faith in Arab unity and which work towards the realization of the unified Arab socialist society.

FUNCTIONS

7. The Federation of Arab Republics shall be concerned with the following functions:

    (a) Working out the bases of foreign policy.
    (b) Questions of peace and war.
    (c) Regulating and commanding the defence of the Federation of Arab Republics in the presence of a military command responsible for training and operations. Forces shall be transferred between the Republics by decision of the Presidential Council or such quarters as it will invest with this power during operations.
    (d) Defending national security, and the formulation of bases whereby to regulate measures to safeguard the Federation. In the event of disorders from within or without, in any Republic, which endangers its security, or threatens the safety of the Federation, the government of such Republic shall immediately advise the Federal Government to take the necessary measures within the limits of its powers to preserve peace and order. In cases where the government of any member Republic is in no position to apply for aid from the Federal Government, or where the security of the Federation is jeopardized, the Federal authorities concerned may intervene without request to restore order.
    (e) Planning the national economy, the formulation of joint general development plans, and the direction of the economic institutions of federal character.
    (f) The introduction of an educational policy aimed at the building of a loyal Arab national socialist generation.
    (g) The institution of a federal information policy serving the targets and the strategy of the Federal State in peace and war.
    (h) The establishment of a unified policy of scientific research, and to co-ordinate its agencies in the Republics.
    (i) The admission of new members to the Federation by a unanimous vote of the Federation's Presidential Council.

FEDERATION OF ARAB REPUBLICS

INSTITUTIONS

8. The following institutions will be set up in the Federation of Arab Republics:

(a) A Federation President Council. It shall be the highest authority in the Federation. It shall be made up of the Presidents of Republics. This Council shall elect a Chairman from among its members and make its decisions on a majority vote.

(b) A number of Ministers shall be appointed by the Presidential Council. They shall be responsible to the Council.

(c) A National Assembly in the Federation. It shall legislate for the Federation. It shall be formed of an equal number of representatives from the people's councils of the Republics.

(d) A Federal Constitutional Court to be appointed by a decree from the Federation Presidential Council. It shall be formed of two members representing each Republic and be concerned with deciding on the constitutionality of laws and with settling disputes between the institutions and the authorities of the Federation and Republics.

9. The setting up of the Federation shall not involve any prejudice to the rules of international treaties and agreements concluded between the Republics in the Federation and between each Republic and other countries. These treaties and agreements shall remain valid within the framework prescribed for them in accordance with the rules of international law.

10. Each Republic may, within its legislative jurisdiction, conclude treaties and agreements with foreign countries and exchange diplomatic and consular representation with them.

11. The General Command of the Armed Forces in each Republic in the Federation shall be assigned to the President of the Republic or to the person specified in the institutions in operation in each Republic.

12. The Republics shall be concerned with all that does not fall within the jurisdiction of the Federation in accordance with these statutes.

13. Until the one Arab movement has been established inside the Federation, the Political Command of each Republic will be responsible for organizing the political activity inside the Republic. Any political organization in any Republic of the Federation is banned from carrying out any political activity in the other Republic of the Federation except through its representatives on the Command of the Political Front which embraces the leaders of the political organizations of the Federation Republics.

14. The declaration of the setting up of the Federation of Arab Republics issued in Benghazi on April 17th, 1971, is considered part and parcel of the basic statutes of the Federation of Arab Republics.

15. The basic statutes of the Federation of Arab Republics cannot be amended unless there is unanimous approval by the Federation's Presidential Council and unless the issue is put up to a referendum and it wins the support of the majority in each Republic.

16. The basic statutes of the Federation of Arab Republics are to be ratified, before they are put to referendum, by the Arab Socialist Union (ASU) High Executive Committee, the ASU Central Committee, the Council of Ministers and the National Assembly in the United Arab Republic, by the Revolution Command Council in the Libyan Arab Republic, and by the Regional Command of the Socialist Baath Party, the Council of Ministers and the People's Council in the Syrian Arab Republic.

Resolution: "With reference to the declaration of the setting up of the Federation of Arab Republics issued on April 17th, 1971, the Presidents agreed that the basic statutes of the Federation of Arab Republics will be put to a referendum in the three Republics of the Federation on September 1st, 1971."

FINANCE

On October 6th, 1972, the Presidential Council approved an administrative budget for the Federation of £2,322,000.

Contributions of the Republics to Federation projects were fixed at £6,000,000.

Investment and credit facilities totalled £15,000,000.

Islamic Conference

Islamic Secretariat, Kilo 6, Mecca Rd., P.O.B. 178, Jeddah, Saudi Arabia

Formally established in May 1971 following a summit meeting of Moslem Heads of State at Rabat, Morocco, in September 1969, and the Islamic Foreign Ministers' Conference in Jeddah in March 1970, and in Karachi, Pakistan in December 1970.

MEMBERS

Afghanistan	Lebanon	Saudi Arabia
Algeria	Libya	Senegal
Bahrain	Malaysia	Sierra Leone
Chad	Mali	Somalia
Egypt	Mauritania	Sudan
Guinea	Morocco	Syria
Indonesia	Niger	Tunisia
Iran	Oman	Turkey
Jordan	Pakistan	United Arab Emirates
Kuwait	Qatar	Yemen Arab Republic

ORGANIZATION

Secretary-General: Tunku Abdul Rahman Putra (Malaysia).

CONFERENCES

Sept. 1969	Summit Meeting of Islamic Heads of State, Rabat.
March 1970	First Islamic Conference of Foreign Ministers, Jeddah.
Dec. 1970	Second Islamic Conference of Foreign Ministers, Karachi.
April 1971	Conference on International Islamic News Agency, Teheran.
June 1971	Conference on Islamic Cultural Centres, Rabat.
June 1971	Conference on the Charter, Jeddah.
Feb./March 1972	Third Islamic Conference of Foreign Ministers, Jeddah.
Aug. 1972	Inaugural Conference on the establishment of an International Islamic News Agency, Kuala Lumpur.
March 1973	Fourth Islamic Conference of Foreign Ministers, Benghazi.

The Fifth Islamic Conference of Foreign Ministers is scheduled to be held in Kabul, Afghanistan, in May 1974.

AIMS

1. To promote Islamic solidarity among member states;
2. To consolidate co-operation among member states in the economic, social, cultural, scientific and other vital fields, and to arrange consultations among member states belonging to international organizations;
3. To endeavour to eliminate racial segregation and discrimination and to eradicate colonialism in all its forms;
4. To take necessary measures to support international peace and security founded on justice.
5. To co-ordinate all efforts for the safeguard of the Holy Places and support of the struggle of the people of Palestine, and help them to regain their rights and liberate their land;
6. To strengthen the struggle of all Muslim people with a view to safeguarding their dignity, independence and national rights; and
7. To create a suitable atmosphere for the promotion of co-operation and understanding among member states and other countries.

ACTIVITIES

1. The establishment of the International Islamic News Agency (IINA).
2. Studies on the possibility of establishing an Islamic International Bank.
3. Efforts to consolidate the activities of the Islamic Cultural Centres in non-Muslim countries.

LANGUAGES

Arabic, English and French.

FINANCES

The Conference is financed by contributions and donations from member states.

PUBLICATIONS

News bulletin, issued three times a week by the International Islamic News Agency (IINA).

The Maghreb Permanent Consultative Committee

(COMITÉ PERMANENT CONSULTATIF DU MAGHREB)
47 ave. Habib Bourguiba, Tunis, Tunisia

A permanent committee for economic co-ordination, established in 1964 by the Economic Ministers of the member countries.

MEMBERS*
Algeria   Morocco   Tunisia

*Libya withdrew from all Maghreb institutions in 1970.

FUNCTIONS

The Maghreb Permanent Consultative Committee has the general aim of studying the whole network of problems bearing on economic co-operation in the Maghreb, and of proposing to the Conference of Economic Ministers, either upon the demand of the latter or in the context of the programme outlined by it, all measures designed to strengthen such co-operation and realize the construction of a Maghreb Economic Community.

The Conference of Economic Ministers is the supreme embodiment of the Maghreb economic organization. It comprises the Economic Ministers of the Maghreb countries and is assisted by delegations of senior officials.

The Maghreb Permanent Consultative Committee exercises tutelar authority over the commissions and specialized organs of which it co-ordinates and directs the activities.

Languages: Arabic and French.

ORGANIZATION

(For the composition of the Maghreb Permanent Consultative Committee and the rules governing its conduct *see* the *Statutes* below.)

Secretariat: f. 1965; each member country is represented by one delegate who exercises his functions permanently at the Headquarters of the Committee; Sec. MUSTAPHA EL KASRI; budget provided by equal donations from the member states.

DEPENDENT BODIES

Maghreb Centre for Industrial Studies: Tangier, Morocco; originally f. 1968 in Tripoli, but transferred to Tangier in 1971, following the withdrawal of Libya; Dir. MOHAMED DAYA (Tunisia).

Maghreb Alfa Bureau: Algiers, Algeria; f. 1965; Dir. LABOUT BELABBES (Algeria).

Maghreb Committee on Tourism: Tunis, Tunisia; f. 1966.

Maghreb Committee on Postal and Telecommunications Co-ordination: seat rotates; f. 1964.

Maghreb Commission for Transport and Communications: Tunis, Tunisia; f. 1965; has four subsidiary committees:

Maghreb Committee for Air Transport, Rabat.
Committee for Maghreb Railways, Algiers.
Maghreb Committee on Shipping.
Maghreb Committee on Road Transport.

Maghreb Committee on Employment and Labour: Rabat; f. 1970.

Maghreb Committee on Normalisation: Algiers; f. 1970.

Maghreb Committee on Insurance and Re-insurance: Rabat; f. 1970.

RECORD OF EVENTS

1964 October	First meeting of the Economic Ministers of the four Maghreb countries, Tunis. The creation of the permanent consultative committee was decided upon. It was recommended that the four countries should work towards the establishment of a tariff union and the principle of co-ordinating export and industrial policies was affirmed.	November	Second Conference of Ministers, Tangier. The decision was taken to establish a centre for industrial studies and it was recommended that Maghreb co-ordination on tourism, transport, posts and telecommunications, manpower and development finance should be developed.

[*cont. on next p.*

THE MAGHREB PERMANENT CONSULTATIVE COMMITTEE

1965

March — First meeting of the Permanent Consultative Committee, Algiers. Inner organization and operation of the Committee: three commissions appointed: one to draw up a schedule of the economies of the four countries, in order to be able eventually to establish relations with the important economic communities; a foreign trade commission to consider means of co-ordinating the export of citrus fruits, wines, esparto and olive oil, and to study the problems of duty-free trade within the Maghreb; and a commission to study the co-ordination of industry and energy, and to seek markets for Maghrebi industrial products.

May — Third meeting of the Maghreb Economic Ministers, Tripoli. Plans agreed for the co-ordination of exports of citrus fruits, wines, esparto and olive oil. An esparto bureau established in Algiers to handle the exports of all four countries. Special commissions set up for statistics, accounting, and the steel industry, and it was agreed to study improvement of telecommunication links. Secretariat for the Consultative Committee established.

October — Meeting of Maghreb Committee on Tourism, Algiers. Meeting of Commission on Transport and Communications, Tunis.

November — Signing of convention setting up Committee on Railways.

December — Meeting of Consultative Committee, Algiers. Studied reports on co-ordination of transport and tourism in the Maghreb, and on industry and postal and telecommunications agreements.

1966

February — Fourth annual meeting of the Maghreb Economic Ministers, Algiers. Plans agreed for establishment of a permanent secretariat in Tunis. The Ministers charged the Committee with the examination of the obstacles hindering the development of inter-Maghreb trade. Reports drawn up by the Committee on tourism, national accounts and statistics, and transport and communications were adopted.

July — Meeting of Commission on Trading Relations, Tunis. Discussion of liberalisation of Maghreb reciprocal trade relations.

August — Robert Gardiner, Exec.-Sec. of UN ECA, announced that the proposed Maghreb Secretariat with additional UN staff was to replace the Consultative Committee.

September — Permanent Maghreb Committee on Tourism created in Algiers.

November — Meeting of Maghreb Air Transport Committee, Algiers; agreement for study group to examine constitution of a Maghreb Airlines Company.

1967

January — Meeting of Permanent Consultative Committee, Rabat; discussion of possible negotiations with EEC and inter-Maghreb trade relations.

March — Indefinite postponement of Maghreb Economics Ministers meeting originally planned for May 1966.

July — Meeting of the Advisory Committee on Education, Algiers.

October — Agreement between presidents of National Airlines to form a single company, to be called "Air Maghreb".

November — Fifth meeting of Economic Ministers in Tunis. Decision to draft a new five-year agreement on general economic co-operation. The agreement to be based on the reduction of exchange barriers, the harmonization of customs policies towards third countries and an agreed list of industries whose products would benefit from freedom of movement and from a common external tariff.

1968

January — Meeting of Maghreb Air Transport Committee, Rabat. Agreement on the creation of "Air Maghreb" and on other co-operation projects concerning air transport.

First meeting of the Administrative Council of the Centre for Industrial Studies, Tripoli. Approval of study programmes on fertilizers, desalinization of seawater and training of skilled manpower.

April — Meeting of Commission on Transport and Communications, Tunis. Recommendation for a master plan to be drawn up of transport in the Maghreb region.

May — Meeting in Algiers of Mixed Commission on Frontier Formalities. Recommendations were made on facilitating the movement of travellers between Maghreb countries by road and rail.

July — Meeting of representatives of Insurance Companies of the Maghreb countries. Decision to create a Maghreb Committee on Insurance and Re-insurance.

Meeting in Tunis of trade union leaders of the Maghreb countries. Decision to hold annual meetings and to organize joint seminars.

October — Meeting of experts in Tunis to examine reports on problems of customs, commerce and external payments.

November — Meeting of experts in Rabat on agricultural exchanges.

Ordinary session of Committee on Railways.

1969

March — Meeting of experts in Algiers to examine study on industry.

May — Second extraordinary session of Centre for Industrial Studies.

Meeting of government delegates to study synthesis report on economic co-operation.

1970

March — Sixth meeting of Economic Ministers postponed because of absence of Libya.

THE MAGHREB PERMANENT CONSULTATIVE COMMITTEE

1970 July — Sixth Conference of Economic Ministers held in Rabat. Meeting held without participation of Libya, who later in summer announced withdrawal from organization. The Ministers agreed to readjust and strengthen the whole Maghreb project. Programme for 1970–71 drawn up: studies on co-operation in tourism, national infrastructures, transport, export policies, etc. The Conference decided to create specialized committees on normalization, insurance and reinsurance, employment and labour, and compensation. Mauritania attended meeting as an observer.

(No meetings have been reported since July 1970.)

STATUTES

Signed at Tunis, October 1st, 1964, by the Economic Ministers of the four member-states.

Article 1. The Permanent Consultative Committee is an organism in which representatives of the four countries of the Maghreb are brought together. It is composed of a President and eight members, of whom four are titulary representatives and four are deputies.

Article 2. The President of the Permanent Consultative Committee must have the rank of Minister. The Presidency is entrusted to each of the member states in turn for the duration of one year.

Article 3. The President may arrange to be assisted by a Vice-President who will be the titulary representative of the country which is holding the Presidency.

Article 4. The Government of each of the countries of the Maghreb will appoint a deputy titulary member with the rank of Director of Central Administration.

The representatives of each country will be able to command the help of these experts in case of need.

Article 5. The Permanent Consultative Committee is provided with a Permanent Secretariat headed by an Administrative Secretary appointed by the President.

The location of the Secretariat will vary according to the location of the Presidency.

Article 6. The Permanent Consultative Committee will have correspondents in each member state appointed by the government concerned. These correspondents must establish a Central Administration, and preferably some organizations and services with the object of planning economic programmes.

Article 7. Meetings of the Permanent Consultative Committee will be held at least once every three months when called by the President. At the same time as the President calls members of the Committee to meetings, he will present them with a programme embodying the proposals which he has received from the member countries.

Article 8. The proceedings of every session of the Permanent Consultative Committee must be recorded in Minutes drawn up by the President in office. These minutes must receive the unanimous approbation of the members of the Committee.

Article 9. The President will supply each of the members of the Committee with a copy of all documents brought to his attention, as well as any document likely to be of value to the Committee.

Article 10. The President will submit the budget planned to cover the expenses of the Permanent Consultative Committee for the approbation of the Maghreb Council of Economic Ministers.

Organization of Arab Petroleum Exporting Countries

P.O.B. 20501, Al-Soor Street, Kuwait

Established 1968 to safeguard the interests of members and determine ways and means for their co-operation in various forms of economic activity in the petroleum industry.

MEMBERS

Abu Dhabi	Egypt	Qatar
Algeria	Iraq	Saudi Arabia
Bahrain	Kuwait	Syria
Dubai	Libya	

ORGANIZATION

COUNCIL

Supreme authority of the Organization, responsible for drawing up its general policy, directing its activities and laying down its governing rules. Meets twice yearly as a minimum requirement and may hold extraordinary sessions. Chairmanship on annual rotation basis.

Chairman: Yousuf Ahmed Al-Shirawi.

BUREAU

Assists the Council to direct the management of the Organization, approves staff regulations, reviews the budget, and refers it to the Council, considers matters relating to the Organization's agreements and activities and draws up the agenda for the Council. Each member country is represented on the Bureau, Chairmanship of which is by rotation. The Bureau convenes four times a year as a minimum requirement.

Chairman: Khalifa Al-Khalifa (Bahrain).

SECRETARIAT

Secretary-General: Abdul Aziz Al-Turki (acting).

Technical Department: Deals with technical matters in petroleum, including exploration, production and processing.

Legal Department: Responsible for all legal studies and reports.

Economic Department: Responsible for all economic studies.

Public Relations Section: Responsible for carrying out programmes, and covering the Organization's projects and activities.

Office of the Secretary-General: Assists the Secretary-General in implementing and following up the resolutions and recommendations of the Council, as well as other matters.

Administration and Financial Department: Deals with personnel matters, budget and accounting, record keeping and archives.

RECORD OF EVENTS

1968
Sept. — First meeting of the Council, Kuwait.
Dec. — First meeting of the National Oil Companies, Riyadh.

1969
Jan. — Second meeting of the Council, Kuwait.
March — Second meeting of the National Oil Companies, Tripoli.
July — Third meeting of the Council, Vienna.

1970
Jan. — Fourth meeting of the Council, Kuwait.
May — Extraordinary meeting of the Council to consider applications for membership of Abu Dhabi, Algeria, Bahrain, Dubai, and Qatar. The applications were approved. Held in Kuwait.
June — Fifth meeting of the Council, Algeria, at which decision was taken to establish a dry dock for large crude carriers.
Dec. — Sixth meeting in Kuwait failed to admit Iraq as a member of the Organization. Members agreed to create a jointly owned tanker company and petroleum services company.

1971
June — Seventh meeting of Council in Kuwait ended early after disagreement on Iraq's proposed admission, support to be given to Algeria in dispute with France, and policy towards EEC and EFTA.
Oct. — Meeting in Kuwait postponed until December because of dispute over Iraq's proposed admission.
Dec. — Eighth meeting of Council in Abu Dhabi. Decided to alter constitution to allow membership of Egypt and Syria.

1972
May — Members sign agreement establishing an Arab Maritime Petroleum Transport Company.
June — Second extraordinary meeting held in Beirut to assist Iraq and Syria in their dispute with the Iraq Petroleum Company.
Nov. — Ninth Council meeting held in Kuwait.

1973
Jan. — Council met in Kuwait as the constituent General Assembly of the Arab Maritime Petroleum Transport Company.

Organization of the Petroleum Exporting Countries—OPEC

Dr. Karl Lueger-Ring 10, 1010 Vienna, Austria

Established 1960 to unify and co-ordinate members' petroleum policies and to safeguard their interests generally.

MEMBERS

Abu Dhabi	Iraq	Qatar
Algeria	Kuwait	Saudi Arabia
Indonesia	Libya	Venezuela
Iran	Nigeria	

ORGANIZATION

THE CONFERENCE

Supreme authority of the Organization, responsible for the formulation of its general policy. It consists of representatives of member countries, decides upon reports and recommendations submitted by Board of Governors. Meets at least twice a year, the first meeting being in Vienna, and the second in the capital of a member country. It approves the appointment of Governors from each country and elects the Chairman of the Board of Governors. It works on the unanimity principle.

CONSULTATIVE MEETING OF CHIEF REPRESENTATIVES

Meetings held by chief representatives for the formulation of recommendations to the Conference concerning current issues.

THE BOARD OF GOVERNORS

Directs management of the Organization; implements resolutions of the Conference; draws up an annual Budget. It consists of one Governor for each member country, appointed for two years, and meets at least twice a year.

Chairman (1973): MUSTAFA MANSOURI (Iran).

THE ECONOMIC COMMISSION

A specialized body operating within the framework of the Secretariat, with a view to assisting the Organization in promoting stability in international oil prices at equitable levels; consists of a Board, national representatives and a commission staff; the Board meets at least twice a year.

SECRETARIAT

Secretary-General: Dr. ABDERRAHMAN KHENE (Algeria).

Administration Department: Deals with personnel matters, budget and accounting, filing and archives, conference services, general correspondence and clerical services.

Economics Department: Consists of Financial, Supply and Demand, and General Economics Sections; is responsible for all economic studies and reports.

Information Department: Responsible for a programme of general and technical publications and periodicals, appropriate relations with other oil industry institutions with a view to expanding the Information Centre of the Organization.

Legal Department: Consists of Concessions and Special Studies sections; is responsible for all legal studies and reports.

Technical Department: Carries out studies mainly on petroleum technical matters, including exploration, production and processing.

Statistics Unit: Collects, edits, collates and analyses statistical information from both primary and secondary sources.

Office of the Secretary General: Assists him in matters of protocol and implementation of the recommendations and decisions of the Conference calling for action by member countries.

ORGANIZATION OF THE PETROLEUM EXPORTING COUNTRIES

RECORD OF EVENTS

1960
September — Baghdad — First OPEC Conference held at invitation of Iraq. Concern expressed over fluctuating oil prices. Resolutions passed to hold twice-yearly meetings and form a Secretariat.

1961
January — Caracas — Second OPEC Conference. Qatar admitted as new member. Board of Governors created and set of Statutes passed (outlined under "Organization"). Budget drawn up. FUAD ROUHANI appointed as first Chairman of Board of Governors and Secretary-General.

October-November — Teheran — Third OPEC Conference. Iraq absent. Conference supports Iraq's position in her dispute with oil companies; approves 1962 Budget.

1962
April (first session) and June (second session) — Geneva — Fourth OPEC Conference. Iraq absent. Indonesia and Libya admitted to membership. Resolutions adopted on price and royalty policies.

November — Riyadh — Fifth OPEC Conference (first session). FUAD ROUHANI's term as Secretary-General renewed for 1963. 1963 budget approved.

1963
December — Riyadh — Fifth OPEC Conference (second session). Dr. ABDUL RAHMAN BAZZAZ appointed as Second Chairman of Board of Governors and Secretary-General. 1964 budget approved.

1964
July — Geneva — Sixth OPEC Conference. Reviewed latest offer by the oil companies in reply to the Member Countries' Resolution IV.33 concerning royalties.

November — Djakarta — Seventh OPEC Conference. With the exception of Iraq, the Member Countries concerned accepted the oil companies' offer for settlement of the royalty issue. The OPEC Economic Commission was established.

1965
April — Geneva — Eighth OPEC Conference (extraordinary). Considered the report of the OPEC Economic Commission; passed resolution concerning measures to halt the decline in crude oil prices; approved a revised Statute of the Organization; appointed FAHD AL-KHAYYAL of Saudi Arabia as Chairman of the Board for one year; appointed ASHRAF LUTFI as OPEC's third Secretary-General.

July — Tripoli — Ninth OPEC Conference. Agreement to move headquarters from Geneva to Vienna. Established a production programme as a transitory measure to stabilize prices.

December — Vienna — Tenth OPEC Conference. Appointed ALIRIO PARRA as Chairman of the Board for one year; extended term of ASHRAF LUTFI until December 1966; supported Libyan Government in dispute with certain companies; asked for study of posted prices.

1966
April — Vienna — Eleventh OPEC Conference. Recommended complete elimination of the allowance, and that posted prices should apply for determining tax liabilities of oil companies.

December — Kuwait — Twelfth OPEC Conference. Appointed MUHAMMAD SALEH JOUKHDAR as OPEC's fourth Secretary-General. Term of ALIRIO PARRA as Chairman of the Board extended until December 31st, 1967; 1967 budget approved; organizational structure revised.

1967
September — Rome — Thirteenth OPEC Conference (extraordinary). Middle East members, except Iraq, represented. Discussed negotiations for elimination of royalty discounts and for higher royalty payments; special Economic Commission set up to study oil exports situation after Middle East crisis.

November — Vienna — Fourteenth OPEC Conference. Discussed effects on oil exports of the closure of the Suez Canal; examined progress of negotiations for elimination of discounts and for higher royalties; recommended the formation of a uniform petroleum code on royalties, concessions and arbitration; Abu Dhabi admitted to membership; FRANCISCO R. PARRA appointed as OPEC's fifth Secretary-General.

1968
January — Beirut — Fifteenth OPEC Conference (extraordinary). Accepted offer on elimination of discounts submitted by oil companies following negotiations held in Teheran in November 1967.

June — Vienna — Sixteenth OPEC Conference (extraordinary). Adopted a resolution on uniform principles for a petroleum policy in member countries.

ORGANIZATION OF THE PETROLEUM EXPORTING COUNTRIES

November	Baghdad	Seventeenth OPEC Conference. IBRAHIM HANGARI appointed Chairman of the Board of Governors and ELRICH SANGER appointed Secretary General for 1969.
1969		
April		Algeria applied for membership of OPEC.
July	Vienna	Eighteenth Conference unanimously admitted Algeria as tenth member of OPEC; discussed the principles of participation and accelerated relinquishment as well as the subject of existing disparities in post or tax-reference prices of member countries' crude oil.
December	Qatar	Nineteenth OPEC Conference adopted several resolutions expressing full support for any appropriate measures taken by the Algerian and Libyan governments to safeguard their legitimate interests in oil resources. NADIM PACHACHI appointed as Chairman of the Board for one year; OMAR EL BADRI appointed as OPEC's seventh Secretary-General.
1970		
June	Algiers	Twentieth OPEC Conference. Resolutions adopted on production programmes, integration of oil industry in members' national economies, negotiations on the revision of the fiscal regime of the French oil companies operating in Algeria and the position of Iraqi companies with respect to the level of production of the existing concessionaires and with the implementation of the royalty expensing formula.
December	Caracas	Twenty-first Conference decided to raise to 55 per cent the minimum level of tax on the net income of companies operating in the OPEC member states. Decision to support Libya's complaints about the "unjustified slowness" on exploration and development operations by some companies and to make special allowances reflecting her privileged geographical position for maritime transport. Resolution passed calling for negotiations on Gulf oil prices.
1971		
January	Vienna	Meeting of Permanent Commission.
	Teheran	Meeting of OPEC member states with representatives of the oil companies on negotiation of Gulf oil prices. Negotiations break down and OPEC members prepare to legislate unilaterally to set posted prices and tax rates.
February	Teheran	Twenty-second OPEC Conference. Resolutions passed made public on February 7th: OPEC threatens oil companies with total embargo if the minimum requirements of the Gulf states are not met by February 15th.
		Five-year agreement between 23 international oil companies and the six producing countries in the Gulf.
July	Vienna	Twenty-third OPEC Conference (extraordinary). Discussion on measures to implement a Joint Production Programme.
		Twenty-fourth OPEC Conference. Nigeria admitted as eleventh member.
September	Beirut	Twenty-fifth OPEC Conference (extraordinary). Discussed and approved the recommendations of the Ministerial Committee for the drawing up of the bases for the effective implementation of participation by member countries in existing concessions.
December	Abu Dhabi	Twenty-sixth OPEC Conference. Discussion on securing member governments' participation in their respective oil concessions and on new oil prices following dollar devaluation.
1972		
January	Geneva	Meetings held between OPEC member countries' representatives and representatives of the international oil companies. Oil companies agreed to adjust the oil revenues for six of the largest oil producing countries of the Middle East caused by changes in exchange values of international currencies.
March	Beirut	Twenty-seventh OPEC Conference (extraordinary). Resolution adopted that in case any oil companies fail to comply with any action taken by a member country in accordance with decisions of OPEC' the Organization shall take appropriate action against said company.
June	Beirut	Twenty-eighth OPEC Conference (extraordinary). Resolution adopted supporting the Iraqi nationalization of the Iraq Petroleum Company.
	Vienna	Twenty-ninth OPEC Conference. Financial Statements for 1971 approved.
October	Riyadh	OPEC discusses the agreement reached between five Arab oil exporting states and Western oil companies on government participation in the oil industry.

ORGANIZATION OF THE PETROLEUM EXPORTING COUNTRIES

1972 November	Lagos	Thirtieth OPEC Conference establishes a $22m. fund to aid member states in difficulty with their oil policy. Support for Iraq's policy reaffirmed.
1973 March	Beirut	OPEC members meet to discuss demands for compensation following the 10 per cent devaluation of the U.S. dollar.
April	Cairo	OPEC members and oil companies meet to discuss the OPEC demand for compensation for the devaluation of the dollar.
	Vienna	An OPEC Ministerial Committee meets oil company representatives to discuss increases in oil prices. No agreement reached.
May	Tripoli	OPEC members have talks with oil companies on increases in oil prices. No agreement reached.
	Vienna	Extraordinary conference of OPEC to discuss the deadlock in the oil price talks with the oil companies.
	Geneva	Negotiations with the oil companies reopen and are successfully concluded (on June 1st) by an agreement under which the posted prices of crude oil are raised by 11.9 per cent and a mechanism is installed whereby prices are adjusted monthly in future.

BUDGET

Budget for 1972: $1,225,971.

Regional Co-operation for Development—RCD

5 Vassal Shirazi, North of Boulevard Elizabeth, P.O. Box 3273, Teheran, Iran
Telephones: 638614, 636152, 638045

Established in 1964 as a tripartite arrangement aiming at closer economic, technical and cultural co-operation and promoting the economic advancement and welfare of over 180 million people of this region.

MEMBERS

Iran   Pakistan   Turkey

ORGANIZATION

MINISTERIAL COUNCIL

Established 1964 as the highest decision-making body of the RCD; composed of the Foreign Ministers of the three countries; considers and decides on measures for regional co-operation among the three countries.

REGIONAL PLANNING COUNCIL

Established 1964; composed of the Heads of the three Planning Organizations; makes recommendations to the Ministerial Council on measures for regional co-operation among the three countries.

Working Committees: Industry, Petrol and Petrochemicals, Trade, Transport and Communications, Technical Co-operation and Public Administration, Social Affairs, Co-ordination Committee.

SECRETARIAT

Permanently established in Teheran in 1965; staff consists of Secretary-General, three Deputy Secretaries-General, six Directors and supporting staff, drawn from nationals of the member countries.

Secretary-General: VAHAP AŞIROĞLU (Turkey).

RECORD OF EVENTS

1964 July	Meeting of Foreign Ministers of the three countries, Ankara. Agreement on collaboration in communications, agriculture, industry, mineral resources, education, health, and regional development, outside the framework of CENTO. Meetings of the Heads of State of Iran, Pakistan and Turkey at Istanbul. Agreement on economic and cultural co-operation. Ministerial Council and Regional Planning Council established.
August	Meeting of working committees, Teheran. Fields of study: trade, shipping, air transport, road and rail transport, telecommunications, petroleum, banking, cultural affairs, tourism.
September	Meetings of Regional Planning Council and Ministerial Council, Teheran. Agreement to set up a joint international airline, a joint shipping company, joint petroleum organizations, and a regional cultural institute. Asphalt roads and rail links to be completed by 1968. Reduction planned of postal charges, insurance rates, and tariffs. Joint action to be taken to develop regional tourism. Secretariat established in Teheran. New committees on joint industrial ventures and technical co-operation set up.
1965 March	Meetings of Regional Planning Council and Ministerial Council, Islamabad, Pakistan.
	Agreement to set up a tripartite Shipping Conference. Air mail surcharges on letters between the countries to be reduced to the internal level. General agreement on technical co-operation. Joint industrial enterprises identified. Agreements on establishment of an RCD Chamber of Commerce, collaboration between news agencies.
July	Meetings of Regional Planning Council and Ministerial Council, Ankara. RCD Joint Chamber of Commerce and Industry established in Teheran. RCD Insurance Centre established in Karachi.
1966 February	Meetings of Ministerial Council and Regional Planning Council, Teheran.
May	Meeting of the Regional Planning Council and the Ministerial Council, Teheran. RCD Shipping Services started operations on intra-regional routes.
August	Iran and Pakistan signed agreement providing for setting up of a joint aluminium plant.
1967 January	Meeting of Regional Planning Council and Ministerial Council, Ankara. Agreement to set up a joint Bank Note Paper project in Pakistan. Decision to form a Payments Union among the three countries.

REGIONAL CO-OPERATION FOR DEVELOPMENT

1967 March	The following three Regional Reinsurance Pools started operations: *Accident*, managed by Iran; *Marine* (*Hull and Cargo*), managed by Pakistan; *Fire*, managed by Turkey.	1970 June	Twelfth Sessions of Regional Planning Council and of Council of Ministers, Bursa, Turkey.
April	Agreement providing for the RCD Union for Multilateral Payments Arrangements signed at Ankara.	July	Twelfth meeting of the RCD Ministerial Council at Bursa.
July	Summit conference held at Ramsar, Iran. Working Group set up to examine possibilities of widening and strengthening collaboration.	August	Conference of Press/Information Officers of Member Countries stationed in Europe at Vienna.
		October	RCD Experts Group on Agriculture at Teheran. Expert Group meeting on Plan Harmonization at Ankara.
August	Seventh session of Council of Ministers and Regional Planning Council held at Islamabad, Pakistan.	November	Meeting of Export Promotion Representatives at Karachi.
October	Meeting of Press and/or Information Officers of the RCD countries stationed in Europe.	December	Experts Group meeting on UNCTAD Report at Teheran.
November	Agreement signed on public and private investment in joint enterprises.	1971 January	Thirteenth meeting of the Co-ordination Committee at Dacca. Thirteenth meeting of the Regional Planning Council at Dacca. Thirteenth meeting of the Ministerial Council at Dacca.
December	Meeting of the Executive Committee of Chambers of Commerce in Teheran.		
1968 January	Agreement to establish joint Jute Manufacturing Project in East Pakistan.		
April	Eighth Session of the Council of Ministers and the Regional Planning Council, Teheran.	March	Mr. Masarrat Husain Zuberi completed his term as Secretary-General of RCD.
	Two more Regional Reinsurance Pools, *Aviation* and *Engineering*, started operations.	April	Meeting of Experts Group on Trade at Teheran.
June	Operator Trunk Dialling System introduced between Ankara, Teheran and Karachi.	May	Mr. Vahap Asiroglu took over as Secretary-General of RCD. Experts Group meeting on UNCTAD Report at Ankara. Experts Group meeting on Tourism at Ankara. RCD Tour Operators Meeting at Istanbul. RCD Shipping Management Body meeting at Teheran. Meeting of RCD Heads of Industrial Development Banks at Teheran.
August	Agreement signed for the establishment of a joint Ball Bearing Plant in Pakistan.		
September	Meeting of Commerce and Economy Ministers in Teheran. Decision to carry out study, with the assistance of UNCTAD, for identifying barriers impeding intra-regional trade.		
November	Agreement to establish joint Tungsten Carbide Plant in Turkey.		
December	Meeting of Regional Planning Council and Ministerial Council, Ankara. Summit Conference, Karachi.	June	Experts Group Meeting on Allowances of trainees and experts under the Technical Co-operation Programme. Expert Group meeting on Telecommunication at Teheran.
1969 February	Meeting of Heads of Iran Air, PIA and Turkish Airlines at Karachi to consider feasibility of forming a joint airline to operate large subsonic and supersonic aircraft.		
		August	Fourteenth Sessions of Regional Planning Council and of Council of Ministers at Teheran and Esfahan.
March	Agreement signed on the establishment of an Ultra-Marine Blue project in Pakistan. Meeting of Regional Planning Council and Ministerial Council, Islamabad.	September	First railway link between Iran and Turkey inaugurated.
July	Agreement signed between IRANAIR and PIA for pooling traffic in Karachi-Teheran sector.	1972 April	Co-ordination Committee, Regional Planning Council and Ministerial Council meetings in Izmir.
December	Eleventh Sessions of the Regional Planning Council and of Council of Ministers, Teheran. Establishment of joint purpose enterprise for production of High-Tension Porcelain Insulators agreed; to be sited in Turkey.	July	Experts Group on RCD Trade Liberalization Measures meeting in Islamabad.
		1973 January	Regional Planning Council meeting in Islamabad.

REGIONAL CO-OPERATION FOR DEVELOPMENT

JOINT UNDERTAKINGS

RCD Cultural Institute: RCD Secretariat, Teheran, Iran.

RCD Insurance Centre: Pakistan Insurance Building, Bunder Rd., P.O.B. 4777, Karachi, Pakistan.

RCD Joint Chamber of Commerce and Industry: RCD Secretariat, Teheran, Iran.

RCD Shipping Services: on intra-regional routes, Tesvikiye, Sisli, P.O.B. 35, Istanbul, Turkey.

Five Regional Reinsurance Pools: Accident and Engineering, managed by Iran; *Marine (Hull and Cargo and Aviation),* managed by Pakistan; *Fire,* managed by Turkey.

Industry: About fifty joint industrial projects have been approved for establishment, of which seventeen are in various stages of implementation. Fifteen of these have already gone into production: Bank Note Paper Plant, Machine Tools, Methanol, Urea Formaldehyde, Gear Box and Differentials, Borax and Boracic Acid, Machinery for Tea Industry, Tungsten Carbide, Filters for the Chemical Industry, Locomotive Diesel Engines, Polystyrene, Glycerine (two) and Tetracycline. Six more projects are nearing completion and are all expected to go into production by the end of 1972.

Steps are being taken by member governments to encourage the participation of the private sector in joint ventures.

A study was recently completed by UNIDO on the establishment of RCD Heavy Engineering and Electrical Corporation(s) in order to evolve an integrated approach, wherever practicable. It is hoped that this study would help in adequately setting up and distributing heavy engineering projects in the region.

In the field of petroleum and petrochemicals co-operation amongst the RCD countries is progressing satisfactorily. Measures are being taken for exploration, drilling, exploitation, refining, transportation and distribution for petroleum and natural gas in the region. The Izmir Oil Refinery project is progressing very well. The question of constructing a pipeline to carry oil from Iranian fields to a Mediterranean port in Turkey is at an advanced stage of negotiations. Furthermore, exchange of petrochemicals on joint enterprise basis and setting up of joint petrochemical plants are under consideration of member governments.

Trade and Finance: Measures include the establishment of the RCD Chamber of Commerce and Industry, the RCD Shipping Services, Agreement on the RCD Union for Multilateral Payments Arrangement, preparation of the RCD Banking Manual, the creation of the RCD Reinsurance Pools, and the RCD Agreement on Trade to promote intra-regional trade.

In pursuance of the decision of the RCD Commerce and Economy Ministers held in Teheran in September 1968, a study was entrusted to UNCTAD with a view to identifying all barriers impeding intra-regional trade and making recommendations for the liberalization and expansion of trade. This study has been submitted by UNCTAD and is under the active consideration of the three governments. The last Izmir Summit meeting in May 1970 issued directive to respective Commerce/Economy Ministers for taking effective decisions towards the reduction of tariff barriers and relaxation of quantitative restrictions and other non-tariff obstacles. The member governments are also considering the establishment of a preferential arrangement for the region. The drawing up of a preferential arrangement will go a long way in promoting trade in the region. Meanwhile member governments are taking administrative action such as barter arrangement and single-country licensing to increase the flow of intra-regional trade.

The possibilities of establishing an RCD Commercial Bank and a joint Development Bank are being explored.

In the field of insurance, the RCD Insurance Manual has already been published by the RCD Insurance Centre and the Reinsurance Pools have been functioning effectively and several national companies have joined the pools. During 1969, the Reinsurance Pools had done over U.S. $1,791,189 worth of business. During 1970, the insurance business in the region is estimated to amount to U.S. $2,056,111.

Transport and Communications: The construction of the RCD Highway linking Ankara-Teheran and Karachi is making reasonably good progress. The Pakistan railway system extends up to the Iranian city of Zahidan, the railway link between Teheran and Kashan is already in operation and the section Kashan-Yazd-Kerman is expected to be completed shortly. The Teheran-Ankara rail link became operational in September 1971. The RCD Shipping Services started operating on intra-regional routes and from U.S. ports to Turkey and Pakistan in 1966. The three airlines are considering the possibility of establishing a fourth airline to operate subsonic and supersonic aircraft. Operator trunk dialling system has been introduced between Teheran, Ankara and Karachi. An agreement has been reached between Turkey and Iran for the routing by Turkey of a telephone circuit Ankara-New York through Iran's new Earth Station at Asadabad. Postage, telephone and telegraphic rates have been reduced within the region.

Technical Assistance: A Regional Technical Assistance Programme was launched in 1965. Between 1965 and 1970, 1,737 students and trainees and 168 experts were provided for under the programme and 32 seminars had been organized on subjects such as financing of development programmes, management research, status of women, family planning, control and eradication of quarantinable diseases, water resource development, Islamic architecture, etc. Four joint courses on public administration were held in 1967 and 1970 and a fifth was held in September of 1971. A Programme of Technical Co-operation for 1971 provides for the exchange of 19 experts and 395 trainees.

Tourism: Visas were abolished for nationals of member countries in 1964.

Scientific Research: The setting up of a Regional Advisory Council is being considered. The Heads of the Atomic Energy organization of the member countries were scheduled to meet in 1971 to undertake co-operation in the peaceful uses of atomic energy.

Cultural Co-operation: The Regional Cultural Institute is engaged in systematic research into the common historical and cultural heritage of the RCD countries. It has published a number of translations, in various languages of the region, of classics and well-known works of the member countries.

The RCD Annual Cultural Exchange Programme includes exchange of professors, writers and artists and the holding of art and cultural exhibitions.

Information: Collaboration is encouraged between national news agencies. A joint documentary film on general aspects of RCD emphasizing cultural and social developments in the region is being planned. RCD countries participated jointly in Expo 1970 at Osaka.

AIMS OF REGIONAL CO-OPERATION FOR DEVELOPMENT

Enunciated in Istanbul, July 23rd, 1964, by the Foreign Ministers of the Member States

1. The emergence of regional economic groupings enjoying a community of interest is an outstanding feature of our time for accelerating the pace of economic growth. Efforts directed towards regional economic collaboration have gained international acceptance and the present move to promote collaboration amongst countries of the region is directed towards the same aim, *viz.*, the strengthening of their development efforts through active and sustained collaboration on a regional basis. This is particularly true in the case of Iran, Pakistan and Turkey since the desire and basis for such a close collaboration and co-operation exist amongst them and will continue in view of the cultural and historic ties of friendship amongst the peoples of the three countries, and further because increasing regional economic co-operation has become a necessity. Economic and cultural collaboration amongst them is therefore most desirable, and should be raised to the highest possible level. There are great possibilities for such collaboration to the mutual benefit of the three countries which should be achieved expeditiously.

Measures

2. The measures for economic collaboration suggested in the following paragraphs may be broadly divided into two categories—(*a*) Those which can be worked out and implemented forthwith and (*b*) Those which will require detailed study and scrutiny by Regional Planning Council.

3. A Regional Planning Council composed of the Heads of the Planning Organizations is established. It will be assisted by advisers and could meet in any of the regional countries, preferably by rotation.

4. The Council will study the development plans and production potential of countries of the region with a view *inter alia* to making recommendations on joint purpose projects and long-term purchase agreements. Joint purpose projects will feed the requirements of the three countries. There are several projects for which none of these countries can provide a sufficient domestic market yet they can be valuable projects if the total requirements of the three countries are taken into consideration.

5. The Council may also make proposals regarding the harmonization of the national development plans in the wide interest of accelerated regional development.

6. The Council will submit its reports to the Ministerial meetings. The first report is to be submitted to the next such meeting.

7. Efficient and effective means of communication and transport are essential for the promotion of the regional economic and cultural collaboration. The preparation of recommendations in this field and their implementation should be given the highest priority.

Air Transportation

8. A Committee on air transportation is set up to study measures required to—(*a*) improve the transport services in the region so that quick and frequent movement of passengers and freight within the region be possible; (*b*) establish a strong and competitive international airline among the three countries; (*c*) foster co-operation among the civil and commercial aviation authorities of the three countries.

The report of the Committee should be available for the next Ministerial meeting.

Shipping

9. Collaboration among the countries of the region in shipping is highly desirable. A Committee on shipping is set up to investigate the possibility of securing a close co-operation in this field including the establishment of a joint maritime line.

Roads and Railways

10. Committees on road, railways and telecommunications are established immediately. The Committee will *inter alia* study and report on the following:
    (*a*) The measures which should be taken to complete expeditiously the rail and road links among the countries of the region.
    (*b*) Whether any additional rail and road links are considered necessary.
    (*c*) Reduction of telephone rates.
    (*d*) Establishment of P.T.T. offices in border areas.
    (*e*) Feasibility of providing services such as direct dialling between the countries of the region and telecommunication, etc.

11. It is agreed that the postal and telegraph rates among Iran, Pakistan and Turkey be reduced to the levels of internal rates within the respective countries. The implementation of this decision is entrusted to the P.T.T. authorities of the three countries.

12. The construction of roads from the western and central parts of Iran to Zahidan and from Karachi to Zahidan should be given consideration by Iran and Pakistan so that the two countries are effectively linked by road. The Zahidan-Kashan rail link should be given further consideration with a view to developing it as early as possible.

Trade

13. Economic collaboration should provide for effective measures to build up and promote trade since expansion of inter-regional trade, apart from being highly desirable, in itself tends further to promote regional economic growth and amity.

14. A Committee on trade is established to study, report and recommend *inter alia* on the following measures on which agreement in principle has been reached:
    (*a*) Free or freer movement of goods among the countries of the region through practicable means such as the conclusion of trade agreements, etc.;
    (*b*) transit trade arrangements;
    (*c*) establishment of closer collaboration between existing chambers of commerce and establishment of a joint chamber of commerce;
    (*d*) establishment of halls and showrooms, provision of special customs facilities for exhibitions and increased participation in each other's fairs;

(e) dissemination of information on a large scale of the export and import potential of the three countries and investigation of the possibilities of joint publicity and joint marketing policy outside the region for similar exportable products.

Petroleum

15. A Committee on petroleum is established to consider measures for co-operation among the three countries in the field of petroleum and natural gas and for their exploration drilling; exploration; refining; transportation; distribution, etc. Collaboration in this field could be developed to mutual advantage.

Petrochemicals

16. A Committee on petrochemical industries is established for development of these industries in the region.

Tourism

17. A Tourist Agreement will be signed at an early date among the countries of the region with a view to promoting tourist traffic among themselves and to increase the flow of tourists from other countries. A Committee on tourism should be established immediately to prepare an agreement on tourism which should *inter alia* cover co-operation in publicity, group or package tourist arrangements. Promotion of inter-regional travel, substitutes of passports by documents valid for travelling in the three countries. Efforts with the aim of exchanging and training of tourist personnel, technicians, tourist investments, tourist propaganda and utilization of the services and facilities of their tourist organizations, travel bureaux and other agencies in their countries and abroad. As economic collaboration grows, inter-regional travel should increase considerably; it does however need a special effort if it is to be developed to a substantial degree in the immediate future.

Abolition of Visas

18. The abolition of visas for travel purposes by their nationals in the three countries is accepted in principle; the procedure for the implementation of this decision should be worked out by the Committee on tourism.

Banking and Insurance

19. A Committee on Banking and Insurance is established for collaboration in these fields.

Technical Co-operation

20. The countries of the region should provide technical assistance to each other in the form of exports and training facilities. Such a programme will, apart from intrinsic utility, promote regional understanding and harmony. The Planning Council will be directly responsible for progress in this matter.

Joint Purpose Enterprises

21. The Committee carries out feasibility studies in regard to the development of some industries on a joint purpose basis.

Cultural Co-operation

22. Iran, Pakistan and Turkey are bound to one another by historical and cultural ties, they share a common heritage. Their cultural ties go far back in history and their national cultures owe much to continuous exchanges which have gone on for centuries. In the modern world they must integrate their traditional cultures with the new scientific outlook.

23. Co-operation in the field of education, science and culture is necessary to develop consciousness of the common cultural heritage and to promote social and economic development and political collaboration.

24. During the last few years a certain measure of progress has been achieved in cultural relations through bilateral programmes. However, there is considerable scope for further action. At the same time there is strong need for a joint sponsorship of many cultural activities under a regional programme.

Cultural Relations

25. The programme of cultural relations should be particularly oriented towards the following aims: (a) creating mass consciousness of the common cultural heritage. To this end the three countries should jointly sponsor an institute for initiating studies and research in this field and bringing out clearly those traditions which bind the people of the region together. Further, school books should be carefully reviewed to eliminate misleading interpretations of history and to promote greater understanding of their common interests; (b) disseminating information about history, civilization and culture of the people of the region. To this end each country should consider: (1) establishment of chairs for the study of its language, history, civilization and culture in universities of the other countries; (2) increasing substantially the number of scholarships for the students of other countries to enable them to study together in their educational institutions; (3) establishment of cultural centres in the other two countries; (4) provision as far as possible of facilities for the teaching of international language in the schools of other member countries; the media of mass communications, radio, films, television, etc., should be extensively used for the propagation of information and ideas aimed at a closer understanding of the people of the region.

26. Cultural co-operation may also be extended through: (a) exchanges in the field of fine arts; (b) exchanges of visits by teachers, scientists, educational administrators, writers, artists, journalists, etc.; (c) exchanges of information on educational techniques, experiences, and programmes; (d) collaboration in regard to programmes for radio, films and television; (e) elimination of obstacles in the way of free exchange of books, films and other printed materials of an educational and cultural character; (f) organization of regional tournaments; (g) co-operation in the field of joint production of films.

Organization

27. The organizational arrangements for planning and promoting economic and cultural collaboration amongst Iran, Pakistan and Turkey should be simple and effective. As the scope of co-operation widens these arrangements could be modified as required.

28. The highest decision-making body for regional co-operation shall be a Council of Ministers consisting of the Ministers nominated by each of the three countries concerned. It shall consider and decide upon measures for regional economic and cultural co-operation. It will also follow the programmes in the implementation of its decisions. The Council shall meet once in four months and more frequently if necessary. The Chairman of the Council shall be the Head of State or Head of Government of the host country.

29. The Council will be assisted by a Regional Planning Council composed of the Heads of the three Planning Organizations. They will deal with work relating to regional collaboration including detailed preparatory negotiations and preparation of recommendations for submission to the Council. The Committee will be assisted by Sub-committees which will report to it. If necessary the Committee may engage expert consultants to examine particular subjects for regional co-operation.

30. The host country will for the time being provide secretarial facilities (including office accommodation, etc.). The officials of the countries deputed by their Governments to serve on the Secretariat will draw their emoluments and allowances from their own Governments.

31. After 12 months the Council of Ministers will review the position and decide upon the setting up of a permanent Secretariat.

Other Regional Organizations

AGRICULTURE, FORESTRY AND FISHERIES

African Agricultural Credit Commission: Rabat, Morocco; f. 1966 to study agricultural finance problems. Mems.: Algeria, Ivory Coast, Libya, Morocco, Senegal, Tunisia, Upper Volta and Zaire.

Afro-Asian Rural Reconstruction Organization (AARRO): C/117-118, Defence Colony, New Delhi-3, India; f. 1962 to launch concrete and wherever possible co-ordinated action to reconstruct the economy of the rural peoples of Afro-Asian countries and to revitalize their social and cultural life. Mems.: governments of 28 African and Asian countries.

Pres. A. A. MUNUFIE (Ghana); Sec.-Gen. H.E. KRISHNAN CHAND (India); Dir. and Programme Co-ordinator M. R. KAUSHAL. Publ. *Rural Reconstruction* (quarterly).

International Olive Growers Federation (*Fédération internationale d'oléiculture*): Agustina de Aragón 11, Madrid 6, Spain; f. 1934 to promote the interests of olive growers and to effect international co-ordination of efforts to improve methods of growing and manufacturing and to promote the use of olive oil. Mems.: organizations and government departments in Algeria, Argentina, France, Greece, Israel, Italy, Lebanon, Libya, Morocco, Portugal, Spain, Syria, Tunisia.

Pres. PIERRE D. BONNET (France). Publs. *Informations oléicoles internationales* (quarterly).

THE ARTS

Afro-Asian Writers' Permanent Bureau: 104 Kasr el-Aini St., Cairo, Egypt; f. 1958 by Afro-Asian Peoples' Solidarity Organization; conferences of Asian and African writers have been held at Tashkent (1958), Cairo (1962), Beirut (1967), New Delhi (1970). Mems.: 78 writers' organizations.

Sec.-Gen. YOUSSEF EL-SEBAI (Egypt). Publ. *Lotus Magazine of Afro-Asian Writings* (quarterly in English, French and Arabic).

ECONOMICS AND POLITICS

African Institute for Economic Development and Planning: Dakar, Senegal (*see* under ECA in the chapter *UN in the Middle East and North Africa*).

Afro-Asian Organization for Economic Co-operation (AFRASEC): Chamber of Commerce Building, Midan al Falaki, Special P.O. Bag, Cairo, Egypt; f. 1958 to speed up industrialization and implement exchanges in commercial, financial and technical fields. Mems.: Central Chambers of Commerce in 45 countries.

Pres. ZAKAREYA TEWFIK; Sec.-Gen. Mrs. NARGUIS HEBEISHA. Publ. *Afro-Asian Economic Review*.

Afro-Asian Peoples' Solidarity Organization (AAPSO): 89 Abdel Aziz al Saoud St., Manial, Cairo, Egypt; f. 1957 as the Organization for Afro-Asian Peoples' Solidarity; acts as a permanent liaison body between the peoples of Africa and Asia and aims to ensure their economic, social and cultural development. Mems.: national committees and affiliated organizations in 75 countries.

Sec.-Gen. YOUSSEF EL-SEBAI (Egypt). Publs. *Afro-Asian Bulletin* (monthly), *Afro-Asian Women's Bulletin* (irregular), etc.

Arab Common Market: (*see* chapter *The Arab League*).

Arab Economic Council: (*see* chapter *The Arab League*).

Arab Financial Institution for Economic Development: to encourage economic development through private and public projects in the Arab states (*see* chapter *The Arab League*).

Comité International de la Gauche pour la Paix au Moyen-Orient (*International Committee of the Left for Peace in the Middle East*): 15 rue des Minimes, Paris 3e, France; f. 1969 to analyse the true causes of the Israeli-Arab conflict and seek for a solution through the organization of meetings between progressive Israelis and Arabs on the one side and Palestinians and Israelis on the other; to mobilize the left internationally against extremists on both sides by the creation of a Palestinian State and the recognition of an Israeli State by all Arab peoples.

Cttee. Mems. MAURICE CLAVEL, JEAN-FRANCOIS REVEL, MAREK HALTER, ARNOLD WESKER, ANGUS WILSON, ANDRE SCHWARTZ-BART, JACQUES DEROGY. Publs. *Elements* (quarterly), paperback collection.

Council of Arab Economic Unity: to co-ordinate economic, financial and social policies in the Arab states (*see* chapter *The Arab League*).

Jewish Agency for Israel: P.O.B. 92, Jerusalem, Israel; f. 1897 as an instrument through which world Jewry could build up a national home. Is now the executive arm of the World Zionist Organisation. Mems.: Zionist federations in 61 countries.

Pres. Dr. NAHUM GOLDMANN; Chair. and Treas. L. A. PINCUS; Dir.-Gen. MOSHE RIVLIN. Publs. *Israel Digest* (fortnightly), *Israel Features Service* (weekly).

Union des Banques Arabes et Françaises—UBAF (*Union of French and Arab Banks*): "La France", 4 rue Ancelle, 92 Neuilly S/Seine, France; f. 1970 to group together 22 banks of 16 Arab countries (with 60 per cent of share capital), the Crédit Lyonnais of France (32 per cent share capital) and the Banque Française du Commerce Extérieur (8 per cent share capital) with the aim of contributing primarily to the development of financial, commercial, industrial and economic relations between Europe and the Arab countries, particularly between France and the Arab countries.

Chair. MOHAMED MAHMOUD ABUSHADI; Gen. Man. JACQUES FRANÇOIS MERIE.

World Zionist Organisation (*see* entry *Jewish Agency for Israel*, above).

EDUCATION AND DEVELOPMENT

Afro-Asian Housing Organization (AAHO): 28 Ramses St., Cairo, Egypt; f. 1965 to promote co-operation between African and Asian countries in housing, reconstruction, physical planning and related matters.

Sec.-Gen. ABDEL HAMID EL ZANFALY (Egypt).

Alliance Israélite Universelle: 45 rue La Bruyère, F. 75425 Paris CEDEX 09, France; f. 1860 to work for the emancipation and moral progress of the Jews; maintains 71 schools in the Mediterranean area; library of 100,000 vols. Mems.: 12,000 in 40 countries; local committees in six countries.

Pres. RENÉ CASSIN (France); Sec.-Gen. EUGENE WEILL (France). Publs. *Cahiers de l'Alliance Israélite Universelle*, *The Alliance Review*, *Les Nouveaux Cahiers*, *La Revista de la Alliance*.

OTHER REGIONAL ORGANIZATIONS

Arab Development Fund for Economic and Social Development: c/o Kuwait Ministry of Finance; f. 1972; finances economic and development projects in the Arab countries. Mems. 15 countries.

Association of Arab Universities: Scientific Computation Centre, Tharwat St., Orman P.O.-Giza, Egypt; f. 1964. Mems.: 26 universities.

Publs. magazine, directory of Arab universities.

Centre Africain de Formation et de Recherches Administratives pour le Développement (CAFRAD) (*African Training and Research Centre in Administration for Development*): 19 rue Victor Hugo, B.P. 310, Tangier, Morocco; f. 1964 by agreement between Morocco and UNESCO, final agreement signed by 19 member states; undertakes research into administrative problems in Africa, documentation of results, provision of a consultation service for governments and organizations; holds frequent seminars. Mems.: Algeria, Cameroon, Central African Republic, Egypt, Ghana, Ivory Coast, Kenya, Liberia, Libya, Mauritania, Morocco, Niger, Nigeria, Senegal, Somalia, Sudan, Togo, Tunisia and Zambia; aided by UNESCO and the UN Development Programme; library of 10,000 vols.

Pres. LOUAFI SKALLI; Dir.-Gen. J. E. KARIUKI; Publs. *Cahiers Africains d'Administration Publique/African Administrative Studies* (twice a year), *CAFRAD News* (irregularly in English and French).

International Institute for Adult Literacy Methods: P.O.B. 1555, Teheran, Iran; f. 1968 by UNESCO and the Government of Iran; carries out comparative studies of the methods, media and techniques used in literacy programmes; maintains documentation service and library on literacy; arranges seminars.

Acting Dir. Dr. A. FATTAHIPOUR. Publs. *Literacy Discussion* and *Literacy Work* (quarterlies in English and French), *Literacy Documentation* (quarterly in English).

International Planned Parenthood Federation: Middle East and North Africa Office, P.O.B. 1567, Beirut, Lebanon; aims to advance planned parenthood through education and scientific research and to attain a favourable balance between population and natural resources; Regional Office covers Afghanistan*, Algeria, the Arabian peninsula, Cyprus*, Egypt*, Iran*, Iraq*, Jordan*, Lebanon*, Libya, Morocco*, Sudan*, Syria, Tunisia* (member asscns. with asterisk).

Near East Foundation, 54 East 64th St., New York 21, N.Y., U.S.A.; f. 1930. Aims: to conduct agricultural and educational programmes and demonstrations in order to improve standards of living in underdeveloped areas of the world, primarily the Near East, with technicians at work in Asia and Africa.

Chair. CLEVELAND E. DODGE; Vice-Chair. J. B. SUNDERLAND; Pres. HERRICK YOUNG; Exec. Dir. Dr. DELMER J. DOOLEY.

Regional Centre for Educational Planning and Administration in the Arab Countries (*Centre Régional de Planification et Administration de L'Education pour les Pays Arabes*): B.P. 5244, Bir Hassan, Beirut, Lebanon; f. 1961; offers advanced training in educational planning and administration in the Arab countries.

Dir. AHMED SALMI; Assistant Dir. MOUNIF MAALOUF. Publs. *Revue de la Planification de l'Education dans les Pays Arabes* (quarterly), *Panoramas de l'Education dans les Pays Arabes*.

Regional Centre for Functional Literacy in Rural Areas for the Arab States (ASFEC): Sirs-el-Layyan, Menoufia, Egypt; f. 1952 for the training of specialists, production of prototype educational materials, research in functional literacy and literacy teaching; advisory service to member states.

Dir. Dr. BASHIR AL-BAKRI.

Unesco Regional Office of Education in the Arab Countries (*Bureau Régional de l'Unesco pour l'éducation dans les pays arabes*): B.P. 5244, Cité Sportive, ave. Bir Hassan, Beirut, Lebanon; f. 1973; part of the Secretariat of Unesco, the Regional Office trains education personnel (especially planners and administrators), provides advisory services, information and documentation, and carries out studies and research.

Dir. CHIKH BEKRI. Publs. *Review Education* (quarterly), *Bulletin du Liaison*.

LABOUR

Afro-Asian Institute for Co-operative and Labour Studies: P.O.B. 16201, Tel-Aviv; f. 1960 by Histadrut. Aims: advanced training of union workers, co-operators, government executives and higher education teachers in the theory and practice of economic and social development problems, labour economics, trade unionism and co-operation; English-speaking courses: Aug.-Dec.; French-speaking courses: Dec.-April; special courses on request: May-Aug.

Chair. Dr. ELIAHU ELATH; Dir. AKIVA EGER.

Arab Federation of Petroleum, Mining and Chemicals Workers (*Fédération arabe des travailleurs du pétrole, des mines et des industries chimiques*): 5 Zaki St. Cairo, Egypt; f. 1961; owns and manages the Arab Petroleum Institute for Labour Studies, Cairo; 18 affiliated unions in 11 countries.

Pres. GHAZI NASSIF (Syria); Sec.-Gen. ALI SAYED ALI (Egypt). Publ. *Arab Petroleum* (monthly; English, Arabic and French editions).

International Confederation of Arab Trade Unions (ICATU): Ramses Building, Ramses Square (P.O.B. 1041), Cairo, Egypt; f. 1956. Mems.: 15 unions in 13 countries.

Pres. ABDULLAH EL-ASNAG; Sec.-Gen. Dr. FAWZY EL SAYED (Egypt). Publs. *Arab Worker* (Arab, French and English editions monthly).

MEDICINE

Middle East Neurosurgical Society: Dr. FUAD S. HADDAD, Neurosurgical Department, Orient Hospital, Beirut, Lebanon; f. 1958; mems. in Egypt, Greece, India, Iraq, Jordan, Lebanon, Pakistan, Syria and Turkey.

Society of Haematology and Blood-Transfusion of African and Near Eastern Countries: Tunis, Tunisia; f. 1965 for the promotion and co-ordination of scientific research in the field of haematology.

Pres. Dr. SY BABA (Ivory Coast); Vice-Pres. Dr. BENABADJY (Algeria); Sec.-Gen. Dr. ALI BOUJNAH (Tunisia).

MILITARY AFFAIRS

Arab Joint Defence Council (*see* chapter *The Arab League*).

Arab Permanent Military Commission (*see* chapter *The Arab League*).

PRESS, RADIO AND TELECOMMUNICATIONS

African Postal Union (*Union postale Africaine—UPAF*): 5 26th July St., Cairo, Egypt; f. 1961 to improve postal services between member states, to secure collaboration between them and to create other useful services. Mems.: Algeria, Egypt, Ghana, Guinea, Mali Morocco and Sudan.

Sec.-Gen. ENG. MOHAMED IBRAHIM SOBHI (Egypt). Publ. *African Postal Union Review* (quarterly).

OTHER REGIONAL ORGANIZATIONS

Arab States Broadcasting Union (*see* chapter *The Arab League*).

Arab Postal Union: 28 Adly Street, Cairo, Egypt; f. 1954; ancillary body of the Arab League; 20 member nations.

Dir. Dr. ANOUAR BAKIR (*see* chapter *The Arab League*).

Arab Telecommunications Union (*see* chapter *The Arab League*).

Federation of Arab News Agencies (*see* chapter *The Arab League*).

Union of African News Agencies (UANA): Algérie Presse Service, 7 blvd. de la République, Algiers, Algeria; f. 1963; meets annually; has proposed the creation of a Pan-African News Agency within aegis of OAU.

Pres. MUHAMMAD BOUZID (Algeria); Sec.-Gen. HAMED SGHAL (Tunisia).

United Arab Press: Cairo, Egypt; f. January 1967 to replace Middle East News Agency.

Dir. M. H. HEIKAL.

RELIGION

Agudath Israel World Organization (AIWO) (*Organisation mondiale Agudas Israel—OMAI*): Hacheruth Square, P.O.B. 326, Jerusalem; f. 1912 to protect the interests of Jewish communities and to further religious education, in the spirit of traditional Judaism; Mems.: affiliated organizations totalling 300,000 mems. in 21 countries.

Chair. Rabbi I. M. LEWIN (Israel); Sec.-Gen. ABRAHAM HIRSCH.

Bahá'í International Community: Office of UN Representative, 345 East 46th St., New York, N.Y. 10017, U.S.A.; f. 1844 in Persia to promote the teachings of the Bahá'í religion; to promulgate the unity of the human race; to work for the elimination of all forms of prejudice and for equality of men and women; to establish basic education schools for children; to maintain adult programmes in basic literacy and community training. Mems. in 69,500 centres in 330 countries and territories. Governing body: The Universal House of Justice, Bahá'í World Centre, Haifa, Israel.

Rep. to UN Dr. VICTOR DE ARAUJO (U.S.A.); Alternate Mrs. ANNAMARIE HONNOLD (U.S.A.). Publs. *The Bahá'í World* (quadrennial), *Bahá'í News* (monthly), publications in 571 languages and dialects.

International Council of Jewish Women: Beith Rothschild, 142 Hanassi Ave., Haifa, Israel; f. 1912 to promote friendly relations and understanding among Jewish women throughout the world. It exchanges information on community welfare activities, promotes volunteer leadership, sponsors field work in social welfare and fosters Jewish education. It has consultative status with UN, ECOSOC and with the UNICEF Executive Board. Mems.: 27 affiliates totalling 700,000 members in 21 countries.

Pres. Mrs. SHOSHANA HARELI (Israel); Sec. Mrs. LILY COHEN (Israel). Publ. *Newsletter* (3 a year; English, Spanish, Persian).

International Hebrew Christian Alliance, The: Shalom, Brockenhurst Rd., Ramsgate, Kent, England; f. 1925. Objects: to unite Hebrew Christians throughout the world, to maintain and extend the Christian faith among those of Hebrew birth and to help them and their families in need.

The Alliance is at work in Great Britain, America, Argentina, South Africa, Iran, Israel and many European countries.

Pres. HABIB YUSEFZADEH; Exec. Sec. and Treas. Rev. HARCOURT SAMUEL. Publ. *The Hebrew Christian* (quarterly).

International Muslim Union (*Union Musulmane Internationale*): Grande Mosquée de Paris, Place du Puits de l'Ermite, Paris 5e, France; f. 1968. Objects: to assist the needy, defend the Muslim community, spread the knowledge of Islamic civilization and to organize Islamic worship wherever necessary.

Sec.-Gen. Dr. BOUBAKEUR DALIL.

World Jewish Congress (*Congrès Juif Mondial*): 1 rue de Varembé, Geneva, Switzerland; f. 1936. It is a voluntary association of representative Jewish bodies, communities and organisations throughout the world. Aims: to assure the survival and to foster the unity of the Jewish people. Mems.: Jewish communities in over 63 countries.

Pres. Dr. N. GOLDMANN; Sec.-Gen. Dr. GERHART M. RIEGNER. Publs. *World Jewry* (bi-monthly, London), *L'Information Juive* (monthly, Paris), *Jewish Journal of Sociology* (bi-annual, London), *Gesher* (Hebrew quarterly, Israel).

World Sephardi Federation: New House, 67-68 Hatton Garden, London, EC1N 8JY; f. 1951 to strengthen the unity of Jewry and Judaism among Sephardim, to defend and foster religious and cultural activities of all Sephardi Communities and preserve their spiritual heritage, to provide moral and material assistance where necessary and to co-operate with other similar organizations. Mems.: 50 communities and organizations in 30 countries.

Sec. MICHAEL MARCHANT.

SCIENCE AND TECHNOLOGY

Inetrnational Meteorological Institute: Cairo; f. 1966 to carry out meteorological research and to provide training for Middle Eastern and African personnel engaged in meteorological work; the building of this project is being executed by World Meteorological Organization (WMO).

Mediterranean Social Sciences Research Council: American University of Beirut, Beirut, Lebanon; f. 1960 to promote research on problems concerning the social and economic development of the land and peoples of the Mediterranean Basin. Mems.: Research Centres and individuals in 19 countries.

Chair. Prof. D. J. DELIVANIS (Greece); Sec.-Gen. Prof. N. ZIADEH (Lebanon).

Middle Eastern Regional Radioisotope Centre for the Arab Countries: Sh. Malaeb El Gamaa, Dokki, Cairo, Egypt; f. 1963; trains specialists in the applications of radioisotopes, particularly in the medical, agricultural and industrial fields; conducts research in hydrology, tropical and subtropical diseases, fertilisers and entomology; promotes the use of radioisotopes in the Arab countries.

UNESCO Regional Centre for Science and Technology for the Arab States: 8 Sh. el Salamlik, Garden City, Cairo, Egypt (*see* chapter *United Nations in the Middle East and North Africa*).

SOCIAL SCIENCES

Congress of Arab and Islamic Studies (*Congrès des études arabes et islamiques*): c/o Prof. F. M. Pareja, Limite 5, Ciudad Universitaria, Madrid 3, Spain; f. 1962; Congresses: Cordoba 1962, Cambridge 1964, Ravello 1966, Coimbra 1968, Brussels 1970, Stockholm 1972. Next Congress: Göttingen 1974.

Sec.-Gen. Prof. F. M. PAREJA (Spain).

OTHER REGIONAL ORGANIZATIONS

European Union of Arabic and Islamic Scholars (*Union Européenne d'Arabisants et d'Islamisants*): Limite 5, Madrid 3, Spain; f. 1970 to organize a Congress of Arabic and Islamic Studies. Mems.: about 120.

Sec. Prof. F. M. PAREJA (Spain).

TRADE AND INDUSTRY

General Union of Chambers of Commerce, Industry and Agriculture for Arab Countries (*Union générale des chambres de commerce, industrie et agriculture des pays arabes*): P.O.B. 2837, Beirut, Lebanon; f. 1951 to foster Arab economic collaboration, to increase and improve production and to facilitate the exchange of technical information in Arab countries. Mems.: 18 Chambers of Commerce in 18 countries.

Pres. IBRAHIM K. KANOO (Bahrain); Gen. Sec. BURHAN DAJANI. Publ. *Arab Economic Report* (Arabic and English).

TRANSPORT AND TOURISM

Arab Association of Tourism and Travel Agents—A.A.T.T.A.: P.O.B. 5196, Beirut, Lebanon; f. 1952; groups Tourist and Travel Agents operating in the Arab world to promote tourism in the region. Mems.: 250.

Pres. MOHAMMED S. GIABER; Senior Vice-Pres. SALIM KHEIREDDIN; Gen. Man. SALIM ISSA. Publ. *Arab World Tourism* (monthly).

Arab Tourist Union: P.O.B 2354, Amman, Jordan; f. 1954. Mems.: Nat. Tourist orgs. of 18 Arab states, and 4 Assoc. mems. in private sector.

Pres. FAWZI BEN HAMIDAH (Tunisia). Publs. *Arab Tourism* (bi-monthly, Arabic), *Tourist Supplement* (bi-monthly, Arabic), *Press Bulletin* (bi-monthly, English).

Trans-Sahara Road Committee: c/o Ministry of Public Works, 135 rue Didouche Mourade, Algiers, Algeria; f. 1964; mems.: Algeria, Mali, Niger and Tunisia; this technical committee was formed to study the proposed trans-Saharan road route, the favoured scheme being a road from El Golea to Tamanrasset in Algeria branching towards Gao in Mali and In Gall in Niger. Tunisia will have access to the route via existing communications. The estimated cost for a tarred road 7 metres wide, 2,900 km. long, is U.S. $86.0 million and the road will take about eight years to build. The pre-feasibility study of the whole route has been completed under the auspices of the UN Development Programme.

PART THREE
Country Surveys

Afghanistan

PHYSICAL AND SOCIAL GEOGRAPHY

W. B. Fisher

Occupying an area of approximately 250,000 square miles (estimates range between 240,000 and 270,000 square miles) Afghanistan has the shape of a very irregular oval with its major axis running N.E.-S.W. and extending over roughly 700 miles, and the minor axis at right angles to this, covering about 350 miles. The country is in the main a highland mass lying mostly at an altitude of 4,000 ft. (1,200 metres) or more, but it presents a highly variable pattern of extremely high and irregular mountain ridges, some of which exceed 20,000 ft. (6,000 metres); ravines and broader valleys, parts of which are very fertile; and an outer expanse of undulating plateau, wide river basins, and lake sumps.

Politically, Afghanistan has two frontiers of major length: one on the north with the Turkmen, Uzbek and Tadzhik Republics of the U.S.S.R., the other (on the south and east) with Pakistan.

This frontier follows what was once termed the Durand Line (after the representative of British India, Sir Mortimer Durand who negotiated it in 1893 with the Ruler of Afghanistan). So long as the British occupied India, it was generally accepted as forming the Indo-Afghan frontier, but in 1947 with the recognition of Pakistan as a successor to the British, the Afghan government recalled that for much of the eighteenth century, Peshawar and other parts of the Indus Valley had formed part of a larger Afghan state, and were moreover occupied largely by Pathans, who are of closely similar ethnic character to many Afghans. Accordingly, the Durand Line frontier was denounced by Afghanistan, and claims were made that the territories as far as the line of the Indus, including Chitral, Swat, and Peshawar, and continuing as far as the Pathan areas of the North-west Frontier Province and Baluchistan, ought to be recognized as an autonomous state, "Pashtunistan" (from the root word "Pathan"). This remains a topic of dispute between Afghanistan and Pakistan.

There are shorter but no less significant frontiers on the west with Iran, and on the north-east with Kashmir and with China. This last was fully agreed only in 1963, and the precise location of others in the south and west has not been fully delimited: an indication of the extreme difficulties of terrain, and an explanation of the uncertainty regarding the actual area of Afghanistan. It is noteworthy that, in order to erect a "buffer" between the then competing Empires of Russia and India, under the Durand treaty of 1893 the Wakhan district, a narrow strip of land 200 miles long and under 10 miles wide in its narrowest part, was attached to Afghanistan. This strip controls the Baroghil pass over the Pamir, and avoids having a Russian-Indian joint frontier.

PHYSICAL FEATURES

The main typographical feature of Afghanistan is a complex of irregular highlands that is relatively broad and low in the west, and very much higher and also narrower towards the east. In this eastern part the mountains form a group of well-defined chains that are known by the general name of the Hindu Kush (Hindu destroyer), and are linked further eastward first to the Pamirs and then to the main Himalaya system. The Eastern Hindu Kush ranges form the southern defining limit of the Wakhan strip whilst a short distance to the north and east, a small but high ridge, the Little Pamir, forms the topographic link between the Hindu Kush and the main Pamir. From maximum heights of 20,000–24,000 ft. (6,000–7,000 metres) the peaks decline in altitude westwards, attaining 15,000–20,000 ft. (4,500–6,000 metres) in the zone close to Kabul. Further west still, the ridges are no more than 12,000–15,000 ft. (3,500–4,500 metres) and in the extreme west they open out rather like the digits of a hand, with the much lower Parapamisus ridges (proto-Pamir) forming the last member of the mountain complex. The various ridges are distinguished by separate names. The Hindu Kush, which has a general altitude of about 15,000 ft. (4,000 metres) with peaks 7,000–10,000 ft. higher still, is however narrow, and crossable by quite a number of passes, some of which are indirect and snow-bound for much of the year.

In geological structure, Afghanistan has close affinities both to Iran further west, and, as has just been stated, to the massive Himalayan system further east. Development of present-day land-forms has been greatly influenced by the existence of several large, stable masses of ancient rocks, which have acted as cores around which rock series of younger age first developed and were then closely wrapped as fold structures. Most important of these ancient massifs, or "shield" areas so far as Afghanistan is concerned, is the plateau of the Deccan, the effect of which was to "bunch" a series of tight folds in a double loop or garland on its northern side. In this way can be explained the existence of the "knot" or "bunch" of fold structures lying partly in Afghanistan, and comprising the Pamir which forms the eastern limb and the Hindu Kush that makes up the western segment of the "garland". The abrupt change of direction and swinging of the fold structures from an east-west to, in some places, a north-south direction are a direct result of the presence of the resistant mass of the Deccan. The fold ranges themselves are composed in part of sediments mainly laid down under water, and include limestones with some sandstones, and are of Cretaceous and later age, Eocene especially. Extensive heat and pressure in some regions have metamorphosed original series into schists and gneiss; and there has been much shattering and cracking of the rock generally, with the consequent development of fault-lines and overthrust zones. A further feature in much of Afghanistan has been a good deal of differential earth movement, uptilting, downwarping and local adjustment which make the region particularly susceptible to earth tremors, which occur frequently, usually on a small scale. Occasionally, however, a major disaster occurs, the latest being at Tashkent just north of Afghanistan in 1965.

As a consequence of frequent crustal disturbance, the rise of magma from the earth's interior has produced lava-flows, and minor volcanos. Most of these are in a stage of old age—being merely fissures from which emanate gas, steam and mud flows; and the presence of soft volcanic debris adds considerably in places to soil fertility.

As far as river drainage is concerned, Afghanistan forms a major watershed, from which rivers flow outward. The Amu Darya (Oxus) rises on the north side of the Hindu Kush and flows northwestwards into the U.S.S.R. Here, away from the mountains the presence of loess (a yellowish soil of high fertility) in small pockets offers scope for agiculture. The Hari Rud rises a short distance only from the Amu Darya, but flows westward through Herat to terminate in a salt, closed basin on the Iranian frontier. From the south and west of the Hindu Kush flow a number of streams that become tributaries of the Indus; and in the extreme south-west the Helmand river flows through to end like the Hari Rud in a closed basin that is partly within Iranian territory. The Helmand basin is of interest in that because of a curious balance in water-level at its lowest part, the river here reverses its flow seasonally, and remains for much of its length non-brackish instead of becoming progressively more saline, as is normal when there is no outlet to the sea. The Helmand basin thus offers distinct potential for agricultural improvement, and in fact schemes for irrigation are in process of development. But political difficulties (part of the lower basin is Iranian territory) and remoteness are inhibiting factors.

The areas of lower, and in the main more densely peopled areas occur either as a series of peripheral zones to north and south, or as a series of interior valleys and basins between the main mountain ridges of the centre. Largest of these areas is the piedmont lying on the northern flanks of the mountains, and dropping northwards in altitude to merge into the steppelands of Russian Central Asia. This is Bactria, a region of, in places, light yellowish loessic soils. An interior situation, shut off from the sea by mountains means that rainfall is deficient, and falls mainly over the mountains. Streams fed partly by mountain snow-melt straggle across the plain, to lose themselves in the sand, feed salt swamps, or in a few cases, join others to form larger rivers such as the Hari Rud. Much of Bactria thus consists of semi or full desert with sheets of sand and gravel in many places, with, nearer the mountains, outwash of larger, coarser scree. Given stable political conditions this area with its areas of highly fertile loess soils and moderate water supplies offers much scope for economic development. For long inhabited by pastoral nomads, and disputed politically between various claimants: Afghan, Iranian and Russian, this northern zone is now developing rapidly with irrigated cotton growing as a main element. Links with the U.S.S.R. are considerable, and the two chief towns of Herat in the west and Mazar-i-Sharif in the north have grown considerably in size over the past few years.

On the south, towards the east, is the Kabul basin, which is a relatively flat zone hemmed in closely by steep mountain ridges. Some distance away to the north-west, and reachable through two major passes is the narrower Vale of Bamian; whilst south-east of Kabul occurs another fertile lowland zone around Jellalabad. Here lower elevation and southerly situation produce warmer conditions, especially in winter, as compared with most of the rest of Afghanistan.

In the south-west, extending through Ghazni as far as Kandahar, there is another series of cultivated zones; but the extent of this piedmont area is much smaller than the corresponding one we have just described as Bactria. To the west, aridity, the price of declining altitude, increases, so the lowland passes into the desertic areas of Registan and the Dasht-i-Mayo. Registan has seasonal flushes of grass, which support relatively large numbers of pastoral nomads, who however, are becoming increasingly sedentarized following irrigation development on the Helmand and Arghandab rivers.

Two other regional units may be mentioned. South of the Parapamisus and Kuh-i-Baba mountain ranges are a number of parallel but lower massifs, with narrow valleys between. Here because of altitude there is relatively abundant rainfall, but owing to topography, the region is one of remoteness and difficulty. This is the Hazarat, so called from the name of the Hazara inhabitants; and it still remains despite a central position one of the least known and visited parts of the country. Another equally remote highland, this time located north-east of Kabul, is Nuristan, again high and mountainous, but well-wooded in places, and supporting a small population of cultivators and pastoralists who use the summer pastures of the high hills, and move to lower levels in winter.

CLIMATE

Climatically, Afghanistan demonstrates a very clear relationship with Iran and the Middle East, rather than with Monsoon Asia, in that it has an almost arid summer, a small amount of rainfall which is largely confined to the winter season, and considerable seasonal variation in temperature. The monsoonal condition of heavy summer rainfall does not occur, despite Afghanistan's nearness to India. Annual rainfall ranges from 4-6 in. (10-15 cm.) in the drier, lower areas of the west and north, to 10-15 in. (25-40 cm.) in the east; and on the highest mountains there is more still. Kabul, with an average of 13 in. per annum, is typical of conditions in the east, and Herat with 5 in. typical of the west. Almost all this falls in the period December to April, though there can be a very occasional downpour at other times, even in summer, when a rare damp monsoonal current penetrates from the Indian lowlands. Temperatures are best described as extreme. In July, the lowlands experience temperatures of 110°F., (43°C.) with 120° not uncommon—this is true of Jellalabad on the edge of the Indus lowlands. But the effects of altitude are important, and Kabul, at an elevation of 6,000 ft. does not often experience temperatures of over 100°F. (38°C.). Winter cold can be bitter, with minima of −10° to −15°F. (−22° to −26°C.) on the higher plateau areas; and as a result there are heavy blizzards in many mountain areas. The January mean at Kabul is 25°F. (−4°C.). Generally speaking, a seasonal temperature range of 80-100°F. is characteristic of many areas (cf. 26°F. for London). A further difficulty is the prevalence of strong winds, especially in the west, where a persistent and regular wind blows almost daily from June to September and affects especially the Sistan area of the lower Helmand basin, where it is known as the *Wind of 120 Days*.

With highly varied topography and climate, Afghanistan has a wide range of plant life—a good deal of which is not yet fully recorded. Conditions range from Arctic and Alpine type flora on the highest parts to salt-tolerant arid zone species in the deserts. Woodland occurs in a few areas, but much has been used for fuel in a country that has cold winters.

PEOPLE AND ACTIVITIES

The considerable variation in the types of terrain, and the considerable obstacles imposed by high mountains and deserts, have given rise to marked ethnic and cultural differences, so that heterogeneity in human populations is most characteristic. The Pathans live mainly in the centre, south and east of the country, and are probably numerically the largest group. The Ghilzais, also of the areas adjacent to Pakistan, are thought to be of Turkish origin, like the Uzbeks who live in the north, mainly in the Amu Darya lowlands. Another important element are the Tadzhiks or Parziwans who are of Persian origin, and in the opinion of some represent the earliest inhabitants of the country. Other groups, such as the Hazari (who are reputed to have come in as followers of Ghenghis Khan), and the Chahar Aimak may have Mongol ancestry, but they now speak Persian and the Hazari are Shi'a Muslims. In the north-east, the presence of fair-haired groups has suggested connection with Europe. Another possibly indigenous group of long-standing, is the Nuristani or Kafirs, now small in number. Most Afghans (the Hazari and Qizilbashi of Kabul excepted) are Sunni.

For long a difficult topography, extreme climate with a generally deficient rainfall, and political instability inhibited economic progress. Small communities lived by cultivation where water and soil were available, and there were relatively numerous pastoralists, mostly nomads, who formed an important section of the community. Even today, it is estimated that about 15 per cent of the population is nomadic, and tribal organization is strong.

Over the last few years developments have taken place on a significant scale. A series of three Five-Year Development Plans, 1956–72, gave encouragement to cereal cultivation (wheat, barley and maize), olive cultivation in the eastern provinces, sericulture in the north, and the improvement of commercial crops such as cotton and sugar beet. As part of a general attempt to improve animal husbandry fodder crops (alfalfa and lucerne) are given prominence, and improved strains of traditional fruit and vegetables (apricots, apples, peaches, melons, vines, squashes, potatoes, etc.) are replacing the older species in many areas.

The Third Five Year Plan (1967–72) has latterly encountered considerable difficulties due in the first place to deficient rainfall between 1968–71, amounting in many areas to severe drought over three years. This has led to economic disaster, not only for the 80 per cent of the total population that still lives directly by agriculture, but, as well, through restriction on water supplies and purchasing power for developing manufacturing activities. Soil deterioration has accelerated due to overuse in those areas where drought has been less severe. Moreover, deficiencies in organization held back development of necessary services: roads, utilities, education, health, etc. As a result, many objectives of the Plan were not realized; and the Fourth Plan, now inaugurated, aims at remedying defects and failures in infrastructure projects, and improving yields from existing agriculture and industry, rather than by introducing major new construction. By also attempting improvements in the administration sector it is hoped to tackle the fundamentals of national economic planning on a realistic basis rather than, as in the recent past, attempting to develop without adequate infrastructure and on overly theoretical lines.

Irrigation has developed markedly within the last ten years. The major scheme so far is in the Helmand basin where two storage dams and a series of distributary canals offer potential development for about a quarter of a million acres (100,000 hectares) of arid land. Irrigation development is also taking place on the Arghandab river in the same region. Other schemes are in existence near Jellalabad, and on the Amu Darya; and there is a much more ambitious scheme for this last river which will involve both extension of irrigation and large-scale generation of electric power, in co-operation with the U.S.S.R.

Because of Afghanistan's former location as a buffer between Russia and British India, railways approached from various sides, but none actually penetrated the country, and so Afghanistan is one of the few parts of the world still to be totally without railways. At the same time, the narrowness (despite the great height) of the mountain barrier as compared with the Himalayas, has made Afghanistan a traditional routeway between north and south, and at present, helped by various foreign agencies and governments, there is a programme for considerable road improvement and development. Given the difficulties of terrain, Afghanistan now possesses a reasonably good road system, with some very good sections. Air transport is also an important factor.

HISTORY
M. C. Gillett

It will be convenient to refer to Afghanistan throughout this essay, though the word (which means "The Country of the Afghans"—i.e. Pashtuns or Pathans) only goes back to 1747 and the name Afghan first appears in the tenth century. A better name would be "The Country of the Hindu Kush". For this range not only gives our area, where Central Asia, India and Persia meet, its special character but also helps to elucidate much of its history. The Hindu Kush forms a boundary between the nomadic and the settled lands: a boundary, but not a barrier. For at its eastern end are several practicable passes of the order of 10,000 feet above sea level and it can be turned at its western end near Herat. It serves as a backbone that encourages the formation of states astride itself. And it is the reservoir of the area: it is the winter snows in the Hindu Kush that provide the water for irrigation so vital to settled life in an area with an average annual precipitation of less than twelve inches. Further, the rivers rising in the Hindu Kush provide convenient routes of communication much frequented by traders and invaders during the ages when land transport predominated. In conjunction with the east-west ways along the Oxus valley and the passes through the Hindu Kush these routes explain why Afghanistan is at the centre of Professor Toynbee's *Central Asian Roundabout*. The valley of the Hari Rud turns the Hindu Kush to the west. The Helmand-Arghandab-Tarnak system leads from the frontiers of Persia to within a hundred miles of the headwaters of the Kabul river. And the line of the Kabul river provides the easiest access to the Indian sub-continent from the north and west. French excavations at Mundigak near Kandahar (virgin soil about 3,000 B.C.) suggest these routes were of importance already in prehistoric times; and they fitted into that great Eurasian caravan route sometimes called "The Silk Road". They were probably used by the Aryans, and certainly used by Alexander and by the Sakas, on their way to India. Though the Hindu Kush is now but a key to India it was formerly *the* key; and the holders of this key seldom failed to use it, lured on, often to the detriment of their interests in Afghanistan, by the great wealth of the sub-continent.

EARLY HISTORY

Afghanistan first appears in history during the reign of Darius I (6th century B.C.) not as a political entity, but divided among at least three of the Achaemenian satrap. It remained under the Achaemenians till the defeat of Darius III by Alexander at Guagamela in 331 B.C. After Darius's death a sort of national resistance to the Greeks developed in Afghanistan and Transoxiana.

Greeks: Alexander, Seleucids, Graeco-Bactrians

Alexander spent three years in and about Afghanistan pacifying and organizing the country, where he established five cities. He marched on India in 327 B.C. and did not return to Afghanistan. During the confused period that followed Alexander's death in 323 B.C. Afghanistan was at first controlled by Antigonus Cyclops but by 305 B.C. it had come into the hands of Seleucus, another of Alexander's generals. The main centre of power then lay to the west so the Seleucids tended to neglect their eastern territories. In 302 B.C. Seleucus himself ceded south-eastern Afghanistan to the Maurya emperor Chandragupta in exchange for the five hundred elephants that contributed to the important victory at Ipsus in the following year. Southeastern Afghanistan remained under Maurya control till that empire declined after the death of Asoka, the encourager of Buddhism. Seleucid preoccupation with the west encouraged their Satrap of Bactria, Diodotus, to declare himself independent of Antiochus II in about 255 B.C. Diodotus and the Graeco-Bactrian rulers who succeeded him (they were not all of his blood: three frequently inimical families of rulers are known) were tough, able men who were able to maintain their independence. And helped by the weakening of the Seleucid and Maurya empires they enlarged their kingdom till it extended from the Zarafshan to the Punjab. But their quarrels weakened them. The rise of Parthia cut them off from the west. And the lure of India was strong. So their guard on their nomadic frontier ultimately failed. Between 140 and 130 B.C. Bactria fell to the nomads, and the Kabul region and the rest of southern Afghanistan (Parthia had already occupied Herat and western Afghanistan) followed suit a century later. Greek influence persisted well into the Christian era, and petty kings of Greek descent probably continued to rule for at least as long in inaccessible places.

Kushans

Between 177 and 170 B.C. the nomadic Hsiungnu, or Huns (probably proto-Turk) inflicted two crushing defeats on the Yüehchih, a nomadic Indo-European people in what is now the Kansu-Ninghsia border area. The Yüehchih fled west driving before them the Saka tribes living astride the Alai mountains (another Indo-European people). What actually happened when the Greek kingdom of Bactria fell to the nomads is not clear. But we do know the Yüehchih ultimately occupied the Balkh region. And the Sakas turned the Hindu Kush to the west, occupied Seistan (Seistan is but a corruption of Sakasthan) and spread up the river system mentioned in paragraph one towards northern India. The chronology of this period is uncertain, but it was probably in the first century A.D. that the Kushans became the leading tribe in the Yüehchih confederacy. Under King Kujula Kadphises they moved south of the Hindu Kush, splitting the Sakas in two and driving part of them down into India. Under some able kings, prominent among whom was Kanishka, the Kushans built up an empire extending from the Oxus to Mathura (Muttra). They were an interesting people who developed a considerable degree of culture. They adapted Greek letters for writing the language they used in Afghanistan. The stability their empire afforded greatly facilitated trade along the "Silk Road" and its important feeder down to India at a time when only the Kushans and the Parthians lay between flourishing Han China and the Roman Empire. From Kanishka onwards the Kushan kings became patrons of Buddhism, probably from policy as much as from conviction, for the southern parts of their empire had been strongly Buddhist ever since Asoka's time. Under them Buddhism spread along the trade routes northwards across the Hindu Kush then eastwards through Central Asia towards China. The Kushan empire, with its capital at Peshawar, started to decline about the middle of the third century. The Sassanians, who replaced the Parthians in Persia in 226, came to control western Afghanistan (including Seistan) and, according to some, may even have exercised suzerainty over the later Kushans. And about the middle of the fifth century the Kushans were replaced in our area by the Kidarites (also of Yüehchih stock) who controlled the country south of the Oxus between Balkh and Merv.

Hephthalites

At the beginning of the fifth century High Asia was controlled by two powerful Turco-Mongol confederacies, both apparently under Mongol leadership. In the east were the Juanjuan; to the west, centred on the Altai, were the Hephthalites, who seem to have been always in some sort vassals of the Juanjuan. During the second quarter of the fifth century the Hephthalites (also known as "Huna" and "White Huns" though with little connection with Attila and his tribes) started to expand westwards. They occupied Soghdia, replaced the Kidarites in Bactria, and in 484 attacked Persia and killed the Sassanian King Firuz. Then, while continuing to harry Persia, they turned to the south-east, occupied Afghanistan and invaded north-west India. The Hephthalites remained nomadic and barbaric, destroyed much, and were particular enemies to Buddhism.

Tuchüeh

When the Juanjuan ruler Anakuei put a slight upon one of his vassals, Bumin, Chief of the Tuchüeh, or Turks, they revolted and, with the help of the Turkish rulers of north China (Wei dynasty), defeated the Juanjuan in 552. Bumin died in the year of this victory and the Turks divided into two: the Eastern Turks under Bumin's son; and the Western Turks under Bumin's able brother, Istämi. The two confederacies continued friendly for a while, but later were often at enmity. About 565 the Western Turks allied themselves with the Sassanians and smashed the Hephthalites, who disappeared as a political entity. Their territory was divided between the allies, roughly along the line of the Oxus, and Afghanistan became part of the Sassanian empire for some twenty years. Later the Turks split with the Sassanians (profits from the transit trade along the "Silk Road" contributed to the quarrel) and allied themselves with Byzantium. The Turks invaded Bactria in 558/9 and by 597/8 they controlled the whole of Afghanistan. Their power was at its peak in 630, when the celebrated Chinese pilgrim Hsüan Tsang passed through their territories. Many Turks adopted Buddhism, which the Hephthalites had failed to eradicate. And some Turks seem to have become partially sedentary in Afghanistan.

Chinese

Between 659 and 661 T'ang China, who had already defeated the Eastern Turks in 630, crushed the Western Turks. The Chinese took over the Turkish territories and started to set up an administration in them, which never had time to develop as the Tibetans occupied the Tarim basin for twenty-four years after 670 and thus cut China off from her westernmost dependencies.

THE COMING OF ISLAM

The Arabs, in their astonishing expansion, now enter our area. At the battle of Nehavend in 642 they completed the destruction of the Sassanians. In 651, they occupied Herat, and the following year they raided Balkh. Civil wars halted this Arab expansion for a time, but it was renewed early in the eighth century under Qutayba b. Muslim, the Ommayad Viceroy of Khorassan. The Western Turks never recovered from their defeat by the Chinese. The Eastern Turks had briefly revived their empire between about 683 and 743 but were never in a position to help their western congeners. And, though the Chinese had recaptured the Tarim basin by 694 and were able to start a forward policy again by 715 (the year of Qutayba's death), they suffered a crushing defeat on the Talas in July 751. So the rulers of Afghanistan, not all of whom were Turks, had no outside help in their resistance to the Arabs. They put up a tough struggle: parts of eastern Afghanistan were not converted to Islam till the ninth century, and the centre not till the beginning of the eleventh century. But ultimately the bulk of Afghanistan became part of the Abbassid Caliphate.

Tahirids, Saffarids and Samanids

By the time of the Abbassids the dilution of the Arab element in Islam by conquests and conversions was already marked. This dilution continued to increase; and the Abbassids came to rely more and more on mercenary armies chiefly composed of Turkish Ghulams, or slaves, rather than on Arabs. And with the decline of the Caliphate there was an increasing tendency for the formation of local dynasties owing but nominal allegiance to the Caliph. Such, in our area, were the Tahirids who ruled Khorassan for about fifty years from 820; the Saffarids from Seistan who overthrew the Tahirids in the second half of the ninth century and added Herat and Balkh to their dominions; and, most important, the Samanids who established their capital in Bokhara in 874, subjugated the Saffarids about 900, and at the height of their power controlled Transoxiana, the greater part of Persia, and much of Afghanistan. The Samanids were brought down by the Qarakhanid Turks in 999.

Ghaznavids

Under the Samanid, Abdalmalik I, a Turkish Ghulam called Alptegin was Captain of the Guard. By shrewd use of the political arts of the time he had made himself Governor of Khorassan and was in the way of becoming the most powerful man in the kingdom when the death of Abdalmalik and the accession of Mansur I ruined his prospects. In 962 he fled to Ghazni, displaced the local ruler, became himself almost independent, and founded the important Ghaznavid dynasty which lasted for 200 years. The greatest Ghaznavid was Mahmud who, building on the foundations laid by his grandfather Alptegin and his father Sabuktegin (977-997), extended his sway till he controlled much of Persia, most of Afghanistan, and northern India. Actuated partly by religious zeal and partly by the desire for loot Mahmud aimed at an annual winter campaign in India, into which he made seventeen expeditions. Towards the north he was less successful but though he was unable to take Transoxiana from the Qarakhanids he managed to hold his own against them and against the Ghuzz. Mahmud adopted the title of Sultan. His court was a brilliant one, frequented by people such as Firdausi, the poet, and Al Biruni, the polymath. Mahmud died in 1030. His successors lacked his abilities and they were under constant pressure from the Seljuks, a tribe of the Ghuzz, to whom the Ghaznavids ultimately became tributary. In 1152 Sultan Bahram Shah was defeated by Alauddin of Ghor, who sacked Ghazni. And Bahram Shah's son Kusru, the last of the Ghaznavids to rule in Afghanistan, was forced down to India by the Ghuzz.

Seljuks

Towards the end of the tenth century a nomadic Turkish people, the Oghuz or Ghuzz, appear in Transoxiana, moving slowly towards the south and west and playing their part in the fighting that accompanied the decline of the Samanids. The bulk of them remained nomadic, as their descendants, the Turcomans, have remained to this day. But one clan, the Seljuks, appreciated the advantages of civilization, became orthodox muslims and ultimately became sedentary. Under Toghrul Beg the senior branch of the Seljuks took Khorassan from the Ghaznavids between 1038 and 1040, when they defeated Masud near Merv. Toghrul Beg's brother occupied Khwarezm. By the middle of the century the Seljuks were the masters of most of Persia; and in 1058 Toghrul Beg displaced the Shi'a Buyids to become Temporal Vicar of the Abbassid Caliph. With the help of an able Persian Vizier known as Nizam-ul-Mulk (the friend of Omar Khayyam) Toghrul Beg's two successors Alp Arslan (1063-72) and Malik Shah (1072-92) were able to hold onto their possessions in Persia and to deal with the traditional fissiparous tendencies of their people. Malik Shah took Balkh from the Ghaznavids. His son, Sultan Sinjar, who became ruler of Khorassan in 1095, played an important part in our area and in 1117 reduced the Ghaznavids to vassalage. He died in 1157, after trouble with the untamed Ghuzz in the Balkh area, without being able to establish a stable Turco-Persian kingdom.

Ghorids

The hill-country up the Hari Rud from Herat, known as Ghor, for long remained in isolation because of its poverty and difficulty of access. The Achaemenians seem to have penetrated there. And Masud, while Governor of Khorassan under his father Mahmud of Ghazni, undertook the systematic reduction of the area to vassalage, and its conversion. At that time the country was divided among a number of *Maliks*, or petty kings. But by the end of the eleventh century a central authority had developed and in 1099 Masud III of Ghazni was able to recognize one Izzuddin Hussain as Prince of Ghor. Izzuddin, who died about the middle of the twelfth century, managed to balance fairly successfully the often conflicting claims of his Ghaznavid suzerains and the powerful Seljuks in Khorassan. His son and successor, Saifuddin Suri, delegated some of his power to two half-brothers. Fakhruddin got Bamian where he founded the Shanshabanid dynasty, which lasted till the Mongol invasion; and Qutbuddin got the hill country. Some family quarrel drove Qutbuddin down to Ghazni where he was poisoned by Sultan Bahram Shah in 1146. Saifuddin marched on Ghazni to avenge his brother, took the town and held it for a couple of years, when he assumed the title of *Sultan*. But in 1149 Bahram Shah drove him out of Ghazni, captured him and ignominiously executed him. A fourth brother died on the way to attack Ghazni. It was left to the fifth brother, Alauddin Hussein (1149-56), to rout Bahram Shah at Taginabad on the Helmand and to sack Ghazni, which earned him the epiteth of *Jahansoz*, or *World Burner*. Alauddin did not hold Ghazni, and Bahram Shah reoccupied it till his death. Alauddin was less successful against the Seljuks, by whom he was defeated in 1152 and held prisoner a while. His son and successor was killed in 1163 near Merv while attacking the Ghuzz and the army gave allegiance to his nephew Ghiyasuddin. This was the Ghiyasuddin who built the beautiful minaret near Jam. Closely supported by his brother Muizuddin (also known as Mohammed Ghori) Ghiyasuddin brought Ghor to its brief period of glory, with an empire stretching from Herat to Ajmir in India. Muizuddin, who had been made Sultan of Ghazni on driving the Ghuzz out of that town in 1173, proved unequal to ruling alone after Ghiyasuddin died in 1203. In 1204 he was defeated by the Khwarezm Shah near Andkhui. And when he was assassinated in 1206 while returning from dealing with a revolt in the Punjab the Ghorid empire collapsed. The Indian territories became independent, and the rest of the kingdom was incorporated in the Khwarezmian empire between 1206 and 1215.

Khwarezm Shahs

The rulers of the Khiva oasis long made use of the title of Khwarezm Shah, which was later appropriated by the Seljuk governors of Khorassan. Shah Atsiz (1127/8-56), son of a Seljuk governor of Khorassan and grandson of a Turkish slave, tried to declare his independence of the Seljuks but was defeated by Sinjar in 1138. In 1141 the Qarakhitai defeated Sinjar and invaded Khwarezm. These Qarakhitai were a strongly sinicized Mongol *élite* who had been driven from Peking some twenty years before by a revolt of their vassals, the Tungusic Jurchen. They fled westward and founded a new state at the expense of the Qarakhanid Turks of Transoxiana and Sinkiang. They were not muslims. Khwarezm remained tributary to the Qarakhitai till the reign of Shah Atsiz's grandson, Alauddin Mohammed (1200-20); and it was with the help of his overlords that he defeated Muizuddin, as related above. Between 1207 and 1210 this Muhammad of Khwarezm threw off the yoke of the Qarakhitai, whose *Gurkhan*, or ruler, Yeh-Liu Ch'e-Lu-Ku was having trouble with rebellion in the east. The Khwarezm Shahs had got control of Khorassan towards the end of the twelfth century, occupied Transoxiana after defeating the Qarakhitai, and by taking Ghazni in 1215-16 completed their occupation of Afghanistan. So by 1217 Muhammad of Khwarezm seemed to have effected the task in which Sinjar had failed: the creation of a strong Turco-Persian state in eastern Islam. But the strength of this empire was illusory. It was based on locally-powerful landowners and a mercenary army, and depended for its strength chiefly on the character of the ruler. Mohammed of Khwarezm was unequal to his task. He offended Genghiz Khan in 1218, and by the time he died, two years later, a broken-hearted fugitive, his empire had disintegrated.

Mongols

Genghiz Khan, the great Mongol leader, had consolidated his power over Mongolia by 1206 and then started to expand. By 1216 he had defeated the Qarakhitai in what is now Sinkiang so his territories marched with those of the Khwarezm Shah. Genghiz Khan, seemingly impressed by the apparent strength of the Khwarezm Shah, was willing to enter into commercial and diplomatic relations. But in 1218 the Khwarezmian governor of Otrar pillaged a Mongol caravan and massacred its muslim merchants and the Mongol envoy accompanying it. The Khwarezm Shah refused any reparation so the following year Genghiz Khan attacked. The Khwarezmians put up little effective resistance, though Mohammed's son Jalaluddin did inflict two defeats on the Mongols in Afghanistan before being finally defeated himself. By 1222 Afghanistan was in Mongol hands. The towns were destroyed, the urban population massacred, the dams on the Helmand wrecked, and the country became a sort of no-man's-land without any proper government. It took one hundred and fifty years before Afghanistan even started to recover from these disasters. Some sort of administration was set up in Möngkä's reign (1251-59) when Afghanistan was divided, the western parts going to the Ilkhans of Persia and the eastern parts forming part of the Jaghatai Khanate. Afghanistan further suffered in the Mongol dynastic wars when the Ilkhans supported the Great Khan Kublai while the Jaghataids did not.

Karts

In 1245 one Shamsuddin Kart, related on his mother's side to Ghiyasuddin of Ghor, inherited the rulership of Ghor, which had suffered less from the Mongols than the rest of Afghanistan. In 1251 he was invested by Möngkä with the province of Herat under the suzerainty of the Ilkhan Hülägü. Shamsuddin laid such solid foundations during his reign of twenty-five years that, despite many difficulties, the Kart dynasty for one hundred and thirty years ruled from Herat over a territory that at its greatest extent comprised western Afghanistan and much of Khorassan.

Timurids

Eastern Afghanistan, as we have seen, formed part of the Ulus of the Mongol prince Jaghatai. When, at the beginning of the fourteenth century, the Jaghatai Khan, Kebek, discovered the delights of urban life in Transoxiana and his successor adopted Islam the Khanate was split in two: in the east Mogholistan, where the Mongols continued their nomadic traditions, and Transoxiana in the west, where the ancient Turkish nobility, notably the Amir Qazghan, held the real power. From this nobility there arose the Barlas Turk known as Tamerlane. By 1365 he had secured control of Transoxiana from the Jaghataids and by 1370 he controlled eastern Afghanistan. For ten years Tamerlane was preoccupied elsewhere but in 1381 he took Herat from the Karts and in the next three years he completed his control over Afghanistan including Seistan. Most of Tamerlane's astonishing career lies outside the scope of this note. He died in 1405 and by 1407 his fourth son Shah Rukh emerged victor from the struggle for succession and for forty years ruled from Herat over the bulk of the Timurid empire—west Persia had been lost to the Black Sheep Turcomans—either directly, or as suzerain over his nephews. Timurid decline began under Ulugh Beg, Shah Rukh's scholarly son, who was murdered by his son in 1449, when the Timurid territories were under serious threat from the Uzbegs. These were a predominantly Turkish horde under Mongol leadership who had started moving southwards in 1428. Within twenty years the Timurid empire had disintegrated under pressure from the Uzbegs in the north and the White Sheep Turcomans in the west. All that remained was Khorassan and parts of western Afghanistan ruled by Hussain Baiqara from Herat till his death in 1507. Hussain Baiqara's court was of great intellectual and artistic brilliance, but he was little of a statesman. His son, the last Afghan Timurid, was driven from Herat by the Uzbegs in 1507.

Safavids, Mughals, Uzbegs

For the next two hundred years the history of Afghanistan is the arid and confusing story of struggles of the Safavids with the Uzbegs for Khorassan and Herat and with the Mughals for Kandahar. The Safavids were a national dynasty that arose in Persia at the beginning of the sixteenth century. The Mughal empire was founded by that fascinating character Babur, Timurid prince of Ferghana who had been driven out of his patrimony by the Uzbegs. He was unable to persuade Hussain Baiqara to join him against the Uzbegs. But in 1502 he occupied Kabul (where he is buried), in 1522 he took Kandahar, and at the battle of Panipat in 1526 he laid the foundation of the Mughal empire.

MODERN HISTORY

Between 1708 and 1730 occurred the first, though brief, emergence of the Pathans as a political power when the Ghilzai Mir Wais revolted from the declining Safavids and for a short time he and his successors ruled Persia itself.

Nadir Shah of Persia

The Safavids were helped against the Ghilzais by Nadir Kuli Khan, a bandit chief, who proclaimed himself ruler of Persia in 1736. Within two years he had extended his rule over southern Afghanistan. In 1739 he carried out his great raid into India and sacked Delhi. And in 1740 he took northern Afghanistan from the Uzbeg ruler of Bokhara. He was assassinated in 1747.

Durranis

Sadozais. Unlike the Safavids, Nadir Shah encouraged Afghans in his service. In the confusion following his assassination an Afghan of the Sadozai clan (the Khan Khel, or Royal Clan) of the important Abdal tribe rallied his countrymen and led them back to Kandahar. Here the chiefs elected him King with the style of Dur-i-Duran (Pearl of the Age), from which the Abdals are now known as Durranis. This Ahmed Shah was a very capable man and created the Afghanistan we now know. His dominions included Afghanistan, Kashmir and north-west India, and Khorassan, Sind and Baluchistan became tributary to him. He undertook regular winter campaigns into India but, though he smashed the Marathas at Panipat in 1761, they brought him little permanent extension of territory, and he met with increasing trouble from the Sikhs. On Ahmed Shah's death he was succeeded by his son Timur who during a reign of twenty years was able to hold the territories he had inherited and who moved the capital from Kandahar to Kabul. But he left more than twenty sons, whose unedifying struggle for the throne brought about the dissolution of the Sadozai kingdom. Zaman, Mahmud, Shuja-Ul-Mulk, and again Mahmud occupied the throne in succession. The Uzbeg north and much other territory fell away from the Sadozais. Mahmud acquired the throne a second time with the help of Fatteh Khan, leader of another important clan, the Barakzais (or Mohammedzais). When Mahmud and his son Zaman barbarously murdered Fatteh Khan his brothers united and drove the Sadozais to Herat, where Sadozai rule came to an end with the death of Kamran in 1842.

Barakzais (Mohammedzais). When the Sadozais were driven west in 1818 Dost Mohammed, youngest of the twenty-one Barakzai brothers, was allotted Ghazni, to which he soon added Kabul. His position was difficult. His brothers were not readily submissive. The Sikhs took Peshawar in 1823. And the British, who had become the leading power in a still nominally Mughal India were inevitably interested in Afghanistan, the key to India. This interest led to the First Afghan War (1838–42) when the British thought they could best secure their northwestern approaches against the Russian threat by replacing Dost Mohammed by the Sadozai, Shuja-ul-Mulk, on the throne of Kabul. The project was ill-conceived, ended in a major disaster, and left an understandable legacy of bitterness. When the British evacuated Afghanistan in 1842 they released the Dost, who returned to Kabul and set about extending his control over the whole country. He died at Herat in 1863 soon after completing his task by taking the town. The Dost appealed particularly to the Afghans, who call him Amir-i-Kabir (The Great Amir). For the last eighteen years of his reign he maintained friendship with the Government of India. He nominated his third son, Shere Ali, to succeed him. The two older brothers, and Abdurrahman, son of the eldest brother, did not accept this and it was not till 1868 that Shere Ali was secure.

At first he continued his father's old policy of friendship with Britain, but as time went on a coolness developed and in 1878 the Second Afghan War started. The underlying cause was again British fear of Russian intentions. The actual crisis came when the Afghans refused to accept a British mission but publicly accepted a Russian one. Shere Ali fled before the invaders and died in Mazar in February 1879. In May his son and acknowledged successor, Yakub, signed the Treaty of Gandamak, which gave the British most of what they wanted. But when the envoy whom Yakub had agreed to accept was massacred together with his escort, the British had to return. When they occupied Kabul in November Yakub gave himself up. Though British arms were generally successful, despite the Maiwand disaster (27 July 1880), the political situation was unsatisfactory, particularly after a change of ministry in London led to the abandonment of the Forward Policy. So when Shere Ali's nephew Abdurrahman returned from exile early in 1880 the British took a gamble (which succeeded) and recognized him as Amir of Kabul.

The British evacuated Kabul early in 1881. They, wisely, no longer insisted on a resident envoy in Afghanistan; but they gained some territory (including the Khyber Pass) and agreed to help the Amir against unprovoked foreign aggression provided he followed their advice on foreign policy. After the British left Abdurrahman spent ten years imposing a despotic centralized government on Afghanistan. In 1895 he occupied, and forcibly converted, Nuristan. Abdurrahman thought Afghanistan's interests best served by loyal friendship with Britain even though this led to certain difficulties with Russia. By the time he died in 1901 the boundaries of modern Afghanistan were largely settled and partially demarcated. Amir Habibullah succeeded his father without any civil war. During his reign Anglo-Russian tension over Afghanistan was lessened as part of a wider diplomatic settlement. But he had to face the complications caused by the First World War. Habibullah was assassinated in 1919, being succeeded after a brief struggle, by his third son Amanullah, one of whose first acts was an abortive attack on India. But by the peace treaty of August 1919 freedom of action in foreign affairs was restored to Afghanistan, which entered into diplomatic relations with several countries, including the U.S.S.R. and Britain in 1921. Amanullah was an erratic character and his precipitate zeal for reform alienated powerful tribes and religious leaders. In May 1929 he fled the country. Kabul was briefly held by a Tadzhik bandit leader known as Bachha-i-Saqao.

Mohammedzai (Yahya Khel). In October, 1929, Nadir Khan, a cousin of Amanullah and a former Minister of War, returned from exile and with the help of his equally able brothers Hashim Khan, Shah Wali Khan and Mahmud Khan (*the Musahiban Brothers*) defeated the Bachha and occupied Kabul. He was soon elected as King Nadir Shah. He was making good progress towards restoring conditions in Afghanistan when he was assassinated in 1933 and was succeeded by his son, the present king, H.M. Mohammed Zahir Shah, the second Durrani to ascend the throne without any civil war. Down to the end of the Second World War King Zahir Shah had the benefit of a wise and experienced Prime Minister in his uncle, Sardar Hashim Khan. The next Prime Minister Sardar Shah Mahmud, for all his ability and integrity was not at home in the changed situation after the war, marked by the British abdication in India and the emergence of the two super-powers, the U.S.S.R., which has a long common frontier with Afghanistan, and the U.S.A., half the world away. At this time the royal family was still effectively the ruling authority in Afghanistan, and the democratic institutions laid down in Nadir Shah's constitution were chiefly consultative. The younger members of the royal family thought that Shah Mahmud was not dealing with Afghanistan's two major problems forcibly enough.

These men were part of the first generation of Afghans to have received some of their education in the west. By the autumn of 1953 they had generated sufficient support within the family to secure the resignation of Shah Mahmud and his replacement by his nephew, Sardar Daud. Internally Daud's administration was less liberal than its predecessor. It kept a firm grip on the country and had little trouble except for some tribal disturbances in the Khost area and a nasty, but short-lived riot in Kandahar. The important problem of modernization was attacked with energy and success. A Ministry of Planning was set up, with Daud holding the portfolio, and a series of Five-Year Plans was initiated. Much of the finance for the Plans came from abroad. Soon after the Flag Incident (*see below*) the U.S.S.R. made a loan of U.S. $10 million, and the U.S.A. and other powers were not long in following this example. Under the Plans due attention was paid to social services, including education. And in 1959 Daud was successful in abolishing the compulsory veiling of women in public. In foreign affairs Daud had his younger brother Sardar Naim as Foreign Minister, who pursued an active and generally successful policy. Diplomatic relations were entered into with many countries and full use was made of the facilities of the United Nations. Politically Afghanistan voted with the muslim members of the Afro-Asian bloc. A UN Technical Assistance Mission was also accepted. But the administration failed to solve the most immediate of its foreign problems, that of the Pathan tribes in Pakistan, which had been separated from Afghanistan during the nineteenth century, first by Sikh then by British action, but who remain of great interest to the predominantly Pathan Government of Afghanistan. When the sub-continent was partitioned the Afghans resented the Pathans there being given the sole choice of acceding to either India or Pakistan. Instead of trying to solve the problem by co-operation with Pakistan, the viability of which they then doubted, the Afghan Government encouraged a latent irredentism and pressed for the establishment of a quasi-independent area, or Pashtunistan. Daud was an ardent supporter of this policy. In 1955 the Flag Incident occurred, when Afghan mobs attacked the Pakistani Embassy and Consulates. This nearly brought down the Daud administration; but the Afghans apologized and relations were patched up. The Pashtunistan Campaign continued, causing an increasing deterioration in Afghan-Pakistan relations and coolness between Afghanistan and the West. One result of this was that the U.S.A. could not help modernize the Afghan armed forces, which had to rely on Soviet help after 1955. The last step was when Afghanistan broke off diplomatic relations with Pakistan in September 1961.

The economic and fiscal results of this break were disastrous and led to the fall of the Daud administration in March 1963. The new Prime Minister, Dr. Yusuf, was not only not a member of the royal family, he was not even a Pathan. His first administration was generally well-received. Its chief achievement was the promulgation of a new, and remarkably liberal, constitution on October 1st, 1964. It also made possible a resumption of relations with Pakistan. Dr. Yusuf's second administration, elected under the new constitution, was not so successful. There were troubles, including student riots in Kabul, which led to his resignation. He was replaced by Mr. Maiwandwal, a Pathan. In 1968 Mr. Maiwandwal resigned on grounds of ill-health and was succeeded by Mr. Nur Ahmed Etemadi, another Pathan and connected with the Royal Family. There has been considerable progress in modernization. In this Afghanistan has been helped by substantial aid from both Communist countries and the West.

Political development has inevitably been slower. For democratic rights granted from above are never so easy to work as those won from below, particularly in a country where scarcely half the population has any tradition of the public discussion of public affairs. The Pathans have their *Jirgas* where such discussions take place; the other peoples are accustomed to live under authority. The result of this has been that the three Prime Ministers since Sardar Daud have all been administrators rather than politicians, while the elected legislators have tended to be critical rather than constructive. And so far no political parties have been formed, as permitted by the 1964 Constitution, though Mr. Maiwandwal was on the way to creating a "tail", rather than a political party as we understand it, when he retired. Ever since the fall of Dr. Yusuf's administration students have been very conscious of their political power: this led to the University and colleges being closed for a while during 1969. One important step forward has been made. The Supreme Court, envisaged in the 1964 Constitution and intended primarily to administer secular law rather than the muslim *shariat* has now been set up. Elections were held in October 1969, for seats to the House of the People and for one third of the seats in the House of Elders.

Events since October 1969

(*by the Editor of* The Middle East and North Africa)

After the 1969 elections, in which all candidates stood as Independents and represented various regional interests, a new government was formed with Nur Ahmed Etemadi again Prime Minister. His government experienced great difficulty in having Bills passed by Parliament, and he resigned in May 1971 when a majority of the members of Parliament had threatened to pass a vote of no confidence in him.

In June 1971 Dr. Abdul Zahir, a former President of the House of the People and Minister of Health, was appointed Prime Minister. The Government continued to maintain good relations with both Britain and the U.S.S.R., with the King and Dr. Shafiq (Foreign Minister) visiting Britain in December 1971, and Dr. Zahir visiting Moscow in March 1972.

During 1972 the serious drought which had taken place since 1970 in central and northern Afghanistan, caused difficulties for the Government. In December 1972 a majority of the House of the People expressed a lack of confidence in Dr. Zahir for allegedly failing to deal with the resultant famine promptly. He was therefore forced to resign, and was succeeded by the former Foreign Minister, Dr. Musa Shafiq. In a coup in Kabul on July 17th, 1973, Sardar Daud ousted his cousin and brother-in-law, King Mohammed Zahir Shah, and proclaimed a republic.

ECONOMIC SURVEY

Arthur Paul

About 18 million people live in the Kingdom of Afghanistan. A full census of the population has yet to be completed, but the round figure cited is one that is based on official estimates. These indicate that from 1966 to 1971 the population increased from 15.5 to 17.5 million. The calculations used for these estimates assume an annual rate of increase of 2.3 per cent.

Of the total population, 85 per cent live in rural areas. Rural migration is augmenting the natural increase in population in urban areas so that this percentage may soon change. Nearly 70 per cent of the people live in villages scattered throughout the mountain or desert countryside. They are too remote from the urban centres to take much part in the market economy. This 70 per cent includes about 2,800,000 Kuchis, many of whom are nomads.

Kabul, the capital city, with a rapidly increasing population that has reached almost 500,000, is the dominant financial and commercial centre of the country. Other large cities are Herat, a trading centre near the Iranian border, with a population of 104,000 people and Kandahar, in the wool and fruit producing area of the south-west, with 130,000 inhabitants. The smaller provincial centres include Mazar-i-Sharif, in the northern karakul country where natural gas has recently been found, Kunduz and Pul-i-Kumri in the cotton country, and Jalalabad in the east. Only in recent years have these and other urban centres been linked to each other and with the capital city by adequate transportation and communication systems. A more unified national economy is now emerging from what had been a group of relatively isolated trading centres located in provincial areas largely devoted to agriculture carried on at close to a subsistence level. These areas were, nevertheless, nearly self-sufficient.

Afghanistan's economy has in the past been based almost entirely on agricultural production. Probably two-thirds of the agricultural production still does not enter the market economy. Of the other third, roughly half is sold for urban consumption and the other half for export. The mainstays of the economy and the chief earners of foreign exchange are still the traditional products of Afghanistan: the production of wool and of karakul skins obtained from a unique breed of sheep that graze in the northern provinces, and the cultivation of cotton. Dried fruit and hand-woven carpets, are also important factors in the Afghan economy.

Industrial production in the modern sense started in Afghanistan with the establishment of a cotton textile plant in 1934. This industry expanded rapidly and is today the largest in the country. It was followed by the building of wool factories, sugar refineries, cement plants, and other processing industries. Engineering industries are small and relatively new. Excluding handicrafts and utilities, industrial production accounts for only about 5 per cent of the total production of the country.

Although the existence of large mineral resources has been known for many years, it is only recently that economic exploitation of some of these resources has become possible. This is due to the discovery of natural gas in the northern part of Afghanistan and to the building of facilities for making use of the large reserves of this new source of energy. The export of natural gas started in 1967 and shipments through a pipeline to the U.S.S.R. accounted for nearly 15 per cent of the country's total export earnings in 1969/70.

Sufficient statistical data are not available to make more than rough estimates of the gross domestic product (G.D.P.) of Afghanistan. Two separate studies for the year 1959 produced estimates varying from Afs. 28,000 million to 39,000 million. The most recent comparable information furnished by Afghan authorities is that the G.N.P. (gross national product) for the year 1970–71 was the equivalent of U.S. $1,500 million at the official exchange rate of Afs. 45 to U.S. $1. During this period the exchange rate in the free market continuously exceeded Afs. 80 to the U.S. dollar. Using the above extimate and converting the figure at the official exchange rate, per capita income in 1971 would be about U.S. $106.

A rough estimate of the rate of growth of output of the Afghan economy for the period 1967 to 1970 is that it averaged less than 3 per cent per annum.

AGRICULTURE

In past years Afghanistan produced enough food to fill the needs of its own people and to supply substantial amounts, particularly of fresh and dried fruits, to the Indian sub-continent. But in recent years, the population has grown at a more rapid rate than food production, so that it became necessary to import large quantities of wheat, sugar and vegetable oils. Some shifting in the use of land from wheat to cotton has contributed to this change in the pattern of agricultural production.

Of the total land area, which is 64.7 million hectares, only 22 per cent, or 14 million hectares, is suitable for cultivation. Of this, 7.8 million hectares are today considered crop land, 6.0 million hectares are irrigable, but only 60 per cent of this irrigable land is actually cropped because of lack of water. Some of the non-irrigable crop land is dry farmed, but not all of it.

Grain Crops

Grains are the most important crops. Estimates of production (in metric tons) for 1971–72 were: wheat, 1,900,000 tons; maize, 670,000 tons; barley, 355,000 tons; and rice 350,000 tons. The wheat crop has varied by large amounts from year to year. This is partly due to periodic recurrences of rust damage and to the shifting of land to cotton. The low yields of wheat obtained in Afghanistan are attributable to a steady reduction in soil fertility and to the primitive methods of cultivation that have been used throughout the country. In recent years, the introduction of improved seeds and the use of chemical fertilizers have increased the yields of wheat and other crops in some areas. 1971–72 was a year of drought so that it was necessary to import 226,000 tons of wheat.

Cotton

Cotton is a major crop in the northern provinces, but in recent years its cultivation has commenced in the Helmand Valley and near Herat. A well planned and intensive effort to encourage cotton cultivation was very effective during the period of 1962-1965. This resulted in a doubling of the production of raw cotton in a remarkably short time. It rose from 52,000 tons in 1961 to 110,000 tons in 1963. But ginning capacity became a bottleneck; furthermore, diseases and seed degeneracy were encountered. Added to these problems was the urgent need for wheat created by the shift in land use. The combination of these factors caused a falling off in the production of cotton, which dropped back to 55,000 tons by 1967. A new cotton programme has recouped a small part of the former gains. The production of seed cotton in 1971–72 reached 63,700 tons.

More than half of Afghanistan's ginned cotton is exported, with the largest shipments going, under barter contracts, to the U.S.S.R.

Other Crops

The estimated production of other important crops in 1971–72 was: sugar beet, 60,000 tons; sugar cane, 50,000 tons; and vegetable oil seeds (excluding cotton seeds) 55,000 tons. None of these crops was sufficient to meet the needs of the country, so that substantial amounts of sugar and vegetable oils were imported.

The climate of Afghanistan is very favourable for the production of a wide variety of fruits. Grapes are the most important of the fruits and account for more than half of the estimated total of 650,000 tons of fruits produced in 1971–72. Afghan fruits are exported in both the fresh and dried states. Traditionally India and Pakistan were the markets for these goods, but shipments now go to the U.S.S.R. and China, and more recently to Germany. The installation of modern facilities for cleaning and packing raisins has made it possible for Afghanistan's dried fruits to enter the European market.

Vegetable production has been neglected in the past, but the use of new seeds and better methods of cultivation are increasing the level of production, which was estimated at 725,000 tons in 1971–72. With the installation of new facilities for handling vegetables, including canning and cold storage plants, vegetable crops will be more important in the future and may even enter the European market.

Afghan melons are famous for their flavour, but the ratio of weight to value and the hazards of spoilage in transit make it impossible to export them except to nearby Pakistan. Pomegranates are also an important crop. The use of concentrated pomegranate juice as a blend in soft drinks is an interesting new export possibility. Pistachios and almonds grow in widely scattered areas and substantial quantities are exported.

Livestock

Two of Afghanistan's leading exports, karakul skins and wool, depend on the raising of sheep. The sale of karakul skins to European and American buyers alone accounts for a large part of the convertible foreign exchange earnings of the country. Karakul, which is more popularly known as Persian lamb, is widely used in the manufacture of fur coats and other garments. Afghan skins generally command a higher price than competing products, which come from South West Africa and the U.S.S.R. The number of karakul sheep is estimated to be 6.8 million, all located in the northern provinces. In recent years the foreign exchange obtained from the export of karakul skins has ranged from U.S. $10 million to U.S. $16 million annually. This industry is very important to the Afghan economy but it is not expanding; in fact, considerable efforts are nedeed to maintain the present volume. In 1970–71 export sales amounted to U.S. $13.2 million.

The number of sheep in Afghanistan, excluding the karakul flock, was estimated in 1971 to be roughly 10 million, a considerable decline due to recent periods of drought. Sheep are the main source of meat for the country. and they produce enough wool to export from 5,000 to 6,000 tons annually, most of which is sent to the U.S.S.R. under barter agreements.

To help make up a deficiency of protein in the Afghan diet, there are important projects for increasing poultry production which is today quite small. A fisheries programme has also been started. In addition, great efforts are being made to improve the local breeds of cattle in order to increase the very low output of dairy products.

A basic problem of the livestock industries of Afghanistan is the limited amount of pasture land and the difficulties which over-grazing causes. The demand for meat and dairy products is expanding much more rapidly than the supply of these products.

MINERAL RESOURCES

Exploratory drilling carried on with Soviet assistance has located supplies of petroleum in the northern provinces, but the commercial production of oil is not yet possible. This exploration work is continuing, and the search for oil has been extended to the southern part of the country as well.

The situation in regard to natural gas is very different. There are proven reserves of more than 60,000 million cubic metres in a large field near Mazar-i-Sharif. The estimate of the total of all reserves is 300,000 million cubic metres.

The availability of natural gas in Afghanistan will have farreaching effects on the economy of the country. The construction of a pipeline to carry natural gas to the U.S.S.R. made it possible to start exporting this commodity in 1967. Contracts with the U.S.S.R. called for delivery of 1,700 million cu. metres in 1968–69, but actual exports were only about half of that amount. By 1971–72 total exports had risen to 2,635 cu. metres and income from this resource may soon exceed that of any other commodity. Relatively small amounts of natural gas have as yet been allocated for domestic uses, which could include the supply of energy for thermal electric plants and for the manufacture of chemical fertilizer.

Iron Ore: unexploited deposits

The discovery of natural gas in Afghanistan raises important questions regarding its uses, one of which could be as a source of energy for the reduction of iron ore and its conversion to steel. The major iron ore deposits are in the Hajikak area, 125 km. west of Kabul and directly south of the natural gas field. The ore is too distant from the sea to be sold competitively on the international market, but efficient, low-cost reduction or conversion to steel prior to shipment would change the economic factors that determine its marketability.

The estimates of the extent of the iron ore deposits are that the proven reserves amount to 10 million tons. In addition, there are 314 million tons of partially drilled reserves, and the general geological prognosis is that the total deposits exceed 2,000 million tons. Analysis of the ore indicates that it is high grade and of a type suitable for reduction by natural gas.

Other mineral resources that have been located, but which are not yet exploited, include deposits of copper, lead, zinc, beryl, gold, barytes and sulphur.

Coal, Salt, Lapis Lazuli

Commercial mining operations have so far been confined to the production of coal, salt and lapis lazuli.

Coal mining was started in 1939 and is entirely a governmental activity. The production of the Karkar and the Ishpushta Coal Mines, both near enough to Kabul to supply most of the needs of the capital city and its industrial environs, has now reached a total annual volume of 150,000 tons. But the reserves of these mines are relatively small, 13 million tons in the case of Karkar, and 2 million tons for Ishpushta. The largest deposits of coal are in the north at the Darrah-i-Soof mines, which have proven reserves of 75 million tons and where the actual reserves may be several hundred million tons. Another coal deposit is at the Sabzak mines near Herat, where the known reserves are 3 million tons. These mines are being prepared for active production and are expected in the near future to add 30,000 tons each to the country's annual production of coal. Because of the size of its reserves, the Darrah-i-Soof mine will play a large role in the future.

Afghanistan produces much of the salt that it consumes, but the methods used for this production are still primitive. New mines equipped for modern methods will soon be in operation and may eliminate any need for importing salt.

Afghanistan's lapis lazuli is famous throughout the world. The mining of these gem stones has been carried on for thousands of years. The chief deposits are in the province of Badakhshan.

ENERGY

At the present time the consumption of energy in Afghanistan is, by Western standards, very low. A calculation based on 1970 estimates shows that the per capita use of energy in the United Kingdom was 200 times that of Afghanistan. Nearly two-thirds of the total energy available is supplied by imported petroleum products. These provide the fuel for transportation, and small quantities of oil are also used in diesel plants producing electricity. In 1964, the imports of petroleum products, most of which came from the U.S.S.R., exceeded 150,000 tons and the amounts purchased are increasing yearly.

Hydroelectric Power

Hydroelecticity is next in importance as a source of energy. Total electric power production in 1971–72 reached 422.6 million kWh and was steadily rising. Several new hydroelectric projects are now nearing completion so that the country's energy capacity should soon exceed 500,000 kWh.

Other Sources

Coal and wood are the other sources of energy used in the country. In 1964 about 100,000 tons of each were consumed for fuel. There are extensive plans for increasing coal production. The target set for the early 1970s is 350,000 tons. However, the supply of wood, which is still extensively used for cooking and heating, is steadily decreasing because of the destructive lumbering practices employed in the few remaining forests.

INDUSTRY

Afghanistan's first modern industrial venture, a cotton textile plant started at Jebel-i-Seraj in 1934, has grown into a large and important enterprise. This business, which is partly owned and managed by the Banke Millie, a private commercial bank, now operates two large-scale spinning and weaving plants, one at Pul-i-kumri and the other, a quite modern plant, at Gulbahar, where it has also installed finishing equipment for dyeing and printing cloth. The basic equipment for textile production now installed in these plants is 77,000 spindles and 2,100 power looms, more than half of which are automatic. In 1971–72, the production of cloth (cotton and rayon) was 72.5 million metres, which is still below the needs of the people. Imports in excess of 35 million metres yearly have added to the supply, but the demand for cloth is not fully satisfied. Consequently the production of the Gulbahar plant has been expanded, and plans have been made to build new textile plants which will be located in Kabul, Nangarhar, Herat, and Balkh.

Woollen textiles have been produced in small quantities for many years, but this industry has not yet become important. Annual production was 663,400 metres in 1969–70.

Processing Industries

Cement production, which was started on a small scale by the Afghan Cement Company at Jebel-i-Seraj in 1958, has been expanded by the building of a large government-owned plant near Pul-i-kumri. In 1971–72 the combined production of the two plants was 173,000 tons. Plans have been made to construct a third plant, for which Herat will be the site.

There are a number of newly established industrial plants for processing agricultural products. A recently built raisin cleaning plant is now operating at its full capacity, which is about 6,000 tons per year. The success of this venture has led to the making of plans for building several new plants of similar capacity. The Spinzar Company operates a large cotton ginning plant at Kunduz with branches throughout the cotton producing provinces. It produces vegetable oil as a by-product, and a new oil extraction plant has been constructed in the Helmand Valley, at Bost. In Kandahar there is a plant for handling and preserving fresh fruits. Other processing or handling industries include leather tanning, the preparation of casings for export, and cold storage and refrigeration facilities for vegetables, fruits and meat.

Sugar refining was started many years ago. The present annual production of beet sugar is only 8,000 tons, but total output of refined sugar is planned to reach more than 20,000 tons.

Other Industries

Among the smaller industries are some plants producing consumer goods such as pottery, glassware, shoes and knitted goods, but the production of these articles is small.

The most important handicraft industry is the weaving of carpets and rugs. Handwoven Afghan carpets are well known in western and other markets and command high prices because of their quality and distinctive designs. Federal Germany and the United Kingdom are the largest customers. This trade earns about U.S. $7 million of foreign exchange annually and is therefore important to the economy of the country. To improve the quality of Afghan carpets, a plant for washing carpets locally, before export, will be built in the near future.

The engineering industries of Afghanistan have confined their operations to the repair of automotive equipment and some assembly work on trucks and motors. Plans for the development of metallurgical industries await the completion of studies of the feasibility of building an iron smelter.

Stimulation of Industrial Expansion

In 1967, a new Foreign and Domestic Private Investment law was passed. This has stimulated interest in industrial enterprises. By 1971, out of 188 investment applications submitted under the law, 153 had been approved and 61 new industrial concerns were already in operation. Of these, eighteen were rayon weaving factories and nine were raising processing plants. Other fields of activity include pharmaceuticals, wine making, animal casings processing, tile making and the manufacture of metal furniture. An Industrial Development Bank may soon be established. The project now awaits the conclusion of negotiations for foreign participation. The completion of these plans will hasten the expansion of industry in many fields in Afghanistan.

TRANSPORT AND COMMUNICATIONS

By using a substantial portion of the foreign aid received in recent years on the building of roads and airports, Afghanistan has greatly expanded and vastly improved its transportation system. Nearly 2,000 km. of asphalt and concrete roads were completed between the years 1957 and 1967. Good roads now connect all of the main cities of the country with Kabul and with each other. The most dramatic achievement of the programme was the reduction of time needed to travel by automobile and for truck services between Kabul and the northern provinces. This has been accomplished by building a high altitude tunnel near the Salang Pass of the Hindu Kush mountain range. A journey from Kabul to Kunduz that formerly required several days of rough driving now takes six or seven hours on a fine road. To complete this project was a spectacular feat of engineering, carried out with Soviet aid and Soviet technical assistance.

Important extensions and spurs for the roads already constructed will soon be completed. These will include the Herat to Islam Qala road which joins Afghanistan's highway system with Iran's. Another important project is the building of a direct road from Herat to Kabul through the central provinces; this will eventually be part of the Asian Highway sponsored by the United Nations.

There are large modern airports at Kabul and Kandahar which can accommodate jet traffic. Local airports are now in use in the north at Kunduz, Faizabad, Mazar-i-Sharif, and Maimana and at Herat in the west and Jalalabad in the southeastern part of the country.

Ariana Airlines, the Afghan national line, in which Pan American Airways has a minority interest and a management contract, provides passenger and cargo service to Iran, Beirut, and the West, as far as London. A service which is shared with Indian Airlines carries traffic to New Delhi.

There are no railroads in Afghanistan, nor are there any plans to build one. From time to time, however, consideration has been given to the desirability of constructing a rail line from the Hajikak area to carry iron ore or iron products to the rail head at Chaman on the border of Pakistan.

Telephone Communications

Automatic telephones were installed in Kabul in 1950. The initial 5,000 line exchange has been replaced by one with 13,000 lines. Automatic equipment is now in use in many of the provincial cities and the installations will be considerably expanded in the near future. Most of the telephone equipment is of German origin, the Afghan Government's communications programme having been assisted by the Federal Republic of Germany.

Access to the Sea

Afghanistan is a land-locked country. The shortest land routes to the sea are through Pakistan to the port of Karachi. There is a rail line from Chaman which runs across western Pakistan to Karachi, a distance of 950 km. A spur of 8 km. from Chaman to the new rail head at Spin Baldack inside the Afghan border near Kandahar will connect this line with the present Afghan highway system. Goods shipped from Kabul usually go by truck to Peshawar and thence by rail to Karachi.

Afghanistan's foreign trade is dependent on transit rights through neighbouring countries. When political difficulties caused the closing of the border between Afghanistan and Pakistan in the early 1960s, it became necessary to use different routes to the sea. One of these was through Iran to the port of Khorramshahr on the Persian Gulf; the other was across Russia to the Baltic sea. Since the reopening of the border, the shorter and less costly routes through Pakistan are again in use.

New transit agreements recently concluded with Turkey and with Iran will soon make through transportation by truck possible from Western Europe to Afghanistan.

FOREIGN TRADE AND BALANCE OF PAYMENTS

The cost of the imported goods and services which Afghanistan requires in order to sustain an economic development programme that will create a modestly rising standard of living exceeds the current value of exports by substantial amounts. In 1962–63 imports cost U.S. $115.9 million, whereas the proceeds from the sale of exports were only $58.9 million. By 1969–70 imports had risen to $124.7 million and exports to $81.9 million. The export-import gap, which had widened to nearly $72 million in 1967–68, amounted to $42.8 million in 1969–70.

The balance of payments problems created by this gap have been met by the reduction of Afghanistan's liquid assets to minimum working balances and by commodity loans and grants from aid-giving countries, chiefly the United States and the U.S.S.R. Short-term credits obtained from the International Monetary Fund have also helped to ease the financial difficulties caused by the imbalance of trade. But the present indications are that the trade gap will continue for some time to come.

These circumstances create difficult problems for those who are planning the future of Afghanistan's economy and for aid-giving countries and the international lending agencies. The burden of an increasing annual foreign debt service, (which by 1971, had reached U.S. $25 million), compounds the difficulties. Important among the factors which may change the future prospects are the rapidly increasing exports of natural gas and the possibility that the use of this new source of energy will expedite the exploitation for export purposes of the iron ore reserves.

Afghanistan's pattern of export trade has shown only minor variations in recent years. More than one-third of the exports were delivered under barter contracts (mainly to the U.S.S.R.) which provide for payments by credits usable only in the country to which the goods were shipped. Exports to India and Pakistan accounted for 25 per cent of the total. Payments for these shipments were made in rupees the use of which was restricted under bilateral agreements. The remaining exports were sold in western markets for convertible currencies. The chief purchasers were the U.S.A., United Kingdom and Federal Germany.

MONEY AND BANKING

Due to a succession of fiscal deficits, the supply of money (bank notes and demand deposits) in Afghanistan increased from a total of Afs. 3,205 million in March 1962 to Afs. 6,785 million in March 1972. The growth rate of the monetized sector of the economy has in recent years exceeded the rate of increase in money supply. The volume of credit extended to both the public and private sectors of the economy also increased substantially. In the past, the growth rates for both monetary supply and credit have not been excessive, and, in general, the fiscal and monetary policies of the country have been conservative. The most recent figures, however, show evidence of inflationary pressures within the economy.

The chief banking institution in Afghanistan is Da Afghanistan Bank, a government-owned central bank, which also engages in commercial operations. As of March 1970, its international reserves amounted to U.S. $45 million. In addition to its main offices in Kabul, it has 57 provincial branches as well as offices in London and New York.

There are two other banks in Afghanistan, the older of which is the Banke Millie (Afghan National Bank), founded in 1932. It conducts a commercial banking business and acts as a holding company with controlling interests in some of the leading industries, including the Textile Company. The other commercial bank, the Pashtany Tejaraty Bank, is affiliated to the Da Afghanistan Bank. It started its commercial operations in 1954, and as of March 1971 had total resources of Afs. 2,249 million and capital and reserves of Afs. 356 million. No foreign banks have been permitted to open in Afghanistan.

PUBLIC FINANCE

Government revenues have risen from Afs. 2,120 million in the fiscal year 1962–63 to Afs. 5,823 million in 1971–72 (not including loans from the Central Bank of Afs. 548.5 million and grants from foreign countries). More than half of the revenues are raised by taxes on business transactions, customs duties on imports being by far the largest source. Income taxes on individuals and corporations account for less than 10 per cent of the total revenue. Direct taxes on land are nominal.

The ordinary expenses of government plus the developmental expenditures incurred by the Government of Afghanistan amounted to Afs. 3,531 million in 1962–63. By 1972–73 the figure had risen to Afs. 8,372 million. which included about Afs. 1,500 million for national defence. Deficits have been financed by credits from the Central Bank, by expansion in the supply of money, and by the sale of commodities supplied under foreign aid grants and loans.

For many years the funds for developmental projects have far exceeded the amounts charged as expenditures in Afghanistan's fiscal accounts. The additional costs were covered by funds received from foreign countries in the form of loans and grants.

FOREIGN AID

Foreign aid to Afghanistan started in 1950 when the Export-Import Bank of the U.S. granted a loan for the development of the Helmand Valley. The U.S. has continued to support this land development programme which has included extensive irrigation and hydroelectric projects.

Up to June 30th 1968, the total aid furnished by the U.S. to Afghanistan amounted to nearly U.S. $400 million. Forty-five per cent of the American aid was used to improve transportation, mainly road building; 25 per cent was spent in the Helmand Valley, and 12 per cent on education. Smaller amounts were used for technical assistance in agriculture, government management and planning.

Soviet aid has exceeded the amounts furnished by the U.S. Details of its use are not available, especially those in respect of military assistance, which has been substantial. The most spectacular Soviet projects are the building of the tunnel through the Hindu Kush mountain range at the Salang Pass, the erection of giant-sized silos in Kabul for the storage of wheat and the Nangahar hydroelectric and rural development projects.

During the period covered by the Second Five-Year Plan (1962 to 1966–67), Afghanistan received a total of U.S. $362 million in the form of project loans and grants from foreign countries. Of this amount, 65 per cent came from the U.S.S.R., 23 per cent from the U.S.A. and 9 per cent from the Federal Republic of Germany.

In addition to these project loans and grants, the Government of Afghanistan realized U.S. $71.1 million from the sale of commodities furnished under grants and loans. Of the total, 47 per cent (almost entirely in the form of grants) came from the U.S., 37 per cent (all under loan agreements) came from the U.S.S.R. and 13 per cent (grants) from Germany. Technical assistance furnished during this period in the amount of U.S. $50 million brings the total aid received by Afghanistan for its Second Five Year Plan to U.S. $483 million. Debt service paid to donor countries during the period amounted to $28.1 million.

By the end of the Third Five-Year Plan in 1972, the total foreign aid received by Afghanistan since 1950 will have amounted to over U.S. $1,600 million of which about $1,000 million will have come from the U.S.S.R.

The United Nations has maintained a large staff in Afghanistan which has furnished a wide variety of technical assistance, which has been especially effective in the field of public health.

Afghanistan is counting heavily on the continuance of foreign aid in order to achieve its developmental objectives. A serious problem for the future is the steadily increasing size of the requirements for debt service payments.

AFGHANISTAN—(Statistical Survey)

STATISTICAL SURVEY

AREA AND POPULATION

Total Area	Estimated Mid-Year Population				Density (per sq. km.) 1971
	1968	1969	1970	1971	
250,000 sq. miles (647,497 sq. km.)	16,330,000	16,700,000	17,087,000	17,480,000	27.0

Ethnic Groups (1963)

Pathans or Pashtuns	Tadzhiks	Uzbeks	Hazarahs	Nomads
8,800,000	4,300,000	800,000	444,000	650,000

PROVINCES
('000—1969 est.)

Province	Population*	Capital	Province	Population*	Capital
Kabu	1,267	Kabul	Faryab	423	Maimana
Kandahar	724	Kandahar	Jauzjan	419	Shiberghan
Herat	669	Herat	Takhar	482	Talokan
Balkh	345	Mazar-i-Sharif	Badakhshan	335	Faizabad
Nangarhar	574	Jalalabad	Parwan	865	Charikar
Paktia	714	Gardez	Bamian	337	Bamian
Ghazni	1,175	Ghazni	Uruzgan	515	Uruzgan
Helmand	309	Bost	Ghor	315	Ghakhcharan
Kunduz	395	Kunduz	Samangan	202	Aibak
Katagan	607	Baghlan	Zabul	349	Kalat
Chakhansur	119	Zaranj	Wardak	404	Maidan
Logar	301	Baraki-Barak	Laghman	216	Meterlam
Kapisa	335	Togab	Badghis	312	Kala-i-Now
Runar	322	Chakhasarai			
Kochi	2,607	—	Total	15,944	
Farah	306	Farah			

*Unrevised.

PRINCIPAL CITIES
(population at July 1st, 1971)

Kabul (capital)	318,094*		Herat	103,915
Kandahar	133,799		Tagab	102,028
Baghlan	105,944			

* Population 498,821, including suburbs.

Other towns (1964 population): Gardez 46,000; Jalalabad 44,000; Mazar-i-Sharif 40,000.

Births and Deaths: Average annual birth rate 50.5 per 1,000; death rate 26.5 per 1,000 (UN estimates for 1965–70).

Employment (1970): Total economically active population 6,000,000, including 4,890,000 in agriculture (ILO and FAO estimates).

AFGHANISTAN—(Statistical Survey)

AGRICULTURE

LAND USE, 1968
('000 hectares)

Arable Land	7,844
Permanent Crops	136
Permanent Meadows and Pastures	6,020
Forest Land	2,000
Other Areas	48,750
TOTAL	64,750

Source: FAO, *Production Yearbook 1971.*

PRINCIPAL CROPS

	Area ('000 hectares)				Production ('000 metric tons)			
	1968	1969	1970	1971	1968	1969	1970	1971
Wheat	2,063	2,105	2,100*	2,000*	2,354	2,401	2,230*	1,915
Barley	316*	319*	320*	315*	361	365	360	355§
Maize	553	559	560*	550*	773	785	770	730*
Rice (Paddy)	205	206	200*	200*	402	407	340	350§
Sugar Cane†	2	2	3	3*	57	57	60	50§
Sugar Beets†	5	5	5	5*	67	62	68	60§
Grapes‡	60	61	61*	n.a.	200	204	210*	n.a.
Cotton Seed	} 55	65	73	73* {	47	57	63	64§
Cotton (Lint)					24	29	31	29

*FAO estimate. † Crop year ending in year stated.
‡ Production of raisins (in '000 metric tons): 32 in 1968; 32 in 1969; 33* in 1970; 33* in 1971. § 1971–72.

Source: mainly FAO, *Production Yearbook 1971.*

1971 estimates ('000 metric tons): Total fruit 650; total vegetables 725; other oilseeds 55.

LIVESTOCK
('000)

	1967–68	1968–69	1969–70	1970–71
Cattle	3,600	3,605	3,608	3,700
Sheep†	21,453	21,668	21,880	22,900
Goats	3,186	3,187	3,219	3,300
Horses	402	410	414	300
Asses	1,328	1,341	1,360	1,275
Mules	32	33	33	25*
Buffaloes	33	33	33	35*
Camels	299	299	301	300

* FAO estimate. † Including Karakul sheep, numbering 6.8 million in 1971.

Source: FAO, *Production Yearbook 1971.*

AFGHANISTAN—(STATISTICAL SURVEY)

LIVESTOCK PRODUCTS
(metric tons)

	1968	1969	1970	1971
Beef, Veal and Buffalo Meat†	32,000*	32,000*	32,000*	33,000*
Mutton, Lamb and Goats' Meat†	118,000*	118,000*	118,000*	120,000*
Cows' Milk	303,000*	311,000*	311,000*	315,000*
Sheep's Milk	212,000	215,000	218,000	220,000*
Goats' Milk	49,000	50,000	51,000*	52,000*
Buffaloes' Milk	4,000	4,000	4,000	4,000*
Hen Eggs	11,500*	11,900*	12,300*	13,000*
Wool: Greasy	27,500	29,500	30,000*	31,000*
Clean	15,100	16,200	16,500*	17,000*

* FAO estimate.

† Meat from indigenous animals only, including the meat equivalent of exported live animals. The estimates are based on earlier years' official figures, the scope of which was unspecified, and may refer to commercial meat production only, excluding farm slaughter.

Source: FAO, *Production Yearbook 1971*.

FORESTRY
('000 cubic metres)

	ROUNDWOOD REMOVALS			SAWNWOOD PRODUCTION		
	1968	1969	1970	1968	1969	1970
Coniferous (soft wood)	1,300	1,300	1,500	550	550	630
Broadleaved (hard wood)	5,800	6,100	6,300	100	163	154
TOTAL	7,100	7,400	7,800	650	713	784

Source: United Nations *Statistical Yearbook 1971*.

OTHER FOREST PRODUCTS
(metric tons)

	1967	1968	1969
Bark and other tanning materials	200	200	220
Materials for plaiting (excluding bamboo)	260	n.a.	320

Source: FAO, *Yearbook of Forest Products*.

Inland Fishing (1964–70): Total catch 1,500 metric tons each year (FAO estimate).

INDUSTRIAL AND MINERAL PRODUCTION

	Unit	1968–69	1969–70	1970–71	1971–72
Ginned Cotton	'000 tons	13.9	27.0	30.5	16.8
Cotton Fabrics	million metres	48.7	49.4	57.1	62.0
Woollen Fabrics	'000 metres	445.8	663.4	433.3	284.0
Rayon Fabrics	,, ,,	2,818.0	2,520.0	8,272.0	10,547.0
Cement	'000 tons	90.6	103.5	94.3	73.0
Electricity	million kWh	317.4	358.8	395.0	422.6
Wheat Flour	'000 tons	58.5	40.4	51.2	92.3
Sugar	,, ,,	5.3	6.1	8.6	8.5
Vegetable Oil	,, ,,	3.0	2.8	4.1	4.0
Coal	,, ,,	124.9	136.6	164.4	135.0
Natural Gas	million cu. metres	1,681.1	2,029.0	2,583.0	2,635.4

Source: Department of Statistics, Kabul, *Survey of Progress 1971–72*.

AFGHANISTAN—(Statistical Survey)

FINANCE

100 puls = 2 krans = 1 afghani.
Coins: 25 and 50 puls; 1, 2 and 5 afghanis.
Notes: 10, 20, 50, 100, 500 and 1,000 afghanis.
Exchange rates (February 28th, 1973): £1 sterling = 111.9 afghanis (official rate) or 194.3 afghanis (free rate); U.S. $1 = 45.00 afghanis (official rate) or 78.13 afghanis (free rate).
1,000 afghanis = £5.15 = $12.80 (free rates).

BUDGET

GOVERNMENT REVENUE AND EXPENDITURE
(million afghanis, years September to August)

Revenue	1969/70	1970/71 (est.)	1971/72 (est.)
Tax on Income and Wealth	328	381	440
Land Tax	84	88	88
Import Duties	1,869	2,074	2,194
Export Duties	188	182	178
Transaction and Consumption Taxes	1,339	1,379	1,264
Licences, Stamp Duties, etc.	97	122	114
Other Tax Revenue	73	84	95
Total Tax Revenue	3,978	4,310	4,373
Other Revenue	1,107	1,408	1,326
TOTAL REVENUE	5,085	5,718	5,699
Deficit	4,010	1,167	2,476
	9,095	6,885	8,175

Expenditure*	1969/70	1970/71 (est.)	1971/72 (est.)
Defence†	1,491	1,260	n.a.
Economic Services	318	337	281
Social Services	880	947	1,125
Other Current Expenditure	1,860	2,388	4,436‡
Total Current Expenditure	4,549	4,932	5,842
Investment §	4,546	1,953	2,333
TOTAL	9,095	6,885	8,175

* Including debt service.
† Excluding foreign aid.
‡ Including defence.
§ Development expenditure, including foreign assistance in 1969/70.

Source: United Nations, *Quarterly Bulletin of Statistics for Asia and the Far East*, December 1971.

Budget (1972-73): Total expenditure Afs. 8,372 million

GOLD RESERVES
BANK OF AFGHANISTAN
('000 U.S. dollars* at December 31st)

1969	32,990
1970	32,980
1971	33,630
1972	35,410

* Beginning December 1971, gold is valued at $38 per troy ounce.

Source: IMF, *International Financial Statistics*.

CURRENCY IN CIRCULATION
(million afghanis at March 21st)

1969	5,238
1970	6,144
1971	6,532
1972	6,785

November 21st, 1972: 7,423 million afghanis.

Source: IMF, *International Financial Statistics*.

AFGHANISTAN—(Statistical Survey)

COST OF LIVING
Index Numbers of Consumer Prices
(Twelve months ending March 20th. Base: 1961–62 = 100)

	1966–67	1967–68	1968–69	1969–70	1970–71	1971–72
All Items	214	264	208	207	270	310
Cereals	247	336	234	219	318	395
Meat	217	212	191	214	223	204
Fruits	188	177	199	232	268	225
Vegetables	157	156	173	241	248	239
Other Food Articles	151	152	146	146	147	161
Non-Food Items	111	111	105	115	117	120

Source: Department of Statistics, Ministry of Planning, Kabul, *Survey of Progress 1971–72.*

FOREIGN AID
(million U.S.$)

Source	1968–69	1969–70	1970–71	1971–72
U.S.A.	4.79	1.45	3.00	2.35
U.S.S.R.	30.52	28.90	17.62	22.47
Germany, Federal Republic	6.47	2.30	2.66	4.04
United Nations	2.11	6.24	2.61	2.66
China, People's Republic	5.53	5.56	1.10	—
Total (including others)	50.20	44.22	27.58	34.32

EXTERNAL TRADE
(million afghanis, twelve months ending March 20th)

	1965–66	1966–67	1967–68	1968–69	1969–70	1970–71
Imports*	9,407	11,271	10,454	9,267	9,410	6,258
Exports	5,025	4,835	5,018	5,348	6,180	7,110

*Including imports under commodity loans and grants from foreign countries and international organizations. In recent years the value of these imports (in million afghanis) was: 4,383.5 in 1968–69; 3,940.1 in 1969–70.

AFGHANISTAN—(STATISTICAL SURVEY)

PRINCIPAL COMMODITIES
(million afghanis)

IMPORTS	1967–68	1968–69	1969–70
Food	1,917.02	1,118.63	1,607.29
Wheat Meal and Flour, etc.	989.41	266.82	0.16
Sugar	394.20	70.39	289.64
Tea	365.11	706.19	705.04
Petroleum Products	404.47	477.17	563.43
Vegetables Oils and Fat	236.01	328.24	292.49
Chemicals	360.77	370.26	573.74
Medicinal and Pharmaceutical	191.98	186.26	260.83
Rubber Tyres and Tubes	288.42	211.23	230.08
Textile Yarn and Thread	202.20	335.48	647.79
Cotton Fabrics	266.32	206.67	222.85
Miscellaneous Fabrics	388.49	270.81	484.63
Machinery and Transport Equipment	624.01	600.46	752.18
Road Motor Vehicles and Parts	330.78	278.29	407.90
TOTAL (incl. others)*	10,454.45	9,266.80	9,409.79

* Includes imports not distributed by commodity, valued (in million afghanis) at 4,866.55 in 1967–68; 4,120.68 in 1968–69; and 2,964.28 in 1969–70. These were most of the imports obtained under commodity loans and grants.

1970/71 (million afghanis): Tea 702.0; Rubber Tyres and Tubes 264.0; Cotton Fabrics 219.0; Miscellaneous Fabrics 453.0.

EXPORTS	1967–68	1968–69	1969–70*
Food	2,079.21	2,102.86	2,225.78
Fresh Fruits	611.79	} 596.67	668.50
Prepared and Preserved Fruits	9.42		
Edible Nuts	513.06	593.17	521.87
Dried Fruits	841.59	814.40	891.85
Hides and Skins	155.17	152.18	194.50
Fur Skins, undressed	1,086.99	636.49	1,004.44
Karakul	1,077.55	629.10	991.09
Oil-Seeds, Oil Nuts and Kernels	67.86	208.50	193.78
Wool and Other Animal Hair	367.06	520.65	505.64
Cotton	593.87	438.02	426.89
Natural Gas	221.25	672.76	915.96
Carpets, etc., of wool and hair	390.91	336.75	470.83
TOTAL (incl. others)	5,017.57	5,348.32	6,160.62

* Provisional figures. Revised total is 6,180 million afghanis.

1970/71 (million afghanis): Hides and Skins 163.0; Wool 527.3; Raw Cotton 670.7; Carpets and Rugs 427.7.

AFGHANISTAN—(STATISTICAL SURVEY)

PRINCIPAL TRADING PARTNERS
(million afghanis)

IMPORTS*	1967–68	1968–69	1969–70
China, Peoples' Republic	424.49	689.64	790.78
Germany, Federal Republic*	846.98	838.27	524.98
India	478.25	850.52	863.07
Iran	215.68	367.72	269.42
Japan	802.99	892.40	1,100.88
Pakistan	246.50	227.44	269.85
U.S.S.R.*	5,025.71	3,561.19	3,145.81
United Kingdom	271.09	238.09	390.97
U.S.A.*	1,340.75	783.74	526.67
TOTAL (incl. others)	10,454.45	9,266.80	9,409.79

* Includes imports under commodity loans and grants (million afghanis):
Total 4,383.51 in 1968–69; 3,940.08 in 1969–70; of which:
Federal Republic of Germany 548.84 in 1968–69; 188.98 in 1969–70;
U.S.S.R. 2,519.56 in 1968–69; 2,201.79 in 1969–70;
U.S.A. 583.52 in 1968–69; 179.58 in 1969–70.

EXPORTS	1967–68	1968–69	1969–70*
Czechoslovakia	170.66	133.14	122.17
India	816.38	1,173.67	1,200.26
Lebanon	144.41	178.72	132.57
Pakistan	416.29	427.31	401.51
Switzerland	284.25	222.97	348.19
U.S.S.R.	1,667.86	1,978.37	2,320.69
United Kingdom	805.06	552.98	965.52
U.S.A.	420.16	341.77	185.35
TOTAL (incl. others)	5,017.57	5,348.32	6,160.62

* Provisional figures. Revised total is 6,180 million afghanis.

Source for Trade tables: United Nations, *Yearbook of International Trade Statistics.*

TOURISM
INTERNATIONAL TOURIST ARRIVALS BY COUNTRY

	1968	1969	1970
Australia	1,242	1,879	2,072
France	2,266	4,709	6,536
Germany, Federal Republic	2,791	3,916	5,472
Pakistan	19,867	26,175	51,250
United Kingdom	5,143	8,080	9,309
U.S.A.	6,034	7,644	9,572
Others	7,196	10,686	16,022
TOTAL	44,539	63,089	100,233

Receipts from Tourism: U.S. $4.3 million in 1969; $7.8 million in 1970.
Source: Afghan Tourist Organization, Kabul.

AFGHANISTAN—(STATISTICAL SURVEY)

TRANSPORT
CIVIL AVIATION
Total Scheduled Services

	1968	1969	1970
Aircraft Departures	4,359	3,618	3,993
Kilometres Flown	2,588,000	2,872,000	3,605,000
Passengers Carried	66,626	67,271	84,688
Passenger-km.	95,770,000	84,888,000	115,037,000
Cargo Carried: metric tons	2,225	2,359	5,599
Cargo tonne-km.	5,296,000	7,253,000	7,886,000
Mail tonne-km.	79,000	72,000	101,000

Source: ICAO, *Digest of Statistics.*

ROAD TRAFFIC
Motor Vehicles in Use

	1969–70	1970–71	1971–72
Cars	30,788	31,884	33,408
Lorries	15,770	15,890	16,162
Buses	2,443	2,611	2,849

COMMUNICATIONS MEDIA

Telephones in use: 18,000 (est.) in 1971/72.
Radio sets in use: 248,000 in 1968.
Books published: 83 titles in 1969.
Daily newspapers: 18 in 1970 (total circulation 101,000).

EDUCATION
(1970)

	Institutions	Pupils
Primary Schools	1,189	421,163
Village Schools	1,852	119,353
Middle Schools	403	81,699
Lycées	133	25,910
Commercial, Agricultural and Technical Schools	15	7,646
Teacher Training Colleges	25	3,987
Universities and Higher Institutes	16	7,397

Note: Teachers in all institutions totalled 18,158 in 1970.

Source (unless otherwise indicated): Department of Statistics, Ministry of Planning, Kabul.

THE CONSTITUTION*

A new Constitution was published in 1964, of which the following are the chief provisions:

Chapter I. The State

Afghanistan is a constitutional monarchy. The State religion is Islam. Religious freedom is assured. The State languages are Pashtu and Dari Persian. The flag is a tricolour of black, red and green, with symbolic emblems on the centre stripe. The State capital is Kabul.

Chapter II. The Sovereign

The King must be of Afghan nationality, and a Muslim of the Hanafi sect. He has the following rights and duties:

Supreme command of the armed forces,
Power to declare war and peace,
Power to inaugurate sessions of Parliament,
Power to inaugurate and terminate extraordinary sessions of Parliament,
Power to dissolve Parliament and to call for fresh elections, which must take place within three months,
Approval and proclamation of laws,
Making and dissolution of international agreements,
Appointment and dismissal of the Prime Minister, and of Ministers on the recommendation of the Prime Minister,
Appointment of Elders, and of the President of the House of Elders with the approval of the House,
Appointment of judges and heads of diplomatic missions,
Proclamation and annulment of national emergency,
Granting of amnesty.
Coin is minted, and the Khutba is read, in the name of the King. Royal expenditure is fixed in the State Budget.

The abdication of the King shall be subject to acceptance by the Loya Jirgah. Tenancy of the throne on the death of the King shall pass to his son, or failing that to his brother. If the King has no brother the Senate shall elect a successor from among male members of the Royal House. Members of the Royal House cannot be members of a political party and may not become Prime Minister, Members of Parliament or members of the Supreme Court.

Chapter III. The People

The people have equal rights and obligations before the law. No person may be punished except under a law already in effect. No Afghan may be deported or extradited. Residence and property are inviolable. Foreign nationals may not own immovable property in Afghanistan. Privacy of communication and freedom of thought and expression are guaranteed. Rights of assembly and to form political parties are assured. Education is a right and shall be provided free.

Chapter IV. Parliament

Parliament shall consist of two Houses, the House of Elders and the House of the People. Members of the House of the People are elected by universal secret ballot for four years. Of the members of the House of Elders, one-third are appointed by the King for five years, one-third are elected by the Provincial Councils for three years, and one-third elected by the residents of each Province for four years.

Members of the House of the People must be literate Afghan citizens of 25 years of age or more. They shall be protected from legal action while carrying out their duties. Members of the Government may attend sessions of either House. Debates are open, unless secrecy is requested by the Head of the Government, the President of the House, or by ten or more members of the House. Decisions are by simple majority.

The following are among the powers of Parliament: Ratification of treaties, Despatch of armed forces, Introduction of bills, Approval of the Budget.

Chapter V. The Loya Jirgah

The Loya Jirgah shall consist of all Members of Parliament, and the Chairmen of Provincial Councils. The President of the House of the People shall preside over its sessions.

Chapter VI. Executive Government

Government consists of a Prime Minister and a cabinet of Ministers. The Prime Minister is appointed by the King. Ministers are presented to the House of the People by the Prime Minister for approval, before being appointed by the King.

The Government shall fall in the event of: resignation or death of the Prime Minister; a vote of no confidence in the Government in the House of the People; a charge of high treason against the Prime Minister or the Government; the dissolution of Parliament, or the end of the legislative term.

The Prime Minister and Ministers are collectively responsible to the House of the People.

Chapter VII. The Judiciary

The judiciary is an independent organ of the State, consisting of a Supreme Court and other courts established by law. Judges are appointed by the King on the recommendation of the Chief Justice. Execution of the death sentence is alone subject to the approval of the King. All other sentences are mandatory.

Chapter VIII. The Administration

Each Province shall have its own Council elected by direct and universal secret ballot; so shall each Municipality.

Chapter IX. State of Emergency

The King may under certain circumstances announce a State of Emergency. However, for a period of more than three months, the concurrence of the Loya Jirgah is required. Should the Parliamentary term end during this time the Loya Jirgah shall be suspended and new elections shall be held immediately following the removal of the State of Emergency. During a State of Emergency the Constitution may not be amended.

Chapter X. Amendment of the Constitution

The Constitution may not be amended so as to affect Islamic principles or the supremacy of the idea of constitutional monarchy. Proposed amendments shall be discussed in the Loya Jirgah and if accepted by majority vote, there shall be fresh elections, after which the amendment shall become law on a second vote of the Loya Jirgah.

Chapter XI. Transitionary Provisions

Following signing of the Constitution there shall be general elections for a new Parliament. The Supreme Court shall be inaugurated one year later.

---

* The republican régime is expected to introduce a new constitution (August 1973).

AFGHANISTAN—(The Government, Diplomatic Representation)

THE GOVERNMENT

HEAD OF STATE
Sardar Mohammed Daoud Khan (also Minister of Defence and Foreign Affairs).

THE CABINET*
(*July* 1973)

Prime Minister and Minister of Foreign Affairs: Mohammad Musa Shafiq.
Minister of Education: Dr. M. Yasin Azim.
Minister of National Defence: Gen. Khan Mohammad.
Minister of the Interior: Nehmatullah Pazhwak.
Minister of Justice: (to be appointed).
Minister of Planning: Abdul Wahid Sarabi.
Minister of Finance: Mohd. Khan Djalalar.
Minister of Economic Affairs: (to be appointed).
Minister of Public Works: Gen. Khwazak Zalmay.
Minister of Information and Culture: Sabahudin Koschkaki.
Minister of Communications: Engineer Nasratullah Malekyar.
Minister of Public Health: (to be appointed).
Ministry of Industry: Engineer Ghulam Dastagir Azizi.
Minister of Agriculture and Irrigation: Dr. Abdul Wakil.
Minister of Tribal Affairs: (to be appointed).

* The above Cabinet is the Royalist Cabinet of ex-King Mohammed Zahir Shah. Details of the Republican Cabinet were unavailable at the time of going to press.

DIPLOMATIC REPRESENTATION
EMBASSIES AND LEGATIONS ACCREDITED TO AFGHANISTAN
(Kabul unless otherwise stated).
(E) Embassy; (L) Legation.

Argentina: Teheran, Iran (E).
Australia: Islamabad, Pakistan (E).
Austria: Zarghouna Wat (E); *Ambassador:* Dr. Georg Seyffertitz.
Belgium: Teheran, Iran (L).
Brazil: Teheran, Iran (E).
Bulgaria: Wazir Mohammad Akbar Khan Mina (E); *Ambassador:* Ivan Hristov Karatzanov.
Burma: New Delhi, India (E).
Canada: Islamabad, Pakistan (E).
China, People's Republic: Sardar Shah Mahmoud Ghazi Wat (E); *Ambassador:* Hsieh Pang-chih.
Czechoslovakia: Taimani Wat, Kale Fathullah (E); *Ambassador:* Jan Suchanek.
Denmark: Teheran, Iran (E).
Egypt: Wazir Mohammad Akbar Khan Mina (E); *Ambassador:* Ezzeddin Ramzy.
Finland: Ankara, Turkey (E).
France: Sardar Mohammad Hashim Khan Wat (E); *Ambassador:* Eugene Wernert.
Germany, Federal Republic: Wazir Mohammad Akbar Khan Mina (E); *Ambassador:* Dr. Richard Breuer.
Ghana: New Delhi, India (E).
Greece: Teheran, Iran (E).
Hungary: Teheran, Iran (E).
India: Malalai Wat (E); *Ambassador:* K. L. Mehta.
Indonesia: Wazir Mohammad Akbar Khan Mina (E); *Ambassador:* Suyoto Suryo-Di-Puro.
Iran: Malekyar Wat (E); *Ambassador:* Djahanguir Tafazoli.
Iraq: Malalai Wat, Shar-e-Nau (E); *Ambassador:* N. A. Kadar Hadissi.
Italy: Khwaja Abdullah Ansari Wat (E); *Ambassador:* Italo Papina.
Japan: Nawai Wat (E); *Ambassador:* Kenji Nakao.
Jordan: Teheran, Iran (E).
Kuwait: Teheran, Iran (E).
Lebanon: Teheran, Iran (E).
Malaysia: Teheran, Iran (E).
Mexico: New Delhi, India (E).
Mongolia: Moscow, U.S.S.R. (E).
Morocco: Teheran, Iran (E).
Nepal: New Delhi, India (E).
Netherlands: Teheran, Iran (E).
Norway: Teheran, Iran (E).
Pakistan: Zarghouna Wat (E); *Ambassador:* Mr. Isphahani.
Philippines: New Delhi, India (E).
Poland: Guzargah Wat (E); *Ambassador:* Tadeusz Martynowicz.
Romania: Teheran, Iran (E).
Saudi Arabia: Wazir Mohammad Akbar Khan Mina (E); *Ambassador:* Mohammad Al-ahmad Al-Shobaili.
Spain: Ankara, Turkey (E).
Sri Lanka: New Delhi, India (E).
Sudan: Islamabad, Pakistan (E).
Sweden: Teheran, Iran (E).
Switzerland: Teheran, Iran (E).
Syria: New Delhi, India (E).
Thailand: New Delhi, India (L).

AFGHANISTAN—(Diplomatic Representation, Parliament, etc.)

Turkey: Shahabuddin Ghouri Wat (E); *Ambassador:* Paruk Sahinbas.

U.S.S.R.: Dar-ul-Aman Wat (E); *Ambassador:* Sergei P. Kiktev.

United Kingdom: Parwan Mina (E); *Ambassador:* J. K. Drinkall.

U.S.A.: Khwaja Abdullah Ansari Wat (E); *Ambassador:* Robert G. Neumann.

Yugoslavia: Wazir Mohammad Akbar Kan Mina (E); *Ambassador:* Vojo Sobajic.

PARLIAMENT*

HOUSE OF ELDERS
MESHRANO JIRGAH

President: Abdul Hadi Dawi.

84 members appointed by H.M. the King for life.

*See also *Constitution* above.

HOUSE OF THE PEOPLE
WOLESI JIRGAH

President:

215 Members elected every four years.

Elections under the new Constitution took place in October 1965 and from August 29th to September 11th, 1969.

POLITICAL PARTIES

Voting at the 1965 elections was by personal choice of candidate. A Statute, under which political parties are to be established, has been passed by both Houses of Parliament (March 1969), but no officially authorized parties had been formed by early 1973.

JUDICIAL SYSTEM

The judiciary of Afghanistan is an independent organ of the State. The Supreme Court is the highest judicial authority and has administrative powers within the framework of the judicial organization. There is no jury in the Western sense but two lawyers may be called by the parties to handle the case before the court.

Supreme Court. Kabul; Chief Justice Dr. A. Hakim Ziayee.

High Courts. There are three High Courts.

Court of Appeal. There is one central Court of Appeal.

Provincial Courts. There are 28 Provincial Courts. Persons convicted in these courts may appeal to the High Court.

Primary Courts. There are 216 Primary Courts.

Special Courts. There are a number of Special Courts.

RELIGION

The official religion of Afghanistan is Islam. The great majority (almost 90 per cent) are Muslims of the Sunni (Hanafi) sect, and the remainder belong to the Shi'a sect. About 20,000 Hindus are living in different parts of the country.

THE PRESS

PRINCIPAL DAILIES

Anis (*Friendship*): Kabul; f. 1927; evening; Independent; news and literary articles; Persian and Pashtu; circ. 25,000; Editor-in-Chief M. Shafi Rahgozer; Editor Abdul Hamid Mubariz.

Heywad: Kabul; f. 1949; Pashtu; Editor Mir Said Bariman; circ. 5,000.

Islah (*Reform*): Kabul; f. 1929; morning; Independent; but co-operating with the Government; Persian and Pashtu; circ. 25,000; Chief Editor Habiburrahman Jadeer.

Kabul Times: Kabul; f. 1962; English; Editor-in-Chief S. Rahel; circ. 5,000.

Badakshan: Faizabad; f. 1945; Persian and Pashtu.

Bedar: Mazar-i-Sharif; f. 1920; Persian and Pashtu; circ. 1,500.

Daiwan: Shiberghan.

Ettifaqi-Islam: Herat; f. 1920; Persian and Pashtu; circ. 1,500.

Ettehadi-Baghlan: Baghlan; f. 1921; Persian and Pashtu.

Helmand: Bost; f. 1953; Pashtu.

Nangrahar: Jalalabad; f. 1918; Persian and Pashtu; circ. 1,500.

Seistan: Farah; f. 1947.

Tuloi-Afghan: Kandahar; f. 1924; circ. 1,500.

Wolanga: Gardiz; f. 1941; Pashtu; circ. 1,000.

PERIODICALS

Adab: Kabul; f. 1953; organ of the Faculty of Literature, Univ. of Kabul.

Afghan Journal of Public Health: Institute of Public Health, Ansari Wat, Kabul; 2 per month; Editor A. Satar Ahmadi, M.D.

Afghan Mellat: Kabul; f. 1966; organ of Social Democrat Party; Editor Qudratullah Haddad.

Afghan Tebbi Mojalla: Faculty of Medicine, Kabul University; monthly.

Afghanistan: Kabul; f. 1946; quarterly; English and French; historical and cultural; Historical and Literary Society of the Afghanistan Academy, Kabul.

Akhbare Erfani: Ministry of Education, Kabul; f. 1952; fortnightly.

Aryana: Kabul; monthly; (Pashtu and Persian) cultural and historical; produced by the Historical and Literary Society of the Afghanistan Academy; Editor Dr. K. Wafaie.

Badany Rauzana: Department of Physical Education, Kabul University; quarterly.

Eqtesad: National Chamber of Commerce, Kabul; monthly.

Hawa: Afghan Air Authority, Kabul; f. 1957.

Irfan: Ministry of Education, Kabul; f. 1923; monthly; Persian.

Kabul: Pashtu Tolana, Kabul; f. 1931; 2 per month; Pashtu; literature, history, social sciences; Editor Rohili.

Kabul Pohantoon: Kabul University; monthly.

Karhana: Kabul; f. 1955; monthly; produced by the Ministry of Agriculture; circ. 2,500; Editor M. Y. Aina.

Kocheniano Zhaqh: Ministry of Education, Kabul; f. 1957; monthly.

Mairmun: Kabul; f. 1955; Persian and Pashtu; produced by the Women's Welfare Association.

Mokhaberet: Ministry of Communications, Kabul; f. 1957; monthly.

Pamir: Kabul; f. 1951; organ of the Municipality; fortnightly.

AFGHANISTAN—(THE PRESS, PUBLISHERS, RADIO, FINANCE)

Pashtun Zhaqh: Ansari Wat, Kabul; f. 1940; programmes of broadcasts; issued by Kabul Radio; 2 per month.
Payame Haq: Ministry of Information, Kabul; f. 1953; monthly.
Payame Wejdan: Kabul; f. 1966; weekly; Editor ABDUL RAUF TURKMAN.
Sera Miasht: Red Crescent Society, Kabul; f. 1958.
Talim wa Tarbia: Kabul; f. 1954; monthly; published by Institute of Education.
Urdu: Kabul; f. 1922; monthly; military journal; issued by the Ministry of National Defence.
Zhwandoon: Kabul; Persian; illustrated; circ. 10,000; Editor MOHAMMED BASHIR RAFIQ.
Zeru: Pashtu Tolana, Kabul; f. 1949; weekly.

NEWS AGENCIES

Bakhtar News Agency: Kabul; f. 1939; Pres. GHULAM H. KUSHAN.

FOREIGN BUREAUX

The following Foreign Agencies are represented in Kabul: Agence France-Presse (AFP), Deutsche Presse-Agentur (DPA), and Tass.

PRESS ASSOCIATION

Journalists' Association: c/o Department of Press and Information, Sanaii Wat, Kabul.

PUBLISHERS

Afghan Historical Society: Kabul; f. 1943 by Department of Press and Information; mainly historical works and two quarterly magazines of which one is in English and French.
Afghan Kitab: Kabul; f. 1969 by K. Ahang; books on various subjects and translations of foreign works on Afghanistan.
Baihaqi Book Publishing Institute: Kabul; f. 1971 by Government Press, Ministry of Information and Culture.
Book Publishing Institute: Kabul; f. 1966 by co-operation of the Government Press, Bakhtar News Agency and leading newspapers.
Book Publishing Institute: Herat; f. 1970 by co-operation of Government Press and citizens of Herat; books on literature, history and religion.
Book Publishing Institute: Kandahar; f. 1970 by citizens of Kandahar, supervised by Government Press; mainly books in Pashtu language.
Educational Publications: Ministry of Education, Kabul; text-books for primary and secondary schools in the Pashtu and Dari languages; also two monthly magazines, one in Pashtu and the other in Dari.
Government Press: Kabul; f. 1870 under supervision of the Ministry of Information and Culture; four daily newspapers in Kabul, one in English; sixteen journals of the private press, one of them a daily; weekly, fortnightly and monthly magazines, one of them in English and French; books on Afghan history and literature, as well as text-books for the Ministry of Education; thirteen daily newspapers in thirteen provincial centres and one journal and also magazines in three provincial centres.
Institute of Geography: Faculty of Letters, Kabul University; geographical and related works.
Pashto Tolana: Kabul; f. 1937 by the Department of Press and Information; research works on Pashtu language.

RADIO

Radio Afghanistan: Ansari Wat, Kabul; Pres. Dr. A. L. JALALI; Prog. Chief G. H. KUSHAN; the Afghan Broadcasting station is under the supervision of the Ministry of Information and Culture; Home service in Dari and Pashtu; Foreign service in Urdu, English, Russian, German, Dari and Pashtu.

Number of radio receivers: 248,000 in 1968.

There is no television.

FINANCE

(cap.=capital; p.u.=paid up; res.=reserves; m.=million; Afs.=Afghanis.)

BANKING
CENTRAL BANK

Afghanistan Bank (Da): Jadeh Ibne Sina Wat, Kabul; f. 1939; the central bank; main functions: banknote issue, foreign exchange control and operations, credit extensions to banks and leading enterprises and companies, government and private depository, government fiscal agency; 57 local brs.; cap. Afs. 480m.; dep. 7,426m. (April 1973); Gov. HABIBULLAH MALI ACHACZAI; Deputy Gov. Dr. MOHAMMED NAWAZ; First Deputy Gov. MOHAMMED HAKIM; Second Deputy Gov. FAQIR MOHAMMED MUNIF; Sec. ABDULLAH HABASHZADAH.

Overseas Corporations:
The Trading Company of Afghanistan Inc.: 122 West Thirtieth, New York, U.S.A.
The Trading Company of Afghanistan Ltd.: Friars House, New Broad St., London, E.C.2, England.

Pashtany Tejaraty Bank (*Afghan Commercial Bank*): Mohammad Jan Khan Wat, Kabul; f. 1954 to provide long- and short-term credits, forwarding facilities, opening letters of credit, purchase and sale of foreign exchange, transfer of capital, issuing travellers' cheques; cap. p.u. Afs. 250m.; total resources Afs. 2,249m. (March 1971); Pres. JANNAT KHAN GHARWAL; Vice-Pres. A. R. VALL; brs. in Afghanistan and abroad.
Agricultural Development Bank of Afghanistan: Kabul; f. 1955; *Agricultural and Cottage Industry Bank* until 1970; makes available credits for farmers, co-operatives and agro-business; aid provided by IBRD and UNDP; auth. share cap. Afs. 1 billion; Pres. A. AFZAL.
Banke Millie Afghan (*Afghan National Bank*): Head Office: Jada Ibn Sina, Kabul; f. 1932; brs. throughout Afghanistan and in Pakistan; London Office: (as Afghan National Bank Ltd.) 22 Finsbury Square, E.C.2; offices in New York and Hamburg; cap. Afs. 500m.; dep. 761m. (March 1968); Pres. A. GHANI GHAUSSY.
Mortgage and Construction Bank: 2 Jade' Maiwand, Kabul; f. 1955 to provide short and long term building loans; cap. Afs. 60m.; Pres. ESMATOLLAH ENAYAT SERAJ.
Industrial Development Bank: Kabul; f. 1965; provides loans for industrial devt.; Pres. Dr. MOHD. AMAN (acting).

There are no foreign banks operating in Afghanistan.

INSURANCE

There is one national insurance company:

Afghan Insurance Co.: P.O.B. 329, 26 Mohd. Jan Khan Wat, Kabul; f. March 1964; marine, aviation, fire, motor and accident insurance; cap. p.u. Af. 15m.; Pres. ABDUL RASHID; Gen. Man. N. H. SIMONDS.

Three foreign insurance companies are operating in the country: *Ingosstrakh* (Russian National Company) and the *Commercial Union Group* (Head Office: 24 Cornhill, London, E.C.3, England) are represented by agents; *Sterling General Insurance Co. Ltd.* (Head Office: Scindia House, P.O.B. 12, New Delhi 1, India) maintains a branch office.

TRADE AND INDUSTRY

CHAMBER OF COMMERCE

Afghan Chamber of Commerce: Darul Aman Wat, Kabul; Pres. A. GHAFOOR SERAJ.

TRADING CORPORATIONS

Cotton Export Corporation: Kabul; formed to facilitate cotton production, improve methods of cultivation, install modern ginning and pressing plants, and export cotton.

Kandahar Woollen Factory: Kandahar; formed for the export of wool.

Livestock Improvement Organization: Kabul; f. 1952; formed to improve the quality of Karakul, campaign against animal diseases and to fix buying prices in the interests of producers.

Pashtoon Food Processors Inc.: P.O.B. 3025, Kabul; f. 1934 for the export of fresh, dry and canned fruit; 64 mems.; Pres. A. MOOSA.

Textile Company: Kabul; cotton, rayon and synthetic fibres manufacturing company.

Herat Pistachio Company: Herat; formed for the export of pistachio nuts.

Balkh Union: export and import agency handling exports of wool, hides and karakul.

Wool Company: deals with wool exports.

Carpet Export Company: Kabul.

State Co-operative Depot: Kabul; deals with export and imports of all commodities.

Government Officials' Co-operative: Kabul; export and import company.

Office S. M. Azam Azimi: P.O.B. 498, Kabul; f. 1972; carries out import-export transactions.

TRADE UNIONS

There are no trade unions in Afghanistan.

TRANSPORT AND TOURISM

RAILWAYS

There are no railways in Afghanistan.

ROADS

Ministry of Communication and Ministry of Public Works: Kabul; there are about 6,700 km. of all-weather tarmac and gravel roads. A modern highway from Kandahar to Kabul was completed in 1966, and the Salang road tunnel beneath the Hindu Kush opened in 1964. Road development continues with the aid of Soviet and American loans.

Afghan Motor Service and Parts Co.: Zendabanon Workshops, P.O.B. 86, Kabul; passenger services in Kabul; long-distance freight and passenger services from Kabul to most parts of the country; trucking services in all towns; Pres. HAFIZULLAH RAHIMI; Vice-Pres. KHAWJA MOENODDIN.

INLAND WATERWAYS

River ports on the Oxus are linked by road to Kabul.

CIVIL AVIATION

Civil Aviation Authority: Ansari Wat, Kabul; Pres. H.R.H. SARDAR SULTAN MAHMOUD GHAZI.

There are modern international terminals at Kandahar and Kabul.

NATIONAL AIRLINE

Ariana Afghan Airlines Co. Ltd.: P.O.B. 76, Kabul; f. 1955; internal services between Kabul and Kandahar; international services to London, Frankfurt, Istanbul, Beirut, Teheran, New Delhi, Lahore, Amritsar, Tashkent, Paris, Rome, Baghdad and Damascus; Pres. H.R.H. Sardar Sultan MAHMOUD GHAZI; Exec. Vice-Pres. CHARLES H. BENNETT; Comptroller S. G. HAZRAT; Dir. of Operations AZIZ A. MALIKYAR; Commercial Dir. ESHAN GRAN.

The following airlines also operate services to Afghanistan: Aeroflot, IAC, Iran Air, Pakistan International Airways, TMA (cargo).

KLM, Lufthansa, TWA, BOAC, SAS and Pan American are also represented in Kabul.

Bakhtar Afghan Airlines: Ansari Wat, P.O.B. 3058, Kabul; f. 1968; internal services between Kabul and 17 regional locations; Pres. A. A. ETEMADI; Dir. of Operations Capt. R. NAWROZ.

TOURISM

Afghan Tourist Organization: Mohammed Jan Khan Wat, Kabul; f. 1958; Pres. A. W. TARZI; Vice-Pres. R. A. SULTANI.

Afghan Tour: Kabul; official travel agency; Gen. Man. ANWARULHAQ GRAN.

ATOMIC ENERGY

Atomic Energy Commission: Faculty of Science, Kabul University, Kabul; Pres. of Commission and Dean of Faculty Dr. A. G. KARKAR.

Under an agreement signed in September 1963 the U.S.S.R. was to provide Afghanistan with a nuclear reactor. No further details have yet been announced (1972).

EDUCATION

The traditional system of education in Afghanistan is religious instruction by mullahs in the mosques, leading to higher religious education in the Ulema schools. These centres are still active, but a modern educational system has been built up over the past sixty-five years.

The broad objectives and guidelines for the development of education are set out in Article 34 of the Constitution:

"Education is the right of every Afghan and shall be provided free of charge by the State to the citizens of Afghanistan; the aim of the State in this sphere is to reach a stage where suitable facilities for education will be made available to all Afghans, in accordance with the provisions of the law, the Government is obliged to prepare and implement a programme for balanced and universal education in Afghanistan. . . ."

Under the Rule of King Mohammed Zahir Shah a large number of primary, middle and secondary schools have been opened all over the country. The development of education since 1961 has been rapid especially at the primary level where enrolment has risen from 231,000 to 573,000 by 1972. In 1972 there were 3,232 primary schools, a 6 per cent increase over 1971. By 1972 the number of

Middle schools had risen to 497, a 21 per cent increase over 1971, and the number of lycées had risen to 188, a 41 per cent increase over 1971. The number of vocational schools has been falling (they numbered 37 in 1972), but this has been compensated for by an expansion of other forms of technical education.

Teacher training began on an organized scale in the early 1950s with the establishment of an Institute of Education and the setting up of 8 colleges for the training of primary school teachers. In 1962 the Faculty of Education of the University of Kabul inaugurated a 4-year degree course of teacher training for the lycées and a higher teachers college, established in 1963, with 2-year training courses in science, social science and languages for teaching in middle schools. The University of Kabul was founded in 1932, when the Faculty of Medicine was established: in 1939 the Faculty of Law and Political Science was added; the Faculty of Science was opened in 1942; the Faculty of Letters and Humanities in 1944; the Faculty of Theology in 1951; the Faculty of Engineering and Agriculture in 1957; of Economics in 1957, of Pharmacy in 1958, of Veterinary Medicine, an Institute of Education in 1961 and finally a Faculty of Education and Home Economics in 1962. In 1963 a second university was established, in Jalalabad, Nangarhar Province; again the nucleus was provided by a Medical Faculty. Students enrolment has grown from 2,000 in 1960 to 8,744 in 1971–72.

Progress is also being made in women's education, and girls' schools are now found in all major cities of Afghanistan. In addition to providing free teaching facilities, textbooks and materials are also provided free of charge by the Government.

As for future developments, the Fourth Five-Year National Development Plan will be launched which envisages a twofold increase in primary school enrolment and improvement in the quality of education at higher levels through better teaching methods, training, curriculum reform, in addition to improved textbooks, a science emphasis, and better evaluation techniques.

UNIVERSITIES

Kabul University: Kabul; 924 teachers, 6,314 students.

University of Naugrahar: Jalalabad; 61 teachers, 410 students.

BIBLIOGRAPHY

GENERAL

AFGHAN TRANSPORT & TRAVEL SERVICE. Afghanistan—Ancient Land with Modern Ways (London, 1961).

CAROE, OLAF. The Pathans.

GRASSMUCK, GEORGE, and ADAMEC, LUDWIG (editors) Afghanistan: Some new approaches (Center for Near Eastern and North African Studies, University of Michigan, 1969).

GREGORIAN, VARTAN. The Emergence of Modern Afghanistan (Stanford University Press, Stanford, 1969).

GRIFFITHS, JOHN C. Afghanistan (Pall Mall Press, London, 1967).

KABUL TIMES YEAR BOOK 1967.

KESSEL, FLINKER and KLIMBURG. Afghanistan (photographs, 1959).

KING, PETER. Afghanistan, Cockpit in Asia (Bles, London, 1966, Taplinger, N.Y., 1967).

KLIMBURG, M. Afghanistan (Austrian UNESCO Commission, Vienna, 1966).

SHALISI, PRITA K. Here and There in Afghanistan.

WATKINS, MARY B. Afghanistan, an Outline (New York, 1962).

Afghanistan, Land in Transition (Van Nostrand, Princeton, N.J., 1963).

WILBER, DONALD N. Afghanistan (New Haven, Conn., 1956).

Annotated Bibliography of Afghanistan (New Haven, Conn., 1962).

TOPOGRAPHY AND TRAVELS

BURNES, Sir ALEXANDER. Cabool (John Murray, London, 1842).

BYRON, ROBERT. Road to Oxiana.

ELPHINSTONE, M. An Account of the Kingdom of Caubul and its Dependencies in Persia, Tartary and India (John Murray, London, 1815).

FERRIER, J. P. Caravan Journeys.

HAHN, H. Die Stadt Kabul und ihr Umland (2 vols., Bonn, 1964–65).

HAMILTON, ANGUS. Afghanistan (Heinemann, London, 1906).

HUMLUM, J. La Géographie de l'Afghanistan (Gyldendal, Copenhagen, 1959).

MASSON, CHARLES. Narrative of various journeys in Balochistan, Afghanistan and the Punjab (Bentley, London, 1842).

MOHUN LAL. Journal.

WOLFE, N. H. Herat (Afghan Tourist Organization, Kabul, 1966).

WOOD, JOHN. A Personal Narrative of a Journey to the Source of the River Oxus by the Route of Indus, Kabul and Badakshan (John Murray, London, 1841).

HISTORY

ADAMEC, LUDWIG W. Afghanistan 1900–1923 (University of California, Berkeley, 1967).

BOSWORTH, C. E. The Ghaznavids (Edinburgh University Press, 1963).

CAMBRIDGE HISTORY OF INDIA, Vols. I, III, IV, V, VI.

DOLLOT, RENÉ. Afghanistan (Payot, Paris, 1937).

FLETCHER, ARNOLD. Afghanistan, Highway of Conquest (Cornell and Oxford University Presses, 1965).

FRASER-TYTLER, Sir W. KERR. Afghanistan (Oxford University Press, 1950, 3rd edn., 1967).

GOVERNMENT OF INDIA. The Third Afghan War, 1919 (Calcutta, 1926).

GREGORIAN, VARTAN. The Emergence of Modern Afghanistan—Politics of Reform and Modernization 1880–1946 (Stanford University Press, 1970).

GROUSSET. L'Empire des Steppes.

KHAN, M. M. S. M., Editor. The Life of Abdur Rahman, Amir of Afghanistan (John Murray, London, 1900).

KOHZAD, A. A. Men and Events (Government Printing House, Kabul).

MACRORY, PATRICK. Signal Catastrophe (Hodder & Stoughton, London, 1966).

MASSON, V. M., and ROMODIN, V. A. Istoriya Afghanistana (Akad. Nauk, Moscow, 1964–65).

MOHUN LAL. Life of the Amir Dost Mohammed Khan of Kabul (Longmans, London, 1846).

NORRIS, J. A. The First Afghan War, 1838–42 (Cambridge University Press, 1967).

SYKES, Sir PERCY. A History of Afghanistan (Macmillan, London, 1940).

TATE, G. P. The Kingdom of Afghanistan (London, 1911).

ECONOMY

ASIAN CONFERENCE ON INDUSTRIALIZATION. Industrial Development: Asia and the Far East (Report of Manila Conference, 1965, published by ECAFE, Bangkok).

MALEKYAR, ABDUL WAHED. Die Verkehrsentwicklung in Afghanistan (Cologne, 1966).

RHEIN, E. and GHAUSSY. A. GHANIE. Die wirtschaftliche Entwicklung Afghanistans, 1880-1965 (C. W. Leske Verlag, Hamburg 1966).

Algeria

PHYSICAL AND SOCIAL GEOGRAPHY

D. R. Harris

Algeria is the largest of the three countries in northwest Africa that comprise the Maghreb, as the region of mountains, valleys and plateaux that lies between the sea and the Sahara desert is known. It is situated between Morocco and Tunisia, with a Mediterranean coastline of nearly 600 miles and a total area of some 900,000 sq. miles, over four fifths of which lies south of the Maghreb proper and within the western Sahara. Its extent, both from north to south and west to east, exceeds 1,200 miles. The Arabic name for the country, *al Jazair* (the Islands), is said to derive from the rocky islands along the coastline, which have always constituted a danger to ships approaching the harbours.

In the 1966 census the population was 12,101,994 and the overall density was 13.4 per sq. mile. However, a vast majority of the inhabitants live in the northern part of the country, particularly along the Mediterranean coast where both the capital, Algiers (population, with suburbs, now over one million), and the second largest town, Oran (about 325,000), are located. The population is almost wholly Muslim, of whom a majority speak Arabic and the remainder Berber, the language of the original inhabitants of the Maghreb. Most educated Algerians, however, speak French. Nearly all the European settlers, who numbered about 1 million in 1960, have left the country since it attained its independence from France in 1962.

PHYSICAL FEATURES

The primary contrast in the physical geography of Algeria is between the mountainous, relatively humid terrain of the north, which forms part of the Atlas mountain system, and the vast expanse of lower, flatter desert to the south, which is part of the Saharan tableland. The Atlas Mountains trend from south-west to north-east across the whole of the Maghreb. Structurally they resemble the "Alpine" mountain chains of Europe north of the Mediterranean and, like them, they came into existence during the geologically recent Tertiary era. They are still unstable and liable to severe earthquakes, such as that which partially destroyed the town of Orléansville in 1954. They consist of rocks, now uplifted, folded and fractured, that once accumulated as submarine deposits beneath an ancestral Mediterranean sea. Limestones and sandstones are particularly extensive and they often present a barren appearance in areas where a cover of soil and vegetation is only thin or absent altogether.

In Algeria the Atlas mountain system is made up of three broad zones running parallel to the coast: the Tell Atlas, the High Plateaux and the Saharan Atlas. In the north, and separated from the Mediterranean by only a narrow and discontinuous coastal plain, is the complex series of mountains and valleys that comprise the Tell Atlas. Here individual ranges, plateaux and massifs vary in height from about 1,500 to 7,500 feet, and are frequently separated from one another by deep valleys and gorges which divide the country into self-contained topographic and economic units. Most distinctive of these are the massifs of the Great and Little Kabyle between Algiers and the Tunisian frontier, which have acted as mountain retreats where Berber ways of village life persist.

South of the Tell Atlas lies a zone of featureless plains known as the High Plateaux of the Shotts. To the west, near the Moroccan frontier, they form a broad, monotonous expanse of level terrain about 100 miles across and over 3,500 feet high. They gradually narrow and fall in height eastward and end in the Hodna basin, a huge enclosed depression, the bottom of which is only 1,375 feet above sea-level. The surface of the plateaux consists of alluvial debris derived from erosion of the mountains to north and south, and only here and there do minor ridges project through the thick mantle of alluvium to break the monotony of the level horizons. The plateaux owe their name to the presence of several vast basins of internal drainage, known as shotts, the largest of which is the Hodna basin. During rainy periods water accumulates in the shotts to form extensive shallow lakes which give way, as the water is absorbed and evaporated, to saline mud flats and swamps.

The southern margin of the High Plateaux is marked by a series of mountain chains and massifs that form the Saharan Atlas. They are more broken than the Tell Atlas and present no serious barrier to communications between the High Plateaux and the Sahara. From west to east the chief mountain chains are the Ksour, Amour, Ouled Naïl, Ziban and Aurès. The latter is the most impressive massif in the whole Algerian Atlas system and includes the highest peak: Djebel Chelia, 7,638 feet. The relief of the Aurès is very bold, with narrow gorges cut between sheer cliffs surmounted by steep bare slopes, and to the east and north of the Hodna basin its ridges merge with the southernmost folds of the Tell Atlas. North-eastern Algeria forms, therefore, a compact block of high relief in which the two Atlas mountain systems cease to be clearly separated. Within it there are a number of high plains studded with salt flats but their size is insignificant compared with the enormous shotts to the west.

CLIMATE AND VEGETATION

The climate of northernmost Algeria, including the narrow coastal plain and the Tell Atlas southward to the margin of the High Plateaux, is of "Mediterranean" type with warm wet winters and hot dry summers. Rainfall varies in amount from over 40 inches annually on some coastal mountains exposed to rain-bearing winds to less than 5 inches in sheltered, lee situations, and most of it occurs during the winter when depressions pass across the western Mediterranean most frequently. Complete drought lasts for three to four months during the summer and at this time too, the notorious sirocco occurs. It is a scorching, dry and dusty south wind blowing from the Sahara and is known locally as the Chehili. It blows on 40 or more days a year over the High Plateaux but nearer the coast its frequency is reduced to about 20 days. When it sets in, shade temperatures often rise rapidly to over 100°F. and vegetation and crops, unable to withstand the intensity of evaporation, may wither and die within a few hours. As a result of low and uneven rainfall combined with high rates of evaporation the rivers of the Tell tend to be short and to suffer large seasonal variations in flow. Many dry out completely during the summer and are only full for brief periods following heavy winter rains. The longest perennially flowing river is the Oued Chélif which rises in the High Plateaux and crosses the Tell to reach the Mediterranean east of Oran. In October 1969, however, severe flooding affected the Aurès area (and much of Tunisia), the cause being exceptionally heavy rain over a very short period.

Along the northern margin of the High Plateaux, which approximately coincides with the limit of 16 inches mean annual rainfall, "Mediterranean" conditions give way to a semi-arid or steppe climate in which summer drought lasts from five to six months and winters are colder and drier. Rainfall is reduced to between 16 and 8 inches annually and tends to occur in spring and autumn rather than in winter. It is, moreover, very variable from year to year, and under these conditions the cultivation of cereal crops without irrigation becomes quite unreliable. South of the Saharan Atlas annual rainfall decreases to below 8 inches and any regular cultivation without irrigation becomes impossible. There are no permanent rivers south of the Tell Atlas and any surface run-off following rain is carried by temporary watercourses towards local depressions, such as the shotts.

The soils and vegetation of northern Algeria reflect the climatic contrast between the humid Tell and the semi-arid lands farther south, but they have also suffered widely from the destructive effects of over-cultivation, over-grazing and deforestation. In the higher, wetter and more isolated parts of the Tell Atlas relatively thick soils support forests of Aleppo pine, cork-oak and evergreen oak, while the lower, drier, and more accessible slopes tend to be bare or covered only with thin soils and a scrub growth of thuya, juniper and various drought-resistant shrubs. Only a few remnants survive of the once extensive forests of Atlas cedar which have been exploited for timber and fuel since classical times. They are found chiefly above 5,000 feet in the eastern Tell Atlas. South of the Tell there is very little woodland except in the higher and wetter parts of the Saharan Atlas. The surface of the High Plateaux is bare or covered only with scattered bushes and clumps of esparto and other coarse grasses.

SAHARAN ALGERIA

South of the Saharan Atlas, Algeria extends for over 900 miles into the heart of the desert. Structurally, this huge area consists of a resistant platform of geologically ancient rocks against which the Atlas Mountains were folded. Over most of the area relief is slight, with occasional plateaux, such as those of Eglab, Tademaït and Tassili-n-Ajjer, rising above vast spreads of gravel such as the Tanezrouft plain and huge sand accumulations such as the Great Western and Eastern Ergs. In the south-east, however, the great massif of Ahaggar rises to a height of 9,850 feet. Here erosion of volcanic and crystalline rocks has produced a lunar landscape of extreme ruggedness. Southward from the Ahaggar the massifs of Adrar des Iforas and Aïr extend across the Algerian frontier into the neighbouring countries of Mali and Niger.

The climate of Saharan Algeria is characterized by extremes of temperature, wind and aridity. Daily temperature ranges reach 90°F. and maximum shade temperatures of over 130°F. have been recorded. Sometimes very high temperatures are associated with violent dust storms. Mean average rainfall is everywhere less than five inches, and in some of the central parts of the desert it falls below half an inch. It is, however, extremely irregular and often torrential; a fall of several inches in one day may be followed by several years of absolute drought. These rigorous conditions are reflected in the extreme sparseness of the vegetation and in a division of the population into settled cultivators, who occupy oases dependent on permanent supplies of underground water, and nomadic pastoralists who make use of temporary pastures which become available after rain.

HISTORY

Algeria as a political entity is a phenomenon of the last four hundred years: the history of its peoples, however, is of considerably greater antiquity. Little is known of the origin of the Berber people who have comprised the majority of the population of this part of Africa since the earliest times, but they had long been established there in numerous nomadic tribes when, at the time of the Punic Wars, the first ephemeral state-organizations may be distinguished in the area. The most important of these states was Numidia (208–148 B.C.), established by the chieftain Masinissa, which occupied most of present-day Algeria north of the Sahara. With the destruction of Carthage in 146 B.C., Numidia, greatly reduced in extent, was transformed into a Roman vassal-state. By the time of Augustus, Numidia was merely a senatorial province of the empire, while the rest of the area formed a loose confederacy of more or less independent tribes. Roman rule lasted until the fifth century. In the coastal centres of trade and culture a certain degree of assimilation to Roman ways took place, but in the mountains and deserts of the interior the Berber tribes maintained their independence by frequent revolt.

The adoption of Christianity as the official religion of the Roman Empire, in the early part of the fourth century, provided a convenient ideological framework for Berber separatism: in particular, their adherence to the Donatist heresy provoked violent civil war and religious strife throughout this period. Under the impact of barbarian invasions, the Roman Empire in the west slowly disintegrated in the course of the fifth century, towards the end of which its rule in North Africa was replaced by the transient dominion of the Vandals. A nomadic people of Germanic origin, they established themselves in the east of present-day Algeria, but failed, like the Romans before them, to gain any real control over the Berber tribes of the hinterland. In A.D. 531, Roman, or rather Byzantine, rule was restored in North Africa, with the conquest by the emperor Justinian of the provinces of Africa (the modern Tunisia) and Numidia, and the establishment of a tenuous hold on the coast as far west as the region of modern Algiers. Elsewhere the Berber confederacies, centred in the Aurès and the Kabyle, maintained their independence.

The rise of Islam in Arabia, and its rapid expansion after the death of the Prophet (632), leading to the Arab conquest of Syria and Egypt, was quickly followed by the penetration of North Africa. The first Arab raids into North Africa (or the Maghreb, as the region comprising the present states of Morocco, Algeria, and Tunisia now came to be called) took place about the middle of the seventh century. The foundation of Kayrawan in 670 provided a permanent base for their operations, which remained for a time little more than raids. The towns remained under Byzantine control, while the Berber tribes, uniting against the invaders, killed the Arab leader, Ukba ibn Nafi (682), and set up a Berber state centred in the eastern Maghreb. Increasing Arab immigration towards the end of the seventh century finally put an end to Berber resistance, under its heroic and legendary warrior-queen Kahina (692). At the same time the last Byzantine garrisons were dislodged from their coastal strongholds, and the whole of the area was incorporated into the Ummayad Empire. The Berbers, for their part, became converted *en masse* to Islam, and, enrolling in its armies, went on with them to the conquest of the western Maghreb and of Spain.

BERBER UNREST

This new-found Islamic unity of North Africa did not long endure. Dissatisfied with their inferior position as non-Arabs in what was in fact an Arab empire, the Berbers adopted Muslim heresies as eagerly as they had previously embraced Christian ones.

The first signs of unrest appeared early in the eighth century, part of a general movement of discontent among the non-Arab peoples of the empire, which in the course of the succeeding years was to bring about the downfall of the Ummayad dynasty (750). By this time the Berbers had become converted to Kharijism, an esoteric left-wing Muslim sect, and in 756 under its auspices they destroyed completely the authority of the recently-established Abbasid Caliphate throughout the Maghreb. In the east of the area imperial authority was restored in 761, ushering in a period of forty years' anarchy and civil war. In the centre and west of the Maghreb, an area comprising much of present-day Algeria, a number of small, mostly heretical states arose. Later, in the ninth century, the focal point of Berber Kharijism was transferred from Tlemcen to Tiaret. Meanwhile, in the west, the authority of the caliphs had been superseded by that of an independent dynasty, the Aghlabids, who, ruling from Kayrawan, attempted to extend their control into the central Maghreb. In opposition to their rule the Berbers of the Kabyle now embraced Shi'i doctrines—in contrast with their previous adoption of Kharijism—a move which led in 910 to the establishment of the Fatimid dynasty in the central Maghreb. Fatimid rule, however, was not undisputed. From 943 to 947 they were faced with the terrible revolt of Abu Yazid, known as "The man with a donkey", and from then on Fatimid interest in and power over the central Maghreb declined. After several attempts the capital of the dynasty was in 973 transferred to Egypt, while power in the Maghreb was again disputed between various Berber confederacies. In the centre and the east the Sinhaja tribes, the successors to the Kutama who had established the Fatimids, supported the minor dynasty of the Zirids; in the west the more nomadic Zenata established themselves under the remote suzerainty of the Spanish Ummayads. In the early eleventh century the Sinhaja Banu Hammad rose to the status of a local dynasty, ruling as neighbours of the kingdom of Kayrawan.

An event of some importance in the history of the

Maghreb occurred c. 1050: the invasion of the Banu Hilal, a confederation of Arab tribes dislodged from Egypt. These nomads severely damaged the economy of North Africa, and represent the only considerable Arab immigration into the Maghreb since the original Arab conquest of the area. A period of anarchy ensued, but some order was restored by the Berber dynasty of the Almoravids who, coming from Morocco, brought the area of modern Algiers and Oran under their rule. The Banu Hammad, meanwhile, had become established at Bougie. Almoravid power rapidly declined, and c. 1147 they were succeeded by the Almohads. This dynasty, perhaps the most important to rule in North Africa in the medieval Islamic period, unified the whole of the Maghreb together with Muslim Spain. This was a time of cultural and economic prosperity for North Africa, especially at Tlemcen, and witnessed the expansion of trade with the northern shores of the Mediterranean, but the precarious unity of the Maghreb was short-lived. By 1250 the area was again in a condition of political chaos and instability, with the Zenata Banu 'Abd al-Wad exercising such power as existed. A general decline set in, which was to last for over two centuries, during which time the general prevalence of the Berber language gradually gave way to Arabic, a further legacy of the Hilali invasions.

Throughout this period the chief seat of political power was at Tlemcen. In the interior various minor princes asserted their independence, while the coastal towns, including the minor port of Algiers, organized themselves into independent republics, the chief support of which came from piracy. This state of affairs, which lasted throughout the fourteenth century, was terminated by the sudden involvement of Algiers in matters of more than local significance.

OTTOMAN RULE

The Spanish monarchy, bringing to completion its task of driving Muslim power from the Iberian peninsula with the conquest of Granada in 1492, now carried its crusade across the Mediterranean to North Africa. The fragmented political state of that area offered little obstacle to its progress. Mers el-Kebir was captured in 1505, Oran in 1509, and Bougie in 1510, while Algiers, at that time a small port of little importance except as a centre for piracy, was reduced to submission in the same year. On the death of Ferdinand of Castile in 1516 the Algerines, in an attempt to throw off Spanish rule, sent envoys to the Turkish corsair Aruj, seeking his assistance. Aruj took possession of the town, together with other places on the littoral and Tlemcen in the interior, and caused himself to be proclaimed sultan. In 1518 Aruj was killed, and was succeeded by his brother Khayr al-Din Barbarossa, who, in order to consolidate his position, placed all the territories which he controlled under the protection of the Ottoman sultan. This decisive act, which brought together under a single jurisdiction the whole of the coast of North Africa and its immediate hinterland between Constantine and Oran, may be said to mark the emergence of Algeria as a political concept. Meanwhile, the struggle for North Africa, one aspect of the conflict between Ottoman and Hapsburg which ranged from the western Mediterranean to Hungary and the Indian Ocean, continued. In 1529 Khayr al-Din drove the Spaniards from the Peñon, the fortified rock which overlooks Algiers, while throughout the next decade constant Spanish efforts were made to re-establish their position in the area. Finally, in 1541, a great expedition led by the Emperor Charles V in person, failed miserably in its objectives, and after that Algeria was left for three centuries to the Muslims. Ottoman rule in Algiers had already been further strengthened. In 1533 Khayr al-Din had been summoned to Istanbul to take charge of the Ottoman fleet. In his place a more regular administration was set up, under a succession of *beylerbeys* responsible directly to the sultan. The regime of the *beylerbeys* lasted in Algiers until 1587, when it was replaced by a government headed by a series of *pashas*, who were appointed for a term of three years. These again were succeeded in power in 1659 by the *aghas* (or commanders) of the corps of janissaries, replaced later by the *deys*, who retained their power until the French occupation in 1830. All these changes were, however, very much on the surface. From the mid-sixteenth century actual Ottoman supervision of Algerian affairs became increasingly a convenient fiction, perpetuated in the interests of both the Algerines themselves and the imperial authorities at Istanbul. The real power in Algiers gradually came into the hands of two main bodies. One, the nominal representative of Ottoman power, was the janissary corps, who were for the most part of Anatolian origin; the other, the so-called *taife-i ruesa*, was the guild of corsair captains, men of widely differing origins, who for over three centuries were the main financial support of the state.

The Regency of Algiers reached the peak of its prosperity in the course of the seventeenth century. During this period the rulers of the state entered into diplomatic relations with the leading maritime states of western Europe—England, Holland and France, while these countries maintained their consuls or agents at Algiers. The profitable trade of piracy flourished throughout the century, bringing to Algiers great wealth in the form of captured ships, cargoes and men, and great notoriety as the centre of the North African slave trade. Throughout the seventeenth and eighteenth centuries Algiers looked outwards to the sea. Despite some early Turkish attempts to control the interior, many of the Berber tribes, especially in the Aurès and the Kabyle, maintained their independence throughout the period of Turkish rule; others, more accessible to Algiers, paid to the *dey* a grudging tribute, or unwillingly recognized his suzerainty. With the eighteenth century, and the growth of European seapower in the Mediterranean, conditions became less favourable for corsair activity, and a period of decline set in. From a former figure of 100,000, the population of the city itself dropped to less than thirty thousand at the beginning of the nineteenth century, while in the interior, never firmly controlled by the Turks, the tribal chiefs extended their authority and a period of relative economic prosperity ensued.

In the period of the Napoleonic wars piracy and the economy of Algiers both underwent a certain revival, but this renewal of prosperity was shortlived. On the restoration of peace the European powers called upon the *dey* to abandon piracy, and in 1816 the British fleet bombarded Algiers. It was obvious that before long one of the European powers would take advantage of the growing anti-slavery movement in Europe, and the increasing weakness of Algiers itself, to go beyond naval demonstrations, and to land forces in the country. In the event, the conquest of Algiers was the work of France.

THE FRENCH CONQUEST

The excuse for intervention was an insult offered by the *dey* to the French consul in 1827: the real cause was the pressing need of Polignac, the chief minister under Charles X, to secure some credit for his administration in the eyes of the French public. On July 5th, 1830, Algiers fell to a French expedition, the *dey* and most of the Turkish officials being sent into exile. But the Polignac administration was unable to gather the fruits of its triumph, for before further plans for the consolidation of French rule, and its extension to other coastal towns, could be put into effect, the Bourbon dynasty and its government were overthrown by revolution. A further casualty in the revolution was Polignac's plan for handing over the rest of the country, and the decision on its future, to a European congress; instead, for four years, the problem of what to do with Algiers now that it was in French hands was left to mark time. Away from Algiers itself the absence of any central authority strengthened still further the prestige of the tribal chiefs. Finally, in 1834, following the report of a special commission, the further conquest and annexation of Algeria was decided upon, and a governor-general appointed to put the new plans into effect.

The history of Algeria for the next quarter of a century is mainly concerned with the gradual reduction of the country by France, against bitter and continuing opposition. Constantine, the last stronghold of Turkish rule, was captured in 1837, and by 1841 French rule had been consolidated in most of the ports and their immediate environs. By 1844 most of the eastern part of Algeria had been brought under French control, but in the west the conquerors were faced with the formidable power of Abd el-Kadir. This Berber leader, a skilful diplomat and a military commander of genius, had at first concluded treaties with the French, which consolidated his position as leader of the Berber confederacies in the west. But in 1839 he declared war on France, achieving widespread unity between Berbers and Arabs against the invaders. He held out until 1847, when he was finally defeated by the persistence and ruthless tactics of the French general Bugeaud, the real architect of French rule in Algeria. During the late 1840s and 1850s the tribes on the edge of the Sahara were pacified, while the virtual end of the conquest was achieved by the submission of the hitherto independent Berber confederacies of the Kabyle, in 1857. Further rebellion was to occur, however, throughout the nineteenth century, and especially after France's defeat at the hands of Prussia in the war of 1870–71.

Meanwhile, a policy of colonization, with widespread confiscation of land and its transference to settler groups, had been pushed forward. Bugeaud had at first encouraged colonization in the coastal plains; after 1848 the influx of colonists was much increased, with the approval of the governments of the Second Republic and, in its early years, the Second Empire. A further stimulus to colonization was provided by the widespread confiscation of lands resulting from the unsuccessful rebellion of 1871. By 1860 much of the best land in Algeria was in French hands, and was the scene of considerable subsequent agricultural development, while the French settlers themselves rapidly became the dominant power in the land. This was well seen some ten years later. Napoleon III had been favourably disposed towards the Algerian Muslim population, and had taken steps to protect tribal lands against settler encroachments, at the same time securing for Muslims the right to acquire French nationality. These measures had provoked strong opposition among the settlers, and in 1870, in the confusion of the Franco-Prussian War, the French colonists in Algeria expelled the imperial agents and set up a revolutionary commune.

After the confusion of the period of "commune" rule, and the subsequent Muslim revolt of 1871, the situation was regularized by the new French administration under Thiers. A civil administration with the status of a French *département* was set up for much of Algeria, while the amount of territory under military rule steadily declined. From then until the end of the nineteenth century Algeria was the scene of considerable economic progress, and increasing European immigration, especially from Italy. A feature of this period was the growth of large-scale agricultural and industrial enterprises, which concentrated still more power in the hands of the most powerful members of the settler groups. In 1900 Algeria secured administrative and financial autonomy, to be exercised through the so-called "Financial Delegations", composed of two-thirds European and one-third Muslim members, and empowered to fix the annual budget and to raise loans for further economic development.

In seventy years the Muslim people of Algeria had been reduced from relative prosperity to economic, social and cultural inferiority. Three million inhabitants had died, tribes had been broken up and the traditional economy altered during the prolonged "civilizing" campaigns. In particular, the production of wine for export had replaced the traditional production of cereals for home consumption. The settlers, however, experienced a high level of prosperity and economic progress in the years before the First World War. For the present, the French ascendancy seemed assured.

BIRTH OF NATIONALISM

The spirit of nationalism was spreading throughout the Middle East, however, and it emerged among the Algerian Muslims as a force to be reckoned with after the First World War. Nationalist aspirations began to be voiced not only by Algerian veterans of the war in Europe but also by Algerians who went to France to study or take up employment. In 1924 one of these students, Messali Hadj, founded in Paris the first Algerian nationalist newspaper, in collaboration with the French communist party; the link with the communists was severed in 1927, however. Messali Hadj and his movement were driven underground by the French Government, but reappeared in 1933 as sponsors of a congress on the future of Algeria which called for total independence, the recall of French troops, the establishment of a revolutionary government, large-scale reforms in land ownership and the nationalization of industrial enterprises.

More moderate doctrines were put forward in the post-war years by an influential body of French-educated Muslims, formalized in 1930 as the Federation of Muslim Councillors. Under the leadership of Ferhat Abbas, this group called for integration with France on a basis of complete equality. The victory of the Popular Front in the French elections of 1936 gave rise to the hope that at least some of these aspirations might be peaceably achieved. The Blum-Viollet Plan, which would have granted full rights of citizenship to an increasing number of Algerian Muslims, was, however, dropped by the French Government in the face of fierce opposition from the French settlers and the Algerian civil service.

The years immediately prior to World War II were marked by growing nationalist discontent, in which Messali Hadj, released from prison in 1936, played a significant part with the formation of the Party of the Algerian People (PPA). The outbreak of war in 1939 temporarily put an end to the nationalists' activities, but the war greatly strengthened their hand for the future. Although the Vichy administration in Algeria, strongly supported by the French settlers, was antipathetic to nationalist sentiment, the Allied landings in North Africa in 1942 provided an opportunity for the Algerian nationalists to put forward constitutional demands. A group headed by Ferhat Abbas on December 22nd, 1942, presented to the French authorities and the Allied military command a memorandum calling for the post-war establishment of an Algerian constituent assembly, to be elected by universal suffrage. No demand was made for Algerian independence outside the French framework, however.

These proposals, to which the French authorities remained unresponsive, were followed early in 1943 by the "Manifesto of the Algerian People", which called for immediate reforms, including the introduction of Arabic as an official language. Further proposals submitted in May envisaged the post-war creation of an Algerian state with a constitution to be determined by a constituent assembly, and looked forward to an eventual North African Union, comprising Tunisia, Algeria and Morocco. The newly-established Free French administration in Algiers rejected the Manifesto and the subsequent proposals out of hand.

In the face of growing Muslim discontent, and following a visit to Algiers by General de Gaulle, a new statute for Algeria was put into effect in March 1944. It was an attempt at compromise which satisfied neither the Algerian nationalists nor the European settlers. Membership of the French electoral college was opened to 60,000 Muslims, but there were still 450,000 European voters, and in the event only 32,000 Muslims accepted inscription. The Muslim share of the seats in the *communes mixtes* was restricted to 40 per cent. All further discussion of Algeria's future relationship with France was ruled out.

Ferhat Abbas shortly afterwards founded the Friends of the Manifesto of Freedom (AML), to work for the foundation of an autonomous Algerian republic linked federally with France. The new movement was based mainly on the support of middle-class Muslims, though it also gained a certain following among the masses. At the same time, Messali Hadj's PPA gained many followers among the masses during 1944 and 1945.

FRENCH INTRANSIGENCE

All possibility of an evolutionary settlement was destroyed by blunders of post-war French policy and the opposition of the French settlers to any concessions to Muslim aspirations. The ruthless suppression of the riots at Sétif in May 1945, which claimed the lives of some 15,000 Muslims, and the subsequent arrest of Ferhat Abbas and the dissolution of the AML drove many of the nationalist leaders to regard force as the only means of gaining their objective.

Nevertheless, attempts to reach a compromise solution continued for some time. In March 1946 Ferhat Abbas, released under an amnesty, launched the Democratic Union of the Algerian Manifesto (UDMA), with a programme providing for the creation of an autonomous, secular Algerian state within the French Union. Despite successes in elections to the French Assembly, the UDMA failed to achieve any of its objectives. It withdrew from the Assembly in September 1946 and refused to participate in the next elections. The breach was filled by the more radical Movement for the Triumph of Democratic Liberties (MTLD), the party formed by Messali Hadj at the end of the war, which demanded the creation of a sovereign constituent assembly and the evacuation of French troops—aims which stood no chance of adoption.

In another attempt at compromise the French Government introduced a new constitution which became law on September 20th, 1947. This gave French citizenship, and therefore the vote, to all Algerian citizens, including women, and recognized Arabic as equal in status to French. The proposed new Algerian Assembly, however, was to be divided into two colleges, each of 60 members, one to represent the 1½ million Europeans, the other the 9 million Muslims. Other provisions ruled out all possibility of anti-European legislation.

The new constitution was never brought fully into operation. Following MTLD successes in the municipal elections of October 1947, the elections to the Algerian Assembly were openly and clumsily interfered with, many candidates being arrested, election meetings forbidden and polling stations improperly operated.

As a result only a quarter of the members returned to the second college in April 1948 were MTLD or UDMA; the remainder, nominally "independent", were nonentities. Such methods continued to be employed in local and national elections during the next six years, as well as in the Algerian elections to the French National Assembly in June 1951. Some of the ameliorative provisions of the 1947 constitution were never put into effect. The aim was to destroy, or at least render harmless, opposition to French rule; the result was to drive the main forces of nationalism underground.

As early as 1947 several of the younger members of the MTLD had formed the "Secret Organization" (OS), which collected arms and money from supporters and built up a network of cells throughout Algeria in preparation for armed insurrection and the establishment of a revolutionary government. Two years later the OS felt itself strong enough to launch a terrorist attack in Oran. The movement was subsequently discovered and most of its leaders were arrested. A nucleus survived, however, in the Kabyle region, ever a stronghold for dissident groups, and the organizer of the attack, Ben Bella, escaped in 1952 to Cairo.

A decisive split was taking place in the ranks of the MTLD, and the veteran Messali Hadj, now embracing nebulous doctrines of pan-Arabism, was gradually losing control of the party organization to more activist members. The first open breach occurred in 1953, and in March the following year nine former members of the OS set up the Revolutionary Council for Unity and Action (CRUA) to prepare for an immediate revolt against French rule.

WAR OF INDEPENDENCE

Plans for the insurrection were worked out at a series of CRUA meetings in Switzerland between March and October 1954. Algeria was divided into six *wilaya* (zones) and a military commander appointed for each. When the revolt was launched on November 1st the CRUA changed its name to the National Liberation Front (FLN), its armed forces being known as the National Liberation Army (ALN). Beginning in the Aurès, the revolt had spread by early 1955 to the Constantine area, the Kabyle and the whole of the Moroccan frontiers west of Oran. By the end of 1956 the ALN was active throughout the settled areas of Algeria.

Ferhat Abbas and Ahmed Francis of the more bourgeois UDMA and the religious leaders of the Ulema joined the FLN in April 1956, making it representative of all shades of Algerian nationalist feeling apart from Messali Hadj's Algerian National Movement (MNA). In August a secret congress of the FLN, held at Soummam in the Kabyle, formed a central committee and the National Council of the Algerian Revolution; drew up a socialist programme for the future Algerian republic; and approved plans for the launching of a terrorist offensive in Algiers.

In the early stages of the war the French Government was convinced that only external support kept the FLN offensive going. The Foreign Minister was therefore despatched to Cairo in an attempt to persuade President Nasser to withdraw his support for the Algerian revolution. This mission was in vain, and Guy Mollet, the French Prime Minister, then resorted to collusion with the Israelis and the British in the abortive invasion of Egypt at the end of October 1956. The Suez operation not only did not topple Nasser, nor stop the Algerian struggle, it actually strengthened the FLN's position by increasing support from newly independent and non-aligned states.

Between September 1956 and June 1957 bomb explosions engineered by the FLN caused much loss of life. This terrorism was brought to a stop only by severe French repression of the Muslim population, including the use of torture and internment, measures which aroused condemnation of French policy both at home and abroad. Guerrilla activities continued but electrified barriers were set up along the Tunisian and Moroccan borders and ALN bands attempting to cross into Algeria met with heavy losses.

In June 1957 the Bourges-Manoury administration in France, which had replaced that of Mollet the previous month, put forward legislation intended to link Algeria indissolubly with France, but the bill was never passed. Following the Soummam conference, a joint Moroccan-Tunisian plan had been put forward for the establishment of a North African federation linked with France. FLN leaders began negotiations in Morocco in October 1957. However, Ben Bella and his companions were kidnapped on their way from Morocco to Tunisia, when the French pilot of their plane, which the Sultan of Morocco had chartered for them, landed it at Algiers. The French authorities could hardly reject this *fait accompli*, and the hijacked leaders were arrested and interned in France. Neither the internment of FLN leaders nor the bombing by French aircraft, in February 1958, of the Tunisian border village of Sakhiet, in which 79 villagers were killed, had any effect on the FLN's capacity to continue fighting, and the failure of these desperate measures only made the possibility of French negotiations with the FLN more likely. This in turn provoked a backlash from the Algerian Europeans (only half of whom were of French origin).

In May 1958 they rebelled and set up committees of public safety in the major Algerian towns. Supported by the army and exploiting the widespread fear of civil war, the colonists caused the overthrow of the discredited Fourth French Republic and General De Gaulle's return to power, believing that he would further their aim of complete integration of Algeria into France. They were very soon to be bitterly disappointed. Although De Gaulle did step up military action against the FLN by the 500,000 French troops in Algeria, this was only at the cost of increased terrorism in Algiers and of growing tension on the Tunisian and Moroccan borders. The FLN responded in August 1958 by establishing in Tunis the Provisional Government of the Algerian Republic (GPRA), headed by Ferhat Abbas and including Ben Bella and the other leaders who had been interned in

France. De Gaulle was already beginning to recognize the strength of Algerian nationalism and was moving cautiously towards accepting FLN demands.

NEGOTIATIONS AND THE COLONISTS' LAST STAND

Initially De Gaulle's public statements on Algeria were vague. When he did make an unequivocable pronouncement, in September 1959, and upheld the right of Algerians to determine their own future, the colonists did not take long to react. In January 1960 they rebelled again, this time against De Gaulle, and erected barricades in Algiers streets. However, without the support of the army the insurrection collapsed within nine days. The first exploratory talks between French and FLN delegates took place in secret near Paris in the summer of 1960 but were abortive.

In November de Gaulle announced that a referendum was to be held on the organization of government in Algeria, pending self-determination, and in December he visited Algeria himself to prepare the way. In the referendum the electorate were asked to approve a draft law providing for self-determination and immediate reforms to give Algerians the opportunity to participate in government. There were mass abstentions from voting in Algeria, however, and in February 1961 new French approaches to the FLN were made through the President of Tunisia. Secret talks led to direct negotiations between French and FLN representatives at Evian, on the Franco-Swiss border. These began in May but were finally broken off in August over the question of the Sahara and because of the French attack on Bizerta.

Europeans in Algeria and segments of the French army had meanwhile formed the Secret Army Organization (OAS) to resist a negotiated settlement and the transfer of power from European hands. On April 22nd, 1961, four generals, Chalel, Zeller, Jouhaud and Salan, organized the seizure of Algiers, but this attempt at an army *putsch* proved abortive, most regular officers remaining loyal to de Gaulle. Offensive operations against the Algerian rebels, which had been suspended when the Evian talks began, were resumed by the French Government in response to rebel pressure, and fighting continued, though on a reduced scale. At the same time the OAS began its campaign of indiscriminate terrorism against native Algerians. The Mayor of Evian had already been killed by an OAS bomb, and attacks were now also mounted in Paris.

Secret contacts between the French government and the FLN were re-established in October. Negotiations were resumed in December 1961 and January 1962 in Geneva and Rome, the five members of the GPRA interned in France taking part through a representative of the King of Morocco. Meetings at ministerial level were held in strict secrecy in Paris in February and the final stage of the negotiations was concluded at Evian on March 18th with the signing of a ceasefire agreement and a declaration of future policy. The declaration provided for the establishment of an independent Algerian state after a transitional period, and for the safeguarding of individual rights and liberties. Other declarations issued the following day dealt with the rights of French citizens in Algeria and with future Franco-Algerian cooperation. In the military sphere, France was to retain the naval base at Mers el Kebir for 15 years and the nuclear testing site in the Sahara, together with various landing rights, for five years.

In accordance with the Evian agreements a provisional government was formed on March 28th, with Abderrahman Farès as provisional President and an executive composed of FLN members, other Muslims and Europeans. Ben Bella and the other detained Algerian leaders had been released on March 18th and flown to Morocco. The Soviet Union, the East European and many African and Asian countries quickly gave *de jure* recognition to the GPRA.

The signing of the Evian agreements was the signal for a final desperate fling by the OAS. A National Council of French Resistance in Algeria was set up, with General Salan as Commander-in-Chief, and OAS commando units attempted by attacks on the Muslim population and the destruction of public buildings to provoke a general breach of the ceasefire. After the failure of the OAS to establish an "insurrectional zone" in the Orléansville area and the capture of General Salan on April 20th, and with a renewal of FLN terrorist activity and reprisals, increasing numbers of Europeans began to leave Algeria for France. Abortive secret negotiations by OAS leaders with the FLN, aimed at securing guarantees for the European population, which began in May, disclosed a split in the OAS which heralded the virtual end of European terrorist activity. By the end of June over half the European population of Algeria had left.

The final steps towards Algerian independence were now taken. In a referendum on July 1st, 91 per cent of the electorate voted for independence, which was proclaimed by General de Gaulle on July 3rd, 1962.

THE INDEPENDENT STATE

The achievement of power by the FLN revealed serious tensions and weaknesses within the government, while the problems facing the new state after eight years of civil war were formidable.

The dominant position in the GPRA of the "centralist" group, headed by Ben Khedda and consisting of former members of the MTLD, was threatened by the release of the five GPRA members who had been detained in France—Ben Bella, Mohammed Khider, Mohammed Boudiaf, Ait Ahmed and Rabah Bitat. Boudiaf and Ait Ahmed rallied temporarily to the support of Ben Khedda, while the others formed yet another opposition faction besides that of Ferhat Abbas, who had been dropped from the GPRA leadership in 1961.

The ALN leadership was also split. The commanders of the main armed forces in Tunisia and Morocco were opposed to the politicians of the GPRA, and the commanders of the internal guerrilla groups were opposed to all external and military factions.

Serious differences had appeared when the National Council of the Algerian Revolution (CRNA) met in Tripoli in May 1962 to consider policies for the new state. A commission headed by Ben Bella produced a programme which included large-scale agrarian reform, involving expropriation and the establishment of peasant cooperatives and state farms; a state monopoly of external trade; and a foreign policy aimed towards Maghreb unity, neutralism and anti-colonialism, especially in Africa. Despite the opposition of Ben Khedda's group, the Tripoli programme became the official FLN policy.

When independence came on July 3rd the GPRA cabinet, with the exception of Ben Bella, flew to Algiers, where they installed themselves alongside the official Provisional Executive, and Ben Khedda attempted to reassert control over the ALN by dismissing the Commander-in-Chief, Col. Boumedienne. Ben Bella, however, flew to Morocco to join Boumedienne and on July 11th they crossed into Algeria and established headquarters in Tlemcen. Here Ben Bella set up the Political Bureau as the chief executive organ of the FLN and a rival to the GPRA. After negotiations he was joined by some of the GPRA leaders; this left Ben Khedda isolated in Algiers, with Boudiaf and Ait Ahmed in opposition.

Several of the *wilaya* leaders, however, felt that, having provided the internal resistance, they represented the true current of the revolution, and they were opposed to the Political Bureau and Boumedienne. While ALN forces loyal to the Bureau occupied Constantine and Bône in the east on July 25th, Algiers remained in the hands of the leadership of *wilaya* IV, who refused the Bureau entry. When Boumedienne's forces marched on Algiers from Oran at the beginning of September there were serious clashes with *wilaya* IV troops. Total civil war was averted, however, partly because of mass demonstrations against the fighting which were organized by the Algerian General Workers' Union (UGTA).

The struggle for power had gone against Ben Khedda. Before the elections were held on September 20th, 1962, a third of the 180 candidates on the single list drawn up in August were purged, including Ben Khedda himself, and their places filled with lesser-known figures. Although the elections failed to produce much public enthusiasm, some 99 per cent of the electorate were declared to have voted in favour of the proposed powers of the Constituent Assembly. The functions of the GPRA were transferred to the Assembly when it met on September 25th, and Ferhat Abbas was elected its President. The Algerian Republic was proclaimed and the following day Ben Bella was elected Prime Minister, with a cabinet drawn from his personal associates and former ALN officers.

BEN BELLA IN POWER

The new government immediately set about consolidating its position. Messali Hadj's PPA (formerly the MNA), the Algerian Communist Party, largely discredited because of its role in the war, and Boudiaf's Party of the Socialist Revolution were all banned in November; the *wilaya* system was abolished the following month, and, apart from the UGTA, all organizations affiliated to the FLN were brought firmly under control.

The economic plight of the country was severe. Some 90 per cent (one million) of the Europeans, representing virtually all the entrepreneurs, technicians, administrators, teachers, doctors and skilled workers had left the country. Factories, farms and shops had closed, leaving 70 per cent of the population unemployed. Public buildings and records had been destroyed by the OAS. At the end of the war, in which over a million had died, there had been two million in internment camps and 500,000 refugees in Tunisia and Morocco. Food, money and clothing were sent by many countries to alleviate the immediate suffering. In December 1962 an emergency austerity plan was drawn up and the government was enabled to continue functioning by large loans and technical assistance from France.

By packing the first UGTA congress with FLN militants and unemployed, the FLN managed in January 1963 to gain control of the UGTA executive, which had been opposed to the dictatorial nature of the new government. The decrees of March legalized the workers' committees which, aided by the UGTA, had taken over the operation of many of the deserted European estates in the summer and autumn of 1962. The system of workers' management known as *autogestion*, under which the workers elected their own management board to work alongside a state-appointed director, became the basis of "Algerian socialism".

In April 1963 Ben Bella increased his powers by taking over the post of general secretary of the FLN, ousting Mohammed Khider, who later went into exile but retained control of FLN funds in Switzerland. In August Ben Bella secured the adoption by the Assembly of a draft constitution providing for a presidential régime, with the FLN as the sole political party. The new constitution was approved in a referendum and on September 13th Ben Bella was elected President for a period of five years, assuming the title of commander-in-chief as well as becoming head of state and head of government.

These moves towards dictatorial government aroused opposition. Ferhat Abbas, the leading spokesman for a more liberal policy, resigned from the presidency of the Assembly and was subsequently expelled from the FLN. In the Kabyle, where discontent was accentuated by Berber regionalism, a revolt broke out during the late summer led by Ait Ahmed's Front of Socialist Forces (FFS) and former *wilaya* chief Col. Mohand Ou El Hadj. After some clashes Ben Bella reached agreement with Mohand but Ait Ahmed remained in the *maquis*. In October, partly in an attempt to regain popularity, Ben Bella nationalized the remaining European estates, placing them under *autogestion*, and suppressed the remaining French-controlled newspapers.

Long-standing disputes between Algeria and Morocco over areas on their common frontiers deteriorated into open conflict in October 1963, a fact which had made the need for agreement with Col.

Mohand Ou El Hadj all the more pressing. The hostilities, near the strategic posts of Hassi-Beida and Tinjoub, were not on a large scale and were soon brought to an end through the mediation of interested African states, but they left a legacy of bitterness between the two countries. The tension between Algeria and its neighbours lessened, however, as a result of the Arab summit conference in Cairo in January 1964 and the implementation of an agreement settling the border dispute between Algeria and Morocco in March.

THE FALL OF BEN BELLA

In the last year of its existence the Ben Bella régime appeared to be achieving both a certain measure of internal stability and an improvement in the country's external relations. In April 1964 Ben Bella visited the Soviet Union where he obtained financial aid for the construction of a metallurgical plant at Bône and assistance for other technical and educational projects. A World Bank loan towards the cost of the Arzew gas liquefaction plant, to exploit the extensive resources of natural gas beneath the Sahara, was also obtained. The plant was opened in September and the following month the first cargo of liquefied methane gas was discharged in England, under a trade agreement.

Relations with Morocco improved during 1964. Prisoners were exchanged in April; a demilitarized zone was delimited by a joint commission drawn from Ethiopia and Mali; the border was reopened in June; and, following discussions on economic and technical cooperation, a trade agreement with Morocco was signed on November 25th. The heads of state of Algeria, Morocco and Tunisia had met together for the first time at the Organization of African Unity conference in Cairo in July, and in November their economic ministers decided in Rabat to establish a permanent joint consultative committee to coordinate economic policies.

At the long-awaited first Congress of the FLN in April 1964, despite opposition from the right and silence from army delegates, Ben Bella secured acceptance of the "Algiers Charter", which criticized past mistakes of the FLN, defined relations between party, state and army, and attempted to formulate a theoretical basis for "Algerian socialism", centred on *autogestion*. This was the last occasion on which most of the "historic chiefs" met together. Soon afterwards Ait Ahmed's FFS again led a revolt in the Kabyle and Col. Chabaani, the army commander in the south, also rebelled against the Government. Both Chabaani and Ait Ahmed were eventually captured; the former was executed but the latter was reprieved in view of his popularity. Most of the other "historic chiefs" were eliminated from public life during 1964.

In the early months of 1965 the Algerian Government was preoccupied with preparations for an Afro-Asian conference, planned for the tenth anniversary of the Bandung Conference and due to open in Algiers on June 29th, when Ben Bella was to stand revealed both as the undisputed leader of Algeria and a force to be reckoned with in Afro-Asian affairs. The conference was not to take place. On June 19th Ben Bella was deposed and arrested in a swift and bloodless military *coup d'état*, led by Col. Houari Boumedienne whose army had brought Ben Bella to power in 1962.

The *coup* successfully pre-empted Ben Bella's own plans for a political takeover to coincide with the opening of the Afro-Asian conference. Ben Bella's takeover would have brought a shift to the left and the introduction of Marxist structures of political control. Ait Ahmed would have been freed and some right-wing ministers and Boumedienne detained. Ben Bella had been preparing for this for some time; he had announced that a popular militia was to be created, and he had dismissed Medeghri, the Minister of the Interior and one of Boumedienne's supporters. Finally, at the end of May, he had attempted to force the resignation of Bouteflika, the Foreign Minister, who was closely associated with Boumedienne. In the face of Algeria's poor economic situation and Ben Bella's dictatorial tendencies, many administrators and politicians were not averse to the *coup*, and his elimination of most of the traditional leaders, his repeated attacks on the UGTA and his failure to turn the FLN into a broadly-based party left him without organized support once the army had turned against him.

Bereft of its leader, the FLN accepted the *coup*, and the UGTA, while expressing no real support for Boumedienne, did not oppose it. A number of known left-wingers, including former officials of the banned Algerian Communist Party, were arrested in September 1965 and the most militant of the opposition groups, the Organization of Popular Resistance was broken up. Although rapid Chinese recognition of the new régime had given rise to conjectures of a move to the left in Algeria's international relations, this did not materialize. Relations with Cairo, with which Ben Bella's links had been close and where concern for his safety had been voiced, became more distant, though not unfriendly.

THE BOUMEDIENNE RÉGIME

Supreme political authority in Algeria was taken over by a Council of the Revolution, consisting mostly of military figures and presided over by Col. Boumedienne. Under the Council's authority a new Government of 20 members was announced on July 10th, with Boumedienne as Prime Minister and Minister of Defence, besides being President of the Council; Rabah Bitat as Minister of State; and Bouteflika continuing as Foreign Minister. Nine members of the Government, which included technocrats and members of the radical wing of the FLN, had held office under Ben Bella. To ensure a satisfactory relationship between the government and the FLN, a five-man party secretariat under Cherif Belkacem was set up on July 17th.

The aims of the new régime, as described by Boumedienne, were to re-establish the principles of the revolution, to remedy the abuses of personal power associated with Ben Bella, to end internal divisions, and to create an "authentic socialist "society" based on a sound economy. To those who feared that it was intended to nationalize land under private ownership and to abolish private property he was reassuring, stating that the traditional sector of the economy would be modified only by the formation of non-compulsory cooperative societies. In international relations a policy of non-alignment would be pursued and support for people struggling for freedom and independence would continue. Beyond this, Algeria was committed to the realization of Mahgreb and Arab unity and to the strengthening of ties with the socialist camp.

The remainder of 1965 was taken up with domestic consolidation and attempts to break out of the diplomatic isolation which had followed the *coup*. The conclusion of a treaty with France on July 23rd providing for the exploitation of Algeria's oil and natural gas was followed by a visit to Paris by Bouteflika for talks with President de Gaulle on future cooperation. Subjects discussed included French aid, the vacant properties in Algeria abandoned by Europeans, guarantees against nationalization to tempt back French capital, the sale of Algerian wines to France, and the future of the base at Mers el Kebir. Relations with both the Soviet Union and the United States were also improved. Boumedienne visited Moscow in December 1965, and in January 1966 American aid, in surplus wheat and technical assistance, which had been in abeyance since June 1965, was resumed.

Although the army remained the basis of Boumedienne's power, an attempt was made in 1966 to strengthen the FLN party organization and, despite general apathy, to recruit new members. Boumedienne stated that under the one-party system contradictions between army and government should not arise, the task of the FLN being to "animate and direct". Feeling against the new régime, shown in demonstrations and student strikes in Algiers in January and February, became less apparent, particularly after a number of arrests of trade union leaders in July.

Signs that discord remained, however, were provided by the defection in August of Hadj Smain, Minister of Reconstruction and Housing before his resignation in April, and of Ahmed Mahsas and Bechir Boumaza, Ministers of Agriculture and Information respectively, in September and October. Slimane Rebba, national secretary of the UGTA, also defected in October. Ait Ahmed, in detention since 1964, had escaped from Algeria in April. Boumedienne nevertheless dismissed the opposition groups in exile as "out of circulation". When Mohammed Khider was assassinated in Madrid in January 1967, it was suggested that he had been killed to prevent him handing over the FLN funds under his control to three of these groups—the Clandestine Organization of the Algerian Revolution (OCRA), the Socialist Forces Front (FFS) and the Committee for the Defence of the Revolution (CNDR)—on condition that they merged.

Apart from preparations for elections to the Communal Councils, the régime showed no signs of seeking a popular mandate and the Algerian National Assembly remained in abeyance. New penal and civil legal codes were promulgated in 1966, the judiciary was Algerianized and tribunals to try "economic crimes" with powers to impose the death penalty were set up in July. New conditions of service and training schemes for public employees were introduced with the aim of improving the standard of administration. A new university, at Oran, was opened in December.

In accordance with its socialist policies, the régime increased state participation during 1966 in fields previously left to private enterprise. A state-owned construction company was set up, and it was decided in March that the distribution of the income of the oil and gas industry, both inside and outside Algeria, should be subject to government supervision. In May the nationalization was announced of eleven foreign-owned mines and of property of absentee owners, and all insurance activities were placed under state control. A National Bank of Algeria, specializing in short-term credit for the nationalized sector of the economy, was inaugurated in July.

Industrial activity continued at a low level and the country remained heavily dependent on external aid for industrial development. A mission from the World Bank investigated development possibilities and bilateral agreements were signed with several countries in 1966. A new investment code, designed to attract both domestic and foreign capital and promulgated in September, contained assurances of indemnification in the event of nationalization. Agriculture was depressed and a poor wheat harvest made necessary substantial purchases on the world market. State loans were made available in October to peasant farmers and cooperatives for the purchase of seed and equipment in an attempt to increase production, and land redistribution was postponed.

CAUTION IN FOREIGN POLICY

The need to consolidate and build up national strength which influenced its domestic policies also caused Boumedienne's Government to conduct Algeria's foreign relations with caution, although it remained committed to "anti-imperialism" and a militant stand on the Palestine question. Caution was shown when an aircraft carrying Moïse Tshombe, the former President of the Congo, was hijacked and landed in Algeria in 1967; Tshombe was detained in Algeria until June 1969 (when he died of a heart attack), despite Congolese demands for his extradition to Kinshasa where he would have faced a death sentence. Again, when Arab commandos forced an Israeli aircraft to land at Algiers in August 1968 the Algerian government released the aircraft the following month in view of the international furore the incident occasioned.

The relationship with France, Algeria's main customer and the source of substantial assistance, remained paramount. In April 1966 an agreement was concluded which provided for French technical and educational assistance for 20 years. Another agreement with France in July covered the setting-up of a new television system. Oil prospecting in the

Sahara by the joint French-Algerian oil concern, ASCOOP, resulted in a new find in November. On December 23rd an agreement was signed which cancelled Algeria's pre-independence debts and reduced indebtedness to France to DA 400 million. Relations with France subsequently deteriorated, however. Domestic pressures caused the French government to revoke the 1964 agreement on Algerian wine exports in 1967, there was increasing Algerian criticism of French petroleum interests because of the slow growth of Algerian oil production, and French fears of the Soviet navy being allowed to use the Mers el Kebir base, handed over by France on January 31st, 1968, led to the cancellation of a visit of the French Foreign Minister towards the end of the year.

The following year saw an improvement: French relations with the Arab world in general were growing more cordial and Algeria seemed to desire a continuation of its links with the former colonial power, possibly as a counterbalance to growing Soviet influence. The French cultural influence remained; there were still many French teachers, although the teaching of Arabic was being extended in the schools; large numbers of Algerians worked in France; there was a preference for such French consumer goods as were still being imported; and France continued to give assistance, including training and equipment for Algeria's armed forces.

Algerian involvement in the six-day Palestine war in June 1967 was small. Several squadrons of MiGs and some troops were sent to Egypt, and, when it was falsely alleged that Britain and the United States were militarily involved in support of Israel, action was taken against their interests in Algeria. When the ceasefire came, however, there were street demonstrations against Nasser's "treason" and also against the Soviet Union for lack of support for the Arab countries. At the Khartoum conference and also at the United Nations, Algeria's voice was one of the most belligerent, calling for a people's war such as had been fought against the French, and as a token of support detachments of Algerian troops were maintained in the Suez Canal area until August 1970.

Boumedienne visited Moscow after the Palestine war in an attempt to get a clearer understanding of Soviet policy over Israel. Algeria's economic and military ties with the Soviet Union were growing closer. Soviet advisers were playing a leading role in the development of Algeria's small industrial base and its considerable mineral resources, and Soviet agreement in 1968 to take approximately half the country's wine exports was a major relief for the agricultural sector. The Algerian army was receiving training and equipment from the U.S.S.R., while Soviet naval units made use of the harbours of Algiers and Oran and the Soviet air force enjoyed access to facilities in the interior formerly used by the French, the base at Tamanrasset in the south being especially useful as a staging post.

A highly critical, often openly hostile attitude to the United States was maintained, and diplomatic relations were severed in 1967. Nevertheless, American oil expertise was respected and encouraged; a substantial American investment in Algeria's oil industry remained, and a contract to sell liquefied natural gas to the United States was signed in 1969.

In Africa the Boumedienne Government took a consistently anti-colonial line, breaking relations with Britain over Rhodesia in 1965 (but restoring them in 1968), and providing training and other facilities for the liberation movements of southern Africa, as well as to the Eritrean Liberation Front and the National Liberation Front of Chad. A determined effort was made to improve relations with neighbouring countries in the Mahgreb. In January 1969 President Boumedienne paid his first official visit to Morocco for talks with King Hassan, and the following June frontier posts were reopened for the first time since 1963. In May 1970 King Hassan and President Boumedienne signed an agreement at Tlemcen settling the long-standing border dispute and pledging mutual cooperation on the question of the Spanish presence in North Africa. Further agreements were signed between the two leaders in June 1972, one defining the Algerian—Moroccan border, the other providing for joint exploitation of the Gara-Djebilet mines in the border regions. Algeria ratified her border settlement with Morocco in May 1973. An agreement with Mauritania was signed in December 1969 and a friendship treaty with Tunisia agreeing on common borders in January 1970. Whilst Algeria welcomed the Libyan revolution in 1969, the subsequent orientation of the Libyan leaders towards Egypt and the Sudan rather than the Mahgreb, was not conducive to close relations between the two régimes; nevertheless, an agreement to coordinate oil policies was signed.

INTERNAL OPPOSITION OVERCOME

The uneasy alliance between opponents of Ben Bella which had enabled Boumedienne to take over in 1965 broke down in 1967. Boumedienne's main support came from the "Oujda group"—Bouteflika, Medeghri, Kaid Ahmed and Cherif Belkacem; ex-members of the GPRA, such as Ben Yahia, Lamine Khane and Belaid Abdessalam; and the new professionals in the administration and the army. Opposition came from certain left-wing ministers, such as Ali Yahia and Abdelaziz Zerdani, the UGTA, the students, and some sections of the army, notably the former *wilaya* leaders. These feared the imposition of a technocratic and centralized form of socialism, different from the syndicalist concepts embodied in *autogestion*, and felt that collegial rule was being supplanted by the dictatorship of the small group round Boumedienne.

During the first half of 1967 the conflict was muted. There was student unrest in February and May, and in the communal elections in February, in which the opposition elements urged abstention, although a turn-out of 71 per cent was officially claimed there were reports of low polls in the Kabylie and Oran regions and of no more than a 50 per cent poll in the Algiers region. Unity brought about by the Palestine war was short-lived. When Abdessalem, Minister of

Industry and Energy, attacked union officials and left-wing employees in the socialist sector at the end of June, the UGTA threatened to call a general strike, which was averted only by Boumedienne's mediation and the appointment of a committee of enquiry. In the autumn Ali Yahia resigned from the Ministry of Agriculture over the refusal of Kaid Ahmed, Minister of Finance to supply funds to help the *autogéré* sector of agriculture. A demand by former *wilaya* leaders for a meeting of the Council of the Revolution was refused by Boumedienne, who was uncertain of getting a majority. In December Kaid Ahmed was put in charge of the FLN, replacing the executive of Cherif Belkacem and several former *wilaya* leaders.

On December 14th, 1967, Col. Tahar Zbiri, army chief of staff and a prominent former *wilaya* leader, launched an armed rising in the Mitidja. It was put down two days later, but Zbiri was not captured and was joined in hiding by Abedlaziz Zerdani, the Minister of Labour, and other supporters. Cols. Mohand Ou El Hadj, Salah Boubnida and Katib Youcef also disappeared. The rising had failed because the key posts in the army were held by the younger professionals loyal to Boumedienne, and it was followed by a wave of arrests in the unions and the administration, and selective dismissals in the FLN and the army in order to secure his position. On March 7th Boumedienne appointed three well-known supporters to vacant ministerial offices: Cherif Belkacem (Finance), Tayebi Larbi (Agriculture) and Mohand Said Mazouni (Labour).

Opposition to Boumedienne was by no means crushed, however. FLN attempts in February 1968 to impose a new loyal student committee at Algiers University provoked a long strike by students and teachers, and in the spring there were numerous reports of guerrilla activity in the Aurès and the Kabyle. The Organization of Popular Resistance (ORP) appeared to be active both in these areas and among the students. An attempt to assassinate Boumedienne was made on April 25th in Algiers, but he escaped with only minor injuries.

In the latter part of 1968 there were signs that the Government's position had strengthened and President Boumedienne made several visits to the provinces without special security precautions. In March 1969 a number of secret trials were held and numbers of less important prisoners were subsequently released. The second stage of the reform of governmental institutions (the first being the 1967 communal elections) was put into operation in May 1969 when elections were held for the 15 administrative districts (*wilaya*) and 72 per cent of the electorate voted for candidates on a single FLN list. In June 1970, following the celebration of his first five years in power, Boumedienne undertook an extensive tour of western Algeria, and when cabinet changes were made in July, his key colleagues retained their places, a fact which served to emphasize the regime's stability. On the anniversary of the revolution in November 1970 he felt able to amnesty 100 people, including three close associates of Ben Bella arrested in 1965—Hadji Ben Alla, Mohamed Nekkache and Abderahmane Sherif; Ben Bella himself remained in detention, however. Others freed included three leaders of the ORP, one being Bachir Hadj Ali, former secretary of the Communist Party, and more recent opponents of the régime who had been tried in 1969. The release of these former enemies gave some indication of the weakness of the underground opposition.

Only among school and university students did discontent remain in evidence. A school strike in December led to violent clashes with the police, and in January 1971 the arrest of eight Algiers university students resulted in a strike at the university, the dissolution by the government of the National Union of Algerian Students (UNEA), the introduction of a university security force and the banning of all meetings, demonstrations and distributions of leaflets on the campus. Six of the students arrested were accused of having connections with the Party of the Socialist Vanguard (PAGS) formed from the remnants of the ORP. The attitude of many students otherwise sympathetic to the aims and achievements of the FLN was doubtless affected by poor employment prospects.

TAKE-OVER OF FRENCH OIL INTERESTS

The improvement in President Boumedienne's position at home enabled him to adopt a more militant attitude towards France. He could afford to demand more for Algerian oil, and the resultant dispute over the price to be paid by the French oil companies culminated in the decision to take control of them by nationalization.

The two companies concerned, the Compagnie Française de Pétroles (CFP) and the Compagnie de Recherches et d'Activités Pétrolières (ERAP), were responsible for some two-thirds of Algeria's total production. In the first half of 1970 the Algerian government pressed them to accept an increase in the price at which each barrel exported was assessed for fiscal purposes (the tax reference price). Negotiations broke down and in July the government unilaterally decided on a new price of $2.85 per barrel, 77 cents above the former level. Talks were resumed at government level in September but, given Algeria's determination to become a "Mediterranean Cuba" rather than submit to what she regarded as French neo-colonialism, no progress was made and they were abandoned on February 4th, 1971. After the agreement of February 14th in Teheran between the international oil companies and the Gulf states, which raised posted prices by only 35 cents, the French thought they were in a stronger position, but on February 24th Boumedienne announced the takeover by the Algerian government of a 51 per cent holding in CFP and ERAP and the complete nationalization of the companies' gas and pipeline interests.

The French Government regarded this move as a breach of the 1965 agreement but could only ask for fair compensation. The subsequent Algerian offer was found unacceptable and in April 1971 France discontinued negotiations. Relations appeared to have reached their lowest ebb. It was announced that many French technicians and teachers were to leave Algeria, and attacks were made on some of the 700,000 Algerians in France. The French Government applied a boycott against Algerian oil and tried to get other major consumers to do the same. Talks between the two French companies and SONATRACH, the Algerian state oil concern, were resumed, however, and agreements were reached in June and September under which the role of CFP and ERAP became that of minority partners of the Algerian state in return for guaranteed oil supplies. After approval by the two governments a final agreement, which also provided for compensation and reduced back claims of taxes, was signed on December 15.

The agreement was the culmination of Algerian measures to gain control by nationalization of all major French industrial and commercial interests in the country and the "privileged relationship" between Algeria and France, provided for in the 1962 Evian agreements, was at an end. In addition, by the end of 1971, the Boumedienne government had nationalized or otherwise assumed control of other foreign oil, industrial and commercial interests in Algeria, including those of Britain and the United States.

THE PALESTINE QUESTION

The Boumedienne Government's stand on the Palestine question remained uncompromisingly militant, despite the decreasing support of other Arab states for the Palestine guerrillas. Algeria accepted neither the 1967 UN resolution nor the ceasefire, and when, after the hostilities along the Suez Canal in 1969 and 1970, a further ceasefire was agreed in August 1970, Algerian troops were withdrawn. Radio stations of Palestine liberation movements banished from Cairo in July 1970 were allowed to broadcast from Algiers and the Jordanian Government was blamed for the fighting between the army and guerrillas in Jordan; American peace proposals made in May 1971 were scouted. Relations with Jordan were broken off in June 1971 following the Jordanian Government's final onslaught on the remaining Palestinian guerrilla bases, and the condemnation of King Hussein remains a feature of Col. Boumedienne's public statements. In February 1973 he again condemned the king, this time for the arrest of the Palestinian leader, Abu Daoud.

Despite Algeria's policy towards Palestine and the welcome accorded to almost any exiled foreign opposition group, it continued to co-operate in the economic field with any state willing to do so. A visit to Algeria by the Soviet Prime Minister, Mr. Kosygin, in October 1971 resulted in increased Soviet economic and technical co-operation. Later in the year Japanese and Canadian assistance in industrial development was announced. Above all, relations with the U.S.A. improved. Two hijackings of American airliners ended in Algeria in June and August 1972. In both cases, although the Algerian Government granted the hijackers asylum, it arranged for the return of the substantial ransom payments that had been extorted from the airlines. The return of this money and the Algerians' doubts about whether the hijackers were genuine supporters of the Black Panther Movement or just gangsters, as the Americans claimed, led to sharp exchanges between Eldridge Cleaver, the Panther leader in Algiers, and Col. Boumedienne. Eventually, Cleaver left Algeria, and, in a deliberate snub to the Algerian Government, the Panthers elected one of the hijackers his successor. Though co-operative over the hijackings, the Algerians continued to criticize U.S. policy in Vietnam, especially when the bombing of Hanoi in October later that year damaged the Algerian mission building. Nevertheless, in 1973 another contract for the sale of natural gas to the U.S.A. was signed, and in April the visit to Algeria of David Newsom, the American Assistant Secretary of State for African Affairs, further patched up relations between the two countries.

ECONOMIC SURVEY

Algeria covers an area of 2,381,743 square kilometres of which a large part is desert. At the census of 1966 the population was returned at 12.1 million and it grew to an estimated 14.6 million by mid-1971. The great majority of Europeans had returned to France by the early 1960s (an estimated 65,000 remained in mid-1965); prior to this exodus, 82 per cent of Europeans and 27 per cent of Muslims lived in towns. The number of Muslims in towns is rising rapidly as migration from the rural areas quickens. The largest towns are Algiers, the capital (1,200,000, including the suburbs), Oran (440,000 with its suburbs), Constantine (280,000), Annaba (Bône) (180,000) and Sidi-Bel-Abbès (101,000). By 1972 the population was growing at an estimated rate of 3.5 per cent a year, and in October the National Census Office forecast that the population could reach 24.6 million by 1986 in view of the current birth rate of 48 per thousand. In an effort to reduce the flow of peasants to the towns, the Government announced, in the summer of 1971, and began to implement in early 1972 a programme of land reform and redistribution.

Algeria has varied natural resources. In the coastal region are highly fertile plains and valleys, where profitable returns are made from cereals and vineyards. However, the rest of the country serves little agricultural purpose, though in the mountains, grazing and forestry bring a small income for the population. Mineral resources are abundant and the discovery of oil and gas deposits was extremely important.

GOVERNMENT STRATEGY

After independence in 1962, the Government of M. Ahmed Ben Bella moved to the left, under pressure from the extremist elements of his party. While official policy was of a socialist character, full-scale nationalization was avoided. The Government of Col. Boumedienne also proclaims a socialist policy. During his first year in power this was little evident, but in 1966 he brought in additional nationalization measures, nationalizing foreign-owned mines, unoccupied lands (left by Europeans at independence) and insurance companies. These were followed in 1968 by further measures directed against the private sector of industry.

The Government's strategy for development is laid down in the Four-Year Plan for 1970 to 1973, which emphasizes the establishment of a capital-intensive sector, involving the hydrocarbon, iron and steel, chemical and engineering industries, which is to serve as the basis for economic growth. The heavy industries are all state-run, while consumer-goods industries, which are not a priority in the 1970–73 plan, remain largely in private hands for the time being, although parts of the textile, leather and food industries have already been nationalized. In brief, all key sectors are run by the state, which intends eventually to control all internal transport, domestic wholesale trade, and foreign trade. In 1970 and 1971 a total of 150,000 new jobs was created outside agriculture, and the Government hopes to solve the massive unemployment problem by 1980. About a quarter of the male workforce was unemployed in 1971. The austerity of the present period is reflected in the 1970 trade figures, where investment goods, semi-finished products, and raw materials accounted for 70 per cent of total imports compared with 43 per cent in 1966.

The Government has a mixed attitude towards foreign investment. It knows that Algeria cannot progress without foreign help, but it will not accept foreign domination of the economy. Foreign investment is only likely to be acceptable in the future if the Government is allowed a controlling share. The Government is either taking over completely or taking a controlling interest in most foreign-owned companies. It took control of the whole of the hydrocarbon sector in the spring of 1971.

The country's gross domestic product, at current prices, rose from 13.3 billion dinars in 1964 to 19.8 billion dinars in 1969, equivalent to an annual average growth of over eight per cent. Per capita income in 1969 was about 1,500 dinars. A growth rate of about 8.9 per cent was achieved in 1970, and similar rates were reached in the two years following. The Government envisages that in 1973 the G.D.P. will increase by a further 10 per cent to total 26.5 billion dinars. The Algerian economy, bolstered by expanding oil production, has been undergoing a radical transformation. It has been moving away gradually from an agricultural emphasis to industrialization, the authorities having accepted that industrialization is the best long-term means of solving the country's two major economic problems—re-organization of agriculture and utilization of surplus and underemployed manpower. According to the last census in 1966, the active work force was put at 2.5 million, of which 1.5 million (55 per cent) were in the agricultural sector, while 200,000 were employed by industry. The same census put unemployed at 610,000 and the young in search of their first job at 262,000. A large part of those classed as unemployed were chronically unemployed.

AGRICULTURE

Algeria is still mainly an agricultural country. There are 13.3 million hectares of agricultural land, of which 6.2 million are arable, c. 230,000 are devoted to vines, 200,000 are orchards and 5.2 million are pastures (often desert or semi-desert). Most of the Sahara is devoted to semi-desert pasturage. The most valuable crop is the grape harvest; whilst wheat, barley and oats, grown for local consumption, cover a large area. Other crops include maize, sorghum, millet, rye and rice, as well as citrus fruit, olives, figs and dates, and tobacco. Algeria is a major date-producer with an output of 100,000 tons of dates and figs in 1970. Agricultural development is restricted by problems such as erosion, primitive methods of production, overpopulation and underemployment.

Before independence, roughly 30 per cent of the cultivated land and most of the irrigated areas were owned by Europeans, but this situation has been changed by the departure of most of the Europeans from Algeria and by the state takeover of much of their land as part of the general policy of socialization of land. The immediate effect of the loss of European technical know-how was detrimental to Algerian economic development. Agriculture is also vulnerable to adverse weather conditions, especially droughts and floods. Severe flooding in October 1969, particularly in the Aurès area, left over 150,000 people homeless and largely destroyed the date crop.

In the 1970–73 Four-Year Plan nearly 4,300 million dinars, or 16 per cent of total investment, is allocated to agriculture. This is a relatively low proportion considering that about 70 per cent of the country's population is employed in agriculture. The 1974–77 plan is expected to invest more in agriculture and related sectors. Expansion will take place particularly in the food-processing industries and the production of agricultural equipment.

LAND REFORM

The first regulations, under which settlers were able to hold and transfer land, were introduced in October 1962. From that date the state took over any property declared vacant; at the same time all property transactions were made illegal in order to prevent profiteering by Muslims. The area of land abandoned and taken over by the state under these first regulations was estimated at 2.5 million acres. Under French Government pressure a guarantee fund was set up to provide compensation for expropriated settlers.

Under the first decree, the settlers remained the legal owners of the land, while the state "used" it. Six months later, however, in March 1963, another Government decree declared that the state was taking over ownership of abandoned land. This was probably a political move, since nothing material was gained.

A number of large French landowners subsequently had their land taken away, although it was still occupied. The measure was not aimed purely at the French—it also affected Muslim and other property owners. Small landowners in occupation, whether French or Muslim, remained untouched. In May 1966 all remaining unoccupied property which had been evacuated by settlers was finally taken over by the state.

The land expropriated by the state is managed by workers' committees (*comités de gestion*) as state farms. By September 1963, 1,525 such organizations had been established, of which 411 were in Oran, 234 in Constantine and 41 in Kabyle. The area under *autogestion* at this date was about 1.7 million ha. After the total nationalization of French land in October 1963, state farm land accounted for 2.3 million ha., roughly half the cultivable land in Algeria. The socialist agricultural sector employs 100,000 workers and their families out of a total peasant population of 7 million (of which 2 million men are of working age). However, it accounts for 75 per cent of the country's agricultural production and over 60 per cent of its exports (excluding oil). State farms account for 85 per cent of the area under the vine.

In July 1971 President Boumedienne announced an agrarian reform programme which provided for the break-up of large, Algerian-owned farms and their re-organization into co-operatives. There were provisions for compensation, and small-landowners were to continue undisturbed. The reform programme became law in November, and the first stage of its implementation, the registration of land ownership, began in March 1972. The Government has made great efforts to explain the programme to the rural population and is proceeding cautiously to avoid stirring up discontent. Since March 1972 some Government-owned land has been distributed to peasants, and many absentee landlords in government service have voluntarily handed over land to the state. Following the completion of the census in May 1973, the next scheduled stage in the programme is the appropriation of privately-owned land.

CROPS

The coastal areas of the Mediterranean produce grapes. Vines have been grown in Algeria since antiquity merely for local consumption; however, after the coming of the French in 1830, vine growing received substantial encouragement and wines still represent the principal agricultural export. In terms of quantity, Algeria has for many years been the world's largest wine exporter, mainly of low quality wine marketed in France. Exports fell sharply after independence, production of wine dropping from 18.6 million hectolitres in 1960 to only 8 million in 1970, largely as a result of the withdrawal of European skill and capital. In 1971 total production was between 8.0 and 8.5 million hectolitres, of which five million hectolitres were sold to the U.S.S.R., 24,000 hectolitres to Poland and only 500,000 hectolitres to the EEC as a whole. French purchases almost completely stopped because of the objections of French wine growers and because of the French quarrel with the Boumedienne régime over the nationalization of French oil companies.

The Boumedienne régime regards agricultural dependence on wine as incompatible with real political independence. Thus it is tearing up the least productive vines and converting the land to cereal and dairy farming, and to forestry—Algeria had only 860,000 cattle in the autumn of 1971 and has at present to import most of its dairy products. The target for 1980 is 140,000 hectares under vines, which required the tearing up of 25,000 hectares in both 1971 and 1972.

Foreign ownership of wheat land was particularly resented by the Algerian peasantry, and practically all settler cultivators of cereals have now left the country. Grown principally in the Constantine, Annaba, Sétif and Tiaret areas, wheat in 1970 covered 2,250,000 hectares. Production has fluctuated considerably since independence, falling as low as 700,000 tons in drought years but reaching 1,800,000 tons in 1963–64. In 1970 it was 1,500,000 tons. The area under barley in 1970 was 700,000 hectares. Production was 847,000 tons in 1961 but it has failed to reach this level since, totalling 500,000 tons in 1970. Rice, maize (400,000 tons in 1970) and sorghum are also grown. Although cereals production in 1972 reached a record figure (25 million quintals), an agreement was announced in September 1972, under which Canada will supply 92 million bushels of wheat over a five-year period in addition to the eight million bushels a year already being supplied.

Olives are grown in the western coastal belt. Production fluctuates because of the two-year flowering cycle of the olive. In 1970 150,000 tons of olives were produced, yielding 18,000 tons of oil.

The citrus crop, grown in the coastal districts, totalled 507,000 tons in 1970, oranges, tangerines and clementines accounting for 487,000 tons. About half of citrus production is exported, mainly to Western Europe and to the U.S.S.R.

Tobacco is the main industrial crop, employing about 13,000 people. Some 10–12,000 tons of leaf are processed annually, producing 3,500 tons of tobacco.

LIVESTOCK, FORESTRY AND FISHING

Sheep and goats are raised on a small scale. In 1970/71 there were 8,400,000 sheep in Algeria. Cattle, donkeys, horses, pigs and goats are also kept. Livestock-raising was severely hit by the military policy of regrouping rural communities, and has not been able to recover.

The area covered by forests has dropped from 3.04 million hectares in 1961 to only 2.4 million hectares in 1970, and the Government is trying to increase this figure, partly to protect cultivable land against erosion. Though largely brushwood, there are large areas of cork-oak trees, Aleppo pine, evergreen oak and cedar; dwarf palm is grown in the plains and alfa on the table-land.

The Government feels that Algeria is not exploiting its fishing potential and hopes to raise annual production to over 40,000 tons. The catch has remained at around 20,000 tons for the last ten years. The fishing fleet is being expanded steadily. Sardines, anchovies, sprats and tunny fish are caught.

SUMMARY

Algerian agriculture suffers considerably from bureaucratic control that is both excessive and inefficient. In the autumn of 1971 there were bitter complaints in the press about the lack of co-ordination between the government departments controlling agriculture. An index of total food production in Algeria, which uses the average 1952–6 production figure as the base year of 100, shows food production in 1971 at 97, compared with 94 in 1970 and a low figure of 68 in 1966. Per capita food output (1952–56 = 100) came to 65 in 1970 and 1971 compared with a low of 53 in 1966.

MINERALS

Algeria has rich mineral resources and these are already an important item in the country's foreign trade. The future promises even larger exports, as petroleum and gas are exploited more intensely. Since before the petroleum era, Algeria has mined and exported high grade iron ore, phosphates, lead, zinc, and antimony. Production generally has fluctuated over recent years. An index of mining production, excluding oil and gas (1963=100), reached 127 in 1968. In May 1966 the government nationalized eleven foreign-owned iron-ore, lead, copper and zinc mines, promising compensation, and mining is now controlled by the state enterprise SONAREM.

Iron ore is found at Beni-Saf, Zaccar, Timezrit and near the eastern frontier at Quenza and Bou Khadra. The average grade of ore is between 50 and 60 per cent. Lack of transport facilities prevents the exploitation of substantial deposits at Tindouf in the Sahara. Production has fluctuated greatly since independence but reached 1,599,000 metric tons in 1969. The deposits at Ouenza represent 75 per cent of total production. Italy is the biggest customer, followed by the United Kingdom. Production of bituminous coal, mined at Colomb Béhar-Kenadza and Ksiksou, has dropped steadily from 153,000 tons in 1958 to 16,800 tons in 1967 and very little in 1968 and 1969, owing mainly to the lack of adequate and regular transport. Most of this coal is consumed locally, though a little is exported to Morocco. A feasibility study is being carried out on the possible development of coal deposits at Abadla, near Colomb-Béhar.

The most important zinc deposit is found on the Algerian-Moroccan frontier at El-Abed-Oued Zounder, which is an extension of the Moroccan deposits. Two forms of zinc are found in Algeria—blende and calamine. Since 1960 production has been around 60,000 tons, with occasional fluctuations. Most of this production is exported to France, Spain, Belgium and Federal Germany. In August 1972 the U.S. Dravo Corporation agreed to expand the production capacity of the El-Abed lead and zinc mine from 800 to 3,300 tons a day by drilling a new extraction shaft and installing extra equipment.

Exploitation of large phosphate deposits at Djegel-Onk, 340 km. from Annaba, began in 1960 and reached 600,000 tons in 1971. It is planned to increase it to 2.40 million tons a year by 1980. Total phosphate production has clearly recovered from the slump which followed independence and which meant production of only 72,000 tons in 1964. France and Spain are the principle export markets for Algerian phosphates.

Lead is mined at El Abed on the Moroccan border; production in 1969 was 7,900 tons. Other mineral resources include antimony, tungsten, manganese, mercury, copper and salt. Under study are plans for an aluminium smelter, possibly at Mostaganem.

SONAREM, the state mining concern, forecast that in 1972 it would produce four million tons of iron ore, 900,000 tons of phosphates, 90,000 tons of lead, zinc and copper concentrate, 300 tons of mercury, 100,000 tons of salt and 160,000 tons of other minerals. An agreement providing Soviet help for a major minerals exploration programme was signed in May 1971.

PETROLEUM

Production of crude oil in the Sahara on a commercial scale began in 1958. The original principal producing areas were at Hassi Massaoud in Central Algeria and round Edjeleh-Zarzaitine in the Polignac Basin near the Libyan frontier. In 1966 production was boosted by substantial quantities of crude from fields at Gassi Touil, Rhourde el Baguel and Rhourde Nouss with the opening of the third pipeline to the coast. Subsequent discoveries of oil have been made at Nezla, Hoaud Berkaoui, Ouargla, Mesdar and El Borma, and more recently at Hassi Keskessa, Guellala and Tin Fouyé. In 1969 Algeria joined the Organization of Petroleum Exporting Countries (OPEC).

From 1.2 million tons in 1959, Algerian production of crude oil rose to a ceiling of 26 million tons in 1964 and 1965, limited by the capacity of the two pipelines to the coast, one from the eastern fields through Tunisia to La Skhirra, and the other from Hassi Messaoud to Bejaia on the Algerian coast. The Hassi Messaoud pipeline also serves other fields further inland. The combined capacity of these two pipelines is now over 30 million tons, as a result of the installation of additional pumping stations. The government set up its own company, *Société Nationale pour la Recherche, la Production, le Transport, la Transformation et la Commercialisation des Hydrocarbures* (SONATRACH) to be responsible for the construction of a third pipeline 28-inch in diameter and 805 km. long from Hassi Messaoud to Arzew on the coast. This pipeline came into operation early in 1966, reaching its maximum capacity of 22 million tons per year in 1970. The new pipeline permitted a steady increase in total production to 48.2 million in 1970. Production in 1971 dropped to 36.5 million tons because of the dispute with French companies. In 1972 oil production recovered to reach 52 million tons and should increase to 56 million tons in 1973.

Algeria's fourth oil pipeline, from Mesdar to Skikda,

was completed in May 1972 with an initial capacity of 12 million tons a year which may be increased to 30 million tons a year.

In 1966 SONATRACH bought BP's distribution network and its share in the Algiers refinery. A year later the Esso and Mobil marketing organizations were nationalized, and in May 1968 the nine remaining networks (mostly French except for *Shell Algérie*) were also taken over and SONATRACH became the sole domestic distributor. SONATRACH acquired majority control of the Algiers refinery (capacity 2.5 million tons per year) in 1969, when it took over Total's holding. It has since gained complete control by taking over the Algerian operations of the other shareholders, CFP and Shell. Crude supplies are delivered by a 135 km. spur from the main pipeline to Bejaia. A small 100,000 tons per year refinery at Hassi Messaoud supplies the Saharan market. Refineries at Arzew (completed in June 1973) and Shikda (under construction), each with a capacity of 2.5 million tons, are both owned by SONATRACH.

In 1970 SONATRACH signed a number of contracts for the development of the petroleum industry with the U.S.S.R. organization Technoexport. The first contract relates to long-term petroleum exploitation with systematic research of the Algerian sub-soil; the contract sets an annual production target of 100 million tons of petroleum. The second concentrates on the improvement of production from existing deposits, notably that of Hassi-Messaoud; it aims to increase the deposit's annual output from 20 million tons to 30 million tons. The third contract relates to commencing production of mixed deposits of petroleum and gas which has hitherto never interested companies with concessions.

Natural gas will become more valuable to Algeria than oil. Reserves are currently estimated at three million million cubic metres, and production could reach 60,000 million cubic metres a year by the late seventies. A pipeline from Hassi R'Mel, one of the world's largest gas fields, to Arzew, Algiers and Oran was opened in 1961. The *Cie. Algérienne du Méthane Liquide* (CAMEL) has a liquefaction plant at Arzew, and shipments of natural gas in liquefied form in specially constructed tankers to the U.K. began in October 1964 and to France in March 1965. The U.K. takes 0.7 million tons and France 0.3 million tons annually under contract. Natural gas is currently produced from fields at Hassi R'Mel, Hassi Messaoud, Nord In Amenas and Rhourde el Baguel. In March 1968 a new field with estimated reserves of 30,000 million cubic metres was discovered at Gassi-El-Adem, some 60 miles south of Hassi Messaoud.

In June 1967 an agreement in principle was signed covering the sale of 3,500 million cubic metres of natural gas annually to France, as outlined in the 1965 agreement between the two countries. The contract, for 15 years, was to have begun in 1971 but was later postponed to 1972. In recent years sales have increased rapidly. Contracts were signed with Distrigas of the U.S. for the delivery of 436 million cubic metres a year starting in 1971 and of 1,200 million cubic metres a year starting in 1975. At the end of 1970 two major deals were arranged with El Paso, another American company, under which SONATRACH will export 15,000 million cubic metres a year for 25 years from the winter of 1975. In the spring of 1972 Gas Natural of Spain agreed to buy 1,500 million cubic metres a year from 1974, and a consortium of European companies contracted to buy 10,000 million cubic metres a year for 20 years commencing in 1977, with the option of buying a further 2,000 million cubic metres a year, and Escogas of the U.S. agreed to buy 6,000 million cubic metres a year for 25 years starting in 1975. The demand for Algerian oil is divided between Europe and the U.S., in accordance with the Algerian Government's wishes. The Algerians have ordered studies on the possibility of building gas pipelines to Europe to increase sales there further. By the end of 1972 SONATRACH should have obtained buyers for more than 40,000 million cubic metres of gas a year.

To fulfil these commitments Algeria is investing heavily in pipelines, liquefaction plants and tankers. New major liquefaction plants are being built at Skikda and Arzew and in May 1972 the 40-inch pipeline from Hassi R'Mel to Skikda was opened. The pipeline, 577 kilometres long and built at a cost of AD 500 million, will have its capacity doubled to 12,000 million cubic metres a year when five pumping stations are finished. The El Paso deal alone involves the building of pipelines and of an Arzew liquefaction plant and the purchase of nine line tankers and will therefore require investment of about $600 million. Although in late 1972 and early 1973 some additional orders were received and existing contracts modified, for instance the contract with European companies was modified to involve a possible 15,500 million cubic metres of gas a year, making it the largest single gas deal ever, the chief development of the period was the removal of obstacles to fulfilment of the contracts. By the end of March 1973 the U.S. Federal Power Commission had given final approval for the El Paso deals after nearly a year of delay caused by the objections of U.S. companies to price restrictions on Algerian gas originally imposed by the FPC. After protest these restrictions were modified. In addition a $557 million loan for SONATRACH had been obtained through the U.S. Export Import Bank for Algerian investments in pipelines, liquefaction plants and tankers. It is significant that in July 1972 a State Department official prophesied that the U.S.A. could be taking half of Algeria's natural gas output even as late as 1985. Regarding European deals, favourable feasibility reports have been received on the possibility of building submarine gas pipelines to Europe, and the Governments involved in the 15,500 million cubic metres a year deal have approved it.

Tokyo Engineering was awarded a $93 million contract in October 1971 to build a petrochemical complex at Skikda for completion in 1975, and in May 1972 President Boumedienne opened a fertilizer factory at Annaba which uses phosphate ore from Djebel Onk. A fertilizer factory at Arzew was opened in 1970.

Algeria intends greatly to expand its condensate production, which in 1970 totalled only 585,000 tons.

A major deal was concluded with Commonwealth Refining of Puerto Rico at the end of 1971 under which Algeria will deliver an increasing quantity of condensate to the U.S.—700,000 tons in 1972 rising to 13 million tons in 1976. This sale will require investment of $260 million on a recycling plant and ancillary units. With the crude oil also to be delivered, the Commonwealth sale is worth a total of $8,000 million.

In June 1970 the local interests of Shell, Phillips, Elwerath, and AMIF were nationalized, following protracted negotiations which failed to achieve agreement on tax reference prices. The four companies, which together produced about 5 million tons of crude annually, were merged into SONATRACH, which thus became Algeria's largest producer.

In February 1971, Algeria nationalized the French oil companies operating in the country, as well as pipeline networks and natural gas deposits. This decision followed a long period of tension in relations with France which began in July 1970, when the government announced that the taxation reference price was to be increased. Since that time, negotiations had been in progress almost constantly and, for a period, it seemed that relations were improving as a result of the French order to its petroleum companies to pay an advance on back taxation. On April 13th, 1971 President Boumedienne issued a decree laying down the conditions under which foreign oil companies could operate in Algeria. Concession-type agreements were banned. Talks were held with the French companies on compensation terms and on the future mode of their activity in Algeria, the negotiations ended in an agreement with CFP at the end of June and a settlement with Elf-ERAP in November. The basic provisions of these agreements were that the companies would provide some investment funds and technical help in exchange for oil and that compensation payments were largely cancelled out by the tax debts of the companies to Algeria. By the end of 1971, after six years of rapid expansion, SONATRACH controlled almost 80 per cent of Algeria's oil production, compared with only 31 per cent in 1970.

Despite a law of April 1972 requiring companies wishing to explore in Algeria to form a joint company with SONATRACH, in which the latter should have a controlling interest, co-operation with foreign oil firms is increasing. For instance the U.S. firm Getty Oil has operated effectively as a minority partner of SONATRACH, and in April 1973 Sun Oil signed an agreement under which, with SONATRACH, it will search for oil in the Sahara. A similar agreement was concluded earlier in the year with the Brazilian firm, Petrobras.

INDUSTRY

Industrialization is the keynote of the government's economic policy and the major investment effort in the 1970–73 plan is devoted to this end. Of the $5,200 million investment over the plan period, about 45 per cent will go to industry, resulting, hopefully, in an industrial growth rate of 13 per cent a year compared with the 8–9 per cent achieved in the 1965–69 period. In the 1970–73 plan, heavy industry is scheduled to grow at 25 per cent a year while the food-processing sector should grow by a more modest 7 per cent a year.

The Algerian industrial sector was very small in 1962, being confined mainly to food-processing, building materials, textiles and minerals. The Government was anxious to industrialize the country and under the Constantine Plan large tax concessions were offered for industrial projects. But it was hard for Algeria to recover from the loss of demand, capital and technical skill caused by the departure in 1962 of French soldiers and settlers, and progress was slow.

The Constantine Plan involved mainly the development of small-scale industries but it did include three major projects—the Algiers refinery, the Arzew liquefaction plant and the iron and steel complex at Annaba which were finished. At the latter, the smelter and pipe-mill were opened after several delays in June 1969 and the steelworks and hot rolling mill were opened in May 1972. The cold rolling mill has not yet been finished. The U.S.S.R., which was responsible for most of the building of the steelworks, has offered help for further expansion. In the east of the country it is planned to build a 40,000 tons a year zinc plant and a 100,000 tons a year aluminium plant.

Foreign firms became increasingly reluctant to invest in Algeria because of the danger of nationalization. In May and June 1968 over 40 companies in the food, chemical, mechanical and construction material sectors were taken over. Renault closed its Maison-Carrée car assembly plant in 1971 after a dispute with the government on imports and later in the year a contract under which Renault was to have built a car assembly plant in Oran was cancelled. Algeria is nevertheless expanding its vehicle industries. In February 1972 work began on the construction by Berliet of a heavy vehicle factory at Rouiba, and a West German firm is building a tractor and diesel engine factory near Constantine for completion in 1976. A motor cycle plant is also being built. A major project, for which tenders were invited in the autumn of 1972, is the building of a £75 million car plant, probably at Oran. Citröen, Fiat, General Motors, Volkswagen, British Leyland and Renault are all interested. The latter has settled its dispute with the Government over the Maison Carrée factory but contests the legality of the cancellation of the original Oran contract.

The mechanical and engineering industries are growing quickly. The Government intends to establish a major shipyard at Oran and a metal works was opened at Meftah in January 1972. West German firms are setting up an electrical goods factory at Tizi Ouzou which will cost 250 million Deutsch Marks and are building a battery factory at Setif to open in 1973. Other growth areas are the paper industry—Sonic, the state paper company, has plans for eight new factories, four of which are already being built—building materials and textiles. Expansion work at the Batna textile complex began in February 1972. The textile industry employed 6,200 people and produced 40 million metres in 1970.

Recent industrial developments include the opening

of a paint factory at Bakhdaria in September 1972, and two plastics factories at Sety. Work has begun on a 55 million dinar printing complex, which will be the largest in Africa.

TRADE

Ever since 1948 until recently Algerian foreign trade figures have consistently shown a surplus of imports over exports; this feature was reversed only in 1967 and 1968. The collapse of the domestic market after the departure of the French army and most of the French settlers reduced imports sharply. In 1962 petroleum exports were included in Algerian figures for the first time, i.e. after the two Saharan departments joined Algeria. Oil and natural gas exports have transformed Algerian export figures, as in the case of Libya where oil has only comparatively recently been discovered and where similarly exports were previously limited to agricultural products and some minerals. Algerian exports used to be about 2,000 million dinars but in 1970 totalled 4,980 million dinars, while imports reached 6,205 million dinars. In the past Algeria's other main exports have been lime, citrus fruit and iron ore, but export markets for wine are now difficult to find. In recent years exports of petroleum products and natural gas have become increasingly important. Other exports include vegetables, tobacco, hides and skins, dates and phosphates. Imports consist increasingly of capital equipment, semi-finished goods and raw materials. Imports of food and consumer goods are declining in importance. Oil now accounts for about 70 per cent of all exports.

Before independence France took 81 per cent of Algeria's exports and provided 82 per cent of its imports. This dominance declined steadily as Algeria tried to break free from dependence on the colonial power but in 1970 France still took 54 per cent of Algeria's exports and supplied 43 per cent of its imports. The 1971 oil crisis made Algeria even more determined to diversify its trade partners but this policy met with only limited initial success. In the first nine months of 1971 France provided 42 per cent of Algerian imports and took 26 per cent of its exports. The drop in Algerian exports to France was caused primarily by a French refusal to buy, not an Algerian ability to find markets elsewhere. Federal Germany, Italy, the U.S. and Britain have become increasingly important trading partners for Algeria (Federal Germany is SONATRACH's best customer). British exports to Algeria in particular increased substantially in 1971 despite Algerian import restrictions caused by the oil dispute. Although important trade agreements were signed in 1971 with China and the U.S.S.R., the communist states have not yet become important in Algerian trade. In the first nine months of 1971 the states of Eastern Europe took only 13.8 per cent of Algerian exports and provided 6.9 per cent of its imports.

Algerian trade stagnated during 1971 because the failure to export oil meant the Government had also to cut back on imports. Imports totalled AD 4,331 million in the first nine months of 1971 and exports came to AD 2,568 million. More recent figures are not available, but the Minister of Commerce has stated that in 1973 imports will be worth AD10,000 million with consumer goods accounting for only a quarter of this figure. Algeria's economic links with France are continuing to weaken, and in 1972 imports from France fell by a further 14 per cent to 2,383 million francs. In the same year British trade with Algeria rose substantially, with both exports and imports rising by £6 million to £33.8 million and £22.9 million respectively.

Since very soon after independence Algeria has been trying to reach an agreement on trade and economic co-operation with the European Economic Community, and by 1972 it seemed that real progress had been made. However, nothing has yet been signed, as Algeria refuses to agree to the restrictions which the EEC requires on importing Algerian wine and refined oil products. At the beginning of 1973 Algeria abolished the trading preferences enjoyed by EEC states.

FINANCE

Until independence, Algeria was mostly dependent on France for its central banking and monetary system, though some of the usual central banking functions were carried out by the *Banque d'Algérie*. The *Banque Centrale d'Algérie*, the sole bank of issue of the new Algerian franc, which started its operations on January 1st, 1963, has all the usual central banking powers. The Algerian Dinar which in 1964 replaced the franc, remained at par with the French franc, until the devaluation of the French franc in 1969, when the parity of the Algerian dinar remained unchanged. After the dollar devaluation of December 1971, the parity of the dinar to gold was left unchanged at AD 1.0=180 milligrams of gold. The banking system has been largely taken over by the state, various restrictions having discouraged private banks (almost all of which were foreign owned, most being subsidiaries of French companies) from continuing their operations in the country. A state monopoly on all foreign financial transactions was imposed in November 1967; this followed a similar monopoly imposed on insurance in June 1966. There are several co-operative agricultural banks, assisted by government funds.

The main sources of budgetary revenue are income tax, turnover tax, customs and indirect taxes, and, more recently, petroleum receipts. The 1973 Investment Budget provides for expenditure of 12,000 million dinars, a 24 per cent increase on the 1972 figure, while the Operating Budget totals 6,430 million dinars, an increase of 17 per cent. Spending will be financed mainly by oil revenues (over 40 per cent) and foreign loans, although domestic saving, which is high in Algeria, will also be important. Investment will be concentrated primarily on industry, while education is the largest single item in the Operating Budget.

The Government is proud of the fact that much of Algeria's investment is financed by domestic saving and Finance Minister Ismail Mahroug, who has said that he wants Algerians to become "Japanese-style savers", has argued that only 18 per cent of Algeria's investments in 1971 were financed by loans from companies undertaking contracts in Algeria or by the Socialist bloc. Nevertheless, Algeria has not found it hard to borrow money in addition to the AD 500 million and the AD 250 million loans from the U.S.S.R. and China respectively which were obtained some time ago. (These loans are thought not to have been fully utilized). Algeria's political stability and its oil revenues have made many countries willing to lend. In 1972 and 1973 loans from American and Western European financial institutions and from Eastern Europe proliferated and appeared fairly easy to obtain. The loans, of which U.S. aid for the El Paso deal was the most important, aided many sectors of Algeria's industry including rail and air transport.

The 1970–73 development plan envisaged investments totalling AD26,400 million and an annual growth rate of nine per cent, but these targets proved conservative. Actual investment in the plan period should reach AD35,000 million. In the plan, industry was allocated 45 per cent of investments and agriculture only 15 per cent. Industrial investment was concentrated in hydrocarbons, iron and steel and other heavy industries. In 1970, to protect the balance of payments, strict limits were imposed on the currency which Algerians could take abroad, and severe import restrictions were introduced. Algeria's achievement in fulfilling the provisions of the plan is all the more remarkable in view of the dislocation which the 1971 nationalization of the French oil companies involved.

STATISTICAL SURVEY

AREA AND POPULATION

Total Area	Arable	Pasture	Vineyards	Fruit	Forests	Scrub	POPULATION April 4th, 1966
2,381,741	62,000	96,000	3,700	2,000	35,000	383,750	11,821,679*

Area (sq. km.)

* Includes European population estimated at 80,000; excludes Algerian nationals living abroad, numbering 268,868 in 1966.

In 1972 over 700,000 Algerians were estimated to be living in France.

Estimated Population (April 1971): 14,644,000 (rural 7,850,000; urban 6,794,000) excluding nationals living abroad.

POPULATION BY DEPARTMENTS
(1966 Census)

Algiers	1,629,019	
Annaba	939,378	
Aurès	748,970	
Constantine	1,469,106	
El Asnam	775,692	
Médéa	864,799	
Mostaganem	766,216	
Oasis*	501,375	
Oran	946,567	
Saida	236,338	
Saoura*	209,850	
Sétif	1,164,636	
Tiaret	360,920	
Tizi-Ouzou	776,588	
Tlemcen	432,225	
TOTAL	11,821,679	

* Enumeration took place between December 22nd, 1965, and January 20th, 1966.

CHIEF TOWNS
POPULATION (1966 Census)

Algiers (capital)	903,530*	Skikda	88,000‡
Oran	327,493†	Mostaganem	74,876
Constantine	243,558	El Asnam	69,580
Annaba	152,006	Batna	68,856
Sidi Bel Abbès	105,000‡	Bejaia	65,012
Sétif	98,384	Biskra	59,052
Tlemcen	96,072	Médéa	53,951
Blida	93,000‡	Tizi Ouzou	53,291

* 1973 estimate 1,200,000 (including suburbs).
† 1973 estimate 325,000.   ‡ Estimates.

ALGERIA—(Statistical Survey)

AGRICULTURE

PRINCIPAL CROPS
('000 metric tons)

	1968	1969	1970	1971
Wheat	1,534	1,326	1,435	1,235
Barley	538	466	571	340
Wine	1,001	871	869	825*
Olives	150*	137	130*	220*
Citrus Fruit	431	492	507	471
Dates	161	79	100	n.a.
Figs	45	24	30*	n.a.

* FAO estimate.

LIVESTOCK
(FAO Estimates)
(1970-71—'000)

Sheep	8,400
Goats	2,100
Cattle	860
Pigs	2
Camels	174
Chickens	12,800

FISHING
('000 metric tons)

1969	22.9
1970	25.7
1971	23.7

MINING

	Unit	1967	1968	1969	1970
Coal	'000 metric tons	17	n.a.	17	15
Iron Ore	,, ,, ,,	1,386	1,684	1,599	1,546
Antimony	metric tons	137	19	n.a.	n.a.
Copper Ore	,, ,,	1,000	800	600	600
Lead Ore	,, ,,	3,800	5,100	7,900	6,500
Zinc Ore	,, ,,	6,700	15,400	20,900	17,000
Phosphate Ore	'000 metric tons	198	361	420	492

Source: United Nations, *Statistical Yearbook 1971*.

PETROLEUM AND NATURAL GAS PRODUCTION

		1968	1969	1970	1971*
Crude Oil	'000 metric tons	42,904	44,784	48,205	36,346
Natural Gas (a)†	million cu. metres	3,462	4,242	4,224	6,684
(b)‡	,, ,, ,,	2,652	2,904	2,904	n.a.

* Provisional.   † According to Algerian published statistics.   ‡ According to UN published statistics.

Source: UN(ECA) *Summary of Economic Data (Algeria)*, November 1972.

FINANCE

100 centimes = 1 Algerian dinar.
Coins: 1, 2, 5, 10, 20 and 50 centimes.
Notes: 5, 10, 50 and 100 dinars.
Exchange rates (April 1973): £1 sterling = 9.90 dinars; U.S. $1 = 4.093 dinars.
100 Algerian dinars = £10.101 = $24.435.

ALGERIA—(STATISTICAL SURVEY)

BUDGET 1972
(million AD)

Current Budget	5,500
of which:	
Ministry of Primary and Secondary Education	1,233
Ministry of Defence	492
Ministry of Public Health	406
Ministry of Interior	406
Construction Budget	3,495
of which:	
Education	685
Irrigation	504
Agriculture and rural development	381
Special programmes	355

1973 Current Budget Expenditure: 6,430 million AD.

INVESTMENT EXPENDITURE

	1970	1971
Agriculture	793	1,010
Industry	3,100	3,100
Infrastructure	494	1,543
Education	784	825
Housing and Health	238	220
Others	714	390
TOTAL	6,507	7,088
Add Current Expenditure	4,447	4,915
TOTAL EXPENDITURE	10,954	12,003

Investment expenditure for 1972: 9,000 million dinars; for 1973: 12,000 million dinars.

FOUR-YEAR DEVELOPMENT PLAN 1970–73
PRODUCTION

	Unit	1969 Production (Estimate)	1973 (Target)
Crude Petroleum	million tons	46	65
Natural Gas	million cu. metres	2,500	6,500
Liquefied Natural Gas	" " "	2,000	5,500
Iron Ore	'000 tons	3,500	3,700
Zinc Concentrates	tons	43,000	127,000
Phosphates	"	520,000	1,470,000
Electricity	million kWh.	1,500	2,800
Crude Steel	tons	—	430,000
Sulphuric Acid	"	61,000	100,000
Manufactured fertilizers	"	120,000	700,000
Refined Sugar	"	—	160,000
Cement	"	950,000	1,800,000
Paper Pulp	"	17,000	70,000
Cotton, Synthetic and Wool Fabrics	million sq. metres	53	110

DEVELOPMENT PLAN 1970–73
EXPENDITURE (million AD)

Agriculture	4,140
Mineral Prospecting	1,577
Industry	10,218
Electricity	735
Dams and Water	850
Transport and Communications	2,177
Education and Training	3,307
Health and Welfare	934
Tourism	700
Housing and Urban Affairs	2,282
Administration	870
TOTAL	27,740

Source: UN (ECA) *Summary of Economic Data (Algeria),* November 1972.

A new Four-Year Development Plan for the period 1974 to 1977 envisages a total expenditure of some 52,000 million AD. Priorities will be light industries and labour intensive projects and social objectives. State investment is expected to reach 50,000 million AD.

ALGERIA—(Statistical Survey)

EXTERNAL TRADE
(million AD)

	1966	1967	1968	1969	1970	1971*	1972*
Imports	3,354	3,154	4,023	4,981	6,205	5,100	5,800
Exports	3,070	3,572	4,098	4,611	4,980	3,200	6,800

* Estimates.

COMMODITIES
(million AD)

	Imports 1969	Imports 1970	Imports 1971	Exports 1969	Exports 1970	Exports 1971
Food, Drink and Tobacco	653	625	755	929	985	514
Energy and Lubricants	78	132	210	3,291	3,505	3,149*
Crude Products	308	421	428	203	158	180
Semi-finished Goods	1,362	1,781	1,608	70	194	123
Capital Goods	1,515	2,238	2,264	69	88	198
Consumer Goods	1,065	1,008	743	49	50	43

* Includes exports of crude petroleum to the value of 2,972 million AD.

Source: UN (ECA) *Summary of Economic Data (Algeria)*, November 1972.

COUNTRIES
('000 AD)

Imports	1969	1970	1971*
France	2,200,066	2,631,278	2,273,000
Germany, Fed. Rep.	457,777	619,807	568,000
U.S.A.	438,471	497,948	503,000
Italy	419,243	451,509	515,000
U.S.S.R.	181,529	224,591	242,000
Belg.-Lux.	164,326	215,631	168,000
United Kingdom	135,084	207,488	331,000

Exports	1969	1970	1971*
France	2,510,791	2,667,180	991,000
Germany, Fed. Rep.	695,018	640,296	1,014,000
U.S.S.R.	254,544	242,045	278,000
United Kingdom	200,284	204,784	153,000
Italy	169,648	209,737	317,000
Belg.-Lux.	128,200	101,464	206,000
Spain	47,000	125,000	170,000
Brazil	30,000	99,000	154,000

*Provisional.

TRANSPORT

Railways (1971): Passenger-km. 1,144m., Freight ton-km. 1,363m.

Roads (1971): Cars 149,339, Lorries and Vans 85,324, other vehicles 36,833.

International Shipping (1970): Vessels entered 29,029,000 net registered tons; Freight entered 2,920,000 tons; Freight cleared 36,890,000 tons.

Civil Aviation (1971 International traffic through Algerian airports): Passengers 1,613,000; Freight loaded 44,212 metric tons, Freight unloaded 7,836 metric tons; Mail 1,495 metric tons.

TOURISM
Number of Tourist Arrivals: (1970) 235,900, (1971) 367,700.

EDUCATION
(1971–72)

	Schools	Pupils	Teachers
Primary	6,500	1,851,000	49,879 (of whom 44,839 Algerians)
Secondary	670	287,700	12,305 (of whom 5,152 Algerians)
University	3	22,568	n.a.

In 1968–69 there were 5,738 students in teacher-training colleges, and 820 students followed courses of higher education abroad, including 355 in France.

Source (unless otherwise stated): Direction Générale du Plan et des Etudes Economiques, Ministère de l'Economie Nationale, Algiers.

ALGERIA—(THE CONSTITUTION)

THE CONSTITUTION

(Approved by popular referendum, September 1963)

Articles 1–11; Main Aims and Principles

Algeria is a Democratic and Popular Republic. It forms part of the Arab Maghreb, the Arab World and of Africa. Islam is the official religion, but the State guarantees freedom of opinion and belief and free expression of religion. Arabic is the official language of the State. The capital of Algeria is Algiers, headquarters of the National Assembly and the Government. The National Popular Army ensures the defence of territory and takes part in the country's social and economic activities. The basic administrative unit of the Republic is the Commune.

The main aims of the Republic are to build a socialist democracy; to fight discimination, in particular that based on race or religion and to strive for peace in the world. The Republic conforms to the Universal Declaration of the Rights of Man.

Articles 12–22; Fundamental Rights

All citizens of both sexes have the same rights and the same duties. All citizens over 19 years have the right to vote. Domicile cannot be violated and secrecy of correspondence is guaranteed to all citizens. No one can be arrested or tried except for legal offences and according to legal procedure. The Family, main unit of society, is under State protection. Education is compulsory. The Republic guarantees freedom of the Press and other means of information, freedom of association, freedom of speech and public discourse and freedom to hold meetings. Trade unionism, the right to strike, and the participation of workers in the administration of business will be upheld within the framework of the relevant laws. The Republic guarantees political asylum to all who fight for freedom.

The rights and freedoms referred to may not be used to hinder national independence, or to affect territorial integrity, national unity, the institution of the Republic, the socialist aims of the people or the principle of unity of the F.L.N.

Articles 23–26; The National Liberation Front (F.L.N.)

The F.L.N. achieves the objectives of the revolution and establishes socialism in Algeria.

Articles 27–38; Sovereign Rights—The National Assembly

Sovereign rights belong to the people. They are exercised by representatives in the National Assembly, nominated by the F.L.N. and elected for five years by direct and secret ballot.

The President of the National Assembly occupies the second highest position in the State.

The President of the Republic and Members of the Assembly have the power to initiate laws. All members of the Government have the right to attend debates and to address the Assembly. Control over Government acts is exercised by: hearings of Ministers in Committees; written questions; oral questions with or without debate.

Articles 39–59; The Executive

The executive power lies with the Head of State, the President of the Republic. He is nominated by the Party, and is elected by universal direct and secret ballot, for a five-year term. Any Moslem of Algerian origin having all civil and political rights and being 36 years of age or older, may be elected President of the Republic.

The President: signs, ratifies (in consultation with the Assembly), and ensures the execution of Treaties and other International Agreements; is Supreme Leader of the Armed Forces; declares war and draws up terms for peace, with the approval of the National Assembly; presides over the Higher Councils of Defence and the Law; exercises the right to grant a legal reprieve; nominates Ministers, of whom two-thirds must be members of the Assembly; has sole responsibility before the Assembly; defines and directs Government policies; proclaims and publishes Laws and ensures that they are executed; appoints all civil servants and defence personnel.

The President must promulgate Laws within ten days of their formal transmission by the National Assembly. Within this time limit the President can ask the Assembly to deliberate a second time, and this request cannot be refused. The period of ten days can be reduced at the request of the Assembly in matters of urgent necessity. If the President of the Republic does not proclaim the Laws within the time limit, the President of the Assembly shall do so.

A motion of censure may be tabled against the President if signed by one-third of the members of the Assembly. A majority vote in the Assembly on such a motion shall entail the resignation of the President and the automatic dissolution of the Assembly. This vote by public ballot shall take place after five clear days have expired from the time of tabling the motion.

In the case of emergency, the President can take exceptional measures to safeguard national independence and the Institutions of the Republic. The National Assembly then has the full right to meet automatically.

Articles 60–62; Justice

Judges obey only the Law and the interests of the Socialist Revolution. Their independence is guaranteed by Law and by the existence of a Higher Council of Law.

Articles 63–64; The Constitutional Council

The Constitutional Council consists of the President of the Supreme Court, the Presidents of the Civil and Administrative Chambers of the Supreme Court, three nominated members of the National Assembly and a member nominated by the President of the Republic.

Articles 65–70; Higher Organizations

The Higher Council of the Law consists of the President, the Minister of Justice, the President and Attorney General of the Supreme Court, a Lawyer of the Supreme Court, two Magistrates, one of whom is a judge, elected by their colleagues, and six Members of the Assembly elected by the permanent Committee of Justice.

The Higher Council of Defence consists of the President, the Ministers of National Defence, the Interior, and Foreign Affairs, the President of the Assembly's Commission for National Defence, and two Members nominated by the President of the Republic.

The Higher Economic and Social Council consists of five Members of the Assembly, the Director of Economic Planning, the Governor of the Central Bank of Algeria, members of the national organizations and representatives of major national economic and social activities appointed by the President. It elects its own President.

Articles 71–74; Constitutional Alterations

The initiative for altering the Constitution lies jointly with the President of the Republic and the National

ALGERIA—(THE CONSTITUTION, THE GOVERNMENT, DIPLOMATIC REPRESENTATION)

Assembly. Two readings and two votes with absolute majority must be given at an interval of two months, to draft any bill. This draft shall then be submitted for approval to the People by referendum. A bill approved by the People shall be proclaimed Law within eight days of the referendum.

Articles 75–78; Temporary Measures

The national hymn is *Kassamen* until such time as an extra-constitutional law shall fix a new national hymn.

The use of French in education shall continue only until the realisation of all-Arabic education becomes possible.

After approval of the Constitution by popular referendum it shall be promulgated within eight days. The election of the President of the Republic shall take place within one month of the approval of the Constitution.

THE GOVERNMENT

REVOLUTIONARY COUNCIL

Set up in June 1965 following the arrest of President Ben Bella. With Col. HOUARI BOUMEDIENNE as its President the Council has the following members:

AHMED BELHOUCHET	BOUHADJAR BENHADDOU	AHMED DRAIA	YAHYAOUI MOHAMMED
CHERIF BELKACEM	CHEDLI BENJEDID	AHMED KAID	SALAH
MOHAMMED BEN AHMED	ABDERRAHMAN BEN SALEM	TAYEBI LARBI	SALAH SOUFI
AHMED BENCHERIF	ABDELAZIZ BOUTEFLIKA	AHMED MEDEGHRI	

COUNCIL OF MINISTERS

(*August* 1973)

Prime Minister and Minister of Defence: Col. HOUARI BOUMEDIENNE.
Minister of State: CHERIF BELKACEM.
Minister of State for Transport: RABAH BITAT.
Minister of the Interior: AHMED MEDEGHRI.
Minister of Justice: BOUALEM BEN HAMOUDA.
Minister of Industry and Energy: BELAID ABDESSALEM.
Minister of Foreign Affairs: ABDELAZIZ BOUTEFLIKA.
Minister of Finance: ISMAIL MAHROUG.
Minister of Agriculture and Agrarian Reform: TAYEBI LARBI.
Minister of Primary and Secondary Education: ABDELKRIM BEN MAHMOUD.
Minister of Higher Education and Scientific Research: MOHAMMED BEN YAHIA.
Minister of Health: OMAR BOUDJELLAB.
Minister of Public Works: ABDELKADER ZAIBEK.
Minister of Posts and Telecommunications: SAID AYAT MASSAOUDEEN.
Minister of Commerce: LAYECHI YAKER.
Minister of Labour and Social Affairs: MOHAND SAID MAZOUNI.
Minister of Youth and Sports: ABDALLAH FADEL.
Minister of Tourism: ABDELAZIZ MAAOUI.
Minister for Harbours: MOULOUD KASSEM.
Minister for Ex-Servicemen: MAHMOUD GUENNEZ.
Minister of Information: AHMED TALEB.
Under-Secretary of State for Planning: KAMEL ABDULLAH KHODJA.
Under-Secretary of State: ABDULLAH ARBAOUI.

DIPLOMATIC REPRESENTATION

EMBASSIES ACCREDITED TO ALGERIA

(In Algiers unless otherwise stated)

Albania: 50 rue Oukil Mohammed, Birmandréis; *Ambassador:* RIZA TAUSHANI.
Argentina: 7 rue Hamani; *Ambassador:* MARIO RAÚL PICO.
Austria: Cité Dar el Kef, rue Shakespeare, El Mouradia; *Ambassador:* Dr. PAUL ZEDTWITS.
Belgium: 18 ave. Claude Debussy; *Ambassador:* PAUL DENIS.
Brazil: 48 blvd. Mohammed V; *Ambassador:* DAVID SILVEIRA DA MOTA.
Bulgaria: 13 blvd. Bougara Mohammed; *Ambassador:* A. P. PACHEV.
Cameroon: 28 chemin Sheikh Bachir Brahimi; *Ambassador:* FERDINAND LEOPOLD AYONO.
Canada: *Ambassador:* CHRISTIAN HARDY.
Central African Republic: 15 Lotissement Brausifour; *Chargé d'Affaires:* M. BAKOUZOU.
Chile: *Ambassador:* EDUARDO YAZIGI.
China, People's Republic: 34 blvd. des Martyrs; *Ambassador:* LIN CHING.
Congo (Brazzaville): 115 rue Ziad Abdelkader; *Ambassador:* RAPHAEL ELENGA.
Cuba: 14 rue Claude Barndard, Le Golf; *Ambassador:* RAUL FORNEL DELGADO.
Czechoslovakia: Villa Malika, Parc Gattlif; *Ambassador:* VACLAV PLESCOT.
Denmark: 23 blvd. Zirout Youcef; *Ambassador:* DIPLEV GORGEN SCHEEL.

ALGERIA—(Diplomatic Representation, National Assembly)

Egypt: chemin de la Madeleine, Hydra; *Ambassador:* NAGUIB H. EL SADR.
Finland: 2 blvd. Mohammed V.; *Ambassador:* OSSI SUNEL.
France: rue Larbi Alik, Hydra; *Ambassador:* JEAN SOUTOU.
German Democratic Republic: (address not available); *Ambassador:* SIEGFRIED KAMPF.
Germany, Federal Republic: 165 Chemin Findga; *Ambassador:* Dr. G. MOLTMANN.
Ghana: 62 rue Parmentier, Kubba; *Ambassador:* YAW ALBERT OSEBRE.
Greece: 38 rue Didouche Mourad; *Ambassador:* DIMITRI COSMADOPOULOS.
Guinea: 43 blvd. Central Said Hamdine, Hydra; *Ambassador:* NAINE NABE.
Hungary: 18 ave. Lyautey; *Ambassador:* ZSIGMOND ZOLTAN.
India: 119 rue Didouche Mourad; *Ambassador:* (vacant).
Indonesia: rue Etienne Baillac, Mouradia; *Ambassador:* SOE MARMAN.
Iran: 60 rue Didouche Mourad; *Ambassador:* DJAHANGUIB TAFAZOLI.
Iraq: 4 rue Areski, Abri-Hydra; *Ambassador:* A. EL YASSINE.
Italy: 37 chemin Sheikh Bachir Brahimi; *Ambassador:* A. M. SAREDO.
Ivory Coast: Parc Paradou, Hydra; *Ambassador:* (vacant).
Japan: 3 rue du Lucien Reynard; *Ambassador:* YUKIHISA TAMURA.
Jordan: 25 blvd. Colonel Amirouche; *Chargé d'Affaires:* TARIK EL MADI.
Kenya: Cairo, Egypt.
Korea, Democratic People's Republic: 49 rue Salvandy; *Ambassador:* O YEN GINE.
Kuwait: rue Didouche Mourad; *Ambassador:* NOURI ABD-AL-SALAM SHUWAIB.
Lebanon: 9 rue Kaid Ahmed el Biar; *Ambassador:* KHALIL AITANI.
Libya: 15 chemin Bachir Brahimi; *Ambassador:* MUHAMMED BUSAIRI.
Madagascar: rue Abdelkadir Aonis; *Ambassador:* BESY ARTHUR.
Mali: Paris, France.
Mauritania: 33 rue Vercors Bouzariah; *Ambassador:* SAAD BOUH KANE.
Mexico: Cairo, Egypt.
Mongolia: rue Marcel Suites, Hydra; *Ambassador:* BAT OCHYRIN GOTOV.
Morocco: 6 rue des Cèdres; *Ambassador:* MUHAMMED SIJILMASSI.
Nepal: Cairo, Egypt.
Netherlands: 23 blvd. Zirout Youcef; *Ambassador:* GERHARD WOLTER.
Niger: *Ambassador:* DODO BOUKARI.
Nigeria: 2 rue de l'Abrevoir; *Chargé d'Affaires:* SOKOYA JAMES.
Norway: Tunis, Tunisia.
Pakistan: 14 ave. Souidani Boudjemâa; *Ambassador:* ZAHIR MUHAMED FAROOQI.
Peru: 47 blvd. Mohamed V; *Ambassador:* E. DE LOS HEROS.
Poland: 37 ave. Mustafa Ali Khodja, El Biar; *Ambassador:* ANTONI KARAS.
Romania: 24 rue Si Areski, Hydra; *Ambassador:* MIHAT G. STEFAN.
Saudi Arabia: chemin des Glycines; *Ambassador:* RIAD AL KHATIB.
Senegal: 50 ave. Souidani Boudjemâa; *Ambassador:* THIERNO DIOP.
Somalia: *Ambassador:* (vacant).
Spain: 10 rue Tirman; *Ambassador:* R. SOBREDO-RIOBOO.
Sudan: 27 rue de Carthage, Hydra; *Ambassador:* EL AMINE EL BACHIR.
Sweden: 4 blvd. Mohammed V; *Ambassador:* BENGT GUSTAVE JEAN-JACQUES DE DARDEL.
Switzerland: 27 blvd. Zirout Youcef; *Ambassador:* JEAN-DENIS GRANDJAN.
Syria: chemin de la Madeleine, El Biar; *Chargé d'Affaires:* ANOIR EL ATTAR.
Tanzania: Paris, France.
Tunisia: 11 rue du Bois de Boulogne, Hydra; *Ambassador:* AHMAD NOURREDEEN.
Turkey: Villa dar el Ouard, blvd. Colonel Bougara; *Ambassador:* FAIK MELEK.
U.S.S.R.: chemin du Prince d'Annam, El Biar; *Ambassador:* SERGE GROUZINOV.
United Kingdom: 7 chemin des Glycines; *Ambassador:* RONALD BURROUGHS.
United Nations: 19 ave Debussy; HANS EHRENSTRALE.
Upper Volta: Hydra le Paradou, Immeuble du Bosquet; *Ambassador:* (vacant).
Vatican: 1 rue de la Basilique; *Pro-Nuncio:* Mgr. SANTE PORTALUPI.
Venezuela: (address not available); *Ambassador:* AQUILES CERTAD.
Viet-Nam, Democratic Republic: rue de Chenoua, Hydra; *Ambassador:* VAN BA KIEM.
Yemen A.R.: 74 rue Bouraba; *Ambassador:* ABDALLAH BARAKAT.
Yemen, P.D.R.: rue Pasquiet Brondt, Birmondréis; *Chargé d'Affaires:* MOHSEIN ALI YASSER.
Yugoslavia: 7 rue d'Anjou, Hydra; *Ambassador:* OSMAN DJICKIL.
Zaire: rue 1, 12 les Crêtes, Hydra; *Chargé d'Affaires:* PAUL MOTO.

Algeria also has diplomatic relations with Afghanistan, Gabon and the Provisional Revolutionary Government of South Viet-Nam.

NATIONAL ASSEMBLY

General Elections were held in September 1964 when a single list of candidates presented by the FLN was returned unopposed. The Assembly has not met since 1966.

In October 1969 President Boumedienne announced that a general election would be held during 1970; none was in fact held, and by summer 1973 no firm date for an election had been announced.

There are twelve Permanent Commissions.

ALGERIA—(Political Parties, Defence, Judicial System, Religion, The Press)

POLITICAL PARTIES

Government is based on a one-party system.

Front de Libération Nationale (FLN): place Emir Abdelkader, Algiers; f. 1954; socialist in outlook, the party is divided into a Secretariat, a Central Committee, Federations, Dairas and Kasmas; Secretariat: Secretary (vacant); Col. Boumedienne has announced his intention of reorganizing the FLN.

There are several small opposition groups; all are proscribed and in exile in France or in other Arab countries.

DEFENCE

Commander-in-Chief of the Armed Forces: Col. Houari Boumedienne.
Defence Budget (1971): 490 million dinars.
Military Service: compulsory national service for both sexes since 1969.
Total Armed Forces: 60,200: army 53,000; navy 3,200; air force 4,000.
Paramilitary Forces: 8,000.

JUDICIAL SYSTEM

The highest court of justice is the Supreme Court in Algiers. Justice is exercised through 132 courts grouped on a regional basis. Three special Criminal Courts have been set up in Oran, Constantine and Algiers to deal with economic crimes against the state. From these there is no appeal. A "Revolutionary Court" was established late in 1968 with jurisdiction over political offences.

President of Supreme Court: M. Gaty.
Procurator-General: M. Mostefaï.
President of Revolutionary Court: Major Abdelghani.

RELIGION

Islam is the official religion and it is estimated that 12 million Algerians are Muslims. The Europeans, and a few Arabs, are Christians, mostly Roman Catholics.

Archbishop of Algiers: H.E. Cardinal Leon-Etienne Duval; 13 rue Khelifa Boukhalfa, Algiers.

SUFFRAGAN BISHOPS

Constantine: Jean Scotto.
Laghouat: Jean-Marie Raimbaud.
Oran: Bertrand Lacaste.

THE PRESS

DAILIES

Algiers

al Chaab: 1 Place Maurice Audin; f. 1962; National informative journal in Arabic.
el Moudjahid: 20 rue de la Liberté; f. 1965; F.L.N. journal in French; circ. 130,000.

Constantine

an Nasr: 100 rue Larbi Ben M'Hidi; Arabic language.

Oran

al Joumhouria—La République: 6 rue Ben Schouer; f. 1962; French language.

WEEKLIES AND TWICE WEEKLIES

Algiers

Algérie Actualité: 20 rue de la Liberté, Algiers; f. 1965; French language weekly; Dir. R. C. Youcef Ferhi.
Bulletin Officiel des Annonces des Marchés Publics Algériens et du Registre du Commerce Algérien: 9 rue Trollier; twice weekly; Dir. Rémi Saint-André.
al Moudjahid: 20 rue de la Liberté; f. 1965; FLN journal in Arabic; weekly.
Office des Nouvelles Algériennes (O.N.A.): 52 rue Didouche Mourad, Algiers; weekly; Dir. Ahmed Khelil.
Révolution Africaine: 9 blvd. Khemisti, Algiers; F.L.N. journal in French; weekly; Socialist.
Révolution et Travail: Maison du Peuple; journal of U.G.T.A. in Arabic and French editions; weekly; Dir. Bennikous Abdelkader.
La Voix de la Mosquée: rue Pêcherie.

Constantine

el Hadef: 100 rue Larbi ben M'Hidi; f. 1972; weekly; sports; in French.

PERIODICALS

L'Algérie Economique: 7 blvd. de la République, Algiers; summary of items and commentaries issued by the State news agency; every two months.
el Djeich: Office de l'Armée Nationale Populaire, Algiers; f. 1963; monthly; Algerian army review; Arabic and French.
Journal Officiel de la République Algérienne: 9 rue Trollier; f. 1962.
Nouvelles Economiques: 6 blvd. Anatole-France, Algiers; bulletin of the Algiers Chamber of Commerce; every two months.
Santé: Fédération Nationale de la Santé, U.G.T.A. Maison du Peuple, place du 1 Mai, Algiers; f. 1956; devoted to the cause of medical progress in Algeria; twice monthly; French; edited by Fédération Nationale de la Santé.
al Shabab: Algiers; f. 1970; published by the F.L.N. youth organization.
Situation Economique: 6 blvd. Anatole-France, Algiers; annual.

PRESS AGENCIES

Algérie Presse Service (A.P.S.): 6 rue Jules Ferry Algiers; f. 1962; Dir. Mohamed Bouzid.

Foreign Bureaux

Algiers

ANSA: 6 rue Abdelkrim Khattabi; Bureau Chief Adriana Antonioli Bouti.
Associated Press: B.P. 769; Bureau Chief Michael Goldsmith.
Bulgarian Telegraph Agency (BTA): Zaatcha 5, Muradia; Bureau Chief Goran Gotev.
Czechoslovak News Agency (Četeka): 7 rue Lafayette, Imm. Lafayette.
Middle East News: 10 ave. Pasteur, B.P. 800.
Novosti: B.P. 24, Muradia.

The following are also represented: Agence France-Presse, Deutsche Presse-Agentur (DPA), Maghreb Arabe Presse, Prensa Latina, Reuters, Tass, UPI.

PUBLISHER

All privately owned publishing firms have been replaced by a single national organization:

Société Nationale d'Edition et de Diffusion (SNED): 3 blvd. Zirout Youcef, Algiers; f. 1966; publishes books of all types, and is sole importer, exporter and distributor of books and periodicals; also holds state monopoly for commercial advertising.

RADIO AND TELEVISION

RADIO

Radiodiffusion Télévision Algérienne (R.T.A.): Imm. RTA, 21 boulevard des Martyrs, Algiers; Government controlled; Dir. MOHAMMED REZZOUG.
Arabic Network: stations at Algiers, Oran, Constantine.
French Network: stations at Algiers, Constantine, Oran.
Kabyle Network: station at Algiers.
Supplementary Network: stations at Bouira, Tlemcen, Sétif, Souk Ahras, Batna, Bejaia, Touggourt, Laghouat.

There are 700,000 radio receivers.

TELEVISION

Radiodiffusion Télévision Algérienne (R.T.A.): Algiers; stations at Algiers, Oran, Tizi-Ouzou, Chrea and Constantine; the national network was completed during 1970. Television is taking a major part in the national education programme. Dir. (vacant).

There are 121,000 television receivers.

FINANCE

(cap. = capital; dep. = deposits; m. = million; AD = Algerian Dinars; Fr. = French Francs.)

BANKING

ALGIERS

CENTRAL BANK

Banque Centrale d'Algérie: 8 boulevard Zirout-Youcef, Algiers; f. 1963; cap. 40m. AD; took over the role of the Banque de l'Algérie, Jan. 1st 1963, as the central bank of issue; Gov. SEGHIR MOSTAFAÏ.

From November 1967 only the following nationalized banks were authorized to conduct exchange transactions and to deal with banks abroad, and by May 1972 these three banks had absorbed all foreign and private banks.

Banque Extérieure d'Algérie: 11 blvd. Colonel Amirouche, Algiers; f. 1967 by transfer of the assets of Crédit Lyonnais, Société Générale, Barclays Bank France (Ltd.), Crédit du Nord, and Banque Industrielle de l'Algérie et de la Méditerranée in Algeria; chiefly concerned with foreign trade transactions and the financing of industrial development in Algeria; cap. 20m. AD; brs. in Algiers and ten other principal cities in Algeria; Pres. and Gen. Man. BOUASRIA BELGHOULA.

Banque Nationale d'Algérie: 8 blvd. Ernesto Ché Guévara, Algiers; f. 1966 by transfer of the assets in Algeria of Crédit Foncier d'Algérie et de Tunisie, Banque de Paris et des Pays Bas, and other foreign banks; cap. 20m. AD; dep. 3,161m. AD; 138 brs.; Pres. and Gen. Man. ABDELMALEK TEMAM.

Crédit Populaire d'Algérie: 2 blvd. Colonel Amirouche, Algiers; f. 1966; re-grouping of former credit banks; brs. in Algiers, Constantine, Oran and Annaba.

SAVINGS BANK

Caisse Nationale d'Epargne et de Prévoyance: 40-42 rue Larbi Ben M'Hidi, Algiers.

INSURANCE

A state monopoly on insurance transactions was introduced on June 1st, 1966.

Caisse Algérienne d'Assurance et de Réassurance: 48 rue Didouche Mourad, Algiers; f. 1963 as a public corporation; Admin.-Gen. C. BENELHADJ SAID.

Caisse Centrale de Réassurance des Mutuelles Agricoles: 24 blvd. Victor Hugo, Algiers; Dir. T. BOUDJAKDJI.

Société Algérienne d'Assurances: 5 blvd. de la République, Algiers; f. 1963; state sponsored Company; Chair. and Man. Dir. MOHAMED BENSALEM.

TRADE AND INDUSTRY

CHAMBERS OF COMMERCE

Chambre de Commerce d'Alger: 6 blvd. Anatole France, Algiers; Administrator HACHEMI LARABI.

Chambre de Commerce et d'Industrie d'Annaba: Palais Consulaire, 4 rue du Cénra, Annaba; Pres. AMARA AMAR.

Chambre de Commerce de Bejaia: B.P. 105, Bejaia; f. 1892; 11 mems.; Pres. BENCHEIKH ABDERRAHMANE; Sec.-Gen. MAHDI YOUNÉS.

Chambre de Commerce et d'Industrie de Constantin: 2 ave. Zebane, Constantine; Pres. BEN MATTI ABDESSELAM.

Chambre de Commerce d'Oran: 8 boulevard de la Soummam, Oran; 16 mems.; Pres. TAÏEB BRAHIM MOKHTAR; Sec.-Gen. ABDELHAK NOR'EDDINE; publs. *Rapport Economique Mensuel, Bulletin Trimestriel d'Informations Economiques.*

Chambre de Commerce et d'Industrie de Mostaganem: avenue Bénaïed Bendehiba, Mostaganem; f. 1901; 8 mems.; Pres. MOHAMED BELHADJ; Sec.-Gen. HARRAG BENBERNOU.

Chambre de Commerce et d'Industrie de Skikda: avenue Sauren Pinelli-Port, Skikda; f. 1844; 12 mems.; Pres. NADJEH MOHAMED.

Chambre de Commerce Espagnole: 8 rue Amjère, Algiers.

Chambre de Commerce Italienne: 6 rue Hamami, Algiers.

Jeune Chambre Economique d'Alger: rue de Nîmes, Algiers; Pres. M. DONNEAUD.

There are also Chambers of Commerce at Colomb-Béchar, Ghordaia and Tlemcen.

EMPLOYERS' ORGANIZATIONS

Confédération Générale Economique Algérienne—CGEA: 1 rue de Languedoc, Algiers; the principal employers' organization; also Chambre française de Commerce et d'Industrie.

Union Générale des Commerçants Algériens: Place des Martyrs, Algiers.

PRINCIPAL TRADE UNIONS

Union Générale des Travailleurs Algériens—UGTA: Maison du Peuple, Algiers; f. 1956; 300,000 mems.; Sec.-Gen. ABDELKADER BENIKOUS; publ. *Révolution et Travail* (weekly).

AFFILIATES

Fédération des Travailleurs de l'Alimentation et du Commerce (*Federation of Food and Commerce Workers*): Maison du Peuple, Algiers; f. 1965; 14,000 mems.; Gen. Sec. DJEBIENE MAHMOUD.

ALGERIA—(Trade and Industry)

Fédération du Bois, du Bâtiment, des Travaux Publics et des Activités Annexes (*Federation of Building Trades Workers*): Maison du Peuple, Algiers; f. 1964; 17,000 mems.; Gen. Sec. Belhadj Bukir.

Fédération des Travailleurs de l'Education et de la Culture—FTEC (*Federation of Teachers*): Maison du Peuple, Algiers; f. 1962; 13,000 mems.; Gen. Sec. Bouamrane Chaikh.

Fédération Nationale des Cheminots (*National Federation of Railwaymen*): 3 rue Alexandre Dumas, Algiers; Sec.-Gen. Azzi Abdelmoudjid.

Fédération Nationale de l'Energie Electrique et du Gaz d'Algérie—FNEEGA (*National Federation of Utility Workers*): Maison du Peuple, Place du 1er Mai, Algiers; f. 1963; 5,000 mems.; Gen. Sec. Chabane Labou.

Fédération des Travailleurs des Mines et Carrières (*Federation of Mine and Quarry Workers*): Maison du Peuple, Algiers; f. 1965; Sec.-Gen. Ouali Mahoud Kahar.

Fédération des Travailleurs Municipaux d'Algérie (*Federation of Municipal Employees*): Maison du Peuple, Algiers; 15,000 mems.; Gen. Sec. Ahmed Zitouni.

Fédération des Travailleurs du Pétrole, du Gaz et Assimilés (*Federation of Oil and Gas Workers*): 21 boulevard Colonel Amirouche, Algiers; f. 1964; 8,000 mems.; Gen. Sec. Benyounes Mohand Arab.

Fédération des Ports, Docks et Aéroports (*Federation of Dock and Airport Workers*): Maison du Peuple, Algiers; f. 1964; 2,500 mems.; Gen. Sec. Said Oukali.

Fédération des Postes et Télécommunications (*Federation of Postal and Telecommunications Workers*): Maison du Peuple, Algiers; f. 1964; 6,000 mems.; Gen. Sec. Yssaad Abdelkadar.

Fédération Nationale de la Santé (*Federation of Hospital Workers*): Maison du Peuple, Algiers; f. 1962; 15,000 mems.; Gen. Sec. Djeffal Abdelaziz.

Fédération Nationale des Travailleurs de la Terre—FNTT (*Federation of Farm Workers*): 4 rue Arago, Algiers; f. 1964; Gen. Sec. Benmeziane Daoud.

DEVELOPMENT

Caisse Algérienne de Développement: Villa Joly, ave. Franklin Roosevelt, Algiers; f. 1963; Government-sponsored Development Fund to finance industrial and commercial enterprises and exercise credit control by means of medium- and long-term credits in the private sector.

Caisse Centrale de Coopération Economique (C.C.C.E.): 22 rue Larbi Alik, Hydra, Algiers; f. 1968; Dir. Jean Gambette.

Caisse Nationale des Marchés de l'Etat: 4 blvd. Mohammed V, Algiers; f. 1962; Dir. M. André.

Office Algérien d'Action Commerciale—O.F.A.L.A.C.: 40–42 rue Benmehidi Larbi, Algiers; f. 1962; quality control and technical advice to exporters; Dir. H. Hanouz.

Organisme de Coopération Industrielle—O.C.I.: Imm. Colisée, rue Ahmed Bey, B.P. 801, Algiers; f. 1965 to carry out the duties of the *Organisme Saharien* in the field of industry; loans granted 1,000 m. A.D.; Pres. Abderrahmane Khene; Dir.-Gen. Gabriel Van Laethem.

Société Centrale pour l'Equipment du Territoire—S.C.E.T. Coopération: 8 rue Sergent Addoun, Algiers; Dir. A. Gambrelle.

Société Nationale d'Etudes de Gestion, de Réalisations et d'Exploitations Industrielles—S.N.E.R.I.: 50 rue Khélifa Boukhalfa, Algiers.

NATIONALIZED INDUSTRIES

Office Algérien des Pêches: Algiers; state trawling organization; to acquire 80 trawlers under the 1970–73 Four-Year Plan.

Société Nationale Algérienne de Construction Mécanique (SONACOME): Algiers; sole manufacturer and importer of motor vehicles, agricultural equipment and allied products.

Société Nationale d'Edition et de Publicité (SNEP): 1 Ave. Pasteur, Algiers.

Société Nationale des Industries Textiles (SONITEX): 5 rue Abane Ramdane; f. 1966; 6,237 employees; Dir. Gen. M. Berber.

Société Nationale Métallique: Algiers; f. 1968.

Société Nationale des Matériaux de Construction: Algiers; f. 1968.

Société Nationale de Recherches et d'Exploitations Minières (SONAREM): 127 Blvd. Salah Bouakouir, Algiers; Pres. Tahar Hamdi.

STATE TRADING ORGANIZATIONS

Since 1972 all international trading has been carried out by state organizations, of which the following are the most important:

Office Algérien Interprofessionel des Céréales (OAIC): Algiers; f. 1962; monopoly of trade in wheat, rice, maize, barley and products derived from these cereals.

Office des Fruits et Légumes d'Algérie (OFLA): 12 ave. des Trois Frères Bouadou, Birmandréis, Algiers; f. 1969; division of the Ministry of Agriculture and Agrarian Reform; collects the produce from worker-controlled farms, and exports vegetables, fresh and dried fruit and associated by-products to Europe.

Office National de Commercialisation (ONACO): 31 rue Larbi Ben M'hidi, Algiers; f. 1963; monopoly of bulk trade in basic foodstuffs except cereals; brs. in over forty towns and under the fair development plan is to open a wholesale market in each *wilaya* to serve retailers.

Office National de Commercialisation des Produits Viti-Vinicoles: 112, Quai-Sud, Algiers; f. 1968; monopoly of importing and exporting products of the wine industry; exports amounted to 483,000 hectolitres in 1970, of which 224,000 hl. went to France and 179,000 hl. to the Soviet Union; Dir.-Gen. H. A. Kara Terki.

Société Nationale des Tabacs et Allumettes (SNTA): Algiers; monopoly of trade in tobacco and matches.

Société Nationale de la Sidérurgie (SNS): 2 rue du Chenova, Hydra-Algiers; sole importer of most semi-finished and manufactured metal products; commissioned feasibility study of an aluminium smelter for Algiers February 1970; Dir. Gen. Mohammed Liassine.

Other state buying organizations exist for dairy products, wood and wood products, textiles, footwear, and hides and skins, and more are being set up.

TRADE FAIR

Foire Internationale d'Alger: Palais des Expositions, Pins Maritimes, B.P. 571, Algiers; annual; fortnight in September.

OIL

Sonatrach (*Société nationale pour la recherche, la production, le transport, la transformation et la commercialisation des hydrocarbures*): Immeuble Maurétania, Agha, Algiers; f. 1963; state-owned organization for exploration, exploitation, transport, refining and marketing of oil and gas and their products. Became the sole marketing organization in May 1968, when the state took over all foreign marketing interests, and since April 1972 has been the sole organization with exploration rights. Built and controls oil pipelines to the coast: from Hassi Messaoud to Arzew (capacity 18 million tons p.a., to be increased to 23 million); from Hassi Messoud to Bejaia (capacity 15.4 million tons p.a.); from In Amenas to la Skirra (capacity 9.6 million tons p.a.); and, completed in 1972, from Mesdar to Haoud el Hamra (6 million tons p.a., to be increased to 18 million) to Skikda (12 million tons p.a., to be increased to 30 million); Dir. SID AHMED GHOZALI.

ALREP: f. 1971; 51 per cent owned by SONATRACH, 49 per cent owned by French company CFP, represented by *Total-Algérie*; operates oil interests formerly owned by CFP.

L'Association Coopérative (ASCOOP): 126 rue Didouche Mourad, Algiers; f. 1966 as the body controlling exploitation of Saharan oil and gas; owned by SONATRACH (51 per cent) and SOPEFAL of France, which acts through ERAP.

Société Nationale de Recherche et d'Exploitation des Pétroles en Algérie (S.N. REPAL): chemin du Réservoir, Hydra, Algiers; f. 1946; 1,663 mems.; Pres. N. AÏT LAOUSSINE; oil exploration, and development, mainly in Northern Algeria and Sahara; SONATRACH has an interest of about 37 per cent following its acquisition of the Shell interests in Algeria in 1970.

NATURAL GAS

Société d'Exploitation des Hydrocarbons de Hassi-R'Mel (SEHR): concession at Hassi-R'Mel; estimated reserves 900,000 million cubic metres equivalent to a possible annual production of 25,000 million cubic metres.

Compagnie Algérienne du Méthane Liquide (CAMEL): B.P. 11, Arzew; promotes export of liquid natural gas.

TRANSPORT

RAILWAYS

Société Nationale des Chemins de Fer Algériens: 21 blvd. Mohammed V, Algiers; f. 1959; 3,951 km. of track, of which 2,690 km. are of standard gauge (299 km. electrified), and 1,261 of metre gauge; 25 diesel electric locomotives were due to be delivered in the spring of 1973; daily passenger services from Algiers to the principal provincial cities, and a service to Casablanca via Oran; Dir. Gen. SADDEK BENMEHDJOUBA.

ROADS

There are about 82,000 km. of roads and tracks, of which 18,500 km. are main roads and 19,000 km. are secondary roads. The total is made up of 55,000 km. in the north, including 24,000 km. of good roads, and 27,000 km. in the south, including 3,200 km. with asphalt surface. The French administration built a good road system, partly for military purposes, which since independence has been allowed to deteriorate in parts, and only a small percentage of roads are surfaced. New roads have been built linking the Sahara oil fields with the coast, and the trans-Saharan highway is a major project. Algeria is a member of the Trans-Sahara Road Committee, organizing the building of this road, now renamed the "Road of African Unity". The first 360-km. stretch, from Hassi Marroket to In Salah, was opened in April 1972, and work has begun on the next section, which will include 420 km. inside Algeria and run into Niger.

Société Nationale des Transports Routiers: 27 rue des 3 Frères, Bouaddon, Algiers; f. 1967; holds a monopoly of goods transport by road; Dir.-Gen. DJELFAOUI MOHAMMED.

MOTORISTS' ORGANIZATION

Touring Club d'Algérie: Algiers.

SHIPPING

Algiers is the main port, with 13-16 fathoms anchorage in the Bay of Algiers, and anchorage for the largest vessels in Agha Bay. The port has a total quayage of 27,500 feet in three basins; the Old Port with 8-39 feet depth alongside, Mustapha Basin 23-36 feet depth alongside, and the Agha Basin.

Annaba's 120 acre harbour has 31-36 feet depth with 400 feet of quayage for petrol tankers. The Inner Port (Grande Darse) has 6,450 feet of quayage with 30 feet depth alongside. Oran's 300 acre harbour has 9,270 feet of quayage with 24-39 feet depth alongside, accommodating vessels of up to 550 feet. Arzew has 6,070 feet of quayage of which a third has 26 feet depth alongside. There are also important ports at Bedjaia, Djidjelli, Ghazaouet, Skikda (for oil), and Mostaganem.

Compagnie Nationale Algérienne de Navigation (CNAN): quai d'Ajaccio, B.P. 280, Algiers; f. 1964; State-owned company managing its own fleet and vessels on time charter; concerned in the transport of oil, gas, wine, early fruit and other goods; 5 vessels; agencies and monopoly of handling facilities in all Algerian ports; office in Marseilles and reps. in Paris, all French ports and the principal ports in many other countries.

Cie. des Bateaux à Vapeur du Nord: 9 rue Jacques Bingen, Paris 17e; f. 1853; tonnage 5,790 d.w.; Pres. JEAN POIGNY; cargo services to Algerian ports.

Cie. Charles le Borgne: 29 rue Maréchal Soult, Algiers; Paris Office: 97 ave. des Champs-Elysées; f. 1735; cargo services to all destinations; offices in Oran and Annaba.

Cie. Générale Transatlantique: Head Office: 6 rue Auber, Paris 9e; Algiers, 6 boulevard Carnot; regular passenger and cargo services from Marseilles to Algiers and Oran.

Cie. de Navigation Mixte: 1 la Canebière, Marseilles; f. 1850; tonnage 39,292 gross; Pres. G. DE CAZALET; Dir.-Gen. J. L. MASSIERA; passenger and cargo service to Algiers and Oran.

Société d'Armement et de Navigation Ch. Schiaffino & Cie.: 90 rue de Miromesnil, Paris 8e; tonnage 52,300; Dir. LAURENT SCHIAFFINO.

CIVIL AVIATION

Algeria's main airport, Dar el Beïda at Algiers, is a class A airport of international standing. At Constantine, Annaba and Oran are smaller modern airports able to accommodate jet aircraft, and there are also 65 aerodromes of which 20 are public, and a further 125 air-strips connected with the oil industry.

Air Algérie: 1 place Maurice Audin, B.P. 858, Algiers; f. 1946; internal services and extensive services to Europe and North Africa; operating fleet of 4 Caravelles, 4 Convair 640, 2 Boeing 727.

Foreign Lines

The following foreign airlines operate services to Algiers: Aeroflot, Air France, Alitalia, Aviaco (Spain), Balkan (Bulgaria), ČSA (Czechoslovakia), EgyptAir, Interflug (German Democratic Republic), Royal Air Maroc, Saudi Arabian Airlines, Swissair, Tunis Air.

TOURISM

Agence Touristique Algérienne: 2 Place Ben Badis, Algiers; f. 1962; branches in Paris, Frankfurt and Stockholm.

The first Pan African Cultural Festival was held in Algiers in July 1969. Thirty-five African states were represented by over 4,000 artists.

THEATRE

Théâtre National Algérien: Opéra Municipal, Algiers; performances in Arabic and French in Algiers and all main cities.

ATOMIC ENERGY

Institut d'Etudes Nucléaires d'Alger: B.P. 1147, Algiers; f. 1958; research into nuclear physics, solid and electronic physics; two Van de Graaff accelerators, 3 MeV and 2 MeV; one Sames accelerator 600 KeV and one isotope separator of the Saclay type; Dir. Prof. M. ALLAB.

EDUCATION

Education in Algeria continues broadly to follow the pattern laid down during the French administration, but its scope has been greatly extended. Over 40 per cent of school-age children still receive no schooling at all, but current plans envisage education facilities for all by 1978. By early 1972 over two million children attended primary schools, compared with about 800,000 in 1962. Facilities for secondary education are still limited, although they, too, have improved greatly in the decade, and accommodated nearly 300,000 pupils in 1972 compared with 45,800 in 1962. Whereas before independence most teachers were French, now nearly 90 per cent of the primary school staffs are Algerians, as are about 40 per cent of staffs in secondary and higher education, where teaching is still mostly in French. In 1971 there were about 700 French teachers in Algeria paid by the French Government, but by the end of the 1972–73 school year all French personnel in schools will have left, to be replaced eventually by Algerians. In the meantime the complement will be made up by teachers from Egypt, Syria, Tunisia and other Arab countries. For several years Arabic has been used increasingly in primary education, and this has been made possible by the recruitment of foreign Arabic-speaking teachers and of Algerian *moniteurs*. At higher levels scientific and technical subjects are being given priority. There are a number of technical colleges and three universities, at Oran, Constantine and Algiers, the latter being the oldest in North Africa. A further number of students go abroad to study, especially to France. Adult illiteracy is being combatted by a large-scale campaign, in which instruction is given in some cases by young people who have only recently left school, and in which the broadcasting services are widely used.

UNIVERSITIES

Université d'Alger: 2 rue Didouche Mourad, Algiers; 500 teachers, 9,500 students.

Université d'Oran: rue du Colonel Lotfi, Oran.

Université de Constantine: rue Ben M'hidi, Constantine; 100 teachers, *c.* 1,600 students.

BIBLIOGRAPHY

ALAZARD, J. and others. Initiation à l'Algérie (Paris, 1957).

ALLAIS, M. Les Accords d'Evian, le référendum et la résistance algérienne (Paris 1962).

AMIN, SAMIR. The Maghreb in the Modern World: Algeria, Tunisia, Morocco. (Penguin, Harmondsworth, 1970).

ARON, RAYMOND. La Tragédie Algérienne (Paris, 1957).

BALOUT, L. Algérie Préhistorique (Algiers, 1958).

BEHR, EDWARD. The Algerian Problem (London, 1961).

BOURDIEU, PIERRE. The Algerians (Boston, 1962).
Sociologie de l'Algérie (Que Sais-je, Paris, 1958).

BRACE, R. and J. Ordeal in Algeria (New York, 1960).

CHALIAND, G. L'Algérie, est-elle Socialiste? (Maspéro, Paris, 1964).

DE GAULLE, CHARLES. Mémoires d'espoir: Le Renouveau 1958-1962 (Plon, Paris, 1970).

DE GRAMMONT, H. Histoire d'Alger sous la Domination Turque (Paris, 1887).

ENCYCLOPAEDIA OF ISLAM. Algeria (New Edition, Vol. I. London and Leiden, 1960).

FANON, FRANZ. Les Damnés de la Terre (Maspéro, Paris, 1961).

FAVROD, CH.-H. Le F.L.N. et l'Algérie (Paris, 1962).

FERAOUN, MOULOUD. Journal, 1955-1962 (Paris, 1963).

FIRST, RUTH. The Barrel of a Gun: Political Power in Africa and the Coup d'Etat (Allen Lane, The Penguin Press, London, 1970).

FISHER, G. Barbary Legend (Oxford, 1957).

GILLESPIE, JOAN. Algeria (Benn, London, 1960).

GORDON, DAVID. North Africa's French Legacy, 1954-1963 (London, 1963).
The Passing of French Algeria (Oxford, 1966).

HENISSART, PAUL. Wolves in the City: The Death of French Algeria (Hart-Davis, London, 1971).

HUMBARACI, ARSLAN. Algeria—A Revolution that Failed (Pall Mall, London, 1966).

JEANSON, C. and F. L'Algérie hors la Loi (Paris 1955).

JEANSON, F. La Révolution Algérienne; Problèmes et Perspectives (Milan, 1962).

JOESTEN, JOACHIM. The New Algeria (New York, 1964).

JULIEN, CHARLES-ANDRÉ. Histoire de l'Algérie contemporaine, conquête et colonisation, 1827-1871 (Presses Universitaires de France, Paris, 1964).

KRAFT, JOSEPH. The Struggle for Algeria (New York, 1961).

LACHERAF, MOSTEPHA. L'Algérie Nation et Société (Maspéro, Paris, 1965).

LAFFONT, PIERRE. L'Expiation: De l'Algérie de papa à l'Algérie de Ben Bella (Plon, Paris, 1968).

LEBJAOUI, MOHAMED. Vérités sur la Révolution Algérienne (Gallimard, Paris, 1970).

LESCHI, L. Algérie Antique (Algiers, 1952).

MANDOUZE, ANDRE. La Révolution Algérienne par les Textes (Paris, 1961).

MANSELL, GERARD. Tragedy in Algeria (Oxford, 1961).

MARÇAIS, G. Algérie Médiévale (Algiers, 1957).

MARTIN, CLAUDE. Histoire de l'Algérie Française 1830-1962 (Paris, 1962).

MOUILLESEAUX, LOUIZ. Histoire de l'Algérie (Paris, 1962).

M'RABET, FADELA. Les Algériennes (Maspéro, Paris, 1967).

NYSSEN, HUBERT. L'Algérie en 1970 (1970).

O'BALLANCE, EDGAR. The Algerian Insurrection 1954-62 (Archon, Hamden, Conn., and Faber, London, 1967).

OPPERMANN, THOMAS. Die Algerische Frage (Frankfurt, 1960).

OTTAWAY, DAVID and MARINA. Algeria. The Politics of a Socialist Revolution (Berkeley, University of California Press, 1970).

OUZEGANE, AMAR. Le Meilleur Combat (Julliard, Paris, 1962).

QUANDT, WILLIAM B. Revolution and Political Leadership: Algeria, 1954-1968 (M.I.T. Press, 1970).

REUDY, JOHN D. Land Policy in Colonial Algeria: The Origins of the Rural Public Domain (University of California Press, Berkeley, 1967.).

ROBSON, P. and LURY, D. The Economies of Africa (Allen & Unwin, London, 1969).

ROY, JULES. The War in Algeria (New York, 1961).

SA'DALLAH, A. Q. Studies on Modern Algerian Literature (Al Adab, Beirut, 1966).

SOUSTELLE, J. La Drame Algérienne et la Décadence Française: Réponse à Raymond Aron (Paris, 1957).

SULZBERGER, C. L. The Test, de Gaulle and Algeria (London and New York, 1962).

THOMAS, BENJAMIN E. Trade Routes of Algeria and the Sahara (London, 1958).

BIBLIOGRAPHY

ALLARD, J. and others. Initiation à l'Algérie (Paris, 1957).
ALLIX, M. Les Accords d'Evian: la fédération et le résultat référendum (Paris, 1962).
AMIN, SAMIR. The Maghreb in the Modern World: Algeria, Tunisia, Morocco. (Penguin, Harmondsworth, 1970).
ANON. BAYNARD. La Vérité Algérienne (Paris, 1957).
BALOUT, L. Algérie Préhistorique (Algiers, 1958).
BEHR, EDWARD. The Algerian Problem (London, 1961).
BODRUMAN, PIERRE. The Algerians (Boston, 1964).
— Sociology of Algeria (Chicago, Paris, 1958).
BRACE, R. and J. Ordeal in Algeria (New York, 1960).
CAMUS, ALBERT. Algerie: essais et chroniques d'Algerie, Paris 1958, 1967).
DE CARTIER, CHARLES. Mémoires d'Algérie: Les témoignages 1958-1962 (Plon, Paris 1970).
DE GRAMMONT, H. Histoire d'Alger sous la Domination turque (Paris, 1887).
ENCYCLOPAEDIA OF ISLAM. Algeria (New Edition, Vol. I, Luzac and Co., London, 1960).
FANON, FRANTZ. Les Damnés de la Terre (Maspero, Paris, 1961).
FAVROD, CH.-H. Le F.L.N. et l'Algérie (Paris, 1962).
FERAOUN, MOULOUD. Journal, 1955-1962 (Paris, 1963).
PIERRE, FOUIN. The Marxist of a Quasi-Political Blanco in Africa and the Coup d'Etat (Allen Lane, The Penguin Press, London, 1970).
FISHER, G. Barbary Legend (Oxford, 1957).
GILLESPIE, JOAN. Algeria (Benn, London, 1960).
GORDON, DAVID. North Africa's French Legacy, 1954-1962 (London, 1963).
— The Passing of French Algeria (Oxford, 1966).
HENISSART, PAUL. Wolves in the City: The Death of French Algeria (Hart-Davis, London, 1971).
HUMBARACI, ARSLAN. Algeria—A Revolution that Failed (Pall Mall, London, 1966).
JEANSON, C. and F. L'Algérie hors la Loi (Paris 1955).
JEANSON, F. La Révolution Algérienne: Problèmes et Perspectives (Milan, 1962).
JOESTEN, JOACHIM. The New Algeria (New York, 1964).
JULIEN, CHARLES-ANDRÉ. Histoire de l'Algérie contemporaine, conquête et colonisation, 1827-1871 (Presses Universitaires de France, Paris, 1964).

KRAFT, JOSEPH. The Struggle for Algeria (New York, 1961).
LACHERAF, MOSTEFA. L'Algérie, Nation et Société (Maspero, Paris, 1965).
LAFITTE, PIERRE. L'Expédition De l'Amiral de 1930 à l'Action de Ben Bella (Pen, Paris, 1966).
LAHOUARI ADDI, MAMAMED. Verités sur la Révolution Algérienne (Gallimard, Paris, 1970).
LASSUS, L. Algérie Antique (Algiers, 1971).
MANDOUZE, ANDRÉ. La Révolution Algérienne par les Textes (Paris, 1961).
MERAD, GHERKO. L'agadé, in Algérie (Oxford, 1968).
MORGAN, C. Algeria Medieval (Algeria, 1955).
MARTIN, CLAUDE. Histoire de l'Algérie Française 1830-1962 (Paris, 1963).
MONTAGNAC, LIONEL. Histoire de l'Algérie (Paris, 1967).
M'RABET, FADELA. Les Algériennes (Maspero, Paris, 1967).
NYSSEN, HUBERT. L'Algérie en 1970 (1970).
O'BALLANCE, EDGAR. The Algerian Insurrection 1954-62 (Archon, Hamden, Conn., and Faber, London, 1967).
OPPERMAN, THOMAS. The Algerian Press (Frankfurt, 1960).
OTTAWAY, DAVID and MARINA. Algeria: The Politics of a Socialist Revolution (Berkeley, University of California Press, 1970).
OUZEGANE, AMAR. Le Meilleur Combat (Julliard, Paris, 1962).
QUANDT, WILLIAM B. Revolution and Political Leadership: Algeria 1954-1968 (M.I.T. Press, 1970).
RUEDY, JOHN D. Land Policy in Colonial Algeria: The Origins of the Rural Public Domain (University of California Press, Berkeley, 1967).
ROBSON, P. and LURY, D. The Economies of Africa (Allen & Unwin, London, 1969).
ROY, JULES. The War in Algeria (New York, 1961).
SA'DALLAH, A. Q. Studies on Modern Algerian Literature (Al-Adab, Beirut, 1966).
SOUSTELLE, J. La Drame Algérienne et la Décadence française: Réponse à Raymond Aron (Paris, 1957).
SULZBERGER, C. L. The Test, de Gaulle and Algeria (London and New York, 1962).
THOMAS, BENJAMIN E. Trade Routes of Algeria and the Sahara (London, 1956).

Bahrain

GEOGRAPHY

The Bahrain Archipelago lies near Qatar off the west coast of the Gulf.

The total area of the Bahrain group of islands is 255 square miles. Bahrain itself, the principal island, is 30 miles long and 10 miles wide. To the north-east of Bahrain, and linked to it by a causeway and motor road, lies Muharraq island, which is approximately 4 miles long. The archipelago comprising the State of Bahrain consists of thirty-three islands, including Nabih Salih, Jeddah, Hawar and Umm Suban.

The total population is 225,000. The port of Manama, the capital and seat of government, has a population of approximately 90,000 (including several hundred foreigners, mainly businessmen). The town of Muharraq has a predominantly Arab population of approximately 35,000. Both Sunni and Shi'ite Moslems are represented in the indigenous population, the Ruling Family belonging to the Sunnis.

HISTORY

After several centuries of independence Bahrain passed firstly under the rule of the Portuguese (1521 to 1602) and then it occasionally came under Iranian rule (1602 to 1782). The Iranians were expelled in 1783 by the Utub tribe from Arabia whose paramount family, the Al-Khalifas, became the independent Sheikhs of Bahrain and have ruled Bahrain ever since, except for a short break before 1810. Iranian claims based on the Iranian occupation of the islands in the seventeenth and eighteenth centuries nevertheless continued to be made from time to time.

In the nineteenth century European powers began to interest themselves in the Gulf area, and Britain was principally concerned to prevent French, Russian and German penetration towards India, and to suppress the slave and arms trades. In 1861, in consequence of political claims put forward by Iran and Turkey, the Sheikh of Bahrain undertook to abstain from the prosecution of war, piracy and slavery by sea in return for British support against aggression. In 1880 and 1892 the Sheikh further undertook not to cede, mortgage or otherwise dispose of parts of his territories to anyone except the British Government, nor to enter into any relationship with a foreign government other than the British without British consent.

Bahrain was naturally affected by the general post-war ferment in the Arab world. A tentative step towards democratic institutions was taken in February 1956, when elections were held for members of an Education and Health Council, the first election in Bahrain being held in 1919 for the Municipal Council. Shortly afterwards there was a strike in the oil refinery, said to be partly a protest against the paternalistic attitude of the British adviser to the Sheikh. There were further disturbances at the time of the Suez crisis. Meanwhile, further symbols of Bahrain's growing independence were the establishment of Bahraini as opposed to British legal jurisdiction over a wide range of nationalities (1957), the issue of Bahrain's own stamps (1960), and the introduction of a separate currency (1965). A small-scale distribution of village lands was started in 1960, and among economic developments the construction of a new town, Isa Town, which is being built to Western standards of amenity, has been prominent; its first stage was completed and formally inaugurated in November 1968. Bahrain also pioneered free education and health services in the Gulf, and good electricity and water services are available. There was another major strike in 1965 lasting from March 19th to April 30th, the principal cause being a fear of redundancies in the oil companies. In May 1966 Britain announced that her principal base in Arabia would be transferred from Aden to Bahrain in 1968, and a more realistic rent was agreed with the Bahrain Government for the military establishment. However, in 1968 the Wilson government announced that all forces "East of Suez"—including those in the Gulf—would be withdrawn by the end of 1971, a decision later confirmed by the Heath government in March 1971.

Extensive administrative and political reforms came into effect in January 1970. A twelve-member Council of State became the State's supreme executive authority, this being the first formal delegation of the sheikh's powers. Only four of the initial twelve "Directors" were members of the royal family, but all were Bahrainis, and the British advisers were officially reduced to civil servant status. Equal numbers of Sunni and Shi'ite Muslims were included (the royal family apart) to represent Bahrain's religious balance. The reform was claimed to bring Bahrain closer to the Kuwait form of government rather than that in the Trucial sheikdoms. In August 1971 the Council of State became the Cabinet of the State of Bahrain, authorized to direct the internal and external affairs of the State.

After 1968 Bahrain was officially committed to membership of the embryonic Federation of Arab Emirates, but with over half the Federation's population and high educational and social welfare standards built up over 40 years, Bahrain disagreed with the richer but more backward sheikdoms further down the Gulf over the terms of the federal constitution (especially those relating to method of government), the allocation of common finances, etc. Bahrain's position was strengthened in May 1970 when Iran accepted the United Nations' report on Bahrain's future. The UN representatives visited the island in April and found that popular opinion overwhelmingly favoured a complete independence rather than union with Iran. Teheran nevertheless expressed misgivings about the safety of the Iranian community in Bahrain, which it claims is much larger than the 4 per cent figure given in the official census.

By the summer of 1971 Bahrain was ready to go it alone. On August 14th, 1971, full independence was proclaimed, the treaty arrangements with Britain being terminated, and a new treaty of friendship was signed with Britain the next day. On August 17th Sheikh Isa took the title of Amir. In September Bahrain became a member of the Arab League and the UN. In December 1972 elections were held for a Constituent Assembly, whose first task was to study proposals for, and produce within six months, a draft Constitution. This task was completed on June 2nd, 1973.

ECONOMICS

Agriculture and cattle breeding are practised throughout the islands, the main crops being vegetables, lucerne, fodder crops and some dates. Traditional occupations such as dhow building, fishing and pearling continue but on a much smaller scale than before. In recent years several soft drink factories and brick making plants have been established. The Bahrain Fishing Company, 40 per cent British owned and 60 per cent Bahraini, has now been operating successfully for several years, exporting frozen prawns to the U.S.A. and Japan.

Oil in commercial quantity was found in 1932. The concession is held by the Bahrain Petroleum Company, which is owned jointly by the Standard Oil Company of California and Texaco Inc.; it extends over the whole of Bahrain and expires in 2024. The Company is registered in Canada. It was announced in December 1952, that the agreement between the Sheikh and the Company had been modified to allow a fifty-fifty profit-sharing arrangement. The State's revenue from oil was thereby doubled. Bahrain became a member of OAPEC (the Organization of Arab Petroleum Exporting Countries) in May 1970. In 1970 The Superior Oil Company took over the exploring rights on a 1,500 square mile offshore area formerly held by the Continental Oil Company.

The second largest refinery in the Middle East is at Bahrain. In 1971 it refined a record total of over 94 million barrels; although this figure includes crude oil piped from Saudi Arabia, the Bahrain Petroleum Company itself produced 27.3 million barrels in 1971. In 1972 plans were laid for the construction of a £26 million desulphurization plant as part of a general expansion programme for the refinery. This new plan, in which Japanese interests are participating, is to provide pollution-free petroleum products for the Japanese market. Production from Abu Saafa, a new offshore field between Bahrain and Saudi Arabia, began in 1968 at the rate of 1,500,000 tons per annum.

In December 1971 the new Bahrain International Airport Terminal Building was opened. The first Terminal designed specifically for Jumbo Jets, this building can handle the passengers of two 747s simultaneously and is equipped with four airbridges and all the equipment required for the handling of the largest aircraft planned from now until the end of the century.

A new four-lane causeway and bridge between the two main islands of Bahrain is almost completed; the final bridge-work is due to be finished by early 1974.

In the first half of 1962 new port installations were completed at Mina Sulman, which enables the port to handle up to six vessels of 30 ft. draught simultaneously.

The port has, unlike the majority of other Gulf ports, never had any surcharge imposed by International Shipping Conferences. It also has storage and refrigeration facilities for the transit trade. A slipway and modern marine and engineering workshops adjacent to the port and under separate commercial management were completed during 1963. Bahrain has a free zone in which many British, American and local concerns have their headquarters; the island is a major entrepôt market for the neighbouring Gulf states.

The Ministry of Development and Engineering Services offers inducements to foreign investors in industrial and commercial projects, notably in the form of relief from taxation, freedom to repatriate profits, and cheap power (Bahrain has a large surplus of low cost natural gas). The concern for industrial development is stronger than in the other Gulf states, owing to the greater educational advancement of the population and the small scale of the islands' oil production and reserves. The majority of new industrial concerns established under this programme have been built in the Free Zone. Besides the ship repair facilities and the fishing company referred to above, other companies are now producing offshore oil wellhead structures, manufactured domestic and industrial plastic products, assembly of air-conditioning units and furniture assembly.

A £60 million aluminium smelter, under construction since 1969, began production in 1970 with an estimated capacity of 120,000 tons per annum. The Bahrain Government has a 27½ per cent share in the consortium, Aluminium Bahrain (ALBA); the rest of the capital has been subscribed by a variety of European and American interests. Under a twenty-year contract production of natural gas was begun in 1971 by the Bahrain Petroleum Company to provide fuel for the turbine complex of the plant. Another long-term contract was signed with Western Australian interests to provide alumina for the Smelter. Ancillary industries are now being established—a factory to produce aluminium powder (Bahrain Atomizers) is now in production and plans for an extrusion plant are in hand.

The departure of the British forces has had no adverse effect on the economy as was feared. In fact the influx of foreign companies since independence has more than compensated for any loss incurred.

STATISTICAL SURVEY

AREA AND POPULATION

Area sq. km.	Population (1971 census)		
	Total	Manama (capital)	Muharraq Town
369.6	216,078	89,399	37,732

(1972 population estimate 225,000).

EMPLOYMENT
(1971)

Agriculture and fishing	3,990
Mining and Manufacturing	4,152
Oil	4,312
Public Utilities	1,705
Construction	10,404
Wholesale and retail trade, and catering	7,706
Transport, storage and communications	7,743
Finance, business services, community and social services	13,182
Public administration and defence	5,206
Other	817
TOTAL	60,301

CRUDE OIL PRODUCTION
('000 metric tons)

1968	1969	1970	1971	1972
3,686	3,800	3,750	3,800	3,500

REFINERY PRODUCTION
(Output in million barrels)

1968	1969	1970	1971	1972
79.9	83.3	88.2	89.9	83.5

Note: 1 metric ton equals approx. 7.3 barrels.

Industry: Building materials, clothing, soft drinks, plastic products, industrial gases, boat building, air conditioning manufacture, flour mills and an aluminium plant.

FINANCE

1,000 fils = 1 Bahrain dinar (BD).
Coins: 1, 5, 10, 25, 50, 100, 250 and 500 fils.
Notes: 100, 250 and 500 fils; 1, 5 and 10 dinars.
Exchange rates (April 1973): £1 sterling = 980.5 fils; U.S. $1 = 394.74 fils.
100 Bahrain dinars = £101.99 = $253.44.

BUDGET
(1973—'000 Bahrain dinars)

REVENUE		EXPENDITURE	
Oil Payments	11,400	Ordinary Expenditure	23,700
Customs	3,500	Construction Expenditure	3,900
Other Items	17,600	Development Expenditure	4,900
TOTAL	32,500	TOTAL	32,500

Currency in Circulation (Sept. 1972): BD 23,278,690. The Bahrain dinar is accepted in other Gulf States.

BAHRAIN—(Statistical Survey)

EXTERNAL TRADE
(B.D. '000)

	1969	1970	1971
Imports	57,939	80,126	105,005
Exports and Re-exports (excl. oil)	19,874	25,156	28,405

COMMODITIES

Imports	1970	1971
Food and live animals	13,457.4	14,536.3
Beverages and tobacco	2,634.5	2,531.8
Inedible raw materials (not fuels)	1,160.2	1,424.9
Mineral fuels, lubricants etc.	860.9	1,125.2
Animal and vegetable oils and fats	141.0	178.8
Chemicals	3,143.9	7,134.7
Manufactured goods	22,936.5	30,624.5
Machinery and transport equipment	23,958.2	33,332.0
Miscellaneous manufactured articles	11,431.0	13,983.3
Unclassified groups and transactions	403.2	133.4
Total	**80,126.9**	**105,004.9**

Re-Exports	1967	1968	1969	1970
Household goods	1,732	2,207	1,701	1,133
Cotton piece goods	1,276	2,031	1,323	1,778
Garments	1,378	2,019	2,906	2,390
Silk and silk piece goods	1,114	2,000	2,273	2,773
Provisions	730	1,586	n.a.	n.a.
Machinery and oilwell supplies	961	980	1,231	1,908
Spices	1,008	695	751	915
Rice	967	679	547	1,238
Haberdashery and hosiery	436	559	n.a.	n.a.

PRINCIPAL COUNTRIES

Imports	1968	1969	1970	1971
United Kingdom	12,735	14,269	24,904	31,754
India	2,516	2,839	3,347	3,031
United States	6,289	6,171	5,812	12,630
Japan	8,248	8,269	9,972	12,793
German Federal Republic	2,239	2,394	2,684	4,155
Netherlands	1,499	1,692	3,817	5,671
Pakistan	2,455	2,260	2,915	2,438
Italy	1,383	1,255	1,580	3,204
China, People's Republic	2,435	3,799	4,091	5,867
Hong Kong	1,785	2,241	2,495	2,790

BAHRAIN—(Statistical Survey, The Constitution)

COUNTRIES—continued

Exports and Re-Exports	1969	1970	1971
Saudi Arabia	9,924	12,544	14,016
Qatar	2,309	1,320	1,648
Iran	658	902	1,043
Dubai	1,257	1,510	1,442
Abu Dhabi	977	466	639
Kuwait	1,733	2,993	3,518

TRANSPORT
ROADS

Type of Licence	1969	1970	1971
Private Cars	8,156	8,960	10,400
Taxi Cabs	911	915	908
Vans and Lorries	2,682	2,999	3,439
Private Buses	344	381	419
Public Buses	140	142	145
Motor Cycles	1,377	1,529	1,772
TOTAL (excl. motor cycles)	12,233	13,397	15,311

EDUCATION
GOVERNMENT EDUCATION 1970–72

	Schools/Colleges*		Pupils/Students	
	1970–71	1971–72	1970–71	1971–72
Primary	73	75	36,113	36,952
Intermediate	25	21	7,288	7,266
Secondary	7	11	5,242	5,322
Technical, Commercial, Religious	3	3	1,079	1,372
Higher (incl. Teacher Training Colleges)	5	5	289	312
TOTAL	113	115	50,011	51,224

* There are also 7 private schools and 3 kindergartens under the supervision of the Ministry of Education.
The total number of pupils in Private Schools in 1971–72 was 3,473.
The total number of teaching staff under the Ministry of Education was 2,247 in 1971–72.

Source: Statistical Bureau, Finance Department, Bahrain Government.

THE CONSTITUTION

A new 108-article constitution was ratified in June 1973. It states that "all citizens shall be equal before the law" and guarantees freedom of speech, of the Press, of conscience and religious beliefs. Other provisions include the outlawing of the compulsory repatriation of political refugees. The constitution also states that the country's financial comptroller should be responsible to Parliament and not to the Government, and allows for national trade unions "for legally justified causes and on peaceful lines". Compulsory free primary education and free medical care are also laid down in the constitution. It is to remain in force for a minimum of five years.

BAHRAIN—(Government, Diplomatic Representation, Judicial System, Religion, etc.)

THE GOVERNMENT

Amir: Sheikh Isa bin Sulman al-Khalifa, K.C.M.G.
Heir Apparent: Sheikh Hamed bin Isa al-Khalifa.

THE CABINET
(*July* 1973)

Prime Minister: Sheikh Khalifa bin Sulman al-Khalifah.
Minister of Defence: Sheikh Hamad bin Isa al-Khalifah.
Minister of Finance and National Economy: Sayed Mahmood al-Alawi.
Minister of Foreign Affairs and Acting Minister for Information: Sheikh Mohamed bin Mubarak al-Khalifa.
Minister of Education: Sheikh Abdul Aziz Muhamed al-Khalifa.
Minister of Health: Dr. Ali Mohamed Fakhro.
Minister of Justice: Sheikh Khalid bin Mohamed al-Khalifa.
Minister of Development and Engineering: Yousif Ahmed al-Shirawi.
Minister of Labour and Social Affairs: Ibrahim Mohamed Hasan Humaydan.
Minister of Municipalities and Agriculture: Sheikh Abdulla bin Khalid al-Khalifa.
Minister of State for Legal Affairs: Dr. Hussain Mohamed al-Baharna.
Minister of State for Cabinet Affairs: Jawad Salim al-Urrayed.

DIPLOMATIC REPRESENTATION

Embassies accredited to Bahrain
(Manama unless otherwise stated)

Egypt: 3105/7 Adliya (E); *Ambassador:* Mohamed Abdul Salan Jaludin.
France: Kuwait City, Kuwait (E).
India: Government Rd. (E); *Ambassador:* Roy Axel Khan.
Iran: 107 Sh. Isa Rd. (E); *Ambassador:* Manuchehr Sepahbodi.
Iraq: 371/7 Sh. Isa Rd. (E); *Ambassador:* Yaakoub Kazim Hamdani.
Japan: Kuwait City, Kuwait (E).
Jordan: Sh. Isa Rd. (E); *Ambassador:* Dr. Suliman al-Dajani.
Kuwait: Qudhaibiyya, nr. the new Palace (E); *Ambassador:* Sulieman Majed al-Shahen.
Lebanon: Kuwait City, Kuwait (E).
Morocco: (E); *Ambassador:* Ahmad Bin Limlaith.
Netherlands: Kuwait City, Kuwait (E).
Pakistan: Sh. Essa Rd. (E); *Ambassador:* Ghoulam Ghouth Khan.
Saudi Arabia: Al-Mahooz (E); *Ambassador:* Shaikh Abdullah al-Fadhel.
Somalia: Jeddah, Saudi Arabia (E).
Spain: Kuwait City, Kuwait (E).
Sudan: Kuwait City, Kuwait (E).
Tunisia: Kuwait City, Kuwait (E).
United Kingdom: Al-Mathaf Square (E); *Ambassador:* Robert Tesch.
U.S.A.: Kuwait City, Kuwait (E).
Yemen Arab Republic: Kuwait City, Kuwait (E).

Bahrain also has diplomatic relations with Afghanistan, Chad, the People's Republic of China, the Republic of China, Federal Republic of Germany, Democratic People's Republic of Korea, Mongolia, Oman, Qatar, Syria, the United Arab Emirates and the U.S.S.R.

DEFENCE

The armed forces number 1,100. Their equipment includes armoured cars and patrol boats.

JUDICIAL SYSTEM

Minister of Justice: Sheikh Khalid bin Mohamed al-Khalifa.

Since the termination of British legal jurisdiction in 1971, intensive work has been in progress on the legislative requirements of Bahrain. The Criminal Law is at present contained in various Codes, Ordinances and Regulations.

Judges, both Bahraini and Arab, are all fully qualified, as are the lawyers that appear before the courts.

Since the end of 1971 all nationalities are subject to the jurisdiction of the Bahrain Courts which guarantee equality before the Law irrespective of nationality or creed.

CONSTITUENT COUNCIL

In December 1972 22 members were elected to seats in the 44-member Constituent Council. The remaining 22 seats are occupied by nominees of the Amir and members of the Cabinet.

Speaker: Ibrahim al-Arrayed.

RELIGION

The great majority of the people are Muslims of the Sunni and Shi'ite sects. The ruling family is Sunni.

Religious affiliation (1971 Census):

Muslims	206,708
Christians	6,590
Others	2,780
Total	**216,078**

PRESS AND RADIO

Al Bahrain Al-Yom (*Bahrain Today*): P.O.B. 253, Manama; Radio monthly; Arabic; published by the Ministry of Information Dept.; Manama; Editor Ahmed Kamal; circ. 4,000.
al Adhwaa: Arab Printing and Publishing Establishment, P.O.B. 250, Tijjar Rd., Manama; f. 1965; Arabic; weekly; Editor Mahmoud Al-Murdi, circ. 5,000.
Akhbar Al-Bahrain: f. 1972; free distribution, published by the Ministry of Information.
Arab Markets: P.O.B. 604, Bahrain; monthly; English and Arabic; Editor Abdu F. Bushara.
Awali Evening News: Published by the Bahrain Petroleum Co. Ltd.; daily; English; circ. 1,000.
Awali Magazine: Published by the Bahrain Petroleum Co. Ltd.; monthly; English; circ. 1,000.

BAHRAIN—(Radio, Finance, Trade and Industry, Transport)

Bahrain Trade Directroy: P.O.B. 524, Manama; Publisher and Man. Dir. A. E. ASHIR.

al Hiya al Tijariya (*Commerce Review*): P.O.B. 248, Manama; English and Arabic; published by Bahrain Chamber of Commerce and Industry.

Al-Mujtama Al-Jadid: P.O.B. 590; Editor MUSTAFA.

Commerce Review: P.O.B. 248, Manama; Chamber of Commerce Journal; monthly.

Gulf Weekly Mirror: P.O.B. 455, Manama; f. 1971; weekly; English; also circulates in Oman, Qatar, United Arab Emirates and eastern Saudi Arabia; Editor STEFAN KEMBALL.

Huna al Bahrain (*Bahrain Calling*): P.O.B. 253, Manama; Radio monthly; Arabic; published by the Information Dept., Manama; Editor (vacant); circ. 4,000.

al Jarida al Rasmiya (*Official Gazette*): Information Department, Government of Bahrain, Manama; f. 1957; Arabic; weekly.

al Murshid: Arabian Printing and Publishing House, P.O.B. 553, Bahrain; monthly guide, including "What's on in Bahrain"; English and Arabic; Editor M. SOLIMAN.

al Najmar al Asbuia (*Weekly Star*): Awali; Arabic; weekly; published by The Bahrain Petroleum Co. Ltd.; circ. 8,000.

The New Society: P.O.B. 590, Manama; weekly.

Sada Al Usbou: P.O.B. 549, Bahrain; f. 1969; Arabic; weekly; Owner and Editor-in-Chief ALI SAYYAR.

Bahrain Broadcasting Station: P.O.B. 253, Manama; f. 1955; state-owned and operated enterprise; two 2kW. transmitters; programmes are in Arabic only, and include news, plays and talks; Dir. of Broadcasting IBRAHIM KANOO.

English language programmes broadcast by the U.S. Air Force in Dhahran and by ARAMCO can be received in Bahrain, as can the television service provided by the latter. The station is currently being expanded and its power increased. A colour television service is planned for 1973.

In 1971 there were approximately 90,000 receiving sets.

FINANCE

BANKING

(cap. = capital; dep. = deposits; m. = millions; B.D. = Bahrain Dinars)

Bank of Bahrain: P.O.B. 106, Manama; f. 1957; cap. p.u. (1972) B.D. 750,000; reserves B.D. 575,000; dep. B.D. 20.4m.; Chair. AHMED ALI KANOO; Gen. Man. A. S. WOOD.

Foreign Banks

Arab Bank Ltd.: Amman, Jordan; P.O.B. 395, Manama; Man. ADNAN N. BSEISU.

Bank of Bahrain and Kuwait: Suk-al-Tuggar, P.O.B. 597, Manama; cap. p.u. 1m B.D. subscribed by Bahraini citizens and the six largest finance institutions in Kuwait.

Bank of Cairo: Manama.

Bank Melli (Iran): Teheran; Government Rd., P.O.B. 785, Manama; 1 br.

British Bank of the Middle East: London; P.O.B. 57, Manama; Man. F. X. PAUL.

The Chartered Bank: London; P.O.B. 29, Manama; dep. B.D. 63,678,000 (Dec. 71); Chief Man. V. R. WINTON.

Chase Manhattan Bank: New York; Manama; Man. JOHN HOUSE.

First National City Bank: New York; P.O.B. 548, Manama; 1 br.; Man. DONALD L. BYRAM.

Habib Bank (Overseas) Ltd.: Karachi; Government Road, Manama; Man. CH. SAJJAD ALI.

Rafidain Bank: Baghdad; f. 1969; P.O.B. 607, Manama; Man. T. AL-KHATIB.

United Bank Ltd.: Karachi; Government Road, Manama; Man. S. M. AKHTAR.

INSURANCE

Bahrain Insurance Co.: f. 1971; general accident, fire and life insurance; cap. B.D. 270,000; 66⅔ per cent Bahrain owned; 33⅓ per cent Iraq owned.

About fourteen foreign insurance companies are represented.

TRADE AND INDUSTRY

Bahrain Chamber of Commerce and Industry: P.O.B. 248, Manama; f. 1939; 1,200 mems.; Pres. KHALIL IBRAHIM KAMEL; Dir. YUSUF MUHAMMAD SALEH.

Michael Rice Group—Middle East: P.O.B. 551, Manama; consultants to the Governments of Bahrain and Oman and to numerous local and foreign businesses trading in Bahrain, the Gulf area, Saudi Arabia and Kuwait.

There are no Trade Unions in Bahrain.

OIL

The Bahrain Petroleum Company (BAPCO) Ltd.: Awali; the sole oil producer in Bahrain; owned jointly by Texaco and Standard Oil of California; also operates the Bahrain refinery and holds a contract to supply natural gas to the ALBA aluminium smelter; Pres. W. O. STOLZ.

TRANSPORT

ROADS

Most inhabited areas of Bahrain are linked by bitumen-surfaced roads. Public transport consists of taxis and privately owned bus services. A modern network of dual highways is being developed; the length of the paved road system rose from 4,300 metres in 1964 to 30,000 metres in 1968. In 1967 the rule of the road was changed from left to right.

SHIPPING

Director-General of Customs and Ports: Sheikh DAIJ BIN KHALIFA AL-KHALIFA.

Harbour Master: Captain J. A. DUCK.

Cargo Manager: HASSAN SHAMS.

Numerous shipping services link Bahrain and the Gulf with Britain and with Europe (Strick Line, V.N.S. "Kerk" Line, Hansa Line, Nationale Compagnie Havraise Peninsulaire and Compagnie Maritime Belge, Kuwait Shipping Company, Iraqi Maritime Transport Corporation, Lauro Line, Yugo-Linea, Polish Ocean Lines); with the East and West Coasts, of U.S.A. (Concordia Line, Nedlloyd Line); with Pakistan, India, Japan and the Far East and Australia (P & O, British & India Steam Navigation Company,

BAHRAIN—(Transport, Education, Bibliography)

Maersk Line, Everett Johnson Line, "K" Line of Japan, etc.). Though predominantly cargo operators, most of the foregoing lines have some passenger accommodation available; the British India Line operates a mail service between Bombay, Karachi, Bahrain and other Gulf Ports, carrying passengers in Saloon and Deck classes; the Mogul line operates mail and passenger services between Bombay and the Gulf, and the Pan Islamic Steamship Co. between Karachi and the Gulf ports.

The deep water harbour of Mina Sulman was opened in April 1962; it has six berths capable of taking vessels of draughts up to 30 ft. In the vicinity are two slipways able to take vessels of up to 1,000 tons and 240 ft. in length, with services available for ship repairs afloat. A trawler basin is the centre of a flourishing shrimping industry, the packaged produce being exported primarily to Europe and North America.

In November 1972 OAPEC approved Bahrain as the site for a £40 million dry dock large enough to accept super-tankers of up to half a million tons. Engineering consultants for the scheme were due to be appointed in July 1973.

CIVIL AVIATION

Bahrain Airport has a first-class runway, capable of taking the largest aircraft in use. A new Jumbo Jet Airport Terminal was opened in December 1971.

Gulf Air: P.O.B. 138, Bahrain Island; f. 1950; jointly owned by the governments of Bahrain, Qatar, Abu Dhabi, Oman, and by BOAC; services from Bahrain to Kuwait, Abu Dhabi, Bandar Abbas, Dhahran, Doha, Dubai, Muscat, Sharjah, Shiraz, Karachi and Bombay; the fleet consists of two BAC 1-11, three F27, three Skyvans, two Islanders, two Beechcraft B80 and one chartered VC 10 on Gulf-London services.

Bahrain is served by the following foreign airlines: Air India, BOAC, Iran Air, Iraqi Airways, Kuwait Airways, MEA, Malaysia-Singapore Airlines, PIA (Pakistan), Qantas, Saudia, TMA.

EDUCATION

Education is free in Bahrain. From the ages of six to twelve children attend primary school. The next intermediate stage lasts two years and the secondary stage three years. There are three higher educational establishments, a Men's Teacher Training College, a Women's Teacher Training College and the Gulf Technical College. Expenditure on education was BD 4.2 million in 1972, 16.2 per cent of the budget.

Gulf Technical College: Isa Town, Bahrain; f. 1969; 220 full-time and 242 part-time students.

BIBLIOGRAPHY

Adamiyat, Fereydoun. Bahrain Islands: A Legal and Diplomatic Study of the British-Iranian Controversy (New York, Praeger, 1955).

Albaharna, H. M. The Legal Status of the Arabian Gulf States (Manchester University Press, 1968).

Busch, B. C. Britain and the Persian Gulf 1894–1914 (University of California Press, 1967).

Fact Sheets on Eastern Arabia (Private Information Center on Eastern Arabia, Heldenplein, 12-1800 Vilvoorde, Belgium).

Faroughby, Abbas. The Bahrain Islands (New York, 1951).

Hakima, A. M. The Rise and Development of Bahrain and Kuwait (Beirut, 1965).

Hay, Sir Rupert. The Persian Gulf States (Middle East Institute, Washington, 1959).

Marlowe, John. The Persian Gulf in the 20th Century (Cresset Press, London, 1962).

Miles, S. B. The Countries and Tribes of the Persian Gulf (3rd edition, Cass, London, 1970).

Wilson, Sir A. T. The Persian Gulf (Oxford University Press, 1928).

Cyprus

PHYSICAL AND SOCIAL GEOGRAPHY

W. B. Fisher

The island of Cyprus, some 3,572 sq. miles in area, is situated in the north-eastern corner of the Mediterranean Sea, closest to Turkey (which is easily visible from its northern coast), but also under 100 miles from the Syrian coast. Its greatest length, including the long, narrow peninsula of Cape Andreas, is 140 miles. The population was estimated at 639,000 in 1971, 523,000 Greeks and the rest Turks.

PHYSICAL FEATURES

Cyprus owes its peculiar shape to the occurrence of two ridges that were once part of two much greater arcs running from the mainland of Asia westwards towards Crete. The greater part of these arcs has disappeared, but remnants are found in Cyprus and on the eastern mainland, where they form the Amanus Range of Turkey. In Cyprus the arcs are visible as two mountain systems—the Kyrenia Range of the north, and the much larger and imposing Troödos Massif in the centre. Between the two mountain systems lies a flat lowland, open to the sea in the east and west and spoken of as the Mesaoria. Here also lies the chief town, Nicosia.

The mountain ranges are actually very different in structure and appearance. The Kyrenia Range is a single narrow fold of limestone, with occasional deposits of marble, and its maximum height is 3,000 ft. As it is mainly porous rock, rainfall soon seeps below ground; and so its appearance is rather arid, but very picturesque, with white crags and isolated pinnacles. The soil cover is thin. The Troödos, on the other hand, has been affected by folding in two separate directions, so that the whole area has been fragmented, and large quantities of molten igneous rock have forced their way to the surface from the interior of the earth, giving rise to a great dome that reaches 6,000 ft. above sea-level. As it is impervious to water, there are some surface streams, rounder outlines, a thicker soil, especially on the lower slopes, and a covering of pine forest.

CLIMATE

The climate in Cyprus is strongly "Mediterranean" in character, with the usual hot dry summers and warm, wet winters. As an island with high mountains, Cyprus receives a fair amount of moisture, and up to 40 in. of rain falls in the mountains, with the minimum of 12 to 15 inches in the Mesaoria. Frost does not occur on the coast, but may be sharp in the higher districts, and snow can fall fairly heavily in regions over 3,000 ft. in altitude. In summer, despite the nearness of the sea, temperatures are surprisingly high, and the Mesaoria in particular can experience over 100° F. A feature of minor importance is the tendency for small depressions to form over the island, giving a slightly greater degree of changeability in weather than is experienced elsewhere in the Middle East.

Relatively abundant rainfall together with high average temperatures were in the past responsible for a heavy incidence of malaria in the island. After World War II, however, an energetic campaign was waged against mosquitoes, and Cyprus is now entirely free from the disease.

Cyprus is noteworthy in that between 50 and 60 per cent of the total area is under cultivation—a figure higher than that for most Middle Eastern countries. This is partly to be explained by the relatively abundant rainfall; the expanses of impervious rock that retain water near the surface; and the presence of rich soils derived from volcanic rocks which occur round the Troödos Mountains. The steadily developing tourist trade and the export markets in wine and early vegetables add to the incentives to development.

HISTORY

EARLY HISTORY

Cyprus first became important in recorded history when the island fell under Egyptian control in the second millennium B.C. After a long period during which the Phoenicians and the people of Mycenae founded colonies there, Cyprus, in the eighth century B.C., became an Assyrian protectorate, at a time when the Greeks of the mainland were extending their settlements in the island. From the sixth century B.C. it was a province of the Persian empire and took part in the unsuccessful Ionian revolt against Persian rule in 502 B.C. Despite the Greek triumph over Xerxes in 480 B.C., subsequent efforts by the Greek city states of the mainland to free Cyprus from Persian control met with little success, largely because of dissension amongst the Greek cities of Cyprus itself. For more than two centuries after 295 B.C. the Ptolemies of Egypt ruled in Cyprus until it became part of the Roman Empire.

Under the enlightened rule of Augustus the island entered upon a long period of prosperity, for trade flourished while the Romans kept the seas clear of piracy. When Jerusalem fell to the Emperor Titus in A.D. 70, many Jews found refuge in Cyprus where they became numerous enough to undertake a serious revolt in A.D. 115. Christianity, apparently introduced into the island in the reign of Emperor Claudius (A.D. 41-54), grew steadily in the next three centuries, during which Cyprus, isolated from a continent frequently ravaged by barbarian inroads, continued to enjoy a relative degree of prosperity. From the time of Constantine the Great, Cyprus was a province governed by officials appointed from Antioch and formed part of the diocese of the East. In the reign of Theodosius I (379–395) the Greek Orthodox Church was firmly established there and in the fifth century proved strong enough to resist the attempt of the Patriarchs of Antioch to control the religious life of the island.

The Arab attack of 649 began a new period in the history of Cyprus which now became, for more than three hundred years, the object of dispute between the Byzantines and the Muslims. In the time of the Caliph Abd al-Malik (685–705) the revenues of the island were divided between the two Empires but in 691 hostilities were renewed after large numbers of Christians from Cyprus had moved to a new settlement on the shores of the Hellespont. In 747 the Byzantines crushed a determined Muslim effort to seize the island but were less successful in repelling serious attacks in the reign of the Emperor Nicephoras I (802–811). For a brief space Byzantium recovered effective possession of the island in the time of Basil I (867–886) but, whenever the Byzantine fleet was weak, Cyprus remained a doubtful possession of the Empire. From the decisive Byzantine reconquest of 964–5 Cyprus now enjoyed for more than two centuries a period of relative calm disturbed only by occasional revolts.

WESTERN RULE

Only with the Third Crusade did Cyprus begin a new chapter of its long story. In 1192 Richard Coeur-de-Lion, having conquered the island from the Greek usurper Comnenus, bestowed it on Guy de Lusignan, formerly King of Jerusalem. There now began almost four hundred years of Western rule, which saw the introduction of Western feudalism and of the Latin Church into a land which hitherto had been Greek in its institutions and Orthodox in its religious beliefs.

In the period from 1192 to 1267 (when the direct line of the Lusignan house became extinct) the new régime was gradually elaborated. The Lusignan monarchy was limited in character, for the royal power was effective only in the military sphere, all other important business of State being decided in a High Court which consisted of the nobles, the fief-holders, and the great officers of State. This Court applied to the island a highly developed code of feudal law derived from the Assizes of Jerusalem, the Cypriots being allowed to retain their own laws and customs in so far as these did not conflict with the feudal law. The period is also marked by the determined efforts of the Latin clergy, supported by the Papacy, to establish a complete control over the Orthodox Church, a policy carried out with much harshness which the Crown and the feudal nobility often sought to mitigate in order to keep the loyalty of the subject population. The dominance of the Latin Church was finally assured by the Bulla Cypria of Pope Alexander IV (1260).

During the second half of the thirteenth century the kingdom of Cyprus (now ruled by the house of Antioch-Lusignan) played an important role in the last struggle to maintain the Latin States in Syria against the Mamluk offensive. The influence of the monarchy was further strengthened in this period, and when in 1324 Hugues IV became king, the great age of feudal Cyprus had begun. Cyprus was now of great importance in the commerce which the Italian republics maintained with the East, and Famagusta became a flourishing port. The Papacy, however, always anxious to weaken the power of Mamluk Egypt, placed on the trade of the Italian republics with that State severe limitations and charged Cyprus and Rhodes with their enforcement. Thus began a conflict between the kings of Cyprus and the great republics of Venice and Genoa which did not endanger Cyprus so long as the Papacy could mobilize sentiment in the West to support the crusading State of the Lusignans. When, as the fourteenth century advanced, the Papacy lost its power to command such support in the West, Cyprus was left to face unaided the ambitions of Genoa and Venice, which she was powerless to withstand.

Before this decline began Cyprus enjoyed, in the mid-fourteenth century, a brief period of great brilliance under her crusading King Peter I (1359–69). In 1361 he occupied the port of Adalia on the south coast of Asia Minor, then held by the Turkish emirate of Tekke; and in the years 1362–65 toured Europe in an effort to win adequate support for a new crusade. His most memorable exploit came in 1365 when he captured Alexandria in Egypt, sacking it so completely that even as late as the sixteenth century it had not recovered its former splendour. In 1366 he repelled a Turkish attack on Adalia and in the next year ravaged the coast of Syria, seizing and pillaging Tripoli; but, seeing at last that no help was to be expected from the West, he made peace with Egypt. With his assassination in 1369 the great period of the Lusignan house was ended.

The reign of King Janus I (1398–1432) was a long struggle to drive out the Genoese, who had seized Famagusta during the war with Cyprus in 1372–74, and to repel the attacks of Mamluk Egypt, which had become weary of the repeated sea-raids undertaken from the ports of Cyprus. After plundering Larnaca and Limassol in 1425 the Mamluks crushed the army of Cyprus in a battle at Khoirakoitia in 1426, King Janus himself being captured, and his capital Nicosia sacked. The King was released in 1427, when he had promised the payment of a large ransom and of an annual tribute. The last years of Lusignan power were marked by dissension in the ruling house and by the increasing domination of Venice which, with the consent of Caterina Cornaro, the Venetian widow of the last Lusignan king, annexed Cyprus in 1489.

TURKISH RULE

Venice held Cyprus until 1570 when the Ottoman Turks began a campaign of conquest which led to the fall of Nicosia in September 1570 and of Famagusta in August 1571. The Turks now restored to the Orthodox Greek Church its independence and ended the former feudal status of the peasantry. The Cypriots paid a tax for their freedom to follow their own religion and were allowed to cultivate their land as their own and to hand it to their descendants on payment of a proportion of the produce, which varied from one-fifth to one-tenth according to the locality. About thirty thousand Turkish soldiers were also given land in the island, thus forming a Turkish element in the population which was later reinforced by a certain amount of immigration from Asia Minor.

The seventeenth and eighteenth centuries were a melancholy period in the history of Cyprus. Repeated droughts and ravages of locusts preceded a famine in 1640 and an outbreak of plague in 1641. In 1660 the Ottoman government, in order to limit the extortions of its officials and of the tax-farmers, recognized the Orthodox Archbishop and his three suffragans as guardians of the Christian peasantry, but this step did not prevent revolts in 1665 and 1690. A great famine in 1757–58 and a severe attack of plague in 1760 reduced the numbers of the peasantry very considerably, causing a widespread distress which culminated in the revolt of 1764–66. Cyprus from 1702 had been a fief of the Grand Vizier who normally sold the governorship to the highest bidder, usually for a period of one year. This practice created opportunities of financial oppression which were rarely allowed to pass unused. Perhaps the most striking development of the period was the continued rise in the power of the Orthodox bishops whose influence was so great in the late eighteenth century that the Turkish administration depended on their support for the collection of the revenues. The Turkish elements in Cyprus, who resented the dominance of the Orthodox bishops, accused them in 1821 of having a secret understanding with the Greeks of the Morea who had revolted against Turkish rule, and carried out a massacre of the Christians at Nicosia and elsewhere, which brought the supremacy of the bishops to an end.

In 1833 the Sultan granted Cyprus to Muhammad Ali, Pasha of Egypt, who was forced, however, to renounce possession of it in 1840 at the demand of the Great Powers. During the period of reforms initiated by Sultan Mahmud II (1808–39) and continued by his immediate successors, efforts were made to improve the administration of the island. The practice of farming out the taxes was abolished (although later partially reintroduced) and the Governor now became a salaried official ruling through a divan half-Turkish and half-Christian in composition.

BRITISH RULE

In 1878 Great Britain concluded an agreement with the Sultan by which Cyprus was given over to British control. Great Britain intended to use the island as a base from which the Ottoman Empire might be protected against the ambitions of Russia, a defence then all the more important in that the opening of the Suez Canal (1869) had made the East Mediterranean an area of great strategic importance. Under the agreement of 1878 Cyprus remained legally a part of the Ottoman Empire, to which a tribute was paid consisting of the surplus revenues of the island, calculated at a sum rather less than £93,000 per annum.

From 1882 until 1931 the island had a Legislative Council partly nominated and partly elected. Various reforms were carried out in this first period of British rule: the introduction of an efficient judicial system and of an effective police force, and considerable improvements in agriculture, roads, education and other public services.

Cyprus was offered to Greece in 1915 provided Greece joined the Allies in the war, but the offer was refused and did not remain open. In 1925 the island became a Crown Colony, at a time when the discontent of the Greek Cypriots was beginning to assume more serious proportions.

In the period since 1931 the desire to achieve self-government within the Commonwealth grew stronger, but the *Enosis* movement remained a strong influence in the political life of the island. Cypriot troops performed valuable services in the war of 1939–45, for example in Libya under Lord Wavell and in the Greek campaign of 1941. Later Cyprus was used as a place of detention for illegal Jewish immigrants into Palestine, the last of such detention camps being closed in 1949.

CONSTITUTIONAL PROPOSALS

In July 1954 Great Britain made known its intention to prepare a restricted form of constitution for Cyprus, with a legislature containing official, nominated and elected members. The Greek Cypriots, insisting that their ultimate goal was *Enosis*, viewed the proposed constitution with disfavour, whereas the Turkish Cypriots declared their readiness to accept it. The Greek Government at Athens now brought the problem of Cyprus before the UN. Great Britain, however, urged that the question was one with which she alone was competent to deal. The result was that, in December 1954, the UN resolved to take no immediate action in the matter.

The more extreme advocates of *Enosis*, grouped together in the EOKA (National Organization of the Struggle for the Freedom of Cyprus) now began a campaign of terrorist activities against the British administration. A conference including representatives from Great Britain, Greece and the Turkish Republic met in London in August 1955. The British offer of substantial autonomy for Cyprus failed to win the approval of Greece, since it held out no clear prospect of self-determination for the island, and the conference therefore ended in frustration.

A new and more violent wave of terrorism swept Cyprus in November 1955. A state of emergency was declared on November 27th whereby the death penalty was imposed for the bearing of arms, life imprisonment for sabotage and lesser sentences for looting and the harbouring of terrorists. All public assemblies of a political nature were forbidden; the British troops in Cyprus (about 10,000 in all) assumed the status of active service in war time. The Governor now ruled the island through an executive council consisting of four officials from the administration, two Greek Cypriots and one Turkish Cypriot.

At the beginning of 1956 the Governor, Sir John Harding, discussed the situation with Archbishop Makarios, head of the Greek Orthodox Church in the island. Since Great Britain was now willing to accept the principle of ultimate independence for Cyprus, agreement seemed to be within reach. In March 1956, however, the discussions were broken off and Archbishop Makarios, implicated in the activities of the EOKA, was deported to the Seychelles Islands.

THE RADCLIFFE PROPOSALS

Great Britain, confronted with a general strike in Cyprus, with a renewed and more intense campaign of terrorism and with the first ominous signs of strife between the Greek and Turkish communities in the island, now appointed Lord Radcliffe, in July 1956, as Commissioner for Constitutional Reform. His report, published in December of that year, proposed that defence, foreign affairs and internal security should be reserved to the Governor, other spheres of rule being under the control of a cabinet of Cypriot Ministers responsible to an elected legislature. Lord Radcliffe laid down careful safeguards for the Turks in Cyprus—no laws affecting the domestic affairs of the Turks would be valid without the consent of two-thirds of the Turkish members in the legislature.

Meanwhile, in June 1956, Greece appealed once more to the United Nations. Great Britain, asserting that the internal affairs of Cyprus fell solely within her own competence, complained to the UN in October about the aid forthcoming from Greece for the EOKA terrorists. There were, however, talks at Athens and Ankara in December 1956, but to no effective end, since Greece rejected the proposals of Lord Radcliffe for constitutional reform in Cyprus. The UN, in February 1957, adopted a resolution urging that a peaceful and democratic settlement be found for the Cyprus problem.

RELEASE OF MAKARIOS

In March 1957 Archbishop Makarios was released from detention in the Seychelles and, since he was not allowed to return to Cyprus, went in fact to Athens. The British authorities also relaxed some of the emergency laws—e.g. the press censorship and the mandatory death penalty for the bearing of arms. These measures facilitated the holding of further discussions, but the progress made by the end of the year was inconsiderable.

The tide of violence ran high in Cyprus during the first half of 1958. EOKA carried out an intensive campaign of sabotage, especially at Nicosia and Famagusta. At the same time strife between the Greek Cypriots and the Turkish Cypriots was becoming more frequent and severe, the outbreaks in June 1958 being particularly serious. There was increased tension, too, between the governments at Athens and at Ankara.

BRITAIN'S SEVEN-YEAR PLAN

It was in this situation that Great Britain, on June 19th, 1958, made public a new scheme for Cyprus. The island was to remain under British control for seven years; full autonomy in communal affairs would be granted, under separate arrangements, to the Greek Cypriots and the Turkish Cypriots; internal administration was to be reserved for the Governor's Council which would include representatives of the Greek Cypriot and Turkish Cypriot communities and also of the Greek and Turkish governments at Athens and Ankara. This scheme came into force on October 1st, 1958.

CYPRUS—(HISTORY)

THE ZÜRICH AND LONDON AGREEMENTS

Negotiations between Greece and the Turkish Republic soon carried the Cyprus problem towards an agreed solution. As the result of a conference held at Zürich, it was announced on February 11th, 1959, that the two states had devised a compromise settlement. A further conference at London led to a full and formal publication of the details.

Cyprus was to become an independent republic with a Greek Cypriot President and a Turkish Cypriot Vice-President. There would be a Council of Ministers (seven Greeks, three Turks) and a House of Representatives (70 per cent Greek, 30 per cent Turkish) elected by universal suffrage for a term of five years. Communal Chambers, one Greek, one Turkish, were to exercise control in matters of religion, culture and education. The Turkish inhabitants in five of the main towns would be allowed to establish separate municipalities for a period of four years.

Cyprus was not to be united with another state, nor was it to be subject to partition. Great Britain, Greece and the Turkish Republic guaranteed the independence, the territorial integrity and the constitution of Cyprus. Greece received the right to station a force of 950 men in the island, and the Turkish Republic, a force of 650 men. Great Britain retained under her direct sovereignty two base areas in Cyprus—at Akrotiri and at Dhekelia.

In November 1959 agreement was attained in regard to the delimitation of the executive powers to be vested in the President and Vice-President of Cyprus. A further agreement defined the composition of the Supreme Constitutional Court. On December 4th, 1959, the state of emergency (in force since 1955) came to an end. Archbishop Makarios, on December 13th, 1959, was elected to be the first President of Cyprus. After long negotiations concluded on July 1st, 1960, Great Britain and Cyprus reached agreement over the precise size and character of the two military bases to be assigned to British sovereignty.

INDEPENDENCE

Cyprus became formally an independent republic on August 16th, 1960, and, on September 20th, a member of the United Nations. The Conference of Commonwealth Prime Ministers, meeting at London, resolved on March 14th, 1961, that Cyprus be admitted as a member of the Commonwealth.

A team of experts from the United Nations visited Cyprus in the autumn of 1960. Its official report was made public on April 5th, 1961. On August 21st, 1961, Archbishop Makarios submitted to the Cyprus House of Representatives the outline of a five-year plan based on the UN report. The Archbishop laid particular emphasis on reform in land-tenure and agrarian methods, on the conservation of existing and the development of new water supplies and on the introduction of long-term loans to farmers.

The Cyprus Government, in June 1961, signed a technical aid agreement with the U.S.A. In November of the same year, the German Federal Republic declared that it would make capital assistance and long-term credits available to Cyprus; it was also prepared to contribute towards the cost of geological and hydrological surveys in the island. December 1961 saw the signing of a contract with a Polish firm for the expansion of port facilities at Famagusta and the conclusion of a reciprocal trade agreement with the Soviet Union. Also in December 1961 Cyprus became a member of the International Monetary Fund and of the International Bank for Reconstruction and Development.

CONSTITUTIONAL PROBLEMS

As Cyprus entered thus into its independence, serious problems began to arise over the interpretation and working of the constitution. There was divergence of opinion between Greek Cypriots and Turkish Cypriots over the formation of a national army, as laid down in the Zürich agreement of 1959 (2,000 men: 60 per cent Greek, 40 per cent Turkish), the main point of dispute being the degree of integration to be established between the two racial components. On October 20th, 1961, the Turkish Vice-President, Dr. Küçük, used his power of veto to ban full integration which President Makarios favoured at all levels of the armed forces.

Difficulties arose also over the implementation of the 70 per cent-30 per cent ratio of Greek Cypriot to Turkish Cypriot personnel in the public services. There was friction too in the House of Representatives, about financial affairs—e.g. customs duties and income tax laws.

The year 1962 saw the growth of a serious crisis over the system of separate Greek and Turkish municipalities in the five main towns of Cyprus—Nicosia, Famagusta, Limassol, Larnaca and Paphos. On December 29th, 1962, the Turkish Communal Chamber passed a law maintaining the Turkish municipalities in the five towns from January 1st, 1963, and also establishing a similar municipality in the predominantly Turkish town of Lefka. President Makarios now issued a decree stating that from January 1st, 1963, Government-appointed bodies would control municipal organizations throughout the island—a decree which the Turkish Cypriots denounced as an infringement of the constitution.

The Constitutional Court of Cyprus, sitting in judgement on the financial disputes, ruled in February 1963 that, in view of the veto exercised by the Turkish members of the House of Representatives since 1961, taxes could be imposed on the people of the island, but that no legal machinery existed for the collection of such taxes. In April the court declared that the Government had no power to control the municipalities through bodies of its own choosing and that the decision of the Turkish Communal Chamber to maintain the separate Turkish municipalities in defiance of the Cyprus Government was likewise invalid.

Negotiations between President Makarios and Vice-President Küçük to resolve the deadlock broke down in May. Accordingly in November Archbishop Makarios put forward proposals for a number of reforms—e.g. that the President and Vice-President of Cyprus should lose their right of veto over certain types of legislation; that separate Greek Cypriot and Turkish Cypriot majorities in the House of Representatives should not be required for financial legislation; and that single municipal councils, with both Greek and Turkish Cypriot members, should replace the separate municipalities in the five chief towns of Cyprus. These proposals proved to be unacceptable to the Turkish Cypriots.

CIVIL WAR

Meanwhile, underground organizations, prepared for violence, had come into being both among the Greek and the Turkish communities. In December 1963 serious conflict broke out. On December 25th Great Britain suggested that a joint force composed of British, Greek and Turkish troops stationed in Cyprus should be established to restore order. The governments at Nicosia, Athens and Ankara gave their assent to this scheme. At this same moment the forces of the Turkish Republic serving in the island occupied, north of Nicosia, a strong position which gave them control of the important road to Kyrenia on the northern coast of Cyprus—a road which was to become the scene of much conflict in the future. As a result of the December crisis co-operation between the Greek Cypriots and the Turkish Cypriots in government and in other sectors of public life came almost to an end.

The general situation was now becoming extremely tense. There was renewed violence in February 1964, especially at Limassol. Arms in considerable quantities were being brought secretly into the island for both sides and the number of armed "irregulars" was increasing rapidly. These developments also gave rise to sharp frictions between Athens and Ankara.

ESTABLISHMENT OF UN PEACE-KEEPING FORCE

Cyprus, in January 1964, had asked the UN to send a representative to the island. On January 16th U Thant, the Secretary-General of the United Nations, nominated Lieutenant-General Prem Gyani of India to act in this role. Later in the same month the Cyprus Government informed U Thant that it would be glad to see a UN force established in the island. The UN Security Council debated the Cyprus question on February 18th, finally adopting a resolution on March 4th authorizing the creation of a United Nations peace-keeping force for Cyprus. U Thant, on March 6th, appointed Lieutenant-General Gyani to command this force. Advance units of the Canadian contingent reached the island later in the month and by May 22nd the UN Headquarters at Nicosia controlled some 7,000 men.

U Thant, on March 25th, announced the appointment of Mr. S. Tuomioja, the Finnish Ambassador to Sweden, as United Nations mediator in Cyprus. Later, on May 11th, U Thant nominated Dr. Galo Plaza, of Ecuador, to be his special representative in the island. After the death of Mr. Tuomioja Dr. Galo Plaza was to become, in September 1964, the UN mediator in Cyprus, Senhor Carlos Bernardes, of Brazil, taking his place as U Thant's Special Representative. The exploratory consultations of the UN officials—at Nicosia, at Athens and at Ankara—failed to achieve real progress in the summer of 1964. The unlikelihood of United Nations success in solving the Cyprus question was underlined when, in June 1964, President Johnson of the U.S.A. resolved to attempt a direct mediation in the dispute. Once again, however, the progress registered was small.

There was more fighting between Greek and Turkish Cypriots in March and April 1964—above all for control of the Nicosia-Kyrenia road, which the troops of the Turkish Republic stationed in Cyprus controlled in the south, near Nicosia, and which Turkish guerrillas operating from St. Hilarion Castle, high in the mountains close to Kyrenia, dominated in the north. The fighting was severe at Ktima on March 7th-9th, 1964. On June 1st the Cyprus House of Representatives passed a Bill establishing a National Guard and making all male Cypriots between the ages of 18 and 59 liable to six months of service in it. Only members of the National Guard, of the regular police and of the army forces would now have the right to bear arms. One purpose of the Bill was to suppress the irregular bands which, as extremist sentiment grew stronger, tended more and more to escape from the control of the established régime.

Under the agreements concluded for the independence of Cyprus in 1959–60 the Turkish Republic maintained a contingent of troops in the island, the personnel of this force being renewed from time to time on a system of regular rotation. A new crisis arose in August-September 1964 when the Government at Nicosia refused to allow such a rotation of personnel. After much negotiation through the UN officials in the island the Cyprus Government agreed to raise its existing blockade of the Turkish Cypriots entrenched in the Kokkina district and to allow the normal rotation of troops for the Turkish force stationed at Cyprus. The Government at Ankara now consented that this force, which dominated the Nicosia-Kyrenia road, should come under the United Nations command in Cyprus.

LEGISLATIVE MEASURES

Towards the end of 1964 the Cyprus House of Representatives passed a number of important measures—a Bill for the creation of unified municipalities in Nicosia, Larnaca, Limassol, Famagusta and Paphos; a law restoring to the Government the right to exact income tax (a right inoperative since 1961 as a result of the veto of the Turkish Cypriot members in the House); and a Bill extending compulsory service in the National Guard for Greek Cypriots from six to twelve months. In July 1965 a new law was approved for unified elections on the basis of a common electoral roll, the communal distinction between Greek Cypriots and Turkish Cypriots being thus abolished.

The UN mediator in Cyprus, Dr. Galo Plaza, resigned in December 1965. A special envoy from U Thant, Señor José Rolz-Bennett, reached Cyprus in February 1966 with the aim of discovering local views on the continuation of the UN mediation effort and to examine the position of the UN peace-force in Cyprus. Little had been done towards mediation since Dr. Galo Plaza published a detailed report in March 1965. Moreover, no clear indication existed at this time as to where the funds would be found to continue the existence of the UN forces in the island. The United Nations was in fact to renew the mandate of these forces in June 1966 and again in December 1966. In addition the UN Secretary-General, U Thant, announced in January 1967 that he had chosen Señor Bibiano Osorio-Tafall, of Mexico, to be his personal representative in Cyprus, Senhor Carlos Bernardes, of Brazil, having resigned the appointment for personal reasons.

GENERAL GRIVAS

There was further tension in Cyprus during March 1966 over the position of General Grivas, the former head of EOKA. The General had returned to the island in June 1964 at a time when it was felt that he might be able, with his high personal prestige, to bring to order the small "private armies" and "irregular bands" which had emerged among the Greek Cypriots and which were violently defying the Cyprus Government.

President Makarios now, in March 1966, attempted to limit the functions of General Grivas in Cyprus and so to end a situation which saw political control vested in himself, while command of the armed forces, both the Greek Cypriot National Guard and also the "volunteer" Greek troops stationed in Cyprus, rested with the General, who took his orders from Athens. The President suggested that the National Guard should be transferred to the control of the Cyprus Minister of Defence—a proposal which found favour neither with General Grivas nor at Athens, where it provoked a sharp political crisis. The whole affair underlined the distrust separating President Makarios and General Grivas and the doubts existing at Athens as to the ultimate intentions of the President.

Meanwhile negotiations in secret had begun anew between Athens and Ankara in June 1966 and continued throughout the rest of the year.

Great Britain, in November 1966, announced her intention to reduce her military establishment in Cyprus. Some

2,000 servicemen would be brought back to Great Britain by the summer of 1967. At the same time there was to be a scaling down in the amount of stores held at the Dhekelia base. The Royal Air Force station at Nicosia had already been run down to care and maintenance status, leaving Akrotiri to function still as a large R.A.F. headquarters.

There was renewed tension in Cyprus during the winter of 1966–67 over the shipment of small arms and machine-guns to the island from Czechoslovakia. Reports current at the time intimated that President Makarios had resolved to create several specialized units within the Cyprus police force. General Grivas was known to have declared to the Greek Government that he would not be responsible for good order in Cyprus, if there were forces in the island bearing arms and yet outside his control. There was serious concern, too, at Ankara that the Turkish Cypriots would be exposed to new dangers, should the Cyprus Government be allowed to arm paramilitary groups independent of the forces now under General Grivas. It was announced from Athens in December 1966 that the arms which had thus far reached Cyprus would be stored on the island in warehouses under the control of Greek troops. Also in December the Turkish Republic informed Czechoslovakia that it would have to review relations between the two countries, if further shipments of arms were sent to Cyprus. The Ankara Government, in February 1967, was urging that the Czechoslovak arms then stored in Cyprus should be surrendered to the custody of the United Nations force in the island.

ATTEMPTS AT A SETTLEMENT

Attempts to settle the dispute over Cyprus continued throughout the spring and summer of 1967. Sufficient progress was made in the course of negotiations between Athens and Ankara to render possible a summit meeting between the Turkish Prime Minister, Mr. Demirel, and the Prime Minister of Greece, Mr. Kollias. The meeting was held on the Turkish-Greek frontier in Thrace, at Kesan and Alexandropolis, in September 1967. Under discussion were proposals involving the union of Cyprus with Greece, but also the establishment in the island of a Turkish base which would safeguard the interests of the Turkish Cypriots. The negotiations at Kesan and Alexandropolis failed, however, to bring about agreement between the Turkish and the Greek Governments.

On October 31st, 1967, Mr. Rauf Denktaş, an exiled leader of the Turkish Cypriots, returned to Cyprus, only to meet with arrest. The Cyprus Government, under pressure from Ankara, released Mr. Denktaş on November 12th and sent him back to the Turkish mainland. This episode led to a swift and, as subsequent events made clear, a dangerous reaction on the part of the Greek Cypriot National Guard under its commander, General Grivas. The Greek Cypriots—in pursuance of a right established earlier with UN approval, but then left in abeyance since April 1967—attempted, in November 1967, to force police patrols through the Turkish Cypriot enclaves of Ayos Theodoros and Kophinou—villages commanding the important roads running from Nicosia to Larnaca and Limassol on the southern shore of the island. Turkish resistance was answered with a full-scale assault by the National Guard on the villages, leading to considerable loss of life amongst the Turks. This renewal of violence led the Turkish Government to threaten massive intervention in Cyprus and along the Turkish-Greek border in Thrace.

The National Guard now withdrew its troops from the Turkish enclaves. Moreover, the Government at Athens recalled General Grivas to Greece, the resignation of the General from his command in Cyprus following hard on the order for his recall. Nonetheless, throughout the last two weeks of November the situation remained tense. Urgent discussions involving Ankara and Athens, the United Nations, the personal ambassador of President Johnson of the U.S.A. and also the Government at Nicosia led eventually to a settlement of the immediate crisis.

The main lines of the settlement embraced the withdrawal from Cyprus of the regular Greek troops introduced there, in the guise of "volunteers", during the course of earlier crises and the end of the large-scale preparations for war which the Turkish Government at Ankara had been making in recent weeks. The Turks also pressed for the dissolution of the Greek Cypriot National Guard, for the handing over of all weapons (including consignments of arms arrived earlier from Czechoslovakia) and for the enlargement of the UN role in Cyprus for the maintenance of law and order there. Between December 8th, 1967, and January 16th, 1968, Greek troops, estimated to number more than 7,000, did in fact leave Cyprus. On January 17th the Greek Government informed the Turkish Government that the withdrawal of all Greek troops, except for the agreed contingent, had been completed.

On December 29th, 1967, the Turkish community set up a "transitional administration" to administer affairs of the Turkish-Cypriot areas "until such time as the provisions of the 1960 Constitution have been fully implemented". The eleven-man administration, with Dr. Küçük as President and Rauf Denktaş (who was permitted to return to Cyprus later, in April) as Vice-President, with assignments similar to those of ministers, was to function as an executive council, with plans for the establishment of a semi-parliamentary House of Representatives.

The subsequent trend of events emphasized the unlikelihood that *Enosis* of Cyprus with Greece would be achieved in the near future. Indeed, the failure of the Turkish-Greek negotiations at Kesan and Alexandropolis in September 1967 had left President Makarios free to pursue a more immediate solution, acceptable now, perhaps, to most of the Greek Cypriots—i.e. to prolong the existence of Cyprus as a sovereign independent state. The Archbishop, in January 1968, announced that a presidential election would be held in February, the objective being to secure a mandate for policies which might lead to a settlement of the differences existing between the Greek and Turkish communities in Cyprus. The opposition elements among the Greek Cypriots, favouring union with Greece, put forward their own candidate for the presidential office. The election thus offered in effect a choice between *Enosis* and continued independence for Cyprus. On February 25th President Makarios was given a massive majority vote in support of his policies.

The Turkish Cypriots announced earlier the same month that in view of the decision of the Greek Cypriot administration to hold elections for the Presidency only, the Turkish Cypriot community had been obliged to hold elections for the Vice-Presidency; Dr. Küçük had been the only candidate and had been declared elected unopposed.

At the same time President Makarios was preparing proposals for constitutional reforms under which the Turkish Cypriots would be accorded special rights and privileges within a unitary state of Cyprus. To prepare the ground for an approach towards future agreement between the two communities, he began to raise the restrictions which had been enforced on the Turkish Cypriots. During the first months of 1968 a series of measures restored to them freedom of movement and freedom to import into their enclaves such essential materials as cement, timber and iron.

During 1968 and early 1969 talks continued to take place between representatives of the Greek and Turkish communities in Cyprus, but little progress was made.

Early in 1969 Mr. Clerides and Mr. Georghadjis announced their intention of forming a new political party, comprising nationalist elements which supported the Cyprus Government, with a wide popular base. The same day Dr. Lyssarides, a left-wing politician, announced the formation of another new party. President Makarios issued a statement approving "the creation of an organized political life" and welcoming "the initiative taken for the creation of one Party for the nationalist front".

ASSASSINATION ATTEMPT AND ELECTIONS

Since early 1969 the National Front, which supports *Enosis* has claimed responsibility for several raids and thefts of arms from police outposts, the shooting and wounding of the Chief of Police, and several unsuccessful bomb attacks on Government ministers. Special legislation was enacted in August 1969 to ban the movement. On March 8th, 1970, an attempt was made on the life of President Makarios as his helicopter took off from the Presidential Palace in Nicosia. Five days later security officials prevented former Minister of the Interior Georghadjis from leaving the island. On the previous day he had been found guilty of illegally possessing two loaded pistols. On March 16th Georghadjis was found shot dead in his car near Nicosia. It was widely believed that Georghadjis was involved in the attempted assassination, and at the trial in November when four Greek Cypriots were found guilty, the suspicion was confirmed by a court ruling. Disturbances continued in May 1970 with a raid on a Limassol police station, when large quantities of arms and ammunition were stolen; fifty members of the banned National Front were arrested, of whom 21 were given prison sentences in December.

Despite these events the Government felt secure enough to hold a general election in July, the first since 1960. The 35 Greek seats in the House of Representatives were contested by 141 candidates. The results showed that the Patriotic (Unified) Party, the leader of the governing coalition, lost ground, whilst the candidates favouring *Enosis* had little success. The Communist AKEL Party won all the nine seats it contested, however, and thus became the second largest party in the chamber. The President had a few days earlier announced the first major cabinet shuffle since he came to power, bringing in six new members. Separate elections were held for the 15 Turkish seats in the House of Representatives and for the 15 communal seats, which together make up the Turkish Communal Chamber; these are unlikely to be considered valid in the event of a settlement being reached between the two communities.

TALKS CONTINUE

The third round of inter-communal talks was resumed on March 23rd, 1970, and continued at weekly intervals. Little affected by the July elections, the talks ended in failure on August 17th, with Turkish demands for regional autonomy still conflicting with Greek fears of partition. Before the fourth round began on September 21st, President Makarios visited Athens and confirmed the Greek Government's support for the further handling of the situation. After a break of over a month to allow consultations between both sides and contacts in the U.S.A., talks continued at fortnightly intervals. A "package deal" solution was proposed by Mr. Clerides in December 1970 and again in January 1971, but on both occasions it was rejected by his Turkish opposite number.

At the same time relations between the Council of Ministers and the House of Representatives became strained when members of the Unified Party rejected certain proposals in the 1971 budget; a constitutional crisis was averted by certain assurances from President Makarios. Hopes of a settlement between the communities rose in February when the Government put forward plans for the rehabilitation of some Turkish Cypriot refugees to their villages on condition that they live under Greek control. Mr. Denktaş rejected this, however, and the talks reached deadlock in April following a speech by President Makarios in which he referred to Cyprus as "a Greek island". He continued, "We shall maintain its unity until we have handed it back to Greece." In an effort to keep the talks open, UN Secretary-General, U Thant, sent a special envoy to meet the Cypriot leaders.

The crisis deepened in July 1971 when the Greek Government put pressure on the Greek Cypriot side to make further concessions, including specifically the appointment of a Turkish Minister in charge of local government, and threatened to seek a solution directly with Ankara. President Makarios reacted strongly to the suggestion of an imposed settlement and, as a result of a visit to Moscow, succeeded in securing Soviet support for his view. The inter-communal talks continued at irregular intervals, reaching deadlock in September, although both sides insisted that efforts to find a solution would continue.

In the same month it was reported that General George Grivas, the former EOKA leader, had disappeared from his home in Athens and had probably returned in secret to Cyprus. As a result, rumours persisted that he may have been planning to overthrow the Makarios Government and that groups supporting his *Enosis* policy were being trained for that purpose. The Cyprus Government reacted by importing 15,000 rifles and automatic weapons from Czechoslovakia in January 1972 and by drawing up plans for a paramilitary force of 1,000 men. This move brought strong opposition from Athens and a demand, which had the support of Britain, Turkey and the UN Secretary-General, that the arms be surrendered to the UN Peace-Keeping Force. The Greek Government also called on President Makarios to dismiss certain members of his cabinet considered hostile to Athens. Makarios eventually agreed to give the UN control of the arms and to reshuffle his cabinet, provided that no attempt be made to remove him by force. In March 1972, three members of the Holy Synod of the Orthodox Church of Cyprus, in a move thought to have the support of Athens, called on Makarios to resign as President, claiming that under the laws of the Church, the Archbishop should not hold temporal power. Encouraged by large demonstrations of support, Makarios persistently rejected the bishops' demand. However, the cabinet reshuffle began in May when Mr. Spyrou Kyprianou, the Foreign Minister and a staunch supporter of President Makarios, resigned under pressure. When President Makarios announced a new Council of Ministers on June 16th, 1972, only three former Ministers remained.

A fourth round of inter-communal talks began after a long delay on June 8th, 1972 in the presence of Dr. Kurt Waldheim, the new UN Secretary-General. His predecessor had secured the agreement of the Greek and Turkish Governments to send technical consultants to attend the meetings, together with Señor Bibiano Osorio-Tafall, the representative of the UN Secretariat in Cyprus. The talks continued throughout 1972 and the first half of 1973, but there was no sign that the two sides were about to reach an agreement. The fact that the talks were in progress has, however, resulted in a respite from intercommunal violence, although tension still remains.

Although there was little intercommunal violence, General Grivas and his supporters were particularly active in the period before the Presidential election in February 1973, when guerrilla activity included the attacking of police posts. Grivas's efforts to cause political instability and thereby jeopardize the electoral prospects of Archbishop Makarios proved fruitless when Makarios was returned unopposed for a further five-year term. Rauf Denktaş, the Turkish Cypriot representative to the intercommunal talks, was elected Vice-President later in February. General Grivas has lost any support that he may once have enjoyed from the Greek Government, but he and his supporters continue to be active, and Archbishop Makarios has accused him of planning a *coup d'état* which was to have taken place on April 1st, 1973 (Independence Day).

Opposition to Archbishop Makarios has continued to come from his three senior Bishops, Bishop Yennadios of Paphos, Bishop Anthimos of Kitium and Bishop Kyprianos of Kyrenia. In March 1973 they again called upon Archbishop Makarios to resign as President, and when he refused, the Bishops announced their decision to unfrock him. Makarios refused to admit the validity of the Bishops' pronouncements, and at a synod of the Eastern Orthodox Churches in the Middle East, the three Bishops were deposed and unfrocked. Opposition from General Grivas continued to trouble Makarios in July and August 1973, when the Cyprus Minister of Justice was kidnapped by Grivas's followers. Makarios refused to give in to blackmail and rejected Grivas's demand for new presidential elections, and for Makarios to choose between church and politics. He challenged Grivas to come out of hiding and face a "democratic confrontation".

ECONOMIC SURVEY

Geographically Cyprus may be divided into four regions distinguished by their natural and climatic features. These are the north coastal belt including the narrow Kyrenia mountain chain; the central plain, known as the Mesaoria, from Famagusta and Larnaca to Morphou Bay; the mountainous area of the south centre, dominated by the Troödos massif with its highest point of Mount Olympus (6,400 feet); and the coastal plain of the south running from a point west of Larnaca to Limassol and Paphos.

Of these areas the most significant in the island's economy are the central plain, which is the most densely populated and the centre of the island's grain production, the mountains, in which are situated the mineral deposits, which form the basis of the important extractive industries, the vineyards and the state forests, and the coastal plain, whose beaches form the principal tourist attraction on Cyprus.

The population of Cyprus has increased rapidly in the period since the island passed under British rule, at a rate of between 1½ per cent and two per cent per annum, and at the end of 1972 had reached an estimated 645,000. This has been the result of a spectacular fall in the death rate, particularly in the infant mortality rate, due to the advances in public health which have virtually eliminated such diseases as malaria and amoebic dysentry. The emergence of a young, mostly literate population, unable to be contained by the old agricultural economy, has been at the root of most of the island's economic and political problems in the last two decades. Income per head has risen from about £200 in 1961 to around £405 in 1972, and is the highest in the area apart from Israel. The third Five-Year Plan was to have begun in 1972, but its start has been delayed and it will not come into operation until 1973. Under the second Plan (1967–71), the Gross Domestic Product increased by 8 per cent a year. It has been estimated that, on current prices, GDP increased by 13 per cent in 1971.

AGRICULTURE

Agriculture is the most important single economic activity in Cyprus. It provides about 21 per cent of domestic production and employs 38 per cent of the labour force. Wheat and barley account for one-third of the cultivated area, but the island is a net importer of cereals. The principal exports are citrus products (£12.6 million in 1971), potatoes (£4.5 million in 1971) and wine and spirits (£3.4 million in 1971); however, the difficulty in marketing recent record crops has led to diversification in production towards "exotic" vegetables such as asparagus, green peppers, aubergines, artichokes, etc. Over 70 per cent of agricultural exports are marketed through co-operatives, which have done much to improve standards of packing and presentation. Viticulture has been an outstanding success in recent years, with steadily increasing exports of wine, grape juice, raisins as well as fresh grapes. Agricultural exports account for just under two-thirds of all exports and the proportion is likely to increase.

About 60 per cent of the land area is cultivated but only 5 per cent of this is irrigable in the hot summer, and because of the extensive fallow system in use on a third of the land only one crop in two years is produced in these areas. A five-year water study completed in 1968 by the UN revealed that the discovery of any new underground water supplies is unlikely. Already uncontrolled pumping has caused an incursion of sea water into some citrus areas. A severe drought in early 1973 caused the failure of the winter grain crop, at a loss of more than £20 million to the economy.

Agricultural output more than doubled over the last ten years. Over the period of the 1967–71 Five-Year Plan, it achieved a growth of 8.5 per cent a year, citrus fruits, cereals, meat, milk and eggs mainly contributing to this success. Production of citrus fruits was 226,000 tons in 1972, of which 184,000 tons were exported. This was a decline in production of 31,000 tons compared with 1971, when an unusually large orange crop was gathered. Cereal production reached a record 205,000 tons in 1971, following the poor crop in 1970 which was affected by drought, but 1972 production is expected to have declined. The value of agricultural exports rose to nearly £29 million in 1971, representing over 60 per cent of total exports. Britain is the island's largest customer and usually taking about a third of the total citrus crop and the majority of the spring crop of potatoes.

Since agriculture is the most important sector of the Cyprus economy, substantial efforts are being made by the government to strengthen it. In March 1969 the House of Representatives passed the Land Consolidation Law, aimed at putting an end to land fragmentation and at establishing economically viable land holdings through the unification and redistribution of existing small plots. Laws and customs of inheritance have led to fragmentation of ownership on a vast scale. The new Law envisaged the creation of a Central Land Consolidation Authority which will direct, organize and co-ordinate *all* activities pertaining to land consolidation. At the end of 1972 land consolidation was being applied in seven different regions. The expectations were that when fully applied, land consolidation will raise the island's agricultural output by 20 per cent, though it should be stressed that this is a long-term programme.

Consolidation is not to be confined only to forming viable units as far as area is concerned. The construction of irrigation channels designed to conserve the use of water, new roads to provide ease of access (farmers and shepherds in many cases have to pay for the right to cross other owners' properties to reach their own), encouragement of terracing in hill farm areas, anti-erosion measures and the provision of windbreaks will be carried out in conjunction with the programme.

The Cyprus Government and the United Nations are also engaged on the "Mixed Farming Project", which aims to integrate animal and crop husbandries in the dry areas, and diversify farming to cut down seasonal unemployment.

INDUSTRY

Industry (consisting of mining, quarrying, manufacturing, electricity, gas and water) accounted for approximately 19 per cent of Gross Domestic Product (net output at current factor cost) and employed 15 per cent of the labour force in 1971. The major sectors of industry in order of importance are manufacturing, mining (mainly copper and iron pyrites) and quarrying, electricity, gas and water. There is a large number of small firms; in fact 32.2 per cent of the labour force in 1971 was employed in establishments with four people or less which account for about 70 per cent of all industrial establishments. This has a bearing on absolute efficiency since bigger establishments are more productive. In 1971 the value added per person engaged in small establishments was £474 whilst that of the large establishments was £1,066. A major factor in limiting the size of the production units is the small size of the domestic market. Value added at current market prices more than doubled in all industrial divisions during the period 1962-71. The real growth, however, as measured by the index of industrial production in physical terms was 83 per cent higher in 1971 as compared with 1962. Mining and quarrying increased by 29 per cent, manufacturing by 109 per cent and electricity and gas by 159 per cent.

The mining and quarrying industry, which contributed approximately 22 per cent to exports offers little prospect of continued growth. Already there has been a contraction in the activity of one leading firm. Cupreous minerals which account for about 70 per cent of the mineral export list are becoming depleted and despite fairly widespread prospecting, no important new reserves have come to light. So far only low grade deposits have been found in any quantity and whether they are worth exploiting depends on prices of metals. The three major copper-producing companies are the Cyprus Mines Corporation, Hellenic Mining Company and Cyprus Sulphur and Copper Company. Asbestos is becoming increasingly important and there are ample reserves. As output and employment have been declining in mining and quarrying so they have been rising slowly in manufacturing and electricity, gas and water. There are, however, no plans to introduce heavy industries.

The index of manufacturing production rose from 100 in 1962 (the base year) to 209 in 1971 whilst the number of people engaged rose from 27,163 to 34,235 in those years. This sector witnessed a great deal of mechanization. In 1967 23 per cent of the manufacturing output was produced by 36 per cent of the manufacturing labour force in establishments engaging under five persons each. On average almost all branches of manufacturing showed some expansion in 1971, but the highest increases were recorded in the footwear and clothing industries.

TRADE

Imports rose from £106.9 million in 1971 to £121.5 million in 1972, while exports rose from £47.3 million to £51.3 million. Manufactured goods, machinery and equipment account for over one-half of total imports and food and fuel another quarter. The agricultural and mineral sectors of the economy account for approximately two-thirds and one-fifth of total exports respectively.

In order to facilitate trade the island's principal port of Famagusta has been improved and expanded and similar extensions are under construction at Limassol and Larnaca. Nicosia International Airport has been modernized and expanded.

Most of the island's trade is with Sterling Area and EEC countries, the U.K. taking between 35 and 40 per cent of Cyprus's exports followed by West Germany with about 10 per cent. Negotiations began early in 1971 to study the island's relationship with the EEC and the possibility of an association. In December 1972 an association agreement with the EEC was signed which came into force on June 1st, 1973. The agreement provides for the elimination of almost all trade barriers during two stages spread over 9½ years. During the first stage, ending on June 30th, 1977, the Community undertakes to reduce import tariffs on Cypriot industrial goods by 70 per cent and on citrus products by 40 per cent. These reductions, together with complete removal of duties on carobs, are to be effective immediately, while Cypriot tariffs on imports of industrial products from the Community are to be reduced by 35 per cent in three stages over a four-year period. Under a separate protocol, trade arrangements between Cyprus on the one hand and the U.K. and the Republic of Ireland on the other are to be maintained during the first stage. It was agreed that Cyprus will be permitted to export 200,000 hectolitres of sherry to the U.K. and the Republic of Ireland each year during 1973 and 1974, without having to respect Community reference prices. This arrangement will continue until the last of the 1974 vintage has been sold.

Diversification of export markets is official policy. Cyprus has trade and payments agreements with most of the east-European countries, but commercial ties with the communist block remain limited. Trade with the U.S.S.R. has tripled in value since 1960 but is still less than 5 per cent of Cyprus's total trade.

The large and widening trade deficit has been more than offset by invisibles and capital inflow, notably tourism, U.K. and other military expenditure and Cypriot expatriate remittances and capital inflows. In 1972 Cyprus's foreign exchange reserves had risen to £125 million.

Tourism has been a major growth industry. The number of visitors to Cyprus has more than trebled between 1967 (68,379) and 1972, when the figure reached over 228,000. In addition many cruise passengers visit the island for short periods. Income from tourism topped £13 million in 1971. From 1966 to early 1970 Cyprus benefited from the U.K. travel allowance which made Sterling Area holidays more attractive for U.K. tourists, who accounted for some 50 per cent of total tourists. Devaluation has also helped. The Cyprus Government has shown its interest in tourism in recent years by granting long-term loans to private tourist enterprises. A £4.5 million government tourist development is to be built.

The purchase of villas or plots of building land by expatriates has become increasingly common in some parts of the island. The buyers are mainly British and the villas are used as homes for retirement or as holiday cottages. Strong demand means that high prices are paid, and this inflow of foreign capital has helped strengthen the balance

CYPRUS—(ECONOMIC SURVEY, STATISTICAL SURVEY)

of payments, as will expenditure by a substantial foreign community.

The U.K. military presence in Cyprus is reckoned to benefit the economy to the extent of £15 million. Dependence on this (and expatriate remittances) is regarded as a structual weakness in the external accounts and growth in exports and tourist revenue is designed to counteract this.

DEVELOPMENT

There was no overall economic planning under British rule, and the first comprehensive Five-Year Plan was launched only in August 1961. By 1966 both unemployment and underemployment in rural areas had been reduced, and the annual rate of growth for G.N.P. and for gross domestic fixed capital formation increased.

The second Five-Year Plan (published in 1968) envisaged an annual growth rate of 7 per cent on the total investment of £200 million. Of this figure government expenditure was to be £57 million with £9.6 million contributed from public corporations. The private sector was to contribute £13.6 million. In contrast to the previous Five-Year Plan, only 9 per cent of the investment was to be derived from foreign sources.

The principal objectives of the 1967-71 Plan were to improve the balance of payments and to expand production in agriculture and in manufacturing and services. Improvements in communications and accelerated tourist development were sought as Cyprus aimed to lessen dependence on the British military presence as a source of foreign exchange. The third Five-Year Plan was to have come into operation in 1972, but its start was delayed until 1973. Expenditure of £360 million is involved.

Two major problems still hamper economic development. First there is the continued reduction of British expenditure on the Cyprus base which has led to unemployment. More important is the communal strife between Greeks and Turks which has dislocated large areas of the island's economy, particularly the tourist trade. There appears to be no economic basis to this conflict, which is purely racial and political, but it has now split the island into two distinct economic units. Moreover, the future of the British base is very problematical and if it goes, expenditures which have in recent years amounted to about one-fifth of the national income will cease. Finally, the conflict has endangered the flow of aid and private investment upon which the success of any plan ultimately depends. In spite of these problems Cyprus in 1973 is enjoying a period of relative prosperity.

STATISTICAL SURVEY

AREA AND POPULATION

AREA (square miles)		POPULATION (1972 estimates)			
TOTAL	CULTIVATED	TOTAL	GREEKS	TURKS	NICOSIA (capital)
3,572	2,300	645,000	528,000	117,000	118,100

Limassol 61,400, Famagusta 44,000, Larnaca 21,800, Paphos 12,000, Kyrenia 5,000. Immigrants: nil; Emigrants: 1,318.

BIRTHS AND DEATHS

	BIRTH RATE (per '000)	DEATH RATE (per '000)
1969	22.4	6.9
1970	21.3	6.8
1971	21.7	6.4
1972	22.0	6.5

EMPLOYMENT

	1970	1971
Agriculture	96,200	96,200
Manufacturing and Construction	63,900	63,600
Mining	5,000	4,200
Commerce and Administration	46,200	30,800
Services	21,100	36,900
Military	6,400	6,400
Other	27,300	14,000

CYPRUS—(Statistical Survey)

AGRICULTURE
PRODUCTION
('000 tons)

	1970	1971	1972*		1970	1971	1972*
Wheat	43	95	80	Olives	8	15	n.a.
Barley	55	110	80	Grapes	180	182	165
Potatoes	205	175	172	Oranges	97	163	139
Carrots	18	15	17	Grapefruit	45	61	55
Carobs	48	32	38	Lemons	28	33	32

* Provisional figures.

EXPORTS (tons)

	1970	1971	1972
Citrus Fruit	130,999	204,255	184,340
Potatoes	158,073	148,403	147,827
Carrots	15,557	12,609	13,538
Grapes	10,114	12,521	11,090
Raisins	6,330	3,652	4,269

EXPORTS OF CITRUS FRUIT (tons)

	1970	1971	1972
Oranges	76,471	133,761	115,766
Grapefruit	33,899	48,586	42,813
Lemons	19,846	21,252	24,487
Others	783	656	1,274

Livestock (1972*): 480,000 sheep, 380,000 goats, 125,000 pigs, 34,000 cattle, 3,450,000 poultry.

* Provisional figures.

Fishing (1970): Value of catch £474,000.

MINING
EXPORTS
(tons)

	1969	1970	1971	1972
Asbestos	18,842	23,752	22,255	27,546
Chromite	26,467	30,752	42,273	23,318
Cupreous concentrates	62,780	53,011	50,633	64,737
Cement copper	9,412	10,961	9,056	5,744
Cupreous pyrites	84,660	94,532	73,336	45,980
Iron pyrites	834,082	805,183	602,177	452,901
Gypsum	9,300	4,508	530	114
Terra umbra	8,731	6,843	6,883	10,265
Yellow ochre	550	444	474	862
Other minerals	12,902	19,552	13,844	12,361

CYPRUS—(Statistical Survey)

INDUSTRY

PRINCIPAL PRODUCTS OF MANUFACTURING AND COTTAGE INDUSTRIES

	Unit	1970	1971	1972
Cement	'000 metric tons	300	300	400
Bricks	million	35.5	37.9	46.4
Tiles	'000 sq. metres	900	1,000	1,000
Cigarettes	'000 lb.	1,960	1,960	2,240
Shoes*	'000 pairs	1,900	2,000	2,000
Beer	million litres	9.3	10.8	12.3
Wines	,, ,,	33.0	34.8	39.7
Intoxicating Liquors	,, ,,	2.6	2.8	2.9

* Excluding plastic and semi-finished shoes.

Gross Output: (1971) Cyprus £73,700,000; (1972) Cyprus £88,500,000*.

* Provisional figure.

FINANCE

1,000 mils = 1 Cyprus pound.

Coins: 1, 3, 5, 25, 50 and 100 mils.

Notes: 250 and 500 mils; 1 and 5 pounds.

Exchange rates (March 1973): £1 sterling = 846.45 mils; U.S. $1 = 345.395 mils.

Cyprus £100 = £118.14 sterling = $289.52.

Note: Prior to the "floating" of sterling in June 1972, the Cyprus pound was at par with £1 sterling.

BUDGET 1972
(Cyprus £)

Revenue		Expenditure	
Direct Taxes	12,776,993	Agriculture and Forests	759,631
Indirect Taxes	23,145,191	Water Development	244,443
Fees, Charges and Reimbursements	6,741,837	Public Works	887,004
Interest on Public Money	4,110,821	Cyprus Army and Tripartite Agreement	153,049
Rents and Royalties	828,772	Customs and Excise	399,047
Fines and Forfeitures	166,447	Public Debt Charges	3,367,729
Lotteries	1,428,983	Pensions and Grants	1,527,665
Miscellaneous	603,704	Cost of Living Allowances	3,465,732
Sales of Immovable Property	28,052	Medical	2,532,082
		Police	2,941,767
		Subsidies, Subventions and Contributions	6,607,867
		Education Grants	4,879,594
		Other	14,529,483
Total	48,831,800	Total	42,295,093

1973 Budget: Revenue £49,711,177; Expenditure £43,940,486; Transfer to Consolidated Fund of the Republic £4,155,574.

CYPRUS—(STATISTICAL SURVEY)

DEVELOPMENT BUDGET
(Cyprus £)

	1971	1972
Water Development	1,069,682	1,884,735
Road Network	859,470	1,462,666
Harbours	2,722,231	2,385,751
Agriculture	1,413,383	1,504,027
Commerce and Industry	384,870	512,188
Airports	701,935	352,603

1973 Development Budget: Total expenditure £16,814,271.

NATIONAL ACCOUNTS
(Cyprus £ million)

	1969	1970	1971	1972*
GROSS DOMESTIC PRODUCT	191.3	203.5	232.7	256.7
of which:				
Agriculture	38.9	35.4	45.8	48.8
Construction	14.5	16.9	19.5	22.0
Income from abroad	8.2	9.1	9.9	10.7
GROSS NATIONAL INCOME	213.7	228.3	260.0	288.1
Less depreciation allowances	−9.6	−10.3	−11.7	−13.0
NET NATIONAL INCOME	204.1	218.0	248.3	275.1
Indirect taxes less subsidies	14.2	15.7	17.4	20.7
NET NATIONAL PRODUCT	189.9	202.3	230.9	254.4
Depreciation allowances	9.6	10.3	11.7	13.0
GROSS NATIONAL PRODUCT	199.5	212.6	242.6	267.4
Balance of exports and imports of goods and services, and borrowing	16.8	24.5	24.2	26.0
AVAILABLE RESOURCES	216.3	237.1	266.8	283.4
of which:				
Private consumption expenditure	149.0	162.4	182.8	n.a.
Government consumption expenditure	24.0	26.0	30.2	n.a.
Gross fixed capital formation	45.8	53.4	57.9	n.a.
Increase in stocks	3.5	1.9	3.4	n.a.

* Provisional figures.

CURRENCY IN CIRCULATION
June 30th, 1969: £16,716,000.
June 30th, 1970: £17,891,000.
June 30th, 1971: £20,018,000.

GOLD RESERVES
1972: £6,200,000.

RETAIL PRICE INDEX
(1967 = 100)

	1970	1971	1972
All Items	108.8	113.29	118.77
Food and Drinks	110.1	115.43	123.18
Rent	106.2	113.53	119.92
Fuel and Light	102.5	102.38	102.81
Household Equipment	116.0	118.15	120.99
Household Operations	107.9	115.93	119.94
Clothing and Footwear	104.2	106.95	111.46
Miscellaneous	113.1	116.89	120.65

CYPRUS—(Statistical Survey)

BALANCE OF PAYMENTS
(£ million)

	1969	1970	1971	1972*
Exports f.o.b.	39.6	42.7	45.3	49.4
Imports f.o.b.	−75.3	−86.0	−94.5	−108.2
TRADE BALANCE	−35.7	−43.3	−49.2	−58.8
Invisible Receipts	55.2	60.9	72.3	83.0
Invisible Payments	−24.1	−26.6	−30.2	−33.1
Invisible Balance	31.1	34.3	42.1	49.9
CURRENT ACCOUNT BALANCE	−4.6	−9.0	−7.1	−8.9
Short-term Capital	3.1	5.3	4.0	5.0
Long-term Loans	−3.6	1.7	—	−0.1
Other Private Long-term Capital	6.0	6.1	12.3	12.0
Other Official Long-term Capital	5.3	0.2	1.8	0.2
Net Capital Movement	10.8	13.3	18.1	17.1
Net Errors and Omissions	0.6	6.2	6.9	−0.8
OVERALL BALANCE	6.8	10.5	17.9	7.4

* Provisional figures.

EXTERNAL TRADE
(£'000)

	1966	1967	1968	1969	1970	1971	1972
Imports*	55,368	59,712	70,944	86,462	98,229	106,869	121,480
Exports	29,238	29,697	36,959	40,903	45,189	47,279	51,305

* Excluding NAAFI imports.

COMMODITIES (£'000)

IMPORTS*	1970	1971	1972	EXPORTS	1970	1971	1972
Food	13,726	13,493	16,224	Food	19,230	24,113	26,732
Beverages and Tobacco	1,190	1,233	2,591	Oranges	3,683	7,121	6,685
Crude Materials, Inedible	2,284	2,740	2,787	Potatoes	6,517	4,563	7,092
Mineral Fuels and Lubricants	6,994	8,534	8,432	Beverages and Tobacco	3,849	4,785	5,906
Petroleum Products	6,629	7,160	8,091	Crude Materials, Inedible	14,859	10,389	9,537
Animal and Vegetable Oils and Fats	1,450	1,981	1,659	Iron Pyrites	2,588	1,546	1,061
Chemicals	7,620	8,935	9,366	Cupreous Concentrates	5,257	3,182	3,827
Manufactures	28,459	30,866	34,032	Copper Cement	3,533	2,144	1,176
Iron and Steel	5,740	6,032	7,026	Mineral Fuels and Lubricants	16	14	184
Machinery and Transport Equipment	27,525	28,704	36,277	Animal and Vegetable Oils and Fats	135	89	160
Non-electric Machinery	10,503	11,304	13,011	Chemicals	249	518	703
Electrical Machinery	6,415	7,225	8,992	Manufactures	1,024	1,326	1,191
Transport Equipment	10,607	10,175	14,274	Machinery and Transport Equipment	3,579	3,225	3,807
Miscellaneous Manufactures	6,706	7,927	8,581	Miscellaneous Manufactures	1,563	2,208	2,831
Other Items, n.e.s.	2,275	2,456	1,531	Other Items, n.e.s.	685	612	254
TOTAL	98,229	106,869	121,480	TOTAL	45,189	47,279	51,305

* Excluding NAAFI imports.

CYPRUS—(Statistical Survey)

COUNTRIES (£'000)

Imports*	1970	1971	1972	Exports	1970	1971	1972
Austria	874	983	1,338	Belgium	295	109	274
Belgium	1,771	1,501	2,603	Czechoslovakia	372	675	1,487
France	4,174	5,807	6,821	Denmark	415	286	521
Germany, Fed. Republic	7,085	7,720	9,087	France	1,198	2,120	1,516
Greece	5,226	6,427	6,530	German Dem. Republic	1,014	542	991
India	775	703	984	Germany, Fed. Republic	8,115	5,597	3,212
Israel	2,847	2,110	2,486	Greece	1,242	1,794	1,781
Italy	10,211	10,903	9,662	Israel	296	679	642
Japan	3,788	4,723	6,120	Italy	2,576	1,655	1,379
Lebanon	1,323	1,113	1,498	Lebanon	549	950	1,006
Netherlands	3,275	4,595	3,806	Netherlands	1,404	1,916	1,171
Portugal	780	653	731	Spain	1,031	669	1,323
Sweden	1,606	2,167	2,323	Sweden	383	419	404
Turkey	383	815	818	Turkey	253	441	1,370
U.S.S.R.	2,027	3,863	3,566	U.S.S.R.	2,289	2,189	3,251
United Kingdom	28,874	30,699	33,915	United Kingdom	17,352	19,680	21,234
U.S.A.	6,554	5,997	7,290	U.S.A.	512	417	565
Yugoslavia	1,568	797	757				

* Excluding NAAFI imports.

TRANSPORT

ROADS

	1969	1970	1971	1972
Cars	46,644	52,882	60,351	72,662
Taxis	2,386	2,570	2,941	3,435
Lorries	13,897	13,722	15,760	18,149
Motor Cycles	13,331	13,765	13,647	14,935
Tractors	7,037	7,295	7,782	8,064
Total	83,300	90,234	100,481	117,245

SHIPPING

	1969	1970	1971	1972
Vessels* Entered ('000 net reg. tons)	4,867	4,699	4,716	4,870
Goods Loaded ('000 tons)	1,496	1,527	1,338	1,235
Goods Unloaded ('000 tons)	1,420	1,418	1,505	1,781

* Steam or motor vessels.

CIVIL AVIATION

Cyprus Airways

	1969	1970	1971	1972
Kilometres flown	1,651,000	3,017,000	3,474,000	4,465,000
Passenger arrivals	165,544	174,681	237,724	309,697
Passenger departures	167,309	174,633	238,691	310,002
Freight landed (tons)	1,402	1,644	2,053	2,596
Freight cleared (tons)	3,930	6,119	6,863	8,460

Passenger kilometres: (1971) 187,983,000; (1972) 254,153,000.
Cargo ton-kilometres: (1971) 19,006,000; (1972) 25,374,000.

TOURISM

VISITORS*

	1969	1970	1971	1972
Greece	9,964	9,305	12,327	12,816
Israel	4,718	3,814	7,957	8,322
Lebanon	7,134	8,995	10,708	10,392
United Kingdom	56,132	60,052	78,062	98,136
United States	10,720	10,401	13,880	15,177
TOTAL (incl. others)	118,006	126,580	178,598	228,309

* Excluding one-day visitors.

Tourist Earnings: (1967) £4.3m.; (1968) £5.8m.; (1969) £7.7m.; (1970) £8.1m.; (1971) £13.6m.
Number of Hotel Beds: (1968) 6,612; (1969) 7,244; (1970) 7,823; (1971) 9,413; (1972) 10,532.
Number of Tourist Nights: (1968) 413,007; (1969) 658,840; (1970) 658,322; (1971) 890,952; (1972) 1,144,437.

EDUCATION

(1972–73)

	GREEK Establishments	GREEK Teachers	GREEK Pupils	TURKISH Establishments	TURKISH Pupils
Elementary	555	2,208	63,068	167	16,014
Secondary (Public)	47	1,471	32,387	} 18	7,190
Secondary (Private)	36	541	11,484		
Technical and Vocational	7	296	4,198	6	753
Teacher Training	1	17	267	1	13

Source: Ministry of Finance, Department of Statistics and Research, Nicosia.

CYPRUS—(THE CONSTITUTION)

THE CONSTITUTION

SUMMARY

The Constitution entered into orce on August 16th, 1960, on which date Cyprus became an independent republic. In March 1961 Cyprus was accepted as a member of the Commonwealth.

ARTICLE 1

The State of Cyprus is an independent and sovereign Republic with a presidential régime, the President being Greek and the Vice-President being Turkish, elected by the Greek and the Turkish Communities of Cyprus respectively as hereinafter in this Constitution provided.

ARTICLES 2–5

The Greek Community comprises all citizens of the Republic who are of Greek origin and whose mother tongue is Greek or who share the Greek cultural traditions or who are members of the Greek Orthodox Church.

The Turkish Community comprises all citizens of the Republic who are of Turkish origin and whose mother tongue is Turkish or who share the Turkish cultural traditions or who are Moslems.

Citizens of the Republic who do not come within the above provisions shall, within three months of the date of the coming into operation of this Constitution, opt to belong to either the Greek or the Turkish Community as individuals, but, if they belong to a religious group, shall opt as a religious group and upon such option they shall be deemed to be members of such Community.

The official languages of the Republic are Greek and Turkish.

The Republic shall have its own flag of neutral design and colour, chosen jointly by the President and the Vice-President of the Republic.

The Greek and the Turkish Communities shall have the right to celebrate respectively the Greek and the Turkish national holidays.

ARTICLES 6–35
Fundamental Rights and Liberties

ARTICLES 36–53
President and Vice-President

The President of the Republic as Head of the State represents the Republic in all its official functions; signs the credentials of diplomatic envoys and receives the credentials of foreign diplomatic envoys; signs the credentials of delegates for the negotiation of international treaties, conventions or other agreements; signs the letter relating to the transmission of the instruments of ratification of any international treaties, conventions or agreements; confers the honours of the Republic.

The Vice-President of the Republic as Vice-Head of the State has the right to be present at all official functions; at the presentation of the credentials of foreign diplomatic envoys; to recommend to the President the conferment of honours on members of the Turkish Community which recommendation the President shall accept unless there are grave reasons to the contrary. The honours so conferred will be presented to the recipient by the Vice-President if he so desires.

The election of the President and the Vice-President of the Republic shall be direct, by universal suffrage and secret ballot, and shall, except in the case of a by-election, take place on the same day but separately.

The office of the President and of the Vice-President shall be incompatible with that of a Minister or of a Representative or of a member of a Communal Chamber or of a member of any municipal council including a Mayor or of a member of the armed or security forces of the Republic or with a public or municipal office.

The President and Vice-President of the Republic are invested by the House of Representatives.

The President and the Vice-President shall hold office for a period of five years.

The Executive power is ensured by the President and the Vice-President of the Republic.

The President and the Vice-President of the Republic in order to ensure the executive power shall have a Council of Ministers composed of seven Greek Ministers and three Turkish Ministers. The Ministers shall be designated respectively by the President and the Vice-President of the Republic who shall appoint them by an instrument signed by them both.

The decisions of the Council of Ministers shall be taken by an absolute majority and shall, unless the right of final veto or return is exercised by the President or the Vice-President of the Republic or both, be promulgated immediately by them.

The executive power exercised by the President and the Vice-President of the Republic conjointly consists of:
- Determining the design and colour of the flag.
- Creation or establishment of honours.
- Appointment of the members of the Council of Ministers.
- Promulgation by publication of the decisions of the Council of Ministers.
- Promulgation by publication of any law or decision passed by the House of Representatives.
- Appointments and termination of appointments as in Articles provided.
- Institution of compulsory military service.
- Reduction or increase of the security forces.
- Exercise of the prerogative of mercy in capital cases.
- Remission, suspension and commutation of sentences.
- Right of references to the Supreme Constitutional Court and publication of Court decisions.
- Address of messages to the House of Representatives.

The executive power exercised by the President consists of:
- Designation and termination of appointment of Greek Ministers.
- Convening and presiding of the meetings of the Council of Ministers.
- Right of final veto on Council decisions and on laws or decisions of the House of Representatives concerning foreign affairs, defence or security.
- Right of recourse to the Supreme Constitutional Court.
- Publication of the communal laws and decisions of the Greek Communal Chamber.
- Prerogative of mercy in capital cases.
- Addressing messages to the House of Representatives.

CYPRUS—(The Constitution)

The executive power exercised by the Vice-President consists of:

- Designation and termination of appointment of Turkish Ministers.
- Asking the President for the convening of the Council of Ministers and being present and taking part in the discussions.
- Right of final veto on Council decisions and on laws or decisions of the House of Representatives concerning foreign affairs, defence or security.
- Right of recourse to the Supreme Constitutional Court.
- Publication of the communal laws and decisions of the Turkish Communal Chamber.
- Prerogative of mercy in capital cases.
- Addressing messages to the House of Representatives.

Articles 54–60
Council of Ministers

The Council of Ministers shall exercise executive power in all matters, other than those which are within the competence of a Communal Chamber, including the following:

- General direction and control of the government of the Republic and the direction of general policy.
- Foreign affairs, defence and security.
- Co-ordination and supervision of all public services.
- Supervision and disposition of property belonging to the Republic.
- Consideration of Bills to be introduced to the House of Representatives by a Minister.
- Making of any order or regulation for the carrying into effect of any law as provided by such law.
- Consideration of the Budget of the Republic to be introduced to the House of Representatives.

Articles 61–85
House of Representatives

The legislative power of the Republic shall be exercised by the House of Representatives in all matters except those expressly reserved to the Communal Chambers.

The number of Representatives shall be fifty:

Provided that such number may be altered by a resolution of the House of Representatives carried by a majority comprising two-thirds of the Representatives elected by the Greek Community and two-thirds of the Representatives elected by the Turkish Community.

Out of the number of Representatives 70 per cent shall be elected by the Greek Community and 30 per cent by the Turkish Community separately from amongst their members respectively, and, in the case of a contested election, by universal suffrage and by direct and secret ballot held on the same day.

The term of office of the House of Representatives shall be for a period of five years.

The President of the House of Representatives shall be a Greek, and shall be elected by the Representatives elected by the Greek Community, and the Vice-President shall be a Turk and shall be elected by the Representatives elected by the Turkish Community.

Articles 86–111
Communal Chambers

The Greek and the Turkish Communities respectively shall elect from amongst their own members a Communal Chamber.

The Communal Chambers shall, in relation to their respective Community, have competence to exercise legislative power solely with regard to the following:

- All religious, educational, cultural and teaching matters.
- Personal status; composition and instances of courts dealing with civil disputes relating to personal status and to religious matters.
- Imposition of personal taxes and fees on members of their respective Community in order to provide for their respective needs.

Articles 112–121, 126–128
Officers of the Republic

Articles 122–125
The Public Service

The public service shall be composed as to 70 per cent of Greeks and as to 30 per cent of Turks.

Articles 129–132
The Forces of the Republic

The Republic shall have an army of two thousand men of whom 60 per cent shall be Greeks and 40 per cent shall be Turks.

The security forces of the Republic shall consist of the police and gendarmerie and shall have a contingent of two thousand men. The forces shall be composed as to 70 per cent of Greeks and as to 30 per cent of Turks.

Articles 133–164
The Courts
(See section Judicial System)

Articles 165–199
Financial, Miscellaneous, Final and Transitional Provisions

Note: The following measures have been passed by the House of Representatives since January 1964, when the Turkish members withdrew:

1. The amalgamation of the High Court and the Supreme Constitutional Court.
2. The abolition of the Greek Communal Chamber and the creation of a Ministry of Education.
3. The unification of the Municipalities.
4. The unification of the Police and the Gendarmerie.
5. The creation of a military force by providing that persons between the ages of eighteen and fifty can be called upon to serve in the National Guard.
6. The extension of the term of office of the President and the House of Representatives by one year intervals from July 1965 until elections in February 1968 and July 1970 respectively.
7. New electoral provisions; abolition of separate Greek and Turkish rolls; abolition of post of Vice-President.

CYPRUS—(The Government, Diplomatic Representation)

THE GOVERNMENT

HEAD OF STATE
President: Archbishop MAKARIOS III.

In the presidential elections of February 1973 Archbishop Makarios was re-elected unopposed.

Vice-President: RAUF R. DENKTAŞ (elected February 1973).

COUNCIL OF MINISTERS*
(*July* 1973)

Minister of Foreign Affairs: IOANNIS CHRISTOPHIDES.
Minister of Finance: ANDREAS PATSALIDES.
Minister of Communications and Works: YANGOS ZAMBARLOUKOS.
Minister of Agriculture and Natural Resources: ODYSSEUS IOANNIDES.
Minister of Commerce and Industry: MICHAEL COLOKASSIDES.
Minister of the Interior and Defence: GEORGIOS IOANNIDES.
Minister of Justice: CHRISTOS VAKIS.
Minister of Labour and Social Insurance: MARKOS SPANOS.
Minister of Education: ANDREAS KOUROS.
Minister of Health: (vacant).

* Since the 1963 inter-communal strife the Turks have set up their own separate administration.

The Executive Council of the Turkish Cypriot Administration: *President:* H.E. RAUF R. DENKTAŞ; *Defence:* OSMAN ÖREK; *Finance and Budgetary Affairs:* RÜSTEM TATAR; *Justice and Interior:* NEJAT KONUK; *Health Services:* NIYAZI MANYERA; *Labour, Rehabilitation and Social Affairs:* İSMET KOTAK; *Agriculture and Natural Resources:* OĞUZ RAMADAN; *Works and Communication:* EROL KÂZIM; *Commerce, Industry and Tourism:* VEDAT ÇELIK; *Education and Teaching:* ORHAN ZIHNI.

DIPLOMATIC REPRESENTATION
EMBASSIES AND LEGATIONS ACCREDITED TO CYPRUS
(In Nicosia, except where otherwise stated.)

(E) Embassy; (HC) High Commission; (L) Legation.

Argentina: Rome, Italy (E).
Austria: Athens, Greece (E).
Belgium: Beirut, Lebanon (E).
Brazil: Tel Aviv, Israel (E).
Bulgaria: 15 St. Paul St. (E); *Ambassador:* CONSTANTIN POPOV.
Canada: Tel-Aviv, Israel (HC).
China, People's Republic: (E); *Ambassador:* TAI LU.
Colombia: Jerusalem, Israel (E).
Cuba: Beirut, Lebanon (L).
Czechoslovakia: 5 Glavcos St. (E); *Ambassador:* PANOL MAJLING.
Denmark: Beirut, Lebanon (E).
Egypt: 3 Egypt Ave. (E); *Ambassador:* SALAH EL DIN MOHAMED SHARAWEY.
Finland: Rome, Italy (E).
France: 43 Savvas G. Rotsides St. (E); *Ambassador:* ALBERT VANTHIER.
Germany, Federal Republic of: 10 Nikitaras St. (E); *Ambassador:* Dr. ALEXANDER TÖRÖK.
German Democratic Republic: (E); *Ambassador:* Dr. KURT MERKEL.
Greece: 8–10 Byron Ave. (E); *Ambassador:* EFSTATHIOS LAGACOS.
Hungary: Athens, Greece (E).
India: Beirut, Lebanon (HC).
Israel: 27 Androcleous St. (E); *Ambassador:* RAHAMIM TIMOR.
Italy: 7 Alexander Diomedes St. (E); *Ambassador:* VITTORIANO MANFREDI.
Ivory Coast: Jerusalem, Israel (E).
Japan: Beirut, Lebanon (E).
Lebanon: 1 Queen Olga St. (E); *Ambassador:* MUNIR TAKKIEDIN.
Malta: (H.C.); *High Commissioner:* ARTHUR SCERRI.
Netherlands: Beirut, Lebanon (E).
Nigeria: Rome, Italy (HC).
Norway: Tel-Aviv, Israel (E).
Pakistan: Beirut, Lebanon (HC).
Poland: Athens, Greece.
Romania: 8 Catsonis St. (E); *Chargé d'Affaires:* ION ANGHEL.
Spain: Damascus, Syria (E).
Sudan: Athens, Greece (E).
Sweden: Beirut, Lebanon (E).
Switzerland: Tel-Aviv, Israel (E).
Syria: 28 Stassinos Ave. (E); *Chargé d'Affaires:* MOHAMMAD JOUHEIR ACCAD.
Turkey: 10 Server Somuncuoğlu St. (E); *Chargé d'Affaires:* ASAF INHAN.
U.S.S.R.: 4 Gladstone St. (E); *Ambassador:* ANATOLI A. BARKOVSKY.
United Kingdom: Alexander Pallis St. (HC); *High Commissioner:* STEPHEN OLVER.
U.S.A.: Therissos St. (E); *Ambassador:* ROBERT MCCLOSKEY.
Vatican: 2 Victoria Rd. (Apostolic Nunciature); *Apostolic Delegate:* PIO LAGHI.
Yugoslavia: 2 Vasilissis Olgas St. (E); *Ambassador:* NICOLA MANDIC.

Cyprus also has diplomatic relations with Ethiopia, Ghana, Somalia, Uganda and Zaire.

CYPRUS—(Parliament, Political Parties, British Sovereign Base Areas, etc.)

PARLIAMENT
HOUSE OF REPRESENTATIVES

The House of Representatives consists of 50 members. Thirty-five Greeks are elected by the Greek community and 15 Turks by the Turkish community. Election is for a term of five years.

President: Glavcos Clerides (Greek).

Elections for the Greek Representatives
(July 5th, 1970)

Party	Seats
Unified Party	15
AKEL (Communist Party)	9
Progressive Front	7
EDEK (Unified Democratic Union)	2
Independents (Pro-Government)	2
Total	35

Turkish House of Representatives

The Turkish members have not attended the House of Representatives since January 1964 and have set up their own House consisting of 15 members.

President: Dr. Necdet Ünel.

THE COMMUNAL CHAMBERS

The Greek Communal Chamber was abolished in 1965 and its former functions are now performed by the Ministry of Education.

The Turkish Communal Chamber continues to legislate on matters of a communal nature (e.g. religion, education and social affairs). Members are elected for a five-year term, and the President and Vice-President are elected by the members.

Turkish Chamber:
  President: (vacant).
  Vice-President: (vacant).
  30 elected members.

POLITICAL PARTIES

Unified Party (*Enieon*): Diagoras St., Chanteclair Building, Nicosia; f. 1960; Greek; supporters of Archbishop Makarios; maintains the Hellenic character of the state, right of private ownership; 15 seats in the House of Representatives; Chair. Glavcos Clerides.

AKEL—Progressive Party of the Working People (*Anorthotikon Komma Ergazomenou Laou*): 2 Spyrou Lambrou St., Nicosia; f. 1941; the Communist Party of Cyprus; over 14,000 mems.; 9 seats in the House of Representatives; Sec.-Gen. Ezekias Papaioannou.

Progressive Front (*Proodeftiki Parataxis*): Dionyssios Solomos Sq., Nicosia; f. 1970; sponsored by the right-wing farmers' union; pro-Government; 7 seats in the House; Chair. Dr. Odysseas Ioannides.

EDEK—Unified Democratic Union of the Centre (*Eniea Demokratiki Enosis Kentrou*): f. 1969; moderate left-wing party which supports the Government and stands for nationalization of mining companies and elimination of foreign military bases; 2 seats in the House; Chair. Vassos Lyssarides.

DEK—Democratic National Party (*Demokratikon Ethnikon Komma*): Archbishop Makarios Ave., Nicosia; f. 1968; opposition party, pledged to a policy of union with Greece (*Enosis*); secured 9.8 per cent of votes in the 1970 elections; Gen. Sec. Polycarpos Petrides; publ. *Gnomi*.

United Democratic Youth Organization (*Eniaia Demokratiki Organosis Neolaias—EDON*): P.O.B. 1986, Nicosia; f. 1959; 16,000 mems.; Pres. Panikos Peonides; Gen. Sec. Donis Christofinis; Org. Sec. Nicos Christodoulou.

Ulusal Dayanışma (*National Solidarity*): Nicosia; national organization with political and economic programme under which the 1970 elections were held; Leader R. R. Denktaş.

Cumhuriyetçi Türk Partisi (*Republic Turkish Party*): Nicosia; f. 1970 by those who had lost General Election; Leader A. M. Berberoğlu.

BRITISH SOVEREIGN BASE AREAS
AKROTIRI and DHEKELIA

Administrator: Air Marshal Sir Derek Hodgkinson, K.C.B., C.B.E., D.F.C., A.F.C., R.A.F.

Chief Officer of Administration: W. C. Curtis.

Senior Judge of Senior Judge's Court: W. A. Sime, M.B.E. Q.C.

Resident Judge of Judge's Court: E. R. Harley, C.B.E.

Under the Cyprus Act 1960, the United Kingdom retained sovereignty in two sovereign base areas and this was recognized in the Treaty of Establishment signed between the U.K., Greece, Turkey and the Republic of Cyprus in August 1960. The base areas cover 99 square miles. The Treaty also conferred on Britain certain rights within the Republic, including rights of movement and the use of specified training areas.

UNITED NATIONS PEACE-KEEPING FORCE IN CYPRUS
(UNFICYP)

P.O.B. 1642, Nicosia, Cyprus

Set up for three months in March 1964 (subsequently extended at intervals of three or six months) to keep the peace between the Greek and Turkish communities and help to solve outstanding issues between them.

Commander: Maj.-Gen. D. Prem Chand (India).

Special Representative of the UN Secretary-General: Dr. Bibiano Osorio-Tafall (Mexico).

See page 92.

JUDICIAL SYSTEM

Supreme Court: Nicosia.

  President: Hon. Mr. Justice M. A. Triantafyllides.

  Judges: Hon. Mr. Justice A. S. Stavrinides, Hon. Mr. Justice L. N. Loizou, Hon. Mr. Justice T. Hadjianastassiou, Hon. Mr. Justice A. N. Loizou, Hon. Mr. Justice Y. Ch. Malachtos.

The Supreme Court is the final appellate court in the Republic and the final adjudicator in matters of constitutional and administrative law, including recourses on conflict of competence between state organs on questions of the constitutionality of laws, etc. It deals with appeals from Assize Courts and District Courts as well as from the decisions of its own single judges when exercising original jurisdiction in certain matters such as prerogative orders of *habeas corpus, mandamus, certiorari*, etc., and in admiralty and certain matrimonial causes.

Assize Courts and District Courts:

As required by the Constitution a law was passed in 1960 providing for the establishment, jurisdiction and powers of courts of civil and criminal jurisdiction, i.e. of six District Courts and six Assize Courts.

Ecclesiastical Courts:

There are seven Orthodox Church tribunals having exclusive jurisdiction in matrimonial causes between members of the Greek Orthodox Church. Appeals go from these tribunals to the appellate tribunal of the Church.

Supreme Council of Judicature: Nicosia.

The Supreme Council of Judicature is composed of the Attorney-General, the President and the two senior Judges of the Supreme Court, the senior District Court President, the senior District Court Judge and a practising advocate of at least twelve years practice.

It is responsible for the appointment, promotion, transfer, etc., of the judges exercising civil and criminal jurisdiction in the District Courts and the Assize Courts.

Turkish Cypriot Judicial System:

In the areas administered by the Cyprus Turkish Administration there is a parallel system of Supreme Court, Assize and District Courts and Supreme Council of Judicature.

Supreme Court: Ataturk Square, Nicosia.
  President: Hon. Mr. Justice M. NECATİ MÜNİR.
  Judges: Hon. Mr. Justice ULFET EMİN, Hon. Mr. Justice AHMED IZZET.

Turkish Communal Courts:

Civil disputes relating to personal status of members of the Turkish Community are dealt with by two Communal Courts. There is also a communal appellate court to which appeals may be made from the decisions of the courts of first instance.

RELIGION

Greeks form 80 per cent of the population and most of them belong to the Orthodox Church. Most Turks (18 per cent of the population) are Muslims.

Greek Orthodox	449,000
Muslims (Turks)	104,000
Armenian Apostolic	3,500
Maronite	3,000
Anglican }	
Roman Catholic }	18,000
Other	

(1960 census).

The Orthodox Church of Cyprus: Archbishopric of Cyprus, P.O. Box 1130, Nicosia; f. 45 A.D.; the Autocephalous Orthodox Church of Cyprus, a part of the Eastern Orthodox Church, enjoys the privilege of independence with the right to elect its own Archbishop; 500,000 members.

Archbishop of Nova Justiniana and all Cyprus: Archbishop MAKARIOS III.
Metropolitan of Paphos: (vacant).
Metropolitan of Kitium: (vacant).
Metropolitan of Kyrenia: (vacant).
Suffragan Bishop of Constantia: Bishop CHRYSOSTOMOS.
Suffragan Bishop of Amathus: Bishop KALLINIKOS.

Islam: Most of the adherents in Cyprus are Sunnis of the Hanafi Sect. The religious head of the Muslim community is the Mufti.

The Mufti of Cyprus: Dr. R. M. RİFAT.

Other Churches: Armenian Apostolic, Catholic (Maronite Rite), Roman Catholic and Church of England.

THE PRESS

The establishment and general running of newspapers and periodicals is defined in the Press Law, consisting of Chapter 79 of the pre-independence Code of Law, later amended by Law 69 in 1965. Article 19 of the Constitution declares in connection with the rights of the Press: "Every person has the right to freedom of speech and expression in any form. This right includes freedom to hold opinions and impart information and ideas without interference by any public authority and regardless of frontiers." This freedom is subject to legally specified conditions and restrictions in the interest of state security, public safety, order, public health and morals, the protection of the reputation and the rights of others and the preservation of the authority and impartiality of the Judiciary.

Cyprus has a small but vigorous Press, catering for all political viewpoints in the twofold community, and constituting the most influential of the communications media. Most newspapers are owned by private individuals but *Patris* is owned by a limited company.

Of the fourteen dailies, ten are in Greek, two in Turkish and two in English. The *Cyprus Mail* appears each day but all the Greek and some of the Turkish dailies do not publish a Monday edition, when most of the weekly papers appear.

Philelephtheros, Agon and *Makhi* (linked with the weekly *Tharros*) tend to be pro-government, while *Haravghi* (associated with the weekly *Nei Keri*) reflects the views of the extreme left, and *Patris* those of the political right. The moderate-liberal *Eleftheria*, a paper of some prestige, is politically independent, like the *Cyprus Mail*. *Bozkurt* and *Halkın Sesi* are the main Turkish Cypriot dailies. Both are independent, nationalist right. The English language *Special News Bulletin* is the mouthpiece of the Turkish Community, reflecting the views of the Turkish Cypriot Administration. *Eleftheria, Philelephtheros* and the *Cyprus Mail* are the dailies most respected for their serious news coverage. *Makhi* and *Haravghi* are also very influential, being very widely read. Though low by West European standards, their readership is high in comparison with other Middle East circulation figures. Precise, reliable circulation figures are virtually unobtainable.

Among the most respected weekly newspapers are the moderate *Kypros* and *Aliithia*, though *Tharros* and *Nei Keri* are very popular. There are also a number of trade union papers, headed by *Ergatiko Vima*, the organ of the Pancyprian Federation of Labour. The Turkish Cypriot Trade Union movement and the Co-operative movement are represented by periodicals *Türk-Sen* and *Kooperatif* respectively.

CYPRUS—(THE PRESS)

Both Communities have their own *Official Gazette* in which laws, regulations and other official notifications are published in their own language.

DAILIES

Agon (*Struggle*): 238 Ledra St., P.O.B. 1417, Nicosia; f. 1964; morning; Greek; nationalist; Owner and Editor N. Koshis; circ. 12,000.

Apogeumatini (*Afternoon*): P.O.B. 1094, Nicosia; f. 1972; afternoon; Greek; pro-Government; Editor M. Hadjiefthymiou; circ. 5,000.

Bozkurt (*Grey Wolf*): 142 Kyrenia St., Nicosia; f. 1951; morning; Turkish; Independent; Editor Sadi C. Togan; circ. 5,000.

Cyprus Mail: P.O.B. 1144, Vasiliou Voulgaroctonou St. 24, Nicosia; f. 1945; English; Independent; Editor C. H. W. Goult; circ. 5,740.

Eleftheria (*Freedom*): P.O.B. 1050, 30 Plutarch St., Nicosia; f. 1906 as bi-weekly, 1936 daily; Greek; Independent; Editor G. J. Hadjinicolaou; circ. 13,250.

Ethniki (*National*): Nicosia; f. 1959; organ of Democratic Union; Greek; edited by a Committee; circ. 5,000.

Gnomi (*Opinion*): P.O.B. 2137, 6 Archbishop Makarios III Ave., Nicosia; organ of the Democratic National Party; circ. 5,000.

Halkın Sesi (*Voice of the People*): 172 Kyrenia St., Nicosia; f. 1942; morning; Turkish; Independent Turkish Nationalist; Editor Akay Cemal; circ. 5,000.

Haravghi (*Dawn*): P.O.B. 1556, Bouboulinas 25, Nicosia; f. 1956; left-wing; Greek; Editor Andreas Fantis; circ. 13,500.

Makhi (*Battle*): P.O.B. 1105, Grivas Dighenis Ave., Nicosia; f. 1960; morning; Greek; Owner and Editor N. Sampson; circ. 12,000.

Mesimvrini: 73 Germanou Patron St., Nicosia; f. 1970; Greek; afternoon; Editor G. Hadjinicolaou.

Philelephtheros (*Liberal*): P.O.B. 1094, Ledras 250-252, Nicosia; nationalist; Greek; morning; Editor N. Pattichis; circ. 12,750.

Special News Bulletin: Nicosia; f. 1963; morning; English; published by Public Information Office of Turkish Cypriot Administration; circ. 1,500.

Ta Nea (*The News*): 4 Leonidas St., Nicosia; Greek; morning; f. 1970; Editor Chr. Savvides; circ. 4,000.

WEEKLIES

Alithea (*Truth*): P.O.B. 1605, 26 Apollon St., Nicosia; f. 1951; Greek; Pancyprian; Liberal; Editor Antonios Pharmakides; circ. 14,500.

Athlitiki (*Athletics*): 7 St. Dimitriou St., Nicosia; Editor A. Tsialis; circ. 8,500.

Asyrmatos (*Wireless*): P.O.B. 2082, 26 Apollon St., Nicosia; Greek; Editor Nt. Constantinides; circ. 7,400.

Cyprus Bulletin: Nicosia; f. 1964; weekly; English; published by the Cyprus Public Information Office.

Elephtheron Vima (*Liberal Tribune*): P.O.B. 2408, 166 Ledra St., Nicosia; Greek; Editor C. N. Hadjicostis; circ. 4,300.

Ergatiki Phoni (*Workers' Voice*): P.O.B. 1138, 23 Athanasiou Diakou, Nicosia; f. 1946; Greek; organ of Cyprus Workers' Confederation; Editor Chr. A. Michaelides; circ. 5,300.

Ergatiko Vima (*Workers' Tribune*): P.O.B. 1885, Volonaki St., Nicosia; f. 1956; Greek; organ of the Pancyprian Federation of Labour; Editor-in-Chief George Tsirponouris; circ. 8,300.

Heranan: P.O.B. 355, 43 Kallipolis Ave., Nicosia; Armenian.

Kypros (*Cyprus*): P.O.B. 1491, 10 Apostle Barnabas St., Nicosia; f. 1952; Greek; non-party; circ. 11,800; Editor J. Kyriakidis.

Nei Keri (*New Times*): P.O.B. 1963, 8 Vasiliou Voulgaroktonou St., Nicosia; Greek; Editor Lyssandros Tsimillis; circ. 7,300.

Official Gazette: Printing Office of the Republic of Cyprus, Nicosia; f. 1960; Greek; published by the Government of the Republic of Cyprus.

Patris (*Fatherland*): P.O.B. 2026, 1 Androcleous St., Nicosia; f. 1964; Greek; right wing; Editor K. Kononas; circ. 7,500.

Philathlos: P.O.B. 1543, Nicosia; Greek; sports; Editor C. J. Solomonides; circ. 4,400.

Savaş (*Combat*): 4 İş Hanı, Kyrenia St., Nicosia; f. 1968; Turkish; Independent; Owner and Editor Özker Yaşın; circ. 3,000.

Synagermos: P.O.B. 1061, 217 Ledra St., Nicosia; f. 1964; Greek; Owner and Editor Ph. Constantinides; circ. 4,000.

Tharros (*Courage*): P.O.B. 1105, Grivas Dighenis Ave., Nicosia; f. 1961; Greek; Independent; Propr. and Editor N. Sampson; circ. 9,200.

PERIODICALS

Apostolos Barnabas: Cyprus Archbishopric, Nicosia; twice monthly; Greek organ of the Greek Orthodox Church of Cyprus; Dir. Dr. Andreas N. Mitsides; circ. 1,200.

Countryman: Nicosia; f. 1943; twice monthly; Greek; published by the Cyprus Public Information Office.

Cyprus Medical Journal: P.O.B. 93, Nicosia; f. 1947; monthly; English and Greek; Editor Dr. G. N. Marangos.

Cyprus Today: c/o Ministry of Education, Nicosia; f. 1963; every two months; published in English by the Public Information Office for the Ministry of Education; cultural and general information; Chair. Editorial Board P. Chr. Serghis; Chief Editor N. Panayiotou.

Dimossios Ipallilos: 2 Andreas Demetriou St., Nicosia; fortnightly; published by the Cyprus Civil Servants' Trade Union; circ. 6,000.

Eğitim Bülteni (*Education Bulletin*): Nicosia; f. 1972; monthly; Turkish; published by Office of Member for Education and Teaching of Turkish Cypriot Administration; circ. 2,000.

International Political Review: 21A Nicodimou Mylona, Nicosia; Editor A. Kannaouros; circ. 2,400.

Kooperatif (*Co-operative*): Nicosia; f. 1970; monthly; Turkish; published by Co-operative Development Dept. of Turkish Cypriot Administration; circ. 2,000.

Kypriacos Logos (*Cypriot Word*): 10 Kimon St. Engomi-Nicosia; f. 1969; twice monthly; Editor P. Stylianou; circ. 2,000.

Mathitiki Estia (*Student Hearth*): Pancyprian Gymnasium, Nicosia; f. 1950; monthly; Greek; organ of the Pancyprian Gymnasium students; Editor Chrysanthos Kyprianoy.

Nea Epochi: 11 Stassandrou St., P.O.B. 1581, Nicosia; f. 1959; every two months; Greek; miscellaneous material; Editor Achilleas Pyliotis; circ. 2,500.

Öğretmen (*Teacher*): Nicosia; f. 1972; monthly; Turkish; organ of Cyprus Turkish Secondary Schools Teachers Asscn.; circ. 1,200.

CYPRUS—(The Press, Radio and Television, Finance)

Paediki Hara: 18 Archbishop Makarios III Ave., Nicosia; monthly; published by the Pancyprian Union of Greek Teachers; Editor Theodossios Pieros; circ. 17,800.

Panta Embros: P.O.B. 1156, Nicosia; monthly; published by the Cyprus Scouts' Association; Greek; circ. 3,700.

Pnevmatiki Estia: Nicosia; f. 1960; Greek; literary; monthly.

Radio Programme: Cyprus Broadcasting Corpn., P.O.B. 4824, Nicosia; fortnightly; published by the C.B.C.; circ. 25,000.

Synergatistis (*The Co-operator*): P.O.B. 4537, Nicosia; f. 1961; monthly magazine; Greek; official organ of the Pancyprian Confederation of Co-operatives; Editor G. I. Photiou; circ. 5,700.

Trapezikos: P.O.B. 1235, Nicosia; f. 1960; bank employees' magazine; Greek; monthly; Editor G. S. Michaelides; circ. 17,500.

Türk Sen (*Turkish Trade Unions*): 13-15 Mufti Ziai St., Nicosia; f. 1971; monthly; Turkish; organ of Cyprus Turkish Trade Unions Federation; circ. 5,000.

RADIO AND TELEVISION

RADIO

Cyprus Broadcasting Corporation: P.O.B. 4824, Nicosia; f. 1952; programmes in Greek, Turkish, English and Armenian; two medium-wave transmitters of 20 kW., one of 2 kW. and one of 0.5 kW.; relay stations at Paphos and Limassol; also relays Radio Monte Carlo to the Middle East from a station on Cape Greco; Chair. N. Hadjigavriel; Dir.-Gen. A. N. Christofides; Head of Radio Programmes G. Mitsides; publ. *Radio Programme* (fortnightly).

Radio Bayrak: Ataturk Sq., Nicosia; home service in Turkish, overseas services in Turkish, Greek and English; Dir.-Gen. H. Süha; Dir. of Programmes Mehmet Fehmi.

British Forces Broadcasting Service, Cyprus: British Forces Post Office 53; 120 hours per week in English; Station Controller R. W. Morgan.

In December 1972 there were 170,500 radio receivers in use in Cyprus.

TELEVISION

Cyprus Broadcasting Corporation—TV Division: P.O.B. 4824, Nicosia; began in 1957; two Band III 40/8 kW. V. transmitters on Mount Olympus and Mount Sina Oros give full coverage of the Island; programmes every day from December 1968; Dir.-Gen. A. N. Christofides; Head of Television Programmes Ch. Papadopoulos.

In December 1972 there were 70,000 television receivers in use in Cyprus.

FINANCE

(cap.=capital; p.u.=paid up; dep.=deposits; m.=million)

BANKING

Central Bank

Central Bank of Cyprus: P.O.B. 1087, 36 Metochiou St., Nicosia; f. 1963; became the Bank of Issue in 1966; cap. p.u. £100,000; dep. £83.6m. (Dec. 1972); Gov. C. C. Stephani; publ. *Report* (annual), *Bulletin* (twice monthly).

Cypriot Banks

Bank of Cyprus Ltd.: P.O.B. 1472, Phaneromeni St. 86–90, Nicosia; f. 1899; cap. p.u. £3,000,000; dep. £82.1m. (Dec. 1972); Gov. Dr. Reghinos Theocharis, ph.d.; Chair. C. D. Severis.

Co-operative Central Bank Ltd.: P.O.B. 4537, Nicosia; banking and credit facilities to member societies.

Cyprus Popular Bank Ltd.: cnr. Athens and T.P. O'Connor Streets, Limassol; f. 1924; cap. p.u. £500,000; dep. £3.3m. (March 1970); Chair. Panos Lanitis; Gen. Man. Kikis N. Lazarides.

Cyprus Turkish Co-operative Central Bank, Ltd.: P.O.B. 1861, Mahmout Pasha St., Nicosia; banking and credit facilities to member societies, bodies and individuals; Gen. Man. Mehmet Eshref.

Turkish Bank Ltd.: P.O.B. 1742, Kyrenia St. and Turkish Bank St., Nicosia; f. 1901; cap. p.u. £200,000; dep. £6.3m. (Dec. 1972); Chair. Umit Suleyman; Gen. Man. Madjid M. Ferdi.

Development Bank

Cyprus Development Bank, Ltd., The: Nicosia; f. 1963; cap. p.u. £1,000,000; provides medium or long term loans, working capital requirements or equity share participation supplementary to existing Cyprus enterprises to encourage the development of manufacturing industries, agriculture and tourism in Cyprus; performs related economic and technical research, and acts as investment banker; Chair. G. Papadopoulos; Gen. Man. A. M. Pikis; Sec. S. G. Ambizas; publ. *Annual Report*.

Other Banks

Barclays Bank International Ltd.: 54 Lombard St., London, E.C.3; Local Director's Office, P.O.B. 2081, Metaxas Sq., Nicosia; branches in Nicosia (Metaxas Sq., Ataturk Sq., Nicosia Airport Rd.), Famagusta, Limassol, Larnaca, Morphou, Akrotiri, Dhekelia, Kyrenia and Episkopi; Local Dir. C. Carolides.

Chartered Bank, The: P.O.B. 1047, Evagoras Ave., Nicosia; two brs. each in Nicosia, Limassol, Famagusta; also brs. in Larnaca, Karavas, Paphos, Kyrenia and Morphou.

Lombard Banking (Cyprus) Ltd.: 31 Lombard St., London, E.C.3; General Manager's Office, P.O.B. 1661, Mitsis Building, Metaxas Square, Nicosia; owns a subsidiary, Lombard (Cyprus) Ltd., specializing in hire purchase business; brs. in Nicosia, Limassol and Famagusta; Gen. Man. H. M. Keheyan.

National and Grindlays Bank Ltd.: 23 Fenchurch Street, London, E.C.3; Regional Manager's Office, P.O.B. 2069, Nicosia; brs. in Nicosia, Famagusta, Kyrenia, Larnaca, Lefka, Limassol, Morphou and Paphos; Regional Man. K. O. Dancey.

National Bank of Greece, S.A.: Athens, Greece; Regional Manager's Office, P.O.B. 1191, Makarios III Ave., Nicosia; three brs. in Nicosia, two in Limassol and other brs. in Famagusta, Larnaca, Paphos and Morphou; Regional Man. C. Matsoukis.

Türkiye İş Bankası: Ulus Meydamı, Ankara, Turkey; brs. at Famagusta and Nicosia.

STOCK EXCHANGE

Janus Exchange Co. Ltd.: Nicosia; f. 1961; Man. Dir. N. M. Hadjigavriel.

INSURANCE

General Insurance Company of Cyprus Ltd., The: Bank of Cyprus Bldg., P.O.B. 1668, Nicosia; f. 1951; Chair. M. S. Savides; Vice-Chair. G. C. Christofides.

TRADE AND INDUSTRY

CHAMBERS OF COMMERCE

Cyprus Chamber of Commerce and Industry: P.O.B. 1455, Nicosia; Pres. M. SAVIDES; Vice-Pres. GEORGE ROLOGIS, CHR. MAVROUDES; Sec.-Gen. S. THEOCHARIDES.

Famagusta Chamber of Commerce and Industry: P.O.B. 777, Famagusta; Pres. TAKIS COUNNAS; Vice-Pres. ANDREAS GEORGIS; Sec.-Gen. PAUL VANEZIS.

Larnaca Chamber of Commerce and Industry: P.O.B. 18, Larnaca; Pres. STELIOS DIMITRIOU; Vice-Pres. Dr. ANNIBAS FRANCIS; Hon. Sec. NEOCLIS AG. ONISSIFOROU.

Limassol Chamber of Commerce and Industry: P.O.B. 347, Limassol; Pres. STAVROS GALATARIOTIS; Vice-Pres. KYRIACOS HAMBOULLAS; Hon. Sec. MICHALAKIS DRACOS.

Paphos Chamber of Commerce and Industry: P.O.B. 1, Paphos; Pres. IANGOS NICOLAIDES; Vice-Pres. LOIZOS HAVOUZARIS; Hon. Sec. GEORGE KYPRIANIDES.

Nicosia Chamber of Commerce and Industry: P.O.B. 1455, Nicosia; Pres. ZENON SEVERIS; Vice-Pres. STELIOS GEORGALLIDES; Hon. Sec. EVELTHON GEORGHIADES.

Turkish Cypriot Chamber of Commerce: 99 Kyrenia Ave., Nicosia, P.O.B. 718; Chair. EKREM F. SARPER; Vice-Chair. MEHMET CAN.

EMPLOYERS' ORGANISATIONS

Cyprus Employers' Federation: 4th and 5th Floors, Charalambides Bldg., Grivas-Dhigenis Ave., P.O.B. 1657, Nicosia; f. 1960; 12 member Trade Associations, 285 direct and 540 indirect mems.; Dir.-Gen. C. KAPARTIS; Chair. DIMIS DIMITRIOU; publ. *Newsletter*.

There are also a number of independent employers' associations, among the largest of which are:

Cyprus Building Contractors' Association: 2 Voulgari St., Nicosia; 190 mems.; Sec. G. PARASKEVAIDES.

Limassol Enterprises Contractors' Association: 18 Ipiros St., Limassol; 60 mems.; Sec. O. ECONOMIDES.

Nicosia District Engineering Employers' Association: 103 Eptanisou St., Nicosia; 30 mems.; Sec. C. VARNAVIDES.

Turkish Employers' Association: 99 Kyrenia Ave., Nicosia; f. 1961; 60 mems.; Pres. RAMIZ MANYERA; Vice-Pres. MUSTAFA TURKOĞLU.

TRADE UNIONS

Cyprus Civil Servants' Trade Union: 2 Andreas Demetriou St., Nicosia; f. 1949, registered 1966; restricted to persons in the civil employment of the Govt.; 6 brs. with a total membership of 4,965; Pres. A. PAPANASTASIOU; Gen. Sec. G. IACOVOU; publ. *Dimosios Ipallilos* (Public Servant), fortnightly.

Demokratiki Ergatiki Omospondia Kyprou (*Democratic Labour Federation of Cyprus*): 10 Kimonos St., Engomi, Nicosia; f. 1962, registered 1962; 4 unions with a total membership of 2,500; Gen. Sec. PETROS STYLIANOU; publ. *Ergatikos Agonas* (fortnightly).

Kibris Türk Işçi Sendikalari Federasyonu (*Cyprus Turkish Trade Unions Federation*): 13–15 Mufti-Ziai St., P.O.B. 681, Nicosia; f. 1954, registered 1955; 14 unions with a total membership of 4,554; affiliated to ICFTU and the Federation of Trade Unions of Turkey; Gen. Sec. NECATI TASHKIN; publ. *Türk Sen* (Turkish Trade Unions), monthly.

Pankypria Ergatiki Omospondia (*Pancyprian Federation of Labour*): 32–35 Archemou St., Nicosia; f. 1946, registered 1947; previously the Pancyprian Trade Union Committee f. 1941, dissolved 1946; 16 unions and 225 brs. with a total membership of 38,007; affiliated to the World Federation of Trade Unions; Gen. Sec. A. ZIARTIDES; publs. *Ergatiko Vima* (Workers' Forum), weekly, *Ergasia* (Labour), quarterly.

Pankyprios Omospondia Anexartition Syntechnion (*Pancyprian Federation of Independent Trade Unions*): 1 Menadrou St., Nicosia; f. 1956, registered 1957; has no political orientations; 7 unions with a total membership of 1,134; Pres. COSTAS ANTONIADES; Gen. Sec. KYRIACOS NATHANAEL.

Symospondia Ergaton Kyprou (*Cyprus Workers' Confederation*): 23 Athanasiou Diakou St., P.O.B. 1138, Engomi, Nicosia; f. 1944, registered 1950; 7 Federations, 5 Labour Centres, 41 unions, 13 branches with a total membership of 28,000; affiliated to the Greek Confederation of Labour; Gen. Sec. MICHAEL IOANNOU; publ. *Ergatiki Phoni* (Workers' Voice), weekly.

On December 31st, 1971, there were 22 employers' associations with 1 branch and a total membership of 1,472, 105 unions with 256 brs. and 8 Unions Federations and 5 Confederations with 10 brs. and a total membership of 80,469.

TRADE FAIR

Cyprus International Trade Fair: P.O.B. 1094, Nicosia, annually in September.

TRANSPORT

RAILWAYS

There are no railways in Cyprus.

ROADS

There are 8,699 kilometres of roads, of which 623 kilometres are main roads. There is an extensive network of bus services between Nicosia and the major towns and most villages, and between district centres and villages in each area. There are also taxi services between the principal towns.

Cyprus Automobile Association: Flat 101, Pedhieos Building, Louki Akrita Ave., P.O.B. 2279, Nicosia; f. 1933; Chair. M. S. AGROTIS.

SHIPPING

Famagusta is the main port of the island and has a natural harbour; vessels of an overall length of 430 feet and a maximum draught of 22 feet can be accommodated alongside the quay in the inner harbour; ships with a maximum draught of 30 ft. can be accommodated in the outer harbour. In 1972 461,733 metric tons were loaded there and 711,991 metric tons unloaded. There is open-roadstead accommodation at Larnaca and Limassol, where 168,563 metric tons were loaded and 324,649 unloaded in 1972. The harbour of Paphos offers good anchorage to small vessels and is used mainly for exports, 107,300 metric tons being loaded in 1972 and only 11,912 unloaded. Kyrenia's small harbour is now used chiefly by fishing boats and yachts. There is very little coastal shipping.

Most of the island's oil passes through Larnaca (705,423 metric tons in 1972), although large quantities are discharged at Dhekelia, Vassiliko, Moni and Akrotiri for use in power stations and cement factories. Minerals are exported mainly through Vassiliko and Karavostassi, where a total of 443,941 metric tons was loaded in 1972.

In recent years the number of merchant vessels registered in Cyprus has risen sharply from 314 (1,575,702 g.r.t.) in 1970 to 659 (2,838,811 g.r.t.) in 1972.

Famagusta is also the main passenger port in Cyprus with 59,229 arrivals and 58,647 departures in 1972. In the same year the figures for Limassol were 43,858 and 46,038 and for all other ports 631 and 598 respectively.

There are over sixty lines running cargo and passenger services to Cyprus at approximately weekly, twice monthly and monthly intervals

CIVIL AVIATION

There is an international airport at Nicosia, which can accommodate all types of aircraft, including jets.

Cyprus Airways: Head Office: 21 Athanasiou Diakou St., P.O.B. 1903, Nicosia; f. 1946; Chair. G. ELIADES; Gen. Man. E. SAVVA; routes from Nicosia to Ankara, Athens, Beirut, Cairo, Frankfurt, Istanbul, London, Rome and Tel Aviv; fleet of two Trident 2E.

Cyprus is also served by the following foreign airlines: Aeroflot, Balkan, BEA, BOAC, ČSA, Egyptair, El Al, Interflug, KLM, LOT, MALÉV, MEA, Olympic, Swissair, Syrian Arab Airlines, TAROM, THY and Zambia Airways.

TOURISM

Since earliest times Cyprus has been at a crossroads between east and west, lying on the main trade routes of the Mediterranean and therefore of strategic importance. As a result of the commercial and military interest shown by neighbouring peoples over the centuries Cyprus has gained a wide cultural background which is now one of its chief assets as a tourist centre.

There was a flourishing civilization in neolithic times, already showing contact with neighbouring countries, and during the early Bronze Age, 2300-1900 B.C., relations with the Near East were both cultural and commercial. By the Middle Bronze Age, 1900-1550 B.C., contact with other cultures had become so varied that Cypriot art began to lose its own individual characteristics. The first Greeks came to the island in the Late Bronze Age, 1500-1050 B.C., first as traders then as colonizers; it was they who laid the basis of modern Cyprus, introducing their architecture and town planning, language, writing, religion, political institutions, art, customs, etc. The mingling of styles evolved into what is known as the Levant Mycenaean. Later Cyprus came under Ptolemy's rule, and then became part of the Roman Empire; not much trace remains of the former influence, but many examples of architecture, sculpture, ceramics, etc., survive from the Graeco-Roman period, notably the ruins of Salamis, which include an amphitheatre. Severe earthquakes destroyed the principal centres of civilization in the fourth century A.D.

The influence of Byzantium was strong and some fragments remain of the great basilicas erected from the fourth century onwards. Arab invasions from the seventh to the tenth centuries caused much destruction, but the inhabitants were not driven from the island and it later became a refuge for various minority groups.

Perhaps the main sources of historical interest in Cyprus are the churches, in the Byzantine style, ornamented sometimes by classical frescoes (twelfth century), sometimes by ikons, and influenced by the French Gothic (fourteenth to fifteenth centuries). The three centuries covered by the reigns of the Princes of Lusignan gave rise to some outstanding examples of architecture, such as the Abbey at Bellapais (fourteenth century). Byzantine creative activity virtually came to an end with the Turkish occupation of the island (1570), with only ikon painting surviving until the eighteenth century; the Turks, however, adapted some existing buildings to their own use, such as the cathedral, built mainly to French designs about 1250, which was Nicosia's principal church until the Turks converted it into a mosque in 1570. There was quite considerable intermingling between the Muslim minority and the Greek majority, with many Christians converting to Islam during the Turkish sovereignty, mainly for commercial reasons; this intermingling lasted until the nineteenth century. Little has survived of early private building in Cyprus, but the churches, particularly in the Gothic style, are some of the finest in the world, and there are many notable castles and mosques. Evidence of the successive invasions of Cyprus can be seen in the castle at Kyrenia, which has a Byzantine core, surrounded by a set of ramparts built by the Crusaders (c. 1190) and a further set erected by the Venetians (c. 1490).

Handicrafts in Cyprus have always displayed a good sense of design—spinning and weaving, embroidery and lacemaking, pottery (all still flourishing) and sculpture in wood and silver and gold work (no longer practised). Poetry has a long tradition dating back at least to the time of Homer: Stassinos, reputed to be Homer's father-in-law, wrote the "Cypriot epics", an introduction to the *Iliad*. Further intellectual flowerings came in the fourth century B.C. and the early Christian period.

Tourist earnings increased from £1m. in 1964 to £4.3m. in 1967 and to £13.6m. in 1971.

Cyprus Tourism Organisation: P.O.B. 4535, Nicosia; there are 165 established hotels with 13,000 beds; Chair. FRIXOS PETRIDES; Dir.-Gen. A. G. COROMILAS.

CULTURAL ORGANIZATIONS

E. Ka. Te: Pancyprian Chamber of Fine Arts, P.O.B. 2179, Nicosia; f. 1964; Pres. A. SAVVIDES; Sec. Gen. A. LADOMMATOS; publ. *Bulletin* (monthly).

TH.OK.: Cyprus Theatrical Organization; Dir. NICOS HADJISCOS.

FESTIVALS

Pancyprian Folk Dance, Music, and Song Festival: c/o Municipal Committee, Limassol; Limassol, June.

Orange Festival: Famagusta and Morphou; early Spring.

Lefkara Lace Festival: c/o Lefkara Municipal Council; July.

Lemon Festival: c/o Karavas Municipal Council, Karavas; August.

Cyprus Night: Larnaka; Summer.

Platres Festival: Platres; August-September.

Limassol Carnival: c/o Limassol Municipal Commission; beginning of Lent.

Cyprus Art Festival: c/o Limassol Municipal Commission; late Summer.

Cyprus Wine Festival: c/o Limassol Chamber of Commerce and Industry; September.

During the Summer there are productions of Classical and Modern Drama at the ancient open-air theatres of Salamis and Curium.

EDUCATION

Until 31st March, 1965, each community in Cyprus managed its own schooling through its respective Communal Chamber. Intercommunal education had been placed under the Minister of the Interior, assisted by a Board of Education for Intercommunal Schools of which the Minister was the Chairman. On 31st March, 1965, the Greek Communal Chamber was dissolved and a Ministry of Education was established to take its place. Intercommunal education has been placed under this Ministry.

Greek-Cypriot Education

Elementary education is compulsory and is provided free in six grades to children between 6 and 14 years of age. In some towns and large villages there are separate junior schools consisting of the first three grades. In some large rural centres there are schools where children can take a two-year post-elementary course if they are not proceeding to a secondary school; there are 9 such schools with 387 pupils. Apart from schools for the deaf and blind, and the Lambousa School for juvenile offenders there are also 7 schools for handicapped children and the Ministry runs 9 kindergartens with 732 pupils; most pre-primary education is privately run.

Secondary education is free as from 1972-73 for the first grade of the lower cycle and is fee-paying for the rest, but over 25 per cent of pupils are wholly or partially exempt from payment. There are two types of six-year schools: the Gymnasion-Lykeoin (classical, science and economic sections) and the Vocational-Technical schools (engineering sections) and also the Agricultural Gymnasion. There are five-year vocational (trade) schools and six-year technical schools. There are also 9 foreign-run schools (formerly called "intercommunal") with 199 teachers and 4,120 pupils, and 36 private schools, with 541 teachers and 11,484 pupils.

Post-Secondary education is provided at the Pedagogical Academy, which organizes three-year courses for the training of elementary school teachers. There is also a two-year Forestry College (administered by the Ministry of Agriculture) and a three-year Nurses School and one-year School for Health Inspectors (Ministry of Health). Adult education is conducted through 72 Youth Centres in rural areas, six Foreign Language Institutes in the towns and an apprenticeship scheme for young workers (in co-operation with the Ministry of Labour).

Turkish-Cypriot Education

The Turkish Education Office caters for some 18 per cent of the island's population and administers 10 kindergartens, 167 elementary schools (16,014 pupils), 18 secondary schools (7,190 pupils), 6 technical schools (753 pupils) and 1 teacher-training college (13 students). There are 43 evening institutes for adult education.

BIBLIOGRAPHY

ALASTOS, D. Cyprus in History (London, 1955).

ARNOLD, PERCY. Cyprus Challenge (London: Hogarth Press, 1956).

BARKER, DUDLEY. Grivas (London, Cresset Press, 1960).

BYFORD-JONES, W. Grivas and the Story of EOKA (London, Robert Hale, 1960).

CASSON, S. Ancient Cyprus (London, 1937).

EMILIANIDES, ACHILLE. Histoire de Chypre (Paris, 1963).

ESIN, EMEL. Aspects of Turkish Civilization in Cyprus (Ankara University Press, Ankara, 1965).

FOLEY, CHARLES. Island in Revolt (London, Longmans Green, 1962).
   Legacy of Strife (Penguin, London, 1964).

FOOT, SYLVIA. Emergency Exit (Chatto and Windus, London, 1960).

FOOT, Sir. H. A Start in Freedom (London, 1964).

GRIVAS (DIGHENIS), GEORGE. Guerilla Warfare and EOKA's Struggle (London, Longmans, 1964).
   Memoirs of General Grivas (London, Longmans, 1964).

HARBOTTLE, MICHAEL. The Impartial Soldier (Oxford University Press, 1970).

HILL, Sir GEORGE. A History of Cyprus (4 vols., London, 1940-1952).

JENNES, D. The Economics of Cyprus (Montreal, 1962).

KYRIAKIDES, S. Cyprus—Constitutionalism and Crisis Government (Philadelphia, University of Pennsylvania Press, 1968).

LAVENDER, D. S. The Story of Cyprus Mines Corporation (San Marino, Calif., 1962).

LUKE, Sir H. C. Cyprus under the Turks 1571-1878 (Oxford, 1921).
   Cyprus: A Portrait and an Appreciation (London, Harrap, 1965).

MEYER, A. J. (with S. VASSILIOU). The Economy of Cyprus (Harvard University Press, 1962).

NEWMAN, PHILIP. A Short History of Cyprus (1940).

PAPADOPOULLOS, T. The population of Cyprus (1570-1881) (Nicosia, 1965).

PURCELL, H. D. Cyprus (London, Benn, 1969).

REID-SMITH, E. R. Books and Libraries in Cyprus (London, 1959).

RICE, D. TALBOT. The Icons of Cyprus (London, 1937).

RICHARD, J. Chypre Sous les Lusignan (Paris, 1962).

SPYRIDAKIS, Dr. C. A. Brief History of Cyprus (Nicosia, 1964).

STORRS, Sir RONALD. A Chronology of Cyprus (Nicosia, 1930).

STYLIANOU, A. and J. Byzantine Cyprus (Nicosia, 1948).

THURSTON, HAZEL. The Traveller's Guide to Cyprus (Jonathan Cape, London, 1967).

XYDIS, S. G. Cyprus—Conflict and Conciliation 1945-58 (Ohio State University Press, Columbus, Ohio, 1967).

OFFICIAL BOOKS OF REFERENCE:
   Cyprus: Documents relating to Independence of Cyprus and the Establishment of British Sovereign Base Areas (Cmnd. 1093, H.M.S.O., London, July 1960).
   Cyprus: Treaty of Guarantee, Nicosia, August 16th, 1960.

Egypt

PHYSICAL AND SOCIAL GEOGRAPHY

W. B. Fisher

SITUATION

The Arab Republic of Egypt occupies the north-eastern corner of the African continent, with an extension across the Gulf of Suez into the Sinai region which is usually, but not always, regarded as lying in Asia. The area of Egypt is approximately 386,200 sq. miles (1,002,000 sq. km.); but of this only 4 per cent can be said to be permanently settled, the remainder being desert or marsh. Egypt lies between Lat. 22° and 32° N.; and the greatest distance from north to south is about 674 miles (1024 km.), and from east to west 770 miles (1240 km.), giving the country a roughly square shape, with the Mediterranean and Red Seas forming respectively the northern and eastern boundaries. Egypt has political frontiers on the east with Israel, on the south with the Democratic Republic of the Sudan, and on the west with the Libyan Arab Republic, which, like Egypt, forms part of the Federation of Arab Republics with Syria. The actual frontiers run in general as straight lines drawn directly between defined points and do not normally conform to geographical features (though since June 1967 the *de facto* frontier with Israel has been the Suez Canal.)

Egypt occupies an almost unique place in the world as a region where, in all probability, the earliest developments of civilization and organized government took place. Though many archaeologists would not wholly subscribe to the view of Egypt as actually the first civilized country, there can be no doubt that from very early times the lower Nile Valley has been prominent as possessing strongly marked unity, with a highly specialized and characteristic way of life. Empires with fluctuating boundaries and with varying racial composition have arisen in neighbouring lands of the Middle East, but Egypt has seemed able to stand relatively unchanged, with the facility of absorbing immigrants and outside ideas, of surviving military occupation and defeat, and of maintaining her own culture, finally shaking clear of foreign influence and rule.

PHYSICAL FEATURES

The reasons for this remarkable persistence of cultural cohesion amongst the Egyptian people may be found in the geography of the country. Egypt consists essentially of a narrow, trough-like valley, some 2 to 10 miles wide, cut by the River Nile in the plateau of north-east Africa. At an earlier geological period a gulf of the Mediterranean Sea probably extended as far south as Cairo, but deposition of silt by the Nile has entirely filled up this gulf, producing the fan-shaped Delta region (8,500 sq. miles in area), through which flow two main distributary branches of the Nile—the eastern, or Damietta branch (150 miles long), and the western, or Rosetta branch (146 miles), together with many other minor channels. As deposition of silt takes place large stretches of water are gradually impounded to form shallow lakes, which later became firm ground. At the present there are four such stretches of water in the north of the Delta: from east to west, and, in order of size, Lakes Menzaleh, Brullos, Idku and Mariut.

Upstream from Cairo the Nile Valley is at first 6 to 10 miles in width, and, as the river tends to lie close to the eastern side, much of the cultivated land, and also most of the big towns and cities, lie on the western bank. Towards the south the river valley gradually narrows until, at about 250 miles from the frontier of the Sudan, it is no more than 2 miles wide. Near Aswan there is an outcrop of resistant rock, chiefly granite, which the river has not been able to erode as quickly as the rest of the valley. This gives rise to a region of cascades and rapids which is known as the First Cataract. Four other similar regions occur on the Nile, but only the First Cataract lies within Egypt. The cataracts form a barrier to human movement upstream and serve to isolate the Egyptian Nile from territories farther south. In Ancient Egypt, when river communications were of chief importance, there was a traditional division of the Nile Valley into Lower Egypt (the Delta), Middle Egypt (the broader valley above the Delta), and Upper Egypt (the narrower valley as far as the cataracts). Nowadays it is usual to speak merely of Upper and Lower Egypt, with the division occurring at Cairo.

The fertile strip of the Nile Valley is isolated on the south by the cataracts and by the deserts and swamps of the Sudan; on the north by the Mediterranean Sea; and to east and west by desert plateaux, about which a little more must be said. The land immediately to the east of the Nile Valley, spoken of as the Eastern Highlands, is a complex region with peaks that rise 6,000 to 7,000 ft., but also much broken up by deep valleys that make travel difficult. Owing to aridity the whole region is sparsely populated, with a few partly nomadic shepherds, one or two monasteries and a number of small towns associated chiefly with the exploitation of minerals—petroleum, iron, manganese and granite—that occur in this region. Difficult landward communications mean that contact is mostly by sea, except in the case of the ironfields. The Sinai, separated from the Eastern Highlands by the Gulf of Suez, is structurally very similar, but the general plateau level is tilted, giving the highest land (again nearly 7,000 ft. in elevation) in the extreme south, where it rises in bold scarps from sea-level. Towards the north the land gradually slopes down, ultimately forming the low-lying sandy plain of the Sinai desert which fringes the Mediterranean Sea. Because of its

239

low altitude and accessibility, the Sinai, in spite of its desert nature, has been for many centuries an important corridor linking Egypt with Asia. It is now crossed only by a motor road, the railway having been torn up in 1968 by occupying Israeli forces.

West of the Nile occur the vast expanses known as the Western Desert. Though by no means uniform in height, the land surface is much lower than that east of the Nile, and within Egypt rarely exceeds 1,000 ft. above sea-level. Parts are covered by extensive masses of light shifting sand that often form dunes; but in addition there are a number of large depressions, some with the lowest parts actually below sea-level. These depressions seem to have been hollowed out by wind action, breaking up rock strata that were weakened by the presence of underground water, and most hollows still contain supplies of artesian water. In some instances (as for example, the Qattara depression, and the Wadi Natrun, respectively south-west and south-east of Alexandria) the subterranean water is highly saline and consequently useless for agriculture; but in others—notably the oases of the Fayyum, Siwa, Dakhla, Behariya, and Farafra—the water is sufficiently sweet to allow use for irrigation, and settlements have grown up within the desert.

CLIMATE

The main feature of Egyptian climate is the almost uniform aridity. Alexandria, the wettest part, receives only 8 inches of rain annually, and most of the south has 3 inches or less. In many districts rain may fall in quantity only once in two or three years, and it is apposite to recall that throughout most of Egypt, and even in Cairo itself, the majority of the people live in houses of unbaked, sun-dried brick. During the summer temperatures are extremely high, reaching 100-110°F. at times and even 120° in the southern and western deserts. The Mediterranean coast has cooler conditions, with 90° as a maximum; hence the wealthier classes move to Alexandria for the three months of summer. Winters are generally warm, with very occasional rain; but cold spells occur from time to time, and light snow is not unknown. Owing to the large extent of desert, hot dry sand-winds (called *khamsin*) are fairly frequent particularly in spring, and much damage can be caused to crops; it has been known for the temperature to rise by 35° in two hours, and the wind to reach 90 m.p.h. Another unusual condition is the occurrence of early morning fog in Lower Egypt during spring and early summer. This, on the other hand, has a beneficial effect on plant growth in that it supplies moisture and is a partial substitute for rainfall.

IRRIGATION

With a deficient rainfall over the entire country, human existence in Egypt depends closely on irrigation from the Nile; in consequence it is now necessary to consider the régime of the river in some detail. More detailed reference to conditions outside Egypt is made in the section on the geography of Sudan (below); but it may here be stated in summary that the river rises in the highlands of East Africa, with its main stream issuing from Lakes Victoria and Albert. In the southern Sudan it wanders sluggishly across a flat open plain, where the fall in level is only 1:100,000. Here the shallow waters become a vast swamp, full of dense masses of papyrus vegetation, and this section of the Nile is called the Sudd (Arabic for "blockage"). Finally, in the north of the Sudan, the Nile flows in a well-defined channel and enters Egypt. In Upper Egypt the river is in process of cutting its bed deeper into the rock floor; but in the lower part of its course silt is deposited, and the level of the land is rising—in some places by as much as 4 inches per century.

The salient feature of the Nile is, of course, its regular annual flood, which is caused by the onset of summer rains in East Africa and Ethiopia. The flood travels northward, reaching Egypt during August, and within Egypt the normal rise in river-level used to be over 21 feet, but owing to irrigation works is now only 15 feet. By December the floods have subsided, and the lowest level occurs in May. This cycle has been maintained for several thousand years though the actual maximum of flood-level varies a little each season. However, the flooding had by 1969 become a feature of the past so far as Egypt is concerned (*see* the section on the Aswan High Dam below).

Originally, the flood waters were simply retained in specially prepared basins with earthen banks, and the water could then be used for three to four months after the flood. Within the last century, by the building of large barrages, water is now held all the year round, and so cultivation can take place at any season. With the old system of basin irrigation one or two crops could be obtained annually; with the newer, perennial system, three or even four; and whereas in the past barley and wheat were the main crops, maize and cotton, which can tolerate the great summer heat provided they are watered, now take first and second place. Basin irrigation still prevails in Upper Egypt, but the rest of the country now employs perennial methods.

This change-over has allowed a considerable increase in the population of Egypt, which has risen from about 2½ million in 1800 to 34 million at the present time. This rate of increase shows no sign of slackening—rather, in fact, the reverse—so that already a few districts of Egypt have a population density of over 6,000 per square mile; and as 99 per cent of all Egyptians live within the Nile Valley (only 4 per cent of its area) there is considerable overcrowding and pressure on the land.

With most Egyptians entirely dependent upon Nile water, the point has now been reached that almost all the water entering Egypt is fully utilized. However, there are enormous losses by evaporation which at present amount to some 70 per cent of the total flow. A political problem is concerned with the effects devoting an increased area of the Nile Valley to the growing of commodities for export: cotton, rice and vegetables. Such a change from agricultural self-sufficiency to a cash economy involves the purchase abroad of fertilizers and even foodstuffs, and is inducing considerable social changes within the country. Moreover, so long as only one or two crops were taken per year, the silt laid down by the annual floods maintained soil fertility, but now that three or four crops are taken the import of fertilizer is essential. Hence Egypt has become increasingly sensitive to world trade prices. The position of the merchant and capitalist has greatly improved, often at the expense of the peasant farmer.

Difficulties and opportunities relating to the use of Nile water are exemplified in the High Dam scheme at Aswan. This involves creating a larger reservoir, some 350 miles in length, which has now gradually extended southwards across the Sudanese frontier thereby inundating the town of Wadi Halfa. Some 55–60,000 Sudanese are thus being displaced and these are in process of resettlement at Kashm el Girba, a district lying south-east of Khartoum. Egyptians displaced by the scheme are being rehoused in 33 villages around Kom Ombo; total costs of resettlement will amount to £13.5 million. Prior to 1959 technical and political objections delayed the High Dam scheme; and as the cost of the dam (estimated at £345–400 million) could not be met by the Egyptian Government alone, application was made to the World Bank, America and Britain for a loan, This was refused (Sudanese opposition being one, but only one, factor in this refusal), whereupon Egyptian reaction was to expropriate the Suez Canal Company, in order to finance part of the Aswan scheme.

Soviet offers to assist were made and accepted; and in 1959 a first Soviet credit of £33 million allowed preliminary work to begin in December of the same year. In 1960 further agreement was reached by which the U.S.S.R. supplied credits up to £81 million (making a total of £194 million) together with technical and material assistance; and in 1964 further proposals for credit and loans were made by Mr. Khrushchev. Egypt must thus find at least £200 million in addition to repayments at a later stage of the Russian credits.

In May 1964 the first phase of the High Dam was inaugurated by President Nasser and Mr. Khrushchev. The High Dam is 3,600 metres across, with a girth of 980 metres at the river bed and 40 metres at the top. It holds back the largest artificial lake in the world, stretching 500 km. and finally crossing the Sudanese border. It is making possible the large-scale storing of water from year to year, thus evening out the effects of a bad (dry) season; and its irrigation potential is put at 2 million feddans in Lower Egypt, which, with local possibilities nearer Aswan, will add about 30 per cent to the total cultivable area of Egypt. Besides this, twelve generator units are incorporated in the dam, and these give considerable quantities of electric power at extremely low cost—estimated as below that obtaining in many parts of Europe, and about half of that of electricity in London. This will, it is expected, be a most important aid to industrialization. The High Dam project was started in January 1960, completed in July 1970, and officially inaugurated in January 1971. Details of the likely effect of the High Dam on the Egyptian economy can be found in the Economic Survey. The storage lake behind the dam (Lake Nasser), which is 500 km. long and 10 km. wide, is the centre of a developing fishing industry which is expected to replace the sardine catch in the Mediterranean, lost as a result of building the dam.

Construction has also begun on a new barrage at Girga; and the existing Aswan Dam is currently being raised from 120 to 122 feet in height.

RACE

The racial origins of the Egyptian people present certain problems. In the deserts to east and west of the Nile Valley the population is of unmixed Mediterranean strains; but within the Nile Valley itself there is a special native Egyptian type that would seem to have developed partly from intermixture. The Egyptian peasant is more heavily built and muscular than the nomadic Bedouin, and his colouring is intermediate between the lighter brown of Syrian and Palestinian Arabs and the dark skins of the negroid peoples of the Sudan and Abyssinia. Facial features show some resemblance to those of other Arabs, but despite this there is often more than a hint of the features depicted in ancient monuments. It might thus be reasonable to suggest that there seems to have developed within Egypt a special racial sub-type, basically Mediterranean, with smaller elements both from the south and the north, but also greatly affected by local indigenous conditions which have given rise to a specific Egyptian racial type.

LANGUAGE

Arabic is the language of almost all Egyptians, though there are very small numbers of Berber-speaking villages in the western oases. Most educated Egyptians also speak either French or English, often with a preference for the former. This is a reflection of the traditional French interest in Egypt, which is reciprocated: governmental decrees are sometimes published in French, as well as Arabic, and newspapers in French have an important circulation in Cairo and Alexandria. Small colonies of Greeks and Armenians are also a feature of the larger Egyptian towns. It should perhaps be noted that the Arabic name for Egypt, Misr, is always used within the country itself.

HISTORY

Geography has influenced the history of Egypt from the earliest times. The narrow strip of cultivable land along the banks of the Nile between the First Cataract and the Delta is distinct from the extensive and fertile plain of the Delta itself, but the resultant tendency to separatism has been counterbalanced by the dependence of the people on the annual Nile flood: the control and exploitation of the water and silt have necessitated co-operation and obedience to routine and authority. The eastern and western deserts seal off the lower reaches of the Nile Valley from the neighbouring territories in Africa and Asia. Until recent times communication with the outside world was largely restricted to the route up the river into Nubia, the sea route across the Mediterranean to Syria and the land route to Palestine across the northern fringe of Sinai. The effect of Egypt's relative isolation has been to produce a high degree of cultural individuality.

PHARAONIC EGYPT TO 671 B.C.

Traditionally Egyptian history begins with the semi-legendary Menes, the first ruler of the united kingdom of Upper and Lower Egypt at the end of the fourth millenium B.C. But the flowering of the Old Kingdom came in the third millenium under the IVth Dynasty, which had its capital at Memphis, near the apex of the Delta. The technical and engineering progress of this period is witnessed by the pyramids. These and other works indicate a powerful monarchy commanding great resources.

This efflorescence was followed by a decline. Not until the XIth and XIIth Dynasties (c. 2000 B.C.) does the resurgence of a united Egypt in the Middle Kingdom become clear. The powerful provincial nobles were slowly brought under royal control. Improved conditions were reflected in reclamation works in the Fayyum and temple building at numerous sites. Egyptian armies penetrated into Nubia, a land at that time rich in gold, and the conquest of the region to a point above the Second Cataract was accomplished.

Another obscure period followed and the course of Egyptian history was interrupted by the invasion from Palestine of the Hyksos who established themselves as rulers in the Delta. Although they adopted Egyptian customs, they were never assimilated. About 1620 B.C. a revolt began under a southern prince and ultimately the Hyksos were expelled and Egypt was reunited.

Under the XVIIIth Dynasty, ancient Egypt reached her zenith. This period of the New Kingdom has left its mark up and down the land especially around the capital, Thebes, near the modern Luxor. Abroad the name of the pharaoh was feared in western Asia. The greatest of the conquerors was Thothmes III who established an Egyptian empire in Syria. Egyptian rule was restored and extended in Nubia.

The empire decayed during the reign of Akhenaten (c. 1380–1362), whose religious innovations antagonized the powerful priesthood of Thebes. On his death the old polytheism was restored. The outstanding figure of the XIXth Dynasty was Rameses II (c 1300–1234). He fought the rising power of the Hittites in Syria for twenty years and was both a great builder and a usurper of other men's works.

After him Egypt passed into decline. The XXth Dynasty closed with a long series of insignificant pharaohs and under their successors Egypt was divided between a ruler in the Delta and a priest-king at Thebes. In the eighteenth century B.C. a dynasty originating from Nubia held Upper Egypt and even for a time the Delta. But Egypt was soon to pass under completely alien domination.

EGYPT UNDER FOREIGN RULERS: 671 B.C.–A.D. 640

In 671 the Assyrians conquered Egypt and drove out the Nubian pharaoh. The Assyrians, however, did not long maintain their hold and a native ruler succeeded in reuniting the country. The dynasty which he founded encouraged Greek traders and was supported by Greek mercenaries.

This last native dynasty came to an end in 525, when Persia conquered Egypt. The Persian kings patronized the religion of their subjects and were officially regarded as pharaohs. Darius I (522–485) completed the work of an Egyptian predecessor in cutting a canal linking the Nile and the Red Sea. His successors fought native pretenders to keep Egypt within their empire.

Under Alexander the Great another change of masters occurred. The Persian satrap surrendered in 332 and Alexander was recognized as pharaoh. His visit to the oracle at Siwa shows his fascinated interest in Egyptian religion, while by founding the city of Alexandria he conferred on Egypt a lasting benefit. After Alexander's death, Egypt fell to his general, Ptolemy. The Ptolemaic Dynasty was Greek in origin and outlook. Its capital was Alexandria, which was in effect a Greek rather than an Egyptian city. Egypt was the private estate of the Ptolemies, who taxed its people through a competent bureaucracy.

When Cleopatra committed suicide in 30 B.C., Egypt passed under Roman rule. Although the emperors were regarded as successors of the pharaohs the country sank into a mere province of a great Mediterranean empire. Egyptian Christianity had a distinctive doctrinal character and, by fostering monasticism, originated an important institution. In the dogmatic disputes of the Byzantine period, the adherence of the Coptic church of Egypt to monophysite beliefs in face of the official theology was a form of national self-assertion.

ARAB EGYPT: 640-969

In the early seventh century two great powers dominated the Middle East: the Byzantine empire and the Sasanian empire of the Persians. In 616 the Sasanian army invaded Egypt but Byzantine supremacy was soon restored. Meanwhile a third power was arising, the Arabs, summoned by Muhammad to belief in Islam.

The Prophet's death in 632 was followed by wars against the Byzantines and Sasanians. Egypt, the granary of the Byzantine Empire, soon attracted the Muslim warriors. In the reign of the Caliph Umar I an Arab army under 'Amr ibn al-As took the invasion route from Syria. The frontier towns fell after short sieges and in April 641 the key-fortress near the head of the Delta was captured. Alexandria, the capital, surrendered and was evacuated by the Byzantine garrison. A camp-city at Al-Fustat, again in the strategic position near the apex of the Delta, became the headquarters of the Muslim army and the new capital.

For some centuries Egypt remained an occupied rather than a Muslim country. The Copts, who disliked Byzantine rule, had not opposed the conquest. Under the Arabs they found less oppression and paid lower taxes at first than under Constantinople. In course of time, however, Egypt became an Arabic-speaking country with a Muslim majority. But to this day the Coptic Christian minority remains and uses the ancient language in its liturgy.

For over two centuries Egypt was administered as a province of the Arab Empire. By the middle of the ninth century the remoter territories were slipping from the grasp of the Abbasid caliphs of Baghdad. Egypt was obviously well-fitted to be the domain of an autonomous governor. Two short-lived Sunnite Dynasties, founded by men of central Asian origin, the Tulunids and the Ikhshidids, ruled in virtual independence of the caliph between 868 and 969. Each rapidly degenerated after the death of its founder. Ahmad ibn Tulun in 877 occupied Syria and thus once again created an empire based on Egypt.

THE FATIMIDS AND AYYUBIDS: 969-1250

Ikshidid rule was terminated in 969 by an invasion from Tunisia. Here the rival caliphate of the Fatimids had been set up by Muslims of the Shia sect, who believed that the caliphate could only pass through the direct descendants of 'Ali, the husband of Muhammad's daughter, Fatima. The fourth of these anti-caliphs, Al-Mu'izz, was made the master of Egypt by his general, Jawhar. Jawhar laid out a new capital, just outside Al-Fustat, which has developed into the modern city of Cairo, and was the founder of the mosque of Al-Azhar, the greatest centre of Islamic theological learning.

Under the early Fatimids Egypt enjoyed a golden age. The country was a well-administered absolute monarchy and it formed the central portion of an empire which at its height included North Africa, Sicily, Syria and western Arabia. Agriculture and industry were encouraged. Trade with Europe and India brought prosperity to the land and wealth to the ruler.

Soon, however, Fatimid rule began to decay. Ali Hakim (996-1021) departed from the tolerant policy towards Christians and Jews which was normal in Muslim states. The long reign of Al-Mustansir (1035-94) witnessed the break-up of the Fatimid Empire and the growing insubordination of the slave-soldiery. In 1073 the caliph was obliged to send for Badr al Jamali, the governor of Acre, to take control of the country. This he did and Egypt passed under the government of a military autocracy who kept the Fatimid caliphs under their tutelage. Thus the collapse of the Fatimid state was postponed for nearly a century but, after the death of Al-Mustansir, the six succeeding caliphs had no power.

Meanwhile a new enemy was on the threshold—the Crusaders who after 1098 established feudal, Christian states along the Syrian coast. Neither the Abbasids nor the Fatimids were capable of resisting them but in the later twelfth century the tide began to turn. The Muslim reconquest of Syria was largely due to the energy and ability of the Kurdish leader, Salah al-Din ibn Ayyub, known in European history as Saladin. In 1169 he became minister to the Fatimid caliph. In 1171 the last Fatimid was quietly deposed and Egypt restored to Sunni orthodoxy. The remainder of Saladin's life was a struggle against the crusading states but when he died in 1193 he was sultan over Egypt and practically the whole of the former Crusader territory.

Saladin's Empire was divided amongst his heirs, one branch of which, the Egyptian Ayyubids, reigned in Cairo. Dynastic struggles weakened the family and the Crusaders were able to recover some lost ground. Louis IX of France led an attack directly on Egypt. Damietta was occupied in 1249 but the advance of the Crusaders through the difficult and pestilential Delta was stopped at the battle of Al-Mansura in 1250. Louis was made prisoner but subsequently regained his liberty on paying a ransom and restoring Damietta.

THE MAMLUK SULTANATE: 1250-1517

During this Crusade the Ayyubid sultan, al-Malik al-Salih, died. This was virtually the end of the dynasty. After a short confused period the commander of the forces, a certain Aybak became the first of the Mamluk sultans who ruled Egypt from 1250 to 1517. These sultans were of slave origin. The Ayyubids had built up bodyguards of slave-troops, whose power increased as that of their masters declined. The earlier Mamluks, until 1390, were mainly of Turkish and Mongol origin, while their successors, originally the bodyguard of the former, were mostly Circassians. The Mamluk sultans did not form a dynasty in the hereditary sense but a caste from which successive rulers emerged after election or a struggle for power. The ranks of the Mamluks were replenished by fresh purchases.

The Mamluks were thus an alien element which was never fully assimilated in Egypt. They exploited the land for their own benefit and the Egyptians played a passive role under their domination. Nevertheless they protected Egypt and Syria against the Mongols and the Crusaders. The Mongol threat developed in the middle of the thirteenth century when Hulagu, the grandson of Jenghiz Khan, advanced through Persia. Baghdad was taken and the Abbasid caliphate extinguished in 1258. From Northern Syria the Mongol army advanced southwards until at Ain Jalut, near Nazareth, it was overwhelmed in 1260 by the Mamluk Sultan, Baibars. Spared from the ravages of the Mongols, Egypt became the principal centre of Arab culture. The change in the centre of gravity of Islam was symbolized when Baibars brought to Cairo an 'Abbasid prince, who was formally recognized as titular caliph.

This victory also ensured that the Mamluk sultans would rule over a combined empire of Egypt and Syria. The remaining pockets of Crusader territory were regained by Baibars and his successors. Baibars also intervened in the affairs of the Christian kingdom of Nubia and virtually established a protectorate.

The numerous mosques and public works of the Mamluk period indicate the wealth of Egypt. But from the middle of the fourteenth century the condition of the country declined owing to plague and civil war, while heavy taxation oppressed all classes of the native Egyptians. Another Mongol invasion under Tamerlane in 1401 devastated Syria, although Egypt itself was again spared. The valuable transit trade through Egypt was subjected to a close monopoly, which diminished its flow. Finally Vasco da Gama's voyage to India around the Cape (1496–99) sounded the doom of Egyptian prosperity. European ships henceforward by-passed Egypt and traded directly with the east, while the Portuguese destroyed the Mamluk fleets and harried Arab shipping in the Indian Ocean, Red Sea and Persian Gulf.

OTTOMAN EGYPT: 1517-1798

At the beginning of the sixteenth century a powerful state was created in Persia under the Safavid dynasty, while Anatolia and the Balkan peninsula were ruled by the Ottomans. The Mamluks were by comparison a declining power and sought by a secret understanding with the Persian Shah to hold their own against the expansionist and militant Ottomans.

In 1516 at the battle of Marj Dabiq north of Aleppo the Ottoman Sultan, Selim I, defeated the Mamluks and advanced southwards. A second battle in January 1517, outside Cairo, resulted in the overthrow of the last Mamluk sultan. The whole of his empire fell into Selim's hands and Cairo sank to a provincial status. The Turkish conquest together with the change in international trade-routes marked the beginning of a period of political and economic insignificance. The great mosque of Al-Azhar retained its primacy among the theological schools of Islam but its teaching was set in a conservative tradition that remained unbroken until the nineteenth century.

Selim recognized the individuality of Egypt and his successors usually interfered but little with the administration. The Mamluk soldiery and their leaders, the beys, were allowed to continue receiving their revenues. A garrison of Turkish janissaries was stationed in Egypt but in the course of a few generations they became useless as a military force, while constant recruiting from the slave-markets kept the Mamluks in unimpaired vigour. Ottoman governors were appointed but for the most part they were utterly dependent on the Mamluk beys.

From time to time Mamluk grandees were virtually sovereign in Egypt. The most famous of these was Ali Bey, who ruled from 1761 to 1766, was then driven into exile, but regained power from 1767 to 1772. He made an alliance with a Syrian Arab chief, and contacted a Russian squadron, which was then cruising in the eastern Mediterranean, during the course of hostilities against the Ottoman Empire. A Mamluk force attacked Damascus, and drove out the Ottoman governor, but Ali's general betrayed him, and returned to Egypt. Ali fled to his Syrian friend, but was defeated in an attempt to reconquer Egypt in 1773 and died a prisoner.

Ali Bey's career illustrated the weakness of the Mamluks. They had no roots in Egypt and the Egyptians viewed with indifference their struggles for mastery. Their power to achieve their ambitions was limited by the difficulty of financing their factions and they became unpopular by the extortions which they practised on the native Egyptians. At the end of the century a shock from Europe was to reveal the hollowness of their power.

THE FRENCH IN EGYPT: 1798-1801

During the eighteenth century, the British obtained the chief share of Eastern commerce. With the outbreak of the Revolutionary War between Britain and France, the French decided that the occupation of Egypt and the revival of the transit trade might lead to the disruption of British commerce and the overthrow of British rule in India. Bonaparte landed at Alexandria in July 1798.

His aim was to colonize Egypt, break the Mamluk hold and introduce Western ideas. Although he professed sympathy with Islam, his expedition was essentially inspired by the nationalist and secular ideology of the French Revolution. The Egyptians saw in it a new crusade and Bonaparte's attempts to win support by appeals to Muslim sentiment miscarried.

Defeated in the decisive "Battle of the Pyramids" on July 21st, the Mamluks fled and the sudden collapse of their administration was followed by disorder and pillage in Cairo until the entry of French troops. The following month, however, Bonaparte was cut off from France by the destruction of his fleet by Nelson in the "Battle of the Nile". In September the Ottoman Sultan declared war and news of this, combined with Mamluk intrigues and hostility towards the alien French, led in October to a serious revolt in Cairo, centred around Al-Azhar which was subjected to an artillery bombardment.

Early in 1799 Bonaparte invaded Syria to attack the combined forces of the Mamluks and the Ottomans under the governor of Acre. The latter was supported by a British naval squadron and after besieging Acre for two months Bonaparte withdrew to Egypt, his forces much reduced by fighting and disease. He repulsed a Turkish landing near Alexandria in July and succeeded in August in getting away to France with a few companions. His army held out until 1801 when a British force, subsequently joined by Ottoman troops, compelled them to capitulate.

The shock to Egypt of the French occupation was great. The Mamluk ruling caste was unseated, Egyptian Muslim leaders were associated with the administration and consulted on public matters, and the Copts were placed on an equal footing with the Muslims. The immediate effect was to confuse and irritate Egyptian opinion, but the way to future developments had been opened.

The French did not abandon the idea of gaining control over Egypt and their interest in Egyptian affairs was maintained. French scholars who had accompanied Bonaparte produced monographs which became the basis of modern studies of the country. In the hands of Champollion, the Rosetta Stone was to be the key to the hieroglyphs.

MUHAMMAD ALI PASHA AND HIS SUCCESSORS: 1805-63

The expulsion of the French was followed by a struggle for power in which the victor was an Albanian officer in the Ottoman forces, Muhammad Ali. In 1805 he was recognized by the Sultan as Governor of Egypt. In 1807 he defeated a British force which had occupied Alexandria. In 1811 the Mamluk chiefs were massacred in Cairo. His prestige was increased by the success of his forces in a campaign in Arabia, undertaken between 1811 and 1818 at the request of the Sultan, against the Wahhabi conquerors of the Hijaz, led by the family of Saud, who threatened the Fertile Crescent. Between 1820 and 1822 his army conquered most of the northern Sudan, the source of gold and slaves.

The gaps in his army resulting from these campaigns were made up first by slaves, who were found unsuitable because of their high mortality, and then by the conscription—unprecedented, brutal and unpopular—of native Egyptians. The new army had Turks, Albanians and Circassians for officers and was trained by European military instructors.

In 1824 Muhammad Ali sent his son Ibrahim with an Egyptian force to assist the Sultan to suppress the Greek revolt, but European intervention in 1827 led to the destruction of the Turkish and Egyptian fleets at Navarino. On the rejection by the Sultan of Muhammad Ali's demand that Syria should be given to him in recompense, Ibrahim invaded that country in 1831. War with the Ottomans followed and Ibrahim advanced into Anatolia. A convention in 1833 gave Muhammad Ali the Syrian provinces, which were ruled by Ibrahim for seven years as his viceroy. A second Ottoman war then broke out, and international intervention once again resulted in Ibrahim's defeat.

Muhammad Ali's dominions were restricted to Egypt and the Sudan but his governorship was made hereditary. He died in 1849, having been predeceased by Ibrahim.

Within Egypt Muhammad Ali reformed the administration and controlled the national wealth. An ambitious educational system was organized under European teachers, and Egyptian students were sent abroad, especially to France. A press was set up, primarily for the production of textbooks and manuals. Towards the end of his reign a Western-educated class was emerging and the ferment of ideas characteristic of modern Egyptian intellectual life had begun.

Muhammad Ali was succeeded by his grandson, Abbas I (1849-54), under whom the westernizing trend was reduced, and he by Said (1854-64), Muhammad Ali's surviving son.

THE MAKING OF THE SUEZ CANAL: 1854-69

During Muhammad Ali's reign, Egypt regained importance as a link between Europe and the East. The overland route via Alexandria, Cairo and Suez, which was improved with the construction of a railway by British enterprise, reduced the passage between England and India from five months to forty days. This route was used by passengers and mail but heavy merchandise continued to go by the Cape. The scheme for a maritime canal, regarded by the British Government as a threat to India, was backed by France but Muhammad Ali refused to grant the necessary concession, seeing a canal as a threat to the independence he sought.

Said proved more pliant and in 1854 granted a concession to de Lesseps which included an undertaking to supply labour but required ratification by the Sultan. This was delayed owing to British opposition and work did not begin until 1859, in anticipation of ratification after de Lesseps had gained the support of Napoleon III.

Said was succeeded by Ismail, Ibrahim's son, who inherited something of his grandfather's imagination and his father's energy. At his insistence the concession (and particularly the clause concerning the provision of labour) was modified, but he was obliged to pay £3 million in compensation to the Suez Canal Company after the matter had been submitted to the arbitration of Napoleon III. The canal was opened with great festivities.

At first the British Government tried to ignore the canal and none of the 80,000 shares reserved for Britain (one-fifth of the total) were bought. Ismail, who had originally been allotted 64,000 shares, took up these and others which remained unsubscribed, bringing his total holding to 182,023 shares. Said and Ismail had together paid about £11½ million in connection with the canal which cost approximately £16 million to cut. Ismail was to receive 15 per cent of the net profits, in addition to the interest on his shares.

THE KHEDIVE ISMAIL AND INTERNATIONAL CONTROL: 1863-81

As part of the Ottoman Empire, Egypt was bound by the Capitulations—treaties with European powers giving European communities in Ottoman territories a considerable degree of autonomy under the jurisdiction of their consuls. Originally they had applied to small groups of merchants but with the growth of trade with Egypt in the nineteenth century consular protection came to be enjoyed by sizeable foreign communities, who were exempt from Egyptian jurisdiction and largely free of Egyptian taxation. After prolonged negotiations Mixed Courts, which reduced the scope of consular jurisdiction, were introduced in 1875; these, however, had a majority of European judges and were not insensitive to diplomatic pressures.

Ismail was to deliver Egypt into far greater international control. His ambitions made him careless of financial considerations, and high cotton prices during the American Civil War gave him a false idea of his country's wealth. In 1866 he obtained the title of Khedive. He extended his Sudanese dominions, cut canals, built railways and constructed telegraph lines. No distinction was drawn between the debts of the state and those of the ruler, whose personal expenses were high, and between 1863 and 1876 Egyptian indebtedness rose from £7 million to nearly £100 million. Much of this was in the form of loans from European financial houses at steep rates of interest.

In 1875 Ismail staved off a financial crisis by selling his Suez Canal shares to the British Government for nearly £4 million, a profitable investment by Disraeli who sought to prevent French control. The crisis came in 1876 when Ismail suspended payment of his treasury bills, a declaration of bankruptcy which led to international control. A khedival decree of May 1876 established the "Caisse de la Dette Publique", administered by four foreign members—British, French, Austrian and Italian—to provide for the service of Egyptian debts. When this arrangement proved unsuccessful the French insisted on reform of the fiscal system to provide for repayment of the debts and in 1878 Ismail was forced by France and Britain, in return for a new loan, to surrender his powers and revenues to a ministry, headed by Nubar Pasha, which included a British and a French minister. Ismail chafed under foreign control, aligned himself with Egyptian opposition to it and in May 1879 dismissed the ministry. The French and British Governments retaliated by securing his deposition by the Ottoman Sultan.

Ismail was succeeded by his son Tawfik, who, ostensibly, governed through a responsible Egyptian ministry. Strict financial control was exercised, however, by a French and a British controller, and under the law of liquidation of 1880 an international Debt Commission, consisting of two French and two British members together with one German, one Austrian and one Italian, administered 66 per cent of the country's revenue for the benefit of foreign creditors. Furthermore, a maximum was laid down for government expenditure and the Commissioners were empowered to draw on any surplus administrative revenue. Such was the burden laid upon the Egyptian people by Ismail's improvidence.

THE ARABI EPISODE: 1881-82

Meanwhile a nationalist outlook was developing among those classes who had been touched by Western influences, particularly the younger Egyptian army officers whose way to promotion was barred by Turks and Circassians. Liberal reformers led by Cherif Pasha resented Turkish overlordship and wanted a Western-style constitution. Moslem leaders were opposed to the spread of Christian influence. The great landowners, many of whom were, like the ruling house, Turkish in origin, fought to retain their privileges which were threatened by foreign control. The peasantry, who had been squeezed to pay for Ismail's schemes were being squeezed again to pay his debts. The Khedive, Tawfik, was revealed as a puppet maintained by France and Britain.

By 1881 the country seethed with unrest and a climax was reached in February when, in protest against cuts imposed on the army, a group of officers led by Arabi Pasha forced Tawfik to dismiss his Circassian War Minister. In September, after surrounding his palace, they compelled him to agree to the formation of a new ministry, and to summon the Chamber of Notables, a consultative body originally set up by Ismail. France was opposed to any concession to moderate Egyptian opinion, Britain agreed rather than risk a split with France, and a Franco-British note was sent proclaiming the resolve to maintain the Khedive and the established order.

The effect of the note was to align the Chamber of Notables with Arabi against foreign intervention. In February 1882 the Khedive was forced to dismiss the ministry led by Cherif Pasha and appoint a nationalist ministry with a supporter of Arabi as Prime Minister and Arabi himself Minister for War. The Dual Control ceased to exist and, although anxious to avoid sending an expedition to Egypt, the British and French Governments in May sent naval squadrons to Alexandria as a demonstration. On their arrival Egyptian opinion became so inflamed that in June fanaticism took control and riots broke out in Alexandria and other places in which numbers of Europeans were killed.

At a conference in Constantinople neither Germany nor Turkey would support the sending of an expeditionary force and the French Chamber of Deputies refused to sanction French intervention. On July 11th, the Egyptians having refused to cease work on the fortifications of Alexandria, the British squadron bombarded the forts. The town was evacuated by the Egyptian army, while the Khedive placed himself under British protection and subsequently proclaimed Arabi a rebel. The French ostentatiously dissociated themselves from the British action. A British expeditionary force landed at Ismailia and routed the Egyptian army at Tel el Kebir. Cairo was occupied and Tawfik's prerogatives were restored, to be subsequently exercised under British control.

EGYPT—(HISTORY)

THE RULE OF CROMER AND HIS SUCCESSORS: 1883-1914

The British Government hoped to set Egyptian affairs in order and then to withdraw, but the execution of this policy was frustrated. The Arabi episode had brought Egypt once again to the verge of bankruptcy. Difficulties were increased by a cholera epidemic, a poor Nile, the Mahdist revolt in the Sudan and the unremitting hostility of France. Evacuation was repeatedly deferred and the occupation gradually assumed the character of a veiled protectorate.

From 1883 to 1907 the Egyptian Government was dominated by the British Agent and Consul-General, Sir Evelyn Baring, who in 1891 became Lord Cromer. He was in title only the equal of the other consuls-general and British control was established with diplomatic care, German support being canvassed to counterbalance French obstruction. A policy of severe economy was necessary to satisfy foreign bondholders. In spite of the limitation on his freedom of action, Cromer obtained remarkable results. An international convention in 1885 eased the financial strain by permitting a further loan and modifying the rigidity with which Egyptian revenues were assigned. British financial advisers brought about increased revenues, solvency was restored and taxation reduced. Irrigation works were improved and paid labour replaced the corvée for the annual clearance of the canals. The Aswan dam was constructed. A new Egyptian army was trained by British officers.

In 1892 Tawfik died. He was succeeded by his son, Abbas II, who was barely eighteen at his accession and soon resented Cromer's authority. The possibility of a conjunction between Abbas and a new nationalist movement led by Mustafa Kamil, a young lawyer who had been trained in France, caused the British some anxiety but the Khedive's attempts to assert himself resulted in humiliation which further embittered him against Britain. A series of puppet governments preserved a façade of constitutionalism but educated youth turned increasingly to opposition.

At the turn of the century Britain gained a freer hand in Egypt. The Sudan was reconquered between 1896 and 1898. A clash between British and French at Fashoda on the Upper Nile was narrowly averted and the liquidation of this problem led ultimately to the Entente Cordiale of 1904 and the diminution of French opposition in Egypt. At the same time senior British officials, who had increased in number from about 100 in 1885 to over 1,000 in 1905, were out of touch with the growing strength of national feeling.

Cromer was succeeded in 1907 by Sir Eldon Gorst, who managed to establish better relations with the Khedive and adopted an attitude of informality which contrasted with Cromer's proconsular pomp. On his death in 1911 he was followed by Lord Kitchener, who, as conqueror of the Sudan, was treated with more deference than had been grudgingly accorded to Gorst and whose arrival marked a return to more autocratic methods. Nevertheless a Legislative Assembly was created in 1913 which provided a platform from which the voice of nationalism could make itself heard with constitutional propriety, and it is to the credit of British rule throughout this period that the press was uncensored and the expression of opinion free.

THE FIRST WORLD WAR AND ITS CONSEQUENCES: 1914-22

After Turkey entered the First World War in November 1914 on the side of Germany, Egypt, still nominally a province of the Ottoman Empire, was declared a British protectorate and Britain assumed responsibility for the defence of the Suez Canal. On December 20th Abbas II was deposed and the British Government offered the title of Sultan to Husain Kamil, the brother of Tawfik. When Husain died in 1917 he was succeeded by his brother Fuad.

Under the protectorate the combination of British and Egyptian officials in the administration continued. Kitchener was succeeded by Sir Henry McMahon, the first High Commissioner, and he in turn was succeeded in 1917 by Sir Reginald Wingate, who had served in the Egyptian army under Kitchener and had since 1899 been Governor-General of the Sudan.

The Constantinople Convention of 1888 provided that the Suez Canal should be "always free and open, in time of war as in time of peace, to every vessel of commerce or war, without distinction of flag", but, by a blockade against enemy shipping outside the three-mile limit covered by the Convention, Britain was able to deny the use of the Canal to enemy shipping.

The pressure of military necessity was increasingly felt by the Egyptians. Martial law, censorship, the dearth of officials of good quality, the forcible recruitment of labour and the requisition of animals for the advance into Palestine, rising prices and profiteering all combined to intensify opposition to the protectorate. The nationalist movement, antagonistic to both the British administration and the Sultan, fed on popular discontent and at the end of the war, in November 1918, a delegation, headed by Saad Zaghlul, presented Wingate with a demand for autonomy. The British Government's refusal to deal with the nationalists and the deportation of Zaghlul and three of his associates resulted in riots and murders early in 1919 and order had to be restored by military action.

Wingate, who had given warning of the danger, was superseded by Allenby, fresh from his successful campaign against the Turks. Allenby made overtures to Egyptian opinion and Zaghlul and his friends were released, only to fail to get a hearing at the Peace Conference and to be rebuffed by the recognition of the British protectorate by the United States. Known now as the *Wafd* (i.e. Delegation), they set to work to organize support in Egypt and boycotted the British mission under Lord Milner, sent to report on the situation. Britain was prepared to negotiate a treaty in exchange for the abolition of the protectorate, and discussion between Milner and Zaghlul subsequently took place in Paris. After inciting further unrest in Egypt, Zaghlul was again deported, however.

On February 28th, 1922, the British Government issued a declaration unilaterally announcing the abolition of the protectorate and the recognition of Egypt as an independent sovereign state. Four matters were absolutely reserved to the discretion of the British Government, pending the conclusion of negotiated agreements. These were: the security of the communications of the British Empire in Egypt; the defence of Egypt; the protection of foreign interests and of minorities in Egypt; and the Sudan.

In March 1922 the Sultan, Fuad, took the title of King of Egypt and in April a committee was set up to draft a constitution.

THE TRIANGULAR STRUGGLE: 1922-39

The period after the declaration of independence saw a triangular struggle in Egypt between the King, the Wafd and the British Government. The Wafd was organized to carry out a revolution, not to direct affairs of state. The King owed his throne to the British and his presence guaranteed their interests, yet obvious subservience to them might have enabled the Wafd to rob him of his throne.

The new constitution, which made Egypt a parliamentary monarchy on the Belgian model, was promulgated in 1923. The Wafd triumphed in the elections which were then held and Saad Zaghlul became Prime Minister for a brief period in 1924. In the succeeding years political instability continued as the struggle for power between the Wafd and the throne went on. Elections usually gave the Wafd a majority but a Wafd ministry was unacceptable to King Fuad and in this he normally had the concurrence of the British Government. Hence Palace influence was predominant in the ministries appointed and at times legislation had to be enacted by decree. In 1928 the Parliament was suspended for three years, in 1930 modifications were made to the constitution which altered the electoral law, but in 1935 the original provisions were restored and in elections the following year the Wafd again obtained a majority. The month before the elections King Fuad had been succeeded by his son, Farouk, a minor. The new Prime Minister was Nahas Pasha, who had led the Wafd since Zaghlul's death in 1927.

Until 1936 negotiations for an Anglo-Egyptian treaty invariably broke down over questions of defence and the Sudan. The continued presence of British troops was regarded by Egyptians as denying the reality of independence. The Egyptians also felt that they had been ousted by Britain from dominion over the Sudan and control over their water supply. When the Governor-General of the Sudan was assassinated in Cairo in 1924, Allenby demanded the withdrawal of Egyptian troops from the Sudan, and also the unlimited extension of the irrigation of the Sudan Gezira. Although these demands were later modified, the Egyptian share in the Condominium was to remain nominal.

In 1929 the Nile Waters Agreement allotted the respective shares of Egypt and the Sudan, to Egypt's advantage. The deadlock over a treaty ended in 1936 when the rise of Italian power threatened British and Egyptian interests alike. On August 26th an Anglo-Egyptian treaty of twenty years duration was signed which formally terminated British occupation but empowered Britain to station forces in the Suez Canal zone until the Egyptian army was in a position to ensure the security of the Canal. The Sudan was to continue to be administered as in the past. The protection of foreign interests and of minorities in Egypt was recognized as the exclusive responsibility of the Egyptian Government. The abolition of the Capitulations was secured by the Convention of Montreux in May 1937. In the same month Egypt was admitted to the League of Nations.

THE SECOND WORLD WAR AND ITS CONSEQUENCES: 1939-52

In the Second World War Egypt was a vital strategic factor as the British base in the Middle East. Her treaty obligations were fulfilled but the ruling classes were by no means committed to the Allied cause and on occasions popular support for Germany became manifest. Nevertheless the presence of British forces ensured co-operation.

The young King Farouk, who had assumed full royal powers in 1937, was a popular national figure but as determined as his father to avoid domination by the Wafd. Although still the dominant political party, the Wafd was losing its revolutionary fervour and its appeal to youth was diminishing. Fascist influence appeared in the Greenshirt organization, while the Muslim Brotherhood, a puritanical religious body, developed a terrorist wing and threatened the established authorities.

The critical year was 1942. Alamein had not yet been fought, the King was disposed to appease the Axis powers and the government was under Palace influence. The Wafd, however, favoured co-operation with Britain. In February the British Ambassador, supported by an armed escort, entered the Palace and insisted on the formation of a Wafdist government. Threatened with deposition, Farouk acquiesced and Nahas Pasha became Prime Minister and Military Governor of Egypt.

Nahas held office until 1944. During this period Nuri al-Said, the Prime Minister of Iraq, and King Abdulla of Transjordan separately put forward proposals for a union of Arab states in the Fertile Crescent. These were opposed by Egypt as they seemed to favour Iraqi hegemony. Nahas took the initiative, proposing a broader league of Arab states, and a conference was held which in October 1944 produced the Alexandria Protocol. On this the Arab League was founded the following year. From the beginning Egypt held a position of leadership in the League, which was bitterly hostile to the idea of establishing a Jewish state in Palestine. Previously, preoccupied with her own national problems, Egypt had shown little interest in the Palestine problem.

By 1944 the danger to Egypt had passed. Nahas was no longer indispensable and his government fell, discredited by co-operation with the British and by the corruption which had flourished during its tenure of office. The struggle between the Wafd and the

Palace revived. Communism, made attractive, especially among students, by the Russian successes in the war, gained new adherents, and the Muslim Brotherhood continued its subversive activities.

Negotiations in the immediate post-war years for a new treaty with Britain broke down over the questions of the British occupation of the Canal Zone and the future of the Sudan. A provisional agreement concluded between Ernest Bevin and Sidki Pasha in 1946 proved abortive owing to Sudanese resentment at a reference to "the unity between the Sudan and Egypt under the common crown of Egypt". The British Government affirmed its intention that the Sudanese should freely decide their own future status. In 1949 Nokrashi Pasha submitted the Egyptian case to the United Nations where the problem was shelved.

In Palestine Britain's renunciation of the Mandate on May 14th, 1948, was followed immediately by the declaration of the State of Israel and military action by Egypt, Iraq, Syria and Jordan. The Egyptian army was badly defeated. Although the fact was long concealed from the Egyptian public, it eventually recoiled on the ruling classes. The King's early popularity had vanished; military failure and the scandal of the supply of faulty arms, in which members of the Palace clique were implicated, undermined the loyalty of the army, which was his last support.

The fall of the discredited regime did not come immediately. The Communists, although widespread, lacked the means to capture the administration. A terrorist campaign by the Muslim Brotherhood was suppressed and the organization driven underground in 1949. Nahas, again in power, made a last bid for royal and popular support in 1951 by abrogating the Treaty of 1936 and the Condominium Agreement and proclaiming Farouk "King of Egypt and Sudan". New British proposals on the Sudan were rejected, as also were proposals on defence, involving the creation of an Allied Middle East Command with Egyptian participation, put forward jointly by Britain, France, Turkey and the United States. Terrorism and economic sanctions were then employed in an attempt to force the withdrawal of British forces from the Canal Zone. Clashes occurred, resulting in many deaths, and on January 26th, 1952, an anti-British demonstration in Cairo developed into rioting, looting and a conflagration, brought to an end only by army intervention.

THE REVOLUTION: 1952-56

On July 23rd, 1952, a group of young army officers, the "Free Officers", who had long been planning a *coup d'état*, seized power in Cairo. They invited the veteran politician, Ali Maher, to form a government under their control, and secured the abdication of King Farouk in favour of his infant son, Ahmed Fuad II, on July 26th. Farouk sailed to exile.

General Muhammad Neguib, an associate of the Free Officers who had incurred the enmity of King Farouk and who had earlier made himself popular by his condemnation of the British action in 1942, was made Commander-in-Chief of the armed forces and head of the military junta. A Council of Regency was formed in August. On September 7th, after an attempt by the Wafd and other parties to resume the political battle on their own terms, a new cabinet with General Neguib as Prime Minister was substituted for that of Ali Maher. Real power, however, lay with the nine officers who formed the Revolutionary Command Council.

The Revolution soon gained momentum. In September 1952 land ownership was limited to 300 acres in any one family and the power of the feudal class which had for so long dominated Egyptian political life was destroyed. Land owned by the royal family was confiscated. On December 10th the constitution was abolished and on January 16th, 1953, all political parties were dissolved. It was announced that there would be a three-year transition period before representative government was restored. On June 18th the monarchy was abolished and Egypt declared a republic, with Neguib as President and Prime Minister as well as Chairman of the Revolutionary Command Council. Colonel Gamal Abdel Nasser, who, although leader of the Free Officers, had hitherto remained in the background, became Deputy Prime Minister and Minister of the Interior, and Abdel Hakim Amer was appointed Commander-in-Chief of the armed forces.

A revolutionary court was set up and a number of persons, including the old politicians most identified with the failure of the Palestine campaign, were tried amid much publicity, on charges of corruption and opposition to the new regime. Action was taken involving widespread arrests and detentions to suppress two potential sources of opposition to the revolutionary government: the Communists and the Muslim Brotherhood.

A struggle for power soon developed between General Neguib, whose personal tendencies were Islamic and conservative, and Colonel Nasser. On February 25th, 1954, Neguib was relieved of his posts as President, Prime Minister and Chairman of the Revolutionary Command Council and accused of having attempted to concentrate power in his own hands. Nasser became Prime Minister and Chairman of the Revolutionary Command Council in his place for a few days but Neguib was restored as President and took back both the other posts. He announced that elections would be held for a constituent assembly, martial law and press censorship were abolished and freedom for political parties was restored. Opponents of the regime, including Nahas and Al-Hudaibi, the leader of the Muslim Brotherhood, were released from prison. Nasser, however, supported by both the army and newly-formed workers' organizations, was able to regain the premiership and the chairmanship of the Revolutionary Command Council in April; Neguib had suffered a defeat and his liberal measures were rescinded. When in October a member of the Muslim Brotherhood attempted to assassinate Nasser, its leaders and several thousand alleged supporters were arrested and in subsequent trials a number of death sentences were passed. On November 14th, 1954, General Neguib was relieved of the office of President and accused of being involved in a Muslim Brotherhood conspiracy against the regime. He was placed under house arrest and Colonel Nasser became acting head of state.

A settlement of the Sudan and Suez problems had been facilitated by the expulsion of King Farouk. The claim to the joint monarchy of Egypt and the Sudan was dropped and negotiations with Sudanese leaders were helped by the fact that Neguib himself was half-Sudanese and popular in the Sudan. An Anglo-Egyptian agreement, signed on February 12th, 1953, ended the Condominium and offered the Sudanese the choice of independence or union with Egypt. Egyptian expectation that they would choose the latter was disappointed; the overthrow of Neguib and the suppression of the Muslim Brotherhood fed the century-old suspicion of Egyptian motives.

An Anglo-Egyptian agreement on Suez was signed on October 19th, 1954; this provided for the withdrawal of British troops from the Canal Zone within twenty months. Certain installations were to be maintained by British civilian technicians and the Egyptian Government would assume responsibility for the remainder of the base. The base might be reactivated by Britain in the event of an armed attack by an outside power on any of the Arab League states or Turkey. The agreement recognized the international importance of the Suez Canal (which was described as "an integral part of Egypt") and expressed the determination of both parties to uphold the 1888 convention.

Under Nasser Egypt began to assert her importance in world affairs. He sought influence in three circles: the Islamic, the African and the Arab, and his visit to the Bandung conference in 1955 added a fourth: the "non-aligned". Egypt led the opposition among certain Arab states to the Baghdad Pact (on which was founded the Central Treaty Organization). In October 1955 Egypt concluded defence agreements with Syria and with Saudi Arabia and in April 1956 a military pact was signed between Egypt, Saudi Arabia and the Yemen. Tension with Israel remained high, and raids and counter-raids across the border of the Gaza Strip called for unceasing vigilance on the part of the United Nations observers stationed on the frontier. In September 1955 Nasser announced an arms deal with Czechoslovakia which was to supply large quantities of military equipment, including Soviet tanks and aircraft, in return for cotton and rice. In July 1956 he had talks with Marshal Tito of Yugoslavia and Pandit Nehru of India and subsequently maintained close relations with these two countries.

In 1956 a constitutional basis for Colonel Nasser's authority was established. A new constitution providing for a strong presidency was proclaimed in January and on June 23rd approved in a plebiscite in which the citizens of the Egyptian Republic also elected Nasser as President.

THE SUEZ CRISIS AND ITS CONSEQUENCES: 1956-57

President Nasser's policy of non-alignment, which implied willingness to deal with both power blocs, was followed in the Egyptian attempt to obtain funds for the ambitious High Dam project at Aswan. By this project the Egyptian Government aimed to increase cultivable land and generate electricity for industrialization, which was seen as the main solution to Egypt's increasing population problem. Following offers of assistance from the United States and Britain and, separately, by the U.S.S.R., the International Bank for Reconstruction and Development offered a loan of $200 million in February 1956, on condition that the United States and Britain lent a total of $70 million and that the agreement of the riparian states to the scheme was obtained; Egypt was to provide local services and material.

The last British troops were withdrawn from Egypt in June 1956, in accordance with the 1954 agreement. Relations with the West were not helped, however, by Egyptian opposition to the Baghdad Pact and strong propaganda attacks on Britain, France and the United States. On July 20th the United States and Britain withdrew their offers of finance for the High Dam, pointing out that agreement between the riparian states had not been achieved and that Egypt's ability to devote adequate resources to the scheme was doubtful. The U.S.S.R. made no compensating move. On July 26th President Nasser announced that the Suez Canal Company had been nationalized and that revenue from the Canal would be used to finance the High Dam.

Britain, France and the United States protested strongly at this action and after an international conference had met in London in August a committee under the chairmanship of Mr. Menzies, the Prime Minister of Australia, went to Cairo to submit proposals for the operation of the Canal under an international system. These were rejected by the Egyptian Government. At a second London conference, in September, a Suez Canal Users' Association took shape and was later joined by sixteen states. On October 13th the UN Security Council voted on an Anglo-French resolution embodying basic principles for a settlement agreed earlier between the British, French and Egyptian Foreign Ministers in the presence of the UN Secretary-General. The first part of this, setting out the agreed principles, was adopted unanimously; the second, endorsing the proposals of the first London conference and inviting Egypt to make prompt proposals providing no less effective guarantees to users, was vetoed by the U.S.S.R.

Britain and France, thus frustrated in their attempts to retain some measure of control over the Suez Canal, at this stage reached a secret understanding with Israel involving military action. Following the disclosure on October 24th that a unified military command had been formed by Egypt, Jordan and Syria, Israeli forces on October 29th crossed into Sinai, ostensibly to attack Egyptian *fedayeen* bases, and advanced towards the Suez Canal. On October 30th France and Britain called on Israel and Egypt to cease warlike action and withdraw their forces from either side of the Canal; Egypt was requested to agree to an Anglo-French force moving temporarily into key positions at Port Said, Ismailia and Suez. Israel agreed but Egypt refused. The same day in the UN Security Council Britain and France vetoed United

States and Soviet resolutions calling for an immediate Israeli withdrawal and calling on all UN members to refrain from the use of force or the threat of force.

Anglo-French air operations against Egypt began on October 31st but paratroops and seaborne forces landed in the Port Said area only on November 5th. Meanwhile, on November 2nd, the UN General Assembly called for a cease-fire and two days later adopted a Canadian proposal to create a United Nations Emergency Force to supervise the ending of the hostilities. On November 6th, following heavy United States pressure, the British Prime Minister, Sir Anthony Eden, announced that, subject to confirmation that Egypt and Israel had accepted an unconditional cease-fire, the armed conflict would end at midnight.

The organization of the UN force was rapidly put in hand and the first units reached Egypt on November 15th. The withdrawal of the Anglo-French forces was completed the following month. The Israelis, who had occupied the entire Sinai peninsula, withdrew from all areas except the Gaza strip, which they wished to prevent becoming a base for more raids, and Sharm el-Sheikh at the entrance to the Gulf of Aqaba, which commanded the seaway to the port of Eilat. These areas were returned to Egyptian control in March 1957 after pressure on Israel by the United States.

The Suez Canal, which had been blocked by the Egyptians, was cleared by a UN salvage fleet and reopened at the end of March 1957. The Egyptian Government rejected in February a plan proposed by Britain, France, Norway and the United States, for the Canal to be operated by Egypt but the tolls collected by an outside agency. The Egyptian terms, announced on March 18th, which users of the Canal were subsequently obliged to accept, were full control by the Egyptian Canal Authority and respect for the Constantinople Convention of 1888. Disputes would be settled in accordance with the UN Charter or referred to the International Court of Justice.

UNION OF EGYPT AND SYRIA

Elections to the Egyptian National Assembly, provided for in the 1956 constitution, were held in July 1957. Only candidates approved by President Nasser and his colleagues were permitted to stand and it was clear that the 350 members elected (who included women) were not expected to exert much influence on the government. The first sitting of the assembly was held on July 22nd, against the background of the disclosure of an alleged plot to assassinate President Nasser in April. In a speech to the assembly the President mentioned with favour the idea of a federation between Egypt and Syria.

Following the defence agreement in 1955, discussions had been held the following year and in 1957 on union between the two states. Both countries were aligned against the West and looked to the U.S.S.R. and other Communist states for support, and in Syria pro-Egyptian elements were in the ascendant. On February 1st, 1958, following a visit to Cairo by President Quwatly and other Syrian leaders, the union of Egypt and Syria under the title of the United Arab Republic (U.A.R.) was announced. Both parliaments formally approved the union on February 5th and seventeen principles on which the constitution of the U.A.R. would be based were proclaimed. A plebiscite, held in both countries on February 21st, confirmed the union and made Nasser the first President of the United Arab Republic.

Under the provisional constitution issued on March 5th the President was head of state and supreme commander of the armed forces. He was authorized to appoint four Vice-Presidents, a Cabinet and an Assembly of 400 members, at least half of whom were to be drawn from the parliaments at Cairo and Damascus. The President could convene and dissolve the Assembly, the chief functions of which were to approve government laws and decisions, and he could himself legislate when it was not sitting. The two Regions of Egypt and Syria were each to have an Executive Council, appointed by the President. A National Union, to be formed on lines laid down by the President, was to replace existing political parties and to mobilize efforts to build the nation on a sound basis.

The implementation of the union took time, and it was not until July 21st, 1960, that the first National Assembly of the U.A.R. was opened in Cairo by President Nasser. It consisted of 400 deputies from Egypt and 200 from Syria, appointed by him from candidates nominated by the National Union. Over half the deputies were former members of the dissolved national assemblies of Egypt and Syria. Early in 1961 the President entrusted the National Assembly with the task of drawing up a permanent constitution for the U.A.R.

EXTERNAL RELATIONS: 1958-61

During this period President Nasser was actively concerned with changes in the rest of the Arab world.

An invitation was extended to other Arab states to join the new Union and in March 1958 the U.A.R. and the Yemen entered into a loose association referred to as the United Arab States, under which separate governments were to be maintained but policies coordinated through a supreme council. This association did not prosper, however, and was terminated by the U.A.R. in December 1961.

The reaction of the Hashemite monarchies of Iraq and Jordan to the new relationship between Egypt and Syria (both of which had been accused of complicity in an attempted *coup d'état* in Jordan in 1957) was immediately to form a federation themselves, styled the Arab Union. This was subjected to U.A.R. propaganda attacks which stigmatized its formation as a hostile move inspired by the West. It did not survive the revolution in Iraq in July 1958.

In the Lebanon, where the government of President Chamoun was attacked by U.A.R. propaganda for pro-Western policies but where popular opinion was sympathetic to the U.A.R., a serious insurrection occurred in May 1958. The government alleged infiltration of arms and men from Syria into rebel-controlled areas and appealed to the UN Security Council which sent observers.

The military revolution in Iraq in July, in which the royal family and the Prime Minister, Nuri al-Said, were murdered, destroyed the only Arab regime in the Middle East to have identified itself explicitly with the West. The immediate dispatch of American troops to the Lebanon and British forces to Jordan drew strong protests from the U.A.R. which were echoed by the U.S.S.R. The U.S.A. and Britain gave warning of the grave consequences of any conflict between their forces and those under the control of Egypt and Syria. President Nasser visited Moscow and on his return received in Damascus a delegation from the new republican regime in Baghdad. A joint communiqué on July 19th declared that the U.A.R. and Iraq would assist each other to repel any foreign aggression. A United Nations resolution sponsored by Arab states in August, which welcomed assurances that they would refrain from action calculated to change each other's system of government, prepared the way for the withdrawal of the British and American forces.

A conference at Damascus in February 1959, attended by Jordan, the Lebanon, the U.A.R. and Saudi Arabia, led to the settlement of differences between Syria and the Lebanon, where the neutralist General Chehab had succeeded President Chamoun.

U.A.R. propaganda voiced support for a revolt which broke out at Mosul in Iraq in March 1959, and there were mass demonstrations in Cairo and Damascus in sympathy with the rebels. The Iraqi Government of General Kassem countered with the accusation that the revolt had been engineered from Syria. The political committee of the Arab League met at Beirut in April in an attempt to reduce the prevailing tension but Iraq took no part in the principal activities of the League until 1960 when relations with the U.A.R. improved.

Diplomatic relations between the U.A.R. and Jordan, severed at the time of the Iraqi revolution, were resumed in August 1959, but there were further violent propaganda exchanges in 1960, the U.A.R. criticizing Jordan for continuing to accept aid from Britain and the United States and Jordan accusing the U.A.R. of complicity in the assassination of the Jordanian Prime Minister in Amman.

Agreement between Egypt and the Sudan on the sharing of the Nile waters after the completion of the Aswan High Dam was reached in November 1959 and a trade and customs convention was also signed.

President Nasser's hostility to the West found favour with the U.S.S.R., with which the U.A.R. established closer ties during these years. He made a state visit to Moscow in the spring of 1958 and in a joint communiqué on May 15th endorsed the broad objectives of Soviet policy whilst the U.S.S.R. declared support for Arab unity. Purchases of arms, military aircraft and industrial equipment were made from the Soviet Union at favourable prices and three submarines were bought from Poland. Soviet aid for the construction of five airfields and for industrial projects in Egypt was announced in December 1958 and the same month an agreement was concluded which ensured Soviet assistance for the building of the Aswan High Dam. Nevertheless, President Nasser was not inhibited from denouncing Communist activities in the Syrian region and from taking measures to circumscribe them. Work on the first stage of the High Dam began in January 1960 and it was announced that the U.S.S.R. had agreed to participate in the second stage, due to begin in 1962. Soviet assistance for shipyard construction at Alexandria and for industrial projects, including steel and engineering plants, irrigation schemes, and oil, chemical, food and textile enterprises, was announced early in 1960.

Relations with the West improved during 1959 and 1960. Through the mediation of the International Bank for Reconstruction and Development an agreement with Britain was signed on March 1st, 1959, providing for the payment by the U.A.R. of £27½ million as compensation for British private property taken over at the time of the Suez crisis in 1956. Diplomatic relations with Britain were resumed at chargé d'affaires level in December 1959 and raised to ambassadorial level early in 1961. A $56.5 million loan from the International Bank was announced in December 1959 for improvement to the Suez Canal. Financial aid agreements between the U.A.R. and the U.S.A. were signed in March 1960, providing for the supply of surplus U.S. farm products and loans totalling $32.5 million for economic development.

SYRIAN WITHDRAWAL FROM U.A.R.

President Nasser replaced the two Regional Executive Councils and the Central Cabinet of the U.A.R. with a single Central Government in August 1961. By this time, however, the increasing subordination of Syria was breeding resentment and the issue of decrees in July of that year nationalizing most large-scale industrial and commercial concerns had provoked further Syrian discontent. Colonel Seraj, a Syrian Vice-President of the U.A.R., resigned on September 26th and on September 28th the Syrian army seized control in Damascus and Syria withdrew from the U.A.R. President Nasser at first called for resistance to the Syrian *coup d'état* but, when the rebels were seen to be in firm control, said on October 5th that he would not oppose recognition of Syria's independence.

The loss of Syria was a bitter blow to President Nasser and his Egyptian colleagues who now set about a re-examination of their policies. In a speech on October 16th Nasser spoke of the illusion that "reconciliation with reaction on a patriotic basis" was possible. "Reaction" had infiltrated into the National Union, which must be converted into "a revolutionary means for the national masses alone"; the machinery of the state must be reorganized. Measures against "reactionaries", including arrests and the sequestration of property, were announced three days later; expropriations by the end of the year affected nearly 1,000 persons who included Syrians and Lebanese.

The U.A.R. Government (Egypt retained the full title) was re-formed on October 18th and a National

Congress of Popular Forces, consisting of 1,750 delegates, representing not geographical areas but economic and professional interests and other social groups, met in Cairo on May 21st, 1962. President Nasser presented the National Congress with a draft National Charter outlining his programme for developing the U.A.R. on Arab socialist lines. The Charter states that imperialists must be evicted, the power of feudalists destroyed and state control of finance and industry established. A new democratic system of government was proposed, based on the Arab Socialist Union (replacing the National Union) and including popular councils at least half the members of which would be workers or *fellahin*. The President emphasized the need to increase the national income and stressed the importance of birth control to contain the alarming growth in the population. As for inter-Arab relations, the Charter placed "unity of objectives before unity of ranks". The National Congress approved the Charter on June 30th and then dispersed.

MORE ATTEMPTS AT UNION

Syrian complaints of Egyptian interference in her internal affairs provoked angry exchanges at a meeting of the Arab League Council in August 1962, as a result of which the U.A.R. boycotted all League activities and withdrew financial support until the downfall in March 1963 of the regime which had brought about Syria's secession. Normal relations were then resumed.

The Syrian *coup d'état* had been preceded by the overthrow in February 1963 of the regime of General Kassem in Iraq. These changes in power brought Syria and Iraq into closer alignment with Egypt and it was announced on April 17th that agreement had been reached on the formation of a federation of the three countries under the name of the United Arab Republic. During the first two years government was to be in the hands of a President and a Presidential Council of six members from each country. It was widely expected that a referendum, to be held within five months, would give Colonel Nasser the post of President with wide powers. Rivalries, however, arose in both Baghdad and Damascus between supporters of the Baath Party and "Nasserists" and by August President Nasser had withdrawn from the agreement, claiming that the Baathists had set up one-party dictatorships in Syria and Iraq and ignored his insistence on wider nationalist representation.

A month later President Arif of Iraq called for a Baathist union of the three countries, but after the expulsion of Baath leaders from Iraq in November 1963 and the consolidation of power in Arif's hands the unity movement between Iraq and Syria fell apart and Iraq and Egypt again moved closer together. An agreement was concluded on May 25th, 1964, to establish a joint Presidency Council, consisting of the two Presidents and six members from each country, with a secretariat and committees in Cairo. A Unified Political Command was set up in December 1964 to bring about political unity and co-ordinate foreign policy, the armed forces, national security, economic planning and education.

The first meeting of the United Political Command was held in Cairo in May 1965 but the succeeding year saw little progress towards unity. In Iraq an attempted *coup* against President Arif, by the Prime Minister, Abdul Razzaq (who subsequently took refuge in Cairo), and elements favouring immediate and complete union with Egypt, failed. Visits to Cairo were made by the new Iraqi Prime Minister, Dr. Bazzaz, in October 1965 and by President Arif the following February, but the United Political Command did not meet again until March 1966. There were signs that this Iraqi Government preferred a looser relationship with Egypt to the integration favoured by Iraqi "Nasserists". Suspicions of Egyptian intentions were strengthened in June 1966 when Abdul Razzaq attempted a second *coup*, which also failed but which provided evidence of Egyptian complicity.

President Nasser took an important initiative in Arab League affairs following the announcement by Israel in 1963 of her intention to take water for irrigation purposes from the River Jordan where it runs through Lake Tiberias. Neighbouring Arab states had for a number of years refused to agree, on political grounds, to the planned use of the Jordan waters and Israel had proceeded unilaterally with a major irrigation project. At President Nasser's invitation a conference of Arab heads of state met in Cairo in January 1964 to discuss what should be done to counter the Israeli move. This Arab summit conference recommended Arab diversion of the Jordan headwaters, and at the same time agreed that Arab states should follow a policy of "live and let live" among themselves.

A second Arab summit meeting, held in Alexandria in September 1964, decided that a dam should be built on the Yarmuk River, a tributary of the Jordan forming the border between Jordan and Syria, and an irrigation scheme developed in Jordan. A fund would be established to strengthen the armies of Syria, the Lebanon and Jordan over the next five years against possible Israeli reprisals. The U.A.R., Saudi Arabia, Libya, Morocco and the Yemen were to make annual financial contributions for this purpose and the three armies were to have a unified command under the Egyptian General Ali Amer, although movement across the frontiers of friendly states was not to be an automatic right. A further £E 1 million was set aside for the formation of a Palestine Liberation Organization.

The Arab reconciliation and presentation of a united front lasted until the spring of 1965. Iraq, Kuwait, Yemen (Republic), Algeria and the Lebanon continued to follow President Nasser's lead, only Syrian critics complaining that U.A.R. policy was not sufficiently anti-Israeli. U.A.R. relations with Jordan improved strikingly and, after a conference of heads of Arab governments in Cairo in January 1965 to discuss co-ordination of Arab policies, King Hussein, previously the object of U.A.R. attacks and derision, himself paid a visit to Cairo. State visits to Cairo were made by President Bourguiba of Tunisia in February and King Hassan of Morocco in March. Only King Faisal of Saudi Arabia remained aloof, seeing the presence of Egyptian troops in the Yemen, in support of the republicans in the civil war which had begun in 1962, as evidence of U.A.R. expansionism and a threat to the Saudi position as the dominant power in the Arabian peninsula.

The general atmosphere of cordiality was shattered in April 1965 by President Bourguiba who criticized Arab policy on Israel as unrealistic and suggested negotiation with Israel on the basis of the 1947 UN partition plan (which would have involved Arab recognition of Israel, Israeli withdrawal to the borders proposed in the plan and the return of the Palestinian Arab refugees). This was attacked by the U.A.R. as a betrayal of the agreement at Alexandria in 1964 that the Arabs should work in concert. Further statements by President Bourguiba, who was not supported on this issue by any other Arab state, were followed by riots in Cairo and Tunis and the breaking of diplomatic relations with U.A.R.

At the third Arab summit conference, at Casablanca in September 1965, President Nasser found himself on the defensive, in the face of charges made by President Bourguiba (who did not attend the conference) of attempting to dominate the Arab world and interfering in the internal affairs of other Arab states. The conference re-emphasized the need for Arab solidarity and called upon Arab countries not to interfere in each other's domestic affairs by encouraging subversive movements or by attacks in the press.

In the Yemen, despite Egyptian support, the republican regime seemed no closer to victory over the royalists, who held the mountainous regions of the north-east and were assisted by Saudi Arabian finance and supplies of arms. This military stalemate and the financial burden of maintaining some 50,000 troops in the Yemen moved President Nasser to attempt to disengage. On August 24th, 1965, after a two-day conference at Jeddah, he and King Faisal reached agreement on a peace plan to end the civil war. A cease-fire was to be declared immediately, a national conference of Yemeni leaders was to meet to form a provisional government, Saudi Arabia was to cease supplying arms to the royalist forces, and Egyptian troops were to be withdrawn by November 1966.

The conference of republicans and royalists at Haradh in November 1965 ended in deadlock, however, owing to republican intransigence, and the Egyptian troops remained in the Yemen. On February 22nd, 1966, the day the British Government announced that British forces would leave Aden and South Arabia when that territory became independent in 1968, President Nasser stated that Egyptian troops would not be withdrawn until the revolution in the Yemen could "defend itself against the conspiracies of imperialism and reactionaries".

CHANGES OF INTERNATIONAL ALIGNMENT

The years 1964 and 1965 saw a deterioration of U.A.R. relations with the West and increasing dependence on the Soviet Union.

Relations with the United States were adversely affected by U.A.R. support for the Stanleyville rebels in the Congo during the winter of 1964–65, and following the airlift of Belgian paratroops in U.S. aircraft in the Stanleyville rescue operation the U.S.I.S. library in Cairo was burned down. This led to an embargo by the U.S. Government on supplies of surplus wheat, badly needed by the U.A.R. Diplomatic relations with Britain, already worsened by Egyptian encouragement of dissident elements in South Arabia, were severed by the U.A.R. in December 1965 over the Rhodesia issue, in common with eight other members of the Organization of African Unity. The new elasticity of Gaullist policy led to improved relations between the U.A.R. and France, however, and in 1965 official visits were exchanged and French financial aid was made available.

With West Germany relations deteriorated after the discovery of an arms agreement between that country and Israel. When in February 1965 the East German Premier, Herr Ulbricht, visited the U.A.R., where he was accorded full honours, West Germany reacted by stopping further economic aid to the U.A.R. and entering into diplomatic relations with Israel. In retaliation the U.A.R. broke off diplomatic relations with West Germany, as did the other Arab states except Libya, Morocco, and Tunisia, and relations were established with East Germany.

Relations with the U.S.S.R. had been strengthened in May 1964 when the Soviet Premier, Nikita Khruschev, made a sixteen-day visit to Egypt to attend the ceremony marking the completion of the first stage of the Aswan High Dam, being built with Soviet aid. President Nasser paid his third visit to the U.S.S.R. in August 1965 and (Khruschev having been overthrown the new Soviet Premier, Alexei Kosygin, visited the U.A.R. in May 1966, expressing support for U.A.R. policies and again demonstrating Soviet interest in the Middle East.

DOMESTIC TROUBLES

Although President Nasser obtained over 99 per cent of the votes cast in the presidential referendum in March 1965, there were subsequently more signs of discontent in the U.A.R. than at any time since he had come to power. In a speech to Arab students during his visit to Moscow in August 1965, he disclosed that a plot against his life had been discovered. Widespread arrests were later made and changes in the Ministry of the Interior were announced. In the trials which followed, in which the accused included about 200 members of the banned Muslim Brotherhood, seven persons were sentenced to death, and many others to long terms of imprisonment, for plotting to assassinate Nasser and overthrow his government.

In September 1965 a new government headed by Zakaria Mohieddin replaced that of Ali Sabri, who became Secretary-General of the Arab Socialist Union. Thereafter, administrative changes were made and the security system was tightened up. Taxation was increased and measures of retrenchment were introduced because of increasing economic difficulties, particularly the acute shortage of foreign exchange. United States wheat supplies were continued, credits from France, Japan and Italy and a loan from Kuwait were obtained and there were increased drawings from the International Monetary Fund. Nevertheless the level of imports, particularly food to feed the growing population, and the debt service burden resulting from the first five-year plan caused a continuing drain on foreign exchange reserves and the U.A.R. faced a balance of payments crisis. A mission from the International Bank for Reconstruction and Development, which visited Cairo in January 1966, subsequently made recommendations for stabilization and missions of Egyptian bankers and finance officials visited Western countries, including Britain, to discuss credits and debt repayment. The second five-year plan was revised and extended over seven years and President Nasser gave public warnings that sacrifices were necessary in every field as Egypt lacked the foreign currency to pay for imports. He refused, however, to abandon the expensive commitment in the Yemen. Zakaria Mohieddin's replacement in September 1966 by Sidki Soliman (a technocrat who retained his post as Minister of the High Dam) was seen as the outcome of disagreement over retrenchment measures. When the U.A.R. defaulted on repayments due to the International Monetary Fund in December 1966, the country was seen to be on the verge of bankruptcy.

WIDENING RIFT WITH SAUDI ARABIA

The year 1966 saw a rapprochement between the U.A.R. and Syria. A trade, payments and technical co-operation agreement was concluded in July and on November 4th a five-year joint defence agreement was signed. This provided for a joint defence council and a joint command, military operations being under the overall control of the U.A.R. Chief of Army General Staff, and stated that armed aggression against either country would be considered as aggression against both.

The rift between the U.A.R. and Saudi Arabia widened. President Nasser in February 1966 expressed opposition to an Islamic grouping which King Faisal was promoting, and in the succeeding months propaganda warfare between the two countries was intensified. In the middle of the year the President gave notice that he would not attend an Arab summit conference with Saudi Arabia and Jordan, both of whom he stigmatized for obtaining British and United States military aid, and called for the indefinite postponement of the conference planned for September. A majority of Arab states agreed, but in October Tunisia broke off relations with the U.A.R. over continued differences on Arab League policies.

In the Yemen Egyptian forces had been withdrawn from northern and eastern areas and concentrated in the triangle between Sana'a, Hodeida and Taiz. Egyptian control over the republican armed forces and administration was increased and when, in September 1966, after President Sallal had returned to the Yemen from a year's absence in Cairo, the republican Prime Minister, Hassan al-Amri, and seven senior members of his cabinet visited Egypt to make a plea for greater independence, they were arrested and detained there. The following month about 100 senior Yemen officials were dismissed and arrests and executions were carried out.

In November 1966 Egyptian aircraft carried out raids on Saudi Arabian villages near the Yemen border. In January 1967, after air attacks with bombs and rockets on royalist-held areas in the Yemen, the village of Kitaf was bombed and over 100 deaths caused, allegedly, by poison gas.

February 1967 saw the closing of two Egyptian banks in Saudi Arabia and the seizure of Saudi property (including King Faisal's) in the U.A.R. In the same month, following President Nasser's accusation that Jordan and Saudi Arabia were "lackey and reactionary regimes" serving the interests of imperialism and allied with the Muslim Brotherhood in Egypt, the Jordanian ambassador was withdrawn from Cairo.

WAR WITH ISRAEL

The events of May 1967 were to transform the Middle East scene. There had been an increase of Syrian guerrilla activities in Israel during the previous six months and on April 7th the tension had led to fighting in the Tiberias area in which six Syrian aircraft had been shot down. Israeli warnings to the Syrian Government, culminating on May 12th in the threat by Premier Eshkol of severe reprisals if terrorist activities were not controlled, evoked Syrian allegations that Israel was about to mount a large-scale attack on Syria. President Nasser, who had been reproached for not aiding Syria in the April fighting in accordance with the mutual defence agreement, responded immediately, moving large numbers of troops to the Israel border. He secured the dissolution of the UN Emergency Force, whose presence on the Egyptian side of the frontier depended on Egyptian permission, and re-occupied the gun emplacement at Sharm el Sheikh on the Straits of Tiran. He later justified these steps by claiming that he had received Syrian and Soviet warnings that Israeli troops were concentrated on the Syrian border (an allegation subsequently disproved by reports of UN truce observers) and an invasion of Syria was imminent.

When on May 23rd President Nasser closed the Straits of Tiran to Israeli shipping, thereby effectively blockading the Israeli port of Eilat, his prestige in the Arab world reached an unparalleled height. Britain and the United States protested that the Gulf of Aqaba was an international waterway; Israel regarded the blockade of the Straits as an unambiguous act of war. A British attempt to produce a declaration by the maritime powers on freedom of passage through the Straits met with little enthusiasm when it became clear that only by force would the blockade be lifted. As tension increased, with frequent belligerent pronouncements from Arab leaders and the threat by President Nasser that any aggressive act by Israel would lead to an all-out battle in which the Arab aim would be Israel's destruction, King Hussein of Jordan concluded a mutual defence pact with the U.A.R.

which was immediately joined by Iraq. Gestures of support were made to Nasser by all Arab leaders, including President Bourguiba and King Faisal.

On the morning of June 5th Israel launched large-scale air attacks on Egyptian, Jordanian, Syrian and Iraqi airfields and Israeli ground forces made rapid advances into the Gaza Strip, Sinai and western Jordan; there was also fighting on the Israeli-Syrian border. The outcome was decided within hours by the air strikes, which destroyed the bulk of the Arab air forces, and the Israeli ground forces were everywhere successful. By June 10th, when all participants had accepted the UN Security Council's call for a cease-fire, Israeli troops were in control of the Sinai peninsula as far as the Suez Canal (including Sharm el Sheikh), the west bank of the Jordan (including the Old City of Jerusalem), the Gaza Strip and Syrian territory extending twelve miles from the Israel border. The Suez Canal was blocked by Egypt in the course of the fighting, and Britain and the United States were falsely accused by President Nasser and King Hussein of giving air support to Israel. The allegation was withdrawn by King Hussein a few days later but not before an embargo had been applied by the oil-producing Arab states against Britain and the United States, and also the Federal Republic of Germany.

On June 9th, the day after he had accepted the cease-fire, President Nasser announced his resignation in a speech in which he assumed full responsibility for the nation's plight, but the following day, in response to huge street demonstrations of popular support, he agreed to continue in office. A number of senior army officers were immediately replaced and on June 19th Nasser took over the duties of Prime Minister and Secretary-General of the Arab Socialist Union.

The implications of the catastrophe were only gradually realized. It was estimated that the loss of revenue from the Suez Canal, from oil produced in Sinai and from tourism amounted to some £12.5 million a month, or almost half Egypt's foreign currency earnings. Also, the withdrawal of a large part of the Egyptian force in the Yemen reduced Nasser's ability to influence affairs both in that country and in Aden and South Arabia (which became independent as the Republic of Southern Yemen on November 30th, 1967, after the withdrawal of British troops).

The Soviet Union, which had given the Arab cause strong verbal support throughout the crisis, continued to take a strong pro-Arab stand at the United Nations and President Podgorny paid a lengthy visit to Cairo to discuss future Egyptian policy. Although the Soviet resolutions were rejected in both the Security Council and the General Assembly, Soviet assistance took the more concrete form of quickly replacing about half the lost Egyptian aircraft and providing other military supplies. By the end of October it was estimated that about 2,500 Russian military instructors had been sent to Egypt. Despite this military aid, Soviet leaders seemed anxious to discourage hopes of a resumption of hostilities, however. Further economic assistance was also offered by the Soviet Union and in May 1968 an agreement was announced for the construction of a steel complex at Helwan.

Israel demanded direct negotiations with the Arab states for a peace settlement but the fourth conference of Arab heads of state, held in Khartoum at the end of August 1967, decided against recognition or negotiation with Israel. At this conference, in which Syria did not participate, it was agreed that the embargo on oil supplies to Western countries should be lifted, that the Suez Canal should remain closed until Israeli forces were withdrawn, and that Saudi Arabia, Kuwait and Libya should give special aid of £95 million a year to the U.A.R. (and also £40 million a year to Jordan) until the "effects of the aggression" were eliminated. King Faisal and President Nasser announced their agreement on a peace plan for the Yemen under which Egyptian troops were to be withdrawn within three months and Saudi Arabia was to stop supplying the royalists; the withdrawal was subsequently completed by December (President Sallal being deposed by republican leaders in November).

In October, following repeated violations of the cease-fire by both Egyptian and Israeli forces in the Suez Canal area, Egyptian patrol boats sank the Israeli destroyer *Eilat* off the Sinai coast; Israel replied with an artillery bombardment of Egyptian oil refineries and other installations at Suez, causing such extensive damage that Egyptian oil had to be sent to Aden to be refined. The Security Council condemned all violations of the cease-fire and on November 22nd adopted a British resolution laying down principles for a just and lasting peace in the Middle East and authorizing the appointment of a special UN representative to assist in bringing about a settlement. Dr. Gunnar Jarring was appointed the following day and subsequently had separate discussions with Israeli and Arab leaders, including President Nasser, which continued at various times throughout 1968 and into 1969.

U.A.R. AFTER THE JUNE WAR

Meanwhile President Nasser faced daunting economic difficulties and a disturbed political situation in Egypt. An austerity budget had been framed in July 1967. The cost of re-equipping the armed forces forced a cut in investment, in spite of Soviet aid and assistance from other Arab governments. Socialist policies were still followed, as was shown by the decision to nationalize the wholesale trade, announced in October. The continuing shortage of foreign exchange made desirable an improvement in the U.A.R.'s relations with the West and in December diplomatic relations with Britain were resumed. A bridging loan from British, West German and Italian banks, obtained in February 1968, enabled the U.A.R. to make the repayments to the International Monetary Fund which had been due since the end of 1966, and in March the IMF approved further drawings. Another hopeful development was the increased production of oil from Egyptian oilfields, which made up for the loss of Sinai.

As a result of the military débâcle the Egyptian army was subjected to major reorganization, involving the dismissal of large numbers of officers. The reaction of Field-Marshal Abdel Hakim Amer was to plan a *coup d'état*, but his intentions became known. His arrest, together with other senior army officers, on August 30th was followed by the arrests of a former Minister of the Interior, Abbas Radwan, and the chief of the central intelligence department. The suicide of Amer was announced by the U.A.R. Government on September 15th. At the end of October senior officers of the air force were put on trial and in February 1968 the former air force commander was imprisoned for fifteen years; other senior air force officers also received prison sentences. In January 1968 the armed forces supreme command was reorganized.

Widespread demonstrations of students and workers took place in Cairo, Helwan and other main centres, towards the end of February. Initially, in protest at the leniency of sentences on air force officers, they revealed widespread popular disillusion and discontent to a degree unprecedented since the revolution of 1952. A number of persons were killed in clashes with police, and the universities were closed; nevertheless President Nasser realized the need for immediate conciliatory action. Re-trials were ordered and sweeping cabinet changes announced, a number of civilian experts in various fields being brought in. Ali Sabry, who had been reinstated as Secretary-General of the Arab Socialist Union in January, was also included but Zakaria Mohieddin left the government. President Nasser continued to exercise the functions of Prime Minister.

On March 30th President Nasser announced a new plan for building a modern state in Egypt based on democracy, science and technology. The single party would remain but there would be free elections from top to bottom of the Arab Socialist Union and changes were promised among leaders in all spheres. An announcement of the distribution to the people of land taken over by the state or reclaimed was made on April 6th. In a plebiscite on May 2nd the "Declaration of March 30th" was overwhelmingly approved. The first Arab Socialist Union elections were held in June; the 75,000 persons chosen then elected a national congress in July; this in turn chose a central committee which then chose the party's higher executive. These proceedings however, did not appear to arouse much public interest. President Nasser dissolved the U.A.R. National Assembly on November 14th and elections for a new Assembly were held on January 8th 1969.

November 1968 saw further student riots, resulting in many injuries and some deaths, in Alexandria and Mansoura. The universities were again closed. Although these disturbances were officially attributed to the activities of an Israeli agent arrested by the police and to indignation at the continued occupation of Sinai by Israeli forces, they were seen by many observers as further evidence of frustration with the restrictions imposed by President Nasser's government and of disillusion with its performance, particularly in relation to Israel. Moreover, in uncertain health, his popularity diminished, the President appeared in 1968 to be increasingly isolated and exposed.

Deprived of foreign exchange by the continued closure of the Canal and the drop in the tourist trade, the U.A.R. remained dependent on the regular aid payments from Saudi Arabia, Kuwait and Libya and on Soviet assistance, both humiliating to a people strongly nationalist in outlook. There were signs that the civilian economic ministers favoured some relaxation of over-rigid state control in industry and more encouragement of private enterprise and foreign investment. Military expenditure in 1968 and 1969 remained high. Soviet arms deliveries continued, as also did the presence of about 3,000 Russian military advisers and instructors.

Two heavy exchanges of artillery fire across the Suez Canal in September and October 1968, reportedly begun by U.A.R. forces in an effort to raise Egyptian morale, were followed by an Israeli airborne commando raid some 230 kilometres north of Aswan in which a bridge over the Nile and an important transformer station at Nagh Hammadi were seriously damaged. The oil refinery at Suez, shelled by Israeli guns in October 1967, remained out of action and the greater part of the population of Suez, Ismailia and Port Said were evacuated. Despite these reverses the U.A.R. Government showed little sign of changing its stance on the Arab-Israel question. Even if it had wished to do so it would have been hampered by the popular support shown in Egypt and elsewhere in the Arab world for the Palestinian guerrillas, the fedayeen, whose activities against Israel were attracting much publicity. In fact, in a speech to the National Assembly on January 20th, 1969, President Nasser said that the U.A.R. unconditionally placed its resources at the disposal of the fedayeen.

The efforts of Dr. Jarring, the representative of the UN Secretary-General, to bring Israel, the U.A.R. and Jordan closer together had, by the end of 1968, yielded little success. In April 1969, following initiatives by the U.S.S.R. and France, those two countries together with Britain and the United States, as permanent members of the Security Council, began talks at the United Nations in New York in an attempt to promote a settlement. These talks, after a recess between July and December 1969, were resumed in December 1969, but no settlement was reached.

In December 1969 President Nasser attended an Arab Summit meeting at Rabat, the capital of Morocco. Differences between the Arab leaders hindered collaboration and the meeting ended without any communiqué being issued. After the ending of the summit meeting President Nasser met the leaders of Libya and the Sudan in Tripoli, and at later talks in Cairo produced plans for military and economic co-operation between the three countries. In February 1970 President Nasser met with the leaders of Jordan, Syria, Sudan and Iraq in Cairo, where they affirmed anew "their determination to liberate violated Arab territories".

Against the background of these developments, artillery exchanges across the Suez Canal began again in March and April 1969. Two Egyptian commando raids on Israeli positions were made in April and were followed by another, less successful, Israeli raid on bridges, the barrage and transmission lines in the Nagh Hammadi area. This pattern of sporadic action involving artillery duels, commando raids and also air combat continued throughout 1969 and into 1970, with growing Soviet involvement in Egypt's defence. In the summer of 1970 the U.S. Secretary of State, Mr. William Rogers, put forward a set of proposals for solving the continuing Middle East crisis. After lengthy negotiations and a visit by President Nasser to Moscow, both Egypt and Israel agreed to a 90 days ceasefire in August 1970. Talks between the U.A.R. and Jordan on the one hand and Israel on the other began later in August in New York under the guidance of the UN mediator Gunnar Jarring. They soon broke down following accusations from both sides of violations of the ceasefire agreement, but despite this the ceasefire was renewed, on its expiry, for another three months.

EGYPT AFTER NASSER

Although President Nasser had had his differences with the Palestinian guerrillas over their rejection of the U.S. peace proposals and the hijackings of the western airliners at the beginning of September, one of his last acts was to secure agreement in Cairo between King Hussein and Yassir Arafat for an end to the fighting between the Jordanian army and the guerrillas.

Nasser's death on September 28th, 1970 came as a profound shock and it was feared by many that it would materially lessen chances of achieving peace in the Middle East. However, his death made it easier for the Jordanian government to proceed with crushing the Palestine commando bases throughout the rest of 1970 and the first half of 1971.

A close associate of Nasser, and Vice-President at the time of his death, Anwar Sadat, was immediately appointed provisional president by the Cabinet and Party, being later elected President in a national referendum, and by mid-1971 he was firmly in control of the government of Egypt.

Meanwhile, the ceasefire on the Suez Canal was extended in February 1971 for only thirty days, but on its expiry fighting was not resumed. Although Egypt was ostensibly preparing for war and, for example, formed a military union with Syria, she also maintained diplomatic efforts to secure a basis for peace negotiations which, in the spring and summer of 1971, centered on various proposals for reopening the Suez Canal as a first step towards a settlement.

In November 1970 President Sadat (whose mother is Sudanese) had agreed to the federation of the U.A.R. with Sudan and Libya. Sudan, however, later postponed her membership of a union and it was Syria who in April became the third member of the Federation. The federation proposals, together with Sadat's plan for the reopening of the Canal, precipitated a crisis in the leadership which led to a comprehensive purge by Sadat of opponents at all levels of the government. Ali Sabri, one of the two Vice-Presidents, and strongly pro-Moscow, was the first to go, on May 2nd, just before U.S. Secretary of State, William Rogers, arrived in Cairo. On May 13th, President Sadat, convinced of an impending coup, dismissed six other ministers and important Party and National Assembly members. In July new elections were held, not only for all levels of the Party, but also for trade unions and professional bodies. A new constitution, the first permanent one since the 1952 revolution, was voted in September. It contained important clauses governing personal freedoms and discarded at last the name of United Arab Republic, the state being known henceforward as the Arab Republic of Egypt.

The year 1971 was marked by repeated Egyptian declarations of the intention to fight Israel—but only when the time was ripe—and Egypt mounted an extensive diplomatic campaign to state her case in the West. One result of this activity was a move towards reconciliation with West Germany. In September 1971 came the first large-scale military operations on the canal since the August 1970 ceasefire and in December the UN passed a resolution calling for the resumption of the Jarring peace mission.

Egypt was becoming increasingly dependent on the U.S.S.R., both militarily and economically. In spite of Russian assurances that aid would be continued, the Egyptians were becoming very dissatisfied. This was partly because they felt the arms deliveries were not up to standard, and partly because of the frustration engendered in the country by the prolonged state of uncertainty. Student riots at the beginning of 1972 brought assurances from President Sadat that an armed confrontation with Israel was definitely intended. Against this background of increasing internal uneasiness Egypt intensified efforts to diversify sources of development aid and armaments. The Suez-Alexandria (Sumed) pipeline received promises of Western backing and in May 1972 a five-year preferential trade agreement was concluded with the EEC. Relations with West Germany, too, on the whole improved.

CRISIS IN EGYPTIAN-SOVIET RELATIONS

The most striking event of 1972 was the dismissal of Soviet military advisers from Egypt in July and the manning of installations by Egyptians. This did not lead to a rupture in Egyptian-Soviet relations but neither did it result in any significant rapprochement with the West, anti-American feeling remaining very strong. A new round of diplomatic visits to state Egypt's case, particularly in the West and the Far East, was embarked upon and arms supplies requested from France and Britain. With the announcement on August 2nd, 1972, of Egypt's plan to merge with Libya, France stated that supplies of Mirage fighters to Libya would continue, Libya not being in direct conflict with Israel.

Contacts with the U.S.S.R. continued and economic relations appeared unaffected by the events of July but it was clear that the U.S.S.R. was looking elsewhere to maintain its presence in the Mediterranean. Prime Minister Aziz Sidqi visited Moscow in October but no conclusive results came of his visit. It was unclear to what extent Sadat's hand had been forced in ordering the Soviet withdrawal. The dismissal in November of the War Minister, General Sadeq, and other high-ranking officers in the armed forces pointed to disagreements between the military and Sadat and to a desire for reconciliation with the U.S.S.R.

INTERNAL UNREST

A law passed in August 1972 provided for penalties up to life imprisonment for offences endangering national unity, including opposing the Government by force and inciting violence between Muslims and the Coptic minority. Clashes between these two communities were growing more frequent and, along with increasing student unrest, were seen as an expression of dissatisfaction with the state of "no-peace-no-war". The Government, in the unenviable position of being unable to remedy the situation without either a fatal confrontation with Israel, or surrender, resorted to repeated assurances of military preparations. In December 1972, Sadat in fact ordered preparations for fighting, after strong criticism in the People's Assembly of the Government's policies. Another cause of uneasiness was the merger with Libya, which many people felt might give Colonel Gaddafi too much control over Egypt's destiny.

January 1973 saw violent clashes between police and students and the universities had to be closed for a short time. In February a number of left-wing elements, among them many journalists, were expelled from the ASU, student unrest continued and in March President Sadat took over from Aziz Sidqi as Prime Minister. The new administration's policies were approved by the People's Assembly but the Government was criticized for failing to follow a clear-cut economic policy, particularly with regard to the five-year plan.

Egypt's diplomatic offensive in Europe continued into May and June and relations with France and West Germany improved significantly.

ECONOMIC SURVEY

The Egyptian economy has been functioning under war conditions since 1967. Temporary measures taken to deal with the emergency have gradually turned into permanent fixtures. The Suez Canal remains closed; Sinai, with its oil fields, remains under enemy occupation; the important urban centres of Port Said, Ismailia, Suez, Port Fuad and Port Tewfik have had to be evacuated after suffering much damage from enemy shelling; vital economic targets such as the refineries and petro-chemical complex at Suez and power transmission lines have been hit; an internal refugee problem has developed in the Canal area; tourism is at a low ebb, and expenditure on the war effort constrains that on development.

The new difficulties, coming on top of chronic economic ills, would have crippled the economy were it not for generous aid from communist countries, with whom trade ties have strengthened still further; some promising oil discoveries made in co-operation with Western interests; direct financial assistance from the oil-rich countries of Kuwait, Libya and Saudi Arabia; and perhaps also higher efficiency inspired by the atmosphere of emergency.

In normal circumstances, official data about the economy tended to lag one or two years behind events and for obvious reasons, the gap has been growing wider. However, in spite of the present unsettled conditions, the Egyptian economy shows many structural features which are unlikely to undergo fundamental change except in the long run, and these receive special attention in the present survey.

GENERAL

The total area of Egypt is about 1,000,000 square km., but 96 per cent of the country is desert. With no forested land, and hardly any permanent meadows or pastures, the arable land available is greatly overcrowded. Relating the population, numbering 34.1 million in 1971, to the inhabited area, a density of over 1,000 persons per square kilometre gives 5.5 persons per acre of arable land, representing one of the highest man/land ratios in the world. At the root of Egypt's poverty lies its expanding population, which advances at about 2.6 per cent annually. Thanks to the recent launching of a major birth control campaign, this rate, the Government claims, has now been cut to 2.24 per cent a year, with a further one-half per cent expected in six years. In 1970, according to figures published by the World Bank, G.N.P. per capita was $210.

Despite this low level of income, certain aspects of the Egyptian economy indicate a relative state of advance, but overpopulation still tends somewhat to neutralize the effects of social and economic progress. Among the comparatively advanced areas of the Egyptian economy are the infrastructure of communications, the irrigation system, public administration and education. Although the illiteracy rate remains high (the 1960 population census showed an illiteracy rate of 69.7 per cent among people of over ten years of age) both secondary and higher education are quite developed and Egypt is a net exporter of skills, especially to other Arab countries. The diet of the average Egyptian is poor and contains little animal protein, but average calorie intake exceeds requirements by a comfortable margin. During the 1918-39 period, when the Egyptian pound was tied to sterling and a fairly free trade policy was being pursued, manufacturing industry had little chance of developing and agricultural production, though expanding, could not keep up with the rapidly rising population. A gradual deterioration of living standards set in. This trend did not change direction until the immediate post-war period, when cotton prices improved. These reached their greatest heights during the Korean boom of 1951–52, when "soft-currency cotton", including Egyptian cotton, enjoyed high premia over dollar-cotton. But the collapse of the boom, the easing up of the world dollar scarcity and the beginning of American subsidization of cotton exports in the mid-1950s, marked a turning point in raw cotton terms of trade which, until quite recently, showed a declining trend.

The régime which assumed power in 1952 and ended the monarchy gave urgent attention to Egypt's economic problems. Its policies included measures of agrarian reform, land reclamation, the High Dam, and a programme of industrialization which was accelerated in 1960 by the formation of a comprehensive social and economic development plan.

Egypt's first five-year plan aimed at increasing real national income by 40 per cent between 1960 and 1965, this being advertised as the first lap of a ten-year programme to double real national income by 1970. The five-year growth target was virtually fulfilled, so that the second lap was initially replaced by a more ambitious plan to double real income in seven years (i.e. by 1972). Lack of finance, however, frustrated this new plan, and after two years of uncertainty, a three-year "accomplishment" plan, beginning July 1967, was proclaimed. This was to aim at a target growth rate of 5 per cent per annum (compared with 7.2 per cent under the first five-year plan) with a total investment of £E1,085 million (against £E1,513 million in 1960–65), and would concentrate on completing projects already started, rather than initiating new ones. This plan was dropped as a result of the 1967 war and was substituted by annual development appropriations (£E320 million in 1968–69 and £E350 million in 1969–70). Apart from a few select new projects, the whole emphasis of Egyptian planning was turned towards rationalizing the existing industries, and introducing incentives to improve their performance.

This plan was, however, to be superseded by a more ambitious ten-year scheme under a Programme of National Action, proclaimed by President Sadat in July 1971. The ten-year programme was to be implemented under two consecutive five-year plans, the first starting in July 1972. The target of the Programme was to double national income within ten years to £E5,000 million, with investments totalling £E8,400 million of which 3,200 million were to be spent on the first Five-Year Plan. Industry was due to receive 31.2 per cent of the five-year allocations, agriculture 12.5 per cent, transport and communications 21.9 per cent, electric power 6.3 per cent, housing 10.2 per cent, public utilities 4.1 per cent and social services 7 per cent.

President Sadat's Programme had not, however, come to life by mid-1973. Its inauguration had been postponed until the beginning of 1973, but when the 1973 budget was announced there was no mention in it of the Programme. Committees still meet to discuss the Programme, but early in 1973 members of the People's Assembly were asking the Government publicly whether it had decided to shelve the Plan, since details had not even been presented to the Assembly. These demands were not even acknowledged.

The development budget for 1971–72 was set at £E350 million and was presented as a means of raising G.D.P. in real terms by 5 per cent. Following the decision to alter the fiscal year from its present July-June basis to a calendar year basis, to conform with arrangements in Syria and Libya, the other two partners in the Federation of Arab Republics, it was announced that the 1971–72 fiscal year would be extended until the end of 1972. The 1973 development plan provides for £E430 million in investments, in addition to £E50 million to be invested in the private sector. Its aim is less ambitious than the 1971–72 plan, which is believed to have been only partly fulfilled; despite greater investment the projected growth rate of the 1973 plan is only 3 per cent.

In the present conditions of warfare it is difficult to forecast the future development of the Egyptian economy (or indeed the other economies of the Middle East). Without the Palestinian conflict, the Egyptian economy, which has often shown unexpected resilience in the past, would have come very near to realizing self-sustained growth by the end of the present decade. Besides the large-scale waste of resources, the conflict may well lead to the development of a new ideology in the entire area.

AGRICULTURE

Under the impact of industrialization the structure of the Egyptian Economy has been changing, and the relative contribution of agriculture to the domestic product, once predominant has been declining. According to the National Bank of Egypt in 1969–70 agriculture generated 25.1 per cent of G.D.P., industry and mining 21.2 per cent, electricity and construction 7.5 per cent, the distributive sectors 14.6 per cent and the services sectors 31.6 per cent. In some respects, however, agriculture remains the leading sector of the economy, employing about 52 per cent of the labour force and earning, through cotton exports, most of the country's foreign exchange. In spite of the diminishing stress on agriculture in Government plans, the volume of agricultural production has been increasing, although population growth has cancelled out most of the benefits of this increase. Indices compiled by FAO show that, taking the average 1952–56 yearly production figures as a base, agricultural production in 1971 stood at 176. But on a per capita basis, the index reaches only 116.

The entire arable land available is just under 6 million feddans (one feddan=1.038 acres). The extension of this area through reclamation has been slow difficult and costly. The increasing pressure of people on the land has led to an intensification of cultivation almost without parallel anywhere. Dams, barrages, pumps and an intricate network of canals and drains (in 1960 there were 25,000 km. of canals and 13,000 km. of drains) bring perennial irrigation to almost the whole area. The strict pursuit of crop rotation, lavish use of commercial fertilizer and pesticides, and the patient application of manual labour, not only make multiple cropping possible, but also raise land yields to exceptionally high levels.

The Government has announced that under the ten-year plan another 604,000 feddans will be reclaimed, and allocations for the scheme will total £E86 million. The plan also aims at completing the utilities for servicing 120,000 feddans of already reclaimed land at a cost of £E122 million. Officials hope that at the end of the ten-year period, a total of 1.5 million feddans will have been added to the 6 million feddans now under cultivation. The declared aim of the plan is to transform the whole irrigation pattern of Upper Egypt, the agricultural heartland of the country, from a basin irrigation system to a perennial irrigation system. The IBRD has approved a long-term interest-free loan of $26 million to finance a drainage scheme in the delta and was reported in mid-1973 to have agreed to provide another $36 million for a similar scheme in Upper Egypt.

As the yields of land are already very high, increased use of manual labour, or practically any other means of production with the exception of land, encounters rapidly diminishing returns. Since the expanding industrial sector, with its use of modern capital-intensive techniques, can offer relatively few opportunities for increased employment, the incidence of both unemployment and under employment in the economy at large is likely to grow as the economy advances, at least for some time. In spite of the steady flow of workers from agriculture to the cities (where 40 per cent of the population lived in 1966, and where employment is far from full), agriculture is still suffering from a surfeit of unnecessary labour. In 1959–60 the Planning Commission estimated that out of a total of 4,220,000 persons engaged in agriculture (excluding dependent female labour), no less than 975,000 were completely redundant. The growth of redundant labour is a constant threat to labour productivity, not only in agriculture, but also in manufacturing industry and service activity. Emigration out of Egypt has recently intensified, but the number of people involved (several thousands every year) is relatively small. The emigrants, however, tend to be highly qualified professionals whom the economy can ill afford to lose.

The bulk of agricultural production is intended for the market place and not for subsistence. Nearly three-quarters of agricultural income comes from field crops, the remainder deriving from fruit, vegetables, livestock and dairy products. Long-staple cotton is the most important field crop; it absorbs a great deal of the available labour, occupies about a quarter of the arable land and provides up to 40 per cent of the value of field crops and 50–60 per cent of the proceeds of visible exports.

Rice is another important crop and now comes second to cotton as a foreign currency earner. Rice yields have also been improving steadily and more is being cropped in spite of lower acreage. The area under rice fell from 502,000 hectares (about 1.2 million feddans) in 1969 to 480,000 hectares in 1972 (about 1.14 million feddans), but output rose from 2,561,000 tons in 1969 to 2,590,000 tons in 1972. Of the 2,605,000 tons produced in 1971, a total of 2,040,000 tons were exported at a value of £E34.2 million. By 1970 Egypt had become the world's third largest rice exporter after the United States and Thailand, accounting for 12.5 per cent of total world exports, but this proportion fell to 9.3 per cent in 1971. Other important grain crops grown include wheat, maize, millet and barley, of which production amounted to 1,616,000 tons, 2,550,000 tons, 854,000 tons (1971) and 107,000 tons respectively. Population pressure has resulted in Egypt becoming occasionally, i.e. in years of drought, a net importer of cereals, mostly wheat. Cereals and milling products imported in 1970, a good year, cost £E30.5 million while exports of these products brought in £E34.4 million, a balance of £E3.8 million in favour of exports.

Another high-yielding crop is sugar-cane (6.93 million tons were produced on an area of 186,000 feddans in 1970). It is nurtured by an expanding sugar industry, supplying the bulk of national requirements. Other crops include lucerne, a nitrogen-fixing fodder, beans, potatoes and onion and garlic. The last three crops in particular have become significant export items, bringing in £E3.7 million, £E7.3 million and £E2.4 million respectively in export proceeds in 1970.

The many kinds of fruit, vegetables and horticultural products grown are capable of great expansion and are potentially important as exports. Special efforts are being made to promote the production of these items, especially citrus fruit, and special areas are being allocated along the Mediterranean coast for their cultivation. In 1970 about 750,000 tons of citrus fruit were produced, compared with about 600,000 tons in 1968 and only an average of 263,000 tons a year in the early 1950s. Recent attention has been given to animal husbandry in an attempt to raise dairy and meat production. Egypt has become a net importer of meats and only recently were restrictions on meat consumption, imposed in 1967, removed.

Egypt is the world's principal producer of long-staple cotton, followed by Sudan and Peru. Many factors combine to give the high yields and excellent quality of Egyptian cotton. Among these should be mentioned climatic, soil and labour conditions, and a long experience with careful planting, watering and picking. Government assistance, which has increased of late, has always been important. The development of new varieties, seed distribution, area selection, timing of farm operations and marketing are all carried out under strict government supervision. Fertilizers and pesticides have long been distributed through the government-sponsored Agricultural Credit Bank, lately converted into a public organization; more recently this task has been undertaken by government-administered agricultural co-operatives which are multiplying and expanding their area of activity. All the cotton ginning industry and the cotton exporting business had been nationalized by 1963. The cotton exchanges were closed, and the Government undertook to guarantee prices to regulate internal trade. A public organization for cotton has been set up to regulate all aspects of cotton growing, marketing and manufacturing. Total cotton exports reached 884,483 bales in the 1971–72 season. Exports in the calendar year 1971 stood at £E174.8 million, accounting for 51 per cent of all exports. In 1970 Egypt's exports of 285,300 tons of lint accounted for 8.6 per cent of world exports, and in 1971 output of 536,000 tons accounted for 4.5 per cent of world production. The yield per acre in 1969–70 was 709 lb., compared with 441 in the United States.

Egypt produces about 40 per cent of the world crop of long-staple cotton (1⅛in. and longer), although this latter percentage fell to 33 in 1969–70. Demand for this type of cotton has been shifting away towards man-made fibres, a fact which has tended to weaken Egypt's previous position of pre-eminence, and consequently the premia Egyptian cotton commanded over rival cottons. In the past the government attempted to reduce cotton production to gain monopoly profits in the export markets but the result was a drastic loss in market shares. Consequently all restrictions on cotton cultivation have been abandoned, save for rotational purposes and for safeguarding food supplies. For many years the government has operated a system of price supports and the farmers find cotton cultivation highly profitable. The shortage of land, however, together with the increasing requirements of the domestic textile industry (190,000 tons in 1970–71 or 38 per cent of production) set a limit on the quantity available for export. It is noteworthy that average annual exports of raw cotton from Egypt have remained roughly constant since the turn of the century when population was less than a third of its present level.

About half of Egypt's cotton exports has gone to Communist countries in recent years under various bilateral agreements. This proportion dropped suddenly in 1967/68 (to 38 per cent) possibly to allow Egypt to earn foreign exchange in the West, but went back to previous levels in the following years. The Communist countries took 47.4 per cent of Egyptian cotton exports in 1968–69, 62.2 per cent in 1969–70 and 56.5 per cent in 1970–71. Egyptian preference for trading with the Western countries, with which Egypt has a balance of payments deficit, has tended to be frustrated by a number of factors, including U.S. trade restrictions (on raw cotton imports), the decline of the high-grade sections of the European cotton industries, political considerations and shortage of finance. The availability of credits (to finance imports) from the Communist countries and the flexibility with which these countries conduct their relations with Egypt, have also tended to divert Egyptian foreign trade towards the Communist states.

AGRARIAN REFORM

Immediately after the Egyptian Revolution of 1952 an experiment in land reform was started. This has been quite successful. Among other measures, a limit of 200 feddans was imposed on individual ownership of land. This limit was lowered to 100 feddans in 1961 and again to 50 feddans in 1969. The primary aim of this reform was the destruction of the feudal power of the old politicians, an aim which was easily realized. In 1952, 5.8 per cent of all landowners held 64.5 per cent of the total area, but only a quarter of the national acreage (some 1.5 million feddans) was in plots of over 100 acres each. By 1961, however, this area had dwindled to about 1 million feddans, nearly all of which had been appropriated by the Ministry of Agrarian Reform and redistributed to landless peasants. The 1969 land reform affected a further 1.13 million feddans owned by some 16,000 landowners.

Other measures of agrarian reform included rent control; the regulation of land tenure; consolidation of fragmented holdings for production purposes; and the drive to build co-operatives. Under Government supervision both the number and activities of agricultural co-operatives increased. By 1963 there were 4,897 such co-operatives (compared with 1,727 in 1952) which offered more than £E46 millions in loans to 920,000 borrowers. The value of services provided by the agrarian reform co-operatives (set up to help the recipients of land under the land reform programme) increased more than fivefold between 1958 and 1965 and the activities provided covered the supply of seeds, sacks, fertilizer, insecticides and pest-control machinery. However, co-operatives were not a complete success since they readily lent themselves to corruption. Also in the process of dispossessing the large landowners and promoting co-operatives, the authorities unwittingly helped to eliminate many highly efficient medium-sized farmers. On balance, however, the redistribution of land was accompanied by improved land productivity and not the reverse.

Since land reform affected only about one-sixth of the total land, the main structure of land-ownership remained unaffected; in 1965, 5.4 per cent of the owners still held 49.3 per cent of the land while 94.6 per cent of the owners shared the other half. But the average ownership of the first group was only 18.05 feddans, and the national average, 1.95 feddans. The fundamental land tenure problem was not so much one of distribution but an overal scarcity.

The Government sees only two ways out of the impasse: an end to fragmentation of holdings and the replacement of archaic methods of production. It recently stated that there were still about 2 million farmers who possessed less than one feddan each. In addition to the projected large-scale spending on improving agricultural methods and the educational and health standards in the ten-year plan, it is proposing to amalgamate smaller holdings in voluntary joint stock companies of at least 30,000 feddans each where crop specialization could be practised. This would also ease the introduction of mechanization, and it is proposed to attach processing plant to each company.

Given the land shortage, special attention has naturally been paid to increasing the arable area. In view of the fact that the land to be reclaimed is often arid desert, reclamation is a costly process requiring substantial capital outlays, and the question has to be asked whether new investment should not be directed to the development of manufacturing industry instead, where returns to the scarce capital may well be higher.

THE HIGH DAM

The decision to invest more than £E400 million in the High Dam project (including initial Russian credits of £E113 million, supported subsequently by another loan of £E81 million for the later stages) was, therefore, taken with an eye also on the development of cheap hydro-electric energy for industry. The project was started in January 1960, completed in July 1970, and officially inaugurated in January 1971. From 1964 onwards various parts of the project matured, but all work ceased when the last of the twelve turbines in the dam's power station had been installed. The station's generating capacity, at 10,000 million kWh., exceeds by a considerable margin the 6,012 million kWh. produced in all Egypt in 1967 mostly from thermal stations with some hydro-electric energy from the old Aswan dam. Transmission lines carry the current from the Dam site to Cairo and further north, and a major scheme aiming at the complete electrification of Egypt's villages has already started. The storage lake behind the dam, which is 500 km. long and 10 km. wide, is the centre of a developing fishing industry which is expected to replace the sardine catch in the Mediterranean, lost as a result of building the dam.

As much as 144,000 feddans were reclaimed annually in the period 1960–65; by the end of 1972 another 1.2 million feddans should have been reclaimed and 700,000 feddans have already been converted from basin (i.e. cultivated once a year) to perennial irrigation. By 1980 a total of 465,000 feddans will have been reclaimed in the Nubariyya region including 300,000 feddans with Russian assistance. The Public Organization for Desert Development is also carrying out an ambitious programme of land reclamation in the Western Desert with the help of underground water. Despite all these activities the man/land ratio is unlikely to improve in the foreseeable future in view of the rapid growth of population.

MANUFACTURING INDUSTRY

Excluding the attempts at industrialization in the early nineteenth century, the history of Egypt's manufacturing industry may be said to begin with World War I. Isolation and increased demand gave rise then to a number of small-scale industries, but many of these had to close down in the face of foreign competition during the 1920s when international trade was resumed. When the commercial treaties holding Egypt to a virtually free-trade policy came to an end in 1930, a protective tariff was established to give shelter to a widening spectrum of nascent industry. The establishment of Bank Misr, and the group of companies it supported in the twenties, coincided with a rising tide of Egyptian nationalism and it became patriotic to buy Egyptian industrial products. A number of manufacturing industries, mainly catering for domestic consumption and with cotton textiles at their head, came to be established and grew rapidly.

On the eve of World War II local industry satisfied a substantial part of the domestic demand for textiles, cement, sugar, edible oils, soap and other consumer products. In 1937 industrial employment in establishments employing 10 persons and over totalled 155,000; two years later, however, the contribution of mining, manufacturing and public utilities to the national product was still only about 8 per cent.

The war greatly stimulated Egyptian industry which, in conditions of acute shortages, especially of equipment and raw materials, strove to meet the expanded demand. A wide variety of goods came to be produced and sometimes exported to neighbouring countries. Considerable expansion took place in the production of textiles, chemicals, building materials and processed foods, while entirely new industries sprang up, including rubber and pharmaceutical manufacturing. By 1947, and in spite of some decline in activity, industrial employment in establishments employing 10 persons and over had risen to 278,000. Industrial growth slowed down after the war owing to a period of relatively free trade, although industry was immensely encouraged by the opening up of foreign sources of machinery. Industrial production continued to expand, however, and in 1951 it reached about 140 per cent of its level in 1938. Throughout the decade of the 1950s industrial production grew steadily at an average rate of about 7 per cent per annum, helped by the chronic deficit which developed in the balance of external payments. The exchange controls that have ruled during most of the post-war period have given Egyptian industry added protection. A great drive toward self-sufficiency after the 1956 war resulted in an intensive industrialization programme which began tentatively in 1957, but was later incorporated in the first five-year economic and social development plan, 1960–65. In the six years from 1959–60 to 1965–66, gross value added by industry and mining rose, at constant prices, at an average rate of 9.5 per cent per annum.

In recent years manufacturing industry has been held back by lack of foreign exchange, and some excess capacity has resulted from shortages of spare parts and raw materials. An acute recession hit the industrial sector in the latter half of 1967, but recovery has been rapid since then. The total value of industrial production (including mining and electricity) has been increasing steadily and advanced from £E1,245 million in 1967 to £E2,500 million in 1971–72, double the 1967 figure, according to Government Ministers. In 1970, 29.4 per cent of the value of manufactured output was contributed by food processing, 28.7 per cent by spinning and weaving, 12.1 per cent by engineering industries, 11 per cent by chemical industries and 8.1 per cent by the growing petroleum industry. At the end of 1969 a total of 587,585 persons were employed by 2,689 industrial establishments with 25 or more employees. The value added in these establishments totalled £E133 million. Official data for employment in 1969–70 indicate a work force of 916,100 in mining and manufacturing industry, 22,800 in electricity and 387,900 in construction, totalling 16 per cent of employed labour compared with 48.9 per cent for agriculture. Production indices show big increases in the manufacturing and mining sector. Compared with 1959–60 (the base year) the index in 1969–70 was 455.4 for crude oil, 205.6 for iron ore, 174.7 for refined sugar, 167.1 for cotton yarn, 140.9 for cotton fabrics, 1,074.2 for pharmaceutical products, 316.7 for paper, 2,615.8 for cars, 2,530 for bicycles, 436.5 for radios, 712.6 for refrigerators and 337.1 for generated power. In terms of value added the industrial sector is roughly of the same order as the leading sector, agriculture: in 1968–69 value added by agriculture amounted to £E644.4 million, whilst value added in the industrial sector was £E598.4 million (£E488.9 million manufacturing industry, £E27.8 million electricity and £E81.7 million construction).

Under the ten-year plan the Government is envisaging investments of £E3,000 million in industrial development of which £E1,184 million is expected to be spent during the first five years. The major project during the first five years, at a cost of £E340 million, is the expansion of the Helwan iron and steel complex, christened "the second High Dam". Other important projects to be implemented by 1977 are a phosphorus complex (£E66.2 million), an aluminium plant £E60 million), a sodium carbonate and caustic soda plant (£E14.8 million) and the exploitation of the Hamrawin phosphate deposits (£E18 million). Three of these projects—the Helwan iron and steel complex, the aluminium plant, and the phosphorus complex—are to be powered by electricity generated by the High Dam, using 3,600 kWh. of electricity a year. This, in addition to the plan to extend electric power to all Egypt's rural communities by 1982, has underlined the need for more power generation than that supplied by the High Dam. The Government is therefore studying the possibility of constructing a nuclear power station which would possibly also serve Libya. The Government hopes that on completion of the ten-year plan steel output will have risen from the present 450,000 tons a year to 2 million tons a year, cement from 3.6 million tons to 6 million, crude oil from 15 million tons to 60 million, oil products from 2.5 million tons to 16 million, fertilizers from 1.6 million tons to 4.5 million and electric power from 7,000 million kWh. to 19,000 million kWh. Most of the industrial development projects are to be implemented with financial and technical aid from Eastern Europe, mostly the Soviet Union, but the development of the oil sector is being entrusted almost exclusively to Western interests, mainly American.

OIL AND GAS

More than 60 per cent of the 130,000 barrels a day of crude petroleum produced in Egypt in 1966 originated in Sinai (mainly from the Belayim onshore and offshore fields), now under enemy occupation and said to be producing 90,000 b/d. Average Egyptian production in 1971 outside Sinai was 300,000 b/d, about 80 per cent of which came from the rich offshore field of Morgan in the Gulf of Suez operated by the Gulf of Suez Petroleum Company (a 50–50 partnership between the Egyptian General Petroleum Corporation and Amoco-Egypt, a subsidiary of Standard Oil of Indiana). Some 30,000 b/d are produced by the Egyptian General Petroleum Company from a number of small fields on the western coast of the Gulf of Suez. A promising discovery, the Alamein field, has been developed by the Western Desert Petroleum Company (an equal partnership between EGPC and Phillips) but production which reached 43,000 b/d early in 1970 declined to about 13,000 b/d early in 1972. All this output does not add up to much in world oil terms. But 1972 appears to be the year of the oil breakthrough in Egypt. Following the discovery of the Abu Gharadeq field in the Western Desert by Amoco in 1971, the company early in 1972 discovered an even richer field at al-Razzaq, a nearby location. This field, which has already been linked by pipeline to the Mediterranean, is expected to produce up to 60,000 b/d or up to 3 million tons a year of high quality crude. The Abu Gharadeq field has proved disappointing as far as oil is concerned but natural gas deposits found there have proved to be significant. Amoco has signed a $100 million agreement under which it will finance the development of Morgan, and the building of a pipeline from Abu Gharadeq to the Mediterranean and a gas pipeline from Abu Gharadeq to industrial centres near Cairo.

These discoveries have led to hopes that by 1976, when the oil and gas from these fields will become available in commercial quantities, Egypt will become a major oil and gas producer. Two other important fields, Yidma and Maliha, have been discovered by Phillips, and the intensive search for oil continues with a production target of 60 million tons a year by 1982 compared with 16.4 million tons produced in 1970–71.

Three new U.S. oil companies joined the scene in 1972–73. The agreement by Esso to invest $50 million in oil exploration in Egypt and by Mobil to invest another $23 million was considered a major success after the failure of the Government to attract much interest when it called for bids for exploration offshore in the Mediterranean west of Alexandria. Both the Esso and Mobil concessions, under which any eventual oil finds would be exploited jointly with EGPC, are for offshore Mediterranean areas east of Alexandria. A third U.S. concern, Trans-World Oil, a small independent company, obtained a small offshore concession in the Red Sea and agreed to invest $6 million in exploration. A new survey is believed to be under way for the area stretching west of Alexandria as far as the Libyan border, which will be used as a basis for a fresh call for tenders. In addition to the Americans, Japanese, French, Italian, Spanish and Brazilian interests are involved in Egyptian oil exploration, but Soviet involvement with drilling in the Siwa oasis has failed to produce results and has been reduced substantially.

The destruction of Egypt's main refineries at Suez upset the balance between crude supply and products demand. The two defunct refineries, with a total capacity of 144,000 b/d or 7.2 million tons/year, were located where the bulk of crude was produced. With the Suez Canal closed the Morgan oil is too far from the Mex refinery (near Alexandria) with a capacity of only 65,000 b/d (3.25 million tons/year). Undamaged units from the Suez refineries have been moved to the Musturud refinery near Cairo, which is now producing 3 million tons a year. A new refinery has been built at Amiriya near Alexandria with a capacity of 1.5 million tons a year, bringing Egyptian refining capacity up to just over the pre-1967 level.

Exploration for oil has revealed promising sources of gas in addition to those discovered at Abu Gharadeq, whose proven reserves stand at 63,000 million cu. metres. Associated gas at the Morgan fields is estimated to amount to 300 million cubic feet a day and this will be used either to make l.p.g. or as an input for a petro-chemical complex. Natural gas has been discovered in various parts of the delta, notably in the Abu-Qir area (offshore as well as onshore) by Phillips (wells yielding 27 million and 7.8 million cubic feet a day respectively together with condensates). A joint ENI/Egyptian gas strike near Abu Madi in 1970 is being developed for use as fuel by the large industrial centres in the north and west delta, and a 750,000 tons a year fertilizer plant is also projected to make use of this gas.

The closure of the Suez Canal and the development of super-tankers have led to the decision to construct a crude oil pipeline linking Suez to the Mediterranean, near Alexandria (SUMED). A consortium of European contractors, lead by the French company Batignolles, have won the bidding for this $210 million project which has been backed by offers of finance from West Germany, France, Britain, Italy, Spain, the Netherlands and others. The project was due to be launched late in 1971 but agreement over financial arrangements and related minimum forward bookings by the oil companies were only finalized by mid-1973. By that time the construction consortium was asking for a 50 per cent price increase to compensate for inflation and the Government was refusing to bow to this demand. The two sides had to reach agreement before the end of September, the date by which other agreements would lapse automatically if no progress is achieved. The future of SUMED appeared very much in the balance in June 1973, although Egyptian officials still believed that the pipeline would be built. Reports early in 1973 that a "second" Suez canal, west of the present one, was under consideration were vehemently denied in Cairo.

FINANCE

British Treasury bills were used as a cover to the Egyptian currency issued by the National Bank of Egypt, then the bank of issue before 1947, when the sterling connection was severed completely. Since 1948 Egyptian government securities have complemented the gold reserves as currency backing, and Egypt has followed a policy of money management based on a separation between the balance of payments and domestic money supply.

The most recent series of reorganizations of the banking system, in late 1971, resulted in three of the banks merging into others and each of the rest being entrusted with specialized functions. The National Bank of Egypt was entrusted with foreign trade, the Bank of Port Said merged into Misr Bank which was to deal with home trade, including agricultural finance, the Industrial Bank merged into the Bank of Alexandria which was to deal with manufacturing, the Mortgage Credit Bank merged with the *Credit Foncier Egyptien* and was to deal with construction and housing and the Bank of Cairo left to deal with operations of the public sector. A new bank, the Nasser Social Bank has been created to deal with pensions and other forms of social security. The Egyptian International Bank for Foreign Trade and Development was also created in 1971 to promote foreign trade and attract foreign investment but was later transformed into the Arab International Bank for Foreign Trade and Development with each of Egypt and Libya holding £10 million of its £30 million capital and the rest offered to other Arab investors. These banks are additional to the Central Bank of Egypt, which was created from the issue department of the National Bank of Egypt in 1960, and the Public Organization for Agricultural Credit and Co-operatives, which the *Crédit Agricole* became in 1964.

Compared with an average rate of growth for the real economy of 5–7 per cent a year since the early 1960s, money supply has been increasing on average by about 9 per cent a year. This has been accompanied by a growing share in the economic life of the community of the public sector which has proved to be a great user of means of exchange. The traditional anti-inflationary devices (e.g. devaluation, used in 1962 to bring the Egyptian pound down to $2.30 from $2.838) have had little effect on effective demand and hence the balance of payments disequilibrium, since most of the credit created by the banking system is for use by the public sector. There were two dollar devaluations, one in 1971 and one in 1972, but a revaluation against the dollar in February 1973 brought the Egyptian pound up to $2.56. In April 1971 the share of the public sector in the use of credit facilities amounted to 68.0 per cent of the total created in the entire economy. As at the end of 1967, 53.1 per cent of total credit facilities granted went to industry, 27.8 per cent to trade, 7.6 per cent to agriculture and 11.5 per cent to other activity. Spinning and weaving obtained about 25 per cent of the credit used by industry. Since then money supply has accelerated, with much of the increase being in the form of a rise in currency in circulation. Wholesale prices fell by about 2 per cent in the course of 1969, but rose by 6 per cent in 1970. Consumer prices, on the other hand, rose by about 3 per cent in 1969 and by 8 per cent in 1970.

At the end of 1971 Egypt's foreign debts, excluding Soviet military aid, were estimated by foreign observers at over $2,000 million, of which half was owed to Western nations. Egyptian officials have publicly acknowledged that Soviet military aid has so far amounted to £2,000 million (about $5,600 million) and some reports have suggested that none of this has been paid back. If both estimates are true, this would bring Egypt's foreign debts up to a phenomenal $7,600 million. However, the outlook for

Egypt and its credit worthiness do not seem as bleak as the figures may first suggest. Most debts to Western nations have been rescheduled recently in an effort to normalize financial relations with those states and open the door to more economic co-operation; and the Soviet Union does not seem to be pressing Egypt for repayment.

Although Egypt technically draws up six budgets, in practice they can be grouped together. An account showing the sources of financing expenditure can show these as originating from "Special Finance Fund" (Arab support mainly), domestic and foreign loans, taxes, and surpluses of enterprises, etc. In the 1971–72 budget, another system was devised whereby productive sectors were said to have been separated from the public services, but the same principles seem to have been retained. In 1971–72 gross public expenditure was estimated at £E2,784 million, of which £E350 million was allocated for investment expenditure. Defence and national security appropriations for the year were set at £E649.5 million. With the decision to change the fiscal year to conform with the calendar year, some budgetary alterations were expected, but the 1973 budget has been kept secret so far, although it was announced shortly after its approval by the People's Assembly that major cuts would be made in expenditure. There was even some confusion about the announced figures, for the total was given variously as £E4,895.4 million and £E3,233.2 million. This had led to a suspicion that double counting had been employed somewhere, especially since it was stated that public expenditure during the year would stand at £E2,459 million. One suspicion was confirmed in 1972 when the Government, under pressure in the Assembly, admitted that expenditure on defence stood at about £E1,000 million a year. The 1971–72 budget showed defence and security appropriations at only £E650 million.

FOREIGN TRADE AND PAYMENTS

The external trade deficit has persisted without interruption for the whole of the past two decades. There was an unusual surplus of £E47.4 million in 1969 but this gave way to a deficit of £E11 million in 1970 and £E57 million in 1971. The Government keeps a constant vigil on all external payments, permitting only the most essential imports, but the pressure of population on resources helps to keep the balance of external payments in a critical state. The problem is unlikely to be solved without a breakthrough in the pattern of imports and exports which may be brought about by the development of the petroleum sector.

Imports in 1971 totalled £E400 million, compared with £E342 million in 1970 and £E277 million in 1969. Machinery, vehicles and metal products formed 33.7 per cent of imports, fuels, chemicals and other raw materials 30.5 per cent, and food products 29.7 per cent. The value of exports in 1971 was £E343.2 million, of which cotton, yarn and textiles alone accounted for 71 per cent. Raw cotton exports for the year stood at £E175 million, accounting for 51 per cent of the total.

In 1971, 33 per cent of imports and 60 per cent of exports were traded with Eastern European countries, compared with 29 per cent and 56 per cent respectively in the previous year. It should be noted, however, that Egyptian trade figures include Greece, Turkey, Finland and Cyprus under this heading. Communist Eastern Europe therefore accounted in 1971 for 26.8 per cent of exports. Trade with the Arab countries is small but growing under official encouragement. Exports to Arab countries reached 8.2 per cent of the total in 1971 and imports 7 per cent.

There was normally a surplus on the current account of invisible trade which helped to redress part of the deficit on merchandise trade, but this surplus was turned into a deficit after the closure of the Suez Canal in June 1967 and the decline in tourist revenue. Canal dues received were £E86.2 million in 1965, £E95.3 million in 1966 and £E47.0 million in (the first five months of) 1967. Payments and receipts for shipping and insurance have been fairly balanced at about £E10 million each way. Interest and dividends acquired were £E12.6 million in 1971, according to provisional estimates, compared with £E14.1 million in 1970. The servicing of foreign loans rose from £E29.4 million in 1970 to £E32.5 million in 1971, and government expenditure abroad reached £E35.7 million in 1971. The Central Bank estimated the deficit on current transactions at £E211.1 million in 1971, compared with £E200.7 million in 1970.

Significant transfer payments on government account appear on the credit side of the balance of payments representing financial assistance from other Arab states, mainly Saudi Arabia, Kuwait and Libya. These, £E134 million in 1970 and £E121.3 million in 1971, reduced the current deficit to £E66.7 million in 1970 and £E89.8 million in 1971.

For a long period previously, little capital movement had appeared in the Egyptian balance of payments, but after the financial settlements with the Suez Canal Company, the French and British Governments (in respect of nationalized property and war damage claims), the Sudan (regarding the redemption of Egyptian banknotes and coins circulating there, and the flooding of land on building the High Dam) and other foreign countries, large outgoing capital transfers figured prominently. On the other hand, credits obtained from Communist countries, and to a lesser extent and for shorter terms for some Western countries and Japan have in recent years, except for 1969, flowed inward and helped to finance much of the gap in current external payments (see Balance of Payments table in Statistical Survey).

ECONOMIC POLICY

According to the Permanent Constitution of 1971 the economy of Egypt is one based on socialism with the people controlling all means of production. In practice this means that the Government owns or controls practically every economic unit in the economy worth controlling. Although the doctrine of socialism was invoked from the first land reform in 1952, the economy remained largely in private hands until 1961, except for the nationalization of the Suez Canal company in 1956 and that of British and French property during the Suez attack. During 1961, all cotton exporting firms were nationalized, and the Alexandria futures market was closed; 275 industrial and trading concerns were taken over by the state in whole or in part; taxation was made so progressive that individual income was virtually limited to the official maximum of £E5,000; the maximum limit on land ownership was reduced from 200 to 100 feddans (before it was reduced again in 1969); individual shareholding was limited to £E10,000; 25 per cent of the net profits of industrial companies was to be distributed to the workers, who were to be represented on the boards of directors, and to work only a 42-hour week.

Other nationalization measures followed, so that the only sectors of the economy remaining outside complete government ownership are agriculture and urban real estate, but even these are overwhelmingly regulated by laws and decrees. Concerns are grouped under boards and boards under Chairmen and Ministers, and a constant stream of directives helps to bring the activities of all the controlled units in line with Government policies.

After 1967 the Government introduced yet more restricting measures aiming at curbing consumer demand including a variety of taxes, forced savings and compulsory contributions out of wages and salaries. There have been some recent moves, however, to give encouragement to the private sector, particularly with regard to the export trade.

STATISTICAL SURVEY

AREA AND POPULATION

AREA (sq. km.)		POPULATION (Census of May 30th, 1966)				
Total	Inhabited	Total	Cairo	Alexandria	Giza	Port Said	Suez
1,001,449	55,039	30,075,858	4,219,853	1,801,056	571,249	282,977	264,098

Total Population (estimated): 34,583,000 (April 1st, 1972).
Population of Cairo (1972 estimate): 5,384,000.
Population of Alexandria (1972 estimate): 2,146,000.

GOVERNORATES*
(1965)

GOVERNORATE	AREA (sq. km.)	CAPITAL	GOVERNORATE	AREA (sq. km.)	CAPITAL
Cairo	214.2	Cairo	Munufia	1,532.1	Shibin el-Kom
Alexandria	2,679.4	Alexandria	Behera	4,589.5	Damanhur
Port Said	72.1	Port Said	Giza	1,009.5	Giza
Ismailia	1,441.6	Ismailia	Beni Suef	1,321.7	Beni Suef
Suez	17,840.4	Suez	Fayum	1,827.2	Fayum
Damietta	589.2	Damietta	Menia	2,261.7	Menia
Dakahlia	3,470.9	Mansura	Asyut	1,553.0	Asyut
Sharkia	4,179.6	Zagazig	Suhag	1,547.2	Suhag
Kalyubia	1,001.1	Benha	Kena	1,850.7	Kena
Kafr el-Sheikh	3,437.1	Kafr el-Sheikh	Aswan	678.5	Aswan
Gharbia	1,942.2	Tanta			

* Excluding the four sparsely-populated "frontier districts".

EGYPT—(STATISTICAL SURVEY)

AGRICULTURE
PRINCIPAL CROPS

	AREA ('000 feddans*)				PRODUCTION ('000 metric tons)			
	1967/68	1968/69	1969/70	1970/71†	1967/68	1968/69	1969/70	1970/71†
Wheat	1,432	1,265	1,312	1,349	1,526	1,277	1,519	1,729
Maize	1,560	1,491	1,508	1,522	2,300	2,368	2,397	2,342
Millet	535	476	500	494	907	814	874	854
Barley	155	148	88	70	126	117	84	76
Rice	1,208	1,196	1,142	1,137	2,591	2,961	2,605	2,534
Clover	2,682	2,732	2,748	2,770	43,616	4,400	45,177	45,539
Beans‡	310	340	302	261	284	299	278	256
Lentils	52	46	47	65	35	24	33	50
Onions‡	45	65	47	54	448	568	451	582
Sugar Cane	156	170	186	193	6,074	6,867	6,934	7,486

* 1 feddan = 1.038 acres. † Preliminary.
‡ Dry crop and the production of onions includes interplanted crop.

Livestock: (1970 estimates—'000) Cattle 2,088, Buffaloes 2,075, Camels 132, Goats 1,152, Sheep 1,968, Horses 40, Donkeys 1,306.

Eggs: (1969–70) 18 million.
Honey: Production (1970) 5,359 tons.

AREA AND PRODUCTION OF COTTON

	1968–69		1969–70		1970–71	
	'000 feddans*	'000 kantars†	'000 feddans*	'000 kantars†	'000 feddans*	'000 kantars†
Menoufi	339	1,783	376	2,050	363	1,916
Dandara	170	705	130	546	117	723
Ashmouni	189	979	176	795	137	838
Others	924	5,927	945	5,523	908	5,527
TOTAL	1,622	9,394	1,627	8,914	1,525	9,004

* 1 feddan = 1.038 acres. † 1 metric kantar = 157.5 kg.
Total cotton production for 1970–71 10.2 million kantars.

MINING AND INDUSTRY
('000 tons)

COMMODITY	1968	1969	1970	1971
Crude oil ('000 cu. metres)	9,890	14,245	18,945	17,010
Benzine ('000 cu. metres)	767	443	495	695
Kerosene ('000 cu. metres)	629	411	516	740
Mazout ('000 cu. metres)	3,045	1,428	1,624	2,572
Asphalt	143	41	59	73
Phosphate	1,441	660	582	574
Manganese	4	4	4	4
Common salt	622	385	444	398
Iron ore	447	460	n.a.	n.a.
Refined sugar	380	487	547	633
Cottonseed oil	92	125	137	117
Super phosphate	306	344	411	487
Caustic soda	20	20	20	18
Cement	3,147	3,613	3,684	3,921
Woollen fabrics	3	3	4	4
Cotton yarn	157	162	164	171
Cotton cloth	102	91	110	110
Electricity (million kWh.)	6,735	7,134	7,592	7,595

EGYPT—(Statistical Survey)

PRODUCTION CO-OPERATIVES

	1967	1968	1969
Agriculture	4,865	4,902	4,955
Sea Food	56	53	54

FINANCE

1,000 millièmes = 100 piastres = 1 Egyptian pound (£E).
Coins: 1, 2, and 5 millièmes; 1, 2, 5 and 10 piastres.
Notes: 5, 10, 25 and 50 piastres; 1, 5 and 10 pounds.
Exchange rates (April 1973): £1 sterling = 973.9 millièmes; U.S. $1 = 391.3 millièmes.
£E100 = £102.68 sterling = $255.56.

BUDGET ESTIMATES
(£E million)
EXPENDITURE
(Twelve months ending June 30th)

	Current Expenditure 1970–71	Current Expenditure 1971–72	% 1970–71	% 1971–72	Investment Expenditure 1970–71	Investment Expenditure 1971–72	% 1970–71	% 1971–72
Agriculture and Irrigation	122.9	146.5	6.5	7.3	42.2	55.9	14.1	16.0
Electricity and High Dam	45.1	54.7	2.4	2.7	27.2	25.1	9.1	7.2
Industry, Petroleum and Mineral Wealth	306.8	302.3	16.3	15.1	109.6	122.0	36.5	34.9
Transport and Communications	170.1	175.7	9.0	8.8	42.7	54.2	14.2	15.5
Trade and Supply	265.1	275.0	14.1	13.8	7.3	7.8	2.4	2.2
Housing and Public Utilities	25.9	28.2	1.4	1.4	18.1	21.6	6.0	6.2
Health, Social and Religious Services	93.4	106.5	4.9	5.3	3.2	4.4	1.1	1.3
Education, Culture and National Guidance	162.2	170.4	8.6	8.5	12.0	14.1	4.0	4.0
Defence, Security and Justice	299.6	312.6	15.9	15.6	1.9	1.9	0.6	0.5
Local Administration	43.8	47.3	2.3	2.4	5.5	5.4	1.8	1.5
Non-distributed Investments	—	—	—	—	28.6	33.0	9.6	9.4
Others*	351.9	381.6	18.6	19.1	1.7	4.6	0.6	1.3
Total	1,886.8	2,000.8	100.0	100.0	300.0	350.0	100.0	100.0

Current Revenues: (1970–71) £E1,782.3 million; (1971–72) £E1,922.0 million.
* Includes tours, presidency services and finance.

PLANNING

A ten-year Development Plan was due to begin on January 1st, 1973. The Plan calls for total investments of £E 8,400 million, of which 38 per cent will be invested in the first five years. It aims at doubling G.N.P. by 1982 at an annual G.N.P. growth rate of 7.2 per cent.

RESERVES AND CURRENCY IN CIRCULATION
(million £E at year end)

	1968	1969	1970
Gold Reserves	40.6	40.6	36.0
Currency in Circulation	489.0	517.0	546.0

EGYPT—(STATISTICAL SURVEY)

BALANCE OF PAYMENTS ESTIMATES
(million U.S.$)

	1965	1966	1967	1968	1969	1970
Balance of Goods and Services:						
Trade balance	−392	−356	−360	−185	−227	−374
Transportation (incl. Suez Canal)	205	217	106	− 3	− 5	− 9
Government	− 74	− 69	− 45	− 51	− 50	− 58
Other	− 1	23	1	− 9	− 22	− 22
	−262	−185	−298	−248	−304	−463
Transfers and Capital Movements:						
Transfers: Private	10	6	12	3	8	4
Government	10	6	122	251	288	304
Capital movements: Private	− 16	− 13	− 14	− 17	− 15	− 10
Government	147	128	108	19	− 66	15
	151	127	228	256	215	313
Changes in Assets and Liabilities:						
Commercial banks	12	60	− 12	− 4	34	32
Monetary gold	7	46	—	—	—	8
IMF accounts	− 14	− 25	4	− 2	− 21	24
Other assets and liabilities	100	− 24	81	− 14	80	104
Net errors and omissions	6	− 1	− 3	12	4	− 18
	111	58	70	− 8	89	150

Source: International Monetary Fund.

EXTERNAL TRADE
(£E million)

	1966	1967	1968	1969	1970	1971
Total Imports	465.5	344.4	289.6	277.3	341.1	400.0
Total Exports	263.1	246.2	270.3	323.9	331.2	343.2

PRINCIPAL COMMODITIES

IMPORTS	£E Million			
	1968	1969	1970	1971
Cereals and Milling Products	62.8	39.8	30.5	70.7
Animal and Vegetable Oils	12.3	12.4	16.9	23.2
General Grocery	7.1	3.3	11.1	6.2
Tobacco	7.0	7.4	7.5	8.1
Textiles	6.8	2.2	3.6	2.5
Paper and Paper Products	7.0	6.4	7.6	9.6
Pottery and Glassware	2.6	3.5	3.4	3.9
Clocks, Watches, Scientific Apparatus	2.2	2.7	2.8	2.7
Mineral Products	49.6	49.3	68.2	75.9
Chemical Products	29.6	37.5	37.4	44.5
Wood, Hides and Rubber	9.6	12.5	23.9	24.6
Machinery and Electrical Apparatus	42.2	40.9	57.1	55.1
Transport Equipment	26.1	23.1	27.5	32.3
Crude Petroleum	8.6	6.7	7.2	13.0
Iron and Steel	16.9	15.6	24.9	28.2

EGYPT—(Statistical Survey)

PRINCIPAL COMMODITIES—*continued*]

EXPORTS	1969 'ooo tons	1969 £E million	1970 'ooo tons	1970 £E million	1971 'ooo tons	1971 £E million
Cotton, raw	253	130.7	285	147.9	333	175.0
Cotton Yarn	48	36.3	43	35.6	42	35.6
Cotton Piece Goods	22	16.0	23	18.1	22	17.5
Rice	n.a.	55.3	n.a.	34.2	n.a.	24.5
Potatoes	81	2.5	90	3.7	61	2.0
Onions	142	7.8	97	7.3	92	5.8
Edible Fruits	101	6.8	110	7.2	145	9.3
Manganese and Phosphates	410	1.7	319	1.4	282	1.2
Crude Oil	1,574	7.4	3,579	15.3	529	1.9
Benzine, Kerosene and Mazout	140	0.8	52	0.5	41	0.3
Cement	820	4.2	345	1.7	1,362	5.9

EXPORTS OF COTTON
(kantars; one kantar = 99.05 lb.)

PRINCIPAL COUNTRIES	EXPORTS FOR WHOLE SEASON 1969–70	EXPORTS FOR WHOLE SEASON 1970–71
China, People's Republic	215,525	295,615
Czechoslovakia	348,708	427,083
France	187,177	169,020
Fed. Repub. of Germany	137,076	254,353
India	593,976	646,666
Italy	304,198	288,730
Japan	484,329	577,632
Poland	223,033	223,873
Romania	297,592	245,249
U.S.S.R.	2,439,990	1,945,009

VARIETIES	EXPORTS FOR WHOLE SEASON 1969–70	EXPORTS FOR WHOLE SEASON 1970–71
Giza 45	458,338	495,519
Menoufi	1,698,734	1,924,263
Giza 68	1,123,684	1,249,173
Giza 69	903,939	860,081
Giza 67	1,706,007	1,259,165
Dandara	357,858	n.a.
Giza 66	83,655	133,987
Others	105,574	150,916
TOTAL	6,437,789	6,073,104

PRINCIPAL COUNTRIES
(£E million)

IMPORTS	1968	1969	1970†	1971
Saudi Arabia	0.2	0.1	0.6	0.5
U.S.S.R.	46.2	37.6	34.9	54.0
Czechoslovakia	10.4	8.9	13.6	17.7
German Democratic Republic	14.1	12.8	8.4	15.8
Yugoslavia	7.0	6.2	8.9	6.2
United Kingdom	8.8	12.1	13.5	14.1
German Federal Republic	19.1	19.3	26.6	28.1
Italy	14.5	16.3	22.6	22.3
Japan	4.5	2.5	5.2	5.1
India	11.3	16.1	27.2	19.2
U.S.A.	16.2	19.6	20.9	22.2
Poland	7.6	6.0	9.9	8.6
Romania	18.6	5.5	11.3	9.9
France	33.2	28.5	25.3	20.7
China, People's Republic	8.9	5.6	6.7	7.7

† Excludes crude petroleum.

EGYPT—(STATISTICAL SURVEY)

PRINCIPAL COUNTRIES—*continued*]

EXPORTS	1968	1969	1970	1971
U.S.S.R.	75.9	107.0	122.4	136.2
Czechoslovakia	14.2	15.3	15.8	17.7
German Democratic Republic	9.8	14.6	19.7	11.2
Yugoslavia	5.1	9.8	8.2	4.1
United Kingdom	6.3	6.7	6.2	7.1
German Federal Republic	10.5	13.3	8.9	9.6
Italy	9.1	12.7	11.0	9.7
Japan	9.9	12.2	10.6	13.3
India	20.3	16.7	18.0	20.9
U.S.A.	5.8	4.8	2.7	2.9
Saudi Arabia	2.9	2.2	1.6	1.6
Poland	8.7	12.3	7.5	12.4
Romania	7.7	6.0	8.1	7.6
France	5.4	7.5	6.5	5.6
China, People's Republic	7.2	6.1	7.7	11.5

TRANSPORT

RAILWAYS

	1969–70	1970–71
Total Freight (million ton km.)	3,333	3,340
Total Passengers (million passenger km.)	6,529	6,772
Track Length (km.)	4,234	4,233

ROADS
(Licences issued at end of each year)

	1969	1970	1971
Buses	6,129	6,888	7,358
Lorries	21,976	23,178	27,351
Cars	122,155	131,104	141,974
Motor Cycles	21,968	25,025	27,494

SHIPPING
SUEZ CANAL TRAFFIC

YEAR	No. OF VESSELS	NET TONNAGE ('000)	No. OF PASSENGERS ('000)	RECEIPTS (£E '000)
1964	19,943	227,991	270	77,697
1965	20,289	246,817	291	85,792
1966	21,250	274,250	300	95,187
1967: Jan.–May	9,652	127,825	157	44,000

CIVIL AVIATION
(tons)

	1967	1968	1969	1970	1971
Cargo	10,064	12,185	14,512	15,269	17,433
Mail	1,216	1,266	1,379	1,151	1,201

TOURISM

	Total Visitors	Arabs	Europeans	Americans	Others	Total (guest-nights) ('000)
1969	345,343	193,977	85,463	32,769	33,134	4,396
1970	357,661	230,803	65,985	25,427	35,446	4,574
1971	428,062	260,169	94,540	30,051	43,302	5,988
1972	540,880	n.a.	n.a.	36,003	n.a.	n.a.

Tourist Accommodation (1969): 17,730 hotel beds in 232 hotels under the supervision of the Ministry of Tourism. Other Tourist Accommodation (1969): 25,753 hotel beds in 725 hotels.

EDUCATION
(1970–71)

	Classes	Teachers	Pupils
Primary	88,056	96,693	3,740,551
General and Technical Preparatory	21,797	27,868	851,936
General Secondary	7,757	13,424	297,867
Technical Secondary	8,072	13,401	271,638
Teacher Training	748	2,113	25,526
Higher Education	n.a.	4,570	227,463

Sources: Central Agency for Public Mobilization and Statistics, Cairo; Research Department, National Bank of Egypt, Cairo; International Monetary Fund.

THE CONSTITUTION

The Permanent Constitution of the Arab Republic of Egypt was approved by referendum on September 11th, 1971. There are six chapters with 193 articles, many of them based on the 1964 Interim Constitution, but chapters 3 and 4 show a considerable degree of liberalization of the former statutes.

CHAPTER 1
The State

Egypt is an Arab Republic with a democratic, socialist system based on the alliance of the working people and derived from the country's historical heritage and the spirit of Islam.

The Egyptian people are part of the Arab nation, who work towards total Arab unity.

Islam is the religion of the State; Arabic is its official language and the Islamic code is a principal source of legislation. The State safeguards the freedom of worship and of performing rites for all religions.

Sovereignty is of the people alone which is the source of all powers.

The protection, consolidation and preservation of the socialist gains is a national duty: the sovereignty of law is the basis of the country's rule, and the independence of immunity of the judiciary are basic guarantees for the protection of rights and liberties.

The Arab Socialist Union is the political organization of the State which represents the alliance of the working forces of the people; the farmers, workers, soldiers, the intelligentsia and national capitalism.

CHAPTER 2
The Fundamental Elements of Society

Social solidarity is the basis of Egyptian society, and the family is its nucleus.

The State ensures the equality of men and women in both political and social rights in line with the provisions of Moslem legislation.

Work is a right, an honour and a duty which the State guarantees together with the services of social and health insurance, pensions for incapacity and unemployment.

The economic basis of the Republic is the socialist based on sufficiency and justice. It is calculated to prevent exploitation and to level up differences between classes.

The people control all means of production and regulate the national economy according to a comprehensive development plan which determines the role of Arab and foreign capital.

Property is subject to the people's control.

Property shall be expropriated only by law and against fair compensation. Nationalization shall also be by law for public interest considerations or socialist objectives.

Agricultural holding may be limited by law.

The State follows a comprehensive central planning and compulsory planning approach based on quinquennial socio-economic and cultural development plans whereby the society's resources are mobilized and put to the best use.

The public Sector assumes the leading role in the development of the national economy. The State provides absolute protection of this Sector as well as the property of co-operative societies and trade unions against all attempts to tamper with them.

Chapter 3
Public Liberties, Rights and Duties

All citizens are equal before the law. Personal liberty is a natural right and no one may be arrested, searched, imprisoned or restricted in any way without a court order.

Houses have sanctity, and shall not be placed under serveillance or searched without a court order with reasons given for such action.

The law safeguards the sanctities of the private lives of all citizens; so have all postal, telegraphic telephonic and other means of communication which may not therefore be confiscated, or persued except by a court order giving the reasons, and only for a specified period.

Public rights and freedoms are also inviolate and all calls for atheism and anything that reflects adversely on divine religions is prohibited.

The freedom of opinion, the press, printing and publications and all information media are safeguarded.

Press censorship is forbidden, so are warnings, suspensions or cancellations through administrative channels. Under exceptional circumstances as in cases of emergency or in war time, censorship may be imposed on information media for a definite period.

Egyptians have the right to permanent or provisional emigration and no Egyptian may be deported or prevented from returning to the country.

Citizens have the right to private meetings in peace provided they bear no arms. Egyptians also have the right to form societies which have no secret activities or are hostile to the government. Public meetings are also allowed within the limits of the law.

Chapter 4
Sovereignty of the Law

All acts of crime should be specified together with the penalties for the acts.

Recourse to justice, it says, is a right of all citizens, and those who are financially unable, will be assured of means to defend their rights.

Arrested persons may protest against their detention and their protests should be decided upon within a prescribed period otherwise they should be released.

Chapter 5
System of Government

The President, who must be at least 40 years old, is nominated by at least one-third of the members of the People's Assembly, approved by at least two-thirds, and elected by popular referendum. His term is for six years and he 'may be re-elected for another subsequent term.' He may take emergency measures in the interests of the state but these measures must be approved by referendum within 60 days.

The People's Assembly, elected for five years, is the legislative body and approves general policy, the budget and the development plan. It shall have 'not less than 350' elected members, at least half of whom shall be workers or farmers, and the President may appoint up to ten additional members. In exceptional circumstances the Assembly, by a two-thirds vote, may authorize the President to rule by decree for a specified period but these decrees must be approved by the Assembly at its next meeting.

The Assembly may pass a vote of no confidence in a Deputy Prime Minister, a Minister or a Deputy Minister, provided three days' notice of the vote is given, and the minister must then resign. In the case of the Prime Minister, the Assembly may "prescribe" his responsibility and submit a report to the President: if the President disagrees with the report but the Assembly persists, then the matter is put to a referendum: if the people support the President the Assembly is dissolved; if they support the Assembly the President must accept the resignation of the government. The President may dissolve the Assembly prematurely, but his action must be approved by a referendum and elections must be held within 60 days.

Executive Authority is vested in the President, who may appoint one or more vice-presidents and appoints all ministers. He may also dismiss the vice-presidents and ministers. The President has 'the right to refer to the people in connection with important matters related to the country's higher interests.' The Government is described as 'the supreme executive and administrative organ of the state'. Its members, whether full ministers or deputy ministers, must be at least 35 years old. Further sections define the roles of Local Government, Specialized National Councils, the Judiciary, the Higher Constitutional Court, the Socialist Prosecutor General, the Armed Forces and National Defence Council and the Police.

Chapter 6
General and Transitional Provisions

No law shall normally have retroactive effect, but this may be changed, except in criminal matters, with the approval of a majority of the Assembly. Articles of the constitution may be revised, at the suggestion of the President or one-third of the Assembly, but the revision must be submitted for approval by a public referendum. The term of the present President shall date from his election as President of the United Arab Republic.

THE GOVERNMENT

THE PRESIDENCY
President: Col. Anwar Sadat.
Vice-Presidents: Husain Shafei, Mahmoud Fawzi.

COUNCIL OF MINISTERS
(July 1973)

Prime Minister: Anwar Sadat.
Deputy Premier and Minister of Culture and Information: Dr. Mohamed Abdul Hatem.
Deputy Premier and Minister of the Interior: Mamdouh Salem.
Deputy Premier and Minister of Finance, Economy and Commerce: Abdul Aziz Higazi.
Deputy Premier and Minister of Religious Affairs: Abdel Aziz Kamel.
Minister of War: Gen. Ahmed Ismail Ali.
Minister of Foreign Affairs: Mohamed Hassan el Zayyat.
Minister of Information: Dr. Mourad Ghaleb.
Minister of Communications: Dr. Mahmoud Riad (namesake of present Sec.-Gen. of Arab League).
Minister of Power: Ahmed Sultan.
Minister of Civil Aviation: Ahmed Nouh.
Minister of Social Affairs: Aisha Rateb.
Minister of Education: Ali Abdul Razek.
Minister of Irrigation: Aziz Youssef Saad.
Minister of Culture: Youssef el Sebai.
Minister of Agriculture and Agrarian Reform: Dr. Mohamed Moheb Zaky.
Minister of Health: Dr. Mahmoud Mohamed Mahfouz.
Minister of Planning: El Sayed Gaballa el Sayed.
Minister of Housing and Construction: Dr. Mahmud Amin Abdul Hafez.
Minister of Military Production: Lt.Gen. Ahmed Kamel al Badri.
Minister of Justice: Fakhri Mohamed Abdel Nabi.
Minister of Petroleum and Mineral Resources: Ahmed Ezzedine Hassan Hilal.
Minister of Industry: Ibrahim Salem Mohamdein.
Minister of Land Reclamation: Dr. Osman Adly Badran.
Minister of Labour: Salahedine Mohamed Gharib.
Minister of Tourism: Ismail Fahmi.
Minister of Higher Education: Mohamed Kamel Leila.
Minister of Marine Transport: Gen. Abdel Moti el Arabi.
Minister of Supply and Home Trade: Gen. Ahmed Mohamed Thabet.
Minister of Al Azhar Affairs: Abdul Aziz Issa.
Minister of Insurance: Hassan el Sherif.
Minister of Transport: Al Hussein Abdul Latif.
Minister of State for Planning: Ismail Sabri Abdullah.
Minister of State for Youth: Ahmed Kamal Aboul Magd.
Minister of State for Local Government and Popular Organizations: Ahmed Fouad Moheiddin.
Minister of State for Relations with the National Assembly: Albert Barsoum Salama.
Minister of State for Cabinet Affairs: Abdul Fateh Abdullah.

DIPLOMATIC REPRESENTATION

EMBASSIES AND LEGATIONS IN CAIRO
(E) Embassy; (L) Legation.

Afghanistan: 59 Sh. Oroba (Heliopolis) (E); *Ambassador:* Shamsuddin Magruh.
Albania: 29 Sh. Ismail Muhammad (Zamalek) (E); *Ambassador:* Ajet Simixhiu.
Algeria: 14 Sh. Brézil (Zamalek) (E); *Ambassador:* Boualem Bessaieh.
Argentina: 8 Sh. As-Saleh Ayoub (Zamalek) (E); *Ambassador:* Paulino Musacchio.
Australia: 1097 Corniche el Nil (Garden City) (E); *Ambassador:* K. R. Douglas-Scott.
Austria: 21 Sh. Sadd El-Aaly (Dokki) (E); *Ambassador:* Heinz Standenat.
Belgium: 8 Rue Abdel Khalek Saroit (E); *Ambassador:* Pierre Ancieux Henri de Faveaux.
Bolivia: 6 Rue Nawal (Dokki) (E); *Ambassador:* (vacant).
Brazil: 27 Rue El Guézira El Wosta (Zamalek) (E); *Ambassador:* Luiz Bastian Pinto.
Bulgaria: 141 Rue El Tahrir (Dokki) (E); *Ambassador:* Gueorgui Tanev.
Burma: 24 Rue Muhammad Mazhar (Zamalek) (E); *Ambassador:* Zahre Lian.
Burundi: 9 Rue Mahmoud Hassan (Heliopolis) (E); *Ambassador:* Isaac Rwasa.
Cameroon: 14 Sh. Wodi El Nil (Dokki) (E); *Ambassador:* William Forcho Lima.
Canada: 6 Sh. Muhammad Fahmy El Sayed (Garden City) (E); *Ambassador:* David Stansfield.
Chile: 5 Sh. Chagaret El-Dorr (Zamalek) (E); *Ambassador:* Mario Prieto Serviere.
China, People's Republic: 14 Sh. Bahgat Aly (Zamalek) (E); *Ambassador:* Chai Tse-Min.
Colombia: 15 Sh. Aboul Feda (Zamalek) (E); *Ambassador:* Dr. Jaime R. Echavarría.
Congo People's Republic: 16 Sh. Téba, Cité des Ingénieurs (Dokki) (E); *Ambassador:* Leon Albert Angor.
Cuba: Villa No. 1, Sh. Sennan (Dokki) (E); *Ambassador:* Dr. Carlos Varela.

EGYPT—(DIPLOMATIC REPRESENTATION)

Cyprus: 3 Sh. Nabil El-Wakkad (Dokki) (E); *Ambassador:* ANTIS G. SOTERIADES.
Czechoslovakia: 43 Sh. Muhammad Mazhar (Zamalek) (E); *Ambassador:* MECISLAV JABLONSKY.
Denmark: 12 Sh. Hassan Sabri (Zamalek) (E); *Ambassador:* EYVIND BARTELS.
Dominican Republic: Maison Jacques, Midan Mustafa Kamel (L).
Ecuador: 15 Sh. Aboul Feda (Zamalek) (E); *Chargé d'Affaires:* LEONARDO ARIZAGA.
El Salvador: *Ambassador:* HUGO LINO.
Ethiopia: 12 Midan Bahlawi (Dokki) (E); *Ambassador:* ATO MALLAS MIKAEL ANDOM.
Finland: 2 El-Malek El-Afdal (Zamalek) (E); *Ambassador:* BABBA MALINEN.
France: 29 Sh. Guizeh (E); *Ambassador:* BRUNO DE LEUSSE DE SYON.
German Democratic Republic: 13 Sh. Hussein Wassef (Dokki) (E); *Ambassador:* HANS-JOACHIM RADDE.
Germany, Federal Republic of: (E); *Ambassador:* HANS-GEORG STELTZER.
Ghana: Villa 24, Sh. 22 (Dokki) (E); *Ambassador:* Maj.-Gen. CLENLAND COFIE BRUCE.
Greece: 18 Sh. Aïcha El-Taïmouria (Garden City) (E); *Ambassador:* ANTOINE KORANTIS.
Guatemala: *Ambassador:* ANGELO ASTURA RIVERA.
Guinea: 46 Sh. Muhammad Mazhar (Zamalek) (E); *Ambassador:* M'TEMPA BANGOURA.
Hungary: 29 Sh. Muhammad Mazhar (Zamalek) (E); *Ambassador:* JENO RANDE.
India: 5 Mahad El Swissri (Zamalek) (E); *Ambassador:* ASHOK BALKRISHNA BHADKAMKAR.
Indonesia: 13 Sh. Aïcha El-Taïmouria (Garden City) (E); *Ambassador:* MOHAMED SHARIF PADMADISASTRA.
Iran: 11 Sh. Okhab (Dokki) (E); *Ambassador:* KHOSROV KHOSROVANI.
Iraq: 9 Sh. Muhammad Mazhar (Zamalek) (E); *Ambassador:* SAMIR ABDUL AZIZ AL-NAJM.
Italy: Sh. El Salamlik (Garden City) (E); *Ambassador:* FELICE CATALANO DI MELILLI.
Japan: 10 Sh. Ibrahim Naguib (Garden City) (E); *Ambassador:* MICHITOSHI TAKAHASHI.
Jordan: 6 Sh. El-Gohainy (Dokki) (E); *Ambassador:* Maj.-Gen. ALI AL HIYARI.
Kenya: 7 Ahmed El Meleky St. (Dokki) (E); *Ambassador:* F. M. HINAWY.
Khmer Republic: 2 Sh. Tahawia (Giza) (E); *Ambassador:* SARIN CHHAK.
Korea, Democratic Peoples' Republic: (E); *Ambassador:* KIM BYONG HO.
Kuwait: 12 Sh. Nabil El-Wakkad (Dokki) (E); *Ambassador:* HAMAD ISSA EL-RUJAIB.
Lebanon: 5 Sh. Ahmed Nessim (Guizeh) (E); *Ambassador:* Dr. HALIM ABUIZZEDDIN.
Liberia: 2 Sh. 22, Cité Awkaf (Dokki) (E); *Ambassador:* JOHN W. GRIGSBY.
Libya: 7 Sh. Saleh Ayoub (Zamalek) (E); *Ambassador:* SAAD EL DIN BUSHWEIRAB.
Malaysia: 34 Sh. El Messaha (Dokki) (E); *Ambassador:* TUAN HAJI ABDUL KHALID.
Mali: 4 Sh. Margil (Zamalek) (E); *Ambassador:* BOUBACAR DIALLO.
Mauritania: 37 Sh. Ismail Muhammad (Zamalek) (E); *Ambassador:* MOHAMMED OULD GIDDO.
Mexico: 5 Sh. Dar El Shifa (Garden City) (E); *Ambassador:* CELSO HUMBERTO DELGADO RAMÍREZ.

Mongolian People's Republic: 46 Sh. Gameat El Dowal El Arabia (Dokki) (E); *Ambassador:* DEMIDDAGVA.
Morocco: 10 Sh. Saleh El Dine (Zamalek) (E); *Ambassador:* MAHDI MRANI ZENTAR.
Nepal: 24 Sh. Syria (Dokki) (E); *Ambassador:* JHARENDRA NARAYAN SINGH.
Netherlands: 18 Sh. Hassan Sabri (Zamalek) (E); *Ambassador:* FRANZ VON OVEN.
Nigeria: 13 Sh. Gabalaya (Zamalek) (E); *Ambassador:* H. MUSA.
Norway: 2 Sh. Chafik Mansour (Zamalek) (E); *Ambassador:* TANCRED IBSEN.
Pakistan: 22 Sh. Mansour Muhammad (Zamalek) (E); *Ambassador:* MOHAMED ISLAM MALIK.
Panama: Villa No. 20 Sh. 75 (Maadi) (E); *Ambassador:* M. HERRERA.
Peru: 9 Sh. El Kamel Muhammad (Zamalek) (E); *Ambassador:* FELIPE VALIVIESO BELAUNDE.
Philippines: 5 Sh. Ibn El-Walid (Dokki) (E); *Ambassador:* YUSUP ABUBAKAR.
Poland: 5 Sh. Aziz Osman (Zamalek) (E); *Ambassador:* ALBERT MORSKI.
Romania: 6 Sh. El Kamel Muhammad (Zamalek) (E); *Ambassador:* PETRU BURLACU.
Saudi Arabia: Villa 12, Sh. El Kamel Mohamed (Zamalek) (E); *Ambassador:* SHAIKH FUAD AHMAD NAZIR.
Senegal: 2 Sh. Ahmed Ragheb (Garden City) (E); *Ambassador:* MUSTAFA CISSE.
Sierra Leone: 56 Sh. Amman (Dokki) (E); *Ambassador:* (vacant).
Singapore: 6 Sh. Nawal (Dokki) (E); *Ambassador:* Dr. HAJI AHMEN BIN MUHAMMAD IBRAHIM.
Somalia: 9 Sh. Rawakeh (Engineer's City) (E); *Ambassador:* ABDULLAHI ADAN AHMED.
Spain: 28 Ahmed Hechmat St. (Zamalek) (E); *Ambassador:* MANUEL ALABARAT.
Sri Lanka: 8 Sh. Yehia Ibrahim (Zamalek) (E); *Ambassador:* RANAWAKA ARATCHIE PERERA.
Sudan: 3 Sh. El Ibrahimi (Garden City) (E); *Ambassador:* MUHAMMAD MIRGHANI MUBARAK.
Sweden: 4 Sh. Sadd El Aali (Dokki) (E); *Ambassador:* LARS PETRUS FOLKE VON CELSINE.
Switzerland: 10 Sh. Abdel Khalek Saroit (E); *Ambassador:* HANS CARL FREY.
Syria: 17 Sh. Ahmad Sabry (Zamalek) (E); *Ambassador:* Dr. SAMI DROUBI.
Tanzania: 18 Sh. Ahmed Hechmat (Zamalek) (E); *Ambassador:* CHRISTOPHER P. NGUIZA.
Thailand: 2 Sh. El Malek El Afdal (Zamalek) (E); *Ambassador:* NIBHON WILAIRAI.
Trinidad and Tobago: Addis Ababa, Ethiopia (E).
Tunisia: 26 Sh. El Guezira (Zamalek) (E); *Chargé d'Affaires:* MUHAMMAD IBN FADL.
Turkey: Avenue El Nil (Giza) (E); *Ambassador:* SEMIH GUNVER.
Uganda: 9 Midan El Missaha (Dokki) (E); *Ambassador:* Capt. YOUNIS KHAMIS WENN.
U.S.S.R.: 95 Sh. El Giza (Giza) (E); *Ambassador:* VLADIMIR VINOGRADOV.
United Arab Emirates: (address not available) (E); *Ambassador:* TARIM OMRAN TARIM.
United Kingdom: Kasrah El Dubara (Garden City) (E); *Ambassador:* Sir PHILIP ADAMS.
Uruguay: 6 Sh. Loutfallah (Zamalek) (E); *Ambassador:* M. S. FLORES.

EGYPT—(Diplomatic Representation, People's Assembly, Political Party, etc.)

Vatican City: 5 Sh. Muhammad Mazhar (Zamalek) (Apostolic Nunciature); *Nuncio:* Mgr. Bruna Heim.
Venezuela: 5 Sh. Mansour Muhammad (Zamalek) (E); *Ambassador:* Dr. Germán Nava Carrillo.
Democratic Republic of Viet-Nam: 21 Sh. Giza (Giza) (E); *Ambassador:* Nguyen Xuan.
Viet-Nam, Republic of: *Ambassador:* Tran Van Hoa.
Yemen Arab Republic: 28 Sh. Amin El Rafei (Dokki) (E); *Ambassador:* Moustapha Ahmed Yacoub.
Yemen People's Democratic Republic: Sh. Hassanein Higazi (Dokki) (E); *Ambassador:* Abdel-Malik Ismail Muhammad Hasan.
Yugoslavia: 33 Sh. El Mansour Muhammad (Zamalek) (E); *Ambassador:* Mihalo Javorski.
Zaire: 23 Sh. Mecca El-Mokarrama (Dokki) (E); *Ambassador:* Giano Biano Te Wapimda.
Zambia: 30 Sh. Montazah (Zamalek) (E); *Ambassador:* Matiya Nealande.

Egypt also recognizes the Central African Republic, Chad, Korea (D.P.R.), Madagascar, Mauritius and Rwanda.

PEOPLE'S ASSEMBLY

Elections

Elections October 27th and November 3rd, 1971

Of the 360 seats 53 per cent were won by farmers and workers.

Speaker: Hafez Badawi.

POLITICAL PARTY

Arab Socialist Union: Cairo; f. 1957 as the *National Union*, renamed 1961; the sole political party; Chair. President Sadat; Sec.-Gen. of Central Committee: Muhammad Hafez Ghanem; there is a Higher Exec. Cttee., a Central Cttee. and a Nat. Congress. Large-scale expulsions were made from the Arab Socialist Union in February 1973.

DEFENCE

Supreme Commander of the Armed Forces: President Anwar El-Sadat.
Chief of Staff of the Army: Gen. Saad-al-Din al-Shazli.
Commander of the Air Force: Air Vice-Marshal Husni Mubarak.
Defence budget 1971: £E650 million.
Military service: 3 years.
Total armed forces: 325,000: army 285,000; navy 15,000; air force 25,000. Paramilitary forces (National Guard): 120,000. Missile Command: 4,000.

JUDICIAL SYSTEM

The Courts of Law in Egypt are basically divided into four categories as follows:
1. *The Supreme Court* (called *The Court of Cassation*)
2. *The Courts of Appeal*
3. *The Primary Tribunals*
4. *The Summary Tribunals*

Each Court contains criminal and civil chambers.

1. The Supreme Court

The highest Court of Law in Egypt. Its sessions are held at Cairo and its jurisdiction covers the whole Egyptian territory.

Final judgements rendered in criminal and civil matters may be referred to the Supreme Court—by the accused or the Public Prosecution in criminal matters, and by any of the litigants in civil matters—in cases of misapplications or misinterpretations of the law as applied by the competent court in final judgement, as well as in cases of irregularity in the form of the judgement or the procedures having effect on that judgement.

The Supreme Court is composed of the Chief Justice, four Deputy-Chief Justices and thirty-six Justices.

2. Courts of Appeal

There are six Courts of Appeal situated in the more important Governorates of Egypt: Cairo, Alexandria, Asyut, Mansura, Tanta, and Beni Suef. Each of these courts contains a criminal chamber, *The Assize Court*, to try cases of felonies, and a civil chamber to hear appeals filed by any of the litigants in civil matters against a judgement rendered by the primary tribunal, where the law so permits.

President in Cairo: M. Mahmoud Abd-el-Latif.

3. Primary Tribunals

In each Governorate, there is a Primary Tribunal, each of which contains several chambers. Each chamber is composed of three Judges. Some of these chambers try criminal cases, whilst others hear civil litigations.

Primary Tribunals sit as Courts of Appeal in certain cases, according to circumstances.

4. Summary Tribunals

Summary Tribunals are branches of the Primary Tribunals and are situated in the different districts of Egypt. Each of these tribunals is composed of a single Judge.

Summary Tribunals hear civil and criminal matters of minor importance according to certain details.

The *Sharia Courts* or courts of Islamic Law, and the religious courts maintained by non-Muslim minorities have been abolished since 1955.

The Public Prosecution

The Public Prosecution is headed by the Attorney-

General and consists of a large number of Attorneys, Chief Prosecutors and Prosecutors, who are distributed among the various districts of Egypt. The Public Prosecution is represented at all criminal Courts and also at litigation in certain civil matters. Furthermore, the enforcement of judgement rendered in criminal cases is controlled and supervised by the Public Prosecution.

Attorney-General: AHMAD MUSA.

The Supreme Judicial Council

This Council exists to guarantee the independence of the judicial system from outside interference. Under the presidency of the Chief Justice, the Supreme Judicial Council contains the following members:
  the Chief Justice
  two Deputy Chief Justices
  the Under-Secretary of State for the Ministry of Justice
  the Attorney-General
  the President of the Court of Appeal in Cairo
  the President of the Primary Tribunal in Cairo.

All matters concerning the promotion, discipline or otherwise of the members of the judicial system are referred to this Council.

An Arbitration Bureau was set up in 1966 to investigate cases between state and public sector organizations.

RELIGION

Over 90 per cent of Egyptians are Muslims, and almost all of these follow Sunni tenets. The four tenets are represented in Egypt and all follow the Holy Koran and the Sunna. Villagers adhere strictly to Islamic rites and teachings. Since the Fatimide dynasty Egyptians have attached great importance to the decoration of their mosques. St. Mark is considered to be the first founder of the Coptic Church after Jesus. The Coptic Church is known historically as the Church of Alexandria or the Egyptian Coptic Orthodox Church, and is still considered the main Eastern church. There are over a million Copts in Egypt forming the largest religious minority, there is no discrimination of any kind against them, and they have contributed greatly to the cultural life of Egypt. Besides the Copts there are other Christian minorities numbering about a quarter of a million and consisting of Greek Orthodox, Roman Catholics, Armenians and Protestants. There is also a small Jewish minority.

Sheikh of Al Azhar: MUHAMMAD EL FAHHAM.
Grand Mufti of Egypt: Sheikh KHATIR MUHAM MUHAMMAD

Coptic Orthodox Church: Azbakia, Cairo; f. 61 A.D.; Leader Pope SHANOUDA.

Coptic Catholic Church: Patriarch Cardinal STEPHANOS I. SIDAROUSS, 34 Sh. Ibn Sandar, Koubbeh Bridge, Cairo; 4 dioceses; 120,000 mems.; publ. *Al Salah*.

Greek Catholic Patriarchate: P.O.B. 50076 Beirut, Lebanon; 16 rue Daher, Cairo; Patriarch of Antioch, of Alexandria and of Jerusalem His Beatitude MAXIMOS V HAKIM; 750,000 mems. in the Middle East.

Greek Orthodox Church: Patriarch CHRISTOPHOROS II.

Armenian Apostolic Church: 179 Ramses Ave., Cairo, P.O.B. 48-Faggala; Archbishop MAMPRE SIROUNIAN.

Armenian Catholic Patriarchate: 36 Mohammed Sabri Abou Alam Street, Cairo; Archbishop RAPHAEL BAYAN.

Maronite Church: Archbishop PIERRE DIB.

Jewish Community: Office of the Chief Rabbi, Rabbi HAIM DOUEK; 13 Sebil-el-Khazindar St., Abbassia, Cairo.

THE PRESS

Despite a high illiteracy rate the Egyptian press is well developed. Cairo is the biggest publishing centre in the Middle East.

Several of the Cairo newspapers and magazines have important circulations in other Arab countries although entry in Saudi Arabia, Jordan and Tunisia is at present either restricted or altogether banned for political reasons.

Newspapers were placed under the control of the National Union (later reformed as the Arab Socialist Union) by a decree issued by President Nasser in May 1960. Journalists were obliged to obtain licences from the National Union and publishing houses, hitherto free, were placed under its control. All the important newspapers and magazines are now owned and controlled by the Government, although the four big publishing houses of al-Ahram, Dar al-Hilal, Dar Akhbar al-Yom and Dar al-Gomhouriya, operate as separate entities and compete with each other commercially. The Government allows the publishing houses a considerable amount of freedom in dealing with domestic affairs but comment on foreign affairs entirely reflects the views of the Government. Dar al-Hilal is concerned only with magazines and publishes *al-Mussawar*, *Hawa'a* and *al-Kawakeb*. Dar Akhbar al-Yom publishes the daily newspaper *al-Akhbar*, the weekly newspaper *Akhbar al-Yom* and the weekly magazines *Akher Saa* and *Al Guil el Gedid*.

Dar al Gomhouriya publishes the daily *al-Gomhouriya*, the daily English language paper *Egyptian Gazette*, the daily French newspaper *Le Progrès Egyptien* and the afternoon paper *al-Misaa*.

The most authoritative daily newspaper is the very old established *al-Ahram*. Other popular large circulation magazines are *Rose al-Youssef*, *Sabah al-Kheir* and *al Izaa w'al Television*. Minority language groups are catered for by the Greek language papers *Tachydromos* and *Phos* and the Armenian language papers *Arev* and *Houssaper*.

DAILIES

ALEXANDRIA

Barid al-Charikat: P.O.B. 813; f. 1952; Arabic; evening; commerce, finance, insurance and marine affairs, etc.; Editor S. BENEDUCCI; circ. 15,000.

al-Ittihad al-Misri: 13 Sharia Sidi Abdel Razzak; f. 1871; Arabic; evening; Propr. ANWAR MAHER FARAG; Dir. HASSAN MAHER FARAG.

Journal d'Alexandrie, Le: 1 Sharia Rolo; French; evening; Editor CHARLES ARCACHE.

Phare Egyptien, Le: 26 Avenue Hourriya; f. 1926; Greek-owned, French language; morning; independent; Editor ANTOINE GERONIMO.

EGYPT—(THE PRESS)

Réforme, La: 8 Passage Sherif; f. 1895; French; noon; Propr. Comte AZIZ DE SAAB; circ. 7,000.

al-Safeer: 4 El-Sahafa St.; f. 1924; Arabic; evening; Editor MOSTAFA SHARAF.

Tachydromos-Egypts: 4 Sharia Zangarol; f. 1882; Greek; morning; liberal; Publisher PENY COUTSOUMIS; Editor DINOS COUTSOUMIS; circ. 11,000.

CAIRO

al-Ahram (*The Pyramids*): United Arab Press, Gallaa St.; f. 1875; Arabic; morning; independent; Editor MUHAMMAD HASSANEIN HEIKAL; circ. 260,000.

al-Akhbar: Dar Akhbar al-Yom, Sharia al-Sahafa; f. 1952; Arabic; independent; Editor MUSA SABRI; circ. 250,000.

Arev: 3 Sharia Soliman Halaby; Armenian; evening; Editor AVEDIS YAPOUDJIAN.

Egyptian Gazette: 24 Sharia Galal; f. 1880; the only English daily; morning; Editor Dr. AMIN MOHAMED ABOUL-ENEIN; circ. 10,000.

al-Gomhouriya (*The Republic*): 24 Sharia Zakaria Ahmed; f. 1953; Arabic; morning; official organ of the Arab Socialist Union; Chief Editor M. B. BADAWI; circ. 250,000.

Houssaper: Armenian; circ. 1,500.

Journal d'Egypte, Le: 1 Borsa Suedida St.; f. 1950; French; morning; Propr. and Editor EDGARD GALLAD; circ. 11,000.

al-Misaa: 24 Sharia Zakaria Ahmed; Arabic; evening; Editor N. MESTIKAOUI; circ. 40,000.

Phos: 14 Zakaria Ahmed St.; f. 1896; Greek; morning; Editor S. PATERAS; Man. BASILE A. PATERAS; circ. 20,000.

Progrès Egyptien, Le: 24 Sharia Zakaria Ahmed; f. 1890; French; morning including Sundays; Editor MAURICE YACCARINI; circ. 14,500.

PERIODICALS
ALEXANDRIA

al Ahad Al Gedid: 88 al-Tatwig Street; Editor-in-Chief MAHMUD ABDEL MALAK KORITAM; General Manager MUHAMMAD KORITAM.

Alexandria Medical Journal: 4 G. Carducci; English, French and Arabic; quarterly; publ. by Alexandria Medical Asscn.; Editor G. E. HANNO; circ. 1,500.

Amitié Internationale: 59 Avenue Hourriya; f. 1957; publ. by Asscn. Egypt. d'Amitié Inter.; Arabic and French; quarterly; Editor Dr. ZAKI BADAOUI.

L'Annuaire des Sociétés Egyptiennes par Actions: 23 Midan Tahrir; f. 1930; annually in December; French; Propr. ELIE I. POLITI; Editor OMAR EL-SAYED MOURSI.

L'Echo Sportif: 7 rue de l'Archevêché; French; weekly; Propr. MICHEL BITTAR.

L'Economiste Egyptien: 11 rue de la Poste, Alexandria; P.O. Box 847; f. 1901; weekly; Propr. MARGUERITE HOSNY.

Egypte-Sports-Cinéma: 7 Avenue Hourriya; French; weekly; Editor EMILE ASSAAD.

Egyptian Cotton Gazette: P.O.B. 433; organ of the Alexandria Cotton Exporters Association; English; three times yearly; Editor M. HASSOUNA.

Egyptian Cotton Statistics: English; weekly.

Gazette d'Orient, La: 5 rue de l'Ancienne Bourse; Propr. MAURICE BETITO.

Guide des Industries: 2 Sharia Adib; French; annual; Editor SIMON A. BARANIS.

Informateur des Assurances: 1 Sharia Adib; f. 1936; French; monthly; Propr. ELIE I. POLITI; Editor SIMON A. BARANIS.

Journal Suisse d'Egypte, Le: 18 Sharia Saleh El-Dine; Editor M. MAURICE FIECHTER.

Médecine d'Egypte: 298 rue Port Said, Cléopatra; Editor HUBERT DE LEUSSE; French.

Réforme Illustrée, La: 8 Passage Sherif; f. 1925; French; weekly; Propr. Comte AZIZ DE SAAB; circ. 20,000.

Répertoire Permanent de Législation Egyptienne: 27 Ave. El Guesch, Chatby-les-Bains; f. 1932; French and Arabic; Editor V. SISTO.

Revue des Questions Douanières: 2 Sharia Sinan; Arabic; monthly; economics and agriculture; Propr. ALY MUHAMMAD ALY.

Revue Economique Trimestrielle: c/o Banque de Port-Said, 18 Talaat Harb St., Alexandria; French (f. 1929) and Arabic (f. 1961) editions; quarterly; Editor: MAHMOUD SAMY EL ADAWAY (Arabic and French editions).

Sanaet El-Nassig (*L'Industrie Textile*): 5 rue de l'Archevêché; Arabic and French; monthly; Editor PHILIPPE COIAS.

L'Universitaire—Science et Techniques: 298 Sharia Port Said, Cléopatra; French; scientific and technical; quarterly; Editor HUBERT DE LEUSSE.

Voce d'Italia: 90 Sharia Farahde; Italian; fortnightly; Editor R. AVELLINO.

CAIRO

Actualité: 28 Sharia Sherif Pasha; French; weekly; Dir. and Propr. GEORGES TASSO.

Akhbar al-Yom: 6 Sharia al-Sahafa; Arabic; weekly; Editor IHSAN ABDUL QADDOUS; circ. 650,000.

Akher Saa: Dar Akhbar al-Yom, Sharia al-Sahafa; f. 1934; Arabic; weekly; independent; Editor-in-Chief AHMED EL-SAWI MUHAMMAD; circ. 150,000.

al-Ahd al-Goumhouri: 132 Sharia Kalaa; Editor ABDEL-KHALEK TAKIA.

al Ahram Al Iqtisadi: United Arab Press, Gallaa St.; economic and political affairs; owned by *Al Ahram*; circ. 12,000.

al-Azhar: Sharia al-Azhar; Arabic; Dir MUHAMMAD FARID WAGDI.

al-Doctor: 8 Hoda Shaarawy St.; f. 1947; Arabic; monthly; Editor Dr. AHMAD M. KAMAL; circ. 30,000.

al-Fussoul: 17 Sharia Sherif Pasha; Arabic; monthly; Propr. and Chief Editor MUHAMMAD ZAKI ABDEL KADER.

al-Garida al-Togaria al-Misriya: 25 Sharia Nubar Pasha; f. 1921; Arabic; weekly; circ. 7,000.

al-Hilal: Dar al-Hilal, 16 Sharia Muhammad Ezz El-Arab; f. 1895; Arabic; monthly; Editor EMILE ZEIDAN.

al-Izaa wal-Television: 13 Sharia Muhammad Ezz El-Arab; f. 1935; Arabic; weekly; Editor RAGA EL AZABI; circ. 120,000.

al-Kawakeb (*The Stars*): Dar al-Hilal, 16 Sharia Muhammad Ezz El-Arab; f. 1952; Arabic; film magazine; Editor FAHIM NAGIB; circ. 38,500.

al-Mukhtar: Dar Akhbar al-Yom, Sharia al-Sahafa; f. 1956; Arabic edition of *Readers' Digest*; Editor MOHAMED ZAKI ABDEL KADER; circ. 50,000.

al-Mussawar: Dar al-Hilal, 16 Sharia Muhammad Ezz El-Arab; f. 1924; Arabic weekly; Editor AHMED BAHA-EDDINE; circ. 50,000.

EGYPT—(THE PRESS)

al-Sabah: 4 Sharia Muhammad Said Pasha; f. 1922; Arabic; weekly; Editor MOSTAFA EL-KACHACHI.

al-Tahrir: 5 Sharia Naguib-Rihani; Arabic; weekly; Editor ABDEL-AZIZ SADEK.

al-Talia (*Vanguard*): f. 1965; left wing; monthly.

Ana Wa Inta: Sharia Central; Arabic; monthly; Editor MOHAMED HASSAN.

Arab Observer: published by the Middle East News Agency, 11 Sh. Sahafa; f. 1960; weekly international news magazine; English; has now incorporated *The Scribe*; Editor-in-Chief Dr. ABDEL HAMID EL-BATRIK.

Contemporary Thought: University of Cairo; quarterly; Editor Dr. Z. N. MAHMOUD.

Echos: 15 Sharia Mahmoud Bassiouni; f. 1947; French; weekly; Dir. and Propr. GEORGES ORFALI.

Egyptian Chamber of Commerce Bulletin: 4 Midan Falaki.

Egyptian Directory, The: 19 Sharia Abdel Khalek Sarwat, B.P. 500; f. 1887; French and English; annual; Man. and Editor TAWHID KAMAL.

Egyptian Mail: 24 Sharia Zakaria Ahmed; f. 1910; English; weekly; Editor Dr. AMIN ABOUL-ENEIN.

Egypt's Medical Digest: 56 Sharia Abdel Khalek Sarwat, monthly; English; Editor Dr. KAMEL MIRZA.

Femme Nouvelle, La: 48 Sharia Kasr-el-Nil; French; twice yearly; Editor DORIA SHAFIK.

Gazette of the Faculty of Medicine: Sharia Kasr El-Aini; Kasr El-Aini Clinical Society; English; quarterly.

German-Arab Trade: 2 Sharia Sherif Pasha; German, English, Arabic; Editor KLAUS BALZER; circ. 6,000.

al Guil el Gedid: Dar Akhbar al-Yom, Sharia al-Sahafa; f. 1945; Arabic; weekly; Editor MOUSSA SABRI; circ. 50,000.

Ghorfet al-Kahira (*Journal of Cairo Chamber of Commerce*): 4 Midan Falaky; Arabic; monthly.

Hawa'a (*Eve*): Dar al-Hilal, 16 Sharia Muhammad Ezz El-Arab; women's magazine; Arabic; weekly.

Images: Dar Al-Hilal, 16 Sharia Muhammad Ezz El-Arab; French; illustrated; weekly; Editors EMILE and CHOUCRI ZEIDAN.

Industrial Egypt: P.O.B. 251, 26A Sharia Sherif Pasha, Cairo; f. 1924; Bulletin of the Federation of Egyptian Industries; English and Arabic; quarterly; Editor Eng. GAMIL EL-SABBAN.

Industry and Trade Information: 13 Sharia Abdel Hamid Said; English; weekly; commercial and industrial bulletin; Dir. and Propr. NICOLAS STAVRI; Editor N. GHANEM.

Informateur Financier et Commercial: 24 Sharia Soliman Pasha; f. 1929; weekly; Dir. HENRI POLITI; circ. 15,000.

Kitab al-Hilal: 16 Sharia Muhammad Ezz El-Arab; monthly; Proprs. EMILE and CHOUKRI ZEIDAN.

Lewa al-Islam: 11 Sharia Sherif Pasha; Arabic; monthly; Propr. AHMED HAMZA; Editor MUHAMMAD ALY SHETA.

Lotus Magazine (*Afro-Asian Writings*): 104 Kasr El Eini St.; f. 1968; quarterly; English, French and Arabic; Editor YOUSSEF EL SEBAI.

Magalet al-Mohandeseen: 28 Avenue Ramses; f. 1945; published by The Engineers' Syndicate; Arabic and English; ten times a year; Editor and Sec. MAHMOUD SAMI ABDEL KAWI.

Megakkah al-Zerayia: monthly; Arabic; agriculture; circ. 30,000.

The Middle East Observer: 8 Chawarby St.; f. 1955; weekly; English industrial, maritime and commercial; Propr. AHMED FODA; Chief Editors ADEL MAGDI, AHMED SABRI; circ. 30,000.

Phos-Chronos: 14 Sharia Galal; Greek; Editors B. PATÈRAS, S. PATÈRAS.

Progrès Dimanche: 24 Sharia Galal; French; weekly; Editor M. YACCARINI.

Riwayat al-Hilal: 16 Sharia Muhammad Ezz El-Arab; Arabic; monthly; Proprs. EMILE and CHOUKRI ZEIDAN.

Rose el Youssef: 89A Kasr el Ainei St.; f. 1925; Arabic; weekly; political; circulates throughout all Arab countries, includes monthly English section, Chair. KAMEL ZOHEIRY; Editor ABDUL RAHMAN AL-SHARQAWI; Editor English section IBRAHIM EZZAT; Man. ABDEL GHANI ABDEL-FATTAH; circ. 35,000.

Sabah al-Kheir: Arabic; weekly; light entertainment.

Tchehreh Nema: 14 Sharia Hassan El-Akbar (Abdine); f. 1904; Iranian; monthly; political, literary and general; Editor MANUCHEHR TCHEHREH NEMA MOADEB ZADEH.

Up-to-Date International Industry: 10 Sharia Galal; Arabic and English; foreign trade journal.

NEWS AGENCIES

Middle East News Agency: 4 Sharia Sherrufin, Cairo; f. 1955; regular service in Arabic, English and French; Chair. MAHMUD EL-HAWARI AHMED.

Misr Egyptian News Agency: 43 Sharia Ramses, Cairo.

FOREIGN BUREAUX

Agence France Presse: 33 Kasr El Nil St., Cairo; Chief JEAN-PIERRE JOULIN.

ANSA: 19 Sh. Abdel Khalek Sarwat, Cairo; Chief GIOVANNI CAMPANA.

AP: 33 Kasr El Nil, Cairo; Chief CHRISTOPHER C. MINICLIER.

Bulgarian Telegraph Agency: 13 Sh. Muhammad Kamel Morsi, Aguza, Cairo; Chief DIMITER MASLAROV.

Četeka (Czechoslovak News Agency): 7 Sh. Hasan Asem, Zamalek, Cairo.

Deutsche Presse Agentur (dpa): 33 Kasr el Nil St., Apt. 13/4, Cairo.

Kyodo News Service: Flat 12, 33 Abdel Khalek Tharawat, Cairo; Chief HIDEO YAMASHITA.

Reuters: Apt. 43, Immobilia Bldgs., 26 Sh. Sherif Pasha, Cairo, P.O.B. 2040.

UPI: 4 Sh. Eloui, P.O.B. 872, Cairo; Chief RAY N. MOSELEY.

Antara and DPA also have bureaux in Cairo.

PUBLISHERS

Egyptian General Organization for Publishing and Printing: 117 Corniche el Nil St., Cairo; affiliated to the Ministry of Culture.

ALEXANDRIA

Alexandria University Press: Shatby.

Artec: 10 Sharia Stamboul.

Dar Nashr ath-Thagata.

Egyptian Book Centre: A. D. Christodoulou and Co., 5 Sharia Adib; f. 1950.

Egyptian Printing and Publishing House: Ahmed El Sayed Marouf, 59, Safia Zaghoul; f. 1947.

Maison Egyptienne d'Editions: Ahmed El Sayed Marouf, Sharia Adib; f. 1950.

Maktab al-Misri al-Hadith li-t-Tiba wan-Nashr: 7 Nobar St.; Man. AHMAD YEHIA.

Munshaat al Marif.

CAIRO

Akhbar El Yom Publishing House: 6 Sharia al-Sahafa; f. 1944; publishes *al-Akhbar* (daily), *Akhbar al-Yom* (weekly), and magazine *Akher Saa*; Man. Dir. Dr. KASSEM FARAHAT.

Al-Hilal Publishing House: 16 Sharia Muhammad Ezz El-Arab; f. 1895; publishes *Al-Hilal*, *Riwayat Al-Hilal*, *Kitab Al-Hilal* (monthlies); *Al Mussawar*, *Al Kawakeb*, *Hawa* (weeklies).

Dar al-Gomhouriya: 24 Sharia Galal; publications include the dailies, *al-Gomhouriya*, *al-Misaa*, *Egyptian Gazette* and *Le Progrès Egyptien*; Pres. KAMEL EL HENNAWI.

Dar al-Hilal: Al Hilal Bldg., 16 Sharia Mohammed Ezz El-Arab; f. 1892; publishes magazines only, including *al-Mussawar*, *Hawa'a* and *al-Kawakeb*; Dir. EMILE and CHOUKRI ZEIDAN.

Dar al Kitab al Arabi: Misr Printing House, Sharia Noubar, Bab al Louk, Cairo; f. 1968; Man. Dir. Dr. SAHAIR AL KALAMAWI.

Dar al Maaref Egypt: 1119 Cornich El-Nil St.; f. 1890; Arabic books in all fields; distributor of books in English, French and German; Man. Dir. Dr. SAYED ABUL NAGA.

Documentation and Research Centre for Education (Ministry of Education): 33 Falaky St.; f. 1956; Dir. Mrs. ZEINAB M. MEHREZ; bibliographies, directories, information and education bulletins.

Editions Horus: 1 Midan Soliman Pasha.

Editions le Progrès: 6 Sharia Sherif Pasha; Propr. WADI CHOUKRI.

Editions et Publications des Pères Jésuites: 1 rue Boustan al Maksi, Faggala; scientific and religious publications; Dir. H. DE LEUSSE.

Editions Universitaires d'Egypte, Les: Alla El-Dine El-Chiati and Co.; 41 Sharia Sherif Pasha.

Higher University Council for Arts, Letters and Sciences: University of Cairo.

Imprimerie Argus: 10 Sharia Galal; Propr. SOCRATE SARRAFIAN.

Lagnat al Taalif Wal Targama Wal Nashr (*Committee for Writing, Translating and Publishing Books*): 9 Sharia El-Kerdassi (Abdine).

Librairie La Renaissance D'Egypte (Hassan Muhammad & Sons): 9 Adly St., P.O.B. 2172; f. 1930; Man. HASSAN MUHAMMAD; religion, history, geography, medicine, architecture, economics, politics, law, children's books, atlases, dictionaries.

Maktabet Misr: P.O.B. 16, Faggalah, Cairo; f. 1932; publ. wide variety of fiction, biographies and textbooks for schools and universities; Man. AMIR SAID GOUDA A SAHHAR.

Middle East Publishing Co.: 29 Rue Abdel Khalek Sarwat.

Mohamed Abbas Sid Ahmed: 55 Sharia Nubar.

National Library Press (*Dar al Kutub*): Midan Ahmed Maher; bibliographic works.

New Publications: J. Meshaka and Co., 5 Sharia Maspero.

The Public Organization for Books and Scientific Appliances: Cairo University, Orman, Ghiza; f. 1965; state organization publishing academic books for universities, higher institutes, etc.; also imports books, periodicals and scientific appliances; Chair. KAMIL SEDDIK; Vice-Chair. FATTHY LABIB.

Senouhy Publishers: 54 Sharia Abdel-Khalek Sarwat; f. 1956; Dirs. LEILA A. FADEL, OMAR RASHAD.

Other Cairo publishers include: *Dar al-Fikr al-Arabi*, *Dar al-Fikr al-Hadith Li-t-Tab wan-Nashr*, *Dar wa Matabi*, *Dar al-Nahda al-Arabiya*, *Dar al-Misriya Li-t-Talif wat-Tardjma*, *Dar al-Qalam*, *Dar ath-Thagapa*, *Majlis al-Ala Li-Riyyat al-Funun*, *Maktaba Ain Shams*, *Maktaba al-Andshilu al-Misriya*, *Maktabat al-Chandshi*, *Maktabat al-Nahira al-Hadith*, *Markaz Tasjil al-Athar al-Misriya*, *Matbaat ar-Risala*, *al-Qaumiya li-t-Tibaa wan-Nashr Wizarat az-Ziraa Maslahat al-Basatin*.

RADIO AND TELEVISION

Egyptian Radio and Television Corporation: Cairo; f. 1971; supervised by Dep. Prime Minister and affil. to Ministry of Culture and Information.

Egyptian Publicity (Advertisements) Co.: 24-26 Sharia Zakaria Ahmed, Cairo; f. 1906; handles all advertising media in Egypt, including radio and television; affil. to Publication and Printing House; Dep. Dir.-Gen. KHEDR MOHAMED ABD EL-SALEM.

RADIO

Egyptian Broadcasting Corporation: Corniche el Nil, Cairo; f. 1928; 169 hours daily; Chair. MOHAMED MAHMOUD SHAABAN; Dir.-Gen. Arabic Programmes SAFIA EL MOHANDES; Dir.-Gen. Foreign Programmes MOHAMED ISMAIL MOHAMED.

Home service programmes in Arabic, English, French, Armenian, German, Greek and Italian; foreign services in Hebrew, Persian, Spanish, Bengali, Turkish, Folani, Malawi, Shona, Lingala, Yoruba, Dankali, English, Swahili, Urdu, Indonesian, Hindi, Somali, Russian, Sosotho, Sindebek, Amharic, Wolof, French, Hausa, German, Siami, Pushtu, Portuguese, Italian, Zulu, Nianja, Thai, Bambra, Arabic. *Broadcasting and TV* (weekly), *Broadcasting Art* (quarterly).

Middle East Radio: Société Egyptienne de Publicité, 24-26 Sharia Zakaria Ahmed, Cairo; f. 1964; commercial service with 500-kW. transmitter; U.K. Agents: Radio and Television Services (Middle East) Ltd., 21 Hertford St., London, W.1.

In 1971 there were 4,500,000 radio receivers and 560,000 television sets.

TELEVISION

Egyptian Television Organization: Corniche el Nil, Cairo; f. 1960; 150 hours weekly (two channels); Chair. ABDEL HAMID YOUNES; Dir.-Gen. Programmes Mrs. SAMIHA AB EL-RAHMAN.

FINANCE

BANKING
(cap.=capital; p.u.=paid up; dep.=deposits; m.=million; amounts in £ Egyptian)

The whole banking system was nationalized in 1961.

CENTRAL BANK
Central Bank of Egypt: 31 Sharia Kasr-el-Nil, Cairo; f. 1961; cap. 3.0m., dep. 499 m. (June 1972); Governor AHMED ZANDO.

COMMERCIAL BANKS
Arabic Real Estate Bank: Cairo; Vice-Pres. HANAFY LABIB HUSEIN.

Egyptian Real Estate Bank: Cairo; Gov. MOHAMED KAMEL ABASS.

Bank of Alexandria, S.A.E.; 6 Salah Salem St., Alexandria; f. 1864; p.u. cap. 3m.; 80 brs.; incorporated Industrial Bank 1971; Pres. AHMED ABDEL GHAFFAR.

Banque du Caire: 22 Sharia Adly Pasha, P.O.B. 1495, Cairo; f. 1952; cap. and reserves 2.5m., dep. 182m. (Dec. 1972); Chair. HASSAN ZAKI AHMED; Man. Dir. ABDEL LATIF DAHABA.

Banque Misr, S.A.E.: 151 Sharia Mohamed Farid, Cairo; f. 1920; nationalized 1960; incorporated Bank of Suez and Banque Collectivité Financière 1964; absorbed Banque de Port Said 1971; 197 brs.; cap. 2m., res. 27.4m. (June 1970); Chair. and Man. Dir. AHMED FOUAD; publ. *Economic Bulletin*.

National Bank of Egypt, S.A.E.; 24 Sharia Sherif Pasha, Cairo; f. 1898; nationalized 1960; incorporated Banque de Commerce 1964; cap. and reserves 12.2m., dep. 248m. (June 1972); 90 brs.; Chair. Dr. HAMED A. EL SAYEH; publ. *Quarterly Economic Bulletin*.

DEVELOPMENT BANKS
Arab African Bank: 44 Abdel-Khalek Sarwat St., Cairo; f. 1964; cap. 10m.; undertakes all banking activities through its branches in Egypt free zones and abroad, and participates in development programmes in Arab and African countries; Chair. and Man. Dir. SULAIMAN AHMED AL HADDAD; branches in Beirut and Dubai.

Arab International Bank: Cairo; f. 1971 as Egyptian International Bank; aims to promote trade and investment in Egypt, Libya and other Arab states; Chair. ABDUL-MONEIM KAISSOUNI.

Egyptian General Agricultural and Co-operative Organisation: 110 El-Kasr El-Eini St., Cairo; f. 1964; formerly *Agricultural Credits and Co-operative Bank*.

OTHER BANK
Nasser Social Bank: Cairo; f. 1971.

STOCK EXCHANGES
Cairo Stock Exchange: 4A Cherifein St., Cairo; f. 1883; Pres. SHOUHDI AZER.

Alexandria Stock Exchange: Pres. M. HASSAN HAGGAG.

INSURANCE
Misr Insurance Company: 78 Sharia Talaat Harb, Cairo; Chair. MOHAMED ALI ARAFA.

Al Chark Insurance Company, S.A.E.: Cairo; 15 Sharia Kasr-el-Nil; f. 1931; Chair. AHMED ZAKI HELMI; general and life; incorporates *Nile Insurance Co.*, *Al Mottahida Insurance Co.*, and *Africa Insurance Co.*

Commercial Insurance Company of Egypt, S.A.E.: 7 Midan E. Tahrir, Cairo; f. 1947; life, fire, marine, accident; Managing Dir. AHMED ZAKY HELMY.

The Egyptian Reinsurance Company, S.A.E.: 28 Talaat Harb St., P.O.B. 950, Cairo; f. 1957; Chair. FATHI MOHAMED IBRAHIM.

L'Epargne, S.A.E.: Immeuble Chemla Sharia 26 July, P.O.B. 548, Cairo; all types of insurance.

Al Iktisad el Shabee, S.A.E.; 11 Sharia Emad El Dine, P.O.B. 1635, Cairo; f. 1948; Man. Dir. and Gen. Man. W. KHAYAT.

Al Mottahida: 9 Sharia Soliman Pasha, P.O.B. 804, Cairo; f. 1957.

National Insurance Company of Egypt, S.A.E.: 33 Sharia Nabi Danial, P.O.B. 446, Alexandria; f. 1900; cap. 750,000; Chair. MOSTAFA EL-SAYED EL-ESNAWY.

Provident Association of Egypt, S.A.E.: 9 Sharia Sherif Pasha, P.O.B. 390, Alexandria; f. 1936; Man. Dir. C. G. VORLOOU.

TRADE AND INDUSTRY

CHAMBERS OF COMMERCE
ALEXANDRIA
Egyptian Chamber of Commerce, Alexandria: El-Ghorfa Eltegareia St.; Pres. ABDEL HAMIED SERRY; Vice-Pres. ABEDEL SATTAR ARAFAH, MOSTAFA KAMAL BARAKAT; Treas. ALY ALY EL KATA, TAWFIC EL MELEIGY; Sec. AHMED EL ALFI MUHAMMAD; Gen. Dir. MUHAMMED FATHY MAHMOUD.

Camera di Commercio Italiana di Alessandria: P.O.B. 1763; f. 1885; 173 mems.; Pres. Cav. LUIGI F. POLVARA; Vice-Pres. Ing. ROBERT MITROVICH, Sig. EMILIO LINDI; Sec. of Council Ing. CARLO SCARPOCCHI; Treas. PIER LUCA CAPPIEILO; Sec.-Gen. PIERO FAZZI; publ. *Rivista degli Scambi Italo-Egiziani*.

Chambre de Commerce Hellénique: 19 Sharia Sherif Pasha; f. 1901; Pres. YANKO CHRYSSOVERGHI; Vice-Pres. C. GEORGIAFENDIS, C. NANOPOULOS; Treas. CHR. KOKKINOS; Hon. Sec. ALEX M. CASULLI.

Chambre de Commerce Turque: 9 Sharia Sherif Pasha; Hon. Pres. TAHA CARIM; Pres. ILHAMI CAKIN; Vice-Pres. IZZET LEVENDER and KASSIM KUTAY; Treas. HABIB ALEX. DIAB; Sec.-Gen. ZIYA SÖNMEZ.

EGYPT—(TRADE AND INDUSTRY)

CAIRO

Egyptian Chamber of Commerce, Cairo: El Falaki St.; Pres. MUHAMMAD SAYED YASSIN; Vice-Pres. ALY EL BEREIR, AHMED ABDEL-NABI EL-ISKANDARANI; Sec.-Gen. KAISSAR BOULOS GAD-EL-KARIM; Treas. MUHAMMAD A. R. SAMAHA; publ. *Monthly Bulletin*.

Cairo Chamber of Commerce: 4 Midah El Falaki St.; f. 1913; Pres. MUHAMMAD ALI SHETA; Vice-Pres. IBRAHIM SALEM ABDEL-AZIZ EL-TOKHI; Treas. ABDEL MENEM MOHMOUD EL-SHERIF; Gen. Sec. MUHAMMAD SAYED ABDEL MONEM; 150,000 mems.; publs. *Protesto Review* (weekly), *Monthly Bulletin*.

Camera di Commercio Italiana per l'Egitto: 33 Sharia Abdel Khalek Sarwat, P.O. Box 19; f. 1947; Pres. GIUSEPPE SCHIRALLI; Vice-Pres. Ing. ITALO RAGNI; 130 mems.; publs. *Rivista degli Scambi Italo-Egiziani* (every three months).

Chambre de Commerce Hellénique du Caire: 17 Sharia Soliman El Halabi; f. 1923; Pres. P. ARSLANOGLOU; Vice-Pres. CH. EGYPTIADIS, Sec. G. SAMARAS.

German-Arab Chamber of Commerce: 2 Sharia Sherif Pasha, Cairo; f. 1951; Pres. RUDI STAERKER; Sec.-Gen. Assessor KLAUS BALZER; publ. *German Arab Trade*.

Representation of Federal Chamber of Foreign Trade of Yugoslavia: 47 Sharia Ramses, P.O.B. 448, Cairo; f. 1954; Sec.-Gen. D. STANKOVIĆ.

OTHER TOWNS

Egyptian Chamber of Commerce for Aswan Governorate: Abtal El-Tahrir St., Aswan.

Egyptian Chamber of Commerce for Asyut Governorate: Asyut.

Egyptian Chamber of Commerce for Behera Governorate: Gomhouriya St., Damanhoru.

Egyptian Chamber of Commerce for Beni-Suef Governorate: Mamdouh St., Moqbel El-Guedid, Beni-Suef.

Egyptian Chamber of Commerce for Dakahlia Governorate, Mansura: El-Saleh Ayoub Square, Mansura.

Egyptian Chamber of Commerce for Damietta Governorate: Damietta.

Egyptian Chamber of Commerce for Fayum Governorate: Fayum.

Egyptian Chamber of Commerce for Gharbia Governorate: Tanta.

Egyptian Chamber of Commerce for Giza Governorate: El-Saa Square, Giza.

Egyptian Chamber of Commerce for Ismailia Governorate: Ismailia.

Egyptian Chamber of Commerce for Kafr-el-Sheika Governorate: Kafr-el-Sheikh.

Egyptian Chamber of Commerce for Kena Governorate: El-Gamil Street, Kena.

Egyptian Chamber of Commerce for Menia Governorate: Menia.

Egyptian Chamber of Commerce for Manufia Governorate: Sidi Fayed Street, Shibín-El-Kom.

Egyptian Chamber of Commerce for Port Said Governorate: Port Said.

Egyptian Chamber of Commerce for Kalyubia Governorate: Benha.

Egyptian Chamber of Commerce for Sharkia Governorate: Zagazig.

Egyptian Chamber of Commerce for Suez Governorate: Suez.

Egyptian Chamber of Commerce for Suhag Governorate: Suhag.

NATIONALIZED ORGANIZATIONS

General Organization under the Ministry of War:

Armed Forces: 90 Sh. Al-Azhar, Cairo.

General Organizations under the Ministry of Industry, Petroleum and Mineral Wealth:

Food Industries: 6 Salem Salem St., Agouza, Cairo; 24 companies; products include most basic foodstuffs, tobacco, sugar, soft and alcoholic drinks, confectionery, essential oils, essences, soap, perfumery and cosmetics; 90,000 workers; Dir. Prof. Dr. HASSAN ASHMAWI.

Spinning and Weaving: 5 Tolombat St., Garden City, Cairo; 28 companies.

Egyptian General Organization for Engineering, Electric and Electronic Industries: 28 Talaat Harb St., Cairo; 22 companies.

Chemical Industries: 49 Kasr El Nil St., Cairo; 29 companies.

Building Materials and Ceramics: 49 Kasr El Nil St., Cairo; 13 companies.

Metal Industries: 5 July 26th St., Cairo; 9 companies.

Egyptian Organization for Geological Researches and Mining: Pres. RUSHDY SAYED FARAG; Dir. Gen. GALAL EL DIN MOSTAFA.

General Organization under the Ministry of Military Production:

Egyptian General Organization for Military Factories and Industries of Aviation: 8 Gemaee St., Garden City, Cairo.

General Organizations under the Ministry of Marine Transport:

Maritime Transport: 8 Nasser St., Alexandria; 7 affiliated companies.

General Organization under the Minister of Treasury:

Social Insurance General Organization: 126 July St., Cairo.

General Organizations under Ministry of Economy and Foreign Trade:

Egyptian General Organization of Foreign Trade: 2 companies for exporting agricultural products, 2 for engineering and one for cars.

Egyptian General Organization of Cotton: 25 Nasser St., Alexandria.

General Organization under Ministry of Health:

Egyptian General Organization for Drugs, Chemicals and Medical Equipment: 11 companies.

General Organizations under Ministry of Housing and Construction:

Egyptian General Organization of Housing and Rehabitation: 4 Latin America Street, Garden City, Cairo; 10 companies.

General Organization of Co-operative Housing and Construction: Nasr City, Cairo.

Civil Contracting Company: 14 Talaat Harb, Cairo.

General Organizations under Ministry of Culture and Information:

Egyptian General Organization for Tourism and Hotels: 4 Latin America St., Garden City, Cairo.

Egyptian Broadcasting and T.V. Corporation: Corniche el Nil, Cairo.

EGYPT—(Trade and Industry)

General Organizations under the Ministry of Land Reclamation:

General Egyptian Organization of Land Reclamation: Dokki; 6 companies.

Executive Council of Desert Projects.

General Organizations under Ministry of Agriculture:

Co-operative Agriculture: Misr Insurance Bldg., Giza; Dir.-Gen. Abdul Maksoud Ezzat Mohamed Ezzat.

Poultry: Misr Insurance Bldg., Giza.

Meat: 14 El Gamhouria Sq., Abdin, Cairo.

Maritime Wealth.

General Organization under Ministry of Aviation:

Misr Organization for Aviation.

General Organizations under the Suez Canal Authority:
  7 affiliated companies.

OIL

Egyptian General Organization of Petroleum: Cairo; state supervisory authority for the development of the national oil resources; has entered into 50:50 partnership agreements with a number of foreign companies; Pres. Ahmad Izz-al-Din Hilal; Dir.-Gen. Mohamed Hassan Mohamed Tawfik El-Dawi.

Egyptian Marine Petroleum: Cairo; f. 1970; partnership between EGPC and North Sumatra Oil Development Corporation (an amalgam of Japanese interests, the largest being the Japanese Petroleum Development Corp.); has concession in the Ras Gharib area in the Gulf of Suez.

Compagnie Orientale des Pétroles: Cairo; partnership between EGPC and International Egyptian Oil Company (owned principally by ENI of Italy); developed the Sinai oilfields now occupied by Israel.

Suez Gulf Petroleum Company: Cairo; partnership between EGPC and Pan American Oil (a subsidiary of Standard Oil of Indiana); developed the Morgan oilfield on the western side of the Red Sea, producing 300,000 barrels per day in early 1970; also holds exploration concessions for territory in the Western Desert and the Nile delta.

Western Desert Operating Petroleum Company: Alexandria; f. 1967 as partnership between EGPC and Phillips Petroleum; developed Alamein field in the Western Desert, producing approx. 40,000 barrels per day in early 1970; Chair. Dr. Mahmoud Amin.

EMPLOYERS' ORGANIZATIONS

Federation of Egyptian Industries: P.O.B. 251, 26A Sharia Sherif Pasha, Cairo, and P.O.B. 1658, 65 Horia Rd., Alexandria; f. 1922; Pres. Dr. Eng. Mahmoud Aly Hassan; represents the industrial community in Egypt.

Affiliated Organizations

Chamber of Food Industries: Pres. Dr. Hassan Ashmawi.

Chamber of Building Materials and Construction: Pres. Eng. Hassan Muhammad Hassan.

Chamber of Cereals and Related Products Industry: Pres. Dr. Fawzi Youssef Refai.

Chamber of Chemical Industries: Pres. Dr. Hassan Ibrahim Badawi.

Chamber of Engineering Industries: Pres. Eng. Muhammad Abdel Baki El-Kosheiry.

Chamber of Leather Industry: Pres. Dr. Hassan Ibrahim El-Sissy.

Chamber of Metallurgical Industries: Pres. Eng. Ali Morsi.

Chamber of Petroleum and Mining: Pres. Dr. Ahmed Tewfik.

Chamber of Printing, Binding and Paper Products: Pres. Eng. Youssef Moustafa Bahgat.

Chamber of Spinning and Weaving Industry: Pres. Hamed el-Maamoun Habib.

Chamber of Woodworking Industry: Pres. Hassan Soliman Muhammad.

TRADE UNIONS

Egyptian Federation of Labour (EFL): 70 Gomhouriya St., Cairo; f. 1957; 27 affiliated unions; 1.5 million mems.; affiliated to the International Confederation of Arab Trade Unions and to the All-African Trade Union Federation; Pres. Ahmed Fahim; Sec.-Gen. Abdel-Latif Boultia; publ. *Misrlab News* (monthly, English).

Arab Federation of Food Workers (AFFW): P.O.B. 877, Cairo; 500,000 mems.; Gen. Sec. Saad Muhammad Ahmed.

Federation of Arab Engineers: Cairo; budget 1965–66 £E 15,000; Sec. Muhammad Saka.

General Trade Union of Agriculture: 31 Mansour St., Bab al-Louk, Cairo; 350,000 mems.; Pres. Salah Al Din Abu Al-Magi; Gen. Sec. Nasr Al Din Mustapha.

General Trade Union of Banking and Insurance: 2 Al Qadi al Fadl St., Cairo; 32,000 mems.; Pres. Muhammad Fathi Fouda; Gen. Sec. Munir Habash.

General Trade Union of Building Industries: 9 Emad el Din St., Cairo; 46,000 mems.; Pres. Abd al Mutale Salem; Gen. Sec. Hamed Hussain Barakat.

General Trade Union of Business and Management Services: 387 Port Said St., Bab al Khalk, Cairo; 46,000 mems.; Pres. Awad Abd Al Qader; Gen. Sec. Abl Al Rahman Khedr.

General Trade Union of the Chemical Industries: 76 Gomhouria St., Cairo; 60,000 mems.; Pres. Muhammad Asaad Rageh; Gen. Sec. Hamya Ali Mahjoub.

General Trade Union of Engineering, Electrical and Metal Industries: 118 Mohamed Farid St., Cairo; 70,000 mems.; Pres. Muhammad Abu Khalil; Gen. Sec. Said Gomaa Ali Mansour.

General Trade Union of Nutritional Industries: 3 Hosni St., Qubba al Hadaek, P.O.B. 2230, Cairo; 125,000 mems.; Pres. Mohamed Abdou Gomaa; Vice-Pres. Mahmoud el Askhri.

General Trade Union of Railways: 47 Al Tera al Boulaquiya St., Cairo; 46,000 mems.; Pres. Muhammad Atito; Gen. Sec. Ahmad Fawzi Ali.

General Trade Union of Textiles: 327 Shoubra St., Cairo; f. 1960; 250,000 mems.; Pres. Salah Gharid.

EGYPT—(Transport, Tourism)

TRANSPORT

RAILWAYS

Egyptian General Organization of Passenger Transport: Alexandria; f. 1852; Mileage and gauge: 2,803 miles, 4 ft. 8½ in., main lines; 1,614 miles, 4 ft. 8½ in., auxiliary lines; Pres. ALI HOSNI MAHMOUD.

Alexandria Region Passenger Transport Organisation: 21 Place Saad Zaghloul, P.O.B. 466, Alexandria: controls tramways, buses and 27 miles of suburban electric railway (4 ft. 8½ in.); Chair. AHMED ZAKY.

Heliopolis Company for Housing and Inhabiting: 28 Ibrahim El Lakkany St., Heliopolis, Cairo; 35 miles; 176 railcars; Pres. MOHAMED MOUNIR ALI MOURAD.

A 6¼-mile underground railway is under consideration in Cairo.

ROADS

Egyptian General Organization of Inland Transport for Provinces Passengers: Sharia Kasr-el-Aini, Cairo; Pres. HASAN MOURAD KOTB.

There are good metalled main roads as follows: Cairo-Alexandria (desert road); Cairo-Benna-Tanta-Damanhur-Alexandria; Cairo-Suez (desert road); Cairo-Ismailia-Port Said or Suez; Cairo-Fayum (desert road); in 1970 there were over 13,000 miles of good metalled roads.

Automobile et Touring Club D'Egypte: 10 rue Kasr-el-Nil, Cairo; f. 1924; 476 mems.; Hon. Pres. Ing. HASSAN NAGI; Pres. Maj.-Gen. Dr. MOHAMMED ABDEL HAMID MORTAGHI.

SHIPPING

Egyptian Maritime Co.: 3 rue de l'Ancienne Bourse, Alexandria; f. 1930; services Alexandria/Europe, Canada, Black Sea, Adriatic Sea and Africa; fleet of 39 vessels; Chair. M. Y. RAMADAN.

American Eastern Trading and Shipping Co., S.A.E.: 17 Sharia Sesostris, Alexandria; Pres. M. E. WAGNER; Manager, Egypt, AHMED LABIB TAHIO.

Egyptian Stevedoring and Shipping Co., S.A.E.: 17 Sharia Sesostris, Alexandria; f. 1946; Pres. J. H. CHALHOUB; Manager MUHAMMAD FAHMY TAHIO.

Thebes Shipping Agency: P.O. Box 45, 41 Sharia Nebi Daniel, Alexandria; maritime transport.

THE SUEZ CANAL

Suez Canal Authority (*Hay'at Canal Al Suess*): 6 Lazokhli St., Garden City, Cairo; Pres. Eng. MASHHOUR AHMED MASHHOUR.

Length of Canal: 107 miles; maximum permissible draught: 38 ft.; maximum width (at water level): 660 ft.; minimum width (at depth of 36 ft.): 300 ft. The Canal has been closed since the war in June 1967.

CIVIL AVIATION

EgyptAir: Head Office: Cairo International Airport, Heliopolis, Cairo; f. 1932 as Misr Airwork; operates internal services in Egypt and external services throughout the Middle East, Far East, Africa and Europe; Chair. ABDEL HAMID MAHMOUD; fleet of four Boeing 707, three Il-62, four comet 4C, three Il-18, three An-24, two Cessna.

The following foreign airlines serve Egypt: Aeroflot, Air France, Air India, Alia, Alitalia, AUA, BEA, BOAC, British Caledonian, ČSA, Cyprus Airways, Ethiopian Air Lines, Garuda, Ghana Airways, Interflug, Iraqi Airways, JAL, JAT, Libyan Arab Airlines, KLM, Kuwait Airways, LOT, Lufthansa, MALÉV, MEA, Olympic Airways, Pan Am, PIA, Qantas, Sabena, SAS, Saudia, Sudan Airways, Swissair, TAROM, TWA and UTA.

TOURISM

Ministry of Tourism: 110 Sh. Kasr-el-Aini, Cairo; f. 1965 to replace the *State Tourist Administration*, f. 1935; branches at Alexandria, Port Said, Suez, Luxor and Aswan; Minister of Tourism Dr. ZAKI HASHEM.

General Organization for Tourism and Hotels: 4 Latin America St., Garden City, Cairo; f. 1961; affiliated to the Ministry of Tourism.

Authorized foreign exchange dealers for tourists include the principal banks and the following:

American Express of Egypt Ltd.: 15 Kasr-el-Nil St., Cairo; f. 1919.

Thomas Cook and Son: 4 Sharia Champollion, Cairo.

CULTURAL ORGANIZATION

Ministry of Culture and Information: Cairo; Pres. Dr. MOHAMED ABDUL HATEM.

PRINCIPAL THEATRES AND ORCHESTRA

Pocket Theatre: Cairo; f. 1961.

Egyptian General Organization of Cinema, Theatre and Music: Ministry of Culture and Information.

Departments include the following:

Opera Lyric Troupe.

Opera Ballet.

Opera Chorale.

Cairo Symphony Orchestra.

Members frequently take part in performances with visiting opera companies.

National Puppet Theatre: Cairo.

NATIONAL DANCE TROUPES

National Folklore Dance Troupe: Cairo; frequently performs on tours abroad.

Reda Folklore Dance Troupe: 50 Kasr-el-Nil St., Cairo; f. 1959; frequently performs on tours abroad; Dirs. MAHMOUD REDA, ALI REDA; Principal Dancers FARIDA FAHMY, MAHMOUD REDA; Composer and Conductor ALI ISMAIL.

ATOMIC ENERGY

Atomic Energy Organization: Dokki, Cairo; f. 1955; Dir. Dr. SALAH HEDAYET. First reactor with 2,000 kW. power, opened at Inchass in 1961.

Regional Radioisotope Centre: Cairo; f. 1957; eleven laboratories for research and development in scientific, medical, agricultural and industrial fields; in 1963 the Centre was transformed into a Regional Centre for the Arab countries of the Middle East, in co-operation with UN I.A.E.A.

The Institute of Nuclear Engineering at Alexandria University is to use a loan of £E 250,000 from Kuwait to purchase an atomic reactor and laboratory facilities.

EDUCATION

Great importance has been attached to the development of educational facilities by the Egyptian Government since 1952. Its educational policy states that education is free and should play an indispensable part in the life of every citizen. It was realised that the first and most essential step in the programme of educational expansion was the construction of an adequate number of new schools. In 1952 a Ten Year Plan was inaugurated whereby an organization known as "The Schools Premises Foundation" was given the responsibility of constructing 400 new schools each year. Education, particularly technical education, has continued to be a primary concern of the Government and in the 1970–71 budget £E107 million was allocated to education.

Primary Education

This is extended to all children between the ages of six and twelve, and is free and compulsory. Four hundred primary schools are being constructed annually. The number of pupils in the primary stage in the year 1952 amounted to 1,540,202 (997,490 boys and 541,708 girls), compared with 3,740,595 in 1970–71 (2,318,333 boys and 1,422,262 girls). In the latter year the pupils were organized into 88,056 classes.

Preparatory Education

This is an intermediate stage between primary and secondary education. There were two main different types of preparatory school, general and technical, but the technical schools are being phased as separate institutions at this level. In 1970–71 there were 21,797 preparatory classes attended by about 852,000 children (two-thirds being boys).

Secondary Education

(a) General schools: here the emphasis is placed on academic studies. The aim is to develop the abilities of pupils best qualified for a university education. The number of students in 1970–71 was about 298,000 (203,000 boys and 95,000 girls).

(b) Technical Schools: a vocational training is given in these schools, in agriculture, industry or commerce. To ensure a knowledge of the machinery used in local production, students of industrial schools are given a practical training inside the factories. Owners of large factories are obliged to run training centres on the premises for their own workers. In 1970-71 there were 271,000 pupils in technical schools of various kinds. There were also about 26,000 pupils in teacher training establishments.

University Education

In addition to the old and famous Al-Azhar University, which opened its gates to women students in 1962, there are the universities of Cairo, Alexandria, Ain Shams and Assiut.

Cairo University was founded privately in 1908; in 1928 it became the State University. The American University at Cairo was founded in 1919, Alexandria University in 1942, and Ain Shams in 1950. Another university has been founded at Assiut, and was opened in time for the academic year 1957–58. Most universities include the following faculties: Agriculture, Commerce, Dental Surgery, Medicine, Pharmacy, Engineering, Law, Arts and Science.

In addition there are various post-graduate courses of study, and many students are sent abroad to complete their higher education. More, however, come from other countries to study in Egypt. In terms of student numbers the leading universities are amongst the world's largest (65,000 students at Cairo University) but the facilities are mostly very overcrowded.

Adult Education

A campaign to promote literacy and adult education is being directed and financed by the Ministry of Education, supported by the continuous co-operation of UNESCO. In 1970–71 new councils for literacy and adult education were formed, consisting of members representing the following sectors of the community: planning, production, local administration and the Arab Socialist Union. The Ministry of Education and the Arab League are co-operating on a Regional Literacy project.

UNIVERSITIES

Ain Shams University: Kasr el Zaafran, Abbasiyah, Cairo; 1,025 teachers, 38,200 students.

Alexandria University: Shatby, Alexandria; 2,350 teachers, 49,234 students.

Al-Azhar University: Cairo; 705 teachers, 16,852 students.

American University in Cairo: 113 Sh. Kasr el Aini, Cairo; 150 teachers, 1,500 students.

University of Assiut: Assiut; 13,177 students.

University of Cairo: Orman, Ghiza; 2,892 teachers, 64,606 students.

BIBLIOGRAPHY

GENERAL

ABDEL-MALEK, ANWAR. Egypte, société militaire (Paris, 1962).
— Idéologie et renaissance nationale/L'Egypt moderne (Paris, 1969).
AHMED, J. M. The Intellectual Origins of Egyptian Nationalism (London, Royal Institute of International Affairs, 1960).
ALDRIDGE, JAMES. Cairo: Biography of a City (Macmillan, London, 1970).
AYROUT, H. H. The Egyptian Peasant (Boston, 1963).
BADDOUR, ABD. Sudanese-Egyptian Relations. A Chronological and Analytical Study (Nijhoff, The Hague, 1960).
BADEAU, J. S. The Emergence of Modern Egypt (New York, 1953).
BAER, GABRIEL. A History of Landownership in Modern Egypt 1800–1950 (Oxford University Press, London, 1962).
— The Evolution of Landownership in Egypt and the Fertile Crescent, the Economic History of the Middle East 1800–1914 (University of Chicago Press, Chicago and London, 1966).
BERGER, MORROE. Bureaucracy and Society in Modern Egypt: a Study of the Higher Civil Service (Princeton University Press, 1957).
BERQUE, JACQUES. Egypt: Imperialism and Revolution (Faber, 1972).
BOKTOR, AMIN. The Development and Expansion of Education in the U.A.R. (The American University, Cairo, 1963).
CACHIA, P. Taha Husain: His Place in the Egyptian Literary Renaissance (London, 1956. Verry, Connecticut, 1956).
COULT, LYMAN H. An Annotated Bibliography of the Egyptian Fellah (University of Miami Press, 1958).
CROMER, EARL OF. Modern Egypt (2 vols., London, 1908).
DODWELL, H. The Founder of Modern Egypt (Cambridge, 1931, reprinted 1967).
DRIAULT, E. L'Egypte et l'Europe (5 vols., Cairo, 1935).
ELISOFAN, E. The Nile (New York, 1964).
GARZOUZI, EVA. Old Ills and New Remedies in Egypt (Dar al-Maaref, Cairo, 1958).
HARRIS, C. P. Nationalism and Revolution in Egypt: the Role of the Muslim Brotherhood (Mouton and Co., The Hague, 1964).
HARRIS, J. R. (Ed) The Legacy of Egypt (2nd ed. Oxford University Press, 1972).
HOLT, P. M. Egypt and the Fertile Crescent (Longmans, London, 1966).
HOPKINS, HARRY. Egypt, The Crucible (Secker and Warburg, London, 1969).
HURST, H. E. The Nile (London, 1952).
— The Major Nile Projects (Cairo, 1966).
LACOUTURE, JEAN and SIMONNE. Egypt in Transition (London, Methuen, 1958).
LANDAU, JACOB M. Parliaments and Parties in Egypt (Israel Publishing House, Tel-Aviv, 1953).
LAUTERPACHT, E. (Editor). The Suez Canal Settlement (Stevens and Sons, London, 1960, under the auspices of the British Institute of International and Comparative Law).
LENGYE, EMIL. Egypt's Role in World Affairs (Public Affairs Press, Washington, D.C., 1957).
LITTLE, TOM. Modern Egypt (Ernest Benn, London, 1967, Praeger, New York 1967).
LLOYD, LORD. Egypt since Cromer (2 vols., London, 1933–34).
MAHMOUD, ZAKI NAGIB. Modern Egyptian Thought (London, 1946).
MARLOWE, J. Anglo-Egyptian Relations (London, 1954).
MORINEAU, RAYMOND. Egypte (Lausanne, 1964).
MUHAMMAD, NAJIB. Egypt's Destiny (Gollancz, London, 1955).
NASSER, ABDEL GAMAL. Egypt's Liberation: The Philosophy of the Revolution (Washington, 1955).
NEGUIB, MOHAMMED. Egypt's Destiny: A Personal Statement (New York, 1955).
OWEN, ROBERT and BLUNSUM, TERENCE. Egypt, United Arab Republic, The Country and its People (Queen Anne Press, London, 1966).
RIAD, HASSAN. L'Egypte Nassérienne (Editions de Minuit Paris, 1964).
RUSSELL PASHA, Sir THOMAS. Egyptian Service, 1902–1946 (London, 1949).
STEVENS, GEORGIANA G. Egypt Yesterday and Today (New York, 1963).
STEWART, DESMOND. Cairo (Phoenix House, London, 1965).
VAUCHER, G. Gamal Abdel Nasser et son Equipe, 2 vols. (Brill, Leiden, 1950).
VIOLLET, ROGER and DORESSE, JEAN. Egypt (New York, Cromwell, 1955).
WATERFIELD, GORDON. Egypt (Thames & Hudson, London, 1966).
WATT, D. C. Britain and the Suez Canal (London, Royal Institute of International Affairs, 1956).
WAVELL, W. H. A Short Account of the Copts (London, 1945).
WILBUR, D. N. The United Arab Republic (New York, 1969).
WILSON, JOHN A. The Burden of Egypt (Chicago, 1951).
WYNN, WILTON. Nasser of Egypt: The Search for Dignity (Cambridge, Mass., 1959).
YOUSSEF BEY, AMINE. Independent Egypt (London, 1940).

ANCIENT EGYPT

ALDRED, CYRIL. Egypt to the End of the Old Kingdom (Thames and Hudson, London, 1965).
BREASTED, JAMES HENRY. A History of Egypt from the Earliest Times to the Persian Conquest (Harper and Row, New York, 1959).
DE LUBICZ, A. S. The Temples of Karnak (2 vols., London, 1961).
ERMAN, ADOLF. The Ancient Egyptians; a Sourcebook of their Writings (trans. A. M. BLACKMAN, Harper, New York, 1966).
FISCHEL, WALTER J. Ibn Khaldun in Egypt (University of California Press, 1967).
FORSTER, E. M. Alexandria: a History and a Guide (Doubleday, New York, 1961).
GARDINER, Sir ALAN HENDERSON. Egypt of the Pharaohs (Clarendon Press, Oxford, 1961).
GLANVILLE, S. R. K. (editor). The Legacy of Egypt (Oxford, 1942).

GREENER, L. The Discovery of Egypt (Cassell, London 1966, Viking Press, New York, 1967).

JOHNSON, ALLAN C. Egypt and the Roman Empire (Ann Arbor, 1951).

MEYER-RANKE, PETER. Der Rote Pharao (Christian Wegner Verlag, Hamburg, 1964).

MONTET, PIERRE. Das Leben der Pharaonen (Frankfurt/Berlin/Vienna, 1970).

PIRENNE, JACQUES. Histoire de la Civilization de l'Egypte antique (Neuchâtel, 1966).
La Religion et la Morale de l'Egypte antique (La Baconnière, Neuchâtel, 1966).

POSENER, G. (Ed.). A Dictionary of Egyptian Civilization (Methuen, London, 1962).

MODERN HISTORY

AVRAM, BENNO. The Evolution of the Suez Canal State 1869–1956. A Historico-Juridical Study (Librairie E. Droz, Libraire Minard, Geneva, Paris, 1958).

BARAWAY, RASHED EL. The Military Coup in Egypt (Cairo, Renaissance Bookshop, 1952).

BARRACLOUGH, GEOFFREY, Ed. Suez in History (London, 1962).

BLUNT, WILFRED SCAWEN. Secret History of the English Occupation of Egypt (Martin Secker, London, 1907).

CONNELL, JOHN. The Most Important Country. The Story of the Suez Crisis and the Events leading up to It (Cassell, London, 1957).

EFENDI, HUSEIN. Ottoman Egypt in the Age of the French Revolution (trans. and with introduction by Stanford J. Shaw) (Harvard Univ. Press, Cambridge, 1964).

FARNIE, D. A. East and West of Suez. The Suez Canal in history, 1854–1956 (Oxford University Press, 1969).

HILL, R. Egypt in the Sudan 1820–1881 (Oxford University Press, London and New York, 1959).

HOLT, P. M. Political and Social Change in Modern Egypt (Oxford University Press, 1967).

HRAIR DEKMEJIAN, R. Egypt Under Nasir (University of London Press, 1972).

ISSAWI, CHARLES. Egypt in Revolution (Oxford, 1963).

JOESTEN, JOACHIM. Nasser: The Rise to Power (London, Odhams, 1960).

KINROSS, LORD. Between Two Seas: The Creation of the Suez Canal (John Murray, London, 1968).

LANE-POOLE, S. History of Egypt in the Middle Ages (4th edn., reprinted, Frank Cass, London, 1967).

LOVE, K. Suez: the Twice-fought War (Longman, 1970).

MANSFIELD, PETER. Nasser's Egypt (Penguin Books London, 1965).
Nasser (Methuen, London, 1969).
The British in Egypt (Weidenfeld and Nicolson, London, 1971).

MARLOWE, JOHN. Cromer in Egypt (Elek Books, London, 1970).

NUTTING, ANTHONY. No End of a Lesson; the Story of Suez (Constable, London, 1967).
Nasser (London, Constable, 1972).

O'BALLANCE, E. The Sinai Campaign 1956 (Faber, London, 1959).

ROWLATT, MARY. Founders of Modern Egypt (Asia Publishing House, London, 1972).

ROYAL INSTITUTE OF INTERNATIONAL AFFAIRS. Great Britain and Egypt, 1914–51 (London, 1952).

SADAT, ANWAR AL. Revolt on the Nile (London, Allen Wingate, 1957).

SAFRAN, NADAV. Egypt in Search of Political Community. An analysis of the intellectual and political evolution of Egypt, 1804–1952 (Harvard University Press, Cambridge, Mass., Oxford University Press, London, 1961).

SAYYID, AFAF LUTFI AL. Egypt and Cromer: A Study in Anglo-Egyptian Relations (John Murray, London, Praeger, New York, 1968).

SHAW, STANFORD J. Ottoman Egypt in the Eighteenth Century (Harvard University Press, 1962).

STEPHENS, R. Nasser (Allen Lane The Penguin Press, London, 1971).

TIGNOR, R. L. Modernization and British Colonial Rule in Egypt 1882-1914 (Princeton, 1966).

VATIKIOTIS, P. J. A Modern History of Egypt (Praeger, New York, 1966: Weidenfeld and Nicholson, London, 1969).
The Egyptian Army in Politics (Indiana University Press, Bloomington, 1961).

WAVELL, A. P. Allenby in Egypt (London, 1944).

ZAKI, ABDEL RAHMAN. Histoire Militaire de l'Epoque de Mohammed Ali El-Kebir (Cairo, 1950).

ZIADEH, FARHAT J. Lawyers, The Rule of Law, and Liberalism in Modern Egypt (Hoover Institution, Stanford. 1968).

ECONOMY

EL GHONEMY, M. RIAD. Economic and Industrial Organization of Egyptian Agriculture since 1952, Egypt since the Revolution (Allen and Unwin, London, 1968).

EL KAMMASH, M. M. Economic Development and Planning in Egypt (London, 1967).

EL NAGGAR, S. Foreign Aid and the Economic Development of the U.A.R. (Princeton, New Jersey, 1965).

HANSON, BENT and MAZOUK, GIRGIS. Development and Economic Policy in the U.A.R. (Egypt) (North Holland Publishing Co., Amsterdam, 1965).

KARDOUCHE, G. S. The U.A.R. in Development (Praeger, New York, 1967).

MEAD, DONALD C. Growth and Structural Change in the Egyptian Economy (Irwin, Homwood, Ill., 1967).

O'BRIEN, PATRICK. The Revolution in Egypt's Economic System 1952-65 (Oxford, 1966).

SAAB, GABRIEL S. The Egyptian Agrarian Reform 1952–1962 (Oxford University Press, London and New York, 1967).

WARRINER, DOREEN. Land Reform and Economic Development (Cairo, 1955).
Land Reform and Development in the Middle East—A Study of Egypt, Syria and Iraq (2nd ed. Oxford University Press, London, 1962).

Iran
(PERSIA)

PHYSICAL AND SOCIAL GEOGRAPHY

W. B. Fisher

SITUATION

The kingdom of Iran is bounded on the north by the Caspian Sea and by the Transcaucasian and Turkistan territories of the U.S.S.R., on the east by Afghanistan and Pakistan, on the south by the Persian Gulf and Gulf of Oman, and on the west by Iraq and Turkey.

PHYSICAL FEATURES

Structurally, Iran is an extremely complex area; and owing partly to political difficulties and partly to the difficult nature of the country itself, complete exploration and investigation have not so far been achieved. In general, it can be stated that Iran consists of an interior plateau, from 3,000–5,000 ft. in height, that is ringed on almost all sides by mountain zones of varying height and extent. The largest mountain massif is that of the Zagros, which runs from the north-west of Iran, where the frontiers of Iran, Russia, Turkey and Iraq meet, first south-westwards to the eastern shores of the Persian Gulf, and then eastwards, fronting the Arabian Sea, and continuing into Baluchistan. Joining the Zagros in the north-west, and running along the southern edge of the Caspian Sea, is the narrower but equally high Elburz range; whilst along the eastern frontier of Iran are several scattered mountain chains, less continuous and imposing than either the Zagros or the Elburz, but still sufficiently high to act as a barrier.

The Zagros range begins in north-west Iran as an alternation of high tablelands and lowland basins, the latter containing lakes, the largest of which is Lake Urmia. This lake, having no outlet, is saline. Further to the south-east the Zagros becomes much more imposing, consisting of a series of parallel hog's-back ridges, some of which reach over 14,000 ft. in height. In its southern and eastern portions the Zagros becomes distinctly narrower, and its peaks much less high, though a few exceed 10,000 ft. The Elburz range is very much narrower than the Zagros, but equally, if not more, abrupt, and one of its peaks, the volcanic cone of Mt. Damavand (18,700 ft.), is the highest in the country. There is a sudden drop on the northern side to the flat plain occupied by the Caspian Sea, which lies nearly 90 ft. below sea-level, and is shrinking rapidly in size. The eastern highlands of Iran consist of isolated massifs separated by lowland zones, some of which contain lakes from which there is no outlet, the largest being the Hirmand Basin, on the borders of Iran and Afghanistan.

The interior plateau of Iran is partly covered by a remarkable salt swamp (termed *kavir*) and partly by loose sand or stones (*dasht*), with stretches of better land mostly round the perimeter, near the foothills of the surrounding mountains. In these latter areas much of the cultivation of the country is carried on, but the lower-lying desert and swamp areas, towards the centre of the plateau, are largely uninhabited. The Kavir is an extremely forbidding region, consisting of a surface formed by thick plates of crystallized salt, which have sharp, upstanding edges. Below the salt lie patches of mud, with, here and there, deep drainage channels—all of which are very dangerous to travellers, and are hence unexplored. Because of this great handicap from the presence of an unusually intractable "dead heart", it has proved difficult to find a good central site for the capital of Iran—many towns, all peripheral to a greater or lesser degree, have in turn fulfilled this function, but none has proved completely satisfactory. The choice of the present capital, Teheran, dates only from the end of the eighteenth century.

Iran suffers from occasional earthquakes, which can cause severe loss of life, damage to property and disruption of communications. A particularly bad example occurred in the north-eastern Khurasan province in August and September 1968; estimates placed the toll from this disaster at up to 20,000 deaths and severe damage over 750 square miles.

The climate of Iran is one of great extremes. Owing to its southerly position, adjacent to Arabia and near the Thar Desert, the summer is extremely hot, with temperatures in the interior rising possibly higher than anywhere else in the world—certainly over 130° F. has been recorded. In winter, however, the great altitude of much of the country and its continental situation result in far lower temperatures than one would expect to find for a country in such low latitudes. Minus 20° F. can be recorded in the north-west Zagros, and 0° F. is common in many places.

Another unfortunate feature is the prevalence of strong winds, which intensify the temperature contrasts. Eastern Iran in particular has a violent visitation in the so-called "Wind of 120 Days", which blows regularly throughout summer, reaching at times over 100 m.p.h. and often raising sand to such an extent that the stone walls of buildings are sometimes scoured away and turn to ruins.

Most of Iran is arid; but in contrast, parts of the northwest and north receive considerable rainfall—up to 80 inches along parts of the Caspian coast, producing very special climatic conditions in this small region, recalling conditions in the lower Himalayas. The Caspian shore has a hot, humid climate and this region is by far the most densely populated of the whole country. Next in order of population density comes the north-west Zagros area,—the province of Azerbaizhan, with its capital, Tabriz, the second city of Iran. Then, reflecting the diminished rainfall, next in order come the central Zagros area, and adjacent parts of the interior plateau, round Isfahan, Hamadan, Shiraz, and Kermanshah, with an extension as far as Teheran. The extreme east and south, where rainfall is very scanty are practically uninhabited.

ECONOMIC LIFE

Owing to the difficulties of climate and topography there are few districts, apart from the Caspian plain, that are continuously cultivated over a wide area. Settlement tends to occur in small clusters, close to water supplies, or where there are especially favourable conditions—a good soil, shelter from winds, or easy communications. Away from these cultivated areas, which stand out like oases among the barren expanses of desert or mountain, most of the population live as nomads, by the herding of animals. The nomadic tribesmen have had great influence on the life of Iran. Their principal territory is the central Zagros, where the tribal system is strongly developed; but nomads are found in all the mountain zones, though their numbers are very few in the south and east. Reza Shah (see "History") made considerable efforts to break the power of the nomadic tribes and to force them to settle as agriculturalists; but since his death there has been a recrudescence of tribal activity. However, the Iranian oilfields lie within tribal territories, and an important change is taking place as nomads accept employment as labourers in the oil industry. This may in time accomplish much of what Reza Shah attempted to do.

Economic activity has suffered from the handicaps of topography and climate, prolonged political and social insecurity (with constant pressure by foreign powers), and widespread devastation in the later Middle Ages by Mongol invaders, from which Iran has never fully recovered. Agricultural methods in particular are primitive, so that yields are low; but the drawbacks to efficient production mentioned in the general introduction to this volume—archaic systems of land tenure, absentee landlords, lack of education, and shortage of capital—are gradually being overcome. In the north and west, which are by far the most productive, a wide variety of cereals (including wheat, barley, and rice) and much fruit are grown, but in the south and east the date is the principal source of food. Some Iranian fruit is of remarkable quality (especially the apricots and grapes) and melons of over 100 lbs. weight are known.

Iran has a number of mineral resources, some of which are exploited on a commercial scale. Iranians have always had a high reputation as craftsmen—particularly in metal work and in carpet-making; and Reza Shah attempted to develop modern mechanized industry by placing State owned factories in most of the big towns. Some of these have proved successful, others not, but bazaar manufactures still remain the more important. Teheran has now become a sizeable manufacturing centre, with brick- and cement-making, light engineering, processing of foodstuffs and manufacture of consumer goods as chief activities. Carpet making remains important in Iran owing to considerable demand from the U.S.A. and Europe (especially West Germany) where Persian rugs are a status symbol.

The adverse nature of geographical conditions has greatly restricted the growth of communications in Iran. The country is very large in relation to its size of population—it is 1,400 miles from north-west to south-west—and because of the interior deserts, many routes must follow a circuitous path instead of attempting a direct crossing. Then, too, the interior is shut off by ranges that are in parts as high as the Alps of Europe, but far less broken up by river valleys. Road construction is everywhere difficult, and few hard-surfaced tracks exist, although road construction is now being undertaken both by the Plan Organization of Iran and the Central Treaty Organization. An important link is the railway constructed at great effort before the Second World War, between the Caspian coast and Teheran and the Persian Gulf. Other rail links with bordering countries are slowly being built. Though there are mountain streams, many flowing in deep inaccessible gorges, only one, the Kharun River, is at all navigable. The Caspian ports suffer rapid silting, whilst in the south most harbours are either poorly sheltered or else difficult of access from the interior. During the last few years, however, with greater strategic and economic interest in the south and east of Iran, parts of the Gulf, especially Bushire, are in process of development as more direct outlets for the interior. A CENTO plan has resulted in the development of roads into Turkey and Pakistan; and in some slight measure the north-east of Iran is less remote, distant provinces being reachable only through Teheran.

RACE AND LANGUAGE

Iran has numerous ethnic groups of widely differing origin. In the central plateau there occurs a distinctive sub-race, termed by some anthropologists Iranian or Irano-Afghan. The distinguishing qualities are a moderate to rather tall stature, a moderately round head, pronounced features, but less so than among Armenoids, and a colouring generally lighter than that of many surrounding peoples. In the mountain districts there are many other smaller groups of separate racial composition. A number of nomads, including the Bakhtiari tribes, would seem to be of Kurdish stock; whilst Turki (Mongoloid) strains are apparent in others, such as the Qashqai tribes. Smaller groups from the Caucasus (Georgians and Circassians) are represented in Azerbaijan and the Caspian provinces, whilst Turki influence is again apparent in the racial composition of the eastern districts of Iran, especially round Meshed. The southern Zagros near the Arabian Sea has a small population that tends to be of mixed Iranian, Afghan, and Hindu stock. Some observers have suggested that in this region there may also be representatives of a primitive negrito race, related to the hill-tribes of India and of south-east Asia.

With so many differing ethnic groups, it is not surprising to find that several languages are current in Iran. Persian, an Indo-Aryan language related to the languages of western Europe, is spoken in the north and centre of the country, and is the one official language of the State. As the north is by far the most densely peopled region of Iran, the Persian language has an importance somewhat greater than its territorial extent would suggest. Various dialects of Kurdish are current in the north and central Zagros mountains, and alongside these are found several Turki-speaking tribes. Baluchi occurs in the extreme south-east. English and French are spoken by most of the educated classes.

HISTORY

EARLY HISTORY

The Achaemenid empire, the first Persian empire, was founded by Cyrus who revolted against the Median empire in 533 B.C. After the defeat of the Median empire Babylon was taken in 539 B.C., and in 525 B.C. under Cambyses, the successor of Cyrus, Egypt was conquered. The period of conquest was rounded off by Darius who reduced the tribes of the Pontic and Armenian mountains and extended Persian dominion to the Caucasus. The main work of Darius, however, lay not in the conquest but in the organization which he gave to the empire. During his reign wars with Greece broke out and in 490 B.C. the Persian army suffered a major defeat at Marathon; an expedition under Xerxes, the successor of Darius, which set out to avenge this defeat was, after initial successes, defeated at Salamis in 480 B.C. The empire was finally overthrown by Alexander who defeated the Persian army at Arbela in 331 B.C. and then burnt Persepolis, the Achaemenid capital; the last Darius fled and was killed in 330 B.C. Alexander thereafter regarded himself as the head of the Persian empire. The death of Alexander was followed by a struggle between his generals, one of whom, Seleucus, took the whole of Persia, apart from northern Media and founded the Seleucid empire. About the year 250 B.C. a reaction against Hellenism began with the rise of the Parthian empire of the Arsacids. Although by origin nomads from the Turanian steppe, the Arsacids became the wardens of the north-east marches and were largely preoccupied in defending themselves in the east against the Scythians who, with the Tocharians and Sacae, repeatedly attacked the Parthian empire, while in the west they were engaged in fending off attacks by the Romans.

The Arsacids were succeeded by the Sasanians, who, like the Achaemenids, came from Fars and, like them, were Zoroastrians. Ardashir b. Babak, after subduing the neighbouring states (c. A.D. 212), made war on the Arsacid, Artabanus V, whom he eventually defeated. The empire which he founded largely continued the traditions of the Achaemenids, although it never equalled the Achaemenid empire in extent. The monarchy of the Sasanian period was a religious and civil institution. The monarch who ruled by divine right was absolute but his autocracy was limited by the powers of the Zoroastrian hierarchy and the feudal aristocracy. In the reign of Qubad (A.D. 488–531) a movement of revolt, partly social and partly religious, led by Mazdak, gained ground. Under Qubad's successor Anushiravan (531–679) orthodoxy was restored, but at the cost of the imposition of a military despotism. Like the Arsacids before them the Sasanians were occupied in the west with wars with Rome and in the east with repelling inroads of the nomads from Central Asia.

MUSLIM PERSIA

By the beginning of the seventh century A.D. Persia had been greatly weakened by these wars, and when the Muslim Arabs attacked, little effective resistance was offered. The decisive battles were fought at Qadisiyya (A.D. 637) and Nihavand (c. A.D. 641). Persia did not re-emerge as a political entity until the sixteenth century A.D., although with the decline of the Abbasid empire semi-independent and independent dynasties arose in different parts of Persia and at times even incorporated under their rule an area extending beyond the confines of present day Persia. As a result of the Arab conquest Persia became part of the Muslim world. Local administration remained largely in the hands of the indigenous population and many local customs continued to be observed. In due course a new civilization developed in Persia, the unifying force of which was Islam.

With the transfer of the capital of the Islamic empire from Damascus to Baghdad (c. A.D. 750) Persian influence began to be strongly felt in the life of the empire. Islam had already replaced Zoroastrianism and by the tenth century modern Persian, written in the Arabic script and including a large number of Arabic words in its vocabulary, had established itself. Its emergence was of immense importance; the literary tradition for which it became the vehicle has perhaps more than any other factor kept alive a national consciousness among the Persians and preserved the memory of the great Persian empires of the past, however much the details became blurred and even distorted in the course of transmission.

By the eighth century A.D. the Abbasid caliphate had begun to disintegrate and when in the eleventh century control of the north-eastern frontiers broke down, the Ghuzz Turks invaded Persia. This movement, of which the Seljuqs became the leaders, was ethnologically important since it altered the balance of population, the Turkish element from then on being second only to the Persian in numbers and influence. Secondly, it was in the Seljuq empire that the main lines of the politico-economic structure, which was to last in Persia in a modified form down to the twentieth century A.D., were worked out. The basis of this structure was the land assignment, the holder of which was often virtually a petty territorial ruler, who was required, when called upon to do so, to provide the ruler with a military contingent. This system was to some extent forced upon the Seljuqs and others after them, because they were unable to establish an effective system of direct administration or to exercise financial control over their military forces and because they could not integrate the settled and semi-settled elements of the population; the weakness of the system was that whenever the central control slackened, the empire tended to split up into independent or semi-independent units.

The Seljuq empire itself broke up in the twelfth century into a number of succession states; the thirteenth century saw the Mongol invasion and in 1258 Hulagu, the grandson of Chinghiz (Jenghiz) Khan, sacked Baghdad and destroyed the caliphate. For some years the Ilkhan dynasty, founded by Hulagu, ruled Persia as vassals of the Great Khan in Qaraqorum, but from the reign of Abaqa (1265–1281) onwards they became virtually a Persian dynasty. Their empire, like that of the Seljuqs before them—and for very much the same reasons—broke up at the beginning of the fourteenth century into a number of succession states. Towards the end of the century Persia again fell under the dominion of a military conqueror, when Timur, who had started his career as the warden of the marches in the Oxus-Jaxartes basin against the nomads of Central Asia, undertook a series of military campaigns against Persia between 1381 and 1387. The kingdom founded by him was short-lived and rapidly disintegrated on the death of his son Shahrukh, the western part falling first to the Turkomans of the Black Sheep and then to the Turkomans of the White Sheep, while Transoxania passed into the hands of the Uzbegs.

THE PERSIAN MONARCHY

The sixteenth century saw the foundation of the Safavid empire, which was accompanied by an eastward movement of the Turkomans from Asia Minor back into Persia. For the first time since the Muslim conquest Persia re-emerged as a political unit; her frontiers became more or less fixed, although there was a general movement of contraction in the eighteenth and nineteenth centuries notably in the north-west and north-east. The foundations of the Safavid empire were laid by Isma'il Safavi (1502-24). He deliberately fostered a sense of separateness and of national unity vis-à-vis the Ottoman Turks with whom the Safavids were engaged in a struggle for supremacy in the west, and the main weapon he used to accomplish his purpose was Shi'ism. Not only the Turks but the majority of his own subjects were at the time Sunni—nevertheless he imposed Shi'ism upon them by force and created among the population of his dominions, many of whom, especially among his immediate followers, were Turks, a sense of national unity as Persians. Apart from a brief interlude under Nadir Shah, Shi'ism has since then remained the majority rite in Persia and is the official rite of the country at the present day. Under Shah Abbas (1587-1629) the Safavid empire reached its zenith and Persia enjoyed a power and prosperity which she has not since achieved.

GREAT POWER RIVALRY

During the Safavid period, intercourse with Europe increased. Various foreign embassies interested mainly in the silk trade reached the Safavid court via Russia and via the Persian Gulf. In the latter area in the early years of the sixteenth century a struggle for supremacy developed between the British and the Dutch. "Factories" were established by the East India Company in the Gulf from the early sixteenth century.

Under the later Safavids internal decline set in and from 1722-30 Persia was subject to Afghan invasion and occupation while in the west and north she was threatened by Turkey and Russia. After the death of Peter the Great there was a temporary slackening of Russian pressure, but the Turks continued to advance and took Tabriz in 1725, peace being eventually made at Hamadan in 1727. The Afghans were finally evicted by Nadir Shah Afshar whose reign (1736-47) was remarkable chiefly for his military exploits. The Afsharids were succeeded by Karim Khan Zand (1750-79) whose relatively peaceful reign was followed by the rise of the Qajars who continued to reign until 1925. Under them the capital was transferred from Isfahan to Teheran. During the Qajar period events in Persia became increasingly affected by Great Power rivalry until not only Persia's foreign policy was dominated by this question, but her internal politics also.

With the growth of British influence in India in the late eighteenth and early nineteenth centuries the main emphasis in Anglo-Persian relations, which during the sixteenth and seventeenth centuries had been on commerce, began to shift to strategy. Persia and the Persian Gulf came to be regarded as one of the main bastions to India and the existence of an independent Persia as a major British interest. In the early nineteenth century fear of a French invasion of India through Persia exercised the mind of the British in India and Whitehall. French envoys were active in Persia and Mesopotamia from 1796 to 1809, and to counter possible French activities Captain (afterwards Sir John) Malcolm was sent to Persia in 1800 by the Governor General of India; he concluded a political and commercial treaty with Fath Ali Shah, the main purpose of which was to ensure that the Shah should not receive French agents and would do his utmost to prevent French forces entering Persia. With the defeat of Napoleon in Egypt the matter was no longer regarded as urgent and the agreement was not ratified. Subsequently the French made proposals to Persia for an alliance against Russia and in 1807 Persia concluded the Treaty of Finkenstein with France after which a military mission under General Gardanne came to Persia. In 1808 another British mission was sent under Malcolm. Its object was "first, to detach the Court of Persia from the French alliance and to prevail on that Court to refuse the passage of French troops through the territories subject to Persia, or the admission of French troops into the country. If that cannot be obtained, to admit English troops with a view of opposing the French army in its progress to India, to prevent the creation of any maritime post, and the establishment of French factories on the coast of Persia". Malcolm's task was complicated by the almost simultaneous arrival of a similar mission from Whitehall. In 1809 after the Treaty of Tilsit, which debarred the French from aiding the Shah against Russia, Gardanne was dismissed.

WARS WITH RUSSIA AND TURKEY

Meanwhile the formal annexation of Georgia by Russia in 1801 had been followed by a campaign against Russia. This proved disastrous to Persia and was temporarily brought to an end by the Treaty of Gulistan (1813) by which Persia ceded Georgia, Qara Bagh and seven other provinces. British policy continued to be exercised over the possibility of an invasion of India via Persia and in 1814 the Treaty of Teheran was concluded with Persia by which Great Britain undertook to provide troops or a subsidy in the event of unprovoked aggression on Persia. Although the treaty provided for defence against any European power it was primarily intended to provide against the designs of Russia. In fact it proved ineffective and when the Perso-Russian war recommenced in 1825 Great Britain did not interfere except as a peacemaker and discontinued the subsidy to Persia, who was technically the aggressor. The war was concluded in 1828 by the Treaty of Turkomanchai, under the terms of which Persia ceded Erivan and Nakhjivan and agreed to pay an indemnity; in addition, she was prohibited from having armed vessels on the Caspian.

During this period Persia was also engaged in hostilities with Turkey. Frontier disputes in 1821 culminated in the outbreak of war, which was concluded by the Treaty of Erzerum (1823).

By the nineteenth century the Persian Government had ceased to exercise effective control over the greater part of Khurasan. Russian policy, which became conciliatory towards Persia during the twenty-five years or so after the Treaty of Turkomanchai, encouraged the Shah to reimpose Persian rule on the eastern provinces. British policy, on the other hand, having come to regard Afghanistan as an important link in the defence of India, urged moderation upon the Persian Government. Nevertheless a Persian expedition set out, took Quchan and Sarakhs and laid siege to Herat; on the death of Abbas Mirza, the heir apparent and commander of the Persian forces in the east at the time, the siege was raised. After the accession of Muhammad Shah in 1834, a new expedition was sent against Herat. The sending of this, too, was encouraged by Russia while the Barakzai chiefs of Kandahar also offered the Persians assistance against their Saduzai rivals in Herat. The siege of Herat began in 1837 but was raised when the Shah was threatened with British intervention. Subsequently local intrigues headed by Sa'id Muhammad had enabled the Persians to enter Herat, and when Muhammad Yusuf Saduzai seized Herat some years later in 1855 and put Sa'id Muhammad to death, relatives of the latter went to Teheran to enlist the support of the Shah who thereupon ordered the governor of Meshed to march on Herat. The seizure of the city by Persia led to the outbreak of the Anglo-Persian war in 1856, which was terminated by the Treaty of Paris (1857) after a British force had occupied the island of Kharg in the Persian Gulf.

In the second half of the century the subjection of the

Turkoman tribes by Russia, her capture of Marv in 1854, and the occupation of the Panjeh, meant that Russian influence became dominant in Khurasan in the same way as the advance of Russia to the Araxes after the Persian wars in the early part of the nineteenth century had made Russian influence dominant in Azerbaizhan.

INCREASED FOREIGN INTERVENTION

Internally the second half of the nineteenth century was remarkable chiefly for the beginnings of the modernist movement, which was stimulated on the one hand by internal misgovernment and on the other by increased intervention in the internal affairs of the country by Russia and Britain. Towards the end of the century numerous concessions were granted to foreigners largely in order to pay for the extravagances of the court. The most fantastic of these was the Reuter concession. In 1872 a naturalised British subject, Baron de Reuter, was given by the Shah a monopoly for seventy years of railways and tramways in Persia, all the minerals except gold, silver and precious stones, irrigation, road, factory and telegraph enterprises, and the farm of customs dues for twenty-five years. Eventually this concession was cancelled and permission instead given for the foundation of a Persian state bank with British capital, which was to have the exclusive right to issue banknotes; and accordingly in September 1889 the Imperial Bank of Persia began business. In the same year Dolgoruki obtained for Russia the first option of a railway concession for five years. In November of the following year the railway agreement with Russia was changed into one interdicting all railways whatsoever in Persia. In 1889 after negotiations for foreign loans Belgian officials were put in charge of the customs administration. By the turn of the century there had been "a pronounced sharpening of Anglo-Russian hostility as a consequence of a whole series of Russian actions, not only in northern Persia where Russian ascendancy to a large extent had to be admitted, but as well in southern and eastern Persia which had hitherto been predominantly British preserves". In 1900 a Russian loan was given, to be followed by another in 1902 secured on the customs (excluding those of Fars and the Gulf). Subsequently various short term advances and subsidies from the Russian treasury including advances to the heir apparent, Muhammad Ali, were made so that by 1906 some £7½ millions were owing to the Russians. Under the 1891 Russo-Persian tariff treaty, trade between the two countries had increased, and when under the 1901 Russo-Persian commercial treaty a new customs tariff was announced in 1903, Russian exports to Persia were considerably aided and up to 1914 Russian commerce with Persia continued to grow.

The grant of these various concessions to foreigners and the raising of foreign loans gave rise to growing anxiety on the part of the Persian public. Further, large numbers of Persians had fled the country and were living in exile. When a tobacco monopoly was granted to a British subject in 1890, various elements of the population, including the intellectuals and the religious classes, combined to oppose it. Strikes and riots threatened and the monopoly was rescinded. No effective steps, however, were taken to allay popular discontent. In 1901 protests were made against the loans and mortgages from Russia which were being contracted to pay for Muzaffar ud-Din Shah's journeys to Europe. By 1905–6 the demand for reform had grown in strength and finally on August 5th, 1906, after 12,000 persons had taken sanctuary in the British legation, a constitution was granted. A long struggle then began between the constitutionalists and the Shah. The Cossack Brigade, formed during the reign of Nasir ud-Din Shah, which was under Russian officers and was the most effective military force in the country, played a major part in this struggle and was used by Muhammad Ali Shah to suppress the National Assembly in 1908. Civil war ensued and Muhammad Ali Shah's abdication was forced in 1909.

Meanwhile in 1907 the Anglo-Russian convention had been signed. The convention, which included a mutual undertaking to respect the integrity and independence of Persia, divided the country into three areas, that lying to the north of a line passing from Qasri Shirin to Kakh where the Russian, Persian and Afghan frontiers meet in the east, that lying to the south of a line running from Qazik on the Perso-Afghan frontier through Birjand and Kerman to Bandar Abbas on the Persian Gulf, and that lying outside these two areas. Great Britain gave an undertaking not to seek or support others seeking political or economic concessions in the northern area; Russia gave a similar undertaking with reference to the southern area. In the central area the freedom of action of the two parties was not limited and their existing concessions (which included the oil concession granted to D'Arcy in 1901) were maintained. The conclusion of this convention—which had taken place partly because of a change in the relative strength of the Great Powers and partly because the British Government hoped thereby to terminate Anglo-Russian rivalry in Persia and to prevent further Russian encroachments—came as a shock to Persian opinion which had hoped much from the support which the British Government had given to the constitutional movement. It was felt that Persian interests had been bartered away by Great Britain for a promise of Russian support in the event of a European war. In fact, the convention failed in its object. Russian pressure continued to be exercised on Persia directly and indirectly. In 1909, 1911 and 1912 Russian troops occupied Tabriz and other towns in north Persia; and in 1911 as a result of Russian pressure the National Assembly was suspended and the resignation forced of the American Administrator-General of the Finances, Shuster, who had been appointed in the hope of bringing order into the finances of Persia.

THE FIRST WORLD WAR

During the 1914–18 War Persia was nominally neutral but in fact Turkish; British and Russian forces and German agents were active in the country, and on the conclusion of the armistice between Russia and Turkey in 1917 two British expeditionary forces set out for Russia through Persia on what proved to be abortive missions. By the end of the war the internal condition of Persia was chaotic. To the British Government the restoration of order was desirable and with this end in view the Agreement of 1919 was drawn up whereby a number of men were to be lent to reorganize the Persian army and to reform the Ministry of Finance and a loan of £2 million was to be given. There was opposition to this agreement in the U.S.A. and France and in Persia, and the treaty was not ratified. A coup d'état took place in 1921, Reza Khan (later Reza Shah) becoming Minister of War. In February 1921 the Soviet-Persian Treaty was signed whereby the U.S.S.R. declared all treaties and conventions concluded with Persia by the Tsarist Government null and void. Under Article VI the U.S.S.R. was permitted "to advance her troops into the Persian interior for the purpose of carrying out the military operations necessary for its defence" in the event of a third party attempting "to carry out a policy of usurpation by means of armed intervention in Persia, or if such a Power should desire to use Persian territory as a base of operations against Russia...." In a letter dated December 12th, 1921, from the Russian diplomatic representative at Teheran to the Persian Minister for Foreign Affairs, it was stated that this article was intended to apply "only to cases in which preparations have been made for a considerable armed attack upon Russia or the Soviet Republics allied to her, by the partisans of the régime which has been overthrown or by its supporters among those foreign Powers which are in a position to assist the enemies of the Workers' and Peasants' Republics and at the same time to possess themselves, by force or by underhand methods, of part of the Persian territory, thereby establishing a base of operations for any attacks—made either directly or through the counter-revolutionary forces—which they might meditate against Russia or the Soviet Republics allied to her".

REZA SHAH 1925–1941

In 1923 Reza Khan became Prime Minister and finally in 1925 the crown of Persia was conferred upon him. His first task was to restore the authority of the central government throughout the country, and the second to place Persia's relations with foreign countries on a basis of equality. All extra-territorial agreements were terminated from 1928. Lighting and quarantine duties on the Persian littoral of the Persian Gulf, hitherto performed by Great Britain, were transferred to the Persian Government in 1930. The Indo-European Telegraph Company, which had been in operation since 1872, had almost entirely been withdrawn by 1931 and the British coaling stations were transferred from Basidu and Henjam to Bahrain in 1935.

In 1932 the cancellation of the Anglo-Persian Oil Company's concession was announced by Persia. The original concession obtained by D'Arcy in 1901 had been taken over by the Anglo-Persian Oil Company (later the Anglo-Iranian Oil Company) in 1909 and the British Government had acquired a controlling interest in the company in 1914. Thenceforward the main emphasis of British policy towards Persia had been on oil rather than strategy, though from 1941 onwards the strategic aspect again became important. The Persian Government's action in cancelling the concession was referred to the League of Nations. Eventually an agreement was concluded in 1933 for a new concession whereby the concession area was materially reduced and the royalty to be paid to the Persian Government increased. The concession was to run to 1993.

Internally Reza Shah's policy aimed at modernization and autarchy. In the later years of his reign the Government became increasingly totalitarian in its nature. Compulsory military service was introduced and the army much increased in size. Communications were greatly improved; the construction of a trans-Persian railway was begun. Education was remodelled on western lines. Women were no longer obliged to wear the veil after 1936. Foreign trade was made a state monopoly, currency and clearing restrictions were established. These arrangements fitted in with the economy of Germany and by the outbreak of World War II, Germany had acquired considerable commercial and political influence in Persia.

On the outbreak of war Persia declared her neutrality. In 1941 the Allies demanded a reduction in the number of Germans in the country, and when no satisfaction was obtained sent another communication demanding the expulsion of all German nationals, except such as were essential to Persian economy and harmless to the Allies. This demand was not complied with and on August 26th, 1941, Persia was invaded. Hostilities lasted some two days. On September 16th Reza Shah abdicated in favour of his son Muhammad Reza. In January 1942 a Tripartite Treaty of Alliance was concluded with Great Britain and the U.S.S.R. whereby Great Britain and the U.S.S.R. undertook jointly and severally "to respect the territorial integrity, sovereignty and political independence of Persia" and "to defend Persia by all means in their command from aggression" and the Persian Government undertook to give the Allies for certain military purposes the unrestricted right to use, maintain and guard, and in the case of military necessity, to control, all means of communications in Persia. Allied forces were to be withdrawn not later than six months after the conclusion of hostilities between the Allied Powers and Germany and her associates. In so far as the establishment of communications with the U.S.S.R. was concerned the Treaty was effective; its operation in other respects was less satisfactory. In the Russian zone of occupation the Persian authorities were denied freedom of movement and effective administration made impossible. American advisers were appointed by the Persian Government in 1942 and 1943 in the hope of reorganising certain aspects of the administration. Their efforts were for a variety of reasons in no case attended by more than a limited measure of success and in due course their services were terminated.

In 1943 a British company applied for an oil concession in south-east Persia and in 1944 the Socony Vacuum and Sinclair Oil Companies made various proposals to the Persian Government. In September the Persian Cabinet issued a decree deferring the grant of oil concessions till after the war. The U.S.S.R. meanwhile asked for an oil concession in the north and brought heavy, though unavailing, pressure to bear on the Persian Government to accede to this demand. Persian security forces were prevented by Soviet forces from entering Azerbaizhan or the Caspian Provinces and an autonomous government was set up in Azerbaizhan with Russian support in December 1945. In January 1946 the Persian Government had recourse to the Security Council. In March the Tripartite Treaty expired and British and American forces evacuated Persia, Soviet forces remaining. The Persian Government again presented a note to the Security Council. In April an oral understanding, confirmed by an exchange of letters between the Persian Prime Minister and the Soviet Ambassador, was arrived at whereby a joint Soviet-Persian company to exploit the oil in the northern provinces was to be formed. In May Soviet forces evacuated the country. Soviet pressure, however, continued to be exerted through the Tudeh party, the Democrat movement in Azerbaizhan, and the Kurdish autonomy movement, and the Persian Government was unable to re-enter Azerbaizhan until December. In the following October, the Soviet Oil Agreement was presented to the National Assembly but was not ratified. In October 1947 an agreement was signed with America, providing for a U.S. military mission in Persia to co-operate with the Persian ministry of war in "enhancing the efficiency of the Persian army".

NATIONALIZING THE OIL INDUSTRY

Meanwhile unrest and discontent at internal misgovernment increased, culminating in the Nationalist movement of 1950/51. In July 1949 a Supplemental Oil Agreement with the Anglo-Iranian Oil Company was initialled. Opposition to this agreement (whereby Persia was offered considerable financial gains) was strong. In November 1950 the oil commission of the National Assembly recommended its rejection. Meanwhile Persia had received a loan of $25 m. from the Export & Import Bank of Washington and a grant of $500,000 under the Point IV allocation. Subsequently in 1952 the Point IV aid programme was expanded. In April 1951 the National Assembly passed a Bill for the nationalization of the oil industry, and in May, Dr. Musaddiq, who had led the campaign for nationalisation of the oil industry, became Prime Minister. The Company and the British Government severally filed petitions with the International Court, the former asking the Court to declare Persia bound by the 1933 agreement to agree to accept the Company's request for arbitration and the latter asking the Court to nominate an arbitrator. The Persian Government declined to recognize the Court's jurisdiction. Eventually the British Government referred the dispute to the Security Council, which decided on October 19th, 1951, to defer consideration of the Persian case pending a final pronouncement of the International Court. The *status quo* however, could not be maintained in Persia and the Anglo-Iranian Oil Company evacuated the country, being unable to continue operations.

On July 22nd, 1952, the International Court found that it had no jurisdiction in the oil dispute. This decision, however, was not a decision on the merits of the case. The Company accordingly maintained its claim to be entitled to all crude oil and oil products derived from the area covered by its concession agreement, and stated its intention to take such action as was necessary to protect its interests. American policy showed an increasing interest in Persian affairs. During the period August to October, 1952, considerable correspondence passed between the British, American and Persian Governments in the oil dispute, culminating in a joint offer by Sir Winston Churchill and President Truman, making proposals concerning the assessment of the compensation to be paid to the Anglo-Iranian Oil Company and the re-starting of the flow of oil to world markets. The Persian Government rejected these proposals and put forward counter proposals which were unacceptable. On October 22nd the Persian Government broke off diplomatic relations with Great Britain. Further Anglo-American proposals for an oil settlement were put forward in February 1953, which the Persian Government rejected. Meanwhile dissension between Musaddiq and some of his supporters broke out, and a rift also developed between him and the Shah. The economic situation of the country began to deteriorate rapidly. Disorders became more frequent. At the end of February the Shah announced his decision to leave the country. The Tudeh party thereupon appealed for a united front against the court, but in response to demonstrations of loyalty the Shah abandoned his decision. In April it was announced that the dissension between Musaddiq and the Shah had been removed. Unrest nevertheless continued, and opposition to Musaddiq in the *majlis* grew. The economic situation of the country continued to worsen. In June President Eisenhower announced that the U.S. would give Persia no further aid unless the oil dispute was settled or referred to an international body. In July there were several resignations from the *majlis* in protest against Musaddiq's conduct of affairs. Musaddiq meanwhile held a "referendum", claimed that this showed a majority in favour of the dissolution of the *majlis* and dissolved it forthwith. On August 16th there was an abortive attempt by the Imperial Guards to arrest Musaddiq. The Shah and the Queen fled the country. Three days later, General Zahedi, who had received an imperial *firman* appointing him Prime Minister a few days before the abortive *coup*, assumed control. Musaddiq and other members of his Government were arrested. The Shah returned and asked for immediate help to restore the economic stability of the country. In September an emergency grant of $45 million was made by the U.S. and the continuation of military and technical assistance was promised. Musaddiq was tried and sentenced to three years solitary confinement for trying to overthrow the régime and illegally dissolving the *majlis*.

The new Government resumed diplomatic relations with Great Britain in December 1953, and negotiations with British and American oil interests began for the solution of the oil problem. In September 1954 an agreement was signed, and ratified by the *majlis* and senate in October, granting a concession to a consortium of eight companies (subsequently increased to seventeen) on a percentage basis.

It was also agreed that the claims of the Anglo-Iranian Oil Company and the Persian Government against each other were to be settled by the payment of a lump sum to the Company, which was also to receive compensation from the other members of the consortium. The profits arising within Persia from the oil operations were to be equally shared between the Persian Government and the consortium. The agreement was for a period of twenty-five years with provision for three five-year extensions, conditional upon a progressive reduction of the original area. The National Iranian Oil Company was to operate the Naft-i Shah oilfield and the Kermanshah refinery to meet part of Persia's own needs and to handle the distribution of oil products in Persia and to be responsible for all facilities and services not directly part of the producing, refining, and transport operations of the two operating companies set up under the agreement. The greater part of the cost of these facilities and services, which would include industrial training, public transport, road maintenance, housing, medical care, and social welfare, would be recovered by the NIOC from the operating companies.

GROWING POWER OF THE SHAH

Internally order was restored. The Tudeh party was proscribed, but continued to exist underground, and in January and August 1954, Tudeh conspiracies were uncovered. The failure of the Government to push forward actively with reform, however, led in due course to a reappearance of unrest and discontent. In April 1955 Zahedi resigned and was succeeded by Ala, the Shah henceforward taking a more active part in the administration. In October, Persia joined the Baghdad Pact. The change of Government, however, did not materially lessen the mounting discontent, and in November an attempt was made on the Prime Minister's life. Meanwhile, the country had not recovered from the financial difficulties brought on by the Musaddiq régime, in spite of the considerable financial aid granted to Persia by the U.S. to enable the country to carry on until oil revenues began to come in. U.S. aid has continued during the years that oil revenues have been coming in, and over 800 million U.S. dollars were poured into Iran between the end of the Second World War and September 1960. On March 5th, 1959, a bilateral defence agreement was signed in Ankara between the United States and Iran. Under the agreement the government of the United States "will, in case of aggression, take such appropriate action, including the use of armed force, as may be mutually agreed, and as envisaged in the Joint Resolution to promote peace and security in the Middle East". (The Joint Resolution refers to the "Eisenhower Doctrine").

Relations with the U.S.S.R. in the years following the fall of Musaddiq were not cordial, but in December 1954 an agreement providing for (1) the repayment by the U.S.S.R. of her war debts to Persia for goods supplied and services rendered, and (2) mapping of the revised frontiers was signed. In 1956 the Shah made a state visit to the U.S.S.R. The joint Soviet-Iranian frontier demarcation commission, which began working in August 1955, completed its task in April 1957, when protocols were signed defining the frontiers in detail.

On April 3rd, 1957, Hussein Ala resigned and was succeeded as Prime Minister by Dr. Manoutchehr Egbal, who formed a new Government. Immediately after taking office Dr. Egbal issued a decree ending martial law and declared his intention of forming a democratic two-party system, in accordance with the desires of the Shah. In February 1958, the formation of a Government-Nation-Party was announced. An Opposition-People's-Party had been formed in 1957. Elections contested by both these political parties were held for the first time in August 1960, but after accusations that electoral irregularities had enabled the Government party to secure an overwhelming majority the Shah declared the elections annulled, and the Prime Minister Dr. Egbal, resigned. A new cabinet was formed under the leadership of Jafar Sharif Emami, the former Minister of Mines and Industries. New elections were held in January 1961 but National Front supporters alleged that the elections had again been rigged. Dr. Emami was again elected Prime Minister, but it was generally agreed that the existing electoral law was unsatisfactory and the Shah, in his speech to the new *majlis*, stated that its first task must be the passing of a new electoral law.

In May 1961, however, Dr. Emami resigned as a result of criticism of his handling of a teachers' strike, and the Shah called upon Dr. Ali Amini, the leader of the opposition, to form a new government.

Dr. Amini quickly took stern measures to halt the political and economic chaos in Iran. A drive against corruption in the Government and civil service was coupled with policies of land reform, decentralization of administration, control of Government expenditure and limitation of luxury imports. Both Houses of Parliament were dissolved pending the passing of a new electoral law which would make free and fair elections possible. Postponement of elections, in July 1962, led to disorder in Teheran, and the added difficulty of producing a reasonably balanced budget led Dr. Amini to tender his resignation.

A new government was quickly formed by Mr. Assadollah Alam, the leader of the *Mardom* (People's) Party. Mr. Alam, one of Iran's largest landowners and administrator of the Pahlevi Foundation, had previously distributed much of his land voluntarily amongst the peasants. He stated that Iran would remain closely linked to the West, and that he would continue the land reform programme and the struggle against internal political corruption. A reform programme was approved by a national referendum held in January 1963. Presenting the new budget in April, Mr. Alam announced that elections restoring the country to a parliamentary government would be held in June or July 1963.

Iran suffered as the result of a serious earthquake in September 1962; about 10,000 people were killed and many more thousands injured over a large area of north-west Iran.

REFORMS OF THE SHAH

Since 1950 the Shah has been distributing his estate amongst the peasants. By the end of 1963 he had disposed of all his Crown Properties and in future he will receive only the sums allotted in the civil list. The Pahlevi Foundation was established in 1958 and has received considerable gifts from the Shah for the purpose of improving standards of education, health and social welfare amongst the poorer classes. In October 1961 the Shah created the £40 million Pahlevi Dynasty Trust, the income of which is being used for social, educational and health services for the Iranian people.

In January 1963 a referendum was held, as a result of which overwhelming approval was given to the Shah's six-point plan for the distribution of lands among the peasants, the promotion of literacy, the emancipation of women, etc. The break-up of great estates began almost immediately, and the programme was finally completed in September 1971; another important measure was the formation of the Literacy Corps (and later of the Health Corps), in which students could serve their period of national service as teachers, working in the villages. This aspect of the Shah's reforms was widely publicized, and in September 1965 an international anti-illiteracy conference was held in Teheran, attended by a number of Ministers of Education. In May 1966 the Shah donated £250,000, or one day's defence expenditure, to the world campaign against illiteracy.

A court statement of March 14th, 1958, announced the divorce of the Shah and Queen Soraya. The Shah and the Queen, who were childless, were married in 1951. The announcement said that the Shah had been unanimously advised by his Privy Councillors that the heir to the throne must be in direct descent from the Sovereign, in order to safeguard national interests. The Shah has a daughter by his previous marriage to Princess Fawzia of Egypt which was dissolved in 1948. In December 1959, the Shah married Farah Diba, an Iranian architectural student, and in October 1960 Riza Kurush, a son and heir, was born. A daughter, Princess Maasoumeh Farahnaz, was born in March 1963, and another son in May 1966.

Early in June 1963 there were riots by political and religious groups protesting against the land reforms and the emancipation of women. Martial law was imposed and the leaders of the riots were arrested, and a return to normal conditions was quickly effected. Some friction was caused with the United Arab Republic, which the Shah accused of fomenting the riots. The accusation was denied in Cairo.

The elections scheduled for July 1963 eventually took place in September of that year. The result was an overwhelming victory for the National Union of Mr. Alam; his party was in fact a coalition of several political groups, all pledged to support the reform programme of the Shah. The elections, in which for the first time women were allowed to vote, were held in the face of strenuous opposition from the left-wing parties of Iran, notably the National Front and the Communist Tudeh party, which called unsuccessfully for a boycott. The new Parliament—the first since both houses were dissolved by Dr. Amini in May 1961—was opened in October; in a speech from the throne, the Shah called on Parliament to inaugurate a new 20 year programme of economic and social reform and political development; he stressed the importance of drastic judicial and administrative reorganization, of educational expansion, and of a system of democratic local government. These reforms, said the Shah, were vital to the future existence of the nation. He announced a second phase of the land reform programme, whereby it was hoped that another 20,000 villages would be added to the 10,000 already handed over to the tenants. Queen Farah accompanied the Shah at the opening—the first Queen ever to do so. The Alam government continued until March 1964, when without tendering any reason, Mr. Alam resigned. The new leader was Hassan Ali Mansur, a former Minister and founder of the Progressive Centre, which had played a prominent part in the coalition of Mr. Alam the previous year. In December 1963 he had formed the New Iran Party, which by now had the support of some 150 members of the *majlis*. In his policy statement, Dr. Mansur said that the major objectives of his party would be the implementation of the Shah's reform programme, the protection and expansion of home industries, and the diversification of Iran's export trade, which hitherto had consisted of little more than oil. The second stage of the land reform plan was placed before the *majlis* in May; this aimed to break down the great estates more thoroughly; the maximum permissable size was to be from 120 hectares in arid regions to 30 hectares in more fertile areas. In spite of fears that the necessary credit would not be forthcoming, the programme was pressed forward by the knowledge that there was impatience among the peasantry and some lack of enthusiasm to undertake new works by landlords who were to be dispossessed.

REGIONAL CO-OPERATION

After preliminary talks by their Foreign Ministers in Ankara earlier in the month, the three Heads of State of Iran, Turkey, and Pakistan met on July 21st–22nd in Istanbul and issued a statement which affirmed the need for increased regional co-operation between the three countries, and announced the formation of a new tripartite scheme of collaboration to be known as 'Regional Co-operation for Development'. The scheme provided for regular thrice-yearly meetings between the Foreign Ministers of the countries concerned, with the possible addition at a later date of Afghanistan; there would be close collaboration in the economic and technical spheres, and many projects could be undertaken together in the fields of communications, agriculture, industry, education, health, tourism and regional development; cultural links, based on the common Islamic heritage of the three nations, would be strengthened, especially at University level. It was emphasised that although the scheme was to exist independently of the Central Treaty Organization, it was not intended to usurp its functions; a large area existed outside the province of CENTO in which collaboration on national projects was possible. The incentive for the project seemed to have come from President Ayub Khan of Pakistan, and was clearly generated by the impatience which had been shown, especially in Iran and Pakistan, with the slow progress of CENTO-sponsored economic development projects. The addition of Afghanistan to the group would create an important new power-bloc in the Middle East, with a total population of 150 million as against the 100 million of the Arab bloc.

On January 21st, 1965, Mr. Mansur was the victim of an armed attack in Teheran, by a young man who fired four shots at him at point-blank range; he died five days later in hospital. The assassin, Muhammad Bokharai, was arrested on the spot, together with two alleged accomplices. The three men, together with another who was said to have incited them to the crime, and nine others who were also implicated, were all members of the extreme right-wing religious sect Fedayan Islam, which was strongly opposed to the liberal policies of the Mansur government. There was no suggestion that the murder was other than an internal affair. The accused men were tried *in camera* by a military tribunal in Teheran and on 9th May the four principal accused were sentenced to death by firing squad. The others received varying terms of imprisonment.

Amir Abbas Hoveida, the Finance Minister, was immediately appointed Acting Premier, and became Prime Minister on the day following Mr. Mansur's death, retaining his post at the Finance Ministry. He pledged himself to the continuation of his predecessor's policies, and was given the massive support of the *majlis*. More active than some of his predecessors, he made a particular point of visiting the provinces in order to study their problems at first-hand. Mr. Hoveida has continued as Prime Minister right through into 1973, although elections took place in 1967 and 1971 and several Cabinet re-organizations have been made.

In April 1965 an attempt was made on the Shah's life. The trial of the six people accused of organizing the attempt attracted world wide publicity; two received a death sentence, but these sentences were eventually reduced to life imprisonment. All six were apparently members of a militant Communist sect.

Several more trials followed; 55 men were accused of plotting armed insurrection, and their leader was sentenced to death; thirteen former Tudeh leaders were sentenced to death *in absentia;* and in February 1966 Khalil Maleki, a former Tudeh leader who broke away to form a moderate socialist group, was sentenced to three years' imprisonment in another public trial. In April 1966 the discovery of another Tudeh network was announced.

FOREIGN RELATIONS

The good relations between Iran and the Soviet Union have continued since 1964–65, when various mutually beneficial trading and technical agreements were signed, and a regular air service between Teheran and Moscow was inaugurated. It had been an avowed part of Mr. Mansur's policy that Iran should be as much interested in maintaining links with the Soviet Union as with the West. In June 1965 the Shah visited Moscow, and in October an agreement was signed for the construction by Soviet engineers of a steel mill. Relations with other countries were mainly commercial, including the U.S.A., Federal Germany, Japan, Romania, Hungary and Czechoslovakia.

The Shah also took seriously his role as a mediator, remaining firmly neutral in the Pakistan–India dispute of September 1965, and discussing the Viet-Nam situation with Averell Harriman in January 1966. Only with Iraq were relations strained during the winter, when the long-standing disagreement over the Shatt-al-Arab erupted into a series of border incidents, protest notes, and popular demonstrations. By the spring of 1966 the situation had eased, discussions expected to start in April were postponed by the death of President Arif.

The policy of strengthening international relations continued throughout 1966 and 1967, with visits by the Shah to Yugoslavia and Morocco in June 1966, and Bulgaria, Hungary and Poland in September, and by the Prime Minister to Romania in November; these resulted in economic and cultural agreements. In April 1967 the King and Queen of Thailand paid a state visit to Iran, and in May the Turkish Prime Minister and King Hussein of Jordan both visited Tehran. At the end of May the Shah and the Queen paid a visit to West Germany, where in spite of elaborate precautions by the police, Iranian students succeeded in carrying out demonstrations of protest. This was followed by a visit to France, cut short because of the Middle East crisis. On May 31st the Government issued a statement of support for the claims of the Palestinian Arabs in accordance with the principles laid down by the United Nations.

A large number of countries from West and East Europe, Asia and America have participated in various aspects of Iran's economic development, most notable being plans for U.S.S.R. assistance in the exploitation of natural gas resources in the north. Iran is also to co-operate in the construction and operation of an oil refinery at the Sudanese port of Port Sudan.

The most publicized event of 1967 was the coronation of the Shah on October 26th, twenty-six years after his accession to the throne. An appropriate atmosphere had been built up by frequent stress in publicity inside and outside Iran on the claim that the Iranian monarchy was the oldest in the world, having been established 2,500 years ago. The long-delayed coronation was also hailed as the crowning glory of the "white revolution" inaugurated by the Shah in 1963. Immediately after placing the crown on his head, the Shah crowned Queen Farah—the first woman to receive this honour in Iranian history—in an act symbolizing the emancipation of Iranian women. By an earlier act of a Constituent Assembly, meeting on September 7th, the Queen had been nominated as Regent in the event of the Shah being unable to carry out his duties before the Crown Prince's twentieth birthday.

The stability of Iran was emphasized, not only by economic development and expansion and by the organization of international gatherings ranging from the Regional Co-operation Organization for Development (in which Iran continued to be an active partner) to the International Congress of Iranian Art and Archaeology, but also by the formal ending on November 29th of United States economic aid under the "Point Four" scheme. Iran, which had been the first country to accept this aid in 1951, was now the second (after the Republic of China) to find herself able to dispense with it. Military aid, however, was to continue. At the same time economic co-operation with the U.S.S.R. was developed, and an agreement was made for the purchase of £40,000,000 of munitions, the first time the Soviet Union had concluded an arms transaction with a member of the Western bloc.

In January 1968 the British Government announced its decision to withdraw all its forces from the Gulf by the end of 1971. Since these forces had apparently helped to preserve the local status quo, a revival of the ancient rivalry between Arabs and Persians over supremacy in the Gulf then seemed a likely prospect following their removal. The Iranian government's reiteration of its claim to Bahrain in February 1968 did not help relations with the Arab world, and the Shah's official visit to Saudi Arabia was abruptly cancelled later that month. However, the political climate in the Gulf improved as the year progressed, partly owing to Iran's reduction of emphasis on the Bahrain question and to its cautious welcome for the proposed Federation of Arab Emirates (which it was thought would incorporate Bahrain). In October the government signed an agreement with Saudi Arabia delineating the continental shelf between the two countries; this was hailed as a major step forward as the ownership of the shelf had become an important issue since the discovery of large offshore oil deposits in 1965. In November the Shah was able to make his state visit to Saudi Arabia, including the pilgrimage to Mecca and Medina, and the occasion was acclaimed as a significant move towards Muslim unity.

The Bahrain dispute was submitted to the United Nations early in 1970, and a special mission visited the island in the spring. As was generally expected, it found that the large Arab majority overwhelmingly preferred full independence to joining Iran or remaining a British protectorate. Iran had previously agreed to accept the mission's findings, and it did so without complaint, though expressing concern for the future of Iranians in the Gulf states. In June 1970 a dispute with other Gulf states also arose over Iran's claim to the islands of Abu Musa and the Tumbs belonging to Sharjah and Ras al Khaimah respectively. The dispute was only settled at the beginning of December 1971. The Sheikh of Sharjah agreed to share his island of Abu Musa with Iran. The Sheikh of Ras al Khaimah was less accommodating, so Iran invaded his possessions of the Greater and Lesser Tumbs and took them by force. Seven people were killed and all the Arab inhabitants expelled to the mainland. Britain's treaty of protection with Ras al Khaimah was about to expire, as a prerequisite of the formation of the United Arab Emirates, and the British therefore took no action, causing strong reactions from Iraq and Libya in particular. Since occupying Abu Musa and the Tumbs Iran has been developing them as military bases to command the straits of Hormuz which lie at the neck of the Gulf.

Relations with the more radical Arab states have been less friendly. These states have long been suspicious of Iran's close ties with the West, and especially of the generous American military aid to the powerful Iranian armed forces. The Iranian attitude to Israel is now, for them, an even greater cause for concern. Though no formal diplomatic ties exist, Iran maintains normal trading links with Israel, of which oil supplies and landing rights for Israeli airlines are thought to be particularly important. Israeli expertise is playing an active part in Iran's development programme, and some reports have even hinted at a limited military co-operation. The National Iranian Oil Company is thought to be the principal user of Israel's oil pipeline running from Eilat to the Mediterranean, which opened early in 1970.

Iran's only frontier with an Arab state is with Iraq. Near the Gulf the border is delineated by the Shatt al Arab waterway, and, by the terms of the 1937 treaty, it actually runs along the eastern, i.e. Iranian bank; thus Iraq legally has sovereignty over the whole waterway. Iran has long resented this position and in April 1969 it decided to abrogate the treaty by sending Iranian vessels flying the national flag through the waterway, whilst heavy naval forces stood by. The aim was apparently to force a re-negotiation of the treaty, but there has been no sign of this as yet. In September 1969, there were further armed clashes on the border—reports differed as to the extent of the casualties. In January 1970, Iraq accused the Iranian Government of backing the abortive coup in Iraq, and diplomatic relations between the two countries were broken. The situation both on the border and at governmental level remained tense throughout 1970. Iraq expelled some 15,000 Iranian residents over this period, and Iran was widely thought to be giving aid to the Kurdish rebels in northern Iraq. Iraq again broke off diplomatic relations in December 1971 in protest against Iranian actions in the Gulf, and more than 60,000 Iranians were expelled from Iraq, including some 4,000 who considered themselves Iraqi nationals. Relations with Iraq continued to be strained, and there were several border clashes in the early months of 1973, when Iran was very critical of Iraq's role in the Iraq-Kuwait border dispute.

Internally, signs of opposition to the Shah's régime, never far from the surface of Iranian life, became more and more evident as the celebrations for the 2,500th anniversary of the Persian monarchy were in preparation for October 1971. The combination of the very unequal distribution of the enormous earnings from oil and the suppression of any sign of dissent was made more politically explosive as the lavishness of the celebrations (estimates of the cost range from $50 million to $300 million) and the massiveness of the security precautions (600–1,000 people were interned in the few months before October) began to make their impact. The underground opposition movements carried out a series of guerrilla attacks, most notably assassinating the Chief of Military Justice, Zia Farsiou, in April 1971. The government response became even more draconian and gave some indication of the seriousness of the guerrilla threat to the government. In 1971, 13 people were executed before verdicts in their cases were even announced. By May 1972, 28 more people had been executed in the first five months of the year.

At the close of the CENTO meeting of foreign ministers, held in Teheran in June 1973, Mr. Nassir Assar, the Iranian Secretary-General of CENTO, described the danger of insurgency in the Gulf as "a real tangible threat", and drew attention to alleged subversion in Pakistan. Iranian anxiety over a Baluchistan independence movement, both in Pakistan and in Iran, had led to the formation of a bilateral defence pact with Pakistan in May 1973.

ECONOMIC SURVEY

At the census of 1966 the population was returned at 25,781,000. Of this total, some 9,800,000 were urban residents, of whom 2,700,000 were located in Teheran and some 1,500,000 in the major cities of Isfahan, Meshed, Tabriz and Shiraz. With a growth rate of 2.7 per cent per annum, the population had risen to an estimated 30,284,000 by 1972. Since the mid-1930s there has been an accelerating migration from rural to urban areas, and the rapid growth of urban population has been particularly marked in Teheran where the population reached an estimated 3,400,000 in 1972. Much of the population is concentrated in the fertile northern areas of the country and the central desert lands are sparsely populated. The rise in the rate of population growth is attributable chiefly to the reduction in deaths due to malnutrition and famine consequent upon the use of vehicles to transport agricultural crops from surplus to famine areas; to great advances in public health, particularly the virtual eradication of malaria over wide areas; and to improved nutrition standards. There has been a relative decline in the size of the nomadic population which since the 1940s has been settling in villages or taking to a semi-nomadic rather than a fully nomadic existence. Whereas the urban population had achieved over 65 per cent literacy by the beginning of the 1970s, the rural population had reached only 15 per cent literacy.

AGRICULTURE

Out of a total surface area of 165 million hectares, 19 million (11.5 per cent) are under cultivation and over half is classified as uncultivable, non-agricultural land. About 4,800,000 hectares of agricultural land are fed with perennial irrigation water supplies, mainly from the ancient system of qanats (underground water channels) or from modern water-storage systems. Rain-fed agriculture is important in the western provinces of Kermanshah, Kurdestan and Azerbaizhan. Agriculture is the principal economic activity of the Iranian people. However, whilst agriculture employs nearly half of the total labour force, it accounts for well under 30 per cent of national income, and as a result the incomes of farm workers remain low. The average annual income of each peasant is calculated at £60, which, divided among his family gives a *per capita* income of less than £20 for the farming community. The structure of agriculture has remained basically unchanged in the twentieth century, although there has been a general tendency over the past forty years away from subsistence farming to the production of cash crops. A large variety of crops are cultivated in the diverse climatic regions of Iran. Grains are the chief crops, including wheat (the major staple), barley and, in the Caspian provinces, rice. Cotton, sugar-beet and tea are of commercial importance and a variety of fruits, nuts and vegetables, as well as tobacco, are also grown. Over recent years the production of grains has usually been largely sufficient for domestic consumption needs.

The agricultural sector remains the least developed sector of the economy despite its importance. The chief factors limiting the size of agricultural production are inadequate communications, limiting access to markets; poor seeds, implements and techniques of cultivation; lack of water and under-capitalization, which is a result chiefly of the low income of the peasant. Attempts have been made, and continue to be made, to overcome these problems, under the development plans and the land reform laws. Rural roads are provided for under the fourth development plan; agricultural research stations and colleges, often with U.S. support, have been established; and the fourth plan provides for the increase of 4,915,000 cubic metres in reservoir capacity.

Although land reform and the introduction of mechanization and fertilizers has contributed to an increase in the size of harvests over recent years, much of this increase has been a result of increasing the area under cultivation. Nevertheless, Iran's agricultural potential has been barely tapped and as a result of changes during the 1960s and early 1970s particularly land reform—the agricultural sector should be much better placed to meet Iran's growing needs for food and raw materials.

Before the Land Reform Act of 1962 about 70 per cent of the fertile land was owned by a small number of large landowners. This led to a situation in which a share-cropping peasant cultivated the land on behalf of an absentee landlord. Until 1962 various attempts at land reform failed because of the dominance of the landlord element in the *Majlis*. In 1962, during the absence of a *Majlis*, a new land reform law was promulgated, limiting landholding to one village. All land above this was to be sold to the peasants. It was recognized that many peasants would lack the knowledge and capital to work their own land independently, so the project was accompanied by a drive to organize the peasants into co-operatives through which state land might be channelled. The second phase of reform was implemented from 1965. This was a much more conservative measure, involving the redistribution of all land in excess of a maximum varying according to soil fertility between 30 and 150 hectares (hectare—2.5 acres approx.). The effect of the programme was somewhat cushioned by escape clauses which allowed landlords, for a transitional period, to keep up to 500 hectares of "mechanized land" and an unlimited further amount of land if it could be shown that this was virgin land which the farmer had himself brought under mechanization. These measures had the double advantage of softening the blow for the richer landlords, and encouraging the continued use of mechanized farming with hired labour. The government would also pay to the landlord one-third of the price of any land sold to a peasant, in cash, which was to be repaid by the peasant over 14 months; and there were further financial inducements to landlords designed to speed the process of changeover. The first and second phases, which were concerned largely with land redistribution, were followed by a third phase, implemented slowly from 1967 onwards and aimed at encouraging mechanization and the consolidation of fragmented holdings. In 1971, when the land reform programme was officially completed, the government claimed that 761,931 families had benefited from phase I of the reform and 1,535,510 from phase II. By March 1972 8,450 co-operatives with a membership of 1,854,000 persons had been set up.

The principal products of the nomad sector of Iranian agriculture are livestock products—dairy produce, wool, hair and hides. Livestock retains considerable importance in the rural economy and its relative importance will probably increase as a result of measures taken during the fourth plan period. About 40 per cent of sheep and goats are raised by semi-nomadic tribal herdsmen. In the late 1960s there were 33,000,000 sheep, 14,000,000 goats and 5,500,000 cattle. Production is limited by the prevalence of animal pests and the apparently inevitable lower productivity of pastoral as compared with domestic stock breeding. There have been attempts by the Government and the Plan Organization to improve breeds and to eliminate pests and diseases and attempts to settle the nomads which have been pursued vigorously since the time of Reza Shah (1923–41) have been achieving gradual success.

Eleven per cent of Iran is under forest or woodland, including the Caspian area—the main source of commercial timber—and the Zagros Mountains. Forestry in an economic sense is a recent activity and it is only since the nationalization of forest land in 1963 that effective attempts have been made under the Forestry Commission at protection, conservation and reafforestation.

Although Iran has direct access to both the Caspian Sea and the Gulf, fishing remains poorly developed in both areas. The Caspian fisheries are chiefly noted for an annual production of over 200 tons of caviar. Production in the Gulf amounts to about 5,000 tons per year and is largely consumed by the fishing community itself. The relative importance of caviar as a fishery export has been increasing in recent years to account for nearly 90 per cent by value of total fish exports. The Government intends to increase the fishing fleet and build canning and fish-meal plants along the Gulf coast. One survey has estimated that when fully developed, Iran's southern fisheries could earn as much as U.S. $200 million annually, chiefly from high-grade shrimp and prawn.

THE OIL INDUSTRY

The major industry of Iran is the oil industry to which the second largest town of Abadan owes its entire existence. The history of commerical exploitation dates back to 1901, when W. K. D'Arcy was granted a sixty-year monopoly of the right to explore for and exploit oil in Iran, with the exception of the five northern provinces which fell within the sphere of Russian influence. Oil was eventually discovered in commercial quantities at Masjid-i-Sulaiman in 1908 and in 1909 was formed the Anglo-Persian Oil Company, renamed Anglo-Iranian in 1935 and British Petroleum in 1954. A long series of disputes between the Iranian Government and Anglo-Iranian ended with the nationalization of the oil industry by Iran in 1951 and the replacement of Anglo-Iranian by what is generally known as the Consortium. The Consortium is an amalgam of interests (British Petroleum 40 per cent; American interests 40 per cent; Royal Dutch Shell 14 per cent; *Compagnie Française des Pétroles* 6 per cent) formed to produce oil in the area of the old Anglo-Iranian concession as redefined in 1933. The Consortium's concession was to have lasted until 1979 with the possibility of a series of extensions under modified conditions for a further fifteen years. Ownership of oil deposits throughout Iran and the right to exploit them or to make arrangements for their exploitation is vested in the National Iranian Oil Company, an Iranian State enterprise.

The terms of Iran's agreement with the Consortium are discussed in "Oil in the Middle East" (*see* page 70). The revenues derived from the Consortium have formed by far the greatest part of Iran's oil revenue, which amounted to U.S. $853 million in 1968, $964 million in 1969, $1,143 million in 1970 and $2,111 million in 1971. Over the period 1966 to 1971 Iran's share of world oil production rose from 6.4 per cent to 9.4 per cent.

Until 1973 Iran had a leasing agreement* with the Consortium, but at a time when Middle Eastern governments were seeking participation agreements with commercial oil companies, the Iranian Government gave the Consortium an ultimatum: under no circumstances would Iran extend its lease, and the companies could either continue under existing arrangements until 1979 and then become ordinary arms-length buyers, or negotiate an entirely new "agency" agreement immediately.

The Consortium opted for the latter plan, and on 24th May, 1973 a contract was signed in Teheran under which the National Iranian Oil Company (NIOC) formally took over operations in the Consortium area, agreeing to provide all investment capital for expansion, while the Consortium was to set up a new operating company, Iranian Oil Services, which would act as production contractor for NIOC. In return the western companies were granted a 20-year supply of crude as privileged buyers, which they would take in proportion to their shareholding in the Consortium. As production had already been scheduled to increase to 8 million barrels per day by 1978, the companies were able to calculate their offtake to within 200,000 barrels per day over the next 20 years. NIOC kept a share of the crude, thought to be about 20 per cent of total production, for its own arms-length sales or downstream operations.

---

* For an explanation of the various types of agreements between oil companies and governments *see* Oil in the Middle East and North Africa, pages 63–81.

The National Iranian Oil Company has partnership and service contract agreements with various other oil companies and groups (see page 78), but production from these companies is small in comparison with Consortium production. In 1971, for example, total production of crude oil in Iran amounted to 227 million metric tons, and Consortium production accounted for 207 million metric tons of this.

OTHER MINERALS

The mineral resources of Iran have not been surveyed completely. Lead-zinc is mined at Bafq near Yazd, at Khomein, west of Isfahan and at Ravanj near Qum, with a combined potential of 600 tons of concentrates daily, though current plans for development are limited to Bafq. Chrome from the Elburz mountains and near Bandar Abbas, red oxide from Hormuz in the Persian Gulf and turquoise from Nishapur are all produced for export. Coal and iron ore are produced for domestic consumption, the former from deposits near Teheran and in Eastern Mazanderan (total production was 300,000 tons) and the latter from deposits in the Elburz, in Yezd, Kerman and at Isfahan. Sulphur and salt are produced on the coast of the Gulf, near Bandar Abbas. Deposits of copper ore have been found in Azerbaizhan, Kerman and in the Yezd and Anarak areas. About 10,000 tons of copper ore is mined annually in Azerbaizhan; it is planned to treble production in the next few years. A very important deposit of copper has been found at Sar Chesmeh near Kerman, where reserves are estimated at some 300 million tons. Following the failure of negotiations in 1971 between the government and foreign mining groups for an agreement on the development of these deposits, it was announced that these reserves would be exploited under purely national auspices and that the Government would allocate $350-400 million towards their development. A small copper deposit has also been discovered at Mazraeh Ahar, northeast of Tabriz; development is scheduled to start in 1973. Prospecting for copper is continuing in several areas, particularly around Kerman where large reserves were discovered in 1967. These are now estimated to be between 400 and 800 million tons of ore with an average of 1.12 per cent copper content and extractable traces of molybdenum. The cost of production in this remote and arid area has proved a formidable obstacle, but with direct government participation it is hoped that smelting can begin in 1977. All mining activities are regulated by the Ministry of Industries and Mines and provision has been made in economic planning for the further development of Iran's mineral resources.

OTHER INDUSTRIES

The industry and mining sector of the Iranian economy has grown extremely rapidly over the period 1963 to 1973. Since 1967 the average annual growth in this sector has been about 15 per cent and it now accounts for 14 per cent of the gross domestic product. The largest cotton-producing area is Isfahan and this is the centre of cotton textile production, followed by Shahi in Mazanderan and Behshahr in Gurgan. Isfahan is also the centre of woollen production, drawing supplies from the nomad producers of the area. Tabriz, in Azerbaijan, is also a big woollen centre. Jute and silk are also produced in Mazanderan. The famous carpet industry is still entirely a handicraft industry: in 1970, some 1.8 million square metres of carpets, worth some $60 million, were exported. Food processing includes sugar refining, flour milling, canning, and industrial alcohol. The building industry has also expanded considerably in recent years and further growth is likely to keep up with local needs. Cement production has grown tenfold to around 1,500,000 tons over ten years.

Industry concentrated initially on transforming local or imported raw materials into goods for the home market. These industries can be divided into three groups: textiles, food processing and construction materials. Despite the declared policy of spreading industrial development widely throughout the country by exploiting local sources of raw materials, only recently have new industrial centres been created in the provinces. Of 4,430 factories in Iran in 1960 nearly half were in Teheran. Iranian industrial development is still characterized by small-scale units of production. Only twenty-nine Iranian factories employed more than 500 people in 1960. Nonetheless, industrial development has played a big role in developing Iranian agriculture, forcing up wages by offering alternative employment.

Another industrial sector comprises assembly plants for electrical goods, cars and buses. Until recently, parts were imported but nowadays these are also manufactured in Iran. Among other industries are those which manufacture basic chemicals both from local and imported raw materials. Under a $286 million credit agreement made with the Soviet Union, Iran's first steel mill was established in Isfahan with an initial capacity of 600,000 tons, and in 1971 Soviet participation in its expansion to a capacity of 4 million tons per year were proposed as part of the Government's programme for a heavy industrial base during the fifth plan period. A heavy-equipment plant may be added to the complex. An aluminium plant (capacity 50,000 tons per year) at Arak had gone into production by the beginning of 1973. Partners in the project are the Iranian and Pakistani governments and Reynolds Metals. Tractor, machine tool, diesel engine and paper plants have recently gone into production or are at the planning stage. Most recent plans include investment in steel sheeting, iron bars, glass and cement.

TRADE AND COMMUNICATIONS

Iran's principal imports are vehicles, iron and steel (both crude and manufactured), machinery, chemicals, pharmaceuticals and electrical goods. Imports of vehicles have been declining in recent years, as Iran builds up her own industry. Her principal exports are oil, raw cotton, fruit, nuts, shoes, soap products and mineral ores. The export trade is dominated by oil. Trade figures for 1972–73 show that Iranian exports, excluding oil, amounted to 22,065 million rials, with imports in the same period totalling 134,214 million rials. Oil exports totalled 150,659 million rials.

There have been a number of important developments in Iran's external communications recently. Under the auspices of CENTO, railway lines are planned, or have been constructed, to link the Iranian system to the European system by building a line from Sharafkhaneh in West Iran to Mus in East Turkey and to the South Asian system by building a line from Yazd to Zahedan. The $90 million link with Turkey was inaugurated in 1971 and it is hoped to complete the extension to join the Pakistani network by 1976. In addition two roads are under construction to link Iran with Pakistan, one from Kerman to Quetta and the second from Bandar Abbas to Karachi via Mekran, to be part of the Asian Highway. The Sari-Shah Pasand, the Quchan-Meshed and the Mashad-Islam Qaleh sections had been completed by 1971. The agreement with the U.S.S.R. in December 1962 to re-open the old land route through Russia for Iran's trade with Europe will also have important consequences, shortening the distance by 3,000 miles. In November 1963 the U.S.S.R. agreed to give a 25 per cent tariff discount on Iranian goods in transit to Europe. This prompted a new transit agreement with Turkey in February 1964, cutting transit rates and times and extending the privileges of both Iranian and Turkish transportation companies on Irano-Turkish routes.

FIFTH DEVELOPMENT PLAN

In March 1973 Iran embarked upon her Fifth Development Plan (1973–78). Whereas the main thrust for the Fourth Plan had been concentrated on oil and industry, the emphasis in the Fifth Plan is on education and social reform, closely followed by agriculture. Total expenditure is planned at U.S. $35,500 million, which is greater than the combined investment of the previous four plans put together. The Government's share of this expenditure will be 1,560,000 million rials ($22,700 million), while the private sector, mainly housing, industry and oil, will account for the difference.

The Shah has been showing great determination to bring about social justice, and the priorities of the Fifth Development Plan fully reflect this. For the past ten years the bulk of Iran's effort had gone into oil and industrialization and it was felt that the private sector would continue to invest heavily in this. Education therefore forms the largest single item in the public sector allocations (230,000 million rials), with agriculture in second place (208,000 million rials). Rural development has been allocated 36,000 million rials, urban development 33,000 million rials and protection of the environment 22,200 million rials.

Industry, however, has not been forgotten. During the period of the plan industrial development will receive 183,900 million rials from development allocations, with the private sector expected to put up 326,800 million rials. It is aimed to achieve an annual growth rate of 14 per cent, with industrial output rising from 509,000 million rials in 1973 to 972,000 million rials in 1978.

IRAN—(Statistical Survey)

STATISTICAL SURVEY*

AREA AND POPULATION

AREA	POPULATION			Estimate (mid-1971)
	Census (November 1st.–20th, 1966)			
	Males†	Females†	Total	
1,648,000 sq. km.*	12,981,665	12,097,258	25,785,210	29,783,000

Total Population: 30,284,000 (March 31st, 1972).

* 636,300 square miles.

† Excluding nomadic tribes (totalling 462,146) and other unsettled population (244,141).

CHIEF TOWNS
POPULATION (1967)

Teheran (capital)	2,719,730	Shiraz	269,278	Rezaieh	110,749
Isfahan	424,045	Ahwaz	206,375	Kerman	85,404
Meshed	409,616	Kermanshah	187,930	Khoramabad	59,578
Tabriz	403,413	Rasht	143,557	Sanandaj	54,578
Abadan	272,976	Hamadan	124,167	Shareh Kord	23,757

Teheran (1972 estimate): 3,400,000.

* The Iranian year begins in March.

ECONOMICALLY ACTIVE POPULATION‡
(1966 Census)

	MALES	FEMALES	TOTAL
Agriculture, Forestry, Hunting and Fishing	2,965,287	203,228	3,168,515
Mining and Quarrying	25,911	401	26,312
Manufacturing	758,799	508,801	1,267,600
Construction	507,703	2,075	509,778
Electricity, Gas, Water Supply	52,165	693	52,858
Commerce	543,096	8,927	552,023
Transport, Storage and Communications	221,531	2,555	224,086
Services	759,718	169,967	929,685
Others (not adequately described)	114,203	13,336	127,539
TOTAL IN EMPLOYMENT	5,948,413	909,983	6,858,396
Unemployed†	635,844	89,845	725,689
TOTAL	6,584,257	999,828	7,584,085

‡ Excluding nomadic tribes and other unsettled population.

† Including persons seeking work for the first time.

IRAN—(Statistical Survey)

INDUSTRIAL EMPLOYMENT 1972

	Number of Establishments	Number of Employees
Food Manufacturing	28,853	159,939
Beverages	89	4,555
Tobacco	3	5,385
Textiles, Carpets, etc.	49,577	239,798
Clothing	47,462	145,207
Wood and Furniture	14,324	32,958
Paper and Cardboard	297	4,612
Printing and Binding	1,239	12,041
Leather and Hides	1,497	12,027
Rubber and Rubber Products	1,244	10,088
Chemicals	1,447	21,613
Non-metallic Minerals	6,655	48,153
Petroleum	15	1,440
Base Metals	944	19,634
Metal Products	29,058	111,162
Non-electrical Machinery	1,653	13,652
Electrical Machinery	3,924	30,146
Transport Equipment	13,788	44,888
Miscellaneous	7,077	18,700
Total	**209,146**	**935,998**

AGRICULTURE

PRODUCTION
('000 metric tons)

	1969	1970	1971
Wheat	4,030	4,000	4,800
Milled Rice	1,020	1,060	1,046
Barley	860	880	800
Sugar Beet	3,480	3,850	4,000
Cotton	520	500	450
Tea	19	20	13
Tobacco	18	17	16

LIVESTOCK
('000)

	1969–70	1970–71
Sheep	35,000	35,000
Goats	12,600	12,500
Cattle	5,200	5,100
Asses	2,100	2,000

Source: FAO Production Yearbook 1971.

Fishing: Persian Gulf 14,000 tons, Caspian Sea 3,250 tons (incl. 2,000 tons of sturgeon and over 200 tons of caviar)—annually.

MINING
('000 metric tons)

	1969–70	1970–71	1971–72
Iron Ore	10.0	150.0	98.0
Copper Ore	2.6	2.8	3.0
Lead	89.0	99.0	77.0
Zinc	97.0	66.0	89.0
Chromite	222.0	152.0	120.0
Barite	77.0	79.0	80.0
Coal	530.0	600.0	1,000.0

OIL

CRUDE OIL PRODUCTION
('000 long tons)

	Total	Export
1967	120,900	99,500
1968	127,325	105,329
1969	165,694	139,942
1970	185,630	162,102
1971	222,181	193,831

IRAN—(Statistical Survey)

INDUSTRY

	Unit	1969	1970	1971
Sugar (refined)	'000 m. tons	512	567	663
Edible Oils (refined)	'000 m. tons	150	167	160
Cigarettes	million	12,104	11,898	13,331
Tobacco	m. tons	18,000	17,000	16,000
Ice	'000 m. tons	1,509	1,651	n.a.
Cement	'000 m. tons	2,342	2,587	2,819

FINANCE

100 dinars = 1 Iranian rial.
Coins: 5, 10, 25 and 50 dinars; 1, 2, 5 and 10 rials.
Notes: 5, 10, 20, 50, 100, 200, 500, 1,000, 5,000 and 10,000 rials.
Exchange rates (March 1973): £1 sterling = 167.50 rials (selling rate); U.S. $1 = 68.175 rials (par value).
1,000 Iranian rials = £5.97 = $14.67.

Note: Prior to February 1973 the exchange rate was U.S. $1 = 75.75 rials (1 rial = 1.32 U.S. cents). In terms of sterling the rate between November 1967 and June 1972 was £1 = 181.80 rials.

BUDGET
(million rials)

Revenue	1970	1971	1972
Direct Taxes	26,838	30,587	36,771
Indirect Taxes	44,988	54,405	60,829
Monopolies, Government Undertakings	95,327	154,873	188,041
Government Service Revenues	13,008	14,870	17,020
Loans, Aids	58,764	61,062	84,255
Profit-making Enterprises	25,362	40,871	50,887
Commercial Agencies	169,755	213,413	249,049
Social Welfare Institutions	6,343	8,088	9,297
Total	440,385	578,170	696,149

Expenditure	1970	1971	1972
General Services	26,487	32,762	36,539
Defence and Security	58,349	78,593	100,941
Social Services	49,477	66,049	83,094
Economic Services	91,733	117,739	138,140
Debt Repayments	12,879	20,655	28,202
Profit-making Enterprises	25,362	40,871	50,887
Commercial Agencies	169,755	213,413	249,049
Social Welfare Institutions	6,343	8,088	9,297
Total	440,385	578,170	696,149

OIL REVENUES

Total oil revenues received by Iran, in U.S. $ million: (1968) 853.5, (1969) 964.6, (1970) 1,143.5, (1971) 2,111.0.

IRAN—(Statistical Survey)

FIFTH DEVELOPMENT PLAN 1973–78
('000 million rials)

	PUBLIC SECTOR			PRIVATE SECTOR
	Development Allocations	Current Allocations	Fifth Plan Total	Projected Investment
Agriculture	208.0	58.9	266.9	50.0
Water	108.0	2.7	110.7	4.0
Industry	183.9	10.6	194.5	326.8
Mining	46.5	0.9	47.4	5.2
Oil	130.7	—	130.7	139.7
Gas	29.0	—	29.0	47.0
Electricity	53.5	1.0	54.5	—
Communications	180.0	20.2	200.2	4.0
Telecommunications	41.2	18.2	59.4	—
Rural Development	36.0	1.8	37.8	2.5
Urban Development	33.0	0.8	33.8	—
Government Construction	90.8	0.4	91.2	—
Housing	82.8	0.4	83.2	308.8
Education	230.0	175.0	405.0	2.6
Arts and Culture	9.4	6.5	15.9	0.4
Tourism	7.7	1.3	9.0	12.2
Health	52.0	64.5	116.5	9.2
Public Welfare	16.0	38.5	54.5	—
Physical Culture	10.0	20.9	30.9	—
Statistics	6.2	10.5	16.7	—
Regional Development	5.3	0.6	5.9	—

EXTERNAL TRADE

IMPORTS AND EXPORTS
(million rials)

	1970–71	1971–72	1972–73
Imports	128,260	157,058	134,214
Exports (excluding oil)	21,192	26,270	22,065
Oil Exports	164,040	196,483	150,659

OIL EXPORTS
('000 long tons)

	1969	1970	1971	1972
Crude Oil	139,942	162,102	193,831	220,752
Crude Oil Run to Abadan Refinery	19,954	20,549	17,741	15,872
Export of Oil Products	15,190	15,462	14,808	14,546

IRAN—(Statistical Survey)

COMMODITIES
(million rials)

	1970–71	1971–72	1972–73
Iron and Steel	23,382	29,402	20,778
Motor Vehicles and Parts	10,526	10,362	10,486
Electrical Machinery and Apparatus	12,608	19,300	14,388
Boilers and other Machinery	28,051	33,807	31,885
Chemicals and Pharmaceuticals	6,244	6,694	6,217
Textiles	5,672	5,962	6,369
Wool and Animal Hair	2,403	2,414	2,867
Animal and Vegetable Fats	3,244	3,471	2,223
Paper, Paperboard, etc.	3,656	3,497	3,155
Rubber and Products	2,390	2,769	2,972
Sugar and Confectionery	549	869	1,620
Cereals	344	7,752	4,052

Principal Exports (excl. Oil)	1970–71	1971–72	1972–73
Raw cotton	4,313	5,142	2,761
Wool	15	41	38
Hides and leather	1,102	1,311	1,496
Fruit	3,236	2,880	2,338
Gum Tragacanth	291	361	231
Carpets	4,104	5,761	4,785
Mineral ores	1,499	1,259	1,183
Oil-bearing seeds	658	610	700

PRINCIPAL COUNTRIES
(million rials)

	1968–69 Imports	1968–69 Exports (excl. Oil)	1969–70 Imports	1969–70 Exports (excl. Oil)	1971* Imports	1971* Exports (excl. Oil)
Czechoslovakia	1,035	561	1,258	858	1,486	716
France	6,894	301	6,483	427	4,715	586
German Federal Republic	22,383	2,380	23,288	2,690	21,717	2,958
India	2,018	147	3,167	129	1,651	95
Italy	6,347	289	5,150	421	5,092	471
Japan	10,025	420	12,621	705	14,330	981
U.S.S.R.	3,376	3,013	8,785	4,357	9,302	3,358
United Kingdom	13,623	608	14,243	731	11,904	517
United States	17,579	1,692	15,904	1,923	14,446	1,655

*(21 Mar.–21 Dec.)

TRANSPORT

RAILWAYS

		1970–71	1971–72
Passengers	('000)	3,502	4,016
Passenger-kilometres	(millions)	1,774	1,875
Freight tons carried	('000)	3,008	3,363

ROADS
('000)

	1970	1971
Cars	261.0	285.4
Goods Vehicles (incl. Buses)	87.6	96.3
Motor Cycles and Scooters	144.1	203.9

SHIPPING

		1970	1971
Ships entered		3,021	5,034
Freight loaded	('000 m. tons)	1,079	974
Freight unloaded	('000 m. tons)	2,500	4,107

CIVIL AVIATION

		1969–70	1970–71
Passenger-km.	('000)	623,321	653,209
Cargo	('000 ton-km.)	3,597	4,033

COMMUNICATIONS MEDIA

	1968–69
Radio Receivers	2,933,000
Television Receivers	198,000
Telephones	268,980
Books Published (titles)	1,757
Daily Newspapers	22
Total Circulation	200,000

EDUCATION
(1970–71)

	Number of Schools	Number of Pupils ('000)
Elementary Schools	15,202	3,003
Education Corps Schools	10,556	504
Secondary Schools	2,509	1,013
Technical and Vocational Schools	189	31
Primary Teacher Training Colleges	79	5
Universities and Colleges	n.a.	74

TOURISM

	1971	1972
Number of Visitors	426,934	453,881
Approximate Money Spent (million rials)	4,212	4,673

Sources (except where otherwise stated): Ministry of Finance, Teheran; General Department of Trade Statistics, Ministry of Economy, Teheran; Ministry of Education, Teheran; Iranian State Railways, Teheran; National Iranian Oil Co., London.

THE CONSTITUTION

On August 15th, 1906, an Imperial Decree was issued to convoke a Constituent Assembly. This Assembly adopted the Constitution of Iran on December 30th of that year.

THE EXECUTIVE POWER

The executive power rests in the Shah. He appoints the Prime Ministers, who must be approved by the *Majlis*. In addition to their individual responsibility for their departments, ministers have a joint responsibility for the affairs of the country.

In 1949 an amendment to the Constitution was made whereby the Shah was granted the right to dissolve the *Majlis* when it was deemed necessary, provided that a new election was ordered to take place soon afterwards.

THE LEGISLATIVE POWER

According to the Constitutional Law the legislative power comprises the Senate and the National Consultative Assembly (the *Majlis*). The latter Assembly consists of over 200 members elected for four years; the number of members rises with the growth of the population and by the July 1971 elections had reached 268. The Senate, which was convened for the first time in February 1950, comprises 60 Senators: 30 elected and 30 nominated by the Shah, 15 representing Teheran, and 15 representing the provinces. Senators must be Muslims. Their term of office is four years.

PROVINCIAL DIVISIONS

Iran is divided into fourteen provinces (*Ostan*). They are administered by Governors-General (*Ostandar*), who are directly responsible to the central Government. These provinces are sub-divided into counties (*Shahrestan*), municipalities (*Bakhsh*), and rural districts (*Dihestan*).

All towns have a municipal administration, the director of which is chosen by the town council. The nomination must be approved by the Ministry of the Interior.

IRAN—(The Government, Diplomatic Representation)

THE GOVERNMENT

THE HEAD OF STATE

H.I.M. Mohammad Reza Pahlavi Aryamehr, Shahanshah of Iran
(succeeded to the throne on the abdication of his father, September 16th, 1941).

THE CABINET
(July 1973)

Prime Minister: Amir-Abbas Hoveida.
Deputy Prime Minister: Eng. S. Asfia.
Minister of Interior: Mohamed Sam.
Minister of Economy: Dr. Hooshang Ansari.
Minister of Education and Training: Mrs. F. Parsa.
Minister of Finance: Dr. Jamshid Amuzegar.
Minister of Culture and Art: Mehrdad Pahlbod.
Minister of Foreign Affairs: Abbas Ali Khalatbari.
Minister of Health: Dr. Manouchehr Shahgholi.
Minister of Information: Hamid Rahnema.
Minister of Agriculture: Mamsur Rouhani.
Minister of Justice: Sadeq Ahmadi.
Minister of Labour and Social Affairs: Ghasem Moini.
Minister of Posts, Telegraph and Telephone: Eng. Fathollah Sotoudeh.
Minister of Roads: Eng. Hassan Shalchian.
Minister of War: Gen. Reza Azimi.

Minister of Water and Power: Iraj Vahadi.
Minister of Co-operatives and Rural Affairs: Abdul Azim Valian.
Minister of Science, Technology and Higher Education: Hossein Kazemzadeh.
Minister of Development and Housing: Kuros Amuzegar.
Director of Budget Bureau: Ali Hezareh.
Minister of State without Portfolio and Director of Civil Services: Dr. Mahmoud Kashfian.
Minister of State without Portfolio: Dr. Mohamedi Nassiri.
Minister of State: H. Hedayati.
Minister of State and Chief of Plan Organization: Dr. M. Majidi.
Minister of the Imperial Court: Assadollah Alam.
Assistants to the Prime Minister: Gen. Nematollah Nassiri, Cyrus Farzaneh, Yadollah Shahbazi, Dr. Hossein Tadayyon, Ghavam Sadri, Gen. Hojjat Kashefi.

DIPLOMATIC REPRESENTATION

EMBASSIES AND LEGATIONS ACCREDITED TO IRAN
(Teheran unless otherwise stated.)
(E) Embassy; (L) Legation.

Afghanistan: Pahlavi Ave. (Yussefabad), 16 Ebn-Sina Ave., Kucheh Rassia (E); *Ambassador:* (vacant).
Algeria: Baghdad, Iraq (E).
Argentina: Pahlavi Ave. (Tajrish), No. 560 (E); *Ambassador:* (vacant) (also accred. to Afghanistan).
Australia: 23 Ave. Arak, P.O.B. 3408 (E); *Ambassador:* H. D. White.
Austria: Takhte Jamshid, Forsat Ave. (E); *Ambassador:* Dr. Albert Filz.
Bahrain: 31 Ave. Vozara (E); *Ambassador:* Abdul Aziz Abdulrahman Buali.
Belgium: Ave. Takht-e-Tavous, 41 Ave. Daryaye Noor (E); *Ambassador:* Marc Taymans (also accred. to Kuwait).
Brazil: Pahlavi Ave., Tajrish No. 69 (E); *Ambassador:* Paulo Braz Pinto da Silva.
Bulgaria: Aramehr Ave. Hijdah Metri Sevon, No. 23 (E); *Ambassador:* Varban Tsanev.
Burma: Islamabad, Pakistan.
Canada: Takhte Jamshid Ave. Forsat, P.O.B. 1610 (E); *Ambassador:* James George (also accred. to Iraq and Kuwait).

Chad: Moscow, U.S.S.R. (E).
Chile: Ankara, Turkey (E).
China, Republic (Taiwan): Pahlavi Ave. No. 647 (E); *Ambassador:* Chen Hsin-jen.
Czechoslovakia: Sarshar No. 61 (E); *Ambassador:* Dr. Jan Straka.
Denmark: Copenhagen Ave. 13 (E); *Ambassador:* Ole Bernhard Olsen (also accred. to Afghanistan).
Egypt: 123 Ave. Abassabad, Ave. Park, P.O.B. 22 (E); *Ambassador:* Muhammad Samih Anwar.
Ethiopia: Ankara, Turkey (E).
Finland: Ankara, Turkey (E).
France: France Ave. (E); *Ambassador:* Robert de Souza.
German Democratic Republic: (E); *Ambassador:* Ferdinand Thun.
Germany, Federal Republic: Ferdowsi Avenue (E); *Ambassador:* Dr. Georg von Lilienfeld.
Greece: Kheradmand Ave., Kucheh Salm, No. 43 (E); *Ambassador:* George Papadopoulos.
Guinea: Cairo, Egypt (E).

IRAN—(Diplomatic Representation, Parliament)

Hungary: Television Ave. No. 7, Rue Sizdahom (E); *Ambassador:* BALINT GAL.

Iceland: Bonn, Federal Republic of Germany.

India: N. Saba Ave. No. 166 (E); *Ambassador:* RAMCHANDRA DATTATRAYA SATHE.

Indonesia: Shah Abbas Kabir Ave., Magndia Ave. No. 1 (E); *Ambassador:* H. A. A. ACHSIEN.

Italy: France Ave. 81 (E); *Ambassador:* LUIGI COTTAFAVI.

Japan: Northern Saba Ave. 53 (E); *Ambassador:* KEISUKE ARITA.

Jordan: Bukharest Ave. No. 16th Ave. No. 55 (E); *Ambassador:* SALEH AL-KURDI (also accred. to Afghanistan).

Korea, Republic: Kakh Ave., Heshmatoddowleh No. 427 (E); *Ambassador:* CHONG KYU KIM.

Kuwait: Maikadeh Ave., 3-38 Sazman-Ab St. (E); *Ambassador:* Shaikh NASSER MUHAMMAD AHMAD AL-JABER AL-SABAH.

Lebanon: Bukharest Ave. No. 12 (E); *Ambassador:* KHALIL AL-KHALIL.

Malaysia: Bukharest Ave. No. 8 (E); *Ambassador:* MUHAMMAD YUSOFF BIN ZAINAL.

Malta: London, U.K. (E).

Mexico: Ankara, Turkey.

Mongolia: Moscow, U.S.S.R. (E).

Morocco: Dorahiye Yussofabad, Muhammad Reza Shah Ave. (E); *Ambassador:* MUHAMMAD LARBI EL-ALAMI (also accred. to Turkey).

Nepal: Islamabad, Pakistan (E).

Netherlands: Takhte Tavous, Near Pahlavi Ave. Rue Moazami Rue Jahansouz No. 36 (E); *Ambassador:* P. A. E. RENARDEL DE LAVALETTE.

Norway: Aban Ave. 3 (E); *Ambassador:* NILS ANTON JORGENSEN (also accred. to Afghanistan).

Oman: Bukharest Ave. No. 17th Ave. No. 10; *Chargé d'Affaires:* ISMAIL KHALIL AL-RASSASI.

Pakistan: 199 Iranshah Ave. (E); *Ambassador:* HAMED NAVAZ KHAN.

Philippines: Islamabad, Pakistan (E).

Poland: 140 Takhte Jamshid Ave. (E); *Ambassador:* BRONISLAW MUSIELAK.

Portugal: Rodsar Ave. No. 41; *Ambassador:* C. H. F. LEMONDE DE MACEDO.

Qatar: Ave. Abbas Abad, Ave. Télévision, Second Ave. 14-16 (E); *Ambassador:* AHMED HAMD AL-ATEYAH.

Romania: Fakhrabad Ave. 12 (E); *Ambassador:* ALEXANDRU BOABĂ (also accred. to Kuwait).

Saudi Arabia: Ave. Aban, P.O.B. 2903 (E); *Ambassador:* ARAB SAID HASHEM.

Senegal: Ave. Vozara, 8th St. No. 4 (E); *Ambassador:* MASSAMBA SARRE.

Spain: Fisherabad Ave., Khoshbin St. 29 (E); *Ambassador:* JOSÉ MANUEL DE ABAROA.

Sri Lanka: Islamabad, Pakistan (E).

Sudan: Qatar (E).

Sweden: Takhte Jamshid Ave., Forsat Ave. (E); *Ambassador:* Comte GUSTAF BONDE (also accred. to Afghanistan).

Switzerland: Pasteur Ave. (E); *Ambassador:* DANIEL GAGNEBIN (also accred. to Afghanistan).

Syria: Shiraz Ave. Roudsar Ave. No. 69 (E); *Ambassador:* (vacant).

Thailand: Bou Ali Sina Ave. Park Amine-Dowleh No. 4 (E); *Ambassador:* Rear-Admiral CHAREN PLENWIDYA.

Tunisia: Saltanatabad (E); *Ambassador:* TAOUFIK SMIDA.

Turkey: Ferdowsi Ave. No. 314 (E); *Ambassador:* SADI ELDEM.

U.S.S.R.: Churchill Ave. (E); *Ambassador:* V. Y. EROFEEV.

United Arab Emirates: Ave. Vozara, 8th St. (E); *Ambassador:* Sheikh AL-MAKTOUM.

United Kingdom: Ferdowsi Ave. (E); *Ambassador:* Sir PETER RAMSBOTHAM.

U.S.A.: Takhte Jamshid Ave., Roosevelt Ave. (E); *Ambassador:* RICHARD M. HELMS.

Vatican: France Ave. 97 (Apostolic Internunciature); *Ambassador:* Mgr. Dr. ERNESTO GALLINA.

Venezuela: Aban Ave. No. 90 (E); *Ambassador:* (vacant).

Viet-Nam: Ankara, Turkey (E).

Yugoslavia: Ave. Arak, rue Shahrivar (E); *Ambassador:* LASLO BALA.

PARLIAMENT

THE SENATE

President: Eng. JA'AFAR SHARIF-EMAMI.

The Senate consists of 60 members, 30 of which are appointed by the Shah, and 30 are elected (15 from Teheran and 15 from the Provinces). The term of office is four years.

NATIONAL CONSULTATIVE ASSEMBLY
(The Majlis)

President: Eng. A. RIAZI.

Elections to the 23rd session of the Majlis were held in July 1971.

ELECTIONS JULY 1971

	SENATE	MAJLIS
Iran Novin Party	26	228
Mardom Party	9	36
Independent	24	2
Vacant	1	2
TOTAL	60	268

IRAN—(POLITICAL PARTIES, DEFENCE, JUDICIAL SYSTEM, RELIGION)

POLITICAL PARTIES

Iran Novin Party (*New Iran Party*): Teheran; governing party since 1960; Sec. MANOUCHEHR KALALI.

Mardom Party (*People's Party*): Teheran; f. 1957; programme includes agrarian reform, limitation of land ownership and labour welfare; Sec.-Gen. (vacant).

Pan Iranist Party: Teheran; f. 1949; nationalist; Leader MOHSEN PAZESHKPUR.

Tudeh Party (*Party of the Masses*): Communist; *proscribed since* 1949; Leader Dr. REZA RADMANESH.

Iran Liberation Movement: offshoot of Mussadeq's National Front.

Saka: revolutionary Communist organization.

DEFENCE

Defence Budget 1972: 70,151 million rials.
Military service: 2 years.
Total armed forces: 191,000: army 160,000; navy 9,000; air force 22,000.

JUDICIAL SYSTEM

Prosecutor-General: Dr. ABDUL HUSSEIN ALIABADI.
Chief Justice of the Supreme Court: EMAD-E-DIN MIRMOTAHARI.

SUPREME COURT

The jurisdiction of the Supreme Court in Teheran includes disputes about the competence of Government departments in relation to the existing laws, and it also acts as a Court of First Instance when ministers are prosecuted, either for personal offences or in respect of the affairs of their department. It is also the highest court of appeal. In exceptional cases, at the request of the Prosecutor-General, the Supreme Court deals with criminal cases.

PROVINCIAL COURTS

Courts of Appeal and Central Criminal Courts are established in each province.

OTHER COURTS

There are Courts of First Instance in the towns. The Arbitration Council was established in 1966 to examine and rule on all petty offences. The courts of lowest jurisdiction are those of the Justices of the Peace, which are established in most villages and small towns and deal with small civil cases and petty offences. On June 30th, 1966, the Arbitration Council was added to the judicial organs of the state. This Council is competent to deal with all complaints and petitions filed by businessmen and craftsmen, claims for damages and losses sustained in driving accidents, and domestic disputes, up to a claimed amount of ten thousand Rials in all cases. The Arbitration Council also examines and rules on petty offences (misdemeanour and felony) for which punishment does not exceed two months and/or one thousand two hundred Rials fine. Trials and examinations in such cases are undertaken free of charge.

SPECIAL TRIBUNALS

Special tribunals include Ecclesiastical Courts, which have a limited jurisdiction on matters of marriage and personal status; the Civil Servants' Criminal Court, in Teheran; and Permanent and Temporary Military Courts. Permanent Military Courts exist in all provinces and deal with treasonable offences; Temporary Military Courts are established whenever martial law is declared in a region, and are competent to hear certain cases which are normally within the jurisdiction of the ordinary courts.

RELIGION

MUSLIMS

The great majority of the Iranian people are Shi'i Muslims, and Iran with Iraq and the Yemen Arab Republic are notable as the only countries in the world where Shi'i adherents are in a majority. About five per cent of the population are Sunni Muslims, but there is complete religious toleration. Iran is thus in many ways the centre of the Shi'i faith, and pilgrimage to Iranian shrines is an important activity; Qum and Meshed are in particular regarded as holy cities.

ZOROASTRIANS

There are about 21,000 Zoroastrians, a remnant of a once widespread sect. Their religious leader is MOUBAD. Zoroastrianism was once the State religion of ancient Iran. Many adherents were compelled by Arab persecution to emigrate, and the main centre of their faith is now Bombay.

OTHER COMMUNITIES

Communities of Armenians, and somewhat smaller numbers of Jews, Assyrians, Greek Orthodox, Uniates and Latin Christians are also found, and the Baha'i faith, which originated in Iran, has about 60,000 adherents.

Baha'i faith: Shirtat-i-Nawnahalan, Manuchehri Avenue, Teheran; 1,854 centres, 1 school.

Roman Catholic Archbishop of Urmia, Bishop of Salmas and Metropolitan of Iran: Archbishop's House, Rezaieh; Most Rev. ZAYA DACHTOU.

Anglican Bishop in Iran: Rt. Rev. HASSAN BARNABA DEHQANI-TAFTI, Bishop's House, P.O.B. 12, Isfahan. Diocese founded 1912.

Synod of the Evangelical (Presbyterian) Church in Iran: Assyrian Evangelical Church, Khiaban-i Shapur, Khiaban-i Aramanch, Teheran; Moderator Rev. ADLE NAKHOSTEEN.

THE PRESS

The working of the Iranian Press is set out in the 1955 Press Law as modified in 1963. This legislation defines the qualities of education and character required in persons intending to publish newspapers; and stipulates that no newspaper may be banned without a court order, except for criticism of religion or the monarchy, for disclosing military information or for provoking the people to oppose government troops. With the exception of scientific, cultural and government publications, newspapers with less than 3,000 circulation and magazines with less than 5,000 are illegal, but this point has not been fully implemented as no official circulations bureau exists.

In 1965 the cabinet approved the Reporters' Code of Journalism which required reporters to be licensed by the Ministry of Information, prevented them accepting government service and prohibited the reporting or photography of specified military areas and closed court sittings, etc. All communist publications are prohibited in Iran.

Teheran dominates the press scene as almost all daily papers are published there and the bi-weekly, weekly and less frequent publications in the provinces generally depend on the major metropolitan dailies as a source of news. In the city are published some 20 daily and 21 weekly newspapers, and 27 weekly and 44 monthly magazines. There are at least 85 registered provincial papers.

Few, if any, newspapers are financed by sales revenue alone. Most papers' budgets depend heavily on revenues from advertising, of which a large portion comes from the Government.

With the exception of a small number of political organs and official publications, all newspapers are owned by private individuals. The chief party organs are the dailies *Nedaye Iran Novin* (New Iran Party) and *Mehre Iran* (Mardom Party) and the weekly *Khak-o-Khun* (Pan-Iranist Party).

The major dailies have each published other papers and periodicals so forming small publishing groups which are still largely family concerns. The *Ettela'at Group* (Prop. ABBAS MASSOUDI) includes *Ettela'at* with two foreign language daily and two weekly newspapers and four popular weekly magazines, including one for women and two for children. The *Kayhan Group* (Prop. Dr. M. MESBAZADEH) includes *Kayhan* with its English daily, a weekly sports paper, two popular weekly magazines and a medical magazine. The *Echo of Iran Group* (Prop. JAHANGIR BEHROUZ) includes the daily, weekly and monthly *Echo of Iran*, the monthly *Iran Trade* and the annual *Almanac*, all in English.

Among the most influential and respected dailies are the *Echo of Iran* which gives summarized news and opinion, and the two wide circulation papers: *Kayhan*, with its sister English paper *Kayhan International*, and *Ettela'at*, with its English and French co-publications *Tehran Journal* and *Journal de Tehran*. *Bourse* is the national financial daily. Among the most respected weekly publications are *Khandaniha*, *Tehran Mossavar* and the satirical paper *Towfiq*. Two of the most popular weekly magazines are *Zan-E-Ruz* for women and *Javanan* for youth.

PRINCIPAL DAILIES

Alik: Naderi Ave., Teheran; f. 1931; morning; political and literary; Armenian; Prop. Dr. R. STEPANIAN; circ. 10,000.

Ayandegan: Shah Ave., 322 Guiti Sq., Teheran; morning; political; Prop. Dr. H. AHARI.

Azhang: Roosevelt St., Teheran; f. 1954; airmail edition *Azhang Havaii*; Editor KAZEM MASOUDI; circ. 10,000.

Azhang: Roosevelt St., Teheran; airmail edition *Azhang Havaii*; Editor KAZEM MASOUDI.

Bourse: Kh. Sevom Esfand, Ku. Mobarshakat, Teheran; f. 1961; financial; Editor Dr. Y. RAHMATI.

Echo of Iran: Ave. Shiraz, Kuche Khalkhali No. 4, P.O.B. 2008, Teheran; f. 1952; English; political and economic press review; circ. 6,000; Editor JAHANGIR BEHROUZ.

Erfan: Isfahan; f. 1924; literary; Editor Mrs. MALEK ERFAN; circ. 3,000.

Ettela'at: Kayyam Ave., Teheran; f. 1925; evening; political and literary; Editor HASSAN SADR HAJ SAYYED JAVADI; circ. 100,000.

Ettela'ate Hawaei: Air edition of above; Editor HAMID MASHOUR; circ. 6,000.

Farman: 69 Manuchehri Ave., Teheran; political; Editor A. SHAHANDEH; circ. 15,000.

Iran Presse: Ave. Kheradmand, Ku. Tahbaz No. 19, Teheran; French; Editor S. FARZAMI.

Kayhan Hava: Political and social; Editor M. SEMSAR; circ. 80,000.

Kayhan International: Ferdowsi Ave., Kuche Atabak, Teheran; political; morning; English; circ. 15,000; Editor W. DUZZFORCE.

Keyhan: Ferdowsi Ave., Teheran; evening; political; Propr. Dr. M. MESBAHZADEH.

Khovassen: Meshed; f. 1948; circ. 15,000; Owner and Editor MUHAMMAD SADEGH TEHRANIAN.

Koushesh: Forughi Ave., Teheran; morning; political and scientific; Editor SHOKRULLAH SAFAVI.

Le Journal de Tehran: Kayyam Ave., Teheran; f. 1934; morning; French; Editor AHMAD CHAHIDI; circ. 8,000.

Mahde Azadi: Tabriz; political and social; Prop. ESMAIL PEYMAN.

Marde Mobarez: Kh. Manouchehri; political and social; Propr. ASSAD RAZMARA.

Mehre Iran: Zhaleh Ave., Teheran; affiliated to Mardom Party; morning; Editor MOHSEN MOVAGHAR.

Nedaye Iran-Novin: Fisherabad Ave. 41, Sepand St., Teheran; affiliated to New Iran Party; Editor M. A. RASHTI.

Peyghame Emrouz: Kh. Qavam Saltaneh, Teheran; evening; political and social; Dr. ABDOLRASUL AZIMI; circ. 23,000.

Poste Teheran: Kh. Shahabad, Teheran; political evening; circ. 8,000; Editor MUHAMMAD ALI MASSOUDI.

Sedaye Mardom: Kh. Hafez, Teheran; political and literary; morning; Publisher MUHAMMAD HUSSEIN FARIPOUR; Editor FEREIDOON FARIPOUR.

Tehran Journal: Kayyam Ave., Teheran; f. 1954; morning; English; Editor VAHE PETROSSIAN; circ. 10,000.

PRINCIPAL PERIODICALS

Aftabe Shargh: Meshed; weekly; political; Prop. Mrs. NARGESS AMOOZEGAR.

Al-Akha: Khayyam Ave., Teheran; f. 1960; Arabic; weekly; Dir. Sen. ABAS MASSOUDI; Editor NAZIR FENZA.

Asiaye Javan: Kh. Opera, Teheran; weekly; Editor CYRUS BAHMAN; circ. 4,000.

IRAN—(THE PRESS)

Assr Novin: Shah-Bakhti Ave., Tabriz; f. 1951; weekly; Editor A. BANI-AHMAD; circ. 20,000.

Bamshad: Pich Shemran, Teheran; weekly; Editor E. POURVALI; circ. 4,000.

Bourse Monthly: Sevom-Esfand Ave., Kuche Bakht 15, Teheran; f. 1963; economic; Editor Dr. Y. RAHMATI.

Daneshkade Pezeshki: Faculty of Medicine, Teheran University; medical magazine; monthly; Editor Dr. M. BEHESHTI.

Donya: Istanbul Ave., Teheran; weekly; Editor A. K. TABATABA'I.

Doyaye Varzesh: Khayyam Ave., Teheran; f. 1970; weekly sport magazine; Editor BIJAN RAFIEI.

Ettela'at Banovan: Kayyam Ave., Teheran; women's weekly magazine; Editor Mrs. PARI ABASALTI; circ. 40,000.

Ettela'at Javanan: Khayyam Ave., Teheran; f. 1958; youth weekly; Editor R. ETTEMADI.

Ettela'at Kodekan: Khayyam Ave., Teheran; f. 1957; teenage weekly; Editor NADER AKHVAN HEYDARI.

Ferdowsi: Ramsar Ave., Teheran; weekly; Editor N. JAHANBANOIE; circ. 8,000.

Film-Va-Honar: Roosevelt Ave., Teheran; weekly; Editor A. RAMAZANI.

Iran Tribune: P.O.B. 11/1244, Teheran, Iran; monthly; socio-political-business; English.

Iran Trade and Industry: Echo of Iran, P.O.B. 1228, Shiraz Ave., Teheran; f. 1965; monthly economic periodical; Editor HASSAN SHAIDA; circ. 10,000.

Javanan: Ave. Sepah, Teheran; weekly magazine for young people; circ. over 10,000.

Kayahan Bacheha: Kh. Ferdowsi, Teheran; children's magazine twice weekly; Editor DJAAFAR BADII; circ. 65,000.

Kayhan Varzeshi: Kh. Ferdowsi, Teheran; sport weekly; Editor Dr. M. MEZBAZADEH; circ. 60,000.

Khandaniha: Kh. Ferdowsi; f. 1939; weekly; circ. 25,000; Editor A. A. AMIRANI.

Khorassan Banovan: Plasco Bldg., Stanbul Ave., Teheran; weekly; published in Meshed.

Khusheh: Safi Ali Shah Avenue, Teheran; f. 1954; weekly; Editor Dr. AMIR HOUSHANG ASKARI.

Music Iran: 1029 Amiriye Ave., Teheran; f. 1951; monthly; Editor BAHMAN HIRBOD; circ. 7,000.

Navaye-Khorasan: Meshed; political; weekly; Prop. H. MAHBODI.

Nedaye Pezeshkan: Teheran; f. 1942; medical monthly; Editor AHMAD PAKRAVAN.

Omide Iran: Kh. Ferdowsi; weekly; Editor A. SAFIPOUR.

Pars: Shiraz; twice weekly; circ. 3,500; Editor F. SHARGI.

Rahnejat: Darvazeh Dowlat, Isfahan; political and social weekly; Prop. N. RAHNEJAT.

Rowshanfekr: Ramsar Ave., Teheran; f. 1953; political weekly; circ. 32,000; Editor Dr. R. MOSTAFAVI.

Sepahan: Baharestan Square, Teheran; literary; weekly.

Sepid va Siyah: Kh. Ferdowsi; popular monthly; Editor Dr. A. BEHZADI; circ. 30,000.

Setareye Cinema: Lalezar-Now Ave., Teheran; film weekly; Editor P. GALUSTIAN.

Setareye Esfahan: Isfahan; political; weekly; Prop. A. MEHANKHAH.

Sobhe Emroug: Ferdowsi Ave., Teheran; Editor Mrs. AMIDI-NURI.

Sokhan: Hafiz Ave., Zomorrod Passage, Teheran; f. 1943; literary monthly; Editor Dr. P. N. KHANLARI; circ. 5,000.

Sport: P.O.B. 342, Ebne Sina St., Park Aminoddole, Kakhe Markazi Taj; Teheran; sports, weekly.

Taraqqi: Kh. Sevvom Esfand, Teheran; f. 1927; weekly; Editor L. TARRAQQI; circ. 21,000.

Teheran Chamber of Commerce Monthly Journal: Teheran; Farsi; circ. 5,000; also **Weekly Bulletin,** circ. 5,000; both distributed mainly to members.

Tehran Economist: 99 Sevom Esfand Ave., Teheran; f. 1953; Persian and English; weekly; Editor Dr. B. SHARIAT; circ. 12,000 Persian, 4,500 English.

Tehran Messavar: Ave. Jaleh, Teheran; popular weekly; Editor ABDULLAH VALA; circ. 35,000.

Towfigh: Istanbul Ave., Teheran; f. 1921; satirical weekly; Editor HASSAN TOWFIGH; circ. 65,000; also **Towfigh Monthly;** f. 1961; humorous; circ. 37,000; Editor HOSSEYN TOWFIGH.

Vezarate Keshavarzi: Teheran; agriculture; monthly.

Zan-E-Ruz (*Women Today*): Kh. Ferdowsi, Teheran; women's weekly; circ. 150,000; Editor Mrs. F MESBAZADEH.

NEWS AGENCIES

International Press Agency of Iran: Teheran Ghvansaltaneh Square, P.O.B. 1125, Teheran.

Pars News Agency: General Department of Publications and Broadcasting, Maidan Ark, Teheran; f. 1936; Pres. NASSER SHIRZAD.

FOREIGN BUREAUX

A.F.P.: P.O.B. 1535, Teheran; Correspondent JEAN-CLAUD BRARD.

A.N.S.A.: Ave. Hafez, Kuche Hatef 11, Teheran; Chief GINA CARUSO.

A.P.: 7 Fifth St., Television Ave., Teheran; Correspondent PARVIZ RAEIN.

Reuter: P.O.B. 1607, Teheran; Correspondent ALI MEHRAVARI.

Tass: Kheyaban Hamid, Kouche Masoud 73, Teheran; Correspondent VLADIMIR DIBROVA.

U.P.I.: P.O.B. 529, Teheran; Correspondent YUSEF MAZANDI.

PRESS UNIONS

United Press Front: Teheran; f. 1960; without politica affiliation but pro-Constitutional; formed of 20 newspapers; Chair. MOHAMMED-BAQER HEJAZI; Sec. JAMAL ASHTIANI.

Press Club of Iran: Teheran; f. 1961; Chair. ABBAS MASSOUDI; Sec. Gen. Dr. M. MESDAZADEH.

Press Association of Iran: Teheran; f. 1960; includes about 40 newspapers and journals; Praesidium of 9 leading journalists; Sec. ESMAIL PURVALI.

Writers and Press Reporters Syndicate: Teheran.

PUBLISHERS

Ali Akbar Elmi: Shahabad Ave.; Dir. ALI AKBAR ELMI.

Amirkabir: Avenue Shahabad; Dir. ABDULRAHIM JAFARI.

Boroukhim: Avenue Ferdowsi, Teheran; dictionaries.

Bungah Tarjomeh va Nashr Ketah: Teheran; affiliated to the Pahlavi foundation.

Bungah Safi Ali Shah: Avenue Safi Ali Shah, Teheran.

Danesh: 357 Ave. Nasser Khosrow, Teheran; f. 1931 in India, transferred to Iran in 1937; literary and historical (Persian); imports and exports books; Man. Dir. NOOROUAH IRANPARAST.

Ebn-e-Sina: Meydane 25 Shahrivar, Teheran, f. 1957; educational publishers and booksellers; Dir. EBRAHIM RAMAZANI.

Eghbal Publishing Co.: Shahabad Ave., Teheran; Dir. DJAVAD EGHBAL.

Franklin Book Programs Inc.: 2 Alborz Ave., Shahreza Ave., Teheran; f. 1952; a non-profit organization for International Book Publishing Development; main office in New York; Dir. ALI ASGHAR MOHAJER.

Ibn-Sina: Shahabad St. Teheran.

Iran Chap Company: Ave. Khayyam, Teheran; f. 1966; newspapers, books, magazines, colour printing and engraving; Man. Dir. FARHAD MASSOUDI.

Kanoon Marefat: 6 Lalehzar St., Teheran; Dir. HASSAN MAREFAT.

Khayyam: Shahabad Avenue; Dir. MOHAMMAD ALI TARAGHI.

Majlis Press: Avenue Baharistan, Teheran.

Nil Publications: Mokhberoddowleh Sq., Koutcheh Rafahi, Teheran. Dir. A. AZIMI.

Pirouz: Shahabad Avenue; Dir. MIRMOHAMMADI.

Safiali Shah: Baharistan Square, Dir. MANSOUR MOSHFEGH.

Taban Press: Ave. Nassir Khosrow, Teheran; f. 1939; Propr. A. MALEKI.

Teheran Economist: Sevom Esfand Ave. 99, Teheran.

Teheran University Press: Avenue Shah-Reza.

Towfigh: Istanbul Ave., Teheran; publishes humorous Almanac and pocket books; distributes humorous and satirical books; Dir. Dr. FARIDEH TOWFIGH.

Zowar: Shahabad Avenue; Dir. AKBAR ZOWAR.

RADIO AND TELEVISION

RADIO

Radio Iran: Ministry of Information, Meidan Ark, Teheran; f. 1940; Home service programmes broadcast in Persian; foreign service programmes are broadcast in Urdu, Arabic, Turkish, English, Russian, French, Armenian and Assyrian; Gen. Man. M. R. ATEFI; publs. *Iran Today* (quarterly magazine in English, French, German), *Facts About Iran* (weekly bulletin in English, French, Arabic), *Press Conferences of His Majesty the Shah, Guides to Historical Sites and Cities, Radio Iran Monthly.*

There are twelve regional services, at Ahwaz, Gorgan, Isfahan, Kerman, Kermanshah, Meshed, Rasht, Reza'ieh, Sanandeh, Shiraz, Tabriz and Zahedan. The most powerful transmitters are at Ahwaz, Kermanshah and Zahedan; these broadcast in Arabic, in Kurdish, and in Baluchi and Urdu respectively.

Number of radio receivers: 1,810,000.

TELEVISION

National Iranian Television: Ave. Jam Jam, P.O.B. 33-200, Teheran; f. 1967; state-owned network with limited advertising; 30 transmitting stations; broadcasts for about 60 hours weekly; Man. Dir. R. GHOTBI.

Television of Iran: P.O.B. 1015, Ave. Pahlavi, Teheran; f. 1958; a private commercial company with stations in Teheran, Ahwaz (relay station), and Abadan; Pres. IRAJ SABET; Man. Dir. PARVIS PARTOVI; Chief Engineer DAVID LINFORD.

Number of television receivers (1972): 250,000.

American Forces Radio and Television: Teheran; f. 1954; recordings and films of American programmes.

FINANCE

(cap.=capital; p.u.=paid up; dep.=deposits; m.=million; all figures stated in Rials)

BANKING

CENTRAL BANK

Bank Markazi Iran (*Central Bank of Iran*): Ferdowsi Ave., Teheran; f. 1960; central note-issuing bank of Iran; cap. 3,600m., dep. 53,500m.; Gov. Dr. ABDUL ALI JAHANSHAHI; Deputy Gov. Dr. CYRUS SAMII.

Bank Asnaf Iran (*Guilds Bank of Iran*): Baharestan Square, Teheran; f. 1957; cap. p.u. 100m.; Chair. Gen. ALI AKHBAR ZARGHAM; Gen. Man. GHOLAM REZA ZAERIN.

Bank Bazargani Iran (*Commercial Bank of Iran*): Maidan Sepah, Teheran; reps. abroad in London, England and Hamburg, German Federal Republic; f. 1950; cap. p.u. 250m., dep. 15,906m. (March 1972); 204 brs.; Chair. and Man. Dir. Senator MOSTAFA TADJADOD.

Bank Bimeh Bazerganan (*Merchants Insurance Bank*): Ave. Bouzerjomehri, Teheran; f. 1952; cap. 220m.; dep. 784m.; Chair. H. E. A. A. SEPEHR; Gen. Man. ALI MOHAMED SHERAFETIAN.

Bank Bimeh Iran (*Iran Insurance Bank*): Teheran; under auspices of government-sponsored Sherkate Sahami Bimeh Iran (Insurance Company of Iran); cap. p.u. 422.5m.

IRAN—(FINANCE)

Banque Etebarate Iran (*Iran Credit Bank*): 50 Ave. Sevom Esfand, Teheran; f. 1958; cap. p.u. 400m., dep. 6,107m. (March 1972); Chair. and Man. Dir. H.E. AHMED CHAFIK.

Bank Etebarat Sanati (*Industrial Credits Bank*): Khiaban Ateshkadeh, Teheran; f. 1956; stock owned by the Plan Organization and two subsidiary companies; cap. p.u. 3,110m., dep. 1,840.8m. (1971); Chair. H.E. Eng. AHMAD ZANGENEH; Man. Dir. Dr. ALINAGHI FARMAN-FARMAIAN.

Bank Kar: Ave. Hafez, Teheran; f. 1958; cap. 400m., dep. 3,219m.; Man. ARSEN BARKHORDARIAN.

Bank Kargosha'i Iran (*Pawn Bank*): Moulavi Ave., Teheran; cap. provided by Bank Melli Iran; Principal Officer ESMAIEL TAHERI.

Bank Keshavarzi Iran (*Agricultural Bank of Iran*): Khiaban Park Shahr (North), Teheran; f. 1933; cap. p.u. 9,334.2m.; Government Bank; Pres. H.E. Eng. R. SADAGHIANI.

Bank Melli Iran (*The National Bank of Iran*): Ferdowsi Ave., Teheran; state-owned bank; brs. abroad in Frankfurt, Sharjah, Paris, Bahrain, Jeddah, Hong Kong, London, Hamburg, New York and Dubai; f. 1928; cap. p.u. 3,000m., dep. 144,137m., res. 1,951.5m. (March 1973); affiliation Bank Tedjarat Kharedji Iran; 1,700 brs. throughout Iran; Pres. YOUSSOF KHOSHKISH.

Bank of Iran and the Middle East: Kucheh Berlin, Ave. Ferdowsi, P.O.B. 1680, Teheran; f. 1959; brs. at Khorrashar, Abadan and Teheran (17); The British Bank of the Middle East owns 40 per cent of the issued capital; 60 per cent is held by Iranian interests; cap. p.u. 400m., dep. 5,510m.; Chair. Dr. G. H. KHOSHBIN; Gen. Man. M. H. VAKILY; Adviser to the Board D. PATTERSON.

Bank of Teheran: 25 Pahlavi Ave., Teheran; f. 1953; cap. p.u. 400m., dep. 14,007.6 (March 1973); Pres. MOSTAFA FATEH; Man. Dir. BAHMAN BEHZADI.

Bank Omran (*Development Bank*): Teheran; f. 1952 to provide technical guidance and financial support to farmers of distributed Crown villages; also acts as a commercial bank; 144 brs.; Pres. HOUSHANG RAM.

Bank Pars: Avenue Takht-Jamshid, Teheran; f. 1952; cap. p.u. 250m.; Chair. and Pres. E. NIKPOUR.

Bank Rahni Iran (*The Mortgage Bank of Iran*): Ferdowsi Street, Teheran; f. 1939; Government bank (affiliate of Ministry of Development and Housing) which grants loans for building houses; cap. p.u. 5,423m., total assets 21,089m. (March 1973); Chair. and Man. Dir. Eng. A. BEHNIA.

Bank Refah Kargaran (*Workers' Welfare Bank*): 125 Roosevelt Ave., Teheran; f. 1960; cap. p.u. 1,000m.; 55 brs.; state-owned bank; Chair. Dr. MEHDI A. ALIABADI.

Bank Russo-Iran: Jonoobe Park Shahr (South), Teheran; cap. 300m., reserves 45m.

Bank Saderat Iran (*The Export Bank of Iran*): 124 Ave. Shah, Teheran; P.O.B. 2751; f. 1951; cap. p.u. 1,500m.; dep. 51,538m. (March 1972); 3,000 brs. in Iran; brs. in Dubai, Abu Dhabi, Fujaireh, Ras Al Khaimah, Ajman (United Arab Emirates), Qatar; offices in London, Hamburg, Paris, Beirut; agency in New York; Man. Dir. Eng. M. A. MOFARAH.

Bank Sepah (*Army Bank*): Ave. Sepah, Teheran; f. 1925; state-owned bank; cap. p.u. 1,500m., dep. 31,332m. (March 1972); 365 brs. and agencies; Pres. Gen. F. AGH EVLI; Deputy Pres. DJALIL SASSINI.

Bayerische Vereinsbank: Munich, German Federal Republic; Ave. Rudsar 29, P.O.B. 2437, Teheran; Rep. PETER SCHMID-LOSSBERG; Berliner Bank A.G. and Vereinsbank in Hamburg.

Distributors' Co-operative Credit Bank: 37 Ave. Ferdowsi, Teheran; f. 1963; cap. 600m., dep. 4,472 (1973); Chair. SEIFULLAH RASHIDIAN; Pres. ASSADULLAH RASHIDIAN.

Foreign Trade Bank of Iran (*Bank Tedjarat Kharedji Iran*): Avenue Saadi, Teheran; f. 1960; jointly owned by Bank Melli Iran, Bank of America, Banca Comerciale Italiana and Deutsche Bank A.G.; cap. 275m., dep. 2,997m., reserves 208m. (March 1970); Man. Dir. ASHOT SAGHATELIAN.

Industrial and Mining Development Bank of Iran (IMDBI): 133 Shiraz St., Teheran, P.O.B. 1801; f. 1959 by private investors from Iran, the United States, the United Kingdom, France, Belgium, Germany, Holland and Italy; aims: to stimulate private industrial development in Iran by making medium- and long-term loans and by investing in share capital; cap. 1,500m.; total assets 18,573m. (March 1972); Man. Dir. A. GHASSEM KHERADJOU.

International Bank of Iran and Japan: 750 Ave. Saadi, P.O.B. 1837, Teheran; f. 1959; cap. 500m.; 35 per cent Japanese owned; Chair. MOSTAFA MESBAH-ZADEH; Gen. Man. ABDOLLAH TAHERI.

Iranians' Bank: 184 Takht Jamshid Ave., Teheran; f. 1960; cap. 500m., dep. 3,127m. (1973); associated with First National City Bank; Chair. A. H. EBTEHAJ; Pres. C. SAMII.

Irano-British Bank: Avenue Saadi, P.O. Box 1584, Teheran; f. 1959; affiliated with the Chartered Bank and the Eastern Bank; cap. p.u. 200m.; Gen. Man. W. T. WATSON.

Mercantile Bank of Iran and Holland: Ave. Saadi, P.O.B. 1522, Teheran; f. 1959; affiliated with Algemene Bank Nederland N.V., Amsterdam; cap. p.u. 300m., dep. 3,123m.; 11 brs. in Teheran, 1 in Ahwaz, 1 in Isfahan; Chair. SOLEYMAN VAHABZADEH; Man. Dir. AHMAD VAHABZADEH; Resident Dir. W. M. BROUWER.

Bankers' Association of Iran: Teheran; Pres. Gen. FARAJOLLAH AQEVLI.

STOCK EXCHANGE

Teheran Stock Exchange: Teheran; f. 1968.

INSURANCE

Sherkate Sahami Bimeh Iran (*The Insurance Co. of Iran*): Avenue Saadi, Teheran; f. 1935; Government-sponsored insurance company; all types of insurance; cap. p.u. 200m.; Chair. and Man. Dir. Dr. FARHANG MEHR.

Alborz Insurance Co. Ltd.: Alborz Bldg., 250 Sepahbod Zahedi Ave., Teheran; f. 1959; most classes of insurance except livestock insurance; five brs.; p.u. cap. 150m.; Management Habibollah Nahai and Brothers.

Omid Insurance Co. Ltd.: Philips Building, 315 Ave. Shahreza, Teheran; f. 1960.

Pars, Société Anonyme d'Assurances: Avenue Saadi, Teheran; f. 1955; fire, marine, motor vehicle and personal accident insurance; Gen. Man. MADJID MALEK; Tech. Man. YERVANT MAGARIAN.

Sherkate Sahami Bimeh Arya (*Arya Insurance Co. Ltd.*): 213 Soraya Ave., Teheran; f. 1952, re-named 1968; cap. 100m.; Chair. Dr. G. H. JAHANSHAI; Man. Dir. MOHAMMAD ALI HANDJANI.

Sherkate Sahami Bimeh Asia (*Asia Insurance Co. Ltd.*): Hafez Shomali Ave., 37 Esfandiary St., Teheran; f. 1960; Man. Dir. R. SHAMS.

Sherkate Sahami Bimeh Melli (*The National Insurance Co. Ltd.*): Shah Reza/Villa Ave., P.O.B. 1786, Teheran; f. 1956; all classes of insurance; Chair. H. E. AHMED CHAFIK; Managing Dir. EDWARD JOSEPH.

Sherkate Sahami Bimeh Omid: Ferdowsi Ave., Sabt St. 3, Teheran; f. 1960.

All insurance companies are members of the Syndicate of Iranian Insurance Companies.

OIL

National Iranian Oil Company (NIOC), Takhte Jamshid Ave. (P.O.B. 1863), Teheran

A state organization controlling all oil and gas operations in Iran.

NIOC

The National Iranian Oil Company (NIOC) was incorporated April 1951 on nationalization of oil industry to engage in all phases of oil operations; auth. cap. 10,000 million rials, in 10,000 shares, 50 per cent paid up; all shares held by Iranian Government and are non-transferable; Chair. of Board and Managing Dir. H.E. Dr. MANOUTCHEHR EGHBAL; Dirs. H.E. M. FOUROUGHI, H.E. A. K. BAKHTIAR, H.E. Dr. R. FALLAH, H. FARKHAN; Alternate Dirs. Dr. P. MINA, LATIF RAMZAN-NIA.

In October 1954 an agreement was concluded between the Iranian Government and NIOC on the one hand and eight major oil companies (subsequently increased to fourteen) on the other, to operate the southern oilfields (as defined) on behalf of NIOC. These companies are collectively known as the Consortium, for which *see below*. The agreement was for twenty-five years with provision for three five-year extensions, at the option of the Consortium under specific terms and conditions, NIOC being responsible for non-industrial activities in the agreement area. It directly operated the Naft-i-Shah oilfield, the Kermanshah refinery and Teheran refineries; it also carried out exploration and drilling in all parts of the country not subject to special agreements. NIOC is solely responsible for internal distribution of petroleum products and has laid over 3,500 km. of pipeline throughout Iran. The Petroleum Act of 1957 empowered NIOC to divide Iran into a number of petroleum districts, to invite bids for their exploitation, and to sign agreements. NIOC signed a series of agreements: in 1957 with AGIP Mineraria (an Italian company); in 1958 with Pan American Petroleum Corpn.; in 1965 with six groups listed below, for exploration of offshore areas. In all eight of the companies formed, NIOC had 50 per cent participation. In September 1966 agreement was reached with the French state organization Entreprise des Recherches et d'Activités Pétrolières (ERAP) to operate as a contractor on behalf of NIOC in exploration both on and offshore.

In December 1966 the Consortium relinquished one-quarter of the Agreement Area, comprising three parcels totalling 25,069 sq. miles, one in the north-west and two in the south-east, to NIOC. A major change took place in 1973, however, when the Consortium was issued with an ultimatum—the oil companies could either remain in the country until the existing 25-year contract expired in 1979 (with the proviso that they doubled production), after which they would get no more preferential treatment than any other foreign company, or alternatively, the Consortium could agree to be taken over immediately and then make preference agreements with the Government on a long-term basis. The latter course was agreed in March, and under a preliminary agreement signed in May 1973 between Iran and the Consortium, the Consortium will be guaranteed a supply of oil over a 20-year period. The Iranian Oil Exploration and Producing Company will become a services company registered in Iran and will operate as a contractor to the National Iranian Oil Company. The operation of Abadan refinery will pass to NIOC who will sell the products to the oil companies.

The decision was due partly to the Iran Government's need for greatly increased funds for the Fifth Development Plan, but also to its aim to gain as much control over foreign oil companies as had been achieved by other Arab states such as Kuwait, Qatar and Saudi Arabia in October 1972.

The company has formed two subsidiaries to represent it in two associated fields—The National Iranian Petrochemical Company and The National Iranian Gas Company. The latter has signed an agreement to supply the Soviet Union with large quantities of natural gas, beginning in 1970.

Société Irano-Italienne des Pétroles (SIRIP): Ave. Abbas Abad 30, P.O.B. 1434, Teheran; f. 1957; owned jointly by NIOC and AGIP S.p.A.; Man. Dir. Dr. G. F. GINO.

Iran-Pan American Oil Co. (IPAC): 315 Takhte Jamshid Avenue, Teheran; f. 1958; owned jointly by NIOC and Amoco Iran Oil Co.; to exploit Persian Gulf offshore deposits in their agreement area; Man. S. A. ANTONIUK.

Iranian Marine International Oil Company (IMINOCO): 128 Roodsar Ave., Teheran; f. 1965; formed with Phillips Petroleum Co., AGIP (a subsidiary of the Italian ENI) and Hydrocarbons India Pvt. Ltd. (a subsidiary of the Oil and Natural Gas Commission of India); Chair. A. FARHI; Man. Dir. GAETANO PERROTTI.

Lavan Petroleum Company (LAPCO): 3 Elizabeth II Boulevard, Teheran; f. 1965; formed with Atlantic Richfield, Murphy Oil Corporation, Sun Oil Co., and Union Oil Co. of California, who own 50 per cent interest, and the National Iranian Oil Co., who own the remaining 50 per cent; Man. Dir. N. E. DIETZEL.

Iranian Offshore Petroleum Company (IROPCO): P.O.B. 3257, Teheran; f. 1965; formed with CEPSA, and Cities Service Co., Kerr-McGee Corpn., Atlantic-Richfield Co., Skelly Oil Co., Superior Oil Co., and Sunray D.X. Oil Co.; Chair. E. SALJOOGHI; Man. Dir. ROBERT H. ROBIE.

Persian Gulf Petroleum Company (PEGUPCO): Teheran; f. 1965; formed with Deutsche Erdoel, Preussag, Wintershall, Deutsche Schachtbau und Tiefbohrgesellschaft, Gelsenkirchener Bergwerke, Gewerkschaft Elwerath, and Scholven-Chemie; Man. Dir. W. WESCHE.

Sofiran: P.O.B. 3220, Teheran; French oil interests. A subsidiary of Elf. ERAP.

Continental Oil Co. of Iran: P.O.B. 1511, 26 17th St., off Bucharest, Teheran; signed agreement with NIOC in April 1969 for exploration and development of a 5,000 square mile area in South Iran; Pres. J. M. SAUNDERS.

ERAP: Teheran; holds a 32 per cent share in a consortium exploring a 10,000 square mile area in Fars province;

IRAN—(OIL, TRADE AND INDUSTRY, TRANSPORT)

ENI has a 28 per cent share, Hispanoil 20 per cent, Petrofina 15 per cent and OMV of Austria 5 per cent.

Iran Nippon Petroleum Company (INPECO): 130 Ave. Shah Abbas Kabir, Teheran; f. 1971; partnership—50 per cent NIOC, 50 per cent Japanese group.

Hormuz Petroleum Company (HOPECO): 290 Ave. Villa, IBM Building, Teheran; f. 1971; partnership—50 per cent NIOC, 50 per cent Mobil.

Bushehr Petroleum Company (BUSHCO): 41 Ave. Daryaye Noor, between Takhte Tavoos and Abbasabad, Teheran; f. 1971; partnership—50 per cent NIOC, 50 per cent Amerada Hess.

THE CONSORTIUM

Consortium members, with percentage shareholdings: Gulf Oil Corporation (7%), Mobil Corporation (7%), Exxon (7%), Standard Oil Co. of California (7%), Texaco Inc. (7%), The British Petroleum Co. Ltd. (40%), Bataafse Petroleum Maatschappij N.V. (14%,) Compagnie Française des Pétroles (6%), the remaining 5 per cent being divided amongst the following six American companies: The American Independent Oil Co., The Atlantic Richfield Co., Charter Oil Co., Getty Oil Co., The Standard Oil Company (Ohio), and Continental Oil Co. Two operating companies, both incorporated under the laws of the Netherlands, were formed by the Consortium although these companies will change under the agreement signed in May 1973 (see above):

Iraanse Aardolie Exploratie en Productie Maatschappij (*Iranian Oil Exploration and Production Co.*): P.O.B. 1065, Khiaban Shah, Kucheh Yaghma, Teheran; solely responsible for exploration and production in a defined area in south Iran; Chair. J. P. VAN REEVEN.

Iraanse Aardolie Raffinage Maatschappij (*Iranian Oil Refining Co.*): P.O. Box 1065, Khiaban Shah, Kucheh Yaghma, Teheran; solely responsible for the operation of the refinery at Abadan and the NGL refinery at Bandar Mahshahr; Chair. J. P. VAN REEVEN.

While the NIOC owns the fixed assets of the oil industry in south Iran, the Operating Companies have the unrestricted use of them during the period of the agreement. The Operating Companies do not themselves buy or sell oil, their function being solely confined to producing and refining it. Each of the Consortium members is represented in Iran by a Trading Company which purchases crude oil from NIOC and resells it to customers for export, either as crude or as products. The Trading Companies deal individually and independently of one another. The net effect of the financial aspects of the sale of oil by the NIOC to the Trading Companies for export is to bring about an equal sharing between Iran and each Trading Company of the profits arising in Iran from the Trading Companies' operations.

REFINERIES' THROUGHPUT
(million barrels)

Year	Abadan	Masjid-i-Sulaiman
1968	150.3	12.5
1969	149.5	10.0
1970	153.8	9.5
1971	154.2	16.7
1972	152.2	12.2

TRADE AND INDUSTRY

CHAMBERS OF COMMERCE

Iran Chamber of Commerce, Industries and Mines: 254 Ave. Takht-Jamshid, Teheran; f. 1970; supervises the affiliated 17 Chambers in the provinces; Pres. Sen. Dr. TAHER ZIAI.

R.C.D. Joint Chamber of Commerce: Teheran; f. 1965 with Pakistan and Turkey under auspices of Regional Co-operation for Development.

EMPLOYERS' ASSOCIATION

Association des Employeurs Industriels de l'Iran: Teheran.

LABOUR ORGANIZATIONS

All Trade Unions were dissolved in 1963, and syndicates of workers must be registered with the Government. In March 1963 there were 67 syndicates representing various trades, of which the largest included the *National Iranian Oil Company Workers' Syndicate* with 6,000 members.

CO-OPERATIVES

Central Organization for Rural Co-operatives of Iran (C.O.R.C.): Teheran; Man. Dir. MANOUCHEHR MA'REFAT. Following the implementation of the Land Reform Act, the C.O.R.C. was established by the Government in 1963. The aim of the organization is to offer educational, technical and credit assistance to rural co-operative societies and their unions. The C.O.R.C. will gradually transfer its stocks to rural co-operative unions and become the National body for Rural Co-operatives. By Dec. 1970, 8,224 rural co-operatives societies and 117 unions with a combined total membership of 1,549,202 had availed themselves of the C.O.R.C. facilities. The share capital of the societies is 1,852m. rials.

TRADE FAIR

Iran International Fairs and Exhibitions Corpn.: P.O.B. 22, Tajrish, Teheran; principal event in 1973 is: Teheran International Trade Fair 22-28 September 1973; Dir.-Gen. M. SHEEDFAR; publ. *Exhibition News*.

TRANSPORT

RAILWAYS

Iranian State Railway: Head Office: Teheran; f. 1938; Pres. Eng. PARVIZ AVINI; Financial Gen. Dir. MOHAMMADIAN; Administrative Gen. Dir. H. MALEKI.

The Iranian railway system includes the following main routes:

Trans-Iranian Railway runs 1,440 km. from Gorgan, in the north, through Teheran, and south to Bandar Shahpur on the Persian/Arabian Gulf.

  South Line links Teheran to Khorramshahr via Ghom, Arak, Dorood, Andimeshk and Ahwaz; 937 km.

  North Line links Teheran to Gorgan via Garmsar, Firooz Kooh and Sari; 499 km.

  Teheran-Tabriz Line linking with the Azarbaijan Railway (736 km.).

IRAN—(TRANSPORT, TOURISM)

Garmsar-Meshed Line connects Teheran with Meshed, via Semnan, Damghan, Shahrud and Nishabur; 812 km.

Ghom-Zahedan Line when completed will be an intercontinental line linking Europe and Turkey, through Iran, with India. Zahedan is situated 91.7 km. west of the Baluchistan frontier, and is the end of the Pakistani broad gauge railway. The section from Ghom to Kashan is open, and that from Kashan to Yazd is under construction. A branch line from the Kashan-Yazd line is under construction which will run through Isfahan and the Riz Lendjan where the Iranian Steel Corporation is to be installed.

Ahwaz-Bandar Shahpur Line connects Bandar Shahpur with the Trans-Iranian railway at Ahwaz (123 km.).

Azarbaizhan Railway extends from Tabriz to Julfa (146.5 km.), meeting the Caucasian railways at the Soviet frontier with a branch line connecting with Sharaf-Khaneh on Lake Rezaiyeh; also administers shipping on Lake Rezaiyeh.

The total length of main lines in January 1972 was 4,560 km. The rail link between Iran and Turkey was opened in September 1971 (344 km.).

ROADS

Ministry of Roads: Ministry of Roads and Communications, Teheran; Minister Eng. H. SHALCHIAN.

There are about 42,000 km. of roads, of which some 11,000 km. had asphalt or paved surfaces by 1972. The Asian (CENTO) Highway now provides a good surface running from Teheran across Turkey to join up with the European road system.

MOTORISTS' ORGANIZATIONS

Touring and Automobile Club of Iran: 37 Varzesh Ave., Teheran; f. 1935.

INLAND WATERWAYS

Principal waterways:

Lake Rezaiyeh (Lake Urmia) 50 miles west of Tabriz in North-West Iran; and River Kharun flowing south through the oilfields into the River Shatt al Arab thence to the head of the Persian/Arabian Gulf near Abadan.

Lake Rezaiyeh: From Sharafkhaneh to Golmankhaneh there is a twice-weekly service of tugs and barges for transport of passengers and goods.

River Karun: Regular cargo service is operated by the Mesopotamia-Iran Corpn. Ltd. Iranian firms also operate daily motor-boat services for passengers and goods.

SHIPPING

Persian Gulf: Principal ports are Khorramshahr, Bushire, Bandar Abbas, Bandar Shahpur. Oil exports from the Abadan refinery are now handled by the new Mahshahr installations (opened December 1967) and Kharg Island terminal in the Persian/Arabian Gulf. Bushire is being developed to supplement the facilities at Khorramshahr, while the capacity of Bandar Abbas has recently been increased.

Caspian Sea: Principal port Bandar Pahlavi.

Arya National Shipping Lines: 2 Pahlavi Ave., Khorramshahr; 13 vessels; liner services between the Persian/Arabian Gulf and Europe.

CIVIL AVIATION

Iran National Airlines Corporation (*Iran Air*): 44 Villa Ave., Teheran; f. 1962; replaces Iranian Airways Co.; serves Iran, the Middle East and Europe, Karachi, Kabul and Bombay; Chair. Gen. M. KHATAMI; Man. Dir. Lt.-Gen. ALI M. KHADEMI; fleet of two Boeing 707, four Boeing 727, three Boeing 737 and three DC-6; two Concordes were bought in October 1972, to be delivered by February 1977.

Teheran is also served by the following foreign lines: Aeroflot, Air France, Air India, Alia, Alitalia, Ariana Afghan Airlines, BOAC, CSA, El Al, Iraqi Airways, JAL, KLM, Kuwait Airways, Lufthansa, MEA, PAA, Qantas, Sabena, SAS, Swissair, Syrian Arab Airlines.

TOURISM

Iran National Tourist Organization (INTO): 174 Elizabeth Blvd., Teheran; f. 1963; Dir. CYRUS FARZANEH. Publications: *Iran Travel News* (monthly), *INTO News Bulletin* (weekly), *Monthly Statistics Bulletin*, brochures, tourist guide books, road maps, posters.

During 1971–72 more than 350,000 tourists visited Iran, showing an increase of some 27,000 over the previous year. The estimated income from tourists over this period was U.S. $49.22 million.

CULTURAL ORGANIZATIONS

Ministry of Culture and Arts: Kh. Kamal-ol-Molk, Teheran; f. 1964 to replace the Fine Arts Administration; depts. of Music, Cinematography, Arts Education (Dramatic Arts, Music, Ballet, Decorative Arts, Plastic Arts, National Arts), Archaeology and Ethnography, Museums and Historical Monument Preservation, Artistic Creation, Libraries, Iranian Academy of Language, Cultural Relations, Arts Exhibitions, Superior Council of Culture and Arts; has under its direction Rudaki Hall (opera, ballet, concerts), ballet, dance, dramatic and folklore troupe, an orchestra, an International Film Festival, etc.; Minister of Culture and Arts MEHRDAD PAHLBOD.

Teheran Symphonic Orchestra: Kh. Kamal-ol-Molk, Teheran; 75 mems.; Leader HESHMAT SANJARI.

Fine Arts Theatre Group: c/o Ministry of Culture, Teheran; produces weekly programmes for television.

Music Council of Radio Iran: Maidan Ark, Teheran; supervises all music programmes, both Persian and Western (popular and classical), broadcasts on two AM stations and one FM station in Teheran; also serves in advisory capacity all provincial stations; Chair. Dr. H. FARHAT.

Shiraz-Persepolis Festival of Arts: Shiraz; f. 1967; plays, films and music representing both Eastern and Western culture; held for a short fortnight at end of Aug. and beginning of Sept.; partly staged in the ruins at Persepolis; Pres. Dr. MEHDI BOUSHEHRI; publs. various books and brochures in Persian on music and drama, festival brochure annually.

ATOMIC ENERGY

National Iranian Atomic Energy Commission: Ministry of Economy, Teheran; co-ordinates nuclear research, and is undertaking construction of a small research reactor; Sec. Eng. A. SEIRAFI.

Teheran University Nuclear Centre: P.O.B. 2989, Teheran; f. 1958; research in nuclear physics, electronics, nuclear chemistry, radiobiology and health physics; training and advice on nuclear science and the peaceful applications of atomic energy; a 5-MW pool-type research reactor on the new campus of Teheran University went critical in November 1967; a 3-MeV Van de Graaff-type accelerator became operational in 1972; Dir. Dr. H. ROUHANINEJAD.

EDUCATION

The ten years before 1939 saw a great expansion in education in Iran. In 1934 the University of Teheran was established, and 25 Normal Schools were opened, to train annually 750 elementary teachers of both sexes as the first step in bringing education to the people.

In 1941, Reza Shah Pahlavi abdicated, and the succession of his son initiated a more democratic régime, which has been reflected in educational matters. Cultural relations were established with many countries, including the Allied Powers, the University was freed from politics, and scholarships for study abroad, which had been suspended, were resumed after the war. Education is now entirely free at elementary schools and to a great extent at secondary level. Many of the public secondary schools charge small tuition fees to provide funds for the better equipment of schools, repairing of school buildings and financial aid to needy students. Under a new scheme the majority of students in public universities have to pay the equivalent of $130 per annum (two semesters). Tuition fees at private universities are higher. Top students are either awarded scholarships or are exempted from paying fees. In addition to the increasing number of working-class children who are receiving elementary education, almost all the middle class send their children to school. Many of the children of wealthy people go to schools and colleges in Europe or America.

Aware of the need to overhaul and modernise Iran's outmoded educational system, the Government has laid down a twenty-five-year period of improvement at the end of which the standard of education should be on the same level as that of other fully developed countries. Iran's latest development plan (1973-78) is concentrating particularly upon education, with expenditure of 230,000 million rials. Though the basic system will remain unchanged, it is planned to extend primary education, which is six years at present, to eight years, develop a good system of secondary vocational schools, increase the number and quality of teachers and launch a major adult literacy programme. The new system of education which is gradually being implemented is divided into three stages, the first of which covers five years and is compulsory and free for all school-age children in cities and rural areas. The second stage, lasting three years, will be declared compulsory when the first stage has been fully implemented. The third stage will consist of two types of secondary education: academic schools for talented and qualified students and technical and vocational schools offering a range of courses in different fields of industry, agriculture, commerce, etc.

Since the establishment of the Education Corps programme in 1962 about 39,000 corpsmen have been sent to villages throughout the country. Working as teachers and village leaders, they have brought many new ideas to backward communities and have raised the rural literacy rate by 5 per cent. However, illiteracy is still a major problem extending to some seven million adults, mostly in rural areas.

Primary Schools. In 1943 the Government passed a law providing for the general establishment over a period of six years of compulsory and free education for both sexes. This has not yet been fully implemented in rural areas owing to the shortage of schools and teachers. In 1971-72 the number of primary schools reached 15,000, with 3 million students. There were also 11,000 education corps schools with 504,000 students. These figures mean that 55 per cent of the country's eligible children are receiving education. The elementary schools are mostly State schools, and often co-educational, but there are also private schools which receive grants-in-aid. The basic curriculum is standard for all types of school, and consists of six years' general education, with the addition of practical subjects suited to the environment. At the age of twelve, pupils sit for a Government examination which entitles them to enter a secondary school.

Secondary Schools. Secondary education is not compulsory, but most of the schools are free or charge only small fees. In 1964 there were 369,000 pupils receiving secondary education; by 1972 enrolment had risen to over a million (18 per cent of eligible children).

Technical Education. In 1971 there were 189 technical and vocational schools, representing a 15.2 per cent growth rate over the previous year, with 31,000 students (a 34.8 per cent growth rate).

On the higher education level there is the Polytechnic Institute of Teheran which offers four-year courses, in 8 different fields, to the graduates of the mathematics course of secondary schools or the graduates of technical schools with certain academic achievements. The Institute of Technology, one of the 8 departments, is exclusively a teacher-training centre for technical and trade schools. Another institute is the Higher Institute of Business Education which offers a regular four-year course. The Polytechnic Institute has been equipped with the aid of the United Nations' Special Fund.

Foreign Schools. Many schools, at all levels, were started by foreign missions during the nineteenth century. American, British, French, and German missions predominated. With the exception of two French schools, the remaining schools have been run by the Ministry of Education since 1940.

Minorities. A number of minorities is officially recognised in Iran. There are the Assyrians and Armenians, both Christian sects, the Zoroastrians, who preserve the ancient Parsee religion, and the Jews, who are found scattered through the bigger towns. These minorities all run their own schools, but before the war were compelled to adhere strictly to the official curriculum. Now, greater freedom is allowed. The Armenians teach in their own language, and the Jews place particular emphasis on the teaching of foreign languages.

Tribal and Fundamental Teaching: Some tribes in Iran are nomadic, and so itinerant schools were founded in 1955. Seven Primary School Teachers' Training Colleges have been established in different provinces, to train the staff for these itinerant schools. In the academic year 1966–67 there were 725 itinerant classes where 22,634 students were receiving instruction. Fundamental education has been rapidly expanded owing to the establishment of the extension corps programme. Under the new scheme two types of agricultural agencies are helping Iranian farmers to increase their productivity. One type consists of permanent government officials who are selected from among agricultural secondary school graduates and have undergone an intensive one-year course in agriculture. The other comprises extension corpsmen. They are either agricultural faculty or agricultural secondary school graduates who work in villages for about 14 months. This is considered as part of their military service.

Teachers' Training. Prospective elementary teachers can take the three-year training course after either three or five years' secondary education. To teach in a secondary school the student must take a university degree simultaneously with his pedagogic training at the University Institute of Education. In 1971 there were 79 Primary Teacher Training Schools, with 5,000 students.

Higher Education. The tradition of University education in Iran goes back some eight hundred years. However, in the middle of the nineteenth century this was remodelled on the French system. A number of university colleges were established in Teheran, and functioned independently until 1934, when they were united to form the University of Teheran. There are also university colleges at Isfahan, Meshed and Shiraz (medicine), and Tabriz. The Honar-Saraye Ali provides advanced studies in engineering. In 1955–56 agricultural colleges were opened at Shiraz, Ahwaz and Tabriz and colleges of literature at Meshed and Shiraz. The University of Ahwaz (Gondishapour University) was opened in 1957. Recent steps towards the expansion of higher education include the founding of a private university, Arya Mehr Industrial University, and new colleges of dentistry and pedagogy in Teheran and some provincial universities. The total number of university and college students in 1970-71 was 74,708. As a result of a law passed in 1928, many students receive scholarships to study abroad, either in Europe or America.

Adult Education/Literacy Corps. A start was made in adult education in 1907, but it was not until 1936 that a serious effort was made to combat illiteracy. Evening classes and part-time day schools were set up, especially in rural areas. By 1965–66 there were 142,000 adult students in the evening classes of education corpsmen. In addition the armed forces, in co-operation with the Ministry of Education, are giving their personnel instruction at an average rate of 80,000 men a year. By 1973 50 per cent of the population in the age group 10-14 were literate.

Since 1962 selected national servicemen have been trained, at the rate of 3,500 per annum, as teachers to be sent out to villages and nomadic groups all over the country. Education Corpsmen have assisted villagers not only with basic teaching in literacy but with self-improvement schemes such as school-building, road and well construction and provision of medical facilities.

UNIVERSITIES

University of Isfahan: Isfahan; 315 teachers, 3,400 students.
Jundi-Shapur University: Ahwaz, Khouzestan Province; 161 teachers, 2,370 students.
University of Meshed: Meshed; 269 teachers, 3,363 students.
National University of Iran: Ewin, Teheran; 426 teachers, 6,089 students.
Pahlavi University: Shiraz; 200 teachers, 3,200 students.
University of Tabriz: Tabriz; 287 teachers, 3,441 students.
University of Teheran: Ave. Shah Reza, Teheran; 1,436 teachers, 16,893 students.
Arya Mehr Industrial University: Karadj Rd., Teheran; 162 teachers, 1,500 students.

BIBLIOGRAPHY

GENERAL

ABDALIAN, S. Damavand (Iran) (Teheran, 1943).
BARTH, F. Nomads of South Persia (London, 1961).
CAMBRIDGE HISTORY OF IRAN.
   Volume I: The Land of Iran.
   Volume V: The Saljuq and Mongol Periods.
   (Both Cambridge University Press, 1968).
CURZON, LORD. Persia and the Persian Question (2 vols., London, 1892).
DE PLANHOL, X. Recherches sur la Géographie humaine de l'Iran Septentrional (Paris, 1964).
ELGOOD, CYRIL. A Medical History of Persia and the Eastern Caliphate (London, 1951).
ELWELL-SUTTON, L. P. Modern Iran (London, 1941).
   A Guide to Iranian Area Study (Ann Arbor, 1952).
   Persian Oil: A Study in Power Politics (London, 1955).
ENGLISH, P. W. City and Village in Iran (Wisconsin, 1967).
ESKELUND, KARL. Behind the Peacock Throne (Alvin Redman, New York, 1965).
FIELD, HENRY. Contributions to the Anthropology of Iran (Chicago, 1939).
FRYE, RICHARD N. Persia (Allen and Unwin, London, 3rd ed. 1969).
FURON, RAYMOND. L'Iran (Paris, 1952).
   Géologie du Plateau iranien (Paris, 1941).
   La Perse (Paris, 1938).
GAIL, MARZIEH. Persia and the Victorians (London, 1951).
GRAVES, PHILIP. The Life of Sir Percy Cox (1941).
GROSECLOSE, ELGIN. Introduction to Iran (New York, 1947).
HAAS, WILLIAM S. Iran (New York, 1946).
HANDLEY-TAYLOR, GEOFFREY. Bibliography of Iran (Fifth Edition, St. James Press, London, 1969).
HUOT, JEAN LOUIS. Persia Vol. I (Muller, London, 1966).
IQBAL, MUHAMMAD. Iran (London, 1946).
   Iran Almanac (Echo of Iran, Teheran, annually).
   Iran: A Selected and Annotated Bibliography (Washington, 1951).
KEDDIE, NIKKI R. Historical Obstacles to Agrarian Change in Iran (Claremont, 1960).
KEMP, N. Abadan (London, 1954).
LAMBTON, A. K. S. Landlord and Peasant in Persia (New York, 1953).
   Islamic Society in Persia (London, 1954).
   A Persian Vocabulary (Cambridge, 1961).
MARLOWE, JOHN. Iran, a Short Political Guide (Pall Mall Press, London and New York, 1963).
MEHDEVI, A. S. Persian Adventure (New York, 1954).
   Persia Revisited (London, 1965).
MILLSPAUGH, A. C. Americans in Persia (Washington, 1946).
MOTTER, T. H. VAIL. The Persian Corridor and Aid to Russia (Washington, 1952).
SANGHVI, RAMESH. Aryamehr: The Shah of Iran (Macmillan, London, 1968).
SHAH OF IRAN. Mission for My Country (Hutchinson, London 1961).
SHEARMAN, I. Land and People of Iran (London, 1962).
SIRDAR, IKBAL ALI SHAH. Persia of the Persians (London, 1929).
SMITH, A. Blind White Fish in Persia (New York, 1953).
STARK, FREYA. The Valleys of the Assassins (London, 1934).
   East is West (London, 1945).
THARAUD, JÉRÔME. Vieille Perse et Jeune Iran (Paris, 1947).
VREELAND, H. H. Iran (Human Relations Area Files, 1957).
WARD, PHILIP. Touring Iran (Faber & Faber, London, 1971).
WICKENS, G. M. and SAVORY, R. M. Persia in Islamic Times, a practical bibliography of its history, culture and language (Institute of Islamic Studies, McGill University, Montreal, 1964).
WILBER, DONALD N. Iran: Past and Present (Princeton University Press, 1955).
   Iran: Oasis of Stability in the Middle East (Foreign Political Association, Inc., New York, 1959).
ZABIH, SEPEHR. The Communist Movement in Iran (University of California Press 1967).

CIVILIZATION AND LITERATURE

ARBERRY, A. J. (ed.). The Legacy of Persia (London and New York, 1953).
   Shiraz: The Persian City of Saints and Poets (Univ. of Oklahoma Press, 1960).
   Tales from the Masnavi (London, 1961).
   More Tales from the Masnavi (London, 1963).
   (ed.). The Cambridge History of Iran (Cambridge University Press 1969).
BAUSANI, A. Der Perser: von den Anfängen bis zur Gegenwart (Kohlhammer, Stuttgart, 1965).
BELL, GERTRUDE L. Persian Pictures (London, 1928).
BROWNE, E. G. A Literary History of Persia (4 vols., Cambridge, 1928).
COLLEDGE, M.A.R. The Parthians (Thames and Hudson, London, 1968).
CULICAN, WILLIAM. The Medes and the Persians (1965).
DUCHESNE-GUILLEMIN, JACQUES. The Hymns of Zarathustra (trans. with commentary) (Beacon, L. R., Boston, Mass., 1963).
ELWELL-SUTTON, L. P. Colloquial Persian (London, 1941).
   Persian Proverbs (London, 1954).
   Elementary Persian Grammar (Cambridge, 1963).
GHIRSHMAN, R. L'Iran: des Origines à Islam (Paris, 1951).
   Iran from the Earliest Times to the Islamic Conquest (London, 1954).
   Arts of Ancient Persia from the Origins to Alexander the Great (London, 1963).
   Iran (New York, 1964).
HERZFELD, E. Iran in the Ancient East (Oxford, 1941).
KAMSHAD, H. Modern Persian Prose Literature (Cambridge, 1966).
LEVY, REUBEN. The Persian Language (New York, 1952).
   Persian Literature (1928).
LOCKHART, L. Famous Cities of Iran (London, 1939).
   The Fall of the Safavi Dynasty and the Afghan Occupation of Persia (Cambridge University Press, 1958).

MONTEIL, V. Les Tribus du Fars et la sédentarisation des nomades (Mouton, Paris and The Hague, 1966).
OLMSTEAD, A. T. History of the Persian Empire, Achaemenid Period (Chicago, 1948).
POPE, ARTHUR. Survey of Persian Art from Prehistoric Times to the Present. Vols. 1–6 (Oxford University Press, 1938–58).
RICE, CYPRIAN. The Persian Sufis (Allen and Unwin, London, 1964).
ROSS, Sir DENISON. Eastern Art and Literature (London, 1928).
The Persians (London, 1931).
STOREY, C. A. Persian Literature (London, 1927).
SYKES, Sir PERCY. Persia (Oxford, 1922).
A History of Persia (2 vols.; 3rd edition, with supplementary essays) (London, 1930).
WIDENGREN. Die Religionen Irans (Kohlhammer, Stuttgart, 1965).
WULFF, H. E. The Traditional Crafts of Persia (M.I.T. Press, Cambridge, Mass., 1966).

RECENT HISTORY

BANANI, AMIN. The Modernization of Iran, 1921–1924 (Stanford, 1961).
BUNYA, ALI AKBAR. A Political and Diplomatic History of Persia (Teheran, 1955).
COTTAM, R. W. Nationalism in Iran (Pittsburgh University Press, 1964).
FATEMI, NASROLLAH S. Diplomatic History of Persia 1917–1923 (New York, 1952).
HAMZAVI, A. H. K. Persia and the Powers: An Account of Diplomatic Relations, 1941–46 (London, 1946).
ISSAWI, CHARLES. The Economic History of Iran, 1800–1919 (University of Chicago Press, 1972).
LENCZOWSKI, GEORGE. Russia and the West in Iran (Cornell Univ. Press, 1949).
NAKHAI, M. L'Evolution Politique de l'Iran (Brussels, 1938).
RAMAZANI, ROUHOLLAH K. The Foreign Policy of Iran 1500–1941 (University Press of Virginia, Virginia, 1966).
SKRINE, Sir CLARMONT. World War in Iran (Constable, London, 1926).
STEPPAT, FRITZ. Iran zwischen den Grossmächten, 1941–48 (Oberursel, 1948).
UPTON, JOSEPH M. The History of Modern Iran: An Interpretation (Harvard University Press, 1960).

ECONOMY AND OIL

ABOLFAZI, ADLI. Aussenhandel und Aussenwirtschaftspolitik des Iran (Duncker and Humblot, Berlin, 1960).
AMUZEGAR, JAHANGIR. Technical Assistance in Theory and Practice: the Case of Iran (Praeger Special Studies in International Economics, New York, 1966).
AMUZEGAR, JAHANGIR and ALI FEDRAT, M. Iran: Economic Development under Dualistic Conditions (University of Chicago Press, 1972).
BALDWIN, GEORGE B. Planning and Development in Iran (Johns Hopkins Press, Baltimore, 1967).
BHARIER, JULIAN. Economic Development in Iran 1900–1970 (Oxford University Press, London, 1971).
FATEH, MOUSTAFA KHAN. The Economic Position of Persia (London, 1926).
GHOSH, SUNIL KANTI. The Anglo-Iranian Oil Dispute (Calcutta, 1960).
GORELIKOV, SEMEN GERASIMOVICH IVAN. A study in the Geography and Economics of Persia (Russian text), (Moscow, 1961).
GUPTA, RAJ NARAIN. Iran: An Economic Study (New Delhi, 1947).
I.L.O. SECRETARIAT. Labour Conditions in the Oil Industry in Iran (Geneva, 1950).
MASON, F. C. Iran: Economic and Commercial Conditions in Iran (H.M.S.O., London, 1957).
NAHAI, L. and KIBELL, C. L. The Petroleum Industry of Iran (Washington: U.S. Department of the Interior, Bureau of Mines, 1963).
NIRUMAND, BAHMAN. Persien, Modell eines Entwicklungslande, oder Die Diktatur der freien Welt (Rowohlt-Verlag, Reinbek-bei-Hamburg, 1967).
SOTOUDEH, H. L'Evolution Economique de l'Iran et ses Problèmes (Paris, 1957).
WILLIAMSON, J. W. In a Persian Oilfield (London, 1930).

MODERN IRAN

ARASTEH, REZA. Educational and Social Awakening in Iran (E. J. Brill, Leiden, 1962).
Man and Society in Iran (Leiden, 1964).
AVERY, PETER. Modern Iran (Benn, London, 1967).
BINDER, LEONARD. Iran, Political Development in a Changing Society (University of Calif. Press, 1962).
VON BLÜCHER, WIPERT. Zeitenwende in Iran: Erlebnisse und Beobachtungen (Biberach an der Riss, 1949).
BROWNE, E. S. The Press and Poetry of Modern Persia (Cambridge, 1914).
A Year Amongst the Persians (London, 1950).
GRAEFE, A. VON. Iran, Das neue Persien (Berlin, 1937).
NIRUMAND, BAHMAN. Iran: the new imperialism in action (Modern Reader Paperbacks, New York and London, 1971).
RAJPUT, A. B. Iran Today (Lion Publications, 1946).
RODKIN, ANGELA. Unveiled Iran (London, 1942).
WILBER, D. N. Contemporary Iran (New York, 1963).
WOODSMALL, RUTH. Moslem Women Enter a New World (London, 1936).

Iraq

PHYSICAL AND SOCIAL GEOGRAPHY

W. B. Fisher

Iraq is bounded on the north by Turkey, on the east by Iran, on the south by Kuwait and the Persian Gulf, on the south-west by Saudi Arabia and Jordan, and on the north-west by Syria. The actual frontier lines present one or two unusual features. In the first place, there exists between Iraq, Kuwait, and Saudi Arabia a "neutral zone", rhomboidal in shape, which was devised to facilitate the migrations of pastoral nomads, who cover great distances each year in search of pasture for their animals and who move regularly between several countries. Hence the stabilization or closing of a frontier could be for them a matter of life and death. Secondly, the frontier with Iran in its extreme southern portion below Basra follows the course of the Shatt al-Arab channel, but instead of running midway down the river course, as is more usual, the frontier lies at the left (east) bank, placing the whole of the river within Iraq. Thirdly, the inclusion of the northern province of Mosul within Iraq was agreed only in 1926. Because of its oil deposits, this territory was in dispute between Turkey, Syria, and Iraq. Again the presence of large numbers of migratory nomads journeying each season between Iran, Turkey, Syria and Iraq was a further complicating factor.

PHYSICAL FEATURES

The old name of Iraq (Mesopotamia=land between the rivers) indicates the main physical aspect of the country—the presence of the two river valleys of the Tigris and Euphrates, which merge in their lower courses. On the eastern side of this double valley the Zagros Mountains of Persia appear as an abrupt wall, overhanging the riverine lowlands, particularly in the south, below Baghdad. North of the latitude of Baghdad the rise to the mountains is more gradual, with several intervening hill ranges, such as the Jebel Hamrim. These ranges are fairly low and narrow at first, with separating lowlands, but towards the main Zagros topography becomes more imposing, and summits over 10,000 ft. in height occur. This region, lying north and east of Baghdad, is the ancient land of Assyria; and nowadays the higher hill ranges lying in the extreme east are called Iraqi Kurdistan, since many Kurdish tribes inhabit them.

On the western side of the river valley the land rises gradually to form the plateau which continues into Syria, Jordan, and Saudi Arabia, and its maximum height in Iraq is about 3,000 ft. In places it is possible to trace a cliff formation, where a more resistant bed of rock stands out prominently, and from this the name of the country is said to be derived (Arabic *Iraq*=cliff). There is no sharp geographical break between Iraq and its western neighbours comparable with that between Iraq and Iran; the frontier lines are artificial.

THE RIVERS

It remains to describe the valley region itself and the two rivers. The Tigris, 1,150 miles in length (1,850 km.), rises in Turkey, and is joined by numerous and often large tributaries both in Turkey and Iraq. The Euphrates, 1,460 miles in length (2,350 km.), also rises in Turkey and flows first through Syria and then Iraq, joining the Tigris in its lower course at Qurna, to form the stream known as the Shatt al-Arab, which is 115 miles (185 km.) in length. Unlike the Tigris, the Euphrates receives no tributaries during its passage of Iraq. Above the region of Baghdad both rivers flow in well-defined channels, with retaining valley-walls. Below Baghdad, however, the vestiges of a retaining valley disappear, and the rivers meander over a vast open plain with only a slight drop in level—in places merely 8 or 10 feet in 100 miles. Here the rivers are raised on great levees, or banks of silt and mud (which they themselves have laid down), and now lie several feet above the level of the surrounding plain. One remarkable feature is the change in relative level of the two river beds—water can be led from one to the other according to the actual district, and this possibility, utilised by irrigation engineers for many centuries, still remains the basic principle of present-day development. At the same time, the courses of both rivers can suddenly alter. A flood may breach the wall of the levee, and the water then pours out on to the lower-lying plain, inundating many square miles of territory. Ultimately, the river finds a new course and builds a fresh levee. Old river channels, fully or partially abandoned by the river, are thus a feature of the Mesopotamian lowland, associated with wide areas of swamp, lakes, and sandbars. The Tigris, though narrower than the Euphrates, is swifter, and carries far more water.

As the sources of both rivers lie in the mountains of Turkey, the current is very fast, and upstream navigation is difficult in the middle and upper reaches. In spring, following the melting of snows in Asia Minor, both rivers begin to rise, reaching a maximum in April (Tigris) and May (Euphrates). The spring is a very anxious time, since floods of 12 to 20 feet occur, and 32 feet is known—this in a region where the land may fall only 10 feet or less in level over 50 miles. Immense areas are regularly inundated, levees often collapse, and villages and roads, where these exist, must be built on high embankments. The Tigris is particularly liable to sudden flooding, and can rise at the rate of one foot per hour. Contrasts with the Nile of Egypt will be noted. The latter river is confined in a steep-sided valley over most of its length, and floods do not spread far away from the river. In lower Iraq, on the other hand, wide expanses are inundated every year, e.g. as in early 1954 when a flood of 30 ft. occurred and many thousands were rendered homeless.

CLIMATE AND ECONOMIC ACTIVITY

The summers are overwhelmingly hot, with shade temperatures of over 110°F.; and many inhabitants retire during the heat of the day to underground rooms. Winters may be surprisingly cold: frost, though very rare at Basra, can be severe in the north. Sudden hot spells during winter are another feature in the centre and south of Iraq. Rainfall is scanty over all of the country, except for the north-east (Assyria), where 15 to 25 inches occur—enough to grow crops without irrigation. Elsewhere farming is entirely dependent upon irrigation from river water. The great extent of standing water in many parts of Iraq leads to an unduly high air humidity, which explains the notorious reputation of the Mesopotamian summer.

The unusual physical conditions outlined present a number of obstacles to human activity. The flood waters are rather less "manageable" than in Egypt, and there is less of the regular deposition of thick, rich silt that is such a feature of the Nile. The effects of this are strikingly visible in the relatively small extent of land actually cultivated—at most, only one-sixth of the potentially cultivable territory and 3 per cent of the total area of the country. The population, of about 8 million, is about a quarter of that of Egypt. Because of the easy availability of agricultural land, wasteful, "extensive" farming methods are often followed, giving a low yield. On the whole, Iraq is underpopulated, and could support larger numbers of inhabitants.

A feature of the last few years has been the use of oil royalties (over £300 million per annum until March 1972) for development schemes, particularly in irrigation. New barrages are in construction along the main rivers and their tributaries, the most important recent works being the Wadi Tharthar Scheme, the Dokan Dam, and the Derbendi Khan Dam; besides providing irrigation water this scheme allows the drawing off of flood waters and has effectively reduced any further risk of disastrous flooding. With the completion of Phase I of the Wadi Tharthar scheme, the liability to flooding has been greatly diminished. This has meant great changes, especially in the Baghdad region. Buildings and roads need no longer always be placed on embankments.

The unusual physical conditions have greatly restricted movement and the development of communications of all kinds. In the upper reaches of the rivers boat journeys can only be made downstream, whilst nearer the sea the rivers are wider and slower but often very shallow. Roads are difficult to maintain because of the floods, and the railways have two differing gauges—standard and metre; the latter is however in process of replacement and with decreasing risk of flooding, standard gauge has been laid between Baghdad and Basra via Kut. The effect has been to leave in isolation many communities that have differing ways of life and even differing languages and religious beliefs. Numerous minority groups are hence a feature of Iraq.

THE PEOPLE

In the marshes of the extreme south there are communities of Arabs who spend most of their lives in boats and rafts. Other important minorities live in, or close to, the hill country of the north: the Kurds, who number over one million and migrate extensively into Syria, Turkey, and Iran; the Yazidis of the Jebel Sinjar; the Assyrian Christians (the name refers to their geographical location, and has no historical connection); and various communities of Uniate and Orthodox Christians. As well, there were important groups of Jews—more than in most other Muslim countries—though since the establishment of the State of Israel much emigration has taken place. It should also be noted that whilst the majority of the Muslims follow Shi'a rites, the wealthier Muslims are of Sunni adherence.

Ethnically, the position is very complicated. The northern and eastern hill districts contain many racial elements—Turki, Persian, and proto-Nordic, with Armenoid strains predominating. The pastoral nomads of western Iraq are, as might be expected, of fairly unmixed Mediterranean ancestry, like the nomads of Syria, Jordan, and Saudi Arabia; but the population of the riverine districts of Iraq shows a mixture of Armenoid and Mediterranean elements. North of the Baghdad district the Armenoid strain is dominant, but to the south, it is less important, though still present.

Arabic is the official and most widely used language. Kurdish and dialects of Turkish are current in the north, whilst variants of Persian are spoken by tribesmen in the east. An estimate, probably over-generous to the Arabic speakers, puts the relative numbers at: Arabic, 79 per cent, Kurdish, 16 per cent, Persian, 3 per cent, and Turkish, 2 per cent of the total population.

HISTORY

Iraq was one of the earliest centres of civilization. Before 3000 B.C. the Sumerians, a people of problematical origin, had established a complete civilization in the marshy alluvial areas at the head of the Persian/Arabian Gulf. Here a number of city states developed, cities like Eridu, Uruk, Ur, Kish and Lagash. These states were supported by a highly developed agricultural economy, based on an intricate irrigation system.

Around 2500 B.C., Lagash gained ascendency over several other cities, until, not long afterwards, Lugalzaggisi, the governor of Umma, overran Uruk and embarked on a career of widespread conquest. Lugalzaggisi was in turn defeated by Sargon of Agade, who united the whole of Mesopotamia under Akkadian rule and conquered Elamite Susa, and whose armies penetrated as far as the Mediterranean. Akkadian dominions were extended even further under his successors, but the Sumerians of the south took every opportunity to revolt and attacks by Elamites and mountain tribesmen, the Gutians, caused the empire to collapse around 2200 B.C. After a period of chaos, a new Sumerian kingdom, centered at Ur (the Third Dynasty of Ur) established supremacy over the south, lasting through the twenty-first century B.C. It was finally sacked by invaders from Elam, and by the Amorites from the north-west, and was never again of great historical importance.

The Amorites were Semites, whose homeland was Arabia. They came into conflict with the Elamites in Sumer, and in the eighteenth century B.C. Hammurabi created an extensive empire famous for the splendour of its civilization. Pressure from the Caucasian tribes, Hurrians and Kassites, was increasing, but the empire finally crumbled before the onslaught of the Hittites, who sacked Babylon in the seventeenth century B.C.

In the north, new powers were emerging, notably the Mitanni, who occupied northern Iraq. At last their rule disintegrated under constant pressure from the Hittites of Asia Minor, whose influence, in the years following the reign of their great king Subbiluliuma (c. 1390–1350 B.C.), was advanced almost to the Persian/Arabian Gulf. Meanwhile, on the higher reaches of the Tigris, the warlike Assyrians, who hastened the decline of the Mitanni and the Hittite empire, embarked from time to time on a career of conquest destined to be of brief duration, as under Adad-nirari I (c. 1300 B.C.) and Tiglath-pileser I (c. 1200 B.C.). In the reign of Ashur-nasir-pal II (883–859 B.C.) Assyrian ambition burst forth once more, re-establishing control over northern Mesopotamia. Syria and Cilicia were subdued under Shalmaneser III (860–825 B.C.) and the Assyrian empire in its heyday comprised Van and other Armenian territories, Babylonia, Syria, Egypt and large areas of Persia. An army of unprecedented efficiency, mass deportations on a vast scale, relentless cruelty, a régime of rigid and despotic centralization—these features of Assyrian rule evoked the bitter enmity of the subject peoples, who, when the empire weakened as a result of incessant warfare and of Scythian invasion from the north, rose in combined revolt and sacked Nineveh in 612 B.C. Iraq now became the centre of a neo-Babylonian state which, under Nebuchadnezzar (604–562 B.C.) included much of the Fertile Crescent, but was soon to fall before the Persians, who seized Babylon in 539–538 B.C.

Thereafter, Iraq was a mere province of the vast Achaemenid empire, which extended from Asia Minor to the Punjab in north-west India and from southern Russia to Egypt. Alexander the Great brought Persian rule to an end in a series of brilliant campaigns (334–327 B.C.). After his death in 323 B.C., one of his generals, Seleucus, controlled most of the Asiatic lands which the conqueror had dominated. The Seleucids maintained their hold on Iraq for more than a hundred years and then, in the course of prolonged warfare, lost it to the Parthians, who during the third and second centuries B.C. founded a powerful state in Persia.

Under the Parthians Iraq was a frontier province over against the might of Rome. To the north and west of Mesopotamia a line of strong fortresses, e.g., Carrhae (Harran), Edessa (modern Urfa), Diyarbakir, Dara, Nisibin, marked the ground where the rival armies fought. At Carrhae, in 54 B.C., the Parthian horsemen severely defeated the Romans but from the time of Augustus until the reign of the Emperor Trajan there was no major war between the two states. Between A.D. 113 and 117, Trajan conquered much of Iraq, yet his successor, Hadrian, felt that it would be too expensive to defend the new territories and so abandoned them. Rome resumed the offensive under Marcus Aurelius (162–166), Septimius Severus (195–199) and Caracalla (216–218), her rule being now extended from the middle Euphrates to the Khabur river.

The Parthian domination came to an end in 224 owing to internal revolt in Persia; the emergence of the Sasanid régime now began. In 260 Sapor I crushed the Romans in battle near Edessa and captured the Emperor Valerian. The endless frontier hostilities flared out once more into violent war under Diocletian, Constantius and Julian (third-fourth centuries), the Romans being forced back behind the line of the Euphrates. The conflict then died down for more than a hundred years and was not resumed on a large scale until the Sasanid state recovered much of its old vigour under Kobad I (488–531) and Khusrau Anushirvan (531–579). The prolonged warfare of the sixth–seventh centuries came to an end with the brilliant campaigns of the Byzantine Emperor Heraclius in Armenia and Iraq (622–628). Byzantium and Persia were by now exhausted and in the meantime a formidable danger had arisen in the far south.

THE RISE OF ISLAM

The prophet Muhammad (d. 632) had created at Mecca and Medina a religious and political organization that aroused powerful forces long latent in Arabia.

The Arab nomads of the great desert, united within the community of Islam, were forbidden to pursue their ancient tribal feuds. The restless energy thus concentrated in the Muslim state found an outlet in war outside Arabia and the Arabs overran Syria and Egypt. By 634 the Arab warriors had begun the conquest of Iraq. The battle of Qadisiya in 635 led to the fall of the Persian capital, Ctesiphon, in June of that year. A further battle at Jalula in 637 marked the end of Sasanid power in Iraq, although resistance continued in the north until the Arabs took Mosul in 641. Kufa and Basra became the two great garrison cities on which Muslim rule in Iraq was to be based for the next hundred years.

The murder of the Caliph 'Uthman in 656 brought about a civil war between his successor, 'Ali, and Mu'awiya, a kinsman of 'Uthman, who had long been governor of Syria. After an indecisive battle at Siffin in 657 the two rivals had recourse to arbitration, as a result of which, at Adhruh in January 659, both men were deposed from their respective positions, a judgment which deprived 'Ali of his real status as Caliph and Mu'awiya of a pretension to that office which as yet he had not ventured openly to avow. The outcome of the conflict remained uncertain during the next two years, until at length the murder of 'Ali at Kufa in January 661 left the way clear for Mu'awiya to become Caliph. The war revealed that effective power within the new empire was passing from Mecca and Medina to the great garrison cities where the main Arab armies were stationed. 'Ali had been obliged to go from the Hijaz to Iraq, his chief support coming from Kufa. Mu'awiya relied for his success on the strength of Syria. The real issue had been whether Iraq or Syria should be the metropolitan province of the empire. With the emergence of Mu'awiya as Caliph in 661, the question was decided, for almost a hundred years, in favour of Syria.

During the period of the Umayyad dynasty (661–750) Iraq became the centre of the movement known as Shi'atu 'Ali, i.e. "the party of 'Ali". Born amongst the Arabs themselves, it assumed at first the form of a "legitimist" opposition to Umayyad rule, asserting that the Caliphate should of right belong to the descendants of 'Ali, the son-in-law of the Prophet. As a purely Arab and political faction, resting to a large degree on the bitter dislike of Iraq for the hegemony of Syria, it was to meet with failure, for the armies of Kufa and Basra could not overcome the military pre-eminence of the Syrians. At Karbala, in October 680, Husain, the son of 'Ali, fell in battle against the Umayyad forces in Iraq. This event, by giving to the Shi'a an illustrious martyr, inaugurated a new and rapid growth of the party, not on the political level but as a religious sect.

UMAYYAD RULE

The Umayyad state was based on the fundamental assumption that a vast subject population, non-Muslim and non-Arab, would continue indefinitely to yield tribute to a dominant Arab and Muslim warrior aristocracy, the revenues derived from the conquered territories and from the *jizya*, i.e. the poll-tax imposed on those who did not belong to the faith of the Prophet, being shared out amongst the members of that aristocracy. Whether from a genuine acceptance of the new religion or from motives of self-interest, e.g. to escape the poll-tax and to secure the financial, economic and social privileges of the Arab Muslims, the subject peoples began to adopt Islam. The revenues of the state fell and the decline could not be made good through the acquisition of rich new lands, for the age of rapid conquest was over. Since Muhammad had declared all Muslims to be equal, the new converts, or Mawali, demanded that the Arabs concede to them a due participation in the rewards of empire. When it became clear that the Arab aristocracy meant to defend its pensions, privileges and other exclusive rights—the available resources of the state were insufficient to meet the claims of the ever-increasing numbers of Mawali—a crisis of the first magnitude threatened the Umayyad régime.

The Mawali now gave their allegiance to the Shi'a, transforming the movement into a means for the expression of their social and economic grievances against the established order and, at the same time, remoulding it as a religious sect which embraced ideas not of Muslim origin but derived from their previous Christian, Jewish and Zoroastrian traditions. This radical change in the Shi'a was already visible in the years 685–687, when a serious revolt occurred at Kufa in the name of Muhammad ibn al-Hanafiya, a son of 'Ali by a wife other than Fatima, the daughter of the Prophet.

The Umayyad Caliph 'Umar II (717–720) introduced a series of financial reforms designed to conciliate the Mawali, a policy which met only with a transient success, for the ultimate effect of his measures was to increase the expenditure and lower the revenue of the state. Disillusionment grew apace amongst the non-Arab Muslims. An efficient propaganda machine, known under the name of the Hashimiya, made its appearance in Iraq, its task being to disseminate extreme Shi'i ideas. In 716 control of this organization fell into the hands of Muhammad ibn 'Ali ibn al-'Abbas, descended from an uncle of the Prophet. Its chief centre of activity was in the great frontier province of Khurasan, in north-east Persia, where Arab colonies from Basra and Kufa had settled in about 670. Abu Muslim, a Persian Mawla of Iraq, was sent to Khurasan as confidential agent of the Hashimiya in 743 and there raised the standard of revolt against the Umayyads. Syria, long since weakened by fierce tribal feuds amongst the Arabs, could not withstand the storm. In 750 Umayyad rule came to an end and was replaced by that of the 'Abbasid dynasty, while Iraq at last achieved her ambition of becoming the dominant province of the empire.

'ABBASID RULE

The 'Abbasid caliphs had now an immediate and urgent task to perform. It was impossible for them to govern as the representatives of the more advanced elements in the Shi'a, when most of their Muslim subjects were of the Sunni or orthodox faith. The second 'Abbasid, al-Mansur (754–775), the real founder of the new régime, therefore abandoned the extremists who had done so much to bring his house to power. He also built a new garrison city in Iraq for his main army, the hard core of which consisted largely of regiments from Khurasan. This capital of the 'Abbasid empire, Baghdad, soon developed into a great emporium of trade and a political centre of vast importance. An autocratic caliph, claiming divine authority for his power, which rested on regular armed forces and was exercised through a paid bureaucracy; a cosmopolitan ruling class of officials and landowners, of merchants and bankers; the 'Ulama, i.e. the hierarchy of religious scholars, jurists, teachers and dignitaries—these were the main characteristics of the 'Abbasid Caliphate, which for a time brought to Iraq and, indeed, to the Islamic state as a whole a splendid prosperity derived from a flourishing agriculture and industry and from the lucrative transit trade between India and the Mediterranean.

It was in regard to political unity that the 'Abbasid empire proved most vulnerable. The relative cohesion which the Muslim state had enjoyed owing to the dominance of the Arab warrior aristocracy did not survive the revolution of 750. The new dynasty sought to use the Muslim faith itself as a means of binding together the varied ethnic and social elements of the population, but the attempt was soon shown to be a failure. After the death of Harun ar-Rashid (786–809), whose reign marked the apogee of 'Abbasid power as well as fostering a great flowering of Arabic culture, civil war broke out between his sons Amin and Ma'mun, the former depending largely on the support of Iraq, the latter on the strength of Persia and, above all, on the troops of Khurasan. The conflict was, in one sense, a battle between Persia and Iraq for pre-eminence within the empire. Ma'mun conquered Baghdad in 813, but for a time considered the idea of making Marv in Khurasan his capital, a project which he abandoned only when he realized that it would lead to repeated revolt in Iraq. In August 819 he returned to Baghdad.

Persia, disappointed in its hopes, now began to break away from the caliphs of Baghdad. Local dynasties made their appearance in the east, the Tahirids in 820, the Saffarids in 867, the Samanids in c. 892. A similar process occurred in the west, Spain after 756, Morocco after 788, Tunisia after 800 being virtually independent of Baghdad. In 868 the dynasty of the Tulunids arose in Egypt. The more extreme elements of the Shi'a were also active, especially in Persia and the neighbouring regions, inspiring repeated insurrections against the 'Abbasid régime. Southern Iraq suffered heavily in the Zanj Rebellion (869–883), when one Ali ibn Muhammad founded a state of Negro slaves at Basra, which was sacked in 871. The Qarmatians, a religious movement of communistic and revolutionary tendencies, founded a strong régime of their own in the province of Bahrain (now called al-Hasa) and for most of the tenth century carried out frequent raids into Iraq. Meanwhile, at Baghdad, the power of the army was growing. The corps gathered for the Caliph's protection consisted of slaves (mamluks), mostly of Turkish origin, commanded by free officers. Since the reigns of al-Mu'tasim (833–842) and al-Wathiq (842–847), their officers had also been Mamluks. As power fell more and more into the hands of the army, the Mamluks were able to appoint and depose the caliphs at will. Iraq fell at length under the domination of Daylamite mountain dwellers from the region south of the Caspian Sea, Shi'i in religion and led by a family of *condottière* chieftains, the Buwaihids, who, after subduing most of western Persia, occupied Baghdad in 945. Buwaihid rule—a period of the deepest degradation for the Caliphate, since the Commander of the Faithful was now a mere puppet obedient to the orders of a Shi'i— lasted until 1055. It then collapsed before the assault of Turks from the steppe lands beyond the Oxus, who, led by the Seljuqs, a family also of *condottière* origin, overran Persia and then seized Baghdad under Tughril Beg. The Seljuq Turks were Sunni Muslims and their success was not unwelcome amongst the orthodox, who regarded it as a liberation from the yoke of the Shi'i Buwaihids. Yet the Caliph, although treated with deference, was still only in name the head of the state, all effective power being concentrated in the hands of the Seljuq Sultan.

After the death of Malik Shah in 1092, dynastic dissension and revolt amongst the Turkish tribesmen brought about a rapid decline of the new régime and the rise of succession states ruled by princes or by officers of the Seljuq house. In Iraq a series of nine Seljuq sultans ruled from 1118–94, almost all of them fated to die a violent death in conflict with rival claimants or with their Atabegs, i.e. amirs, who were the most powerful figures in the land. Some of these Atabegs established independent principalities of their own, e.g. the Zangid dynasty at Mosul, which played an important role in arousing the Muslims to defend Islam against the Christian Crusaders in Syria. The last Seljuq Sultan of Iraq, Tughril (1177–94), was defeated in battle with the Turkish ruler of Khwarizm (the region of Khiva, south of the Aral Sea). The victor, Takash (1172–1200), and his successor, 'Ala'ad-Din Muhammad (1200–20), sought to extend their rule over Iraq, but, before this ambition could be realised, the Mongols destroyed the power of the Khwarizm shahs.

THE MONGOL INVASIONS

By 1220 the great conqueror Jenghiz Khan had overrun all Transoxania and was threatening to invade Persia. His death in 1227 led to a long pause in the Mongol advance. In 1253 Hülakü, a grandson of Jenghiz Khan, moved westward in force, captured Baghdad in 1258 and thus made an end of the Abbasid caliphate. Subordinated henceforth to the Mongol Khan of Persia, Iraq became a mere frontier province, bereft of all its former wealth and splendour and much neglected by its rulers. On the death of the Mongol Khan Abu Sa'id in 1335, Iraq, after a brief period of confusion, passed into the hands of a new dynasty, the Jala'irids, who ruled over the land until the early years of the fifteenth century. During this period Iraq was again overrun by Mongols and in

1401 Timur Beg sacked Baghdad with merciless severity. The Jala'irid régime did not long outlast the death of Timur in 1405.

To the north of Iraq, around Lake Van, a powerful Turcoman confederation, known as the Black Sheep (Kara Koyunlu) was rising into prominence. The Turcomans defeated the last Jala'irid, Ahmed, and created a new state which, under Jihan Shah (1444–67), extended from Tabriz to the Shatt al-'Arab. The power of the Kara Koyunlu soon collapsed in war with a rival Turcoman confederation, that of the Ak Koyunlu (White Sheep), who, led by their famous chieftain, Uzun Hasan (1423?–78), crushed Jihan Shah and took over the territories which he had ruled. Dynastic quarrels brought about a rapid disintegration of the White Sheep ascendancy.

In the years 1499–1508 the now crumbling Ak Koyunlu régime was destroyed by the Safavid, Isma'il. (His ancestors were hereditary masters of a powerful religious order notable for its advanced Shi'i teaching and, from their main centre at Ardabil near the Caspian Sea, had fashioned their numerous adherents amongst the Turcoman tribes of Asia Minor into a formidable military movement). Isma'il made himself Shah of Persia and also conquered Iraq. To the Ottoman Sultan, the dissemination of Shi'i beliefs among the tribes of Anatolia was a menace which had to be eliminated, for it threatened to undermine his own control in that region, the Ottomans being Sunni, i.e. orthodox Muslims. Selim I made war on Shah Isma'il in 1514 and so began a protracted conflict between the Ottomans and the Safavids which was to last, with long intervals of precarious peace, until 1639. Sultan Suleyman, in the course of his first campaign against Persia, conquered Baghdad in 1534–35.

OTTOMAN IRAQ

The Ottomans were to find Iraq a most difficult and expensive province to administer. Religious animosities proved to be a constant source of trouble. Northern Iraq and Kurdistan followed largely the Sunni faith; Baghdad itself was divided in its allegiance between Sunni and Shi'i Islam; southern Iraq was a region under strong Shi'i influence. The task of restraining nomad tribes from raiding the settled lands was an endless and wearisome business. Moreover, the tribes of the delta marshlands and of the mountainous areas close to the frontier with Persia were ever liable to rise in revolt against the administration. From time to time Iraq was the scene of warfare between the Ottomans and the Safavids, e.g., in the years 1578–90, and indeed came once more under Persian control, when Shah Abbas (1587–1629) seized Baghdad in 1623 and retained it in the face of a determined Ottoman counter-offensive in 1625/26. After a second attempt at reconquest in 1629/30 had failed, the Ottomans at last recovered Baghdad in 1638 and in the next year made peace with the Safavids.

As the Ottoman state fell into decline, the Sultan at Istanbul became less able to dominate the course of events in so distant a province as Iraq. From about 1625 until 1668, Basra and the Delta marshlands were in the hands of local chieftains independent of the Ottoman administration at Baghdad, a state of affairs which recurred in the period 1694–1701. The appointment of Hasan Pasha to command at Baghdad in 1704 marked a new phase in the history of Ottoman Iraq. The pashalik was to pass from himself to his son, then to the husbands of his grand-daughters, and thereafter to a series of Mamluk governors raised and trained in the household of his immediate successors. From 1704 to 1831, therefore, the Sultan failed to enforce at Baghdad an appointment of his own choice.

Hasan Pasha died in 1723, just at the moment when the Ottomans had become involved in a new war against Persia. The last of the Safavids had been deposed in 1722 by the Afghan Mir Mahmud. Hasan Pasha's son, Ahmed Pasha, occupied Kermanshah, which Hasan himself had seized in the first stage of the conflict, and then overran Hamadan and Luristan, but these lands were lost once more to Persia when Nadir Shah, in the years after 1729, drove out the Afghans and invaded Iraq. Baghdad itself withstood a siege in 1733 and Mosul underwent the same experience in 1743. The war brought much suffering to Iraq, the province falling, as a result of frequent revolt amongst the restless tribesmen and the devastation caused by repeated campaigns, into a state of anarchy. None the less, Ahmed Pasha remained throughout this period in firm control of Baghdad and Basra and also exercised a strong influence over the affairs of Mosul and Kirkuk. He lived to see peace made with Persia in 1746 on terms which restored the general position to what it had been before the war. A few months later in 1747, he died, leaving no son to succeed him.

The palace household which his father had created and which he himself had further developed contained Mamluks recruited for the most part from Georgia, converted to Islam and trained in their youth for subsequent service in the administration of Iraq. After a brief interval of confusion, in which the Porte tried to impose its own nominee but soon had to admit failure, Suleyman Agha, one of the Mamluks whom Hasan Pasha had bought and educated, became the governor of Baghdad and Basra, an office which he held with great success for twelve years until his death in 1762. Yet another Mamluk, 'Umr Agha, ruled Iraq from 1764 to 1775. Internal strife and a frontier war which led to a Persian occupation of Basra marked the period immediately following his death.

At length, in 1780, the most famous of the Mamluk pashas, Suleyman the Great, assumed the government of Baghdad and Basra. Much of his time was spent in curbing the Kurdish chieftains in the north and the Arab tribes, above all the powerful Muntafiq confederation in the south of Iraq. From about 1790 he had to face the enmity of the formidable Wahhabi state recently founded in central Arabia. The raids of the Wahhabi tribesmen into Iraq intensified until in 1801 the great Shi'i sanctuary of Karbala was taken and sacked. The death of Suleyman in the next year threw Iraq into even greater confusion. There were further Wahhabi *razzias*, e.g. against Najaf in 1803 and Basra in 1804, and constant trouble with the tribes along the Persian border. It was only in 1817 that the last of the Mamluk pashas, Da'ud, secured control of the province and restored some semblance of order by repeated punitive campaigns against the Kurds and the nomads of the desert lands.

Meanwhile, reforms were being introduced at Istanbul which foreshadowed the end of the Mamluk régime in Iraq. Selim III (1789–1807) and Mahmud II (1808–39) sought to refashion the administration and the military forces of the empire on European lines. The moment when the Ottoman Sultan would attempt to end the Mamluk system and regain direct possession of Iraq was now at hand. Mahmud II sent 'Ali Ridha Pasha to perform this task in 1831. A severe outbreak of plague crippled the resistance of the Mamluks, Da'ud Pasha was deposed and the Mamluk regiments were at once exterminated. A new phase in the history of Iraq was about to begin.

WESTERN INFLUENCE

Although some of the European nations had long been in contact with Iraq through their commercial interests in the Persian/Arabian Gulf, western influences were slow to penetrate into the province. By 1800 there was a British Resident at Basra and two years later a British Consulate at Baghdad. France also maintained agents in these cities. French and Italian religious orders had settlements in the land. It was not, however, until after 1831 that signs of more rapid European penetration became visible, such as steam-boats on the rivers of Iraq in 1836, telegraph lines from 1861 and a number of proposals for railways, none of which was to materialise for a long time to come. The Ottoman government did much in the period between 1831 and 1850 to impose direct control over Kurdistan and the mountainous areas close to the Persian border, but the introduction of reforms was not, in fact, begun until in 1869 Midhat Pasha arrived at Baghdad. Much of his work, performed in the brief space of three years, proved to be superficial and ill-considered, yet he was able to set Iraq on a course from which there could be no retreat in the future. A newspaper, military factories, a hospital, an alms-house, schools, a tramway, conscription for the army, municipal and administrative councils, comparative security on the main routes and a reasoned policy of settling tribesmen on the land—these achievements, however imperfect, bear solid witness to the vigour of his rule. After his departure in 1872, reform and European influence continued to advance, although slowly. Postal services were much developed, a railway from Baghdad to Samarra was completed in 1914 (part of the projected *Baghdadbahn*, which betokened the rapid growth of German interest in the Ottoman Empire) and the important Hindiya Barrage on the Euphrates was rebuilt between 1910 and 1913. The measures of reform and improvement introduced between 1831 and 1914 must indeed be judged as belated and inadequate—the Iraq of 1900 differed little from that of 1500—yet a process of fundamental change had begun, which no régime, however inept, could reverse.

In November 1914 Britain and the Ottoman Empire were at war. British troops occupied the Shatt al-Arab region and, under the pressure of war needs, transformed Basra into an efficient and well-equipped port. A premature advance on Baghdad in 1915 ended in the retreat of the British forces to Kut, their prolonged defence of that town and, when all attempts to relieve it had failed, the capitulation to the Ottomans in April 1916. A new offensive launched from Basra in the autumn of that year brought about the capture of Baghdad in March 1917. Kirkuk was taken in 1918, but, before the Allies could seize Mosul, the Ottoman government sought and obtained an armistice in October. For two years, until the winter of 1920, the Commander-in-Chief of the British Forces, acting through a civil commissioner, continued to be responsible for the administration of Iraq from Basra to Mosul, all the apparatus of a modern system of rule being created at Baghdad—e.g., departments of Land, Posts and Telegraphs, Agriculture, Irrigation, Police, Customs, Finance, etc. The new régime was Christian, foreign and strange, resented by reason of its very efficiency, feared and distrusted no less by those whose loyalties were Muslim and Ottoman than by important elements who desired self-determination for Iraq.

The last phase of Ottoman domination in Iraq, especially during the years after the Young Turk Revolution in 1908, had witnessed a marked growth of Arab nationalist sentiment. Local circles in Iraq now made contact with the Ottoman Decentralization Party at Cairo, founded in 1912, and with the Young Arab Society, which moved from Paris to Beirut in 1913. Basra, in particular, became a centre of Arab aspirations and took the lead in demanding from Istanbul a measure of autonomy for Iraq. A secret organization, al-'Ahd (the Covenant) included a number of Iraqi officers serving in the Ottoman armies. The prospect of independence which the Allies held out to the Arabs in the course of the war strengthened and extended the nationalist movement. In April 1920 Britain received from the conference at San Remo a mandate for Iraq. This news was soon followed by a serious insurrection amongst the tribesmen of the south. The revolt, caused partly by instinctive dislike of foreign rule but also by vigorous nationalist propaganda, was not wholly suppressed until early in the next year. In October 1920 military rule was formally terminated in Iraq. An Arab Council of State, advised by British officials and responsible for the administration, now came into being and in March 1921 the Amir Faisal ibn Husain agreed to rule as King at Baghdad. His ceremonial accession took place on August 23rd, 1921.

The Najdi (Saudi Arabian) frontier with Iraq was defined in the Treaty of Mohammara in May 1922. Saudi concern over loss of traditional grazing rights resulted in further talks between Ibn Saud and the U.K. Civil Commissioner in Iraq, and a Neutral Zone of 7,000 sq. km. was established adjacent to the western tip of the Kuwait frontier. No military or permanent buildings were to be erected in the zone and the nomads of both countries were to have unimpeded access to its pastures and wells. A further agreement concerning the administration of this zone was signed between Iraq and Saudi Arabia in May 1938.

MODERN IRAQ

Despite the opposition of the more extreme nationalists, an Anglo-Iraqi Treaty was signed on October 10th, 1922. It embodied the provisions of the mandate, safeguarded the judicial rights of foreigners and guaranteed the special interests of Britain in Iraq. Subsidiary agreements were to be made covering military co-operation, the status of British officials and also matters of justice and finance. An Electoral Law, published in May 1922, prepared the way for the choice of a constituent assembly, which met in March 1924 and, in the face of strong opposition by the nationalists, ratified the treaty with Britain. It accepted, too, an Organic Law declaring Iraq to be a sovereign state with a constitutional hereditary monarchy and a representative system of government. In 1925 the League of Nations recommended that the *vilayet* of Mosul, to which the Turks had laid claim, be incorporated into the new kingdom, a decision finally implemented in the treaty of July 1926 between the interested parties, Britain, Turkey and Iraq. By this year a fully constituted Parliament was in session at Baghdad and all the ministries, as well as most of the larger departments of the administration, were in effective control. Moreover, the state now possessed a competent judicial organization, a small army of about 7,500 men and a police force well equipped to deal with the refractory desert tribesmen. In 1930 a new treaty was signed with Britain, which established between the two countries a close alliance for a period of 25 years. The agreement provided for full consultation in foreign affairs and mutual aid in time of war. Iraq undertook to grant free passage for British troops and all other needful facilities, recognizing the importance to Britain of its "essential communications" in the region. British forces were also to hold two air bases at Shu'ayba and Habbaniya. On October 3rd, 1932 Iraq entered the League of Nations as an independent power, the mandate being now terminated.

The difficulties which confronted the Kingdom in the period after 1932 required much time and effort for their solution: e.g. the animosities between the Sunni Muslims and the powerful Shi'i tribes on the Euphrates, which tended to divide and embitter political life; the problem of relations with the Kurds, some of whom desired a state of their own, and with other minorities like the Assyrians; the complicated task of reform in land tenure and of improvement in agriculture, irrigation, flood control, public services and communications. As yet the Government itself consisted of little more than a façade of democratic forms concealing a world of faction and intrigue. The realities of the political scene were a xenophobe press often ill-informed and irresponsible; "parties" better described as cliques gathered around prominent personalities; a small ruling class of tribal sheikhs; landowners; and the intelligentsia—lawyers, students, journalists, doctors, ex-officers—frequently torn by sharp rivalries. It is not surprising, therefore, that the first years of full independence showed a rather halting progress towards efficient rule. The dangerous nature of the tensions inside Iraq was revealed in the Assyrian massacre of 1933 carried out by troops of the Iraq army. Political intrigue from Baghdad had much to do with the outbreak of tribal revolt along the Euphrates in 1935/36. The army crushed the insurrection without much trouble and then, under the leadership of General Bakr Sidqi and in alliance with disappointed politicians and reformist elements, brought about a *coup d'état* in October 1936. The new régime failed to fulfil its assurances of reform, its policies alienated the tribal chieftains and gave rise to serious tensions even within the armed forces, tensions which led to the assassination of Bakr Sidqi in August 1937.

Of vast importance for Iraq was the rapid development of the oil industry during these years. Concessions were granted in 1925, 1932 and 1938 to the Iraq, Mosul and Basra Petroleum Companies. Oil had been discovered in the Kirkuk area in 1927 and by the end of 1934 the Iraq Petroleum Company was exporting crude oil through two 12-inch pipelines, one leading to Tripoli and the other to Haifa. Exploitation of the Mosul and Basra fields did not begin on a commercial scale until after World War II.

In 1937 Iraq joined Turkey, Persia and Afghanistan in the Sa'dabad Pact, which arranged for consultation in all disputes that might affect the common interests of the four states. A treaty signed with Persia in July 1937 and ratified in the following year provided for the specific acceptance of the boundary between the two countries as it had been defined in 1914. Relations with Britain deteriorated in the period after 1937, mainly because of the growth of anti-Zionist feeling and of resentment at British policy in Palestine. German influence increased very much at this time in Iraq, especially amongst those political and military circles associated with the army group later to be known as the Golden Square. Iraq severed her diplomatic connections with Germany at the beginning of World War II, but in 1941 the army commanders carried out a new *coup d'état*, establishing, under the nominal leadership of Rashid 'Ali al-Gaylani, a régime which announced its non-belligerent intentions. A disagreement over the passage of British troops through Iraq left no doubt of the pro-German sympathies of the Gaylani government and led to hostilities that ended with the occupation of Basra and Baghdad in May 1941. Thereafter Iraq co-operated effectively with the Allied war effort and became an important base from which aid was sent northward through Persia to Russia. In 1943 Iraq declared war on the Axis powers and in 1945 signed the Charter of the United Nations.

Iraq, during the years after World War II, was to experience much internal tension and unrest. Negotiations with Britain led to the signing at Portsmouth in January 1948 of a new Anglo-Iraqi agreement designed to replace that of 1930 and incorporating substantial concessions, amongst them the British evacuation of the airbases at Shu'ayba and Habbaniya and the creation of a joint board for the co-ordination of all matters relating to mutual defence. The animosities arising from the situation in Palestine called forth riots at Baghdad directed against the new agreement with Britain, which were sufficiently disturbing to oblige the Iraqi Government to repudiate the Portsmouth settlement.

ARAB-ISRAEL WAR 1948

With anti-Jewish and anti-Western feeling so intense, it was inevitable that troops should be sent from Iraq to the Arab-Israeli war which began on May 15th, 1948. The Iraqi troops shared in the hostilities for a period of just over two months, their participation terminating in a truce operative from July 18th. Their final withdrawal from Palestine did not commence, however, until April 1949. Subsequently, there was a considerable emigration of Jews from Iraq to Israel, especially in the years 1951-52.

The expense of the war against Israel, bad harvests, the general indigence of the people—all contributed to bring about serious tensions resulting in rioting at Baghdad in November 1952 and the imposition of martial law until October 1953. None the less, there were some favourable prospects for the future—notably a large expansion of the oil industry. New pipelines were built to Tripoli in 1949 and to Banias in Syria in 1952; the oil-fields of Mosul and Basra were producing much crude petroleum by 1951-52. A National Development Board was created in 1950 and became later, in 1953, a national ministry. An agreement of February 1952 gave to the Iraq Government 50 per cent of the oil companies' profits before deductions for foreign taxes. Abundant resources were thus available for development projects of national benefit (e.g. the flood control and irrigation works opened in April 1956 on the Tigris at Samarra and on the Euphrates at Ramadi).

THE BAGHDAD PACT

Iraq, in the field of foreign relations, was confronted during these years with a choice between the Western powers, eager to establish in the Middle East an organized pattern of defence, and the Soviet Union, entering at this time into a diplomatic propaganda and economic drive to increase her influence in the Arab lands. Baghdad, in February 1955, made with Ankara an alliance for mutual co-operation and defence. Britain acceded to this pact in the following April, agreeing also to end the Anglo-Iraqi agreement of 1930 and to surrender her air bases at Shu'ayba and Habbaniya. With the adherence of Pakistan in September and of Iran in October 1955 the so-called Baghdad Pact was completed: a defensive cordon now existed along the southern fringe of the Soviet Union. It was resolved, in November 1955, to form a permanent Council of the Baghdad Pact and, in April 1956, to create an organization which would counter Communist penetration and activities in the Middle East. The U.S.A. also declared its wish to enter into close political, military, economic and technical liaison with the Council of the Baghdad Pact and its subordinate committees.

CONSEQUENCES OF THE SUEZ CRISIS

The outbreak of hostilities between Israel and Egypt on October 29th, 1956, and the armed intervention of British and French forces against Egypt (October 31st–November 6th) led to a delicate situation in Iraq, where strong elements were still opposed to all connections with the Western Powers. Iraq, indeed, broke off diplomatic relations with France on November 9th and announced that, for the immediate future at least, it could give no assurance of taking part in further sessions of the Council of the Baghdad Pact, if delegates from Britain were present.

The attitude of the Baghdad Government during the Suez crisis had provoked unrest in Iraq. Disturbances at Najaf and Mosul resulted in some loss of life. Student demonstrations against the Anglo-French intervention in Egypt and the Israeli campaign in Sinai led the Iraqi Government to close colleges and schools. Martial law, imposed on October 31st, 1956, was not raised until May 27th, 1957.

The tension born of the Suez crisis persisted for some time to come. President Eisenhower, concerned over the flow of Soviet arms to Syria and Egypt, sought from Congress permission to use the armed forces of the United States to defend nations exposed to danger from countries under the influence of international communism. He also requested authorization to disburse 200 million dollars in economic and military aid to the Middle East states prepared to co-operate with the West. This programme received the formal approval of the Congress and Senate of the United States in March 1957. On March 16th the U.S.A. pledged some $12,500,000 of the funds available under the "Eisenhower Doctrine" to the Muslim members of the Baghdad Pact and also made it known that it would participate actively in the work of the military committee of the Pact.

RELATIONS WITH SYRIA AND JORDAN

At the time of the Suez crisis there had been sharp tension between Iraq and Syria. Pumping-stations located inside Syria and belonging to the Iraq Petroleum Company were sabotaged in November 1956 with the result that Iraq suffered a large financial loss through the interruption in the flow of oil to the Mediterranean coast. Not until March 1957 did Syria allow the Iraq Petroleum Company to begin the repair of the pipelines.

Since the Suez crisis of 1956 troops of Iraq and Syria had been stationed in Jordan as a precaution against an Israeli advance to the east. Iraq, in December 1956, announced that her troops would be withdrawn; the Syrian forces, however, still remained in Jordan. The fear that Syria might intervene in favour of the elements in Jordan opposed to King Hussein brought about further recriminations between Baghdad and Damascus. The danger of an acute crisis receded in April 1957, when the U.S.A. declared that the independence of Jordan was a matter of vital concern and underlined this statement by sending its Sixth Fleet to the eastern Mediterranean.

THE ARAB FEDERATION, 1958

The creation of the United Arab Republic embracing Egypt and Syria induced Iraq and Jordan to join together in the so-called Arab Federation on February 14th, 1958. The articles of federation allowed King Faisal of Iraq and King Hussein of Jordan to retain their sovereign power over their respective territories, but envisaged the unification of their armed forces, foreign policies, diplomatic corps, educational systems and customs administration. Members chosen in equal numbers from the Parliaments of Iraq and Jordan would unite to form a Federal Legislature. The federal constitution was proclaimed in Baghdad and Amman on March 19th, 1958. At the beginning of August 1958 and as a result of events which had occurred meanwhile in Iraq (see below) King Hussein of Jordan made an official announcement, declaring that the Arab Federation was at an end.

OVERTHROW OF THE MONARCHY

King Faisal II, together with the Crown Prince of Iraq and General Nuri as-Sa'id, lost their lives in the course of a *coup d'état* begun on July 14th, 1958, by units of the Iraqi Army stationed near Baghdad. Iraq was now to become a Republic. Power was placed in the hands of a council of sovereignty exercising presidential authority and of a cabinet led by Brigadier 'Abd al-Karim Kassem, with the rank of Prime Minister. By the first week in August the new regime in Iraq had received international recognition from most states, whether of the East or of the West.

A struggle for power was now to develop between the two main architects of the July *coup d'état*—Brigadier (later General) Kassem, the Prime Minister, and Colonel Aref, the Deputy Premier and Minister of the Interior. Colonel Aref was associated with the influential Baath Party and had shown himself to be a supporter of union between Iraq and the United Arab Republic. Now, in September 1958, he was dismissed from his offices and, in November, was tried on a charge of plotting against the interests of Iraq. As reconstituted in February 1959 the new régime might be described as hostile to the United Arab Republic and inclined to favour a form of independent nationalism with left-wing tendencies.

On March 8th, 1959, Colonel Shawwaf, commanding the Iraqi forces at Mosul, banned a gathering of communist "peace-partisans". Violent conflict followed in the streets of Mosul between the Communists and the Arab nationalists. A rebel "government" was now established at Mosul which called for the support of the nationalist elements. On March 9th, however, the Iraqi Air Force bombed Mosul and the revolt was suppressed almost immediately.

General Kassem announced the withdrawal of Iraq from the Baghdad Pact on March 24th, 1959. Since the revolution of July 1958 Iraq's adherence to the Pact had been little more than nominal. One result of this withdrawal was the termination of the special agreement existing between Britain and Iraq since 1955 under the first article of the Baghdad Pact. On March 31st it was made known that the Royal Air Force contingent at Habbaniyah would be recalled.

PROBLEMS OF THE KASSEM RÉGIME

Earlier in 1959 the Communist elements in Iraq had been refused representation in the government. The Communists operated through a number of professional organizations and also through the so-called People's Resistance Force. Communist elements had infiltrated into the armed forces of Iraq and into the civil service. General Kassem now began to introduce measures which would limit Communist influence inside the government and administration of the country. In July 1959 fighting occurred at Kirkuk between the Kurds (supported by the People's Resistance Force) and the Turcomons, with considerable loss of life. General Kassem, accusing the Communists of being responsible for this outbreak, now disarmed and disbanded the People's Resistance Force. How strong the internal tensions had become in Iraq was underlined when, on October 7th, 1959, an attempt was made on the life of General Kassem.

There was friction, too, in the field of external relations. In December 1959 Iraq claimed the return to herself of certain waterways outside the Iranian ports of Abadan, Khorramshahr and Khorzabad on the Shatt al-Arab. Iranian sovereignty over these waterways had been recognized by Iraq in a treaty of July 1937. Iran now rejected the Iraqi demand for their return.

General Kassem, in June 1961, laid claim to Kuwait on the ground that Kuwait, in former times, had been included in the Ottoman province of Basra. Reports of Iraqi troop movements in the region of Basra induced the Shaikh of Kuwait to appeal for armed assistance from Great Britain. At the beginning of July 1961 the Security Council of the United Nations met to consider a complaint from Kuwait to the effect that Iraq was threatening her independence and territorial integrity.

REBELLION OF THE KURDS

Much more important for the government at Baghdad was the fact that, in March 1961, a considerable section of the Kurdish population in northern Iraq rose in rebellion under Mustafa Barzani, the President of the Democratic Party of Kurdistan—a party established in 1958 after the return of Barzani from an exile occasioned by an earlier unsuccessful revolt in 1946. The refusal of the central regime at Baghdad to grant the reiterated Kurdish demands for an autonomous status had contributed greatly to bring about the new insurrection. Mustafa Barzani in March 1961, proclaimed an independent Kurdish state. By September 1961 the rebels controlled some 250 miles of mountainous territory along the Iraqi-Turkish and Iraqi-Persian frontiers, from Zakho in the west to Sulaimaniya in the east. The Kurds were able to consolidate their hold over much of northern Iraq during the course of 1962. Military operations tended, in these years, to follow a regular pattern—a spring and summer offensive by the government forces, with the ground then won being lost again to the

Kurds in the autumn and winter. The Kurds used guerrilla tactics with much success to isolate and deprive of supplies the government garrisons in the north. By December 1963 Kurdish forces had advanced south towards the Khanaqin area and the main road linking Iraq with Iran. The government troops found themselves in fact confined to the larger towns such as Kirkuk, Sulaimaniya and Khanaqin. Negotiations for peace began near Sulaimaniya in January 1964 and led to a cease-fire on February 10th. The national claims of the Kurds were to be recognized in a new provisional constitution for Iraq. Moreover, a general amnesty would be granted by the Iraqi Government. The Kurdish tribesmen, however, refused to lay aside their arms until their political demands had been given practical effect. Despite the negotiation of this settlement it was soon to become clear that no final solution of the Kurdish problem was as yet in sight.

FALL OF KASSEM

A military coup carried out in Baghdad on February 8th, 1963, overthrew the régime of General Kassem, the General himself being captured and shot. The coup arose out of an alliance between nationalist army officers and the Baath Party. Colonel Aref was now raised to the office of President and a new cabinet created under Brigadier Ahmed Bakr. The Baath Party, founded in 1941 (in Syria) and dedicated to the ideas of Arab unity, socialism and freedom, drew its main support from the military elements, the intellectuals and the middle classes. It was, however, divided in Iraq into a pro-Egyptian wing advocating union with the United Arab Republic and a more independent wing disinclined to accept authoritarian control from Egypt. The coup of February 1963 was followed by the arrest of pro-Kassem and of Communist elements, by mass trials and a number of executions, by confiscations of property and by a purge of the officer corps and of the civil service.

A number of efforts were made, during the years 1963–65, to further the cause of Arab unification. An agreement signed at Cairo on April 17th, 1963, envisaged a federation of Egypt, Syria and Iraq. On September 2nd a communiqué stated that Syria and Iraq would create new committees to hasten defence co-operation between the two states. A Supreme Defence Council for the forces of Syria and Iraq was in fact established on October 8th with General Ammash (Defence Minister of Iraq) as Commander-in-Chief. On May 26th, 1964, Iraq signed with the U.A.R. an agreement establishing a Joint Presidency Council, with a secretariat at Cairo. Later in the same year, on October 16th, President Aref of Iraq and President Nasser of the U.A.R. made it known that a unified political command would be created between their two states. A further announcement of December 20th, 1964, revealed that such a unified command had in fact been brought into being. The subsequent course of events in 1965 was to demonstrate that these measures to advance the cause of Arab unification had little prospect of achieving much immediate practical effect.

MANOEUVRES OF THE BAATH PARTY

These same years saw in Iraq itself a conflict for control between the extremist and the more moderate Baath elements. At the end of September 1963 the extremists dominated the Baath Regional Council in Iraq. An international Baath Conference held at Damascus in October 1963 strengthened the position of the extremists through its support of a federal union between Syria and Iraq and its approval of more radical social and economic policies. A further Baathist conference at Baghdad in November 1963 enabled the moderates to elect a new Baath Regional Council in Iraq with their own adherents in control. At this juncture the extremists attempted a *coup d'état*, in the course of which air force elements attacked the Presidential Palace and the Ministry of Defence.

On November 18th, 1963, President Aref assumed full powers in Iraq, with the support of the armed forces, and a new Revolutionary Command was established at Baghdad. Sporadic fighting occurred (November 18th–20th) between the government troops and the pro-Baathist National Guard. A main factor in the sudden fall of the Baathists was the attitude of the professional officer class. Officers with Communist, Kassemite or pro-Nasser sympathies, or with no strong political views, or of Kurdish origin, had all been removed from important commands and offices. The privileged position of the National Guard caused further resentment in the army. The long drawn-out operations against the Kurds, the known dissensions within the Baathist ranks in Iraq and the intervention of Baath politicians from abroad in Iraqi affairs also contributed to discredit the extreme elements amongst the Baathists. On November 20th, 1963, a new Cabinet was formed at Baghdad, consisting of officers, moderate Baathists, independents and non-party experts.

THE ARAB SOCIALIST UNION

On July 14th, 1964, President Aref announced that all political parties would be merged in a new organization known as the "Iraqi Arab Socialist Union". At the same time it was revealed that all banks and insurance companies, together with thirty-two important industrial concerns, would undergo nationalization. The firms now nationalized included steel, cement and tobacco concerns, flour mills, food industries, building material firms and tanneries.

In July 1965 a number of pro-Nasser ministers handed in their resignations. At the beginning of September 1965 a new administration came into being with Brigadier Aref Abd al-Razzaq as Prime Minister. The Brigadier, reputed to be pro-Nasser in his sympathies, attempted to seize full power in Iraq, but his attempted *coup d'état* failed and, on September 16th, he himself, together with some of his supporters, found refuge in Cairo. On April 13th, 1966, President Abd al-Salam Aref of Iraq was killed in a helicopter crash. His brother Major-General Abd al-Rahman Aref succeeded him as President with the approval of the Cabinet and of the National Defence Council. In late June 1966 Brigadier Aref Abd al-Razzaq, who had staged the unsuccessful *coup d'état* of September 1965, led a second abortive coup, which was foiled by the prompt action of President Aref.

KURDISH NATIONALISM

The war against the Kurds, halted only for a short while by the cease-fire of February 1964, dragged out its inconclusive course during 1964–66. Some of the fighting in December 1965 occurred close to the Iraq-Iran border, leading to a number of frontier violations which gave rise to sharp tension between the two states during the first half of 1966. In June of 1966 Dr. Abd al-Rahman al-Bazzaz, Prime Minister of Iraq since September 1965, formulated new proposals for a settlement of the conflict with the Kurds. Kurdish nationalism and language would receive legal recognition; the administration was to be decentralized, allowing the Kurds to run educational, health and municipal affairs in their own districts; the Kurds would have proportional representation in Parliament and in the Cabinet and the various state services; the Kurdish armed forces (some 15,000 strong) were to be dissolved. Mustafa Barzani, the Kurdish leader, declared himself to be well disposed towards these proposals.

This entente was implemented only to a limited extent. The cabinet formed in May 1967 contained Kurdish elements, and President Aref, after a visit to the north in late 1967, reaffirmed his intention to make available to the Kurds appointments of ministerial rank, to help with the rehabilitation of the war-affected areas in Kurdistan, and to work towards effective co-operation with the Kurds in the Government of Iraq. This state of quiescence was, however, broken in the first half of 1968 by reports of dissension amongst the Kurds themselves, with open violence between the adherents of Mustafa Barzani and the supporters of Jalal Talabani, who had co-operated with the Government.

RAPPROCHEMENT WITH IRAN

Relations with Iran, always strained, had not been helped by the Kurdish conflict. During the second half of 1966, however, there was a marked improvement in the relations between Iraq and Iran. Incidents on the common frontier of the two states died down with the lull in the fighting between Iraqi troops and the Kurdish insurgents. President Aref of Iraq made an official state visit to Teheran in March 1967. A communiqué of March 19th declared that the two countries had agreed to continue negotiations for a joint oil exploration in the Naft Khaneh and Naft-i Shah border regions. Details of agreements on other issues, e.g. navigation rights and the collection of tolls in the Shatt al-Arab, demarcation of the Gulf continental shelf (important for the control of potential oil resources) and the status of Iranian nationals in Iraq, would be worked out by a joint committee. A cultural and trade agreement was also to be concluded between the two states.

OIL DISPUTES AND THE JUNE WAR

The winter of 1966–67 witnessed a dispute between Syria and the Iraq Petroleum Company—a dispute which was to have a serious effect on the oil revenues accruing to Iraq. The government at Damascus claimed that it had not been receiving from the IPC the full amount of revenue due to it under an agreement reached in 1955. To compensate for the alleged loss of revenue, levied on oil carried across Syria from the IPC fields in northern Iraq to ports on the Mediterranean coast, the Damascus Government demanded large back payments, increased the transit charges, and envisaged also the imposition of a surcharge. The Iraqi Government was also considering a request to the IPC that oil production in Iraq be raised 10 per cent. It was embroiled, moreover, in a long argument with the IPC over concession areas confiscated from the company five years earlier, but as yet unsettled by the national oil organization created to take them over. On December 8th, 1966, Syria impounded the property of the Iraq Petroleum Company within its territories. The assets impounded embraced some 300 miles of pipeline, several pumping stations and the terminal installations at Banias on the coast of Syria. On December 12th–13th Iraqi oil ceased to flow across Syria to Banias and to Tripoli. Iraq was thus confronted with a potential loss of revenue amounting to about £8 million per month. Several delegations from Baghdad went to Damascus in order to urge that a settlement be found for the dispute. Not until the beginning of March 1967, however, was a new agreement signed between the IPC and the Syrian Government. It was announced early in May 1967 that the IPC had also reached agreement in principle with the Iraqi Government on the royalties payable for the first quarter of 1967, when the pipeline across Syria was out of use.

When the Arab-Israeli war broke out in June 1967, the movement of Iraqi oil was again affected. Problems connected with its production and export constituted a major preoccupation of the Baghdad Government during the period immediately following the war. Iraq had at the outset severed diplomatic relations with the U.S.A. and Britain after Arab charges that the two states had aided Israel in the war and she also banned the export of oil to them. When, at the end of June, supplies of Iraqi oil began to be moved once more from the pipeline terminals on the Mediterranean, this embargo remained. In August Iraq, Syria and the Lebanon resolved to allow the export of Iraqi oil to most of the countries of Europe, the United Kingdom being still subject, however, to the embargo.

Relations with the West improved slightly during the autumn and winter of 1967. The remaining oil embargoes were gradually removed, and in December General Sabri led a military delegation to Paris. This was followed by President Aref's official visit to France in February 1968, and in April France agreed to supply Iraq with 54 Mirage aircraft over the period 1969–73. In May diplomatic relations with the United Kingdom were resumed.

THE 1968 COUP AND ITS AFTERMATH

Throughout the first half of 1968 the régime conspicuously lacked popular support, being commonly thought to be both corrupt and inefficient, and the sudden bloodless *coup d'état* of July 17th did not surprise many observers. General Ahmed Hassan al-Bakr, a former Prime Minister, became President; the deposed President Aref went into exile and his Prime Minister, Taher Yahya, was imprisoned on corruption charges. The new government, though still composed of Baath Party members, was expected to follow a moderate line within the Arab context, and the coup elicited a hostile reaction from Cairo and Damascus. Two ministers were influential Kurds, which was also thought to be a significant development.

Nothing came of this, however, for on July 30th the entire cabinet was dismissed by the President, who accused it of "reactionary tendencies". He then appointed himself Prime Minister and Commander-in-Chief and chose a new cabinet in which Generals Hardan Takriti and Saleh Ammash (formerly Interior Minister) were seen as the other major figures.

During the second half of 1968 the internal political situation deteriorated steadily. By November there were frequent reports of a purge directed against opponents of the new régime, and freedom of verbal political comment seemed to have disappeared. Numerous Western teachers and professional people were expelled. A former Foreign Minister, Dr. Nasser al Hani, was found murdered, and a distinguished former Prime Minister, Dr. al Bazzaz, and other members of former governments were arrested as "counter-revolutionary leaders"; most were later given long jail sentences. Open hostilities with the Kurds broke out in October 1968 for the first time since the June 1966 ceasefire, and continued on an extensive scale throughout the winter. Early in March 1969 the rebels shelled the IPC's installations at Kirkuk, inflicting considerable damage. Iraqi army and air force attempts to enforce the writ of the Baghdad Government had little success; the régime claimed that the rebels were receiving aid from Iran and Israel. Fighting continued unabated through 1969, the Kurds demanding autonomy within the state and asking for UN mediation.

In January 1969 a special revolutionary court passed death sentences on fourteen men accused of espionage for Israel and of seeking to overthrow the régime. Their execution and the subsequent much publicized display of their corpses in Baghdad and Basra aroused world-wide comment. Particular attention was drawn to the fact that nine of the executed men were Jewish, and to the various restrictions imposed on the Jewish community. The régime denied all accusations of anti-Semitism, and it was noted that all eight of a further group of Iraqis convicted and executed on similar charges in February were Muslims. Some commentators saw the hangings as mainly intended as a warning for the régime's opponents. By the end of 1969 over fifty executions had taken place.

Nevertheless, it remained clear that the life for the Jewish minority in Iraq had become steadily more difficult since the rise of Zionism and the establishment of the State of Israel. The community numbered some 250,000 in 1939, widely spread throughout Iraq both geographically and occupationally; thirty years later estimates put its size at a mere 2,500 people, virtually confined to a ghetto in Baghdad. Large-scale emigration, mainly to Israel had taken place in the early 1950s.

In January 1970 a group of army and police officers attempted to overthrow the régime, but their plans were discovered and about twenty alleged conspirators were promptly executed, whilst numerous others were imprisoned. Iranian complicity in the plot was widely reported; Baghdad claimed that the U.S. and other "imperialist" powers were also involved.

SETTLEMENT WITH THE KURDS

The most important event of 1970 was the settlement with the Kurds when, in March, a fifteen-article peace plan was announced by the Revolutionary Command Council and the Kurdish leaders. The plan conceded that the Kurds should participate fully in the Government; that Kurdish officials should be appointed in areas inhabited by a Kurdish majority; that Kurdish should be the official language, along with Arabic, in Kurdish areas; that development of Kurdish areas should be implemented; and that the provisional constitution should be amended to incorporate the rights of the Kurds.

The agreement was generally accepted by the Kurdish community and fighting ceased immediately. The war had been very expensive for Iraq, in terms of both lives and money, and it had seriously delayed the national development programme. It had also absorbed a large part of Iraq's army, which consequently became available for service on Israel's eastern front—joining the Iraqi force already stationed in Jordan—or for defensive duties on the Iranian frontier.

Although Mustafa Barzani retained his 15,000 troops as an official Iraqi frontier force, the legal status of Kurdistan still remained to be settled. A census should have been held to determine which parts of northern Iraq had a predominantly Kurdish population to qualify for the promised autonomy, but this was postponed. The Kurds claimed that this was to allow Arabs to emigrate to the rich oil-bearing area of Kirkuk. The Government, on its side, pointed to the thousands of Kurds who returned from Iran when hostilities ceased.

The Kurdish settlement, although not entirely satisfactory, did introduce an element of stability into life in Iraq and allowed a number of reforms to be initiated. In October 1970 the state of emergency, in operation almost continuously since July 1958, was lifted. Many political detainees, including former ministers, were released. Censorship of mail was abolished at the end of the year, having lasted for over thirteen years, and a month later the censorship of foreign correspondents' cables was brought to an end after a similar period.

At the same time, however, the Government maintained its ruthless attitude towards possible new opponents. Salah Umar Ali, Minister of Information and Culture and member of the Council of Command of the Revolution was dismissed in July 1970; Vice-President Hardan al Takriti in October. Both dismissals arose from internal policy differences, and only limits of the wranglings inside the Baath Party at the time reached the outside world. "Reactionaries" and communists alike were the victims of press campaigns or purges. The reported drive against communists in southern Iraq in January 1971 prompted adverse press comment in the Soviet Union, especially when two detained members of the Iraq Communist Party died in a Baghdad prison.

Kurdish unity was boosted in February 1971 by the decision of the Kurdish Revolutionary Party to merge with the Kurdish Democratic Party of Mustafa Barzani and in July 1971 a new provisional constitution was announced, which embodies many of the points contained in the 1970 settlement. The Kurds were directed by the Supreme Committee for Kurdish Affairs to give up their arms by August 1971 and the situation in the north continued to be normal.

Evidence of unrest, however, was growing both in Kurdistan and in the Government itself. In July 1971 an attempted coup by army and air force officers was put down by the Government but dissatisfaction continued to be reported. The Kurds were beginning to show discontent with the delays in implementing the 1970 agreement. Their demand for participation in the Revolutionary Command Council was refused and in September 1971 an attempt was made on Barzani's life. Also in September, while President Bakr was in hospital, another coup was said to have been attempted but this was denied. Vice-President Salih Mahdi Ammash and the Foreign Minister, Abd-al-Karim Shaikhli, were dismissed soon afterwards, indicating the extent of the power struggles within the Council.

THE CONTINUING KURDISH PROBLEM

During 1972, possibly because of increasing preoccupation with foreign affairs, dissension within the Government was less in evidence. Clashes with the Kurds, however, became more frequent and there was another plot to assassinate Barzani in July. The Baath Party's deteriorating relations with the Kurds brought a threat from the Kurdish Democratic Party to renew the civil war. One of the main Kurdish grievances was that the census agreed upon in 1970 had still not taken place. The two sides met to discuss their differences, the Kurdish side pointing to the unfulfilled provisions of the 1970 agreement and the Baath reiterating the various development projects carried out in Kurdish areas. In December 1972, a break appeared in the Kurdish ranks when it was reported that a breakaway party was to be set up in opposition to Barzani's party.

FOREIGN RELATIONS 1968-71

The more radical section of the Arab world had initially greeted the July 1968 coup with disfavour and the new régime was at pains to prove itself as militant an exponent of Arab nationalism as its predecessor. The régime gradually became an accepted member of the nationalist group, but there was some Arab criticism of its policies, notably the public hangings and their effect on world opinion. In March 1969, a joint Eastern Command was established comprising Jordan, Syria and Iraq. This was made possible by changes in the Syrian leadership in the spring of 1969, the Damascus régime having previously had very poor relations with Iraq.

Like Algeria, on the opposite flank of the Arab world, Iraq took a hard line on the Palestinian problem (having moved substantial forces into Jordan on the outbreak of war in 1967). All peace proposals—American, Egyptian and Jordanian—were rejected. In theory total support was given to the Palestine liberation movement but, despite a threat to the Jordanian Government at the beginning of September 1970 to intervene in Jordan on behalf of the Palestinian guerrillas, the Iraqi forces stationed there did not take part in the fighting. In January 1971, most of Iraq's 20,000 troops were withdrawn from both Jordan and Syria. In March it was reported in Cairo that Iraq's monthly contribution to the Palestine Liberation Army had ceased. Iraq's attitude to Middle East peace proposals opened up a rift with Egypt even before President Nasser's death and her contempt for the proposed Egypt-Libya-Syria federation, as well as for any negotiated settlement with Israel, kept her well isolated from Egypt and almost all the other Arab states. In July 1971 there were signs that Iraq wished to reduce her isolation, offering to co-operate again with the Arab states if they abandoned attempts to negotiate with Israel, but the renewal of hostilities between the Jordanian Government and the guerrillas caused a break in relations with Jordan. Iraq closed the border, called for Jordan's expulsion from the Arab League and banned her from participating in the Eighth International Baghdad Fair. Sudan broke off relations after Iraq's recognition of the short-lived revolutionary take-over at the end of July 1971 and there were differences with Syria. A certain rapprochement was, however, achieved with Kuwait.

Meanwhile, relations with Iran continued to be poor. Iraq frequently accused the Teheran Government of assisting the Kurdish rebellion and had responded by mass expulsions of Persians resident in Iraq. In April 1969 the Shatt al-Arab waterway again caused a minor confrontation. Iraq has benefited by a 1937 treaty (engineered by the British Government which then effectively controlled Iraq, but not Iran) which gave it control of the waterway. Iran tried to force a re-negotiation of the treaty by illegally sending through vessels flying the Iranian flag. Being unwilling (or politically unable) to yield any of its sovereignty, and unable to challenge Iran militarily, Iraq was obliged to accept this situation. Iraq proposed referring the dispute to the International Court of Justice, but Iran rejected the suggestion. Minor border clashes between the two sides' forces continued to occur sporadically. The Shah's Government was generally thought to have been a party to the attempted coup in January 1970, some of whose leaders were apparently in exile in Teheran. In December 1970, it was the turn of the Iranians to accuse Iraq of sponsoring an attempt to stage a coup in Teheran. Not surprisingly, the two countries were also divided on policy towards the Gulf States. Iraq broke off diplomatic relations with Iran (and Britain) after Iran's seizure of the Tumb Islands in the Persian/Arabian Gulf in November 1971. The deportation of ever larger numbers of Iranians from Iraq was reported at the end of 1971 and their expulsion continued into 1972.

Relations with the Western world, and the U.S.A. in particular, remained poor, several people arrested or expelled in late 1968 being accused of spying for the Americans. The friendship with the Soviet Union remained the major factor in Iraq's foreign policy, particularly since the U.S.S.R. was supplying the bulk of Iraq's military equipment. Partly as an extension of this friendship and partly as a gesture of disapproval for the German Federal Republic's relationship with Israel, Iraq recognized the German Democratic Republic at ambassador level in May 1969.

THE PROBLEM OF OIL

Relations between the Government and the IPC had continued to be strained, the Government continually maintaining its intention of eventually exploiting its own oil resources. An agreement reached in March 1972 provided for a 20 per cent Government participation in the concessions of the Iraq, Basra and Mosul Petroleum Companies but the details of the agreement were left for further negotiation. The North Rumeila field, expropriated from the IPC in 1962, started production in April 1972, its development having been financed by a Russian loan. Nevertheless, Iraq was still dependent on Western oil interests and the Government was anxious that output should be maintained at a high level in order to safeguard revenues. Thus the cutback in production from the northern oilfields in early 1972 caused the Government to protest. In June 1972 IPC's interests were nationalized and the company immediately announced that it would take legal action to prevent the marketing of the oil.

It had been assumed that Iraq's oil exports would be very seriously affected by the difficulties of finding markets for oil after the nationalization. In the event, Iraq was able to make a number of agreements almost immediately for the sale of oil. Among them were, as might have been expected, a number of barter deals with Eastern Bloc countries and the Soviet Union, and several agreements to repay loans in crude oil.

Immediately after the break with IPC, Iran concluded an agreement with France for the sale of 23.75 per cent of oil from the nationalized Kirkuk field. This was, the Government explained, in token of France's continued friendly attitude towards the Arab World. Contacts were also made with Spain, Italy, Greece, India, Japan and Brazil. By the end of 1972 it was clear that Iraq was maintaining sales, although the situation was marred by a dispute over transit dues for use of the IPC pipeline which Syria had nationalized on June 2nd, 1972. Syria was insisting on higher rates than those originally paid by IPC and an agreement was only reached in January 1973.

Meanwhile, contacts between IPC and the Government to determine compensation had continued, and IPC had repeatedly postponed its deadline for beginning legal proceedings. With the mediation of Nadim Pachachi of OPEC and Jean Duroc-Danner of CFP, an agreement was finally reached on February 28th, 1973. The company agreed to settle Iraqi claims for back royalties by paying £141 million, and to waive its objections to Law No. 80 under which the North Rumeila fields were seized in 1961. The Government agreed to deliver a total of 15 million tons of crude from Kirkuk, to be loaded at Eastern Mediterranean ports, to the companies as compensation. The Mosul Petroleum Company agreed to relinquish all its assets without compensation and the Basrah Petroleum Company, the only one of the group to remain operational in Iraq, undertook to increase output from 32 million tons in 1972 to 80 million tons in 1976. This agreement was regarded on the whole as a victory for the Iraqi Government, although the companies were by no means net losers by it.

With the IPC dispute out of the way, Iraq showed its unwillingness to continue indefinitely with exporting oil on a barter basis to the Eastern Bloc countries. The Government has made it clear that it will press for a cash basis to future agreements.

FOREIGN RELATIONS FROM 1972

The nationalization of IPC brought expressions of approval from a number of countries, including Arab States and the Soviet Union. The 15-year friendship treaty with the Soviet Union, signed in March 1972, was ratified in July and Iraq's relations with the Eastern Bloc states continued to be good. President Bakr visited Moscow in September for talks on increased economic and military aid and in October Iraq applied to join COMECON. Despite this, however, the Government was well aware of the dangers of too close and exclusive a relationship with the Soviet Bloc. France was specifically singled out as the Western country most friendly towards the Arabs and the President's fourth anniversary speech in July revealed that Iraq would not be unwilling to open up friendly relations with Western countries. Although diplomatic relations with the United States were still severed, the U.S.A. established an "interests section" in Baghdad.

The beginning of 1973 saw a number of disputes between Iraq and its immediate neighbours. Continuing strained relations with Iran found expression in border clashes. In February, a great sensation was caused by the discovery of arms in Iraq's Islamabad embassy. This led to a temporary severance of diplomatic relations with Pakistan and there were reports that the arms were intended either for Baluchistan or for rebels within Iran.

In March 1973, there was a clash with Kuwait, arising out of Iraq's desire to safeguard the military base at Um Qasr and the narrow oil export routes via the Gulf. Iraqi forces occupied the border post of Sameta but later withdrew.

In July 1973 an abortive coup took place, led by the security chief, Nazim Kazzar, in which the Minister of Defence, General Hammad Shehab, was killed.

ECONOMIC SURVEY

Iraq is traditionally an agricultural country, but its economic development has been largely attributable to its oil industry, which accounts for four-fifths of the country's foreign exchange receipts (and over nine-tenths of its export earnings), two-thirds of government revenue and one-fifth of gross domestic product. Accordingly Iraq's chief opportunity for development consists in the large revenues accruing from the operations of the oil companies in her territory. These revenues were stagnant in the early sixties at ID120–135 million but in the year ending March 31st, 1971 they had risen to ID230 million and for the year to March 31st, 1972, oil revenues have been estimated at ID354 million. This rapid rise is attributed to revisions to agreements with the oil companies together with a sharp increase in production. The improvement in oil revenues was short-lived, however, for on June 1st, 1972, the long-standing disputes between Iraq and the oil companies culminated in the nationalization of the assets of the Iraq Petroleum Company (IPC) the largest producing company in Iraq.

The nationalization move and the events leading up to it resulted in a severe loss of production throughout 1972 and necessitated a temporary curtailment of the development programme. The programme was reinstituted on the announcement of the settlement of the dispute on February 28th, 1973. The terms of the agreement are expected to increase oil receipts to at least ID500 million by 1976. Iraq's economic potential remains great for alone of the oil-producing countries of the Middle East she has enough land and water to enable her to spend her oil revenue in a productive manner.

Iraq is also an underpopulated country which, according to both historical evidence and present estimates of possible expansion could support a population of, perhaps, twice the size of her present ten million. She has millions of acres of cultivable land that could be irrigated from the generous (though in the past dangerously undisciplined) waters of the Tigris and the Euphrates.

These great advantages have indeed certain limitations placed upon them by the nature of the country and the degree of social evolution attained by its people. Salination of the soil and the spreading of malaria as a result of big irrigation projects are dangers that have to be guarded against. The two great rivers, the Tigris and Euphrates, which must be the basis of the country's entire system of irrigation, are, in the words of Lord Salter "temperamental and difficult to control". In addition, the country, with the exception of its northern area, is extremely flat and only a little above sea-level. This makes drainage and irrigation difficult and explains why most of the land at present consists largely of either desert or swamps. On the human side there may be a shortage of labour, and, particularly at the present moment, of the skilled labour that will be required to accomplish and operate the vast and up-to-date schemes of agricultural and industrial development that are contemplated or actually in process of execution.

The total population was estimated at 9.75 million in mid-1971, mostly living in the alluvial plain of the Tigris and Euphrates or the foothills of the north-east. Between 1965 and 1971 the population increased by 3.3 per cent annually. The working population was estimated at 3 million in 1970. Though many women work in agriculture, women are not generally employed elsewhere and at the present time cannot be regarded as making a substantial contribution to the non-agricultural labour force. Some idea of the employment situation may be formed from the table in the Statistical Survey.

Iraq's gross domestic product rose from ID 826 million in 1964 to ID 1,039 million in 1969, the latest year for which detailed estimates are available. This increase represents an annual average growth of 5.8 per cent. Per capita G.D.P. amounted to 107 dinars in 1969.

The currency unit of Iraq is the dinar (of 1,000 fils). Iraq left the Sterling Area in 1959 but the dinar was maintained at parity with the pound until the U.K. devaluation of November 1967, which Iraq did not follow. The dinar remained at a par rate equal to U.S. $2.80 until the currency realignment of December 1971 when, with its gold parity unchanged, it was effectively revalued by 8.57 per cent against the U.S. dollar to a new par of $3.04. As a result of the international currency crisis in February 1973 the Iraqi dinar was further revalued by 11.2 per cent against the U.S. dollar to a new par of $3.38.

AGRICULTURE

Agriculture is the main source of employment and, next to oil, the most important sector. The country's latest development plan (1970–74) gives high priority to agriculture; the aim is to produce an agricultural surplus for export by reducing dependence on weather conditions and solving the salinity problems which affect irrigated land. Iraq has a total area, including territorial waters and counting half the neutral zone, of 438,446 square kilometres. Of this the North Desert, South Desert and Al-Jazira Desert comprise about 200,000 square kilometres, so that the total area of the fourteen Liwas (administrative units) of urban and agricultural land into which the country is divided is 238,000 square kilometres, or 95,000,000 dunums. At present about 23 million dunums of this total are utilized for agricultural purposes.

The land tenure system is extremely complex, embracing privately owned land, public land (mainly desert), waqfs (religious endowments), and three types of government-owned land. By far the greater part of registered land is that which is government-owned and previously without established tenancy.

The effect of the land registration programme, which lasted from 1932 until 1958, was to create a large landowner class and a landless peasantry. Despite the fertility of many areas of the country, the development of agricultural techniques and productivity has been inhibited by the lack of security in rural areas arising from the disruptive activities of large landowners and, more recently, the land reform agencies.

The first attempts to reform the system of land tenure resulting from the 1932 legislation concentrated upon the distribution of government land among peasant smallholders with the aim of creating communities of landowners with an improved standard of living and practising agriculture by modern methods. In October 1958 the Government announced a new and more radical land reform project. This provided for the break-up of large estates whose owners were to be compelled to forfeit their "excess" land to the Government which would redistribute the land to new peasant owners. Under the terms of the reform the largest holding permitted on flow-irrigated land is 1,000 dunums (about 600 acres), on land watered by rainfall it is 2,000 dunums. The estates broken up were to be allotted to farmers in holdings of a maximum of 60 or 120 dunums, according to the type of land, and the formation of agricultural co-operatives was planned to help the new owners with capital, machinery and technical advice. Landowners losing land were to be compensated in state bonds (in 1969 all the state's liabilities to recompense landowners were cancelled). It was hoped that the reform would take only five years to complete but the application of the law was initially mismanaged and the expropriation of land consistently ran ahead of the ability of the administration to distribute it. By the end of 1972 some 4.73 million dunums had been requisitioned from landlords and distributed to 100,646 families, but considerable areas of land remain awaiting distribution.

Meanwhile, in 1967, plans were drawn-up to re-invigorate the co-operative movement. At the end of 1965 there were still only 75 co-operative societies registered, with a membership of 12,464 persons; by 1969 there were 608 registered societies taking in a membership of 76,609. A new Agrarian Reform Law of 1970 strengthened the move towards co-operative agriculture and by the end of 1972 there were 1,049 societies and 145,000 members. More recently the Government has been experimenting with the creation of collective farms—for both ideological and practical reasons. At the beginning of 1971 there were 22 such units and at the beginning of 1972 there were 61. Membership of the collectives now totals some 8,400 families jointly owning 300,000 dunums. Although the Government expects all co-operative units to be converted eventually into collective farms, attention is currently being focused on areas of land reclamation and land resettlement outside the traditional farmlands, and the older co-operatives are being left to function.

The general system of cultivation is fallow farming and crop rotations are rare. Despite changes in recent years, the most common type of farm operation is by share tenancy, the farmer surrendering to the landowner a share of his crop—usually 50 per cent in return for pump irrigation, water and other facilities. Other forms of operation are: (1) plantation farming, when the landowner or tenant of a rented farm employs paid labour; and (2) individual peasant proprietorships, when the farmer owns or rents his land and works it himself with his family.

The farm worker is concerned primarily with subsistence and grows crops and keeps animals to provide for himself and his family. Cash crops are grown by plantation farmers and peasant proprietors. Types of agriculture vary considerably but the largest and most commonly grown crops are barley and wheat. Together with lentils, vetch and linseed they constitute the main winter crops. Normally Iraq produces an exportable surplus of barley, though in years of low rainfall barley exports are not possible. After several years poor harvest there was a successful cereal crop in 1972 with a total of 3.5 million tons of cereals being harvested of which 1.75 million tons were exported. Summer crops are much smaller but in recent years have all shown healthy increase in size. The principal summer crops include rice, dates, tobacco and sesame, and these are grown much more extensively where better irrigation is available, as in the northern zone between Fallujah, Baghdad and Diyalah. Among fruit trees the date palm is by far the commonest and the best. Year by year Iraq alternates with Egypt as the world's largest date-producing country. In 1972 Iraq exported 265,416 tons of dates earning the country ID8.1 millions; dates are, after oil, the biggest export earner. Also an agreement has been signed for 1,200 tons of Iraqi tobacco to be sold to Egypt. Cotton is also grown on a small scale in central Iraq. Around the major towns a comparatively sophisticated market gardening organization has developed.

Generally, agricultural output varies according to rainfall, flooding and political disturbances. In recent years harvests have proved poor, the weather has been unfavourable and fears of massive land collectivization by the Government have caused uncertainty, while the Government's promises of greatly increased aid for agricultural development have not been fulfilled.

Wheat and barley production have been falling in recent years, and the area under barley has contracted considerably. The average yield of wheat has fallen from 228.2 kg. per meshara in 1968 to 175.7 kg. per meshara in 1970. The average yield of barley fell from 274.6 kg. per meshara in 1968 to 253.6 kg. per meshara in 1970. As an indication of the problems of the agricultural sector, some 200,000 tons of Australian wheat was imported in 1971. However there was a good harvest in 1972 so no cereal imports were necessary—saving the country ID 8.78 million on the previous year's imports. The successful harvest is thought to be largely due to the new high yielding varieties of seed used. It is estimated that these new varieties were sown over 20,000 dunums in 1972, and it is hoped that they will be sown over some 420,000 dunums in the 1973 harvest and so increase the crop yield further. In the 1973 budget ID15 million were allocated to be spent on agriculture. These funds are to be concentrated on improving the level of mechanized farming, to extend the use of the higher yielding seeds and to expand the fishing industry.

RIVER CONTROL AND IRRIGATION

River control policy in Iraq has three main objects: the provision of water for irrigation, the prevention of devastating floods, and the creation of hydro-electric power. It is southern and central Iraq that are affected in all three cases, since northern Iraq is rain-fed and for the most part the terrain is unsuitable for large-scale irrigation from the stored water of major dams. Minor local reservoirs and tube wells are enough to supplement the rain in the north.

At present the main systems providing flow irrigation are based on the Euphrates (serving nearly 3 million dunums), the Tigris (1.7 million dunums), the Diyalah River and the Lesser Zab River. Pumps are used extensively along both the Euphrates and the Tigris. Four dams, barrages or reservoirs (at Samarra, Dokan, Derbendi Khan and Habbaniyah) provide security against flood dangers. When the waters of the Euphrates and Tigris are fully utilized through dams and reservoirs, the area of cultivated land in Iraq will be almost doubled.

Great importance has been placed on the country's need for improved irrigation and an agreement has been signed with the U.S.S.R. for joint co-operation in irrigation affairs. Soviet experts are studying the Bakhma, Hindujah, Haditha, Fallujah and Kirkuk irrigation projects. The current development plan envisages further outlays on a number of other major water storage and control schemes of which the most important are the Euphrates dam, the Himrin dam, the Eski-Mosul dam and the Bekhme dam, while work on smaller scale canal, drainage and diversion works will also form a continuing element in the overall water control programme. Recent irrigation schemes to have received funds from the Iraqi Government include the Eski-Kalat, the Kirkuk-Haiwijah and the Badrah, Jassan and Zarbatiyah irrigation projects. Construction of the Tharthar-Euphrates canal and the Halapcha storage schemes has begun. Work has begun on the lower Al-Khalis irrigation scheme at an estimated cost of ID21.3 million (half of which will be provided by the World Bank). An area of 362,000 dunums will be supplied with water and 50,000 peasant families will benefit from this scheme.

OIL

The oil industry is the country's principal source of wealth and provides the bulk of capital for all state and municipal industries. In 1970 Iraq was the eighth largest oil producer in the world. This production has hitherto come almost exclusively from the Iraq Petroleum Company (IPC) and its associated companies, the Mosul Petroleum Company and the Basra Petroleum Company. The IPC group represents a consortium of British, Dutch, French and American oil companies together with the Gulbenkian interest. Under an agreement signed on February 28th, 1973 the IPC group conceded the nationalization of its assets in Iraq with the exception of the BPC operation which remains independent for the present.

The major oil field previously controlled by the IPC group is at Kirkuk with subsidiary production from the Jambur and Bai Hassan fields. Export from these and from the small fields previously controlled by MPC at Ain Zalah and Butmah is by pipeline, through Syria and the Lebanon, to the port terminals of Banias (890 km. from Kirkuk) and Tripoli (854 km. from Kirkuk) on the East Mediterranean coast. The output of BPC is from its Rumaila and Zubair fields in southern Iraq and exports are piped to the Gulf and shipped from the deep water terminal at Khor al-Amaya and from Fao. There is also a pipeline from Kirkuk to Baghdad, completed in 1966, which carries natural gas and liquid petroleum gas for use in Baghdad's power stations and industries. Production from the state-owned North Rumaila field began in the second quarter of 1972 and the first full year's production was 4.3 million tons.

Of the total IPC group output in 1970, 73.3 million tons was exported (56.2 million tons by pipeline to the Mediterranean coast) and 3.3 million tons was delivered to oil refineries owned and operated by the Iraqi Government. Iraq's refinery capacity in 1969 was estimated at 5.1 million metric tons. In August of 1971 the Soviet Union undertook to construct a refinery in Mosul capable of handling 30,000 barrels a day.

The IPC concession in Iraq dates from 1925. Relations between the oil companies and the Government were first comprehensively formalized in 1952. The companies undertook to pay the Government 50 per cent of their theoretical profit (based on posted prices) as well as certain other revenues, and guaranteed revenue and production minima. In December 1961, after prolonged negotiations for a revision of concession agreements had broken down, the Government passed Law No. 80, under which the companies' area of operations was restricted to their producing oilfields, equivalent to less than 0.5 per cent of their previous area, and the remainder of their concessions withdrawn. Negotiations over the revision of Law No. 80 resulted in a draft agreement concluded in

1965, but never ratified, which reportedly provided for the oil companies to retain their current producing areas and as much acreage again (including the newly discovered North Rumaila field).

However, by Law No. 97 of 1967, the Government's oil policy changed direction. Under this law the Iraq National Oil Company (INOC), a state oil company formed in 1964, was given exclusive rights over all areas except those left to IPC in Law 80. INOC was to be allowed to operate jointly in association with foreign companies, if it wished, as long as no concession was awarded. Accordingly, a contract was signed between INOC and *l'Entreprise de Recherches et d'Activités Petrolières* (ERAP), a French state company. The French company acts as contractor in four areas where oil has not been proven. INOC will contribute financially only if oil is found. All oil will belong to INOC, while ERAP will be permitted to buy a share at a privileged price. ERAP began drilling in 1968 near Basra and has since discovered oil at Buzurgan, Abu Gharab and Siba. However, the development of these fields has been delayed for some two years by disputes between ERAP and the Iraqi Government. Negotiations on the price of the crude extracted by ERAP have now been resumed and an agreement seems more likely now that the IPC dispute has been settled.

Despite negotiations with several foreign companies, INOC finally announced, early in 1968, that it would develop the rich field of North Rumaila by itself. This field, discovered by IPC but expropriated under Law 80, is thought to be capable of 40 million tons per year. The Alrafidain Bank agreed to extend a loan of ID 6 million to INOC to finance the first stage of the exploitation of the field. Five major international companies are reported to be bidding for a contract worth up to $30 million to extend the terminal at Fao to cope with 40 million tons a year. In July 1969 the U.S.S.R. and Iraq signed an agreement under which Soviet aid worth some £28 million would be given to INOC to develop North Rumaila and other proven oilfields. In August 1971 a new protocol on economic and technical co-operation was signed in Moscow. It was agreed to proceed with the second stage of the North Rumaila field, so as to achieve an annual output of 18 million tons, to explore other new fields, and to link the Nahr Umr field to the pipeline from North Rumaila to Fao. The Soviet Union also agreed to participate in a major project to link the new fields in southern Iraq with the Mediterranean port-terminals by a pipeline of 1,250 km. in length and 48 inches in diameter; it has been suggested that the pipeline would have an annual capacity of 50 million tons and would cost some $420 million. In 1972 production began on the North Rumaila field, at an initial rate of 5 million tons a year. INOC has been active in the past year negotiating long term trade agreements for its crude oil output. New contracts of particular note include an agreement to supply India with a total of 112 million tons of oil over the twelve year period beginning in 1976. In addition Iraq has given India credits of $50 million in order to finance purchases of crude oil before the implementation of the major contract. Austria is to buy 4 million tons of crude over next 3 years at a value of £39 million. Spain has also agreed to buy 6 million tons at competitive prices over the next 3 years. These contracts are in addition to deals previously announced with the Soviet Union and other Eastern Bloc countries, Italy, Ceylon and Brazil.

Recent developments have included an agreement (February 1972) signed between INOC and an East German firm to allow some two-thirds of an ID 30 million loan from East Germany to be repaid in Iraqi crude oil. The loan is being used for a number of industrial projects in Iraq. A similar agreement was signed with the Romanian Government at the end of 1971. INOC secured a $35 million Romanian loan, bearing an interest rate of 2.5 per cent, to be repaid in oil in seven annual instalments. Romanian organizations will carry out oil exploration and exploitation operations, supply oil equipment and services, and assist in training Iraqi technicians. In northern Iraq the Hungarian organization Chemokomplex is drilling on the Jambur field, and INOC is itself drilling to the west of the North Rumaila field.

INOC's activities extend beyond the exploration for and production of crude oil. In 1972 it established a Directorate of Crude Oil Tankers as an autonomous company, to be responsible for the operation and management of a tanker fleet. Five of seven tankers ordered from Spanish yards have been delivered. A state-owned sulphur recovery plant has been operating at Kirkuk since 1968 producing 120,000 tons per year of sulphur from associated gas from the Kirkuk field. The by-product gases are sent by pipeline to Baghdad.

Total oil production in Iraq was 22 million tons in 1957 and 47.3 million tons in 1960. By 1970 output had reached 76.4 million tons, only marginally more than the previous year, but in 1971 it increased sharply to 83.8 million tons following agreements between the Government and the oil companies on higher production targets for the southern oilfields. A sharp decline in production in 1972 to an estimated 69 million tons was caused by the disputes between IPC and the Government. This 17 per cent decline was despite production of some 3 million tons from the new field at North Rumaila.

In February 1971 Iraq participated in the Teheran agreement (*see* p. 72 for full text) between the Western oil companies and the six oil-producing companies of the Gulf. The agreement provided for a 35 cents per barrel increase in posted prices on oil shipped from the Gulf as well as for a higher (55 per cent) tax rate on relevant company profits, and also incorporated escalation clauses to take account of the rise in the price of petroleum products on world markets and of changes in the terms of trade experienced by the oil-producing countries.

In June 1971 the Iraqi Government reached an agreement with IPC, after protracted negotiations, whereby the posted price of all Iraqi oil shipped from the Mediterranean terminals was to be raised;

additionally the tax rate on the companies operating in northern Iraq was also raised to 55 per cent, and the companies agreed to monthly instead of quarterly tax and royalty payments.

In January of 1972 the signatories of the Teheran agreement, meeting at Geneva, agreed to a further increase (of 8.57 per cent) in posted prices at the Gulf to offset the effect of the dollar devaluation that resulted from the currency realignment of December 1971. The postings for Iraqi and Saudi Arabian crude oil at East Mediterranean terminals were similarly increased. The additional payments will be linked to an index reflecting changes in the values of nine industrial countries' currencies and will vary with the appreciation or depreciation of the dollar as measured by this index. The oil producing countries later claimed payments in excess of this index which they contended did not sufficiently account for the effects on their revenue of the currency realignments of February 1973. The oil companies finally agreed to meet the full demands of the producing countries early in June 1973.

As a result of these agreements and the increased volume of output, the revenue from oil production accruing to the Iraqi Government has increased rapidly in the past few years. Total oil revenue in fiscal year ending March, 31st 1970 amounted to ID 169 million; in the year ending March 1971 it rose to ID230 million and for the year ending March 1972 oil revenue had increased sharply to an estimated ID354 million. Although oil receipts in 1972 were adversely affected by the disputes between Government and oil companies the settlement announced in February 1973 is expected to raise receipts to at least ID500 million by 1976.

The already poor relations between the Government and the oil companies deteriorated when the companies further cut back production in the northern fields by some 45 per cent in March and April compared with the two preceding months. IPC claimed that the cut-back was necessitated, for purely commercial reasons, by the widened cost differential between crude oil shipped from East Mediterranean and Gulf terminals which followed the June 1971 agreement on Mediterranean posted prices. Compared with an average difference in tax burden of around 35 cents per barrel between oil shipped through the Mediterranean and through the Gulf, the difference in freight rates is only some 10 cents per barrel in favour of the Mediterranean terminals. This difference was further widened by higher tax payments to Syria and the Lebanon for transit dues to East Mediterranean terminals.

This cut-back revived, with increased bitterness, the disputes which had continued since 1961, and on June 1st, 1972, the Iraqi Government announced that by decree Law No. 69 the assets of IPC had been nationalized. The Syrian Government then announced that it had similarly nationalized all IPC assets in Syria. After protracted negotiations an agreement was finally announced in Baghdad on 28th February, 1973 which settled all outstanding disputes between the Government and the IPC group. Under the settlement the IPC conceded the loss of its Kirkuk oilfields in return for a total of 15 million tons of crude oil, worth some £128 million, to be loaded at Eastern Mediterranean ports, free of all charges and at the rate of at least one million tons a month starting on March 1st, 1973. The IPC agreed to waive its objection to Law 80 under which the North Rumaila fields were seized in 1961 and also agreed to pay the Government the sum of £141 million as settlement of all Government claims on the group. The agreement further announced that the MPC had agreed to hand over all its assets and installations to the Government as of March 31st, 1973 without seeking any compensation.

The IPC pipeline and port facilities in the Lebanon were also scheduled to be handed over to the Iraq Government but Lebanon refused to allow this and a subsequent agreement, signed in Beirut on March 5th, 1973, provided for a Lebanese takeover of the pipeline and loading installations.

The terms of the agreement also require BPC, the only member of the IPC group to remain operational in Iraq, to increase output from the 1972 level of 32 million tons to 80 million tons in 1976. In addition BPC is to relinquish its concession in the Mosul field without compensation. It is likely that Iraq will acquire a 25 per cent stake in BPC rising to 51 per cent in 1982 thus staying in line with the recent participation agreements signed by the major international oil companies and the Gulf States. This is believed to be one of the reasons for the anxiety of BPC to increase production as rapidly as possible in order to reap the full benefits before the major share of profits goes to the State. Work on the BPC terminal facilities at Khar-al-Amaya has been speeded up so that facilities for the projected 1975 output of 65 million tons will be ready this year.

INDUSTRY

Iraq has not the same impelling reasons for rapid and large-scale industrialization as countries with a surplus and increasing population that is too large to be supported by agriculture. The policy of the Government and the Ministry of Planning aims therefore at an industrial development that will not be so accelerated as to outrun seriously the available surplus of skilled labour required. It also prescribes that the industries to be encouraged should be carefully selected as based upon domestic resources and assured of a domestic market.

Apart from oil (which stands in a category by itself) Iraq has few industries of any size. In greater Baghdad the larger enterprises are electricity and water supply, brick and cement manufacture. In addition there is a large number of smaller-unit industries concerned with food and drink processing (date-packing, breweries, etc.), cigarette-making, spinning and weaving, chemicals, furniture, shoe-making, jewellery and various metal manufacturers. The Government controls most of manufacturing industry and mining through the General Industrial Organization, set up in 1964. Most large current or planned projects are in the public sector but following government encouragement for private industry the Industrial Development Department announced that during the first six months of 1972, 51 schemes were given licences to operate involving a total private investment of ID6.5 million.

The industrial census of March 1966 showed that, of 1,742 manufacturing establishments, 276 were large-scale public entities and the remainder were small private workshops. Total civilian employment in 1967 was officially reported at 319,000. Government employment was 312,000, and of this total 165,000 were classified in the services sector.

Major state factories include a bitumen plant at Qaiyarah, south of Mosul, which produces 60,000 tons of asphalt per year and employs 250 workers; a £3 million textile factor at Mosul, equipped with 644 looms, employing 1,200 workers, and producing 25 million square yards per year of calico from locally grown cotton; and two cement factories, each with a daily output of 350 tons. Total cement output is some 1 million tons, which more than covers Iraqi demand. A sugar factory with an annual production of 35,000 tons is in production at Mosul and further expansion is planned. Two further plants at Kerbela and Sulaimaniyah are under construction. A fertilizer factor at Basra has an initial annual output of 120,000 tons of ammonium sulphate as well as uric and sulphuric acid. It uses sulphur from the Kirkuk plant and natural gas from the Rumaila field. Other projects include a paper board factory at Basra. A rayon plant at Hindiyah opened in 1968 and another is planned. Shoe and cigarette factories serve the domestic market. Special attention is being paid to the private sector in the four-year plan (1970–74) and to the development of the northern part of Iraq. Projects under construction include plants of fruit drying and processing dairy products and a cement works.

The Soviet Union has assisted with the construction of eleven factories, including a steel mill and an electrical equipment factory at Baghdad, a drug factory at Samarra and an agricultural machinery plant at Musayib. A large share of industrial development is expected to take place in co-operation with Eastern bloc countries and several agreements have been signed. These include loans from Bulgaria, to pay for complete industrial plants and technical aid in mineral exploration, which will be repaid in crude oil shipments, and a loan from Hungary, some two-thirds of which is also repayable in oil. The U.S.S.R. is to receive oil to the value of ID 50 million in return for services in connection with industrial projects and, on a similar contract, Czechoslovakia is to build an oil refinery at Basra. In addition, the U.S.S.R. has provided a ID 80 million loan to finance Russian-built projects including an oil refinery and pipeline, two hydro-electric power stations, a phosphate mine and a fertilizer plant, while contracts, each valued at ID 7 million have been signed under which the U.S.S.R. will provide agricultural and road-building equipment. In December 1972 an agreement was signed with the Soviet Union whereby the total amount of loans to Iraq will be repaid in oil (against the 70 per cent originally agreed).

Two trade agreements have been completed with China. Under the terms of the first, Iraq will supply 100,000 tons of sulphur each year over a five-year period while China will make available ID 14 million to Iraq for the purchase by China of 250,000 tons a year of chemical fertilizer from the Basra fertilizer plant. In 1971 the Kuwait Fund for Arab Economic Development promised a loan of ID 3.8 million to cover half the costs of an extension of cement works' capacity. Early in 1972, work on an extension to the Mosul textile mill was completed and the second phase of the Ramadi glass factory was commissioned.

There are deposits of iron ore, chromite, copper, lead and zinc in the north, where test drilling is now being carried out, and important deposits of limestone, gypsum, salt, dolomite, phosphates and sulphur have also been located. The main sulphur deposit, discovered at Mishraq in North Central Iraq, is to be developed by the state Iraq National Minerals Company, which awarded the contract to the Polish state firm, Centrozap. The plant was commissioned early in 1972; output will begin at a rate of 250,000 tons a year and a rate of 1.5 million tons annually is the eventual target. A large proportion of the electricity generated by the new hydroelectric station on the Samarra barrage will be utilized by the Mishraq sulphur complex; a power line costing ID 2.3 million will directly connect Samarra and Mishraq. Polish help will also be given to develop Iraqi phosphate deposits in return for phosphate fertilizers and crude oil deliveries to Poland.

Many new industrial plants have been started or are planned for the future. A steel rolling mill is to be constructed at Khor-Al-Zubair at a cost of ID 30 million. The planning board has given permission for a petrochemical plant at Basra which will produce 120,000 tons of plastic annually. This plant will use the by-product gas from crude oil production in Southern Iraq, most of which is now burnt off. The new sulphur plant at Kirkuk started production in May 1972 at a capacity of 400 ton/day. The sulphur output supplies the Basrah fertilizer plant, and the Hindujah artificial fibres factory. While desulphurized gas will be sent to al-Taji in dry gas and LPG form for domestic and industrial use. Gas will also be available for power stations and in other industry in Baghdad.

Along with growth in the industrial base there is a continuing increase in the generation and consumption of electricity. In the years 1953–65 consumption of electricity rose substantially from 343 to 1,200 million kWh. Consumption in Baghdad rose from 206.4 million kWh. in 1960/61 to 1,383.5 million kWh. in 1968/69. The capacity of the power station on the Lesser Zab, near Kirkuk, will eventually be raised to 150,000 kW., when it will supply Mosul, Kirkuk, Arbil and Sulaimaniyah. Baghdad's power station is similarly raising its capacity to 200,000 kW. There are other hydro-electric stations at Basra, and based on the Samarra barrage, and more are planned at Dokan and Derbendi.

The commercial banks (which were nationalized in 1964) provide short-term credit, while longer term credit and aid for industry and agriculture is provided by several state-owned agencies—the Industrial, Agricultural, Mortgage and Co-operative banks. The Industrial Bank, whose board is appointed by the Council of Ministers, is a shareholder in several large plants and in the private Light Industries Company which is establishing plants for the manufacture or assembly of kerosene heaters, cookers, radio sets, animal fodder, bicycles and electric wire.

COMMUNICATIONS

The Public Works Department is responsible for the control and maintenance of public roads in Iraq, but major road and bridge construction is the responsibility of the Ministry of Planning. The main artery runs from the Jordanian frontier through Baghdad to the Iranian border but the road system is under complete reconstruction with the assistance of a World Bank loan of $23 million as part finance for a $54 million building programme. In 1972 the Government announced schemes for 272 km. of major roadways to be built at a cost of ID 1.64 million. The 1973/74 investment programme envisages the construction of 10 bridges at a cost of ID 17.5 million and a road building programme of ID 6.25 million.

Iraq's main port is at Basra; a new port has been constructed at Um Qasr and also BPC is going ahead with building offshore and onshore loading facilities at the Khor-al-Amaya terminal. A new terminal is to be built at Fao at an estimated cost of ID 25 million to deal with the expected increase in INOC's output. The continuing dispute with Iran over the approaches to Basra on the Shatt el Arab river has made it increasingly necessary to develop Um Qasr as an alternative post and military base. Iraq has been extremely anxious to secure the approaches to Um Qasr which lies at the head of a lagoon whose entrance is controlled by Kuwait. River navigation is of some importance, particularly on the Tigris between Basra and Baghdad.

There are major international airports at Basra and Baghdad and civil airports at Mosul (which is being developed to take international services) and Kirkuk, as well as an IPC field at Kirkuk. A new airport is being constructed at Baghdad.

The Railways Administration is a semi-autonomous body operating under a Director-General who is responsible to a government-appointed board. The principal lines run from Baghdad through Mosul to Tel Kotchek (529 km.) and from Basra to Baghdad (569 km.). In 1971 work was completed, with Russian assistance, on the realignment and conversion of the latter to standard gauge. A line is being built to link Shaiba and Um Quasr and work is to begin on a line from Kirkuk to Salaimaniyah. Eventually the Government hopes to expand the railway system to provide links with Kuwait, Saudi Arabia, Lebanon and Iran.

Improvements are planned for the telecommunications system. The Government has been granted a World Bank loan of $27.5 million towards a major plan, costing $61 million, which includes the provision of subscriber-trunk-dialling services, a micro-wave link between major towns and the establishment of a satellite ground station.

FINANCE

Development spending is a potential cause of inflation but until the past three years the rate of price increase, as measured by available indices, was very modest. At the end of 1968 consumer prices were less than 3 per cent higher than their level of five years earlier. Since then prices have risen comparatively sharply, partly as a result of the poor performance of the agricultural sector, and by the first half of 1971 inflation was a cause of some concern to the Government, anxious for its political popularity. Increased imports and tighter price controls resulted in a fall in prices in the second half of 1971 and by the end of that year inflation appeared to be under control. The consumer price index stood at 127.5 in November 1972 showing an increase of 5.3 per cent on the 1971 level. The most recent statistics indicate that national income amounted to ID 909 million in 1969, having increased at an annual average rate of 6.3 per cent since 1965.

The budgeting procedure has been rationalized in recent years and a consolidated account consisting of the Ordinary Budget, the Development Plan Budget, and the Budget for the Autonomous Agencies, is now presented. Despite the receipt of 50 per cent of all state oil revenues the budget has tended to show a deficit. Total Government income for 1970–71 was approximately ID 287 million in the Ordinary Budget and ID 110 million in the Development Budget, together showing an increase of ID 55 million or 16 per cent over the previous year. This was mainly attributable to a rise in oil revenues. Total expenditure during 1970–71 was estimated at about ID 264 million in the Ordinary Budget and ID 202 million in the Development Budget. In the 1971–72 budget Government income was approximately ID 334 million in the Ordinary Budget.

On external account Iraq usually runs a deficit on trade (excluding oil) which is more than offset by foreign exchange earnings from the oil sector. The payments surplus generated by the oil industry is needed to meet payments on foreign borrowing for Iraq's development programme. A balance of payments surplus of ID 68 million has been estimated for the year 1970–71 and a strengthening external position is indicated by the rise in gold and foreign exchange reserves held by the Iraq Central Bank, from $462 million at end-1970 to $742 million in December 1972.

DEVELOPMENT AND PLANNING

The bulk of financing for development comes from the Government's oil revenues, supplemented by the net profits from government agencies and by external loans. In recent years Eastern bloc countries have been an increasingly important source of external finance; the Soviet Union has been the major lender here, but other communist countries have provided sizeable loans; an East German loan amounting to $84 million was granted in 1969 to be repaid over a twelve-year period at an interest rate of 2.5 per cent, in Iraqi commodities and crude oil. It will be used to finance cement, starch and sugar factories.

In 1970, the broad outlines of the five-year plan for the period 1970–74 were published. An annual growth rate in gross domestic product of 7.1 per cent was the target for the plan period; with agriculture growing at a rate of 5 per cent per annum and industry at 12 per cent. Emphasis was placed on the development of the agricultural sector (with a view to slowing down the drift to the towns). Total expenditure was estimated at around ID 1,000 million and of this central government investment was forecast at ID 537 million with the bulk (ID 490 million) coming from oil revenues. Total public sector investments were expected to account for some 75 per cent of the total expenditure in the plan period. During the dispute with the oil companies in 1972 and under the resulting austerity régime, the implementation of plans in the 1972–73 development programme was severely curtailed and current expenditure squeezed. The investment allocation for the financial year 1972–73 was cut from ID 242 million to ID 119 million. The settlement of the dispute with IPC has made this austerity unnecessary and the Government has announced a record State Budget for 1973–74 of ID 1,375 million with the investment allocation at ID 296 million. With oil income expected to be well in excess of ID 500 million by 1976 and with Iraq's foreign-exchange position strong, expenditure on development and imports in general is expected to increase substantially over the medium term.

STATISTICAL SURVEY

AREA AND POPULATION

Total Area	Arable	Population (1971)	Baghdad (capital)	Mosul	Basra
438,446 sq. km.	75,364 sq. km.	9,750,000	1,884,151*	343,121*	420,145*

* 1968 estimate.

A neutral zone of 7,000 sq. km. between southern Iraq and northern Saudi Arabia is administered jointly by the two countries. Nomads move freely through it, but there are no permanent inhabitants.

POPULATION BY PROVINCE (MUHAFADHA)
(1971)

Naynawa	839,047	Babil	.	531,490
Sulaimaniya	487,479	Kerbela	.	473,007
Arbil	432,430	Qadisiyah	.	413,141
Kirkuk	546,480	Maysan	.	356,007
Diyala	454,729	Dhiqar	.	529,207
Anbar	353,213	Basra	.	825,253
Baghdad	2,838,330	Muthanna	.	145,180
Wasit	364,813	Duhok	.	159,791

EMPLOYMENT
(1971)

Agriculture	1,434,700
Mining	16,500
Manufacturing	160,000
Electricity, Gas and Water	13,400
Construction	69,000
Commerce	155,000
Transport	154,000
Services	310,000
Others	280,000
Unemployed	166,500
Total Labour Force	2,759,100

IRAQ—(Statistical Survey)

AGRICULTURE

AREA AND PRODUCTION OF PRINCIPAL WINTER CROPS

Crop	1968–69 Area ('000 dunums)	1968–69 Production ('000 tons)	1969–70 Area ('000 dunums)	1969–70 Production ('000 tons)	1970–71 Area ('000 dunums)	1970–71 Production ('000 tons)
Wheat	6,645.6	1,183.1	7,034.1	1,235.6	3,793.2	822.3
Barley	3,381.0	963.2	2,690.4	682.2	1,584.3	432.4
Linseed	64.9	11.5	68.9	14.2	37.8	6.1
Lentils	39.0	6.5	42.1	4.5	33.5	3.9
Vetch (Hurtman)	3.4	0.8	37.8	0.9	26.9	0.6
Broad Beans	67.2	17.7	71.2	20.1	78.6	18.5

AREA AND PRODUCTION OF PRINCIPAL SUMMER CROPS

Crop	1969 Area ('000 dunums)	1969 Production ('000 tons)	1970 Area ('000 dunums)	1970 Production ('000 tons)	1971 Area ('000 dunums)	1971 Production ('000 tons)
Rice	558.7	284.2	298.0	180.1	436.3	306.7
Sesame	68.4	12.0	73.1	13.3	82.2	13.9
Maize	16.1	4.8	19.6	5.9	37.5	16.0
Green grams	53.5	9.0	61.3	12.9	61.0	10.0
Millet	5.7	1.3	11.0	2.8	22.3	4.8
Giant millet	12.5	2.4	17.2	5.4	44.4	13.3

Livestock (1970): Sheep 13,831,000; Goats 2,412,000; Cattle 1,830,000; Donkeys 566,000; Horses 124,000; Buffaloes 288,000; Camels 252,000; Chickens 5,677,000.

DATE CROP
(tons)

1966–67	1968–69	1969–70	1970–71
380,000	260,000	480,000	300,000

AREA AND PRODUCTION OF COTTON

	1969	1970	1971
Area (dunums)	87,900	134,600	135,600
Production (tons)	29,100	41,500	42,840

IRRIGATION

	1967–68	1968–69	1969–70	1970–71
Number of Pumps	11,612	13,066	13,769	14,135
Total Horse Power	328,680	357,099	366,751	350,335

IRAQ—(STATISTICAL SURVEY)

OIL
PRODUCTION OF CRUDE OIL
('000 long tons)

Company	1967	1968	1969	1970	1971	1972*
Iraq Petroleum Co. Ltd.	37,625	54,828	55,441	56,893	51,100	
Basra Petroleum Co. Ltd.	20,049	16,511	16,587	17,067	30,100	69,000
Mosul Petroleum Co. Ltd.	1,264	1,281	1,281	1,281	1,300	
Total	58,938	72,620	73,309	75,241	82,500	69,000

* estimate.

INDUSTRY
('000 units)

	1965	1966	1967	1968	1969
Leather tanning:					
Upper leather (sq. ft.)	5,300.6	6,140.0	6,110.9	6,738.6	n.a.
Toilet Soap (tons)	4.6	7.2	5.9	7.6	7.3
Vegetable oil (tons)	46.7	43.1	50.2	52.9	58.0
Woollen textiles:					
Cloth (metres)	902.4	937.7	87.9	835.6	n.a.
Blankets (number)	461.7	510.9	506.8	447.5	611.0
Cotton textiles (metres)	32,541.7	33,131.9	34,046.5	31,805.7	32,447.0
Beer (litres)	4,803.1	5,639.8	5,523.2	6,064.1	n.a.
Matches (gross)	1,102.5	1,031.0	1,275.3	1,371.0	1,686.4
Cigarettes (million)	5.1	5.2	4.9	5.1	5.2
Shoes (pairs)	5,203.6	5,363.5	5,145.0	5,619.5	n.a.

FINANCE

1,000 fils = 20 dirhams = 5 riyals = 1 Iraqi dinar (I.D.).
Coins: 1, 5, 10, 25, 50 and 100 fils.
Notes: 250 and 500 fils; 1, 5, and 10 dinars.
Exchange rates (March 1973): £1 sterling = 728.29 fils; U.S. $1 = 296.05 fils.
100 Iraqi dinars = £137.31 = $337.78.

Note: Prior to December 1971 the Iraqi dinar was valued at U.S. $2.80. Between December 1971 and February 1973 the value was $3.04. In terms of sterling, the exchange rate between November 1967 and June 1972 was £1 = 857.14 fils (£7 = 6 dinars).

Ordinary Budget 1970-71: Revenue I.D. 287 million; Expenditure I.D. 264 million.
Development Budget 1970-71: Revenue I.D. 110 million; Expenditure I.D. 202 million.

The new 1970-74 Development Plan calls for total investment of I.D. 953 million, of which I.D. 829 million will accrue from oil revenues. I.D. 336 million will be invested in agriculture, and I.D. 207 million will be devoted to industry.

INTERNATIONAL LIQUIDITY
(Central Bank Gold and Foreign Exchange Holdings. $ million end-period).

	1967	1968	1969	1970	1971
Gold	114.8	192.6	192.7	143.5	155.8
Foreign Exchange	253.4	240.0	263.7	318.7	430.1
	368.2	432.6	456.4	462.2	585.9

IRAQ—(STATISTICAL SURVEY)

CONSUMER PRICES INDEX (IFS)
(1963=100)

1966	1967	1968	1969	1970	1971	1972
98.9	101.3	102.6	111.9	116.8	121.0	127.5

EXTERNAL TRADE

TOTAL TRADE
('000 I.D.)

Year	Imports	Exports*	Re-exports	Transit
1969	157,169	22,002	3,937	20,356
1970	181,651	22,566	2,164	27,942
1971	247,870	22,780	n.a.	n.a.
1972	234,680	23,214	n.a.	n.a.

* Exports of crude oil are not included.

EXPORTS OF CRUDE OIL
('000 I.D.)

1967	1968	1969	1970	1971
273,541	344,154	346,185	368,065	523,191

COMMODITIES
('000 I.D.)

Imports	1968	1969	1970	Exports	1968	1969	1970
Tea	6,098	7,061	6,052	Barley	667	1,278	538
Sugar	6,268	8,151	7,927	Dates	6,439	7,444	9,278
Pharmaceutical products	3,118	5,816	5,481	Straw and fodder	452	305	27
Clothing	15,162	1,247	664	Raw wool	1,234	1,591	1,530
Boilers and engines	10,981	30,194	28,808	Raw cotton	879	1,204	174
Automobiles and parts	58,715	8,143	12,076	Hides and skins	1,482	1,699	1,694
Timber	2,853	3,024	2,910	Cement	4,357	2,142	2,569

EXPORTS OF CRUDE OIL BY COUNTRY
(million long tons)

	1968	1969	1970	1971
United Kingdom	3.1	3.2	2.5	3.4
France	15.7	14.8	11.8	16.1
Italy	17.6	18.0	22.0	18.5
Netherlands	5.1	6.7	5.1	5.0
German Federal Republic	2.5	2.1	2.8	2.8
Japan	1.4	0.2	—	—
Belgium	3.2	1.3	1.0	2.0
Brazil	2.9	3.1	3.2	3.0
Greece	1.7	3.0	3.5	4.1
South Africa	1.9	1.9	2.2	2.2
Spain	1.8	2.0	1.8	2.0
Turkey	2.0	2.0	2.8	2.4
TOTAL (incl. others)	69.3	69.7	72.2	78.1

IRAQ—(Statistical Survey)

COUNTRIES
('000 I.D.)

Imports	1969	1970	1971
Australia	748	2,458	15,444
Belgium	5,270	9,271	6,338
Bulgaria	2,397	3,487	3,631
Canada	845	1,700	16,293
China, People's Republic	7,093	8,174	7,446
Czechoslovakia	3,187	4,710	12,496
Egypt	3,697	3,421	2,789
France	7,988	10,715	15,344
German Democratic Republic	1,447	2,877	3,665
Germany, Federal Republic	5,867	6,459	8,218
India	4,809	5,281	4,184
Italy	12,304	5,461	7,972
Japan	12,645	5,606	7,482
Lebanon	3,745	4,971	5,484
Malaysia	3,547	6,746	7,822
Netherlands	2,495	4,006	3,257
Pakistan	1,072	2,221	4,253
Poland	2,205	5,129	7,044
Sri Lanka	5,236	3,846	4,997
Sweden	4,613	7,410	6,873
U.S.S.R.	15,514	19,263	29,605
U.K.	18,814	21,822	22,626
U.S.A.	5,783	6,532	12,096

Exports (excluding oil)	1969	1970	1971
China, People's Republic	1,871	1,440	1,070
India	1,268	1,333	1,197
Kuwait	2,331	2,647	3,002
Lebanon	3,914	2,825	2,829
Syria	1,130	1,430	3,809
U.S.S.R.	1,467	2,029	1,194
U.A.R. (now Egypt)	2,640	3,301	3,299

TRANSPORT

RAILWAYS

	1967–68	1968–69	1969–70
Passenger km. ('000)	366,716	366,847	368,743
Freight ton km. ('000)	1,123,215	1,032,140	1,193,857

ROADS
Licensed Vehicles ('000)

	1968	1969	1970	1971
Cars	61.5	65.0	67.4	71.8
Goods Vehicles	31.3	32.5	32.7	33.7
Buses	9.2	9.3	9.2	10.9
Motor Cycles	5.9	6.6	6.9	7.5

Source: International Road Federation.

INLAND WATERWAYS

	1967–68	1968–69	1969–70
Total net reg. tonnage	218,051	135,698	137,911
Number of Vessels	1,322	1,271	1,285

IRAQ—(Statistical Survey)

SHIPPING
Movement of Ocean-going Merchant Vessels at the Ports of Basra and Um Qasr.

Year	No. of Passengers (Arrivals and Departures)*	No. of Vessels Loaded (Entered and Cleared)	No. of Vessels In Ballast (Entered and Cleared)	Tonnage of Cargo (excluding Crude Oil) Imported	Tonnage of Cargo (excluding Crude Oil) Exported
1967*	8,002	1,006	578	1,088,502	411,391
1968	8,127	955	615	1,156,200	461,820
1969	6,462	793	491	1,031,021	597,413
1970	5,610	661	395	1,082,215	438,945

* Port of Basra only.

In 1972 passenger arrivals at Basra were 2,956 and departures 3,257.

SHIPPING OF CRUDE OIL
Export by Tanker from Ports of Abadan and Khor Al-Amaya.

	1968	1969	1970
Number of ships docking	590	602	604
Net registered tonnage	6,835,069	7,018,061	7,544,388
Tonnage of cargo	16,196,902	16,357,918	17,037,667

CIVIL AVIATION
Flights through Baghdad and Basra Airports.

	No. of Flights Iraqi Airways	No. of Flights Total	No. of Passengers Disembarked	No. of Passengers Embarked	No. of Passengers Transit	Cargo (kg.) Off-Loaded	Cargo (kg.) Loaded
1968	1,892	4,085	111,563	110,542	8,614	2,113,987	465,742
1969	2,060	4,132	119,772	116,725	9,065	2,442,518	493,956
1970	1,527	3,198	110,172	111,841	8,071	2,615,722	528,542
1971	2,346	4,031	127,404	126,760	n.a.	2,463,596	820,156

TOURISM

	1969	1970	1971
Number of Visitors	429,654	359,929	589,857

EDUCATION
(1972–73)

Level	Number of Schools	Number of Pupils
Primary	3,654	1,298,422
Secondary (General)	1,032	348,648
Vocational	60	11,248
Teacher Training	5	7,405
Universities	5	48,073*

* 1971–72.

Source: Central Statistical Organization, Ministry of Planning, Baghdad.

PROVISIONAL CONSTITUTION

The following are the principal features of the Provisional Constitution issued on September 22nd, 1968:

The Iraqi Republic is a popular democratic state. Islam is the state religion and the basis of its laws and constitution.

The political economy of the state is founded in socialism.

The state will protect liberty of religion, freedom of speech and opinion. Public meetings are permitted under the law. All discrimination based on race, religion or language is forbidden. There shall be freedom of the Press, and the right to form societies and trade unions in conformity with the law is guaranteed.

The national rights of the Kurdish people are guaranteed within the framework of the unity of Iraq.

The highest authority in the country is the Council of Command of the Revolution, which will promulgate laws until the election of a National Assembly. The (five) members of the Council of Command of the Revolution are nominated Vice-Presidents of the State.

Two amendments to the constitution were announced in November 1969. The President, already Chief of State and head of the government, also became the official Supreme Commander of the Armed Forces and President of the Command Council of the Revolution. Membership of the latter body, was to increase from five to a larger number at the President's discretion.

Earlier, a Presidential decree replaced the 14 local government districts by 16 governates, each headed by a governor with wide powers.

The fifteen-article agreement which ended the Kurdish war was issued on March 12th, 1970. A new provisional constitution was announced in July 1970 which took account of this agreement. It had 67 articles, the most prominent being the article which further defined the Revolutionary Command Council. This now has 12 members, all members of the National Command Party. The President is elected by a two-thirds majority of the Council; he is responsible to the Council and the Vice-Presidents and Ministers will be responsible to him.

In November 1971 President Bakr announced a National Charter as a first step towards a permanent constitution. A National Assembly and popular councils are features of the Charter.

In July 1973, under amendments to the Constitution, President Bakr was given powers to appoint and dismiss every minister or official from the Vice-President downwards.

THE GOVERNMENT

HEAD OF STATE
President: Field-Marshal AHMED HASSAN AL BAKR.

REVOLUTIONARY COMMAND COUNCIL
President: Field-Marshal AHMED HASSAN AL BAKR
Vice-President: SADAM HUSSAIN TAKRITI
Members: The President, the Vice-President, and twelve other members.

COUNCIL OF MINISTERS
(July 1973)

Prime Minister: Field-Marshal AHMED HASSAN AL BAKR.
Minister of Foreign Affairs: MURTADHA AL-HADITHI.
Minister of the Interior: Gen. SAADOUN GHAIDAN.
Minister of Health: Dr. IZZAT MUSTAFA.
Minister of Industry: TAHA AL-JEZRAWI.
Minister of Transport: NIHAD FAKHRI AL-KHAFFAF.
Minister of Agriculture and Agrarian Reform: IZZAT AL-DOURI.
Minister of Information and Culture: HAMID AL-JIBOURI.
Minister of Youth: ADNAN AYOUB SABRI.
Minister of Agriculture: NAFIZ JALAL.
Minister of Irrigation: MUKARRAM AL-TALABANI.
Minister of Labour and Social Affairs: ANWAR ABDUL QADIR AL-HADITHI.
Minister of Education: Dr. AHMED A. S. AL-JAWARI.
Minister of Higher Education and Scientific Research: Dr. HISHAM AL-SHAWI.
Minister of Planning: Dr. JEWAD HASHIM.
Minister of the Economy: HIKMAT AL-AZAWI.
Minister of Oil and Minerals: Dr. SAADOUN HUMMADI.
Minister of Communications and Acting Minister of Defence: Dr. RASHID AL-RAFAIE.
Minister of Justice: HUSSAIN AL-SAFI.
Minister of Finance: AMIN ABDUL KARIM.
Minister of Municipal and Rural Affairs: IHSAN SHIRZAD.
Minister of Public Works and Housing: NOURI SHAWIS.
Minister of Northern Reconstruction: MUHAMMAD MAHMOUD.
Minister of Unity and the North: Dr. ABDULLA AL-KHUDAIRI
Ministers of State: SALIH AL-YOUSIFI, AZIZ SHARIF, NAZAR AL-TABAQCHALI, AMIR ABDULLA, ABDULLAH SALLOUM SAMARRAI.

DIPLOMATIC REPRESENTATION

EMBASSIES AND LEGATIONS ACCREDITED TO IRAQ
(In Baghdad unless otherwise stated.)
(E) Embassy; (L) Legation.

Afghanistan: 28/10 Waziriyah (E); *Ambassador:* Prof. KHALILLULLAH KHALILI.
Algeria: Karradat Mariam (E); *Ambassador:* OTHMANE SAADI.
Austria: Masbah (E); *Ambassador:* NOREBERT LINHART.
Bangladesh: (E); *Ambassador:* RASHID AHMAD.
Belgium: Abu Nawas St., Kard el Pasha (E); *Ambassador:* MARCEL VAN DE KERCKHOVE.
Brazil: (E); *Ambassador:* ROBERTO ASSUMPCAO DE ARAUJO.
Bulgaria: 35/1 Karradat Mariam (E); *Ambassador:* PENU IVANOV DOKOUZOV.
Canada: Teheran, Iran (E).
China, People's Republic: Karradat Mariam (E); *Ambassador:* HU CHENG-FANG.
Cyprus: (E); *Ambassador:* A. SOTERIADIS.
Czechoslovakia: 1/7 Karradat Mariam (E); *Ambassador:* JAN GAZIK.
Denmark: 204 Nidhal St., Alwiyah (E); *Ambassador:* S. SANDAGER JEPPESEN.
Egypt: (E); *Ambassador:* ABDEL MONEIM EL-NAGAR.
Ethiopia: Cairo, Egypt (E).
Finland: Masbah 37/7/35 (E); *Chargé d'Affaires:* MARTII LINTULAHTI.
France: Kard el Pasha 9/G/3 (E); *Ambassador:* PIERRE CERLES.
Germany, Democratic Republic: (E); *Ambassador:* HANS JURGEN WEITZ.
Greece: Beirut, Lebanon (E).
Hungary: 40/35 Masbah (E); *Ambassador:* JOSSEF FERRÓ.
India: Taha St., Najib Pasha, Ahmadiya (E); *Ambassador:* K. R. B. SINGH.
Indonesia: 22/9/21 (E); *Ambassador:* MALIKOESWARI M. P. MANGKUNEGARA.
Italy: Karradat Mariam (E); *Ambassador:* ROMUALDO MASSA BERNUCCI.
Japan: 40/7/35 Masbah (E); *Ambassador:* SEIICHI SHIRA.
Jordan: (E); *Chargé d'Affaires:* N.S. AL-KADI.
Korea (D.P.R.): (E); *Ambassador:* KIM QYO NAM.
Kuwait: (E); *Ambassador:* KHALID A. L. AL-MUSALLAM.
Lebanon: 11/35 Masbah (E); *Chargé d'Affaires a.i.:* H. HACHACHE.
Libya: Saadoun Park (E); *Ambassador:* SALEH AL-SENUSSI ABDUL SAYED.
Mauritania: (E); *Ambassador:* MOHAMMED OULD JIDDOU.
Mongolia: (E); *Ambassador:* JAMBYN NYAMA.
Morocco: 3/1/37 Masbah (E); *Ambassador:* MOHAMED NACIRI.
Nepal: (E); *Ambassador:* JHARENDRAS SINGHA.
Netherlands: (E); *Ambassador:* J. G. N. DE HOOP SCHEFFER.
Norway: Ankara, Turkey (E).
Nigeria: (E); *Ambassador:* ALHAJ OSMAN AHMDU SUKA.
Poland: Karrada al-Sharkiya, Masbah (E); *Ambassador:* LUCJAN LIK.
Qatar: (E); *Ambassador:* AHMED ALI MAARIFIYA.
Romania: (E); *Chargé d'Affaires a.i.:* VLADIMIR VISINESCU.
Saudi Arabia: Waziriyah (E); *Ambassador:* ALI A. EL-SUGAIR.
Somalia: Cairo, Egypt (E).
Spain: Saadoun Park 162/2 (E); *Ambassador:* MANUEL THOMÁS DE CARRANZA.
Sri Lanka: 10 B/6/12 Alwiyah (E); *Chargé d'Affaires a.i.:* A. T. MOORTHY.
Sudan: 51/5/35 Masbah (E); *Chargé d'Affaires:* SAYID SHARIF AHMED.
Sweden: 132/2 Al Nidhal St. (E); *Ambassador:* GUNNAR GERRING.
Switzerland: 3/1/2 Saadoun St. (E); *Chargé d'Affaires a.i.:* Dr. M. VOGEL-BACHER.
Syria: 160/2 Saadoun Park (E); *Ambassador:* IZZELDIN NAISSA.
Turkey: 2/8 Waziriyah (E); *Ambassador:* NAZIF CUHRUK.
U.S.S.R.: 140 Mansour St., Karradat Mariam (E); *Ambassador:* VENIAMIN ANDREEVICH LIKHATCHEV.
United Arab Emirates: (E); *Ambassador:* RASHID SULTAN AL-MUKHAWI.
United Kingdom: Sharia Salah Ud-Din, Karkh (E); *Ambassador:* HUGH G. BALFOUR-PAUL.
Vatican: Karrada al-Sharkiya, Saadoun St. (Apostolic Nunciature); *Apostolic Pro-Nuncio:* JEAN RUPP.
Venezuela: Cairo, Egypt (E).
Viet-Nam, Democratic Republic: Damascus, Syria.
Vietnam, Republic of: (E); *Ambassador:* HUYNH PHAN.
Yemen Arab Republic: Karradat Mariam (E); *Ambassador:* AHMED HUSSEIN AL-MURWENI.
Yemen P.D.R.: (E); *Chargé d'Affaires a.i.:* ABDULLAH AL-SALEH.
Yugoslavia: 10/11/1 Asfar Quarter, Battaween (E); *Ambassador:* REDZO TERZIC.

Iraq also has diplomatic relations with Cuba, Malta, Pakistan and Tanzania.

NATIONAL ASSEMBLY

No form of National Assembly has existed in Iraq since the 1958 revolution which overthrew the monarchy. The existing provisional constitution contains provisions for the election of a new 100-member assembly at a date to be determined by the Government, now expected to be October 1973.

POLITICAL PARTIES

Baath Party: Baghdad; revolutionary Arab socialist movement, founded in Damascus in 1947; has ruled Iraq since July 1968; Regional Sec.-Gen. AHMED HASSAN AL BAKR; Vice Regional Sec.-Gen. SADAM HUSSAIN TAKRITI.

Kurdish Democratic Party: seeks special status for the Kurdish minority in north-eastern Iraq.

DEFENCE

Estimated defence expenditure 1970-71: 84,700,000 dinars.
Military service: 2 years.
Total armed forces: 101,800; army 90,000; navy 2,000; air force 9,800. Paramilitary forces: 18,000.

JUDICIAL SYSTEM

Courts in Iraq consist of the following: The Court of Cassation, Courts of Appeal, First Instance Courts, Peace Courts, Courts of Sessions, Shara' Courts and Penal Courts.

The Court of Cassation: This is the highest judicial bench of all the Civil Courts; it sits in Baghdad, and consists of the President and a number of Vice-Presidents and not less than fifteen permanent judges, delegated judges and reporters as necessity requires. There are four bodies in the Court of Cassation, these are: (a) The General body, (b) Civil and Commercial body, (c) Personal Status body, (d) The Penal body.

A Technical Bureau has been established which is related to the Court of Cassation and is carrying out the work of abstracting and classifying the legal principles which are contained in the judgments issued by it.

Courts of Appeal: The country is divided into five Districts of Appeal: Baghdad, Mosul, Basrah, Hilla, and Kirkuk, each with its Court of Appeal consisting of a President, Vice-Presidents and not less than three members, who consider the objections against the decisions issued by the First Instance Courts of first grade.

Courts of First Instance: These courts are of two kinds: Limited and Unlimited in jurisdiction.

Limited Courts deal with Civil and Commercial suits, the value of which is five hundred Dinars and less; and suits, the value of which cannot be defined, and which are subject to fixed fees. Limited Courts consider these suits in the final stage and they are subject to Cassation.

Unlimited Courts consider the Civil and Commercial suits irrespective of their value, and suits the value of which exceeds five hundred Dinars with first grade subject to appeal.

First Instance Courts consist of one judge in the centre of each *Liwa*, some *Qadhas* and *Nahiyas*, as the Minister of Justice judges necessary.

Revolutionary Courts: These deal with major cases that would affect the security of the state in any sphere: political, financial or economic. In December 1968 the death penalty was introduced for espionage; a special three-man court was then set up to try such cases.

Courts of Sessions: There is in every District of Appeal a Court of Sessions which consists of three judges under the presidency of the President of the Court of Appeal or one of his Vice-Presidents. It considers the penal suits prescribed by Penal Proceedings Law and other laws. More than one Court of Sessions may be established in one District of Appeal by notification issued by the Minister of Justice mentioning therein its headquarters, jurisdiction and the manner of its establishment.

Shara' Courts: A Shara' Court is established wherever there is a First Instance Court; the Muslim judge of the First Instance Court may be a *Qadhi* to the Shara' Court if a special *Qadhi* has not been appointed thereto. The Shara' Court considers matters of personal status and religious matters in accordance with the provisions of the law supplement to the Civil and Commercial Proceedings Law.

Penal Courts: A Penal Court of first grade is established in every First Instance Court. The judge of the First Instance Court is considered as penal judge unless a special judge is appointed thereto. More than one Penal Court may be established to consider the suits prescribed by the Penal Proceedings Law and other laws.

One or more Investigation Court may be established in the centre of each *Liwa* and a judge is appointed thereto. They may be established in the centres of *Qadhas* and *Nahiyas* by order of the Minister of Justice. The judge carries out the investigation in accordance with the provisions of Penal Proceedings Law and the other laws.

There is in every First Instance Court a department for the execution of judgments presided over by the Judge of First Instance if a special President is not appointed thereto. It carries out its duties in accordance with the provisions of Execution Law.

There is a Notary Public for the swearing of contracts and he carries out his duties in accordance with the provisions relating to Notaries Public.

RELIGION

ISLAM

Over 90 per cent of the population are Muslims. The Arabs of northern Iraq, the Bedouins, the Kurds, and some of the inhabitants of Baghdad and Basra, are mainly of the Sunni sect, the remaining Arabs south of the Diyala, belong to the Shi'i sect. Leaders: Mr. ALWAIDH (Sunni), Prof. ABDUL QASSEM AL MOUSAWI AL KHOUI (Shi'i).

CHRISTIANITY

There are Christian communities in all the principal towns of Iraq, but their principal villages lie mostly in the Mosul district. The Christians of Iraq fall into three groups: (a) the free Churches, including the Nestorian, Gregorian, and Jacobite; (b) the churches known as Uniate, since they are in union with the Roman Catholic Church including the Armenian Uniates, Jacobite Uniates, and Chaldeans; (c) mixed bodies of Protestant converts, New Chaldeans, and Orthodox Armenians.

Catholic:

Latin Rite: Archbishop of Baghdad: Most Rev. MAURICE PERRIN; approx. 2,000 adherents.

Armenian Rite: Archbishop of Baghdad: Most Rev. NERSES TAYROYAN.

Chaldean Rite: Patriarch of Babylon of the Chaldeans: His Beatitude PAUL II CHEIKHO, with 13 Archbishops and Bishops in Iraq, Iran, Syria and Lebanon. Approx. 330,000 adherents.

Syrian Rite: Archbishop of Mosul: Most Rev. EMANUEL BENNI; Archbishop of Baghdad: Most Rev. ATHANASE J. D. BAKOSE; approx. 25,000 adherents.

Orthodox Syrian Community: 12,000 adherents.

Orthodox (*Gregorian*) **Community:** 12,000 adherents, mainly Armenians; Acting Bishop of Baghdad: KRIKOR HAGOPIAN.

JUDAISM

The Jewish community numbered some 250,000 in 1939, but most Jews have left the country since the Second World War, particularly during the nineteen-fifties; unofficial estimates put the present size of the community at 2,500, almost all living in Baghdad.

OTHERS

About thirty thousand Yazidis and a smaller number of Turcomans, Sabeans, and Shebeks make up the rest of the population.

Sabean Community: 20,000 adherents; Head Sheikh DAKHIL, Nasiriyah; Mandeans, mostly in Nasiriyah.

Yazidis: 30,000 adherents; TASHIN BAIK, Asifni.

THE PRESS

DAILIES

Baghdad Observer: P.O.B. 257, Karantina, Baghdad; f. 1967; English; Editor-in-Chief FUAD YOUSIF QAZANCHI; circ. 5,000.

al Jumhuriya (*The Republic*): Karantina, Baghdad; f. 1963, re-founded 1967; Editor-in-Chief SA'AD QASSIM HAMMOUDI; circ. 25,000.

al Taakhi (*Brotherhood*): P.O.B. 5717, Baghdad; re-founded 1968; organ of the Democratic Kurdistan Party; Editor-in-Chief DARA TAWFIQ; circ. 25,000.

al Thawra (*Revolution*): Aqaba bin Nafi's Square, P.O.B. 2009, Baghdad; f. 1968; organ of Baath Party; Chief Editor TARIK AZIZ; circ. 70,000.

The Sportsman: Baghdad; f. 1971; published by Ministry of Youth.

WEEKLIES

al-Ahwaz: Basra; f. 1971; published twice weekly by Popular Front for the Liberation of Arabistan.

al-Aswaq al-Tijariya (*The Commercial Markets*): 28/13 Sharia Hassan Ben Thabit, Baghdad; f. 1951; economic and commercial; Propr. and Editor JAMAL DAWOOD; circ. 3,000.

al-Fikr al-Jadid (*New Thought*): f. 1972; weekly; political; Editor HUSAIN QASIM AL-AZIZ.

Alif Ba: Baghdad; published by Ministry of Information; circ. 2,000.

al-Iqtisad al-Iraqi (*The Iraq Economy*): Baghdad; economic affairs; weekly; Editor A. B. MAHMUD AL-UMAR.

al-Kashkal: Mosul; humorous.

al-Mutafarrij: Rashid St., Hayderkhana, P.O.B. 409 Baghdad; f. 1965; satirical; Editor MOUJIB HASSOON.

al-Nahdha: Sulaymaniya; Arabic and Kurdish; general interest.

L'Opinion de Baghdad: L'Etablissement Général de la Press et de l'Imprimerie, B.P. 580, Baghdad; f. 1970; French; Editor-in-Chief ALI SMIDA.

Saut al Fallah: Baghdad; organ of Peasants' Federation; circ. 5,000.

Saut al-Ummal: Karradat Mariam, Baghdad; organ of General Federation of Iraqi Trade Unions.

al Shuoun al Zirayah wol Iqtisadiyah: Baghdad.

Waee Ul-Omal (*Workers of Conciousness*): Headquarters of General Federation of Trade Unions in Iraq, Abu Nawas St., P.O.B. 2307, Baghdad; Iraq Trades Union organ; Chief Editor MOHMMAD AYESH.

al Watan al-Arab: Baghdad.

PERIODICALS

al Adib: Mosul; political; fortnightly.

al Amilun fil Naft: Baghdad; petroleum news; monthly; Editor FAKHRI KHALIL AZIZ.

al Aqlam (*The Pen*): Baghdad; literary; monthly; Ministry of Culture and Information; f. 1964.

Commerce: Chamber of Commerce, Baghdad; f. 1938; quarterly; commercial and economic; circ. 2,000; also a weekly bulletin dealing in commodity prices and market conditions; circ. 2,000.

al-Fikr al-Arabi: Mosul; political; fortnightly.

al-Hadaf: Mosul; political; fortnightly.

al-Idaa'h Wal-Television: Iraqi Broadcasting, Television and Cinema Establishment, Salihiya, Baghdad; radio and television programmes and articles; fortnightly.

Iraq Government Gazette, The: Ministry of Information, Baghdad; f. 1922; Arabic edition irregular, English edition weekly; legal and official; circ. Arabic 4,000, English 500.

Journal of the Faculty of Medicine, The: College of Medicine, University of Baghdad, Baghdad; f. 1941; quarterly; Arabic and English; medical and technical; published by the Faculty of Medicine, Baghdad; Edited by Prof. YOUSIF D. AL NAAMAN, M.D., D.SC.

Majallat al-Ziraa al-Iraqiyah (*Magazine of Iraq Agriculture*): Baghdad; quarterly; agricultural; published by the Ministry of Agriculture.

Majallat-al-Majma al-'Ilmi al-Iraqi: Iraqi Academy, Waziriyah, Baghdad; f. 1947; quarterly; scholarly magazine on Arabic Islamic culture.

al-Mu'allem al-Jadid: Ministry of Education, Baghdad; f. 1935; quarterly; educational, social, and general; owned and published by the Ministry of Education; Editor ATIF AL-EZZI.

Mujalat Huwat al Tuwabiya al Iraqiyah: Baghdad; monthly.

Nation, The: Mid-East House, Shahrah; f. 1960; monthly; English; Editor MUMTAZ TARIQ.

Review of Arab Petroleum and Economics: Baghdad; English and Arabic; monthly.

IRAQ—(THE PRESS, PUBLISHERS, RADIO AND TELEVISION, FINANCE)

al-Sinai (*The Industrialist*): P.O.B. 11120, Baghdad; publ. by Iraqi Federation of Industries; Arabic and English; quarterly.

Sumer: Directorate-General of Antiquities, Jamal Abdul Nasr Street, Baghdad; f. 1945; archaeological, historical journal; publ. by the Directorate-General of Antiquities; Chair. of Ed. Board Dr. FAISAL EL-WAELY (Dir.-Gen. of Antiquities); twice yearly.

Tourism in Iraq: Tourism and Resorts Administration, Ministry of Information, Baghdad; bi-monthly; Editor FAKHRI KHALIL AZIZ.

NEWS AGENCIES

Iraqi News Agency: Abu Nawwas St., P.O.B. 3084, Baghdad; f. 1959; gathers and circulates news and photographs for use at home and abroad; independent in financial and administrative affairs; has contracts and agreements with various international commercial agencies and government newsagencies; Board of Directors includes representatives from the Ministries of Culture and Information, Foreign Affairs, Dir. of Military Intelligence, Dir.-Gen. of Broadcasting and Television, of P.T.T., representative of Revolutionary Command Council, Chair. of Al-Jamahir Press House; offices in Beirut, Amman, Cairo, Rabat and Kuwait and correspondents in the Arab and other countries; Dir.-Gen. (acting) TAHA YASEEN AL-BASRI.

FOREIGN BUREAUX

AFP (*France*): P.O.B. 5699, South Gate, Baghdad; Chief NAGIB FRANGIEH.

MENA (*Egypt*): Rasheed Str., al-Morabaa, Zaki Gamil Building, P.O.B. 2, Baghdad.

D.P.A. and Tass also have offices in Baghdad.

PUBLISHERS

al Ahliya: Mutanabi St., Baghdad.

Dar al Basri: Amin Square, Rashid Street, Baghdad.

Dar al Bayan: Mutanabi Street, Baghdad.

al Irshad: Baghdad; Arab literature.

Jamahir Publishing House: Baghdad; f. 1971; government publishing house.

al Jumhuriyah Printing and Publishing Co.: Waziriya, Baghdad; f. 1963; the principal Iraqi publishers of newspapers and books.

al Ma'arif Ltd.: Mutanabi Street, Baghdad; f. 1929; publishes periodicals and books in Arabic, Kurdishi Turkish, French and English.

al Muthanna: Mutanabi St., Baghdad.

al Nahdah: Mutanabi St., Baghdad; politics, Arab affairs.

Dar al Nathir: North Gate, Baghdad.

Dar al Shafik: Baghdad; art books.

RADIO AND TELEVISION

RADIO

Broadcasting Station of the Republic of Iraq: Iraqi Broadcasting and Television Establishment, Salihiya, Baghdad; home service broadcasts in Arabic, Kurdish and Turkuman; foreign service in French, German, English, Russian, Persian, Turkish and Urdu; there are 4 medium wave and 13 short wave transmitters; Dir.-Gen. M. S. AL-SAHAF.

Idaa'h Baghdad: f. 1936; 22 hours daily.

Idaa'h Sawt Al-Jamahir: f. 1970; 21 hours daily.

Idaa'h Dar Al-Salam: f. 1971; commercial; 4 hours daily.

Number of radio receivers (1972): 1.7 million.

TELEVISION

Baghdad Television: Ministry of Information, Iraqi Broadcasting and Television Establishment, Salihiya, Karkh, Baghdad; f. 1956; government station operating 7 hours daily; Dir.-Gen. MOHAMMED S. AL-SAHAF.

Kirkuk Television: f. 1967; government station; commercial; 6 hours daily.

Mosul Television: f. 1968; government station; commercial; 6 hours daily.

Basrah Television: f. 1968; government station; commercial; 6 hours daily.

Number of TV receivers (1972): 200,000.

FINANCE

All banks and insurance companies, including all foreign companies, were nationalized in July 1964. The assets of foreign companies were taken over by the state.

(cap.=capital; p.u.=paid up; dep.=deposits; res.=reserves; m.=million; amounts in Iraqi dinars.)

BANKING

CENTRAL BANK

Central Bank of Iraq: Banks St., Baghdad; f. 1947 as National Bank of Iraq; brs. in Mosul and Basra; has the sole right of note issue; cap. p.u. 25m., dep. 71.2 (March 1973); Gov. FAWZI AL-QAYSSI; publs. *Quarterly Bulletin, Annual Report*.

COMMERCIAL BANKS

Commercial Bank of Iraq: New Banks' St., P.O.B. 66, Baghdad; f. 1953; nationalized 1964; 44 brs.; cap. p.u. 3.75m., res. 1.9m., dep. 81.3m. (Dec. 1972); absorbed the Baghdad Bank and the Credit Bank of Iraq in 1970; Chair. and Gen. Man. ADNAN AL TAYYAR; Assistant Gen. Mans. I. H. SHAWKI, SABIH SADIQ, JAMIL KADHIM; publs. *Al-Masarafi* (The Banker, monthly), *Al-Masarafi* (weekly).

IRAQ—(Finance, Oil and Gas, Trade and Industry)

Rafidain Bank: Banks St., Baghdad; f. 1941; cap. 6.6m., res. 5.5m., dep. 155m. (1972); 71 brs. in Iraq, 6 overseas brs.; Chair. and Gen. Man. Atta Al-Dhahi.

SPECIALIZED BANKS

Agricultural Bank of Iraq: Rashid St., Baghdad; 24 branches; cap. p.u. 6.4m.; Gen. Man. Abdul Razzak al-Hilali.

Estate Bank of Iraq: Hassan ibn Thanit St., Baghdad; f. 1949; 18 branches; gives loans to assist the building industry; cap. p.u. 25m.; acquired the Co-operative Bank in 1970; Dir.-Gen. Labeed al-Karagully.

Industrial Bank of Iraq: Industrial Bank Building, Baghdad; 5 branches; f. 1940; cap. p.u. 4.75m.; Gen. Man. Dr. Farhang Jalal; publ. *Annual Report*.

INSURANCE

Iraqi Life Insurance Co.: Shabander Bldg., New Banks' St., Baghdad; f. 1960; cap. p.u. 325,000; Chair. and Gen. Man. Bedi Ahmed al-Saifi.

Iraq Reinsurance Company: Reinsurance Building, Khullani Square, P.O.B. 297, Baghdad; f. 1961; to transact reinsurance business on the international market; Chair. and Gen. Man. Dr. Mustafa Rajab; London Office: 5 Fenchurch St., E.C.3.

National Insurance Co.: Al-Aman Bldg., Al-Khulani St., P.O.B. 248, Baghdad; f. 1950; cap. p.u. 1m.; state monopoly for all direct non-life insurance; Chair. and Gen. Man. Abdulbaki Redha.

OIL AND GAS

Iraq National Oil Company (INOC): P.O.B. 476, Saadoun St., Baghdad; f. 1967 to operate in all stages of the oil industry outside and within the country. With Cabinet approval INOC may form or participate in other companies and contract loans. The Government will pay 50 per cent of INOC's net annual profits until INOC has recovered its capital, when the payment shall be 75 per cent. The Company runs two production operations, the small Khanaqin oil field and the North Rumaila field which came on stream in April 1972. With Russian and Hungarian help other new finds are being investigated. INOC is to participate in the building of a Central European crude oil pipe-line to carry Iraqi oil to Yugoslavia, Hungary and Czechoslovakia. Chair. Adnan Qassab; Deputy-Chair. Ali Hadi al Jabir; board of 5 mems.

Iraq Company for Oil Operations (ICOO): state-owned company formed in June 1972 to take over the operations of the nationalized Iraq Petroleum Company. It manages production from the Kirkuk, Bai Hassan and Jambur fields (formerly IPC run), and from the Ain Zalah and Butmah fields (turned over to the Government by IPC in February 1973); Chair. Abd.-al-Fattah al-Yasin.

Entreprise des Recherches et d'Activités Petroliers (ERAP): signed a contract with INOC in 1968 under which it acts as contractor to INOC. It operates a 10,800 km. onshore/offshore area. Oil has been discovered but is not yet on stream.

Gas Distribution Administration (G.D.A.): Baghdad; f. 1964 to supervise all gas projects, and to distribute and market natural and liquid gas all over Iraq. The sulphur recovery plant at Kirkuk utilizes gas supplied by the Kirkuk oilfield. Two gas pipelines are being laid from Kirkuk to Baghdad, and a liquid gas processing plant (12,000 b/d) has been erected at Taji, north of Baghdad.

Government Oil Refinery Administration: Baghdad; operates refineries at Baghdad, Khanaqin, Kirkuk, Hadithah and Qayyarah; capital investment I.D. 30m.; annual turnover I.D. 25m. approx.

Iraq Petroleum Company: Office: 33 Cavendish Square, London, W1M 0AA; Chair. C. M. Dalley; Man. Dir. G. G. Stockwell; Exec. Dirs. H. C. Goff, R. Milne, G. B. Wepsala.

In 1951 Iraq Petroleum Company and its associated companies signed an agreement with the Iraqi Government to share the profits from oil production and export on a 50-50 basis, the first comprehensive agreement since the first concession made in 1925. In 1961, under Law no. 80, the Government expropriated 99.5 per cent of IPC's concession area, including the prolific North Rumaila oilfield, although the Company reserved its ownership rights. In June 1972 the Company's oil fields were nationalized, intensifying the dispute which had continued since 1961. However, on February 28th, 1973 a wideranging agreement was signed, under which IPC was to drop all claims outstanding since 1961, and accept, along with BPC, the seizure of the Consortium's non-producing assets in 1961. In settlement the companies would receive 15 million tons of crude oil over the next two years, an assurance of BPC's continued operations in the south, and the inclusion of IPC's Lebanon pipeline as part of the compensation. But the Iraqi Government would receive £141 million to meet its accumulated claims against the Companies, and take over the Mosul Petroleum Company.

Basrah Petroleum Co. Ltd.: an affiliate of IPC with the same officials (*see above*); on November 30th, 1938, the Company was granted a concession over southern Iraq, south of latitude 33°, for 75 years. Oil was found in 1948 at Zubair and in 1953 at Rumaila. The Feb. 28 agreement between the Iraq Government and IPC meant that BPC was the only remaining non-nationalized foothold of the Consortium. Under the agreement the company is to raise oil production to 80 million tons a year by 1976. Production in 1972 was about 32 million tons.

TRADE AND INDUSTRY

CHAMBERS OF COMMERCE

Federation of Iraqi Chambers of Commerce: Mustansir St., Baghdad; f. 1969; all Iraqi Chambers of Commerce are affiliated to the Federation; Pres. Shaban J. al-Rajab; Sec.-Gen. Kadhim A. al-Mhaidi; publs. *Bulletin*, *Monthly News*, *Annual Report* and brochures.

Amarah Chamber of Commerce: Al-Amarah; f. 1950; Pres. Haj J. al-Ammar; Sec. R. Al-Saffar.

Arbil Chamber of Commerce: Arbil; f. 1966; Pres. Shekheel Haj Hassan; Sec. Muhammad Dazah (*ad interim*).

Baghdad Chamber of Commerce: Mustansir St., Baghdad; f. 1926; 14,296 mems.; Pres. SHA'ABAN JASSIM AL RIJAB; Sec. MOHAMMAD NAYEF AL-SHIBLI; Dir.-Gen. MUNIER SAID; publs. *Weekly Bulletin*, *Commerce* (quarterly magazine), *Trade Directory*.

Basra Chamber of Commerce: Basra; f. 1926; Pres. AMER AL-TIKRITI; Sec.-Gen. HARITH AL-MAKZOMY; publ. *al Tajir* (monthly).

Diwaniya Chamber of Commerce: Diwaniya; f. 1961; Pres. ABDULLAH AL-KHAFAJI; Sec. AMIN AL-ASADI.

Diyala Chamber of Commerce: Diyala; f. 1966; Pres. ADNAN AL-SARAH; Sec. ABDUL SATTAR HILMI.

Hillah Chamber of Commerce: Hillah; f. 1949; Pres. SAMI ALI AL-SULTAN; Sec. SHAHID AL-KHRIBAWI.

Karbala Chamber of Commerce: Karbala; f. 1952; Pres. JAWAD ABULHAB; Sec. MUDHER QUANDI; Man. SAHIB H. HILME.

Kirkuk Chamber of Commerce: Kirkuk; f. 1957; Pres. HASSANI AL-HADITHI; Sec. SAMI BUNI.

Mosul Chamber of Commerce: Nineveh St., P.O.B. 35, Mosul; f. 1926; 4,000 mems.; Pres. ABDUL GHANI AL ANNAZ; Vice-Pres. ABDUL MAJEED AL NAFOUSSI; Sec. ABDUL JAWAD AL NEAIMI.

Najaf Chamber of Commerce: Najaf; f. 1950; Pres. MUHAMMAD ALI AL-BALAGHI; Sec. ABDUL MAHDI SHLAL.

Nasiriya Chamber of Commerce: Nasiriya; f. 1958; Pres. SHAIL ABID AL-YASIN; Sec. SATTR SALMON.

Sulaimaniya Chamber of Commerce: Sulaimaniya; f. 1967; Pres. SHAFIQ AHMED AL-CHALABI; Sec. AMIN MOLOOD.

EMPLOYERS' ORGANIZATION

Iraq Federation of Industries: Credit Bank Bldg., 5th Floor, Bank St., Baghdad; f. 1956; 2,126 mems.; Pres. HATAM ABDUL RASHID; publs. *Al Sinai* (quarterly), Directory of Iraqi Industries and monthly reports.

INDUSTRIAL ORGANIZATIONS

General Establishment for Industry: Baghdad; state organization controlling most of Iraq's industry; organized into 5 departments covering (1) Clothing, Hides and Cigarettes, (2) Construction industries, (3) Weaving and Textiles, (4) Chemicals and Foodstuffs, (5) Engineering.

Iraqi Dates Organization: Baghdad; responsible for date exports; Dir. Dr. BAHA SHUBBAR.

National Iraqi Minerals Co.: P.O.B. 2330, Alwiyah, Baghdad; f. 1969; 1,210 mems.; responsible for exploiting all minerals in Iraq except oil; Pres. Dr. SHAKIR AL-SAMARRAI.

TRADE UNIONS

General Federation of Iraqi Trade Unions: Karradat Mariam, Baghdad; f. 1964; 19 unions, with a membership of 250,000, are affiliated to the General Federation and registered with the Ministry of Labour and Social Security Affairs; Pres. HASHIM ALI MOHSIN; Sec.-Gen. NOURI NAJIM; publ. *Saut al-Ummal*.

Union of Teachers: Baghdad; Pres. IBRAHIM MARZOUK.

Union of Palestinian Workers in Iraq: Baghdad; Sec.-Gen. SAMI AL SHAWISH.

CO-OPERATIVES

By the end of 1970 there were 805 agricultural co-operatives with 110,472 members. Collective farms are now being developed and at the beginning of 1972 there were 61.

PEASANT SOCIETIES

General Federation of Peasant Societies: Baghdad; f. 1959; has 734 affiliated Peasant Societies.

TRADE FAIR

Baghdad International Fair: Damascus St., Al Mansoor, Baghdad; administered by Directorate-General of Fairs and Trade Centers; held annually in October; f. 1964; 192 foreign companies from 23 countries took part in the 1972 Fair.

TRANSPORT

RAILWAYS

Iraqi Republic Railways: Baghdad Central Station Building, Baghdad; total length of track (1971): 2,528 km., consisting of 1,234 km. of standard gauge, 1,294 km. of one-metre gauge; Dir.-Gen. ABDUL JABBAR SA'ADI; Chief of Traffic HAMID ABDUL MAJEED AL-ANI.

A metre-gauge line runs from Basra through Baghdad, Khanaqin and Kirkuk to Erbil. The standard gauge line covers the length of the country from Rabiyah on the Syrian border via Mosul, Baghdad and Basrah to Um-Qasr. From here it is proposed to extend the track through Kuwait to Dhahran in Saudi Arabia, thus connecting Europe with the Persian Gulf. The standard gauge line between Baghdad and Basra is intended to eventually replace the metre gauge line between the two cities. Most trains are now hauled by diesel-electric locomotives. As well as the internal services there is also a regular express between Baghdad and Istanbul.

ROADS

The most important roads are: Baghdad–Mosul–Tel Kotchuk (Syrian border), 521 km.; Baghdad–Kirkuk–Arbil–Zaho (border with Turkey), 544 km.; Kirkuk–Sulaimaniya, 109 km.; Baghdad–Amara–Basra–Safwan (Kuwaiti border), 595 km.; Baghdad–Rutba–Syrian border, 555 km.; Baghdad–Babylon–Diwaniya, 181 km.

Under the 1970–75 Development Plan $91 million have been allocated to rebuilding and extending the present road system. The World Bank has made a $19 million loan towards the project. In 1972 a total of 9,240 km. of paved road had been completed and a further 1,368 km. were under construction.

Iraq Automobile and Touring Association: Al Mansoor, Baghdad; f. 1931; 3,500 mems.; Chair. ALADDIN EL-BAKRI; Sec.-Gen. NAFIE FAJIR AL QASIR.

INLAND WATERWAYS

Directorate-General of Navigation: Basra; Dir.-Gen. (vacant); in 1972 there were 1,041 registered river craft, 65 motor vessels and 106 motor balams.

SHIPPING

Iraqi Ports Administration: Basra; Dir.-Gen. ADNAN AL-QASAB.

The Ports of Basra and Um Qasr are the commercial gateway of Iraq. They are connected by various ocean routes with all parts of the world, and constitute the natural distributing centre for overseas supplies. The Iraqi Maritime Company maintains a regular service between Basra, the Gulf and north European ports. Other shipping lines operate cargo and passenger services from Basra and Um Qasr to all parts of the world. There are fast mail and passenger services from Basra to Bombay via Khorramshahr, Bushire, and Karachi, connecting at Bombay with the Peninsula and Orient Mail Services to England, Australia, South Africa, and the Far East.

At Basra there is accommodation for 12 vessels at the Maqal Wharves and accommodation for 7 vessels at the buoys. There is room for 3 vessels at Um Qasr.

In 1971–72 the revenue of the Iraq Ports Administration was I.D. 13,653,019 against a general expenditure of I.D. 13,953,721 (including capital works). Expenditure on planning schemes was I.D. 3,597,243. In 1972 the port of Basrah was visited by 819 cargo ships; the total tonnage exported was 454,391 and imported tonnage totalled 1,167,221. Um Qasr port handled 57 cargo vessels, imports were 216,108 tons and exports 454,391.

There are deep water tanker terminals at Fao and Khor Al-Amaya for 4 and 2 vessels respectively. In 1972 34,206,419 long tons of crude oil were exported in 543 tankers.

Iraqi Maritime Transport Co.: P.O.B. 3052, Baghdad; f. 1952; 6 cargo vessels; total g.r.t. 15,559.65 (1973); Dir.-Gen. (acting) EDGAR SARKIES.

CIVIL AVIATION

A new international airport, ten miles from Baghdad, was opened in January 1970. Another airport at Bamerni, in the province of Dhok was opened in August 1972. There is also an international airport at Basra. Internal flights connect Baghdad to Basra and Mosul.

Iraqi Airways: Al Kharkh, Baghdad; f. 1945; Dir.-Gen. ABDUL MUHSEN ABUE AL KHAIL; regular services from Baghdad to Amman, Bahrain, Basra, Beirut, Berlin, Cairo, Damascus, Dhahran, Doha, Frankfurt, Geneva, Istanbul, Kuwait, London, Mosul, Paris, Prague, Teheran, Vienna, Copenhagen, Karachi, New Delhi, Dubai, Moscow, Warsaw; fleet: 3 Tridents, 3 Viscounts.

In 1970 the following airlines also operated services to Iraq: Aeroflot, Air France, Ariana Afghan, Balkan, BOAC, ČSA, Egyptair, Interflug, KLM, Kuwait Airways, LOT, Lufthansa, MEA, PIA, Saudia, Swissair, Syrian Arab.

TOURISM AND CULTURE

Ministry of Information, Tourism and Resorts Administration: Khulani Sq., Baghdad; f. 1956; Dir.-Gen. Dr. ALI GHALIB AL-ANI; publs. *Tourism in Iraq* (bi-monthly), guide books, posters, tourist maps and pamphlets.

THEATRE GROUPS
1. OFFICIALLY SPONSORED

National Group for Acting: Department for Cinema and Theatre, Ministry of Culture and Information, Baghdad.

Rashid National Group: Department for Cinema and Theatre, Ministry of Culture and Information, Baghdad; folklore group providing dancing and singing concerts.

2. PRIVATE

Baghdad Theatre Group: Baghdad; f. 1967.

Contemporary Theatre Group: Baghdad; f. 1966.

Folklore Group: Baghdad; f. 1965.

Free Theatre Group: Baghdad; f. 1965.

14 July Theatre Group: Baghdad; f. 1966.

Modern Art Group: Baghdad; f. 1967.

Theatre Arts Group: Baghdad; f. 1967.

United Artists' Group: Baghdad; f. 1967.

ATOMIC ENERGY

Atomic Energy Commission: Baghdad; f. 1957; Sec.-Gen. Dr. MOYASSAR YAHIA AL MALLAH; an atomic reactor, built with Soviet aid at Tuwaitha, south of Baghdad, was inaugurated in 1968. The reactor will provide isotopes for teaching and civilian research.

EDUCATION

Since the establishment of the Republic in 1958 there has been a marked expansion in education at all levels. Spending on education has increased substantially since 1958, reaching I.D. 78 million in the 1973 budget—over five times the 1958 figures. Apart from private schools and universities, education in Iraq is entirely free. Pre-school education is expanding although as yet it reaches only a small proportion of children in this age group. Primary education, lasting six years, is now officially compulsory, and there are plans to extend full-time education to nine years as soon as possible. At present, secondary education, which is expanding rapidly, is available for six years. In 1970 French was officially adopted as the second language to be taught in schools.

Science, Medical and Engineering faculties of the universities have undergone considerable expansion, although technical training is less developed. Two branches of Baghdad University at Basra and Mosul became independent universities in 1967. A private university, al Mustansiriya University, partly Government assisted, offers evening courses and full-time tuition.

UNIVERSITIES

University of Baghdad: Baghdad; 968 teachers, 20,066 students.

Basra University: Basra; 126 teachers, 3,213 students.

al Hikma University of Baghdad: P.O.B. 2125, Baghdad; 65 teachers, 610 students.

al Mustansiriya: Baghdad; 450 teachers, 9,716 students.

Mosul University: Mosul; 149 teachers, 3,275 students.

University of Sulaimaniya: Sulaimaniya; 74 teachers, 1,130 students.

BIBLIOGRAPHY

GENERAL

BELL, Lady FLORENCE (Ed.). The Letters of Gertrude Lowthian Bell (2 vols., London, 1927).

BURGOYNE, ELIZABETH (Ed.). Gertrude Bell, from her personal papers, 1914-26 (London, 1961).

HARRIS, GEORGE L. Iraq, Its People, Its Society, Its Culture (HRAF Press, New Haven, 1958).

LLOYD, SETON F. H. Iraq: Oxford Pamphlet (Bombay, 1943).
    Twin Rivers: A Brief History of Iraq from the Earliest Times to the Present Day (Oxford, 1943).
    Foundations in the Dust (Oxford, 1949).

LONGRIGG, S. H. and STOAKES, F. Iraq (Ernest Benn, London, 1958).

MEZERIK, A. G. Kuwait-Iraq Dispute, 1961 (New York, 1961).

QUBAIN, FAHIM I. The Reconstruction of Iraq 1950-57 (Atlantic Books, London, 1959).

SALTER, Lord, assisted by PAYTON, S. W. The Development of Iraq: A Plan of Action (Baghdad, 1955).

STARK, FREYA. Baghdad Sketches (John Murray, London, 1937).

STEWART, DESMOND, and HAYLOCK, JOHN. New Babylon: a Portrait of Iraq London, (Collins, 1956).

VERNIER, B. L'Irak d'Aujourd'hui (Paris, 1962).

ANCIENT HISTORY

BRAIDWOOD, R. J. and HOWE, B. Prehistoric Investigation in Iraqi Kurdistan (Chicago, 1961).

CAMBRIDGE ANCIENT HISTORY (Vols. I and II, New Ed., Cambridge, 1962).

CHATERJI, S. Ancient History of Iraq (M. C. Sarkar, Ltd. Calcutta, 1961).

FIEY, J. M. L'Assyrie Chrétienne (Imprimerie Catholique, Beirut, 1965).

FRANKFORT, H. Archæology and the Sumerian Problem (Chicago, 1932).
    The Birth of Civilization in the Near East (Anchor, New York, 1951).

LLOYD, SETON F. H. The Art of the Ancient Near East (London, 1961).
    Ruined Cities of Iraq (Oxford, 1945).
    Mesopotamia (London, 1936).
    Mounds of the Near East (Edinburgh, 1964).

MALLOWAN, M. E. L. Early Mesopotamia and Iran (Thames and Hudson, London, 1965).

OATES, E. E. D. M. Studies in the Ancient History of Northern Iraq (British Academy, London, 1967).

OPPENHEIM, A. LEO. Ancient Mesopotamia (Chicago U.P., 1964).
    Letters from Mesopotamia (Chicago U.P., 1967).

PARROT, A. Nineveh and Babylon (London, 1961).
    Sumer (London, 1961).

PIGGOTT, S. (Ed.) The Dawn of Civilization (London, 1962).

ROUX, GEORGES. Ancient Iraq (London, 1964).

SAGGS, H. W. F. The Greatness that was Babylon (Sidgwick and Jackson, London, 1962).

STARK, FREYA. Rome on the Euphrates (John Murray, London, 1966).

WOOLLEY, Sir C. L. Abraham (London, 1936).
    Mesopotamia and the Middle East (London, 1961).
    The Sumerians (Oxford, 1928).
    Ur of the Chaldees (London, 1950).
    Ur Excavations. 8 vols. (Oxford, 1928-).

ISLAMIC PERIOD

CRESWELL, K. A. C. Early Muslim Architecture (3 vols., Oxford, 1932-50).

HITTI, P. K. A History of the Arabs (2nd ed., London, 1940).

LE STRANGE, GUY. The Lands of the Eastern Caliphate (Cambridge, 1905).

LOKKEGAARD, FREDE. Islamic Taxation in the Classical Period, with a Special Reference to Circumstances in Iraq (Copenhagen, 1950).

RECENT HISTORY

ADAMSON, DAVID. The Kurdish War (London, 1964).

AL-MARAYATI, ABID A. A Diplomatic History of Modern Iraq (Speller, New York, 1961).

BRADDON, RUSSELL. The Siege (Jonathan Cape, London, 1969).

DANN, URIEL. Iraq under Qassem: A Political History 1958-63 (Praeger, New York, 1969).

FOSTER, H. A. The Making of Modern Iraq (London, 1936).

GALLMAN, W. J. Iraq under General Nuri (Johns Hopkins Press, 1964).

HALDANE, Sir J. A. L. The Insurrection in Mesopotamia, 1920 (Edinburgh, 1922).

HASANI, ABDUL RAZZAQ. Ta'rikh al-'Iraq al-Siyasi al-Hadith (Political History of Modern Iraq) (Sidon, 1948).

KHADDURI, MAJID, Independent Iraq 1932-58, A Study in Iraqi Politics (2nd edition, Oxford University Press, 1960).
    Republican Iraq: A study in Iraqi Politics since the Revolution of 1958 (Oxford University Press, 1970).

LONGRIGG, S. H. Four Centuries of Modern Iraq (Oxford, 1925).
    Iraq 1900-1950: A Political, Social and Economic History (London, 1953).

MILLAR, RONALD. Kut: The Death of an Army (London 1969).

MOBERLY, F. J. The Campaign in Mesopotamia, 1914-1918 (4 vols., London, 1923-27).

PAIFORCE: the official story of the Persia and Iraq Command, 1941-1946 (London, 1948).

WILSON, Sir A. T. Loyalties: Mesopotamia, 1914-17 (London, 1930).
    Mesopotamia, 1917-20: a Clash of Loyalties (London, University Press, 1931).

ZAKI, SALIH. Origins of British Influence in Mesopotamia (New York, 1941).

ECONOMY

AINSRAWY, ABBAS. Finance and Economic Development in Iraq (Praeger, New York, 1966).

LANGLEY, KATHLEEN M. The Industrialisation of Iraq (Harvard University Press, 1961).

LONGRIGG, S. H. Oil in the Middle East (London, 1954).

IRAQ—(BIBLIOGRAPHY)

MINORITIES

ARFA, HASSAN. The Kurds (Oxford University Press, Oxford, 1966).

BADGER, G. P. The Nestorians and their Rituals (2 vols., London, 1888).

BLUNT, A. T. N. Bedouin Tribes of the Euphrates (2 vols., London, 1879).

DAMLUJI, S. The Yezidis (Baghdad, 1948) (in Arabic).

DROWER, E. S. Peacock Angel (Being some account of Votaries of a Secret Cult and their Sanctuaries) (London, 1941).
The Mandeans of Iraq and Iran (Oxford, 1937).

EMPSON, R. H. W. The Cult of the Peacock Angel. (A Short Account of the Yezidi Tribes of Kurdistan) (London, 1928).

FIELD, H. Arabs of Central Iraq: Their History, Ethnology, and Physical Characters (Chicago, 1935).
The Anthropology of Iraq (4 vols., 1940, 1949, 1951, 1952, Chicago (first 2 vols.), Cambridge, Mass. (last 2 vols.).

KINNANE, DIRK. The Kurdish Problem (Oxford, 1964).
The Kurds and Kurdistan (Oxford, 1965).

LUKE, Sir H. C. Mosul and its Minorities (London, 1925).

SALIM, S. M. Marsh Dwellers of the Euphrates Delta (New York, 1961).

THESIGER, WILFRED. The Marsh Arabs (London, 1964).

Israel

PHYSICAL AND SOCIAL GEOGRAPHY

W. B. Fisher

The pre-1967 frontiers of Israel are defined by armistice agreements signed with neighbouring Arab states, and represent the stabilization of a military front as it existed in late 1948 and early 1949. These boundaries are thus in many respects fortuitous, and have little geographical basis. It may be pertinent to recall that prior to 1918 the whole area now partitioned between Syria, Israel and the kingdom of Jordan formed part of the Ottoman Empire, and was spoken of as "Syria". Then after 1918 came the establishment of the territories of the Lebanon, Syria, Palestine, and Transjordan—the frontier between the last two lying for the most part along the Jordan river.

The present State of Israel is bounded on the north by the Lebanon, on the north-east by Syria, on the east by the Hashemite Kingdom of Jordan, and on the south and south-west by the Gulf of Aqaba and the Sinai Desert, now an occupied territory. The so-called "Gaza strip", a small piece of territory some 25 miles long, formed part of Palestine, but was, under the Armistice Agreement of February 1949, then left in Egyptian control. The territories occupied after the war of June 1967 are not recognized as forming part of the State of Israel, although it seems unlikely that she will give up her annexation of the Old City of Jerusalem. The geographical descriptions of these territories are, therefore, given in the chapters on the countries which controlled them before June 1967.

Because of the nature of the frontiers, which partition natural geographical units, it is more convenient to discuss the geography of Israel partly in association with that of its neighbour, Jordan. The Jordan Valley itself, which is divided territorially between the two states, is dealt with in the chapter on Jordan, but the uplands of Samaria-Judaea, from Jenin to Hebron, and including Jerusalem, which form a single unit, will be discussed below, though a large part of this territory lies outside the frontiers of Israel.

PHYSICAL FEATURES

The physical geography of Israel is surprisingly complex and though the area of the state is small, a considerable number of regions are easily distinguished. In the extreme north the hills of the Lebanon range continue without break, though of lower altitude, to form the uplands of Galilee, where the maximum height is just under 4,000 ft. The Galilee hills fall away steeply on three sides: on the east to the well-defined Jordan Valley (see Jordan), on the west to a narrow coastal plain, and to the south at the Vale of Esdraelon or "Emek Yezreel". This latter is a rather irregular trough formed by subsidence along faults, with a flat floor and steep sides, and it runs inland from the Mediterranean south-eastwards to reach the Jordan Valley. At its western end the vale opens into the wide Bay of Acre, 15 to 20 miles in breadth, but it narrows inland to only a mile or two before opening out once again where it joins the Jordan Valley. This lowland area has a very fertile soil and an annual rainfall of 16 inches, which is sufficient, with limited irrigation, for agriculture. Formerly highly malarial and largely uncultivated, the vale is now very productive. For centuries it has been a corridor of major importance linking the Mediterranean coast and Egypt with the interior of south-west Asia, and has thus been a passage-way for ethnic, cultural, and military invasions.

South of Esdraelon there is an upland plateau extending for nearly 100 miles. This is a broad upfold of rock, consisting mainly of limestone and reaching 3,000 ft. in altitude. In the north, where there is a moderate rainfall, the plateau has been eroded into valleys, some of which are fertile, though less so than those of Esdraelon or Galilee. This district, centred on Jenin and Nablus, is the ancient country of Samaria, now part of Jordan. Further south rainfall is reduced and erosion is far less prominent; hence this second region, Judaea proper, stands out as a more strongly defined ridge, with far fewer streams and a barer open landscape of a more arid and dusty character. Jerusalem, Bethlehem and Hebron are the main towns. Towards the south-east rainfall becomes scanty and we reach the Wilderness of Judaea, an area of semi-desert. In the extreme south the plateau begins to fall in altitude, passing finally into a second plateau only 1,000 to 1,500 ft. above sea level, but broader, and broken by occasional ranges of hills that reach 3,000 ft. in height. This is the Negev, a territory comprising nearly half of the total area of Israel, and bounded on the east by the lower Jordan Valley and on the west by the Sinai Desert. Agriculture, entirely dependent on irrigation, is carried on in a few places in the north, but for the most part the Negev consists of steppe or semi-desert. Irrigation schemes are now being developed in those areas where soils are potentially productive.

Between the uplands of Samaria-Judaea and the Mediterranean Sea there occurs a low-lying coastal plain that stretches southwards from Haifa as far as the Egyptian frontier at Gaza. In the north the plain is closely hemmed in by the spur of Mount Carmel (1,800 ft.), which almost reaches the sea; but the plain soon opens out to form a fertile lowland—the Plain of Sharon. Further south still the plain becomes again broader, but with a more arid climate and a sandier soil—this is the ancient Philistia. Ultimately the plain becomes quite arid, with loose sand dunes, and it merges into the Sinai Desert.

ISRAEL—(Physical and Social Geography)

One other area remains to be mentioned—the Shephelah, which is a shallow upland basin lying in the first foothills of the Judaean plateau, just east of the Plain of Sharon. This region, distinguished by a fertile soil and moister climate, is heavily cultivated, chiefly in cereals.

CLIMATE

Climatically Israel has the typical "Mediterranean" cycle of hot, dry summers, when the temperature reaches 90° to 100° F., and mild, rainy winters. Altitude has a considerable effect, in that though snow may fall on the hills, it is not frequent on the lowlands. Jerusalem can have several inches of snow in winter, and Upper Galilee several feet. The valleys, especially Esdraelon and adjacent parts of the upper Jordan, lying below sea-level, can become extremely hot (over 100°) and very humid.

Rainfall is very variable from one part of Israel to another. Parts of Galilee receive over 40 inches annually, but the amount decreases rapidly southwards, until in the Negev and Plain of Gaza, it is 10 inches or less. This is because the prevailing southwesterly winds blow off the sea to reach the north of Israel, but further south they come from Egypt, with only a short sea track, and are hence lacking in moisture.

RACE AND LANGUAGE

Discussion over the racial affinities of the Jewish people has continued over many years, but there has been no unanimity on the subject. One view is that the Jewish people, whatever their first origin, have now taken on many of the characteristics of the peoples among whom they have lived since the Dispersal—e.g., the Jews of Germany were often closely similar in anthropological character to the Germans; the Jews of Iraq resembled the Arabs; and the Jews of Abyssinia had a black skin. Upholders of such a view would largely deny the separateness of ethnic qualities amongst the Jews. On the other hand, it has been suggested that the Jews represent an intermixture of Armenoid and other Middle-Eastern racial strains, with the former predominating—and evidence for this may be found in the headform and facial appearance of many Jews, which are often strongly Armenoid. The correctness of either viewpoint is largely a matter of personal interpretation.

Under British mandatory rule there were three official languages in Palestine—Arabic, spoken by a majority of the inhabitants (all Arabs and a few Jews); Hebrew, the ancient language of the Jews; and English. This last was considered to be standard if doubt arose as to the meaning of translation from the other two.

Since the establishment of the State of Israel the relative importance of the languages has changed. Hebrew is now dominant, Arabic has greatly declined following the flight of Arab refugees, and English is also less important, though it remains the first foreign language of most Israelis.

Hebrew, once widely current in biblical days, underwent considerable eclipse after the dispersal of Jewish people by the Romans, and until fairly recently its use was largely restricted to scholarship, serious literature and religious observance. Most Jews of Eastern and Southern Europe did not employ Hebrew as their everyday speech, but spoke either Yiddish or Ladino, the former being a Jewish-German dialect current in East and Central Europe; the latter being a form of Spanish. Immigrants into Israel since 1890 have, however, been encouraged to use Hebrew as a normal everyday speech, and Hebrew is now the living tongue of most Israeli Jews. The revival has been a potent agent in the unification of the Israeli Jewish people because, in addition to the two widely different forms of speech, Yiddish and Ladino, most Jewish immigrants usually spoke yet another language according to their country of origin, and the census of 1931 recorded over sixty such languages in habitual use within Palestine.

It is only by a revival of Hebrew that the Jewish community has found a reasonable *modus vivendi*—yet this step was not easy, for some devout Jews opposed the use of Hebrew for secular speech. Furthermore, there was controversy as to the way Hebrew should be pronounced but the Sephardic pronunciation was finally adopted.

HISTORY

Tom Little

For most Jews the creation of the State of Israel in 1948 was the fulfilment of Biblical prophecy; to some in this more secular age it is a country justifiably won by political skill and force of arms in a world that denied them one for nearly 2,000 years; but, however regarded, it is seen as the fulfilment of Jewish history.

Although clearly a more ancient people from east of the Euphrates, the Jews trace their descent from Abraham, the first of the Patriarchs, who departed from Ur, the centre of the ancient Chaldean civilization, about 2,000 years B.C. Oral tradition as recorded in the Old Testament states that he was instructed by God to leave Chaldea with his family and proceed to Canaan (Phoenicia), or Palestine, the land of the Philistines, where he would father a great nation which would play an important part in human history. The authors of the Old Testament were primarily concerned to establish the descent of the Jewish people from Abraham under the guidance of God but in so doing they preserved the ancient history of the Jews which archaeology has tended to confirm within a debateable chronology.

Abraham's nomad family eventually reached Canaan and grazed their flocks there for a time before crossing Sinai to the richer pastures of Egypt. They remained in Egypt probably about 400 years and multiplied greatly, but their separateness in race, religion and customs at last excited the fears of the pharaohs, who enslaved them. Moses, who had escaped this slavery because he was brought up an Egyptian, fled with the Jews from the country (c. 1,200 B.C.) and gave them his law (the Torah) proclaiming the absolute oneness of God and establishing the disciplines of His worship.

They wandered for some decades in the wilderness before reaching the river Jordan. Moses' successor, Joshua, led some of the families (or tribes) across it and conquered Canaan. It was a stormy occupation of constant conflict with the indigenous peoples until the warrior Saul triumphed and became the first 'king'. His successor, David, completed the subjugation of the Israelites' enemies and briefly united all the tribes. King Solomon, his son, raised the country to its peak and built the Temple of Jerusalem which came to be recognized as the temple of all the Jews and the focal point of worship. His magnificence burdened the people, and this and his tolerance of the worship of idols provoked a successful revolt of the ten northern tribes under Jereboam who established Israel as his own kingdom. This division into two parts, Israel and Judah (which contained Jerusalem), was disastrous, for Israel was soon overcome by the Assyrians and its people were taken into captivity and lost to history. About 100 years later Judah fell victim to the Babylonians and its people were also taken captive, but their community endured to become an important element in the future of Judaism. The Babylonians destroyed Solomon's temple.

When the Persian leader Cyrus conquered Babylon he gave the Jews permission to return to Jerusalem, and some did so. There they set about rebuilding the Temple which was completed about 500 B.C. and in 200 years of relative tranquility their religion was consolidated by a series of great teachers. Palestine was in turn conquered by Alexander the Great and it and the Jews became part of his empire; but Alexander was tolerant, as were his successors in Egypt, the Ptolemies, with the result that Alexandria became the centre of a learned school of Hellenic Judaism.

The results were tragic in the successor Roman empire. The Jews rebelled against the oppressive Roman rule and Nero sent his greatest general, Vespasian, and his son, Titus, to suppress them. The conquest was completed by Titus, Jerusalem and the second temple were destroyed (c. 70 A.D.), and the Diaspora which began with the Assyrian conquest of Israel was complete. A small community of Jews remained in Jersualem and the surrounding countryside, and devoted themselves to their religion, producing their version of the Talmud, the repository of Judaic history, learning and interpretation which, with the Torah and the Old Testament, became the essence of the faith, but it was the version of the Talmud produced by the Babylonian scholars which became the accepted document.

Scattered across the world, throughout Arabia, Asia as far as China, North Africa and Europe as far as Poland and Russia, Jewish communities continued to exist, sometimes powerful, often persecuted, but held in their exclusiveness and survival by religion and certain central themes: their belief in the oneness of God, his promise to Abraham, the promise of the 'return', and the Temple as the temple of all Jews. In terms of time their occupation of Palestine was relatively short and for even less of that time did they hold or rule it all, but the scattered communities continued to look towards Jerusalem.

THE ZIONIST MOVEMENT

In the late nineteenth century there were affluent and even powerful groups of Jews in Europe but the people as a whole were usually treated as second-class citizens in the countries where they lived. The large, pious and orthodox groups in Eastern Europe, in particular, were subject intermittently to persecution, and in 1881 there was a series of pogroms in Russia which stirred the conscience of world Jewry into forming plans for their escape. For the eastern Jews there could be only one destination: Palestine. The pogroms lead directly to the formation in Russia of a movement called the Lovers of Zion (*Hovevei Zion*), and within that movement another was formed, called the *Bilu*, by a large community of young Jews in the Kharkov region. In 1882 a *Bilu* group in Constantinople issued a manifesto demanding a home in Palestine. They proposed that they should beg it from the Sultan of Turkey, in whose empire Palestine lay, and that if he would not give them absolute possession he should at least let them have an autonomous 'State within a larger State.'

The word Zionism was coined by a Russian about a decade later as a spiritual-humanitarian concept but Theodor Herzl, who became the leader of the movement, defined its aim specifically at the Basle Congress of 1897 (see Documents on Palestine, p.46): 'Zionism', he said, 'strives to create for the Jewish people a home in Palestine secured by public law'. He wrote in his journal after the congress: 'At Basle I founded the Jewish State ... perhaps in five years, and certainly fifty, everyone will know it'. He is recognized as the founder of political Zionism.

He was concerned essentially with the creation of a safe refuge for the suffering communities of Eastern Europe and thought that their migration and settlement could and should be financed by prosperous Jews. When he failed to get help from the Sultan he considered other possible 'homes' as far apart as Uganda and Latin America, but even safe places could never have the appeal to orthodox Jews as had Palestine, sanctioned in their scriptures and 'promised' to them by God. Some of the Jews of Russia and Poland escaped persecution to make their own way to Palestine and became the earliest immigrant communities there.

When the Turkish empire was destroyed by Allied forces in the 1914–18 war new possibilities of getting their 'home' or State in Palestine opened up before the Zionists. In the years 1915–16 Sir Mark Sykes for Britain and M. Charles Georges-Picot for France had, in fact, drafted an agreement (see Documents on Palestine, p.46) in which, while undertaking 'to recognize and protect an independent Arab State or Confederation of Arab States', the two powers in effect carved the Middle East into their respective spheres of influence and authority pending the time of its liberation from Turkey. (Russia had been party to the Sykes-Picot pact but, publicly withdrew after the 1917 revolution, embarrassing the powers, particularly Britain which had entered into undertakings with the Arabs that conflicted with it). Influential Zionists, notably Dr. Chaim Weizmann, saw their opportunity to press Britain for a commitment to provide a home for the Jews in Palestine and secured the help of Judge Louis Brandeis, a leading United States Zionist and principal adviser to President Woodrow Wilson, in bringing the U.S. into the war on the side of the Allies in April 1917. The outcome was the Balfour Declaration (see Documents on Palestine, p.47) which was contained in a letter from Arthur James Balfour to Lord Rothschild on behalf of the Zionist Federation, dated November 2nd, 1917. It stated:

"His Majesty's Government view with favour the establishment in Palestine of a national home for the Jewish people, and will use their best endeavours to facilitate the achievement of this object, it being clearly understood that nothing shall be done which may prejudice the existing civil and religious rights of existing non-Jewish communities in Palestine, or the rights and political status of Jews in other countries".

The San Remo Conference decided on April 24th, 1920 to give the Mandate under the newly formed League of Nations to Britain (the terms of which were approved by the United States, which was not a member of the League) before they were finally agreed by the League Council on July 24th, 1922. The terms (see Documents on Palestine, p.50) included a restatement of the Balfour Declaration and provided that "an appropriate Jewish agency" should be established to advise and cooperate with the Palestine Administration in matters affecting the Jewish national home and to take part in the development of the country. This gave the Zionist organization a special position because the mandate stipulated that it should be recognized as such an agency if the mandatory authority thought it appropriate. Britain took over the mandate in September of the following year.

THE MANDATE

Herzl's first aim had thereby been achieved: the national home of the Jewish people had been "secured by public law"; but major obstacles were still to be overcome before the home, or State, became a reality. When the Mandate was granted, the Arabs constituted 92 per cent of the population and owned 98 per cent of the land in Palestine, and it could clearly not be a home unless the demography and land ownership were changed in favour of the Jews. It was to these ends that the Zionist movement now directed itself, but Britain and it had different views concerning what was meant by "favouring" the establishment of the home, both in the matter of boundaries and immigration, even though Britain was consistently sympathetic to the enterprise. This was important, for although she was nominally under the supervision of the Mandates Commission of the League, she was able to run Palestine very much as a Crown Colony and administered it through the Colonial Office.

The World Zionist Organization had presented a memorandum to the Paris Peace Conference in 1919 setting forth its territorial concept of the home, as follows:

The whole of Palestine, southern Lebanon, including the towns of Tyre and Sidon, the headwaters of the Jordan river on Mount Hermon and the southern portion of the Litani river; the Golan Heights in Syria, including the town of Quneitra, the Yarmuk river and Al-Himmeh hot springs; the whole of the Jordan valley, the Dead Sea, and the eastern highlands up to the outskirts of Amman, thence in a southerly direction along the Hedjaz railway to the Gulf of Aqaba; in Egypt, from El-Arish, on the Mediterranean coast, in a straight line in a southerly direction to Sharm as-Sheikh on the Gulf of Aqaba.

The League of Nations and the Peace settlement did not accept these boundaries but the mandate given to Britain included Transjordan, the territory East of the river and beyond Amman. Britain allotted Transjordan as an Emirate to Emir Abdullah in 1921 and with the grant of full independence in 1946 it became a kingdom.

The Arabs bitterly opposed the Balfour Declaration and Jewish immigration and called for the prohibition of land sales to Jews. Britain would neither accede to their demands nor to Jewish claims to a majority in Palestine. There were intermittent outbreaks of Arab violence, notably in 1922 and 1929, which brought the Arabs into conflict with the mandatory government and there were four British Commissions of Inquiry and two White Papers were issued (see Documents on Palestine, p.51) on the situation before 1936, none of which envisaged a Jewish majority. In 1936 there was an effective six-months general strike of the Arab population followed by a large scale rebellion which lasted until the outbreak of the Second World War and in 1939 another Commission issued the third White Paper (see Documents on Palestine, p.53) which stated that Britain would not continue to develop the Jewish national home beyond the point already reached, proposed that 75,000 more Jews should be admitted over five years and then Jewish immigration would cease. Finally, it proposed that self-governing institutions should be set-up at the end of the five years. This would have preserved the Arab majority in the country and its legislature.

THE BILTMORE PROGRAMME AND AFTER

The world emotional context at that time was conditioned by the horrifying Nazi policy of exterminating Jews—a policy which was to reach even more frightful proportions after the outbreak of war. Zionists and Jews generally regarded the White Paper as a betrayal of the terms of the Mandate and when Mr. Ben Gurion, Chairman of the Jewish Agency Executive, was in New York in 1942 an Extraordinary Zionist Conference held at the Biltmore Hotel utterly rejected the White Paper and reformulated Zionist policy. The declaration of the conference (see Documents on Palestine, p.54) issued on May 11th, 1942 concluded as follows:

> The conference urges that the gates of Palestine be opened; that the Jewish Agency be vested with control of immigration into Palestine and with the necessary authority for upbuilding the country, including the development of its unoccupied and uncultivated lands; and that Palestine be established as a Jewish Commonwealth integrated into the new structure of the democratic world.

This policy brought the Jews into head-on collision with the Palestine Government before the war was over. Those in Europe who escaped the Nazi holocaust were herded into refugee camps and some who could do so with organized Zionist help tried to reach Palestine, but the British authorities, in accordance with the 1939 policy, tried to prevent their entry.

The British failed. The Jewish population which had been 56,000 at the time of the Mandate was 608,000 in 1946 and was estimated to be 650,000 on the eve of the creation of Israel, or about two-fifths of the entire population. Further, the Jewish Agency had formed its own military organizations, the Haganah and its units of shock troops, the Palmach, which were strengthened by those Jews who had fought on the side of the British during the war, and supported by two smaller extremist groups, the Irgun Zvaei Leumi and the Stern Gang. Towards the end of the war they embarked on a policy of violence designed to impose the Biltmore programme. They successfully made the Mandate unworkable and Britain referred it to the United Nations (which had replaced the League) on April 2nd, 1947.

The UN General Assembly sent a Special Commission (UNSCOP) to Palestine to report on the situation and its report issued on August 31st, 1947 proposed two plans: a majority plan for the partition of Palestine into two States, one Jewish and one Arab, with economic union; and a minority plan for a federal State. The Assembly adopted the majority plan (see Documents on Palestine, p.55) on November 29th by 33 votes for and 13 against, with ten abstentions. The plan divided Palestine into six principal parts, three of which, comprising 56 per cent of the total area were reserved for the Jewish State and three, with the enclave of Jaffa, comprising 43 per cent of the area, for the Arab State. It provided that Jerusalem would be an international zone administered by the UN as the holy city for Jews, Moslems and Christians. The Arabs refused to accept this decision and in the subsequent disorders about 1,700 people were killed. In April 1948 the Jewish forces swung into full-scale attack and by the time the Mandate was terminated on May 14th, 400,000 Arabs had evacuated their homes to become refugees in neighbouring Arab countries.

THE STATE ESTABLISHED

The Mandate was relinquished by Britain at 6 p.m. Washington time; at 6.01 the State of Israel was officially declared by the Jewish authorities in Palestine; at 6.11 the United States accorded it recognition and immediately afterwards Russia did likewise. Thus Israel came into existence only one year late on Herzl's 50-year diary prophecy. The Arab States belatedly came to the help of the Palestinian Arabs but their attempt to overthrow it failed and Israel was left in possession of more territory than had been allotted to her under the UN partition plan. It included new (non-Arab) Jerusalem and she rejected the proposed internationalization of the city, for the Jews considered the return to Jerusalem to be at the heart of the divine promise to them.

A provisional government was formed in Tel-Aviv the day before the Mandate ended with Ben Gurion as Prime Minister and other members of the Jewish Agency Executive in leading ministerial posts. The constitution and electoral laws had already been prepared and the first general elections were held in January 1949 for a single-chamber Knesset (or parliament) elected by proportional representation. This enabled several parties to gain representation with Mapai usually in the majority but never predominant. The result has been that government was conducted afterwards by uneasy coalitions—except when military confrontation with the Arabs was involved.

After the war another 400,000 Arabs fled from the additional territory conquered by Israel and in the course of another year about 300,000 more left the impoverished Arab West Bank for Transjordan. (In 1950 King Abdullah held a referendum in which the West Bank Arabs agreed to be part of his kingdom which then became known as Jordan.) The Israeli Government maintained the mandatory military control, established in the earlier disorders, over those Arab populations which remained within its territory but allowed "co-operative" Arabs to be elected to the Knesset; four were elected to the first parliament.

A gigantic programme of immigration was launched immediately the Provisional Government took over and within three years the Jewish population was doubled. This result, unparalleled in history, was assisted by Iraq which expelled the larger part of its age-old Jewish communities. The 1961 census gave Israel's population as 2,260,700, of whom 230,000 were Arabs. The two-millionth Jew arrived in May 1962 and the three-millionth early in 1972. A massive plan for land development to provide for the new people was executed concomitantly with the early immigration programme; the Jewish National Fund took over 3,000,000 dunums of former Arab land and used heavy mechanical equipment to bring it rapidly back into production. This was made possible by the stupendous support from abroad which came in the form of private gifts from world Jewry, State loans and aid, and private Jewish investments. The United States was both privately and publicly the major contributor but by agreement at the Hague in 1952, West Germany agreed to pay reparations for Nazi crimes which amounted to £216 million in Deutschemarks and about £100 million in oil from Britain before payments were concluded in 1966. The effect of this influx of unearned money from all sources was to cause serious inflation which in 1962 forced devaluation of the Israel £ to one-fifth of its original value and was still a grave problem in mid-1972 (*see* Economic Survey). Israel remains by far the greatest per-capita recipient of aid in the world.

Israel was admitted to the United Nations, albeit on conditions concerning Jerusalem and refugees which were contrary to her overall policy and were never fulfilled. Her relations with the Arab States were governed by a series of armistice agreements reached in Rhodes in 1949 which, in effect, established an unsteady truce without an Arab commitment to permanent peace. The Arabs continued to insist that the creation of Israel was a usurpation of Arab territory and right and a denial of UN principles. Defence policy therefore dominated Israel's political thinking and firmly established the principle that she would remain militarily superior to any combination of Arab States. In the early 1950s, however, it was the Palestinian refugees who caused intermittent frontier trouble, mainly from Syria and Jordan but to some extent from the Gaza strip which, since the 1948 war, had been administered by Egypt.

Whenever one of the frontiers became too troublesome, Israel mounted a massive retaliatory raid *pour décourager les autres*. On the principle that Nasser's Egypt was the only serious danger, Mr. Ben Gurion ordered a raid which on February 28th, 1955, wiped-out the small Egyptian garrison at Gaza and the reinforcements travelling by road to its support. The result was contrary to Ben Gurion's intention; Nasser determined to secure adequate military strength and to that end entered into the "Czech" arms agreement in August 1955 by which he bartered cotton and took credits from Russia for substantial quantities of arms and planes which began to arrive quickly. The threat to Israel was therefore increased.

SUEZ

On July 26th, 1956, Nasser nationalized the Suez Canal company of which Britain and France were the principal shareholders (*see* Egypt) and the two European powers prepared to retake control of it. Neither could expect any support from the two super-powers, or from world opinion in general, for open invasion, but in October Ben Gurion entered into a secret pact with them by which Israel would invade Sinai and thus justify Britain and France intervening to keep the combatants apart. The Israelis invaded on October 29th, with powerful armoured columns and rapidly advanced towards the canal and 24 hours later Britain and France issued their ultimatum that both sides should withdraw to 20 miles from the canal. Israel had by this time taken almost all of the Sinai, including the Gaza strip and Sharm as-Sheikh at the entrance to the Gulf of Aqaba, and she readily agreed to do so, but Egypt refused on the grounds that she was being asked to withdraw from her own territory.

The Anglo-French force thereupon invaded the Port Said area and advanced some miles along the Suez Canal. There it was halted by Sir Anthony Eden, the British Prime Minister, in face of the forthright condemnation of the UN and financial sanctions threatened by the U.S.; a decision which the French Prime Minister, M. Guy Mollet, reluctantly accepted. Both countries withdrew their troops before the year was out. This was a severe blow to Mr. Ben Gurion who had counted on holding at least a security buffer zone on a line from El Arish, on the Mediterranean coast, to Sharm as-Sheikh (the Zionist 1919 frontier proposal). Therefore Israel delayed her final withdrawal from Egypt until January, and from the Gaza strip until March 1957 when a UN Emergency Force proposed by Canada and accepted by Egypt, was completely established on the Sinai frontier and at Sharm as-Sheikh. Even so, Egypt kept detaining ships in the Suez Canal and confiscating cargoes bound for Israel, against which Mrs. Golda Meir, then Foreign Minister, strongly protested to the United Nations in September 1959.

ISRAEL—(HISTORY)

A development of great consequence to Israel at this time was Russia's more active policy in the Middle East, founded on relations with Egypt which had begun with bulk purchases of cotton and the arms deal in 1955. The U.S.S.R. took no less than 50 per cent of Egyptian exports in 1957 and in 1958 agreed to finance the foreign currency requirements of the mammoth High Dam at Aswan and to direct the building of it. In keeping with this policy Russia adopted a strongly pro-Arab and anti-Israeli line and steadily rearmed Nasser's forces.

Mr. Ben Gurion resigned "for personal reasons" in June 1963 and was succeeded by Mr. Levi Eshkol, his Finance Minister and continuously a minister since he joined the provisional government from the Jewish Agency in 1948. He was in modern terminology a "dove", inclined to a more conciliatory policy which he hoped would in time erode Arab enmity. This was opposed by many in the ruling hierarchy, notably the veteran Ben Gurion and Moshe Dayan, who had commanded the Israeli forces in their brilliant victory in 1956 and was now in the cabinet. Ben Gurion emerged from retirement to become Minister of Defence early in 1967 intent to counter Egypt's President Nasser, whom he considered the serious menace to Israel's security. There had also been a notable increase in Arab guerrilla activity across the frontiers of Egypt, Jordan and Syria and the Palestinians had formed a guerrilla organization called Al-Fatah for which the Syrian premier had publicly declared his support in 1966.

Israel countered with occasional massive "strikes", notably one against the Jordanian village of Samu in November 1966. The Syrian frontier became more active in January and the situation became serious enough for the UN Secretary-General, U Thant, to seek—unsuccessfully—to reconvene the lapsed Syrian-Israeli Mixed Armistice Commission. The border clashes took on even graver proportions in April, with aircraft engaged on both sides, and in May Israel warned that it would invade Syria to overthrow its Baathist Government if guerrilla raids did not cease.

President Nasser warned that he would have to activate the Egypt-Syrian Joint Defence Agreement if Israel's "aggression" did not cease. In May, King Hussein brought Jordan into the agreement and in that same month Nasser received information, which proved later to be untrue, that Israeli troops were massing on the Syrian frontier. In response Nasser ordered the withdrawal of the United Nations Emergency Force from the Gaza strip, the Sinai Desert and Sharm as-Sheikh. U Thant immediately obeyed, and Nasser then imposed a total blockade on Israeli shipping in the Straits of Tiran, although Israel had always made it plain that this would be considered a *casus belli*.

U Thant flew to Cairo on May 22nd, but by that time Nasser had already strengthened his forces in the Sinai and called up his reserves. Israel, Jordan and Syria had also mobilized. Israel formed a national government by bringing to the cabinet one representative of each of the three opposition parties. General Moshe Dayan, the victor of the 1956 Sinai campaign, was brought in as Defence Minister.

THE JUNE WAR

Israel made its preemptive strike in the early hours of June 5th when her armoured forces moved into Sinai. At 0600 hours GMT Israeli planes attacked 25 airfields in Egypt, Jordan, Syria and Iraq, destroying large numbers of planes on the ground and putting the runways out of action, thus effectively depriving the Egyptian and Jordanian ground forces of air cover. There were some fierce armoured battles in the Sinai but Israeli forces were in position along the Suez Canal on June 8th. They took Sharm as-Sheikh without a fight. On the eastern front, they reached the Jordan river on June 7th and entered and conquered Old (Arab) Jerusalem on the same day. Their main forces destroyed, President Nasser and King Hussein accepted a cease-fire on the 8th. Israel then turned its attention to the Syrian fortifications on the Golan Heights from which Israeli settlements were being shelled. In a brilliant but costly action, armour and infantry captured the heights. Syria accepted a cease-fire on the 9th but Israel ignored it until the 10th, by which time her troops were in possession of Quneitra, on the road to Damascus. The "six-day war", as it became known, was over; Israel had achieved a victory more sweeping even than that of 1956.

Israel had recovered Jerusalem and access to the Western Wall of the Temples of Solomon and Herod, which were the most sacred places of worship for all Jews but to which they had been denied access since the division of the city between the Arabs and Israel in 1948. Israel immediately tore down the barriers, reunited the city, put the administration of Arab Jerusalem under her existing city administration, and effectively annexed it. The UN General Assembly passed a resolution on July 4th, which Israel disregarded, calling on her to rescind all the measures taken and to desist from any further action that would change the status of the holy city. Israel made it plain from the beginning that there could be no question of returning Old Jerusalem to Arab possession in any peace settlement.

The United Nations and the world powers busied themselves with the search for peace. On August 29th the heads of the Arab States began a Summit conference in Khartoum at which they decided to seek a political settlement but not to make peace with or recognize Israel or to negotiate directly with her and meanwhile "to adopt necessary measures to strengthen military preparation to face all eventualities". The UN Security Council agreed to Resolution 242 after many attempts on November 22nd which stated that the establishment of a just and lasting peace in the Middle East should include the application of the following principles:

(i) withdrawal of Israeli armed forces from territories occupied in the recent conflict; and (ii) termination of all claims or states of belligerency and respect for and acknowledgement of the sovereignty, territorial integrity, and political independence of every State in the area, and their right to live in peace within secure and recognized boundaries free from threats or acts of force. The

ISRAEL—(HISTORY)

Council affirmed also the necessity for (a) guaranteeing freedom of navigation through international waterways in the area, and (b) achieving a just settlement of the refugee problem.

The Secretary-General designated Ambassador Gunnar Jarring of Sweden as Special Representative to assist the process of finding a peaceful settlement on this basis.

The essential ambiguity of the Council resolution was contained in the phrase "withdrawal... from territories occupied..." (which in the French translation became "les territoires"), and the Israeli Government has contended ever since that it meant an agreed withdrawal from some occupied territories "to secure and recognized boundaries". This was, in Israel's view, precluded by the Arab States' Khartoum resolution and their insistence that Resolution 242 meant total withdrawal from the 1967 occupied territories. Further, Israel insisted that she would only negotiate withdrawal directly with Egypt and the Arab States as part of a peace settlement and that the function of Jarring was to bring this about and not to initiate proposals of his own for a settlement.

UNEASY SECURITY

Meanwhile Israel based her policy on retention of the occupied territories as warranty of her security. The 1967 defeat had severely damaged Russia's prestige in the Arab world and to repair her position she began immediately to restore the Egyptian armed forces, including the air force. Meanwhile President de Gaulle imposed in 1967 an arms embargo on Israel and refused to deliver 50 supersonic Mirage IV fighters which Israel had ordered and paid for. Israel therefore turned to the United States, arguing that the balance of military power must, for her security, be maintained in her favour. This point was conceded by the U.S. in 1968 with a contract to deliver 50 Phantom jet fighter-bombers, which brought Cairo within range and were more powerful than any MiGs in Egypt.

Russia established powerful artillery West of the canal with which Nasser began in 1968 a "war of attrition" in order to force Israel to accept his terms. Relatively heavy casualties were caused to the Israeli troops, notably in July and October, but throughout the period Israel retaliated punitively with air and artillery attacks which forced Egypt to evacuate the canal zone towns. Suez and its oil refineries were destroyed. The zone remained disturbed until 1970 then it reached a climax in February. This time Israel retaliated by bombing a factory 10 miles from Cairo, killing 80 workers and another raid into the delta killed children in a school. The Israeli targets were Soviet Sam-II missile installations.

President Nixon, who had taken office in the United States, supported an initiative by his Secretary of State, William Rogers, "to encourage the parties to stop shooting and start talking". This was announced on June 25, 1970, and was unfavourably received in the Arab world. Nasser flew to Moscow with a proposal to accept it on condition that Russia supplied SAM-III missiles capable of destroying low-flying aircraft. He returned to Cairo and stunned Egypt and the Arab world with an unconditional acceptance of the Rogers plan and its related canal zone 90 day ceasefire. King Hussein immediately associated Jordan with Nasser's acceptance. Israel was surprised by this turn of events and did not accept the Rogers plan until August 7th; but within hours she complained that Egypt had broken the ceasefire agreement by moving SAM-III missile sites into the 30-mile wide standstill area along the canal. Nothing was done by the United Nations or the U.S. to remedy the situation in the zone but the U.S. restored the balance of power by increasing the supply of Phantoms to Israel.

President Nasser died suddenly on September 28th but President Sadat, who succeeded him, sustained his policy. Although he only agreed to extend the ceasefire for another 90 days, it was again renewed in February 1971 and continued indefinitely. The American effort was directed towards securing an interim agreement by which Israel would withdraw from the Suez Canal and allow it to be reopened but Israel, again on the basic principle of her security, would only consider a limited withdrawal and would not agree that Egyptian troops should cross the canal, terms which Egypt would not accept. U.S.-Israeli relations, vital to Israel, were uneasy during most of 1971 while the State Department pressed the Tel-Aviv Government to concede unacceptable terms of withdrawal from the canal. President Sadat gave the end of the year as a deadline for "peace or war", but before the year was out Mrs. Golda Meir secured a commitment to Israeli security from President Nixon firmer than any obtained in the past; the Rogers plan thereupon died but 1972 dawned without the threatened outbreak of war from Egypt.

An upsurge of Palestinian guerrilla activity disturbed Israel after the 1967 war. People in frontier villages and settlements were forced to sleep in underground shelters. Although security was more than adequate to secure the State, it could not prevent isolated raids and terrorist acts which reached their peak in 1969, but in the end the problem was largely solved by the disunity within the Palestinian movement itself. Two left-wing guerrilla groups, the Popular Front for the Liberation of Palestine (PFLP) and its offshoot, the Popular Democratic Front (PDFLP) embarked on a series of terrorist acts against Israeli planes and passengers at European airports and challenged the authority of King Hussein within Jordan. The King proceeded to drive the guerrillas out of his country, an operation which was not finally concluded until July of the following year (see Jordan). Israel's troubles along the Jordan frontier thereupon ceased. There were intermittent raids from Syria and Lebanon but Israel was able to control these disturbances by retaliatory attacks and the dangers within the country greatly declined. In May 1972 the PFLP returned to the airport terrorist acts. A Sabena plane was hijacked to Lod airport by two men and two women of the movement who held the crew and passengers hostage for the release of 100 Palestinian prisoners in Israel. Israeli commandos recaptured the plane, killing or capturing the guerrillas. Three weeks later a three-man Japanese "Red Army" suicide squad sent by the PFLP landed at Lod in an Air France plane and indiscriminately shot to death 28 people in the airport and wounded 80 before two of them were killed and the third captured. A new Palestinian terrorist group calling itself Black September (*see* Jordan) seized the Israeli team at the Munich Olympics on September 5th; eleven of the team and four terrorists were killed in a battle with West German police who captured the remaining three terrorists. There were a number of letter-bomb attacks on Israelis in Europe in the last quarter of the year but it soon became evident that Israeli security services were retaliating when fourteen PLO members were killed or wounded by similar attacks in the space of a few weeks. It developed into a silent war between the Palestinian terrorists and a terrorist wing of the Israeli secret service, and by mid-1973 five Arabs and five Israeli agents had been murdered in European capitals and Cyprus.

Punitive raids were made on the Syrian Golan Heights on January 2nd and 8th, in which 125 Syrian civilians were killed and 80 wounded, and on February 21st, 30 Arabs were killed in raids on two camps in northern Lebanon. That same day an Israeli Phantom shot down a Libyan airliner which had strayed over Sinai, causing 108 deaths, including some French crew members. This caused a world outcry which was muted ten days later when eight Palestinians seized the Saudi Arabian Embassy in Khartoum and held the retiring U.S. Ambassador and his successor, the Belgian Chargé d'Affaires, the Saudi Ambassador and the Jordanian Chargé d'Affaires as hostages for the release of Palestinians in several countries. They killed the American and European diplomats before surrendering to the Sudanese authorities.

The stated objective of Israeli punitive raids on Syria and Lebanon was to compel both countries to prevent the Palestinian resistance groups from mounting raids from within their borders, whether against Israel or in other countries. This objective seemed most successfully achieved in Lebanon on April 10th by a daring commando raid into the heart of Beirut, where the raiders killed three resistance leaders, while other commando units attacked two refugee camps outside the city and destroyed the PDFLP headquarters, killing one of its leaders. The Israeli authorities were able to make a number of arrests in the occupied territories from information gained in this raid. It caused a political crisis in Lebanon and led to open conflict between Palestinian groups and the Lebanese Army, which only came to an end when the Palestinian leaders agreed to revise the Cairo agreement of 1970, by which they had had virtual autonomy within the refugee camps. Israel received its most serious condemnation from the UN Security Council for this raid but rejected it, as it had done in the case of other critical resolutions.

THE OCCUPIED TERRITORIES

About 380,000 Arabs fled from the West Bank to Jordan, but nearly a million remained under Israeli occupation; of these, the 70,000 in East (Arab) Jerusalem, which was annexed, were treated as Israeli citizens and the remainder brought under military administration. This was of necessity strict for the first three years because of help given to Palestinian guerrillas by the Arabs in the occupied territories and, in some instances, in Israel proper. The Gaza strip was by far the most troublesome and it was not until the end of 1971 that Israeli security operations, including the clearance of one large refugee camp which had proved particularly difficult, brought the area under control. It was announced in March 1973 that the strip would be incorporated into Israel, that Jewish settlement in the strip would continue and that Arab inhabitants could circulate freely in Israel during the day. Higher living standards enjoyed by the Arabs under the occupation, 60,000 of whom found work in Israel itself, the inevitable growth of collaboration with the Israeli authorities and, finally, the disarray in which the Palestinian movement found itself by late 1970 rendered the security problem inside the country minimal during 1971. In March of the following year the Israeli military authorities successfully held elections for the mayors and municipalities in the main Arab towns, despite guerrilla threats of reprisals against any Arabs taking part.

Government policy was officially that in a peace settlement there would be substantial territories returned to the Arabs but there was no clear consensus in the Government or the country as to what they would amount to, except to the extent that Israel should have "secure frontiers". However, statements by Ministers made it clear that in addition to East Jerusalem, The Gaza strip, and Sharm as-Sheikh, the strategic headland overlooking the Gulf of Aqaba, all of which had been effectively annexed, the Golan Heights of occupied Syria and substantial parts of the Jordanian West Bank would not be returned. There was also increasing evidence on the ground. An extensive building programme to house immigrants was rapidly being executed in and around Jerusalem; 48 settlements had been established by mid-1973, including 11 along the West Bank of the Jordan river; and a Jewish quarter had been built in the Arab town of Nablus. The replanning of Jerusalem was the subject of dispute inside and outside the country.

Defence Minister Moshe Dayan caused controversy early in 1973 by contending that there would not be any settlement for at least a decade and the Government should conduct itself accordingly. He also suggested that individual Israelis should be allowed to buy land in the occupied areas. The Government rejected this proposal but in fact the Jewish National Fund and the Israeli Lands Administration had between them acquired 15,000 acres of Arab land and the army was in occupation of another 20,000 acres. A plan advanced by Deputy Prime Minister Yigal Allon, although not publicly approved by the Government, seemed to be in process of *de facto* execution. He proposed that a chain of Israeli settlements should be established along the Jordan river, which was effectively being done, a second chain along the

Samarian Hills on the West bank, and a third along the road from Jerusalem to Jericho, in order to establish Israel's security. The rest of the West Bank and the main towns, excepting Jericho, would then be returned to Jordan.

The virtue of the Allon plan for most Israelis was that it would absorb few Arabs, for the core of the dispute within Israel remained the question of demographic balance between Arabs and Jews which would be changed in the Arabs' favour by the absorption of territory in which there were many of them resident. For that reason, the Government refused the request, submitted by the newly elected mayors of the Arab towns on the West Bank, that those Arabs who had fled the area after the 1967 war should be allowed to return. To restore the population balance the Jewish Agency, which was responsible for organizing immigration, concentrated upon Jews in Soviet Russia who were the largest reservoir of would-be immigrants. Russia began to relax its stringent opposition to Jewish emigration in 1971, with the result that tens of thousands of Soviet Jews began to arrive in Israel. In 1972, 32,000 Jews from Russia entered the country. This created great social and economic problems (see Economic Survey).

Arab-Israeli relations remained deadlocked despite hopes early in 1973 that the United States, freed from its military commitments in Viet-Nam, would work positively for a settlement. UN Secretary-General Kurt Waldheim reported on the problem in May and suggested that a commission appointed by the Security Council should try to find a solution. Surprisingly, Israel responded with the suggestion that the Jarring Mission, about which it had never been enthusiastic, should be maintained and continue to work on the basis of the Security Council's Resolution 242 of 1967. One cause for anxiety in Israel was the increasing dependence of the United States on Arab oil supplies, which might enable the Arab States to put pressure on the White House. There was so far no evidence of this. On December 31st, 1972, President Nixon agreed to resume deliveries of the powerful F4 Phantom fighter-bombers and other strike aircraft. Israel celebrated its 25th anniversary on May 7th with a formidable display of its military hardware, including missiles, rifles and artillery of her own manufacture. President Sadat of Egypt continued to insist that war was inevitable but the restraint upon it was this power that Israel could mount against the disunited Arab States and the opposition to its renewal manifest both in the United States and Russia.

Professor Ephraim Katzir, a biophysicist, was elected President on April 10th in place of 84-year-old Professor Zalman Shazar, who had served ten years, the maximum allowed by law. President Katzir was inaugurated on May 24th.

ECONOMIC SURVEY

The continuous flow of immigrants, as well as the hostility of both the natural and human environment in the eastern Mediterranean have not only affected Israel's political progress. They have also left a deep imprint on her economy and its development.

Large-scale immigration calls not only for heavy financial outlay to transport the future citizen to the shores of the new state and to maintain him during the early period of his stay, but also for extensive capital investments in order to absorb him into the economic life of the country. Similar problems have had to be overcome with respect to the establishment of a productive agricultural—and later industrial—economy.

The continued tension between Israel and her Arab neighbours entails the maintenance of a costly defence system. At the same time, the boycott operated through the Arab League reinforces a certain intrinsic isolation from world markets—interfering with Israel's lines of communication, hampering her foreign trade, and restricting the natural outlets for her products and services.

Yet despite these difficulties, Israel's economy has expanded at a very rapid rate and shows substantial achievements in practically every branch of production: agriculture and fisheries, industry and mining, building and construction, transport and communications, trade and services. At the same time, a high rate of capital formation has been sustained.

One of the basic problems of Israel's economy, however, has been a tendency towards overheating—inflation—and in turn, towards too rapid contraction. In fact in 1971 and 1972 inflation ran at the high rate of 12–13 per cent per annum, stimulated primarily by a large increase in money supply. The last low point in Israel's economic cycle occurred in 1966 and early 1967 when economic growth fell to nil. Unemployment increased sharply, as did emigration.

By mid-1967, however, it was evident that the economic picture was improving; this trend was confirmed by the war "boom" which followed the Arab-Israeli fighting of that year. Production and employment returned to their former levels, helped by large military orders, as well as by the revival of the home market. The occupied territories provided additional markets as well as a labour source. As a result economic growth showed an 11 per cent rise in 1968 and 12.3 per cent in 1969.

Some signs of a falling off of this high level of economic expansion were discernible in 1970, when the overall G.N.P. growth rate fell to 9 per cent, largely because sufficient financial or human resources were not available to sustain further increases. Capital inflow and immigration have been maintained through 1971 and 1972 with the result that growth in real terms continued at an annual rate of 9 per cent.

AREA AND POPULATION

The total area of the State of Israel within its 1948 armistice frontiers amounts to 7,993 square miles; the territories occupied in 1967 (i.e. Sinai, the West Bank and the Golan Heights) multiplied fourfold the original area of Israel. This compares with the area of Palestine under British mandate which totalled 10,249 square miles. The *de jure* population by the end of 1971 totalled 3,095,100 of whom 2,636,000 were Jews and the remainder mostly Arabs. Preliminary results from the 1972 census show that the population had grown to 3,200,500 by the end of 1972. In addition, there were one million persons in the area brought under Israeli administration as a result of the 1967 war.

The population density of Israel was 153 per square kilometre in 1972. The population is heavily concentrated in the coastal strip, with about three-quarters of the Jewish and nearly two-thirds of the non-Jewish population located between Ashkelon and Naharia. The Tel-Aviv—Jaffa area, which had a population of some 1,000,000 in 1972, is the most densely populated area of the country and accounts for 33 per cent of the total population. A further 18 per cent live in the central area between Tel-Aviv and Jerusalem, 15 per cent around Haifa, 15 per cent in the northern area and some 11 per cent around Jerusalem. Large desert areas are uninhabited except for nomadic Bedouin tribes numbering about 38,000 people in 1970. Over 82 per cent of the population was classified as urban in 1972, the urban population being made up of 2,268,000 Jews and 188,400 non-Jews.

The main reason for the growth of the Jewish population was immigration. Immigration accounted for 60 per cent of the yearly increase in the Jewish population between 1958 and 1970. In 1970, 54 per cent of the Jewish population had been born abroad. Twenty-eight per cent was born in Europe and America, 14 per cent in Africa and 12 per cent in Asia. Of the 1,182,800 Israeli-born Jews, only 17 per cent were second generation Israelites. Immigration up to 1948 totalled 452,158 persons, of whom nearly 90 per cent came from Europe and America. The biggest wave of immigrants—over 576,000—arrived during the first six years of the new State. These were refugees from war-torn Europe, followed by Jews emigrating from the Arab States. Large numbers have come from North Africa as a result of political developments there and during 1955-64 a total of over 200,000 emigrated from Africa into Israel. Since 1956 immigration from Eastern Europe has been resumed. After the mid-1960s immigration began to decline, falling from 54,716 in 1964 to 14,327 in 1967, but the level of immigration picked up considerably after the 1967 war bringing the total numbers of immigrants between 1965 and 1972 to over 200,000. The bulk of these came from Europe and America and this source accounted for 55 per cent of the 36,928 immigrants in 1970. The level of immigration rose to 45,000 in 1971, and is estimated to have been between 60,000 and 70,000 in 1972, primarily as a direct reversal of Soviet policy towards Jewish emigration.

The Jewish birth rate was around 27 per thousand in 1972 compared with a rate almost twice as high for non-Jews, but the infant mortality rate was much higher for the latter. The total yearly rate of increase (including immigration) of the Jewish population was 5.0 per cent in 1972, compared with a peak annual rate of increase of 23.7 per cent during 1948-51.

The Israeli civilian labour force in 1972 totalled 1,047,000, or slightly below 50 per cent of the population aged 14 years and over, and was made up of roughly 30 per cent women and 70 per cent men. The growth in the labour force from 735,800 in 1960 has been due chiefly to the rise in total population, since the participation rate has declined slightly.

An important characteristic is the relatively high proportion of dependents in the population, with one-third aged 14 years and under. As a result of this, the ratio of the labour force to total population—under 35 per cent—is low by European and American standards.

In 1972 some 24 per cent were employed in manufacturing and mining, 8 per cent in agriculture and about 13 per cent in commerce.

As is apparent from these figures, only about half of the labour force is employed in the truly "productive" branches of the economy. Efforts are being made to improve this distribution, which is considered unsatisfactory and which, to a certain extent, is the result of a tendency of many of the immigrants to continue, if possible, in their former professions—mostly in the field of trade and services. Large-scale building projects and public works and the compulsory national service for both sexes in the armed forces have also taken a large share of the labour supply available, while the availability of economic assistance and other forms of unilateral transfers from abroad has also prevented the weeding-out of "non-productive" economic branches.

AGRICULTURE

The agriculture sector is relatively small, accounting for just over 6 per cent of domestic product and employing 8 per cent of the labour force. In spite of this, Israeli agriculture has attracted a great deal of international attention. Agriculture, more than any other sector of the economy, has been the focus of ideological pressure. For centuries Jews in the Diaspora were barred from owning land and the Zionist movement therefore saw land settlement as one of the chief objectives of Jewish colonization. Since the establishment of the State, government agricultural policy has centred chiefly on the attainment of self-sufficiency in foodstuffs, in view of military considerations and Israel's possible isolation from its chief foreign food supplies; on the saving of foreign exchange through import substitution and the promotion of agricultural exports; and on the absorption of the large numbers of immigrants in the agricultural sector. In line with these objectives, the promotion of mixed farming and of co-operative farming settlements has also been an important element in government policy. Although the increase in agricultural production has resulted in Israel becoming largely self-sufficient in foodstuffs—it is seriously deficient only in grains, oils and fats—and important savings have been made in foreign exchange, government intervention in the agricultural sector has been criticized as having resulted in a misallocation of resources and in impairment of the economic efficiency of agriculture.

Cultivation has undergone a profound transformation and from an extensive, primitive and mainly dry-farming structure it has developed into a modern intensive irrigated husbandry. A special feature of Israel's agriculture is its co-operative settlements which have been developed to meet the special needs and challenges encountered by a farming community new both to its surroundings and its profession. While there are a number of different forms of co-operative settlements, all are derived from two basic types: the *moshav* and the *kibbutz*. The *moshav* is a co-operative smallholders' village. Individual farms in any one village are of equal size and every farmer works his own land to the best of his ability. He is responsible for his own farm, but his economic and social security is ensured by the co-operative structure of the village, which handles the marketing of his produce, purchases his farm and household equipment, and provides him with credit and many other services.

The *kibbutz* is a collective settlement of a unique form developed in Israel. It is a collective enterprise based on common ownership of resources and on the pooling of labour, income and expenditure. Every member is expected to work to the best of his ability; he is paid no wages but is supplied by the *kibbutz* with all the goods and services he needs. The *kibbutz* is based on voluntary action and mutual liability, equal rights for all members, and assumes for them full material responsibility.

During the years following the establishment of the State a large-scale expansion of the area under cultivation took place. This was caused by the heavy influx of immigrants and the recultivation and rehabilitation of the area from which the Arabs had been forced to flee. The cultivated area increased from 400,000 acres in the crop year 1948–49 to over one million acres in 1971–72, of this some 480,000 acres are irrigated. Total water consumption at present amounts to 1,500 million cubic metres, of which 1,200 million cubic metres is consumed by agricultural users.

Without taking into consideration the cost or availability of irrigation water, it is estimated that the land potential ultimately available for farming under irrigation is 5,284 million dunums, while 4,096 dunums is the figure given for the area potentially available for dry farming. There are also 8.5 million dunums available for natural pasture and 0.9 million dunums for afforestation.

The main factor limiting agricultural development is not land, but the availability of water.

Since on average 800 cubic metres of water are needed per annum to irrigate one dunum of cultivated area, it is obvious that Israel must harness all water resources. For this reason, the Government established a special Water Administration headed by a Water Commissioner who has statutory powers to control and regulate both the supply and the consumption of water.

The Water Administration has been charged, among other tasks, with the implementation of the national water project. The purpose of this project is to convey a substantial part of the waters of the Jordan River and of other water sources from the north to southern Judea and to the Negev, to store excess supplies of water from winter to summer and from periods of heavy rainfall to periods of drought, and to serve as a regulator between the various regional water supply systems. The backbone of the national water project is the main conduit from Lake Tiberias to Rosh Haayin (near Tel-Aviv), known as the National Water Carrier, which has an annual capacity of 320 million cubic metres. Two other large schemes, also in operation, are the Western Galilee-Kishon and the Yarkon-Negev projects. Small desalination plants have been built at Eilat and elsewhere, and will be used more extensively if costs are eventually reduced. Desert farming in the Negev, using brackish water found underground, has achieved considerable success on an experimental basis.

Cultivation of citrus fruits is one of the principal agricultural branches and produces the main export crop. The varieties grown are "shamouti" oranges, "late" oranges, grapefruit, lemons, tangerines, and citrons. A Citrus Marketing and Control Board supervises all aspects of the growing and marketing of the fruit, particularly exports. Not only have new plantings led to an expansion of the area under cultivation (some 425,000 dunums at the beginning of 1971), but stress has also been laid on the introduction of modern methods and techniques both in the groves and in the packing houses.

The 1971–72 citrus crop was some 1,552,800 tons. Of this total 936,000 tons were exported. Chief markets were West Germany, the United Kingdom and France. The total value of Israeli citrus fruit exports in 1971 was $114 million.

Of the remaining area under cultivation at the beginning of 1972—some 3,900,000 dunums—about 2,900,000 dunums are producing field crops, 450,000 are planted with other fruit crops, 400,000 dunums are being used for assorted vegetables, potatoes, melons and pumpkins, 54,000 dunums are devoted to fish ponds and the remainder for miscellaneous purposes. Of the last, increasing emphasis is being laid on the growing of floral plants, produce from which is exported directly to Western Europe as cut flowers.

There has been a steady increase in the number of cattle, raised mainly for dairy farming. However, government policy from 1970 through 1972 has led to a shift towards increasing beef cattle production, this in turn has created a shortage of milk. Government controls on dairy herds have therefore been relaxed, and grants of I£50 million are being made available to farmers for improving and increasing their dairy herds. Milk production for 1973 is expected to reach

470 million litres against a demand of 550 million litres. At the end of 1971 cattle in Israel totalled 262,000 head, of which 72,000 were beef animals. The keeping of poultry has become one of the basic branches of agriculture: laying hens, geese, ducks and turkeys in Israel now total about 10,150,000 and poultry now provides the main source of animal protein for the population. It is of particular importance for the absorption of new immigrants as the raising of poultry is eminently suitable for new settlers who have as yet little experience of farming.

Supplies of fish are derived from three sources: Mediterranean Sea fishing (trawling, in-shore and deep-sea fishing), lake fishing (Lake Tiberias) and fish breeding ponds. Sea fishing has been expanding in recent years and Israeli fleets operate from the Canary Islands to the Indian Ocean, and also off the South African Cape. Breeding of fish in ponds has become highly developed and provides the largest part of the total catch. In 1972, the fish catch totalled 27,000 tons, about half of which came from Israeli ponds.

INDUSTRY

Israel derives more of its national income—some 27 per cent—from industry than does any other Middle Eastern country and the relative importance of industry is steadily increasing. From 1950 to 1970 industrial production rose by over 500 per cent—or over 10 per cent per year—and the value of industrial output in 1972 reached I£19,100 million, compared with I£15,700 million in 1971. Industrial growth has been particularly vigorous since 1967. Output in the period 1968-72 in real terms rose by 80 per cent while exports have risen over five years by 124 per cent. The expansion has been particularly rapid in the more sophisticated industries—electrical and electronic equipment, transport equipment, machinery and metal products.

In 1970 there were some 18,653 industrial establishments in Israel (including self-employed persons) of which about 244 employed more than 100 persons and about 117 more than 300 persons. Whilst over two-thirds of the industrial labour force was employed in establishments employing over 30 persons, nearly 12 per cent worked in establishments employing fewer than 5 persons and which accounted for nearly 70 per cent of the total number of industrial establishments.

Israel's industry originally developed by supplying such basic needs as soap, oil and margarine, bread, ice, printing and electricity. It used raw materials available locally to produce citrus juices and other citrus by-products, canned fruit and vegetables, cement, glass and bricks. In order to save foreign exchange, imports of manufactured goods were curtailed, thus giving local industry the opportunity of adding local labour value to the semi-manufactures imported from abroad.

To stimulate investment and encourage the inflow of foreign capital the Law for the Encouragement of Capital Investments was enacted in 1950, broadened in 1959 and amended in 1967. The Law sets up an Investment Centre and provides for the approval of projects contributing to the development of industrial potential, the exploitation of natural resources, the creation of new sources of employment—particularly in development areas—and to the absorption of new immigrants. Among the concessions granted to approved projects, particularly those financed in foreign currency, are remittance of profits and withdrawal of capital, and tax benefits in respect of income tax, indirect taxes and depreciation allowances.

Although most of Israel's industrial production, about 85 per cent, still goes for home consumption, industrial exports now constitute about half of all Israeli exports. Here again there has been a very rapid expansion as a result of tax and investment incentives from the Government. Israeli industrial exports, worth $18 million in 1950, had risen to $946 million by 1972.

Israel's most important industrial export product is diamonds, most of the expertise for the finishing of which was supplied by immigrants from the Low Countries. In 1972 Israel exported some $426 million worth of diamonds; the country's share of international trade in polished diamonds has risen to 30 per cent and as high as 80 per cent in medium-sized stones, in which she specializes.

Israel Aircraft Industries, employing some 14,000, is Israel's largest single industrial enterprise. At its main plant adjacent to Lod Airport it produces the first wholly Israeli-designed aircraft—the Arava, a twin-turboprop passenger/cargo transport—and the Commodore Jet, a 10-place twin-jet executive aircraft, as well as the Gabriel sea-to-sea missile. It also overhauls, maintains and repairs almost every type of aircraft. Subsidiary and integrated plants design and make a large variety of aviation products.

The food, beverage and tobacco industries account for about 15 per cent of manufactures and employ some 35,000 persons. About 90 per cent of output is sold on the local market; the rest, such as juices, wines, chocolate and coffee, goes abroad.

The textiles and clothing industry, which was developed chiefly because of its low capital-labour ratio, accounts for about 15 per cent of total industrial production and employs some 50,000 persons. In 1970, it exported goods worth some $96 million—about 15 per cent of total output.

There is also a small but rapidly expanding electronics industry, specializing in equipment for military and communications purposes. Exports by this sector have been increasing by some 20 to 30 per cent a year and in 1970 were worth in the area of $14,623,000.

In view of the heavy power needs of irrigation and the water installations, agriculture as well as industry are large-scale consumers of electricity. As both irrigation and industry have been expanding, sales of electric power are constantly increasing. By the end of 1972, generating capacity had increased to over 1,500,000 kW. This will be further increased to 2,070,000 kW. by the end of 1973 when the Eshkol C power station unit one commences operation. Production of electricity in 1971 was some 6,769 kWh. of which some 1,945 kWh. was sold to industry, 1,382 kWh. to users in water pumping and irrigation, and 2,525 kWh. to other consumers.

MINERALS

The Petroleum Law of 1952 regulates the conditions for the granting of licences for oil prospecting, divides the country into petroleum districts and fixes a basic royalty of 12.5 per cent. Oil was discovered in 1955 at the Heletz-Bror field on the coastal plain and later at Kokhav, Brur and Negba. Although 34 wells in Israel are now producing, their output is less than 100,000 tons a year. The current level of production in Egyptian territory occupied by Israel is about 5 million tons a year: estimates of potential production range as high as 40 million tons a year. In 1971 Israel made a major oil strike in the occupied Egyptian area of the Gulf of Suez. Estimates of the size of output varied from 24,000 to 70,000 barrels per day.

Output of gas from Rosh-Zohar in the Dead Sea area, Kidod, Hakanaim and Barbur is transported through a 29 km. 6-inch pipeline to the Dead Sea potash works at Sodom and through a 49 km. 4-inch and 6-inch line to towns in the Negev and to the Oron phosphate plant.

Despite these finds, Israel has in the past lacked large resources of fuel and power and has been dependent on imports (mainly crude oil and fuel oil) amounting in 1970 to over $70 million a year. The imported crude oil is refined at the Haifa oil refinery, which has a capacity of over 6.0 million tons per year. Actual throughput in 1972 was 6.15 million tons, of which 912,000 tons were exported. Roughly a third of its output is exported. Dependent on the Haifa refinery is a growing petrochemicals industry, which represents an investment of some $20 million. A new chemical terminal was inaugurated at the end of 1972. The terminal covering an area of 200 dunums is reserved for the import of liquified chemicals and was built at a cost of I£5 million. Further expansion is planned.

The closure of the Suez Canal and the new oil supplies encouraged the Israeli authorities to go ahead with a scheme for a new large 42-inch pipeline, 160 miles in length, from Eilat to Ashkelon on the Mediterranean coast. The first crude oil flowed through the pipeline early in 1969. Initial throughput was about 13 million tons, this was increased to 25 million tons in 1972, and it is anticipated that this will rise to 35–40 million tons in 1973. Provision has been made for an eventual increase in the line's capacity to 60 million tons a year. The source of the crude oil put through the pipeline is thought to be Iran, though some may come from the Sinai fields. A refinery with a capacity of 3.5 million tons per year has been built at Ashdod, ten miles north of the pipeline terminal at Ashkelon. Initial production started in early 1973. An Israeli-owned tanker fleet is now under construction, gross tonnage totalled over 1.0 million tons by the end of 1972 and will rise to 1.8 million tons in 1973.

The Dead Sea, which contains potash, bromides, magnesium and other salts in high concentration, is the country's chief source of mineral wealth. The potash works on the southern shore of the Dead Sea, are owned by Dead Sea Works Ltd. The works are linked by road to Beersheba, from where a railway runs northward. Production capacity by the end of 1972 stood at 1.4 million tons.

Phosphates are mined at Oron in the Negev. New plant has improved the concentration of the ore to 38 per cent. The plant has now a production capacity of 600,000 tons a year and a new railway line from the Oron phosphate area to Eilat is planned. New deposits of phosphates estimated at 8 million tons have been found in the Arava of the Negev. Production from Oron and Arava amounted in 1972 to 946,000 tons, and is expected to rise to 1.25 million tons in 1973.

At Timna, in the southern Negev near Eilat, geological surveys have located proven reserves of 20 million tons of low-grade copper ore (about 1.5 per cent Cu) and a further 50 million tons of probable reserves. The building of a mill to make use of these ores and for producing copper-cement was completed in 1958. The capacity was recently doubled to 3,000 tons per day. The ore is mined by open-cast and underground methods. In 1972, copper production from the Timna complex exceeded 12,000 tons.

FINANCE

The problems confronting Israel make a certain degree of inflationary financing unavoidable, and it is reflected in the country's financial statistics. In the early years of the State, when the Government financed its deficits through the printing press and banks expanded their credits, efforts were made to maintain a low level of prices by means of controls and rationing. The result was a large surplus of purchasing power in the hands of the public. The attempt of the public to expand this surplus gave rise to a black market in controlled goods and to a sharp rise in the prices of uncontrolled goods and services.

Government deflationary measures and a credit squeeze were not effective in slowing down the rise in prices until 1967. In November 1967, the occasion of the British devaluation of sterling was taken for a further devaluation of the Israeli pound. The Israeli pound was devalued again in August 1971, following the imposition by the U.S. of an import surcharge. The U.S. in fact was forced to devalue the dollar in December 1971 amidst considerable international currency uncertainty, which culminated in a further devaluation of the U.S. dollar in February 1973 along with the currencies of other countries including Israel.

The size and composition of the Israeli budget reflect, perhaps better than any other economic indicator, the special conditions and problems confronting Israel's economy. To begin with, the Israeli budget generally accounts for more than 40 per cent of the national income—a situation made possible on the one hand by the direct receipt from abroad of grants-in-aid, reparations and loans; and on the other, because it has been the practice to channel these very large revenues directly into development projects.

The budget consists of two main parts: the ordinary budget and the development budget. The first makes provision for current expenses, for example on defence (always a very large item), social and economic services, administration and debt servicing. Its main sources of revenue are direct and indirect taxation. The development budget makes provision for the capital investment required to implement development projects. Its main sources are external and internal loans, reparations received from West Germany (ended in 1964-65 and now replaced with credits), U.S. development assistance and proceeds of food surpluses received from the U.S.

The 1973-74 Israeli budget lists expenditures of I£22,415 million, with nearly half of revenues deriving from property and income tax as well as from taxes on expenditure, the remainder being made up of War bond sales, gifts and transfers.

Main items of revenue outlay are defence and security, social services and "economic purposes". Reflecting yet another of the problems of inflationary financing is expenditure on debt servicing and repayment.

That the Israeli payments position is at present in surplus (some I£142 million in 1972) is the result of capital movements to Israel totalling more than $10,000 million since the establishment of the State. Against these funds may be set the inevitable loss on current account ($1,075 million in 1972). Transfer payments—proceeds from the United Jewish Appeal and similar campaigns, personal restitutions, as well as institutional and personal remittances—comprised about 70 per cent of this total, the remainder coming from overseas short and long-term loans and investments, including about $80 million from the sale of State of Israel bonds.

Israel's foreign exchange obligations at the end of 1972 amounted to some $4,000 million, following particularly heavy borrowing throughout 1970-73 (a net increase in the period of almost $1,800 million).

TRADE

Israel's balance of trade inevitably shows a heavy deficit, reflecting its dependence on foreign consumer and capital goods—if not foodstuffs—and raw materials. Although exports have increased dramatically, from $28 million in 1949 to $199 million in 1959 and $1,101 million in 1972, imports have stayed well ahead. In 1949, Israel's imports were worth $252 million, in 1959, $427 million; in 1972 Israel imported goods and services to a total value of $1,957 million. The trade deficit of $855 million in 1972 shows a marginal improvement on 1971 which totalled $896 million.

Imports of consumer goods amounted to some $212 million (or 10.8 per cent of the total) in 1972. Capital goods amounted to some $478 million (or 24.5 per cent of the total) in 1972. However, when aircraft and ships are excluded imports of capital goods total $415 million. By far the largest import sector, however, was that which covered raw materials and production inputs at $1,258 million. This includes the import of diamonds which amounted to $336 million in 1972.

The focus of Israel's foreign trade is mainly Europe and North America. Thus the progress towards regional economic integration in Western Europe is of considerable concern. In May 1964, a three-year agreement was concluded with the European Economic Community providing for tariff reductions of from 10 to 40 per cent on about 20 items, mostly industrial goods. This expired in 1967, but a five-year preferential trade agreement with the EEC was signed in June 1970. This agreement included a 45 per cent cut in EEC tariffs on certain agricultural and industrial items, a 40 per cent cut for citrus fruit and a 300 ton per year quota for textiles. In return, Israel is granted tariff cuts of from 10 to 25 per cent on industrial and processed agricultural imports. It has also been agreed with the EEC that Israeli access to the United Kingdom (which became a member of the EEC on January 1st, 1973) shall remain on the pre-entry basis while further agreements are negotiated for 1974-75.

BANKING, TRANSPORT AND TOURISM

Israel possesses a highly-developed banking system, consisting of the central bank (the Central Bank of Israel), 28 commercial banks, 14 credit co-operatives and 35 other financial institutions. Long-term credits are granted by mortgage banks, the Israel Agricultural Bank, the Industrial Development Bank and the Maritime Bank. As of mid-1971, the amount of outstanding bank credit to the public was I£6,739 million.

The function of the Central Bank is to issue currency, to accept deposits from banking institutions in Israel (and extend temporary advances to the Government), act as the Government's sole fiscal and banking agent, and manage the public debt. Its Governor supervises the liquidity position of the commercial banks and regulates the volume of bank advances.

As of June 1973, the total assets of the Central Bank were I£13,933 million. Currency in circulation totalled I£2,376 million and gold and foreign currency assets were I£6,994 million.

The Israeli pound (divided into 100 agorot) was first issued in 1948 by the Bank Leumi le-Israel B.M.— then the Anglo-Palestine Bank Ltd.—in exchange for the Palestine pound, a colonial sterling currency issued in London. Since December 1st, 1954, the Bank of Israel has taken over the issue of currency. As cover for its issue, the Bank holds gold, foreign exchange, Government Land Bills, Treasury Bills and other government obligations.

The continued severance of all lines of communication with her Arab neighbours has not only intensified Israel's dependence on sea and air communications, but has also given great impetus to the establishment of a national merchant marine and airline.

ISRAEL—(Economic Survey, Statistical Survey)

Since 1949, Israel has operated its own international air carrier—El-Al Israel National Airlines Ltd. Regular scheduled services to West Europe, U.S.A., Cyprus, Iran, and parts of Africa and Asia are maintained; in addition, some 14 international airlines call at Lod, the airport of Tel-Aviv.

Domestic services are provided by Arkia, a national carrier which in 1972 carried over 400,000 passengers from Tel-Aviv to Jerusalem, Eilat, Haifa, Rosh Pina and Massada, as well as to points in the occupied territories.

Israel's merchant navy at present consists of some 120 vessels with a total deadweight of some 3.3 million tons. At the beginning of 1971, some 52 new ships were on order for delivery by the end of 1974, when total capacity will exceed 4.5 million tons, composed of all types of vessels. Most of these will be built abroad, but a shipyard is now being built in Haifa where there are already floating and dry-dock facilities. In the north, the port of Haifa and its Kishon harbour extension provide Israel's main port facilities. The south is served by the port of Eilat—Israel's only non-Mediterranean port—at the head of the Gulf of Aqaba, and by a new deep-water port at Ashdod, some 30 miles south of Tel-Aviv.

About I£70 million have so far been invested in Israel's railways, which by 1970 operated some 416 miles of main lines and 205 miles of branch lines. The service extends from Nahariya, north of Haifa, to Jerusalem, and then southwards through Beersheba. In 1965 it reached Dimona and in 1970 the phosphate works at Oron; ultimately, an extension to Eilat is envisaged. Traction is wholly by diesel locomotives. In 1971–72 traffic consisted of 38 million passenger-kilometres and 490 million ton-kilometres of freight.

Roads are the chief means of transport. In 1972 there were some 2,600 miles of paved roads in Israel, 92 miles of which were four-lane motorways, and 1,786 miles of which were main or regional roads. Travelling them were 147,000 private vehicles—nearly 49 per thousand of the Israeli population.

In 1972, some 727,500 tourists visited Israel, bringing foreign exchange earnings from tourism to $212.7 million, an increase of 19 per cent on 1971. The country has more than 300 hotels graded from five-star to one-star, and including guest-houses at the *kibbutzim*, pilgrims' hospices and youth hostels. Overall administration of Israeli tourism is carried out by the Ministry of Tourism, which maintains 20 offices abroad. It is also in charge of regulating tourist services in Israel, including the arrangement of "package" tours and the provision of multilingual guides.

STATISTICAL SURVEY

AREA AND POPULATION

Area (sq. miles)	Population Dec. 1972	Birth Rate (per '000) 1972	Marriage Rate (per '000) 1972	Death Rate (per '000) 1972
7,993	3,200,500	27.2	9.4	7.2

* This includes the population of the Old City of Jerusalem and the surrounding areas (68,000 inhabitants), which Israel annexed in 1967.

ADMINISTERED TERRITORIES
(1972)

	Area (sq. miles)	Population
Golan	444	n.a.
Judea and Samaria	2,270	639,300
Gaza	140	} 390,700
Sinai	23,622	
Total	26,476	1,030,000

POPULATION OF CHIEF TOWNS
(May 1972–Estimates)

Jerusalem (capital)	304,500	Holon	98,000
Tel-Aviv—Jaffa	362,200	Petach-Tikva	92,400
Haifa	217,400	Beersheba	84,100
Ramat Gan	120,100	Bene Beraq	74,100

ISRAEL—(STATISTICAL SURVEY)

GROWTH OF POPULATION AND JEWISH IMMIGRATION, 1959–72

End of Year	Permanent Population	Jews	Others	Immigration
1959	2,088,685	1,858,841	229,344	23,895
1960	2,150,400	1,911,200	239,200	24,510
1961	2,234,200	1,981,700	252,500	47,638
1962	2,331,800	2,068,900	262,900	61,328
1963	2,430,100	2,155,500	274,600	64,364
1964	2,525,600	2,239,000	286,400	54,716
1965	2,598,400	2,299,100	299,300	30,736
1966	2,657,400	2,344,900	312,500	15,730
1967*	2,773,900	2,383,600	390,300	14,327
1968*	2,841,100	2,434,800	406,300	20,544
1969*	2,919,200	2,496,600	422,700	23,510
1970*	3,001,400	2,561,400	440,000	20,624
1971*	3,095,100	2,636,600	458,500	41,930
1972*	3,200,500	2,723,600	476,900	55,888

* These figures exclude the population of the areas occupied by Israel since June 1967 and now known in Israel as the "Administered Territories" (*see* above), but include the population of the Old City of Jerusalem and the surrounding areas, which Israel annexed in 1967 and regards as Israeli territory (the UN Security Council and General Assembly have declared this annexation invalid).

EMPLOYMENT
('000)

	1969	1970	1971	1972
Agriculture, Forestry and Fishing	91.3	84.8	84.5	83.4
Mining, Quarrying and Manufacturing	226.1	233.3	239.6	248.3
Electricity, Gas and Water	10.6	11.3	11.0	8.8
Construction	75.9	80.1	88.3	99.3
Trade, Restaurants and Hotels	125.0	125.0	126.4	137.0
Transport, Storage and Communications	74.7	72.2	74.0	76.9
Financing, Insurance and Business Services	48.5	49.7	56.7	60.2
Community, Social and Personal Services	290.3	303.8	314.1	328.7
Others	3.4	3.0	2.5	4.4
Total	945.8	963.2	997.1	1,047.0

AGRICULTURE
AGRICULTURAL LAND USAGE
('000 dunums or '00 hectares)

	1969–70	1970–71	1971–72	1972–73
Field Crops	2,655	2,695	2,650	2,670
Fruit incl. citrus	855	835	845	860
Vegetables, potatoes, etc.	346	370	396	415
Nurseries, flowers, fish ponds, etc.	264	240	239	240
Total Cultivated Area	4,120	4,140	4,130	4,185

ISRAEL—(Statistical Survey)

PRODUCTION
(metric tons)

	1968–69	1969–70	1970–71	1971–72
Wheat	155,800	125,000	199,500	301,400
Barley	20,500	13,600	17,600	32,800
Sorghum	16,400	10,900	20,600	40,400
Hay	139,900	137,300	141,200	132,500
Groundnuts	12,400	18,700	21,200	19,800
Cotton Lint	39,200	35,300	36,700	40,300
Cottonseed	61,000	58,600	69,000	65,000
Sugar Beet	214,600	237,000	258,600	248,500
Melons and Pumpkins	119,900	131,500	132,900	161,700
Vegetables	443,000	472,300	490,400	502,600
Potatoes	114,600	137,100	142,000	143,100
Citrus Fruit	1,178,100	1,261,900	1,513,500	1,552,800
Other Fruit	304,800	288,800	307,700	359,800
Milk (kl.) (incl. sheep and goat milk)	456,000	487,700	497,500	519,200

PRODUCTION OF CITRUS FRUIT
(metric tons)

	1969–70	1970–71	1971–72
Grapefruit	284,300	361,300	334,300
Lemons	39,800	46,400	39,900
Oranges: Shamouti	677,900	746,500	842,200
Lates	207,600	298,100	273,500
Other varieties	52,300	61,200	62,900
Total	1,261,900	1,513,500	1,552,800

LIVESTOCK
(thousands)

Animal	1970	1971	1972
Cattle	251	253	275
Poultry	8,800	9,600	10,150
Sheep	189	184	188
Goats	136	134	135
Work Animals	24	23	n.a.

FISHERIES
(tons)

1968–69	1969–70	1970–71	1971–72
21,900	21,800	26,100	27,100

INDUSTRIAL OUTPUT
(I£ million at market prices)
(Establishments employing 5 or more people)

Major Branch	1968	1969	1970	1971
Non-Metallic Mineral Products	362	395	503	638
Foodstuffs, Beverages and Tobacco	1,724	1,966	2,257	2,766
Textiles and Clothing	1,116	1,255	1,515	1,854
Metals and Machinery	1,263	1,583	1,863	2,322
Chemicals and Petroleum Products	537	590	714	901
Diamond Industry	614	563	518	634
Wood and Wood Products	315	329	379	484
Transport Equipment	353	441	657	816
Electrical and Electrical Equipment	399	625	776	960
Rubber and Plastics	356	408	479	605
Printing and Publishing	215	246	275	336
Leather and Leather Products	90	104	109	123
Mining and Quarrying	181	222	264	323
Paper and Cardboard	201	209	265	351
Miscellaneous	92	106	117	153

ISRAEL—(STATISTICAL SURVEY)

FINANCE

100 agorot (singular, agora) = 1 Israeli pound (I£).
Coins: 1, 5, 10, 25 and 50 agorot; 1 pound.
Notes: 1, 5, 10, 50 and 100 pounds.
Exchange rates (March 1973): £1 sterling = I£10.40; U.S. $1 = I£4.20.
I£100 = £9.615 sterling = $23.81.

CENTRAL GOVERNMENT BUDGET
(I£ million, twelve months ending March 31st)

REVENUE	1971–72	1972–73	1973–74*
Ordinary Budget:			
Income Tax and Property Tax	3,075.5	3,851.0	4,493.0
Customs and Excise	2,645.5	3,455.5	4,067.0
Purchase Tax	969.8	1,325.0	1,786.0
Other Taxes	432.0	596.0	774.0
Interest	434.9	492.0	553.4
Loans	1,129.9	1,145.0	1,399.0
Other Receipts	614.0	674.6	679.6
TOTAL	9,301.6	11,539.1	13,752.0
Development Budget:			
Foreign Loans	2,488.8	2,406.0	3,276.0
Internal Loans	1,619.8	2,410.0	2,259.5
Other Receipts	1,071.2	1,460.4	512.5
TOTAL	5,179.8	6,276.4	6,048.0
TOTAL REVENUE	14,481.4	17,815.5	19,800.0

EXPENDITURE	1971–72	1972–73	1973–74*
Ordinary Budget:			
Ministry of Finance	114.9	132.4	166.0
Ministry of Defence	5,546.6	5,458.0	6,065.4
Ministry of Health	295.6	n.a.	n.a.
Ministry of Foreign Affairs	105.2	115.1	142.0
Ministry of Education and Culture	816.9	995.8	1,433.3
Ministry of Police	183.2	205.8	264.0
Ministry of Social Welfare	100.4	107.0	163.5
Other Ministries	458.6	572.8	751.9
Interest	1,151.7	1,740.0	2,000.1
Transfers to Local Authorities	428.1	520.3	671.9
Subsidies	1,249.4	1,347.0	1,550.0
Other Expenditures	453.6	1,798.3	1,921.9
TOTAL	10,904.2	12,892.5	15,130.0
Development Budget:			
Industry and Crafts	209.5	277.8	285.0
Transport	174.4	199.3	254.4
Communications	240.2	304.8	330.0
Housing	1,142.6	969.1	934.8
Public Buildings	189.9	241.1	373.6
Debt Repayment	1,138.2	2,125.0	2,028.2
Other Expenditures	339.8	805.9	464.0
TOTAL	3,434.6	4,923.0	4,670.0
TOTAL EXPENDITURE	14,338.8	17,815.5	19,800.0

* Forecasts.

ISRAEL—(Statistical Survey)

GENERAL CONSUMER PRICE INDEX
(1969 = 100)

1969	1970	1971	1972
100.0	106.1	118.8	134.1

MONEY SUPPLY
(million I£ at year end)

	1969	1970	1971	1972
Currency held by the public	1,128.9	1,281	1,584	1,974
Demand deposit at banks	1,841.2	2,102	2,757	3,613
TOTAL MONEY SUPPLY	2,970.1	3,383	4,341	5,587

EXTERNAL TRADE
('000 U.S.$)

YEAR	IMPORTS	EXPORTS	BALANCE
1965	814,523	406,095	408,428
1966	817,091	476,926	340,165
1967*	756,935	517,245	239,690
1968*	1,093,192	602,105	491,087
1969*	1,304,376	688,697	615,679
1970*	1,433,497	733,622	699,875
1971*	1,811,605	915,061	896,544
1972*	1,957,538	1,101,892	855,646

* Excluding trade with the administered territories.

COMMODITIES
('000 U.S. $)

IMPORTS	1970	1971	1972
Diamonds, rough	174,785	240,264	336,589
Boilers, machinery and parts	172,355	197,818	242,198
Electrical machinery	88,568	96,342	127,959
Iron and steel	140,705	144,672	151,162
Vehicles	87,569	96,972	133,445
Chemicals	101,040	117,520	134,627
Crude oil	64,568	84,589	97,308
Cereals	81,846	83,908	77,077
Textiles and textile articles	64,609	74,201	72,980
Ships, boats, etc.	58,437	189,850	64,516

EXPORTS	1970	1971	1972
Diamonds, worked	244,586	303,379	426,867
Edible fruits	94,941	124,474	123,372
Textiles and textile articles	102,278	119,154	121,364
Fruit and vegetable products	39,447	50,120	62,202
Resins and plastics	9,312	9,858	12,163
Fertilizers	25,552	29,801	29,699
Rubber, including synthetic	16,820	18,772	20,847
Organic chemicals	13,926	12,524	15,379
Mineral products	5,356	3,906	3,402
Plywood	6,673	6,412	6,287

ISRAEL—(Statistical Survey)

COUNTRIES
('000 U.S. $)

	1970 IMPORTS	1970 EXPORTS	1971 IMPORTS	1971 EXPORTS	1972 IMPORTS	1972 EXPORTS
Australia and New Zealand	4,259	5,492	4,018	7,158	7,203	7,839
Austria	14,040	5,270	12,716	7,654	13,124	8,662
Belgium-Luxembourg	62,835	38,420	75,265	43,886	122,351	46,151
Canada	14,455	15,068	21,355	15,885	27,313	18,682
Denmark	9,014	4,389	9,774	4,157	8,822	6,903
Finland	15,061	6,705	17,843	7,643	20,920	8,491
France	61,352	39,663	85,972	42,453	95,155	54,716
German Federal Republic	174,928	66,861	237,888	90,585	228,232	103,455
Hong Kong	1,739	37,197	1,881	45,268	2,592	60,982
Iran	2,695	22,291	2,608	32,913	2,258	44,617
Italy	76,204	14,809	85,161	22,734	166,291	28,860
Japan	61,934	32,299	57,949	48,351	47,286	71,608
Netherlands	71,836	45,519	79,598	57,875	82,827	65,064
Romania	26,491	11,023	26,476	10,745	25,304	10,707
South Africa	10,221	10,689	7,973	9,398	11,591	8,819
Sweden	28,515	11,623	28,613	13,113	37,200	13,784
Switzerland	49,033	33,060	62,087	42,770	70,299	62,083
Turkey	3,727	2,624	5,619	2,482	13,683	2,813
United Kingdom	227,741	81,389	277,157	97,515	365,362	112,892
U.S.A.	324,298	149,114	426,568	185,548	373,235	223,892
Yugoslavia	15,784	9,426	11,211	8,261	18,905	7,560

TRANSPORT

RAILWAYS

	1970	1971	1972
Passengers ('000)	4,117	4,232	4,424
Freight ('000 metric tons)	3,419	3,200	3,136

ROADS 1972
MOTOR VEHICLES ('000)

Private Cars	197.4
Trucks, Trailers	79.7
Buses	4.94
Taxis	3.73
Motorcycles, Motorscooters	39.3
Other Vehicles	2.80
TOTAL	327.9

SHIPPING
('000 tons)

	1970	1971	1972
Cargo Loaded	3,336	3,376	3,464
Cargo Unloaded	4,261	4,635	4,926

CIVIL AVIATION (El Al revenue flights only)
('000)

	1970	1971	1972
Kilometres flown	29,471	31,825	30,362
Passenger-km.	2,531,248	3,213,940	3,488,457
Cargo ton-km.	332,000	404,000	419,000
Mail (tons)	745	745	746

ISRAEL—(STATISTICAL SURVEY)

TOURISM
NUMBER OF TOURIST ARRIVALS

1968	432,000
1969	409,000
1970	441,294
1971	656,756
1972	727,532

COMMUNICATIONS MEDIA
(1971–72)

Radios licensed	n.a.
Televisions licensed	n.a.
Telephones	586,500
Daily Newspapers	26

EDUCATION
(1971–72)

	NUMBER OF SCHOOLS	NUMBER OF PUPILS
JEWISH:		
Kindergarten	3,560	115,679
Primary Schools	1,197	366,591
Secondary Schools	200	54,333
Vocational Schools	288	60,039
Agricultural Schools	29	7,189
Teachers' Training	36	5,381
Others (Evening, Handicapped)	282	17,996
ARAB:		
Kindergarten	232	14,271
Primary Schools	281	95,130
Secondary Schools	46	7,912
Vocational	18	1,120
Agricultural Schools	2	461
Teachers' Training	2	390
Others (Evening, Handicapped)	11	296

Source: Central Bureau of Statistics, Jerusalem.

THE CONSTITUTION

There is no written Constitution. In June 1950, the Knesset voted to adopt a State Constitution by evolution over an unspecified period. A number of laws, including the Law of Return (1950), the Nationality Law (1952), the State President (Tenure) Law (1952), the Education Law (1953) and the "Yad-va-Shem" Memorial Law (1953) are considered as incorporated into the State Constitution. Other constitutional laws are: The Law and Administration Ordinance (1948), the Knesset Election Law (1951), the Law of Equal Rights for Women (1951), the Judges Act (1953), the National Service and National Insurance Acts (1953), and the Basic Law (The Knesset) (1958).

The President

The President is elected by the Knesset for five years.

Ten or more Knesset Members may propose a candidate for the Presidency.

Voting will be by secret ballot.

The President may not leave the country without the consent of the Government.

The President may resign by submitting his resignation in writing to the Speaker.

The President may be relieved of his duties by the Knesset for misdemeanour.

The Knesset is entitled to decide by a two-thirds majority that the President is incapacitated owing to ill-health to fulfil his duties permanently.

The Speaker of the Knesset will act for the President when the President leaves the country, or when he cannot perform his duties owing to ill-health.

The Knesset

The Knesset is the parliament of the State. There are 120 members.

It is elected by general, national, direct, equal, secret and proportional elections.

Every Israel national of 18 years or over shall have the right to vote in elections to the Knesset unless a court has deprived him of that right by virtue of any law.

Every Israel national of 21 and over shall have the right to be elected to the Knesset unless a court has deprived him of that right by virtue of any law.

The following shall not be candidates: the President of the State; the two Chief Rabbis; a judge (*shofet*) in office; a judge (*dayan*) of a religious court; the State Comptroller; the Chief of the General Staff of the Defence Army of Israel; rabbis and ministers of other religions in office; senior State employees and senior Army officers of such ranks and in such functions as shall be determined by law.

The term of office of the Knesset shall be four years.

The elections of the Knesset shall take place on the third Tuesday of the month of Cheshven in the year in which the tenure of the outgoing Knesset ends.

Election day shall be a day of rest, but transport and other public services shall function normally.

Results of the elections shall be published within fourteen days.

The Knesset shall elect from among its members a Chairman and Vice-Chairman.

The Knesset shall elect from among its members permanent committees, and may elect committees for specific matters.

The Knesset may appoint commissions of inquiry to investigate matters designated by the Knesset.

The Knesset shall hold two sessions a year; one of them shall open within four weeks after the Feast of the Tabernacles, the other within four weeks after Independence Day; the aggregate duration of the two sessions shall not be less than eight months.

The outgoing Knesset shall continue to hold office until the convening of the incoming Knesset.

The members of the Knesset shall receive a remuneration as provided by law.

The Government

The Government shall tender its resignation to the President immediately after his election, but shall continue with its duties until the formation of a new Government.

After consultation with representatives of the parties in the Knesset, the President shall charge one of the Members with the formation of a Government.

The Government shall be composed of a Prime Minister and a number of Ministers from among the Knesset Members or from outside the Knesset.

After it has been chosen, the Government shall appear before the Knesset and shall be considered as formed after having received a vote of confidence.

Within seven days of receiving a vote of confidence, the Prime Minister and the other Ministers shall swear allegiance to the State of Israel and its Laws and undertake to carry out the decisions of the Knesset.

ISRAEL—(The Government, Diplomatic Representation)

THE GOVERNMENT

HEAD OF THE STATE

President of the State of Israel: Ephraim Katzir.

THE CABINET
(July 1973)

Prime Minister: Mrs. Golda Meir (Labour Party).

Deputy Prime Minister and Minister for Education and Culture: Gen. Yigal Allon (Labour Party).

Minister of Foreign Affairs: Abba Eban (Labour Party).

Minister of Defence: Gen. Moshe Dayan (Labour Party).

Minister of Social Welfare: Mikhail Hazani (Nat. Religious Party).

Minister of Housing: Ze'ev Sharef (Labour Party).

Minister of Agriculture and Development: Haim Gvati (Labour Party).

Minister of Religious Affairs: Zerah Warhaftig (Nat. Religious Party).

Minister of Labour: Joseph A. Almogi (Labour Party).

Minister of Justice: Ya'acov Shimshon Shapiro.

Minister of Finance: Pinhas Sapir (Labour Party).

Minister of Commerce and Industry: Haim Bar-Lev (Labour Party).

Minister of the Interior: Shlomo Yosef Burg (Nat. Religious Party).

Minister of Police: Shlomo Hillel (Labour Party).

Minister of Health: Victor Shemtov (Mapam).

Minister of Posts and Transport and Communications: Shimon Peres.

Minister of Tourism: Moshe Kol (Independent Liberal).

Minister of Immigrant Absorption: Nathan Peled (Mapam).

Minister without Portfolio: Israel Galili (Labour Party).

DIPLOMATIC REPRESENTATION

EMBASSIES AND LEGATIONS ACCREDITED TO ISRAEL

(E) Embassy; (L) Legation.

Argentina: 33 Shaul Hamelekh St., Tel-Aviv (E); *Ambassador:* Jorge E. Casal.

Australia: 145 Hayarkon St., Tel-Aviv (E); *Ambassador:* Rawdon Dalrymple.

Austria: 11 Herman Cohen St., Tel-Aviv (E); *Ambassador:* Dr. Johanna Nestor.

Barbados: London, United Kingdom (E).

Belgium: 76 Ibn Gvirol St., Tel-Aviv (E); *Ambassador:* Frans Willems.

Brazil: 53 Sderoth Hen, Tel-Aviv (E); *Ambassador:* Luiz de Almeida Nogueira Porto.

Burma: 12 Mateh Aharon St., Ramat Gan (E); *Ambassador:* Ba Ni.

Canada: 84 Hashmonaim St., Tel-Aviv (E); *Ambassador:* T. Paul Malone.

Central African Republic: 40 Hantke St., Jerusalem (E); *Ambassador:* Victor N'Gawe.

Chile: 10 Brenner St., Jerusalem (E); *Ambassador:* Carlos Diemer.

Colombia: 22 Jabotinsky St., Jerusalem (E); *Ambassador:* Ramon Martinez Valle.

Costa Rica: 4 Mevo Yoram St., Jerusalem (E); *Ambassador:* Mrs. Carmen Naranjo.

Cuba: 12 Einstein St., Herzliya-Pituah (L); *Minister:* Ricardo Subirano y Lobo.

Dahomey: (see Ivory Coast).

Denmark: 23 Bnei Moshe St., Tel-Aviv (E); *Ambassador:* Sigvald Alexander Kristensen.

Dominican Republic: 3 Bustanay St., Jerusalem (E); *Ambassador:* José Villanueva.

Ecuador: 37 Jabotinsky St., Jerusalem (E); *Ambassador:* Dr. Ernesto Valdivieso.

El Salvador: Rome, Italy (E).

Finland: 224 Hayarkon St., Tel-Aviv (E); *Ambassador:* A. von Heiroth.

France: 112 Tayeleth Herbert Samuel, Tel-Aviv (E); *Ambassador:* Francis Huré.

Gabon: 8 Shoshana St., Kiryat Moshe, Jerusalem (E); *Ambassador:* Marcel Sandoungout.

Germany, Federal Republic of: 16 Soutine St., Tel-Aviv (E); *Ambassador:* Jesco von Puttkamer.

Ghana: 37 Brandeis St., Tel-Aviv (E); *Ambassador:* Maj.-Gen. S. J. A. Otu.

Greece: 31 Rachel Imenu St., Jerusalem (L); *Diplomatic Representative:* Dimitri Petrou.

Guatemala: 3 Azza St., Jerusalem (E); *Ambassador:* Carlos Manuel Pellecer (also accred. to Greece).

Haiti: 31 Ramat Hagolan St., Jerusalem (E); *Ambassador:* Musset Pierre Jerome.

Honduras: Paris, France (E).

Iceland: Oslo, Norway (E).

Italy: 24 Huberman St., Tel-Aviv (E); *Ambassador:* Vittorio Cordero di Montezemolo.

Ivory Coast: 20 Rachel Imenu St., Jerusalem (E); *Ambassador:* Anoma Kanie (also accred. to Cyprus).

Japan: 10 Huberman St., Tel-Aviv (E); *Ambassador:* Eiji Tokura.

Kenya: Addis Ababa, Ethiopia (E).

Khmer Republic: 20 Rashba St., Jerusalem (E); *Ambassador:* Keo Kim San.

ISRAEL—(Diplomatic Representation, Parliament, Political Parties)

Korea: Rome, Italy (E).
Laos: Paris, France (E).
Liberia: Binyan Gad, Hassoreg St., Jerusalem (E); *Ambassador:* J. Edwin Morgan.
Malagasy Republic: 4 Mevo Yoram St., Jerusalem (E); *Ambassador:* Alfred Rajaonarivelo.
Malawi: Addis Ababa, Ethiopia (E).
Malta: London, United Kingdom (E).
Mexico: 22 Huberman St., Tel-Aviv (E); *Ambassador:* Mrs. Rosario Castellanos.
Nepal: Paris, France (E).
Netherlands: Beth Yoel, 33 Yaffo St., Jerusalem (E); *Ambassador:* Gerrit Jan Jongejans.
Nicaragua: Rome, Italy (E).
Norway: 21 Hess St., Tel-Aviv (E); *Ambassador:* Peter Graver (also accred. to Cyprus).
Panama: 6 Yeshayahu Press St., Jerusalem (E); *Ambassador:* Elio V. Ortiz.
Peru: 19 Weizmann St., Tel-Aviv (E); *Chargé d'Affaires:* Jorge Velásquez de la Torre.
Philippines: 4 Keren Hayessod St., Herzliya-Pituah (E); *Ambassador:* Mrs. Rafaelita Soriano.

Romania: 24 Adam Hacohen St., Tel-Aviv (E); *Ambassador:* Ioan Covaci.
Sweden: 198 Hayarkon St., Tel-Aviv (E); *Ambassador:* Sten Sundfeldt.
Switzerland: 228 Hayarkon St., Tel-Aviv (E); *Ambassador:* Hansjoerg Hess (also accred. to Cyprus).
Thailand: Rome, Italy (E).
Turkey: 20 Bialik St., Tel-Aviv (L); *Chargé d'Affaires:* Melih Akbil.
United Kingdom: 192 Hayarkon St., Tel-Aviv (E); *Ambassador:* Bernard Ledwige, C.M.G.
U.S.A.: 71 Hayarkon St., Tel-Aviv (E); *Ambassador:* Kenneth Keating.
Upper Volta: (see Ivory Coast).
Uruguay: Gad Building, Hassoreg St., Jerusalem (E); *Ambassador:* Yamandú Laguarda.
Venezuela: 28 Rachel Imenu St., Jerusalem (E); *Ambassador:* Napoleón Giménez.
Zaire: 23 Hovevei Zion St., Jerusalem (E); *Ambassador:* Gen. N'Kulufa Lombindo Lonjali.

Israel also has diplomatic relations with Botswana, Jamaica, Lesotho, Rwanda, Sierra Leone, Singapore, Swaziland and Republic of Viet-Nam.

PARLIAMENT

Speaker of the Knesset: Yisrael Yeshayahu.

The state of the parties in the 7th Knesset, following the General Election of October 1969, was as follows:

Party	Votes	Percentage	Seats
Labour-Mapam Alignment	632,035	46.22	56
Herut-Liberal Bloc	296,294	21.67	26
National Religious Party	133,238	9.74	12
Arab Lists (affiliated to Labour)	47,989	3.51	4
National List	42,654	3.11	4
Independent Liberals	43,933	3.21	4
Agudat Israel	44,002	3.22	4
New Communist List	38,827	2.84	3
Poalei Agudat Israel	24,968	1.83	2
Ha'olam Hazeh	16,853	1.23	2
Free Centre	16,393	1.20	2
Israel Communist Party	15,712	1.15	1

There was an 82 per cent poll from the 1,758,685 people eligible to vote in the 1969 elections. The Knesset is elected by proportional representation by universal suffrage for four years.

POLITICAL PARTIES

Israel Labour Party: P.O.B. 36, Tel-Aviv; formed in 1968 as a merger of the three former Labour groups, Mapai, Rafi and Achdut Ha'avoda; Zionist Social Democratic party, membership 300,000, including most of Kibbutz (collective) and Moshav (co-operative) villages. In 1969 elections, in alignment with another Zionist Socialist party, Mapam, gained 65.17% in Histadrut (General Federation of Labour) and, together with affiliated Arab and Druze factions, 60 out of 120 Knesset (Parliament) seats. Holds all central cabinet positions and heads almost all important municipalities.

Gahal (the Herut Movement and Liberal Party Bloc): formed in 1965 as the result of an agreement between:

The Herut (*Freedom*) **Movement:** P.O.B. 23062, Tel-Aviv; was founded in 1948 by the Irgun Zvai Leumi, which played an activist part in the underground struggle against the British in the closing years of the Mandate.

The Herut Party strives to extend the present frontiers of Israel to its historic boundaries extending on both sides of the Jordan. The party stands for

ISRAEL—(Political Parties, Defence)

private initiative; 61,000 mems.; Founder and Chair. Menachem Begin, M.K.

The Liberal Party of Israel: 68 Ibn Gvirol St., Tel-Aviv; f. 1961 by merger of the General Zionists' and Progressive Parties; "Includes all strata of Israel's society. Its basic principles are those of the liberal philosophy. It strives for: national unity, political and economic consolidation of the state, safeguarding its security and integrity; unceasing efforts to achieve a durable peace with our neighbours; a community based on democracy and social justice; insuring freedom of the individual and his liberties; stimulation of private enterprise; reform of the tax system; narrowing the social and educational gap between the various strata of the nation; extensive immigration and complete material and social integration of newcomers; equal rights and chances for all citizens of the state." Party Chair. Dr. E. S. Rimalt; Exec. Chair. S. Ehrlich.

National Religious Party: f. 1956; stands for strict adherence to Jewish religion and tradition, and strives to achieve the application of the religious precepts of Judaism in everyday life. It is also endeavouring to establish the constitution of Israel on Jewish religious law.

The United Workers' Party—Mapam (*Mifleget Hapoalim Hameuchedet*): P.O. Box 1777, Tel-Aviv; f. January 1948.

Mapam is a left-wing Socialist-Zionist party, participating in the coalition government; membership: urban workers, professionals, 75 *Kibbutzim*; aims: public-owned enterprise, guaranteed real wages, progressive taxation, independence of labour movement from state control, large-scale Jewish immigration equal rights for Arabs, neutralist foreign policy, atomic demilitarization of Israel-Arab region, a negotiated Israel-Arab peace; branches in North and South America, Europe and Australia; in January 1969 formed an "alignment" with the Israel Labour Party (see above).

The Kibbutz Artzi Federation of collective settlements (affiliated with Mapam) maintains *Hashomer Hatzair*, which educates Jewish youth to pioneer life in Israel, and operates *Sifriat Poalim* (*The Workers' Library*) and *Hadfus Hehadash* (*The New Press*).

Daily newspaper *Al Hamishmar*; weeklies in Arabic, Yiddish, Bulgarian, Persian and Romanian.

Gen. Sec. Meir Yaari; Political Sec. Naphtali Feder; Organizing Sec. Naphtali Ben-Moshe; International Sec. Peretz Merhav.

Independent Liberal Party: P.O.B. 23076, Tel-Aviv; f. 1965 by 7 Liberal Party Knesset members after the formation of the Herut Movement and Liberal Party Bloc; 20,000 mems.; Chair. Moshe Kol; Gen. Sec. Itzhak Barkai; publs. *Temurot* (Hebrew, monthly), *Die Liberale Rundschau* (German, monthly), *Igeret* (Hebrew, quarterly).

Ha'olam Hazeh (New Force): 12 Carlebach St., Tel-Aviv; f. 1965; supports an Israeli-Arab federation, separation of religion and state, civil rights and freedom of speech and the press; Pres. Uri Avnery.

Communist Party of Israel (MAKI): P.O.B. 1843, Tel-Aviv; f. 1919; originated from the Palestine Communist Party; opposes Soviet policy; aims include non-alignment of Israel; peace with the Arab States based on mutual recognition of the just national rights of Israeli and Arab peoples; defence of working class interests and formation of Left alignment for social progress. Publishes the Hebrew weekly *Kol Haam* and Arabic *Sout el Shaab* (monthly). Other weeklies in Yiddish, Romanian, Bulgarian; monthlies in English and French.

New Communist List of Israel: broke away from the *Communist Party of Israel* in 1965.

The National List: f. 1969 by former members of Rafi.

Agudat Israel and **Poalei Agudat Israel** are also Orthodox Judaist parties, the membership of the Poalei Agudat Israel being drawn largely from wage-earners.

The official organ of Agudat Israel is the daily *Hamodia*; that of the Poalei Agudat Israel is the daily *Shearim*.

Pres. of Poalei Agudat Israel Dr. K. Kahana.

Co-operation and Fraternity Party: an Arab party associated with the *Mapai* party; has two seats in the 7th Knesset.

Progress and Development Party: an Arab party associated with the *Mapai* party; has two seats in the 7th Knesset.

DEFENCE

The General Staff

This consists of the Chiefs of the Manpower, Logistics and Intelligence Branches of the Defence Force, the Commanders of the Air Force and the Navy, and the officers commanding the three Regional Commands (Northern, Central and Southern). It is headed by the Chief of Staff of the Armed Forces.

Chief of Staff of the Armed Forces: Lt.-Gen. David Elazar.

Commander of the Air Force: Maj.-Gen. Binyamin Peled.

Commander of the Navy: Maj.-Gen. Binyamin Telem.

Defence Budget (1972-73): I£5,300 million.

Military Service (Jewish population only): Men under 29 and women under 26 are called for regular service of up to 36 months for men and 20 months for women. Physicians may be called up to the age of 34.

Total Armed Forces: 95,250: 75,000 regular cadre and conscripts, this can be raised to 300,000 by mobilizing reservists within 48-72 hours; army 11,500 regular, 50,000 conscripts (275,000 when fully mobilized); navy 3,500 regular, 1,000 conscripts (8,000 when fully mobilized); air force 8,000 regular, 1,000 conscripts (17,000 conscripts when fully mobilized).

Paramilitary Forces: 10,000.

THE JEWISH AGENCY FOR ISRAEL
P.O.B. 92, Jerusalem.

Organization:
The governing bodies are the Assembly which determines basic policy, the Board of Governors which manages the Agency between Assembly meetings and the Executive responsible for the day to day running of the Agency.

Chairman, Executive Committee: (Vacant).

Chairman of Board of Governors: MAX M. FISHER.

Director-General: MOSHE RIVLIN.

History:
Article Four of the League of Nations' Mandate provided for the establishment of a Jewish agency to co-operate with the administration in the economic and social development of the Jewish national home. The Zionist Organization served as this agency until 1929, when the Jewish Agency was finally constituted, with the admission of non-Zionists as well as Zionists to its Council. The Zionist Congress of 1925 bound the Agency to the following "inviolable principles": a continuous increase in the volume of Jewish immigration, the recovery of the land as Jewish public property, agricultural colonization based on Jewish labour, and the promotion of the Hebrew language and Hebrew culture.

When the State of Israel was established in 1948, the provisional Government was formed from the members of the Executive of the Va'ad Leumi (the representative organ of Palestinian Jewry) and members of the Jewish Agency Executive resident in Palestine at the time. The division of tasks between the Jewish Agency and the Government was defined in the Status Law of 1952 and in a Covenant entered into in 1954.

During 1967-71 discussions on reconstituting the Jewish Agency were conducted between the World Zionist Organization and the fund raising organizations of World Jewry. In June 1971, an agreement for the reconstitution of the Agency came into force, separating the functions of the World Zionist Organization from those of the Agency.

Functions:
According to the Agreement of 1971, the Jewish Agency undertakes the immigration and absorption of immigrants in Israel, including absorption in agricultural settlement and immigrant housing, social welfare and health services in connection with immigrants, and education, youth care and training.

Revenue and Expenditure:
The Jewish Agency's chief source of revenue are the voluntary fund-raising campaigns throughout the world. Approximately two-thirds of the campaign income is derived from the U.I.A. Inc. in the United States, and the rest from campaigns conducted under the auspices of or in cooperation with the Foundation Fund (Keren Hayesod). The Agency also received 18 per cent of German Reparations from 1952–66.

Expenditure abroad, apart from debt service, includes transport of immigrants, aid to Jewish education and cultural activities as well as purchases of equipment and stocks for the new settlements established by the Agency.

Budget: (1972–73) I£1,953 million; (1973–74) I£1,974 million.

JUDICIAL SYSTEM

The law of Israel is composed of Ottoman law, British law, Palestine law, applicable in Palestine on May 14th, 1948, when the independence of the State of Israel was declared, the substance of the common law and doctrines of equity in force in England, as modified to suit local conditions, and religious law of the various recognized religious communities as regards matters of personal status, in so far as there is nothing in any of the said laws repugnant to Israeli legislation and subject to such modifications as may have resulted from the establishment of the State of Israel and its authorities, and also of the laws enacted by the Israeli legislature of which there are already over 1,000. The pre-1948 law is increasingly being replaced by original local legislation.

CIVIL COURTS

The Supreme Court is the highest judicial instance in the State. It has jurisdiction as an Appellate Court from the District Courts in all matters, both civil and criminal (sitting as a Court of Civil Appeal or as a Court of Criminal Appeal), and as a Court of First Instance (sitting as a High Court of Justice) in matters in which it considers it necessary to grant relief in the interests of justice and which are not within the jurisdiction of any other court or tribunal. This includes applications for orders in the nature of *habeas corpus, mandamus,* prohibition and *certiorari,* and enables the court to supervise the legality of acts of administrative authorities of all kinds.

President of the Supreme Court: S. AGRANAT.

Permanent Deputy President of the Supreme Court: Y. SUSSMAN.

Justices of the Supreme Court: M. LANDAU, Z. BERINSON, A. WITKON, H. COHN, E. M. MANNY, I. KISTER, M. ETZIONI, I. KAHAN.

The District Courts: Jerusalem, Tel-Aviv-Jaffa, Haifa, Beersheba, Nazareth. They have unlimited jurisdiction as Courts of First Instance in all civil and criminal matters not within the jurisdiction of a Magistrates' Court, all matters not within the exclusive jurisdiction of any other tribunal, and matters within the concurrent jurisdiction of any other tribunal so long as such tribunal does not deal with them, and as an Appellate Court in appeals from judgments and decisions of Magistrates' Courts and judgments of Municipal Courts and various administrative tribunals.

Magistrates' Courts: There are 26 Magistrates' Courts, having criminal jurisdiction to try contraventions and misdemeanours, and civil jurisdiction to try actions concerning possession or use of immovable property, or the partition thereof whatever may be the value of the subject matter of the action, and other civil actions where the amount of the claim, or the value of the subject matter, does not exceed I£10,000.

ISRAEL—(JUDICIAL SYSTEM, RELIGION)

Labour Courts: Established in 1969. Regional Labour Courts in Jerusalem, Tel-Aviv, Haifa and Beersheba, composed of Judges and representatives of the Public. One National Labour Court in Jerusalem, presided over by Judge Z. Bar-Niv. The Courts have jurisdiction over all matters arising out of the relationship between employer and employee; between parties to a collective agreement; matters concerning the National Insurance Law and the Labour Law and Rules.

Municipal Courts: There are 5 Municipal Courts, having criminal jurisdiction over any offences against municipal regulations and by-laws and certain other offences, such as town planning offences, committed within the municipal area.

RELIGIOUS COURTS

The Religious Courts are the Courts of the recognized religious communities. They are competent in certain defined matters of personal status concerning members of their community. Where any action of personal status involves persons of different religious communities the President of the Supreme Court will decide which Court shall have jurisdiction. Whenever a question arises as to whether or not a case is one of personal status within the exclusive jurisdiction of a Religious Court, the matter must be referred to a Special Tribunal composed of two Justices of the Supreme Court and the President of the highest court of the religious community concerned in Israel.

The judgments of the Religious Courts are executed by the process and offices of the Civil Courts.

Jewish Rabbinical Courts: These Courts have exclusive jurisdiction in matters of marriage and divorce of Jews in Israel who are Israeli citizens or residents. In all other matters of personal status they have concurrent jurisdiction with the District Courts with the consent of all parties concerned.

Muslim Religious Courts: These Courts have exclusive jurisdiction in matters of marriage and divorce of Muslims who are not foreigners, or who are foreigners subject by their national law to the jurisdiction of Muslim Religious Courts in such matters. In all other matters of personal status they have concurrent jurisdiction with the District Courts with the consent of all parties concerned.

Christian Religious Courts: The Courts of the recognized Christian communities have exclusive jurisdiction in matters of marriage and divorce of members of their communities who are not foreigners. In all other matters of personal status they have concurrent jurisdiction with the District Courts with the consent of all parties concerned. But neither these Courts nor the Civil Courts have jurisdiction to dissolve the marriage of a foreign subject.

Druze Courts: These Courts, established in 1963, have exclusive jurisdiction in matters of marriage and divorce of Druze in Israel, who are Israeli citizens or residents, and concurrent jurisdiction with the District Courts in all other matters of personal status of Druze with the consent of all parties concerned.

MILITARY COURTS

Courts-Martial: A Court-Martial is competent to try a soldier within the meaning of the Military Justice Law, 1955, who has committed an act constituting a military offence, without prejudice to the power of any other Court in the State to try him for that act if it constitutes an offence under any other law. A Court-Martial is also competent to try a soldier for any offence which is not a military offence, but the Attorney General may order that he be tried by another Court if he is of the opinion that the offence was not committed within the framework of the Army or in consequence of the accused's belonging to the Army.

RELIGION

JUDAISM

Judaism, the religion evolved and followed by the Jews, is the faith of the great majority of the population, although certain features of Jewish traditional ritual and observance are less rigidly maintained by sections of the community than in European Jewish life of former centuries. Its basis is a belief in an ethical monotheism.

There are two main Jewish communities: the Ashkenazim and the Sephardim. The former are the Jews from Eastern, Central, or Northern Europe, while the latter originate from the Balkan countries, North Africa and the Middle East. Although they have separate synagogues, and differ somewhat in their ritual and pronunciation of Hebrew, there is no doctrinal distinction. The prevailing influence is that of the Ashkenazim Jews, who are more modern and westernized, but the recent Hebrew revival has been based on the Sephardi pronunciation of the ancient Hebrew tongue.

The supreme religious authority is vested in the Chief Rabbinate, which consists of the Ashkenazi and Sephardi Chief Rabbis and the Supreme Rabbinical Council. It makes decisions on interpretation of the Jewish law, and supervises the Rabbinical Courts. There are 8 regional Rabbinical Courts, and a Rabbinical Court of Appeal presided over by the two Chief Rabbis.

According to the Rabbinical Courts Jurisdiction Law of 1953, marriage and divorce among Jews in Israel are exclusively within the jurisdiction of the Rabbinical Courts. Provided that all the parties concerned agree, other matters of personal status can also be decided by the Rabbinical Courts.

There are 185 Religious Councils, which maintain religious services and supply religious needs, and about 380 religious committees with similar functions in smaller settlements. Their expenses are borne jointly by the State and the local authorities. The Religious Councils are under the administrative control of the Ministry of Religious Affairs. In all matters of religion, the Religious Councils are subject to the authority of the Chief Rabbinate. There are 365 officially appointed rabbis. The total number of synagogues is about 4,000.

Head of the Ashkenazi Community: The Very Rev. The Chief Rabbi SHLOMO GOREN.

Head of the Sephardic Community: The Very Rev. The Chief Rabbi OVADIA YOSEF.

Two Jewish sects still loyal to their distinctive customs are:

The Karaites, a sect which recognizes only the Jewish written law and not the oral law of the Mishna and Talmud. The community of about 12,000 many of whom live in or near Ramla, has been augmented by immigration from Egypt.

ISRAEL—(Religion, The Press)

The Samaritans, an ancient sect mentioned in 2 Kings xvii, 24. They recognize only the Torah and the Book of Joshua. The community in Israel numbers about 100; they live in Holon, where a Samaritan synagogue is now being built. Their High Priest lives in Nablus, near Mt. Gerizim, which is sacred to the Samaritans.

ISLAM

The Muslims in Israel are in the main Sunnis, and are divided among the four rites of the Sunni school of Muslim thought: the Shafe'i, the Hanbali, the Hanafi, and the Maliki. Before June 1967 they numbered approximately 175,000.

CHRISTIAN COMMUNITIES

The Greek Catholic Church, P.O.B. 279, Haifa; numbers about 35,000 and Haifa is the seat of the Archbishop of Acre, Haifa, Nazareth and all Galilee; Archbishop JOSEPH M. RAYA; publ. *Ar-Rabita* (Arabic monthly; circ. 4,000).

The Greek Orthodox Church in Israel has approximately 16,000 members. The Patriarch of Jerusalem is His Beatitude BENEDICTOS.

The Latin (Roman Catholic) Church has about 7,000 native members in Israel plus about 3,000 Polish and Hungarian Catholic refugees. The Latin Patriarch of Jerusalem is His Beatitude ALBERTO GORI.

The Maronite Community, with approximately 4,000 members, has communal centres in Haifa, Nazareth and Jaffa. The Maronite Patriarch resides in the Lebanon.

The Evangelical Episcopal Church in Israel, which belongs to the Anglican Communion, has 1,000 members and was officially recognised by Israel in April 1970; it comes under the jurisdiction of the Archbishop in Jerusalem (The Most Rev. GEORGE APPLETON, St. George's Close, Jerusalem).

Other denominations include the *Armenian Church* (900 members), the *Coptic Church* (700 members), the *Russian Orthodox Church*, which maintains an Ecclesiastical Mission, the *Ethiopian Church*, and the *Baptist Lutheran* and *Presbyterian Churches*.

THE PRESS

Tel-Aviv is the main publishing centre, only three dailies being published in Jerusalem. Largely for economic reasons there has developed no local press away from these cities; hence all papers regard themselves as national. Friday editions, Sabbath eve, are increased to up to twice the normal size by special weekend supplements, and experience a considerable rise in circulation. No newspapers appear on Saturday.

Most of the daily papers are in Hebrew, and others appear in Arabic, English, French, Polish, Yiddish, Hungarian and German. The total daily circulation is 500,000–600,000 copies, or twenty-one papers per hundred people, although most citizens read more than one daily paper.

Most Hebrew morning dailies have strong political or religious affiliations. *Lamerhav* is affiliated to Achdut Ha'avoda, *Al Hamishmar* to Mapam, *Hatzofeh* to the National Religious Front—World Mizrahi. *Davar* is the long-established organ of the Histadrut. Mapai publishes the weekly *Ot* but no daily. Although the revenue from advertisements is increasing, very few dailies are economically self-supporting; most depend on subsidies from political parties, religious organizations or public funds. The limiting effect on freedom of commentary entailed by this party press system has provoked repeated criticism.

The Jerusalem Arabic daily *Al Anba* has a small circulation (8,000) but an increasing number of Israeli Arabs are now reading Hebrew dailies. The daily, *Al Quds*, was founded in 1968 for Arabs in Jerusalem and the West Bank; the small indigenous press of occupied Jordan has largely ceased publication or transferred operations to Amman.

There are around 400 other newspapers and magazines including some 50 weekly and 150 fortnightly; over 250 of them are in Hebrew, the remainder in eleven other languages.

The most influential and respected dailies, for both quality of news coverage and commentary, are *Ha'aretz*, characterized by its sober but proudly independent editorials, and the Union paper, *Davar*, which frequently has articles by government figures. These are the widest read of the morning papers, exceeded only by the popular afternoon press, *Ma'ariv* and *Yedioth Aharonoth*. The *Jerusalem Post* gives detailed and sound news coverage in English.

The Israeli Press Council, established in 1963, deals with matters of common interest to the Press such as drafting the recently published code of professional ethics which is binding on all journalists.

The Daily Newspaper Publishers' Association represents publishers in negotiations with official and public bodies, negotiates contracts with employees and purchases and distributes newsprint, of which Israel now manufactures 75 per cent of her needs.

DAILIES

Al-Anba: P.O.B. 428, Hachavazelet St., Jerusalem; f. 1968; published by Jerusalem Publications Ltd.; Editor YAACOV HAZMA; circ. 8,000.

Al Hamishmar (*The Guardian*): Hamishmar House, 4 Ben Avigdor St., Tel-Aviv; f. 1943; morning; organ of the United Worker's Party (Mapam); Editor YA'AKOV AMIT; circ. 25,000.

Al Quds (*Jerusalem*): Jerusalem; f. 1968; Arabic; Editor ABU ZALAF.

Chadshot Hasport: Tushia St., P.O.B. 20011, Tel-Aviv 61200; f. 1954; sports; independent; circ. 30,000.

Davar (*The Word*): P.O.B. 199, 45 Sheinkin St., Tel-Aviv; f. 1925; morning; official organ of the General Federation of Labour (Histadrut); Editor HANNAH ZEMER; circ. 50,000.

Ha'aretz (*The Land*): 56 Mazeh St., Tel-Aviv; f. 1918; morning; liberal, independent; Editor GERSHOM G. SCHOCKEN; circ. 50,000 (week-days), 70,000 (weekends).

Hamodia: Kikar Hacheruth, P.O.B. 1306, Jerusalem; organ of Agudat Israel; morning; Editor YEHUDA L. LEVIN; circ. 8,000.

Hatzofeh: 66 Hamasger St., Tel-Aviv; f. 1938; morning; organ of the National Religious Front; Editor S. DANIEL; circ. 11,000.

L'Information d'Israel: 7 Chodal Street, P.O.B. 741, Tel-Aviv; f. 1957; supports Israel Labour Party; daily; French; Editor NATHANEL GRYN; circ. 8,000; also overseas weekly selection; circ. 10,000.

Israelski Far Tribuna: 113 Givat Herzl St., Tel-Aviv; became daily in 1959; Bulgarian.

ISRAEL—(THE PRESS)

Jerusalem Post (formerly *Palestine Post*): P.O.B. 81, Romema, Jerusalem; f. 1932; morning daily except Saturdays; independent; English; Editor TED R. LURIE; circ. 32,000 (weekdays), 43,000 (weekend edition); there is also a weekly overseas edition (q.v.).

Lamerhav: 1 Nahal Ayalon St., Tel-Aviv; f. 1954; morning; socialist; Chief Editor DAVID PEDAHZUR; circ. 18,000.

Letzte Nyess (*Late News*): 52 Harakevet St., Tel-Aviv; f. 1949; Yiddish; morning; Editor M. TSANIN; circ. 23,000.

Ma'ariv: Ma'ariv House, P.O.B. 20010, Tel-Aviv; f. 1948; evening; independent; Editor ARIE DISSENTSHIK; circ. daily 160,000, Friday 210,000.

Nowiny i Kurier: 52 Harakevet St., Tel-Aviv; f. 1952; Polish; morning; Editor S. YEDIDYAH; circ. 10,000.

Omer: 45 Sheinkin St., Tel-Aviv; Histadrut popular vowelled Hebrew paper; f. 1951; Chief Editor MEIR BARELI; circ. 10,000.

Sha'ar: 4A Hissin St., Tel-Aviv 64284; economy and finance; Hebrew and English.

Shearim: 64 Frichman St., Tel-Aviv; organ of Poalei Agudat Israel; Editor YEHUDA NAHSHONI; circ. 5,000.

Uj Kelet: 52 Harakevet St., Tel-Aviv; f. 1918; morning; Hungarian; independent; Editor Dr. G. MARTON; circ. 20,000.

Viata Noastra: 52 Harakevet St., Tel-Aviv; f. 1950; Romanian; supports the Israel Labour Party; morning; Editor MEIR ZAIT; circ. 30,000.

Yedioth Aharonoth: 5 Yehuda Mozes St., Tel-Aviv; f. 1939; evening; independent; Editor Dr. H. ROSENBLUM; circ. 140,000, Friday 195,000.

Yedioth Hadashot: P.O.B. 1585, 66 Harakevet St., Tel-Aviv; f. 1935; morning; German; independent; Editor Dr. I. LILIENFELD; circ. 18,000.

Yom Yom: Tel-Aviv; f. 1964; morning; economy and finance; Editor P. MERSTEN.

WEEKLIES AND FORTNIGHTLIES

Al Ta'awun: P.O.B. 303, Tel-Aviv; f. 1961; published by the Arab Worker's Dept. of the Histadrut and the Co-operatives Dept. of the Ministry of Labour; co-operatives quarterly; Editor TUVIA SHAMOSH.

Adevarul: 21 Hasharon St., Tel-Aviv; f. 1949; Romanian; weekly; Editor IEHUDA MAERSON-SEVERIN.

Al Harriya: 38 King George St., Tel-Aviv; Arabic weekly of the Herut Party.

Al-Ittihad: P.O.B. 104, Haifa; f. 1944; Arabic; journal of the Israeli Communist Party; Chief Editor EMILE TOUMA.

Al Marsad: P.O.B. 736, 4 Ben Avigdor St., Tel-Aviv; Mapam; Arabic.

Bama'alah: P.O.B. 303, Tel-Aviv; journal of the young Histadrut Movement; Editor N. ANAELY.

Bamahane: Military P.O.B. 1013, Tel-Aviv; f. 1948; military, illustrated weekly of the Israel Army; Editor-in-Chief IZHAK LIVNI.

Bitaon Heyl Ha'avir (*Air Force Magazine*): Doar Zwai 2704; f. 1948; Editor M. HADAR; Managing Editor Y. OFFER; circ. 33,000.

Dvar Hashavua: 45 Sheinkin St., Tel-Aviv; f. 1946; popular illustrated; weekly; published by Histadrut, General Federation of Labour; Editor O. ZMORA; circ. 50,000.

Economic Review: 17 Kaplan St., Tel-Aviv; economic and social problems of immigration and absorption; Editors Dr. L. BERGER, CHAYA LAZAR; circ. English edition 3,500, Spanish edition (*Reseña Económica*) 2,000, French edition (*Revue Economique*) 2,000.

Ethgar: 75 Einstein Street, Tel-Aviv; twice weekly; Editor NATHAN YALIN-MOR.

Frei Israel: P.O.B. 8512, Tel-Aviv; Yiddish, progressive weekly, publ. by Asscn. for Popular Culture; Editor I. LIPSKI.

Glasul Populurui: Eilath Street, P.O.B. 2675, Tel-Aviv; weekly of the Communist Party; Romanian; Editor M. HARSGOR.

Hamis'har (*Commerce*): P.O.B. 852, Tel-Aviv; f. 1932; Hebrew; economic and commercial; Chamber of Commerce Tel-Aviv-Yafo; Editor Dr. E. W. KLIMOWSKY; circ. 39,000.

Haolam Hazeh: P.O.B. 136, 8 Glikson St., Tel-Aviv; f. 1937; independent; illustrated news magazine; weekly; Man. Editor URI AVNERY; Editor ELI TAVOR.

Hed Hahinukh: 8 Ben-Saruk Street, Tel-Aviv; f. 1926; weekly; educational; published by the Israeli Teachers' Union; Editor ZVI ARAD; circ. 26,000.

Illustrirte Weltwoch: P.O.B. 2571, Tel-Aviv; f. 1956; Yiddish; weekly; Editor M. TSANIN.

The Israel Digest: P.O.B. 92, Jerusalem; f. 1957; independent; fortnightly digest of news and views; circ. 20,000; Editor ZVI SOIFER.

Jerusalem Post Overseas Weekly: P.O.B. 81, Romema, Jerusalem; f. 1959; English; Overseas edition of the *Jerusalem Post* (q.v.); circ. 35,000 to 95 countries.

Kol Ha'am (*Voice of the People*): 37 Eilath St., P.O.B. 2675, Tel-Aviv; f. 1947; organ of the Communist Party of Israel; Editor MOSHE SNEH.

Laisha: P.O.B. 28122, 7 Fin St., Tel-Aviv; f. 1946; Hebrew; women's magazine; Editor DAVID KARASSIK.

Liawladina: Arabic Publishing House, P.O.B. 28049, Tel-Aviv; f. 1960; children's; fortnightly; Board of Editors ELIAHU AGHASSI, MISHEL HADDAD, WALID HUSSEIN, AIDA SABBAGH.

Maariv Lanoar: 2 Carlebach St., Tel-Aviv; f. 1956; weekly for the youth; Editor YANAI REUBEN; circ. 25,000.

MB (formerly *Mitteilungsblatt*): P.O.B. 1480, Tel-Aviv; f. 1932; German; journal of the Irgun Olei Merkas Europa; Editor Dr. HANS TRAMER.

Min Hayesod: Tel-Aviv; fortnightly; Hebrew; news and political commentary.

Ot: P.O.B. 36, 10 Dov Hoz St., Tel-Aviv; f. 1971; weekly organ of the Israel Labour Party; Editor DAVID SHAHAM.

Reshumot: Israel Government Printer, Jerusalem; f. 1948; Hebrew and Arabic; official Government gazette, edited by the Ministry of Justice.

Sada-A-Tarbia (*The Echo of Education*): published by the Histadrut and Teachers' Association, P.O.B. 303, Tel-Aviv; f. 1952; Arabic; educational; fortnightly; Editor TUVIA SHAMOSH.

El Tiempo: P.O.B. 671, Tel-Aviv; weekly; Ladino.

MONTHLY AND QUARTERLY PERIODICALS

Al-Bushra: P.O.B. 6088, Haifa; f. 1935; monthly; Arabic; organ of the Ahmadiyya movement; Editor FAZL ILAHI BASHIR.

Al Hamishmar: 20 Yehuda Halevy Street, Tel-Aviv; Bulgarian monthly of United Workers' Party.

ISRAEL—(THE PRESS)

Al Jadid: P.O.B. 104, Haifa; Arabic; literary monthly; Editor HANA NAKARA.

Ariel: Cultural and Scientific Relations Division, Ministry for Foreign Affairs, Jerusalem; f. 1962; quarterly review of the arts and letters in Israel; Editor T. CARMI.

Avoda Ubituach Leumi: P.O.B. 915, Jerusalem; f. 1949; monthly review of the Ministry of Labour, and the National Insurance Institute, Jerusalem; Editor Z. HEYN; circ. 3,000.

Christian News from Israel: 23 Shlomo Hamelech St., Jerusalem; quarterly issued by the Ministry of Religious Affairs; in English, French, Spanish; Acting Editor SHALOM BEN-ZAKKAI; circ. 20,000.

Dapim Refuiim: 101 Arlosoroff St., P.O.B. 16250, Tel-Aviv; f. 1935; eight times a year; medical; Hebrew with English and French summaries; circ. 5,000; Editor Dr. M. DVORJETSKI.

Divrei Haknesset: c/o The Knesset, Jerusalem; f. 1949; records of the proceedings of the Knesset, published by the Government Printer, Jerusalem; Editor D. NIV; circ. 300.

Dvar Hapoelet: P.O.B. 303, Tel-Aviv; f. 1934; monthly journal of the Council of Women Workers of the Histadrut; Hebrew; Founder and Past Editor Mrs. RACHEL SHAZAR; Editor SHULAMIT OR; circ. 11,000.

Folk un Zion: P.O.B. 92, Jerusalem; f. 1950; monthly; current events relating to Israel and World Jewry; circ. 6,000; Editor MOSHE HORVITZ.

Gazit: 8 Zvi Brook St., P.O.B. 4190, Tel-Aviv; f. 1932; monthly; Hebrew and English; art, literature; Publisher G. TALPHIR.

Goldene Keit, Die: 30 Weizmann St., Tel-Aviv; f. 1949; Yiddish; literary quarterly; published by the Histadrut; Editor A. SUTZKEVER; Co-Editor E. PINES; Man. Editor M. KARPINOVITZ.

Hameshek Hahaklai: 21 Melchett St., Tel-Aviv; f. 1929; agricultural; Editor ISRAEL INBARI.

Hamizrah Hehadash: (*The New East*): The Hebrew University of Jerusalem; f. 1949; quarterly of the Israel Oriental Society; Hebrew with English summary; Middle Eastern, Asian and African Affairs; Editor YEHOSHUA PORATH.

Hamlonai (*The Hotelier*): 13 Montefiore Street, P.O.B. 2032, Tel-Aviv; f. 1962; monthly of the Israel Hotel Association; Hebrew and English; Editor Dr. K. LICHT.

Hapraklit: P.O.B. 788 Tel-Aviv: f. 1943; quarterly; published by the Israel Bar Association; Editor A. POLONSKY; Editorial Sec. J. GROSS; circ. 5,000.

Harefuah: 39 Shaul Hamelech Blvd., Tel-Aviv; f. 1920; with English summary; fortnightly journal of the Israeli Medical Association; Editor I. SUM, M.D.; circ. 6,000.

Hassadeh: 25 Lilienblum St., Tel-Aviv; f. 1920; monthly; review of mixed farming; Editor J. M. MARGALIT; circ. 10,000.

Hataassiya (*Israel Industry*): 13 Montefiore St., P.O.B. 2032, Tel-Aviv; f. 1941; monthly review of the Manufacturers' Asscn. of Israel; Man. Dir. Z. PELTZ.

Hed Hagan: 8 Ben Saruk St., Tel-Aviv; f. 1935; educational; Editor Mrs. ESTHER RABINOWITZ; circ. 3,500.

International Monetary Issues: 37 Harbour St., Haifa; f. 1969; monthly; English; gold, gold shares, finance and investment; Editor G. ALON.

Israel Annals of Psychiatry: Jerusalem Academic Press, Givat Saul, P.O.B. 2390, Jerusalem; f. 1963; quarterly; Editor-in-Chief Prof. H. Z. WINNIK.

Israel Economist: P.O.B. 7052, 6 Hazanowitz St., Jerusalem; f. 1945; monthly; English; political and economic; independent; Editor J. KOLLEK, M.JUR.; also publishes *The Tel-Aviv Stock Exchange Information Card Service*.

Israel Exploration Journal: P.O.B. 7041, Jerusalem; f. 1950; quarterly; Editor Prof. M. AVI-YONAH; Associate Editor Dr. D. BARAG; circ. 2,000.

Israel Export and Trade Journal, The: 13 Montefiore Street, P.O.B. 2032, Tel-Aviv; f. 1949; monthly; English; commercial and economic; published by Israel Periodicals Co. Ltd.; Editor YOANNE YARON; Man. Dirs. F. A. LEWINSON and ZALMAN PELTZ.

Israel Industry and Commerce: P.O.B. 1199, Tel-Aviv; English; monthly; serves Israeli exporters; Editor SH. YEDIDYAH.

Israel Journal of Medical Sciences: P.O.B. 1345, Jerusalem; incorporating *The Israel Journal of Experimental Medicine* and *The Israel Medical Journal*; f. 1965; monthly; Editor-in-Chief Dr. M. PRYWES; circ. 5,500.

Israels Aussenhandel: 13 Montefiore Street, Tel-Aviv; f. 1967; monthly; German; commercial; Editor N. PELTZ.

Iyyun: Jerusalem Philosophical Society, c/o The Hebrew University, Jerusalem; f. 1945; quarterly; Hebrew (English summaries); Editor EDWARD I. J. POZNANSKI.

Kalkalan: 8 Akiva St., P.O.B. 7052, Jerusalem; f. 1952; monthly; Hebrew commercial and economic; independent; Editor J. KOLLEK, M.JUR.

Kirjath Sepher: P.O.B. 503, Jerusalem; bibliographical quarterly of the Jewish National and University Library, Jerusalem; f. 1924.

Labour in Israel: 93 Arlosoroff St., Tel-Aviv; periodic bulletin of the Histadrut; English, Swedish, French, Portuguese and Spanish.

Leshonenu: Academy of the Hebrew Language, P.O.B. 3449, Jerusalem; f. 1929; quarterly; for the study of the Hebrew language and cognate subjects; Editor S. ABRAMSON.

Leshonenu La'am: Academy of the Hebrew Language, P.O.B. 3449, Jerusalem; f. 1945; popular Hebrew philology; Editors E. ETAN, M. MEDAN.

Ma'arachot: Ha'Kirya, 1 Rechov Gimmel, Tel-Aviv; f. 1939; military; Editor Col. GERSHON RIVLIN.

Mada: Weizmann Science Press, P.O.B. 801, Jerusalem; f. 1956; popular scientific bi-monthly in Hebrew; Editor-in-Chief KAPAI PINES; circ. 10,000.

Mibifnim: 27 Sutin St., P.O.B. 16040, Tel-Aviv; f. 1924; quarterly of the United Collective Settlements (Hakibbutz Hameuchad); Editor ZERUBAVEL GILEAD; circ. 8,000.

Molad: P.O.B. 1165, Jerusalem; f. 1948; bi-monthly; independent political and literary review; Hebrew; published by Miph'ale Molad Ltd.; Editor EPHRAIM BROIDO.

Monthly Bulletin of Statistics: Israel Central Bureau of Statistics, Jerusalem; f. 1949.

   Monthly Statistics of the Administered Territories: f. 1971; Hebrew and English.

   Foreign Trade Statistical Quarterly: f. 1969; Hebrew and English.

   Monthly Statistics of Tourism and Hotel Services: f. 1973; Hebrew and English.

   Monthly Price Statistics: f. 1949; Hebrew.

   Monthly Foreign Trade Statistics: f. 1949; Hebrew and English.

ISRAEL—(THE PRESS)

Moznayim (*Balance*): P.O.B. 7098, Tel-Aviv; f. 1929; literature and culture; monthly; circ. 2,500; Editor M. SHAMIR.

Ner: Ihud, P.O.B. 451, Jerusalem; f. 1948; monthly on political and social problems; advocates Arab-Jewish reconciliation; Hebrew, English, Arabic; circ. 1,500.

New Outlook: 8 Karl Netter Street, Tel-Aviv; f. 1957; monthly; circ. 10,000; Editor SIMHA FLAPAN.

Proche-Orient Chrétien: B.P. 19079, Jerusalem; f. 1951; quarterly.

Quarterly Review of the Israel Medical Association (*Mif'al Haverut Hutz*—Non-resident Fellowship of the Israel Medical Association): 39 Shaul Hamelekh Blvd., Tel-Aviv; English; also published in French and Spanish; quarterly; Editor Dr. V. RESNEKOV.

Refuah Veterinarit: P.O.B. 18, Beit Dagan, Tel-Aviv; f. 1943; quarterly review of veterinary surgery; Editor Dr. F. G. SULMAN.

La Revue de l'A.M.I. (Non-resident Fellowship of the Israeli Medical Association): 39 Shaul Hamelekh Blvd., Tel-Aviv; French, English and Spanish; quarterly; Editor Dr. S. ZALUD.

Scopus: Hebrew University of Jerusalem; f. 1946; published by Department of Information and Public Affairs, Hebrew University of Jerusalem; twice yearly; English; Editor D. A. SUSMAN.

Shituf (*Co-operation*): 24 Ha'arba St., Tel-Aviv, P.O.B. 7151; monthly; Hebrew co-operative journal; published by the Central Union of Industrial, Transport and Service Co-operative Societies; Editor L. LOSH.

Sinai: P.O.B. 642, Jerusalem; Torah, science and literature; Editor Dr. YITZHAK RAPHAEL.

Sindbad: P.O.B. 28049, Tel-Aviv; f. 1969; children's monthly; Editors ELIAHU AGHASSI, WALID HUSSEIN.

Sion: P.O.B. 14001, Jerusalem; f. 1866; bi-monthly of religion, literature and philology; official organ of the Armenian Patriarchate of Jerusalem; circ. 1,200; Editor His Beatitude Patriarch Y. DERDERIAN.

Sulam: 2 Ben Yehuda St., Jerusalem; political; monthly; Editor Y. SHAIB.

Tarbitz: Magnes Press, the Hebrew University, Jerusalem; f. 1929; quarterly; for Jewish studies; Editor E. E. URBACH; circ. 750.

Terra Santa: P.O.B. 186, Jerusalem; f. 1921; monthly; published by the Custody of the Holy Land (the official custodians of the Holy Shrines); Italian, Spanish, French and Arabic editions published in Jerusalem, by the Franciscan Printing Press, English edition in Washington, German edition in Vienna, Maltese edition in Valletta.

Teva Vaarez: 25 Lilienblum Street, P.O.B. 4, Tel-Aviv; f. 1958; monthly; review of agriculture, nature and geography; Editor Dr. DANIEL RIMON.

Tmuroth: 48 Hamelech George St., P.O.B. 23076, Tel-Aviv; f. 1960; organ of the Liberal Labour Movement; monthly; Editor D. SHLOMI.

Urim La-Orim: 93 Arlosoroff St., P.O.B. 303, Tel-Aviv; educational problems in the family; monthly; Editor HAYIM NAGID.

Vilner Pinkas: P.O.B. 28006, Tel-Aviv; f. 1968; periodical review of current affairs for Vilna-Jews the world over, and for the history of Yerushdayim Delito; Yiddish; Editor M. KARPINOVITZ.

WIZO Review: Women's International Zionist Organization, 38 Sderoth David Hamelekh, Tel-Aviv; English, Spanish and German editions; Editor SYLVIA SATTEN BANIN; circ. 50,000.

Yam: Israeli Maritime League, P.O.B. 706, 2 Hanamal St., Haifa; f. 1937; review of marine problems; Editer Z. ESHEL; Pres. S. TOLKOWSKY; circ. 4,000.

Zion: P.O.B. 1062, Jerusalem; f. 1935; research in Jewish history; quarterly; Hebrew and English; Editors I. F. BAER, B. DINUR, H. H. BEN-SASSON, S. ETTINGER.

Zraim: 7 Dubnov Street, P.O.B. 20126, Tel-Aviv; f. 1935; journal of the Bnei Akiva (Youth of Hapoel Hamizrachi) Movement; Editor SHLOMO SAMSON.

Zrakor: 37 Harbour St., Haifa; f. 1947; monthly; Hebrew; news digest, trade, finance, economics, shipping; Editor G. ALON.

The following are all published by Weizmann Science Press Israel, P.O.B. 801, Jerusalem 91000; Exec. Editor L. LESTER.

Israel Journal of Botany: f. 1951; Editor Prof. LEONORA REINHOLD; quarterly.

Israel Journal of Chemistry: f. 1951; Editor Prof. Y. ELIAZER; bi-monthly.

Israel Journal of Earth-Sciences: f. 1951; Editor Y. WEILER; quarterly.

Israel Journal of Mathematics: f. 1951; Editors B. WEISS, A. PAZI; monthly, 3 vols. of 4 issues each per year.

Israel Journal of Technology: f. 1951; Editor Prof. D. ABIR; 8 issues per year.

Israel Journal of Zoology: f. 1951; Editor Y. WERNER; quarterly.

PUBLISHERS' ASSOCIATION

Daily Newspaper Publishers' Association of Israel: P.O.B. 2251, 4 Kaplan St., Tel-Aviv; safeguards professional interests and maintains standards, supplies newsprint to dailies; negotiates with trade unions, etc.; mems. all daily papers except *Ha'aretz*; affiliated to International Federation of Newspaper Publishers.

NEWS AGENCIES

Jewish Telegraphic Agency (JTA): Israel Bureau, Jerusalem Post Building, Romema, Jerusalem 94467; Dir. DAVID LANDAU.

Israeli News Agency (INA): Israel Affiliate of JTA; 59 Sheinkin St., Tel-Aviv; 9 Havazelet St., Jerusalem; London Office: 182 Fleet St., London, E.C.4; f. 1923; Dir. A. SCHWARTZ; publ. *Hebrew News Bulletin* (daily).

ITIM, News Agency of the Associated Israel Press: 10 Tiomkin Street, Tel-Aviv; f. 1950; co-operative news agency; Dir. and Editor HAYIM BALTSAN.

FOREIGN BUREAUX

Agence France-Presse: 7 Schderot Kheu, Tel-Aviv; Chief NATHAN GURDUS.

ANSA: 20 29th November Street, Jerusalem; Bureau Chief REPHAEL MIGDAL.

Middle East Bureau: Jerusalem Post Bldg., Jerusalem 94 467.

The following are also represented: AP, DPA, North American Newspaper Alliance, Reuters, Tass.

ISRAEL—(PUBLISHERS)

PUBLISHERS

Achiasaf Ltd.: 13 Yosef Hanassi St., Tel-Aviv; f. 1933; general; Man. Dir. SCHACHMA ACHIASAF.

Am Hassefer Ltd.: 9 Bialik St., Tel-Aviv; f. 1955; Man. Dir. DOV LIPETZ.

"Am Oved" Ltd.: 22 Mazah Street, Tel-Aviv; f. 1942; fiction, scientific, sociology; textbooks, children's books; Man. Dir. N. URIELI.

Amichai Publishing House Ltd.: 5 Yosef Hanassi St., Tel-Aviv; f. 1948; Man. Dir. YEHUDA ORLINSKY.

Arabic Publishing House: 17A Hagra Street, P.O.B. 28049, Tel-Aviv; f. 1960; established by the Histadrut (trade union) organization; periodicals and books; Dir. and Gen. Editor ELIAHU AGHASSI.

Bialik Institute, The: P.O.B. 92, Jerusalem; f. 1935; classics, encyclopaedias, criticism, history, archaeology, art, reference books, Judaica; Dir. CHAIM MILKOV.

Carta: Mazie St., P.O.B. 2500, Jerusalem; f. 1958; the principal cartographic publisher; Man. Dir. EMANUEL HAUSMAN.

Dvir Publishing Co. Ltd., The: 58 Mazah St., Tel-Aviv; literature, science, art, education; Man. Dir. ALEXANDER BROIDO.

Eked Publishing House: 29 Bar-Kochba St., Tel-Aviv; f. 1959; poetry; Dirs. ITAMAR YAOZ-KEST, MARITZA ROSMAN.

Gazit: 8 Zvi Brook St., Tel-Aviv, P.O.B. 4190; art publishers; Editor GABRIEL TALPHIR.

Haifa Publishing Co. Ltd.: P.O.B. 407, Haifa; f. 1960; fiction and non-fiction.

Hakibbutz Hameuchad Publishing House Ltd.: P.O.B. 16040, Pumbadita St., Tel-Aviv; f. 1940; general; Dir. YAAKOV MOSSEK.

Hamenorah Publishers Ltd.: 24 Zangwill St., Tel-Aviv; f. 1958; books in Hebrew and Yiddish; Dir. MORDECHAI SONNSCHEIN.

Israel Program for Scientific Translations Ltd.: 2 Hameiri Blvd., P.O.B. 7145, Jerusalem; f. 1958; original and translated works in all fields of science and humanities, published in English, French, German, other European languages and Hebrew; publishing imprints: Israel Universities Press, Keter Books, Encyclopaedia Judaica; Man. Dir. YITZHAK RISCHIN.

Israeli Music Publications Ltd.: 105 Ben Yehuda St., P.O.B. 6011, Tel-Aviv; f. 1949; books on music and musical works; Dir. Dr. PETER E. GRADENWITZ.

Izre'el Publishing House Ltd.: 76 Dizengoff St., Tel-Aviv; f. 1933; Man. ALEXANDER IZRE'EL.

Jerusalem Academic Press: Shattner Industrial Centre, P.O.B. 2390, Jerusalem; f. 1959; scientific and technical publications; Gen. Man. ITZHAK LAHAD.

Jerusalem Publishing House: 39 Tchernechovski St., Jerusalem, P.O.B. 7147; f. 1967; history, archaeology, art and other reference books; Dir. SHLOMO S. GAFNI.

Jewish Agency Publishing Department: P.O.B. 704; Jerusalem; f. 1945; Palestinology, Judaism, scientific, classics, and publicity brochures; Dir. M. SPITZER.

Karni Publishers Ltd.: 11 Yehuda Halevi St., Tel-Aviv; f. 1951; children's and educational books; Dir. SAMUEL KATZ.

Kiryath Sepher: 15 Arlosorov St., Jerusalem; f. 1933; dictionaries, textbooks, maps, scientific books; Dir. SHALOM SIVAN (STEPANSKY).

Lewin-Epstein Ltd.: 9 Yavneh St., Tel-Aviv; f. 1930; general fiction, education, science; Man. Dir. ABRAHAM GOTTESMANN.

Magnes Press, The: The Hebrew University, Jerusalem; f. 1929; general studies; Dir. CHAIM TOREN.

Massada Ltd.: 21 Jabotinsky St., Ramat Gan; f. 1931; art, encyclopaedias, literature; Chair. Mrs. BRACHA PELI; Man. Dir. ALEXANDER PELI.

Ministry of Defence Publishing House: Hakiriya, Tel-Aviv; f. 1939; military literature; Dir. AHARON NIV. MA'ARACHOT.

M. Mizrachi Publishers: 19 Y. L. Peretz, Tel-Aviv; f. 1960; children's books; Dir. MEIR MIZRACHI.

Otsar Hamoreh: 8 Ben Saruk, Tel-Aviv; f. 1951; educational; Dir. MENACHEM LEVANON.

Y. L. Peretz: 31 Allenby Rd., Tel-Aviv; f. 1956; mainly books in Yiddish; Man. Dir. MOSHE GERSHONOWITZ.

Rubin Mass: Marcus St., P.O.B. 990, Jerusalem; Tel-Aviv branch: Allenby 62; f. 1927; Hebraica, Judaica; Dir. RUBIN MASS.

Schocken Publishing House Ltd.: P.O.B. 2316, Tel-Aviv; f. 1938; general; Dir. Mrs. RACHELI EDELMAN.

Sifriat-Ma'ariv Ltd.: Ma'ariv House, 2 Carlebach St., Tel-Aviv; f. 1954; general; Man. YAKIR WEINSTEIN.

Sifriat Poalim Ltd.: 73 Allenby St., P.O.B. 526, Tel-Aviv 65-171; f. 1939; textbooks; Gen. Man. YAAKOV ZVIELI.

Sinai Publishing Co.: 72 Allenby Rd., Tel-Aviv; Hebrew books and religious articles; Dir. AKNAH SCHLESINGER.

Tarbut Ve'Hinuch Publishers: 93 Arlozorov St., Tel-Aviv; f. 1956; educational; Man. IZAAK KOTUNSKY.

Tarhish Books: P.O.B. 4130, Jerusalem 91-040; f. 1940; plays, poetry, bibliophile, classics; Man. Dir. Dr. MOSHE SPITZER.

Weidenfeld and Nicolson Jerusalem Ltd.: 19 Herzog St., P.O.B. 7545, Jerusalem; branch of the London publishing company; established in Israel 1969; Man. Dir. ASHER WEILL.

Weizmann Science Press of Israel: 33 King George Ave., P.O.B. 801, Jerusalem 91000; f. 1951; publishes scientific books and periodicals; Man. Dir. RAMI MICHAELI; Exec. Editor L. LESTER.

Yachdav United Publishers Co. Ltd.: 29 Carlebach St., Tel-Aviv; f. 1960; educational; Chair. MORDECHAI BERNSTEIN; Dir. BENJAMIN SELLA.

Yavneh Ltd.: 4 Mazeh St., Tel-Aviv; f. 1932; general; Dir. YEHOSHUA ORENSTEIN.

S. Zack and Co.: 2 King George St., Jerusalem; f. c. 1930; reference books; Dirs. DAVID and MICHAEL ZACK.

Israel Book Publishers Association: 29 Carlebach St., Tel-Aviv; f. 1939; mems.: approx. 100 publishing firms; Chair. MORDECHAI BERNSTEIN; Sec.-Gen. BENJAMIN SELLA.

Jerusalem International Book Fair: P.O.B. 1508, Jerusalem 91000; takes place in alternate years; 900 publishing firms from 30 countries were represented in 1971.

RADIO AND TELEVISION

RADIO

I.B.A.: The Israel Broadcasting Authority; f. 1948; station, Jerusalem with studios in Tel-Aviv and Haifa; Dir.-Gen. S. ALMOG. I.B.A. broadcasts five programmes for local and overseas listeners on medium, shortwave and VHF/FM in twelve languages; Hebrew, Arabic, English, Yiddish, Ladino, Romanian, Hungarian, Moghrabit, Persian, French, Russsian and Georgian.

Number of radio receivers: 700,000.

TELEVISION

Programmes for schools started in spring 1966, and programmes for the general public, run by the Israel Broadcasting Authority, began in 1967.

Instructional Television Centre: Ministry of Education and Culture, Tel-Aviv; f. 1963 by Hanadiv (Rothschild Memorial Group) as Instructional Television Centre; began transmissions in 1966; now broadcasts on a national scale to 1,300 schools with 540,000 pupils, 70 per cent of the high school population; the programmes form an integral part of the syllabus in a wide range of subjects.

Number of TV receivers: 430,000.

FINANCE

(cap.=capital; p.u.=paid up; dep.=deposits; m.=million; I£=Israeli £; brs.=branches.)

BANKING

CENTRAL BANK

Bank of Israel: Mizpeh Building, 29 Jaffa Rd., Jerusalem, P.O.B. 780; f. 1954 as the Central Bank of the State of Israel; (Dec. 1972) cap. I£10m., dep. I£8,956m.; Gov. MOSHE SANBAR; Dir.-Gen. Dr. E. SHEFFER, Mans. M. HETH, Y. J. TAUB, S. LEVI, Z. SUSSMAN, M. MEIREV, S. PELED; 2 brs.; publs. *Annual Report, Economic Review, Banking Statistics* (monthly).

ISRAELI BANKS

Arab Israel Bank Ltd.: 2 Shivat Zion Street, Haifa; f. 1959 to serve primarily the Arab sector of the economy; cap. p.u. I£3.5m., dep. I£63.9m. (Dec. 1972); Chair. B. YEKUTIELI; Gen. Man. S. SHAUL.

Bank Hapoalim B.M.: 50 Rothschild Blvd., Tel-Aviv; f. 1921; cap. p.u. I£81.9m., dep. I£9,140m. (Dec. 1972); Man. Dirs. J. LEVINSON (Chair.), E. AVNEYON, A. DICKENSTEIN, E. MARGALIT, B. RABINOW, M. OLENIK; 202 brs.

Bank Lemelacha Ltd.: 9 Carlebach St., Tel-Aviv; f. 1953; cap. p.u. I£13.3m., dep. I£96.8m. (Dec. 1972); Chair. DOV KANTOROWITZ; Gen. Man. A. FEIN; 14 brs.

Bank Leumi le-Israel B.M.: 24-32 Yehuda Halevy St., Tel-Aviv; f. 1902; cap. p.u. I£90.1m., dep. I£10,136.3m. (1972); Chair. E. LEHMANN; Man. Dir. and Chief Exec. E. I. JAPHET; 218 brs.; publ. *Review of Economic Conditions in Israel* (quarterly).

First International Bank of Israel Ltd.: 39 Rothschild Blvd., P.O.B. 2110, Tel-Aviv; f. 1972 as a result of a merger between *The Foreign Trade Bank Ltd.* and *Export Bank Ltd.*; Chair. of Board MARK MOSEVICS; Man. Dir. DAVID GOLAN; 34 brs.

Israel American Industrial Development Bank Ltd.: 50 Rothschild Blvd., Tel-Aviv; f. 1956; cap. p.u. I£12m.; dep. I£179m. (Dec. 1972); Chair. A. DICKENSTEIN; Gen. Man. H. DUVSHANI.

Israel Bank of Agriculture Ltd.: 83 Hashmonayim St., Tel-Aviv; f. 1951; cap. p.u. I£171.8m., dep. I£500.2m. (March 1973); Chair. Prof. H. HALPERIN; Man. Dir. D. CALDERON.

Israel British Bank Ltd.: 20 Rothschild Blvd., Tel-Aviv; f. 1929; cap. p.u. I£11.3m., dep. I£340m. (Dec. 1971); Chair. HARRY LANDY; Man. Dirs. JOSHUA BENSION, DAVID HERSHKOVITZ; 8 brs.

Israel Discount Bank Ltd.: 27-29 Yehuda Halevy St., Tel-Aviv; f. 1935; cap. p.u. I£60m., dep. I£7,998m. (Dec. 1972); Chair. DANIEL RECANATI; Vice-Chair. RAPHAEL RECANATI; 133 brs.

Israel General Bank Ltd.: 28 Achad Ha'am St., Tel-Aviv; f. 1964; cap. p.u. I£4.5m., dep. I£197.4m. (Dec. 1972); Chair. Baron EDMOND DE ROTHSCHILD; Man. Dir. DAVID SHOHAM; 3 brs.

Israel Industrial Bank Ltd.: 13 Montefiore St., Tel-Aviv; f. 1933; cap. p.u. I£12.05m., dep. I£139.8m. (Dec. 1972); Chair. A. FROMCENKO; Man. Dir. A. D. KIMCHI; 9 brs.

Israel Loan and Savings Bank Ltd.: 21 Herzl St., Tel-Aviv; cap. I£10.3m.; Chair. E. AVEYNON; Man. Dir. I. GAFNI.

Japhet Bank Ltd.: 11 Rothschild Blvd., Tel-Aviv; f. 1933; subsidiary of Bank Hapoalim B.M.; cap. p.u. I£7m., dep. I£378.1 m.(Dec. 1972); Chair. E. MARGALIT; Man. Dir. P. ALROY; 13 brs.

Kupat Am Bank Ltd.: 13 Ahad Ha'am St., P.O.B. 352, Tel-Aviv; f. 1918; cap. p.u. I£2m., dep. I£165.8m (Dec. 1972); Chair. B. YEKUTIELI; Man. Dir. M. GEFEN; 14 brs.

Mercantile Bank of Israel Ltd.: 24 Rothschild Blvd., Tel-Aviv; f. 1924; subsidiary of Israel Discount Bank; cap. p.u. I£2m., dep. I£102m. (Dec. 1972); Chair. DANIEL RECANATI; Gen. Man. SHLOMO MAGRISO.

Union Bank of Israel Ltd.: 6-8 Ahuzat Bait St., P.O.B. 2428, Tel-Aviv; f. 1951; subsidiary of Bank Leumi le-Israel B.M.; cap. p.u. I£13.8m., dep. I£1,260.9m. (Dec. 1972); Chair. E. I. JAPHET; Gen. Mans. W. HAUCK, M. MAYER; 14 brs.; publ. *Newsletter* (monthly).

United Mizrahi Bank Ltd.: 48 Lilienblum St., Tel-Aviv; f. 1923; cap. p.u. I£22.7m., dep. I£913m. (Dec. 1972); Chair. N. FEINGOLD; Gen. Man. A. MEIR; 42 brs.

MORTGAGE BANKS

General Mortgage Bank Ltd.: 13 Ahad Ha'am St., Tel-Aviv; f. 1921; subsidiary of Bank Leumi le-Israel B.M.; cap. p.u. I£18.2m., dep. I£455.8m. (Dec. 1971); Chair. E. LEHMANN; Gen. Mans. Y. BACH, M. KAHAN.

ISRAEL—(FINANCE)

Housing Mortgage Bank Ltd.: 115 Allenby St., Tel-Aviv; f. 1951; subsidiary of Bank Hapoalim B.M.; cap. p.u. I£12.0m., dep. I£230.2m. (Dec. 1971); Chair. A. OFFER.

Israel Development and Mortgage Bank Ltd.: 16 Simtat Beit Hashoeva, Tel-Aviv; f. 1959; subsidiary of Israel Discount Bank Ltd.; Gen. Mans. K. REICH, A. VREEDENBURG.

Tefahot, Israel Mortgage Bank Ltd.: 9 Heleni Hamalka St., Jerusalem; f. 1945; cap. p.u. I£42m.; Chair. DAVID TANNE; Man. Dir. MOSHE MANN.

Unico Mortgage and Investment Bank Ltd.: Shalom Tower, 9 Ahad Ha'am Street, Tel-Aviv; f. 1961.

FOREIGN BANKS

Barclays Discount Bank Ltd.: 103 Allenby Rd., Tel-Aviv; f. 1971 in association with Israel Discount Bank Ltd. incorporating former brs. of Barclays Bank International Ltd.; cap. p.u. I£11m.; Chair. DANIEL RECANATI; Gen. Man. RAPHAEL MOLHO; 49 brs. *Affiliated bank:* **Mercantile Bank of Israel Ltd.,** 24 Rothschild Blvd., Tel-Aviv.

Exchange National Bank of Chicago: 9 Ahad Ha'am St., Shalom Tower, Tel-Aviv 65251; f. 1970; Vice-Pres. and Gen. Man. AVIEZER CHELOUCHE; 1 br.

STOCK EXCHANGE

Tel-Aviv Stock Exchange: 113 Allenby Rd.; Chair. Dr. E. LEHMANN; Vice-Chair. D. RECANATI; Exec. Dir. D. OTENSOOSER; publs. *Official Quotations* (daily, monthly, annually), *Financial Structure and Performance of Companies Listed on the Tel-Aviv Stock Exchange* (annual).

INSURANCE

Ararat Insurance Company Ltd.: Ararat House, 32 Yavneh St., Tel-Aviv; f. 1949; Man. Dir. PHILIP ZUCKERMAN.

Aryeh Insurance Co. Ltd.: Shalom Tower, Tel-Aviv; f. 1948; Chair. AVINOAM M. TOCATLY.

Hassneh Insurance Co. of Israel Ltd.: 115 Allenby St., P.O.B. 805, Tel-Aviv; f. 1929; Chair. MICHAEL NUSSBAUM.

Israel Phoenix Assurance Company Ltd., The: 30 Levontin St., Tel-Aviv; f. 1949; Chair. of Board and Man. Dir. DAVID J. HACKMEY.

Israel Reinsurance Company Ltd., The: 7 Shadal St., P.O.B. 2037, Tel-Aviv; f. 1951; Chair. Board of Dirs. A. SACHAROV; Man. S. JANNAI.

Maoz Insurance Co. Ltd.: 36 Lilienblum St., Tel-Aviv; f. 1945; formerly Binyan Insurance Co. Ltd.; Chair. Y. GRUENGARD.

Mazada Insurance Service Ltd.: 3 Ahuzat Bait St., Tel-Aviv; f. 1932; Mans. S. SPIGELMAN, A. SPIGELMAN.

Menorah Insurance and Reinsurance Company Ltd.: Menorah House, 73 Rothschild Blvd., Tel-Aviv; f. 1935; Gen. Man. DAVID HIRSCHFELD.

Migdal-Binyan Insurance Co. Ltd.: 53 Rothschild Blvd., Tel-Aviv; f. 1934; Chair. A. LEHMAN; Man. Dir. J. GRUENGARD.

Palglass Palestine Plate Glass Insurance Co. Ltd.: 30 Achad Ha'am St., Tel-Aviv; f. 1934; Gen. Man. AKIVA ZALZMAN.

Sahar Insurance Company Ltd.: Sahar House, 23 Ben-Yehuda St., Tel-Aviv; f. 1949; Chair. and Man. Dir. A. SHAROV.

Samson Insurance Co. Ltd.: 27 Montefiore St., P.O.B. 29277, Tel-Aviv; f. 1933; Chair. M. NUSSBAUM.

Sela Insurance Co. Ltd.: 6 Ahuzat Bait St., Tel-Aviv; f. 1938; Man. Dir. S. P. LUSTIG.

Shiloah Company Ltd.: 2 Pinsker St., Tel-Aviv; f. 1933; Gen. Man. R. S. BAMIRAH; Man. Mme BAMIRAH.

Yardenia Insurance Company Ltd.: 22 Maze Street, Tel-Aviv; f. 1948; Gen. Man. S. LEBANON, H. LEBANON.

Yuval Insurance Co. of Israel: 27 Keren Hayesod, Jerusalem; f. 1962; Dir. J. KAPLAN.

Zigug Glass Insurance Co. Ltd.: 34 Sheinkin St., Tel-Aviv; f. 1952; Chair. D. HIRSCHFELD.

Zion Insurance Company Ltd.: 120 Allenby Rd., Tel-Aviv; f. 1935; Chair. HAIM TAIBER.

ISRAEL—(THE HISTADRUT)

THE HISTADRUT

Hahistadrut Haklalit shel Haovdim Beeretz Israel, 93 Arlosoroff Street, Tel-Aviv

(GENERAL FEDERATION OF LABOUR IN ISRAEL)

Secretary-General: YITZHAK BEN-AHARON.

The General Federation of Labour in Israel, usually known as the Histadrut, is the largest voluntary organization in Israel, and the most important economic body in the State. It is open to all workers, including members of co-operatives and of the liberal professions, who join directly as individuals. The Histadrut engages in four main fields of activity: trade union organization; economic development; social insurance based on mutual aid; and educational and cultural activities. Dues—between 3 per cent and 4.5 per cent of wages (up to I£700)—cover all its trade union, health and social services activities. The Histadrut was founded in 1920.

ORGANIZATION

In 1971 the Histadrut had a membership of 1,124,000, including over 275,000 in collective, co-operative and private villages (*kibbutzim*, *moshavim* and *moshavot*), affiliated through the Agricultural Workers' Union, and 279,400 wives (who have membership status); 62,000 of the members were Arabs. In addition some 110,000 young people under 18 years of age belong to the Organization of Working and Student Youth, a direct affiliate of the Histadrut. The main religious labour organizations, *Histadrut Hapoel Hamizrahi* and *Histadrut Poalei Agudat Israel*, belong to the trade union section and welfare services, which thus extend to 90 per cent of all workers in Israel.

All members take part in elections to the Histadrut Convention (*Veida*), which elects the General Council (*Moetsa*) and the Executive Committee (*Vaad Hapoel*). The latter elects the 19-member Executive Bureau (*Vaada Merakezet*), which is responsible for day-to-day implementation of policy. The Executive Committee also elects the Secretary-General, who acts as its chairman as well as head of the organization as a whole and chairman of the Executive Bureau. Nearly all political parties are represented on the Histadrut Executive Committee. Throughout Israel there are 65 local Labour Councils.

The Executive Committee has the following departments: Trade Union, Arab Affairs, Mutual Aid, Organization, International, Finance, Legal, Employment, Vocational Training, Absorption and Development, Academic Workers, Pensions, Religious Affairs and Higher Education.

TRADE UNION ACTIVITIES

Collective agreements with employers fix wage scales, which are linked with the retail price index; provide for social benefits, including paid sick leave and employers' contributions to sick and pension and provident funds; and regulate dismissals. Dismissal compensation, until recently fixed by collective agreements, is now regulated by law. The Histadrut actively promotes productivity through labour management boards and the National Productivity Institute, and supports incentive pay schemes.

There are unions for the following groups: clerical workers, building workers, teachers, engineers, agricultural workers, technicians, textile workers, printing workers, diamond workers, metal workers, food and bakery workers, wood workers, government employees, seamen, nurses, civilian employees of the armed forces, actors, musicians and variety artists, social workers, watchmen, cinema technicians, institutional and school staffs, pharmacy employees, medical laboratory workers, X-ray technicians, physiotherapists, social scientists, microbiologists, psychologists, salaried lawyers, pharmacists, physicians, occupational therapists, truck and taxi drivers, hotel and restaurant workers, workers in Histadrut-owned industry, garment, shoe and leather workers, painters and sculptors and industrial workers.

OFFICERS AND PUBLICATIONS

The principal officers engaged in the Histadrut are as follows:

Secretary-General: YITZHAK BEN-AHARON.

Deputy Secretary-General: S. G. YERUHAM MESHEL.

Secretary of Labour Economy (Hevrat Odim): ASHER YADLIN.

Chairman of Trade Union Department: URIEL ABRAHAMOVICZ.

Chairman of Mutual Aid and Insurance: AHARON EFRAT.

Chairman of Culture and Education Department: RAPHAEL BASH.

Chairman of Sports and Youth Department: ISRAEL KEISAR.

Treasurer: YEHOSHUA LEVI.

Chairman of Organization Department: AHARON HAREL.

The principal newspapers and periodicals published by the Histadrut are as follows:

Davar (*The Word*) (daily), *Al-Yaum* (Arabic, daily), *Omer* (daily), *Dvar Hashavua* (illustrated weekly), *Davar Liyeladim* (children's weekly), *Bahistadrut* (monthly review), *Devar Hapoalet* (women's monthly), *Israel au Travail* (French, monthly), *Labour in Israel* (English, monthly), *Trabajo en Israel* (Spanish, monthly). (See also Press section.)

ECONOMIC ACTIVITIES

General Co-operative Association of Labour in Israel (*Hevrat Ovdim*): Every member of the Histadrut is simultaneously a member of Hevrat Ovdim, and therefore a part-owner in its economy, whether or not he works within its framework. This labour economy includes a variety of structural forms, falling into two main types: co-operative societies run by their own members, such as all *kibbutzim* and *moshavim* and the producer, service, transport and consumer co-operatives; and the collectively-owned enterprises which are initiated by Hevrat Ovdim. The following are among the enterprises controlled by Hevrat Ovdim.

ISRAEL—(THE HISTADRUT)

Industry and Production

Koor Industries Ltd.: 8 Shaul Hamelech Blvd., Tel-Aviv; f. 1944; a group of 43 plants, including chemical works, engineering works, foundries, cement factories, rubber products, plastics, plywood, and light industry, electronic plants, vehicles, cardboard containers; Gen. Man. General MEIR AMIT.

Hamashbir Hamerkazi l'Ta'asiah (*Co-operative Society for Industry*): 60 Salame Road, Tel-Aviv.

Tiyyus (*Establishment of Industries in Development Areas*): 33 Lilienblum Street, Tel-Aviv.

The Co-operative Centre of Producers, Transport and Public Services: 24 Ha'arba St., Tel-Aviv.

Agriculture

YAKHIN Agricultural Company Ltd.: 2 Kaplan St., P.O.B. 332, Tel-Aviv.

Nir Ltd.: 28 Rothschild Boulevard, Tel-Aviv P.O.B. 1294.

Nachson Ltd.: 1 Nathan St., Haifa; fishing company.

Yona Ltd.: 1 Nathan St., Haifa; fishing company.

Marketing and Services

Hamashbir Hamerkazi Co-operative Wholesale Soc. Ltd.: 76 Giborey-Israel Rd., Tel-Aviv; main supplier of the *kibbutzim* and *moshavim*.

Hamashbir Latzarchan Consumers' Co-operative Association: 58 Salame Rd., Tel-Aviv; department store chain company with 18 branches throughout Israel.

Tnuva, Co-operative Centre for Marketing of Agricultural Produce in Israel Ltd.: 17 Yehuda Halevi St., P.O.B. 265, Tel-Aviv; f. 1927; markets two-thirds of all farm produce in Israel, and is increasingly active in exports.

Histour: 32 Ben Yehuda St., P.O.B. 3341, Tel-Aviv; travel and tourism agency.

Finance and Insurance

Bank Hapoalim B.M.: 50 Rothschild Blvd., Tel-Aviv (*see* entry under banks).

Ampal, American Israel Corporation: 17 East 71st St., New York, U.S.A.

Hassneh Insurance Co. Ltd.: 115 Allenby St., Tel-Aviv; f. 1929; Chair. M. NUSSBAUM.

Co-operative Savings and Loan Society: 5 Hehoshmal St., Tel-Aviv.

Building and Housing

Solel Boneh Ltd.: 111 Allenby Rd., P.O.B. 1267, Tel-Aviv; f. 1923; as the largest Histadrut concern has carried out projects in Africa, Asia and the Middle East in building and related industrial work; organized into seven units: Soleh Boneh Building and Public Works Co. Ltd.—Building, Manufacturing, Road and Public Works Divisions, Solel Boneh Overseas and Harbour Works Co. Ltd., Herouth Ltd. Electrical and Sanitary Engineering, Even Vesid Ltd., Diur B.P. Ltd.; Man. Dir. ZVI RECHTER.

Shikun Ovdim Ltd.: 21 Leonardo da Vinci St., Tel-Aviv; f. 1956; Workers' Housing.

Transport and Haulage

Arkia Israel Inland Air Lines Ltd.: 88 Ha'hashmonaim St., Tel-Aviv.

Ophir Fishing Society Ltd.: 19 Jaffa Rd., Haifa.

Tarshish Navigation Co. Ltd.: 60 Atzmaut St., Haifa.

Egged Ltd.: 3 Finn St., Tel-Aviv; road transport.

Dan Ltd.: 17 Arlosoroff St., Tel-Aviv; road transport.

The Centre for Producers, Service and Transport Co-operatives: 24 Arbra'al St., Tel-Aviv.

Special Services

Mekorot: f. 1937; for exploration for water and the exploitation of discovered sources for large scale irrigation.

The Histadrut is also an important partner in *Zim*, the Israel Navigation Company, and in *El Al*, Israel Air Lines.

SOCIAL WELFARE

All the Histadrut's social welfare institutions are based on the principal of mutual aid, and over 75 per cent of membership dues is allocated to them.

Kupat Holim (*The Workers' Sick Fund*): 14 Ben Ami Street, Tel-Aviv; the largest health organization in Israel; over 850 clinics, 14 hospitals, 17 convalescent homes; also conducts preventive health services; serves 77 per cent of the population.

Mishan: 27 Bloch St., Tel-Aviv; grants loans to needy members and maintains old-age homes and children's institutions.

Dor l'Dor: 27 Bloch St., Tel-Aviv; assists elderly workers, in particular those not covered by a regular pension scheme.

Matsiv: 93 Arlosoroff Street, Tel-Aviv; assists dependents of deceased members.

Seven central pension and provident funds operate within the Histadrut framework, with contributions coming from both their members and the employers. In addition to providing a wide range of benefits, these funds constitute the principal source of savings of the population. These long-term savings are directed to the development of the economy; moreover, by absorbing monies, they also act as an anti-inflationary influence. Accumulated funds total I£2,150 million.

EDUCATION AND CULTURE

The Centre for Education and Culture: 93 Arlosoroff Street, Tel-Aviv; initiates, plans and co-ordinates activities on a national scale, among them immigrant education courses, evening courses for adults, a theatre company, and numerous choirs, folk-dance groups and popular art circles; arranges theatrical performances and concerts in rural centres, supplies films weekly to agricultural villages and produces its own documentary films.

Amal: 93 Arlosoroff Street, Tel-Aviv; a special Histadrut department to operate and co-ordinate a network of 32 technical high schools.

The Organization of Working and Student Youth: 91 Hachashmonaim St., Tel-Aviv; for young people under the age of 18 who have commenced work or are still at secondary school; 110,000 mems.

Hapoel: 8 Haarba St., P.O.B. 7170, Tel-Aviv; f. 1926; the Histadrut sports organization; 600 brs. with 92,500 mems.

The Women Workers' Council (*Moetzot Hapoalot*) **and Union of Working Mothers** (*Irgun Imahot Ovdot*): 93 Arlosoroff Street, Tel-Aviv; cover both women workers and women members who do no paid outside work but actively help in the absorption of immigrants, the welfare of children of members, the promotion of education programmes for women, including the eradication of illiteracy, good citizenship courses and consumers' activities, etc.; 700 summer camps for 20,000 children; vocational and agricultural training for 6,500 boys, girls and women; over 100 women's club rooms for both Jewish and Arab women.

397

ISRAEL—(THE HISTADRUT, TRADE AND INDUSTRY)

INTERNATIONAL RELATIONS

The Histadrut is affiliated to the International Confederation of Free Trade Unions, is active in the International Labour Organization and the International Co-operative Alliance, and has active and friendly relations with labour movements all over the world. Most of its national unions are affiliated to their respective International Trade Secretariats.

Afro-Asian Institute for Co-operation and Labour Studies: P.O.B. 16201, Tel-Aviv; f. 1960; has conducted courses for over 3,500 participants from 87 countries.

Centre for Labour and Co-operative Studies for Latin America: f. 1962; has conducted courses for some 400 participants from all the countries of Latin America, and from the Caribbean.

TRADE AND INDUSTRY

CHAMBERS OF COMMERCE

Joint Representation of the Israeli Chambers of Commerce: P.O. Box 501, Tel-Aviv; co-ordinates the Tel-Aviv, Jerusalem and Haifa Chambers of Commerce; Sec. F. B. WAHLE.

Jerusalem Chamber of Commerce: P.O.B. 183, 10 Hillel St., Jerusalem; f. 1908; about 300 mems.; Pres. M. H. ELIACHAR; Vice-Pres. A. P. MICHAELIS, A. DASKAL, Y. PEARLMAN, A. ASHBEL, E. BODENKIN; publ. *Bulletin* (Hebrew and English).

Haifa Chamber of Commerce and Industry (*Haifa and District*): P.O.B. 176, 53 Haatzmaut Rd., Haifa; f. 1921; 700 mems.; Pres. JOSEPH ROSH; Gen. Sec. A. MEHOULAL.

Chamber of Commerce, Tel-Aviv-Jaffa: P.O.B. 501, 84 Hachashmonaim St., Tel-Aviv; f. 1919; 1,200 mems.; Pres. A. BENYAKAR; Secs. D. GRAJCAR, F. B. WAHLE; publ. *Hamishar*.

Association of Bi-National Chambers of Commerce in Israel: 82 Allenby Rd., Tel-Aviv; federates the following bi-national chambers of commerce: Israel-America Chamber of Commerce and Industry; Anglo-Israel Chamber of Commerce; Australia-Israel Chamber of Commerce; Chamber of Commerce and Industry Israel-Africa and the Malagasy Republic, Canada-Israel Chamber of Commerce and Industry; Israel-Danish Chamber of Commerce; Chambre de Commerce Israel-France; Camera di Commercio Israel-Italia; Israel-Japan Chamber of Commerce; Israel-Latin America Chamber of Commerce; Netherlands-Israel Chamber of Commerce; Israel-Norway Chamber of Commerce; Handelskammer Israel-Schweiz; Israel-South Africa Chamber of Commerce; Israel-Sweden Chamber of Commerce; Chair. A. CHELOUCHE; Exec. Dir. H. ZUCKERMAN, O.B.E.; and also incorporates Bi-National Chambers of Commerce existing in 22 foreign countries with Israel.

Anglo-Israel Chamber of Commerce (Israel): 82 Allenby Rd., Tel-Aviv, P.O.B. 1127; f. 1951; 400 mems.; Joint Pres. Dr. A. S. ARNON, C.B.E., A. S. COHEN, C.B.E.; Chair. E. IZAKSON.

TRADE AND INDUSTRIAL ORGANIZATIONS

Agricultural Union, The: Tchlenov 20, Tel-Aviv; consists of more than 50 agricultural settlements and is connected with marketing and supplying organizations, and Bahan Ltd., controllers and auditors.

Central Union of Artisans and Small Manufacturers: P.O.B. 4041, Tel-Aviv; f. 1907; has a membership of 40,000 divided into 70 groups according to trade; the union is led by a seventeen-man Presidium; Chair. JACOB FRANK; Gen. Sec. PINHAS SCHWARTZ; publ. *Hamlakha*; 30 brs.

Citrus Control and Marketing Boards: 69 Haifa Road, Tel-Aviv; the government-established institution for the control of the Israel citrus industry; Boards made up of representatives of the Government and the Growers. Functions: Control of plantations, supervision of picking and packing operations; marketing of the crop overseas and on the home markets; shipping: supply of fertilisers, insecticides, equipment for orchards and packing houses and of packing materials, technical research and extension work; long-term financial assistance to growers.

Farmers' Federation: P.O. Box 209, Tel-Aviv; has a membership of 7,000 independent farmers and citrus growers; Pres. ZVI IZACKSON; Dir.-Gen. ITZHAK ZIV-AV; publ. *The Israeli Farmer* (monthly).

General Association of Merchants in Israel: 6 Rothschild Boulevard, Tel-Aviv; the organization of retail traders; has a membership of 30,000 in 60 brs.

Histadrut: 93 Arlosoroff St., Tel-Aviv; f. 1920; membership of the Histadrut is open to all wage-earners and self-employed persons with no staff under them; Sec.-Gen. YITZHAK BEN-AHARON (Labour Party).

Israel Diamond Exchange Ltd.: P.O.B. 3222, Ramat Gan; f. 1937; production, export, import and finance facilities; estimated exports (1972) U.S. $300m.

Israel Journalists' Association Ltd.: 4 Kaplan St., Tel-Aviv; Sec. MOSHE RON.

Manufacturers' Association of Israel: 13 Montefiore St., P.O.B. 29116, Tel-Aviv; Pres. MARK MOSEVICS; Gen. Man. Col. PELEG TAMIR; Gen. Sec. A. Z. CRYSTAL, F.C.C.S.; publ. *News Bulletin* (every two months).

TRADE UNIONS

Histadrut: (see *The Histadrut* section above).

Histadrut Haovdim Haleumit (*National Labour Federation*): 23 Sprinczak St., Tel-Aviv; f. 1934; 84,000 mems.; publs. *Hazit Ha'Oved*, *Lapid*.

Histadrut Hapoel Hamizrahi (*Mizrahi Workers' Organization*): 108 Ahad Haam St., Tel-Aviv; has 55,000 members in 75 settlements.

Histadrut Poalei Agudat Israel (*Agudat Israel Workers' Organization*): Geula Quarter, Corner Yehezkel St., Jerusalem; has 19,000 members in 12 settlements.

ISRAEL—(TRANSPORT, TOURISM)

TRANSPORT

RAILWAYS

Israel Railways: P.O. Box 44, Haifa; a department of the Ministry of Transport and Communications. All its lines are managed and operated from Haifa. The total length of mainline track in operation is 598 km. Traction is wholly diesel.

All lines in operation are standard gauge (4 ft. 8½ in.).

The main flow of traffic is from Haifa Port and from the oil installations and industrial centres in the vicinity of Haifa and of minerals from Beersheba, Dimona and Oron, to the north. The bulk of freight traffic consists of grain, cement and building materials, heavy bulk imported commodities, minerals, phosphates and potash, and oils. Passenger traffic is operated between the main towns: Jerusalem, Tel-Aviv, Haifa, Beersheba, Dimona and Nahariya.

Gen. Man. Col. Y. RESHEF; Principal Asst. LEA STEINMETZ.

UNDERGROUND RAILWAYS

Haifa Underground Funicular Railway: Haifa; opened 1959; 2 km. in operation; Man. D. SCHARF.

Tel-Aviv Rapid Transit: Municipal Offices, Tel-Aviv-Jaffa Municipality; a feasibility study has been made on the possibility of building a 48 km. rapid transit line (11 km. underground).

ROADS

Ministry of Labour, Public Works Dept., Jerusalem.

There are 3,700 km. of metalled main roads not including roads in towns and settlements. Under a five-year plan ending in 1975 the following works will be completed:

One hundred km. new roads to be built, 25 km. additional two-lanes for existing roads, 400 km. widening and improving existing roads.

In addition, a 150-mile long first-class road was built between Eilat and Sharm as-Sheikh during 1970-71.

Automobile and Touring Club of Israel (ATCI): 19 Petah Tiqva Rd., P.O.B. 36144, Tel-Aviv 66183; f. 1949; over 11,000 mems.; Sec.-Gen. Mrs. C. NAHMIAS; publ. *Memsi* (monthly).

SHIPPING

The Israel Ports Authority: Maya Building, 74 Petah Tiqva Rd., Tel-Aviv; f. 1961; to plan, build, develop, administer, maintain and operate the ports. In 1973-74 investment will amount to I£77m. for the Development Budget in Haifa, Ashdod and Eilat Ports. Cargo traffic in 1972-73 amounted to 8.4m. tons (oil excluded).

ZIM Israel Navigation Co. Ltd.: 209 Hameginim Ave., P.O.B. 1723, Haifa; f. 1945; runs cargo services in the Mediterranean and to N. Europe, N. and S. America, Far East, Africa and Australia; Chair. M. TZUR; Man. Dir. M. KASHTI.

Cargo Ships "El-Yam" Ltd.: P.O.B. 182, Haifa; f. 1952; Man. Dir. RAPHAEL RECANATI; a world-wide cargo tramp service.

Maritime Fruit Carriers Co. Ltd.: 53 Shderot Hameginim, P.O.B. 1501, Haifa; refrigerated cargo services; Chair. YAACOV MERIDOR; Man. Dir. MILA BRENER.

Haifa and Ashdod are the main ports in Israel. The former is a natural harbour, enclosed by two main breakwaters and dredged to 37 ft. below mean sea-level. An auxiliary harbour was opened in 1955. In 1965 the new deep water port was completed at Ashdod which has a capacity of about 4 million tons per year. The Tel-Aviv/Jaffa ports were closed down in 1965 as their facilities were no longer adequate for Israel's needs.

Israel has a merchant fleet of more than 100 ships, with a displacement of over 1,600,000 tons.

The port of Eilat is Israel's gate to the Red Sea. It is a natural harbour, operated from a wharf. A new port, to the south of the original one, started operating in 1965.

CIVIL AVIATION

El Al Israel Airlines Ltd.: P.O.B. 41, Lod Airport, Tel-Aviv; f. 1949; daily services to most capitals of Europe; over twenty flights weekly to New York; services to Johannesburg, Teheran, Nairobi, Addis Ababa, Nicosia, Istanbul, Bucharest and Montreal; fleet of two Boeing 720B, three Boeing 707-420, three Boeing 707-320B, two Boeing 707-320C, two Boeing 747B; Pres. M. BEN-ARI.

Arkia, Israel Inland Airlines Ltd.: 88 Ha'Hashmonaim St., Tel-Aviv; f. 1950; scheduled services from Tel-Aviv and Jerusalem to Eilat, Rosh Pina, Haifa, Massada, Abu Rodes, Sharm as-Sheikh and Santa Katarina; fleet of four Viscounts, five Heralds; Man. Dir. L. BIGON.

The following airlines also serve Israel: Air France, Alitalia, AUA, BEA, BOAC, Canadian Pacific, Cyprus Airways, KLM, Lufthansa, Olympic Airways, Sabena, SAS, Swissair, Tarom, THY, TWA.

TOURISM

Ministry of Tourism: Hakirya, P.O. Box 1018, Jerusalem; information offices at Jerusalem, Tel-Aviv, Haifa, Nazareth, Safed, Lod International Airport, Beersheba, Tiberias, Ashkelon, Arad, Bethlehem, Acre, Netanya, Nahariya and Eilat; Minister of Tourism MOSHE KOL; Dir.-Gen. H. GIVTON; publs. *Annual Report, Statistical Year-Book.*

There are also offices in the following countries: England (London), France (Paris), German Federal Republic (Frankfurt), Italy (Rome), Netherlands (Amsterdam), Switzerland (Zürich), Sweden (Stockholm), U.S.A. (New York, Chicago, Boston, Beverly Hills, Atlanta), Argentina (Buenos Aires), Canada (Montreal, Toronto), Denmark (Copenhagen), Belgium (Brussels), South Africa (Johannesburg), Brazil (São Paulo), Australia (Sydney).

CULTURAL ORGANIZATIONS

The Israel Festival: 52 Nachlat Benjamin St., Tel-Aviv, P.O.B. 29874; organizes the Israel Festival which takes place in July/August in Caesarea, Jerusalem and Tel-Aviv; Dir. A. Z. PROPES.

ISRAEL—(TOURISM, ATOMIC ENERGY)

Israel Music Institute: P.O.B. 11253, Tel-Aviv; f. 1961; publishes and promotes Israeli music and musicological works abroad; member since 1969 of International Music Information Centre; Chair. URI TOEPLITZ; Man. Dir. WILLIAM ELIAS.

The National Council of Culture and Art: Hadar Daphna Bldg., Shaul Hamelech Blvd., Tel-Aviv.

PRINCIPAL THEATRES

Cameri Theatre: Tel-Aviv; f. 1944; public trusteeship; repertory theatre; tours abroad.

Habimah National Theatre of Israel: P.O.B. 222, Tel-Aviv; f. 1918 in Russia, moved to Palestine 1928; Jewish, classical and modern drama.

Israel National Opera and Israel National Opera Ballet: 1 Allenby St., Tel-Aviv; f. 1947 by Edis de-Philippe (Dir.); classical and modern opera and ballet; open 50 weeks of the year.

PRINCIPAL ORCHESTRAS

Haifa Symphony Orchestra: 50 Pevsner St., Haifa; Music Dir. AVI OSTROWSKY.

Israel Chamber Orchestra: 103 Ibn Gvirol St., Tel-Aviv; f. 1965; 35 mems.; Artistic Dir. GARY BERTINI.

Israel Philharmonic Orchestra: Frederic R. Mann Auditorium, Tel-Aviv; f. 1936 by Bronislaw Huberman; 106 mems.; frequent tours abroad; 35,000 subscribers; Musical Adviser ZUBIN MEHTA; Concertmasters CHAIM TAUB, URI PIANKA.

The Israel Broadcasting Symphony Orchestra: Israel Broadcasting Authority, P.O.B. 1082, Jerusalem; f. 1938; 70 mems.; Dir. YEHUDA FICKLER; Chief Conductor LUKAS FOSS.

DANCE TROUPES

Bat-Dor Dance Company: 30 Ibn Gvirol St., Tel-Aviv; Dir. BATSHEVA DE ROTHSCHILD.

Batsheva Dance Company: 9 Sderoth Hahaskala, Tel-Aviv.

Inbal Dance Theatre: Tel-Aviv; f. 1949; modern Israeli dance theatre specializing in their traditional folk art, with choreographic themes from the Bible; frequent tours abroad; Founder and Artistic Dir. SARA LEVI-TANAI.

FESTIVALS

Israel Festival of Music and Drama: Caesarea; international festival; of music, dance and drama; f. 1961; one month annually July-August; organized by Israeli Festival Association.

Ein Gev Music Festival: Kibbutz Ein Gev, Kinneret; international festival; annually for one week at Passover.

Zimriya: World Assembly of Choirs, comprising Israeli and international choirs; f. 1952; triennial; next assembly 1976.

ATOMIC ENERGY

Israel Atomic Energy Commission: 26 Rehov Ha Universita, Ramat Aviv, Tel-Aviv; and P.O.B. 17120, Tel-Aviv; f. 1952; advises the Government on policies in nuclear research, supervises the implementation of approved policies and represents Israel in its relations with scientific institutions abroad and international organizations engaged in nuclear research and development (Israel is a member of IAEA); Chair. The PRIME MINISTER; Dir.-Gen. SHALHEVETH FREIER.

The Atomic Energy Commission has two research and development centres: the Soreq Nuclear Research Centre and the Negev Nuclear Research Centre near Dimona. The main fields of research are: nuclear physics and chemistry, reactor physics, reactor engineering, radiation research and applications, application of isotopes, metallurgy, eletronics, radiobiology, nuclear medicine, nuclear power and desalination. The centres also provide national services: health physics including film badge service, isotope production and molecule labelling, activation analysis, irradiation, advice to industry and institutions, training of personnel, technical courses, documentation.

Soreq Nuclear Research Centre: Yavne; f. 1952; equipped with a swimming pool type research reactor IRR-1 of 5 MW thermal; Dir. Prof. I. PELAH.

Negev Nuclear Research Centre: Dimona; equipped with a natural uranium fuelled and heavy water moderated reactor IRR-2 of 26 MW thermal; Dir. JOSEPH TULIPMAN.

Weizmann Institute of Science: Rehovot; in the field of atomic energy, the Institute's equipment includes a 15 MeV Van de Graaff accelerator and a product on-scale plant for the separation of O^{17} and O^{18} from O^{16} Dirs. Prof. IGAL TALMI (Nuclear Physics), Prof. FRITZ KLEIN (Isotope Research), Prof. MICHAEL FELDMAN (Cell Biology).

The Hebrew University of Jerusalem: Jerusalem; engages in atomic research and teaching in chemistry, physics biology and medicine.

Technion: Israel Institute of Technology: Haifa; the Dept. of Physics engages in teaching and research in experimental and theoretical nuclear physics, elementary particle and high energy physics; the Dept. of Nuclear Science undertakes teaching and graduate work in applied nuclear science and engineering; research groups work in the fields of theoretical and experimental nuclear reactor physics, neutron physics, nuclear desalination, heat transfer, nuclear chemistry and technology and applications of nuclear radiations; Head, Nuclear Science Dept. Prof. W. ROTHENSTEIN.

EDUCATION

The present-day school system is based on the Compulsory Education Law (1949), the State Education Law (1953) and on some provisions of the 1933 Education Ordinance dating back to the British Mandatory Administration. The former introduced free compulsory primary education for all children between the ages of 5 and 14 (one kindergarten, eight years elementary schooling); in addition, those aged 14–18 who have not completed their elementary schooling have to attend special evening classes until they reach the necessary standard.

The State Education Law abolished the old complicated Trend Education System, and vested the responsibility for Primary Education in the Government, thus providing a unified State-controlled elementary school system. The law does, however, recognise two main forms of Primary Education—(a) State Education; (b) Recognised Non-State Education. State Education may be sub-divided into two distinct categories of schools—State Schools and State Religious Schools for Jews, and State Schools for Arabs. Schools and kindergartens of the State system are in the joint ownership of the State and the Local Authorities, while the recognized non-State institutions are essentially privately-owned, although they are subsidised, and supervised by the State and the Local Authorities. The standard curriculum for all elementary schools is laid down by the Ministry of Education and Culture, but supplementary subjects, comprising not more than 25 per cent of the syllabus, may be included at the discretion of the school authorities, subject to prior approval by the Minister.

The two largest non-State school systems are the Agudat Israel Schools (of an ultra-orthodox religious character) and the boarding schools, mostly agricultural, for young immigrants, run by various voluntary bodies. The tendency is to strengthen the State System at the expense of the private schools, the possibility of opting out of the State System existing out of deference to the democratic rights and liberties of the citizen.

State Primary Education is financed by a partnership of the Central Government and the Local Authorities. Since 1953 the salaries of all teachers and kindergarten mistresses of State Schools have been paid by the Central Government, whilst the cost of maintenance and of maintenance services, and the provision of new buildings and equipment have been the responsibility of the Local Authorities. The State does not impose an Education Tax but local authorities may, with the Ministry's approval, levy a rate on parents for special services.

School supervision is the prerogative of the Ministry of Education and Culture through the Director-General of the Ministry, and there are six District Inspectors and a varying number of School Inspectors. No supervision is carried out by the Local Authorities, except over property and supplies. Two "Pedagogical Secretariats", one for primary and one for post-primary schools, co-ordinate educational work and deal with problems arising in the various branches of the Educational System.

The State provides different schools for the Jewish and Arab children, because of the distribution of population and the language difference. Nevertheless many Arab children attend Jewish primary, secondary, vocational, agricultural and even teacher-training colleges. In the Jewish sector there is a distinct line of division between the secular State schools and the Religious State Schools, which are established on the demand of parents in any locality, provided that a certain minimum number of pupils have first been enrolled. In the Arab Schools all instruction is in Arabic, and there is a special department for Arabic Education in the Ministry of Education and Culture. Some 90 per cent of the Arab children attend school regularly, but while almost all the boys attend school, there is still reluctance on the part of some Arab parents to send girls to school. This reluctance has been overcome to a great extent by dividing the girls into separate classes and schools.

Particular attention is paid to retarded children, and special classes are provided for them in the ordinary schools, besides the moderate-sized schools for backward and handicapped children which have been established by the Ministry.

Working Youth Schools are provided for boys and girls, between the ages of 14–17, who have not completed their primary education. These schools provide a four-year course, their grades corresponding to grades 5–8 in the primary schools, but there are also two preparatory classes for beginners, mostly for the children of new immigrants.

Post Primary Education is of three main types: Secondary, Vocational and Agricultural. Secondary Education is under the jurisdiction of the Ministry of Education and Culture. The other two categories were administered by the Ministries of Labour and Agriculture respectively, but passed over to the Ministry of Education in September 1960.

Secondary Schools. In 1970–71 the Ministry of Education and Culture had under its supervision 200 Hebrew and 46 Arab secondary schools, with 59,000 and 7,000 pupils respectively. No direct financial aid is given by the State to secondary schools, except building loans. On the other hand the central government and local authorities assist children who have passed a preliminary test to pay their school fees. This assistance is given on a sliding scale according to the parents' means and obligations, and may even cover the total cost. An official proposed syllabus has been published by the Ministry, for use in these schools.

Vocational Training. There are three types of training available in this section of the Education System: Vocational Schools, Apprenticeships and Vocational Training Courses for Adults.

In the school year 1970–71 there were 265 Hebrew and 19 Arab vocational schools with 54,000 and 1,000 pupils respectively. Almost all the courses extend over a period of three or four years, and the students are boys and girls between the ages of 14 and 18. The curriculum consists of some 20 hours practical training, and 24 hours instruction on industrial and general subjects, each week.

Apprenticeship is regulated by the Apprenticeship Act of 1953, and all apprentices must attend apprenticeship schools one day a week. In 1961 there were 13,000 apprentices in industrial trades and crafts. There is no apprenticeship in agriculture; most trades require 3–4 years apprenticeship, which normally applies to youths from 14–18 years of age.

A programme of Pre-Vocational Training for pupils in the last two grades of the Government Primary Schools was launched in 1955. This programme includes training in various trades, handicrafts and agriculture, and was intended to enable pupils continuing in the Vocational Schools to begin their studies in the second year of those schools. In fact they are now absorbed in the two-year secondary schools and thus get four years of a mixed general and vocational education. The training is given in addition to the Primary School curriculum.

Vocational training for adults is divided into two sections: basic trade courses (day courses) which are intended for persons who have had no previous vocational training or have to change their occupation (mostly new immigrants), and supplementary training courses (evening classes), intended for the further education of already skilled workers. The courses are from 3–18 months.

Agricultural Schools: there are various kinds of schools offering training in agriculture, ranging from the Faculty of Agriculture of the Hebrew University, and the Rupin Institute courses for adults to the agricultural secondary schools and other training centres for youth.

In 1970–71 there were 31 agricultural schools of which one was for Arab pupils, including a fishing school, a school of horticulture, and an agricultural technical institute providing a diploma-course. Five of these (including the fishing school and the technical institute) are government schools; the others are financed by various organizations such as the Women Workers' Council, Women's International Zionist Organization, etc.

In 1968–69 there were over 7,500 Hebrew and 400 Arab pupils. Most schools have well-developed farms in which the pupils work for 3–4 hours a day. A 3-year course is usual and only a few have a 4-year course. Some 2-year courses are being opened in regional schools for farm-youth.

Teachers' Training. As the enrolment in schools throughout the country increases by about 20,000 pupils each year, the need for additional teachers is keenly felt. There are 50 Hebrew and one Arab teacher training colleges with 5,000 Hebrew and 358 Arab students respectively. To qualify as a teacher the student must have taken 14 years of study. Pupils normally complete the 12-year secondary school course and then go to a teachers' training college for a further two years. In these two years the student has practical teaching experience before sitting for the examination of the Ministry of Education and Culture.

Adult Education. Numerous facilities for adult education are offered both by institutions of higher learning and by various organizations. Special attention is being paid to the study of the Hebrew language and new immigrants have the opportunity to study Hebrew in intensive 5–6 month courses (*ulpanim*) some of which are conducted in agricultural settlements where students work for half the day to cover their living expenses.

The Occupied Territories. The educational system in the occupied parts of the adjacent Arab countries has been taken over with few changes. In the west bank 830 schools (200 run by UNRWA) had 6,200 teachers and 170,000 pupils. In the Gaza strip were 80 state and 100 UNRWA schools with 2,700 teachers and an enrolment of approximately 100,000, while there were 8 schools with 40 teachers and 1,000 pupils in Golan. Many of the textbooks have been replaced where material critical of Jews, Zionism or the State of Israel was discovered; at first, teachers and students refused to return to schools under Israeli control, but this school strike gradually lost force and within a year of the occupation most schools in the occupied territories were operating more or less normally.

UNIVERSITIES

Bar-Ilan University: Ramat-Gan; 850 teachers, 5,500 students.

Haifa University: Mount Carmel, Haifa; 652 teachers, 5,000 students.

The Hebrew University of Jerusalem: Jerusalem; 1,955 teachers, 16,000 students.

University of the Negev: P.O.B. 2053, Beersheba; 385 teachers, 3,200 students.

Tel-Aviv University: Ramat-Aviv, Tel-Aviv; 2,086 teachers, 16,384 students.

Technion, Israel Institute of Technology: Haifa; 1,300 teachers, 6,150 undergraduate, 2,781 graduate students.

BIBLIOGRAPHY

GENERAL

ARENDT, HANNAH. Eichmann in Jerusalem (New York, 1963).

AVNERY, URI. Israel without Zionists (Collier-Macmillan, London, 1969).

EDELMAN, MAURICE. Ben Gurion, a Political Biography (Hodder and Stoughton, London, 1964).

GLUECK, NELSON. The River Jordan (Philadelphia, 1946.) Rivers in the Desert (London, 1959).

HILLEL, MARC. Israel en danger de paix (Fayard, Paris, 1969).

KOHN, HANS. Nationalism and Imperialism in the Hither East (London, 1932).

KOLLEK, TEDDY, and PEARLMAN, MOSHE. Jerusalem, Sacred City of Mankind (Weidenfeld and Nicholson, London, 1968).

MALLISON, W. T. (Jr.) The Zionist-Israel Juridical Claims to Constitute "The Jewish People" Nationality Entity and to Confer Membership of it. (*George Washington Law Review*, Vol. 32, No. 4-June 1964).

MARMORSTEIN, EMILE. Heaven at Bay: The Jewish Kulturkampf in the Holy Land (Oxford University Press, 1969).

ORNI, E. and EFRAT, E. The Geography of Israel (Darey, New York, 1965).

ORON, YITZHAK. Middle East Record, Vol. II (Daniel Davey and Co., New York, 1966).

PARKES, J. W. The Emergence of the Jewish Problem, 1878-1939 (Oxford, 1946).

A History of Palestine from A.D. 135 to Modern Times (Gollancz, London, 1949).

End of Exile (New York, 1954).

Whose Land? A History of the Peoples of Palestine (Pelican, Harmondsworth, 1970).

ISRAEL—(BIBLIOGRAPHY)

PATAI, R. Israel Between East and West (Philadelphia, 1953).
  Culture and Conflict (New York, 1962).
SHAPIRO, HARRY L. The Jewish People: a biological history (UNESCO, 1960).
TOYNBEE, ARNOLD J. Survey of International Affairs, Vol. I (London, 1925).
TUCHMAN, BARBARA W. Bible and Sword (Redman, London, 1957; Minerva, New York, 1968).
WEINGROD, ALEX. Reluctant Pioneers, Village Development in Israel (Cornell University Press, New York, 1966).
ZANDER, WALTER. Israel and the Holy Places of Christendom (Weidenfeld and Nicolson, 1972).

ANCIENT HISTORY

DE VAUX, R. Ancient Israel: Its Life and Institutions (New York, 1961).
ORLINSKY, H. M. Ancient Israel (Cornell University Press).
SMITH, Sir G. A. Historical Geography of the Holy Land (24th ed., London, 1931).
YADIN, YIGAEL. Message of the Scrolls (Grosset and Dunlap, New York).
  Masada (Weidenfeld and Nicholson, London, 1966).
YEWIN, S. A Decade of Archaeology in Israel 1948-58 (Istanbul, 1960).

RECENT HISTORY

ALLON, YIGAL. The Making of Israel's Army (Mitchell Valentine, London, 1970).
BARBOUR, NEVILL. Nisi Dominus: a survey of the Palestine Controversy (Harrap, London, 1946, reprinted by the Institute for Palestine Studies, Beirut, 1969).
BENTWICH, NORMAN and HELEN. Mandate Memories, 1918-1948 (Hogarth Press, London, 1965).
BERMANT, CHAIM. Israel (Thames and Hudson, London, 1967).
BERGER, EARL. The Covenant and the Sword, Arab-Israel Relations 1948–56 (University of Toronto Press, Toronto, 1965).
BURNS, E. L. M. Between Arab and Israeli (Harrap, London, 1962; Astor-Honor, New York, 1963).
CATTAN, HENRY. Palestine, the Arabs and Israel (Longmans Green, London, 1969).
CHURCHILL, RANDOLPH and WINSTON. The Six Day War (Heinemann/Penguin, London, 1967).
CROSSMAN, R. H. S. Palestine Mission (London, 1947).
DOUGLAS-HOME, C. The Arabs and Israel (Bodley Head, 1968).
DRAPER, T. Israel and World Politics: Roots of the Third Arab-Israeli War (Secker and Warburg, London, 1968).
ESCO FOUNDATION FOR PALESTINE, Palestine: A Study of Jewish, Arab and British Policies (2 vols., New Haven, 1947).
FURLONGE, GEOFFREY. Palestine is my Country: The Story of Musa Alami (John Murray, London, 1969).
GABBAY, RONY E. A Political Study of the Arab-Jewish Conflict, the Arab Refugee Problem (Geneva and Paris, 1959).
HADAWI, SAMI, Palestine, Loss of Heritage (San Antonio, Texas, 1963).
HOWARD, M., and HUNTER, R. Israel and the Arab World (Institute of Palestine Studies, Beirut).
HUTCHISON, Cmdr. E. H. Violent Truce (New York, Devin-Adair, 1956).
JIRYIS, SABRI. The Arabs in Israel (Institute for Palestine Studies, Beirut, 1968).
KADER, RAZZAK ABDEL. The Arab-Jewish Conflict (1961).
KHALIDI, WALID. From Haven to Conquest: Readings in Zionism and the Palestine Problem until 1948 (Institute for Palestine Studies, Beirut, 1971).
KIMCHE, JON and DAVID. Both Sides of the Hill: Britain and the Palestine War (Secker and Warburg, London, 1960).
KOESTLER, ARTHUR. Promise and Fulfilment: Palestine, 1917-1949 (London, 1949).
  Thieves in the Night (New York and London, 1946).
LANDAU, JACOB M. The Arabs in Israel (Oxford University Press, London, 1969).
LAQUEUR, WALTER. The Road to War 1967 (Weidenfeld and Nicolson, London, 1968).
  The Israel-Arab Reader (Weidenfeld and Nicolson, London, 1969).
LILIENTHAL, ALFRED M. The Other Side of the Coin: An American Perspective of the Arab-Israeli Conflict (New York, 1965).
LORCH, N. The Edge of the Sword: Israel's War of Independence 1947-49 (Putnam, New York, 1961).
MARLOWE, JOHN. The Seat of Pilate, An Account of the Palestine Mandate (Cresset, London, 1959; Dufour, Philadelphia, 1958).
O'BALLANCE, E. The Arab-Israeli War (New York, Praeger, 1957).
PERETZ, DON. Israel and the Palestine Arabs (The Middle East Institute, Washington, 1958).
RIZK, EDWARD. The Palestine Question, Seminar of Arab Jurists on Palestine, Algiers, 1967 (Institute for Palestine Studies, Beirut, 1968).
RODINSON, MAXIME. Israel and the Arabs (Penguin Books, Harmondsworth, 1968; Pantheon, New York, 1969).
ROULEAU, ERIC and HELD, JEAN-FRANCIS. Israel et les Arabes (Editions du Seuil, Paris, 1967).
ROYAL INSTITUTE OF INTERNATIONAL AFFAIRS. Great Britain and Palestine 1915-45 (London, 1946).
SHARABI, HISHAM B. Palestine and Israel: The Lethal Dilemma (Van Nostrand Reinhold, New York, 1969).
SYKES, CHRISTOPHER. Crossroads to Israel (Collins, London, 1965).
ZURAYK, C. N. Palestine, the Meaning of the Disaster (Beirut, 1956).

THE STATE

BADI, JOSEPH. Fundamental Laws of the State of Israel (New York, 1961).

ISREAL—(BIBLIOGRAPHY)

BARUTH, K. H. The Physical Planning of Israel (London, 1949).

BEN GURION, D. Rebirth and Destiny of Israel (New York, 1954).

BENTWICH, NORMAN. Fulfilment in the Promised Land 1917-37 (London, 1938).

Judæa Lives Again (London, 1944).

Israel Resurgent (Ernest Benn, 1960).

The New-old Land of Israel (Allen and Unwin, 1960).

BENTWICH, J. S. Education in Israel (Routledge and Kegan Paul, London, 1965).

BERNSTEIN, MARVER H. The Politics of Israel (London, 1958).

COMAY, JOAN. Everyone's Guide to Israel (New York, 1962).

Introducing Israel (London, Methuen, 1963).

COMAY, JOAN and PEARLMAN, MOSHE. Israel (New York, 1965).

CROSSMAN, R. H. S. A Nation Reborn (London, Hamish Hamilton, 1960).

DAVIS, MOSHE (Ed.). Israel: its Role in Civilisation (New York, 1956).

DAYAN, SHMUEL. The Promised Land (London, 1961).

DE GAURY, GERALD. The New State of Israel (New York, 1952).

DRABKIN-DARIN, H. Housing in Israel (Tel-Aviv, Gadish Books, 1957).

EBAN, A. The Voice of Israel (New York, Horizon Press, 1957).

HALPERIN, HAIM. Changing Patterns in Israel Agriculture (London, 1957).

THE ISRAEL ECONOMIST. Jerusalem (annual).

JANOWSKY, OSCAR I. Foundations of Israel: Emergence of a Welfare State (Anvil Nostrand Co., Princeton, 1959).

KRAINES, O. Government and Politics in Israel (Allen and Unwin, London, 1961).

MEDDING, PETER. Mapai in Israel: Political Organisation and Government in a New Society (Cambridge U.P., London, 1972).

MEIR, GOLDA. This is our Strength (New York, 1963).

PATINKIN, D. The Israel Economy; the first decade (Jerusalem, 1960).

PEARLMAN, Lt.-Col. MOSHE. The Army of Israel (New York, 1959).

PREUSS, W. Co-operation in Israel and the World (Jerusalem, 1960).

RUBER, A. The Economy of Israel (Frank Cass, London, 1960).

SACHAR, H. M. ALIYAH, The Peoples of Israel (New York, 1962).

SAFRAN, NADAV. The United States and Israel (Harvard U.P., 1963).

SAMUEL, The Hon. EDWIN. Problems of Government in the State of Israel (Jerusalem, 1956).

SEGRE, V. D. Israel: A Society in Transition (Oxford U.P., London, 1971).

SHATIL, J. L'économie Collective du Kibboutz Israëlien (Paris, Les Editions de Minuit, 1960).

SITTON, SHLOMO. Israël: Immigration et Croissance 1948-58 (Editions Cujas, Paris, 1963).

WAAGENAAR, S. Women of Israel (New York, 1962).

ZIONISM

BEIN, ALEX. Theodor Herzl (East and West Library, London, 1957).

COHEN, ISRAEL. A Short History of Zionism (London, Frederick Muller, 1951).

FRANKL, OSCAR BENJAMIN. Theodor Herzl: The Jew and Man (New York, 1949).

GOLDWATER, RAYMOND (ed.). Jewish Philosophy and Philosophers (McGraw, London, 1962).

LIPSKY, L. A Gallery of Zionist Profiles (New York, Farrar, Straus and Cudahy, 1950).

LOWENTHAL, MARVIN (ed. and trans.) Diaries of Theodor Herzl (Grosset and Dunlap, New York, 1965).

PETUCHOWSKY, J. J. Zionism Reconsidered (Twayne, New York, 1966).

SCHECHTMAN, J. Rebel and Statesmen: the Jabotinsky Story (New York, Thomas Yoseloff, 1956).

SOKOLOW, NAHUM. History of Zionism (2 vols., Longmans, London, 1919; Ktav, New York, 1969).

STEIN, LEONARD and YOGEV, GEDILIA (Editors). The Letters and Papers of Chaim Weizmann; Volume I 1885-1902 (Oxford University Press, 1968).

SOKOLOW, NAHUM. History of Zionism (2 vols., London, 1919).

WEISGAL, MEYER, and CARMICHAEL, JOEL. Chaim Weizmann—a Biography by Several Hands (London, Weidenfield and Nicholson, 1962).

WEIZMANN, Dr. CHAIM. The Jewish People and Palestine (London, 1939).

Trial and Error: the Autobiography of Chaim Weizmann (Hamish Hamilton, London, 1949; Schocken, New York, 1966).

OFFICIAL PUBLICATIONS

Report of the Palestine Royal Commission, 1937 (Cmd. 5479), London.

Report of the Palestine Partition Commission, 1938 (Cmd. 5854), London.

Statement of Policy by His Majesty's Government in the United Kingdom (Cmd. 3692), London, 1930; (Cmd. 5893), London, 1938; (Cmd. 6019), London, 1939; (Cmd. 6180), London, 1940.

Government Survey of Palestine (2 vols., 1945-46), Jerusalem. Supplement, July 1947, Jerusalem.

Report of the Anglo-American Committee of Enquiry, Lausanne, 1946.

Report to the United Nations General Assembly by the UN Special Committee on Palestine, Geneva, 1947.

Report of the UN Economic Survey Mission for the Middle East, December 1949 (United Nations, Lake Success, N.Y.; H.M. Stationery Office).

Annual Yearbook of the Government of Israel.

Israel Government. The Arabs in Israel (1952).

Jewish Agency for Palestine. Documents Submitted to General Assembly of UN, relating to the National Home (1947).

The Jewish Plan for Palestine (Jerusalem, 1947).

Statistical Survey of the Middle East (1944).

Statistical Abstract of Israel. Central Bureau of Statistics (annual).

Jordan

PHYSICAL AND SOCIAL GEOGRAPHY

W. B. Fisher

The Hashemite Kingdom of Jordan (previously Transjordan) came officially into existence under its present name in 1947 and was enlarged in 1950 to include the districts of Samaria and part of Judaea that had previously formed part of Arab Palestine. The country is bounded on the north by Syria, on the north-east by Iraq, on the east and south by Saudi Arabia, and on the west by Israel. The total area of Jordan is approximately 37,500 sq. miles (The territory west of the Jordan river—some 2,165 sq. miles—has been occupied by Israel since June 1967).

PHYSICAL FEATURES

The greater part of the State of Jordan consists of a plateau lying some 2-3,000 ft. above sea-level, which forms the north-western corner of the great plateau of Arabia (see "Arabia"). There are no natural topographical frontiers between Jordan and its neighbours Syria, Iraq, and Saudi Arabia, and the plateau continues unbroken into all three countries, with the artificial frontier boundaries drawn as straight lines between defined points. Along its western edge, facing the Jordan Valley, the plateau is up-tilted to give a line of hills that rise 1-2,000 ft. above plateau-level. An old river course, the Wadi Sirhan, now almost dry with only occasional wells, breaks up the plateau surface on the south-east and continues into Saudi Arabia.

The Jordanian plateau consists of a core or table of ancient rocks, covered by layers of newer rock (chiefly limestone) lying almost horizontally. In a few places (e.g. on the southern edge of the Jordan Valley) these old rocks are exposed at the surface. On its western side the plateau has been fractured and dislocated by the development of two strongly marked and parallel faults that run from the Red Sea via the Gulf of Aqaba northwards to the Lebanon and Syria. The narrow zone between the faults has sunk, to give the well-known Jordan rift valley, which is bordered both on the east and west by steep-sided walls, especially in the south near the Dead Sea, where the drop is often precipitous. The valley has a maximum width of 14 miles.

The floor of the Jordan Valley varies considerably in level. At its northern end it is just above sea-level; the surface of Lake Tiberias (the Sea of Galilee) is 686 ft. below sea-level, with the deepest part of the lake 700 ft. lower still. Greatest depth of the valley is at the Dead Sea (surface 1,300 ft. below sea level, maximum depth 1,298 ft.).

Dislocation of the rock strata in the region of the Jordan Valley has had two further effects: firstly, earth tremors are still frequent along the valley (Jerusalem has minor earthquakes from time to time); and secondly, considerable quantities of lava have welled up, forming enormous sheets that cover wide expanses of territory in the State of Jordan and southern Syria, and produce a desolate, forbidding landscape. One small lava flow, by forming a natural dam across the Jordan Valley, has impounded the waters to form Lake Tiberias.

The River Jordan rises just inside the frontiers of Syria and the Lebanon—a fruitful source of dispute between the two countries and Israel. The river is 157 miles long, and after first flowing for 60 miles in Israel it lies within Jordanian territory for the remaining 95 miles. Its main tributary, the Yarmuk, is 25 miles long, and close to its junction with the Jordan forms the boundary between Jordan State, Israel and Syria. A few miles from its source, the River Jordan used to open into Lake Huleh, a shallow, marsh-fringed expanse of water which was for long a breeding ground of malaria, but which has now been drained. Lake Tiberias, also, like Huleh, in Israel, covers an area of 122 sq. miles and measures 14 miles from north to south, and 16 miles from east to west. River water outflowing from the lake is used for the generation of hydro-electricity.

The river then flows through the barren, inhospitable country of its middle and lower valley, very little of which is actually, or potentially, cultivable, and finally enters the Dead Sea. This lake is 40 miles long and 10 miles wide. Owing to the very high air temperatures at most seasons of the year evaporation from the lake is intense, and has been estimated as equivalent to $8\frac{1}{4}$ million tons of water per day. At the surface the Dead Sea water contains about 250 grams of dissolved salts per litre, and at a depth of 360 feet the water is chemically saturated (i.e. holds its maximum possible content). Magnesium chloride is the most abundant mineral, with sodium chloride next in importance; but commercial interest centres in the less abundant potash and bromide salts.

Climatically, Jordan shows close affinity to its neighbours. Summers are hot, especially on the plateau and in the Jordan Valley, where temperatures up to 120° F. have been recorded. Winters are fairly cold, and on the plateau frost and some snow are usual, though not in the lower Jordan Valley. The significant element of the climate of Jordan is rainfall. In the higher parts (i.e. the uplands of Samaria and Judaea and the hills overlooking the eastern Jordan Valley) 15 to 25 inches of rainfall occur, enough for agriculture; but elsewhere as little as 8 inches or less may fall, and pastoral nomadism is the only possible way of life. Only about 25 per cent of the total area of Jordan is sufficiently humid for cultivation.

Hence the main features of economic life in Jordan are subsistence agriculture of a marginal kind, carried on in Judaea-Samaria and on the north-eastern edge of the plateau, close to Amman, with migratory herding of animals—sheep, goats, cattle and camels—over the remaining and by far the larger portion of the country. As a result, the natural wealth of Jordan is small and tribal ways of life exist in many parts. Before the June 1967 War tourism (with which must be included religious pilgrimage, mainly to the Holy Christian places of Jerusalem) had developed into a very important industry but this has been seriously jeopardized by the Israeli occupation of the west bank territory and annexation of Jerusalem.

RACE AND LANGUAGE

A division must be drawn between the Jordanians living east of the River Jordan, who in the main are of pure Mediterranean stock, ethnically similar to the desert populations of Syria and Saudi Arabia, and the Arabs of the Jordan Valley and Samaria-Judaea. These latter are slightly taller, more heavily built, and have a broader head-form. Some authorities suggest that they are descendants of the Canaanites, who may have originated far to the north-east, in the Zagros area. An Iranian racial affinity is thus implied—but this must be of very ancient date, as the Arabs west of the Jordan Valley have been settled in their present home for many thousands of years. Besides the two groups of Arabs there are also small colonies of Circassians from the Caucasus of Russia, who settled in Jordan as refugees during the nineteenth and twentieth centuries A.D.

Arabic is spoken everywhere, except in a few Circassian villages, and, through the contacts with Britain, some English is understood in the towns.

HISTORY

Jordan, as an independent State, is a twentieth-century development. Before then it was seldom more than a rugged and backward appendage to more powerful kingdoms and empires, and indeed never had any separate existence. In Biblical times the area was covered roughly by Gilead, Ammon, Moab and Edom, and the western portions formed for a time part of the kingdom of Israel. During the sixth century B.C. the Arabian tribe of the Nabataeans established their capital at Petra in the south and continued to preserve their independence when, during the fourth and third centuries, the northern half was incorporated into the Seleucid province of Syria. It was under Seleucid rule that cities like Philadelphia (the Biblical Rabbath Ammon and the modern Amman) and Gerasa (now Jerash) rose to prominence. During the first century B.C. the Nabataeans extended their rule over the greater part of present-day Jordan and Syria; they then began to recede before the advance of Rome, and in A.D. 105-6 Petra was incorporated into the Roman Empire. The lands east of the Jordan shared in a brief blaze of glory under the Palmyrene sovereigns Odenathus (Udaynath) and Zenobia (al-Zabba') in the middle of the third century A.D., and during the fifth and sixth centuries formed part of the dominions of the Christian Ghassanid dynasty, vassals of the Byzantine Empire. Finally, after fifty years of anarchy in which Byzantine, Persian and local rulers intervened, Transjordania was conquered by the Arabs and absorbed into the Islamic Empire.

For centuries nothing more is heard of the country; it formed normally a part of Syria, and as such was generally governed from Egypt. From the beginning of the sixteenth century it was included in the Ottoman *vilayet* of Damascus, and remained in a condition of stagnation until the outbreak of the Great War in 1914. European travellers and explorers of the nineteenth century rediscovered the beauties of Petra and Gerasa, but otherwise the desert tribes were left undisturbed. Even the course of the war in its early stages gave little hint of the upheaval that was to take place in Jordan's fortunes. The area was included in the zone of influence allocated to Britain under the Sykes-Picot Treaty of May 1916 (*see* Documents on Palestine, p. 46), and Zionists held that it also came within the area designated as a Jewish National Home in the promise contained in the Balfour Declaration of November 1917. Apart from these somewhat remote political events the tide of war did not reach Jordanian territory until the capture of Aqaba by the Arab armies under Faisal, the third son of King Hussein of the Hijaz, in July 1917. A year later, in September 1918, they shared in the final push north by capturing Amman and Deraa.

The end of the war thus found a large area, which included almost the whole of present-day Jordan, in Arab hands under the leadership of Faisal. To begin with, the territory to the east of the River Jordan was not looked on as a separate unit. Faisal, with the assistance of British officers and Iraqi nationalists, set up an autonomous government in Damascus, a step encouraged by the Anglo-French Declaration of November 7th, 1918, favouring the establishment of indigenous governments in Syria and Iraq. Arab demands, however, as expressed by Faisal at the Paris Peace Conference in January 1919, went a good deal further in claiming independence throughout the Arab world. This brought them sharply up against both French and Zionist claims in the Near East, and when in March 1920 the General Syrian Congress in Damascus declared the independence of Syria and Iraq, with Faisal and Abdullah, Hussein's second son, as kings, the decisions were denounced by France and Britain. The following month the San Remo Conference awarded the Palestine Mandate to Britain, and thus separated it effectively from Syria proper, which fell within the French share. Faisal was forced out of Damascus by the French in July and left the country.

THE KINGDOM OF TRANSJORDAN

The position of Transjordania was not altogether clear under the new dispensation. After the withdrawal of Faisal the British High Commissioner informed a meeting of notables at Es Salt that the British Government favoured self-government for the territory with British advisers. In December 1920 the provisional frontiers of the Mandates were extended eastwards by Anglo-French agreement so as to include Transjordania within the Palestine Mandate, and therefore presumably within the provisions regarding the establishment of a Jewish National Home. Yet another twist of policy came as the result of a conference in Cairo in March 1921 attended by Winston Churchill, the new British Colonial Secretary, Abdullah, T. E. Lawrence and Sir Herbert Samuel, High Commissioner for Palestine. At this meeting it was recommended that Faisal should be proclaimed King of Iraq, while Abdullah was persuaded to stand down in his favour by the promise of an Arab administration in Transjordania. He had in fact been in effective control in Amman since his arrival the previous winter to organize a rising against the French in Syria. This project he now abandoned, and in April 1921 was officially recognized as *de facto* ruler of Transjordan. The final draft of the Palestine Mandate confirmed by the Council of the League of Nations in July 1922 contained a clause giving the Mandatory Power considerable latitude in the administration of the territory east of the Jordan (*see* Documents on Palestine, p.50). On the basis of this clause a memorandum was approved in the following September expressly excluding Transjordan from the clauses relating to the establishment of the Jewish National Home, and although many Zionists continued to press for the reversal of this policy, the country thenceforth remained in practice separate from Palestine proper.

Like much of the post-war boundary delineation, the borders of the new state were somewhat arbitrary. Though they lay mainly in desert areas they frequently cut across tribal areas and grazing grounds with small respect for tradition. Of the three or four hundred thousand inhabitants only about a fifth were town-dwellers, and these confined to four small cities ranging in population from 30,000 to 10,000. Nevertheless Transjordan's early years were destined to be comparatively peaceful. On May 15th, 1923, Britain formally recognized Transjordan as an independent constitutional State under the rule of the Amir Abdullah with British tutelage, and with the aid of a British subsidy it was possible to make some slow progress towards development and modernization. A small but efficient armed force, the Arab Legion, was built up under the guidance of Peake Pasha and later Glubb Pasha; this force distinguished itself particularly during the Iraqi rebellion of May 1941. It also played a significant role in the fighting with Israel during 1948. Other British advisers assisted in the development of health services and schools.

The Amir Abdullah very nearly became involved in the fall of his father, King Hussein, in 1924. It was in Amman on March 5th, 1924, that the latter was proclaimed Caliph, and during the subsequent fighting with Ibn Sa'ud Wahhabi troops penetrated into Transjordanian territory. They subsequently withdrew to the south, and in June 1925, after the abdication of Hussein's eldest son Ali, Abdullah formally incorporated Ma'an and Aqaba within his dominions. The move was not disputed by the new ruler of the Hijaz and Najd, and thereafter the southern frontier of Transjordan has remained unaltered.

INDEPENDENCE

In February 1928 a treaty was signed with Great Britain granting a still larger measure of independence, though reserving for the advice of a British Resident such matters as financial policy and foreign relations. The same treaty provided for a constitution, and this was duly promulgated in April 1928, the first Legislative Council meeting a year later. In January 1934 a supplementary agreement was added permitting Transjordan to appoint consular representatives in Arab countries, and in May 1939 Britain agreed to the conversion of the Legislative Council into a regular Cabinet with ministers in charge of specified departments. The outbreak of war delayed further advances towards independence, but this was finally achieved in name at least by the Treaty of London of March 22nd, 1946. On the following May 25th Abdullah was proclaimed king and a new constitution replaced the now obsolete one of 1928.

Transjordan was not slow in taking her place in the community of nations. In 1947 King Abdullah signed treaties with Turkey and Iraq and applied for membership of the United Nations; this last, however, was thwarted by the Russian veto and by lack of American recognition of Transjordan's status as an independent nation. In March 1948 Britain agreed to the signing of a new treaty in which virtually the only restrictive clauses related to military and defence matters. Britain was to have certain peace-time military privileges, including the maintenance of airfields and communications, transit facilities and co-ordination of training methods. She was also to provide economic and social aid.

Transjordan had, however, not waited for independence before making her weight felt in Arab affairs in the Middle East. She had not been very active before the war, and, in fact her first appearance on the international scene was in May 1939, when Transjordanian delegates were invited to the Round Table Conference on Palestine in London. Transjordan took part in the preliminary discussions during 1943 and 1944 that led finally to the formation of the Arab League in March 1945, and was one of the original members of that League. During the immediately following years it seemed possible that political and dynastic differences would be forgotten in this common effort for unity. Under the stresses and strains of 1948 however, the old contradictions began to reappear. Abdullah had long favoured the project of a "Greater Syria", that is, the union of Transjordan, Syria, and Palestine, as a step towards the final unification of the Fertile Crescent by the inclusion of Iraq. This was favoured on dynastic grounds by various parties in Iraq, and also by some elements in Syria and Palestine. On the other hand it met with violent opposition from many Syrian nationalists, from the rulers of Egypt and Saudi Arabia—neither of whom were disposed to favour any strengthening of the Hashemite house—and of course from the Zionists and the French. It is in the light of these conflicts of interest that developments subsequent to the establishment of the State of Israel must be seen.

FORMATION OF ISRAEL

On May 14th–15th, 1948, British troops were withdrawn into the port of Haifa as a preliminary to the final evacuation of Palestine territory, the State of Israel was proclaimed, and Arab armies entered the former Palestinian territory from all sides. Only those from Transjordan played any significant part in the fighting, and by the time that major hostilities ceased in July they had succeeded in occupying a considerable area. The suspicion now inevitably arose that Abdullah was prepared to accept a *fait accompli* and to negotiate with the Israeli authorities for a formal recognition of the existing military boundaries. Moreover, whereas the other Arab countries refused to accept any other move that implied a tacit recognition of the *status quo*—such as the resettlement of refugees—Transjordan seemed to be following a different line. In September 1948 an Arab government was formed at Gaza under Egyptian tutelage, and this was answered from the Transjordanian side by the proclamation in December at Jericho of Abdullah as King of All-Palestine. In the following April the country's name was changed to Jordan and three Palestinians were included in the Cabinet. In the meantime armistices were being signed by all the Arab countries, including Jordan, and on January 31st, 1949, Jordan had at last been recognized by the United States.

On the three major problems confronting the Arab States in their dispute with Israel, Jordan continued to differ more or less openly with her colleagues. She refused to agree to the internationalization of Jerusalem, she initiated plans for the resettlement of the Arab refugees, and she showed a disposition to accept as permanent the armistice frontiers. In April 1950, after rumours of negotiations between Jordan and Israel, the Arab League Council in Cairo succeeded in getting Jordan's adherence to resolutions forbidding negotiations with Israel or annexation of Palestinian territory. Nevertheless in the same month elections were held in Jordan and Arab Palestine, the results of which encouraged Abdullah formally to annex the latter territory on April 24th, 1950. This step was immediately recognized by Britain.

At the meeting of the Arab League that followed, Egypt led the opposition to Jordan, who found support, however, from Iraq. The decisions reached by the Council were inconclusive; but thereafter Jordan began to drift away from Arab League policy. Jordan supported the United Nations policy over Korea, in contradistinction to the other Arab states, and signed a Point Four agreement with the United States in March 1951. Though there was at the same time constant friction between Jordan and Israel the unified opposition of the Arab States to the new Jewish State seemed to have ended, and inter-Arab differences were gaining the upper hand.

ABDULLAH ASSASSINATED

On July 20th, 1951, King Abdullah was assassinated in Jerusalem. Evidence brought out at the trial of those implicated in the plot showed that the murder was as much as anything a protest against his Greater Syria policy, and it was significant that Egypt refused to extradite some of those convicted. Nevertheless the stability of the young Jordanian State revealed itself in the calm in which the King's eldest son Talal succeeded to the throne, and the peaceful elections held shortly afterwards. In January 1952 a new constitution was promulgated. Even more significant, perhaps, was the dignity with which, only a year after his accession, King Talal, whose mental condition had long been giving cause for anxiety, abdicated in favour of his son, Hussein, still a minor. In foreign policy Talal had shown some signs of a reaction against his father's ideas in favour of a *rapprochement* with Syria and Egypt, one step being Jordan's signature of the Arab Collective Security Pact which she had failed to join in the summer of 1950.

This policy was continued during the reign of his son, King Hussein, notably by the conclusion of an economic and financial agreement with Syria in February 1953, and a joint scheme for the construction of a dam across the Yarmuk River to supply irrigation and hydro-electric power. At the same time Hussein maintained the family ties with Iraq, state visits being exchanged with King Faisal II immediately after the former's formal accession in May 1953.

During the year there was a recrudescence of trouble along the frontier with Israel. A temporary agreement reached under UN auspices in June seemed to have eased matters, but in October an Israeli attack on the Jordanian village of Qibya aroused violent emotions in the Arab countries. In March, 1954, the position was reversed with an Arab attack on an Israeli bus in the Scorpion Pass, an incident that led to a temporary breakdown in the truce arrangements and to a series of further frontier violations. Another problem that still remained unsolved was the elaborate scheme sponsored by the United States for the sharing of the Jordan waters between Jordan, Iraq, Syria and Israel, which could make no progress in the absence of political agreement. In May, amid mounting tension, the cabinet of Fawzi al-Mulqi resigned, and a new government was formed by Tawfiq Abu'l-Huda, which was re-organized on October 25th, 1954, after the elections of October 16th.

During December a financial aid agreement was signed in London with the United Kingdom, and the opportunity was taken to discuss the revision of the Anglo-Jordanian Treaty of 1946. Agreement over this was not possible owing to British insistence that any new pact should fit into a general Middle East defence system. In May 1955 Abu'l-Huda was replaced by Sa'id al-Mufti, while an exchange of state visits with King Sa'ud hinted at a *rapprochement* with Saudi Arabia. Nevertheless, in November Jordan declared its unwillingness to adhere either to the Egyptian-Syrian-Saudi Arabian bloc or to the Baghdad Pact.

DISMISSAL OF GLUBB PASHA

On December 15th, following a visit to General Sir. G. Templer, Chief of the Imperial General Staff, Sa'id al-Mufti resigned and was replaced by Hazza al-Majali, known to be in favour of the Baghdad Pact. The following day there were violent demonstrations in Amman, and on December 20th Ibrahim Hashim became Prime Minister, to be succeeded on January 9th by Samir Rifai. In February 1956 the new Prime Minister visited Syria, Lebanon, Iraq, Egypt and Saudi Arabia, and shortly after his return, on March 2nd, King Hussein announced the dismissal of Glubb Pasha, commander-in-chief of the Jordanian armed forces, and replaced him by Major-General Radi 'Annab. The Egyptian-Syrian-Saudi Arabian bloc at this juncture offered to replace the British financial subsidy to Jordan; but the latter was not in fact withdrawn, and King Hussein and the Jordanian government evidently felt that they had moved far enough in one direction, and committed themselves to a policy of strict neutrality. In April, however, the King and the Prime Minister paid a visit to the Syrian President in Damascus, and in May Major-General Annab was replaced by his deputy, Lt.-Colonel Ali Abu Nuwar, generally regarded as the leader of the movement to eliminate foreign influence from the Jordanian army and government. This coincided with the reappointment of Sa'id al-Mufti as Prime Minister. During the same period discussions culminated in agreements for military co-operation between Jordan and Syria, Lebanon and Egypt, and in July Jordan and Syria formed an economic union. At the beginning of the same month al-Mufti was replaced by Ibrahim Hashim.

RELATIONS WITH ISRAEL AND WITH THE OTHER ARAB STATES

Meanwhile relations with Israel, including the problem of the Arab refugees, the use of Jordan waters, the definition of the frontier, and the status of Jerusalem, continued to provide a standing cause for anxiety. Early in July there was a further series of frontier incidents, which lasted well into the autumn. October saw the development of military relations with Iraq; however a plan to move Iraqi troops into Jordan was stopped by the stiff reaction of the Israeli government. Tension between Jordan and Israel was further increased after the Israeli, British and French military action in Egypt. A new cabinet, headed by Suleiman Nabulsi, had taken office early in October, and new elections were followed by the opening of negotiations for the abrogation of the Anglo-Jordanian Treaty of 1948, and the substitution of financial aid from the Arab countries. At a conference held in Cairo on January 18th and 19th, 1957, between King Sa'ud, King Hussein, President Nasser and the Syrian and Jordanian Prime Ministers, an agreement was signed providing for an annual payment of £E 12,500,000 (£12,800,000 sterling) to Jordan over the next ten years. Saudi Arabia and Egypt were each to contribute £E 5,000,000 and Syria £E 2,500,000. Owing to subsequent political developments, however, the shares due from Egypt and Syria were not paid. On March 13th, 1957, an Anglo-Jordanian agreement was signed abrogating the 1948 treaty, and by July 2nd the last British troops had left. In the meantime Nabulsi's evident leanings towards the Soviet connection, clashing with the recently-enunciated Eisenhower doctrine, led to his breach with King Hussein and his resignation on April 10th. Two weeks of cabinet crises, demonstrations and riots preceded the formation of a new government under Ibrahim Hashim. All political parties were suppressed, and plans to establish diplomatic relations with Russia were dropped. Gen. Ali Abu Nuwar was removed from the post of Commander-in-Chief, and the United States announced its determination to preserve Jordan's independence—a policy underlined by a major air-lift of arms to Amman in September in response to Syria's alignment with the Soviet Union. In May Syrian troops serving under the joint Syro-Egypto-Jordanian command were withdrawn from Jordanian territory at Jordan's request, and in June there was a partial rupture of diplomatic relations with Egypt.

On January 18th, 1958, an agreement was reached between Israel and Jordan for the implementation of the 1948 agreement on the Mount Scopus demilitarized zone.

On February 14th, the merger of the Kingdoms of Iraq and Jordan in a federal union to be known as the Arab Federation was proclaimed in Amman by King Faisal of Iraq and King Hussein. This new federation, made in response to the formation of the United Arab Republic a fortnight before, was dissolved by decree of King Hussein on August 2nd, following the revolution in Iraq. Samir Rifai became Prime Minister of Jordan in May, on the resignation of Ibrahim Hashim who took up the appointment of Vice-Premier in the short-lived Arab Federation. On July 22nd, Hashim was assassinated by the mob in Baghdad during the rioting that followed the revolution.

British troops were flown to Amman from Cyprus on July 17th, in response to an appeal by King Hussein. They had all been withdrawn by the beginning of November—under UN auspices—and in the two years that followed Jordan settled down to a period of comparative peace. Hazza' al-Majali succeeded Rifai at Prime Minister on May 6th, 1959. Firm measures were taken against communism and subversive activities (defence and internal security accounted for rather more than half of the 1960–61 budget) and collaboration with the West was, if anything, encouraged by the country's isolation between Iraq, Israel and the two halves of the United Arab Republic. American loans continued to arrive at the rate of about $50,000,000 a year, and there was also technical aid of various kinds from Britain, Western Germany and other countries. An important development was the official opening of the port of Aqaba on the Red Sea, virtually Jordan's only outlet.

Relations with Jordan's Arab neighbours continued to be uneasy, though diplomatic relations with the United Arab Republic, broken off in July, 1958, were resumed in August 1959. Incidents on the Syrian border were almost as frequent as on the Israeli, and there were no signs of a rapprochement with Iraq. In January 1960, both the King and the Prime Minister condemned the Arab leaders' approach to the Palestine problem, and in February Jordanian citizenship was offered to all Arab refugees who applied for it. On the other side of the balance sheet, King Hussein paid a flying visit to King Saud in February, 1960, and in March strongly anti-Zionist statements appeared in the Jordanian press. Nevertheless there seemed to be no change in the general position that Jordan wished for formal recognition of her absorption of the Palestinian territory west of the Jordan, while the United Arab Republic and other Arab countries favoured the establishment of an independent Palestine Arab government.

On August 29th, 1960, the Jordanian Prime Minister, Hazza al-Majali, was assassinated by the explosion of a time-bomb in his office. Jordan was quick to attribute the outrage to persons in the United Arab Republic. A curfew was imposed, but after a cabinet reshuffle comparative stability was restored, with Bahjat Talhouni as Prime Minister.

In the last few months of 1960 relations between Jordan and Iraq gradually improved, culminating, in December, in the resumption of diplomatic relations between the two countries.

There were also signs of some relaxing of the tension between Jordan and the United Arab Republic, with an exchange of letters between King Hussein and President Nasser during the first half of 1961. In September, however, Jordan was quick to recognize the independent status of Syria, and in the following month relations with the United Arab Republic were broken off.

United States aid continued to reach Jordan on a substantial scale, and relations with the United States were further strengthened by the visit of King Hussein to New York in October 1960, when he addressed the United Nations Assembly and talked with President Eisenhower, and by a trade agreement in February 1961.

INTERNAL DEVELOPMENTS

The calm and even enthusiasm with which the King's marriage to an English girl in May 1961 was received by the Jordanian population was generally seen as a sign of the strength of the Throne.

The King visited Morocco and Saudi Arabia in the summer of 1962, and subsequently conversations were begun with the latter with a view to improving relations. Meanwhile in January 1962, Wasfi al-Tal had taken over the premiership, and in December after the completion of elections, the formation of political parties was once again permitted.

Mr. Al-Tal's government was short-lived. In March 1963 he was replaced by Samir Rifai, a nominee of the King. But shortly after the news of a plan to federate Egypt, Syria and Iraq, rioting broke out against Mr. Rifai who resigned on April 20th after only twenty-three days in office. A transitional government was appointed by the King with the task of dissolving the Lower House and holding new elections; these were duly held in July, when the caretaker government of Sherif Hussein bin Nasser, the king's great-uncle, was confirmed in office. The relaxing of tension at home was followed by a conciliatory policy abroad. In January 1964 King Hussein himself represented Jordan at the Cairo conference held to discuss joint Arab measures to deal with the Jordan waters dispute, which had flared up again with the rumour of Israeli plans to take unilateral action in the continued absence of any international agreement. The opportunity was taken to resume diplomatic relations between Jordan and the United Arab Republic.

In July 1964 King Hussein demonstrated his personal control over the Government when Hussein bin Nasser resigned, and Bahjat Talhouni was asked to take over once again. Talhouni, who had previously been head of the Royal Cabinet and the official representative of the King since the Arab summit conference in January 1964, stated that his government would work "in accordance with the spirit of the Arab summit conference and based on King Hussein's instruction". Also in July, Jordan recognized the Republican régime in the Yemen, and relations with the United Arab Republic were improved by an exchange of visits between the U.A.R. First Vice-President, Abdul Hakim Amer, and King Hussein. In August Jordan signed the Arab Common Market agreement, and in September the King attended the Arab Summit Conference in Alexandria, at which the problem of the Jordan waters was one of the main topics of discussion. Talhouni resigned in February 1965, and was replaced by Wasfi al-Tal. In April a constitutional uncertainty was resolved, with the nomination of the King's brother Hassan as Crown Prince; the infant son of the formerly British Princess Muna was thus excluded.

In May 1965, Jordan, in common with nine other Arab states, broke off diplomatic relations with West Germany as a protest against the latter's establishment of relations with Israel.

WAR WITH ISRAEL

During the latter part of 1966 Jordan's foreign relations became increasingly worsened by the widening breach with Syria. Charges and counter-charges were made of plots to subvert each other's governments, and while the U.A.R. and the U.S.S.R. supported Syria, Jordan looked for backing to Saudi Arabia and the U.S. This situation made it increasingly difficult for Jordan's relations with Israel to be regularized. In July 1966 Jordan suspended support for the Palestine Liberation Organization, accusing its secretary Shukairy of pro-Communist activity, and this move was copied by Tunisia in October. In November an Israeli reprisal raid aroused bitter feeling in Jordan and elsewhere. While Jordan introduced conscription and Saudi Arabia promised military aid, Syria and the Palestine Liberation Organization called on the Jordanians to revolt against King Hussein. Negotiations to implement the resolution of the Supreme Council for Arab Defence that Iraqi and

Saudi troops should be sent to Jordan to assist in her defence broke down in December. This was followed by clashes on the Jordan/Syria frontier, by PLO-sponsored bomb outrages in Jordan (resulting in the closure of the PLO headquarters in Jerusalem), and by worsening relations between Jordan and the U.A.R. and a ban by the latter on aircraft carrying British and American arms to Jordan. In retaliation Jordan withdrew recognition of the Sallal régime in Yemen, and boycotted the next meeting of the Arab Defence Council. On March 5th Wasfi al-Tal resigned and was succeeded by Hussein bin Nasser at the head of an interim government.

As the prospect of war with Israel drew nearer, King Hussein composed his differences with Egypt, and personally flew to Cairo to sign a defence agreement. Jordanian troops, together with those of the U.A.R., Iraq and Saudi Arabia, went into action immediately on the outbreak of hostilities in June. By the end of the Six Days War, however, all Jordanian territory west of the River Jordan had been occupied by Israeli troops, and a steady stream of west-bank Jordanians began to cross the River Jordan to the east bank. Estimated at between 150,000 and 250,000 persons, they swelled Jordan's refugee population and presented the government with intractable social and economic problems. In August, although Jordan had reached no settlement with Israel, a small percentage of the refugees were enabled to return to the west bank under an agreement mediated by the International Red Cross. By June 1968 about 105,000 of the new refugees remained in temporary camps. Jordan had so far refused to ask UNRWA to extend its mandate to the refugees of the June war.

King Hussein formed a nine-man Consultative Council in August 1967, composed of former premiers and politicians of varying sympathies, to meet weekly and to participate in the "responsibility of power". Later a Senate was formed consisting of fifteen representatives from the inhabitants of the west bank area, and fifteen from eastern Jordan. Several changes of government took place. Saad Jumaa had succeeded as Prime Minister on April 23rd, 1967, after general elections, and on July 15th, after first resigning, was entrusted with the formation of a new cabinet. On October 7th, however, he resigned again, and was succeeded by Bahjat Talhouni; a feature of this reconstruction was that the King took over personal command of the country's armed forces. King Hussein was also active in the diplomatic field, visiting Britain, the United States, France, Italy, Turkey, Pakistan and the U.S.S.R. to gain sympathy and support for his country's cause. U.S. arms shipments to Jordan were resumed on February 14th, 1968.

Meanwhile the uneasy situation along the frontier with Israel persisted, aggravated by the deteriorating economic situation in the country. Reprisal actions by Israel after numerous commando raids directed against her authority in Jerusalem and the west bank and operating from Jordanian territory culminated in a major attack in March with the object of destroying an alleged guerrilla camp at Karameh. Further major attacks were made at Irbid and Essalt in June and August respectively; following the latter attack, Jordan appealed for UN intervention. In June 1969 Israeli commandos blew up the diversion system of the Ghor Canal, Jordan's principal irrigation project.

THE GUERRILLA CHALLENGE

The instability in Amman after the June War was reflected in the short life of Jordanian cabinets—it became rare for one to remain unchanged for more than three months. A careful balance had to be struck between the Palestinians and the King's traditional supporters. Thus, in the new cabinet announced after the June 1970 crisis, Palestinians were given more of the key ministries, including that of the Interior. Abdul Munem Rifai, Jordan's senior diplomat, became Prime Minister for the second time.

The main factor in Jordan's internal politics between June 1967 and 1971 was the rivalry between the official government and the guerrilla organizations, principally Al Fatah. These organizations gradually assumed effective control of the refugee camps and commanded widespread support amongst the Palestinian majority of Jordan's present population. They also received arms and training assistance from other Arab countries, particularly Syria, and finance from the oil-rich Gulf states. Some camps became commando training centres, the younger occupants of these, almost all unemployed, welcoming the sense of purpose and relief from idleness and boredom that recruitment into a guerrilla group offered. The fedayeen movement virtually became a state within a state. Its leadership has stated that "We have no wish to interfere in the internal affairs of Jordan provided it does not place any obstacles in the way of our struggle to liberate Palestine". In practice, however, its popularity and influence represented a challenge to the government, whilst its actions attracted Israeli reprisals that did serious damage to the east bank, now the only fertile part of Jordan, and generally reduced the possibilities of a peace settlement on which Jordan's long-term future depended.

A major confrontation between the two forces occurred in November 1968, after massive demonstrations in Amman on the anniversary of the Balfour Declaration. Extensive street fighting broke out between guerrillas and the army, which, being mainly Bedouin, has little in common with the Palestinians anyway, and for a short period a civil war seemed possible, but both sides soon backed down. Some sources attributed the trouble to the government's attempt (subsequently abandoned) to disarm the refugee camps; others pointed out that small extremist groups had led the fighting which was discouraged by the more responsible Al Fatah leadership. Similar confrontations followed in February and June 1970, and on both occasions the Government was forced to yield to Palestinian pressures. In February the cabinet soon had to abandon an attempt to restrict the carrying of arms by guerrillas. June saw the most serious crisis. A week's fighting in Amman and the surrounding district resulted in an estimated 100 deaths, an assassination attempt on the King and a partial evacuation of the Western community in the capital. King Hussein and Yasser Arafat, the Al Fatah leader (whose own position was threatened by the rise of small extremist groups in Jordan), jointly drew up and signed an agreement redefining their respective spheres of influence. The guerrillas appeared to have granted little or nothing, but Hussein was forced to dismiss his Commander-in-Chief and a cabinet minister, both relatives. These were regarded as the leaders of the anti-fedayeen faction, which remained strong amongst the Bedouin sheikhs. Despite the agreement, the tension between the government and the guerrillas continued, aggravated by opposition to the government's concessions from hard-line army officers.

A new and dangerous stage in the relations between the two sides in Jordan was reached in July with the acceptance by the government of the American peace proposals for the Middle East. The guerrilla groups, with few exceptions, rejected these, and, as the cease-fire between the U.A..R and Israel came into operation on August 7th, it was clear that the Jordanian Government was preparing for a full-scale confrontation with them. The top command of the army was strengthened and measures were taken to bolster the defences of Amman. At the same time there was fighting between some of the guerrillas themselves over attitudes to the Rogers plan.

CIVIL WAR

Bitter fighting between government and guerrilla forces broke out at the end of August. In the first part of September the violence was increased by two factors: the assassination attempt on King Hussein and the hijackings by PLFP of four Western Airliners. The threat of intervention on the side of the commandos by Iraq and Syria; the transference of Libyan aid from the Jordanian government to the guerrillas; a succession of cease-fire agreements between the two sides; the release of all but 54 hostages taken from the aircraft to secure the release of Palestinian commandos held by Western governments; none of these developments were enough to prevent the escalation into full civil war in the last half of the month, and thousands of deaths and injuries. (Estimates of deaths up to the first week in October vary between 500 and 3,500.) The continued detention of any hostages by the PFLP was a direct challenge to the government's authority. On September 16th a military cabinet was formed under Brig. Muhammad Daoud—in any case martial law had been in force since the end of the June 1967 war—and immediately Field Marshal Habis Majali replaced as Commander-in-Chief Lt.-Gen. Mashour Haditha, who had been sympathetic to the commandos and had tried to restrain their severest opponents in the army.

In the fighting that followed the guerrillas claimed full control in the north, aided by Syrian forces and, it was later revealed, three battalions of the Palestine Liberation Army sent back by President Nasser from the Suez front. The Arab states generally appealed for an end to the fighting. Libya threatened to intervene and later broke off diplomatic relations; Kuwait stopped its aid to the government; but the Iraqi troops stationed on the Eastern front against Israel notably failed to intervene. On the government side talks were held with the U.S.A. about direct military assistance—on what scale is not known, but there were rumours of a plan for joint American and Israeli intervention if Hussein looked in danger of being overthrown. In the event such a dangerous widening of the Palestinian confrontation was avoided by the scale of the casualties in Jordan and by the diplomacy of Arab heads of state (reinforced by President Nasser's reported threat to intervene on the guerrillas' behalf) who prevailed upon King Hussein and Yasser Arafat to sign an agreement in Cairo on September 27th ending the war. A follow-up committee of three members was established under the Tunisian premier, Bahi Ladgham, to oversee the implementation of the agreement. The previous day a civilian cabinet had been restored under Ahmed Toukan. Five military members were retained.

A definitive agreement, very favourable to the liberation organizations, was signed by Hussein and Arafat on October 13th in Amman, but this proved to be simply the beginning of a phase of sporadic warfare between the two parties, punctuated by new agreements, during which the commandos were gradually forced out of Amman and driven from their positions in the north back towards the Syrian frontier. At the end of October a new government, still containing three army officers, was formed under Wasfi Tal. By January 1971 army moves against the Palestine guerrillas had become so blatant that Ladgham threatened to resign from the follow-up committee and the U.A.R., Syria and Algeria all issued strong protests at the Jordanian Government's attempt to "liquidate" the liberation movements. All but two brigades of Iraqi troops were, however, withdrawn from Jordan.

By April the Jordanian Government seemed strong enough to set a deadline for the guerrillas' withdrawal of their remaining men and heavy armaments from the capital. Later in the month King Hussein was able to state that "security" had been restored, and to ban trade unions, student unions and other organizations backed by the guerrillas. Isolated outbreaks of fighting between government and commando forces were still being reported from the north, however. More important was the declaration issued on June 5th by seven commando organizations, including even the more moderate Fatah, calling for the overthrow of Hussein. However, it was the Jordanian authorities who in July moved first to resolve the contest for political power in Jordan. On July 13th a major Government attack began on the guerrillas entrenched in the Jerash-Aljoun area. Four days later it was all over. The Government claimed that all the bases had been destroyed and that 2,300 of 2,500 guerrillas in them had been captured. About 100 sought refuge in Israeli-occupied territory. Most of the Palestinians taken prisoner by the Jordanian government were released a few days later, either to leave for other Arab states or to return to normal life in Jordan.

The "solution" (in King Hussein's word) of the guerrilla "problem" provoked strong reaction from other Arab governments. Iraq and Syria closed their borders with Jordan; Algeria suspended diplomatic relations; and Egypt, Libya, Sudan and both Yemens voiced public criticism. Relations with Syria deteriorated fastest of all. In August there were three days of clashes on the border between Syrian and Jordanian tanks and artillery, which appeared to have been the result of a simple mistake escalating out of all proportion, and Syria broke off diplomatic relations. The closure of the border was more serious for Jordan than the actual breach in relations, because the trade route through Syria from Beirut was now denied and all Jordan's imports had to be directed to her only port, Aqaba, on the Red Sea. However, Iraq soon began to ease the restrictions on movements across her border and airspace, and by February 1972 normal trading relations between her and Jordan had resumed.

In the meantime, Saudi Arabia had been attempting to bring together guerrilla leaders and Jordanian Government representatives to work out a new version of the Cairo and Amman agreements. Meetings did take place in Jeddah but were fruitless, and the Palestinians responded in their own way to the events of July. Three unsuccessful attempts were made in September to hijack Jordanian airliners. Then, on September 28th, Wasfi al-Tal, the Prime Minister and Defence Minister, was assassinated by members of a secret Palestinian guerrilla group, the Black September Organization. Tal was shot in the back as he walked into a hotel in Cairo, where he was attending meetings of the Arab League Defence Council. The day after his death Hussein appointed his Minister of Finance, Ahmed Lawzi, to take Tal's place, and the Minister of Transport, Anis Muashshir took on the additional responsibility of Finance.

Many Arabs, especially Palestinians in East Jerusalem and on the West Bank, greeted the news of Tal's death with joy, and the Arab governments which expressed any regrets did so in a reserved manner. The Black September Organization later claimed that it had received the approval of the Egyptian Government for the plan to kill Tal. That many Arabs, including governments, tacitly supported the action became clear at the opening of the trial of the four alleged assassins in Cairo in February 1972. Dozens of eminent lawyers from various Arab states offered to defend the accused; the Presidents of Algeria, Libya and Iraq offered their personal sureties for the release of the men; and they were eventually freed on bail.

In December 1971 the Black September Organization had made two further assassination attempts. In one the

Jordanian Ambassador to the United Kingdom, Zaid al-Rifai, escaped with a wounded hand from a gun attack in London. In the other the Jordanian Ambassador to Switzerland was sent a parcel bomb which exploded when opened by police, seriously injuring three people.

HUSSEIN'S ANSWER

Throughout the period since the liquidation of the guerrillas in July 1971 Hussein had been seeking to strengthen his political position. In August he announced the creation of a tribal council—a body of sheikhs or other notables, appointed by him and chaired by the Crown Prince—which was to deal with the affairs of tribal areas. A month later the formation of the Jordanian National Union was announced. This (renamed Arab National Union in March 1972) was to be Jordan's only legal political organization. It was not to be a party in the usual sense; proponents of "imported ideologies" were debarred from membership; the King became President and the Crown Prince Vice-President; and appointed the 36 members of the Supreme Executive Committee. Around the same time as these developments there were reports of election-rigging by the Government to place its candidates in office in the trade unions. By May 1972 the General Federation of Jordanian Workers, operating from Damascus, claimed that over 150 trade unionists were in prison in Jordan for opposing the government's actions.

However, the King's boldest political move, and an obvious attempt to regain his standing in the eyes of Palestinians, was his unfolding of plans for a United Arab Kingdom in March 1972. This kingdom was to federate a Jordanian region, with Amman as its capital and also federal capital, and a Palestinian region, with Jerusalem as its capital. Each region was to be virtually autonomous, though the King would rule both and there would be a federal council of ministers.

Outside Jordan there was almost universal criticism of this plan from interested parties—Israel, the Palestinian organizations and Egypt, which in the following month broke off diplomatic relations. Jordan's isolation in the Arab world had never been more complete.

Throughout the rest of 1972 and the first half of 1973 Hussein has continued to stand by his original plans for a United Arab Kingdom, but at the same time insisting that peace with Israel can only come within the framework of UN Resolution 242 (see Documents on Palestine, page 56) and hotly denying suggestions from other Arab states that he was considering signing a separate peace treaty with Israel.

The internal security of Jordan was threatened in November 1972 when an attempted military coup in Amman by Major Rafeh Hindawi was thwarted. It was alleged that the attempted coup had the support of Libya and the Palestinian guerrillas. In February 1973 Abu Daoud, one of the leaders of Al Fatah, and 16 other guerrillas were arrested on charges of infiltrating into Jordan for the purpose of subversive activities. It was alleged that they intended to kidnap the Prime Minister and other Cabinet Ministers and hold them hostage, and seize government buildings.

The latter affair took place while King Hussein was on a visit to the U.S.A. requesting defence and financial aid. President Nixon agreed to provide two squadrons of F.5 fighter bombers. In May 1973 Hussein's Prime Minister, Ahmed Lauzi, resigned for health reasons and a new government under Zaid al-Rifai was formed. Rifai is known to be firmly against the Palestinian guerrillas and was the target of a bomb attack when he was Ambassador to London in 1971.

ECONOMIC SURVEY

Jordan's economy has twice been completely disrupted by war between the Arabs and the Israelis, first in 1948, and then in 1967. While Jordan in 1948 acquired some 2,165 square miles of new territory—the vast salient which juts out into Israel west of the River Jordan—the country's population also increased more than threefold. In 1948, before the war broke out, the country's population was perhaps 400,000. The number of those living on the West Bank of the River Jordan in the territory acquired in 1948 was well over 800,000. This territory was occupied by the Israelis in 1967, but perhaps 350,000 of the inhabitants fled to non-occupied Jordan. According to the latest estimates, the population of Jordan in late 1972 was 2,497,000, of which about 40 per cent lived in the Amman district.

The absorption of the refugees of 1948 and of 1967 into Jordan's economy has presented the country with problems for which few precedents could be found in modern times. These problems were accentuated by ethnic, cultural and religious differences. Jordanians before 1948 were mainly Bedouin and mostly engaged in pastoral, and even nomadic, activities. They therefore had little in common with the Palestinians, many of whom established themselves in Jordan as traders and professional men. The vast majority of the country's original inhabitants were Sunni Muslims, but until 1967 at least there were also 180,000 Christians. Also in 1967 some 53 per cent of the population was classified as urban.

Again, the loss of the West Bank of the Jordan to Israel in the summer of 1967 created a whole series of new problems. For the result was the loss not only of some efficiently farmed agricultural land, but also of the important and growing tourist industry, and the large sums in foreign exchange received from the people who annually visited the old city of Jerusalem and Bethlehem. Some of the immediate problems brought by the war of 1967 were met by aid from Arab countries, but Jordan's economic future in the long run will obviously depend on the nature of any settlement which may be reached with Israel.

The area of the country, including the 2,165 square miles of the West Bank territory, was about 25,000 square miles. A large part of it however consisted of desert which spreads eastwards from a narrow, fertile strip of country running south from the Syrian frontier to Ma'an, and probably no more than about 5 per cent of the country's total area was cultivable. East of the Jordan river the country is mostly plateau, averaging about 2,000 ft. above sea level. The climate is of the Mediterranean variety, but, owing perhaps to the height above sea level, the extremes of heat and cold are greater than on the Levantine littoral. West of the Hedjaz railway there is an abundant and fairly regular rainy season, beginning in October or November and ending in April, and following the same pattern as in Israel. East of the railway line the annual rainfall tends to decrease very rapidly. From May to September there is generally no rainfall at all.

AGRICULTURE

Agriculture is the most important sector of the economy accounting for 20 per cent of the gross domestic product and employing over three-quarters of the settled population. Great improvements were achieved in the years prior to the 1967 war but the war and the consequent instability in the East Bank resulted in almost complete disruption. With the defeat of the Palestinian guerrillas in the September 1970 civil war, the economic situation in the East Bank has returned to normal although sanctions against Jordan by other Arab states resenting the Government's attitude to the guerrillas have slowed down the anticipated recovery, including that of agricultural production.

From the little data available it is clear that the size of the average agricultural holding is very small. One can also distinguish between agricultural conditions on the two sides of the River Jordan. On the West Bank the land is poor but well farmed. At least until June 1967, most of the cultivable land was cultivated, and about a third of the area was sown to fruit and vegetables. On the East Bank, methods of farming have been less developed, and much of the land has suffered severely from erosion. The shortage of capital has been an obstacle to extensive irrigation and even to terracing, and, though there is evidence that in ancient times the land supported a much larger population than it does today, further development depends on the realization of international schemes of irrigation such as those referred to below. Generally speaking, stock-raising by the Bedouin is the principal occupation, and the overwhelming majority of settled farmers follow the hard life of subsistence agriculture.

Crop-raising has been improved, however. There were 2,758 tractors in use on the East Bank alone at the end of 1970, compared with 2,000 in the whole of Jordan four years earlier. Similarly in 1966 the farmers bought about 10,000 tons of inorganic fertilizers compared with 3,000 tons in 1962, but the total for the East Bank fell to 3,500 tons in 1970. Before 1967, cereals were one of the mainstays of agriculture and in a good year the wheat harvest could produce well over 200,000 tons and that of barley about 70,000 tons. The year 1967 saw a bumper crop of 240,000 tons of wheat and 78,000 tons of barley. But although the farmers on the East Bank produced 159,300 tons of wheat and 42,500 tons of barley under conditions of strain in 1969, the civil war of 1970 reduced the output to 54,100 tons of wheat and 5,300 tons of barley. The return of stability resulted in a more than threefold increase in production in 1971 when 168,200 tons of wheat and 26,200 tons of barley were produced. A cereal crop of this size is not, however, enough to feed the country. The bulk of the grain needed by Jordan always has to be imported, the value of flour and grain imported amounting, in some years, to more than the value of the whole of Jordan's exports.

Much success was achieved between 1948 and 1967 in the cultivation of fruit and vegetables, particularly on the West Bank. Tomatoes became especially important as an article of export. Other important crops were citrus fruits, chickpeas, lentils, and grapes in addition to the traditional olive groves and the olive oil of the West Bank which had always been an important export item. The loss of the West Bank had an even more disastrous effect on these crops since it meant the loss of 80 per cent of the fruit-growing area, 45 per cent of the vegetable-growing area and 25 per cent of the area under cereals. With the political improvements after the 1970 civil war tomato production on the East Bank reached 147,600 tons in 1971 compared with 259,700 tons in 1967, that of other vegetables 89,800 tons compared with 282,200 in 1967, olives 18,500 tons compared with 64,000, grapes 18,600 tons compared with 71,600, citrus fruits 20,000 tons (1972) compared with 61,400, melon and water melon 28,000 tons compared with 118,400 and other fruits 14,500 tons compared with 64,800.

The basis of Bedouin stockfarming is the sheep and goat. Cattle are much less important.

There are still several important forests, particularly in the north around Ajlun and near Ma'an, but timber production is negligible.

INDUSTRY AND MINING

Industry, which is almost entirely of recent origin and accounts for about 10 per cent of the Gross National Product, is concentrated around Amman and in Nablus on the West Bank. About 65 per cent of all factories produce food products or clothing but the major industrial income derives from the three heavier industries—phosphate extraction, cement manufacture and petroleum refining. Most plant is small and industry is mostly concerned with assembly and processing rather than manufacturing.

The country's mineral wealth appears to be small, although there are possibilities of finding useful deposits of copper, iron ore, nickel and manganese. Concessions have been granted to various groups for oil prospecting, but so far none has been found in commercial quantities. A new company is being formed to exploit clay and felspar deposits and another will shortly start producing ceramics from locally extracted materials.

Rich beds of phosphates exist at Rusaifa, a few miles north-east of Amman, and have been exploited since 1963 by a local company financed partly by the government. There is also a deposit of phosphates, estimated to amount to about 30 million tons, in the Wadi Hasa area, south of Amman, and this has been developed by American and Italian interests. By 1968 the country's total production of natural phosphates was 1,162,000 tons, more than five times the production in 1956. Production fell however to 651,100 tons in 1971, mainly as a result of the closure of the

Syrian borders to Jordanian traffic, but rose again to 715,000 tons in 1972 with the return of normality. Phosphates have become Jordan's largest export commodity. Phosphate exports in 1968 were valued JD 4.2 million, or 24.4 per cent of total exports. This fell to JD 2.2 million in 1970 but rose again in the following two years to reach JD 3.5 million in 1972, representing 27.8 per cent of total exports. The Wadi Hasa valley, which leads into the southern end of the Dead Sea, appears to be comparatively rich in other minerals, e.g. gypsum and manganese ore.

Production of cement increased from a monthly average of 31,000 tons in 1966 to 40,000 tons in 1969, fell during the troubles of 1970, but rose again in the following two years to reach a record 661,600 tons in 1972. There are small concerns canning fruit and vegetables, making soap and matches, and refining olive oil. A government-run mineral oil refinery produced 605,100 tons of petroleum products in 1972. The Gulf of Aqaba abounds in fish and, if capital were available, a flourishing fishing industry might be developed.

TRANSPORT

The development of the Jordanian economy is hampered by the difficulty of communication. The only railway, the Hedjaz line, is single-track, and runs from Damascus to Naqb Ishtar, via Amman. From Ma'an it used to run on to Medina and Mecca in Saudi Arabia, but the Saudi section has been derelict since the First World War and rebuilding financed by the Jordanian, Saudi Arabian and Syrian Governments has recently been suspended because of political differences between the three governments. Work started in 1972 on building a 120-kilometre railway linking the Hedjaz line with Aqaba, mainly to carry phosphates for shipment from the port. Two loans totalling over £16 million for the construction of this line were provided by Federal Germany in 1972. At the moment Aqaba, Jordan's only port, is over 200 miles by road from the capital, and, though there is a good road from Amman to Beirut through Syria, the transport costs of this route are heavy. Aqaba, which in 1966 handled an average of about 100,000 tons of cargo a month, was by 1970 handling only 32,000 tons, but this figure rose again to over 100,000 tons in 1972. Phosphate exports in 1972 accounted for more than half the tonnage handled.

EXTERNAL TRADE

The war of 1967 disrupted the country's foreign trade less, perhaps, than might have been expected. By 1970 imports had recovered to 65.8 million, roughly the level of 1966, and in 1972 reached a record JD 95.3 million. The value of domestic exports, which had been rising steadily in the years up to 1968, declined in the following three years but recovered in 1972 to reach JD 17.0 million compared with JD 11.3 million in 1968.

In 1972 food and live animals, mainly citrus fruits and tomatoes, accounted for 37.9 per cent of the value of Jordan's exports, with raw materials, mainly phosphates, accounting for another 29.5 per cent and manufactured goods, mainly cement, accounting for a further 19 per cent. Three commodities, phosphates, tomatoes and cement, accounted for 62.7 per cent of all Jordanian exports in 1972. Phosphates and tomatoes used to dominate exports alone but cement has now joined them and, although this is a healthy development of diversification, the Jordanian export trade is still too dependent on a very few commodities. By far the greatest proportion of Jordan's exports used to be sold to Iraq, Lebanon and Syria which together absorbed as much as 89 per cent of exports in 1953. But by 1972 the proportion of her exports taken by all the other Arab countries had fallen to 72 per cent, with India taking another 11 per cent and Japan 5 per cent.

The import trade is naturally more varied. In most years manufactured goods (19.9 per cent of the total in 1972) and machinery and transport equipment (16.4 per cent) together form a large part of total imports. The value of imports in these two categories alone represents three times the value of all exports. Owing mainly to the loss of the West Bank and other war effects, the largest single import category in 1972, as in the previous few years, was food and live animals. The value of such imports reached JD 27.3 million in 1972 or 28.6 per cent of total imports.

Imports in 1972 at JD 95.3 million were 24.4 per cent up on 1971 and the biggest ever. The main beneficiary of the increase in recent years has been the United States, which is now Jordan's biggest supplier, accounting for 17.7 per cent of total imports in 1972. Britain accounted for 9 per cent of all imports in 1972 and the European Economic Community (pre-U.K. entry) accounted for 18.2 per cent. The changing pattern here is a direct reflection of changing aid patterns, with the United States and the Federal Republic of Germany replacing Britain as the main Western providers of aid and, consequently, of imports. The proportion of imports from the Arab countries has been declining in recent years and reached 17.1 per cent in 1972 compared with 22.9 per cent in the previous year. Imports from Eastern Europe, China and Japan have been increasing in recent years. The main sources of supplies in 1972 in order of importance were the United States, the Federal Republic of Germany, Britain, Lebanon, Japan and Syria.

FINANCE

The only important invisible export on current account before 1967 had been the net earnings from the tourist trade and the net income from private donations, including those from religious, charitable and similar organizations. Many people visited Bethlehem (now occupied by Israel) and the Old City of Jerusalem (now annexed by Israel), and sent money from abroad to help maintain the various foundations. By 1972 net income from tourism had fallen to JD 3.39 million and, although this was an improvement on the previous year, there was actually a deficit on the travel account of JD 5 million compared with a surplus of JD 6 million in 1966 when income from tourism reached JD 11.3 million.

There was a similar fall in the net income from private transfers into Jordan after 1967 and from oil transit dues, but these were almost back to pre-1967 levels in 1972. These invisible payments do much to offset the heavy adverse balance of visible trade. In 1972 the trade deficit had almost reached JD 95 million and the deficit on current account stood at only JD 3.5 million.

For many years this deficit has been made good mainly by capital imports and subventions. Before 1967 these used to come principally from Britain and the United States but since 1967 there have been similar payments from Saudi Arabia and other Arab states (see below). These subventions have enabled the country's exchange reserves to be maintained and even increased. At the end of 1972 net foreign assets stood at JD 97.6 million compared with JD 64.2 million at the end of 1966, and Central Bank reserves stood at $271.3 million compared with $167.7 million at the end of 1966.

As the country's economy was, until 1956, mainly financed by the United Kingdom, it was natural that Jordan should remain a member of the sterling area. The Jordanian dinar of 1,000 fils was held at parity with sterling until the devaluation of the pound in November 1967. On this occasion, the dinar did not follow sterling, with the result that the parity for sterling changed to 857 fils to the £1, i.e. JD 1 = £1.17p. But, with increased dependence on U.S. aid, the Government decided to maintain the parity of its currency with the U.S. dollar at JD 1 = $2.80 when the latter was devalued early in 1972. The U.S. dollar's later devaluation resulted in an increase of the value of the dinar against the dollar to $3.11 in February 1973. Currency in circulation at the end of February 1973 was JD 83.1 million. The Arab Bank, which possesses branches in most of the countries that are members of the Arab League, has its head office in Amman, but the other commercial banks are British, namely National and Grindlays and the British Bank of the Middle East. There is, however, a Development Bank of Jordan for long-term development and an Agricultural Bank in both of which the Government has interests.

Before 1967 most of Jordan's financial support had come from the United Kingdom and the United States. After the June 1967 war Kuwait, Saudi Arabia and Libya undertook to pay Jordan quarterly sums of U.S. $112 million. These budgetary grants were suspended in the autumn of 1970 in protest against the Government's treatment of the Palestinian guerrillas, and revenue from foreign grants fell from JD 37.6 million in 1969 to JD 33 million in 1970, the only two years when subventions to the Government were exclusively from Arab sources. The United States, whose direct budgetary support ceased altogether in 1968, one year after Britain's, stepped in again in 1971 to make up the deficit. Of the JD 66 million received by the Government from foreign sources in 1972, and recorded in the preliminary balance of payments figures, JD 23.2 million came from Arab Governments, JD 23.4 million came from the United States Government, JD 6.8 million from the United Nations Relief and Works Agency for Palestine Refugees (UNRWA) and JD 12.5 million from unspecified other foreign governments. Of this total JD 40.8 million was received in grants (budgetary support); the Three-Year Plan (see below) estimates this figure at an average JD 45 million a year during 1973–75. Saudi Arabia is the main Arab provider, others including Abu Dhabi, Oman and Qatar, while Kuwait is providing development loans.

Largely as a result of the 1967 war, there has been a noteworthy increase in state expenditure from something of the order of JD 70 million a year immediately before the war to just under JD 100 million in 1972. Of the 1972 total 45.3 per cent was spent on defence and security. This proportion is similar to that of previous years but, as a result of the increase in expenditure, it represented, at JD 45.1 million, double such expenditure in 1966 (JD 22.2 million). Receipts for 1972 stood at JD 91.1 million, according to provisional figures issued by the Central Bank. Of these JD 38.5 million consisted of domestic revenue, with almost two-thirds coming from indirect taxation. Since 1969 the Government has resorted to domestic borrowing to help meet cash shortages, mainly in the form of sales of Treasury Bills and Government Bonds. This accounted for JD 12.1 million of income in 1971 and JD 5 million in 1972.

Economic development in Jordan has been severely handicapped by the 1948 and 1967 wars with Israel, and by the civil war of 1970. The hundreds of thousands of refugees from the Israelis are the ultimate responsibility of UNRWA, which pays out about JD 3.3 million a year for rations for them, and also employs probably the largest number of people in Jordan—some 2,500. But Jordan has still had to devote most of her own scanty resources to the solution of pressing short-term problems. The 1966–73 Seven-Year Plan was suspended after the 1967 war and a new Three-Year Plan covering the period 1973–75 was outlined to a conference of aid givers and supporters in Amman in November 1972. The JD 179 million development plan was ambitious but well thought out and offered incentives to both local and foreign investors. The public sector was due to provide 55.6 per cent of total investment of which more than half are to come from foreign grants and loans. This was thought to be a reasonable aim given the support expressed by the West, especially the United States and West Germany. But reservations have been expressed about the ability of the Jordanian private sector to provide JD 79.4 million towards investment under the plan, although this figure included JD 8 million in foreign loans and assistance. The Government, however, says that gross private fixed capital formation should reach JD 22.9 million in 1973, JD 25.6 million in 1974 and JD 30.9 million in 1975 and that this was not too ambitious since it had actually reached JD 22.7 million in 1969, fell to JD 17.8 million in 1970 and was estimated at JD 23 million in 1971.

The plan aims at an investment of JD 114 million in the economic sector (the economically productive sector as distinct from the unproductive social sector). Of this JD 71.8 million was to be invested by the public sector. Transport was to receive JD 35.8 million from both sectors, industry and mining JD 26.1 million, irrigation JD 14.6 million, agriculture JD 13 million, electric power JD 9.8 million, tourism JD 7.2 million and communications JD 6.7 million. Of social sector allocations of JD 65 million, JD 34.9 million were to go towards housing and government buildings, JD 14.8 million towards municipal and rural affairs, JD 10.9 million towards education and JD 1.5 million towards health. The plan aims at creating 70,000 new jobs, increasing the gross domestic product by 8 per cent a year to JD 273.5 million in 1975, developing the socio-economic superstructure, raising the ratio of domestic revenues to total state revenues from 42 per cent in 1972 to 57 per cent in 1975, strengthening the balance of payments and reducing the deficit in the trade balance.

The external public debt rose to JD 60.55 million at the end of 1972 and another JD 21.1 million had been committed by foreign governments and institutions but undisbursed. Of the total debt, 28.8 per cent was owed to Britain, 16.2 per cent to West Germany, 15 per cent to the United States, 14.1 per cent to Kuwait, 8.9 per cent to Saudi Arabia and 6.9 per cent to the International Development Association (IDA) of the World Bank. Of the undisbursed loans, JD 11.5 million was to come from West Germany, JD 4.7 million from Kuwait, JD 3.4 million from the IDA and JD 1.5 million from the U.S. By the middle of 1973, these commitments had been augmented by a DM 4 million loan from West Germany, two IDA loans totalling $18.9 million, aid from the United Nations Development Programme (UNDP) for the Three-Year Plan set at $15 million, a $10 million loan from the United States Agency for International Development (AID) and a British pledge of £10 million in aid for the Three-Year Plan. Saudi Arabia also granted Jordan an additional subsidy of JD 8 million early in 1973 and the U.S. Government proposed to grant $65 million in budget support and another $39 million in military aid during the same year. The figure for U.S. military aid was revealed for the first time at Congressional hearings in Washington and it is not known how this military aid is accounted for under the Jordanian budget.

Gross domestic product at factor cost in 1971 was JD 202.6 million, according to preliminary estimates. Indirect taxes brought the G.D.P. at market prices to JD 223.4 million. Net factor income from abroad at JD 13.2 million meant that the gross national product for the year stood at JD 236.6 million at market prices.

STATISTICAL SURVEY

AREA AND POPULATION

Total Area	Arable Land	Pastures	Forest	Population (1972 est.)
94,500 sq. km.	10,695 sq. km.	75,000 sq. km.	1,250 sq. km.	2,497,000

Amman (capital) (1972 est.): 560,000.
1972: Births 80,327, Deaths 6,261, Marriages 11,039.

Refugees: For details of Refugees see section on UNRWA, page 89

AGRICULTURE
PRINCIPAL CROPS

	Area ('000 dunums)			Production ('000 metric tons)		
	1970	1971	1972	1970	1971	1972
Barley	408.5	524.5	605.6	5.3	26.2	34.0
Maize	3.4	2.8	2.5	0.1	0.8	0.3
Sesame	6.4	11.1	12.5	0.2	0.2	0.3
Wheat	2,228.4	2,438.6	2,236.7	54.1	168.2	211.4
Broad Beans	7.3	2.3	2.7	n.a.	0.1	0.1
Chick Peas	12.8	7.1	30.9	0.3	0.6	2.0
Kersenneh	82.8	69.1	71.0	2.5	5.3	6.8
Lentils	205.8	205.3	284.1	5.0	20.8	22.4

JORDAN—(STATISTICAL SURVEY)

FRUIT AND VEGETABLES
('000 metric tons)

	1970	1971	1972		1970	1971	1972
Almonds	0.5	1.2	1.0	Tomatoes	137.4	147.6	152.7
Apples and Pears	0.5	0.6	2.9	Eggplants	23.1	50.2	32.5
Apricots	—	0.3	0.4	Onions and Garlic	3.3	1.5	0.7
Citrus Fruits	3.8	9.3	20.9	Cauliflowers and Cabbages	10.9	5.4	13.2
Figs	3.0	2.9	2.2	Watermelons and Melons	22.5	28.0	63.0
Bananas	8.2	4.2	6.7	Potatoes	2.1	0.4	0.9
Plums and Peaches	0.5	0.3	0.1	Broadbeans (green)	5.1	4.2	5.1
				Cucumbers	6.8	10.2	17.7

LIVESTOCK
('000)

	1970	1971	1972
Camels	9.5	17.3	16.1
Cattle	32.1	38.8	45.9
Sheep and Goats	1,013.7	1,051.9	1,128.2

FORESTRY

	1969	1970
Area newly planted ('000 dunums)	1,936	1,949
Timber production (cu. metres)	1,666	1,392

FISHING

	1970	1971	1972
Quantity of fish landed at Aqaba and on Jordan and Yarmuk rivers (tons)	122.5	152.4	134.8

INDUSTRY
('000 tons)

	1969	1970	1971	1972
Phosphates	1,089.0	912.7	651.1	714.9
Cement	480.6	377.5	418.9	661.6
Alcohol ('000 litres)	260.8	228.3	192.6	208.2
Beer ('000 litres)	n.a.	n.a.	1,734.7	1,753.4
Tobacco (Kg.)	9,634	8,294	8,224.0	7,517.0
Cigarettes (Kg.)	1,818,062	1,609,827	1,533,291.0	1,511,336.0
Electricity (million kWh.)	199.8	187.4	210.1	n.a.

JORDAN—(STATISTICAL SURVEY)

FINANCE

1,000 fils = 1 Jordanian dinar (J.D.).
Coins: 1, 5, 10, 20, 25, 50, 100 and 250 fils.
Notes: 500 fils; 1, 5 and 10 dinars.
Exchange rates (March 1973): £1 sterling = 803 fils (selling rate); U.S. $1 = 321.43 fils (central rate).
100 Jordanian dinars = £124.53 = $311.11.

BUDGET 1970
(J.D. '000)

REVENUE		EXPENDITURE	
Internal Revenue	30,260	Defence and Police	37,860
Foreign Grants	37,481	Administration	14,189
Foreign Borrowing	4,459	Social Services	10,158
Internal Borrowing	4,200	Economic Services	14,578
Loans Repaid	—	Transport and Communications	4,975
TOTAL	76,400	TOTAL	81,760

1971 Budget: Revenue J.D. 78.8 million; Expenditure J.D. 85 million.
1972 Budget: Balanced at J.D. 124.8 million.
1973 Budget: Balanced at J.D. 148.6 million.

NATIONAL ACCOUNTS
(million J.D.)

	1970	1971	1972
GROSS DOMESTIC PRODUCT (at factor cost)	189.56	202.58	217.00

DEVELOPMENT EXPENDITURE ESTIMATES
1973–75
(million J.D.)

Agriculture	13.020
Irrigation	14.636
Mining and Industry	26.120
Tourism and Antiquities	7.170
Electricity	9.781
Transportation	35.812
Communications	6.712
Trade	0.775
Education	10.914
Public Health	1.480
Social Welfare and Labour	1.455
Housing and Government Buildings	34.890
Municipal and Village Affairs	14.758
Miscellaneous	1.477
TOTAL	179.000

Source: National Planning Council.

JORDAN—(Statistical Survey)

EXTERNAL TRADE
('000 J.D.)

	1968	1969	1970	1971	1972
Imports	55,048	67,700	65,882	76,627	95,310
Exports	11,327	14,700	12,170	11,440	17,005

COMMODITIES
('000 J.D.)

Imports	1970	1971	1972
Animals and Products	4,538.4	4,139.1	5,574.8
Grains and Legumes	6,162.0	4,029.5	4,580.6
Vegetables	1,092.2	914.8	719.5
Fruits	1,912.6	2,778.4	2,552.4
Spices	1,692.0	2,094.2	1,858.4
Other Agriculture	55.6	1,798.3	2,248.5
Forestry Products	1,344.1	491.2	837.7
Mining and Quarrying	454.8	4,271.8	4,973.9
Food Manufactures	3,626.5	7,289.3	12,675.2
Textiles	4,864.5	6,186.4	8,081.1
Clothing	2,309.4	1,659.5	1,762.4
Wood and Cork	51.0	553.4	564.9
Paper and Products	1,227.5	1,070.5	1,902.3
Printing and Publishing	175.2	415.4	406.1
Rubber and Products	863.4	766.6	1,137.0
Chemical Products	2,171.7	3,982.4	6,089.5
Petroleum (refined)	1,132.6	719.5	1,193.0
Non-Metallic Minerals	595.1	1,292.5	1,401.2
Metallic Minerals	5,807.9	3,741.4	7,300.6
Non-Electric Machines	4,264.0	2,891.6	4,988.5
Electric Machines	2,186.5	2,181.2	3,989.4
Transport Equipment	4,502.9	11,418.6	6,473.7

Exports	1970	1971	1972
Phosphates	2,236.7	2,238.8	3,497.1
Tomatoes	1,569.7	1,183.3	724.3
Lentils	537.0	335.2	918.8
Water Melons	75.4	28.2	38.5
Other vegetables and fruit	1,833.5	1,435.0	2,145.0
Cigarettes	519.1	367.9	397.7
Bananas	147.8	78.5	105.9
Raw Hides and Skins	166.2	66.2	130.1
Electric Accumulators	303.7	332.6	432.7
Olive Oil and Prepared Olives	210.9	392.9	376.2

COUNTRIES

Imports	1970	1971	1972
United Kingdom	8,815.9	6,783.0	8,645.2
U.S.A.	7,380.5	18,133.0	16,887.3
Germany, Fed. Repub.	5,911.5	4,524.6	8,693.3
Lebanon	4,409.1	5,319.3	5,045.5
Japan	3,868.7	4,190.9	4,598.0
Syria	3,191.9	2,313.9	4,143.7
Saudi Arabia	2,543.1	4,172.5	3,379.0
Italy	2,235.4	1,824.0	2,677.6
China, People's Repub.	1,496.7	1,555.6	1,997.2
France	1,648.0	2,333.3	2,284.3
U.S.S.R.	2,342.1	996.6	1,117.4
Netherlands	1,271.7	1,635.5	2,441.9
Egypt	2,052.1	3,651.6	2,446.1
India	1,634.7	1,071.4	1,396.5
Romania	1,386.8	745.2	1,886.5

Exports	1970	1971	1972
Kuwait	1,318.4	1,334.9	1,685.2
Iraq	1,312.3	747.0	1,504.9
Lebanon	1,433.8	964.4	1,529.8
Saudi Arabia	1,578.9	1,535.9	2,140.5
India	252.8	956.5	1,404.9
Syria	1,477.5	1,496.1	1,611.9
Yugoslavia	787.6	463.3	201.2
Turkey	359.6	166.2	247.5
China	201.4	—	—
Czechoslovakia	193.4	122.6	210.6

JORDAN—(Statistical Survey)

TRANSPORT

RAILWAYS

	1970	1971	1972
Passengers carried	16,757	16,450	n.a.
Freight carried (tons)	77,547	55,111	56,305

ROADS

	1970	1971	1972
Cars (private)	10,059	10,356	11,173
Taxis	3,509	4,391	4,785
Buses	501	504	470
Lorries and Vans	5,110	5,387	5,243
TOTAL (with others)	22,743	24,220	24,320

SHIPPING
(Aqaba port)

	1970	1971	1972
Number of vessels calling	220	254	327
Freight loaded ('000 tons)	186.3	387.2	704.9
Freight unloaded ('000 tons)	195.6	278.1	518.6

CIVIL AVIATION
('000)

	1969	1970	1971
Passengers	121,300	119,400	125,900
Freight (tons)	1,164.1	1,132.2	1,622.6

TOURISM

	1970	1971	1972
Visitors to Jordan	321,657	256,775	292,041

COMMUNICATIONS MEDIA

Number of telephones (1971)	19,150
Number of radio sets (1969)	150,000
Number of cinemas (1972)	32

EDUCATION

Year	Number of Schools and Universities (East Bank)	Number of Teachers (East Bank)	Number of Pupils (East and West Bank)
1970–71	1,531	11,947	611,735
1971–72	1,712	13,136	630,235

Source: Department of Statistics, Amman.

THE CONSTITUTION

(Revised Constitution approved by King Talal I on January 1st, 1952)

The Hashemite Kingdom of Jordan is an independent, indivisible sovereign state. Its official religion is Islam; its official language Arabic.

Rights of the Individual. There is to be no discrimination between Jordanians on account of race, religion or language. Work, education and equal opportunities shall be afforded to all as far as is possible. The freedom of the individual is guaranteed, as are his dwelling and property. No Jordanian shall be exiled. Labour shall be made compulsory only in a national emergency, or as a result of a conviction; conditions, hours worked and allowances are under the protection of the State.

The Press, and all opinions, are free, except under martial law. Societies can be formed, within the law. Schools may be established freely, but they must follow a recognized curriculum and educational policy. Elementary education is free and compulsory. All religions are tolerated. Every Jordanian is eligible to public office, and choices are to be made by merit only. Power belongs to the people.

The Legislative Power is vested in the National Assembly and the King. The National Assembly consists of two houses; the Senate and the House of Representatives.

The Senate. The number of Senators is one-half of the number of members of the House of Representatives. Senators must be unrelated to the King, over 40, and are chosen from present and past Prime Ministers and Ministers, past Ambassadors or Ministers Plenipotentiary, past Presidents of the House of Representatives, past Presidents and members of the Court of Cassation and of the Civil and Sharia Courts of Appeal, retired officers of the rank of General and above, former members of the House of Representatives who have been elected twice to that House, etc. . . . They may not hold public office. Senators are appointed for four years. They may be reappointed. The President of the Senate is appointed for two years.

The House of Representatives. The members of the House of Representatives are elected by secret ballot in a general direct election and retain their mandate for four years. General elections take place during the four months preceding the end of the term. The President of the House is elected by secret ballot each year by the Representatives. Representatives must be Jordanians of over 30, they must have a clean record, no active business interests, and are debarred from public office. Close relatives of the King are not eligible. If the House of Representatives is dissolved, the new House shall assemble in extraordinary session not more than four months after the date of dissolution. The new House cannot be dissolved for the same reason as the last.

General Provisions for the National Assembly. The King summons the National Assembly to its ordinary session on November 1st each year. This date can be postponed by the King for two months, or he can dissolve the Assembly before the end of its three months' session. Alternatively, he can extend the session up to a total period of six months. Each session is opened by a speech from the throne.

Decisions in the House of Representatives and the Senate are made by a majority vote. The quorum is two-thirds of the total number of members in each House. When the voting concerns the Constitution, or confidence in the Council of Ministers, "the votes shall be taken by calling the members by name in a loud voice". Sessions are public, though secret sessions can be held at the request of the Government or of five members. Complete freedom of speech, within the rules of either Houses, is allowed.

The Prime Minister places proposals before the House of Representatives; if accepted there, they are referred to the Senate and finally sent to the King for confirmation. If one house rejects a law while the other accepts it, a joint session of the House of Representatives and the Senate is called, and a decision made by a two-thirds majority. If the King withholds his approval from a law, he returns it to the Assembly within six months with the reasons for his dissent; a joint session of the Houses then makes a decision, and if the law is accepted by this decision it is promulgated. The Budget is submitted to the National Assembly one month before the beginning of the financial year.

The King. The throne of the Hashemite Kingdom devolves by male descent in the dynasty of King Abdullah Ibn al Hussein. The King attains his majority on his eighteenth lunar year; if the throne is inherited by a minor, the powers of the King are exercised by a Regent or a Council of Regency. If the King, through illness or absence, cannot perform his duties, his powers are given to a Deputy, or to a Council of the Throne. This Deputy, or Council, may be appointed by *Iradas* (decrees) by the King, or, if he is incapable, by the Council of Ministers.

On his accession, the King takes the oath to respect and observe the provisions of the Constitution and to be loyal to the nation. As head of the State he is immune from all liability or responsibility. He approves laws and promulgates them. He declares war, concludes peace and signs treaties; treaties, however, must be approved by the National Assembly. The King is Commander-in-Chief of the Navy, the Army and the Air Force. He orders the holding of elections; convenes, inaugurates, adjourns and prorogues the House of Representatives. The Prime Minister is appointed by him, as are the President and members of the Senate. Military and civil ranks are also granted, or withdrawn, by the King. No death sentence is carried out until he has confirmed it.

The King exercises his jurisdiction by *Iradas*. These are signed by the Prime Minister and the Minister concerned, and the King places his signature above the others.

Ministers. The Council of Ministers consists of the Prime Minister, President of the Council, and of his Ministers. Ministers are forbidden to become members of any company, to receive a salary from any company, or to participate in any financial act of trade. The Council of Ministers is entrusted with the conduct of all affairs of State, internal and external. Oral or written orders of the King do not release Ministers from their responsibility.

The Council of Ministers is responsible to the House of Representatives for matters of general policy. Ministers may speak in either House, and, if they are members of one House, they may also vote in that House. Votes of confidence in the Council are cast in the House of Representatives, and decided by a two-thirds majority. If a vote of "no confidence" is returned, the Ministers are bound to resign. Every newly-formed Council of Ministers must present its programme to the House of Representatives and ask for a vote of confidence. The House of Representatives can impeach Ministers, as it impeaches its own members.

Titles. By an order of the Regency Council (August 1952) all titles, e.g. those of Pasha and Bey, have been abolished. All subjects are now addressed as Assayed.

In March 1972 King Hussein announced plans for a new federal constitution.

THE GOVERNMENT

HEAD OF STATE
KING HUSSEIN IBN TALAL; proclaimed King by a decree of the Jordan Parliament on August 11th, 1952; crowned on May 2nd, 1953.

CABINET
(August 1973)

Prime Minister, Minister of Foreign Affairs and Defence: ZAID AL-RIFAI.
Minister of Reconstruction and Development: Dr. SUBHI AMIN A'AMR.
Minister of Culture and Information: ADNAN ABU-ODEH.
Minister of Agriculture: OMAR NABULSI.
Minister of Islamic Affairs: ISHAQ FARHAN.
Minister of Justice: SALIM AL-MASA'ADEH.
Minister of Tourism and Antiquities: GHALEB BARAKAT.
Minister of Public Works: AHMAD SHAWBAKI.
Minister of Transport: NADEEM AL-ZARU.
Minister of Education: MODAR BADRAN.
Minister of Finance: MOHAMMAD NOURI SHAFIQ.
Minister of Health: FOUAD KEILANI.
Minister of Interior: AHMAD ABDUL-KAREEM TARAWNEH.
Minister of Communication: MUHIEDDIN HUSSEINI.
Minister of National Economy: KAMEL ABU JABER.
Minister of Social Affairs and Labour: YUSUF THUHNI.
Minister of Interior for Municipalities: MARWAN AL-HUMOUD.
Minister of State for Foreign Affairs: ZUHAYR MUFTI.
Minister of State for the Occupied Land: TAHER NASHAT MASRI.

ADMINISTRATIVE PROVINCES (LIWAS)

Province	Location
Ajlun	Northern Jordan, between the River Yarmuk and Wadi Zerqa.
Balqa	Between Wadi Zerqa and Wadi Mujib.
Kerak	Between Wadi Mujib and the edge of the desert.
Ma'an	Southern Jordan, including Aqaba on the Red Sea.
Nablus*	Includes the towns of Tulkarm and Jenin.
Jerusalem Governorate*	Includes Jerusalem, Ramallah, Jericho and Bethlehem.
Hebron*	Central Jordan.
Amman Governorate	Includes Amman and Zarka.

* Indicates a province which has been occupied by Israel since the war of June 1967.

DIPLOMATIC REPRESENTATION
EMBASSIES AND LEGATIONS ACCREDITED TO JORDAN
(E) Embassy; (L) Legation.

Afghanistan: Jeddah, Saudi Arabia (L).
Algeria: Amman (E); *Ambassador:* (vacant).
Argentina: Beirut, Lebanon (L).
Austria: Beirut, Lebanon (L).
Belgium: Beirut, Lebanon (E).
Brazil: Beirut Lebanon (E).
Bulgaria: Amman (E); *Ambassador:* PETAR ILIEV.
Canada: Beirut, Lebanon (E).
Chad: Beirut, Lebanon (E).
Chile: Amman (E).
China, Republic of (Taiwan): Amman (E); *Ambassador:* SHU-MING WANG.
Czechoslavakia: Beirut, Lebanon (E); *Chargé d'Affaires* in Amman: KAREL HOTAREK.
Denmark: Beirut, Lebanon (E).
Finland: Beirut, Lebanon (E).
France: Amman (E); *Ambassador:* JEAN-MARIE MERILLON.
Germany, Federal Republic: Amman (E); *Ambassador:* ALOIS SCHEGL.
Greece: Damascus, Syria (L).
Guinea: Cairo, Egypt (E).
Haiti: Amman (E); *Ambassador:* Dr. JOSEF YOUNIS.
India: Beirut, Lebanon (E).
Indonesia: Jeddah, Saudi Arabia (E).
Iran: Amman (E); *Ambassador:* MANSOUR GHADAR.
Italy: Amman (E); *Ambassador:* DANTE MATACOTTA.
Japan: Beirut, Lebanon (E).
Korea, Republic of: Ankara, Turkey (E).
Kuwait: Amman (E); *Ambassador:* MUHAMMAD SADDAH.
Lebanon: Amman (E); *Ambassador:* ABDEL RAHMAN SAMI SOLH.
Malaysia: Jeddah, Saudi Arabia (E).
Morocco: Amman (E); *Ambassador:* MUHAMMAD TAZI.
Nepal: Cairo, Egypt (E).
Netherlands: Beirut, Lebanon (E).

JORDAN—(Diplomatic Representation, Parliament, Political Parties, Defence, etc.)

Nigeria: Jeddah, Saudi Arabia (E).
Norway: Cairo, Egypt (E).
Pakistan: Amman (E); *Ambassador:* Mahdi Masud.
Romania: Beirut, Lebanon (E).
Saudi Arabia: Amman (E); *Ambassador:* Sheikh Ahmed al-Kuheimy.
Somalia: Jeddah, Saudi Arabia (E); *Ambassador:* Ahmad Issa.
Spain: Amman (E); *Ambassador:* Don Juan Duran-Loriga.
Sri Lanka: Cairo, Egypt (E).
Sweden: Beirut, Lebanon (E).
Switzerland: Amman (E); *Ambassador:* Dr. Marcel Luy.
Turkey: Amman (E); *Ambassador:* Sahin Uzgören.
U.S.S.R.: Amman (E); *Ambassador:* Alexey Voronin.
United Kingdom: Amman (E); *Ambassador:* Hugh Balfour Paul.
U.S.A.: Amman (E); *Ambassador:* Dean Brown.
Venezuela: Beirut, Lebanon (L).
Viet-Nam, Republic of: Ankara, Turkey (E).
Yugoslavia: Damascus, Syria (L).

PARLIAMENT

THE SENATE
President: Said al Mufti.

The Senate consists of 30 members, appointed by the King.

HOUSE OF REPRESENTATIVES
Speaker: Kamil Arikat.

Elections to the 60-seat House of Representatives took place in April 1967. There were no political parties.

POLITICAL PARTIES

Political parties were banned before the elections of July 1963. In September 1971 King Hussein announced the formation of a Jordanian National Union. This is the only political organization allowed and represents both East and West Banks. Communists, Marxists and "other advocates of imported ideologies" are ineligible for membership. In March 1972 the organization was renamed the Arab National Union. It is estimated that there are about 100,000 members.

Secretary-General: Jumaa Hamad.

DEFENCE

Commander-in-Chief of the Armed Forces: Field-Marshal Habis Majali.
Chief-of-Staff of the Armed Forces: Major-General Zaid bin Shakar.
Defence Budget (1971): 32.3 million dinars.
Military Service: 2 years.
Total Armed Forces: 69,250: army 65,000; navy 250; air force 4,000.

Paramilitary Forces: 37,500 (7,500 Gendarmerie and 30,000 National Guard).

Since the disastrous losses of the June War, when the Jordanian air force was totally destroyed and many tanks and artillery lost, the air force has been re-equipped, largely by the U.S.A. and Britain.

JUDICIAL SYSTEM

With the exception of matters of purely personal nature concerning members of non-Muslim communities, the law of Jordan was based on Islamic Law for both civil and criminal matters. During the days of the Ottoman Empire, certain aspects of Continental law, especially French commercial law and civil and criminal procedure, were introduced. Due to British occupation of Palestine and Trans-Jordan from 1917 to 1948, the Palestine territory has adopted, either by statute or case law, much of the English common law. Since the annexation of the non-occupied part of Palestine and the formation of the Hashemite Kingdom of Jordan, there has been a continuous effort to unify the law. This process of unification is now virtually completed, with the promulgation of new laws to replace older laws on both sides of the River Jordan.

Court of Cassation. The Court of Cassation consists of seven judges, who sit in full panel for exceptionally important cases. In most appeals, however, only five members sit to hear the case. All cases involving amounts of more than J.D. 100 may be reviewed by this Court, as well as cases involving lesser amounts and cases which cannot be monetarily valued. However, for the latter types of cases, review is available only by leave of the Court of Appeal, or, upon refusal by the Court of Appeal, by leave of the President of the Court of Cassation. In addition to these functions as final and Supreme Court of Appeal, the Court of Cassation also sits as High Court of Justice to hear applications in the nature of habeas corpus, mandamus and certiorari dealing with complaints of a citizen against abuse of governmental authority.

JORDAN—(Judicial System, Religion, The Press, Publishers)

Courts of Appeal. There are two Courts of Appeal, each of which is composed of three judges, whether for hearing of appeals or for dealing with Magistrates' Courts judgments in chambers. Jurisdiction of the two Courts is geographical, with the Court for the Western Region sitting in Jerusalem (which has not sat since June 1967) and the Court for the Eastern Region sitting in Amman. The regions are separated by the River Jordan. Appellate review of the Courts of Appeal extends to judgments rendered in the Courts of First Instance, the Magistrates Courts, and Religious Courts.

Courts of First Instance. The Courts of First Instance are courts of general jurisdiction in all matters civil and criminal except those specifically allocated to the Magistrates' Courts. Three judges sit in all felony trials, while only two judges sit for misdemeanor and civil cases. Each of the seven Courts of First Instance also exercises appellate jurisdiction in cases involving judgments of less than J.D. 20 and fines of less than J.D. 10, rendered by the Magistrates' Courts.

Magistrates' Courts. There are fourteen Magistrates' Courts, which exercise jurisdiction in civil cases involving no more than J.D. 250 and in criminal cases involving maximum fines of J.D. 100 or maximum imprisonment of one year.

Religious Courts. There are two types of Religious Courts: The Sharia Courts (Muslims); and the Ecclesiastical Courts (Eastern Orthodox, Greek Melkite, Roman Catholic and Protestant). Jurisdiction extends to personal (family) matters, such as marriage, divorce, alimony, inheritance, guardianship, wills, interdiction and, for the Muslim community, the constitution of Waqfs (Religious Endowments). When a dispute involves persons of different religious communities, the Civil Courts have jurisdiction in the matter unless the parties agree to submit to the jurisdiction of one or the other of the Religious Courts involved.

Each Sharia (Muslim) Court consists of one judge (Qadi), while most of the Ecclesiastical (Christian) Courts are normally composed of three judges, who are usually clerics. Sharia Courts apply the doctrines of Islamic Law, based on the Koran and the Hadith (Precepts of Muhammad), while the Ecclesiastical Courts base their law on various aspects of Canon Law. In the event of conflict between any two Religious Courts or between a Religious Court and a Civil Court, a Special Tribunal of three judges is appointed by the President of the Court of Cassation, to decide which court shall have jurisdiction. Upon the advice of experts on the law of the various communities, this Special Tribunal decides on the venue for the case at hand.

RELIGION

Over 80 per cent of the population are Sunni Muslims, and the king can trace unbroken descent from the Prophet Muhammad. There is a Christian minority, living mainly in the towns, and smaller numbers of non-Sunni Muslims.

Prominent religious leaders in Jordan are:

Sheikh Abdullah Ghosheh (Chief Justice and President of the Supreme Muslim Secular Council).

Sheikh Mohammed Fal Shankiti (Director of Sharia Courts).

Sheikh Abdullah Qalqili (Mufti of the Hashemite Kingdom of Jordan).

THE PRESS

DAILIES

Al-Destour (*The Constitution*): P.O.B. 591, Amman; f. 1967; Arabic; publ. by the Jordan Press and Publishing Co.; circ. 14,000.

Al-Rai: Amman; government-controlled.

PERIODICALS

Amman al Masa'a: P.O.B. 522, Amman; f. 1961; Arabic; weekly; political and cultural; circ. 12–15,000; Editor Arafat Higazi.

Al Aqsa: Amman; armed forces magazine; weekly.

Huda El Islam: Amman; f. 1956; monthly; Islamic; scientific and literary; published by the Department of Islamic Affairs; Editor Abdullah Kalkeli.

Huna Amman (*Amman Calling*): f. 1961; monthly; published by the Television Corporation; circ. 5,000.

Jordan: P.O.B. 224, Amman; f. 1969; published quarterly by Jordan Tourism Authority; circ. 5,000.

Military Magazine: Army Headquarters, Amman; f. 1955; quarterly; dealing with military and literary subjects; published by Armed Forces.

Official Gazette: Amman; f. 1923; weekly; circ. 8,000; published by the Jordan Government.

Rural Education Magazine: P.O.B. 226, Amman; f. 1958; published by Khadouri Agricultural College, Teachers' Training College at Beit Haninah and Teachers' Training College at Howwarah (jointly).

Sharia: P.O.B. 585, Amman; f. 1959; fortnightly; Islamic affairs; published by Sharia College; circ. 5,000.

Al Usra: Amman; Arabic; monthly; womens' magazine.

NEWS AGENCIES

Jordanian News Agency: Amman; Dir. (vacant).

FOREIGN NEWS BUREAUX

D.P.A. and Tass maintain bureaux in Amman.

PUBLISHERS

Jordan Press and Publishing Co. Ltd.: Amman; f. 1967 by owners of the former *al-Manar* and *Falastin*; cap. J.D. 100,000, of which 25 per cent held by govt.; publishes *al-Destour*.

Other publishers in Amman include: *Dairat al-Ihsaat al-Amman, George N. Kawar, al-Matbaat al-Hashmiya* and *The National Press*.

RADIO AND TELEVISION

The Hashemite Jordan Broadcasting Service (H.B.S.): P.O.B. 909, Amman; f. 1959; station at Amman broadcasts daily 19½ hours in Arabic to the Arab World, 7 hours in English to Europe and 1 hour in Arabic to Europe; Dir.-Gen. MARWAN DUNIN.

Jordan Television Corporation: P.O.B. 1041, Amman; f. 1968; government station broadcasting for 48 hours weekly in Arabic and English; advertising accepted; Dir.-Gen. M. KAMAL.

Number of radio receivers: 155,000.
Number of TV receivers: 85,000 (East Bank only).

FINANCE

(cap.=capital; p.u.=paid up; dep.=deposits; m.=million; J.D.=Jordan dinars; L£=Lebanese £; I.D.=Iraq dinars.)

BANKING

CENTRAL BANK

Central Bank of Jordan: P.O.B. 37, Amman; f. 1964; cap. J.D. 2m.; dep. 20.2m (1972); Gov. Dr. KHALIL SALIM; Deputy Gov. MUHAMMAD TOUKAN.

NATIONAL BANKS

Agricultural Bank: P.O.B. 77, Amman; f. 1970; government-owned credit institution; Dir. Gen. M. O. QUR'AN.

Arab Bank Ltd.: King Faisal St., Amman, P.O.B. 68; f. 1930; cap. p.u. and reserves J.D. 15.7m.; dep. 146.6m. (1972); branches in several Arab countries, and in U.K., Germany, Switzerland and Nigeria; Chair. ABDUL HAMEED SHOMAN.

Bank of Jordan Ltd.: P.O.B. 2140, Jabal Amman on 3rd Circle, Amman; f. 1960; cap. p.u. J.D. 533,360; dep. 6.1m. (December 1972); Chair. and Gen. Man. MUHAMMAD TOUKAN.

Cairo Amman Bank: P.O.B. 715, Shabsough St., Amman; f. 1960; cap. J.D. 750,000; dep. 13.6m. (1971); 7 brs.; Chair. JAWDAT SHASHA'A; Gen. Man. HAIDAR CHUKRI; associated with Banque du Caire, Cairo, and succeeded their Amman Branch.

Industrial Development Bank: Amman; f. 1965; cap. J.D. 3m. of which J.D. 1m. owned by the government.

Jordan National Bank S.A.: P.O. Box 1578, Amman; f. 1956; cap. p.u. J.D. 1m.; dep. J.D. 12.7m. (Dec. 1972); 7 brs. in Jordan, 3 brs. in Lebanon; Chair. and Gen. Man. H.E. SULEIMAN SUKKAR; Deputy Gen. Man. H.E. ABDUL-KADER TASH.

FOREIGN BANKS

British Bank of the Middle East: 20 Abchurch Lane, London, EC4N 7AY; Amman; f. 1889; Chair. C. E. LOOMBE, C.M.G.; Area Man. F. J. ROBBINS.

National and Grindlays Bank: 26 Bishopsgate, London, E.C.2; Amman; acquired the Ottoman Bank interests in Jordan in 1969; brs. in Aqaba, Irbid (sub-branch in Northern Shouneh) and Zarka; Gen. Man. in Jordan J. C. HENDRY.

Rafidain Bank: Baghdad; Amman; f. 1941; cap. I.D. 6.4m.; Chair. and Gen. Man. ATTA AL-DHAHI.

INSURANCE

Al Chark Insurance Co.: P.O. Box 312, Amman.

Jordan Insurance Co. Ltd.: P.O.B. 279, King Hussein St., Amman; cap. p.u. J.D. 350,000; brs. in five Arab countries and the U.K.

Many of the larger British and American insurance companies have branches or agents in Jordan.

TRADE AND INDUSTRY

CHAMBERS OF COMMERCE

Chamber of Commerce, Amman: King Abdullah St., P.O.B. 287, Amman; f. 1923; Pres. MUHAMMAD ALI BDEIR; Dir. SAID MATOUK.

Chamber of Commerce, Irbid: P.O. Box 13; f. 1950; Pres. MUFLEH HASSAN GHARAIBEH; Dir. HASSAN M. MURAD.

PUBLIC CORPORATION

East Ghor Canal Natural Resources Authority: P.O.B. 878, Amman; the 50-mile canal is now completed, and work is in progress on the irrigation system; the U.S.A. has provided $12m. towards the cost of the canal; the project provides irrigation for some 20,000-30,000 acres. Israeli attacks on the canal in June and August 1969 seriously damaged the irrigation system, but the canal is now in operation again and most of the irrigation system has been completed. An additional 6 miles of main canal and irrigation system have been completed with an additional irrigated area of 5,000 acres, financed by Kuwait Government grants of $3m.

TRADE UNIONS

The General Federation of Jordanian Trade Unions: Wadi as-Sir Road, P.O. Box 1065, Amman; f. 1954; 15,000 mems.; member of Arab Trade Unions Confederation; Gen. Sec. MOHAMMAD H. JAWHAR.

There are also a number of independent unions, including:

Drivers' Union: P.O. Box 846, Amman; Sec.-Gen. SAMI MANSOUR.

Union of Petroleum Workers and Employees: P.O. Box 1346, Amman; Sec.-Gen. BRAHIM HADI.

OIL

Oil has yet to be discovered in commercial quantities in Jordan. In April 1969 INA, a Yugoslavian consortium, was granted a 25-year exploration concession on a 16,000 square kilometre area on Jordan's eastern frontier. "Significant traces" of oil were reported in November, 1969.

TRANSPORT AND TOURISM

TRANSPORT

RAILWAYS

Hedjaz Jordan Railway: (administered by the Ministry of Transport): P.O.B. 582, Amman; f. 1902; length of track 366 km.; Gen. Man. M. R. QOSEINI.

This was formerly a section of the Hedjaz railway (Damascus to Medina) for Muslim pilgrims to Medina and Mecca. It crosses the Syrian border and enters Jordanian territory south of Dera'a, and runs for approximately 366 km. to Naqb Ishtar, passing through Zarka, Amman, Qatrana and Ma'an. Some 523 miles of the line, from Ma'an to Medina in Saudi Arabia, have been abandoned for the past fifty years. Reconstruction of the Medina line, begun in 1965, was scheduled to be completed in 1970 at a cost of £15 million, divided equally between Jordan, Saudi Arabia and Syria. However, due to some misunderstanding between the interested Governments, the reconstruction work has been suspended. A new 115 km. extension to Aqaba is to be financed by a J.D. 12 million loan from the German Federal Republic; currently being re-examined, the project is hoped to be completed in the next few years. The extension will mainly be used for transporting phosphates and will connect Aqaba to Beirut.

As at the end of 1972 there were 17 locomotives, 344 goods wagons, 45 oil tank wagons and 8 passenger cars.

ROADS

Ministry of Public Works: Amman.

Amman is linked by road with all parts of the kingdom and with neighbouring countries. In addition, several thousand miles of tracks make all villages in the kingdom accessible by motor transport in summer. At the end of 1971 Jordan had 1,717 km. of main roads, 1,538 km. of secondary roads and 2,438 km. of other roads. 80 per cent of the roads are metalled.

Royal Automobile Club of Jordan: P.O.B. 920, Jebel Lweibdeh, Amman; Head Office: Wadi Seer Cross Roads, Telephone 22467, 44261; f. 1953; affiliated to the F.I.A.; Pres. of Honour H.M. King HUSSEIN; Gen. Man. D. H. LEDGER.

SHIPPING

The port of Aqaba is Jordan's only outlet to the sea and has two general berths of 340 metres and 215 metres, with seven main transit sheds, covered storage area of 4,150 sq. metres, an open area of 50,600 sq. metres and a phosphate berth 210 metres long and 10 metres deep.

PIPELINES

Two oil pipelines cross Jordan. The Iraq Petroleum Company pipeline, carrying petroleum from the oilfields in Iraq to Haifa, has not operated since the Arab-Israeli hostilities commenced. The 1,067-mile pipeline, known as the Trans-Arabian Pipeline (TAPLINE) carries petroleum from the oilfields at Dhahran in Saudi Arabia to Sidon on the Mediterranean seaboard in Lebanon. It traverses Jordan for a distance of 110 miles and Jordan receives about £1½ million per annum in royalties. The company also paid the Government an outstanding amount of £5m., by an agreement reached in March 1962. Tapline has frequently been cut by hostile action.

CIVIL AVIATION

In addition to Jordan's international airport of Amman, a new airport at Aqaba was opened in May 1972.

Alia (The Royal Jordanian Airline): Head Office: P.O.B. 302, Arab Insurance Building, First Circle, Jabal, Amman; f. 1963; became a corporation in 1968, entirely owned by the Government of Jordan; services to Middle East, Europe and Pakistan; fleet of three Caravelle, one Boeing 707, two Boeing 720; Man. Dir. ALI GHANDOUR.

The following airlines also serve Jordan: Alitalia, EgyptAir, Iraqi Airways, KLM, Kuwait Airways, MEA, Saudia.

TOURISM

Jordan Tourism Authority: P.O.B. 224, Amman; f. 1952; Chair. GHALEB BARAKAT; Dir. MANSOUR EL-BATAINEH; publ. *Jordan* (quarterly).

CULTURAL ORGANIZATION

The Department of Culture and Arts: Ministry of Culture and Information, P.O.B. 6140, Amman; aims to encourage artistic movements throughout the Kingdom, promote growth of talents and prepare specialists in all fields of culture and fine arts. Consists of six Divisions:

Division of Culture: publishes books, issues literary magazines (*Afkar* and *Resalat al-Urdon*) and collaborates with men of letters in the Kingdom.

Division of Folklore Arts: aims to carry out research into and promote the traditional customs of folkloric arts; organizes folklore festivals in different parts of the Kingdom.

Division of the Dramatic Arts: aims to train actors; produces plays and encourages playwrights.

Division of Painting and Sculpture: aims to encourage painting and sculpture and to offer all assistance to improve and widen talents in these fields; arranges local art exhibitions.

Division of Music: aims to develop musical talents on a sound and educational basis; a teaching institute has been established.

Jordanian Folklore Dancing: This group revives folk dancing in Jordan and organizes festivals in different parts of the world and in neighbouring Arab Countries.

EDUCATION

Education in Jordan is both centralized and decentralized. The Ministry of Education prescribes textbooks and curricula for all schools, both public and private. On the other hand, Jordan is divided into 15 districts of education, called directorates (5 are located in the West Bank), each headed by a Director who takes many decisions without reference to the Ministry of Education.

Ministry of Education schools and institutes of higher education accommodated about 67 per cent of total school enrolment in 1972-73. One per cent of school enrolment was in the schools of the Ministry of Defence, Ministry of Public Health, Ministry of Social Affairs and Labour, and the Department of Inalienable Properties. The University of Jordan offered 0.78 per cent of total student enrolment, while UNRWA provided education for about 21 per cent of the student population. Foreign and national private schools took about 10 per cent of the school enrolment. Most of the foreign private schools are run by religious bodies, while the national private schools are run by secular as well as religious bodies.

Children normally start the six years of elementary education at the age of seven. The elementary cycle is followed by three years of the preparatory cycle (junior high). The nine years of the elementary and preparatory cycles are compulsory. At the end of the compulsory years of education, all students sit for the Public Preparatory Education Examination. According to the Education Act of 1964, education terminates for those who do not pass the examination. Those who do pass are entitled to pursue their education in the three-year secondary cycle education schools (senior high) depending upon the number of vacancies available in the tenth grade (the first secondary year) in the various districts.

Higher secondary education is provided either by secondary general schools or secondary vocational schools. Students of both types of secondary schools sit for the public secondary education examination. Those who pass are entitled to pursue their education in institutes of higher learning, both in Jordan and abroad.

In 1971-72 the Ministry of Education budget was J.D. 7.13 million, or 6.7 per cent of the total national budget. For details of number of pupils, etc., *see* Statistical Survey.

UNIVERSITY

University of Jordan: near Jubaiha, Amman; 218 teachers, *c.* 3,600 students.

BIBLIOGRAPHY

ABDULLAH OF TRANSJORDAN, KING. Memoirs, trans. G. Khuri, ed. P. Graves (London and New York, 1950).

ABIDI, A. H. H. Jordan, a Political Study, 1948–1957 (Asia Publishing House, Delhi, 1966).

ALLEGRO, J. M. The Dead Sea Scrolls (Penguin, Harmondsworth, 1961).

AURAL, A., and COVIFELD, P. Palestine and Transjordan Who's Who (Jerusalem, 1946).

CROSS, FRANK M. (Jr.). Ancient Library of Qumran (Anchor Books, New York).

DEARDEN, ANN. Jordan (Hale, London, 1958).

GLUBB, J. B. The Story of the Arab Legion (London, 1948).
A Soldier with the Arabs (Hodder and Stoughton, 1957).
Britain and the Arabs: A Study of Fifty Years 1908–1958 (Hodder and Stoughton, London, 1959).
War in the Desert (London, 1960).
Syria, Lebanon, Jordan (London, 1967).

GOICHON, A. M. L'Eau: Problème Vital de la Région du Jourdain (Brussels, Centre pour l'Etude des Problèmes du Monde Musulmane Contemporain, 1964).

GRANQVIST, HILMA. Birth and Childhood among the Arabs: Studies in a Muhammadan Village in Palestine (Helsinki, 1947).
Family Life among the Arabs.
Marriage Conditions in a Palestinian Village.

HACKER, JANE M. Modern Amman: a social study (Durham, 1960).

HARRIS, G. L. Jordan, Its People, Its Society, Its Culture (Human Relations Area Files, New Haven, 1958).

THE HASHEMITE KINGDOM OF JORDAN: NUTRITION SURVEY, April-June 1962. A report by the Interdepartmental Committee on Nutrition for National Defense (Amman, 1963).

HUSSEIN, HIS MAJESTY KING. Uneasy Lies the Head (London, 1962).

HUTCHISON, Cmdr. E. H., Violent Truce (New York, Devin-Adair, 1956).

INTERNATIONAL BANK FOR RECONSTRUCTION AND DEVELOPMENT. The Economic Development of Jordan (Baltimore, Johns Hopkins Press, 1957).

IONIDES, M. G. and BLAKE, G. S. The Water Resources of Transjordan and their Development (Government of Transjordan, London, 1940).

JARVIS, C. S. Arab Command: the Biography of Lt.-Col. F. W. Peake Pasha (London, 1942).

KENNEDY, Sir ALEXANDER. Petra: Its History and Monuments (London, 1925).

KENYON, KATHLEEN M. Archaeology in the Holy Land (Frederick Praeger, New York, 1960).

KOHN, HANS. Die staats- und verfassungsrechtliche Entwicklung des Emirats Transjordanien (Tübingen, 1929).

KONIKOFF, A. Transjordan: An Economic Survey (2nd edn., Jerusalem, 1946).

LUKE, Sir HARRY C., and KEITH-ROACH, E. The Handbook of Palestine and Transjordan (London, 1934).

LYAUTEY, PIERRE. La Jordanie Nouvelle (Juilliard, Paris, 1966).

MINISTRY OF EDUCATION, AMMAN. Education in Jordan (Amman, 1952).

MINISTRY OF FOREIGN AFFAIRS, AMMAN. Jordan: Some aspects of its growing importance in the Middle East (Amman, 1951).

MORRIS, JAMES. The Hashemite Kings (Faber, London, 1959).

PALESTINE GOVERNMENT. Memorandum on the Water Resources of Palestine (Jerusalem, 1947).

PATAI, R. The Kingdom of Jordan (Princeton, 1958).

PEAKE, F. G. History of Jordan and Its Tribes (Univ. of Miami Press, 1958).

PEROWNE, STEWART. The One Remains (London, 1954).
Jerusalem and Bethlehem (A. S. Barnes Ltd., South Brunswick, New Jersey, 1966).

PHILLIPS, PAUL G. The Hashemite Kingdom of Jordan: Prolegomena to a Technical Assistance Programme (Chicago, 1954).

SANGER, RICHARD H. Where the Jordan Flows (Middle East Institute, Washington, 1965).

SHWADRAN, B. Jordan: A State of Tension (Council for Middle Eastern Affairs, New York, 1959).

SMITH, Sir G. A. Historical Geography of the Holy Land (24th ed., London, 1931).

SPARROW, GERALD. Hussein of Jordan (the authorized biography) (Harrap, London, 1961).
Modern Jordan (Allen and Unwin, 1961).

TOUKAN, BAHA UDDIN. A Short History of Transjordan (London, 1945).

U.S. GOVERNMENT PRINTING OFFICE. Area Handbook for the Hashemite Kingdom of Jordan (Washington, D.C., 1970).

VATIKIOTIS, P. J. Politics and the Military in Jordan 1921-57 (Praeger, New York, 1967).

VERDES, JACQUES MANSOUR. Pour les Fidayine (Paris, 1969).

WALPOLE, G. F. Land Settlement in Transjordan (M.E. Supply Centre Agricultural Report No. 6).

YOUNG, P. Bedouin Command with the Arab Legion (London, William Kimber, 1956).

Kuwait

PHYSICAL AND SOCIAL GEOGRAPHY

Kuwait lies at the head of the Persian Gulf bordering Iraq. The area of Kuwait State is approximately 15,000 sq. km., and the population according to the 1970 census was 738,662, having risen rapidly since the 1965 census which recorded a population of 467,000. The 1972 estimate is 914,000. The inhabitants of the principal town and harbour, Kuwait Town, are estimated at over half the population.

For long it was generally held that the Gulf extended much further north, but geological evidence suggests first, that the coastline has remained broadly at its present position, and second, that the immense masses of silt brought down by the Tigris and Euphrates cause irregular downwarping at the head of the Gulf. Local variation in the coastline is therefore likely, with possible changes since ancient times. Kuwait grew up because it has a zone of slightly higher, firmer ground that gives access from the Gulf inland to Iraq, and because it has a reasonably good and sheltered harbour in an area that elsewhere has many sandbanks, and further south, coral reefs. In recent years owing to Kuwait's rapid economic development the city of Kuwait has been almost totally rebuilt on a much grander scale.

The territory of Kuwait is mainly almost flat desert, with a few oases. With an annual rainfall of one to seven inches, almost entirely between October and April, there is a spring "flush" of grass. Summer shade temperature may reach 125°F., while in January, the coldest month, temperatures range between 45° and 60°, with a rare frost. There is little drinking water within the state, and supplies are largely distilled from sea water.

Immediately to the south of Kuwait, along the Gulf, is a Partitioned Zone of 5,700 sq. km. which is divided between Kuwait and Saudi Arabia. Each country administers its own half, in practice as an integral part of the state. However, the oil wealth of the whole Zone remains undivided and production from the on-shore concessions in the Partitioned Zone is shared equally between the two states' concessionaires (Aminoil and Getty).

HISTORY

Although Kuwait is situated on the fringe of the Mesopotamian basin it has always belonged rather to the nomadic desert of Arabia than to the settled populations of the plains watered by the Euphrates and Tigris rivers. Thus the successive rule of the Abbasid Caliphate of Baghdad (750–1250), the Mongols (1250–1546) and the Ottoman Turks (1546–1918) had little direct influence on the area around Kuwait.

The origin of the present town of Kuwait is usually placed about the beginning of the 18th century, when a number of families of the famous Anaiza tribe migrated from the interior to the Arabian shore of the Gulf. These migrants included such important families as Al Sabah, Al Khalifa, Al Zayed, Al Jalahima and Al Ma'awida, from whom many of the present Kuwaitis are descended.

The foundation of the present Sabah ruling dynasty dates from about 1756 when the settlers of Kuwait decided to appoint a Sheikh to administer their affairs, provide them with security and represent them in their dealings with the Ottoman Government. The town prospered and in 1765 it was reported to contain some 10,000 inhabitants possessing 800 vessels and living by trading, fishing and pearling.

In 1776 war broke out between Persia and Turkey and the Persians captured Basra, which they held until 1779. During this time the East India Company moved the southern terminal of its overland mail route to Aleppo from Basra to Kuwait, and much of the trade of Basra was diverted to Kuwait. Sheikh Abdullah bin Sabah was reported to have been well disposed to the British, who for their part held him in high regard as being a man of his word.

About this time Kuwait was repeatedly threatened by raids from the Wahhabis, fanatical tribesmen from central Arabia, and the need for protection against these enemies led to closer contacts with the East India Company, who had a depot in the town. Ottoman dominion over the mainland was accepted in return for recognition of British trading interests over the route from the Mediterranean to India through the Gulf. The depredations of pirates and the threat from the Wahhabis caused Kuwait's prosperity to decline in the early years of the 19th century, but the British Navy restored peace to the Gulf, and by 1860 prosperity had returned.

In order to retain their autonomy the Kuwaitis had to maintain good relations with the Turks. Although not under direct Turkish administration the Sheikh of Kuwait recognised a general Ottoman suzerainty over the area by the payment of tribute and Sheikh Abdullah bin Sabah al Jabir (1866–92) accepted the title of *Qaimaqam* (Commandant) under the Turkish *Vali* (Governor) of Basra in 1871. His successor, Sheikh Mubarak "the Great", feared that the Turks would occupy Kuwait, and in 1899, in return for British protection, he signed an agreement with the British not to cede, mortgage or otherwise dispose of parts of his territories to anyone except the British Government, nor to enter into any relationship with a foreign government other than the British without British consent. This agreement prevented Germany securing Kuwait as a terminal for her projected Berlin to Baghdad railway.

The reign of Sheikh Mubarak from 1896 to 1915 marked the rise of Kuwait from a Sheikhdom of undefined status to an autonomous state. In 1904 a British political agent was appointed, and in 1909 Great Britain and Turkey opened negotiations which, although never ratified because of the outbreak of the First World War, in practice secured the autonomy of Kuwait.

Sheikh Mubarak's second son, Sheikh Salem, who succeeded to the Sheikhdom in 1917, supported the Turks in the World War, thus incurring a blockade of Kuwait. Sheikh Salem was succeeded in 1921 by his nephew Sheikh Ahmad al Jabir. Kuwait prospered under his rule and by 1937 the population had risen to about 75,000.

Under Sheikh Ahmad the foundation of Kuwait's great oil industry was laid. After considerable prospecting, he granted a concession in 1934 jointly to the Gulf Oil Corporation of the U.S.A. and the Anglo-Persian Oil Co. of Great Britain who formed the Kuwait Oil Co. Ltd. Deep drilling started in 1936, and was just beginning to show promising results when war broke out in 1939. The oil wells were plugged in 1942 and drilling was suspended until the end of the war.

After the war the oil industry in Kuwait was resumed on an extensive scale (*see* Economic Survey) and in a few years the character of Kuwait Town was changed from an old-fashioned dhow port to a thriving modern city supported by the revenues of the oil industry. In 1950 Sheikh Ahmad died and was succeeded by Sheikh Abdullah al Salem. His policy was to use the oil revenues substantially for the welfare of his people, and in 1951 he inaugurated a programme of public works and educational and medical developments which has turned Kuwait into a planned and well-equipped country.

THE MODERN STATE

The economic aspects of post war development are dealt with in the survey following. Here it should be noted that Kuwait has gradually built up what are probably the most comprehensive welfare services in the world, very largely without charge, at least to native Kuwaitis. Education is completely free in Kuwait, and this includes free food and clothing for students. Medical attention is also free to all and the health service is generally considered to be of a very high standard. A heavily subsidized housing programme has now provided accommodation for most residents meeting the country's generous criteria of "poverty". Even local telephone calls are free.

In June 1961 the United Kingdom and Kuwait terminated the 1899 agreement which had given the U.K. responsibility for the conduct of Kuwait's foreign policy, and Kuwait therefore became a fully independent state. In July Kuwait was admitted as a member of the Arab League.

Shortly after attaining independence, Kuwait was threatened by an Iraqi claim to sovereignty over the territory. British troops landed in Kuwait in response to a request from the Amir for assistance. The Arab League met in July and agreed that an Arab League Force should be provided to replace the British troops as a guarantee of Kuwait's independence. This force, composed of contingents from Saudi Arabia, Jordan, the United Arab Republic and the Sudan, arrived in Kuwait in September 1961. The United Arab Republic contingent was withdrawn in December 1961, and those of Jordan, Saudi Arabia and Sudan before the end of February 1963. On May 14th, 1963, Kuwait became the 111th member of the United Nations.

In December 1961, for the first time in Kuwait's history, an election was held to elect 20 members of the Constituent Assembly (the other members being Ministers). This Assembly drafted a new Constitution which was published on November 11th, 1962. Under the new Constitution a National Assembly of 50 members was elected in January 1963, and the first session was held on January 29th, with Sheikh Sabah al-Salem al-Sabah, brother of the Amir and Heir-Apparent, as the Prime Minister of a new Council of Ministers.

In October 1963 the new Iraqi government announced that it had decided to recognize Kuwait's complete independence; Iraq wanted to clear her relations with Kuwait and remove the atmosphere created by the Kassem régime. Kuwait is thought to have made a substantial grant to Iraq to improve relations at this juncture. In February 1964 an agreement (never implemented) was subsequently signed whereby Iraq would supply to Kuwait 120 million gallons of water daily; and in November the two countries concluded a Trade and Economic Agreement which virtually abolished customs duties between them.

In January 1965 a constitutional crisis reflecting the tension between the paternalist ruling house and the democratically-minded National Assembly, resulted in the formation of a strengthened cabinet under the Heir Apparent, Sheikh Sabah al Salem. In May that year Kuwait was one of ten Arab countries, which broke off diplomatic relations with West Germany as a consequence of the formal establishment by that country of diplomatic relations with Israel. Two months later Kuwait decided not to ratify the agreement to set up an Arab Common Market with Iraq, Jordan, Syria and the U.A.R. There was strong feeling in the National Assembly that such an association would be disadvantageous to Kuwait.

On November 24th, 1965, Sheikh Abdullah died and was succeeded by Sheikh Sabah. His post as Prime Minister was taken over by another member of the ruling family, Sheikh Jabir al Ahmad, who became Heir Apparent in May 1966.

In the developments of 1966 and 1967 within the Arab community Kuwait continued to play a neutral role, and in particular tried to act as mediator in inter-Arab disputes such as the Yemen and South Arabian problems. Sheikh Sabah paid visits to Iraq and Lebanon, and Kuwait supported Syria in the dispute with the Iraq Petroleum Company. The progress of Kuwait's own oil industry was marked by the acquisition by the Kuwait National Petroleum Company of a Danish subsidiary with storage facilities at Copenhagen. In October the University of Kuwait and its Institute of Social and Economic Planning were opened.

Kuwait declared her support for the Arab countries in the war with Israel, and joined in the oil embargo on the United States and Great Britain. No Kuwaitis had, however, reached any theatre of war before the ceasefire was announced. The government donated KD 25 million to the Arab war effort. At the Khartoum Conference in September 1967 Kuwait joined Saudi Arabia and Libya in offering financial aid to the U.A.R. and Jordan whilst their economies recovered from the June war. The Kuwaiti share of this amounted to KD 55 million annually.

On May 13th, 1968, it was announced that the agreement of June 1961—whereby Britain had undertaken to give military assistance to Kuwait if asked to do so by her ruler—would terminate on May 13th, 1971. This followed an earlier announcement that Britain would withdraw all troops from the Gulf region by the end of 1971. After the election of a Conservative government in June 1970, however, Britain investigated the possibility of reconsidering this decision, but the Kuwaiti Government stressed its belief that there was no need for the presence of British forces in the Gulf region. In this connection, Kuwait continually encouraged the formation of a federation of Bahrain, Qatar and the Trucial States but her qualities as a go-between were insufficient to persuade the first two states to join what eventually became the United Arab Emirates.

Since the June 1967 war Kuwait has no longer been a frequent target of radical Arab criticism. Its financial support for the countries hit by the war and other generous economic assistance have no doubt contributed to this, while the lavish financing of the Palestinian guerrillas has been even more important. A factor behind this assistance is the large Palestinian community, said to be over 70,000 strong, in Kuwait; many of the most able and educated Palestinians have made a career in the country in recent years. Financial aid to Jordan, however, was cut off in September 1970 following the war between government and guerrilla forces; although resumed in December, it was again suspended in January 1971 as fighting in Jordan continued, and has not been resumed again since.

The main domestic problem is the difference in status between native-born Kuwaitis and immigrants, the latter now comprising around 53 per cent of the population. Whilst the living conditions of the immigrants are very good by Arabian standards, most senior positions are reserved for Kuwaitis, as is the suffrage and free use of some welfare services. The creation of sufficient employment opportunities to avoid the unsettling effects of idleness and boredom, a social problem even with generous unemployment benefits, is a major difficulty now confronting the Government.

In March 1973 Iraqi troops and tanks occupied a Kuwaiti outpost at Samtah, on the 100-mile border with Iraq. Iraq later withdrew her troops, but by July 1973 the border dispute was still unsettled. In May 1973 it was announced that Kuwait was to buy arms worth almost £200 million from the U.S.A. in order to strengthen her defensive position in the Gulf.

ECONOMIC SURVEY

The State of Kuwait has an area of 16,918 square kilometres. It consists mainly of desert with no natural land frontiers. There is practically no rainfall, and the humidity is lower than it is farther down the Gulf. The temperature is exceedingly high in spring and summer; there is occasionally a frost in winter. Until oil was produced, the only town was the harbour of Kuwait on the Gulf. But for some 150 years this port was of some significance because it was a centre for pearl fishing and the building of dhows or "booms"; and several of the plans for building a railway across Mesopotamia envisaged Kuwait as the eastern terminus.

The rapid development of the oil industry since about 1950 has dramatically changed all this. Kuwait is now known to possess about 10 per cent of the proven reserves of the entire world, and its production in 1972 was the fifth largest outside Soviet Russia, even though the Kuwait Government limited production in 1972 so that the increase over 1971 was only 2.8 per cent. The revenue from oil, estimated to reach KD 513 million in 1972–73, has brought to the area a prosperity unimaginable twenty years ago. Crude oil and natural gas accounted for over half of the 1969/70 Gross National Product of £1,147 million.

The population, estimated at 914,000 by the middle of 1972, has more than trebled in ten years as the result of immigration from the surrounding countries, resulting from higher wages and better working conditions than anywhere else in the Middle East; of the total of 733,000 recorded at the 1970 census, less than half, some 346,000, were Kuwaitis. An important part of the annual revenue from oil has been spent on health, education and other social services such as the distillation of fresh from sea water, and as a result the standard of living in Kuwait is at present probably the highest in the world. Most of the social services, such as education and health, are free; it has been said that, as a welfare state, Kuwait now probably has no parallel. In recent years the Government has distributed some of its wealth to other parts of the Arab world by loans and grants.

OIL

In 1933 the Anglo-Persian Oil Company, now the British Petroleum Company Limited, and Gulf Oil Corporation applied jointly to the Ruler of Kuwait for a concession to explore the territory. The two companies formed an operating company, Kuwait Oil Company, each holding 50 per cent of its share capital, and a concession was granted for 75 years in December 1934, extended for a further 17 years in 1951. A large oilfield was discovered at Burgan, about 25 miles south of the town of Kuwait, in 1938, but the onset of World War II delayed development until 1945. By 1948 six million tons were produced, but the main impetus to speed up development was supplied by the Abadan affair in 1951, which in effect denied Iranian production to the rest of the world for three years. By 1956 Kuwait's production had increased to 54 million tons, and was then the largest in the Middle East. Further fields were found by the company, notably at Raudhatain, north of Kuwait, and the company's production had reached over 148 million tons by 1972, although large areas of the original concession have been relinquished to the State in accordance with the Agreement. To handle this vast production, a huge tanker port has been constructed at Mina al Ahmadi, not far from the Burgan field, which from a terminal some 10 miles offshore can now handle the largest tankers. At Ahmadi there is also a town of more than 20,000 inhabitants, of whom about 5,000 are employees of the company, and there is a refinery with an annual throughput capacity of 12 million tons.

An agreement was signed in December 1972 providing for an eventual 51 per cent participation by the State of Kuwait in this concession, but this agreement has still to be ratified by the National Assembly.

Two other companies have been permitted by Kuwait and Saudi Arabia to operate in the Partitioned Zone, and produce oil. These are Aminoil, which has a joint operating agreement with Getty Oil Co. under which Aminoil and Getty bear one half of certain expenses such as drilling; and Arabian Oil Company in which Japanese interests own 80 per cent of the share capital, the governments of Kuwait and Saudi Arabia each holding 10 per cent. So far the production of these companies is small compared with that of the Kuwait Oil Company. In 1971 the Arabian Oil Company produced nearly 20 million tons, entirely from offshore wells, and Aminoil about 8 million tons, making the total production in 1972 of Kuwait and the Kuwaiti half share of the Partitioned Zone about 162 million tons. The Royal Dutch-Shell group has a concession to explore for oil offshore, but its operations have been held up by the problem, so far unsolved, of determining what are Kuwaiti waters. A Spanish state oil company, Hispanoil, was granted a concession in Kuwait during 1967 on territory relinquished by the Kuwait Oil Company. Of this concession, the Kuwait National Petroleum Company (KNPC) owns 51 per cent, but KNPC is not obliged to pay any of the costs of exploring until oil is discovered in commercial quantities. In addition KNPC, which is owned as to 60 per cent by the government of Kuwait and 40 per cent by Kuwait public shareholders, markets in Kuwait oil products produced by the Kuwait Oil Company, and owns a refinery at Shuaiba with an annual capacity of 4.75 million tons. However, in 1969 the refinery operated at well below this figure, with an average throughput of 64,000 barrels per day (3.2 million tons), causing the company to make a loss of £4.6 million. With an increase in throughput and improvements in administration and facilities, the situation improved in 1970.

The government derives its income from the oil industry through the so-called fifty-fifty agreements signed by the operating companies with many host countries in the early 1950s. The principle of these agreements was that when the operating company exported its crude oil, it paid a royalty to the host government amounting to $12\frac{1}{2}$ per cent of the value of the oil at the "posted" price less the cost of production, then paying income tax at $37\frac{1}{2}$ per cent of the total value of the oil at that price, the host government thus receiving 50 per cent of the value. As the companies were free to fix the posted price they exerted their right to reduce it when the price at which they were able to sell the oil fell below the posted price. This of course had the effect of unilaterally diminishing the revenues of the host governments, although because the realized price was lower than the posted price, the host governments were receiving more than 50 per cent of the actual revenue per barrel.

The outcry in the Middle East against this practice was such that the last time the posted price was reduced was in August 1960. In order to increase their "take", the host countries, Kuwait among them, persuaded the companies to agree in 1964 that the $12\frac{1}{2}$ per cent should be "expensed". This meant that, in addition to the cost of production, the amount of the royalty was to be deducted from the posted price, but the tax of 50 per cent was to be charged on the balance, thus increasing the payment to the host country from 50 to $56\frac{1}{4}$ per cent of the posted price. But as the price realized by the companies has continued almost uninterruptedly to fall below the posted price, the division of profits is now nearer to 70–30, the latter being the companies' share, which is often less. However, so great has been the increase of Kuwait's production that its revenue, estimated at KD 370 million in 1971–72, has doubled since 1958. The co-operation between the host countries referred to above was achieved largely through the Organization of Petroleum Exporting Countries (OPEC), formed in 1960. Of this body Kuwait was a founder-member. Kuwait was also a founder-member of the Organization of Arab Petroleum Exporting Countries (OAPEC), formed in 1968, which has its headquarters in Kuwait, and has grown rapidly in membership.

In November 1970, the Kuwait Oil Company agreed to an increase of 9 U.S. cents in the posted price of crude oil, bringing it to $1.68 per barrel, and to an increase of 5 per cent in the rate of income tax payable. However, following the OPEC conference held in Caracas in December, tough negotiations began between OPEC and the major oil companies regarding further price increases. A final settlement was reached on February 14th, when it was agreed to stabilize the rate of income tax at 55 per cent and to increase the posted price by a uniform 35 cents per barrel, with a new system of gravity differentials and an allowance for upward adjustments in four of the five years of the agreement. From June 1971 the terminal price of the Kuwait Oil Company's crude oil was $2.187 per barrel. To offset the effects of the dollar devaluation, agreements were reached in Geneva in January 1972 and June 1973 to raise the posted price to $2.776 per barrel.

In April 1972, the Kuwait Finance and Oil Ministry instructed that the Kuwait Oil Company's production for that year be limited to an average of 3 million barrels per day; the output during the first three months had topped 3,100,000 barrels. This move followed reports that Kuwait's oil reserves might be considerably less than usually estimated and could well last only 15 years. The Government also brought in American experts to make a new estimate of the reserves.

OTHER INDUSTRIES

The government has done much to foster the growth of other industries in order to diversify the economy and to provide an alternative source of employment to oil. A law of 1965 empowers it to grant exemption from import duties on capital goods, subsidized rates for water and power, and preference in government purchases for locally manufactured products. An Industrial Development Committee assists the development of local industry. A Petrochemical Industries Company was formed in 1963 to manufacture fertilizers, and in 1964 a larger concern, Kuwait Chemical Fertilizer Company, was set up, with 60 per cent of the share capital owned by the Petrochemical Industries Company, the balance being held equally by BP and Gulf Oil until they were bought-out in 1973. An industrial area has been developed at Shuaiba, between the town of Kuwait and Ahmadi close to KNPC's refinery. With a new fertilizer plant at Shuaiba owned by KNPC, Kuwait now has a potential production capacity of 1.5 million tons a year.

There are several factories in Kuwait supplying consumer requirements, such as processed food and soft drinks, and there is a flour mills company. The construction industry is of some importance, owing to the vast amount of house and office building there has been in the last decade, not to mention the construction of public works such as roads, power stations, schools and hospitals, much of this work having been undertaken, however, by foreign contractors. According to the industrial census of 1963, nearly 22,000 persons were then employed in industrial establishments excluding oil, or 14 per cent of the labour force at that time. The number has no doubt increased since 1963, but these industries naturally provide a small proportion of the G.N.P. when compared with the oil industry.

PUBLIC UTILITIES

To support the increase of population brought by the development of oil, a vast infrastructure of public works had to be created. There are desalination plants in Kuwait town and the Shuaiba industrial area, and production from them is expected to amount shortly to 52 million gallons a day. Important sources of fresh water have been found at Raudhatain and Al Shigaia. Kuwait's production of thermal power is now about 560,000 kWh. The harbour of Kuwait town has been completely reconstructed; four deep water berths have been provided, and an international airport has been built. There is a national airline with an international service, Kuwait Airways Corporation, which is owned by the State. All these facilities were created at the expense of the Government, the oil ports at Mina al Ahmadi and nearby at Mina al Abdullah having been made by the Kuwait Oil Company. However, there are several shipowning companies owned by the private sector, including Kuwait Oil Tanker Company, which owns six tankers with a total deadweight tonnage of about 800,000 tons, and Kuwait Shipping Company.

AGRICULTURE AND FISHERIES

Owing to the present lack of water, little grain is grown, and most of the food consumed in Kuwait has to be imported. Of the total area of Kuwait, only 3 per cent consists of land suitable for agriculture, and at the end of 1969 there were only 70 farms. However the government has done much to encourage animal husbandry, the main activity before the development of the oilfields of the bedouin, who still rear camels, sheep and goats. There is an experimental farm of 90 acres owned by the government, and in the private sector there is a growing poultry and dairy industry. Fishing, on the other hand, is of some importance, because the Gulf, and particularly Kuwait's territorial waters, abound in fish, notably prawns and shrimps. There were four fishing companies based on the abundance of fish in Kuwait's territorial waters, until they were amalgamated into Kuwait United Fisheries in 1972; prawns, some of which are exported to the U.S.A., and shrimps are the main catch.

FOREIGN TRADE AND BALANCE OF PAYMENTS

Well over 90 per cent of the value of Kuwait's exports consists of oil. Total exports in 1972 were valued at KD 496 million, having shown an uninterrupted and very substantial increase since oil was first produced. About two thirds of the volume of the oil exported goes to European destinations. In 1972, over 17 per cent of the Kuwait Oil Company's exports went to the United Kingdom, over 16 per cent to Japan, over 12 per cent to France, 11 per cent to the Netherlands and 10 per cent to Italy.

Kuwait has the highest per capita level of imports in the world, at U.S. $823 in 1971. The total value of imports in 1970 dropped slightly to KD 223 million, having risen steadily for many years except in 1964, when there was something of a recession owing apparently to overstocking. Imports in 1971 totalled KD 232 million. The most important item, as might be expected when industrial development is proceeding so rapidly, is machinery, accounting for something like 25 per cent of the total imports by value, with transport equipment accounting for another 13 per cent. Foodstuffs account generally for about 18 per cent, and textiles for about 15 per cent, but the range of imports is naturally very wide owing to the comparatively unimportant part played in Kuwait's economy at present by agriculture and domestic manufacture. For the first time, in 1970, Japan took over from the United States as Kuwait's principal supplier with about 15 per cent of total imports. The U.S.A. regained its leading position in 1971, when it accounted for more than KD 33 million of Kuwaits total imports of KD 232 million.

According to the third Annual Report of the Central Bank of Kuwait the balance of payments of Kuwait during the fiscal year ending March 1972 revealed a payments surplus of KD 252 million, which is the changes in the net foreign assets of monetary authorities and the banking system. The official account, which measures the net changes in the assets of monetary authorities, showed a surplus of KD 195 million. Official and banking net foreign assets amounted to KD 1078 million at the end of March 1972, 27 per cent more than the previous year. The net foreign assets held by the commercial banks was KD 320 million. Accurate data on the volume and composition of foreign assets held by the private sector is not known.

CURRENCY, BANKING AND FINANCE

The currency in circulation is the Kuwait dinar. Kuwait was a member of the sterling area, and the Kuwait dinar was for many years held at parity with the £ sterling. However, it remained steady after the devaluation of the pound in 1967 and the dollar in 1971, and the floating of the pound in 1972, with the result that the exchange rates are now set daily. The currency was for years managed by a currency board which included a British member, but in April 1969 a Central Bank was established and took over these functions. The currency in circulation at the end of 1971 amounted to KD 56 million, compared with KD 49 million at the end of 1970 and KD 33 million at the end of 1963.

The only foreign bank previously allowed to operate in Kuwait, the British Bank of the Middle East, was taken over by the Government in 1971 and now manages the Bank of Kuwait and the Middle East under agreement. However, there are a number of commercial banks financed by local capital, and the management of one of these, the Al Ahli Bank, is provided by the French Credit Lyonnais. Of the local banks, by far the largest is the National Bank of Kuwait, founded in 1953, the total assets of which at the end of 1969 amounted to KD 295 million. The other banks include the Gulf Bank and the Commercial Bank of Kuwait, founded respectively in 1960 and 1961. The United Bank of Kuwait, founded in London in 1966, represents the National Bank, the Commercial Bank and the Gulf Bank, which hold part of its share capital. The net foreign assets of the commercial banks at the end of 1971 amounted to KD 374 million. In 1960 the Government founded a Savings and Credit Bank with a paid-up capital now of KD 2.1 million, all provided by the State, to promote savings and to provide finance for small industries, agriculture, property, and small businesses.

There is now an active stock market in Kuwait, and for some time the State has been active in encouraging investment. In 1962 a Kuwait Investment Company was created, of which the State owns half the capital, to engage in portfolio investment and in property dealing in Kuwait. A similar concern, the Kuwait Foreign Trading & Investment Company was established by the State, which owns 98 per cent of the share capital, to undertake business transactions abroad, and reference has already been made to the reserves of the State overseas. There is no official information about the amount of private portfolio investment overseas by Kuwaitis, but it is known to be substantial, and the estimate of the country's balance of payments for 1967–68 puts the income derived therefrom in that year at KD 30 million.

PUBLIC FINANCE

The ordinary budget of the State for the year ended March 31st, 1973, estimated revenue at KD 536 million, of which KD 506 million or 94 per cent was to be provided by the oil industry, KD 386 million in the form of income tax and KD 120 million in that of royalties. There is no personal income tax or estate duty. The other more important sources of ordinary revenue were customs and excise duties, KD 7.8 million, income from the electricity and water services, and transport, KD 7.1 and 6.5 million respectively. Of the total ordinary revenue, namely KD 536 million, KD 123 million was allocated to reserve, KD 101 million was allocated to development projects and the further acquisition of property, and KD 310 million to ordinary expenditure. Of the last named, KD 47 million was to be spent on education—there are now about 120,000 attending the Ministry's schools—KD 31 million on defence, KD 28 million on the Ministry of the Interior, KD 22 million on public health, KD 14 million by the Ministry of Public Works, KD 12 million on electricity and water plants, and KD 8 million went to the Amir. However, there was an allocation of KD 86 million to miscellaneous expenditure and the support of independent budgets, including those of the Municipality of Kuwait, the Shuaiba Industrial Board and the new University of Kuwait, founded in 1966, and now attended by about 1,300 students. The development budget included KD 39 million for public works, KD 30 million for the Ministry of Electricity and Water, and KD 25 million for the acquisition of property.

The amount of the State's reserve overseas in 1968 stood at £396 million, much of which is believed still to be held in London; and for 1967–68 the ordinary budget included KD 25 million under the heading interest from investments. However, in 1961 the government set up a Kuwait Fund for Arab Economic Development (KFAED) to provide loan capital for development projects in the other Arab countries. KFAED has an authorized capital of KD 200 million, of which less than half has been paid up, and it has powers, not yet used, to borrow twice its paid-up capital. During 1971 KFAED made loan agreements of KD 500,000 to Bahrain for construction of a grain silo and flour mill, a further KD 500,000 to Bahrain for construction of the causeway linking Bahrain with Muharraq, KD 900,000 to Tunisia for the construction of a 300 km. gas pipeline, KD 3.8 million to Iraq for the expansion of the Samaweh Cement Plant and the construction of a new grinding mill at Um Qasr, and KD 330,000 to the Yemen Arab Republic for an agricultural survey. In addition to this, the Government has from time to time made loans to other Arab countries directly from its own reserves, and by the end of 1968 commitments of this kind totalled KD 196 million. These must certainly have included the payments which Kuwait undertook at the Khartoum conference of August 1967 to make to the Arab countries affected by the Arab-Israeli war of that year.

DEVELOPMENT

The efforts of the last few years to diversify the economy have had some success. In 1963 the GNP of Kuwait was estimated to be KD 500 million. Of this KD 444 million, or 89 per cent was provided by the oil industry. For the year 1968–69 the GNP was estimated to be KD 793 million, of which KD 559 million, or only just over 70 per cent was due to oil. During the last few years, it is true, there have been slight setbacks to those parts of the economy which do not depend directly on oil, and the years 1968 to 1970 are regarded as a period of relative recession. The cause of this lay mainly in the June 1967 war, after which Kuwait undertook to pay large subsidies to the U.A.R. and Jordan. At the same time, the slowing down of the growth in oil production necessitated restraints in public spending. The greatly increased oil revenues of 1971 seem to have brought Kuwait out of this period of stagnation. All the same, efforts to diversify the economy and maximize the increase of the GNP continue. In 1965 work started on a five-year plan for economic development covering the years 1966–71 and providing for the expenditure by the public and private sector of KD 915 million during the period. Of this KD 187 million was to be spent on housing, KD 162 million on transport and communications, KD 156 million on industry, of which KD 70 million on oil, mainly by the companies, KD 137 million on electricity and water supply, and KD 94 million on the building of new schools, training centres, hospitals and clinics. Preparations are being made to introduce a similar plan, but for ten years, and excluding projects to be financed by the private sector, except for commitments made under the earlier plan.

The 1966–71 plan provided for total expenditure of KD 915 million. Of this no less than KD 281 million was allocated to social services (KD 187 million to housing).

KUWAIT—(Statistical Survey)

STATISTICAL SURVEY
AREA AND POPULATION

Area (sq. km.)		Population (Census of April 19th, 1970)			
Kuwait	Partitioned Zone*	Total	Kuwaitis	Foreigners	Males	Females
16,918	5,700	733,000†	346,000	387,000	417,000	316,000

Estimated Population: 914,000 (July 1st, 1972).

* The Partitioned Zone lies south-east of Kuwait and is partitioned between Kuwait and Saudi Arabia.
† Revised total 738,662, excluding 754 Kuwaiti nationals abroad.

ECONOMICALLY ACTIVE POPULATION*
(1970 Census)

	Males	Females	Total
Agriculture, Hunting, Forestry and Fishing	4,051	9	4,060
Oil and Natural Gas, Mining and Quarrying	6,455	716	7,171
Manufacturing	31,973	115	32,088
Electricity, Gas and Water Supply	7,236	16	7,252
Construction	33,606	68	33,674
Trade, Restaurants and Hotels	28,954	329	29,283
Transport, Storage and Communications	11,997	141	12,138
Finance, Insurance, Property and Business Services	3,506	242	3,748
Community, Social and Personal Services	89,320	14,816	104,136
Other Activities (not adequately described)	795	26	821
Total in Employment	217,893	16,478	234,371
Unemployed	4,782	118	4,900
Total	222,675	16,596	239,271

* Including Kuwaiti nationals outside the country.

OIL

KUWAIT (Kuwait Oil Co.)

Year	Production (long tons)
1967	113,355,644
1968	120,162,473
1969	127,502,203
1970	135,494,480
1971	144,468,129
1972	148,711,076

KUWAIT/SAUDI ARABIA PARTITIONED ZONE
(American Independent Oil Co. and Getty Oil Co.)

Year	Production (long tons)
1968	6,636,777
1969	6,493,592
1970	8,940,000
1971	9,910,000
1972	8,190,464

KUWAIT/SAUDI ARABIA PARTITIONED ZONE OFFSHORE
(Arabian Oil Co.)

Year	Production (long tons)
1968	15,316,000
1969	16,150,000
1970	16,960,000
1971	18,690,000
1972	20,000,000*

* Approximate.

KUWAIT—(Statistical Survey)

OIL EXPORTS
Export of Oil Products by Region
(1971)

DESTINATION	CRUDE OIL* million U.S. barrels	%	REFINED PRODUCTS million U.S. barrels	%	LIQUEFIED PETROLEUM GAS million U.S. barrels	%
Western Europe	603.3	59.6	10.4	7.5	0.3	1.9
Asia and Oceania	365.8	36.1	78.1	56.3	14.8	96.2
North and South America	38.1	3.7	7.8	5.6	0.3	1.9
Arab and Other Countries	5.8	0.6	42.4	30.6	—	—
TOTAL	1,013.0	100.0	138.7	100.0	15.4	100.0

* Excludes American Independent Oil Company production of crude oil, which is included in the refined products figure for the company.

Kuwait Oil Company Crude Oil Exports by Destination

DESTINATION	1969 tons	%	1970 tons	%	1971 tons	%	1972 tons	%
United Kingdom	19,602,763	17.3	25,236,126	21.2	25,842,332	20.2	24,070,928	17.9
Japan	12,163,417	10.8	15,353,896	12.9	17,783,685	13.9	22,465,540	16.7
Netherlands	13,531,653	12.0	10,812,790	9.1	12,015,376	9.4	14,872,166	11.0
Italy	14,758,426	13.0	12,374,513	10.4	11,954,502	9.3	13,526,299	10.0
France	9,367,952	8.3	10,697,850	9.0	11,117,512	8.7	16,599,045	12.3
Ireland	8,194,332	7.2	10,515,043	8.8	10,445,691	8.2	6,668,442	5.0
Singapore	4,675,820	4.1	4,377,414	3.7	6,183,626	4.8	7,884,940	5.9
South Korea	3,207,755	2.8	2,416,540	2.0	5,894,861	4.6	5,380,114	4.0
Federal Germany	1,308,558	1.2	4,110,392	3.4	4,427,435	3.5	4,360,783	3.2
Taiwan	3,757,194	3.3	2,764,286	2.3	3,166,073	2.5	2,813,214	2.1
Belgium	4,295,911	3.8	2,958,250	2.5	2,555,098	2.0	496,908	0.4
Other Countries	18,460,741	16.2	17,521,860	14.7	16,671,833	12.9	15,563,501	11.5
TOTAL	113,324,522	100.0	119,138,960	100.0	128,058,024	100.0	134,701,880	100.0

ARABIAN OIL COMPANY
CRUDE OIL EXPORTS BY DESTINATION, 1971
(long tons)

DESTINATION	
Europe	921,157
Japan	15,617,100
Australia	246,853

KUWAIT—(Statistical Survey)

AMERICAN INDEPENDENT OIL COMPANY EXPORTS OF REFINED PRODUCTS
(U.S. barrels)

Year	Barrels
1967	12,766,080
1968	11,886,830
1969	12,805,358
1970	28,640,259
1971	30,551,116

KUWAIT NATIONAL PETROLEUM COMPANY PRODUCTION EXPORTS OF REFINED OIL PRODUCTS
(U.S. barrels)

Product	1970	1971
Light Distillates	13,260,425	11,786,382
Gasoline Premium	2,431,377	2,366,210
Gas Oil	18,814,287	18,164,374
Fuel Oil	44,866,491	42,315,787
Aviation Kerosene	818,544	810,056
Kerosene	315,565	422,082
Asphalt	186,801	169,416
Light Benzine	540,068	608,059
Diesel	1,733,061	1,835,263

NATURAL GAS PRODUCTION
(million cu. ft.)

Year	Gas Produced	Used by Companies	Used for Injection	Used by State	Total Gas Used
1968	478,958	83,945	53,679	33,966	171,590
1969	513,094	86,769	49,353	44,869	180,991
1970	570,374	90,000	45,339	52,706	188,045
1971	643,710	93,830	69,469	63,222	226,521

INDUSTRY

	Unit	1969	1970	1971
Motor Spirit	'000 metric tons	830	1,192	—
Kerosene	,, ,, ,,	555	726	—
Distillate Fuel Oils	,, ,, ,,	6,491	6,955	—
Residual Fuel Oil	,, ,, ,,	7,855	10,246	—
Ammonium Sulphate	metric tons	35,205	71,198	65,450
Electricity Generated	million kW.	2,012	2,213	2,636
Potable Water	million galls.	5,865	6,683	7,675
Brackish Water	,, ,,	5,578	5,755	5,507
Sodium Chloride	tons	3,910	4,653	4,731
Chlorine	,,	1,528	1,661	1,674
Caustic Soda	,,	1,724	1,876	1,890
Hydrochloric Acid	galls.	124,163	160,709	126,774
Lime-Sand Bricks	'000	46,032	33,544	55,878
Milling (Kuwait Flour Mills Co.)	tons	82,755	83,735	94,528

KUWAIT—(Statistical Survey)

FINANCE

1,000 fils = 1 Kuwait dinar (KD).
Coins: 1, 5, 10, 20, 50 and 100 fils.
Notes: 250 and 500 fils; 1, 5 and 10 dinars.
Exchange rates (March 1973): £1 sterling = 728.29 fils; U.S. $1 = 296.05 fils.
100 Kuwait dinars = £137.31 = $337.78.

BUDGET
(1972–73)

Revenue	KD	Current Expenditure	'000 KD
Income Tax	386,906,000	Head of State	8,000
Production and Consumption Taxes and Fees	128,699,300	Information	6,769
		Public Works	14,224
Services Revenues	17,416,944	Posts, Telegraphs and Telephones	7,642
Miscellaneous Revenues and Dues	1,603,756	Education	47,115
Incidental Revenues	1,600,000	Foreign Affairs	3,600
		Interior	28,568
		Defence	30,694
		Public Health	22,976
		Social Affairs and Labour	8,161
		Electricity, Water, Power and Water Distillation Plant and Chlorine Plant	15,340
		Finance and Oil, including Customs and Ports and Housing	14,191
		Unclassified and Transferable	86,565
		Other Expenditure	16,721
Total	536,226,000	Total	310,566

1973–74: Revenue 568.1m.; Expenditure 470.1m. (est.).

EXTERNAL TRADE
(million KD)

	1967	1968	1969	1970	1971
Imports	210.0	218.3	230.8	223.3	232.3
Exports*	13.0	20.8	23.1	26.4	34.4

* Export figures exclude oil.

COMMODITIES
('000 KD)

	Imports			Exports		
	1969	1970	1971	1969	1970	1971
Food and Live Animals	34,012	37,804	40,924	3,382	5,481	6,561
Beverages and Tobacco	5,904	5,724	6,094	1,237	1,247	913
Crude Materials, inedible, except fuels	4,294	3,400	4,015	870	1,280	748
Mineral Fuels, Lubricants and Related Materials	2,121	1,588	2,154	194	349	339
Animal and Vegetable Oils, Fats	764	609	1,117	57	48	36
Chemicals	11,126	10,354	10,684	4,857	5,177	6,484
Manufactured Goods	50,405	47,515	51,340	3,122	2,658	4,194
Machinery and Transport Equipment	85,620	80,070	77,501	7,167	7,778	12,537
Miscellaneous Manufactured Articles	36,183	35,823	37,980	1,590	1,772	1,968
Others	349	381	497	597	593	602

KUWAIT—(Statistical Survey, The Constitution)

PRINCIPAL COUNTRIES
('000 KD.)

Imports	1969	1970	1971	Exports*	1969	1970	1971
Australia	4,171	5,267	6,475	Bahrain	598	603	1,069
Belgium	2,737	2,507	3,599	Egypt	267	417	800
China, People's Republic	8,920	7,269	7,629	India	774	1,750	654
France	7,175	10,696	14,002	Iran	3,913	3,399	2,501
Federal Germany	23,867	18,690	17,598	Iraq	2,636	2,902	3,814
India	11,043	8,337	7,384	Jordan	403	530	1,277
Iran	2,843	3,795	4,047	Lebanon	897	1,498	2,360
Italy	11,411	10,733	9,782	Pakistan	n.a.	502	1,131
Japan	33,782	33,946	32,789	Qatar	794	900	923
Lebanon	8,173	9,743	10,654	Saudi Arabia	3,327	3,896	6,803
Netherlands	5,150	5,523	5,649	United Arab Emirates	4,006	3,012	2,845
Switzerland	4,000	3,541	3,429	United Kingdom	776	1,214	2,523
United Kingdom	29,132	26,411	26,841	U.S.A.	403	862	1,159
United States	34,277	29,589	33,597				

* Excludes oil exports (see OIL above).

TRANSPORT

Shipping (1971): *Arrivals:* 3,474 ships; passenger arrivals 15,490; passenger departures 20,498.

Vehicles: Total (1968) 124,192; (1969) 136,622; (1970) 149,150; (1971) 157,876.

Civil Aviation: Kuwait Airport, total aircraft movements (1968) 15,438; (1969) 13,379; (1970) 14,088; (1971) 13,998.

EDUCATION*
(1972-73)

	Number of Schools	Number of Teachers	Number of Students
Kindergarten	49	882	12,786
Primary	96	3,758	69,241
Intermediate	78	3,675	52,399
Secondary	28	2,256	21,278
Commercial	3	192	1,173
Industrial College	1	214	739
Religious Institute	1	38	270
Special Training Institutes	11	271	1,385
Teacher Training Colleges	4	219	960

* Data for government schools only; in 1971-72 there were 1,527 teachers, 32,467 pupils at private schools.

Sources: Central Statistical Office, Planning Board, Kuwait; Ministry of Finance and Oil, Kuwait; Ministry of Education, Kuwait; National Bank of Kuwait, S.A.K.; Kuwait Oil Co. Ltd., Ahmadi, Kuwait.

THE CONSTITUTION
(Promulgated November 16th, 1962)

The principal provisions of the Constitution are as follows:

SOVEREIGNTY

Kuwait is an independent sovereign Arab State; her sovereignty may not be surrendered, and no part of her territory may be relinquished. Offensive war is prohibited by the Constitution.

Succession as Amir is restricted to heirs of the late Mubarak al-Sabah, and an Heir Apparent must be appointed within one year of the accession of a new Amir.

EXECUTIVE AUTHORITY

Executive power is vested in the Amir, who exercises it through a Council of Ministers. The Amir will appoint the Prime Minister "after the traditional consultations", and will appoint and dismiss Ministers on the recommendation of the Prime Minister. Ministers need not be members of the National Assembly, though all ministers who are not Assembly members assume membership *ex-officio* in the Assembly for the duration of office. The Amir also lays

KUWAIT—(THE CONSTITUTION, THE GOVERNMENT)

down laws, which shall not be effective unless published in the *Official Gazette*, The Amir sets up public institutions. All decrees issued in these respects shall be conveyed to the Assembly. No law is issued unless it is approved by the Assembly.

LEGISLATURE

A National Assembly of 50 members will be elected for a four-year term by all natural-born literate Kuwait males over the age of 21, except servicemen and police, who may not vote. Candidates for election must possess the franchise and be over 30 years of age. The Assembly will sit for at least eight months in any year, and new elections shall be held within two months of the last dissolution of the outgoing Assembly.

Restrictions on the commercial activities of Ministers include an injunction forbidding them to sell property to the Government.

The Amir may ask for reconsideration of a Bill passed by the Assembly and sent to him for ratification, but the Bill would automatically become law if it were subsequently passed by a two-thirds majority at the next sitting, or by a simple majority at a subsequent sitting. The Amir may declare Martial Law, but only with the approval of the Assembly.

The Assembly may pass a vote of no confidence in a Minister, in which case the Minister must resign. Such a vote is not permissible in the case of the Prime Minister, but the Assembly may approach the Amir on the matter, and the Amir shall then either dismiss the Prime Minister or dissolve the Assembly.

An annual budget shall be presented, and there shall be an independent finance control commission.

CIVIL SERVICE

Entry to the Civil Service is confined to Kuwait citizens.

PUBLIC LIBERTIES

Kuwaitis are equal before the law in prestige, rights and duties. Individual freedom is guaranteed. No one should be seized, arrested or exiled except within the rules of law.

No punishment shall be administered except for an act or abstaining from an act considered a crime in accordance with a law applicable at the time of committing it, and no penalty shall be imposed more severe than that which could have been imposed at the time of committing the crime.

Freedom of opinion is guaranteed to everyone, and each has the right to express himself through speech, writing or other means within the limits of the law.

The Press is free within the limits of the law, and it should not be suppressed except in accordance with the dictates of law.

Freedom of performing religious rites is protected by the State according to prevailing customs, provided it does not violate the public order and morality.

Trade unions will be permitted and property must be respected. An owner is not banned from managing his property except within the boundaries of law. No property should be taken from anyone, except within the prerogatives of law, unless a just compensation be given.

Houses may not be entered, except in cases provided by law. Every Kuwaiti has freedom of movement and choice of place of residence within the state. This right shall not be controlled except in cases stipulated by law.

Every person has the right to education and freedom to choose his type of work. Freedom to form peaceful societies is guaranteed within the limits of law.

THE GOVERNMENT

HEAD OF STATE

Amir of Kuwait: His Highness Sheikh SABAH AS-SALIM AS-SABAH, (succeeded on the death of his brother, November 24, 1965).

COUNCIL OF MINISTERS
(August 1973)

Prime Minister: Sheikh JABIR AL-AHMAD AL-JABIR.
Minister of Education: JASIM KHALID AL-MARZOUQ.
Minister of Public Works: HUMMOUD YOUSUF AL-NUSUF.
Minister of Social Affairs and Labour: HAMAD MUBARAK AL-AYYAR.
Minister of Interior and Defence: Sheikh SA'AD AL-ABDULLAH AL-SALEM AL-SABAH.
Minister of Foreign Affairs and Acting Minister of Information: Sheikh SABAH AL-AHMAD AL-JABIR.
Minister of Trade and Industry: KHALID SULAIMAN AL-ADSANI.
Minister of Awqaf and Islamic Affairs: RASHID ABDULLAH AL-FARHAN.

Minister of Finance and Oil: ABDURRAHMAN SALEM AL-ATIQI.
Minister of Public Health: Dr. ABDURRAZAQ MISHARI AL-ADWANI.
Minister of Posts, Telephones and Telegraphs: ABDUL AZIZ AS-SARAWI.
Minister of Electricity and Water: ABDULLAH YOUSUF AL-GHANIM.
Minister of Justice: MUHAMMAD AHMAD AL-HAMID.
Minister of State for Cabinet Affairs: ABDUL AZIZ HUSAIN.
Special Adviser to the Amir: Sheikh ABDULLAH AL-JABIR AL-SABAH.

PROVINCIAL GOVERNORATES

Ahmadi: Sheikh JABIR ABDULLAH JABIR AL-SABAH.
Hawalli: Sheikh NAWAF AL-AHMAD AL-JABIR.
Kuwait: Sheikh NASSER SABAH AL-NASSER AL-SABAH.

KUWAIT—(Diplomatic Representation)

DIPLOMATIC REPRESENTATION
EMBASSIES AND LEGATIONS ACCREDITED TO KUWAIT
(In Kuwait unless otherwise indicated)
(E) Embassy; (L) Legation.

Afghanistan: (E); *Ambassador:* Khalilallah Khalili.
Algeria: Istiqlal St. (E); *Ambassador:* Muhammad Y. Al-Ghassiri.
Argentina: Beirut, Lebanon.
Austria: Beirut, Lebanon (E).
Belgium: Beirut, Lebanon.
Brazil: Beirut, Lebanon (E).
Bulgaria: (E); *Ambassador:* Zdravko Zelenogradski.
Canada: Teheran, Iran (E).
China, People's Republic of: (E); *Ambassador:* Sun Chieng-Wei.
Colombia: Beirut, Lebanon (E).
Costa Rica: Beirut, Lebanon (E).
Cyprus: *Ambassador:* (vacant).
Czechoslovakia: No. 14, Diyya Quarter (E); *Ambassador:* Ladislav Tisliar.
Denmark: Beirut, Lebanon (E).
Egypt: Mussa'ed al Saleh Bldg., Istiqlal St., (E); *Ambassador:* Izz-Al Arab Amin Ibrahim.
Finland: Beirut, Lebanon (E).
France: Kuwait Bldg. 4th Floor No. 202, Fahad al-Salem St. (E); *Ambassador:* Paul Carton.
German Democratic Republic: (E); *Ambassador:* Hans-Jurgen Weitz.
Germany, Federal Republic: (E); *Ambassador:* Hans Freundt.
Greece: Beirut, Lebanon (E).
Guinea: Cairo, Egypt (E).
Hungary: Baghdad, Iraq (E).
India: Ring Rd. No. 1 (E); *Ambassador:* R. Axel-Khan.
Indonesia: Baghdad, Iraq (E).
Iran: Haj Abdulla Dashti Bldg., Istiqlal St. (E); *Ambassador:* Dr. Fereydun Zand-Fard.
Iraq: 37 Istiqlal St. (E); *Ambassador:* Muhammad Sabri Al-Hadeethi.
Italy: (E); *Ambassador:* Romano Rossetti.
Japan: Al-Khalid Bldg., Fahad-al-Salem St. (E); *Ambassador:* Ryoko Ishikawa.
Jordan: Mansour Qabazard Bldg. Istiqlal St. (E); *Ambassador:* Touqan Al Hindawi.
Kenya: Cairo, Egypt (E).
Lebanon: (E); *Ambassador:* Samih al-Baba.
Libya: (E); represented by Egypt's ambassador.

Malaysia: Jeddah, Saudi Arabia (E).
Mali: Cairo, Egypt. (E).
Malta: (E); *Ambassador:* (vacant).
Mauritania: Jeddah, Saudi Arabia (E).
Morocco: Ville No. 7, Rd. 14, Shuwaikh (E); *Ambassador:* Ahmad Ben Lamih.
Nepal: Cairo, Egypt (E).
Netherlands: Baghdad, Iraq (E).
Nigeria: Jeddah, Saudi Arabia (E).
Norway: Ankara, Turkey (E).
Oman: (E); *Ambassador:* Ahmad M. Al-Nabuani.
Pakistan: Salah Jamal Bldg., No. 7, Nuzha St. (E); *Ambassador:* Shahryar Khan.
Poland: 48 Istiqlal St. (E); *Ambassador:* Zdzislaw Tadeusz Wojcik.
Qatar: (E); *Ambassador:* Muhammad M. Al-Khelaifi.
Romania: Beirut, Lebanon (E).
Saudi Arabia: Sheikh Fahad al-Salem Bldg., al-Hilali St., Sharq (E); *Ambassador:* Humoid Fahad Al-Zaid.
Senegal: Jeddah, Saudi Arabia (E).
Somalia: Jeddah, Saudi Arabia (E).
Spain: (E); *Ambassador:* Ramón Armengod.
Sudan: Badr al-Mulla Bldg., Fahad al-Salem St. (E); *Ambassador:* Ibrahim M. Ali.
Sweden: Baghdad, Iraq (E).
Switzerland: Amman Jordan (E).
Syria: Thounayan al-Ghanim Bldg., Fahad al-Salem St. (E); *Ambassador:* Hajj Abdullah Razouq.
Tunisia: Ghanim al-Shaheen al-Ghanim Bldg., Istiqlal St. (E); *Ambassador:* Habib Nouira.
Turkey: Beirut, Lebanon (E).
United Arab Emirates: (E); *Ambassador:* Rashid A. A. Al-Makhawi.
United Kingdom: Arabian Gulf St. (E); *Ambassador:* Arthur John Wilton.
U.S.A.: Bnaid Al-Gar (E).
U.S.S.R.: Sheikh Ahmad al-Jaber al-Sabah Bldg., No. 5 Dasman District (E); *Ambassador:* Nikolai Tupitsyn.
Venezuela: Beirut, Lebanon (E).
Yemen Arab Republic: (E); *Ambassador:* Abdullah Ali Al-Dhabi.
Yugoslavia: Baghdad, Iraq (E).

Kuwait also has diplomatic relations with Tanzania, Uganda and Upper Volta.

KUWAIT—(NATIONAL ASSEMBLY, DEFENCE, JUDICIAL SYSTEM, ETC.)

NATIONAL ASSEMBLY

In elections held for the third time under the new Constitution on January 23rd, 1971, 184 candidates were nominated for the 50 seats (5 seats in each of 10 districts). There are no official political parties, the candidates standing as individuals. In the 1971 elections, however, five members of the radical Arab Nationalist Movement were returned. The vote is limited to natural-born Kuwaiti males over 21 who are able to read and write (about 40,000 voters).

Secretary: IBRAHIM AL-KHREIBIT.
Speaker: KHALID SALIH AL-GHUNAIM.
Deputy-Speaker: YOUSUF AL-MUKHLID.

DEFENCE

Estimated Defence Expenditure 1972-73: 30,694,860 dinars.
Total Armed Forces: 9,200; army 7,000; navy 200; air force 2,000.

In May 1973 Kuwait was negotiating to buy almost £200 millions worth of tanks, planes, missiles and military construction assistance from the U.S.A., and in June 1973 it was announced that mandatory military service would be introduced.

JUDICIAL SYSTEM

There is a codified system of law based largely upon the Egyptian system. In criminal matters, minor contraventions are dealt with by Magistrates Courts, felonies by Criminal Assize Courts. Appeal in the case of misdemeanours is to a Misdemeanours Court of Appeal.

Civil cases are heard by a General Court within which are separate chambers dealing with commercial cases, other civil cases and matters of personal status. Appeal is to a High Court of Appeal. Matters of personal status may go beyond the High Court of Appeal to a Court of Cassation.

In criminal cases, investigation of misdemeanours is the responsibility of the police, while responsibility for the investigation of felonies lies with the Attorney-General's Office.

RELIGION

MUSLIMS

The inhabitants are mainly Muslims of the Sunni and Shiite sects.

CHRISTIANS

Anglican Chaplain in Kuwait: Rev. JOHN PRAGNELL, c/o Kuwait Oil Co. Ltd., 3 Ninth Avenue, Ahmadi 6, Kuwait.

Roman Catholic: Right Rev. Mgr. V. SAN MIGUEL, O.C.D., Administrator Apostolic of Kuwait, Bishop's House, P.O.B. 266, Kuwait.

National Evangelical Church in Kuwait: Rev. YUSEF ABDUL NOOR, Box 80, Kuwait; a United Protestant Church founded by the Reformed Church in America; services in Arabic, English and Malayalam.

There are also Armenian, Greek, Coptic and Syrian Orthodox Churches in Kuwait.

THE PRESS

DAILIES

Akhbar al-Kuwait (*Kuwait News*): P.O.B. 1747, Shuwaikh, Kuwait; f. 1961; Arabic; independent; Editor ABDULAZIZ FAHAD AL-FULAIJ; circ. 4,000.

Al-Qabas: P.O.B. 21,800, Ahmad al Jabir St., Kuwait; f. 1972; Arabic; Editor JASSIM AHMAD AL-NUSUF; circ. 5,000.

Al-Siyasa: P.O.B. 2270, Kuwait; f. 1965; Arabic; political; Editor AHMED AL-JARALLAH; circ. 10,000.

Ar Rai al-Amm (*Public Opinion*): P.O.B. 695, International Airport Road, Shuwaikh Industrial Area, Kuwait; f. 1961; Arabic; political, social and cultural; Editor FAHAD AL-MASSA'ID; circ. 15,000.

Daily News: P.O.B. 695, International Airport Rd., Shuwaikh Industrial Area, Kuwait; f. 1963; English; political, independent; Editor-in-Chief FAHAD AL MASSA'ID; circ. 10,000.

Kuwait Times: P.O.B. 1301, Fahed Al Salem Ave., Kuwait; f. 1961; English; political; Owner and Editor-in-Chief YOUSUF ALYAN; circ. 4,000.

KUWAIT—(The Press, Radio and Television, Finance)

WEEKLIES AND PERIODICALS

Kuwait Al-Youm (*Kuwait Today*): P.O.B. 193, Kuwait; f. 1954; Sunday; the "Official Gazette"; Amiri Decrees, Laws, Govt. announcements, decisions, invitations for tenders, etc.; published by the Ministry of Information; circ. 5,000.

Adhwa al-Kuwait: P.O.B. 1977, Kuwait; f. 1962; literature and arts; Arabic; weekly; free advertising magazine; Editor MYRIN AL HAMAD; circ. 5,000.

Al-Arabi: P.O.B. 748, Kuwait; f. 1958; Arabic; science, history, arts; monthly; published by the Ministry of Information; Editor Dr. AHMED ZAKI; circ. 125,000.

Al-Balagh: Kuwait; weekly.

Al-Hadaf (*The Aim*): P.O.B. 1142, Al Sur St., Kuwait; weekly; f. 1961; Arabic; political and cultural; Editor-in-Chief M. M. SALEH; Proprietor D. M. SALEH; circ. 8,000 (also monthly supplement: *Economic Review*).

Al-Ittihad: P.O.B. 13189, Kuwait; monthly organ of the National Association of Kuwait Students.

Al Kuwaiti: Ahmadi; fortnightly journal of the Kuwait Oil Co. Ltd. (also in English edition: *The Kuwaiti*).

Al-Mujtama'a: P.O.B. 4850, Kuwait; f. 1969; Arabic weekly issued by the Social Reform Society.

Al Nahdha (*The Renaissance*): P.O.B. 695, International Airport Road, Shuivaikh Industrial Area, Kuwait; f. 1967; weekly; Arabic; Editor YOUSSUF AL-MASSAEED; circ. 8,000.

Ar Ressaleh (*The Message*): P.O.B. 2490, Shuwaikh, Kuwait; f. 1961; weekly; Arabic; political, social and cultural; Editor JASSIM MUBARAK.

Ar-Raid (*The Pioneer*): P.O.B. 11259, Cairo Rd., Kuwait; f. 1969; weekly; issued by Kuwaiti Teachers' Association; circ. 4,000.

At-Tali'a: P.O.B. 1082, Mubarak al-Kabir St., Kuwait; f. 1962; weekly; Arabic; Editor SAMI AHMED AL-MUNAIS; circ. 10,000.

Al-Watan (*The Homeland*): P.O.B. 1774, Kuwait; f. 1964; political weekly circ. 1,000.

Al-Yaqza (*The Awakening*): P.O.B. 1617, Kuwait; f. 1966; political weekly; circ. 1,000.

Hayatuna (*Our Life*): P.O.B. 1708, Kuwait; f. 1968; medicine and hygiene; Arabic; fortnightly; published by Al-Awadi Press Corporation; Editor Dr. ABDUL RAHMAN AL-AWADI; circ. 6,000.

Journal of the Kuwait Medical Association: P.O.B. 1202, Kuwait; f. 1967; English; quarterly; published by Medical Assoc.; Editor Dr. ABDUL RAZZAK AL YUSUF; circ. 1,500.

Kuwait Chamber of Commerce and Industry Magazine: P.O.B. 775, Kuwait; f. 1960; monthly; circ. 4,900.

Mejallat al-Kuwait (*Kuwait Magazine*): P.O.B. 193, Kuwait; news and literary articles; Arabic; fortnightly illustrated magazine; published by Ministry of Information.

Saut al-Khaleej (*Voice of the Gulf*): P.O.B. 659, Kuwait; f. 1962; political weekly; Editor BAQER KHRAIBITT; circ. 9,000.

Usrati (*My Family*): P.O.B. 2995, Kuwait; women's magazine; Arabic; fortnightly; Editor Mrs. GHANIMA AL-MARZOOG; circ. 10,000.

NEWS AGENCIES

FOREIGN BUREAUX

AFP: Sayyid Nabeel Shami, P.O.B. 193, Kuwait.
Hsinhua: P.O.B. 22168, nr. Dasman Palace, Kuwait.
Middle East News Agency: P.O.B. 1927, Fahd El-Salem St.
Reuters: P.O.B. 5616, Kuwait.
Tass: P.O.B. 1455, Kuwait.

RADIO AND TELEVISION

RADIO

Kuwait Broadcasting Station: P.O.B. 397, Kuwait; f. 1951; broadcasts in Arabic and English; short wave (250 kW.), medium wave (750 kW.) and F.M. stereo transmitters; Asst. Under-Sec. for Broadcasting Affairs ABDUL AZIZ MOHAMED JA'FFER; Asst. Under-Sec. for Engineering Affairs ABDUL-RAHMAN IBRAHIM AL-HUTY.

Number of radio receivers (1971): 110,000.

TELEVISION

Television of Kuwait, Ministry of Information: P.O.B. 621, Kuwait; f. 1961; broadcasts in Arabic; three transmitters are used, and broadcasts reach Saudi Arabia, southern Iraq, and other Gulf States; advertising is accepted, and colour television is planned for 1974; Asst. Under-Sec. of TV Affairs MUHAMMAD SANOUSSI; Programme Controller IBRAHIM AL-YUSUF.

Number of television receivers (1971): 120,000.

FINANCE

(cap.=capital; p.u.=paid up; dep.=deposits; m.=million; amounts in Kuwait Dinars)

BANKING

NATIONAL BANKS

Central Bank of Kuwait: P.O.B. 526, Kuwait; f. 1969; replaced Currency Board in administering currency and credit policies; cap. 2m., reserves 3m.; Governor (vacant); Deputy Governor HAMZAH ABBAS HUSSEIN; publ. *Annual Report*.

National Bank of Kuwait, S.A.K.: Abdullah Al-Salim St., P.O.B. 95, Kuwait; f. 1952; cap. and res. 22.1m., total assets 356.5m. (Dec. 1972); 21 brs.; Chair. YACOUB YOUSUF AL HAMAD; Gen. Man. C. D. FEARS.

Alahli Bank of Kuwait K.S.C.: Commercial Centre 5, P.O.B. 1387, Kuwait; 10 brs.; cap. p.u. 2m.; Gen. Man. P. DUJARDIN.

Commercial Bank of Kuwait, S.A.K.: Mubarak Al Kabir St., P.O.B. 2861, Kuwait; cap. and res. 7.3m., dep. 151m. (Dec. 1972); 19 brs.; Chair. ABDUL AZIZ AL AHMAD AL BAHAR; Gen. Man. H. T. GRIEVE.

Gulf Bank K.S.C.: P.O.B. Safat 3200 Abdullah Al-Salim St., Kuwait; f. 1961; cap. p.u. 2,970m.; 12 brs.; Chair. KHALID YUSUF AL-MUTAWA; Gen. Man. R. SINCLAIR.

Savings and Credit Bank: Arabian Gulf St., P.O.B. 1454, Kuwait; f. 1960; cap. p.u. 35m., dep. 24.9m. (June

KUWAIT—(Finance, Oil, Trade and Industry)

1973); 11 brs. throughout Kuwait; Chair. AHMED Z. AL-SERHAN; Dir.-Gen. YOUSEF M. SHAIJI.

FOREIGN BANK

Bank of Kuwait and the Middle East K.S.C.: P.O.B. Safat 71, Kuwait; 51 per cent owned by the Government; began operations in Dec. 1971 with former branches of the British Bank of the Middle East; cap. p.u. 2m.; Chair. FAHAD AL BAHAR; Gen. Man. L. J. MCLERY.

INSURANCE
NATIONAL COMPANIES

Al Ahleia Insurance Co., S.A.K.: P.O.B. 1602, Ali Al-Salim St., Kuwait; f. 1962; covers all classes of insurance; cap. K.D. 1m.; Chair. MUHAMMAD Y. AL-NISF; Man. Dir. ABDULLA A. AL-RIFAI; Gen. Man. Dr. RAOUF H. MAKAR.

Gulf Insurance Co. K.S.C.: P.O.B. 1040, Kuwait; f. 1962; cap. 900,000; Gen. Man. ELIAS N. BEDEWI.

Kuwait Insurance Co.: Abdullah Al-Salim St., P.O.B. 769, Kuwait; f. 1960; cap. p.u. 525,000; Gen. Man. SHAKIB S. SHAKHSHIR.

FOREIGN COMPANIES

Some 20 Arab and other foreign insurance companies are active in Kuwait.

OIL

Kuwait National Petroleum Co., K.S.C.: P.O.B. 70, Kuwait; f. 1960; 60 per cent state-owned; refining, exploring and marketing company; a large new refinery at Shuaiba opened in May 1968; p.u. cap. 15m.; Chair. AHMAD ABDUL MOSHIN AL MUTAIR.

Kuwait Oil Co.: Ahmadi, Kuwait; f. 1934 and jointly owned by BP Exploration Company (Associated Holdings) Ltd. and Gulf Kuwait Company. It had 692 wells producing at end of 1972; oil production in 1972 was 148.7 million long tons. The original concession area covered all of Kuwait, including territorial waters to a six-mile limit. In May 1962 exploratory rights to 9,262 square kilometres, roughly 50 per cent of the original concession area, were voluntarily relinquished to the state. Further offshore areas were relinquished in 1967 and 1971; in 1973, as a result of the Participation agreement of October 1972, the Kuwaiti Government took a 25 per cent share of KOC with an option to raise its shareholding by 5 per cent in 1979, 1980, 1981 and 1982, and by 6 per cent in 1983—giving a majority interest of 51 per cent. As of June 1973 the agreement had been signed by the Government but not yet ratified by the National Assembly; Man. Dirs. K. R. HENSHAW, J. A. STRAND.

Kuwait Shell Petroleum Development Co. (*Royal Dutch Shell*): Fahad al-Salim St., Kuwait; has concession, signed January 1961, of 2,160 sq. miles offshore from Kuwait; operations suspended pending clarification of the offshore boundary disputes with Iraq, Iran and Saudi Arabia.

Kuwait Spanish Petroleum Co.: P.O.B. 20467, Kuwait; f. 1968; 51 per cent owned by Kuwait National Petroleum Co., 49 per cent by Hispanoil of Spain; holds concessions of 910,000 hectares (about half the land area of Kuwait) for a period of 35 years from 1968; drilling began in 1970.

American Independent Oil Co.: Main Office 50 Rockefeller Plaza, New York, N.Y.; Kuwait Office P.O.B. 69, Kuwait: shares with Getty Oil Co. (from Saudi Arabia) concessions in Kuwait/Saudi Arabia Partitioned Zone onshore; combined oil production in 1972 was 8,190,464 long tons.

Arabian Oil Co.: Head Office Tokyo; Kuwait Office P.O.B. 1641, Kuwait; Field Office Ras Al-Khafji, Kuwait Partitioned Zone; a Japanese company which has concessions offshore of the Partitioned Zone; there are 56 producing wells as well as four flow stations in operation; in 1971 crude oil production reached 18,690,000 long tons.

TRADE AND INDUSTRY

CHAMBER OF COMMERCE

Kuwait Chamber of Commerce and Industry: P.O.B. 775, Chamber's Bldg., Ali Salem St., Kuwait State; f. 1959; 3,500 mems.; Pres. ABDUL AZIZ AL-SAGER; Vice-Pres. YOUSEF AL-FULEIJ and MOHAMAD A. AL-KHARAFI; Gen. Sec. HAYTHAM MALLUHI; publs. *Monthly Magazine* (circ. 4,900) and annual economic and administrative reports.

DEVELOPMENT

Kuwait Chemical Fertilizer Co. K.S.C.: P.O.B. 3964, Kuwait; f. 1964; government enterprise (with British Petroleum and Gulf Oil Co. holding minority interests) for manufacture of liquid ammonia, sulphuric acid, urea and ammonium sulphate.

Kuwait Foreign Trading, Contracting and Investment Co.: P.O.B. 5665, Kuwait; f. 1965; overseas investment company; 80 per cent government holding; total assets KD 27.4m. (1972); Man. Dir. ABDULAZIZ AL-BAHAR.

Kuwait Fund for Arab Economic Development: Al-Mutanabbi St., P.O.B. 2921, Kuwait; cap. KD 200m.; wholly Government owned; assists other Arab governments with development loans; Chair. ABDULREHMAN SALEM AL-ATEEQY; Dir. Gen. ABDLATIF Y. AL-HAMAD.

Kuwait Investment Co. S.A.K.: P.O.B. 1005, Kuwait; f. 1961; cap. KD 7.5m.; investment banking institution owned 50 per cent by the Government and 50 per cent by Kuwaiti nationals; international banking and investment; Man. Dir. ABDUL LATIF Y. AL-HAMAD.

Kuwait National Industries Company: Kuwait; f. 1960; 51 per cent Government owned company with controlling interest in various construction enterprises.

Kuwait Planning Board: Kuwait City; f. 1962; supervises the 1967–68/1971–72 Five-Year Plan; through its Central Statistical Office publishes information on Kuwait's economic activity; Dir.-Gen. AHMED ALI AL DUAIJ.

Shuaiba Area Authority: P.O.B. 4690, Kuwait; f. 1964; an independent public body developing a new town with dockyard and industrial estate.

TRANSPORT

ROADS

Roads in the towns are metalled and the most important are dual carriageway. There are metalled roads to Ahmadi, Mina Al-Ahmadi and other centres of population in Kuwait, and to the Iraqi and Saudi Arabian borders.

Automobile Association of Kuwait and the Gulf: P.O.B. Safat 2100, Kuwait; f. 1964; Pres. H. E. Sheikh NASSER ATHBI AL-SABAH.

Gulf Automobile Association: P.O.B. 827, Fahad al Salem St., Kuwait.

Kuwait Automobile and Touring Club: Airport Rd., Khaldiah, P.O.B. Safat 2100, Kuwait; f. 1956; Pres. H. E. Sheikh NASSER AL ATHBI AL SABAH.

Kuwait International Touring and Automobile Club: P.O.B. Safat 2100, Kuwait; f. 1966; Gen. Man. A. W. MONAYES.

Kuwait Transport Co. S.A.K.: Kuwait; provides internal bus service; regular service to Iran inaugurated December 1968.

SHIPPING

A modern port has been built at Shuwaikh, two miles west of Kuwait Town, which is capable of handling simultaneously up to eight large cargo ships and several smaller ships. Ships of British and other lines make regular calls.

A second port is under construction at Shuaiba to the south of Kuwait.

The oil port at Mina al-Ahmadi, 25 miles south of Kuwait Town, is capable of handling the largest oil tankers afloat, and oil exports of over 2 million barrels per day.

Kuwait Oil Tanker Co. S.A.K.: P.O.B. 810, Kuwait; f. 1957; 1,500 shareholders; cap. KD 11.5m.; owns 6 vessels totalling 800,000 deadweight tons; sole tanker agents for Mina al-Ahmadi and agents for other ports.

Kuwait Shipping Co. S.A.K.: P.O.B. Safat 3636, Kuwait; f. 1965; 76.9 per cent government owned; services to Europe, the Far East, America and Australia; 23 vessels totalling 250,000 tons; fully paid cap. KD 6m.; Man. Dir. NOURI MUSAED AL SALEH; Gen. Man. D. H. TOD.

CIVIL AVIATION

Kuwait Airways Corporation: Kuwait Airways, Fahd al Salim St., P.O.B. 394, Kuwait; f. 1954; government owned; services to Cairo, Beirut, Damascus, Amman, Baghdad, Aden, Teheran, Abadan, Abu Dhabi, Bahrain, Dhahran, Doha, Dubai, Karachi, Bombay, Delhi, London, Muscat, Sana'a, Paris, Rome, Geneva, Athens and Frankfurt; fleet of six Boeing 707; Chair. FAISAL SAOUD AL-FULAIJ; Man. Dir. JASSIM YOUSUF AL-MARZOOK; publs. *Alboraq* (magazine), *KAC News*.

Kuwait is also served by the following airlines: Air France, Air India, Alia, Alitalia, BOAC, CSA (Czechoslovakia), Democratic Yemen Airlines, EgyptAir, Gulf Aviation, Iranair, Iraq Airways, KLM, Lufthansa, MEA, PIA (Pakistan), Saudia, Syrian Arab Airlines and Yemen Airways.

EDUCATION

Within the last few years a comprehensive system of kindergarten, primary, intermediate and secondary schools has been built up, and compulsory education between the ages of 6 and 14, was introduced in 1966–67. However, many children spend two years before this in a kindergarten, and can go on to complete their general education at the age of 18 years. At present there are over 160,000 pupils enrolled in some 270 schools staffed by over 11,000 teachers. The general policy of the Government is to provide free education to all Kuwaiti children from kindergarten stage to the University. Almost all Kuwaitis are Muslims and speak Arabic, so there is no language problem. Pupils are also provided, free of cost, with food, textbooks, clothing and medical treatment. There are 66 private schools in Kuwait with an enrolment of 34,171 pupils and staffed by 1,577 teachers (1973).

Children may spend two preliminary years at a kindergarten, and at the age of 6 commence their compulsory education at a primary school. This lasts four years, after which the pupils move on to an intermediate school where they stay for another four years. Secondary education, which is optional and lasts four more years, is given mainly in general schools, but there are also a technical college for boys, a technical school for boys and a religious institute (with intermediate and secondary stages). There are also eleven institutes for handicapped children. Adult education centres have 23,091 students.

Two-year courses at post-secondary teacher training institutes provide teachers for kindergartens and primary schools and the University provides for intermediate and secondary schools. The number of graduates is not enough to meet all the teaching staff requirements and so the Ministry of Education meets this shortage by recruiting teachers from other Arab countries.

Scholarships are granted to students to pursue courses which are not offered by Kuwait University, especially medicine, pharmacy and engineering. In 1972–73 there were 792 Kuwaiti scholarship students studying in Egypt, Lebanon, U.K. and the U.S.A. There were also 575 pupils from Arab, African and Asian states studying in Kuwait schools on Kuwait Government scholarships. Kuwait University also provides scholarships for a number of Arab, Asian and African students.

In 1970–71 the education budget totalled KD 47 million (this figure does not cover building new schools) representing 8.8 per cent of the total state budget.

UNIVERSITY

Kuwait University: P.O.B. 5969, Kuwait; f. 1966; 1,988 students (1971); 58 professors.

BIBLIOGRAPHY

Berreby, Jean-Jacques. Le Golfe Persique; mer de légende-réservoir de pétrole (Payot, Paris 1959).

Bureau of Foreign Commerce. A Trade List of Kuwait Business Firms (Washington).

Central Office of Information. The Arab States of the Persian Gulf (London).

Daniels, John. Kuwait Journey (White Crescent Press, Luton, England, 1972).

Department of Social Affairs. Annual Report (Kuwait).

Dickson, H. R. P. Kuwait and her Neighbours (Allen and Unwin, London, 1956).

El Mallakh, Ragaei. Economic Development and Regional Co-operation: Kuwait (University of Chicago Press, 1968).

Freeth, Z. Kuwait was my Home (Allen and Unwin, London, 1956).

Government Printing Press. Education and Development in Kuwait (Kuwait).
Port of Kuwait Annual Report (Kuwait).

Hakima, A. A. The Rise and Development of Bahrein and Kuwait (Beirut, 1964).

Hay, Sir Rupert. The Persian Gulf States (Middle East Institute, Washington, 1959).

International Bank for Reconstruction and Development. The Economic Development of Kuwait (Johns Hopkins Press, Baltimore, 1965).

Kochwasser, Friedrich H. Kuwait. Geschichte, Weren und Funktion einer modernen Arabischen Staates (Tübingen, Eldmann, 1961).

Kuwait Government, Ministry of Guidance and Information. Kuwait Today (Quality Publications Ltd., Nairobi, 1963).

Kuwait Oil Co. Ltd. The Story of Kuwait (London).

Marlowe, John. The Persian Gulf in the 20th Century (Cresset Press, London, 1962).

Mezerik, Avraham G. The Kuwait-Iraq Dispute, 1961 (New York, 1961).

Samīr Shammā. The Oil of Kuwait, Present and Future. Translated from Arabic. (Middle East Research and Publishing Centre, Beirut, 1959).

Wilson, Sir A. T. The Persian Gulf (Oxford University Press, 1928).

Lebanon

PHYSICAL AND SOCIAL GEOGRAPHY

W. B. Fisher

The creation, after 1918, of the modern State of the Lebanon, first under French Mandatory rule and then as an independent territory, was designed to recognize the nationalist aspirations of a number of Christian groups that had lived for many centuries under Muslim rule along the coast of the eastern Mediterranean and in the hills immediately adjacent. At least as early as the sixteenth century A.D. there had been particularist Christian feeling that ultimately resulted in the grant of autonomy, though not independence, to Christians living in the territory of "Mount Lebanon", which geographically was the hill region immediately inland and extending some 20–30 miles north and south of Beirut. The territory of Mount Lebanon was later expanded, owing to French interest, into the much larger area of "Greater Lebanon" with frontiers running along the crest of the Anti-Lebanon mountains, and reaching the sea some miles north of Tripoli to form the boundary with Syria. In the south there is a frontier with Israel, running inland from the promontory of Ras an-Nakura to the head of the Jordan Valley. In drawing the frontiers so as to give a measure of geographical unity to the new State, which now occupies an area of 4,015 square miles, large non-Christian elements of Muslims and Druzes were included, so that at the present day the Christians of the Lebanon form only about half the total population. Many Christians have emigrated to North and South America, and the relatively higher birth-rate of the non-Christian groups is a further factor in altering the balance of numbers.

PHYSICAL FEATURES

Structurally, the Lebanon consists of an enormous simple upfold of rocks that runs parallel to the coast. There is, first, a very narrow and broken flat coastal strip —hardly a true plain—then the land rises steeply to a series of imposing crests and ridges. The highest crest of all is Qurnet as-Sauda, just over 10,000 ft. high, lying south-east of Tripoli; Mount Sannin, north-east of Beirut, is over 9,000 ft. A few miles east of the summits there is a precipitous drop along a sharp line to a broad, troughlike valley, known as the Bekaa (Biqa), about 10 miles wide and some 70 to 80 miles long. The eastern side of the Bekaa is formed by the Anti-Lebanon mountains, which rise to 9,000 ft., and their southern continuation, the Hermon Range, of about the same height. The floor of the Bekaa Valley, though much below the level of the surrounding mountain ranges, lies in places at 3,000 ft. above sea-level, with a low divide in the region of Baalbek. Two rivers rise in the Bekaa— the Orontes, which flows northwards into Syria and the Gharb depression, ultimately reaching the Mediterranean through the Turkish territory of Antioch; and the River Litani (Leontes). This latter river flows southwards, and then, at a short distance from the Israeli frontier, makes a sudden bend westwards and plunges through the Lebanon mountains by a deep gorge. Plans are now partly complete to develop the waters of the Litani in this region for irrigation and hydro-electric power.

There exists in the Lebanon an unusual feature of geological structure which is not present in either of the adjacent regions of Syria and Israel. This is the occurrence of a layer of non-porous rocks within the upfold forming the Lebanon mountains; and, because of this layer, water is forced to the surface in considerable quantities, producing large springs at the unusually high level of 4,000 to 5,000 ft. Some of the springs have a flow of several thousand cu. ft. per second and emerge as small rivers; hence the western flanks of the Lebanon mountains, unlike those nearby in Syria and Israel, are relatively well watered and cultivation is possible up to a height of 4,000 or 5,000 ft.

With its great contrasts of relief, and the configuration of the main ranges, which lie across the path of the prevailing westerly winds, there is wide variety in climatic conditions. The coastal lowlands are moderately hot in summer, and warm in winter, with complete absence of frost. But only 5 or 10 miles away in the hills there is a heavy winter snowfall, and the higher hills are covered from December to May, giving the unusual vista for the Middle East of snow-clad peaks. From this the name Lebanon (*laban*— Aramaic for "white") is said to originate. The Bekaa has a moderately cold winter with some frost and snow, and a distinctly hot summer, as it is shut off from the tempering effect of the sea.

Rainfall is on the whole abundant, but it decreases rapidly towards the east, so that the Bekaa and Anti-Lebanon are definitely drier than the west. On the coast, between 30 and 40 inches fall annually, with up to 50 inches in the mountains, but only 15 inches in the Bekaa. As almost all of this annual total falls between October and April (there are three months of complete aridity each summer) rain is extremely heavy while it lasts, and storms of surprising intensity can occur. Beirut, for example, has slightly more rain than Manchester, but on half the number of rainy days. Another remarkable feature is the extremely high humidity of the coastal region during summer, when no rain falls. The sultry heat drives as many as can afford it to spend the summer in the hills.

ECONOMIC LIFE

The occurrence of high mountains near the sea, and the relatively abundant supplies of spring water have had a marked influence on economic development within the Lebanon. Owing to the successive levels of terrain, an unusually wide range of crops can be grown, from bananas and pineapples on the hot, damp coastlands, olives, vines and figs on the lowest foothills, cereals, apricots and peaches on the middle slopes, to apples and potatoes on the highest levels. These latter are the aristocrats of the Lebanese markets, since they are rarest, and, with the growing market in the oilfield areas of Arabia and the Persian Gulf, they fetch the highest price. Export of fruit is therefore an important item. Then, too, abundant natural water has led to the growth of pinewoods and evergreen groves, which add greatly to the already considerable scenic beauty of the western hill country. There has hence grown up an important tourist trade, centred in the small hill villages, some of which have casinos, luxury hotels, and cinemas. Main activity is during the summer months, when wealthy Middle Easterners and others arrive; but there is a smaller winter sports season, when ski-ing is carried on.

In addition, the geographical situation of the Lebanon, as a "façade" to the inland territories of Syria, Jordan, and even northern Iraq and southern Turkey, enables the

LEBANON—(Physical and Social Geography, History)

Lebanese ports to act as the commercial outlet for a very wide region. The importance of Beirut as a commercial centre is due in large part to the fact that the Lebanon is a free market. Over half of the volume of Lebanese trade is transit traffic, and the Lebanon handles most of the trade of Jordan. Her own exports are mostly agricultural products. Byblos claims to be the oldest port in the world; Tyre and Sidon were for long world-famous, and the latter is now reviving as the Mediterranean terminal of the Tapline (Trans-Arabian Pipe Line) from Saudi Arabia. Another ancient centre, Tripoli, is also a terminal of the IPC pipeline from Iraq. Beirut is now, however, the leading town of the country, and contains one-quarter of the total population. Though local resources are not in general very great (there are no minerals or important raw materials in the Lebanon) the city lives by commercial activity on a surprising scale, developed by the ingenuity and opportunism of its merchant class. The opening in 1951 of a commercial airport designed for jet airliners, before any such aircraft were actually in use in the world, is typical of the forward-looking attitude of many Lebanese.

Beirut has of recent years come to serve as a financial and holiday centre for the less attractive but oil-rich parts of the Middle East. Transfer of financial credit from the Middle East to Zürich, Paris, London, New York and Tokyo; a trade in gold and diamonds; and some connexion with the narcotic trade of the Middle East—all these give the city a very special function. In addition, the town provides discreet distraction for all types of visitor.

RACE AND LANGUAGE

It is difficult to summarize the racial affinities of the Lebanese people. The western lowlands have an extremely mixed population possibly describable only as "Levantine". Basically Mediterranean, there are many other elements, including remarkably fair individuals—Arabs with blonde hair and grey eyes, who are possibly descendants of the Crusaders. The remaining parts of the country show a more decided Armenoid tendency, with darker colouring, broader head-form, and more pronounced facial features. In addition, small refugee groups, who came to the more inaccessible mountain zones in order to escape persecution, often have a different racial ancestry, so that parts of the Lebanon form a mosaic of varying racial and cultural elements. Almost all Middle Eastern countries are represented racially within the Lebanon.

Arabic is current over the whole country, but owing to the high level of education (probably the highest in any Middle Eastern country) and to the considerable volume of temporary emigration, English, French and even Spanish are widely understood. French is probably still the leading European language (though English is tending to replace it) and some of the higher schools and one university teach basically in this language. In addition, Aramaic is used by some religious sects, but only for ritual—there are no Aramaic speaking villages as in Syria.

HISTORY

ANCIENT AND MEDIEVAL HISTORY

In the Ancient World the Lebanon was important for its pine, fir, and cedarwood, which neighbouring powers, poorly supplied with timber resources, coveted so much that during the long period of Egyptian, Assyrian, Persian, and Seleucid rule, the exploitation of the forests of the Lebanon was normally a royal privilege. The area was also mined for its iron and copper in the time of the Ptolemies and the Romans. Gradually the Lebanon came to have a distinct history of its own, for the mountainous character of the region prevented any complete subjugation to outside authority. It is probable that the Arab conquest of Syria did not include the "mountain", to which fled all those who, for one reason or another, were opposed to the Arab domination. The Caliph Mu'awiya (661–80) made some effort to assert a greater control, but the resistance of the native Aramaean Christians was reinforced by the arrival of the Mardaites from the fastnesses of the Taurus and the Amanus. These Christian nomads, led by Byzantine officers, made determined advances into the Lebanon, late in the seventh century, and seem to have united with the Maronite Christians who were later to become a Uniate Church of the Roman communion and to have a predominant role in the history of the Lebanon. The Caliph Abd al-Malik (685–705) paid tribute to Byzantium in return for a withdrawal of most of the Mardaite forces; but it is clear that the "mountain" had begun to assume its historic function of providing a sure refuge for racial and religious minorities.

The Lebanon maintained its Christian character until the ninth century when, amongst other elements, the Arab tribe of Tanukh established a principality in the region of al-Gharb, near Beirut, and acted as a counterpoise to the Maronites of the North Lebanon, and as a bulwark against Byzantine threats from the sea. Gradually, Islam and, more slowly still, the Arabic language penetrated the "mountain" where, however, Syriac lingered on in the Maronite districts until the seventeenth century (it is still spoken in three villages of the Anti-Lebanon). In the ninth and tenth centuries Muslim sects began to take root in the "mountain" as, for example, the Shi'i, known in the Lebanon under the name of Mitwali and, in the eleventh century, the Druse faith, which won a firm hold in the South Lebanon.

The Crusaders established in this area the County of Tripolis and the lordships of Gibelet and Batron which enjoyed considerable support from the Christian population of the North Lebanon and were protected by a network of fortresses, the most famous of which is Hisn al-Akrad (Crac des Chevaliers). In the Mamluk period the rulers of the Lebanon continued to practise the art of political manoeuvring, thus maintaining for themselves a considerable degree of autonomy. The Tanukhid Amirs, after a long period in which they had played off the Crusaders against the Muslim amirates, had eventually taken the Mamluk side. In the North Lebanon the Maronites, under their bishop, maintained contact with the Italian Republics and also with the Roman Curia. Less fortunate were the Druses and the Mitwali who, in the last years of the thirteenth century, took advantage of the Mamluk preoccupation with the Mongol threat from Persia and began a protracted revolt which led to widespread devastation in the Central Lebanon.

THE OTTOMAN PERIOD

In the sixteenth century the Turcoman family of Assaf and, after them, the Banu Saifa rose to prominence in the area from Beirut to the north of Tripoli; while in the south the Druse house of Ma'an supplanted the Tanukhid amirs.

LEBANON—(HISTORY)

After the conquest of 1516–17, the Ottoman Sultan Selim I had confirmed the amirs of the Lebanon in their privileges and had imposed only a small tribute; yet not infrequently there was open conflict with the Ottomans, as in 1584–5 when, after an attack on a convoy bearing the tribute from Egypt to Constantinople, the Sultan Murad III sent a punitive expedition to ravage the lands of the Banu Saifa and of the Druses.

The power of the House of Ma'an now reached its zenith in the person of Fakhr ad-din II (1586–1635), who by every possible means—bribery, intrigue, foreign alliance, and open force—set out to establish an independent power over the whole of the Lebanon and parts of Palestine to the south. To this end he entered into close relations with the Grand Duke of Tuscany, negotiating in 1608 a commercial agreement which contained a secret military clause directed against the Sultan. In 1613 a naval and military expedition sent from the Porte compelled Fakhr ad-din to seek refuge with his Tuscan ally; but, returning in 1618, he rapidly restored his power and within a few years was virtual ruler from Aleppo to the borders of Egypt. The Sultan, heavily engaged in repressing revolt in Anatolia, and in waging a long struggle with Persia, could do no more than recognise the *fait accompli*. Fakhr ad-din now embarked on an ambitious programme of development for the Lebanon. He sought to equip a standing army with arms imported from Tuscany. Italian engineers and agricultural experts were employed to promote a better cultivation of the land and to increase the production of silk and olives. The Christian peasantry were encouraged to move from the North to the South Lebanon. Beirut and Sidon flourished as a result of the favour he showed to commerce; and religious missions from Europe—Capuchins, Jesuits, Carmelites—were allowed to settle throughout Syria, a development of great importance for France which strove to assert a "protectorate" over all the Catholic and other Christian elements in the Ottoman Empire. However, the ambitions of Fakhr ad-din were doomed to failure when by 1632 the Sultan Murad IV assumed effective control at Constantinople. The Pasha of Damascus, supported by a naval squadron, began a campaign to end the independent power of the Lebanon, and in 1635 Fakhr ad-din was executed at Constantinople.

In 1697, the Ma'an family became extinct, and was succeeded by the House of Shihab, which maintained its predominance until 1840. In the course of the eighteenth century, the Shihab Amirs gradually consolidated their position against the other factions of the "Mountain" and for a while recovered control of Beirut. While normally they took care to remain on good terms with the Turkish Pashas of Tripoli, Sidon and Damascus, the Pashas, for their part, strove to exercise an indirect control by fomenting the family rivalries and religious differences which always marked the course of Lebanese politics. With the advent of Bashir II (1788–1840) the House of Shihab attained the height of its influence. Not until the death of Ahmed Jazzar, Pasha of Acre (1804), was he free to develop his power, which he maintained by the traditional methods of playing off one Pasha against the other, and by bribing the officials of the Porte whenever it seemed expedient. In 1810 he helped the Ottomans to repel an invasion by the Wahhabi power of Arabia; but in 1831 he sided openly with Muhammad Ali of Egypt, when that ruler invaded Syria. Holding the Lebanon as the vassal of Egypt, he was compelled, however, to apply to the "Mountain" the unpopular policy imposed by Ibrahim Pasha, the son of Muhammad Ali, with the result that a revolt broke out, which, after the Egyptian withdrawal of 1840, led to his exile. The age of the Lebanese Amirs was now at an end, for the Ottomans assumed control of the "Mountain", appointing two Kaimakams to rule there, one Druse and the other Maronite, under the supervision of the Pashas of Sidon and Beirut.

The period of direct Ottoman rule saw the rapid growth, between the Druses and the Maronites, of a mistrust already visible during the time of the Egyptian dominance, and now fostered by the Ottomans as the only means of maintaining their influence over the Lebanon. As a result of social and economic discontent, due to the slow disintegration of the old feudal system which had existed in the Lebanon since the Middle Ages, the Maronite peasantry revolted in 1858 and destroyed the feudal privileges of the Maronite aristocracy, thus clearing the way for the creation of a system of independent smallholdings. The Druse aristocracy, fearing the consequences of a similar discontent among their own Maronite peasantry, made a series of attacks on the Maronites of the North Lebanon, who, owing to their own dissensions, could offer no effective resistance. The dubious attitude of the Turkish Pashas, in the face of these massacres of 1860, led to French intervention, and in 1864 to the formation of an organic statute for the Lebanon, which was now to become an autonomous province under a non-Lebanese Ottoman Christian governor, appointed by the Sultan and approved by the Great Powers. He was to be aided by an elected administrative council and a locally recruited police force. The statute also abolished legal feudalism in the area, thus consolidating the position won by the Maronite peasantry in 1858. The period from 1864 to 1914 was one of increasing prosperity, especially among the Christian elements, who also played an important role in the revival of Arab literature and Arab national feeling during the last years of the nineteenth century.

THE FRENCH MANDATE

The privileged position of the Lebanon ended when the Turks entered the war of 1914–18; and by 1918 the coastal areas of the Lebanon were occupied by British and French forces. In September 1920 the French created the State of the Greater Lebanon which included not only the former autonomous province but also Tripoli, Sidon, Tyre and Beirut, some of which had in earlier times been under the control of the amirs of the Lebanon. The period from 1920–36 was for the Lebanon one of peaceful progress. A constitution was devised in 1926, which proved unworkable and was suspended in 1932, from which time the President of the Republic carried on the administration. He was, by convention, a Christian, while the Prime Minister was a Muslim, and both worked towards the achievement of a careful balance between the various religious communities of the new State. The Lebanon was not unaffected by the growth of the nationalist movement in Syria, some sections of which demanded the reduction of the Lebanon to its pre-war limits and even the abolition of its existence as a separate State. These demands found some support amongst the Sunni Muslims of the areas added to the Lebanon proper in 1920, with the result that the Syrian revolt of 1925–26 spread to parts of the southern Lebanon. The Maronite Christians, on the whole, supported the idea of a separate Lebanon, but were not united in their attitude towards France on the one hand, and the Arab States on the other. The Franco-Lebanese Treaty of 1936 differed little from that which France negotiated at the same time with Syria, the chief difference being that the military convention gave France wider military powers in the Lebanon than in Syria. A reformed constitution was promulgated in 1937; but the French refusal to ratify the treaty in 1938, and the advent of war prolonged a situation which, if outwardly calm, concealed a considerable discontent beneath the surface. In November 1941 the Free French Commander, General Catroux, formally proclaimed the Lebanon a sovereign independent State. In September

1943 a new Parliament which had a strong nationalist majority soon came into conflict with the French authorities over the transfer of the administrative services. When, in November 1943, the Lebanese Government insisted on passing legislation which removed from the constitution all provisions considered to be inconsistent with the independence of the Lebanon, the French Delegate-General arrested the President and suspended the constitution. The other Arab States, together with Great Britain and America, supported the Lebanese demands and in 1944 France began to transfer to Lebanese control all important public services, save for the *Troupes Spéciales*, i.e. local levies under French command, whose transfer the French authorities at first made conditional on the signing of a Franco-Lebanese Treaty. But in 1945 the *Troupes Spéciales* were handed over to the Lebanon without such conditions, and an agreement between France and the Lebanese Government in 1946 provided for the withdrawal of French troops.

MODERN HISTORY

Since 1946 the Lebanon has continued to view with great reserve all projects for a Greater Syria, or for the union of Syria and Iraq; and has striven to maintain a neutral role in those disputes which have rendered the unity of the Arab League largely illusory. Like the other Arab States, the Lebanon was at war with the new State of Israel from May 1948; but negotiated an armistice in March 1949. Just as in Syria the ill-success of the Arab arms had led eventually to the *coup d'état* of March 1949, so in the Lebanon the widespread disillusionment of Arab nationalist hopes prepared the ground for a conspiracy against the Government. This conspiracy was easily suppressed in June 1949 and its leader, Antun Sa'ade, was executed in July.

In internal affairs, the Lebanese Government had to face considerable economic and financial difficulties soon after the end of the 1939-45 war. When, in January 1948, France devalued the franc (to which both the Lebanese and the Syrian currencies were linked) the Lebanon, economically weaker than Syria, felt obliged to sign a new agreement with France (February 1948). Syria refused to do so and began a long and complicated dispute with the Lebanon over the precise nature of the economic and financial arrangements which were to exist between the two States. In March 1950 the Lebanese Government refused a Syrian demand for full economic and financial union between Syria and the Lebanon. The severance of economic relations which now ensued did not end until the signing, in February 1952, of an agreement which arranged for the division of royalties due from oil companies, and for the status, for customs purposes, of agricultural and industrial products passing between the two states.

In recent years American influence has increased in the Lebanon as in the other states of the Middle East and the Lebanon now receives considerable revenues from the oil companies whose pipe-lines bring the oil of Iraq and Saudi Arabia through Lebanese territory. Negotiations with the oil companies, in the spring of 1952, foreshadowed an increase in such revenues.

In September 1952 the Lebanon had to face a severe crisis in her internal affairs. Political and economic unrest brought about the fall of the Lebanese Government and the resignation of President al-Khuri, who had held office since 1943. Charges of corruption were made against the President. During his long tenure of power he had indeed used all the arts of political influence and manoeuvre in order to impose a real degree of unity on a state where the divergent interests of Maronites, Sunni and Shi'i Muslims, Druses, and other religious communities underlined the need for firm and coherent rule.

To an even greater degree, however, the crisis was due to causes of an economic order. The Lebanon had attained its independence in the period of war-time prosperity. The end of the war meant a progressive diminution of foreign expenditure in the Lebanon, e.g., by the French and British forces stationed there, and the gradual disappearance of war shortages which had favoured Lebanese trade. The devaluation of the French franc, the unsuccessful war with Israel, and above all the economic rupture with Syria gave rise to further difficulties. The break with Syria hit the Lebanon hard, for Syria was the chief provider of agricultural goods to the Lebanon and the chief customer for Lebanese industrial products. The effect of these developments was the more serious in that the Lebanon has a permanent adverse balance of trade, her annual deficit being largely covered by the revenues accruing to her from a wide variety of financial, commercial and transit services and by royalties paid to her by the oil companies. By 1952 there was much discontent arising from the high cost of living and from considerable unemployment. It was in fact a loose coalition of all the elements of opposition, both political and economic which brought about the fall of the al-Khuri régime.

CONSTITUTIONAL REFORM

As a result of the crisis Camille Chamoun became the new President of the Republic. The new administration, with the Amir Khalid Chehab as Prime Minister, bound itself to introduce reforms, including changes in the electoral laws, the grant of the vote to women, revision of the Press laws and the reorganization of justice. The elections held in July 1953 led to the formation of a Chamber of Deputies, 44 in number and divided as follows: 13 Maronites, 9 Sunni Muslims, 8 Shi'i Muslims, 5 Orthodox Christians, 3 Greek Catholics, 3 Druses, 2 Orthodox Armenians and one member for other minorities.

Negotiations between Syria and the Lebanon over common economic problems continued throughout these years. The agreement of February 1952 had been prolonged for a period of one year. This agreement was renewed for a further six months in February 1953 and again for a similar period in August 1953.

The elections held in the Lebanon during the summer of 1953 were carried out under the provisions of the electoral law of November 1952. Since the foundation of the republic, all seats in the Chamber of Deputies had been distributed among the various religious communities in proportion to their numerical strength. Parliament was thus an institution reflecting in itself the religious and social structure of the state and capable of harmonious function, provided that the electoral system which maintained a delicate balance between the communities suffered no violent and prejudicial change. At the same time, it contained a strong "feudal" element—the tribal and religious leaders who, with their trusted retainers, formed powerful groups within the Parliament and were often criticised as being "anti-national" in their aims and methods. To end or at least weaken this "feudalisation" of Lebanese political life, without, however, impairing the vital equilibrium between the Muslim and Christian communities, had long been the purpose of those who advocated a reasonable and well-considered policy of reform. The law of 1952 created 33 electoral districts (during the previous life of the republic the number had been, as a rule, five) and allotted to eleven of them two seats, and to the remainder one seat each. Of the sum-total of 44 seats the Maronites were now to receive 13, the Sunni Muslims 9, the Shi'i Muslims 8, the Greek Orthodox Christians 5, the Druses 3, the Greek Catholics 3, the Armenian Catholics 2 and the other confessions (Protestant, Jewish, Nestorian, etc.) 1 seat.

The election of 1953 did in fact bring defeat to some of the Shi'i lords of the south. It would seem, however, that something more than electoral reform will be needed, if the "feudal" aspects of the present régime are to be eliminated. In the course of time such a change might perhaps come about through the growth of well-organized political parties which cut across confessional lines. None the less it remains an open question whether a government more "national" in character would succeed in preserving Lebanese unity and concord as well as the old order, grounded in the traditions of the past, has so far been able to do.

FOREIGN RELATIONS 1953-56

In the period 1953-56 financial and economic relations with Syria remained on a provisional basis much the same as that which had prevailed in the years 1950-53, earlier short-term arrangements being renewed from time to time, as need arose. Discussions with Syria in November 1953 over problems of currency, loan policy, banks and exchange difficulties made no effective progress. The Lebanese Government was more successful, however, in its efforts to promote internal development. It was announced in August 1955 that the International Bank had granted to the Lebanon a loan of 27 million dollars for the Litani river scheme which, when completed, was expected to more than double the electric power available within the republic and also to irrigate a large acreage in the coastal region. The Lebanon signed a number of commercial treaties at this time, which bore witness to the growing penetration of Soviet influence into the Arab lands: with Russia itself in April 1954, with Eastern Germany in November 1955, with Communist China in December 1955 and with Poland in January 1956.

At the Asian-African conference held at Bandung in April 1955 the Lebanese delegates expressed themselves in terms unfavourable to Communism. Since that time the Beirut government has not allowed its relations with Russia and her allies to pass beyond the limits of normal commercial intercourse. In regard to the Baghdad Pact, concluded between Iraq and the Turkish Republic in February 1955, the Lebanon adopted a neutral attitude. When, in March 1955, Egypt, supported by Saudi Arabia and (although with some hesitation) by Syria, attempted to form an alliance of Arab states from which Iraq was to be excluded, the Lebanese Government declined to enter into the proposed scheme, but also assured Cairo that it did not intend to join the Baghdad Pact. Its efforts were in fact directed, and not unsuccessfully, towards allaying, at least for the immediate future, the sharp tension then existing between Egypt and Iraq. Moreover, as the visit of President Chamoun to Ankara at the end of March, and the return visit of President Bayar to Beirut in June revealed, the Lebanon, while anxious not to compromise the cause of Arab unity, saw no reason to avoid diplomatic endeavours which might bring about more amicable relations between the Turkish Republic and the Arab world.

In the winter of 1955/56 the Lebanon discussed with Syria the possibilities of a defence pact between the two countries. The talks were broken off, however, in January 1956. The Lebanon wanted the proposed agreement to be local in its scope, whereas Syria desired it to have wider international implications. Moreover, the Lebanese Government insisted on direct control of such Syrian troops as might be sent into the Lebanon in case of need and on the stipulation that the pact itself should be operative only in time of war. The Foreign Minister of the Lebanon visited Saudi Arabia in February. The two states reaffirmed their decision not to join the Baghdad Pact and also resolved to work for a solution of the Palestine problem and for the furtherance of Arab unity and progress. In the same month a Soviet technical mission arrived at Beirut; its role was stated, however, to be purely consultative in character. The Foreign Minister of the U.S.S.R. came to the Lebanon in June. According to reports issued at the time, his visit led to an exchange of views and to an offer of Soviet economic assistance to the Lebanon. It was announced, also in June, that the U.S.A. had decided to furnish the Lebanon with financial aid, amounting to 3,670,000 dollars, for the improvement of the international airport at Beirut and of communications between the Lebanon and Syria.

The Lebanese Government had entered into negotiation with the Iraq Petroleum Co. in regard to an increase of the royalties paid on oil passing through the Lebanon to the Mediterranean coast. No agreement could be reached, however, and the talks were broken off in January 1956, an event which led Iraq to offer her mediation in the dispute. The Iraq Petroleum Co. stated that, in the circumstances, it might not be able to continue with its plans for increasing the flow of oil to Lebanese ports. A renewed offer of mediation came from Baghdad in April, but achieved no effective result. The Lebanon now passed a law imposing taxes, retrospective to the beginning of 1952, on oil companies which operated pipelines through her territories. Although the Lebanese Government expressed its readiness to resume negotiations, the Iraq Petroleum Co. stated in October that its decision to build a new pipeline to the Syrian port of Baniyas instead of to the Lebanese port of Tripoli was final.

THE EISENHOWER DOCTRINE

A state of emergency was declared in the Lebanon during the Sinai-Suez crisis at the end of October 1956. The Chamber of Deputies announced its support of Egypt, but the Lebanon did not break off diplomatic relations with Great Britain and France. In November there were disturbances, however, at Tripoli and Beirut against the attitude of the Government. Reports issued at this time intimated that the Egyptian military attaché at Beirut had been implicated in the recent disorders. The "Eisenhower Doctrine", a new programme, made known in January 1957, of financial, economic and military aid by the United States to those countries of the Middle East which were prepared to accept it, evoked a favourable response in Lebanese official circles. The Foreign Minister of the Lebanon declared that the government was willing to collaborate closely with the U.S.A. in the implementation of the programme. During the visit to Beirut in March of Mr. Richards, special adviser to President Eisenhower on Middle Eastern affairs, it was announced that the Lebanon would co-operate with the United States in the task of opposing the growth of Communist influence in the area and would receive, under the new programme, assistance to the amount of some 20 million dollars. The United States was also to help in the strengthening of the Lebanese armed forces. Some of the political groups in the Lebanon protested against this pro-Western alignment, asserting that it could not fail to isolate the Lebanon from the other Arab states and thus impair Arab solidarity. None the less, in April, the government obtained from the Chamber of Deputies a vote of confidence in its policies.

The problem of electoral reform had been under consideration in the Lebanon in the course of 1956. The main proposal now to be given effect was that the number of seats in the Chamber of Deputies should be raised from 44 to 66. As election time drew near in the summer of 1957, riots occurred at Beirut, the government being compelled to call out troops for the maintenance of order. According to reports current at this time more than one hundred

Communists were arrested for their share in the disturbances. The tense electoral campaign of June 1957 was fought out between two blocs, the one supporting the government, the other opposing it in the form of a United National Front. When the election results were made known, it became clear that the government had won a marked triumph. A first provisional estimate suggested that it might count on the adherence of some three-quarters of the deputies in the new Chamber. Of the sum-total of 66 seats the Maronites now received 20, the Sunni Muslims 14, the Shi'i Muslims 12, the Greek Orthodox Christians 7, the Druses 4, the Greek Catholics 4, the Orthodox Armenians 3, the Armenian Catholics 1 and the other religious minorities (Protestants, Jews, etc.) also 1 seat.

It was announced in July 1957 that the Lebanon would receive from the United States, under the Eisenhower Doctrine, economic and military aid to the value of approximately 15 million dollars in the course of the fiscal year 1958. Military equipment granted under the Doctrine had in fact begun to reach Beirut in June 1957. The Lebanese Government reiterated in August 1957 its firm desire to continue co-operation with the United States. In October, the King of Saudi Arabia and, in December, the Shah of Iran, visited Beirut, communiqués being issued, of which the first pledged Saudi Arabia and the Lebanon to support of the Arab cause, while the second gave assurances that both Iran and the Lebanon would work for peace in the Middle East.

There had been sharp disturbances in the Lebanon at the time of the elections held in June 1957. It became clear that unrest, especially amongst those elements of the population which opposed the pro-Western policies of the Lebanese Government and favoured an alignment with Egypt and Syria, was in no wise dead, when further incidents (bomb outrages, assassinations) occurred in November 1957. The government, in its desire to halt these subversive activities, now imposed a close control over all Palestine refugees in the Lebanon. Indeed, after renewed outbreaks of violence in December, the northern area of the Lebanon was declared to be a military sector. It was also announced in January 1958 that a national guard would be formed for the protection of important installations.

The Lebanese Government stated in March 1958 that it would not join the United Arab Republic (Egypt and Syria), the Arab Federation (Iraq and Jordan) or indeed any association which might limit its own independence and sovereignty. Large sections of the Muslim population, both in the north (at Tripoli) and in the south (at Tyre and Sidon), were inclined to be pro-Arab rather than pro-Lebanese in sentiment—a mood greatly stimulated by the emergence of the new United Arab Republic and by the propaganda emitted from Cairo and Damascus for the return to Syria of those predominantly Muslim areas which had been joined to the old Lebanon in the time of the French Mandate. There was conflict, too, between those who, although reluctant to see the Lebanon lose its separate political existence, were none the less strongly opposed to the pro-Western attitude of the Lebanese Government and those who, fearing the possible absorption of the Lebanon into the framework of a larger Arab state, felt themselves bound to support fully the policies of the Beirut régime. The danger was real that these complex tensions might explode in the form of a "confessional" conflict between Muslims and Christians, in which, if not the continued independence, then at least the entire political orientation of the Lebanon would be at stake.

THE CRISIS OF 1958

A reorganization of the government, carried out in March 1958 and designed to remove certain members who were critical of the pro-Western policies of the Lebanon and favoured closer co-operation with the United Arab Republic, brought no relief to the grave situation then developing. Serious disturbances, originating in Tripoli and the northern areas adjacent to the Syrian border, broke out in the second week of May and spread rapidly to Beirut and also to Tyre and Sidon in the southern Lebanon. The Druse population in the south-east was involved, too, in the disorders, being sharply divided into pro- and anti-government factions. Hostile demonstrations led to the destruction of the United States Information Service centres at Tripoli and Beirut. At the request of the Lebanese Government, the United States agreed to dispatch in all haste supplies of arms and police equipment and decided at the same time to reinforce the American 6th Fleet stationed in the Mediterranean. The U.S.S.R. now accused the United States of interference in Lebanese affairs and declared that Western intervention might have grave consequences. The Lebanese Government itself charged the United Arab Republic with interference in its internal affairs and appealed for redress to the Arab League which, meeting at Benghazi in June, failed to agree on a course of action. The problem was now brought before the United Nations which resolved to send an Observer Corps to the Lebanon. The Secretary General of U.N.O., Dr. Hammarskjöld, also visited the Middle East, conferring both with leaders in the Lebanon and with President Nasser at Cairo.

The Lebanese Government was now, in fact, confronted with a widespread insurrection, in which the Muslim elements in the population were ranged against the Christian elements. The forces opposed to the existing régime controlled parts of Beirut, Tripoli and Sidon, as well as large areas in the north and the south of the Lebanon. Attempts to negotiate a settlement led to no favourable result. The Prime Minister, Sami al-Sulh, gave an assurance that President Chamoun did not intend to ask for a constitutional amendment which would enable him to seek re-election to his office in September 1958, the date when his present tenure of it was due to end. To this assurance the leaders of the insurrection replied with a firm demand for the immediate resignation of the President, who made it clear, however, that he would not relinquish his office until September.

On July 14th—the date of the *coup d'état* which led to a change of régime in Iraq—President Chamoun requested the United States to send American troops into the Lebanon with a view to the maintenance of security and the preservation of Lebanese independence. By July 20th, some 10,000 men of the United States forces were stationed in and around Beirut. Meanwhile, Mr. Robert Murphy of the American State Department had come to the Lebanon with the aim of discussing the situation with leaders of both sides in the conflict. The United States also made it known that action on the part of forces under the control on the United Arab Republic against American troops in the Lebanon might lead to most serious consequences. At this juncture, the U.S.S.R. and the Chinese People's Republic made strong protests against the American intervention and asked for the prompt withdrawal of the United States forces landed in the Lebanon. In August 1958, the General Assembly of the United Nations met to discuss the problem. On August 18th, the United States gave a written undertaking to withdraw its troops, either at the request of the Lebanese Government, or in the event that the United Nations took appropriate measures to ensure the integrity and peace of the country. The General Assembly thereupon adopted a resolution, framed by its Arab members, which provided for the evacuation of American troops under the auspices of the United Nations and of the Arab League.

LEBANON—(HISTORY)

PRESIDENT CHEHAB, 1958-64

Meanwhile, the Lebanese Chamber of Deputies had, on July 31st, elected as the new President of State General Fuad Chehab, the Commander-in-Chief of the Lebanese Army—a choice supported by members from both sides involved in the internal conflict. He assumed office on September 23rd, in succession to President Chamoun and at once invited Rashid Karami, the leader of the insurgents at Tripoli, to become Prime Minister. An agreement was made on September 27th to the effect that the United States forces were to leave the Lebanon by the end of October.

It seemed for a time, however, that a new period of violence was about to begin. There was much resentment amongst the Christian elements of the population and, above all, the adherents of the former régime, that General Chehab should have chosen one of the most notable leaders in the insurrection as Prime Minister. On September 25th, the National Liberal, Falangist and National Bloc parties formed around ex-President Chamoun a united opposition, with a view to refusing the new government a vote of confidence. At the end of September and in the beginning of October, spasmodic clashes occurred at Beirut and Tripoli. The danger of a fresh conflict, with the roles of the former opponents now reversed, was in the end avoided through the formation, on October 15th, of a new Cabinet representing in equal proportions the two sides in the recent conflict. Of the four ministers who constituted this Cabinet, two were Muslim and two were Christian. On October 17th, the Chamber of Deputies gave a vote of confidence to the Prime Minister, Rashid Karami, and the three other members of the Cabinet.

In October 1959 the Lebanese Cabinet was increased from four to eight members, so that greater representation might be given to the various political groups. The Chamber of Deputies approved in April 1960 an Electoral Reform Bill, which imposed for the first time the principle of the secret ballot in Lebanese elections and also enlarged the Chamber itself from 66 to 99 deputies—a total figure that maintained the existing ratio (laid down in 1943) of six Christian to every five Muslim (including Druse) deputies in the Chamber. The Chamber was dissolved by the President of the Lebanon on May 5th, 1960, the government of Mr. Rashid Karami resigning nine days later. A general election was then held in four separate stages on June 12th, 19th and 26th and July 3rd, 1960.

The election took place in an atmosphere of complete calm, strict security measures being enforced throughout the various stages of the electoral process. In the new Chamber of Deputies there were 30 Maronite Christians, 20 Sunni Muslims, 19 Shi'i Muslims, 11 Greek Orthodox Christians, 6 Greek Catholics, 6 Druses, 4 Armenian Orthodox Christians, 1 Armenian Catholic, 1 Protestant and 1 member representing other elements. A large number of the "rebel" personalities prominent in the events of 1958 and hitherto not seated in the Chamber were now returned as members. Of the Deputies who had formed the previous Chamber 31 (out of 66) retained their seats. Some of the traditional "feudal" notabilities also recovered their places in the Chamber.

President Chehab announced on July 20th, 1960, that he intended to resign his office. He was persuaded, however, to reverse his decision. A new government, under the leadership of Mr. Saeb Salam, took the oath of office on August 2nd, 1960. The Cabinet, which included several personalities active on one side or the other in the troubles of 1958, was prompt to reaffirm the traditional policies of non-expropriation, of minimal government intervention in private enterprise, of encouragement for private investment both foreign and domestic, and of currency convertibility. Economic trends during 1960 revealed that the Lebanon had recovered almost completely from the effect of the disturbances in 1958. One adverse development of considerable importance involved the Litani River project, work on which, begun in 1959, came to a standstill as a result of major technical difficulties. A French firm was invited in December 1960 to re-examine the Litani scheme, to analyse the existing situation and to prepare a plan of future action.

The Lebanon, during 1961, had to face complaints from the United Arab Republic to the effect that some of the numerous exiles who had fled from Syria, between 1949 and 1958, to find refuge in the Lebanon were serving, as volunteers and as mercenaries, in guerrilla and sabotage attacks emanating from Jordan against Syria—the tension between these two states during the first three months of the year was indeed rather acute. The U.A.R. made a number of sharp protests against this exploitation of the Syrian exiles living in the Lebanon. To the Lebanese government, ever inclined to remain neutral in the face of inter-Arab disputes and anxious to ensure normal relations with Syria, involvement in the friction between Syria and Jordan was most unwelcome. A private meeting of Mr. Saeb Salam, Prime Minister of the Lebanon, with President Nasser of the U.A.R. at Damascus on March 5th, 1961, helped to ease the animosities of the preceding months.

CABINET REFORM

It had come to be felt, since August 1960, that the Lebanese Cabinet, 18 members strong, was too large for the maintenance of an efficient administration. Internal dissension, having weakened the Cabinet for some time past, brought about a crisis leading to the resignation of six ministers on May 9-10th, 1961. On May 22nd, the Prime Minister established a new Cabinet consisting of eight ministers only. Mr. Salam, as the result of a dispute with some members of his government, notable amongst them being Mr. Jumblatt, the Druse leader, who was Minister of Works and Planning, resigned his office on October 24th, 1961. Mr. Rashid Karami, a former Prime Minister, formed a new government on October 31st, 1961.

Military elements, acting in conjunction with civilians described as supporters of the extremist National Social Party, made an unsuccessful attempt, on December 31st, 1961, to overthrow the Lebanese government. The National Social Party was in fact the old Parti Populaire Syrien founded in the 1930s by Antoine Saadé with the aim of uniting several Arab States into a Greater Syria. Its present leader, Dr. Abdallah Saadé, was now arrested and the party itself dissolved by the Lebanese government on January 1st, 1962. The rebels, failing in their purpose, fled towards the Metn region in the hope of finding assistance there, the National Social Party having enjoyed considerable favour in that area. The Lebanese government took firm action against all the elements suspected of implication in the revolt. Military operations continued throughout the first days of January 1962. By January 10th, the rebellion was over save for a few remnants of rebel resistance still to be found in the Akkar and Hermel mountains.

EXTERNAL AGREEMENTS

In February 1962 the Lebanese Government entered into an agreement with the Tunisian Government envisaging co-operation between the two states in the fields of educational, cultural and technical assistance. During the remainder of 1962 the Lebanon entered into various agreements with the Egyptian half of the United Arab Republic, Niger, Cameroon, Guinea and Senegal. These agreements were mainly on technical and cultural co-operation.

The dispute, now six years old, over payments connected with the pipelines passing oil through the Lebanon to the Mediterranean coast was at last brought to an end. At Beirut in August 1962 a settlement was made between the Lebanese Government and the Trans-Arabian Pipeline Company (Tapline), an American organization. In return for facilities relating to the transit of oil, to the loading of the oil and to the security of the pipelines the Lebanon was to receive about $4,500,000 (as against $1,250,000 under earlier agreements). The new and higher rate of payment included a sum of $500,000 in lieu of supplies of oil at reduced prices which Tapline had undertaken to make available to the national oil refineries in Syria and Jordan— the Lebanon itself does not possess such oil refineries. Tapline also promised to pay the sum of $12,500,000 in settlement of all past claims made by the Lebanese Government. Of this latter amount $865,000, together with a portion of the new payments to be made to the Lebanon in respect of facilities for the loading of oil would be withheld until the full implications of a former agreement between the Lebanon and Syria had been made clear, such agreement having envisaged that whatever advantage the Lebanon might obtain in its relations with Tapline should be shared with Syria.

During the course of 1963 the government negotiated new economic and commercial agreements with Poland (April), the German Federal Republic (May), Sweden (October), and the U.S.S.R. (November). Syria and Lebanon agreed in September to ease restrictions in travel, employment, trade and finance between their respective territories and also reached an understanding in regard to their protracted dispute over the sharing of oil-transit dues. A brief period of sharp tension ensued, however, during the second half of October, as the result of a frontier clash between Syrian and Lebanese troops, which led to the death of several Lebanese soldiers. Syrian and Lebanese delegations met in January, 1964, to discuss questions relating to their common frontier and in particular the delimitation of certain areas hitherto not clearly demarcated.

On February 19th, 1964, the Cabinet led by Rashid Karami (which had held office for the last two years) resigned, after President Chehab had signed a decree dissolving the Chamber of Deputies (elected in 1960) and ordering elections to be held on four successive Sundays from April 5th, 1964 to May 3rd, 1964. A caretaker cabinet was appointed to supervise the elections for the new Chamber of Deputies.

PRESIDENT HÉLOU

General Chehab, whose six-year term of office as President of the Republic was due to end in September 1964, rejected all appeals that he should submit himself as a candidate for a second time. Even when the Chamber of Deputies passed a motion in favour of an amendment to the Constitution which would enable him to stand for a further term of office, General Chehab persisted (June 3rd, 1964) in his refusal. On August 18th, 1964, M. Charles Hélou, Minister of Education in the caretaker administration, succeeded General Chehab as President. M. Hélou pledged himself to follow the policies and reforms introduced under General Chehab.

On September 25th, 1964, Hussein Oweini, the Head of the caretaker Cabinet in office since February of that year, formed an administration at the request of President Helou. The new administration aroused dissatisfaction, however, in the Chamber of Deputies, since, deriving from the Cabinet appointed originally to act as a caretaker during the period of the 1964 elections, it was in fact composed wholly of non-members of the Chamber. Having resigned on November 13th, 1964, Oweini now, on November 18th, 1964, gathered together a new Cabinet which, save for himself and the Foreign Minister, consisted of members drawn from the Chamber of Deputies and reflected in itself all the main trends of opinion within the Chamber.

FOREIGN RELATIONS

On July 20th, 1965, the Prime Minister, Mr. Hussein Oweini, resigned. There had been much debate in the Chamber of Deputies about a proposed agreement to guarantee private American investment in the Lebanon against expropriation, war or revolution—an agreement construed in some political circles as giving to the United States a possible excuse for intervention, at need, in Lebanese affairs. Acrid discussion had also occurred in the Chamber over bills intended to bring about reforms in the judicial system and in the civil service. On July 26th, Rashid Karami became the new Prime Minister, with nine Cabinet Ministers to assist him, all chosen from outside the Chambers of Deputies.

There was friction during the first months of 1965 between Federal Germany and the Arab States because of the decision by Bonn to enter into formal diplomatic relations with Israel. Anti-German demonstrations occurred at Tripoli and Beirut and on May 13th, 1965 the Lebanon broke off diplomatic relations with Federal Germany. In May 1965 Lebanon signed an agreement on trade and technical co-operation with the European Economic Community (EEC). There was some friction between Israel and the Lebanon over border incidents during the summer and autumn of 1965. Members of the Palestinian guerrilla organization, al-Fatah, raided into Israel, provoking Israeli reprisals against the Lebanese village of Noule.

FINANCIAL CRISIS

Rashid Karami modified his cabinet in December 1965 and January 1966, these changes arising from difficulties which hindered the full implementation of an administrative and judicial reform programme, one of the main advocates of which was President Hélou. A number of senior judges had to accept a forced retirement in December 1965, and a similar fate overtook several ambassadors and senior diplomats in January 1966. By the end of March an estimated 150 officials including 100 civil servants had been compelled to withdraw from public life. This sustained attempt to curb corruption and the abuse of office in government circles and to ensure efficient and honest administration inevitably caused considerable tension. There was strong pressure in the Chamber of Deputies for a return to a cabinet chosen mainly from the Chamber itself. This and other difficulties obliged Karami to offer his resignation to President Hélou who appointed Dr. Abdallah al-Yafi as the new Premier.

Dr. al-Yafi assembled a ten-man Cabinet drawn entirely from the Chamber of Deputies with the exception of himself and M. Philippe Takla, the new Foreign Minister. The constitution of the cabinet represented a balance between the various religious interests and, from the point of view of politics, between the left-wing and right-wing elements in the Chamber of Deputies.

In October 1966 the Intra Bank of the Lebanon was compelled to close its doors because of a run of withdrawals amounting to more than £11 million in the preceding month. The Lebanese Cabinet, on October 16th, met to discuss methods of ensuring that the banks of the Lebanon had available adequate supplies of liquid cash. It also ordered all Lebanese banks to discontinue operations for a period of three days. Later in the same month the Cabinet decided to place before Parliament a bill seeking special powers which would enable the government to take measures of safeguarding of the interests of small depositors at the Intra Bank. A crisis of confidence was a serious affair for a state where banking activities are of the highest importance. The bill presented to the Parliament envisaged the establishment of an insurance company, jointly owned by the government and the banks, to guarantee small deposits. A special commission would supervise the activities of the banks in the Lebanon. A further result of that financial crisis was that the Government resolved to discourage the creation of new commercial banks, foreign or Lebanese, for a period of five years. Hitherto there had been an almost complete freedom to establish new banks in the Lebanon and there had been a large expansion of the banking system based on the flow into the Lebanon of vast oil revenues from Saudi Arabia and from the states of the Persian Arabian Gulf.

On December 2nd the Prime Minister of the Lebanon, Dr. Abdullah al-Yafi, offered the resignation of his government to President Hélou. Mr. Rashid Karami formed a new administration on December 7th, 1966. It was composed of men drawn from outside Parliament, six of whom held ministerial posts for the first time.

In April 1967 the Lebanon obtained an increase of more than 50 per cent in the royalties which it received from the Iraq Petroleum Company for the transit and loading of Iraq oil.

In June 1967 the Lebanese Government aligned itself with the Arab states then engaged in war against Israel. On June 8th the Government asked the Ambassadors of Britain and the U.S.A. to leave the Lebanon. Pro-Egyptian demonstrations at Beirut in June caused some damage to British and American properties there. Some trouble was also reported from Tripoli, where a West German cultural centre was subjected to attack. However, the months following the war witnessed a gradual easing of the tensions arising out of the conflict, and in September 1967 the Lebanese Cabinet agreed to reinstate its ambassadors in Washington and London.

POLITICAL INSTABILITY

Rashid Karami's Cabinet resigned from office in February 1968. President Hélou then asked Dr. Abdallah al-Yafi to form an interim administration, whose main task was to be the preparation and conduct of the general election in March 1968. The two most successful parties in the Chamber of Deputies elected were the Maronite-dominated Triple Alliance, of a right-wing complexion, and the Democratic Block aligned further to the left. However, Dr. al-Yafi's interim administration remained in office until October, when it was forced to resign, owing to bitter rivalry between the two main political groups, the "Chamounists" and the "Chebabists" (both named after former Presidents), disputes over sectional representation in the Cabinet, and the Government's inability to command a majority in the Chamber of Deputies. After a week of confusion, during which the President, Charles Hélou, offered his own resignation, a new four-man government was announced on October 20th, still headed by Dr. al-Yafi. The political situation remained fluid; in November the new ministry offered to resign, apparently over student unrest, but withdrew the offer the following day.

THE GUERRILLAS AND ISRAEL

May 1968 had seen the first clash between Lebanese and Israeli forces on the border for over two years. But as the activities of the Palestinian guerrillas increased, so the Lebanon became more and more the scapegoat for Israel's grievances against the Palestinians. On December 26th an Israeli airliner was machine-gunned by Arab guerrillas at Athens airport, causing two casualties (one fatal). Two days later Israeli commandos raided Beirut airport and destroyed thirteen aircraft, all belonging to Lebanese lines, without loss of life. Israel said the raid should be seen as a reprisal for the Athens attack, a warning to the Arab world not to make any repetition of it, and a further warning to the Lebanon to police the activities of the fedayeen movement in the country more effectively. The financial cost to the Lebanon was relatively small as most were insured abroad. The major after-effects of the raid were, firstly, the widespread criticism it attracted even from countries normally favourable to Israel. The Lebanon was seen as a country which had taken little active part in the campaign against Israel, while the *fedayeen* within it were only enjoying the freedom available to them in Lebanon's open, tolerant society. The UN Security Council unanimously condemned Israel for the raid. The second effect was the fall of the Government on January 7th, 1969, its alleged lack of preparedness for Israeli aggression being the final blow to bring down a weak administration. After much political manoeuvring, a new ministry was formed on January 20th headed by Mr. Rashid Karami, Prime Minister for the seventh time.

This government was immediately confronted with the basic problems underlying the Lebanese situation. Foremost amongst these is the Christian-Muslim balance; in theory both religions are equally represented in the Lebanon, but no census has been held since 1939 mainly because the authorities fear that the balance has shifted to a 60 per cent Muslim predominance, which would seriously affect the political situation. The Christian community has a disproportionate share of the wealth and important positions, and is the mainstay of the modest armed forces; it is generally conservative by Arab standards and takes a moderate position on the Israel question. The less privileged Arab majority is more in favour of both domestic reform (Lebanon has, for example, only the beginnings of a welfare state) and of a more militant position towards Israel. Early in 1969 numbers of Syrian guerrillas entered the country and apparently spent as much time in action against the Lebanese army as against Israel. Unrest also appeared amongst the 260,000 Palestinian refugees in the Sidon camp; part of the frontier with Syria was eventually closed. Numerous strikes and demonstrations continued. The Karami government felt unable to maintain the necessary coalition from the two communities and their various factions and resigned on April 25th, but it continued to function as a caretaker administration as no stronger government could be formed.

In the late summer of 1969 a number of guerrilla groups were reported to have moved to new bases better sited for attacks on Israel, which continued to raid these bases in reprisal; the combination of these factors created some friction between the guerrillas and the Lebanese army. In October the army apparently attacked some of these camps in an attempt to restrict or direct their activities. This triggered off a crisis that continued through the second half of October and threatened to develop into a full-scale civil war. The caretaker government resigned, claiming that it had not authorized the army's actions, and the President and the armed forces administered the country directly. Radical elements and guerrillas took over Tripoli, the second largest city, for several days, and most of the Palestinian refugee camps became fully converted into military training and equipment centres. Militant support for the guerrillas was voiced throughout the Arab world, and there were threats of military intervention by Syria and Iraq. Despite the tension, no extensive fighting occurred and there were few deaths.

On November 2nd the Lebanese Commander-in-Chief and Yassir Arafat, the leader of Al Fatah, signed a ceasefire agreement in Cairo. This limited the guerrilla freedom of movement to certain areas; as further defined in January 1970, it also provided that camps had to be set up some distance from towns, that military training must cease in refugee camps, and that guerrillas must enter Israel before starting to shoot. The intention was not to prevent guerrilla attacks, but to stop innocent Lebanese getting hurt, or their property being damaged, by Israeli counter-attacks.

The calmer atmosphere that followed the ceasefire enabled Mr. Karami to form another cabinet towards the end of November. There was much concern about the weakness of the country's southern defences, and in January 1970 the new ministry felt strong enough to fire the Commander-in-Chief, appointing instead Brigadier Jean Njeim. In March there was a series of street battles in the Beirut area between the Palestinian guerrillas and militant right wing Falangist groups, but the Government and the army managed to avoid becoming involved. In May Israel launched a major air and ground attack on guerrilla positions in southern Lebanon, a substantial area being occupied for nearly two days. Syria sent air assistance for the small Lebanese air force. The result of the raid was as usual disputed.

Throughout the remainder of 1970 and during 1971 and 1972 the Israelis continued to launch periodic attacks against guerrilla bases in the Lebanon, and the Lebanese continued to lodge their complaints with the UN, as in January 1971, when the Israelis struck deep into Lebanese territory. After July 1971 when the Jordanian Government eliminated the last of the guerrilla bases from its territory, the Lebanon's position in regard to Israel became even more vulnerable, for the Lebanon was now the only area where Palestinian guerrillas could operate freely. Fatah closed its office in Beirut in August, having decided to continue its activities underground, but Israel still held the Lebanese Government responsible for these activities. A four-day Israeli attack on Lebanon in February 1972 caused much damage and injury, and left Israeli units entrenched inside the Lebanese frontier. As in August 1970, the injuries to civilians provoked strong pressure from villages in the south of the Lebanon for the Government to exercise greater control over the guerrillas. In March 1972 this pressure secured the positioning of Lebanese army units in the vulnerable areas and the restriction of guerrillas to the woods, away from the villages.

Far more serious Israeli reprisals followed the attack at Lydda airport on May 30th, 1972, by three Japanese members of the PFLP, who killed 25 passengers and wounded 78. The remoteness of the connection with the Lebanon of the attackers did not prevent Israel from holding that state responsible in the UN Security Council the next day. The expected Israeli military counter-attack soon followed, but with more than usual ferocity: 36 Lebanese civilians were killed and 80 wounded, and 30 guerrillas killed and 50 wounded in land and air attacks around Hasbaya; earlier five Syrian officers travelling with the Lebanese army in the Lebanon well away from the fighting were kidnapped by the Israelis. On June 26th the UN Security Council condemned "the repeated attacks of Israeli forces on Lebanese territory and population", called for an end to the attacks, and demanded measures leading to the release of the captured officers.

The election of Sulaiman Franjiya as President in August 1970 and the formation of a new cabinet, by Saeb Salam, from outside Parliament in October changed noticeably little. The ban on extremist parties (the Lebanese Communist Party, Parti Populaire Syrien, pro-Iraq Baath Party, etc.) was rescinded in October. Censorship of press, radio and television was also lifted in October, but was reimposed on television in the following April. Relations with Iraq were strengthened, necessitating consultations with Syria, whose Baath Party is at loggerheads with its Iraqi counterpart. The spring of 1971 brought evidence of domestic unrest. On top of the activities of the Palestine commandos (including their infighting), there was fighting between the Falangists and the Parti Populaire Syrien, extensive student strikes and widespread dissatisfaction, especially in Tripoli, with the high unemployment rate and cost of living. Extensive security measures were taken for the visit in May of American Secretary of State, William Rogers, in order that Beirut should present as calm an appearance as possible. In the parliamentary elections held in three stages in April 1972, not only was there a discernible left-wing swing but also nearly half of the 99 deputies in the Chamber failed to achieve re-election.

The killing of 11 Israeli athletes by Arab terrorists at the Munich Olympic Games in September 1972 provoked heavy air attacks by the Israel Air Force against guerrilla bases in the Lebanon. This was later followed by further raids into Lebanese territory against the guerrillas by Israeli ground forces in which the Lebanese army admitted to losing 61 men. The Lebanese Government then attempted to persuade the guerrillas to suspend their activities across the southern border with Israel, although their failure to do so resulted in clashes between Lebanese regular troops and the guerrillas in December.

In February 1973 Israeli commandoes penetrated 100 miles into the Lebanon in an action against two Palestinian Arab guerrilla training bases, and in April Israeli troops in civilian dress raided Beirut and shot dead three top-ranking guerrilla leaders. Later in April two oil-storage tanks at the Zahrani (Sidon) terminal of the Trans-Arabian Pipeline Co. were blown up, but on this occasion it was not thought to be the work of the Israelis but of a dissident Palestinian commando group—the Lebanese Revolutionary Guard.

The Israeli raid on Beirut resulted in the resignation of Saeb Salam's government three days later (April 13th), and on April 18th Dr. Amin Hafez undertook to form a new Government. The new Government was formed a week later and within the following week fierce fighting developed between the Lebanese army and the Palestinian guerrillas. It had become evident that the Lebanese Government could no longer tolerate the presence of "an army of occupation", as they put it. After considerable fighting, in the course of which Dr. Hafez resigned and was persuaded to remain as Prime Minister, an agreement was eventually reached between the guerrillas and the Lebanese Government, although no details have been made public. On June 14th Dr. Hafez resigned for a second time, on this occasion because of a crisis concerning the partnership or effective participation in the government of Sunni Muslims.

On June 21st President Franjiya asked Mr. Takieddin Solh, a prominent Muslim politician from Beirut, to form a new Government. The new Government was finally formed on July 8th. The delay was caused because of conflict between right- and left-wing parties over the allocation of the Ministry of the Interior.

ECONOMIC SURVEY

The area of the Lebanon is 10,400 square kilometres. Before independence after the war, the Lebanon formed a part, with Syria, of a much larger economic unit that had already established itself. After the two countries decided in March 1950 to dissolve the economic partnership by which they were bound together, there were few who would have believed that the Lebanon, divorced as she was from the Syrian hinterland, could survive as an economic unit. In the event, not only did the Lebanon manage to survive, but within a few years Beirut had made itself the commercial and financial capital of the Middle East.

According to estimates published by the IMF, the population of the Lebanon in mid-1971 was 2.87 million, almost equally divided between Muslims and Christians. Of the total population, just over a third live in the four big towns of Beirut, Tripoli, Sidon and Zahlé. Exactly how many refugees from Palestine are living in the Lebanon is not certain, but it is significant that between 1947 and 1960 the population of the country increased by over a third, while the natural rate of increase was believed to have been in the region of 2 per cent per annum.

The total labour force in the Lebanon stood at 572,000 in November 1970, according to a survey carried out by the Ministry of Planning. The survey showed that those actually employed at the time were 538,000, leaving 32,000, or 6 per cent, unemployed. Of the total employed, 55 per cent were working in the services sector, including government administration, 18.9 per cent were working in agriculture and 17.7 per cent in industry. Of the total labour force, 364,620 or 63.8 per cent were either illiterate or had not completed primary education and they did not form a disproportionate number of the unemployed. The survey, however, did not take into account the large number of immigrant workers—mainly Palestinian refugees and Syrian expatriates—whose number is estimated at at least 100,000.

Of the total area of the country, just over half (52 per cent) consists of mountain, swamp or desert, and a further 7 per cent of forest. Only 23 per cent of the area is cultivated, but there is a further 17 per cent which it is considered could be cultivated given suitable conditions. The coastal strip enjoys a Mediterranean climate and is exceedingly fertile, producing mainly olives, citrus fruits and bananas. Many of the steep valleys leading up from the coastal plain are carefully terraced and very productive in olives and soft fruit, especially mulberries, and in the Zahlé and Shtaura regions there are well-known vineyards. Cotton, in particular, and onions are grown in the hinterland of Tripoli. The main cereal-growing district is the Bekaa, the fertile valley between the Lebanon and the Anti-Lebanon ranges. In the north of this valley is the source of the river Orontes. The river Litani also flows southwards through the Bekaa before it turns west near Merjayoun to flow into the Mediterranean just north of Tyre. This valley is particularly fertile, and cotton is now grown there with some success. Throughout the country the size of the average holding is exceedingly small and, even so, a smallholding, particularly in the mountains, may be broken up into several fragments separated from each other by a considerable distance.

AGRICULTURE

The country's principal grain crop is wheat, which in good years reaches 70,000 tons, but in bad years can fall to 40,000 tons. The 1971 yield was 50,000 tons. The only other important cereal crop is barley which rarely exceeds about 30,000 tons in a good year, and which in 1970 was very small indeed. Thus the country is far from being self-supporting in cereals, and grain and flour continue to constitute one of the most important items which the Lebanon has to buy from abroad. It is also in this respect especially that the Lebanon has suffered from the economic divorce which has separated her from Syria, for in most years Syria has an exportable surplus of cereals.

Lebanon's production of fruit is almost more important to her economy than that of grain. Production has increased substantially over the last two decades and the citrus crop has risen from an annual average in the years 1948–52 of 75,000 tons to 280,000 tons in 1971. There was a rush to plant apple trees in the 1950s but overproduction and lower prices have led to a reduction in output, and production fell from about 163,000 tons in 1968 to 90,000 tons in 1970, rising again to about 100,000 tons in 1971. The production of fresh grapes has flourished in recent years, and in 1969 amounted to 77,000 tons. That of figs amounts to about 15,000 tons a year, but bananas constitute perhaps a more important cash crop, production having increased from an annual average of 16,000 tons during the years 1948–52 to 29,000 tons in 1969. Much progress has recently been made in the production of sugar beet, which reached 120,000 tons in 1970–71.

Other important vegetable crops are potatoes, onions, apples, pears and melons. Cotton and tobacco are also grown. The forests are well regulated, but have been greatly thinned by the ravages of the goat, as elsewhere in the region, and the number of the famous cedars of Lebanon has sadly diminished. Stock-raising is not so important in the Lebanon as elsewhere in the Middle East, but Lebanese dairy produce is now of excellent quality. There were about 84,000 head of cattle in the Lebanon in 1971. Seasonal migration from winter to summer pastures in the mountains and vice versa continues to be one of the chief characteristics of stock-raising in the Lebanon, as elsewhere in the Middle East.

Poultry production has recently become a major source of agricultural income and, although modern methods are used, more primitive handling methods are said to be the cause of an 18 per cent death rate for newly hatched chickens. A record 24.9 million chicks were hatched in 1971 but only about 18 million of these survived. Of the total, 15.8 million were set aside for flesh and 2.1 million for egg laying. Egg production in 1971 reached 576 million of which 309 million eggs were exported. The difficulties of chicken production are a good example of the problems facing producers in all sectors of the Lebanese economy where modern production techniques are imported but the lack of know-how renders these techniques less efficient.

INDUSTRY

The mineral wealth of the Lebanon does not appear to be great. There are deposits of bitumen near Hasbaya, but in spite of intensive prospecting, no oil has yet been found in commercial quantities. However, the Lebanon is of great importance to the oil industry of the Middle East because it is crossed by two highly important pipelines, that from the recently nationalized Kirkuk oil wells in Iraq to the Mediterranean at Tripoli, and Tapline which runs from Aramco's oilfields in Saudi Arabia to Sidon. There are two important refineries, one at the terminal of each of the pipelines, and the Lebanese and Saudi Governments have now agreed to co-operate in building a third refinery. Income received by the Government from royalties on the two pipelines were estimated at £L42.7 million and were expected to rise to £L64.5 million in 1972 following the conclusion of new agreements with both companies. But the nationalization by Iraq and Syria on June 1st, 1972, of IPC assets in their territories resulted in a reduction of Lebanese Government royalties from the IPC pipeline. A dispute with IPC resulted from the settlement of differences between Iraq and the company which gave Iraq the right to take over the IPC pipeline in Lebanon. The Lebanese Government took over both the pipeline and refinery in its territory under protest from IPC although the company continued to operate both. The Government crisis in mid-1973 left the dispute between Lebanon and the company unsettled but the refinery was generally expected to be handed back to IPC on terms which may leave the company as leaseholder but not owner of the refinery. A dispute with the American-owned Mediterranean Refining Company (Medreco) which processes Saudi crude, is still to be settled. Both refineries processed a total of 2,040,000 tons of crude oil in 1972, compared with 1,730,000 tons in 1967, reflecting increasing local demand. But a Lebanese-Saudi joint refinery project under discussion for several years was still to be implemented in mid-1973 although feasibility studies by two teams, one French and one American, had been completed by the beginning of the year.

Manufacturing industry has for many years been highly developed in the Lebanon compared with other states in the Middle East. Industrial investment rose by £L200 million in the three years 1970-72 to £L1,200 million and labour employed in industry had risen during the two years 1971 and 1972 by 30,000 to 100,000. The value of industrial production has also been rising steadily. It increased from £L1,059 million in 1964 to £L1,697 million in 1970 and the 1971 figure is estimated at about £L2,000 million. In 1970 industry contributed 13.6 per cent of the gross domestic product, coming second after trade (31.4 per cent) but ahead of agriculture (9.2 per cent). Industrial growth can best be measured by looking at industry's contribution to the G.D.P. This rose from £L410.6 million in 1964 to £L661.2 million in 1970, a 61 per cent increase. There are few large-scale industrial establishments, and the average capital of these does not exceed £L200,000, each employing an average of 20 workers. Individually owned enterprises are the majority (54 per cent). Partnerships account for 37 per cent of the total and companies with limited liability only 3 per cent. Mechanical industries account for 7 per cent of the total, food processing and yarn and textile firms 44 per cent and wood and furniture 29 per cent. The rest is divided among cement, ceramics, pharmaceutical and plastics industries. About 25 per cent of the industrial establishments are located in Beirut and 55 per cent in the Mount Lebanon region near Beirut. Raw materials are mainly imported. Imports by industrial establishments are estimated at about £L800 million a year, accounting for about 40 per cent of all imports. Semi-processed commodities account for 61 per cent of the imports by these establishments, raw materials account for 24 per cent and machinery and equipment 15 per cent. Industrial exports reached £L337.5 million in 1972. In 1971 when they stood at £L262.8 million, they represented 26.6 per cent of total exports. The value of industrial exports stood at only £L46 million in 1964 and they had therefore increased more than fivefold in eight years.

Perhaps one indication of economic growth is the production and consumption of electric power. Production reached 1,548 million kWh. in 1972, registering a 12.6 per cent increase over the previous year. This compares with a total production of only 288 million in 1962. The lack of adequate sources of power had hindered the development of industry in the 1960s, but with constantly increasing production, Lebanon now has excess capacity and in 1972 started supplying power through a 100 million kWh. line to southern Syria, and was proposing to set up a similar line to supply central Syria.

With the exception of the oil companies, the largest industrial employers are probably the food-processing industries, including sugar refineries and biscuit and confectionery factories. These are followed by the well developed textile industries, but perhaps more important is the cement industry whose average monthly production has risen from 21,900 tons in 1951 to 126,580 tons in 1971. The Government is exerting increasing efforts towards promoting industrial expansion and in March 1972, in a measure similar to one of 1954, all industries created between 1971 and 1976 were exempted from income tax for six years. Industries created before 1971 were to benefit from a partial tax holiday if they expanded their activities before the end of 1975. The Government has also been inviting foreign capital to participate in industrial development and, with the help of the United Nations Industrial Development Organization (UNIDO), organized contacts between Lebanese and foreign investors in June 1972 with the aim of securing $14.7 million foreign participation in 46 projects requiring a total investment of $48.5 million. The Government has also created a new bank to finance industrial expansion, the National Bank for the Development of Industry and Tourism, with a capital of £L60 million of which 51 per cent is subscribed by the state.

EXTERNAL TRADE

Lebanon has suffered from an adverse balance of visible trade for many years, the ratio between the value of imports and of exports now being between three and four to one. There has been a remarkable expansion of external trade since the 1950s. The value of imports increased from £L298.4 million in 1951 to £L2,452 million in 1971 and that of exports from £L89.7 million in 1951 to £L815.6 million in 1971, about a tenfold increase in both cases. These figures do not include re-exports, worth £L176 million in 1971, nor the highly important transit trade through the free port of Beirut to Syria, Jordan, Iraq, Saudi Arabia and the Gulf States which is estimated to have contributed £L275.1 million to the Lebanese balance of payments in 1969, a net gain exceeding in real terms the contributions of both exports and re-exports.

The principal articles of export are fruit and vegetables, and the total value of Lebanon's exports of citrus fruit, bananas, apples, pears and fresh vegetables accounted for over 13 per cent of total exports in 1971 with much of the fruit and vegetables flown to the large communities working in the oilfields of the Gulf States. Among the other important exports are precious stones, metals and coins, mineral products, electrical goods, textiles, beverages and tobacco, transport equipment, base metals and their products and chemical and pharmaceutical products. Reflecting Lebanon's strategic position as a centre of transport and communications, the country's second largest export outlet is supplies of ships and planes. These accounted for 12.2 per cent of exports in 1971. The most important import by far now is precious stones and metals which are worked and re-exported to other parts of the Middle East, Asia and Africa. These accounted for 12.1 per cent of imports in 1971. They were followed by electrical equipment and machinery (11.2 per cent), textiles (11.1 per cent), vegetable products (9.7 per cent), base metals and their products (7.8 per cent), transport equipment and mineral products (7.6 per cent each) beverages and tobacco (6.1 per cent) and livestock and animal products (4.8 per cent). A Ministry of Planning survey has shown that increasing industrialization is gradually changing the structure of Lebanese imports. Consumer goods accounted for 36.8 per cent of imports in 1965 but only 32 per cent in 1971. Capital goods, however, increased their share of imports from 11.2 per cent in 1965 to 14 per cent in 1971 and goods imported for processing increased their share from 47.6 per cent in 1965 to 54 per cent in 1971.

In 1971 some 60 per cent of Lebanon's exports went to the Arab countries, about 14 per cent going to Saudi Arabia alone. Western Europe took 13 per cent of exports, Eastern Europe 5 per cent and the Americas 4 per cent. Lebanon's leading suppliers in the same year were France (10.5 per cent of total imports), the United States (10.4 per cent), West Germany (9.8 per cent), Switzerland (9.1 per cent), Britain (7.9 per cent) and Italy (7.7 per cent). Western Europe supplied more than half the requirements of the Lebanese market in 1971, accounting for 55.8 per cent of total imports. This share was expected to increase with the signing of a preferential trade agreement with the European Economic Community in December 1972. Eastern Europe supplied 13.9 per cent of Lebanese imports in 1971, the Americas supplied 13 per cent and the Arab states 11.3 per cent.

The heavy adverse balance of visible trade is generally made good by the large net invisible exports which the Lebanon's position as the chief *entrepôt* and distributing centre of the Middle East has enabled her to earn, and by the remittances from the Lebanese overseas, of whom there are large numbers, especially in the United States, South America and West Africa. The latest balance of payments figures, relating to the year 1969, show an adverse visible balance of trade amounting to £L1,033.9 million, in addition to £L10 million in the deficit for the trade in non-monetary gold. But against this can be set the net earnings of tourism and travel (£L235.6 million), transport (£L175.3 million), interest and dividends (£L137.8 million), government expenditure (£L125.3 million) and other services, of which 50 per cent comes from the transit trade (£L 234.1 million). This brought the deficit on the goods and services account down to £L135.8 million, but the current account deficit was further reduced to £L50.8 million by an income of £L85 million from donations and transfers.

CURRENCY AND FINANCE

Gold and foreign exchange reserves, which amounted to U.S. $232 million at the end of 1964, steadily increased to U.S. $675 million at the end of 1972. The purchasing power of the currency remained relatively stable at the same time and the cost of living, up to 1971, was rising according to official figures by an annual average of 2.5 per cent only. The official index, however, showed a rise of 4.9 per cent in consumer prices in 1972 and labour leaders claim that the rise was nearer 7 per cent.

Nearly all dealings in the Lebanese pound in recent years have been at the "free" rate, and, although a "provisional legal parity" of £L3.08 was established with the U.S. dollar in 1965, in practice the Lebanese pound has depreciated against the dollar and averaged £L3.30 to the dollar early in 1970. But the dollar troubles during the last two years have meant an improvement in the value of Lebanese currency and the exchange rate stood at £L2.70 to the U.S. dollar in March 1973. The rate for sterling in the same month was £L6.70.

The importance of Beirut as the commercial and financial centre of the Middle East has derived from the almost complete absence of restriction on the free movement of goods and capital, and from the transference of the Middle Eastern headquarters of many foreign concerns from Cairo to Beirut after 1951. Moreover, large sums were being earned in the Gulf by Arabs who were seeking investment locally, especially in property, and for them Beirut was a convenient centre. There were at one time over eighty officially recognized banks established in Beirut, including branches or representatives of very many major international banks. Among them are the British Bank of the Middle East, The Eastern Bank, the Moscow Narodny Bank, and several leading German and American banks.

Early in 1966 the Government introduced new regulations governing the establishment of new banks (notably a minimum capital of £L3 million) and subjected the opening of additional branches to the consent of the central bank. The failure of the Intra Bank, the largest purely Lebanese bank, in 1966 resulted in a thorough reform of the banking system, and some smaller commercial banks of local origin were merged into larger concerns.

The stability of the Lebanese banking system had in 1972 and 1973 resulted in an embarrassingly large liquidity surplus, for deposits had risen from £L3,357 million in 1969 to £L5,138 million at the end of 1971 with no equivalent increase in investment opportunities inside the country. Another 12 per cent rise was recorded in 1972. Loans during 1969-71 rose from £L2,301 million to £L3,038 million but a 21 per cent increase in 1972 was considered a considerable improvement. This same banking stability had led to increasing confidence in the Lebanese pound as a relatively stable international currency and for the first time at the end of 1972 a Lebanese currency loan was granted to a foreign borrower by Lebanese banks. Lebanese currency foreign loans had reached £L162 million by June 1973 of which £L75 million was lent to the World Bank.

COMMUNICATIONS AND TOURISM

The growth in importance of Beirut as a centre for air communications has been remarkable. Civil aviation, which includes Beirut International Airport and the two national airlines, employed 8,210 persons in August 1971. The sector is estimated to have generated £L219 million in income in 1970 and that the value added to the balance of payments in that year by the operations of the civil aviation companies amounted to £L67 million. In addition the Lebanon has been successfully developed as the tourist centre of the Middle East. Many large modern hotels have been built in recent years and the invisible income the country has earned from tourism has been of great importance. The tourist trade has now fully recovered from the setback of the June 1967 war and the total number of visitors to Lebanon in 1971 reached 2,257,405, an increase of 34 per cent over the previous year. Income from tourism in 1971 has been estimated at £L580 million compared with £L430 million in 1970. The number of visitors increased only slightly in 1972 to 2,281,066, but one significant change was that whereas the total number of Arab tourists had declined, the number of visitors from Europe and the Americas had increased by about a quarter.

PUBLIC FINANCE AND DEVELOPMENT

The 1973 ordinary budget estimates put total expenditure for the first time above £L1,000 million at £L1,077 million, a rise of 9.9 per cent over the planned £L980 million budget for the previous year. Although the state has traditionally suffered from a budget deficit, a surplus of £L50 million was achieved in 1971 and another £L84 million recorded in 1972. Of the expenditure forecast for 1973, 22.9 per cent was to be spent on defence, 18.7 per cent on education, 15.4 per cent on public works and transport, 7.7 per cent on the Interior Ministry and 4.1 per cent on health.

Except in the refugee camps, where Arabs driven out of Palestine are maintained largely by UNRWA, the general standard of living in the Lebanon is higher than in most of the other Arab countries of the Middle East. According to the latest estimates, made available by IMF, the national income in 1970 was £L4,411 million, compared with £L2,861 million in 1964. Per capita national income, however, was rising at the slow rate of 0.5 per cent a year between 1960 and 1970 although at $590 in 1970 it was the highest in the Arab world outside the oil-rich states.

The Government has now worked out a six-year plan under which a total of £L7,200 million is to be spent, of which the public sector will contribute £L1,740 million. According to the plan outline published early in 1972, of the public sector allocations, 15.6 per cent is to be spent on developing municipal and co-operative services, 14.3 per cent on roads, 14.3 per cent on education, 11.6 per cent on irrigation and another 3.4 per cent on agriculture, 10.6 per cent on power, 8.8 per cent on communications, 5.8 per cent on airports and harbours, 4.2 per cent on public health and 2.6 per cent on industry. A separate £L200 million plan for the modernization and expansion of the armed forces was approved by parliament in 1971. The Government hopes that the plan will only increase the public debt by £L200 million to £L560 million. Parliament does not have to approve the plan as a whole, but separate allocations will have to be approved individually. The Government hopes that the plan will provide the necessary infrastructure for the development of industry, agriculture, tourism and transport and that the private sector will contribute actively to the success of the plan with the help of the newly created Development Bank and with participation from foreign investors.

STATISTICAL SURVEY

AREA AND POPULATION

AREA
(hectares)

Total	Cultivated	Irrigated	Marginal and Grazing	Forest	Waste
1,040,000	270,000	72,000	128,800	73,200	549,200

POPULATION

Total*	Beirut* (capital)	Tripoli*	Births (1972)	Marriages (1972)	Deaths (1972)
2,600,000	800,000	150,000	74,980	17,359	30,718†

* 1972 estimate.

† Large increase due to registration of hitherto unregistered deaths prior to 1972 parliamentary elections.

AGRICULTURE
PRINCIPAL CROPS

	Area ('000 hectares) 1969	Area 1970*	Area 1971*	Production ('000 tons) 1969	Production 1970*	Production 1971*	Yield (tons per hectare) 1971*
Wheat	43.2	60.0	60.0	33.0	50.0	50.0	0.8
Barley	8.3	9.0	10.0	7.8	8.0	10.0	1.0
Sugar Beet	2.2	2.0	2.5	94.0	94.0	120.0	48.0
Potatoes	9.0	8.0	9.0	86.6	75.0	85.0	9.4
Onions	1.9	2.0	n.a.	30.0	30.0	n.a.	n.a.
Tobacco	6.6	7.0	7.0	6.7	7.3	7.3	1.0
Citrus Fruit	11.3	n.a.	n.a.	208.5	270.0	285.0	n.a.
Apples	14.1	n.a.	n.a.	66.5	90.0	100.0	n.a.
Grapes	16.6	17.0	n.a.	76.6	80.0	n.a.	n.a.
Olives	27.7	n.a.	n.a.	46.3	20.0	n.a.	n.a.
Tomatoes	5.7	6.0	n.a.	70.0	75.0	n.a.	n.a.

* FAO estimates.

LIVESTOCK
('000)

	1968	1969	1970	1971
Goats	357	348	330	318
Sheep	200	213	214	218
Cattle	86	86	85	84
Donkeys	28	28	26	25
Poultry	16,538	17,463	17,800	n.a.

LEBANON—(STATISTICAL SURVEY)

INDUSTRY

	Unit	1969	1970	1971	1972
Tobacco Manufactures	tons	2,650	2,281	3,122	3,250
Refined Sugar	,,	31,613	—	—	—
Fertilizers	,,	52,870	—	—	—
Timber	cu. metres	46,342	46,545	48,793	57,748
Cement	'000 tons	1,252	1,339	1,499	1,626
Electricity	million kWh.	1,139	1,230	1,375	1,548

OIL REFINING
('000 tons)

	1966	1967	1968	1969	1970	1971	1972
Crude Oil intake	1,652	1,730	1,803	1,849	1,992	2,001	2,039
Petrol	310	303	347	347	374	397	446
Paraffin	154	180	190	207	212	218	155
Gas Oil	232	269	281	318	338	343	329
Fuel Oil	883	891	897	884	958	947	1,082
Butane	23	21	24	23	22	24	26

FINANCE

100 piastres = 1 Lebanese pound (£L).
Coins: 1, 2½, 5, 10, 25 and 50 piastres.
Notes: 1, 5, 10, 25, 50 and 100 pounds.
Exchange rates (March 1973): £1 sterling = £L6.70; U.S. $1 = £L2.70.
£L100 = £14.93 sterling = $37.04.

ORDINARY BUDGET ESTIMATES
(Expenditure 1972—million £L)

Defence	212.7
Education	172.0
Public Works and Transport	144.9
Ministry of the Interior	n.a.
Debt Servicing	n.a.
Hydro-electric Resources	n.a.
Total (including others)	980.0

1973 Budget: £L1,077 million.

EXTERNAL TRADE*
(£L'000)

	1966	1967	1968	1969	1970	1971
Imports	1,913,707	1,769,992	1,865,087	2,006,431	2,252,177	2,451,922
Exports	369,465	453,347	510,261	554,301	650,619	815,619
Transit Trade†	1,050,015	957,715	1,532,938	1,348,894	1,272,105	2,429,687

* Based on the rate of free market prices of the U.S. dollar.
† Through the free port of Beirut; includes crude oil pumped through the Lebanon.

LEBANON—(Statistical Survey)

PRINCIPAL COMMODITIES
(£L '000)

Imports	1970	1971
Precious Metals, Stones, Jewellery and Coins	432,947	304,584
Vegetable Products	234,795	237,959
Machinery and Electrical Apparatus	239,336	282,274
Textiles and Products	222,125	284,802
Non-precious Metals and Products	184,301	202,642
Transport Vehicles	129,115	170,396
Animals and Animal Products	126,264	122,916
Industrial Chemical Products	152,820	182,041
Mineral Products	129,112	139,487
Beverages and Tobacco	97,435	142,273

Exports*	1970	1971
Vegetable Products	99,459	121,598
Precious Metals, Stones, Jewellery and Coins	62,256	51,413
Animals and Animal Products	37,286	55,050
Machinery and Electrical Apparatus	65,701	98,702
Non-precious Metals and Products	53,288	80,230
Textiles and Products	57,247	79,527
Beverages and Tobacco	54,758	49,445
Transport Vehicles	48,290	57,997

* Including re-exports.

PRINCIPAL COUNTRIES
(£L '000)

Imports	1969	1970	1971
Belgium	38,930	44,216	54,773
Czechoslovakia	35,947	37,971	41,384
France	161,299	211,030	266,549
German Federal Rep.	187,131	197,630	264,295
Iraq	75,729	91,923	98,017
Italy	142,431	149,663	187,269
Japan	74,691	87,618	103,370
Jordan	18,683	19,560	13,895
Netherlands	43,603	42,495	56,897
Saudi Arabia	37,696	22,473	32,983
Switzerland	165,104	273,223	228,307
Syria	91,591	66,907	35,312
Turkey	22,393	33,787	56,574
United Kingdom	255,590	258,168	198,054
U.S.A.	180,407	223,990	250,408

Exports	1969	1970	1971
France	10,770	12,673	13,896
German Federal Rep.	7,578	9,413	13,496
Greece	3,060	2,593	2,083
Iraq	33,181	36,974	68,641
Italy	13,405	13,000	14,855
Jordan	36,328	37,022	37,843
Kuwait	60,729	79,528	88,690
Saudi Arabia	117,258	125,157	125,387
Spain	1,132	1,007	1,207
Syria	42,290	43,432	75,654
U.S.S.R.	7,592	11,159	9,404
United Kingdom	20,135	14,533	26,508
U.S.A.	22,102	24,261	23,164

TRANSPORT

RAILWAYS

	Passengers (Thousands) Number	Passengers (Thousands) Passenger-Kms.	Goods (Thousands) Tons	Goods (Thousands) Ton-Kms.	Revenue ('000 £L) Passengers	Revenue ('000 £L) Goods	Revenue ('000 £L) Total
1968	88	6,691	489	37,036	148	3,067	3,215
1969	78	7,278	313	24,455	178	2,018	2,196
1970	76	7,430	258	20,082	187	1,916	2,103
1971	71	7,187	325	26,789	184	2,236	2,420
1972	55	5,004	417	33,116	134	2,313	2,447

LEBANON—(Statistical Survey)

ROADS

	1968	1969	1970	1971	1972
Motor cars (taxis and private)	123,891	129,674	136,016	146,270	164,790
Buses	1,645	1,763	1,794	1,905	2,067
Lorries	13,404	14,473	14,795	15,656	17,130
Motor cycles	11,291	12,004	9,800	9,731	10,734

SHIPPING IN BEIRUT

	Ships Entered — Number	Ships Entered — Tonnage	Merchandise (Metric Tons) — Entered	Merchandise (Metric Tons) — Cleared
1968	2,879	4,146,000	1,916,000	654,000
1969	3,126	4,361,512	1,995,000	700,000
1970	3,128	4,428,491	2,289,321	728,144
1971	3,320	4,837,003	2,456,517	626,384
1972	3,586	6,197,000	2,665,000	678,000

TRAFFIC THROUGH THE INTERNATIONAL AIRPORT IN BEIRUT

	Aircraft Using Airport	Passengers Using Airport	Freight Through Airport (metric tons)
1968	41,082	1,512,599	51,238
1969	42,733	1,571,667	53,594
1970	41,553	1,558,246	57,691
1971	39,643	1,832,514	69,742
1972	38,735	2,090,634	87,991

TOURISM

	1969	1970	1971	1972
Total Foreign Visitors (except Syrians)	777,135	822,347	1,015,772	1,048,163
of which:				
Visitors from Arab countries	459,858	534,250	619,171	577,186
Visitors from Europe	172,462	149,518	213,698	250,914
Visitors from the Americas	76,964	67,190	94,076	116,153
Syrian Visitors	810,050	863,833	1,241,633	1,232,903
Total	1,587,185	1,686,180	2,257,405	2,281,066

EDUCATION
(1971–72)

	Number of Schools	Number of Pupils	Number of Teachers
Public Education:			
Primary, Kindergarten and Upper Primary	1,278	273,092	14,763
Secondary	39	10,531	1,618
Private Education:			
Primary and Kindergarten	} 1,501	{ 406,789	} 21,083
Upper Primary and Secondary		{ 90,032	

Source: Direction Centrale de la Statistique, Ministère du Plan, and Direction Générale des Douanes, Beirut.

THE CONSTITUTION

(Promulgated May 23rd, 1926; amended October 27th, 1927, May 8th, 1929, November 9th and December 7th, 1943.)

According to the Constitution, the Republic of the Lebanon is an independent and sovereign State, and no part of the territory may be alienated or ceded. Lebanon has no State religion. Arabic is the official language. Beirut is the capital.

All Lebanese are equal in the eyes of the law. Personal freedom and freedom of the Press are guaranteed and protected. The religious communities are entitled to maintain their own schools, provided they conform to the general requirements relating to public instruction as laid down by the State. Dwellings are inviolable; rights of ownership are protected by law. Every Lebanese citizen who has completed his twenty-first year is an elector and qualifies for the franchise.

Legislative Power

Legislative power is exercised by one house, the Chamber of Deputies, with 99 seats, 54 of which are allocated to Christians and 45 to Muslims (for full details of allocation, *see* Parliament, p. 469). Its members must be over 25 years of age, in possession of their full political and civil rights, and literate. They are considered representatives of the whole nation, and are not bound to follow directives from their constituencies. They can only be suspended by a two-thirds majority of their fellow-members. Secret ballot was introduced in a new election law of April 1960.

The Chamber holds two sessions yearly, from the first Tuesday after March 15th to the end of May, and from the first Tuesday after October 15th to the end of the year. The normal term of the Chamber of Deputies is four years; general elections take place within sixty days before the end of this period. If the Chamber is dissolved before the end of its term, elections are held within three months of dissolution.

Voting in the Chamber is public—by acclamation, or by standing and sitting. A quorum of two-thirds and a majority vote is required for constitutional issues. The only exceptions to this occur when the Chamber becomes an electoral college, and chooses the President of the Republic, or Secretaries to the Chamber, or when the President is accused of treason or of violating the Constitution. In such cases voting is secret, and a two-thirds majority is needed.

Executive Power

The President of the Republic is elected for a term of six years, and is not immediately re-eligible. He and his ministers deal with the promulgation and execution of laws passed by the Chamber of Deputies. The Ministers and the Prime Minister are chosen by the President of the Republic. They are not necessarily members of the Chamber of Deputies, although they are responsible to it and have access to its debates. The President of the Republic must be a Maronite Christian and the Prime Minister a Sunni Muslim; and the choice of the other Ministers has to reflect the division between the communities in the Chamber.

The President himself can initiate laws. Alternatively, the President may demand an additional debate on laws already passed by the Chamber. He can adjourn the Chamber for up to a month, but not more than once in each session. In exceptional circumstances he can dissolve the Chamber and force an election. Ministers can be made to resign by a vote of no confidence.

THE GOVERNMENT

HEAD OF STATE

President of the Republic: SULAIMAN FRANJIYA (took office September 23rd, 1970).

THE CABINET

(*August* 1973)

Prime Minister and Minister of Finance: TAKIEDDIN SOLH.
Minister of Foreign Affairs: FUAD NAFAA.
Deputy Prime Minister, Minister of Public Works and Transport: FUAD GHUSN.
Minister of Interior: BAHIJ TAKIEDDIN.
Minister of Defence: NASRI MAALOUF.
Minister of Economy and Trade: Dr. NAZIH BIZRI.
Minister of Health: OTHMAN DANA.
Minister of Information: FAHMI SHAHIN.
Minister of Social Affairs and Labour: EMILE ROUHANA SAQR.
Minister of Education: EDMOND RIZQ.

Minister of Posts and Communications: TONY FRANJIYA.
Minister of Agriculture: SABRI HAMADA.
Minister of Justice: KAZEM KHALIL.
Minister of Co-operatives and Housing: MICHEL SASSIN.
Minister of Tourism: SOUREN KHANAMERIAN.
Minister of Power and Hydroelectric Resources: JOSEPH SKAFF.
Minister of Oil and Industry: TAUFIQ ASSAF.
Minister of Planning: Dr. HASSAN RIFAI.
Ministers of State: MAJID ARSLAN, Dr. ALI KHALIL, JOSEPH SHADER, Dr. ALBERT MUKHAIBER.

In the Lebanon the President must be a Maronite and the Prime Minister a Sunni Muslim. The rest of the Cabinet represents other faiths.

LEBANON—(Diplomatic Representation)

DIPLOMATIC REPRESENTATION

EMBASSIES AND LEGATIONS ACCREDITED TO LEBANON (Beirut unless otherwise indicated)
(E) Embassy; (L) Legation.

Afghanistan: Rue Verdun, Imm. Belle-Vue (E).
Algeria: Jnah (opposite Coral Beach) (E); *Ambassador:* Muhammad Yazid.
Argentina: 149 Ave. Fouad 1er (E); *Ambassador:* Raúl A. Medina Muñoz.
Australia: Rue Mgr. Chébil et Kantari, Imm. Sfah (E); *Ambassador:* Peter Bruce Norman.
Austria: Quartier Sursock, Rue Négib Trad, Villa Nocolas Cattan (E); *Ambassador:* Dr. Walter R. Backes.
Belgium: 15th Floor, Centre Verdun, Rue Dunant (E); *Ambassador:* Le Comte de Lichterville.
Bolivia: Place de l'Etoile, Imm. Naffah (E).
Brazil: Rue Verdun, Imm. Mahmassani (E); *Ambassador:* Carlos da Ponte Ribeiro Eiras.
Bulgaria: Boulevard Chish-Hedoth, Imm. Lati (E); *Ambassador:* Vulko Shivaroff.
Cameroon: Cairo, Egypt (E).
Canada: Rue Hamra, Centre Sabbagh (E); *Ambassador:* Jacques Gignac.
Chad: Bid Solh, Forêt Kfoury, Imm. Kalot Frères (E); *Ambassador:* Maroun Haimari.
Chile: Rue Maamari, Imm. Lion's (E); *Ambassador:* Guillermo Ovalle Blanchet.
China, People's Republic: Rue 62, Nicolas Ibrahim Sursock, Ramlet El-Baida (E); *Ambassador:* Hsu Ming.
Colombia: Chouran, Imm. Jaber al-Ahmad al-Sabbah (E); *Ambassador:* Alberto Losada Larra.
Congo, People's Republic: Cairo, Egypt (E).
Costa Rica: Rue Hamra (E); *Chargé d'Affaires:* Riad Abdel-Baki.
Cuba: Rue Jnah, Imm. Sélim Abboud (E); *Ambassador:* Dr. Carlos E. Alfaras Varela.
Cyprus: Cairo, Egypt (E).
Czechoslovakia: Rue Fouad 1er, Imm. Kayssi (E); *Ambassador:* Dr. Karel Blazek.
Denmark: Rue Clemenceau, Imm. Minkara (E); *Ambassador:* Mogens Warberg.
Egypt: Rue Ramlat el-Baida (E); *Ambassador:* Ahmad Loutfi Moutawalli.
Ethiopia: Cairo, Egypt (E).
Finland: Centre Gefinor, Rue Clemenceau (E); *Ambassador:* Carolus Lassila.
France: Rue Clemenceau (E); *Ambassador:* Michel Raul Guillaume Fontaine.
German Democratic Republic: (E); *Ambassador:* Gerhard Herder.
German Federal Republic: Rue Hamra, Imm. Arida (E); *Ambassador:* Hans Christian Lankes.
Ghana: Jnah, Imm. Cheikh Sabah Ahmad Al-Sabah (E); *Chargé d'Affaires a.i.:* Joseph Kodjo Arthur.
Greece: Rue de France (E); *Chargé d'Affaires:* Spyridon Adamopoulos.
Guinea: Cairo, Egypt (E).
Haiti: Rue du Fleuve, Imm. Sarkis (E); *Ambassador:* Pierre Sarkis.

Hungary: Jnah, Imm. Cheikh Salem Al-Sabah (E); *Ambassador:* Janos Veres.
India: Rue Kantari, Imm. Samharini (E); *Ambassador:* A. S. Mehta.
Indonesia: Corniche Mazraa, Imm. Khaouam (E); *Ambassador:* Muhammad Sharif Padmadisastra.
Iran: Jnah, Imm. Sakina Mattar (E); *Ambassador:* Rokneddine Achtiany.
Iraq: Ramlat al-Baida, Imm. Ali Arab (E); *Ambassador:* Younes Hassan Al-Mosleh.
Italy: Rue Makdissi, Imm. Cosmidis (E); *Ambassador:* Cesare Regard.
Ivory Coast: Avenue Sami Solh, Imm. Georges Tazbek (E); *Ambassador:* Amadou Bocoum.
Japan: Corniche Chouran, Imm. Olfat Nagib Salha (E); *Ambassador:* Jiro Inagawa.
Jordan: Rue Verdun, Imm. Belle-Vue (E); *Ambassador:* Akram Zoaiter.
Kenya: Cairo, Egypt (E).
Kuwait: Bir Hassan, The Stadium Roundabout (E); *Ambassador:* Muhammad Youssef Al-Adassani.
Liberia: Rome, Italy (E).
Libya: Jnah, Imm. Cheikh Abdallah Khalifé Al-Sabbah (E); *Ambassador:* Ismail al-Siddiq Ismail.
Malaysia: Cairo, Egypt (E).
Mali: Cairo, Egypt (E).
Malta: Achrafié, Rue Marian Geahchan, Imm. Varkés Sarafian (L); *Minister:* Umberto Turati.
Mauritania: Cairo, Egypt (E).
Mexico: Rue Hamra, Imm. Arida (E); *Ambassador:* Dr. Francisco Apodaca.
Morocco: Corniche Masraa, Imm. Chamat (E); *Ambassador:* Ahmed Bensouda.
Nepal: Cairo, Egypt (E).
Netherlands: Rue Kantari, Imm. Sahmarani (E); *Ambassador:* Adrianus Cornelis Vroon.
Nigeria: Cairo, Egypt (E).
Norway: Cairo, Egypt (E).
Pakistan: 2699 Rue de Lyon (E); *Ambassador:* Dr. S. M. Koreshi.
Panama: address unavailable (L).
Peru: Cairo, Egypt (E).
Poland: Furn el-Chebbak, Rue Asile des Veillards, Imm. Haddad Frères (E); *Ambassador:* Dr. Tadeusz Wujek.
Portugal: Rue Beyhum, Villa Omar Beyham (E); *Ambassador:* Dr. Augusto Henrique de Almeida Coelho-Lopes.
Qatar: Dibs Building, Chouran Street (E); *Ambassador:* Muhammad ben Hamad al Thani.
Romania: Avenue Sami el-Solh, 215 Forêt Kfouri, Imm. Boutros et Chammah (E); *Ambassador:* Dr. Mihail Levente.

LEBANON—(Diplomatic Representation, Parliament, Political Parties)

Saudi Arabia: Rue Bliss, Manara (E); *Ambassador:* Sheikh Muhammad al-Mansour al-Rumaih.

Senegal: Corniche Mazraa, Rue Ibn el-Assir, Imm. Kholy el-Kataby (E); *Ambassador:* Alphonse N'Diaye.

Singapore: Cairo, Egypt (E).

Spain: Ramlet el Baida, Imm. White Sands (E); *Ambassador:* José Luis Florez-Estrada.

Sri Lanka: Cairo, Egypt (E).

Sudan: Rue Verdun, Imm. Mahmassani (E); *Ambassador:* Salah Ahmed.

Sweden: Rue Clemenceau, Imm. Moukarzel et Rubeiz (E); *Ambassador:* Ake A. Jonsson.

Switzerland: Avenue Perthuis, Imm. Achou (E); *Ambassador:* Charles-Albert Dubois.

Thailand: Rue Hamra, Sebbag Centre (E); *Ambassador:* Somchai Anuman-Rajadhon.

Tunisia: Ramlet el-Baida, Imm. Rock and Marble (E); *Ambassador:* Slaheddin Abdellah.

Turkey: Rue Bliss, Imm. Dr. Nassif (E); *Ambassador:* Necmettin Tunal.

U.S.S.R.: Rue Mar Elias el-Tina (E); *Ambassador:* Sarvar Azimov.

United Arab Emirates: Massabili & Serhal Bldg., Cairo Street (E); *Ambassador:* Said Ahmad el-Ghabbash.

United Kingdom: Avenue de Paris, Ain el-Mreissé (E); *Ambassador:* P. H. G. Wright, c.m.g., o.b.e.

United States of America: Avenue de Paris (Corniche), Imm. Ali Reza (E); *Ambassador:* William B. Buffum.

Uruguay: Rue John Kennedy (E); *Ambassador:* Rodolfo Comas Amaro.

Vatican: Rue Georges Picot; Apostolic Nuncio: Mgr. Alfredo Bruniera.

Venezuela: Rue Kantari, Imm. Sahmarani (E); *Ambassador:* Dr. Rafael Armando Rojas.

Viet-Nam, Republic of: (information unavailable).

Yemen, Arab Republic: Bld. Khaldé-Quzai, Imm. Ingénieur Ryad Amaiche (E); *Ambassador:* Ahmed Basha.

Yemen, People's Democratic Republic: Corniche Mazra, Imm. Najij (E); *Chargé d'Affaires a.i.:* Muhammad Nasser Muhammad.

Yugoslavia: Rue Chouran, Sakiet el-Janzir, Imm. Hindi (E); *Ambassador:* Milic Bugarcic.

Zaire: Cairo, Egypt (E).

Zambia: Cairo, Egypt (E).

Lebanon also has diplomatic relations with Central African Republic, Dahomey, Dominican Republic, Ecuador, El Salvador, Gabon, German Democratic Republic, Guatemala, Honduras, Ireland, Khmer Republic, Luxembourg, Madagascar, Monaco, Nicaragua, Niger, Paraguay, Philippines, Sierra Leone, South Africa, Togo, Upper Volta.

PARLIAMENT

CHAMBER OF DEPUTIES

The electoral reform bill of April 1960 maintained the existing ratio of 6 Christians to 5 Muslims in the Chamber of Deputies. It is the custom for the President of the Chamber of Deputies to be a Shi'i Muslim.

President of Chamber: Kamal Asaad.

Deputy President of Chamber: Nasim Majdalani.

Religious Groups

Maronite Christians	30
Sunni Muslims	20
Shi'i Muslims	19
Greek Orthodox	11
Greek Catholics	6
Druses	6
Armenian Orthodox	4
Armenian Catholics	1
Protestants	1
Others	1
Total	**99**

There was a General Election in May 1972, but the diversity of allegiance in the Chamber makes a strict analysis by party groupings impossible. The distribution of seats among religious groups is laid down by law.

POLITICAL PARTIES AND GROUPS

Baath Party: Beirut; Lebanese branch of Arab reformist party.

Constitutional Party (Destour): Leader Sheikh Michel el Khoury.

Democratic Socialist Party: southern Muslims; Leader Kamel al Assad.

Lebanese Communist Party: Beirut; legalized August 1970; Third Congress held in Beirut Jan. 1972 and attended by delegates from over 30 foreign Communist parties, as well as from the Baath parties of Iraq and Syria, the Egyptian Arab Socialist Union, the Kurdish Democratic Party and the Palestinian Liberation Movement; Sec.-Gen. Nicolas Chaoui.

Mouvement de l'Action Nationale: f. 1965; Leader Uthman Dana.

National Bloc: Leader Raymond Eddé.

National Liberal Party: Leader Camille Chamoun.

Organization of Communist Action in Lebanon: f. 1971.

Phalangist (Kata'eb) Party: Place Charles Hélou, P.O.B. 992, Beirut; f. 1936; democratic social party; 63,000 mems.; Leader Pierre Gemayel; Vice-Pres. Joseph Chader; Gen. Sec. Joseph Saade; publs. *Al-Amal* (Arabic daily), *Action—Proche Orient* (French political and scientific monthly).

Progressive Socialist Party: Zkak-el-Blat, P.O.B. 2893, Beirut; f. 1949; over 16,000 mems.; Principal Officer: Kamal Jumblatt; publ. *Al-Anba'* (weekly).

Social Nationalist Party (Partie Populaire Syrienne): resumed operations in 1969; advocates a "Greater Syria"; has collective leadership.

Tachnag Party: right-wing Armenian party.

LEBANON—(Defence, Judicial System, Religion)

DEFENCE

Commander-in-Chief of the Armed Forces: Gen. A. Ghanem.

Defence Budget (1972): £L212.7 million.

Military Service: At present voluntary, but proposals have been made to introduce compulsory military training.

Total Armed Forces: 14,250: army 13,000; navy 250; air force 1,000. Paramilitary Forces: 2,500 Gendarmerie. A National Guard of 5,000 is being formed.

JUDICIAL SYSTEM

Law and justice in the Lebanon are administered in accordance with the following codes, which are based upon modern theories of civil and criminal legislation:

(1) Code de la Propriété (1930).
(2) Code des Obligations et des Contrats (1932).
(3) Code de Procédure Civile (1933).
(4) Code de Commerce (1942).
(5) Code Maritime (1947).
(6) Code de Procédure Pénale (Code Ottoman Modifié)
(7) Code Pénal (1943).
(8) Code Pénal Militaire (1946).
(9) Code d'Instruction Criminelle.

The following courts are now established:

(a) Fifty-six "Single-Judge Courts", each consisting of a single judge, and dealing in the first instance with both civil and criminal cases; there are seventeen such courts at Beirut and seven at Tripoli.

(b) Eleven Courts of Appeal, each consisting of three judges, including a President and a Public Prosecutor, and dealing with civil and criminal cases; there are five such courts at Beirut.

(c) Four Courts of Cassation, three dealing with civil and commercial cases and the fourth with criminal cases. A Court of Cassation, to be properly constituted, must have at least three judges, one being the President and the other two Councillors. The First Court consists of the First President of the Court of Cassation, a President and two Councillors. The other two civil courts each consist of a President and three Councillors. If the Court of Cassation reverses the judgment of a lower court it does not refer the case back but retries it itself.

First President of the Court of Cassation: Badri Meouchi.

(d) The Council of State, which deals with administrative cases. It consists of a President, Vice-President and four Councillors. A Commissioner represents the Government.

President of the Court of the Council of State: Abou Khair.

(e) The Court of Justice, which is a special court consisting of a President and eight judges, deals with matters affecting the security of the State.

In addition to the above, Islamic, Christian and Jewish religious courts deal with affairs of personal status (marriages, deaths, inheritances, etc.).

There is also a Press Tribunal.

RELIGION

Principal Communities

Maronites	424,000
Greek Orthodox	149,000
Greek Catholic	91,000
Sunni Muslim	286,000
Shi'i Muslim	250,000
Druzes	88,000

It will be seen that the largest single community in the Lebanon is the Maronite, a Uniate sect of the Roman Church. The Maronites inhabited the old territory of Mount Lebanon, i.e. immediately east of Beirut. In the south, towards the Israeli frontier, Shi'i villages are most common whilst between the Shi'i and the Maronites live the Druzes (divided between the Yazbakis and the Jumblatis). The Bekaa has many Greek Christians, whilst the Tripoli area is mainly Sunni Muslim. Altogether, of all the regions of the Middle East, the Lebanon probably presents the closest juxtaposition of sects and peoples within a small territory. As Lebanese political life is organized on a sectarian basis, the Maronites also enjoy much political influence, including a predominant voice in the nomination of the President of the Republic.

Patriarch of Antioch of the Maronites: H.E. Cardinal Paul Pierre Meouchi.

Patriarch of Cilicia of the Armenians: Rt. Rev. Mgr. Ignace Pierre XVI Batanian.

Patriarch of Antioch and all the East, of Alexandria and of Jerusalem (*Melkite-Greek Catholic*): P.O.B. 50076, Beirut; Maximos V. Hakim.

Union of the Armenian Evangelical Churches in the Near East: P.O. Box 377, Beirut; Moderator Prof. Hov P. Aharonian; the Union includes some thirty Armenian Evangelical Churches in Syria, Lebanon, Egypt, Cyprus, Greece, Iran and Turkey.

LEBANON—(The Press)

THE PRESS

With 96 newspapers, some 40 of them dailies, serving a readership drawn from a population of only two and a half million, the Lebanese Press is highly competitive. It is also relatively free from external controls, compared with most of the other Middle East countries. Freedom of the press, along with freedom of expression and association, is guaranteed, within the limits of the law, by article 13 of the Constitution. However, the legal limitations on the expression of opinion are somewhat restrictive, so that, for example, it is an offence to defame a foreign head of state, or print false reports about government policies. The basic press law is that of 1948, under which all papers and periodicals have to be licensed by the Ministry of the Interior. The licence can be withdrawn if a paper ceases publication temporarily within six months of its inception, or if circulation drops below 1,500 for thirty days. The editor must have a university qualification, and must deposit a security. The 1948 law also made journalists subject to the judgements of a tribunal of discipline. After a period of conflict between the Government and the Press, the existing law was revised by the press law of 1958, which abolished the procedure for detaining journalists pending investigations, and, with certain exceptions, made it possible for persons convicted of infringement of press regulations to lodge an appeal.

The most important dailies are *Al-Hayat* and *An-Nahar*, which have the highest circulations, *The Daily Star*, *Al-Jaryda* and *L'Orient-Le Jour*, the foremost French paper. The latter two are owned by Georges Naccache, former Lebanese ambassador to France, and tend to take a pro-government line. In a country where most of the élite speak French the other French daily, *Le Soir*, is also influential, and, for the same reason, the twice-weekly publication *Le Commerce du Levant* occupies an important place in the periodical press.

The Lebanese Press has benefited indirectly from Beirut's status as by far the most important base for foreign correspondents covering the Middle East—by 1970 there were more than 120 of these. Long-distance communications have consequently been developed to a high standard.

DAILIES

al-Amal: Place Charles Hélou, P.O.B. 992, Beirut; f. 1939 as a weekly, 1946 as a daily; Phalangist Party; Arabic; circ. 14,000; Editor Georges Omeira.

al-Anwar: Dar Assayad, P.O.B. 1038, Beirut; f. 1959; independent; Arabic; published by Dar Assayad S.A.L.; (has weekly supplements); Prop. Said Freiha; Editor Issam Freiha; circ. 62,200.

al-Bairaq: Rue Sursock, Beirut; National Bloc; Arabic; Editors Assad and Fadel Akl; circ. 3,000.

Beirut al-Masa: Place des Capucins, P.O.B. 1203, Beirut; Arabic; Editor Abdallah Mashnuq; circ. 6,000.

al Dastour: Beirut; Editor Muhyeddine Midani; circ. 3,000.

al Dunia: P.O.B. 4599, Beirut; f. 1953; Arabic; political; also publishes books; Chief Editor Suliman Abou Zaid.

al-Dyar: Place Tabaris, P.O.B. 959, Beirut; f. 1941; independent; Arabic; Editor G. W. Skaff; circ. 22,300.

al Hadaf: Rue Béchir, Immeuble Esseilé, P.O.B. 39, Beirut; Arabic; Editor Zouhair Osseiran.

al-Hayat: Rue Al-Hayat, P.O.B. 987, Beirut; f. 1946; independent; Arabic; circ. 25,000.

al-Jaryda: Place Tabaris, P.O.B. 220, Beirut; f. 1953; independent; Arabic; circ. 22,600; Editor Georges Skaff.

al-Kifah: Rue Mère Gelas, P.O.B. 1462, Beirut; f. 1950; Arabic; Editor Riad Taha; circ. 21,000.

Lissan-ul-Hal: Rue Chateaubriand, P.O.B. 4619, Beirut; f. 1877; Arabic; Editor Gebran Hayek; circ. 29,000.

al Moharrer: P.O.B. 5366, Beirut; Arabic; nationalist; Propr. and Editor Hisham Abu Dahr; circ. 4,000.

an-Nahar: Rue Banque du Liban, Hamra; Press Co-operative Building, P.O.B. 226, Beirut; f. 1933; Arabic; independent; circ. 64,397; Publisher and Editor-in-Chief Ghassan Tueni.

Nida: P.O.B. 4744, Beirut; Arabic; Communist; Editor Suheil Yamout; circ. 1,500.

an-Nidal: Rue Mère Yilas, Beirut, P.O.B. 1354; f. 1939; independent; Arabic; Editor Mustapha Moqaddam; circ. 25,000.

Rakib al-Ahwal: Rue Patriarche Hoyek, P.O.B. 467, Beirut; Arabic; Editor Sima'n Farah Seif.

ar-Rawwad: Rue Mokhalsieh, P.O.B. 2696, Beirut; Arabic; Editor Beshara Maroun.

as Safa: P.O.B. 9192, Beirut; French; published by Soc. Nat. de Presse et d'Édition S.A.L.; Editor Rushdi Malouf; circ. 15,000.

Saout Al Ourouba: P.O.B. 3537, Beirut; Arabic.

al Shaab: P.O.B. 5140, Beirut; Arabic; nationalist; Propr. and Editor Muhammad Amin Dughan; circ. 4,000.

al-Sharq: Rue de la Marseillaise, P.O.B. 838, Beirut; f. 1945; Arabic; Editor Khairy Al-Ka'ki.

Telegraph-Beirut: Rue Béchara el Khoury, P.O.B. 1061, Beirut; f. 1930; Arabic; political, economic and social; Editor Tewfiq el Metni; circ. 15,500 (5,000 outside Lebanon).

al Yaum: P.O.B. 1908; Beirut; Arabic; Editor Afif Tibf.

az-Zaman: Rue Boutros Karameh, Beirut; Arabic; Editor Robert Abela.

Ararat: Nor Hagin, Beirut; Hunchag Party; Armenian; Editor Krikor Jabuliano.

Aztag: Rue Zokak El-Blatt, P.O.B. 587, Beirut; Tachnak Party; Armenian; Editor Haik Balyan.

Daily Star, The: Rue Al-Hayat, P.O. Box 987, Beirut; f. 1952; independent; English; circ. 8,250; Editor George S. Hishmeh.

Le Orient-Le Jour: Rue Banque du Liban, P.O.B. 2488, Beirut; f. 1924; independent; French; circ. 20,000.

Le Soir: Rue de Syrie, P.O.B. 1470, Beirut; f. 1947; political independent daily; French; circ. 16,500; Gen. Man. Dikran Tosbath; Chief Editor André Kécati.

Zartonk: Rue de l'Hôpital-Français, P.O. Box 617, Beirut; f. 1937; official organ of Armenian Liberal Democratic Party; Armenian; Editor P. Toumassian.

WEEKLIES

Achabaka: Dar Assayad, P.O. Box 1038, Beirut; f. 1956; society and features; Arabic; Prop. Said Freiha; Editor George Ibrahim El-Khoury; circ. 120,000.

al-Ahad: Rue Mère Gelas, P.O.B. 1462, Beirut; Arabic; Riad Taha; circ. 32,000.

al-Anba': Rue Maroun Naccache, P.O.B. 2893, Beirut; Progressive Socialist Party; Arabic; Editor Kamal Jumblatt.

LEBANON—(The Press)

al-Anwar Supplement: P.O.B. 1038, Beirut; cultural-social; every Sunday; supplement to daily *al-Anwar*; Editor ISSAM FREIHA; circ. 66,900.

al-Ash-Shir': 144 Rue Gouraud, Beirut; f. 1948; Catholic; Arabic; Editor Father ANTOINE CORTBAWI.

al Awassef: Homs Bldg., P.O.B. 2492, Beirut; f. 1953; Arabic; Trade union news; Dir. DAHER KHALIL ZEIDAN; circ. 8,000.

al Hawadess: P.O.B. 1281, Beirut; f. 1911; Arabic political; Chair. and Gen Man. SALIM LOZI; circ. 90,000.

al-Hurriya: P.O.B. 857, Beirut; f. 1960; voice of Arab Nationalist Movement; Arabic; Chief Editor MUHSIN IBRAHIM; circ. 12,000.

al-Iza'a: Rue Selim Jazaerly, P.O.B. 462, Beirut; f. 1938; politics, art, literature and broadcasting; Arabic; circ. 11,000; Editor FAYEK KHOURY.

al-Liwa: Rue Abdel Kaim Khalil, P.O.B. 2402, Beirut; Arabic; Propr. ABDEL GHANI SALAAM.

al-Jamhour: Mustapha Naja St., Mussaïtbeh, P.O.B. 1834, Beirut; f. 1936; Arabic; illustrated weekly news magazine; Editor FARID ABU SHAHLA; circ. 45,000, of which over 30,000 outside Lebanon.

al Rassed: P.O.B. 2808, Beirut; Arabic; Editor GEORGE RAJJI.

al-Usbua al-Arabi: P.O.B. 1404, Beirut; f. 1959; Arabic; Publishers Les Editions Orientales, S.A.L.; Editor ASSAD MOKADDEM; circ. 147,500 (circulates throughout the Arab world).

Argus: Bureau des Documentations Libanaises et Arabes, P.O.B. 3000, Beirut; circ. 1,000.

Assayad: Dar Assayad, P.O.B. 1038, Beirut; f. 1943; Prop. SAID FREIHA; Editor RAFIQUE KHOURY; circ. 64,400.

Combat: Beirut; French; Editor GEORGES CORBAN.

Commerce du Levant, Le: P.O.B. 687, Kantari St., SFAH Bldg., Beirut; f. 1929; twice weekly; also publishes monthly edition; commercial; French; circ. 10,000; Editor: Société de la Presse Economique; Pres. E. S. SHOUCAIR.

Dabbour: Museum Square, Beirut; f. 1922; Arabic; Editors MICHEL RICHARD and FUAD MUKARZEL; circ. 12,000.

Kul Shay': Rue Béehara el Khoury, P.O.B. 3250, Beirut; Arabic.

Magazine: P.O.B. 1404, Beirut; in French; Publ. Les Editions Orientales S.A.L.; Editor MILAD SALAME; circ. 8,345.

Massis: Place Debbas, Beirut; f. 1949; Armenian; Catholic; Editor F. VARTAN TEKEYAN; circ. 2,000.

an-Nahda: Abdul Aziz St., P.O.B. 3736, Beirut; Arabic; independent; Man. Editor NADIM ABOU-ISMIL.

Revue du Liban: Rue Allenby, Beirut; f. 1928; French; Editor EMILE MAKHLOUF; circ. 7,000.

OTHER SELECTED PERIODICALS

Note: published monthly unless otherwise stated.

al-Adib: P.O.B. 878, Beirut; f. 1942; Arabic, artistic, literary, scientific and political; Editor ALBERT ADIB.

al-Afkar: Rue Mère Gelas, Beirut; international; French; Editor RIAD TAHA.

al-Intilak: c/o Michel Nehme, al-Intilak Printing and Publishing House, P.O.B. 4958, Beirut; f. 1960; literary; Arabic; Chief Editor MICHEL NEHME.

al-'Ulum: Dar al Ilm Lil Malayeen, rue de Syrie, P.O.B. 1085, Beirut; scientific review.

Lebanese and Arab Economy: Allenby Street, P.O. Box 1801, Beirut; f. 1951; fortnightly; Arabic, English and French; publisher Beirut Chamber of Commerce and Industry and SAMI N. ATIYEH; Editor and Dir. ABDEL-WAHAB RIFA'I.

L'Economie des Pays Arabes: B.P. 6068, Beirut; f. 1969; French; published by Centre d'Etudes et de Documentation Economiques Financières et Sociales S.A.L.; Dir. Dr. CHAFIC AKHRAS; circ. 5,000.

Majallat al Izaat al Loubnaniat: Lebanese Broadcasting Corporation, Beirut; Arabic; broadcasting affairs.

Naft al Arab: Beirut; f. 1965; monthly; Arabic; oil; Publisher ABDULLAH AL TARIQI.

Nous Ouvriers du Pays: 144 Rue Gouraud, Beirut; Catholic; English-French; social welfare; Editor Father ANTOINE CORTBAWI.

Rijal al Amal (*Businessmen*): P.O.B. 220, Cornishe Square, Beirut; business magazine; Arabic, with special issues in English and French; Editor G. W. SKAFF; circ. 12,000.

Sawt al-Mar'ah: Dar al-Kitab, P.O.B. 1284, Beirut; Lebanese Women's League; Arabic Editor: Mrs. J. SHEIBOUB.

Tabibok: P.O.B. 4887, Beirut; f. 1956; medical, social, scientific; Arabic; Editor Dr. SAMI KABANI; circ. 78,000.

Welcome to Lebanon and the Middle East: Tourist Information and Advertising Bureau: Starco Centre, North Block 711, P.O.B. 4204, Beirut; f. 1959; on entertainment, touring and travel; English; Editor SOUHAIL TOUFIK ABOU-JAMRA; circ. 6,000.

Alam Attijarat (*Business World*): Strand Bldg., Hamra St., Beirut; f. 1965 in association with Johnston International Publishing Corpn., New York; bi-monthly; commercial; Editor NADIM MAKDISI; international circ. 13,600.

NEWS AGENCIES

FOREIGN BUREAUX

AP: Antoine Massoud Building, Rue Mgr. Chebli, No. 12, Beirut; Chief of Middle East Services ROY ESSOYAN.

Četeka (Czechoslovak News Agency): P.O.B. 5069, Beirut; Chief Middle East Correspondent VLADIMIR OTRUBA.

Middle East News Agency: 72 Al Geish St., P.O.B. 2268, Beirut.

North American Newspapers Alliance: Palm-Beach Hotel, Beirut; Chief ANDREW J. NASH.

UPI: Press Co-operative Building, Rue Hamra, Beirut; Bureau Man. GERARD LOUGHRAN.

DPA, Iraq News Agency and Reuters also have offices in Beirut.

PRESS ASSOCIATION

Lebanese Press Syndicate: P.O.B. 3084, Beirut; f. 1911; 12 mems.; Pres. RIAD TAHA; Vice-Pres. DICRAN TOSBAT; Sec. HISHAM ABU-ZAHR.

PUBLISHERS

Dar al Adab: Beirut; literary and general.

Dar al Ilm Lil Malayeen: Rue de Syria, P.O.B. 1085, Beirut; f. 1945; dictionaries, textbooks, Islamic cultural books; owners: MUNIR BA'ALBAKY and BAHIJ OSMAN.

Dar-Alkashaf: P.O.B. 2091, Pres. A. Malhamee St., Beirut; f. 1930; publishers of *Alkashaf* (Arab Youth Magazine), maps and atlases; printers and distributors; Propr. M. A. FATHALLAH.

Dar al-Kitab al-Jadid: Hamra St., Hindi Building, P.O.B. 1284, Beirut; political studies; owner: FUAD BADR.

Dar al-Makshouf: Rue Amir Beshir, Beirut; scientific, cultural and school books; owner: Sheikh FUAD HOBEISH.

Dar Al-Maaref Liban S.A.L.: P.O.B. 2320, Esseily Bldg., Riad Al-Solh Square, Beirut; f. 1959; textbooks in Arabic, English and French; Gen. Man. JOSEPH NASHOU.

Dar Al Mashreq (Imprimerie Catholique): P.O.B. 946, Beirut; f. 1853; religion, art, literature, history, languages, science, philosophy, school books, dictionaries and periodicals; Dir. PAUL BROUWERS, SJ.

Dar An-Nahar S.A.L.: B.P. 226, Beirut; f. 1967; publishes *Kadaya Moua'ssira* (quarterly), circ. 7,000; Gen. Man. CHARLES RAAD.

Dar Assayad S.A.L.: P.O.B. 1038, Beirut; f. 1943; publishes *Al-Anwar* (daily), circ. 58,000, *Assayad* (weekly), circ. 64,400, *Al-Tayar* (monthly), circ. 62,200, *Achabaka* (weekly), circ. 120,000; has offices and correspondents in Arab countries and most parts of the world; Chair. SAID FREIHA; Man. Dir. BASSAM FREIHA.

Dar Beirut: Librairie Beyrouth, Immeuble Lazarieh, rue Amir Bechir, Beirut; f. 1936; Prop. M. SAFIEDDINE.

Institute for Palestine Studies, Publishing and Research Department: Ashqar Bldg., Clémenceau St., P.O.B. 7164, Beirut; f. 1963; private non-profit making research organization; to promote better understanding of the Palestine problem; publishes research papers, documentary material, yearbook (in Arabic), *Bulletin* (fortnightly, Arabic), *Journal of Palestine Studies* (quarterly, English); library: 5,000 vols.; Chair. CONSTANTINE ZURAYK; Exec. Sec. WALID KHALIDI.

The International Documentary Center of Arab Manuscripts: Syria St., Salha and Samadi Bldg., P.O.B. 2668, Beirut; f. 1965; publishes and reproduces ancient and rare Arabic texts; Propr. ZOUHAIR BAALBAKI.

Khayat Book and Publishing Co. S.A.L.: 90-94 rue Bliss, Beirut; history, literature, economy, language, Arabic reprints; Man. Dir. PAUL KHAYAT.

Librairie du Liban: Sq. Riad Solh, Beirut; languages and general books.

Middle East Publishing Co.: Beirut, Rue George Picot, Imm. El Kaissi; f. 1954; publishes *Medical Index* and *Revue Immobilière* (Real Estate); Man. Editor ELIE SAWAF.

New Book Publishing House: Beirut.

Rihani Printing and Publishing House: Jibb En Nakhl St., Beirut; f. 1963; Propr. ALBERT RIHANI; Man. DAOUD STEPHAN.

Other publishing houses in Beirut include: *Dar al-Andalus, Dar Majalaat Shiir, Imprimerie Catholique, Imprimerie Universelle, Al Jamiya al Arabi, Al Kitab al Arabi, Librairie Orientale, Al Maktab al-Tijari, Middle East Stamps Inc., Mu'assasat al-Marif, Nofal and Bait at Hikmat, Saidar.*

RADIO AND TELEVISION

RADIO

Lebanese Broadcasting Station: rue Arts et Métiers, Beirut; is a part of the Ministry of Information; f. 1937; Dir.-Gen. K. HAGE ALI; Technical Dir. J. ROUHAYEM; Dir. of Programmes N. MIKATI; Head of Administration A. AOUN.

The Home Service broadcasts in Arabic on short wave, the Foreign Service broadcasts in Portuguese, Arabic, Spanish, French and English.

Number of radio receivers: 605,000.

TELEVISION

Compagnie Libanaise de Télévision (C.L.T.): P.O.B. 4848, Beirut; f. 1959; commercial service; programmes in Arabic, French and English on four channels; Pres. Dir.-Gen. General S. NOFAL; Technical Man. M. S. KARIMEN; Programme Dir. PAUL TANNOUS.

Télé Orient: P.O.B. 5054, Beirut; f. 1960; Compagnie de Télévision du Liban et du Proche-Orient (S.A.L.); commercial service; programmes in Arabic, French and English on two channels (11 and 5); Acting Gen. Man. CLAUDE SAWAYA.

Number of TV receivers: 325,000.

FINANCE

(cap.=capital; p.u.=paid up; dep.=deposits; m.=million; L£=Lebanese £; res.=reserves.)

Beirut has for long been the leading financial and commercial centre in the Middle East, as can be seen from the extensive list of banking organizations given below. However, public confidence in the banking system was strained by the closing of the Intra Bank, the largest domestic bank, late in 1966 when its liquid funds proved insufficient to cope with a run of withdrawals. The bank obtained enough guarantees to re-open in January 1968, though it is now an investment bank managed by a New York company. Before this crisis the government had passed a law stipulating a minimum capital of £L 3 million for all banks. This was followed in 1967 by a new law authorising a government take-over of a private bank facing difficulties threatening the interests and deposits of its clients; all depositors are to be paid in full by the State. This law was invoked in June 1968 when the Banque al-Ahli was taken over. The new Bank Control Commission has taken over a number of small banks and assisted in the liquidation of several others. The major foreign-owned banks now have a much larger proportion of deposits than before the Intra crisis, and a number of the major American banks have acquired interests in Beirut.

CENTRAL BANK

Banque du Liban: rue Masraf Loubnane, Beirut; P.O.B. 5544, Beirut; f. 1964; central bank; cap. L£15m.; total resources L£1,792m.

DEVELOPMENT BANK

National Development Bank for Industry and Tourism: Beirut; f. 1971; 51 per cent government-owned.

PRINCIPAL LEBANESE BANKS

Bank Almashrek S.A.L.: Bank Almashrek Bldg., Riad El Solh St. 52, Beirut; Affil. with Morgan Guaranty Trust; cap. L£15m., dep. L£64.4m. (1973); Chair. FAHD ALBAHAR; Man. Dir. RODNEY B. WAGNER.

Bank of Beirut and the Arab Countries S.A.L.: Allenby Street, P.O.B. 1536, Beirut; f. 1957; cap. L£5m., dep. L£108.3m. (1972); Chair. TOUFIC S. ASSAF; Vice-Chair. and Gen. Man. NASHAT SHEIKH EL-ARD; Joint Gen. Man. AMIN M. ALAMEH.

Banque al-Ahli (Banque Nationale) Foncière, Commerciale et Industrielle S.A.L.: Rue Foch, Beirut, P.O.B. 2868; f. 1953; cap. L£3.16m.; Pres. and Gen. Man. BOUTROS EL KHOURY (*see note above*).

Banque Audi S.A.L.: rue Al Arz, Imm. Beydoun, P.O. Box 2560; f. 1928 as Oidih and Joseph Audi, since 1962 known as Banque Audi S.A.L.; cap. p.u. L£10m.; dep. L£173.2m. (1972); Gen. Man. GEORGES OIDIH AUDI.

Banque de Crédit Agricole, Industriel et Foncier: Beirut; f. 1954; Dir.-Gen. Sheikh BOUTROS EL KHOURY; took over several banks in 1967–68, including Banque de l'Economie Arabe, Banque d'Epargne and Union National Bank.

Banque de Crédit National S.A.L.: rue Allenby, Beirut, P.O. Box 204; f. 1959 (f. 1920 as Banque Jacob E. Safra); cap. and reserves L£4.1m.; dep. L£20.7m. (Dec. 1972); Pres. and Gen. Man. EDMOND J. SAFRA; Dep. Gen. Man. HENRI KRAYEM.

Banque de l'Industrie et du Travail, S.A.L.: B.P. 3948, rue Riad Solh, Beirut; f. 1960; cap. L£10m.; dep. L£65m. (1972); Chair. NADIA EL-KHOURY; Gen. Man. W. F. GOSLING, O.B.E.

Banque du Liban et d'Outre-Mer (S.A.): ave. Foch, P.O.B. 1912, Beirut; f. 1951; cap. p.u. L£8m., dep. L£187.5m. (Dec. 1971); Chair., Gen. Man. Dr. NAAMAN AZHARI.

Banque de la Méditerranée S.A.L.: P.O.B. 348, Beirut; f. 1944; cap. L£5m.; dep. L£74m. (1972); Pres. JOSEPH S. NAGGEAR; Gen. Man. JOSEPH A. EL-KHOURY.

Banque Française pour le Moyen-Orient S.A.L.: P.O.B. 393, Imm. Starco, Rue Omar Daouk, Beirut; f. 1971 to take over branches in Lebanon of Société Centrale de Banque; affil. to Banque de l'Indochine; cap. L£5m.; total resources L£212.7m. (Dec. 1971); Pres. and Gen. Man. RENÉ BOUSQUET.

Banque Libanaise pour le Commerce S.A.L.: P.O.B. 1126, rue Riad El-Solh, Beirut; f. 1950; cap. L£5m.; res. L£11.7m. (Dec. 1971); Man. JEAN FARES SAAD ABI-JOUADE.

Banque Libano-Bresilienne S.A.L.: P.O.B. 3310, Maarad St., Beirut; f. 1962; cap. L£3m.; res. L£44,399 (Dec. 1971); Gen. Man. J. A. GHOSN.

Banque Libano-Française S.A.L.: P.O.B. 808, Sehnaoui Building, Riad el Solh St., Beirut; f. 1968; took over Lebanese branches of Compagnie Française de Credit de Banque; cap. L£5m., dep. L£264.5m. (Dec. 1971); Chair. JEAN GILBERT; Gen. Man. FARID RAPHAEL.

Banque Sabbag S.A.L.: P.O.B. 144, Sabbag Centre, Hamra, Beirut; f. 1880 as H. Sabbag et Fils, since 1950 a joint stock company with Banque de L'Indochine and Banca Commerciale Italiana; cap. L£6m.; dep. L£126m. (1972); Chair. PAUL-MARIE CRONIER.

Banque Saradar S.A.L.: Kassatly Bldg., Fakhry Bey St., Beirut, P.O.B. 1121; f. 1948; cap. L£3m.; dep. L£56.3m. (1972); Pres.-Gen. Man. JOE MARIUS SARADAR; Asst. Gen. Man. ABDO I. JEFFI.

Banque G. Trad (Crédit Lyonnais) S.A.L.: Weygand St., Beirut; f. 1951; cap. L£3m.; dep. L£167.3m. (Dec. 1971); Pres. G. G. TRAD.

Beirut-Riyad Bank S.A.L.: Beirut-Riyad Bank Bldg., Riad Solh St., P.O.B. 4668, Beirut; f. 1959; cap. p.u. L£12.5 m.; dep. L£131.2m. (Dec. 1972); Pres. and Gen. Man. HUSSEIN MANSOUR.

Continental Development Bank, S.A.L.: Beydoun Bldg., Arz St., Beirut, P.O.B. 3270; f. 1961; cap. L£8m.; total resources L£122m. (Dec. 1971); Chair. LEO C. DE GRIJS; Gen. Man. RICHARD K. O. CAREY.

Federal Bank of Lebanon S.A.L.: Parliament Square, P.O.B. 2209, Beirut; f. 1952; cap. L£10m.; Pres. M. SAAB; Vice-Pres. A. FARID M. SAAB; Mans. G. A. KHOURY, A. B. ATAMIAN.

MEBCO BANK—Middle East Banking Co. S.A.L.: B.P. 3540, Beydoun Bldg., Beirut; f. 1959; cap. p.u. L£6.25m.; dep. L£48m. (1973); Chair. M. J. BEYDOUN.

Rifbank S.A.L.: Head Office: P.O.B. 5727, rue Kantari Beirut; f. 1965; in association with Commerzbank A.G., The National Bank of Kuwait S.A.K., The Commercial Bank of Kuwait S.A.K.; cap. p.u. L£4m.; dep. L£105m. (1972); Chair. A. A. BASSAM; Man. G. H. CLAYTON, F.I.B.

Société Bancaire du Liban S.A.L.: rue Allenby, Beirut; P.O.B. 435; f. 1899; cap. p.u. and reserves L£3.8m.; dep. L£36.7m. (Dec. 1971); Chair. S. S. LEVY.

Société Générale Libano-Européenne de Banque S.A.L.: P.O.B. 2955, Beirut; f. 1953; cap. p.u. L£5m., dep. L£185m. (1972); Chair. A. M. SEHNAOUI; Gen. Man. GÉRARD GLORIEUX.

Société Nouvelle de la Banque de Syrie et du Liban S.A.L.: P.O.B. 957, Beirut; f. 1963; cap. p.u. L£10.4m.; Pres. PHILIPPE DUPERON.

Trans Orient: Beirut; f. 1966; cap. p.u. L£3m.; joint venture with the International Bank of Washington and Lebanese private investors.

PRINCIPAL FOREIGN BANKS

Algemene Bank Nederland N.V. (*General Bank of the Netherlands*): Amsterdam; P.O.B. 3012, Beirut; brs. in Saudi Arabia (Jeddah, Dammam, Alkhobar).

Arab Bank Ltd.: Amman; P.O.B. 1015, Beirut; f. 1930.

Banco del Atlántico: Barcelona 8, Spain; Arab Bank Bldg., Riad Solh St., Beirut.

Banco di Roma: Rome, Italy; Beirut.

Bank of America (National Trust and Savings Asscn.): San Francisco; f. 1904; P.O.B. 3965, Beirut; Man. C. HOLLANDER.

Bank of Nova Scotia: Toronto, Ont.; Riad el Solh St., P.O.B. 4446, Beirut.

Bank of Tokyo: Tokyo; Arab Bank Bldg., P.O.B. 1187, Beirut; Reps. Y. MORIMOTO, K. KATO.

LEBANON—(Finance, Trade and Industry)

Bank Saderat Iran: Teheran, Iran; Beirut Branch, P.O.B. 5126, Beirut.

Bankers Trust Co.: New York, U.S.A.; Shaker Oueini Bldg., Place Riad Solh, P.O.B. 6239, Beirut; f. 1903; Vice-Pres. Resident Rep. MUHAMMAD SALEEM.

Banque Libano-Française-Beyrouth: 1 Rue Riad El Solh; f. 1968; cap. p.u. L£5m.; dep. L£305m. (Dec. 1972); Pres. and Chair. JEAN GIBERT; Dir. and Gen. Man. FARID RAPHAEL.

Banque pour le Développement Commercial: Geneva, Switzerland; Beirut.

Bayerische Vereinsbank: Munich; K.L.M. Bldg., rue de l'Armee, Beirut; Rep. PETER SCHMID-LOSSBERG; also representing Berliner Bank A.G., Frankfurter Bank, Norddeutsche Kreditbank A.G., Westfalenbank A.G.

Berliner Bank: Berlin; Beirut (see Bayerische Vereinsbank).

British Bank of the Lebanon: rue Trablos, P.O.B. 7048, Beirut; f. 1971; dep. L£30m. (1972); owned by British Bank of the Middle East; Chair. J. C. KELLY, O.B.E.; Man. Z. N. AUDEH.

British Bank of the Middle East: London; Beirut; brs. at Ras Beirut, St. George's Bay, Mazra'a and Tripoli.

Chase Manhattan Bank, N.A.: New York; P.O.B. 3684, Beirut; Vice-Pres. ADOLF KNUL; Rep. CHARLES L. WIDNEY.

Chemical Bank: 20 Pine St., New York 10015; P.O.B. 7286, Riad el Solh St., Beirut; Rep. MICHAEL DAVIS.

Commercial Bank of Czechoslovakia Ltd.: Prague, Czechoslovakia; Middle East Office: B.P. 5928, Beirut.

Commerzbank A.G.: Düsseldorf, Frankfurt, Hamburg, Berlin, German Federal Republic; P.O. Box 3246, Beirut; Rep. KLAUS TJADEN.

Dresdner Bank A.G.: Frankfurt/Main, Federal Republic of Germany; Imm. Starco, B.P. 4831, Beirut; Reps. M. S. HADDAD and REINER AURICH.

First National City Bank: New York, N.Y. 10022; P.O.B. 3648, Beirut; Gen. Man. MICHAEL A. CALLEN.

Frankfurter Bank: Frankfurt, German Federal Republic; P.O.B. 3247, Beirut (see Bayerische Vereinsbank).

Habib Bank (Overseas) Ltd.: Karachi, Pakistan; Beirut.

Jordan National Bank, S.A.: Amman, Jordan; Beirut, Tripoli and Saida.

Manufacturers Hanover Trust Co.: New York; B.I.T. Bldg., Riad el-Solh St., Beirut; Rep. HASSAN HUSSEINI.

Morgan Guaranty Trust Co.: New York, U.S.A.; P.O.B. 5752, Beirut-Riyad Bank Bldg., rue Riyad Solh, Beirut; Rep. in Middle East P. J. DE ROOS.

Moscow Narodny Bank Ltd.: Head Office: London, E.C.4; Beirut Branch: P.O.B. 5481, Beirut; Man. in Beirut T. ALIBEKOV.

National Bank of China: the Government of the People's Republic of China announced in January 1972 that a branch was to be opened in Beirut.

Norddeutsche Kreditbank: Bremen, German Federal Republic; Beirut (see Bayerische Vereinsbank).

Rafidain Bank: Head Office: Baghdad, Iraq; Beirut Branch: Bazirkan Souk, Beirut, P.O.B. 1891; f. 1941.

Royal Bank of Canada (Middle East) S.A.L.: Lebanon; P.O.B. 2520, SFAH Bldg., Kantari, Beirut.

Saudi National Commercial Bank: Jeddah, Saudi Arabia; P.O.B. 2355, Beirut; f. 1938.

Société Tunisienne de Banque: Tunis, Tunisia: Place Riad Solh, Imm. Shaker Oueyni, Beirut; f. 1957; Dir. in Lebanon T. MOALLA.

The Chartered Bank: London; P.O.B. 3996, Riad el Solh St., Beirut; Man. in Beirut G. R. LOVELL.

Westfalenbank: Bochum, German Federal Republic; Beirut (see Bayerische Vereinsbank).

Association of Banks in Lebanon: Army St., P.O.B. 967, Beirut; f. 1959; 87 mems.; Pres. JOSEPH GEAGEA; Gen. Sec. Dr. PIERRE NASRALLAM.

INSURANCE

NATIONAL COMPANIES

"La Phenicienne" (S.A.L.) (formerly al Ahli): Centre Géfinor, rue Clemenceau, P.O.B. 5652, Beirut; f. 1964; Chair., Gen. Man. ANTOINE K. FEGALY; Dep. Gen. Man. NICOLAS MAASSAB.

al-Ittihad al-Watani: Head Office: Immeuble Fattal, P.O.B. 1270, Beirut; Chair. DESIRÉ KETTANEH.

Arabia Insurance Co. Ltd. S.A.L.: Arabia House, Phoenicia St., P.O.B. 2172, Beirut; Gen. Man. BADR S. FAHOUM.

Commercial Insurance Co., S.A.L.: Starco Centre, P.O. Box 4351, Beirut; f. 1962; Chair. J. SABET; Gen. Man. R. M. ZACCAR.

Compagnie Libanaise d'Assurances (S.A.L.): Riad El Solh Street, P.O. Box 3685, Beirut; f. 1951; Managing Dir. JEAN F. S. ABIJAOUDÉ; Man. PEDRO J. S. ABIJAOUDÉ.

Some twenty of the major European companies are also represented in Beirut.

TRADE AND INDUSTRY

CHAMBERS OF COMMERCE AND INDUSTRY

Beirut Chamber of Commerce and Industry: Ayass Bldg., Allenby St., P.O.B. 1801, Beirut; f. 1898; 7,000 mems.; Pres. KAMAL JABRE; Gen. Dir. WALID AHDAB; publ *The Lebanese and Arab Economy* (twenty issues per annum).

Tripoli Chamber of Commerce and Industry: Tripoli.

Sidon Chamber of Commerce and Industry: Sidon.

Zahlé Chamber of Commerce and Industry: Zahlé; f. 1939; 497 mems.; Pres. ALFRED SKAFF.

Association des Industriels du Liban: Beirut.

EMPLOYERS' ASSOCIATIONS

Association of Lebanese Industrialists: Immeuble Asseily, Rue Tripoli, Beirut.

Conseil National du Patronat: Beirut; f. 1965.

TRADE UNION FEDERATIONS

Confédération Générale des Travailleurs du Liban (C.G.T.L.): Beirut; confederation of the following four federations; Pres. GABRIEL KHOURY.

Federation of Independent Trade Unions: Central Bldg., rue Mère Galace, Beirut; f. 1954; estimated 6,000 mems in 7 trade unions; affiliated to Confed. of Arab T.U.'s; Pres. MOHAMED EL-ASSIR; Sec.-Gen. ALI HOURANI; publ. *Sawt al 'Amel*.

LEBANON—(Trade and Industry, Transport)

Federation of Unions of Workers and Employees of North Lebanon: Al-Ahram Building, Abu-Wadi Square, Tripoli; f. 1954; affiliated to Confed. of Arab T.U.'s; 3,700 mems. in 14 trade unions; Pres. MOUSTAFA HAMZI; Sec.-Gen. KHALED BARADI; publ. *Al A'mel*.

Ligue des Syndicats des Employés et des Ouvriers dans la République Libanaise (*League of Trade Unions of Employees and Workers in the Lebanese Republic*): Immeuble Rivoli Place des Canons, Beirut; f. 1946; estimated 6,000 mems. in 21 trade unions; affiliated to ICFTU; Pres. HUSSEIN ALI HUSSEIN; Vice-Pres. HALIM MATTAR; Sec.-Gen. FOUAD KHARANOUH; Foreign Sec. ANTOINE CHIHA; Del. to ICFTU and mem. of Exec. Cttee. ANTOINE CHIHA; publ. *Al-Awassef*.

United Unions for Employees and Workers: Imm. Waqf Bzoummar, rue Béchara el Khoury, Beirut, B.P. 3636; f. 1952; affiliated to ICFTU; 16,000 mems. in 21 trade unions; Pres. GABRIEL KHOURY; Sec.-Gen. ANTOINE AOUN; publ. *La Gazette*.

RESEARCH CENTRE

ICFTU Trade Union Research Centre: P.O.B. 3180, Beirut; f. 1964.

TRANSPORT

RAILWAYS

Office des Chemins de Fer de l'Etat Libanais et du Transport en Commun de Beyrouth et de sa Banlieue: Head Office: Beirut; since 1960, all railways in Lebanon have been state-owned. There are 208 miles of standard-gauge railway and 51 miles of narrow-gauge local lines; Dir.-Gen. ANTOINE BAROUKI.

ROADS

Lebanon has 7,100 km. of roads, of which 1,990 km. are main roads. Most are generally good by Middle Eastern standards. The two international motorways are the north-south coastal road and the road connecting Beirut with Damascus in Syria. Among the major roads are that crossing the Bekaa and continuing South to Bent-Jbail and the Chtaura-Baalbek road. Hard-surfaced roads connect Jezzine with Moukhtara, Bzebdine with Metn, Meyroub with Afka and Tannourine.

Automobile et Touring Club du Liban: Immeuble Fattal, rue du Port, P.O.B. 3545, Beirut.

SHIPPING

Beirut is the principal port of call for the main shipping and forwarding business of the Levant. Tripoli, the northern Mediterranean terminus of the oil pipeline from Iraq (the other is Haifa), is also a busy port, with good equipment and facilities. Saida is still relatively unimportant as a port.

There are many shipping companies and agents in Beirut. The following are some of the largest:

"Adriatica" S.p.A.N.: Rue Riad E. Solh, Immeuble Gellad, Beirut, P.O.B. 1472; Dir. ALDO SILLI.

American Lebanese Shipping Co. S.A.L.: P.O.B. 215, Imm. Fattal, rue du Port, Beirut; f. 1951; Pres. P. PARATORE.

American Levant Shipping & Distributing Co.: P.O.B. 1429, Rue Patriarch Hoyek, Immeuble Anwar Dassouki & Co.; agents for: Holland America Line, Lykes Bros. Steamship Co., Prudential Steamship Corpn., Chevron Shipping Co., Ciro Pellegrino & Figlio, Bermare—Marittima di Navigazione; branches and correspondents throughout Middle East; Man. Dir. SAMIR ISHAK.

Arab Shipping and Chartering Co.: P.O.B. 1084; agents for China National Chartering Corpn., China Ocean Shipping Co., Kiu Lee Shipping Co. Ltd., Chinese-Tanzanian Joint Shipping Co.

Ets. René Balgis: Port St., P.O.B. 806; agents for: Hellenic Mediterranean Lines Ltd. (Piraeus), Linea "C" (Genoa), Home Lines (Genoa), Sun Lines (Athens), Uiterwyk Shipping Ltd., Tampa, Florida and many other companies.

Catoni & Co. S.A.L.: P.O.B. 800, rue du Port; f. 1960; Chair. H. J. BEARD; agents for: British Maritime Agencies (Levant) Ltd., Royal Netherlands Steamship Co., Lloyd's.

Ets. Derviche Y. Haddad: rue Derviche Haddad, P.O.B. 42; agents for: Armement Deppe, Antwerp and Compagnie Maritime Belge, Antwerp.

Daher & Cie. S.A.L.: Byblos Bldg., Place des Martyrs, P.O.B. 254; agents for: Cie. de Navigation Daher, Concordia Line, Navale et Commerciale Havraise Peninsulaire, Société Maritime des Petroles B.P., Cie Navale des Petroles, Cie. Générale Transatlantique, Nouvelle Cie. de Paquebots, Sudcargos.

O. D. Debbas & Sons: Head Office: Sahmarani Bldg., Kantary St., P.O.B. 3, Beirut; Man. Dir. ELIE O. DEBBAS.

British Maritime Agencies (Levant) Ltd.: rue du Port, agents for: Ellerman and Papayanni Line Ltd., Ellerman's Wilson Line Ltd., Prince Line Ltd., etc.

Fauzi Jemil Ghandour: P.O.B. 1084; agents for: Denizçilik Bankası T.A.O. (Denizyolları), D.B. Deniz Nakliyatı T.A.Ş. (Dbcargo), Iraqi Maritime Transport Co.

T. Gargour & Fils: rue Foch, P.O.B. 371; f. 1928; agents for: Assoc. Levant Lines S.A.L.; Dirs. NICOLAS T. GARGOUR, HABIB T. GARGOUR.

Henry Heald & Co. S.A.L.: Im. Fattal, Rue du Port, P.O.B. 64; f. 1837; agents for: Canadian Pacific Lines, Nippon Yusen Kaisha, P. & O. Group, Royal Mail Lines, Scandinavian Near East Agency, Vanderzee Shipping Agency, Worms and Co.; Chair. J. L. JOLY; Dirs. G. HANI, M. J. H. MOFFETT.

Hitti Frères: Parliament Square, P.O. Box 511; agents for: General Steam Navigation Co. Ltd. of Greece (Greek Line), United States Lines, Royal Mail Line, Canadian Pacific Lines.

Khedivial Mail Line: Rue du Port.

Raymond A. Makzoumé: rue de la Marseillaise, P.O.B. 1357; agents for: Jugoslav Lines, Italian Lines, Hellenic Lines Ltd. (New York), Fenton Steamship Co. Ltd. (London).

Mena Shipping and Tourist Agency: El Arz St., Modern Bldg., P.O.B. 884, Beirut.

Messageries Maritimes: Rue Allenby, P.O. Box 880.

Rudolphe Saadé & Co., S.A.L.; Freight Office: P.O.B. 2279, Rue de la Marseillaise; Travel Office: Ave. des Français; agents for American Export Lines, Rosade Lines and Syrian Arab Airlines; f. 1964; Pres. JACQUES R. SAADE.

Union Shipping & Chartering Co. S.A.L.: P.O.B. 2856; agents for Yugoslav vessels.

CIVIL AVIATION

MEA (*Middle East Airlines, Air Liban*): MEA Bldgs., Airport Blvd., Beirut, P.O.B. 206; f. 1945; regular services throughout Europe, the Middle East and Africa; fleet of 3 Boeing 707, 13 Boeing 720, 1 Comet 4C, one Caravelle 6R; Pres. and Chair. Sheikh NAJIB ALAMUDDIN; Gen. Man. ASAD NASR; publs. *Lebanon Fortnightly*.

Trans-Mediterranean Airways (TMA): Beirut International Airport, P.O.B. 3018, Beirut; f. 1953; world-wide cargo services between Europe, Middle East, S.-E. Asia, the Far East and U.S.A., including a round-the-world cargo service; Pres. and Chair. MUNIR ABU-HAIDAR; Exec. Vice-Pres. M. V. RICHMOND.

The following foreign companies also operate services to Lebanon: Aeroflot, Air Algérie, Air France, Air India, Alia, Alitalia, Ariana Afghan Airlines, AUA, BOAC, CSA, EgyptAir, Ethiopian, Garuda, Ghana Airways, Iberia, Interflug, Iranair, Iraqi Airways, JAL, JAT, KLM, Kuwait Airways, Libyan Arab Airlines, LOT, Lufthansa, Malev, Olympic Airways, Pan American, PIA, Sabena, SAS, Saudia, Sudan Airways, Swissair, Syrian Arab Airlines, Tarom (Romania), THY (Turkey), TWA, UTA, Varig, Viasa and Yemen Republic Airlines.

TOURISM

Ministry of Tourism: P.O.B. 5344, Beirut, f. 1966; official organization; Dir.-Gen. Dr. HASSAN EL HASSAN.

National Council of Tourism: P.O.B. 3544, rue de la Banque du Liban, Beirut; government-sponsored autonomous organization; overseas offices in New York, Paris, Frankfurt, Stockholm, Brussels and Cairo; Pres. CHEIKH HABIB KAYROUZ; Vice-Pres. SELIM SALAM.

THEATRES

Baalbek Festival Modern Theatre Group: Baalbek; Dir. MOUNIR ABU-DEBS.

National Theatre: Beirut; Dir. NIZAR MIKATI.

EDUCATION

Until 1952 facilities for public education were provided only at the primary stage and they were considerably outnumbered by foreign and private institutions. Since the end of the French mandate in 1944, public education has greatly developed and now reaches all levels of instruction. However, private institutions still provide the main facilities for secondary and university education. Private schools enjoy almost complete autonomy except for a certain number which receive government financial aid and are supervised by the Ministry's inspectors.

The primary course lasts for five years. It is followed either by the seven-year secondary school, or by the four-year higher primary school. The baccalaureate examination is taken in two parts at the end of the sixth and seventh years of secondary education, and a public examination is taken at the end of the higher primary course. Technical education is provided mainly at the National School of Arts and Crafts, which offers three-year courses in electronics, mechanics, architectural and industrial drawing, and other subjects. There are also public Vocational schools providing courses for lower levels.

Higher education is provided by eleven institutions, including five universities. In 1969–70 35,521 students attended these centres, of whom 43.1 per cent were Lebanese citizens. Teacher training is given at various levels. A three-year course which follows the upper primary school trains primary school teachers and another three-year course which follows the second part of the baccalaureate trains teachers for the upper primary school. Secondary school teachers are trained at the Higher Teachers' College at the Lebanese University. Two Agricultural Schools provide a three-year course for pupils holding the upper primary school degree.

For the year 1972 the budget of the Ministry of National Education amounted to £L172 million or 15.9 per cent of state expenditure. Free primary education was introduced in 1960 and by 1971–72 there were altogether 1,317 public schools and 1,501 private schools, containing over 780,000 pupils and 37,464 teachers.

UNIVERSITIES

American University of Beirut: Beirut; 590 teachers, 4,100 students.

Beirut Arab University: Eltareek Elguidida, P.O.B. 5020, Beirut; 163 teachers, 23,000 students.

Université Libanaise (*Lebanese University*): UNESCO Building, Beirut; 698 teachers, 14,018 students.

Université Saint Joseph: B.P. 293, Beirut; 2,192 students.

Université Saint-Esprit De Kaslik: Jounieh; 88 teachers, 365 students.

BIBLIOGRAPHY

Abouchdid, E. E. Thirty Years of Lebanon and Syria (1917–47) (Beirut, 1948).

Agwani, M. S. (Ed.). The Lebanese Crisis, 1958: a documentary study (Asia Publishing House, 1965).

Ansari, A. Die Verfassungen des Libanon, der Vereinigten Arabischen Republik und des Irak (Metzner Verlag, Frankfurt am Main, Berlin, 1960).

Atiyah, E. An Arab tells his Story (London, 1946).

Besoins et Possibilités de Développement du Liban, Étude Préliminaire, 2 Vols. (Lebanese Ministry of Planning, Beirut, 1964).

Binder, Leonard (Ed.). Politics in Lebanon (Wiley, New York, 1966).

Burckhard, C. Le Mandat Français en Syrie et au Liban (Paris, 1925).

Cardon, L. Le Régime de la propriété foncière en Syrie et au Liban (Paris, 1932).

Catroux, G. Dans la Bataille de Méditerranée (Julliard, Paris, 1949).

Chamoun, C. Les Mémoires de Camille Chamoun (Beirut, 1949).

Churchill, C. The City of Beirut (Beirut, no date).

Corm, G. C. Politique Economique et Planification au Liban 1953–63 (Beirut, 1964).

Dagher, J. Bibliographie du Liban (Beirut, 1945).

Eddé, Jacques. Géographie Liban-Syrie (Beirut, 1941).

Fedden, R. Syria (London, 1946) (also covers the Lebanon).

France, Ministère des Affaires Etrangères. Rapport sur la Situation de la Syrie et du Liban (Paris, annually, 1924–39).

Ghattas, Emile. The monetary system in the Lebanon (New York, 1961).

Gulick, John. Social Structure and Culture Change in a Lebanese Village (New York, 1955).

Hachem, Nabil. Liban: Sozio-ökenomische Groundlagen (Opladen, 1969).

Hachette World Guides. Lebanon (Hachette, Paris, 1965).

Haddad, J. Fifty Years of Modern Syria and Lebanon (Beirut, 1950).

Harding, G. Lankester. Baalbek, a New Guide (Beirut, 1964).

Harik, Iliya F. Politics and Change in a Traditional Society—Lebanon 1711–1845 (Princeton University Press, 1968).

Hepburn, A. H. Lebanon (New York, 1966).

Himadeh, Raja S. The Fiscal System of Lebanon (Khayat, Beirut, 1961).

Hitti, Philip K. Lebanon in History (3rd ed., Macmillan, London 1967).

Hourani, Albert K. Syria and Lebanon (London, 1946).

Hudson, Michael C. The Precarious Republic: Political Modernization in the Lebanon (Random House, New York, 1968).

Jidejian, Nina. Byblos Through the Ages (Dar El-Mashreq, Beirut, 1968).

Katin, Vladimir Konstantinovich. Lebanese Economy and Foreign Trade (Russian Text) (Vneshtorgizdats, Moscow, 1961).

Longrigg, S. H. Syria and Lebanon under French Mandate (Oxford University Press, 1958).

Mills, Arthur E. Private Enterprise in Lebanon (American University of Beirut, 1959).

Pearse, R. Three Years in the Levant (London, 1949).

Penrose, S B. L. That They Have Life: the story of the American University of Beirut 1866–1941 (Princeton, New Jersey, U.P., 1941).

Puaux, G. Deux Années au Levant; souvenirs de Syrie et du Liban (Hachette, Paris, 1952).

Qubain, Fahim I. Crisis in Lebanon (Middle East Institute, Washington, D.C., 1961).

Rondot, Pierre. Les Institutions Politiques du Liban (Paris, 1947).

Saba, Elias S. The Foreign Exchange Systems of Lebanon and Syria (American University of Beirut, 1961).

Safa, Elie. L'Emigration Libanaise (Beirut, 1960).

Salibi, K. S. The Modern History of Lebanon (Praeger, New York, and Weidenfeld & Nicolson, London, 1964).

Sayigh, Y. A. Entrepreneurs of Lebanon (Cambridge, Mass., 1962).

Siksek, Simon G. Preliminary Assessment of Manpower Resources and Requirements in Lebanon (American University of Beirut, 1960).

Stewart, Desmond. Trouble in Beirut (Wingate, London, 1959).

Studies on the Government of The Lebanon. (Compiled by the Dept. of Public Admin., American University of Beirut, 1956.)

Suleiman, M. W. Political Parties in Lebanon (Cornell University Press, Ithaca, N.Y., 1967).

Sykes, John. The Mountain Arabs (Hutchinson, London, 1968).

Thubron, C. The Hills of Adonis (Heinemann, London, 1968).

Tibawi, A. L. A Modern History of Greater Syria, including Lebanon and Palestine (Macmillan, London, 1969).

Ward, Philip. Touring Lebanon (Faber and Faber, London, 1971).

Ziadeh, Nicola. Syria and Lebanon (Praeger, New York, 1957).

Libya

PHYSICAL AND SOCIAL GEOGRAPHY

W. B. Fisher

Libya, until recently three Federated States, is bounded on the north by the Mediterranean Sea, on the east by Egypt and the Sudan, on the south and south-west by Chad and Niger, on the west by Algeria, and on the north-west by Tunisia. The three component areas of Libya are: Tripolitania, in the west, with an area of 110,000 sq. miles; Cyrenaica, in the east, area 350,000 sq. miles; and the Fezzan, in the south, area 220,000 sq. miles—total for Libya, 680,000 sq. miles. The independence of Libya was proclaimed in December 1951; before that date, following conquest from the Italians, Tripolitania and Cyrenaica had been ruled by a British administration, at first military, then civil; and the Fezzan had been administered by France. The revolutionary government which came to power in September 1969 has formally re-named the three regions: Tripolitania became known as the Western provinces, Cyrenaica the Eastern provinces, and the Fezzan the Southern provinces.

PHYSICAL FEATURES

The whole of Libya may be said to form part of the vast plateau of North Africa, which extends from the Atlantic Ocean to the Red Sea; but there are certain minor geographical features which give individuality to the three component areas of Libya. Tripolitania consists of a series of regions of different level, rising in the main towards the south, and thus broadly comparable with a flight of steps. In the extreme north, along the Mediterranean coast, there is a low-lying coastal plain called the Jefara. This is succeeded inland by a line of hills, or rather a scarp edge, that has several distinguishing local names, but is usually alluded to merely as the Jebel. Here and there in the Jebel occur evidences of former volcanic activity—old craters, and sheets of lava. The Jefara and adjacent parts of the Jebel are by far the most important parts of Tripolitania, since they are better watered and contain most of the population, together with the capital town, Tripoli.

South of the Jebel there is an upland plateau—a dreary desert landscape of sand, scrub, and scattered irregular masses of stone. After several hundred miles the plateau gives place to a series of east-west running depressions, where artesian water, and hence oases, are found. These depressions make up the region of the Fezzan, which is merely a collection of oases on a fairly large scale, interspersed with areas of desert. In the extreme south the land rises considerably to form the mountains of the central Sahara, where some peaks reach 12,000 ft. in height.

Cyrenaica has a slightly different physical pattern. In the north, along the Mediterranean, there is an upland plateau that rises to 2,000 ft. in two very narrow steps, each only a few miles wide. This gives a bold prominent coastline to much of Cyrenaica, and so there is a marked contrast with Tripolitania where the coast is low-lying, and in parts fringed by lagoons. The northern uplands of Cyrenaica are called the Jebel Akhdar (Green Mountain), and here, once again, are found the bulk of the population and the two main towns Benghazi and Derna. On its western side the Jebel Akhdar drops fairly steeply to the shores of the Gulf of Sirte; but on the east it falls more gradually, and is traceable as a series of ridges, only a few hundred feet in altitude, that extend as far as the Egyptian frontier. This eastern district, consisting of low ridges aligned parallel to the coast is known as Marmarica, and its chief town is Tobruk.

South of the Jebel Akhdar the land falls in elevation, producing an extensive lowland, which except for its northern fringe, is mainly desert. Here and there occur a few oases—Aujila (or Ojila) Jalo, and Jaghbub in the north; and Jawf, Zighen, and Kufra (the largest of all) in the south. These oases support only a few thousand inhabitants and are of much less importance than those of the Fezzan. In the same region, and becoming more widespread towards the east, is the Sand Sea—an expanse of fine, mobile sand, easily lifted by the wind into dunes that can sometimes reach several hundred feet in height and over 100 miles in length. Finally, in the far south of Cyrenaica, lie the central Saharan mountains—the Tibesti Ranges, continuous with those to the south of the Fezzan.

The climate of Libya is characterised chiefly by its aridity and by its wide alternation of temperatures. Lacking mountain barriers, the country is open to influences both from the Sahara and from the Mediterranean Sea, and as a result there can be abrupt transitions from one kind of weather to another. In winter, it can be fairly raw and cold in the north, with sleet and even light snow on the hills. In summer it is extremely hot in the Jefara of Tripolitania, reaching temperatures of 105°–115° F. In the southern deserts conditions are hotter still. Garian once (incorrectly) claimed the world record in temperature, but figures of over 120°F are known. Several feet of snow can also occur here in winter. Northern Cyrenaica has a markedly cooler summer of 80°–90°, but with high air humidity near the coast. A special feature is the *ghibli*—a hot, very dry wind from the south than can raise temperatures in the north by 30° or even 40° in a few hours, sometimes giving figures of 70° or 80° in January. This sand-laden, dry wind may blow at any season of the year, but spring and autumn are the most usual seasons. Considerable damage is done to growing crops, and the effect even on human beings is often marked.

The hills of Tripolitania and Cyrenaica receive annually as much as 15 to 20 inches of rainfall, but in the remainder of the country the amount is 8 inches or less. A special difficulty is that once in every five or six years there is a pronounced drought, sometimes lasting for two successive seasons. Actual falls of rain can also be unreliable and erratic.

ECONOMIC LIFE

Such conditions impose severe restriction on all forms of economic activity. Although oil has been found in considerable quantities in Libya, physical and climatic conditions make exploitation difficult, and the remote situation of the country, away from the currents of international trade, is a further handicap. But production of crude oil has increased rapidly and in 1971, though production was cut back, it reached 132,000 metric tons. The availability of oil revenues has now begun to transform the economic situation of Libya. Plans for extensive development are being drawn up by foreign consultants, with the aim of improving housing, and the fostering of consumer goods industry. Roads, electricity, better water supplies and re-organized town planning are in process of being achieved.

In the better-watered areas of the Jafara, and to a smaller extent in northern Cyrenaica, there is cultivation of barley, wheat, olives, and Mediterranean fruit.

The Fezzan and the smaller oases in Cyrenaica are almost rainless, and cultivation depends entirely upon irrigation from wells. Millet is the chief crop, and there are several million date palms, which provide the bulk of the food. Small quantities of vegetables and fruit—figs, pomegranates, squashes, artichokes, and tubers—are produced from gardens. Along the northern coast, and especially on the lower slopes both of the Tripolitanian Jebel and the Jebel Akhdar, vines are widely grown, chiefly for wine-making. An edict imposing complete prohibition upon Libyan Muslims has, however, led to a restriction of production.

Over much of Libya pastoral nomadism, based on the rearing of sheep and goats, and some cattle and camels, is the only possible activity. In Cyrenaica nomads outnumber the rest of the population, and animal products account for 60 per cent of the total trade, but in Tripolitania main emphasis is on agriculture, though herding is still important. The latter region also has a number of small local industries, whilst there are very few of these in Cyrenaica, and none in the Fezzan.

The original population of Libya seems to have been Berber in origin, i.e. connected with many of the present-day inhabitants of Morocco, Algeria, and Tunis. The establishment of Greek colonies from about 650 B.C. onwards seems to have had little ethnic effect on the population; but in the ninth and tenth centuries A.D. there were large-scale immigrations by Arabic-speaking tribes from the Najd of Arabia. This latter group, of relatively unmixed Mediterranean racial type, is now entirely dominant, ethnically speaking, especially in Cyrenaica, of which it has been said that no other part of the world (central Arabia alone excepted) is more thoroughly "Arab".

A few Berber elements do, however, survive, mainly in the south and west of Libya; whilst the long-continued traffic in Negro slaves (which came to an end less than thirty years ago) has left a visible influence on peoples more especially in the south but also to some extent in the north.

Arabic, brought in by the tenth century invaders, is now current as the one official language of Libya, but a few Berber-speaking villages remain.

HISTORY

Until very modern times, the history of Libya consisted basically of a series of local histories of small cities, and it is difficult to obtain a clear conspectus of the history of the country as a whole.

Where harbours and roadsteads existed in Libya, which had more or less fertile immediate hinterlands, and which were conveniently sited with respect to the northern ends of caravan routes trading from the interior of Africa, those peoples of the Mediterranean who from time to time were active as seamen and traders, established, or maintained, "emporia"—small city colonies. These conditions existed in Libya only at the west and the east ends of the bleak and forbidding Gulf of Sirte where the desert reaches to the sea and separates the modern provinces of Tripolitania and Cyrenaica by a vacuum 250 miles across.

Where there was desert, there was nothing; where the semi-desert lay, and around the distant oases of the interior, there were the nomads and the semi-nomads, whose way of life changed little throughout the centuries and in whose history the main event was their conversion to Islam. Intolerant of all external controls, they seem perpetually to have resented the civilizing influences from without which clung to the two extremities of the Mediterranean coastline around Sabratha, Tripoli, Leptis at the west end, and ancient Cyrene, Barca, Berenice (now Benghazi) and Derna at the east. When the coastal cities were in strong hands, their civilizing influence was pushed inland to the limits of cultivable land. When they were in weak hands, their influence stopped at their city gates, and the very sands of the desert invaded what under stronger rulers of the cities bore crops of corn, olives and grapes.

From the evidence of Herodotus, and also from that of modern archaeological research, it appears that in the earliest historical times two races inhabited Libya—the "Libyans" and the "Ethiopians"—the former, of Mediterranean stock, inhabited the coastal areas; the latter, of negroid and African stock, inhabited the interior. They used neolithic stone instruments. They knew how to cultivate. The Garamantes of the Fezzan raised cattle over a thousand years before Christ, when Phoenician sailors from the cities of Tyre and Sidon in Syria began to visit Libya to trade for gold and silver, ivory, apes, and peacocks. The perils of their voyages in little ships and the advantages of having emporia at or near the northern ends of the caravan routes led the Phoenicians eventually to establish permanent colonies on the coast, at Leptis, Uai'at (Tripoli) and Sabratha, where more or less safe roadsteads existed. Their most famous colony, Carthage, lay to the west of the boundary of what is now called Libya. But this city, in its maritime and commercial struggle with the ancient Greeks, extended its influence eastward and by 517 B.C. had incorporated the three cities into its Empire.

By this time the Greeks had colonized Cyrene (about 600 B.C.) and raised it to be a powerful city. The Carthaginians, sensitive to competition in Libya, not only drove off an attempt by the son of a Spartan King to found a colony near Leptis, but advanced to contact with Cyrene, where, some time about the beginning of the fourth century B.C., a firm frontier was established against the Cyrenaicans at the Mounds of Philainos, where Mussolini's "Marble Arch" now stands. Cyrene herself fell under the domination of Alexander the Great, and although he was never able to carry out his threat of marching against Carthage, Ptolemy I Soter, heir to Alexander's Egyptian conquests, conquered Cyrenaica for Egypt and extended his empire westwards as far as Sirte.

By about 250 B.C. Carthage was at the height of her power. Her monopolistic policy in commercial and foreign relations reduced the three "emporia" to political non-entity, although their agriculture flourished.

By this time the Romans had substituted themselves for the Greeks as the most powerful Europeans in the Mediterranean. During the struggle between Rome and Carthage which followed, the Tripolitanian half of Libya fell into the power of the Numidians under Massinissa, who allied

LIBYA—(HISTORY)

himself with Rome. After the destruction of Carthage, the three emporia remained under nominal Numidian suzerainty, but in ever closer trading relationship with Italy, until Caesar's war against Pompey, when, after his victory at Thapsus over the Pompeians and their Numidian allies, Caesar created the Roman province of Africa Nova. Augustus set this province under a proconsul responsible to the Senate who also commanded the Legio III Augusta. Meanwhile Cyrenaica had passed under Roman sovereignty by the testament of the last of her Ptolemaic Kings—Ptolemy Apion—and was eventually created a province about 75 B.C.

The Pax Romana extended itself during the first century after Christ from the Mediterranean to the Fezzan. The second century was for Libya a period of prosperity, peace and civilization, the like of which she has never seen again. In particular under Septimius Severus, himself born in Leptis, and the successors of his family, the cities, and especially Leptis, attained the height of their splendour.

This condition did not last. Decline had set in by the middle of the fourth century. The general economic disease which was affecting Roman civilization affected also Africa. Christianity had challenged the spiritual values of the classical world but was itself too full of schisms to provide unity and strength. Libya itself was the scene of fierce internecine struggles caused by the Donatist heresy. Barbarians broke into the province, devastating the countryside, destroying its agricultural system, and spreading insecurity which caused depopulation through flight to the towns. In A.D. 431, Genseric and his Vandals appeared, overran the country, beat down the city walls, and brought ruin in their train. They were the first to introduce that piracy for which its harbours in a later age became notorious. A hundred years later the Emperor Justinian's general Belisarius found little difficulty in reconquering the country for the Byzantine Empire. There was a temporary revival of prosperity but continual rebellions by the Berber tribes soon reduced the country to anarchy.

THE MUSLIM PERIOD

In this condition the first Arab invaders found it. In the Caliphate of Omar, Amr ibn al-As, the conqueror of Egypt, overran the country as far as the Fezzan and Tripoli, the walls of which city he razed. This was in A.D. 643. There followed successive expeditions, mostly for booty, fiercely resisted by the Berbers, in the course of which Oqba ibn Nafi founded Qairawan (A.D. 670) and actually reached the Atlantic. The majority of the Berbers rapidly embraced Islam, but for the most part in its schismatic forms as Kharijites, Ibadites, and Shi'ites. An outlet for their turbulence was found in joining them with the Arabs in the invasion of Spain (A.D. 711).

Schism and continual rebellion induced the Caliph of Baghdad, Harun ar-Rashid, to appoint, in A.D. 800, Ibrahim ibn al-Aghlab as Governor with capital at Qairawan. He founded the Aghlabid dynasty, which became virtually independent of the Abbasid Caliph of Baghdad, but which brought little peace to Libya. A hundred years later a Shi'ite rising overthrew the Aghlabids and founded the Shi'ite Fatimid Dynasty, which from Tunisia conquered Egypt, transferred the seat of their Government to Cairo in A.D. 972, and made Bulukkin ibn Ziri Governor of Ifriqiya. He in turn set up a dynasty under which the land enjoyed considerable prosperity. But, at the beginning of the eleventh century, the Zirid Amir returned to orthodox Sunnism and acknowledged the sovereignty of the Caliph of Baghdad.

The Fatimid Caliph of Egypt, Al-Mustansir, reacted by sending against Libya two nomad Arab tribes which had been kept in Upper Egypt—the Banu Hilal and the Banu Suleim (A.D. 1049). This invasion was a final catastrophe for medieval Libya. The country was devastated, agriculture abandoned. The fortified cities, and in particular Tripoli, alone retained some vestiges of civilization. The next two centuries tell of little but intertribal wars, and the gradual fusion of the Arab and Berber races. Nor do the fourteenth and fifteenth centuries offer much more to record in "Ifriqiya". Murabit dynasts from Morocco contended with Muwahhid dynasts from the Balearic Islands. From these struggles emerged a dynasty in Tunisia called the Hafsids, whose power declined into a weak and anarchic state that attracted the attention of the new, crusading and imperialistic power of Christian Spain which could not overlook the fact that the cities of the northern coast of Africa had become dens of pirates.

Ferdinand the Catholic sent an expedition under Cardinal Ximenes and Don Pietro of Navarre which took Oran, Bugia, Algiers, and Tunis, and then, in 1510, Tripoli. These conquests produced a profound impression on the Muslim world, which at that time had become more united under the Ottoman Turks than it had been since the Abbasid Caliphs were at their zenith six hundred years earlier. The people outside the cities resisted the Spanish with Ottoman encouragement. Within the cities the Spanish were exposed to the dangers of conspiracy. Moreover they could make little effort to extend their power inland since, after the accession of the Emperor Charles V, Spain became heavily involved in European politics. The citizens of Tripoli intrigued unsuccessfully with the corsair Khair ad-Din, known as Barbarossa, who had made himself Lord of Algeria and had later become the Admiral of the Ottoman Sultan.

In these circumstances, the Emperor Charles V confided (A.D. 1530) the Lordship and the defence of Tripoli to the Knights Hospitallers of St. John (later to be known as the Knights of Malta) who had in A.D. 1522 lost Rhodes to the Ottoman Sultan, Suleyman the Magnificent. The Knights were able to maintain themselves there for only 21 years and then Sinan Pasha, who had been sent to reduce Malta but had failed in the attempt, invaded the town and forced the Knights to capitulate.

The Ottoman rulers of Constantinople now proceeded to organise their North African possessions into three Regencies—Algeria, Tunisia, and Tripoli, the last including also Cyrenaica and the Fezzan—each under a Pasha. But their organization contained from the first the germs of the disease to which it ultimately succumbed. The population of the interior was left almost unadministered. Tribute was levied and collected by a few regular troops, and by the "Maghzen" tribes from the remaining tribes, in return for the privilege of exemption from tithe and capitation tax. The system gave obvious opportunities for oppression and rebellion, and the division of the people into feudal lords and serfs. Worse still was the hardening of the professional soldiery of the garrisons, the Janissaries, of slave origin, into a military caste in which promotion was by seniority alone, and the retired officers of which had the right to a seat in the Pasha's Divan, or Council. The Janissaries became a power within the state. No less dangerous was the influence of the pirate captains—the corsairs. The Pashas subsidized them with arms and equipment and took their recognized share of their prizes. The Captains' Guild, called at-Ta'ifa, also became a power within the State. As early as A.D. 1595 the Divan was conceded by the Sultan the right of deciding foreign affairs and taxation. At the beginning of the seventeenth century the Janissaries introduced the custom of electing a "Dey" who sometimes reduced the Ottoman Pasha to a nonentity, sometimes shared with him the power, and sometimes was himself both Dey and Pasha. The history of the seventeenth and eighteenth centuries is one of intrigue, rebellion, sudden death, occasional outbreaks of pestilence, and of a country supported mainly by the depredations of the corsairs upon the merchant-fleets of Christian powers and the enslavement of their crews. In A.D. 1654 Admiral Blake was the first to bombard Tripoli in reprisal for such piracies. The great de Ruyter of Holland followed in 1669 and again in 1672.

In 1711 a local notable, Ahmed Karamanli, of Ottoman origin, and an officer of Janissaries, was proclaimed Dey. He succeeded not only in killing the former Dey and in defeating and killing the new Pasha sent from Constantinople, but also in persuading the Sultan Ahmed III to recognise him as Pasha. For the first time Libya had some sort of autonomous existence. The Karamanli dynasty lasted until 1835. Several of these rulers, and in particular the first and the last (Yusuf ibn Ali Karamanli, who was in power during the period of the Napoleonic wars) were men of strong personality, and capable statesmen who controlled the whole of Libya and improved the political and economic condition of the country. Like the former Pashas, they relied for much of their revenue on piracy. But the Karamanlis learned to make treaties with the maritime powers, bargaining with them to refrain from attacking their ships for a consideration, and for the most part restraining their Captains from breaking such treaties. When they failed to do so the powers would take strong action, as did the United States of America in 1805. The lesser powers naturally suffered most from the corsairs.

Such vast profits had the rulers of the Barbary coast made from piracy during the Napoleonic wars that the smaller powers made the abolition of piracy and of the enslavement of Christians points for discussion at the Congress of Vienna. England was entrusted with the suppression of these evils. It took ten years of naval and diplomatic action on the part of England and the Kingdom of the Two Sicilies to effect this. The suppression of piracy spelt the ruin of the Karamanlis. Yusuf Pasha fell into dire financial straits from which his expedients of adulterating the currency, of state trading, and of pledging in advance the already exorbitant taxes, so far from rescuing him served only to ruin both him and Libya. In 1830 French pressure compelled him to give up even the payments formerly exacted from Christian States for the right to maintain Consuls in Tripoli and for the right to unmolested navigation. In desperation, Yusuf demanded a special "aid" from both Jews and Muslims and this was the signal for revolt.

Probably through fear of the extension of French power in Algiers and Tunis, the Sultan decided to reoccupy Libya and to bring it once more under the direct rule of the Porte. This was in 1835. The rest of Libya's story in the nineteenth century is similar to that of most of the possessions of "The Sick Man of Europe"—corruption, oppression, revolts and their suppression—the towns alone being held by the Turks, with an occasional more energetic or more honest Governor. The period was, however, marked by the diffusion of Sanusi influence. The Sanusi were a religious brotherhood, founded by one Muhammad ibn Ali al Sanusi who settled in Cyrenaica on Jebel al Akhdar in 1834. From there the order spread, founding fraternities (*zawia*) throughout Libya and North Africa. In 1855 the Sanusi headquarters were transferred to Jaghbub to avoid opposition to the order of the Turks and, to some extent, Europeans. Al Sanusi was succeeded on his death in 1859 by his son Muhammad al Mahdi, who led the brotherhood until 1901.

ITALO-TURKISH CONFLICTS

On September 29th, 1911, Italy declared war on Turkey for causes more trivial than those which twenty-four years later led to her war with Ethiopia and her denunciation as an aggressor. After a short bombardment Italian troops landed at Tripoli on October 3rd. Italy knew the Turks to be involved in the Balkans, and knew, through her commercial infiltration of Libya, their weakness in Africa. But her attack on Libya was not the easy exercise she expected. The Turks withdrew inland. But the Libyans organized themselves and joined the Turks, to whom the Porte sent assistance in the form of arms and of two senior officers, Ali Fethi Bey and Enver Pasha. The presence in the Italian army of Eritrean troops was a spur to the pride of the Libyans. In October and November a number of actions were fought around Tripoli in which the Italians had little success. A seaborne Italian force then descended on Misurata and seized it, but could make no progress inland. At Ar-Rumeila they suffered a considerable reverse. Turkey, however, defeated in the Balkan War, was anxious for a peace, which was signed on October 18th, 1912. One of the conditions of this peace was that the Libyans should be allowed "administrative autonomy". This was never realized.

Peace with Turkey did not, however, mean for the Italians peace in Libya. Although most of the Tripolitanians submitted and were disarmed within two years, the Sanusiya of Cyrenaica under Sayyid Ahmad ash-Sharif, and their adherents in the Fezzan and Tripolitania, refused to yield. The Sanusiya maintained a forward post at Sirte under Sayyid Ahmad's brother, Sayyid Safi ad-Din as-Sanusi. What contact there was between this Sayyid and one Ramadan as-Sueihli of Misurata is obscure. Ramadan had been in the resistance to the Italians and two years later had appeared to be submissive. At all events, he found himself commanding Libyans in an action started by the Italians at Al-Qaradabia in 1914, to push back Sayyid Safi ad-Din. Ramadan and his Misuratis changed sides in this action to the discomfiture of the Italians. By the time that the First World War had started, the Italians held only the coast towns of Tripoli, Benghazi, Derna and Tobruk, and a few coast villages near Tripoli.

The First World War gave Turkey and her German allies the opportunity of fermenting trouble against Italy in Libya. Arms and munitions were sent by submarine. Nuri Pasha from Turkey and Abdurrahman Azzam (late Secretary-General of the Arab League) from Egypt joined Sayyid Ahmad ash-Sharif in Cyrenaica. Ramadan as-Sueihli became head of a government at Misurata. The Sultan, to prevent quarrels, sent as Amir Osman Fu'ad, grandson of Sultan Murad; and Ishaq Pasha as commander in chief in Tripolitania. The strategical objective of these efforts was to tie up Italian forces in Libya and British forces in the Western Desert. The climax of Nuri Pasha's efforts with the Sanusi was their disastrous action in the Western Desert against the British, as a result of which Sayyid Ahmad ash-Sharif handed over the leadership to Sayyid Muhammad Idris. He was compelled to make the treaty of az-Zawiatna with the British and the Italians who recognised him as Amir of the interior of Cyrenaica, provided he desisted from attacks on the coastal towns and on Egypt.

The end of the war in 1918 left Italy weak and the Libyans, deserted by the Turks, weary. The Tripolitanians attempted to form a republic with headquarters at Gharian and with Abdurrahman Azzam as adviser. The Italians made a truce with them at Suani ibn Adam, permitting a delegation to go to Rome and entertaining the idea of "administrative independence". Ramadan as-Sueihli visited Tripoli. In Cyrenaica, Sayyid Muhammad Idris as-Sanusi likewise attempted to come to terms. In 1921 at Sirte the Tripolitanian leaders agreed with him to join forces to obtain Libya's rights and to do homage to him as Amir of all Libya. Meanwhile the delegation to Rome had returned empty-handed and Ramadan as-Sueihli had been slain in a tribal fight.

ITALIAN COLONIZATION

The advent of the Fascists to power in Italy (1922) coincided with the appointment in Tripoli of a vigorous Governor, Count Volpi. Thereafter, it took them until 1925 to occupy and pacify the province of Tripolitania and disarm the population. In Cyrenaica, however, the famous Sayyid Omar al-Mukhtar, representing the Amir Muhammad Idris, whose health had broken down, kept up the struggle. The Italians realized that the only effective policy was to deprive the Sanusiya of their bases, the oases of the South. Jaghbub was occupied in 1925, Zella, Ojila and Jalo in 1927. In 1928 Marshal Badoglio was appointed Governor General and in 1929 he occupied Mizda in the Fezzan. Omar Mukhtar still resisted. The Italians removed into concentration camps at al-Aqeila the tribes of the Jebel Akhdar. In 1930 Graziani was appointed to Cyrenaica, and the famous barbed-wire fence was erected along the frontier of Egypt. Finally, in 1931, cut off from all support, Omar Mukhtar, now an aged man, was surrounded, wounded, captured, and hanged.

Starting in the early 1920s, the Italians proceeded to colonize, in the sense of that word which is now in disrepute, those parts of Libya which they had occupied, and which geographical and ecological conditions rendered profitable for development. They enlarged and embellished the coastal towns. They extended throughout the cultivable areas a most excellent network of roads. They bored wells. They planted trees, and stabilized sand-dunes. But their civilizing policy was weighted heavily in favour of their own race. The object was clearly the settlement in Africa of as much as possible of Italy's surplus peasant population. These were encouraged to come in large numbers. Skilled cultivators of olives, vines, tobacco, barley, they needed the best lands and were provided with them. The priority given to the progress of the Libyans was a low one. Primary education for the Libyans was encouraged and schools provided for them. But the main medium of instruction was Italian. Very few Libyans were accepted into Italian secondary schools. To prevent Muslim Libyans seeking higher education in Egypt and elsewhere, a small Muslim Higher College was founded in Tripoli. The Libyans avoided sending their children to school, although attempts at compulsion were made. They feared lest their children lose their Islamic faith and way of life.

INDEPENDENCE

There followed the Second World War, and the occupation in 1942 of Cyrenaica and Tripolitania by a British Military Administration and of the Fezzan by French Forces. Thereafter until 1950 the country was administered with the greatest economy on a care and maintenance basis. Its final fate was long in doubt, until the United Nations decreed its independence by 1952. On December 24th, 1951, Libya was declared an independent United Kingdom with a federal constitution under King Idris, the former Amir Muhammad Idris, hero of the resistance.

According to the Constitution promulgated in October 1951, the state of Libya was a federal monarchy ruled by King Muhammad Idris al-Mahdi al-Sanusi and his heirs, and divided into the three provinces of Tripolitania, Cyrenaica and the Fezzan. The Federal Government consisted of a bicameral legislature, i.e., a Chamber of Deputies, to which was responsible a Council of Ministers appointed by the King, and a Senate of 24 members, 8 for each province. The King had the right to nominate half the total number of Senators, to introduce and to veto legislation, and to dissolve the Lower House at his discretion. The Constitution also provided that Provincial Legislatures should be created for the subordinate provinces of the new realm.

On the attainment of full independence serious political, financial and economic problems confronted Libya. Not the least of these was the task of fostering amongst the population a sense of national identity and unity. The loyalties of the people were still given to the village and the tribe, rather than to the new federal state. Poor communications and the great spaces of desert land, together with the lack of trained personnel and lingering provincial rivalries, were great obstacles to the establishment of a stable and efficient modern administration.

These rivalries revealed themselves in the next two years. The Party of Independence, which supported the constitution, won control in the February 1952 elections for the Federal Chamber of Deputies. The National Congress Party of Tripolitania, however, was opposed to the federal principle and advocated a unitary state with proportional representation (which would have given Tripolitania the main voice). Disorders arising from this disagreement led to the outlawing of the Tripolitania party and the deportation of its leader al-Sa'adawi. A Legislative Council for Tripolitania was formed in 1952 but had to be dissolved in 1954 because of continued friction with the Federal Government and the King.

Matters were further aggravated at the end of 1954 when a sharp crisis occurred in the affairs of the ruling house, the King being compelled to declare a state of emergency in Cyrenaica and to banish seven members of his family to the southern desert.

About 80 per cent of the population of Libya was engaged in agriculture; but owing to the low rainfall, the hot desert winds and primitive farming methods, the average yield was small. There were no important mineral resources and only a few industries, most of them in Italian hands. Since 1945 exports had sufficed to meet only about 50 per cent of the cost of imports, most of which had been in the form of consumer goods needed to maintain the already low standards of life, and not of capital equipment and machinery. Income from foreign military establishments had been estimated as being 50 per cent above the total value of exports. Drought in Cyrenaica (1952) and Tripolitania (1953) meant a diminished yield of olives, citrus, cereals and the like, and caused a sharp fall in the livestock of the new state. Moreover, the world market prices for esparto grass, a main export from Libya, declined rapidly in 1953; while by that year the stores of war-time scrap, hitherto an important source of revenue, were almost exhausted. The financial situation was reflected in the fact that during the first budgetary period of the new realm, i.e., April 1952–March 1953, Cyrenaica alone spent £1 million more than it could provide from its own revenues and its share of foreign aid.

Efforts were undertaken, with Western technical aid, to increase the economic resources of Libya, e.g., to improve irrigation and initiate schemes for water catchments, to extend reafforestation, to teach better methods of farming, and to explore the possibilities of extending industries which could process local products and raw materials such as edible oils, fruits, vegetables, fish, etc.

FOREIGN RELATIONS IN THE 1950s

The first important development in the sphere of foreign relations was the admission of Libya to the Arab League in March 1953. The second development reflected the economic difficulties of the new state and its close links with Western Europe. In July 1953 Libya concluded a twenty-year treaty with Britain. In return for permission to maintain military bases in Libya, Britain undertook to grant the new state £1 million annually for economic development and a further annual sum of £2,750,000 to meet budgetary deficits. The financial obligations of the treaty were subject to review after five years.

In September 1954 a similar agreement was signed with the United States. A number of air bases were granted to the U.S. in return for economic aid amounting to $40 million over twenty years, which amount was later substantially increased. Libya also consolidated relations with France and Italy, signing a friendship pact with France in 1955 and a trade and financial agreement with Italy in 1956. In addition Libya was attempting to cement relations with her Arab neighbours. In May 1956 Libya concluded a trade and payments pact with Egypt, arranging the exchange of Libyan cattle for Egyptian foodstuffs. At the time of the Suez crisis Libya was obliged, however, to ask the Egyptian military attaché to leave on the grounds that he was engaged in "harmful activities". Libya signed a treaty of friendship with Tunisia in January 1957 envisaging collaboration between the two states in cultural and economic matters.

The critical problem for Libya was to ensure that enough funds from abroad should be available to meet the normal expenses of the Government and to pay for much-needed improvements. At this time, her strategic position was all Libya had to sell, hence her involvement with the Western military alliance and in particular with Britain, France, Italy, Turkey and the United States. The Libyan attitude to the Communist world was much more reserved. A Soviet ambassador was accredited to Tripoli in January 1955, but a Soviet offer of economic aid was rejected the following year. In 1955, too, Libya was admitted to membership of the United Nations.

Reliance on income from foreign military bases continued, therefore, to dominate foreign policy. In April 1958 the Prime Minister, Abd al Majid Kubar, who had taken office in May 1957 on the resignation of his predecessor, Mustafa ibn Halim, went to London to discuss the financial assistance that would be given to Libya during the five years 1958–63 under the terms of the Anglo-Libyan agreement signed in 1953. He announced to the Libyan Parliament in May 1958 that in the five-year period ending on April 1st, 1963, Great Britain would provide subsidies to the amount of £3,250,000 per annum, would make available light arms and equipment for 5,000 Libyan troops and would also continue the programme of free military training. He also stated that the British Government would no longer give £1 million per annum to the Libyan Development Agency, as it had done since 1953, and that the United States intended to contribute to the Agency $5.5 million during the next five years.

In September 1958 Libya became a member of the International Monetary Fund and of the International Bank for Reconstruction and Development. Official sources stated in May 1959 that Libya would henceforward receive financial aid from the United States, not through the various aid organizations of the United States, but directly from the United States Government. In June 1959 the U.S. Development Loan Fund made available to Libya $5 million for electric power generation and transmission facilities designed to serve Tripoli and the surrounding region. During the course of 1958 and 1959 a number of discoveries of oil were made in various areas of Libya.

In August 1960 the Libyan Government announced that the U.S.A. had agreed to pay $10 million per annum for the use of military bases in Libya. An agreement for technical and economic co-operation was signed at Tripoli on July 8th, 1960, between Libya and the Federal German Government. German experts were to be sent to Libya in order to advise on matters connected with agriculture, irrigation and fisheries, with health services, with training facilities in mechanical and electrical engineering, and with the development of tourism. In August 1961 the Federal German Government announced that it would grant to Libya a long-term loan amounting in value to over £5,000,000 for agricultural and industrial projects.

OIL DISCOVERIES

After 1955–56, when Libya granted concessions for oil exploration to several American companies, the search for oil resources became one of the main interests of the Libyan Government. By the end of 1959 some fifteen companies held oil concessions in Libya. An oilfield at Zelten in Cyrenaica was discovered in June 1959. Before the year was out, six productive wells had been found in Tripolitania, four in Cyrenaica and one in the Fezzan. On May 24th, 1960, the Libyan Government promulgated a law establishing a Council of Development (Majlis al-I'mār) to examine the natural resources of Libya and to consider projects and policies of an economic and social character. By the beginning of July 1960 there were thirty-five oil wells in production, yielding altogether a little less than 93,000 barrels of oil per day. The development of the oilfields is dealt with in greater detail in the *Economic Survey* which follows this history.

The International Bank for Reconstruction and Development made public in July 1960 a general report on the Libyan economy. This report expressed the view that oil discoveries would not suffice, at least in the immediate future, to solve the basic economic problems of Libya. No large yield of revenues from oil could be foreseen within the next five years. Agriculture was of vital importance, but the lack of water set great obstacles in the path of improvement; indeed, of the entire Libyan territories perhaps only about 10 per cent could be regarded as cultivable. Fishing and tourism, if suitably fostered, might be able to make an appreciable contribution towards the needs of the Libyan people (estimated as being 35 per cent urban, 40 per cent rural and 25 per cent nomadic in their mode of life).

However, in August 1964 British Petroleum discovered large oil reserves in eastern Libya, not far from the Egyptian frontier, and stated that a pipeline would be built to Tobruk for the exploitation of this field. The Esso Libya corporation confirmed in November that it intended to construct a gas liquefaction plant at Mersa Brega. December 1964 witnessed the opening of a pipeline from the Hofra oilfield to a new loading terminal at Ras Lanuf on the Gulf of Sirte. Oil production showed a tremendous increase in the 1962–66 period, with exports rising from 8 million tons in 1962 to over 70 million in 1966.

A UNITARY REALM

A general election was held in Libya on January 17th, 1960. Most of the 55 seats were contested, but there was no party system in operation. The election was fought mainly on a personal basis. Secret ballotting, limited in earlier elections to the urban areas, was now extended to the rural districts. The Prime Minister, Abd al Majid Kubar, and the other members of his Cabinet retained their seats.

Libya's increasing wealth was making the business of government more complex and several changes of administration ensued between 1960 and 1963. Finally, in March 1963, a new cabinet under the premiership of Dr. Mohieddin Fekini was appointed.

Dr. Fekini stated in April 1963 that his government intended to introduce legislation designed to transform

Libya from a federal into a unitary state—a change which would mean increased efficiency and considerable economies in administration. On April 15th the Prime Minister presented to the Chamber of Deputies a Bill which contained a number of important reforms: (1) the franchise was to be granted to women; (2) Libya would have (as before) a bicameral parliamentary system, but henceforward the King was to nominate all the 24 members of the Senate (heretofore half nominated and half elected); (3) the Kingdom of Libya would cease to be a federal state comprising three provinces (Tripolitania, Cyrenaica and Fezzan), becoming instead a unitary realm divided into ten administrative areas; (4) the administrative councils established in each of the three provinces were to be abolished, the exercise of executive power residing now in the Council of Ministers. Libya became a unitary state by royal proclamation on April 27th, 1963. Each of the ten new administrative areas was to come under the control of a government-appointed administrator, aided by local advisory councils for matters relating to health, labour, education, agriculture and communications.

THE REALITY OF INDEPENDENCE

In the field of foreign relations, Libya was by now helped by the prospect of financial independence and was making her voice heard in international affairs, particularly in Africa. As a result of decisions taken at the Addis Ababa conference of African Heads of State in May 1963 Libya closed her air and sea ports to Portuguese and South African ships. The signing of pacts with Morocco (1962) and Algeria (1963) meant that Libya now had closer links with all the Maghreb countries. Libya was also showing signs of throwing off her dependence on the West. The 1955 agreement with France had allowed France to retain in Libya certain military facilities—notably in the field of communications—for the defence of her African territories. The future of this agreement was raised by Dr. Fekini in November 1963. He expressed the view that the recently acquired independence (1960) of Libya's southern neighbours, Niger and Chad, rendered the agreement obsolete and he thought that the whole matter should be considered anew.

The question of foreign military bases in Libya now came to the fore. On January 22nd, 1964, Dr. Fekini resigned his office of Prime Minister after student demonstrations at Benghazi and Tripoli. The new Prime Minister was Mahmud Muntasser, hitherto Minister of Justice. The Government issued a statement on February 23rd to the effect that it did not propose to renew or extend its military **agreements with Great Britain and the United States and that it supported the other governments of the Arab world in the resistance to imperialism.** Mr. Muntasser defined the aim of his government as the termination of the existing agreements with Great Britain and the United States and the fixing of a date for the evacuation of the bases in Libya. The Chamber of Deputies now passed a resolution calling for the achievement of this aim and providing that, if negotiations were unsuccessful, the Chamber would pass legislation to abrogate the treaties and close the bases.

The Anglo-Libyan treaty of 1953 was due to expire in 1973. Under the treaty Great Britain maintained a Royal Air Force staging post near Tobruk, an Air Force detachment at Idris airport in Tripoli and Army District Headquarters at Tripoli and Benghazi. The American-Libyan agreement of 1954 was to expire in 1971. Near Tripoli was situated the largest American air-base outside the United States. Under the treaties Libya had received large amounts of financial, economic and military aid from the United States and from Great Britain. Libyan dependence on such aid had diminished, however, as a result of the swift development of the oil fields, which provided the state with increasing revenues. Great Britain offered to withdraw from her military positions in Tripolitania, the western region of the Kingdom.

At a conference of Economic Ministers held in Tunis on August 30th–September 1st, 1964, Algeria, Morocco, Tunisia and Libya signed an agreement stating their readiness in principle to create a system of special relationships amongst themselves in the field of trade exchanges, economic co-operation and the harmonization of tariff policies. During the course of a subsequent conference held at Tangier in November 1964 it was decided to establish between the four states a joint and permanent consultative committee which would serve to harmonize in general the development plans envisaged by the participating governments. The Committee would have an administrative secretariat and a number of specialized commissions. It was also resolved to create an industrial studies centre with a permanent headquarters at Tripoli. The centre was intended to co-ordinate the industrialization projects of the member states.

At elections for the Libyan Parliament held in October 1964 moderate candidates won most of the 103 seats. Women received the right to vote in this election. King Idris dissolved the Parliament, however, on February 13th, 1965, as the result of complaints about irregularities in the election procedure of October 1964.

The Prime Minister resigned, to be succeeded by Husayn Maziq, Minister for Foreign Affairs. A new election for Parliament was held on May 8th, 1965, over two hundred candidates contesting the 91 seats, 16 members being returned unopposed.

The withdrawal of the British troops stationed in Tripolitania took place in February and March 1966. Britain retained certain facilities at Idris airport near Tripoli, small detachments at Benghazi, Tobruk and the R.A.F. staging post of El Adem, to the south of Tobruk. Discussions on the eventual withdrawal of the remaining British and American forces stationed in Libya were initiated in the latter part of 1967.

The outbreak of the six-day Arab-Israeli war in June 1967 was followed by serious disturbances in Tripoli and Benghazi, in which port and oil workers and students, inflamed by Egyptian propaganda, played a prominent part. The British and United States embassies were attacked and the Jewish minorities were subjected to violence and persecution which resulted in the greater part of them emigrating to Italy, Malta and elsewhere. The Prime Minister, Husayn Maziq, proved unable to control the situation and was dismissed by the King on June 28th. Firm measures by his successor, Abdul Qadir Badri, brought a return to order but the antagonisms he aroused forced him to resign in turn in October. He was succeeded as Prime Minister on October 28th by the Minister of Justice, Abdul Hamid Bakkush, a Tripoli lawyer.

An immediate result of the June war was a fall in the Libyan output of crude oil of about 80 per cent because of the boycott of oil supplies from Arab countries to Britain, the United States and Federal Germany. There was a gradual return to full production in the months following the conflict, however, and the ban on the export of oil was lifted in September. The closure of the Suez Canal brought about a considerable increase in Libya's oil exports and general prosperity, although the Libyan Government agreed to make annual aid payments totalling £30 million to the U.A.R. and Jordan to alleviate the consequences of the war. Libya's oil output increased by about 50 per cent in 1968 and the country became after only $7\frac{1}{2}$ years the second largest producer in the Arab world with the great advantage, as a supplier to Europe, of being on the right side of the Suez Canal.

The new Prime Minister, Abdul Hamid Bakkush, was a progressive. His relatively young and well-educated administration immediately embarked on a programme of rapid change, seeking to modernize Libya's administration, reform the civil service and improve the educational system. He also sought to provide the armed forces with up-to-date equipment, and under a contract announced in April 1968 the purchase from a British firm of a surface-to-air missile defence system costing £100 million was arranged. An agreement to buy British heavy arms, notably the advanced Chieftain tanks, followed in spring 1969. In September 1968, however, Mr. Bakkush was replaced as premier by Wanis el Qaddafi, the pace of his reforms having apparently alienated some conservative elements. Both ministries enjoyed close relationships with the Western countries but played little part in Arab politics.

THE 1969 COUP

On September 1st, 1969, a military coup was staged in Tripoli whilst the King was in Turkey for medical treatment. Within a few days the new régime gained complete control of the entire country. The coup was remarkable for the absence of any opposition, relatively few arrests, virtually no fighting and no deaths at all being reported. The "Revolutionary Command Council" (RCC) initially remained anonymous but was soon revealed as a group of young army officers, the leader, Muammar Gaddafi, being only 27. The aged King refused to abdicate but accepted exile in Egypt when it became obvious that the revolution had been completely accepted by his people. The RCC announced its personal respect for the monarch, and declared that he would be allowed to return to Libya as a private citizen whenever he wished. However, a substantial number of royal advisers were arrested or obliged to leave the country.

The provisional constitution announced in November stated that supreme power would remain in the hands of the RCC which appoints the cabinet; there was no mention of any future general election or of a National Assembly, and the royal ban on political parties continued. A largely civilian cabinet was appointed under close military supervision. The Ministers of Defence and of the Interior were accused of organizing an abortive counter-revolution in December, and were tried and sentenced in 1970. In January Col. Gaddafi himself became Prime Minister and several of his colleagues also joined the cabinet.

The principal force underlying the régime's policies was undoubtedly the professed one of Arab nationalism. Internally this led to the strict enforcement of the royal law requiring businesses operating in Libya to be controlled by Libyans—banks being particularly affected. The remaining British military establishment in Libya, requested to leave as soon as possible, was finally removed in March 1970, and the much larger U.S. presence at Wheelus Field followed suit in June. Most of the European and American managers, teachers, technicians and doctors were replaced by Arabs, mainly from Egypt. English translations disappeared from street signs, official stationery and publications, and most hoardings, the use of Arabic alone being permitted; similarly, the Islamic prohibitions on alcoholic drinks and certain Western clothes were officially revived. In July 1970 the property of all Jews and Italians still living in Libya—some 25,000 people—was sequestrated by the Government, and both communities were encouraged to leave without delay; some Jews were, however, offered compensation in government bonds. With regard to the Italians, Col. Gaddafi said "the Libyan people are receiving back the property usurped by the Fascists who came to impose their tyranny". In the same month the three main oil marketing companies—Shell, Esso and an ENI subsidiary—had their distribution facilities nationalized.

Another anti-government plot was reported crushed in July 1970. In the autumn two ministers resigned and there were signs of a power struggle developing in the Revolutionary Command Council. The internal dissension apparently increased in the first part of 1970 over the proposed federation with the U.A.R., Syria and Sudan, and over President Gaddafi's promises of a constitution, and political institutions, including an elected president. A step towards introducing these was the announcement in June 1971 that an Arab Socialist Union was to be created as the state's sole party. Such a development would also presumably assist integration with the U.A.R. and Sudan.

FOREIGN POLICY AFTER THE COUP

The new régime almost immediately received recognition—indeed acclaim—from the radical Arab countries and the U.S.S.R., and the rest of the world also granted recognition within a few days. As would be expected from the Arab nationalist inspiration behind the revolution, the monarchy's close ties with the Western powers were abandoned in favour of close relations with the Arab world and Egypt in particular; this friendship became the basis of an important triple alliance announced late in 1969, the Sudan being the third member. The alliance was intended to develop both politically—as a strong bulwark against Israel and the West—and economically, in that the economies of the three countries complemented each other to a considerable extent. However, when a federation agreement was signed in April 1971, it was Syria which became the third member. Libya also adopted a militant position on the Palestine question, and this created some diplomatic problems regarding arms contracts.

The royal government's contract to buy a British missile defence system, implicitly aimed against Egypt, was duly cancelled; fulfilment of another major British contract, for the advanced Chieftain tanks, was delayed by Britain, which feared that the tanks might reach the Palestine front. Colonel Gaddafi's government itself ordered over 100 French Mirage jet fighters. There were widespread fears in the West that Egyptian pilots would fly the Mirages, which might then be used to escalate the campaign against Israel. Deliveries of Soviet tanks were reported in the summer of 1970.

Although in July 1970 the Libyan Government followed Egypt in accepting the American proposals for a cease-fire with Israel, it continued its militant statements on the Middle East problem. President Gaddafi stated that a peaceful solution was impossible and rejected the UN Security Council resolution on which the Rogers initiative was based. During the fighting between Palestine guerrillas and the Jordanian army in September 1970, Libya redirected its financial aid from the Government to the guerrillas and broke off diplomatic relations with Hussein's government. It also criticized the failure of the Iraqi troops stationed in Jordan to assist the guerrillas. But Libyan threats to intervene in Jordan on the guerrillas' behalf proved empty, and the conference of heads of state Gaddafi called at the end of July 1971 to discuss the Jordanian Government's final assault on the commando bases only issued more threats.

Nearer home, the coup appeared to have reorientated Libya away from the Maghreb; in the summer of 1970 Libya withdrew from the Maghreb Permanent Consultative Committee. Relations with Tunisia improved in the last half of 1970, after initial concern in Tunis in 1969 at the radical leanings of the new régime, and President Gaddafi headed a delegation which visited Tunisia in February 1971. Relations with Morocco were severed in July 1971 after the Libyan Government prematurely gave its support to an attempt to overthrow King Hassan, which failed within twenty-four hours.

There was little evidence of any closer relationship with the communist power, although China was recognized in June 1971 and the U.S.S.R. was given due credit for its Middle East policies. But communism was regarded in Libya as a "foreign" ideology, antipathetic to more "progressive" Arab socialism (as in Sudan). Hence, in July 1971, Gaddafi was ready to help President Nemery of Sudan to regain power after a coup led by communists had ousted him. A regular BOAC flight from London to Khartoum was forced down over Libya and two leaders of the coup, one of whom, Major al-Nur, was travelling back to become head of state, were taken from the plane and handed over to Sudan. They were almost immediately executed by the restored régime.

OIL POWER

In April 1971 the negotiations with the oil companies operating in Libya, which had begun soon after the 1969 coup, finally ended in a new five-year agreement raising the total posted price for Libyan crude to $3.447 per barrel. In the last stage of the negotiations, conducted in Tripoli, the Libyan Government also represented the interests of the Algerian, Iraqi and Saudi Arabian Governments. Threats of an embargo on the export of crude oil were used as a lever in the negotiations.

In ten years Libya's position had changed from one of penury and dependence to one of power based entirely on her ability to cut off oil supplies. The pronouncements of President Gaddafi were therefore, by now of great moment to the West. In July 1971, the Deputy Prime Minister, Major Abd al Salam Jalloud, visited West Germany, France and Britain. Germany, which buys a particularly large proportion of its crude oil from Libya, needed to maintain good relations. France was anxious over the use to which Libya would put the Mirage jet fighters being supplied under the 1970 agreement. The same anxiety was revealed in Britain over the supply of armaments, but none of these countries could afford to alienate Libya.

In December 1971, avowedly in retaliation for Britain's failure to prevent the Iranian occupation of the Tumb islands in the Gulf, Libya nationalized the assets of British Petroleum. This move was, apparently, not unopposed by some members of the Libyan Government. Libya was expelled from the Sterling Area. British Petroleum subsequently took legal action against those who attempted to buy BP oil from Libya. This move was followed by lengthy talks with the Italian state company, ENI. Finally, on September 30th, an agreement was reached under which Libya took a 50 per cent share in ENI's operations and AGIP, a subsidiary of ENI, became responsible for marketing the oil from ENI's concessions. Libya had originally asked for a 51 per cent share and it was thought possible that arms agreements with Italy might have influenced the situation. The ENI agreement then became the basis for Libya's negotiations with other companies, and, in October 1972, the Government demanded a 50 per cent share in Bunker Hunt's Sarir operations. This dispute eventually went to arbitration. In talks in May and June 1973 with the Oasis group, the Amoseas group and Occidental, the Prime Minister was reported to have demanded 100 per cent control of foreign oil company operations.

Relations with Egypt and Syria were somewhat strained at the end of 1971, the cause of the friction being largely Gaddafi's uncompromising hard line on the Arab/Israel conflict. In October, President Sadat and Gaddafi met for talks on the problem and Gaddafi continued to press for all-out war.

Relations with Britain were also very much strained in the winter of 1971/72, not only because of the nationalization of BP but also because of Libyan intervention in the dispute with Malta over the British bases there. Libya had for some time been actively fostering relations with Malta, talks on possible Libyan aid being held in August 1971. In January 1972 the British naval training mission was ordered to leave Libya. And in February the 1954 agreement with the United States was abrogated.

Libya's attitude towards the Soviet Union had remained cool, and the Government was violently opposed to the Iraqi/Soviet treaty, signed in April 1972. Nevertheless, in February 1972, Major Jalloud visited Moscow and in March an agreement on oil co-operation was signed. It was also reported that the U.S.S.R. might supply arms to Libya.

At home, President Gaddafi continued to attempt to run the legislature and the Government entirely in accordance with Islamic principles. At the end of March 1972 the Arab Socialist Union held its first national congress. At subsequent sessions of the ASU resolutions were passed clarifying its position and policies, and abolishing censorship of the Press, while at the same time maintaining financial control of newspapers.

In July 1972 disagreement within the RCC led to Maj. Jalloud taking over as Prime Minister from Gaddafi, a new cabinet being formed in which all but two of the ministers were civilians.

PROPOSED MERGER WITH EGYPT

Presidents Gaddafi and Sadat announced in August 1972 that complete union between Egypt and Libya by September 1st, 1973, had been agreed. Joint committees were set up on constitutional affairs, political organizations, defence, economics, legislation, administration, finance, education and information. The capital of the new union was to be Cairo.

The move was generally welcomed in the Arab world, at least officially, but King Hussein of Jordan and the Lebanese Phalange leader, Pierre Gemayel, expressed doubts about the union's staying power. The constitution of the Federation of Arab Republics, between Syria, Egypt and Libya, had already come into effect on January 1st, 1972. Abroad the merger was seen as a response both to Egypt's need for capital and as a following of a more Arab line of policy as a consequence of Sadat's dismissal of the Soviet advisers in July. The union agreement passed, in fact, virtually without comment from the Soviet Union. The merger increased the possibility of Libya's oil being used as a political weapon against the West, particularly in discouraging support for Israel. Gaddafi had already asked U.S. oil companies to use their influence with the U.S. Government.

Later in the year, when it was evident that Syria was reinforcing ties with the Soviet Union this, and the fact that Soviet/Egyptian relations were becoming somewhat warmer, was seen as hindering the merger, and the work of the joint committee progressed only very slowly. By July 1973 prospects of the proposed merger taking place by September 1st, 1973, seemed slender.

FOREIGN AFFAIRS

The basis of Libyan foreign policy was non-alignment, with the Government announcing its intention of maintaining good relations with both East and West, provided neither tried to dominate or interfere with Libya. The most striking feature of Libya's foreign dealings, however, was the large amount of aid given to revolutionary movements in other countries, notably the U.S.A., Northern Ireland, Morocco, Tunisia and Uganda. The President's interference in the affairs of other states was productive of a good deal of hostility and ridicule. These activities reached such a pitch in 1972 that it was impossible even for other Arab countries to disregard their implications. In September 1972, Libyan aircraft bound for Uganda to aid General Amin were stopped from flying over Sudan.

Gaddafi's attitude to the Arab/Israel conflict underwent some change in 1972. In an important speech in October he denounced the failure of Arab unity in the conflict and maintained that Libya was not to be regarded as a source of unlimited monetary handouts. In January 1973 he made an unprecedented attack on the Palestinian resistance. Whereas previously he had called for all-out fighting, he now denounced hasty action, praised the restraint of President Sadat of Egypt and criticized the lack of fedayeen action. He went even further in February and actually praised Israel's courage and resolution, contrasting it with the spirit shown by the Arab states.

When on February 21st, 1973, a Libyan airliner was shot down over Sinai by Israeli fighters, Libyan Government reaction was notably slow and mild. There were many demonstrations in Libya, and the Egyptians were attacked because of their failure to help the aircraft. The RCC, however, announced that any criticism of the merger with Egypt would be considered high treason.

LIBYA'S CULTURAL REVOLUTION

In April 1973 President Gaddafi made a speech in which he denounced the Libyan reluctance to contribute to national development, particularly mentioning qualified personnel who chose to work abroad. He announced a five-point plan designed to place the running of the country on a wholly Islamic basis. The plan also involved the revision of all existing laws, purging the country of the politically "sick", arming the masses "to defend the revolution" and a complete overhaul of the administration. Popular committees were to be set up in villages, offices and work places in order to return power to the people, and it is known that by June 1973 these committees had already been set up in some of the oil companies.

ECONOMIC SURVEY*

Oil has transformed the Libyan economy. Before its discovery in commercial quantities in the 1950s, agriculture was the basis of the economy and domestic revenue covered only about half of the Government's ordinary and development expenditure. But between 1962 and 1968, national income increased by 344 per cent from LD 131 million to LD 798 million and gross national product increased by 458 per cent from LD 163 million to LD 909 million. The deciding factor was the increase in the value of oil exports during the period—by 835 per cent. Exports accounted for 51 per cent of gross domestic product in 1968.

The structure of G.D.P. was also profoundly affected by the advent of oil and in some ways was distorted by it so that while other sectors grew absolutely, their importance declined relatively. As a whole, G.D.P. (at constant prices and factor cost) increased by 365 per cent between 1962 and 1968. The value of agriculture grew by almost 30 per cent, wholesale and retail trade increased by 231 per cent, construction by 385 per cent, manufacturing by 90 per cent and ownership of dwellings by 29 per cent. At the same time, the value of mining and quarrying decreased from 9 to 3 per cent of G.D.P., trade from 9 to 6 per cent, transport and communication from 6 to 3 per cent, manufacturing from 6 to 2 per cent, and ownership of dwellings from 17 to 5 per cent; only the value of construction actively maintained its share of G.D.P. at 7 per cent. The share of mining increased from 28 to 61 per cent of G.D.P.

In foreign trade 99.6 per cent of exports are petroleum and products and a healthy trade surplus is being maintained. This surplus was LD 643.8 million in 1970 and LD 331.3 million in the first six months of 1972.

---

* *Note:* In August 1971 the Libyan Government changed the name, but not the value, of the Libyan pound (£L) to the Libyan dinar (LD).

Government ordinary and development allocations have grown enormously: for 1972–73 they were set at LD 599 million (the Libyan financial year begins on April 1st). Since the 1969 revolution, state intervention in the economy has increased, in line with President Gaddafi's ideas of "Islamic socialism". The Government has at least a 51 per cent share in a number of sectors including banking and insurance, public transport, some sections of the construction industry and some manufacturing concerns. There is also a state petroleum company, the Libyan National Petroleum Corporation (LINOCO). At present, however, almost all oil production is in private hands but rigorously overseen by the Ministry of Petroleum.

Until the country's oil resources began to be exploited not more than 25 per cent of the population lived in the towns. This is no longer true, and the drift to the towns has caused a serious problem. Something like half of the rest of the population are settled in rural communities, and the other half are semi-nomads, who follow a pastoral mode of life. The Western provinces are the smallest, but they include Tripoli, which is the business capital of Libya, the population of Tripoli town being 353,982 at the end of 1972. The main town of Cyrenaica is Benghazi, the population of the Benghazi district in 1964 being 278,826, but Cyrenaica is an area three times the size of Tripolitania. The Fezzan is about twice as large as Tripolitania, and its chief town is Sebha. The overwhelming majority of the population of Libya is Arab or Berber by race, with Negroid races predominating in the Fezzan. The population is growing rapidly and by the end of 1971 was estimated at 2,084,000.

AGRICULTURE

Agriculture dominated the economy until the discovery of oil. Even now the oil industry gives direct employment to no more than a small fraction of the population, so although the prosperity brought by oil has attracted many people to the towns, agriculture is still of some importance. This is despite only a very small proportion of the total area of the country being cultivable. Moreover, in some areas a high percentage of this cultivable land is used for grazing. The area under irrigation has increased steadily and had reached about 501,000 hectares in 1968, according to a UN estimate. The present Government is now sponsoring several land reclamation and irrigation projects including the Kufra project to irrigate 10,000 hectares and the Tawurgha project to reclaim 3,000 hectares. In mid-1970 all Italian-owned land and property in Libya, including 37,000 hectares of cultivated land, was confiscated and plans were made to distribute the expropriated lands to Libyan farmers with government credits for seed, fertilizers and machinery. In addition, the Government is undertaking a major road-building effort which includes 2,400 kilometres of new rural roads and 1,200 kilometres of new highways.

Animal husbandry is the basis of farming in Libya. The sheep are mainly of the fat-tailed Barbary type; like the goats they are used for meat, milk and wool. Cattle are used principally for draught and transport, like the donkeys and camels. All in all, livestock has been the most important single source of income to the farmers. Of the cereal crops, barley, which is the staple diet of most of the population, is far and away the most important. Production fluctuates widely with the rainfall.

Olives and citrus fruit are next in importance by value, both being grown mainly in Western province. Dates are grown in oases in the Southern province and on the coastal belt, and form an important article of food. Other important food crops are tomatoes, almonds, castor beans and groundnuts, which are grown mainly in Western province. An important crop is that of esparto grass (*stipa tenacissima*) which grows wild in the Jebel. It is used for the manufacture of high qualities of paper and bank-notes, and was formerly the most important article of export. It is handled by the National Esparto Development Corporation, of which the Government owns 80 per cent of the shares. It is curious that the plant *silphium*, which made Cyrene famous in antiquity and which is well known from Herodotus and from the celebrated Arkesilaos vase in Paris, has not been identified with any certainty.

Oil revenues have enabled the Government to provide vast aid to agriculture. After a successful year in 1972–73, as far as the implementation of investment projects was concerned, the Government decided to make a great effort in agriculture, allocating to it a sum of LD 416 million for the period April 1st, 1973, to March 30th, 1975. In 1972–73 the allocation was just LD 53 million and most of this was actually spent. Investment is designed especially to increase meat, dairy and fruit production.

Consumption of fertilizers is increasing. In 1970–71 a total of 4,500 tons of nitrogenous fertilizers were used (3,300 tons in 1969–70) as well as 7,500 tons of phosphates (4,900 tons in 1969–70) and 1,000 tons of potash (400 tons in 1969–70). In 1971 the food production index rose to 241 compared with 209 in 1970; the per capita food production index rose to 134 from 120; and the agricultural production index rose to 233 from 204. (The base figure of 100 was calculated on the average production between 1952 and 1956.) All these movements reflected the heavy investment in agriculture by the Libyan Government.

The agricultural situation as a whole, however, is not satisfactory. The olive crop has declined since President Gaddafi came to power and only 14,000 tons of olive oil was produced in 1970. In the same year only 53,000 tons of barley was grown compared with 124,000 tons the year before. Moreover, agricultural expansion is hindered by the lack of trained technicians and administrators. However, output is increasing as projects are completed and new ones begun. For instance, the Yugoslav firm, Abrejoproject, was awarded a LD 32 million contract in April 1973 to build 1,000 new farms near Qarrah Boli as part of the Al Jeffara scheme. Between the beginning of March 1973 and the end of May, agricultural contracts worth over LD 116 million were awarded. Projects completed include dam schemes at Wadi Qattera and Wadi Majanin which were finished in 1972. Development continues of the fertile but isolated Kufra oasis, discovered by Occidental Oil in 1968 and run by a state company since January 1972.

FORESTRY AND FISHING

Some attempts have been made by the Government at reafforestation, including a successful small-scale experiment in 1971 to stabilize the soil with a synthetic rubber spray and then plant eucalyptus saplings.

The off-shore waters abound in fish, especially tunny and sardines, but most of the fishing is done by Italians, Greeks or Maltese. Of special importance are the sponge-beds along the wide continental shelf off the Libyan coast. These are exploited by foreign fishermen and divers, mainly Greeks from the Dodecanese. During 1971 it was agreed to set up a joint Tunisian-Libyan fishing company to exploit the waters west of Misurata. Two sardine-packing plants are being built, at Zuwarah and Khums, by a German firm.

OIL

That oil was present in both Tripolitania and Cyrenaica had long been suspected, and for several years after Libya became independent, a large number of the bigger oil companies carried out geological surveys of the country. In 1955 a petroleum law came into force setting up a petroleum commission, which was empowered to grant concessions on the basis that any profits would be divided equally between the Government and the operating company, and that parts of each concession had to be handed back to the Government after a given period of years. Under this law, still in effect but with amendments, concessions were granted to many American companies and to British, French and other foreign groups. By 1972 eleven groups, involving 21 companies, held concession rights.

Important oil strikes first began to be made in 1958, and ten years later Libya was already the fourth largest exporter in the world. The growth of the oil industry has been particularly rapid since the closing of the Suez Canal in 1967. The oil industry still employs only a relatively small proportion of the Libyan population: in 1969, 6,395 persons, of whom 2,627 were foreigners.

Exports take place from five different ocean terminals connected to the various fields by pipeline built by the five groups which have made the major finds. The pipeline system and the terminals are, however, available to other groups which are producing oil. The earliest of the five ocean terminals to be opened was that at Mersa Brega in the Gulf of Sirte in 1961. The pipeline was built to Bir Zelten, some 200 miles south of Benghazi, where Esso Standard (Libya) had found oil in 1959. This group also operates a refinery at Mersa Brega and a gas liquefaction plant to prepare gas for shipment to Italy and Spain. Another terminal is that at Ras el Sidr, to the west of Mersa Brega, built by the Oasis group. Oasis's original find was at Hofra, from which the pipeline runs to the sea at Ras el Sidr. A third group consisting of Mobil and the German firm Gelsenberg also found oil near Hofra, but built another pipeline to a terminal at Ras Lanuf, just east of Ras el Sidr. From a fourth terminal at Mersa el Hariga, near Tobruk, a pipeline some 320 miles long runs to Sarir, near which British Petroleum and its American partner, Bunker Hunt, had made an important find in 1964, and another two years later. The latest terminal is at Zuetina, about 150 miles south of Benghazi. This was opened in 1968, as the terminal for a pipeline about 135 miles long to two fields at Augila and Idris. Here an American Company, Occidental Oil, which did not even obtain its concession until early in 1966, had found oil in large quantities. Outside the five main oil groups, the only other group of any importance is the Amoseas group, in which two American companies, Standard of California and Texaco are equal partners. This group is producing oil from the Nafoora field, not far from Augila, and has a pipeline connected to the ocean terminal at Ras Lanuf.

In 1965 a law was passed bringing the arrangements under which the producing companies pay tax and royalties to the Libyan Government into line with those in force in the other Middle Eastern members of OPEC, which Libya joined in 1962. Hitherto the price used by the companies to calculate the profits on which tax was assessed had been the price they actually realized on world markets. The new law stipulated amongst other things that the price used should be the so-called posted price instead, which for many years had been much higher; this the operating companies eventually accepted. Negotiations began in the autumn of 1969 between the Government and the companies with the object of increasing the posted price, and came to fruition in April 1971 with the signing of the Tripoli agreements which raised the base posted price per barrel of 40° API crude to $3.07 with temporary adjustments bringing the total posted price per barrel to $3.447.

The agreement also included annual incremental price rises until 1975; settlement of company income tax rates at 55 per cent (except for Occidental Oil); an assured reinvestment in exploration, secondary recovery or gas projects; and a guaranteed supply of crude to LINOCO, sufficient for local consumption.

LINOCO is the Government's instrument for developing the oil industry. It has already taken over the marketing of oil products in Libya and has concluded agreements for co-operation in exploitation for oil with six foreign countries. These are ERAP and ENI, two concerns owned respectively by the French and Italian Governments, and Ashland, an American oil company. In 1971 LINOCO awarded contracts for a LD 25 million refinery at Zawia and for a petrochemical complex near Mersa Brega.

Libya is a leader of those oil-producing states which demand participation in oil-company activities. It negotiated with ENI in September 1972 an agreement under which Libya received an immediate 50 per cent share in ENI's Libyan activities. ENI was induced to make this agreement by Libya's refusal to allow exports from Concession 100, the Italian company's first source of Libyan oil, and by the awarding of a contract for the construction of a refinery at Zawia to an ENI subsidiary. Libya, for its part, reduced its initial demand, which was for a 51 per cent share, perhaps because of an Italian agreement to supply weaponry to the Gaddafi régime. Libya was thought to be seeking similar agreements with two other companies, Oasis and Bunker Hunt, negotiations with the former resuming in May 1973. The Bunker Hunt matter is to go to arbitration and production of the company's oil from its only Libyan well at Sarir was reported to have stopped by early 1973. However, the situation may have radically changed in May 1973 when Prime Minister Jalloud demanded that Libya should have a 100 per cent share in foreign oil companies. He made this point during talks with Oasis, Libya's largest producer, which is a consortium made up of Continental, Amerada Hess, Marathon and Shell, and it is unclear whether the demand for 100 per cent control is part of the bargaining process or a serious request. Talks on participation have also commenced with the Amoseas group and Occidental.

So far the Government has refrained from any general nationalization measures but in December 1971 it took over British Petroleum's Libyan interests in retaliation for the British Government's failure to prevent the Iranian takeover of the three Gulf islands of Abu Musa and the two Tumbs. BP had operated the 400,000 barrels-a-day Sarir field in Libya with Bunker Hunt and Libya set up the Arabian Gulf Exploration Company to operate BP's half of the field. Production at the field dropped to a little over 200,000 barrels a day and BP warned that it would take legal action against any buyer of Sarir oil from AGEC. In January 1972 ownership of a shipload of Libyan oil sent to Italy for refining became the subject of legal action, with BP claiming that it held legal title to the cargo. The court rejected this claim in March 1973. AGEC is believed to have sold most of the oil produced at Sarir since December 1971 to East European buyers.

A central feature of the oil policy of the Gaddafi Government has been its willingness to impose restrictions on oil production on the grounds that reserves may run out leaving Libya still a backward country. It is hoped that new discoveries will match production in the near future and the Government plans that the oil sector should grow by only 7.5 per cent a year until 1975. In fact oil output has fallen since 1969. In 1971 it fell by 17.1 per cent to 132 million metric tons and in 1972 by a further 20.5 per cent to 105 million tons. As a result of Government actions, companies have become increasingly reluctant to invest in Libya and the number of drilling rigs in operation has dropped to single figures.

One hindrance to good company—Government relations was removed at the beginning of May 1972 when agreement was reached in principle on an 8.49 per cent increase in posted prices to offset the realignment of world currencies in December 1971. Detailed agreements on this issue had been concluded by early June with all the oil companies in Libya except Mobil/Gelsenberg and Esso. Libya's disagreement with the latter stems from the Government's argument, not accepted by Esso, that the 8.49 per cent price increase should apply also to liquefied natural gas produced from the Brega Liquefaction plant. A further agreement on a new formula for adjusting oil prices was signed between Libya and the oil companies in Geneva in June 1973.

Esso is believed to have lost as much as $200 million on the Brega project due to building and technical difficulties and price quarrels with the Government. The plant cost $350 million and was completed in June 1970 but deliveries to Spain, the first customer, did not begin until March 1971 and to Italy until the summer of 1971.

In 1972 Libya produced 3,160,410 barrels of refined oil but plans to increase output. LINOCO intends to build a 130,000 barrels-a-day refinery at Tobruk. A factor to package and blend lubricating oil is being built by Mothercat at Zawia and two 47,000-ton tankers for LINOCO have been ordered from Spain.

INDUSTRY

Manufacturing industry is largely confined to processing local agricultural products. These include carpet weaving, tanning and leather working, shoes, building materials (gypsum and cement), matches and soap and detergent manufacture. Food processing includes a government tobacco and cigarette factory, a date-packing plant, four tomato-canning plants, castor- and olive-oil presses, several flour mills, and soft drinks firms. There are also a number of service industries with government participation. These include all insurance firms and commercial banks, a contracting firm and nation-wide public transport. Plans are also in hand to build a whole range of factories in the near future ranging from prefabricated construction materials to cables, glass and pharmaceuticals.

The Government is now settling down to getting Libyan development going again after a period of stagnation during which the Gaddafi régime re-examined the projects approved by King Idris. Contracts have been awarded mainly to West European companies for the expansion of the building material and textile industries. Ports and airfields are being improved and a LD 10.7 million contract has been awarded to Nippon Electric of Japan for the installation of a microwave network for telephones and telecommunications. This was the first major contract awarded in Libya to a Japanese firm. At the end of 1972 a £30 million contract was awarded to a Turkish firm for the expansion of Tripoli port and an Egyptian company is to improve the port at Derna. A steel pipe factory is being built in Benghazi by Aresta of Spain. Public utilities are being improved with Westinghouse building a desalination plant at Tuara. The building of a nuclear desalination plant is being studied. Libya plans to increase its power production to 700,000 kilowatts by 1984 and has contracted with Alsthom of France for a power station and two desalination plants at Tripoli and with Deutsche Babcock Wilcox for a power station and a desalination plant at Benghazi. A nuclear power station may be built with Egypt. The U.S.S.R. has agreed to build twelve clinics and a Libyan firm is building a LD 23.5 million hospital in Benghazi. There are plans to build 18,000 houses a year. More flour mills and fish processing plants, as well as Libya's first shoe factory and tyre plant, are being built.

The three-year plan covering the period ending in March 1975 provided for growth in the industrial, electric power, housing, transport and communication sectors of 14.5 per cent a year. The main difficulties which Libya will face in implementing its plan are a lack of administrators and technicians, which makes it hard for projects to be started and organized on schedule, and a shortage of skilled labour. Both problems were made more severe by President Gaddafi's expulsion of Italian settlers. Industry now accounts for about 10 per cent of the national income and employs about a sixth of the working population.

EXTERNAL TRADE

Until production of oil began, Libya's exports consisted almost entirely of agricultural products, and its imports of manufactured goods. In 1960, for instance, imports were valued at LD 60.4 million and exports at LD 4.0 million, leaving an adverse balance of LD 56.4 million (although LD 21 million of the total value of imports in 1960 was accounted for by goods imported for the account of the oil companies). Oil was first exported in the autumn of 1961, and by 1969 imports totalled LD 241.3 million and exports LD 773.9 million, of which LD 771.2 or over 99 per cent, was accounted for by oil. The minute proportion of remaining exports were mainly hides and skins, groundnuts, almonds, metal scrap and re-exports.

Imports consist of a wide variety of manufactured goods such as textiles and motor vehicles, but also of timber, chemicals and other raw materials. In addition, many foodstuffs have to be imported, such as tea, sugar, coffee and, in years of drought, wheat and flour. The principal suppliers are Italy, the U.S.A., West Germany and the United Kingdom.

The year 1962 was the last time Libya showed a deficit on balance of trade (LD 23.4 million). Since then there has been a surplus which has steadily increased. The surplus for 1970 totalled LD 643.8 million and for 1971 it totalled LD 712.2 million, an indication of the fact that Libya had more foreign exchange than it could use. However, the surplus was reduced to LD 331.3 million in the first half of 1972, because of the enlarged investment programme, and this process should continue. Imports in the first half of 1972 rose by 42 per cent compared with the corresponding period in 1971, a rise which was accounted for largely by increased purchases of investment goods. Libya's best oil customers are Britain, France, the Federal Republic of Germany, Italy and the U.S.A. Sales to Italy have been stimulated by the ENI settlement and to the U.S.A. by the much-publicized American fuel crisis. Oil exports rose by 1.5 per cent in value in the first half of 1972 but only because increased oil prices more than offset a decreased volume of sales. In the whole of 1972 oil exports averaged 2.2 million barrels a day. In March 1972 the foreign exchange reserves and gold assets of the Central Bank of Libya totalled $2,783.4 million.

FINANCE

Before the 1969 coup most Libyan banks were subsidiaries of foreign banks. However, amongst the first decrees issued by the Revolutionary Council was one which required 51 per cent of the capital of all banks operating in Libya to be owned by Libyans; the majority of directors, including the chairman, of each bank had to be Libyan citizens. The royal Government had followed a similar policy without compulsion, and a number of foreign banks had accordingly already "Libyanized" themselves. In December 1970, all commercial banks were nationalized, with government participation set at 51 per cent of bank shares. In addition, all foreign-held shares of banks entirely owned by Libyans continue to operate. There are now only five commercial banks in the country including one formed at the same time by the amalgamation of the former commercial section of the central bank with two small Libyan banks.

The development of the oil industry has enabled Libya to maintain a high degree of stability in the external value of its currency. Until December 1971 Libya was a member of the Sterling Area, but the nationalization of BP and the withdrawal of deposits of £200 million from British banks resulted in her expulsion from it.

The massive growth in oil revenue has also allowed the Government to devote about half its income to development expenditure. It has even been able to give generous aid abroad, in particular to Egypt, Syria and Jordan. Aid to these countries was decided on at Khartoum in 1968 in the aftermath of the June War, but was cut off from the Jordanian Government in September 1970 when it attacked the Palestinian guerrillas. In 1972 and 1973 Libya gave increased attention to the Mediterranean and Africa. Thus increased economic co-operation was organized with Malta, Chad and Uganda and some aid was provided to these states.

At the end of April 1972 the Government published a one-year development budget to cover the period ending March 31st, 1973, and a three-year development budget to end on March 31st, 1975. The one-year budget involved total spending of LD 367 million, a record figure (the 1970-71 budget totalled LD 300 million), and the three-year programme called for expenditure of LD 1,165 million. Despite the fact that many of the allocations in the 1972-73 budget were not spent (in some sectors probably less than half the funds available were utilized), the Government was sufficiently encouraged by its experience to revise the three-year plan dramatically. In the spring of 1973 the three-year budget was amended to provide for a LD 800 million increase in spending to bring the three-year total to LD 1,965 million. Increased emphasis was placed on agriculture and LD 2.5 million was singled out for administrative development. Industry's allocation rose to LD 238 million while oil received LD 164.5 million. The plan envisages LD 278 million being spent on housing, while electricity, transport and communications and education each receive LD 190 million. These increases make it likely that the targets of the original plan, a rise in the gross domestic product of 10.5 per cent a year and a per capita income of LD 2,684 in 1975, will be achieved. Per capita income in 1971 was LD 2,247.

Editorial Note: A series of important events took place in Libya in June, July and August 1973, after this volume had gone to press. In the sphere of oil activities, Libya nationalized the assets of the American oil company, Nelson Bunker Hunt on June 11th. Early in August, after prolonged talks, Libya announced 51 per cent nationalization of Occidental Petroleum's assets, and on August 16th it was announced that the independent members of the Oasis group (Marathon, Continental Oil and Amerada Hess) had agreed to Libya's 51 per cent nationalization demands.

In July, Colonel Gaddafi, rendered impatient by the apparent failure of his talks with President Sadat on the proposed union with Egypt, briefly resigned, but was persuaded to withdraw his resignation by the threatened resignation of the Revolutionary Command Council and the Cabinet. Meanwhile, thousands of Libyans set off on a march to Cairo calling for the total merger of Libya with Egypt by September 1st. They were turned back, however, before they could reach Cairo. By mid-August, after further negotiations, it was apparent that Gaddafi had yielded on his insistence for a complete merger by September 1st, and it appeared that all that will take place on September 1st will be a declaration of principle on the merger.

STATISTICAL SURVEY

AREA AND POPULATION

AREA (sq. km.)	POPULATION 1964 Census	POPULATION 1971 Estimate
1,759,500	1,564,369	2,084,000

About 30 per cent of the population are nomadic or semi-nomadic according to 1964 census.

POPULATION BY DISTRICT
(1964 Census)

Tripoli	379,925	Khoms		136,679
Benghazi	278,826	Jebel Akhdar		88,016
Zavia	190,708	Darna		84,112
Jebel Gharbi	180,883	Sebha		47,436
Misurata	145,894	Ubari		31,890

AGRICULTURE

DISTRIBUTION OF LAND
(1960 census—'000 hectares)

	TRIPOLITANIA	CYRENAICA	FEZZAN
Arable	1,605	742	28
Pasture	1,121	15	—
Permanent Crops, Forests	154	37	7

LIVESTOCK
(Estimates—'000)

	1970	1971
Sheep	2,163	2,284
Goats	1,234	1,141
Cattle	108	101
Camels	163	120

PRINCIPAL CROPS
(tons)

	1970	1971	1972
Barley	52,808	32,127	116,395
Wheat	21,112	17,726	41,585
Olives	71,154	5,000	94,533
Citrus Fruits	20,050	24,918	27,138
Groundnuts	10,685	11,075	13,692
Almonds	3,787	3,560	4,515
Tomatoes	136,413	130,816	170,038
Dates	49,111	66,190	59,544
Potatoes	9,982	22,813	49,046

Tobacco leaf production (1970) 2 million kilos, manufactured tobacco production 170,000 kilos. Grapes are also grown in quantity (about 7,000 metric tons in 1970).

LIBYA—(Statistical Survey)

INDUSTRY
(Value of Output in LD'000—Large establishments only)

	1970	1971
Food Manufacturing	8,258	10,221
Beverage Industries	2,174	2,252
Tobacco Manufactures	9,219	11,286
Chemicals and Products	5,060	4,916
Textiles	1,743	2,011
Cement and Products	2,371	2,786
Fabricated Metal Products	1,828	1,747
Total (incl. others)	30,653	38,323

OIL
CRUDE OIL PRODUCTION
(metric tons)

1965	58,378,000
1966	72,645,000
1967	83,477,000
1968	125,539,000
1969	149,728,000
1970	161,708,000
1971	132,400,000
1972	105,000,000

FINANCE

1,000 dirhams (formerly millièmes) = 1 Libyan dinar (LD).
Coins: 1, 5, 10, 20, 50 and 100 millièmes (dirham coins have not yet been issued).
Notes: 250 and 500 dirhams; 1, 5 and 10 dinars.
Exchange rates (March 1973): £1 sterling = 728.29 dirhams; U.S. $1 = 296.05 dirhams.
100 Libyan dinars = £137.31 = $337.78.

Note: The dinar is equivalent to the former Libyan pound, which it replaced in 1971.

DEVELOPMENT BUDGET
(1971-72: LD'000)

Agriculture and agrarian reform	50,400
Industry	32,000
Education and National Guidance	27,150
Information and Culture	27,000
Public Health	17,000
Transport and Communications	39,800
Municipalities	29,150
Housing	40,000
Public Works	21,500
Total (including others)	300,000

Development Budget 1972-73: LD 367 million.

ORDINARY BUDGET
(1971-72: LD million)

Education and National Guidance	46.3
Defence	n.a.
Police and Public Security	n.a.
Total (including others)	201.0

DEVELOPMENT COUNCIL THREE-YEAR PLAN

In March 1972 a three-year development budget was published, to run until the end of March 1975. In the Spring of 1973 this budget was revised to bring the three-year total expenditure to LD 1,965 million.

EXTERNAL TRADE
(LD'000)

	1968	1969	1970	1971	1972
Imports	230,200	241,301	198,002	250,352	343,204
Exports	669,800	772,765	841,829	959,918	966,307

LIBYA—(Statistical Survey)

SELECTED COMMODITIES
(LD'000)

Imports	1970	1971	1972
Food and Live Animals	39,326	47,574	53,128
Beverages and Tobacco	2,532	2,484	1,201
Mineral Fuel	3,618	5,770	7,393
Animal and Vegetable Oils and Fats	2,777	5,539	2,786
Inedible Crude Materials excluding Fuel	6,300	8,307	9,980
Chemicals	11,415	15,123	16,646
Manufactures	42,384	52,025	81,220
Machinery	58,708	72,963	117 780
Miscellaneous	30,942	40,557	53,069

Exports	1970	1971	1972
Crude Petroleum	841,134	959,392	948,230
Groundnuts	—	235	408
Hides and Skins	202	284	1,247
Castor Oil Seed	5	3	16
Wool and other Animal Hair	488	—	311

PRINCIPAL COUNTRIES
(LD'000)

Imports	1969	1970	1971	1972
Italy	54,788	42,712	57,712	88,352
U.S.A.	45,152	27,307	17,323	21,635
U.K.	29,768	18,579	24,866	29,911
German Federal Republic	21,426	17,950	23,167	32,825
Netherlands	8,871	6,190	7,600	10,135
France	12,015	12,724	21,402	24,206
Belgium	3,318	2,212	—	—
Japan	11,747	11,116	15,193	19,930
China, People's Republic	5,388	3,781	6,444	8,433
Lebanon	3,726	5,628	7,335	11,149
Other Countries	n.a.	50,003	53,847	96,628

EXPORTS OF CRUDE OIL
(LD'000)

Country	1969	1970	1971	1972
U.K.	106,405	127,697	157,230	129,620
German Federal Republic	167,732	147,305	168,260	238,332
Italy	178,618	218,090	230,526	185,714
France	89,871	113,344	119,492	84,619
Netherlands	78,457	79,627	56,928	44,063
U.S.A.	39,548	22,251	57,746	74,867
Belgium	30,327	32,634	23,550	11,132
Spain	38,503	38,363	39,060	24,107
Total (incl. others)	771,857	841,134	956,867	948,231

TRANSPORT
ROADS

	1969	1970	1971
Private Cars	86,814	95,762	110,312
Lorries	39,947	44,582	50,435
Buses	727	820	877
Taxis	3,884	4,367	4,703

SHIPPING

	Ships ('000 N.R.T.) Entered	Cleared	Cargo ('000 metric tons) Loaded	Unloaded
1969	4,908	4,886	27	3,099
1970	4,381	4,357	39	2,600
1971	4,559	4,487	18	3,004
1972	4,792	4,801	22	5,649

CIVIL AVIATION

	1970	1971	1972
Number of Passengers Entering	165,369	128,005	274,243
Leaving	170,854	124,356	237,548
Cargo Unloaded (tons)	8,835	12,111	13,808
Cargo Loaded (tons)	2,459	2,412	2,763

EDUCATION
(1971–72)

State Schools	Schools	Students	Teachers
Primary	1,413	407,805	14,421
Preparatory	203	43,790	3,039
Secondary	39	9,642	1,007
Teacher-Training	20	5,984	518
Technical	9	3,202	376

Source: Census and Statistical Dept., Ministry of Economy and Trade, Tripoli.

THE CONSTITUTION

A new provisional constitution of 37 articles was proclaimed in December 1969. The following is a summary of its principal features:

Libya is a democratic and free Arab Republic with sovereignty of the people who constitute part of the Arab nation and whose objective is comprehensive Arab unity.

The official religion of the state is Islam but the state guarantees religious freedom.

Supreme authority is vested in the Revolutionary Command Council which has power to appoint the Council of Ministers, to sign and modify treaties and to declare war. It retains power over the armed forces and the diplomatic corps.

All citizens are equal and the foundations of the country are built on family unity.

The state will aim to achieve socialism by means of social justice which forbids all forms of exploitation. It will work towards the liberation of the national economy from every foreign influence, guiding it towards productivity and stability.

The property of the state is also the property of the public. Private property cannot be exploited and is guaranteed by the state. It can only be expropriated as laid down by law.

Freedom of speech is guaranteed as long as it does not transgress the principles of the revolution.

The extradition of political prisoners is forbidden.

All titles, including those granted by the previous government, have been revoked.

Medical care is a guaranteed right for all citizens; education will be compulsory until the end of primary stage (now at the age of nine).

THE GOVERNMENT

REVOLUTIONARY COMMAND COUNCIL

Chairman: Col. MUAMMAR AL GADDAFI.

Members: Lt.-Col. ABU BAKAR YUNIS JABER, Maj. ABDUL SALAM JALLOUD, Maj. BASHIR AL SAGHIER HAWADY, Maj. ABDUL MONIEUM AL TAHER AL HUNY, Maj. AL KHOWEILDY AL HAMIDY, Maj. MUSTAFA AL KHARROBY, Maj. MUKHTAR ABDULLAH AL GERWY, Maj. MUHAMMED NAJIM, Maj. AWAD ALI HAMZA.

LIBYA—(THE GOVERNMENT, DIPLOMATIC REPRESENTATION)

CABINET
(May 1973)

Prime Minister: Maj. ABDUL SALAM JALLOUD.
Minister of Defence: (vacant).
Minister of Education: MOHAMED AHMED AL CHERIF.
Minister of Housing and Public Services: MUHAMMAD AHMAD MANQOUSH.
Minister of Communications and Electricity: TAHA SHARIF BIN AMIR.
Minister of Justice: MUHAMMAD ALY AL JADY.
Minister of Health: Dr. MEFTAH AL USTA OMAR.
Minister of Agriculture and Agrarian Reform: MUHAMMAD ALI TABOU.
Minister of State for Agricultural Development: ABDUL MAJID JAUD.
Minister of Petroleum: EZZEDIN MABROUK.

Minister of Labour and Acting Minister of Foreign Affairs: ABDUL ATY AL ABEIDY.
Minister of the Interior: Maj. AL KHUWAILDI AL HUMAIDI.
Minister of Information and Culture: ABOU ZEID OMAR DOURDA.
Minister of the Economy: ABU BAKR AL CHERIF.
Minister of the Treasury: MOHAMED AL ZARROUK RAGAB.
Minister of Industry and Mineral Resources: GABALLAH AZOUZ TALHI.
Minister of Youth and Social Affairs: ABDEL HAMID AL ZINATI.
Minister of Planning: ABDUL KARIM BALLO.
Minister of the Civil Service: MOHAMED ABU BAKR BEN YOUNIS.
Minister of Agricultural Development: ABDUL MAJED AL QAOWD.

DIPLOMATIC REPRESENTATION

EMBASSIES ACCREDITED TO LIBYA
(Tripoli unless otherwise stated)
(E) Embassy.

Afghanistan: Cairo, Egypt (E).
Algeria: Sharia Qayrouan 12 (E); *Ambassador:* 'ALI KAAFI.
Argentina: Algiers, Algeria (E).
Austria: Tunis, Tunisia (E).
Belgium: Sharia Sidi 'Isa (E); *Chargé d'Affaires:* ALBERT F. DURRE.
Brazil: Tunis, Tunisia (E).
Bulgaria: Sharia Murad Agha (E); *Ambassador:* STYKO NEDELCHEV.
Canada: Cairo, Egypt (E).
Chad: Sharia Bin 'Ashur; *Chargé d'Affaires:* JUSTIN DE GARABAYE.
Chile: Cairo, Egypt.
China: Sharia al-Hadi Ka'bar (E); *Ambassador:* TSAI PA (Taiwan).
Czechoslovakia: Sharia Mahmud Shaltut (E); *Ambassador:* Dr. STEFAN UHER.
Denmark: Tunis, Tunisia (E).
Egypt: Sharia Bin 'Ashur (Relations Office); *Ambassador:* GAMAL AL-DIN SHUAIR.
Finland: Algiers, Algeria.
France: Sharia Huper (E); *Ambassador:* GUY GEORGY.
German Democratic Republic: (E); *Chargé d'Affaires:* ALFRED HENGELHAUPT.
Germany, Federal Republic: Sharia Hassan al-Masha (E); *Ambassador:* Dr. GUNTHER F. WERNER.
Greece: Sharia Jalal Bayar, 18; *Ambassador:* DIMITRI A. PAPADAKIS.
Guinea: Cairo, Egypt (E).
Hungary: Cairo, Egypt (E).
India: Sharia Mahmud Shaltut (E); *Ambassador:* HOMI J. H. TALEYARKHAN.
Iran: Tunis, Tunisia (E).

Iraq: Sharia Nasser (E); *Ambassador:* (vacant).
Italy: Sharia 'Oran 1 (E); *Ambassador:* ALDO CONTE MAROTTA.
Japan: Cairo, Egypt (E).
Kuwait: Sharia Bin Yassir (E); *Ambassador:* YUSIF AL-MENAISI.
Lebanon: Sharia Bin Yassir (E); *Ambassador:* MUHAMMAD MALEK.
Mali: Cairo, Egypt (E).
Malta: Sharia Bin Ka'ab, 13 (E); *Ambassador:* (vacant).
Mauritania: Sharia Bin Ka'ab (E); *Ambassador:* YAATHA OULD SIDI AHMED.
Morocco: Sharia Bashir al-Ibrahimi (E); *Ambassador:* (vacant).
Netherlands: Cairo, Egypt (E).
Niger: Sharia Bin 'Ubaydallah (E); *Ambassador:* OUMAROU AMADOU.
Nigeria: Cairo, Egypt (E).
Norway: Rabat, Morocco (E).
Pakistan: Sharia al-Khitabi (E); *Ambassador:* ABDUR RAUF KHAN.
Poland: Cairo, Egypt (E).
Saudi Arabia: Sharia al-Qayrouan 2 (E); *Ambassador:* ABD AL-MUSHIN AL-ZAYD.
Senegal: Cairo, Egypt (E).
Somalia: Cairo, Egypt (E).
Spain: Sharia al-Jazayri (E); *Ambassador:* JOSÉ M. MORO.
Sri Lanka: Cairo, Egypt (E).
Sudan: Sharia Donato Suma (E); *Ambassador:* RASHID TAHIR.
Sweden: Tunis, Tunisia (E).
Switzerland: Tunis, Tunisia (E).

LIBYA—(Diplomatic Representation, Parliament, Political Party, Defence, etc.)

Syria: Sharia Muhamed Rashid Rida, 4 (Relations Office); *Head:* 'Adam Kilani.
Tunisia: Sharia Bashir al-Ibrahimia (E); *General Commissioner:* Amor Fezzani.
Turkey: Sharia al-Fatah 36 (E); *Ambassador:* Ozdemir Yigit.
Uganda: Cairo, Egypt (E).
U.S.S.R.: Sharia Solaroli (E); *Ambassador:* Ivan N. Yakushin.
U.K.: Sharia al-Fatah (E); *Ambassador:* Peter Tripp.
U.S.A.: Sharia al-Nasr (E); *Ambassador:* (vacant).
Yemen Arab Republic: Cairo, Egypt (E).
Yemen People's Democratic Republic: Sharia Bin 'Ashur (E); *Ambassador:* Ali Ahmed al-Sulami.
Yugoslavia: Sharia Bashir al-Ibrahimi (E); *Ambassador:* Boris Rafajlovski.

PARLIAMENT

The Senate and House of Representatives were dissolved after the *coup d'état* of September 1969, and the provisional constitution issued in December 1969 made no mention of elections or a return to Parliamentary procedure. However, in January 1971 Col. Gaddafi announced that a new Parliament would be appointed, not elected; no date was mentioned. All political parties other than the Arab Socialist Union, are banned.

POLITICAL PARTY

Arab Socialist Union: f. 1971; the only legal party; there are 366 basic units; elections to them began in November 1971; Sec.-Gen. Major Bashir Hawady.

DEFENCE

Chief of Staff of Armed Forces: Maj. Abu Bakr Younis.
Defence Budget (1972): LD 40 million.
Military Service: voluntary.
Total Armed Forces: 25,000: army 20,000; navy 2,000; air force 3,000.

JUDICIAL SYSTEM

President of the Supreme Court: Abdul Aziz Najar.

The law of the Judicial System of 1954 established the following courts: the Federal Supreme Court, the Courts of Appeal, the Courts of First Instance and the Summary Courts. Sittings are in public, unless the court decides to hold them *in camera* in the interests of decency or public order. Judgment is in all cases given in public. The language of the courts is Arabic, but there is a translation office attached to each Court to help non-Arabic speaking parties, judges or lawyers.

In October 1971 the Revolutionary Command Council decreed that all legislation should conform with the basic principles of Islamic Law and set up committees to carry this out.

The **Supreme Court** consists of a President and judges appointed by the Revolutionary Command Council. Final judgements passed by the Courts of Appeal or Courts of First Instance sitting as appellate courts are executable despite any relative objection for cassation before the Supreme Court.

Courts of Appeal exist in each of the three provinces, consisting of a President, Vice-President and three judges; judgments must be given by three judges. Each Court of Appeal includes a Court of Assize with of three judges.

Courts of First Instance are set up in the provinces, consisting of a President, Vice-President and a number of judges; judgment in these courts is given by one judge.

Summary Courts, composed of one judge, exist within the territorial jurisdiction of every Court of First Instance. Appeal includes a Court of Assize with three judges.

The People's Court is a special court set up by decree in October 1969. It deals with any crimes the Revolutionary Command Council sees fit to refer to it, but is particularly concerned with cases of political or administrative corruption.

RELIGION

Muslims: The Libyan Arabs practically without exception follow Sunni Muslim rites.
Chief Mufti of Libya: Sheikh Taher Ahmed al Zawi.
Christians: The Christian community numbered about 35,000, mostly Italian Roman Catholics, before the 1969 revolution; its numbers have been greatly reduced by the departure of the Italians during 1970. The Roman Catholic Cathedral in Tripoli was transformed into a mosque in November 1970.

THE PRESS

DAILIES

Tripoli

Al-Fajr al-Jadid: Maidan 9 August; f. 1969; official journal; Editor Omar al Hamdi.
Al Balagh.

Benghazi

Al Kifah.

PERIODICALS

Tripoli

al Hadaf: Badri Bldg., Sharia 24 December, P.O.B. 6135, Tripoli; weekly; sports.
Al Jundi: Libyan Army Publication, weekly.
The Libyan Arab Republic Gazette: published by the Ministry of Justice; legal; weekly.
Al Wahdah.

NEWS AGENCIES

Libyan News Agency: Tripoli; f. 1965; attached to Ministry of Information and Culture. Serves the Libyan radio network, newspapers and Government departments (name changed to Arab Revolution News Agency, June 1973).

Foreign Bureaux

DPA, Reuters and Tass have offices in Tripoli.

PUBLISHER

Dar Libya Publishing House: P.O.B. 2487, Benghazi; f. 1966; general books.

RADIO AND TELEVISION

Libyan Broadcasting and TV Service: P.O.B. 333, Tripoli; P.O.B. 274, Benghazi; f. 1957 (TV 1968); broadcasts in Arabic and English from Tripoli and Benghazi; from September 1971 special daily broadcasts to Gaza and other Israeli-occupied territory were begun; under the direction of the Minister of Information and Culture; Dir.-Gen. SAAD MOJBER.

Number of radio receivers: 90,000.

A National Television Service was inaugurated in December 1968. There are now 2,000 sets.

People's Committees took over the running of Tripoli and Benghazi radio and television stations in June 1973, but it is thought the popular committees are under the tight control of the Revolutionary Command Council.

FINANCE

On November 14th, 1969, the Revolutionary Command Council published a decree requiring that all banks should become locally registered with 51 per cent Libyan ownership. Several foreign banks had already taken this step; of the remaining four banks, Barclays D.C.O., the largest bank in Libya, was bought by the state and renamed Masraf al Gumhouria in February 1970. All banks in Libya were completely nationalized on December 22nd, 1970, several being merged to form larger units.

BANKING
(cap.=capital; p.u.=paid up; dep.=deposits; LD=Libyan Dinar; m.=million)

CENTRAL BANK
Central Bank of Libya: Fatah St., P.O.B. 1103, Tripoli; br. at Benghazi; f. 1955; central bank with facilities for commercial business; cap. p.u. LD 1m.; dep. LD 868.6m.; Gov. K. M. SHERLALA.

Wahda Bank: P.O.B. 3427, Sharia Istiklal, Tripoli; f. 1970 to take over Bank of North Africa, Commercial Bank, S.A.L., Nadha Arabia Bank and Soc. Africaine de Banque; cap. and res. LD 3.6m.; dep. LD 34m. (Dec. 1971); Chair. and Gen. Man. BASHIR M. SHARIF.

Masraf al Gumhouria: Giaddat Istiqlal, P.O.B. 3224, Tripoli; f. Nov. 1969 as successor to Barclays Bank D.C.O. in Libya; government owned; 18 brs., at Benghazi (3), Tripoli (7), Agedabia, Beida, Derna, Tobruk, Misurata, Zavia and Zliten; cap. LD 1.5m.; dep. LD 30.3m. (Sept. 1971); Chair. AHMED EL SHERIF.

National Commercial Bank: P.O.B. 4647, Tripoli; Chair. and Gen. Man. BASHIR M. SHARIF.

Sahara Bank: P.O.B. 270, 1st September St., Tripoli; f. 1964; Chair. and Gen. Man. FARAG A. GAMRA.

Umma Bank S.A.L.: P.O.B. 685, 1 Giaddet Omar Mukhtar, Tripoli; brs. in Benghazi, Sebha, Kufra, Hoon; f. 1969; cap. LD 2.25m.; dep. LD 27m.; Chair. and Gen. Man. YOUSEF I. AGHIL.

INSURANCE
Some twenty of the major European insurance companies, and some from other Arab countries, are represented in Libya. In December 1970 the state took over a 60 per cent share in all insurance companies, domestic and foreign, operating in Libya.

OIL

Petroleum affairs in Libya are dealt with entirely by the reorganized Ministry of Petroleum which is charged, in accordance with Article 2 of Law 170 of 1970, with organization, control, follow-up and supervision of petroleum resources within the limits of the State's general policy, development plan and regulations in force concerning petroleum matters.

Ministry of Petroleum: P.O.B. 256, Tripoli.

Libyan National Oil Corporation (LINOCO): P.O.B. 2655, Tripoli; f. 1970 as successor to the Libyan General Petroleum Corporation, to undertake joint ventures with foreign companies; to build and operate refineries, storage tanks, petrochemical facilities, pipelines and tankers; to take part in arranging specifications for local and imported petroleum products; to participate in general planning of oil installations in Libya; to market crude oil and to establish and operate oil terminals; Chair. ANIS A. ISHTEIWY.

The following are the principal foreign companies operating in Libya:

American Overseas Petroleum Ltd. (AMOSEAS): P.O.B. 693, Tripoli; equally owned by Texaco and Standard of California; Gen. Man. WARREN J. GLOSS.

Amoco Libya Oil Co.: P.O.B. 982, Tripoli; Pres. and Resident Man. J. L. FRENCH.

Aquitaine Libye: P.O.B. 282, Tripoli; subsidiary of Société Nationale des Pétroles d'Aquitaine; operates in association with Hispanoil, Murphy Oil and Elf Libye; shares concession with Elf Libye; operates joint venture with Libyan National Oil Corporation (LINOCO) and Elf Libye.

Arabian Gulf Exploration Co.: P.O.B. 263, Benghazi; f. 1971 after nationalization of BP interests; Chair. and Gen. Man. ABDEL RAHIM M. NAAS.

Esso Sirte Inc.: P.O.B. 565, Tripoli; Pres. and Board Chair. H. H. GOERNER.

Esso Standard Libya Inc.: P.O.B. 385, Tripoli; exploration, production, transportation, refining, marketing of crude oil and other hydrocarbons; transportation and marketing of petroleum products and related specialities; Pres. and Board Chair. H. H. GOERNER.

Gelsenberg A.G.: P.O.B. 2537, Tripoli; Gen. Man. Dr. J. HOFFMANN-ROTHE.

Mobil Oil Libya Ltd.: P.O.B. 690, Tripoli; Gen. Man. K. W. WISEMAN.

Nelson Bunker Hunt: P.O.B. 20, Benghazi.

Occidental of Libya Inc.: P.O.B. 2134, Tripoli; runs a pipeline from the Intisar field to a terminal at Zuetina; present production 600,000 BPD; Pres. and Dir. R. H. ESPEY.

Oasis Oil Company of Libya Inc.: P.O.B. 395, Tripoli; operator for Continental, Marathon, Amerada and Shell companies; Chair. and Chief Exec. W. E. SWALES.

Agip, a subsidiary of the Italian state company ENI, has formed a company to participate with the Libyan National Oil Corporation (LINOCO).

TRADE AND INDUSTRY

CHAMBERS OF COMMERCE

Tripolitania Chamber of Commerce and Industry: Sharia Al Jumhouria, Tripoli; f. 1952; Pres. ABDUL LATIF KEKHIA; Sec.-Gen. KAMIL AREIBI; 30,000 mems.; publs. *Quarterly Bulletin*, *Commercial Directory* (annual, English and Arabic).

Cyrenaica Chamber of Commerce, Industry and Agriculture: P.O.B. 208-1286, Benghazi; f. 1953; Pres. ABDALLAR H. LABBAR; Vice-Pres. ABDU I. ABDUNNABI; 4,517 mems.; publ. *Commerce and Economy* (quarterly, Arabic and English).

DEVELOPMENT

Industrial and Real Estate Bank of Libya: Tripoli and Benghazi; f. 1965; state industrial development and house-building finance agency, cap. LD 10m.; Dir. MOHAMED RABEI.

Kufrah Agricultural Project Authority: Ministry of Agriculture, Tripoli; f. 1970 to develop the Kufrah Oasis in south-east Libya.

National General Organization for Industrialization: P.O.B. 4388, Tripoli; f. March 1970; Chair. ABDEL SALAM JALOOD; Deputy Chair. ABU-BAKR SHERIF.

NATIONALIZED INDUSTRIES

State Tobacco Monopoly: P.O.B. 696, Tripoli; develops the production and curing of tobacco; leaf production (1971) 1.75 million kilos, manufactured tobacco production 2.3 million kilos per year.

TRADE UNIONS

National Trade Unions' Federation: (affiliated to ICFTU); P.O.B. 734, 2 Sharia Istanbul, Tripoli; f. 1952; Sec.-Gen. SALEM SHITA; 30,000 mems.; Publ. *Attalia* (weekly).

Engineering Union: Tripoli; f. 1971; membership open to foreign engineers working in Libya, as well as Libyans.

Union of Petroleum Workers of Libya: Tripoli; also branch in Benghazi.

TRADE FAIR

Tripoli International Fair: P.O.B. 891, Tripoli; annual fair March 1st–20th; Chair. and Dir.-Gen. AHMED MURTADI.

TRANSPORT

ROADS

The most important road in Libya is the national coast road, 1,822 km. in length, which runs the whole way from the Tunisian to the Egyptian border, passing through Tripoli and Benghazi. This road has recently been widened and re-surfaced. It has a second link between Barce and Lamluda, which is 141 km. long. The other federal road completed (in 1962) runs from a point on the coastal road 120 km. south of Misurata through Sebha (capital of Fezzan) to Ghat near the Algerian border (total length of 1,250 km.). There is a branch 260 km. long running from Vaddan to Sirte. There is a new road crossing the desert from Sebha to the frontiers of Chad and Niger.

In addition to the national highways, Tripolitania has about 1,200 km. of black-top and macadamized roads and Cyrenaica about 500 km. Practically all the towns and villages of Libya, including the desert oases, are accessible by motor vehicle, but the going is sometimes rough.

General Corporation for Public Transport (GCPT): Tripoli; f. 1971 to manage public transport utilities throughout the country.

SHIPPING

Principal ports are Tripoli, Benghazi, Port Brega and the Oasis Marine Terminal at Es-Sider. Port Brega was opened to oil tankers in 1961. A 30-inch crude oil pipeline connects the Zelten oilfields with Marsa El Brega. Another pipeline joins the Sarir oilfield with Marsa Hariga, the port of Tobruk, and a new pipeline from the Sarir field to Zuetina was opened in 1968. There is another oil port at Ras Lunuf.

Maritime Transport Corporation: Tripoli; f. 1970 to handle all projects dealing with maritime trade.

The following shipping companies are among those operating services through Libyan ports:

Abdurrahman R. Kikhia and Co. (Shipping Division): f. 1968; offices in Tripoli: P.O.B. 401; Benghazi: P.O.B. 157; Tobruk: P.O.B. 16.

The Libyan Transport Co.: Benghazi; Sharia Omar El Mukhtar, P.O.B. 94; f. 1949; brs. at Beida, Tobruk, Marsa Brega and Cairo; Dirs. A. S. FERGIANI, A. T. BUZER, A. F. JIAFAR.

Mitchell Cotts & Co. (Libya) Ltd.: Tripoli: Sharia Sidi Aissa, P.O.B. 393; Benghazi: P.O.B. 202.

Giaber Agency: f. 1946; membership 25; Head Office: Tripoli, 12-16 Jebba St.

National Navigation Co. of Libya: Tripoli: 67 Bagdad St., P.O.B. 2437; Benghazi: P.O.B. 139; f. 1964; regular services from Tunisian, French, Spanish, Moroccan, Algerian, Turkish and Italian ports to Tripoli and Benghazi; Man. L. TAKTAK.

The Tripolitania Enterprises Co. (T.E.C.O.): Ben Basi Bldg., Omer Muktar St., P.O.B. 149, Tripoli; f. 1948; Man. Dir. A. M. MEKATI.

The Tripolitania Shipping Agency: Tripoli: Sharia Istiklal 8-10-12, P.O.B. 2299.

Tirrenia, Società per Azioni di Navigazione: Tripoli: c/o Libyan Shipping and Travel Agency, Sharia Istiklal, Badri Bldg., P.O.B. 985; Benghazi: G. Gabriel, c/o Libyan Transport Co., Sharia Omar El Mukhtar 19.

CIVIL AVIATION

There are four civil airports:

The International Airport, situated at Ben Gashir, 21 miles from Tripoli.

Benina Airport, 12 miles from Benghazi.

Sebha Airport.

Misurata Airport (domestic flights only).

Libyan Arab Airlines: P.O.B. 2555, Tripoli; f. 1965; services to Benghazi, Tripoli, Athens, Cairo, Rome, Tunis, Malta, Paris, Beirut, Belgrade, London, Khartoum, Damascas, Algiers, Casablanca; domestic services throughout Libya; fleet includes two Boeing 727, three Caravelle 6R aircraft and four Fokker F-27; Chair. ABDULGADER GEBANI; Vice-Chair. and Gen. Man. HASSAN KUNIALI.

Libyan Aviation Ltd.: Benghazi; Domestic services.

Linair (*Libyan National Airways*): P.O.B. 3583, Tripoli; f. 1962; domestic services; Pres. Z. Y. LENGHI, Gen. Man. P. W. BAKKER.

Libya is also served by the following foreign airlines: Aeroflot, Air Algérie, Alitalia, British Caledonian, ČSA, EgyptAir, JAT, KLM, Lufthansa, Malta Airlines, Saudia, Sudan Airways, Swissair, Syrian Arab, Tunis Air, UTA.

TOURISM

General Board of Tourism: Tripoli; f. 1964.

Tourism is so far largely undeveloped in Libya, but major potential attractions include the superb Roman remains at Leptis Magna, Sabratha and Cyrene, the fine climate and hundreds of miles of unspoilt beaches.

EDUCATION

One of the consequences of Libya's long history of successive foreign occupations and subjugation to foreign domination has been the extreme paucity of educational facilities for the indigenous peoples.

In 1921 only four Arab primary schools were in existence in Tripolitania, with a total of 611 pupils, and there was a similar lack of development in respect of native education in Cyrenaica.

During the following years some expansion took place, and by 1939 there were in Tripolitania 70 Italo-Arab primary schools with 6,884 Arab and 170 Italian pupils, 13 girls' trades schools with 944 pupils, a secondary school, and an arts and crafts school with 85 students. In addition, evening classes were started for adult Arab illiterates, and in 1928 Arabs were permitted to join Italian secondary schools. Small numbers of Arabs also gained admittance to Italian and Egyptian universities. Koranic schools also increased in numbers from 52 with 1,792 pupils in 1921 to 496 schools with 10,165 pupils in 1939. For Jews there were 19 primary schools (2,645 students), 2 trade secondary schools with 101 pupils, and 15 private schools catering for 1,939 pupils.

Up to the year 1939 the educational system for Arabs in Cyrenaica was similarly under-developed. At that time not more than 37 elementary schools were in existence with a total of 2,600 Arab pupils, and for Jews there were 5 elementary schools with 621 students.

Due to the destruction of towns and communications and to the evacuation of many people to the interior during the Second World War, education was badly disrupted, and at the end of the war there was a great demand for educational facilities. Secondary education was no longer limited to the few places permitted in Italian schools and Libyan schools of all grades rapidly increased in number. A steady expansion of all educational services occurred between 1943 and 1949, followed by a considerable acceleration after the United Nations' decision of November 21st, 1949.

The numbers attending kindergarten, primary and secondary schools increased from a total of 6,808 in 1943–44 to 396,000 in 1970–71. The number of teachers rose similarly, from 219 in 1943–44 to 16,300 in 1970–71. Elementary education is compulsory for children of both sexes, although a few children in the smallest most scattered villages in Fezzan do not yet attend school.

In 1958 the University of Libya opened in Benghazi with Faculties of Arts and Commerce, followed the next year by the Faculty of Science near Tripoli. Faculties of Law, Agriculture, Engineering, Teacher Training, and Arabic Language and Islamic Studies have since been added to the University, which had 309 teachers and 3,488 students in 1970.

In the 1971–72 Ordinary Budget LD 46.3 million were allocated to education and national guidance, or about one-quarter of the total budget.

UNIVERSITY

University of Libya: Benghazi; f. 1955; 540 teachers, 12,813 students (1972–73).

BIBLIOGRAPHY

DI AGOSTINI, Col. ENRICO. La popolazione della Tripolitania (2 vols.; Tripoli, 1917).
    La popolazione della Cirenaica (Benghazi, 1922-23).
    Amministrazione Fiduciaria all'Italia in Africa (Florence, 1948).
    Archivio bibliografico Coloniale (Libia) (Florence, 1915-21).

BARUNI, OMAR. Spaniards and Knights of St. John of Jerusalem in Tripoli (Arabic) (Tripoli, 1952).

BERLARDINELLI, ARSENIO. La Ghibla (Tripoli, 1935).

BLUNSUM, T. Libya: the Country and its People (Queen Anne Press, London, 1968).

CACHIA, ANTHONY J. Libya under the Second Ottoman Occupation, 1835-1911 (Tripoli, 1945).

CECCHERINI, UGO. Bibliografia della Libia in continuazione .... de F. Minutilli (Rome, 1915).

COLUCCI, MASSIMO. Il Regime della Proprieta Fondiaria nell'Africa Italiana: Vol. I. Libia (Bologna, 1942).

CORÒ, FRANCESCO. Settantasei Anni di Dominazione Turca in Libia (Tripoli, 1937).

CUROTTI, TORQUATO. Gente di Libia (Tripoli, 1928).

DESPOIS, JEAN. Géographie Humaine (Paris, 1946).
    Le Djebel Nefousa (Paris, 1935).
    La Colonisation italienne en Libye; Problèmes et Méthodes (Larose-Editeurs, Paris, 1935).

EPTON, NINA. Oasis Kingdom: The Libyan Story (New York, 1953).

EVANS-PRITCHARD, E. E. The Sanusi of Cyrenaica (London, 1949).

FARLEY, RAWLE. Planning for Development in Libya (Pall Mall, London, 1971).

FISHER, W. B. Problems of Modern Libya (*Geographical Journal*, June 1953).

FORBES, ROSITA. The Secret of the Sahara: Kufara (London, 1921).

FRANCA, PIETRO, and others. L'Italia in Africa: Incivilimento e Sviluppo dell'Eritrea, della Somalia, e della Libia (Rome, 1947).

GNECCO, ALBERT. Aspetti di Diretto Agrario Libico (Milan, 1939).

HAJJAJI, S. A. The New Libya (Tripoli, 1967).

HERRMANN, GERHARD. Italiens Weg zum Imperium (Goldman, Leipzig, 1938).

HESELTINE, NIGEL. From Libyan Sands to Chad (Museum Press, London, 1960).

HILL, R. W. A Bibliography of Libya (University of Durham, 1959).

JONGMANS, D. G. Libie-land van de dorst (Boom, Meppel, 1964).

JUIN, A-P. Le Maghreb en Feu (French) (Paris, Librairie Plon, 1957).

KHADDURI, MAJID. Modern Libya, a Study in Political Development (Johns Hopkins Press, 1963).

KHALIDI, I. R. Constitutional Developments in Libya (Beirut, Khayat's Book Co-operative, 1956).

KUBBAH, ABDUL AMIR Q. Libya, Its Oil Industry and Economic System (The Arab Petro-Economic Research Centre, Baghdad, 1964).

LeBLANC, M. E. Anthropologie et Ethnologie (du Fezzan) (1944-45).

LEGG, H. J. Libya: Economic and General Conditions in Libya (London, 1952).

LETHIELLEUX, J. Le Fezzan, ses Jardins, ses Palmiers: Notes d'Ethnographie et d'Histoire (Tunis, 1948).

LINDBERG, J. A General Economic Appraisal of Libya (New York, 1952).

MICACCHI, RODOLFO. La Tripolitania sotto il dominio dei Caramanli (Intra, 1936).

MINUTILLI, FEDERICO. Bibliografia della Libia (Turin, 1903).

Missione Scientifica della Reale Accademia d'Italia a Cufra (Rome, 1934-39).

MURABET, MOHAMMED. Tripolitania: the Country and its People (Tripoli, 1952).

NORMAN, JOHN. Labour and Politics in Libya and Arab Africa (Bookman, New York, 1965).

OWEN, R. Libya: a Brief Political and Economic Survey (London, 1961).

PELT, ADRIAN. Libyan Independence and the United Nations (Yale U.P., 1970).

PICHOU, JEAN. La Question de Libye dans le règlement de la paix (Paris, 1945).

Lord RENNELL. British Military Administration of Occupied Territories in Africa during the years 1941-47 (London, H.M.S.O., 1948).

RIVLIN, BENJAMIN. The United Nations and the Italian Colonies (New York, 1950).

ROYAL INSTITUTE OF INTERNATIONAL AFFAIRS. The Italian Colonial Empire (London, 1940).

ROSSI, P. Libya (Lausanne, 1965).

RUSHDI, MUHAMMAD RASIM. Trablus al Gharb (Arabic) (Tripoli, 1953).

SCARIN, Prof. La Giofra e Zella (Florence, 1938).
    L'Insediamento Umano nella Libia Occidentale (Rome, 1940).
    Le Oasi Cirenaiche del 29° Parallelo (Florence, 1937).
    Le Oasi del Fezzan (2 vols.; Florence, 1934).

SCHMEIDER, OSKAR and WILHELMY, HERBERT. Die faschistische Kolonisation in Nordafrika (Quelle and Meyer, Leipzig, 1939).

STEELE-GREIG, A. J. History of Education in Tripolitania from the Time of the Ottoman Occupation to the Fifth Year under British Military Occupation (Tripoli, 1948).

VILLARD, HENRY S. Libya: The New Arab Kingdom of North Africa (Ithaca, 1956).

WARD, PHILIP. Touring Libya. 3 vols. (1967–69).
    Tripoli: Portrait of a City (1970).

WILLIAMS, G. Green Mountain, an Informal Guide to Cyrenaica and its Jebel Akhdar (London, 1963).

WILLIMOTT, S. G. and CLARKE, J. I. Field Studies in Libya (Durham, 1960).

WRIGHT, JOHN. Libya (Ernest Benn, London, and Praeger, New York, 1969).

Morocco

PHYSICAL AND SOCIAL GEOGRAPHY

D. R. Harris

The Kingdom of Morocco is the westernmost of the three north African countries known to the Arabs as Djezira el Maghreb or "Island of the West". Intermediate in size between Algeria and Tunisia, it occupies some 172,000 square miles and has an extensive coastline facing both the Atlantic and the Mediterranean. However, as a result of both its position and the existence of massive mountain ranges within its borders, Morocco has remained relatively isolated from the rest of the Maghreb and has served as a refuge for descendants of the original Berber-speaking occupants of north-west Africa.

The population at the 1971 census was 15,379,259, and the overall density was 27 per square kilometre. About 35 per cent of the total are Berber-speaking peoples, living mainly in mountain villages, while the Arabic-speaking majority is concentrated in towns in the lowlands, particularly in Casablanca, which is the largest city in the Maghreb, in Marrakesh, the old southern capital, and in Rabat (population: 367,620), the modern administrative capital. There were some 450,000 Europeans living in Morocco before the country attained its independence from the French in 1956 but since then their number has greatly diminished.

PHYSICAL FEATURES

The physical geography of Morocco is dominated by the highest and most rugged ranges in the Atlas Mountain system of north-west Africa. They are the result of a phase of mountain-building that took place in the geologically recent Tertiary era when sediments deposited beneath an ancestral Mediterranean Sea were uplifted, folded and fractured. The mountains remain geologically unstable and Morocco is liable to severe earthquakes, such as the appallingly destructive one that took place at the port of Agadir in 1960.

In Morocco the Atlas Mountains form four distinct massifs which are surrounded and partially separated by lowland plains and plateaux. In the north, in the zone of the former Spanish Protectorate, the Rif Atlas comprise a rugged arc of mountains that rise steeply from the Mediterranean coast to heights of over 7,300 feet. Their limestone and sandstone ranges are difficult to penetrate and have functioned as an effective barrier to east-west communications. They are inhabited by Berber farmers who live in isolated mountain villages and have little contact with the Arabs of Tetuan (population: 139,105) and Tangier (population: 187,894) at the north-western end of the Rif chain.

The Middle Atlas lie immediately south of the Rif from which they are separated by the Col of Taza, a narrow gap which affords the only easy route between western Algeria and Atlantic Morocco. They rise to nearly 10,000 feet and form a broad barrier between the two countries. They also function as a major drainage divide and are flanked by the basins of Morocco's two principal rivers, the Oum er Rbia which flows west to the Atlantic and the Moulouya which flows north-east to the Mediterranean. Much of the Middle Atlas consists of a limestone plateau dissected by river gorges and capped here and there by volcanic craters and lava flows. Semi-nomadic Berber tribesmen spend the winter in valley villages and move to the higher slopes in summer to pasture their flocks.

Southward the Middle Atlas chain merges into the High Atlas, the most formidable of the mountain massifs, which rises to over 13,000 feet and is heavily snow-clad in winter. The mountains are aligned in a chain from south-west to north-east, and they rise precipitously from both the Atlantic lowland to the north and the desert plain of Saharan Morocco to the south. The contrast between the two sides is very striking; the northern slopes are covered by forest and scrub while the southern slopes consist of bare, sunbaked rock. Eastward the chain loses height and continues into Algeria as the Saharan Atlas. The central part of the massif is made up of resistant crystalline rocks which have been eroded by former glaciers and present streams into a wilderness of sharp peaks and steep-sided valleys, but elsewhere limestones and sandstones give rise to more subdued topography. There are no easily accessible routes across the High Atlas, but numerous mountain tracks make possible the exchange of goods by pack animal between Atlantic and Saharan Morocco. A considerable Berber population lives in the mountain valleys in compact, fortified villages.

The Anti Atlas is the lowest and most southerly of the mountain massifs. Structurally it forms an elevated edge of the Saharan platform which was uplifted when the High Atlas were formed. It consists largely of crystalline rocks and is joined to the southern margin of the High Atlas by a mass of volcanic lavas which separates the valley from the river Sous, draining west to the Atlantic at Agadir, from that of the upper Draa, draining south-east towards the Sahara. On the southern side of the chain barren slopes are trenched by gorges from which cultivated palm groves extend like green tongues out into the desert.

The only extensive area of lowland in Morocco stretches inland from the Atlantic coast and is enclosed on the north, east and south by the Rif, Middle and High Atlas. It consists of the Gharb plain and the wide valley of the River Sebou in the north and of the plateaux and plains of the Meseta, the Tadla, the Rehamna, the Djebilet and the Haouz farther south. Most of the Arabic-speaking people of Morocco live in this region.

CLIMATE

Northern and central Morocco experiences a "Mediterranean" type of climate, with warm wet winters and hot dry summers, but this gives way southward to semi-arid and eventually to desert conditions. In the Rif and the northern parts of the Middle Atlas mean annual rainfall exceeds 30 inches and the summer drought lasts only 3 months, but in the rest of the Middle Atlas, in the High Atlas and over the northern half of the Atlantic lowland rainfall is reduced to between 30 and 16 inches and the summer drought lasts for 4 months or more. During the summer intensely hot winds from the Sahara, known as the Sirocco or Chergui, occasionally cross the mountains and sweep across the lowland desiccating all that lies in their path. Summer heat on the Atlantic coastal plain is tempered however by breezes that blow inland after they have been cooled over the cold waters of the Canaries current offshore.

Over the southern half of the Atlantic lowland and the Anti Atlas semi-arid conditions prevail and rainfall decreases to between 16 and 8 inches a year. It also becomes very variable and is generally insufficient for the regular cultivation of cereal crops without irrigation. East and south of the Atlas Mountains, which act as a barrier to rain-bearing winds from the Atlantic, rainfall is reduced still further and regular cultivation becomes entirely dependent on irrigation.

VEGETATION

The chief contrast in the vegetation of Morocco is between the mountain massifs, which support forest or open woodland, and the surrounding lowlands which, when uncultivated, tend to be covered only by scrub growth of low, drought-resistant bushes. The natural vegetation has however been widely altered, and in many places actually destroyed, by excessive cutting, burning and grazing. This is particularly evident in the lowlands and on the lower mountain slopes where such scrub species as juniper, thuya, dwarf palm and gorse are common. There is little doubt that cork oak covered a large part of the Atlantic lowland but today only the "forest" of Mamora remains to suggest the former abundance of this valuable tree. The middle and upper slopes of the mountains are often quite well wooded, with evergreen oak dominant at the lower and cedar at the higher elevations. The lowlands to the east and south of the Atlas Mountains support distinctive types of steppe and desert vegetation, in which esparto grass and the argan tree (which is unique to south-western Morocco) are conspicuous.

Since Morocco gained its independence territorial disputes have arisen with Algeria, Mauritania and the Spanish Sahara. During the period of French occupation the south-eastern frontier with Algeria was never precisely defined and the Moroccan government has claimed an area beyond it which extends into all three neighbouring countries. The claim is based on the fact that in medieval times Moroccan rule was effective over much of the western Sahara and it is associated with the recent discovery of large iron ore deposits in the area together with the expectation of finding valuable reserves of oil. An agreement on the border with Algeria was finally ratified in May 1973.

HISTORY

The Phoenicians and after them the Carthaginians established staging posts and trading factories on the coasts of Morocco. Still later, the Romans established in what is now northern Morocco the province of Mauritania Tingitana, the frontier or *limes* passing a little to the south of Rabat, Meknès and Fez. Muslim warriors raided into Morocco under Uqba b. Nafi in A.D. 684–85. It was not, however, until the first years of the eighth century that the Muslims began to bring Morocco under durable control, their forces, under Musa b. Nusair, reaching the Tafilalet and the Wadi Draa. The Berber tribesmen of Morocco rallied to the cause of Islam and had a large share in the Muslim conquest of Spain after A.D. 711. Religious ideas of a heterodox character—i.e., the ideas of the Khawarij, who constituted the first of the great schismatic movements inside Islam—won much support among the Berbers of Morocco. The spread of Kharijite beliefs, the fierce particularism of the Berbers and their refractoriness towards all forms of political control, led to a great rebellion in 739–40, which had as its chief consequence the fragmentation of Morocco into a number of small Muslim principalities.

It was Idris, a descendant of al-Hasan, the son of the Caliph 'Ali and of Fatima, the daughter of the Prophet Muhammad, who, fleeing westward after an unsuccessful revolt against the Abbasid Caliph in Iraq, founded the first of the great Muslim dynasties ruling in Morocco. The Idrisid régime lasted from 788–89 to 985–86. Idris, the founder of the new state, died in 792–93, after reducing most of Morocco and also Tlemcen to obedience with the aid of the Berber tribesmen who had rallied to his cause on his arrival in the western Maghreb. His son, Idris II, founded Fez, the capital of the Idrisids and a notable centre of Muslim life and civilisation in the Maghreb. After the death of Idris II (d. 828–29) the régime fell into decline. Morocco now endured for some two hundred years a long period of internecine conflict, of tribal revolt and of warring principalities. At the same time it had to face external danger in the form of pressures from the Umayad Caliphate of Cordoba in Spain (at the apogee of its power and splendour in the reigns of Abd al-Rahman III (912–61) and al-Hakam II (961–76)) and also from the Fatimid Caliphate established and consolidated in Ifriqiya (i.e. modern Tunisia and eastern Algeria) during the years 908–69.

It was after this long period of turmoil and fragmentation that Morocco entered into the most splendid phase of its medieval history. There now arose, amongst Berbers of Sanhaja descent who followed a nomadic mode of life in the regions near the Senegal, the religious movement of the Almoravids (al-Murabitun—"people of the ribat", i.e., of a fortified abode devoted to spiritual retreat and also to jihad or war against the infidel). The chieftain of these Berbers, Yahya b. Ibrahim, brought back from Mecca Abd Allah b. Yasin to spread the true doctrine of Islam among his people. The Almoravids soon passed over from the pursuit of the ascetic life to war on behalf of the true faith. The tide of conquest in Morocco gathered momentum under the amir Abu Bakr and led, after his death, to the establishment of a vast Almoravid state in the time of Yusef b. Tashufin (d. 1106), who in 1062 founded Marrakesh and extended the domination of the Almoravids over all Morocco and much of Algeria. In 1086 he halted the southward advance of the Christian *riconquista* in Spain and then annexed the Muslim lands there to the Almoravid territories in North Africa. His successor Ali b. Yusuf (d. 1142) consolidated and maintained the empire, but thereafter the power of the Almoravids fell into a rapid decline. The Saharan nomads who had been the dynamic force behind the movement became absorbed, as it were, into the rich milieu of Andalusian Muslim civilization. Dynastic discord and incompetence among the Almoravid amirs hastened the collapse of the régime. The Christians in Spain took Saragossa in 1118 and began a new phase of their *riconquista*. And in the Atlas mountains of Morocco a new religious force was preparing to burst out over the Moroccan scene. Seven years later, in Morocco, the Almohads rose in revolt against the Almoravids and after 22 years of stubborn conflict took Marrakesh in 1147.

A religious leader, Muhammad b. Tumart (d. 1130), who had studied at Cordoba, Mecca and Baghdad, taught amongst the Masmuda Berbers of the High Atlas doctrines of a strict unitarian character and assumed for himself the designation of al-Mahdi, "the rightly guided one". Amongst the Masmuda he gathered around himself a nucleus of Berber adherents—the "Unitarians", i.e., al-Muwahhidun or Almohads. After the death of Ibn Tumart in 1130 one of his ardent disciples, a Berber of the Kumiya tribe named Abd al-Mumin, became the Khalifa of the Mahdi. Under the guidance of Abd al-Mumin (d. 1163) the Almohads took

MOROCCO—(HISTORY)

Marrakesh in 1147 and then in the years 1151-59 overran the rest of Morocco and the North African lands as far east as Tripolitania and Cyrenaica. The Almohads reached the summit of their splendour in the reign of al-Mansur (1184-98), who brought Muslim Spain under Almohad control and checked the menacing advance of the Christians at the battle of Alarcos (1196). Under his successor Muhammad al-Nasir (1199-1214) the Almohads suffered a serious defeat in battle against the Christians of Spain at Las Navas de Tolosa (1212). Thereafter the Almohad empire began to decline. The Hafsids made themselves independent in Ifriqiya (1235-56). Much of the Central Maghreb came under the control of the Abd al-Wadid amirs ruling at Tlemcen. At the same time a new Berber house—the Merinids, of Zenata Berber origin—rose into prominence, conquering Fez in 1248 and Marrakesh in 1269 and thus bringing to an end the last remnants of Almohad rule.

THE MERINIDS

The Merinids, whose effective power lasted for about one hundred years, came from eastern Morocco, overran first the northern regions of Morocco and then the lands in the south. Their attempts to reconstitute the empire of the Almohads met with no durable success. Revolt against their domination was not infrequent in the southern regions of Morocco. Several campaigns undertaken to regain control of the eastern Maghreb brought no more than transient gains, both Ifriqiya and Tlemcen escaping from their domination. Nor could the Merinids establish themselves in Spain, although their interventions there did hinder the Christian *riconquista* and gave the Muslim state of Grenada enough time to consolidate its resources and thus gain the strength to resist the Christians until 1492. The decline of the Merinid régime saw the culmination of a process long since in train. Nomadic tribes of Arab origin—the Hilal and the Sulaym—penetrated into the Maghreb during the course of the 11th and 12th centuries. Other Badawi elements infiltrated through the northern reaches of the Sahara during the later phases of Almohad rule. With the gradual disintegration of the Merinid state the Badawi tribes thrust westward through the Atlas mountains and penetrated into the heart-lands of Morocco. These Badawi invasions, although causing widespread disruption and confusion, contributed much to the arabisation of Morocco and the neighbouring lands. During the years of Merinid decline, dynastic quarrels led to political disintegration, with the result that rival states came into being at Fez and Marrakesh. Morocco, until 1465, was a prey to prolonged internal discords, which ended, at least in part, only with the emergence of another régime of Zenata Berber origin—the Wattasid régime (1465-1549). The Wattasids had no long pre-eminence, their failure to halt the progress of the Portuguese and the Spaniards, who had begun to establish themselves along the Atlantic and the Mediterranean shores of Morocco, being one of the main reasons for their rapid decline.

THE LINE OF SHARIFS

A new movement of resistance to the intrusions of the Spaniards, and, above all, of the Portuguese (by 1500 the masters of Ceuta, Tangier, Arcila, Agadir, Mazagan and Safi on the western coast of Morocco) was born amongst the religious confraternities, amongst the *marabouts* and the "shorfa" (descendants of the Prophet) in Morocco, who now led the Jihad, or war on behalf of the Muslim faith, against the Christians. Out of this situation arose the Saadian régime, originating in a line of Sharifs from the region of the Wadi Draa on the Saharan side of the Atlas mountains. The Saadians took Fez in 1520 and Marrakesh in 1548. Their prestige was due to their status as descendants of the Prophet and to their success in driving the Portuguese from most of their possessions on the Atlantic littoral of Morocco—a success which culminated in their defeat of the Portuguese at the battle of Alcazarquivir in 1578. The most famous of the Sharifs, Ahmad al-Mansur (1578-1603) resisted the pressure of the Ottoman Turks on his eastern frontier with Algeria and in 1591 sent out a large expedition which seized Timbuktu and Goa on the Western Sudan, returning with rich plunder in the form of slaves and gold. Al-Mansur, realising that his house had no strong tribal support, such as earlier dynasties had owned, organised the Saadian régime on a new foundation (the Makhzan)—a system under which various Arab tribes enjoyed exemption from taxes in return for armed service to the state. Much depended, in such a system, on the character of the Sultan. If he were strong and able, all might be well, but in practice the political influence of the sultans tended to fluctuate in accordance with their skill or incompetence. The tribal rivalries would break out anew, the endless tensions between the nomadic and the settled elements in the population became intensified whenever the central government was weak or ill-directed. At such times the "Bled as-Siba" (the areas of dissidence—in particular the Atlas Mountains) set their tribal autonomies against the forces of the "Bled al-Makhzan" (the controlled areas). The period of Saadian rule, which ended in 1668, was, however, one of considerable prosperity for Morocco. Sugar cane culture was encouraged; gold brought by caravan from the Sudan added to the resources of the régime; close commercial contact was made with the lands of southern and western Europe, amongst them England.

Yet another wave of popular religious sentiment brought to power a new house—known under the designations Alawi, Hasani or Filali—which still reigns in Morocco. The Alawi Sharifs had their origin amongst the Berbers located in the oases of Tafilalet, i.e., Saharan Morocco. Under the guidance of the Alawi house Berber forces took Fez in 1644 and Marrakesh in 1668. The reigns of Rashid II (1664-72) and, above all, of Mulai Ismail (1672-1727) established the Alawi régime on a firm basis and saw Morocco more thoroughly pacified and more solidly united than it was ever to be again until the time of the French occupation. Ismail used as one of his main instruments of rule a powerful corps of negro troops, some stationed close to his capital, Meknès, others established in a network of Qasbahs (fortresses) which covered most of the land. He also had at his command a strong force of European renegades. Among the main achievements of Mulai Ismail must be numbered the occupation, in 1684, of Tangier (English since 1662) and the capture, in 1689, of Larache (Spanish since 1610). Mulai Ismail concluded with France in 1682 a commercial agreement, which was confirmed later in 1787, precedence being then accorded to the consuls of France over the consuls of all other nations.

Mulai Ismail had managed to thrust back the pressure of the Sanhaja Berbers, who were beginning to move down from the Middle Atlas into the lowland areas of Morocco. His successors did not win the same degree of success, with the result that, after the death of Ismail in 1727, a period of confusion ensued in Morocco until the rise of yet another able prince, the Sharif Muhammad b. Abdallah (1757-1790). Muhammad founded Mogador in 1765 and drove the Portuguese from Mazagan in 1769. He entered into a pact of friendship and commerce with Spain in 1767. A brief period of conflict with Spain followed in 1774, but a new agreement was negotiated between Morocco and Spain in 1780.

Muhammad b. Abdallah and his immediate successors, Mulai Sulaiman (1792-1822) and Mulai Abd al-Rahman (1822-59) made strenuous efforts to maintain the control of the central régime in the face of tribal dissidence, and to ward off the possibilities of foreign intervention in the affairs of Morocco. The French conquest of Algiers in 1830 was bound, however, to have repercussions in Morocco. Mulai Abd al-Rahman gave assistance to Abd al-Qadir, the amir who led the Muslim resistance to France in Algeria during the years 1832–47. During the course of their campaigns against Abd al-Qadir the French met and defeated a Moroccan force at Wadi Isly in 1844.

A dispute over the limits of the Ceuta enclave, which was under Spanish rule, led in 1860 to a brief war between Morocco and Spain. Spanish troops under General O'Donnell defeated the Moroccans at Los Castillejos and seized Tetuan. A further engagement at Wadi Ras in March 1860 brought the war to a close. A peace settlement followed, under the terms of which the Ceuta enclave was enlarged and Spain was given indemnities amounting to 100 million pesetas. Morocco also granted to Spain a territorial enclave on the Atlantic coast opposite the Canaries (Santa Cruz de Mar Pequeña, now Ifni).

FRENCH RULE

France, with her hold on Algeria secure, began to turn her eyes towards the Western Maghreb—but the rivalries among the great Powers long hindered the establishment of a French protectorate over Morocco. In April 1904, however, Great Britain agreed to recognise the pre-eminence of French interests in Morocco in return for a similar recognition of English interests in Egypt. A convention between France and Spain in October 1904 assigned to Spain two zones of influence, one in northern and the other in southern Morocco. The Germans now sought to intervene in Moroccan affairs and at the conference of Algeciras in 1906 secured the adherence of the Great Powers to the economic "internationalisation" of Morocco. A sharp crisis in 1911, when the German gun-boat *Panther* appeared at Agadir, ended in a Franco-German settlement, the Germans now recognising Morocco as a French sphere of influence in return for territorial concessions in the Congo. In March 1912 Morocco became a Protectorate of France, with a French Resident-General empowered to direct foreign affairs, to control defence and also to introduce internal reforms. A new convention of 1912 between France and Spain revised the earlier agreement of 1904: Spain now received her zones of influence in Morocco (though somewhat diminished in extent)—but from France as the protecting power and *not* from the Sultan.

The first French Resident-General in Morocco was General Lyautey (1912–25). He established effective control, before 1914, over the plains and lower plateaux of Morocco from Fez to the Atlas mountains south of Marrakesh; then, before 1918, over the western Atlas, the Taza corridor connecting with Algeria and some areas of the northern highlands. French troops helped Spain to subdue the formidable rebellion (1921–26) of the Rif tribesmen under Abd al-Krim. This success meant the subjugation of the northern mountains and allowed the French to turn with unimpeded vigour to the reduction of the Middle Atlas and the Tafilalet—a task accomplished by 1934, when the pacification of the whole of Morocco could be regarded as complete.

It was at this time that nationalist sentiment began to make itself felt in Morocco. A "Comité d'Action Marocaine" now asked for a limitation of the protectorate. This "Comité" was dissolved in 1937, but nationalist propaganda continued against the French régime. Morocco rallied to the cause of France in 1939 and to the Free French movement in 1942. A Party of Independence (Istiqlal), formed in 1943, demanded full freedom for Morocco, with a constitutional form of government under Sultan Muhammad b. Yusuf, who supported the nationalist movement. The Istiqlal, strong in the towns, did not find great favour at this time among the conservative tribesmen of Morocco, who tended to concentrate their resistance to reform on western lines around Thami al-Glawi, the Pasha of Marrakesh. The tensions between the new and the old ideas in Morocco became much sharper in 1953. Sultan Muhammad b. Yusuf had long adhered to the aims of the Istiqlal movement. He had fallen into disagreement with the French administration, refusing to issue *dahirs* (decrees) authorising various measures that the French desired to see in force. In May 1953 a number of Pashas and Caids, with al-Glawi, the Pasha of Marrakesh, at their head, asked for the removal of the Sultan. Berber tribesmen began to converge in force towards the main urban centres in Morocco such as Rabat, Casablanca and Fez. On August 20th, 1953, the Sultan agreed to go into exile in Europe, but not to abdicate. Muhammad b. Arafa, a prince of the Alawi house, was now recognised as Sultan. Attempts to assassinate him occurred in September 1953 at Rabat and again in March 1954 at Marrakesh. The situation continued to be tense, with outbreaks of violence occurring here and there throughout Morocco in 1954–55 and nationalist fervour running high.

INDEPENDENCE—1956

Sultan Muhammad b. Arafa renounced the throne and withdrew to Tangier in 1955. Muhammad b. Yusuf, on November 5th in that year, was recognised once more as the legitimate Sultan. A joint Franco-Moroccan declaration of March 2nd, 1956, stated that the Protectorate agreement of 1912 was obsolete and that the French government now recognised the independence of Morocco. A Protocol of the same date covered the transitional phase before new agreements between France and Morocco, still to be negotiated, could come into effect. The Sultan would now have full legislative powers in Morocco. Henceforward a High Commissioner was to represent France in the new state. France undertook also to aid Morocco with the organization of its armed forces and to assist in the re-assertion of Moroccan control over the zones of Spanish influence, the sole legal basis for which was the Franco-Spanish convention of 1912. On November 12th, 1956, Morocco became a member of the United Nations.

In August 1956 the Istiqlal proclaimed the need to abrogate the Convention of Algeciras (1906), which had "internationalised" the economic life of Morocco, and also to secure the withdrawal of all foreign troops from the land. An international conference met at Fedala, near Casablanca, in October 1956, to consider the future of Tangier, administered since 1912 under an international régime. In October 1956 Tangier was restored to Morocco. A Royal Charter of August 1957 maintained in general the former economic and financial system in force at Tangier, including a free money market, quota-free trade with foreign countries and a low level of taxation. In 1959 Tangier lost its special status and was integrated financially and economically with Morocco, but a Royal decree of January 1962 made it once more a free port. The Istiqlal, in 1956, had envisaged the creation of a "Great Morocco" which, according to a map published in July of that year, would include certain areas in South-West Algeria, the Spanish territories in North-West Africa and also Mauritania, together with the French Sudan (i.e., the Republic of Mali). The Sultan of Morocco and his government reiterated these claims in the years which followed the achievement of Moroccan independence. Moreover, in 1958, a number of personalities prominent in the political life of Mauritania, amongst them the Amir of Trarza in the extreme south-west of the Republic, withdrew to Morocco and found a welcome there. Morocco began in 1960 an intensive propaganda and diplomatic campaign against Mauritania, asking, in August 1960, that the question of Mauritania be placed on the agenda of the United Nations. The Political Committee of the UN General Assembly debated the question in November, but without agreeing to a formal resolution.

The problem of the Spanish territories in North-West Africa also came to the fore at this time. During the course of a visit which Sultan Muhammad b. Yusuf made to Madrid in April 1956, soon after Morocco became independent, Spain had recognised the independence of Morocco, renouncing also the northern zone of the protectorate assigned to her in Morocco under the terms of the Franco-Spanish convention of 1912. One factor in the general situation was the existence in the western Sahara of irregular Moroccan forces (the "Armée de Libération du Grand Sahara") reputed to have some connection with the Istiqlal. These irregular forces attacked the Spanish enclave of Ifni in Southern Morocco on November 23rd, 1957, but after some stiff fighting had to withdraw in the first week of December. During the first three months of 1958 irregular bands also raided into the Spanish territories of Saguia al-Hamra and Rio de Oro and into the northern fringes of Mauritania. A combined Franco-Spanish operation cleared the irregulars from the Spanish territories and the adjacent lands by the beginning of March. The Moroccan government had declared that it was not responsible for these incursions. Negotiations between Morocco and Spain, held at Cintra in Portugal, led in April 1958 to an agreement under which Spain, in accordance with the settlement reached in April 1956, relinquished to Morocco the southern zone of her former protectorate.

KING HASSAN II AND ROYAL DOMINANCE OF GOVERNMENT

On July 9th Prince Moulai Hassan was proclaimed heir to the throne and on August 15th, 1957, Sultan Muhammad assumed the title of king. The prince, on the death of King Muhammad in January 1961, ascended the throne as Hassan II. In November 1962 King Hassan announced details of a new constitution (later approved through a referendum held in December 1962). The Kingdom of Morocco was declared to be a sovereign state—monarchical, constitutional, democratic and social in its form of government. The state religion was Islam; the official language, Arabic. All adult men and women would have the franchise. To all citizens the constitution guaranteed freedom of movement, speech and opinion and the right to join political and trade union organizations. The King was empowered to appoint and dismiss the Prime Minister and the Ministers of State, and to preside over the Cabinet. Morocco would have a House of Representatives, elected by universal direct suffrage for a term of four years, and a House of Councillors (i.e., a Senate), two-thirds of its members chosen by an electoral college consisting of members drawn from the provincial, prefectural and communal councils, and one-third selected by the trade unions and by the Chambers of Handicrafts, of Commerce and Industry and of Agriculture.

An election for the House of Representatives (chosen under a system of single member constituencies) was held on May 17th, 1963. The Front for the Defence of Constitutional Institutions (FDIC)—a pro-government organization—had been formed in March 1963. The main opposition came from the left-wing National Union of Popular forces (UNFP) and from the conservative Istiqlal. The UNFP had been formed in September 1959 following a split in the ranks of the Istiqlal between the young militants (led by people like Mehdi Ben Barka) and the old guard. As a result of the election the distribution of seats in the new House of Representatives was: FDIC, 69 seats; Istiqlal, 41 seats; UNFP, 28 seats; Independents, 6 seats. The FDIC had shown itself to be the strongest in the eastern and southern areas of Morocco; the UNFP had found its best support in the main towns such as Casablanca, Rabat, Agadir and Tangier; while the Istiqlal did well in the former Spanish (northern) zone and the adjacent areas, and also in the region of Marrakesh. The elections to the House of Councillors, held on October 13th, 1963, gave 107 seats to the FDIC, 11 to Istiqlal and two seats to Independent members. King Hassan opened the first Parliament of Morocco on November 18th, 1963.

The chances of a parliamentary victory by the UNFP were virtually finished off in July 1963 when most of the leaders were arrested in connection with an alleged *coup* attempt. Many of them were held in solitary confinement, tortured, and eventually sentenced to death. In 1965, however, the death sentences were commuted to life imprisonment. The UNFP had had its opportunity of running the Government between December 1958 and May 1960, when the King summarily dismissed Abdullah Ibrahim; Istiqlal received similar treatment from the monarch in January 1963. The opposition was now factionalized, and the King was able to sponsor a series of nominally independent, but in reality royalist, parties, like the FDIC, in order to maintain the democratic façade of government.

RELATIONS IN THE MAGHREB

Moroccan troops, in July 1962, had entered the region south of Colomb-Béchar in Algeria—a region never officially demarcated. The Moroccan press also launched a strong campaign in support of the view that the Tindouf area in the extreme south-west of Algeria should belong to Morocco—a claim of some importance, since the area contains large deposits of high-grade (57 per cent) iron ore and also considerable resources of oil and natural gas. King Hassan paid an official visit to Algeria in March 1963, as a result of which, in March and again in April, the two states entered into a number of agreements relating to technical, economic, administrative and cultural matters. Morocco and Algeria came into violent conflict, however, in October 1963. Morocco and France, in the Lalla-Marnia agreement of 1845 had defined their common frontier from the coast southward to Teniet al-Sassi (a distance of some 80 miles), the frontier to the desert lands to the South remaining undemarcated. French forces from Algeria occupied the Touat oases, however, in 1899–1900 and also Colomb-Béchar in 1901. An agreement of 1912 defined the border from Teniet al-Sassi to Colomb-Béchar (the "Varnier Line", which the Sultan of Morocco recognized in 1928 as the administrative and financial frontier). French forces from Algeria occupied the Tindouf area in 1934. Morocco now, in the years after the attainment of her independence, recognized as valid only the agreement of 1845.

In September 1963 Moroccan auxiliaries began to move southward from Tagounit into the region of Hassi-Beida and Tinjoub, about 250 miles south-west of Colomb-Béchar and 200 miles north-east of Tindouf. There was sharp fighting in this area from October 8th to November 4th, 1963. With the mediation of President Keita of Mali a ceasefire was signed at Bamako on October 30th. The Council of Foreign Ministers of the OAU (Organization for African Unity) met at Addis Ababa on November 18th and created an arbitration commission, which thereafter (December 3rd-5th, 1963 to January 23rd-27th, 1964) held discussions at Abidjan in the Ivory Coast and at Bamako in Mali, Morocco and Algeria submitting evidence in support of their respective territorial claims. On February 20th, 1964, an agreement was reached on the establishment of a demilitarized zone.

Relations between Morocco and Algeria improved in the course of 1964. April 1964 witnessed an exchange of prisoners taken in the late hostilities and also the withdrawal—its work completed—of the joint Mali-Ethiopia Commission. Morocco and Algeria resumed normal diplomatic relations in May 1964. At Tlemcen, also in May, a joint technical commission reached agreement on a number of points—on the re-opening of the common frontier (achieved on June 8th 1964), on freedom for the nationals of either state, expelled from the other, to return to their homes, on compensation for such expelled nationals, on the ending of all measures of detention directed against the citizens of either state as a result of the pre-existing dispute, and on further discussions designed to explore the possibilites of technical, economic, financial and administrative co-operation between the two countries. The Special Commission of Arbitration established by the OAU in November 1963 continued its work in 1964, meeting on a number of occasions in Morocco and Algeria. A more amicable relationship also became evident between Morocco and Mauritania. The Ministers of Information of these two states met at Cairo in July 1964 during the course of an African Summit Conference. An understanding was reached to bring an end to the 'war' of radio propaganda and criticism hitherto active between Morocco and Mauritania.

King Hassan II paid an official visit to Tunisia in December 1964—a visit which marked the full renewal, between Morocco and Tunisia, of the good relations disturbed when, in 1960, Tunisia had recognized the independence of Mauritania. Diplomatic relations between Morocco and Tunisia had been restored somewhat earlier in May 1964.

In May 1964 Morocco concluded with UNESCO an agreement to establish at Tangier an administrative training and research centre for Africans, with special emphasis on the training of senior personnel for development projects. At Tunis, on September 9th-October 1st 1964, the Economic Ministers of Morocco, Algeria, Tunisia and Libya agreed to create special relationships between their respective countries in the field of economic co-operation, trade exchanges and the co-ordination of tariff policies. A further conference at Tangier in November 1964 led to the formation of a permanent joint consultative committee served by an administrative secretariat and by a number of subordinate and specialized commissions (see separate Chapter in Part I). The Committee, which would meet at least once a quarter, under the chairmanship of each state in rotation, was to harmonize the development programmes of the participating countries. At this same time it was also resolved to establish an Industrial Studies Centre, with its headquarters at Tripoli and with the co-ordination of industrial projects in the member states as its main function. King Hassan, in December 1964, inaugurated the work of a Superior Council for National Promotion and Planning, a consultative organ of Government, as envisaged in the Constitution of Morocco. A three-year programme (1965-1967) now came under discussion, the main emphasis resting on agriculture, on industrial projects connected with the preserving and treatment of agricultural products, on the training of civilian personnel and also on the advantages to be drawn from tourism.

INTERNAL UNREST

In August 1964 there was a reorganization of the Moroccan Government. The new Cabinet, under the leadership of M. Hajj Ahmad Bahnini, consisted in the main of members chosen from the FDIC. This reorganization was interpreted as foreshadowing a possible attempt of King Hassan to broaden the basis of Government through close co-operation with members of the Opposition—i.e., with the Istiqlal and with the UNFP. Istiqlal held its national congress at Casablanca on February 14th, 1965. M. Allal al-Fassi was re-elected as its President. The congress adopted resolutions for the economic liberation of Morocco and for an increased measure of agrarian reform. It also asked for new political elections free from Government intervention. In October 1965 the UNFP lost its main inspiration, Ben Barka, when he disappeared in France, never to be seen again. Gen. Oufkir, one of the King's sturdiest supporters, was found guilty in France in his absence of complicity in Ben Barka's disappearance, and a period of very strained Moroccan-French relations ensued.

The first half of 1965 was a time of political tension in Morocco. A circular from the Minister of Education, issued in March 1965, imposed on all students over seventeen years of age some form of technical training. To numerous students it seemed that the circular might lead to their exclusion from professional and civil service careers. At Casablanca, on March 23rd, demonstrations amongst the students developed into riots with the rapid participation of workers, amongst whom rising prices and growing unemployment had caused much unrest. Police and troops had to fire on the demonstrators before order could be restored: over 100 people were estimated to have been killed.

At the opening of a new session of Parliament on May 3rd, 1965, the King made an appeal for the formation of a government of National Union. He had begun discussions earlier, on April 20th, with the leaders of the political parties, with the Presidents of the two Chambers of the Parliament and also with prominent political figures. The King proposed a programme of development for Morocco—a programme which emphasized the need for industrial advance with the aid of foreign capital, the introduction of measures designed to encourage investment, the stabilization of the cost of living and the limitation of the birth-rate. Amongst the reforms now put forward was the suggestion that the Government should take over all lands granted by former Sultans to the various tribes, dedicated as religious endowments, or owned formerly by the French Government and by French colonists, and share them out amongst the peasant population, the beneficiaries receiving in addition financial and technical assistance from the state. There were proposals, too, for administrative reform: the Civil Service would be recruited through a system of competitive examinations, and a special court, established under a law promulgated in April 1965, would sit in judgement on officials accused of corrupt practices.

The appeal of King Hassan II to the main political parties met with no pronounced success. Dissension continued inside Parliament. M. Hajj Ahmad Bahnini, the Prime Minister, resigned from the Democratic Socialist Party, of which he was President, on June 4th, 1965. On June 7th King Hassan proclaimed a state of emergency, under which he himself assumed full legislative and executive power within Morocco. New elections, it was stated, would be held, after the Constitution had been revised and submitted to a referendum. On July 1st, the King announced the nationalization of the export trade of citrus fruit, vegetables, fish products and handicraft goods, under the *Office Chérifien de Contrôle et d'Exportation*. Together with the phosphate industry, over 60 per cent of Moroccan export trade was now nationalized. Further nationalization was carried out in 1966 and 1967.

In July 1967, King Hassan relinquished the post of Prime Minister to Dr. Mohammed Benhima, and in 1967 and 1968 there were eight major cabinet reshuffles. Considerable student unrest continued in this period.

There was a gradual return to full political activity in 1969, though still under royal direction. Municipal and rural communal elections were held in October, although these were boycotted by opposition parties and the successful candidates mostly stood as independents. Following this Dr. Mohammed Benhima, Prime Minister since July 1967, was replaced by Dr. Ahmed Laraki, formerly Foreign Minister. A national referendum on a new constitution was at last held in July 1970; official figures claimed that over 98 per cent of the votes were affirmative, despite general opposition from the main political parties, trade unions and student organizations. Elections for a new single chamber legislature were held in August. Of the 240 members, 90 were elected by direct suffrage, 90 by local councils and 60 by an electoral college. The results were that 158 elected members were Independents, 60 were of the government party *Mouvement Populaire* and 22 from opposition parties.

In July 1971 there was an unsuccessful attempt by a section of the army to overthrow the King and establish a republic. The attempt was led by Gen. Mohammed Medbouh, Minister of the Royal Military Household and Col. Muhammad Ababou. Together with some 1,400 military cadets, they attacked the King's palace at Skhirate while he was celebrating his birthday with members of the government, foreign diplomatic corps and many other guests. Although the rebels at one point had captured the King and his ministers, and controlled the radio station and the Interior Ministry, they were soon overwhelmed. Many of their own men apparently rallied to the King, while the rest of the army counter-attacked quickly. The revolt was suppressed in under 24 hours. Over 150 of the rebels were killed in the fighting. The King escaped unhurt but some of his generals, a minister and an ambassador were among those killed, and other guests were wounded. The King later said that there had been foreign involvement in the abortive *coup*, which he described as "Libyan-style". A few hours after the revolt had begun, the Libyan Government had alerted its armed forces to be ready to defend the Moroccan "revolution". Relations between the two countries were later severed. The *coup* attempt appeared to have been engineered by right-wing army officers, angered by the level of corruption in the royal administration and by the King's too lenient treatment of dissent on the left. The King's response was to reshuffle the cabinet, giving General Oufkir a much enhanced position, and to begin to attack corruption in the ranks of state employees, civil servants and former ministers. The leaders of the attack on the Skhirate Palace had been killed in the fighting or summararily executed immediately afterwards, but more than a thousand other army officers and men were brought before the military tribunal at Kenitra in January 1972 and charged with complicity, and they were sentenced to imprisonment lasting variously from one year to life.

During the months following the Skhirate *coup*, a series of conciliatory talks was held between the Government and members of the National Front opposition parties, Istiqlal and the *Union Nationale des Forces Populaires*, who were invited by the King to co-operate with the Government. Meanwhile, the trial at Marrakesh of 193 UNFP supporters charged with treason, which had been in progress since early 1970 was completed in September 1971, and sentences passed included five of the death penalty and six of life imprisonment. Talks continued into 1972, by which time all but 30 of the UNFP detainees had been released, but both Istiqlal and the UNFP refused to compromise with government policies.

In February 1972 King Hassan announced a new Constitution, under which executive power would be vested in the Government and the Assembly, and two-thirds of the Assembly's members were to be elected by universal suffrage compared to half under the previous constitution. The National Front urged a boycott of the constitution referendum and accused the Government of rigging the results, according to which 93 per cent of voters took part and approved the constitution in 98.75 per cent of valid votes cast. The constitution was promulgated in March, and in April a new cabinet, substantially the same as its predecessor was appointed to organize elections. On April 30th, however, King Hassan announced that Parliament, which was due to be reopened, would remain dissolved, and that elections for the new assembly were being postponed until new electoral lists had been drawn up.

In August 1972 King Hassan survived another attempt on his life, when fighter planes of his air force tried to shoot down the plane in which he was travelling and strafed the airport and the royal palace in Rabat. The assassination attempt had apparently been planned by General Oufkir, the Minister of Defence and Army Chief of Staff, whose death occurred immediately afterwards. The King himself took over the command of the armed forces and defence matters and did not appoint a new Defence Minister until March 1973. He approached the opposition parties again, asking for their co-operation in supervising general elections and collaboration with the Government. However, both Istiqlal and the UNFP demanded that a number of far-reaching reforms be introduced, which were unacceptable to the King, as they included curtailing the King's powers and guaranteeing political freedom. The elections, which had been postponed until October, were further postponed indefinitely, and a new cabinet was formed in November without National Front participation.

At the beginning of March 1973 armed attacks on army posts were reported in the Atlas at Moulay-Bouazza and on the edge of the Sahara at Goulmina, and two groups of armed men were discovered and taken prisoner by the armed forces. The Government blamed the military régime in Libya for the incidents and accused the UNFP of being involved. On March 9th arrests were made, including that of Omar Benjelloun, a member of the UNFP Commission, and on March 21st others followed, including two UNFP militants acquitted in the 1971 Marrakesh trial. The Minister of the Interior announced that as a result of these arrests, information had come to light, which had led to the discovery of large caches of arms and explosives in Rabat, Casablanca and Olijda and to the identification of those responsible for several recent violent crimes. A government statement condemned the Rabat branch of the UNFP as merely a cover for subversive activity, and the party was banned. Decrees issued shortly afterwards controlled the right of assembly, limited public meetings and imposed press censorship. On June 25th the trial of 157 people, including UNFP militants, accused of plotting against the monarchical régime opened before the Kenitra military tribunal, and Abderrahim Bouabid, a former minister and the leader of the Rabat branch of the UNFP, was refused the right to appear for the defence. The prisoners were accused of belonging to a secret organization set up in 1966 in Oran and Paris to plot against the régime, of having had guerilla training in Algeria and being responsible for various terrorist incidents including those of March 1973. In mid-August sentences passed included 25 of the death penalty and 30 more of life imprisonment.

In March 1973 the King introduced several nationalist measures: foreign-held lands, mainly holdings of French settlers, were to be recouped, important sectors of the economy were to be morocconized, and the territorial waters were to be extended from 12 to 70 miles. The first two reforms are to be introduced gradually, but the last came into effect immediately and led to a series of disputes with Spain, involving minor clashes between the naval and air forces of the two countries in support of their respective fishing fleets. The measures are interpreted as being an attempt by King Hassan to counterbalance popular discontent.

FOREIGN RELATIONS 1966-73

In June 1966 Morocco signed two agreements with Yugoslavia—the one for joint participation in oil prospecting, the other for the exploitation of potash deposits. Oil exploration has not so far been promising. Some oil (about 100,000 tons a year) is available at two small fields—at Sidi Rhalem and at Harisha. Morocco also made with Yugoslavia in 1966 arrangements for the working of some potash, copper, lead and zinc resources.

During 1966-67 Morocco viewed with unease the arrival, in Algeria, of Soviet planes, guns and tanks. The Moroccan government felt that the flow of arms into Algeria was creating a serious military imbalance in North Africa. Some of the new equipment which Algeria had received from the U.S.S.R. had been sent, so it was said, to the western areas of Algeria, where the Tindouf region was still a matter of dispute between Morocco and Algeria. In November 1966 Morocco acquired from the U.S.A. a number of military jets which formed a counterpoise to Soviet planes known to have reached Algeria. The King visited the United States in February 1967. Reports current at the time intimated that the U.S.A. was prepared to make available arms worth some 15 million dollars in order to strengthen the defences of Morocco. In March 1967 King Hassan urged Algeria to discontinue its military programme and to enter into negotiations with Morocco or else to accept the suggestion that a United Nations disarmament commission should visit Morocco and Algeria.

In the Arab-Israeli war in June 1967, the Moroccan government gave voice to its support of the Arabs' anti-Zionist cause, but did not commit its troops to the fighting. After the Arab defeat brief outbursts of public demonstration were followed by an unofficial commercial boycott of the 70,000 strong Jewish community in Morocco. The government condemnation of this boycott was unpopular with trade unionists and was challenged by the General Secretary of the U.M.T., Mahjoub Ben Seddiq, who was promptly arrested and sentenced to eighteen months' imprisonment on a charge of undermining the respect due to the authority of the state.

In October 1967 the Moroccan government signed an agreement with the U.S.A. which would make available to her some 34 million dollars of economic aid. In February 1968 Herr Brandt, the Federal German Foreign Minister, visited Rabat for talks. Among matters discussed were a number of economic projects which it is hoped, with German assistance, to undertake in Morocco. King Hassan himself visited Iran in April 1968 in order to discuss economic co-operation.

One principal event of the undisturbed political scene since the Palestine war was the Spanish surrender of the small coastal enclave of Ifni. Spain's possession of Ifni, Ceuta, Melilla and the Spanish Sahara to the south of Morocco has long been a cause of friction between the two countries; the Moroccan Government has made much of the apparent inconsistency between the Spanish campaign against Gibraltar and Spain's determined retention of its African colonies. Ifni, held by Spain since 1860, is a poor territory with little obvious economic or strategic potential, and its Spanish population is small. It might well have been handed over before but for Moroccan insistence on negotiating on the other territories. Ceuta and Melilla are Spanish populated and rich phosphate deposits have been discovered in the Sahara, so a voluntary Spanish surrender of these colonies appears unlikely. Morocco officially took over Ifni on June 30th, 1969.

Moroccan diplomacy achieved several notable successes in the 1969-70 period. Rabat was host to both the Islamic summit conference held in September 1969 following the fire at the Al Aqsa mosque in Jerusalem, and to the fifth Arab summit conference in December 1969. Morocco did not take a very active part in either meeting—just as it did not participate in the hostilities in Palestine—but its official acceptance of Mauritania's presence in September was to lead to the dropping of her claim to that country later in the year. Full diplomatic recognition and an exchange of ambassadors followed in January 1970; in June 1970, a treaty of solidarity, good neighbourliness and co-operation was signed between the two countries. Relations with France improved following the general pattern in the Arab world, and the diplomatic missions in Paris and Rabat were returned to full ambassadorial status for the first time since the Ben Barka affair in 1966. Relations were further improved with the visit to Morocco by the French Foreign Minister, M. Schumann in December 1970. As a result of talks, a Franco-Moroccan intergovernmental commission was set up, to meet at least once a year.

In May 1970 final agreement was reached in the frontier dispute with Algeria, and a joint commission mapped out a delineation maintaining the boundaries of the colonial period. The disputed region of Gara-Djebilet, rich in iron ore deposits, thus became the property of Algeria, but Morocco will have a share in a joint company to be established to exploit these deposits. In June 1972 the OAU Heads of State Assembly was held in Rabat, and King Hassan was elected Chairman. At the close of this meeting the Algerian-Moroccan border was agreed by both heads of state, and the agreement was ratified on May 17th, 1973.

Recently, Morocco has further consolidated relationships with both the other Maghreb States and with Mauritania. In January 1972 an agreement was made with Algeria and Mauritania to present a united front against Spain in the Sahara, and further agreements were concluded between Morocco and Mauritania on trade, transport and education. Relations with Spain, already tense over her possessions in the Sahara, became more strained by the fisheries dispute in 1973, but talks are in progress to find a solution. In May, 1973 King Hassan announced that he would send an expeditionary force to help the Arab cause in Syria, but in general, Morocco has not taken an active part in the Arab-Israel conflict. Relations with Libya continue to be very poor, but it is not known to what extent President Gadaffi is supporting opponents of the Moroccan régime.

ECONOMIC SURVEY

Morocco has a congenial climate, varied soils with good agricultural potential and important mineral resources. There is an emerging industrial sector, a small, but growing managerial class and the beginnings of an industrial force. The economic infrastructure (transport, communications, electric energy) is at an advanced stage. The beauty of the country and its climate offer opportunities for the growth of tourism. However, the movement out of the country of capital and trained personnel in the period immediately before and after independence was a severe setback to economic growth, and the G.N.P. fell to 8,530 million dirhams in 1959. This was followed by an extremely poor harvest in 1961, although thanks to favourable capital movements, growth was more satisfactory in 1962, when the gross national product reached 10,650 million dirhams. This improvement continued in the period 1963–69, when the G.N.P. rose at an annual average rate of 3.9 per cent in real terms to 16,110 million dirhams in the latter year. Of the major total sectors of production, only mining and industry grew faster than the national average in 1968–69 (by 4.3 per cent and 4.3 per cent a year respectively). Agricultural production rose by less than 1 per cent annually over this period, as did the activity in the various service sectors while construction and public works showed a decline. A five-year plan came into operation in 1968 which aimed at an annual growth rate of 4.3 per cent. The plan got off to a good start, and there was growth of five per cent in 1969, but agriculture was set back by severe floods in early 1970. The fourth year of the plan, 1971, was marked by a fall in investment due mainly to political instability, but there was a slight recovery in 1972, and the overall growth exceeded the target. Production went up by about five per cent, the largest increases being in the mining, public works and power sectors. Agricultural output went up by about four per cent, barely enough to offset the population increase.

The problems that Morocco has had to face are familiar ones for those countries called "underdeveloped"—a fast-rising population (3.3 per cent per annum), nourished for the most part by an out-of-date agricultural system, and to a considerable extent dependent on foreign capital for financing any substantial increase in the country's productive capacity. In 1970 G.N.P. totalled 17,010 million dirhams at current prices and G.D.P. 14,970 million dirhams at current prices (11,960 million at 1960 prices). The population totalled 15.3 million, giving a low per capita income of 1,112 dirhams. In 1971 the GNP came to approximately 1,883 million dirhams. The population could reach 28 million by 1990. The wealth of the country is most unequally distributed between the landowners and the small number of urban industrialists and merchants on the one hand, and the rural masses and small but growing proletariat on the other.

The share of G.N.P. devoted to investments is about 13.5 per cent, a low level by world standards.

Unemployment is a serious problem; it is estimated that 40 per cent of the youth between the ages of 20 and 30 are unemployed. A substantial trade deficit has been built up and deficits continue, requiring to be balanced by foreign loans and aid. The Government hopes to borrow 980 million dirhams from abroad in 1973.

The five-year plan for 1973–77 involves investment of 26,000 million dirhams, more than twice the corresponding figure in the 1968–72 plan. The new plan aims at an annual growth rate of 6.5 per cent, and like its predecessor, it puts substantial emphasis on development in agriculture, tourism and vocational education. However, when full details of the plan are published, it is expected that they will reveal a greater effort to establish labour-intensive industries, so that the unemployment problem can be alleviated.

Morocco has a great need for investment, and it must receive the assistance of private industry, as well as of foreign governments and international agencies, in helping it to expand its assets and to use them to best advantage. The country has features which should help considerably towards its development, including a convenient geographical position, considerable natural resources, an excellent communications system and a booming tourist industry. The number of tourists entering Morocco has increased rapidly in recent years to 1,191,033 in 1972, which is slightly less than the target figure of 1,150,000.

AGRICULTURE AND FISHERIES

Agriculture is the key to the economy of Morocco. Three-quarters of Morocco's population of 15 million people live in the countryside, and 65 per cent of the active labour force is engaged in agriculture, livestock-raising and fishing. Thus agriculture provides the means of livelihood of the majority of the population, supplies about 90 per cent of the country's domestic food requirements and in the region of 50 per cent of the country's total merchandise exports. The agricultural sector contributed 31 per cent of the gross domestic product in 1970.

Changing climatic conditions cause substantial year-to-year variations in agricultural output. In years with bumper harvests the contribution of agriculture to the gross domestic product rises to over 30 per cent, whereas in years with particularly poor crops the corresponding contribution is in the region of 20 per cent.

The principal crops are cereals, especially wheat and barley; beans and chick peas and other legumens, canary seed, cumin and coriander, linseed, olives, almonds and citrus fruits. Esparto grass is put to several uses including the manufacture of vegetable horsehair and is exported for paper making. Recently, vast areas of esparto grass have been brought into economic use by the establishment of a pulp industry based on this grass and on the eucalyptus tree. Forest resources, almost entirely under state control, include cork (covering approximately 310,000 hectares), cedar, argon, oak and various conifers. Tizra wood is exported for tanning.

Since 1967, as a result of difficulties in the sale of wine, particularly to France, till then the largest client, Morocco has been looking for other wine markets, and reducing the area of its vineyards by converting them to orange groves. In 1972 wine production amounted to 1.2 million hectolitres, of which 850,000 hectolitres were exported.

Livestock numbers are declining, the quality of the herds is poor, and pasture is often thin. The country is largely self-sufficient in foodstuffs though it needs to import sugar, dairy products and wheat.

Agricultural goods account for a varying but substantial proportion of total exports—51.3 per cent in 1968, 48.3 per cent in 1969, 50.6 per cent in 1970 and 47.7 per cent in 1971. The main items involved are citrus fruits, mainly oranges, and tomatoes. Tomato exports were worth 180.2 million dirhams in 1970 and went almost entirely to France. Citrus sales in the same year were worth 357.3 million dirhams and again France was the most important outlet, although West Germany, the U.S.S.R. and Britain also took substantial amounts. Wine exports were worth only 19 million dirhams in 1971. Under its 1969 treaty of association with the European Economic Community, Moroccan citrus exports enter the EEC paying only a little duty but they face severe competition from Spanish and Israeli fruit. Morocco is the world's second largest exporter of citrus, selling abroad about 550,000 tons of its 700,000 ton orange crop in an average year. It is also trying to build up a fruit juice industry and exported about 35,000 tons worth 37.9 million dirhams in 1970. Citrus production in 1971 fell because of poor weather. Because of the higher prices prevailing in Europe, however, the value of exports remained constant. In 1972/73 Morocco's citrus exports totalled 447,358 tons, most of which went to Europe. In April 1973 citrus sales to the EEC were suspended for a week as part of a Moroccan protest against alleged violations of EEC price regulations by Spain and Israel.

Fishing is an important industry and catches average about 220,000 tons of sardines, 10,000 tons of mackerel, 10,000 tuns of tunny fish and 2,000 tons of anchovies a year. Agadir has taken over from Safi as the main fishing port although Casablanca and Eassaouira are also important. Most fish is processed before being consumed or exported, and in 1970 44,300 tons of canned fish were exported worth 127.3 million dirhams. Moroccan sardines are renowned on the world market for their flavour and high quality. There are also substantial exports of fish meal and other products for use as fertilizers and animal foodstuffs. In recent years catches have been declining and Moroccan fishermen blame European boats, especially from Spain, for catching too many fish and depleting stocks.

There were further developments in the fishing dispute with Spain following King Hussan's announcement in March 1973 that Morrocco was extending its jurisdiction over territorial waters from 12 to 70 miles.

Foreign fishing vessels are no longer allowed into the 70-mile area unless their government has a fishing agreement with Morocco. Spain has refused to accept this measure, and several incidents involving the Spanish and Moroccan navies have occurred. Nevertheless, negotiations continue, and the latest round of talks was held in May 1973.

The agricultural sector is one of contrasts: on the one side, a system of holdings inherited from, and in many cases still owned by, European farmers, with an emphasis on cash and export crops; and, on the other, the Muslim farmers, who are much less prosperous, and who raise crops mainly for their own consumption. The traditional arable farming comprises 800,000 to 1,000,000 holdings covering approximately 4 million hectares and is characterized by the small size of the holdings, the legal complexity of rights governing their tenure, low productivity, and the predominance of cereals and stock-raising. Not all animal husbandry is carried on by Moroccans,—15 per cent of stock in the 1960 animal census was owned by Europeans. Irrigation plans have not made great headway due to the conservatism of the farmers and the complexity of the legal situation (much of farming and grazing land is owned by the state, tribes and religious communities—individual ownership formalized by title deeds is still relatively unusual but is spreading. This situation will change shortly, as in March 1973 King Hassan announced that the 250,000 hectares of agricultural land owned by foreigners would be nationalized. About 2,000 settlers, mostly French, are involved, and the question of compensation is still being studied, so that the nationalization decree will take effect only when a policy on compensation has been drawn up.

Cereals are grown on more than 80 per cent of the cultivated land. In 1971 a total of 2.2 million tons of wheat was grown compared with 1.8 million tons in 1970. The citrus crop, which totalled 887,000 tons in 1969/70, fell to 832,000 tons in 1970/71 because of poor weather. Morocco is far from self-sufficient in wheat production and the Government is trying hard to increase output. Some changes are planned for the 1973–74 season. The Minister of Agriculture has said that the area producing wheat is to be increased by 281,000 hectares to 2,186,000 hectares, yielding an expected 6.0–6.5 million quintals of hard wheat. The area under barley will decrease by 100,000 hectares to 1.6 million hectares, with expected production between 9 and 11 million quintals. The area under maize will be diminished from 468,000 to 450,000 hectares, producing between 2.5 and 3.5 million quintals. However, it is probable that 10 million quintals of wheat will have to be imported during the season. In the year ending June 30th, 1972, the U.S.A. provided Morocco with food aid worth $30 million, of which wheat accounted for over 80 per cent.

The Government has strongly pressed for increases in sugar beet production, and by 1965 sugar beat was being grown on over 11,500 hectares. In 1971/72 the sugar beet crop came to 1.7 million tons. In 1972/73 it should reach two million tons, producing 290,000 tons of refined sugar, 70 per cent of total domestic demand. Market gardening, especially in irrigated areas yields more income per unit of land than most other crops. Output of tomatoes and miscellaneous green vegetables is fairly constant, but potato output fluctuates widely from one year to another. A year of weak prices can be disastrous for small market gardeners, who are nevertheless unwilling to submit to output controls. Output of pulses especially broad beans and chick peas has expanded fairly steadily. In 1971 42,000 tons of dry peas were produced, 190,000 tons of broad beans, 100,000 tons of chick peas and 22,000 tons of lentils. Production of olive oil came to only 40,000 tons in the 1972/73 season, a drop of 15,000 tons on the production of the previous year.

A total sum of £63 million was allocated to dams and irrigation networks under the five-year plan (1968–72) with a view to increasing the irrigated area by 158,000 hectares. The first of a series of six dams to be built during the plan period was completed in November 1970. The dam, located at Ait Aidel on the River Tersaout, will increase the irrigated area in the Haouz plain from 3,000 to 30,000 hectares. A hydro-electric plant with a capacity of 60 million kWh. a year is also planned. In May 1972 the Mansour Eddahbi dam in southern Morocco was inaugurated and in April 1971 the Hassan Eddakhil Dam was finished, which should irrigate a total area of 40,000 hectares. By the end of the 1973–77 plan Morocco should have 671,000 hectares under permanent irrigated cultivation.

MINING AND INDUSTRY

The most important mineral deposits are phosphates —Morocco is the second most important producer after the United States and the largest exporter in the world—and they represent about half the value of total production of minerals in Morocco. In addition, Morocco is the fourth largest world producer of cobalt and sixth among the manganese-producing countries. Morocco also possesses important deposits of lead and zinc and lesser resources of several other metals, including copper and tin.

The chief phosphate deposits are at Khouribga and Youssoufia and are controlled by the state *Office Chérifien des Phosphates* (OCP). National consumption of phosphates, however, is very small at the moment and is coped for by a factory for super-phosphates and hyper-phosphates in the Safi complex near Casablanca, which produces about 100,000 tons a year. At present, the bulk of production is exported and provided 25 per cent of total Moroccan exports in 1971. The main clients are France, Holland, Spain Britain and Poland. The value of phosphate exports has risen steadily from 430 million dirhams in 1962 to 600 million dirhams in 1971. However, in recent years the world supply of phosphates has outstripped demand and prices have been depressed. Phosphate ore production has increased greatly in recent years, reaching 16.6 million tons in 1972 and an anticipated 18.5 million tons in 1973. In 1972 about 14.5 million tons was exported. A phosphate calcination plant is under construction, and a phosphoric acid plant is planned. This continued development of the country's phosphate deposits clearly offers enormous prospects for increased economic expansion though there is going to be stiff competition from the vast deposits in the Spanish Sahara which Spain began exploiting in April 1972. Talks are being held with Spain on the controlled expansion of phosphate exports from Spanish Sahara, so that Moroccan sales should not suffer.

Most of the other mineral products have not shown such a dynamic growth since independence as has phosphates. Iron is mined in Ait Amar and Uixan. Production, 1,577,000 tons in 1960, was only 623,257 tons in 1971. The lack of a steel industry within the country has not encouraged high activity in this sector. Manganese is the chief dollar earner; 35 per cent of production is treated in the Sidi Marouf factory. Lead and zinc are often found together in deposits e.g. at Boukber, Touissit, Aouli and Mikbladen. The output of zinc, 101,000 tons in 1959, was down to 72,000 tons ten years later. About 30 per cent of lead production goes through the lead foundry at Oued el Heimer. Production totalled 120,911 tons in 1970 and 122,521 tons in 1971. Lead used to be a valuable export, and sales of MD 64.7 million were recorded in 1969. However, the world price of lead has dropped and exports were worth only MD 27.5 million in 1970. Cobalt is also produced from Bou Azzer (14,097 tons in 1969), and copper (12,000 tons in 1970). The total value of mining exports in 1971 was 833 million dirhams, compared with 840 million in 1970. Recent developments include a Soviet project to develop lead, zinc and silver deposits in the Great Atlas; and also extensive copper ore prospecting in the Anti-Atlas area of south Morocco, undertaken by Occidental Petroleum Inc. of Los Angeles, under an agreement signed with the Ministry of Industry and Mines in 1967. Output from the largest domestic iron ore deposit near Nador and Melilla on the Mediterranean coast has dropped sharply since 1967, when the Moroccan Government bought out Spanish interests in *Minas del Rif*.

Morocco also has coal and small quantities of petroleum. The coal deposits are at Djerada south of Oujda and are controlled by the Government mining organization, BRPM. The theoretical production capacity of Djerada's anthracite mines is 600,000 tons per year but this has not been achieved for a long time, production in 1971 totalling just 474,000 tons, and the outlook for coal must remain black for the forseeable future. To a certain extent the coal industry has been affected by the concentration in electricity projects on hydro electricity at the expense of thermal generation, although the Soviet Union has agreed to build a 60 MW. anthracite-fired power station at Djerada to provide 1,150 million kilowatt hours by 1977 or 1978. Thermal plants accounted for half of electricity production in 1953 but only for 10 per cent in 1965. Total production in 1971 came to just over two million kilowatt hours and in 1972 increased by nearly 13 per cent. Production and distribution are state-controlled through *Energie Electrique du Maroc*; the frequency is 50 cycles per second.

Small deposits of petroleum have been found but despite prospecting in the Doukkala, Draa and Tarfaya areas no important discovery has been made since 1962, when oil was found at Sidi Rhalem in the Essaouira region. Esso Exploration Inc., started activity in 1967, on off-shore permits south of Agadir. All Morocco's production is refined in the country in a topping unit jointly owned by the government agency, SAMIR, and the Italian oil firm, ENI, set up in 1961 at Mohammedia and in another refinery inherited from the French at Sidi Kacem. However, a great part of the refineries' need for crude oil is satisfied by imports, and oil continues to be an expensive import item. Oil production in 1971 came to only 23,000 tons and in 1972 it was declining to almost zero as deposits became exhausted.

The Bureau of Mining Research and participation (BRPM) is undertaking large-scale prospecting for hydro-carbons both alone and in association with private partners. Encouraging results have been found by Esso in the province of Tarfaya. In early 1970 a team of Soviet technicians discovered a deposit of cobalt in the region of Ouarzazate. Two Japanese companies, Mitsui Metal and Mining and Nittetsu Mining, have agreed to form a consortium with the Moroccan Government and a French company (Omnium Nord Africain de France) to build a factory to process copper extracted from a mine 130 kilometres to the east at Casablanca. The factory will have a capacity to treat between 800 tons and 1,000 tons of ore per day and should have come into operation in mid-1972. The Japanese companies will import about half the factory's production. In August 1972 an agreement was reached with French and American companies for oil exploration in the Gharb area. It is hoped to sign further contracts for exploration along the Atlantic coast.

Several projects are proceeding for the exploitation of deposits of copper ores, fluorine and silver, and notably the Upper Moulaya lead zinc mines to be opened up by Zellidja with the BRPM.

The mining industry has been placed on the list of industries which benefit under the Investment Code from a series of incentives and advantages designed to promote private investments, according to a decree published in December 1969. Another decree virtually abolished the export tax on minerals by lowering it from 5 per cent *ad valorem* to 0.5 per cent on iron, antimony, cobalt, manganese, barytine and fluorine ores, fullers earth, lead zinc and silver metals. For lead, zinc and copper ores the tax is reduced on a variable scale related to world prices of these minerals.

Industry is perhaps the least stagnant sector of the economy and certainly promises the highest rate of growth in the immediate future. The industrial sector including building accounted for 28 per cent of the Gross Domestic Product in 1970. Even so, the extent of manufacturing is still relatively small, accounting for 17 per cent of G.N.P. in 1968. The growth of manufacturing in Morocco (5 per cent a year on average during 1960-68) has been directed largely towards the light industries. Although the majority of the population has very little purchasing power, there is nevertheless a fairly large market for many consumer goods among the two to three million people who are better off. Encouraged by government promotion, many new enterprises have been established to produce goods that formerly had to be imported. An export-orientated industry has also emerged during the past few years, particularly in the field of food-processing. This consists mainly of fruit juice plants and canneries (fish and vegetables) as well as the edible oil industry. Of special importance for the domestic market are the flour-milling, sugar refining and tobacco processing industries. Next to the food industries in importance are the textile and leather industries. A metal products industry is also well established, while in the chemical sector the most significant plants are a crude oil refinery and the Safi plant which processes Morocco's most important mineral, phosphate. The country's timber industry is also expanding rapidly. All the cork output was exported as well as 36,000 tons of alfa grass and 46,000 tons of cellulose.

Several foreign companies contribute to the country's manufacturing capacity; General Tire and Rubber Co. of Morocco, the SAMIR/ENI refinery and the *Société Marocaine de Constructions Automobiles*. An extension doubling the capacity of the SAMIR refinery to 2.5 million tons a year was opened by King Hassan in May 1972. A new $17 million tyre plant has been completed by Goodyear near Casablanca. The Safi chemical complex produces sulphuric acid (1,300 tons daily), phosphoric acid (450 tons daily), triple super-phosphates (200,000 tons a year), and diammonium phosphate (150,000 tons a year). This helps to supply the country's great need for agricultural fertilizers. A MD 14 million chemical plant built by the West German Hoechst concern was opened in Casablanca in May 1972 to produce plastics, medicines and other chemical goods. Morocco has its own car assembly company, which intends to increase its output of cars by 20 per cent in 1973 to 22,000.

Morocco is at present heavily dependent on imported textiles but considerable investment (some of it from a World Bank loan granted in 1962) has been made in increasing the capacity of the local industry, especially in cotton cloth. Industrialization plans for the future include projects for the manufacture of vegetable oil, PVC, iron and steel, artificial fibres and fertilizer. Increased demand for fertilizers will justify the installation of a second chemical plant for the processing of ammonium phosphate. Particularly worthy of note is Morocco's long-term sugar plan which is designed to promote national sugar production in such a way as to bring about a steady reduction in imports. According to the plan, an integrated sugar industry will be formed, through the addition of sugar work to the existing refineries and through the development of sugar crops, notably beet, which is already being grown successfully in some parts of the country. There are at present seven sugar mills with several more planned, and Morocco hopes eventually to become self-sufficient in sugar.

About half of the industrial labour force is concentrated in Casablanca. There is substantial unemployment and after the last shipments of agricultural exports this is swelled by the seasonal laying off of workers (packers, etc.). The 1971 census revealed that 8.7 per cent of the active labour force was unemployed. Many workers emigrate for lack of employment opportunities and recently the pace of this emigration has stepped up, mostly to France. Some Moroccans are working in Gibraltar, and substantial employment opportunities may open up there owing to the withdrawal of the Spanish labour force. The remittance of these workers' wages helps to strengthen the balance of payments. Fez and Marrakesh contain most of the artisans.

The conditions under which Morocco's industrial development surged forward since 1945 explain to some extent the present structure of industry. Some sections such as fish canning and edible oils and fats are over-equipped, while others are under-equipped. The textile industry, for instance, meets only about 35 per cent of local demand. Often the equipment is not fully integrated or balanced; for example, textiles have had an imbalance between spinning and weaving capacity. Recent trends indicate that many of these problems are being faced. The latest modern equipment is being installed to improve quality and increase profits.

"Moroccanization" of the country's business is taking place gradually. In April 1971 King Hassan II outlined that several hundred enterprises owned by foreigners in Morocco would gradually be transferred to Moroccan control. The King has taken particular care to point out that Moroccanization does not mean nationalization. Instead he sees it as the negotiated transfer of private enterprises from foreign to Moroccan hands with adequate immunities paid. In March 1973 King Hassan indicated that the pace of Moroccanization was to be accelerated. In April the details were published of the requirements for a "Moroccan" company: the chairman, the managing director, a majority of the board and at least half of the shareholders must be Moroccan. Under a timetable published in May 1973 wholesale and retail businesses, import agencies and industrial concerns must be Moroccanized by April 31st, 1974, and the banking and insurance sectors will be taken over within the following year. Ten of the foreign banks in Morocco have anticipated the move by taking in Moroccan shareholders, two of them majority holdings.

TRADE AND PAYMENTS

Morocco runs a deficit in her trade with other countries. The chief reason for the disappointing export results has been a levelling-off in phosphate rock exports, valued at 554 million dirhams in 1969, almost 25 per cent of total exports. The export effort otherwise depends on agricultural produce such as citrus fruit, tinned fish, wine, fresh tomatoes, and on metalliferous ores. France still remains by far the largest customer and sales to France recovered satisfactorily from the heavy fall noted in the immediate post-independence period. The amount of Morocco's exports absorbed by France has risen while France's share of the Moroccan market has fallen steadily. Morocco still retains her quotas in the French market and recently the prospects for an increase in her wine exports improved as a result of a French decision to upgrade the classification of Moroccan wines. Federal Germany, the U.S.A. and Britain follow France in trading importance, but at a considerable distance.

In 1969 Morocco concluded a treaty of association with the European Economic Community which provided for duty-free entry into the EEC of Moroccan goods. Restrictions were lowered on Moroccan exports of certain food products including citrus fruits, olive oil and fish. In return Morocco reduced duties on manufactured goods from the EEC. Tomatoes, wine and some preserved foods were excluded from the agreement. The treaty runs out in March 1974 but it will probably be renegotiated before then. Morocco hopes to conclude a new arrangement which will provide trade advantages for more Moroccan goods and will include provisions on financial and technical aid. The EEC is currently trying to develop a coherent Maghreb policy towards Algeria, Morocco and Tunisia together. One step forward was taken in February 1973, when Morocco conducted an agreement amending its treaty with the EEC to take into account the entry into the Community of Britain, Denmark and Ireland. The enlarged EEC will account for over half Morocco's imports and exports.

In 1971 both imports and exports stagnated. Imports went up by only 1.2 per cent and totalled MD 3,532 million. Exports, at MD 2,526 million, increased by 2.2 per cent. Food accounted for 20.1 per cent of all imports (16.1 per cent in 1970) and imports of industrial equipment fell by 10 per cent in value. Trade with France rose slightly in 1971, imports totalling MD 1,083 million and exports MD 917.9 million. Imports from the U.S.A., mainly food, rose by 27 per cent to MD 501.2 million. Substantial rises were recorded in exports to China (up by 156.3 per cent to MD 93.8 million) and to the U.S.S.R. (up by 25.9 per cent to MD 89.0 million). Austerity measures succeeded in narrowing the trade gap in 1972 to 624 million dirhams compared with 1,007 million dirhams in 1971. Imports rose hardly at all, by only about one per cent, while exports rose by over 15 per cent.

More and more state control has been introduced into the export trade as the country's financial position has deteriorated. The export of phosphates is controlled by the *Office Chérifien des Phosphates*, and the export of citrus fruit, other agricultural products, fish products and handicraft goods by the *Office Chérifien de Contrôle d'Exportation* which controls 35 per cent of the nation's exports.

Over the last few years various austerity measures have been resorted to: increases in direct taxation and corporation taxation and restrictions on credit facilities. The Government has also sought to diversify its trading products, to open up new markets, and to obtain more foreign aid for development.

TRANSPORT AND COMMUNICATIONS

The road network of Morocco is well developed. In December 1970 there were 24,775 km. of roads, of which 85 per cent were paved. There were 14 km. of modern motorway and 7,125 km. of main roads. Most public transport is by road. The paved highway system is the second longest in Africa (after South Africa), and most of the roads are built to design standards well in advance of the traffic which they are currently carrying. Many of these were built by the French army, primarily for strategic purposes. In 1968, there were over 278,000 vehicles in Morocco, more than twice as many as in 1957. The tonnage transported on Moroccan roads in 1971 was 7.2 million tons. In October 1970 an agreement was concluded between the French Renault company and the Moroccan Government on the establishment of an assembly factory near Casablanca. The factory will employ about 500 people and initial production will be 12,500 vehicles per day. A similar agreement was signed with the French Peugeot company in the same month. These decisions are the result of the growing demand for private and commercial vehicles in Morocco.

The *Société Marocaine de Construction Automobile* (Somaca) assembles Renault, Simca, Fiat, Opel and Chrysler vehicles and production is currently running at about 23,000 vehicles a year. Volvo lorries are also assembled in Morocco, some of which are exported to China.

The country's railway network is good, there being 1,756 km. of track, 730 km. of which are electrified. Traction is by electric or diesel locomotives. Casablanca is connected by a track that continues through Algeria to Tunis. The only line that shows a profit, however, is the western network of the *Compagnie des Chemins de Fer du Maroc* (CFM), which stretches from Sidi Kacem to Casablanca, Marrakesh and Safi. This is almost entirely on account of the large shipments of minerals particularly phosphates. The latter accounted for 10.5 million tons out of 16.2 million tons of all Moroccan freight hauled in 1968, and provided nearly 40 per cent of income.

Morocco currently has eleven commercial airfields, of which seven are served by regular schedules. The major traffic is international, the most important international airports being Casablanca-Anfa and Casablanca-Nouaceur and Rabat-Salé. Substantial runway and terminal improvements are being carried out at major airfields to encourage the tourism industry. With the opening of the new runway at Tangier on May 4th, 1972, Morocco acquired its fourth airport, which can accommodate the Boeing 747 and other large jets. Moroccan air transport, both domestic and international, is now mainly provided by Royal Air Maroc, which is an autonomous corporation in which the Moroccan State has a 68.85 per cent share and Air France 17.53 per cent, the remainder being held either by private transportation companies or by individuals. The number of passengers carried has shown a steady upward trend, numbering 602,592 in 1968 compared with only 437,000 in 1967. It is interesting to note that a new air company, Royal Air-Inter, which serves only Morocco's internal lines, hitherto largely covered by Air France, came into operation in April 1970. Royal Air Maroc has an 80 per cent holding in the company. During 1969, the country's internal airlines were used by 35,652 passengers, 22 per cent more than in 1968.

On its 2,000 km. of coastline, Morocco has a dozen ports of greatly varying importance. The coast is generally not very favourable for port installations since it is particularly rocky and the Atlantic swell is one of the strongest in the world. In 1967, the ports handled over 15 million tons of cargo. Of this total over 60 per cent went through Casablanca, about 20 per cent through Safi, and in the region of 7 per cent through Mohammedia. The volume of cargo shipped has increased by between 3 and 4 per cent annually in recent years (although with considerable variations between the different ports). In fact, Morocco has two major phosphate ports, Casablanca and Safi. Under the Five-Year Plan for 1968–72, Safi is to be expanded. At present it can receive tankers of 45,000 tons from which oil is purified 6 km. away at the SAMIR refinery. It is now anticipated that after the installation of new pipelines the port will be able to receive and pump oil from tankers of 60,000 tons. Mohammedia is the principal petroleum port at present. Maritime passenger traffic is concentrated at Tangier and Casablanca, with most at the former being based on the ferry service across the Straits of Gibraltar, and most at the latter on cruise visitors on relatively short stays. Studies commenced in March 1970 for a bridge link between Morocco and Gibraltar. The studies are being undertaken by the Moroccan Government and an international specialist.

FINANCE AND FOREIGN AID

As in most other countries at a similar stage of economic development customs duties and indirect taxes each contribute more to budget income than direct taxation. About a third of budget income is on capital account and derives from profits from the exploitation of the mines run by the *Office Chérifien des Phosphates*, treasury bills and advances from the banks, and foreign grants and loans. To an increasing extent the banking system has been financing the deficits; in 1965 total advances outstanding to the Government were almost four times that in 1958. However, in another way, things are better recently following the restoration of French aid in 1962; this aid being usually tied to a certain extent to the purchase of French goods. Combined with certain difficulties on the production side budgetary troubles have produced inflationary symptoms. The Government has pledged general wage rises when the cost of living index increases by more than 6 per cent, but this pledge has only partly been fulfilled and on occasions when the Government has tried to implement it, it has met with protests involving civil disturbances. The cost of living rose by an average of almost 6 per cent a year in the 1962–64 period, but during 1965–69 the trend moderated to an average annual rate of 3 per cent. Foreign aid in 1971 totalled 840 million dirhams compared with 651 million dirhams in 1966. The agreement for financial co-operation between France and Morocco was not renewed in 1967. The 1973 ordinary budget provides for administrative spending of 3,476 million dirhams, investment of 1,801 million dirhams and debt repayments of 482 million dirhams, thus increasing total expenditure by 557 million dirhams compared with the previous year. Revenue should rise by 3.6 per cent to 6,175 million dirhams, because of heavier duties on imports and on alcohol. The investment budget for 1973 provides for investment in new projects of 1,817 million dirhams, an increase of 159 million dirhams on 1972. The Government will borrow 980 million dirhams from abroad to finance the investment budget.

The 1970 balance of payments showed a surplus on private capital movements of 246.8 million dirhams. In the public domain there was a capital movement surplus of 477.4 million dirhams which included commercial credits of 335.5 million. The total balance of payments surplus came to MD 169.9 million dirhams. The cost of living index rose by 5.9 points in 1971 to 131.4 (1960=100) and this caused industrial unrest which was only partly alleviated by wage increases announced by King Hassan in the winter of 1971. The balance of payments surplus has continued to grow since 1971, partly because of foreign aid, but also because revenues from tourism have risen steadily, totalling 380 million dirhams in the first nine months of 1972. This represented a 5.3 per cent increase on the 1971 figure. Morocco's international reserves at the end of October 1972 came to 1,205 million dirhams.

DEVELOPMENT

The Five-Year Plan launched in 1968 had the same development objectives as the previous Three-Year Plan (1965–67). Total investment of 12,500 million dirhams was envisaged for the plan period, to provide an anticipated annual growth rate of 4.3 per cent. About 40 per cent of planned investment was to be financed by foreign loans, in particular from the World Bank. In recent years much financial assistance has been given to Morocco by the United States, the Federal Republic of Germany, Italy, Belgium, Kuwait and the U.S.S.R.

The plan for 1973–77 involves investment of 26,000 million dirhams, and, as before, priorities include the development of tourism, agriculture and education. However, more emphasis than in former plans is placed on industry and on housing, with plans to build 60,000 homes during the five-year period.

STATISTICAL SURVEY

AREA AND POPULATION

Area (sq. km.)	Population (Census of July 20th, 1971)		
	Total	Moroccans	Aliens
446,550	15,379,259	15,267,000	112,000

CHIEF TOWNS

Population (1971 Census)

Casablanca	1,506,373	Oujda		175,532
Rabat (capital)	367,620	Saié		155,557
Marrakesh	332,741	Kénitra		139,206
Fez	325,327	Tétuan		139,105
Meknès	248,369	Safi		129,113
Tangier	187,894			

517

MOROCCO—(Statistical Survey)

AGRICULTURE
('000 tons)

	1969–70	1970–71	1971–72
Wheat	1,800	2,188	2,162
Barley	1,953	2,572	2,466
Maize	320	390	368
Olives	160	506	n.a.
Dates	90†	90†	n.a.
Pulses	392	354	414
Tomatoes	250†	250†	112*
Potatoes	300†	300†	81*
Citrus Fruit	887	832	852
Sugar Beet	1,114	1,584	1,677
Cotton	19	19	27
Wine ('000 hectolitres)	1,253	1,150	1,500‡

* Amount exported.   † FAO estimate.   ‡ Official estimate.

Livestock (1971): Cattle 3,630,000; Sheep 17,500,000; Goats 8,850,000; Camels 230,000; Horses 400,000; Pigs 14,000; Poultry 15,800,000.

Fishing (1971): The total catch was 228,700 metric tons, of which sardines comprised 183,000 tons.

MINING
('000 tons)

	1970	1971	1972
Phosphates	11,424	12,030	15,105
Iron Ore	872	623	234
Coal	433	475	547
Manganese	112	160	96
Lead	121	124	146
Petroleum	46	23	28
Zinc	32	22	36
Cobalt	6	10	11

INDUSTRY*

	Unit	1968	1969	1970	1971
Cement	'000 tons	1,011	1,165	1,405	1,481
Processed Lead	,, ,,	24	27	20	18
Refined Sugar	,, ,,	425	409	399	424
Soap	tons	29,472	27,593	28,771	n.a.
Paint	,,	8,252	9,714	11,219	n.a.
Textiles	,,	31,690	37,153	40,446	n.a.
Electricity (hydraulic and thermal)	'000 kWh.	1,538	1,693	1,830	1,962
Cars	number	n.a.	n.a.	n.a.	n.a.
Tyres (tubes)	,,	308,000	363,000	411,000	n.a.
Shoes	'000 pairs	5,127	5,537	4,494	n.a.
Flour	tons	667,218	625,426	818,000	817,700
Refined Petroleum	'000 tons	1,322	1,470	1,506	1,473
Superphosphate	,, ,,	253	281	180	n.a.

* Major industrial establishments only.

MOROCCO—(STATISTICAL SURVEY)

FINANCE

100 Moroccan francs (centimes) = 1 dirham.
Coins: 1, 2, 5, 10, 20 and 50 francs; 1 and 5 dirhams.
Notes: 5, 10, 50 and 100 dirhams.
Exchange rates (March 1973): £1 sterling = 10.08 dirhams (selling rate); U.S. $1 = 4.195 dirhams (par value).
100 dirhams = £9.92 = $23.84.

ORDINARY BUDGET
(million dirhams)

Revenue: (1971) 4,432; (1972) 5,799; (1973) 6,175. **Expenditure:** (1971) 4,432; (1972) 6,197; (1973) 6,632.

FIVE-YEAR DEVELOPMENT PLAN 1973-77
INVESTMENT*

	million dirhams
Agriculture	2,300
Industry	1,120
Mining	1,000
Energy	1,000
Transport	1,000
Housing	600
Tourism	600
Posts and Telecommunications	500
Education	450
Administration	310
Hospitals	225
Youth and Sports	85
TOTAL	26,000

* Provisional figures.

Currency in Circulation (Note issue at year end): (1969) 2,123m. dirhams; (1970) 2,262 dirhams; (1971) 2,473 dirhams.

BALANCE OF PAYMENTS—ALL FOREIGN COUNTRIES
(million dirhams)

	1971 Credit	1971 Debit	1971 Balance	1972 Credit	1972 Debit	1972 Balance
Goods and Services:						
Merchandise f.o.b.	2,518.4	3,207.1	−688.7	2,946.7	3,241.6	−294.9
Gold for Industry	—	4.3	−4.3	—	11.5	−11.5
Transport and Insurance	174.0	403.6	−229.6	221.3	431.5	−210.2
Travel	760.0	300.0	460.0	893.3	388.2	505.1
Income from Investments	69.8	310.4	−240.6	59.9	323.7	−263.8
Government n.i.e.	195.9	312.7	−116.8	194.4	309.9	−115.5
Other services	81.7	112.2	−30.5	80.4	104.9	−24.5
Transfer Payments	842.6	293.3	549.3	980.7	349.1	631.6
CURRENT BALANCE	4,642.4	4,943.6	−301.2	4,396.0	4,811.3	−415.3
Capital and Monetary Gold:						
Public Sector:						
Commercial Credits	432.1	155.1	277.0	284.6	242.7	41.9
Foreign Exchange Loans	311.9	140.9	171.3	217.6	90.3	127.3
Loans in Dirhams	4.2	18.2	−14.0	0.7	18.4	−17.7
Others	7.6	1.0	6.6	6.1	1.3	4.8
Private Sector:						
Commercial Credits	165.9	76.8	89.1	24.9	65.9	−41.0
Loans and Investments	168.8	49.7	119.1	160.7	94.1	66.6
Others	13.9	63.4	−49.5	78.8	197.2	−118.3
CAPITAL BALANCE	1,104.4	504.8	599.6	773.4	719.2	54.2
Special Drawing Rights				61.0	—	61.0
TOTAL	5,746.8	5,448.4	298.4	6,211.1	5,879.6	331.5

MOROCCO—(Statistical Survey)

EXTERNAL TRADE
(million Dirhams)

	1966	1967	1968	1969	1970	1971	1972
Imports	2,418	2,620	2,790	2,844	3,471	3,532	3,577
Exports	2,168	2,146	2,278	2,455	2,469	2,526	2,953

PRINCIPAL COMMODITIES
(million Dirhams)

Imports	1970	1971	1972
Milk, Butter and Cheese	71	73	71
Coffee	49	32	35
Tea	90	84	86
Wheat	130	243	137
Sugar	138	149	170
Petroleum	114	145	172
Timber (raw and prepared)	102	105	102
Paper and Products	48	47	71
Cotton Textiles	108	86	43
Motor Vehicles and Parts	182	193	212

Exports	1970	1971	1972
Tomatoes	180	163	179
Fresh Vegetables and Potatoes	87	81	122
Cotton	28	23	40
Citrus Fruits	357	389	429
Preserved Fish	127	148	134
Wine	43	19	35
Phosphates	572	588	673
Iron Ore	29	23	11
Lead Ore	71	69	90
Zinc Ore	14	7	10
Cork and Cork Products	21	15	25

PRINCIPAL COUNTRIES
(million Dirhams)

Imports	1970	1971	1972
China, People's Republic	n.a.	60	86
Cuba	n.a.	74	45
France	1,074	1,083	1,111
Germany, Federal Republic	304	267	268
Italy	187	210	200
Netherlands	n.a.	102	111
U.S.S.R.	166	142	142
United Kingdom	161	144	160
U.S.A.	392	501	270

Exports	1970	1971	1972
Belgium/Luxembourg	n.a.	100	121
France	904	918	964
Germany, Federal Republic	227	214	265
Italy	163	119	265
Netherlands	116	80	110
Poland	n.a.	51	66
Spain	n.a.	107	164
U.S.S.R.	n.a.	89	113
United Kingdom	138	126	136

MOROCCO—(Statistical Survey)

TRANSPORT

ROADS

	1969	1970
Tonnage Transported	6,187,000	6,619,000
Cars	207,028	222,460
Lorries and Vans	79,253	83,899
Motor Cycles	14,741	14,670

In 1971 the Tonnage Transported was 7,168,000.

SHIPPING

Freight	Unit	1971	1972
Tonnage Loaded	'000 tons	13,354	16,367
Tonnage Unloaded	,, ,,	5,198	4,871

Source: Institut National de la Statistique et des Etudes Economiques, Paris, *Données Statistiques.*

CIVIL AVIATION

	1971	1972
Total passengers	1,124,140	1,191,033
Freight (metric tons)	11,142	14,461

TOURISM

Country of Origin	1970	1971	1972
Algeria	60,238	66,632	91,578
Belgium	21,585	21,775	25,906
France	174,050	188,175	210,625
Federal Germany	55,405	70,702	95,272
Italy	18,462	17,904	125,147
Scandinavia	12,105	8,621	9,454*
Spain	41,969	42,789	76,107
Switzerland	10,116	12,591	19,091
U.K.	84,411	80,882	107,733
U.S.A.	117,820	136,677	194,071
Others	150,692	176,168	208,469
Total	746,860	822,916	1,063,453
Cruise Passengers	105,505	91,376	127,580
Grand Total	852,365	914,292	1,191,033

* Denmark only.

Hotel Capacity (1972): 52,000 beds.

EDUCATION

	Primary School Pupils	Secondary School Pupils	Students Engaged in Higher Education
1970–71	1,175,277	298,880	13,572
1971–72	1,231,436	313,424	15,148
1972–73	1,277,660	334,959	n.a.

Sources (unless otherwise stated): Direction de la Statistique, Rabat; Banque Marocaine du Commerce Extérieur.

THE CONSTITUTION

(Promulgated March 10th, 1972, after having been approved by national referendum.)*

Preamble: The Kingdom of Morocco, a sovereign Moslem State, shall be a part of the Great Maghreb. As an African State one of its aims shall be the realization of African unity. It will adhere to the principles, rights and obligations of those international organizations of which it is a member and will work for the preservation of peace and security in the world.

General Principles: Morocco shall be a constitutional, democratic and social monarchy. Sovereignty shall pertain to the nation and be exercised directly by means of the referendum and indirectly by the constitutional institutions. All Moroccans shall be equal before the law, and all adults shall enjoy equal political rights including the franchise. Freedoms of movement, opinion and speech and the right of assembly shall be guaranteed. Islam shall be the state religion.

The Monarchy: The Crown of Morocco and its attendant constitutional rights shall be hereditary in the line of H.M. King Hassan II, and shall be transmitted to the oldest son, unless during his lifetime the King has appointed as his successor another of his sons. The King is the symbol of unity, guarantees the continuity of the state, and safeguards respect for Islam and the Constitution. The King shall have the power to appoint and dismiss the Prime Minister and Cabinet Ministers and shall preside over the Cabinet. He shall promulgate legislation passed by parliament and have the power to dissolve the House of Representatives; is empowered to declare a state of emergency and to initiate revisions to the Constitution. The Sovereign is the Commander-in-Chief of the Armed Forces; makes appointments to civil and military posts; appoints Ambassadors; signs and ratifies Treaties; presides over the Council for National Development Planning and the Supreme Judiciary Council; and exercises the right of pardon.

Parliament: Parliament shall consist of a single assembly, the House of Representatives, which shall comprise 240 members elected for a four-year term. Two thirds of the members shall be elected by direct universal suffrage, and one third by an electoral college composed of councillors in local government and employers' and employees' representatives. Parliament shall pass legislation, which may be initiated by its members or by the Prime Minister; authorize any declaration of war; and approve any extension beyond thirty days of a state of emergency.

Government: The Government shall be responsible to the King and the House of Representatives and shall ensure the execution of laws. The Prime Minister shall be empowered to initiate legislation and to exercise statutory powers except where these are reserved to the King. He shall put before parliament the Government's intended programme and shall be responsible for co-ordinating ministerial work.

Relations between the Authorities: The King may request further consideration of legislation by parliament before giving his assent; submit proposed legislation to a referendum by decree; and dissolve the House of Representatives if a Bill rejected by parliament is approved by referendum. He may also dissolve the House of Representatives by decree, but the succeeding House may not be dissolved within a year of its election. The House of Representatives may defeat the Government either by refusing a vote of confidence moved by the Prime Minister or by passing a censure motion; either eventuality shall involve the Government's collective resignation.

Judiciary: The Judiciary shall be independent. Judges shall be appointed on the recommendation of the Supreme Council of the Judiciary presided over by the King.

* For the most part the Constitution is unchanged from the one drawn up by King Hassan II and promulgated in 1962. This provided for two houses of parliament, one elected by universal suffrage and one by electoral colleges, and was superceded by that of June 1970, which introduced a unicameral parliament, of which one-quarter of the members were to be elected by universal suffrage, and it increased the powers of the monarch.

THE GOVERNMENT

HEAD OF THE STATE

H.M. King Hassan II (*accession February 26th, 1961*).

CABINET
(*June 1973*)

Prime Minister and Minister of National Defence: Ahmed Osman.
Minister of State: Hadj M'Hamad Bahnini.
Minister of Justice: Bel Abbès Taarji.
Minister of the Interior: Mohamed Haddou Shiguer.
Minister of Foreign Affairs: Ahmed Taïbi Benhima.
Minister of Finance: Bensallem Guessous.
Minister of Trade, Industry, Mines and Merchant Shipping: Abdelkader Benslimane.
Minister of Agriculture and Agrarian Reform: Abdeslam Berrada.
Minister of Education: Dey ould Sidi Baba.

Minister of Posts, Telegraph and Telecommunications: Gen. Dris Ben Omar El Alami.
Minister of Information: Ahmed Majid Benjelloun.
Minister of Administrative Affairs and Secretary General to the Government: Hamid Benyakhlef.
Minister of Labour, Social Affairs, Youth and Sport: Mohammed Arsalane El Jadidi.
Minister of Public Works: Salah M'Zili.
Minister of Town Planning, Housing and the Environment: Hassan Zemmouri.
Minister of Health: Dr. Abderrahman Touhami.
Minister of Tourism: Abderrahman El Kouhen.

MOROCCO—(The Government, Diplomatic Representation)

Minister of Waqfs and Islamic Affairs: Mohamed Mekki Naciri.

Secretary of State at the Prime Minister's Office for Planning, Regional Development and Professional Training: Abd-Al-Latif Imani.

Secretary of State at the Prime Minister's Office for National Promotion, National Co-operation and Crafts: Abdallah Gharnit.

Under-Secretary of State at the Prime Minister's Office for Higher Education: Abd-Al-Krim Halim.

Under-Secretary of State at the Prime Minister's Office for Primary and Secondary Education: Muhammad Bouamoud.

Under-Secretary of State at the Prime Minister's Office for Youth and Sport: Mounir Doukkali.

Director-General of the Royal Cabinet: Abbès El Kaissi.

DIPLOMATIC REPRESENTATION

EMBASSIES AND LEGATIONS ACCREDITED TO MOROCCO
(in Rabat unless otherwise stated)
(E) Embassy; (L) Legation.

Algeria: 46 blvd. Front l'Oued (E); *Ambassador:* Ferhat Tayeb Hamida.

Argentina: 4 blvd. Moulay Hassan (E); *Ambassador:* Florencio Méndez Gazariego.

Austria: 2 rue de Tedders (L); *Ambassador:* Ernst Hessenberger.

Belgium: 6 avenue de Marrakech (E); *Ambassador:* Baron Roland D'Anethans.

Brazil: 34 rue Lamartine (E); *Ambassador:* Silvio Ribeiro.

Bulgaria: 6 rue Blaise Pascal (E); *Ambassador:* Arsène Petrov Tarkov.

Cameroon: (address not available) (E); *Ambassador:* Ferdinand Leopold Oyono.

Canada: Madrid, Spain.

Czechoslovakia: 4 rue Normand (E); *Ambassador:* Dr. Joseph Soltesz.

Chile: rue Docteur Laraki, Quartier Souissi (E); *Chargé d'Affaires:* José Mario.

China, People's Republic: 6 rue Joachim du Bellay (E); *Ambassador:* Yang Chi-liang.

Cuba: 4 rue El Jabarti (E); *Ambassador:* Enrique Rodríguez Loeches.

Denmark: 5 ave. de Marrakech (E); *Ambassador:* M. Viggo Jensen (also accred. to Libya and Senegal).

Egypt: 31 rue d'Alger (E); *Ambassador:* Izz-al-din Ramzi.

Ethiopia: Hotel Rex (E); *Ambassador:* Gen. Makonnen Deneke.

Finland: (E); *Ambassador:* Hanikainen Heikki Juhani.

France: ave. Mohammed V (E); *Ambassador:* Claude Lebel.

Gabon: (E); *Ambassador:* Joseph Megnier Mbo.

German Democratic Republic: (E); *Ambassador:* Walfred Kitler.

Germany, Federal Republic of: 2 blvd. Front d'Oued (E); *Ambassador:* Heinrich Kendus.

Ghana: (E); Abidjan, Ivory Coast.

Greece: 9 rue de Kairouan (E); *Ambassador:* G. Warsamy.

Guatemala: (E); *Ambassador:* Doroteo Reyes Santa Cruz.

Guinea: (E); *Ambassador:* Camara Nabiyaya.

Hungary: 12 rue de Talda (E); Laszlo Guyaros.

India: 11 rue Descartes (E); *Ambassador:* Valliath Madhavan-Nair.

Indonesia: 29 rue Zankat Al Jaseir (E); *Ambassador:* Ahmed Janus Mokiginta.

Iran: 7 rue Montaigne (E); *Ambassador:* Abbes Nayeri Iram.

Iraq: 17 ave. de la Victoire (E); *Ambassador:* Dr. Hamad Dali al-Arbouli.

Italy: 9 ave. Franklin Roosevelt (E); *Ambassador:* Giovanni Ludovico Borromeo.

Ivory Coast: 21 rue de Tedders (E); *Ambassador:* Amadou Thiam.

Japan: 7 rue de Midelt (E); *Ambassador:* (vacant).

Jordan: 1 rue de Kairouan (E); *Ambassador:* Nazir Rashid.

Korea, Republic: 9 ave. de Meknès (E); *Ambassador:* Shi Hak Hyun.

Kuwait: 48 ave. Pasteur (E); *Ambassador:* Muhallal Al-Mudif.

Lebanon: 5 rue de Tedders (E); *Ambassador:* Abdul Rahman Adra.

Libya: 1 ave. A.-Derraq (E); *Ambassador:* Mohammed Tlissi.

Luxembourg: (*see* Netherlands).

Malaysia: (E); *Ambassador:* Tan-Sri Abd-Al-Latif.

Mali: (E); *Ambassador:* Amadou Diababa.

Mauritania: (E); *Ambassador:* (vacant).

Mexico: (E); *Ambassador:* Ernesto Madeno.

Netherlands: 38 rue de Tunis (E); *Ambassador:* Jonkheer Jan-Derck van Karnebeek (also represents Luxembourg).

Norway: 20 ave. Yarmouk (E); *Ambassador:* Olav Moltke-Hausen.

Pakistan: route des Zaërs (E); *Ambassador:* Maqbul Abid.

Peru: 2 ave. Moulay Youssef (E); *Ambassador:* Valdiviesco Belaúnde.

Poland: rue Omar Slaoui (E); *Ambassador:* (vacant).

Portugal: 45 rue Maurice Pascouet (E); *Ambassador:* (vacant).

Qatar: *Ambassador:* Abdullah Youssef Al-Jida.

Romania: 10 rue d'Ouezzane (L); *Ambassador:* Coronel Purtica.

Saudi Arabia: 45 place Ibn Said (E); *Ambassador:* Fakhry Sheikh el Adhr.

MOROCCO—(Diplomatic Representation, National Assembly, Political Parties, etc.)

Senegal: 3 rue Descartes (E); *Ambassador:* Massambadou Diouf.
Spain: 1 ave de Marrakech (E); *Ambassador:* Adolfo Martín Gamero y Gonza.
Sudan: Cairo, Egypt.
Sweden: 6 rue Slaouane (E); *Ambassador:* Bo Siegbahn (also accred. to Libya and Senegal).
Switzerland: square Condo de Sabriano (E); *Ambassador:* Jean Strohlin.
Syria: (E); *Ambassador:* Suhail Al-Ghazi.
Tunisia: 5 rue Montaigne (E); *Ambassador:* Natib Bouzibt.
Turkey: 6 rue El Yarmouk (E); *Ambassador:* Kamuran Acet.
U.S.S.R.: 18 ave. Abderrahmane Aneggai (E); *Ambassador:* Louca Balamartchouk.
U.K.: 28 ave. Allal Ben Abdullah (E); *Ambassador:* Ronald Bailey.
U.S.A.: 45 ave. Allal Ben Abdullah (E); *Ambassador:* Stuart Wesson Rockwell.
Uruguay: 18 rue Descartes (E); *Ambassador:* Julio Pons.
Venezuela: (E); *Ambassador:* Pedro Barradas.
Viet-Nam, Republic: 5 ave. de Meknès (E); *Chargé d'Affaires:* Buu-Kinh.
Yugoslavia: 10 rue de Djebli (E); *Ambassador:* Milan Venisnik.
Zaire: (E); *Ambassador:* (vacant).
Zambia: (E); Mativa N'Galante.

Morocco also has diplomatic relations with Afghanistan, Albania, Mongolia, Niger, Nigeria, Oman and the Vatican.

NATIONAL ASSEMBLY

Although the constitution of March 1972 provides for a new form of Assembly, elections for this have been postponed indefinitely, and parliament remains dissolved.

POLITICAL PARTIES

Mouvement Populaire: Leader Mahjoubi Aherdan; had 60 seats in Chamber of Representatives.

Progrès Social: represents salaried workers' groups; 10 seats in former Chamber of Representatives.

Istiqlal: f. 1944; aims to raise living standards, to confer equal rights on all, stresses the Moroccan claim to Mauritania and the Spanish Sahara; formed a National Front with UNFP July 1970; 9 seats in former Chamber of Representatives; Pres. Allal El Fassi; publs. *Al Alam* (daily) and *L'Opinion* (daily).

Union National des Forces Populaires—UNFP (*National Union of Popular Forces*): B.P. 747, Casablanca; f. 1959 by Mehdi Ben Barka from a group within Istiqlal; left wing; opposition party; formed National Front with Istiqlal July 1970; 2 seats in former Chamber of Representatives; in July 1972 the national administrative committee suspended the 10-man secretariat general and rejected the 3-man political bureau for failing to arrange a third congress and acting autocratically; five permanent committees have replaced them.

Union National des Forces Populaires—UNFP (Rabat section): Rabat; f. 1972 by the political bureau of the UNFP when the party split in July; Leader Abderrahim Bouabid. (In April 1973 this section of the party was banned for terrorism and treason and many arrests made including that of Bouabid.)

Parti Démocratique Constitutionnel: Leader Mohammed Hassan Wazzani; 1 seat in former Chamber of Representatives.

DEFENCE

Defence Budget: (1972): 568 million dirhams.
Military Service: 18 months.
Total Armed Forces: 53,500: army 48,000; navy 1,500; air force 4,000. Paramilitary Forces: 23,000 (2,250 Gendarmerie, 750 Royal Guards and 20,000 Auxiliaries).

MOROCCO—(JUDICIAL SYSTEM, RELIGION, THE PRESS)

JUDICIAL SYSTEM

The **Supreme Court** (*Majlis el Aala*), created on September 27th, 1957, is responsible for the interpretation of the law and regulates the jurisprudence of the courts and tribunals of the Kingdom. The Supreme Court sits at Rabat and is divided into four Chambers:

1 Civil Chamber (the First Chamber).
1 Criminal Chamber.
1 Administrative Chamber.
1 Social Chamber.

First President and Attorney-General: BRAHIM KEDDARA.

There are 20 Counsellors and 4 General Advocates.

Three Courts of Appeal. The Fez Court covers all the former Southern Zone and comprises:

8 Regional Tribunals.
11 Sadad Tribunals and branch chambers.

The Court of Appeal at Marrakesh comprises:

4 Regional Tribunals.
7 Sadad Tribunals and branch chambers.

The Court of Appeal at Casablanca comprises:

4 Regional Tribunals.
9 Sadad Tribunals and branch chambers.

The **Sadad Tribunals** pass judgment, without possibility of appeal, in personal, civil and commercial cases involving up to 300 dirhams. These tribunals also pass judgment, subject to appeal before the Regional Tribunals, in the same cases up to 900 dirhams, in disputes related to the personal and successional statutes of Moroccan Muslims and Jews, and in penal cases involving misdemeanours or infringements of the law.

The **Regional Tribunals** deal with appeals against judgments made by the Sadad Tribunals; and pass judgment in the first and last resort in cases of personal property of 900 to 1,200 dirhams or property producing a yield of up to 80 dirhams. The Regional Tribunals also pass judgment, subject to appeal before the Court of Appeal, in actions brought against public administrations in administrative affairs, and in cases of minor offences in penal matters.

Labour Tribunals settle, by means of conciliation, disputes arising from rental contracts or services between employers and employees engaged in private industry. There are 14 labour tribunals in the Kingdom.

A special court was created in 1965 in Rabat to deal with corruption among public officials.

RELIGION

MUSLIMS
Most Moroccans are Muslims.

CHRISTIANS
There are about 400,000 Christians, mostly Roman Catholics.

Archbishop of Rabat: JEAN MARCEL CHABBERT, 1 rue de l'Evêché, B.P. 258, Rabat.

Archbishop of Tangier: FRANCISCO ALDEGUNDE DORREGO; 55 S. Francisco, B.P. 2116, Tangier.

JEWS
There are between 60,000 and 80,000 Jews.

Grand Rabbi of Casablanca: 167 blvd. Ziraoui, Casablanca; CHALOM MESSAS, President of the Rabbinical Court of Casablanca, Palais de Justice, Place des Nations Unies.

THE PRESS

DAILIES
Casablanca

Maghreb Informations: 16 rue de Foucauld; f. 1966; organ of U.M.T.; suspended by government 1968–71; Dir BOUBKER MONKACHI.

Maroc Soir: 88 blvd. Mohammed V; f. Nov. 1971 to replace *La Vigie Marocaine*, closed down by the Government; French; Dir. MOULAY AHMAD ALAWI; circ. 30,000.

Le Matin: rue Mohammed Smiha; f. Nov. 1971 to replace *Le Petit Marocain*, closed down by the Government; French; Dir. AHMED BENKIRANE; circ. 45,000.

Rabat

Al Alam (*The Flag*): ave. Allal ben Abdullah 11; organ of the Istiqlal Party and of National Front (formed by Istiqlal Party and UNFP); f. 1946; Arabic; Dir. M. A. GHALLAB; circ. 30,000; also *Al Alam Book*.

Al Anba'a (*Information*): rue Hamdani, B.P. 65; Arabic; Dir. ALI ALAOUI; circ. 5,000.

L'Opinion: ave. Allal Ben Abdullah 11; f. 1965; Istiqlal party newspaper; French; Dir. ABDELHAMID AOUAD; circ. 50,000.

Tangier

Diario España: Calle Cervantes; f. 1938; Spanish; independent; Pres. LUIS ZARRALUQUI; Dir. MANUEL CRUZ.

PERIODICALS
Casablanca

Al Ahdaffe: left-wing weekly; Dir. AHMED AL KHARRASS.

Akbar Al-Dounia: Arabic, weekly, independent, satirical.

At Talia: Arabic; organ of U.M.T.; weekly; Editor MAHJUB BEN EL SEDDIQ.

L'Avant Garde: 222 ave. de l'Armée Royale; French and Arabic; trade union affairs; weekly; Dir. MOHAMMED TIBARY; circ. 10,000.

Bulletin Africain: 61 blvd. de Bordeaux; f. 1946; French and periodically German; monthly technical and economic revue; Editor J. AXELROD.

Al Fallah: 49 rue Tizi Ougli, Ain Sebâa; agricultural; fortnightly; Dir. AHMED NEJJAI.

525

MOROCCO—(THE PRESS, PUBLISHERS, RADIO AND TELEVISION)

Index Analytique de la Production Marocaine: 61 blvd. de Bordeaux; Industrial directory; French, English and German; Editor J. AXELROD.

Al Kifah al-Watani: 32 rue Ledru-Rollin, B.P. 152; Arabic and French; weekly; Dir. ALI YATA.

Lamalif: French; monthly; non-political features and cultural magazine.

Maroc-Demain: 248 blvd. Mohammed V; French; weekly; Editor A. CHABAN.

Maroc-Médical: Immeuble Liberté, 287 Bd. de la Liberté; f. 1920; French; monthly medical journal; Dir. E. LEPINAY; Editor Prof. Agr. J. CHENEBAULT.

Al Mohirrin (*The Liberator*): 46 rue de la Garonne; organ of UNFP (Rabat section); Dir. OMAR BENJELLOUN (arrested March 1973).

L'Opinion: published by the Istiqlal Party; f. 1962; circ. 50,000.

Al Oummal (*The Workers*): 10 ave. de l'Armée Royale; trade union affairs (U.G.T.M.); Arabic; weekly.

Tahrir: 13 rue Soldat Roche; Arabic.

La Vie Economique: 5 ave. Abdallah Ben Yacine; f. 1921; French; weekly; Editor MARCEL HERZOG.

Fez

Al-Siassa (*Politics*): 10 rue de l'Angleterre; Arabic; f. 1967 as successor to Al-Doustour (f. 1963); weekly; Man. Dir. MOHAMMED HASSAN QUAZZANI.

Rabat

Achaab (*The People*): 2 rue Parmentier, B.P. 364; independent; twice weekly; Arabic; Founder and Editor M. MEKKI NACIRI; Dir. MUSTAPHA BELHAJ; circ. 25,000.

Action Africaine: 10 place Mohammed V; popular; circ. 3,000.

Atlas: ave. Mohammed V; Arabic; fortnightly; illustrated; political and general information.

Chenguit: Arabic; weekly.

Al Fellah: Chamber of Agriculture; on agricultural affairs; weekly; Arabic.

Al Idaa al Watania: Arabic; monthly.

Al Janoub: Ministry of State for Mauritanian and Saharan Affairs, 6 ave. Moulay Hafid; southern affairs; Dir. KHALIFA MAHFOUD; circ. 30,000.

Al Maghreb al Arabi: 8 place Mohammed V; weekly.

Al Manarat: 281 ave. Mohammed V; F.D.I.C. weekly; Arabic.

Maroc-65: Ministry Representative of H.M. the King; f. 1965.

Al Nidal (*The Fight*): ave. Allal Ben Abdullah 18; political; weekly; Arabic; liberal; independent.

Sahraouna: 6 rue Moulay Hafid; Arabic; weekly.

Sawt al Maghreb (*Voice of the Maghreb*): 1 rue Pierre Parent; organ of the R.T.M.; Arabic; monthly.

La Voix des Communautés: 12 Sh. el Amir Moulay Abdullah; monthly organ of the Jewish Community; French; Dir. DAVID AMAR.

Tangier

Al Mitak: Kasba 39; f. 1962; religious; fortnightly; Dir. Prof. ABDALLAH GUNNOUN.

Journal de Tanger: B.P. 420; French; weekly; Dir. R. DELAUNAY.

Tanjah: 8 place de France, B.P. 1055; f. 1956; French and Arabic; weekly; Dir. MOHAMMED MEHDI ZAHDI.

NEWS AGENCIES

Maghreb Arabe Presse: imm. Karrachou, rue ibn Aicha, Rabat; f. 1959; Arabic, French and English; independent; Casablanca, Tangier; Man. Dir. MEHDI BENNOUNA.

Morrocan National News Agency: Rabat; became Government-owned 1973.

FOREIGN BUREAUX

AFP (*France*): place Mohammed V, B.P. 118, Rabat; f. 1920; French; Dir. DAVID DAURE; Sec. and Editor MANOUBI MEKNASSY.

ANSA (*Italy*): c/o "MAP", rue Henri Gaillard (immeuble Karrachou), Rabat; Chief CLAUDIO ANTONIOLI.

DPA, Reuters and Tass also have bureaux in Rabat.

PUBLISHERS

Dar El Kitab: Place de la Mosquée, B.P. 4018, Casablanca, philosophy, law, etc., Arabic and French, Dir. BOUTALEB ABDELHAY.

Imprimerie Artistique: 31 avenue Es-Sellaoui, Fez.

Imprimerie de Fedala: rue Ibn Zaidoun Mohammedia; f. 1949; education, history, theology.

RADIO AND TELEVISION

RADIO

Radiodiffusion Télévision Marocaine: 1 Zenkat Al Brihi, Rabat; Government station; Network 1 in Arabic, Network 2 in French, Spanish and English, Network 3 in Berber; Foreign Service in Arabic, French and English; Dir. Radio and TV A. BENNOUNA; publ. *Sawt al Maghreb*.

Number of radios (1971): 1,002,090.

Voice of America Radio Station in Tangier: Voice of America, Washington, D.C. 20547, U.S.A.

TELEVISION

Radiodiffusion Télévision Marocaine: 11 rue Al Brihl, Rabat; f. 1962; 31½ hours weekly; French and Arabic; linked with Eurovision in 1964; carries commercial advertising; Dir.-Gen. M. ABDELWAHAB BENMANSOUN.

Number of television sets (1971): 222,557.

FINANCE

(amounts in Dirhams unless otherwise indicated.)

BANKING

CENTRAL BANK

Banque du Maroc: 277 ave. Mohammed V, Rabat; f. 1959; cap. 20m.; dep. 486m. (Dec. 1971); Gov. Prince MOULAY HASSAN BEN MEHDI; Vice-Gov. AHMED BENNANI.

MOROCCAN BANKS

Algemene Bank Nederland (Maroc) S.A.: Place du 16 Novembre, Casablanca; branch in Tangier; f. 1948; wholly owned subsidiary of Algemene Bank Nederland N.V., Amsterdam, Netherlands; cap. 5m.; Man. B. HANSEN.

Banco Español en Marruecos, S.A.M.: blvd. Mohammed V, Casablanca; f. 1964; affil. to Banco Exterior de España, Madrid; cap. 2.5m.; dep. 62.5m. (Dec. 1971); Chair. MANUEL ARBURÚA DE LA MIYAR; Gen. Man. JOSÉ-MARIA BRAVO IBÁÑEZ.

Banque Americano Franco-Suisse pour le Maroc: 26 ave. de l'Armée Royale, B.P. 972, Casablanca; f. 1951; affil. to Swiss Banking Corporation, Crédit Commercial de France and Continental Illinois National Bank & Trust Co. of Chicago; cap. 4.5m.; Man. ROLAND FREY.

Banque Commerciale du Maroc S.A.: 1 rue Idriss Lahrizi, Casablanca; f. 1911; affiliated to Crédit Industriel et Commercial, Paris, France; cap. 10m., dep. 538m. (Dec. 1972); Pres. R. BELIN; Gen. Man. A. ALAMI; 5 brs.

Banque de Paris et des Pays-Bas (Maroc): 79 avenue Hassan II, Casablanca; f. 1968; cap. 5m.; Gen. Man. F. JOURDAN.

Banque Marocaine du Commerce Extérieur: 241 boulevard Mohammed V, Casablanca; f. 1959; took over Société de Banque du Maghreb, oldest-established foreign bank, 1971; partly state-owned; cap. 20m., res. 29m. (Dec. 1971); Chair. and Chief Exec. HADJ ABDEL MAJID BENGELLOUN; Man. Dir. DRISS GUEDDART; 42 brs. in Morocco, one in Paris, France.

Banque Marocaine pour le Commerce et l'Industrie: 26 place Mohammed V, Casablanca, P.O.B. 573; f. 1964; cap. 10m., res. 16m. (Dec. 1971); Pres. HENRI GILET; Gen. Man. MOHAMED BENKIRANE; 23 brs.

Banque A Mas: 51 ave. Hassan-Seghir, Casablanca.

Banque Nationale pour le Développement Economique: B.P. 407, place des Alaouites, Rabat; f. 1959; cap. p.u. 3.2m.; Pres. and Gen. Man. MUSTAPHA FARES; publ. *Rapport annuel*.

British Bank of the Middle East (Morocco): 80 ave. Lalla Yacout, P.O.B. 880, Casablanca; f. 1948; wholly-owned subsidiary of the British Bank of the Middle East, London, England; 3 brs. in Casablanca, 1 in Tangier; Chair. C. E. LOOMBE, C.M.G.

Compagnie Marocaine de Crédit et de Banque S.A.: 1 ave. Hassan II, Casablanca; f. 1964; affiliated to Compagnie Française de Crédit et de Banque, Paris, France; cap. 14.5m., res. 4.1m.; Pres. ALI KETTANI; Gen. Man. MOHAMED AMINE BENGELOUN; 46 brs.

Credit du Maroc S.A.: B.P. 579, 48–58 blvd. Mohammed V, Casablanca; f. 1963; cap. 8m., res. 9m. (Dec. 1970); Pres. M. KARIM-LAMRANI; Dir.-Gen. JAWAD BEN BRAHIM.

Société Générale Maraocine de Banques: 84 blvd. Mohammed V, B.P. 90, Casablanca; f. 1962; cap. 11m., res. 9m. (Dec. 1971); Chair. JACQUES FERRONNIÈRE; Man. Dir. YVES BONDIL; 14 brs.

Unión Bancaria Hispano Marroquí: 69 rue de Prince Moulay Abdullah, Casablanca; f. 1958; cap. 16m., dep. 229m. (Dec. 1971); Pres. ANTONIO SAEZ DE MONTAGUT; Gen. Man. PEDRO LANDRA VELON; 15 brs.

Worms et Cie. (Maroc): 81 rue Colbert, Casablanca, B.P. 602; f. 1960; cap. 6,048,000; brs. in Rabat and Casablanca; Pres. ROBERT DUBOST; Gen. Man. JEAN PINEILL.

FOREIGN BANKS

Arab Bank Limited: Amman, Jordan; Casablanca and Rabat.

Several Spanish banks have branches in Ceuta.

BANK ORGANIZATIONS

Groupement Professionnel des Banques du Maroc: 27 ave. Hassan II, B.P. 577, Casablanca; f. 1967; groups all commercial banks for organization, studies, inquiries of general interest, and connection with official authorities; Pres. Hadj ABDELMAJID BENGELLOUN.

Association Professionelle des Intermédiaires de Bourse: 27 ave Hassan II, B.P. 577, Casablanca; f. 1970; groups all banks and brokers in the stock-exchange of Casablanca, for organization, studies, inquiries of general interest and connection with official authorities; Pres. Hadj ABDELMAJID BENGELLOUN.

STOCK EXCHANGE

Bourse des Valeurs de Casablanca: Chamber of Commerce Building, 98 boulevard Mohammed V, Casablanca; f. 1929; Dir. ABDERRAZAK LARAQUI; publ. *Bulletin de la Côte*.

INSURANCE

Atlanta: 243 blvd. Mohammed V, Casablanca; f. 1947; Dir. M. POIRRIER.

Atlas: 44 rue Mohammed Smiha, Casablanca; Dir. M. POIRRIER.

Cie. Africaine d'Assurances: 123 blvd. Rahal el Meskini, Casablanca; Dir. M. ROUTHIER.

Cie. Nordafricaine et Intercontinentale d'Assurances (C.N.I.A.): 157 ave. Hassan II, Casablanca; cap. 1.8m.; Pres. ABDELKAMEL RERHRHAYE.

Cia. Marroqui de Seguros: 62 rue de la Liberté, Tangier; Dir. M. BUISAN.

COMAR Paternelle-Prévoyance: 42 avenue de l'Armée Royale, Casablanca; cap. 3.1m.; Gen. Man. BERNARD PAGEZY.

L'Empire: 45 rue du Cdt. Lamy, Casablanca; Dir. M. LÓPEZ.

L'Entente: 2 rue Mohammed Smiha, Casablanca; f. 1960; Pres. PIERRE ESTEVA; Man. Dir. MAURICE FLEUREAU.

Mutuelle Agricole Marocaine d'Assurances: 14 rue Abou Faras El Marini, Rabat; Dir. Gen. YACOUBI SOUSSANE.

La Providence Marocaine: 1 rond-point St. Exupéry, Casablanca; Dir. M. DE ROQUEFEUIL.

La Royale Marocaine d'Assurance: 67 ave. de l'Armée Royale, Casablanca; cap. 1.1m.; Dir.-Gen. M. BECERRA.

Es Saada, Cie. Générale d' Assurances et de Réassurances: 123 ave. Hassan II, Casablanca.

Société Centrale de Réassurance: P.O.B. 435, 31 boulevard des Alaouites, Rabat; f. 1961; Dir. MOHAMED AIMARAH.

Société Marocaine d'Assurances: 1 rond-point Saint Exupéry, Casablanca; Dir. M. GIUSTINIANI.

Fédération Marocaine des Sociétés d'Assurances et de Réassurances: 300 rue Mustafa el Maani, Casablanca; Pres. M'HAMED BEN JILALI BENNANI; Sec. MOHAMED IBN KHAYAT.

… MOROCCO—(Trade and Industry, Transport)

TRADE AND INDUSTRY

CHAMBERS OF COMMERCE

Chambre de Commerce et d'Industrie de Casablanca: 98 blvd. Mohammed V, B.P. 423, Casablanca; Pres. ABDELLAH SOUIRA.

Chambre Française de Commerce et d'Industrie du Maroc (CFCI): 15 avenue Mers Sultan, B.P. 73, Casablanca; Pres. J. P. HAINAUT; Dir. PIERRE ROUSSELOT.

La Fédération des Chambres de Commerce et d'Industrie du Maroc: B.P. 218, 11 ave. Allal Ben Abdullah, Rabat; f. 1962; groups the 15 Chambers of Commerce and Industry; Pres. ABDELLAH SOUIRA; publ. *Revue Trimestrielle*.

DEVELOPMENT ORGANIZATIONS

Bureau d'Etudes et de Participations Industrielles (BEPI): 8 rue Michaux-Bellaire, Rabat; f. 1958; a state agency to develop industry.

Bureau de Recherches et de Participations Minières (BRPM): 27 Chana Moulay Hassan, Rabat; f. 1928; a state agency to develop the mining industry; Dir.-Gen. YAHIA CHEFCHAOUNI.

Caisse Marocaine des Marchés (*Marketing Fund*): Casablanca.

Caisse Nationale de Crédit Agricole (*Agricultural Credit Fund*): B.P. 49, Rabat.

Crédit Immobilier et Hôtelier: 159 ave. Hassan II, Casablanca; f. 1920; cap. 20m.; Dir. Gen. MOHAMED BENCHEKROUN.

Office de Commercialisation et d'Exportation (OCE): 45 ave des F.A.R., Casablanca; f. 1965; turnover (1970–71) 1,300m. Dirhams; takes part in productivity planning, industrialization and overseas trade; Dir. SBIHI ABDELHADI.

STATE ENTERPRISES

Complexe Textile de Fes (COTEF): B.P. 267, Fez; f. 1967; 90 per cent state participation; a plant for weaving up to 45 million sq. metres of cloth per annum, started full activity in Jan 1972.

Minas del Rif: Nador; nationalized 1967; two iron mines produce 1 m. tons of ore per annum for the Nador iron and steel complex.

Office Chérifien des Phosphates (OCP): Rabat; f. 1921; a state company to produce and market rock phosphates and derivatives; Dir.-Gen. MOHAMMED KARIM LAMRANI.

Office National de l'Electricité: B.P. 498, Casablanca; state electrical authority.

EMPLOYERS' ORGANIZATIONS

Association Marocaine des Industries Textiles: 58 rue Lugherim, Casablanca; f. 1958; mems. 300 textile factories; Pres. MOHAMED DRISSI; publ. *Bulletin* (weekly).

Association des Producteurs d'Agrumes du Maroc (ASPAM): 44 rue Mohamed Smiha, Casablanca; links Moroccan citrus growers; has its own processing plants.

Confédération Générale Economique Marocaine (C.G.E.M.): 23 blvd. Mohammed Abdouh, Casablanca; Pres. MOHAMMED AMOR; Sec.-Gen. M. FAYÇAL CHRAÏBI.

Office Chérifien Interprofessionelle des Céréales: Casablanca; Dir. MOHAMMED BRICK.

Union Marocaine de l'Agriculture (U.M.A.): rue Michaux-Bellaire, Rabat; Pres. M. NEJJAI.

TRADE UNIONS

Union Générale des Travailleurs du Maroc (U.G.T.M.): 9 rue du Rif, angle Route de Médiouna, Casablanca; associated with Istiqlal; supported by unions not affiliated to U.M.T.; Sec.-Gen. ABDERRAZZAQ AFILAL.

Union Marocaine du Travail (U.M.T.): Bourse du Travail, 222 avenue de l'Armée Royale, Casablanca; left wing and associated with UNFP (Rabat); most unions are affiliated; 700,000 mems.; Sec. MAHJOUB BEN SEDDIQ; publs. *Maghreb Informations* (daily), *L'Avant Garde* (French weekly), *At Talia* (Arabic weekly).

Union Syndicate Agricole (U.S.A.): agricultural section of U.M.T.

Union Marocaine du Travail Autonome: General union disassociated from U.M.T.

Syndicat National Libre: blvd. Hansali (prolongé), Casablanca; f. 1958; 69,000 mems.; Sec.-Gen. MEEKI IBRAHIMY.

Union Agricole pour le Progrès Rural: Agricultural union; associated with *Mouvement populaire*.

Union Marocaine de l'Agriculture (U.M.A.): Pres. M. NEJJAI.

TRADE FAIR

Foire Internationale de Casablanca: 11 rue Jules Mauran, Casablanca; international trade fair; alternate years usually for two weeks in April–May; next fair will be 1975.

TRANSPORT

RAILWAYS

Railways cover 1,756 km. of which 161 km. are double track; 730 km. of lines are electrified and diesel locomotives are used on the rest. All services are nationalized.

Office National des Chemins de Fer du Maroc (ONCFM): 19 ave. Allal Ben Abdallah, Rabat; f. 1963; runs all Morocco's railways; Pres. SALAH M'ZILY; Dir. MOUSSA MOUSSAOUI.

ROADS

There are about 52,000 km. of roads of which 42 per cent are surfaced. In 1972 there were 14 km. of modern motorway and 7,620 km. of main roads. Road length increases by about 300 km. a year. Most public transport is by road.

Compagnie Auxiliaire de Transports au Maroc (C.T.M.): 303 blvd. Brahim Roudani, Casablanca; Agencies in Tangier, Rabat, Meknès, Oujda, Marrakesh, Agadir, El Jadida, Safi, Essouira, Ksar-Es-Souk and Ouarzazate.

MOTORISTS' ORGANIZATIONS

The Royal Moroccan Automobile Club: place des Nations Unies, P.O.B. 94, Casablanca; f. 1913; 10,000 mems.; offices at Kenitra, Meknès, Fez, Oujda, Tangier, El Jadida, Safi, Marrakesh, Agadir, Taza, Khouribga, Youssoufia and Tétuan; Pres. MOHAMMED M'JID.

Touring Club du Maroc: 3 ave. de l'Armée Royale, Casablanca; 645 mems., 10,021 associate mems.; Pres. LARBI LAMRANI.

MOROCCO—(Transport, Tourism)

SHIPPING

The chief ports of Morocco are Tangier, Casablanca, Safi, Mohammedia, Kenitra and Agadir. In January 1962 the port of Tangier became an International Free Zone. Tangier is the principal port for passenger services.

A governor for the Port Area of Casablanca was appointed for the first time in 1967, to improve the operational efficiency of the port; Casablanca handles 70 per cent of Morocco's trade; Gov. of Casablanca Port Area MOHAMMED LYOUSSI.

Bland Line: 21 blvd. Pasteur, Tangier; also at Casablanca and Marrakesh; regular air and sea services Tangier to Gibraltar.

Compagnie Marocaine de Navigation: 28 rue de Lille, Casablanca; f. 1946; Pres., Dir.-Gen. A. BOUAYAD.

Compagnie Chérifienne d'Armement: 5 ave. de l'Armée Royale, Casablanca; f. 1929; Pres. BENNANI-SMIRES; regular lines to North France and Europe.

Compagnie Maritime des Chargeurs Réunis: Agence Paquet, 65 ave. de l'Armée Royale, B.P. 60, Casablanca.

Limadet-ferry: 3 rue H. Regnault, Tangier; operates between Malaga and Tangier.

Normandy Ferry Co.: Casablanca; regular car ferry service to Lisbon and Southamption.

Transmediterranea S.A., Cia: 39 rue du Mexique, Tangier and at Casablanca; daily services Algeciras to Tangier.

Voyages Paquet: 65 ave. de l'Armée Royale, Casablanca; 21 ave. d'Espagne, Tangier.

CIVIL AVIATION

There are international airports at Casablanca, Rabat and Tangier.

NATIONAL AIRLINE

Royal Air Maroc: Aéroport International Casablanca, Nouasseur; f. 1953; 67.7 per cent owned by the Government; domestic flights and services to Algeria, Belgium, France, Federal Germany, Italy, Libya, Netherlands, Senegal, Spain, Switzerland, Tunisia and U.K.; fleet of two Boeing 727, four Caravelles and two SF-260; Chair. AHMED LASKY; Gen. Man. SAID BEN ALI.

Royal Air Inter: Aéroport Casablanca-Anfa; f. 1970; operates domestic services from Casablanca to Agadir, Al Hoceima, Fez, Ksar-es-Souk, Marrakesh, Ouarzazate, Oujda, Rabat, Tangier and Tetouan; fleet of two F-27; Dir. Gen. HASSAN YACOUBI SOUSSANE.

Casablanca is served by the following foreign airlines: Air Afrique, Air Algérie, Air France, Air Mali, Alitalia, Balkan, British Caledonian, Iberia, KLM, Lufthansa, Pan American, Sabena, Saudia, Swissair and Tunis Air. In addition, Aeroflot and ČSA fly to Rabat, and BEA and Gibair to Tangier.

COMMUNICATIONS

The first commercial communications centre in Africa was opened in December 1969 at Ain-el-Aouda, 20 miles south-west of Rabat. The station initially carries 9 channels, but will eventually expand to over 100 channels.

TOURISM

Office National Marocain de Tourisme: B.P. 19, 22 ave. d'Alger, Rabat; f. 1946; Dir. ABDELLATIF AMOR; publ. *Maroc-Tourisme* (quarterly).

CULTURAL ORGANIZATIONS

Direction des Affaires Culturelles: Ministry of Education and Fine Arts, Jardin de la Mamounia, Rabat; consists of three departments: Cultural Activities, Fine Arts and Folklore, Historical Monuments and Antiquities, which together administer all national cultural activities; Publs. *Bulletin d'Archéologie Marocaine, Etudes et Travaux d'Archéologie Marocaine.*

Association des Amateurs de la Musique Andalouse: Casablanca; directed and subsidized by the Ministry of Education and Fine Arts; Dir. Hadj DRISS BENJELLOUN.

PRINCIPAL THEATRES

Théâtre National Mohammed V: Rabat; Morocco's national theatre with its own troupe, subsidized by the state; Dir. M. A. SEGHROUCHNI.

Théâtre Municipal de Casablanca: blvd. de Paris, Casablanca; f. 1922, reorganized 1934 and 1949; 1,022 seats; formerly presented a limited number of French productions; now presents a large number of foreign and national productions; maintained by the Casablanca Municipality; Dir. TAIB SADDIKI; Gen. Administrator ALI KADIRI.

PRINCIPAL ORCHESTRAS

Orchestre Symphonique du Conservatoire National de Musique: Rabat; European classical music and Andalusian (Arabic) music using internationally accepted notation; chamber orchestra.

Orchestre du Conservatoire de Tétouan: Tetuan; specializes in Andalusian (Arabic) music; Dir. M. TEMSEMANI.

Orchestre du Conservatoire Dar Adyel: Fez; specializing in traditional music; Dir. Hadj ABDELKRIM RAIS.

FESTIVAL

Folklore Festival: Marrakesh; national festival of folk dancing; annually April–May; organized by the Ministry of Tourism under the direction of the Ministry of Education and Fine Arts.

EDUCATION

Since Independence in 1956 Morocco has had to tackle a number of educational problems: a youthful and fast-growing population, an urgent need for skilled workers and executives, a great diversity of teaching methods between French, Spanish, Muslim and Moroccan Government schools, and, above all, a high degree of adult illiteracy. Morocco spends one-fifth of her national budget on education of which a considerable proportion is devoted to constructing buildings for higher studies and technical education. In many small towns and villages, local craftsmen have co-operated together in the building of elementary schools.

In 1972-73 there were 1,277,660 pupils in primary schools. At this level nearly 95 per cent of instruction is given in government schools, where syllabuses have been standardized since 1967. Great progress was made in providing new schools between 1957 and 1964, but since then the increase in the number of places has slowed down. A decree of November 1963 made education compulsory for children between the ages of seven and thirteen, and this has now been applied in most urban areas, but throughout the country only 51 per cent of the age-group attended school in 1970–71. That year there were 5,034 government primary schools with 32,050 teachers, all Moroccan, trained in the 18 regional teacher training colleges. Instruction is given in Arabic for the first two years and in Arabic and French for the next three years, with English as the first additional language.

Secondary education lasts for three or four years, depending on the type of course, and in 1972–73 provided for 334,952 pupils. Approximately a quarter of these pupils attended technical schools, where reforms have taken place since 1970 to attract more pupils and to provide relevant training to meet the country's need for technical manpower. In 1971 there were 12,364 qualified teachers in secondary schools, of whom just under half were Moroccan and most of the rest French. Instruction is given mainly in French, but about a third of teachers use Arabic, and this trend is increasing.

Higher education has a long history in Morocco. The Islamic University of Al Qarawiyin at Fez celebrated its eleventh centenary in 1959-60. The Mohammed V University opened in Rabat in 1957 and now has about 14,000 students in four faculties. The new University Ben Youssef in Marrakesh has over 1,000 students. In addition there are institutes of higher education in business studies, agriculture, mining, law, and statistics and advanced economics. An African Centre for Research into Administrative Training for Development opened in Tangier in 1964 with financial backing from UNESCO and the UN Economic Commission for Africa.

Adult education is being tackled through the means of radio, simplified type, a special newspaper for the newly literate, and the co-operation of every teacher in the country. Another notable development in recent years has been the increasing attention given to education for girls. There are now a number of mixed and girls' schools, and the proportion is now growing yearly, especially in urban areas.

UNIVERSITIES

Al Quarwiyin University: 27 rue St. Pierre et Miquelon, Rabat; f. 859 A.D.; 422 students.

Université Mohammed V: ave. Moulay Chérif, Rabat; f. 1957; 6,000 students.

Université Ben Youssef de Marrakech: Cité Universitaire, Marrakesh; 1,100 students.

BIBLIOGRAPHY

Amin, Samir. The Maghreb in the Modern World (Penguin, Harmondsworth, 1971).

Ashford, D. E. Political Change in Morocco (Princeton U.P., 1961).
  Perspectives of a Moroccan Nationalist (New York, 1964).

Ayache, A. Le Maroc (Editions Sociales, Paris, 1956).

Barbour, Nevill. Morocco (Thames and Hudson, London, 1964).

Belal, Abdel Aziz. L'investissement au Maroc (1912–1964) et ses enseignements en matière de développement économique (Mouton, Paris, 1968).

Ben Barka, Mehdi. Problèmes de l'édification du Maroc et du Maghreb (Plon, Paris, 1959).
  Option Révolutionnaire en Maroc (Maspéro, Paris, 1966).

Bennett, Norman Robert. A study guide for Morocco (Boston, 1970).

Bernard, Stéphane. Le Conflit Franco-Marocain 1943–1956, 3 vols. (Brussels, 1963; English translation, Yale University Press, 1968).

Berque, Jaques. Le Maghreb entre deux guerres (Eds. du Seuil, Paris, 1962).

Bovill, E. W. The Golden Trade of the Moors (London, 1958).

Clasen, Dirk. Stauffacher-Reiseführer Marokko (Stauffacher Verlag, Zürich, 1964).

Cohen, M. I., and Hahn, Lorna. Morocco: Old Land, New Nation (Praeger, New York, 1964).

Coulau, Julien. La paysannerie marocaine (Paris, 1968).

Hall, L. J. The United States and Morocco, 1776–1956 (Scarecrow Press, Metuchen, N.J., 1971).

Halstead, John P. Rebirth of a Nation: the Origins and Rise of Moroccan Nationalism (Harvard University Press, 1967).

Kininmonth, C. The Travellers' Guide to Morocco (Jonathan Cape, London, 1972).

Lacouture, J. and S. Le Maroc à l'épreuve (du Seuil, Paris, 1958).

Landau, Rom. The Moroccan Drama 1900–1955 (Hale, London, 1956).
  Morocco Independent under Mohammed V (Allen and Unwin, London, 1961).
  Hassan II, King of Morocco (Allen and Unwin, London, 1962).
  The Moroccans—Yesterday and Today (London, 1963).
  Morocco (Allen & Unwin, London, 1967).

Landau, Rom and Swann, Wim. Marokko (Cologne, 1970).

Le Tourneau, Roger. Evolution politique de l'Afrique du Nord musulmane (Armand Colin, Paris, 1962).

Maxwell, Gavin. Lords of the Atlas (Longmans, London, 1966).

Metcalf, John. Morocco—an Economic Study (First National City Bank, New York, 1966).

Perroux, F. and Barre, R. Développement, croissance, progrès—Maroc-Tunisie (Paris, 1961).

Robert, J. La monarchie marocaine (Librairie générale de droit et de jurisprudence, Paris, 1963).

Spencer, William. The Land and People of Morocco (Lipincott, Pennsylvania, 1965).

Stewart, Charles F. The Economy of Morocco 1912-1962 (Oxford Univ. Press, 1965).

Terrasse, H. Histoire du Maroc des origines à l'établissement du protectorat français, 2 vols. (Casablanca, 1949–50) (English trans. by H. Tee, London, 1952).

Tiano, André. La politique économique et financière du Maroc indépendant (Presses universitaires de France, Paris, 1963).

Trout, Frank E. Morocco's Saharan Frontiers (Geneva, 1969).

Waterson, Albert. Planning in Morocco (Johns Hopkins, 1963).

Waterbury, John. The commander of the Faithful. The Moroccan political élite (London, 1970).

World Bank. The Economic Development of Morocco (Johns Hopkins Press, Baltimore, 1966).

Zartman, I. W. Morocco: Problems of New Power (Atherton Press, New York, 1964).

BIBLIOGRAPHY

Abun-Nasr, J., *A History of the Maghrib in the Modern World* (Penguin Harmondsworth, 1971).

Ashford, D. E., *Political Change in Morocco* (Princeton U.P., 1961).

——, *Perspectives of a Moroccan Nationalist* (New York, 1964).

Ayache, A., *Le Maroc* (Éditions Sociales, Paris, 1956).

Barbour, Nevill, *Morocco*, Thames and Hudson, London, 1965.

Benani, Ahmed Azij, *L'Investissement au Maroc (1912–1964) et ses enseignements en matière de développement économique* (Mouton, Paris, 1968).

Ben Barka, Mehdi, *Problèmes de l'édification du Maroc et du Maghreb* (Éd.) Paris, 1959.

——, *Option Révolutionnaire au Maroc* (Maspéro, Paris, 1966).

Bidwell, Robin, *Morocco; A Study Guide for Morocco* (Boring, 1973).

Bernard, Stephane, *Le Conflit Franco-Marocain 1943–1956*, 3 vols. (Brussels, 1963; English translation, Yale University Press, 1968).

Berque, Jacques, *Le Maghreb entre deux guerres* (Éds. du Seuil, Paris, 1962).

Bovill, E. W., *The Golden Trade of the Moors* (London, 1970).

Evans, Dirk, *Staatliche Rekodifizierung in Marokko* (Stanbacher Verlag, Zürich, 1967).

Epton, N. F., and Hahn, Lorna, *Morocco, Old Land, New Nation* (Praeger, New York, 1964).

Goulas, Julien, *L'expansion du Maroc–cité* (Paris, 1958).

Hall, L. J., *The United States and Morocco, 1776–1956* (Scarecrow Press, Metuchen, N.J., 1971).

Halstead, John P., *Rebirth of a Nation; the Origins and Rise of Moroccan Nationalism* (Harvard University Press, 1967).

Kininmonth, C., *The Traveller's Guide to Morocco* (Jonathan Cape, London, 1972).

Lacouture, J. and S., *La Maroc à l'épreuve* (du Seuil, Paris, 1958).

Landau, Rom, *The Moroccan Drama 1900–1955* (Hale, London, 1956).

——, *Morocco Independent under Mohammed V* (Allen and Unwin, London, 1961).

——, *Hassan II, King of Morocco* (Allen and Unwin, London, 1961).

——, *The Moroccans — Yesterday and Today* (London, 1963).

——, *Morocco* (Allen & Unwin, London, 1967).

Lapham, Rom and Swann, Wim, *Marokko* (Cologne, 1970).

Le Tourneau, Roger, *Évolution politique de l'Afrique du Nord musulmane* (Armand Colin, Paris, 1962).

Maxwell, Gavin, *Lords of the Atlas* (Longmans, London, 1966).

Mezran, John, *Morocco — an Economic Study* (First National City Bank, New York, 1963).

Paenson, I., and Hayes, R., *Development, croissance*. *Tunisie–Maroc–Algérie* (Paris, 1961).

Robert, J., *La monarchie marocaine* (Librairie générale de droit et de jurisprudence, Paris, 1963).

Spencer, William, *The Land and People of Morocco* (Lippincott, Philadelphia, 1965).

Stewart, Charles F., *The Economy of Morocco 1912–1962* (Oxford Univ. Press, 1964).

Terrasse, H., *Histoire du Maroc des origines à l'établissement du protectorat français*, 2 vols. (Casablanca, 1949–50; English trans. by H. Tee, London, 1952).

Tiano, André, *La politique économique et financière du Maroc indépendant* (Presses universitaires de France, Paris, 1963).

Trout, Frank E., *Morocco's Saharan Frontiers* (Geneva, 1969).

Waterbury, Albert, *Farming in Morocco* (Johns Hopkins, 1972).

Waterbury, John, *The commander of the Faithful, The Moroccan political élite* (London, 1970).

World Bank, *The Economic Development of Morocco* (Johns Hopkins Press, Baltimore, 1966).

Zartman, I. W., *Morocco, Problems of New Power* (Atherton, New York, 1964).

Oman

GEOGRAPHY

The Sultanate of Oman lies at the extreme south-east of the Arabian peninsula and is flanked by the United Arab Emirates on the extreme north, by the *Rub al Khali* (or Empty Quarter) of Saudi Arabia on the north and west, and by Southern Yemen on the extreme west. Its sea coast extends for over 1,000 miles and its total area (including Dhofar) is about 107,000 square miles, but the frontier with Saudi Arabia in particular is very ill-defined. The whole area is known as Oman (of which Muscat is the capital), and it includes the province of Dhofar which comprises the south-west of Oman. The population of the whole area is estimated at about 750,000 and the population of Muscat at 6,200.

At Muscat the mean annual rainfall is 3.94 inches and the average mean temperature varies between 69°F. and 110°F. Although most of the region is arid the coastal plain of Batina, east of the Jabal Akhdar ridge, is relatively fertile, and so also is the Dhofar plateau in the south-west. The *Rub al Khali*, on Oman's northern border, is a rainless unrelieved wilderness of shifting sand, too difficult for occupation even by nomads.

HISTORY

Little is known about Muscat and Oman before the capture of its capital by the Portuguese in 1508. For almost 150 years the Portuguese maintained a naval station and factory at Muscat controlling trade in the Persian Gulf area. In 1650 they were turned out by local Arabs. The importance and power of the Arab rulers of Muscat were gradually extended, until, by 1730, they had conquered the Portuguese settlements in East Africa, including Mogadishu, Mombasa and the islands of Mafia and Zanzibar. A brief Iranian invasion (1741–43) was terminated by the rise of the present dynasty, the Al Abu Saids. On the death of Saiyid Said in 1856, his territories were divided between his two sons through British mediation, an agreement being concluded in 1861 under which Zanzibar agreed to pay an annual subsidy of 86,400 rupees to Muscat, and each ruler was accorded the style of Sultan.

In the early 19th century Muscat was the main market for slaves imported from the East African territories of the Sultan of Muscat and Oman but in 1822 Britain concluded a treaty with the Sultan of Muscat prohibiting the trade in slaves between his dominions and those of Christian countries. Towards the end of the 19th century the European powers showed increased interest in the Persian Gulf area generally, and in 1891 the Sultan of Muscat signed an agreement with the British not to dispose of any of his territory. But this agreement is now regarded as having lapsed. The only formal link between Muscat and Oman and the United Kingdom has been the successive Treaties of Friendship and Commerce signed in 1891, 1939 and 1951. The Treaty of 1951 provides for reciprocal treatment of each other's nationals and most-favoured nation treatment between the signatories for commerce, shipping and taxation. The Treaty ran for 15 years from May 1952 and now continues in effect unless notice to terminate is given by either party. The Sultan of Muscat relies on the United Kingdom to help him resist aggression.

In 1920 the Sultan agreed to allow the Imam his traditional measure of temporal authority over his Omani followers, the Sultan's sovereignty over the entire Sultanate remaining unimpaired. The Imam resided at Nizwa and most of the tribes of the interior acknowledged his authority as far north as Ibri, at the southern end of the Dhahirah. He also had some influence over the tribes in the desert west of the mountains.

For many years there was harmony between successive Sultans and their vassals, which was demonstrated when the Imam Muhammad Kahili provided military assistance to his overlord in 1952 when the Sultan was assembling an army for the purpose of expelling Saudi Arabian intruders from the Buraimi Oasis. But after the death of the old Imam in 1954 his successor, Ghalib, sought, with foreign help, to establish a separate principality. In December 1955, forces under the Sultan's control entered the main inhabited centres of Oman without resistance. The former Imam was allowed by the Sultan to retire to his village but his brother, Talib, escaped to Saudi Arabia and thence to Cairo. An "Oman Imamate" office was set up there and the cause of the Imam was supported by Egyptian propaganda.

OMAN AND THE UN

When in the summer of 1957 Talib returned and established himself with followers in the mountain areas north-west of Nizwa, he was supported by Suliman bin Himyar. The Sultan appealed for British help in July and in August 1957 the end of the rising was announced; but fighting continued and the rebels were able to maintain themselves in the Jebel Akhdar until early 1959, when the Sultan's authority was fully re-established. (On September 4th, 1958, the Sultan of Muscat ceded to Pakistan, in exchange for £3 million, the Persian Gulf port of Gwadur, which had been in Muscat hands for 150 years.)

In October 1960 ten Arab countries secured the placing of the "question of Oman" on the agenda of the General Assembly of the United Nations, despite British objections. A draft resolution calling for the "independence of Oman" failed, however, to secure the necessary majority in December 1961. A UN Commission of Inquiry led by the Swedish diplomat Mr. H. de Ribbing visited Muscat and Oman in May and June 1963, where they interviewed government officials, *walis* and tribal leaders. The Commission also interviewed the Imamate leaders in Cairo. Their report to the UN General Assembly, debated in the late autumn, refuted the Imamate charges of oppressive government and strong public feeling against the Sultan. But the Arab countries succeeded in obtaining sufficient support for the setting up of an *ad hoc* Committee to examine "the question of Oman". The Committee, composed of Afghanistan, Costa Rica, Nepal, Nigeria and Senegal, submitted its report to the General Assembly in October 1965. In December 1965 a resolution was adopted by the General Assembly which amongst other things considered that the colonial presence of the United Kingdom prevented the people from exercising their rights of self-determination and independence, called for the elimination of British domination in any form and invited the Special Committee on the Granting of Independence to Colonial Peoples to examine the situation further. The question was raised again in the United Nations on several occasions, until, nearly two years after Sultan Qabus' accession, Oman became a member of the UN early in 1972.

THE SULTANATE SINCE 1967

In the spring of 1968 there were reports that the Sultan was preparing to make a number of co-operative arrangements with Abu Dhabi, which might have helped to forge further links with the proposed Federation of Arab Emirates, which lies on the country's northern border. This possible break in Oman's traditional isolation was perhaps caused by the announcement of the intended withdrawal of British forces from the Gulf by 1971, since these forces had helped to protect Sultan Said in the past. The R.A.F. retains a staging post on Masirah island, but Britain has no other troops stationed in the area. The Sultan's armed forces have British citizens serving under contract as officers, however, and the oil revenues have recently enabled the Government to buy modern British arms including jet fighters.

By 1970 Sultan Said's government had come to be regarded as the most reactionary and isolationist in the area, if not the world—slavery was still common, and many mediaeval prohibitions were in force. The Sultan's refusal to use the oil revenues for any purpose other than the building up of his armed forces had particularly embarrassed Britain, the oil companies and most neighbouring states, and this attitude had provided ideal conditions for the rebellion in Dhofar province and elsewhere. On July 24th, 1970, the Sultan was deposed by a coup led by his son, Qabus bin Said, at the royal palace in Salalah; wounded in a brief skirmish, he was flown to a hospital in Britain after abdicating. Qabus, aged 28 and trained at Sandhurst, thus became Sultan to general acclaim both within the Sultanate and abroad, including support from the army; reports of British complicity in the coup were strongly denied by London. The new Sultan announced his intention to transform the country by using the oil revenues for development, following the example of the Gulf shiekhdoms to the north. He asked the rebels for their co-operation in developing the country, but only the Dhofar Liberation Front reacted favourably. The Popular Front for the Liberation of the Occupied Arabian Gulf (reported to control much of Dhofar, and to be receiving Chinese aid through the Yemen P.D.R.) and its ally the National Democratic Front for the Liberation of the Occupied Arabian Gulf appeared to think that the palace coup changed little.

In August 1970 "Muscat" was dropped from the title of the country, which became simply the "Sultanate of Oman". Sultan Qabus appointed his uncle, Tariq bin Taimur, as Prime Minister. Other ministerial appointments were made during August, and two Britons were named, one for the key post of Defence. At the same time three leading officials of the old régime were dismissed. Government policy is aimed at providing the basic social and economic infrastructure which the former Sultan was rigidly opposed to—housing, education, communications, health services, etc. (Before the coup there were only three primary schools and one hospital). In addition, restrictions on travel have been lifted, many prisoners released, and many Omanis have returned from abroad. However, more than half the annual budget is still devoted to defence and to quelling the Dhofar insurgency.

Oman's recent admission to the UN has been achieved in face of opposition from the Yemen P.D.R., which supports the PFLOAG. Oman's relationship with Britain also compromised Oman's candidature for UN membership. Britain still supplies arms and ammunition to the Oman Government and officers on secondment or contract. In February 1972 the two nationalist liberation fronts announced their unification under the title Popular Front for the Liberation of Oman and the Arabian Gulf. The progress achieved since the palace coup of 1970 has had some impact on the insurgents' following (more than 680 by May 1973), with a number of defections to the Sultan's forces. But fighting between the Sultan's forces and the Yemen-based rebels continues. Omani forces attacked the border area of the Yemen P.D.R. for the first time in May 1972, the guerrillas having increasingly operated from beyond the border as the Sultan's forces advanced into Dhofar. During 1972 and 1973, the Oman Government has received military assistance from the governments of Jordan, Saudi Arabia, Iran and Pakistan. This additional assistance has enabled the Sultan's armed forces successfully to extend their operation against the guerrilla forces.

ECONOMIC SURVEY

Dhofar, in the south, the district around Nizwa and the Batina coastal plain in the north are the principal areas of cultivation. Cereal crops are grown for local consumption, while dates, pomegranates and limes are the chief export crops. Cattle breeding is extensively practised in the fertile province of Dhofar, and the Oman camel, bred in all parts of the country, is highly valued throughout Arabia. One of the most urgent problems facing the country is the shortage of water. If this can be overcome by exploiting and harnessing all available supplies, then there will be great possibilities of further agricultural development through-

OMAN—(Economic Survey, Statistics)

out the area. Agricultural experimental stations have been set up at Nizwa Rumais, Wadi Quriyat and Sohar where research is being carried out on irrigation and fertilization techniques and on the cultivation under local conditions of improved varieties of wheat, sorghum, fruit, vegetables, pulses and cotton.

There are, as yet, no local industries of any importance, but oil has been discovered in commercial quantities in Oman. In 1937 Petroleum Concessions (Oman) Ltd., a subsidiary of the Iraq Petroleum Co., was granted a 75-year oil concession extending over the whole area except the district of Dhofar. A concession covering Dhofar was granted in 1953 to Dhofar Cities Service Petroleum Corporation; it expires in 25 years from the date of commercial production, with option to renew for another 25 years.

In 1964 Petroleum Development (Oman) Ltd., reformed in 1967 and now a subsidiary of Royal Dutch Shell (with an 85 per cent interest), Compagnie Française des Pétroles (with 10 per cent) and Gulbenkian interests with their traditional 5 per cent, announced that drilling had proved sufficient reserves for the company to go into commercial production. The production of oil began in 1967 at a rate of 200,000 barrels per day and expanded to 360,000 barrels per day by the end of 1969. However, since late 1970 and early 1971 technical difficulties have affected production and the 1971 production of 105.56 million barrels was 15 million down on 1970. Total oil exports in 1972 were 103,184,721 barrels. Crude is exported by pipeline through the Sumail gap to a headquarters and oil-loading terminal at Mina al Fahal, a few miles to the west of Muscat town. The principal oilfields in production at present are (going north-east from the Saudi frontier) at Al Huwaisah, Yibal, Fahud and Natih. The German Wintershall company heads a consortium exploring an offshore concession in the Gulf of Oman.

Sultan Said's conservative policy severely restricted economic development. Since Sultan Quabus took over, a number of new projects have been started and by mid-1972 extensive redevelopment of Muscat and Muttrah was in progress: electricity supplies, piped drinking water, new port facilities and other amenities were being introduced or greatly extended. Major projects included a £20 million contract to develop Matrah port; a 200 km. road linking Muscat with Sohar in the north; the development of Seeb International airport; and the building of a new industrial and commercial town near Matrah at Ruwi.

In 1973 a new government planning organization was set up under the title of the Organization for General Development. This organization has overall responsibility for the Center for Economic Planning and Development including national planning and statistics; the Department of Petroleum and Mineral Affairs; the Department of Commerce and Industry; the Department of Agriculture and Water Resources and the Department of Municipal Affairs which includes town planning.

STATISTICS

Area: 82,000 square miles.

Population: 750,000 (estimate for mid-1973); Muscat (capital) 6,200, Matrah 14,000. Estimated number of employed: 150,000: agriculture 109,000; fisheries 15,000; government 10,000; construction 6,000; oil banking, services 5,000; others 5,000.

Agriculture: Land utilization 1971 (hectares): Batinah 13,800; Interior 19,920; capital area 1,080; Musandam 400; Dhofar 800. Crops include dates, lucerne, limes, onions, pomegranates, wheat, bananas, mangoes, tobacco, chickpeas and coconuts.

Currency: 1,000 baiza = 1 rial Omani (formerly called the rial Saidi). Coins: 2, 5, 10, 25, 50 and 100 baiza. Notes: 100, 250 and 500 baiza; 1, 5 and 10 rials. Exchange rates (March 1973): £1 sterling = 855 baiza; U.S. $1 = 345.4 baiza; 100 rials Omani = £116.96 = $289.52.

Budget: Revenues depend almost entirely on oil royalties and other payments by oil companies; in 1969 these were estimated at over £30 million.

External Trade: Exports (1971): £53.7 million, of which £53.2 million were oil exports. Imports (1971): £31 million (estimate).

EXTERNAL TRADE
IMPORTS*
(Omani rials)

	1971	1972
Australia	969,852	1,068,843
Burma	1,095,536	365,862
Germany, Fed. Repub.	352,661	654,437
Japan	847,003	1,949,435
India	971,405	1,124,468
Iran	801,501	429,003
Netherlands	498,337	957,427
U.A.E.	2,457,225	3,920,822
United Kingdom	2,707,558	3,872,289
Others	n.a.	4,342,595
TOTAL	10,699,078	18,713,181

* Total of non-oil and non-government imports.

NON-OIL EXPORTS
Non-oil Exports consist mainly of limes, fish and tobacco: (Omani Rials) 1970 388,500; 1971 429,804; 1972 391,327.

OIL PRODUCTION
(million tons)

1968	12.1
1969	16.1
1970	17.2
1971	14.7
1972	13.6

Oil: The main oilfields are at Fahud, Natih and Yibal. Output in 1971 was 14.7 million tons; the Government receives 50 per cent of the net income, plus 12.5 per cent of total oil exports.

Education

	PRIMARY		SECONDARY	
	BOYS	GIRLS	BOYS	GIRLS
1970–71	3,008	470	—	—
1971–72	13,450	2,351	—	—
1972–73	25,414	4,774	623	128

THE GOVERNMENT

Head of State and Premier:
Sultan QABUS BIN SAID.

CABINET
(*June* 1973)

Deputy Premier and Minister of Health: Dr. ASSIM JAMALI.
Minister of Communications and Public Services: ABD-AL-HAFIZ SALIM RAJAB.
Minister of Foreign Affairs: SAYD FAHAD BIN MAHMOUD AL-SAID.
Minister of the Interior and Justice: HILAL BIN HAMAD AL-SAMMAR.
Minister of Land Affairs: MUHAMMAD BIN AHMED.
Minister of Social Affairs and Labour and Acting Minister of Education and Culture: KHALFAN NASSIR AL-WAHAIBI.
Deputy Minister of Defence: SAYYID FAHAR BIN TAIMUR.

DIPLOMATIC REPRESENTATION

EMBASSIES ACCREDITED TO OMAN
(Muscat unless otherwise stated)

India: (E); *Ambassador:* J. SINGH.
Italy: Kuwait City, Kuwait (E).
Japan: Kuwait City, Kuwait (E).
Jordan: (E); *Ambassador:* Lt.-Gen. MUHAMMAD KHALIL ABDED DAIEM.
Kuwait: (E); *Ambassador:* (vacant).
Morocco: (E); *Ambassador:* AHMAD BIN LIMAITH.
Qatar: (E); *Ambassador:* MOHAMED SAAD FUHAID.
Saudi Arabia: (E); *Ambassador:* Sheikh SALAH AL SUQAIR.
Spain: Kuwait City, Kuwait (E).
Tunisia: Kuwait City, Kuwait (E).
United Kingdom: (E); *Ambassador:* DONALD HAWLEY.
U.S.A.: Manama, Bahrain (E).

Oman also has diplomatic relations with Algeria, France Iran, Lebanon and Syria.

JUDICIARY AND RELIGION

Legal System: Jurisdiction is exercised by the Sharia Courts, applying Islamic Law. Local courts are officered by *Qadhis* appointed by the Sultan. The Chief Court is at Muscat. Appeals from the Chief Court go to the Sultan.

Religion: The majority of the population are Ibadhi Muslims; about a quarter are Sunni Muslims.

PRESS

Al-Watan: Muscat; weekly newspaper.
Gulf Weekly Mirror: P.O.B. 455, Manama, Bahrain; weekly English newspaper for the Southern Gulf; Editor STEPHEN KEMBALL.

RADIO

Radio Oman: Muscat; f. 1970; transmissions 7 hours daily; Dirs. SALIM AL-FAHID, Shaikh ABDULLAH AL-AMRI.

The British Broadcasting Corporation has built a powerful new medium-wave relay station on the island of Masirah, off the Oman coast. It is used to expand and improve the reception of the B.B.C.'s Arabic, Farsi and Urdu services.

FINANCE

BANKING

British Bank of the Middle East: London; f. 1889; P.O.B. 234, Muscat; handles government finance; branches in Matrah, Mina Al-Fahal, Salalah, Sohar and Nizwa; Man. P. F. H. MASON.
The Chartered Bank: P.O.B. 210, Muscat; Man. Dir. A. H. DEVERELL; brs. in Matrah and Sur.
National and Grindlays Bank: London; P.O.B. 91, Muscat; Man. R. MURRAY.
National Bank of Oman: Muscat.

INSURANCE

Gray, Mackenzie and Co. Ltd.: Muscat; representatives of several British insurance companies.

OIL

Petroleum Development (Oman) Ltd.: P.O.B. 81, Muscat; f. 1937; since 1967 85 per cent owned by Shell, 10 per cent by Compagnie Française de Pétroles and 5 per cent by Gulbenkian interests; exports oil from the Fahud, Yibal and Natih and Al-Huwaisah oilfields via a pipeline to a terminal at Mina al Fahal, near Muscat; production (1972) 103 million barrels.

Wintershall AG: P.O.B. 155, Muscat; holds offshore exploration concession in the Gulf of Oman; drilling since 1968; Wintershall heads consortium with 50 per cent, Shell 24 per cent, Deutsche Schachtbau 10 per cent, and Partex 7 per cent.

In February 1973 an agreement was signed with a group of four companies (two Canadian, one German, one American) to explore an offshore area of 13,000 km.

TRANSPORT

Pack animals, especially camels, remain the favoured means of transport for most of the population, but the number of motor vehicles is rapidly increasing.

ROADS

On the coastal plain there is a graded motor road from Sohar to Sharjah and to Buraimi through the Wadijizi. The Oil Company and the Development Department also maintain several graded motor roads in the interior linking Muscat with the Sharqiyah to the south-east, with Nizwa to the west, and with Ibri and Buraimi to the north-west, covering approximately 500 miles. The Government is now constructing a macadamized road from Muscat to Sohar on the coast (232 km.), at a cost of £10.5 million. It is due to be completed in 1973, and will serve as the main land link between Oman and the Trucial States of the Gulf.

SHIPPING

The construction of Port Qabus, a new port at Matrah costing £20 million, is due to be completed by 1974; it will be able to accommodate the largest freighters in the Gulf. About 200 cargo vessels call annually, and regular calls are also made by the Bombay–Gulf passenger vessels. All vessels at present discharge into lighters off Matrah.

Other ports for small craft only are Murbat, Sohar, Kuburah, Sur and Salalah.

Gray, Mackenzie and Co. Ltd.: P.O.B. 70, Muscat; shipping, clearing and forwarding agents and general merchants.

CIVIL AVIATION

All domestic and international flights now operate from Seeb International Airport; the terminal building is still under construction and expected to be completed by the end of 1973. From Muscat Gulf Aviation operates 16 flights to Bahrain, Dubai, Abu Dhabi, Doha, Bombay, Karachi and London, and a bi-weekly service to Salalah, a military airfield in the south. International flights are also operated by BOAC, MEA, KAC, PIA and Air India. Use of the airfield by unscheduled aircraft is subject to at least 72 hours notice and the permission of the Oman Government.

Gulf Aviation Co. Ltd.: Head Office: P.O.B. 1388, Bahrain; f. 1950; shareholders: Governments of Bahrain, Qatar, Abu Dhabi and the Sultanate of Oman with 19 per cent each, and British Airways Associated Companies Ltd. with 23 per cent; fleet: two BAC 1-11 400, three Fokker F.27, three Skyvan, one Skyliner, two Queen Air B80, two BN-2A Islander; Chair. G. H. C. LEE.

BIBLIOGRAPHY

FACT SHEETS ON EASTERN ARABIA (Private Information Center on Eastern Arabia, Heldenplein 12, 1800 Vilvoorde, Belgium).

KELLY, J. B. East Arabian Frontiers (Faber and Faber, London).

LANDEN, R. G. Oman Since 1856 (Princeton University Press, 1967).

MILES, S. B. The Countries and Tribes of the Persian Gulf (3rd edition, Frank Cass, London, 1966).

MORRIS, JAMES. Sultan in Oman (Faber, London, 1957).

PHILLIPS, WENDELL. Unknown Oman (Longmans, London, 1966).
Oman. A History (Longmans, London, 1967).

ROYAL INSTITUTE OF INTERNATIONAL AFFAIRS. Sultanate and Imamate in Oman (Oxford University Press, 1959).

THESIGER, WILFRED. Arabian Sands (Longmans, London, 1959).

WILSON, Sir A. T. The Persian Gulf (London, 1928).

Qatar

GEOGRAPHY

The Sheikhdom of Qatar is a peninsula roughly 100 miles in length, with a breadth varying between 35 and 50 miles, on the west coast of the Persian Gulf. The total area is 4,000 square miles. There are over 170,000 inhabitants, two-thirds of whom are concentrated in the town of Doha, on the east coast. Two other ports, Zakrit on the west coast and Umm Said on the east, owe their existence to the discovery of oil. Zakrit is a convenient, if shallow, harbour for the import of goods from Bahrain, and Umm Said affords anchorage to the deep-sea tankers and freighters.

Qatar is stony, sandy and barren; limited supplies of underground water are unsuitable for drinking or agriculture because of high mineral content. Over half the water supply is now provided by sea water distillation processes. The inhabitants have traditionally lived from pearl-diving, fishing and nomadic herding.

HISTORY

Owing to the aridity of the peninsula the early history of Qatar is of little interest. In 1916 Great Britain, in order to exclude other powers from the area, made an agreement with the Sheikh of Qatar, who undertook not to cede, mortgage or otherwise dispose of parts of his territories to anyone except the British Government, nor to enter into any relationship with a foreign government other than the British without British consent. Similar agreements had been concluded with Bahrain in 1880 and 1892, with the Trucial States in 1892 and with Kuwait in 1899. In return Britain undertook to protect Qatar from all aggression by sea, and to lend her good offices in case of an overland attack.

The discovery of oil in the 1930s promised greater prosperity for Qatar, but because of the Second World War production did not begin on a commercial scale until 1949 (see below). An ambitious development programme is now being put into operation with the revenues from the production and export of oil. The Sheikhdom has taken a leading part in moves towards the formation of a Gulf Federation; it also enjoys close relations with Saudi Arabia. In January 1961 Qatar joined the Organization of Petroleum Exporting Countries, and in May 1970 it also became a member of OAPEC (the Organization of Arab Petroleum Exporting Countries).

In April 1970 a provisional constitution was announced which, it was said, would assist Qatar's entry into the Federation of Arab Emirates. The first cabinet was formed in May; the Ruler became Prime Minister with responsibility for oil, and six of the other nine members were also members of the Royal Family. However, Qatar decided to remain outside a Gulf Federation and became independent on September 1st, 1971. Qatar and the United Kingdom immediately signed a new treaty of friendship. In the same month Qatar was first admitted as a member of the Arab League, and then to membership of the United Nations. Sheikh Ahmad bin Ali Al Thani became Amir on September 4th, but apparently took little interest in affairs of the State. He was deposed on February 22nd, 1972 in a bloodless coup staged by his cousin Sheikh Khalifa bin Hamad Al Thani. Sheikh Khalifa seized power with the support of the ruling Al Thani family, although his avowed purpose included some of the vast family's privileges. The coup also curtailed the ambitions of the deposed Amir's son, Sheikh Abdul Aziz, who went into exile.

Moves made immediately after the February coup, affecting salaries in the public sector, housing and Royal appropriations, suggested that the new ruler was about to introduce an era of steadier social and political reform. In accordance with the 1970 constitution, Sheikh Khalifa decreed the first Advisory Council, to complement the ministerial government. Its 20 members, appointed initially, should eventually be elected representatives. The Advisory Council's constitutional entitlements include power to debate legislation drafted by the Council of Ministers before ratification and promulgation. It also has power to request ministerial statements on matters of general and specific policy inclusive of the draft budget.

ECONOMIC SURVEY

Qatar has almost no agriculture and outside the capital most of the population is employed in the oil industry, which is the state's principal source of wealth. Fishing, apart from shrimp fishing and processing, is carried on to supply local demands. Unlike many of the other Sheikhdoms, Qatar has no entrepôt trade.

Interest in the petroleum possibilities of Qatar was first stimulated by the entry of Standard of California into Bahrain in 1930. Shortly after this date the Anglo-Iranian Company received permission from the ruler to make a surface survey of his territories, and in 1935 they were granted a concession. This gave them exclusive petroleum rights in the Sheikhdom and its territorial waters for 75 years. Payments were to be 400,000 rupees upon signature; an annual rental of 150,000 rupees for the first 5 years and 300,000 rupees thereafter; and a royalty of 3 rupees per long ton. The concession was later transferred to Petroleum Concessions Ltd., which formed an operating company, Petroleum Development (Qatar) Ltd.

Petroleum Development started exploration in 1937 and oil was discovered in 1939. Field activities were interrupted during the war, but resumed in 1947. By 1949 the Company had completed a drilling programme, the laying of a pipeline system from the field of Dukhan, on the west coast to Umm Said, and the construction of terminal facilities. At the end of that year the first shipment was made from the

Umm Said offshore berths. Since 1963 production has stagnated at a little over nine million tons a year but expanded rapidly during 1971 to reach 10.4 million tons, and the increase was maintained in 1972, when production reached 11.4 million tons.

In 1951 the royalty rate was raised to 10 rupees, and in 1952 a profit-sharing scheme was adopted. A year later the name of the Company was changed to Qatar Petroleum Company Ltd.

An offshore grant was awarded to the "Shell" Overseas Exploration Company in 1952. This covers an area of approximately 10,000 square miles and it expires in 2027. A down payment of over £260,000 was made and exploration started in 1953. The first and second exploratory wells failed to find oil and were abandoned in 1955 and 1956 respectively. The operating company, the Shell Company of Qatar Ltd., lost their original drilling platform in a storm in 1956. This was replaced and drilling operations recommenced in December 1959. Test production from the offshore field at Idd el Shavgi through temporary facilities began in January 1964. Construction of permanent facilities on Halul Island, some 60 miles off the coast of Qatar, were completed early in 1966. This also enabled production to be commenced from Shell's second field in Maydam Mazam. Shell Qatar began commercial production of oil in 1966 at an annual rate of more than 5,000,000 long tons, and this had increased to 11.5 million tons by 1972. In 1963 the Continental Oil Company of Qatar was granted a concession over land and offshore areas relinquished by the Qatar Petroleum Company and the Shell Company of Qatar, and over a strip of territory in the south of the peninsula not previously included in any concession. In March 1969 a Japanese consortium was granted an exploration concession in the south-eastern offshore area, and made its first strike in May 1971. In 1971 the Belgian Oil Corporation was granted a 30 year exploration concession in an area of 12,000 square km. onshore and offshore, covering the whole of the Qatar peninsula except for the Dukhan field.

In April 1972 the Amir signed a law to create the Qatar National Petroleum Co., with power to carry out a comprehensive range of production, refining and marketing functions. In January 1973 the Qatar Government signed participation agreements with both local crude-producing companies—Qatar Petroleum Co. Ltd. and Shell Company of Qatar Ltd.—whereby it will acquire a 52 per cent share of the operations of each by 1982.

The revenue derived from the production and export of oil comprises the principal source of income; by 1971 this revenue amounted to £75 million per annum. A high percentage of this is being used by the Government to finance an ambitious development programme. So far development has been concentrated in Doha, the capital. Part of the substantial income of the country is being expended on building and equipping schools and hospitals. A 130-bed hospital which was built in Doha at a total cost of £3.5m., claims to be one of the most modern hospitals in the world. Early in 1971 the Qatar Petroleum Company announced a £25 million project to process and export natural gas; the liquid gas will pass by pipeline to the terminal at Umm Said. Any surplus is to be supplied, free of charge, to the Qatari Government. Natural gas, piped from Dukhan to Doha, is also used to distil sea-water and to run a 30-MW power station. Doha has a piped water supply which will eventually carry over two million gallons a day. Doha airport is of international standard. Dredging of a four-mile channel, twenty-seven feet deep, into Doha Bay was completed in 1966.

In order to avoid complete dependence on oil the Government planned to diversify the economy, encouraging such projects as gas-based petrochemical industries, fish-processing, cement, and intensified agriculture. The Department of Agriculture has already succeeded in making the country self-sufficient in vegetables, production of which was negligible as recently as 1960; fruit production and the planting of forest trees is making rapid progress. Some vegetables, mainly tomatoes, marrows and cucumbers, are now exported to other Gulf states.

The Qatar National Fishing Company formed in 1966 as a partnership between the government (with 60 per cent interest) and the British Ross Group, started shrimp processing in 1968. Its catch exceeded 500 tons in 1970. A freezing plant has been constructed near the new Doha harbour. Seventy-five per cent of the government interest has been sold to private Qatari interests. The Qatar National Cement Manufacturing Company at Umm Bab began production at the rate of 100,000 tons a year early in 1969 and in late 1972 work on doubling its capacity was nearing completion. It is the state's largest non-oil enterprise. A major ammonia and urea fertilizer plant, based on the conversion of waste gas, was completed at Umm Said in 1972 and inaugurated in February 1973 with an output of 430,000 tons annually.

Following the seizure of power by Sheikh Khalifa in February 1972, a larger share of the state's rapidly growing oil revenues will be assigned to development projects. Development expenditures were expected to exceed £10 million per year. Numerous projects were introduced, including improvements to the harbour at Doha, an HQ building for the Qatar Police Force, new seawater distillation plants, improvements to electricity supply, a plan for the development of Doha International Airport, and extensions to Doha's sewerage system.

In May 1973 the Monetary Agency of Qatar announced the issue of its own Qatari currency, the Qatar riyal (QR) with the same parity and exchange value as the old currency, the Qatar/Dubai riyal.

QATAR—(STATISTICAL SURVEY)

STATISTICAL SURVEY

AREA AND POPULATION

AREA	POPULATION (1972 Estimates)	
	TOTAL	DOHA (capital)
4,000 sq. miles	170,000	130,000

OIL

QATAR PETROLEUM COMPANY CRUDE OIL PRODUCTION

YEAR	LONG TONS	YEAR	LONG TONS
1963	9,096,000	1968	9,018,000
1964	9,978,000	1969	9,366,000
1965	9,158,000	1970	8,882,000
1966	9,059,000	1971	10,400,000
1967	9,070,000	1972	11,368,000

SHELL QATAR CRUDE OIL PRODUCTION

YEAR	LONG TONS (million)
1970	7.4
1971	9.9
1972	11.5

FINANCE AND TRADE

In May 1973 Qatar issued its own currency, the Qatar riyal (QR) with the same parity and exchange value as the old currency, the Qatar/Dubai riyal. Value in this Statistical Survey is expressed in the old currency.

100 dirhams = 1 Qatar riyal (QR).
Coins: 1, 5, 10, 25 and 50 dirhams.
Notes: 1, 5, 10, 25, 50 and 100 riyals.

Exchange rates (July 1973): £1 sterling = 10.23 QR; U.S. $1 = 3.947 QR.
100 QR riyals = £9.77 = $25.333.

Budget: The budget for the Muslim year 1392 (February 16th, 1972, to February 3rd, 1973) totalled **700 million Q/D riyals**, of which 300 million were allocated to capital projects.

OIL REVENUES
('000 Q/D riyals)

	1970–71 (1390)	1971–72 (1391)
Payments by Qatar Petroleum Co.	327,985	517,911
Payments by Shell Qatar	267,016	429,200

541

QATAR—(Statistical Survey)

EXTERNAL TRADE
Imports ('000 Q/D riyals)

1969	252,179
1970	305,491
1971	515,869
1972	607,000*

* provisional.

Exports: Non-oil exports are negligible, and the customs do not provide figures, but there is a flourishing re-export trade with other Gulf States.

IMPORTS
('000 Q/D riyals)

Principal Countries	1969	1970	1971	1972
United Kingdom	56,894	73,939	193,213	160,575
U.S.A.	31,606	30,865	50,298	63,149
Japan	19,365	28,492	54,108	76,108
Germany, Federal Republic	17,563	17,053	23,532	31,856
Lebanon	15,317	19,949	28,394	42,033
India	11,293	18,583	14,727	12,453
Bahrain	10,866	6,991	8,421	11,871
Iran	9,355	10,429	6,232	12,576
France	9,116	11,954	12,343	50,682
Netherlands	8,326	9,516	12,188	12,416

EXPORTS
('000 Q/D riyals)

Principal Countries	1972
Saudi Arabia	37,366
United Arab Emirates	14,153
Iran	3,669
Kuwait	2,794
Bahrain	1,887
Oman	1,696
Lebanon	1,627
Japan	1,431

EDUCATION

Stage	Number of Pupils 1969/70	Number of Pupils 1970/71	Number of Teachers 1969/70	Number of Teachers 1970/71
Primary	13,665	14,479	762	752
Preparatory General	2,183	2,537	120	141
Secondary General	769	911	62	80
Teacher Training	205	237	24	38
Commercial School	74	66	10	10
Technical School	170	143	34	34
Religious Institutions	157	158	16	16

THE CONSTITUTION

A new provisional constitution came into effect in July 1970. Executive power is put in the hands of the Cabinet, which will appoint three members to a twenty-three member Consultative Assembly; the other twenty members are to be elected. All fundamental democratic rights are guaranteed.

THE GOVERNMENT

HEAD OF STATE
Amir: Sheikh KHALIFA BIN HAMAD AL-THANI.

COUNCIL OF MINISTERS
(*July* 1973)

Prime Minister and Minister of Finance: Sheikh KHALIFA BIN HAMAD AL-THANI.
Minister of Finance and Petroleum: Sheikh ABDUL-AZIZ BIN KHALIFA AL-THANI.
Minister of Foreign Affairs: Sheikh SUHEIM BIN HAMAD AL-THANI.
Minister of Education, Culture and Youth Care: Sheikh JASIM BIN HAMAD AL-THANI.
Minister of Public Health: KHALED BIN MOHAMMED AL-MANAI.
Minister of the Economy and Commerce: Sheikh NASSER BIN KHALID AL-THANI.
Minister of Power and Water: Sheikh JASIM BIN MUHAMMAD AL-THANI.
Minister of Justice: Sheikh ABDEL RAHMAN BIN SAUD AL-THANI.
Minister of the Interior: Sheikh KHALID BIN AHMED AL-THANI.
Minister of Industry and Agriculture: Sheikh FAISAL BIN THANI AL-THANI.
Minister of Public Works: KHALID BIN ABDULLAH AL-ATIYYAH.
Minister of Information: ISA GHANI AL-KUWARI.
Minister of Municipal Affairs: Sheikh MOHAMMED BIN JABER AL-THANI.
Minister of Labour and Social Affairs: ALI BIN AHMAD AL-ANSARI.
Minister of Transport and Communications: ABDULLAH BIN NASSER AL-SUWAIDI.

DIPLOMATIC REPRESENTATION
EMBASSIES ACCREDITED TO QATAR

Egypt: *Ambassador:* AHMAD FOUAD HILAL.
France: *Chargé d'Affaires:* PIERRE VERMET.
Iran: *Ambassador:* HOUSHING MOKADDAM.
Iraq: *Ambassador:* DAHHAM AL-ALOUSI.
Jordan: *Ambassador:* HASHIM ABU AMARA.
Kuwait: *Ambassador:* SULAIMAN SANEH.
Lebanon: *Ambassador:* MARCELLE NAMMOOR.
Saudi Arabia: *Ambassador:* Sheikh AHMED BIN ALI AL-MUBARAK.
Sudan: *Ambassador:* MOHAMMAD UTHMAN SHENDI.
Tunisia: *Ambassador:* MAHMOOD SHARSPHOOR.
United Kingdom: *Ambassador:* EDWARD HENDERSON.
Yemen Arab Republic: *Ambassador:* ABDULLA HIJIRI.

Qatar also has diplomatic relations with Chad, Japan, Pakistan, Syria and the United States.

JUDICIAL SYSTEM

Justice is administered by five courts (Higher Criminal, Lower Criminal, Civil, Appeal and Labour) on the basis of codified laws. In addition traditional Sharia courts apply the Holy Law in certain cases. Non-Muslims are invariably tried by a court operating codified law. Independence of the judiciary is guaranteed by the provisional Constitution.

RELIGION

The indigenous population are Muslims of the Sunni sect, most being of the strict Wahabi persuasion.

PRESS

Al-Doha Magazine: Ministry of, P.O.B. 2324, Doha; f. 1969; monthly; Arabic.
al Ouroba: Arabian Newspaper Printing and Publishing House, Doha; f. 1969; weekly; Arabic.

RADIO AND TELEVISION

Radio Qatar: P.O.B. 1414, Doha; f. 1968; government service, transmitting for 12 hours daily in Arabic; an English language programme was introduced early in 1972.
Qatar Television: P.O.B. 1944, Doha; f. 1970; two 5 kW transmitters began beaming programmes throughout the Gulf in March 1972.

FINANCE
BANKING

Qatar Monetary Agency: P.O.B. 1234, Doha; f. 1966 as Qatar and Dubai Currency Board; became Qatar Monetary Agency 1973 when Qatar issued its own currency, the Qatar riyal; currency in circulation (June 1973) QR 116 million; Governor ABDUL GALEL EL-EMARI.
Qatar National Bank, S.A.Q.: Doha, P.O.B. 1000; f. 1965; cap. and res. Q/D riyals 48.9m.; dep. 203m. (1972); Chair. Sheikh ABDUL AZIZ BIN KHALIFEH ALTHANI.
Arab Bank Ltd.: Amman, Jordan; Doha, P.O.B. 172; Man. SHARIF AL JA'ABARY.
British Bank of the Middle East, The: Doha, P.O.B. 57; Man. R. R. REES.
Chartered Bank: London; P.O.B. 29, Doha.
First National City Bank: P.O.B. 2309, Doha.
National and Grindlays Bank Ltd.: London; Doha, P.O.B. 2001; Man. L. B. CANT.
United Bank of Pakistan: P.O.B. 242, Doha.

INSURANCE

Qatar Insurance Co.: P.O.B. 666, Doha; f. 1964; assets and reserves 5m. Q/D riyals (1971); branch in Dubai; Man. FATHI I. GABR.

COMMERCE

Qatar Chamber of Commerce: P.O.B. 402, Doha; f. 1963; 13 mems. appointed by decree; Pres. AHMED MUHAMMAD AL SOWAIDI; Sec. KAMAL ALI SALEH.

OIL

Qatar National Petroleum Company: f. April 1972; owns 20 per cent of shares of *Qatar Petroleum Co.* and *Shell Qatar*, and 50 per cent of shares of *Qatar Oil Co. (Japan)*; in line with OPEC policy the Government is to acquire a greater share in QPC and Shell Qatar (52 per cent by 1982), according to an agreement signed in January 1973. It has taken over the National Oil Distribution Co., which handles distribution and marketing.

Qatar Oil Co. Ltd (Japan): Doha; formed by a consortium of Japanese companies; granted an 8,500 square mile offshore concession in March 1969; drilling began in January 1971.

Qatar Petroleum Co.: Doha; an associate of Iraq Petroleum Co. and 75 per cent shareholder in the operating Company producing and exporting crude oil from the Dokhan oilfield (onshore). Total production in 1972: 88.8 million barrels. A Government participation agreement was signed in January 1973 (see above).

Shell Company of Qatar: P.O.B. 47, Doha; holds an offshore concession. A Government participation agreement was signed in January 1973 (see above); Man. Dir. B. R. SUTTIL.

TRANSPORT

ROADS

There are some 450 miles of surfaced road linking Doha and the oil centres of Dukhan and Umm Said with the northern end of the peninsula. A 65-mile long road from Doha to Salwa was completed in 1970, and joins one leading from Al Hufuf in Saudi Arabia, giving Qatar land access to the Mediterranean. A 260-mile highway, built in conjunction with Abu Dhabi, links both states with the Gulf network.

PIPELINES

Oil is transported by pipeline from the oilfield at Dukhan to the loading terminal at Umm Said. Natural gas is brought by pipeline from Dukhan to Doha where it is used as fuel for a power station and water distillation plant.

SHIPPING

Qatar National Navigation and Transport Co. Ltd.: P.O.B. 153, Doha; shipping agents, lighterage contractors ship chandlers, clearing and forwarding agents at the ports of Qatar.

Doha Port: A four-berth quay costing £10 million was completed in 1969; it is linked with Doha Town by a causeway. A new expansion project is expected to almost double the size of the port.

Umm Said Harbour: Although accommodating smaller tankers (up to 60,000 d.w.t.) Umm Said still has the country's main oil terminal. A 220,000 ton capacity tank farm is connected by a series of pipelines with QPC's three main gathering stations. A 700 ft. wide jetty is linked to a grain mill and a newly constructed fertilizer plant.

CIVIL AVIATION

Doha international airport is equipped to receive jumbo jets, its runway was extended to 15,000 ft. in 1970.

Gulf Air Co. Ltd.: jointly owned by Bahrain, Qatar, Abu Dhabi and B.O.A.C. (*see* Bahrain—Civil Aviation).

Gulf Helicopters: 75 per cent owned by Gulf Air, 25 per cent by a British Airways Group; fleet of two Sikorsky S6A's.

Doha is served by the following airlines: Alia (Jordan), BOAC, EgyptAir, Gulf Air, Iranian Airways, Iraqi Airways, Kuwait Airways, MEA, Pakistan International Airlines, Saudia, Syrian Arab Airlines, TMA, Yemen Airlines.

EDUCATION

All education within Qatar is free and numerous scholarships are awarded for study overseas. The state education system was inaugurated in 1956, when 1,400 boys attended 17 primary schools; by 1972–73 some 23,500 children (13,000 boys and 10,000 girls) attended primary school. The six-year primary stage is followed by a three-year preparatory stage (2,228 boys and 1,544 girls in 1972–73) and a further three-year secondary stage. General secondary education facilities are complemented by a teacher-training institute, a technical school, a school of commerce and an institute of religious studies. 938 boys and 521 girls received general secondary education in 1972–73, while there were 306 trainee teachers enrolled. A number of Qataris are at present enrolled in higher education institutions abroad, almost all in other Arab countries, Britain, or the U.S.A. The number of schools (93 in 1973) and of teachers (1,350), together with expenditure under the 1970–71 budget of about £290 per pupil indicates the importance given to education in Qatar. In October 1973 the first two Higher Teacher Training Colleges will be started. Education there will be at the university level. The Ministry of Education has made substantial efforts to mitigate the effects of social deprivation on equal educational opportunity.

BIBLIOGRAPHY

See Bibliography on Bahrain, p. 212, and United Arab Emirates, p. 718.

Saudi Arabia

PHYSICAL AND SOCIAL GEOGRAPHY OF THE ARABIAN PENINSULA

The Arabian peninsula is a strongly marked geographical unit, being delimited on three sides by sea—on the east by the Persian Gulf and Gulf of Oman, on the south by the Indian Ocean, and on the west by the Red Sea—and its remaining (northern) side is occupied by the deserts of Jordan and Iraq. This isolated territory, extending over more than one million square miles, is, however, divided politically into several states. The largest of these is Saudi Arabia, which occupies over 900,000 sq. miles; to the east and south lie much smaller territories where suzerainty and even actual frontiers are in some instances a matter of doubt. Along the shores of the Persian Gulf and Gulf of Oman there are first the State of Kuwait, with two adjacent patches of "neutral" territory; then, after a stretch of Saudi coast, the island of Bahrain and the Qatar peninsula, followed by the United Arab Emirates and the much larger state of Oman. The People's Democratic Republic of Yemen (composed of the former British colony of Aden and former British-protected South Arabian Federation) occupies most of the southern coastline of the peninsula. To the north of it, facing the Red Sea, lies the Yemen Arab Republic. The precise location of frontiers between these states and Saudi Arabia, which adjoins them all, is still in some doubt, and atlases show varying positions. The granting of oil concessions and continued discoveries of oil may ultimately lead to a more accurate delimitation.

PHYSICAL FEATURES

Structurally, the whole of Arabia is a vast platform of ancient rocks, once continuous with north-east Africa. In relatively recent geological time a series of great fissures opened, as the result of which a large trough, or rift valley, was formed and later occupied by the sea, to produce the Red Sea and Gulf of Aden. The Arabian platform is tilted, having its highest part in the extreme west, along the Red Sea; and it slopes gradually down from west to east. Thus the Red Sea coast is often bold and mountainous, whereas the Persian Gulf coast is flat and low-lying being fringed with extensive coral reefs that make it difficult to approach the shore in many places.

Dislocation of the rock strata in the west of Arabia has led to the upwelling of much lava, which has solidified into vast barren expanses known as *harras*. Volcanic cones and flows are also prominent along the whole length of the western coast as far as Aden, giving peaks that rise well above 10,000 ft. The maximum height of the mountains is attained in the south, in the Yemen Arab Republic, where summits reach 14,000 ft.; and the lowest part of this mountain wall occurs roughly half-way along its course, in the region of Jeddah, Mecca, and Medina. One main reason for the presence of these three towns is the geographical fact that they offer the easiest route inland from the coast, and one of the shortest routes across Arabia.

Further to the east the ancient platform is covered by relatively thin layers of younger rocks. Some of the strata have weathered away to form shallow depressions; others have proved more resistant, and now stand out as ridges. This central area, diversified by shallow vales and upstanding ridges and covered in many places by desert sand, is called the Najd, and is spoken of as the homeland of the Wahhabi sect, which now rules the whole of Saudi Arabia. Farther east still practically all the land lies well below 1,000 ft. in altitude, and both to north and south lie desert areas. The Nefud in the north has some wells, and even a slight rainfall, so life is possible for a few oasis cultivators and pastoral nomads. But south of the Najd lies the Rub' al-Khali, or Empty Quarter, a rainless, unrelieved wilderness of shifting sand, too difficult for occupation even by nomads.

Though most of the east coast of Arabia (termed al-Hasa) is low-lying, there is an exception in the imposing ridge of the Jebel Akhdar of Oman, which also produces a fjord-like coastline along the Gulf of Oman. One other feature of importance is the presence of several large river valleys, or *wadis*, cut by river action at an earlier geological period, but now almost, or entirely, dry and partly covered in sand. The largest is the Wadi Hadhramaut, which runs parallel to the southern coast for several hundred miles; another is the Wadi Sirhan, which stretches from the Nefud north-westwards into Jordan.

CLIMATE

Because of its land-locked nature, the winds reaching Arabia are generally dry, and almost all the area is arid. In the north there is a rainfall of 4 to 8 inches annually; further south, except near the coast, even this fails. The higher parts of the west and south do, however, experience appreciable falls—rather sporadic in some parts, but copious and reliable in the Yemen Arab Republic. There are even small, regularly flowing streams in the higher parts of the Yemeni mountains, but none manages to reach the sea. The Jebel Akhdar (Green Mountain) of Oman, as its name indicates, also has more rainfall than the surrounding districts.

Because of aridity, and hence relatively cloudless skies, there are great extremes of temperature. The summer is overwhelmingly hot, with maxima of over 120° F., which are intensified by the dark rocks, whilst in winter there can be general severe frost and even weeks of snow in the mountains—sheepskins are worn in the Yemen Arab Republic. Another feature, due to wide alternations of temperature, is the prevalence of violent local winds. Also, near the coast, atmospheric humidity is very high, and this makes living conditions extremely unpleasant. The coasts of both the Red Sea and Persian Gulf are notorious for their humidity.

Owing to the tilt of the strata eastwards, and their great elevation in the west, rainfall occurring in the hills near the Red Sea apparently percolates gradually eastwards, to emerge as springs along the Persian Gulf coast. This phenomenon, borne out by the fact that the flow of water in the springs greatly exceeds the total rainfall in the same district, would appear to indicate that water may be present underground over much of the interior. Hence irrigation schemes to tap these supplies have been developed, notably in Najd at al-Kharj. Results are, however, fairly limited.

ECONOMIC LIFE

Over much of Arabia life is dependent on the occurrence of oases. Many wells are used solely by nomads for watering their animals, but in some parts, more especially the south, there is some regular cultivation. The Yemen Arab Republic, in particular, has a well-developed agriculture, showing a gradation of crops according to altitude, with cereals, fruit, coffee and *qat* (a narcotic) as the chief products. Other agricultural districts occur in Aden and the Hadhramaut (in Yemen P.D.R.), in Oman, and in the large oases of the Hijaz (including Medina and Mecca). Despite this, however, it must be emphasized that in the main, conditions in Arabia are harsh, and human life depends for existence partly on resources brought in from outside—the revenues from pilgrimage, trading by dhow in the Indian Ocean, or trading in the East Indies. A major change in the economy of Saudi Arabia and the Gulf states has taken place following the exploitation of oil, the revenues from which are transforming these states, and *inter alia* allowing the import of food for Arab oil workers.

RACE

The inhabitants of the centre, north, and west are of almost unmixed Mediterranean stock—lightly built, long-headed, and dark. In coastal districts of the east, south, and south-west intermixture of broader-headed and slightly heavier peoples of Armenoid descent is a prominent feature; and there has been some exchange of racial type with the populations on the Persian shores of the Persian Gulf and Gulf of Oman. Owing to the long-continued slave trade, negroid influences from Africa are also widespread. On this basis it is possible to delimit two ethnic zones within Arabia: a northern, central and western area, geographically arid and in isolation, with a relatively unmixed racial composition; and the coastlands of the south, south-west, and east, showing a mixed population.

LANGUAGE

Arabic is the only language of Arabia. Unlike many other parts of the Middle East, European languages are not current.

HISTORY

ANCIENT AND MEDIEVAL HISTORY

Although there is some support for the belief that Arabia was at one time a land of great fertility, there is little evidence of this in historical times. For the most part Arabian history has been the account of small pockets of settled civilization, subsisting mainly on trade, in the midst of an ocean of nomadic tribes whose livelihood was derived mainly from camel-breeding and raiding. The earliest urban settlements developed in the south-west, where the flourishing Minaean kingdom is believed to have been established as early as the twelfth century B.C. This was followed by the Sabaean and Himyarite kingdoms, which lasted with varying degrees of power until the sixth century A.D. The term "kingdom" in this connection implies rather a loose federation of city states than a centralized monarchy. As an important trading station between east and west, southern Arabia was brought into early contact with the Persian and Roman empires, whence spread the influence of Judaism, Zoroastrianism, and later Christianity. Politically, however, the south Arabian principalities remained independent, though there was an abortive Roman expedition in A.D. 24, and two brief periods of Abyssinian rule in the fourth and sixth centuries A.D.

By the end of the sixth century the centre of gravity had shifted to the west coast, to the Hijaz cities of at-Ta'if, Mecca and Medina. While the southern regions fell under the somewhat spasmodic control of the Sasanid rulers of Persia, the Hijaz grew in independence and importance as a trade route between the Byzantine Empire, Egypt, and the East. From the fifth century onwards Mecca was dominated by the tribe of Quraish, through whose extensive commercial activities influences from Byzantine, Persian, Aramaic and Judaic sources began to make themselves felt. Meanwhile the central deserts remained obstinately nomadic, and the inhospitable east coast formed for the most part a corner of the Persian sphere of influence.

It is not necessary here to relate in detail the events that led to the spectacular outbreak of the Arabs from the Arabian peninsula and their political and social domination within a century of an area extending from Spain to northern India. Ostensibly the driving force behind this great movement was the Islamic religion preached by Muhammad, a humble member of the Quraish tribe; and so powerful was its appeal that not only was the faith itself widely adopted, but even the language of its holy book, the Koran, has left an indelible impression on the speech of all the peoples it reached.

But this flowering and development of Arabism was to proceed for the most part outside the confines of the Arabian peninsula itself. The Islamic unification of the Near and Middle East reduced the importance of the Hijaz as a trade route. Mecca retained a unique status as a centre of pilgrimage for the whole Muslim world, but Arabia as a whole, temporarily united under Muhammad and his successors, soon drifted back into disunity. The Yemen was the first to break away from the weakening Abbasid Caliphate in Baghdad, and from the ninth century onwards a variety of small dynasties established themselves in Sana'a, Zabid, and other towns. Mecca also had its semi-independent governors, though their proximity to Egypt made them more cautious in their attitude towards the Caliphs and the later rulers of that country, particularly the Fatimids of the tenth to twelfth centuries. In Oman in the south-east a line of spiritual Imams arose who before long were exercising temporal power; to the north the Arabian shores of the Persian Gulf provided a home for the fanatical Carmathian sect whose influence at times extended as far as Iraq, Syria, Mecca, and the Yemen.

THE OTTOMAN PERIOD

Arabia continued to be restless and unsettled until the beginning of the sixteenth century, when the whole peninsular came nominally under the suzerainty of the Ottoman Sultans at Istanbul. It was a hold that was never very strong, even in the Hijaz, while in Oman and the Yemen native lines of Imams were once again exercising unfettered authority before the end of the century. More important for the future of the peninsula was the appearance of European merchant adventurers in the Indian Ocean and the Persian/Arabian Gulf. The Portuguese were the first to arrive in the sixteenth century, and they were succeeded in the seventeenth and eighteenth centuries by the English, Dutch and French. By the beginning of the nineteenth century Britain had eliminated her European rivals and had established her influence firmly in the Gulf and to a lesser extent along the southern coast.

The political structure of Arabia was now beginning to take the shape it has today. The Yemen was already a virtually independent Imamate; Lahej broke away in the middle of the eighteenth century, only to lose Aden to Britain in 1839 and to become the nucleus of the Aden Protectorate. To the north of the Yemen was the principality of the Asir, generally independent, though both countries were occupied by the Turks from 1850 to the outbreak of the Great War. The Hijaz continued to be a province of the Ottoman Empire. In 1793 the Sultanate of Oman was established with its capital at Muscat, and during the nineteenth century all the rulers and chieftains along the Persian Gulf coast, including Oman, the sheikhdoms of the Trucial Coast, Bahrain and Kuwait, entered into close and "exclusive" treaty relations with the British Government. Britain was principally concerned to prevent French, Russian and German penetration towards India and to suppress the slave and arms trades.

Meanwhile the Najd in the centre of Arabia was the scene of another upheaval with religious inspirations. The puritanical and reforming Wahhabi movement, launched in the middle of the eighteenth century, had by 1800 reached such strength that its followers were able to capture Kerbela and Najaf in Iraq, Damascus in Syria, and Mecca and Medina in the Hijaz. They were defeated by Muhammad Ali of Egypt, acting in the name of the Ottoman Sultan, in 1811–1818 and again in 1838; but the Wahhabi ruling house of Sa'ud continued to rule in the interior. Towards the end of the century they were in danger of being eclipsed by the Shammar line of Rashid to the north, who had Turkish support; but in 1902 Abd al-Aziz ibn Sa'ud, the late ruler of Saudi Arabia, succeeded in recapturing the Wahhabi capital of Riyadh, and by the outbreak of the Great War was master of the whole of central Arabia, including the Hasa coast of the Persian Gulf. In 1910, with the aim of reviving the ideals of the Wahhabi movement, he established the *Ikhwan* or Brethren and proceeded to settle them in colonies throughout the Najd, thus forming the basis of a centralized organization that was to prove a powerful instrument in later years.

MODERN HISTORY

When Turkey entered the war on the side of Germany in October 1914 Arabia inevitably became a centre of intrigue, if not necessarily of military action. British influence was paramount along the eastern and southern coasts, where the various sheikhs and tribal chiefs from Kuwait to the Hadhramaut lost no time in severing their last slender connections with the Ottoman Empire. On the other hand, the Turks had faithful allies in Ibn Rashid of the Shammar to the north of the Najd, and in Imam Yahya of the Yemen; they also retained their garrisons along the west coast, both in the Asir, whose Idrisi ruler was impelled by his long-standing enmity with the Imam of the Yemen to intrigue against them, and in the Hijaz, where Sharif Hussein of Mecca still acknowledged Ottoman suzerainty. In the centre Ibn Sa'ud, who had accepted Turkish recognition in 1913 of his occupation of the Hasa coast, was in close and friendly relations with the Government of India.

British military strategy developed as the war dragged on into a two-pronged thrust against the Turks from both Egypt and the Persian Gulf. In the implementation of this plan opinions were divided on the extent to which use could be made of the Arab population. The Indian Government on the eastern wing, while favouring the pretensions of Ibn Sa'ud, preferred to see the problem in purely military terms, and opposed any suggestion of an Arab revolt. This, however, was the scheme favoured by the Arab Bureau in Cairo, whose views eventually prevailed in London. They were alarmed at the Ottoman declaration of a *Jihad* (Holy War) and possible repercussions in Egypt and North Africa. Negotiations were started at a very early stage with Arab nationalist movements in Syria and Egypt, but these met with comparatively little success. More progress was made when the British negotiators turned their attentions to the Sherif of Mecca, Hussein, member of the Hashimi family that had ruled in Mecca since the eleventh century A.D. The support of such a religious dignitary would be an effective counter to Turkish claims. Hussein was inclined to favour the Allied cause, but was reluctant to act independently, and it was only after he had elicited from the British (in the MacMahon correspondence—see DOCUMENTS ON PALESTINE, p. 46) promises which he believed would meet Arab nationalist aspirations that he decided to move. On June 5th, 1916, he proclaimed Arab independence and declared war on the Turks. By November things had gone so well that he felt able to claim the title of King of the Hijaz. Military operations continued throughout the winter, and in July 1917 the port of Aqaba was captured and the Hijaz cleared of Turkish troops except for a beleaguered and helpless garrison in Medina.

Arabia thereafter remained comparatively peaceful, and was not even greatly disturbed by the complicated post-war political manoeuvres in the Middle East. Hussein played a somewhat ineffectual role in maintaining the Arab point of view at the peace conferences and over the allocation of mandates, and as a result forfeited the favour of the British Government. When, therefore, he was unwise enough to challenge the growing power of his old enemy Ibn Sa'ud, he found himself entirely without support. Ibn Sa'ud's stature had been steadily growing since the end of the war. In November 1921 he had succeeded in eliminating the house of Ibn Rashid and annexing the Shammar, and a year later he was recognized by the Government of India as overlord of Ha'il, Shammar and Jawf. On March 5th, 1924, King Hussein laid claim to the title of Caliph, vacant by the deposition of the Ottoman Sultan. His claims were nowhere recognized, and Ibn Sa'ud, declaring him a traitor, overran the Hijaz in a campaign of a few months, captured Mecca and forced Hussein's abdication. Hussein's eldest son, Ali, continued to hold Jeddah for another year, but was then driven out, and on January 8th, 1926, Ibn Sa'ud proclaimed himself King of the Hijaz, so formally marking the establishment of the Saudi Arabian kingdom.

THE KINGDOM OF SAUDI ARABIA*

Ibn Sa'ud's new status was recognized by Britain in the Treaty of Jeddah of 1927, while Ibn Sa'ud in his turn acknowledged his rival Hussein's sons, Abdallah and Faisal, as rulers of Transjordan and Iraq, and also the special status of the British-protected sheikhdoms along the Gulf coast. The northern frontier of his domains had previously been established by the Hadda and Bahra agreements of November 1925, which set the Mandate boundaries as the limit of his expansion; while the border war with Yemen was, after protracted negotiations and a brief war, settled in 1934. (For a fuller account of this, see the Yemen Arab Republic chapter, History.)

During the years that followed, the new king continued to be absorbed in his primary task of unifying and developing his country. The colonization policy begun in 1910 was pursued vigorously; land settlements were established and Bedouin unruliness was suppressed. A start was made at the modernization of communications, and the need for economic development along modern lines was emphasized by the falling-off in the pilgrimage during the early 1930s. The serious crisis that this produced might indeed never have been averted had it not been for the discovery of oil in Bahrain in 1932 and the subsequent extension of prospecting to the mainland.

Saudi Arabia's chief sufferings during the war were economic, though there was an Italian air raid on Dhahran (and also on Bahrain) in October 1940. The pilgrimage traffic dropped away almost to extinction, and in April 1943 it was found necessary to include Saudi Arabia in the benefits of Lease-Lend. Up to September 1946 $17,500,000 had been received, and in August of that year there was a further £10,000,000 from the Export-Import Bank. Two years later, however, as a protest against American policy over Palestine, an American loan of $15,000,000 was turned down. But by this time the oil industry alone was enough to establish the Saudi Arabian economy firmly on its feet.

In January 1944 the California Arabian Standard Oil Company, owned jointly by the Standard Oil Company of California and the Texas Company, was re-formed as the Arabian American Oil Company. This was reconstructed once more in December 1948 to include the Standard Oil Company of New Jersey and Socony Vacuum—a move that brought protests from the French Government. Under an agreement of 1928 shareholders in the Iraq Petroleum Company, who included the latter two American companies as well as French and British interests, had agreed not to secure rival concessions within an area including the Arabian peninsula. A settlement was finally reached at the end of 1948, by which this so-called "Red Line" clause was abandoned. Meanwhile production had been mounting steadily as new fields were developed; a refinery was opened at Ras Tanura in October 1945, and two years later work was started on a pipeline to connect the Arabian fields with the Mediterranean. In spite of a year's suspension owing to events in Palestine, the task was completed before the end of 1950, and oil first reached the Lebanese port of Sidon on December 2nd of that year. In the same month a new "fifty-fifty" agreement was signed with the Arabian American Oil Company which was to set an interesting example to other foreign oil interests in December 1951. In 1955 Saudi Arabia was involved in a dispute with Aramco over its decision to grant oil transportation concessions to the Greek shipowner Aristotle Onassis. In 1956 a government-owned National Oil Company was formed to exploit areas not covered by the Aramco concession.

---

* For subsequent developments in the rest of the Arabian Peninsula, see separate chapters on Bahrain, Kuwait, Oman, Qatar, United Arab Emirates, Yemen Arab Republic and Yemen People's Democratic Republic.

Saudi Arabia was an original member of the Arab League formed in 1945, and to begin with played a loyal and comparatively inconspicuous part. Ibn Sa'ud sent a small force to join the fighting against Israel in the summer of 1948. When the solidarity of the League began to show signs of cracking, it was natural that he should side with Egypt and Syria rather than with his old dynastic enemies, the rulers of Iraq and Jordan. In course of time, however, he began to turn once more to internal development, and to forget his political quarrel with the United States in his need for economic advice and aid. The $15,000,000 Export-Import Bank loan was finally taken up in August 1950; in January 1951 a Point Four Agreement was signed, and in June a Mutual Assistance Pact. But the real basis of development was the revenue from the ever-expanding oil industry. This was sufficient to justify the announcement in July 1949 of a $270,000,000 Four Year Plan, in which an ambitious programme of railway development was the main item. A railway now links the oilfields in the east with Riyadh in the centre, and extends to the port of Dammam. For the rest the King's policy was one of cautious modernization at home, and the enhancement of Saudi Arabian prestige and influence in the Middle East and in world affairs generally.

AFTER IBN SA'UD

On November 9th, 1953, King Ibn Sa'ud died at the age of 71, and was succeeded peacefully by the Crown Prince, Sa'ud. It was assumed that there would be no major changes, but the policy already adopted of strengthening the governmental machine and of relying less on one-man rule was continued by the formation of new ministries and of a regular cabinet. In March 1958 King Saud conferred upon his brother, the Amir Faisal, full powers over the foreign, internal and economic affairs of Saudi Arabia, with the professed aim of strengthening the machinery of government and centralizing responsibilities. In December 1960, however, the Amir Faisal resigned, and the King took over the office of Prime Minister himself. In the following month a High Planning Council, with a team of international experts, was set up to survey the country's resources, and thereafter there has been slow but steady progress in the modernization of the country.

Throughout his reign the King had seen his role as that of a mediator between the conflicting national and foreign interests in the Arab Middle East. He refused to join either the United Arab Republic or the rival Arab Federation. Relations with Egypt ranged from the mutual defence pacts between Egypt, Syria and Saudi Arabia in October 1955 (to which Yemen and Jordan adhered the following year) to the open quarrel in March 1958 over an alleged plot to assassinate President Nasser. Subsequently, relations improved, and the King visited Cairo in September 1959. Contacts with the United States have always been close, owing to the extensive American oil interests. In 1957 King Sa'ud visited America, and in 1959 he made an extensive tour of Europe. The Saudi Arabian Government also played a leading role in bringing the Arab governments together after Egypt's nationalization of the Suez Canal in July 1956 and the Israel, British and French military action in the Sinai peninsula in November. In 1961 Saudi Arabia supported the Syrians in their break with the United Arab Republic, and in general relations with the U.A.R. deteriorated (diplomatic relations were severed in November 1962, shortly before they were resumed with the United Kingdom). By 1964, however, in spite of the tensions over the Yemen revolution, there were signs of improved relations. King Sa'ud attended the Cairo conference on the Jordan waters dispute in January, and in March, after a meeting in Riyadh, diplomatic relations with the United Arab Republic were resumed. In September Prince Faisal attended the Arab Summit Conference in Alexandria, and afterwards had talks with President Nasser on the Yemen situation.

THE REIGN OF KING FAISAL

Meanwhile, in March 1964 King Sa'ud had relinquished all real power over the affairs of the country to his brother, Crown Prince Faisal, who had again acted as Prime Minister intermittently during 1962, and continuously since the middle of 1963. The rule of Prince Faisal was expected to result in many concessions to "Westernization" such as more cinemas and television, with more profound social and economic reforms to follow. The division of the country into provinces, each with a thirty-man council, was under study early in 1964. The change of power, by which King Sa'ud retired as active monarch, was supported in a statement by the *ulema* council of religious leaders "in the light of developments, the King's condition of health, and his inability to attend to state affairs". In November 1964 Sa'ud was formally deposed, and Faisal became King, as well as head of the Council of Ministers with the exclusive power of appointing and dismissing Ministers. His younger brother Khalid was appointed Crown Prince. On August 24th, 1965, King Faisal confirmed his stature as an important Arab leader, when he concluded an agreement at Jeddah with President Nasser of the U.A.R. on a Peace Plan for the Yemen. King Sa'ud went into exile, living principally in Athens, where he died in February 1969.

Although the Yemen problem remained unsolved, there was evidence of Saudi Arabia's genuine anxiety that a solution should be found, even though in April 1966 the construction of a military airfield near the frontier brought protests from the Yemeni Republican Government and the U.A.R. Representatives of Saudi Arabia and the U.A.R. met in Kuwait in August 1966 in an attempt to implement the Jeddah agreement. But relations with both the U.A.R. and the Arab League continued to be tense, and no progress was evident. Matters were not improved by the appearance in Cairo of ex-King Sa'ud, with a public declaration of his support for U.A.R. policy in Yemen.

During 1966 King Faisal undertook an extensive series of visits abroad, including Iran, Jordan, Sudan, Pakistan, Syria, the United States, Turkey,

Morocco, Guinea, Mali, and Tunisia. A trade and financial agreement with Morocco was the chief concrete result of these tours. In May 1967 he paid a state visit to the United Kingdom, and discussed the South Arabian situation with British ministers. Saudi Arabian troops moved into Jordanian territory at the beginning of June, and collaborated with Jordanian and Iraqi forces in hostilities against Israel. At a summit conference of Arab leaders held in Khartoum at the end of August 1967 Saudi Arabia agreed to put up £50 million of a total £135 million fund to assist Jordan and the U.A.R. in restoring their economic strength after the hostilities with Israel. At the same time an agreement was concluded with President Nasser on the withdrawal of U.A.R. and Saudi military support for the warring parties in the Yemen. By way of recompense for these concessions the Saudi Arabian Government persuaded the other Arab states that it was in their best interests to resume production of oil, shipments of which to western countries had been suspended for political reasons after the war with Israel.

EVENTS SINCE THE 1967 WAR

Though outwardly calm, the internal political situation was apparently disturbed by abortive coups in June and September 1969. Plans for both are presumed to have been discovered in advance, the only visible evidence of the attempts being the arrests of numbers of army and air force officers. A flight of private capital abroad was also reported. Some observers drew parallels with developments in Libya. In the Yemen the Royalist cause which the Saudi Government had strongly supported appeared to be within sight of victory early in 1968, but by mid-1969 its remaining adherents had largely been driven into exile and the civil war seemed to have come to an end, although further hostilities were reported during the 1969-70 winter. Dissension amongst the Royalists, which led to the withdrawal of Saudi assistance, was a principal factor in this decline. Discussions between Sana'a representatives and Saudi officials took place at Jeddah in March 1970, and the Yemen Republic was officially recognized in July. Relations with Southern Yemen deteriorated, however, and an extensive battle on the disputed frontier took place in December 1969, with Saudi Arabia apparently winning easily owing mainly to its superior air power. Since then the Aden Government has accused Saudi Arabia of backing the mercenaries of the National Deliverance Army.

The important relationship with Iran, under some strain at the beginning of 1968 over the Bahrain question, improved greatly later in the year. In October the two countries signed a treaty which at last delineated their offshore boundaries. In November the Shah paid a state visit to Saudi Arabia; the occasion, which included a pilgrimage, was acclaimed as symbolic of Muslim unity. The Saudi Government took a favourable view of the proposed Gulf federation, and gave financial assistance for the road linking the Trucial sheikhdoms. Together with Kuwait the government was closely involved in 1971 in the diplomatic efforts to secure Bahrain's and Qatar's membership of a nine-member Gulf federation, but the two sheikhdoms eventually decided to remain apart from the Trucial States, which formed the United Arab Emirates.

As principal guardian of Muslim interests, Saudi Arabia was particularly concerned by the fire at the Al Aqsa mosque in Jerusalem in August 1969, and hence it was the leading instigator of the Islamic summit conference held to condemn Israel in Rabat the following month. Relations with other Muslim countries were strengthened by King Faisal's state visits to Afghanistan, Algeria, Indonesia and Malaysia in June 1970, but the closure of the Tapline pipeline in May and Syria's refusal to allow repairs to be carried out, strained relations with some of Saudi Arabia's neighbours. After Tapline had agreed to increased transit fees, the Syrian Government allowed repairs to be carried out, and the oil flow resumed in January 1971.

Relations with Sudan have become closer since the communist-inspired *coup* attempt there in July 1971, and President Nemery visited Saudi Arabia in November 1971 and April 1972. Saudi Arabia has also played a leading role in attempting to bring about agreement between the Palestinian guerrillas and the Jordanian Government since the final confrontation between them in north Jordan in July 1971. Aided by Egypt, the Saudi Government managed to arrange a series of talks between the representatives of the two sides in Jeddah during the last half of the year. President Sadat visited Jeddah in August, Yassir Arafat in October, but despite the intense diplomatic activity, no agreement was reached, though in January 1972 a Saudi Government spokesman said hope of success in mediation had not been abandoned.

In 1972 and 1973 Faisal visited a large number of countries, including Morocco, Italy, Algeria, Tunisia, Egypt, France, Uganda, Chad, Senegal, Mauritania and Niger. The growing tension in the Gulf area generally was illustrated by an agreement with the U.S.A. in May 1973 for the supply of Phantom jets to Saudi Arabia, and the signing of a £250 million contract in June 1973 for British Aircraft Corporation to supply Saudi Arabia with air defence support systems. Saudi Arabia, however, has warned the United States that she might be prepared to withhold oil supplies unless the U.S.A. changed her attitude in the Arab-Israeli dispute.

Despite the great improvement in communications, welfare services and the standard of living in general over recent years, Saudi Arabia remains the most traditional and conservative of the Arab countries; the ancient restrictions on smoking, alcohol, dress, etc., are still very largely observed, as are the Muslim calendar and religious festivals.

SAUDI ARABIA—(Economic Survey)

ECONOMIC SURVEY

AREA AND POPULATION

The area of Saudi Arabia has been estimated at some 875,000 square miles, but the borders have not all been defined and therefore no precise figure can be arrived at. A census of the entire population is difficult because the Bedouin shift from one area of the country to another; but it is estimated that more than 50 per cent of the population is Bedouin, about 25 per cent urban dwellers, and the rest settled cultivators. The total population is not known accurately and estimates vary considerably. A UN estimate gave the population as 8.2 million in 1972. The largest towns are Riyadh, estimated at 300,000, and Jeddah, estimated at 250,000.

AGRICULTURE

Agriculture contributes about 8 per cent of G.N.P. and employs some three-quarters of the population. Cultivation is confined to oases and to irrigated regions: the remaining agricultural land is used for low-grade grazing. The chief crops cultivated on irrigated or cultivated soil are wheat, lucerne, millet and maize, while fruits of many varieties, particularly dates, grow in abundance in oases. Sheep and goats are bred extensively, both for meat and for wool; camels are also bred.

The Government has recognized the importance of developing agriculture as a means of reducing the dependence on imported food, and as a means of diversifying the economy and of raising rural living standards. Since scarcity of water constitutes the chief factor limiting the development of agriculture, the Government has launched an ambitious programme to overcome this obstacle. Execution of this programme—which includes surveys for underground water resources, construction of dams, irrigation and drainage networks, combined with distribution of fallow land, settlement of Bedouin and the introduction of mechanization—is aimed at eventually raising agricultural production to the level of near self-sufficiency in food. Consequently, budgetary allocations for the agricultural sector have increased by nearly 55 per cent during the period from 1964-65 until 1970-71, rising from 149 million to 230 million riyals per year. The Economic Development Plan covering 1970-75 projects a total outlay of 1,317.5 million riyals for agriculture and water resources. Agricultural production is expected to grow by 27 per cent from a preliminary level of 1,177 million riyals to 1,496 million riyals by the end of the plan period. Wheat production is expected to increase by 71 per cent, fodder by 35 per cent, vegetables by 35 per cent, barley by 55 per cent and dairy products and fish by 20 per cent each.

During the 1960s, surveys were carried out over 393,800 square miles—45 per cent of the total area of the country—on behalf of the Government by foreign consulting firms. The reports indicated a large potential for considerably increasing agricultural production in nearly all areas under cultivation by improving water distribution and drainage systems. Three other important projects which have been undertaken by the Government include the al-Hasa irrigation scheme, the Faisal Model Settlement scheme and the Wadi Jizan dam project.

The al-Hasa irrigation and drainage scheme, inaugurated in December 1971, was completed over five years at a cost of 260 million riyals and will result in the reclamation of 12,000 hectares. It is the country's biggest agricultural scheme and about 50,000 persons will benefit from it. The Faisal Model Settlement scheme had almost been completed by the end of 1971. The scheme, which cost 100 million riyals, has involved extensive land reclamation and irrigation and will be used for the settlement of 10,000 Bedouin. The Wadi Jizan dam, which was inaugurated in March 1971, has a capacity of 71 million cubic metres of water and was built at a cost of 42 million riyals. It constitutes the first stage in a plan for the development of Wadi Jizan which will increase the irrigated area by 8,000 hectares and will contribute about 8.8 million riyals annually to agricultural and livestock production. Other agricultural projects include the construction of two desalination plants, including the plant at Jeddah which has a production capacity of 5 million gallons of water per day. Projects under way in early 1972 included a dam at Abha costing 24.7 million riyals, the establishment of an agricultural college at Buraida, flood protection projects and desalination plants.

OIL

The most important industry in Saudi Arabia is the production of crude oil and petroleum products. In 1972 the country produced more oil than any other country in the Middle East and ranked third in world crude oil output, following the U.S.A. and the U.S.S.R. Proven Saudi oil reserves stood at 138 billion barrels at the end of 1972 or just 20 per cent of the world total.

In 1933 a Saudi concession was granted to Standard Oil Company of California to explore for oil. The operating company, the Arabian American Oil Company (Aramco), has the following ownership: the Saudi Arabian Government 25 per cent, Exxon Corporation 22½ per cent, Standard Oil Company of California 22½ per cent, Texaco Inc. 22½ per cent Mobil Oil Corporation 7½ per cent. The Saudi Arabian Government acquired its 25 per cent participation as a result of the participation agreement signed in Riyadh on December 20th, 1972.

The operating company began exploring for oil in 1933 and drilling in 1935. It discovered oil in commercial quantities in 1938. By the end of the Second World War it had discovered four oil fields and had established the necessary facilities, including a large refinery, to meet post-war demands for crude oil and refined products.

SAUDI ARABIA—(Economic Survey)

At the end of 1972, Aramco's proven resources of crude oil were estimated to be 93.0 billion barrels.* Production comes from twelve major oilfields: Ghawar, Abqaiq, Safaniya, Abu Hadriya, Abu Sa'fah, Qatif, Fadhili, Manifa, Khursaniyah, Dammam, Berri and Khurais. Of these the three first-named are by far the most important. Ghawar is generally accepted as the world's largest oilfield and Safariya is the world's largest offshore field. Two more fields—the Marjan and Zuluf—were being brought into production in 1972. Production has mounted steadily each year since 1956 to reach 1,642 million barrels in 1971. Aramco's payments to the Government increased by 43.4 per cent to $2,677.9 million in 1972 from $1,866.4 million in 1971. The Ras Tanura refinery on the Gulf, which was completed in 1945, processed 205 million barrels of crude oil, natural gasoline and raw liquified petroleum gas in 1972.

A 30/31-inch pipeline system, 1,068 miles long, runs from Aramco's oil fields to the Mediterranean port of Sidon, Lebanon. It was brought into operation in 1950 and by 1958 its capacity was 470,000 barrels per day. The western 754 miles are operated by the affiliated Trans-Arabian Pipe Line Company (Tapline), the capital of which is held by the Aramco companies and the rest by Aramco. The pipeline normally carries around 8 per cent of Aramco's production.

The oilfields contain vast quantities of natural gas and Aramco has developed the capacity in the Abqaiq and Ghawar fields to reinject 405,000,000 cubic feet per day in order to conserve the gas for future use and to reinforce the underground pressure necessary for oil recovery.

The area of Aramco's original concession was about 673,000 square miles. The company has, however, agreed to relinquish progressively parts of its concession areas. Following relinquishments in 1960, 1963 and 1968, its concession has been reduced to 105,000 square miles and is expected to be progressively reduced to 20,000 square miles by 1993.

In 1949 the Saudi Arabian government granted the Getty Oil Corporation a 60-year exclusive concession covering its undivided half interest in the Saudi Arabian-Kuwait Neutral Zone. The American Independent Oil Company (Aminoil, covering Kuwait's undivided half interest) is the operating company and it discovered oil in commercial quantity in 1953 in the Wafra field. Reserves there have been estimated to be 6,500 million barrels. First shipments of oil were made there in 1954. Japanese interests which had obtained concessions from Saudi Arabia and Kuwait in 1957 and 1958 covering an offshore area of the neutral zone of the Gulf, found oil in 1969 which is now being exploited by the Arabian Oil Co.

In 1972 Arabian Oil Company paid the Saudi Arabian Government $68.7 million in tax and royalty, and Aminoil paid $28.0 million. The total revenue derived by the Government from all three companies (for Aramco payments see above) in 1972 was $2,779.3 million, including $4.7 million paid by companies not yet producing. Saudi Arabia's oil revenue will rise substantially in coming years as a result of new agreements made with the producing companies.

In 1965 the French state company Auxerap concluded an agreement for offshore exploration in the Red Sea. The agreement provided for the Saudi Arabian state organization Petromin (General Petroleum and Mineral Organization) to participate in exploitation of any commercial discoveries. In December 1967 two further important agreements were signed. One was between Petromin and the Italian state oil corporation, ENI, by which the latter was permitted to explore for oil during a period of six years in some 77,000 square km. of the Rub'al-Khali and 9,600 square km. in the Eastern Province. The other was between Petromin and two American corporations, Sinclair Oil Co. and Natomas, under which the latter were granted similar rights in the Red Sea area. In both cases the prospecting concerns were to act as contractors for Petromin which retained the legal title to the concessions.

OTHER INDUSTRIES

The development of modern industry is at a very early stage. In 1971 there were 283 industrial units employing around 10,000 persons. Besides 41 electricity plants, these were largely small-scale concerns catering for domestic needs, distributed as follows: tile-making (45), furniture-making (30), printing and publishing (27,) metal goods (25), food (18) and soft drinks (12). Eighty-three of these enterprises were located in Jeddah and 54 in Riyadh.

In terms of output, construction has been the most important industry after oil in recent years, contributing around 4.5 per cent to net domestic product in 1969-70 compared with 2 per cent for other branches of manufacturing. Consumption of cement has risen by 315 per cent during 1960-70, with nearly 60 per cent being produced domestically compared with 25 per cent in 1960. However, other branches of manufacturing have grown by over 40 per cent in real terms over the period 1967-70, compared with only 2 per cent for the construction industry.

The chief instrument of industrial development is Petromin, set up in 1962 to implement the long-run objective of diversifying the economy through the establishment of industries based on petro-chemicals and minerals. Three important projects initiated by Petromin have started production. The most important of these is the $7 million steel rolling mill at Jeddah, which started production in 1968 with an annual capacity of 45,000 tons of bars and sheet steel. Second, the Jeddah oil refinery began production in 1968 with a production capacity of 12,000 barrels per day. The third project is the $40 million Saudi Arabian Fertilizer Co. (SAFCO) plant which began production in 1969 with an initial capacity of 1,100 tons of urea and 35 tons of sulphur.

Petromin is to play a key role in the development of minerals and manufacturing under the current Economic Development Plan and has a planned investment of 5,113 riyals during the period 1970-75.

---

* 1 barrel = 42 U.S. gallons, 34.9726 Imperial gallons; 1 billion = 1 thousand million.

SAUDI ARABIA—(Economic Survey)

Twenty-five per cent of this total will be contributed by the Government through equity participation or loans and the remainder is to be raised from domestic and foreign investors. Fifteen million riyals were assigned to projects already under way: the Petromin Lubricating Oil Co. (Petrolube) at Jeddah, which has an annual capacity of 75,000 barrels; and the sulphuric acid plant at Damman which has a capacity of 50 tons of sulphuric acid per day. A further 548 million riyals is assigned for the expansion of the Jeddah oil refinery from 12,000 to 45,000 barrels per day, the construction of a 15,000-barrels-per-day refinery at Riyadh and the expansion of the Jeddah rolling mill from 45,000 to 100,000 tons capacity. Some 4,550 million riyals is for a variety of petrochemical and mineral projects and the Uthmaniya–Riyadh pipeline.

The Directorate-General of Mineral Resources has been pursuing a programme for the discovery and exploitation of mineral resources. Geological studies and exploration missions have been undertaken in several parts of the country and an economic feasibility study is planned for the iron-ore deposit in Wadi Fatima, estimated at 50 million tons. Although mineral industry is non-existent, apart from oil and a small output of salt, gypsum and limestone, mineral prospects are thought to be good, particularly for phosphates along the Jordan border and for iron ore along the Red Sea coast. Government sources have stated that minerals may account for as much as 30 per cent of G.N.P. in the long-term future.

Apart from developments under the auspices of Petromin, it is proposed under the Economic Development Plan to establish 31 new industrial concerns, involving a total investment of 236 million riyals. The cement, food and beverage, textile and clothing and paper industries will account for nearly 70 per cent of the investment in new enterprises under the plan.

TRANSPORT

Until 1964 the only surfaced roads, besides those in the oil network, were in the Jeddah-Mecca-Medina area. Since then roads have been given priority with 20 per cent of the development budget. By 1970 there were over 4,705 miles of asphalted road, compared with 4,262 miles at the end of the previous year, and nearly 1,300 miles were under construction. In addition the total length of rural road reached over 2,450 miles compared with 1,574 miles in the previous year. Under the Economic Development Plan, 3,918.7 million riyals, or 58 per cent of 57,092 million riyals allocated to the transport and communications sector, are to be spent on the construction of roads. Under the plan, 2,680 miles of main road and 1,240 miles of rural road are to be built during 1970-75, bringing the total length of main road to nearly 7,400 miles and that of rural road to 3,700 miles.

There are three chief ports: Jeddah and Yanbou on the Red Sea and Dammam on the Gulf. During 1969 a total of 1,851 ships called at these ports with a cargo of 2 million tons. These ports have been undergoing expansion and improvement in recent years. Jeddah, for example, has been modernized with the construction of six new piers at a cost of 134 million riyals. Projects are in hand for the development of al-Qatif and Jubail ports. Under the Economic Development Plan, 823 million riyals will be spent on the development of ports and major projects include the expansion of the annual capacities of Jeddah and Damman ports to 1.7 and 2.8 million tons respectively.

The chief international airports are Jeddah, Dhahran and Riyadh. Although both Jeddah and Riyadh have been considerably improved in recent years, schemes are under way for the future development of Riyadh and the building of a new airport to the north of Jeddah at a total cost of some $150–200 million. The Government operates Saudia–Saudi Arabian Airlines which links important Saudi cities, with regular flights to many foreign countries. The airline flew 226 million passenger-km. in 1968.

The government operates a modern railway system connecting the port of Dammam on the Gulf with Riyadh, the capital, some 370 miles inland. Work is proceeding on the rebuilding of the historic Hejaz railway, which ran from Damascus through what is now Jordan to Mecca, but little progress has been made since the 1967 Palestine war.

FOREIGN TRADE

The total value of the country's exports in 1971 amounted to 17,302 million riyals. Exports consist almost entirely of oil: in 1970 oil exports amounted to 10,877 million riyals. Western Europe is the major market for Saudi oil and accounted for 44 per cent of total exports in 1970, of which two-thirds went to EEC countries. Exports to Asia were about 31 per cent of the total, of which over two-thirds went to Japan. Other important sources of foreign exchange derive from the local expenditure of Aramco and from the pilgrimage traffic.

In 1971 the total value of imports was 3,667 million riyals compared with 3,197 million in 1970. Imports cover a wide range of manufactured goods, particularly machinery, vehicles and transport equipment (accounting for 29 per cent of total imports in 1971) and foodstuffs (29 per cent). Other significant imports are building materials (13 per cent), chemical products (6 per cent) and textiles and clothing (5 per cent). The pattern of imports reflects the Saudi development effort and the country's poor agricultural resources. The U.S.A. has been the leading exporter to Saudi Arabia in recent years, accounting for 16.8 per cent of Saudi imports in 1971, followed by Japan and U.K. (11.3 per cent and 8.9 per cent) and West Germany (7.9 per cent). Lebanon, which accounted for 12.9 per cent of imports in 1971, has an important entrepôt trade with Saudi Arabia. There was a surplus on current account of $59 million in 1970, in contrast with an average current account deficit of $114 during the two preceding years. The rapid rise in oil exports and other receipts (chiefly Aramco royalties and the pilgrimage traffic) of 17.4 per cent in 1970 exceeded the rise in investment income payments and government expenditure abroad, which were also partly offset by the decline in imports. The capital account for 1970 shows an inflow of direct investment capital of $3 million plus $101 million in suppliers' credits, which were largely offset by an increase in the foreign exchange reserves of SAMA and the commercial banks plus errors and omissions representing an unrecorded excess of payments over receipts.

FINANCE

The unit of currency is the riyal, subdivided into 20 qursh and 100 halalah. Halalah coins were first issued in December 1972, and qursh coins are gradually being withdrawn from circulation. New riyal notes were introduced in June 1961, replacing the "Pilgrims Receipts" which had previously been in circulation. The Saudi Arabian Monetary Agency, established in 1952, is the Central Bank, its total holdings of gold and foreign exchange in September 1970 amounting to 2,917 million riyals, compared with 2,916 million in September 1969 and 3,373 million in September 1968.

In 1971 Saudi Arabia's quota in the IMF stood at $134 million and its subscription to the World Bank at $114 million. Most of the country's international financial business is transacted in Jeddah.

The largest Saudi commercial bank, the National Commercial Bank, has branches in most of the principal towns. The Agricultural Bank has five branches, and, since its establishment in 1964, it has granted 17,458 loans totalling 69.6 million riyals for investment in the agricultural sector. The Saudi Credit Assistance Bank, set up with the purpose of granting interest-free loans to persons of limited means unable to borrow through normal banking channels, was chartered in 1971 with an initial authorized capital of 5 million riyals.

BUDGET AND ECONOMIC DEVELOPMENT PLAN

A very large part of the government's revenue consists of tax and royalty in oil. Thus the budget for the fiscal year 1971-72 provided for a total revenue of 10,782 million riyals. Of this, oil royalties amounted to 2,227 million riyals, or nearly 20 per cent of the total, while income tax, much of it from the oil industry, amounted to 7,728 million riyals, or nearly 72 per cent of the total. This was a balanced budget and expenditure included 1,138 million riyals for Ministry of Defence and National Guards (10.5 per cent of the total), 5,036 million riyals for Development Projects (46.7 per cent of the total), 1,031 million riyals for the Ministry of Education and Schools (9.6 per cent of the total), 850 million riyals for the Ministry of the Interior (7.9 per cent of the total) and 250 million riyals for the Ministry of Health (2.3 per cent of the total). The 1972-73 budget is balanced at 13,200 million riyals.

The first Economic Development Plan, which covers the period 1970-75, aims at diversifying the Saudi economy and lessening its dependence on oil. It envisages a 9.8 per cent annual increase in gross domestic product during the plan period to 26 billion riyals in 1975. A total of 41,314 million riyals have been earmarked for expenditure under the plan, with projects spending accounting for 18,383 million riyals and recurrent expenditures for 22,931 million riyals.

SAUDI ARABIA—(Statistical Survey)

STATISTICAL SURVEY

AREA AND POPULATION

Area (estimated)	Mid-year Population (UN estimates)†					
	1967	1968	1969	1970	1971	1972
830,000 sq. miles*	7,119,000	7,317,000	7,524,000	7,740,000	7,965,000	8,199,000

* 2,149,690 square kilometres.
† A census was held in 1962–63 but the results have been officially repudiated.

PRINCIPAL TOWNS
(estimated population in 1965)

Riyadh (royal capital)	. .	225,000
Jeddah (administrative capital)	. .	194,000
Mecca	. .	185,000

Medina: 72,000 in 1962.

SAUDI ARABIA–IRAQ NEUTRAL ZONE

The Najdi (Saudi Arabian) frontier with Iraq was defined in the Treaty of Mohammara in May 1922. Later a Neutral Zone of 7,000 sq. km. was established adjacent to the western tip of the Kuwait frontier. No military or permanent buildings were to be erected in the zone and the nomads of both countries were to have unimpeded access to its pastures and wells. A further agreement concerning the administration of this zone was signed between Iraq and Saudi Arabia in May 1938.

SAUDI ARABIA–KUWAIT PARTITIONED ZONE

A Convention signed at Uqair in December 1922 fixed the Najdi (Saudi Arabian) boundary with Kuwait. The Convention also established a Neutral Zone of 5,770 sq. km. immediately to the south of Kuwait in which Saudi Arabia and Kuwait held equal rights. The final agreement on this matter was signed in 1963. Since 1966 the Zone has been divided between the two countries and each administers its own half, in practice as an integral part of the state. However, the oil wealth of the whole Zone remains undivided and production from the on-shore oil concessions in the Partitioned Zone is shared equally between the two states' concessionaires (Aminoil and Getty).

AGRICULTURE AND INDUSTRY

Agriculture (estimates, metric tons): Wheat 15,000, Maize 21,000, Millet and Sorghum 6,000, Barley 13,000, Rice 2,000, Dates 200,000. Other crops include alfalfa, vegetables, coffee and henna.

Livestock: Sheep 3,600,000, Goats 1,900,000, Asses 22,000.

Industry: Building, Date Packing, Cement (703,000 tons in 1971–72), Soap, Sugar, Rugs, Marble, Gypsum, Nails, Soft Drinks, Industrial Gases, Electricity (763 million kWh. in 1971–72).

OIL

CRUDE OIL PRODUCTION BY COMPANY
(million barrels)

	Total	Aramco	Getty Oil	Arabian Oil
1938	0.5	0.5	—	—
1946	59.9	59.9	—	—
1955	356.6	352.2	4.4	—
1965	804.8	739.1	32.6	33.1
1966	950.0	873.3	30.2	46.5
1967	1,023.8	948.1	25.1	50.6
1968	1,114.0	1,035.8	23.2	55.0
1969	1,173.9	1,092.4	22.7	58.8
1970	1,386.3	1,295.3	28.3	62.7
1971	1,740.8	1,641.6	33.7	65.5
1972	2,201.7	2,098.4	28.3	75.0

SAUDI ARABIA—(Statistical Survey)

OIL REVENUES BY SOURCE
(million U.S. $)

	Total	Aramco	Getty Oil	Arabian Oil	Other Companies
1939	3.2	3.2	—	—	—
1946	10.4	10.4	—	—	—
1955	340.8	338.2	2.6	—	—
1965	662.6	618.4*	23.8	20.4	—
1966	789.7	745.5*	20.6	22.3	1.3
1967	909.1	859.4*	17.8	31.8	0.1
1968	926.8	872.0	13.6	34.3	6.9
1969	949.0	895.2	15.2	37.1	1.5
1970	1,149.7	1,088.4	17.2	40.3	3.8
1971	1,944.9	1,866.4	20.6	44.2	13.7
1972	2,779.3	2,677.9†	28.0	68.7	4.7

* Including certain special payments.
† Including $45.2 million for the value of royalty oil delivered to PETROMIN.

FINANCE

100 halalah = 20 qursh = 1 Saudi riyal.
Coins: 1, 5, 10, 25 and 50 halalah; 1, 2 and 4 qursh.*
Notes: 1, 5, 10, 50 and 100 riyals.
Exchange rates (March 1973): £1 sterling = 9.13 Saudi riyals; U.S. $1 = 3.73 Saudi riyals.
100 Saudi riyals = £10.95 = $26.81.

* The coins of 1, 2 and 4 qursh are being gradually withdrawn from circulation.

BUDGET
(million riyals)

Revenue	1971-72	1972-73
Oil Royalties	2,227	2,529
Income Tax (inc. tax on oil receipts)	7,728	9,674
Customs	314	315
Other Items	513	682
Total	10,782	13,200

Expenditure	1971-72	1972-73
Defence	1,138	1,427
Interior	850	1,071
Education	1,031	1,300
Health	250	375
Development Projects	5,036	6,718
General Budgetary Reserve	250	300
Other Items	2,227	2,009
Total	10,782	13,200

DEVELOPMENT EXPENDITURE
(million riyals)

	1969	1970	1971
Transport and Communications	792.3	700.6	603.5
Agriculture, Livestock, and Water	398.8	300.0	230.1
Petroleum and Minerals	56.2	57.7	39.6
Industry and Commerce	14.4	8.7	9.2
Labour and Social Affairs	8.0	8.7	8.2
Education	51.0	33.0	24.9
Health and Red Crescent	13.7	13.5	10.9
Municipalities	300.9	252.4	190.1
Holy Mosques	15.0	15.8	16.9
Hajj Affairs	6.6	2.8	2.9
Information	50.9	53.5	28.2
Others	862.2	1,235.3	1,431.5
Total	2,570.0†	2,682.0†	2,596.0†

† In addition there were allocations of 13.9 million riyals in 1969, 15.6 million riyals in 1970, and 25.7 million riyals in 1971, for projects of public corporations from the third chapter of the budget.

SAUDI ARABIA—(Statistical Survey)

Currency in Circulation (million riyals): 1968–69, 1,446.1; 1969–70, 1,566.9; 1970–71, 1,655.8; 1971–72, 1,788.2; 1972–73, 2,163.9.

NATIONAL ACCOUNTS
(million riyals—at current factor cost)

	1967–68	1968–69	1969–70*	1970–71*
Agriculture, Forestry, Fishing	895.7	974.4	1,002.7	1,035.9
Mining and Quarrying:				
Crude petroleum and natural gas	6,772.9	7,201.0	8,238.0	11,350.3
Other mining and quarrying	39.8	41.9	42.1	44.5
Manufacturing:				
Petroleum refining	870.6	946.5	1,207.8	1,440.5
Other manufacturing	265.6	299.0	332.0	371.8
Construction	796.1	837.8	841.4	890.0
Electricity, Gas, Water, and Sanitary Services	181.3	196.0	212.5	231.6
Transport, Storage and Communications	1,060.1	1,198.1	1,307.1	1,433.7
Wholesale and Retail Trade	988.9	1,180.4	1,252.3	1,322.7
Banking, Insurance, and Real Estate	93.0	102.7	109.7	117.7
Ownership of Dwellings	545.0	601.0	654.5	712.8
Public Administration and Defence	1,096.3	1,195.1	1,247.0	1,313.3
Services:				
Education	413.1	426.0	453.2	508.8
Medical and health	135.4	140.2	141.2	143.8
Other services	304.3	320.6	329.6	358.9
Gross Domestic Product at Factor Cost	14,458.1	15,660.7	17,371.1	21,276.3
less: Net factor income payments to the rest of the world	3,204.0	3,390.3	3,961.0	5,346.6
Gross National Product	11,254.1	12,270.4	13,410.1	15,929.7
less: Depreciation	1,125.4	1,227.0	1,341.0	1,593.0
National Income	10,128.7	11,043.4	12,069.1	14,336.7

* Provisional.

BALANCE OF PAYMENTS
(million U.S. $—estimates)

	1969	1970	1971
Receipts:			
Exports, f.o.b.	1,845	2,180	3,622
Oil royalties from companies other than Aramco	54	66	78
Pilgrimage	94	102	114
Miscellaneous	70	90	105
Total	2,063	2,438	3,919
Payments:			
Imports, c.i.f.	893	891	988
Non-monetary gold	13	18	21
Investment income payments	721	893	1,433
Government expenditures abroad, n.i.e.	278*	268*	274*
Travel and personal transportation, n.i.e.	104	123	144
Tapline expenditures abroad	23	16	47
Other services	150	166	147
Total	2,182	2,375	3,054
Current Balance	−119	63	865
Capital and Financing Account:			
Direct investment capital	−5	−3	−109
Other capital	−10	−99	138
Gold, foreign exchange holdings, and investments of SAMA	−127	87	794
Commercial banks' net foreign position	10	23	23
Errors and Omissions	13	55	19
Capital Balance	−119	63	865

* Includes $140 million in aid paid to Arab countries.

SAUDI ARABIA—(STATISTICAL SURVEY)

EXTERNAL TRADE
(million riyals—Muslim calendar)

	1966–67	1967–68	1968–69	1969–70	1970–71*
Imports	2,288	2,212	2,804	3,213	3,465
Exports	7,654	7,853	8,953	9,449*	10,600

* Provisional.

(million riyals—Gregorian calendar)

	1968	1969	1970	1971
Imports	2,578	3,377	3,197	3,667
Exports	9,118	9,496	10,907	17,302

PRINCIPAL COMMODITIES
(million riyals)

IMPORTS	1967–68	1968–69	1969–70	EXPORTS	1968–69	1969–70	1970–71
Foodstuffs	666	894	865	Crude Oil	7,087.5	7,596.0	8,222.0
Textiles and Clothing	147	154	157	Refined Oil	1,260.0	1,305.0	1,701.0
Machinery, Transport	709	880	1,022				
Building Materials	199	430	413				
Chemical Products	111	159	238				
Miscellaneous	380	287	518				
TOTAL	2,212	2,804	3,213	TOTAL (incl. others)	8,952.9	9,449.2*	10,600.0*

* Provisional

PRINCIPAL COUNTRIES
(million riyals)

	IMPORTS 1970	IMPORTS 1971	EXPORTS 1970	EXPORTS 1971
North America	575.6	629.2	146.4	733.3
U.S.A.	568.5	615.1	97.8	589.5
Western Europe	1,080.8	1,218.3	4,820.3	8,386.1
Belgium	65.0	90.6	248.2	351.0
France	88.0	78.6	691.6	1,661.8
Federal Germany	312.8	289.0	222.3	577.8
Italy	142.8	161.0	1,178.6	1,767.4
Netherlands	139.7	169.3	992.5	1,568.8
Spain	3.5	4.0	465.7	453.1
United Kingdom	230.9	327.7	827.6	1,510.2
Middle East	636.2	810.0	608.6	805.7
Bahrain	46.8	78.7	511.7	646.4
Jordan	45.5	40.7	31.5	51.6
Lebanon	362.9	473.9	30.4	69.9
Africa	127.4	152.4	473.7	758.9
Asia	610.8	711.9	3,339.4	4,413.7
India	102.1	68.5	130.9	222.1
Japan	314.2	414.2	2,323.4	2,783.1
Malaysia	23.8	21.9	211.1	83.9
South America	1.0	1.0	445.0	973.9

SAUDI ARABIA—(Statistical Survey)

PILGRIMAGE TO MECCA
NUMBER OF PILGRIMS BY COUNTRIES
(Muslim years)

	1387 (1967–68)	1388 (1968–69)	1389 (1969–70)	1390 (1970–71)	1391 (1971–72)	1392 (1972–73)
Afghanistan	5,841	8,744	9,125	13,663	10,744	17,447
Egypt	7,143	12,413	10,875	11,490	29,171	39,606
Indonesia	17,569	17,062	10,615	14,633	22,753	22,659
India	15,826	16,154	16,057	16,470	16,657	18,306
Iran	22,903	13,642	15,132	48,367	30,299	45,298
Iraq	19,475	24,875	24,902	19,482	17,628	24,681
Jordan	4,449	5,179	6,376	10,909	15,933	25,819
Libya	10,444	16,565	13,547	11,835	16,861	23,774
Malaysia	6,236	6,591	8,353	10,361	10,650	10,395
Morocco	8,208	9,449	10,943	10,640	15,463	22,425
Nigeria	10,790	16,177	24,185	35,187	44,061	48,981
Pakistan	25,052	27,402	28,535	38,256	23,344	95,968*
Sudan	18,035	21,649	20,495	14,865	29,004	29,506
Syria	14,521	12,814	22,383	42,329	27,045	31,777
Turkey	41,998	51,055	56,578	13,269	23,922	27,235
Yemen	31,489	51,577	54,658	50,269	60,358	60,250
Others	58,528	63,436	73,554	69,245	85,476	101,055
Total	318,507	374,784	406,295	431,270	479,339	645,182

* Including 6,595 pilgrims from Bangladesh.
Source: General Directorate of Passports and Nationality, Ministry of Interior.

TRANSPORT

Roads (1970): 42,161 cars, 3,833 buses and coaches, 30,662 goods vehicles.

Railways (1966): 52.1 million kilometre tons, 96,000 passengers; length of track 610 km. standard gauge (1972).

EDUCATION
(Academic year 1971–72)

Type of Education	Schools	Teachers	Pupils
Kindergarten	45	192	6,349
Elementary	2,154	19,577	475,007
Intermediate	486	4,193	83,729
Secondary	141	944	23,014
Teacher Training	63	949	14,453
Technical	7	257	899
Schools for Deaf, Dumb, Blind	10	299	1,287
Adult Education	624	*	46,034
Higher Education	19	975	9,471
Night Schools	†	†	†

* Includes day school teachers teaching in other schools.
† Included in figures for day schools, by level.
Educational budget for financial year 1971–72: 1,150m. riyals.
Educational budget for financial year 1972–73: 1,585m. riyals.

SAUDI ARABIA—(THE CONSTITUTION, THE GOVERNMENT)

THE CONSTITUTION

After Ibn Saud had finally brought the whole of present-day Saudi Arabia under his control in 1925, the territory was made into a dual kingdom.

Six years later, in 1932, the realm was unified by decree and became the Kingdom of Saudi Arabia. Saudi Arabia as a whole has in practice been developing, in the last six years or so particularly, from monarchical towards ministerial rule. The power of the Cabinet was further increased in May 1958, when several ministries were delegated to the Crown Prince. In December 1960, however, the Crown Prince resigned and King Saud assumed the Prime Ministership. In 1962, Prince Faisal resumed the Prime Ministership. In 1964 King Saud was relieved of his duties and his brother Prince Faisal was proclaimed King.

The organs of local government are the General Municipal Councils, the District Council and the tribal and village councils. A General Municipal Council is established in the towns of Mecca, Medina and Jeddah. Its members are proposed by the inhabitants and must be approved by the King. Functioning concurrently with each General Municipal Council is a General Administration Committee, which investigates ways and means of executing resolutions passed by the Council. There are also elected district councils under the presidency of local chiefs, consisting of his assistant, the principal local officials and other important persons of the district. Every village and tribe has a council composed of the sheikh, who presides, his legal advisers and two other prominent personages. These councils have power to enforce regulations.

The principal administrative divisions are as follows:

Najd: capital Riyadh. Najd is sub-divided as follows:
1. The principality of Riyadh, to which are associated Wadi al-Dawasir, al-Aflaj, al-Hariq, al-Kharj, al-'Aridh, al-Washm and Sudair.
2. The principality of al-Qasim, comprising 'Unaizah, Buraidah, al-Ras and their villages, and al-Mudhannab and its dependencies.
3. The Northern principality (capital Hayil). This includes the tribes of Shammar, 'Anzah, al-Dhafir and Mutair, the Town of Taima in the south and some northerly towns.

Hijaz: capital Mecca. Includes the principalities of Tabuk, al-'Ula, Dhaba, al-Wajh, Amlaj, Yanbu', Medina, Jeddah, al-Lith, al-Qunfundhah, Baljarshi and Tayif.

'Asir: capital Abha. Includes Abha, Qahtan, Shahran, Rijal Alma', Rijal al-Hajr, Banu Shahr, Mahayil, Bariq and Bisha.

Najran and its villages.

Eastern Province (*Al Hasa*): capital Dammam. Includes Hofuf, Al-Mubarraz, Qatif, Dhahran, Al-Khobar and Qaryat al-Jubail.

THE GOVERNMENT

HEAD OF STATE
H.M. KING FAISAL IBN ABDUL AZIZ AL SA'UD, G.B.E., K.C.M.G.
(Acceded to the throne November 2nd, 1964)
Crown Prince: KHALID IBN ABDUL AZIZ.

COUNCIL OF MINISTERS
(*July* 1973)

Prime Minister and Foreign Minister: H.M. King FAISAL IBN ABDUL AZIZ.

Deputy Prime Minister: H.R.H. Prince KHALID INB ABDUL AZIZ.

Second Deputy Prime Minister and Minister of the Interior: H.R.H. Prince FAHD IBN ABDUL AZIZ.

Minister of Finance and National Economy: H.R.H. Prince MUSA'ID IBN ABDUL RAHMAN.

Minister of Defence and Aviation: H.R.H. SULTAN IBN ABDUL AZIZ.

Minister of Oil and Mineral Wealth: Sheikh AHMED ZAKI YAMANI.

Minister of Agriculture and Water: Sheikh HASSAN AL MUSHARI.

Minister of Pilgrimage Affairs and Endowments: HASSAN KUTBI.

Minister of Communications: Sheikh MUHAMMAD UMAR TAWFIQ.

Minister of Education: Sheikh HASAN IBN ABDULLA AL ASH-SHAYKH.

Minister of Labour and Social Affairs: Sheikh ABDUL RAHMAN ABA AL-KHAYL.

Minister of Commerce and Industry: Sheikh MUHAMMAD ALI AL AWADI.

Minister of Justice: Sheikh MUHAMMAD AL-HARAKAN.

Minister of Health: JAMIL AL-HUJAILAN.

Minister of Information: Sheikh IBRAHIM AL-ANGARI.

Special Councellor to H.M. King Faisal: Dr. RASHAD FAROUN.

Minister of State for Finance and National Economy: Sheikh ALI ABA AL KHAIL.

Minister of State for Foreign Affairs: SAYID OMAR AL SAKKAF.

Ministers of State without Portfolio: HISHAM MUHYI AL DIN NAZIR, ABDUL AZIZ AL KURAISHI, ABDUL WAHHAB AHMAD ABDUL WASI, SALIH BIN ABDUL RAHMAN AL HUSAIN.

DIPLOMATIC REPRESENTATION

EMBASSIES IN JEDDAH

Afghanistan: *Ambassador:* Sayed Tajuddin.
Algeria: *Ambassador:* Mohamed Kadri.
Argentina: *Ambassador:* (vacant).
Austria: *Ambassador:* Dr. Heinrich Winter.
Belgium: *Ambassador:* René Vanhenten.
China, Republic (Taiwan): *Ambassador:* Tien Pao-tai.
Egypt: *Ambassador:* Khaled Fawzi.
Ethiopia: *Ambassador:* Johanes Tsuai Ajzy.
France: *Ambassador:* Georges de Boutellier.
Ghana: *Ambassador:* Osborne Heney Kwest Brew.
Greece: *Ambassador:* Georgios Yannie Kalitsounakis.
Guinea: *Ambassador:* Toure Fodé Mamadou.
India: *Ambassador:* Trotilla Cato Abdullah.
Indonesia: *Ambasasdor:* H. Rus'an.
Iran: *Ambassador:* Jaafar Raed.
Iraq: *Ambassador:* Ahmad Dhafar Mahmoud al-Ghailani.
Italy: *Ambassador:* Massimo Cassilli D'Aragona.
Japan: *Ambassador:* Kanji Takasugi.
Jordan: *Ambassador:* Sheikh Muhammad Amin Shanqiti.
Kenya: *Ambassador:* Farid Mburak Aly Hinawy.
Kuwait: *Ambassador:* Miqren Ahmad al-Hamad.
Lebanon: *Ambassador:* Rashid Fakhouri.

Libya: *Ambassador:* Mohieddin Messaudi.
Malaysia: *Ambassador:* Ahmad Bin Mohamed Hashim.
Mauritania: *Ambassador:* Wild Jado.
Morocco: *Ambassador:* Abdul Rahman Badu.
Netherlands: *Ambassador:* Jacopus Johannes Derksen.
Nigeria: *Ambassador:* Haj Bello Mallabo.
Oman: *Ambassador:* Sulaiman Bin Ali-Khalili.
Pakistan: *Ambassador:* (vacant).
Qatar: *Ambassador:* Abdul Aziz Muhammad Rashid.
Senegal: *Ambassador:* Mustafa Ahmad Cisse.
Somalia: *Ambassador:* Ahmad Sheikh Muhammad Issa.
Spain: *Ambassador:* Alberto de Mestas.
Sudan: *Ambassador:* Al Khitm al-Sanoussi.
Switzerland: *Ambassador:* Max Casanova.
Syria: *Ambassador:* Medhar Bittar.
Tunisia: *Ambassador:* Muhammad Ruwaisi.
Turkey: *Ambassador:* Ciladet Qiyassi.
United Kingdom: *Ambassador:* Alan Keir Rothnie.
U.S.A.: *Ambassador:* Nicholas Thacher.
Venezuela: *Ambassador:* Francisco Nillan Delpretti.
Yemen Arab Republic: *Ambassador:* Ismail Ahmad al-Jarafi.

Saudi Arabia also has diplomatic relations with Canada, Chad, Denmark, Mali, Mexico, Norway, the Philippines and Sierra Leone.

DEFENCE

Defence Budget (1972–73): 1,427m. riyals.
Military Service: voluntary.
Total Armed Forces: 40,500; army 36,000; navy 1,000; air force 3,500.
Paramilitary Forces: 30,000.

JUDICIAL SYSTEM

Justice throughout the kingdom of Saudi Arabia is administered according to Islamic law by a Chief Judge, who is responsible for the Department of Sharia Affairs. Sentences in the kingdom are given according to the Koran and the Sunna of the Prophet.

The judicial system provides for three grades of court and a Judicial Supervisory Committee:

The Judicial Supervisory Committee. The Committee consists of three members and a president appointed by the King. It supervises all the other courts and is situated at Mecca.

Chief Justice, Mecca: Sheikh Abdullah ibn Hassan.

Courts of Appeal (Courts of Cassation). There are several courts of appeal in Hijaz and Najd, having jurisdiction to hear appeals from the *Mahkamat al-Sharia al-Koubra*.

Mahkamat al-Sharia al-Koubra. The competence of these courts extends to all cases not covered by the above. They are situated in Mecca, Medina and Jeddah. Appeal may be made to the Courts of Cassation.

Mahkamat al-Omour al Mosta'jalah. These courts, which are held throughout the country, deal with cases of minor misdemeanours and actions in which the value does not exceed S.R. 30. Other branches of these courts deal exclusively with affairs of the Bedouin tribes with the same competence. The decisions of these courts are final.

RELIGION

Arabia is the centre of the Islamic faith and includes the holy cities of Mecca and Medina. Except in the Eastern Province, where a large number of people follow Shi'a rites, the majority of the population are of the Sunni faith. The last fifty years have seen the rise of the Wahhabi sect, who originated in the eighteenth century, but first became unified and influential under their late leader King Ibn Saud. They are now the keepers of the holy places and control the pilgrimage to Mecca.

Mecca: Birthplace of the Prophet Muhammad, seat of the Great Mosque and Shrine of Ka'ba visited by a million Muslims annually.

Medina: Burial place of Muhammad, second sacred city of Islam.

Chief Qadi and Grand Mufti: (Vacant).

THE PRESS

Since 1964 most newspapers and periodicals have been published by press organizations administered by boards of directors with full autonomous powers, in accordance with the provisions of the Press Law. These organizations, which took over from small private firms, are privately owned by groups of individuals widely experienced in newspaper publishing and administration (see Publishers).

There are also a number of popular periodicals published by the government and by the Arabian American Oil Co. and distributed free of charge. The press is subject to no legal restriction affecting freedom of expression or the coverage of news.

DAILIES

al-Bilad: King Abdul Aziz St., Jeddah; f. 1934; Arabic; published by al-Bilad Publishing Corporation; Editor ABDULMAJID AL-SHUBUKSHI; circ. 20,000.

al-Medina al-Munwara: Jeddah, P.O.B. 807; f. 1937; Arabic; published by al-Medina Publishing Organization; Editor OSMAN HAFEZ; circ. 20,000.

al-Nadwah: Mecca; f. 1958; Arabic; published by Mecca Press and Information Organization; Editor HAMED MUTAWI'E; circ. 10,000.

Replica: P.O.B. 2043, Jeddah; English; daily newsletter from Saudi newspapers and broadcasting service.

al-Riyadh: P.O.B. 851, Riyadh; Arabic; published by Yamamah Press Organization; Editor AHMED HOSHAN; circ. 10,000.

al Ukadh: Jeddah; circ. 3,500.

WEEKLIES

Akhbar al-Dhahran (*Dhahran News*): Dammam; f. 1958; Editor 'ABD AL-AZIZ AL-ISA; circ. 1,500.

al-Dawa: Riyadh; Arabic.

al-Jazirah: P.O.B. 354, Apt. 88, Municipality Bldg., Safat, Riyadh; Arabic; circ. 5,000.

al-Khalij al-'Arabi (*The Arabian Gulf*): Al-Khobar; f. 1958; Editor 'ABD ALLAH SHUBAT; circ. 1,200.

Arabian Sun: Aramco, Dhahran; English; published by the Arabian American Oil Co.

News from Saudi Arabia: Press Dept., Ministry of Information, Jeddah; f. 1961; news bulletin; English; Editor IZZAT MUFTI; circ. 22,000.

News of the Muslim World: Mecca; English and Arabic; published by Muslim World League; Editor FUAD SHAKER.

Oil Caravan Weekly: Aramco, Dhahran; Arabic; published by the Arabian American Oil Co.

al-Qasim: Riyadh; f. 1959; Editor 'ABD ALLAH AL SANE'; circ. 1,000.

Quraish: Mecca; f. 1959; Editor AHMED SIBA'I; circ. 1,000.

al-Ra'id: Jeddah; f. 1959; Editor 'ABDUL-FATTAH ABU MADYAN; circ. 2,000.

al-Riyadhah: Mecca; f. 1960; for young men; Editor MUHAMMAD 'ABD ALLAH MALIBARI; circ. 500.

Umm al-Qura: Mecca; f. 1924; Editor ABDUL RAHMAN SHIBANI; published by the Government; circ. 5,000.

al-Yamamah: Riyadh; f. 1952; Dir. AHMED EL-HOSHAN; circ. 1,000.

al-Yaum (*Today*): P.O.B. 565, Dammam; f. 1965; Dir. ABDUL AZIZ AL-TURKY.

PERIODICALS

al-Manhal: 44 Arafat Street, Jeddah; f. 1937; monthly; literary; Editor 'ABDUL QUADDOS ANARIS; circ. 3,000.

al-Mujtama: P.O.B. 354, Apt. 88, Municipality Bldg., Safat, Riyadh; f. 1964; Arabic; monthly; Dir.-Gen. SALEH SALEM.

al-Tijarah: Jeddah; f. 1960; monthly; for businessmen; Editor AHMAD ISA TAHKANDI; circ. 1,300.

Hajj (*Pilgrim*): Mecca; f. 1947; Arabic and English; Editor MUHAMMAD SAID AL 'AMOUDI; published by the Government Ministry of Pilgrimage and Endowments; circ. 5,000.

PUBLISHERS

al-Bilad Publishing Organization: King Abdul Aziz St., Jeddah; publishes *al-Bilad*; Dir.-Gen. ABDULLAH DABBAGH.

Dar al-Yaum Press and Publishing Establishment: P.O.B. 565, Damman; publishes *al-Yaum*; Dir.-Gen. OMAR ZAWAWI.

al-Jazirah for Press Printing and Publishing: P.O.B. 354, Riyadh; f. 1964; 28 mems.; publishes *al-Jazirah* (weekly) and *al-Mujtama* (monthly); Dir.-Gen. SALEH SALEM.

al-Medina Publishing Organization: P.O.B. 807, Jeddah; publishes *al-Medina al-Munwara*; Dir.-Gen. AHMED SALAH JAMJOON.

Saudi Publishing House: 30–31 Shurbatly Bldg., Gabel St., P.O.B. 2043, Jeddah; books in Arabic and English; Man. Dir. MUHAMMAD SALAHUDDIN.

Yamamah Press Organization: Riyadh; publishes *al-Riyadh*, *al-Yamamah* and *New Eve*; Dir.-Gen. AHMED HOSHAN.

RADIO AND TELEVISION

RADIO

Saudi Arabian Broadcasting Co.: Ministry of Information, Airport Rd., Jeddah; three stations at Jeddah, Riyadh and Dammam broadcast programmes in Arabic and English; overseas service in Urdu, Indonesian, Persian and Swahili; Dir.-Gen. Sheikh A. F. GHAZAWI.

ARAMCO Radio: Dhahran; broadcasts programmes in English for the entertainment of employees of Arabian American Oil Company.

There are about 87,000 radio receivers.

SAUDI ARABIA—(Finance, Trade and Industry, Oil)

TELEVISION

Saudi Arabian Government Television Service: Information Ministry, Riyadh; stations at Riyadh, Jeddah, Medina, Dammam, and Qassim operate 6 hours daily; major stations and relay points are under construction to serve all principal towns; Dir.-Gen. A. S. Shobail.

ARAMCO-TV: P.O.B. 96, Dhahran; f. 1957; non-commercial, private company; 12 kW. transmitter at Dhahran, limited range transmitter at Hofuf; Producer S. A. Al-Mozaini; 4-5 hours a day.

There are about 120,000 TV sets.

FINANCE
BANKING

The Saudi Arabian banking system consists of the Saudi Arabian Monetary Agency as central note-issuing and regulatory body, three national banks, one specialist bank (The Agricultural Credit Bank) and ten foreign banks. Charter for an industrial Bank and a Bank for people of small means have been drawn up; both are expected to be set up in the near future.

Saudi Arabia had no central monetary authority until 1952. Previous to this, foreign merchant companies (Gellatly Hankey, Netherlands Trading Society) had acted as bankers to the government, with such functions as the issue of currency being the responsibility successively of the General Finance Agency (set up in the late 1920s) and the Ministry of Finance (established 1932).

The rising volume of oil revenues imposed a need for modernization of this system, and in 1952 on American advice the Saudi Arabian Monetary Agency (SAMA) was established in Jeddah, SAMA complies with a Muslim law prohibiting the charging of interest. Instead, its services are paid for by a commission charged on all transactions. SAMA's functions include: bankers to the government; stabilization of the value of the currency; administration of monetary reserves; issue of coin and notes; and regulation of banking.

From 1959 all banks were obliged to hold with SAMA a sum equivalent to 15 per cent of their deposit liabilities. This figure was reduced to 10 per cent between 1962 and 1966, when a new banking law came into force, which reintroduced the 15 per cent level. This could, however, be varied, at the Agency's discretion within the limits of 10 and 17.5 per cent. In addition every bank must maintain a liquid reserve of not less than 15 per cent of its deposit liabilities, which may be increased to 20 per cent by the SAMA. In addition banks must be organized as limited liability companies, and may not trade for purposes other than banking. A minimum of RIs 2.5m. equivalent is set for paid-up capital; banks' deposit liabilities may not exceed 15 times their paid-up capital and reserves; and all banks must plough back 25 per cent of profits before dividends to build up their reserve funds.

The intention of the 1966 law, besides strengthening the control of SAMA, is to encourage foreign banks to open branches in Saudi Arabia in an atmosphere of financial stability and assured growth potential.

(cap.=capital; p.u.=paid up; dep.=deposits; m.=million; amounts in Saudi Riyals)

Central Bank

Saudi Arabia Monetary Agency: P.O.B. 394, Airport St., Jeddah; f. 1952; gold, foreign exchange and investments 10,309m. (Nov. 1972); Pres. and Gov. Anwar Ali; Vice-Gov. Sheikh Khalid Mohammad Algosaibi; Controller-Gen. Abdul Wahab M. S. Sheikh; publs. *Statement of Affairs* (bi-weekly), *Annual Report, Statistical Summary*; 10 brs.

Agricultural Credit Bank: Jeddah; f. 1964; cap. 31.5m.; Dir.-Gen. Izzat Husni Al-Ali.

Ibrahim I. Zahran Bank: Jeddah.

National Commercial Bank: P.O.B. 104, King Abdulaziz St., Jeddah; f. 1938; cap. 30m.; Partners Sheikh Saleh Abdullah Mosa Alkaaki, Sheikh Abdulaziz Muhammad Alkaaki, Sheikh Salim Bin Mahfooz (Gen. Man.); cap. and res. 66m.; 22 brs.

Riyad Bank Ltd.: P.O.B. 1047, Jeddah; f. 1957; cap. p.u. 37.5m.; dep. 339m. (Aug. 1971); Chair. H.E. Sheikh Abdulla ibn Adwan; Man. Dir. H.E. Sheikh Abdul Rahman Al-Sheikh; Gen. Man. J. A. Court; 21 brs.

Foreign Banks

Algemene Bank Nederland, N.V.: P.O.B. 67, Jeddah; Alkhobar; Dammam; head office: Amsterdam, Netherlands.

Arab Bank Ltd.: Amman, Jordan; Jeddah; 6 brs.

Bank Melli Iran: Ferdawsi Ave., Tehran; Jeddah.

Banque de l'Indochine: Paris; Jeddah; P.O.B. 1.

Banque du Caire: Cairo; Riyadh; 2 brs.

Banque du Liban et d'Outre-Mer S.A.: Beirut, Lebanon; Jeddah.

British Bank of the Middle East: head office: 20 Abchurch Lane, London EC4N 7AY; Jeddah; Dammam; Al-khobar.

First National City Bank: New York; Riyadh, P.O.B. 833, Al Batha St.; Man. W. L. Roberts, Jr.; Jeddah, P.O.B. 490; Man. M. Y. Wyskiel; 2 brs.

National Bank of Pakistan: Karachi; Jeddah; principal foreign branches in London, New York, Hong Kong (2), Birmingham and Manchester; Man. Sheikh Inayat Ali.

United Bank Ltd.: Dammam.

INSURANCE COMPANY

Saudi National Insurance Co. Ltd.: P.O.B. 106, Al-Khobar; f. 1958; Pres. Hamad Ahmad Algosaibi; Gen. Man. A. A. Algosaibi.

TRADE AND INDUSTRY
CHAMBERS OF COMMERCE

Chamber of Commerce and Industries: Jeddah, P.O.B. 1264; f. 1950; Pres. (vacant); Dir. Yousuf M. Bannan; publ. *Al-Tijara*.

Chamber of Commerce and Industry: S. G. Saleh Tuimi, P.O.B. 596, Riyadh; f. 1961; acts as "arbitrator" in business disputes; Chair. Sheikh Abdul Aziz Muqairen; publ. monthly journal.

Dammam Chamber of Commerce: P.O.B. 719, Dammam.

Mecca Chamber of Commerce: P.O.B. 2, Mecca.

Medina Chamber of Commerce: P.O.B. 443, Medina.

CO-OPERATIVE SOCIETIES

Trade unions are prohibited but since 1962 several Co-operative Societies have been formed by workers in particular trades.

OIL

General Petroleum and Mineral Organization (PETROMIN): Riyadh; f. 1962 to establish oil and mineral industries and collateral activities in Saudi Arabia; Gov. Dr. Abdul Hadi Taher.

SAUDI ARABIA—(OIL, TRANSPORT)

The following projects have been set up by Petromin:

Arabian Drilling Co.: f. 1964; shareholding 51 per cent, remainder French private capital; undertakes contract drilling for oil, minerals and water; working offshore concessions in Neutral Zone and Red Sea coast areas.

Arabian Geophysical Survey Co. (ARGAS): f. 1966; shareholding 51 per cent, remainder provided by *Cie. Générale de Géophysique*; exploration and discovery of natural resources; is setting up a nation-wide geodetic survey network.

Jeddah Refining Co.: Jeddah; f. 1968; shareholding 75 per cent, remainder held by Saudi Arabian Refining Co. (SARCO); the refinery at Jeddah, Japanese-built and American-staffed, has a capacity of 12,000 bbl./day; distribution in the Western Province is undertaken by Petromin's **Department for Distribution of Oil Products.**

Petromin Oil Lubricating Co.: Jeddah; f. 1968; joint venture with Mobil to set up a blending plant handling 75,000 bbl./year.

Saudi Arabian Fertilizer Co. (SAFCO): Dammam; f. 1965; 49 per cent shareholding, remainder open to public subscription; the plant at Dammam has a capacity of about 1,100 tons of urea and 35 tons of sulphur a day; construction and management have been undertaken by Occidental Petroleum Co. of U.S.A.

Agreements have also been concluded with Jefferson Lake Sulphur Co. to set up a sulphur extraction plant at **Abqaiq** in Eastern Province, with Richard Costain to build **a steel rolling mill** in Jeddah using local iron ores (completed Nov. 1967), with McDermot Co. of U.S.A. for construction **of a naval oil installation**, and with United Tankers of U.S.A. to set up **Petromin Tankers** with two ships of 100,000 tons capacity each.

Petromin has exploration concessions in the Empty Quarter (being operated by the Italian state enterprise **AGIP**) and along the Red Sea coast (operated by an American-Pakistani consortium).

FOREIGN CONCESSIONAIRES

Arabian-American Oil Co. (Aramco): Dhahran; f. 1933; present name 1944; holds the principal working concessions in Saudi Arabia, covering approx. 85,000 square miles; production (1972) 2,098.4 million barrels; Pres. F. JUNGERS; Chair. L. F. HILLS.

Arabian Oil Co. Ltd.: P.O.B. 335, Riyadh; f. 1958; holds concession for offshore exploitation of Saudi Arabia's half interest in the Kuwait-Saudi Arabia Partitioned Zone; production (1972) 75 million barrels; Chair. T. ISHIZAKA; Dir. in Saudi Arabia TAKASHI HAYASHI.

Getty Oil Co.: P.O.B. 363, Riyadh; office in Mina Saud; f. 1928; present name 1956; holds concession for exploitation of Saudi Arabia's half-interest in the Saudi Arabia-Kuwait Partitioned Zone, both on-shore and in territorial waters; total Zone production (1972) 28.3 million barrels; Pres. J. P. GETTY.

REFINERIES

The following refineries are in operation:

LOCATION	CAPACITY (bbl./day)
Ras Tanura	255,000
Mina Saud	50,000
Khafji	30,000
Jeddah	12,000
Projected but not built:	
Riyadh	15,000

TRANSPORT

RAILWAYS

Saudi Government Railroad Organization: Dammam; Gen. Man. KHALID M. ALGOSAIBI.

The Saudi Government Railroad is a single track, standard gauge line 610 km. long. The main line, 577 km. long, connects the Port of Dammam and the Gulf with the capital Riyadh. The Organization is an independent entity with a board of directors headed by the Minister of Communications. In addition to working the railways the Organization is also responsible for managing the Port of Dammam.

The historic Hedjaz railway running from Damascus to Medina has been the subject of a reconstruction project since 1963; however, little progress has been made since the war of June 1967.

ROADS

Asphalted roads link Jeddah to Mecca, Jeddah to Medina, Medina to Yanbu, Taif to Mecca, Riyadh to al-Kharj, and Dammam to Hofuf as well as the principal communities and certain outlying points in Aramco's area of operations. Work is proceeding on various other roads, including one which will link Medina and Riyadh, and one from Taif to Jizan in the south, near the Yemeni border. 1967 saw completion of the trans-Arabian highway, which links Damman, Riyadh, Taif, Mecca and Jeddah. In 1971 there were 8,759 kilometres of asphalted roads.

SHIPPING

The deep-water port of Jeddah is the main port of the kingdom and the port for pilgrims to Mecca. An expansion scheme providing for nine new piers for large ships, costing £20 million was completed in January 1973. Yanbu, the port of Medina, has been extended and modernized, with new docks, storage space and a special Pilgrim centre; other ports on the Red Sea are Muwaih, Wejh and Rabigh. On the Gulf there are the small ports of Alkhobar, Qatif and Uqair, suitable only for small local craft, and a deep-water port at Ras Tanura built by the Arabian American Oil Co. for its own use. The deep-water Dammam Port, which was also built by the Arabian American Oil Co. and is operated by the Saudi Government Railroad, lies approximately 12 km. from the coast and is connected to the mainland by a railway causeway. Expansion of the port was completed in 1961 at a cost of over U.S. $20 million. Further expansion is planned.

Khedivial Steamship Co.: Jeddah; services to Egypt.

Saudi Lines: P.O.B. 66, Jeddah; regular cargo and passenger services between all Red Sea ports and transport of pilgrims from the Philippines, Bangkok and Thailand; 2 cargo and 3 passenger ships.

CIVIL AVIATION

In August 1971 the government announced that an international airport was to be constructed near Hail in the centre of Saudi Arabia.

Saudia-Saudi Arabian Airlines: Head Office: SDI Bldg., P.O.B. 620, Jeddah; f. 1945; regular internal services to all major cities of Saudi Arabia; regular international services to London, Frankfurt, Geneva, Beirut, Rabat, Algiers, Tunis, Tripoli, Bombay, Karachi, Istanbul, Port Sudan, Khartoum, Cairo, Kuwait, Baghdad, Damascus, Amman, Doha and Asmara; fleet of 24 aircraft, principally Boeing 707, Boeing 720B, Boeing 737, Douglas DC-9, DC-6, and Convair 340; Dir.-Gen. Sheikh KAMIL SINDI; Asst. Dir.-Gen. MELVIN L. MILLIGAN; Gen. Man. Technical T. MORGAN; Gen. Man. External Affairs RIDA HAKEEM.

Saudi Arabia is also served by the following foreign airlines: Air France, ALIA, Alitalia, AUA, BOAC, CSA, EgyptAir, Iranair, Iraqi Airways, KLM, Lufthansa, MEA, PIA, Sabena, Sudan Airways, and Syrian Arab Airlines.

ATOMIC ENERGY

Saudi Arabia joined the International Atomic Energy Agency in January 1963. Radioisotopes are used in the oil industry and are being introduced into state-controlled agricultural schemes.

EDUCATION

In recent years Saudi Arabia has made important progress in the field of education. Budgetary grants for education increased by about 15 per cent per year in the 1960s, and in the financial year 1972–73 will reach 1,585m. riyals. Primary education covers six years, from the ages of 6 to 12. Many students go straight to three-year intermediate schools of commerce, industry and agriculture. The industrial schools cover a wide range of traditional crafts as well as metal working, car mechanics and electric fitting. The agricultural schools have modern laboratory facilities and testing grounds. Secondary education, covering the ages 15 to 18 is split up between academic and technical branches. The first foreign language learnt is English, which is usually compulsory in intermediate and secondary schools and is often used as the medium of instruction in higher education. Teacher training has received special attention from the Ministry of Education and a number of specialized schools have been opened in recent years. Nevertheless the shortage of trained teachers remains a major problem. At present there are about 27,000 teachers of whom roughly two-thirds are non-Saudi, and despite an intensive teacher training programme, the Ministry of Education estimates that it will not be able to meet its own requirements until 1981 at the earliest. All schools are segregated, and far fewer girls than boys are receiving education at all levels.

In 1973 there were about 9,500 students at higher educational establishments in Saudi Arabia, and about 1,900 studying abroad, about half in the U.S.A. The first university was founded in 1957 in Riyadh, and others have since been established in Medina and Jeddah. There is a considerable emphasis on technical subjects, which extends to several technical institutes of which those in Riyadh and Dhahran are particularly important. Women were first admitted to universities in 1964.

Besides academic education, great importance is attached to industrial, commercial, and agricultural instruction and attention is also given to the teaching of the handicapped. Progress has also been made in the field of evening schools. These have been instituted in order to make further education available for those who have discontinued their education.

UNIVERSITIES

Islamic University: Medina; f. 1961; 57 teachers, 1,007 students.

Riyadh University: Riyadh; f. 1957; 365 teachers, 4,369 students.

King Abdulaziz University: P.O.B. 1540, Jeddah; f. 1967; Rector Dr. AHMAD ALI; 163 teachers (1971–72).

BIBLIOGRAPHY

ARMSTRONG, H. C. Lord of Arabia (Beirut, 1962).

BENDIST-MÉCHIN, S. Ibn Séoud ou la naissance d'un royaume (Albin Michel, Paris, 1955).

BROWN, E. HOAGLAND. The Saudi-Arabia-Kuwait Neutral Zone (Beirut, 1964).

BUTLER, GRANT C. Kings and Camels: An American in Saudi Arabia (The Devin-Adair Co., New York, 1960).

DE GAURY, GERALD. Faisal (Arthur Barber, London, 1966).

DEQUIN, HORST. Saudi Arabia's Agriculture and its Development Possibilities (Frankfurt, 1963).

GHARAYBEH, A. Saudi Arabia (London, 1962).

HOWARTH, DAVID. The Desert King: Ibn Sa'ud (McGraw Hill, New York, 1964).

LEBKICHER, ROY, RENTZ, GEORGE, and STEINCKE, MAX. Saudi Arabia (New York, 1952).

LIPSKY, GEORGE A., and others. Saudi Arabia: Its People, Its Society, Its Culture (New Haven, 1959).

VAN DER MEULEN, D. The Wells of Ib'n Saud (John Murray, 1957).

PHILBY, H. ST. J. B. Arabia and the Wahhabis (London, 1928).
Arabia (London, Benn, 1930).
Arabian Jubilee (London, 1951).
The Empty Quarter (London, 1933).
The Land of Midian (London, 1957).
A Pilgrim in Arabia (London, 1946).
Saudi Arabia (London, 1955).

SOULIÉ, G. J. L., Le Royaume d'Arabie Séoudite face à l'Islam révolutionnaire 1953-64 (Armand Colin, Paris, 1966).

TWITCHELL, KARL S., with the co-operation of JURJI, EDWARD J. Saudi Arabia (Princeton, 1953).

WILLIAMS, K. Ibn Sa'ud: the Puritan King of Arabia (London, Cape, 1933).

WINDER, R. BAYLY. Saudi Arabia in the Nineteenth Century (Macmillan, London, 1965).

Spanish North Africa

SPANISH SAHARA   CEUTA AND MELILLA

Spanish Sahara

GEOGRAPHY

The Spanish Sahara consists of an arid tract of country, some 100,000 square miles in area, which extends from the southern boundary of Morocco along the Atlantic coast for over 500 miles to the Mauritanian frontier at Cape Blanc. Inland it reaches 300 miles into the Sahara to its eastern frontier with Mauritania. Only about 60,000 people live in the territory, most of whom are nomadic pastoralists of Moorish or mixed Arab-Berber descent with some negro admixture. They are divided into a number of tribes and depend for their existence on herds of camels, sheep and goats which they move seasonally from one pasture to another. The only towns are the capital, al-Aiún, and Villa Cisneros. The latter stands on a narrow peninsula half-enclosing the bay of Río de Oro and its harbour suffers from severe silting.

The relief of most of Spanish Sahara is gentle. The coast is backed by a wide alluvial plain overlain in the south by extensive sand dunes aligned from south-west to north-east and extending inland over 150 miles. Behind the coastal plain the land rises gradually to a plateau surface diversified by sandstone ridges that reach 1,000 feet in height. In the north-east, close to the Mauritanian frontier, isolated mountain ranges, such as the Massif de la Guelta, rise to over 2,000 feet. There are no permanent streams in Spanish Sahara and the only considerable valley is that of the Saguia el Hamra which crosses the northernmost part of the country to reach the coast at al-Aiún north of Cape Bojador. The whole of Spanish Sahara experiences an extreme desert climate. Nowhere does mean annual rainfall exceed 4 inches and over most of the territory it is less than 2 inches. In 1964 a vast subterranean fresh-water lake was discovered which is thought to extend some 60 miles inland from Villa Cisneros. Vegetation is at present restricted to scattered desert shrubs and occasional patches of coarse grass in most depressions. Along the coast summer heat is tempered by air moving inland after it has been cooled over the waters of the cold Canaries current which flows off shore from north to south.

Spanish Sahara formerly extended in the north as far as the River Draa in southern Morocco, but this strip of territory was ceded to Morocco in 1958. Morocco, however, lays claim to the whole country. This claim is based on the fact that Moroccan rule was effective over the whole area in medieval times and the claim has been pressed more strongly since the discovery of phosphates in the territory.

HISTORY

Cape Bojador on the north-west coast of Africa is named in a Catalan map of 1375. The Portuguese rounded the Cape in 1434 and two years later discovered an inlet which became known to them as Rio do Ouro, i.e. in Spanish, the Río de Oro. The voyage of 1436 would seem to have been the first occasion when the Portuguese brought back to Europe negro slaves acquired from the Sanhaja Berbers. Thereafter the Portuguese began to penetrate into the interior, establishing a trading-post at Wadan, not far from Atar, in 1487. Spanish attempts thereafter to colonise the coastal area from the Canaries had little success. It was not until 1884 that Spain occupied Río de Oro itself, the site of the future Villa Cisneros, and claimed at the same time a protectorate over the coastal zone from Cape Bojador southward to Cape Blanco. An agreement of June 1900 between France and Spain marked out the frontier between Río de Oro and Mauritania, but the border lands in the direction of Morocco remained ill-defined. Two further conventions of 1904 and 1912 dealt with these lands. The southern frontier of Morocco was situated on the Wadi Draa. Beyond the Draa southward as far as latitude 27° 40′ N. the area known as Tarfaya became the southern zone of the Spanish Protectorate in Morocco. The region of Cape Juby was occupied in 1916; La Güera, in the extreme south of the Río de Oro, in 1920; and Smara in the interior only in 1934. It was in 1934 that Spain reorganised the territories lying beyond the southern zone of her Protectorate in Morocco—i.e. the Spanish Sahara. The region between 27° 40′ N. and 26° N. became known as Saguia el Hamra the main centres being the capital, al-Aiún and Smara. All the lands south of it constituted the Río de Oro, with its capital at Villa Cisneros.

Between 1934 and 1958 the Spanish Sahara (i.e. Saguia el Hamra and Río de Oro) formed one centralised administration with Tarfaya and Ifni, under a military Governor located at Sidi Ifni, the capital of the Ifni enclave. Three delegates represented the Governor in the southern territories and local administration was in the hands of military officials called *interventores*. On January 14th, 1958, it was announced at Madrid that these territories would be formed into two provinces: Ifni and the Spanish Sahara. No mention was made of the Tarfaya region. The two provinces now came under the control of the Director-General of African Provinces at Madrid. Command over all the troops in Ifni and the Spanish Sahara was entrusted to the Captain-General of the Canaries, but each province had its own Governor-General with headquarters at Sidi Ifni and at al-Aiún.

Morocco, which became independent in March 1956, laid claim thereafter to all the Spanish possessions in North-West Africa and also to the Islamic Republic of Mauritania.

SPANISH NORTH AFRICA—SPANISH SAHARA

The existence in the western Sahara of Moroccan irregular forces soon gave rise to serious trouble. These irregular bands, which attacked Ifni in November-December 1957, made raids into Tarfaya, Saguia el Hamra and Río de Oro and also into the northern areas of Mauritania, finding some support amongst such nomads as the Riqaibat, the most powerful of the tribes in the western Sahara. Actions of some considerable size had to be fought near Villa Cisneros on January 3rd and near al-Aiún on January 12th–13th, 1958. A joint Franco-Spanish campaign was waged against the irregulars in February. A French column from Fort Trinquet in Mauritania and Spanish forces from Villa Bens, the capital of Tarfaya, and from al-Aiún converged on Smara in Saguia el Hamra. Further south French troops from Fort Goureaud in Mauritania and Spanish forces from Villa Cisneros drove the irregulars out of Río de Oro. Operations which the French undertook from Fort Trinquet and from Tindouf in Algeria pacified the northern borders of Mauritania. By the beginning of March 1958 the western Sahara had been restored to order.

Spain, in April 1956, had renounced the northern zone of the Protectorate in Morocco assigned to her under the terms of the Franco-Spanish convention of 1912. And in April 1958, after discussions held at Cintra in Portugal, Spain relinquished to Morocco the southern zone of her Protectorate (also assigned to her in 1912), i.e. the region of Tarfaya. Morocco, since that time, has continued to assert her claim to the territories still under Spanish control in North-West Africa. For instance King Hassan II, during a visit in February 1965 to the province of Agadir in the south of Morocco, met representatives of the tribes located in Río de Oro, who, it was said, then re-affirmed their allegiance to Morocco. At the United Nations in December 1965 the Moroccan delegate expressed the hope that the Moroccan claim to the Spanish Sahara and to Ifni might be settled through amicable negotiation. On December 16th, 1965, the United Nations adopted a resolution calling on Spain to liberate the Spanish Sahara and Ifni, and to enter into negotiations which would decide their future. The situation was rendered more complex by the fact that Mauritania had in October 1964 informed the U.N. Special Committee on Colonization of its desire to initiate direct discussions with Spain over the territories constituting the Spanish Sahara—a demand which the Ambassador of Mauritania at Washington reiterated in February 1966. A further complication was discernible inside Morocco itself, where some of the political organizations, above all the right-wing Istiqlal, had long maintained that Mauritania itself was an integral part of Morocco. Indeed, the Istiqlal, during the troubles of February 1966 in Mauritania, urged the government of Morocco to intervene on behalf of the Muslims in what it described as "our usurped province".

In September 1967 the Foreign Minister of Morocco went to Madrid in order to discuss the future of the Spanish territories in North Africa. The following December, the United Nations passed a new resolution urging Spain to organize, in consultation with Morocco and Mauritania and under UN auspices, a referendum which would allow the people of Spanish Sahara to determine its future. The Spanish Government accepted the principle of self-determination, but a fundamental difference in approach to the problem became apparent at the meetings in May and June 1970 at Nouakchott and Rabat between the Spanish Foreign Minister and Moroccan leaders. Positions hardened later in the same month after riots at al-Aiún were quelled with loss of life. Accusations of interference and oppression were made by both sides and in July Spain held military exercises along the Spanish Sahara coast. On a visit to the area the Spanish Minister of Housing declared that Spain would never abandon the people of Spanish Sahara. On the other side the leaders of Mauritania, Morocco and Algeria met at Nouadhibou and pledged themselves to co-operate in the decolonization of Spanish Sahara.

In December 1970 the UN Committee on Trusteeship again called for a referendum in the territory, while in Algeria an organization working for Spanish Saharan liberation, "Nidam", claimed responsibility for the June riots at al-Aiún. However, diplomatic relations have been maintained at a high level between the most interested parties. In 1971 the Spanish Foreign Minister exchanged visits with his Moroccan and Mauritanian counterparts. On each occasion great stress was laid on the importance of consultation in the settlement of all outstanding problems, but no agreement was reached. In February 1973 the General Assembly of the United Nations passed a resolution calling on Spain to grant the territory independence in consultation with Morocco and Mauritania.

ECONOMICS AND STATISTICS

Spanish Sahara is to a major extent a military territory, and policing operations by the forces stationed there account for a quarter of the province's budgetary expenditure. In 1961 the province received a considerable boost from petroleum exploration when the expenditure of the prospecting companies helped to offset the costs of maintaining the province. However, hopes of valuable petroleum finds have been disappointed and the main new element in the economic life of the area is the introduction of phosphate mining. There is also tourism, though this is at the moment on a very reduced scale.

In the Sahara the land is too poor and the population too small to generate any economic wealth. By 1970 the European population was estimated at 16,300 (the majority being Spanish soldiers), while the number of the indigenous population, most of whom have a nomadic way of life, was put at 50,000, though many more nomads enter the territory during the rainy season. The northern part of the province parallel to the River Draa on the northern boundary is fairly mountainous, but none of the rivers is of any permanence; most of the territory is desert.

Settled agriculture is consequently slight; small quantities of barley and maize are grown, but most of the population is engaged in animal husbandry. In 1970 there were 56,287 camels, 145,408 goats and 17,975 sheep. Live camels and animal skins are sometimes exported to the Canary Islands. From Cabo Bojador down to La Güera, lobsters and other fish are caught by the Canaries fleet and sometimes by the Huelva fleet and by members of the Imeraguen tribe. The tonnage landed fluctuates from year to year, but is usually 3,500 to 4,500 tons. At La Güera, the centre of this activity, there are two fish-processing plants. This is virtually the only industrial activity except for local crafts and a U.S.-financed desalting plant producing flavoured mineral water for local consumption. The production of electricity was 5,508 thousand kWh. in 1970. Communications in the Sahara are limited to 6,500 km. of poor-quality roads and a number of small airports served by the Spanish airline Iberia. In 1970 there were 3,289 cars, 284 commercial vehicles and 48 tractors.

In 1961 the restrictions on foreign capital investment were modified and the Saharan province experienced a brief

SPANISH NORTH AFRICA—SPANISH SAHARA

boom as a result of the lure of mineral wealth. Nine U.S. and three Spanish firms took up concessions for petroleum prospecting. However, by the end of 1963 nearly all of the companies ran down operations and the only ones to remain were Gulf Oil (allied with the Spanish CEPSA), Texaco of Spain Inc. and the State-controlled INI. By 1964 60 per cent of the area of the concessions had been investigated at an approximate cost of 5,000 million pesetas, with no favourable results. The discovery of oil in mainland Spain probably precludes any revival of interest in the Spanish Sahara for some time to come. Oil companies were thought to be holding on to the concessions there only to put themselves in a better position to compete for concessions in mainland Spain. The only mineral sources proved so far are iron, situated in the north of the province (the INI, which carried out the survey, claimed that the deposits are considerable and of 65 per cent iron content) and phosphates, commercially workable deposits of which were found in 1963.

The phosphate deposits are now known to be amongst the richest in the world. In March 1967 the development contract was awarded to a consortium led by the International Minerals and Chemical Corporation of America (with a 25 per cent interest). French and German interests took 20 per cent, and the Spanish Government the remaining 55 per cent. However, early in 1968 the American interests withdrew from the project, mainly because Spain insisted on sending the phosphates to a new factory in Spain itself. The Spanish state-controlled company Empresa Nacional Minera del Sahara S.A. (ENMINSA) is now in complete control of the venture and has signed up several subcontractors from other European countries to construct the various facilities required, with financial guarantees provided by the Spanish Government. Desert roads have been cut, and Spain has built a village for 500 workers at Bu-Craa. A conveyor belt has been built to carry ore to the sea. Production started in 1972 and is expected to reach an annual rate of 3 million tons by 1974.

It was announced from al-Aiún in May 1966 that a commission was to be formed which would prepare a plan for the social and economic development of the Spanish Sahara. The opening up of the phosphate mines at Bu-Craa, near the Moroccan border, has increased the desire of both Morocco and Mauritania to annexe the Spanish Sahara. Morocco is herself an important producer of phosphates, and she might expect to suffer commercially from this development.

A potential source of income, which has been exploited only on a very small scale as yet, is the tourist trade. In 1972 there were 21,163 visitors to the country and these mostly came on day excursions from the Canary Islands, for the country has little hotel accommodation to offer. Probably the most important economic breakthrough of recent years was the discovery in 1964 of a vast subterranean lake of fresh water thought to extend some 60 miles inland from Villa Cisneros. Rationally tapped, this water opens up a number of development possibilities. The fading prospects of oil may encourage attention to the joint development of water and agriculture.

STATISTICS

Area: approx. 266,000 square km. (Río de Oro 184,000 sq. km.; Saguia el Hamra 82,000 sq. km.).

Population (Census of December 31st 1970): 76,425, including about 16,300 Europeans. There are about 15,000 Spanish soldiers. al-Aaiún (capital) 24,048 (12,238 non-Europeans, 11,810 Europeans); Villa Cisneros 5,454; the number of nomads entering the territory during the rainy season is indeterminable.

Agriculture (1970): 700 palm trees.

Livestock (1970): 56,287 camels, 145,408 goats, 17,975 sheep, 400 cows, 2,397 asses.

Fishing (1969): Weight of catch 6,661 tons.

Mining: Phosphate deposits at Bu-craa estimated at 1,700 million tons are exploited by Fosfatos de Bu-craa, S.A., a state-controlled company. In April 1972 the first shipment of phosphate ore was loaded at el-Aiún. Production is expected to reach a yearly rate of 3m. tons in 1974.

Industry (1970): Production of electric energy: 5,508,000 kWh.

Finance: Spanish currency: 100 céntimos=1 peseta. Coins: 10 and 50 céntimos; 1, 2½, 5, 25, 50 and 100 pesetas. Notes: 100, 500 and 1,000 pesetas. Exchange rates (March 1973): £1 sterling=144.25 pesetas; U.S.$1 =58.03 pesetas; 1,000 Spanish pesetas=£6.93=$17.23.

Budget (1972): Expenditure 1,214,783,421 pesetas. The territory receives substantial aid from Spain.

External Trade (1970): Imports ('000 pesetas): 388,302 (Foodstuffs 127,095, Manufactures 261,207; Exports are negligible).

Transport: *Roads:* 6,500 km. roads and tracks; *Shipping* (1969): Passengers disembarked 11,229, freight entered 108,423 tons; *Civil Aviation* (1969): Passengers entered 47,064, Passengers leaving 47,821; Freight (metric tons), unloaded 13,999, loaded 16,077.

Tourism (1971): 21,163 tourists.

Education (1972): *Pre-primary:* 368 pupils; *Primary:* 3,405 Spanish, 614 Saharan pupils; 84 Spanish and 60 Saharan teachers; *Secondary:* about 1,500 pupils at al-Aiún and Villa Cisneros.

THE GOVERNMENT

Spanish Sahara was recognized as a Province in 1958. It is divided into two regions: Saguia el Hamra (82,000 sq. km.) and Río de Oro (184,000 sq. km.). A *Yemáa* (General Assembly) of 103 members (Pres. JATRI ULD SAID ULD YUMANI) and a *Cabildo* or local council (Pres. SEILA ULD ABEIDA) are the main representative bodies of the province. The province is represented in the Spanish *Cortes* by 6 *procuradores*.

There was an election to the General Assembly in January 1971.

Governor-General: Gen. FERNANDO DE SANTIAGO Y DÍAZ DE MENDIVIL.

Director-General for Promotion of the Sahara: D. EDUARDO JUNCO MENDOZA (resident in Madrid).

Religion: Muslim; the Europeans are nearly all Catholics.

Radio: *Radio Sahara*, Apt. 7, al-Aiún; government station; Dir. EDUARDO GONZÁLEZ RUIZ.

Radio Villa Cisneros, Apt. 60, Villa Cisneros; government station; Dir. E. PONCE RAMOS.

Television: retransmission stations in al-Aiún and Smara.

Transport: Airfields at Villa Cisneros (the chief seaport) and al-Aiún, with passenger services to Madrid and Las Palmas operated by Iberia. There are also landing-strips at La Güera, Hagunía, Auserd, Aargub, Bir Enzarán, Anech and Agracha. A 3,500 metre loading pier has been constructed at al-Aiún to handle phosphate exports. A 60-mile conveyor brings the phosphate ores from the mines at Bu-craa.

Ceuta and Melilla

GEOGRAPHY

CEUTA

The ancient port and walled city of Ceuta is situated on a rocky promontory in north-western Morocco overlooking the Strait of Gibraltar. It was retained by Spain as a *plaza de soberania* when Morocco became independent in 1956 and is administered as part of Cádiz Province. The Portuguese first established a fort at Ceuta in 1415 and it was ceded to Spain by Portugal in 1668. It developed as a military and administrative centre for the former Spanish Protectorate in Morocco and now functions as a bunkering and fishing port. In 1971 its population was 66,900.

MELILLA

Melilla is situated on a small peninsula jutting out into the Mediterranean in north-eastern Morocco. It was retained by Spain as a *plaza de soberania* when Morocco became independent in 1956 and is administered from Málaga. It was annexed by Spain in 1471 and served as a military stronghold up to the present. In 1971 it had a population of 64,307 and it is an active port which exports over 1 million tons of iron ore annually from mines inland at Kelata, Morocco.

PEÑÓN DE VELEZ, PEÑÓN DE ALHUCEMAS AND CHAFARINAS

These three rocky islets, situated respectively just west and east of Alhucemas and east of Melilla off the north coast of Morocco, are governed as integral parts of Spain.

HISTORY

Ceuta, Melilla and the island dependencies are known as the Plazas de Soberanía—i.e. *presidios*, or fortified enclaves, over which Spain has full sovereign rights. Children born in these dependencies, whether Christian or Muslim, are Spanish citizens and subjects. Both Ceuta and Melilla have municipal councils (*ayuntamientos*). Since Morocco became independent in 1956, supreme civil power in the *presidios* has rested in the hands of the Governor-General of the Plazas de Soberanía, who is himself responsible to the Directorate-General of African Possessions. In respect of ecclesiastical and judicial affairs Ceuta is integrated with the province of Cádiz, and Melilla with the province of Málaga in Spain.

Morocco, since 1956, has laid claim on a number of occasions to the Spanish possessions in North-West Africa. Spain, indeed, renounced in April 1956 the protectorate in northern Morocco which had been assigned to her under the terms of the Franco-Spanish convention of November 1912. No mention was made, however, of Melilla. Two years later, in April 1958, after discussions held at Cintra in Portugal, Spain handed over the protectorate in southern Morocco (sometimes known as Tarfaya) which had also been allotted to her in 1912. Recent events have made it clear that Spain would be most reluctant to cede Ceuta and Melilla—towns which she has now held for some centuries and which are largely Spanish in population and character. The Moroccan government has drawn a parallel with the situation in Gibraltar and pointed to the apparent inconsistency in the policies of the Spanish government. However, Moroccan attention is now focused on the much more important Saharan territory ruled by Spain.

CEUTA

Ceuta is situated on the African shore opposite Gibraltar, the Straits being here about 16 miles wide. The Portuguese took Ceuta in 1415. On the union of the crowns of Spain and Portugal in 1580 Ceuta passed under Spanish rule and in 1694, when Portugal was formally separated from Spain, asked to remain under Spanish control. During the sixteenth, seventeenth and eighteenth centuries Ceuta had to endure a number of sieges at the hands of the Muslims. Ahmad Gailan, a chieftain in northern Morocco, blockaded the town in 1648–55. The Sultan of Morocco, Mulai Ismail (1672–1727), attacked Ceuta in 1674, 1680 and 1694, after which he maintained a blockade against the town until 1720. Ahmad Ali al-Rifi, a chieftain from northern Morocco, made yet another unsuccessful assault in 1732. A pact of friendship and commerce was negotiated between Spain and Morocco at Aranjuez in 1780, a peaceful agreement following in the next year over the boundaries of the Ceuta enclave. There was in 1844–45 a sharp dispute once more about the precise limits of Ceuta. Further disagreement in 1859 led to the war of 1860. Spanish forces, after an engagement at Los Castillejos, seized Tetuán from Morocco. After another battle at Wadi Ras in March 1860 the conflict came to an end. A settlement was now made which enlarged the enclave of Ceuta and obliged Morocco to hand over to Spain 100 million pesetas as war indemnities. In 1874 the town became the seat of the Capitanía General de Africa.

MELILLA

Spain secured control of Melilla in 1496, the town being infeudated thereafter to the ducal house of Medina Sidonia, which was empowered to appoint the governor and seneschal with the approval of the Spanish Crown. The Rif tribesmen attacked Melilla in 1562–64. Later still, the Sultan of Morocco, Mulai Ismail (1672–1727) assaulted the town in 1687, 1696 and 1697. Sultan Muhammad b. Abdallah (1757–90) besieged Melilla in 1771 and 1774. An agreement concluded between Spain and Morocco in 1780 at Aranjuez led, however, in the following year, to a peaceful delimitation of the Melilla enclave. There was a brief period of tension in 1844 and then, in 1861, under the terms of an agreement signed at Madrid, after the Spanish-Moroccan campaign of 1860, Melilla received an extension of its boundaries. Trouble with the Rif tribesmen gave

SPANISH NORTH AFRICA—CEUTA, MELILLA

rise in 1893–94 to the so-called "War of Melilla", which ended with a settlement negotiated at Marrakesh. It was not until 1909 that Spanish forces, after a hard campaign, occupied the mountainous hinterland of Melilla between the Wadi Kert and the Wadi Muluya—a region in which, some ten miles behind Melilla, are situated the rich iron mines of Beni Bu Ifrur. In July 1921 the Rif tribes, under the command of Abd al-Krim, defeated a Spanish force near Anual and threatened Melilla itself. Only in 1926, with the final defeat of the Rif rebellion, was Spanish control restored over the Melilla region. Melilla was the first Spanish town to rise against the Government of the Popular Front on July 17th, 1936, at the beginning of the Spanish Civil War. Since 1939 both towns have been ruled as integral parts of Spain.

OTHER POSSESSIONS

The Chafarinas Islands, lying about 2½ miles off the Cabo de Agua, came under Spanish control in 1847. Peñon de Alhucemas is situated some three-quarters of a mile from the coast opposite Ajdir. It was occupied in 1673. Peñon de Vélez de la Gomera, about 50 miles farther west, came under Spanish rule in 1508, was then lost not long afterwards and reoccupied in 1564.

ECONOMICS

CEUTA AND MELILLA

Ceuta and Melilla, both free ports, are in fact of little economic importance, while the other possessions, with a population of 530, mostly fishermen, are of negligible significance. The basic reason for Spanish retention of these areas is their overwhelmingly Spanish population. For instance, in the Melilla census of 1960 (the latest complete figures available), of a total population of 79,056 only 6,300 Muslims and 3,100 Jews were recorded. The 80,000 population of Ceuta was similarly composed. Ceuta's population has fallen to 66,900 since 1960 owing to the lack of economic opportunities in the town. The hinterland of the two cities is small: the total extent of Ceuta is 19 square kilometres, and of Melilla 12 square kilometres. Accordingly most of the population's food needs have to be imported, with the exception of fish which is obtained locally. Sardines and anchovies are the most important items, in an annual catch of about 16,000 tons. Ceuta is the stronger in terms of fish-processing, and in a census taken in 1955 eight firms produced 1,419 tons of tinned fish; in Melilla the production figure for the same year was 709 tons. The fishing fleet here numbers 70 boats, landing an average of 9,000 tons a year. A large proportion of the tinned fish is sold outside Spain. More important to the economies of the cities is the port activity; most of their exports take the form of fuel supplied—at very competitive rates—to ships. Most of the petroleum fuels come from the Spanish refinery in Tenerife. Ceuta's port is the busiest, visited by 9,234 vessels in 1969, but apart from the ferries from Málaga in Spain, Melilla's port is not so frequented and its exports are correspondingly low—3.6 million pesetas in 1962. But it figures importantly as an export point for the iron ore mined in the Uixan mines of the Moroccan Rif. Ceuta, on the other hand, was able to show exports of 73 million pesetas in the same year. Ceuta exports wood, cork, foodstuffs and beverages. Imports—largely of fuels—were 94 million pesetas to Ceuta and 16 million to Melilla in 1962. Industry is limited to meeting some of the everyday needs of the cities. In both cities less than two per cent of the working population are employed in agriculture. Most of the industry is located in the port area. The total labour force in Ceuta in 1962 numbered 13,080 (construction 2,083, textiles 1,276, fishing 1,384 and commerce 1,768). Unemployment in both towns is about 600-700. Business and port activity are sufficiently high to permit the municipalities budgets which, by Spanish standards, are high in relation to the numbers of population; in 1964 these were 70 million pesetas for Ceuta and 90 million pesetas for Melilla.

STATISTICS

CEUTA

Area: 19 square km.

Population (1971): 66,900.

External Trade: Ceuta is a duty-free port. Trade is chiefly with Spain, the Balearic and Canary Islands and Melilla.

Transport: Much of the traffic between Spain and Morocco passes through Ceuta; there are ferry services to Algeciras, Spain.

Education (1970): Primary: 205 schools, 6,750 pupils; Secondary: 2,206 pupils.

Government: A Mayor administers the town and he is also a member (under the title *Procurador*) of the Spanish Parliament in Madrid. Procurador: SERAFINO BECERRA.

Religion: Most Africans are Muslims; Europeans are nearly all Catholics; there are a few Jews.

Radio: *Radio Ceuta*, Alfau 20, Ceuta; commercial; owned by Sociedad Española de Radiodifusión.

SPANISH NORTH AFRICA—CEUTA, MELILLA, OTHER POSSESSIONS

MELILLA

Area: 12.3 square km.

Population (1971): 64,307.

External Trade: Melilla is a duty-free port. Most imports are from Spain but over 90 per cent of exports go to non-Spanish territories. Chief exports: fish and iron ore from Moroccan mines.

Transport: There is a daily ferry service to Málaga and a weekly service to Almería. Melilla airport is served by a daily service to Málaga, operated by Iberia.

Education (1970): Primary: 196 schools, 6,174 pupils; Secondary: 2,675 pupils.

Government: A Mayor administers the town.

Radio: *Radio Melilla*, O'Donell 26, Melilla; commercial; owned by Sociedad Española de Radiodifusión.

OTHER POSSESSIONS

Peñón de Vélez de la Gomera and Villa Sanjurjo on the Mediterranean coast between Ceuta and Melilla—and the Chafarinas Islands lying east of Melilla near the Algerian border. Peñón de Vélez de la Gomera and Villa Sanjurjo are small towns. The Chafarinas Islands have no permanent inhabitants.

BIBLIOGRAPHY

Areilza, J. Ma. de, and Castiella, F. Ma. Revindicaciones de España (Madrid, 1941).

Boucher, M. Spain in Africa (3 articles, *Africa Institute Bulletin*, May–July 1966).

Caro Baroja, J. Estudios Saharianos (Madrid, 1955).

Habsbourg, Otto D. E. Européens et Africains: L'Entente Nécessaire (Hachette, Paris, 1963).

Hernández Pacheco, E. and F. El Sahara Español (Instituto de Estudios Africanos, Madrid, 1947).

Lodwick, J. The Forbidden Coast: the Story of a Journey to Río de Oro (London, 1956).

Pacheco, F. Hernandez, and Torres, J. Ma. Cordero. El Sahara Español (Madrid, 1962).

Pélissier, René. Los Territorios Españoles de Africa (Madrid, 1964).

Servicio Informativo Español. España en el Sahara (Madrid, 1968).

The Sudan

PHYSICAL AND SOCIAL GEOGRAPHY

L. Berry

THE NILE

The Democratic Republic of the Sudan is the largest state in Africa (2,500,000 sq. km.), stretching across nearly 18° of latitude and from sub-equatorial forest to some of the driest desert in the world. These vast spaces of contrasting terrain are, however, linked by the unifying Nile. Any account of Sudan should perhaps start with the river, so vital is it to the republic. The Nile enters Sudan from Uganda in the south and the "Bahr el Jebel" is fed by a number of streams draining the south-west of the country. Some miles north of Mongalla, the river enters the Sudd region where seasonal swamps cover a large part of the area. The White Nile drains the Sudd region northward, though half of the flow is lost by irrigation in the Sudd. The Blue Nile drains a large part of the Ethiopian Highlands and joins the White Nile at Khartoum. The two rivers are very different. In August the Blue Nile is in flood and, rising seven metres above its low level, makes up nearly 90 per cent of the total discharge at Khartoum (7,000 cu. m. per sec.). At low water the more regularly flowing White Nile provides 83 per cent of the discharge and the Blue Nile is reduced to a mere 80 cu. m. per second. North of Khartoum the Nile is the focus of most agricultural activity and pump irrigation along its banks provides a green strip through the desert to Wadi Halfa and Lake Nasser. The Atbara, which is the only tributary north of Khartoum, flows for about six months of the year and then dries up into a series of pools.

PHYSICAL FEATURES

Away from the Nile Sudan is mainly a plainland and plateau country, although there are a number of important mountain ranges such as the Imatong and the Nuba Mountains (rising to over 1,500 m.) in the south; Jebel Marra, a largely extinct volcano (over 3,500 m.) in the west; and the Red Sea Hill ranges (over 2,000 m.) in the north-east. Elsewhere the plainlands, diversified in places by smaller hill ranges, slope gently to the north and towards the Nile.

CLIMATE

Sudan has a range of tropical continental climates, with a marked climatic gradient from south to north and from the Ethiopian plateau north-westwards. In the south the rainy season lasts up to eight months, producing over 1,000 mm. of precipitation, while at Atbara, north of Khartoum, there is a one-month rainy season in August and only 50 mm. of rainfall. In the north high summer temperatures are common, mean daily maxima reaching about 104°F. in Khartoum in May and June, though there is usually a marked diurnal range (about 68°F.). In the south temperatures are lower (average daily maxima 86°F.), the hottest months being February and March.

VEGETATION AND SOILS

Vegetation types are related to the climatic gradient. Tropical rain forest is found only in the uplands of the extreme south; and the south-east is dominated by a wooded-grassland complex, which merges northwards in Kordofan, Darfur and Blue Nile Provinces to a "low woodland savannah", dominated by acacia and with large areas of short grassland. Northward is a gradation through semi-desert to desert. The pattern is broken in the south by the large swamp grasslands of the Sudd area.

In the south-east areas from east of Khartoum to Juba alkaline clay soils dominate, and the south-western part of the country has red latosols, but elsewhere soils are predominantly sandy with pockets and strips of finer materials along the water courses.

POPULATION

The population of Sudan, projected from the 1956 census, was about 16,000,000 in 1971 and seems to be increasing rapidly. The total is small in relation to the size of the country, but there is a very uneven distribution, with over 50 per cent of the people concentrated in 15 per cent of the total national area. High densities occur along the Nile and around Khartoum, but parts of Kordofan near the railway line, the Nuba mountains and parts of Bahr el Ghazal and Darfur have average densities of 15 per sq. km. with much higher local concentrations. The people of northern Sudan are of mixed Arabic and African origin and traditionally are nomadic or semi-nomadic; in the south Nilotic peoples predominate, the Nuer, the Dinka and the Shilluk being the most important.

The major towns are the provincial centres, with the three towns of Khartoum, Omdurman and Khartoum North forming by far the largest urban centre. The Khartoum urban complex, with a population of about 700,000, is the main industrial, commercial, communication and administrative centre, and handles 90 per cent of the external trade. Of the other towns Atbara the centre of the railway industry, Wad Medani, first town of the Gezira, El Obeid and Juba, are the most important. Sudan has a well-developed railway system which now provides good links with the most populated parts of the country. The road system is poorly developed, and outside the main towns well maintained roads are rare, except in the extreme south.

HISTORY

Muddathir Abdel Rahim

The geographic position of the Sudan, between the Mediterranean-Middle Eastern world on the one hand and Central Africa on the other, has played an important part in determining the character and politics of the country since Biblical times at least. In almost all the contacts between the Sudan and the outside world Egypt has been the most important link, and, especially since the rise of Islam, the dominant one. Thus the Pharaohs, the Persians, the Greeks, the Romans, the Arabs, the Turks and the British, all those who governed or conquered Egypt in the past, have in turn found it either necessary or desirable to extend their influence, if not their power, beyond the traditional boundaries of Egypt (between the first and second cataracts) into the lands which now constitute the Republic of Sudan. Conversely, the inhabitants of those lands, or at any rate those of them who lived in the northern parts of the country, have always had to choose between three alternative policies: domination by Egypt; independence from their neighbours; or conquest of Egypt; at one time or another each of these possibilities was actually realized. At no time, however, could either of the two countries ignore the other—a fact which, with modern Egyptian nationalists, became the justification for making the Unity of the Nile Valley for many years the *raison d'être* of Egyptian foreign policy.

ANCIENT AND MEDIEVAL

From the time of Tuthmosis I (1530–1520 B.C.) until the eighth century B.C. northern Cush (as the area as far as the Gezira was called in ancient times) was, for the most part, under the effective control of the Pharaohs. And even after the political supremacy of the Pharaohs had been completely shaken off the Cushites continued to be so thoroughly Egyptianized that, at times, they regarded themselves as the champions of true Egyptian culture.

The political mastery of the Pharaohs in Cush gradually diminished from the tenth century onwards, and by 725 B.C. the balance of power was finally turned by a series of competent Cushite leaders who established themselves as the twenty-fifth Pharaonic dynasty. The most renowned Pharaoh of this Cushite dynasty was Tirhaka (688–663 B.C.) under whose leadership the empire extended from Cush to Syria and whose wars in Syria and Judea are recorded in the Bible. Tirhaka's empire, however, did not last long; a number of setbacks led to his final defeat by the Assyrians in 666 B.C. The kingdom of Cush survived for a thousand years, during which it expanded to the south, the capital being transferred from Napata, near the fourth cataract, to Meroe, near Kaboshiya, about 100 miles north of Khartoum. But under the pressure of Nubian migrants from the south-west and the new power of Axum in the east, the Meroitic kingdom declined and there was little of its former glory left when the first Christian king of Axum raided the Nile valley in A.D. 350.

From this cataclysm emerged three Nuba kingdoms into which Christianity was introduced from Egypt under the patronage of the Empress Theodora early in the sixth century A.D.

By A.D. 639, when the Arab Muslims invaded Egypt, two Christian Nuba kingdoms occupied approximately the territory formerly covered by the Meroitic realm. With the more northerly of these the Arab invaders made a treaty which subsisted for six hundred years. There was little Arab penetration into the Nuba country and the Sudan as a whole until the rise in Egypt of the Bahri Mamluk Sultans about A.D. 1250. These both encouraged southern emigration by the Bedouin and interfered in the politics of the northern Nuba Kingdom, which eventually disintegrated through Arab infiltration and intermarriage. The more southerly kingdom survived until A.D. 1504, when it was overthrown by the invasion of Negroid newcomers from the south called the Funj, who also defeated the infiltrating Arabs.

The Islamic Sultanate of The Funj, otherwise known as "the Black Sultanate", was, in effect, a confederation of smaller Sultanates or tribal chieftainships, each ruled by a "mek", or prince, who owed allegiance to the Sultan at Sennar, the new capital city on the Blue Nile, about 170 miles south of Khartoum. The authority of the Sultan at Sennar was recognized throughout the former lands of Cush and Nubia, including the Gezira, but was contested in Kordofan by the dynasty of Sultan Suleiman Solong, which established itself in Darfur in 1596. Largely as a result of internecine warfare and wars with the Furs in the west and the Abyssinians in the east the energies of the Funj were sapped and, by the nineteenth century, when Muhammad Ali Pasha of Egypt challenged them, their Sultanate was already in decline.

THE NINETEENTH CENTURY

Muhammad Ali had two main objectives in the Sudan: gold and slaves, both of which he needed in order to build an Egyptian-Arab empire independent of that of the Sultan in Istanbul. His ambitions in this respect were frustrated by the European powers and his dreams about gold were proved to be false. But Muhammad Ali did succeed in establishing an empire in the Nile Valley which lasted from 1821, when the last of the kings of Sennar surrendered, until 1885 when Khartoum fell to the Mahdi. Kordofan and Darfur were subsequently added to Sennar and, under his successors, principally Khedive Ismail, the boundaries of the empire were extended to the Great Lakes, and by 1877 the Somali coast as far as Ras Hofun was also recognized as Egyptian territory under the suzerainty of the Sultan.

Within this vast but loosely organized empire the Sudan was, at first, viewed as a province of Egypt but its administration, centred on the new capital of Khartoum, was afterwards decentralized and put under a Hakimdar (or Governor General) to whom provincial governors were responsible. And the provinces were likewise divided into smaller units which tended to follow the traditional tribal and territorial boundaries of the Funj period. The personnel of the new regime was a mixture of Circassian, Turkish, European and Armenian officers of the Ottoman-Egyptian army who were assisted, especially at the lower levels, by Sudanese sheikhs and tribal leaders.

Like its counterparts in other parts of the later Ottoman empire the Sudan administration was corrupt and far from efficient. Its difficulties, arising from the general malaise of the declining empire, were further accentuated, on the one hand by frequent and arbitrary interference from Cairo and, on the other, by the policy of rapid but poorly organized expansion which was followed by Muhammad Ali's successors, especially Khedive Ismail. Ismail furthermore was determined to abolish slavery in his own lifetime. Slavery had been part of the social system throughout the Nile Valley including the southern Sudan. But trading rights in the newly opened south had been sold to armed adventurers, and searching for slaves was carried to extremes which were in many cases reminiscent of the barbarities of the triangular slave trade. Ismail hoped to mitigate these evils by administrative means and through the agency of European expatriates such as Sir Samuel Baker and General Charles Gordon. But the violent methods used by these men in order to abolish the slave trade alienated large sections of the population, caused considerable social and economic dislocation and to that extent weakened the government's control over the country and played into the hands of the Sudanese religious rebel Muhammad Ahmed Abdulla. In March 1881, Abdulla declared that he was the Mahdi and called upon the people to rally with him against the Turks and for the reformation of Islam. This was not, at first, taken seriously by the government. The Mahdi on the other hand showed remarkable skill in manoeuvre and organization, and under his able leadership the apparently minor rebellion was rapidly transferred into a nation-wide "jihad" which by January 1885 resulted in the fall of Khartoum. Thus began a new chapter in the history of the country during which the Sudan was governed by Sudanese; first under the Mahdi and after his death in June 1885, by the Khalifa Abdullahi whose rule lasted for more than thirteen years.

In the meantime Britain had occupied Egypt and assumed effective, but indirect, control of its government. This, in 1883, the Government of the Khedive, acting on what was officially described as the advice of the British Government, concluded that it could not hold the Sudan against the Mahdists and therefore decided to evacuate the country and concentrate, instead, on the development of Egypt's own resources. It was in order to execute this policy that Gordon was sent to Khartoum where he was killed when the town fell to the Mahdi. The Egyptian nationalists greatly resented this policy of evacuation which they felt was dictated by British, not Egyptian, interests.

Ten years later Britain, in order to safeguard its own position in Egypt and to ward off the Italians, the Belgians and, most importantly, the French—all engaged in the general scramble for Africa, including the Upper Nile—decided that the Sudan also should be brought under its effective control. But since conquest would have brought Britain in direct conflict with the French and the other European powers in Central Africa, the British Government decided that the conquest should be done in the name of the Khedive and Egypt who, it was contended, were now in a position to reaffirm their control over what was described as Egyptian territory which had been temporarily disrupted by the Mahdist rebellion. The reconquest, as it was called, was as unpopular with the Egyptian nationalists as the policy of evacuation had been ten years previously—and for the same reasons. Opposition notwithstanding, the reconquest was executed by combined Egyptian and British forces under the general command of General Herbert Kitchener. It took three years: from 1896 to 1898, when, on September 2nd, the last of the Mahdist forces were destroyed at the battle of Omdurman.

THE CONDOMINIUM

The Anglo-Egyptian Agreement of 1899 laid the foundations of the new régime in the Sudan. The important, but thorny question of sovereignty over the country was however deliberately left out of the Agreement. For, from Britain's point of view, the acceptance, as binding law, of the theory that the new régime was a restoration of the Ottoman—Egyptian régime overthrown by the Mahdi was undesirable because it would have left Britain without legal basis for its presence in the Sudan, while the alternative—the theory that Britain was sovereign or had a share in sovereignty over the Sudan—would have aroused the hostility, not only of the Egyptians and the Sultan, but also of the French and the other European powers, and was therefore similarly undesirable. While emphasizing the claims which accrued to Britain by virtue of her participation in the reconquest, therefore, the Agreement was silent as to the juridical positions of the two conquering powers in the Sudan. This allowed Britain considerable scope for political and diplomatic manoeuvre. Thus, when the French questioned Britain's presence in the Sudan the British government insisted that it was acting on behalf of the Khedive; when the Egyptian nationalists raised the same question they were reminded of Britain's role in the reconquest; and when they protested their inferior position in the administration of the country, though they had contributed the larger share of men and money during the reconquest and almost all the expenses of the administration, Britain maintained that this was only fair as the country was reconquered in the name of Egypt which, however, was unable to govern itself let alone the Sudan. This was perhaps illogical but from a practical point of view, it made little difference so long as Britain was in effective control of Egypt as well as the Sudan. After Egypt's independence in 1922 however, and especially after the abolition of the Caliphate, in whom sovereignty over the Sudan had theoretically resided during the

Ottoman-Egyptian régime, the silence of the Agreement as to the subject of sovereignty became a source of increasing embarrassment to Britain.

The juridical dispute aside, the Agreement established in the Sudan an administration which was nominally Anglo-Egyptian but was actually a British colonial administration. Like the Ottoman-Egyptian administration it was headed by a Governor-General in whom all civil and military authority was vested. He was appointed by Khedivial decree but on the recommendation of the British government, without whose consent he could not be dismissed. Nothing was mentioned in the Agreement about his nationality but it is not surprising that all the Governors-General of the Sudan—like the Province Governors and District Commissioners who assisted them—were British. The British character of the régime became more obvious after 1924, when the Egyptian troops, officers and civilians who had hitherto acted as intermediaries between the British and the Sudanese were evacuated from the Sudan following the murder in Cairo of Sir Lee Stack, the then Governor-General of the Sudan and Sirdar (i.e. C.-in-C.) of the Egyptian Army. The administration of the country was until then based on the principle of Direct Rule and was, especially before the First World War, carried out along military lines. This was necessitated by the fact that resistance to the new régime did not cease after the battle of Omdurman and risings against it occurred annually. By the end of the war, however, the process of pacification, except in the south, was completed, and the last stronghold of Mahdism was taken when, in 1916, Sultan Ali Dinar of Darfur was killed and his Sultanate made a province of the Sudan.

INDIRECT RULE

The evacuation of the Egyptians from the Sudan in 1924 was generally unpopular with the Sudanese, especially the non-Mahdists and the small but influential educated class, who sympathized with the Egyptians on grounds of common language and religion, and saw in Egypt a natural ally against the British. Demonstrations were therefore organized in order to show solidarity with the Egyptians, and a Sudanese battalion mutinied and clashed with British troops. The rising was however ruthlessly crushed. Relations between the Sudan government and educated Sudanese deteriorated rapidly and a period of intense bitterness began which lasted well into the 1930s and was much aggravated by the depression and the subsequent retrenchment of salaries.

It was against this background that Indirect Rule, through the agency of tribal sheikhs and chiefs, was introduced, which soon replaced Direct Rule as the guiding principle in administration. Tribalism, which had been greatly weakened during the Mahdiyya, was revived and encouraged not only for purposes of administrative decentralization but also, and more importantly, as an alternative to bureaucratic government which necessitated the creation and employment of more and more educated Sudanese. These, because of their education, however limited, were politically more conscious than tribal leaders and therefore more difficult to control. Simultaneously with the stimulation of tribalism and tribal institutions therefore, training centres such as the military college were closed down; courses for training Sudanese administrators were discontinued; and harsh discipline which "savoured strongly of the barracks" was introduced in the Gordon College—an elementary institution which had been opened in 1902 for the training of artisans and junior officials. In general, the period from 1924 to the mid-thirties may be described as the golden age of Indirect Rule, or Native Administration; but from the point of view of education—always, under the British, closely connected with policy and administration—it was, in the words of a distinguished British scholar, "a period of utter stagnation". Economically however it was notable for the development of the Gezira scheme, whose cotton crops were largely responsible for the growth of the government's revenue from £1,654,149 in 1913, when the budget was balanced for the first time since the reconquest, to over £S4 million in 1936 and nearly £S46 million in 1956. Today the scheme covers over 1,500,000 acres and is the basis of the country's prosperity.

The introduction of Native Administration in the Northern Sudan after 1924 was paralleled in the south, by the launching of the government's new "Southern Policy". Until then official policy in the south was, apart from the maintenance of law and order, largely limited to the provision of various forms of assistance to Christian missionary societies which, in the words of an official Annual Report, worked for the proselytization of the population and "teaching these savages the elements of common sense, good behaviour, and obedience to government authority". After the rising of 1924 which, incidentally was led by an officer of southern (Dinka) origin, the "Southern Policy" was introduced. It had two main objectives: the prevention of the spirit of nationalism, which had already taken root in Egypt, from spreading across the Northern Sudan to the south and to other East African "possessions"; and the separation of the three southern provinces from the rest of the country with a view to their eventual assimilation by the government of neighbouring British territories which, it was hoped, would then emerge as a great East African Federation under British control. Accordingly, Muslim and Arabic speaking people in the south, whether they were of Egyptian, northern Sudanese or west African origins, were evicted from the region while stringent systems of permits and "Closed Districts" were introduced to prevent others from entering. Southerners, on the other hand, were discouraged from visiting or seeking employment in the north, and those among them who had adopted the Muslim religion or used Arabic names, clothes or language were persuaded, by administrative means (which sometimes involved the burning of Arab clothes) to drop them and use, instead, Christian, English or native equivalents. Whereas education was then stagnating in the north and had so far been neglected in the south it was now enthusiastically supported by the government—but along lines calculated to eradicate all traces of Islamic and Arabic culture, and thus gradually sever relations between the northern and southern provinces.

TOWARDS SELF-GOVERNMENT

As may be expected the Southern Policy, like Native Administration, was most unpopular with the nationalists who, by the mid-1930s, had recovered from the shocks they had suffered after the failure of 1924. Encouraged by the challenge which the Axis powers were then presenting to Britain and by the restoration of Egypt's position in the Sudan in 1936, itself largely the result of the changing international scene, they began to mobilize themselves and prepared to resume their offensive. The Graduates' Congress, representing the *literati* of the country, was established early in 1938. Stimulated by the war, the Atlantic Charter and the open competition of the Egyptian and Sudan governments for their sympathy and support, the graduates, in 1942, submitted to the government a famous Memorandum in which they demanded, *inter alia*, the abolition of the Closed Districts Ordinance; the cancellation of subventions to missionary schools and the unifications of syllabuses in the north and the south; an increase in the share of the Sudanese in the administration of their country and the issue of a declaration granting the Sudan the right of self-government directly after the war. The government rebuffed the graduates by refusing to receive their Memorandum but nevertheless proceeded to react, on the local level, by the gradual transformation of Native Administration into a modern system of local government and, in central government administration, by launching, in 1943, an Advisory Council for the Northern Sudan which was replaced, in 1948, by a Legislative Assembly for the Sudan as a whole. The development of local government, however, was a very slow process (the first comprehensive local government Ordinance being promulgated as late as 1951); and it was in any case peripheral to the main wishes of the nationalists. The Advisory Council and the Legislative Assembly on the other hand failed to satisfy them because among other things, they had very little power to exercise (in the case of the Council no power at all), while their composition, largely based on the principle of appointment rather than free elections, only partially reflected political opinion in the country.

The limitations of the Council and the Assembly notwithstanding, the promulgation of these institutions had the effect of accentuating differences within Congress and eventually splitting it into two rival groups. Some worried about Egypt's continued claims over the Sudan, and feeling that independence could best be achieved by co-operating with the government, thought that Congress should participate in the Council and the Assembly however defective they were. This group, led by the Umma Party, was supported by the Mahdists, and their motto was "The Sudan for the Sudanese". Others being more distrustful of the British, felt that independence could best be achieved through co-operation with Egypt which was an Arabic-speaking and Muslim neighbouring country and, like the Sudan, despite its formal independence, a victim of British imperialism. They therefore stood for "The Unity of the Nile Valley" and, supported by the Khatmiyya, the chief rival of the Mahdists among the religious fraternities, boycotted both the Council and the Assembly.

In the meantime successive negotiations between the British and Egyptian governments led from one deadlock to another and the unhappy schism between "the Unionists" and "the Independence Front" continued until the outbreak of the Egyptian Revolution in July 1952. The new régime promptly disowned the king and the Pasha class with whom "The Unity of the Nile Valley under the Egyptian Crown" was a basic article of political faith, and thus cleared the way for a separate settlement of the Sudan question. Neguib, Nasser and Salah Salem, all of whom had served in the Sudan and knew the Sudanese well, then staged a diplomatic *coup* which put the initiative in their hands.

The British had consistently justified their continued presence in the Sudan in terms of their desire to secure self-determination for the Sudanese as opposed to imposing on them a unity with Egypt which many Sudanese were prepared to resist by force of arms if necessary. Having got rid of the king the new Egyptian régime now declared that it was equally willing to grant the Sudanese the right of self-determination. On the basis of this declaration an Anglo-Egyptian Agreement was signed in 1953. This Agreement provided, among other things, for the Sudanization of the police and the civil service and the evacuation of all British and Egyptian troops in preparation for self-determination within a period of three years. Elections, held under the supervision of an international commission, resulted in the victory of the National Unionist Party, whose leader Ismail El Azhari became the first Sudanese Prime Minister in January 1954 and proceeded to put the terms of the Agreement into effect. The Egyptians had supported the NUP during the elections and it was naturally expected that Azhari would try to lead the country in the direction of union with Egypt. However, by the time the Sudanization programme was completed and the Egyptian and British troops had left the country, it was clear that he stood for independence. Several reasons led to this apparent reversal of attitude. Among these was the fact that the overwhelming majority of the NUP had looked upon solidarity with the Egyptians as a means for achieving the independence of the Sudan. Besides, the official opening of Parliament of March 1st, 1954, witnessed a violent demonstration by the Mahdists of their determination to split the country if the government wanted to lead the Sudan along the path of unity with Egypt rather than independence. Several people were killed and the ceremony to which guests from many countries, including Gen. Neguib, had been invited, was postponed. It then became obvious that independence would not only satisfy the aspirations of the Sudanese but would also save the country from civil war. One thing, however, could still frustrate the country's progress to independence: namely the mutiny of southern troops at Juba in August 1955. This was the prelude to an attempted revolt in the south in which nearly three hundred northern Sudanese officials, merchants and their families were massacred. The disorders, except for some sporadic outbursts, did not spread to the two provinces of Upper Nile and Bahr El Ghazal but were centred in Equatoria. Order was restored in due course but the political problem of the south which, springing from the geographic and social differences between the northern and southern provinces, had been greatly accentuated by the "Southern Policy" of the British administration, continued to present a serious challenge to the Sudanese and the unity of the Sudan. Before they could vote for independence southern members of Parliament insisted that their request for a federal form of government be given full consideration. This they were duly promised.

The agreement had prescribed a plebiscite and other protracted procedures for self-determination. Azhari, supported by all Sudanese parties, decided to sidestep these arrangements, and on December 19th, 1955, Parliament unanimously declared the Sudan an independent republic and, at the same time, resolved that a committee of five elected by Parliament to exercise the powers of the Head of State in place of the Governor-General. Faced with this *fait accompli* Britain and Egypt had no choice but to recognize the Sudan's independence, which was formally celebrated on January 1st, 1956.

INDEPENDENT SUDAN

Immediately after independence the Sudan sought to establish itself in the international field and was soon afterwards unanimously accepted as a member of the UN, and in regional organizations such as the Arab League and later the OAU. Internally, the social services were expanded; the University College of Khartoum was raised to full university status; railway extensions on the Blue Nile south of Sennar and from Darfur to El De'ain were completed; and the first stages of the Managil extensions began operating, in July 1958, with a gross irrigable area of 200,000 acres, the whole scheme, involving some 800,000 acres, being completed in 1961. The administration, despite the difficulties which inevitably followed the rapid Sudanization programme, overcame the increased responsibilities with which it was charged. But financial and economic problems arising from rapid expansion on the one hand and difficulty in selling the cotton crops of 1957 on the other began to embrace the whole country and, coupled with difficulties on the political plane, resulted, in 1958, in the replacement of parliamentary government by the military regime of General Ibrahim Abboud.

The political problems in which the country was involved soon after independence began with a split which took place within the ruling N.U.P. between the Khatmiyya and the non-sectarian elements in the party. This was accompanied by an agreement between the leaders of the two religious fraternities, the Mahdists and the Khatmiyya, which was reflected in the political field by the final replacement of Azhiri by a coalition government which was formed by the Umma Party, representing the Mahdists, and the newly formed Peoples Democratic Party, the political organ of the Khatmiyya. The new Prime Minister was Sayed Abdalla Khalil, the secretary of the Umma Party and a retired officer of the Sudan Defence Force.

The unprecedented coalition of Mahdists and Khatmiyya at first seemed to work reasonably well but difficulties soon began to appear. One of these was the traditional difference of attitude towards Egypt which had always existed between the two but had been temporarily forgotten during the final stages of the country's progress towards independence. During the Suez crisis for example the P.D.P. felt that the Sudan should have given greater support to Egypt than the Prime Minister was prepared to give. And when a minor dispute arose between Egypt and the Sudan in February 1958 the P.D.P. was in turn accused by some Umma spokesmen of softness towards, if not actual complicity with, the Egyptians. Another point of difference arose over the constitutional future of the country. For while the Umma Party favoured a presidential form of government and felt that its patron, Sayed Abdel Rahman Al Mahdi, should be the first president, the P.D.P. and, behind them, the Khatmiyya, could not agree. A third difficulty arose from the deteriorating financial and economic situation which having initially resulted from failure to dispose of the cotton crop of 1957 was made even worse by an exceptionally poor crop in 1958. With the country's reserves falling rapidly, severe and unpopular restrictions had to be imposed and foreign aid sought. But the P.D.P., already worried by what it considered was the unduly pro-Western foreign policy of the Prime Minister, opposed acceptance of American aid.

Elections held in February 1958 resulted in no change and the already strained Umma-P.D.P. coalition was restored to power. If either party had been able to win a sufficient number of seats to form a government of its own the course of subsequent events would have been different. After hard negotiations the N.U.P. and the Umma Party agreed, on November 16th, 1958, to form a new government. But Abdalla Khalil did not view this move with favour, and having been an officer and having therefore close relations with the army, he consulted with a group of senior officers about the possibility of an army *coup*.

MILITARY GOVERNMENT

The *coup d'état* was launched on November 17th, 1958. To the people in general it came as a relief after the wrangling and differences of the parties. Gen. Abboud assured the country that his aim was restoration of stability and sound administration at home, and the fostering of cordial relations with the outside world, especially the U.A.R. For the politicians and those Sudanese who prized the Sudan's democratic institutions, however, the *coup*, followed by the suspension of the constitution and the dissolution of parliament and the parties, was a serious setback. But there was at first no sign of active opposition and the two leaders, Al Mahdi and Al Mirghani, gave their blessing to the new regime on the understanding that the army would not stay in power longer than was necessary for the restoration of stability.

The military régime made a good start in the economic field by following a realistic cotton sales policy which ensured the sale of both the carry-over from the past seasons and the new crop. Loans from various international institutions and aid from the U.S.A., the U.S.S.R. and other sources were successfully negotiated. The money was used to finance such projects as the completion of the Managil extension and the construction of the Roseires Dam on the Blue Nile and the Khashm Al Girba Dam on the Atbara, the latter being used for the purpose of irrigating an area for the resettlement of the people of Halfa, whose ancient town has now been submerged by waters of the High Dam at Aswan.

In spite of these efforts discontent soon began to grow. Prompting this was the feeling that too many officers—encouraged by the absence of democratic procedures of control and accountability—had become corrupt and used public funds for private gain. The result was that when the country was again gripped by financial and economic difficulties in 1964 the public was convinced that this could not be accounted for in terms of the poor cotton crop of that year, nor in terms of over-ambitious economic development schemes; in a word, they no longer trusted the government.

In the field of administration other than financial, the military regime was again unfortunate. In July 1961 a new system of provincial administration not unlike Pakistan's "Basic Democracies" was inaugurated. This was crowned in 1962 by the creation of the Central Council which met for the first time in November 1963. The idea was to train the people in responsible self-government through institutions which, it was said, would be more suitable to their genius than imported ones such as Westminster-type parliaments and the administrative system inherited from the pre-independence era. While this was, to most people, perfectly acceptable in principle, the actual working of the new system—under the close supervision and control of military personnel—turned out to be very different from the professed ideal. Friction between army officers on the one hand, and civil servants and other professional administrators on the other, resulted in the alienation of this important section of Sudanese society. Therefore, when the civil service was called to join the judiciary, university staff, workers and others in the general strike which took place after the outbreak of the revolution in October 1964, the response was both complete and enthusiastic.

THE CIVILIAN COUP

The immediate cause of the revolution was the Government's heavy-handed administration in the southern provinces. This was based on the mistaken idea that the problem of the southern Sudan was a military, not a political, problem and that it was mainly the result of the activities of the missionaries who had participated in the implementation of the "Southern Policy" of the British administration. But the expulsion of the missionaries in February 1964 dramatized the problem for the outside world rather than helped to solve it, while military action against both the *Anaya Nya* rebels and the civilian villagers who were sometimes obliged to give them food and shelter, had the effect of forcing thousands of southerners to live as refugees in neighbouring countries and convinced many that the only solution of the problem was for them to have a separate and independent state in the south. Concerned for the unity of the country, politicians, university students and others started campaigning for the view that the country could not be saved except by the removal of the military from authority and the restoration of democratic government. Orders forbidding public discussion of the southern problem and other political matters were issued but were defiantly disregarded by students. On October 21st the police, determined to break up such a discussion, opened fire on students within the precincts of the university. One of the students died, and thus the revolution was set into motion. A general strike brought the country to a standstill and General Abboud was forced to start negotiations with a Committee of Public Safety to which he subsequently agreed to surrender political power. His decision was partly dictated by the fact that the army was known to be divided, and the younger officers especially were reluctant to open fire on unarmed civilian demonstrators with whom they generally sympathized.

A transitional Government, in which all parties, including for the first time the Communist Party and the Muslim Brotherhood, were respresented, was sworn in on November 1st. The Prime Minister was Sirr Al Khatim Al Khalifa, of the Ministry of Education. He had worked for many years in the south and was much respected by southerners. The ministers of interior and communications were southerners. As a result of the inclusion as ministers of representatives of the communist-dominated Workers' and Tenants' Trades Unions and certain front organizations, the cabinet as whole was dominated by the Communist Party, which had played an active part in mobilizing opinion against the military regime.

After restoring the freedom of the press, raising the ban on political parties, and starting a purge of the administration (which was subsequently abandoned on account of its being carried along partisan lines), the new government turned to the most important problem facing it: the problem of the southern Sudan. One of the first acts of the government had been a declaration of a general amnesty in the south which was accompanied by an appeal to southern leaders inside and outside the country to help solve the problem by peaceful means.

On March 16th, 1965, a Round Table Conference in which northern and southern parties participated was opened in Khartoum. It was also attended by observers from seven African states. The northern parties proposed to set up a regional government in the south which would have its own parliament, executive, public service commission, development committee and university. The southern parties which attended the conference were divided. Some wanted federation; others a separate state; while the unionists (who were not represented in the conference because the two other groups threatened to boycott it if they were allowed to participate) favoured the status quo. The federalists and the separatists eventually agreed to demand a referendum to enable southern voters to choose between the three alternatives of regional government, federation and separation. By March 30th however no general agreement between the northern and southern parties was reached over the constitutional future of the country, and the subject was referred to a Twelve Man Committee, on which all parties (except the Southern Unionists) were represented. In the meantime the conference agreed on a constructive programme of immediate action which included the repatriation of refugees and the restoration of order, freedom of religion and unrestricted missionary activity by Sudanese nationals, and the training of southerners for army, police and civil service.

Externally the transitional government broke with the traditional neutralism which had characterized Sudanese foreign policy since independence, and supported national liberation movements in Southern Arabia, in the Congo, and among the Eritreans in Ethiopia. But this, like the purging of the administration, was controversial and was especially disliked by the leaders of the two main traditional parties, the Umma and the N.U.P., who together with the Islamic Charter Front (at the core of which was the Muslim Brotherhood) formed a front against the more left-wing P.D.P. and the Communist Party. The former felt that elections should be held as soon as possible so that a representative and responsible government could be formed, while the latter, who could not hope to improve their position in the country through elections, favoured the continuation of the new policies.

Elections were held in June 1965. They were boycotted by the P.D.P. but were heavily contested by all other parties, including the Communists. The Umma Party won the greatest number of seats, 76, followed by the N.U.P. who won 53. Neither party was however in a position to form a government on its own. The Communists won 11 out of the 15 seats in the graduates' constituency and had the further distinction of having among their representatives the first Sudanese woman M.P. Other seats were won by the Islamic Charter Front (7) and, for the first time, tribal groups representing the Beja (10) and the Nuba of Kordofan (11).

COALITION GOVERNMENT

It was obvious that the new government had to be a coalition. After some discussion the Umma and N.U.P. agreed to form a government in which Mohamed Ahmed Mahgoub (Umma) became Prime Minister and Azhari the permanent President of the Committee of Five which collectively acted as Head of State.

The new coalition at once ran into difficulties over the southern question. In July there was serious rebel activity at Juba and Wau, and large numbers of southerners were killed in the course of reprisals by Government troops. There were also severe difficulties in retaining southern representation on the Government; two members appointed by SANU, the leading southern nationalist party, were withdrawn when Buth Dieu, Secretary of the Southern Liberal Party, was appointed Minister of Animal Resources in August.

Personal animosity between the President of the Supreme Council, Al Azhari, and the Umma Party, Premier Mahgoub, led to a crisis within the coalition in October, which was only solved by the mediation of the young Umma Party President, Sadik el Mahdi. Government policies meanwhile became increasingly right-wing, as when, in November 1965, the Communist Party was banned and its members unseated from the Assembly. This act was contested in the courts, which in December 1966 ruled that it was illegal. But the Constituent Assembly, acting in its capacity as constitution-maker, overruled the courts' judgement. A crisis in which the judiciary and the Assembly confronted one another was thereby precipitated, but this was finally resolved in favour of the Assembly.

In order to pacify Ethiopian opinion, which had been provoked by the discovery in the Sudan of a consignment of arms from Syria destined for the Eritrean rebels, and the Chad Government, which was concerned about the possibility of a conspiracy being hatched against it on Sudanese soil, the new Prime Minister hastened to affirm his government's adherence to the Accra pledges of non-interference (in the case of Ethiopia signing a border pact in June 1966). This was followed by a number of visits to neighbouring countries with the purpose of confirming the new government's position in this respect and, at the same time, making arrangements whereby the return of Sudanese refugees from these countries would be facilitated.

SADIK EL MAHDI ELECTED PREMIER

In the meantime a serious split was developing between the right wing of the Umma Party, led by Imam el Hadi (Sadik's uncle), which supported Premier Mahgoub, and the younger and more moderate elements who looked to Sadik for more effective leadership. Sadik, however, was reluctant to accept the Premiership not only on account of his young age (30), but also because failure (which was likely, in view especially of the mounting financial and security problems of the country) would prejudice his political future. But events, particularly the growing split within his party, and the pressure of his supporters, finally obliged him to change his mind. After a heavy defeat in a vote of censure, on July 25th, 1966, Mahgoub resigned and Sadik was then elected Premier. His government was also a coalition of Umma and N.U.P. but included, as Minister of Finance an independent expert of Khatmiyya background, Hamza Mirghani, who in 1961 had resigned his post as Principal Under-Secretary of the Ministry of Finance, and had since worked with the IBRD. There were also two southern Ministers.

The new government at once addressed itself to the two major problems of the country. With the help of stringent controls, on the one hand, and loans from the IBRD and IMF, the economy gradually began to recover, and the country's reserves of foreign currency, which had dropped to the alarming level of £S14 million, began to improve. Meantime the Twelve Man Committee had made considerable progress towards the settlement of the southern problem on the basis of regional government. A "Parties Conference" continued the Committee's work and, in April 1967, submitted a report in which it also recommended a regional solution. By this time the long-awaited supplementary elections in the south had been held, bringing 36 members to the Constituent Assembly, of whom 10, led by William Deng, represented SANU, the leading southern party. It was now possible to speed up the process of drafting the permanent constitution and the settlement, *inter alia,* of the southern problem.

The relative success of Sadik's nine-month-old administration, however, coupled with the announcement that he would stand for the post of President under the proposed constitution, resulted in the break-up of the coalition between his wing of the Umma Party and the N.U.P., whose leader, Azhari, like the leader of the Ansar, Imam el Hadi, also aspired to the Presidency. Thus, on May 16th, 1967, Sadik was defeated in the Assembly (111 against 93) and Mahgoub was, once again, elected Premier.

MAHGOUB RETURNS TO POWER

Under his leadership the new coalition of NUP and El Hadi's branch of Umma pursued a vigorous foreign policy, particularly in the Middle East after the Six Days War. As a result, the first Arab Summit Conference after the war was convened in Khartoum (August 1967) and Mahgoub, together with Iraqi and Moroccan colleagues, was subsequently entrusted with the task of finding a formula for the settlement of the Yemeni dispute. Deterioration of relations with the Western Powers, culminating in the severance of diplomatic relations with the United Kingdom and the U.S.A. after the June War, was accompanied by the development of closer relations with the Eastern bloc, and the conclusion of an arms deal with the U.S.S.R. resulted in the lifting, without formal announcement, of the ban which had previously been imposed on the Sudanese Communist Party.

The internal affairs of the country, particularly the already precarious financial situation, had in the meantime been somewhat neglected. The result was that when the Constituent Assembly was reconvened after the prolonged recess which followed the outbreak of hostilities in the Middle East, the opposition under the vigorous leadership of Sadik El Mahdi and William Deng (who, together with the ICF, now formed the New Forces Congress), was able to defeat the Government on several occasions. This, together with the growing PDP and Communist opposition to the Draft Permanent Constitution based on Islam, regionalism and a strong executive on the presidential model, induced the Government to dissolve the Constituent Assembly on January 7th, 1968, following a mass resignation of government members in the Assembly. Sadik and his allies contested the constitutionality of this act in the courts. Before any judgement was pronounced, however, new elections were held in April, which were contested for the first time since 1958 by the PDP now merged with the NUP in the new Democratic Unionist Party. This won the largest number of seats, 101, followed by Sadik's Umma, who won 38, and El Hadi's Umma, with 30 seats. As the DUP did not command a majority on its own, a new coalition, also with Imam El Hadi's faction of the Umma Party, and under the leadership of Mahgoub, was formed when the Assembly was convened on May 27th.

Mahgoub's third government, however, was unable to improve the economic and financial conditions of the country and the situation in the southern provinces continued to deteriorate. Mahgoub, moreover, fell ill and the situation was aggravated by the cabinet crisis of April-May over the reallocation of ministerial responsibilities between the Umma and Democratic Unionist Parties. In the circumstances few people were surprised when, on May 25th, 1969, the Government was overthrown by a group of officers led by Col. (later Maj.-Gen.) Jaafir al-Nemery.

NEMERY'S REVOLUTIONARY GOVERNMENT

The new régime which was thereby ushered in declared that it was committed to a policy of "Sudanese Socialism" and gave the country the new name of the "Democratic Republic of the Sudan". The Transitional Constitution, Supreme Council of State and Constituent Assembly were abolished. Pending the promulgation of a new constitution, power was vested in a Revolutionary Council headed by Gen. Nemery. The only civilian member of the Council, Babiker Awadallah, a former Chief Justice, was appointed Prime Minister of a twenty-one-man cabinet, of whom at least five were full members of the Sudanese Communist Party. But he was subsequently replaced as Prime Minister by Gen. Nemery who was also Chairman of the Revolutionary Council.

All political organizations were later dissolved and several former ministers were tried on charges of bribery and corruption rumours of which had been rife before the coup. The property of certain persons, including the Mahdi family, was confiscated. Following an attempt on the life of Gen. Nemery the chief source of opposition to the régime in its early days, the Imam al-Mahdi (who had for some time been gathering weapons and supporters at Aba Island in the White Nile) was eliminated in March 1970. Imam al-Mahdi himself was killed on his way to Ethiopia, and Sadiq, who had previously been arrested, was exiled to Egypt. Azhari, who had also been arrested, died while awaiting trial in Khartoum.

The régime was now able to turn more of its attention to the reshaping of the economy and the administration in the light of its professed policy of Sudanese Socialism. Considerable attention was given to the problem of the southern Sudan in particular. In June 1969 Gen. Nemery declared his government's policy of solving the problem by introducing regional autonomy in the southern provinces. A special Ministry of Southern Affairs was subsequently created to spell out the details of this policy. The first Minister of Southern Affairs was Joseph Garang, a Catholic southern Sudanese and a member of the Communist Party. Under his leadership considerable effort was directed to the formation of political cadres, but a certain amount of progress was also achieved in reconstruction and development. Several southerners were also appointed to ministerial, ambassadorial and administrative posts.

With growing self-assurance, particularly towards the end of its second year in office, the régime began to reconsider the extensive and controversial purges which had been enforced—largely under the influence of the Communist Party—in the early days of the régime. And Gen. Nemery began to publicly criticize the manner in which nationalized firms were being run.

In the field of foreign affairs, the policies of the régime were, above all, characterized by its militant support for the Arab cause over the Palestine question and by close cooperation with Libya and Egypt in particular. Thus one of the first decisions taken by the régime was to recognize the German Democratic Republic because of its position over the Palestine issue, and to refuse considering the re-establishment of relations with either Federal Germany or the U.S.A. owing to their support of Israel. The Rogers Plan was accepted, the fighting in Jordan deplored and Gen. Nemery headed the conciliation committee which secured a ceasefire between the Jordanian army and the Palestinian Liberation Organization in September 1970. In the meantime closer diplomatic and trade relations were forged with China and, until the coup and counter-coup of July 1971, with the U.S.S.R. and her closer Eastern European allies.

The coup of July 19th, 1971, was apparently engineered by a group of left-wing officers (principally Maj. Hashim al-Atta, Col. Babiker al-Nour and Maj. Farouq Hamadallah) who had been dropped from the Revolutionary Council, and by the Communist Party. Some of the Party's leading members had joined Nemery and apparently accepted his advocacy of Sudanese Socialism, but the bulk of the Party (led by Secretary-General Abdel-Khaliq Mahgoub) refused to follow suit and were particularly critical of Nemery's decision, in November 1970, to unite the Sudan with Libya and Egypt into one federal Arab Republic. A swift mid-day operation, personally led by Hashim al-Atta removed Nemery from office for three days during which supporters and opposers of the coup, within the armed forces and outside, fought each other. Among the dead were about thirty pro-Nemery officers who were machine-gunned while waiting, unarmed, in one of the official guest houses: an act which strongly influenced Nemery's handling of the insurgents after the collapse of the coup. This was partly brought about through the intervention of Col. Gaddafi of Libya. For while Col. al-Nour and Maj. Hamadallah were returning from London to take command of the revolution, the BOAC plane carrying them was forced to land in Libya. They were taken off and the Libyan Government later handed them over to President Nemery who had regained power in a counter-coup three days after being ousted. (An Iraqi plane bringing Baathist and other supporters of the coup to Sudan crashed on the way killing all aboard). A massive purge of communists followed and fourteen people were executed. Apart from Maj. al-Atta, who set the coup in motion in Khartoum, and the two leaders back from London, the Communist Party's Secretary-General, Abdel-Khaliq Mahgoub, the Secretary-General of the Federation of Sudanese Workers Union, al-Shafie Ahmad al-Shaikh and Joseph Garang were executed after trials before a military tribunal.

The events of July 1971 constituted an important landmark in the internal development and foreign relations of the Sudan.

In the field of foreign relations, the manner in which Nemery dealt with his adversaries after his return to power brought condemnation in unusually strong terms from the Soviet and East European governments. This, coupled with the apparent enthusiasm, if not active support, of Soviet and East European diplomats working in Khartoum for the communist-inspired coup, strained relations between the Sudan and these countries, though diplomatic ties remained intact. There was a corresponding softening of attitude towards the U.S.A., though, in view of its continued support for Israel, diplomatic relations have not been reopened. In the circumstances Sudanese foreign policy became mainly directed to forging closer relations with Arab countries—including Kuwait, Saudi Arabia and Abu Dhabi, from which much needed loans and aid were later forthcoming—and with neighbouring non-Arab African countries—especially Uganda after the expulsion of the Israelis by General Idi Amin, and Ethiopia, whose emperor played an important role in facilitating the conclusion of the Addis-Ababa Agreement of April 1972 between representatives of the Sudan Government and leaders of the southern Sudanese Anya Nya rebels.

Internally, Nemery's victorious return to power, followed by his election, by an overwhelming majority of the population, as the first President of the Sudan, greatly strengthened his own position in the country. To reinforce this and, in order to provide the régime as a whole with an organized popular base, the Sudanese Socialist Union was established. In the absence of communists, the leadership of the SSU passed to more pragmatic elements, including proponents of Arab Socialism who would, however, prefer closer relations with Egypt than President Nemery is inclined to accept.

But, by far the most crucial development in Sudan's internal affairs since July 1971, was the conclusion of the Addis-Ababa Agreement. Among other things, this provided for the return and rehabilitation of southern Sudanese refugees abroad, the reintegration of Anya Nya rebels into the Sudanese armed forces and the establishment of administratively autonomous institutions for the southern provinces within the boundaries of the Sudan. (*By mid-1973 much of the Addis Ababa agreement had been implemented. The Office of the UN High Commissioner for Refugees con-*

sidered that by June 1973 the repatriation of about 180,000 refugees from the southern provinces would have been completed. Under the new permanent Constitution (see page 597), *which was ratified by the People's Assembly in April 1973, the autonomy of the three southern provinces was confirmed.*—EDITOR)

ECONOMIC SURVEY

Ali Ahmed Suliman

THE MAIN CHARACTERISTICS OF THE ECONOMY

It hardly needs stating that Sudan is an agricultural and pastoral country. Agriculture, including livestock and forestry products, contributed more than 50 per cent of the gross domestic product in 1962–63. Animal wealth, though very undeveloped, contributes about 10 per cent of the G.D.P., while the share of forestry products in the G.D.P. is about the same. However, the contribution of fish and marine products is only about 2 per cent. The significance of agriculture in the Sudanese economy is also reflected in the distribution of manpower among the different economic sectors. About 85 per cent of those economically active (according to 1955–56 figures) are engaged in primary production. Manufacturing industries contributed only about 2 per cent of the G.D.P. up to 1962–63, while the share of minerals is less than 1 per cent. No important minerals have yet been found in Sudan in significant enough quantities to be exploited economically. In the late 1960s agriculture contributed about 40 per cent, while manufacturing contributed much less than 10 per cent of G.D.P. Sudan not only depends on agriculture, but on one main crop for its exports. In fact the share of extra-long staple cotton in the exports of Sudan reaches more than 70 per cent in some years. Such dependence on one major export crop, with wide fluctuations in price and quantity exported, has caused political, as well as economic, instability.

Furthermore, about 48 per cent (on 1962–63 figures) of the G.D.P. is produced in the traditional sector, and about 25 per cent, it is estimated, is produced and consumed in the subsistence sector. With such a traditional agricultural sector it is not surprising that Sudan has a low per capita income, which was only U.S. $97 in 1963–64, rising a little to $104 by 1968–69. For the last ten years or so the Sudanese economy has been growing at an annual rate of about 4 per cent, while the population has been growing annually at a rate of about 2.8 per cent.

The average density of population in Sudan is low and there is no population pressure on the available resources at present. Open unemployment is very insignificant. In fact, Sudan suffers from a shortage of labour, particularly during the cotton-picking season. Sometimes this problem is solved by immigrant labour from neighbouring countries. The Sudan is a large country with large unproductive areas. Unfortunately it is these vast unproductive parts which are close to the Red Sea, whereas the more productive regions are separated from the sea and from Port Sudan by distances ranging between 500 and 1,500 miles. Their remoteness was a major factor in retarding economic development in the past. For the present, inadequacy of transport is one of the important bottle-necks in the economy.

Perhaps one of the most striking features of the Sudanese economy is the dominant role which is played by the public sector in all important economic activities. The government, aside from its day-to-day administrative, financial and fiscal efforts, owns the majority of modern capital establishments in the economy. In the ten-year plan the share of the government was £S337 million out of the total investment of £S565 million. In the period 1955/56–1962/63 the share of the government in gross fixed capital formation ranged between a half and two-thirds. The government is not only the chief investor in public utilities, but it is the main promoter of industries such as sugar, cotton-ginning, food-processing, tanning and printing. Governmental efforts to develop the country have expanded to such an extent that all large hotels in the various parts of Sudan are owned and managed by the government. With the nationalization of all commercial banks and several leading commercial firms in May and June 1970 the economic significance of the public sector has become even greater.

AGRICULTURE

The availability of water is the governing factor for agriculture in Sudan. In most parts of the rainlands of Sudan drinking water for humans and animals is a crucial factor, especially before the rainy season, when land is prepared for cultivation, and after it during harvest time. However, land does not impose any constraint on the agricultural development of the country. The cultivable land is estimated to be about 200 million feddans (one feddan=1.038 acres). Only about 8 per cent of this cultivable land is being utilized in agriculture, and less than four million feddans are under irrigation. Half of this area is in the Gezira scheme (with its Managil extension), and the rest is irrigated by the flood waters of two small rivers in eastern Sudan, Gash and Baraka, by the flood waters of the Nile and by pumps.

Prior to the Nile Waters agreement of 1959 the distribution of water between Sudan and the U.A.R. was governed by the Nile Waters agreement of 1929, which allocated four milliard cubic metres to Sudan.

However, with the 1959 agreement and the construction of the Roseires and Khashm el Girba dams, the water problem has been solved. Sudan is now entitled to draw 18.5 milliard cubic metres at Aswan High Dam or the equivalent of about 20.5 milliard cubic metres in Sudan, and the way has been opened for considerable expansion of irrigated agriculture. At present Sudan is drawing about half of its entitlement—about ten milliard cubic metres annually—but with the development of new areas along the White and Blue Nile, Atbara River and the Main Nile, as well as the intensification of the Gezira scheme by reducing fallow, and its diversification by such crops as wheat, groundnuts and *philipesara* vegetables, Sudan is expected to utilize all its entitlement within the coming five years or so. One of the main development projects in Sudan is the Rahad project, which will need about four milliard cubic metres of water for an area of about half a million feddans. The Sukki project, which has also started, may reach an area of 170,000 feddans, while the pump-irrigated areas of the Northern Province may increase by about 165,000 feddans within a few years to come.

In spite of the significant role played by irrigation (particularly gravity irrigation) in the economic development of Sudan, the rainlands are more important. In 1970–71 the total cropped area of main crops increased by 4.9 per cent from the previous year's level of 9,820,793 feddans to 10,305,118 feddans. Rain-grown and flooded areas under cultivation both decreased from 7,900,000 and 150,000 feddans in 1969–70 to 2,400,000 and 130,000 respectively in 1970–71. The total area under irrigation continued to increase and reached 2.8 million feddans in 1970–71. With the exception of cotton, pulses and a proportion of groundnuts, Sudan's foodstuffs and most exported agricultural products come from the rainlands. In fact Sudan is self-sufficient in the essential foods: millet, meat, edible oils and salt. However, the output per feddan in the rainlands is low. Rainlands agriculture is a somewhat risky business and to some extent this has probably deterred investment and modernization. The government has already taken steps to encourage large farming units and agricultural mechanization. This type of cultivation is mainly practised in the Gedaref area, in Kassala Province and the Dali and Mazmoum regions of the Blue Nile Province. The total area has increased considerably since 1955–56. In peak years, the total area reaches about 1.5 million feddans. The area shows considerable fluctuations, which are mainly due to changes in the prices of durra. In these areas durra is the main crop, but sesame and American cotton are also grown.

The agricultural sector of the Sudan does not face any serious land tenure problems. The rainlands, in particular, are very free from such problems, and also enjoy the advantage of relatively low production costs. The present government has already started an anti-thirst campaign and has promised the economic and social development of those areas. The Ten-Year Plan (1961/62–1970/71) was more concerned with the modern sector and the irrigated lands.

Sudan has animal wealth which contributes about 10 per cent of G.D.P. annually. It was estimated in 1970–71 as 12.6 million cattle, 10.6 million sheep, 7.4 million goats and 2.5 million camels, although FAO estimates are somewhat higher. Its annual share in Sudan's exports (animals, hides and skins) was about 4 per cent between 1969 and 1971.

In the year 1962–63 forest reserve estates, which are completely owned by the government, increased by 7,000 feddans to a total of 2,574,000 feddans. Beside gum arabic, the other important forest products are the various types of timber which are processed by the forest department of the ministry of agriculture. In 1968–69 the forest department produced 112,000 railway sleepers, 390,000 poles and 4,500 tons of sawn timber. The main consumer of these products is the government itself.

Sudan is rich in fish and other aquatic resources. The inland fisheries cover more than 20,000 sq. km., while marine fisheries extend for a distance of about 700 km. along the Red Sea. It is estimated that the annual total value of the output of fish and aquatic resources in Sudan is about £S10 million. The output of fish from the Nile is 60,000 tons annually but only a small percentage of this wealth is utilized at present. Since the actual output of fish from inland fisheries is estimated at around 20,000 tons annually, therefore about 40,000, valued at £S4 million, are wasted.

The contribution of fisheries to Sudan's exports is small. The share of salted fish and shells (mother of pearl and torchus) is much less than 1 per cent of the total exports.

Cotton is the most important crop in Sudan from the economic point of view. It is the major export crop, the chief exchange earner and the main generator of income in the Sudan. A proportion of it is consumed locally by the textile industry. Its average share of exports over the five years 1965–69 was 53 per cent, not including its by-products, and 63 per cent including them. The cotton is of two types: long-staple varieties, Skallarides and its derivatives (commonly known as *Sakel*), and short-staple varieties, which are mainly American types and are consumed locally. The *Sakel* varieties are exclusively for export and are grown in the large schemes of the Gezira and the Gash and Tokar deltas, while the American types are grown in the rainlands of Equatoria, the Nuba mountains, Gedaref and also in some of the pump schemes in the Northern Province. The volume of output of the American types fluctuates more than the *Sakel*, but is generally increasing at a faster rate. In 1970–71 the total production of *Sakel* was 618,314 tons, while the total production of American types was 108,212 tons.

Durra includes various types of sorghum millets. It is the most important staple food in Sudan and is mainly grown in the rainlands. Sudan produces annually about 1.5 million tons of durra, which is usually sufficient for domestic consumption. It is not an export crop, though in good years some is exported, as, for example, in 1962–63, when 68,635 tons were exported. In bad years the government may need to import some durra. However, there are still no adequate storage facilities for offsetting bad years against good years. So far there are only two grain silos in Sudan with a storage capacity of 150,000 tons.

With urbanization and social development the consumption of bread made out of wheat flour is increasing by about 10 per cent annually. There seems to be a shift in consumption from *kisra* made out of durra to bread made out of wheat. Wheat is grown mainly as a cash crop. A small proportion of rural people use wheat flour in their diet. To meet the rapidly expanding demand of the urban population the government is growing wheat in the Gezira scheme and other suitable areas. It is also paying a subsidy to encourage its production and at the same time keep the price of bread reasonably low. The government buys a ton of wheat from the farmer at £S38 and then sells it to the flour mills at £S28.7.

Sudan gums have been known in trade for at least two thousand years. Gum arabic, which constituted about 10 per cent of Sudan's exports in 1969 and 9 per cent in 1970 was for many years the second export crop, until overtaken by groundnuts in 1971. It is the most important forest product and, though collected in the traditional sector, it is a purely cash crop. It is almost entirely exported, as the confectionery industry manufactures only a very small percentage of it. Sudan is the world's largest source of gum arabic, producing about 92 per cent of the total world consumption (1962–66). Two types of gum are produced in Sudan, *Hashab* from *Acacia Senegal* and *Talh* from *Acacia Seyal*. The former is of a superior quality. The annual production of *Hashab* gum in normal years ranges between 40,000 and 50,000 tons and that of *Talh* between 2,000 and 4,000 tons. Kordofan and Darfur provinces in western Sudan are the main production centres. The chief market for gum is at El Obeid in Kordofan Province, where it is sold by auction. In order to stabilize the price of gum, the government formed the Gum Traders' Association in 1962 which was made responsible for buying any gum left in the market at a price not less than 288 piastres per kantar.* A levy of 35 piastres was paid by exporters on every kantar of gum exported, to enable the Gum Traders' Association to pay the minimum price. This system was an improvement on previous methods but it was not satisfactory. In September 1969 the government formed the Gum Arabic Company Ltd., a public concession company in which government participation is 30 per cent of the capital. The company is now handling all the gum trade of Sudan with the objectives of promoting it, maximizing the returns to the country and to the producer and stabilizing gum prices.

INDUSTRY

Industrialization usually starts in one of two basic ways, either with the processing of exports which were previously exported in their crude form, or with the manufacturing of import substitutes for an expanding home market, a surplus perhaps being exported later.

The ginning of cotton encouraged the beginning of industry in Sudan early in this century. With the expansion of cotton production the number of ginning factories have increased until the Gezira Board alone has the largest ginning enterprise under single management in the world. The processing of cotton has not gone beyond ginning. Cotton seeds are partly decorticated, while the exports of cotton-seed oil and oil cakes are increasing. Groundnuts are also shelled for export. In 1969 24,685 tons were exported in shell, while 57,456 tons were exported shelled. Minerals (copper, iron, mica and chromite), which constitute less than 1 per cent of exports, are exported in the crudest form.

However, the story of import substitution is different. This type of industry, though of more recent origin than the industries which process for export, has made more progress, and is expected to play a more important role in the economic development of the country. With the exception of the soap, soft drinks and oil-pressing industries, large industries manufacturing import substitutes started only after 1960. The government was not involved in any industry until 1959, with the exception of the Zande scheme, which involved a cotton mill at Nzara for promoting the social development of the Zande tribe. From 1960 the involvement in industry began to increase and in 1962 the government formed an industrial development corporation to look after the large factories of the public sector. By 1968 the Industrial Development Corporation was managing nine manufacturing factories, in which the government has invested £S23.7 million. There are also factories in the public sector managed by the ministries, such as the government printing press and the mint.

The first factory to be established was the Guneid sugar factory, which, in response to the great increase in the consumption of sugar in the 1950s, came into production in November 1961 with a capacity of 60,000 tons of refined sugar annually. A second factory was needed to meet the local demand and in 1963 Khashm el Girba sugar factory was started, with a capacity similar to that of Guneid. In addition to a tannery, opened in November 1961, the government also has five food processing plants: one cannery and one date factory in Kareima, another cannery in Wau, an onion dehydrating plant in Kassala and a milk factory in Babanousa. What is very striking about these food processing industries is that the supply of raw materials is not high enough to match the productive capacity, and therefore, the weakness in these factories is not technical but agricultural.

The private sector has also played an important role in the industrial development of this country. In the period 1960–69 the private sector invested £S35.9 million in industries of which £S16.1 million was Sudanese and £S19.8 foreign capital. The foreign capital is mainly savings of foreign residents accumulated from the profits of the import and export trade. The bulk of the investment has gone into the textile,

---

* Gum is weighed in small kantars. Cotton is weighed in big kantars. 1 small kantar=44.928 kilogrammes. 1 big kantar=141.523 kilogrammes.

soap, oil-pressing, footwear, soft drinks, printing, packing, flour, and knitwear industries.

The government has encouraged industrialization in Sudan by various means. The Approved Enterprises (Concessions) Act, 1959, gave generous concessions to infant industries. The Organisation and Promotion of Industrial Investment Act, 1967, has been even more generous to industry. It gives exemption from the business profits tax for a number of years, depending on the size of the invested capital, allows very high rates of depreciation, gives very fair treatment to losses, reduces import duties on imported machinery and materials, protects domestic production by high tariffs and import restrictions and allocates building lands at reduced prices. In addition to this, the Industrial Bank, which was established in 1961, assists in the financing of private industrial enterprises with up to two-thirds of the capital required. By the end of 1968 the value of loans given by the bank amounted to £S3.9 million. In 1972 the Ministry of Industry brought in new legislation to encourage industrial investment. The new act is very similar to that of 1967. However, the Organization and Promotion of Industrial Investment Act of 1967 seems to favour large-scale investment, since under it enterprises whose capital is £S one million or more are exempted from the Business Profits Tax for ten years, while under the 1972 act they are exempted for the first five years and during the second five years, 10 per cent of the profits only are free from taxation.

FOREIGN TRADE

The value of Sudan's exports rose from £S63.4 million in 1960 to £S114.4 million in 1971, while the value of imports rose from £S63.7 million to £S115.4 million. Thus both exports and imports rose by 50 per cent, greater increases in exports occurring more recently, so that although Sudan has faced a deficit every year since 1960, the balance of payments has now become a less serious problem. This must be due at least in part to the Government's policy of clamping down on imports and encouraging exports. There are import restrictions and high import duties on a large number of goods, but export taxes are light and no licence is required for export, with the exception of goods consumed locally and in short supply.

Merchandise trade dominates the current account, while the net balance on the invisible account is usually negative.

Sudan's main exports are primary agricultural products, and since the establishment of the Gezira scheme in 1925, cotton has dominated. Between 1960 and 1971 the share of lint cotton alone ranged between 46 and 65 per cent. In 1971 the U.S.S.R. was the largest buyer of Sudan's cotton, followed closely by India, the People's Republic of China, whose share had doubled since the previous year, and the EEC. In the last ten years, due to the expansion of production in the traditional sector, the relative importance of oil seeds as exports has increased and in 1971 groundnuts formed the second most important export crop with a share of about 8 per cent of exports.

The EEC is the largest buyer of Sudan's groundnuts (60 per cent). The east European countries buy about 20 per cent of the groundnuts and the rest go to various west European countries. Gum arabic was overtaken in importance by groundnuts in 1971 to become the third export product, making up 7 per cent of total exports.

The major imports are vehicles, transport equipment, machinery, appliances and textiles. The growth of industries which are manufacturing import substitutes has affected the pattern of imports since the mid-1960s. The imports of sugar, footwear and cigarettes are declining in relative and absolute terms.

Perhaps a more striking change has taken place in the pattern of suppliers and buyers, if the late 1960s are compared with the early 1950s. The U.K. used to be the largest seller and buyer from the Sudan (30–40 per cent before independence). In 1971 only 4.5 per cent of Sudan's exports went to the U.K., and only 12.6 per cent of imports were brought from the U.K. However, the U.K. continues to have a large share of Sudan's imports of machinery, appliances, vehicles, transport equipment, chemicals, pharmaceutical products and cigarettes. Trade with socialist countries has been increasing since independence, and especially in recent years, as a result of several bilateral agreements. In 1960–69 the Sudan signed agreements with Bulgaria, Czechoslovakia, the German Democratic Republic, Yugoslavia, Hungary, Poland, China and others. The share of socialist countries in Sudan's trade is about 20 per cent of both exports and imports. Trade with the Arab countries has been expanding in recent years and exports to them have reached about 10 per cent, but imports from these countries form a smaller percentage. The Arab countries are a good market for Sudan's animals. Trade between the Sudan, Egypt and Libya is developing further as a result of an agreement on economic integration signed in May 1970. Furthermore, the summit conferences of east and central African heads of state and governments may increase trade between Sudan and east and central African countries in the near future.

FOREIGN AID 1960–1969

The Ten-Year Plan of Economic and Social Development, 1961/62–1970/71, was the country's first experience in planning, although there had been three previous attempts to develop Sudan in a systematic manner: 1946–51, 1951–56 and the Managil extension programme. In contrast to the Ten-Year Plan, the development programmes were not comprehensive, being concerned only with some projects in the public sector and depending on finance from savings of the public sector.

The total gross investment of the plan was estimated to be £S565 million, of which 40 per cent (£S228 million) was to be sponsored by the private sector and 60 per cent (£S337 million) by the public sector. Out of the total investment £S415.9 million was to be financed by domestic savings and £S219.7 million from foreign financial assistance. The £S415.9

would consist of £S219.7 million public savings and £S196.2 million private savings.

The amount of foreign aid which was actually received in the period 1960–69 did not fall very much short of the target of the plan. While £S150 million of foreign aid was forecast for the period 1961/62, 1970/71, £S141 million of aid in the form of grants, long-term and medium-term loans and in kind was received in the period 1960–69. However, in spite of the small difference between projected and realized foreign aid, the plan could not be properly implemented, mainly because of a shortage of domestic and foreign finance.

The Khashm el Girba and Roseires dams could not be utilized fully because the lack of finance prevented the associated works being completed. Additional reasons, such as wastage and corruption, also contributed to hampering the completion of projects of the public sector. Foreign aid of about £S60 million was needed in 1970 to complete the basic association projects, which will enable Sudan to utilize its investment reasonably well.

It is clear from the sources of foreign aid over the period 1960–69 that the International Bank for Reconstruction and Development has played an important part in the financing of development projects in Sudan. About 16 per cent of all foreign aid in the 1960–69 period has come from it. The Bank has financed very vital projects such as the Roseires Dam, mechanized farming, Sudan Railways extension and dieselization, and the Managil Extension. American aid, mainly given in non-project commodities, has also been important, constituting about 14 per cent of the total between 1960 and 1969. American aid to Sudan ceased when Sudan severed diplomatic relations with the U.S.A. in June 1967. Cumulative withdrawals up to the end of 1967 totalled £S23.3 million.

Aid to Sudan from Yugoslavia included a tannery, a cardboard factory and three ships, which constitute the Sudan Shipping Line. The U.S.S.R. has provided Sudan with two grain elevators, factories for processing agricultural and dairy products, a hospital and veterinary laboratories. Federal Germany also played an important role in financing the economic development of Sudan between 1960 and 1969 by contributing to the financing of the Roseires Dam; and credit from German firms helped in financing the Guneid and Khashm el Girba sugar factories.

The June War (1967), which brought about closer relations between the Arab countries, has increased the flow of Arab aid to Sudan. By the end of 1969 the drawings on Arab aid had reached £S42.4 million—more than 30 per cent of the total foreign aid received between 1960 and 1969. In addition to this Sudan received £S15 million from the United Arab Republic, not as aid, but as compensation for the resettlement of Halfa town, caused by the construction of the Aswan High Dam.

The financing of public sector projects has mainly come from various governments, but firms have also played a part. For example, Italian contractors granted a credit of £S2.6 million to cover a part of the cost of the construction of Khashm el Girba dam and three Fokker aeroplanes were obtained on a three-year credit from the suppliers.

During 1960–69 the Sudan government obtained short-term loans from the IMF and some Dutch commercial banks. The Dutch commercial banks provided £S0.9 million to finance about 90 per cent of the cost to the Sudan government of importing telecommunication equipment from Holland.

There is no information about foreign loans to the private sector, but the two textile mills in the country were financed by foreign loans from the U.S.A. and Japan.

At the end of 1969 the net foreign debt outstanding in respect of government loans amounted to £S109.3 million. This figure includes £S18 million representing obligations to the IMF, but it excludes the amounts received under the different American aid programmes, before such aid was stopped in 1967. At the end of 1971 the net foreign debt in respect of government loans amounted to £S110.6 million.

Repayment of loans in 1969 amounted to £S10.9 million, of which £S6.7 million was for principal and £S3.9 million was interest. In 1968 and 1969 the Sudan Government secured sizeable short-term and medium-term loans which had the effect of increasing the debt servicing burden immediately. The ratio of debt servicing to export proceeds rose from 6.9 per cent in 1967 to 12.5 per cent in 1969. In 1971 it reached 20 per cent. Such a high ratio of debt servicing indicates that the Sudan has reached a critical limit.

The total amount of external resources received in 1970 amounted to £S12.8 million compared to £S26.1 in 1969. In 1971 the total amount of external resources received amounted to £S10.8 million. This sum includes £S2.7 million of Sudan's allocation of Special Drawing Rights (short-term loan from the IMF), and the drawing of £S100,000 on suppliers' credit.

PUBLIC FINANCE

The Sudan government, like governments in many other underdeveloped countries, depends heavily on indirect taxes as a major source of revenue. In the fiscal year 1969–70 indirect taxes contributed 44 per cent of the central government's revenue, while in 1968–69 they yielded about 50 per cent. In these two years the relative share of indirect taxes declined because of increased import restrictions, and also because of the increased revenue from direct taxes and proceeds from government agricultural enterprises, particularly in 1969–70. The main source of revenue from indirect taxation is import duties. Because of balance of payments deficits in recent years the government has been trying to restrict imports of consumer goods, particularly luxuries, and those which bear the highest rates. Excise duties are growing in importance because of the growth of industries producing import substitutes. Thus, the share of excise duties in revenue from indirect taxation, 5 per cent in 1964–65, rose to 18 per cent in 1966–67.

This change is also reducing the rate of increase of revenue from indirect taxation. Excise duties are of lower rates than import duties on the same goods, and they are more difficult to collect.

The revenue from export taxes declined from £S3.8 million in 1966–67 to £S3 million in 1969–70. The majority of export taxes, which were an important feature of the tax system of Sudan, were cancelled, together with royalties, in November 1968, with the exception of those on gum and cotton, in an attempt to encourage exports. This action has not proved effective and the revenue of the government from export taxes has been greatly reduced. The taxes were reintroduced in November 1969, but at lower rates.

The revenue from direct taxes was about 13 per cent of the total revenue of the central government in 1969–70, having been 2.7 per cent in 1963–64. The present direct taxes of Sudan (1969–70) are: income taxes, an emergency tax and a stamp duty. The income taxes comprise a personal income tax on monetary earnings, fringe benefits and interest; a business profits tax; and a tax on income from rent (as laid down by the Income Tax Act, 1967). The top rate is 50 per cent, when total income reaches £S25,000. Dividends are not normally taxable in the Sudan, since companies pay a business profits tax; shareholders do not pay an income tax on their dividends. Nevertheless, a holding company which receives dividends from its subsidiaries pays a business tax on aggregate profits, after getting a tax credit for the tax paid by the subsidiary. An emergency tax was introduced in August 1969 to absorb part of the wage and salary increases given to employees in the public sector in 1968 by the previous government. The yield of the emergency tax is estimated to be £S7 million in 1969–70. Stamp duty is considered as a direct tax in Sudan and its revenue is less than £S2 million.

In addition to the revenue from taxation, fees, charges and profits from agricultural enterprises, the central government may borrow internally to meet current expenditure. Under the Bank of Sudan Act, 1959, amended in 1962, the government, its boards and agencies, are permitted to borrow from the Central Bank up to 15 per cent of the ordinary revenue of the government, defined to include the central government, provincial and local government bodies, government boards, government banks and enterprises owned by the government or in which the government participates. For the fiscal year 1967–68 the maximum limit of such borrowing was fixed at £S21.4 million, while the total advances from the Central Bank at the end of June 1968 amounted to £21.2 million. The revenue for the fiscal year 1968–69 for all the units in the public sector was estimated at £S171,878,116, and the maximum limit of borrowing by the government from the Central Bank was fixed at £S24.5 million, while the actual borrowing of the government during that fiscal year was £S24.3 million.

Furthermore, according to the Treasury Bill Act, 1966, the government may borrow by means of treasury bills, provided that the value of such bills outstanding at any time shall not exceed £S5 million. The bulk of treasury bills have already been bought by the commercial banks. At the close of 1968 the value of commercial banks' holdings of treasury bills amounted to £S4.85 million, and £S150,000 was held by other financial institutions in the private sector.

Since the mid-1960s the Sudan government has been finding it more and more difficult to make all its local cash payments, whether wages and salaries or payment to contractors, in time. This seems to be the result of two main factors: underestimation of expenditure and ineffective financial control of government accounts. This problem of the illiquidity of the public sector has forced the government to seek various ways to increase revenue and reduce expenditure, but it has not yet been solved.

The expenditure of the central government has been rising very fast since independence in 1956. In 1949 the total current expenditure of the central government was £S10 million; by 1970–71 it was £S158 million, an increase of more than fifteen times in a period of twenty years. Besides the rise in prices and the normal expansion in government services, increased expenditure on education, national defence and the rise in wages and salaries of the employees of the public sector have accentuated the rate of increase of the total current expenditure in recent years. The expenditure of the Ministry of Defence increased from £S14.1 million in 1965–66 to £S38 million in 1970–71, while the expenditure of the Ministry of Education increased from £S5.8 million in 1965–66 to £S8.6 million in 1970–71. This increase is a direct result of the continued crisis in the Middle East and a strong popular demand for more education. In 1968 the government raised the wages and salaries of its employees by 5–15 per cent and thus wages and salaries amounted to 41 per cent of the expenditure of the Central Government for 1968–69.

LABOUR AND WAGES

The number of persons five years of age and over reported in the 1955–56 census, as mainly engaged in economic activity, was 3,800,000 out of a population of 10.2 million. In addition, it is estimated, on the basis of detailed tabulations of the census returns, that 1,116,000 persons, whose main activity was not economic, took part in subsidiary economic activity. So the total number engaged to any degree in economic activity is approximately 4,916,000 or 48 per cent of the population. Sudan's labour force is overwhelmingly male. Men make up 56 per cent of the total economically active population, women 24.7 per cent, boys 14.4 per cent and girls 4.9 per cent.

Of all the males and females in the labour force 86.7 per cent are primary producers, 3.3 per cent secondary producers and 10 per cent tertiary producers. All these percentages of sex and industrial distribution of the Sudan's labour force have not, it is thought, changed very much since 1955–56.

Beyond 1956 it is difficult to get any reasonably accurate data in order to assess the labour situation in Sudan. However, the number of wage-earners at present is estimated to be about one million—excluding agricultural workers. About half a million workers are engaged in the public sector and about the same number are employed by the private sector.

Until about 1965 one of the country's major problems was considered to be the shortage of skilled workers. There was heavy dependence on expatriates of Greek and Armenian descent, who filled a high proportion of skilled jobs and managerial and executive posts.

However, by 1965 the major development projects were finished. The most important factories in both private and public sectors, as well as Khashm el Girba and Roseires dams, were finished by that year. In the early 1960s institutes of technical education and training centres were established and by 1965 their graduates could meet the demand for skilled labour. The Khartoum Senior Trade School was opened in 1960 to teach electronics, commerce, electrical installation, machine shop, automobile and diesel mechanics, carpentry, cabinet making, brickwork and draughtsmanship. The Khartoum Technical Institute (Polytechnic) was opened in 1950, but the total enrolment was only 25 in 1950–51. At that time it taught only civil engineering. By 1960 the enrolment had risen to 569 and the institute syllabus included courses in civil engineering, mechanical and electrical engineering, surveying, secretarial work and commerce. An up-grading centre was established in Khartoum in 1960 by the Labour Department to improve the skills of workers already employed in both public and private sectors, and an apprenticeship centre was also established in Khartoum by the government, with German aid, in 1962. Another apprenticeship centre was established in Kosti in 1967.

In fact, after 1965, unemployment began to appear among skilled workers in the towns, and some economists and businessmen began to believe that the shortage of skilled workers was no longer a serious problem to the industrialization of Sudan. Sudan has already started to export skilled workers, clerical staff and teachers to the Arab countries.

The only available figures on unemployment come from the registrations at employment exchanges in major towns. In 1967–68 31,919 were registered as unemployed. In 1970–71 registered unemployment totalled 58,022. However, it is obvious that this figure does not represent total open unemployment in Sudan. Not all the workers register themselves when they are unemployed, particularly unskilled workers. On the other hand, some workers may register more than once, while, when other workers find a job, neither they nor their employers report to the employment exchanges. Therefore, the present figures of unemployment in Sudan should be viewed with great caution.

There is no legal minimum wage in Sudan. However, in the public sector the minimum monthly wage paid for permanent employment is £S11.8, while it is about £S6 in the private sector. The daily minimum wage ranges between 25 and 50 piastres, depending on the region and the season. During the cotton-picking season in the Gezira the daily minimum wage may rise as high as 50 piastres per day. Wages and salaries are higher in the public sector than in the private sector, with the exception of modern and large firms in the private sector, who only employ a very small percentage of the labour force engaged in the modern sector.

Although wages in the public sector are higher than wages in the private sector, they have declined in real terms over the last twenty years or so. At best, money wages increased by 40 per cent between 1951 and 1970. A wage increase was given in 1965 and 1968, but the cost of living increased by at least 70 per cent between 1951 and 1970, and therefore real wages declined by about 30 per cent in that period. Most wages in the private sector have lagged behind wages in the public sector.

PLANNING AND DEVELOPMENT

The first development plan was a ten-year plan, 1961–62 to 1970–71. Then a five-year plan 1970–71 to 1974–75 was published in 1970 and later in the year it was revised. Because of nationalization, the share of the public sector in investment increased from £S200 million to £S215 million. The private sector's share in capital investment has been fixed at £S170 million. The major targets of the plan are: to increase G.D.P. at an average rate of 7.6 per cent annually; to increase the revenue of the Government to £S953 million compared to £S516.5 million for the previous five years; to increase the share of commodity production to 65 per cent in 1974–75 as against 61.1 per cent in 1969–70; to increase industrial production by 57.4 per cent, and to increase the volume of agricultural production by 60.8 per cent.

The general aim of the plan is to promote welfare through an increase in productivity, realization of full employment and an expansion of public services. The number of projects in the plan for the public sector was 276, of which 239 projects have actually been started. In 1970–71 40 projects (17 per cent of the total planned) were completed.

In the Development Budget for 1970–71 £S18.3 million was approved for development expenditure. However, only £S13.1 million was spent in that fiscal year on economic development, so that in financial terms the plan was only implemented by about 70 per cent in its first year. Poor execution of the development plan during 1970–71 was most apparent in the Ministry of Industry (37 per cent), the Ministry of Animal Resources (41.4 per cent), and the Agricultural Development Corporation (38.7 per cent). There is no information as to the fulfilment of the plan by the private sector, but the latter has not been very active in Sudan for the last three years or so.

POWER AND TRANSPORT

The installed generating capacity of the Sudan in 1970 was 96,685 kW. thermal and 29,220 kW. hydro. The total power generated in 1969 was 310,051,000 kWh. The number of consumers is 68,529 residential and commercial, 558 agricultural and 844 industrial. All the main towns of Sudan are supplied with electricity and some of the small towns which lie near to

THE SUDAN—(Statistical Survey)

the transmission lines, such as Kamlin, also enjoy this facility. Seventeen towns in Sudan are provided with electricity.

The volume of electricity used by industry is 118,200,000 kWh., while the volume of electricity used by agriculture for pumps is 26,200,000 kWh. The electricity consumption of industry does not include that of ginning factories, the large oil mills and Guneid and Khashm el Girba sugar factories. All these generate their own electricity from by-products. The grain silos at Gedaref and Port Sudan have their own generating sets.

Sudan depends mainly on railways for transport. Steamers and motor transport play only a secondary role. All-weather roads are very limited. The total length of asphalt main roads in Sudan is 208 miles, of which Khartoum Province has 178 miles. The length of cleared tracks covered with gravel is 3,210 miles. The length of just cleared tracks is 7,810 miles and these make up the main network of roads in Sudan. However, they are usually impassable immediately after the rains. Road bridges cross the Blue and White Niles at four points, and four dams on the river also carry traffic.

The rail transport facilities are still far from adequate. In 1969–70 the railway network was 4,756 km. In 1970 the average density of railways for the whole country was only 1.9 km. per 1,000 sq. km. The river fleet comprises 386 low-speed old steamers of various types. River transport is mainly used between Kosti and Juba (1,435 km.) and between Dongola and Kareima (187 km.); these routes are navigable all year round. The total length of the river navigation routes is about 2,445 km., of which 1,723 km. are open all the year and the rest are seasonal. River transport between Wadi Halfa and Shellal, which lies partly on Lake Nasser, is under development at present. As far as sea transport is concerned, the government company, the Sudan Shipping Line, owns four dry cargo ships of 5,000 tons each. At present, only 5 per cent of exports and imports are carried by domestic vessels. Two additional dry cargo ships of 20,000 tons each, which are being built in Yugoslavia, were to be delivered in 1972–73.

The government-owned Sudan Airways, formed in 1947, operates internal and international services. It connects Khartoum with twenty important Sudanese towns as well as with Europe, the Middle East and Africa. In 1968–69 it carried 122,574 passengers and 1.8 million ton/km., while in 1970–71 it carried 65,116 passengers and 3.3 million ton/km.

STATISTICAL SURVEY

AREA AND POPULATION

Total Area	Arable Land	Pasture	Forest	Total Population (July 1st, 1972)
967,500 sq. miles*	71,000 sq. kilometres	240,000 sq. kilometres	914,999 sq. kilometres	16,489,000

* 2,505,813 sq. kilometres.

PROVINCES
(July 1st, 1971)

	Area (sq. miles)	Population		Area (sq. miles)	Population
Bahr el Ghazal	82,530	1,499,000	Khartoum	8,097	922,000
Blue Nile	54,880	3,315,000	Kordofan	146,930	2,954,000
Darfur	191,650	1,779,000	Northern	184,200	1,190,000
Equatoria	76,495	1,369,000	Upper Nile	91,190	1,346,000
Kassala	131,528	1,712,000	Total	967,500	16,087,000

THE SUDAN—(Statistical Survey)

PRINCIPAL TOWNS

Town	Population (1971)
Khartoum (capital)	280,431
Omdurman	273,268
El Obeid	76,420
Wadi Medani	79,364
Port Sudan	116,366
Khartoum North	138,014
Atbara	58,939

Because of the flooding of the Wadhi Halfa and adjacent areas by the Aswan High Dam, over 50,000 inhabitants have been resettled in Khashm el Girba, on the Atbara River.

Employment (1970): Total economically active population 5,016,000, including 4,007,000 engaged in agriculture (ILO and FAO estimates).

AGRICULTURE
COTTON CROP
(1 feddan = 1.038 acres = 4,201 sq. metres)

	Area (feddans) 1968–69	1969–70	1970–71	Production (tons) 1968–69	1969–70	1970–71
Long Staple	775,159	824,662	828,306	548,707	566,667	618,314
Medium Staple	138,917	138,041	184,953	78,361	82,234	89,675
Short Staple	240,867	295,208	200,729	28,548	33,583	18,537
Total	1,154,943	1,257,911	1,213,988	655,616	682,484	726,526

Production of lint (metric tons): 184,000 in 1968; 225,000 in 1969; and 225,000 in 1970.

OTHER CROPS
(metric tons)

	1968	1969	1970	1971
Wheat	88,000	123,000	115,000	135,000
Maize	16,000	36,000	23,000	40,000*
Millet	267,000	384,000	460,000	325,000
Sorghum (Durra)	870,000	1,499,000	1,529,000	2,152,000
Rice	1,000	3,000	6,000	7,000*
Sugar Cane†	969,000	939,000	780,000*	750,000*
Potatoes	25,000*	26,000*	26,000*	26,000*
Sweet Potatoes and Yams	11,000*	11,000*	12,000*	n.a.
Cassava (Manioc)	132,000	140,000	140,000	n.a.
Onions	18,000	20,000*	20,000*	n.a.
Dry Beans	4,000	6,000	6,000*	6,000*
Dry Broad Beans	13,000	11,000	12,000*	13,000*
Chick-Peas	2,000	2,000	2,000*	2,000*
Other Pulses	42,000*	43,000*	40,000*	46,000*
Oranges and Tangerines	1,000*	1,000*	1,000*	1,000*
Dates	70,000	72,000*	72,000*	n.a.
Bananas	10,000*	10,000*	10,000*	n.a.
Groundnuts (in shell)	197,000	383,000	353,000	381,000
Cottonseed	334,000	421,000	420,000	428,000*
Sesame Seed	122,000	201,600	282,000	271,000
Castor Beans	15,000	12,000	18,000	18,000*

1968: Mangoes 15,000 tons; Guavas 4,000 tons.

* FAO estimate.   † Crop year ending in year stated.

THE SUDAN—(STATISTICAL SURVEY)

LIVESTOCK
('000)

	1968–69	1969–70	1970–71
Cattle	13,326	13,500*	13,650*
Sheep	12,678	13,000*	13,200*
Goats	10,036	10,050*	10,100*
Pigs	6*	7*	7*
Horses	20*	20*	19*
Asses	610*	630*	640*
Camels	2,918	3,000*	3,100*
Chickens	18,200*	18,500*	18,800*

* FAO estimate.

Source: FAO, *Production Yearbook 1971.*

LIVESTOCK PRODUCTS
(FAO estimates, metric tons)

	1968	1969	1970
Cows' Milk	1,330,000	1,350,000	1,360,000
Sheep's Milk	120,000	125,000	130,000
Goats' Milk	425,000	440,000	450,000
Beef and Veal	129,000	142,000	140,000
Mutton, Lamb and Goats' Meat	64,000	71,000	72,000
Poultry Meat	10,000	10,000	10,000
Edible Offal	40,000	43,000	43,000
Other Meat	52,000	54,000	56,000
Tallow	6,000	6,000	6,000
Hen Eggs	16,200	16,400	16,700
Cattle Hides (salted)	11,760	11,840	11,760
Sheep Skins (dry)	2,760	3,120	3,280
Goat Skins (dry)	360	368	360

1971 (metric tons): Cows' Milk 1,370,000; Sheep's Milk 140,000; Goats' Milk 450,000; Hen Eggs 17,000.

Source: FAO, *Production Yearbook 1971.*

GUM ARABIC PRODUCTION
(tons)

Season	Gum Hashab	Gum Talh	Total
1965–66	47,960	2,444	50,404
1966–67	42,713	2,296	45,009
1967–68	58,896	2,649	61,545
1968–69	40,955	4,592	45,547
1969–70*	30,000	4,000	34,000

* Estimates.

FISHING
(metric tons)

	1967	1968
Inland waters	19,200	20,700
Sea	800	800
Total Catch	20,000	21,500

Source: FAO, *Yearbook of Fishery Statistics*

THE SUDAN—(Statistical Survey)

MINING
PRODUCTION

	Unit	1966	1967	1968	1969
Iron Ore*	'000 tons	14	39	—	—
Manganese Ore*	tons	2,500	1,500	5,000	850
Chromium Ore*	,,	25,000	17,391	22,086	23,944
Gold	ounces	—	111	29	—
Magnesite	tons	4,000	4,000	7,000	1,000
Unrefined Salt	'000 tons	57	43	50	51

1971: Salt 63,000 tons.

* Figures relate to gross weight. Metal content (in metric tons) was as follows:

Iron: 20,000 in 1966; 7,000 in 1967.
Manganese: 600 in 1966; 600 in 1967; 2,000 in 1968; 340 in 1969; more than 500 in 1970.
Chromium oxide: 10,100 in 1966; 9,043 in 1967; 11,485 in 1968; 12,451 in 1969; 13,866 in 1970.

INDUSTRY
PRODUCTION

	Unit	1967–68	1968–69	1969–70	1970–71
Cement	'000 tons	128.7	140.7	194.0	229.0
Flour of Wheat	,,	48.8	51.5	111.6	176.0
Sugar	,,	93.3	82.1	75.3	72.5
Soap	,,	18.4	19.3	23.7	27.9
Wine	'000 litres	1,634.6	1,453.0	2,450.0	3,357.0
Beer	,, ,,	7,447.6	7,159.0	4,534.0	7,245.0
Cigarettes	'000 kilos	660.9	532.0	660.9	741.8
Matches	billion	4.0	3.9	4.9	4.4
Shoes	million pairs	9.5	10.7	6.7	8.5
Textiles	yards	93,122.0	101,350.0	n.a.	n.a.
Alcohol	'000 litres	552.6	464.0	n.a.	n.a.
Oil	'000 tons	36.0	46.0	n.a.	n.a.

PETROLEUM PRODUCTS
(metric tons)

	1967	1968	1969	1970
Motor Spirit	82,000	62,000	70,000	90,000
Naphtha	34,000	12,000	25,000	26,000
Jet Fuels	57,000	70,000	} 76,000	82,000
Kerosene	19,000	53,000		
Distillate Fuel Oils	428,000	184,000	234,000	234,000
Residual Fuel Oils	233,000	195,000	224,000	239,000
Liquefied Petroleum Gas	1,000	1,000	2,000	2,000

Source: United Nations, *Statistical Yearbook 1971.*

593

THE SUDAN—(Statistical Survey)

FINANCE

1,000 millièmes = 100 piastres = 1 Sudanese pound (£S).
Coins: 1, 2, 5 and 10 millièmes; 2, 5 and 10 piastres.
Notes: 25 and 50 piastres; £S1, £S5 and £S10.
Exchange rates (January 31st, 1973): £1 sterling = 812.00 millièmes; U.S. $1 = 348.24 millièmes.
£S100 = £123.153 sterling = $287.156.

BUDGET ESTIMATES FOR CURRENT REVENUE AND EXPENDITURE
(£S, twelve months ending June 30th)

Revenue	1969–70	1970–71	Expenditure	1969–70	1970–71
Direct Taxation	17,500,000	18,870,000	Ministry of Agriculture and Forests	3,558,739	3,655,280
Indirect Taxation	63,201,000	73,636,797	Ministry of Communications and Tourism	4,239,999	4,258,324
Fees and Charges, etc.	8,129,786	10,289,597	Ministry of Education	9,803,319	8,667,390
Proceeds from Government Enterprises	42,395,227	43,542,204	Ministry of Health	6,585,877	7,910,532
Interest and Dividends	1,217,037	1,169,460	Ministry of Works		
Pension Contributions	1,373,964	1,554,000	Works	3,826,839	2,046,554
Reimbursement and Inter-Departmental Services	7,203,271	7,208,673	Mechanical Transport	2,434,941	2,494,414
Other Sources	1,093,435	1,745,629	Ministry of Irrigation	3,852,513	4,037,261
			Department of Stores and Equipment	1,104,171	915,310
			Other Ministries and Departments	65,083,411	77,558,732
			General Administration	40,623,911	38,781,043
			Koranic Studies	—	91,520
			Total Expenditure	141,113,720	150,416,360
			Surplus	1,000,000	7,600,000
Total Revenue	142,113,720	158,016,360		142,113,720	158,016,360

1972–73 Budget Estimate: Revenue £S191.3m.; Expenditure £S255.5m.
1973–74 Budget Estimate: Revenue £S220.8m.; Expenditure £S217.1m.

Five-Year Plan (1970–75): £S217.3 million capital investment by public sector.

NATIONAL ACCOUNTS
(£S'000, years ending June 30th)

	1968/69	1969/70
Wages and Salaries	366,460	286,948
Operating Surplus	125,791	186,676
Domestic Factor Incomes	492,251	473,624
Wages and Salaries Paid Abroad (net)	−2,412	−1,500
Property and Entrepreneurial Income Paid Abroad (net)	−3,689	−1,600
Indirect Taxes	59,960	88,242
Less Subsidies	−3,742	−9,027
National Income at Market Price	542,369	550,739
Other Current Transfers to the Rest of the World (net)	−1,616	−1,100
National Disposable Income	540,752	549,639
National Disposable Income per capita (£S)	37.3	37.9

FIVE-YEAR PLAN 1970/71–74/75

The Plan has as its main objectives a sustained annual growth rate of the G.N.P. of 7.6 per cent; the raising of per capita income to £S46.6 by 1974/75; increasing agricultural output by 60.8 per cent; increasing the level of investment in education and culture by 60 per cent, in health by 82 per cent and in public utilities by 58 per cent; developing urban and rural water networks; increasing livestock production by 75.5 per cent; increasing the volume of trade by value to £S340 million.

Total Investment, by Public Sector by 1974/75
(£S '000)

Agriculture	80,000
Industry and Power	49,200
Transport and Communications	29,630
Education and Culture	14,580
Health and Public Utilities	21,420
Central Administration	6,440
Technical Assistance and Grants	9,800
Unallocated and Others	3,930
Total	215,000

THE SUDAN—(Statistical Survey)

BALANCE OF PAYMENTS ESTIMATES
(£S million)

	1970–71	1971–72*
Receipts:		
Cotton exports	61.3	47.2
Other exports	45.3	41.7
Invisible	16.4	13.8
Foreign loans	12.1	11.8
Other short-term capital	18.0	10.0
	153.1	124.5
Payments:		
Government imports	43.8	28.4
Private sector imports	75.3	68.7
Invisible	27.4	23.7
Repayments of capital	11.5	7.0
	158.0	127.8
Deficit	4.9	3.3

* July to April.

EXTERNAL TRADE
(£S million)

	1967	1968	1969	1970	1971	1972*
Imports	74.3	83.8	89.3	100.1	115.4	108.2
Exports	74.6	85.6	86.2	103.4	114.4	101.2

* Estimate.

PRINCIPAL COMMODITIES
(£S '000)

Imports	1969	1970	1971
Sugar	2,715	5,143	9,247
Tea	2,210	4,955	4,004
Coffee	453	1,907	1,635
Wheat Flour	1,125	657	226
Textiles	16,561	15,119	26,462
Clothing	749	672	911
Footwear	585	127	102
Sacks and Jute	2,611	3,013	3,694
Cement	47	33	70
Fertilizers	1,397	1,658	1,937
Machinery, Apparatus, Vehicles	22,790	28,788	23,312
Tyres	1,485	1,384	1,937
Petroleum Products	8,809	9,025	8,918
Pharmaceuticals	2,200	3,387	2,760
Iron and Steel	4,594	4,612	4,794

Exports	1969	1970	1971
Animals	2,332	2,317	1,959
Cotton, Ginned	49,498	65,052	69,424
Cotton Seed	1,489	1,728	1,422
Cotton Seed Oil	920	771	4,501
Durra	43	60	1,136
Groundnuts	5,991	5,466	9,324
Gum Arabic	8,699	8,969	8,425
Oilseed Cake	3,879	n.a.	n.a.
Sesame	8,017	5,087	7,996
Hides and Skins	1,803	1,590	1,806

THE SUDAN—(Statistical Survey)

COTTON EXPORTS BY COUNTRIES
(tons)

	1969	1970	1971
Germany, Federal Republic	21,034	15,769	13,328
India	29,913	30,462	37,001
Italy	28,596	28,509	13,620
Japan	15,663	15,900	11,260
United Kingdom	15,038	14,670	10,581
People's Republic of China	13,735	17,821	35,221
U.S.A.	935	2,388	2,549
U.S.S.R.	8,319	57,564	39,158
Romania	6,126	2,221	7,437
France	2,925	7,006	4,834
Netherlands	859	1,006	328
Hungary	3,124	4,981	4,983
Poland	4,839	4,999	6,593
Total (all countries)	172,425	203,296	206,903

PRINCIPAL COUNTRIES
(£S '000)

	Imports 1968	1969	1970	1971	Exports* 1968	1969	1970	1971
Belgium	1,830	2,094	2,076	1,708	2,206	1,957	1,996	2,080
China, People's Republic	5,993	4,876	4,030	7,733	4,838	6,430	6,000	10,785
Egypt	3,516	3,848	5,323	6,814	2,402	3,914	4,981	5,700
France	3,325	3,351	1,716	4,234	2,061	1,307	2,223	3,090
Germany, Federal Republic	4,647	5,771	7,802	7,069	12,256	10,142	9,855	8,779
India	9,342	9,063	14,226	22,677	7,946	10,133	14,226	11,997
Italy	4,990	4,327	2,430	2,351	9,713	10,777	10,190	9,775
Japan	8,113	7,153	5,629	4,796	6,652	8,010	9,250	8,332
Netherlands	2,346	3,512	2,892	3,038	4,276	3,359	3,319	4,155
Poland	1,498	1,789	1,916	1,873	1,786	1,544	1,660	2,111
U.S.S.R.	6,223	4,486	8,328	7,858	4,818	3,389	17,242	18,351
United Kingdom	15,831	16,944	17,929	15,757	4,800	5,762	5,834	4,885
U.S.A.	1,945	2,605	2,822	2,910	2,760	3,010	4,026	3,014
Yugoslavia	639	770	1,140	2,201	831	989	986	1,006
Others	19,471	21,887	30,774	24,417	13,489	14,901	9,827	20,314
Total	89,709	92,476	109,033	115,436	80,834	85,624	101,615	114,374

* Excluding re-exports.

TRANSPORT

SHIPPING

	1966	1967	1968	1969	1970
Number of Ships calling at Port Sudan	1,223	1,004	845	770	760
Total Inward Tonnage	1,427,743	1,528,183	1,594,019	1,582,369	1,845,215
Total Outward Tonnage	941,317	866,948	952,449	950,975	1,014,757

EDUCATION
(1969)

	TEACHERS	STUDENTS		
		BOYS	GIRLS	TOTAL
Pre-Primary	266	7,927	7,958	15,885
Primary	12,370	410,023	200,775	610,798
Secondary: General	9,030	126,617	45,869	172,486
Vocational	151	1,181	—	1,181
Teacher-Training	156	1,439	852	2,291
Tertiary	1,107	10,304	1,387	11,691

Source: United Nations, *Statistical Yearbook 1971.*

Source: Department of Statistics, H.Q. Council of Ministers, Khartoum, except where otherwise stated.

THE CONSTITUTION

In December 1955 a Transitional Constitution was adopted, under which the highest authority was vested in a Supreme Commission of five members, who were responsible for appointing the Prime Minister and his Cabinet from amongst the members of Parliament.

This Transitional Constitution was suspended following the military *coup d'état* of 1958, but the provisional Government which took office after the overthrow of the military regime in October 1964, announced its intention of governing under the terms of the 1955 Constitution.

The Constituent Assembly, whose term had been extended in 1968, was abolished by the new regime in May 1969.

A Provisional Constitution was introduced by the Revolutionary Command Council in August 1971. A People's Council, including various categories of the people's working forces, was called to draft and ratify a permanent constitution. It was endorsed by the People's Assembly in April 1973 as the Permanent Constitution of the Sudan.

The President

The President must be a Sudanese of at least 35 years of age. He is nominated by the Sudanese Socialist Union, is Head of State, and is responsible for maintaining the Constitution. He may appoint Vice-Presidents, a Prime Minister and Ministers who are responsible to him. He is the Supreme Commander of the People's Armed Forces and Security Forces, and the Supreme Head of the Public Service.

If satisfied that a national crisis exists, the President may declare a State of Emergency, which may entail the suspension of any or all freedoms and rights under the Permanent Constitution other than that of resort to the courts. In the event of the President's death, the First Vice-President will temporarily assume office for a period not exceeding 60 days.

The People's Assembly

The President may appoint up to a tenth of the members of the Assembly. The duration of a sitting is four years and sittings are held in public. A quorum consists of half the number of members. Amendments to the Constitution may be proposed by the President or one third of the membership of the People's Assembly. An amendment to the Constitution must have a two-thirds majority of the People's Assembly and the assent of the President.

Judiciary

The State is subject to the rule of law which is the basis of government. The judiciary is an independent body directly responsible to the President and judges are appointed by the President.

Religion

Unrestricted freedom of religion is allowed and mention is specifically made of the Islamic and Christian religions.

Southern Region

Under the Regional Constitution for the Southern Sudan, the three southern provinces form a single region, with its own regional executive in Juba headed by a president who is also a Vice-President of the whole Republic. The regional executive will be responsible for all matters outside national defence, external affairs, communications, currency and foreign trade regulation. The regional President will be appointed by and responsible to a regional People's Assembly, although, pending the election of such an assembly in October 1973, he was initially appointed by Pres. Nemery after consulting representative southern Sudanese. The Assembly may postpone legislation of the central Government which it considers adverse to the interests of the South, though the President is not compelled to accede to its request. The Constitution can be amended only by a four-fifths majority of the central People's Assembly, where southerners will be proportionally represented.

THE GOVERNMENT

President: Maj.-Gen. JAAFIR AL NEMERY (*elected October* 1971).
First Vice-President: Maj.-Gen. MUHAMMAD AL-BAQIR AHMAD.
Vice-President and President of the High Executive Council for the Southern Region: ABEL ALIER.

CABINET MINISTERS
(*August* 1973)

Prime Minister and Minister of Defence: Maj.-Gen. JAAFIR AL-NEMERY.
Minister of Foreign Affairs: Dr. MANSOUR KHALID.
Minister of Local Government and Community Development: Dr. GAAFAR BAKHEIT.
Minister of Finance and National Economy: IBRAHIM MONEIM MANSOUR.
Minister of Education: Sir EL KHATIM EL KHALIFA.
Minister of Agriculture, Food and Natural Resources: WADIE HABASHI.
Minister of Culture and Information: OMER HAG MUSA.
Minister of Health and Social Care: ABU EL GASIM MOHAMED IBRAHIM.
Minister of Transport and Communications: Dr. BASHIR ABADI.
Minister of Industry and Mining: MUSA AWAD BALLAL.
Minister of Interior: ABDULLAHI EL HASSAN.
Minister of Construction and Public Works: MUBARAK SINADA.
Minister of Public Service and Administrative Reform: ABDUL RAHMAN ABDALLAH.
Attorney General: Dr. ZAKI MUSTAFA.
Minister of State for Presidential Affairs: SALAH ABDEL AAL MABROUK.

MINISTERS OF STATE
Minister of State for Irrigation: YAHIA ABDEL MAGID.
Minister of State for Local Government: SAMUEL LUPAI.
Minister of State for Culture and Information: BONA MALWAL.
Minister of State for Trade: HASSAN MOHAMED ALI BILEIL.
Minister of State for Agricultural Production: Dr. KAMAL ABDALLA AGABAWI.
Minister of State for General Education: Dr. MOHAMED KHEIR OSMAN.
Minister of State for Cabinet Affairs: Dr. BAHAA EL DIN M. IDRIS.
Minister of State for the Government Secretariat: AHMED BABIKER BISA.
Minister of State for Agricultural Research and Services: Dr. HUSSEIN IDRIS.

HIGH EXECUTIVE COUNCIL FOR THE SOUTHERN REGION
There are eleven Regional Ministers.
President: ABEL ALIER.
Secretary-General: CLETO HASSAN.

PROVINCE COMMISSIONERS FOR THE NORTHERN REGION

COMMISSIONER	PROVINCE
AHMED EL SHERIF EL HABIB	Khartoum
AHMED SALAH BUKHARI	Kordofan
EL TAYEB EL MARDI	Darfur
HUSSEIN SHARFI	Northern Province
KARRAR AHMED KARRAR	Blue Nile
MOHAMED ABDEL GADER	Kassala
KARAMALLA EL AWAD	Red Sea

DIPLOMATIC REPRESENTATION

EMBASSIES ACCREDITED TO SUDAN
(In Khartoum unless otherwise stated)

Algeria: Junction Mek Nimr St. and 67th St., P.O.B. 80; *Ambassador:* ABDEL AZIZ BEN HUSAIN.
Austria: Cairo, Egypt.
Belgium: St. 3, New Extension, P.O.B. 969; *Chargé d'Affaires a.i.:* GUY EID.
Bulgaria: El Mek Nimr St. South 7, P.O.B. 1690; *Chargé d'Affaires a.i.:* NIKOLA NIKOLOV.
Central African Republic: Africa Rd., P.O.B. 1723; *Ambassador:* GILBERT BANDIO.
Chad: St. 47, New Extension; *Ambassador:* EL HADJ ABDERAHMAN MOUSSA.
China, People's Republic: 69 31st St., P.O.B. 1425; *Ambassador:* YANG SHOU-CHENG.
Czechoslovakia: 1, 5GE, Khartoum Central, P.O.B. 1047; *Ambassador:* MIROSLAV NOVOTNÝ.
Egypt: Mogram St.; *Ambassador:* MOHAMMED EL TABIE MOHAMMED.
Ethiopia: 6, 11A St. 3, New Extension, P.O.B. 844; *Ambassador:* DAWIT ABDOU.
France: 6H East Plot 2, 19th St., P.O.B. 377; *Ambassador:* HENRI COSTILHES.
German Democratic Republic: P4(3)B2, Khartoum West, P.O.B. 1089; *Ambassador:* KURT BOETTGER.
Germany, Federal Republic: 53 Abdel Rahman El Mahdi St., P.O.B. 970; *Ambassador:* MICHAEL JOVY.
Greece: Block 74, 31st St., P.O.B. 1182; *Ambassador:* NICOLAS KARANDREAS.
Hungary: Block 11, Plot 12, 13th St., New Extension, P.O.B. 1033; *Ambassador:* LAJOS BENCEKOVITS.
India: El Mek Nimr St., P.O.B. 707; *Chargé d'Affaires:* N. K. GHOSE.
Iraq: St. 5, New Extension; *Ambassador:* (vacant).
Italy: 39th St., P.O.B. 793; *Ambassador:* CARLO DE FRANCHIS.

THE SUDAN—(Diplomatic Representation, People's Assembly, Political Party, etc.)

Japan: 14-16, Block 5HE, P.O.B. 1649; *Chargé d'Affaires a.i.:* Shigeru Nomoto.
Jordan: 25 7th St., New Extension; *Chargé d'Affaires:* Adli El Nasir.
Korea, Democratic Republic: 2-10 BE, 7th St., New Extension, P.O.B. 332; *Ambassador:* Kim Dok Su.
Kuwait: 9th St., New Extension; *Ambassador:* Jasim Mohammed Borsuly.
Lebanon: 60 St. 49; *Ambassador:* Bulind Beydoun.
Libya: Africa Rd. 50, P.O.B. 2091; *Ambassador:* Younis Abu Ageila El Omrani.
Netherlands: P.O.B. 391; *Chargé d'Affaires a.i.:* J. W. Bertens.
Niger: St. 1, New Extension, P.O.B. 1283; *Ambassador:* El Hag Omarou Adamou.
Nigeria: P.O.B. 1538; *Ambassador:* El Haji Nuhu Mohammed.
Pakistan: 29, 9AE, St. 3, New Extension, P.O.B. 1178; *Ambassador:* S. A. H. Ahsani.
Poland: 73 Africa Rd., P.O.B. 902; *Chargé d'Affaires:* Jan Klioszewski.
Qatar: St. 15, New Extension; *Ambassador:* Ali Abdul Rahman Muftah.
Romania: St. 47, Plot 67, P.O.B. 1652; *Ambassador:* (vacant).
Saudi Arabia: Central St., New Extension, P.O.B. 852; *Ambassador:* Abdallah El Malhoug.
Somalia: Central St., New Extension; *Ambassador:* Abdullahi Farah Ali.
Spain: 52 39th St., P.O.B. 2621; *Chargé d'Affaires a.i.:* Julian Ayesta.
Switzerland: Cairo, Egypt.
Syria: 3rd St., New Extension; *Ambassador:* Chteioui Mahmoud Seifo.
Tanzania: Cairo, Egypt.
Turkey: 71 Africa Rd., P.O.B. 771; *Ambassador:* Besir Balcioglu.
Uganda: Cairo, Egypt.
United Arab Emirates: St. 3, New Extension; *Ambassador:* Mohammed Ali El Shurafa.
United Kingdom: New Abulela Bldg., P.O.B. 801; *Ambassador:* R. G. A. Etherington-Smith.
U.S.S.R.: B1, A10 St., New Extension, P.O.B. 1161; *Ambassador:* Felix Fedotov.
U.S.A.: Gumhouria Ave.; *Ambassador:* William D. Brewer.
Vatican: El Safeh City, Shambat, P.O.B. 623; *Apostolic Pro-Nuncio:* Ubaldo Calabresi.
Yemen Arab Republic: St. 35, New Extension; *Ambassador:* Mohammed Abdul Wasse.
Yemen, People's Democratic Republic: Cairo, Egypt.
Yugoslavia: St. 31, 79-A, Khartoum 1, P.O.B. 1180; *Ambassador:* Ljubomir Drndić.
Zaire: Gumhouria Ave.; *Ambassador:* Matonda Sakala.

Sudan also has diplomatic relations with Afghanistan, Argentine, Brazil, Cameroon, Canada, Chile, Cyprus, Denmark, Finland, Guinea, Indonesia, Malaysia, Mali, Mauritania, Norway, Senegal, Sri Lanka, Sweden, Democratic Republic of Viet-Nam, and Zambia.

PEOPLE'S ASSEMBLY

A People's Assembly is provided for under the Permanent Constitution, but elections to it are not due till February 1974.

POLITICAL PARTY

Sudanese Socialist Union: Khartoum; f. 1971; inaugural conference held Jan. 1972; Sudan's only recognized political party; consists of National Conference, Central Committee, Political Bureau and Secretariat-General.

Political Bureau: Maj.-Gen. Jaafir al-Nemery,* Maj.-Gen. Muhammad al-Baqir Ahmad,* Abel Alier, Maj. Abdul El Gasim Mohammed Ibrahim,* Dr. Gaafer Mohammed Ali Bakheit,* Dr. Mansour Khalid,* Peter Gatkouth,* Ahmed Abdel Halim,* Mahdi Mustafa El Hadi,* Luigi Adwok, Tobi Madot, Hilary Logali, Dr. Lawrence Wol, Joseph Oduho, Omer El Hag Musa,* Ibrahim Moniem Mansour,* Col. Salah Abdel Aal Mabrouk,* Nifisa Ahmed El Amin,* El Rasheed El Taher,* Izzedin El Sayed,* Abdulla El Hassan, Wadie Habashi, Abdel Rahman Abdalla,* Badr Eddin Suliman,* Mubarak Sinadah.*

* Member also of the Secretariat-General.

JUDICIAL SYSTEM

The administration of justice is the function of the Judiciary, as a separate and independent department of state. The general administrative supervision and control of the Judiciary is vested in the Chief Justice.

Civil Justice: is administered by the Courts constituted under the Civil Justice Ordinance, namely the Supreme Court, Court of Appeal and Other Courts. The Supreme Court consists of a President and one or more Vice-Presidents and sufficient number of judges. It is the custodian of the Constitution under the Permanent Constitution of the Sudan of 1973.

Criminal Justice: is administered by the Courts constituted under the Code of Criminal Procedure, namely Major Courts, Minor Courts and Magistrates' Courts. Serious crimes are tried by Major Courts which are composed of a President and two members and have power to

THE SUDAN—(Judicial System, Religion)

pass the death sentence. Major Courts are as a rule presided over by a Judge of the High Court appointed to a Provincial Circuit, or a Province Judge. There is a right of appeal to the Chief Justice against any decision or order of a Major Court and all findings and sentences of a Major Court are subject to confirmation by him.

Lesser crimes are tried by Minor Courts consisting of three Magistrates and presided over by a Second Class Magistrate and by Magistrates' Courts consisting of a single Magistrate, or a bench of lay Magistrates.

Local Courts: try a substantial portion of the Criminal and Civil cases in the Sudan and work in parallel to some extent with the State Courts.

Chief Justice: UTHMAN AS SAYID.

MUHAMMADAN LAW COURTS

Justice in personal matters for the Muslim population is administered by the Muhammadan Law Courts, which form the Sharia Division of the Judiciary. These Courts consist of the Court of Appeal, High Courts and Qadis' Courts, and President of the Sharia Division is the Grand Qadi. The religious Law of Islam is administered by these Courts in matters of inheritance, marriage, divorce, family relationships and charitable trusts.

Grand Qadi: Sheikh YAHYA ABDEL GASIM.

RELIGION

The majority of Sudanese are vigorous followers of Islam—it will be remembered that the Mahdi of 1896 was a religious leader—but some communities in the south remain untouched by Islam and practise animism or fertility worship. The cultural contrast between the Muhammadan north and centre, and the non-Muslim south, with differences in race, language, religion and outlook, gives rise to one principal political problem of the Sudan. It is estimated that there are more than 9 million Muslims and over 400,000 Catholics.

MUSLIM COMMUNITY
(Mainly divided into the following sects:)

Qadria: Heads of important local sub-sections include:
Sheikh AHMED EL GAALI.
Sheikh IBRAHIM EL KABASHI.
YOUSIF EL SHEIKH OMER EL OBEID.
KHALIFA BARAKAT EL SHEIKH.
Sheikh HAMAD EL NIL ABD EL BAGI.
Sheikh ABD EL BAGI EL MUKASHFI.

Shadhlia: Heads of local sub-sections include:
Sheikh EL MAGDOUB EL BESHIR.
Sheikh GAMAR EL DAWLA EL MAGDOUB.

Idrisia: Heads of local sub-sections include:
Sheikh EL HASSAN EL IDRISI.

Khatmiya: MUHAMMAD OSMAN EL MIRGHANI.

Sammania: Sheikh FATEH GHARIBALLA.

Ismaila: Sayed JAYAL ASFIA EL SAYED EL MEKKI.

Ansari.

CHRISTIAN COMMUNITIES

Coptic Orthodox Church: Bishop of Nubia, Atbara and Omdurman: Rt. Rev. BAKHOMIOS.
Bishop of Khartoum, S. Sudan and Uganda: Rt. Rev. ANBA YOUANNIS.

Greek Orthodox Church: Metropolitan of Nubia: Archbishop SINESSIOS.

Greek Evangelical Church.

Evangelical Church: P.O.B. 57, Khartoum; Chair. Rev. RADI ELIAS; about 500 mems.

Episcopal Church in the Sudan: Clergy House, P.O.B. 135, Khartoum; Bishop in the Sudan: The Rt. Rev. OLIVER C. ALLISON; Asst. Bishops: The Rt. Rev. YEREMAYA DOTIRO; The Rt. Rev. ELINANA NGALAMU, The Rt. Rev. BUTRUS SHUKAI, The Rt. Rev. BENJAMINA YUGUSUK.

Catholic Church:

Roman Rite:

Vicariate Apostolic of Khartoum: P.O.B. 49, Khartoum; Rt. Rev. Bishop AUGUSTINE BARONI.

Vicariate Apostolic of Wau: P.O.B. 29, Wau; Rt. Rev. Bishop IRENEUS WIEN DUD.

Vicariate Apostolic of Juba: P.O.B. 32, Juba; Rt. Rev. PAOLINO DOGGALE, Apostolic Administrator.

Vicariate Apostolic of El Obeid: P.O.B. 386, El Obeid, Rt. Rev. Mgr. FRANCO CAZZANIGA, Apostolic Administrator.

Vicariate Apostolic of Rumbek: Catholic Church, Rumbek; Rev. Fr. DOMINIC MATONG, Vicar Del.

Prefecture Apostolic of Malakal: P.O.B. 27, Malakal; Rt. Rev. Mgr. PIUS YUKWAN.

Prefecture Apostolic of Mupoi: Catholic Church, Tombora; Rt. Rev. Msgr. JOSEPH GASI, Apostolic Administrator.

Maronite Church: P.O.B. 244, Khartoum; Rev. Fr. YOUSEPH NEAMA.

Greek Catholic Church: P.O.B. 766, Khartoum; Archimandrite: BASILIOS HAGGAR.

Jewish Community: Chief Rabbi: (vacant).

THE SUDAN—(The Press, Publishers, Radio and Television, Finance)

THE PRESS

The Press was nationalized on August 27th, 1970. A General Corporation for Press, Printing and Publications was set up with two publishing houses, the Al-Ayam (P.O.B. 363, Khartoum), and the Al-Rai Al-Amm (P.O.B. 424, Khartoum). These two houses publish all the following newspapers and magazines with the exception of those produced by other ministries.

DAILIES

Al-Ayam: P.O.B. 363, Khartoum; Arabic.
Al-Sahafa: P.O.B. 424, Khartoum; f. 1961; Arabic.
Sudan Standard: P.O.B. 424, Khartoum; English.

PERIODICALS

El Guwat El Musallaha: armed forces publication; weekly.
Huna Omdurman: f. 1942; Arabic; weekly; Sudan Broadcasting Service Magazine; published by Ministry of Communications.
Khartoum: P.O.B. 424, Khartoum; Arabic; monthly.
Nile Mirror: English; weekly; published by High Executive Council for the Southern Region.

El Rai El Amm: P.O.B. 424, Khartoum; Arabic; weekly.
Sudan Cotton Bulletin: P.O.B. 1672, Khartoum; English; monthly; published by Cotton Public Corporation.
Sudan Cotton Review: P.O.B. 1672, Khartoum; English; annually; published by Cotton Public Corporation.
El Sudan El Gadid: P.O.B. 363, Khartoum; Arabic; weekly.
Sudanese Economist: Khartoum; English; monthly; economic and commercial review.

NEWS AGENCIES

Sudan National News Agency: P.O.B. 624, Khartoum; f. 1971; daily and weekly summaries in English and Arabic; Man. Abdul Karim Osman el Mahdi.

Foreign Bureaux

Middle East News Agency: Dalala Bldg., P.O.B. 740, Khartoum.

Tass also has a bureau in Khartoum.

PUBLISHERS

African Printing House: Press House, P.O.B. 1228, Khartoum; f. 1960; publishers of *al-Sahafa*; also African News Service; Gen. Man. Abdul Rahman Mukhtar.
Ahmed Abdel Rahman El Tikeina: P.O. Box 299, Port Sudan.
Al Ayam Press Co. Ltd.: Aboul Ela Building, United Nations Square, P.O. Box 363, Khartoum; f. 1953; Man. Dir. Beshir Muhammad Said; newspapers, pamphlets and books.
Al-Rai Al-Amm: P.O.B. 424, Khartoum.
Al Sahafa Publishing House: government publications and short stories.

Al Salam Co. Ltd.: P.O.B. 197, Khartoum.
Central Office of Information: Khartoum; government publishing office; publications include the *Sudan Almanac*.
Claudios S. Fellas: P.O. Box 641, Khartoum.
Fuad Rashed: Wadi Halfa.
Khartoum University Press: P.O.B. 321, Khartoum; f. 1967; scholarly works; Dir. Mohd. Ibrahim Shoush, ph.d.
McCorquodale and Co. (Sudan) Ltd.: P.O. Box 38, Khartoum.
Mitchell Cotts and Co. (ME) Ltd.: P.O. Box 221, Khartoum.

RADIO AND TELEVISION

Sudan Broadcasting Service: P.O.B. 572, Omdurman; a government-controlled radio station which broadcasts daily in Arabic and English; Dir. El Tigani El Tayib.

There are 200,000 radio receivers.

Sudan Television Service (STS): P.O.B. 1094, Omdurman; f. 1962; thirty-five hours of programmes per week; Dir.-Gen. Mekki Awad.

There are 50,000 television receivers.

FINANCE

BANKING

(cap.=capital; p.u.=paid up; dep.=deposits; m.=million)

Under the Nationalization of Banks Act 1970, all banks have been nationalized.

Central Bank

Bank of Sudan: P.O. Box 313, Khartoum; f. 1960; acts as banker and financial adviser to the Government and has sole right of issue of Sudanese banknotes; cap. p.u. £S1.5m.; Chair. Ibrahim Nimir; Deputies El Faki Mustafa, El Baghir Yousif Mudawi; 7½brs; publ. *Economic and Financial Bulletin* (quarterly), *Foreign Trade Statistical Digest* (quarterly), *Annual Report*.

Commercial Banks

El Nilein Bank: P.O.B. 466, Khartoum; f. 1965 as a partnership between the Bank of Sudan and the Crédit Lyonnais; cap. p.u. £S53m.; 8 branches Chair. Dr. Mohamed Mekki Kanani.

THE SUDAN—(Finance, Trade and Industry)

Juba Commercial Bank: P.O.B. 1186, Khartoum; formerly the Commercial Bank of Ethiopia; especially concerned with the non-Muslim south and with trading relations with African countries; 2 brs.; Gen. Man. EL DIRDEERI IBRAHIM.

Omdurman National Bank: Khartoum; formerly the Ottoman (National and Grindlays) Bank; 10 brs; Chair. a.i. and Gen. Man. ZAKARIA MOHAMED ABDO.

People's Co-operative Bank: P.O.B. 922, Khartoum; formerly the Misr Bank; 6 brs.; deals with all operations and facilities of the Sudan co-operative movement; Gen. Man. AHMED ABDEL RAHMAN.

Red Sea Commercial Bank: Khartoum; formerly the Arab Bank; 3 brs.

State Bank for Foreign Trade: P.O.B. 1008, Khartoum; formerly Barclays Bank D.C.O.; £S35,551,000 (Dec. 1972); 24 brs.; Gen. Man. HUSSEIN ABDEL GADIR.

Sudan Commercial Bank: P.O.B. 1116, Khartoum; f. 1960; cap. p.u. £S1,099,611; dep. £S8,280,000; Chair. and Gen. Man. MOHAMED SALIH YAHIA; 6 brs.

DEVELOPMENT BANKS

Agricultural Bank of Sudan: P.O. Box 1363, Khartoum; f. 1957; cap. £S7m.; provides agricultural credit; Chair. and Man. Dir. MIRGHANI EL AMIN EL HAG.

Estate Bank of Sudan: Khartoum.

Industrial Bank of Sudan: P.O.B. 1722, Khartoum; f. 1962; cap. £S 2m.

INSURANCE COMPANIES

There are over forty foreign insurance companies operating in the Sudan.

TRADE AND INDUSTRY

Sudan Gezira Board: H.Q. Barakat; Sales Office, P.O.B. 884, Khartoum; Chair. and Man. Dir. Dr. ABBAS ABDEL MAGID; Deputy Man. Dir. MAHMOUD MOHD. ALI; Financial Controller ABDALLA IMAM; Agricultural Man. HASSAN ABDALLA HASHIM; Sales Man. BESHIR MEDANI; Sec. YOUSIF EL KARIB.

The Sudan Gezira Board is responsible for Sudan's main cotton producing area. Starting in 1911 as a company enterprise, it was nationalized in 1950 and has since then been run by a Board of Directors, consisting of 8 to 11 members. In 1969 the Revolutionary Government formed a temporary Board of Directors consisting of six officials and a tenant farmers' representative pending an extensive reorganization of the Board.

The Gezira Scheme represents a partnership between the Government, the tenants and the Board. The Government, which provides the land and is responsible for irrigation, receives 36 per cent of the net proceeds; the tenants (who numbered about 100,000 in 1971 and who do the actual cultivation) receive 49 per cent. The Board receives 10 per cent, the local Government Councils in the Scheme area 2 per cent and the Social Development Fund, set up to provide social services for the inhabitants, 3 per cent.

The total possible cultivable area of the Gezira Scheme is over 5 million acres and the total area under systematic irrigation is now almost 2 million acres. In addition to cotton, groundnuts, sorghum, wheat and millet are grown for the benefit of tenant farmers.

Publications: *Annual Report, Annual Statement of Accounts, El Gezira News Paper* (weekly), *Weekly Bulletin*.

State Cotton Marketing Corpn.: P.O.B. 1672, Khartoum, Sudan; f. June 1970; the Corporation now supervises all cotton marketing operations through the following four main cotton companies:

> **Port Sudan Cotton and Trade Co. Ltd.:** P.O.B. 590, Khartoum.
>
> **National Cotton and Trade Co. Ltd.:** P.O.B. 1552, Khartoum.
>
> **Sudan Cotton Trade Co. Ltd.:** P.O.B. 2284, Khartoum.
>
> **Alaktan Trading Co. Ltd.:** P.O.B. 2607, Khartoum.

Offices Abroad:

> Democratic Republic of Sudan Consulates, Sudan Cotton Section, 3 rue de Marché, 1204 Geneva, Switzerland.
>
> Sudan Cotton Centre, P.O.B. 152, Osaka, Japan.

State Trading Corporation: Gen. Man. MOHAMED ABDEL KARIM ABBAS.

The Food Industries Corporation: P.O.B. 2341, Khartoum; produces dehydrated onion and pepper, dried vegetables, gum arabic, etc; dates, canned fruit and vegetables; wheat bran and sweets.

CHAMBER OF COMMERCE

Sudan Chamber of Commerce: P.O.B. 81, Khartoum f. 1908; Pres. ABDEL SALAM ABOUL ELA; Hon. Treas. TH. APOSTOLOU; Hon. Sec. SAYED SALEH OSMAN SALEH.

TRADE UNIONS

FEDERATIONS

Federation of Sudanese Workers' Unions (F.S.W.U.): P.O.B. 2258, Khartoum; f. 1963; includes 135 affiliates totalling 450,000 mems.; affiliated to the International Confederation of Trade Union Federations and the All-African Trade Union Federation; Pres. AWADALLA IBRAHIM; Sec.-Gen. (vacant); publs. *Al Talia* (Arabic, weekly), *Bulletin* (English and Arabic, monthly).

Federation of Workers' Trade Unions of the Private Sector: Khartoum; f. 1965; Pres. SALIH ABDEL RAHMAN.

Federation of Workers' Trade Unions of the Public Sector: Khartoum; f. 1965.

PRINCIPAL UNIONS

In 1958 all Trade Unions were dissolved, but legislation in 1961 permitted registration of Trade Unions satisfying certain conditions. The larger ones are:

Central Electricity and Water Administration Trade Union: P.O.B. 1380, Khartoum; 3,000 mems.; Pres. ALI SAID; Sec.-Gen. MAHJUB SID AHMAD.

Department of Agriculture Trade Union: Khartoum Workers' Club, Khartoum; 1,170 mems.; Pres. ABDAL-KARIM SADALLAH; Sec.-Gen. ABDULLAM IBRAHIM.

Egyptian Irrigation Department Trade Union: Khartoum; 1,210 mems.; Pres. FADL ABD-AL-WAHAB; Sec.-Gen. MUHAMMAD AL SAIYID MUHAMMAD.

Forestry Department Trade Union: c/o Forests Department, Al Suke; f. 1961; 2,510 mems.; Pres. IMAN UMAR; Sec.-Gen. MUHAMMED IBRAHIM AHMED.

Gezira Board Non-Agricultural Workers' Union: c/o Gezira Board, Wad Medani; f. 1961; 6,600 mems.; Pres. SULAYMAN ABD-AL-FARAJ; Sec.-Gen. MIRGHANI ABD-AL-RAHIM.

THE SUDAN—(Trade and Industry, Transport and Tourism)

Khartoum Municipality Trade Union: c/o Khartoum Municipal Council, P.O. Box 750, Khartoum; 891 mems.; Pres. Muhammad Abdullah Ahmad; Sec.-Gen. Uthman Muhammad Al Shaikh.

Khartoum University Trade Union: Khartoum University, P.O.B. 321, Khartoum; f. 1947; 1,400 mems; Pres. Mahjub Ahmad Al-Zubayr.

Mechanical Transport Department Trade Union: Khartoum Workers' Club, P.O.B. 617, Khartoum; 2,593 mems.; Pres. Madarri Muhammad Ayd; Sec.-Gen. Ibrahim Baballah.

Ministry of Education Trade Union: Khartoum Workers' Club, Khartoum; 679 mems.; Pres. Muhammad Hamdan; Sec.-Gen. Uthman Al-Siddiq.

Ministry of Health Trade Union: c/o Khartoum Hospital, Khartoum; 3,592 mems.; Pres. Abdal Raziq Ubayd; Sec.-Gen. Ibrahim Umar Alhaj.

Ministry of Irrigation and Hydro-Electric Power Trade Union: Medani Workers' Club, Wad Medani; 15,815 mems.; Pres. Yahya Hasan Al-Rau.

Ministry of Public Utilities Trade Union: Khartoum Workers' Club, Khartoum; 607 mems.; Pres. Awadallah Ibrahim; Sec.-Gen. Hassan Abdel Gadir.

Posts and Telegraphs Trade Union: Khartoum Workers' Club; 700 mems.; Pres. Abd-Al-Moneim Ahmad; Sec.-Gen. Fadl Ahmad Fadl.

Sudan Textile Industry Employees Trade Union: Khartoum North; f. 1968; 3,750 mems.; Sec. Mukhtar Abdalla.

Sudan Railway Workers' Union (S.R.W.U.): Sudan Railway Workers' Union Club, Atbara; f. 1961; 28,000 mems.; Pres. Musa Ahmed Muttai; Sec. Muhammad Osman Ali el Mudir.

CO-OPERATIVE SOCIETIES

There are some 600 Co-operative Societies in the Sudan, of which 570 are formally registered. Of these 206 are Consumers' Societies, 152 are Agricultural Co-operative Societies, 41 General Purpose, 107 Marketing and Credit, 15 Flour Mill and 49 other types.

TRANSPORT AND TOURISM

TRANSPORT
RAILWAYS

Sudan Railways: Atbara; Gen. Man. Abdel Moneim Abbas.

The total length of railway in operation is 4,756 route-kilometres. The main line runs from Wadi Halfa, on the Egyptian border to El Obeid, via Khartoum. Lines from Atbara and Sennar connect with Port Sudan on the coast. Since independence two new lines have been built, one from Sennar to Roseires on the Blue Nile (225 km.), opened in 1954, and one from Aradeiba to Nyala, in the south-western province of Darfur (689 km.), opened in 1959. A railway branching from this line, at Babanousa, to Wau in Bahr el Ghazal province (445 km.) has now been completed.

ROADS

Ministry of Communications: P.O.B. 300, Khartoum; Dir. of Works Ibrahim Mohd. Ibrahim.

Roads in the Northern Sudan, other than town roads, are only cleared tracks and often impassable immediately after rain. Motor traffic on roads in the Upper Nile Province is limited to the drier months of January–May. There are several good gravelled roads in the Equatoria and Bahr el Ghazal Provinces which are passable all the year round, but in these districts some of the minor roads become impassable after rain. Rehabilitation of communications in the Southern Sudan is a major priority as the Civil War completely destroyed 1,000 miles of roads and 70 bridges.

The through route from Juba to Khartoum is open from mid-November to mid-April.

Over 30,000 miles of tracks are classed as "motorable", but only 208 miles are asphalt.

INLAND WATERWAYS

Ministry of Communications: P.O.B. 300, Khartoum.

The total length of navigable waterways served by passenger and freight services is 4,068 km. From the Egyptian border to Wadi Halfa and Khartoum navigation is limited by cataracts to short stretches but the White Nile from Khartoum to Juba is navigable at almost all seasons. The Blue Nile is not navigable. River transport was badly hit by the Civil War. A new harbour is to be constructed at Suakin.

The Sudan Railways operate 2,500 km. of steamer services on the navigable reaches of the Nile, touching Juba, Gambeila, Wau, Shellal (in Egyptian territory), and Dongola. These services connect with the Egyptian main railway services and the Nile river services of Kenya and Uganda.

The construction of the Egyptian High Dam has flooded the Wadi Halfa. The Sudan and Egypt operate river services in the Wadi Halfa/Aswan reach by deep-draught vessels suitable to sail in the big lake thus created.

SHIPPING

Sudan Railways: Atbara; responsible for operating Port Sudan.

Port Sudan, on the Red Sea, 490 miles from Khartoum, is the only seaport. There are eleven fully equipped berths, with a total length of 5,718 feet, and two secondary berths. There are also two berths with a total length of 1,200 feet.

River Navigation Corporation: Khartoum; f. 1970; jointly owned by the Egyptian and Sudan governments; operates services between Aswan and Wadi Halfa.

Sudan Shipping Line: P.O.B. 426, Port Sudan; f. 1960; four vessels operating between the Red Sea, North Europe and the United Kingdom; Gen. Man. Yousif Bakheit Arabi.

CIVIL AVIATION

Sudan Airways: Gumhouria Ave., P.O.B. 253, Khartoum; f. 1947; this airline is owned by the Sudan Government; regular services throughout the Sudan and external services to Aden, Chad, Egypt, Ethiopia, Greece, Italy, Lebanon, Libya, Saudi Arabia, and the U.K.; Charter and Survey based at Khartoum; fleet of 2 Boeing 707, 5 Fokker F-27A, 1 DC-3, and 3 Twin Otters; Gen. Man. M. E. El Amir.

The Sudan is also served by the following foreign airlines: Aeroflot, Alitalia, BOAC, EgyptAir, Ethiopian, Interflug, Libyan Arab, Lufthansa, MEA, Saudia and Swissair.

TOURISM

Sudan Tourist Corporation: P.O.B. 2424, Khartoum; Dir. Abdul Rahman I. Kebeda.

EDUCATION

The education system in Sudan has been under review since 1972, and new laws governing education are being drafted. Recent education policy has aimed to help make attainable the ideals of the new Socialist State established after the May (1969) Revolution. The administrative machinery of supervision and control is conducted through the Ministries of Education and Higher Education. General policy is executed through different technical and administrative bodies under the control of the Ministry. A technical "professional" Inspectorate at headquarters is responsible for the day-to-day application of curricula in the Higher Secondary Schools and similar Inspectorates exist at provincial levels for Primary and General Secondary Schools.

Under the new Five-Year Plan 1970/71–1974/75, education is being reconstructed and all curricula revised to relate the educational system more effectively to the new economic and social needs of the country. While the duration of formal schooling remains the same as before, i.e. 12 years, the Primary Level (*see* below) has been lengthened by two years; the six years secondary stage has been into a lower level or General Secondary and an upper level or Higher Secondary, each of three years duration. The Higher Secondary Level is in turn divided into an Academic and a Vocational/Technical/Higher Secondary stage, the latter being one year longer than the former. In 1970/71 £S20.92 million was allocated for education representing 18.4 per cent of the National Budget. Over the whole Plan period, i.e. 1970/71–1974/75, £S9,800,000 has been granted to the Ministries of Education and Higher Education and Scientific Research representing 4.9 per cent of the total Five-Year Development Budget.

Pre-Primary Education. With the exception of a few pilot projects, pre-primary education is still in the hands of voluntary bodies, e.g. Christian Mission schools. However, attempts are being made to bring these under the control of the Ministry of Education.

Primary Education. Several important developments have taken place in primary education. The most important are those in connection with the implementation of the New Plan including the extension of this level from four to six years and the expansion of classes; the completion of a scheme to raise all rural subgrade (3 year) schools to the level of primary (6 year) schools. By September 1970 a total of 615 such schools, of which 208 were girls schools, had been raised to the level of 6-year primary schools and had nearly 2,900 teachers. As regards the curricula, notable features included the introduction of "Environmental Studies", "Citizenship Education" and "National Subjects" comprising civics, history and geography.

Academic Secondary and Vocational Education. Two essential developments have taken place: firstly the introduction of the "Selective System" whereby students in the two final years specialize in one of three alternative groups of subjects: Literary, Science and Mathematics or Commercial subjects. The second change is that students sit only for those subjects included in their specialization whether literary, scientific or commercial. New curricula changes include the introduction of New Mathematics projects, Sociology and Psychology at the Higher Secondary level and French as an alternative foreign language.

Technical Education. In March 1970 a scheme for the reorganization of Technical Education was officially announced. The new system comprises schools for unskilled workers, skilled workers, technical assistants, technicians and professional engineers, etc. Higher Technical education is provided at the Khartoum Technical Institute and in other new post-secondary, two-year institutions, for different technical and vocational specializations throughout the country. Agricultural education is being stressed and new agricultural schools and institutes are being built.

Higher Education. The Policy regarding Higher Education has been guided by two main principles: co-ordination and centralization. With regard to the University of Khartoum, the Amended Law (1970) was passed which included basic changes in the role and administration of the University, for example, the Head of State now becomes the Chancellor with the right to appoint the Vice-Chancellor, greater participation by students and the public has been granted in the running of the University's internal affairs and more democratic means are utilized in the running of academic affairs including departments.

Teacher Training. A number of crash programmes for training new teachers have been implemented following the introduction of the New Plan. The raising of the status of subgrade schools to primary schools status has created the need for at least 2,000 primary teachers who would be in charge of teaching the additional fifth class in the new primary schools. Student teachers are hence selected from the Secondary School Certificate holders.

Adult and Non-Vocational Education. Projects for increasing literacy among adults have been in progress for several years. Experiments in the improvement of syllabuses have begun and new Adult Education curricula will be introduced and taught in the teacher training institutes.

UNIVERSITIES

University of Khartoum: P.O.B. 321, Khartoum; f. 1956; 440 teachers, 6,650 students.

Cairo University Khartoum Branch: P.O.B. 1055, Khartoum; f. 1955; 80 teachers, 5,100 students.

BIBLIOGRAPHY

GENERAL

ABDEL RAHIM, MUDDATHIR. Imperialism and Nationalism in the Sudan: A Study in Constitutional and Political Developments 1899–1956 (Oxford University Press, 1969).

ALBINO, OLIVER. The Sudan, a southern viewpoint (Oxford, 1969).

AMMAR, ABBAS, and others. The Unity of the Nile Valley, its Geographical Basis and its Manifestations in History (Cairo, 1947).

BARBOUR, K. M. The Republic of the Sudan: A Regional Geography (University of London Press, London, 1961).

BESHIR, M. O. The Southern Sudan: Background to Conflict (C. Hurst, London, 1968, Praeger, New York, 1968).

BONN, GISELA. Das doppelte Gesicht des Sudan (F. A. Brockhaus, Wiesbaden, 1961).

BOUSFIELD, L. Sudan Doctor (London, 1954).

BUDGE, Sir E. A. T. W. The Egyptian Sudan: Its History and Monuments (2 vols., London, 1907).
By Nile and Tigris (London, 1920).

BUXTON, J. C. Chiefs and Strangers (Oxford, 1963).

EGYPTIAN SOCIETY OF INTERNATIONAL LAW. Documents of the Sudan 1899–1953 (Cairo, 1953).

FADL, EL S. H. Their Finest Days (Rex Collings, London, 1969).

FAWZI, S. ED DIN. The Labour Movement in the Sudan, 1946–55 (Oxford University Press, London, 1957).

GAITSKELL, ARTHUR. Gezira: A Story of Development in the Sudan (Faber, London, 1959).

HAMILTON, J. A. DE C. The Sudan: the Road Ahead (London, 1945).
The Anglo-Egyptian Sudan from Within (London, 1935).

HENDERSON, K. D. D. The Sudan Republic (Benn, London, 1965).

HERZOG, ROLF. Sudan (Kurt Schroeder, Bonn, 1958).

HILL, R. A Bibliography of the Anglo-Egyptian Sudan from the earliest times to 1937 (Oxford, 1939).
A Bibliographical Dictionary of the Anglo-Egyptian Sudan (new edition, Frank Cass, London, 1967).
Egypt in the Sudan 1820–1881 (Oxford University Press, London and New York, 1959).
Slatin Pasha (Oxford University Press, London, 1964, New York, 1965).
Sudan Transport: a History (London, 1965).

HODGKIN, R. A. Sudan Geography (London, 1951).

HURST, H. E. and PHILIPS, P. The Nile Basin, 7 vols. (London, 1932–38).

JACKSON, H. C. The Fighting Sudanese (London, 1954).
Sudan Days and Ways (London, 1954).

KNIGHT, R. L., and BOYNS, B. M. Agricultural Science in the Sudan (1950).

LANGLEY, M. No Woman's Country: Travels in the Anglo-Egyptian Sudan (New York, 1951).

LEBON, J. H. C. Land Use in Sudan (Geographical Publications Ltd., Bude, U.K., 1965).

NASRI, A. R. EL-. A Bibliography of the Sudan 1938–1958 (Oxford University Press, 1962).

NEWBOLD, Sir D. The Making of the Modern Sudan; the Life and Letters of Sir Douglas Newbold (London, Faber and Faber, 1953).

ODUHO, JOSEPH, and DENG, WILLIAM. The Problem of the Southern Sudan (Oxford University Press, 1963).

SUDANESE GOVERNMENT. Ten Year Plan of Economic and Social Development 1961-62—1971-72 (Khartoum, Ministry of Finance and Economics, 1962).

TRIMINGHAM, J. S. Islam in the Sudan (London, 1949).

ANTHROPOLOGY

CUNNISON, IAN. Baggara Arabs (Oxford University Press, New York, 1966).

EVANS-PRITCHARD, E. E. Kinship and Marriage among the Nuer (London, 1951).
The Nuer (London, 1940).
Witchcraft, Oracles and Magic among the Azande (London, 1937).

GRIFFITHS, V. L., and TAHA, ABDEL RAHMAN ALI. Sudan Courtesy Customs (Sudan Government, 1936).

HABER, HUGO. Das Fortleben nach dem Tode im Glauben westsudanischer Völker (Mödling, 1951).

NADEL, S. F. The Nuba: an Anthropological Study of the Hill Tribes of Kordofan (London, 1947).

PAUL, A. A History of the Beja tribes of the Sudan (Cambridge, 1954).

SELIGMAN, C. G. Pagan Tribes of the Nilotic Sudan (London, 1932).

HISTORY

ABBAS, MEKKI. The Sudan Question: the Dispute about the Anglo-Egyptian Condominium, 1884-1951 (London, 1952).

ARKELL, A. J. Outline History of the Sudan (London, 1938); History of the Sudan to 1821 (2nd. ed., London, 1961).

BOAHEN, A. ADU. Britain, the Sahara and the Western Sudan 1788-1816 (Oxford University Press, New York and London, 1964).

COLLINS, ROBERT O. The Southern Sudan 1883-1898 (Yale University Press, 1962).

COLLINS, ROBERT O and TIGNOR, R. L. Egypt and the Sudan (Prentice, New York, 1967).

CORBYN, E. N. Survey of the Anglo-Egyptian Sudan, 1898-1944 (London, 1946).

FABUNMI, L. A. The Sudan in Anglo-Egyptian Relations (Longmans, London, 1965).

GRAY, RICHARD. History of the Southern Sudan 1839–89 (Oxford, 1961).

HASSAN, YUSUF FADL. The Arabs and the Sudan (Edinburgh University Press, Edinburgh, 1967).

THE SUDAN—(BIBLIOGRAPHY)

HENDERSON, K. D. D. Survey of the Anglo-Egyptian Sudan, 1898-1944 (London, 1946).

HOLT, P. M. The Mahdist State in the Sudan: 1881-98 (Oxford University Press, 2nd edn., 1970).

    A Modern History of the Sudan (Weidenfeld and Nicolson, London, 1962, Praeger, New York, 1963).

MACMICHAEL, Sir H. A. A History of the Arabs in the Sudan (2 vols., Cambridge, 1922; reprinted Frank Cass, London and Barnes & Noble, New York, 1967).

    The Anglo-Egyptian Sudan (London, 1935).

    The Sudan (London, 1954).

SABRY, M. Le Soudan Egyptien, 1821-98 (Cairo, 1947).

SANDERSON, G. N. England, Europe and the Upper Nile (Edinburgh University Press, Edinburgh, 1965).

SHIBEIKA, MEKKI. The Sudan in the Century 1819-1919 (Cairo, 1947).

    British Policy in the Sudan: 1882-1902 (London, 1952).

    The Independent Sudan: The History of a Nation (New York, 1960).

SHINNIE, MARGARET. A Short History of the Sudan up to A.D. 1500 (Khartoum, 1954).

SHINNIE, P. L. Meroe (Thames and Hudson, London, 1967).

THEOBALD, A. B. The Mahdiya: A History of the Anglo-Egyptian Sudan, 1881-1899 (New York, 1951).

Syria

PHYSICAL AND SOCIAL GEOGRAPHY

W. B. Fisher

Before 1918 the term "Syria" was rather loosely applied to the whole of the territory now forming the modern States of Syria, the Lebanon, Israel, and Jordan. To the Ottomans, as to the Romans, Syria stretched from the Euphrates to the Mediterranean, and from the Sinai to the hills of southern Turkey, with Palestine as a smaller province of this wider unit. Though the present Syrian Arab Republic has a much more limited extension, an echo of the past remains to colour the political thinking of a few present-day Syrians, and from time to time there are references to a "Greater Syria" as a desirable but possibly remote aspiration.

The frontiers of the present-day State are largely artificial, and reflect to a considerable extent the interests and prestige of outside Powers—Britain, France, and the United States—as these existed in 1918–20. The northern frontier with Turkey is defined by a single-track railway line running along the southern edge of the foothills—probably the only case of its kind in the world; whilst eastwards and southwards boundaries are highly arbitrary, being straight lines drawn for convenience between salient points. Westwards, the frontiers are again artificial, though less crudely drawn, leaving the headwaters of the Jordan river outside Syria and following the crest of the Anti-Lebanon hills, to reach the sea north of Tripoli.

PHYSICAL FEATURES

Geographically, Syria consists of two main zones: a fairly narrow western part, made up of a complex of mountain ranges and intervening valleys; and a much larger eastern zone that is essentially a broad and open platform dropping gently towards the east and crossed diagonally by the wide Euphrates Valley.

The western zone, which contains over 80 per cent of the population of Syria, can be further subdivided as follows. In the extreme west, fronting the Mediterranean Sea, there lies an imposing ridge rising to 5,000 feet, and known as the Jebel Ansariyeh. Its western flank drops fairly gradually to the sea, giving a narrow coastal plain; but on the east it falls very sharply, almost as a wall, to a flat-bottomed valley occupied by the Orontes river, which meanders sluggishly over the flat floor, often flooding in winter, and leaving a malarial marsh in summer. Farther east lie more hill ranges, opening out like a fan from the south-west, where the Anti-Lebanon range, with Mount Hermon (9,000 ft.), is the highest in Syria. Along the eastern flanks of the various ridges lie a number of shallow basins occupied by small streams that eventually dry up or form closed salt lakes. In one basin lies the city of Aleppo, once the second town of the Ottoman Empire, and still close to being the largest city of Syria. In another is situated Damascus, irrigated from five streams, and famous for its clear fountains and gardens—now the capital of the country. One remaining sub-region of western Syria is the Jebel Druse, which lies in the extreme south-west, and consists of a vast out-pouring of lava, in the form of sheets and cones. Towards the west this region is fertile, and produces good cereal crops, but eastwards the soil cover disappears, leaving a barren countryside of twisted lava and caverns, for long the refuge of outlaws, bandits, and minority groups. Because of its difficulty and isolation the Jebel Druse has tended socially and politically to go its own way, remaining aloof from the rest of the country.

The entire eastern zone is mainly steppe or open desert, except close to the banks of the rivers Euphrates, Tigris, and their larger tributaries, where local irrigation projects have allowed a little cultivation. The triangularly-shaped region between the Euphrates and Tigris rivers is spoken of as the Jezireh (Arabic *Jazira*=island), but it is in no way different from the remaining parts of the east.

The presence of ranks of relatively high hills aligned parallel to the coast has important climatic effects. Tempering and humid effects from the Mediterranean are restricted to a narrow western belt, and central and eastern Syria show marked continental tendencies: that is, a very hot summer with temperatures often exceeding 100° or even 110° F., and a moderately cold winter, with frost on many nights. Very close to the Mediterranean, frost is unknown at any season, but on the hills altitude greatly reduces the average temperature, so that snow may lie on the heights from late December to April, or even May. Rainfall is fairly abundant on the west, where the height of the land tends to determine the amount received; but east of the Anti-Lebanon mountains the amount decreases considerably, producing a steppe region that quickly passes into true desert. On the extreme east, as the Zagros ranges of Persia are approached, there is once again a slight increase, but most of Syria has an annual rainfall of under ten inches.

ECONOMIC LIFE

There is a close relationship between climate and economic activities. In the west, where up to 30 or even 40 inches of rainfall occur, settled farming is possible, and the main limitation is difficult terrain; but from the Orontes Valley eastwards natural rainfall is increasingly inadequate, and irrigation becomes necessary. The narrow band of territory where annual rainfall lies between 8 and 15 inches is sometimes spoken of as the "Fertile Crescent", since it runs in an arc along the inner side of the hills from Jordan through western and northern Syria as far east as Iraq. In its normal state a steppeland covered with seasonal grass, the Fertile Crescent can often be converted by irrigation and efficient organisation into a rich and productive territory. Such it was in the golden days of the Arab Caliphate; now, after centuries of decline, it is once again reviving. Even within ten years a marked change can be observed and thanks to small-scale irrigation schemes and the installation of motor pumps to raise water from underground artesian sources, large areas of the former steppe are producing crops of cotton, cereals and fruit. Syria has now a surplus of agricultural production, especially cereals, and this allows her to export to Jordan and the Lebanon, neither of which are self-sufficient in foodstuffs. Production will increase further when the Euphrates Dam is completed in 1974.

Because of its relative openness and accessibility and its geographical situation as a "waist" between the Mediterranean and the Persian Gulf, Syria has been a land of passage, and for centuries its role was that of an intermediary, both commercial and cultural, between the Mediterranean world and the Far East. From early times until the end of the Middle Ages there was a flow of traffic east and west that raised a number of Syrian cities and ports to the rank of international markets. Within the last twenty or so years, following a long period of decline and eclipse resulting from the diversion of this trade to the sea, one can again note a revival due to the new elements of air transport and the construction of oil pipelines from Iraq.

RACE AND LANGUAGE

Racially, we can distinguish many elements in the Syrian people. The nomads of the interior deserts are unusually pure specimens of the Mediterranean type, isolation having preserved them from intermixture. To the west and north there is a widely varying mosaic of other groups: Armenoids, such as the Kurds and Turkish-speaking communities of the north, and the Armenians themselves, who form communities in the cities; groups such as the Druses, who show some affinity to the tribes of the Persian Zagros, and many others.

As a result, there is a surprising variety of language and religion. Arabic is spoken over most of the country, but Kurdish is widely used along the northern frontier and Armenian in the cities. Aramaic, the language of Christ, survives in three villages.

HISTORY

ANCIENT HISTORY

From the earliest times, Syria has experienced successive waves of Semitic immigration—the Canaanites and Phoenicians in the third millennium B.C., the Hebrews and Aramaeans in the second, and, unceasingly, the nomad tribes infiltrating from the Arabian peninsula. This process has enabled Syria to assimilate or reject, without losing its essentially Semitic character, the alien invaders who, time and again, in the course of a long history, have established their domination over the land. Before Rome assumed control of Syria in the first century B.C., the Egyptians, the Assyrians and the Hittites, and, later, the Persians and the Macedonian Greeks had all left their mark in greater or lesser degree. Damascus is claimed to be the oldest capital city in the world, having been continuously inhabited since about 2000 B.C., and Aleppo may be even older. Under Roman rule the infiltration and settlement of nomad elements continued, almost unnoticed by historians, save when along the desert trade routes a Semitic vassal state attained a brief importance as, for example, the kingdom of Palmyra in the Syrian desert, which the Emperor Aurelian destroyed in A.D. 272 or, later still, when the Byzantines ruled in Syria, the Arab State of Ghassan, prominent throughout the sixth century A.D. as a bulwark of the Byzantine Empire against the desert tribes in the service of Sasanid Persia.

ARAB AND TURKISH RULE

When, after the death of the Prophet Muhammad in A.D. 632, the newly-created power of Islam began a career of conquest, the populations of Syria, Semitic in their language and culture and, as adherents of the Monophysite faith, ill-disposed towards the Greek-speaking Orthodox Byzantines, did little to oppose the Muslims, from whom they hoped to obtain a greater measure of freedom. The Muslims defeated the Byzantine forces at Ajnadain in July 634, seized Damascus in September 635, and, by their decisive victory on the River Yarmuk (August 636), virtually secured possession of all Syria. From 661–750 the Umayyad dynasty ruled in Syria, which, after the conquest, had been divided into four military districts or junds (Damascus, Homs, Urdun, i.e. Jordan, and Palestine). To these the Caliph Yazid I (680–83) added a fifth, Kinnasrin, for the defence of northern Syria, where in the late seventh century, the Mardaites, Christians from the Taurus, were making serious inroads under Byzantine leadership. Under Abd al-Malik (685–705) Arabic became the official language of the State, in whose administration, hitherto largely carried out by the old Byzantine bureaucracy, Syrians, Muslim as well as Christian, now had an increasing share. For Syria was now the heart of a great Empire, and the Arab Army of Syria, well trained in the ceaseless frontier warfare with Byzantium, bore the main burden of imperial rule, taking a major part in the two great Arab assaults on Byzantium in 674–8 and in 717-18.

The new regime in Syria was pre-eminently military and fiscal in character, representing the domination of a military caste of Muslim Arab warriors, who governed on the basic assumption that a large subject population, non-Muslim and non-Arab in character, would continue indefinitely to pay tribute. But this assumption was falsified by the gradual spread of Islam, a process which meant the progressive diminution of the amount of tribute paid to the State, and the consequent undermining of the fiscal system as a whole In theory, conversion meant for the non-Arab convert (*Mawla*; in the plural, *Mawali*) full social and economic equality with the ruling caste, but in practice it was not enough to be a Muslim, one had to be an Arab as well. The discontent of the *Mawali* with their enforced inferiority expressed itself in an appeal to the universal character of Islam, an appeal which often took the form of religious heresies, and which, as it became more widespread, undermined the strength of the Arab régime.

To the ever present fiscal problems of the Arab State and the growing discontent of the *Mawali* was added a third and fatal weakness: the hostility between those Arab tribes which had arrived in Syria with or since the conquest, and those which had infiltrated there at an earlier date. The Umayyad house strove to maintain a neutral position over and above the tribal feuds; but from the moment when, under the pressure of events, the Umayyads were compelled to side with one faction to oppose the other (battle of Marj Rahit 684), their position was irretrievably compromised.

When in A.D. 750 with the accession of the Abbasid dynasty the centre of the Empire was transferred to Iraq, Syria, jealously watched because of its association with the former ruling house, became a mere province, where in the course of the next hundred years, several abortive revolts, inspired in part by the traditional loyalty to the Umayyads, failed to shake off Abbasid control. During the ninth century Syria was the object of dispute between Egypt and Baghdad. In 878 Ahmad ibn Tulun, Governor of Egypt, occupied it and, subsequently, every independent ruler of Egypt sought to maintain a hold, partial or complete, over Syria. Local dynasties, however, achieved from time to time a transitory importance, as did the Hamdanids (a Bedouin family from Northern Iraq) who, under Saif ad-Daula, ruler of Aleppo from 946–967, attained a brief ascendancy, marked internally by financial and administrative ineptitude, and externally by military campaigns against the Byzantines which did much to provoke the great Byzantine reconquest of the late tenth century. By the treaty of 997, northern Syria became Byzantine, while the rest of the country remained in the hands of the Fatimid dynasty which ruled in Egypt from 969. Fatimid control remained insecure and from about 1027 a new Arab house ruled at Aleppo—the Mirdasids, who were soon to disappear before the formidable power of the Seljuq Turks. The Seljuqs, having conquered Persia, rapidly overran Syria (Damascus fell to them in 1075) but failed to establish there a united State. As a result of dynastic quarrels, the Seljuq domination disintegrated into a number of amirates: Seljuq princes ruled at Aleppo and Damascus, a local dynasty held Tripoli and, in the south, Egypt controlled most of the littoral.

This political fragmentation greatly favoured the success of the First Crusade which, taking Antioch in 1098 and Jerusalem in 1099, proceeded to organise four feudal States at Edessa, Antioch, Tripoli and Jerusalem, but did not succeed in conquering Aleppo, Homs, Hama, and Damascus. From the death of Baldwin II of Jerusalem in 1131, the essential weakness of the crusading States began to appear. Byzantium, the Christian State of Lesser Armenia, and the Latin principalities in Syria never united in a successful resistance to the Muslim counter-offensive which, initiated by the energetic Turkish general Zangi Atabeg of Mosul, developed rapidly in the third and fourth decades of the century. Zangi, who seized Aleppo in 1128, and the Latin State of Edessa in 1144, was succeeded in 1146 by his able son Nur ad-Din, who by his capture of Damascus in 1154 recreated in Syria a united Muslim Power. On Nur ad-Din's death in 1174, the Kurd Saladin, already master of Egypt, assumed control at Damascus and, in 1183, seized Aleppo. His victory over the Crusaders at Hittin (July 1187) destroyed the kingdom of Jerusalem. Only the partial success of the Third Crusade (1189-92) and, after his death in 1193, the disintegration of Saladin's Empire into a number of separate principalities, made it possible for the Crusaders to maintain an ever more precarious hold on the coastal areas of Syria. The emergence in Egypt of the powerful Mamluk Sultanate (1250) meant that the end was near. A series of military campaigns, led by the Sultan Baibars (1260-77) and his immediate successors, brought about the fall of Antioch (1268) and Tripoli (1289), and, with the fall of Acre in 1291, the disappearance of the crusading States in Syria.

Before the last crusading States had been reduced, the Mamluks had to encounter a determined assault by the Mongols, in the course of which Aleppo and Hama were sacked, and Damascus besieged; until, in 1260, the Mongol army of invasion was crushed at the battle of Ain-Jalut, near Nazareth. The Mongol Il-Khans of Persia made further efforts to conquer Syria in the late thirteenth century, negotiating for this purpose with the Papacy, the remaining crusader States, and Lesser Armenia. In 1280 the Mamluks defeated a Mongol army at Homs; but in 1299 were themselves beaten near the same town, a defeat which enabled the Mongols to ravage northern Syria and to take Damascus in 1300. Only in 1303, at the battle of Marj as-Suffar, south of Damascus, was this last Mongol offensive finally repelled.

The period of Mamluk rule in Syria, which endured until 1517, was on the whole one of slow decline. Warfare, periodical famine, and not least, the plague (there were four great outbreaks in the fourteenth century, and in the fifteenth century fourteen more recorded attacks of some severity) produced a state of affairs which the financial rapacity and misrule of the Mamluk governors and the devastation of Aleppo and Damascus by Timur (1400-01) served only to aggravate.

The ill-defined protectorate which the Mamluks asserted over Cilicia and considerable areas of southern Anatolia occasioned, in the late fifteenth century, a growing tension with the power of the Ottoman Turks, which broke out into inconclusive warfare in the years 1485-91. When to this tension was added the possibility of an alliance between the Mamluks and the rising power of the Safavids in Persia, the Ottoman Sultan Selim I (1512-20) was compelled to seek a decisive solution to the problem. In August 1516 the battle of Marj Dabik, north of Aleppo, gave Syria to the Ottomans, who proceeded to ensure their continued hold on the land by conquering Egypt (1517). Turkish rule, during the next three centuries, although unjustly accused of complete responsibility for a decay and stagnation which appear to have been well advanced before 1517, brought only a temporary improvement in the unhappy condition of Syria, now divided into the three provinces of Damascus, Tripoli, and Aleppo. In parts of Syria the Turkish pashas in reality administered directly only the important towns and their immediate neighbourhood; elsewhere, the older elements—Bedouin emirs, Turcoman chiefs, etc.—were left to act much as they pleased, provided the due tribute was paid. The pashas normally bought their appointment to high office and sought in their brief tenure of power to recover the money and bribes they had expended in securing it, knowing that they might, at any moment, be replaced by someone who could pay more for the post. Damascus alone had 133 pashas in 180 years. As the control of the Sultan at Constantinople became weaker, the pashas obtained greater freedom of action, until Ahmed Jazzar, Pasha of Acre, virtually ruled Syria as an independent prince (1785-1804).

The nineteenth century saw important changes. The Ottoman Sultan Mahmud II (1808-39) had promised Syria to the Pasha of Egypt, Muhammad Ali, in return for the latter's services during the Greek War of Independence. When the Sultan declined to fulfil his promise, Egyptian troops overran Syria (1831-33). Ibrahim Pasha, son of Muhammad Ali, now gave to Syria, for the first time in centuries, a centralised government strong enough to hold separatist tendencies in check and to impose a system of taxation which, if burdensome, was at least regular in its functioning. But Ibrahim's rule was not popular, for the land-owners resented his efforts to limit their social and political dominance, while the peasantry disliked the conscription, the forced labour, and the heavy taxation which he found indispensable for the maintenance of his regime. In 1840 a revolt broke out in Syria, and when the Great Powers intervened on behalf of the Sultan (at war with Egypt since 1839), Muhammad Ali was compelled to renounce his claim to rule there.

Western influence, working through trade, through the protection of religious minorities, and through the cultural and educational efforts of missions and schools, had received encouragement from Ibrahim Pasha. The French Jesuits, returning to Syria in 1831, opened schools, and in 1875 founded their University at Beirut. The American Presbyterian Mission (established at Beirut in 1820) introduced a printing press in 1834, and in 1866 founded the Syrian Protestant College, later renamed the American University of Beirut. Syria also received some benefit from the reform movement within the Ottoman Empire, which, begun by Mahmud II, and continued under his successors, took the form of a determined attempt to modernise the structure of the Empire. The semi-independent pashas of old disappeared, the administration being now entrusted to salaried officials of the central government; some effort was made to create schools and colleges on Western lines, and much was done to deprive the landowning classes of their feudal privileges, although their social and economic predominance was left unchallenged. As a result of these improvements, there was, in the late nineteenth century, a revival of Arabic literature which did much to prepare the way for the growth of Arab nationalism in the twentieth century.

MODERN HISTORY

By 1914 Arab nationalist sentiment had made some headway among the educated and professional classes, and especially among army officers. Nationalist societies like *Al-Fatat* soon made contact with Arab nationalists outside Syria—with the army officers of Iraq, with influential Syrian colonies in Egypt and America, and with the Sharif Husein of Mecca. The Husein-McMahon Correspondence (July 1915–January 1916) encouraged the Arab nationalists to hope that the end of the Great War would mean the creation of a greater Arab kingdom. This expectation was disappointed, for as a result of the Sykes-Picot Agreement, negotiated in secret between England, France, and Russia in 1916 (*see* Documents on Palestine, page 46), Syria was to become a French sphere of influence. At the end of the war, and in accordance with this agreement, a provisional French administration was established in the coastal districts of Syria, while in the interior an Arab government came into being under Amir Faisal, son of the Sharif Husein of Mecca. In March 1920 the Syrian nationalists proclaimed an independent kingdom of Greater Syria (including the Lebanon and Palestine); but in April of the same year the San Remo Conference gave France a mandate for the whole of Syria, and in July, French troops occupied Damascus.

By 1925 the French, aware that the majority of the Muslim population resented their rule, and that only amongst the Christian Maronites of the Lebanon could they hope to find support, had carried into effect a policy based upon the religious divisions so strong in Syria. The area under mandate had been divided into four distinct units; a much enlarged Lebanon (including Beirut and Tripoli), a Syrian Republic, and the two districts of Latakia and Jebel Druse. Despite the fact that the French rule gave Syria a degree of law and order which might render possible the transition from a medieval to a more modern form of society, nationalist sentiment opposed the mandate on principle, and deplored the failure to introduce full representative institutions and the tendency to encourage separatism amongst the religious minorities. This discontent, especially strong in the Syrian Republic, became open revolt in 1925-26, during the course of which the French twice bombarded Damascus (October 1925 and May 1926).

The next ten years were marked by a hesitant and often interrupted progress towards self-government in Syria, and by French efforts to conclude a Franco-Syrian treaty. In April 1928 elections were held for a Constituent Assembly, and in August a draft Constitution was completed; but the French High Commissioner refused to accept certain articles, especially Article 2, which, declaring the Syrian territories detached from the old Ottoman Empire to be an indivisible unity, constituted a denial of the separate existence of the Jebel Druse, Latakia, and the Lebanese Republic. After repeated attempts to reach a compromise, the High Commissioner dissolved the Assembly in May 1930 and, on his own authority, issued a new Constitution for the State of Syria, much the same as that formerly proposed by the Assembly, but with those modifications which were considered indispensable to the maintenance of French control. After new elections (January 1932) negotiations were begun for a Franco-Syrian treaty, to be modelled on that concluded between England and Iraq in 1930, but no compromise could be found between the French demands and those of the nationalists who, although in a minority, wielded a dominant influence in the Chamber and whose aim was to limit both in time and in place the French military occupation, and to include in Syria the separate areas of Jebel Druse and Latakia. In 1934 the High Commissioner suspended the Chamber indefinitely. Disorders occurred early in 1936 which induced the French to send a Syrian delegation to Paris, where the new Popular Front Government showed itself more sympathetic towards Syrian aspirations than former French governments had been. In September 1936 a Franco-Syrian treaty was signed which recognised the principle of Syrian independence and stipulated that, after ratification, there should be a period of three years during which the apparatus of a fully independent State should be created. The districts of Jebel Druse and Latakia would be annexed to Syria, but would retain special administrations. Other subsidiary agreements reserved to France important military and economic rights in Syria. It seemed that Syria might now enter a period of rapid political development; but the unrest caused by the situation in Palestine, the crisis with Turkey, and the failure of France to ratify the 1936 treaty were responsible, within two years, for the breakdown of these hopes.

In 1921 Turkey had consented to the inclusion of the Sanjak of Alexandretta in the French mandated territories, on condition that it should be governed under a special regime. The Turks, alarmed by the treaty of 1936, which envisaged the emergence of a unitary Syrian State including, to all appearance, Alexandretta, now pressed for a separate agreement concerning the status of the Sanjak. After long discussion the League of Nations decided in 1937 that the Sanjak should be fully autonomous, save for its foreign and financial policies which were to be under the control of the Syrian Government. A treaty between France and Turkey guaranteed the integrity of the Sanjak, and also the Turco-Syrian frontier. Throughout 1937 there were conflicts between Turks and Arabs in the Sanjak, and in Syria a widespread and growing resentment, for it was clear that sooner or later Turkey would ask for the cession of Alexandretta. The problem came to be regarded in Syria as a test of Franco-Syrian co-operation, and when in June 1939, under the pressure of international tension, Alexandretta was finally ceded to Turkey the cession assumed in the eyes of Syrian nationalists the character of a betrayal by France. Meanwhile, in France itself, opposition to the treaty of 1936 had grown steadily; and in December 1938 the French Government, anxious not to weaken its military position in the Near East, declared that no ratification of the treaty was to be expected.

Unrest in Syria led to open riots in 1941, as a result of which the Vichy High Commissioner, General Dentz, promised the restoration of partial self-government; while in June of the same year, when in order to combat Axis intrigues the Allies invaded Syria, General Catroux, on behalf of the Free French Government, promised independence for Syria and the end of mandatory rule. Syrian independence was formally recognized in September 1941, but the reality of power was still withheld, with the effect that nationalist agitation, inflamed by French reluctance to restore constitutional rule, and by economic difficulties due to the war, became even more pronounced. When at last elections were held once more, a nationalist government was formed, with Shukri Kuwatly as President of the Syrian Republic (August 1943).

Gradually all important powers and public services were transferred from French to Syrian hands; but conflict again developed over the *Troupes Spéciales*, the local Syrian and Lebanese levies which had existed throughout the mandatory period as an integral part of the French military forces in the Levant, and which, transferred to the Syrian and Lebanese Governments, would enable them to form their own armies. Other points of dispute were the so-called "Common Interests" (i.e. departments dealing with matters of concern to both Syria and the Lebanon), and the control of internal security, hitherto in French hands. Strongly supported by the newly-created Arab League, Syria refused the French demand for a Franco-Syrian Treaty as the condition for the final transfer of these administrative and military services which had always been the main instruments of French policy. In May 1945 disturbances broke out which ended only with British armed intervention and the evacuation of French troops and administrative personnel. The *Troupes Spéciales* were now handed over to the Syrian Government, and with the departure of British forces in April 1946 the full independence of Syria was at last achieved.

UNSTABLE INDEPENDENCE

Since the attainment of independence Syria has passed through a long period of instability. She was involved in a complicated economic and financial dispute with the Lebanon (1948–50) and also in various schemes for union with Iraq—schemes which tended to divide political opinion inside Syria itself and, in addition, to disrupt the unity of the Arab League. Syria, in fact, found herself aligned at this time with Egypt and Saudi Arabia against the ambitions of the Hashemite rulers of Iraq and Jordan. These rivalries, together with the profound disappointment felt at Damascus over the Arab failures in the war of 1948–49 against Israel, were the prelude to a series of *coups d'état* in Syria: in March 1949, under Colonel Husni Za'im; in August of the same year, under Colonel Sami Hinnawi; and in December 1949, under Lieut.-Colonel Shishakli. Dislike of continued financial dependence on France, aspirations towards a greater Syria, the resentments arising out of the unsuccessful war against the Israelis—all help to explain the unrest inside Syria.

The intervention of the army in politics was itself a cause of further tension. Opposition to the dominance of the army grew in the Syrian Chamber of Deputies to such an extent that yet another *coup d'état* was carried out in December 1951. Syria now came under the control of a military autocracy with Colonel Shishakli as head of the state. The Chamber of Deputies was dissolved in December 1951; a decree of April 1952 abolished all political parties in Syria. After the approval of a new constitution in July 1953 General Shishakli became President of Syria in August of that year. The formation of political parties was now allowed once more. Members of the parties dissolved under the decree of April 1952 proceeded, however, to boycott the elections held in October 1953, at which President Shishakli's Movement of Arab Liberation obtained a large majority in the Chamber of Deputies. Politicians hostile to the regime of President Shishakli established in November 1953 a Front of National Opposition, refusing to accept as legal the results of the October elections and declaring as their avowed aim the end of military autocracy and the restoration of democratic rule. Demonstrations at Damascus and Aleppo in December 1953 led soon to the flight of Shishakli to France. The collapse of his regime early in 1954 meant for Syria a return to the Constitution of 1950. New elections held in September 1954 brought into being a Chamber of Deputies notable for the large number of its members (81 out of 142) who might be regarded as independents grouped around leading political figures.

INFLUENCE FROM ABROAD

There was still, however, much friction in Syria between those who favoured union or at least close co-operation with Iraq and those inclined towards an effective *entente* with Egypt. In August 1955 Shukri al-Kuwatli became President of the Republic. His appointment was interpreted as an indication that pro-Egyptian influence had won the ascendancy in Syria. On October 20th, 1955, Syria made with Egypt an agreement for the creation of a joint military command with its headquarters at Damascus.

The U.S.S.R., meanwhile, in answer to the developments in the Middle East associated with the Baghdad Pact, had begun an intensive diplomatic, propaganda and economic campaign of penetration into the Arab lands. In the years 1954–56 Syria, the only Arab state where the Communist Party was legal, made a number of barter agreements with the Soviet Union and its associates in eastern Europe. A report from Cairo intimated, in February 1956, that Syria had joined Egypt in accepting arms from U.S.S.R.

At the end of October 1956 there occurred the Israeli campaign in the Sinai peninsula, an event followed, in the first days of November, by the armed intervention of Great Britain and France in the Suez Canal region. On October 30th the President of the Syrian Republic left Damascus on a visit to the Soviet Union. A state of emergency was declared in Syria. Reports from Beirut revealed on November 3rd that Syrian forces had put out of action the pipelines which carried Iraqi oil to the Mediterranean. The damage that Syrian elements had done to the pipelines earned the sharp disapproval of such Arab states as Iraq and Saudi Arabia, both of whom were now faced with a severe loss of oil revenues. The Syrian Government declared that it would not allow the repair of the pipelines until Israel had withdrawn her troops from Gaza and the Gulf of Aqaba. Not until March 1957 was it possible to restore the pipelines, Israel having in the meantime agreed to evacuate her forces from the areas in dispute.

In April 1957 a crisis took place in Jordan where the Palestinian elements in political circles, with some support from the army, sought to draw Jordan into alignment with Egypt and Syria. At the time of the Sinai-Suez crisis in November 1956 contingents of Syrian troops had been stationed in Jordan. These troops were still on Jordanian soil. There were also reports that reinforcements might be sent to the Syrian forces in Jordan. It seemed that a major intervention in the affairs of Jordan was imminent. On April 24th the U.S.A. announced that it regarded the independence and integrity of Jordan as a matter of vital concern. The United States Sixth Fleet was now ordered to the eastern Mediterranean with instruction to assist Jordan, if aid were requested. At the same time the U.S. Government deplored the flow of Soviet arms and equipment to Egypt and Syria. In May 1957 Syria stated that, in compliance with a request from Amman, she would withdraw her forces from Jordan.

UNION WITH EGYPT

The Syrian National Assembly, in November 1957, passed a resolution in favour of union with Egypt. Earlier in the year there had been discussions concerning proposals for a customs union between the two countries and for the co-ordination of their currencies and of their economic policies. The formal union of Egypt and Syria to constitute one state under the title of the United Arab Republic received the final approval of the Syrian National Assembly on February 5th, 1958. President Nasser of Egypt, on February 21st, became the first head of the combined state. A central cabinet for the U.A.R. was established in October 1958, also two regional executive councils, one for Syria and one for Egypt. A further move towards integration came in March 1960, when President Nasser announced the formation of a single National Assembly for the whole of the U.A.R. The Assembly, consisting of 400 deputies from Egypt and 200 from Syria, held its first meeting at Cairo on July 21st, 1960.

The more extreme elements of the right and of the left—e.g. the conservative class of landowners and also the Communist following in Syria—had viewed with distrust the union of Syria and Egypt. Amongst the Baath Socialists, who had played an important role in bringing about the merger with Egypt in 1958, dissatisfaction grew as a result of the small progress made with schemes for the socialization of the Syrian economy. There was disillusionment, too, in the Syrian armed forces over the more and more frequent transfer of Syrian officers to Egypt and of Egyptian officers to Syria. Administrators and officials of Egyptian origin had come, moreover, to hold a large number of the most influential positions in the Syrian Region of the U.A.R. Syria still retained, however, at the end of 1960 and in the first months of 1961, a considerable measure of autonomy in most economic matters.

August 1961 saw the abolition of the regional executive councils for Syria and Egypt created in 1958. This attempt to hasten the integration of the two countries was the prelude to a new crisis at Damascus. On September 28th, 1961, there occurred in Syria a military *coup d'état* which aimed—successfully—at the separation of Syria from Egypt and at the dissolution of the United Arab Republic. Political figures representing most of the parties which existed in Syria before the establishment of the U.A.R. in 1958 met at Damascus and Aleppo on October 3rd, 1961, issuing a declaration of support for the new regime and calling for free elections to a new legislature. Syrian members of the National Assembly of the U.A.R. gathered at Damascus on October 4th to denounce the arbitrary and dictorial character of the control previously exercised from Cairo over Syrian affairs. President Nasser now, on October 5th, recognized the *fait accompli*. Most foreign states made haste to grant formal recognition to the government at Damascus. On October 13th, 1961, Syria became once more a member of the United Nations. A provisional constitution was promulgated in November and elections for a Constituent Assembly took place on December 1st, 1961.

The regime thus established in Syria rested on no sure foundation. At the end of March 1962 the Syrian Army intervened once more, bringing about the resignation of Dr. Nazim Kudsi, the President of the Republic, and also of the ministers who had taken office in December 1961. After demonstrations at Aleppo, Homs and Hama in April 1962, Dr. Kudsi was reinstated as President, but further ministerial resignations in May of that year pointed to the existence of continuing tensions within the government.

THE REVOLUTION OF 1963

A military junta, styled the National Council of the Revolutionary Command, seized control in Damascus on March 8th, 1963. During March and April 1963 tension was visible between those elements which advocated a close association with Egypt and those Baathist circles which tended to oppose such a programme. In May 1963 the Baathists took measures to purge the armed forces and the administration of personnel known to favour a close alignment with Egypt. A new government, formed on May 13th and strongly Baathist in character, carried out a further purge in June and at the same time created a National Guard recruited from members of the Baath movement. These measures led the pro-Egyptian elements to attempt a *coup d'état* at Damascus on July 18th, 1963. The attempt failed, however, with a considerable loss of life.

There were, in the second half of 1963, a number of moves designed to bring about some form of union between Syria and Iraq. In August it was announced that the two countries would establish committees empowered to promote effective co-operation in matters of defence; in September proposals for a federation of Syria and Iraq came under discussion; in October a Supreme Defence Council was established under General Ammash, the Defence Minister of Iraq; and, also in October, at an international conference of al-Baath held in Damascus, a resolution was adopted calling for the union of Syria and Iraq. The aspirations embodied in this resolution were doomed, however, to disappointment; a *coup d'état* at Baghdad in November 1963 swept aside the Baath regime in Iraq.

BAATH SOCIALISM

The Syrian Government, in May 1963, had nationalized all Arab-owned banks in Syria and in August of that year proceeded to order their reduction into fewer but larger units with new boards set in charge of them. Government decrees issued in April 1964 nationalized a number of textile factories at Aleppo. The factories would henceforward be under the control of elected representatives of the employees, together with representatives of the Government, of al-Baath and of the trade unions. The principle of "self-management" in industrial concerns, and also in agriculture, had received approval at the international Baath conference of October 1963.

The nationalization of the banks and of various industrial enterprises, also the transfer of land to the peasants—all had contributed to bring about much dissatisfaction in the business world and amongst the influential landed elements. The Baath regime depended for its main support on the armed forces (purged of the personnel opposed to the policies of the government). These forces, however, had been recruited in no small degree from the religious minorities in Syria, including adherents of the Shi'i (Alawi) faith—most Syrians being, in fact, of Sunni or orthodox Muslim allegiance. In general, conservative Muslims tended to oppose the Baath government under guidance of the *'ulama* and of the Muslim Brotherhood. The mass of the peasant population was thought to have some pro-Nasser sympathies; the working class (small in number) was divided between pro-Nasser and Baathist adherents; the middle and upper classes opposed the domination of al-Baath.

The unease arising out of these frictions and antipathies took the form of disturbances at Banias and Homs (February 1964), at Aleppo (March 1964) and finally of open revolt—soon suppressed—at Hama (April 1964). After the Hama rising came a wave of anti-government demonstrations and a strike of shopkeepers in all the main towns—e.g. Damascus, Hama, Homs, Aleppo—of central and northern Syria, except Latakia (an Alawi centre). The government now used pressure to bring about a resumption of normal business activities—pressure which threatened confiscation and trial for sabotage as the penalties for resistance.

Meanwhile, on April 25th, 1964, a provisional constitution had been promulgated, describing Syria as a democratic socialist republic forming an integral part of the Arab nation. A Presidential Council was established on May 14th, 1964, with General Hafiz as head of the state.

A government decree of December 23rd, 1964, nationalized the as yet undeveloped petroleum and other mineral resources of Syria. Early in January 1965 the Syrian Government placed under national control, wholly or in part, industrial concerns connected with cement, dyes, textiles, sugar, canning, food production, chemicals and soap. On January 7th, 1965, a special military court was created with sweeping powers to deal with all offences, of word or deed, against the nationalization decrees and the socialist revolution. These new measures evoked once more a series of demonstrations and a strike of shopkeepers in Damascus (January 24th, 1965). Further government decrees now confiscated the goods and properties of merchants held to be responsible for the disorders. General Hafiz denounced the *'ulama* and the Muslim Brotherhood as being involved in the demonstrations. On February 19th, 1965, further decrees nationalized about forty pharmaceutical importing establishments at Damascus and

Aleppo, together with a number of other trading companies. The official Importing and Exporting Organization was now alone able to import basic commodities such as tea, tinned meats, fish, rubber, iron, timber, textiles, tractors, cars, drugs, fertilizers, salt, tobacco and paper. Reports current at the beginning of March 1965 stated that the government had ordered the nationalization of nine oil companies estimated to control between them some two-thirds of the total fuel consumption in Syria.

The autumn of 1965 saw a number of important changes inside Syria. A National Council, almost one hundred strong, was established in August with the task of preparing a new constitution which would be submitted to a public referendum. Meeting for the first time on September 1st, 1965, it created a Presidency Council, of five members, which was to exercise the powers of a head of state.

RADICAL REACTION

The tensions hitherto visible in al-Baath were, however, still active. Two groups stood ranged one against the other—on the one hand the older more experienced politicians in al-Baath, less inclined than in former years to insist on the unrestrained pursuit of the main Baathist objectives, socialism and pan-Arab union, and on the other hand the extreme left-wing elements, doctrinaire in their attitude and enjoying considerable support amongst the younger radical officers in the armed forces.

The tensions thus engendered found expression in a new *coup d'état* on February 23rd, 1966. A military junta representing the extreme radical elements in al-Baath seized power in Damascus and placed under arrest a number of personalities long identified with al-Baath and belonging to the international leadership controlling the organization throughout the Arab world—amongst them Mr. Michael Aflaq, the founder of al-Baath; General Hafiz, the chairman of the recently established Presidency Council; and Mr. Salah al-Din Bitar, the Prime Minister of the displaced administration.

The new Prime Minister of Syria, Dr. Zeayen, visited the Soviet Union in April 1966. Russia then granted Syria a loan of about £50 million for the construction of a great dam, about a mile long, on the River Euphrates at Tabqa in northern Syria. The dam—being built with Soviet technical assistance—is a major factor in a long-term project of development designed to irrigate an additional million and a half acres of land, i.e. to double in extent the present irrigated area in Syria and to make possible a notable increase in the production of cotton. The dam will also be able to produce large quantities of hydro-electric power.

Reports current in July 1966 indicated that the government at Damascus had arrested a number of politicians, amongst them personalities associated with the former National and People's Parties. On September 6th the Syrian Government announced that it had discovered and foiled a conspiracy against itself. The conspiracy was said to have been prepared by Baathist elements representing the regime evicted from power in the *coup d'état* of February 1966. Of the personalities charged with involvement in the conspiracy the most prominent were Mr. Michel Aflaq, the founder of al-Baath; Mr. Salah al-Din Bitar, a former Prime Minister; and Dr. Munif al-Razzaz, at one time the Secretary-General of the International Baathist Organization. Also said to be implicated in the conspiracy were military elements supporting General Hafiz, the head of the preceding regime.

A delegation led by Dr. Yusuf Zeayen, the Prime Minister of Syria, visited Cairo on November 1st, 1966. On November 4th the United Arab Republic and Syria entered into a defence agreement for military co-ordination between the two countries. The agreement stipulated that aggression against either state would be considered as an assault on the other, to be repelled by the armed forces of the U.A.R. and of Syria acting together. A defence council and a joint military command were to be established under the terms of the agreement.

ARAB-ISRAELI WAR

The friction ever present along the frontier between Syria and Israel had flared out from time to time during recent years into violent conflict—e.g. in March 1962 (Lake Tiberias), August 1963 (Huleh), November 1964 (Dan), August 1965 (Khirbet, north of Lake Tiberias), February 1966 (al-Dardara), May 1966 (Lake Tiberias) and July 1966 (again in the region of Lake Tiberias). Now, in the winter of 1966–67, the tension along the border began to assume more serious proportions. Israel, in October 1966, complained to the Security Council of the United Nations about guerilla activities from Syria across the frontier into Israeli territory. There was renewed violence near Lake Tiberias in January 1967. U Thant, in this same month, urged Syria and Israel to act with restraint and suggested that a special meeting be arranged of the Syrian-Israeli mixed armistice commission. This commission—which had not been convened since 1959—began its new discussions on January 25th, 1967. With further incidents occurring along the border, these discussions made no significant progress and came to an end on February 17th, 1967. There was a more serious outbreak of violence during April 1967, tanks, mortars, cannon and air force units from Syria and Israel being involved in fighting south-east of Lake Tiberias.

The continuing tension on the Syrian-Israeli frontier was now to become a major influence leading to the war which broke out on June 5th, 1967, between Israel and her Arab neighbours Egypt, Syria and Jordan. During the course of hostilities which lasted six days Israel defeated Egypt and Jordan and then, after some stubborn fighting, outflanked and overran the Syrian positions on the hills above Lake Tiberias. With the breakthrough accomplished, Israeli forces made a rapid advance and occupied the town of Quneitra about forty miles from Damascus. On June 10th Israel and Syria announced their formal acceptance of the United Nations proposal for a cease-fire. UN observers were stationed on both sides of the line then existing between the Israeli and Syrian forces. The UN truce supervision control was established at Quneitra.

During the period following the war, Syria opposed all attempts to reach a compromise solution and in effect boycotted the Arab summit conference held at Khartoum in August 1967. In September, the Baath party of Syria rejected all idea of a compromise with Israel, expressed its full support for the Yemen Republic and for the Arab nationalists in South Arabia and called on the Arab states in general to maintain a diplomatic, economic and cultural boycott of the United States, the United Kingdom and the German Federal Republic.

In the same month Israeli elements began to settle in some of the lands taken from the Arab states in the course of the war, particularly in Banias on the Syrian plateau. At the same time a number of small incidents occurred along the frontier between Israel and the adjacent Arab states, apparently the work of sabotage organizations trained and supported by Syria. On 4th November there was a brief conflict between Israeli forces and Syrian troops who crossed the cease-fire line on the Golan heights (located in the territories which Israel had taken over from Syria in June 1967).

A British resolution urging the withdrawal of the Israelis from the lands occupied by them during the June war and the ending of the belligerency which the Arab governments had up till then maintained against Israel, was adopted by the U.N. Security Council in November 1967. However, the resolution was immediately rejected by Syria, which alone maintained its commitment to a reunified Palestine.

STRUGGLE FOR POWER 1968-71

The ruling Baath Party had for some years been divided into two main factions. Until October 1968 the dominant faction had been the "progressive" group led by Dr. Atassi and Dr. Makhous, the Premier and Foreign Minister respectively. This group was distinguished by its doctrinaire and Marxist-orientated public pronouncements (not always put into effect despite its control of the government) and by the strong support it received from the U.S.S.R. It held that the creation of a strong one-party state and economy along neo-Marxist lines was of paramount importance, overriding even the need for a militant stand towards Israel and for Arab unity.

By October 1968 the government felt particularly insecure, partly owing to a feud with the new Baath régime in Iraq, and at the end of the month a new cabinet was formed including several members of the opposing "nationalist" faction. This group took less interest in ideological questions and favoured a pragmatic attitude to the economy, improved relations with Syria's Arab neighbours and full participation in the campaign against Israel, including support for the fedayeen movement. Its leader was General Hafez Assad, who assumed the all-important Ministry of Defence. His critical attitude to the powerful Soviet influence on the government, seen by some "nationalists" as tantamount to colonialism in restricting Syria's freedom of action, led to a prolonged struggle with the "progressive" leadership. Cabinet reshuffles took place in March and again in May, but both Dr. Atassi and General Assad retained their positions. During the spring of 1969 a number of Communists were arrested or sent into exile, and the leader of the Syrian Communist Party (still technically an illegal organization) flew to Moscow.

General Assad attempted to take over the government in February 1969 but was forestalled by Soviet threats that if he did so all military supplies (including spares), economic and technical aid, and trade agreements would end. This would have brought about a major disruption in the national economy and the armed forces, and the "nationalists" were obliged to yield. In May General Mustafa Tlas, the Army Chief of Staff and General Assad's right-hand man, led a military delegation to Peking to buy arms. Some Chinese weapons were reported to be delivered in July. The incident indicated a new independence of Moscow. Some observers also saw this independence in the creation of a joint military command with Iraq (with whom relations improved during the spring) and Jordan. Relations with the Lebanon worsened, owing to Syria's support of the Lebanese fedayeen movement, which has many Syrian members. In the 1968-70 period this appeared to direct much of its activity towards bringing down the precarious Lebanese Government, presumably in the hope that a more militantly anti-Israel ministry would take power. Syria did, however, grant diplomatic recognition to the German Democratic Republic (East Germany) in June, and refused to resume diplomatic relations with Britain and the U.S.A. In May it was announced that a general election would be held in September, the first for seven years, but in August the elections were postponed indefinitely.

During the year 1969-70 there was some revival of activity on the front with Israel. Several air battles took place, and there was an extensive surface conflict involving tanks in June 1970; as usual, both sides claimed sweeping victories. Syria consistently supported the guerrilla forces in their struggle with the Jordan government, although guerrillas on Syrian territory seem to be allowed little freedom to manoeuvre.

In the spring of 1970 the Syrian section of the Tapline pipeline was put out of action, apparently by an accident. Syria refused to allow repairs, claiming that these operations would be dangerous as the section affected lies near Israeli-occupied territory. Since the pipeline and the crude oil it transports are American owned, the refusal was commonly seen as an attempt to put pressure on the United States and its Middle East policy. There was no official American reaction, but Saudi Arabia, as the oil producer affected and in any case at the opposite extreme to Syria in ideology, responded by threatening to abandon the use of Tapline altogether. This would have lost Syria (and the Lebanon and Jordan) considerable sums in transit dues. King Faisal also threatened to cease paying subventions to Egypt and Jordan, in the hope that these countries would then put pressure on Damascus to allow repairs. In January Syria allowed repairs to the pipeline to be started, after increased transit fees had apparently been conceded by Tapline.

In November 1970, following a reported *coup* attempt backed by Iraq in August, the struggle between the two factions of the Baath Party came to a head when General Assad seized power. Dr. Atassi, who was in hospital at the time, was placed under guard and General (retired) Salah Jadid, Assistant Secretary-General of the Baath Party and leader of the civilian faction, was arrested. Other members of the civilian wing were arrested or fled to the Lebanon. The coup was precipitated by attempts of Jadid and his supporters (culminating at the emergency session of the Tenth National Pan-Arab Congress of the Party) to oust Assad and Tlas from their posts. This power struggle had become acute as a result of differences over support for the Palestine guerrillas during the fighting with the Jordanian army in September. Jadid and Yousef Zayyen, a former Prime Minister, controlled the Syrian guerrilla organization, Saiqa, and supported the movement of tanks from Syria into Jordan to support the Palestinian guerrillas' efforts against the Jordanian army. This Assad and the military faction opposed. Their approach to the Palestinian problem was more akin to Nasser's and they wanted to avoid giving any provocation to Israel, because they considered the Syrian armed forces to be unready to offer adequate resistance.

ASSAD IN POWER

There was no obvious opposition to the army takeover. Ahmed Khatib became acting President and General Assad Prime Minister and Party Secretary-General. A new Regional Command of the Baath Party was formed. The old leaders were removed from their posts in a purge which stretched into the new year. Following amendments to the 1969 provisional constitution in February 1971, General Assad was elected President for a seven-year term in March. In the following month General Abdel Rahman Khlefawi became Premier and Mahmoud Ayoubi was appointed Vice-President. In February, the first legislative body in Syria since 1966, the People's Council, was formed. Of its 173 members, 87 represented the Baath Party.

The Nasserite leanings of the new régime in foreign policy soon became apparent (and presumably helped Assad establish some kind of *modus vivendi* with the U.S.S.R.). Although Syria continued to reject the November 1967 UN Security Council resolution, relations with the U.A.R. and Jordan improved, and Syria's isolation in the Arab world was soon reduced. Syria's willingness to join a union with the U.A.R., Sudan and Libya almost immediately became apparent and agreement on federation with Libya and the U.A.R. was reached in April 1971. In the same month the Syrian Government advised the Palestinian guerrillas not to initiate any more operations from the Syrian front.

SYRIA—(History, Economic Survey)

In September the Federation of Arab Republics was established, following a referendum covering all three countries. In Syria 96.4 per cent of the voters were in favour.

Since coming to power, the Assad régime had increased the army's control over Saiqa. In April 1971 guerrilla operations against Israeli positions from the Syrian front were banned by the Government. Then, at the beginning of July, some guerrilla units were forced out of Syria into south Lebanon and arms destined for them and arriving from Algeria were seized by the Syrian authorities. Yet after the Jordanian Government's final onslaught on the Palestinian guerrillas in north Jordan in July Syria closed her border and in August broke off diplomatic relations when the tension had become so great that tank and artillery clashes developed between the two armies. Egyptian mediation reduced the chances of any more serious conflict developing but diplomatic links remained severed with Jordan (and seem likely to continue that way following Hussein's announcement in March 1972 of plans for a United Arab Kingdom, and Egypt's subsequent breaking off of diplomatic relations with Jordan). At about the same time as the dispute with Jordan, the Syrian Government was itself attempting to mediate between Sudan and the Soviet Union in the wake of the abortive communist-led *coup* against President Nemery in July. Relations with the U.S.S.R. improved a lot during the last half of 1971 and in 1972, and in May Marshal Grechko, the Soviet Defence Minister, visited Damascus. Syria was not prepared, however, to sign a friendship treaty with the U.S.S.R. like Egypt and Iraq. On the other hand, the Syrian Government, which had been broadened in March 1972 to include representatives of parties other than the Baath like the communists, did not follow Egypt's example in July and expel its Soviet advisers. Syria's estrangement from her two partners in the Federation of Arab Republics was increased in August 1972 by the announcement of the proposed merger between Egypt and Libya.

At the beginning of June 1972, a few hours after the Iraq Government nationalized the Iraq Petroleum Company, the Syrian Government nationalized all IPC installations in Syria and demanded increased payments from the Iraq Government for oil pumped accross Syria by pipeline. A new price agreement was finally negotiated in January 1973.

In December 1972 Maj.-Gen. Khleifawi resigned from the post of Prime Minister for health reasons and a new Government was formed by Mahmoud al-Ayoubi, the Vice-President, with 16 out of 31 government portfolios going to the Baath Party. At the end of January 1973 a draft Constitution was approved by the People's Council and confirmed by a referendum in March. The Sunni Muslims were dissatisfied that the Constitution did not recognize Islam as the State religion, and as a result of their pressure an amendment was passed declaring that the President must be a Muslim. Under the Constitution freedom of belief is guaranteed, with the State respecting all religions, although the Constitution recognizes that Islamic jurisprudence was "a principal source of legislation". In May 1973 elections took place for the new People's Council, and 140 out of the 186 seats were won by the Progressive Front (a grouping of the Baath Party and its allies, while 42 seats were won by Independents and 4 by the Opposition.

ECONOMIC SURVEY

Youssef Azmeh

Syria is a land of frustrated economic promise. Rich in agricultural resources and entrepreneurial and artisan skills, it has after almost a quarter of a century of political instability been unable to initiate the expected economic take-off. Alternate revolution and counter-revolution and their consequent reversals of economic policy have been the norm since the first military coup in 1949, only three years after independence from France. Periods of economic boom were hastily replaced by lengthy slumps and with each new government attempting to repair what it thought were the economic mistakes of the previous one, a state of economic chaos has ensued. This resulted in a loss of confidence in the country's economic future which led in its turn to a mass exodus of capital and skills and a state of lethargy among those who remained. The gradual take-over by the state since the late 1950s of the "dominant heights" of the economy had led some to assume that state control might fill the vacuum left by the departing land-owners, entrepreneurs, technicians and administrators. But inexperience, inefficiency and ineptitude, coupled with constant changes that did not give the new men a chance to gain experience, did not allow state-control to succeed where others had failed. The ruling Baath Party came to power in 1963 and on the face of it it would appear that Syria as a result has had almost ten years of political stability. But the in-fighting within the Party and the numerous palace *coups*, the last of which in November 1970 brought the then Minister of Defence, General Hafez Assad, to power, has not radically altered the picture. During its two and a half years in power the Assad régime has initiated many measures to liberalize political and economic life while retaining a firmly centralized system of control. The relative success of these reforms has generated confidence in the ability of the régime. The failure of right-wing traditionalists to use religious conservatism as a vehicle for gaining power resulted in a further strengthening of the régime, especially after its success at the polls early in 1973. The Assad régime has also been successful in fostering foreign confidence in the Syrian economy. With the maturation of the Baath bureaucracy after ten years in power real progress towards the consolidation of a stable political régime is being achieved. While the Government's economic ideology remains a constant factor the prospects for the economy appear to be improving.

AREA AND POPULATION

Syria covers an area of about 72,000 square miles (185,180 sq. km.), under three-quarters of the size of England, Wales and Scotland. About 45 per cent of the total area is considered arable and the rest consists of bare mountain, desert and pastures suitable only for nomads. Of the total cultivable area of 8.7 million hectares, only 5.9 million hectares, or 68 per cent was cultivated in 1970, making the area under cultivation only 32 per cent of the total area. Official figures put the population at the end of 1969 at 6,471,074, indicating a 39 per cent increase in ten years since the population at the end of 1959 was put at 4,656,688. Of the total in 1969, 2,735,817, or 40 per cent, were classified as urban compared with 35 per cent in 1959. Comparing figures of urban population one notes an increase of 60 per cent in the ten-year period, reflecting the continued movement from village to town amply illustrated by the growth of shanty towns along the edges of large urban centres such as Damascus and Aleppo. The population of Damascus has risen from 475,399 in 1959 to 813,008 in 1969 and that of Aleppo from 466,026 to 639,000 (1970). The total labour force in November 1969 was put at 1,970,940 of whom 85,305 or 4.3 per cent were unemployed. Of the total labour force 1,262,349, or 64 per cent, were illiterate and 13,983 had a university education. Agriculture employed 67 per cent of the labour force, manufacturing and extraction industries 7.6 per cent, construction 3.7 per cent, transport and communications 2.3 per cent, trade and catering 6.7 per cent and financial and other services 10 per cent.

AGRICULTURE

Agriculture is still the mainstay of the Syrian economy in spite of the existence of a traditionally strong trading sector and relatively successful efforts at industrialization in recent years. It accounts for at least one fifth of the G.D.P. and employs two-thirds of the labour force. The main areas of cultivation are a narrow strip of land along the coast from the Lebanese to the Turkish frontiers which enjoys a Mediterranean climate, is exceedingly fertile and produces fruit, olives, tobacco and cotton. East of this strip lies the northward continuation of the Lebanon range of mountains, which falls sharply on the east to the Orontes River valley whose marshes were recently reclaimed to form one of Syria's most fertile areas. This valley joins in central Syria the 100-mile wide steppe-plain which runs from the Jordanian borders northeastwards towards the Euphrates valley and is separated by a range of hills from the plain's northern reaches. The plain is traditionally Syria's major agricultural area, mainly grains-producing, in which are located the main cities, Damascus, Homs, Hama and Aleppo. The importance of this plain is now being rivalled by the Jezira area which lies between the Euphrates in Syria and the Tigris in Iraq. Although fertile lands along the banks of the Euphrates and its tributaries in Syria had previously been cultivated, the Jezira only came into its own in the early 1950s when large scale cotton cultivation was introduced in former pasture lands. This area will vastly increase in importance on the completion of the Euphrates dam now under construction.

Agriculture in general has, however, been experiencing a decline on two fronts, the area of land under cultivation and productivity. Agriculture's share of the G.D.P. fell from 32.2 per cent in 1962 to 20.3 per cent in 1970 but rose to 25.6 per cent in 1972, a year of bumper cereals crops. The gross product of the agricultural sector stood at £S2,213.9 million in 1972 compared with £S1,380.3 million in 1970, a rise of 60 per cent in two years. The year 1970, however, was particularly bad for agriculture and the share of agriculture in the G.D.P. in 1969 was 25.6 per cent, the same as in 1972. Indices collated by the Food and Agriculture Organization of the United Nations (FAO) show that total agricultural production actually fell between 1962 and 1972, from 166 to 131 (base calculated on average yearly production 1952–56). Calculated on a per caput basis, the index fell from 132 in 1962 to 83 in 1970. Both indices, improved slightly in 1971 with that of agricultural production rising to 144 and the per caput index rising to 87.

The Government appears to realize that the economic well-being of the state is closely linked to the development of agriculture. The Third Five-Year Plan (1971–75) allocates 34.8 per cent of investments to agricultural projects, although the Euphrates Dam project, which gets the lion's share of appropriations (24.7 per cent of the total), is not of exclusively agricultural interest since it will provide much of Syria's future power needs. Public-sector investment in agriculture, irrigation and the dam under the Plan was set at £S2,241 million out of total allocations of £S6,447 million. The dam is to receive £S1,593 million, irrigation and land reclamation are to receive £S211.7 million and £S436 million was allocated to agriculture. A total of 38,700 hectares should be reclaimed under the plan, but the Euphrates dam project should add a total of 550,000 hectares to the area under irrigation by 1990. This would mean providing an additional 100,000 hectares by 1975 to the area under cultivation in 1970. The main factors affecting the decline in agriculture are political. They stem from political instability and the resulting reluctance of farmers to invest in their land, and even in some cases resulting in farmers refraining from cultivating their land. The basic reason has been the suspicion of Government intentions in relation to land ownership since the first agrarian reform law of 1958 and the inadequacy of credit and other facilities where the traditional channels, the large land-owners in the villages and the money-lenders in the towns, has been suppressed. The situation has improved recently with the more liberal interpretation of the agrarian reform law of 1958 and later amendments by the Assad régime leading to a relative stabilization of the situation in the countryside. But the major problem facing Syrian agriculture remains unresolved: that of the under-use of potential. Traditionally between one quarter and one-third of cultivable land is kept fallow every year for purposes of conservation and crop rotation. The additional area of unused cultivable land, however, remains large by any standard. It increased from 1,892,000 hectares in 1963 to 2,825,000 hectares, or 32.5 per cent of total cultivable area in 1970. This adds up to a staggering 62 per cent of the cultivable land remaining unused for different reasons in 1970. Some of this land does suffer from the lack of water resources in years of drought and this problem could be partly solved with the coming availability of water from the Euphrates Dam, which is now due to be completed in 1974, one year ahead of schedule, and from the Government drive to find and extract underground reserves.

Cotton has for some years replaced grains as Syria's most valuable crop for although the area under cotton in 1970, for example, was one tenth of the area sown with grains, the value of cotton production was more than double that of grains and cotton provided almost half of Syria's total export earnings. Medium-staple cotton has been grown in the country for many years, but the high price of cotton after the Second World War, especially during the Korean War, gave a great stimulus to cotton production in the early fifties and the previously neglected Jezira area was opened up for large-scale agriculture on a new capital intensive basis relatively free from the traditional agricultural relations, still semi-feudal in the rest of the country. Cotton production grew from 38,000 tons in 1949, to 100,000 tons in 1950, 175,500 tons in 1951 and 220,800 tons in 1954. The area under cotton grew from 25,300 hectares in 1949 to 78,000 hectares in 1950 and 217,400 hectares in 1951, levelling off after that. In 1972-73 the area under cotton was about 240,000 hectares and the output reached 424,000 tons compared with 396,000 in the previous season. Ginned cotton production in the 1971-72 and 1972-73 seasons averaged 155,000 tons. Of the ginned cotton production for 1972, 75 per cent was exported as raw cotton for £S373 million, which represented 34 per cent of the year's total export earnings of £S1,098 million. Exports of other cotton products raised cotton's share of total export earnings to about 42 per cent in that year.

The grain crop is of great importance, for bread is the country's staple diet and in normal years there is an exportable surplus of grains. The size of the harvest, however, depends heavily on weather conditions and lack of adequate rainfall in several recent years resulted in disastrous droughts and grains had to be imported in large quantities. The year 1972, however, saw a bumper cereals crop but early indications for 1973 were not very encouraging. With the relative return of agricultural stability, the area under cereals was up to the levels of the early sixties in 1970 and reached 2,476,000 hectares, a near normal acreage, which is just under half of the total sown area. Total cereal output was 884,000 tons. 1971 saw another drastic reduction of the area sown. Cereals were down to 1,744,000 hectares and the harvest was reduced despite better weather. Early in 1973 figures were not yet available for the area sown with cereals in 1972 but it is thought to have been similar to that of 1970. The 1972 crop, however, was an all-time record. The wheat crop reached 1,950,000 tons, more than treble the previous year's total of 662,000 tons. Barley production in 1972 was estimated at 735,000 tons compared with 123,000 tons in the previous year. Exports of wheat during the year were worth £S82 million and exports of barley £S10.6 million compared to total cereal exports of £S136,000 in 1971. Some cereal imports were still necessary in 1972, especially during the first half of the year before the harvest was gathered. Imports of wheat were worth £S66.3 million while those of barley only £S2.8 million compared with cereals imports of £S231.7 million in 1971.

Syria, however, does not depend only on cotton and cereals and produces abundant quantities of dry legumes, fruit, vegetables and tobacco. Taking figures for 1969, a better year for comparison than 1970 or 1971, we see that the total value of agricultural production was £S1,052 million of which industrial crops (mainly cotton) accounted for 32 per cent, cereals 26.1 per cent, fruit 16.9 per cent, vegetables 15 per cent and dry legumes 6.2 per cent. The major products after cotton and cereals are tobacco, sugar beet, sesame, olives, grapes, figs, apricots, apples, melon, pistachio nuts, walnuts, lentils, chick peas, vetch, broad beans, tomatoes, onion, garlic, potatoes, egg plant and other soft vegetables. Stockraising is another important branch of agriculture and there are large flocks grazed by nomads in the pasture lands along the edges of the Syrian Desert. There were 5.2 million sheep in 1971, 701,000 goats and 436,000 head of cattle. There were also 4.9 million chickens. Sheep and goats are usually exported for flesh and so is their wool, hair and hides.

OIL

Syria was at one time thought to have no oil. The Iraq Petroleum Company group had rights throughout Syria which it abandoned in 1951 after failing to find oil in commercial quantities. A concession was granted in 1955 to an independent American operator who discovered the Karachuk field in the northeastern corner of the country. The oil was of extremely low quality, a density of 19° API and a sulphur content of 4.5 per cent. The operator's concession was cancelled later to make way for state exploitation of the find but commercial production has not yet started on a significant scale. Another concession was granted in 1956 to a West German-led consortium which discovered the richer Suweidiya field whose deposits, although of low quality also, are at 25° API and 3.5 per cent sulphur content a much better commercial proposition than Karachuk oil. A third field was discovered at Rumelan, not far from Suweidiya, but Suweidiya is so far the only field producing significant quantities of crude. The concession of the German consortium was also cancelled later and in 1964 the Government decided that concessions should only be granted to the state-owned agency, the General Petroleum Authority and its offshoot, the Syrian General Petroleum Company.

The oilfields were actually developed with Soviet assistance. Commercial production from Suweidiya started in July 1968 when, out of production for the year of one million metric tons, 833,000 tons were exported. The Government estimated early in 1969 that Suweidiya production would reach five million tons in that year of which 3.6 million tons would be exported. Actual production that year was 3.2 million tons of which 2.3 million tons were exported. Output in 1970 also did not reach expectations. Six million tons were expected to be produced but output reached only 4.7 million tons and 3.5 million tons were exported, 200,000 tons more than expected. Output reached 5.8 million tons in 1971 and 6.3 million tons in 1972 and exports reached 3.4 million tons in 1971 and 3.9 million tons in 1972. The Karachuk field was supposed to start producing 500,000 tons in 1969 rising to one million tons in 1970, all of which would be exported, but production has not started on this scale yet. No serious move has yet been made to start production from the Rumelan field.

The failure to reach aims in oil production and exports is mainly attributable to difficulties in marketing the Syrian crude abroad, although the Suweidiya crude is suitable for blending with lighter crudes originating in Algeria or Libya to produce fuel oils. The high sulphur content of the Karachuk crude makes it especially suitable for the production of good quality asphalt. In its marketing efforts, Syria has concentrated mainly on sales to Western Europe in order to acquire sorely needed hard currencies. Barter deals have been concluded with some Western European buyers, such as a barter deal with Italy in 1969 to exchange crude oil for tractors, and agreements have been concluded with Eastern European countries, mainly the Soviet Union, but these have not exceeded one million tons a year. The main reason for Syria's lack of success in marketing its crude in Europe is believed to be the reluctance of the major oil companies, which control most of the sales outlets, to allow the success of the Syrian experiment in state-exploitation of oil reserves, the first of its kind in the Middle East.

In spite of disappointments in the development of oil in Syria, the fact that oil has become a major export commodity is a measure of its importance to the economy. The value of oil exports in 1971 was £S176 million representing about 25 per cent of total exports. The value rose to £S200 million in 1972, representing 18 per cent of total exports. The decreasing proportion reflects the relative slow rate of growth in relation to other exports. But still more important are the royalties paid by the oil companies for the transit of their crude through Syrian territory. One pipeline was built in 1934 from the Iraq Petroleum Company installations at Kirkuk crossed Syria to a terminal at Tripoli in Lebanon but a parallel line, completed in 1952, branches off at Homs in central Syria to a terminal on the Syrian coast at Banias. The other pipeline is that of the Trans-Arabian Pipeline Company (Tapline) which carries Saudi Arabian crude to a terminal near Sidon in Lebanon and crosses about 100 miles of Syrian territory although most of it since 1967 passes through Israel-occupied territory. Under agreements signed in 1971 royalties received from the two pipelines were to reach £S342 million a year (£37.6 million). But the royalties due from IPC are now to come from Iraq as a result of the nationalization of IPC in both countries on June 1st, 1972, and a new agreement with Iraq revising the royalties is expected to bring total oil royalties nearer £S400 million a year. Discussions are under way with Iraq about the building of a second pipeline to carry crude oil produced from southern Iraqi fields to the Mediterranean and the two countries have already agreed to increase the capacity of the former IPC pipeline.

INDUSTRY

A remarkable industrial boom, mainly based on textiles, occurred in Syria shortly after independence and was the main cause of the dissolution of the customs union with Lebanon in 1951 since the protectionist policies adopted by the Syrian Government to safeguard this growth came into direct conflict with Lebanon's free-trade tradition. Since then the industrial sector has grown steadily until in 1970, for the first time, the manufacturing and mining sector replaced agriculture as the main generator of wealth with this sector accounting for 20.5 per cent of the gross domestic product compared with 20.3 for agriculture. Industrial production has more than trebled since the early fifties and in money terms, the index of industrial production rose to 360.3 in 1970, taking 1953 as a base year. Funds for industrialization originally came from the rich trading and agricultural sectors, but by 1965, the main industries had been nationalized and industry now is mainly a state concern.

The gross output of Syrian industry in 1971 was valued at £S2,621 million of which 32.9 per cent was contributed by food processing and tobacco, 31.9 per cent by textiles, yarn and clothing, 8.9 per cent by chemicals, 6.5 per cent by mining and quarrying, 5 per cent by basic metallic industries and 4.1 per cent each by non-metallic products industries (mainly cement and glass), electricity and water. There are also rubber and paper industries, a sugar refinery, tanneries and a nitrogenous fertilizers plant, assembly plants for vehicles and electrical equipment such as refrigerators and television sets. A steel rolling mill is planned. Syria was thought to possess few minerals of commercial value apart from oil but phosphates have now been discovered in significant quantities in the desert near Palmyra and production started there in 1972. There are other mineral deposits but they are not of significance.

The principal industries centre round the major towns, Damascus, Aleppo, Homs and the port of Latakia and although no exact figures are available about the number of persons employed in industry, official classifications show that 316,203 persons or 16 per cent of the labour force, were employed in manufacturing, mining, transport and communications in November 1969.

EXTERNAL TRADE

Commerce has traditionally been a major occupation of Syria's towns, especially Damascus and Aleppo as they lie on the main east-west trade route. It has declined in importance with the increasing role played by Government in economic affairs and the resulting exodus of leading merchants and their firms who have transferred the centre of their activities, mainly to Beirut. But the country's foreign trade in general has been expanding rapidly. The value of exports increased from £S271 million in 1951 to £S721 million in 1961 but stabilized during the next decade, reaching £S743 million in 1971. The following year, however, saw an unprecedented jump of 47.6 per cent in Syrian exports, reaching £S1,098 million. The main expansion has been in the value of imports, which meant a rising deficit in the trade balance. The value of imports increased from £S291 million in 1951 to £S644 million in 1961 and a record £S2,060 million in 1972 compared with £S1,677 in the previous year. The public sector accounted for 79 per cent of exports and 71 per cent of imports in 1971.

Raw cotton, as mentioned above, is Syria's principal export and at £S373 million in 1972, it amounted to over a third of total exports. The growing importance of oil is reflected in the fact that crude oil exports in 1972 accounted for 18 per cent of the total compared with 10 per cent in 1969. Grain is exported in normal years but drought in the last few years has resulted in large net imports of this commodity. The other major export commodities are textiles and live animals, mainly sheep and goats, which account for more than 10 per cent of exports.

The main imports are usually industrial raw materials, machinery and manufactured articles but with the poor grain harvest, cereals worth £S265 million were imported in 1971 but the good harvest of 1972 cut this item to only £S130 million. Imports of food and live animals as a whole accounted for £S467 million including in addition to cereals, sugar worth £S116 million, fruit and vegetables worth £S85 million and dairy products worth £S56 million. Other major import categories in 1972 were chemicals worth £S244 million of which pharmaceuticals accounted for £S104 million; manufactured goods totalled £S566 million, of which £S169 million went towards textiles, yarn and ready-made clothing and £S207 million towards iron and steel; imports of mineral fuels and lubricants were worth £S92 million of which £S91 million was for crude oil; machinery and transport equipment totalled £S463 million of which £S80 million was for transport equipment, £S96 million for electrical equipment and £S287 million for other machinery. Another £S42 million was spent on imports of lumber and wood.

The trading pattern has altered appreciably since the fifties and by 1970, the Communist countries, mainly the Soviet Union, had become Syria's leading suppliers. Syria is, however, trying hard to reduce its dependence on these countries and in 1972 member states of the European Economic Community and the European Free Trade Association (EFTA) accounted for 37.6 per cent of Syria's imports and 21.8 per cent of its exports. The Soviet Union and other countries of Eastern Europe in that year accounted for 17.2 per cent of imports and 32.2 per cent of exports. The Arab states took 25.1 per cent of Syria's exports in 1972 and supplied 14.7 per cent of its imports. Italy was again Syria's main supplier followed by West Germany, the Soviet Union, Lebanon, Japan, France and Britain. Its main markets were the Soviet Union followed by Lebanon, Italy, Greece, China, Bulgaria, Iraq, France, West Germany and East Germany.

The Government has put into effect a five-year foreign trade plan (1971–75) but very few details have been revealed. Official pronouncements have, however, indicated that the plan aims at altering the structure of exports in a way that will reduce exports of local raw materials, replacing them with exports of processed or semi-processed products. It also aims at reducing the volume and value of imports in favour of locally-produced goods. It limits the annual growth of imports to 5 per cent and restricts the import of luxury and non-essential goods, encouraging their replacement by Syrian-produced commodities, even if they are of inferior quality. It gives priority to equipment, machinery and other capital goods, encouraging direct import from the country of manufacture to eliminate middlemen's commissions. The plan also envisages a minimum 6.5 per cent average annual increase in exports over the five-year period.

FINANCE

The marked increase in Syrian exports in 1972 was one of the major results of a reform in the foreign exchange regulations. All exports other than cotton and crude oil were shifted to the parallel (free) market which meant a *de facto* devaluation of Syrian currency in relation to most transactions. The controlled rate stood at £S3.82 to the U.S. dollar in March 1973 compared with £S4.32 on the parallel market. Figures published by the Central Bank of Syria show a provisional balance of payment deficit of £S288 million in 1971 but this had been reduced to £S84.5 million by June 1972. Agricultural exports during the second half of 1972 may result in a reduced deficit for the whole year but the liberalization of imports could reverse the trend. The commitment by Saudi Arabia, Kuwait and other Gulf states to provide subsidies to Syria along the line of those provided to Egypt and Jordan since 1967 should also help the balance of payments position.

Banking, as well as other major economic activities, has been nationalized and the Commercial Bank of Syria is responsible for all trade transactions. There are also an Industrial Bank, an Agricultural Bank, a Real Estate Bank and a Popular Credit Bank.

There has been a steady increase in state expenditure during the past few years and ordinary budget expenditure, about half of which goes to defence, has risen from £S205 in 1953 to £S552 in 1962 and £S1,670 million in the 1973 estimates. There is also a development budget which in 1973 was for the first time allocated more than the total allocated for the general state budget and stood at £S1,743 million, bringing total state expenditure to £S3,413 million. Of the general state budget, £S786.3 million, or 70 per cent, was allocated for defence. Of the development budget, 33.6 per cent was allocated for industry, petroleum and power, 31.2 per cent for agriculture and irrigation and 22 per cent for communications and public works.

ECONOMIC DEVELOPMENT

The most ambitious of the projects contained in the five-year plans is the Euphrates Dam project. This is a scheme for constructing a huge dam on the Euphrates connected with a power station having an initial capacity of 200,000 kWh., and the digging of certain canals which would lead to the irrigation of about 1,640,000 acres of land. The difficulties which this plan faces are not only financial but political, for it would of course be necessary to reach agreement with the other riparian states, Turkey and Iraq, on how the waters of the Euphrates would be shared before the project could be finally realized. Notwithstanding these problems, in 1963, the West German authorities agreed to provide credits of up to DM 350 million towards meeting the foreign exchange costs. Perhaps because of the worsening of relations between Germany and the Arab world arising out of the problem of Israel, the German offer of finance was dropped in 1965. In April 1966, however, an agreement was reached with the U.S.S.R., which consented to give the Syrians technical and financial assistance on the first phase of the scheme. It was estimated that this phase would cost some £S1,000 million or about $260 million, of which the U.S.S.R. would lend the Syrians £S600 million, or $157 million, to cover the foreign exchange costs. The whole scheme and its associated hydro-electrical project was estimated at the time to cost about £S2,400 million, or about $628 million. Work began on the dam in the spring of 1968 with the assistance of large numbers of Soviet experts; by 1969 considerable progress was reported, and in that year some 22 per cent of the development budget was appropriated. Preparations were under way throughout the first half of 1973 for a ceremony in July during which the course of the Euphrates was to be diverted marking the end of the first stage of work on the main body of the dam and the start of power generation from some of the dam's turbines.

STATISTICAL SURVEY

AREA AND POPULATION

Total Area	Arable Land	Pastures	Forest	Population*
185,180 sq. km.	87,240 sq. km.	54,340 sq. km.	4,400 sq. km.	6,661,000

* July 1st, 1972.

	Births	Marriages	Deaths
1969	181,925*	56,268	26,327
1970	191,728	82,222	29,783
1971	207,564	50,495	29,014

* The drop in 1969 is due to an increase in the number of non-registered births.

CHIEF TOWNS
(1970)

Damascus (capital)	836,000	Latakia . . . 126,000
Aleppo	639,000	Deit-ez-Zor . . . 66,000
Homs	216,000	Hasakeh . . . 32,000
Hama	137,000	

SYRIA—(Statistical Survey)

AGRICULTURE
AREA AND PRODUCTION OF PRINCIPAL CROPS

	1970 Hectares	1970 Metric tons	1971 Hectares	1971 Metric tons
Wheat	1,341,000	625,000	1,274,000	662,000
Barley	1,126,000	235,000	435,000	123,000
Maize	5,600	7,900	6,500	8,500
Millet	25,800	13,500	25,300	19,400
Lentils	139,600	57,500	111,500	61,300
Cotton	249,300	382,600	250,400	407,900
Tobacco	10,200	6,700	12,983	7,500
Sesame	6,200	2,700	10,000	4,300
Grapes	66,000	206,000	67,000	209,000
Olives	124,000	85,000	125,000	117,000
Figs	23,000	44,000	20,000	55,000
Apricots	10,000	22,000	10,000	31,000
Apples	7,000	17,700	8,000	34,200
Sugar Beet	9,000	227,500	8,600	232,200
Pomegranates	2,900	16,400	3,300	24,500
Onions	6,100	65,300	7,300	90,400
Tomatoes	16,400	192,400	20,200	248,400
Potatoes	5,900	65,300	5,900	72,500

LIVESTOCK
('000 head)

	1969	1970	1971
Cattle	363	385	368
Horses	64	68	66
Camels	6	3.9	8.6
Asses	243	235	244
Sheep	5,963	6,112	5,230
Goats	770	771	701
Hens and Chickens	3,585	3,669	4,785

DAIRY PRODUCE

		1969	1970	1971
Milk	'000 tons	524	451	441
Cheese	tons	27,418	24,355	27,758
Butter	,,	1,819	1,827	2,045
Honey	,,	257	202	279
Ghee	,,	10,097	7,197	5,530
Eggs	'000	354,338	274,119	301,801

INDUSTRY

	Unit	1970	1971	1972
Cotton Yarn	'000 tons	20.0	23.4	27.9
Silk and Cotton Textiles	,, ,,	27.0	29.1	n.a.
Woollen Fabrics	million metres	6.1	5.7	n.a.
Cement	'000 tons	964.0	910.0	1,004.0
Natural Asphalt	,, ,,	23.6	24.6	21.0
Glass	,, ,,	15.9	15.2	15.8
Soap	,, ,,	21.2	23.3	25.9
Sugar	,, ,,	123.7	130.4	137.2
Salt	,, ,,	46.3	13.5	49.5
Edible Oils	,, ,,	25.1	26.2	27.4
Manufactured Tobacco	,, ,,	4.2	4.4	4.7
Electricity	million kWh.	946.9	1,049.0	1,223.0
Beer	'000 litres	3,047.8	3,470.0	3,784.8
Wine	,, ,,	235.0	269.6	n.a.
Arak	,, ,,	548.0	654.3	n.a.

SYRIA—(STATISTICAL SURVEY)

FINANCE

100 piastres = 1 Syrian pound (£S).
Coins: 2½, 5, 10, 25 and 50 piastres; 1 pound.
Notes: 1, 5, 10, 25, 50, 100 and 500 pounds.
Exchange rates (April 1973): £1 sterling = £S9.501 (official rate) or £S9.998 (free rate);
U.S. $1 = £S3.825 (official rate) or £S4.025 (free rate).
£S100 = £10.525 sterling = $26.144 (official rates).

ORDINARY BUDGET*
(£S million)

	1969	1970	1971
National Defence	661.6	671.6	675.5
Cultural and Social Affairs	251.2	285.2	318.5
Communications and Public Works	32.3	48.1	29.0
Economic Affairs and Planning	137.4	250.7	265.0
Administrative Affairs	116.5	128.9	107.0
TOTAL	1,199.0	1,384.5	1,395.0

* The Syrian budget is published at the end of the year in question.

CONSOLIDATED BUDGET
(£S million)

A new consolidated budget has been issued incorporating both ordinary and development budgets

	1970	1971	1972
Justice and Public Authorities	45.2	62.9	71.6
National Security	679.3	690.6	795.0
Culture and Information	293.4	324.5	364.3
Social Welfare	59.3	71.0	84.1
Economy and Finance	276.2	304.7	282.2
Agriculture and Land Reclamation	554.5	523.2	536.5
Industry and Mining	443.6	517.4	500.3
Public Works, Utilities and Communications	371.6	343.0	473.7
Other Expenditure and Revenue	56.9	48.2	80.3
TOTAL	2,780.0	2,886.2	3,188.0

The 1973 budget totalled £S3,413 million.

SYRIA—(Statistical Survey)

THIRD FIVE-YEAR PLAN
(1971–75—£S million)

Sector	Investment (Public Sector)	%
Euphrates Dam Project	1,593.0	24.7
Irrigation and Land Improvement	211.7	3.3
Agriculture	436.1	6.8
Industry	1,173.0	18.2
Power and Fuel	1,013.8	15.7
Transport and Communications	783.0	12.1
Towns and Buildings	585.9	9.1
Public Services	525.8	8.2
Local Trade	124.7	1.9
Total	6,447.0	100.0

OIL

FLOW OF OIL ACROSS SYRIA
('000 long tons)

Year	Total	To Banias	To Sidon (Lebanon)	To Tripoli (Lebanon)
1968	73,389	29,533	23,543	20,313
1969	68,351	29,875	16,138	22,338
1970	60,679	29,977	8,036	22,666
1971	64,544	27,712	16,407	20,425
1972	50,477	22,213	21,053	7,193

EXTERNAL TRADE
(£S '000)

	1967	1968	1969	1970	1971	1972
Imports	1,009,091	1,193,635	1,411,324	1,374,637	1,677,038	2,060,648
Exports	591,271	673,978	789,918	775,343	743,353	1,097,601

SYRIA—(Statistical Survey)

COMMODITIES (£S million)

Imports	1969	1970	1971	1972
Cotton textiles, other textile goods and silk	158.9	120.6	112.2	202.3
Mineral fuels and oils	144.9	106.9	102.3	91.4
Lime, cement and salt	16.6	8.5	27.6	28.0
Cereals	28.5	146.0	231.7	96.8
Vegetables and fruit	50.8	60.1	81.3	81.0
Oilseeds and medical plants	7.4	4.7	6.0	8.3
Machinery, apparatus and electrical materials	226.3	174.1	222.2	374.8
Precious metals and coins	7.3	3.4	3.5	2.7
Base metals and manufactures	212.7	207.7	201.2	308.1
Vehicles	104.1	57.5	50.1	65.0
Chemical and pharmaceutical products	64.5	73.3	74.5	112.0
Preserved foods, beverages and tobacco	49.1	69.7	141.1	169.0
Other products	340.2	342.1	423.3	521.2

Exports	1969	1970	1971	1972
Cotton (raw, yarn, textiles)	325.9	332.1	} 412.1	536.2
Other textile goods	58.3	57.2		
Cereals	39.8	22.2	0.1	94.9
Vegetables and fruit	46.0	24.1	39.1	51.2
Precious metals	0.8	0.6	0.5	0.3
Preserved foods, beverages and tobacco	44.8	47.2	35.8	63.4
Live animals	99.6	70.8	25.2	60.0
Dairy products	4.0	2.7	0.9	2.1
Other Products	170.7	218.4	229.6	289.5

Oil Exports: (1971) £S176 million; (1972) £S200 million.

COUNTRIES (£S million)

Imports	1969	1970	1971	1972
Belgium	26.2	25.0	31.1	50.3
Cuba	20.1	33.9	52.3	86.4
France	93.7	64.3	99.0	119.6
German Federal Republic	99.4	93.7	107.7	160.0
Iraq	88.1	88.7	101.6	83.7
Italy	123.1	89.5	116.4	166.3
Japan	59.6	80.2	72.9	130.8
Lebanon	72.1	86.5	143.5	138.4
Netherlands	28.4	24.4	42.5	48.1
U.S.S.R.	125.9	105.7	104.9	154.3
United Kingdom	64.9	54.2	55.5	99.0
U.S.A.	50.9	47.2	112.1	92.4

Exports	1969	1970	1971	1972
China	43.7	60.6	24.2	70.3
Czechoslovakia	11.4	11.5	9.2	24.7
France	26.4	39.7	29.0	35.7
German Federal Republic	7.6	17.3	29.3	33.3
Italy	96.6	167.0	208.8	116.7
Japan	11.3	54.3	20.9	16.3
Jordan	41.7	29.1	15.0	18.5
Kuwait	21.3	13.5	9.9	13.9
Lebanon	112.2	89.2	55.8	150.5
Romania	22.0	4.9	4.5	7.6
Saudi Arabia	12.4	4.3	14.7	24.6
U.S.S.R.	136.0	67.6	112.4	221.3
United Kingdom	8.9	3.4	3.3	22.0
U.S.A.	5.1	2.9	5.8	7.5

SYRIA — (Statistical Survey, The Constitution)

TRANSPORT

RAILWAYS

	1970	1971
Passenger-km.	86,459	83,735
Freight, '000 tons	1,406	1,136

ROADS

	1970	1971
Passenger Cars	30,592	31,476
Buses	1,760	1,639
Lorries, Trucks, etc.	17,793	17,598
Motor-cycles	8,122	8,580

SHIPPING
PORT OF LATAKIA

	1968	1969	1970	1971
Number of steam vessels entering harbour	1,527	1,697	1,642	1,629
Number of sailing vessels entering harbour	206	216	258	134
Cargo unloaded ('000 tons)	1,612	1,597	1,847	1,717
Cargo loaded ('000 tons)	364	526	478	264

CIVIL AVIATION
(Damascus Airport)

	1969 ARRIVE	1969 DEPART	1970 ARRIVE	1970 DEPART	1971 ARRIVE	1971 DEPART
No. of Planes	3,640	3,644	4,640	4,639	5,282	5,284
No. of Passengers	124,607	123,662	118,726	116,240	139,598	139,633

TOURISM

	Jordanians and Lebanese	Total Visitors
1967	576,794	864,600
1968	471,348	772,452
1969	524,596	797,272
1970	504,692	870,276
1971	943,011	1,322,862

Tourist Accommodation: 19,952 tourist hotel beds (1969).

EDUCATION
(1970–71)

	Pupils Public Sector	Pupils Private Sector	Teachers Public Sector	Teachers Private Sector
Pre-School	—	26,438	—	723
Primary	868,957	32,842*	23,298	1,216
Preparatory	211,928	15,185*	12,226	897
Secondary	71,511	7,983		
Vocational	10,089	42	1,124	3
Teacher Training	2,424	—	250	
Universities	38,734	—	1,123	

* Excluding UNRWA schools.

Source: Statistical Yearbook of Damascus and Aleppo Universities.

Source: Central Bureau of Statistics, Office of the Prime Minister, Damascus.

THE CONSTITUTION

A new and permanent constitution was endorsed by 97.6 per cent of the voters in a national referendum on March 12th, 1973. The 157-article constitution defines Syria as a "Socialist popular democracy" with a "pre-planned Socialist economy". Under the new constitution, Lt.-Gen. al-Asad remains President, with the power to appoint and dismiss his Vice-President, Premier and Government Ministers, and also becomes Commander-in-Chief of the armed forces, secretary-general of the Baath Socialist Party and President of the National Progressive Front. This is the country's first permanent constitution since 1961, when Syria ended its union with Egypt. The provisional constitution introduced in 1969 was never formally promulgated.

THE GOVERNMENT

HEAD OF STATE

President: HAFIZ AL-ASAD (elected March 12th, 1971, for a seven-year term).
Vice-President: MAHMOUD AL-AYOUBI.

CABINET
(June 1973)

(B) Baath, (SU) Socialist Union, (ASU) Arab Socialist Union.

Prime Minister: MAHMOUD AL-AYOUBI (B).
Deputy Prime Minister and Minister of Foreign Affairs: ABDEL HALIM KHADDAM (B).
Deputy Prime Minister and Minister of Agriculture and Agrarian Reform: MOHAMED HAIDAR (B).
Minister of Municipal and Rural Affairs: ABDEL RAZZAK ABDEL BAKI (SU).
Minister of the Economy and External Trade: MOHAMED IMADI (Independent).
Minister of Justice: ADIB AL-NAHAWI (ASU).
Minister for the Euphrates Dam: MUNIR WANNOUS (B).
Minister of Education: HAFEZ AL JAMAIL (B).
Minister of Defence: Maj.-Gen. MUSTAFA TLAS (B).
Minister of Health: Dr. MADANI AL KHYAMI (Independent).
Minister of Information: AHMAD AL-ASSAD (B).
Minister of the Interior: Brig. ALI ZAZA (B).
Minister of Supply and Internal Trade: ABDEL KARIM ADI.
Minister of Public Works and Water Resources: ABDLE-GHANI KANNOUT (ASU).
Minister of Higher Education: SHAKIR FAHHAM (B).
Minister of Petroleum, Electricity and Mineral Resources: FAYEA NASSER (B).
Minister of Finance: NOURALLAH NOURALLAH (Independent).
Minister of Culture and National Guidance: FAWZI KAYYALI (ASU).
Minister of Labour and Social Affairs: HUSSEIN AHMED KOUEIDER (B).
Minister of Local Administration: ADIB MELHEM (B).
Minister of Industry: HASSAN AL KHATIB (B).
Minister of Religious Affairs: Sheikh ABDEL SATTAR AL-SAYED (Independent).
Minister of Communications: Ing. OMAR SIBAI (Communist).
Minister of Tourism: ABDALLAH AL KHANI (Independent).
Minister of State for Village Affairs at the Front: MOUAYEN JAZZAN (B).
Minister of Planning: MOUSTAPHA HALLAJE (SU).
Minister of State for the Premiership: MARWAN SABBAGH (B).
Ministers of State: ZOUHAIR ABDEL SAMAD (Communist), ALI HACHEM (Independent), ANWAR HAMADEH (ASU).

DIPLOMATIC REPRESENTATION

EMBASSIES ACCREDITED TO SYRIA
(Damascus unless otherwise stated)

(E) Embassy

Algeria: Rue Nouri Pacha (E); *Ambassador:* ALARABI SAADOUNI.
Argentina: Raouda, Rue Ziad ben Abi Soufian, Imm. Ab Kérim Abul (E); *Ambassador:* ENRIQUE LUPIZ.
Austria: Beirut, Lebanon (E).
Belgium: Rue Ata Ayoubi, Imm. Hachem (E); *Ambassador:* LUC SMOLDEREN.
Brazil: 76 Rue Ata Ayoubi (E); *Ambassador:* ROBERTO DE ARAÚJO.
Bulgaria: 4 Rue Chahbandar (E); *Ambassador:* PETER ILIEVE.
Canada: Rue Clemenceau, Imm. Alpha (E); *Ambassador:* JACQUES GIGNAC.
Chad: (E); *Ambassador:* MARON HAYMARI.
Chile: Beirut, Lebanon (E); *Ambassador:* GUILLERMO OVALLE.
China, People's Republic: Avenue Al Jala'a (E); *Ambassador:* CHIN CHIA-LIN.
Cuba: 81 Avenue Al Jala'a (E); *Ambassador:* CARLOS ALVAREZ VARELA.
Czechoslovakia: Place Aboul-Alaa (E); *Ambassador:* MIROSLAV POKORNY.
Denmark: Beirut, Lebanon (E); *Ambassador:* MOGENS WARBERG.
Egypt: Rue Misr, Imm. Malki (E); *Ambassador:* MAMDOUH GOBBA.
France: Rue Ata Ayoubi (E); *Ambassador:* ANDRÉ NÈGRE.
German Democratic Republic: 60 Avenue Adran el Malki (E); *Ambassador:* WOLFGANG KONSCHEL.
Greece: 57 Rue Ata Ayoubi (E); *Ambassador:* JEAN TSAOUSSI.
Hungary: 13 Rue Ibrahim Hanano (Imm. Roujoulé) (E); *Ambassador:* JANOS VERES.
India: 40/46 Avenue Al Malki (E); *Ambassador:* PRANAB KUMAR GUHA.
Indonesia: 19 Rue Al-Amir Ezzeddine (E); *Ambassador:* BAHRUDDIN UBANI.
Iran: Avenue Al-Jala'a, Imm. Wazzan (E); *Ambassador:* ARDACHIR NOURAZAR.

Iraq: Avenue Al Jala'a (Imm. Coudsi) (E); *Ambassador:* AUDA AHMED AL-BAYATI.
Italy: 82 Avenue Al Mansour (E); *Ambassador:* UBERTO BOZZINI.
Japan: 62 Rue Rawdak (E); *Ambassador:* SHIGETO NIKAI.
Korea, Democratic People's Republic: 89 Avenue Al Jala'a (E); *Ambassador:* LI SEUNG-HI.
Kuwait: Rue Ibrahim Hanano (E); *Ambassador:* AHMED HUSSEIN.
Libya: Place Al Malki, 10 Avenue Mansour (E); *Ambassador:* MUHAMMAD RAMADAN MAHMOUD.
Mauritania: (address not available) (E); *Ambassador:* ABDALLAHI OULD EREBIH.
Morocco: Abou Roumaneh (E); *Ambassador:* IDRIS BENOUNA.
Netherlands: Rue Ziad Ben Abi Soufian (E); *Ambassador:* ANDRÉ M. E. BRINK.
Pakistan: Avenue Al Jala'a (E); *Ambassador:* MUHAMMAD SALIMALLA.
Poland: Rue Georges Haddad, Imm. Chahine (E); *Ambassador:* LONGIN ARABSKI.
Romania: (address not available) (E); *Ambassador:* EMILIAN MANIER.
Saudi Arabia: Avenue Al Jala'a (E); *Ambassador:* MUHAMMAD ABDULLA AL-MUTLAQ.
Spain: 14 Rue Misr (E); *Ambassador:* NUNO AGUIRE DE CARCER.
Sudan: Rue Hanano (E); *Ambassador:* HASSAN EL HASSAN.
Sweden: Damascus (E); *Ambassador:* AAKE JONSSON.
Switzerland: 12 Rue Georges Haddad (E); *Ambassador:* ALBERT DUBOIS.
Tunisia: (to be appointed).
Turkey: 58 Avenue Ziad Bin Abou Soufian (E); *Ambassador:* FAHIR ALACAM.
U.S.S.R.: Boustan El-Kouzbari, Rue d'Alep (E); *Ambassador:* NOUREDDIN MOHIEDDINOV.
United Arab Emirates: (address not available) (E); *Ambassador:* MUHAMMAD ABDER-RAHMAN AL-BAKR.
Vatican: Rue Nasr (*Apostolic Nunciature*): RAPHAEL FORNI.
Venezuela: Abou Roomaneh, Rue Nouri Pacha (E); *Chargé d'Affaires:* J. QUINTANA.
Viet-Nam, Democratic Republic: (E); *Ambassador:* HOANG DUC PHONG.
Yemen Arab Republic: Avenue Al Jala'a (E); *Ambassador:* YAHYA MUDWAHI.
Yugoslavia: Avenue Al Jala'a (E); *Ambassador:* MIRKO JALEC.

Syria also has diplomatic relations with: Austria, Cyprus, Colombia, Finland, U.K., Uruguay and Venezuela.

PEOPLE'S COUNCIL

A new People's Council was elected in May 1973 under the terms of the new Constitution. 140 out of the 186 seats were won by the Progressive Front, a grouping of the parties listed below, 42 seats were won by Independents, and the remainder by the Opposition.

Chairman: MUHAMMAD AL-HALABI.

POLITICAL PARTIES

The National Progressive Front, headed by President Asad, was formed in March 1972 by the grouping of the five parties listed below:

Baath Party: Arab socialist party; in power since 1963; supports militant Arab unity; Sec.-Gen. Pres. HAFIZ AL-ASAD.

Syrian Arab Socialist Union: Nasserite; Leader Dr. JAMAL ATASI; Sec.-Gen. FAUZI KAYYALI.

Socialist Union: Leader SAMI SOUFAN.

Arab Socialist Party: a breakaway socialist party; Leader ABDEL GHANI KANNOUT.

Communist Party of Syria: Sec.-Gen. KHALID BAGDASH.

DEFENCE

Chief of Staff of the Armed Forces: Maj.-Gen. YUSUF SHAKKUR.

Defence Budget (1972): £S960 million.

Military Service: 30 months (Jewish population exempted).

Total Armed Forces: 111,750: army 100,000; navy 1,750; air force 10,000.

Paramilitary Forces: 9,500 (8,000 Gendarmerie, 1,500 Internal Security Camel Corps).

JUDICIAL SYSTEM

Court of Cassation: Damascus; is the highest court of appeal.

Courts of Appeal: 13 Courts of Appeal in the 13 Prefectures try all criminal cases subject to appeal, as well as all other cases within their competence by virtue of the law in force; some of them are composed of several chambers; decisions are given by three judges, one of them being the President.

SYRIA—(Judicial System, Religion, The Press)

Summary Courts: 110 Summary Courts try civil, commercial and penal cases within their competence; a Summary Court is constituted by one judge known as a "Judge of the Peace".

First Instance Courts: 14 First Instance Courts, constituted by one judge, deal with all cases other than those within the competence of special tribunals. In some Prefectures are several Chambers.

Chief Justice of Syria: Ibrahim Al Faraji.

PERSONAL STATUS COURTS

For Muslims: each court consists of one judge, the "Qadi Shari'i", who deals with marriage, divorce, etc.

For Druzes: one court consisting of one judge, the "Qadi Mazhabi".

For non-Muslim Communities: for Catholics, Orthodox, Protestants, Jews.

OTHER COURTS

Courts for Minors: their constitution, officers, sessions, jurisdiction and competence are determined by a special law.

Military Court: Damascus.

RELIGION

In religion the majority of Syrians follow a form of Sunni orthodoxy. There is also a considerable number of religious minorities: Muslim Shi'ites; the Ismaili of the Salamiya district, whose spiritual head is the Aga Khan; a large number of Druzes, the Nusairis or Alawites of the Jebel Ansariyeh and the Yezidis of the Jebel Sinjar.

Muslims

Grand Mufti: Ahmad Kuftaro.

Most Syrians are Muslims. Nearly all are Sunnites with a small number of Ismailis and Shi'ites.

Christians

Greek Orthodox Patriarch: Ghofrail Faddoul.

Greek Catholic Patriarch: H.E. Maximos V. Hakim; Bab-Sharki, Damascus; P.O.B. 7181, Beirut, Lebanon.

Syrian Orthodox Patriarch: His Holiness Ignatius Yacob III.

THE PRESS

Since the coming to power of the Baath Arab Socialist Party the structure of the press has been modified according to socialist patterns. Most publications are published by organizations such as political, religious, or professional associations, trade unions, etc. and several are published by government ministries. Anyone wishing to establish a new paper or periodical must apply for a licence.

The major dailies are *al-Baath* (the organ of the party) and *al-Thawrah* in Damascus, *al-Jamahir al-Arabia* in Aleppo, and *al-Fida* in Hama.

PRINCIPAL DAILIES

Aravelk: Aleppo; Armenian; morning; Editor Dr. A. Angykian; circ. 3,500.

al-Baath (*Renaissance*): rue el Barazil, Damascus; Arabic; morning; organ of the Baath Arab Socialist Party; circ. 20,000.

Barq al-Shimal: rue Aziziyah, Aleppo; Arabic; morning; Editor Maurice Djandji; circ. 6,400.

al-Fida: rue Kuwatly, Hama; political; Arabic; morning Publishing concession holder Osman Alouini; Editor A. Aulwani; circ. 4,000.

al-Jamahir al-Arabia: El Ouedha Printing and Publishing Organization, Aleppo; political; Arabic; Chief Editor Mortada Bakach; circ. 10,000.

al-Shabab: rue al Tawil, Aleppo; Arabic; morning; Editor Muhammad Talas; circ. 9,000.

al-Thawrah: El Ouedha Printing and Publishing Organization, Damascus; political; Arabic; morning; circ. 20,000.

WEEKLIES AND FORTNIGHTLIES

al-Ajoua: Compagnie de l'Aviation Arabe Syrienne, Damascus; aviation; Arabic; fortnightly; Editor Ahmad Allouche.

Arab Press Digest: Syrian Documentation Papers, P.O.B. 2712, Damascus.

al-Esbou al-Riadi: ave. Firdoisse, Tibi Bldg., Damascus; sports; Arabic; weekly; Publisher Mounir Bakir; Dir. and Editor Kamel El Bounni.

Hadarat al-Islam: B.P. 808, Jadet Halbouni, Jadet El Raby, Damascus; religious; Arabic; fortnightly; Publisher Moustapha Essibai; Dir. Ahmad Farhat; Editor Muhammad Adib Saleh.

Homs: Homs; literary; Arabic; weekly; Publisher and Dir. Adib Kaba; Editor Philippe Kaba.

Jaysh al-Shaab: P.O.B. 3320, blvd. Palestine, Damascus; f. 1946, took present title 1967; army magazine, Arabic; weekly; published by the Political Department.

Kifah al-Oummal al-Ishtiraki: Fédération Générale des Syndicats des Ouvriers, Damascus; labour; Arabic; weekly; Published by General Federation of Trade Unions; Editor Said El Hamami.

al-Majalla al-Batriarquia: B.P. 914, Syrian Orthodox Patriarchate, Damascus; f. 1962; religious; Arabic monthly; Dir. and Editor Samir Abdoh; circ. 3,000.

al-Maukef al-Riadi: El Ouehda Organization, Damascus; sports; Arabic; weekly; Published by El Ouehda Printing and Publishing Organization; circ. 5,000.

al-Nass: B.P. 926, Aleppo; f. 1953; Arabic; weekly; Publisher Victor Kalous.

Nidal al-Fellahin: Fédération Générale des Laboureurs, Damascus; peasant workers; Arabic; weekly; Published by General Federation of Workers; Editor Mansour Abu El Hosn.

Revue de la Presse Arabe: 67 Place Chahbandar, Damascus; twice weekly.

al-Riada: B.P. 292, near Electricity Institute, Damascus; sports; Arabic; weekly; Dir. Noureddine Rial; Publisher and Editor Ourfane Ubari.

al-Sakafe al-Isboui: B.P. 2570, Soukak El Sakr, Damascus; cultural; Arabic; weekly; Publisher, Dir. and Editor Madhat Akkache.

Saut al-Fellah (*Voice of the Peasant*): Ministry of Agriculture, Damascus; agriculture; Arabic; fortnightly.

al-Talia (*Vanguard*): B.P. 3031, the National Guard, Damascus; Arabic; fortnightly; Editor Sohdi Khalil.

al-Tamaddon al-Islami: Darwichillé, Damascus; religious; Arabic; fortnightly; Published by Tamaddon al-Islami Association; Dir. Muhammad El Khatib; Editor Ahmad Mazar El Adme.

al-Thawrah al-Ziraia: Ministry of Agrarian Reform, Damascus; f. 1965; agriculture; Arabic; fortnightly; circ. 7,000.

al-Yanbu al-Jadid: al-Awkaf Bldg., Homs; literary; Arabic; weekly; Publisher, Dir. and Editor Mamdou El Kousseir.

SYRIA—(Press, Publishers, Radio and Television)

MONTHLIES

al-Dad: rue El Tital, Wakf El Moiriné Bldg., Aleppo; literary; Arabic; Dir. Riad Hallak; Publisher and Editor Abdallah Yarki Hallak.

Ecos: P.O.B. 3320, Damascus; monthly review; Spanish.

Flash: P.O.B. 3320, Damascus; monthly review; English and French.

al-Irshad al-Zirai: Ministry of Agriculture, Damascus; agriculture; every two months.

al-Kalima: Al-Kalima Association, Aleppo; religious; Arabic; Publisher and Editor Fathalla Sakal.

al-Kanoun: Ministry of Justice, Damascus; juridical; Arabic.

al-Maarifa: Ministry of Culture and National Guidance, Damascus; f. 1962; literary; Arabic; Editor Adib El Lajmi.

al-Majalla al-Askaria: P.O.B. 3320, blvd. Palestine, Damascus; f. 1950; official military magazine; Editor Nakhli Kallas.

al-Majalla al-Toubilla al-Arabilla: Al-Jalla's St., Damascus; Published by Arab Medical Commission; Dir. Dr. Shamseddin El Jundi; Editor Dr. Adnan Takriti.

al-Majma al Ilmi al-Arabi: The Arab Academy, Bab el Barid, Damascus; f. 1921; Islamic culture and Arabic literature (three a year).

Monthly Survey of Arab Economics: B.P. 2306, Damascus and B.P. 6068, Beirut; f. 1958; English and French editions; published Centre d'Etudes et de Documentation Economiques, Financières et Sociales; Dir. Dr. Chafic Akhras.

al-Mouallem al-Arabi (*The Arab Teacher*): Ministry of Education; Damascus; f. 1948; educational and cultural; Arabic.

al-Mouhandis al-Arabi: 8 Parliament St., Damascus; published by Union of Asscns. of Syrian Engineers; engineering, scientific and cultural; Dir. Samih Fakhoury; Editor Kassem Shawaf.

al-Moujtama al-Arabi al-Ishtiraki: Ministry of Social Affairs, Damascus; social security; Arabic; Editor Sami Atfe.

al-Oumran: Ministry of Municipal and Rural Affairs, Damascus; fine arts; Arabic.

Rissalat al-Kimia: B.P. 669, El Abid Bldg., Damascus; scientific; Arabic; Publisher, Dir. and Editor Hassan El Saka.

Saut al-Forat: Deir-Ezzor; literary; Arabic; Publisher, Dir. and Editor Abdel Kader Ayach.

al-Shourta: Directorate of Public Affairs and Moral Guidance, Damascus; juridical; Arabic.

Souriya al-Arabilla: Ministry of Information, Damascus; publicity; in four languages.

Syrie et le Monde Arabe: P.O.B. 3550, Place Chahbandar, Damascus; economic and political review.

al-Yakza: Sisi St., Al Yazka Association, Aleppo; f. 1935; Dir. and Editor Paul Genadri.

QUARTERLY

Les Archives Litteraires du Moyen Orient: Syrian Documentation Papers, P.O.B. 2712, Damascus.

ANNUALS

Bibliography of the Middle East: Syrian Documentation Papers, P.O.B. 2712, Damascus.

General Directory of the Press and Periodicals in the Arab World: Syrian Documentation Papers, P.O.B. 2712, Damascus.

PRESS AGENCIES

Agence Arabe Syrienne d'Information: Damascus; f. 1966; supplies bulletins on Syrian news to foreign news agencies.

Agence Nouvelle de l'Orient Arabe: Damascus; Dir. Fawzi Allaf.

Foreign Bureaux

ANSA: P.O.B. 827, rue Salhié, Immeuble Tibi-Selo; f. 1962; Chief Khalil Nabki.

UPI: 3 Argentine St., Hafez Bldg.; Chief Adnan Inayeh.

DPA, Reuter and Tass also have bureaux in Damascus.

PUBLISHERS

Arab Advertising Organization: 28 Moutanabbi St., P.O.B. 2842 and 3034, Damascus; f. 1963; publishes Directory of Commerce and Industry and other advertising material; Dir.-Gen. George Khoury.

Bureau des documentations syriennes et arabes: B.P. 451, 67 place Chahbander, Damascus; f. 1948; affiliated with the *Office arabe de presse et de documentation* (see below) in 1966, Dir.-Gen. Samir A. Darwich, publs. include *Répertoire Permanent des Lois et Réglements Syriens, Tarif Permanent des Douanes de Syrie, Recueil des Accords Internationaux conclus par la Syrie* and monographs, legislative texts and other documents concerning Syria and the Arab world.

Damascus University Press: Damascus; art, geography, education, history, engineering, medicine, law, sociology, school books.

Office Arabe de Presse et de Documentation: P.O.B. 3550, Damascus; f. 1964; numerous periodical books and surveys on political and economic affairs; Dir.-Gen. Samir A. Darwich.

al-Ouedha Printing and Publishing Organization (*Institut al-Ouedha pour l'impression, édition et distribution*): Damascus and Aleppo; published *al-Jamahir al-Duroubah* and *al-Thawrah* (dailies) and *al-Maukef al-Riadi* (weekly).

Syrian Documentation Papers: P.O.B. 2712, Damascus; f. 1968 by Louis Farès; publishers of *Bibliography of the Middle East* (annual), *General Directory of the Press and Periodicals in the Arab World* (annual), *Les Archives Littéraires du Moyen Orient* (quarterly), *Arab Press Digest* (weekly), and numerous publications on political, economic and social affairs and literature and legislative texts concerning Syria and the Arab world; Dir.-Gen. Louis Farès.

al-Tawjih Press: P.O.B. 3320, Palestine St., Damascus.

Other publishers include: *Dar El-Yakaza El-Arabia, Dar El-Hahda El-Arabia, Dar El-Filez, Dar El-Fatah, Dubed, El-Mouassassa El-Sakafieh*.

RADIO AND TELEVISION

General Directorate of Broadcasting and Television: Omayyad Square, Damascus; f. 1945; Gen. Dir. Ahmad Korneh; Dirs. Ahmad Ayass, Bachar Akhrass, George Boulad; publ. *Here is Damascus* (fortnightly).

RADIO

Broadcasts in Arabic, French, English, Russian, German, Spanish, Polish, Turkish, Bulgarian.

There were 1,616,538 receivers in use in February 1972.

TELEVISION

Services started in 1960. Dir. KHODR AL SHA'AR.
There were 1,616,538 receivers in use in February 1972.

FINANCE

BANKING

(cap.=capital; p.u.=paid up; dep.=deposits; m.= millions; amounts in £S)

CENTRAL BANK

Central Bank of Syria: 29 Ayar Square, Damascus; f. 1956; cap. 10m.; Gov. NASSOUH DACEAK; Sec. Gen. Dr. ABDEL CHAFI ALAMY; 7 brs.

OTHER BANKS

Agricultural Bank: Baghdad Street, Damascus; f. 1924; Dir.-Gen. Dr. HANNA KHOURY.

Commercial Bank of Syria S.A.: P.O.B. 933, Moawia St., Damascus; f. 1967 by a merger of the five commercial banks nationalized in 1963: Arab Orient Bank, Arab World Bank, Banque de l'Unité Arabe, Omayad Bank, Syria and Overseas Bank; 20 brs.; cap. 50m.; total resources 1,555m. (1973); Pres. and Gen. Man. BASHIR ZOUHAIRI.

Industrial Bank: Damascus; f. 1959; nationalized bank providing finance for industry; cap. 12.5m., dep. 53.4m., total investments (Feb. 1971) 106.8m.; brs. in Aleppo and Homs; Chair. and Gen. Man. Dr. A. S. KANAAN.

Popular Credit Bank: Darwishieh, Harika, P.O.B. 2841, Damascus; f. 1967; governmental bank; cap. 3m., dep. 90.5m. (June 1973).

Real Estate Bank: Damascus; f. 1966; cap. 25m.

INSURANCE

Société d'Assurances Syrienne: Taghiz St., Damascus; f. 1953; operates throughout Syria, with branches in Jordan and Lebanon; Chair. and Gen. Man. MAMDOUH RAHMOUN.

TRADE AND INDUSTRY

CHAMBERS OF COMMERCE

Damascus Chamber of Commerce: B.P. 1040, Mou'awiah St., Damascus; f. 1914; 3,800 mems.; Pres. BADREDDINE SHALLAH; Gen. Dir. MUHAMMAD THABET; publ. *Economic Bulletin* (quarterly).

Aleppo Chamber of Commerce: Al-Moutanabbi, Aleppo; f. 1885; Pres. KASSEM NOUR-EL-DINE; Dir. FADEL ANIS.

Hama Chamber of Commerce and Industry: Sh. Bachoura, Hama; f. 1934; Pres. ABDUL-HAMID KAMBAZ.

Homs Chamber of Commerce: Sh. Aboul-Of, Homs; Pres. ABDUL HASIB RUSLAN.

Latakia Chamber of Commerce: Sh. Al-Hurriyah, Latakia; Pres. JULE NASRI.

CHAMBERS OF INDUSTRY

Aleppo Chamber of Industry: Sh. Wara el-Jameh, Aleppo; Pres. SAMI AL-DAHR.

Damascus Chamber of Industry: P.O.B. 1305, Harika-Mouawiya St., Damascus; Vice-Pres. SHAFIC SOUCCAR; Man. ABDUL HAMID MALAKANI; publ. *Al Siniye* (Industry) (irregularly).

EMPLOYERS' ORGANIZATIONS

FEDERATIONS

Fédération Générale à Damas: Damascus; f. 1951; Dir. TALAT TAGLUBI.

Fédération de Damas: Damascus; f. 1949.

Fédération des Patrons et Industriels à Lattaquié: Latakia; f. 1953.

TRADE UNIONS

Ittihad Naqabat al-'Ummal al-'Am fi Suriya (*General Federation of Labour Unions*): Qanawat Street, Damascus; f. 1948; Pres. FAWZI BALI; Sec. MAHMUD FAHURI.

FEDERATIONS

Fédération de la Mécanique: Aleppo; f. 1956.
Fédération de l'Electricité: Damascus; f. 1956.
Fédération de l'Imprimerie: Damascus; f. 1956.
Fédération des Administrations de L'Etat: Damascus; f. 1955.
Fédération des Chemins de Fer de L'Etat: Damascus; f. 1951.
Fédération des Tabacs: Damascus; f. 1949.
Fédération du Pétrole: Homs; f. 1956.
Fédération du Tissage à Bras: Damascus; f. 1956.
Fédération du Tissage Mécanique: Damascus; f. 1956.
Teachers' Federation: Damascus; Chair. AHMED AL KHATIB.

TRADE

Foire Internationale de Damas: 67 blvd. de Baghdad, Damascus; held annually from August 25th to September 20th.

OIL

General Petroleum Company: P.O.B. 2849, Damascus; f. 1958; state agency; holds the oil concession for all Syria; exploits the Suwadiyah, Karachuk and Rumaila oilfields; production in 1971 5.26 million metric tons; also organizes refining, storage and distribution of petroleum; Dir. Engineer GHASSAN MOUHANNA.

TRANSPORT AND TOURISM

TRANSPORT

RAILWAYS

Syrian Railways: Registered Office: B.P. 182, Aleppo; Pres. of the Board of Administration Ing. OMAR SIBAI; Gen. Man. ABDELJABBAR KOUNDAKJI.

The present railway system is composed of the following network:

Meydan Ekbez (Turkish frontier)–Aleppo; Çobanbey (Turkish frontier)–Aleppo; Qamishliya (Turkish frontier)–Jaroubieh (Iraq frontier); Aleppo–Homs; (Lebanese frontier); Tartous–Akkari; there are 555 km. of normal gauge and 313 km. of narrow gauge track. Lines from Latakia to Aleppo and Djezira are under construction, and work on a line between Homs and Damascus (204 km.) is due to begin in the second half of 1973.

Syrian Railways:
  Northern Lines: 248 km.
  Southern Lines: 295 km.

Hejaz Railways (narrow gauge): 301 km. in Syria; the historic railway to Medina is the subject of a reconstruction project jointly with Jordan and Saudi Arabia, but little progress has been made since the June 1967 war.

ROADS

Arterial roads run across the country linking the north to the south and the Mediterranean to the eastern frontier.

The main arterial networks are as follows: Sidon (Lebanon)-Quneitra-Sweida-Salkhad-Jordan border; Beirut (Lebanon)-Damascus - Khan Abu Chamat - Iraq border - Baghdad; Tartous - Tell Kalakh - Homs - Palmyra; Banias - Hama - Salemie; Latakia-Aleppo-Rakka-Deirezzor-Abou Kemal-Iraq border; Tripoli (Lebanon)-Tartous-Banias-Latakia; Turkish border - Antakya; Amman (Jordan) - Dera'a - Damascus-Homs-Hama-Aleppo-Azaz (Turkish border); Haifa (Palestine)-Kuneitra-Damascus-Palmyra-Deirezzor-Hassetche-Kamechlie.

Asphalted roads: 6,000 kms.

Macadam roads: 1,300 kms.

Earth roads: 6,000 kms.

Touring Club de Syrie: P.O.B. 28, Aleppo; f. 1950; the principal Syrian motoring organization; Pres. ALFRED GIRARDI.

PIPELINES

The oil pipelines which cross Syrian territory are of great importance to the national economy, representing a considerable source of foreign exchange. One of the pipelines runs from the Iraq Petroleum Company's installations in Kirkuk to Tripoli in the Lebanon, cutting through approximately 300 miles of Syrian territory. Another line also crosses Syria *en route* to Sidon (Lebanon). Another line, completed in 1968, runs from Karatchouk, through Homs to a terminal at Tartous.

Following the Iraq Government's nationalization of the Iraq Petroleum Company, the Syrian Government nationalized the IPC's pipelines, pumping stations and other installations in Syria, setting up a new company to administer them:

Syrian Company for Oil Transport (SCOT): Dir.-Gen. HANNA HADDAD.

SHIPPING

The port of Latakia has developed and the construction of a deep water harbour, which began in 1953, was completed in 1959. 1,642 ships entered Latakia in 1970. A new port at Tartous is under construction.

The Iraq Petroleum Company has built a harbour at Banias to handle the oil transported in underground pipelines from Kirkuk.

CIVIL AVIATION

A new international airport for Damascus was opened in the summer of 1969.

Syrian Arab Airlines: P.O.B. 417, Red Crescent Bldg., Yousef-Al-Azmeh Square, Damascus; f. 1946, refounded 1961 after revocation of merger with Misrair forming U.A.A.; domestic services and routes to Cairo, Teheran, Kuwait, Baghdad, Sharjah, Dahran, Doha, Rome, London, Karachi, Delhi, Athens, Paris and Munich; Chair. LOUIS DAKKAR; Gen. Man. Brig.-Gen. ZOUHAIR AKIL.

FOREIGN COMPANIES OPERATING SERVICES THROUGH SYRIA

The following foreign airlines serve Syria: Aeroflot, Air France, Alitalia, Ariana Afghan Airlines, Balkan (Bulgaria), BOAC, ČSA, EgyptAir, Interflug, Iraqi Airways, KLM, Kuwait Airways, Lufthansa, Malev, Pan American, Pakistan International Airlines, Qantas, SAS, Saudia and Swissair.

TOURISM

Ministry of Tourism: Abou Firas St., Damascus; f. 1958; Minister of Tourism ABDALLAH KHANI; Vice-Minister B. KASSAB HASSAN.

Youth Tourism and Travel Organization: Av. 29 Mai, B.P. 201, Damascus; f. 1966; Dir. MOHAMED D'ADOUCH; 3 brs.

EDUCATION

Compulsory schooling lasts six years up to the age of 14, and text books are issued free in the primary sector. Both primary and secondary education are expanding rapidly.

Technical schools prepare students mainly for work in agriculture and are open to the sons of peasants. Higher education is provided by the Universities of Damascus and Aleppo, and the Damascus Institute of Technology.

The main language of instruction in schools is Arabic, but English and French are widely taught and are used for instruction in the University of Aleppo.

The budget of the Ministry of Education in the fiscal year 1971 amounted to £S222 million, or 7.5 per cent of the national budget, while the budget of the Ministry of Higher Education reached £S49 million, or 1.7 per cent of the national budget.

UNIVERSITIES

University of Aleppo: f. 1960; 350 teachers; 5,792 students.

Damascus University: Damascus; f. 1923; 677 teachers; 31,071 students.

BIBLIOGRAPHY

Abu Jaber, Kamal S. The Arab Baath Socialist Party (Syracuse University Press, New York, 1966).

Asfour, Edmund Y. Syrian Development and Monetary Policy (Harvard, 1959).

Directory of Commerce and Industry for the Syrian Arab Republic (Arab Advertising Organization, Damascus, 1969).

Fedden, Robin. Syria: an Historical Appreciation (London, 1946).
 Syria and Lebanon (John Murray, London, 1966).

Glubb, J. B. Syria, Lebanon, Jordan (Thames and Hudson, London, 1967).

Haddad, J. Fifty Years of Modern Syria and Lebanon (Beirut, 1950).

Helbaoui, Youssef. La Syrie (Paris, 1956).

Hitti, Philip K. History of Syria; including Lebanon and Palestine (New York, 1951).

Homet, M. L'Histoire secrète du traité franco-syrien (New Ed., Paris, 1951).

Hopwood, Derek. The Russian presence in Syria and Palestine 1843–1914 (Oxford, 1969).

Hourani, Albert H. Syria and Lebanon: A Political Essay (New York, 1946).

International Bank for Reconstruction and Development, The. The Economic Development of Syria (Baltimore, 1955).

Lloyd-George, D. The Truth about the Peace Treaties, Vol. II (London, 1938).

Longrigg, S. H. Syria and Lebanon Under French Mandate (Oxford University Press, 1958).

Rabbath, E. Unité Syrienne et Devenir Arabe (Paris, 1937).

Report of the United States-Syria Agricultural Mission (Washington, 1947).

Runciman, Steven. A History of the Crusades (London, Vol. I 1951, Vol. II 1952).

Sauvaget, J. Les monuments historiques de Damas (Beirut, 1932).

Seale, Patrick. The Struggle for Syria (London, 1965).

Sharif, A. A. Sources of Statistics in Syria (B.D.S.A., Damascus, 1964).

Springett, B. H. Secret Sects of Syria and the Lebanon (London, 1922).

Stark, Freya. Letters from Syria (London, 1942).

Sultanov, A. F. Souremennaya Siriya (Izdatel'stvo Vostochnoi Literaturni, Moscow, 1958).

The Syrian Five Year Plan for Economic and Social Development 1960–65 (Ministry of Planning, Damascus, 1963).

Thubron, C. A. Mirror to Damascus (Heinemann, London, 1967).

Tibawi, A. L. Syria (London, 1962).
 American Interests in Syria 1800–1901 (Oxford University Press, New York, 1966).
 A Modern History of Syria (Macmillan, London, 1969).

Torrey, Gordon H. Syrian Politics and the Military (State University, Ohio, 1964).

Tritton, A. S. The Caliphs and their Non-Muslim Subjects (London, 1930).

Weulersse, J. Paysans de Syrie et du Proche Orient (Paris, 1946).

United Arab Republic, Ministry of Culture and National Guidance. A Bibliographical List of Works about Syria (National Library Press, Cairo, 1965).

Yamak, L. Z. The Syrian Social Nationalist Party (Harvard University Press, Cambridge, Mass., 1966).

Ziadeh, N. Syria and Lebanon (New York, Praeger, 1957).

Tunisia

PHYSICAL AND SOCIAL GEOGRAPHY

D. R. Harris

Tunisia is the smallest of the four countries that comprise the "Maghreb" of north Africa but it is more cosmopolitan than either Algeria or Morocco. It forms a wedge of territory, some 48,200 square miles in extent, between Algeria and Libya. It includes the easternmost ridges of the Atlas Mountains but most of it is low-lying and bordered by a long and sinuous Mediterranean coastline that faces both north and east. Ease of access by sea and by land from the east has favoured the penetration of foreign influences and Tunisia owes its distinct national identity and its varied cultural traditions to a succession of invading peoples: Phoenicians, Romans, Arabs, Turks and French. It was more completely Arabized than either Algeria or Morocco and remnants of the original Berber-speaking population of the Maghreb are confined, in Tunisia, to a few isolated localities in the south.

In 1966 the population was 4,533,341 and the overall density was 92.5 per square mile. Most of the people live in the more humid, northern part of the country and nearly one sixth of the total are concentrated in the sprawling city of Tunis (population 789,787). Situated strategically where the Sicilian Channel links the western with the central Mediterranean and close to the site of ancient Carthage, Tunis combines the functions of capital and chief port. No other town approaches Tunis in importance but on the east coast both Sousse (population 90,000) and Sfax (population 100,000) provide modern port facilities, as does Bizerta (population 70,000) on the north coast, while some distance inland the old Arab capital and holy city of Kairouan (population 50,000) serves as a regional centre.

The principal contrasts in the physical geography of Tunisia are between a humid and relatively mountainous northern region, a semi-arid central region of low plateaux and plains and a dry Saharan region in the south. The northern region is dominated by the easternmost folds of the Atlas mountain system which form two separate chains, the Northern and High Tell, separated by the valley of the River Medjerda, the only perennially flowing river in the country. The Northern Tell, which is a continuation of the Algerian Tell Atlas, consists mainly of sandstone and extends along the north coast at heights of between 1,000 and 2,000 feet. South of the Medjerda valley the much broader Tell Atlas, which is a continuation of the Saharan Atlas of Algeria, is made up of a succession of rugged sandstone and limestone ridges. Near the Algerian frontier they reach a maximum height of 5,065 feet in Djebel Chambi, the highest point in Tunisia, but the folds die away eastward towards the Cape Bon peninsula which extends north-east to within 90 miles of Sicily.

South of the High Tell or Dorsale ("backbone") central Tunisia consists of an extensive platform sloping gently towards the east coast. Its western half, known as the High Steppe, is made up of alluvial basins rimmed by low, barren mountains, but eastward the mountains give way first to the Low Steppe, which is a monotonous gravel-covered plateau and ultimately to the flat coastal plain of the Sahel. Occasional watercourses cross the Steppes but they only flow after heavy rain and usually fan out and evaporate in salt flats, or sebkhas, before reaching the sea.

The central Steppes give way southward to a broad depression occupied by two great seasonal salt lakes or shotts. The largest of these, the Shott Djerid, lies at 52 feet below sea level and is normally covered by a salt crust. It extends from close to the Mediterranean coast near Gabès almost to the Algerian frontier and is adjoined on the north-west by the Shott el Rharsa which lies at 69 feet below sea level. South of the shotts Tunisia extends for over 200 miles into the Sahara. Rocky, flat-topped mountains, the Monts des Ksour, separate a flat plain known as the Djeffara which borders the coast south of Gabès, from a sandy lowland which is partly covered by the dunes of the Great Eastern Erg.

The climate of northern Tunisia is "Mediterranean" in type with hot, dry summers followed by warm, wet winters. Average rainfall reaches 60 inches in the Kroumirie Mountains, which is the wettest area in north Africa, but over most of the northern region it varies from 16 to 40 inches. The wetter and least accessible mountains are covered with forests in which cork oak and evergreen oak predominate, but elsewhere lower rainfall and overgrazing combine to replace forest with meagre scrub growth. South of the High Tell rainfall is reduced to between 16 and 8 inches annually, which is insufficient for the regular cultivation of cereal crops without irrigation, and there is no continuous cover of vegetation. Large areas of the Steppes support only clumps of wiry esparto grass, which is collected and exported for paper manufacture. Southern Tunisia experiences full desert conditions. Rainfall is reduced to below 8 inches annually and occurs only at rare intervals. Extremes of temperature and wind are characteristic and vegetation is completely absent over extensive tracts. The country supports only a sparse nomadic population except where supplies of underground water make cultivation possible, as in the famous date-producing oasis of Tozeur on the northern edge of the Shott Djerid.

HISTORY

Although the creation of the present-day independent Republic of Tunisia has been a phenomenon of the post-war period, the history of this small but important part of North Africa has displayed a certain continuity since the earliest times. From the early days of Phoenician settlement in the course of the ninth century B.C., the region has alternated between being itself a focus of political control (the Carthaginian Empire, or the period of medieval Islam, for example) reaching out to colonize or dominate the adjacent shores of the Mediterranean; and being the object of imperial aggrandizement (Rome, the Ottoman Empire, France) on the part of the dominant Mediterranean power of the time. On top of this pattern must be superimposed the conquest of North Africa by the Arabs in the course of the seventh century A.D., which has determined the basic characteristics of Tunisia ever since.

The history of Tunisia may be said to begin with the establishment there of colonies of Phoenician settlers, and the rise of the Carthaginian Empire. Emerging, in the course of the sixth century B.C., from the mists of its legendary foundation by the semi-mythical Queen Dido, by c. 550 B.C. Carthage had reached a position of commercial and naval supremacy in the Mediterranean, controlling part of Sicily, and with trading colonies established as far as what is now southern Portugal. The empire reached its height in the course of the fourth century, but shortly afterwards became involved with the rising power of the Roman Republic in a bitter struggle for the hegemony of the Mediterranean. The Punic Wars (264–241; 218–201; 149–146), of which the second is memorable for Hannibal's invasion of Italy, ended in the utter destruction of Carthage as a political entity, and the incorporation of its domains within the growing empire of Rome.

After one and a half centuries of abandonment, the ancient site of Carthage was rebuilt by Augustus at the dawn of the Christian era: intensive colonization from this time onward brought to what had become the Province of Africa a new prosperity, and the blessings of Roman civilization. During the first two centuries A.D. Carthage was generally accounted the second city of the Empire after Rome, but with the decline of the Empire in the west in the course of the fourth century, the great days of Roman Carthage were over. In A.D. 439 the city was lost to the Vandals, a nomadic people of Germanic origin, and became the capital of their ephemeral state, to be recovered for the Byzantine Empire in 533–34.

For the next two hundred and fifty years the history of Tunisia cannot be separated from the larger account of North Africa. Although Byzantine rule was better established in Tunisia than in the rest of the area, it was by no means secure. The tendency of the local governors to free themselves of the control of Constantinople was echoed by religious dissensions among the native population, who, largely Berber in origin, adopted various Christian heresies as tokens of their opposition to Imperial rule.

It was from another quarter, however, that the final challenge to Byzantine rule was to come The foundation in Arabia of the power of Islam, and its rapid expansion after the death of the Prophet (632), led quickly to the Arab conquest of Egypt and Syria, and to the shattering of the precarious unity of the Byzantine Empire. The first Arab raids into North Africa soon followed (647). After a confused period, in which the Arabs, the Berbers, and the forces of Byzantium all contested for the control of North Africa, Arab control over the area was finally established (698) with the conquest of Carthage, and the foundation of the town of Tunis. Islam now spread rapidly amongst the Berbers, but did not prevent them from making further attempts to regain their independence, merely providing them with new and more convenient pretexts for revolt in the shape of new Islamic religious heresies. The greater part of the eighth century is taken up with Berber-supported Kharijite risings, manifestations of extreme left-wing Islam against the central government, and with constant revolts among the occupying Arab forces. In the last years of the Ummayad dynasty (overthrown 748–50) Tunisia escaped completely from Imperial control: the new dynasty of the Abbasids, ruling from Iraq, made strong efforts to recapture the province. Kayrawan, founded in 670 as the centre of Arab rule in the Maghreb, was retaken, but lost in 767, when a period of complete anarchy ensued. After a period of rule by petty chieftains, Tunisia was restored to Abbasid control in the year 800, in the person of Ibrahim ibn Aghlab. As a reward for his services, and as a means of maintaining the form if not the actuality of imperial control over the area, the caliph Harun al-Rashid thereupon appointed him as tributary ruler of al-Ifrikiya—corresponding more or less to the Roman Province of Africa, and to the present-day state of Tunisia.

The period of Aghlabid rule is one of great importance for the history of Tunisia. For the major part of the ninth century the country enjoyed a relatively stable and prosperous existence, while the importance of the dynasty was early recognized by the arrival of an embassy from the Emperor Charlemagne. Some years later, returning in a different way the interest of Europe, Aghlabid forces began the conquest of Sicily (827–39). The middle of the ninth century was the zenith of Aghlabid rule, and was signalized by the emir Ahmed with the construction of great mosques in the major cities, and the building of an elaborate system of dams and reservoirs to supply the capital of Kayrawan. From 874 the power of the Aghlabid state began to decline; despite the virtual completion of the conquest of Sicily (878) the dynasty was finally overthrown in the course of a religious revolution from the west. Between 905 and 909 Tunisia was brought under the control of the Fatimids, adherents and fanatical propagators of the heretical doctrines of Shi'ism. Established in their new capital of Mahdiya, on the Tunisian coast, the Fatimids pursued a vigorous policy of expansion and conquest. Expeditions were sent against Egypt, and Sicily was once more ruled from North Africa, while by 933 Fatimid rule was established throughout the Maghreb. A serious threat to the regime, posed in 943–47 by the terrible Berber revolt led by "the man with the donkey", was overcome, and for the next twenty-five years Tunisia enjoyed a certain degree of prosperity. Fatimid power meanwhile was expanding in the east. In 969–70 the dynasty gained control of Egypt and Syria: three years later the caliph al-Muizz abandoned Mahdiya for his new capital of Cairo, and handed over the government of Tunisia to the Zirids, a family of Berber princes who had long supported the Fatimid regime. Under Zirid rule Tunisia enjoyed great prosperity, in which the arts and sciences, commerce and industry, all flourished, but this golden age was suddenly brought to an end in 1050 by the Zirids transferring their allegiance from Cairo to the orthodox caliph at Baghdad. Fatimid revenge was terrible. In 1051 hundreds of thousands of Hilali Arab nomads were sent against Ifrikiya from Egypt. Under the devastating impact of these marauding nomads the economy crumbled, along with the political power of the Berbers, and the country as a whole lapsed into political fragmentation. Further troubles now came from another quarter. In 1087 forces from the rising Italian city-states of Pisa and Genoa took Mahdiya, allowing the Zirids, who had held out there against the Hilali invasion, to continue as its rulers. Early in the twelfth century the Zirids renewed their loyalty to Cairo, and attempted to restore the shattered fragments of their state, but were interrupted by the Normans, who, having previously conquered Sicily and Malta, in 1148 drove the last Zirid from Mahdiya.

Norman rule in Tunisia was short-lived. By 1160 they had been ejected from their last coastal stronghold, and for the next fifty years Tunisia formed part of the empire of the caliphs of Marrakesh (the Almohads). With the thirteenth century the authority of Baghdad was briefly restored over Tunisia. In 1207 the Abbasid caliph al-Nasir set up a strong provincial government under a member of the Berber family of the Hafsids, who, having held the governorship of Tunis since 1184, were to continue as the main political force in the area until the Ottoman conquest late in the sixteenth century.

For the most of the thirteenth century the Hafsids ruled over North Africa from Tripoli to central Algeria, and maintained close diplomatic and commercial relations with the trading ports and city-states of the northern shores of the Mediterranean. European interest in Tunisia had never disappeared since the temporary Norman conquest of the twelfth century: with the weakening of Hafsid rule in face of tribal and Arab unrest, Jerba came once more into Christian hands (1284–1337). In the reign of Abu'l-Abbas (1370–94) the fortunes of the dynasty once more improved, and further Christian attempts to seize coastal places were repelled. His son held off repeated Sicilian and Catalan attempts to capture Jerba, and in 1428 went on the offensive, becoming involved in operations against Malta. The last Hafsid ruler of note was Abu Amr Uthman (1435–88). Shortly after his death the Hafsid Empire began to disintegrate, and at the same time Tunisia became involved in the wider struggle between the resurgent forces of the newly-unified Spanish monarchy and the Ottoman Empire for control of the Mediterranean, the outcome of which conflict was to determine the future of Tunisia for the next four centuries, and to mark its emergence as a definite political entity.

OTTOMAN RULE

With the completion of the *reconquista* in 1492 by the incorporation of the Muslim kingdom of Granada, Spain turned her attentions to the conquest of Muslim North Africa. The first place in the crumbling Hafsid territories to fall under her control was Bougie, in 1510, and then Tripoli, in the same year. Ten years later the strategic place of Jerba also fell. But these events had already produced a reaction. In 1516 Algiers had come into the possession of the Turkish corsair Aruj. His brother, Khayr ed-Din Barbarossa, who had succeeded him in 1518, had in 1533 been summoned to Istanbul to act as high admiral of the Ottoman fleet. In this new capacity he drove the compliant Emir al-Hasan from Tunis (1534), and placed the town under Ottoman control. In the following year a great Spanish naval expedition retook the town, and al-Hasan returned as the Emperor's vassal, handing over la Goleta to Spain as the price of his restoration. Further coastal strongholds subsequently passed into Spanish hands, while in 1542 al-Hassan was deposed by his son Ahmed, who, with the not disinterested help of the Turkish corsair chiefs, made a final attempt to reunite Tunisia against Spain. After a long drawn-out struggle Ahmed fell at the siege of Malta, 1565, which, together with the Spanish naval victory of Lepanto six years later, marks the climax and virtual end of their struggle with the Ottomans for control of the sea. As far as Tunisia was concerned, the sole beneficiaries of the struggle were the Ottomans. Already well established at Algiers, in 1569 the Pasha of Algiers, Uluj Ali, placed a garrison in Tunis, only to be driven out briefly (1572) in the aftermath of the Spanish victory at Lepanto. The unfortunate Hafsid was restored for the last time as nominal ruler, but in 1574 an Ottoman expedition put an end to Spanish power in Tunis, and to the Hafsid dynasty itself.

Direct Ottoman rule in Algiers lasted only seventeen years. The provincial administration set up in 1574 took its orders at first from Algiers, and later from the Porte itself, but a military revolt in 1591 reduced the power of the Pasha, the actual representative of the sultan, to a cypher, and the affairs of the state were taken over by one of the forty *deys* or high officers of the Ottoman army of occupation. By c. 1600 a situation had arisen analogous to that in Algiers, the *diwan*, or governing council, coming to share a pre-eminent place with the *taifa*, or guild of the corsair chiefs. By 1606 the *de facto* independence of Tunisia had been recognized by the dispatch of a French embassy, under orders to negotiate commercial privileges with Tunis without reference to the Porte. Nevertheless, for the next two and a half centuries and more, Tunisia was regarded as part of the Ottoman Empire, a convenient fiction both flattering to the government at Istanbul, and useful to the *deys* in safeguarding their rule and bolstering their reputation with outside powers.

In the first half of the seventeenth century the situation of Tunis was fairly flourishing. Trade and commerce, especially with Marseilles and Livorno, prospered, while commercial relations were entered into with states as far distant as England and the Netherlands. From *c.* 1650 the power of the *deys* declined, and authority in the state gradually passed to the *beys*, originally subordinate in rank. Hammuda, *bey* from 1659 to 1663, became master of the entire country, and assured the maintenance of power in his family—the Muradids—until 1702. This was a period of decline, with tribal unrest away from Tunis, and incursions from the direction of Algiers. With the accession of Huseyn Ali Turki in 1705 a new line of *beys* brought some semblance of order to the country. The remainder of the eighteenth century passed fairly uneventfully for Tunisia, with a certain amount of quiet prosperity, despite the uncertainty of relations with Algeria, and the growing naval power of Europe in the Mediterranean.

With the aftermath of the Napoleonic Wars came the first real impact of Europe on Tunisia. The European powers, in congress at Vienna and Aachen (1815–17) forced upon the *bey* Mahmud (1814–24) the suppression of the corsairs and their piratical activities, which had provided a considerable part of the revenues of the state. The French occupied Algiers in 1830, and subsequently reduced the whole of Algeria to colonial status. The next fifty years witnessed desperate but unavailing efforts by Tunisia to avoid the same fate. Increasingly the influence of France and Britain, and later Italy, came to be manifest through the activities of their consuls. The *bey* Ahmed (1837–55) attempted to reform the army on western lines, and to liberalize the institutions of society: his efforts merely increased the financial dependence of Tunisia on France. Under Muhammad (1855–59) a proclamation of reform and equality based on the Ottoman Hatti-Sherif of 1839 was promulgated under European pressure: his successor Muhammad al-Sadik (1859–82) promulgated a Constitution (suspended 1864) which attempted to separate executive from legislative power, to codify the laws, and to guarantee the independence of the judiciary.

Nevertheless, Tunisia's position deteriorated. Increased taxes, imposed from the mid-fifties, provoked tribal rebellion, and the growing dependence on foreign loans led to foreign intervention. Annual debt charges eventually exceeded revenue and in 1869 the *bey* was obliged to accept international financial control by France, Britain and Italy. By 1881 the imminence of financial collapse decided France to intervene, especially as at the Congress of Berlin three years earlier Britain, confronted by French hostility to the Cyprus Convention between Britain and Turkey, had indicated that it would not contest French influence in Tunisia, which Germany actually encouraged. French forces invaded Tunisia in April 1881, the immediate occasion being incidents on the frontier with Algeria. They encountered no serious resistance and the *bey* was forced to accept the terms of the Treaty of Kassar Said (also known as the Treaty of Bardo) under which he remained the nominal ruler of his country while French officials took over the direction of military, financial and foreign affairs.

FRENCH PROTECTORATE

The French presence once established, French control was soon extended. In 1883 Ali IV, the successor to Muhammad al-Sadik, was forced to sign the Treaty of Mersa, which formally established a French protectorate over Tunisia and brought the actual government of the country under French control. Although the office of *bey* was preserved, the real power passed to the French Resident-General. The international control commission was abolished in 1884, the currency was reformed on French lines in 1891, and the extra-territorial privileges of other Europeans were abrogated. Encouraged by large-scale grants of land, there was a considerable influx of settlers from France, and also from Italy, especially after 1900. Besides being confronted with the task of sustaining the economy by something better than the proceeds of piracy, which they tackled by investment in the development of the country's resources, the French were faced with rivalry from Italy, whose ambitions in North Africa were not extinguished until the collapse of the Fascist regime in the Second World War, and with the rise of Tunisian nationalism.

Tunisian cultural and political life absorbed many French ideas but was also influenced by movements in other parts of the Islamic world. An attempt to emulate the Young Turk reformers in the Ottoman Empire was seen in the Young Tunisian movement (1908) which called for the restoration of the authority of the *bey* together with reforms on democratic lines. The achievement of independence in eastern Arab countries after the Second World War, and the example of the nationalist movement in Egypt, inspired Tunisians with a greater national consciousness and in 1920 the Destour (Constitution) movement was formed under the leadership of Shaikh al-Tha'libi, one of the founders of the pre-war Young Tunisians.

The Destour called for a self-governing constitutional regime with a legislative assembly. French attempts to conciliate opinion by administrative reforms, beginning in 1920 with economic councils on which Tunisians were represented, did not satisfy the more radical elements, however, and in the face of further nationalist activity repressive measures were resorted to. Shaikh al-Tha'libi was exiled in 1923 and in 1925 the Destour movement was broken up. It revived in the years after the Depression but soon split, the old Destour leaders being accused of collaboration with France by younger members eager for political action on a broad front. In 1934, led by Habib Bourguiba, a Tunisian lawyer, these created the Néo-Destour (New Constitution) Party. The new party employed methods of widespread political agitation as a result of which Bourguiba was exiled. With the victory of the Popular Front in France in 1936 he returned to Tunisia but little was achieved in direct negotiations with the new French government, from which much had been expected in the way of reforms. The Néo-Destour was built up into a powerful organization, its influence extending into all parts of the country, and its strength was proved in a successful general strike in 1938. Widespread clashes with the police followed, martial law was proclaimed, some 200 nationalists were arrested and both the Destour and Néo-Destour parties were dissolved.

When the Second World War broke out in the following year Tunisian opinion rallied in favour of France and when Italy entered the war some 23,000 Italians in Tunisia were interned. With the fall of France Tunisia came under Vichy rule and Bizerta, Tunis and other ports were used by Germany and Italy to supply their armies in Libya. The country became a theatre of war until the defeat of the Axis forces by the Allies in 1943 brought about the eventual restoration of French authority. The *bey*, Muhammad al-Monsif, was accused of collaboration with the Axis powers and deposed; he was replaced by his cousin, Muhammad al-Amin, who reigned until Tunisia became a republic in 1957.

GROWING AUTONOMY

The virtual restoration of peace-time conditions in 1944 brought a relaxation of political restrictions and the years immediately following saw renewed agitation for political changes. French action to repress this obliged Habib Bourguiba to remove himself to Cairo in 1945 but his chief lieutenant, Salah ben Youssef, was able to remain in Tunisia. The French authorities turned their attention to political reforms and by Beylical decrees in 1945 the Council of Ministers and the Grand Council (an elected body with equal French and Tunisian representation) were reorganized, the authority of the latter being extended. These moves did not satisfy the nationalists, however, who in August 1946 at a national congress unequivocally demanded complete independence. Later in the year a ministry was formed under Muhammad Kaak which included an increased number of Tunisians (moderate leaders being appointed, the Destour and Néo-Destour having refused to participate); the French retained overriding control.

Bourguiba returned to Tunisia in 1949. In April 1950 Néo-Destour proposals were put forward for the transfer of sovereignty and executive control to Tunisian hands, under a responsible government with a Prime Minister appointed by the *bey* and an elected National Assembly which would draw up a democratic constitution. Local French interests would be protected by representation on municipal councils, and Tunisia would co-operate with France on terms of equality. These proposals were met with a reasonable response in France and a new Tunisian government was formed in August 1950, composed of an equal number of Tunisian and French ministers, with Muhammad Chenik as Chief Minister and Salah ben Youssef Minister of Justice. The object of the new Government was stated to be the restoration of Tunisian sovereignty in stages, in co-operation with France. Despite strong opposition to these developments from the European settlers (some 10 per cent of the population), who opposed all concessions to nationalist demands, further reforms were effected in September 1950 and February 1951, when French advisers to the Tunisian ministers were removed and the Resident-General's control over the Council of Ministers was diminished.

Peaceful progress towards autonomy came to a halt, however, with growing settler opposition, procrastination on the part of the French government and consequent alienation of the nationalists. Franco-Tunisian negotiations in 1951 came to nothing and Tunisian resentment erupted in strikes and demonstrations early in 1952. In February 1952 Bourguiba and other Néo-Destour leaders were arrested on the order of a new Resident-General, de Hautecloche, and a wave of violence spread throughout the country, culminating in the arrest and removal from office of the Chief Minister and the imposition of French military control.

A new Government was formed under Salaheddine Baccouche, a French-inspired scheme of reforms designed to lead to eventual internal autonomy was announced in April, and a temporary easing of tension followed, although the now-proscribed Néo-Destour took their case to Cairo and the UN General Assembly. Against a background of increasing terrorism, countered by French repressive action, and in face of opposition from both the Néo-Destour and the settlers, little in the way of reform could be achieved. The *bey* at first refused to sign French reform decrees and when he yielded in December 1952 under the threat of deposition the proposals were promptly repudiated by the Néo-Destour.

Terrorist activities continued and a secret settler counter-terrorist organization, the "Red Hand", came into prominence. The situation, which approached civil war in 1953, with bands of *fellagha* active in the western highlands and around Bizerta, and terrorism and counter-terrorism in the towns, did not improve until July 1954, when the newly-formed Mendès-France government in France offered internal autonomy for Tunisia with responsibility only for defence and foreign affairs being retained by France. The French proposals were accepted and in August a new Tunisian government headed by Tahar ben Ammar, which contained moderate nationalists but also three Néo-Destour members, was formed. Negotiations with the French government began at Carthage in September 1954 and although they had reached deadlock when the Mèndes-France government fell in February 1955 they were resumed in March and a final agreement was signed in Paris on June 2nd.

The agreement gave internal autonomy to Tunisia while at the same time protecting French interests and preserving the close links with France. France retained responsibility for foreign affairs, defence (including the control of frontiers) and internal security.

Although it was supported by a majority of the Néo-Destour, the extremist wing, headed by the exiled Salah ben Youssef, and the old Destour and Communist elements, opposed it, as also did the settlers' organizations. An all-Tunisian cabinet was formed in September 1955 by Tahar ben Ammar, with Néo-Destour members holding six of the twelve posts.

Habib Bourguiba had returned from three years' exile in June 1955, to be followed by Salah ben Youssef in September. In October, however, ben Youssef was expelled from the party for opposition to the recent agreement and for "splitting activities". A Néo-Destour party congress at Sfax in November 1955 confirmed the expulsion and re-elected Bourguiba as party president. The congress accepted the agreement but at the same time reaffirmed that it would be satisfied only with independence and demanded the election of a constituent assembly. Clashes between "Bourguibist" and "Youssefist" factions followed and in December a conspiracy to set up a terrorist organization to prevent the implementation of the agreement was discovered. Salah ben Youssef fled to Tripoli in January 1956 and many suspected "Youssefists" were placed in detention. At the same time *fellagha* activity revived, rebel bands becoming active in the remoter parts of the country and acts of terrorism being committed against both Frenchmen and members of the Néo-Destour.

INDEPENDENCE

Against the background of these events a Tunisian delegation led by Bourguiba began independence negotiations with the French Government in Paris on February 27th, 1956. In a protocol signed on March 20th France formally recognized the independence of Tunisia and its right to exercise responsibility over foreign affairs, security and defence, and to set up a national army. A transitional period was envisaged during which French forces would gradually be withdrawn from Tunisia, including Bizerta.

Elections for a Constituent Assembly, immediately held on March 25th, resulted in all 98 seats being won by candidates of the National Front, all of whom acknowledged allegiance to the Néo-Destour. The elections were boycotted by the "Youssefist" opposition. The ministry of Tahar ben Ammar resigned and Habib Bourguiba became Prime Minister on April 11th, leading a government in which 16 of the 17 ministers belonged to the Néo-Destour.

In the early years of independence Tunisia's relations with France were bedevilled by the question of the evacuation of French forces. A Tunisian demand for their withdrawal was rejected in July 1956 by a French government preoccupied with a deteriorating situation in Algeria. Bourguiba visited Paris in September in an attempt to promote a mediated settlement in Algeria based on French recognition of Algeria's right to independence but hopes of progress in this direction were shattered by the French kidnapping in October of five leading Algerian nationalists on their way from Morocco to Algeria. Tunisia immediately severed diplomatic relations with France, anti-French riots broke out and there were clashes between French troops and Tunisian demonstrators resulting in deaths on both sides.

Moves were made early in 1957 to strengthen Tunisia's relations with her neighbours. In January a treaty of good-neighbourliness was signed with Libya and proclaimed to be a step towards establishing a "Greater Arab Maghreb", and in March, at the end of a visit by Bourguiba, a twenty-year treaty of friendship was concluded with Morocco.

The *bey*, Muhammed al-Amin, had for long been the object of criticism from Tunisian nationalist leaders who saw him as having been unwilling to participate actively in the struggle for independence and apt to rely on French support. After independence his remaining powers were whittled away and on July 25th, 1957, the Constituent Assembly decided to abolish the monarchy, proclaim Tunisia a republic and invest Bourguiba with the powers of Head of State.

RELATIONS WITH FRANCE

Although diplomatic relations with France had been resumed in January 1957, differences between the two governments in connection with the Algerian revolt soon worsened. In May France suspended economic aid; Tunisia retaliated by abrogating the customs union with France and concluding trade agreements with Yugoslavia and Switzerland. In the same month French troops in Tunisia attempted to drive back into Algeria several thousand Algerian refugees who had crossed the border. Clashes between French forces and Tunisian national guards followed and Bourguiba called for negotiations for the withdrawal of all French troops to Bizerta. The French government's proposal to withdraw 10,000 out of the 25,000 French troops in Tunisia was cautiously welcomed, but at the same time the French claimed, and in September began to exercise, the right to pursue Algerian rebel bands across the Tunisian frontier. Bourguiba, now President, declared a state of emergency along the border with Algeria on September 9th and relations with France once more neared breaking point.

A further difference arose over the question of arms supplies. A French refusal in May 1957 to supply military equipment to Tunisia led President Bourguiba to look elsewhere. French attempts to prevent Tunisia from obtaining arms from any country other than France proved unsuccessful and in November the United States and Britain announced, to French protests, that they would proceed with deliveries.

During October and November 1957 discussions between President Bourguiba, the King of Morocco and Algerian rebel leaders resulted in an offer by Tunisia and Morocco of their good offices in an attempt to achieve a settlement which would combine sovereignty for Algeria with the safeguarding of French interests. This was accepted by the rebel leaders but rejected by the French government.

The most serious Franco-Tunisian incident of the Algerian war occurred in February 1958 when French aircraft from Algeria attacked the Tunisian border village of Sakhiet Sidi Youssef, the scene of several clashes the previous month, killing 79 people, injuring

130 and destroying many buildings. The Tunisian government's reaction was to break off diplomatic relations with France, to forbid all French troop movements in Tunisia, to demand the immediate evacuation of all French bases, including Bizerta, and to take the matter before the UN Security Council. French troops were blockaded in their barracks and the extra-territorial status of Bizerta, from which French warships were banned, was abolished. In addition some 600 French civilians were expelled from the frontier area and five of the seven French consulates closed.

British and United States mediation was accepted and on April 15th it was agreed that all French troops would be evacuated in accordance with a jointly-agreed timetable and Tunisian sovereignty over Bizerta recognized; at the same time the French consulates would be reopened and the cases of the expelled French civilians examined. When further clashes between Tunisian and French forces occurred in May, a state of emergency covering the whole country was proclaimed and Tunisia again took the matter to the Security Council and also requested further arms supplies from the United States and Britain.

A new phase in Franco-Tunisian relations began with the accession to power of General de Gaulle in June 1958. An agreement was concluded on June 17th under which French troops stationed outside Bizerta were to be withdrawn during the next four months, while negotiations for a provisional agreement on Bizerta were to follow. Restrictions on French troops were removed and diplomatic relations resumed. By October the only French troops remaining in Tunisia were in Bizerta.

Further elimination of French interests had meanwhile commenced. In June the French-owned transport services and in August the electricity services of Tunis were nationalized. On November 29th President Bourguiba announced proposals for purchasing by 1960 all agricultural land in Tunisia owned by French citizens, for distribution to landless Tunisians.

POLITICAL CONSOLIDATION

With the improvement of relations with France the Tunisian government felt free to consolidate its internal position, by reforming the party structure of the Néo-Destour and by taking court proceedings against members of the former regime and "Youssefist" opponents. Prince Chadly, the eldest son of the ex-*bey*, and the former Prime Ministers, Tahar ben Ammar and Salaheddine Baccouche, were among those tried in the latter part of 1958 on charges which included the misuse of public funds and collaboration with the French authorities; sentences imposed ranged from heavy fines to imprisonment and loss of civic rights. Salah ben Youssef (*in absentia*) and 54 of his supporters were charged with plotting the death of President Bourguiba, smuggling arms from Libya, and aiming to overthrow the government; ben Youssef and several others were sentenced to death and most of the remainder received long prison sentences.

This trial reflected a widening breach between Tunisia and the United Arab Republic, from where ben Youssef had been conducting his activities. In October 1958 Tunisia had joined the Arab League, only to withdraw from a meeting of its Council ten days later after accusing the U.A.R. of attempts at domination. Diplomatic relations with the U.A.R. were severed the same month on the grounds of Egyptian complicity in the "Youssefist" attempt to assassinate President Bourguiba, and on the eve of ben Youssef's trial the President announced the capture of Egyptian officers who had secretly entered Tunisia to assist subversive elements to overthrow his government.

A further step in the establishment of a presidential system of government was taken with the promulgation on June 1st, 1959, of a new constitution for Tunisia, which provided for the election of the President for five years and permitted his re-election for three consecutive terms. The President was empowered to lay down the general policy of the state, choose the members of the government, hold supreme command of the armed forces and make all appointments to civil and military posts. The constitution also provided for the election of a National Assembly for five years and required the approval of the Assembly for the declaration of war, the conclusion of peace and the ratification of treaties. In elections which followed on November 8th President Bourguiba was unopposed and all 90 seats in the Assembly went to the Néo-Destour, their only opponents being the Communists.

THE BIZERTA CRISIS

During 1959 and 1960 Tunisian relations with France gradually improved. A trade and tariff agreement was signed on September 5th, 1959, and further agreements on technical co-operation and the transfer of French state property in Tunisia to the Tunisian government were concluded. In October 1959 President Bourguiba announced his support for President de Gaulle's offer of self-determination for Algeria, and Tunisia was subsequently able to act as intermediary between France and the Algerian rebels in moves towards a negotiated settlement. A meeting in Paris in February 1961 between Presidents Bourguiba and de Gaulle, at the latter's invitation, was regarded as a significant step forward in relations between the two countries.

At the same time the Tunisian claim for the handing-back of the Bizerta base was maintained and the issue came to a head on July 5th, 1961, when President Bourguiba made a formal demand for its return and repeated the claim, first put forward in 1959, to Saharan territory in Algeria adjacent to the south-western part of Tunisia. Demonstrations then took place against the continued French occupation of Bizerta and on July 17th President Bourguiba referred in the National Assembly to plans to "express our will to restore the Tunisian soil in both north and south".

Fighting between Tunisian and French troops began around the Bizerta base and in the disputed area of the Sahara on July 19th, 1961, diplomatic relations were again severed, and Tunisia called for a meeting of the UN Security Council. The fighting ended on July 22nd with the French in firm control of the base and town of Bizerta, over 800 Tunisians having been killed. In the south a Tunisian attempt to seize the fort of Garat el-Hamel also failed. A subsequent visit to Bizerta by the UN Secretary-General, Mr. Hammarskjöld, in an attempt to promote a settlement, was unsuccessful. A French statement on July 28th said that France wished to continue to use the base whilst a state of international tension persisted but was prepared to negotiate with Tunisia about its use during this period.

The immediate results of the Bizerta crisis were a rapprochement between Tunisia and other Arab states, a cooling of relations with the West and an improvement of relations with the Communist bloc. Diplomatic links were re-established with the U.A.R., a move facilitated by the unexplained murder of Salah ben Youssef in Frankfurt in August. The Tunisian Foreign Minister visited the U.S.S.R., Poland and Czechoslovakia and a technical assistance agreement with the U.S.S.R. was signed. Following censure of France in the UN General Assembly in August, talks on the interim use of the base were commenced and on September 29th the French agreed to evacuate the town of Bizerta and retire to positions held before July 19th.

The final settlement of the Bizerta dispute occupied the remainder of 1961 and much of 1962, talks being held in both Rome and Paris. The Algerian cease-fire in March 1962 had an immediately beneficial effect on Franco-Tunisian relations and the French base installations at Menzel Bourguiba, near Bizerta, were handed over to Tunisia on June 30th. In March 1963 agreement was reached on the transfer of some 370,000 acres of French-owned agricultural land to the Tunisian government. Other agreements, on trade and finance, were designed to reduce Tunisia's balance of payments deficit with France.

Although Algerian independence had been warmly welcomed by Tunisia the extremist doctrines of the new state conflicted with Tunisian moderation and relations quickly deteriorated. In January 1963 the Tunisian ambassador was recalled from Algiers on the grounds of alleged Algerian complicity in an unsuccessful attempt the previous month on the life of President Bourguiba in which "Youssefists" in Algeria, as well as supporters of the old Destour and army elements, were implicated. Moroccan mediation led to a conference of the Maghreb states in Rabat in February 1963 at which the Tunisians demanded the cessation of "Youssefist" activities in Algeria, and after further negotiations a frontier agreement between Tunisia and Algeria was signed in July. Algerian, and also Egyptian, leaders attended celebrations in December of the final French evacuation of Bizerta which had taken place two months earlier.

EXPROPRIATION

Despite agreement with France in February 1964 on the provision of loans and credits, it was claimed that the March 1963 agreement on the transfer of French-owned land had placed too great a strain on Tunisian financial resources and had also resulted in over-exploitation of the land held by settlers, who had been given up to five years before relinquishing it. On May 11th the Tunisian National Assembly enacted legislation authorizing the expropriation of all foreign-owned lands; this affected the proprietors of some 750,000 acres. The French immediately suspended, then cancelled, all financial aid.

This nationalization of foreign-owned land was also seen as a step towards the development of socialism in the agrarian sector of the economy. The Néo-Destour's commitment to "Tunisian socialism" was emphasized in the change of the party's name to the Partie Socialiste Destourien (PSD) at the time of the presidential and general elections in November 1964, in which President Bourguiba was again elected unopposed and the PSD, the only party to present candidates, filled all 90 seats in the National Assembly. Subsequent cabinet changes included the appointment of the President's son, Habib Bourguiba, Jr., as Foreign Minister.

From 1964 onwards internal political conditions became more settled and the attention of the government was turned to the tasks of economic development. The hold of the PSD on the country was strengthened and President Bourguiba's dominating position was unchallenged. In 1966 the setting-up was announced of a Council of the Republic, consisting of members of the government and of the political bureau of the PSD, to ensure continuing stability, one of its functions being to nominate an interim President in the event of the President's death.

FOREIGN POLICIES

Externally, Tunisia's relations with the world beyond the Arab states and Africa since 1964 have tended to be influenced by the need for foreign aid, most of which has been received from Western countries (particularly from the United States but also from Federal Germany) where the moderation of Tunisian policies has inspired confidence. Towards the Communist world Tunisian gestures have been cautious. Some economic assistance has been obtained from the Soviet Union without Tunisia having shifted her non-aligned stance, and although a visit by Chou En-lai in January 1964 was followed by the establishment of diplomatic relations between Tunisia and the Chinese People's Republic, President Bourguiba nevertheless publicly criticized Chinese policies, including the encouragement of revolution in Africa. On African issues Tunisia has taken a moderate line and inside the Organization of African Unity has exercised a responsible influence. In 1965, in the course of a tour of French-speaking African states, President Bourguiba suggested the formation of a francophone African "Commonwealth"; the idea had a mixed reception, however, and interest soon waned.

Relations with the rest of the Arab world have been President Bourguiba's main foreign preoccupation and here his initiatives have resulted in bitter controversy. In April 1965 he openly criticized Arab League policy on Palestine and advocated a more flexible approach, with direct negotiations with Israel on the UN partition plan of 1948. This provoked severe attacks from the U.A.R. and other Arab states (excepting Morocco, Libya and Saudi Arabia), and after violent demonstrations in Cairo and Tunis both countries withdrew their ambassadors. Tunisia's refusal at the end of April to follow the example of other Arab League states in breaking off relations with Federal Germany, which had exchanged ambassadors with Israel, increased the rift. A conference of Arab heads of state at Casablanca in May at which Tunisia was not represented, categorically rejected President Bourguiba's proposal that Israel should be asked to cede territory to the Palestine refugees in return for recognition by the Arab states, and reaffirmed their determination to bring about the complete overthrow of Israel. In an open letter to those attending, President Bourguiba accused President Nasser of attempting to use the Arab League as an instrument of U.A.R. national policy and of interfering in the affairs of every Arab state; Tunisia was not prepared to take part in the debates of the Arab League in the light of this situation. In October 1966, after accusations by President Bourguiba that the U.A.R. was waging a campaign of insults against Tunisia, the severance of diplomatic relations with the U.A.R. was announced. In January 1967 Tunisia joined Saudi Arabia in protesting to the UN Secretary-General at the use of poison gas by Egyptian aircraft in a bombing attack in the Yemen, where the U.A.R. was virtually in control of the republican regime in the civil war with the royalists; Tunisian recognition of the republican regime was revoked the following month.

RECENT DEVELOPMENTS

The six-day war between Israel and the Arab states in June 1967 brought immediate reconciliation in the Arab world despite long-standing differences. Tunisian troops were dispatched to the front but the Israeli success was so swift and the cease-fire came so soon that they were recalled before they had reached the scene of the fighting. Diplomatic relations between Tunisia and the U.A.R. were resumed and Tunisia was represented at the Arab summit meeting in Khartoum in September, which agreed not to recognize nor to negotiate with Israel. Untrue allegations of United States and British intervention on the side of Israel, made by Egypt and Jordan at the time of the Arab-Israel hostilities, resulted in serious rioting in Tunis where the British Embassy was sacked. Strict measures were taken by the Tunisian authorities to deal with the rioters and a student leader was subsequently sentenced to twenty years' imprisonment. After further disorders in March 1968, when his appeal was heard, 134 students and lecturers were arrested. They were tried in September on charges of plotting against the security of the state and attempting to overthrow the government. Most of them were given prison sentences, but President Bourguiba later threw out hints of possible clemency.

The reconciliation between Tunisia and other Arab countries was short-lived. In May 1968, following an attack on President Bourguiba by the Syrian Prime Minister, who charged him with having betrayed the Arab struggle in Palestine, the Syrian chargé d'affaires and his staff in Tunis were accused of inciting Tunisian citizens to undertake subversive activities and ordered to leave the country. The Arab League, at a meeting in Cairo on 1st September refused to hear a statement from the Tunisian delegate criticising the Arab attitude over Israel, and particularly that of the U.A.R. On 26th September the Tunisian Government announced its intention of boycotting future meetings of the League. The statement reproached the U.A.R. with having sought to dictate to the Arab states and with having followed policies which had led to successive defeats at the hands of the Israelis and excessive dependence on communist countries; Tunisia could not subscribe to the continuation of such policies which would lead only to greater disasters, but nevertheless affirmed its support for the Palestinian guerrillas whom it would provide with material and moral aid. The Tunisian Government would continue to co-operate bilaterally with all Arab states desiring good relations, including Egypt.

Earlier, there had been an improvement in Tunisia's relations with Algeria and an agreement had been signed in April 1968 on the demarcation of their common frontier. There was a subsequent deterioration, however, following Algerian criticism of statements made by President Bourguiba during a visit to Canada and the United States in May (on the Arab/Israel question and on the growth of Soviet naval forces in the Mediterranean) and because the Tunisian Government granted asylum in June to the former Algerian Chief of Staff, Colonel Zbiri, who stood accused of leading an unsuccessful *coup d'état* against President Boumedienne in December 1967 (and who subsequently left for Europe). President Bourguiba did not attend the annual meeting of the Organisation of African Unity which was held in Algiers in September. A visit to Tunis by the Algerian Foreign Minister in March 1969, however, which was followed by a visit to Algiers by Habib Bourguiba, Jnr., in April, brought about an improved climate for negotiation on economic matters, especially those arising from the nationalization by each country of properties owned by nationals of the others, and on the boundary question.

THE FALL OF AHMED BEN SALAH

In September 1969 a cabinet reshuffle was announced. Its principal feature was the demotion of Ahmed Ben Salah, Minister of Finance and Planning for almost ten years and as such the unchallenged controller of the economy; still only 43, he had been generally regarded as the most brilliant member of the cabinet and a possible successor to the ageing President. He remained Minister of Education until November, but was then stripped of all office; subsequently arrested, he was tried and found guilty on a variety of charges in May 1970, and was finally sentenced to ten years' hard labour. Ben Salah escaped from prison in February 1973, and it is thought took refuge in a European country, via Algeria.

Ben Salah was the leading force behind the ruthless drive towards co-operative farming that had been the major feature of Tunisian life in preceding years. The programme had aroused massive opposition throughout the areas affected; evidence at the trial also indicated that the existing farms had operated very inefficiently and lost large sums of money, which Ben Salah, as Minister of Finance, had reimbursed from the Treasury. No new co-operatives were formed after 1969 and some land was returned to the peasants. The unprecedented floods in the autumn of 1969 exacerbated the problems of Tunisia's rural economy.

President Bourguiba was re-elected without opposition in November 1969, but then spent much time in France, the U.S.A. and Switzerland receiving medical treatment. In his absence the main point of interest was the struggle to succeed him. Until November 1970 Bahi Ladgham, the Prime Minister, seemed to be in the strongest position. He was chairman of the Supreme Follow-Up Committee, set up to supervise the implementation of the Cairo agreement between King Hussein and the Palestine liberation organizations. This committee had developed from the initiatives towards mediation started by President Bourguiba's suggestion in September 1970 for a conference of Arab heads of state to discuss the Jordanian situation. However, Ladgham's success on the committee and the wide publicity he received throughout the Arab world, combined with his running of Tunisia for six months in Bourguiba's absence, apparently lost him favour with the President. While Ladgham was in Jordan in October, Hedi Nouira was appointed interim Prime Minister, and in November his post was officially confirmed. By October 1971 Bourguiba was prepared to declare that Nouira would be his successor when the time came. In March 1973 Ladgham resigned from all his political posts.

With the doubt about the succession receding in 1971 the question of the nature of political life in Tunisia got more attention, and the campaign of Ahmad Mestiri, the Interior Minister, for some immediate liberalization of government eventually resulted in his dismissal from the cabinet in September 1971, and expulsion from the Party in January 1972 and the National Assembly in May 1973.

After 1970 relations with the more radical Arab states and with radical powers outside the area improved. Normal relations were resumed with the U.A.R. and Syria, and Tunisia took up again membership of the Arab League. Relations with China and North Viet-Nam also improved. In May 1973 Bourguiba stressed the need for dialogue between Arabs, Palestinians and Israelis, in the search for an "honourable compromise" in the Arab-Israeli dispute. There was some speculation that Bourguiba might be willing to act as mediator, but he later said that this was a misunderstanding.

ECONOMIC SURVEY

Tunisia covers an area of 165,150 square kilometres. At the last census in 1966 the population was 4,533,351 and in 1972 it was estimated at 5.2 million with over half under 25 years old. The annual rate of increase in the population in recent years has averaged 2.1 per cent, with emigration offsetting a natural rate of increase slightly above this rate. Most of the towns, and also the greater part of the rural population are concentrated in the coastal areas. In the centre and the south, the land is infertile semi-desert, the population scattered, the standard of living very low, and the rate of growth of the population even higher than in the north.

The capital and main commercial centre is Tunis (population, including suburbs, around 800,000) which, together with the adjacent La Goulette is also the chief port. There are about 50,000 Europeans in Tunis, mainly French and Italians, their numbers having decreased rapidly since independence. Other towns of importance are Sfax (100,000), which is the principal town in the south, the second port and the centre for exports of phosphates and olive oil, Sousse (90,000), Bizerta (70,000) and Khairouan (50,000). There is a special petroleum port at La Skhovia. Approximately 60 per cent of the population depend directly on the agricultural sector, and of the total workforce of some 1.3 million approximately 50 per cent are employed in agriculture, which contributed only 17 per cent of the total Gross National Product in 1972. Much of agricultural employment is seasonal, bearing a large body of unskilled labourers without employment for part of the year.

Tunisia is not lacking in natural resources. However, until recently, they have been poorly exploited. Agricultural production, still the mainstay of the economy, is subject to fluctuations in output which have repercussions on the rest of the domestic economy and on foreign trade. The specialization in certain regions on a particular crop, which is necessary for reasons of productivity and the limitations of soil and climate, increases the dependence on agriculture, whereas the growth of the phosphates and petroleum industries offsets it. The very severe floods in September 1969 and the preceding three years of drought caused grave economic damage reflected in a worsening balance of trade and a sharp increase in the rate of inflation, which the Government had to restrain by direct price controls. However, in 1971 and in 1972 Tunisia had two exceptionally good harvests with cereal and fruit crops showing an overall increase of 50 per cent and 60 per cent respectively. Principally as a result of the exceptional harvests, but also because of production increases in manufacturing, transport, telecommunications and tourism, G.D.P. increased by more than 18 per cent in 1972, double the rate of growth achieved in 1971.

Mineral resources are large and there is plenty of room for development. Phosphates are the most important mineral, followed by iron ore. The 1969 floods cut the Gafsa–Sfax railway, making phosphate exports impossible for several months and also the iron mines at Djerissa inaccessible. Generally speaking, with the exception of the Djerissa iron mines where the high metal content of the ore and ease of working have favoured exploitation, mining concerns in the past have often been under-equipped and frequently only exploited intermittently. There are substantial undeveloped deposits of iron, lead and zinc. A major hope for the future is oil which was first found in commercial quantities in 1964. Production began in 1966, and an estimated four million tons were produced in 1972. A natural gas field was discovered at Abder Rahmane in Cap Bon with reserves of 200 million cubic metres, which are sufficient to supply Tunis for 20 years.

Industry generates only a small part of national income, its development having been retarded by Tunisia's dependence on France and her market. The Government's policies on development are contained in the plans for 1962–64, 1965–68, 1969–72 and, currently, 1973–76. Encouragement is given to public and private sectors, with the latest plan emphasizing the Government's concern to attract private foreign capital for investment in export-orientated industries. Tunisia normally runs a considerable trade deficit which is covered by tourism receipts, remittances from abroad, and by foreign grants and loans of which the principal donors are the U.S.A., Federal Germany, Canada, France and the World Bank. Tunisia has, however, been successful in attracting aid from a large number of multilateral and bilateral sources. The servicing of foreign loans in recent years has required about 25 per cent of the gross receipts from exports and services. Though autonomous development is the ultimate aim, Tunisia continues to welcome foreign aid from any source. Without it, the successful implementation of the plan would be impossible.

The Tunisian economy is at a decisive stage in its development. Having suffered several setbacks over the last few years, the outlook is now much more favourable and there seems to be a more determined effort to formulate an economic policy which will stimulate growth and reduce the trade deficit. G.N.P. grew by over 18 per cent in 1972 compared with about 8 per cent in 1971 and only 4 per cent in 1970. An overall rate of growth of 5 per cent has been set as a target in the 1973–76 development plan. Attention is being focused towards industries which promise a quick return on investment and away from large and problematical projects. Recent oil finds also give grounds for optimism in the longer term.

AGRICULTURE

About two-thirds of the total area of Tunisia is suitable for farming. For agricultural purposes the country is composed of five different districts—the north with its mountains, having large fertile valleys; the north-east including the Cap Bon, where the soil is especially suitable for the cultivation of oranges and other citrus fruit; the Sahel where the olives grow; the centre with its high tablelands and pastures; and the south with oases and gardens where dates are prolific. Harvests vary considerably in size, depending on the uncertain rainfall, since cultivation is largely by dry farming and irrigation is as yet limited. The main cereal crops are wheat, barley, maize, oats and sorghum; fruit is also important—grapes, olives, dates, oranges and figs are grown for export as well as for the local market.

In good years there is a surplus of cereal for export but in the late '60's a series of poor harvests necessitated wheat and flour imports. In 1970 agricultural production increased by 3 per cent, which represented a satisfactory recovery from the devastation of the previous year's floods. Exceptional weather conditions and improved irrigation in 1971 and 1972 resulted in excellent agricultural yields with cereal production up some 50 per cent and orange production up 60 per cent, while the olive crop more than doubled. The prospects for 1973 are more moderate; severe flooding of the Medjerda valley means that cereal production will be some 10–30 per cent down on the 1972 level, while the olive crop is expected to be considerably below the freak 1971–72 season's yield. It is hoped that citrus fruit production will equal the record levels of 1972. Over the period of the 1973–76 plan the Government hopes for a 22 per cent increase in production.

Under the 1969–72 plan the Government allocated 21 per cent of total investment to agriculture. It is hoped that the country will become self-sufficient in foodstuffs and that expansion in agriculture will be sufficient for the sector not to act as a drag on the rest of the economy. The means by which this should be achieved has been the cause of political conflict in the past decade. From 1960 until 1969, under the Minister of Planning, Ahmed Ben Salah, the basis of the Government's agrarian reform programme lay in the formation of collective "agricultural units". These units, consisting of 500 hectares at least, were to be operated as collectives in order to consolidate small peasant holdings and, later, to exploit land expropriated from French farmers or to be acquired eventually from owners of large or medium-sized farms. Usually each unit was divided up between various crops, such as hard-wheat, soft-wheat, olives and almonds, as well as livestock and fallow. It was aimed to introduce water and electricity as resources allowed and to provide other communal facilities. The system was controlled through credits provided by the Agricultural Bank. By 1968 some 220 state co-operatives were in existence and several hundred more were being put together. However, there was then a pause for consolidation as "bottlenecks" and rural opposition were becoming widespread while political pressure was mounting from owners of the larger estates whose turn was now coming for collectivization. Questions were raised about the efficiency of the system and there were revelations of unsatisfactory performance, heavy debts and misappropriation of state funds. These discoveries were instrumental in the downfall and disgrace of Ben Salah, whose position was weakened by the displeasure of foreign aid donors with his agricultural policies (especially the World Bank which had previously given some support, including an $18 million loan in 1967).

Following Ben Salah's downfall farmers were given a chance to opt out of the state system which was soon dismantled. Nonetheless a law was passed providing for the eventual break-up of large private estates which cover about 750,000 hectares. They are to be split among individual farmers or private co-operatives over which the state intends to maintain some control through agricultural advisers and central marketing agencies. The Government has also taken a number of measures to stimulate output, including providing funds for mechanization, reducing taxes, and subsidizing fertilizers and seed purchases. In mid-1970 approximately half the cultivated area was in private hands, a further 30 per cent was worked by co-operative farm groups and the remainder was in large estates or under forest.

The Government has also taken steps to encourage the fishing industry. Sfax is the main centre of the industry which lands 30,000 tons of fish annually (compared with only half that ten years ago). The International Development Association has advanced $2 million to help replace sailing vessels with motorized boats. In November 1971 delivery was taken of 10 new Spanish-built boats, part of an order for over 300 vessels. Early in 1972 the Government signed an agreement with Libya to establish a joint fishing company.

Tunisia's main crops are wheat, barley, grapes, olives, citrus fruit and dates.

Grown in a belt across the northern part of the country, wheat is the most important cereal crop. In good years, wheat is exported but in bad years imports of wheat become necessary. The Government guarantees the price to the grower and, amongst other incentives, pays the transport costs of merchants. Wheat is now sold at world market prices, which are lower than the prices which used to be obtained in the French market. Production rose in 1970 and is now back almost to its 1965 level, although wheat imports are still required. The Government has encouraged the spread of the Mexican dwarf wheat and this variety now accounts for over one-tenth of output.

Production of barley fluctuates according to the rainfall, and in recent years has been only about half the record levels (around 200,000 tons) reached earlier.

Grapes are grown around Tunis and Bizerta. Over the last seven years wine production has declined and in 1971 fell by 30 per cent from the previous year to 600,000 hectolitres. In March 1969 an agreement was signed between the EEC and Tunisia which allowed Tunisia partial association to the Community. Favourable concessions were granted to olive oil, fruit and vegetable exports, but wine is excluded from Community preferences although it receives privileged access to the French market. Wine used to represent Tunisia's second most important export, but in 1971 it ranked only seventh. In 1972 the value of wine exports trebled to TD 3 million from the 1971 figure.

The size of olive harvests varies considerably, partly due to the two-year flowering cycle of the tree. In 1971 there was a dramatic rise over 1970 to well over 100,000 tons. In 1972 there was an exceptionally good crop of 167,000 tons of which 129,000 tons were exported, earning TD 46.3 million in foreign exchange compared with about 90,000 tons and TD 21 million in 1971. Thus olive oil temporarily displaced petroleum oil as the country's main export earner in 1972. Olive oil is likely to slip back to second place in 1973 as provisional estimates for production are put at 66,000 tons only. Domestic trade in olive oil is controlled by a State monopoly but the private sector is involved in export sales.

Citrus fruit is grown on the north-eastern coast. In 1971 77,000 tons of citrus fruits were grown, of which about 24,000 tons were exported. In 1972 production rose to 104,600 tons, of which 37,472 tons were exported, and an equally good tonnage is expected in 1973. Production of dates had fallen steadily and was only 18,000 tons in 1970. Exports have fallen even more precipitately because of increased domestic consumption. Experimental planting of cotton and sugar beet has been tried. Sugar beet is used by the sugar refinery near Beja, which has a capacity of 1,850 tons per day. Other crops being tried include bananas, strawberries and pistachio nuts.

Tunisia's livestock includes some 3.10 million sheep, half a million cattle, 98,000 horses, 60,000 mules and 280,000 camels. The Government is anxious to improve cattle-stock and milk production. In 1971 an agreement was signed with Austria for technical and financial assistance in setting up a cattle-rearing scheme at Bou Salem. Of the TD 135 million to be spent on agriculture in the 1973–76 plan a significant amount is allocated to livestock breeding in order to keep pace with the increased demand for meat. Some 20,000 hectares of grazing land in the North will be improved and a further 50,000 hectares of grazing land created.

Some progress has been made in the last decade towards the diversification of crops, mechanization, irrigation and increased use of fertilizers. Two new irrigation schemes should improve output; the Oued Nebhana dam, near Kairouan, which cost 23 million dinars, will irrigate 5,000 hectares and assist in flood prevention; and in 1971 work began on the Bou Heurtma dam in Jendouba. Federal Germany is providing finance for this latter project which will irrigate 20,000 hectares when it reaches completion probably in 1974. The Council of Ministers has approved investments totalling TD 50 million for water and irrigation projects and by the end of 1976 it is hoped that the area of irrigated land will have increased to 61,000 hectares and some 23,000 hectares which is at present under-utilized will be brought under intensive cultivation.

The World Bank is to provide $8 million for several schemes aimed at increasing milk production, and wheat output, providing farm machinery and developing date plantations and a new oasis in the south. In January 1973 a U.S. loan of $11 million was announced for financing agricultural projects. In addition it was announced that the U.S. Agency for

International Development agreed to lend Tunisia TD 1.4 million to be used for a water purification plant in Tunis and for irrigation in the Shanshou region.

Fishing. Fishing employs 13,807 men and over 4,000 boats. In October 1962 territorial waters were extended from 3 to 6 miles and fishing limits to 12 miles off shore. The fishing industry is being expanded—the catch rose to 23,000 tons in 1962, nearly double the 1956 figure, but the subsequent rate of expansion has varied. The 1972 catch was about 35,000 tons, but it is expected that the annual fish catch will increase to 54,000 tons by the end of 1973. Exports of sea food were unable to keep pace with demand in 1972 and reached TD 2.2 million.

MINERALS

Tunisia has several rich mineral deposits and is one of the world's largest producers of phosphates. Although their quality is not as good as Morocco's, phosphates are nevertheless one of the country's most important exports. Iron ore is also mined and lead, zinc, potash and salt. Oil was discovered close to the Algerian border in May 1964 and gas has also been found. Some 13,000 persons are employed in the mining industry.

The current plan recognizes the present importance of the mining industry to the economy. It encourages the processing of minerals in Tunisia, which at present are exported in their raw state, particularly phosphates. The plan also proposes the exploitation of the iron ore deposits at Djebel Ank and further exploration for minerals. Production of phosphates and iron ore is expected to show a rising trend while output of lead and zinc ores may fall. Recent discoveries indicate a bright future for the petroleum industry. Considerable expansion in mineral production has taken place in the last decade, but there have been fluctuations in output, especially when operations were interrupted by the floods, in 1969. Output was again disappointing in 1972; although phosphate production increased by some 15 per cent, the industry remained depressed because of low grade ores and because of poor worldwide demand while petroleum production was virtually stagnant. There was a decline in zinc and iron ore production, but the output of lead increased over the 1971 level. The *Office National des Mines* is responsible for exploration for fresh mineral deposits, for the reactivation of deposits which have ceased production, for the carrying out of an elaborate modernization programme in mining methods and in the improvement of productivity. A further task is to promote exploration for oil.

Tunisia is the fourth largest producer in the world of calcium phosphates, which are mined mainly from six large deposits in central Tunisia. Production recovered after the floods to 3 million tons in 1970, increased by 4.6 per cent in 1971 to 3.2 million tons and in 1972 stood at 3.7 million tons. Exports of phosphates in 1971 were valued at TD 21.3 million and provisional estimates for 1972 put receipts somewhat lower at about TD 20.4 million. Some 60 per cent of Tunisian phosphate exports are for Western markets, particularly France while the balance goes to Eastern European countries and China. The Tunisian phosphate industry is undergoing some major changes in policy under the new 1973–76 plan. The main objectives under the new policy plan is to develop new resources and to concentrate efforts on the local manufacture of highly profitable fertilizer and phosphoric acid. Phosphate is used by the fertilizer industry to produce hyperphosphate, superphosphate and triple superphosphate. Phosphate mining is now concentrated in the hands of a single concern, the Sfax-Gafsa Co., which operates under the overall financial control of the Government. The company has announced a wide range of plans of modernization of output and new refining projects, as well as changes in the location of mining activities. New mechanical processes are to be introduced in order to speed up the growth of productivity. The Sfax-Gafsa Co. is in the process of opening two new mines, one at M'rata to replace the Moularies mine and one at Ste'Barba to succeed the Kalaa Jerda mine. The M'rata mine is expected to allow easy working with an annual output of some 1 million tons—double that of the Moularies. The Ste'Barba scheme, currently under study, is expected to cost around 1 million dinars in investment expenditure.

The long-term plan now laid down by the company includes development of a new deposit at Sehib, also in southern Tunisia. Reserves are now reported to be over 60 million tons. Preliminary work on this new deposit, began in December 1970, and capital investment of 14 million dinars is expected, creating 1,200 new jobs.

Tunisia has numerous deposits of rich non-phosphorous iron ore; the two main deposits are at Djerissa and Douaria. Production in 1971 fell by 37 per cent over 1970 to 940,000 tons but rose in 1972 by 29 per cent over the 1971 level to 1,106,000 tons. Exports were valued at TD 2.46 in 1972 and went mostly to markets in Italy, the United Kingdom and Greece. Other deposits may be exploited after the conclusion of studies currently being undertaken.

Lead ore is extracted in the northern coastal region. Production of lead ore rose from 18,840 metric tons of contained lead in 1971 to 25,080 metric tons of contained lead in 1972. Exports of lead ore and products were valued at TD 2 million in 1971 and increased to an estimated TD 2.14 million in 1972. Zinc ore is mined in the north-western corner of Tunisia and production in 1972 equalled the 1971 level of 11,400 metric tons contained zinc. Most zinc exports used to be taken by France but the French share is now falling. About 90 per cent of the salt produced by COTUSAL (300–320,000 tons annually) is exported, principally to Japan.

Intensive exploration for petroleum has been carried out since the discovery of oil in neighbouring Algeria. In May 1964 the subsidiary of the Italian State Hydrocarbons Agency (ENI) found oil at El Borma in the south near the Algerian border. Recoverable reserves are estimated at between 35 and 45 million tons. The field went into production in mid-

1966 and in 1972 output reached 3.6 million tons. It is expected however, that the output from this field will fall to 2.5 million tons in 1973 because of loss of pressure.

In 1968 a second field came into operation at Douleb, 125 miles north of El Borma. This field is operated by a joint French-Tunisian company SEREPT and had an output of 100,000 tons in 1972.

The Tunisian Government took a 50 per cent share in the El Borma operating company when oil was found. Crude oil is taken from El Borma via a spur pipeline which links with the pipeline from the oil fields at Zarzaitine and Edjeleh in Algeria to the terminal at La Skhirra on the Gulf of Gabès. Thence the crude is taken to the refinery at Bizerta (capacity one million tons per year). A second refinery is under study at Sfax though as yet local demand is only 700,000 tons annually.

The *Société de Recherches et d'Exploitations des Pétroles en Tunisie* (SEREPT), in which French interests both public and private have a large share, together with *Aquitaine-Tunisie* (a wholly owned subsidiary of the French company SNPA) works the field at Douleb. A six-inch pipeline has been built to the port of La Skhirra. Production began in May 1968 and totalled 220,000 tons in that year. A small field, named Tamesmida on the Algerian border south-west of Douleb, was joined to the Douleb–La Skhirra pipeline in 1969 and will produce some 30,000 tons per year in order to supply a paper pulp plant at nearby Kasserine. Companies are showing a keen interest in exploration in Tunisia. *Aquitaine* with 4,000 square kilometres is a major exploration permit holder as is SITEP. The French company, *Cie Française des Pétroles* was awarded in 1968 a permit covering 15,000 square kilometres onshore and offshore in the Gulf of Gabes. SEREPT also operates a small gas field in the Cap Bon area which supplies Tunis. Production at Cap Bon amounts to nearly 10 million cubic metres annually. The same company in conjunction with the *Société Nationale des Pétroles d'Aquitaine* found gas at Douleb south-west of Tunis in 1966. A second gas field has been discovered at Bir Ali ben Khalifa near Sfax by a group of U.S. companies. The production rate from one well is estimated at 2.7 million cubic metres annually.

The Ashtart field in the Gulf of Gabes, in a concession held by Aquitaine and Elf/Erap, began production in 1972 and is expected to produce 2 million tons a year. Two other fields became operational in 1972, the Bhirat and the Sidi al-Itayem fields, with annual production targets of 600,000 tons and 500,000 tons respectively.

Total Tunisian oil production in 1970 was 3.2 million tons. In 1971 there was only a 1 per cent increase in output, but oil receipts rose comparatively sharply as a result of the increase in posted prices, and oil remained the principal export for the third year running, accounting for 25 per cent of export revenue. Total output in 1972 was 4 million tons, but although this was less than in the previous two years, revenues rose by 31 per cent to TD 38 million as a result of increased crude oil prices. Oil was overtaken by olive oil as Tunisia's major export in 1972. Prospects for the oil industry are promising. Offshore and onshore operations round the Gulf of Tunis are proceeding and there are hopes of further finds in the Gulf of Gabes. In 1972 the National Assembly passed a bill to set up a state company for petroleum activities, and the Government now has a 50 per cent participation in all the operating fields except for Douleb. Apart from the State oil company and SONATRACH (the Algerian state oil company which has agreed to help in efforts to inject pressure into the El Borma field) five foreign companies are prospecting in Tunisia and together are scheduled to spend TD 47 million on prospecting and TD 22.6 million on development of existing wells.

INDUSTRY

Industrial production in 1972 showed an 8.8 per cent increase over the 1971 level but still contributed only about 15 per cent of G.N.P. and 3 per cent of exports. Industry consists of the processing of local raw materials, minerals, wool (two factories in the Sousse region are under construction), leather and foods—the last named being the most important. There are 20 major flour mills with a total milling capacity of 380,000 tons. Vegetable oil processing is also important and a canning industry is being developed—already over 20 canning factories process fish of all kinds, mostly destined for export. At Beja is a sugar refinery capable of refining 1,850 tons per day, sufficient to cover the country's needs in the near future, though some sugar beet has to be imported. Other factories pasteurize milk and make butter, cheese and yoghourt. Other industries include, amongst other construction materials plants, two cement factories. Production in 1972 was 630,000 tons, which did not meet Tunisia's domestic requirements, and about 100,000 tons will need to be imported in 1973 and 1974. A new cement factory with an annual output of 700,000 tons is to be built at a cost of TD 17 million, and the existing Bizerta plant is to be expanded at a cost of TD 10 million. In addition, factories manufacture glass, metal furniture, batteries, paint and varnish, leather and shoes, clothing, various textiles, biscuits, chocolates, etc. There is also a motor vehicle assembly plant and three small metal foundries. The industrial sector, however, is expanding fast. There is an oil refinery, with a capacity of one million tons, at Bizerta which supplies all local needs in petroleum products except aviation spirit. Built at a cost of 100 million francs, it is owned by *Société Tuniso-Italienne de Raffinage* (STIR), a joint Government/ENI company. A cellulose factory and a paper paste plant at Kasserine uses locally grown esparto grass as raw material. The first phase of a rubber factory near Sfax was opened in March 1973 with a work force of 200, scheduled to reach 450 when the second phase is completed.

Industrial projects include a $30 million nitrogenous fertilizer plant at Gabes and superphosphates plant at Sfax. The triple superphosphate fertilizer plant was initially backed by the IFC and Swedish and

American Companies and is run by N.P.K. Engrais, S.A.T. The plant was designed for a capacity of 180,000 tons of triple superphosphate which was to be produced from local phosphates and imported sulphur and which was all to be exported. Shipments have been made to more than twenty countries including Sweden under long-term sales contracts. The company's production was 165,000 tons in 1970, and target output was 200,000 in 1972. The latest development plan emphasizes the need for expansion of the fertilizer industry in order to obtain full benefits in terms of added value for the country's phosphates deposits. Another major project, the steel complex at Menzel-Bourguiba is supplied with iron ore from Tamera and Djerissa and when it began operations in 1965, had an initial capacity of 120,000 tons of iron bars, wire and small sections. Other industrial capacity includes the glassworks at Megrine, a vehicle (Peugot) and tractor assembly plant, electrical equipment plant and a centre for manufacture of precision tools.

The Government is taking an active interest in the development of the south. Here the first plant producing phosphoric acid in Tunisia came into production at Ghannouch early in 1972, and by the end of the year its exports had earned TD 680,000. The plant is owned by Maghreb Chemical Industries and has a capacity of 120,000 tons a year; its output will be mainly for export. A second plant is already under construction.

Production of electricity in 1972 was 869 million kWh., most of which was produced by thermal means; hydro-electric power is of lesser importance. Power production from this source varies considerably, depending on the availability of water. Altogether there are eighteen power stations. A 40 megawatt power station is being built in the Ghonnouch area and IBRD has approved a loan of $12 million for use in the project by *Société Tunisienne de L'Electricité et du Gaz*. In September 1971 a new electricity generating station was opened at Qirbah.

Plans have been drawn up for building a nuclear reactor costing 15 million dinars at Gabès. It is expected to produce 20,000 cubic metres of desalinized water and 50 megawatts of electricity per day.

In 1971 the World Bank granted Tunisia a loan of 5.2 million dinars to lay a gas pipe from Al-Burmah to the proposed power station at Gabès. The Bank will grant 3.9 million dinars at an interest rate of 7 per cent while the Kuwaiti Fund for Arab Economic Development will provide the remainder.

Tunisia inherited a relatively modern system of road and rail communications from the period of colonial rule. The rail network has approximately 2,300 km. of track and there are 18,000 km. of road. A loan of $24 million from IBRD is to be spent on a major road improvement scheme in the south. In February 1973 the Minister of Planning announced that TD 165 million would be spent on transport in the next four years, of which TD 70 million has been allocated to road transport. In September 1971, the first oil tanker of the Tunisian Navigation Company, was delivered from Spain. The tanker was built at a cost of $2 million. A recent measure taken by the Government to encourage exports should benefit industry. An agency has been established which will assist new companies producing for export. Valuable tax concession, for periods of ten years or longer, will be granted.

The overall index of industrial production registered a 9 per cent increase in 1972, with manufacturing output having grown by 11.3 per cent over 1971.

FINANCE

The *Banque Centrale de Tunisie* is the sole bank of issue of the dinar; it performs all the normal central banking functions. Transfers of foreign exchange to all countries have been subject to control since 1959. Apart from the commercial banks, there are financial institutions such as the *Société Nationale d'Investissement* which specialize in providing finance for investment purposes. SNI, established as a development finance company by the Government in 1959 with assistance from the IFC, was reorganized in 1965 into a privately controlled development finance company. Its objectives are to invest capital, both loan and equity, in private and public enterprise in manufacturing and tourism. The World Bank has so far contributed loans to the value of $49 million to help finance SNI's activities. In June 1970, SNI joined with the IFC and other foreign investors in establishing COFITOUR, a tourism investment holding company.

The dinar was devalued in September 1964 because of the termination of French financial aid after the nationalization of French owned farms, but Tunisia did not devalue with the Franc zone in August 1969 and has maintained the gold parity of the dinar after the currency realignments of December 1971 when the par value of the dinar rose from 0.52 dinars to the dollar to 0.48 dinars to the dollar. As a result of the February 1973 currency crisis the dinar was further revalued to a new par of 0.44 dinars to the dollar. Foreign exchange reserves held by the central bank (including gold, SDR's and Tunisia's IMF position) rose from $147.8 million at the end of 1971 to $260 million by February 1973.

The current budget usually shows a surplus which is directed to capital expenditure. Direct taxation normally accounts for 20 per cent of total revenue and indirect taxes for over 50 per cent. Other sources of Government revenue are profits from state monopolies and receipts from state property and forests; oil is a growing source of Government income. In 1971 the ordinary budget was balanced at 154 million dinars only marginally up from the 1970 level. The 1972 budget increased expenditure by 14 per cent to TD 175 million and in 1973 a further 8 per cent increase in total expenditure to TD 208 million was set. In an attempt to reduce dependence on the agricultural sector, the output of which can vary drastically according to weather conditions, increased emphasis is placed on the development of industry, particularly labour-intensive concerns orientated to both domestic and foreign markets. Some 27 per cent of the 1973 budget is allocated for education.

PLANNING

It was not until 1961, when the Ten-Year Perspective Plan was formulated, that the Government laid down comprehensive plans for development. The broad lines of policy put forward in the Perspective Plan were embodied in the first three-year plan (1962–64), and then in successive four-year plans (1965–68, 1969–72, and, currently, 1973–76). The 1969–72 plan aimed at a 6 per cent growth rate compared with the 3.5–4 per cent rate achieved during the years 1962–68. Total investment was put at $1,200 million, of which $246 million was allocated to agriculture and some $300 million for industrial projects. The overall emphasis was on reducing unemployment, increasing productivity and improving the balance of payments. Again, the plan's objectives were not fully met—not least because of the 1969 floods. Reliance on foreign capital for investment rose to some 50 per cent. In addition to contributions from the United States, Tunisia received aid from Federal Germany, Canada and the World Bank. A consultative group on development assistance to Tunisia, comprised of the country's principal aid donors, met at the end of 1969 to formulate a policy of assistance for recovery from the floods.

Foreign aid requirements continue to run at $10 million annually, and other difficulties confronting the planners are the rapid growth in population and the consistently heavy trade deficit. The main objectives of the 1973–76 plan are to ensure the profitability of investments under earlier plans; to concentrate on short-term productive investments, particularly in export industries; and to encourage private investment. Total expenditure during the 4 years covered by the new plan will be TD 1,000 million, almost the same as the total expenditure in the ten-year period 1962–72. Investments will begin at the rate of TD 200 million in 1973 rising to TD 290 million in 1976. A determined effort will also be made to reduce Tunisia's dependence on foreign aid.

Bizerta will continue to be the main industrial zone with its port, oil refinery and steel complex at Menzel Bourguiba, and other lesser enterprises. The Government hopes to establish a new industrial complex in the south where underemployment is severe. A new port, a fertilizer plant and a power station are planned. The Gabès port development is particularly significant. This will represent Tunisia's most important port complex and will in fact comprise three adjacent ports and an industrial estate. These three ports will be specially built to handle general merchandise, petroleum and other minerals respectively. Costs will be covered in part by development credits from Italy and the World Bank.

EXTERNAL TRADE

Tunisia's foreign trade normally shows a deficit of up to 50 million dinars. Exports show a rise in most years but are still heavily dependent on the success of the harvest and world market conditions for mineral exports. The 1972 trade figures were exceptional with imports rising to an estimated TD 236 million* (the first time they have exceeded TD 200 million) while exports increased to an estimated TD 152 million. The 1972 trade gap of TD 84 million compared with a trade gap of TD 66 million in 1971. Although the increase in value of exports is encouraging it must be remembered that 1972 was an exceptionally good year for agricultural products, accounting for 42 per cent of total exports, and such good crops cannot be relied upon every year. Also it is expected that imports will rise sharply under the new four-year plan. Exports of crude oil which began in 1966 are now making a substantial contribution (about 25 per cent) to total export earnings. Also with the rapid increase in tourism over the last two years tourist receipts have ensured a substantial improvement in the overall payments position.

Olive oil used to be the principal export in the past but phosphates took the lead in 1965 and in turn were replaced by crude oil in 1969—though as a result of the massive crop in the 1971/72 season olive oil regained its position as the principal export in 1972. Olive oil exports in 1972 were a record 128,518 tons worth TD 46.3 million as against 66,823 tons worth TD 24 million in 1971. Crude oil exports were worth TD 38 million during 1972 as against TD 28.7 million in 1971 and it is hoped that they will rise to over TD 40 million in 1973. In 1972 3.7 million tons of phosphates were produced and exports were valued at an estimated TD 20.4 million; also phosphoric acid worth some TD 680,000 was exported in 1972. Iron, lead and citrus fruits are other important export commodities. Wheat used to be an important export, but, since a series of bad harvests began in 1966, in recent years there have been substantial wheat imports. In recent years wine has made an increasingly smaller contribution to export earnings, and in 1971 it ranked only seventh, with receipts of TD 1 million, but in 1972 exports trebled.

In spite of good harvests and increased production food imports increased in 1972 to TD 41.9 million, a rise of 12 per cent over the 1971 level. With increased tourism it is expected that food imports may increase further to average TD 50 million over the next four years. Apart from food, imports consist mainly of machinery, metal goods and transport equipment. Textile imports have declined with increasing domestic production.

France remains Tunisia's principal supplier (accounting for 35 per cent of imports in 1971 and 1972), followed by the U.S.A., Italy, and West Germany. In 1971, however, France was replaced as Tunisia's largest export market by Italy (which took 30 per cent of Tunisia's exports compared with the 29 per cent taken by France), and again in 1972 Italy was the

_____
* See final figures in Statistical Survey.

largest market, taking 29 per cent of Tunisia's exports compared with 21 per cent taken by France. The EEC accounted for nearly 60 per cent of Tunisian exports in 1971, as against 12 per cent of exports going to Eastern Europe.

Much of Tunisia's trade takes place within the framework of bilateral agreements with other countries. Agreements have been renewed or reached in the last two years with Yugoslavia, the U.K., Switzerland, the U.S.S.R., Egypt, Poland and other countries as well as with France and Libya.

TOURISM

Tourism has grown rapidly in Tunisia in recent years and became the nation's largest foreign currency earner in 1968. The industry has boomed since the typhoid and flood setbacks of 1969 and receipts in 1972 were estimated at TD 70 million, representing just under half of total export earnings. Federal Germany is the principal contributor to tourist earnings, followed by France and the United Kingdom. There are four main centres for tourists: Hammamet, Sousse, Djerba, and Tunis. Foreign private investment in the tourist industry is steadily growing and in 1971 Federal German and French companies spent 6 million dinars on hotel construction. In February 1973 a West German development bank granted the Tunisian National Tourism Office a TD 6.5 million loan most of which is to be used for tourist infrastructural projects. This loan was in addition to $12.4 million granted in September 1972 also for tourist infrastructure development. The International Finance Corporation (IFC) is to invest $1.9 million in a $11.4 million tourist project at Skanes. This is a joint British/Tunisian venture in which IFC will have a 10 per cent stake, Tunisian Holidays 40 per cent and Tunisian investors 50 per cent. The project should provide between 460 and 480 jobs and brings IFC's investment in Tunisia to $16.6 million. The *Compagnie Financière et Touristique* (COFITOUR), set up in 1970 with initial capital resources of $39 million, promotes and finances three types of ventures: new hotel construction; modernization of existing hotels; and other activities related to tourism such as transport, housing and real estate.

FOREIGN AID

The principal sources of economic aid obtained by Tunisia continue to be Western countries and international institutions, with over 50 per cent of all aid coming from the U.S.—total U.S. aid between 1957 and 1967 amounted to $528 million.

The World Bank Group (IBRD, IDA and IFC) has been the most important multilateral donor, providing loans and credits for investment in a variety of projects—including participation in the *Société Nationale d'Investissement* and in COFITOUR. Other donors include the Kuwait Fund for Arab Economic Development. Soviet aid has so far been on a limited scale and other East European countries have made limited contributions.

French aid was resumed in 1967 with a major contribution (loans of 93 million francs) being made for development of the Gabès industrial complex. In 1971, following a further easing in relations between Tunisia and France, a 40 per cent increase in the flow of French aid was announced, returning it to near the 1963 level. In 1972 France agreed to lend 15 million francs for investment in small enterprises, of which about 5 million francs was to come directly from the French treasury, the balance being provided by private credits guaranteed by COFACE. During 1973 France is to give Tunisia 25,000 tons of wheat under her foreign aid policy.

A number of loans have been received from Federal Germany including one of DM 40 million granted in 1970. Following a German mission to Tunisia in April 1972, a loan of DM 65 million was announced, together with several agreements for technical assistance in agriculture, tourism and industrial projects. The major part of the loan will be used for infrastructure projects to provide drinking water, electricity and roads (in conjunction with IBRD assistance).

After long negotiations, agreement was reached in 1969 between the European Economic Community and Tunisia under which Tunisia was granted partial association. Full association, which would include aid provisions and the free movement of labour, was thus postponed. Under the partial association agreement, to run for 5 years, the EEC countries will remove all custom duties and quotas on virtually all industrial exports from Tunisia (at present some 60 per cent of Tunisian exports to the EEC). However, there remains a quota of 100,000 tons of petroleum products exported to the EEC without tariff. Custom duties on olive oil and fish are reduced and preference given to hard wheat and various processed agricultural products. Limited preference will be given to citrus fruit. In return Tunisia will give tariff reductions, equivalent to 70 per cent of the preference, previously given to French goods, on 40 per cent of its imports from the EEC. Tunisia is unhappy about the terms of the present agreement (the trade gap with the EEC increased from TD 3.9 million in 1969 to TD 57 million in 1972) and hopes to negotiate favourable revisions.

In the meantime progress towards economic co-operation between the Maghreb countries is slow, though a Maghreb Permanent Consultative Committee and an Industrial Studies Centre have been established. One of the aims is to co-ordinate the four countries' development plans. Co-operation with Libya in the petrochemical industry is expected, following a 1968 agreement under which Tunisia will concentrate on production of superphosphates and phosphoric acid while Libya will devote its efforts to the production of ammonia and its derivatives; joint production of sulphuric acid is envisaged. The recently established joint venture in the fishing industry is a small step in the direction of co-operation. A number of important bilateral and multilateral agreements have been signed in recent years. Tunisia is to co-operate with the Netherlands in establishing several manufacturing plants (to produce bicycles, shirts and shoes). A $6.8 million loan from the U.S.A. was agreed earlier in 1972 to enable Tunisia to purchase 10,000 tons of soya bean oil and 60,000 tons of wheat. A similar loan, for $12 million, had been granted in November 1971. Other major loans agreed in 1972–73 include a TD 1.6 million loan from Sweden for development in olive-growing regions, and a loan of TD 4 million from U.S. AID to be used for transport and irrigation projects. The World Bank agreed in mid-1972 to provide a further 5 million dinars to the *Société d'Investissement*. In 1973 the World Bank approved a further loan of $14 million to SNI to help finance imports needed for the development of industrial and tourism projects. World Bank loans to Tunisia since 1964 now total $155.6 million.

STATISTICAL SURVEY

AREA AND POPULATION

AREA (sq. km.)	POPULATION Total (1971 est.)	Tunis (capital) (1966 census)
164,150	5,179,000	789,787

	1969	1970	1971*
Births	194,940	185,756	182,749
Deaths	52,872	45,435	48,762
Marriages	33,764	34,318	37,642

* Provisional figures.

Chief Towns: Sfax 100,000, Sousse 90,000, Bizerta 70,000, Kairouan 50,000, Gabès 40,000, Monastir 40,000, Menzel-Bourguiba 35,000.

AGRICULTURE
PRINCIPAL CROPS
('000 metric tons)

CROP	1968	1969	1970	1971
Soft Wheat	73	91	150	200
Hard Wheat	310	245	299	400
Barley	130	81	151	140
Esparto Grass	108	74	84	79
Citrus Fruits	66	97	n.a.	77
Dates	39	59	18	39
Sugar Beet	27	34	30	27

LIVESTOCK
(1970—'000)

CATTLE	ASSES	SHEEP	HORSES	MULES	GOATS	CAMELS
670	185	3,100	98	60	450	280

Source: FAO Production Yearbook, 1971.

Fishing: Total catch including Shellfish (1968) 27,972 tons, (1969) 29,668 tons, (1970) 24,376 tons, (1971) 27,040 tons.

TUNISIA—(STATISTICAL SURVEY)

MINING

		1967	1968	1969	1970	1971
Iron Ore	('000 metric tons)	1,003	1,016	945	774	940
Lead Ore	(,, ,, ,,)	28	24	38	35	33
Calcium Phosphate	(,, ,, ,,)	2,810	3,361	2,599	3,021	3,162
Zinc	(metric tons)	5,635	7,165	16,692	21,500	20,800

Petroleum: Production from the El Borma field totalled approximately 3,300,000 tons in 1968, 3,707,000 tons in 1969, 4,151,000 tons in 1970 and 4,096,000 tons in 1971.

INDUSTRY

		1968	1969	1970	1971
Superphosphates	('000 metric tons)	376	333	382	422
Cement	(,, ,, ,,)	491	582	522	554
Lead	(,, ,, ,,)	14	24	22	21
Electric Power	(million kWh.)	546	624	680	768
Natural Gas	('000 cubic metres)	9,443	9,299	4,740	936
Town Gas	(,, ,, ,,)	19.5	19.3	19.1	17.6
Beer	('000 hectolitres)	237	169	201	280
Cigarettes	(millions)	2,975	3,253	3,286	3,549
Wine	('000 hl.)	912	843	559	966
Olive Oil	('000 metric tons)	51	55	25	90

FINANCE

1,000 millimes = 1 Tunisian dinar.
Coins: 1, 2, 5, 10, 20, 50, 100 and 500 millimes.
Notes: 500 millimes; 1, 5 and 10 dinars.
Exchange rates (April 1973): £1 sterling = 1.023 dinars (selling rate); U.S. $1 = 435.2 millimes (par value).
100 Tunisian dinars = £97.75 = $229.78.

BUDGET
('000 dinars)

REVENUE	1969	1970	EXPENDITURE	1969	1970
Direct Taxes	26,819	30,545	Education	35,721	44,367
Indirect Taxes	80,163	81,582	Finances and National Economy	41,630	31,239
Other Taxes	3,448	3,829	Public Health	12,350	13,708
Internal Revenue and Services	6,090	5,528	Interior	10,200	10,637
Revenue from Investments	9,567	18,523	National Defence	7,000	9,509
Others and Reinvestments	5,263	6,493	Public Works and Housing	6,530	6,088
			Others	17,919	30,952
TOTAL	131,350	146,500	TOTAL	131,350	146,500

Budget Estimates: 154 million dinars (1971); 175 million dinars (1972); 208 million dinars (1973).

TUNISIA—(Statistical Survey)

NATIONAL ACCOUNTS
(million dinars, at 1966 prices)

	1969	1970	1971*
Agriculture	77.8	80.1	100.7
Food and Agricultural Industries	20.6	19.3	26.0
Petroleum	22.5	26.0	24.0
Mining	9.1	8.7	9.1
Public Utilities	n.a.	n.a.	n.a.
Other Industry	32.1	33.9	35.8
Building and Public Works	42.9	44.4	49.3
Transport and Telecommunications	45.0	51.3	45.8
Rent	46.7	47.4	48.3
Commerce	56.0	72.5	84.8
Tourism	14.8	16.6	25.2
Other Services including Government	132.8	142.6	145.2
GROSS DOMESTIC PRODUCT AT FACTOR COST	518.6	561.6	615.0
Indirect Taxes	83.7	88.2	94.8
GROSS DOMESTIC PRODUCT AT MARKET PRICES	602.3	649.8	709.8
Imports of Goods and Services *less* Exports	46.0	49.9	57.1
TOTAL RESOURCES	648.3	699.7	766.9
Private Consumption	399.4	421.7	469.9
Government Consumption	110.5	122.9	121.4
Gross Fixed Capital Formation	135.3	145.7	173.4
Increase in Stocks	3.1	9.4	2.2

* Provisional.

EXTERNAL TRADE
('000 dinars)

	1966	1967	1968	1969	1970	1971	1972
Imports	131,224	137,087	114,497	139,777	160,396	179,958	222,200
Exports	73,684	78,355	82,829	86,960	95,804	113,304	150,300

PRINCIPAL COMMODITIES
('000 dinars)

IMPORTS	1968	1969	1970
Machinery, non-electric	15,324	16,818	20,048
Cereals	11,301	15,493	18,016
Iron and Steel	6,530	9,598	10,996
Electric Machinery	8,067	9,402	10,699
Road Transport Equipment	6,332	7,564	9,824
Animal and Vegetable Oils and Fats	3,631	6,182	8,926
Petroleum Products	3,422	6,780	7,704
Sugar and Sugar Preparations	2,927	3,587	4,804

TUNISIA—(STATISTICAL SURVEY)

PRINCIPAL COMMODITIES—*continued*]

EXPORTS	1969	1970	1971
Crustaceans and Molluscs	696	1,131	1,075
Oranges	3,040	1,590	1,302
Dates	990	1,399	2,228
Dried Almonds	638	1,488	1,362
Other Fruit and Nuts	262	215	1,669
Wine	3,443	4,754	1,316
Pulp and Waste Paper	1,856	1,884	1,889
Natural Phosphates	8,699	10,529	11,554
Iron	1,745	1,946	2,834
Crude Petroleum	21,158	23,451	28,733
Motor Spirit and Gas Oil	1,165	1,673	1,450
Other Petroleum Products	1,450	n.a.	n.a.
Olive Oil	9,964	8,394	24,019
Phosphatic Fertilizers	8,161	8,611	9,634
Lead	2,226	3,215	1,925
TOTAL (incl. others)	86,960	95,804	113,304

PRINCIPAL COUNTRIES
('000 dinars)

IMPORTS	1969	1970	1971
Belgium/Luxembourg	1,833	3,059	3,674
Brazil	952	2,303	3,249
France	46,196	55,557	64,827
Germany, Federal Republic	10,512	13,619	12,239
Iraq	2,094	2,584	3,216
Italy	12,489	11,566	15,497
Netherlands	2,522	3,480	3,742
Poland	2,698	4,856	2,970
United Kingdom	4,105	4,557	5,836
U.S.A.	28,208	27,134	26,230
TOTAL (incl. others)	139,777	160,396	179,958

EXPORTS	1969	1970	1971
Algeria	2,236	4,045	1,724
France	23,173	23,383	21,884
Germany, Federal Republic	12,088	9,293	14,857
Italy	11,745	19,781	22,146
Libya	6,362	8,873	11,212
Poland	2,360	3,523	3,459
U.S.S.R.	2,525	1,460	3,721
United Kingdom	2,736	2,503	1,770
TOTAL (incl. others)	86,960	95,804	113,304

TRANSPORT
ROADS

VEHICLES LICENSED	1969	1970	1971
Private Cars	62,280	66,438	72,056
Buses / Lorries / Commercial Vehicles	34,889	37,246	41,506
Motor Cycles	9,808	9,904	10,063

TUNISIA—(Statistical Survey)

SHIPPING

	1968	1969	1970	1971
Vessels Entered* ('000 net reg. tons)	12,379	13,547	13,124	25,137
Passengers (number)	163,700	229,100	213,800	252,200
Goods Loaded ('000 metric tons)	5,147	4,655	4,799	5,043
Goods Unloaded (,, ,, ,,)	2,931	3,417	3,459	3,472

* Including vessels leaving.

CIVIL AVIATION

	1969	1970	1971
Passenger ('000)	695.5	785.0	1,047.2
Freight (metric tons)	4,294	4,475	4,756
Mail (metric tons)	775	896	921

TOURISM

PRINCIPAL NATIONALITIES OF VISITORS
('000)

	1968	1969	1970	1971
Federal Germany	71.7	66.5	84.2	163.7
France	66.6	93.5	113.8	138.1
United Kingdom	48.2	60.8	47.0	73.0
Italy	34.9	50.3	58.6	63.4
Libya	31.7	31.0	36.3	54.4
Sweden	22.6	23.9	17.8	22.5
Switzerland	22.6	27.1	20.6	28.9
Algeria	14.4	7.5	8.9	11.8
U.S.A.	11.8	16.9	17.2	15.5
Morocco	9.7	11.6	5.8	5.1
Total (incl. others)	384.3	455.3	482.0	673.1

Tourist Accommodation: 6,800 beds in officially classified hotels (total capacity in 1971: 42,996 beds including hostels and holiday villages).

Tourist Spending: (1969) 26m. dinars, (1970) 29m. dinars, (1971) 54m. dinars.

EDUCATION

Type	Number of Institutions	Number of Pupils 1968–69	Number of Pupils 1969–70	Number of Teachers 1968–69	Number of Teachers 1969–70
Primary	2,131	859,927	912,646	16,194	18,000
Secondary	88	135,947	163,353	3,818	6,931
Secondary Technical	80	n.a.	n.a.	2,141	
Teacher Training	5	n.a.	n.a.	n.a.	
University of Tunis	1	7,668	9,413	304	539
Students Abroad	—	2,816	n.a.	—	—

The ratio of boys to girls is approx. 2 : 1 in primary schools, 3 : 1 in secondary schools and 4 : 1 at the University.

TUNISIA—(The Constitution, The Government, Diplomatic Representation)

THE CONSTITUTION

Tunisia, which had been a French Protectorate since 1881, achieved full internal autonomy in September 1955, and finally recognized as a fully independent sovereign State by the Protocol of Paris of March 20th, 1956, by which France abrogated the former treaties and conventions.

NATIONAL ASSEMBLY

The Constitution was proclaimed by the Constituent Assembly on June 1st, 1959. Tunisia is a free, independent and sovereign republic. Legislative power is exercised by the National Assembly which is elected (at the same time as the President) every five years by direct universal suffrage. Every citizen who has had Tunisian nationality for at least five years and who has attained twenty years of age has the vote. The National Assembly shall hold two sessions every year, each session lasting not more than three months. Additional meetings may be held at the demand of the President or of a majority of the deputies.

HEAD OF STATE

The President of the Republic is both Head of State and Head of the Executive. He must be not less than forty years of age and is not permitted to serve more than three terms consecutively. The President of the Republic is also the Commander-in-Chief of the army and makes both civil and military appointments.

COUNCIL OF STATE

Comprises two judicial bodies: (1) an administrative body dealing with legal disputes between individuals and State or public bodies; (2) an audit office to verify the accounts of the State and submit reports.

ECONOMIC AND SOCIAL COUNCIL

Deals with economic and social planning and studies projects submitted by the National Assembly. Members are grouped in seven categories representing various sections of the community.

THE GOVERNMENT

HEAD OF STATE

President of the Republic: Habib Bourguiba (*re-elected for a third five-year term on November 2nd, 1969*).

THE CABINET
(*August* 1973)

Prime Minister: Hedi Nouira.
Minister, Director of the President's Office: Habib Chatti.
Minister of Justice: Slaheddine Bali.
Foreign Minister: Mohamed Masmoudi.
Minister of the Interior: Tahar Belkhodja.
Minister of Defence: Abdallah Farhat.
Minister in charge of the Plan: Mansour Moalla.
Minister of Finance: Mohamed Fitouri.
Minister of the Economy: Chedly Ayari.
Minister of Agriculture: Dr. Dhaoui Hannablia.
Minister of Education: Driss Guiga.
Minister of Cultural Affairs and Information: Chedli Klibi.
Minister of Public Health: Mohamed Mzali.

Minister of Public Works and Housing: Mohamed Hédi Khefachai.
Minister of Social Affairs: Farhat Dachraoui.
Minister of Posts and Telecommunications: Habib Ben Cheikh.
Minister of Youth and Sport: Mohamed Sayah.
Secretary of State for the Plan: Mustapha Zaanouni.
Secretary of State for the National Economy: Mekki Zidi.
Secretary of State for Education: Hamed Zghal.
Secretaries of State for Agriculture: Mohamed Ghedira and Abderrahman Ben Messaoud.
Secretary of State for Public Works and Housing: Adbelhamid Sassi.

DIPLOMATIC REPRESENTATION

EMBASSIES ACCREDITED TO TUNISIA
(Tunis unless otherwise indicated)

Algeria: 18 rue du Niger; *Ambassador:* Tedjeni Haddam.
Argentina: Rabat, Morocco.
Austria: 17 ave. de France; *Ambassador:* Hans Pasch.
Belgium: 47 rue du 1er Juin; *Ambassador:* Jacques Gérard.
Brazil: rue Sayouti et rue Tamia; *Ambassador:* (vacant).
Bulgaria: 137 ave. de la Liberté; *Ambassador:* Bogomil Nonev.
Cameroon: 3 ave. de Lesseps; *Ambassador:* Ferdinand Léopold Oyono.

Canada: 3 rue Didon, Notre Dame de Tunis, Cité al Mahdi; *Ambassador:* Henri Gaudefroy.
Central African Republic: 10 rue Imam Muslim, El Menzah; *Ambassador:* Jean Charlie Mokamenede.
China, People's Republic: 41 ave. Lesseps; *Ambassador:* Hou Yeh-Feng.
Czechoslovakia: 98 rue de la Palestine; *Ambassador:* Jan Janik.
Denmark: 138 ave. de la Liberté; *Ambassador:* Ditlov Scheel.

TUNISIA—(Diplomatic Representation, National Assembly, Political Parties, etc.)

Egypt: 1 rue Dr. Calmette; *Ambassador:* Mahmoud Touhami.
Finland: 23 rue Baudelaire, El Omrane; *Ambassador:* Sunnell Juhani Ossi.
France: pl. de l'Indépendance; *Ambassador:* Georges Gaucher.
Gabon: Paris, France.
German Democratic Republic: 16 rue Es-Soyouti, El Menzah; *Ambassador:* Heinz Dieter Winter.
Germany, Federal Republic of: 18 rue Félicien Challaye; *Ambassador:* Dr. Heinz Naupert.
Ghana: 103 ave de la Liberté.
Greece: 78 ave. Mohamed V; *Ambassador:* Georges J. Gavas.
Guinea: Algiers, Algeria.
Hungary: Algiers, Algeria.
India: 13 rue du Dr. Burnet; *Ambassador:* V. M. M. Nair.
Indonesia: Algiers, Algeria.
Iran: 10 rue Dr. Burnet, Belvédère; *Ambassador:* Mahmoud Saleh.
Iraq: 125 ave. de la Liberté.
Italy: 37 rue Abdennasser; *Ambassador:* Salvatore Saraceno.
Ivory Coast: 1 pl. Pasteur; *Ambassador:* Charles Aillot About.
Japan: 16 rue Jugurtha; *Ambassador:* Yasuo Yano.
Jordan: 16 rue El Moutanabi, El Menzah; *Ambassador:* Wajih Kaylani.
Korea, Republic of: 85 ave. de la Liberté; *Ambassador:* Kyu Sap Chung.
Kuwait: rue Jacques Cartier, Belvédère; *Ambassador:* Saoud Abdul Hamidhi.
Lebanon: 18 ave. Charles Nicolle; *Ambassador:* Joseph Salama.
Libya: 48bis rue du 1er Juin; *Commissioner General:* Fraj Ben Gileil.
Mali: Paris, France.
Malta: Tripoli, Libya.
Mauritania: 18 ave. Charles Nicolle; *Ambassador:* Barek Ould Bouna Mokhtar.
Mexico: Rome, Italy.
Morocco: 5 rue Didon Notre Dame; *Ambassador:* Mohamed Snoussi.
Netherlands: 2 rue d'Artois; *Ambassador:* J. D. Van Den Brandeler.
Niger: Algiers, Algeria.
Nigeria: Paris, France.
Norway: 7 ave. Habib Bourguiba; *Ambassador:* Olave Moltthe Hansen.
Pakistan: 20 rue Imam Muslim, El Menzah; *Ambassador:* N. Khan Khattak.
Peru: *Ambassador:* Felipe Valdivieso Belaunde.
Poland: 12 rue Didon, Notre Dame.
Romania: 6 rue Magon, Notre Dame; *Ambassador:* Marin Radoi.
Saudi Arabia: 16 rue de l'Autriche; *Ambassador:* Abdel-Rahman El Bassam.
Senegal: 122 ave. de la Liberté; *Ambassador:* Lt.-Gen. Claude Mademba-Sy.
Spain: 14 ave. des Etats-Unis d'Amérique; *Ambassador:* Román Oyarzún.
Sudan: Cairo, Egypt.
Sweden: 17 ave. de France; *Ambassador:* Marc Giron.
Switzerland: 17 ave. de France; *Ambassador:* René Stoudmann.
Thailand: Madrid, Spain.
Turkey: 47 ave. Mohamed V; *Ambassador:* Adnan Bulak.
U.S.S.R.: 31 rue du 1er Juin; *Ambassador:* S. Afanassiev.
United Kingdom: 5 pl. de la Victoire; *Ambassador:* John Marnham.
U.S.A.: 144 ave. de la Liberté; *Ambassador:* Talcott Williams Seelye.
Viet-Nam, Republic: 23 rue Jacques Cartier; *Ambassador:* Tram Van Minth.
Yugoslavia: 4 rue du Libéria; *Ambassador:* Dragomir Petrovic.
Zaire: 5 rue du Niger; *Ambassador:* Losso Lisongi.

Tunisia also has diplomatic relations with Afghanistan, Chad, Kenya, Madagascar, Monaco, Panama, Somalia, Syria, Uganda, Upper Volta, Vatican, Venezuela, People's Republic of Viet-Nam and Yemen.

NATIONAL ASSEMBLY

President: Sadok Mokaddem.
First Vice-President: Ferdjani Belhadj Ammar.

Election, November 1969

All 101 seats were won by the Destour Socialist Party. There were no opposition candidates, but some seats were contested by more than one member of the governing party.

POLITICAL PARTIES

Destour Socialist Party (*Parti socialiste destourien—PSD*): 10 rue de Rome, Tunis; f. 1934 by Habib Bourguiba, as a splinter party from the old *Destour* (Constitution) Party; moderate left-wing republican party, which achieved Tunisian independence; 8th Congress held Oct. 1971; Pres. Habib Bourguiba.

Political Bureau: 14 members, elected by the Central Committee, including:
President: Pres. Bourguiba.
Secretary: Hadi Nouira.
Deputy Secretary-Generals: Mohamed Masmoudi and Mansour Moalla.
General Treasurer: Abdallah Farhat.
Deputy-General Treasurer: Jellouli Fares.
Director of Party: Mohamed Sayah.

Central Committee: 56 members.

DEFENCE

Estimated Defence Expenditure (1972): 13,800,000 dinars.
Military Service: 1 year (selective).
Total Armed Forces: 24,000: army 20,000; navy 2,000; air force 2,000.
Paramilitary Forces: 10,000 (5,000 Gendarmerie, 5,000 National Guard).

TUNISIA—(JUDICIAL SYSTEM, RELIGION, THE PRESS)

JUDICIAL SYSTEM

Cour de Cassation: Tunis; has three civil and one criminal sections.

There are three Courts of Appeal, at Tunis, Sousse and Sfax, and thirteen courts of First Instance, each having three chambers except the Court of First Instance of Tunis which has eight chambers.

Cantonal Justices have been set up in 48 areas.

RELIGION

The Constitution of 1956 recognizes Islam as the State religion, with the introduction of certain reforms, such as the abolition of polygamy. Minority religions are Jews (20,000), Roman Catholics (20,000), Greek Orthodox and a number of French and English Protestants.

Grand Mufti of Tunisia: Sheikh MOHAMMED HEDI BELCADHI.

Roman Catholic Prelature: 4 rue d'Alger, Tunis; *Titular Archbishop of Mossori:* Mgr. MICHEL CALLENS.

THE PRESS

DAILIES

TUNIS

L'Action: 10 rue de Rome; f. 1932; organ of the Destour Socialist Party; French; Chief Editor ABDELHAY SEGHAÏER; circ. 32,000.

al-Amal (*Action*): 10 rue de Rome; f. 1934; organ of the Destour Socialist Party; Arabic; Chief Editor LARBI ABDERRAZAK; circ. 25,000.

Dar Assabah: 4 rue Ali Bach-Hamba; f. 1951; Dir. HABIB CHEKH ROUHOU; circ. 30,000.

La Presse de Tunisie: 6 rue Ali Bach-Hamba; f. 1936; French; Dir. ABDELHAKIM BELKHIRIA; Chief Editor NOUREDDINE TABKA; circ. 35,000.

PERIODICALS

TUNIS

ach-Chaab: Place M'Hamed Ali; Trade union publication; Arabic; fortnightly.

ach-Chabab: 10 rue de Rome, publ. of the Union of Tunisian youth; Arabic language; monthly.

Bulletin Annuel: Institut National de Statistique, B.P. 65.

Bulletin de la Chambre de Commerce de Tunis: 1 avenue Habib Thameur, Palais Consulaire; monthly; Dir. SLIMANE AGHA.

Conjoncture: Banque Centrale de Tunisie, 7 place de la Monnaie; economic and financial surveys; quarterly.

Il Corriere di Tunisi: 4 rue de Russie; Italian; weekly; Dir. M. FINZI.

Etudiant Tunisien: B.P. 286, 13 rue Gamal Abdel Nasser; f. 1953; French and Arabic; Chief Editor MOUNIR BEJI.

al-Fikr (*Thought*): B.P. 556, 13 rue Dar Djeld; f. 1955; cultural review; Arabic; monthly; Dir. MOHAMED MZALI.

Ibla: 12 rue Jamâa el Haoua; f. 1937; social and cultural review on Maghreb and Muslim-Arab affairs; French and Arabic; twice yearly; Dir. A. DEMEERSEMAN.

al-Idhaa wa Talvaza (*Radio and Television*): 71 ave. de la Liberté; broadcasting magazine; Arabic language; fortnightly; Editor ABDELMAJID ENNAIFAR; circ. 15,000.

al-Jaich: National Defence publication; Arabic language.

Journal Officiel Tunisien: 42 rue du 18 Janvier 1952; the official gazette; f. 1860; French and Arab editions published twice weekly by the Imprimerie Officielle (The State Press); Pres./Gen. Man. MOHIEDDINE DEROUICHE.

al-Maraa (*The Woman*): 56 boulevard Bab Benat; f. 1961; issued by the National Union of Tunisian Women; Arabic; political, economic and social affairs; monthly; circ. 10,000.

Le Sport: 9 ave. de la Liberté; French language; weekly; Pres. MAHMOUD ELLAFI; circ. 20,000.

Statistiques Financieres: Banque Centrale de Tunisie, 7 place de la Monnaie; statistical tables; monthly.

Tunisie Actualités: Centre de Documentation Nationale, 2 rue d'Alger, Tunis; f. 1966; quarterly; French; official journal.

La Tunisie Economique: 32 rue Charles-de-Gaulle; French; every 2 months; published by the Union Tunisienne de l'Industrie, du Commerce et de l'Artisanat; circ. 2,000.

SFAX

Bulletin Economique de la Chambre de Commerce du Sud: 21–23 rue Habib Thameur; f. 1949; monthly; French and Arabic.

SOUSSE

Bulletin de la Chambre de Commerce du Centre: every two months in French and Arabic; Dir. HEDI BOUSLAMA.

NEWS AGENCIES

Tunis Afrique Presse (TAP): 47 ave. Habib Bourguiba, Tunis; f. 1961; operates a news exchange service by cable other than with AFP (France), Reuter (U.K.) and UPI (U.S.A.) with: LNA (Libya), APS (Algeria), MAP (Mahgreb Arab Agency) and EFE (Spain), and by radio with: MENA (Middle East News Agency), HSINHUA (China), DPA (Federal Rep. of Germany), ANSA (Italy), TASS (U.S.S.R.), Tanjug (Yugoslavia), Ager Press (Romania), ADN (German Democratic Republic), CTK (Czechoslovakia), Anadulu Agency (Turkey); Pres. and Dir.-Gen. SLAHEDDINE BEN HAMIDA.

FOREIGN BUREAUX

AFP (*France*): 45 ave. Habib Bourguiba, Tunis; Chief MARIO BIANCHI.

ANSA (*Italy*): rue Caracalla, Tunis; Chief NICOLA RIENZI.

AP (*U.S.A.*): 35 rue Garibaldi, Tunis; Chief F. VENTURA.

Četeka (*Czechoslovakia*): Tunis; Chief A. DAHMANI.

DPA (*Federal Rep. of Germany*): Tunis; Chief A. JEMAÏEL.

Novosti (*U.S.S.R.*): APN office, 108 ave. de la Liberté, Tunis; Chief O. BOGUSHEVICH.

Reuters (*U.K.*): 45 ave. Habib Bourguiba; Chief GUSTAVE DEJEANNE.

Tanjug (*Yugoslavia*): 4 rue du Libéria, Tunis.

TASS (*U.S.S.R.*): 2 rue Gounot, Tunis; Chief VARDAN NADIRIAN.

UPI (*U.S.A.*): 28 rue Essadikia, Tunis; Chief MICHEL DÈVRE.

Visnews: 33 rue Lénine, Tunis.

PUBLISHERS

COPI (Coopérative de Publications et d'Impression): rue Taieb Mehiri, Sfax.

Dar Al Kitab: 5 ave. Habib Bourguiba, Sousse.

Dar Assabah (*Société Tunisienne de Presse, d'Edition et d'Impression*): 37 rue de Marseille, Tunis; f. 1951; 48 mems.; publishes daily papers which circulate throughout Tunisia, North Africa and France.

Hedi Abdelghani: ave. de France, Tunis.

Maison Tunisienne d'Edition (M.T.E.): 70 ave. de la Liberté, Tunis.

Service des statistiques du Secrétariat d'Etat au plan et à l'économie nationale: Tunis; publishes a variety of annuals, periodicals and papers concerned with the economic policy and development of Tunisia.

S.L.I.M. (Société Librairie Imprimerie Messagerie): blvd. Président Bourguiba, El Kef.

Société L'Action d'Edition et de Presse (S.A.E.P.): 10 rue de Rome, Tunis.

Société Anonyme de Papeterie et Imprimerie: 12 rue de Vesoul, Tunis.

Société Nationale d'Edition et de Diffusion: 5 ave. de Carthage, Tunis.

RADIO AND TELEVISION

RADIO

Radiodiffusion Télévision Tunisienne: 71 ave. de la Liberté, Tunis; government station; broadcasts in French, Arabic, English, German and Italian; Dir.-Gen. MIMOUN CHATTI.

Number of radio receivers 388,000.

TELEVISION

Television was introduced in northern and central Tunisia in January 1966, and by 1972 transmission reached all the country. A relay station to link up with European transmissions was built at Ain Drahman in 1967.

Number of television receivers 75,000.

FINANCE

(cap.=capital, p.u.=paid up, dep.=deposits, m.=million)

BANKING

CENTRAL BANK

Banque Centrale de Tunisie: 7 Place de la Monnaie, Tunis; f. 1958; cap. 1.2m. dinars, dep. 54.8m. dinars; Gov. MOHAMED GHENIMA; Dir.-Gen. MOHAMED BOUSBIA; publs. *Conjoncture* (quarterly), *Statistiques Financières* (monthly), *Rapport Annuel*.

Banque de Tunisie: 3 avenue de France, Tunis; f. 1884; cap. 1m. dinars, dep. 31.89m. dinars (Dec. 1972); Pres. and Gen. Man. BOUBAKER MABROUK.

Banque Franco-Tunisienne: 13 rue d'Alger, Tunis; Gen. Man. RACHID MZALI.

Banque Nationale de Tunisie: 19 ave. de Paris, Tunis; f. 1959; cap. p.u. 1.6m. dinars, dep. (1971) 32,394m. dinars; Pres./Gen. Man. ABDELAZIZ LASRAM; Dir.-Gen. TAHAR FARAH; 24 brs.; publ. *Report* (annual).

Banque du Sud: Tunis; f. 1965; cap. 270,000 dinars; Pres. and Gen. Man. SAÏD CHENIK.

Caisse d'Epargne Nationale Tunisienne: blvd. 9 Avril 1938, Tunis.

Compte Cheques Postaux: blvd. 5 Avril 1938, Tunis.

Société Nationale d'Investissement: 68 ave. Habib Bourguiba, Tunis; f. 1959; development bank, now the main source of long term and equity finance for industrial and tourist enterprises; received $35m. loan from World Bank in 1967; cap. 14m. dinars; Pres. and Gen. Man. HABIB BOURGUIBA, Jr.

Société Tunisienne de Banque: 1 ave. Habib Thameur, Tunis; f. 1958; cap. p.u. 3m. dinars (July 1972); Chair. M. HASSEN BELKHODJA.

Union Bancaire pour le Commerce et l'Industrie: 7–9 rue Gamal Abdel Nasser, Tunis; f. 1961; cap. p.u. 1.65m. dinars, dep. 33.6m. dinars; incorporates Banque d'Escompte et de Crédit à l'Industrie en Tunisie; Pres. and Dir.-Gen. MOHAMED BADRA; publ. *Report* (annual).

Union Internationale de Banque: 65 ave. Habib Bourguiba, Tunis; f. 1963 as a merging of Tunisian interests by the Société Tunisienne de Banque with the Crédit Lyonnais and other foreign banks; cap. 2m. dinars; Pres. and Gen. Man. TAOUFIK TORJEMAN.

FOREIGN BANKS

Arab Bank Ltd., Tunis Branch: Amman, Jordan; 21 rue Al-Djazira, Tunis.

British Bank of the Middle East: London; 70 avenue Habib Bourguiba, Tunis.

Crédit Foncier et Commercial de Tunisie: 13 ave. de France, Tunis.

Société Marseillaise de Crédit: Marseilles; 12 avenue de France, Tunis.

A national Stock Exchange was opened during 1967.

INSURANCE

Astrée, Compagnie Franco-Tunisienne d'Assurances Tous Risques et de Réassurances, S.A.: 43–45 ave. Habib Bourguiba, Tunis; f. 1950; Pres. ABDERRAZAK RASSAA; Dir.-Gen. MOHAMMED HACHICHA.

Caisse Tunisienne d'Assurances Mutuelles Agricoles: 6 ave. Habib Thameur, Tunis; f. 1912; Pres. MOKTAR BELLAGHA, Dir.-Gen. SLAHEDDINE FERCHIOU.

Lloyd Tunisien: 7 ave. de Carthage, Tunis; f. 1945; Pres. M. ZERDZERI; fire, accident, liability, marine, life.

Société Tunisienne d'Assurances et de Réassurances: ave. de Paris, Tunis; f. 1958; Pres./Dir-Gen. HEDI NAÏFAR; all kinds of insurance.

FOREIGN COMPANIES

About thirty of the major French, Swiss and British insurance companies are represented in Tunisia.

TRADE AND INDUSTRY

CHAMBERS OF COMMERCE

Tunis

Chambre de Commerce de Tunis: Palais Consulaire, 1 ave. Habib Thameur, Tunis; f. 1925; 25 mems.; Pres. MAHMOUD ZERZERI; publ. *Bulletin* (monthly).

Sousse

Chambre de Commerce du Centre: rue Chadly Khaznadar, Sousse; Pres. HÉDI BOUSLAMA; Sec.-Gen. MOHAMED BEN CHERIFA; publ. *Bulletin Economique* (every two months in French and Arabic).

TUNISIA—(Trade and Industry, Transport, Tourism, Atomic Energy)

Sfax
Chambre de Commerce du Sud: 21–23 rue Habib Thameur; f. 1895; 8 mems.; publ. *Bulletin Economique*.

Bizerta
Chambre de Commerce du Nord: 12 rue Ibn Khaldoun, Bizerte; f. 1903; 8 mems.; Pres. MOHAMED TERRAS; Sec.-Gen. Mme SFAXI RACHIDA; publ. *Bulletin Economique*.

ECONOMIC ORGANIZATION

Union Tunisienne de l'Industrie, du Commerce et de l'Artisanat (U.T.I.C.A.): 32 rue Charles-de-Gaulle, Tunis; f. 1946 by FERDJANI BEN HADJ AMMAR; mems. about 250,000 in 13 regional unions and federations (Industry, Commerce, Handicrafts); Pres. FERDJANI BEN HADJ AMMAR; First Vice-Pres. HABIB MAJOUL; publs. *La Tunisie Economique* (monthly), *Economic Yearbook* (annual).

TRADE UNIONS

Union Générale Tunisienne du Travail (U.G.T.T.): 29 place M'Hamed Ali, Tunis; f. 1946 by FARHAT HACHED; affiliated to ICFTU; mems. 150,000 in 23 affiliated unions; Sec.-Gen. HABIB ACHOUR.

Union Générale des Etudiants de Tunisie (U.G.E.T.): 11 rue d'Espagne, Tunis; f. 1953; 600 mems.; Sec.-Gen. MOHAMED BEN AHMED; publ. *L'Etudiant Tunisien*.

Union Nationale des Femmes de Tunisie (U.N.F.T.): blvd. Farhat Hached; f. 1956; 37,000 mems.; Pres. Mme. RADHIA HADDAD; Sec.-Gen. Mme MONGIA MABROUK.

TRADE FAIR

International Fair in Tunis: Mohammed V St., Tunis; May 25th–June 10th.

TRANSPORT

RAILWAYS

Société Nationale des Transports: Tunis; controls the electrified line from Tunis to La Marsa (39 km.); operates over 100 local and long-distance domestic bus routes.

Société Nationale des Chemins de Fer Tunisiens: 67 blvd. Farhat Hached, Tunis; f. 1957; State organization controlling 1,998 km. of railways; acquired *Chemin de Fer Gafsa* (a line specializing in the transport of phosphate) in Jan. 1967; Pres. ABDELHAKIM SLAMA; publs. monthly and annual reports.

In 1969 the total length of railways was 2,305 km.

ROADS

In 1971 there were 18,267 km. of roads. Of these 10,483 km. were main roads and 5,603 km. secondary roads.

SHIPPING

Tunisia has 4 major ports: Tunis–La Goulette, Bizerta, Sousse and Sfax. There is a special petroleum port at La Skhirra. In October 1972 a complex of three amalgamated ports, with separate facilities for general merchandise, minerals, and oil was completed at Gabès.

La Compagnie Tunisienne de Navigation: P.O. Box 40, 5 avenue Dag Hammarskjoeld, Tunis; brs. at Bizerta, La Skhirra, Sfax and Sousse.

CIVIL AVIATION

A new international airport for Tunis was opened at Skanes-Monastir in April 1968, and can now provide facilities for large jet aircraft. A second airport at Jerba was opened in August 1972, while a new international airport, adjacent to Tunis-Carthage, was inaugurated in late July 1972.

Tunis Air (*Société Tunisienne de l'Air*): 113 ave. de la Liberté, Tunis; f. 1948; flights to Algeria, Belgium, France, Fed. Rep. of Germany, Italy, Libya, Luxemberg, Morocco, Netherlands, Saudi Arabia, Switzerland and U.K. and internal flights; fleet of three Boeing 727, four Caravelles, one Nord 262; Pres. EASSAÂD BEN OSMAN.

Société Tunisienne de Réparations Aéronautiques et de Constructions: Aérodrome de Tunis-Carthage, Tunis; f. 1952; internal charter flights for oil companies.

FOREIGN AIRLINES

Aeroflot, Air Afrique, Air Algérie, Air France, Air India, Alitalia, Austrian Airlines, Balkan, British Caledonian, CSA, EgyptAir, Interflug, JAT, KLM, Libyan Arab, LOT (Poland), Lufthansa, Malev Hungarian, Royal Air Maroc, Sabena, SAS, Swissair, Tabso (Bulgaria), TWA, and UTA also serve Tunis.

TOURISM

Office National du Tourisme et du Thermalisme: ave. Mohammed V, Tunis; Dir. Gen. RIDHA AZZABI.

Direction de l'Information: 2 rue d'Alger, Tunis; Dir. MUSTAPHA MASMOUDI.

Tunisian Hotel and Tourism Association: 2 ave. de France, Tunis; Dir. SAHEB ETTABA; publ. *Voyages* 2,000.

CULTURAL ORGANIZATIONS

Ministry of Cultural Affairs: Tunis; departments organize all national cultural events; Minister CHEDLI KLIBI.

International Cultural Centre: Hammamet; f. 1962; has built an amphitheatre at Hammamet and maintains a summer drama school for actors and students; Dir. NACEUR CHLIOUI.

PRINCIPAL THEATRES

Théâtre Municipal de Tunis: Tunis; has performed twice at the *Théâtre des Nations* festival, Paris; subsidized by the state.

Hammamet Theatre: Hammamet; open air theatre built 1963; organized by International Cultural Centre of Tunis.

CULTURAL FESTIVALS

Carthage Festival: Ministry of Cultural Affairs, Tunis; international festival of arts; held every year at the site of the ancient city and in Tunis; next Festival October, 1974.

Maghreb Theatre Festival: Monastir; f. 1964; open to theatrical groups from Algeria, Libya, Morocco and Tunisia.

ATOMIC ENERGY

Institut de Recherche Scientifique et Technique: Tunis-Carthage; f. 1969; attached institute of the University of Tunis; Dir. TAOUFIK BEN MENA.

EDUCATION

Tunisia is relatively well equipped from an educational point of view. Approximately 60 per cent of children of school age receive an education, and the proportion rises annually. In 1969–70 there were 912,646 children in primary grades, the great majority in state-run schools. At the secondary level, a wide range of schools and lycées gave instruction to 163,000 pupils.

Arabic only is used in the first two years of primary school, but in the higher grades French becomes progressively more important and is used almost entirely in higher education. About 10,000 Tunisians receive some higher education in the country, and a further 3,000 go abroad for University courses. The University of Tunis was opened in 1961-62, and incorporates as its Faculty of Theology the ancient Es Zitouna University of Islamic studies. The University has five Faculties and a number of attached Institutes. A permanent *cité universitaire* is under construction on a site near the Belvedere Park in Tunis.

UNIVERSITY

Université de Tunis: 94 Bvd. du 9 Avril 1938, Tunis; f. 1960; 681 teachers, 10,922 students.

BIBLIOGRAPHY

ANTHONY, JOHN. About Tunisia (London, 1961).

ARDANT, GAVRIEL. La Tunisie d'Aujourd'hui et Demain (Paris, 1961).

ASHFORD, DOUGLAS E. Morocco-Tunisia: Politics and Planning (Syracuse University Press, 1965).

BASSET, ANDRÉ. Initiation à la Tunisie (Paris, 1950).

BOURGUIBA, HABIB. La Tunisie et la France (Paris, 1954). Hadith al-Jamaa (*Collected Broadcasts*) (Tunis, 1957).

BRUNSCHVIG, ROBERT. La Tunisie au haut Moyen Age (Cairo, 1948).

CAMBON, HENRI. Histoire de la régence de Tunisie (Paris, 1948).

DE MONTETY, HENRI. Femmes de Tunisie (Paris, 1958).

DESPOIS, JEAN. La Tunisie, ses Régions (Paris, 1959).

DUVIGNAUD, JEAN. Tunisie (Editions Rencontre, Lausanne, 1965).

DUWAJI, GHAZI. Economic Development in Tunisia (Praeger, New York, 1967).

GARAS, FELIX. Bourguiba et la Naissance d'une Nation (Paris, 1956).

GERMANN, RAIMUND E. Verwaltung und Einheitspartei in Tunisien (Europa Verlag, Zürich, 1968).

GUEN, MONCEF. La Tunisie indépendente face à son économie (Paris, 1961).

KNAPP, W. Tunisia (Thames and Hudson, London, 1972).

LAITMAN, LEON. Tunisia Today: Crisis in North Africa (New York, 1954).

LING, DWIGHT D. Tunisia, from Protectorate to Republic (Indiana University Press, 1967).

MENSCHING, HORST. Tunisien eine geographische Landeskunde (Darmstadt, 1968).

MICAUD, C. A. Tunisia, the Politics of Moderation (New York, 1964).

MOORE, C. H. Tunisia since Independence (University of California Press, Berkeley, 1965).

PERROUX, F. and BARRE, R., Editors. Développement, croissance, progrès: Maroc-Tunisie (Paris, 1961).

RAYMOND, ANDRÉ. La Tunisie (Series *Que sais-je*, No. 318) (Paris, 1961).

ROMERIL, PAUL E. A. Tunisian nationalism: a bibliographical outline (*Middle East Journal* 1960, pages 206-215).

RUDEBECK, LARS. Party and People: A Study of Political Change in Tunisia (C. Hurst, London, 1969).

RUF, WERNER KLAUS, Der Burgismus und die Aussenpolitik der unabhängigen Tunesien (Freiburg, 1969).

SYLVESTER, ANTHONY. Tunisia (Bodley Head, London, 1969).

TLATLI, SALAH-EDDINE. Tunisie nouvelle (Tunis, 1957).

TUNISIA—SECRÉTARIAT D'ÉTAT À L'INFORMATION. Tunisia Works (La Tunisie au travail) (Tunis, 1960).

TUNISIA-SECRÉTARIAT D'ÉTAT AU PLAN ET À L'ECONOMIE NATIONALE. Plan Quadriennal 1965-68 (3 vols.) (Tunis, 1965). Perspectives Décennales de Développement 1962-71 (Tunis, 1962).

UNION TUNISIENNE DE L'INDUSTRIE ET DU COMMERCE. Annuaire économique de la Tunisie 1966/67 (Tunis, 1967).

ZIADEH, NICOLA A. The Origins of Tunisian Nationalism (Beirut, 1962.)

Turkey

PHYSICAL AND SOCIAL GEOGRAPHY

W. B. Fisher

Turkey is in a remarkable sense a passage land between Europe and Asia. Nearly one-half of her 1,630 miles of land frontier is with European States—Greece, Bulgaria, and Soviet Russia; and the remainder with Iran, Iraq, and Syria. The richest and most densely populated west of Turkey looks towards the Aegean and Mediterranean Seas and is very conscious of its links with Europe; whilst in culture, racial origins, and ways of life there are frequent reminders of Turkey's geographical situation primarily as a part of Asia.

Turkey consists essentially of the large peninsula of Asia Minor, which has strongly defined natural limits: sea on three sides (the Black Sea in the north, the Aegean in the west, and the Mediterranean on the south), and high mountain ranges on the fourth (eastern) side. The small region of European Turkey, containing the cities of Istanbul (Constantinople) and Edirne (Adrianople) is on the other hand defined by a purely artificial frontier, the exact position of which has varied considerably over the last century, according to the fluctuating fortunes and prestige of Turkey herself. Another small territory, the Hatay, centred on Iskenderun (Alexandretta) and lying as an enclave in Syrian territory, was acquired as a diplomatic bargain in 1939.

PHYSICAL FEATURES

The geological structure of Turkey is extremely complicated, and rocks of almost all ages occur, from the most ancient to most recent. Broadly speaking, we may say that Turkey consists of a number of old plateau blocks, against which masses of younger rock series have been squeezed to form fold mountain ranges of varying size. As there were several of these plateau blocks, and not just one, the fold mountains run in many different directions, with considerable irregularity, and hence no simple pattern can be discerned—instead, one mountain range gives place to another abruptly, and we can pass suddenly from highland to plain or plateau.

In general outline Turkey consists of a ring of mountains enclosing a series of inland plateaus, with the highest mountains on the east, close to the U.S.S.R. and Iran. Mount Ararat, overlooking the Soviet frontier, is the highest peak in Turkey, reaching 16,915 feet, and there are neighbouring peaks almost as large. In the west the average altitude of the hills is distinctly lower, though the highest peak (Mount Erciyas or Argaeus) is over 13,000 ft. The irregular topography of Turkey has given rise to many lakes, some salt, and some fresh, and generally more numerous than elsewhere in the Middle East. The largest, Lake Van, covers nearly 4,000 sq. kilometres (1,100 sq. miles).

Two other features may be mentioned. Large areas of the east, and some parts of the centre of Asia Minor have been covered in sheets of lava which are often of such recent occurrence that soil has not yet been formed—consequently wide expanses are sterile and uninhabited. Secondly, in the north and west cracking and disturbance of the rocks has taken place on an enormous scale. The long, indented coast of the Aegean Sea, with its numerous oddly shaped islands and estuaries, is due to cracking in two directions, which has split the land into detached blocks of roughly rectangular shape. Often the lower parts have sunk and been drowned by the sea. The Bosphorus and Dardanelles owe their origin to this faulting action, and the whole of the Black Sea coast is due to subsidence along a great series of fissures. Movement and adjustment along these cracks has by no means ceased, so that at the present day earthquakes are frequent in the north and west of Turkey, occasioning at times severe loss of life—most recently in the disaster of March 1970.

Because of the presence of mountain ranges close to the coast, and the great height of the interior plateaus (varying from 2,500 ft. to 7,000 ft.) Turkey has special climatic conditions, characterised by great extremes of temperature and rainfall, with wide variation from one district to another. In winter conditions are severe in most areas, except for those lying close to sea level. Temperatures of minus 20° to minus 40° F. can occur in the east, and snow lies there for as many as 120 days each year. The west has frost on most nights of December and January, and (again apart from the coastal zone), has an average winter temperature below that of the British Isles. In summer, however, temperatures over most of Turkey exceed 85° or 90° F., with 110° F. in the south-east. There can hence be enormous seasonal variation of temperature—sometimes over 100° F., probably the widest in the world.

Rainfall too is remarkably variable. Along the eastern Black Sea coast, towards the Soviet frontier, over 100 inches fall annually (as much as in the wettest parts of the English Lake District, or the Western Isles of Scotland); but elsewhere, amounts are very much smaller. Parts of the central plateau, being shut off by mountains from the influence of sea winds, are arid, with annual totals of under 10 inches, and expanses of salt steppe and desert are frequent. Like Iran, Turkey also has a "dead heart", and the main towns of Anatolia, including Ankara, the capital, are placed away from the centre and close to hills, where rainfall tends to be greater.

It is necessary to emphasize the contrast that exists between the Aegean coastlands, which climatically are by far the most favoured regions of Turkey, and the rest of the country. Round the Aegean, winters are mild and fairly rainy, and the summers hot, but tempered by a persistent northerly wind, the Meltemi, or Etesian wind, which is of great value in ripening fruit, especially figs and sultana grapes.

ECONOMIC LIFE

The variety of geographical conditions within Turkey has led to uneven development, and this unevenness has been intensified by poor communications, due to the broken nature of the topography. Roads are relatively few, railways slow and often roundabout, and whole districts—sometimes even considerable towns—are accessible only by bridle track. Many rivers flow in deep gorges near their sources and either meander or are broken by cascades in their lower reaches, so that none are navigable.

Thus we find that the west of Turkey, situated close to the Aegean Sea, is by far the most densely peopled and the most intensively developed. Since 1923, however, attempts have been made to develop the Anatolian plateau and the districts in the extreme east, which, following the expulsion and massacre of the Armenians in 1914-18, for a time supported only a very scanty population. Development in the central plateau has been aided by the exploitation of several small but on the whole valuable mineral deposits, and by irrigation schemes to improve agriculture. A certain degree of industrialisation (mainly undertaken by state-sponsored and owned organisations) has also grown up, based on Turkish-produced raw materials—cotton, wool, mohair, beet-sugar, olive-oil, and tobacco. The eastern districts present a more intractable problem, and development so far has been slower.

Of recent years, the considerable annual increase of population, now of 3%—one of the highest in the world—has led to intensification of settlement and the bringing in of all available land for cultivation. Henceforth a principal problem for Turkey must be to improve yields from agriculture and industry. Because of the strategic importance of the country, there has been a considerable programme of road-building, largely financed by the U.S.A. and CENTO.

RACE AND LANGUAGE

Racially, the bulk of the Turkish people show an intermixture of Mediterranean and Armenoid strains. In the western half of the country Mediterraneans and Armenoids are more or less equally represented; but further east the proportion of Armenoids steadily increases, until towards the Soviet and Iranian borders, they become almost universal. We can in addition note less important racial elements: there would seem to be small numbers of proto-Nordics in the north and west, and some authorities suggest a racial relationship between Galatia (the modern district of Ankara) and ancient Gaul. The Ottoman Turks were in the main of Turki (western Mongoloid) ancestry, but in the view of some authorities their contribution to the ethnic stocks of Turkey would seem to have been small, since they were really an invading tribal group that became an aristocracy and soon intermarried with other peoples. There are also numbers of Caucasians—particularly Circassians and Georgians—who have contributed to the racial structure of Turkey; and during 1951 a further element was added by the arrival of many thousands of Bulgarian Muslims who had been deported from their own country.

The Turkish language, which is of central Asiatic origin, is spoken over most, but by no means all of the country. This was introduced into Turkey in Seljuq times, and was written in Arabic characters, but as these are not really well adapted to the sound of Turkish, Roman (i.e. European) script has been compulsory since 1928. As well, there are a number of non-Turkish languages. Kurdish has a wide extension in the south-east, along the Syrian and Iraqi frontiers; and Caucasian dialects, quite different from either Turkish or Kurdish, occur in the north-east. Greek and Armenian were once widespread, but following the deportations of the last forty years both forms of speech are now current only in the city of Istanbul, where considerable numbers of Greeks and Armenians still live.

HISTORY

ANCIENT HISTORY

The most ancient written records so far found in Asia Minor date from the beginning of the second millennium B.C. They are in Assyrian, and reveal the existence of Assyrian trading colonies in Cappadocia. These documents, together with a growing amount of archaeological evidence, show an important Copper Age culture in Central Anatolia in the third and early second millennia. Later in the second millennium the greater part of Asia Minor fell under the rule of the Hittites. This people has long been known from references in the Old Testament and other ancient texts, but its full importance was first revealed by the excavations at Boğazköy, the site of the ancient Hittite capital of Hattushash. The Hittite Empire flourished from about 1600 to about 1200 B.C., and reached its apogee in the fourteenth and thirteenth centuries, when it became one of the dominant States of the Middle East. One of the sources of Hittite strength was iron, which was first worked in Anatolia. The production of iron was for long a monopoly of the Hittite kings, but the use of iron implements eventually spread to other parts, and revolutionised agriculture, industry and war.

After the break-up of the Hittite Empire, Asia Minor was split up among a number of dynasties and peoples—Phrygians, Cimmerians, Lydians and others—about whom not very much is known. Towards the end of the Hittite period the Greeks began to invade the Aegean coast, and entered on a long struggle with the native states that is reflected in the story of the Trojan war. Greek culture spread in western Anatolia, which was gradually incorporated into the Hellenic world. A series of political changes, of which the most important are the Persian conquest in 546, the conquest of Alexander in 334, and the constitution of the Roman province of Asia in 133 B.C., did not impede the steady spread of Greek language and culture in the cities.

In A.D. 330, the Emperor Constantine inaugurated the new city of Constantinople, on the site of the old Greek trading settlement of Byzantium. This city at once became the capital of the East Roman and then of the Christian Byzantine Empire. Asia Minor was now the metropolitan province of a great Empire, and grew in wealth, prosperity and importance. Under Byzantine rule Greek Christianity, already firmly established in Roman times, spread over most of the peninsula.

SELJUQS AND OTTOMANS

At the beginning of the eleventh century a new conquest of Anatolia began—that of the Turks. The early history of the Turkish peoples is still obscure. Some references in the ancient biography of Alexander show them to have been established in Central Asia at the time of his conquests, and Turkish tribal confederacies played an important part in the invasions of Europe from late Roman times onwards. The name "Turk" first appears in historical records in the sixth century A.D., when Chinese annals speak of a powerful empire in Central Asia, founded by a steppe people called Tu-Kiu. It is from this state that the oldest surviving Turkish inscriptions have come. From the seventh century onwards the Central Asian Turks came into ever closer contact with the Islamic peoples of the Near East, from whom they adopted the Islamic faith and the Arabic script, and with them much of the complex civilisation of Islam. From the ninth century Turks entered the service of the Caliphate in increasing numbers, and soon came to provide the bulk of its armies, its generals, and eventually its rulers.

From the tenth century whole tribes of Turks began to migrate into Persia and Iraq, and in the eleventh, under the leadership of the family of Seljuq, the Turks were able to set up a great empire comprising most of the eastern lands of the Caliphate. The Muslim armies on the Byzantine frontier had long been predominantly Turkish, and in the course of the eleventh century they began a great movement into Anatolia which resulted in the termination of Byzantine rule in most of the country and its incorporation in the Muslim Seljuq Sultanate. A Seljuq prince, Suleyman ibn Kutlumush, was sent to organise the new province, and by the end of the twelfth century his successors had built up a strong Turkish monarchy in Anatolia, with its capital in Konya (the ancient Iconium). Under the rule of the Anatolian Seljuqs, which in various forms lasted until the fourteenth century, Anatolia gradually became a Turkish land. Masses of Turkish immigrants from further east entered the country, and a Turkish, Muslim civilisation replaced Greek Christianity.

In the late thirteenth century the Sultanate of Konya fell into decay, and gradually gave way to a number of smaller principalities. One of these, in north-western Anatolia, was ruled by a certain Osman, or Othman, from whom the name Ottoman is derived. The Ottoman State soon embarked on a great movement of expansion, on the one hand in Anatolia, at the expense of its Turkish neighbours, on the other in the Balkans. Ottoman armies first crossed to Europe in the mid-fourteenth century, and by 1400 they were masters of much of the Balkan peninsula as well as of almost all Anatolia. The capital was moved first from Bursa to Edirne and then, in 1453, to Constantinople, the final conquest of which from the last Byzantine Emperor completed the process that had transformed a principality of frontier-warriors into a new great empire. Constantinople, called Istanbul by the Turks, remained the capital of the Ottoman Empire until 1922. The wave of conquest was by no means spent. For more than a century Ottoman arms continued to advance into Central Europe, while in 1516–17 Sultan Selim I destroyed the Mamluk Sultanate and incorporated Syria and Egypt into the Empire. During the reign of Sultan Suleyman I (1520–66), called the Magnificent in Europe, the Ottoman Empire was at the height of its power. In three continents the Sultan held unchallenged sway over vast territories. A skilled and highly-organised bureaucracy secured for the peoples of the Empire peace, justice and prosperity; literature, scholarship and the arts flourished; and the Ottoman armies and fleets seemed to threaten the very existence of Western Christendom.

The decay of the Empire is usually dated from after the death of Suleyman. In the West great changes were taking place. The Renaissance and the Reformation, the rapid development of science and technology, the emergence of strong, centralised nation states with constantly improving military techniques, the deflection of the main routes of international trade from the Mediterranean to the open seas, all combined to strengthen Turkey's Western adversaries while leaving her own resources unchanged or even diminished, and helped to relegate her into a backwater of cultural and economic stagnation. An imposing military façade for a while masked the internal decay that was rotting the once all-powerful Empire, but by the end of the seventeenth century the weakness of the Ottoman State was manifest. Then began the struggle of the Powers for pickings of Turkish territory and for positions of influence in the Empire. During the eighteenth century it was Austria and Russia that made the main territorial advances in the Balkans and in the Black Sea area, while England and France were content with commercial and diplomatic privileges. In a succession of wars one province after another was lost, while internal conditions went from bad to worse. During the nineteenth century England and France began to play a more active role. British policy was generally to support the Turks against their impatient heirs. In 1854 Britain and France went to war at the side of Turkey in order to check Russian aggression, and in 1877–78 British diplomatic intervention was effective to the same end. Meanwhile the ferment of nationalist ideas had spread from the West to the subject peoples of the Empire, and one by one the Serbs, Greeks, Romanians and Bulgarians succeeded in throwing off Ottoman rule and attaining independent statehood.

More significant for Turkish history were the first stirrings of a new spirit among the Turks themselves. The first serious attempts at reform were made during the reign of Selim III (1789–1807), and during the nineteenth century a series of reforming sultans and ministers worked on a programme of reform and modernisation which, though it fell short of its avowed objectives, nevertheless transformed the face of the Ottoman Empire and began a process of change, the effects of which are still visible. In 1878 the reforming movement came to an abrupt end, and from that year until 1908 the Empire was subjected to the iron despotism of Abdul-Hamid II, who ruthlessly repressed every attempt at liberal thought and reform. In 1908 the secret opposition group known as the Young Turks seized power, and in a wave of revolutionary enthusiasm inaugurated a constitution, parliamentary government, and a whole series of liberal reforms. Unfortunately the Young Turks had little opportunity to follow up their promising start. First internal dissension, then foreign wars, combined to turn the Young Turk regime into a military dictatorship. In 1911 the Italians suddenly started a war against Turkey which ended with their gaining Libya and the Dodecanese Islands; in 1912–13 a Balkan alliance succeeded in wresting from the dying Empire most of its remaining possessions on the continent of Europe. Finally, in October 1914, Turkey entered the war on the side of the Central Powers. During the reign of Abdul-Hamid German influence had been steadily increasing in Turkey, and the process continued under the Young Turks. It was certainly helped by the growing friendship between the Western Powers and Russia, which threw the Turks into the arms of the only power that seemed ready to support them against Russian designs. German officers reorganised the Turkish Army. German business-men and technicians extended their hold on the economic resources of the country, and German engineers and financiers began the construction of the famous Baghdad railway which was to provide direct rail communication between Germany and the Middle East.

The Turkish alliance was of immense military value to the Central Powers. The Turkish armies, still established in Syria and Palestine, were able to offer an immediate and serious threat to the Suez Canal and to the British position in Egypt. By their dogged and successful defence of the Dardanelles they prevented effective co-operation between Russia and the Western Powers. Their Balkan position assured the supremacy of the Central Powers in that important area. Their position as the greatest independent Muslim State and their prestige among Muslims elsewhere created a series of problems in the British and French Empires.

Despite their weakness and exhaustion after two previous wars, the Turks were able to wage a bitter defensive war against the Allies. At last, after two unsuccessful attempts, one on the Dardanelles and the other in Mesopotamia, a new British attack from Egypt and from India succeeded in expelling the Turks from Palestine, Syria, and most of Iraq. Defeated on all sides, cut off from their allies by the Salonica Expedition, the Turks decided to abandon the struggle, and signed an armistice at Mudros on October 30th, 1918. The outlook for Turkey seemed black. Allied forces controlled Istanbul and the Straits— British forces were in control of the Arab countries, and in 1919 French, Italian and British forces occupied strategic positions in parts of Anatolia itself. In the capital the Young Turk leaders had fled, and a new Government was formed, subservient to the will of the occupying Powers.

For some time the victorious Powers were too busy elsewhere to attend to the affairs of Turkey, and it was not until the San Remo Conference of April 1920 that the first serious attempt was made to settle the Turkish question. Meanwhile the victors were busy quarrelling among themselves. Partly, no doubt, with the idea of forestalling Italian ambitions, the British, French, and American Governments agreed to a Greek proposal for a Greek occupation of Izmir and the surrounding country, and on May 15th, 919, a Greek Army, under cover of allied warships, landed at Izmir. Second thoughts on the wisdom of this step appeared in the allied camp, and in October 1919 the Inter-Allied Commission in Istanbul condemned it as "unjustifiable" and as "a violation of the terms of the Armistice". The consequences of the invasion for Turkey were momentous. Now it was no longer the non-Turkish subject provinces and the Ottoman superstructure of the Turkish nation that were threatened, but the Turkish homeland itself. Moreover, the Greeks, unlike the Western Allies, showed that they intended to stay, and that they were aiming at nothing less than the incorporation of the territories they occupied into the Greek kingdom. The Turkish reaction to this danger was vigorous and immediate. The Nationalist movement, hitherto limited to a small class of intellectuals, became the mass instrument of Turkish determination to preserve the integrity and independence of the homeland. A new leader appeared to organise their victory.

THE RISE OF ATATÜRK

Mustafa Kemal, later surnamed Atatürk, was born in Salonica, then an Ottoman city, in 1880. After a promising career as a regular army officer, he achieved his first active command in Libya in 1911, and thereafter fought with distinction in the successive wars in which his country was involved. After his brilliant conduct of the defence of Gallipoli, he fought on various fronts against the Allies, and at the time of the Armistice held a command on the Syrian front. A month later he returned to Istanbul, and at once began to seek ways and means of getting to Anatolia to organise national resistance. At length he was successful, and on May 19th, 1919—four days after the Greek landing in Izmir—he arrived at Samsun, on the Black Sea coast, ostensibly in order to supervise the disbanding of the remaining Turkish forces. Instead he set to work at once on the double task of organising a national movement and raising a national army.

Meanwhile the Allied Powers were at last completing their arrangements for the obsequies of the Sick Man of Europe. After a series of conferences, a treaty was drawn up and signed by the Allied representatives and those of the Sultan's Government at Sèvres, on August 10th, 1920. The Treaty of Sèvres was very harsh—far harsher than that imposed on Germany. The Arab provinces were to be placed under British and French Mandates, to prepare them for eventual independence. In Anatolia, Armenian and Kurdish States were to be set up in the east, the south was to be divided between France and Italy, and a truncated Turkish Sultanate confined to the interior. The Straits were to be demilitarised and placed under Allied administration, with a Turkish Istanbul surrounded by Allied forces. The rest of European Turkey was to be ceded to Greece, while the Izmir district was to be under "Ottoman sovereignty and Greek administration".

This treaty was, however, never implemented. While the Allies were imposing their terms on the Sultan and his government in Istanbul, a new Turkish State was rising in the interior of Anatolia, based on the rejection of the treaty and the principles on which it was founded. On July 23rd, 1919, Mustafa Kemal and his associates convened the first Nationalist Congress in Erzurum, and drew up a national programme. A second Congress was held in September in the same year, and attended by delegates from all over the country. An executive committee, presided over by Mustafa Kemal, was formed, and chose Ankara, then a minor provincial town, as its headquarters. Frequent meetings were held in Ankara, which soon became the effective capital of the Nationalist movement and forces. It was there that they issued the famous National Pact, the declaration that laid down the basic programme of the Kemalist movement, renouncing the Empire and the domination of the non-Turkish provinces, but demanding the total and unconditional independence of all areas inhabited by Turks. This declaration won immediate support, and on January 28th, 1920, was approved even by the legal Ottoman Parliament sitting in Istanbul. The growth of the Nationalist movement in Istanbul alarmed the Allies, and on March 16th British forces entered the Turkish part of the city and arrested and deported many Nationalist leaders. Despite this setback, followed by a new anti-Nationalist campaign on the part of the Sultan and his political and religious advisers, the Kemalists continued to advance. On March 19th, 1920, Mustafa Kemal ordered general elections, and at the end of April a National Assembly of 350 deputies met in Ankara and voted the National Pact. The Sultan and his government were declared deposed, a provisional Constitution promulgated, and a government set up with Mustafa Kemal as President.

There remained the military task of expelling the invaders. The Greco-Turkish war falls into three stages, covering roughly the campaigns of 1920, 1921 and 1922. In the first the Nationalists, hopelessly outmatched in numbers and material, were badly defeated, and the Greeks advanced far into Anatolia. Turkish resistance was, however, strong enough to impress the Allies, who, for the first time, accorded a certain limited recognition to the Nationalist Government and proclaimed their neutrality in the Greco-Turkish war. The second campaign began with Greek successes, but the Turks rallied and defeated the invaders first at İnönü—from which İsmet Pasha, who commanded the Turkish forces there, later took his surname—and then, on August 24th, 1921, in a major battle on the Sakarya River, where the Turkish forces were under the personal command of Mustafa Kemal. This victory considerably strengthened the Nationalists, who were now generally realised to be the effective Government of Turkey. The French and Italians withdrew from the areas of Anatolia assigned to them, and made terms with the new Government. The Soviets, now established on Turkey's eastern frontier, had already done so at the beginning of the year.

A period of waiting and reorganization followed, during which the morale of the Greek armies was adversely affected by political changes in Greece. In August 1922 the third and final phase of the war of independence began. The Turkish Army drove the Greeks back to the Aegean, and on September 9th reoccupied Izmir. Mustafa Kemal now prepared to cross to Thrace. To do so he had to cross the Straits, still under Allied occupation. The French and Italian contingents withdrew, and, after a menacing pause, the British followed. On October 11th an armistice was signed at Mudanya, whereby the Allied Governments agreed to the restoration of Turkish sovereignty in Eastern Thrace. In November the Sultan's Cabinet resigned, and the Sultan himself went into exile. Turkey once more had only one government, and Istanbul, the ancient seat of Empire, became a provincial city, ruled by a governor appointed from Ankara.

The peace conference opened in November 1922. After many months of argument the treaty was finally signed on July 24th, 1923. It recognised complete and undivided

TURKEY—(HISTORY)

Turkish sovereignty and the abolition of the last vestiges of foreign privilege. The only reservation related to the demilitarisation of the Straits, which were not to be fortified without the consent of the Powers. This consent was given at the Montreux Conference in 1936.

THE TURKISH REPUBLIC

The military task was completed, and the demands formulated in the National Pact had been embodied in an international treaty. There remained the greater task of rebuilding the ruins of long years of war and revolution—and of remedying those elements of weakness in the Turkish State and society that had brought Turkey to the verge of extinction. Mustafa Kemal saw the solution of Turkey's problems in a process of Westernisation—in the integration of Turkey, on a basis of equality, in the modern Western world. To do this it was not sufficient to borrow, as other reformers had done, the outward forms and trappings of Western civilisation. It was necessary to change the very basis of society in Turkey, and to suppress, ruthlessly if need be, the opposition that was bound to come from the entrenched forces of the old order. Between 1922 and 1938, the year of his death, Kemal carried through a series of far-reaching reforms in Turkey. These may be considered under various headings.

The first changes were political. After the deposition of Sultan Vahdeddin in November 1922, a brief experiment was made with a purely religious sovereignty, and Abdul-Mejid was proclaimed as Caliph but not Sultan. The experiment was not successful. Abdul-Mejid followed his predecessor into exile, and on October 29th, 1923, Turkey was declared a Republic, with Kemal as President. The regime of Kemal Atatürk was effectively a dictatorship—though without the violence and oppression normally associated with that word in Europe. A single party—the Republican People's Party—formed the main instrument for the enforcement of Government policy. The Constitution of April 20th, 1924, provided for an elected Parliament which was the repository of sovereign power. Executive power was to be exercised by the President and a Cabinet chosen by him.

The next object of attack was the religious hierarchy, already weakened by the removal of the Sultan-Caliph. In a series of edicts the Ministry of Religious Affairs was abolished, the religious orders disbanded, religious property sequestrated, religious instruction forbidden. With the religious leaders in retreat, the attack on the old social order began. Certainly the most striking reforms were the abolition of the fez and the Arabic alphabet, and their replacement by the hat and the Latin alphabet. But these were probably less important in the long run than the abrogation of the old legal system and the introduction of new civil and criminal codes of law adapted from Europe. In 1928 Islam itself was disestablished, and the Constitution amended to make Turkey a secular State.

Not the least of the problems that faced Mustafa Kemal was the economic one. Turkey is naturally a very rich country, but her resources were for the most part undeveloped, and what development there was had been in foreign hands. To restore the devastation of war, replace the departed foreign investors, and raise the low standard of living of the country, much capital was needed. Rather than risk the independence of Turkey by inviting foreign capital in a time of weakness, Kemal adopted the principle of *Étatisme*, and made it one of the cardinal doctrines of his regime. From 1923 to 1933 the State made its main effort in railway construction, nearly doubling the length of line in that period. At the same time a start was made in establishing other industries. The major effort of industrialization began in 1934, with the adoption of the first five-year plan—completed in 1939. While often wasteful and inefficient, State-sponsored industry was probably the only form of development possible at the time without recourse to foreign aid. The progress achieved stood Turkey in good stead in the critical years that were to follow.

The foreign policy of the Republic was for long one of strict non-involvement in foreign disputes and the maintenance of friendly relations with as many Powers as possible. In 1935-36, however, Turkey co-operated loyally in sanctions against Italy, and thereafter the growing threat of German, and more especially Italian, aggression led to closer links with the West. In 1938 steps were taken to strengthen economic links between Turkey and Britain. A British credit of £16 million was granted to Turkey, and a number of contracts given to British firms by Turkey.

The death of Kemal Atatürk in November 1938 was a great shock to Turkey. Perhaps the best testimony to the solidity of his achievement is that his régime was able to survive that shock, and the stresses and strains of the war that followed shortly after.

He was succeeded as President by İsmet İnönü, who announced his intention of maintaining and carrying on the work of his predecessor. The new President was soon called upon the guide his country through a very difficult time. As early as May 12th, 1939, a joint Anglo-Turkish declaration was issued, stating that "the British and Turkish Governments, in the event of an act of aggression leading to war in the Mediterranean area, would co-operate effectively and lend each other all the aid and assistance in their power". This prepared the way for the formal Anglo-French-Turkish Treaty of Alliance signed October 19th, 1939. It had been hoped that this Treaty would be complemented by a parallel treaty with the U.S.S.R., but the equivocal attitude of the Soviet Government, followed by the Stalin-Hitler Agreement of August 1939, made this impossible, and the Turks proceeded with the Western alliance in the face of clearly expressed Soviet disapproval. They protected themselves, however, by Protocol II of the Treaty, stipulating that nothing in the Treaty should bind them to any action likely to involve them in war with the U.S.S.R.

TURKEY DURING THE SECOND WORLD WAR

The fall of France, the hostile attitude of the Soviet Government, and the extension of German power over most of Europe, led the Turkish Government to the conclusion that nothing would be gained by provoking an almost certain German conquest. While continuing to recognize the Alliance, therefore, they invoked Protocol II as a reason for remaining neutral, and in June 1941, when German expansion in the Balkans had brought the German armies within 100 miles of Istanbul, the Turks further protected themselves by signing a friendship and trade agreement with Germany, in which, however, they stipulated that Turkey would maintain her treaty obligations to Britain.

The German attack on the U.S.S.R., and the consequent entry of that country into the Grand Alliance, brought an important change to the situation, and the Western Powers increased their pressure on Turkey to enter the war. On December 3rd, 1941, President Roosevelt extended lease-lend aid to Turkey; in February 1943, Mr. Churchill visited Turkey and met Turkish statesmen at Adana; in December 1943, President İnönü went to Cairo to meet the British and American leaders. The main consideration holding Turkey back from active participation in the war was mistrust of Russia, and the widespread feeling that Nazi conquest and Soviet "liberation" were equally to be feared. Turkish statesmen foresaw the fate of the East European countries occupied by the Red Army, and evinced no desire to share it. While stopping short of actual belligerency, however, the Turks, especially after 1942, entered into closer economic and military relations with the West and aided the Allied cause in a number of ways. In August 1944 they broke off diplomatic relations with Germany, and on February 23rd, 1945, declared war on Germany in order to comply with the formalities of entry to the United Nations Conference in San Francisco.

The war years subjected Turkey to severe economic strains. These, and the dangers of armed neutrality in a world at war, resulted in the imposition of martial law, of closer police surveillance, and of a generally more authoritarian form of government. An unfortunate impression was made by the discrimination practised against foreigners and non-Muslim citizens in the assessment and collection of the Capital Levy imposed in 1942 to meet the growing financial strain. This measure, which occasioned much criticism both in Turkey and abroad, was quietly abandoned in 1943. And then, between 1945 and 1950, came a further series of changes, no less remarkable than the great reforms of Atatürk. When the Charter of the United Nations came up for ratification in the Turkish Parliament in 1945, a group of members, led by Celâl Bayar, Adnan Menderes, Fuad Köprülü and Refik Koraltan, tabled a motion suggesting a series of reforms in the law and the Constitution which would effectively ensure inside Turkey those liberties to which the Turkish Government was giving its theoretical approval in the Charter. The motion was rejected by the Government, and its sponsors forced to leave the party. In November 1945, however, under pressure of a by now active and informed public opinion, President İnönü announced the end of the single-party system, and in January 1946 the opposition leaders registered the new Democratic Party. Numerous other parties followed, including the National Party (formed July 1948 and reconstituted as the Republic National Party in 1954).

TURKEY UNDER THE DEMOCRATIC PARTY

In July 1946 new elections gave the Democrat opposition 70 out of 416 seats, and there can be little doubt that completely free elections would have given them many more. During the years that followed, the breach in the dictatorship grew ever wider, and a series of changes in both law and practice ensured the growth of democratic liberties. Freedom of the Press and of association were extended, martial law ended, and, on February 15th, 1950, a new electoral law was approved, guaranteeing free and fair elections. In May 1950 a new general election was held, in which the Democrats won an overwhelming victory. Celâl Bayar became President, and a new Cabinet was formed, with Adnan Menderes as Prime Minister and Fuad Köprülü as Foreign Minister. The new régime adopted a more liberal economic policy, involving the partial abandonment of Étatisme and the encouragement of private enterprise, both Turkish and foreign. For a while, the stability and progress of the republic seemed to be threatened by the growing activities of groups of religious fanatics, whose programme appeared to require little less than the abrogation of all the reforms achieved by the Turkish revolution. After the attempt on the life of the liberal journalist Ahmet Emin Yalman in November 1952, the government took more vigorous action against what were called the "forces of clericalism and reaction". Many arrests were made, and in the summer of 1953 the National Party, accused of complicity in reactionary plots, was for a time outlawed and legislation was passed prohibiting the exploitation of religion for political purposes. The relations between the two main parties, after a temporary improvement in the face of the common danger of reaction, deteriorated again in the course of 1953-54, though not to such an extent as to imperil national unity. On May 2nd, 1954, in Turkey's third general election since the war, the Democrats won a resounding victory. Over 80 per cent of the electorate voted, and close on 65 per cent of the votes cast went to the Democratic Party. Owing to the cumulative effect of the electoral system, this gave them 504 out of a total of 541 seats in the new Assembly, as against 407 out of 487 in the previous Assembly. Of the remainder, 28 seats went to the Republican People's Party, 5 to the reconstituted Republican National Party, and 2 to Independents.

Encouraged by this overwhelming reaffirmation of popular support, the Government proceeded to adopt a number of measures which were criticised by the opposition as undemocratic. These included new civil service laws giving the Government greatly increased powers of dismissal and compulsory retirement, and an electoral reform restricted coalition candidatures. These laws, following on the new Press law of March 7th, 1954, embittered relations between Government and opposition. A number of prosecutions of opposition journalists followed, and in September the well-known journalist Hüseyin Cahit Yalçin was fined and condemned to imprisonment. This case aroused widespread indignation both at home and abroad, and despite official insistence that Yalçin had been tried and condemned by due process of law, he was amnestied by the President. Charges against some other opposition journalists were also dropped. Some Republican People's Party leaders, notably Nihat Erim, responded to this more conciliatory attitude of the Government, and on April 17th there was a meeting and an exchange of views between the Prime Minister and the Republican leader İsmet İnönü. Others, however, found the concessions of the Government inadequate, and by the summer, relations between Government and opposition had again been strained by new Press prosecutions. The opposition parties, however, remained active. On June 10th, 1955 the Republican Party organ *Ulus*, which had ceased publication in December 1953, reappeared under the editorship of Hüseyin Cahit Yalçin, and in the same month the National Party held a party congress in Ankara. both opposition parties decided to boycott the provincial council and municipal elections (September and November 1955 respectively), in which therefore the Democrats were opposed only by the very small Peasant Party and by Independents. These were able to score some successes.

In view of the smallness and weakness of the opposition parties, and the immense parliamentary majority of the Democratic Party, it was inevitable that sooner or later splits would appear within it. In October 1955 a serious crisis culminated in the dismissal or resignation from the party of nineteen deputies. These were later joined by some others and formed a new party, the Freedom Party.

Meanwhile, in September 1955, anti-Greek outbreaks occurred in Istanbul and Izmir. Turco-Greek relations had been growing steadily worse because of the Cyprus question, and the riots appeared to have been touched off by a report, later proved false, that Atatürk's house in Salonica had been blown up by a bomb. The riots, which affected other non-Turkish and non-Muslim elements besides the Greeks, did immense damage to property, though injury to persons was very limited. Martial law was at once proclaimed in Istanbul, Izmir and Ankara, several senior officers and officials relieved of their duties, and several cabinet changes made. A new Cabinet, the fourth since the Democrat victory in 1950, was presented to the assembly on December 9th.

These events, and the growing economic difficulties of the country, brought new political tensions, and in the summer of 1956 new amendments to the Press law (June 7th), the law for the protection of the national economy

(June 6th) and the law of public assembly (June 27th) again aroused bitter opposition criticism.

Conflict between the Government and Opposition was sharpened by the decision taken to advance the date of the general elections by more than eight months, to October 27th, 1957. The three Opposition parties—Republicans, Freedom and National Parties—first intended to present a united front, but the electoral law was changed to make this impossible. They were therefore obliged to present separate lists in each constituency, and so, although the combined votes won by Opposition candidates were slightly more than 50 per cent of the total, the Democrats again emerged triumphant, though with a diminished majority. In an enlarged Assembly of 610 seats, the Democrats held 424, the Republicans 178, and the National and Freedom Parties 4 each.

Mr. Menderes announced the new Cabinet—his fifth—on November 26th. It contained two new Ministries, Press and Tourism, and Reconstruction and Town Planning. One of the most significant changes was the appointment of Mr. Fatin Zorlu as Foreign Minister in place of Mr. Ethem Menderes. In September 1958, the resignation of two Ministers led to an extensive reshuffle of the Cabinet.

In the new Assembly the themes of debate continued to centre on the economic condition of the country and what the Opposition considered inroads on liberty. A Bill was passed in December 1957 amending the rules of the Assembly, and laying down a new scale of penalties for their infraction. At the same time a proposal to channel all newspaper advertisements through a single organisation was interpreted as another device for ensuring Government control over the Press. The editors of the political weekly *Akis*, the managing editor and a writer on the staff of *Ulus*, and the managing editor of *Zafer* (a Government paper), were among journalists who suffered imprisonment.

At the end of 1959 the law claimed a victim well known abroad—Mr. Ahmet Yalman, the 71-year old editor of *Vatan*. His offence—shared with other editors—was to have reprinted an article strongly critical of the Government which had appeared in an American newspaper. Mr. Yalman was in Pakistan when sentence was passed on him, and on his return duly went to jail, whence he and other journalists emerged after the *coup d'état* of May, 1960. There is no doubt that its running fight with the Press contributed much to the downfall of the Menderes regime. The new régime, while not immediately sweeping away the old bans, encouraged newspaper owners and editors to draw up a "code of self-control" which was worked out with the assistance of the International Press Institute.

FOREIGN AFFAIRS 1945-60

In foreign affairs, both the People's Party and the Democrat Governments followed a firm policy of unreserved identification with the West in the cold war. Since May 1947 the United States has extended economic and military aid to Turkey on an increasing scale, and in 1950 a first indication of both the seriousness and the effectiveness of Turkish policy was given with the despatch of Turkish troops to Korea, where they fought with distinction. In August 1949 Turkey became a member of the Council of Europe, and early in 1952 acceded to full membership of the North Atlantic Treaty Organisation, in which she began to play an increasingly important part. Thereafter other arrangements were made by which Turkey accepted a role in both Balkan and Middle Eastern defence. On February 28th, 1953 a treaty of friendship and collaboration was signed in Ankara with Greece and Yugoslavia, which prepared the way for a subsequent alliance, and on April 2nd, 1954 a mutual aid pact was signed in Karachi between Turkey and Pakistan, with the blessing of the United States.

Despite her economic problems and her failure to secure the 300 million U.S. dollar loan which she had requested from the United States, Turkey resisted the temptation to follow the example of some other states and play the great powers off against one another. In spite of efforts from both north and south to detach her, Turkey remained faithful to the northern tier alliance, and on November 21st–22nd, 1955, the Turkish Prime Minister attended the inaugural meeting of the council of the Baghdad Pact, in which Turkey thereafter played a major role.

During the Sinai-Suez crisis of November 1956 the representatives of the Turkish Government, meeting with those of the other three Muslim members of the Baghdad Pact (Iraq, Iran and Pakistan), welcomed the withdrawal of the Anglo-French forces from Egypt. In December the Turkish Foreign Minister declared that the Pact had done much to limit and circumscribe the threat to peace in the Middle East. The President of the United States announced in January 1957 a new programme of economic and military assistance for those countries of the area which were willing to accept it. At a further meeting held in Ankara the Muslim states belonging to the Baghdad Pact expressed their approval of this "Eisenhower Doctrine". The United States, in March 1957, made known its decision to join the military committee of the Baghdad Pact. Mr. Richards, special adviser to the President of the United States, carried out a tour of the Middle East in March/April 1957 in order to explain the new doctrine and to distribute the funds assigned to its fulfilment. At the close of his visit to Ankara in March a joint communiqué was issued to the effect that Turkey would co-operate with the United States against all subversive activities in the Middle East and that financial aid would be forthcoming from Washington for the economic projects previously discussed between the members of the Baghdad Pact. On October 18th, 1958, an agreement was signed by the Turkish and Iranian governments for the construction of a 1,000-mile pipe-line from the Iranian oilfields to the Turkish Mediterranean seaboard.

At the time of the Jordan crisis in April 1957 there was a period of tension when Turkish troops were held in readiness for action near the frontier with Syria. The outbreak of civil war in Lebanon in May 1958, and, still more, the *coup d'état* in Iraq of July 14th, gave Turkey fresh cause for anxiety. The events in Iraq took place on the eve of a meeting in Istanbul of Moslem members of the Baghdad Pact, but had the immediate consequence of withdrawing Iraq, in practice if not in name, from membership of the Pact. The staff of the Pact Council, secretariat and military planning organization were subsequently transferred to Ankara. Iraq withdrew formally from the Pact on March 24th, 1959. The Pact had, however, been strengthened a few weeks before by new defence agreements between Turkey, Iran, Pakistan and the United States of America signed on March 5th.

Fidelity to NATO and CENTO remained the basis of Turkey's foreign policy through the next two years. By the beginning of 1960, Turkey, following the examples of some of her allies, decided that such a policy need not be incompatible with less frigid relations towards Russia, and in April a visit to Moscow by Mr. Menderes was announced for July. Before it could take place the Menderes régime was overthrown, but his successors continued a more flexible policy. Soon after the revolution a cordial letter from Mr. Khrushchev to Gen. Gürsel received a cordial reply, in which, however, Turkey's need for active allies was once more emphasised.

TURKEY—(HISTORY)

THE CYPRUS QUESTION

Early in 1957 Great Britain had decided to release Archbishop Makarios from detention in the Seychelles islands. The leaders of the Turkish community in Cyprus visited Ankara in April. Their view was that, ultimately, partition alone would provide an adequate solution for the Cyprus problem. The Archbishop had meanwhile rejected all participation of the Cypriot Turks in future negotiations regarding the island. The Turkish Government itself remained firm in its determination not to allow Cyprus to be handed over unreservedly to the Greeks.

British efforts for a solution of the Cyprus problem increased as conditions inside the island deteriorated. The meeting of the Baghdad Pact Council at Ankara in January 1958, which was attended by the U.S. Secretary of State and the British Foreign Minister, was made the occasion for informal talks. The new Governor of Cyprus, Sir Hugh Foot, arrived to take part in these, but while they were in progress there was serious rioting by Turkish Cypriots in Nicosia and Limassol.

In June 1958 the British Government published a new plan for Cyprus, involving the association of the Greek and Turkish communities directly with the government of the island. Initial Turkish reaction was cold, but in the end it was accepted that the plan was workable, and not incompatible with the eventual solution of partition, which the Turkish Government then favoured. Subsequent efforts by the British Prime Minister, Mr. Macmillan, who paid flying visits to Ankara and Athens in August, and by the Secretary-General of NATO, M. Spaak, were devoted to trying to bring Turkey and Greece together with Great Britain and other interested but "neutral" states in a round-table conference on Cyprus.

The winter of 1958-59 saw a period of intense diplomatic activity and exchanges between Athens and Ankara, as a result of which there began in Zürich on February 5th, 1959, bilateral negotiations between the Prime Ministers and Foreign Ministers of Greece and Turkey. Both countries emphasised that the Zürich conference was called on joint Greco-Turkish initiative. On February 11th, the two Prime Ministers initialled an agreement on the basic structure of a new independent Republic of Cyprus, with a Greek Cypriot President and a Turkish Cypriot Vice-President. There were to be ten Ministers in the Cabinet, three of them Turkish, and a House of Representatives, 30 per cent of whom should be Turkish. The possibility of the union of Cyprus with any other state, or of the partition of it into two independent states, was expressly excluded. On February 11th the two Foreign Ministers came to London from Zürich for preliminary discussions with the British Foreign Secretary, and it was then decided to invite Archbishop Makarios and Dr. Fazıl Küçük, the leader of the Turkish Cypriots, to a conference in London. On February 18th a conference of Prime Ministers, Foreign Ministers and the two Cypriot leaders opened at Lancaster House, London, and it ended on February 19th with the acceptance by all parties of the new Constitution for Cyprus.

The aeroplane bringing Mr. Adnan Menderes, the Turkish Premier, to London crashed on February 17th, and as a result of the injuries he received, Mr. Menderes was unable to attend the conference at Lancaster House, although he initialled the final agreements in a London hospital where he was convalescing.

Prolonged negotiations to implement the London and Zürich agreement were finally completed in Cyprus on July 1st, 1960. Elections were to be held at the end of the month, and Cyprus became an independent republic on August 16th. Turks filled fifteen of the fifty seats in the House of Representatives, and a detachment of Turkish troops was stationed in the island.

THE 1960 REVOLUTION

Economic difficulties continued to be one of the main preoccupations of the Turkish Government. The development plans envisaged since 1950 had been carried forward with financial aid from the United States and from such bodies as the International Bank; farm mechanisation, roads, communication facilities, port development and grain-storage projects were among the chief items of the programme. These policies had been accompanied by inflationary pressures, an unfavourable trade balance, decreased imports, a shortage of foreign exchange and, since the agricultural population was in receipt of subsidies from the Government, a higher demand for consumer goods which aggravated the prevalent inflation. Social and economic unease tended to reveal itself in a drift of people from the villages to the towns, the population of centres like Ankara, Istanbul, Izmir, Bursa and Adana being considerably increased during recent years.

The influences which led to the revolution had been long at work. Hostility between the Democrats in power and the People's Party in opposition grew steadily more marked, and was sharpened towards the end of 1959 by suspicions that the Democrats were planning to hold fresh elections in the near future ahead of time. It was feared that these would, if necessary, be rigged to keep the Democrats in power indefinitely.

In May, 1959, political tension between the two main parties had already broken into violence during a political tour of Anatolia conducted by the opposition leader İsmet İnönü. The Government banned all political meetings. Blows were struck in the Grand National Assembly, and the Opposition walked out.

Much the same pattern of events ushered in the final breakdown a year later. At the beginning of April, 1960, İsmet İnönü undertook another political tour of Anatolia. At one point troops were called on to block his progress. Three of the officers involved in this incident took the strong step of resigning. The Opposition tried, but failed, to force a debate in the Assembly. On their side the Democrats set up a commission of enquiry, composed entirely of their own supporters, to investigate "the destructive and illegal activities of the P.R.P." Again the Grand National Assembly was the scene of violence, and all political activity was suspended for three months.

At this point the students took a hand. The universities had for some time been a focus of anti-government feeling, and in consequence had, like the newspapers, found their liberties attacked. On April 28th students in Istanbul demonstrated against the Menderes Government. Troops were called on to fire; five of the demonstrators were killed and 40 injured. Martial law and a curfew were called in Istanbul and Ankara. There were more demonstrations in Istanbul on May 2nd, in Ankara on May 5th and in Izmir on May 15th. On May 21st cadets from the Ankara War College joined students in a protest march.

As administrator of martial law the Turkish Army found itself, contrary to its traditions, involved in politics. A group of officers decided that their intervention must be complete if Turkey was to return to Kemalist principles. In the early hours of May 27th they struck. President Bayar, Mr. Menderes, most Democratic Deputies and a number of officials and senior officers were arrested. The Government was replaced by a Committee of National Union headed by General Gürsel, a much respected senior officer who had fought with Atatürk at Gallipoli.

The *coup* was immediately successful and almost bloodless, though Dr. Gedik, former Minister of the Interior, committed suicide after his arrest. The accusation against the Menderes régime was that it had broken the constitution and was moving towards dictatorship. The officers insisted that they were temporary custodians of authority and would hand over to the duly constituted civilians. A temporary constitution was quickly agreed, pending the drafting of a final new one. During this interval legislative power was vested in the Committee of National Unity, and executive power in a Council of Ministers, composed of civilians as well as soldiers. On August 25th, however, ten of the eighteen Ministers were dismissed, leaving only three civilians in the Government. General Gürsel was President of Republic, Prime Minister and Minister of Defence. The courts were declared independent. Commissions were set up to inquire into the alleged misdeeds of the Menderes regime.

Although the new régime did not fail to meet political opposition, particularly among the peasants and around Izmir, a stronghold of Mr. Menderes, the main problems facing it were economic. The former régime was shown to be heavily in debt in every field. Austerity measures, including restrictions on credit, had to be put into operation and an economic planning board was set up to work out a long-term investment plan with the aid of foreign experts.

THE COMMITTEE OF NATIONAL UNITY

The Committee of National Unity, which originally consisted of 37 members, was reduced to 23 on November 13th, 1960. The 14 officers dismissed represented a group led by Colonel Turkeş, who had been pressing for the army to retain its post-revolutionary powers and to introduce radical social reforms. They were officially described as "dangerous elements planning to seize power" and were sent out of harm's way to diplomatic posts abroad.

This purge completed, preparations for a return to political democracy continued. A new Assembly, to act as a temporary parliament, was convened at the beginning of January 1961. It consisted of the National Unity Committee of 23, acting jointly with a House of Representatives of 271 members, both elected and nominated. In this the People's Party predominated. At the same time party politics were again legalised and a number of new parties emerged. Some of them proved short-lived, but one, the Justice Party founded by General Ragıp Gümüşpala, who had been Commander of the Third Army at the time of the *coup d'état*, was destined to become formidable by attracting the support of many former adherents of the Democratic Party, now declared illegal.

A special committee of the Assembly was charged with framing a new constitution. It produced a draft of 156 articles, which were debated clause by clause, often with heat, in the Assembly sitting in plenary session. The constitution, as finally ratified on May 26th, 1961, had some significant changes from the 1924 version. It provided for a court to determine the constitutionality of laws, for a two-chambered legislature, and it included a reference to "social justice" as one of the aims of the State.

THE YASSIADA TRIALS

These constitutional developments took place against the background of the trial of the accused members of the Menderes régime. The trial was held on the little island of Yassıada in the Bosphorus, where the accused had been confined after arrest. It began on October 14th, 1960, and continued until August 14th, 1961, thus becoming one of the largest and longest political trials in history. By the end the court, presided over by Judge Selim Basol, had held 203 sittings and heard 1,068 witnesses. Some of the early charges seemed trivial and ill-prepared. By May, however, the main charges, alleging violation of the constitution, had been reached. Impressive witnesses were heard on both sides and some of the accused defended themselves with spirit.

In the final session of the court 633 accused appeared in the dock, of whom nearly 100 had earlier been liberated but not formally acquitted. The prosecutor asked for 228 death sentences, including eight for Mr. Menderes and four for Mr. Bayar. Then followed a month's adjournment, and during this interval an attempt was made to close the national ranks. On September 5th leaders of the five principal parties signed a joint declaration undertaking to avoid destructive speeches and to preserve national unity during the electoral campaign. After a five-day round-table conference, presided over by General Gürsel, they further agreed to reject the "Democrat mentality" and to eschew the coming Yassıada sentences as a subject for public discussion. On September 6th leading newspaper editors followed suit. The sentence of the court was pronounced on September 15th. There were fifteen death sentences, twelve of which, including that on Mr. Bayar, were commuted to life imprisonment. Adnan Menderes, Fatin Zorlu, the former Foreign Minister, and Hasan Polatkan, the former Minister of Finance, were duly hanged.

The trial inevitably absorbed the attention of the country, and there were many reminders that sympathy for the former régime and its leaders was far from dead. In March General Gürsel, who had suffered a slight stroke at the end of November, warned the Opposition parties that they were "playing with fire". There were rumours of a plot to rescue Mr. Menderes from prison, and on May 9th–10th 123 people were arrested and charged with "armed resistance to the régime". The most serious setback for the authorities, however, appeared in the results of the referendum on the new constitution. This was approved by 6,348,191 votes against 3,934,370, and the large minority was taken as an indication of continuing loyalty to the Democrats. However, the authorities made no attempt to disguise the significance of the vote, which was completely free, nor did they allow it to deflect them from their declared aim of handing back power to the civilians after an election to be held before the end of October.

It was to electioneering that the country, still stirred by the execution of Mr. Menderes and his colleagues, turned in the autumn. The campaign, perhaps because Yassıada was ruled out as a subject for discussion, proved unexpectedly quiet. On October 15th, 1961, the elections gave the People's Party 173 seats and the Justice Party 158 seats in the National Assembly, and 36 and 70 respectively in the Senate.

These figures were a blow to the hopes of the People's Party that they would achieve an overall working majority. A coalition became necessary. The election results were also further evidence of latent support for the Democrats.

THE NEW GOVERNMENT

On October 25th, 1961, Parliament opened and the transfer of power from military to civilians was made. The revolutionaries had kept their word and a new epoch began. The next day General Gürsel, the only candidate, was elected President. But forming a government proved a much harder process. On November 10th Mr. İsmet İnönü, leader of the People's Party, was asked to form a government, and after much hesitation and strong pressure from the Army, the Justice Party agreed to join forces with its rival. A Cabinet was formed with Mr. İnönü as Prime Minister, Mr. Akıf İyidoğan, of the Justice Party, as

Deputy Prime Minister, and ten more Ministers from each of the two coalition parties. Mr. Selim Sarper, who had held the same office since the *coup d'état*, remained Foreign Minister (but resigned in March 1962).

Restlessness in the country and within the Army was not, however, at an end. On February 22nd, 1962, there was an abortive revolt by a group of officers inside the Ankara Garrison. This appeared to be the act of some of those who feared that, with the Justice Party sharing power, the revolution was in danger of surrendering to those it had set out to overthrow. The Government remained, as Mr. İnönü said, exposed to a double fire—from those who thought the Army did too much (i.e. that civil liberties were still circumscribed) and those who thought it did too little (i.e. that it did not crush all signs of counter-revolution). The resignation of Mr. İnönü at the end of May weakened the extremists in the Justice Party, who had wanted to grant an amnesty to former supporters of Mr. Menderes. They were now face to face with the Army, the original movers of the 1960 revolution, and many of them felt it wise to moderate their demands.

By the end of June Mr. İnönü had formed a new coalition government composed of twelve Ministers from the Republican People's Party, six from the New Turkey Party, four from the Republican Peasants' Nation Party, and one Independent Minister.

The new government's programme expressed attachment to the principles of Western democracy and to the NATO alliance. It covered almost every sphere of the national life, including education, taxation, employment, and the problems of a rapidly rising birth-rate and an adverse balance of trade.

The somewhat uneasy political balance persisted against a background of rumours of further army intervention, and at times it seemed that only Mr. İnönü's skill and prestige kept Turkey on her chosen parliamentary course. As it was, the second half of 1962 saw scuffles break out on more than one occasion in the Assembly and Senate. The most controversial legislation concerned an amnesty for those convicted at Yassıada. A Bill was passed in October which cut sentences by four years. This automatically released those serving sentences of four years or less. Those with sentences of up to six and a half years were also given their freedom. On October 18th, 280 prisoners were set free. They were allowed to practise their professions but not to take part in public life. This act of clemency did not prevent the Opposition from pressing for a complete amnesty for all still detained, including Celal Bayar.

The Republican People's Party, like the country as a whole, found itself divided between those who favoured caution and those who insisted that the pace of reform should be faster. At its congress in October three leading members of the party, including its former secretary-general, Mr. Kasım Gülek, were expelled for a year. There were in addition some signs of a growing but largely uninformed interest in socialism. A Socialist Cultural Association, composed of politicians, intellectuals and journalists, was formed in December. But an article on socialism in *Cumhuriyet* brought its author arrest—a sign that the identification of socialism with communism was still prevalent.

1962 saw the publication of Turkey's long-awaited first Five-Year Plan (see below, *Economic Survey*). Before the Plan was published there had been considerable controversy over how the amount should be raised (about £2,400 million sterling). Four leading members of the planning organization, who favoured more drastic taxation of landowners and agriculturalists, including the director, Mr. Osman Torun, resigned in September. In January 1963 Mr. Attila Sönmez, director of economic planning, likewise resigned, on the grounds that serious inflation would result if the Plan were carried out as the Government intended. A working group set up in July by OECD in Paris was one answer to the problem of outside contributions to the Plan. This reached agreement in June 1963 and formal signature followed on September 12th. The agreement provided for the association of Turkey with the Common Market in two phases. The first, preparatory, phase was to last from five to nine years, and during it the Turkish economy would be prepared for a customs union by aid, amounting to $175 million, from the Six. Certain staple Turkish exports would, during the period, have privileged entry to Common Market countries. The second, transitional, phase would last twelve years. During it Turkish tariffs would be gradually reduced, leading ultimately to a full customs union. In April 1964 Turkey received a loan from Britain of £3 million.

POLITICAL UNREST

The political climate during 1963 remained unsettled. In February the leading radical of the original Committee of National Unity, Colonel Türkeş, who had been in unofficial exile abroad, returned with plans to set up a new political organization. More immediately threatening to the régime were the disturbances which marked the temporary release of the former President, Celal Bayar, from the prison in Kayseri where he had been since his sentence. A convoy of hundreds of cars escorted the 80-year-old politician to Ankara, where he was welcomed on March 24th by large and enthusiastic crowds. The reception appeared as a direct challenge to the revolution and was countered by violent protests, in which students and members of the armed forces participated, denouncing Mr. Bayar and his supposed supporters in the Justice Party. The Ankara offices of the party and its newspaper were attacked. After five days of liberty Mr. Bayar was taken back into custody, first in hospital and then again to his old prison at Kayseri. He was released again in November, 1964, by which time only a handful of those sentenced with him were left in gaol.

In the early hours of May 21st, 1963, Ankara was the scene of yet another abortive *coup d'état*. The instigator was Colonel Aydemir, who had been responsible for the attempted revolt in February 1962. On this occasion his resort to arms, in which some of the cadets at the Military Academy were involved, was quickly suppressed. One hundred and three men were subsequently put on trial for their part in the insurrection and four of them, including Colonel Aydemir, were sentenced to death. Colonel Aydemir was executed in July, 1964. One result of the attempted *coup* was the imposition of martial law in Ankara, Istanbul and Izmir. Originally proclaimed for one month, martial law was repeatedly prolonged.

Although the Bayar incident and Aydemir *coup* produced divisions inside the ranks of the Justice Party, it showed considerable successes at the local elections in November, the first to be held since 1954. These successes were mainly at the expense of the New Turkey Party and the Republican Peasants' Nation Party, Mr. İnönü's two junior partners in the coalition. They resigned from the government, and after General Gümüşpala, the leader of the Justice Party, had tried and failed to form a Ministry, the President called again on Mr. İnönü, who on December 23rd formed a minority government drawn from members of his own Republican Party and some independents. It received a vote of confidence in the Assembly.

The first months of 1964 were overshadowed by an attempt on the life of Mr. İnönü in February, and by the situation in Cyprus, where the fate of the Turkish minority created strong feeling in the mainland. Mr. İnönü's critics claimed that he had "missed the bus" by failing to intervene on the island with force when the trouble started. There were several subsequent occasions when a Turkish descent on the island appeared imminent, but it never materialised and in the middle of June Mr. İnönü accepted President Johnson's invitation to Washington.

RAPPROCHEMENT WITH U.S.S.R.

This, and other diplomatic efforts towards a solution, failed, and public opinion grew more irritated, not only with Greece, but also with Turkey's western allies, in particular America and Britain, who were accused of being lukewarm in their support for Turkey's case. In August this irritation caused a violent explosion in Izmir, when rioters wrecked the American and British pavilions at the trade fair. Mr. İnönü, though moving with characteristic caution, gave a warning that the alliance with the west, the basis of Turkey's foreign policy since the war, was in danger. To reinforce his warning came several steps designed to improve relations with the U.S.S.R. When the Cyprus problem first flared up again it had appeared that the Soviet Government took the side of Greece, and the Soviet trade pavilion had also been a target for the Izmir hooligans. But feelers were out in both Moscow and Ankara, and at the end of October 1964 Mr. Erkin visited the U.S.S.R.—the first Turkish Foreign Minister to make this journey for twenty-five years. Before leaving he invoked the memory of the early days of friendship between Atatürk and Lenin, and the same precedent was made much of by his hosts, who tactfully did not try to press Turkey into premature neutralism, as they had done in the past. On Cyprus, the U.S.S.R. appeared to have moved closer to the Turkish point of view, the communiqué which ended Mr. Erkin's talks speaking favourably of a solution "by peaceful means on the basis of respect for the territorial integrity of Cyprus, and for the legal rights of the two national communities".

Mr. Erkin's journey was followed up in January, 1965, by the visit to Ankara of a Soviet parliamentary delegation —the first to come for 30 years—led by Mr. Nikolai Podgorny, a member of the Praesidium. This visit too was a success, though some deputies made an angry protest when he was invited to address the National Assembly. A trade pact between the two countries followed in March. In May, Mr. Gromyko, the Soviet Foreign Minister, paid a five-day visit to Turkey, and in August, Mr. Ürgüplü, the Prime Minister, paid a return visit to the U.S.S.R. Both occasions were the first of their kind for a generation, and produced a good deal of cordiality. The Soviet Government promised to supply Turkey with credits worth £71 million for a steel works, an oil refinery, and other industrial enterprises. But over Cyprus it was less forthcoming. Friendly references to the banned Turkish Communist Party at the Communist Party Congress in Moscow in March 1966 revived old suspicions of Soviet motives.

FALL OF MR. İNÖNÜ

For all this, Cyprus continued to give the Opposition ammunition with which to harass the İnönü government. At the Senate elections in June, 1964, the Justice Party won 31 out of the 51 seats contested, thus increasing its already large majority in this House. Its success was clouded by the death of the Party's leader, General Gümüşpala. In November Mr. Süleyman Demirel, aged 40, a trained engineer and a former Director General of the state water organization, was elected leader in his place, though he was without a seat in Parliament. Mr. İnönü survived more than one narrow vote of confidence, but was finally brought down on February 13th, 1965, by an adverse vote (225 to 197) in the Assembly on the Budget—the first time that the life of a Turkish government had been ended in this way. There was some speculation whether the Army would allow the Opposition to form a government: the previous November General Sunay, Chief of Staff of the Armed Forces, had warned Justice Party Deputies against criticizing the army. After a short delay, however, a coalition government was formed, made up from the four parties which had been in Opposition—the Justice Party, the New Turkish Party, the Republican Peasant's Party, and the National Party. An independent senator, Mr. Suat Ürgüplü, who had spent much of his previous career in diplomacy, headed the team as Prime Minister. Mr. Hasan Işık, recently appointed as Ambassador to Moscow, was brought in as Foreign Minister, thereby indicating that the new government intended to continue pursuing better understanding with Russia. There was a sharp exchange with Greece in April, when most of the remaining Greek citizens in Turkey were expelled in retaliation for restrictions imposed on the Turkish community in Nicosia.

Turkey suffered a bitter blow when, in December, the General Assembly of the United Nations passed a resolution urging all states to refrain from intervention in Cyprus. This was seen as directly aimed at Turkey's aid for the Turkish minority there. The Government in Ankara denounced the resolution as being "against right, law, and international agreements". However, in the early months of 1966 the position improved somewhat. Direct contacts between Ankara and Athens led to renewed hopes of a negotiated settlement. Unfortunately nothing had been achieved by the early summer of 1967, when the military *coup* in Athens led to Turkish fears that Greece was entering a new phase of instability and nationalism.

1965 was election year. The general election of October 11th confirmed the growing popularity of the Justice Party. Winning 240 seats in an Assembly of 450, it achieved a majority over all its rivals. The People's Party was reduced to 134 seats, followed by the extreme right-wing National Party with 31, the New Turkish Party with 19, the Turkish Workers' Party with 15, and the Republican National Peasants' Party with 11 seats. The emergence of an organized party of the left was perhaps even more remarkable than the triumph of the Justice Party, heirs of the Menderes tradition. Contrary to some expectations, the armed forces accepted both these unwelcome manifestations without open protest. On its side the Justice Party confirmed its adherence to the principles of the 1960 revolution.

DEMİREL CABINET

Mr. Süleyman Demirel formed his cabinet from members of his own party. Mr. Faruk Sukan became Minister of the Interior, and Mr. İhsan Çağlayangil Minister for Foreign Affairs. Introducing his government to the Assembly, Mr. Demirel declared that its most important task would be to withstand communism "by the realization of social justice and measures of social security". Emphasis was to be put on industrialization. "We have to catch up three centuries in three decades", he said.

In spite of its working majority the Demirel Government proved hardly more successful than its predecessors in getting things done. The Justice Party blamed its poor record of legislation on the obstructionist tactics of the Opposition. There had been filibusters, and several ugly scenes of violence on the floor of the Assembly. However, elections in June 1966 for a third of the seats in the Senate showed that the Justice Party was not losing popularity. It gained an increased share of the votes and 35 seats, compared with 13 for the People's Party, and one each for four other parties, including the Turkish Workers' Party, which thus became represented in the Senate for the first time.

To some extent this success was attributable to the innate conservatism of the Turkish peasantry, who may have been alarmed by Mr. İnönü's statement that the People's Party was left of centre. This position was not approved by all the party—some thought it went too far, others not far enough. A convention of the party in October showed a victory for the left-wingers. Mr. Bülent Ecevit, 41 years old and a former Minister of Labour, was elected general secretary of the party, with the declared intention of turning it into a party of democratic socialism. Six months later 48 senators and congressmen, led by Mr. Turhan Feyzioğlu, a former Minister, resigned from the party on the grounds that it was falling into a "dangerous leftist adventure". This was denied by Mr. Ecevit and Mr. İnönü, who supported him. They claimed that, on the contrary, their progressive policies took the wind out of other left-wing parties' sails, and so was the best barrier against communism.

In May 1967 a majority of dissidents came together to form the new Reliance Party, which proclaimed its opposition to socialism and its belief in the "spiritual values of the Turkish nation." In June Mr. Ecevit forced a fresh election of the People's Party executive, and by securing the elimination of two left-wing representatives on it he was able to emphasise that his party remained left of centre rather than left wing.

The National Party also found itself in trouble when 8 of its 31 deputies resigned. But the real threat to all parties other than the governing Justice Party was the new electoral law. This, which was finally passed in March 1968 against the protests of a united opposition, did away with the so-called "national remainder system"—a change which threatened the electoral chances of all the smaller parties but was thought to be particularly aimed at the Turkish Workers' Party, which was accused by the Government of using communist tactics. Earlier a battle had been fought over the party's stormy petrel, Çetin Altan. In July 1967 a vote was taken to lift his parliamentary immunity so that he could stand trial on a charge of distributing communist propaganda. This decision was quashed by the constitutional court in August.

At the beginning of February, 1966, President Gürsel, whose health had been deteriorating, was flown to America for medical treatment. There he suffered further strokes, and it was decided that he was no longer competent to fulfill the duties of his office. On March 28th, Senator Cevdet Sunay, the former Chief of Staff, was elected fifth President of the Turkish Republic to replace him. The former President died on September 14th, 1966.

FOREIGN POLICY 1966-1969

Turkey's relations with her allies in 1966 deteriorated. There were various demonstrations against the Americans, culminating in March 1966 in a riot in Adana, during which American buildings were attacked and American cars overturned. This was touched off by rumours that American servicemen, of whom there were large numbers near the town, had made improper advances to Turkish women. But in effect it was the consequence of a long campaign in the press against America's military presence, which reflected a general increase in xenophobia.

Parallel with these manifestations against Turkey's formerly most stalwart ally went an effort by the Demirel Government to make its whole foreign policy more flexible. This flexibility was symbolized by many official visits, given and received. In May 1967 Mr. Çağlayangil, the Foreign Minister, went to Romania and Bulgaria, and Mr. Rapacki, the Polish Foreign Minister, visited Turkey. In the following spring the Foreign Minister of Egypt, Mahmoud Riad, the Premier of Bulgaria, Mr. Zhivkov, the President of the Yugoslav Executive Council, Mr. Spiljar, and King Hassan of Morocco pressed hard on each other's heels on the road to Ankara. One outcome of the exchanges with Arab leaders was that at the time of the June war with Israel the Turkish Government expressed its sympathy with the Arab cause. But perhaps the state visit which attracted most attention was that of President Sunay to Britain, where he was the guest of Queen Elizabeth—the first Turkish head of state to be so welcomed since Sultan Abdul Aziz exactly 100 years before.

As usual the touchstone of Turkey's foreign relations continued to be Cyprus. In 1967 this perennial problem oscillated between near settlement and near war. The military régime brought to power in Athens by the *coup* of April 1967 seemed ready to negotiate, and in September a meeting between the two Prime Ministers was held at Alexandropoulos on the Greco-Turkish frontier in Thrace. A communiqué issued on September 10th, however, at the end of the two-day meeting, made it clear that no agreement had been reached. It spoke only of continuing "the exploration of the possibilities of a rapprochement through the appropriate channels".

Later in the year the situation suddenly deteriorated as a result of attacks by Greek Cypriots on the Turkish enclaves on the island on November 15th. Two days later the National Assembly voted by 432 votes to 1 to authorize the Government to send troops to foreign countries—in other words, to fight in Cyprus. There were daily Turkish flights over the island and the prospects of war seemed real. As a result of strong intervention by American and UN go-betweens the worst was avoided. On December 3rd the Greeks undertook to withdraw their troops from the island and the Turks to take the necessary measures to ease tension. By February 1968 the situation had been so far restored that direct efforts to agree on a negotiated settlement for Cyprus were once again under way.

The principal event affecting foreign policy in 1968 was the state visit paid by General de Gaulle in October. The visit aroused considerable popular interest, and was widely seen as an attempt to restore the French language and culture to its former pre-eminence amongst European influences in Turkey. Since the Second World War it has largely been replaced by Anglo-American influences, and English is now the main foreign language taught in Turkey. A new defence agreement with the U.S. was signed in March 1969, which increased and clarified Turkish control over the American bases.

HOME AFFAIRS 1968-70

The basic factors underlying the Turkish political scene came to the surface during recent years. First amongst these factors is the conservatism of a large majority of the Turkish people, principally the peasants; this majority never accepted the necessity of the 1960 revolution, still mourns the execution of Adnan Menderes, and has transferred its support to the ruling Justice Party. Atatürk's reforms were to a considerable extent imposed upon Turkey by his Republican People's Party and the Army; the party is now the principal opposition group in Parliament but has little chance of regaining power by democratic methods, given the traditionalist outlook of the rural electorate. The R.P.P. leadership follows a moderate reformist policy but has recently been overtaken as a radical force by numerous left-wing elements, some within its ranks, some in the Turkish Workers Party and some independent. These elements command substantial support in the main cities, especially amongst students and youth in general, and have been campaigning for socialism and other far-reaching domestic reforms, withdrawal from

TURKEY—(HISTORY)

NATO, and the abolition of the American bases in Turkey. In recent years the main visible result of this campaign has been a series of anti-American riots led by extremists. These have now been countered by right-wing extremist groups with passionate Muslim and nationalist convictions.

The Turkish democracy, already threatened by this polarization of political feeling, faced a fresh crisis in May 1969. The Justice Party had introduced a Bill to restore political rights to the leaders of its predecessor, the Democratic Party, and the Bill had passed its initial parliamentary stages by large majorities which included most of the R.P.P. members. Yet the Bill was withdrawn after the armed forces had made their opposition to it very clear; thus the implied threat of a military *coup d'état* was generally thought to have been responsible for the withdrawal and the natural conclusions about the limits of democratic authority in Turkey were widely drawn. Nevertheless there was some suspicion that political manoeuvring with an eye on the elections due in October was at least partly responsible for the crisis.

FALL OF DEMİREL GOVERNMENT

The 1969 elections duly granted Mr. Demirel's Justice Party another term in office; however, in February 1970 the government resigned after 41 right wing Justice Party members had joined the opposition to vote against the budget. A general election was called for June, but cancelled after the National Assembly gave a vote of confidence to a slightly changed Demirel ministry. Sixteen of the 41 rebels were expelled from the Justice Party for a year, which left the government without an absolute majority and thus in a weak position to deal with the unrest that subsequently developed, due mainly to rising taxation and prices. This unrest led to labour and, more significantly, student agitation which brought about the imposition of martial law in Istanbul and İzmir during June. Growing dissatisfaction with the government caused the situation to grow steadily worse towards the end of the year, by which time clashes between left-wing and right-wing students or between students and police were regular occurrences, and several people had been killed. Measures aimed at restricting political activity and preventing "violence and anarchy" were introduced into the National Assembly, but none dealt successfully with the growing crisis, which was further aggravated by Kurdish separatists and by the establishment of an extreme left-wing underground urban guerrilla movement known as the Turkish People's Liberation Army. In December further resignations from the Justice Party brought Mr. Demirel's majority to one, resigning members later forming their own Democratic Party in opposition.

The disturbances continued into 1971, and in March military leaders presented the Demirel government with an ultimatum stating that it had "driven the country to anarchy, fratricidal strife and social and economic unrest", and demanding the formation of a "strong and credible government", otherwise the armed forces would take over the administration of the state. Mr. Demirel resigned and a new government, with fifteen ministers from outside the National Assembly, was formed under Professor Nihat Erim, promising the restoration of public order and extensive reforms of education, finance, laws, agriculture and land. However, student violence and urban guerrilla activities increased during April with kidnappings, bank raids and clashes between students and police, and martial law was proclaimed in eleven of the country's 67 provinces for one month (extended since that time at two-monthly intervals). It failed to prevent further kidnappings and the murder of the Israeli Consul, both by the People's Liberation Army. However, the disturbances gradually subsided, and in June the government announced certain constitutional amendments aimed at a long-term settlement of the situation.

In September, however, amendments were made to the Constitution aimed at preventing further extremist acts of terror and at enabling the Government to carry out the economic and social reforms demanded by the military leaders.

A new crisis developed in October 1971 when the Justice Party withdrew its members from Dr. Erim's cabinet. Dr. Erim's subsequent resignation was initially rejected by President Sunay, but he resigned once again early in December following the withdrawal of eleven of his ministers. Soon afterwards he formed another reform administration, but this time with the number of ministers from outside Parliament reduced from fifteen to eleven. Although the disturbances of the previous year seemed to have subsided, in March 1972 members of the Liberation Army kidnapped and later murdered three NATO technicians—two British and one Canadian—as a reaction to the death sentences imposed upon three of their colleagues.

The second Erim Government was still unable to gain the support of the political parties for its economic and social reforms, and in April 1972, at a time when terrorist activities seemed likely to increase, Dr. Erim finally gave up the premiership. A new coalition cabinet, this time under Mr. Ferit Melen and including nine non-parliamentarians, was eventually accepted by President Sunay over a month later. Its programme was approved in the National Assembly by an overwhelming majority. However, in November 1972 the Republican People's Party announced that it would no longer support the Government. A crisis was avoided when members decided to resign from the party rather than from the cabinet. They joined a merger of the National Reliance and Republican Parties to form the Republican Reliance Pary.

President Sunay's term of office expired in March 1973, but neither the candidate supported by the armed forces nor those proposed by the political parties could obtain the necessary majority in the presidential elections and Mr. Ariburun, as President of the Senate, became acting Head of State on March 29th. For the fifteenth ballot agreement was reached on a compromise candidate, Senator Korutürk, a former naval officer, and he was elected President on April 6th.

Mr. Melen resigned the following day and Senator Naim Talû formed a new cabinet with a coalition of the Justice Party and the Republican Reliance Party and six other Independents. According to the Constitution certain Ministries must be in the charge of Independents immediately before and during general elections, which are due to be held on October 14th, 1973.

ECONOMIC SURVEY

Turkey is about 1,449 km. long and some 483 km. wide, covering an area of 779,445 sq. kilometres. The 1970 census recorded a population of 35,666,549, an increase of 2.7 per cent annually since 1965. By the end of 1972 the population had increased to 36,160,000. Two-thirds of the population live in rural areas. Of the twenty cities with a population of more than 100,000 the largest and best known are the former capital of Istanbul (2.2 million), the port of Izmir (520,000) on the Aegean Sea, and the capital Ankara (1.2 million). The average population density was 46 per sq. kilometre in 1972.

The country possesses great natural advantages: the land yields good grain and a wide variety of fruit and other products; it is rich in minerals; and it has a number of natural ports. The climate is varied and, on the whole, favourable, but communications are hindered by the mountain ranges that ring the Anatolian plateau to the north, east and south.

In the Europe of the seventeenth and eighteenth centuries Turkish manufactures, such as textiles, were in great demand, but the Ottoman Empire failed to keep pace with the industrial development of the West. As production costs were lowered through machine production, Turkish handwork was swept off the market, even in Turkey, and the country returned to agriculture.

When the republic was founded in 1923, industrial development was undertaken, and textiles, cement and paper were among the first industries to be established. Between 1923 and 1941 the number of industrial establishments increased from 118 to 1,052. During this period the government's policy was one of *"étatisme"*, aimed chiefly at the development of heavy industry. Its main instruments were two state "holding" companies, the Etibank and the Sümerbank, and much was achieved through them. In the post-war years there was a marked decline in economic impetus; it was not until after the victory of the Democratic Party in 1950 that the situation began to be transformed.

Under the Menderes régime, free enterprise was encouraged and there was a considerable private investment in industrial undertakings. Some government monopolies were returned to private hands, and state economic undertakings went into partnership with new enterprises formed with both domestic and foreign private capital. At the same time, there was large-scale official investment in public works schemes, notably in expanding electric power production and communications, with the result that the pace of development was greatly increased. The proportion of national income diverted to investment averaged 12 to 15 per cent between 1950 and 1959.

The Government made great efforts to speed up development and put through a vast industrialization programme. But the consequences of such rapid development with its high level of investment, were serious. Difficulties first made themselves felt in the autumn of 1952, and a severe economic crisis had arisen by the end of 1955. Capital development outran resources, and large imports of heavy industrial goods and machinery, not offset by a corresponding expansion in exports, produced a series of foreign trade deficits, with a consequent acute shortage of foreign exchange, in spite of considerable financial assistance from the United States. At home this led to strong inflationary pressure and high prices. The situation was aggravated by a succession of indifferent harvests and by low export prices for chromium and copper. Another contribution to Turkey's difficulties was the high prices paid to farmers, resulting in wheat and other agricultural produce being offered at higher than world prices. To this must be added the fact that Turkey had met heavy defence commitments, nearly 40 per cent of recent budgetary expenditure having been devoted to this purpose.

In an endeavour to combat inflation and reduce pressure on the country's slender reserves, the Government introduced a number of restrictive measures in 1955 and 1956. These included tight controls over liquidity, credit and foreign trade and strict profit margins. However, inflation continued and the trade position deteriorated still further so that in 1958 further controls were introduced. The 1958 stabilization programme was aimed at correcting the external imbalance by restricting imports and fighting inflation. The most important measures were credit restrictions, the reduction of non-essential investment and the effective devaluation of the Turkish lira. However, the Government's heart was not in its policies and they were not fully applied or completely effective. The Revolutionary Government showed more determination, imposed even more stringent controls and in August 1960 devalued the Turkish lira.

The stabilization programme was continued after 1961 with some success; restrictive measures were gradually being relaxed, though some imports were still limited. Investment policy was then co-ordinated in the Five-Year Plan (1962–67), which called for an annual investment of 18 per cent of gross national product (against an average of under 16 per cent in recent years) to a final total investment of £T59,646 million. It aimed at an annual increase in the Turkish national income of some 7 per cent a year. A second Five-Year Plan (1968–72) followed, again aiming at a 7 per cent annual rise in the gross national product: total investment in it was set at £T111,500 million, in annual instalments rising to £T29,000 million by the last year of the Plan. A third Five-Year Plan (1973–77) commenced in 1973 with a target increase in the Turkish gross national product of 7.9 per cent per annum. Total investment is planned at £T281,000 million, of which manufacturing industry is to receive some £T187,000 million.

From 1963 until 1970 growth in G.N.P. averaged 6.5 per cent annually. There was a downturn in 1969 which, because of bad harvests and the effects on industry of acute shortages of foreign exchange, became more pronounced in 1970. In 1971 the growth rate was 9.2 per cent in real terms, while for 1972 the growth rate of G.N.P. is estimated at 7.3 per cent.

AGRICULTURE

Turkey is still predominantly an agricultural country, with over 60 per cent of the population dependent on the land for a livelihood. In spite of the heavy dependence on agriculture, this sector accounted for only 28 per cent of G.N.P. in 1972. At the beginning of the 1970s 95,470 sq. miles (247,310 sq. kilometres), or 32 per cent of the total area, was under cultivation. Most of the farms are small and the average size of a family farm is only 19 acres (7.7 hectares). In good years the country basically was self-sufficient in foodstuffs, except for wheat. Agricultural products account for 75 per cent of exports, the chief items being cotton, tobacco and nuts, which alone made up over half of the export trade in 1970.

During the period 1963–70, the agricultural growth rate was only 2.5 per cent per annum compared with a target rate of 4.2 per cent under the first five-year plan. This failure is attributed to the insufficient emphasis placed on agriculture in both plans. Agriculture was allocated 17.7 per cent of total investment under the first plan and 15.2 per cent under the second. In fact, actual fixed investment under the first plan amounted to only 15.5 per cent of the national total and this pattern of underachievement was repeated during the first three years of the second plan. There were indications by 1971 that this relative neglect would cease, with land reform aimed at the limitation of individual landholdings, redistribution of land to farmers in co-operatives and the improved utilization of land, machinery and farmer education resources. In fact agricultural production in 1971 increased by some 30 per cent. If the potential for agricultural development is to be exploited, then along with land reform a larger share of government expenditure must be allocated to agriculture than it has received hitherto. Nevertheless, the foundations for the modernization of agriculture have been laid under the first and second plans: for example, the consumption of fertilizer increased from 430,000 tons in 1963 to over 3 million tons in 1971 and the land area under irrigation was increasing at an average rate of 100,000 hectares per annum.

Nearly nine-tenths of the cultivated area is devoted to cereals, the most important of which, wheat, makes up about 60 per cent of the total grain production. The principal wheat-growing area is the central Anatolian plateau, but the uncertain climate causes wide fluctuations in production. Barley, rye and oats are other important crops grown on the central plateau. Maize is grown along the Black Sea coastal regions, and leguminous crops in the Izmir hinterland. Rice, normally sufficient for domestic needs, is grown in various parts of the country. In 1971, thanks to favourable weather conditions, the wheat crop increased by 35 per cent to a new record level of 13.5 million tons.

Cotton has only recently been taken seriously by Turkey, but its cultivation, mainly in the Izmir region and in the district round Adana, in southern Turkey, has been successful and great hopes are placed in it. Production has risen from under 200,000 tons in 1960 to 522,000 tons in 1971, with the result that cotton has become Turkey's single most profitable agricultural export: in 1971, cotton earned $203 million, or approximately 31 per cent of total exports.

Turkey produces a particularly fine type of tobacco. The three principal producing regions are the Aegean district, the Black Sea coast, and the Marmara-Thrace region. The bulk of the crop is produced in the Aegean region, where the tobacco is notable for its light golden colour and mild taste. The finest tobacco is grown on the Black Sea coast, around Samsun. Although a traditional Turkish export, its relative position as an export has been declining in recent years. Exports in 1971 were worth $76 million, or 12 per cent of total exports, most of which came from buyers in the United States and East European countries. The size of the crop fluctuates considerably: in 1967 it reached a record level of 183,000 tons, but by 1969 production had fallen off to only 127,000 tons. In 1971 production amounted to 168,000 tons.

The coastal area of the Aegean, with mild winters and hot, dry summers produce the grape, fig and the olive. The outstanding product, however, is the sultana type of raisin, which is grown also in California and elsewhere. Turkey normally ranks second in the world as a sultana producer, but in good years such as 1970 (when the crop was 128,000 tons) becomes the largest producer in the world. In 1971, some 70,000 tons of sultanas were exported, with a total value of $20 million.

The Black Sea area, notably around the Giresun and Trabzon, produces the greatest quantity of hazel nuts (filberts) of any region in the world: in 1970—which was a record harvest year—a total of 250,000 tons of hazel nuts were harvested. This figure dropped to 171,000 tons in 1972, but is forecast to recover to 220,000 tons in 1973. Exports in 1971 amounted to $115 million. Substantial amounts of walnuts and almonds are also grown.

Tea is grown at the eastern end of the Black Sea, around Rize, and in other areas. Production from state tea plantations reached a record 40,000 tons in 1971.

Turkey is also an important producer of oilseeds, the principal varieties grown being sunflower, cotton, sesame and linseed. Output has expanded considerably, reaching 1.4 million tons in 1971.

Turkey was until 1972 one of the seven countries with the right to export opium under the UN Commission on Narcotic Drugs. Much opium was, however, exported illegally, particularly to the U.S. and Iran; partly as a result of pressure from the U.S. Government, the Turkish Government has made opium cultivation illegal from 1972.

Sheep and cattle are raised on the grazing lands of the Anatolian plateau. Stock-raising forms an important branch of the economy. The sheep population of about 36.8 million is mainly of the Karaman type and is used primarily as a source of meat and milk. The bulk of the clip comprises coarse wool suitable only for carpets, blankets and poorer grades of clothing fabric, but efforts have been made in recent years to encourage breeding for wool and there are some 200,000 Merino sheep in the Bursa region.

The Angora goat produces the fine, soft wool known as mohair. Turkey is the second largest producer of mohair in the world; production averages 9,000 tons per annum.

Livestock production accounts for around 30 per cent of agricultural output and roughly 10 per cent of G.N.P. Increased production is aimed at under the five-year plans to cater for expected growth in home demand and also in export markets.

MINERALS

Turkey has a diversity of rich mineral resources, including large quantities of bauxite, borax, chrome, copper, iron ore, manganese and sulphur. Around 100,000 persons are employed in mining, and mineral products accounted for 4 per cent of total exports in 1971. In spite of the importance of mining—particularly as a foreign exchange earner—investment in mining under the second five-year plan was set at £T4,100 or only 3.7 per cent of total planned allocations. This is attributed partly to the absence of an overall development strategy for the mining industry, where output is divided between the private and public sectors, and to the uneasy balance which has prevailed between the two sectors. About 60 per cent of all mineral output and all coal production is carried out by State enterprises. The most important state enterprise in the mining sector is Etibank, which works through its subsidiaries, Eregli Coal Mines, East Chromium Mines, Turkish Copper, Keban Lead Mines and Keçiborlu Sulphur Mines. The state enterprises increased their predominance over the private sector during the early 1960s with an investment programme backed by the Mining Investment Bank, which was set up in 1962. The policy of encouraging the private sector to play a greater part in the mining industry through the establishment of the Turkish Mining Bank Corporation (TMBC) in 1968 has failed to overcome the general reluctance on the part of private investors to view mining as a worthwhile area for long-term investment, with the result that the private sector is undercapitalized. An additional factor militating against the development of mining has been the long-held suspicion of foreign investment in mining. An important development in the light of these considerations was that in early 1972 there was a bill before the Turkish Parliament for the nationalization of boron minerals and lignite and for the prohibition of foreign investment in mining. When the bill was passed in May 1973, it had been amended to merely restrict foreign participation.

Turkey's mineral resources have not been fully surveyed, but investigations are being carried out by the Mineral Research and Exploration Institute of Turkey (MTA).

Bituminous coal is found at and around Zonguldak on the Black Sea coast. The seams are steeply inclined, much folded, and strongly faulted. The coal is generally mined by the longwall system or a variation of it. These mines constitute the Etibank's largest operation, and the coalfield is the largest in this part of the world, including the Balkans. Most of the seams are of good coking quality, the coke being used in the steel mills at nearby Karabük. Production has risen from around 6,000,000 tons in 1962 to approximately 7,840,000 tons in 1971. It is thought that these reserves may become exhausted by the mid-1980s when Turkey will become dependent on its lignite reserves.

Lignite is found in many parts of central and western Anatolia. Seams located in western Turkey are operated by the West Lignite Mines, whose marketable production now exceeds 2,000,000 tons. Their reserves are estimated at some 1,500 million tons. Total lignite production in 1971 was 9.56 million tons, compared with a production of 8.77 million tons in 1970. The main mines, in addition to those operated by West Lignite Mines are at Soma, Degirmisaz and Tunçbilek.

Practically all of Turkish iron ore comes from the Divrigi mine situated between Sivas and Erzurum in the north-east of the country and run by the Turkish Iron and Steel Corporation. The average grade of ore is from 60 to 66 per cent: reserves have been put at 28 million tons. Output varies with the needs of the Turkish iron and steel industry. Output of iron ore in 1971 amounted to 2,544,000 tons and is expected to register a significant increase when reserves in southern Turkey begin to be worked to serve the country's third major steelworks which is being built at Iskenderum.

Turkey is one of the world's largest producers of chrome. The mineral was first discovered in 1848 near Bursa, in the area around Marmara: chrome deposits have since been discovered in more than 120 different locations. The richest deposits are in Güleman, south-eastern Turkey, in the vicinity of Iskenderun; in the area around Eskisehir, north-west Anatolia; and between Fethiye and Antalya on the Mediterranean coast. The Güleman mines, producing 25 per cent of the country's total, are operated by East Chromium Mines under Etibank. Other mines are owned and worked by private enterprise. Little chromium is used domestically and the mineral is the greatest foreign-exchange earner among mining exports. Production rose to a record figure of 912,000 tons in 1971; exports were valued at $18.5 million in 1971.

Copper has been mined in Turkey since ancient times. Present-day production, conducted entirely by Etibank, comes from the Ergani Mines situated at Maden in Elazig, and the Morgul Copper Mine at Borçka in Çoruh province. The latter mine is smaller, but is equipped with more modern plant. A third copper refinery, with an annual output of 400,000 tons, was completed in 1972. Output of refined copper rose to 14,500 tons in 1972, while production of blister copper amounted to 18,000 tons, most of which was exported to West Germany, the United Kingdom and the United States. Known reserves of copper ore are put at 90 million tons, on which basis an annual production rate of some 50,000 tons is foreseen by the mid-1970s. Studies carried out by MTA have revealed the presence of a promising copper belt along the Black Sea coast, with possible reserves of 300 million tons of medium quality ore.

Eskisehir in north-west Anatolia is the world's centre of meerschaum mining. Meerschaum, a soft, white mineral which hardens on exposure to the sun and looks like ivory, has long been used by Turkish craftsmen for pipes and cigarette-holders, to which may now be added various items of costume jewellery.

Manganese, magnesite, lead, sulphur, salt, asbestos, antimony, zinc and mercury are important mineral resources. Of these, manganese ranks first in importance. Deposits, worked by private enterprise, are found in many parts of the country, but principally near Eskisehir and in the Eregli district. Production of manganese in 1971 amounted to 12,700 tons. Lead is mined at Keban, west of Elazig. In the Konya region a project to mine 40,000 tons of lead and 20,000 tons of zinc has been postponed indefinitely. Production of sulphur from the Keciborlu mine in Isparta province was 23,600 tons in 1971. Antimony is mined in small quantities near Balikesir and Nigde.

The Uludag (Bursa) wolfram deposits, have been calculated at 10,000 tons of tungsten ore, carrying an average grade of 0.43 per cent WO_3. These reserves are among the richest in the world. Etibank and the German firm of Krupp have entered into an agreement on the development of the deposits.

Turkey's bauxite deposits are about to be developed for the first time. An aluminium complex at Seydisehir was nearing completion early in 1973. Built with Soviet aid, the plant will produce 60,000 tons of aluminium and 25,000 tons of semi-finished products. Bauxite will be supplied from the deposits located at Seydisehir, where the reserves are estimated at 30 million tons. When the plant is fully operational 80,000 tons of alumina will be available for export.

Oil was first struck in Turkey in 1950 and all subsequent strikes have been in the same area in the south-east of the country. Production rose from 2,401,000 tons in 1966 to 3,408,000 in 1972; it now meets about half of total Turkish requirements. Four companies produce oil: (1) the Turkish Petroleum Corporation (TPAO), a 51 per cent state-sponsored Turkish company, at Garzan and Ramandag, with recently discovered deposits at Magrip, Batıraman and Kurtalan and the smaller fields at Kurtalan and Çelikli; (2) Mobil at Bulgurdag, Silivanka and Selmo; (3) Shell at Kayaköy, Kurkan, Beykan and Sahaban; and (4) Ersan, a small private Turkish company, at Kahta. In 1972 the largest producer was Shell accounting for 60 per cent of output, followed by TPAO and Mobil. Ersan accounted for only around 50,000 tons. Recent discoveries are reported by the Turkish Government to have raised the country's reserves to some 500 million tons.

The largest oil refinery in Turkey, at Mersin, came on stream in June 1962. Built at a cost of $50 million, it has a capacity of 4,500,000 tons. It is operated by the Anatolian Refinery Company (ATAS), a Turkish-registered company owned by Mobil, Shell and BP. Fifteen per cent of the crude oil processed comes from the Mobil field at Bulgurdag and the Shell field at Karaköy; the remainder is imported from Iraq and Libya. The one million ton refinery at Izmit which came on stream in 1961, is wholly TPAO-owned, following the sale of Caltex's 49 per cent share to TPAO in 1972. The capacity of this refinery is being raised from 2.2 million to 5.5 million tons per annum. The TPAO operates a 660,000 tons per annum refinery at Batman, near Diyarbakır, connected by pipeline to both Garzan and Ramandag. Its capacity is being expanded to 800,000 tons per annum. A fourth refinery, with a 3 million ton per annum capacity, was under construction at Izmir in 1971 with Soviet aid. At present, two further refineries are planned, at Thrace, and at a site on the Black Sea.

TPAO operates a 310-mile, 18-inch diameter pipeline running from the oilfields around Batman to Dörtyol on the Gulf of Iskenderun. Daily throughput capacity is around 10,000 tons, but this may be increased to 16,000 tons. Other companies use the pipeline on a tariff basis.

INDUSTRY

The leading role in the process of inaugurating industrialization has been played by the state economic enterprises. Since 1950, however, private enterprise has been encouraged: although the state enterprises have not been denationalized, by the beginning of the 1970s the private sector accounted for about two-thirds of industrial output and its rate of capital investment had become almost equal to public sector investment. The share of industry in the economy is increasing: whereas in 1952 industry accounted for 12 per cent of domestic product this had increased to 18 per cent by 1970. Simultaneously there has been a change in the structure of industry, away from the production of consumer goods to the production of secondary and even of capital goods. Whereas in 1962 consumer goods industries accounted for over two-thirds of industrial production, by 1969 its share had fallen to under 55 per cent. In the same period the share of the secondary goods industries increased from 17 to 30 per cent and that of capital goods from 12.9 to 14.1 per cent. Turkish industrial development has been protected from overseas competition by tariff and quota restrictions, with the result that Turkish industry is geared principally to the needs of the home market and manufactured goods account for only around 4 per cent of total exports.

The textile industry is Turkey's largest, employing around 275,000 persons and contributing about 16.5 per cent of industrial production at the beginning of the 1970s. The private sector accounts for 35 per cent of textile output. Production in the cotton industry has risen rapidly under the five-year plans, from 98,500 tons of yarn and 547.5 million metres of fabrics in 1962 to 200,000 tons and 950 million metres respectively in 1971. During the same period, exports of cotton yarn and fabrics rose from $0.9 million to $28.4 million. There were 1.34 million cotton spindles in 1971 and this should double by 1976 with yarn exports rising to $55–60 million and fabric exports to $26–30 million by 1977–78, by which time Turkey may begin to compete with developing countries such as Pakistan and Hong Kong. In comparison the development of the wool weaving industry has been slow with output rising from 20,000 tons of yarn and 23.6 million metres of fabrics in 1962 to 28,500 tons and 28 million metres respectively in 1969.

The iron and steel works at Karabük, north-west Anatolia, are run by the state-controlled Turkish Iron and Steel Corporation. Capacity is 570,000 tons. A second iron and steel complex, at Eregli in west Anatolia, produces hot and cold rolled sheets, steel strip and tinplate. Production was disrupted at this plant during 1972 as a result of work to install an additional blast furnace and sintering plant. This should be completed by mid-1974 when plant capacity will be expanded from 600,000 to 1,250,000 tons. A new steel mill with a capacity of 1.2 million tons being built at Iskenderum under a credit agreement with the Soviet Union is planned for completion also in 1974. In 1972 the merger of the Karabük works, the Divigri iron mine and the Iskenderum works was approved by the Turkish Parliament. Forty-nine per cent of the shares of the projected corporation will be sold to the public.

There are 31 cement factories with an annual capacity of nearly 10 million tons; more are under construction or planned. Production has been steadily increasing over recent years and in 1972 amounted to 8,424,000 tons, representing an increase of over 98 per cent on production in 1967.

Among food industries, the state-controlled sugar beet industry is the most important. Sugar production in 1971 totalled 723,000 tons. Production costs are very high and exports have to be heavily subsidized by the domestic market, except when the international price is very high.

The paper and board industry is dominated by the government-owned SEKA corporation which has one old established mill at Izmir with an annual capacity of 126,000 tons of paper and board plus three mills which were opened during 1971 with a combined annual capacity of 226,000 tons. SEKA's output in 1971 amounted to 154,000 tons, or 47 per cent of total paper and board production. SEKA plans to open three more mills in 1973.

The motor vehicle industry was established after 1956 as an import substitute industry and by 1971 had become the largest industrial employer after the textile industry. However, it accounted for only around 5 per cent of total industrial output. The total output of 25,000 trucks, pick-ups and buses and 46,000 saloon cars is fragmented between 15 enterprises with resulting loss of economies of scale. The process of merging of firms (there were 22 in 1967) is expected to continue under the impact of heavier taxation. The comparative efficiency of the Turkish motor industry, which is based on a small and limited home market, is greatest in bus and truck production, which is more labour-intensive than saloon car assembly. Perhaps the most likely possibility of Turkish penetration of foreign markets is as a producer and exporter of bus and truck parts. Turkey's first petro-chemicals complex, situated at Izmit, began production in 1970 in ethylene, polythene, PVC, chlorine and caustic soda. In 1971 plans were under consideration for a second one, also at Izmit. Fertilizer production has increased rapidly in recent years, totalling 835,000 tons in 1971. The state-owned Turkish Nitrates Corporation (TNC) has a nitrates plant at Kutahya with an annual capacity of 350,000 tons of nitrates, as well as a 220,000 tons triple superphosphates plant at Samsun and a superphosphates plant at Elazig also with 220,000 tons annual capacity.

The Mediterranean Fertilizer Corporation's phosphates-nitrates complex at Mershin, based on by-products of the refinery there, began trial production in 1972. The TNC has plans for a plant with 1 million tons capacity in the Marmara region. In the private sector the capacities of the phosphates plants at Iskenderum and Yarimca were doubled in 1971 to 200,000 tons per annum each and converted to triple superphosphates.

Other manufacturing industries include tobacco, chemicals, pharmaceuticals, construction, metal working, engineering, leather goods, glassware and ferrochrome.

Expansion is planned into a variety of fields, including aircraft production, dairy products and fruit-juice extraction.

There has been an extensive development of electrical energy; production in 1972 totalled 10,680 million kWh., of which 70 per cent was supplied by thermal sources and the remainder by hydroelectric plants.

Turkey's most ambitious power project, the Euphrates dam at Keban is due to begin production in 1973. The 670 ft. high dam will hold back a lake 70 miles long at the confluence of the two main branches of the Euphrates. The plant will have an initial capacity of 620,000 kW., rising to 1,240,000 kW. The power generated will go firstly through a 400-mile grid system to the industries of the north-western part of the country; but it is intended that the dam will also serve as the power basis for the development of the eastern part of Turkey, which in the past has lagged in industrial and agricultural wealth. The Gökçekaya hydroelectric station is due for completion in 1973 and the plant at Ambarli near Istanbul is being extended.

FINANCE

The Central Bank (Merkez Bankasi), the sole bank of issue, started its operations on October 3rd, 1931. It controls exchange operations and ensures the monetary requirements of certain state enterprises by the discounting of bonds issued by these establishments and guaranteed by the Treasury.

There are 45 other banks; thirteen are state-controlled and operate under special legislation to promote governmental industrial agricultural and other plans. The largest of these are the Agricultural Bank (Ziraat Bankası), concerned with the development of agriculture; the Emlak Kredi Bankası, a mortgage loan bank; the Sümerbank, founded in 1933 to develop and control government industry; the Etibank, founded in 1935 to develop mines and market minerals, and expand bulk power supply; the Iller Bankası (Provincial Bank); and the Denizcilik Bankası (Maritime Bank), founded in 1952 to run the mercantile marine.

Among leading private banks are the Industrial Development Bank of Turkey, founded in 1950 to promote private industrial enterprise with the help of the International Bank and such commercial banks as Akbank (1948), Demirbank (1953), Is Bankası (1924), and Yapı ve Kredi Bankası (1944). One new commercial bank, Raybank, was formed in 1956, with a nominal capital of £T4,000,000.

The monetary unit is the kurus (piastre) by the law of April 1916. The Turkish lira (pound), which is, in practice, employed as the monetary unit, is made up of 100 kurus.

The principal sources of budgetary revenue are income and wealth tax, transaction tax, customs, consumption tax and revenues from State monopolies. From the beginning of 1962 agricultural incomes were taxed for the first time in recent history.

For the fiscal year 1971–72 estimated total budgetary revenue was £T38,472 million, against which expenditure was to be balanced. £T7,916 million was allocated for investment expenditure, and £T10,534 for capital formation and transfer expenditure, within the public sector, and £T20,022 was allocated for current expenditures. Actual revenue in the fiscal year 1971–72 totalled £T39,645. Some indication of the growth rate which these figures reflect may be seen by comparing them with the fiscal year 1968–69 in which expenditures were £T21,60 million and revenue £T21,000 million. Taxes have been increased by unprecedented amounts over the last two years, partially to counteract the traditional budget deficit, and to reduce the volume of deficit financing.

EXTERNAL TRADE

Before and during World War II, Turkish foreign trade figures showed a surplus of exports over imports. Since 1947 this position has been reversed, and the demands of Turkey's economic development, especially since 1950, have inflated the imports bill without making equivalent short-term additions to the country's exporting strength: in 1972 exports were only $807 million compared with imports of $1,450 million, giving a trading deficit of $643 million.

The main exports by value in 1971 were cotton ($193 million), hazelnuts ($84 million) and tobacco ($86 million); principal imports by value were boilers and machinery ($327 million), iron and steel ($132 million), transportation equipment ($107 million), liquid fuel ($129 million), and medicines and dyes ($108 million). By area, most of Turkey's 1971 exports went to the member countries of the European Economic Community and the European Free Trade Area (39 and 19 per cent respectively) and the East Bloc (14 per cent). Imports in 1971 came primarily from the EEC (35 per cent), the dollar area (11 per cent), EFTA countries (16 per cent) and the East Bloc (12 per cent).

An agreement with the European Economic Community was signed in September 1963 under which Turkey entered into a preparatory association with the Community. Turkey received $175 million in loans and preferential tariff quotas to help strengthen its economy to enable Turkey to meet the obligations involved in developing its association with the EEC. Early in 1973 Turkey entered into the second stage of its Association Arrangement with the EEC, the long-term aim being full membership in 1995.

PLANNING

During the years of the First Plan (1962–67) a real growth rate of 6.6 per cent per annum was achieved. Over 90 per cent of the scheduled investment targets were reached, private sector investment exceeding its target share of 40 per cent of total investment by a considerable margin.

The Second Five-Year Plan, covering the years 1968 to 1972, envisaged an annual growth rate of 7 per cent—the same as that targeted for the First Plan. Investment was planned to reach £T17,000 million in 1969 and to rise by some 11 per cent annually to nearly £T29,000 million by 1972. Total investment through the Second Plan is expected to be £T111,500 million from both the public and the private sectors. Foreign aid increased to $2,338 million by the end of 1970, a lower rate of increase than during the First Plan. Overseas loans of some $247 million in 1968 fell to $230 million in 1972. The long-term target of self-sustained economic growth, i.e. independent of foreign loans, is a prominent aim of the Third Five-Year Plan (1973–77). In addition, a substantial increase in revenues from foreign exchange is sought; for this reason heavy emphasis is now placed on export opportunities and import substitution.

The emphasis of the Second Plan was on industrial development and the reduction of the dependence of agriculture on weather conditions. Of total investment 22.4 per cent was allocated to manufacturing industry, a sum double the amount realized between 1963 and 1967 when certain projects were delayed. The Third Plan also places the emphasis on industrial development, almost 45 per cent of the total investment being allocated to the mining and manufacturing industries. Priority is to be given to providing a modern heavy industry base to promote export opportunities and import substitution.

Government investment will concentrate on the infrastructure and education and health. Manufacturing industry will be mainly the responsibility of the private sector but the government will help out, if the private sector proves reluctant.

TURKEY—(STATISTICAL SURVEY)

STATISTICAL SURVEY

AREA AND POPULATION

TOTAL AREA	THRACE	ANATOLIA	POPULATION (1970 Census)	WORKERS ABROAD (October 1972)
779,452 sq. km.	23,764 sq. km.	755,688 sq. km.	35,666,549	636,800

CHIEF TOWNS
POPULATION (1970 census)

Ankara (capital)	1,208,791	Konya		200,760
Istanbul	2,247,630	Kayseri		167,696
İzmir	520,686	Diyarbakir		138,657
Adana	351,655	Erzurum		134,655
Bursa	275,917	Samsun		134,272
Gaziantep	255,881	Sivas		132,527
Eskişehir	216,330	Malatya		130,340

EMPLOYMENT*
(1970)

	MALE	FEMALE	TOTAL
Agriculture, Forestry, Hunting and Fishing	4,249,184	4,513,539	8,762,723
Mining and Quarrying	101,684	2,041	103,725
Manufacturing Industries	1,004,596	259,028	1,263,624
Construction	409,796	2,267	412,063
Gas, Electricity and Water	16,551	453	17,004
Distributive Trades, Restaurants and Hotels	706,346	30,720	737,066
Transport, Storage and Communications	380,322	18,932	399,254
Financial, Insurance, Real Estate and Business Services	154,283	35,935	190,218
Community, Social and Personal Services	1,448,514	207,448	1,655,962
Activities not Adequately Defined	117,328	15,416	132,744

* Based on a 1 per cent sample of the 1970 census results.

WORKERS ABROAD (1972)

Germany, Federal Republic	528,143
Belgium	4,628*
Netherlands	16,836*
Austria	9,545*
Switzerland	7,781*

Remittances sent back to Turkey by workers abroad:
1967	U.S. $93,000,000	1970	U.S. $273,020,778
1968	U.S. $107,318,285	1971	U.S. $471,370,427
1969	U.S. $140,636,057	1972	U.S. $732,182,858†

* 1971 figures.   † provisional.

680

TURKEY—(Statistical Survey)

AGRICULTURE
UTILIZATION OF LAND

	Area ('000 hectares)				
	1967	1968	1969	1970	1971
Area under cultivation	23,896	24,092	24,672	24,294	24,527
Meadows and grazing lands	26,135	n.a.	n.a.	n.a.	n.a.
Market gardens and truck farms, orchards, olive groves, vineyards, etc.	2,414	2,925	2,961	3,043	3,087
Forests	12,578	18,273	18,273	18,273	18,273
Unproductive area	13,095	n.a.	n.a.	n.a.	n.a.

PRINCIPAL CROPS

Crop	Area ('000 hectares)			Production ('000 metric tons)		
	1969	1970	1971	1969	1970	1971
Cereals:						
Wheat	8,660	8,600	8,700	10,500	10,000	13,500
Rye	685	650	655	817	630	895
Barley	2,687	2,590	2,600	3,740	3,250	4,170
Oats	351	320	309	468	415	455
Maize	659	648	635	1,000	1,040	1,135
Millet and sorghum	39	38	41	56	46	61
Vegetables:						
Dry beans	110	99	102	138	138	153
Broad beans	35	29	31	45	39	42
Chick peas	90	100	110	111	109	133
Lentils	103	108	105	107	92	101
Potatoes	157	155	169	1,936	1,915	2,100
Industrial and other crops:						
Cotton:						
Lint	639	528	688	400	400	522
Seed				640	640	835
Tobacco	315	328	342	147	150	174
Sugar beet	103	124	159	3,356	4,254	5,956
Hemp:						
Seed	8	8	9	3	3	3
Fibre				8	8	8
Sesame seed	67	62	64	41	36	43
Sunflower seed	286	360	396	310	375	465
Flax: Fibre	17	13	11	4	1	2
Seed				12	7	7
Olives*	72,574	73,085	73,950	308	681	326
Olive oil				54	118	52
Opium: Gum	16	10	13	0.127	0.06	0.149
Seed				11	8	14

* Number of trees.

FRUIT PRODUCTION

		1968	1969	1970	1971
Pears	tons	180,000	160,000	180,000	175,000
Apples	,,	700,000	620,000	748,000	780,000
Figs, Fresh	,,	215,000	215,000	214,000	195,000
Grapes	,,	3,725,000	3,635,000	3,850,000	3,853,000
Walnuts	,,	96,000	84,000	103,000	110,000
Lemons	,,	130,000	121,494	126,000	141,500
Oranges	,,	476,000	414,100	445,000	460,000

TURKEY—(STATISTICAL SURVEY)

LIVESTOCK
('000 head)

	1969	1970	1971		1969	1970	1971
Horses	1,110	1,049	1,027	Sheep	36,351	36,471	36,760
Asses	1,938	1,805	1,760	Goats	20,267	19,483	18,863
Mules	291	299	301	Buffaloes	1,178	1,117	1,026
Cattle	13,189	12,756	12,653	Camels	39	31	29
Hens	32,313	32,306	34,612				

MINING
PRODUCTION
('000 tons)

MINERAL	1967	1968	1969	1970	1971
Copper, Blister and Refined	996	984	924	840	912
Chrome Ore	636	612	660	756	912
Iron Ore	1,548	2,220	2,508	2,952	2,544
Coal	7,452	7,500	7,728	7,596	7,848
Lignite	6,648	8,076	8,556	8,772	9,564
Manganese	41.9	25.3	13.7	12.4	12.7
Petroleum	2,748	3,108	3,624	3,540	3,456

* Provisional figures.

INDUSTRY
PRINCIPAL PRODUCTS

ITEM	UNIT	1966	1967	1968	1969	1970	1971
Steel	'000 tons	842.6	996	1,109.4	1,169.7	1,311.9	1,121.8
Crude Iron	,, ,,	823.5	933.7	1,007.7	1,045.6	1,156.4	841.4
Coke	,, ,,	1,452	1,356	1,428	1,596	1,536	1,440
Sulphuric Acid	,, ,,	20.0	23	21.6	23.2	22.2	21.4
Superphosphates	,, ,,	414.3	392.7	326.9	264.7	349.9	450.0
Cement	,, ,,	3,864	4,248	4,728	5,796	6,384	7,548
Paper and Cardboard	,, ,,	112.8	115.0	122.9	122.9	125.6	330.3
Glass*	,, ,,	6.0	7.4	8	10.7	10.8	13.0
Cotton Yarn*	,, ,,	33.2	34.3	37	37.1	46.8	48.0
Cotton Fabric*	million metres	187.4	188.7	208.9	200.8	219.7	222.3
Woollen Fabric*	,, ,,	4.5	5.2	6	5.3	4.7	4.7
Woollen Yarn*	'000 tons	3.5	3.7	3.4	3.2	3.1	3.0
Sugar (refined)	,, ,,	600.6	663.2	717.6	587.2	518.0	723.1
Beer	million litres	38	34.1	38.2	41.5	48.0	55.6
Wines	,, ,,	15.0	17.2	14.9	22.1	19.1	18.1
Raki	,, ,,	7.3	8.1	8.9	8.7	8.4	9.1
Tobacco*	'000 tons	39.4	36.5	38.2	40.3	41.0	46.7
Electric Energy	million kWh.	5,549.3	6,216.0	6,963.6	8,035.2	8,622.0	9,780.0

* Public sector only.

FINANCE

100 kuruş = 1 Turkish lira (TL) or pound.
Coins: 5, 10, 25 and 50 kuruş; 1 and 2½ liras.
Notes: 5, 10, 20, 50, 100 and 500 liras.

Exchange rates (March 1973): £1 sterling = 34.08 liras; U.S. $1 = 14.00 liras.
100 Turkish liras = £2.935 = $7.143.

TURKEY—(STATISTICAL SURVEY)

BUDGET
(TL million)

REVENUE	1970–71	1971–72
Direct Taxes	8,640	11,878
Income Tax	6,573	9,584
Indirect Taxes	14,351	19,538
Production Tax	7,947	10,467
Customs Duties	1,438	1,990
Profits and Taxes on Monopolies	2,276	2,715
TOTAL TAXES	22,982	31,416
Other Normal Revenues	4,028	3,671
Special Revenues and Funds	4,336	4,558
TOTAL REVENUES	31,356	39,645

EXPENDITURE (Main Items)	1968–69	1969–70
Justice	387	419
Defence	4,278	4,270
Police and Security	780	840
Interior	242	263
Finance and Debt Repayments	8,067	10,959
Education	3,144	3,040
Public Works	1,035	1,534
Health	785	845
Agriculture	732	779
Other Expenditure	1,628	1,931
Total Expenditure	21,078	24,880

1971–72 Budget: Revenue and Expenditure: TL 38,472 million.

FIVE-YEAR DEVELOPMENT PLAN
(TL million—at 1965 prices)

SECTOR	1968–72 Investment over 5 Years	Percentage of Total
Agriculture	16,900	15.2
Mining	4,100	3.7
Manufacturing Industry	25,000	22.4
Energy	8,900	8.0
Transportation and Communications	18,000	16.1
Housing	20,000	17.9
Education	7,500	6.7
Health	2,000	1.8
Tourism	2,600	2.3
Other Services	6,100	5.5
Development Fund	400	0.4
TOTAL	111,500	100.0

DEVELOPMENT PERFORMANCE
(Percentage growth per annum)

SECTOR	1963–67 PLAN PLANNED	1963–67 PLAN ACHIEVED	1968–72 PLAN PLANNED
Agriculture	4.2	3.3	4.1
Industry	12.3	9.7	12.0
Building and Public Works	10.7	8.2	7.2
Transport	10.5	7.7	7.2
Services	6.2	8.1	6.0
National Product	7.0	6.7	7.0

TURKEY—(Statistical Survey)

NATIONAL ACCOUNTS
(TL million, at current prices)

	1970*	1971*	1972†
Agriculture and Livestock	37,639.9	46,374.2	52,258.4
Forestry	845.0	1,083.3	1,201.0
Fishing	236.2	316.8	392.1
Mining and Quarrying	2,492.1	3,234.8	4,059.5
Manufacturing	27,463.3	35,943.4	45,756.5
Electricity, Gas and Water Supply	1,760.5	2,346.8	3,581.0
Construction	9,645.1	10,311.3	12,678.4
Wholesale and Retail Trade	13,928.5	18,625.0	23,268.8
Transport and Communications	8,548.9	10,993.7	13,392.1
Financial Institutions	4,277.5	5,217.5	6,308.0
Private Professions and Services	7,370.5	9,426.9	11,482.0
Ownership of Dwellings	7,497.5	8,776.6	10,279.9
Less Imputed Bank Service Charge	−2,352.0	−2,932.3	−3,489.4
Domestic Product of Industries	119,353.0	149,718.0	181,168.3
Government Services	13,323.1	20,029.5	25,530.2
Sub-Total	132,676.1	169,747.5	206,698.5
Import Duties	5,332.1	7,143.3	8,989.4
Gross Domestic Product	138,008.2	176,890.8	215,687.9
Net Factor Income from Abroad	2,285.3	5,469.0	7,667.5
Gross National Product	140,293.5	182,359.8	223,355.4

* Provisional.   † Estimate.

GOLD RESERVES AND CURRENCY IN CIRCULATION
(TL million, at year end)

	1969	1970	1971	1972*
Gold Reserves	1,112	1,834	1,765	1,844
Currency in Circulation	11,264	14,235	17,378	20,460

* Provisional figures.

CONSUMER PRICE INDEX
(Ankara—1968=100)

	1969	1970	1971
Food	109.6	118.2	134.7
Clothing	106.3	120.1	142.2
Household Expenditures	102.5	114.2	135.3
Medical and Personal Care	101.7	104.1	119.6
Transportation	102.7	118.6	131.2
Cultural and Recreational Expenditures	112.0	124.4	149.4

TURKEY—(STATISTICAL SURVEY)

BALANCE OF PAYMENTS
(million U.S.$)

	1968	1969	1970	1971
Imports (c.i.f.)	−764	−801	−948	−1,171
Exports (f.o.b.)	496	537	588	677
Trade Balance	−208	−264	−360	−494
Invisible Items (net)	37	44	188	379
CURRENT BALANCE	−241	−221	−172	−109
Capital Receipts	309	374	571	428
Capital Expenditure	−94	−115	−174	−91
CAPITAL BALANCE	215	259	431	337
Change in Monetary Reserve (−=increase)	6	—	−236	−346
Net Errors and Omissions	20	−38	−23	107
TOTAL BALANCE	−26	38	259	228
Special Drawing Rights	—	—	18	—

EXTERNAL TRADE
(TL million)

	1967	1968	1969	1970	1971
Imports	6,217	6,934	7,275	9,598	17,725
Exports	4,701	4,467	4,832	6,408	9,090

COMMODITIES
(TL '000)

IMPORTS	1969	1970	1971
Live Animals and Animal Products	10,830	17,819	13,931
Vegetable Products	182,246	621,193	77,254
Animal and Vegetable Oils and Fats	18,698	52,119	232,273
Foodstuffs, Beverages and Tobacco	13,127	11,743	31,042
Mineral Products	629,898	782,573	1,979,228
Chemicals	1,362,956	1,554,994	2,599,301
Plastic and Rubber	287,313	383,966	643,818
Hides and Skins	20,287	19,626	46,200
Wood	11,697	36,032	34,340
Paper-making Material	232,053	197,321	577,872
Textiles	339,378	408,258	610,034
Glassware, Ceramics	79,313	95,286	197,381
Base Metals	742,153	1,342,655	2,681,828
Machinery	1,983,442	2,858,283	4,850,333
Vehicles	713,018	1,010,585	1,497,304
Measuring Instruments	135,225	182,338	365,398
All Other Products	513,000*	23,000*	1,251,030
TOTAL	7,275,000*	9,598,000*	17,688,567

* Approximate figures.

685

TURKEY—(Statistical Survey)

COMMODITIES—continued]

EXPORTS	1969	1970	1971
Livestock	102,923	197,196	295,756
Fish	52,880	67,530	122,615
Fruit and nuts	1,432,639	1,501,651	1,859,463
Cereals	2,948	6,882	10,049
Oilseeds	65,417	115,312	146,061
Tannin materials, gums	6,963	7,355	10,280
Cattlecake and foodstuff residues	159,088	227,288	296,664
Tobacco	733,124	782,007	1,064,724
Iron, chrome, manganese and other ores	152,910	232,910	316,339
Hides and skins	60,568	64,963	81,323
Mohair, wool	66,263	56,660	74,424
Cotton	1,126,505	2,015,056	2,842,505
Copper and products	61,322	74,005	49,674
All other products	807,952	1,058,888	1,920,172
TOTAL	4,831,502	6,407,703	9,090,049

COUNTRIES
(TL '000)

	IMPORTS			EXPORTS		
	1969	1970*	1971	1969	1970*	1971
Belgium	134,851	191,261	333,724	139,313	239,062	303,935
Czechoslovakia	112,168	136,427	169,981	124,579	117,710	151,440
France	228,168	348,273	1,101,519	249,071	431,253	651,197
Federal Germany	1,258,527	1,775,440	2,954,511	1,011,957	1,323,530	1,745,217
German Democratic Republic	107,479	117,036	114,900	96,346	98,758	74,529
Italy	667,930	761,153	1,759,179	386,075	430,762	540,626
Japan	79,563	260,333	379,054	113,452	208,830	132,432
Netherlands	164,231	251,051	357,964	147,292	230,669	333,515
Poland	93,323	295,304	97,712	75,945	79,951	131,595
Switzerland	315,030	492,165	864,041	250,187	487,481	855,663
U.S.S.R.	301,869	412,330	969,053	269,713	306,308	443,560
United Kingdom	829,201	945,758	1,655,743	272,578	361,315	423,941
U.S.A.	1,152,964	1,851,965	1,951,630	538,962	587,951	914,646

* The 1970 figures are affected by the devaluation of the lira in August. Imports have been calculated at the rate TL 9.08=U.S. $1 (Jan. 1st–Aug. 9th) and TL 15.15=$1 (Aug. 10th–Dec. 31st); exports at TL 9=$1 (Jan. 1st–Aug. 9th) and both TL 12=$1 and TL 14.85=$1 (Aug. 10th–Dec. 31st).

TOURISM

	1969	1970	1971	1972
Foreign Visitors to Turkey	694,229	724,784	926,019	935,358
Income from Tourism ($'000)	36,554	51,595	57,206*	78,600

* Provisional figure.

Tourist Accommodation (1970): 292 classified hotels, 3 holiday villages.

686

TURKEY—(Statistical Survey)

TRANSPORT

RAILWAYS
(millions)

	1970	1971	1972
Passenger kilometres	5,561	5,738	6,000
Net ton-kilometres	6,080	6,198	6,228

ROADS
(January—'000)

	1968	1969	1970
Passenger Cars	125.4	137.3	147.0
Trucks	62.6	69.5	74.7
Buses	32.9	36.1	37.6
Motor Cycles	47.1	53.0	62.5

SHIPPING

		1968	1969	1970	1971
Vessels Entered*	('000 gross reg. tons)	9,210	9,795	11,092	13,704
Vessels Cleared*	(,, ,, ,, ,,)	9,110	9,708	11,086	13,550
Goods Loaded	('000 metric tons)	2,641	2,870	3,431	3,787
Goods Unloaded	(,, ,, ,,)	7,087	7,672	8,279	11,189

* Includes vessels entered and cleared in ballast and loaded, but excludes coastal shipping.

CIVIL AVIATION
Turkish Airlines.
('000)

	1968	1969	1970	1971
Kilometres Flown	13,069	12,444	13,464	15,696
Passenger-kilometres	418,080	494,112	640,128	966,588
Cargo ton-kilometres	36,216	41,784	56,857	84,276
Mail ton-kilometres	1,092	1,308	1,476	1,428

COMMUNICATIONS MEDIA

	1970	1971	1972
Telephones	376,987	426,377	518,700
Radio Licences	3,136,498	3,855,913	3,942,293
Letters Sent ('000)	567,990	567,377	895,132

EDUCATION
(1971–72)

	Schools	Teachers	Pupils
Primary	39,100	139,981	5,132,786
Secondary	2,467	35,259	1,147,957
Technical and Vocational	838	15,410	262,701
Universities and Colleges	156	9,211	169,672

Source: Ministry of Education, Ankara.

Source: State Institute of Statistics, Prime Minister's Office, Ankara.

TURKEY—(The Constitution)

THE CONSTITUTION

Preamble

Having enjoyed freedom, and fought for her rights and liberties throughout her history, and having achieved the Revolution of May 27th, 1960, by exercising her right to resist the oppression of a political power which had deteriorated into a state of illegitimacy through behaviour and actions contrary to the rule of law and the Constitution, the Turkish Nation, prompted and inspired by the spirit of Turkish nationalism, which unites all individuals, be it in fate, pride or distress, in a common bond as an indivisible whole around national consciousness and aspirations, and which has as its aim always to exalt our nation in a spirit of national unity as a respected member of the community of the world of nations enjoying equal rights and privileges;

With full dedication to the principle of peace at home, peace in the world and with full dedication to the spirit of national independence and sovereignty and to the reforms of Atatürk;

Guided by the desire to establish a democratic rule of law based on juridical and social foundations, which will ensure and guarantee human rights and liberties, national solidarity, social justice, and the welfare and prosperity of the individual and society;

Now, therefore, the Turkish Nation hereby enacts and proclaims this Constitution drafted by the Constituent Assembly of the Turkish Republic, and entrusts it to the vigilance of her sons and daughters who are devoted to the concept of freedom, justice and integrity, with the conviction that its basic guarantee lies in the hearts and minds of her citizens.

Part One

Articles 1–9

The Turkish Republic is a nationalistic, democratic, secular and social State governed by the rule of law, based on human rights.

The Turkish State is an indivisible whole comprising the territory and people. Its official language is Turkish. Its capital is the city of Ankara.

Sovereignty is vested in the nation without reservation and condition. Legislative power is vested in the Turkish Grand National Assembly.

This power shall not be delegated.

The executive function shall be carried out by the President of the Republic and the Council of Ministers within the framework of law.

Judicial power shall be exercised by independent courts on behalf of the Turkish Nation.

Laws shall not be in conflict with the Constitution.

The provision of the Constitution establishing the form of the State as a republic shall not be amended.

Part Two

Articles 10–62

Every individual is entitled, in virtue of his existence as a human being, to fundamental rights and freedoms, which cannot be usurped, transferred or relinquished.

All individuals are equal before the law irrespective of language, race, sex, political opinion, philosophical views, or religion or religious sect.

Status of aliens, personal immunities, freedom of communication, travel, residence, thought, belief, press and publications.

Right to controvert and rebut, to congregate, demonstrate and form associations.

Protection of individual rights.

Part Three

Articles 63–66. Grand National Assembly

The Grand National Assembly of Turkey is composed of the National Assembly and the Senate of the Republic.

The two bodies meet in joint session in such instances as are provided in the Constitution.

The Grand National Assembly is empowered to enact, amend and repeal laws, to debate and adopt the bills on the State budget and final accounts, to pass resolutions in regard to minting currency, proclaiming pardons and amnesties, and to the carrying out of definitive death sentences passed by courts.

Articles 67–69. National Assembly

The National Assembly is composed of 450 deputies elected by direct general ballot. Election qualifications: elections shall be held every four years. The Assembly may hold new elections before the end of the four-year period.

Articles 70–73. The Senate

The Senate of the Republic is composed of 150 members elected by general ballot and 15 members appointed by the President of the Republic. Election qualifications: term of office is six years, one-third of members shall be re-elected every two years.

Articles 74–94. Elections, Members, Debates, Laws, Expenditure

Articles 95–101. The President of the Republic

The President of the Turkish Republic shall be elected for a term of seven years from among those members of the Turkish Grand National Assembly who have completed their fortieth year and received higher education; election shall be by secret ballot, and by a two-thirds majority of the plenary session. In case this majority is not obtained in the first two ballots, an absolute majority shall suffice.

The President is not eligible for re-election.

The President elect shall dissociate himself from his party, and his status as a regular member of the Grand National Assembly shall be terminated.

The President of the Republic is the head of the State. In this capacity he shall represent the Turkish Republic and the integrity of the Turkish Nation.

The President of the Republic shall preside over the Council of Ministers whenever he deems it necessary, shall dispatch the representatives of the Turkish State to foreign states, shall receive the representatives of foreign states, shall ratify and promulgate international conventions and treaties and may commute or pardon on grounds of chronic illness, infirmity or old age the sentences of convicted individuals.

The President of the Republic shall not be accountable for his actions connected with his duties.

All decrees emanating from the President of the Republic shall be signed by the Prime Minister, and the relevant Ministers. The Prime Minister and the Ministers concerned shall be responsible for the enforcement of these decrees.

The President of the Republic may be impeached for high treason upon the proposal of one-third of the plenary session of the Turkish Grand National Assembly, and conviction of high treason shall require the vote of at least a two-thirds majority of the joint plenary session of both legislative bodies.

TURKEY—(THE CONSTITUTION)

Articles 102–109. The Council of Ministers

The Council of Ministers shall consist of the Prime Minister and the Ministers.

The Prime Minister shall be designated by the President of the Republic from among the members of the Turkish Grand National Assembly.

The Ministers shall be nominated by the Prime Minister, and appointed by the President of the Republic from among the members of the Turkish Grand National Assembly, or from among those qualified for election as deputies.

As head of the Council of Ministers, the Prime Minister promotes co-operation among the Ministries, and supervises the implementation of the Government's general policy. The members of the Council of Ministers are jointly and equally responsible for the manner in which this policy is implemented.

Each Minister shall be further responsible for the operations in his field of authority and for the acts and activities of his subordinates. The Ministers are subject to the same immunities and liabilities as the members of the Turkish Grand National Assembly.

Articles 110–111. National Defence

The office of the Commander-in-Chief is integrated in spirit in the Turkish Grand National Assembly and is represented by the President of the Republic.

The Council of Ministers shall be responsible to the Turkish Grand National Assembly for ensuring national security and preparing the armed forces for war.

The Chief of the General Staff is the Commander of the armed forces.

The Chief of the General Staff shall be appointed by the President of the Republic upon his nomination by the Council of Ministers, and his duties and powers shall be regulated by law. The Chief of the General Staff is responsible to the Prime Minister in the exercise of his duties and powers.

The National Security Council shall consist of the Ministers as provided by law, the Chief of the General Staff, and representatives of the armed forces.

The President of the Republic shall preside over the National Security Council, and in his absence this function shall be discharged by the Prime Minister.

Articles 112–125. Administration

Articles 126–131. Economic and Fiscal Provisions

The budget, accounts, development projects, natural resources.

Articles 132–136. The Judiciary

Judges shall be independent in the discharge of their duties. They shall pass judgment in accordance with the Constitution, law, justice and their personal convictions.

No organ, office, agency or individual may give orders or instructions to courts or judges in connection with the discharge of their judicial duty, send them circulars or make recommendations or suggestions.

No questions may be raised, debates held, or statements issued in legislative bodies in connection with the discharge of judicial power concerning a case on trial. Legislative, executive organs, and the administration are under obligation to comply with ruling of the courts. Such organs and the administration shall in no manner whatsoever alter court rulings or delay their execution.

Article 137. The Public Prosecutor

Article 138. Military Trial

Article 139. Court of Cassation

The Court of Cassation is the court of the last instance for reviewing the decisions and verdicts rendered by courts of law. It has original and final jurisdiction in specific cases defined by law.

Article 140. Council of State

The Council of State is an administrative court of the first instance in matters not referred by law to other administrative courts, and an administrative court of the last instance in general.

The Council of State shall hear and settle administrative disputes and suits, shall express opinions on draft laws submitted by the Council of Ministers, shall examine draft regulations, specifications and contracts of concessions, and shall discharge such other duties as prescribed by law.

Article 141. Military Court of Cassation

The Military Court of Cassation is a court of the last instance to review decisions and verdicts rendered by military courts. Furthermore, it shall try specific cases as a court of the first and last instance involving military matters as prescribed by law.

Article 142. Court of Jurisdictional Disputes

The Court of Jurisdictional Disputes is empowered to settle definitively disputes among civil, administrative and military courts arising from disagreements on jurisdictional matters and verdicts.

Articles 143–144. Supreme Council of Judges

Articles 145–152. The Constitutional Court

PARTS FOUR, FIVE AND SIX
Miscellaneous, Temporary and Final Provisions.

AMENDMENTS

Article 73 concerning membership of the Senate of the Republic, and Article 131 concerning the preservation of forests, were amended on April 17th, 1970.

Article 56 concerning financial aid to political parties, and Article 82 concerning the monthly allowances of members of the National Assembly were amended on June 30th, 1971.

On September 22nd, 1971, thirty-five articles were amended and nine temporary articles added. These amendments were aimed at preventing the abuse of liberties by making use of gaps existing in the Constitution, and at providing greater clarity to certain articles.

Five articles (30, 57, 136, 138 and 148) were changed and two temporary articles were added on March 15th, 1973. The addition to Article 36 set up State Security Courts.

TURKEY—(The Government, Diplomatic Representation)

THE GOVERNMENT

THE HEAD OF STATE
President: Admiral Fahri Korutürk (elected April 1973).
Principal Secretary of President's Office: Cihat Alpan.

COUNCIL OF MINISTERS
(A coalition of the Justice Party (A.P.) and the Republican Reliance Party (C.G.P.), with seven Independents, formed April 1973.)

(July 1973)

Prime Minister: Senator Naim Talû (Ind.).
Deputy Prime Ministers: Kemal Satir (C.G.P.), Nizamettin Erkmen (A.P.).
Ministers of State: İlhan Öztrak (Ind.), İsmail Hakki Tekinel (A.P.).
Minister of Justice: Hayri Mumcuoğlu (Ind.).
Minister of Defence: İlhami Sancar (C.G.P.).
Minister of the Interior: Senator Mukadder Öztekin (Ind.).
Minister of Foreign Affairs: Ümit Halûk Bayülken (Ind).
Minister of Finance: Sadik Tekin Müftüoğlu (A.P.).
Minister of Education: Orhan Dengiz (A.P.).
Minister of Public Works: Nurettin Ok (A.P.).
Minister of Commerce: Ahmet Türkel (A.P.).
Minister of Health: Vefa Tanir (C.G.P.).
Minister of Customs and Monopolies: Fethi Çelikbaş (Ind.).
Minister of Agriculture: Ahmet Nurset Tuna (A.P.).
Minister of Communications: Sabahettin Özbek (Ind.).
Minister of Labour: Ali Naili Erdem (A.P.).
Minister of Industry: Nuri Bayar (A.P.).
Minister of Energy and Natural Resources: Kemal Demir (C.G.P.).
Minister of Housing and Reconstruction: Mehmet Nebil Oktay (C.G.P.).
Minister of Tourism and Information: Ahmet İhsan Kirimli (A.P.).
Minister of Rural Affairs: Orhan Kürümoğlu (A.P.).
Minister of Forests: İsa Bingöl (A.P.).
Minister of Youth and Sport: Celâlettin Coşkun (A.P.).

DIPLOMATIC REPRESENTATION

EMBASSIES AND LEGATIONS ACCREDITED TO TURKEY
(In Ankara unless otherwise stated)

(E) Embassy; (L) Legation.

Afghanistan: Yenişehir, Gazi Mustafa Kemal Bulvari 12 (E); *Ambassador:* Serdar G. M. Suleyman.
Albania: Gazi Osman Paşa, Nene Hatun Caddesi 89/2 (E); *Ambassador:* Ulvi Lulo.
Algeria: Baghdad, Iraq (E).
Argentina: Vali Dr. Reşit Cad. 82/3 (E); *Ambassador:* J. E. T. Sanchez Santamaria.
Australia: Gaziosmanpaşa, Nenehatun Cad. 83; *Ambassador:* J. M. McMillan.
Austria: Atatürk Bulvari 197 (E); *Ambassador:* Dr. Franz Herbatschek.
Belgium: Atatürk Bulvari 145 (E); *Ambassador:* André J. A. Wendelen.
Brazil: Esat Cad. 19, Bakanliklar (E); *Chargé d'Affaires a.i.:* Jose Augusto de Macedo Soares.
Bulgaria: Atatürk Bulvari 120 (E); *Ambassador:* Gantchev Vatchov.
Cameroon: Cairo, Egypt (E).
Canada: Vali Dr. Reşit Cad. 52 (E); *Ambassador:* Gerald Francis George Hughes.
Chad: (E); *Ambassador:* Joseph Chédid.
Chile: Çankaya, Şehit Ersan Cad. 34/6 (E); *Ambassador:* Alajandro Jara Lazcano.
China, People's Republic: Çankaya, Nergiz Sok II, (E); *Ambassador:* Liu Chun.
Cyprus: Vali Dr. Reşit Cad. 108, Çankaya (E); (vacant).
Czechoslovakia: Ataturk Bulvari 261 (E); *Ambassador:* Dr. Petr Brudnak.
Denmark: Gaziosmanpaşa Bölük Cad. 14 (E); *Ambassador:* S. A. Sandager Jeppesen.
Dominican Republic: London, England (E).
Egypt: Atatürk Bulvari 39 (E); *Ambassador:* (vacant).
El Salvador: Bad Godesberg, Federal Republic of Germany (E).
Ethiopia: Kavaklıdere, Tunalı Hilmi Cad. 93/5 (E); *Ambassador:* Col. Belachew Jemaneh.
Finland: Vali Dr. Reşit Cad. 15/3 (E); *Ambassador:* Ake J. B. Frey (also accred. to Afghanistan and Iran).
France: Paris Cad. 70, Kavaklıdere (E); *Ambassador:* Roger Vaurs.
Federal Republic of Germany: Atatürk Bulvari 114 (E); *Ambassador:* Dr. Gustav-Adolf Sonnenhol.

TURKEY—(Diplomatic Representation)

Ghana: Rome, Italy (E).
Greece: Fatma Alıye Sok. 1 and Yeşilyurt Sok. (E); *Ambassador:* IOANNIS TZOUNIS.
Hungary: Gazi Mustafa Kemal Bulvarı 10 (E); *Ambassador:* GYÖRGY ZAGOR.
Iceland: Copenhagen V, Denmark (E).
India: Kızılırmak Cad. 50 (E); *Ambassador:* K. R. NARAYANAN.
Indonesia: Çankaya, Abdullah Cevdet Sok. 10 (E); *Ambassador:* H. MOHAMMED ALI MOERSID.
Iran: Tahran Cad. 10 (E); *Ambassador:* DJAMEHID GHARIB.
Iraq: Muhammad Rıza Şah Pehlevi Cad. 47 (E); *Ambassador:* Dr. MAHMOUD ALI EL-DAOUD.
Ireland: Rome, Italy (E).
Israel: Vali Dr. Reşit Cad., Farabî Sok. 43 (L); *Chargé d'Affaires:* SHAUL BAR HAIM.
Italy: Atatürk Bulvarı 118 (E); *Ambassador:* GIORGIO SMOQUINA.
Japan: Gazi Osman Pasa, Resit Galip Cad. 81 (E); *Ambassador:* TATSUO HIROSE.
Jordan: Kavaklıdere, Vali Dr. Reşit Cad. 12 (E); *Ambassador:* ZUHAIR AL-MUFTI.
Korea, Republic of: Vali Dr. Reşit Cad., Alaçam Sok. 9 (E); *Ambassador:* CHAN HYUN PAK (also accred. to Iran and Jordan).
Kuwait: Ankara (E); *Ambassador:* M. Y. ABDUL-AZIZ AL-RUSHEID (also accred. to Bulgaria).
Lebanon: Çankaya, Vali Dr. Reşit Cad. 25/5 (E); *Ambassador:* FAIÇAL SULTAN.
Libya: Çankaya, Ebuzziya Tevfik Sok. 5 (E); *Chargé d'Affaires:* FERHAD ALGHERWI.
Malaysia: Teheran, Iran (E).
Mexico: Vali Dr. Reşit Cad. 41/13 (E); *Ambassador:* ALFONSO CASTRO-VALLE.
Morocco: Teheran, Iran (E).
Nepal: Islamabad, Pakistan (E).
Netherlands: Çankaya, Sehit Ersan Cad. 4 (E); *Ambassador:* COENRADD THEODOR VAN BAARDA.
Nigeria: Berne, Switzerland (E).
Norway: Farabi Sok. 27/7 (E); *Chargé d'Affaires:* ANFIM ULLERN (also accred. to Iraq).

Pakistan: Farabî Sok. 8 (E); *Ambassador:* ENVER MURAD.
Peru: Vienna, Austria (E).
Philippines: Rome, Italy (E).
Poland: Atatürk Bulvarı 251 (E); *Ambassador:* IGNACY LOGA-SOWIŃSKI.
Portugal: Vali Dr. Reşit Cad., Alemdaroğlu Apt. 28/3 (E); *Ambassador:* Dr. A. P. DE MESQUITA DE MELO MEXIA E VASCONCELOS (also accred. to Iran and Iraq).
Romania: Çankaya, Yeşilyurt Sok. 4 (E); *Ambassador:* GHEORGHE MARIN.
Saudi Arabia: Çankaya, Abdullah Cevdet Sok. 18 (E); *Ambassador:* SAMIR S. SHIHABI.
Senegal: Beirut, Lebanon (E).
Spain: Güvenevleri Yeşilyurt Sok. 25 (E); *Ambassador:* M. D. EMILIO GARRIGUES Y DIAZ CANABATE.
Sudan: Baghdad, Iraq (E).
Sweden: Kâtip Çelebi Sok. 5 (E); *Ambassador:* M. L. S. MATHEUS LUNDBORG.
Switzerland: Atatürk Bulvarı 263 (E); *Ambassador:* JEAN-DENIS GRANDJEAN.
Syria: Çankaya, Abdullah Cevdet Sok. 7 (E); *Ambassador:* Dr. SALAH EADINE TARAZI.
Thailand: Vienna, Austria (E).
Tunisia: Vali Dr. Reşit Cad. 11 (E); *Ambassador:* MOHAMMED SLIM BENGHAZI (also accred. to Iran).
U.S.S.R.: Çankaya, Kar Yağdı Sok (E); *Ambassador:* VASSILIY FEDOROVICH GROUBYAKOV.
United Kingdom: Çankaya, Şehit Ersan Cad. 46/A (E); *Ambassador:* Sir HORACE PHILLIPS.
U.S.A.: Atatürk Bulvarı 110 (E); *Ambassador:* WILLIAM B. MACOMBER.
Vatican: Gaziosmanpaşa, Reşit Galip Cad. 94 (Apostolic Internunicature); *Apostolic Internuncio:* Mgr. SALVATORE ASTA.
Venezuela: Kavaklıdere Cad. 23/6 (E); *Ambassador:* LUIS ALBERTO OLAVARRIA.
Viet-Nam, Republic: Vali Dr. Reşit 10 (E); *Chargé d'Affaires:* DANG NGOC TRAN (also accred. to Iran, Jordan and Lebanon).
Yugoslavia: Paris Cad. 47, Kavaklıdere (E); *Ambassador:* EDUARD KLUJN.
Zaire: *Ambassador:* GIALO BINO T. WAPINDA.

Turkey also has diplomatic relations with Barbados, Chad, Cuba, Guinea, Laos, Malawi, Mauritania, Mongolia, Qatar, Sierra Leone, Somalia, Uruguay and Yemen Arab Republic.

GRAND NATIONAL ASSEMBLY

SENATE
President: Tekin Arıburun.

Party	Seats Elections July 1970	April 1973
Justice Party	101	86
Republican People's Party	34	19
*National Reliance Party	11	20
Democratic Party	—	7
*Republican Party	—	—
National Action Party	1	—
Turkish Workers' Party	1	—
Nation Party	—	—
Independents	1	15
Presidential Appointees	15	15
Life Senators	18	18
Vacant	—	—
Ex-Presidents of the Republic	—	3
Total	**183**	**185**

NATIONAL ASSEMBLY
President: Sabit Osman Avcı.

Party	Seats General Election (Oct. 1969)	April 1973	Votes General Election (Oct. 1969)
Justice Party	257	224	4,229,712
Republican People's Party	144	97	2,487,006
Democratic Party	—	41	—
*National Reliance Party	15	44	597,818
*Republican Party	—	—	—
Nation Party	6	4	292,961
Turkish Unity Party	8	2	254,695
National Action Party	1	1	275,091
Turkish Workers' Party	2	—	243,631
New Turkey Party	6	—	197,929
Independent	11	22	511,023
Vacant	—	15	—
Total	**450**	**450**	

* The National Reliance Party merged with the Republican Party in March 1973 to form the Republican Reliance Party.

POLITICAL PARTIES

Justice Party (A.P.): Ankara; f. 1961; Leader Süleyman Demirel; Sec.-Gen. Nizamettin Erkmen; inherited much support from the former Democratic Party; supports private enterprise.

Republican People's Party (C.H.P.): Ankara; f. 1923 by Kemal Atatürk; Leader Bulent Ecevit; Sec.-Gen. Dr. Kâmil Kırıkoğlu; favours a considerable degree of State enterprise along with continuing private enterprise. In recent years the party has moved to the left of centre.

Democratic Party: Ankara; f. 1970 by deputies and senators expelled from the Justice Party; Leader Ferruh Bozbeyli.

Republican Reliance Party (C.G.P.): Ankara; f. 1967 as the National Reliance Party by 45 members of Parliament from the Republican People's Party, who broke away as a result of this party's "left of centre policies"; merged with Republican Party 1973; Leader Prof. Turhan Feyzioğlu.

Nation Party (M.P.): Ankara; f. 1962; traditional and religious in character; Leader Cemal Tural.

New Turkey Party (Y.T.P.): Ankara; f. 1961; moderate right-wing; dissolved itself March 1973 and most of its members joined the Justice Party.

Turkish Workers' Party (T.I.P.): Ankara; f. 1961; left-wing party, formerly having one seat in the Senate and two in the National Assembly but dissolved in July 1971 by the Turkish Constitutional Court for violating the Constitution; Leader Dr. Behice Boran.

Nationalist Movement Party (M.H.P.): 3 Cadde 47, Bahçelievler, Ankara; f. 1954; secularist and nationalist; seeks progressive reform; Leader Alparslan Türkeş; publs. *Devlet* (weekly), *Töre* (monthly).

Turkish Unity Party (T.B.P.): Ankara; f. 1968; Conservative; Leader Mustafa Timisi.

National Welfare Party (M.S.P.): Ankara; f. 1972; right-wing; took place of National Order Party which was closed down by order of the Constitutional Court; 3 mems. in Nat. Assembly since 1973 (fmr. mems. of Nat. Order Party).

DEFENCE

Chief of General Staff: Gen. Semih Sancar.

Defence Budget (1972-73): 8,124 million liras.

Military Service: 20 months.

Total Armed Forces: 449,000: army 360,000; navy 39,000; air force 50,000.

Paramilitary Forces: 75,000 Gendarmerie.

JUDICIAL SYSTEM

Until the foundation of the new Turkish Republic, a large part of the Turkish civil law—the laws affecting the family, inheritance, property, obligations, etc.—was based on the Koran, and this holy law was administered by special religious (Sharia) courts. The legal reform of 1926 was not only a process of secularization, but also a root-and-branch change of the legal system. The Swiss Civil Code and the Code of Obligation, the Italian Penal Code, and the Neuchâtel (Cantonal) Code of Civil Procedure were adopted and modified to fit Turkish customs and traditions.

Constitutional Court: Consists of fifteen regular and five alternate members. Reviews the constitutionality of laws passed by the Turkish Grand National Assembly. Sits as a High Council empowered to try senior members of state. The rulings of the Constitutional Court are final. Decisions of the Court are published immediately in the Official Gazette, and shall be binding on the legislative, executive, and judicial organs of the State.

Court of Cassation: The court of the last instance for reviewing the decisions and verdicts rendered by courts of law. It has original and final jurisdiction in specific cases defined by law. Members are elected by the Supreme Council of Judges.

Council of State: An administrative court of the first instance in matters not referred by law to other administrative courts, and an administrative court of the last instance in general. Hears and settles administrative disputes and expresses opinions on draft laws submitted by the Council of Ministers.

Military Court of Cassation: A court of the last instance to review decisions and verdicts rendered by military courts.

Court of Jurisdictional Disputes: Settles disputes among civil, administrative and military courts arising from disagreements on jurisdictional matters and verdicts.

Supreme Council of Judges: Consists of eighteen regular and five alternate members. Decides all personnel matters relating to judges.

Public Prosecutor: The law shall make provision for the tenure of public prosecutors and attorneys of the Council of State and their functions.

The Chief Prosecutor of the Republic, the Chief Attorney of the Council of State and the Chief Prosecutor of the Military Court of Cassation are subject to the provisions applicable to judges of higher courts.

Military Trial: Military trials conducted by military and disciplinary courts. These courts are entitled to try the military offences of military personnel and those offences committed against military personnel or in military areas, or offences connected with military service and duties. Military courts may try non-military persons only for military offences prescribed by special laws.

Independence of Courts: Judges shall be independent in the discharge of their duties. They shall pass judgment in accordance with the Constitution, law, justice and their personal convictions. No organ, office, agency or individual may give orders or instructions to courts or judges in connection with the discharge of their judicial duty, send them circulars, or make recommendations or suggestions.

No questions may be raised, debates held, or statements issued in legislative bodies in connection with the discharge of judicial power concerning a case on trial. Legislative, executive organs, and the administration are under obligation to comply with ruling of the courts. Such organs and the administration shall in no manner whatsoever alter court rulings or delay their execution.

State Security Courts: Set up by supplement to Article 136 of Constitution in March 1973 to prosecute offences against integrity of the State. Consists of presiding judge, four regular and two substitute judges, a public prosecutor and assistant public prosecutors.

RELIGION

MUSLIMS

Diyanet İşleri Reisi (*Head of the Muslim Faith in Turkey*): LÜTFİ DOĞAN (ad interim).

Over 98 per cent of the Turkish people are Muslims, mainly Sunnis. Under the Republic, from 1923 onwards, action was taken to reduce the influence of religion on state affairs: e.g., its association with the schools was curtailed, mosques and churches were sometimes closed and facilities denied to their adherents, both Muslim and Christian. The Muslim faith was also disestablished. After 1950 there was a change, and religious life was to a certain extent revived. Since the revolution of 1960, however, there has been a return to the more secular republic of Atatürk.

NON-MUSLIMS
Mainly Greek Orthodox, Armenian Christians and Jews.

THE PRESS

Under the Constitution of 1961, "the press is free within the limits of the law". Provision is made for recourse to a constitutional court in issues involving laws affecting the Press.

Following the Revolution of 1960 and the new Constitution, which also introduced a measure of protection for editors, came the Law for Preventive Measures of March 1962. This law provided penalties of imprisonment with forced labour for persons criticizing the 1960 Revolution or for defending the pre-1960 or pre-Atatürk régimes, or suggesting that Turkey is unable to thrive as a democracy.

Political offences affecting the Press and the protection of the State and civil order are treated in Articles 141 and 142 of the Penal Code, the latter providing penalties of up to 15 years imprisonment for Communist propaganda. Articles 158 and 159 penalize defamation of the President, the Republic, the nation and institutions such as the army, parliament and the courts.

The liberal conditions which followed the Revolution led to abuses. In the attempt to develop greater responsibility and self-discipline within the Press, the Press Council or Court of Honour was founded in 1960. Composed of publishers, journalists and private individuals, it censures those violating the voluntary Code of Ethics adopted by editors and owners. Lacking legal power, the Court has the disadvantage of depending on the support of newspaper membership, which may be withdrawn by editors seeking to avoid the Court's moral sanctions.

A stronger incentive of self-discipline was provided in 1961 by the Board of Official Announcements which supervises the just distribution of official announcements and advertising (which serve as an essential subsidy to the Press.) The Board, composed of a broadly chosen group of representatives of different professions, by its power to withhold advertisements, obliges editors to maintain standards and observe the Code of Ethics, and has put an end to the abuses of advertisement distribution of the pre-Revolutionary period.

Formerly most newspapers were family businesses, but recently companies have emerged and newspaper groups are beginning to develop. *Hürriyet, Milliyet* and *Hayat* each head a group of papers. The Hürriyet Group includes *Hürriyet, Günaydın* and several weekly and monthly papers and its own news agency. The Hayat Group, which is the largest group owning periodicals, includes *Hayat, Ses* (the cinema and arts magazine), and several children's periodicals. Most papers are politically independent. A small number, while not being political organs, are indirectly associated with political parties. Noteworthy among these are *Barış*, which supports the Republican People's Party, and *Son Havadis*, which supports the Justice Party.

Almost all Istanbul papers are also printed in Ankara and İzmir on the same day. Among the most serious and influential papers are the dailies *Milliyet* and *Cumhuriyet*. *Akbaba* is noted for its political satire. The most popular dailies are the Istanbul papers *Hürriyet, Milliyet, Tercüman, Son Havadis, Günaydın, Akşam* and *Cumhuriyet; Yeni Asır*, published in İzmir, is the best selling quality daily of the Aegean region. A major popular weekly is the illustrated magazine *Hayat*.

PRINCIPAL DAILIES

ADANA

Çukurova: Kızılay Cad.; f. 1961; political; Editor MEHMET OLGUNBAŞ; circ. 1,950.

Vatandaş: Dörtyolağzı 117 Sok. 11; f. 1951; political; Editor MİTHAT GÜLYAŞAR; circ. 1,700.

Yeni Adana: Kızılay Cad. 65; f. 1918; political; Editor ÇETİN R. YÜREGİR; circ. 2,000.

ANKARA

Adalet: Agâh Efendi Sok.; f. 1962; morning; political, supports the Democratic Party; Editor TURHAN DİLLİGİL; circ. 16,500.

Ankara Ekspres: Rüzgârlı Sok. 21/3; f. 1968; political; Editor YAŞAR AYSEV; circ. 4,150.

Ankara Ticaret Postası: Rüzgârlı Sok., O.W. Han; f. 1954; commercial; Editor CAHİD BAYDAR; circ. 3,000.

Barış: Şinasi Sok., Ulus; f. 1971; morning; political, supports the Republican People's Party; Editor CEMALETTİN ÜNLÜ; circ. 15,700.

Başkent: Rüzgârlı Sok. 21/2; f. 1968; political; Publisher İSMET ÖZKAN; circ. 4,100.

Daily News: Konur Sok. 16, Yenişehir; f. 1961; English language; Publisher-Editor İLHAN ÇEVİK; circ. 5,500.

Ekonomide Egemenlik: Atatürk Bulvarı 137/2; f. 1970; commercial; Editor FEHMİ ANLAROĞLU.

Halkçi: Rüzgârlı Sok. 39; f. 1956; evening; Editor ERDOĞAN TOKATLI; circ. 4,100.

Hür Anadolu: Rüzgârlı Sok. 21; f. 1967; political; Editor MUSTAFA ÖZKAN; circ. 4,050.

İktisadi İnkılâp: Plevne Sok. 12, Ulus; f. 1957; commercial; Editor ÜNSAL ÖZMEN; circ. 1,600.

İktisat ve Piyasa: İzmir Cad. 22/9; f. 1964; commercial; Proprietor ÜLKÜ BİLGİN; circ. 1,900.

İş ve Ekonomi: Rüzgârlı Sok., O.W. Han; f. 1964; Publisher-Editor COŞKUN BÖLÜKBAŞIOĞLU; circ. 2,000.

Memleket: Rüzgârlı Sok. 21/3; f. 1970; political; Editor ŞEMSİ BELLİ.

Resmi Gazete: Başbakanlık Neşriyat, ve Müdevvenat Genel Müdürlüğü; f. 1920; official gazette.

Tasvir: Ulus Han, Kat 5, Ulus; f. 1960; political; Propr. ŞAHİN AYMETE; Man. Dir. ŞAHAP GENSOY; circ. 8,500.

Turizm Ticaret: Çelikkale Sok. 8/12, Kızılay; f. 1970; commercial; Editor MEHMET EREN.

Turkiye Iktisat Gazetesi: Karanfil Sok. 56, Bakanlıklar; f. 1953; commercial; Editor SELAHATTİN TEDMAN.

Vatan: İbrahim Müteferrika Sok. 2/2; f. 1940; evening; Editor TURHAN TÜKEL; circ. 4,000.

Yenigün: Rüzgârlı Sok. 45/8, Ulus; f. 1968; political; Editor KEMAL YAZGAN; circ. 4,000.

Yeni Tanin: Agâh Efendi Sok. 2/A, Ulus; f. 1964; political Editor KEMAL YAZGAN; circ. 4,000.

Zafer: Çankırı Cad. 14; f. 1963; morning; political; Proprietor MUAMMER KIRANER; circ. 11,000.

BURSA

Bursanın Sesi: Yeniyol, Ersan Işhanı; f. 1969; political Editor NECATİ AKGÜN; circ. 800.

Haber: Kümbet Sok. 7; f. 1964; political; Editor TURHAN TAYAN; circ. 1,200.

Hakimiyet: Başak Cad. 5; f. 1950; political; Editor MUSTAFA TAYLA; circ. 5,500.

Millet: Ankara Cad. 59; f. 1960; political; Editor FATMA MAT; circ. 900.

ESKİŞEHİR

İstikbal: Çarşı, Değirmen Sok. 15/A; f. 1950; political; Editor İRFAN UĞURLUER.

TURKEY—(THE PRESS)

Milli İrade: Uygur Sok. 1; f. 1968; political; Editor ERDOĞAN KÂHYA.

Sakarya: Hacet Sok. 3; f. 1947; political; Editor BOZKURT ÜNÜGÜR.

ISTANBUL

Akşam: Mollafenari Sok. 30; f. 1918; independent; Editor İRFAN DERMAN; circ. 42,000; (closed down by the military authorities in February 1972).

Apoyevmatini: Suriye Çarşısı 10, Beyoğlu; f. 1925; Greek language; Publisher TAKVOR ACUN; circ. 3,500.

Babıalide Sabah: Sultanahmet, Adliye Bitişiği; f. 1965; political; Editor SABRİ YILMAZ; circ. 7,300.

Bizim Anadolu: Şeref Efendi Sok., Cağaloğlu; f. 1969; political; Editor ABDÜLKADİR BİLLURCU.

Cumhuriyet: Halkevi Sok. 39, Cağaloğlu; f. 1924; morning; independent political; Editor SAMİ KARAÖREN; circ. 90,000.

Dünya: Narlıbahçe Sok. 15, Cağaloğlu; f. 1952; morning; political; Editor TEKİN GÜZELBEYOĞLU; circ. 14,500.

Ekonomi: Cemal Nadir Sok. 22, Cağaloğlu; f. 1944; commercial; Editor SAFA ÇELİKER; circ. 1,500.

Ekspres: Şeref Efendi Sok. 44, Cağaloğlu; f. 1962; evening; Editor COŞKUM ÖZER.

Embros: Galip Dede Cad. 103, Tünel; f. 1953; Greek language; evening; Editor MİHAL VASILIYADİS; circ. 1,000.

Günlük Ticaret: Çemberlitaş Palas, Çemberlitaş; f. 1947; political; Editor NESRİN TUNÇBİLEK; circ. 1,700.

Günaydın: Alây köşkü Sok. 2; f. 1968; political; Editor RAHMİ TURAN; circ. 272,600.

Haber: Şeref Efendi Sok. 44, Cağaloğlu; f. 1934; political; Editor EROL DALLI; circ. 8,100.

Hergün: Cemal Nadir Sok. 9, Cağaloğlu; f. 1947; evening; Editor UĞUR GÜRTUNCA; circ. 8,300.

Hürriyet: Babıali Cad. 15-17, Cağaloğlu; f. 1948; morning; independent political; Publisher EROL SİMAVİ; Editor SALİM BAYER; circ. 650,000.

İstanbul Postası: Çatalçeşme Sok. 17, Cağaloğlu; f. 1946; commercial; Editor ÇETİN A. ÖZKIRIM; circ. 2,250.

Jamanak: İstiklâl Cad., Narmanlı Yurdu, Beyoğlu; f. 1908; Armenian; Chief Editor MARDİROS KOÇUNYAN; circ. 2,100.

Kelebek: Babıali Cad. 15-17, Cağaloğlu; f. 1972; morning; daily home magazine; Publisher EROL SİMAVİ; Editor ZEYNEP AVCI; circ. 260,000.

Marmara: İstiklâl Cad. 360/12, Tünel; f. 1941; Armenian language; Editor R. HADDECİYAN; circ. 1,700.

Milliyet: Nuruosmaniye Caddesi 65; f. 1950; morning; political; Editor ABDİ İPEKÇİ; circ. 250,000 (weekdays), 300,000 (Sunday).

Son Havadis: Şeref Efendi Sok. 44, Cağaloğlu; f. 1951; supports the Justice Party; Editor CAN KAYA İSEN; circ. 34,500.

Son Saat: Çemberlitaş Palas Kat 1, Cağaloğlu; f. 1956; evening; Editor SELİM BİLMEN; circ. 8,700.

Tercüman: Nuruosmaniye, Cağaloğlu; f. 1961; political; Editor SADETTİN ÇULCU; circ. 266,000.

Yeni Asya: Şeref Efendi Sok. 32, Cağaloğlu; f. 1970; political; Editor A. RAHMİ ERDEM; circ. 9,400.

Yeni İstanbul: Dr. Emin Paşa Sok. 20, Cağaloğlu; f. 1950; independent political; Editor DOĞAN KOLOĞLU; circ. 29,200.

İZMİR

Ege Ekonomi: 2 Beyler Sok. 45/A; f. 1968; commercial; Editor KÂZIM YENİSEY; circ. 2,200.

Ege Telgraf: Atatürk Cad. 150; f. 1960; evening; political; Editor SÜHA SÜKÂTÎ TEKİL.

Ekspres: 856 Sok. No. 46; f. 1952; political; Editor İŞLTHAN ESEN; circ. 52,000.

Ticaret: Gazi Bulvarı 18; f. 1942; commercial and political news; Editor SEZAİ GÜVEN; circ. 7,600.

Yeni Asır: Gazi Osman Paşa Bulvarı 13/A; f. 1895; political; Editor CEMİL DEVRİM; circ. 65,000.

KONYA

Yeni Konya: İş Bankası bitişiği 4; f. 1949; political; Editors GÜLTEKİN and AYHAN GÜCÜYENER; circ. 2,500.

Yeni Meram: Mevlâna Cad. Sağlık Pasajı; f. 1949; political; Editor A. RIDVAN BÜLBÜL; circ. 1,660.

WEEKLIES

ANKARA

Ekonomi ve Politika: Tunus Cad. 12/3 Bakanlıklar; f. 1966; economic and political; Publisher ZİYA TANSU.

Hız: Necatibey Cad., Sezenler Sok.; f. 1965; labour news; Publisher ŞERAFETTİN AKOVA; Editors İSMAİL S. GAŞAN, ERTAN OKTAY; circ. 10,000.

Outlook: Konur Sokak 27/7, Kizilay P.K. 210; f. 1967; English language; Editor M. A. KIŞLALI.

Türkiye Ticaret Sicili: Karanfil Sok. 56, Bakanlıklar; f. 1957; commercial; Editor OKTAY DİZDAROĞLU.

Yarın: İnkılap Sok. 25/2, Yenişehir; f. 1963; political; Publisher-Editor MÜFİT DURU.

Yanki: Konor Suk. 27/7, Bakanlıklar, Kizilay P.K. 210; f. 1970; Editor MEHMET ALİ KIŞLALI.

İSTANBUL

Akbaba: Klodfarer Cad. 8-10, Divanyolu; f. 1923; satirical; Editor KADRİ YURDATAP.

Doğan Kardeş: Türbedar Sok. 22, Cağaloğlu; f. 1945; illustrated children's magazine; Editor SEZAİ SOLELLİ; circ. 40,000.

Durum: Nuruosmaniye Cad., Atasaray Iş Hanı, Kat 1.3, no. 102-302; f. 1964; political; Editor MİTHAT PERİN.

Geçit: Nuruosmaniye Cad., Atasaray Han 408; f. 1966; political; Publisher FÜRÜZAN TEKİL.

Hayat: Türbedar Sok. 22, Divanyolu; f. 1956; general interest illustrated magazine; Publisher ŞEVKET RADO.

İstanbul Ticaret: İstanbul Ticaret Odası, Eminönü-Unkapanı Cad.; f. 1957; commercial news; Publisher İSMAİL ÖZASLAN.

La Vera Luz: Tahtakale Cad., Prevuayans Han 12; f. 1951; Jewish news weekly; Publisher İLYAZER MENDA.

Pazar: Alây Köşkü Cad. 12, Cağaloğlu; f. 1956; illustrated; Publisher HALDUN SİMAVİ.

Resimli Roman: Türbedar Sok. 22, Cağaloğlu; f. 1965; twice weekly; illustrated; Editor SEZAİ SOLELLİ; circ. 120,000.

Şalom: Bereket Han 24/5, Karaköy; f. 1948; Jewish; Publisher AVRAM LEYON.

Ses: Türbedar Sok. 22, Cağaloğlu; f. 1962; illustrated film magazine; Editor ERDOĞAN SEVGİN; circ. 90,000.

Tutum: Nuruosmaniye Cad. 54; f. 1967; political; Editor ERDOĞAN AKKURT.

TURKEY—(THE PRESS)

Yeni Gavroş: Billûr Sok. 10, Karaköy; f. 1945; Armenian news weekly; Publisher Boğos ARTUR.

PERIODICALS
ANKARA

Adalet Dergisi: Adalet Bakanlığı; f. 1909; legal journal published by the Ministry of Justice; Editor HÜSEYIN ERGÜL; circ. 3,500.

Ankara Barosu Dergisi: f. 1944; monthly; journal of the Ankara Bar.

Azerbaycan: Azerbaizhan Cultural Association, P.K. 165; f. 1949; literary; Editor Dr. AHMET YAŞAT.

Bayrak Dergisi: Necatibey Cad., Karakimseli Han; f. 1964; Pub. and Editor HAMI KARTAY.

Çiftlik Dergisi: P.K. 43, Bakanlıklar-Ankara; f. 1960; agricultural; monthly; Publisher VASFİ HAKMAN; circ. 10,000.

Devlet Operası: Devlet Operası Umum Md.; art, opera.

Devlet Tiyatrosu: Devlet Tiyatrosu Um. Md.; f. 1952; art, theatre.

Dost: Menekşe Sok. 16/13, Yenişehir; f. 1947; literary; Editor SALİM SENGİL.

Elektrik Mühendisliği Mecmuası: Ihlamur Sokak 10/1, Yenişehir; f. 1954; published by the Chamber of Turkish Electrical Engineers.

Halkevleri Dergisi: Atatürk Bulvarı 104; f. 1966; art, literary; Publisher KADRİ KAPLAN.

Hisar: P.K. 501; f. 1950; literary; monthly; Editor-in-Chief MEHMET ÇINARLI; Editor SETENAY BATU.

İdare Dergisi: İçişleri Bakanlığı; administrative.

İlk Öğretim: Millî Eğitim Bakanlığı; educational.

İller ve Belediyeler Dergisi: Mithat Paşa Cad. 45/2; f. 1945; monthly journal of the Turkish Municipal Asscn.; Pres. İSMET SEZGİN.

Karınca: Mithat Paşa Cad. 38/A, Yenişehir; f. 1934; monthly revue published by the Turkish Co-operative Society; circ. 6,000.

Maden Tetkik ve Arama Enstitüsü Dergisi: Eskişehir Yolu; f. 1935; bi-annual; publ. by Mineral Research and Exploration Institute of Turkey; English Edition *Bulletin of the Mineral Research and Exploration Institute* (bi-annual).

Meslekî ve Teknik Öğretim: Millî Eğitim Bakanlığı; f. 1942; educational.

Mühendis ve Makina: Çelikkale Sok. 3, Kızılay; f. 1957; engineering monthly; Publ. Chamber of Mechanical Engineers; Dir. ARSLAN SANIR; Editor SELAMİ ÜNER.

Önasya Dergisi: P.K. 605; f. 1965; monthly; cultural; Publisher SADİ BAYRAM; circ. 5,000.

Resmi Kararlar Dergisi: Ministry of Justice, Adalet Bakanlığı; f. 1966; legal; Editor AVNİ ÖZENÇ; circ. 3,500.

T. C. Merkez Bankası Aylık Bülten: Merkez Bank; monthly.

Türk Arkeoloji Dergisi: General Directorate of Antiquities and Museums, Eski Eserler ve Müzeler Genel Müdürlüğü; archaeological.

Türk Dili: Türk Dil Kurumu, Atatürk Bulvarı 221, Kavaklıdere; f. 1951; monthly; literary.

Türk Kültürü: Tunus Cad. 16; f. 1962; cultural studies; Editor Prof. Dr. AHMET TEMİR.

Turkey—Economic News Digest: Karanfil Sok. 56; f. 1960; Editor-in-Chief BEHZAT TANIR; Man. Editor SADIK BALKAN.

Türkiye Bankacılık: P.K. 121; f. 1955; commercial; Publisher MUSTAFA ATALAY.

Türkiye Bibliyografyası: Millî Kütüphane Genel Müdürlüğü, Yenişehir; f. 1934; quarterly; Turkish national bibliography; published by the Bibliographical Institute of the Turkish National Library; Dir. FİLİZ BAŞBUĞOĞLU.

Yeni Yayınlar, Aylık Bibliografya Dergisi (*New Publications, Monthly Bibliographic Journal*):P.K. 440, Kızılay, Ankara; f. 1956; Published by Asscn. of Univ. Library School Graduates; Dir. ÖZER SOYSAL.

Ziraat Dergisi: Posta K. 305; f. 1950; monthly; agriculture.

Ziraat Dünyası: Posta K. 127; f. 1950; monthly; agriculture.

ISTANBUL

Arkitekt: Anadolu Han 32, Eminönü; f. 1931; quarterly; architecture, city planning and tourism; Chair. Dr. Arch. ZEKİ SAYÂR; Sec. KETİ ÇAPANOĞLU.

Bakış: Cağaloğlu Yokuşu; f. 1945; Editor AVNİ ALTINLER.

Banka ve Ekonomik Yorumlar: Erçevik Işhani 316, Sultanahmet, Istanbul; f. 1964; banking, economic, social and management subjects; Publisher NEZİH H. NEYZİ; circ. 2,500.

Deniz: Rıhtım Cad., Veli Alemdar Han, Kat 6/23, Karaköy; f. 1955; monthly; maritime news; Publisher EMEL KAZANLIOĞLU.

Filim: P.K. 307, Beyoğlu; f. 1970; cinema; Editor ONAT KUTLAR.

İktisadi Yükseliş: P.K. 317; f. 1949; economic; Publisher ŞEMSETTİN CURA.

Istanbul, A Handbook for Tourists: Sişli Meydanı, 364; f. 1968; quarterly; published by the Touring and Automobile Club of Turkey; Publisher Dr. NEJAT F. ECZACIBAŞI; Editor ÇELİK GÜLERSOY.

İstanbul Barosu Dergisi: f. 1926; monthly; published by the Istanbul Bar.

İstanbul Ticaret Odası Mecmuası: f. 1884; every two months; journal of the Istanbul Chamber of Commerce; Turkish and English; Editor Dr. YILDIRIM KILKIŞ.

Kadın: Nuruosmaniye Cad., Benice Han 54, Cağaloğlu; f. 1947; serious, political, women's magazine; Publisher İFFET HALİM ORUZ.

Kemalizm: Bankalar Cad., Ankara H. 16; f. 1962; Publisher HÜSEYİN SAĞIROĞLU.

Köy Postası: Nuruosmaniye Cad. 57; f. 1944; Editor KADRİ OĞUZ.

Kulis: Cağaloğlu Yokuşu 10/A; f. 1947; fortnightly arts magazine; Armenian; Publisher HAGOP AYVAZ.

Musiki Mecmuası: Mehtap S. 15, Erenköy, P.K. 666; f. 1948; monthly; music and musicology; Editor ETEM RUHİ ÜNGÖR.

Pirelli: Büyükdere Cad. 151, Gayrettepe; f. 1964; Publisher EMİL ELÂGÖZ.

Polis Dergisi: Kuledibi, Emniyet Sarayı, Karaköy; f. 1954; Publisher ADNAN KİRMAN.

Polis Magazin: İstiklâl Cad. 364/18, Beyoğlu; f. 1958; Publisher MİTHAT ENGİN VİRANYALI.

Ruh ve Madde Dergisi: P.K. 1157; f. 1959; organ of the Metapsychic and Scientific Research Society of Turkey; Publisher ERGÜN ARIKDAL.

TURKEY—(THE PRESS)

Sağlık Âlemi: Divanyolu Cad. Ersoy Pasajı 1, Cağaloğlu; f. 1964; health; Editor ATİLÂ YÜCEL.

Sevgi Dünyası (*World of Love*): Larmartin Cad. 26/3, Taksim; f. 1963; Publisher Dr. R. KAYSERİLİOĞLU; circ. 10,000.

Söz: Piyerloti Cad. 7, Divanyolu; f. 1966; political; Editor GENÇAY GÜN.

Tıb Dünyası: Ankara Cad. 31/3 Küçük Han, Cağaloğlu, P.K. 192; f. 1927; monthly; organ of the Turkish Mental Health and Social Psychiatry Society; Editor Dr. FAHRETTİN KERİM GÖKAY.

Türk Anglo-Amerikan ve Almanya Postası: P.K. 192, Beyoğlu; f. 1947; commercial; Publisher KEMAL ERKAN.

Türk Folklor Araştırmaları: P.K. 46, Aksaray; f. 1949; arts and folklore; Editor İHSAN HINÇER.

Türk Ticaret Almanağı: Mollafenari Sok. 25, Cağaloğlu; commercial; Editor REŞAT TOPALOĞLU.

Turkish Trade Directory: Peykhane Caddesi 14, Daire 1, Cemberlitas; f. 1960; annual; Publisher SERGIO COSTANTE.

Turkish Trade Telex Index: Peykhane Caddesi 14, Daire 1, Cemberlitas; f. 1972; annual; Publisher SERGIO COSTANTE.

Türkiye Turing ve Otomobil Kurumu Belleteni: Halaskargazi Cad. 364, Şişli Meydanı; f. 1930; quarterly; published by the Touring and Automobile Club of Turkey; Publisher Dr. NEJAT ECZACIBAŞI; Editor ÇELİK GÜLERSOY.

Türkiyede ve Dünyada Tarım: P.K. 578; f. 1964; agricultural news; Publisher KEMAL BAYKAL.

Ülkücü Öğretman: Divanyolu Cad. 64, Cağaloğlu; f. 1965; education; Publisher HALİD BERK; Editor-in-Chief TEVFİK MARAL.

Varlık: Cağaloğlu Yokuşu 40; f. 1933; monthly; literary; Editor YAŞAR NABİ NAYIR.

Yeditepe: P.K. 77, Cağaloğlu, Mengene Sok., Yeni Han 21; f. 1950; literary and cultural; monthly; Editor HÜSAMETTİN BOZOK.

Yelken: P.K. 639, Karaköy; f. 1955; arts; Editor RÜKNETTİN RESULOĞLU.

Yeni Sanayi Dünyası: P.K. 515, Beyoğlu; f. 1963; Editor NURETTİN ÖZŞIMŞEK.

İZMİR

Devir Dergisi: Halit Zıya Bulvari 74A; f. 1972; political; weekly; Editor OLTEMUR KILIÇ.

İzmir Barosu Dergisi: f. 1967; monthly; journal of the İzmir Bar; Editor CİHANGİR KUTLAY; Propr. NECDET ÖKLEM; circ. 1,000.

İzmir Ticaret Odası Dergisi: Atatürk Cad. 126; f. 1925; monthly; commercial.

KONYA

Çağrı Dergisi: P.K. 99; f. 1957; literary; monthly; Editor FEYZİ HALICI.

NEWS AGENCIES

Anatolian News Agency: Ankara and Istanbul; f. 1920; Gen. Man. ATTILA ONUK; publ. *Weekly Economical Bulletin*.

Haber Ajansı: Ersoy Han, Cağaloğlu; f. 1963; Dir.-Gen. AYDOĞAN ÖNOL.

İKA Economic and Commercial News Agency: Tunus Cad. 12/3, Bakanlıklar, Ankara; f. 1954; Dir. ZİYA TANSU; publs. *Daily Economic and Commercial Bulletin*, *Investment and Finance Bulletin* (both English and Turkish), *Labour, Law and Social Insurance Bulletin*, *Ekonomi ve Politika*.

Türk Haberler Ajansı (*Turkish News Agency*): Basın Sarayı, Cağaloğlu, Istanbul; f. 1950; 11 brs. in Turkey; Dir.-Gen. KADRİ KAYABAL; Editor in Chief HASAN YILMAER.

FOREIGN BUREAUX

AFP (*France*): P..K 30. Cankaya-Ankara, Güneş Sok. 14; Corr. VINCENT LATÈVE.

ANSA (*Italy*): Gelincik Sok. 7A/6, Ankara; Corr. ROMANO DAMIANI.

AP (*U.S.A.*): Konur Sok. 16, Kizilay, Ankara; Corr. NICHOLAS S. LUDINGTON.

DPA (*Federal Germany*): Ahmet Mithat Efendi Sok. 20/1, Cankaya-Ankara.

UPI (*U.S.A.*): Basın Sarayı, Çağaloğlu; Bureau Chief JOHN LAWTON.

AFP also has representatives in Istanbul and İzmir. Reuters (*U.K.*) and TASS (*U.S.S.R.*) are also represented in Turkey.

PRESS ASSOCIATIONS

Editörler Derneği (*Editors' Union*): Ankara Cad. 93, Istanbul; f, 1950; Pres. REMZİ BENGİ; Sec. RAMAZAN ARKIN.

TURKEY—(Publishers, Radio and Television)

PUBLISHERS

Ağaoğlu Yayınevi: Selvilimesçit Sokak 2, Kurt İş Hanı, Cağaloğlu, Istanbul; translations and literary books; Mustafa Kemal Ağaoğlu.

Akgün Matbaası: Istanbul.

Ark Ticaret Ltd. ŞTİ: P.K. 577, Ankara; f. 1962; imports technical books and exports all kinds of Turkish books, periodicals and newspapers; Gen. Man. Atılan Tümer.

Arkın Kitabevi—Bir Yayınevi: Ankara Cad. 60, P.K. 11, Istanbul; f. 1949; encyclopedias, atlases, children's books, reference; Pres. and Man. Ramazan Gökalp Arkın.

Atlas Kitabevi Yayınevi: Nuruosmaniye Caddesi, Mengene Sokak 7-9, Istanbul: literary.

Ayyıldız Matbaası: Ankara.

Baha Matbaası: Cemal Nadir Sokak 12, Istanbul.

Başkent Yayınevi: Anafartalar Caddesi, Nilüfer Sokak 5A, Istanbul; literary.

Bates Bayilik Teşkilâtı A.Ş.: Molla Fenari Sokak 1, Cağaloğlu, Istanbul; f. 1960; books and periodicals.

Bedri Yayınevi: Istanbul.

Berkalp Kitabevi: Şehir Bahçesi 7/8, Ankara.

Cumhuriyet Mat. ve Gaze T.A.Ş.: Halkevi Sokak 40/41, Cağaloğlu, Istanbul.

De Yayınevi: Vilâyet Han, Kat. 3, Cağaloğlu, Istanbul; literary.

Depas: 56 Cumhuriyet Bulvarı, Izmir.

Elif Kitabevi: Sahaflar Çarşısı 4, Beyazit, Istanbul; f. 1956; all types of publications, especially historical, literary, political, drama and reference; publ. *Elif Yayınları Kitap Belleten* (twice monthly).

Forum Yayınları: Ankara; literary and artistic books.

Gerçek Yayınevi: Istanbul; economic.

İnkılâp Kitabevi: Ankara Caddesi 95, Istanbul; Dir. Nazar Fikri.

İnkılâp ve Aka Kitabevleri Kollektif Şirketi: Ankara Caddesi 95, Istanbul; Dir. Karabet Fikri.

İzel Yayınları: Istanbul; plays.

Kanaat Kitabevi: Ilyas Bayar Halefi, Yakup Bayar, Ankara Caddesi 133, Istanbul; f. 1896; textbooks, novels, dictionaries, posters, maps and atlases.

Kanaat Yayınları Ltd. Şti: Narlıbahçe Sokak 19, Istanbul; f. 1951; maps, school books; Dir. Yakup Bayar.

Kültür Kitabevi: Ankara Cad. 62, Sirkeci, Istanbul; f. 1945; technical books, school books, language books, etc.; Dirs. İzidor and Rene Kant.

Neşriyat A.Ş.: Mollafenari S.1, Cağaloğlu, Istanbul; classics, children's books, novels.

Nil Yayınevi: Istanbul; literary translations.

Nişantaşı Deniz Kitabevi: Nisantas, Istanbul; poetry.

Öğretim Yayınevi: Ankara Cad. 62/2, Sirkeci, Istanbul; f. 1959; English, French, German, Italian and Dutch language courses, guides and dictionaries; Dir. İzidor Kant.

Remzi Kitabevi: Ankara Caddesi 93, Istanbul; f. 1930; school textbooks, novels, fiction, children's, science and art books; Dir. Remzi Bengi.

Sermet Matbaası: Şeref Efendi Sok. 28, Cağaloğlu, Istanbul; f. 1950; books on medicine, statistics, economics, mathematics, dictionaries; Gen. Man. Sermet Arkadaş.

Tifdruk Matbaacılık Sanayii Anonim Şirketi: Topkapı Davutpaşa Caddesi 101, Istanbul; f. 1955; novels, magazines, encyclopaedia; Pres. Kâzım Taşkent.

Türk Dil Kurumu: Atatürk Bulvarı, 221 Kavaklıdere, Ankara; f. 1932; non-fiction.

T.T.K. Basımevi: Ankara.

Türkiye Yayınevi: Ankara Caddesi 36, Istanbul.

Üniversite Kitabevi: Istanbul.

Varlık Yayınevi: Cağaloğlu Yokuşu 40, Istanbul; f. 1946; fiction and non-fiction books; Dir. Yaşar Nabi Nayir.

Yeditepe Yayınları: P.K. 77, Cağaloğlu, Mengene Sok., Yeni Han 21, Istanbul; publishes literature, poetry, translations, etc. and also *Yeditepe* (monthly).

Yeni Zaman Kitabevi: Ankara Caddesi 155, Istanbul; f. 1970; Dir. Rozin Iulia Fikri.

RADIO AND TELEVISION

RADIO

Turkiye Radyo Televizyon Kurumu (T.R.T.): Mithat Paşa Caddesi 37, Ankara; f. 1964; controls Turkish radio and television services; Dir.-Gen. Musa Öğün.

Home Service:

Radio Ankara: LW, 1,200 kW., Dir. Oğuz Yılmaz Hiçyılmaz.

Ankara II Programme: MW, 2 kW., Dir. Oğuz Yılmaz Hiçyılmaz.

Ankara III Programme: FM, 0.25 kW., Dir. Oğuz Yılmaz Hiçyılmaz.

Radio Antalya: MW, 600 kW., Dir. Ayhan Dündar.

Radio Çukurova: MW, 300 kW., Dir. Ali Rıza Erdoğan.

Radio Diyarbakır: MW, 300 kW., Dir. Rıdvan Çongur.

Radio Istanbul: MW, 150 kW., Dir. Alâaddin Göktuğ.

Istanbul II Programme: MW, 2 kW., Dir. Alâaddin Göktuğ.

Radio Erzurum: LW, 100 kW., Dir. Selâhattin Altay.

Radio Izmir: MW, 100 kW., Dir. Nihat Uytun.

İzmir II Programme: MW, 2 kW., Dir. Nihat Uytun.

Radio Kars: MW, 2 kW., Dir. Hasan Kınaş.

Radio Van: MW, 2 kW., Dir. Kadir Kaynar.

Radio Gaziantep: MW, 2 kW., Dir. Adil Dai.

Radio Trabzon: MW, 2 kW., Dir. Kemâl Kolluoğlu.

Radio Hakkâri: SW, 2 kW., Dir. Mehmet Güven.

Foreign Service:

Ankara I: SW, 100 kW.

Ankara II: SW, 250 kW. Nine daily short-wave transmissions in the following languages: Arabic, Bulgarian, English, French, German, Greek, Romanian, Serbo-Croat, Turkish. Dir. Oğuz Yılmaz Hiçyılmaz; also on the above frequency:

Voice of Turkey: broadcasting to Turks in Europe.

Technical University of Istanbul: 0.5 kW., Frequency Modulation; broadcasts for Istanbul; Dir.-Gen. Prof. Dr. A. Ataman.

In 1972 3,941,293 licenced radio receivers were in use.

TELEVISION

Türkiye Radyo Televizyon Kurumu (Ankara TV): Mithat Paşa Caddesi 49, Ankara. A limited television service was set up in 1965, and regular broadcasts for Ankara began in 1968, now transmitting programmes five days a week and four hours a day from 8 transmitters. New studios are to be established in Ankara, Istanbul and İzmir; Head of Television and Dept. of T.V. Programmes Cevdet Karahan; Head of Dept. of TV Studios of TRT: Fahrettin Işıkçı.

In 1972 132,804 licenced television receivers were in use.

FINANCE

(cap. = capital; p.u. = paid up; dep. = deposits; m. = million; brs. = branches)
Amounts in Turkish liras, except where otherwise stated. Figures given for capital and deposits are for the end of the calendar year stated, except where otherwise stated.)

The Central Bank of the Republic of Turkey was originally founded in 1931, and constituted in its present form after the revolution of 1960. The Central Bank is the bank of issue and is responsible also for public deposits, and medium and long-term borrowings of the banks. In addition, all international payments go through the Bank, and all foreign exchange is held by the Bank.

There are some 50 other banks functioning in Turkey. Thirteen had been created by special laws to fulfil specialized services for particular industries. The Sümerbank directs the operation of a number of state-owned factories; Etibank operates primarily in the extractive industries and electric power industries; the Agricultural Bank makes loans for agriculture; the Maritime Bank operates government-owned port facilities, the merchant marine and its own fleet of ships; the Real Estate Credit Bank participates in industrial undertakings and the construction of all types of buildings. Other specialized banks deal with tourism, municipalities and mortgages, etc.

The largest of the 33 private sector Turkish banks is the Türkiye İş Bankası which operates over 500 branches. The private banks borrow at medium- and long-term mainly from the State Investment Bank.

These banks are required to contribute credits to the Bank Liquidation Fund set up by law in December 1960 to liquidate gradually those banks whose financial standing was unsatisfactory. This fund is derived from annual contributions of 0.2 per cent of savings and commercial deposits and since 1960 has been made up to the required amount by the Central Bank.

There are three foreign banks operating branches in Turkey. Apart from these the Ottoman Bank, which was founded in 1863 and is the oldest bank in Turkey, has strong British and French interests, while the Turkish Foreign Trade Bank is partly owned by the Bank of America and the Banca d'America e d'Italia.

There are several other credit institutions in Turkey, including the Industrial Development Bank of Turkey, which encourages private investment in industry by acting as underwriter in the issue of share capital. The Turkiye Sınai Kalkınma Bankası is a privately owned development finance company founded in 1950 with the assistance of the World Bank to stimulate industrial growth in the private sector.

There are numerous co-operative organizations, and in the rural areas there are Agricultural Sale Co-operatives and Agricultural Co-operatives. There are also a number of savings institutions.

BANKING
STATE BANKS

Türkiye Cumhuriyet Merkez Bankası (*Central Bank of the Republic of Turkey*): Bankalar Caddesi 48, Ankara; f. 1931; bank of issue; part of the share capital is owned by the State; cap. p.u. 25m.; dep. 7,712m.; Gov. M. Güpgüpoğlu.

Devlet Yatırım Bankası (*State Investment Bank*): Ankara; f. 1964; loans and guarantees to State enterprises; cap. 1,000m.

Etibank: Atatürk Bulvarı, Cihan Sok., Sihhiye, Posta K. 505, Ankara; f. 1935; Government Bank for mineral, electric-power and banking development; cap. p.u. 2,000m.; Gen. Man. Nezihi Berkkam.

İller Bankası (*Municipal Bank*): Atatürk Bulvarı, Ankara; f. 1945; Government Municipalities Bank; cap. p.u. 2,000m.; Chair. of Board and Gen. Dir. Mazhar Haznedar.

Sümerbank: Ulus Meydanı 2, Ankara; Holdings Bank for governmental industrial undertakings; cap. p.u. 1,500m.; Gen. Man. Hızır Geylan.

Türkiye Cumhuriyeti Turizm Bankası: Ankara; f. 1960; state bank to develop tourism; authorized cap. 500m., cap. p.u. 129.4m; Gen. Man. Ilhan Evliaoglu.

Türkiye Cumhuriyeti Ziraat Bankası (*Agricultural Bank of the Republic of Turkey*): Bankalar Caddesi, Ankara; f. 1863; Government Agricultural Bank; 774 branches; cap. p.u. 1,127m.; dep. 13,730m. (1971); Gen. Man. Nevzat Alptürk.

Türkiye Emlâk Kredi Bankası A.O. (*Real Estate Credit Bank of Turkey*): Atatürk Bulvarı 15, Ankara; f. 1946; cap. p.u. 1,000m. (1971); 123 brs.; Pres. and Gen. Man. Miraç Aktuğ.

Türkiye Sınai Kalkınma Bankası A.Ş. (*Industrial Development Bank of Turkey*): Meclisi Mebusan Cad. 137, Fındıklı, Istanbul; f. 1950; cap. 193.4m.; loans and investments 2,216m. (1972); Chair. Ferid Basmacı; Gen. Man. Reşid Egeli.

Türkiye Vakıflar Bankası T.A.O.: Bankalar Caddesi 52, Ankara; f. 1954; state bank controlling funds of religious foundations; cap. p.u. 50m.; dep. 2,165m. (1972); 149 brs.; Chair. Ziya Kayla; Gen. Man. Cavid Oral.

Denizçilik Bankası T.A.O. (*Turkish Maritime Bank*): Rihtim Caddesi, Posta K. 1387, Istanbul; a semi-public corporation with a 99-year charter, which took over the function of the former State Seaways and Harbours

TURKEY—(FINANCE)

Administration; f. 1952; cap. approx. 1,500m., of which 51 per cent is subscribed by the Government, the rest by private investors and organizations; Gen. Man. CELALETTIN EROL.

PRINCIPAL COMMERCIAL BANKS

Akbank T.A.S.: Eski Gümrük Sokak 2, P.K. 926, Karaköy, Istanbul; f. 1948; cap. p.u. 150m., dep. 6,838m. (Dec. 1972); 326 brs.; Chair. BÜLENT YAZICI; Gen. Man. MEDENİ BERK; publ. monthly bulletin.

Anadolu Bankası A.Ş.: Okçu Musu Caddesi, Karaköy, Istanbul; f. 1962; cap. p.u. 45m., deposits 610m. (1972); successor to Türk Ekspres Bank and Buğday Bankası; Gen. Man. SAİT DARGA.

Demirbank T.A.Ş.: 44–46 Bankalar Caddesi, Karaköy, Istanbul; f. 1953; cap. p.u. 12m., dep. 85.6m. (1972); Pres. TEVFİK ERENGÜL; Gen. Man. NURİ CINGILLIOĞLU.

Egebank, S.A.: Atatürk Avenue 80, P.K. 251, İzmir; f. 1928; cap. p.u. 5m., dep. 23.5m. (1972); Chair. ŞEVKET FİLİBELİ.

İstanbul Bankası T.A.Ş.: Beyoğlu istiklâl Caddesi, Mısır Apart. 309, Galatasaray, Istanbul; f. 1953; cap. p.u. 35m., dep. 210m. (1972); Pres. KEMAL HASOĞLU; Gen. Man. EROL TOKSÖZ.

Osmanlı Bankası (*Ottoman Bank*): Bankalar Caddesi, Karaköy, Istanbul; f. 1863; authorised cap. 10m., cap. p.u. 5m., dep. 112.9m. (1972); Dir.-Gen. J. JEULIN; over 90 brs.

Pamukbank T.A.S.: İstiklâl Caddesi 261, Galatasaray, Istanbul; f. 1955; cap. p.u. 25m., dep. 478.3m. (1972); 65 brs.; Chair. KEMAL ÇELİK; Gen. Man. FETHİ AŞKIN.

Şekerbank T.A.Ş.: Atatürk Bulvarı 55, Ankara; f. 1953; cap. p.u. 40m., dep. 716m. (1972); 106 brs.; Chair. of Board HALİL ATALAY; Gen. Man. ÖMER SUNAR.

Türk Dış Ticaret Bankası A.Ş. (*Turkish Foreign Trade Bank*): Cumhuriyet Caddesi 199-201, Harbiye, P.K. 11, Şişli, Istanbul; f. 1964; cap. p.u. 10m., dep. 320m. (1972); jointly owned by Bank of America, Türkiye İş Bankası and Banca d'America e d'Italia; brs. in Ankara, Istanbul (three) and İzmir; Chair. A. ÜSKÜDAELİ; Gen. Man. NEJAT TÜMER.

Türk Ticaret Bankası A.Ş.: Iskele Caddesi, Hayri Efendi Sokak, Bahçekapı, Istanbul; f. 1914; cap. p.u. 125m., dep. 3,630m. (1972); 211 brs.; Gen. Man. TURGUT SIZMAZOĞLU.

Türkiye Garanti Bankası A.Ş.: 43 Yeni Postahane Caddesi, Bahçekapı, Istanbul; f. 1946; cap. p.u. 100m., dep. 2,305m. (1972); 192 brs.; Chair. CABIR S. SELEK.

Türkiye Halk Bankası A.Ş.: Anafartalar Caddesi 41, Ankara; f. 1938; cap. p.u. 1,000m., dep. 1,788m. (April 1973); 231 branches; Dir.-Gen. HALİT TAŞÇIOĞLU.

Turkiye İmar Bankası T.A.Ş.: Karakoy, Istanbul; f. 1928; cap. p.u. 5m., dep. 137.1m. (1972).

Türkiye İş Bankası A.Ş.: Ulus Meydanı, Ankara; f. 1924; cap. p.u. 40m., dep. 15,866m. (1972); 519 brs., including 2 in Cyprus; Chair. İ. RÜŞTÜ AKSAL; Gen. Man. FERİD BASMACI; publs. annual review, two-monthly economic review.

Türkiye Tütüncüler Bankası A.Ş.: Halit Ziya Bulvarı No. 45, İzmir, P.K. 239; f. 1924; 5 brs.; cap. p.u. 7m., dep. 69.6m. (1972); Chair. REŞAT EKİNCİ; Gen. Man. İSMAİL AKSOY.

Uluslarası Endüstri ve Ticaret Bankası A.Ş.: Cumhuriyet Cad. 7, Taksim, Istanbul; f. 1888 as Selânik Bankası T.C.S.; cap. p.u. 2.7m., res. 27.5m., dep. 439.6m. (1972); Pres. FAHRETTİN ULAŞ; Gen. Man. Dr. MUZAFFER ERSOY.

Yapı ve Kredi Bankası A.Ş.: P.O.B. 250, Istiklal Cad. 285, Beyoğlu, Istanbul; f. 1944; cap. p.u. 150m., dep. 8.776m. (1972); 310 brs.; Chair. FAHRETTİN ULAŞ.

FOREIGN BANKS

Banka Komerçiyale İtalyana: Istanbul branch: Bankalar Cad. 53, Karaköy; Head Office: Milan, Italy; cap. p.u. 2.5m., dep. 201m. (1972).

Banko di Roma: Hayri Efendi Caddesi, Bahçekapı, P.O.B. 464, Istanbul; Head Office: Rome, Italy: cap. 1.5m., dep. 135.6m. (1972); Man. in Istanbul CARLO CAPPI.

Holantse Bank-Üni N.V.: Istanbul branch: P.K. 34, Karaköy; Head Office: Amsterdam, Netherlands; cap. p.u. 1m., dep. 95m. (1972); Man. in Istanbul Dr. J. M. VAN'T HOFF.

STOCK EXCHANGE

Borsa-Komiserliği: Menkul Kıymetler ve Kambiyo Borsası, 4 Vakıf Han, Bahçekapı, Istanbul; f. 1873; 323 mems.; Pres. REFİK T. SELİMOĞLU; publ. *Borsa*.

INSURANCE

Milli Reasürans T.A.Ş.: P.K. 359, Istanbul; f. 1929; state-owned with monopoly of re-insurance; supervises private insurance companies; Chair. SALİH COŞKUN; Gen. Man. SEBATİ ATAMAN.

Sosyal Sigortalar Kurumu: Ankara; Social Insurance Organization.

PRIVATE INSURANCE

Anadolu Anonim Türk Sigorta Şirketi (*Anatolia Turkish Insurance Society*): Galata, Anadolu Sigorta Hanı, P.O.B. Karaköy 1845, Istanbul.

Ankara Sigorta Şirketi (*Ankara Insurance Society*): Bankalar Cad. 80, Ankara Sigorta Hanı, Istanbul; f. 1936; Dir. KEMAL SARİGÖLLÜ.

Atlantik Sigorta A.Ş.: Bankalar Cad. No. 2, Karaköy, Istanbul; f. 1964; fire, marine, accident; Chair. EMİN ANSEN; Gen. Man. ENGİN ASAL.

Destek Reasurans T.S.A.Ş.: Cumhuriyet Caddesi 6a/2, Istanbul; f. 1943; Pres. BÜLENT KOZLU.

Doğan Sigorta A.Ş.: Doğan Sigorta Binası, Karaköy, Istanbul; f. 1942; Chair. EMİN ANSEN; Managing Dir. NAİL MORALI; Gen. Man. ENGİN ASAL; fire, marine, accident and life.

Güven Türk Anonim Sigorta Şirketi: Karaköy, Istanbul; f. 1925; Chair. and Gen. Man. A. FETHİ SOYSAL.

Halk Sigorta T.A.Ş.: Galata, Halk Sigorta Hanı, Söğüt Sokak, Istanbul; f. 1944; Man. SAFFET DEMİR.

Istanbul Umum Sigorta, Anonim Şirketi (*General Insurance Society of Istanbul*): Bankalar Cad. 31/33, Karaköy, Istanbul; f. 1893; Pres. CABİR SELEK; Man. HAŞIM EKENER.

İmtaş İttihadi Milli Türk Anonim Sigorta Şirketi (*Imaşt Insurance Company*): Karaköy, Ünyon Han, Istanbul, P.K. 107; f. 1918; Man. NURETTİN YAMANLAR.

Şark Sigorta Türk Anonim Şirketi (*Orient Turkish Insurance Society*): P.O.B. 111. Karaköy, Bankalar Cad., Şark Han, Istanbul; f. 1923; Chair. İZZET AKOSMAN.

Şeker Sigorta Anonim Şirketi: Meclisi Mebusan Cad. 325, Seker Sigorta Hanı, Fındıklı, Istanbul; all types of insurance.

Tam Hayat Sigorta A.Ş.: Büyükdere Cad., Tamhan, Şişli, Istanbul; general life assurance.

Tam Sigorta A.Ş.: Büyükdere Cad. 15, Tamhan, Şişli, Istanbul; all types of insurance except life.

Türkiye Genel Sigorta Anonim Şirketi: Yeni Postahane Karşışı, Istanbul; f. 1948; Pres. A. SOHTORIK; Gen. Man' A. GÖMEÇ.

TRADE AND INDUSTRY

CHAMBERS OF COMMERCE AND INDUSTRY

Union of Chambers of Commerce, Industry and Commodity Exchanges of Turkey: 149 Atatürk Bulvarı, Ankara; Pres. SEZAİ DIBLAN.

There are Chambers of Commerce and Industry in all towns of the Republic. Among the most important are the following:

Adana Chamber of Commerce: Adana; f. 1893; Pres. KÂZIM KÖSEOĞLU; Sec.-Gen. Â. İRFAN TUĞBERK; 4,000 mems.; publ. *Gazetesi*.

Adana Chamber of Industry: Adana; f. 1966; Pres. SAKIP SABANCI; 230 mems.

Ankara Chamber of Commerce and Industry: Şehit Teğmen Kalmaz Caddesi 20; Pres. NURI CİRİTOĞLU; Gen. Sec. IZZET DURU; publ. *Bulletin* (monthly).

British Chamber of Commerce of Turkey (Inc.): P.O.B. 190, Karaköy, Istanbul; f. 1887; 500 mems.; Sec. and Treas. N. COVEY, M.B.E.; publ. *Journal* (4 to 6 issues a year).

Bursa Chamber of Commerce and Industry: Bursa; f. 1926; 4,582 mems.; Pres. A. OSMAN SÖNMEZ; Sec.-Gen. ERGUN KAĞITCIBAŞI; publ. *Bursa Ticaret Haberleri*, weekly.

Chamber of Industry for the Aegean Region: Cumhuriyet Blv. 136, İzmir; f. 1954 succeeded to the İzmir Chamber of Industry; Pres. SİNASİ ERTAN; Sec.-Gen. NAİM KARAOSMAN; publs. *News Bulletin* (weekly), *Quarterly Review*.

Istanbul Chamber of Commerce: Ragıp Gümüş Pala Cad., Eminönü, Istanbul; and P.K. 377, Istanbul; f. 1882; 43,400 mems.; Pres. EMİR SENCER; Pres. Exec. Board BEHCET OSMANAAĞOĞLU; Sec.-Gen. İSMAİL HÜSREV TÖKİN; publs. *Istanbul Ticaret Odası Mecmuası*, *Istanbul Ticaret*, *Statistical Abstract* (in English), *Monthly Bulletin* (in English).

İstanbul Chamber of Industry: Eminönü, Istanbul; Pres. BEHCET OSMANAĞAOĞLU.

İzmir Chamber of Commerce: Atatürk Caddesi 126, İzmir; f. 1885; 7,163 mems.; Pres DÜNDAR SOYER; Sec.-Gen. Dr. AYDEMİR AŞKIN; publ. *Izmir Ticaret Odası Dergisi* (monthly).

Mersin Chamber of Commerce and Industry: P.O.B. 212, Mersin; f. 1886; 1,711 mems.; Pres. NUREDDIN ALGÜL; Sec.-Gen. ALİ B. AYDENİZ.

Samsun Chamber of Commerce and Industry: Samsun: f. 1923; 9 members; Pres. CENGIZ BALKAN; Gen.-Sec.; CEVDET KARSLI.

TRADE UNIONS

CONFEDERATION

Türkiye İşçi Sendikaları Konfederasyonu-Türk İş (*Confederation of Turkish Trade Unions*): Bayındır Sok. 8, Yenişehir, Ankara; f. 1952; affiliated to I.C.F.T.U.; 29 national unions and 6 federations with 934,000 employees; Chair. SEYFİ DEMİRSÖY; Sec.-Gen. HALİL TUNÇ; Financial Sec. ÖMER ERGÜN; Organizing Sec. ETHEM EZGÜ; publ. *Türk-İş*.

PRINCIPAL UNIONS

Unions affiliated to Türk İş in 1972 with a membership of over 5,000.

Ağaç-İş (**Türkiye Ağaç Sanayii İşçileri Sendikası**) (*Wood and Lumber*): Necatibey Cad. No. 20/22-23, Yenişehir, Ankara; f. 1949; 8,000 mems.; also affil. to IFBWW; Pres. ÖMER DENİZ; Gen. Sec. OSMAN NOGAY

Basın-İş (**Türkiye Gazeteciler ve Basın Sanayii İşçileri Sendikası**) (*Journalists and Press Technicians*): Atatürk Bulvari No. 73/14, Yenişehir, Ankara; f. 1964; 15,000 mems.; Pres. MUSTAFA ULUCAN; Gen. Sec. NURETTİN YERDELEN.

Çimse-İş (**Türkiye Cimento, Seramik ve Toprak Sanayii İşçileri Sendikası**) (*Cement, Ceramic and Soil*): Necatibey Cad. 22/11-12, Yenişehir, Ankara; f. 1963; 15,000 mems.; also affiliated to IFPCW; Pres. HASAN TURKAY; Gen. Sec. ABUZER UCAR.

Deri-İş (**Türkiye Deri, Debbağ, Kundura ve Saraciye Sanayii İşçileri Sendikası**) (*Leather and Shoe*): Nuruosmaniye Cad. 9, Cağaloğlu, Istanbul; f. 1948; 5,000 mems.; also affiliated to ISLWF; Pres. MUSTAFA ŞAHİN; Gen. Sec. ADNAN GÜRKULE.

Dok Gemi-İş (**Türkiye Liman Dok ve Gemi Sanayii İşçileri Sendikası**) (*Port, Dock and Ship Building*): Ordu Caddes, 285, Kat-6, Aksaray, Istanbul; f. 1947; 6,000 mems.; also affiliated to IMF; Pres. ARSLAN SİVRİ; Gen. Sec. GÜNGÖR TARI.

Dyf-İş (**Türkiye Demiryolları İşçi Sendikaları Federasyonu**) (*Railways*): Necatibey Cad., Sezenler Sok. 5/4, Yenişehir, Ankara; f. 1952; 35,000 mems.; also affiliated to ITF; Pres. ŞERAFETTİN AKOVA; Gen. Sec. AHMET ÇATAKÇİNLER.

Genel-İş (**Türkiye Genel Hizmetler İşçileri Sendikası**) (*Public Services*): Süleyman Sırrı Sokak No. 2, Kat-1, Yenişehir, Ankara; f. 1962; 17,665 mems.; also affiliated to PSI; Pres. ABDULLAH BAŞTÜRK; Gen. Sec. HASAN OKYAR.

Ges-İş (**Türkiye D.S.I. Enerji, Su ve Gaz İşçileri Sendikası**) (*State Energy, Gas, Water-Workers*): Süleyman Sırrı Sokak No. 2/14-15, Yenişehir, Ankara; f. 1961; 17,000 mems.; also affiliated to PSI; Pres. OSMAN SOĞUKPINAR; Gen. Sec. EROL AYKAŞ.

Harb-İş (**Türkiye Harb Sanayi ve Yardımcı İşkolları İşçileri Sendikası** (*Defence Industry and Allied Workers*): Adakale Sok., Set Apt. 73/5-8, Kocatepe, Ankara; f. 1956; 26,000 mems.; also affiliated to PSI; Pres. KENAN DURUKAN; Gen. Sec. İLHAMI AÇIKSÖZ; publ. *Türk harb-iş*.

Koop-İş (**Türkiye Tarım Kredi Kooperatifleri Personeli Sendikası**) (*Agricultural Credit Co-operative Employees*): Talâtpaşa Bulvari No. 157/5, Cebeci, Ankara; f. 1964; 6,000 mems.; Pres. İBRAHIM ÇAPAN; Gen. Sec. M. ALİ KIRIKOĞLU.

Likat-İş (**Türkiye Liman ve Kara Tahmil-Tahliye İşçileri Sendikası**) (*Loading and Unloading Workers*): Necatibey Cad. 13/11-12, Yenişehir, Ankara; f. 1963; 14,770 mems.; also affiliated to ITF; Pres. AHMET KURT; Gen. Sec. YAŞAR ATICI.

Metal-İş (**Türkiye Metal, Çelik, Mühimmat, Makina, Metalden Mamul Eşya ve Oto Sanayii İşçi Sendikaları**) **Federasyonu** (*Federation of Turkish Metal, Steel, Metal Goods, Ammunition, Machines and Automobile Industry*

TURKEY—(Trade and Industry)

Workers' Unions): Gazi Mustafa Kemal Bulvarı No. 40/1-2 Maltepe, Ankara; f. 1962; 61,428 mems. in 20 mem. unions; Pres. Enver Kaya; Gen. Sec. Fehmi Işıklar.

OLEYIS (Türkiye Otel Lokanta ve Eğlence Yerleri İşçileri Sendikası) (*Hotel, Restaurant and Places of Entertainment*): Akay Cad. No. 24, Bakanlıklar, Ankara; f. 1969; 26,970 mems.; also affiliated to IUF; Pres. Mukbil Zirtiloğlu; Gen. Sec. Nusret Aydın.

Petrol-İş (Türkiye Petrol, Kimya, Azot ve Atom İşçileri Sendikası) (*Oil, Chemical, Nitrogen and Atomic*): Yıldız Posta Cad., Evren Sitesi, P.K. 37, D-Blok, Gayrettepe, Istanbul; f. 1950; 19,500 mems.; also affiliated to IFPCW; Pres. İsmail Topkar; Gen. Sec. Özkal Yıcı; publ. *Petrol-İş* (fortnightly), *Petrol-İş Magazine* (quarterly).

Sağlık-İş (Türkiye Sağlık İşçileri Sendikası) (*Health Employees*): Necatibey Cad., Başkent Apt. 1-2, Yenişehir, Ankara; f. 1961; 11,400 mems.; also affiliated to PSI; Pres. Mustafa Başoğlu.

Şeker-İş (Türkiye Şeker Fabrikaları İşçileri Sendikası) (*Sugar Industry*): Mithatpaşa Cad. 13/3, Yenişehir, Ankara; f. 1947; 18,500 mems.; Pres. Sadık Side; Gen. Sec. Haydar Özöğretmen; publ. *Şeker-İş* (fortnightly).

Sselüloz-İş (Türkiye Selülloz ve Mamulleri İşçileri Sendikası) (*Celluloid Industry*): Hürriyet Caddesi, Işılay Apt. Kat-1, Kocaeli; f. 1952; 8,400 mems.; Pres. Necati Cansever; Gen. Sec. Salih Güngörmez.

Tarım-İş (Türkiye Tarım ve Tarım Sanayii İşçileri Sendikası) (*Agricultural Workers*): Necatibey Cad. 22/9-12, Yenişehir, Ankara; f. 1961; 10,000 mems.; affiliated to IUF and IFPAAW; Pres. Binali Yağışan; Gen. Sec. Ali Riza Özdemir.

Tek Gida-İs (Türkiye Tütün, Müskirat Gida ve Yardimci İşçileri Sendikası) (*Tobacco, Drink, Food and Allied Workers*): 4. üncü Levent, Konaklar Sokak, Levent, Istanbul; f. 1952; 146,176 mems.; also affiliated to IUF; Pres. İbrahim Denizcier; Gen. Sec. Orhan Sorguç.

Teksif (Türkiye Tekstil, Orme ve Giyim Sanayii İşçileri Sendikası) (*Textile, Knitting and Clothing*): Ziya Gökalp Cad. 80, Yenişehir, Ankara; f. 1951; 100,000 mems.; also affiliated to ITGWF; Pres. Şevket Yılmaz; Gen. Sec. Vahap Güvenç.

Tes-İş (Türkiye Enerji, Su, Gaz ve Devlet S.I. İşçi Sendikaları Federasyonu) (*Energy, Water, Gas and State Water Department*): Meşrutiyet Cad. Karanfil Sokak, Beton Apt. No. 6, Kat-2, Bakanlıklar, Ankara; f. 1963; 17,000 mems.; Pres. Orhan Erçelik; Gen. Sec. Faruk Barut.

Tümtis (Türkiye Motorlu Taşıt İşçileri Sendikası) (*Motor Transport*): Yeniselim Paşa Sok. 62, P.K. 292, Aksaray, Istanbul; f. 1949; 7,163 mems.; also affiliated to ITF; Pres. Mehmet Inhanli; Gen. Sec. D. Zeki Demirel.

Türk Deniz Ulaş-İş (Türkiye Deniz Taşıtmacılığı İşçi Sendikaları Federasyonu) (*Water Transport*): Necatibey Cad., Şeref Han 401, Karaköy, Istanbul; f. 1959; 12,478 mems.; also affiliated to ITF; Pres. Feridun Şakır Öğünç; Gen. Sec. Kerim Akyüz.

Türkiye Maden-İş (Türkiye Maden İşçileri Sendikaları Federasyonu) (*Mine Workers*): Mithatpaşa Cad. 10/11-12, Yenişehir, Ankara; f. 1958; 87,731 mems.; also affiliated to IMF; Pres. Kemal Özer; Gen. Sec. Mustafa Orhan.

Türkiye Maden, Madeni Eşya ve Makine Sanayii İşçileri Sendikası (*Metal, Metal Goods and Machine Industry Workers' Union of Turkey*): Barbaros Bulvarı 58, Kat 2-3-4-5, Beşiktaş, Istanbul; f. 1947; 44,000 mems.; Pres. Kemal Türkler; Gen. Sec. Ruhi Yümlü; publ. *Maden-Is Gazetesi* (fortnightly).

Yapı-İş (Türkiye Yapıcılık Genel Hizmetleri Sanayii İşçileri Sendikası) (*General Construction Services Industry*): Ziya Gökalp Cad. 20/12, Yenişehir, Ankara; f. 1964; 31,005 mems.; also affiliated to IFBWW; Pres. Tahir Öztürk; Gen. Sec. Emrullah Akdoğan.

Yol-İş (Türkiye Karayolu Yapım-Bakım ve Onarım İşçi Sendikaları Federasyonu) (*Highways Construction, Maintenance and Repair Workers*): İzmir Cad. No. 22/7, Yenişehir, Ankara; f. 1963; 29,759 mems.; also affiliated to PSI; Pres. Halit Misirlioğlu; Gen. Sec. R. Rafet Altun.

TRADE FAIR

İzmir Enternasyonal Fuarı (*Izmir International Fair*): Kültürpark, İzmir; f. 1929; August 20th–September 20th annually.

TRANSPORT

RAILWAYS

Türkiye Cumhuriyeti Devlet Demiryolları İşletmesi—TCDD (*Turkish Republic State Railways*): Ankara; f. 1924; operates all railways and connecting ports; the Railway Administration acquired the status of a public corporation in July 1953; Gen. Dir. AHMET SARP; Gen. Sec. FAHİR BİLCE; publ. *Demiryol* (monthly).

The total length of the railways operated within the national frontiers is 9,831 km. (1972), of which 272 km. are electrified. Five-Year Plans for modernizing the railway system were introduced in 1963, with dieselization and electrification projects having since been carried out. A third Five-Year Plan (1973–77) has been prepared and submitted to the Ministry of Communications; it aims at the further rationalization and modernization of the railways.

A rail link built under a CENTO agreement between Turkey and Iran was put into service in September 1971. Soon afterwards, a direct line to Bulgaria (Pehlivanköy to Edirne) was completed and opened.

ROADS

General Directorate of Highways: Ankara; Dir.-Gen. ATALAY COŞKUNOĞLU.

At the beginning of 1971 the total length of expressways was 23 km., the total of all-weather national roads was 31,503 km., there were 13,038 km. of provincial roads and 30,587 km. of village roads. The highway network totalled 124,790 km. In 1968 a ten-year programme of road improvement for eastern Turkey was announced. A 78 km. main road (sponsored by CENTO) runs from Sivelan in south-eastern Turkey to Rezaiyeh on Lake Urmia in Iran. Construction of a TL 1,500m. six-lane bridge across the Bosphorous was started early in 1970, for completion in 1973. It will be the fourth longest in the bridge world and the biggest in Europe, with a centre span of 1,074 metres, and a length of 1,560 metres. The existing ferry services constitute a major traffic "bottleneck" in the Turkish transport system. Construction of a third bridge across the Golden Horn was started at the end of 1971 and will be completed at the end of 1974.

MOTORISTS' ASSOCIATION

Türkiye Turing ve Otomobil Kurumu (*Touring and Automobile Club of Turkey*): Halaskargazi Cad. 364, Şişli, Istanbul; f. 1923; 4,500 mems.; Dir. ÇELİK GÜLERSEY.

SHIPPING

Denizcilik Bankası T.A.O. (*Turkish Maritime Bank*): Genel Müdürlük, Karaköy, Istanbul; f. 1952 by Act of Parliament converting the Turkish State Seaways and Harbour Administration into a corporation controlled and part-owned by the State. The Bank has a capital of TL 1,500m.; four maritime establishments operate passenger, cargo and ferry-boat lines on inter-city, coastal, Adriatic, Aegean and Mediterranean Sea routes; four Port Administrations offer loading, unloading, transfer and warehousing facilities; five ship-yards and dry docks have repair and construction facilities for ships up to 15,000 tons; international concerns such as ship salvage and coastal security; other assets include: six hotels; 73,562 gross tons of shipping, 19 ships and 44,493 gross tons of inter-city communication, 68 ferries.

D.B. Deniz Nakliyatı T.A.Ş.: Fındıklı, Istanbul; associated company of the above, operating R.C.D. joint services to U.S. Atlantic and Gulf ports; regular liner services to Continent and Mediterranean ports; Gen. Man. CEZMİ BİREN; 39 cargo ships, 7 tankers, 21 vessels under construction.

PRIVATE COMPANIES

Denizcilik Anonim Şirketi: Meclisi Mebusan Caddesi, Fındıklı Han Kat 4, Fındıklı, Istanbul; f. 1952; tanker owners and shipbuilders up to 8,000 t.d.w., repair and dry-docking at company's shipyard in Istanbul; Chair. Board of Dirs. HAYRETTİN BARAN; Man. Dir. SABAHATTİN ÜLKÜ; 2 tankers.

Koçtuğ Denizcilik İşletmesi D.İ.: Bankalar Caddesi, Bozkurt-General Han Kat 5, Karaköy, P.K. 884, Istanbul; cargo services to and from Europe and the U.S.A.; Owners S. KOÇMAN, S. GÖKTUG; 6 ships.

Marmara Transport A.S.: Assikürazioni Generali Han Kat 2, Bankalar Cad., Karaköy, Istanbul; international tanker services; Chair. A. KUNT; Man. Dir. S. BIGAT; 1 tanker.

Sadikzade Rusen Oğulları Akif, Talat Sadıkoğlu Kollektif Şirketi: Arlu Han Kat 2, Rhıtım Caddesi, Tophane, Istanbul; cargo services to Europe; Chair. T. SADIKOGLU; Man. Dir. ADNAN ALDORA; 1 cargo vessel.

CIVIL AVIATION

There are airports for scheduled international and internal flights at Yeşilköy (Istanbul), Esenboğa (Ankara) and Adana, while international charter flights are handled by Antalya and Cigli (Izmir). Seventeen other airports handle internal flights only.

Türk Hava Yolları A.O. (THY) (*Turkish Airlines Inc.*): Cumhuriyet Caddesi 199-201, Osmanbey-Istanbul; f. 1934; Gen. Man. REMZİ YELMAN; extensive internal network and flights to Amsterdam, Athens, Beirut, Brussels, Frankfurt, Geneva, London, Milan, Munich, Nicosia, Paris, Rome, Tel-Aviv, Vienna and Zurich; fleet of four Boeing 707, seven DC-9, three DC-10 and five F-28.

Turkey is also served by the following foreign airlines: Aeroflot, Air France, Alia, Alitalia, Ariana, AUA, Balkan, BEA, ČSA, Cyprus Airways, El-Al, Iran National, Iraqi Airways, JAT, KLM, LOT, Lufthansa, MALÉV, MEA, Olympic, Pan American, Pakistan International, Sabena, Saudia, SAS, Swissair and TAROM.

TOURISM

Ministry of Tourism and Information: Gazi Mustafa Kemal Bulvarı 33, Ankara; Dir.-Gen. of Tourism BEYHAN ÖZBAY; Dir.-Gen. of Information AYDIN KEZER.

CULTURAL ORGANIZATION

Fine Arts General Directorate (*Güzel Sanatlar Genel Müdürlüğü*): Education Ministry, Bakanlıklar, Ankara; Dir.-Gen. MÜKERREM KEYMEN.

PRINCIPAL THEATRES

State Theatre General Directorate (*Devlet Tiyatrosu Genel Müdürlüğü*): part of the above; runs eight playhouses; Dir.-Gen. CÜNEYT GÖKÇER.

Büyük Tiyatro (*Great Theatre*): Ankara.

Küçük Tiyatro (*Small Theatre*): Ankara.

Devlet Operası ve Balesi: Ankara; national opera and ballet; permanent classical ballet company of 50 dancers.

There are three other state theatres in Ankara, and five private companies. Istanbul has thirteen private companies.

Istanbul Municipal Theatre: Harbiye, Istanbul; f. 1914; presents wide range of plays, Turkish and international, classical and modern; five playhouses; Artistic Dir. VASFİ RIZA ZOBU; Admin. Dir. BASRİ DEDEOĞLU; publ. *Review*.

Istnabul City Opera: Taksim, Istanbul (burned down, being rebuilt); Dir. MUHSIN ERTUĞRUL.

ORCHESTRAS

Istanbul Municipal Symphony Orchestra: Taksim, Istanbul.

Presidential Symphony Orchestra: Ankara.

ATOMIC ENERGY

Turkish Atomic Energy Commission: Prime Minister's Office, Bestekar Sokak 29, Ankara; f. 1956; controls the development of peaceful uses of atomic energy; 10 mems.; Chair. Hon. DOĞAN KİTAPLI; Sec.-Gen. İBRAHİM DERİNER; publs. *Activity Reports*, *Research Reports*, etc.

There are nuclear research centres at Çekmece, near Istanbul, and at Ankara.

Technical University of Istanbul: graduate school of nuclear engineering.

Institute of Radiobiology: University of Ankara; sub-critical assembly.

Co-operation. Turkey is a member of the International Atomic Energy Agency (IAEA) and the European Nuclear Energy Agency (ENEA). IAEA is providing assistance which includes equipment and technical aid for the universities of Ankara and Istanbul.

Power: Turkey's first nuclear power station, with a capacity of 400 MW, is planned for completion in 1977.

EDUCATION

One of the greatest problems confronting the new Republic was that of modernising and extending the educational system, for at that time only 11 per cent of the population were literate. New schools had to be built and equipped in towns and villages; teachers and inspectors trained, and suitable schemes of training devised for them; technical courses provided to equip skilled workers for industry and agriculture; and, above all, training in reading and writing had to be provided for the millions of peasants who had received no schooling.

Under the Ottoman Empire there had been a dual system of education—religious schools existing side by side with others in which ordinary educational subjects were taught, although religious instruction played a large part. Unity of education was recognised as the first requisite; the theological schools were converted into theological seminaries for the training of clergy, or abolished; the others were secularised. The Ministry of Education was declared the sole authority in all educational matters.

One of the main obstacles to literacy was the Arabic script, which required years of study before proficiency could be attained. In 1928, therefore, a Turkish alphabet was introduced, using Latin characters. At the same time the literary language was simplified, and purged of some of its foreign elements. By 1969–70 the education budget amounted to over £T3,000 million, around 17 per cent of the state budget.

People's Schools

This change of script created a need for schools in which reading and writing in the new alphabet could be taught to adults. Temporary institutions known as "people's schools" or "national schools" were set up everywhere. During the winter months these schools gave instruction in reading and writing and other basic subjects to men and women beyond the normal school age. Between 1928 and 1935 some 2 million people received certificates of proficiency. Since then education in Turkey has made big advances, but although literacy is estimated at 65 per cent in towns, it is still much lower in the villages (30.3 per cent in 1960).

Primary Education

A compulsory school attendance law had been passed in 1913, but only under the Republic were measures taken to enforce this. Primary education is now entirely free, and co-education is the accepted basis for universal education. The number of schools has risen from 12,511 in 1950 to 38,421 in 1971, and the number of teachers from 27,144 to 133,812. In 1970–71, over 5 million children were attending primary schools.

Secondary Education

The reorganization of the system of secondary education began in the early 1920s. Before the reorganization there were two types of secondary schools: state schools, providing one or two educational stages, and local schools corresponding approximately to the modern middle schools. In 1926 the system of co-education was adopted in day schools of the middle-school group.

Present Organization. This period of education lasts six years, and is free.

The secondary schools are divided into two stages: middle schools and *lycées*, and students who intend to proceed to higher educational institutions must pass through both stages, spending three years in the middle school and three in the *lycée*.

The middle school, although complementary to the *lycée*, is a separate unit, designed to give a definite and complete education to those students who at the end of the course will proceed directly to work. The state examination is taken by all students at the end of the third year. Graduates of a middle school are qualified either to take up an unskilled occupation or to enter upon a vocational course at a school of a higher grade.

The *lycée* takes the student up to the age of 17 or 18 years, and those who wish to proceed to an institute of higher education must pass the state matriculation examination. The study of a modern language (English, French or German) is compulsory in middle schools and *lycées*. In addition, Latin and Greek have been taught in some *lycées* since 1940. The number of secondary schools has increased from 343 in 1950 to 2,467 in 1971, including the *lycées*. The number of students in these schools in the 1971–72 school year totalled 1,147,957.

Adult Education. Since 1932, reading-rooms have been established in every town and many villages. They are centres of social and cultural life and provide evening classes. Their libraries, meeting-halls and recreational facilities are open to all. In the towns there are also evening trade schools which provide technical training for adults, and travelling courses are sent out to the villages.

Higher Education. Higher educational institutions in Turkey were founded, and are administered, by the State. These institutions include the universities and the higher professional schools. There are now eight universities and 38 institutes of higher education (including teacher training colleges). Three of the universities specialize in scientific and technical subjects. The number of students at universities and other institutes of higher education rose to nearly 170,000 in the academic year 1971–72.

Technical Education. The events of the past thirty years have shown that vocational education is an all-important factor in the life and progress of all nations, and the 1931 programme of the People's Party therefore accepted the desirability of setting up in Turkey professional and trade schools. The problem of technical education began to be seriously considered first in 1926; specialists were invited from Europe and America, and a plan was drawn up for perfecting the existing vocational schools and for founding new ones to meet the economic needs of each region. In addition, plans were made for evening schools to train craftsmen and for the founding of teachers' technical training colleges. There are two such colleges in Ankara, one for men and one for women. The number of technical and vocational schools and colleges in 1971–72 was 838, the number of instructors was 15,410 and 262,701 students were enrolled.

Teachers' Training. There are five types of teachers' training colleges in Turkey, excluding the universities.

Normal Schools. Graduates of the normal schools are appointed to positions in the primary schools, and are eligible by examination for admission to certain higher teachers' training institutions. There are two types of normal schools—six-year schools, grades 6–11, following the primary school, and three-year schools following the middle school. All normal schools are boarding schools, but day students are accepted. There were 89 normal schools in 1970–71, with a total of 17,419 students.

Secondary Teachers' Training Schools and Pedagogical Institutes. There are ten secondary teachers' training schools and pedagogical institutes: one at Ankara, one at Istanbul, one at Bursa, one at İzmir and others at Balıkeşir, Diyarbakır, Konya, Samsun, Erzurum and Trabzon. These schools are normally boarding schools; the following subjects can be studied at one or other of the ten institutions—literature, science, music, drawing and handicrafts, physical education, German, French, English. The graduates of the pedagogy departments are appointed to be primary school inspectors, or teachers of professional subjects in the normal schools.

Lycée Teachers' Training Colleges. There are two *lycée* teachers' training colleges, one in Istanbul and one in Ankara, offering courses in thirteen subjects—Turkish language and literature, history, geography, philosophy, French, English, German, mathematics–astronomy, mathematics-physics, chemistry-physics, physics-chemistry, natural sciences, and commerce. *Lycée* and commercial *lycée* graduates are admitted to these colleges, and graduates teach in *lycées* and vocational schools of *lycée* standard.

Technical Teachers' Training Colleges for Men and Women. There are three, two for men and one for women; two are in Ankara and one is in Istanbul; the courses are four-year, and graduates to the colleges teach either at boys' trade schools and institutes, or at girls' schools of domestic science and girls' trade schools and institutes.

Commercial Teachers' Training College. The College is at Ankara; it offers a three-year course, and prepares teachers for the commercial *lycées* and commercial middle schools.

Students from the Universities of Istanbul and Ankara may qualify for a teaching certificate by following certain courses, including one on pedagogy.

UNIVERSITIES

Ankara Üniversitesi (*University of Ankara*): Ankara; 1,886 teachers, 16,316 students.

Atatürk Üniversitesi (*Atatürk University*): Erzurum; 345 teachers, 2,779 students.

Boğaziçi Üniversitesi (*Bosphorus University*): Istanbul; f. 1971; formerly Robert College; 130 teachers, 1,261 students.

Ege Üniversitesi (*Aegean University*): Bornova, Izmir; 549 teachers, 6,171 students.

Hacettepe University: Ankara; f. 1967; 5,000 students.

İstanbul Üniversitesi (*Istanbul University*): Bayezita Istanbul; 1,327 teachers, 35,289 students.

İstanbul Teknik Üniversitesi (*Istanbul Technical University*): Beyoğlu, Istanbul; 743 teachers, 7,481 students.

Karadeniz Teknik Üniversitesi (*Black Sea Technical University*): Trabzon; 188 teachers, 1,200 students.

Orta Doğu Teknik Üniversitesi (*Middle East Technical University*): Yenişehir, Ankara; 530 teachers, 5,472 students.

TURKEY—(BIBLIOGRAPHY)

BIBLIOGRAPHY

GENERAL

AKCURA, TUGRUL. Turkey L'Architecture d'Aujourdhui (Paris, 1968).

ALLEN, H. E. The Turkish Transformation (Chicago, 1935).

AND, METIN. A History of the Theatre and Popular Entertainment in Turkey (Forum, Ankara, 1964).

ARMSTRONG, H. C. Grey Wolf: Mustafa Kemal: an Intimate Study of a Dictator (London, 1937).

AUBOYNEAU & FEVRET. Essai de bibliographie pour l'Empire Ottomane (Paris, 1911).

BAHRAMPOUR, FIROUZ. Turkey, Political and Social Transformation (Gaus, New York, 1967).

BEAN, G. E. Aegean Turkey (Benn, London, 1966).
Turkey's Southern Shore (Benn, London, 1968).

BERKES, NIYAZI. The Development of Secularism in Turkey (McGill University Press, Montreal, 1964).

BIRGE, J. K. A Guide to Turkish Area Study (Washington, 1949).

BISBEE, ELEANOR. The New Turks (Philadelphia, 1951).
The People of Turkey (New York, 1946).

BRIDGE, ANN. The Dark Moment (New York, 1952).
The Falcon in Flight (New York, 1951).

COHN, EDWIN J. Turkish Economic, Social and Political Change (New York, Praeger, 1970).

COOKE, HEDLEY V. Challenge and Response in the Middle East: The Quest for Prosperity, 1919-1951 (New York, 1952).

DE PLANHOL, XAVIER. Nomadisme et vie paysanne (Paris, 1961).

DEWONEY, J. C. Turkey (London, 1971).

DODD, C. H. Politics and Government in Turkey (Manchester University Press, 1970).

EDGECUMBE, Sir, C. N. E. Turkey in Europe (Barnes and Noble, N.Y., 1965).

EKREM, SELMA. Turkey: Old and New (New York, 1947).

EREN, NURI. Turkey Today and Tomorrow (New York, 1964).

FREY, F. W. The Turkish Political Elite (M.I.T. Press, Cambridge, Mass., 1965).

GÖKALP, ZIYA. Turkish Nationalism and Western Civilisation (London, 1960).

GOUGH, MARY. The Plain and the Rough Places (London, 1953).

GÜNTEKIN, REŞAT NURI (trans. Sir WYNDHAM DEEDES). Afternoon Sun (London, 1950).
The Autobiography of a Turkish Girl (London, 1949).

HARRIS, GEORGE S. The Origins of Communism in Turkey (Hoover Institution, Stanford, Calif., 1967).

HAYIT, B. Turkestan im XX Jahrhundert (Darmstadt, C. W. Leske Verlag, 1956) (in German).

HEYD, URIEL. Foundations of Turkish Nationalism: the Life and Teachings of Ziya Gökalp (Luzac and Harvill Press, London, 1950).
Language Reform in Modern Turkey (Jerusalem, 1954).

JACKH, ERNEST. The Rising Crescent (New York, 1950).

JÄSCHKE, GOTTHARD. Der Islam in der Neuen Türkei: eine Rechtsgeschichtliche Untersuchung Die Welt des Islams (N.S., Vol. I, Nos. 1-2).
Die Türkei in den Jahren 1942-51 (Wiesbaden, 1954).

KARPAT, KEMAL. Turkey's Politics, The Transition to a Multi-Party System (Princeton, 1959).

KAZAMIAS, A. M. Education and the Quest for Modernity in Turkey (Allen and Unwin, London, 1967).

KELLY, MARIE NOËLE. Turkish Delights: Travels and Impressions of the Turkish Scene, 1946-1949 (London, 1951).

KINNANE, DIRK. The Kurds and Kurdistan (Oxford, 1965).

KINROSS, Lord. Within the Taurus (London, 1954).
Europa Minor: Journeys in Coastal Turkey (London, 1956).
Turkey (303 photogravure illustrations, London, 1960).
Atatürk (Weidenfeld, London, 1964).

KIŞLALI, AHMET TANER. Forces politiques dans la Turquie moderne (Ankara, 1967).

KORAY, ENVER. Türkiye Tarih Yayınları Bibliografyası 1729-1950; A Bibliography of Historical Works on Turkey (Ankara 1952).

KÜRGER, K. Die Türkei (Berlin, 1951).

LAMB, HAROLD. Suleiman the Magnificent: Sultan of the East (New York, 1951).

LEWIS, BERNARD. Turkey Today (London, 1940).
The Emergence of Modern Turkey (Oxford University Press, London and New York, 1968).

LEWIS, G. L. Turkey ("Nations of the Modern World" series) (London, 1955) (3rd edn., Praeger, N.Y., 1965).

LINKE, L. Allah Dethroned (London, 1937).

LUKACH (LUKE), Sir HARRY CHARLES. The Old Turkey and the New (Geoffrey Bles, London, 1955).

MAKAL, MAHMUT. A Village in Anatolia (London, 1953).

MANGO, ANDREW. Turkey (Thames and Hudson, London, 1967).

MARFORI, TERENZIO. La Constituzione della Repubblica Turca (Florence, 1947).

MAYNE, PETER. Istanbul (Dent, London, 1967).

MELLAART, JAMES. Earliest Civilizations of the Near East (Thames and Hudson, London, 1965).
Çatal Hüyük (Thames and Hudson, London, 1967).

MOOREHEAD, A. Gallipoli (New York, Harper, 1956).

MUNTZ, T. G. A. Turkey (New York, 1951).

NEWMAN, BERNARD. Turkish Crossroads (London, 1951).
Turkey and the Turks (Herbert Jenkins, London, 1968).

TURKEY—(BIBLIOGRAPHY)

ORGA, IRFAN. Portrait of a Turkish Family (New York, 1950).
    The Caravan Moves On (Secker & Warburg, London, 1958).

ORGA, IRFAN and MARGARETE. Atatürk (London, 1962).

PARKER, J., and SMITH, C. Modern Turkey (London, 1940).

PLATE, HERBERT. Das Land der Türken (Verlag Styria, Graz, Wien, Köln, 1957).

ROBINSON, RICHARD D. The First Turkish Republic (Harvard University Press, 1963).

SALTER, CEDRIC. Introducing Turkey (Methuen, London, 1961).

STARK, FREYA. Ionia (London, 1954).
    Lycian Shore (London, 1951).
    Riding to the Tigris (London, 1956).

STEINHAUS, KURT. Soziologie der turkischen Revolution (Frankfurt, 1969).

STEWART, DESMOND. Turkey (Life World Library Series, Time Inc., N.Y., 1965).

STIRLING, PAUL. Turkish Village (Weidenfeld and Nicolson, London, 1965).

SZYLIOWICZ, JOSEPH S. Political Change in Rural Turkey: Erdemli (Mouton, The Hague, 1966).

TOMLIN, E. W. F. Life in Modern Turkey (New York, 1946).

TOYNBEE, A. J. The Western Question in Greece and Turkey (Constable, London, 1923).

TOYNBEE, A. J., and KIRKWOOD, D. P. Turkey (London, 1926).
    Lycian Shore (London, 1956).

TUNAYA, T. Z. Atatürk, the Revolutionary Movement and Atatürkism (Baha, Istanbul, 1964).

UNESCO. Emancipation of the Turkish Woman (Columbia University Press, New York).

U.S. DEPARTMENT OF STATE. Problem of Turkish Straits (Dept. of State, Publ. 2752).

VALI, FERENC A. Bridge across the Bosphorus: the Foreign Policy of Turkey (Johns Hopkins Press, 1970).

WARD, BARBARA. Turkey (Oxford, 1942).

WARD, ROBERT E., and RUSTOW, OANKWART A. (eds.). Political Modernizations in Japan and Turkey (Princeton University Press, 1964).

WEBSTER, D. E. The Turkey of Atatürk: Social Progress in the Turkish Reformation (Philadelphia, 1939).

WILLIAMS, GWYN. Turkey: A Travellers Guide and History (Faber and Faber, London, 1967).

YALMAN, A. E. Turkey in my time (University of Oklahoma Press, 1956).

HISTORY

AHMAD, FEROZ. The Young Turks (Oxford University Press, 1969).

AKURGAL, E. Hittite Art (London, 1962).

ALDERSON, A. D. The Structure of the Ottoman Dynasty (Oxford, 1956).

ALLEN, W. E. D., and MURATOFF, P. Caucasian Battlefields: A History of the Wars on the Turco-Caucasian Border, 1828-1921 (Cambridge, 1953).

ANCHIERI, ETTORE. Costantinopoli e gli Stretti nella Politica Russa ed Europea: dal Trattato di Qüciük Kainargi alla Convenzione di Montreux (Milan, 1948).

CAHEN, CLAUDE. Pre-Ottoman Turkey (Sidgwick and Jackson, London, 1968).

CASSELS, LAVENDER. The Struggle for the Ottoman Empire, 1717-1740 (John Murray, London, 1967).

COLES, PAUL. The Ottoman Impact on Europe (Thames and Hudson, London, 1968; Brace and World, New York, 1968).

DAVIDSON, RODERIC H. Turkey (Prentice-Hall, New York, 1968).

DUDA, HERBERT W. Vom Kalifat zur Republik (Vienna, 1948).

FISHER, SYDNEY NETTLETON. The Foreign Relations of Turkey, 1481-1512 (Illinois Studies in Social Science, XXX, 1) (Urbana, 1948).

GURNEY, O. R. The Hittites (London, 1952).

JASCHKE, G. Die Türkei in den Jahren 1952-61 (Otto Harrassowitz, Wiesbaden, 1965).

KEDOURIE, ELIE. England and the Middle East: The Destruction of the Ottoman Empire, 1914-1921 (Cambridge, 1956).

LEWIS, BERNARD. Istanbul and the Civilization of the Ottoman Empire (University of Oklahoma Press, 1963).

LEWIS, GEOFFREY. La Turquie, le déclin de l'Empire, les réformes d'Ataturk, la Republique moderne (Verviers/Belgique, 1968).

LIDDELL, ROBERT. Byzantium and Istanbul (London, 1956).

LLOYD, SETON. Early Anatolia (London, 1956).

MANTRAN, ROBERT. Histoire de la Turquie (Paris, 1952).

MILLER, WILLIAM. The Ottoman Empire and its Successors, 1801-1927 (Cambridge, 1934).

OSTROGORSKY, G. History of the Byzantine State (Oxford, 1956).

PALLIS, A. A. In the Days of the Janissaries (London, 1951).

PFEFFERMANN, HANS. Die Zusammenarbeit der Renaissance Päpste mit den Türken (Winterthur, 1946).

PRICE, M. PHILIPS. A History of Turkey: From Empire to Republic (London, 1956).

PURYEAR, VERNON J. Napoleon and the Dardanelles (Berkeley, 1951).

RAMSAUR, E. E. The Young Turks and the Revolution of 1908 (Princeton University Press, 1957).

RICE, DAVID TALBOT. Art of the Byzantine Era (Frederick A. Praeger, New York, 1963).
    Byzantine Art (Penguin, London, 1962).

RICE, TAMARA TALBOT. The Seljuks (London, 1962).

RUNCIMAN, Sir STEVEN. The Fall of Constantinople, 1453 (Cambridge, 1965).

SUMNER, B. H. Peter the Great and the Ottoman Empire (Oxford, 1949).

THOMAS, L. V., and FRYE, R. N. The U.S.A. and Turkey and Iran (Oxford University Press, 1952).

VAUGHAN, DOROTHY. Europe and the Turk: A Pattern of Alliances, 1350-1700 (Liverpool, 1954).

VERE-HODGE, EDWARD REGINALD. Turkish Foreign Policy, 1918-1948 (2nd (revised) edition, London, 1950).

WALDER, DAVID. The Chanak Affair (Hutchinson, London. 1968).

ECONOMY

CENANI, RASIM. Foreign Capital Investments in Turkey (Istanbul, 1954).

The Economy of Turkey: an Analysis and Recommendations for Development Program: Report of the Mission sponsored by the International Bank for Reconstruction and Development; in collaboration with the Government of Turkey (Baltimore, 1951).

THE FIRST FIVE YEAR DEVELOPMENT PLAN 1963-67, Annual Programme; Central Bank of Republic of Turkey (Ankara 1963).

HERSHLAG, Z. Y. Turkey: the Challenge of Growth (Leiden, 1968).

INTRODUCTION TO TURKISH LAW. Edited by Tuğrul Ansay and Don Wallace Jr. (Society of Comparative Law, Ankara, 1966).

INVESTMENT GUIDE TO TURKEY: Investment Promotion Publication No. E.-13/64 (Union of Chambers of Commerce, Ankara, 1964).

LINGEMAN, E. R. Economic and Commercial Conditions in Turkey (London, 1948).

SHORTER, FREDERIC C. (ed.). Four Studies on the Economic Development of Turkey (Cass, London, 1967; Kelley, New York, 1968).

THORNBURG, MAX, SPRY, GRAHAM, and SOULE, GEORGE. Turkey: an Economic Appraisal (New York, 1949).

United Arab Emirates

ABU DHABI   DUBAI   SHARJAH   RAS AL KHAIMAH   UMM AL QUWAIN   AJMAN
FUJAIRAH

GEOGRAPHY

The coastline of the seven United Arab Emirates extends for nearly 400 miles from the frontier of the Sultanate of Oman to Khor al-Odaid on the Qatar Peninsula in the Persian Gulf. The area is one of extremely shallow seas, with offshore islands and coral reefs, and often an intricate pattern of sandbanks and small gulfs as a coastline. In contrast to the Mediterranean, there is a large tide. The waters of the Gulf contain relatively abundant quantities of fish, large and small, hence fishing plays some part in local life. The climate is arid, with very high summer temperatures; and except for a few weeks in winter, air humidity is also very high. The total area of the U.A.E. has been estimated at approximately 32,000 square miles and it has a rapidly growing population estimated at 210,000, now concentrated in the oil boom areas of Abu Dhabi, the capital of the U.A.E., and Dubai. Many inhabitants are nomadic or settled Arabs. In the coastal towns live also many Persians, Indians, Pakistanis, Baluchis and Negros, the latter being descended from slaves carried from Africa during the course of several centuries of slave trading. The most important port is Dubai and this has a population of about 75,000. Its significance derives from its position on one of the rare deep creeks of the area, and it now has a very large transit trade.

HISTORY

In the early 16th century the Portuguese commercial monopoly of the Gulf area began to be challenged by other European traders eager for a share in the profits from the Eastern trade, first by the Dutch, later by the British. By the end of the century the Portuguese ascendency in the East had declined and in 1650 the Portuguese evacuated Oman losing their entire hold on the Arabian shore. Then followed a period of commercial and political rivalry between the Dutch and the British during which the initial Dutch predominance weakened and in 1766 came practically to an end, while the British were consolidating their supremacy in India.

Both European and Arab pirates were very active in the Gulf during the 17th, 18th and early 19th centuries. Lawlessness reached its height at the beginning of the 19th century when the seafaring Arab tribes were welded together and incited to pillage by Wahhabi emissaries who had established their supremacy over the whole Arabian coast of the Gulf. Attacks on British-flag vessels led to British expeditions against the pirates in 1806 and 1809 and, finally, in 1818 against the pirate headquarters at Ras al Khaimah and other harbours along the 150 miles of "Pirate Coast". In 1820 a General Treaty of Peace for suppressing piracy and slave traffic was concluded between Great Britain and the Arab Tribes of the Gulf. Among the signatories were the principal Sheikhs of the Pirate Coast and the Sheikhs of Bahrain. A strong British squadron was stationed for some time at Ras al Khaimah to enforce the treaty.

Many piratical acts continued to be committed and accordingly, in 1835, the Sheikhs were induced to bind themselves by a "Maritime Truce" not to engage, in any circumstances, in hostilities by sea for a period of six months (i.e. during the pearl-diving season). The advantages of this were so marked that they were easily persuaded to renew the truce and continually did so for increasing periods until, in May 1853 a Treaty of Maritime Peace in Perpetuity was concluded between all the Sheikhs of the "Trucial Coast"—as it was henceforth called—establishing a "perpetual maritime truce". It was to be watched over and enforced by the British Government, to whom the signatories were to refer any breach. The British, however, did not interfere in wars between the Sheikhs on land.

The British concern in stopping the slave trade had also led to contacts with the Trucial Coast, where the Sheikhs had been engaged in carrying slaves from Africa to India and Arabia. By agreements signed with the British in 1838–39 and 1847 the Sheikhs undertook to prohibit the carriage of slaves on board vessels belonging to them or their subjects, and consented to the detention and search of such vessels and to their confiscation in case of guilt.

Towards the end of the 19th century France, Germany and Russia showed increasing interest in the Gulf area and in 1892 Britain entered into separate but identical "exclusive" treaties with the Trucial rulers concluded on different dates, whereby the Sheikhs undertook not to cede, mortgage nor otherwise dispose of parts of their territories to anyone except the British Government, nor to enter into any relationship with a foreign government other than the British without British consent. Britain had already undertaken to protect the states from outside attack in the Perpetual Maritime Treaty of 1853.

In 1820 when the General Treaty was signed, there were only five Trucial States. In 1866, on the death of the Chief Sheikh of Sharjah, his domains were divided amongst his four sons, the separate branches of the family being established at Sharjah, Ras al Khaimah, Dibah and Kalba.

In 1952, Kalba was incorporated into Sharjah when its ruler undertook to accept all the treaties and agreements in force between the United Kingdom and the other Trucial States. These undertakings included recognition of the right of the U.K. Government to fix state boundaries, to settle disputes between the Trucial Sheikhdoms and to render assistance to the Trucial Oman Scouts, a British-officered Arab force set up in 1952. The Ruler of Fujairah also accepted these undertakings when his state was recognized as independent in 1952.

In 1952 on British advice a Trucial Council was established at which all seven rulers met at least twice a year under the chairmanship of the Political Agent in Dubai. It was formed with the object of inducing the rulers to adopt a common policy in administrative matters and in the hope that an eventual federation of the states would ensue.

The advent of commercial production of oil in mid-1962 gave Abu Dhabi a great opportunity for development. The deposition of the Ruler, Sheikh Shakhbut, in 1966 removed a major obstacle to implementing this opportunity, and the history of this sheikhdom since then is a classic example of a society being transformed almost overnight by the acquisition of immense wealth. Dubai has also benefited greatly from the oil boom.

In June 1965 Sheikh Saqr of Sharjah was deposed. In spite of an appeal to the UN Secretary-General, supported by Iraq and the United Arab Republic, the accession of his cousin, Sheikh Khalid, passed off without incident. There was an unsuccessful attempt on the Sheikh's life in July 1970.

After June 1966 Britain gradually built a substantial military base at Sharjah, with the object of replacing Aden as the major base in the Middle East; by July 1968 the force of 3,000 men was also larger than Bahrain's and Sharjah had become the principal base in the Gulf. Early in 1968 the British Government announced that all its forces would be withdrawn from the area by the end of 1971, and this policy was eventually reaffirmed after the Conservative Party's return to power in Britain in June 1970. The Trucial Oman Scouts, a force of some 1,600 men officered and paid for by Britain and based in Sharjah, was proposed as the nucleus of a federal security force after British withdrawal in 1971, but some states, notably Abu Dhabi, were already creating their own defence forces.

It was feared that friction might be aroused by disputes over the ill-defined state borders; those between Qatar, Abu Dhabi and Dubai were settled early in 1970, the settlement being disputed by Saudi Arabia, whose claimed territory overlapped that of Abu Dhabi to a considerable extent. In July 1970 King Faisal requested that a plebiscite be held in the Buraimi district now ruled by Abu Dhabi. Further down the Gulf, offshore rights also caused trouble in the summer of 1970. Rival claims over the island of Abu Musa were made by both Sharjah and Iran when Umm al Quwain's concessionaire, Occidental Petroleum, began drilling there.

The original proposals for the formation of a federation on the departure of British Influence included Bahrain and Qatar, as well as the seven Trucial States, but negotiations on the participation of the larger and more developed states eventually broke down in 1971, and they opted for separate independence. On December 1st, 1971, Britain terminated all existing treaties with the Trucial States. The following day Abu Dhabi, Dubai, Sharjah, Umm al Quwain, Ajman and Fujairah formed the United Arab Emirates and a treaty of friendship was made with Britain.

Ras al Khaimah refused to join the Union until February 1972, when it had become clear that neither Britain or any Arab government was prepared to take action on Iran's seizure of the two Tumb islands in the Gulf belonging to the sheikhdom. In December 1971 the U.A.E. became members of both the Arab League and the United Nations.

In January 1972 the Ruler of Sharjah, Sheikh Khalid was killed by rebels led by his cousin, Sheikh Saqr, who had been deposed as Ruler in 1965. The rebels were captured, and Sheikh Sultan succeeded his brother as Ruler. Sheikh Sultan soon confirmed that he would rule according to the relatively liberal principles of his brother and retain Sharjah's membership of the U.A.E.

In September 1972 the U.A.E. was admitted to the International Monetary Fund and the International Bank for Reconstruction and Development (World Bank).

ECONOMIC SURVEY

ABU DHABI

In Abu Dhabi the oil concession for the greater part of the mainland area is held by Abu Dhabi Petroleum Company (same shareholders as the Iraq Petroleum Company). In 1973, as a result of a Participation Agreement, the Abu Dhabi Government took a 25 per cent stake in ADPC. In 1967, a consortium of Phillips Petroleum, American Independent Oil Company and ENI obtained a concession over part of the area relinquished by ADPC. Further onshore areas are still available. Offshore, the principal concession holder is Abu Dhabi Marine Areas (owned by British Petroleum and *Compagnie Française des Pétroles*). A contract was signed in September 1970 between British Petroleum and four Japanese companies, Abu Dhabi Oil, Qatar Oil, North Slope Oil and Alaska Petroleum Development, for a joint operation to develop the Bunduq oilfield, part of the ADMA concession. The Japanese Abu Dhabi Oil Company (Maruzen Oil, Daikyu Oil and Nippon Mining) obtained a concession covering relinquished offshore areas in December 1967, and plans to start production from its Mubarraz field by the end of 1972; eventual output is likely to reach 200,000 barrels a day. The Murban field started producing in December 1963 and the Bu Hasa field a year later. These fields are both about 75–80 miles west of the town of Abu Dhabi and well inland from the sea. Production in 1971 was 44.5 million tons, an increase of 29 per cent on 1970. In 1971 it was announced that a national oil company was to be set up with an initial capital of £20 million.

The tremendous growth of the oil revenues has already enabled Abu Dhabi to claim to be the richest country in the world, in terms of income per capita. These revenues reached £35 million in 1967, doubled in 1968, and are expected to rise from an estimated £160 million in 1971 to approach £200 million in 1972. The population was estimated at around 17,000 before 1966, but with the considerable number of immigrants since then it was thought to have reached 70,000 in 1972. This explosive growth has inevitably led to shortcomings in such facilities as water and power supplies, accommodation and transport, though money is available to solve these problems. In 1968 Abu Dhabi initiated its first National Plan which envisaged a total expenditure of BD 316.97 million ($662 million) of which over 90 per cent was to be spent on social services and industrial and agricultural projects during the period 1968–73. The pace and pressure of development led to a minor crisis in late 1969 when expenditure began to exceed revenues, partly because the Government had authorized more projects than it could immediately pay for, especially as inflation had driven up the cost of all construction. A policy of consolidation was introduced at the end of 1969, with a resultant slowdown in the rate of development. In the 1970 budget development expenditure was reduced by 35 per cent from the level envisaged under the five-year plan. Since the 1969–70 "freeze" the Government has continued a more cautious policy of "controlled expansion" and in 1972, for the third year running, a surplus was budgeted for. Following an industrial survey to examine ways of reducing the state's dependence on oil production, a $30 million refinery with a capacity of 15,000 barrels a day is to be constructed in Umm Al Nar for the newly established national oil company. Abu Dhabi's development has been made more difficult by the poor port facilities—most trade comes through Dubai as the Gulf waters surrounding Abu Dhabi are extremely shallow. To overcome this dependence on Dubai, deep-water facilities at Abu Dhabi harbour were under construction in 1971. In late 1967 the country joined the Organization of Petroleum Exporting Countries.

In May 1973 the U.A.E. brought uniform currency into circulation, replacing the Bahrain dinar used in Abu Dhabi and the Qatar/Dubai riyal used in Dubai and the other northern states. The new denomination, the dirham, is equal to one Q/D riyal or one-tenth of the Bahrain dinar.

DUBAI

In the offshore area of Dubai (where oil has been discovered) exploitation is carried on by a partnership of Dubai Marine Areas, Dubai Petroleum Company, Deutsche Texaco, Delfzee Dubai Petroleum and Sun Oil. Dubai Marine Areas has 50 per cent, Dubai Petroleum Company 30 per cent, and Delfzee, Texaco and Sun share the remainder. Dubai has been owned solely by *Compagnie Française des Pétroles* since October 1969. Dubai Petroleum Company is a wholly-owned subsidiary of Continental Oil; it also holds land concessions for Dubai, some of which it has assigned to other firms, one German and one American. The offshore concessionaires announced in 1966 that oil had been discovered in commercial quantities, and production started in 1969 at the rate of 30,000 barrels a day rising to 100,000 per day in early 1971. However, the Continental Oil Company is spending £33 million on oilfield development in an attempt to increase production to 300,000 barrels a day, earlier estimates of reserves having been far exceeded. By 1971 oil revenues had risen to £13 million and after the expansion programme is complete in 1973, revenues should rise to £50 million a year.

Dubai has long been the principal commercial centre and entrepôt port for the Emirates, and in consequence has benefited greatly from the oil boom in the area. The basis of the supremacy has been the relatively good facilities for shipping offered by Dubai Creek; this lead is now being consolidated by the construction of a £24 million deep water harbour. This harbour, to be known as Port Rashid, which was approaching completion in early 1972, will be the largest harbour in the Middle East and Dubai will become a free port. Dubai's official import figures are the most reliable index of economic activity in the

Emirates; in 1966 imports totalled £23 million, in 1970 they exceeded £80 million and were expected to rise to about £200 million by the mid-1970s. The sheikhdom has all the characteristics of a boom economy, albeit not in such an extreme form as Abu Dhabi. Massive construction projects absorb most of the local labour force, and immigrants, whose numbers have now had to be restricted, already outnumber natives. All food and manufactured articles have to be imported. Traditional occupations have declined—in Dubai these mainly consisted of fishing and smuggling. Dubai's low tariffs and absence of official restrictions have fostered smuggling to states with higher tariffs in the Gulf, and to India and Pakistan. This used to be particularly true of gold, still thought to be smuggled into India on a large if declining scale; the apparent decline is due to both increasingly vigilant Indian policing and to the safer and equally profitable opportunities now available in legal trade.

THE SMALLER SHEIKHDOMS

Until very recently the other Trucial States had only a traditional and very impoverished economy based on fishing and pearling. Red oxide deposits are exploited in Sharjah and Ras al Khaimah possesses an Agricultural Trials Station operated under British supervision. In 1972 work started on the construction of a $5.6 million cement factory in Sharjah, which has particularly good limestone resources. Another cement plant, with a capacity of 700 tons a day, is under construction in Ras Al Khaimah; it is the first industry of any size to be introduced into the state. Several sheikhdoms have produced colourful series of postage stamps and attempted to tap the world philatelic market, with varying success. All have now signed oil agreements which give the rulers a limited income whilst exploration continues; oil has yet to be discovered outside Abu Dhabi and Dubai, although some oil has been discovered in Sharjah. The ill-defined borders between the states, and the offshore rights which are disputed both amongst themselves and with Iran, are both likely to cause friction should commercial discoveries be made.

Sharjah is the most developed of these five states, owing to the former presence of a British R.A.F. station and the progressive attitude of the late Ruler, Sheikh Khalid. A British withdrawal has meant loss of an important source of revenue and employment, although it may develop into a repair complex for commercial aircraft, and there are plans to exploit the rich fishing grounds from Sharjah's enclave on the Gulf of Oman, around Khor Fakkan. A fisheries station is to be built at Umm Al Qiwain.

STATISTICAL SURVEY

AREA AND POPULATION

AREA (sq. miles)		POPULATION			
Total	Abu Dhabi (estimate)	Total (1972 est.)	Abu Dhabi (1968 Census)	Dubai (1972 est.)	Sharjah (1968 Census)
32,000	25,000	230,000	46,375	75,000	31,480

Population estimates (1970) for the other sheikhdoms are as follows: Ras al Khaimah 24,500, Fujairah 10,000, Ajman and Umm al Quwain 4,000 each.

OIL
PRODUCTION OF CRUDE OIL
(metric tons)

YEAR	ABU DHABI MARINE AREAS LTD.	ABU DHABI PETROLEUM CO. LTD.	DUBAI PETROLEUM COMPANY
1968	8,878,089	15,156,700	—
1969	11,728,264	16,815,000	523,000
1970	12,686,029	20,080,000	4,305,000
1971	16,833,341	27,160,000	6,252,000
1972	22,409,000	28,833,735	7,500,000

UNITED ARAB EMIRATES—(Statistical Survey)

FINANCE

1,000 fils = 1 U.A.E. dirham.
Coins: 1, 5, 10, 25, 50 and 100 fils.
Notes: 1, 5, 10, 50, 100 and 1,000 dirhams.
Exchange rates (June 1973): £1 sterling = 9.868 dirhams; U.S. $1 = 3.947 dirhams.
100 U.A.E. dirhams = £10.133 = $25.333.

Note: The dirham was introduced on May 20th, 1973, replacing the Bahrain dinar in Abu Dhabi and the Qatar riyal in other states.

Budget: The 1973 budget totalled £49 million; among the largest allocations were £10.9 million for development projects, £8.3 million for education, £49 million for defence, £5.3 million for health services and £3.5 million for water and electricity supplies.

EXTERNAL TRADE

Dubai
IMPORTS
('000 Qatar/Dubai riyals)

Commodities	1968	1969	1970	1971
Household Goods	179,411	202,150	179,391	208,137
Foodstuffs	117,634	114,142	132,498	150,080
Garments	147,812	164,910	145,278	134,140
Machinery	150,880	187,173	155,606	102,001
Building Materials	73,947	101,000	139,151	142,154
Electrical, Radio and Allied Goods	30,560	44,021	62,992	54,970
Stationery	5,024	6,980	5,581	7,314
Photographic Goods	2,413	3,969	5,870	3,793
Cosmetics	6,591	6,871	8,925	8,986
Medicines and Chemicals	5,141	8,694	9,230	19,263
Fuel and Oil	12,088	27,979	27,031	26,710
Arms and Ammunition	1,369	5,543	17,622	10,078
Oil Field Materials	25,550	45,192	64,436	90,347
Liquor and Wine	2,657	4,317	6,279	11,063
Total	761,080	922,951	899,880	1,059,021

Principal Countries	1969	1970	1971	1972
Switzerland	105,722	82,678	93,724	110,249
Japan	179,012	162,668	181,699	308,157
United Kingdom	161,227	169,990	186,450	191,314
United States	75,594	88,304	127,394	200,483
India	42,007	56,048	47,010	54,026
Pakistan	34,603	20,721	25,282	29,336
China	32,672	30,111	33,887	46,535
German Federal Republic	39,260	31,514	36,252	43,259
Hong Kong	28,741	32,323	35,562	57,604
Netherlands	19,962	25,743	32,018	41,518
Saudi Arabia	23,443	23,245	22,792	77,399

EXPORTS AND RE-EXPORTS
(Qatar/Dubai riyals)

1969	93,074,606
1970	120,800,256
1971	136,827,297

There is a large and officially authorized trade in gold which is not, however, included in the official trade statistics for Dubai.

UNITED ARAB EMIRATES—(Statistical Survey, The Constitution, etc.)

ABU DHABI

IMPORTS
(Bahrain dinars)

Commodities	1972
Food and Live Animals	6,873,324
Beverages and Tobacco	1,322,442
Crude Materials (excl. oil)	821,420
Gas and Fuels	2,692,447
Chemicals	2,619,487
Machinery and Transport	36,271,769
Manufactured Goods	18,156,141
Animal and Vegetable Fats	447,559

('000 Bahrain dinars)

Countries	1971	1972
Australia	1,070	1,444
Dubai	4,316	n.a.
France	1,009	5,569
German Federal Republic	2,135	436
Italy	1,193	2,002
Japan	2,556	11,786
Lebanon	1,012	2,152
Netherlands	1,649	213
United Kingdom	14,541	18,138
U.S.A.	10,687	10,395

TOTAL IMPORTS
(Bahrain dinars)

1969	59,277,212
1970	35,245,328
1971	46,941,551
1972	75,761,951

THE CONSTITUTION

The Rulers of the United Arab Emirates have absolute control over their own subjects though the Ruler of Abu Dhabi has appointed a cabinet and a National Consultative Assembly.

The Supreme Council of the Union, on which all the Rulers are represented, meets at least twice a year to discuss problems of mutual interest.

THE GOVERNMENT

HEAD OF STATE
President: Sheikh Zaid bin Sultan al-Nihyan.
Vice-President: Sheikh Rashid bin Said al-Maktum.

SUPREME COUNCIL OF THE UNION
(with each ruler's date of accession)

Ruler of Sharjah: Sheikh Sultan bin Muhammad al-Qasimi (1972).
Ruler of Ras al Khaimah: Sheikh Saqr bin Muhammad al-Qasimi (1948).
Ruler of Umm al Quwain: Sheikh Ahmed bin Rashid al-Mu'alla, M.B.E. (1929).
Ruler of Ajman: Sheikh Rashid bin Humaid al-Nuaimi (1928).
Ruler of Dubai: Sheikh Rashid bin Said al-Maktum (1958).
Ruler of Abu Dhabi: Sheikh Zaid bin Sultan al-Nihyan (1966).
Ruler of Fujairah: Sheikh Muhammad bin Hamad al-Shargi (1940).

CABINET
(*August* 1973)

Prime Minister: Sheikh Maktum bin Rashid al-Maktum.
Deputy Prime Minister and Minister of Finance, Economy and Industry: Sheikh Hamdan bin Rashid al-Maktum.
Minister of the Interior: Sheikh Mubarak bin Muhammad al-Nihyan.
Minister of Defence: Sheikh Muhammad bin Rashid al-Maktum.
Minister of Foreign Affairs: Ahmad Khalifa al-Suweidi.
Minister of Health: Sheikh Sultan bin Ahmad al-Mualla.
Minister of Public Works: Sheikh Sultan bin Muhammad al-Qasimi.
Minister of Education: Abdulla bin Umran Taryam.
Minister of Communications: Sheikh Abd-al-Aziz bin Rashid al-Nuaimi.
Minister of Agriculture and Fishing Resources: Sheikh Muhammad bin Hamad al-Sharoi.
Minister of Information: Sheikh Ahmad bin Hamid.
Minister of Water and Electricity: Abdullah bin Hammoud al-Qasimi.
Minister of Planning: Muhammad al-Kindi.
Minister of Housing: Saeed bin Abdullah bin Salman.
Minister of Justice: Ahmed bin Sultan al-Qasimi.
Minister of Youth and Sports: Sheikh Rashid bin Humaid.
Minister of Labour and Social Affairs: Sheikh Sami bin Isa bin Harith.

UNITED ARAB EMIRATES—(The Government, Diplomatic Representation, etc.)

Minister of State for Financial and Economic Affairs: Ahmad bin Sultan bin Sulayim.
Minister of State for Unity and Gulf Affairs: Muhammed Saeed al-Mulla.
Minister of State for the Council of Ministers: Utaiba bin Abdullah al-Utaiba.

ABU DHABI CABINET

Prime Minister and Minister of Defence and Finance: Sheikh Khalifa bin Zayed al-Nihyan.
Deputy Prime Minister and Minister of Public Works: Sheikh Hamdan bin Muhammad al-Nihyan.
Minister of the Interior: Sheikh Mubarak bin Muhammad.
Minister of Municipalities and Agriculture: Sheikh Mahmoud bin Muhammad al-Nihyan.
Minister of Communications: Sheikh Muhammad bin Khalid al-Nihyan.
Minister of Health: Sheikh Saif bin Muhammad.
Minister of Water and Electricity: Sheikh Khalifa bin Muhammad al-Nihyan.
Minister of Justice: Sheikh Surur bin Muhammad.
Minister of Information and Tourism: Sheikh Ahmad bin Hamid.
Minister of Cabinet Affairs: Ahmad bin Khalifa al-Suweidi.
Minister of Labour and Social Affairs: Sheikh Muhammad bin Butti.
Minister of Economy and Trade: Sheikh Khalifa bin Ahmad al-Utaiba.
Minister of Oil and Industry: Mani Saeed al-Utaiba.
Minister of Education: Muhammad Khalifa al-Kindi.
Ministers of State: Muhammad Habrush and Dr. Adnan al-Pachachi.

DIPLOMATIC REPRESENTATION

EMBASSIES ACCREDITED TO THE UNITED ARAB EMIRATES
(Abu Dhabi unless otherwise stated.)
(E) Embassy.

Afghanistan: (E); *Ambassador:* Khalil A. Khalili.
Egypt: (E); *Ambassador:* Sahid D. Mortaba.
France: Kuwait City, Kuwait (E).
India: Kuwait City, Kuwait (E).
Iran: (E); *Ambassador:* Mohogbar Behnam.
Iraq: (E); *Ambassador:* Tawfiq al Moumen.
Japan: Kuwait City, Kuwait (E).
Jordan: (E); *Ambassador:* Abdel al-Shalamaina.
Kuwait: (E); *Ambassador:* Sheikh Badr Muhammad Ahmad al-Sabah.
Lebanon: (E); *Ambassador:* Hassib al-Abdullah.
Libya: (E); *Ambassador:* Muhammad Bashir al-Mughayribi.
Netherlands: Baghdad, Iraq (E).
Pakistan: (E); *Ambassador:* Jamil Eddin Hasan.
Somalia: Jeddah, Saudi Arabia (E).
Sudan: (E); *Ambassador:* Sulaiman Babakr.
Syria: (E); *Ambassador:* Rashid Kailani.
Tunisia: Kuwait City, Kuwait (E).
United Kingdom: (E); *Ambassador:* Donald MacCarthy.
United States: Kuwait City, Kuwait (E).
Yemen Arab Republic: (E); *Ambassador:* Muhammad Said Qubati.

The United Arab Emirates also has diplomatic relations with the Netherlands and the Federal Republic of Germany.

ASSEMBLIES

U.A.E. NATIONAL CONSULTATIVE ASSEMBLY

This met for the first time on February 13th, 1972, when it was opened by the U.A.E. President, Sheikh Zaid.

ABU DHABI CONSULTATIVE ASSEMBLY

Formed on September 1st, 1971, it has 50 members, all nominated by the Ruler, Sheikh Zaid. None of the members belong to the ruling family, though many of them represent tribal interests.

The Assembly can make recommendations on draft laws to the Council of Ministers before they are submitted for the Ruler's approval.

The Assembly met for the first time in October 1971. Its term is two years.

DEFENCE

Total Armed Forces: 9,850: Union Defence Force 1,600; Abu Dhabi 7,000; Dubai 1,000; Ras al Khaimah 250.

JUDICIAL SYSTEM

U.A.E. subjects and citizens of all Arab and Muslim states are subject to the jurisdiction of the local courts.

In the local courts the rules of Islamic law generally prevail. A modern code of law is being produced for Abu Dhabi.

In Dubai there is a court run by a *qadi*, while in some of the other states all legal cases are referred immediately to the Ruler or a member of his family, who will refer to a *qadi* only if he cannot settle the matter himself. In Abu Dhabi a professional Jordanian judge presides over the Ruler's Court.

RELIGION

Most of the inhabitants are Muslims of the Sunni and Shi'ite sects.

THE PRESS

Abu Dhabi Chamber of Commerce Review: P.O.B. 662, Abu Dhabi; monthly; Arabic.
Abu Dhabi News: Department of Information and Tourism, P.O.B. 17, Abu Dhabi; weekly; English.
al-Ittihad (*Unity*): Abu Dhabi; f. 1972; first daily paper in the UAE.
Raj al-Khalij (*Gulf Opinion*): Abu Dhabi; f. 1973; daily; Arabic, with English supplement.

Akhbar Dubai: Department of Information, Dubai Municipality, P.O.B. 1420, Dubai; f. 1965; weekly; Arabic.

UNITED ARAB EMIRATES—(THE PRESS, RADIO AND TELEVISION, FINANCE, OIL)

Dubai External Trade Statistics: P.O.B. 516, Dubai; monthly; English.

Dubai Official Gazette: P.O.B. 516, Dubai; Arabic and English; quarterly or as necessary.

---

al Sharooq (*The Sunrise*): Sharjah; f. 1970; monthly; Dir.-Gen. TAREEM OMRAN; Editor YOUSEF AL HASSAN; circ. 3,000.

Akhbar Ras al Khaimah: Ras al Khaimah; monthly; Arabic.

RADIO AND TELEVISION

There are radio stations in Abu Dhabi and Sharjah and television stations in Abu Dhabi, Dubai and Qatar.

Voice of the United Arab Emirates Radio: f. 1972; broadcasts ten hours a day on medium wave.

Voice of the Coast (*Sawt as Salih*): Sharjah; broadcasts daily in Arabic over a wide area; accepts advertisements.

Forces Radio Station: P.O.B. 627, Sharjah; broadcasts in English; accepts advertisements.

FINANCE
BANKING

Committee of Clearing Bankers: Abu Dhabi; f. 1971 by the banks operating in Abu Dhabi; Chair. HAZIM CHALABI.

Arab Bank: Amman, Jordan; P.O.B. 875, Abu Dhabi; P.O.B. 1650, Dubai; P.O.B. 130, Sharjah; Ras al Khaimah (2 brs.).

Bank of Cairo: P.O.B. 533, Abu Dhabi.

Bank of Oman Ltd.: P.O.B. 2111, Dubai; f. 1967; cap. p.u. 6,750,000 Q/D riyals; P.O.B. 858 Abu Dhabi; brs. in Ajman and Al Bin; Gen. Man. MAJED AL GHURAIR.

British Bank of the Middle East, The: London; brs. in Dubai, Sharjah, Khor Fakkhan, Ras al Khaimah, Abu Dhabi, Fujairah, Kalba.

Commercial Bank of Dubai: P.O.B. 1709, Dubai; f. 1969; owned by Chase Manhattan Bank, Commerzbank A.G. and the Commercial Bank of Kuwait; br. in Sharjah.

Dubai Bank: P.O.B. 545, Deira, Dubai; f. 1970; control is held by local interests, but British, French and American banks are also participating; p.u. cap. 8,686,800 Q/D riyals.

Chartered Bank: London; P.O.B. 240, Abu Dhabi; P.O.B. 999, Dubai; P.O.B. 5, Sharjah.

First National City Bank: New York; P.O.B. 749, Dubai; P.O.B. 346, Sharjah; P.O.B. 999, Abu Dhabi.

Habib Bank (Overseas): Karachi; P.O.B. 888, Dubai; P.O.B. 300, Sharjah.

Melli Bank (Iran): P.O.B. 1894, Dubai; P.O.B. 459, Sharjah.

National and Grindlays Bank Ltd.: London; P.O.B. 241, Abu Dhabi; P.O.B. 225, Ras al Khaimah; P.O.B. 257, Sharjah.

National Bank of Abu Dhabi: P.O.B. 4, Abu Dhabi; f. 1968; p.u. cap 1m. BD; Gen. Man. D. G. SUTCLIFFE.

National Bank of Dubai: P.O.B. 777, Dubai; brs. in Abu Dhabi and Umm al Quwain; Gen. Man. D. W. MACK, M.B.E.

Rafidain Bank (Iraq): Ras al Khaimah.

Sedarat Bank (Iran): P.O.B. 7000, Abu Dhabi; P.O.B. 4182 Dubai; other brs. at Sharjah and Ras al Khaimah.

United Bank: P.O.B. 1000, Dubai; P.O.B. 237, Abu Dhabi; eight other brs.

INSURANCE

Abu Dhabi Insurance Co.: f. 1972; cap. 500,000 BD subscribed by the Government of Abu Dhabi.

Arab Commercial Enterprise (Dubai) Ltd.: P.O.B. 1100, Dubai; Man. TOUFIC H. BARAKEH.

Arab Commercial Enterprises (Abu Dhabi) Ltd.: P.O.B. 585; Man. MANSOUR ABDUL RAHMAN.

Arabia Insurance Co. Ltd.: P.O.B. 1050, Dubai; Rep. WALEED H. JISHI.

Sharjah Insurance Co.: P.O.B. 792, Sharjah; f. 1970; monopoly of local insurance business; cap. 2.5m. Q/D riyals, half subscribed by the Sharjah Government.

A large number of foreign insurance companies are represented in the United Arab Emirates.

COMMERCE

Abu Dhabi Chamber of Commerce and Industries: P.O.B. 662, Abu Dhabi; f. 1969; mems. 700; Pres. AHMED MASSOUD; publ. monthly magazine in Arabic.

Dubai Chamber of Commerce: Gamal Abdul Nasser Square, P.O.B. 1457, Dubai; f. 1965; 2,300 mems.; Pres. SAIF AHMED ALGHURAIR.

Ras al Khaimah Chamber of Commerce: P.O.B. 87, Ras al Khaimah; publ. quarterly magazine in Arabic and English.

Sharjah Chamber of Commerce and Industry: P.O.B. 580 Sharjah; f. 1970; Pres. MOHAMMED BIN OBAID AL-SHAMSI.

DEVELOPMENT

The activities of the former Trucial States Development Office were taken over by the Government in 1972 and assigned to various ministries.

Capital Projects include inter-state roads, urban water and electricity schemes, housing and other urban development, rural water supplies, agricultural extension schemes and harbour works. Investigations into water resources, mineral prospects, soil, agricultural marketing and fisheries have been conducted. An Arab economic development fund, with a capital of BD 50 million, was set up by Abu Dhabi in 1971.

Planning and Co-ordination Department: Abu Dhabi; under Ministry of Cabinet Affairs, supervises Abu Dhabi's Development Programme; Dir. MAHMOUD HASSAN JUMA.

OIL

In line with OAPEC policy the Government is to acquire a 51 per cent holding in all oil concessions by 1983. It is to pay $152 million for its initial 25 per cent share of ADMA and ADPC operations.

ABU DHABI

Department of Petroleum Affairs and Industry: B.P. 9 Abu Dhabi; State supervisory body; Dir. MANI AL OTAIBA.

Abu Dhabi Marine Areas Ltd. (ADMA): P.O.B. 303, Abu Dhabi; British Petroleum is to relinquish 45 per cent of its two-thirds holding (a Japanese Consortium—the Overseas Petroleum Corporation has bought 30 per cent for $780 million), another third is owned by *Compagnie Française de Pétroles*; oil has been found in commercial quantities 88 miles offshore from Abu Dhabi on the Umm Shaif structure, 20 miles east of Das Island, only a mile long and half a mile wide, the operating headquarters and tanker loading terminal. A new field at Zakum was brought into production in 1967. Production (1972) 22,409,000 metric tons; Gen. Man. Dr. A. J. HORAN.

Abu Dhabi Oil Company: Abu Dhabi; consortium of three Japanese oil companies, Maruzen, Daikyo and Nihon Kogyo; holds offshore concession; oil strikes reported in September 1969 and January 1970.

Abu Dhabi Petroleum Company Ltd. (ADPC): P.O.B. 270, Abu Dhabi; a subsidiary of the Iraq Petroleum Company. Export of oil from the Murban Field started on December 14th, 1963. The terminal is at Jebel Dhanna. The annual production capacity was raised to 12 million tons during 1965 by the connection of Bu Hasa field to Jebel Dhanna. Facilities installed to raise annual production capacity to 20 million tons were completed in December 1967; production (1972) 28,836,000 long tons; Chair. C. M. DALLEY; Man. Dir. G. G. STOCKWELL; U.A.E. Government nominated Dir. MANI SAEED AL-UTAIBA; Gen. Man. A. TURNER.

Middle East Oil Company Ltd: Abu Dhabi; formed 1968 by the Mitsubishi group; holds concessions covering some 15,000 square km. on land.

Phillips Petroleum: P.O.B. 6, Abu Dhabi; heads consortium with the Italian AGIP Company (each with a 41.66 per cent interest) and the American Independent Oil Company (with a 16.66 per cent interest); holds 9,686 square km. concession on land; Gen. Man. E. D. COOPER.

United Petroleum Development (Japan): Abu Dhabi; f. 1970; association of four Japanese companies, in association with British Petroleum, to develop the Bunduq oilfield.

DUBAI

Petroleum Affairs Department: P.O.B. 707, Dubai; government supervisory body; Dir. MAHDI AL TAJIR.

Dubai Marine Areas: Dubai; holds offshore concession agreement signed in 1963, with a 50 per cent holding in production; British Petroleum sold its two-thirds interest in the company to *Compagnie Française des Pétroles* in October 1969.

Dubai Petroleum Company: Dubai; subsidiary of Continental Oil Co. (U.S.A.) in partnership with *Compagnie Française des Pétroles*, Hispanoil (Spain), Dubai Sun Oil Co. (U.S.A.), Wintershall AG (Germany); holds offshore concession in "Fateh" oilfield, which began production in 1969; output in 1971 6.2m. tons; 1972 7.7m. tons.

RAS AL KHAIMAH

Union Oil of California has a concession.

SHARJAH

John Mecom Ltd. have held a concession since 1964. In January 1969 the Ruler of Sharjah signed two exploration agreements with *Shell* interests, and in December 1969 he also granted an offshore exploration concession to the *Buttes Oil and Gas Co.* of California.

FUJAIRAH

Bochumer Mineralöl G.m.b.H., owned by the Federal German Bomin Group, has held a concession covering the whole of the land area and territorial waters of the sheikhdom since 1966.

AJMAN

Occidental Petroleum has a concession.

UMM AL QUWAIN

An offshore concession was granted to *Occidental Petroleum* in November 1969. *John Mecom Ltd.* and *Shell* also hold concessions.

TRANSPORT

ROADS

Until very recently there was no proper system of roads except in Dubai town, but the desert tracks are often motorable. In 1965 plans were made for a £1 million all-weather metalled road to be built from Dubai to Ras al Khaimah, to be financed by the Trucial States Development Office. The Dubai/Sharjah section of this was opened in September 1966. Work has now been completed on the Sharjah/Ras al Khaimah section at the expense of the Saudi Arabian Government. In 1968 Abu Dhabi opened a £1 million bridge linking the town with the mainland. The town is also linked with the Buraimi Oasis by a dual-carriageway motor road built mainly for political reasons. The oil companies have constructed roads in the area in which they operate. An underwater tunnel linking Dubai Town and Deira with a dual carriageway and pedestrian subway is to be built by a British firm at a cost of £7.5 million. There is a road linking Dubai and Abu Dhabi, and also a road between Fujairah and Khor Fakkar. Roads between Dhaid (Sharjah) and Fujairah and between Qatar and Abu Dhabi are under construction.

SHIPPING

Dubai is the main port. The British India Steam Navigation Co. Ltd. maintains a weekly scheduled service to Dubai on the Bombay–Basra run. The ships of British India Line and F. Strick & Co. call at Dubai and Abu Dhabi several times a month. Other lines which call regularly are D. D. G. Hansa, Johnson Line, Holland-Persian Gulf, Maersk Line, and Jugolinÿa. Work began in 1970 on a new four-mile channel which will make the port of Abu Dhabi accessible to sea-going vessels including tankers. The Port Rashid project was completed a year ahead of schedule in October 1972; with fifteen deep-water berths it makes Dubai harbour the biggest in the Middle East. A dry dock scheme costing £51 million is expected to be under way in 1973; it will have two docks capable of handling 500,000-ton tankers, seven repair berths and also a third dock able to accommodate one million ton tankers, which will make Dubai the biggest supertanker complex in the whole of the Gulf.

CIVIL AVIATION

The new air terminal at Dubai was opened in 1971 by Sheikh Rashid. The £4m. terminal was the first in the Middle East to have facilities for handling Jumbo Jets. There are smaller international airports at Abu Dhabi and Sharjah.

Gulf Air Co. Ltd.: P.O.B. 138, Bahrain; Dubai National Air Travel Agency, P.O.B. 1515, Dubai; Omeir Travel Agency, Abu Dhabi; Sharjah Aircraft Handling Agency, Sharjah; daily service Bahrain – Doha – Abu Dhabi–Muscat and twice weekly from Dubai to Shiraz, Bandar Abbas, Bombay and Kuwait; four times weekly from Dubai to Karachi and Salalah.

Alia, Air India, BOAC, Iran Air, Kuwait Airways, Middle East Airlines, PIA, KLM, Gulf Air, Iraqi Airways, Saudia, Syrian Arab Airlines and TMA all serve Dubai and Abu Dhabi, while Gulf Air serves Sharjah.

TOURISM

Department of Information and Tourism: Government of Abu Dhabi, P.O.B. 17, Abu Dhabi.

EDUCATION

There are boys' and girls' primary-intermediate schools in all states. There are also trade schools in Sharjah, Dubai, Ras al Khaimah and Abu Dhabi and an agricultural school in Ras al Khaimah. There are secondary schools for boys and girls in Abu Dhabi, Dubai, Sharjah, Ras al Khaimah, Ajman and Umm Al-Quwain. There are three Islamic Religious Institutes in Abu Dhabi, Dubai and Ajman. The United Arab Emirates is drawing up plans for the further development of its educational system.

BIBLIOGRAPHY

ALBAHARNA, H. M. The Legal Status of the Arabian Gulf States (Manchester University Press, May 1969).

BUSCH, B. C. Britain and the Persian Gulf 1894–1914 (University of California Press, 1967).

FACT SHEETS ON EASTERN ARABIA (Private Information Center on Eastern Arabia, Heldenplein 12, 1800 Vilvoorde, Belgium).

HAWLEY, DONALD FREDERICK. Courtesies in the Trucial States (1965).

   The Trucial States (George Allen and Unwin, London 1971).

HAY, Sir RUPERT. The Persian Gulf States (Middle East Institute, Washington, 1959).

MANN, CLARENCE. Abu Dhabi: birth of an Oil Sheikhdom (Khayats, Beirut, 1964).

MARLOWE, JOHN. The Persian Gulf in the 20th Century (Cresset Press, London, 1962).

MILES, S. B. The Countries and Tribes of the Persian Gulf (3rd edition, Cass, London, 1966).

WILSON, Sir A. T. The Persian Gulf (1928).

Yemen Arab Republic

GEOGRAPHY

The Yemen Arab Republic lies at the south-west corner of the Arabian peninsula and comprises two well-defined areas—the highlands inland, and the coastal strip along the Red Sea. The climate of the highlands is considered the best in all Arabia since it experiences a régime rather like that of East Africa, with a warm temperate and rainy summer, and a cool, moderately dry winter with occasional frost and some snow. As stated below (see Yemen P.D.R.) these conditions are thought to be produced by an upper air current that brings very moist air from the Atlantic, giving rise to a minor monsoonal effect of heavy summer rainfall. As much as 35 inches of rain may fall annually on the higher parts of the interior, with 15–20 inches over much of the plateau; but the coast receives under 5 inches generally, and in the form often of irregular downpours. There is therefore the phenomenon of streams and even rivers flowing perennially in the highlands, but failing to reach the coast.

Because of this climatic gradation, from desert to temperate conditions, the Yemen has a similar gradation of crops and vegetation. The highest parts appear as "African", with scattered trees and grassland. Crops of coffee, qat, cereals and vegetables are grown, whilst lower down, "Mediterranean" fruits appear, with millet, and where irrigation water is available, bananas. Finally, near the coast, the date palm becomes the only tree.

The area of the Yemen is approximately 75,000 square miles and its population has been estimated at 6 million. The capitals are Sana'a (on the d'El Jehal plateau, altitude 7,260 ft.) and Taiz (altitude 4,600 ft.), which have populations of 120,000 and 80,000 respectively.

HISTORY

In classical times the Yemen formed part of the south-eastern area of Arabia Felix. One of the best-known kingdoms in that region was that of Sheba, which lasted from 950 to 115 B.C. From then until the sixth century A.D. Arabia Felix was ruled by the Himyarite dynasty, from whom the modern Imams claim descent. In A.D. 525 the Ethiopians conquered the Himyarite Kingdom, and they in turn were overthrown by a Persian invasion in 575. During the seventh century the country nominally accepted Islam and the Sunnis of the Shafi'i rite established their power in the Tihama (the coastal region), and the Zaidis, a moderate branch of the Shia, held the highlands.

During the ninth century the Zaidi Imam Yahya al-Hadi ila'l-Haqq founded the Rassid dynasty of the Yemen, which has survived, with some interruptions, to the present time.

In 1517 the Yemen was conquered by the Ottoman Turks, but their power was continually contested by other European powers, and their authority was not great. Fierce tribal and religious warfare led the Turks to establish in 1872 a full occupation of the country under a Turkish *Vali*. This occupation lasted until the Mudros armistice of 1918, but in 1911 the Imam Yahya had led a full-scale revolt which secured a treaty confirming Turkish suzerainty, but dividing administrative control between the Imam in the highlands and the Turks in the Tihama and on the coast.

During the First World War the Imam had supported the Turks, and the British had therefore supported Idrisi invaders from the small state of the Asir to the north of the Yemen. A succession dispute broke out in the Asir in 1923 in the course of which Imam Yahya of the Yemen had occupied the port of Hodeida and the coastal areas. By the Treaty of Mecca in October 1926 the Sheikh of the Asir was placed formally under the protection of Ibn Sa'ud; this position, however, was never enthusiastically accepted by the Imam, who continued to bait the new king of Arabia and also to encroach on the British-protected territory of the Aden Protectorate. In these activities he seemed to have had the support of Italy, with whom he signed a treaty of friendship in 1926; and a Soviet trade delegation made a brief appearance in the country at this time. In 1930 following on a dispute over his Hijaz borders he encouraged the Sheikh of the Asir to revolt against Ibn Sa'ud; the latter attempted to settle the dispute by peaceful means, and negotiations dragged on until 1934. In April of that year, however, Ibn Sa'ud decided on more drastic action; marching on the Yemen, he drove the Yemeni troops out of Hodeida, and in a bloodless campaign of a month forced them back into Sana'a. The peace treaty of Ta'if allotted Tihama and Najran to Ibn Sa'ud but otherwise left the boundaries of the Yemen undisturbed —a policy of moderation that won him considerable prestige. At the same time Britain formally recognized the independence of the Yemen by treaty, and ended for a time a long series of frontier disputes.

The despotic and conservative Imam Yahya continued to rule until February 1948, when an attempted *coup d'état* by Sayyid Abdullah al-Wazzir resulted in his murder; his eldest son, Saif al-Islam Ahmad, however, succeeded to the throne and drove out the insurgent. Since then the Yemen has been co-operating in international affairs; in January 1951 a start was made on the development of the country with British, American and French technical aid, and at the same time full diplomatic relations were established for the first time with foreign powers, including Britain, the U.S.A. and Egypt. During 1953 agreements were concluded with German and Italian firms for the development of the Yemen's mineral resources, including oil, coal and iron. Turkish, Iraqi, Egyptian and Pakistani advisers have also been employed in connection with financial and military reforms.

In the winter of 1953 Yemen, with Arab support, began pressing before the United Nations her claims to Aden and the territories of the Aden Protectorate, and throughout the summer of 1954, and again in 1955, there was a series of frontier incidents.

In April 1955 an attempted *coup d'état* against the Imam Ahmad was defeated, and the royal conspirators executed; but one consequence may have been the Imam's decision in August of that year to set up a formal cabinet. During 1956 relations were established with the Soviet Union and a military pact was concluded with Egypt, Saudi Arabia and Syria.

In March 1956, Yemen protested against Britain's grant of an oil concession to the B.P. (formerly D'Arcy) Exploration Company on the Red Sea island of Kamaran, claimed by the Yemen. Further protests were made in July 1958 and May 1959.

The frontier dispute between Britain and the Yemen was continued late in December 1956 and in 1957, when Yemeni tribesmen were reported to have attacked villages in the Aden Protectorate. The Crown Prince visited London for talks in November 1957, but hostilities flared up again in the spring of 1958 and the political committee of the Arab League denounced the actions of Great Britain in the Aden territories. Two bomb incidents in Aden itself led to the enforcement in May 1958 of a temporary state of emergency. Unsuccessful talks to settle the dispute were held in July 1958 and May 1959. (For a fuller account of the border dispute see the chapter on Southern Yemen.)

A Yemeni delegation, headed by the Crown Prince, visited Cairo in February 1958 for negotiations which led to a federal union between the United Arab Republic and the Yemen, established by an agreement signed in Damascus on March 8th. The new union was named the United Arab States, and was to have a unified defence and foreign policy, and later a Customs union and common currency. Few practical steps were taken to that end and although, in November 1961, the Yemen renewed the agreement for a further three years, the Federation was formally dissolved by the United Arab Republic in December 1961.

In May 1959 disorders followed the departure of the Imam Ahmad to Europe and the Crown Prince Muhammad al-Badr introduced various reforms, including the innovation of a Representative Council. This policy was reversed on the return of the Imam in August.

CIVIL WAR 1962—1969

In March 1961 there was an unsuccessful attempt to assassinate the Imam, who was wounded in the shoulder. The Imam died in September 1962, and was briefly succeeded by his son Muhammad Badr. But a week later a revolt broke out, led by Colonel Abdullah Sallal, supported by troops from the U.A.R. The new Imam fled into the hills after a series of attempts to regain the capital, and Republican forces gained control of most of the country. The Republic was soon recognized by the U.S.S.R. and the United States, and early in 1963 was admitted to the United Nations. Britain, however, continued to give recognition to the Royalist régime, and stated on a number of occasions that she would only recognize the Republic when U.A.R. forces were withdrawn. Fighting continued throughout the year and did not cease until the summer of 1969, having been particularly severe during the winter of 1963–64 and much of 1968. An Observer Mission dispatched by the United Nations found that an agreement for simultaneous withdrawal of U.A.R. troops and Saudi Arabian military supplies had not been implemented by either side. The Mission operated from July 1963 to September 1964.

The rapprochement between U.A.R. and Saudi Arabia in February 1964 suggested that a solution would not be long delayed, and recognition by Jordan of the Republican régime was a further important step towards complete acceptance of the Revolution and its consequences. Britain, nevertheless, maintained her stand in support of the Royalists; the interest of the U.A.R. in driving British influence out of South Arabia (the Yemen Republican leaders were less vehement in this aim than their Egyptian colleagues) only strengthened the determination of the United Kingdom Government.

In May 1964 a new Republican Government was announced under the terms of a new Constitution published in April. The Prime Minister, Hamud Al Jaifi, soon displayed his command of the situation, which was emphasised by the frequent absences of the President for medical treatment in Cairo and Europe. In a policy statement in June a programme of school, hospital and road building was announced, and in July an agreement was signed in Cairo to establish a U.A.R./Yemen co-ordinating council and a joint military command; 90 per cent of the expenses of these ventures would be provided by Egypt, which had already sent an estimated 40,000 troops into the country in support of the Republicans.

In September the UN military observers left the country, while at the same time Sallal was attending the Arab Summit Conference in Alexandria. Following this meeting President Nasser and King Faisal discussed the Yemen situation, and this led in November to a meeting at Erkwit in the Sudan, at which republican and royalist delegations agreed to a cease-fire and the convening of a national congress. Differences over procedure forced the postponement of this, and in December the royalists resumed the offensive. During January the Imam al-Badr proclaimed a constitutional charter. This military and political offensive led to dissensions in the republican cabinet, culminating in the fall of Hamud Al Jaifi in January 1965, and his replacement by Lieut.-Gen. Hassan Al-Amri with a mandate to stiffen the war effort. In April, however, Lieut.-Gen. Amri resigned, and was replaced by the moderate Muhammad Ahmad Noman, who embarked on a policy of conciliation. The long postponed National Congress met in May in the village of Khamer, though without the participation of the royalists, and on May 9 the text was published of an interim constitution, setting up a supreme Consultative Assembly with power to make laws, remove members of the Republican Council, and nominate the President. Despite the energetic efforts of Mr. Noman to achieve a peace settlement, it was not long before his sympathy for the Baathist cause ran him into opposition from the Egyptian authorities, who retained a measure of financial control over the Yemen. In July Noman resigned and after a few days of uncertainty President Sallal announced a new cabinet headed by Lieut.-Gen. Amri. The return to prominence of the military, pro-Egyptian element coincided with a number of important Royalist advances, and relations between the U.A.R. and Saudi Arabia worsened dangerously as each accused the other once again of complicity in the civil war.

THE SEARCH FOR A SETTLEMENT

In late summer events took a more hopeful turn when President Nasser agreed to discuss the Yemen situation with King Faisal at Jeddah. On August 24th, after their two-day conference, the two leaders concluded an agreement on a plan to bring the war to an end and to establish, within fifteen months, a Yemeni government free from outside interference. The agreement stipulated that a cease-fire was to be declared immediately; Saudi Arabia was to stop supplying arms to the Royalist forces; an interim government of moderate politicians, excluding both the Imam al-Badr and President Sallal, was to be set up within three months; after which the Egyptian forces, numbering about 50,000, were to be withdrawn during the ten-month period ending September 23rd, 1966. By November 23rd, 1966, a plebiscite would be held to enable the Yemenis to choose the political form they wished their state to assume.

Although the immediate effects of the Jeddah agreement were hopeful, including the establishment of a more representative Presidency Council for the Republic, and of a U.A.R./Saudi Arabian Peace Committee, the good intentions of the participants to the agreement were soon eroded. In November 1965 a conference of Republican and Royalist envoys meeting at Haradh reached deadlock over

YEMEN ARAB REPUBLIC—(HISTORY)

the next steps to be taken, and through 1966 the implementation of the agreement seemed less and less likely as relations between Egypt and Saudi Arabia deteriorated. Egyptian troop numbers in the Yemen, far from being reduced, were built up; despite a further U.A.R./Saudi meeting in August in Beirut, chaired by Kuwait, a solution seemed no nearer. Worse still, in September 1966 friction between Lt.-Gen. Amri and President Sallal came into the open when the latter returned to Sana'a. A large delegation, led personally by the Premier, then flew to Cairo to demand complete independence from U.A.R. for the Yemen régime, and the permanent removal of the President. The U.A.R. response to this was to arrest the members of the delegation, and Sallal himself assumed the duties of the premiership. This was followed by a drastic purge of the republican armed forces and administration, and a wave of riots, trials and executions. The dissident republican elements took refuge in the mountains to the north of Sana'a.

During the latter months of 1966 republican and royalist operations began to escalate. Egyptian aircraft were in action, and on several occasions air raids were made on the Saudi Arabian towns of Jizan and Najran. In January allegations were made of the use of poison gas, a charge denied by the U.A.R.

Meanwhile there was considerable diplomatic activity. In January Sallal formed the Popular Revolutionary Union at a meeting attended by Makkawi (see Southern Yemen). Outside Yemen, a Union of Popular Forces was formed, led by Ibrahim al-Wazir, who visited Riyad and Geneva calling for an Islamic State of Yemen, the withdrawal of Egyptian troops, and the ending of Saudi Arabian aid. On February 11th, 1967, Tunisia and Jordan withdrew their recognition of the Sallal régime. However, Jordanian recognition was subsequently restored, in consequence of the diplomatic rapprochement with Egypt at the time of the Arab-Israel war of June 1967.

In July, following a major government reorganization, the Royalists took advantage of the run-down in Egyptian troops to stage one of the fiercest land offensives for two years. Republican forces were driven from Haradh and the port of Maydi, and refugees from the coastal town of al-Luhayya had to be evacuated to the British-administered island of Kamaran. Later in July the Egyptian military build-up was resumed, and these localities were retaken. At the end of the month a Royalist spokesman complained to the United Nations of persistent poison gas attacks by Egyptian forces. U.A.R. denials of the use of poison gas were discredited by an independent International Red Cross inquiry in May 1967, which confirmed the use of such gas in a raid on May 10th.

THE EGYPTIAN WITHDRAWAL

Early in August 1967, on the occasion of the meeting of Foreign Ministers at Khartoum to prepare an agenda for an Arab summit conference, the U.A.R. delegate announced that the Egyptian Government was once again prepared to put into effect the agreement drawn up with King Faisal of Saudi Arabia at Jeddah in August 1965. The supervision of the withdrawal of troops would be entrusted to a committee of three Arab states. According to Radio Sana'a, a principal factor influencing this change of heart by the Egyptians was the British decision on a definite date for the withdrawal of troops from Aden, in January 1968. The implication appeared to be that Egypt saw no further need for the presence of her forces in Yemen after the British withdrawal from South Arabia had taken place. The fact that the U.A.R. was now partially dependent on financial aid from more conservative Arab countries, notably Saudi Arabia, was not mentioned.

On August 31st an agreement on these terms was finally reached by King Faisal and President Nasser at the Arab leaders' conference at Khartoum. Egyptian troops were to be withdrawn within three months; a plebiscite to determine the political future of the Yemen was to be held within a further six months; President Sallal was to lead a transitional government; the whole agreement to be carried out under the supervision of representatives of three independent Arab states, Iraq, Morocco and Sudan. Although President Sallal immediately protested against the peace plan, his opposition did not prove an obstacle.

The Egyptian army, with an estimated strength of up to 80,000 men, had effectively colonized the Republican-held sector of the Yemen, and was in general neither popular nor well regarded for its military prowess. Thus its withdrawal, which was completed by January 1968, was not altogether unwelcome although it naturally encouraged the Royalist forces to become bolder. It also led to the deposition of President Sallal in November, carried out while he was on an official visit to Iraq, and the institution of a three man Presidency Council headed initially by Abdul Rahman al-Iriani. In December 1967 General Hassan Al-Amri, a militant republican, replaced the moderate Muhammad No'man on the Council; shortly afterwards he also became Prime Minister, again replacing a more moderate man. The National Liberation Front, the left-wing force that had come to power in the newly independent territory of Southern Yemen, also came to possess considerable influence in the Yemen at this time.

The Royalist army continued to make progress early in 1968, and for some time the Republican capital of Sana'a was virtually besieged. Its defendants claimed that the Imam was still receiving generous aid from Saudi Arabia, while much of their own equipment had been taken by the Egyptians. In January the Iraqi, Sudani and Moroccan foreign ministers arranged a peace meeting in Beirut, but it proved abortive as the rival factions could not even agree to meet. By April the pressure on Sana'a had relaxed somewhat; a left-wing plot to overthrow the Al-Amri government was unsuccessful. In June the Royalist leader, Imam Muhammad al-Badr, was deposed by his followers in favour of his son (his cousin according to some accounts), Muhammad bin Hussein. A ministerial delegation from Southern Yemen met the leaders of the Republican government in July, apparently for talks regarding the rebels in the hinterland of both countries.

THE END OF THE CIVIL WAR

During the 1968-69 period it became evident that the Royalist military effort was in decline after its major offensive following the Egyptian withdrawal; some accounts claimed that the Royalists ceased to exist as a regular fighting force after a defeat at Hajja in December 1968. By the summer of 1969 the leading members of the Royalist camp were all in exile, and their followers had apparently accepted the Sana'a government. The principal cause of this swift collapse appeared to be a feud within the royal family following the deposition of the Imam. The Saudi Arabian Government's confidence in the Royalists, already weakened by their failure to capture Sana'a, thus diminished further; eventually the Saudis ceased their financial and military assistance on which the Royalists had depended. Since the Republicans were apparently in receipt of substantial arms supplies from other Arab countries and the U.S.S.R. their success was assured.

Nevertheless, there was a short-lived revival of military activity in the north-east during the winter of 1969-70. Rebel tribesmen, said to be opposed to rule from Sana'a rather than positive supporters of the Imam, surrounded the town of Saada for some weeks. This development, plus the massive economic problems faced by the government, led to the resignation of the Prime Minister, Abdallah Kurshoumi, in February 1970, only six months after he had succeeded General Al Amri. Muhsin Al Aini, the Ambassador in Moscow, was then appointed Prime Minister.

In March 1970 the Premier and the Foreign Minister met Saudi Arabian officials privately during the Islamic Foreign Ministers Conference at Jeddah. Although no formal announcement of the outcome was made, it appeared that an informal peace settlement was agreed upon. As a result, the leading Royalists, apart from the Imam and the royal family itself, returned to Sana'a in May 1970 and were offered a number of posts in the administration. Ahmed Al Shami, the former Royalist foreign minister, joined the Presidential Council, four Royalists joined the cabinet, and others were given high diplomatic or civil service posts or became members of the National Assembly.

The government was said to be anxious to open relations with the Western countries which had recognized the Royalist régime; in July 1969 diplomatic relations with Federal Germany were restored at a time when several Arab states followed an opposite policy in recognizing the G.D.R. (East Germany). One result was a generous offer of economic and financial aid from Bonn. In July 1970 Saudi Arabia formally opened diplomatic relations with the republic, and within a few days Britain and France followed suit. Drought created a widespread famine in the summer of 1970, and offers of food and medical supplies were received from many countries.

In December 1970, a new constitution was promulgated, providing for a Consultative Council to replace the National Assembly. Elections were held in March 1971.

In July 1971 there were rumours of an attempt by senior army officers to overthrow the Government, and several officers were dismissed. In September the Prime Minister, Lt.-Gen. Hassan al-Amri, went into exile after reportedly murdering a man in his office. Tension between Sana'a and Aden increased in the first half of 1972 as supporters of FLOSY and the South Arabian League, opponents of the Aden Government, amassed on the borders between the two states.

Serious fighting broke out on the border in September, but an Arab League mission was able to mediate and a ceasefire became effective in October. A peace agreement and an agreement on eventual unification of the two Yemens were signed in Cairo on October 28th. Further details were discussed in Tripoli (Libya) in November by the Presidents of the two Yemens, and it was agreed that the people of Yemen would establish a single state, to be known as the Yemen Republic, with Sana'a as its capital, Islam as the State religion and Arabic as the official language. Committees were set up to discuss details of the unification. In January 1973 it appeared that certain obstacles had arisen in the progress towards union, but in February a new political organization, the Yemeni Union, was formed in Sana'a in anticipation of the forthcoming union. At the end of May fighting again broke out on the border between the two Yemens, and on May 30th, Sheikh Muhammad al-Othman, a member of the three-man Presidential Council, was assassinated by unknown gunmen. Although this incident temporarily soured relations between the two Yemens, it was announced in June that talks on unity would continue.

In December 1972 Mohsin Aini resigned as Prime Minister and a new government was later formed under Abdullah al-Hajari.

ECONOMIC SURVEY

M. Jibb

AGRICULTURE

Yemen contains some of the most fertile land in the Arabian Peninsula, both in the highlands, where agriculture has always been extensively practised, and in the dry coastal plain of the Tihama. Yemen's best-known crop is coffee, grown mainly in the hills behind the Tihama, although it is cultivated in various degrees all over the country. It is Yemen's largest foreign exchange earner, but the amount of land devoted to it has decreased, partly because of fluctuations in demand on the world market, partly because the farmers find the narcotic, qat, to be a more profitable crop. Qat is grown over a very wide area and it is estimated that as much land is devoted to its cultivation as to that of cotton or tobacco. In 1972, however, the Government announced measures to limit the growing of qat, whereby its cultivation was banned on state-owned land or on *Waqf* (religious endowment) land.

Dhurra, Yemen's major cereal crop, is grown at any altitude up to 9,000 feet; other cereals are wheat, barley and maize. Although a comparatively large area is allocated to cereals, the yield is poor and Yemen relies on imports of staple foods. A prolonged drought in the years 1968 to 1970 caused the failure of many crops and the resultant famine obliged the Government to import even larger quantities of wheat and cereals. The 1971 season saw increased yields, but it will take some time for the farmers to recover completely.

The highland areas also produce many fruits and vegetables, citrus fruits, apricots, peaches, grapes, tomatoes and potatoes being the main crops, but others such as cauliflowers, lettuces, peas, cucumbers and water melons are being introduced at the instigation of the Ministry of Agriculture. The hot Tihama plain produces dates, and tobacco and cotton plantations are being established there to form the basis for local industries. Cotton in particular is assuming some importance as a cash crop; production in 1971 totalled 12,000 tons, compared with only 2,000 tons the year before.

The Government plans to introduce Friesian cattle to the upland regions to improve the local stock and breeding stations are being built in Sana'a, Taiz and Hodeida.

Although rain is more abundant in Yemen than elsewhere in the Peninsula, nevertheless it cannot be completely relied upon and, indeed, droughts are frequent. Yemen's major concern is, therefore, to achieve efficient irrigation and water storage schemes and to utilize the ground water which exists in the Tihama.

The largest project now in hand is the $17.5 million agricultural scheme for the Tihama region, assisted by the United Nations. The International Development Association (IDA) is providing a $10.9 million credit and the rest will be contributed by the Kuwait Fund for Arab Economic Development (KFAED) and Yemen itself. The scheme involves irrigation works in the Wadi Zebid area, the development of 60,000 hectares at Wadi Mawr, the establishment of a Tihama Development Authority and providing credit schemes and various other services. Output of cotton and vegetables in the area should almost double when the project is completed and substantially increased yields of cereals and oilseeds are expected. Other UN schemes are a pilot project for the development of a sugar cane industry and the expansion of the government-run model farm near Taiz into an agricultural advisory centre.

INDUSTRY

Yemen's traditional handicraft industries—textiles, leatherwork, basketry, jewellery and glass-making—are beginning to feel the effects of competition from manufacturing industries in other Arab countries, which threaten the export market for Yemeni goods. The towns of Beit el Faqih, Zebid and Hodeida in the Tihama produce textiles of traditional design made from local cotton and indigo dye which, though beautiful, cannot compete in price and durability with modern synthetics and factory-woven fabrics. It is likely, however, that the Government will encourage the traditional crafts, particularly if a tourist industry can be established. Many may well disappear without State patronage.

The existing and projected new industries are based on the traditional occupations and, where possible, local raw materials. There is a state-owned spinning and weaving factory at Sana'a, established under an agreement of 1958 between Yemen and China, and completed in 1967. The plant, the Sana'a Textile Factory, employs 1,240 workers, many of them women, and produces about 6.1 million metres of fabric per year. The Bajil textile factory, set up by French and Syrian interests in the 1950s, encountered financial difficulties and never went into production. A United Nations report of 1968 recommended its urgent rehabilitation and repair, and a Dutch firm has conducted a study. In addition, there are two cotton-cleaning plants in Hodeida, and one in Zebid, and a cotton seed oil and cake plant in Hodeida; these are privately owned. The Government is also considering the establishment of a new complex (location uncertain) to combine cleaning and oil seed production. Clearly the textile industry is the promising line of industrial development in Yemen. The Yemen Cotton Company, owned 51 per cent by the Government, 30 per cent by the Yemeni Bank for reconstruction and development and 19 per cent by private interests, provides the plants with raw cotton, over which it has monopoly rights.

The rock salt factory at Salif, managed by the Ministry of Economy, utilizes local salt deposits, estimated to contain at least 25 million tons. The salt, which is of high quality, is all exported to Japan. The Salt Company has invested about $400,000 to raise production to 500,000 tons a year and the KFAED provided a loan to extend bulk-loading facilities at Salif port. A further KFAED loan of KD 1.2 million was agreed upon in 1972 to exploit the salt deposits further and to raise production to 1 million tons a year by 1974. A Canadian company is developing the mines.

The salt at Salif is the only mineral at present exploited in Yemen on any scale. There are also salt deposits at Marib in the east and at Qumah, near Salif. Other minerals known to exist in Yemen are: coal, copper (at Hamoura, near Taiz), marble, iron, sulphur, lead, zinc, silver, gold and uranium.

In 1970 a joint company, the Yemen Oil and Mineral Industrial Company, was formed by the Yemeni Government with the Algerian state-owned oil concern, SONATRACH. It was announced in 1972 that oil had been found in the Tihama but whether in commercial quantities was not established. The company had to be dissolved in 1972 because of lack of capital but the Government made it known that it would welcome foreign firms who wished to prospect for oil.

Other industries include three soft drinks factories, a cigarette plant at Hodeida, built with Italian aid, an oxygen plant, originally set up by the U.S.S.R. and now state-operated, and a plant making aluminium products. Schemes are in hand to set up an industrial estate in Sana'a with technical aid provided by the UN. The Yemeni Company for Industrial Development was formed to develop light industry, particularly in Sana'a, Taiz and Hodeida but industrialization generally is progressing very slowly.

The Soviet-built cement factory at Bajil, which uses local limestone deposits is one of the more successful ventures. It should eventually achieve an output of 100,000 tons a year, which is thought to be sufficient to meet local demand for the time being.

COMMUNICATIONS

It is only since the revolution in 1962 that Yemen has established regular links with the outside world, and that good roads have been built connecting the main towns. The Sana'a–Hodeida road, completed in 1962, was built by Chinese engineers and is a spectacular achievement. The Sana'a–Saada road, also built with Chinese aid, should be completed by 1974. The Sana'a–Taiz, the Mocha–Taiz and the Sana'a–Ibb–Taiz roads were built with American aid. The repair and maintenance of these roads is proving a problem, since neither the equipment nor the personnel are available locally. Altogether there are estimated to be about 1,650 km. of roads, of which only 600 km. are asphalted. In addition there are a number of gravel feeder roads under construction. These are of great importance for the transport of agricultural produce which otherwise cannot reach centres of distribution.

There are three ports in Yemen: Hodeida, Mocha and Salif, of which the most important is Hodeida. A new harbour was completed there in 1962, built by the U.S.S.R., and it is now being expanded. Mocha cannot be used by ships of any size at present. With the expansion of salt mining at Salif, the harbour is being rebuilt to enable it to take ships of up to 5,000 tons and a bulk petrol plant is also planned.

There are airports at Sana'a, Hodeida and Taiz and smaller airstrips in other towns. Sana'a airport, built by the U.S.S.R. and now being equipped by West Germany, is capable of taking large aircraft, and both Hodeida and Taiz can take international flights. Yemen has its own airline, Yemen Airlines, but the company ran into financial difficulties and was re-organized by the Ministry of Economy. Facilities for air travel are poor by international standards.

Much work is now being done on providing Yemen with a telecommunications system. The three main towns, Sana'a, Taiz and Hodeida are linked by a 600 km. telephone line, built by East German experts, and are also connected to a number of other towns where telephone exchanges are in operation: Bajil, Ibb, Dhamar, Yerim, Manakha, Zebid, Beit-el-Faqih and Hais. East Germany also helped to found a Communications College at Sana'a and is to expand the Sana'a, Taiz and Hodeida exchanges to 4,000 lines each from the present 1,000 lines. A six-channel microwave scatter system linking Sana'a and Taiz is being implemented by the United Nations and Sana'a is linked via Aden with the rest of the world. There are radio transmitters at Sana'a and Taiz and various small wireless communications posts scattered throughout the country. Work has started on a television network to operate from Sana'a.

FOREIGN TRADE

Yemeni foreign trade statistics at present are unreliable and do not conform to the Standard International Trade Classification. No consistent sets of figures exist giving a complete time series but the United Nations has prepared figures based on the SITC for the years 1964 to 1966 which show a steadily-growing trade deficit. Figures for 1967 and 1968 are incomplete, but an attempt has been made to reconcile the 1969 and 1970 statistics, at least for imports, with the S.I.T.C. The trade deficit in both 1970 and 1971 amounted to 163 million riyals.

Yemen's exports consist almost entirely of agricultural produce, salt, skins and products of the artisan industries, such as basketry and textiles. The principal import is food and this has contributed most to the large trade gap. Food imports rose from 30 million riyals in 1966 to over 100 million riyals in 1970 because of the drought and famine experienced during that period, but in 1971 food imports fell to 66 million riyals. A substantial proportion of the remainder of Yemen's imports is made up of finished goods, vehicles, electrical machinery and petrol.

Yemen imports most from Australia, which supplies foodstuffs, the Soviet Union, Japan and, lately, China.

Figures for trade with Yemen P.D.R. are inflated due to the volume of transit trade *via* Aden, but with the development of Hodeida as a port capable of handling all Yemen's trade, the importance of Aden is declining.

The amount of barter trade with the Eastern Bloc is increasing, with China and the Soviet Union taking deliveries of Yemen cotton and coffee in return for aid with industrial projects and the supply of machinery.

FINANCE AND FOREIGN AID

During the civil war there was a considerable inflow of foreign exchange from Saudi Arabia and Egypt. This, coupled with continued remittances from Yemenis living abroad, tended to soften the effects of the decline in agriculture which took place after 1966. These flows resulted, however, in a rise in liquidity which, with increasing government expenditure, led in turn to inflation, a sharp rise in imports and the depreciation of the Yemeni riyal.

Yemen has a very large budgetary deficit, which in 1968–69 amounted to 70 million riyals and reached 83 million riyals in 1971–72 quite apart from foreign loan commitments. The instability of the Government in 1971 meant that no firm measures were taken to deal with the situation. In July 1971 the Government of Muhammad Ahmed Noman resigned because of its inability to deal with the state's financial difficulties. The Government of his successor, Lt.-Gen. Hassan al-Amri lasted only ten days. A new administration under Mohsin el-Aini announced that it would make a sharp reduction in government spending, would do all it could to attract foreign investment and would establish light industry in Yemen to reduce imports.

After the civil war the country had to rely more and more on foreign assistance for development. Extensive aid was offered by China, the Soviet Union and the United Nations and smaller amounts by Hungary, Yugoslavia, Bulgaria and Romania. Western aid came mainly from the United States and West Germany. The richer Arab countries, notably Algeria and Kuwait, also started to take an interest in Yemen, Algeria in oil and mineral exploitation, and Kuwait in the agricultural sector through loans from the Kuwait Fund for Arab Economic Development. Between 1962 and 1969 a total of $141 million was offered by China, the Soviet Union and the United Nations alone and Yemen has since 1956 accumulated a total debt of about $190 million. Even so, aid offered has been in excess of aid drawn and many development projects have been held up for years. This was partly due to the uncertain political situation during the years of the Civil War and partly because the riyal was depreciating rapidly, making the use of foreign aid difficult and expensive.

Nevertheless, Yemen must attract foreign aid and investment or remain backward and underdeveloped. With the stabilization of the Government in 1971/72 many foreign interests showed themselves more ready to invest in and aid Yemen. The Government, for its part, in 1972 published the "Law for the Investment

YEMEN ARAB REPUBLIC—(Economic Survey, Statistical Survey)

of Foreign Capital", first drafted in 1970. Besides aid for industrial and agricultural development, much practical aid in the fields of health, education and social welfare continued to flow in, particularly from China, the U.S.S.R., the World Health Organization and UNICEF. Kuwait and Saudi Arabia and, more recently, the United Arab Emirates have provided schools, hospitals and clinics and many other Arab countries have sent teachers to Yemen. The Arab states appear to be increasingly ready to co-operate with Yemen in providing both financial and practical assistance. Much work still needs to be done to combat the effects of malnutrition, disease and ignorance. The UN has launched a nutrition project aimed at providing school meals and improving the protein content of the average Yemeni's diet. Particular attention is being paid to the development of water resources, both for agriculture and in the towns.

Lack of data in almost every sector is the main obstacle to be overcome, and it is in some cases even more serious than lack of funds. The full resources of the country have not yet been surveyed so that it is difficult to say where its true potential lies. Unless some very large mineral deposit is discovered, Yemen's main source of wealth will continue to be agriculture. Meanwhile, the World Bank is studying the economic situation in detail and helping to reorganize the country's financial and economic institutions.

Political events in 1972 also had an unfortunate effect on the economy, the fighting with the South being most unlikely to inspire confidence in foreign investors. The unity agreement signed at the end of 1972 between North and South Yemen achieved some pause in hostilities, but no firm progress towards implementation was made in the following months.

STATISTICAL SURVEY

AREA AND POPULATION

Area	Total (July 1st, 1972)	Sana'a (capital)	Taiz	Hodeida
195,000 sq. km.	6,062,000	120,000*	80,000*	90,000*

* 1970 estimate.

AGRICULTURE
PRINCIPAL CROPS
Average Annual Production 1965-69

	Area (Hectares)	Gross Yield (metric tons)
Sorghum	} 1,260,000	970,000
Millet		
Wheat	25,000	25,000
Barley	145,000	145,000
Maize	4,000	10,000
All Cereals	1,434,000	1,160,000
Coffee	*	4,500
Cotton	12,000	5,000
Vegetables	8,000	40,000
Tobacco	3,400	2,000
Sugar Cane	600	5,000

* 300,000 plants.

YEMEN ARAB REPUBLIC—(Statistical Survey)

INDUSTRY

Industrial Production 1971
('000 riyals)

Mining and Quarrying	3,579
Food Manufacturing	6,332
Soft Drinks	6,877
Tobacco and Cigarettes	2,062
Textiles	25,352
Wood Products	2,260
Printing and Publishing	1,042
Building Materials	4,178
Metal Products	3,077
Electricity	9,256
Vehicle Maintenance	3,751
Others	1,886

FINANCE

40 buqsha = 1 Yemeni riyal.
Coins: ½, 1 and 2 buqsha.
Notes: 10 and 20 buqsha; 1, 5, 10, 20 and 50 riyals.
Exchange rates (April 1973): £1 sterling = 11.18 Yemeni riyals; U.S. $1 = 4.50 Yemeni riyals.
100 Yemeni riyals = £8.95 = $22.22.

BUDGET
(riyals)

	Revenue	Expenditure
1970–71	97,464	170,672
1971–72	151,274	233,803

LIVESTOCK
1969 ('000 head)

Cattle	1,200
Sheep	3,680
Goats	5,000
Camels	75
Horses	3
Donkeys	600

Source: Ministry of Agriculture.

EXTERNAL TRADE
('000 riyals)

	1966	1969	1970	1971
Imports	56,400	158,128	178,449	184,840
Exports	7,283	17,957	15,759	21,571

YEMEN ARAB REPUBLIC—(Statistical Survey)

PRINCIPAL COMMODITIES
(riyals)

Imports	1971
Foodstuffs	66,847,599
Beverages and Tobacco	14,848,768
Petroleum Products	10,544,543
Chemicals	9,406,572
Manufactured Goods	39,167,487
Machinery	14,127,654
Transport Equipment	15,422,431
Textiles	7,916,018

Exports	1971
Cotton	7,986,195
Coffee	4,582,409
Qat	2,798,095
Rock Salt	2,383,694
Hides and Skins	2,039,483

Source: Central Bank of Yemen.

EXPORTS BY MAIN COUNTRY
(million riyals)

	1970	1971
Yemen P.D.R.	8.1	7.3
Japan	1.9	2.5
U.S.S.R.	5.0	1.9
China	—	8.0

IMPORTS BY MAIN COUNTRY
(million riyals)

	1970	1971
Yemen P.D.R.	41.8	49.5
Japan	10.2	17.4
U.K.	15.1	14.7
Australia	22.3	13.9
U.S.S.R.	21.4	13.5
Singapore	2.5	8.4
Italy	5.9	8.5

Source: Central Bank of Yemen.

TRANSPORT

ROAD TRAFFIC 1970
Private cars 723, motor cycles 3,190, taxis 2,616, trucks 2,994.

SHIPPING

	Vessels Entering Hodeida Port	Tonnage Unloaded
1968	256	217,659
1969	280	275,740

CIVIL AVIATION

	Passengers Carried	Freight (kilos)
1968	24,300	174,300
1969	33,500	295,100

EDUCATION
(1969–70)

	Schools	Teachers	Pupils Boys	Pupils Girls
Primary Schools	744	1,499	60,560	4,966
Intermediate Schools	20	149	2,905	90
Secondary Schools	4	55	939	—

Source (except where otherwise stated): Yemen Arab Republic Central Statistical Office.

THE CONSTITUTION

(*Published December 28th, 1970*)

Yemen is an Islamic Arab independent sovereign Republic, with parliamentary democracy, forming part of the Arab nation. Islam is the state religion and Islamic Law the basis of all legislation. Sana'a is the capital.

The Constitution ensures equality of all before the law, freedom of expression, press, publication, public gatherings and trade union activity within the framework of the law. The people are the source of all authority, through their representatives in the Consultative Assembly.

The Consultative Assembly is composed of 179 members, 20 of whom will be appointed by the President and the rest elected by popular franchise every four years. The Assembly shall issue laws and regulations for the organization of the state, and approve the state budget and treaties and agreements concluded by the Government. The members of the Republican Council will be appointed by the Assembly, and may be withdrawn by a two-thirds majority vote of the Assembly.

The Republican Council may present bills to the Council of Ministers for presentation to the Consultative Assembly. Any motion submitted to the Council will require the support of at least 30 members and must be endorsed by a two-thirds majority. No reports are to be submitted to the President except through the Council of Ministers and all laws, orders and directions from the President will be issued through the Council of Ministers.

The Consultative Assembly will nominate the President. Duties of the President of the Republic include the signing of legislation approved by the Consultative Assembly.

The Council of Ministers, as executive and administrative authority in the state, is responsible *inter alia* for the execution of plans laid down by the follow-up committee of the national peace conference, set up to implement the conference resolutions.

The Constitution provides for an independent judiciary, a supreme Sharia Court, and local organs of government. Other provisions cover human rights and equality for women.

THE GOVERNMENT

HEAD OF STATE

President: QADHI ABDUL RAHMAN AL-IRYANI.
Presidential Council: QADHI ABDUL RAHMAN AL-IRYANI, ABDULLAH AL-HAJARI.

CABINET

(*July* 1973)

Prime Minister: ABDULLAH AL-HAJARI.
Deputy Premier and Minister of Foreign Affairs: MUHAMMAD AHMAD NUMAN.
Deputy Premier and Minister of Economic Affairs: Dr. HASSAN MAKKI.
Minister of Economy: ABDULLAH AL-ASNAG.
Minister of the Treasury: ABD-AL-KARIM AL-JUNAIDI.
Minister of the Interior: Brig. MUHAMMAD AL-ASHWAL.
Minister of Justice: ALI SAMMAN.
Minister of Health: Dr. MUHAMMAD AL-KABARI.
Minister of Education: AHMAD JABIR AFIF.
Minister of Agriculture: ABD-AL-JABIR AL-MUJAHID.
Minister of Information: AHMAD DAHMASH.
Minister of Works: ABDULLAH AL-SAADI.
Minister of Local Administration: ABD-AL-KARIM ARASHI.
Minister of Communications: Brig. ABD-AL-LATIF SAIFALLAH.
Minister of Waqfs: ALI ABDULLAH AL-AMRI.
Minister of State for Presidential Affairs: ABDULLAH HUMRAN.
Minister of State for Development Affairs: AHMAD ABDU SAID.
Minister of State for Supply Affairs: SAID AL HAKIMI.

DIPLOMATIC REPRESENTATION

EMBASSIES AND LEGATIONS ACCREDITED TO THE YEMEN ARAB REPUBLIC

(Sana'a unless otherwise stated)
(E) Embassy; (L) Legation.

Algeria: Ali Abdul Mogni St. (L); *Chargé d'Affaires:* OMER BEN AL-SHIAKH.
Bulgaria: Cairo, Egypt (E).
China: Hodeida Rd. (E); *Ambassador:* CHANG TSAN-MING.
Czechoslovakia: Cairo, Egypt (E).
Egypt: Gamal Abdel Nasser St. (E); *Ambassador:* (vacant).
Ethiopia: Chancery Mustafa Court, Taiz (E); *Ambassador:* Ato WOLD ENDSHAW.
France: (E); *Ambassador:* JEAN LEGRAIN.
German Federal Republic: (address not available); *Ambassador:* A. VESTRING.
Hungary: Cairo, Egypt (E).
India: (E); *Ambassador:* NADHIR HUSAYN.
Iran: Jeddah, Saudi Arabia (E).
Iraq: Gamal Abdul Nasser St. (E); *Ambassador:* MAHDI AL-YASIRI.
Italy: (E); *Ambassador:* ROMALDO MASSA.

Japan: Jeddah, Saudi Arabia (E).
Jordan: Jeddah, Saudi Arabia (E).
Korea, Democratic Republic: Cairo, Egypt (E).
Netherlands: Jeddah, Saudi Arabia (E).
Pakistan: Cairo, Egypt (E).
Poland: Cairo, Egypt (E).
Romania: (E); *Ambassador:* MIRCEA NICOLAESCU.
Saudi Arabia: (E); *Ambassador:* Prince MUHAMMAD AL-SIDAIRI.
Syria: Alzubairi Rd. (L); *Chargé d'Affaires:* YAHIA ALMAHAMIAD.
U.S.S.R.: (E).
United Kingdom: (E); *Ambassador:* JOHN MICHAEL EDES.
United States: (E); *Ambassador:* WILLIAM CRAWFORD.
Viet-Nam, Democratic Republic: Cairo, Egypt (E).
Yugoslavia: Ali Abdul Mogni St. (E); *Ambassador:* DRAGO NOVAK.

The Republic also has diplomatic relations with Afghanistan, Bahrain, Chad, German Democratic Republic, Kuwait, Lebanon, Libya, Morocco, Sweden, Tunisia and Turkey.

CONSULTATIVE COUNCIL

A Consultative Council was established as the supreme legislative body under the 1970 Constitution. It consists of 179 members, of whom 20 are appointed by the President and the remainder elected by popular vote every four years. Elections were first held in March 1971.

Speaker: Shaikh ABDULLAH BIN-HUSAIN AL-AHMAR.

POLITICAL ORGANIZATION

Yemeni Union: Sana'a; f. 1973 in anticipation of merging of two Yemens; Leader President ABDUL RAHMAN AL-IRYANI; Sec.-Gen. ABDULLA ASNAG.

LAW AND RELIGION

President of the People's Tribunal: Col. GHALIB SHARI.
Public Prosecutor: Major ABDULLA BARAKAT.
Sharia Court: Sana'a; f. 1964 to deal with political cases and to try senior government officials.

PRESS AND RADIO

Al Bilad: Sana'a; Arabic; weekly.
Al Iman: Sana'a; Arabic; Editor ABDUL KARIM BIN IBRAHIM AL-AMIR.
Al Nasr: Taiz; Arabic; Editor MUHAMMAD BIN HUSSEIN MUSA.

Saba: Taiz; f. 1949; Arabic; fortnightly; political and social affairs; Editor MUHAMMAD ABDU SALAH AL-SHURJEBI; circ. 10,000.
Al Thawra (*The Revolution*): Sana'a; daily.

Middle East News: Ali Abdel Ghani St., Ali Moh. Hamoud Al-Yamani, Sana'a.
Saba News Agency: Sana'a; f. 1970; Chair. AHMAD MUHAMMAD HADI.

Tass also has a bureau in Sana'a.

Radio Sana'a: Station controlled by the government which broadcasts in Arabic for thirteen hours daily; Dir. Gen. ALI HAMOOD AFIF.

There are 250,000 receiving sets.

BANKING

Central Bank of Yemen: P.O.B. 59, Sana'a; f. 1971; cap. p.u. 10m. riyals; responsible for issuing currency, managing gold and foreign exchange reserves etc.; at end of June 1972 currency in circulation amounted to 321.7m. riyals; Gov. and Chair. ABDUL AZIZ ABDUL GHANI; Dep. Gov. and Dep. Chair. ABDULLA SANABANI; Gen. Man. AHMED MUHAMMAD ALI.

Yemen Bank of Reconstruction and Development: Sana'a; f. 1962; cap. 10m. riyals; government bank; 8 brs.; Pres. ALI LOFT AL-THOWR.

British Bank of the Middle East: 20 Abchurch Lane, London, E.C.4; P.O.B. 932, Hodeida; Man. D. C. HOWELLS; P.O.B. 886, Taiz; Man. I. W. CUTTRESS.

TRADE AND INDUSTRY

NATIONALIZED ORGANIZATIONS

General Cotton Organization: Sana'a.

Hodeida Electricity & Waker Company: Hodeida.

National Tobacco & Matches Co.: P.O.B. 571, Hodeida; f. 1964; monopoly importing and sales organization for tobacco and matches; now building a cigarette factory at Hodieda to use tobacco grown locally on the company's plantations; Chair. A. A. NAGI.

Yemen Company for Foreign Trade: Hodeida.

Yemen Petroleum Co.: P.O.B. 360, Hodeida; the sole petroleum supplier in the Yemen; Chair. HUSSAIN ABDULLAH AL MAKDANI; Gen. Man. ABDUL RAHMAN YOUSEF.

Yemen Printing and Publishing Co.: P.O.B. 1081, Sana'a; f. 1970; publishes ten newspapers (including two government newspapers), and undertakes many kinds of commercial printing; Chair. AHMAD MUHAMMAD HADI.

TRANSPORT

Roads: There are about 1,650 km. of main roads, of which about 450 km. are asphalted and the rest gravelled. Highways run from Hodeida to Sana'a, and from Moka to Taiz, Ibb and Sana'a. A highway from Sana'a to Saada is being built with Chinese aid. The Sana'a-Khamir section was opened in February 1972.

Shipping: Hodeida is a Red Sea port of some importance, and the Yemen Navigation Company runs passenger and cargo services to many parts of the Middle East and Africa.

Adafar Yemenite Line: Hodeida.

Middle East Shipping Co.: P.O.B. 700, Hodeida; br. in Moka.

Civil Aviation: Three airports—Al Rahaba at Sana'a, Al Ganad at Taiz and Hodeida Airport—are classified as being of international standard and are being developed following the end of the civil war. Federal Germany is to give financial assistance towards the construction of a new airport at Sana'a, which is to begin in 1971.

Yemen Airlines: Sana'a; internal services to Sana'a, Hodeida, Taiz, Beida, Hareeb, Barat and Saada, external services to Aden, Asmara, Djibouti and Doha (Qatar); Yemeni Airlines is run by a Cttee. formed from the Ministers of Economy, Development, Communications and Local Administrations.

The following airlines also serve the Yemen: Aeroflot, Democratic Yemen Airlines, Ethiopian Airlines and Saudi Arabian Airlines.

EDUCATION

Education in Yemen is still provided mainly by traditional types of school. A modern graded school system has, however, been introduced recently, providing a six-year primary course, a four-year intermediate course and a three-year secondary course. The religious colleges are located in the mosques, the most important of these being at Bir Al-A'zab, Zabid and Dhamar. They provide tuition in Arabic, philosophy, commentaries on the Koran, Muslim Law, tradition and history for those students who wish to pursue further studies. There is one agricultural school and six vocational schools in the Yemen. There is also a Military Academy, a College for Radio Telecommunications and a College of Aviation.

UNIVERSITY

Islamic University: Taiz.

BIBLIOGRAPHY

ANSALDI, C. Il Yemen nella storia e nella leggenda (Rome, 1933).

ATTAR, MOHAMED SAID EL-. Le sous-développement Economique et Social du Yémen (Editions Tiers-Monde, Algiers, 1966).

BALSAN, FRANÇOIS. Inquiétant Yémen (Paris, 1961).

BETHMANN, E. W. Yemen on the Threshold (American Friends of the Middle East, Washington, 1960).

COLONIAL OFFICE. Aden and the Yemen (H.M.S.O., London, 1960).

DEUTSCH, ROBERT. Der Yemen (Vienna, 1914).

DOE, BRIAN. Southern Arabia (Thames and Hudson, London, 1972).

FAROUGHY, A. Introducing Yemen (New York, 1947).

FAYEIN, CLAUDE. A French Doctor in the Yemen (Robert Hale, London, 1957).

HELFRITZ, H. The Yemen: A Secret Journey (Allen and Unwin, London, 1958).

HEYWORTH-DUNNE, G. E. Al-Yemen: Social, Political and Economic Survey (Cairo, 1952).

INGRAMS, HAROLD. The Yemen; Imams, Rulers and Revolutions (London, 1963).

LUQMAN, FAROUK M. Yemen 1970 (Aden, 1970).

MACRO, ERIC. Bibliography of the Yemen, with Notes on Mocha (University of Miami Press, 1959).

Yemen and the Western World since 1571 (C. Hurst, London, and Praeger, New York, 1968).

O'BALLANCE, EDGAR. The War in the Yemen (Faber, London, 1971).

PAWELKE, GUNTHER. Der Yemen: Das Verbotene Land (Econ. Verlag., Düsseldorf, 1959).

SCHMIDT, DANA ADAMS. Yemen, the Unknown War (Bodley Head, London, 1968).

SCOTT, H. In the High Yemen (Murray, London, 1942).

U.S.G.P.O. Geology of the Arabian Peninsula: Yemen (Washington, 1967).

WENNER, MANFRED W. Yemen: a selected Bibliography of Literature since 1960 (Library of Congress Legislative Reference Service, Washington, D.C., 1965).

Modern Yemen, 1918-1966 (Johns Hopkins Press, Baltimore, U.S.A., 1967).

People's Democratic Republic of Yemen

(Southern Yemen)

PHYSICAL AND SOCIAL GEOGRAPHY

W. B. Fisher

On November 30th, 1967, the People's Republic of Southern Yemen came into existence, formed from the former British Colony and Protectorate of Aden (75 sq. miles and 111,000 sq. miles respectively), together with the islands of Perim (5 sq. miles) and Kamaran (22 sq. miles). Socotra (1,400 sq. miles) elected to join the new state. The Kuria Muria group of islands were returned to Muscat by Britain but the new Republican government revoked this decision. In November 1970 the name of the Republic was changed to the "People's Democratic Republic of Yemen". The capital is Aden. The state is divided into six governorates which replace the twenty-three sheikhdoms and sultanates of the Protectorate. The Republic lies at the southern end of the Arabian peninsula, approximately between longitude 43° and 56°E., with Perim Island a few miles due west, in the strait marking the southern extremity of the Red Sea; Kamaran Island some 200 miles north of Perim; Socotra and the Kuria Muria groups in the extreme east, the former at the entrance to the Gulf of Aden, the latter near the coast of Oman. The Republic has frontiers with the Yemen Arab Republic, Saudi Arabia, and Oman, but none of these frontiers is fully delimited, and in some instances they are disputed. Atlases still show considerable variation in the precise boundaries of all four territories, or sometimes do not indicate them at all.

Physically, the Republic comprises the broken and dislocated southern edge of the great plateau of Arabia. This is an immense mass of ancient granites, once forming part of Africa, and covered in many places by shallow, generally horizontal layers of younger sedimentary rocks. The whole plateau has undergone downwarping in the east and elevation in the west, so that the highest land (over 10,000 ft.) occurs in the extreme west, near the Red Sea, with a gradual decline to the lowest parts (under 1,000 ft.) in the extreme east. The whole of the southern and western coasts of the Republic were formed by a series of enormous fractures, which produced a flat but very narrow coastal plain, rising steeply to the hill country a short distance inland. Percolation of molten magma along the fracture-lines has given rise to a number of volcanic craters, now extinct, and one of these, partly eroded and occupied by the sea, forms the site of Aden port.

An important topographic feature is the Wadi Hadhramaut, an imposing valley running parallel to the coast at 100–150 miles distance inland. In its upper and middle parts, this valley is broad, and occupied by a seasonal torrent; in its lower (eastern) part it narrows considerably, making a sudden turn south-eastwards and reaching the sea. This lower part is largely uninhabited, but the upper parts, where alluvial soil and intermittent flood water are available, are occupied by a farming population.

The details of climate in the Republic are simple to state, but extremely difficult to explain. Rainfall is everywhere scanty, but relatively more abundant on the highlands and in the west. Thus Aden itself has 5 in. of rain annually, entirely in winter (December-March), whilst in the lowlands of the extreme east, it may rain only once in five or ten years. In the highlands a few miles north of Aden, falls of up to 30 in. occur, for the most part during summer, and this rainfall also gradually declines eastwards, giving 15–20 in. in the highlands of Dhofar. Ultimately, to the north and east, rainfall diminishes to almost nil, as the edges of the Arabian Desert are reached. This unusual situation of a reversal in climatic conditions over a few miles is thought to be the result of two streams of air; an upper one, damp and unstable in summer, and originating in the equatorial regions of East Africa; and a lower current, generally drier and related to conditions prevailing over the rest of the Middle East. In this way the low lying coastal areas have a maximum of rainfall in winter, and the hills of both the Yemens a maximum in summer. Temperatures are everywhere high, particularly on the coastal plain, which has a southern aspect: mean figures of 76°F. (Jan.) to 89° (June) occur at Aden town, but maxima of over 100° are common.

Except on the higher parts, which have a light covering of thorn scrub (including dwarf trees which exude a sap from which incense and myrrh are derived), and the restricted patches of cultivated land, the territory of the Republic is devoid of vegetation. Cultivation is limited to small level patches of good soil on flat terraces alongside the river beds, on the floor and sides of the Wadi Hadhramaut, or where irrigation from wells and cisterns can be practised. The most productive areas are: Lahej, close to Aden town; two districts near Mukalla (about 300 miles east of Aden), and parts of the middle Hadhramaut. Irrigation from cisterns hollowed out of the rock has long been practised, and Aden town has a famous system of this kind, dating back many centuries.

HISTORY

ADEN COLONY

When the Portuguese first rounded the Cape of Good Hope (1497–98), Aden was a port of some commercial importance, acting as a rendezvous for ships bound from India to the Red Sea and at the same time enjoying an active local trade with the Persian Gulf and the coast of East Africa. In 1513 the Portuguese, under Albuquerque, tried to capture the town, though without success. The Ottoman Turks, in their endeavour to deny the Portuguese access to the Red Sea, seized Aden in 1538, but their hold on the Yemen proved to be precarious. There was a serious revolt against the Ottoman régime in 1547–51 and a still more dangerous rebellion in 1566–70. When in the course of the seventeenth century the Ottoman state fell into decline, the authority of the Sultan over this distant region became little more than nominal, effective power in the Yemen passing now into the hands of local chieftains, the most notable of whom, after 1735, was the Sultan of Lahej. The discovery of the Cape route to India had greatly diminished the prosperity of Aden as a commercial entrepot, but with the Napoleonic campaign in Egypt in 1798, Aden assumed strategic importance in Britain's plan of containment. In 1799 Britain occupied the island of Perim. Shortage of water compelled a withdrawal to the mainland where friendly relations were established with the Sultan of Lahej with whom later in 1902 a commercial treaty was concluded. However, the need to possess a base in these waters under the British flag doubled with the coming of the steamship. Negotiations began for the purchase of the island of Socotra, which in 1834 was temporarily occupied by the East India Company; they might have succeeded had not the relations with the Sultan suddenly deteriorated in 1837 following the plunder near Aden of a wrecked Indian vessel flying the British flag. The incident was followed by the despatch by the East India Company of a British force from Bombay, under the command of Captain Haines of the Indian navy, which, on January 16th, 1839, captured Aden. By the peace treaty, the Sultan was guaranteed an annual sum of 6,000 dollars and Aden became part of the British Empire, administered by the government of Bombay. The Sultan did not finally abandon his efforts to regain Aden until 1857 when permanent peace was established with Britain. Perim Island was ceded in the same year. The Kuria Muria Islands had already been acquired in 1854 from the Sultan of Oman. With the opening of the Suez Canal and the revival of the Red Sea route, Aden, which had been a free port since 1853, increased in importance. In the twentieth century, with the gradual replacement of coal by oil, Aden, closely linked to the Persian Gulf area, enhanced its historic position as a fuelling station. Aden's strategic value is also based on plentiful supplies of fresh drinking water from the artesian wells at Shaikh Othman.

In 1932, the administration of Aden passed to the Governor-General of India in Council; in April 1937, it was vested in a separately appointed governor, who was also commander-in-chief, and who was assisted by an Executive Council. Crown Colony status had in fact been granted two years previously by the Government of India Act 1935. A Legislative Council for Aden, granted in 1944, was inaugurated in 1947. In 1955 the Aden Colony (Amendment) Order came into force, providing for an elected element in the Council; the first elections were held in December of the same year. Further constitutional changes were made in 1959. On January 4th, 1959, voting took place for the choice of 12 elected members of the Legislative Council. Nine Arabs, 2 Somalis and 1 Indian were elected to the Council. Large numbers of the Arab population boycotted the election.

On January 16th, 1961, Sir Charles Johnston, the Governor of Aden, announced to the Legislative Council of Aden that the (then) Colonial Secretary, Mr. Macleod, had approved a ministerial system of government for Aden and that members of the Executive Council in charge of administrative departments would soon assume ministerial status. The Governor also spoke of a possible closer association with the West Aden Protectorate and in particular with the Federation of Arab Emirates in the South. The Federation was renamed the Federation of South Arabia in April 1962. On November 27th, 1967, Aden and the Federation of South Arabia achieved independence under the name of the People's Republic of Southern Yemen.

SOUTH ARABIAN PROTECTORATE

Behind Aden and stretching some 600 miles along the coast, are the territories of 23 Arab States, whose rulers, between 1882-1914, entered into protective treaty relations with the British Government and acknowledged the authority of the Governor of Aden as Governor of the Protectorate. Many of the States later entered into closer treaty relations, and, while retaining independent control in the internal affairs of their respective territories, the rulers accepted the advice on administration offered by British Agents and Political Officers appointed by the Governor. Britain guaranteed protection to the States and they agreed not to cede territory to foreign powers.

EASTERN PROTECTORATE STATES

Formerly named the Eastern Aden Protectorate, the region covered by the States comprised the Hadhramaut (consisting of the Qu'aiti State of Shihr and Mukalla, and the Kathiri State of Sai'un), the Mahra Sultanate of Qishn and Socotra, the Wahidi Sultanates of Balhaf and Bir'ali, and the Sheikhdoms of Irqa and Haura. At the end of 1960 the total population of the area was estimated at 305,000. The Qu'aiti Sultan first concluded a protectorate treaty with Britain in 1888. In 1918 following an agreement between the Qu'aiti and the Kathiri Sultans, the latter accepted the protectorate treaty as extending to his State. Both Sultans agreed by further treaties, signed in 1937 and 1939, to accept the advice of a British Agent in all matters except those concerning the religion and custom of Islam. The British Agent for the Eastern Protectorate States was stationed at Mukalla in the territory of the premier chief, the Qu'aiti Sultan of Shihr and Mukalla. Both he and the Kathiri Sultan were constitutional rulers and were assisted by State Councils. Close co-operation existed between the two states in constitutional and in economic matters.

In 1949 an advisory treaty was concluded with the Wahidi Sultan of Balhaf. The Mahra Sultan of Qishn and Socotra signed a treaty of protection with Britain in 1866 and by it the Island of Socotra and the Abd Alkuri and Brothers Islands came within the protectorate.

WESTERN PROTECTORATE STATES

The former Western Protectorate comprised 20 states. Population at the end of 1960 was estimated at 355,000. Five of the States, in 1944 and 1945, agreed by advisory treaties with Britain to accept the advice of the Governor of Aden on administrative affairs—the Fadhli, the Lower 'Aulaqi and the Lower Yafa'i Sultans, the Sherif of Beihan and the Amir of Dhala. In 1952 similar treaties were signed by the Upper 'Aulaqi Sheikh and the 'Audhali Sultan; and a joint advisory and protectorate treaty was accepted by the newly elected Sultan of Lahej. The British Political Officers and the Arab Assistant Political Officers for the Western Protectorate States were under the supervision of the Assistant High Commissioner whose headquarters were in Al Ittihad, the Federal capital.

The British authorities, in 1954 and again in 1956 had discussed a plan of federation with local rulers in the West Aden Protectorate. On February 11th, 1959, the rulers of six (out of 20) states in the Western Protectorate signed a Federal Constitution and also a Treaty of Friendship and Protection with Great Britain. The British Government promised financial and military aid which would assist the Federation (embracing 'Audhali, Lower Yafa'i, Fadhli, Dhala, Beihan and Upper 'Aulaqi) to become eventually an independent state. The members of the Federation bound themselves not to enter into foreign relations of whatsoever kind without the approval of Great Britain. Lahej joined the Federation in October 1959, and Lower 'Aulaqi, 'Aqrabi and Dathina in February 1960. The Wahidi States of Balhaf and Bir Ali in the Eastern Aden Protectorate joined in 1962. Aden Colony became a member in January 1963, and Haushabi and Shaib joined in April. In 1965 there were three further accessions: the 'Alawi and Muflahi Sheikhdoms, and the Upper 'Aulaqi Sultanate. The new Federal capital was Al Ittihad near Bir Ahmed.

The U.K. met the cost of defence, including the R.A.F. and Protectorate levy establishments. Beside the security forces maintained by the U.K. Government there were tribal guards in the Western States partially supported by the States, and the Mukalla Regular Army maintained by the Qu'aiti State.

At the end of November 1961 the British Government handed over control of the Aden Protectorate Levies to the Federation of Arab Emirates in the South. The Levies—which would be henceforth the Army of the Federation—had been formed in 1928 to protect Aden on the landward side and to provide garrisons for the Red Sea islands of Perim and Kamaran. An Arab force trained and commanded by British officers, the Levies consisted in 1961 of five infantry battalions, an armoured car squadron, and various signals and administrative units. The Levies came under the control of the Sultan of Lahej, who was Minister of Defence to the Federation, but command of the force still rested in the hands of a British officer as hitherto; for operational purposes the Levies were at the disposal of the G.O.C. Land Forces, Middle East.

ADEN AND THE YEMEN

Relations between the Protectorate and the neighbouring State of the Yemen were at all times delicate. Frequent encroachments led to the demarcation of frontiers which were accepted in a convention signed with the Ottoman government in March 1914. During the first World War, the Turkish troops from Yemen occupied the greater part of the Protectorate, and though in 1919 most of the chiefs resumed their treaty relations with Britain, the Imam of Sana'a, who exercised the principal religious authority in Yemen, being the most powerful of the Chieftains, maintained his claim to the entire territories. He sought to enforce it by occupying the Amiri district including the Radhfan tribes and parts of Haushabi, Sha'ibi and Upper Yafa'i territory, and the Audhali plateau. He also occupied territory not then within the Protectorate, the district of the Beidha Sultan. Britain continually repelled the Imam's advance and in 1928 he was compelled to withdraw from most of the Amiri territory. The Anglo-Yemenite treaty of peace and friendship was signed in February 1934, and was to be valid for 40 years; the two powers agreed to respect the *status quo*, and to negotiate for the classification of frontiers; Britain recognized the independence of the Yemen and the Imam agreed to evacuate the remainder of the Amiri district. In 1950 they agreed further to set up a frontier commission and to exchange diplomatic missions. In 1953 Yemen pressed her claims to the territories of the Aden Protectorate before the United Nations, and in subsequent years there was a series of border incidents. In December 1956 both tribesmen and Yemeni forces were reported to have raided villages in the Protectorate and made invasions into Western Aden. Similar incidents of varying degrees of importance continued until 1959. During this period there was a substantial flow of arms and technicians into the Yemen from the U.S.S.R. and its allies, and in March 1958 a formal union with the U.A.R. was announced. Britain sent troop reinforcements and R.A.F. units to repel these attacks, and in 1958 it established a separate military command in Aden. On two occasions the Yemen brought the dispute before the United Nations on the grounds that the U.K. was committing acts of aggression against her territory.

Incidents along the ill-defined frontier between Aden and the Yemen became less numerous in 1959.

The Governor of Aden paid a visit to Taiz in November 1959 which led to the conclusion of two informal agreements with the Yemen, the first covering civil aircraft flights between Aden and the Yemen, the second establishing local frontier commissions to settle border incidents. The first frontier commission met in February 1960.

In August 1962 the Yemen denounced the agreements reached at the London conference (discussed below), and reiterated its claim to the Aden territories. The revolution which broke out in the Yemen on September 27th, 1962, led to the establishment of a Republic of the Yemen. Colonel Sallal, the leader of the revolution, stated at this time that the new régime did not intend to press a claim to the Aden territories and hoped indeed for friendship with Britain. The U.S.S.R. and the U.A.R. recognized the republican régime almost immediately, and the United States followed suit in December, but Britain refused recognition. The new Yemen government frequently accused Britain of giving assistance to the Royalist resistance during the winter of 1962–63; the British legation at Taiz was closed, there were several minor conflicts in the border area, and another Yemen protest was made at the UN.

British and Federal forces carried out extensive military operations against dissident border tribesmen in 1964 and 1965; officials claimed these measures were necessary mainly because of unrest created by Yemeni agents. Direct clashes with Yemeni forces also occurred; the situation remained complex owing to the continuing presence of Royalist forces in the area. In 1964 Britain proposed that UN observers should patrol the border areas; the republican government, however, would not accept this, claiming that no frontier was necessary as Aden and the Federation all belonged by right to the Yemen. This attitude did not help relations during the independence negotiations or with the new Southern Yemen government.

CONSTITUTIONAL DEVELOPMENTS

In August 1960 Sir Charles Johnston became Governor of Aden in succession to Sir William Luce. The new Governor announced to the Legislative Council of the Aden Colony in January 1961 that a ministerial system was to be introduced into Aden—members of the Executive Council in charge of administrative departments (twelve in all) would soon assume ministerial status. Sir Charles Johnston also noted that efforts were in progress to promote constitutional development within Aden and in particular to bring about a closer association between the West Aden Protectorate and the Federation of Arab Emirates of the South.

A constitutional conference, which included five Ministers from Aden and five from the Federation, met in London (July–August 1962) under the chairmanship of Mr. Duncan Sandys, the Colonial Secretary. The Aden Trade Union Congress and its political wing, the People's Socialist Party (both counted much on the support of Yemenis who worked in Aden, and aimed at the ultimate union of the Yemen, Aden, the Federation and the other territories of the West Aden Protectorate) denounced the conference held in London. On July 23rd, 1962, they called a strike to protest against the composition of the existing Legislative Council of Aden and to demand a general election and the establishment of an autonomous government in Aden before further progress should be made towards union with the Federation of Arab Emirates.

The discussions undertaken in August 1962 led to a White Paper recommending the incorporation of Aden into the Federation as a constituent state. It specified that Britain would retain sovereignty over Aden and responsibility for its defence and internal security. These proposals were the principal features of a draft treaty between Britain and the Federation (re-named the Federation of South Arabia); Perim and the Kuria Muria islands, although administered by the governor of Aden, were to be excluded.

There was considerable opposition in Aden to incorporation into the Federation. Several political parties opposed the move, and strikes and demonstrations directed against it occurred throughout 1962. Serious riots coincided with the Aden Legislative Council's passing of the draft treaty in September. Nevertheless, Britain and the Federation duly signed the agreement in January 1963 and Aden formally became a member of the Federation later that month.

ADEN'S INCORPORATION IN THE FEDERATION

Aden's new government consisted of a nine-member Council of Ministers, all Adenis except for the British Attorney-General. Since its principal economic support remained British forces expenditure—£20 million was spent on capital projects alone in the 1962–65 period—it could hardly expect to escape the suspicions of the radical Arab nationalist movements. In May 1963 representatives of the United Nations Committee on decolonization visited Yemen but were not allowed into Aden or the Federation. In July they issued a report—later adopted by the full committee and eventually the General Assembly—which claimed that most of the population disliked "the repressive laws and police methods" of the government; it accused Britain of attempting to prolong its control whilst most South Arabians wanted union with the Yemen. Britain, of course, rejected the report. In the meantime two more states—the Haushabi Sultanate and the Shaibi Sheikdom—had joined the Federation, now 14 strong; on April 1st all customs barriers were abolished within the Federation, Aden remaining a free port.

In December 1963 an attempt to assassinate the High Commissioner in Aden killed two people and injured over fifty; a state of emergency was declared and large numbers of political activists were detained. Although no charges were made, several weeks elapsed before many activists were released, and much opinion in Aden and beyond clearly thought this police treatment was too harsh.

PEOPLE'S DEMOCRATIC REPUBLIC OF YEMEN—(HISTORY)

MOVES TOWARDS INDEPENDENCE

In June 1964 a constitutional conference was held in London and an agreement was signed whereby the Federation of Saudi Arabia, inclusive of Aden, would become independent not later than 1968. A further conference should have met in London in March 1965 to further these proposals, but a clash of interests between Britain, the Federal Government of South Arabia and the Government of the State of Aden, together with the rivalry between local political parties in Aden and threats from the "National Front for the Liberation of South Yemen", prevented the holding of this conference.

Further discussions took place in London in August 1965, but the talks failed, and violence in Aden increased. It was estimated that between December 1963 and May 1966 60 people had been killed and 350 injured in Aden alone as a result of terrorism, one-third of the casualties being British.

POLITICAL REALIGNMENTS

The political scene in South Arabia, as viewed from the side of the nationalist elements, presented at this time an appearance of increasing confusion. The People's Socialist Party, led by Mr. Abdallah al-Asnag, had merged, in May 1965, with the Committee for the Liberation of Occupied South Yemen and with the South Arabian League to form the Organization for the Liberation of the Occupied South. A further development took place in January 1966, when the Organization for the Liberation of the Occupied South united with the National Front for the Liberation of the Occupied South, an extremist group operating from the Yemen with Egyptian support and responsible for the campaign of terrorism in Aden. Out of this new fusion of interests came the Front for the Liberation of Occupied South Yemen (FLOSY), in which political figures like Mr. Makkawi and Mr. al-Asnag now began to assume positions of prominence. The South Arabian League, however, declined to accept the prospect of complete absorption in a united nationalist movement and resumed its former independence. As an organization it held moderate nationalist views, rejecting the territorial claims of the Yemen, disapproving of terrorism and of influence emanating from Egypt, and aiming in general at a united state of South Arabia which should embrace Aden, the federal states and also the principalities of the East Aden Protectorate. Over against these various nationalist forces stood the "traditionalist" elements, embodied in the sheikhdoms and sultanates of the South Arabia Federation (and also of the East Aden Protectorate).

Of great importance, too, as a factor influencing the affairs of South Arabia was the situation in the Yemen, itself divided between tribesmen loyal to the old Imamate and supported by Saudi Arabia, and the republican régime maintained and controlled by Egypt—a situation, in short, which reflected in itself the confrontation of Egypt and Saudi Arabia for a dominant voice in the affairs of Arabia as a whole.

NEW PROPOSALS FOR ADEN, 1966

The Federation of South Arabia made known in February 1966, proposals which, it was hoped, might serve as a basis for a constitution when South Arabia gained independence in 1968. At the request of the Federal Government in September 1965, two British experts, Sir Ralph Hone and Sir Gawain Bell, had undertaken the task of framing new proposals. Their recommendations now envisaged the creation of a United Republic of South Arabia (including the Hadhramaut area). The republic would be organized on federal lines. Aden, however, together with the federal capital al-Ittihad and the islands of Perim, Kamaran and Kuria Muria, would form within the republic a distinctive "capital territory".

THE DEFENCE QUESTION

In February 1966 the British Government issued a White Paper on Defence, which envisaged large reductions in the use of the armed forces of Great Britain overseas and in the general expenditure on them. The White Paper declared that, when Aden became independent in 1968, all British forces would be withdrawn and concentrated at Bahrain in the Persian Gulf; it also made known that the British Government did not propose to enter into defence agreements with the newly independent state of South Arabia.

This announcement gave grounds for alarm to the sheikhdoms and sultanates embraced within the Federation that the National Guard of the Federation might be confronted in the future with a Yemen able to call on large numbers of Egyptian troops. The federal authorities sent a delegation to London, hoping to persuade the British Government to at least assist with the rapid strengthening of the federal forces and with the provision of equipment. In June the British Government offered to contribute as much as £5,500,000 towards the capital cost of expanding and re-equipping the armed forces of the Federation. It also declared its readiness to continue its contribution (about £5,000,000) to the federal budget each year and to increase, to the extent of some £2,500,000, its share (hitherto about £4,600,000) in the maintenance of the federal troops. This aid was to continue for three years after independence, provided that no radical change occurred in the political situation of an independent South Arabia. The British Government still declined, however, to undertake the defence of South Arabia after it had won independence.

The extreme nationalist organizations had long advocated the acceptance in full of the UN resolutions passed in December 1963. Now, in May 1966, the Federal Government of South Arabia made known its readiness at last to take the resolutions as a basis for future action.

THE UN MISSION

In June 1966 the UN Committee on Colonialism urged that a United Nations Mission be sent to South Arabia to advise on the best means of giving effect to the UN resolutions of 1963 and 1965: resolutions which envisaged the granting of independence to South

Arabia, the withdrawal of British forces, the return of political leaders in exile or in detention and the holding of elections under international supervision. In August 1966 the British Government declared that it welcomed the appointment of such a mission, but it insisted that it could not abandon its responsibilities for the maintenance of good order in South Arabia and that it was bound to observe the agreements which it had made with the local states existing in the area.

Further violence and demonstrations in Aden in February 1967 perhaps hastened the actual appointment, on February 23rd, of the UN Mission to South Arabia to be led by Señor Manuel Pérez-Guerrero, of Venezuela; his two colleagues were Mr. Abd al-Satar Shalizi, of Afghanistan, and Mr. Moussa Léo Keita, of Mali. On April 2nd, 1967, the UN mission arrived in Aden, where violence continued, after passing through London, Cairo and Jeddah. On April 7th the UN mission, accusing the British and the federal authorities of non-co-operation, left Aden for Rome and then Geneva, their task remaining unaccomplished. Their talks later in the month with the British Foreign Minister led to no fruitful result.

PREPARATIONS FOR INDEPENDENCE

Also in April Lord Shackleton, Minister without Portfolio, was sent to South Arabia to assist the High Commissioner in examining the possibilities for the establishment of a "caretaker" régime representing all the interested elements in South Arabia. The nationalist organizations continued, however, to reject all appeals for co-operation with the British and the federal authorities.

On June 20th, 1967, the British Government made known the measures that it intended to bring into effect. The date of independence was to be January 9th, 1968. During the critical months following the grant of independence a naval force, including an attack carrier, was to be assigned to South Arabian waters; a number of V-bombers would also be stationed on the island of Masira, not far from the South Arabian territories. In addition, Great Britain promised financial aid (for aircraft, amongst other items) and undertook to re-equip the federal forces with more modern types of small arms, field guns and armoured cars. A military mission would also be sent from Great Britain to advise the federal authorities. In order to check the growing violence in South Arabia it was proposed to suspend trial by jury in respect of terrorist activities. On the other hand, the ban on the NLF was to be removed and consideration given to the possible release of some detainees. The British Government also declared that it would be willing to accept a draft constitution which the federal régime was now circulating to its member states. This constitution would prepare the ground for eventual elections on a basis of universal adult suffrage and for the establishment, as soon as circumstances allowed, of an administration representative of all the political elements in South Arabia. Regarding the problem of the uncommitted states in the East Aden Protectorate, Great Britain favoured their union with the Federation of South Arabia. It seemed improbable, however, that such a merger, if it did indeed come about, would occur before South Arabia attained its independence. The British Government now made known its readiness to finance, for a period of two years after January 1968, the Hadhrami Legion, an Arab force at present British-paid and British controlled and constituting the main defence of the Eastern Protectorate. Measures would be taken to assist with the establishment of co-ordinated defence arrangements between the Federation and the three states of the East Aden Protectorate.

The tense situation prevailing in Aden became still more complicated when, on June 21st, 1967, some of the South Arabian federal troops mutinied and fought out with the British force a battle which involved considerable loss of life. This trouble was said to have arisen out of tribal rivalries affecting the federal forces, but the suspicion could not be excluded that, under the impact of nationalist sentiments, some of the troops might have weakened in their allegiance both towards the federal régime and towards the protecting power.

During July 1967 Britain continued her efforts to establish in Aden and the associated territories a broad-based provisional administration which should hold office until the moment of independence in January 1968. To facilitate the achievement of this aim the Federal Government consented to invite one of its own members, Mr. Bayumi, to form an interim administration with the aid, if possible, of FLOSY and the NLF. These nationalist organizations remained adamant, however, in their refusal to recognize the federal régime, which, in their view, reflected in its structure pre-eminently the interests of the local sultans. Mr. Bayumi's endeavour to gain the co-operation of the nationalist groups ended in failure and on July 27th the federal authorities relieved him of his appointment as Prime Minister designate.

Meanwhile, in South Arabia itself, during August to October 1967 the authority of the sultans crumbled rapidly before the advancing tide of nationalism. The NLF extended its control over the sheikhdom of Maflahi and over most of the other tribal states. On August 28th Sheikh Ali Musaid al-Babakri, speaking as chairman of the Supreme Council of the South Arabian Federation, admitted that the Federal Government and the Sultans had lost control of events and appealed to the armed forces of South Arabia to take command of the situation. This appeal—which marked in fact the virtual disintegration of the federal régime—was unsuccessful, the South Arabian Army refusing to accept the role thus offered to it. The swift advance of the NLF was due, not least of all, to the alignment on its side of a large measure of support amongst the local tribes against their traditional rulers, and also to the determination of the federal armed forces to maintain a neutral attitude. During September and October the NLF also moved into the territories of the Eastern Aden Protectorate, the sultanates of Qaiti, Kathiri and Mahra now passing under its influence. The High Commissioner annnouced on September 5th that Britain was now prepared to recognize the nationalist forces in general as representative of the local populations and would be willing to enter into negotiations with them.

THE CLASH BETWEEN NATIONALISTS

The collapse of the federal régime left the main nationalist organizations face to face. There had been discussions between them, under Egyptian auspices, at Cairo and in the Yemen, but without much sign of ultimate agreement. Now, the notable success of the NLF had done much to diminish the prospect before the Front for the Liberation of the Occupied South Yemen. This latter organization was under the disadvantage that it operated largely under Egyptian guidance and not in South Arabia itself, but from the Yemen. Its chief support in Aden had come from the numerous Yemeni elements formerly working there. Of adverse effect, too, was the fact that its leaders, Abdallah al-Asnag and Abd al-Qawi Makkawi, had been working from the Yemen as exiles during the past two years. The imminence of an Egyptian withdrawal from the Yemen also contributed to a decline in its influence.

With the federal structure now in ruins, the immediate question was whether or not the two main nationalist groups could be brought into mutual cooperation. Conflict soon broke out, however, between them, and fierce fighting developed in the northern suburbs of Aden during September. The South Arabian Army was able to enforce a brief ceasefire, and the rival organizations met in Cairo in October, but without any agreement. Fresh fighting then began, FLOSY being finally defeated when the Army high command joined forces with the NLF.

The latter then insisted that Britain should regard it as the sole valid representative of the people of South Arabia—a course of action which the authorities in London agreed to take on November 11th, 1967. On November 14th it was announced at Aden that Qahtan al-Shaabi, one of the founders of the NLF, would lead a delegation to Geneva to hold discussions with the representatives of Britain.

The evacuation of British troops from Aden had begun earlier on August 25th, 1967. As the situation unfolded itself in Aden, the British Government resolved to hasten the withdrawal of its forces and to advance the independence of South Arabia from January 9th, 1968, to a date if possible in the second half of November 1967. On November 27th, after the British troops had made over large areas of Aden to the armed forces of South Arabia, the NLF proclaimed the creation of the People's Republic of Southern Yemen. At Geneva, Qahtan al-Shaabi announced on November 28th that agreement had been reached with Great Britain over the cession of Aden and its associated territories. The last British troops in Aden were withdrawn on November 29th, 1967. Qahtan al-Shaabi, with the approval of the NLF, was appointed the first President of the Republic on November 30th.

INDEPENDENCE

The prospect before the new Republic in December 1967 was still a most uncertain one. On the economic side there were great difficulties to be overcome. The withdrawal of the British troops meant a serious loss of revenue. To maintain the armed forces inherited from the era of British control would impose on the Republic a large expenditure. Moreover, the closure of the Suez Canal had brought about a great falling off in the entrepôt trade of Aden and in the bunkering of ships. The continuance, in the immediate future, of financial aid from Britain was therefore of prime importance to the new régime in Aden. During the negotiations in Geneva between Britain and the NLF in November 1967 the British representatives agreed to make available financial aid to South Arabia for a period of six months (December 1st, 1967, to May 31st, 1968) at a rate amounting to about £2 million per month. Talks held in Aden in April 1968 between a British delegation and the government led only to the rejection of a new, though reduced, offer of further financial assistance from Britain.

There was disagreement also between the South Yemen and Britain over the Kuria Muria Islands. These islands, about 40 miles from the south coast of Arabia and 200 miles east of the border between the Republic of the Southern Yemen and the Sultanate of Muscat, had been handed over to Britain in 1854 and, though administered subsequently from Aden, had not been included formally within the Aden Protectorate. On November 30th, 1967, Britain had made known to the United Nations her intention to restore the Kuria Muria Islands to the Sultan of Muscat—a decision which gave rise to much bitterness amongst the members of the new government in Aden, which continued to claim these islands and also Perim and Kamaran.

INTERNAL DISSENSION

The administration of President al-Shaabi had to meet other serious difficulties also. In the first months of 1968 it had carried out a series of "purges" in the armed forces and the police of the Southern Yemen. Discontent amongst the armed forces increased after the annual conference of the NLF convened at Zinjibar, east of Aden, in March 1968. The more extreme elements in the NLF were reported to have put forward at the conference resolutions designed to force the Government of the Southern Yemen further to the left—amongst them resolutions calling for the appointment of political commissars to all army units, for the strengthening of the NLF militia and for the creation of "popular guards". A demand was also made, it would seem, at this conference, for the establishment of popular councils in all six of the governorates of the Southern Yemen—these provincial councils having the right to elect a supreme council which would control the affairs of the new Republic. There was in March 1968 a real danger of conflict between the moderate and the extreme elements in the NLF. On March 20th the army intervened to bring about the dismissal of several ministers identified with the more radical section of the Front. The extremists indeed had been taking matters into their own hands in the eastern areas of the Republic—above all in the fifth and sixth governorates which embrace the former sultanates of Qaiti, Kathiri and Mahra (i.e. the erstwhile Eastern Aden Protectorate). Here the radical elements had established popular councils of their own choice, ignoring the governors appointed from the central régime, ousting members of the armed forces and the police, and seizing the oil installations at Mukalla. The tensions thus generated showed no sign of a rapid abatement, and on May 15th, 1968, there was a short-lived rebellion in the region of Jaar, Abyan and Shuqra—i.e. in the third governorate to the north-east of Aden.

Another more serious uprising occurred at the end of July 1968, when two groups of armed rebels cut roads in the Radfan and Aulaqi districts north and east of Aden. The leaders of this rebellion were named as Colonel Abdullah Saleh al Aulaqi ("Colonel Sabaa"), formerly the NLF commander of security forces, and Brig. Nasser Buraik al Aulaqi, who until independence had been commander of the South Arabian Army. These risings were quickly crushed by NLF forces. Both FLOSY and the rival exiled political organization, the South Arabian League, claimed credit for this threat to the Government of President al-Shaabi. Although several members of the FLOSY High Command were captured during the campaign, the economic difficulties of the country continued to act as a serious threat to the stability of the new régime. These difficulties enforced drastic cuts in government expenditure during the summer of 1968, notably in the salaries of the armed forces and the civil service, which cannot have helped the regime's popularity. The President did succeed in getting offers of aid from Federal Germany, Yugoslavia and several Arab countries, but on a small scale compared with the pre-independence British assistance. All support from Federal Germany was in any case cancelled following Southern Yemen's recognition of the German Democratic Republic in July 1969.

NEIGHBOURING HOSTILITY

Relations with neighbouring states continued to be poor, and the government blamed all unrest within the country on elements operating from these states. FLOSY, operating from Yemen and now without its Egyptian support, the deposed sheikhs and sultans from the Federation (now mostly in Saudi Arabia), and the Sultan of Muscat and Oman with his British advisers were claimed to be the most important of these. There were reports of large supplies of Soviet military equipment reaching Aden, some of which has been displayed in military parades; units of the Soviet fleet frequently visit Aden, which is now rarely used by British or other Western naval vessels.

In June 1969 President al-Shaabi resigned following a reported power struggle; Salem Rubia Ali, a former commando leader who had gone into semi-exile in the provinces after a dispute with the leadership, came to power as Chairman of a new five-man Presidential committee, and a new cabinet was formed which included several other exiles. The new régime was seen as even more left-wing and pro-Soviet than its predecessor.

In November 1969 the government announced the nationalization of 36 foreign firms, including shipping, insurance and commercial companies, but excluding the BP oil refinery at Little Aden.

At this time there were reports of Saudi troops massing on the ill-defined frontier with Southern Yemen, and Saudi sources claimed than an extensive battle took place in December, with Saudi Arabia emerging victorious. Some reports claimed that the clash took place over oil-bearing territory. This occurred again in March 1970 and coincided with a report of an attempted *coup d'état* in Aden.

In November 1970, a new Constitution was promulgated, changing the name of the country to the People's Democratic Republic of the Yemen, with a view to possible Yemeni unity. However, relations with the other Yemen and with other neighbouring states failed to improve, and by the first half of 1972 the People's Democratic Republic seemed threatened on all sides. Omani forces attacked frontier posts of the Aden Government in its drive against the rebels in its Dhofar province. These are grouped under the Popular Front for the Liberation of the Occupied Arab Gulf (PFLOAG) and are supported by the Aden Government, through whom they receive Chinese aid. Forces of FLOSY and the South Arabian League were also reported to be gathering on the Yemeni borders. Saudi Arabia, as well as the Yemen Arab Republic, gives refuge to dissidents from the People's Democratic Republic, mainly because of the Aden Government's ideology.

POSSIBLE YEMENI UNITY

Serious fighting broke out on the border with the Yemen Arab Republic in September 1972, but an Arab League mission was able to mediate and a ceasefire became effective in October. A peace agreement on eventual unification of the two Yemens was signed in Cairo on October 28th. Further details were discussed in Tripoli (Libya) in November by the Presidents of the two Yemens, and it was agreed that the people of the Yemen would establish a single state, to be known as the Yemeni Republic, with Sana'a as its capital, Islam as the state religion and Arabic as the official language. Committees were set up to discuss details of the unification. In January 1973 it appeared that obstacles had arisen in the progress towards union, but in June 1973 the People's Democratic Republic Foreign Minister received the heads of mission of all socialist, Asian and African countries represented in Aden and reiterated his government's determination to implement the Cairo and Tripoli agreements on union.

ECONOMIC SURVEY

M. Jibb

The People's Democratic Republic of Yemen consists of the former British colony of Aden and the former Eastern and Western Aden Protectorates. It is now divided into six governorates, or provinces, whose finances and administration are centrally controlled, although the provincial councils are responsible for planning and finance on a local level. The Governorates vary greatly in size, the smallest being the First Governorate in the west, consisting of Aden district and the offshore islands, and the largest being the Sixth Governorate, the former Mahra Sultanate, situated in the extreme east of the country. Most of the population is concentrated in the west and one of the Government's hardest tasks since independence has been to unite the various regions politically, administratively and economically.

Under British rule, the country was sustained by the position of Aden on the main shipping route to Europe from the Far East, India and East Africa via Suez. The British Petroleum refinery, completed in 1954, was the focus of industry and trade. In addition, the British troops stationed in Aden and the many foreign visitors who came ashore from ships calling at the port provided a market for services and luxury goods which encouraged local merchants and entrepreneurs and brought plenty of foreign exchange into Aden. This prosperity was, in the main, confined to the then Aden Colony where there was a boom in construction work between 1955 and 1965. The British Government was more concerned with maintaining the Aden base and the port installations than with developing the hinterland although certain agricultural areas were developed during this period. The Abyan district, where development started in 1947, became one of the major cotton-producing areas and a similar scheme was carried out in Lahej in the 1960s. In the Hadhramaut, where there are fertile valleys in an otherwise barren area, the Governments of the states of Quaiti and Kathiri financed irrigation schemes and agricultural developments.

The closure of the Suez Canal in 1967 and the withdrawal of British troops in the same year, put an end to the Republic's commercial prosperity. Furthermore, British aid and military expenditure, which amounted to about £11 million in 1960 and had increased to £36 million by 1967 and had more than covered the visible trade deficit, was discontinued after withdrawal, making it impossible for the Government to cover the budget deficit. In such a situation the Republic had no choice but to turn to other countries for sources of finance and technical aid to assist it in the transition from a service economy to one based on agriculture and manufacturing. The favourable terms offered by the Communist countries, coupled with a seeming lack of interest on the part of the West, made it inevitable that the Aden Government should turn to the Eastern bloc.

In November 1969 a decree was issued nationalizing all important foreign assets in the Republic, with the exception of the BP refinery. This development, although a logical one in view of the régime's socialist leanings, nevertheless tended to frighten off firms which might otherwise have risked some investment, and made the Republic more than ever dependent on the Soviet Union, China and East Germany.

The Three Year Development Plan 1971–1974, although limited by shortage of funds, aims at the creation, firstly of a communications network, secondly the expansion of agricultural production and, thirdly, the establishment of small-scale light industries, based on locally produced raw materials. A new Five-Year Plan has been drawn up to start in April 1974.

AGRICULTURE

Only about a quarter of the country's cultivatable land is used at present, and the most intensively cultivated areas are Abyan, east of Aden, and Lahej, north of Aden. The river valleys of the Hadhramaut area in the Fifth Governorate are also fertile and relatively well-developed.

Cotton is produced mainly in Lahej and Abyan. The government-controlled Abyan Board supervises the whole process of growing and marketing and has its own ginnery at El Kad. Cotton is also produced in other areas and the Cotton Producers' Associations were the most flourishing co-operatives in the country. The area under cotton is, however, declining, in spite of cash incentives offered to growers. It is also becoming harder to market and much work needs to be done to improve the varieties grown and to seek suitable export outlets.

The Republic is able, on the whole, to meet local demand for most vegetables but imports onions, potatoes and fruit. The main fruits and vegetables grown are tomatoes, carrots, salad vegetables, bananas and melons. Bananas in particular are produced in quantity and the Food and Agriculture Organization has recommended an expansion of banana-growing, provided export markets can be found. In 1972 the only foreign customer was China.

Wheat is grown mainly in the Hadhramaut and Beihan but is not enough for the country's needs. The balance is imported mainly from Australia. Other cereals produced include barley, millet and sorghum. Tobacco is grown in the coastal areas, mainly in the Ghail Ba Wazir area. Livestock production has remained fairly static for the last ten years and considerable numbers of sheep and goats have to be imported to satisfy local meat demand.

The resources available at present are not sufficient to finance agricultural development schemes over the whole country and efforts are being concentrated in the Lahej, Abyan, Beihan and Hadhramaut areas. In the east, the developments most likely to take place are the expansion of tobacco growing and the development of the fishing industry, with Mukalla as its centre.

FISHERIES

The Arabian Sea fishing grounds are the Republic's greatest potential source of wealth. Most of the 10,000 fishermen fish only in territorial waters, their equipment is often poor and efficient marketing of the catch is impossible with the present state of communications. The main species caught are: anchovy, tunny, sardine, Indian mackerel, crayfish and green turtle. At the beginning of 1973 exports of fish took a very encouraging turn and several foreign countries were involved in developing the industry.

The Soviet Union and Cuba provided modern fishing vessels and equipment and technical aid. A Japanese firm obtained a contract in 1969 to fish in the coastal waters, and a joint Polish/Yemeni company with a capital of $5 million was planned. A $2 million Danish loan was being used to finance development of Nakhtun port, where a Danish firm is supervising refrigeration and storage facilities. The fishing ports of Mukalla and Shihr are to be developed, probably with IDA aid, at a cost of about $3.5 million.

The Soviet Union is providing modern fishing vessels and technical aid, the United Nations is resuming its three-year fisheries survey, begun in 1966 but interrupted in 1967, and a Japanese firm obtained a contract in 1969 to fish in Yemeni coastal waters.

INDUSTRY

The BP refinery accounts at present for over 80 per cent of the country's total industrial output. In spite of the closure of the Suez Canal, output at the refinery continued to expand, partly because of increased demand from Egypt, although exports to Egypt decreased in 1970. The Government intended to spend about YD 2 million on the oil sector in 1972, one of the main projects being the supplying of oil by pipeline from Aden to Mukalla.

Industrial developments are planned to take the form of agro-industries. The Three-Year Development Plan envisaged the establishment of a textile industry based on local cotton; fruit and vegetable processing and canning plants; a cigarette factory; fish-canning plants and a tanning industry. This last will be particularly suitable since skins are at present exported in the raw state and there is much wastage. Some progress was made in 1972/73 towards setting up a textile industry, with the formation of a textile company, and China is building the factory. A cigarette factory is also being built which will produce a million cigarettes a day. Initially raw materials will be imported from Britain but eventually Hadhramaut tobacco will be used. Existing industries (in Aden) are: the manufacture of cement blocks, tiles and bricks for the now-stagnating building industry; salt production; soft drinks bottling and dairy plants. In the western Governorates there are also cotton ginneries, flour mills and seed-crushing plants. Some small fish-canning factories exist in Mukalla. These are to be extended and others built, with Soviet and Japanese aid. A cement plant is planned for the Third Governorate, possibly using the extensive limestone deposits reported to exist to the east of Aden. The German Democratic Republic is helping to set up factories making flour, biscuits, vegetable oil and animal fodder.

Known mineral resources are few but the country has not yet been fully explored. The Southern Yemen Algerian Petroleum Company, a joint venture with the Algerian state oil concern SONATRACH is prospecting for oil in the Hadhramaut.

FOREIGN TRADE

Aden port handles nearly all the Republic's trade, as well as a considerable proportion of that of the Yemen Arab Republic. Transit trade to Yemen however, had declined somewhat owing to the development of Hodeida. The free port of Aden attracted a large volume of traffic and all the commercial activities associated with a large port flourished, providing comfortable livings for the Adeni merchants but contributing little to the development of the other sectors of the economy. The disadvantages of a free port in the changed situation after independence, not least the hindrance to industrial development caused by the lack of protective tariffs, led the Government, after much deliberation, to remove Aden's free port status, although there is still a free zone for transit trade.

The trade deficit continued to grow up to 1969. Government measures and the lack of foreign exchange, reduced imports in 1970 by over £7 million but exports continued at much the same level. The main commodities exported (excluding petroleum products) are cotton, hides and skins, dried fish, rice and coffee. The chief imports (excluding petroleum) are clothing, foodstuffs and livestock. Britain was still in 1970 the Republic's main customer, importing £14.9 million worth of goods, mainly petroleum products, with Japan as the second-largest customer. The leading supplier of crude oil, apart from Iran and Kuwait, was Japan.

By 1971, the few available figures showed increased stagnation in both import and export trade. The drop in petroleum trade was particularly significant as it made reduction of activity at the refinery inevitable with consequent repercussions on the whole fragile economy. In 1966, bunkering made up a third of total exports, but by 1970 this proportion had fallen to less than 7 per cent and petroleum exports were moving to markets in Africa and Asia rather than Europe.

FINANCE AND FOREIGN AID

The Republic's finances have deteriorated steadily since independence. In 1966, gold reserves were $1.41 million and foreign exchange reserves amounted to $64.86 million. By the end of 1970, gold reserves had fallen to $600,000 and foreign exchange to $53.3

million. In the same period, the budget deficit grew from 100,000 dinars to over 4 million dinars. This deficit was substantially cut in 1971, largely because more foreign grants were obtained, but expenditure still had to be held down with very adverse effects on development. The situation was considered to be so serious in 1972 that the salaries of many government employees were cut by anything from 15 to 50 per cent and restrictions were placed on foreign travel.

The abrupt cessation of British aid to the Republic after the withdrawal of troops in November 1967 caused a crisis which more or less forced the Government to turn to the communist bloc. The Soviet Union, under an agreement of February 1969, which included aid specifically for fisheries, undertook to provide technical aid and experts for a number of development projects. A separate agreement, signed in August 1969, covered aid for agriculture and irrigation. The first agreement was extended in February 1970 to include aid in kind worth 5.5 million roubles and, most important of all, a low-interest 7 million rouble loan repayable over 12 years. This loan was significant in that actual financial aid was offered rather than aid in the form of goods or technical assistance. The German D.R. agreed to a loan of $22 million in October 1969 and China granted a $18 million loan in 1970, both part of large aid and trade "package deals". Both cover a wide range of projects, including in the case of the German D.R., the construction of telephone facilities and the establishment of light industries; and in the case of China,

help with the road-building programme. North Korea is providing aid for communications and for one or two light industrial projects. Most of the Eastern bloc countries have promised industrial aid and Romania has lent $5 million, under a 1971 agreement, to irrigate 4,000 hectares of arable land and to set up a poultry farm. The Eastern bloc countries have also provided a good deal of aid for radio and communications projects

The richer Arab countries, too, are providing aid in certain sectors. The Kuwait Fund for Arab Economic Development is to finance a pre-investment study of the Abyan Delta and an economic survey of the whole country. Algeria, as well as participating in oil exploration, has agreed to give $4 million worth of development aid. Libya is considering loans for industrial projects and in 1972 granted a loan of 5.8 million dinars. The Aden Government has approached the Arab League on the subject of compensation for losses incurred as a direct result of the June War. No actual financial compensation has so far been awarded, but the League's Industrial Promotion Centre is undertaking studies in the Republic.

The Republic's relations with the West have deteriorated not only because of the British refusal to continue aid, but as a result of the rapprochement with the Eastern bloc countries. The establishment of ties with the German D.R. caused Federal Germany to break off relations and now the main source of aid other than the socialist countries and the Arab states, is the United Nations.

STATISTICAL SURVEY

AREA AND POPULATION

Area (sq. miles)		Mid-year Population	
Aden	Hinterland	1970	1971
75	111,000	1,436,000	1,475,000

Capital: Madinat ash-Sha'b (population 29,000 in 1967).
Largest City: Aden (population 150,000 in 1964).

EMPLOYMENT
Aden
1967

Total	Port Handling	Building	Oil Refining	Industry	Retail and Wholesale Trade	Government Service	Domestic Servants	Miscellaneous
42,417	5,172	473	2,943	8,425	3,730	12,632	8,000	1,042

In the rest of the country 90 per cent of the population are engaged in agriculture.

PEOPLE'S DEMOCRATIC REPUBLIC OF YEMEN—(Statistical Survey)

AGRICULTURE
(Protectorate states)
Principal Crops

	1965–66 ACRES	1965–66 TONS	1966–67 ACRES	1966–67 TONS
Sorghum } Millets	90,000	25,000	93,600	30,000
Wheat	11,000	9,000	12,000	10,500
Barley	2,500	2,750	3,000	3,500
Sesame	4,000	900	4,300	1,000
Fruit and Vegetables	2,000	30,325		21,850
Cotton Lint } Cotton Seed	40,000	6,116	36,670	7,850

LIVESTOCK
(1970–71)

Cattle	92,000
Sheep	215,000
Goats	870,000
Camels	40,000

Source: FAO Production Yearbook 1971.

FINANCE

1,000 fils = 1 Yemeni dinar (YD).
Coins: 1, 5, 25 and 50 fils.
Notes: 250 and 500 fils; 1, 5 and 10 dinars.
Exchange rates (April 1973): £1 sterling = 835.69 fils; U.S. $1 = 336.97 fils.
100 Yemeni dinars = £119.66 = $296.76.

BUDGET
(million dinars)

	REVENUE	FOREIGN AID	EXPENDITURE
1967–68	8.94	16.49	23.68
1968–69	8.96	4.91	15.83
1969–70	11.11	0.21	15.44
1970–71	13.22	1.85	17.56

THREE-YEAR PLAN 1971–74
('000 dinars)

Transport and Communications	13,184.3
Agriculture	10,495.0
Industry	9,865.3
Education	3,234.0
Geological Surveys	2,300.0
Health	750.0
Culture	7.0
Unallocated Reserve	864.7
	40,700.3

PEOPLE'S DEMOCRATIC REPUBLIC OF YEMEN—(Statistical Survey)

EXTERNAL TRADE
(million dinars)

	1967	1968	1969	1970	1971
Imports	72.1	84.5	90.9	83.7	64.9
Exports	49.0	45.8	59.8	60.8	43.6

COMMODITIES, 1970
(dinars)

	Imports	Exports
Live Animals	1,427,340	—
Dairy Produce, Eggs	2,533,358	72,057
Cereals	8,058,942	1,214,378
Fruit and Vegetables	1,571,888	148,547
Sugar, etc.	2,220,512	163,418
Coffee, Tea, Cocoa, Spices	2,803,054	801,856
Beverages and Tobacco	1,147,535	37,848
Oilseeds, Oil Nuts, etc.	1,277,443	389,440
Petroleum and Petroleum Products	34,390,272	44,991,450
Chemicals	3,029,368	256,496
Textiles	8,210,356	1,768,661
Machinery	1,572,333	117,019
Electrical Machinery	1,265,284	113,386
Transport Equipment	1,517,064	88,413
Manufactured Goods	5,055,902	696,195

COUNTRIES
(dinars)

Imports	1969	1970
Iran	13,545,258	15,252,843
Kuwait	12,327,134	11,106,192
Japan	11,899,701	8,820,657
U.K.	5,078,864	4,579,634
India	4,281,988	3,470,064
Trucial States (now U.A.E.)	3,951,816	4,592,011
Hong Kong	2,496,129	2,239,319

Exports	1969	1970
U.K.	13,117,710	14,945,217
Japan	6,288,104	8,724,919
Australia	4,217,861	3,664,670
Thailand	4,012,614	5,192,631
Ships Bunkers	3,767,533	4,011,144
Canary Is.	2,905,417	3,041,468
Yemen A.R.	2,958,359	2,852,661

PEOPLE'S DEMOCRATIC REPUBLIC OF YEMEN—(STATISTICAL SURVEY)

TRANSPORT

ROADS

	PASSENGER CARS	COMMERCIAL VEHICLES
1962	12,000*	—
1964	11,030	2,269
1965	11,452	2,246

* All classes

SHIPPING
Vessels entering Aden port

	NUMBER	FUEL OIL BUNKERS ('000 long tons)
1966	6,246	3,486
1967	3,100	1,400
1968	1,382	388
1969	1,568	576

CIVIL AVIATION
(1968)

AIRCRAFT MOVEMENTS	PASSENGERS			FREIGHT (kilos)	
	Arrivals	Departures	Transit	Inward	Outward
5,860	53,300	53,161	8,167	998,538	852,898

EDUCATION
NUMBER OF SCHOOLS
(1967–68)

Primary Schools	387
Intermediate Schools	67
Secondary Schools	16
Teachers' Colleges for Males	4
Teachers' Colleges for Females	2
Technical Institute	1

Source: Ministry of National Guidance and Information, Aden.

PEOPLE'S DEMOCRATIC REPUBLIC OF YEMEN—(The Constitution, The Government, etc.)

THE CONSTITUTION

Before the new constitution was drawn up existing ordinances and regulations remained in force, with Presidential authority replacing the powers of the British and Federal Governments. The National Liberation Front general command, which had 41 members, formed the interim legislative authority. The country is divided into six administrative Governates. The two-year term of office granted to the National Liberation Front expired on November 30th, 1969, and was formally renewed for another year. Following the adoption of the new constitution on November 30th, 1970, a Provisional Supreme People's Council took over legislative powers. The 101 members were selected from the NLF, armed forces, professions, etc., with 15 workers elected by trade unions.

THE GOVERNMENT

HEAD OF STATE

President and Supreme Commander of the Armed Forces: Salem Rubai Ali.

PRESIDENTIAL COUNCIL

Chairman: Salem Rubai Ali.
Member and NLF Secretary-General: Abd-Al-Fattah Ismail.
Member: Ali Nasir Muhammad Hasani.

CABINET
(*July* 1973)

Prime Minister and Minister of Defence: Ali Nasir Muhammad Hasani.
Minister of Foreign Affairs: Muhammad Salih Muti.
Minister of the Interior: Saleh Musleh.
Minister of Information (Acting): Rashed Muhammad Thabet.
Minister of Justice and Waqfs: Mustafa Abd-Al-Khaliq.
Minister of Health: Dr. Abd-Al-Aziz Al-Dali.
Minister of Public Works: Haidar Abu Bakr Al-Attas.
Minister of Communications: Anis Hasan Yahya.
Minister of Labour and Social Affairs: Muhammad Ali Amayah.

Minister of Finance (Acting): Fadl Muhsin Abdullah.
Minister of Agriculture and Agrarian Reform: Muhammad Sulaiman Nasir.
Minister of Economy and Industry: Abdel-Aziz Abdel-Wali.
Minister of Culture and Tourism: Abdullah Badib.
Minister of Education: Ahmad Abdullah Abd-Al-Ilah.
Deputy Premier for Economy and Finance: Mahmoud Abdulla Oshaish.
Minister of Planning: Ali Salem Baid.
Minister of State (Presidential Affairs): Abdulla Khameri.

DIPLOMATIC REPRESENTATION

EMBASSIES ACCREDITED TO THE PEOPLE'S DEMOCRATIC REPUBLIC OF YEMEN
(Aden unless otherwise stated)

Bulgaria: *Ambassador:* M. Serafimov.
Egypt: Rock Hotel; *Ambassador:* Samir Abbassi.
China, People's Republic: *Ambassador:* Tsui Chien.
France: Barrack Hill, Tawahi; *Ambassador:* G. Denizeau.
German Democratic Republic: *Ambassador:* Guenther Scharfenburg.

India: Premjee Mansion, Steamer Point; *Ambassador:* J. L. Malhotra.
Korea (Democratic People's Republic): *Ambassador:* Hong Man Pyo.
Somalia: *Ambassador:* Dr. Abdarahman Hussein.
U.S.S.R.: *Ambassador:* Vladimir Polyakov.
United Kingdom: Ras Bradly, Tawahi; *Ambassador:* James Ramage.

The People's Democratic Republic of Yemen also has diplomatic relations with Belgium, Cuba, Denmark, Ethiopia, Iraq, Italy, Lebanon, Mongolia, Netherlands, Norway, Pakistan, Portugal, Sweden, Switzerland and Yugoslavia.

PEOPLE'S DEMOCRATIC REPUBLIC OF YEMEN—(POLITICAL PARTIES, JUDICIAL SYSTEM, ETC.)

POLITICAL PARTIES

National Liberation Front: Aden; f. 1963; socialist and Arab nationalist; Leader ABDUL FATTAH ISMAIL. The Central Committee has 31 members and 14 substitute members—all elected.

POLITICAL BUREAU
Secretary-General: ABD-AL-FATTAH ISMAIL.
Deputy Secretary-General: President SALEM RUBAI ALI.
ALI SALIH OBAID.
ALI SALIM AL-BEIDH.
SALIH MUSLIH.
MUHAMMAD SALIH MUTI.
ALI NASIR MUHAMMAD.

JUDICIAL SYSTEM

The administration of justice is entrusted to the Supreme Court and Magistrates' Courts. In the former Protectorate States Muslim law and local common law (Urfi) are also applied.

President of the Supreme Court: ABD-AL-MAJID ABD-AL-RAHMAN.

RELIGION

The majority of the population are Muslim but there are small Christian and Hindu communities.

THE PRESS

DAILIES

al Akhbar: News House, P.O.B. 435, Aden; f. 1953; Arabic; Editor MUHAMMAD ALI LUQMAN, B.A., M.L.C.

Fatat ul Jezirah: Esplanade Rd., Crater, Aden; f. 1940; Arabic; Editor MUHAMMAD ALI LUQMAN; circ. approx. 10,000.

Fourteenth October: Aden.

WEEKLIES

Aden Chronicle: Esplanade Road, Crater, Aden; English; Editor FAROUK LUQMAN.

al Taleeah: P.O.B. 115, Mukalla; Arabic.

al-Thaqafa Al-Jadida: P.O.B. 1187, Aden; f. Aug. 1970; a cultural monthly review issued by the Ministry of Culture and Tourism; Arabic; circ. 3,000.

MONTHLIES

Angham: P.O.B. 555, Aden; f. 1956; Arabic; Editor ALI AMAN.

B.P. Aden Magazine: B.P. Refinery, P.O.B. 3003, Little Aden; f. 1960; English (publ. in Arabic as **Magallat Adan**); Editor The Public Relations Officer, B.P. Refinery.

NEWS AGENCY

Aden News Agency: Aden.

RADIO AND TELEVISION

RADIO

Democratic Yemen Broadcasting Service: P.O.B. 1264, Aden; transmits 76 hours a week in Arabic; Broadcasting Officer H. M. SAFI; there are about 80,000 receivers in the country.

TELEVISION

Democratic Yemen Broadcasting Service: P.O.B. 1264, Aden; programmes for three hours daily were introduced in 1964 on a commercial basis and extended to 4½ hours in both English and Arabic, plus 2½ hours weekly of programmes for schools. There are about 25,000 receivers.

FINANCE

CENTRAL BANK

Bank of Yemen: P.O.B. 4452, Aden; replaced Yemeni Currency Authority 1972; cap. p.u. 500,000 YD; Publ. *Annual Report*.

BANKS

All foreign banking interests were nationalized in November 1969 and thereafter amalgamated to form the National Bank of Yemen, the only commercial bank operating in the country.

National Bank of Yemen: P.O.B. 5, Crater, Aden; f. 1970 by nationalizing and amalgamating the local branches of the seven foreign banks then in Aden.

INSURANCE

All foreign insurance interests were nationalized in November 1969.

Arabian Trading Co. (Aden) Ltd.: P.O.B. 426, Aden; Dir. TAHER A. A. NABEE.

TRADE AND INDUSTRY

National Chamber of Commerce and Industry: P.O.B. 4345, Crater; Pres. ABDULREHMAN AL-SAILANI; Sec. HUSSEIN ALI ABDO.

Aden Merchants' Association: M. A. Luqman Rd., 1-11 Crater; f. 1932; 209 mems.; Pres. PHEROZESHAW P. PATEL; Secs. SORABJEE P. PATEL, M.B.E., ALI A. SAFFI.

National Company for Home Trade: Crater, Aden; f. 1969; importers of cars, electrical goods, agricultural machinery, building materials and general consumer goods; incorporates the main foreign trading businesses which were nationalized in 1970; Acting Gen. Man. SALEH AHMED SALEH.

EMPLOYERS' ASSOCIATIONS

Aden Hotel Proprietors' Association: c/o Crescent Hotel, Steamer Point, Aden.

Civil Contractors' Association: P.O. Box 307, Aden.

TRADE UNIONS

General Confederation of Workers of the People's Democratic Republic of Yemen: P.O.B. 1162, Maala, Aden; f. 1956; affiliated to W.F.T.U. and I.C.F.T.U.; 35,000 mems.; Gen. Sec. FADHLE ALI ABDULLA; publ. *Sout A Omal* weekly, circ. approx. 4,500.

PEOPLE'S DEMOCRATIC REPUBLIC OF YEMEN—(Trade and Industry, Transport, etc.)

There are fifteen Registered Trade Unions, including the following:

General and Port Workers' Union.
Forces and Associated Organizations Local Employees' Union.
Government and Local Government Employees' Union.
General Union of Petroleum Workers.
Miscellaneous Industries Employees' Union.
Aden Port Trust Employees' Union.
Civil Aviation Employees' Union.
Banks Local Staff Union.

CO-OPERATIVES AND MARKETING

There are 65 co-operative societies, mostly for agricultural products; the movement was founded in 1965 and is now the responsibility of the Ministry for Agriculture and Agrarian Reform.

OIL

Yemeni National Petroleum Co.: P.O.B. 5050, Aden; sole oil concessionaire importer and distributor of oil products in Yemen P.D.R.; in receipt of technical and financial assistance from Algeria; Chair. and Gen. Man. ABDUL KARIM THABET.

TRANSPORT

RAILWAYS

There are no railways.

ROADS

Aden Bus Co. Ltd.: Adbusco Bldg., Ma'alla, P.O.B. 905, Aden; f. 1960; operates services within the Crater, Ma'alla, Steamer Point, Sheikh Othman and Al-Mansoura areas; Chair. and Gen. Man. SAEED FARA SALIM.

A new state transport monopoly, the Yemen Land Transport Company, is being formed to incorporate the Aden Bus Company and all other local public transport.

Aden has 140 miles of roads, of which 127 have bituminous surfacings. There are approximately 2,680 miles of rough tracks passable for motor traffic in the hinterland, but most of the transport is by camel and donkey.

SHIPPING

National Shipping Company: P.O.B. 1228, Steamer Point, Aden; founded by the amalgamation and nationalization of five foreign shipping companies in November 1969; freight and passenger services; branches or agents in Mukalla, Berbera (Somalia) and Mocha and Hodieda (Yemen Arab Republic).

Yemen Ports Corporation: Aden; f. 1889 as Aden Port Trust; name changed January 1972; state administrative body; Aden remained a free port (except for tariffs on petrol, alcohol and tobacco) until 1970, though trade has greatly declined since 1967. Aden Main Harbour has twenty first-class berths. Three of them are Dolphin berths accommodating vessels drawing up to 40 ft., and the remaining seventeen are buoy berths for vessels drawing up to 42 ft. There are 4 second-class berths for vessels drawing up to 28 feet, and four third-class berths for vessels whose draught does not exceed 18 feet. In addition to the above, there is ample room to accommodate vessels of light draught at anchor in the 18-foot dredged area. There is also 600 feet of cargo wharf accommodating vessels of 300 feet length and 18 feet draught. Aden Oil Harbour accommodates four tankers of 55,000 tons and up to 40 feet draught.

A programme of dredging to maintain the advertised depths, and of deepening some channels, began in April 1970 and was completed in 1971.

CIVIL AVIATION

Democratic Yemen Airlines Company: Aden; f. 1971 as wholly owned Corporation by the Govt.

Other companies operating services include the following: Aeroflot, Air Djibouti, Air India, EAAC, EgyptAir, Ethiopian Airways, Kuwait Airways, MEA, Pakistan International Airlines, Somali Airlines Sudan Airways, Yemen Airlines.

Aden Civil Airport is at Khormaksar, 7 miles from the Port. It was established in 1952, and is operated by the Civil Aviation Department.

EDUCATION

The educational system consists of four years of Primary, three years of Intermediate and four to six years of Secondary schooling. There are 225 Government Primary Schools, 29 Intermediate Schools and 6 Secondary Schools, and a Technical Institute at Maalla, Aden, with a branch at Little Aden. Other higher education is received abroad.

In addition there are 12 Government-Aided and 5 Private Primary Schools, and 10 Grant-Aided and 4 Private Intermediate Schools. Teacher-Training Centres provide over 200 places for men and women trainees while adult education is provided by evening classes.

BIBLIOGRAPHY

BRINTON, J. Y. Aden and the Federation of South Arabia (American Soc. of Int. Law, Washington, 1964).

CENTRAL OFFICE OF INFORMATION. Aden and South Arabia (London, H.M.S.O., 1965).

COLONIAL OFFICE. Accession of Aden to the Federation of South Arabia (London, H.M.S.O., 1962).

COLONIAL OFFICE. Treaty of Friendship and Protection between the United Kingdom and the Federation of South Arabia (London, H.M.S.O., 1964).

FEDERATION OF SOUTH ARABIA. Conference on Constitutional Problems of South Arabia (H.M.S.O., 1964).

GEHRKE, Dr. ULRICH. Südarabien, Südarabische Föderation oder Süd-Jemen? (*Orient* Magazine, German Near and Middle East Association, Hamburg, 1967).

GOVERNMENT OF ADEN. Memorandum on the Five-Year Development Plan, 1952-53 to 1956-57 (Aden, 1958).

GOVERNMENT OF ADEN. Report of the Adenisation Committee, 1959 (London, 1959).

HARDING, H. LANKESTER. Archaeology in the Aden Protectorate (London, H.M.S.O., 1964).

HICKINBOTHAM, Sir TOM. Aden (London, Constable, 1959).

INGRAMS, DOREEN. A Survey of the Social and Economic Conditions of the Aden Protectorate (London).

INGRAMS, W. H. A Report on the Social, Economic and Political Conditions of the Hadhramaut, Aden Protectorate (London, 1936).

JOHNSTON, CHARLES. The View from Steamer Point (London, Collins, 1964).

KING, GILLIAN. Imperial Outpost-Aden (New York, Oxford University Press, 1964).

LITTLE, TOM. South Arabia (London, Pall Mall Press, 1968).

MAWER, JUNE KNOX. The Sultans Came to Tea (Murray, London, 1961).

PAGET, JULIAN. Last Post: Aden 1964-67 (Faber and Faber, London, 1969).

QAT COMMISSION OF INQUIRY. Report (Aden, 1958).

TREVASKIS, Sir KENNEDY. Shades of Amber, A South Arabian Episode (London, Hutchinson, 1967).

VAN DER MEULEN, DANIEL. Hadramaut: Some of Its Mysteries Unveiled (Leiden, 1932, reprinted 1964).

WATERFIELD, GORDON. Sultans of Aden (Murray, London 1968).

PART FOUR

Other Reference Material

WHO'S WHO IN THE MIDDLE EAST AND NORTH AFRICA

A

Aamiry, Mohammad Adeeb al-, B.A.; Jordanian politician and educationalist; b. 1907 Palestine; ed. American Univ. of Beirut and Palestine Law Inst.
Teacher 30; Headmaster 34; Ministry of Educ. Insp. 43; Deputy Dir. of Broadcasting Station, Jerusalem 44; Gen. Sec., Ministry of Foreign Affairs 50; Dir. Imports Dept. 51; Under-Sec. at Ministry of Educ. 52, at Ministry of Reconstruction and Devt. 53; Dir. Civil Service Dept. 55-58; Minister of Foreign Affairs Aug.-Oct. 67, of Educ. Oct. 67-April 68; Amb. to U.A.R. May 68; Minister of Culture, Information, Tourism and Antiquities Dec. 68-69; mem. Jerusalem Scientific Org., Cairo, Friends of Archaeology, Amman; Al Kawkab Medal 1st Grade, Al Istiqlal Medal 1st Grade and others.
Publs. *How to Keep Your Health* (2 vols.), *Ray of Light* (short stories), *General Science* (4 vols.), *Plant Families*, *Life and Youth* 67, *Jerusalem: The Arab Heritage* 70, *Palestine: The Arab Heritage* 72.
P.O. Box 1514, Amman, Jordan.

Aba el-Khayl, Sheikh Abdulrahman, B.A.; Saudi Arabian diplomatist and politician; b. 1927; ed. Cairo Univ.
Diplomatic Service 52-, Ministry of Foreign Affairs, Cairo, Beirut 52-58; Dir.-Gen. Ministry of Finance and Nat. Econ. Council 58-60; Senior Adviser, Ministry of Foreign Affairs 60; mem. Admin. Board, Arab Cement Co., Jeddah 60-61; Minister of Labour and Social Affairs 61-.
Ministry of Labour and Social Affairs, Riyadh, Saudi Arabia.

Abaza, Tharwat, LL.B.; Egyptian lawyer, editor and writer; b. 28 June 1927; ed. Monira Primary School, Farouk Secondary School and Cairo Univ.
Lawyer 50-54; Editor *Elmasri* daily newspaper 52-54, *Alkahira* 54-55; Publishing Consultant 56-57, 61-; mem. Cttee. on Fiction, Supreme Council for Arts, Literature and Social Sciences, and of its State Prizes Cttee.; State Prize for Fiction 59; State Decoration Grade I for Literature.
Publs. *Ibn Ammar* (Historical Fiction) 54, *Al Hayat Lana* (Life for Us—play) 55, *Hareb men Alayam* (An Escape from Fate—novel) 56, *Kasr Ala Elnil* (A Palace over the Nile—novel) 57, *Alayam Alkhadra* (Green Days—short stories) 58, *Thoma Toshrelk Alshams* (Then the Sun Rises—novel) 60, *Zhekriat Baida* (Far Echoes—short stories) 61, *Leka Honak* (An Appointment There—novel) 62, *Aldabab* (The Fog—novel) 64, *Shaion men Alkhawf* (A Little Fear—novel) 65, *Hayat El Hayah* (Life of Life—play), *Hathihi Elloba* (This Toy—short stories), *Hina Yamil Al Mizan* (When the Scales are Unbalanced—short stories).
5 Nadi Street, Maadi, Egypt.

Abbadi, Bashir Ahmed, D.SC.; Sudanese politician; b. 1936, Omdurman; ed. Univ. of Khartoum and Northwestern Univ., U.S.A.
Lecturer, Faculty of Eng., Univ. of Khartoum, Head, Dept. of Mechanical Eng. 70-71; mem. Board of Dirs. Sudan Railways 68-69, Chair. 69-70; Minister of Communications Oct. 71-.
Ministry of Communications, Khartoum, Sudan.

Abbas, Ferhat; Algerian politician; b. 1899; ed. Algiers Univ.
Formerly a chemist at Sétif; Leader of *Association des Etudiants musulmans* 26-31; took part in org. of the Algerian People's Union 38; published "Manifesto of the Algerian People" 43; founded Amis du Manifeste et de la Liberté (A.M.L.) 44; under detention May 45-March 46; took part in the formation of the Union Démocratique du Manifeste Algérien (U.D.M.A.) 46; elected rep. to French Constitutional Assembly 46, later mem. of French Union Assembly; elected to Algerian Assembly 48 and 54; Leader of U.D.M.A. 46-56; joined Nat. Liberation Front (FLN) 55; mem. FLN del. to Eleventh Gen. Assembly of UN 57; Prime Minister of Provisional Government of the Algerian Republic (GPRA) in Tunisia 58-61; Pres. of the Chamber of Algeria 62-63; under detention July 64-June 65.
Publs. *Le jeune algérien* 31, *La nuit coloniale* 62.
Konba, Algiers, Algeria.

Abbas, Major-Gen. Khalid Hassan; Sudanese army officer and politician.
Member Revolutionary Command Council 69-71; Chief of Gen. Staff Oct. 69-70; Minister of Defence 69-72; Vice-Pres. 71-72; mem. Political Bureau, Sudanese Socialist Union 71-72; mem. Free Officers Group; led del. to Peking 71.
c/o Sudanese Socialist Union, Khartoum, Sudan.

Abboud, Gen. Ibrahim; Sudanese officer and politician; b. 1900; ed. Gordon Memorial Coll., Khartoum and Military Coll., Khartoum.
Entered Sudan Defence Force; served 39-45 war with Sudanese contingent, British Army in Eritrea, Ethiopia and Libya; Dep. C.-in-C. Sudanese Army 54, C.-in-C. 56-64; Pres. Supreme Military Council, Prime Minister and Minister of Defence 58-64.
Suakin, Sudan.

Abdelkerim, Ahmad Ezzat, D.LITT.; Egyptian historian; b. 19 June 1909; ed. Cairo Univ.
Lecturer, Asst. Prof. of Modern History, Cairo Univ. until 50; Visiting Prof. Univ. of Damascus 46-49; Prof. of Modern History, Ain Shams Univ. 50-64, Dean of Faculty of Arts, Ain Shams Univ. 61-64, Vice-Rector 64-68, Rector 68-71; Visiting Prof., Woodrow School of Foreign Affairs, Univ. of Virginia 52, Univ. of Libya, Benghazi 60-61.
Publs. *History of Education in Egypt under Mohamed Ali* 38, *History of Education in Egypt (From the Reign of Mohamed Ali to the British Occupation*—3 vols.) 44, *Venice, an Aristotic Republic* (trans. from French) 47, *Modern and Contemporary History of the Arab World* 55, *History of Syria in the 18th Century* 58, *Studies in Modern Arab Renaissance* 59.
Abbasiyah, Cairo, Egypt.

Abdel Meguid, Ahmed Esmat, PH.D.; Egyptian diplomatist; b. 22 March 1923, Alexandria; ed. Faculty of Law, Alexandria Univ. and Univ. of Paris.
Attaché and Sec. Egyptian Embassy, London 50-54; Ministry of Foreign Affairs, Head of British Desk 54-56, Asst. Dir. Legal Dept. 61-63, Head, Cultural and Technical Assistance Dept. 67-68; Counsellor, Perm. Mission to European Office of UN, Geneva 57-61; Minister Counsellor, Egyptian Embassy, Paris 63-67; Official Spokesman of Govt. and Head Information Dept. 68-69; Amb. to France 69-70; Minister of State for Cabinet Affairs 70-72; Perm. Rep. to UN 72-; mem. Int. Law Asscn., took part in UN confs. on the Law of the Sea 59, on Consular Relations 63 and on the Law of Treaties 69; Ordre National du Mérite, France 67; Grand Croix 71; 1st Class Decoration, Egypt 70.
Publs. several articles in *Revue Egyptienne de Droit International*.
Permanent Mission of Egypt to the United Nations, 36 East 67th Street, New York, N.Y. 10021, U.S.A.
Telephone: 879-6300.

Abdel-Rahman, Aisha, PH.D. (pen name **Bint el-Shati**); Egyptian writer and university professor; ed. Cairo Univ.
Assistant Lecturer, Cairo Univ. 39-; Literary Critic, *Al Ahram* 42-; Inspectress in Arabic Languages and Litera-

ture, Ministry of Education 42; Lecturer in Arabic, Ain Shams Univ. 50-57, Asst. Prof. 57-62, Prof. of Arabic Literature and Chair. Univ. Coll. for Women 62-; mem. Higher Council of Arts and Letters 60-; State Prize 36; Acad. of Arabic Language Award, for Textual Studies 50, for Short Story 54.
Publs. *Rissalet el Ghofram bv Abul Ala'a* 50, *New Values in Arabic Literature* 61, *The Koran: Literary Interpretation* 62, *Ibn Seeda's Arabic Dictionary* 62, *Contemporary Arab Women Poets* 63; six books on illustrious women of Islam; two novels; four vols. of short stories.
13 Agam Street, Heliopolis, Cairo, Egypt.

Abdel-Rahman, Ibrahim Helmi, PH.D.; Egyptian United Nations official; b. 5 Jan. 1919; ed. Univs. of Cairo, London, Edinburgh, Cambridge and Leiden.
Lecturer in Astronomy and Astrophysics, later Asst. Prof. Cairo Univ. 42-54; Sec.-Gen. Council of Ministers 54-58; Dir. Egyptian Atomic Energy Comm. 54-59; mem. and Sec.-Gen. Nat. Science Council 56-58; mem. Nat. Planning Comm. 57-60; Dir. Inst. of Nat. Planning 60-63; UN Commr. for Industrial Devt. 63-66; Exec. Dir. UN Industrial Devt. Org. (UNIDO) 67-; mem. Egyptian Del. UNESCO Gen. Conf. 48, 52, 54; mem. U.A.R. Del. to Int. Atomic Energy Agency, Vienna 57; mem. numerous UN Missions.
United Nations Industrial Development Organization, Lerchenfelderstrasse 1, A-1070, Vienna, Austria.

Abderrahmane, Iddir; Algerian mining engineer; b. 13 Dec. 1941; ed. Ecole Supérieure des Mines, Nancy, France.
Engineer in charge of mining operations 66; Gen. Man. SONAREM (State Mining Org.) Dec. 72-.
SONAREM, 127 Boulevard Bouakouir, Algiers, Algeria.

Abdessalam, Belaid; Algerian politician.
Former Hon. Pres. Union Générale des Etudiants Musulmans Algériens; in Cabinet of M. Abdelhamid Mehri, Tunisia 60; in Cabinet of M. Ben Khedda 61; in charge of Economic Affairs, FLN Provisional Exec. 62; Pres., Dir.-Gen. SONATRACH 64-65; Minister of Industry and Energy 65-.
Ministry of Industry and Energy, Algiers, Algeria.

Abdoh, Djalal, LL.D.; Iranian diplomatist; b. 1909; ed. Teheran and Paris Univs.
Assistant Dir. Ministry of Justice 37-39; Public Prosecutor, Court of Govt. Employees, Teheran 41-43; Dir.-Gen. Ministry of Justice 43-44; mem. Parl. 44-49; Deputy Perm. Rep. to UN 49-53; Dir.-Gen. of Political Affairs, Ministry of Foreign Affairs 54-55; Acting Head Del. to Bandung Conf. 55; Amb. and Perm. Rep. to UN 56; Act. Rep. Security Council 56; Chair. Iranian Del. Gen. Assembly 58-59; Minister of Foreign Affairs 59; UN Plebiscite Commr., British N. Cameroons 59-60; Amb. at Large 61; Administrator, UN Temporary Exec. Authority (UNTEA), West New Guinea (West Irian) 62-63; Prof., Teheran Univ. 64-65; Amb. to India 65-68, to Italy 68-72.
Publs. *Civil Procedure of Iran, Comparative Law, International Private Law, Eléments psychologiques dans les Contrats, Le Ministère Public, Le régime Pénitentiaire en Iran, The Political Situation in Africa* (Persian), *The Political Situation in The Middle East* (Persian).
c/o Ministry of Foreign Affairs, Teheran, Iran.

Abdulla, Rahmatalla; Sudanese diplomatist; b. 1922; ed. Trinity Coll., Cambridge Univ.
Ambassador to India and Japan 59-60, Nigeria 60-61, France, Netherlands, Belgium, Switzerland and Spain 61-65; Minister of Nat. Educ. 64-65; served as Head of the History Faculty, Sudan Inst. of Educ.; Exec. Sec. and later Asst. Gen. Man., Sudan Gezira Board; Dept. Under-Sec. for Foreign Affairs 65-67; Amb. to France, Netherlands, Switzerland and Spain 68-70, Zaire 70-72; Perm. Rep. to UN 72-; served as Personal Envoy of the Govt. to a meeting of African Heads of State, Del. to many int. confs., including those of the UN, OAU, regional African meetings and the Arab League.
Permanent Mission of Sudan to the United Nations, 757 Third Avenue, 12th Floor, New York, N.Y. 10017, U.S.A.

Abdullah, Abdel Rahman; Sudanese politician; b. 1932, Abu Hamad; ed. Khartoum Univ. Coll.
Joined Ministry of Interior, Sub-Mamour 56; Inspector, Tokar district, later of Kassala Province; joined Halfa People's Settlement Comm. 59; Dir. Inst. of Public Admin. 63-65; Dir. African Admin. Training and Research Inst., Morocco 65; Dir. Nat. Inst. of Public Admin., Libya; Deputy Minister of Local Govt. Aug. 71; Minister of Public Service and Admin. Reform Oct. 71-.
Ministry of Public Service and Administrative Reform, Khartoum, Sudan.

Abdullah al Sheikh, Hassan; Saudi Arabian politician; b. 1932; ed. Shariah Coll., Mecca and Al Azhar Univ., Cairo.
Former mem. Judicial Supervisory Cttee.; Vice-Pres. Judicial Supervisory Cttee.; Minister of Education and Health 62, now Minister of Educ.; High Pres. Riyadh Univ.; Pres. Higher Cttee. for Arts, Sciences and Literature 62-; Chancellor Univ. of King Abdel-ziz; Dir. Archaeological Dept.
Publs. *Duwarna Fi Al-Kufah* (Our Turn in the Struggle), *Brave Ideas, Dignity of The Individual in Islam.*
Ministry of Education, Riyadh, Saudi Arabia.

Abidia, Fathi, B.A.; Libyan diplomatist; b. 21 March 1923; ed. Cairo Univ.
Special Sec. to King Idris I 50-54; Under-Sec. of Royal Divan 54-55; Counsellor, Washington, D.C. 55-57, London 57-61; Chargé d'Affaires, Jeddah 61-62; Dir. of Political Dept., Ministry of Foreign Affairs 62-63; Under-Sec. Ministry of Foreign Affairs 63; Amb. to U.S.A. 63-70; import-export commerce and private business 70-.
P.O. Box 444, Benghazi, Libya.

Abou-Hamad, Khalil; Lebanese politician; b. 1936.
Minister of Foreign Affairs 70-73.
c/o Ministry of Foreign Affairs, Beirut, Lebanon.

Abou Nosseir, Mohamed, B.A.; Egyptian lawyer and politician; b. 1915.
Legal practice 36-39; Advocate, State Legal Dept. 39-44; Advocate, Legal Dept. of Cabinet 44-46; Asst. Councillor and Sec.-Gen. State Council 52; Councillor, State Council, Public Works Section 53; Supervisor, Admin. Contracts Section, State Council 54; Dep. Minister of Commerce and Industry 54; Head of trade mission to Indonesia and Japan 54; mem. official del. to Bandung Conf. for Afro-Asian Countries 55; Head of Trade Missions to China 55, to U.K. 56, and of Economic Mission to Syria 56; Minister of Commerce and Industry 56-58, of Municipal and Rural Affairs 58-61 (Egyptian Regional Govt.); Chair. Board of Dirs., Gen. Egyptian Housing and Urbanism Org. 61-; Minister of Housing and Public Utilities 64-66; mem. Gen. Secr., Arab Socialist Union 66-; Chair. Preparatory Cttee. New Perm. Constitution 66; Minister of Justice 68-69.
4 El Saleh Ayoub Street, Zamalek, Cairo, Egypt.

Abu Hassabu, Abd el Magid Mohamed; Sudanese politician; b. 1 Jan. 1919; ed. Gordon Memorial Coll., Khartoum, Univ. of Alexandria.
Teacher in private schools 50-53; founding mem. Nat. Unionist Party; practising lawyer 57-65; in charge of Press Affairs, N.U.P. 64-65; Minister of Public Works and Mineral Resources 65-66, of Information, Social Affairs and Justice 67-69; publisher *Nidaa* journal 64-; Jordanian Award.
c/o Ministry of Information and Social Affairs, P.O.B. 300, Khartoum, Sudan.

Abu-Izzeddin, Halim Said, B.A., LL.B., LL.D.; Lebanese diplomatist; b. 11 June 1918; ed. American Univ. of Beirut and Faculté de Droit, Univ. de Paris.
Consul-General Cairo 44-46, Counsellor 46-50; Dir. Political Dept., Ministry of Foreign Affairs 50-53, 64-66; Dir.-Gen. Ministry of Information 53-55; Asst. Sec.-Gen. Ministry of Foreign Affairs 55-57; Ambassador to India 57-59; Gov. Northern Lebanon 59-64; Amb. to Egypt 66-71; Amb., Perm. Del. to UNESCO 71-; numerous decorations.
Publs. *Lebanon and its Provinces* (English) 53, *The Foreign Policy of the Lebanon* (Arabic) 66.
UNESCO, 7 and 9 place de Fontenoy, Paris, France; and Abadyeh, Lebanon.

Abu Zeid, Maj. Ma'mun Awad; Sudanese politician b. 6 Dec. 1939, Omdurman; ed. Sudan Military Coll.
Chief Spokesman, National Revolutionary Council 69-71; Head, Nat. Security Service of the Sudan 69-71; Minister of State for Cabinet Affairs 69-71; Sec.-Gen. Sudan Socialist Union 71-72; Order of Bravery, Order of Loyal Son of the Sudan; Grand Cordon of Manalik (Ethiopia).
Sudan Socialist Union, al-Makk Nimir Street, P.O. Box 1850, Khartoum, Sudan.

Abushadi, Mohamed Mahmoud, PH.D., B.COM., A.C.I.P.; Egyptian banker; b. 15 Aug. 1913, Fayoum; ed. Cairo Univ., Chartered Inst. of Patent Agents, and American Univ., Washington, D.C., U.S.A.
Controller-Gen. Insurance Dept., Ministry of Finance 49-52; Dir.-Gen. Govt. Insurance and Provident Funds 53; Chair. and Man. Dir. Development and Popular Housing Co. 54-55; Sub.-Gov. Nat. Bank of Egypt 55-60, Man. Dir. 61-67, Chair. 67-70; Chair. Social Insurance Org. 56-57; Chair. and Man. Dir. Cairo Insurance Co. 56-57; Man. Dir. Cairo Bank 56-57; Chair. Union de Banques Arabes et Françaises, Paris 70-, UBAF Ltd., London 72-; Order of the Repub., 2nd Class, Order of Merit, 1st Class.
Publs. *The Art of Central Banking and its Application in Egypt* 52, *Central Banking in Egypt* 52.
Union de Banques Arabes et Françaises, 4 rue Ancelle, 92 Neuilly sur Seine; Home: 52 avenue Foch, Paris 16e, France.

Abuzeid, Salah; Jordanian politician; b. 21 April 1925; ed. Syrian Univ., Damascus, and Syracuse Univ., New York.
Teacher, Irbid Secondary School 42; Chief, Publicity Dept., Statistical Dept., Amman 50; Sec. Jordan Devt. Bd. 53-56; Controller of Press, Press Dept. 56-57; Asst. Dir.-Gen. Hashemite Broadcasting Service 58-59, Dir.-Gen. 62-64; Asst. Dir.-Gen. Nat. Guidance and Information 59-60, Dir.-Gen. 62, Chief, National Guidance 62-64; Minister of Information 64-65, Culture and Information 67-68, Tourism and Antiquities 67-68; Amb. to the U.K. 69-70; Personal Adviser to H.M. King Hussein 71-72; Minister of Foreign Affairs 72; Arab Renaissance Medal, Jordanian Star, Cedar of Lebanon and several other medals.
Publ. *Al Hussein bin Talal* 58.
c/o Ministry of Foreign Affairs, Amman, Jordan.

Acet, Kamran; Turkish diplomatist; b. 2 March 1917; ed. School of Political Studies, Univ. of Ankara.
With Ministry of Foreign Affairs 41-; served Ankara 41-43, 45-47; Attaché Rio de Janeiro 43-45; Vice-Consul Mytilene, Greece 47-49; First Sec. Helsinki 49-51; Dir. of Section, Dept. of Trade and Trade Agreements 51-53; First Sec. and Counsellor Washington 53-59; Deputy Dir.-Gen. then Dir.-Gen. Dept. of Middle East, Africa and Asia, Ministry of Foreign Affairs 59-62; Amb. to Ghana 62-64, to Morocco 64-66, to Tunisia 67-70; Deputy Sec.-Gen. for Cyprus Affairs and Greece Nov. 70-Nov. 71; Dir.-Gen. Personnel and Admin., Ministry of Foreign Affairs Dec. 71-; mem. Turkish del. to 15th Session of Gen. Assembly of UN and to several meetings of CENTO and NATO; Grand Cordon, Kingdom of Morocco.
c/o Ministry of Foreign Affairs, Ankara, Turkey.

Achour, Habib; Tunisian trade unionist.
Secretary-Gen. Union Générale Tunisienne du Travail 64-65; mem. Political Bureau, Destour Socialist Party Nov. 64-; arrested June 65, sentenced to six months imprisonment March 66.
Destour Socialist Party, 10 rue de Rome, Tunis, Tunisia.

Adams, Michael Evelyn, M.A.; British writer; b. 31 May 1920; ed. Sedbergh School and Christ Church, Oxford.
Commonwealth Fund Fellowship in U.S.A. 54-55; Middle East Corresp. *The Guardian* 56-62; Asst. to Dir. Voluntary Service Overseas 64-67; Dir. of Information, Council for the Advancement of Arab-British Understanding (CAABU) 68-; Editor *Middle East International*.
Publs. *Suez and After* 58, *Umbria* 64, *Voluntary Service Overseas* 68, *Chaos or Rebirth* 68, *Handbook to the Middle East* (Editor) 71.
Council for the Advancement of Arab-British Understanding, 104 Grand Buildings, Trafalgar Square, London, W.C.2, England.

Adams, Sir Philip George Doyne, K.C.M.G.; British diplomatist; b. 17 Dec. 1915, Wellington, New Zealand; ed. Lancing and Christ Church, Oxford.
Vice-Consul, Beirut 39-41; war service 41; Third Sec., Cairo 41-45; Second Sec., Jeddah 45-47; Foreign Office, London 47-51; First Sec., Vienna 51-54; Trade Commr., Khartoum 54-56; Regional Inf. Officer, Beirut 56-59; Foreign Office, London 59-63; Consul-Gen., Chicago 63-66; Amb. to Jordan 66-70; Asst. Under-Sec. Foreign and Commonwealth Office 70; Deputy Sec. Cabinet Office 71-72; Amb. to Egypt 73-.
British Embassy, Kasrah El Dabara, Cairo, Egypt.

Adams, Robert McCormick, A.M., PH.D.; American anthropologist and archaeologist; b. 23 July 1926; ed. Univ. of Chicago.
Archaeological field work at Jarmo, Iraq 50-51; joined staff of Univ. of Chicago 54, Dir. Oriental Inst. 62-68, Prof. of Anthropology 63-, Dean, Div. of Social Science 70-; Field studies of irrigation and settlement patterns in central and southern Iraq 56-58, 60, 67, 68-69, Iran 60-61; excavations in Iran 63, Syria 70; Chair. Assembly of Behavioral and Social Sciences, Nat. Research Council 73-, American Oriental Soc.; Fellow, American Acad. of Arts and Sciences, American Anthropological Asscn., American Asscn. for the Advancement of Science; mem. German Archaeological Inst., Nat. Acad. of Science, Middle East Studies Asscn.
Publs. *City Invincible: a Symposium of Urbanization and Cultural Development in the Ancient Near East* (co-editor with C. H. Kraeling) 60, *Land Behind Baghdad: a History of Settlement on the Diyala Plains* 65, *The Evolution of Urban Society: Early Mesopotamia and Pre-hispanic Mexico* 66, *The Uruk Countryside* (with H. J. Nissen) 72.
The Oriental Institute, 1155 East 58th Street, Chicago, Illinois 60637; and 5201 South Kimbark Avenue, Chicago, Illinois 60615, U.S.A.

Adasani, Mahmoud, B.SC.; Kuwaiti engineer; b. 31 Jan. 1934; ed. Kuwait, American Univ., Beirut and Univ. of Southern California.
Assistant petroleum engineer, Kuwait Oil Co. 58-60, petroleum engineer 60, Dir. 60-; Technical Asst., Gen. Oil Affairs Dept., Ministry of Finance and Oil 60-63, Dir. of Technical Affairs 63-66, Asst. Under-Sec. for Oil Affairs 66-; Man. Dir. Salwa Construction Co.; Dir. Kuwait Metal Pipeline Co. 70-; mem. American Inst. Mechanical Engineers, Kuwait Soc. Engineers.
Publs. *Oil of Kuwait, The Greater Burgan Field, North Kuwait Oil Fields*.
Ministry of Finance and Oil, P.O.B. 5077, Kuwait.

Adib, Albert; Lebanese editor; b. 1 July 1908 Mexico. Editor many magazines, Cairo 27-30, Beirut 30-38; Pres. Acad. of Oriental Music, Beirut 33-38; Gen. Dir. Radio-Levant Broadcasting Station, Beirut 38-43; Editor and proprietor *Al-Adib* review, Beirut 42-; mem. various acads. and foreign cultural insts.; Chevalier of the Order of the Cedar.
Publ. *Liman* (poems) 52.
P.O. Box 878, Beirut, Lebanon.

Adly, Ibrahim, PH.D.; Syrian United Nations official; ed. Damascus Univ., American Univ. Washington D.C. Formerly Dir. of Personnel, Ministry of Finance; Dir.-Gen. Pension and Insurance Fund Inst.; Vice-Pres., Dir. Arab World Bank; Resident Rep. UN Devt. Programme (UNDP), Kuwait 66-72, Libya 72-.
United Nations Development Programme, P.O. Box 358, Tripoli, Libya.

Adwok, Bong Gicomeko, Luigi; Sudanese schoolmaster and public servant; b. 1929; ed. Rumbek Secondary School and Inst. of Education, Bakht Er Ruda.
Schoolmaster 52-58; mem. Parl. March-Nov. 58; Headmaster Tembura Intermediate School 63-64; elected mem. Supreme Council of State Dec. 64, re-elected June 65, resigned June 65; mem. Central Exec. Cttee. Southern Front Party 64-67; mem. Sudan Constituent Assembly 67-69; mem. for Educ., High Exec. Council for the Southern Region April 72-.
High Executive Council for the Southern Region, Juba, Sudan.

Afif, Ahmed Jaber; Yemeni government official; b. 1930; ed. High School, Sana'a.
Director of Schools, Hodeida Province 52-56; Under-Sec. for Educ. 56-58; Dir. Sana'a Hospital 58-60; Under-Sec. for Health 60-63; Amb. to Lebanon and Syria 63-69; Pres. Council of Petroleum Co. 69-; Minister of Educ. 70-.
Al-rayni Street, Sana'a, Yemen Arab Republic.

Afifi, Ahmed; Egyptian agriculturalist; b. 6 March 1910; ed. Abbassia Primary School, Ismail Secondary School, Cairo and London Univs.
Lecturer, Cairo Univ. 34-46; Chief Plant Breeder, Egyptian Agricultural Org. 46-53, Sub-Dir.-Gen. 53-57, Dir.-Gen. 57; mem. board of several orgs. under Ministries of Agric., Econ., and Scientific Research; various awards for agricultural achievements including prize for breeding new variety of cotton in Egypt.
Publs. *Cytological and Genetical Principles of Plant Breeding* (Arabic) 55, and many scientific papers in int. journals of genetics and cytology 33-53.
Exhibition Grounds, P.O.B. 63, Gezira, Cairo, Egypt.

Afshar, Amir Aslan; Iranian government official; b. 21 Nov. 1922; ed. Berlin and Hindenburg Schools, and Univs. of Berlin, Greifswald, Vienna and Geneva.
Joined Ministry of Foreign Affairs 47, Sec., The Hague 50-54; Del. to Bandung Conf., Indonesia 55; Eisenhower Exchange Fellowship 55-56; mem. Parl. 56-61; Del. to UN Gen. Assembly 57, 58 and 60; Adjutant to the Shah 59-66; Plenipotentiary Minister 63; mem. High Political Council 63-66; Pres. Iranian Shipping Lines 60-67; Amb. to Austria 67-70; Amb. to U.S.A. 70-73; Chair. Board of Governors of the Int. Atomic Energy Agency, Vienna; numerous decorations.
Publs. in German: *The Constitution of the Third Reich* 42, *The Administration of the Third Reich* 42, *Possibilities for the Economic Development of Iran* 43; in Persian: *The End of the Third Reich* 48, *God Created the Universe and the Dutch made Holland* 55; in English: *Report on America* 56.
c/o Ministry of Foreign Affairs, Teheran, Iran.

Afshar, Amir Khosrow; Iranian diplomatist; ed. Geneva Univ.
Foreign Service 41-; served Washington, UN, Ministry of Foreign Affairs, London 41-57; Head, Political Section, Ministry of Foreign Affairs 57; fmr. Ambassador to German Fed. Repub.; Ambassador to France 64-66, to U.K. 69-.
Iranian Embassy, 16 Princes Gate, London, S.W.7, England.

Aga Khan IV, H.H. Prince Karim; spiritual leader and Imam of Ismaili Muslims; b. 13 Dec. 1936; ed. Le Rosey, Switzerland, Harvard Univ., U.S.A.
Became Aga Khan on the death of his grandfather, Sir Sultan Mohamed Shah, Aga Khan III, G.C.S.I., G.C.I.E., G.C.V.O. 57; granted title His Highness by Queen Elizabeth II 57, His Royal Highness by the Shah of Iran 59; Commdr. Ordre du Mérite Mauritanien 60; Grand Croix, Ordre Nat. de la Côte d'Ivoire 65, Ordre Nat. de la Haute-Volta 65, Ordre Nat. Malgache 66, Ordre du Croissant Vert des Comores 66; Grand Cordon Ordre du Tadj de l'Empire d'Iran 67; Nishan-I-Imtiaz, Pakistan 70; Hon. LL.D. (Peshawar Univ.) 67, (Univ. of Sind) 70.
1 rue des Ursins, 75004 Paris, France.

Aga Khan, Prince Sadruddin; Iranian UN official; b. 1933; ed. Harvard Univ. and Harvard Univ. Graduate School for Arts and Sciences.
UNESCO Consultant for Afro-Asian Projects 58; Head of Mission and Adviser to UN High Commr. for Refugees 59-60; UNESCO Special Consultant to Dir.-Gen. 61; Exec. Sec. Int. Action Cttee. for Preservation of Nubian Monuments 61; UN Dep. High Commr. for Refugees 62-65, High Commr. 65-; Publ. *The Paris Review*; Founder and Sec. Harvard Islamic Asscn.; Pres. Council on Islamic Affairs, New York City; mem. Inst. of Differing Civilizations, Brussels.
Château de Bellerive, Collonge-Bellerive, Geneva, Switzerland.

Agranat, Shimon, LL.D.; Israeli judge; b. 1906 U.S.A.; ed. Chicago Univ.
Went to Palestine 30; Advocate in private practice 31-40; Magistrate 40-48; Pres. District Court, Haifa 48-50; Judge, Supreme Court, Jerusalem 50-, Dep. Pres. 61-65, Pres. 65-.
62 Nayot Street, Rehavia, Jerusalem; and The Supreme Court, Jerusalem, Israel.

Ahardane, Mahjoubi; Moroccan politician; b. 1922.
Former soldier in the French Army; fmr. Sec.-Gen. Mouvement Populaire; Minister of Defence 63-64; Minister of Agriculture and Agrarian Reform Aug. 64-66; mem. Regency Council July 65; Minister of Nat. Defence 66-67; now leader Mouvement Populaire.
House of Representatives, Rabat, Morocco.

Ahmad, Maj.-Gen. Mohammed al-Baqir; Sudanese army officer and politician; b. 1927, El Sofi; ed. Commercial Secondary School, Khartoum, Military Coll. and Cairo Univ. Commissioned 50; Chief of Staff, Southern Command 58; Mil. Gov. Upper Nile Province 59; Mil. Attaché, London 60-67; Dir. of Training and Chief of Staff, Southern Command 68; Commdr. Mil. Coll. 68-69; Under-Sec. Ministry of Defence June-Dec. 69; First Deputy Chief of Staff of Armed Forces Dec. 69-June 70, Chief of Staff 70-71; Minister of Interior Oct. 71-72; mem. Council, Univ. of Khartoum; del. to several int. confs.; several decorations.
Office of the First Vice-President, Khartoum, Sudan.

Ahmadi, Sadegh; Iranian lawyer; b. March 1920, Kermanshah; ed. Darol-Fonoon High School, Teheran, Univ. of Teheran.
Appointed Judge 46; Asst., Inspectorate Org. of the Prime Minister's Office, later Dir.-Gen.; Public Prosecutor of Teheran; First Asst., State Gen. Inspectorate; mem. Parl.; Under-Sec. in charge of Planning and Studies, Ministry of Justice, Parl. Under-Sec.; Minister of Justice Sept. 71-; mem. Parl. del. to U.S.S.R.; has studied judicial systems in European countries.
Ministry of Justice, Teheran, Iran.

Ahmed, S. Habib, B.A.; Pakistani United Nations official; b. 1 April 1915; ed. Univ. of Delhi.
Administration, Central Govt., India 35-41; Finance and Budget Officer, Tata Iron & Steel Co., India 41-47; Budget Officer, UN 49-50; Public Admin. Adviser UN Commr., Libya 50; Adviser on Public Admin., Ethiopia and Iraq 51-54; Chief Officer for Asia and the Far East, UN Technical Assistance Admin. 55-59; Deputy Dir. Bureau of Tech. Assistance Operations UN Headquarters 59-60; Chief Admin. Officer, UN Mission in the Congo 60-62; Resident Rep. of Tech. Assist. Board, and Dir. of Special Fund Programme, Congo 62-64, Resident Rep. of UN Devt. Programme, Somalia 64-67, Libya 68-71, Syria 71-.
c/o UNDP, P.O. Box 20, Grand Central Station, New York, N.Y. 10017, U.S.A.

Aini, Mohsin A. al; Yemeni diplomatist and politician; b. 1932; ed. Cairo Univ. and Univ. of Paris.
Schoolteacher, Aden 58-60; Int. Confederation of Arab Trade Unions 60-62; Minister of Foreign Affairs, Yemeni Republic Sept.-Dec. 62; Perm. Rep. to UN Dec. 62-65, 65-66, 67-69; Amb. to U.S.A. 63-65, 65-66; Foreign Minister May-July 65; Prime Minister Nov. 67; Personal Rep. of Chair. Republican Council 67; Amb. to U.S.S.R. 68-70; Prime Minister and Foreign Minister 70-Feb. 71; Amb. to France July-Sept. 71; Prime Minister, Minister of Foreign Affairs 71-72.
Publ. *Conspiracy against Yemen.*
c/o Office of the Prime Minister, Sana'a, Yemen Arab Republic.

Ajlouni, Brig. Mazen al-; Jordanian politician; b. 1924, Amman; ed. High School in Jordan and in U.K.
Joined Jordanian Army 48; A.-D.-C. to King Hussein 55; Chief Aide-de-Camp 57; Mil. Attaché, Ankara 57-58; Asst. for Admin., Amman Municipality 64; Gen. Insp., Public Security Dept. 69; Chief Aide-de-Camp 69; Deputy Prime Minister for Mil. Gov.-Gen. Sept. 70; Minister of State, Prime Minister's Office, Sept.-Oct. 70, Oct. 71-; Minister of Interior Oct. 70-May 71; Senator 71-.
c/o Prime Minister's Office, Amman, Jordan.

Akurgal, Ekrem, PH.D.; Turkish archaeologist; b. 1911, Istanbul; ed. Germany.
Lecturer, Univ. of Ankara 41-49, Prof. of Archaeology 49-; has conducted excavations at Smyrna, Sinope, Phokaia, Daskyleion, Pitane and Erythrai 53-, at Izmir 67-; Visiting Prof., Princeton Univ. 61-62; mem. Turkish Historical Soc., Turkish High Comm. for Ancient Monuments; mem. Austrian and German Archaeol. Insts., British, Austrian and Swedish Acads.; Hon. mem. Soc. for Promotion of Hellenic Studies, London, American Inst. of Archaeol.; Dr. h.c. (Bordeaux) 61.
Publs. *Griechische Reliefs aus Lykien* 42, *Remarques Stylistiques sur les reliefs de Malatya* 46, *Späthethitische Bildkunst* 49, *Phrygische Kunst* 55, *Die Kunst Anatoliens von Homer bis Alexander* 61, *Die Kunst der Hethiter* 61, *Orient und Okzident* 66, *Treasures of Turkey* (with Mango and Ettinghausen) 66, *Urartäische und Altiranische Kunstzentren* 68.
University of Ankara, Yildirim Beyazit Meydani, Ankara, Turkey.

Akwaa', Brig. Mohamed Ali al-; Yemeni army officer; b. 1933, Sana'a; ed. secondary school, Mil. Coll., Sana'a.
Participated in the movts. against last three Imams of Yemen, Free Yemenis Revolution 48, attempted coup 55, Revolution of 26 September 1962; leading figure in movt. which ousted Pres. al-Sallal 67; has held several posts in mil. and civil service including Asst. Mil. Commdr. Taiz District, Head Criminal Investigation Dept., Head Nat. Security (Intelligence) Dept.; Chief of Staff, Army Operations, Head S. Yemen Relief Office attached to Presidency; Minister of the Interior 73-.
Bir Al-Azab, Sana'a, Yemen Arab Republic.

Alam, Amir Assadollah; Iranian agriculturalist and politician; b. 1919; ed. Karaj Agricultural College, Univ. of Teheran.
Gov.-Gen. of Baluchistan 45-48; Minister of the Interior 48, of Agriculture 49, of Labour 50; Superintendent of the Pahlavi Estates and mem. of the High Council for their disposal 51; Minister of the Interior 55-57; Leader, Mardom (*People's Party*) 56-60; Prime Minister 62-64; Minister of the Imperial Court 66-; Sec.-Gen. Pahlavi Foundation; Chancellor Pahlavi Univ.
Ministry of the Imperial Court, City Avenue Kakh, Teheran, Iran.

Alami, Musa; Jordanian philanthropist; b. 1897; ed. Trinity Hall Cambridge.
Crown Counsel 26-37; founded Arab Devt. Soc. 43; founded orphanage and farm in desert near Jericho 51; region under Israeli occupation June 67-.
Rabiya, Beirut, Lebanon.

Alamuddin, Sheikh Najib Salim, B.A.; Lebanese airline executive; b. 9 March 1909; ed. American Univ. of Beirut and Univ. Coll. of South West, Exeter, England.
Teacher of Engineering and Mathematics, American Univ. of Beirut 30-33; Insp. of Mathematics, Educ. Dept., Govt. of Trans-Jordan 33-36; Insp.-Gen. of Customs, Trade and Industry, Trans-Jordan 39-40; Chief Sec. Govt. of Trans-Jordan 40-42; founded Near East Resources Co. 42; Gen. Man. Middle East Airlines 52-56, Chair. and Pres. 56-; Minister of Information and Tourism 65; Minister of Public Works and Transport 66, 73; mem. Exec. Cttee. of Int. Air Transport Asscn.; Trustee Emeritus, American Univ. of Beirut; Dir. several Lebanese companies; numerous decorations.
Middle East Airlines, Beirut International Airport, Beirut, Lebanon.
Telephone: 272220, 274440.

Albright, William F., PH.D., LITT.D., D.H.L., TH.D., LL.D., D.H.C.; American orientalist and archaeologist; b. 24 May 1891; ed. Upper Iowa and Johns Hopkins Univs.
Dir. American School of Oriental Research in Jerusalem 20-29 and 33-36; W. W. Spence Prof. of Semitic Languages, Johns Hopkins Univ. 29-58, Prof. Emeritus 58-; Dir. of Excavations at Gibeah of Saul, Tell Beit Mirsim and Bethel; Chief Archaeologist, Sinai 47-48, Beihan (S. Arabia) 50-51; mem. American Philosophical Soc., Nat. Acad. of Sciences. Amer. Acad. of Arts and Sciences; foreign mem. Austrian, Royal Danish, Flemish and Irish Acads.; corresp. mem. Acad. des Inscriptions et Belles Lettres; Pres. Amer. Oriental Soc. 35-36; Pres. Int. Org. Old Testament Scholars 56-59; Trustee American Schools Oriental Research, Inst. Mediterranean Affairs; Corresp. Fellow British Acad.; mem. (hon.) Société Asiatique, Royal Asiatic Soc., British Soc. for Old Testament Study, etc.; Hon. degrees from Yale, Harvard, Trinity Coll. (Dublin), St. Andrews, Utrecht, Oslo, Uppsala, Hebrew Univ. Jerusalem); Gold Medal Archaeological Inst. America 67.
Publs. *Excavation at Gibeah of Benjamin* 24, *The Spoken Arabic of Palestine* 27, *The Archæology of Palestine and the Bible* 32, *The Excavation of Tell Beit Mirsim* 32-43, *The Vocalisation of the Egyptian Syllabic Orthography* 34, *Recent Discoveries in Bible Lands* 36, *From the Stone Age to Christianity* 40, *Archæology and the Religion of Israel* 42, *Archæology of Palestine* 49, *Recent Discoveries in Bible Land,* 56, *The Biblical Period from Abraham to Ezra* 63, *History, Archaeology and Christian Humanism* 64, *The Proto-Sinaitic Inscriptions and their Decipherment* 66, *Yahweh and the Gods of Canaan* 68, Senior Editor *The Anchor Bible* 64.
3401 Greenway, Baltimore, Md. 21218, U.S.A.

Alfozan, Yusuf; Saudi Arabian diplomatist; b. 1913; ed. Bombay and Arabia.
Agent (Personal) to H.M. King Abdulaziz Ibn Saud (Bom-

bay) 38; Saudi Arabian Consul-Gen., Palestine 39-41, Bombay 49-55; Editor *Shubban's Voice* 36-38; Saudi Arabian Minister to India 55-57; Saudi Arabian Ambassador to India 57-65, to Iran 66-68, to Spain 68-.
Saudi Arabian Embassy, Hermanos Bécquer 4, Madrid, Spain.

Ali, Anwar, M.A., F.I.B.A.; Pakistani civil servant; b. 16 Feb. 1913; ed. Islamia Coll., Lahore.
Assistant Financial Adviser and Under-Sec., Ministry of Finance, India 43-47; Dep. Sec. Min. of Finance, Govt. of Pakistan 47-52, Joint Sec. 52-54; Dir. National Bank of Pakistan 49-53; Dir. State Bank of Pakistan 52-54; Dir. Middle Eastern Dept. Int. Monetary Fund, Washington 54-; Gov. Saudi Arabian Monetary Agency 58-; awarded title Sitara-e-Quaid-e-Azam 61 and Sitara-e-Pakistan 67.
Office: Saudi Arabian Monetary Agency, Jeddah; Home: 39 Sharia Ali Ibn Abi Talib, Sharafia, Jeddah, Saudi Arabia.

Ali, Ali Sayed; Egyptian trade union executive; b. 4 July 1925; ed. El Zaher Commercial School, Cairo.
District Sales Man. Nasr Petroleum Co. until 63; petroleum union exec. since 48; Gen. Sec. Arab Fed. of Petroleum, Mining and Chemical Workers 63-; Chair. Workers' Educ. Asscn. 64; mem. Nat. Assembly until 71; Minister of State June 64; ILO Expert on Workers' Educ.
The Arab Federation of Petroleum, Mines and Chemicals Workers, 5 Zaki Street, Tewfikia, Cairo, Egypt.

Ali, Salem Rubia; Yemeni politician; b. 1934 Southern Arabia; ed. in Aden.
Formerly school-teacher and in private law practice; participated in activities of Nat. Front for the Liberation of Occupied Southern Yemen (FLOSY) 63-67; mem. Gen. Command of NLF Nov. 67; in exile 68-69; Chair. Presidential Council June 69-; Pres. Supreme Commdr. of the Armed Forces.
Presidential Council, Aden, People's Democratic Republic of Yemen.

Alier, Abdel, LL.B., LL.M.; Sudanese politician; b. 1933, Bor District, Upper Nile Province; ed. Univs. of Khartoum, London, Yale.
Former advocate; District Judge in El Obeid, Wad Medani and Khartoum until 65; participant in Round Table Conf. and mem. Twelve Man Cttee. to Study the Southern problem 65; mem. Constitution Comms. 66-67, 68; fmr. mem. Law Reform Comm. and Southern Front; Minister of Supply and Internal Trade Oct. 69-June 70; Minister of Works June 70-July 71; Minister for Southern Affairs July-Oct. 71; Vice-Pres. Oct. 71-; Pres. High Exec. Council for the Southern Region April 72-; mem. Board of Dirs., Industrial Planning Corpn.; mem. Nat. Scholarship Board.
People's Palace, Khartoum, Sudan.

Alikhani, Ali Naghi; Iranian economist and politician; b. 1928; ed. Alborz Coll., Teheran, Univ. of Teheran and Univ. of Paris.
Former Econ. Adviser to Nat. Iranian Oil Co. and other orgs.; Minister of Economy 63-69; Chancellor, Univ. of Teheran 69-71; private business 71-.
264, 28th Park Avenue-Abbasabad, Teheran, Iran.

Alireza, Sheikh Mohamed Ibn Abdullah; Saudi Arabian merchant and industrialist; b. 1911; ed. Saudi Arabia and India.
Former Pres. Chamber of Commerce and Industries, Jeddah; mem. Admin. Council, Jeddah 46; Ex-Pres. Jeddah Benevolent Water Supply Cttee.; mem. Board of Trustees of the Benevolent Falah School 34; Leader Saudi Arabian del. to the Int. Islamic Econ. Conf., Pakistan 49; Chair. of Jeddah Port Trust Project 50; Minister of Commerce and Industries 54-58; Ambassador to U.A.R. March-June 64; Pres. Haji Abdullah Alireza & Co. Ltd., Haji Abdullah Alireza Libyan Trading Co., Arabian Italian Engineering Contractors S.p.A., Rome, Arabian Petroleum Supply Co. S.A.; now Amb. to France.
Embassy of Saudi Arabia, rue André-Pascal 1, Paris 16e, France.

Allegro, John Marco; British philologist and archaeologist; b. 17 Feb. 1923; ed. Wallington County Grammar School and Univ. of Manchester.
Royal Navy 41-46; Manchester Univ. 47-52; research in Hebrew dialects, Magdalen Coll., Oxford 52-53; British rep. on Int. Editing Team for Dead Sea Scrolls, Jerusalem 53-; Lecturer in Comparative Semitic Philology and Hebrew, Univ. of Manchester 54-62, in Old Testament and Intertestamental Studies 62-70; Adviser to Jordanian Govt. on Dead Sea Scrolls 61-; Trustee and Hon. Sec. Dead Sea Scrolls Fund 62-70.
Publs. *The Dead Sea Scrolls* 56, 64, *The People of the Dead Sea Scrolls* 59, *The Treasure of the Copper Scroll* 60, 64, *Search in the Desert* 64, *The Shapira Affair* 65, *Discoveries in the Judaean Desert* (Vol. 5) 68, *The Sacred Mushroom and the Cross* 70, *The End of a Road* 70, *The Chosen People* 71, *Lost Languages* 74.
Craigmore, Ballasalla, Isle of Man.

Allon, Brig.-Gen. Yigal; Israeli soldier, agriculturalist and politician; b. 10 Oct. 1918, Kfar Tabor, Lower Galilee; ed. Kadourie Agricultural Coll., Oxford, Hebrew Univ., Jerusalem.
Joined Hagana 31, Commdr. of Palmach Company 41, in Syria and Lebanon with Allies, Dep. Commdr. Palmach 43, C.-in-C. Palmach 45-48; charged with Hagana operations in Palestine 45-47; in command, Upper Galilee, Central Israel, Jerusalem Corridor, the Negev and N. Sinai 47-48; fought in War of Independence 48-49; promoted to rank of Maj.-Gen. 48; Minister of Labour 61-67; Minister for Absorption 67-69; Deputy Prime Minister 67-; Minister of Educ. and Culture 69-; mem. Exec. Cttee. Hakibbutz Hameuchad; fmr. Sec.-Gen. Achduth Ha-avodah Socialist Party; mem. 3rd, 4th, 6th and 7th Knessets.
Publs. *The Story of Palmach* 51 (Book of Palmach), *Curtain of Sand* 60, *The Making of Israel's Army* (in English and German) 70, *Shield of David*, and many essays and articles on political, military, education and cultural subjects in Hebrew, Yiddish, Arabic and English.
Deputy Prime Minister's Office, Ministry of Education and Culture, Jerusalem; and Jewish Quarter, Old City, Jerusalem; Home: Kibbutz Genossar, Israel.

Almogi, Major Joseph; Israeli politician; b. 5 May 1910; ed. secondary school.
Came to Palestine 30; mem. Haganah Command 33-39; Prisoner of War, Germany 41-45; Gen. Sec. Labour Council, Haifa 45-59; Gen. Sec. Mapai Party 59-62; Minister of State 61-62; Minister of Housing and Development 62-65; joined Israel Labour List (Rafi Party) 65; Minister of Labour 68-.
Ministry of Labour, Building B no. 2 Kaplan, Hakirya, Jerusalem; Home: 120 Arlozorov Street, Haifa, Israel.

Al-Nakib, Ahmed Abdul Wahab; Kuwaiti diplomatist; b. 30 July 1930, Kuwait; ed. Adam State Univ., Colorado, U.S.A.
First Sec., Kuwait Embassy, London 62-63; mem. first Perm. Mission of Kuwait to UN 63-66; Consul-Gen., Nairobi, Kenya 66-67; Amb. to Pakistan 67-70, to U.K. 71-.
Embassy of Kuwait, 40 Devonshire Street, London, W1N 2AX, England.

Alparslan, Fehmi; Turkish politician; b. 1918, Ardanuç, Artvin Prov.; ed. Faculty of Law, Ankara Univ.
Worked as judge and general prosecutor in several provs.; private practice 49-; Mayor of Artvin (Republican People's Party—RPP) 50; mem. Constituent Assembly 60; Senator

for Artvin 64; joined Nat. Reliance Party, mem. Exec. Cttee. 67; Minister of Justice 72-73.
National Reliance Party, Ankara, Turkey.

Alpert, Carl; Israeli journalist and university official; b. 12 May 1913; ed. Boston Univ., U.S.A.
Editor *The New Palestine* 40-47; Nat. Pres. American Young Judaea 40-41; Nat. Dir. Educ. Dept. Zionist Org. of America 47-52; emigrated to Israel 52; Dir. Public Relations Dept., Technion Israel Inst. of Technology 52-68; Exec. Vice-Chair. Technion Board of Govs. 62-; Nat. Pres. Asscn. of Americans and Canadians in Israel 57-59; author int. syndicated weekly column in 36 newspapers.
Technion Israel Institute of Technology, Technion City, Haifa, Israel.

Amer, Subhi Ameen, M.D.; Jordanian politician; b. 1912; ed. American Univ. of Beirut.
Physician, Transjordan 38-46, Palestine Govt. 47-48; Dir. Govt. Hospital, Nablus 48-53; Chief Physician, Nablus District 53-57; Asst. Under-Sec. to Minister of Health 57-62; Minister of Health five times 62-67; Minister of Health, Reconstruction and Devt. Oct.-Dec. 62, 68-70, of Health June-Sept. 70, of Reconstruction and Devt. Sept. 70-.
Ministry of Reconstruction and Development, Amman, Jordan.

Amin, Mohamed el Amir; Sudanese airways official; b. 1 June 1919; ed. Gordon Memorial Coll., Khartoum.
Attached to Office of Civil Sec. (now Ministry of Interior) 38-48; Chief of Booking and Freight Office, Sudan Airways 48-54, Sales Supt. Sudan Airways 54-66; Gen. Man. Sudan Airways 66-68, 72-; Adviser-Gen. 68-.
Sudan Airways, P.O. Box 253, Khartoum North, Sudan.

Amin, Osman Muhammad, D. ès L.; Egyptian university professor; b. 1905; ed. Saidia School, Giza, and Univs. of Cairo and Paris.
Member Egyptian Univ. Mission, Paris 31-39; Lecturer, Faculty of Arts, Cairo 39; Asst. Prof. Faculty of Arts, Cairo 48; Prof. of Philosophy, Cairo Univ., Cairo 54-56, Head of Dept. 57; Sec. Egyptian Philosophical Society; Pres. Asscn. Muhammad Abduh.
Publs. *L'Humanisme de F. C. S. Schiller* (French) 39, *Muhammad Abduh* (French) 44, *Towards Better Universities* (Arabic) 52, *Philosophical Essays* (Arabic) 53, *The Pioneer of Egyptian Thought* (Arabic) 55, *Descartes* (Arabic), 4th edn. 57, *Lights on Contemporary Moslem Philosophy* (English) 58, *Schiller* (Arabic) 58, *Stoic Philosophy* (Arabic), 2nd edn. 59; Editor: *Les Classiques de la Philosophie* (Arabic) 42, *Les Chefs-d'oeuvre de la Philosophie Occidentale* (Arabic) 46, *Al-Färäbi* (Classification of Sciences) 49, *Ibn Rushd* (Compendium of Metaphysics) 58; translations of Kant and Descartes.
22a Sharia Muhammad Said, Cairo, Egypt.

Amin, Samir, D.ECON.; Egyptian economist; b. 4 Sept. 1931, Cairo; ed. Univ. of Paris.
Senior Economist, Econ. Devt. Org., Cairo 57-60; Technical Adviser for Planning to Govt. of Mali 60-63; Prof. of Econs., Univs. of Poitiers, Paris and Dakar; Dir. UN African Inst. for Econ. Devt. and Planning 70-.
Publs. *Trois expériences africaines de développement, Mali, Guinée, Ghana* 65, *L'Economie du Maghreb* (2 vols.) 67, *Le développement du capitalisme en Côte d'Ivoire* 68, *Le monde des affaires sénégalais* 68, *Maghreb in the Modern World*, 70, *L'Accumulation à l'échelle mondiale* 70, *L'Afrique de l'Ouest bloquée* 71.
African Institute for Economic Development and Planning, B.P. 3186, Dakar, Senegal.

Amini, Ali, D.ECON. ET IUR.; Iranian politician; b. 1 July 1907; ed. Ecole de Droit, Grenoble, and Faculté de Droit, Paris, France.
Alternative Judge, Court of First Instance, and Penal Branch, Court of Appeal, Teheran 31; Asst. Dir. Opium Admin. Monopoly 33; Asst. Dir. Customs Admin. 34, Dir.-Gen. 36; Economic Dir.-Gen. Ministry of Finance 38, Under-Sec. 40; mem. Chamber of Deputies Teheran and Deputy Prime Minister 40; Iranian rep. Int. Narcotic and Opium Confs. 49 and 50; Minister of Finance 52; led Iranian del. in negotiations with Int. Oil Consortium 54; Minister of Justice 55; Ambassador to U.S.A. 56-58; Prime Minister 61-62.
Publ. *L'institution du monopole de commerce extérieur en Perse.*
Park Aminowleh, Teheran, Iran.

Amir, Rehaveam; Israeli government official; b. 1 Jan. 1916; ed. Hebrew Teachers' Coll., Jerusalem.
Military Gov., Western Galilee 50; joined Ministry of Foreign Affairs 50; Head of Personnel and Asst. Dir.-Gen. Admin. 50-53; Consul-Gen., London 53-58; Minister, Poland 58-63; Adviser on Arab Affairs, Prime Minister's Office 63-65; Dir. Dept. of Educ. and Culture in Diaspora, World Zionist Org. 65-68; Consul-Gen., New York.
56 Hapalnach Street, Jerusalem, Israel.

Amiran-Pougatchov, Emanuel; Israeli composer; b. 1909, Russia.
Arrived in Israel 24; teachers included Yoel Engel and Prof. David Shor (Russia), Prof. S. Rosowsky (Israel), Sir Granville Bantock and Alec Roley (England); co-founder with Prof. Leo Kestenberg of Music Teachers' Seminary, Tel-Aviv; Officer-in-Charge of musical activities Israel Defence Forces 48; Directing Supervisor of Music Educ. in Ministry of Educ. and Culture; Founder and Chair. Les Jeunesses Musicales in Israel; mem. of Board ISME 68-.
Compositions include: *Hashomer* (The Guard) for orchestra, *Evel* (orchestra), *A Symphonic Movement*, *Achrei Moti* (After my death) cantata, *Nachamu Ami* (cantata for mixed choir and orchestra), piano pieces, music for the theatre, and numerous songs which include *Ki Mitsion* (Out of Zion), *Mayim, Mayim* (Water, Water), *Hagez* (Shearing song), *Halleluyah*.
Office: Ministry of Education and Culture, Hadar-Daphna Building, Shderoth Hamelech Shaul, Tel-Aviv; Home: 39 Harav Friedman Street, Tel-Aviv, Israel.

Ammar, Abbas Moustafa, M.A., PH.D.; Egyptian international official; b. 1907; ed. Cairo, Manchester, Cambridge and Columbia Univs.
Asst. Prof. of Social Anthropology and Socio-Economics, Cairo Univ. 42-47; Head of the Petitions Division of the Trusteeship Dept. of UN; Dir.-Gen. Rural Welfare Dept. Ministry of Social Affairs 50-51; Acting Dean Cairo School of Social Work 50-51; Dir. UNESCO Arab States Fundamental Education Centre, Egypt 52; Min. of Social Affairs 52-54; Min. of Education 54; Asst. Dir.-Gen. Int. Labour Organisation 54-64, Deputy Dir.-Gen. 64-; mem. Board of Trustees, Int. Council for Educ. Devt., New York, Higher Cttee. Acad. of Sciences, Egypt.
Publs. Arabic: *Anthropological Study of the Arabs* 46, *Report on Adult Education and People's University for Workers* 47, *Report on Population Situation in Egypt* 53, *Re-organization of the Egyptian Village in a Decentralised Administration* 54; English: *The Peoples of Sharqia: An Anthropo-Socio-Economic Study of the Eastern Province of the Nile Delta* (2 vols.) 46.
2 rue Crespin, 1206 Geneva, Switzerland.
Telephone: 46-03-08.

Ammash, Major-General Saleh Mahdi; Iraqi soldier and politician; ed. Military Coll.
Minister of Defence Feb.-Nov. 63; C.-in-C. Supreme Defence Council of Iraq and Syria Oct.-Nov. 63; Deputy Prime Minister and Minister of the Interior July 68-70; Vice-Pres. 70-71; Amb. to U.S.S.R. Oct. 71-.
Embassy of Iraq, Per Ostrovskogo 8, Moscow, U.S.S.R.

WHO'S WHO IN THE MIDDLE EAST AND NORTH AFRICA

Ammoun, Fouad; Lebanese jurist and politician; b. 26 Nov. 1899; ed. Beirut School of Law and Univ. de Lyon.
President, Court of Appeal and of Cassation, Lebanon 35-42, Attorney-Gen. 42-43; Commr. of Govt. attached to Council of State 43-44; Joined Ministry of Foreign Affairs 44, Legal Expert 44-45, Gen. Sec. 45-56, 60-63; mem. Cttee. drafting Covenant of League of Arab States and numerous int. treaties 44; Minister for Planning and Nat. Economy Feb.-March 64; Minister for Foreign Affairs 64-65; Judge Int. Court of Justice 65-, Vice-Pres. 70-; Chair. Lebanese Nat. Comm. UNESCO 45-55, 60-63 and Cttee. Int. Econ. Relations 60-63; mem. del. to UN seven sessions between 48-63; Dr. h.c. Univ. of Monrovia; Cordon of the Phoenix (Greece).
Publs. several juridical articles, notably a commentary on the *Code Correctionnel Libanais* (with Ph. N. Boulos and W. El Kassar).
The International Court of Justice, The Hague, Netherlands.

Amouzegar, Jamshid, B.C.E., M.S., PH.D.; Iranian politician; b. 25 June 1923; ed. Univs. of Teheran, Cornell, Washington.
United Nations Expert, Mission to Iran 51; Chief, Engineering Dept. 52-55; Deputy Minister of Health 55-58; Minister of Labour 58-59, of Agriculture 59-60; Consulting Engineer 60-64; Minister of Health 64-65, of Finance 65-; Chair. Int. Civil Service Advisory Board of UN.
Tajrish, Teheran, Iran.

Amri, Gen. Hassan al-; Yemeni politician.
Took part in the Revolution against the Imamate 62; Minister of Transport Sept.-Oct. 62, of Communications Oct. 62-April 63; mem. Council of the Revolutionary Command 62-63; Vice-President of Yemen 63-66; mem. Political Bureau 63-66; Prime Minister Jan.-April 65, July 65-Sept. 66; C.-in-C. Yemen Armed Forces 67-71; mem. Presidential Council and Prime Minister April-July 69, Aug.-Sept. 71.
c/o Presidential Council, Sana'a, Yemen Arab Republic.

Amuzegar, Jahangir, PH.D.; Iranian economist and politician; b. 13 Jan. 1920; ed. Univs. of Teheran, Washington and California.
Teaching Asst., Univ. of California, Los Angeles 51-53; Lecturer, Whittier Coll. 53, Univ. of Michigan 53-55; Asst. Prof. Pomona Coll., Claremont, California 55-56; Asst. Prof. Michigan State Univ., E. Lansing, Mich, 56-58; Assoc. Prof. Occidental Coll. and Univ. of Calif., Los Angeles 58-60; Brookings Research Prof. 60-61; Econ. Adviser, Plan Org., Govt. of Iran 56-57; Minister of Commerce, Iran 61-62; mem. Council of Money and Credit 61-62, High Econ. Council 61-62; mem. Board of Dirs. Bank Melli Iran 61-62; Chair. Board, Foreign Trade Co. 61-62; Minister of Finance 62; Chair. High Council of Nat. Iranian Oil Co. 62; Ambassador-at-Large, Chief Iranian Econ. Mission, Washington, D.C. 63-.
Publ. *Technical Assistance in Theory and Practice: The Case of Iran* 66, *Iran: Economic Development under Dualistic Conditions* 71.
Iranian Economic Mission, 5530 Wisconsin Avenue, Chevy Chase, Md. 20015, U.S.A.

Amuzegar, Kuros, M.SC., PH.D.; Iranian politician; b. 15 June 1927, Teheran; ed. Univ. of Teheran and in U.S.A.
Engineering Consultant to Karaj Dam; Technical Consultant to Planning Org.; Under-Sec., Ministry of Devt. and Housing, subsequently Ministry of Labour; mem. Board of Dirs. and Man. Dir. Org. of Social Security; Minister of Devt. and Housing 71-.
Ministry of Development and Housing, Teheran, Iran.

Anderson, James Norman Dalrymple, O.B.E. M.A. LL.D., F.B.A.; British educationalist; b. 29 Sept. 1908; ed. St. Lawrence Coll., Trinity Coll., Cambridge.
Missionary (Egypt GenMission) 32-40; Capt. Liby an Arab Force 40-41; Major (Political Officer for Sanusi Affairs) 41; Lieut.-Col. (Sec. for Arab Affairs, Civil Affairs Branch, G.H.Q., M.E. 43, Political Sec. 43); Col. (Chief Sec., Civil Affairs Branch) 44-45; lectured on Islamic Law in Cambridge 47-50; Lecturer in Islamic Law, School of Oriental and African Studies, Univ. of London 47; Reader in Oriental Laws, Univ. of London 51; Prof. of Oriental Laws Univ. of London 53-; Head of Dept. of Law, School of Oriental and African Studies 53-71; Lecturer in Mohammedan Law, Council of Legal Educ. 53-; Visiting Prof., Princeton Univ. and New York Univ. Law School 58, Harvard Law School 66; Chair. U.K. National Comm. of Comparative Law 58-60; Dir. Inst. of Advanced Legal Studies, Univ. of London 59-; Dean, Faculty of Law, Univ. of London 64-69; Pres. Soc. of Public Teachers of Law 69-70; Chair. House of Laity, Gen. Synod of Church of England 70-; mem. Native Law Advisory Panel 56-, Panel of Advisory Jurists to Northern Nigerian Govt. 58, 62; Vice-Pres. Int. African Law Asscn.; mem. Int. Cttee. of Comparative Law 63-67; Libyan Order of Independence, Class II.
Publs. *The World's Religions* (Gen. Editor) 50, *Islamic Law in Africa* 54, *Islamic Law in the Modern World* 59, *Changing Law in Developing Countries* (Editor) 63, *Family Law in Asia and Africa* (Editor) 68, *Into the World: The need and limits of Christian involvement* 68, *Christianity: the Witness of History* 69, *Christianity and Comparative Religion* 70, *Morality, Law and Grace* 72; contributions on Islamic Law, etc., to various learned journals.
12 Constable Close, London, N.W.11, England.

Aneizi, Dr. Aly Noureddin; Libyan economist and diplomatist; b. 1904, Benghazi; ed. Secondary Agricultural School of Pescia (Tuscany, Italy), Agronomincal Inst. of Florence, Univ. of Naples, Oriental Inst. of Naples and Inst. de Grenoble, Naples.
Secretary, Cyrenaica Govt. 33-35; Dir. "Auqat", Benghazi Prov. 35-41; Councillor, Benghazi Prov. 37-41; fled to Egypt to join nat. movt. for independence of Libya 41-44; Sec. Arab League, Cairo 45-51; mem. Libya House of Reps. 52-55, Vice-Pres.; Finance Minister 53-55; Founder and First Gov. Central Bank of Libya 55-61; Amb. to Lebanon and Jordan 61-62; Petroleum Minister 63-64; Chair. Sahara Bank 64-70, Libya Insurance Co. 64-71, Nat. Navigation Co. May 64-; Pres. Intellectual Soc. of Libya 65-, Libyan Olympic Cttee. 67-69; Highest Libya Independence Decoration 54; High Lebanon and Jordan Decoration 62.
P.O. Box 3760, Tripoli; 2 Kairawan Street, Tripoli, Libya.

Anisimov, Anatoly Vasilyevich; Soviet diplomatist; b. 17 March 1919, Stepanovo Village, Vologda Region; ed. Pokrovsky Pedagogical Inst. of Leningrad.
Attaché, Soviet Embassy, Iran 43-54; First Sec., Dept. for Near East and Middle East Countries, Ministry of Foreign Affairs 54-56; Counsellor, Deputy Head of Dept. for Middle East Countries, Ministry of Foreign Affairs, 56-68, 72-; Amb. to Jordan 68-72; Badge of Honour.
Ministry of Foreign Affairs, Moscow, U.S.S.R.

Ansari, Eng. Abdol Reza; Iranian politician; b. 1923; ed. Karaj Agricultural Coll., Teheran Univ. and U.S.A.
Former Deputy Dir. of Nat. Econ., Ministry of Econ.; Treas. Ministry of Labour; Gov. Khuzistan Province; Minister of the Interior 66-68; Man. Dir. Khuzistan Water and Electricity Authority; founder mem. Melliyun Party; Javid Medal.
Ministry of the Interior, Maidan Ark, Teheran, Iran.

Ansari, Houshang, M.A.; Iranian politician; b. 1928; ed. England, U.S.A. and Japan.
Successively Special Reporter of Int. News Service and Int. News Photos; Press Attaché of Publication and Propaganda Dept. in Japan; Commercial Attaché in Japan,

Econ. Attaché, Tokyo; Chief, Supervisory Comm. of Public Supplies, mem. High Council on Iranian Aviation; Technical Under-Sec., Ministry of Commerce; Special Ambassador in African countries; Amb. to Pakistan and Ceylon 65-66; Minister of Information 66-67; Amb. to U.S.A. 67-69; Minister of Economy 69-.
Ministry of Economy, Maidan Ark, Teheran, Iran.

Anthimos, Mgr.; Cypriot ecclesiastic.
Former Metropolitan of Kitium; Leader of Nat. Front.
c/o Archbishopric of Cyprus, P.O. Box 1130, Nicosia, Cyprus.

Appleton, Most Rev. George, C.M.G., M.B.E., M.A.; British ecclesiastic; b. 20 Feb. 1902, Windsor; ed. County Boys' School, Maidenhead, Selwyn Coll., Cambridge and St. Augustine's Coll., Canterbury.
Ordained deacon 25, priest 26; Curate, Stepney Parish Church 25-27; Missionary in charge S.P.G. Mission, Irrawaddy Delta 27-33; Warden, Coll. of Holy Cross, Rangoon 33-41; Archdeacon of Rangoon 43-46; Dir. of Public Relations, Govt. of Burma 45-46; Vicar of Headstone 47-50; Sec. Conf. of British Missionary Socs. 50-57; Rector of St. Botolph, Aldgate, London 57-62; Archdeacon of London and Canon of St. Paul's Cathedral 62-63; Archbishop of Perth (Australia) 63-69; Anglican Archbishop in Jerusalem 69-.
Publs. *John's Witness to Jesus* 55, *In His Name* 56, *Glad Encounter* 59, *On the Eightfold Path* 61, *Daily Prayer and Praise* 62, *Acts of Devotion* 63, *One Man's Prayers* 67.
St. George's Close, P.O. Box 1248, Jerusalem, Israel; 12 Warwick Square, London, SW1V 2AA, England.

Aqib, Ahmed Abdel Rahman al-, D.MECH.ENG.; Sudanese politician and engineer; b. 1932, Sudri, Kababish; ed. Khartoum Univ. Coll. and Imperial Coll., London.
Trained with English Electric Co. and several Italian and German companies; Technical Man. Sifrian Co. 59-62; Lecturer, Univ. of Khartoum 59, Head, Dept. of Mechanical Engineering 67-69, Dean, Faculty of Engineering 69-71, Prof. 70-; Minister of Industry and Mining 71-72.
c/o Ministry of Industry and Mining, Khartoum, Sudan.

Arafat, Yasser (*pseudonym* of Mohammed Abed Ar'ouf Arafat); Palestinian resistance leader; b. 1929, Jerusalem; ed. Cairo Univ.
Joined League of Palestinian Students 44, mem. Exec. Cttee. 50, Pres. 52-56; formed, with others, Al Fatah movt. 56; engineer in Egypt 56, Kuwait 57-65; Pres. Exec. Cttee. of Palestine Nat. Liberation Movement (Al Fatah) June 68-, now also Pres. Cen. Cttee.; also Chair. Palestinian Nat. Council; Gen. Commdr. Palestinian Revolutionary Forces.
Palestine Liberation Organization, Colombani Street, Off Sadat Street, Dr. Raji Nasr Building, Ras Beirut, Lebanon.

Araji, Ali Muhideen al-; Iraqi civil engineer; b. 9 Aug. 1926; ed. Iraqi primary and secondary schools and Durham Univ., England.
Civil engineer, with Iraq Devt. Board 51-53, Govt. Oil Refineries Admin. (GORA) 53-54, Iraq Petroleum Co. at Kirkuk and Pipeline Stations 54-57; Plant Engineer and Chief Construction Co-ordinator at Dora Refinery, Govt. Oil Refineries Admin. 57-59; Civil and Off-site Engineer Kellogg Int. Corpn., London 59-62; Dir. of Projects, Govt. Oil Refineries Admin. 62-64; Dir.-Gen. Oil Planning and Construction Admin., Ministry of Oil 64-; mem. Iraqi Del. to the Fifth Arab Congress, Cairo 64; attended numerous confs. in connection with major oil projects and refineries.
Oil Planning and Construction Administration, Ministry of Oil, Baghdad, Iraq.

Aram, Abbas; Iranian diplomatist; b. 1906; ed. Teheran and Europe.
Entered diplomatic service 31; Asst. Chief, Third Political Div., Foreign Ministry 43; First Sec. Berne 45; First Sec., Counsellor, and Chargé d'Affaires, Washington 46, 49 and 50; Dir. Fourth Political Div., Foreign Ministry 51; Counsellor, Embassy, Baghdad 53; Chargé d'Affaires and Minister, Washington 53 and 54-56; Dir.-Gen. Political Affairs, Foreign Ministry 58; Ambassador to Japan 58, concurrently to Republic of China; Minister of Foreign Affairs 59-60; Ambassador to Iraq 60-62; Minister of Foreign Affairs 62-67; Ambassador to U.K. 67-69, to People's Repub. of China March 72-.
Imperial Embassy of Iran, Peking, People's Republic of China.

Ardon, Mordechai; Israeli (b. Polish) artist; b. 13 July 1896; ed. Bauhaus, Weimar and Munich Acad. of Fine Arts.
After working in Berlin and teaching in the Itten School of Art, moved to Palestine 33; Principal Bezalel School of Arts 43-52; Adviser on Art to Ministry of Education and Culture, Jerusalem; Israel Prize 63.
Ardon House, Yefoh Nof Quarter, Jerusalem, Israel.

Aref, Lt.-Gen. Abdul-Rahman Mohammed (brother of late Pres. Abdul Salam Aref); Iraqi army officer and politician; b. 1916; ed. Baghdad Military Acad.
Joined Army 36; took part in July 58 Revolution, Chief of Gen. Staff Armoured Corps Dept. 58-61; Commdr. 5th Div. Feb. 63-Nov. 63; assisted in overthrow of Gen. Kassem 63; mem. Regency Council 65; Asst. Chief of Staff Iraqi Armed Forces Dec. 63-64; Acting Chief of Staff 64, Chief of Staff 64-68; Pres. of Iraq April 66-68; also Prime Minister 67.

Arian, Abdullah al-, LL.B., PH.D.; Egyptian diplomatist and lawyer; b. 21 March 1920, Damanhur; ed. Cairo, Harvard and Columbia (N.Y.) Univs.
Assistant District Attorney, Boheirah Province 42-43; Lecturer in Law, Cairo Univ. 43-45, Asst. Prof. of Int. Law and Int. Org., Inst. of Public Admin., Cairo 59-61; Prof. of Int. Law, Div. of Legal Studies, Inst. of Arab Higher Studies, Cairo 59-; Counsellor, Office of Pres. of Egypt 55-56; Counsellor and Legal Adviser, Perm. Mission at UN 57-59; Dir. Dept. of Legal Affairs and Treaties, Ministry of Foreign Affairs 59-68; Amb. and Deputy Perm. Rep. to UN 68-71; Amb. to France 71-; mem. Int. Law Comm. 57-58, 61-65, 66-; del. to numerous UN and OAU confs. and several sessions in UN Gen. Assembly.
Publs. several books and articles on questions of international law and the UN.
Embassy of Egypt, avenue d'Iéna 56, Paris 16e, France.

Ariburun, Gen. Tekin; Turkish politician; b. 1905, Istip, Yugoslavia; ed. Kuleli and Konya Mil. Schools, Harbiye (Mil.) Coll. and War Acad.
Staff Officer in Turkish Air Force; served as first Turkish Air Attaché in Germany, U.S.A.; promoted to rank of Brig.-Gen. 50, Gen. 59; Commdr. Turkish Air Force 59-60, retd.; Senator for Istanbul 64-; Speaker of Senate 70-; Justice Party.
The Senate, Ankara, Turkey.

Arkell, Rev. Anthony John, M.B.E., M.C., D.LITT., F.S.A.; British archaeologist; b. 29 July 1898; ed. Bradfield and Queen's Coll., Oxford.
2nd-Lieut. Royal Flying Corps 16; Flying Off. Royal Air Force 18; Sudan Political Service 20-38; Chief Transport Officer Sudan Govt. 40-44; Commr. for Archæology and Anthropology, Sudan Govt. 38-48; Chair. and Editorial Sec. *Sudan Notes and Records* 46-48; Lecturer in Egyptology, Univ. Coll. London 48-53; Reader in Egyptian Archæology, Univ. of London 53-63; Archæological Adviser to Sudan Govt. 48-54; mem. German Archæological Inst. 53-; British Ennedi Expedition 57.
Publs. *Early Khartoum* 49, *The Old Stone Age in the Anglo-*

Egyptian Sudan 49, *Shaheinab* 53, *History of the Sudan* 55, (2nd edn.) 61, *Wanyanga* 64.
Cuddington, Colam Lane, Little Baddow, Chelmsford, Essex, England.

Armouti, Mohamed Nazzal; Jordanian diplomatist; b. 24 Aug. 1924; ed. Amman Secondary School, Salt Coll.; Univ. of Damascus, and Exeter Univ., England.
Former Sec.-Gen. Ministry of Interior, House of Notables and House of Reps.; fmr. Insp.-Gen. Income Tax Dept.; Legal Adviser to Ministry of Finance; fmr. Gov. of Irbid, Ma'an, Salt, Hebron, Nablus, Kerak and Amman Districts; Under-Sec. Ministry of Interior, then Minister of Interior 64-65; Ambassador to Tunisia, Algeria and Libya 65, to Kuwait 67-70; Chair. Nat. Econ. Devt. Co.; numerous decorations.
c/o National Economic Development Co., P.O. Box 357, Amman, Jordan.

Arslane, Amir Majuid Toufik; Lebanese politician; b. 1905; ed. Beirut.
Minister of Defence 43, 60-64, 69-70, May 72-73; fmr. Minister of Agriculture; Grand Cordon of the Libyan Order of Independence and several foreign decorations.
c/o Ministry of Defence, Beirut, Lebanon.

Arthur, Sir Geoffrey George, K.C.M.G., M.A.; British diplomatist; b. 19 March 1920; ed. Christ Church, Oxford.
War service 40-45; joined H.M. Foreign Service 47, served in Baghdad 48-50, Ankara 50-53, London 53-55, Bonn 56-58, Cairo 59-63; Counsellor, Foreign Office, London 63-67; Amb. to Kuwait 67-68; Asst. Under-Sec. of State, Foreign and Commonwealth Office 68-70; British Political Resident, Bahrain 70-72; Visiting Fellow St. Anthony's Coll., Oxford 72-73; Deputy Under-Sec. of State, FCO 73-.
Foreign and Commonwealth Office, Whitehall, London, S.W.1, England.

Asfia, Safi; Iranian mining engineer and politician; b. 1916; ed. Polytechnic Inst., Ecole des Mines, Paris.
Professor of Economic Geology, Teheran Univ. 39-62; Deputy Dir. Plan Org. 54-61, Man. Dir. 61-68; Minister of State and Deputy Prime Minister 68-70, of Econ. and Devt. 70.
c/o Ministry of Economy, Teheran, Iran.

Asha, Rafik el, M.B.A.; Syrian diplomatist; b. 1910; Damascus; ed. American Univ. of Beirut and New York City Univ.
Former bank official and finance analyst; Prof. of Banking Econs. and Accounting, Baghdad 32-41; joined Syrian Civil Service 41 and served as Deputy Dir.-Gen. of Supplies, Ministry of Supplies, Damascus; Chargé d'Affaires, Cairo 44-45; Acting Consul-Gen., N.Y. 45-47, Consul-Gen. 47-52; First Counsellor, Syrian Embassy, Washington 52, Minister Plenipotentiary June 52, Chargé d'Affaires a.i. Aug. 52; Alternate Gov. Int. Bank for Reconstruction and Devt. 52-55; del. to UN Gen. Assembly 46-60; alternate rep. Security Council 47-48, Acting Perm. Del. 48-51, Chargé d'Affaires, Perm. Del. to UN 53-58; Pres. Trusteeship Council 56-57; Pres. Arab League Council 59; U.A.R. Dep. Perm. Rep. to UN 59-61; Ambassador to Romania 61, to U.S.S.R. 61-62; Sec.-Gen. Ministry of Foreign Affairs 62-64; Syrian Perm. Rep. to UN July 64-65; Senior Financial Adviser to Admin. of UNDP 68-.
c/o UNDP, P.O. Box 2317, Damascus, Syria.

Ashiotis, Costas; Cypriot diplomatist; b. 1908; ed. Pancyprian Gymnasium, Nicosia, and London School of Economics.
Former journalist and editor; Govt. Service 42-; Asst. Commr. of Labour 48; Dir.-Gen. Ministry of Foreign Affairs 60; mem. Cypriot Dels. to UN and Int. Confs.; High Commr. in U.K. 66-; Hon. M.B.E.
Publ. *Labour Conditions in Cyprus During the War Years 1939-45.*
Cyprus High Commission, 93 Park Street, London, W.1, England.

Ashraf Ahmadi, Ali, LL.B.; Iranian judge and politician; b. 1910, Behbahan; ed. High School, Shiraz and Univ. of Teheran.
Chief Magistrate Province of Teheran 47-49; Chief Justice Province of Khoozistan 50; Chief Criminal Court, Teheran 51; Chief Justice, Province of Isfahan 53; Gov. Isfahan 53-55; Judge, Supreme Court 55; Deputy Prime Minister 56-60; Sec. Royal Council 56-61; Minister of State 60-61; Deputy Dir. Pahlavi Foundation 62; Chief 12th Branch Supreme Court 63; Senator 64-; Scientific Order, 1st Class, Taj, 2nd Class, Homayoun, 1st Class.
Publs. *Laws and Justice in Ancient Imperial Iran* 60, *Five Years in the Service of His Majesty the Shahanshah* (2 vols.), *Ten Years' Work and Endeavour*, *12 Years of Efforts for Reconstruction of New Iran*, *Iran in the Past and Present.*
176 Television Avenue, Abbas Abad, Teheran, Iran.

Âşiroğlu, Vahap, L. EN D.; Turkish diplomatist; b. 14 Aug. 1916, Karamursel; ed. Galatasaray Lycée, Istanbul and Faculty of Law, Univ. of Istanbul.
Entered diplomatic service 43; served in Czechoslovakia, Turkish Ministry of Foreign Affairs and Perm. Mission of Turkey at UN 46; Head of Chancery of Turkish Mission to UN 53-59; Minister and Deputy Perm. Rep. to UN 62-65; Amb. to Denmark 65-68, to Indonesia 68-71; Sec.-Gen. Regional Co-operation for Devt. (RCD) May 71-(74); mem. UN Comm. on Human Rights 53-56; Leader, Turkish del. to ICAO Assembly 56; Chair. del., GATT Ministerial meeting, Tokyo 59; Chair. UN Conciliation Comm. for Palestine 62-65.
Regional Co-operation for Development, 5 Los Angeles Avenue, North of Boulevard Elizabeth II, P.O. Box 3273, Teheran, Iran.

Asnag, Abdallah Al-Majid al-; Yemeni trade union official and politician; b. 1933.
Senior Reservation Officer, Aden Airways 51-62; leader, People's Socialist Party, Gen. Sec. Aden Trade Union Congress until Dec. 62, 63-65; imprisoned Dec. 62-Dec. 63; Head of Political Bureau, Front for Liberation of Occupied South Yemen (FLOSY); Minister of Foreign Affairs Aug.-Sept. 71, of the Economy Sept 71-.
Ministry of the Economy, Sana'a, Yemen Arab Republic.

Assaad, Kamel el, L. EN D.; Lebanese politician; b. 1929; ed. Law Faculty, Beirut and Univ. de Paris.
Practising lawyer; Deputy 53-; Mayor of Marjéyoun; Minister of Education 61-64; Pres. Chamber of Deputies 64-65; Speaker 72-; Minister of Water Resources and Health 66.
Hazmieh, Imm. Haddad, Beirut, Lebanon.

Assad, Gen. Hafiz; Syrian army officer and politician; b. 1928.
Minister of Defence and Commdr. of Air Force Feb. 66-Nov. 70; Prime Minister and Sec. Baath Party Nov. 70-; Pres. of Syria Feb. 71-; mem. Pres. Council, Fed. of Arab Repubs. 71-; Pres. Syrian Nat. Progressive Front 72-; Commdr. in Chief of Armed Forces 73-.
Office of the President, Damascus, Syria.

Assar, Nassir; Iranian diplomatist; b. 1926; ed. Univ. of Teheran.
Ministry of Foreign Affairs 45-; Vice-Consul, Stuttgart 49, Hamburg 53; Deputy Dir. Dept. of Int. Org., Ministry of Foreign Affairs 53-55; First Sec. Iranian Embassy to Turkey 56, Counsellor 61; First Sec. Iranian Mission to UN 58, Counsellor 59; Deputy Dir. Dept. of Econ. Affairs, Ministry of Foreign Affairs 60; Deputy Prime Minister, Head of Iranian Public Trust and Endowments 64; Sec.-Gen. Central Treaty Org. (CENTO) 72-.
c/o CENTO, Eski Büyük Millet Meclisi Binasi, Ankara, Turkey.

Atalla, Anton Abden-Nur; Jordanian lawyer, banker and politician; b. 18 Oct. 1897; ed. American Univ. of Beirut and Law School, Jerusalem.

Crown Counsel 24-27, Magistrate 28-31; Senior Magistrate 32-37, Judge of District Court, Palestine 37-43; Senior Partner A. & H. Atalla and Co., Advocates, Jerusalem 43-48; Regional Gen. Manager, Arab Land Bank, Jordan 48-63, 64-, Dep. Gen. Manager 60-63, 64; mem. Jordan House of Reps.; Chair. House Finance Cttee. 54-56; Minister of Foreign Affairs 63-July 64; mem. Senate 63-; Minister of Foreign Affairs June-Oct. 70; Gov. Rotary Int. District, East Mediterranean 66-67; Jordanian Star, First Degree; several foreign decorations.
Arab Land Bank, P.O. Box 6425, Amman, Jordan.

Atassi, Nureddin, M.D.; Syrian politician; b. 1929; ed. Damascus Univ.
Minister of the Interior Aug. 63; Deputy Prime Minister Oct. 64; mem. Syrian Presidential Council May 64-Dec. 65; Pres. of Syria 66-70, also Prime Minister 68-70; Sec.-Gen. Syrian Baath Party 66-Oct. 70; in exile in Libya.

Ateeqy, Abdulreham Salim al-; Kuwaiti diplomatist and politician; b. 5 April 1928; ed. High School, Kuwait.
Secretary-General, Police Dept., Kuwait 49-59; Dir.-Gen. Health Dept. 59-61; Del. to UN 60-61, to WHO, Geneva 61, to UN Gen. Assembly 61; Amb. to U.S.A. 62-63; Under-Sec. Ministry of Foreign Affairs 63-67; Minister of Finance and Oil 67-; Chair. Kuwait Fund for Arab Econ. Devt.
Ministry of Finance and Oil, P.O. Box Safat 9, Kuwait.

Atiya, Aziz Suryal, M.A., PH.D., LITT.D., F.R.HIST.S.; Egyptian historian and writer; b. 7 July 1898; ed. Univs. of Liverpool and London.
Charles Beard Fellow and Univ. Fellow, Univ. of Liverpool 30-32; History Tutor, School of Oriental Studies, Univ. of London 33-34; Prof. of Medieval and Oriental History, Univ. of Bonn 35-38; Prof. of Medieval History, Cairo Univ. 38-42; Prof. of Medieval History and Chair. of History Dept. Alexandria Univ. 42-54; President Higher Institute of Coptic Studies, Cairo; consultant to Library of Congress, Washington, D.C. 50-51; visiting lecturer U.S. Univs., Univ. of Zurich and Swiss Inst. of Int. Affairs 50-51; Medieval Acad. Visiting Prof. of Islamic Studies, Univ. of Michigan, Ann Arbor 55-56; Luce Prof. of World Christianity, Union Theological Seminary, and Visiting Prof. of History, Columbia Univ., New York 56-57; Visiting Prof. of Arabic and Islamic History, Princeton Univ. 57-58; mem. Inst. for Advanced Study, Princeton 58-59; Senior Prof. Language and History, Center for Intercultural Studies, Utah Univ. 59-; corresp. mem. UNESCO Int. Comm. for the Scientific and Cultural History of Mankind; corresp. mem. Coptic Archaeological Soc.; mem. Medieval Acad. of America, mem. Board of Trustees American Asscn. for Middle East Studies.
Publs. *The Crusade of Nicopolis* 34, *The Crusade in the Later Middle Ages* 38, *Egypt and Aragon—Embassies and Diplomatic Correspondence between 1300 and 1330* 38, *Kitab Qawanin al-Dawawin by Saladin's Wazir ibn Mammati* 43, *History of the Patriarchs of the Holy Church of Alexandria* 48, *Monastery of St. Catherine in Mt. Sinai* 49, *The Mt. Sinai Arabic Microfilms* 54, *Crusade, Commerce and Culture* 62, *The Crusades—Historiography and Bibliography* 62, *History of Eastern Christianity* 68, etc. (all books in either English or Arabic).
8 Sharia Wadi el-Nil, Maadi, near Cairo, Egypt; and 1335 Perry Avenue, Salt Lake City, Utah, U.S.A.

Attar, Mohammed Said al-; Yemeni diplomatist; b. 26 Nov. 1927; ed. Ecole Pratique des Hautes Etudes à la Sorbonne, Inst. d'Etudes de Développement Econ. et Social (I.E.D.E.S.), Univ. de Paris.
Research I.E.D.E.S. 60-62; Dir.-Gen. Yemen Bank for Reconstruction and Devt. 62-65; Minister of Econ. March-Aug. 65; Pres. Econ. Comm. Oct. 65-Feb. 66; Pres. Board Yemen Bank and Pres. of Econ. High Comm. March 66-; Minister of Foreign Affairs Nov. 67-69; Vice-Pres. High Cttee. for Planning; mem. Int. Asscn. of Sociology; Perm. Rep. to the UN 69-71; Deputy Premier for Financial Affairs, Minister of the Economy Aug.-Sept. 71; Amb. to U.K. 73-.
Publs. *L'Industrie du gant en France* 61, *L'épicerie à Paris* 61, *Etude sur la croissance économique de l'Afrique Occidentale* 62, *Le marché industriel et les projets de l'Arabie Séoudite* 62, *Le sous-développement économique et social du Yemen (Perspectives de la Révolution Yemenite)* 64, Arabic edn. 65.
Embassy of Yemen Arab Republic, 41 South Street, London, W17 5PD, England.

Attiga, Ali Ahmed, B.SC., M.SC., PH.D.; Libyan economist; b. Oct. 1931, Misurata; ed. Univ. of Wisconsin and Univ. of California, U.S.A.
Assistant Economic Adviser, Nat. Bank of Libya 59-60, Dir. of Research 60-64; Under-Sec. Ministry of Planning and Devt. 64-66, Dir. Econ. Research Div. 66-68; Minister of Planning and Devt. 68-69, concurrently of the Economy 69; Gen. Man. Libya Insurance Co. 70-, Chair. 73-; Chair. Nat. Investment Co. 71-73, Libya Hotel and Tourism Co. 71-; mem. Board of Dirs., Arab Reinsurance Co., Beirut.
P.O. Box 3717, Tripoli, Libya.

Attiyia, Mahmoud Ibrahim, B.SC.; Egyptian geologist; b. 1900; ed. Cairo and Imperial Coll. of Science and Technology, London.
Assistant Lecturer, School of Engineering, Giza 23-25; Geologist, Geological Survey of Egypt 29, Asst. Dir. 39, Dir. 49; Dir.-Gen. Mines and Quarries Dept. 54-56; Tech. Dir. Mineral Wealth Co. and Sinai Manganese Co., Cairo 56-; delegated Prof. of Geology, Cairo Univ.; A.R.C.S. London 29; F.G.S. London 30; mem. Inst. d'Egypte 46; mem. of the Board, Desert Inst. of Egypt 50; mem. Egyptian Acad. of Sciences 50; mem. Conseil d'Administration de la Société de Géographie d'Egypte 51; State Prize in Geological and Chemical Sciences; Order of the Republic (Egypt).
Publs. *Notes on the Underground Water in Egypt* 42, *The Barramiya Mining District* 48, *New Mode of Occurrence of Iron-Ore Deposits* 49, *Iron-Ore Deposits of Egypt* 50, *Ground-Water in Egypt* 53, *Deposits in the Nile Valley and the Delta* 54, *Iron-Ore Deposits of the District East of Aswan* 55.
13 Sharia el-Malek el-Mozaffar, Geziret el-Rada, Cairo, Egypt.

Aulaqi, Sheikh Mohamed Farid al-; see Farid al-Aulaqi.

Avci, Sabit Osman; Turkish politician; b. 1921, Vesir, Artvin Prov.
Head of several depts. of Forestry Operational Management, Artvin; studied forestry related subjects in U.S.A. 53; Deputy for Artvin 61-; Minister of Rural Affairs 65, of Forestry 69, of Power and Natural Resources 69-70; Speaker of Nat. Assembly 70-; Vice-Chair. Justice Party in Nat. Assembly 67; Justice Party.
National Assembly, Ankara, Turkey.

Avidar, Brig.-Gen. Yosef; Israeli soldier and diplomatist, b. 7 May 1906, Keremenitz, Poland.
Came to Palestine 25; with Hagana from 25; mem. Chief Command 37-48; Dir. Mil. Industry 45-46; Deputy Chief, Gen. Staff 46-47, Quartermaster-Gen. I.D.F. 48-49; Brig.-Gen. Commdr. Northern Command 49-52; Commdr. Central Command 52-53; Head, Gen. Staff 54-55; Amb. to U.S.S.R. 55-58; Dir.-Gen. Ministry of Labour 59-60; Amb. to Argentina 61-65; Dir. Govt. Corpns. Authority 66-68; Comptroller of Histadrut 68-71.
5 Mevo Yoram, Jerusalem, Israel.

Avidom (Mahler-Kalkstein), Menahem, B.A.; Israeli composer; b. 6 Jan. 1908; ed. American Univ. Beirut, and in Paris.
Lecturer on theory of music, Hebrew Conservatoire of

Music, Tel-Aviv 36-, and Music Teachers' Training Coll. Tel-Aviv 45-; Sec.-Gen. Israel Philharmonic Orchestra 46-; Vice-Pres. Board of Dirs. Acum Ltd. (Composers and Authors Asscn.), Dir.-Gen. 56-; Dir. Arts Dept. Jerusalem Convention Centre 52; Pres. League of Composers 58-; mem. Nat. Arts Council 62-; mem. Board of Dirs., Artistic Cttee. Israel Festival; recipient of the Israel State Prize in Arts 61, and many other awards for music.
Compositions include: *A Folk Symphony* 47, *Symphony No. 2 David* 48, *Mediterranean Sinfonietta* 51, 2 Piano Sonatinas 49, *Concertino* for violinist Jascha Heifetz, *Concertino* for cellist Gregor Piatigorsky 51, *Alexandra Hashmonaith* (opera in 3 acts) 52, *Jubilee Suite, Triptyque Symphonique, The Crook* (opera in 2 acts) 65, *B-A-C-H Suite* for chamber orchestra, *Sinfonietta* 66, *Twelve Changing Preludes* for piano 68, *Symphonie Variée* for chamber orchestra 69, *The Farewell* (opera in 1 act) 70, *The Independence-Night Dream* (opera in 2 acts) 72, concerto for strings and flute, music for strings, symphonies 3, 4, 5, 6 and 7, psalms and cantatas, septet for woodwind, piano and percussion, string quartet No. 2, quartet for brass instruments, *The Pearl and The Coral* (ballet) 72, *Spring* overture for symphony orchestra 73, *Six Inventions* for piano 73.
30 Semadar Street, Ramat-Gan, Israel.

Avinoam (Grossman), Reuben, B.A.; Israeli writer and educationalist; b. 12 Aug. 1905; ed. New York Univ.
Lecturer in English, Herzlia Hebrew Coll., Tel Aviv 29, Head of Dept. of English 46-49; mem. Exec. P.E.N. Centre in Israel 42-56; del. of Hebrew P.E.N. to Int. P.E.N. Congress, Zürich 47, Venice 49, Dublin 53; Inspector-Gen. of English Studies, Department of Education, Ministry of Education and Culture 50-52, Editor-in-Chief all literary publications in memory of heroes of Israel's War of Liberation (by special appt. of Ministry of Defence) 52-; mem. Exec. of Hebrew Writers' Asscn. 53-56, 60-64.
Publs. *Avbaa Iyim (Four Islands), Av Ubito (Father and Daughter)* 34, Poetry: *Shirim* 31, *Idiliyoth (Idylls)* 34, *Aley Dvai (Leaves of Woe)* 48, *Shirath Enayim Velevav (Song of Eyes and Heart)* 49, *Hebrew Anthology of English Verse* 44, *Hebrew Anthology of American Verse* 53, *Hebrew-English Dictionary, Collected Poems (1930-50)* 50, *Hebrew Anthology of English Verse* (revised and complete edn.) (Tchernichowsky Prize for Model Translations 58) 56, *A Tree I Planted* (poems) 58, *Images of Yore* 64, *Along My Lanes (Poems 1950-1970)* 71; Editor of anthology of works of heroes of Israeli War at request of Prime Minister, 4 vols. 52, 58, 61, 70 and of abridged English edn. *Such Were Our Fighters* 65; Co-editor of Shakespeare's Tragedies in Hebrew and translator of three thereof 59; editor of series of booklets for youth; many translations of English works into Hebrew.
103 Rothschild Boulevard, Tel-Aviv, Israel.

Avni, Tzvi; Israeli composer; b. 2 Sept. 1927, Germany.
Arrived in Israel as a child; studied with Abel Ehrlich, Paul Ben-Haim and Mordecai Seter, Tel-Aviv Acad. of Music, with Aaron Copland and Lukas Foss at Tanglewood, Mass., and electronic music at Columbia Univ.
Compositions include: *Songs for Soprano and Orchestra* 57, *Woodwind Quintet* 59, *Prayer* for string orchestra 61, *Summer Strings* for string quartet 62, *Chaconne for Harp* 62, *Capriccio* for orchestra 63, *Vocalise* (electronic music) 64, *Two Pieces for Four Clarinets* 65, *Meditations on a Drama* for chamber orchestra 66 (ACUM Prize), *Collage* for Mezzo Soprano, Fl., Perc. and electronic tape 67, *Yerushalayim Shel Ma'ala* for mixed choir and orchestra 68, *Churban Habayit* for mixed choir and orchestra 68, *Five Pantomimes* for eight players 68, *Akeda* for chamber groups and narrator 69, *String Quartet No. 2* (Liberson Prize 69), *Requiem for Sounds* (ballet music), *Ein Der* (ballet music) 70, *Holiday Metaphors* for symphony orchestra 70, *All the King's Women* (ballet music) 71, *By the Waters of Babylon* (prelude for small orchestra) 71.
Office: Central Music Library, Huberman Street, Tel-Aviv; Home: 7 Zangwill Street, Tel-Aviv, Israel.

Avriel, Ehud; Israeli diplomatist; b. 19 Oct. 1917; ed. High School Vienna.
Israeli Minister to Czechoslovakia 48, concurrently to Hungary 49; Minister to Romania 50; Dir.-Gen. Prime Minister's Office, Jerusalem 51-57; Ambassador to Ghana and to Liberia 57-60; Ambassador to Congo 60-61; Dep. Dir.-Gen. Ministry of Foreign Affairs 61-65; Ambassador to Italy Feb. 66-68, concurrently accred. to Malta May 66-68; elected Chair. World Zionist Action Cttee., Jerusalem 69-; mem. Knesset 55.
Jewish Agency for Israel, P.O. Box 92, Jerusalem; and Neoth Mordechai, Hagalil Haelyon, Israel.

Awadallah, Babikir; Sudanese jurist; b. 1917; ed. School of Law, Gordon Coll., Khartoum.
District Judge, El Obeid; resigned to become Speaker of Sudanese House of Representatives 54-57; Judge of the Supreme Court 57, Chief Justice Oct. 64-May 67; Prime Minister and Minister of Foreign Affairs May-Oct. 69; Minister of Foreign Affairs 69-70, of Justice 69-71; First Vice-Pres. of Sudan Oct. 71-May 72.
c/o Sudanese Socialist Union, Khartoum, Sudan.

Ayari, Chedly, L. EN D.; Tunisian economist and politician; b. 24 Aug. 1933.
Head of Admin., Tunisian Banking Soc. 58-59; Asst., Faculty of Law and Political and Econ. Sciences, Univ. of Tunis 59-60, Dean 65-67; Econ. Adviser, Perm. Mission to UN 60-64; Exec. Dir. Int. Bank for Reconstruction and Devt. (IBRD), Int. Devt. Asscn. (IDA), Int. Finance Corpn. (IFC) 64-65; Dir. *Ceres* (FAO journal) 67-69; Sec. of State in charge of the Nat. Plan 69-70; Minister of Educ., Youth and Sport 70-71; Amb. to Belgium and Luxembourg Feb.-March 72; Minister of the Nat. Economy March 72-; Pres. UN Industrial Cttee. 62; del. to UN Confs. on Commerce and Devt. 62, 64; Grand Cordon, Order of the Repub.
Publs. Numerous articles in economic journals.
Ministère de l'Economie Nationale, Tunis; and 4 rue Manilius, Le Kram, Tunisia.

Aybar, Mehmet Ali, LL.D.; Turkish politician; b. 1910, Istanbul; ed. Lycée of Galatasaray and Univ. of Istanbul, Faculty of Law, Paris.
Assistant Prof. Int. Law, Univ. of Istanbul; practised as barrister; Judge, Bertrand Russell Tribunal; Leader, Türkiye İşçi Partisi (Turkish Workers' Party) 62-69; Deputy for Istanbul 65-.
Publs. studies on the philosophy of law, lectures on international law; *Bağımsızlık, Demokrasi, Sosyalizm* (political writings and speeches) 45-67, *12 Mart'tan Sonra* (political speeches) 73.
Güneş Sokak 23/6, Kavaklidere, Ankara, Turkey.

Ayyoubi, Mahmoud; Syrian politician; b. 1932.
Former Dir.-Gen. for Admin. Affairs, Euphrates Dept.; Minister of Educ. 69-71, and Deputy Prime Minister 70-71; Vice-Pres. of Syria April 71-; Prime Minister 73-.
Office of the Vice-President, Damascus, Syria.

Azkoul, Karim, PH.D.; Lebanese former diplomatist; b. 15 July 1915; ed. Jesuit Univ. of St. Joseph, Beirut, and Univs. of Paris, Berlin, Bonn and Munich.
Professor of History, Arab and French literature, and Philosophy in various colls. in Lebanon 39-46; Dir. of an Arabic publishing house and of a monthly Arabic review, *The Arab World*, in Beirut 43-45; mem. of the Lebanese del. to UN 47-50; Acting Perm. Del. to UN 50-53; Head of UN Affairs Dept., Ministry for Foreign Affairs 53-57; Head of the Permanent Delegation of Lebanon to UN 57-59;

Consul-General in Australia and N.Z. 59-61; Amb. to Ghana, Guinea and Mali 61-64, to Iran and Afghanistan 64-66; Prof. of Philosophy, Beirut Coll. for Women 68-72, Lebanese Univ. 70-72; mem. Emergency World Council, PEN Club of Lebanon; Order of Cedar (Lebanon), Order of Holy Sepulchre (Jerusalem), Order of St. Marc (Alexandria), Order of the Brilliant Star (Republic of China), Order of Southern Star (Brazil), Order of St. Peter and Paul (Damascus).
Publs. *Reason and Faith in Islam* (in German) 38, and a similar work in Arabic 46, *A Study on Freedom of Association* (French, English, Russian, Spanish) 68; transl. *Consciencism* (Nkrumah) 64; *Arabic Thought in the Liberal Age of Albert Hourani* 69.
Al-Sanayeh Spears Street, Union Building, Beirut, Lebanon.
Telephone: 233250.

B

Baalbaki, Leila Ali; Lebanese novelist; b. 1936; ed. Univ. Saint Joseph, Beirut.
Publs. (novels) *Je Vis, Les Dieux Monstres, Un Bâteau de Tendresse pour la Lune.*
rue Amir Amran, Imm. Tousbahgi, Beirut, Lebanon.

Babikian, Khatchik Diran; Lebanese politician; b. 1924. Cyprus; ed. Collège Italien Beirut, Faculté Française de Droit Beirut, Faculté de Paris, Univ. of London.
Barrister; Deputy for Beirut 57, 60, 64, 68, 72; mem. Parl. Comm. on Justice; Pres. Traffic Comm., Parl. Comm. on Planning, Lebanese Management Asscn. 72; Minister for Admin. Reform 60-61; Minister of Public Health 68-69; Minister of Tourism 69-70, of Information 72-73, of Planning 73.
Ministère du Plan, Beirut; Home: Rue Abrine Achrafié, Beirut, Lebanon.

Bachi, Roberto; Israeli statistician; b. 16 Jan. 1909; ed. Univ. degli Studi, Rome.
Professor of Statistics in Italian universities including Palermo 36, Genoa 37; Prof. of Statistics and Demography, Hebrew Univ. of Jerusalem 45-, Head of Dept. of Statistics 47-60, Dean Faculty of Social Sciences 53-54, Pro-Rector 59-60; planned Central Bureau of Statistics, State of Israel; Govt. Statistician and Scientific Dir. Central Bureau of Statistics 48-71; Fellow, American Statistical Soc., Israel Acad. of Sciences and Humanities; mem. Int. Statistical Inst. and of many int. and nat. learned socs; Szold Prize 67, Bublick Prize (Hebrew Univ.) 72.
Publs. *Mobility of Population in the Large European Towns* (Italian) 32, then about 160 papers and books in English, Italian, Hebrew, French and Spanish on statistical method, demography, health, social and geographical statistics; *Graphical Rational Patterns: a New Approach to Graphical Presentation of Statistics* 68.
Chovevey Zion Street, 19 Jerusalem, Israel.

Badeau, John Stothoff, B.SC., S.T.M., D.D., LL.D.; American educationalist; b. 24 Feb. 1903; ed. Union, Rutgers and Columbia Univs. and Union Theological Seminary.
Prof. of Philosophy, and Dean Faculty of Arts and Sciences, American Univ. at Cairo 36; Regional Chief, Middle East, O.W.I. 43; Pres. American Univ. at Cairo 45-53; Pres. Near East Foundation 53-61; Ambassador to United Arab Republic 61-64; Dir. Middle East Inst., Columbia Univ., New York City 64-67, Emer. Prof. 71-; Lecturer, School of Foreign Service, Georgetown Univ.; Special Consultant, Dept. of Health, Education and Welfare; Trustee, American Univ. of Cairo, Union Theological Seminary, Near East Foundation, and Middle East Inst., Washington, D.C., American Research Centre in Egypt.

Publs. *East and West of Suez* 43, *Emergence of Modern Egypt* 53, *The Lands Between* 57, *The American Approach to the Arab World* 68.
Middle East Institute, Columbia University, New York, N.Y., U.S.A.

Baghdady, Abdel Latif; Egyptian politician; b. 1917; ed. Mansoura School, Cairo and Military Coll., Cairo.
Military and air force instructor and sometime Commdr. Cairo/West Nile Aerodrome; Minister of War 53-54; Minister of Municipal and Rural Affairs 54-57; fmr. Vice-Pres. U.A.R.; Minister of Planning U.A.R. 58-62, in charge of Production and concurrently Minister of Treasury 61-62; mem. Presidency Council 62-64; under house arrest 64.
6 Sharia El Oroba, Heliopolis, Cairo, Egypt.

Baghdady, Hassan; Egyptian horticulturalist and politician; b. 1909; ed. Higher School of Agriculture, Giza and Univ. of California.
Professor of Horticulture, Univ. of Alexandria 41-58; Under-Sec. Ministry of Supply 58-59; Minister of Land Reform, Egyptian Region, U.A.R. 59-61; Rector Univ. of Alexandria.
Publs. many books and articles on horticulture.
Alexandria University, Shatby, Alexandria, Egypt.

Bahar, Abdul Aziz al-, B.A.; Kuwaiti businessman; b. 1929; ed. American Univ., Beirut.
Executive, Ministry of Public Works; Dir.-Gen. of Housing Dept. 55-60; Dir.-Gen. Kuwait Fund for Arab Econ. Devt. 61-62; Chair. Commercial Bank of Kuwait, S.A.K. 62-; Chair. Kuwait Nat. Industries 63-65; Dir. Rifbank, Beirut 67; Dir. United Bank of Kuwait 66-; Chair. Kuwait Foreign Trading, Contracting and Investment Co. 65-; Acting Chair. Commercial Bank of Dubai 69-; Dir. Kuwait Chamber of Commerce 64-; Hon. Consul of Costa Rica.
P.O. Box 460, Kuwait City, Kuwait.

Bahnini, Hadj M'Hammed, L. EN D., L. ÈS L.; Moroccan politician; b. 1914, Fez; ed. Lycée Gouraud (now "Lycée Hassan II"), Rabat.
Sec. Royal Palace; Magistrate, Haut Tribunal Chérifien; Instructor, Collège Impérial and Private Tutor to H.R.H. Crown Prince Moulay El Hassan, Prince Moulay Abdallah, Princess Lalla Aïcha and Princess Lalla Malika; Dir. of the Imperial Cabinet 50-51; Del. Judge, Meknès 51; Exiled Dec. 52-July 54; Sec.-Gen. of the Cabinet 55-; Minister of Justice 58-60; Minister of Admin. Affairs 65-70; Minister of Nat. Defence 70-71; Minister of Justice 71; Vice-Premier and Minister of Justice 72; Minister of State Nov. 72-.
Ministry of Justice, Rabat, Morocco.

Bakdash, Khalid; Syrian politician; b. 1912; ed. Damascus Inst. of Law.
Member of Parl. 54-58; Sec.-Gen. Syrian Communist Party; self-imposed exile in East Europe 58-66; returned to Syria April 66; mem. Cen. Cttee., Syrian Nat. Progressive Front 72-.
Ave. Akrad, Damascus, Syria.

Bakir, Anwar, D. EN D.; Egyptian postal executive; b. 24 Nov. 1914; ed. Univs. of Cairo and Paris.
Former Dir. of Int. Services, Egyptian Postal Service; fmr. Dir. of Posts of Egypt, now mem. Admin. Council; mem. Board of Dirs., Egyptian Postal Org.; Sec.-Gen. Arab Postal Union; del. to numerous confs. of APU and int. postal confs.
General Secretariat, Arab Postal Union, 28 rue Adly, Cairo, Egypt.

Bakoush, Abdel Hamid; Libyan politician; b. 1933. Trained in legal practice; Minister of Justice Jan. 64-Oct. 67; Prime Minister and Minister of Justice 67-Sept. 68; imprisoned 71.
c/o Office of the Prime Minister, Tripoli, Libya.

Bakr, Field Marshal Ahmed Hassan: Iraqi army officer and politician; b. 1914; ed. Military Academy.
Army career 36-58; Commdr. First Infantry Brigade 57; Forced to retire from Iraq Army 58; Prime Minister of Iraq Feb. 63 and Nov. 63; Vice-Pres. of Iraq Nov. 63-Jan. 64; Amb. Jan.-Sept. 64; Pres., Prime Minister and C.-in-C. of Armed Forces July 68-; promoted to rank of Field-Marshal 69.
Office of the President, Baghdad, Iraq.

Bakri, Dr. Bashir el-; Sudanese diplomatist; b. 1918; ed. Univs. of Cairo, Oxford and Paris.
Member of many Sudanese dels. to UN and other int. centres; Ambassador to France 57-61, to the Netherlands, Belgium and Spain 59-61, to Nigeria 61-64; Chair. El Nilein Bank 64-.
c/o El Nilein Bank, P.O. Box 466, Khartoum, Sudan.

Bakri-Wahab, Laman, B.A.; Iraqi cultural official; b. 8 Jan. 1929; ed. Fine Arts Inst., Baghdad and Baghdad Univ.
Editor-in-Chief *New Iraq Magazine* 60-61; Supt. Arabic Press Dept., Ministry of Culture and Guidance 63-64; Man. Nat. Symphony Orchestra 64-66; Dir. Nat. Museum of Modern Art 67-; Dir. of Art Exhibitions 69-.
44/2/55 Sulikh, Ahdamia, Baghdad, Iraq.

Balafrej, Ahmed; Moroccan politician; b. 1908; ed. Univs. of Paris and Cairo.
Secretary-General in Istiqlal (Independence) Party 44-; later exiled by French, returned to Morocco 55; Minister of Foreign Affairs 55-58; Prime Minister May-Dec. 58; Ambassador-at-Large 60-61; Dep. Prime Minister June 61; Minister of Foreign Affairs 61-Nov. 63; Personal Rep. of King with rank of Minister 63-June 72.
c/o The Royal Palace, Rabat, Morocco.

Balial, Musa Awad; Sudanese politician; b. 1931, El Fasher; ed Univs. of Khartoum and Pennsylvania.
Director of Admin., Productive Efficiency Centre 65-67; Deputy Gen. Man. Industrial Devt. Corpn. and Sec.-Gen. Higher Council of Public Sector Corpns. 70; Minister of Supply 71-72, of Industry Oct. 72-.
Ministry of Industry, Khartoum, Sudan.

Barakat, Gamal Eddine, LL.B., B.LITT.; Egyptian diplomatist; b. 1921; ed. Cairo Univ., Acad. of Int. Law, The Hague and Oriel Coll., Oxford.
Third Sec., London 50-52; with Political Dept., Ministry of Foreign Affairs 53-55; Consul-Gen. Aleppo 55-58; Counsellor, Washington 58-60; Head of Service Training Dept., Ministry of Foreign Affairs 61-63; mem. Org. of African Unity Expert Cttee., Addis Ababa 63-64; Ambassador to Uganda 64-68, and to Burundi 67-68; Amb. to Finland Oct. 68-; Order of Merit (4th Grade) 58, Order of the Republic (2nd Grade) 64.
Publs. *Status of Aliens in Egypt* 49, *Lectures on Diplomacy and Diplomatic Terminology in Arabic* 62.
Embassy of the Arab Republic of Egypt, Stenbäckinkatu 22, Helsinki, Finland.

Barakat, Ghaleb, B.A.; Jordanian civil servant; b. 1927; ed. American Univ. Beirut.
Teacher, Nat. Coll., Tripoli 49-50, Teachers' Coll., Tripoli 50-52, Asst. Dir. 51-52; Chief Clerk, Jordan Tourist Dept. 52-53, Press Attaché 53-54; Tourist and Press Attaché, Royal Jordan Embassy, Rome 54-60; Dir. of Tourism 60-; Dir. Jordan Pavilion, Brussels Exhbn. 58; Commr.-Gen. Jordan Pavilion, New York World's Fair 64; Pres. Arab Int. Tourist Union 64, 70; Dir.-Gen. Tourism Authority 66-; Dir.-Gen. Ministry of Tourism and Antiquities 68; Minister of Tourism and Antiquities 72-, concurrently of Transport 72; Jordanian, Belgian and Vatican decorations.
Ministry of Tourism and Antiquities, P.O.B. 224, Amman; Home: P.O. Box 9064, Amman, Jordan.

Baramki, Dimitri Constantine, B.A., PH.D.; Jordanian archaeologist; b. 1909; ed. St. George's School, American Univ. of Beirut, Univ. of London.
Teacher, Jerusalem 25-26; Student Inspector of Antiquities, Palestine 27-28, Inspector 29; Senior Archæological Officer 45; Archæological Adviser and Librarian, American School of Oriental Research, Jerusalem 49-51; Curator of Museums 51-; Asst. Prof. of Ancient History, American Univ. of Beirut 51-53, Associate Prof. 53, Prof. 58-; UNESCO Expert in Prehistoric Archaeology, accred. to Libya 64-65; excavated numerous sites in Palestine.
Publs. Numerous articles in the Quarterly of the Dept. of Antiquities, Palestine and in other publications.
American University of Beirut, Beirut, Lebanon.

Barbour, Walworth, A.B.; American diplomatist; b. 4 June 1908; ed. Harvard Univ.
Served Naples 31, Athens 33, Baghdad 36, Sofia 39, Cairo 41, Baghdad and Cairo 42, with American Rep. to exiled Greek and Yugoslav Govts., Cairo 43, Athens 44; Asst. Chief, Div. of Southern European Affairs, Dept. of State, Washington 45, Chief, Div. of Southeast European Affairs 47; Counsellor with rank of Minister, Moscow 49; Dir. Office of Eastern European Affairs 51; Dep. Asst. Sec. of State for European Affairs 53-55; Minister and Dep. Chief of Mission, American Embassy, London 55-61; Ambassador to Israel 61-73.
Department of State, Washington, D.C., U.S.A.

Bargach, M'Hamed, L. ès D.; Moroccan banker and politician; b. 28 June 1928; ed. Lycée Gouraud, Law School, Montpellier, School of Political Science, Paris and Inst. des Études de Droit International, The Hague.
Former Dir.-Gen. Ministry of Nat. Defence; Chargé d'Affaires, Paris; Chef du Cabinet to the Deputy Prime Minister in charge of Econ. Affairs; High Commr. of the Plan for the Formation of Services; Vice-Gov. Banque du Maroc 67-; Minister of Devt. 64, 67, also of Agriculture July 67-69; Chair., Gen. Man. Nat. Bank for Econ. Devt. 69-.
12 place des Alaouites, Rabat, Morocco.

Bar-Ilan, Tuvia, PH.D., B.CH.E.; Israeli chemist and university administrator; b. 28 Dec. 1912; ed. Polytechnic Inst. of Brooklyn and Hebrew Univ., Jerusalem.
Emigrated to Palestine from U.S.A. 23; research worker, Weizmann Inst. of Science, Rehovot 36-43; War Dept. analyst and British army officer 43-46; Commdr. Scientific Corps, Jerusalem area, Israeli Defence Forces 47-48; manufacturer of plastic products 49-66; Dir. Bar-Ilan Univ., Ramat-Gan 58-63; Dir. Bar-Ilan Univ., Extension Div. (Ashkelon, Nathania, Safed and Jordan Valley) 65-; Pres. B'nei-B'rith, Holon 59-62, 63-; Chair. Exec. Cttee. Nat. Religious Party, Holon 63-66; mem. Board of Higher Studies 61-65; Town Councillor, Holon 69-; mem. Cen. Cttee. for Colleges 72-.
Publs. Articles and patents on organic chemistry and plastics.
3 Azar Street, Holon, Israel.

Bar-Lev, Lieut.-Gen. Haim; Israeli soldier; b. 1924, Austria; ed. Mikhev Israel Agricultural School, Columbia Univ. School of Econs. and Admin., U.S.A.
Joined Palmach Units 42; Platoon Commdr., Beith-Ha'Arava 44; Commdr. D Co., Yesreel 45-46; Commdr. Palmach N.C.O.'s course and C.O. Eight Regt., Negev Brigade 47, Operations Officer 48; Commdr. Armoured Units 48; Instructor and later Commdr., Bn. Commdrs. course 49-52; Chief of Staff, Northern Command 52-53; C.O. Givati Brigade 54-55; Dir. G.H.Q. Training Div. 56; Commdr. Armoured Brigade during Sinai campaign; Commdr. Armoured Corps 65-71; made study tour of armoured corps of Western European countries and U.S.A. 61; visited U.S. army installations and the armies of the

Philippines, Japan, Thailand and S. Viet-Nam; Dir. Gen. Staff, Operations Branch 64-66; Deputy Chief of Staff, Israel Defence Forces 67, Chief of Staff 68-72; Minister of Commerce and Industry 72-.
Ministry of Commerce and Industry, Tel-Aviv, Israel.

Barromi, Joel; Israeli (b. Italian) diplomatist; b. 1920; ed. Univ. of Rome Law School and Hebrew Univ., Jerusalem.
Ministry of Foreign Affairs 51-; First Sec. and Counsellor, Buenos Aires, Chargé d'Affaires *a.i.*, Montevideo and Havana 55-61; Deputy Dir. W. European Div., Ministry of Foreign Affairs 61, Dir. Latin American Div. 62-63; Deputy Perm. Rep. to UN 63-69, concurrently Amb. to Haiti Sept. 63-69; Dir. Div. of Cultural and Scientific Relations, Ministry of Foreign Affairs 70-.
Division of Cultural and Scientific Relations, Ministry of Foreign Affairs, Tel-Aviv, Israel.

Bartur, Moshe; Israeli diplomatist; b. 27 Oct. 1919; ed. Germany and Palestine.
Went to Palestine 38; with Jewish Agency 46-48; joined Ministry of Foreign Affairs 48; Perm. Rep., Office of UN, Geneva 61-65; Amb. to Japan 66-71; Senior Adviser to Major int. and Israeli corpns., Ministry of Foreign Affairs 72-.
Ministry of Foreign Affairs, Jerusalem, Israel.

Barzani, Gen. Mustafa; Iraqi politician; b. 1904.
Founder and leader, Kurdish Democratic Party; led revolts in Kurdistan 34, 43, 45, 46; exiled to U.S.S.R. 46-58; returned at invitation of Gen. Kassem 58; led Kurdish rebellion 65 until settlement 70.
Rania Village, Sulaimaniyah Province, Iraq.

Basher, Sayed Taha; Sudanese medical doctor and politician; b. 2 June 1922, Swakin; ed. Gordon Memorial Coll. and Univ. of Khartoum.
Assistant neurologist 54-56; dipl. in psychiatry, London Univ. 56; psychiatric specialist 57-59; Senior psychiatric specialist 59-69; Minister of Labour May 69-70; Minister of Health 70-71; mem. WHO Scientific Advisory Cttee., Exec. Cttee. of the Int. Union for Psychiatry, Sudanese Medical Board, Exec. Cttee. of Psychiatry Soc. of Africa, Sudanese Philosophical Soc. Council and Nat. Vocational Front.
c/o Ministry of Health, Khartoum, Sudan.

Basmaci, Ferid; Turkish banker; b. 13 Feb. 1911, Istanbul; ed. Faculty of Econs. and Commerce, Istanbul.
Treasurer, Türkiye İş Bankası 53-58, Vice-Pres. 58-60, Man. Galata Branch 60-66, Senior Vice-Pres. 66-67, Pres. 67-; Chair. Sınai Yatırım ve Kredi Bankası 67-, Industrial Devt. Bank of Turkey 69-.
Türkiye İş Bankası A.Ş., Ulus, Ankara; Home: Vali Dr. Reşit Caddesi 73, Çanakaya, Ankara, Turkey.

Basri, Meer S.; Iraqi poet, writer and economist; b. 19 Sept. 1911; ed. Baghdad.
Official, Iraqi Ministry for Foreign Affairs; Chief of Section and Acting Dir. of the Protocol; Dir. *The Iraq Directory* 35; Sec., and later Dir., Baghdad Chamber of Commerce 35-45; Controller Commercial Exchange 37-38; Asst. Iraq Commr. Int. Paris Exhbn. 37; Editor *Chamber of Commerce Journal* 38-45; del. Int. Business Conf., Rye, N.Y. 44; Dir. Eastern Commercial Corpn. Ltd. 45-49; mem. Iraqi PEN Club; mem. Gen. Council and Admin. Council, Baghdad; Dir. of Information, Date Asscn. of Iraq 47; Fellow, Royal Asiatic Soc., London 50; Dir. of various companies 53-.
Publs. *Essays on Iraqi Economy* (Arabic) 48, *Echoes of the Lyre* (poetry), *Men and Shadows* (short stories), *Dictionary of Economic Terms and Theories* (Arabic, English and French), *Travels of Nijeholt* (trans.), *Role of Arab Men of Letters* 69, *Leaders of Thought in Modern Iraq*; poetry, short stories, literary criticism, etc.
18 Aslami Street, Saadoun, Baghdad, Iraq.

Bayani, Mehdi, PH.D.; Iranian librarian; b. 1906; ed. Univ. of Teheran.
Librarian, Nat. Teachers' Coll., and Lecturer, Faculty of Literature, Teheran Univ. 33; Head of Education Dept., Ispahan Province 40; Special Inspector and Asst. Dir. of Education Dept., Ministry of Art and Industry 41; Dir. Nat. Library of Teheran 42; Dir. of Imperial Library 57-; Dir.-Gen. The Nat. Library 57; Prof. Nat. Teachers' Coll. 61-; Prof. Faculty of Art 63-.
Editor: *Nimuneh-Sukhan-i-Farsi* 38, *Rahnemaye Ganjineh Koran* 48, *Specimens of Fine Writing from the National Library*, Teheran 48, *Specimens of Fine Writing from the Imperial Library of Iran* 51, *Ahval va Athare mir Emad* 52, *Khochnevissan* (vol. 1) 66.
Publs. *Three Essays of Sheikh Shahabod-din Suhrawardi* 38-40; *Essay Sawanih-fel-Eshq Ahmad Ghazzali* 43; *Badaya ol-Azman* (Tarikhe Afzal) 47.
Imperial Library, Qolestan Palace, Teheran, Iran.

Bayar, Celal; Turkish politician; b. 1883.
Minister of Nat. Economy 21; Minister of Reconstruction and Settlement (when Turkish and Greek populations were exchanged in accordance with Treaty of Lausanne) 23; founded İş Bank 24; Minister of Nat. Economy 32; Prime Minister 37-39; Vice-Pres. Republican People's Party during Presidency of Kemal Atatürk; undertook leadership of new Democratic Party founded 46; Pres. of the Republic May 50-60; arrested and detained May 60; death sentence passed and changed to life imprisonment 61; released Nov. 64; pardoned 66.
Ankara, Turkey.

Bayoomi, Husain Aly; Yemeni politician.
Former Minister of State, Aden Govt.; Minister of Civil Aviation and Acting Minister of Agriculture, Federal Govt. 65-66; Minister of Nat. Guidance and Information 66-67; nominated to form first Govt. of South Arabian Fed., but withdrew from task 67; Gen. Sec. United Nat. Party.
As Shaab, People's Democratic Republic of Yemen.

Bayramoğlu, Fuat; Turkish diplomatist; b. 1912; ed. School of Political and Administrative Sciences, Istanbul, and Univ. of Liège.
Entered Diplomatic Service 39; mem. Gen. Directorate of Press and Publication Cttee. 43; Head of Secretariat Prime Minister's Office 44-46; Chair. Press Dept. Cttee. 46; Dir. in Foreign Ministry 48; Consul, Cyprus 49; Consul Gen., Jerusalem 51-53; Dir.-Gen. Consular and Claims Dept., Ministry of Foreign Affairs, Ankara 53-57; Ambassador to Norway 57-59, to Iraq 59-60, to Iran 60-62, to Italy 62-63; Sec.-Gen. Ministry of Foreign Affairs 63-64; Ambassador to Belgium 64-67, to Italy 67-69, to U.S.S.R. 69-71; Chair. Inspection Corps, Ministry of Foreign Affairs 71.-72; Sec.-Gen. to the Pres. of Turkey 72-.
Presidential Palace, Ankara, Turkey.

Bayülken, Ümit Halûk; Turkish diplomatist; b. July 1921; ed. Ankara Univ.
Joined Ministry of Foreign Affairs 44, served Frankfurt, Bonn, Dir. Middle East Section 51-53; Political Adviser to UN Del. 53-59; mem. Turkish Del. to Cyprus Joint Cttee., London 59-60; Dir.-Gen. Policy Planning Group, Ministry of Foreign Affairs 60-63, appointed Minister Plenipotentiary; Asst. Sec.-Gen. for Political Affairs 63-64; Sec.-Gen. Ministry of Foreign Affairs 64-66; Ambassador to U.K. 66-69; Perm. Rep. to UN 69-71; Minister of Foreign Affairs Dec. 71-; Head of several overseas dels. since 52, Orden Isobel la Católica, German Grand Cross of Merit, Hon. G.C.V.O. 67.
Publs. several papers on the Cyprus question.
Ministry of Foreign Affairs, Ankara, Turkey.

Beaumont, Sir Richard Ashton, K.C.M.G., O.B.E.; British diplomatist; b. 29 Dec. 1912; ed. Repton Coll. and Oriel Coll., Oxford.
Entered Consular Service 36, served Beirut 36, Damascus

38; war service 41-44; joined Foreign Office 45, served Mosul 46-47; Chargé d'Affaires, Damascus 47-48; Consul-Gen., Jerusalem 48-49, Caracas 50-53, Baghdad 53-58; Imperial Defence Coll. 58-59; Head of Arabian Dept., Foreign Office 59-61; Amb. to Morocco 61-65; Amb. to Iraq 65-67, to Egypt (fmrly. U.A.R.) 69-73; Dir.-Gen. Middle East Asscn. 73-.
Middle East Association, 33 Bury Street, London S.W.1, England.

Becker, Aharon; Israeli labour leader; b. 28 Dec. 1906; ed. secondary school.
Came to Palestine 24; Sec. Histadrut, Ramat Gan 29-32; Sec. Textile Workers Union 33-34; mem. Exec. Labour Council, Tel-Aviv 34-43; Man. Dir. Industrial Dept. Co-op. Wholesale Soc. 43-47; Head, Supply Mission, Ministry of Defence 48-49; Chair. Histadrut Trade Union Dept. 49-61, Sec.-Gen. of Histadrut 61-69; mem. Labour Party Secretariat, Governing Body of ILO, Bank of Israel, Knesset, Exec. Cttee. Histadrut.
Publs. numerous articles and booklets on economic and labour problems.
66 Keren Kayemet Boulevard, Tel-Aviv, Israel.

Bedjaoui, Mohammed; Algerian politician; b. 21 Sept. 1929; ed. Univ. of Grenoble and Institut d'Etudes Politiques, Grenoble.
Lawyer, Court of Appeal, Grenoble 51; research worker at Centre National de la Recherche Scientifique (C.N.R.S.), Paris 55; Legal Counsellor of the Arab League in Geneva 59-62; Legal Counsellor Provisional Republican Govt. of Algeria in Exile 58-61; Dir. Office of the Pres. of Nat. Constituent Assembly 62; mem. Del. to UN 62; Sec.-Gen. Council of Ministers, Algiers 62-63; Pres. Soc. Nat. des chemins de fer algériens (S.N.C.F.A.) 64; Dean of the Faculty of Law, Algiers Univ. 64-; Minister of Justice and Keeper of the Seals 64-70; mem., special reporter, Comm. on Int. Law, UN 65-; Amb. to France 70-; Perm. Rep. to UNESCO 71-; Carnegie Endowment for Int. Peace 56; Ordre du Mérite Alaouite, Morocco; Order of the Repub., Egypt.
Publs. *International Civil Service* 56, *Fonction publique internationale et influences nationales* 58, *La révolution algérienne et le droit* 61, *Succession d'états* 70.
Embassy of Algeria, rue Hamelin 18, Paris 16e, France; and 39 rue des Pins, Hydra, Algiers, Algeria.

Bedri, Abdul-Kader el; Libyan politician.
Minister of Housing and State Property until July 67; Prime Minister July-Oct. 67; sentenced to imprisonment for treason.
c/o Office of the Prime Minister, Tripoli, Libya.

Begin, Menachem, M.JUR.; Israeli politician; b. 1913; ed. Warsaw Univ.
Active in Jewish Youth Movement "Betar"; Chair. "Betar" in Czechoslovakia 36, in Poland 39; confined in Siberian labour camp by Moscow Comm. of N.K.V.D. 40-41; came with Polish army to Palestine 42; C.-in-C. Irgun Zvai Leumi 43, leading revolt against British rule in Palestine; mem. 1st, 2nd, 3rd, 4th and 5th Knessets (Israel Parl.); Leader of the Opposition in Knesset 48-67, 69-; Minister without Portfolio 67-69; Founder and fmr. Chair. Herut (Freedom Movement).
Publs. *The Revolt, personal memoirs of the Commander of Irgun Zvi Leumi* 49, *The White Nights*.
Knesset Building, Jerusalem; and 1 Rosenbaum Street, Tel-Aviv, Israel.

Beheiry, Mamoun Ahmed, B.A.; Sudanese civil servant and politician; b. 1925; ed. Victoria Coll., Alexandria and Brasenose Coll., Oxford.
Former Dep. Perm. Under-Sec. Ministry of Finance and Economics; fmr. Chair. Sudan Currency Board; fmr. Chair. Nat. Technical Planning Cttee. 62; First Gov. Central Bank of Sudan 58-63; Gov. IMF and IBRD for Sudan; Chair. Cttee. of Nine preparing for African Devt. Bank 63; Minister of Finance and Econs. 63-64; Pres. of African Devt. Bank 64-70.
c/o Ministry of Finance, Khartoum, Sudan.

Behnia, Abolhassan; Iranian banker; b. 5 Jan. 1910; ed. Univ. of Paris.
Professor, Technical Faculty, Teheran Univ. 42-67; Dir.-Gen. Ministry of Roads and Communications 46-47; Chair. and Man. Dir. Irrigation Org. 50-55; Minister of Roads and Communications 60; Dir. of Technical Bureau of Plan Org. 61-64; Chair. and Man. Dir. Bank Rahni Iran 65-.
Bank Rahni Iran, Ferdowsi Street, Teheran; and 41 Avenue Heravi, Saltanatabad, Teheran, Iran.

Bekata, Hıfzı Oğuz; Turkish politician; b. 17 March 1911; ed. Ankara Univ.
Deputy for Ankara 43-50, 57-60; mem. Constituent Assembly 61; Minister of State June-Oct. 62, of the Interior 62-63; Senator for Ankara 61-; Gen. Sec. Turkish Asscn. of United Nations; Republican People's Party.
Publs. *Aydın Din Adamları* 62, *Bırıncı Cumhurıyet* 60, *Dağların Ardi* 65, *Hükumet Hakkında Konusmalar* 67, *Türkiyenin Bungünkü Görünüşü* 69.
Atatürk Bulvarı 237/9, Kavaklidere, Ankara, Turkey.

Bel Kacem, Cherif; Algerian politician.
Former mem. Armée de Libération Nationale; Deputy for Tlemcen; Questeur, Nat. Ass.; Minister of Nat. Orientation 63-64; Minister of Education 64-65; mem. Revolutionary Council and Dir. of Information July 65-67; mem. Bureau Politique, F.L.N. 65-67; Minister of Finance and Planning March 68-70; Minister of State 70-.
Palais du Gouvernement, Algiers, Algeria.

Ben Abbes, Youssef, M.D.; Moroccan physician and politician; b. 15 Aug. 1921; ed. Marrakesh, Medical Coll. of Algiers and Paris.
Joined Public Health Service 49, Dir. several hospitals, then Insp.-Gen. of Health; Minister of Health 58-61, of Health and Educ. 61-62, of Educ. 62-65; Mayor of Marrakesh and Pres. Provincial Council; Senator for Marrakesh; Ambassador to U.A.R. 65-66, to Italy 67-69, to Algeria 69-70; Minister of Foreign Affairs Oct. 70-71; Amb. to Spain 71-72, to France Sept. 72-.
Embassy of Morocco, rue Le Tasse 3, Paris 16e, France.

Benabdallah, Abdel-Aziz; Moroccan professor; b. 28 Nov. 1923; ed. Univ. of Algiers.
General Dir. for the Conservation and Registry of Land Properties 57; Dir. of Higher Educ. for Scientific Research 58-61; Dir. of Nat. Arabization Centre 61-68; Dir.-Gen. Perm. Office for the Co-ordination of Arabization in the Arab World, Arab League, Rabat 69-; Prof., Faculty of Arts, Mohamed V Univ., Rabat and also Dar-el-Hadith Inst., al-Qarawiyine Univ., Rabat.
Publs. in Arabic: history, philosophy, geography and linguistics.
Bureau Permanent d'Arabisation, 8 rue Angola, Rabat, Morocco.

Ben-Aharon, Yitzhak; Israeli administrator; b. 1906, Bukovina, Austria; ed. Berlin High School for Political Science and Econs.
Went to Palestine 28; founder of Kibbutz Givat Hayim; Sec. Tel-Aviv Labour Council 38-39; Lieut., British Army, Second World War, prisoner-of-war 41-45; mem. Knesset 49-62; Minister of Transport 59-62; mem. Knesset 69-; Sec.-Gen. Histadrut Dec. 69-.
Publs. *Listen Gentile, Michtavim Leuni, Bepheta Temura*.
Hahistadrut Haklalit shel Haovdim Beeretz Israel, 9 Arlosoroff Street, Tel-Aviv; and Kibbutz Givat Hayim (Meyuhad), Doar Hedera, Israel.

Ben Ammar, Hassib; Tunisian professor and politician; b. 11 April 1924; ed. Coll. Sadiki, Tunis and Faculty of Sciences, Paris.
Active mem. of Destour groups abroad 42-52; mem. Destour Fed., Tunis 54; Sec.-Gen. of the Econ. and Social Board 59; Sec.-Gen. of Destour Youth Movt. 60; Mayor of Tunis 63-65, Gov. 65-69; Amb. to Italy 69; Minister of Defence 70-71; mem. Cen. Cttee., Destour Socialist Party (DSP) 64; mem. Political Bureau DSP, Chair. 69-70, Supreme Cttee. DSP 70-, Council of Nat. Defence 71-; Grand Cordon, Order of Independence, Grand Cordon, Order of the Repub.
Parti socialiste destourien, 10 rue de Rome, Tunis, Tunisia.

Ben-Ari, Mordechai; Israeli (b. Transylvania) airline executive; b. Sept. 1920; ed. Hebrew Univ., Jerusalem.
Arrived in Palestine 40, joined Kibbutz; fought in Israel's War of Independence; later Dir. of Immigration Operations in Austria and E. Europe; joined El Al Israel Airlines 50, Man. of Freight and Mail Dept., Head of Commercial Div. 58, Vice-Pres. (Commercial) 60-67, Pres. of El Al Israel Airlines Ltd. July 67-.
El Al Israel Airlines Ltd., Lod Airport, Israel.

Benawa, Abdul Raouf; Afghan writer and administrator; b. 1913; ed. Ganj Public School, Kandahar.
Member Language Dept. Afghan Acad. 39; mem. Words Dept. Afghan Acad. and Asst. Information Dept. 40; Dir. Publ. Dept. Afghan Acad. 41; Gen. Dir. *Pashtu Tolana*; Sec. Afghan Acad. and Dir. *Kabul* magazine; proprietor of weekly magazine *Hewad*; mem. History Dept. 50, Dir. Internal Publ. Dept. 51, Gen. Dir. 52; Press Attaché India 53-56; Pres. Radio Kabul 56-63; Press and Cultural Counsellor, Cairo 63-.
Publs. *Women in Afghanistan, Mir Wiess Neeka, Literary Sciences, Pushtu Songs, De Ghanamo Wazhai, Pushtoonistan, A Survey of Pushtoonistan, Rahman Baba, Pir Mohammad-Kakar, Khosh-hal Khan se Wai, Pushtoo Killi*, Vol. 4, *Kazim Khan-e-Shaida*; translations: *Mosa-fir Iqbal, Geetan-Jali Tagoor, Da Darmistatar Pushtoo Seerane, Leaders of Pushtoonistan, History of Hootaki, Preshana afkar* (poem), *Da zva khwala, Pashto writers today* (2 vols.), *Pashto reader for schools, Pachakhan* (A leader of Pashtoni), *Landei* (public poems); plays: *I-Zoor gonahgar* (Old criminal), *Ishtebah* (Confusion), *Kari bar asal, Aashyanae aqab, Zarang, Chaoki der khater, Hakoomat baidar*.
Afghan Embassy, Cairo, Egypt; and Ministry of Information and Culture, Kabul, Afghanistan.

Ben Bella, Mohammed; Algerian politician; b. 1916.
Warrant Officer in Moroccan regiment during Second World War (decorated); Chief O.S. rebel military group in Algeria 47; imprisoned 49-52 (escaped); directed Algerian nat. movement from exile in Libya 52-56; arrested Oct. 56; held in France 59-62; Vice-Premier, Algerian Nationalist Provisional Govt., Tunis 62; Leader, Algerian Political Bureau, Algeria 62; Premier of Algeria Sept. 62-June 65, President of Algeria Sept. 63-June 65, concurrently Minister of Interior Dec. 64-June 65; overthrown by military *coup* and imprisoned 65; Lenin Peace Prize 64.
c/o Ministry of Justice, Algiers, Algeria.

Bendor, Shmuel; Israeli diplomatist; b. Belfast 21 June 1909; ed. Liverpool Univ.
Emigrated to Palestine 32; became English teacher, later Vice-Principal, Haifa Reali School 32-48; Military Service 48-49; with Ministry of Education 49; Dir. of U.S. Dept. Foreign Ministry 50-54; Counsellor, Paris 54-57; Minister to Czechoslovakia 57-59, to Rumania 59-61; Dir. Western European Dept., Foreign Ministry 61-63; Deputy Dir.-Gen. Prime Minister's Office 63-66, Dir. Foreign Relations Atomic Energy Comm. 66-69; Dir. Foreign Relations and Sec. Council for Higher Educ., Ministry of Educ. and Culture 69-72; Dir. Israel Acad. of Sciences and Humanities 72-.
Israel Academy of Sciences and Humanities, P.O. Box 4040, Jerusalem, Israel.

Benedictos (Vassilios Papadopoulos); Greek orthodox ecclesiastic; b. 1892; ed. Greek Orthodox Hieratic School, Jerusalem, and Athens Univ.
Clerk, Patriarchal Offices, Jerusalem 14; ordained deacon 14; accompanied the then Patriarch to Damascus during World War I; studies in Law and Theological Schools, Athens Univ. 21-25; rep. of Patriarch of Jerusalem at World Christian Conf. of Faith and Order, Geneva 27; Exarch of the Holy Sepulchre in Athens 29-46; ordained priest and Archimandrite 46; mem. Holy Synod, Jerusalem Patriarchate 46-; Legal Adviser and Chair. Pending Property Cttee. 47; Chair. Financial Cttee. 50; rep. of Patriarch, Internationalisation of Jerusalem Trusteeship Conf. 50; Archbishop of Tiberias 51; Greek Orthodox Patriarch of Jerusalem 57-; Grand Cross of King George of Greece, Grand Cross and Cordon of Patriarchate of Antioch, Jordanian and Lebanese orders.
Publs. Numerous historical and legal works.
Greek Orthodox Patriarchate, P.O. Box 4074, Jerusalem, Israel.

Bénézit, Jacques Charles Victor; French oil executive; b. 7 Oct. 1913; ed. Ecole Polytechnique, Ecole des Mines.
Mining engineer, Nancy, Paris; Dir. Exploration/Production Dept. 55; Dir. Compagnie Française des Pétroles; Pres. and Dir.-Gen. Compagnie Française des Pétroles (Algérie); Chevalier, Légion d'Honneur.
Compagnie Française des Pétroles, 5 rue Michel-Ange, 75781 Paris, France.

Bengelloun, Admed Majid, L. EN D.; Moroccan lawyer and politician; b. 27 Dec. 1927, Fez; ed. Inst. of Political Science, Paris.
Public Prosecutor, Marrakesh 56, later Public Prosecutor of Mil. Tribunal, Meknés, Gen. Counsel, Supreme Court; Public Prosecutor Court of Appeal 60-64; Minister of Information 65-67; Sec.-Gen. Ministry of Justice 67; Minister at the Royal Cabinet 67-71, of Civil Service 71-72, of Information 72-; fmr. Prof. Inst. des Hautes Etudes Juridiques; Prof. Law Faculty, Univ. of Rabat, Ecole Morocaine d'Admin.; mem. Comm. for the Drafting of the Penal Code and Penal Procedure Code; has attended numerous int. judicial confs.; Order of the Throne, and several foreign decorations.
Ministère de l'Information, Rabat, Morocco.

Ben-Gurion, David; Israeli statesman; b. 16 Oct. 1886; ed. privately and Istanbul Univ.
Settled in Palestine 06; exiled by Turks as Zionist 15; went to U.S. where one of organizers of Jewish Legion in which he himself served under Gen. Allenby; mem. Gen. Council Zionist Org. 20; one of organizers of Jewish Labour Party (Mapai) and Gen. Federation of Jewish Labour (Histadrut) and Sec.-Gen. of Federation 21-35; Chair. Jewish Agency for Palestine 35-48; proclaimed independence of Israel May 14th, 1948; founder mem. of Parl. 48-70; Head of Provisional Govt. and Minister of Defence May 48-March 49; Prime Minister and Minister of Defence 49-53, 55-63; leader of Mapai (Labour) Party 48-65, expelled 65; formed Israel Labour List 65; Hon. D.Phil. (Hebrew Univ. of Jerusalem) 57, Hon. LL.D. (Brandeis, Rangoon Univs.); Bialik Literary Prize for Judaica 52; Hadessah Henrietta Szold Award 58.
Publs. *Self-Government of Villayets* 14, *Eretz Israel* 18, *We and our Neighbours* 20, *The Labour Movement and Revisionism* 35, *From Class to Nation* 33, 55, *Mishmarot* (essays on Labour Zionism) 35, *The Struggle* (5 vols.) 47-50, *Israel at War* 50, *Vision and Implementation* (5 vols.) 51-57, *Nezach Israel* 53, *Rebirth and Destiny of Israel* 54, *Mima-*

amad Leam 55, *En la Patria Libre* 54, *The Sinai Campaign* 59, *Israel: Years of Challenge* 63, *Ben-Gurion looks back* 65, *Dvarim Kehavayatam, Talks with Arabs, The Restored State of Israel* (2 vols.), *Michtavim Le Paula, Iyunim Batanach* 69, *Zichronot* (3 vols.) 71-73, *Israel: A Personal History* 71, *Yehud Veye'ud* 71, *Ben-Gurion Looks at the Bible* 72, and many essays and articles.
Kibbutz Sdeh Boker, Israel.

Ben-Haim, Paul; Israeli composer; b. 5 July 1897; ed. State Acad. of Music and Univ. of Munich.
Composer, pianist and conductor in various cities in Germany 20-23; moved to Palestine 33 and settled in Tel-Aviv teaching composition and piano; guest conductor, Jerusalem Radio Orchestra and Israel Philharmonic Orchestra; Dir. New Jerusalem Acad. of Music 49-54; Hon. Pres. Israeli Composers' Asscn.; awarded Engel Prize of Tel-Aviv Municipality for *1st Symphony* 45, and for *2nd Symphony* 53; awarded Israel State Prize 57 for symphonic work *The Sweet Psalmist of Israel*; Cross of Merit (1st Class) of the Fed. Repub. of Germany 68.
Works include two symphonies, *Evocation* for violin and orchestra, *Pastorale* for clarinet and strings, Concerto for piano and orchestra, Concerto for strings, *Liturgical Cantata, The Sweet Psalmist of Israel*, other symphonic works include a violin and a 'cello concerto, cantatas, chamber music, songs, etc.
Aharonovitz Street 11, Tel Aviv, Israel.

Ben Halim, Mustafa; Libyan engineer and politician; b. 1921; ed. The Egyptian Univ., Alexandria.
Began career with Egyptian engineering firm; Minister of Works and Communications in first Cyrenaican Govt. 50; Minister, Province of Cyrenaica 52-54; Federal Minister of Communications 54; Prime Minister 54-57, simultaneously Minister of Foreign Affairs April 55-Nov. 56; Special Adviser to the King 57-58; Ambassador to France 58-60; Chair. Libyan Engineering and Construction Co. Ltd. and other companies; sentenced to imprisonment *in absentia* 71.

Benhima, Ahmed Tahibi (brother of Mohamed Benhima, *q.v.*); Moroccan diplomatist and politician; b. 13 Nov. 1927; ed. Univs. of Nancy and Paris.
Chargé d'Affaires, Paris 56-57, Ambassador to Italy 57-59; Sec.-Gen. of Ministry of Foreign Affairs 59-61; Perm. Rep. to UN 61-64; Minister of Foreign Affairs 64-66; Dir. Cabinet of the King 66-67; Perm. Rep. to UN 67-71; Minister of Foreign Affairs May 72-.
Ministry of Foreign Affairs, Rabat, Morocco.

Benhima, Mohamed, M.D. (brother of Ahmed Benhima, *q.v.*); Moroccan physician and politician; b. 25 June 1924; ed. Faculté de Médecine de Nancy, France.
Chief Medical Officer, Had Court District 54-56; Chief of Central Service for Urban and Rural Hygiene 56-57; Head of Personal Office of Minister of Public Health 57-60; Sec.-Gen., Ministry of Public Health Jan.-June 60; Gov. of Provinces of Agadir and Tarfaya 60-61; Minister of Public Works 61-62, 63-65, 67-69, of Commerce, Industry, Mines, Handicrafts and Merchant Marine 62-63; Minister of Nat. Educ. 65-67; Prime Minister July 67-69; Minister of Agriculture and Agrarian Reform 69; Ministry of Public Health 69-72; Minister of the Interior 72-73; Minister of State for Co-operation and Training 73-; decorations from Govts. of Belgium, Morocco, Sweden, Ethiopia, Tunisia, Liberia and Egypt.
Km. 5,500, Route des Zaërs, Rabat, Morocco.

Benjenk, Munir P., B.SC. (ECON.); Turkish public servant; b. 1924; ed. English Lycée and Robert Coll., Istanbul and London School of Economics.
Worked with B.B.C., Reading 49-51; served with Turkish Army in Korea 51-52; with OEEC (now OECD), Paris 53-63; mem. Perm. Mission to Washington of OEEC 55-57; Dir. Sardinian Village Devt. Project 59-60; Asst. Dir. Devt. Dept., OECD 62-63; with Int. Bank for Reconstruction and Devt. 63-; Head of Econ. Advisory Mission, Algeria 64; Head of North Africa Div. 65-67, Deputy Dir. Middle East and North Africa Dept. 67-68; Deputy Dir. Europe, Middle East and North Africa Dept. 68-69, Dir. 70-72, Vice Pres. 72-; Ordine al Merito della Repubblica Italiana, Order of the Cedars of Lebanon 73.
1308 28th Street, N.W., Washington, D.C. 20007; and International Bank for Reconstruction and Development, 1818 H Street, N.W., Washington, D.C. 20433, U.S.A.

Ben Khedda, Ben Yousef; Algerian politician; b. 1920.
Minister of Cultural and Social Affairs, Algerian Provisional Govt. 58-Jan 60; Missions, Moscow and Peking 60-61; Prime Minister Algerian Provisional Govt., Tunis 61-62, Algiers 62; placed under arrest July 64.
c/o Ministry of Justice, Algiers, Algeria.

Ben Lamlih, Ahmed, B.A.; Moroccan diplomatist; b. 1916; ed. Univ. of Cairo.
Participated in nat. liberation movement at "The Maghreb Office" Cairo 41-56; Minister to United Arab Repub. 56-59; Head, Afro-Asian Dept. at Ministry of Foreign Affairs 59-61; Amb. to Iraq 61-62, to U.A.R. 62-63, to Iran and Turkey 65-68; Head, Middle East and Arab League Dept. at Ministry of Foreign Affairs 68-70; Amb. to Libya 71, to Kuwait and United Arab Emirates 72-.
Embassy of Morocco, P.O. Box 784, Kuwait.

Ben Mansour, Abdelwahab; Moroccan radio official and politician; b. 1920; ed. Al Qarawiyin Univ., Fez.
Political prisoner before leaving school; returned to North Africa, Algeria after Second World War and acted as liaison officer between Algerian and Moroccan Nationalists before independence; after independence, teacher then Head of Arab Services, Radiodiffusion Marocaine; Dir. of Political Affairs, Ministry of the Interior 63; mem., then Head of Royal Cabinet 64; Dir.-Gen. Radiodiffusion Télévision Marocaine 65-; attends numerous int. confs.; numerous awards including named "Historiographer of the Realm" 63.
Radiodiffusion Télévision Marocaine, 11 rue Al Brihl, Rabat, Morocco.

Ben-Natan, Asher; Israeli soldier and diplomatist; b. 15 Feb. 1921; ed. Geneva Univ.
Secretary and Treas. Medorot-Zeraim Kibbutz 38-44; Immigration organizer, Europe 44-47; Ministry of Foreign Affairs 48-51; Gen. Man. Red Sea-Inkodeh Co. 55-56; Rep. of Ministry of Defence 56-59; Dir.-Gen. Ministry of Defence 59-65; Amb. to Fed. Repub. of Germany 65-70, to France 70-; Officier, Légion d'Honneur, Commdr., Ordre Nat. (Ivory Coast), Commdr., Ordre de l'Etoile Equatoriale (Gabon).
Embassy of Israel, avenue de Wagram 143, Paris 17e, France; and 89 University Street, Tel-Aviv, Israel.

Ben Salah, Ahmed; Tunisian politician; b. 13 Jan. 1926; ed. Collège Sadiki, Tunis and Univ. of Paris.
Teacher, Lycée de Sousse 48-51; Del. Tunisian Trade Union Movement at Int. Confederation of Trade Unions, Brussels 51-54; Sec.-Gen. Union Générale Tunisienne du Travail 54-56; Sec. of State for Public Health and Social Affairs 57-60, for the Plan and Finance 61-64, for the Plan and Nat. Economy 64-69, for Educ. Sept. 69-70; Asst. Sec.-Gen. Destour Socialist Party 64-70; imprisoned 70, escaped Feb. 73.
c/o Ministry of Justice, Tunis, Tunisia.

Ben Seddik, Mahjoub; Moroccan trade union leader; b. 1925.
Secretary-General Union Marocaine du Travail 55-; Pres. All-African Trade Union Fed. 61, 64, 66, 71; mem. Secretariat-Gen. Union Nat. des Forces Populaires; imprisoned 52-53, July 67; mem. Admin. Council, ILO.
Union Marocaine du Travail, 222 avenue des Forces Armées Royales, Casablanca, Morocco.

Bentov, Mordechai; Israeli journalist and politician; b. 28 March 1900; ed. Inst. of Technology, Warsaw Univ., Jerusalem Law Classes.
Founder and Chief Editor *Al-Hamishmar* 43-48 and 49-55; Signatory of Declaration of Independence 48; elected mem. Knesset (Israel Parl.) 49, 51, 55, 59, 61; Minister of Labour in Provisional Govt. 48-49; Minister of Development 55-61; Minister of Housing 66-69; mem. Jewish Agency Del. to UN, Lake Success 47; Del. to Zionist Congresses, Round Table Conf., London 38, World Jewish Congress, U.S.A. 44, Geneva 53; mem. Secretariat, United Workers' Party (Mapam); Chair. Economic Affairs Cttee. of the Knesset 51; mem. World Exec. Hashomer Hatzair; Exec. Histadrut and Zionist Action Cttee.
Publs. *The Case for a Bi-National Palestine* 46, *Israel Economy at the Crossroads* 65, *Israel, The Palestinians and the Left* 71.
Kibbutz Mishmar Haemek, Israel.

Ben Yahya, Prince Abdul Rahman; Yemeni Royalist politician.
Deputy Prime Minister until 67; Prime Minister 67-68; mem. Imamate Council 67-68; in exile 68-.

Ben Yahya, Mohammed Sedik; Algerian diplomatist; b. 1934.
Closely associated with Ferhat Abbas in Tunisia and Yazd 59-62; Ambassador to U.S.S.R. 62-65; undertook several missions for President Ben Bella 63-65; Ambassador to U.K. 65; mem. Algerian Del. to UN 65-66; Minister of Information 66-70, of Higher Educ. and Research 70-.
Ministry of Higher Education, Algiers, Algeria.

Berenblum, Isaac, M.D., M.SC.; Israeli pathologist and experimental biologist; b. 26 Aug. 1903; ed. Bristol Grammar School and Leeds Univ.
Riley-Smith Research Fellow, Dept. Experimental Pathology and Cancer Research, Leeds Univ. Medical School 29-36; Beit Memorial Research Fellow, Dunn School of Pathology, Oxford Univ. 36-40; Departmental and Univ. Demonstrator in Pathology, Oxford Univ. 40-48; in charge of Oxford Univ. Research Centre of British Empire Cancer Campaign 40-48; Special Research Fellow, Nat. Cancer Inst., Bethesda, Md., U.S.A. 48-50; Head of Dept. of Experimental Biology, The Weizmann Inst. of Science, Rehovot, Israel 50-71; Visiting Prof. of Oncology, Hebrew Univ., Jerusalem 50-56; mem. Israel Research Council 52-57; Jack Cotton Prof. of Cancer Research, The Weizmann Inst. of Science, Rehovot, Israel 62-71, Emer. Prof. 71-; mem. Israel Acad. of Sciences and Humanities.
Publs. *Science versus Cancer* 46, *Man Against Cancer* 52, *Cancer Research Today* 67.
Weizmann Institute of Science, Rehovot; and 33 Ruppin Street, Rehovot, Israel.

Berger, Morroe, PH.D.; American educator and writer; b. 25 June 1917; ed. Columbia Univ., New York.
Assistant Prof., Princeton Univ. 52-58, Assoc. Prof. 58-61, Prof. of Sociology 62-; Dir. Program in Near Eastern Studies, Princeton Univ. 62-68; mem., Chair. Joint Cttee. of Near and Middle East, of American Council of Learned Socs. and Social Science Research Council 62-69; Consultant to U.S. Office of Educ. 65-68; mem. Governing Boards, American Research Center, Egypt, American Research Inst., Turkey 64-; Pres. Middle East Studies Asscn. 67; Chair. Council on Int. and Regional Studies, Princeton Univ. 68-, Chair. Dept. of Sociology 71-.
Publs. *Equality by Statute* 52, 67, *Bureaucracy and Society in Modern Egypt* 57, *The Arab World To-day* 62, *Madame de Staël on Politics, Literature and National Character* 64, *Islam in Egypt Today* 70; Editor *New Metropolis in the Arab World* 63; numerous articles in learned journals and contributions to encyclopaedias.
422 1879 Hall, Princeton University, Princeton, New Jersey 08540, U.S.A.

Bergman, Shmuel Hugo, PH.D.; Israeli philosopher; b. 25 Dec. 1883; ed. Prague and Berlin Univs.
Philosopher and critic; Dir. Jewish Nat. and Univ. Library in Jerusalem until 35; Prof. of Philosophy Hebrew Univ., Rector 35-38, Dean Faculty of Humanities 52-53; mem. Board of Govs., Hebrew Univ.; Hon. mem. Inst. Int. de Philosophie; Hon. D.Phil. (Hebrew Univ.); mem. Israel Acad. of Sciences and Humanities.
Publs. *Untersuchungen zum Problem der Evidenz der inneren Wahrnehmung* 08, *Das philosophische Werk Bolzanos* 10, *Das Unendliche und die Zahl* 13, *Jawne und Jerusalem* 19, *The Philosophy of Kant* 27, *Der Kampf um das Kausalgesetz in der jüngsten Physik* 29, *The Philosophy of Maimon* 32 (Hebrew, 2nd edn. 67), *Present-day Thinkers* 35, *Theory of Knowledge* 41 (2nd edn. 72), *Pensadores Judios Contemporáneos* 44, *Science and Belief* 45, *Judiska Religions-filosofer i var generation* 50, *Introduction to Logic* 53, *God and Man in Modern Thought* 56, *Believing Thinkers* 59, *Faith and Reason* 61, *Sohelling on the Source of Eternal Truths* 64, *Men and Ways: Philosophical Essays* (Hebrew) 67, *The Philosophy of Solomon Maimon* 67, *Heaven and Earth* 68, English Trans. *The Quality of Faith* 70, *History of Modern Philosophy I* (Hebrew) 70.
51 Ramban Road, Jerusalem, Israel.

Bergmann, Ernst David, PH.D.; Israeli chemist and university professor; b. 18 Oct. 1903; ed. Berlin Univ.
Lecturer Berlin Univ. 28-33; Immigrated to Palestine 33; Scientific Dir. Daniel Sieff Research Inst. (now Weizmann Inst. of Science), Rehovot 33-51; Prof. of Organic Chemistry, The Hebrew Univ., Jerusalem 53-; Dir. Scientific Dept. Ministry of Defence 48-66; Chair. Israel Atomic Energy Comm. 52-66; Chair. Science Section, Israel Acad. of Sciences and Humanities; Hon. Sc.D. (Haifa Inst. of Technology), Hon. Ph.D. (Univ. of Montpellier); Rothschild Prize 62; Israel Defence Prize 66; Israel Prize 68.
Publs. *Organic Chemistry* (with W. Schlenk), *Isomerism and Isomerisation, Acetylene Chemistry* and many articles in scientific journals.
14 Ayn Rogel Street, Jerusalem, Israel.

Berinson, Zvi, SC. DIP., B.A.; Israeli judge; b. 1907; ed. Scots Coll. (Safad, Israel), Jesus Coll. Cambridge, and Gray's Inn, London.
Lecturer, Scots Coll. 29-31; Legal Adviser and Dir. Municipal Dept. Gen. Fed. of Jewish Labour, Palestine 36-49; Dir.-Gen. Ministry of Labour, Israel Govt. 49-53; Justice, Supreme Court 54-; Lecturer on Labour Law and Social Insurance, Hebrew Univ. 53-71; Chair. League of Societies for the Rehabilitation of Offenders in Israel, Council of Israel Opera; Hon. Pres. Public Council for the Prevention of Noise and Air Pollution in Israel; mem. Board of Dirs., Int. Prisoners' Aid Asscn.; Head of Israeli Del. to Int. Labour Conf. 49-53, 58, 59.
The Supreme Court of Israel, Jerusalem, Israel.

Berk, Medenî; Turkish politician.
Fmr. Dir.-Gen. Emlâk Kredi Bankası; Minister of Reconstruction and Town Planning 57-59; Deputy Prime Minister 59-60; arrested May 60; sentenced to life imprisonment, released 65; Dir.-Gen. Akbank T.A.Ş. 66-; Pres. Union of Chambers of Commerce, Chambers of Industry and Commodity Exchanges of Turkey 70-71.
Etiler, Çamlık Sokak 6, Istanbul, Turkey.

Berk, Mükerrem; Turkish musician; b. 1917; ed. Istanbul Conservatoire.
Joined Presidential Symphony Orchestra 37, Principal Flute and Woodwind leader 41-, Admin. Dir. 60-68; Gen. Dir. State Opera and Ballet 69-; many tours in U.S.A., United Kingdom, W. Europe, Scandinavia, Middle East, India, Pakistan and U.S.S.R.
Cumhurbaşkanlığı Senfoni Orkestrası, Talatpaşa Bulvarı 38/A, Ankara, Turkey.

Berk, Nurullah; Turkish artist; b. 1906; ed. Acad. of Fine Arts, Istanbul, Paris Acad. and Léger and Lhote studios, Paris.
Teacher in Acad. of Fine Arts, Istanbul; exhibited UNESCO Int. Art Exhbn., Paris 47, Exhbn. of Turkish Art, Musée Cernuschi, Paris 47, Exhbn. of Turkish Art, Amsterdam 48, Turin Art Club Exhbn. 50.
Publs. *Turkish Sculpture, Leonardo da Vinci, Art in Modern Turkey, La Peinture Turque, Bellinis.*
Kuyulubustan Sokak 19/3, Nişantaç, Istanbul, Turkey.

Berkol, Faruk N., LL.D.; Turkish diplomatist; b. Sept. 1917, Istanbul; ed. Univs. of Istanbul and Paris and School of Political Science, Paris.
Joined Ministry of Foreign Affairs 41; First Sec., Washington 45-50; Counsellor, later Chargé d'Affaires, London 52-56; Chef de Cabinet to Pres. of Turkey 56-60; Amb. to Tunisia 62-67, to Belgium 67-72; UN Disaster Relief Co-ordinator 72-.
Publs. works in Turkish and French on the Balkan *entente*, Turkish economic expansion and the legal status of eastern Mediterranean ports.
UN Disaster Relief, Palais des Nations, Geneva, Switzerland.

Berque, Jacques, D. ès L.; French oriental sociologist; b. 4 June 1910; ed. Univ. of Algiers and Univ. de Paris à la Sorbonne.
Early career as Admin. Officer in Morocco; UNESCO specialist in Egypt 53-55; Dir. of Studies, Ecole des Hautes Etudes, Sorbonne 55-; Prof. of Social History of Contemporary Islam, Coll. de France 56-; Commdr. du Ouissam Alaouite (Morocco), Chevalier Légion d'Honneur and Palmes académiques (France); Commdr. of Merit (Syria).
Publs. *Structures sociales du Haut-Atlas* 55, *Les Arabes* 57, *Les Arabes d'hier à demain* 60, *Le Maghreb entre deux guerres* 62, *Dépossession du monde* 64, *L'Egypte, impérialisme et révolution* 67, *L'Orient Second* 70.
Collège de France, Paris 5e, France.

Berrada, Abdeslam, DIP.SC.AGRI.; Moroccan agronomist; b. 3 Oct. 1931, Fez; ed. secondary schools, Fez, Ecole Nat. d'Agriculture de Grignon, Ecole Nat. des Eaux et Forêts, Nancy, France.
Several posts in Waters and Forests Admin., subsequently Dir. 65; Sec.-Gen. Ministry of Agriculture and Agrarian Reform 71-72, Minister Nov. 72-; Exec. Vice-Pres. Soc. Cellulose du Maroc 72-; rep. to numerous regional and int. confs.
Ministère de l'Agriculture et de la Réforme Agraire, Rabat, Morocco.

Bertini, Gary; Israeli conductor; b. 1 May 1927, Bessarabia; ed. Israel, Conservatorio Verdi, Milan, Conservatoire Nat. Paris and studies under Arthur Honegger.
Founder and Dir. RINAT Chamber Choir 55; Founder Jeunesses Musicales d'Israel; teacher of conducting at Rubin Acad. of Music; Artistic Dir. and Conductor Israel Chamber Ensemble; has conducted many orchestras in Israel and abroad, and has premiered much contemporary Israeli music; composer of symphonic and chamber music, ballets, incidental music to more than 40 plays, and music for films and radio.
Office: The Israel Chamber Ensemble, 103 Ibn Gvirol Street, Tel-Aviv; Home: 5 Basel Street, Tel-Aviv, Israel.

Besse, Antonin Bernard; French company director; b. 22 Feb. 1927.
Chairman Besse group of companies (import, export, finance, maritime affairs) 51-65; Chair. Besse Int. S.A. (finance); mem. Int. Council of United World Colls.; Chevalier de l'Ordre de la Couronne.
P.O. Box 8203, Beirut, Lebanon; 14 avenue de Verzy, Paris 17e, France.

Bierbach, Dr. Martin; German diplomatist; b. 1928.
First Sec. in Ministry of External Affairs 54-55; Counsellor to G.D.R. Embassy in Peking 55-59; Consul-Gen. Cairo, 59-62; Dir. of Arab Affairs, Ministry of External Affairs 62-; Ambassador to Egypt (fmrly. U.A.R.) 69-72.
c/o Ministry of External Affairs, Berlin, German Democratic Republic.

Bilge, Ali Suat, LL.T.; Turkish professor of international law and politician; b. 1921, Istanbul; ed. Univs. of Ankara and Geneva.
Assistant, Faculty of Political Science, Univ. of Ankara 50, Assoc. Prof. 52, Prof. 60-; Hon. Legal Adviser, Ministry of Foreign Affairs 60, First Hon. Legal Adviser 65; Judge, European Court of Human Rights 66; mem. Perm. Court of Arbitration, The Hague 66; mem. UN Cttee. of Human Rights 70; mem. Int. Law Comm. 71-; Minister of Justice Dec. 71-72; Amb. to Switzerland Oct. 72-.
Publs. *Diplomatic Protection of Compatriots* 53, *International Politics* 66.
Kalcheggweg 18, Berne, Switzerland.

Binder, Leonard; American university professor; b. 20 Aug. 1927; ed. Boston Latin School, Harvard Coll. and Harvard Univ.
Assistant Prof. Univ. Calif., Los Angeles 56-61; Assoc. Prof. and Prof. Univ. of Chicago 61-, Chair. Dept. of Political Science 64-67, Chair. Cttee. on Near Eastern Studies 63-65; mem. New Nations Cttee. 61-; Fellow Center for Advanced Studies in the Behavioral Sciences 67-68; Field Research in Pakistan 54-55, in Iran 58-59, in Egypt 60-61, in Lebanon 64, in Tunisia 64, 65, 66, 69. Chair. Research and Training Cttee., Middle East Studies Asscn.
Publs. *Religion and Politics in Pakistan* 60, *Iran: Political Development in a Changing Society* 61, *The Ideological Revolution in the Middle East* 64, Editor, *Politics in the Lebanon* 65, Co-author, *Crises and Sequences in Political Development* 72; also numerous articles in periodicals.
Department of Political Science, University of Chicago, Chicago, Illinois 60637, U.S.A.

Birgi, Muharrem Nuri, LL.B.; Turkish diplomatist; b. 1908; ed. School of Political Sciences, Paris, and Faculty of Law, Geneva.
Joined Ministry of Foreign Affairs 32; served Warsaw 35-39, Ministry of Foreign Affairs 39-41, Paris 41, Madrid 42; Co-Dir.-Gen. First Political Dept., Ministry of Foreign Affairs 44; Dir.-Gen. Dept. of Int. Affairs 45, Dept. of Co-ordination 46, Dept. of Consular Affairs 46, Second Political Dept. 50; Adjutant to Sec.-Gen. Ministry of Foreign Affairs 51; Under-Sec. Ministry of Foreign Affairs 52-54, Sec.-Gen. 54-57; Ambassador to Great Britain 57-60; Perm. Del. NATO 60-72, retd.; head of Turkish del. to London Conference on Suez 56.
Toprakli Sokak, 11 Salacak-Üsküdar, Istanbul, Turkey.

Bishara, Abdulla Yacoub; Kuwaiti diplomatist; ed. Cairo Univ. and Balliol Coll., Oxford.
Second Sec., Kuwait Embassy, Tunisia 63-64; Dir. Office of Ministry of Foreign Affairs, Kuwait 64-71; Perm. Rep. to UN Sept. 71-; del. to numerous int. confs.
Permanent Mission of Kuwait at United Nations, 235 East 42nd Street, 27th Floor, New York, N.Y. 10017, U.S.A.

Bishti, Ahmed; Libyan politician; ed. Italian School, Tripoli and Cairo Univ.
Doctor in Tripoli 55-61; Joined Ministry of Health 61; Dir. of Govt. Hospitals, Tripoli 62-63; Minister of Health 63-64; Ambassador to the Lebanon 64-65; Minister of Foreign Affairs 65-68; Amb. to Turkey 68-71.
c/o Ministry of Foreign Affairs, Tripoli, Libya.

Bitar, Salah Eddine el-; Syrian politician; b. 1912; ed. Damascus and Univ. of Paris.
Secondary school teacher in Damascus 34-42; entered

politics 42; co-founder, with Michel Aflak, of Arab Resurrection Party and Editor of party organ; left Syria after Shishekly coup 52; later returned and took part in merging of Renaissance and Socialist parties to form Baath Party; elected to Parliament after overthrow of Shishakly 54; Minister of Foreign Affairs 56; head of Syrian Del. to UN Gen. Assembly 57; Minister of Culture and Nat. Guidance, U.A.R. 58-59; Prime Minister of Syrian Arab Republic March-May 11, 63, May 13, 63-Nov. 63; concurrently Minister of Foreign Affairs May 63-Nov. 63; Vice-Pres. Council of Revolutionary Commd. Nov. 63-May 64; Prime Minister and Vice-Pres. Council of Presidency May-Oct. 64; Prime Minister and Foreign Minister Jan.-Feb. 66, expelled from Baath Party Oct. 66.
Pacific Hotel, Beirut, Lebanon.

Bitat, Rabah; Algerian politician; b. 1927.
Member Front de Libération Nationale (F.L.N.); imprisoned 55-62; fmr. Minister of State, Algerian Provisional Govt., Tunis, later Algiers; mem. Political Bureau (in charge of Party Org.) July 62-63; Dep. Premier Sept. 62-May 63; Third Deputy Premier May 63-Sept. 63; left Algeria July 64, returned Dec. 64; Minister of State July 65-66; Minister of State in Charge of Transport 66-.
Ministry of Transport, Algiers, Algeria.

Blickenstaff, David; American United Nations official; b. 20 May 1915, Laverne, Calif.; ed. Woodstock School, Landour, Uttar Pradesh, India, Manchester Coll., Indiana, Univ. of Chicago.
Director, Jt. Office for Refugees, Madrid 42-45; Asst. Head of Section, UN Preparatory Comm., London 45-46; Exec. Officer, Head Gen. Assembly Affairs and Admin. Section, Office of UN Sec.-Gen. 47-54; Deputy Principal Sec. UN Comm. in Eritrea 49; Political Officer, UN Mission on Kashmir 51; Principal Sec. UN Observation Group in Lebanon June-Dec. 58; Dir. UN Information Centre, Paris 54-59, New Delhi 60-64; Resident Rep. UN Technical Assistance Board, Dir. Special Fund Programmes, India 60-64; Regional Rep. UN Devt. Programme (UNDP), Malaysia, Brunei, Singapore 64-69, Resident Rep. UNDP Indonesia 69-71, now Resident Rep. UNDP, Tunisia.
United Nations Development Programme, P.O. Box 863, Tunis, Tunisia.

Bouabid, Abderrahim, LIC. EN DROIT; Moroccan lawyer, b. 23 March 1920; ed. schools in Salé, Rabat and Univ. of Paris.
Student and Istiqlal Rep., Paris 45-50; mem. Exec. Comm. of Istiqlal, Dir. *Al Istiqlal* 50-52; Political Officer, Moroccan Trade Union Movt. 50-52; in prison 52-54; Istiqlal Rep. to France 54-55, to Aix-les-Bains Conf. 55; Minister of State, First Moroccan Govt. Nov. 55; mem. Moroccan del. to Independence Conf., Paris 56; Amb. to France April-Nov. 56; Minister of Finance 56-58; took part in left-wing split of Istiqlal, leader of Union Nat. des Forces Populaires (UNFP) 59-, party banned 73; elected mem. Gen. Secr. UNFP by 2nd Congress 62; Deputy for Kénitra 63; lawyer for UNFP in trial for plot against King Hassan II Nov. 63-April 64; Head UNFP del. to Govt. consultations 65; mem. Cen. Cttee., Nat. Front (Koutla Watania) 70; mem. of body negotiating with King Hassan Dec. 71-March 72.
Plateau de Bettana, Salé, Morocco.

Boudiaf, Mohammed; Algerian politician; b. 1929.
Founder mem., Front de Libération Nationale (F.L.N.); imprisoned 56-62; fmr. Minister of State, Algerian Provisional Govt., Tunis, Deputy Premier 61-62; mem. Political Bureau (Guidance and External Affairs); imprisoned June-Nov. 63; Pres. Nat. Cttee. for Defence of the Revolution 64-; sentenced to death *in absentia* 65.
Comité National pour la Défense de la Révolution Algérienne, Paris, France.

Boulares, Habib; Tunisian journalist and politician; b. 1932.
Editor-in-Chief of *As Sabah* 55-60; Dir. Tunis Radio and Television 60-61; Dir. of Information, Agence Tunis-Afrique Presse 61-64; Chief of Press of Destour Socialist Party 64-65; studied in Paris 65-70; Minister of Information 70-71.
Publ. *Murad III* (drama).
c/o Ministry of Information, Tunis, Tunisia.

Boumedienne, Colonel Houari (real name: **Mohammed Boukharouba**); Algerian army officer and politician; b. 1927; ed. Islamic Inst., Constantine, Al Azhar, Cairo, and Military Schools.
Former Teacher, Guelma; Commdr. Armée de Libération Nationale, Tunis 60-62, Algiers 62-; Minister of Nat. Defence 62-; First Vice-Premier 63-65; Head of Revolutionary Council June 65-; Prime Minister July 65-.
Office of the Prime Minister, Algiers, Algeria.

Boumendjel, Ahmed; Algerian politician; b. 1908.
Former lawyer; fmr. mem. Democratic Union of the Algerian Manifesto (U.D.M.A.); Political Adviser to Provisional Govt. of the Algerian Republic; Head, Algerian Del. Melun Conf. June 60, mem. Algerian Del. Evian Conf. May 61; fmr. mem. Algerian Nat. Revolutionary Cttee.; Minister of Reconstruction, Works and Transport Sept. 62-Dec. 64; Officer-in-Charge UN Inst. for Training and Research (UNITAR), Geneva Dec. 65.
Algiers, Algeria.

Bourguiba, Habib Ben Ali; Tunisian politician; b. 3 Aug. 1902; ed. Collège Sadiki, Lycée Carnot, Univ. of Paris, Ecole Libre des Sciences Politiques.
Active in politics and journalism since 28; mem. Destour Party 21, broke away and formed Néo-Destour Party (outlawed by the French) 34; imprisoned by the French 34-36 and 38-43; escaped to Middle East 45, travelled to promote Tunisian independence 45-49, world tour 51 during Tunisian negotiations with French Govt.; arrested 52, placed under surveillance at Tabarka (Jan.), imprisoned at Remada (March), in solitary confinement, Ile de la Galite (May) until 54; released 54, under surveillance in France 54-55, during negotiations; returned to Tunisia following Franco-Tunisian Agreements 55; Pres. Tunisian Nat. Assembly, Prime Minister, Pres. of the Council 56-59, concurrently Minister of Foreign Affairs and Defence 56-59; Pres. of Republic 57-; Pres. Destour Socialist Party; Ordre du Sang, Ordre de la confiance en diamants.
Publs. *Le Destour et la France* 37, *La Tunisie et la France* 54.
The Presidency, Tunis, Tunisia.

Bourguiba, Habib, Jr., L.ès D.; Tunisian diplomatist and politician; b. 9 April 1927; ed. Collège Sadiki, Lycée Carnot de Dijon, Faculté de Droit, Paris and Grenoble Univs.
Collaborated in nat. liberation movement, especially 51-54; lawyer in training, Tunis 54-56; Counsellor, Tunisian Embassy, Washington 56-57; Ambassador to Italy 57-58, to France 58-61, to U.S.A. 61-63, concurrently to Canada and Mexico; Sec.-Gen. to Presidency of the Repub. 64; Asst. Sec.-Gen. Destour Socialist Party 64-; mem. Nat. Assembly 64-; Sec. of State for Foreign Affairs Nov. 64-70.
Villa Al Mahroussa, Avenue Salammbo, Tunis, Tunisia.

Bouri, Wahbi el; Libyan politician and diplomatist; b. 23 Jan. 1916; ed. Univs. of Naples and Sienna.
Deputy Chief of Royal Cabinet, later Master of Ceremonies of Royal Palace, Libya 48-53; Counsellor of Embassy, Cairo 53-56; Under-Sec. of Foreign Affairs 56-57; Minister of Foreign Affairs 57-59; Minister of State for Parliamentary Affairs 59-61; Minister of Justice 61-62; Minister of

Petroleum Affairs 62-63; Perm. Rep. of Libya to UN 63-65, 65-70; Minister of Foreign Affairs March 65-Oct. 65.
c/o Ministry of Foreign Affairs, Tripoli, Libya.

Boustany, Elie J., LIC. EN DROIT; Lebanese lawyer and diplomatist; b. 20 Aug. 1918; ed. Univ. of Saint-Joseph, Beirut.
Chef de Bureau, Office of Pres. of the Repub. 42, Head of Youth Dept. 43; Sec. Lebanese Embassy, Paris 44-45; Head of Legis., Ministry of Justice 47; Counsellor, Lebanese Embassy, Rome 56-58, 62-64, Madrid 58-60, London 60-62; Head Litigation Dept., Ministry of Foreign Affairs 64-66; Amb. to Senegal 66-71, concurrently accred. to Mali, Guinea, The Gambia; Dir. Int. Relations, Ministry of Foreign Affairs 71; Amb. to People's Repub. of China May 72-; Officer Order of Merit of the Repub. (Italy) 58, Commdr. Order of Civil Merit (Spain) 60, Grand Officer Nat. Order (Senegal) 71.
Publs. *Les codes libanais annotés et traduits* (7 vols.), *Recueil des traités* (2 vols.), *Législation libanaise* 1954-56; contribs. to Lebanese magazines and periodicals.
Embassy of Lebanon, Peking, People's Republic of China.

Boustany, Fouad Ephrem, DR.-ès-LETTRES; Lebanese scholar; b. 15 Aug. 1906; ed. Deir-el-Kamar Coll. and Univ. St. Joseph, Beirut.
Teacher in Arab Literature, Islamic Insts. and History of Arab Civilization, Institut des Lettres Orientales 33-; Dir. Ecole Normale 42-53; Prof. of Near Eastern History and Civilizations, Inst. des Sciences Politiques 45-55; Prof. of Arab Literature, Islamic Philosophy and Arab Historv, Acad. Libanaise des Beaux-Arts 47-53; Rector Univ. Libanaise 53-70; Sec.-Gen. Lebanese Nat. Comm. for UNESCO 48-55, Int. Comm. for Translation of Classic Works 49-, Acad. Libanaise; Dr. h.c. Univs. of Lyon 57, Austin, Texas 58, Georgetown, Washington, D.C. 58; decorations from: Lebanon, France, Vatican, Spain, Italy, Iran, Tunisia, Morocco and Senegal.
Publs. *Au temps de l'Emir* 26, *Ar-Rawae* (critical studies) 27, *Pourquoi* 30, *Histoire du Liban sous les Chéhab* of Amir Haïdar Chéhab (with Dr. A. Rustem) 33-35, *Bagdad, capitale des lettres abbassides* 34, *Le rôle des chrétiens dans l'établissement de la dynastie Omayyade* 38, *Le style orale chez les Arabes préislamiques* 41, *Al-Magani al Haditah* (5 vols.) 46-50, *Cinq jours à travers la Syrie* 50, *Les dits des mois* 73, *Encyclopedia Arabica* (10 vols.) 56-73.
Université Libanaise, Beirut, Lebanon.

Boutaleb, Abdelhadi; Moroccan politician; b. 23 Dec. 1923, Fez; ed. Al Qarawiyin Univ., Fez.
Professor of Arabic History and Literature, and Tutor to Prince Moulay Hassan and Prince Moulay Abdallah; Founder-mem. Democratic Party of Independence 44-51; campaigned, through the Party, for Moroccan independence, and for this purpose attended UN Session, Paris 51, and Negotiating Conf. at Aix-les-Bains 54-56; Minister of Labour and Social Questions in Bekkai Govt. 56; Chief Editor of journal *Al Rayal Am* 56-61; Amb. to Syria Feb. 62; Sec. of State, Ministry of Information Nov. 62, Ministry of Information, Youth and Sports Jan. 63; Minister of Information, Youth and Sports June 63; Interim Minister in Charge of Mauritania and Sahara Nov. 63; Minister of Justice 64-67, of Nat. Educ. and Fine Arts 67; Minister of State 68; Minister of Foreign Affairs 69-70; Pres. of Parl. 70-71; decorations from Morocco, France, Spain, Italy, Tunisia and Egypt include Commdr., of the Throne of Morocco, Grand Cordon of the Republic of Egypt and Commdr. du Mérite Sportif, France.
Publs. Many cultural and literary works.
51-55 rue de la Drôme, Casablanca, Morocco.

Boutaleb, Abdelhafid, L. ès L., L. ès D.; Moroccan politician; b. 30 June 1928; ed. Lycée de Fès, Lycée Louis-le-Grand, Paris, the Sorbonne and Faculté de Droit, Paris.
Director-General Ministry negotiating Independence for Morocco 55-56; Lawyer at Casablanca 57-58; Dir., Civil Service Dept. 59-60; Dir. of Admin., Municipal and Local Affairs, Ministry of the Interior 60-64; Dir. Royal Cabinet 64; Under-Sec. of State for the Interior Aug. 64-June 65; Minister of Work and Social Affairs 65-68; Minister of Public Works and Communications 68-69, of Justice 69-70; Minister of Labour, Employment and Professional Training Sept. 70; decorations from Fed. Repub. of Germany, Ghana, Tunisia, Egypt and Liberia.
8 rue Tedders, Rabat, Morocco.

Bouteflika, Abdul Aziz; Algerian politician; b. 1935; ed. Morocco.
Former Capt. Nat. Liberation Army (A.L.N.) and Secretary Gen. Staff; Minister of Sports 62-63; Minister of Foreign Affairs Sept. 63-; mem. F.L.N. Political Bureau 64-; mem. Revolutionary Council 65-.
Ministry of Foreign Affairs, Algiers, Algeria.

Boutros, Fouad; Lebanese lawyer and politician; b. 1918; ed. Coll. des Frères, Beirut and Univ. of Lyon.
Judge, Civil and Mixed Commercial Court, Beirut 43-46; Judge Mil. Tribunal 45-46; Court Lawyer 47-; Govt. Lawyer 51-57; Minister of Nat. Educ. and of the Plan 59-60; mem. Chamber of Deputies 60, Deputy Speaker 60-61; Minister of Justice 61-64; Vice-Pres. of the Council, Minister of Educ. and Defence 66, Minister of Foreign Affairs 68; numerous decorations and honours.
Damascus Street—Al Kamal Building, P.O. Box 5848; Home: Sursock Street, Fouad Boutros Building, Beirut, Lebanon.

Bouvet, Jacques Etienne; French engineer; b. 15 Jan. 1909; ed. Ecole Polytechnique and Ecole des Ponts-et-Chaussées.
Assistant Dir. Public Works, Cameroon 34-40, Dir. Martinique 40-43; Chief Engineer Hydraulic Service, Oran, Algeria 43-46; Engineer with Seine Navigation 46; Dir. S.A.C.T.A.R.D. (Soc. Auxiliaire de Co-ordination des Travaux d'aménagement du Rhône à Donzère-Mondragon) 47-53; Dir. E.G.T.H. (Entreprise des Grands Travaux Hydrauliques) 53-57; Prés. Dir.-Gén. S.O.P.E.G. (Soc. Pétrolière de Gérance) 57-72; Prés. Dir.-Gén. S.O.T.H.R.A. (Soc. de Transport du Gaz Naturel d'Hassi-er-r'Mel à Arzew) 60-67, Dir.-Gén. 67-72; Prés. Dir.-Gén. S.E.T.R.E.L. (Soc. d'études pour le transport du Gaz d'Hassi-r'Mel par Canalisations Transméditerannéennes) 60-64; Pres., Dir.-Gen. S.P.M.R. 69-; Chevalier Légion d'Honneur, Chevalier du Mérite Saharien.
Major engineering works include: enlargement of dry-dock at Fort de France, Martinique; improvement of the fall at Donzère-Mondragon and Montelimar power stations; 24 × 22 inch pipeline Haoud-el-Hamza-Bougie and 24 × 20 inch pipeline Hassi-er-r'Mel/Arzew.
195 avenue Charles de Gaulle, 92 Neuilly, France.

Bouziri, Najib; Tunisian diplomatist; b. 1925; ed. Sorbonne, Paris and Ecole libre des sciences politiques (public and private law).
Joined Néo-Destour Party (now Destour Socialist Party) 41, mem. Central Cttee. 64-; practised law in France; mem. Tunisian del., autonomy negotiations 54-55; served with Home and Foreign Ministries 55-56; Chargé d'Affaires, Paris 56; Chef de Cabinet. Foreign Ministry 57-58; Ambassador to Italy 58-61, to Fed. Repub. of Germany 61-64; Sec. of State for P.T.T. Feb.-Nov. 64; 2nd Vice-Pres. Nat. Assembly 64-65; Amb. to U.S.S.R. March 65-70, concurrently to Poland Feb. 67; Amb. to Belgium and Luxembourg 70-72, to Morocco June 72-; mem. Tunisian del. to confs. on Maritime Law, Geneva 60, Diplomatic Relations, Vienna 61, Consular Relations, Vienna 63; Chair. Admin. and Budgetary Cttee. of UN Gen. Assembly 65.
Embassy of Tunisia, 5 rue Montaigne, Rabat, Morocco.

Bozbeyli, Ferruh; Turkish lawyer and politician; b. 21 Jan. 1927, Pazarcik, Maras Prov.; ed. Univ. of Istanbul. Practised law until 65; mem. Parl. (Justice Party—JP) 61-70; fmr. Vice Pres. JP Parl. Group; Deputy Speaker Nat. Assembly, Speaker 65-70; founded Democratic Party (DP) 70; Leader DP Dec. 70-.
Democratic Party, Ankara, Turkey.

Brahimi, Lakhdar; Algerian diplomatist; b. 1934; ed. Medersa Algiers, Institut des Sciences Politiques, Algiers, and Ecole des Sciences Politiques, Paris.
Student Leader 53-56; Perm. Rep. of F.L.N. and later of Provisional Govt. of Algeria in South East Asia 56-61; Gen. Secretariat Ministry of External Affairs 61-63; Amb. to U.A.R. and Sudan 63-70; Perm. Rep. to Arab League 63-70; Amb. to U.K. July 71-.
Algerian Embassy, 6 Hyde Park Gate, London, S.W.7.

Brown, L. Dean; American diplomatist; b. 1920, U.S.A.; ed. Wesleyan Univ. and Imperial Defence Coll., London. Served in U.S. Army 42-46; joined U.S. Foreign Service 46; postings to Congo, Canada, France, U.K., Morocco, Senegal; Amb. to Senegal and The Gambia 67-70; Amb. to Jordan 70-.
American Embassy, Amman, Jordan.

Btesh, Simon, M.D., M.P.H., F.R.C.P.; Israeli physician; b. 20 April 1906, Jerusalem; ed. schools in Buenos Aires, The American Univ., Beirut and Johns Hopkins Univ., Baltimore, Md.
Medical Officer of Health, Palestine 34; Chief Physician, Govt. Hosp., Haifa 37; Medical Supt., Yarkon Hosp., Tel-Aviv 42; Dir.-Gen. Ministry of Health, Israel 52; Dir. of Research Co-ordination, WHO, Geneva 60; Exec. Sec. Council for Int. Orgs. of Medical Sciences (CIOMS) 70-.
Publs. articles on tropical diseases, medical case administration, public health, etc.
10 Lamartine, Geneva, Switzerland.

Burg, Yosef, DR. PHIL.; Israeli politician; b. 31 Jan. 1909; ed. Univs. of Berlin and Leipzig, Pedagogical Inst., Leipzig, Rabbinical Seminary Berlin, and Hebrew Univ. of Jerusalem.
Directorate, Palestine Office, Berlin 36; Nat. Exec. Mizrachi; Zionist Gen. Council 39-51; mem. Exec. Hapoel Hamizrachi 44-; Deputy Speaker First Knesset (Israeli Parl.) 49-51; Minister of Health, Govt. of Israel 51-52; Minister of Posts and Telegraphs 52-58; Minister of Social Welfare 59-70; Minister of the Interior 70-; Hapoel Hamizrachi (Religious Workers' Party).
Ministry of the Interior, Jerusalem; and 6 Ben Maimon Street, Jerusalem, Israel.

Burgan, Salih Khalil, M.D.; Jordanian politician; b. 1918; ed. American Univ. of Beirut.
Physician, Transjordan Frontier Forces 43-46, Dir. of Arab Physicians, T.F.F. 46-48; Private Physician, Zerka 48-63; M.P. 61-63; Minister of Health April 63-July 64, of Social Affairs and Labour Feb. 66, Sept. 66, 67-69, of Public Health Sept. 66-Aug. 67, of Social, Labour, Home, Municipal and Rural Affairs April 67-69; mem. of Senate 63-69; Regional Dir ILO, Beirut 69-; Al Kawkab Medal (1st Grade); Grand Knight of the Holy Tomb.
ILO, P.O.B. 4656, Beirut, Lebanon.

Burns, Norman, M.A.; American economist and educationalist; b. 14 Nov. 1905; ed. Wittenberg Univ., Ohio, Yale Univ. and Univ. of Montpellier, France.
Assistant Prof. of Econs. American Univ. of Beirut 29-32; U.S. Govt. Service as Foreign trade economist, U.S. Tariff Comm., Dir. Foreign Service Inst. of State Dept., Dep. Dir. for Near East and South Asia, Int. Co-operation Admin., Econ. Adviser, UN Relief and Work Agency, Beirut, Dir. United States Operations Missions, Amman 34-61; Pres. American Univ. of Beirut 61-65; Board of Dirs. American Near East Refugee Inc., Washington 68-; mem. Board of Govs. Middle East Inst., Washington; Hon. LL.D. (Wittenberg Univ.); Commdr. Order of Cedar of Lebanon 65.
Publs. *The Tariff of Syria* 33, *Government Budgets of Middle East Countries* (Editor) 56, *Planning Economic Development in the Arab World* 59, *Education in the Middle East* 65, *Application of Technology and the Cultural Heritage* 65, *Management Factor in Economic Development* 70.
3813 North 37th Street, Arlington, Va. 22207, U.S.A.

Burroughs, Ronald Arthur, C.M.G.; British diplomatist; b. 4 June 1917; ed. St. John's School, Leatherhead and Trinity Coll., Cambridge.
Fleet Air Arm 40-45; Foreign Office 46; Second Sec., Rio de Janeiro 47-49; Consul, Marseilles 49-50; First Sec., Cairo 50-53; Foreign Office 53-55; Canadian Nat. Defence Coll. 55-56; First Sec., Vienna 56-59; Counsellor, Foreign Office 59-62; Counsellor and Head of Chancery, Rio de Janeiro 62-64; Counsellor, Lisbon 64-67; Chargé d'Affaires, S. Yemen 67-68; Asst. Under-Sec. of State, Foreign and Commonwealth Office 68-71; U.K. Govt. Rep., Northern Ireland 70-71; Amb. to Algeria 71-.
British Embassy, 7 Chemin des Glycines, Algiers, Algeria.

Bydany, Abdulrahman al-; Yemeni politician and diplomatist; b. 1926; ed. Univs. of Cairo and Bonn.
Minister to German Fed. Repub. 55-59, to Sudan 59-60; resigned and resided in Cairo 60-62; after Yemen Revolution was Vice-Pres. of Revolutionary Council, Prime Minister, Minister of Economy, Minister of Foreign Affairs, Deputy C.-in-C. 62-63; in Cairo 63-66; Amb. to Lebanon 66-70.
Publs. *Secrets of Yemen, Economy of Yemen.*
c/o Ministry of Foreign Affairs, Sana'a, Yemen Arab Republic.

C

Çağlayangil, Ihsan Sabri; Turkish politician; b. 1908; ed. Faculty of Law, Univ. of Istanbul.
Formerly with Ministry of Interior; Gov. of Antalya 48-53, of Çannakale 53-54, of Sivas 54, of Bursa 54-60; Senator for Bursa 61-; Minister of Labour Feb.-Oct. 65, of Foreign Affairs Oct. 65-March 71; Pres. Senate Foreign Affairs Cttee. 72-; Justice Party.
Kennedy Caddesi 64/2, Ankara, Turkey.

Cahen, Claude Louis Alfred, D. ès L.; French university professor; b. 1909; ed. Sorbonne, Ecole des Langues Orientales and Ecole Normale Supérieure, Paris.
Professor, Faculty of Letters, Univ. of Strasbourg 45-59, Sorbonne, Paris 59-; Lecturer, Ecole des Langues Orientales, Paris 37-54; Dir. *Journal of the Economic and Social History of the Orient*; Schlumberger Prize 45.
Publs. *La Syrie du Nord au temps des Croisades* 40, *Le régime féodal de l'Italie normande* 40, *Histoire générale des Civilisations* III, *Le Moyen Age (chapitres sur l'Islam), Pre-Ottoman Turkey* 68, *Der Islam* (Fischer Weltgeschichte) 68, French edn. *L'Islam* 70; various studies in Turkish history, Islamic economic and social history, and history of the Crusaders.
62 avenue Carnot, Savigny s. Orge (S.et.O.), France.

Caid Essebsi, Beji; Tunisian politician; b. 29 Nov. 1926. Lawyer in Tunis 52-55; mem. Cabinet of Habib Bourguiba 56, Taïeb Mehiri 57-58; Dir. Local and Common Admin. 58-62; Dir. of Tourism 62; Dir. Nat. Guard 63-65; Sec. of State for Interior July 65-69; Minister of Defence 69-70; Grand Cordon Order of the Republic; Commdr. Order of Independence.
c/o Ministry of Defence, Tunis, Tunisia.

Cappelletti, Luciano, J.D., PH.D.; Italian United Nations official; b. 22 Nov. 1930; ed. Univs. of Padua, Ferrara, Bologna and (Berkeley) Calif.
Associate Prof., Univ. of Bologna 60-63; joined UN Devt. Programme (UNDP) 63, has worked in India, Burma, Uganda, Pakistan; now Resident Rep. UNDP, Sudan.
Publs. *Burocrazia e Società* 68, and several articles on public administration in professional journals.
United Nations Development Programme, P.O. Box 913, Khartoum, Sudan.

Carton, Paul Georges; French diplomatist; b. 30 March, 1920; ed. Ecole Libre des Sciences Politiques and Ecole des Hautes Etudes Commerciales.
Joined diplomatic service 43, served Délégation Générale au Levant 43-45, Paris 46, Rabat 46-47, Tangier 47-48, Kabul 48-51, Amman 51-54, Tabriz 54, Ankara 54-55, Jeddah 55-56, Khartoum 56-58, Marrakesh 58-59; Consul-Gen. Aden 59-64; Counsellor, Washington 64-68; Amb. to Kuwait 68-, concurrently to Qatar, Bahrain, United Arab Emirates, Oman 72-; Officier, Légion d'Honneur, Lebanese decorations.
French Embassy, Kuwait Building, 4th Floor No. 202, Fahad al-Salem Street, Kuwait City, Kuwait.

Cayer Rt. Rev. John Aimé, D.D.; Canadian ecclesiastic; b. 1900; ed. Quebec and Montreal Colls. and Innsbruck Univ., Austria.
Ordained priest 26; missionary in Edmonton, Alberta 27-36; apptd. Rector of St. Anthony's Coll., Edmonton 30; Prof. of Theology, R.C. Seminary, Regina, Sask. 40-45; elected Commissary Provincial for the Franciscan Fathers 45, Minister Provincial for the Order in Canada 48; consecrated Bishop of Alexandria and Vicar Apostolic of Egypt, Sept. 49-, and Admin. of the Apostolic Vicariate of Port Said 57-.
Publ. *Mère Marie de Bethanie Beghian* 60.
Archbishop's Residence, 10 Sidi Metwalli, Alexandria, Egypt.

Chaker, Abdelmajid; Tunisian politician.
Secretary of State for Agriculture 62-64, for Information 64-66; Ambassador to Algeria 66-70; mem. Néo Destour, later Socialist Destour Party, Dir. until Nov. 64, mem. Bureau Politique Nov. 64-.
c/o Ministry of Foreign Affairs, Tunis, Tunisia.

Challah, Anwar S., M.S., M.B.A.; Syrian industrialist; b. 1910; ed. American Univ., and Univ. of California.
Former Pres. Syrian Oil Refining and Distribution Co., Damascus Chamber of Industry, Trustee Syrian Univ.; Pres. Juvenile Soc.; Trustee Savings Hospital; mem. Rotary Int.; Pres. Arab World Trade Promotion Centre.
P.O. Box 1618, Beirut, Lebanon.

Chamoun, Camille, LL.D.; Lebanese lawyer; b. 3 April 1900; ed. Coll. des Frères and Law School, Beirut.
Qualified as lawyer 24; mem. Parl. 34-; Minister of Finance 38; Minister of Interior 43-44; Minister to Allied Governments in London 44; Head of Del. to Int. Civil Aviation Conf., Chicago 44, UNESCO Conf. and UN Preparatory Comm. 45; Del. to UN Gen. Assembly, London and N.Y. 46; Lebanese rep. Interim Comm., UN 48; Pres. Lebanese Republic 52-58; leader Liberal Nationalist Party 58-.
Office of the Liberal National Party, Beirut; Home: Saadyat, Lebanon.

Chanderli, Abdelkader; Algerian diplomatist; b. 1915; ed. Univ. of Paris.
Former Foreign Correspondent and Editor; Chief, Public Relations Div. UNESCO 49-55; Rep. of Algerian Front de Libération Nationale (FLN) in U.S.A. 56-62; Perm. Rep. of Algeria to UN 62-64; Vice-Pres. ECOSOC 64-65; Dir.-Gen. Centre for Industrial Studies and Technology, Algiers; Pres. and Gen. Man. CAMEL Petroleum Co.
c/o Ministry of Industry and Energy, Algiers, Algeria.

Chatty, Habib; Tunisian diplomatist; b. 1916; ed. Sadiki Coll., Tunis.
Journalist 37-52, Editor *Ez-Zohra* 43-50, *Es-Sabah* 50-52; imprisoned 52, 53; Head, Press Cabinet of Pres. of Council 54-55, Head, Information Service 55; mem. Nat. Council, Néo-Destour Party 55; Dir. *Al Amal* 56; Vice-Pres. Constituent Nat. Assembly 56; Ambassador to Lebanon and Iraq 57-59, to Turkey and Iran 59-62, to U.K. 62-64, to Morocco 64-70, to Algeria 70-72; Head Cabinet of the Pres. Aug. 72-; Grand Cordon Ordre de la Répub. Tunisienne, several foreign decorations.
Presidential Palace, Carthage, Algeria.

Chaudhuri, Kamal Reheem, F.R.S.A.; Pakistani administrator; b. 1 March 1921; ed. Calcutta Univ., Presidency Coll., Aligarh Muslim Univ., Imperial Agricultural Research Inst. and Edinburgh Univ.
Governor Imperial Coll. of Science and Technology 57-65; Chair. British Commonwealth Scientific Offices, London 58; Assessor British Cttee. for Int. Nature Conservation 58-65; Chair. Commonwealth Agricultural Bureaux 61; Alt. Gov. IAEA 63; Head UNESCO Regional Office for the Arab States 70-; del. to numerous int. scientific and agricultural confs.
Publs. include *Science and Ourselves* 60.
UNESCO Regional Office for the Arab States, 8 Salamlik Street, Garden City, Cairo, Egypt.

Chéhab, Amir Khalid; Lebanese diplomatist and politician; b. 1890; ed. Patriarchal Coll. Damascus.
Mem. comm. for drawing up Lebanese Constitution 26; Minister of Finance 27; elected Deputy 28-55, 60-; Pres. Chamber of Deputies 35; Prime Minister 38; Minister of State 43; Minister to Jordan 47; Prime Minister and Minister of the Interior Oct. 52-April 53; Leader Dar el Fatura.
Rue de Damas, Beirut, Lebanon.

Chéhab, Amir Maurice; Lebanese archaeologist and historian; b. 1904; ed. Univ. St. Joseph, Beirut, Ecole du Louvre, and Ecole des Hautes Etudes Historiques, Paris.
Conservator, Lebanese Nat. Museum 28, Chief of Antiquities Service 37, Dir. 44; Prof. of the History of Architecture, Lebanese Acad. of Fine Arts 42, of Lebanese History, Ecole Normale 42, of Diplomatic and Gen. History, Ecole des Sciences Politiques 45; Prof. of Oriental Archæology, Inst. of Oriental Literature 46; Dir. Tyre and Anjar Excavations 50; Prof. of History and Archæology, Univ. of the Lebanon; Curator of Lebanese Gen. Antiquities 53-59, Dir.-Gen. of Antiquities 59-.
Direction des Antiquités, rue de Damas, Beirut, Lebanon.

Chelli, Tijani; Tunisian politician; b. 23 March 1931, Nabeul; ed. Collège Sadiki, Tunis and in France.
Engineer, Ministry of Public Works, Kef 59-60; Deputy Chief Engineer of Roads and Bridges 60; Dir. of Transport 61; Dir. of Sea and Air Transport 62; Pres., Dir.-Gen. Société Nationale des Chemins de Fer Tunisiens 65-67; Dir. of Industry, Dept. of the Plan and Nat. Economy 67-69; Pres., Dir.-Gen. Industries Chimiques Maghrébines (ICM) Jan.-Nov. 69; Minister of Public Works 69-70, of the Economy 70-72; Pres., Dir.-Gen. Agence de Promotion des Investissements Jan. 73-.
Agence de Promotion des Investissements, 18 avenue Mohamed V, Tunis, Tunisia.

Cherkaoui, Mohamed, LL.B.; Moroccan diplomatist and politician; b. 5 March 1921; ed. Univ. de Toulouse.
Minister of Posts and Telegraphs 60-61; Ambassador to France June 61-Aug. 64; Minister of National Economy 64-65; Minister of Development 65-Feb. 66, of Foreign Affairs Feb. 66-67; Minister of Nat. Defence 67; Pres. Org. for Afro-Asian Co-operation 66-; Pres. Comité Permanent Consultatif du Maghreb 64-; Democratic Constitutional.
c/o Ministry of National Defence, Rabat, Morocco.

Christofides, Andreas N., M.A.; Cypriot broadcasting official; b. 20 Aug. 1937; ed. Pancyprian Gymnasium, Nicosia, Athens Univ. and Columbia Univ., New York.
Teacher at Pancyprian Gymnasium 58-63; Dir. of Radio Programmes of Cyprus Broadcasting Corpn. 64-67; Dir.-Gen. of Cyprus Broadcasting Corpn. 67-.
Publs. include: Essays: *Letters from New York* 65, *Points of View I* 66, *Points of View II* 69 (First Nat. Award Prize), *Introduction to Propaganda* 66, *Love Songs from Cyprus* 64, *An Anthology of Poetry from Cyprus* (with K. Montis) 69, *An Anthology of Short Stories* (with P. Ioannides) 71; Poems: *A Strange Illustration* 69, *Analytical Propositions* 70.
Cyprus Broadcasting Corporation, P.O. Box 1824, Nicosia, Cyprus.

Clerides, Glavkos John, B.A., LL.B.; Cypriot lawyer and politician; b. 1919; ed. Pancyprian Gymnasium, Nicosia, Univ. Tutorial Coll., London, King's Coll., London Univ., Gray's Inn, London.
Served with R.A.F. 39-45; shot down and taken prisoner 42-45 (mentioned in despatches); practised law in Cyprus 51-60; Head of Greek Cypriot Del., Constitutional Comm. 59-60; first Minister of Justice of the Republic 59-60; mem. House of Representatives 60-, Pres. of the House 60-; Acting Pres. of Repub.; Chair. Selection Cttee, Public Accounts Cttee., Attendance of Members Cttee.; Rep. to Consultative Assembly of the Council of Europe; mem. Political Cttee. and Standing Cttee.; leader of Unified Party; Gold Medal Order of the Holy Sepulchre.
56 Metochio Street, Nicosia; House of Representatives, Nicosia Cyprus.

Cohn, Haim H.; Israeli lawyer; b. 11 March 1911; ed. Univs. of Munich, Hamburg and Frankfurt-am-Main, Germany, Hebrew Univ. of Jerusalem, and Govt. Law School, Jerusalem.
Admitted to Bar of Palestine 37; Sec. Legal Council, Jewish Agency for Palestine, Jerusalem 47; State Attorney, Ministry of Justice, Hakirya 48, Dir.-Gen. 49; Attorney-Gen., Govt. of Israel 50; Minister of Justice and Acting Attorney-Gen. 52; Attorney-Gen. 52-60; Justice, Supreme Court of Israel 60-; mem. Perm. Court of Arbitration, The Hague 62-, UN Comm. on Human Rights 65-67; Deputy Chair. Council of Higher Educ., Israel 58-71; mem. Board of Govs., Int. Inst. of Human Rights, Strasbourg; Chair. Exec. Council Hebrew Univ. of Jerusalem; Visiting Prof. of Law, Univ. of Tel-Aviv.
Publs. *The Foreign Laws of Marriage and Divorce* (English) 37, *Glaube und Glaubensfreiheit* (German) 67, *The Trial and Death of Jesus* (Hebrew) 68 English edn. 71, *Jewish Law in Ancient and Modern Israel* 72.
Supreme Court of Israel, Jerusalem; and 36 Tchernihovsky Street, Jerusalem, Israel.

Comay, Michael, B.A., LL.B.; Israeli diplomatist; b. 17 Oct. 1908; ed. Cape Town Univ., South Africa.
Major South African Army 40-45; Special Rep. South African Zionist Fed., attached to Political Dept. Jewish Agency, Jerusalem 46-48; mem. Israel del. to UN 48-, Chair. 60-67; has represented Israel at a number of int. confs.; Dir. British Commonwealth Div., Israel Foreign Ministry 48-51, Asst. Dir.-Gen. 51-53; Amb. to Canada 53-57; Asst. Dir.-Gen. Ministry for Foreign Affairs 57-59; Perm. Rep. to UN 60-67; Political Adviser to Foreign Minister and Amb.-at-Large 67-70; Amb. to U.K. 70-73; Special Adviser to Minister of Foreign Affairs Oct. 73-.
Ministry of Foreign Affairs, Jerusalem, Israel.

Coobar, Abdulmegid; Libyan politician; b. 1909; ed. Arabic and Italian schools in Tripoli, and privately.
With Birth Registration Section, Tripoli Municipal Council and later its Section Head, Adviser on Arab Affairs for the Council 43-44; resigned from Govt. Service 44; mem. Nat. Constitutional Assembly 50, and mem. its Cttee. to draft the Libyan Constitution; mem. of Parl. for Eastern Gharian 52-55, Pres. of Parl. Assembly 52-55; Dep. Prime Minister and Minister of Communications 55-56; again elected for Eastern Gharian to the new Chamber of Deputies 55, Pres. 56; mem. of Council of Viceroy 56; Dep. Prime Minister and Minister of Foreign Affairs 57; Prime Minister 57-60, concurrently Minister for Foreign Affairs 58-60; Independence Award (First Class).
Asadu el-Furat Street 29, Garden City, Tripoli, Libya.

Cosséry, Albert; Egyptian writer; b. 1913; ed. French schools in Cairo.
Went to Paris 30; served in Egyptian Merchant Marine 39-45; has lived in Paris since 45; Edited *Al Tatawwor* weekly 43.
Publs. *Les hommes oubliés de Dieu* 40, *La maison de la mort certaine, Les fainéants dans la vallée fertile, Mendiants et orgueilleux, La violence et la dérision.*
Hôtel de la Louisiane, rue de Seine, Paris 6e, France.

Crawford, William R., Jr., M.A.; American diplomatist; b. 22 April 1928; ed. Harvard Coll. and Univ. of Pennsylvania, U.S.A.
Political Officer, Jeddah, Saudi Arabia 51; Consul, Venice, Italy 53; Chargé d'Affaires, Taiz, Yemen 57, Principal Officer, Aden; Officer-in-Charge Lebanon-Israel Affairs, Washington, D.C. 62; Counsellor, Political Officer, Rabat, Morocco 64; Deputy Head of Mission to Cyprus 68; Amb. to Yemen Arab Repub. 72-; Meritorious Service Award (U.S. Dept. of State) 59, William A. Jump Award 63.
American Embassy, Sana'a, Yemen Arab Republic.

Creswell, Sir Keppel Archibald Cameron, Kt., C.B.E., F.B.A., F.S.A.; British archaeologist; b. 13 Sept. 1879; ed. Westminster School.
Served First World War; Inspector of Monuments, Occupied Enemy Territory (Syria, Palestine) 19-20; lived in Cairo 20-; mem. cttee. Persian Exhibition, London 31; Prof. of Muslim Architecture, Fuad I Univ. 31-51, American Univ., Cairo 56-; Museum of Antiquities 49-55; mem. of Cttee. for the Preservation of Muslim Monuments, Cairo; Order of Ismail (3rd Class); Syrian Order of Merit (1st Class); Hon. D.Litt. (Oxford), Hon. Lit.D. (Princeton), Hon. A.R.I.B.A.
Publs. *Brief Chronology of the Muslim Monuments of Egypt* 19, *Origin of the Cruciform Plan of Cairene Madrasas* 22, *Archæological Researches at the Citadel of Cairo* 24, *The Works of Sultan Bibars in Egypt* 26, *Early Muslim Architecture*, 2 vols., folio, 32-40, *The Muslim Architecture of Egypt*, 2 vols., folio, 52-59, *A Short Account of Early Muslim Architecture* 58, *A Bibliography of the Architecture, Arts and Crafts of Islam* 61.
American University, Cairo; and 2 rue Baehler, Cairo, Egypt.

Cunbur, Fatma Müjgân, DR. PHIL.; Turkish librarian; b. 1926; ed. Lycée and Univ. of Ankara.
Librarian of Faculty of Letters, Univ. of Ankara 52-55, Lecturer in Library Science 60-; Librarian Nat. Library 55-59, Acting Dir. 59, Chief of rare books and manuscripts section 60-65, Gen. Dir. 65-; mem. Turkish Librarians' Asscn., Turkish Language Asscn., Asscn. for Studying Social Life of Women.
Publs. *Türk Kadın Yazarları Bibliyografyası* (Bibliography of Turkish Women Authors) 55, *Fuzuli hakkında bir bibliyografya denemesi* (A Preliminary Bibliography of the Turkish Poet Fuzuli) 56, *Fuzuli divan* (Collected Poems of Fuzuli) 58, *Yunus Emre'nin gönlü* (The Heart of Yunus Emre) 59, *Yusuf Ağa Kütüphanesi Vakfiyesi* (The Endowment of Yusuf Ağa Library) 63, *I. Abdülhamid vakfiyesi ve Hamidiye Kütüphanesi* (The Endowment of Abdülhamid I and the Hamidiye Library) 65, *Başaklarin sesi, Türkhalk sairleri, hayatları ve eserleri* (The Sounds of Corn Ears, Turkish folk poets, their lives and works).
Turkish National Library, Yenişehir, Ankara, Turkey.

D

Dafaalla, El Nazeer, D.K.V.S., DIP.BACT., A.F.R.C.V.S.; Sudanese university professor; b. 1922; ed. Khartoum and Manchester Univs.
Government Veterinary Officer, Khartoum, Malakal and Nyala 46-50; research in England on anaerobic bacteria 50-52; Research Officer, Sudan Veterinary Service 52-54, Senior Research Officer 55-56; Senior Lecturer, Univ. of Khartoum 56-57, Dean Faculty of Veterinary Science 58-60; Deputy Vice-Chancellor 60-62, Prof. of Bacteriology and Vice-Chancellor 62-68; Provost of Agriculture and Veterinary Medicine, Ahmadu Bello Univ., Nigeria 71-72; Speaker People's Assembly 72-; Round Table Conf. for Southern Sudan; mem. FAO Int. Panels of Experts, Nat. FAO Cttee., and various foreign socs.; mem. Admin. Board Int. Asscn. of Univs.; Exec. Vice-Pres. of Asscn. of African Univs.; mem. Exec. Cttee. Sudan Veterinary Asscn. 47-; Chair. Editorial Board, *Sudan Journal of Veterinary Science and Husbandry;* Pres. Sudan Nat. Scientific Council 73, mem. Advisory Panel of Experts on the Emergency Control of Livestock Diseases, Rome May 67; Hon. Fellow, Hanover Univ.; Hon. D.Sc. (Charles Univ., Prague).
Publs. many papers on Veterinary Bacteriology.
People's Assembly, Khartoum, Sudan.

Dagher, Abdallah, S.J.; Lebanese ecclesiastic and university rector; b. 1 June 1914; ed. Secondary School of Univ. St. Joseph, Oriental Seminary of Beirut and Univ. de Paris à la Sorbonne.
Entered Jesuit Noviciate 32; ordained priest 45; Prefect Arabic Studies, Secondary School of Univ. St. Joseph; Dir. Oriental Seminary (Maronite) of Beirut; Rector Maronite Seminary of Ghazir, Lebanon 51-57; Jesuit Provincial for the Near East 57-65; Rector Univ. St. Joseph 65-72, Coll. Notre-Dame de Jamhour 72-; Consultant of Roman Congregation for the Non-Christian Religious (Islam); Officier de la Légion d'Honneur.
Collège Notre-Dame de Jamhour, P.O. Box 2904, Beirut, Lebanon.

Dajani, Ali Taher, B.A.; Jordanian administrator; b. 1911; ed. English Coll., Jerusalem, American Univ. of Beirut.
Assistant Information Officer, Public Information Office, Jerusalem 36-43; Sec. Arab Chamber of Commerce, Jerusalem 43-47; Asst. Commr. of Commerce and Industry, Palestine Govt. 47-48; Admin. Sec. Amman Chamber of Commerce and Industry 50-55; Controller-Gen. Transjordan Electric Power Co., Amman 55-60; Co-manager Wafa Dajani & Sons Co. Ltd. 60-63; commentator on economic activity in Jordan to *Al-Difa'a* newspaper and Jordan corresp. of *Al-Hayat,* Beirut; mem. of Parl. July 63-Dec. 66; Minister of Communications Feb.-July 65; The Star of Jordan 1st class.
Publs. in Arabic: *Pilgrimage to Mecca* 44, *The Economy of Jordan* 55; in English; *Industry of Jordan* 65, 67.
P.O. Box 1791, Amman, Jordan.

Dakhqan, Omar Abdullah, B.SC.; Jordanian politician; b. 1927, Amman.
Assistant Under-Sec. Ministry of Public Works 54; Dir.-Gen. Jordan-Hijaz Railway 56; Dir.-Gen. Central Water Authority 64-66, also Dir. of Geological and Mining Research 65-66; Dir.-Gen. and Deputy Pres. Natural Resources Authority 66-69; Dir.-Gen. Jordan Phosphate Co. 69-70; Minister of Agriculture 70-72.
c/o Arab National Union, Amman, Jordan.

Dalley, Christopher Mervyn, C.M.G., M.A., F.INST.PET., C.ENG.; British petroleum executive; b. 26 Dec. 1913; ed. Epsom College and Queens' Coll., Cambridge.
Royal Navy 39-45; British Petroleum Co. 46, Chief Engineer, B.P. Refinery (Llandarcy) 52; Iranian Oil Operating Companies in Iran 54, Asst. Gen. Man. Dir. 58; Iraq Petroleum Co., Abu Dhabi Petroleum Co., Qatar Petroleum Co. and other associated companies 62, Man. Dir. 63; Pres. Inst. of Petroleum 70; Chair. Iraq Petroleum Co. 70-; Order of Homayoun (Iran) 63.
33 Cavendish Square, London, W.1, England.

Dana, Osman Mosbah el; Lebanese politician; b. 1921; ed. Faculty of Law, Beirut.
Member Chamber of Deputies 60-; Minister of Public Works 60-61; Minister of General Economy 61-64; Minister of Finance 65; Leader Mouvement de l'action nationale 65-; Solicitor-Gen. Beirut Court of Appeal 51-60; Minister of Public Works and Transport 68; Minister of Hydraulic and Electrical Resources 69; Minister of Information 70, of Health 73-.
Ministère de la Santé Publique, Beirut, Lebanon.

Danişman, Rıfkı; Turkish politician; b. 1924, Erzurum; ed. secondary school, Erzurum, School of Higher Studies in Commerce and Econs., Istanbul, Inst. of Public Admin. for Turkey and the Middle East, Ankara.
Served in various posts in State Highways Org., and in Dir.-Gen. of Posts, Telegraphs and Telecommunications, later Sec.-Gen. PTT and mem. Exec. Board; fmr. mem. of Exec. Board, Northern Electric Co.; mem. Parl. (Justice Party) 69-; Minister of Communications 71-73; mem. Nat. Security Council.
National Assembly, Ankara, Turkey.

Daoud Khan, Mohammad (cousin of fmr. King Zahir Shah); Afghan army officer and politician; ed. Habibia Coll. Kabul, Pre-cadet School Kabul, and in France.
Governor of Kandahar 32; Gov. and C.-in-C. Eastern Provinces 34; C.-in-C. Central Forces and Mil. Schools 37; suppressed revolt of 45; Prime Minister 53-63, concurrently Minister of Defence and of the Interior; led coup deposing King Mohammed Zahir Shah July 73; Pres., Prime Minister Repub. of Afghanistan 73-.
Office of the President, Kabul, Afghanistan.

Daouk, Ahmed bey; Lebanese engineer, diplomatist and politician; b. 1893; ed. Univ. of Aix-en-Provence.
Engineer with Sucreries et Raffineries d'Egypte 15-19; technical mission for King Hussein of Hedjaz 19-20; consultant 20-27; held various directorships 27-40; Prime Minister 41, 42, May-Aug. 60; Pres. Nat. Congress 43; Ambassador to France 44-58, to Spain; Head of Missions to U.S.A., South America and Africa; Rep. to Arab League; mem. Dels. to UN and UNESCO 44-58; Pres. Admin. Council of Banks and Socs. 60-; Leader of official dels. overseas 60-; Prime Minister 60; holder of several Lebanese and foreign decorations.
Rue Omar Daouk, Beirut, Lebanon.

Darwish, Dr. Ahmed el Sayed; Egyptian physician; ed. Cairo Univ.
Lecturer, Alexandria Coll. of Medicine until 64, Dean 64-; fmr. Minister of Tourism; Minister of Health and Social Affairs Sept. 71-Jan. 72; Adviser to the Pres. Jan. 72-.
The Presidency, Cairo, Egypt.

Dashti, Ali; Iranian writer, politician and diplomatist; b. March 1895; ed. Iraq.
Former mem. *Majlis,* mem. Senate; fmr. Editor *Shafaq Sorkh* (Red Dawn); Ambassador to Egypt 50, to Lebanon 60-63; Senator 63-.
Publs. Novels, short stories, analytical works on poetry of Hafez and Sa'adi, Omar Khayyam, Rumi, Khaghani and others; *Prison Notebooks, Anglo-Saxon Accomplishments, Sajeh, Self-Help.*
The Senate, Teheran, Iran.

Davachi, Abbas, ING.AGRIC.; Iranian university professor; b. 1906: ed. Teheran, Paris and Montpellier Univs.
Entomologist, Ministry of Agriculture 36, Dir.-Gen. Dept. of Plant Protection 43-46; Pres. Teheran Int. Locust Cttee.

44-46; Prof. of Entomology, Faculty of Agriculture, Teheran Univ. 46-, Dean of Faculty 66-; mem. Agricultural Acad. of France 57; Chair. FAO Nat. Cttee. 58; Légion d'Honneur de France; mem. Agricultural Council.
Publs. *Entomology and Applied Phytopathology*, *Insects Harmful to Plants Cultivated in Iran*, etc.
Faculty of Agriculture, University of Teheran, Teheran, Iran.

Dawalibi, Marouf; Syrian professor and lawyer; b. 1907; ed. Aleppo, Damascus, and Univ. of Paris.
Lawyer Court of Appeal Aleppo 35-39; Prof. Law Faculty, Damascus 47; Minister of Nat. Economy 49-50; Pres. Chamber of Deputies 51; Prime Minister and Minister of Defence 51; Minister of Nat. Defence 54; Prime Minister 61-62; mem. Exec. Council Motamav al Alam al Islami (World Muslim Congress) 65; living in Saudi Arabia 66.
Publs. *La Jurisprudence dans le Droit Islamique* 41, *Introduction au Droit Romain* 47, *Introduction à la science des sources du Droit Musulman* 49, *Précis du Droit Romain* 2 vols. 61, *Histoire Générale du Droit* 61.

Dayan, Gen. Moshe, LL.B.; Israeli soldier and politician; b. 20 May 1915, Degania; ed. agricultural high school, Nahalal, and Staff Coll., Camberley.
Trained in Haganah (Jewish militia) 29; second in command to Capt. Orde Wingate 37; imprisoned by British when Haganah declared illegal 38; released for training as intelligence scout in Syria 41: Colonel after 45; took leading part in war with Arabs 48-49; promoted to Gen. and Commdr. Southern Region Command 50; Commdr. Northern Region Command 51; Chief of Staff 53-58; Minister of Agriculture 59-64; Minister of Defence 67-; fmr. mem. Mapai Party; joined Rafi Party (Labour List) 65; elected to the Knesset 59, 65, 69 (Maarach List).
Publs. *Diary of the Sinai Campaign* 66, *Mapa Hadasha*, *Yahassim Aherim* 69.
Ministry of Defence, Tel-Aviv; and Yoav Street 11, Zahala, Tel-Aviv, Israel.

de Garang, (Enok) Mading; Sudanese politician; b. 1 Jan. 1934, Kongor, Bor; ed. Malek Atar Intermediate School, Rumbek Secondary School, Manchester Coll. of Science and Technology, Inst. of Educ., London Univ.
Managing Editor, *Malakal* 63-65; Deputy Dir. Africa Literature Centre, Kitwe, Zambia 67-69; Dir. Southern Sudan Asscn., Editor *Grass Curtain* 70-72; Principal Political Rep. abroad for Sudanese Liberation Movt. 69-72; Negotiator for SLM, Addis Ababa Peace Talks 72; mem. for Information, Culture, Youth, Tourism, Sports and Social Services, High Exec. Council for the Southern Region April 72-.
Ministry of Information, P.O. Box 126, Juba; Home: Bor District, Upper Nile Province, Sudan.

Deif, Nazih Ahmed, B.COM., M.A., PH.D.; Egyptian economist; b. 4 March 1923; ed. Cairo Univ. and Univ. of Chicago, Ill., U.S.A.
Member Expert Group collaborating with Arthur D. Little Group on Industrialization of Egypt 53; Dir. Econ. Statistics, Ministry of Finance 54; Senior Research Officer, Nat. Planning Comm. 57, Dir.-Gen. 58; Under-Sec. Ministry of Planning, U.A.R. 61-64; Gov. Int. Monetary Fund, U.A.R. 64-66; Minister of Treasury, Egypt 64-68; Prof. Inst. of Statistical Studies and Research, Cairo Univ. 69-70; Exec. Dir. for Middle East, IMF Sept. 70-.
Publs. numerous papers on national planning issues, particularly national accounting, and various UN publs.
International Monetary Fund, Washington, D.C.; and 2 Rollins Court, Rockville, Md. 20852, U.S.A.

Demirel, Süleyman; Turkish hydraulic engineer and politician; b. 1924, Istâmköy, Isparta Prov.; ed. High School, Afyon and Istanbul Technical Univ.
Qualified engineer; worked in U.S.A. 49-51, 54-55; with Dir.-Gen. Electrical Studies, Ankara 50-52; in charge of building various hydro-electric schemes 52-54; Head of Dept. of Dams 54; Dir.-Gen. of Water Control 54-55; first Eisenhower Fellow for Study in U.S.A. 54; Dir. State Hydraulics Admin. 55-60; private practice including Consultant to Morrison-Knudsen, and lecturer Middle East Technical Univ. 61-65; Pres. Justice Party 64-; Deputy Prime Minister Feb.-Oct. 65; Prime Minister Nov. 65-March 71.
Adalet Partisi Genel Müdürlüğü, Ankara, Turkey.

Denktaş, Rauf; Cypriot lawyer; b. 1924; ed. English School, Nicosia, and Lincoln's Inn, London.
Legal practice, Nicosia 47-49; Crown Counsel and Acting Solicitor-Gen., Attorney-Gen.'s Office 49-58; Chair. Fed. of Turkish Asscns. 58-60; Pres. Turkish Communal Chamber 60-; Vice-Pres. Turkish Cypriot Admin. 67-73, Pres. 73-; Vice-Pres. of Cyprus 73-.
6 Ankara Street, Nicosia, Cyprus.

Deriner, İbrahim; Turkish civil engineer; b. 1909; ed. Istanbul Technical Univ.
Formerly in Electrical Power Resources Survey and Planning Admin., Dir.-Gen. 52; Under-Sec. of Power 65; Minister of Power and Natural Resources Nov. 65-67; Sec.-Gen. Turkish Atomic Energy Comm. 67-; Dir.-Gen. Turkish Electricity Authority 70-71.
Turkish Atomic Energy Commission, Bestekar Sok. No. 29, Kavaklidere-Ankara, Turkey.

De Shalit, Meir; Israeli civil servant; b. 1921; ed. Pardess Hana School of Agriculture, Israel.
Infantry officer, Jewish Brigade, British Army, Second World War; Israel Defence Forces 46-49; First Sec. Israel Embassy, Washington 49-54; Deputy Dir.-Gen. Prime Minister's Office 54-59; Dir. Israel Govt. Tourist Corpn. 59-64; Dir.-Gen. Ministry of Tourism 64-70; Chair. of Board, Rassco; dir. of several cos.
76 Rehov HaNassi, Herzliya-on-Sea, Israel.

Desroches-Noblecourt, Christiane; French museum curator; b. 17 Nov. 1913; ed. Lycée Molière and Faculté des Lettres, Univ. of Paris.
Conservator, then Chief Conservator of Nat. Museums; Conservator of Egyptian Antiquities, Louvre Museum; teacher, Ecole du Louvre; Counsellor to UNESCO at Centre de documentation et d'Etudes sur l'Egypte ancienne, Cairo; Chevalier, Légion d'Honneur; Médaille de la Résistance.
Publ. *Toutan Khamon* 66.
3 rue de la Pompe, Paris 16e; and Château de Mondemont, par Cézanne, Marne, France.

Diba, H.I.M. Queen Farah; Empress of Iran; b. 1938; ed. Italian School, Jeanne d'Arc School and Razi School, Teheran and Ecole Spéciale d'Architecture, Paris.
Married H.I.M. the Shah 21 December, 59; son Reza b. 31 Oct. 60, daughter Farahnaz b. 12 March 63, son Ali Reza b. 28 April 66; Patron Farah Pahlavi Asscn. (administration of orphanages in Iran), Iran Cultural Foundation, etc.
The Imperial Palace, Teheran, Iran.

Diba, Fereidun, DR. RER. POL.; Iranian diplomatist; b. 1920; ed. Univs. of Teheran and Rome.
Ministry of Foreign Affairs, successively Library Dept., Dept. of Ministerial Work, First Political Dept., Iranian Consul Shanghai; Second Sec. Nanking; First Sec. Rome; Deputy Dir. Political Dept., Dir. Passport Dept. and Head Nationality Dept., Ministry of Foreign Affairs, Dir. First Political Dept.; Amb. to Syria 63-65, to Belgium and Luxembourg, Head of Mission to EEC 65-67; Dir.-Gen. (for Asian and African Affairs), Foreign Ministry, Teheran 68-70; Amb. to Poland 70-.
Embassy of Iran, Warsaw, Poland.

Dimechkié, Nadim, M.A.; Lebanese diplomatist; b. 5 Dec. 1919; ed. American Univ. of Beirut.
Director-General Ministry of Nat. Economy 43-44; Lebanese del. Joint Supply Board for Syria and Lebanon 42-44; Counsellor, Lebanese Embassy, London 44-49; Consul-Gen., Ottawa 50; Dir. Econ. and Social Dept., Ministry of Foreign Affairs 51-52; Chargé d'Affaires, Cairo 52, Minister 53-55; Minister to Switzerland 55-57; Amb. to U.S.A. 58-62; Dir. Econ. Affairs, Ministry of Foreign Affairs 62-66; Amb. to U.K. 66-; Lebanese Order of Cedars, Syrian Order of Merit, Tunisian Order of Merit, Greek Order of Phoenix, Egyptian Order of Ismail, etc.
Lebanese Embassy, 21 Kensington Palace Gardens, London, W.8, England.

Dimitriou, Nicos George, F.C.I.S.; Cypriot merchant banker, industrialist and politician; b. 16 July 1920; ed. Larnaca Commercial Lyceum, Greek Gymnasium, Athens, and Maiden Erlegh Private School, Reading, England.
Manager and Sec. N. J. Dimitriou Ltd., Merchant Bankers 52-62, Man. Dir. 62-; Man. Dir. Larnaca Oil Works Ltd. 63-; dir. several Cyprus companies; Dir. Bank of Cyprus Ltd. 60-62; Chair. Cyprus Chamber of Commerce 60-63; Pres. Chamber of Commerce and Industry, Larnaca 63-68, Pezoporicos Club, Larnaca 57-68; Pres. Cyprus Soc. of Inc. Secretaries 68; Consul-Gen. of Denmark 61-; mem. Council Cyprus Chamber of Commerce and Industry 63-68; Chair. Cyprus Devt. Corpn. Ltd. 66-68; Minister of Commerce and Industry 68-70; Chair. Electricity Authority of Cyprus 70-, Advisory Board Nat. and Grindlays Bank Ltd. 70-; Commdr. Order of Cedar of Lebanon; Commdr. Order of Dannebrog.
Publ. *Chambers of Commerce—their Objects and Aims.*
Artemis Avenue 39, Larnaca, Cyprus.

Dinitz, Simcha, M.S.; Israeli politician; b. 23 June 1929; ed. Univ. of Cincinnatti and School of Foreign Service, Georgetown Univ.
Director, Office of the Dir.-Gen., Ministry of Foreign Affairs 61-63; Political Sec. to Minister of Foreign Affairs 63-66; Minister, Embassy of Israel, Rome 66-68, Washington 68-69; Political Advisor to the Prime Minister 69, later Dir.-Gen. Office of the Prime Minister; Amb. to U.S.A. 73-; mem. Israeli del. to the UN 63, 64, 65.
Publ. *The Legal Aspect of the Egyptian Blockade of the Suez Canal* (Georgetown Law Journal) 56.
Embassy of Israel, 1621 22nd Street N.W., Washington, D.C. 20008, U.S.A. Home: 40 Nayot, Jerusalem, Israel.

Diringer, David, M.A., D.LITT.; British oriental archæologist and epigraphist; b. 1900; ed. Univ. of Florence.
Lecturer Univ. of Florence 31, Prof. 34; during Second World War held a position with the Foreign Office London; Editor War Office paper *Il Corriere del Sabato* 44; Univ. Lecturer in Semitic Epigraphy, Cambridge Univ. 48-66, Reader 66-68; Deputy Sec.-Gen. First Int. Congress for Etruscan Studies 28; Sec. Perm. Cttee. for Etruria 31; Deputy Sec.-Gen. Italian Congress for Colonial Studies 31, 34, 37; Prize of Royal Italian Acad. for research in Oriental Archæology; in England, lecturer on Biblical archæology, history of writing, oriental philology, and allied subjects, Fellow and mem. various learned socs.; Founder Alphabet Museum and Seminar, Cambridge 59; Alphabet Museum, Tel-Aviv 65.
Publs. In Italian, over 100, including: *The Early Hebrew Inscriptions* 34, *The Alphabet in the History of Civilisation* 37, 69; in English, over 250, including: *The Alphabet, a Key to the History of Mankind* 48, 3rd edn. 66, revised edn. in 2 vols. 68, *The Hand-produced Book* 53, *The Illuminated Book: its History and Production* 58, revised edn. 67, *The Story of the Aleph Beth* 58, *Writing* 62 (also in Swedish, Danish, etc.), *Alphabet* (in Russian) 63, and over 350 articles in scientific periodicals and encyclopedias.
50 St. Barnabas Road, Cambridge, England.

Djamalzadeh, Mohamed Ali, LIC. EN DROIT; Iranian writer; b. 1896, Ispahan; ed. Univ. of Dijon, France.
Member, Cttee. of Iranian Nationalists, Berlin; worked for Int. Labour Org. 31; Cultural Attaché, Iranian Embassy, Geneva.
Publs. *Kaveh, Yéki bond-o-yéki nabond* (Once upon a time) 21, *Gandjé Cháyégan* (Economy of Iran), *History of Russo-Persian Relations*, *Elm-o-Honar* (Science and Art), and several novels and articles; translations in French, German, Russian, Hebrew, etc.
78F Corissant, 1206 Geneva, Switzerland.

Dobkin, Eliahu; Israeli jurist; b. 1898; ed. Kharkov Univ.
Founder of "Hechalutz" World Pioneer Movement 20; mem. Exec. Jewish Agency, World Zionist Organization 35-; mem. Exec. Jewish Federation of Labour 32-; Chair. Board of Dirs. Keren Hayesod 52-; Head of Dept. of Youth and Hechalutz, Jewish Agency; Chair. Board of Dirs., Bezalel National Museum; mem. Board of Dirs. Israel Museum, ZIM Navigation Co.
Publs. *Immigration and Rescue in Years of Disaster*, several articles.
Jewish Agency Buildings, Jerusalem, Israel.

Doğramaci Ihsan, M.D.; Turkish pediatrician and educator; b. 3 April 1915; ed. Istanbul, Harvard, Washington Univs.
Associate Prof. of Pediatrics, Ankara Univ. 49-54, Prof. of Child Health and Head of Dept. 54-63; Dir. Inst. of Child Health, Ankara 58-63; Prof. of Pediatrics and Head of Dept. Hacettepe Faculty of Medicine 63-, Dean of Faculty June 63-Nov. 63; Pres. Ankara Univ. 63-65; Pres. Hacettepe Science Centre, Ankara 65-67; mem. UNICEF Exec. Board 60-, Chair. 68-70; Chair. Board of Trustees, Middle East Technical Univ. 65-67; Pres. Hacettepe Univ. 67-; Chair. Exec. Cttee. Int. Pediatric Asscn. 68-; mem. Bureau of Standing Conf. of Rectors and Vice-Chancellors of the European Univs. 69-; Dir. Int. Children's Centre (Paris) 70-; Fellow, Royal Coll. of Physicians (London) 71; Corresp. mem. Acad. Nat. de Médecine, France 73-; hon. mem. several foreign pediatric socs.; Hon. LL.D. (Nebraska Univ.), Dr. h.c. (Nice Univ.); Chevalier, Légion d'Honneur 73; Editor *The Turkish Journal of Pediatrics*, Consulting Editor *Clinical Pediatrics.* Publs. *Annenin Kitabi* (Mother's Handbook on Child Care) 7 edns. 52-71, *Premature Baby Care* 54, *Porphysis in Childhood* 64, *Care of Mother and Child* 67, various monographs and articles on child health and pediatric topics.
Hacettepe University, Ankara, Turkey.

Dostrovsky, Israel, PH.D.; Israeli atomic energy official and professor of isotope research; b. 1918, Odessa, U.S.S.R.; ed. Univ. Coll., London.
Engaged in research work, Univ. Coll., London 40-43; Lecturer in Chem., Univ. Coll. of N. Wales 43-48; Dir.-Gen. Israel Atomic Energy Comm. 48-; Prof. Isotope Research Dept., Weizmann Inst. of Science; research on reaction mechanisms and separation of isotopes; Acting Pres. Weizmann Inst. 73-; Ramsay Medal, U.K. 44; Weizmann Prize, Israel 52.
Neve Weizmann, Rehovot, Israel.

Driss, Rachid; Tunisian journalist and diplomatist; b. 27 Jan. 1917; ed. Sadiki Coll., Tunis.
Joined Néo-Destour Party 34; journalist exiled in Cairo, and with President Bourguiba founder mem. Bureau du Maghreb Arabe 46-52; returned to Tunisia 55; Editor *El*

Amal; Deputy, Constitutional Assembly 56; Sec. of State Post Office and Communications 57-64; mem. Nat. Assembly 58-, Political Bureau Destour Socialist Party 58-; Amb. to the U.S.A. and Mexico 64-70; Perm. Rep. to UN 70-; Pres. Econ. and Social Council 71; Grand Cordon de l'Ordre de l'Indépendance de la République Tunisienne and foreign decorations.
Permanent Mission of Tunisia to UN, 40 East 71st Street, New York, N.Y. 10021, U.S.A.

Driver, Sir Godfrey, C.B.E., M.C., M.A., F.B.A.; British university professor emeritus; b. 20 Aug. 1892; ed. Winchester Coll. and New Coll., Oxford.
Military and nat. service 15-19, 40-44; Fellow and Classical Tutor Magdalen Coll. Oxford 19-28, Librarian 23-42, Fellow by Special Election 28-62, Hon. Fellow 62; Reader in Comparative Semitic Philology, Univ. of Oxford 28, Prof. of Semitic Philology 38-62, Grinfield Lecturer on the Septuagint 35-38, Curator of Bodleian Library 34-53; Visiting Prof. Chicago Univ. 25, Louvain Univ. 50, Jerusalem Univ. 57; Cadbury Lecturer, Birmingham 58, Walker Lecturer, Belfast 61; Joint Editor *Journal of Theological Studies* 33-47; Joint Dir. of Cttee. revising English Bible 47; assoc. mem. Royal Flemish Acad. of Science, Letters and Arts 54; Pres. Int. Organization of Old Testament Scholars; Hon. Fellow, School of Oriental Studies, London; Hon. D.D. (Aberdeen), Hon.Litt.D. (Durham, Cambridge, Oxford).
Publs. *Letters of the First Babylonian Dynasty* 25, *Grammar of the Colloquial Arabic of Syria and Palestine* 25, *Nestorius, the Bazaar of Heracleides* (with Rev. L. Hodgson) 25, *Assyrian Laws* (with Sir John Miles) 35, *Problems of the Hebrew Verbal System* 36, *Semitic Writing* 48 (3rd edn. 37), *Babylonian Laws I-II* (with Sir John Miles) 54-55, *Aramaic Documents of the 5th century B.C.* 54, *Canaanite Myths and Legends* 56, *The Judaean Scrolls: The problem and a solution* 65.
41 Park Town, Oxford, England.

Duaij, Ahmad Ali al-, B.A.; Kuwaiti civil servant; b. 25 Dec. 1937; ed. Shuwaikh Secondary School, Kuwait, Reading Technical Coll. and Keele Univ., England.
Joined Ministry of Foreign Affairs 62; joined Planning Board as Sec. 62, Sec.-Gen. 63, Dir.-Gen. with rank of Perm. Under-Sec. 64-; Head of Govt. Scholarships Cttee.; mem. Board, Univ. of Kuwait.
Publs. Regular articles in Kuwait, Lebanese and British Press.
The Planning Board, P.O. Box 15, Kuwait.

Duke, Sir Charles Beresford, K.C.M.G., C.I.E., O.B.E.; British former diplomatist and administrator; b. 19 Dec. 1905; ed. Chillon Coll., Montreux, Charterhouse School and Lincoln Coll., Oxford.
Entered Indian Civil Service 28; Asst. Private Sec. to Viceroy of India 34-38; Political Officer, N. W. Frontier of India 38-43; External Affairs Dept., Govt. of India, New Delhi 43-47; transferred to Diplomatic Service 47-61, served in Pakistan, Iran, Egypt and Foreign Office 47-54; Ambassador to Jordan 54-56, to Morocco 57-61; Dir.-Gen. Middle East Asscn., London 64-70.
The Athenaeum, London, S.W.1; Cadenham Grange, Cadnam, Southampton; 32 Sloane Court West, London, S.W.3, England.

Dultzin, Leib (Leon Aryeh); Israeli business executive; b. 31 March 1913, Minsk, Russia.
Lived in Mexico 28-56, Israel 65-; mem. of the executive, Jewish Agency, Treas. 68; Minister without Portfolio, Govt. of Israel 70; Gov. Pal Land Devt. Co. Ltd., Bank Leumi le-Israel; Dir. Rassco Ltd., Yakhim Hakal Co. Ltd., Otzar Hataasiya; mem. World Directorate, Keren Hayesod; mem. of numerous Zionist orgs.
11 Mapu Street, Tel-Aviv, Israel.

Dupont-Sommer, André Louis; French university professor; b. 23 Dec. 1900; ed. Univ. of Paris.
Secretary, Collège de France 34-40; Dir. of Studies, School of Higher Studies 38-; Prof., Univ. of Paris 45-63; Pres. of Inst. of Semitic Studies, Univ. of Paris 52-; Prof. Collège de France 63-71, Hon. Prof. 72; mem. Institut de France 61-; Secrétaire Perpétuel de l'Académie des Inscriptions et Belles-Lettres 68-; Officier de la Légion d'Honneur Commandeur des Palmes académiques.
Publs. *La Doctrine gnostique de la lettre wâw*... 46, *Les Araméens* 49, *Les inscriptions araméennes de Sfiré* 48, *Aperçus préliminaires sur les manuscrits de la mer Morte* 50, *Nouveaux aperçus sur les manuscrits de la mer Morte* 53, *Les Ecrits esséniens découverts près de la mer Morte* 59, 60, 64, and others.
Palais Mazarin, 25 quai de Conti, Paris 6e, France.

Duval, H.E. Cardinal Léon-Etienne; Algerian (b. French) ecclesiastic; b. 9 Nov. 1903; ed. Petit Séminaire, Roche-sur-Foron, Grand Séminaire Annecy, Séminaire français Rome, and Pontifica Universitas Gregoriana.
Ordained priest 26; Prof. Grand Séminaire Annecy 30-42; Vicar-Gen. and Dir. of works, Diocese of Annecy 42-46; consecrated Bishop of Constantine and Hippo 46; Archbishop of Algiers 54-; created Cardinal 65; took Algerian nationality 65; Officier Légion d'Honneur.
Publs. *Paroles de Paix* 55, *Messages de Paix 1955-1962* 62, *Laïcs, prêtres, religieux dans l'Eglise selon Vatican II* 67.
Archbishop's House, 13 rue Khelifa-Boukhalfa, Algiers, Algeria.

E

Eban, Abba, M.A.; Israeli politician; b. 2 Feb. 1915, South Africa; ed. Queens' Coll., Cambridge.
Apptd. Liaison Officer of Allied H.Q. with the Jewish population in Jerusalem 40; Chief Instructor at the Middle East Arab Centre in Jerusalem; entered service of Jewish Agency 46; apptd. Liaison Officer with UN Special Comm. on Palestine 47; apptd. by the Provisional Govt. of Israel as its rep. to the UN 48, permanent rep. with rank of Minister 49; Ambassador to U.S.A. 50-59; Minister without Portfolio 59-60; Minister of Educ. and Culture 60-63; Deputy Prime Minister June 63-66; Minister of Foreign Affairs 66-; Pres. Weizmann Inst. of Science 58-66; Hon. Dr. New York, Maryland, Boston, Chicago, Cincinnati Univs.; foreign mem. American Acad. of Arts and Sciences 60.
Publs. *Maze of Justice* 46, *Social and Cultural Problems in the Middle East* 47, *The Toynbee Heresy* 55, *Voice of Israel* 57, *Tide of Nationalism* 59, *Chaim Weizmann: A Collective Biography* 62, *Israel in the World* 66, *My People* 68, *My Country* 72.
Ministry of Foreign Affairs, Jerusalem, Israel.

Ebtehaj, Abol Hassan; Iranian banker and administrator; b. 1899; ed. Lycée Montaigne, Paris, and Syrian Protestant Coll., Beirut.
Joined Imperial Bank of Iran 20; Govt. Inspector Agricultural Bank and Controller of State-owned companies 36; Vice-Gov. Bank Melli Iran 38; Chair. and Man. Dir. Mortgage Bank 40; Gov. and Chair. Bank Melli Iran (National Bank of Iran) 42-50; Chair. Iranian Del. Middle East Financial and Monetary Conf., Cairo 44; Chair. Iranian Del. Bretton Woods Conf. 44; Iranian Ambassador to France 50-52; Adviser to Man. Dir. Int. Monetary Fund 52-53; Dir. Middle East Dept. Int. Monetary Fund 53; Man. Dir. Plan Org. (Development Board), Teheran 54-59; Chair. and Pres. Iranians' Bank (Private Bank) 59-.
Iranians' Bank, Khiaban, Hafez, Teheran, Iran.

Ecevit, Bülent, B.A.; Turkish journalist and politician; b. 1925; ed. Robert Coll., Ankara and Harvard Univ.
Government official 44-50; Turkish Press Attaché's Office,

London 46-50; Foreign News Editor, Man. Editor later Political Dir. *Ulus* (Ankara) 50-61, Political Columnist, *Ulus* 56-61; M.P. (Republican People's Party) 57-60, Oct. 61-; mem. Constituent Assembly 61; Minister of Labour 61-65; Political Columnist *Milliyet* 65; Sec.-Gen. Republican People's Party 66-71, Chair. 72-.
Publs. *Ortanin Solu* (Left of Centre) 66, *Bu Düzen Değismelidir* (The System Must Change) 68, *Atatürk ve Devrimeilik* (Atatürk and Revolution) 70.
Bade Sokak, Bade Apt. 22/25 Küçükesat, Ankara, Turkey.

Eddé, Raymond, L. en D.; Lebanese lawyer and politician; b. 1913; ed. Univ. Saint Joseph, Beirut.
Member of Parl. 53-57-60-65-68-72; Leader, Nat. Bloc Party 49-; Minister of Interior, of Public Works, of Social Affairs, and of Posts, Telegraphs and Telephones 58-59; stood for Presidency 58; Minister of Public Works, Agriculture, Planning, Water and Power 68-72.
Publs. *Loi sur les Immeubles de Luxe, Loi sur le Secret Bancaire, Loi sur le compte joint.*
Rue Emile Eddé, Quartier Arts et Métiers, Beirut, Lebanon.

Eghbal, Manouchehr, M.D.; Iranian physician and politician; b. 1908; ed. Iran and Univs. of Montpellier and Paris.
Professor of Infectious Diseases, Medical Faculty, Univ. of Teheran 38-53; fmr. Under-Sec. of State for Public Health and acting Minister of Public Health; Minister of Public Health 46; Minister of Posts and Telegraphs 47, of Nat. Education 48; Minister of Roads and Communications, of Health and of Interior 49; Gov.-Gen. of Azerbaijan 50; Teheran Senator 53; Rector, Univ. of Tabriz 51, Univ. of Teheran 54; Minister of the Imperial Court 56-57; Prime Minister 57-60; Prof. Teheran Univ. 60-61; Perm. Iranian Rep. to UNESCO 61-; Chair. of Board and Gen. Managing Dir. Nat. Iranian Oil Co. Oct. 63-; corresp. mem. Acad. of Medicine, Paris; mem. Board of Trustees of several insts., Board of Dirs. of numerous nat. companies and socs.; Dr. h.c. (Lafayette Coll., U.S.A., Paris, Bordeaux, Punjab Univs.); 33 decorations including Grand Croix, Légion d'Honneur; Grand Cross, Order of Danebrog; Order of Merit (China); Order of the Rising Sun (Japan); Das Grossverdienstkreuz mit Schulterband; and many Iranian decorations.
Office: National Iranian Oil Co., Ave. Takhte Jamshid, P.O. Box 1863; Home: Elahieh, Teheran, Iran.

Eisenstadt, Shmuel N., M.A., PH.D.; Israeli professor of sociology; b. 10 Sept. 1923; Warsaw, Poland; ed. Hebrew Univ., Jerusalem and London School of Economics.
Chairman, Dept. of Sociology, Hebrew Univ., Jerusalem 51-68, Prof. of Sociology 59-, Dean, Faculty of Social Sciences 66-68; Visiting Prof., Univ. of Oslo 58, Univ. of Chicago 60, Harvard Univ. 66, 68-69; Carnegie Visiting Prof., Mass. Inst. of Technology 62-63; Chair. Council on Community Devt., Israel 62-66, Israeli Sociological Soc. 69-; Visiting Prof., Univ. of Michigan 70, Univ. of Chicago 70; mem. Advisory Board *International Encyclopedia of the Social Sciences;* Fellow, Royal Anthropological Inst., London, Netherlands Inst. of Advanced Studies 73; mem. Israel Acad. of Sciences and Humanities, Int. Sociological Soc., American Sociological Asscn.; Foreign Hon. mem. American Acad. of Arts and Sciences; Hon. Fellow, London School of Econs.; McIver Award, American Sociological Asscn.
Publs. *The Absorption of Immigrants* 54, *Political Sociology* (editor) 55, *From Generation to Generation* 56, *Essays on Sociological Aspects of Economical and Political Development* 61, *The Political Systems of Empires* 63, *Essays on Comparative Institutions* 65, *Modernization, Protest and Change* 66, *Israeli Society* 68, *The Protestant Ethic and Modernization* 68, *Political Sociology of Modernization* (in Japanese) 68, *Comparative Perceptives on Social Change* (editor) 68, *Charisma and Institution Building: Selections from Max Weber* (editor) 68, *Ensayos sobre el Cambio social y la Modernización* (Spanish) 69, *Modernização e Mudança Social* (Portuguese) 69, *Political Sociology* (editor) 71, *Social Stratification and Differentiation* 71.
The Hebrew University, Jerusalem; Home: Rechov Radak 30, Jerusalem, Israel.

El-Assad, Nassir El-Din, M.A., PH.D.; Jordanian administrator; b. 14 Dec. 1922; ed. Arab Govt. Coll., Jerusalem, and Cairo Univ.
Cultural Attaché League of Arab States, Cairo 54-59; Dean, Faculty of Arts and Educ., Univ. of Libya, Benghazi 59-61; Prof. of Arabic, Univ. of Jordan 62; Pres. Univ. of Jordan 62-68; Cultural Counsellor, League of Arab States, Cairo 68-; Corresp. mem. Arabic Language Acads. in Cairo and Damascus; Istiqlal Decoration, First degree.
Publs. *Sources of Pre-Islamic Poetry and their Historic Value* 56, *Modern Literary Trends in Palestine and Jordan* 57, *Singing and Singing Girls in Pre-Islamic Arabia* 60, *Modern Poetry in Palestine and Jordan* 61, *Diwan Kais Ibn El-Khatim* 62.
League of Arab States, Midan El-Tahrir, Cairo, Egypt.

Elath, Eliahu, PH.D.; Israeli diplomatist; b. 30 July 1903; ed. Hebrew Univ. of Jerusalem and American Univ. of Beirut.
Jewish Agency 34; Jewish Agency observer to San Francisco Conf. 45; Head of Jewish Agency's Political Office in Washington, D.C.; Israeli Amb. to U.S.A. 48-50; Minister to U.K. 50-52, Amb. 52-59; Adviser, Ministry of Foreign Affairs 59-60; Pres. Hebrew Univ., Jerusalem 61-67; Pres. Israel Magen David Adom, Israel Oriental Soc.; Chair. Afro-Asian Inst., Tel-Aviv; Hon. Ph.D.
Publs. *Bedouin, their Life and Manners* 34, *Trans-Jordan* 35, *Israel and Her Neighbours* 57, *The Political Struggle for the inclusion of Elath in the Jewish State* 67, *San Francisco Diary* 71, *British Routes to India* 71.
17 Bialik Street, Beth Hakerem, Jerusalem, Israel.

Elazar, Lieut.-Gen. David; Israeli army officer; b. 1925, Yugoslavia; ed. Hebrew Univ.
Went to Israel 40; entered army 46; served in War of Liberation, Sinai Campaign; Deputy Commdr. Armoured Corps 61; Officer-in-Charge, Northern Command 64; commanded forces of Northern Command during six-day War June 67; Chief, Gen. Staff Branch 69; Chief of Staff and C.-in-C. Israeli Army Dec. 71-.
Ministry of Defence, Jerusalem, Israel.

Elemary, Abdelgaleel; Egyptian financial administrator; b. 1907; ed. Cairo Univ. and Leeds Univ., England
In Ministries of Finance and Commerce; Minister of Finance 52-54; Gov. Central Bank of Egypt 57-60; Pres. and Gen. Man. Alexandria Commercial Co. 60-62; Dir. Industrial Development Bank Service Dept. Int., Finance Corpn. 62-63; Dir. of Investments, Africa, Asia and Middle East, Int. Finance Corpn. 63-65; Dir. Africa Dept., Int. Bank for Reconstruction and Devt. 65-68, Dir. Eastern Africa 68-69, Special Adviser to the Pres. 70-.
International Bank for Reconstruction and Development, Washington, D.C. 20433, U.S.A.

Elias IV Moawad; Greek ecclesiastic; b. 1914; ed. Theological Inst. of Halki, Istanbul.
Greek Orthodox Patriarch of Antioch (Antyarka) and all the East Sept. 70-.
P.O. Box 9, Damascus, Syria.

Elmandjra, Mahdi, PH.D.; Moroccan international official; b. 13 March 1933; ed. Lycée Lyautey, Casablanca, Putney School, Vermont, U.S.A., Cornell Univ., London School of Economics and Univ. de Paris.
Head of Confs., Law Faculty, Univ. of Rabat 57-58; Adviser Ministry of Foreign Affairs, and to Moroccan Del. to UN 58-59; Dir.-Gen. Radiodiffusion Télévision Marocaine 59-60; Chief of African Div., Office of Relations with mem. States, UNESCO 61-63; Dir. Exec. Office of Dir.-Gen. of UNESCO 63-66; Asst. Dir.-Gen. of UNESCO for Social

Sciences, Human Sciences and Culture July 66-Dec. 69; Visiting Fellow, Centre for Int. Studies, London School of Econs. and Political Sciences 70; Asst. Dir.-Gen. of UNESCO for Pre-Programming 71-.
Publ. *The United Nations System: An Analysis* 73.
Office UNESCO, place de Fontenoy, Paris 7e; Home: 12 rue Dufrenoy, 75016 Paris, France, and 20 rue Chenier, Casablanca, Morocco.

Epikman, Refik; Turkish artist and writer; b. 1902; ed. Acad. of Fine Arts, Istanbul and Paris.
Teacher in Gazi Pedagogic Inst., Ankara; exhibited in Exhbns. of Turkish Art, Amsterdam, Paris, Linz and Vth Teheran (Regional) Biennale; f. the Asscn. of Independent Turkish Painters and Sculptors 28; mem. Int. Asscn. of Art Critics.
Publs. *Classical Painters* 45, *17th, 18th and 19th Century World Art* 46, *Tiziano Vecellio's Art* 47, *The Art of Rubens* 51, *Turkish Artist and Archaeologist, The Art of Osman Hamdi* 69.
Gazi Osmanpasa Mahallesi, Nenehatun Cad. 114/1, Kavaklıdere, Ankara, Turkey.

Eralp, Orhan, B.A., LL.B., PH.D.; Turkish diplomatist; b. 28 Jan. 1915; ed. Robert Coll. Istanbul, Univ. Coll., London, and London School of Economics.
Ministry of Foreign Affairs 39-; Sec. Washington 42-48; Adviser to Turkish Del., UN Conciliation Comm. for Palestine 49-51; Perm. Rep. to European Office of UN, Geneva 51; Counsellor, London 52; Dir.-Gen. Second Dept., Ministry of Foreign Affairs 52-56; Ambassador to Sweden 57-59, to Yugoslavia 59-64; Perm. Rep. of Turkey to UN, New York 64-69; Sec.-Gen. Foreign Ministry 69-.
Ministry of Foreign Affairs, Ankara, Turkey.

Erdem, Hasan Hüsnü; Turkish theologian; b. 1889; ed. Univ. of Istanbul.
Teacher of Religion, Royal Middle School, Antalya; Prof. of Theology and Headmaster, Ankara Dârü'l-Hilâfe; Teaching mem. Ministry of Canonical and Pious Endowments; Teacher, Antalya High School; mem. Advisory Cttee. Religious Affairs Dept.; Lecturer in Exegesis and History of Exegesis, Faculty of Divinity, Ankara Univ.; Head of Religious Affairs Dept., Turkish Republic 61-64; mem. Supreme Cttee. of Religious Affairs, Dept. of Religious Affairs 66-.
Publs. Numerous translations from Arabic, and biographical and theological Islamic treatises.
Diyanet İşleri Başkanlığı, Din İşleri Yüksek Kurulu Üyesi, Ankara, Turkey.

Ergin, Sait Naci; Turkish civil servant and politician; b. 1908, Niğde; ed. Faculty of Political Sciences, Istanbul. Joined Ministry of Interior, later Ministry of Finance; studied public finance in France; later Under-Sec. Ministry of Finance, Ankara; mem. Constituent Assembly responsible for drafting 1961 Constitution; Minister of Finance 71-72.
c/o Ministry of Finance, Ankara, Turkey.

Erim, Nihat, PH.D.; Turkish politician; b. 1912, Kandıra, Kocael Province; ed. Lycée of Galatasaray, Istanbul, and Univ. of Istanbul Law School and Univ. of Paris.
Professor of Constitutional and Int. Law, Univ. of Ankara and Legal Adviser, Ministry of Foreign Affairs 42; mem. Parl. 45-50; Minister of Public Works, concurrently Deputy Prime Minister 48-50; Publr. and Editor *Ulus* (organ of the Republican People's Party) 50, subsequently Publr. and Editor of *Halkçi*; mem. for Turkey, European Human Rights Comm.; mem. Parl. 61-; Deputy Chair. Republican People's Party Nat. Assembly Group 61-71; mem. Turkish Parl. Group, European Council 61-70; Prime Minister March 71-March 72; Senator 72-.
Publs. several books on law.
The Senate, Ankara, Turkey.

Erkmen, Hayrettin; Turkish economist and politician; b. 1915; ed. Univs. of Ankara, Lausanne and Geneva.
Reporter, Board of Financial Research, Ministry of Finance 48; Asst. Prof. of Economics, Univ. of Istanbul 49; Minister of Labour 53-55; Pres. Parliamentary Group of Democratic Party; Minister of Labour Nov. 57-58; Minister of Commerce 58-60; Acting Minister of Reconstruction Dec. 59-May 60; arrested 60, sentenced 61, released 65; mem. Management Cttee. Turkish Central Bank 67-.
Publs. *La Participation des Salariés à la Gestion de l'entreprise* 48; trans. in Turkish: J. Marchal, *Le mécanisme des prix*, R. Ramadier, *Le Socialisme et l'exercise de pouvoir*.
Istiklal Cad. Terzi Han 378, Beyoğlu, Istanbul, Turkey.

Erkmen, Nizamettin; Turkish politician; b. 1919, Giresun.
Director of Legal Affairs, Samsun; mem. Parl. for Giresun 61; Sec.-Gen. Justice Party until 73; Minister of State, Deputy Prime Minister 73-; Justice Party.
Office of the Minister of State, Ankara, Turkey.

Erofeyev, Vladimir Yakovlevich; Soviet diplomatist; b. 1909; ed. Moscow Machine Tool Inst.
Diplomatic Service 39-; Deputy Dir. and Chief. of Consular Dept., State Cttee. for Foreign Affairs 39-40; Counsellor to Turkey 40-42; Deputy Chief, Second European Dept., Ministry of Foreign Affairs 42-48, Head of Dept. for Latin American countries 48-49; Counsellor, London 49-52; Counsellor Ministry of Foreign Affairs 52-54; Minister Counsellor, Paris 54-55; Chief. of Second European Dept., Ministry of Foreign Affairs 55-58, of Near East Dept. 58-59; Amb. to the U.A.R. 59-65; on staff Ministry of Foreign Affairs 65-68; Amb. to Iran 68-.
U.S.S.R. Embassy, Churchill Avenue, Teheran, Iran.

Essaafi, M'hamed; Tunisian diplomatist; b. 26 May 1930; ed. Collège Sadiki and Univ. of Paris.
Secretariat of Foreign Affairs, Tunis 56; Tunisian Embassy, London 56-57; First Sec., Washington 57-60; Dir. of American Dept., Secr. of Foreign Affairs, Tunis 60-62, American Dept. and Int. Conf. Dept. 62-64; Amb. to U.K. 64-69; Sec.-Gen. Foreign Affairs, Tunis 69-70; Amb. to U.S.S.R. Sept. 70-; Commandeur de l'Ordre de la République Tunisienne.
Embassy of Tunisia, 28/1 Katchalova Street, Moscow, U.S.S.R.

Ete, Muhlis, M.A., PH.D.; Turkish economist; b. 23 Oct. 1904.
Asst. Instructor 30, later Asst. Prof. Faculty of Law and Economics Istanbul Univ.; Teacher of Statistics School of Political Science, Istanbul, and of Money and Exchange, Higher School of Commerce and Economics Istanbul; Prof. of Business Economics, later of Gen. Principles of Economics, Ankara School of Political Science 40-50; Minister of State Enterprises 50-51; Minister of Economy and Commerce 51-52; Turkish Rep. Council of Europe, Vice-Pres. 53; Pres. Turkish Economic Asscn. and Turkish European Movement; fmr. Chief Editor *Türk Ekonomist*; Pres. of Control Board of State Enterprises 58-61; Minister of Commerce June 62-June 63; mem. of Parl.; Dir. of School of Econs., Istanbul 67-.
Publs. *Transportation, Money and Exchange, Lessons in Business Economics, Administration of Temporary and Permanent Exhibitions, Commerce, Banking and Exchanges, Probleme der Assoziierung der Türkei mit der Europäischen Wirtschaftsgemeinschaft* 63; and numerous translations.
Gözetepe, Yeşil Çeşme Sokak 30/8, Istanbul, Turkey.

Etemadi, Noor Admad; Afghan diplomatist; b. 22 Feb. 1921, Kandahar; ed. Istiqlal Lycée, Kabul, and Kabul Univ.
Joined Ministry of Foreign Affairs 46, Asst. Chief of Protocol, Dir. for Econ. Relations, Dir.-Gen. for Political Affairs 57; diplomatic posts in London and Washington;

Deputy Minister of Foreign Affairs 63; Amb. to Pakistan 64; Minister of Foreign Affairs 65-71, Prime Minister 67-71; Amb. to Italy 71-.
Royal Afghan Embassy, 120 Via Nomentana, Rome, Italy.

Etemadi, Tooryalay, M.A.; Afghan educationist; b. Aug. 1923; ed. Esteklal High School, Kabul, Indiana Univ., U.S.A.
Director of Foreign Cultural Relations, Sec. Afghan Nat. Comm. for UNESCO 53-60; Dean, Colls. of Science, Engineering and Agriculture 56-58, of Agriculture and Engineering 58-60; Pres. Cultural Office, Washington, D.C. 60-63; Pres. of Secondary Educ., Ministry of Educ. 63-64; Pres. Inst. of Educ. 64-65, Kabul Univ. 65-67, Acting Pres. 68-69; Cultural Rep., Beirut 67-68; Cultural Counsellor, Afghan Embassy, Bonn and W. Europe 69-70; Amb., Chef de Cabinet of the Minister of Foreign Affairs 71-; Grosses Verdienstkreuz mit Stern, and several other decorations; Hon. LL.D.
Publs. papers and articles on education.
The Secretariat, Ministry of Foreign Affairs, Kabul, Afghanistan.

Ettinghausen, Richard, PH.D.; American educationist and art curator; b. 5 Feb. 1906; ed. Univs. of Munich, Cambridge and Frankfurt a.M.
Asst. Islamic Dept., State Museum, Berlin 31-33; Asst. to Editor *A Survey of Persian Art* 33-34; Research Assoc., American Inst. for Persian Art and Archæology, N.Y. 34-37; Lecturer on Islamic Art, Inst. of Fine Arts, N.Y. Univ. 36-38; mem. Inst. of Advanced Study, Princeton, N.J. 37-38; Assoc. Prof. of Islamic Art, Univ. of Mich., Ann Arbor 38-44; Assoc. in Near-Eastern Art, Freer Gallery of Art, Smithsonian Inst., Washington, D.C. 44-58, Curator of Near Eastern Art 58-61, Head Curator 61-66; Research Prof. of Islamic Art, Univ. of Mich. 48-67; Editor *Ars Islamica* 38-51; Near-Eastern Editor *Ars Orientalis* 51-58; Editorial Board *The Art Bulletin* 40-, *Kairos* 59-, Assoc. Prof. of Islamic Art, Inst. of Fine Arts, New York Univ. 62-67, Adjunct Prof. of Fine Arts 60-67, Prof. of Fine Arts 67-; Asst. Curator, Near Eastern Art, Los Angeles County Museum of Art 67-; Consultative Chair. Islamic Dept., Metropolitan Museum of Art, N.Y. 69-.
Publs. *The Unicorn* (*Studies in Muslim Iconography I*) 50, *The Paintings of Emperors and Sultans of India in American Collections* 61, *Persian Miniatures in the Bernard Berenson Collection* 63, *Arab Painting* 62; Editor and contributor: *A Selected and Annotated Bibliography of Books and Periodicals in Western Languages dealing with the Near and Middle East, with special emphasis on Medieval and Modern Times* 52, *Aus der Welt der Islamischen Kunst* 59, *Turkish Miniatures from the 13th to the 14th Century* (editor) 65, *Treasures of Turkey* (co-author) 66.
Office: Institute of Fine Arts, New York University, 1 East 78th Street, New York, N.Y. 10021; Home: 24 Armour Road, Princeton, N.J. 08540, U.S.A.

Evans, Trefor Ellis, C.M.G., O.B.E.; British university professor and diplomatist; b. 4 March 1913; ed. Cowbridge, Balliol Coll., Oxford and Hamburg Univ.
Joined Consular Service 37, served Beirut, Alexandria, Cairo, Damascus, Foreign Office; Counsellor, Cairo 52-56, Berne 57-59; Consul-Gen., then Ambassador, Algiers 59-64; Amb. to Syrian Arab Republic 64-67; Amb. to Iraq 68-69; Woodrow Wilson Prof. of Int. Politics, Univ. of Aberystwyth, Wales 69-.
Plas Maes-y-Groes, Talybont, Bangor, Wales.

Evans-Pritchard, Sir Edward Evan, Kt., M.A., PH.D.; British social anthropologist; b. 21 Sept. 1902; ed. Winchester Coll. and Exeter Coll. Oxford.
Expeditions to Central, East and North Africa 26-39; Prof. of Sociology Egyptian Univ. Cairo 30-33; Leverhulme Fellow 34-35; Research Lecturer Oxford 35-40; Active Service 40-45; Reader, Cambridge 45-46; Prof. of Social Anthropology Univ. of Oxford 46-70; Fellow, All Souls' Coll. 46-70; Pres. Royal Anthropological Inst. 49-51; Fellow, British Acad. 56; Hon. mem. American Acad. Arts and Sciences 58, American Philosophical Soc. 68; Hon. Fellow, School of Oriental and African Studies, London 63; Hon. Prof. (Univ. of Wales) 72; Hon. Lecturer (Univ. of Aahus) 72; Hon. D.Sc. (Univ. of Chicago) 67, (Bristol) 69, Hon. D.Litt. (Univ. of Manchester) 69; Chevalier, Légion d'Honneur.
Publs. *Witchcraft, Oracles and Magic among the Azande* 37, *The Nuer* 40, *The Sanusi of Cyrenaica* 49, *Kinship and Marriage among the Nuer* 51, *Social Anthropology* 51, *Nuer Religion* 56, *Essays in Social Anthropology* 62, *The Position of Women in Primitive Societies and Other Essays* 65, *Theories of Primitive Religion* 65, *The Zande Trickster* 67.
The Ark, Jack Straws Lane, Headington, Oxford, England.

Evenari, Michael; Israeli botanist; b. 9 Oct. 1904; ed. Univ. of Frankfurt.
Staff of Botany Dept., Univ. of Frankfurt 27-28, German Univ., Prague 28-31; Staff of Technische Hochschule, Darmstadt 31-33, Lecturer 33; External Teacher, Hebrew Univ., Jerusalem 34-37, Instructor 37-44, Lecturer 44, Chair. Dept. of Botany 45-, Prof. 51-; Vice-Pres. Hebrew Univ., Jerusalem 53-59; Fellow Linnean Soc.; Hon. Fellow American Botanical Soc.; mem. German Acad. of Science. Major Research on ancient desert agriculture and its modern application and studies in germination, physiology and ecology of desert plants.
Department of Botany, Hebrew University of Jerusalem, Jerusalem, Israel.

Eytan, Walter, M.A.; Israeli public official; b. 24 July 1910; ed. St. Paul's School, London, Queen's Coll. Oxford.
Lecturer in German, Queen's Coll., Oxford 34-46; Principal, Public Service Coll., Jerusalem 46-48; Dir.-Gen., Ministry for Foreign Affairs, Israel 48-59; Ambassador to France 60-70; Political Adviser to Minister of Foreign Affairs 70-72; Chair. Israel Broadcasting Authority 72-.
Publ. *The First Ten Years* 58.
18 Balfour Street, 92 102 Jerusalem, Israel.

Eyuboğlu, Bedri Rahmi; Turkish painter and poet; b. 1913; ed. Académie des Beaux Arts, Istanbul, and André Lhote Atelier, Paris.
Exhibited in Turkey with advanced painters' *Group D* 33-37; influenced by Anatolian handicraft designs 41-45; worked on block printing, serigraphy, engraving and textile printing 45-50; mosaic work since 57; Ford Foundation Grant for travel in Europe and U.S.A. 61-63; Prof. Acad. of Fine Arts, Istanbul; has also written poems, essays and travel notes in books, magazines and newspapers; Prize at São Paulo Bienal 56, Gold Medal, Brussels Fair 58; exhbns. in several cities of Europe and U.S.A.
Major works: Panel at Brussels Fair 58, Mosaic panel for NATO Building in Paris 59, Christmas Card for UNICEF 61, mosaic murals in Ankara, Izmir and Istanbul 63-65.
29/3 Manolya Sokak, Kalamis, Kızıltoprak, Istanbul, Turkey.

F

Fahd ibn Abdulaziz, H.R.H. Prince; Saudi Arabian politician; b. 1922.
Brother of H.M. King Faisal; fmr. Minister of Education; Minister of the Interior 62-; Second Deputy Prime Minister.
Ministry of the Interior, Jeddah, Saudi Arabia.

Faisal, H.M. King Malik Faisal ibn Abdulaziz; Saudi Arabian monarch; b. 1906.
Brother of former King Saud; Viceroy of the Hedjaz 26-53;

rep. Saudi Arabia at San Francisco Conf. 45; acclaimed Crown Prince 53; delegated control of Govt. by King Saud March 58-Dec. 60; Prime Minister and Minister of Foreign Affairs 62-; Regent 63-64, declared King 64, also Head of State; Hon. G.B.E., K.C.M.G.; medals and awards from several countries.
Royal Palace, Riyadh, Saudi Arabia.

Fakhreddine, Mohamed; Sudanese diplomatist; b. 12 Oct. 1924; ed. Gordon Memorial Coll., Khartoum, and Univ. of Durham.
Chief of Protocol, Head of UN Section, Ministry of Foreign Affairs, Khartoum 56-58; Counsellor, London 58-60; Ambassador to Pakistan and Afghanistan 60-64, concurrently Ambassador to People's Repub. of China 64-65; Perm. Rep. to UN 65-71; Under-Sec. for Foreign Affairs Nov. 70-71, Deputy Minister 71; Amb. to U.S.S.R. 73-.
Embassy of Sudan, Moscow, U.S.S.R.

Farhan, Staff Brig. Abdul-Karim, B.A.; Iraqi soldier and politician; b. 1922; ed. Military Coll., Baghdad, Staff Coll., Baghdad and Univ. of Baghdad Coll. of Law.
Battalion Commdr., Acting Brigade Commdr. 58-59; Commdr. Baghdad Garrison Feb. 63; Commdr. First Div. Feb.-Nov. 63; Minister of Culture and Guidance Nov. 63-July 65; Sec.-Gen. Arab Socialist Union of Iraq 64-65; mem. Council of Revolutionary Command 64; Minister of Agrarian Reform 67; Acting Minister of Agric. July 67-March 68; Minister of Agric. April-July 68; arrested 68, released Nov. 70; Rafidian Medal (First Grade), Jordanian Star (First Grade) and many other military awards.
Publs. include contributions to military textbooks and *Al Jundi* magazine.
Al-Mansoor, House No. 91/8, Baghdad, Iraq.

Farhan, Ishaq Ahmad, M.SC., M.A., ED.D.; Jordanian educationalist; b. 1934, Ein Karem; ed. American Univ., Beirut, and Columbia Univ., New York.
Science teacher 58-64; with Ministry of Educ., Amman 64-, Dir. of Pedagogical Services and Head, Syllabi Section 69, Dir. of Syllabi 69-70; Minister of Educ. 70-73, of Endowments and Islamic Shrines 73-.
Publs. several school textbooks and articles in scientific and pedagogical journals.
Ministry of Endowments and Islamic Shrines, Amman, Jordan.

Farhat, Abdallah; Tunisian politician; b. 28 Aug. 1914, Ouerdenine; ed. Ecole Supérieure de langue Arabe, Tunis.
Member Parti Néo-Destour 34-; successively Dir. Fédération Nationale des P.T.T. (Post and Telecommunications), Dir. Fédération Générale des Fonctionnaires and Treas.-Gen. Union Générale des Travailleurs Tunisiens 48-56; elected to 2nd Political Bureau 52, re-elected 55; Vice-Pres. Constituent Assembly 56-59; Deputy Nat. Assembly 59-; Dir. Cabinet of the Pres. 56-63, 70-71, Oct. 71-Aug. 72; Pres. and Dir.-Gen. Société Nationale d'Investissement 63-64; Sec. of State for Post and Telecommunications (P.T.T.) 64-69; Sec. of State for Agriculture Sept.-Nov. 69, Minister for Agriculture Nov. 69-Oct. 71; Minister for Nat. Defence Aug. 72-; Grand Cordon Ordre de l'Indépendance, Ordre de la République; many foreign decorations.
Ministère de la Défense Nationale, Tunis, Tunisia.

Farid al-Aulaqi, Sheikh Mohammed; Yemeni politician; b. 1929; ed. Aden Protectorate Coll. for Sons of Chiefs, Government Secondary School, Aden, and Queen's Coll., Oxford.
Joined Protectorate Govt. Service as Asst. Political Officer 50; Political Officer 56-59; Minister of Finance, Fed. of S. Arabia 59-63; Minister of External Affairs 63-67; mem. Presidential Council June 69.
Upper Aulaqi, Fourth Governorate, People's Democratic Republic of Yemen.

Faris, Mustapha, DIPL.ING.; Moroccan economist; b. 17 Dec. 1933; ed. Ecole Nat. des Posts et Chaussées, Paris.
Government Civil Engineer, Dept. of Public Works 56-61; Dir. of Supply, Nat. Irrigation Office 61-65; Dir.-Gen. of Hydraulic Engineering 65-69; Sec. of State for Planning attached to Prime Minister's Office 69-71; Minister of Finance 71-72; Pres., Dir.-Gen. Banque Nationale pour le Développement Economique Dec. 72-; fmr. Vice-Pres. Int. Comm. on Large Dams; Gov. IBRD (World Bank), African Devt. Bank; Ordre du Trône.
Banque Nationale pour le Développement Economique, B.P. 407, Rabat, Morocco.

Farkhan, Hushang; Iranian petroleum engineer; b. 16 Feb. 1914; ed. American Coll., Teheran High School and Colorado School of Mines, U.S.A.
Petroleum Engineer, Anglo-Iranian Oil Co. 39; Officer, Imperial Iranian Army 40-41; Ministry of Finance 42-46; private business 47-48; Petroleum Engineer (Exploration), Iran Oil Co. 49-55; Dir. Iran Oil Co. and mem. Board of Dirs. Irano-Italian Oil Co. 56-60; mem. Board of Dirs. Nat. Iranian Oil Co. (Dir. Oil Operation) 61-63, alt. mem. Board of Dirs. 64-69, mem. Board of Dirs. 69-; Chair. Iran Oil Co. 61-64; Man. Dir. Nat. Iranian Gas Co. 65-69; Chair. Board of Dirs. Dashtestan Offshore Petroleum Co. 65-69; mem. Board of Dirs. and Dir. of Production, Refining and Distribution, NIOC 69-; mem. Board of Dirs. Iranian Oil Exploration and Producing Co. 69-; mem. Iranian Engineering Soc., Iranian Petroleum Inst, (Pres. 64-65); Order of Taadj (Fourth Class), Order of Homayoun (Third Class and Second Class), Coronation Medal, Order of Work (First Class).
National Iranian Oil Company, P.O. Box 1863, Teheran, Iran.

Farmanfarmaian, Khodadad, M.A., PH.D.; Iranian economist and banker; b. 5 May 1928, Teheran; ed. American Univ. of Beirut, and Stanford and Colorado Univs.
Instructor and Research Asst., Dept. of Econs., Colorado Univ. 52-53; Instructor, Dept. of Econs., Brown Univ. 53-55; Research Fellow, Center for Middle Eastern Studies, Harvard Univ. 55-57; Research Assoc., Dept. of Econs. and Oriental Studies, Princeton Univ. 57-58; Dir. Econ. Bureau, Plan Org. 58-61; mem. Tax Comm., Ministry of Finance 58-60; mem. High Econ. Council 59-62: Deputy Man. Dir. Plan Org. 61-62, Man. Dir. 70-73; Deputy Gov., Bank Markazi Iran (Central Bank of Iran) 63-68, Gov. 68-71; medals from govts. of Iran and Belgium.
Publs. *Social Change and Economic Behaviour in Iran, Exploration in Entrepreneurial History* 56; has contributed to *Middle Eastern Journal*.
c/o Bank Markazi Iran, Avenue Ferdowsi, Teheran, Iran.

Farra, Muhammad H. el-; Jordanian diplomatist; b. 20 April 1921; ed. Boston Univ. and Univ. of Pennsylvania.
Director of Arab Affairs, Ministry of Foreign Affairs, Amman 59-60, Dir. Palestine Div. 60-61; Jordan Rep. UN Econ. and Social Council 60-61, Vice-Chair. ECOSOC 62; Minister, Cairo 63; Pres. Arab Council for Econ. Unity 64-65; Perm. Rep. of Jordan to UN 65-70, 70-71; Minister of Culture, Information, Tourism and Antiquities June-Sept. 70; Amb. to Spain 71.
c/o Ministry of Foreign Affairs, Amman, Jordan.

Farrukh, Omar A., PH.D.; Lebanese educationist; b. 8 May 1906; ed. American Univ. of Beirut, and Univs. of Berlin, Leipzig, and Erlangen.
Taught at Al-Najah Nat. High School, Nablus 28-29; Prof. of Islamic Philosophy and Arabic Literature, Maqasid Coll., Beirut 29-; post-graduate work in Germany

and France 35-37; taught at High Training School Baghdad 40-41; Visiting Prof. of History of Muslim Spain, Syrian Univ. Damascus 51-60; Prof. of the History of Arab Science and History of Arab Civilization, Arab Univ. of Beirut 60-; mem. Lebanese Nat. Cttee. 48; mem. Lebanese Del. to UNESCO, Beirut 48; mem. Arab Acad. of Damascus, Arab Acad., Cairo, Islamic Research Asscn., Bombay.
Publs. *Das Bild des Frühislams in der arabischen Dichtung* 37; in Arabic: *Abu Tammam* 35, *Arab Genius in Science and Philosophy* 44, 52 (English edn. 54), *Avempace* 45, *Islam at the Crossroads* (trans.) 46, *Mysticism in Islam* 47, *Greek Philosophy and the Story of its Translation into Arabic* 47, *The Family in Muslim Jurisprudence* 51, *The Incubation of Western Culture in the Middle East* (trans.) 52, *Missions and Imperialism* 52, *The Arabs and Islam in the Western Mediterranean* 59, *A History of Arab Thought* 62, *History of Pre-Islamic Arabia* 64, *A History of Arab Literature I, II and III, A History of Science* 70, etc.
P.O. Box 941, Beirut, Lebanon.

Fasi, Mohammed el; Moroccan university rector; b. 2 Sept. 1908; ed. Al Qarawiyin Univ., Fez, Univ. de Paris à la Sorbonne and Ecole des langues orientales, Paris. Teacher, Inst. des Hautes Etudes Marocaines 35-40; Head Arab manuscript section, Bibliothèque Gén., Rabat 40; Tutor to Prince Moulay Hassan 41-44, 47-52; Rector Al Qarawiyin Univ. 42-44, 47-52; Vice-Pres. Conseil des Uléma 42-; Founder-mem. Istiqlal Party 44; under restriction 44-47, 52-54; Minister of Nat. Educ. 55-58; Rector of the Univ. of Morocco 58-; Pres. Moroccan Del. to Gen. Conf. of UNESCO 56, 58, 60, 64, Vice-Pres. 62, leader of numerous UNESCO Confs. in the Arab World, Pres. Exec. Board of UNESCO 64-; Pres. Conseil d'Administration de l'Association des Universités Partiellement ou Entièrement de Langue Française (AUPELF) 66; Pres. Conseil Exécutif de l'Association des Universités Africains 67; Minister for Cultural Affairs and Nat. Educ. 68; Pres. Conseil Exécutif de l'Association des Universités Islamiques 69; mem. Acad. of Arabic Language, Cairo 58, Acad. of Iraq; Dr. h.c. Univ. of Bridgeport 65, Lagos 68, Djakarta 68.
Publs. Numerous works in Arabic and French including *L'évolution politique et culturelle au Maroc* 58, *La Formation des Cadres au Maroc* 60, *Chants anciens des femmes de Fès* 67.
Ministère des Affaires Culturelles, B.P. 702, Rabat-Agdal; Home: 12 rue Louis Chatelain, Rabat, Morocco.

Fassi, Mohammed Allal el; Moroccan politician; b. 1910, Fez; ed. Univ. of Fez.
Work with Moroccan nationalists 20-; imprisoned briefly 30; Prof. Univ. of Fez 32, forced to leave Morocco (for nationalist activities) 33; returned 34, presented plans for reform and independence to French authorities; imprisoned 35-36; presided first meeting Comité d'Action Marocaine 36; exiled to French Equatorial Africa 37; returned to Morocco 46, became a leader of Istiqlal Party (formed 43); lived abroad 47-53; leader, Istiqlal (Independent Party) 56-; Minister of State 61-63; elected Deputy 63; corresp. mem. Arabic Acad., Damascus, Cairo, Pres. of Cttee.
Publ. *The Independence Movement in Arab North Africa* 54.
Parti Istiqlal, Rabat, Morocco.

Fatemi, Nasrollah, M.A., PH.D.; (b. Iranian); American professor.
Formerly Ed. Bakhtar newspaper, Gov. of Fars, mem. of Majlis, Mayor of Shiraz, and del. to UN (adviser to perm. Iranian del.); Visiting Prof. Asia Inst. and Princeton Univ. 50-55; Prof. of Social Sciences, Fairleigh Dickinson Univ. 55-61, Chair. Social Sciences Dept. 61-65, Dean of the Graduate School 65-71, Distinguished Prof. of Int. Affairs and Dir. of Graduate Inst. of Int. Studies 71.
Publs. *Biography of Hafiz* 36, *Persian Literature in the 16th and 17th centuries* 37, *Modern Persian Literature* 39, *Diplomatic History of Persia* 51, *Oil Diplomacy* 54, *The Dollar Crisis* 64, *The Roots of Arab Nationalism* 65, *Humanities in the Age of Science* 67.
Fairleigh Dickinson University, Teaneck, N.J., U.S.A.

Fawzi, Ahmad; Jordanian politician and engineer; b. 1927; ed. U.S.A. and Baghdad Univ.
District Engineer, Public Works 50-53, Asst. Under-Sec. 53-57, Under-Sec. 57-64; Lord Mayor of Amman 64-; Minister of Interior for Municipal and Rural Affairs 67-68, and Minister without Portfolio 67-68; Minister of Public Works April 68-Aug. 69; Sec. Civil Eng. Union; mem. Devt. Board; Chair. Housing Corpn. Board; Chair. Municipal and Rural Loan Fund; Chair. Hidjaz Railway Reconstruction Cttee.; mem. Arab Cities Org. Exec. Office; Orders of Al-Kawkab (first rank), Al-Istiklal (first rank), Al-Nahda (second rank), Al-Jalalah Asharefah (first rank, Morocco), Tunisian Repub. (first rank), Mallizia, Ethiopian Emperor (first rank).
c/o Municipality of Amman, Amman, Jordan.

Fawzi, Mahmoud; Egyptian diplomatist and politician; b. 1900, Cairo; ed. Univs. of Cairo, Rome, Liverpool and Columbia.
Vice-Consul, N.Y. and New Orleans 26-29; Consul, Kobe, Japan 29-36; Dir. Dept. of Nationalities, Ministry of Foreign Affairs 39-41; Consul-Gen., Jerusalem 41-44; Egyptian rep. Security Council, UN 46; alternate rep. UN Gen. Assembly, N.Y. 47; Perm. Rep. of Egypt to UN 49-51; Ambassador to Great Britain 52; Minister of Foreign Affairs Dec. 52-58; U.A.R. Minister of Foreign Affairs 58-64; mem. Presidency Council 62-64; Dep. Prime Minister of Foreign Affairs 64-67, Vice-Pres. and Presidential Asst. for Foreign Affairs 67-68; Prime Minister 70-72; Vice-Pres. Jan. 72-.
Office of the Vice-President, Cairo, Egypt.

Fawzi, Gen. Mohammed; Egyptian army officer; ed. Military Acad.
Former Dir. Mil. Acad. and Commdr. United Arab Repub. Expeditionary Forces in Yemen; Commdt. of Syrian-Egyptian forces under Defence Pact 67; Chief of Staff of Army and Sec.-Gen. for Mil. Affairs, Arab League until 67; C.-in-C. Joint U.A.R. Forces 67-68; Minister of War 68-70; charged with high treason July 71; sentenced to imprisonment Dec. 71.
Cairo, Egypt.

Fayez, Akef Mithqal al-; Jordanian politician; b. 1924; ed. Aleh Univ. Lebanon.
President Jordanian Agricultural Asscn. 45; Chief of Protocol for Tribes, Royal Palace 46; Co-founder Jordanian People's Party; mem. House of Reps. 47-, Speaker 62-68, successively Minister of Agriculture, Development and Construction, Defence, Communications, and Public Works 57-62; Chair. Nat. Group, Inter-Parl. Union 64-; Deputy Prime Minister, Minister of Interior 69-70; Minister of State for Pres. Council Affairs June-Sept. 70.
House of Representatives, P.O.B. 72. Amman, Jordan.

Federbush, Rabbi Simon; American Jewish leader; b. 1892.
One of leaders of Mizrachi Movement since 18; mem. Seym 22-27; Editor *Jüdische Blätter* 28 and of Hebrew monthly *Mizracha* since 30; fmr. Chief Rabbi of Finland; Cultural Dir. World Jewish Congress, New York; mem. World Zionist Organization Action Cttee.; Chair. World Union for Hebrew Language and Culture; mem. quarterly *Judaism*, N.Y.; Pres. Histadruth Ivrith of America; Literary Prizes of Lamed Foundation 53 and 58; Pres. Hapoel Hamizrachi of America.
Publs. *Ijjunim* 29, *Zion's Wisest Protocol in Saningens Ijus* 35, *Hikre Talmud* 38, *Hamusar Vehamishpat* 48, *Mishpat Hamlucha* 51, *The Jewish Concept of Labor* 56, *Benthivoth Hatalmud* 56, *World Jewry To-day* 59, *Hason Tora Vezion*

60, *Hikre Hayaduth* 64, *History of the Hebrew Language* 67.
2105 Ryer Avenue, Bronx 57, New York City, New York, U.S.A.

Feinberg, Nathan, DR.IUR.UTR.; Israeli university professor; b. 6 June 1895; ed. Univ. of Zürich and Graduate Inst. of Int. Studies, Geneva.
Head of Dept., Ministry of Jewish Affairs, Lithuania 19-21; Sec. Cttee. of Jewish Dels., Paris 22-24; law practice in Palestine 24-27 and 34-45; Lecturer, Univ. of Geneva 31-33; Lecturer, Hebrew Univ., Jerusalem 45-49, Assoc. Prof. 49-52, Prof. of Int. Law and Relations 52-66, Dean of Faculty of Law 49-51, Prof. Emer. 66-; Lecturer Acad. of Int. Law, The Hague 32, 37, 52; mem. Perm. Court of Arbitration; mem. Inst. of Int. Law; Fellow of the Int. Inst. of Arts and Letters; mem. Board of Governors, Hebrew Univ.
Publs. *La Question des Minorités à la Conférence de la paix de 1919-1920 et l'action juive en faveur de la Protection Internationale des Minorités* 29, *La Juridiction de la Cour Permanente de Justice Internationale dans le Système des Mandats* 30, *La Juridiction de la Cour Permanente de Justice dans le Système de la Protection Internationale des Minorités* 31, *La Pétition en Droit International* 33, *Some Problems of the Palestine Mandate* 36, *L'Admission de Nouveaux Membres à la Société des Nations et à l'Organisation des Nations Unies* 52, *The Jewish Struggle Against Hitler in the League of Nations (Bernheim Petition)* (Hebrew) 57, *The Legality of a "State of War" after the Cessation of Hostilities* 61, *Palestine under the Mandate and the State of Israel: Problems of International Law* (Hebrew) 63, *The Jewish League of Nations Societies* (Hebrew) 67, *The Arab-Israel Conflict in International Law* 70, *On an Arab Jurist's Approach to Zionism and the State of Israel* 71, etc.; co-editor: *The Jewish Year Book of International Law* 49; Editor *Studies in Public International Law in Memory of Sir Hersch Lauterpacht* (in Hebrew) 62.
6 Ben Labrat Street, Jerusalem, Israel.

Feki, Ahmed Hassan el-; Egyptian soldier and diplomatist; b. 1911; ed. Cairo Mil. Acad. and Staff Coll., Gunnery Staff Coll. (U.K.).
Army service, reaching rank of Maj.-Gen. 30-54; fmr. Instructor Mil. Acad. and Staff Coll., Mil. Attaché Rome; Ambassador of Egypt to Libya and subsequently of U.A.R. 54-59; Ambassador of U.A.R. to India 59-64, to Canada 64-65; Under-Sec. of State, Ministry of Foreign Affairs 65-67; Deputy Minister of Foreign Affairs Oct. 67; Amb. to U.K. Dec. 67-72.
c/o Ministry of Foreign Affairs, Cairo, Egypt.

Felek, Burhan, L. en D.; Turkish journalist; b. 1889; ed. Scutari Lycée and Istanbul Univ.
Civil servant 08; served in Army Reserve First World War; sports journalist and photographer 19; Editor *Milliyet* (Istanbul daily) 69-; Lecturer Istanbul Univ. Inst. of Journalism 51-; Pres. Asscn. of Turkish Journalists; Pres. Turkish Olympic Cttee.; mem. Int. Press. Inst.; Hon. O.B.E.; NATO Medal, Diplôme Olympique; Greek, Yugoslav, Romanian and Austrian decorations for services to sport; Republican People's Party.
Publs. Works on photography, sport and travel; two collections of humorous stories and one play; translations of novels into Turkish, including *Il Piccolo Mondo di Don Camillo* and *Il Compagno Don Camillo*.
Home: Dost apt. 8/9, M. Kemal Street, Nişantaş, Istanbul (winter), Santral sok., Omerpaşa Caddesi, Erenköy, Istanbul (summer); Office: *Milliyet*, Istanbul, Turkey.

Fernea, Robert Alan, PH.D.; American anthropologist; b. 25 Jan. 1932; ed. Reed Coll., Portland, Oregon, and Univ. of Chicago.
Assistant, Assoc. Prof. of Anthropology, American Univ. in Cairo 59-65, Social Research Center, American Univ. in Cairo 61-65; Dir. Nubian Ethnological Survey 61-65; Visiting Lecturer, Univ. of Alexandria 63, 64; Consultant, Ford Foundation in U.A.R. 63-65; Post-doctoral Fellow, Harvard Univ. 65-66; Prof. of Anthropology, Univ. of Texas at Austin 66-, Dir. Middle East Center, 66-73; Fellow, American Anthropological Asscn., Founding Fellow, Middle East Studies Asscn. of N. America; Trustee, American Inst. of Iranian Studies; Univ. of Chicago Fellow 54, Nat. Science Foundation Fellowship 56, 57, Danforth Fellow 54-59, Faculty Fulbright-Hays Fellow (Afghanistan) 67.
Publs. *Symposium on Contemporary Egyptian Nubia* 67, *Shaykh and Effendi* 70, *Nubians in Egypt: Peaceful People* 73, and numerous anthropological articles.
University of Texas at Austin, Middle East Center, 2609 University Avenue, Social Work Building, Room 326, Texas 78712, U.S.A.

Feyzioğlu, Turhan, LL.D.; Turkish university professor and politician; b. 19 Jan. 1922; ed. Galatasaray Lycée, Istanbul Univ., and Ecole Nat. d'Administration, Paris.
Assistant Prof. Ankara Political Science School 45-47, Assoc. Prof. 47-54; Research, Nuffield Coll., Oxford 54; Co-editor *Forum* 54-58; Prof. Ankara Univ. 55; Dean, Political Science School, Ankara 56; M.P. 57, 61, 65-; mem. Nat. Exec. Cttee. Republican People's Party 57-61; Pres. Middle East Technical Univ. 60; mem. Constituent Assembly 60; Minister of Education 60; Minister of State 61; Deputy Prime Minister 62-63; mem. Turkish High Planning Council 61-63, Asst. Sec.-Gen. Republican People's Party 64, Vice-Pres. Parl. Group 65-66; founded Nat. Reliance Party (now Republican Reliance Party) 67, Pres. 67-; Turkish Rep. Consultative Assembly, Council of Europe 64-66.
Publs. *Administration Law* 47, *Judicial Review of Unconstitutional Laws* 51, *Les Parties Politiques en Turquie* 53, *The Reforms of the French Higher Civil Service* 55, *Democracy and Dictatorship* 57, *The Communist Danger* 69.
Republican Reliance Party, Ankara, Turkey.

Field, Henry, B.A., M.A., D.SC.; American anthropologist; b. 15 Dec. 1902; ed. Eton Coll., and New Coll., Oxford.
Asst. Curator of Physical Anthropology, Field Museum of Natural History (Chicago) 26-34, Curator 34-41; Field Museum Expeditions, Near East 25-26, 27-28, 34; engaged in Govt. research work in Washington 41-45; Research on Anthropology of S.W. Asia 46-47; Univ. of Calif. African Expedition 47-48; Peabody Museum-Harvard Expedition to Near East 50, and to West Pakistan 55; Honorary Associate in Physical Anthropology, Peabody Museum, Harvard 50-; Research in India 69; Annandale Medal, Asiatic Soc. of Bengal 66.
Publs. *Arabs of Central Iraq: their History, Ethnology and Physical Characters* 35; *Contributions to the Anthropology of Iran* 39; *The Anthropology of Iraq, Part I, No. 1* 40, Nos. 2-3 49; *Part II, No. 1* 51, Nos. 2, 3 52; *Contributions to the Anthropology of the Faiyum, Sinai, Sudan and Kenya* 52; *Contributions to the Anthropology of the Caucasus* 53; *The Track of Man* 53; *Ancient and Modern Man in Southwestern Asia* I 56, II 61; *Bibliographies on S.W. Asia,* I-VII 53-63; *An Anthropological Reconnaissance in West Pakistan* 59; *North Arabian Desert Archaeological Survey* 25-50, 60; *"M" Project for F.D.R.: Studies on Migration and Settlement* 62; Editor *Peabody Museum Russian Translation Series,* Vols. I-V 59-70, *Contributions to the Anthology of Saudi Arabia* 72.
3551 Main Highway, Coconut Grove, Miami 33, Florida; Office: Peabody Museum, Harvard University, Cambridge, Mass., U.S.A.

Filali, Abd al-Latif, LL.D.; Moroccan politician and diplomatist; b. 1928, Fez; ed. Univ. of Paris.
Ambassador, Ministry of Foreign Affairs 57; Chargé

d'Affaires UN 58-59; Head, Royal Cabinet 59-60; Chargé d'Affaires, Paris 61; Amb. to People's Repub. of China 65, to Algeria 67; Minister of Higher Educ. 68-69; Amb. to Spain 69-71; Minister of Foreign Affairs Aug. 71-72; mem. Political Bureau, Destour Socialist Party.
c/o Ministry of Foreign Affairs, Rabat, Morocco.

Filali, Abdelaziz, LL.D.; Moroccan judge and administrator; b. 10 June 1924; ed. Lycée Gouraud, Rabat, Lycée Lyautey, Casablanca, Ecole Nat. d'Org. Economique et Sociale, Paris, Grenoble Univ. and Inst. des Hautes Etudes, Rabat.
Practised at the Bar, Casablanca 51-55; First Pres. Int. Tribunal of Tangier, Court of Appeal Tangier and Court of Appeal Rabat 55-; Lecturer Inst. des Hautes Etudes Marocaines, Ecole Marocaine d'Administration, then Asst. Dir. Ecole Marocaine; Pres. Centre Africain de Formation et de Recherche Administratives pour le Développement (C.A.F.R.A.D.), Tangier 64-; mem. Comm. for Arabization of Code of Civil Procedure 63, Comm. for Arabization of Code of Obligations and Contracts 64; Pres. Comm. for Arabization of Code of Commercial Law 65; Dr. h.c. Univ. of Grenoble.
Publs. *Marriage in Moroccan Law* (in Arabic), *Notes Judiciaires* (in French).
Cour d'Appel, Fez, Morocco.

Fisher, Sydney Nettleton, M.A., PH.D.; American university professor and editor; b. 1906; ed. Oberlin Coll., Univ. of Illinois, Princeton Univ. and Univ. of Brussels.
Tutor in Mathematics and English, Robert Coll., Istanbul 28-31, 36-37; Instructor in History, Denison Univ., Granville, Ohio 35-36; Instructor in History, The Ohio State Univ. 37-42, Asst. Prof. 42-47, Assoc. Prof. 47-55, Prof. 55-72, Prof. Emer. 72-; Co-ordinator, Graduate Inst. for World Affairs 62-65; Dir. Near and Middle East Program 67-71; Assoc. Chief, Econ. Analysis Section, Middle East Div., Foreign Econ. Admin., Washington, D.C. 43-44, Country Specialist, Commercial Policy Div., Dept. of State 44-46; Lecturer on World Affairs, Chautauqua Inst., Chautauqua, N.Y. 40, 41 and 42; Visiting Prof. of History and Govt., Stetson Univ., DeLand, Fla. 49; Dir. of Publs. of The Middle East Inst. and Editor *The Middle East Journal*, Washington, D.C. 52-53; Visiting Prof. of History, Univ. of S. Calif., Los Angeles 54, 61; mem. American Historical Asscn., The Middle East Inst., Royal Historical Soc., London, Accademia del Mediterraneo, Asscn. for North American Middle East Studies, etc.
Publs. *The Foreign Relations of Turkey, 1481-1512* 48, *Evolution in the Middle East* 53, *Social Forces in the Middle East* 55, *The Middle East: A History* 59, 69, *The Military in the Middle East* 63, *France and the European Community* 65.
P.O. Box 162, Worthington, Ohio 43085, U.S.A.

Fisher, William Bayne, B.A., DR. DE L'UNIV. (Paris); British university professor; b. 24 Sept. 1916; ed. Univs. of Manchester, Louvain, Caen and Paris.
Research Fellow 37-40; served in Royal Air Force 40-46, commissioned 41, O.C. R.A.F. Liaison Unit, Syria and Lebanon 44-45; Lecturer, Univ. of Manchester 46; Senior Lecturer, Dept. of Geography, Aberdeen Univ. 47-53; Reader and Head of Dept. of Geography, Univ. of Durham 54-56, Prof. 56-, Dir. Inst. of Middle Eastern and Islamic Studies 62-65, Principal Graduate Coll. 65-; Consultant H.M. Govt., Govt. of Libya and Harvard Univ., U.S.A.; Leader Univ. Expedition to Libya 51.
Publs. *The Middle East—a Physical, Social and Regional Geography* 50, 71, *Spain* (with H. Bowen-Jones) 57, *Malta* (with H. Bowen-Jones and J. C. Dewdney), Editor Vol. I *The Cambridge History of Iran* (Land and People) 68, *Populations of the Middle East and North Africa* (with J. I. Clarke) 72.
Abbey View, 42 South Street; and 38 Old Elvet, Durham, England.

Foroughi, Mahmoud; Iranian diplomatist; b. 1915; ed. Teheran Univ.
Iranian Foreign Service 39-, London 43-48, Ministry of Foreign Affairs 48-50; Consul-Gen. in New York, Del. to UN Gen. Assembly 50-56; Ambassador to Brazil 57-62; Under-Sec. for Political Affairs, Ministry of Foreign Affairs 62; Ambassador to Switzerland 62-63, to U.S.A. 63-65, to Afghanistan 66-69.
c/o Ministry of Foreign Affairs, Teheran, Iran.

Franjiya, Sulaiman; Lebanese politician; b. 14 June 1910, Zgharta; ed. coll. at Zgharta, near Beirut.
Elected to Parl. as Independent mem. 60 and 64; Minister of Posts, Telegraphs and Telephones and Minister of Agriculture 60-61; Minister of the Interior 68; Minister of Justice, Minister of Econ., Minister of Public Works, Minister of Nat. Econ. 69-70; head, trade del. to negotiate Soviet-Lebanese trade and payments agreement; Pres. of Lebanon Aug. 70-.
Office of the President, Beirut, Lebanon.

Frei, Ephraim Henrich, D.PHIL.; Israeli professor; b. 2 March 1912, Vienna, Austria; ed. Vienna and Hebrew Univs.
Broadcasting Engineer, British Army; attached to British Embassy, Athens; mem. staff Scientific Dept., Ministry of Defence; Prof. and Head, Dept. of Electronics, Weizmann Inst. of Science; mem. Inst. for Advanced Study, Princeton, N.J. 52; Int. Research Fellow, Stanford Research Inst., Calif. 60; mem. Board of Dirs. Yeda, Advisory Board, Jerusalem School of Applied Science; mem. Board, Silver Inst. of Bio-Medical Engineering; Acad. Board, Hollon Univ. of Technology; Fellow, I.E.E.E.; Weizmann Prize 57.
Publs. scientific papers on electronics and physics.
5 Ruppin Street, Rehovot, Israel.

Freiha, Said; Lebanese newspaper proprietor; b. 1905. Chairman Board Dar Assayad S.A.L. which publishes *Assayad* (weekly) 43-, *Achabaka* (weekly) 56-, *Al-Anwar* (daily) 59-.
Hazmié, P.O.B. 1038, Beirut, Lebanon.

Freund, Mrs. Miriam Kottler, M.A., PH.D.; American Zionist leader; b. 17 Feb. 1906; ed. Hunter Coll., New York Univ.
Teacher high schools, N.Y.C. to 44; Vice-Pres. Women's Comm., Brandeis Univ. 50-52; Nat. Board Hadassah, Women's Zionist Organization 40-, Vice-Pres. 53-56, Pres. 56-60; Chair. Nat. Youth Aliyah 53-56; mem. Actions Cttee., World Zionist Organization 56; Chair. Exec. Cttee. American Zionist Council 60-; mem. Nat. Board Jewish Nat. Fund and Keren Hayesod 47-48; del. 21st Orientalist Congress, Moscow 60; Editor *Hadassah* magazine 66-71, Nat. Ed. Chair. 71-; mem. American Asscn. of Univ. Women, Jewish History Soc., Nat. Council of Nat. Planning Asscn. 70; Vice-Pres. American Zionist Fed. 70-72; mem. Exec. World Council of Synagogues.
Publs. *Jewish Merchants in Colonial America* 36, *Jewels for a Crown: The Chagall Windows* 63.
575 Park Avenue, New York, N.Y. 10021, U.S.A.

Frye, Richard Nelson, PH.D.; American orientalist; b. 10 Jan. 1920; ed. Univ. of Ill., Harvard Univ., and School of Oriental and African Studies, London.
Junior Fellow, Harvard 46-49; visiting scholar, Univ. of Teheran 51-52; Aga Khan Prof. of Iranian, Harvard 57-; Visiting Prof., Oriental Seminary, Frankfurt Univ. 58-59; Hamburg Univ. 68-69; assoc. Editor *Central Asian Journal* and *Indo-Iranica*; Hon. mem. German Archaeological Inst.
Publs. *Notes on the early coinage of Transoxiana* 49, *History of the Nation of the Archers* 52, *Narshakhi, The History of Bukhara* 54, *Iran* 56, *The Heritage of Persia* 62, *The Histories of Nishapur* 65, *Bukhara, the Medieval*

Achievement 65, *Corpus Iranian Inscriptions* 68, 71, *Qasr-i Abu Nasr Excavations* 73; Editor: *Bulletin Asia Institute* (monographs), *Cambridge History of Iran Vol. IV.*
546 Widener Library, Cambridge 38, Mass.; and The Asia Institute, Pahlavi University, Shiraz, Iran.

G

Gaballah, Sayed; Egyptian politician; ed. Cairo and Wisconsin Univs.
Teacher, Cairo Univ., Head Agricultural Econ. Section; Under-Sec. of State for Planning 63-71; Minister for Planning 71-.
Ministry of Planning, Cairo, Egypt.

Gaddafi, Col. Moamar al-; Libyan army officer and political leader; b. 1938, Misurata; ed. Univ. of Libya, Benghazi.
Served with Libyan Army 65-; Chair. Revolutionary Council and C.-in-C. of Armed Forces of Libya Sept. 69-; Prime Minister 70-72; Minister of Defence 70-; mem. Pres. Council, Fed. Arab Repubs. 71-.
Revolutionary Command Council, Tripoli, Libya.

Gaddafi, Wanis; Libyan politician and diplomatist.
Head of Exec. Council in Cyrenaican Provincial Govt. 52-62; Minister of Foreign Affairs Jan. 62-63, of Interior 63-64, of Labour 64; Ambassador to Fed. Repub. of Germany 64-65; Minister of Planning and Devt. 66-68; Minister of Foreign Affairs 68; Prime Minister Sept. 68-69; imprisoned for two years Nov. 71.
Tripoli, Libya.

Galili, Israel; Israeli politician; b. May 1911, Brailov, Ukraine; ed. Ahad Ha'am Primary School.
Went to Palestine 15; later worked on buildings and in printing; f. Asscn. of Working Youth 24; helped establish Kibbutz Na'an 30; Haganah activities 35-48; Deputy Minister of Defence, Israel Govt. 48; mem. Knesset, Minister without Portfolio (in charge of Information Services) 66-69; Minister without Portfolio 69-; Achdut Ha'Avoda.
The Knesset, Jerusalem; Kibbutz "Naan", Israel.

Gat, Dr. Joel R., M.SC., PH.D.; Israeli professor of isotope research; b. 17 Feb. 1926, Munich, Germany; ed. Hebrew Univ., Jerusalem.
Department of Physical Chem., Hebrew Univ. 49-50; Ministry of Defence Laboratories, Jerusalem 50-52; Israel Atomic Energy Comm., Rehovot 52-59; Fellow ISNSE, Argonne Nat. Laboratories and Enrico Fermi Inst., Univ. of Chicago, Ill. 55-56; Fellow, Scripps Inst. of Oceanography, Univ. of Calif. San Diego at La Jolla 64-65; Acting Head, Isotopes Dept., Weizmann Inst. of Science 66-70; Prof. Isotope Research 71-; Deputy Chair. Scientific Council 72-; Walter P. Reuther Chair in the Peaceful Uses of Atomic Energy 68.
3 Hagrast, Rehovot, Israel.

Gazit, Mordechai, M.A.; Israeli diplomatist; b. 5 Sept. 1922; ed. Hebrew Univ., Jerusalem.
Minister, Embassy of Israel to U.S.A. 60-65; Asst. Dir.-Gen. Ministry of Foreign Affairs 65-67; Deputy Dir.-Gen. Ministry of Immigrant Absorption 69-70; Asst. Dir.-Gen. Ministry of Foreign Affairs 70-72, Dir.-Gen. 72-73; Dir.-Gen., Political Adviser Prime Minister's Office 73-.
Office of the Prime Minister, Jerusalem; Home: 1 Rashba Street, Jerusalem, Israel.

Geghman, Yahya Hamoud; Yemeni diplomatist; b. 24 Sept. 1934; ed. Law Schools, Cairo, Paris, Damascus and Boston and Columbia Univs.
Teacher of Arabic Language and Literature, Kuwait 57-59; Dir.-Gen. Yemen Broadcasting System, Special Adviser, Ministry of Foreign Affairs 62-63; Deputy Perm. Rep. to UN 63-66, 67-68; Minister Plenipotentiary, Yemen Arab Repub. (Y.A.R.) Embassy to U.S.A. 63-67; Minister of Foreign Affairs 68; Minister of State, Personal Rep. of the Pres. 69; Deputy Prime Minister 69-71; Minister Extraordinary and Plenipotentiary, Perm. Rep. to UN June 71-; Pres. Supreme Council for Youth's Welfare and Sport 70; Gov. for Y.A.R., Int. Bank for Reconstruction and Devt., Int. Monetary Fund 70-; mem. of del. to Conf. of Arab Heads of Govts. 65, 69, to U.S.S.R. 68, to UN General Assembly 62-; has represented Y.A.R. at many int. functions.
Publs. articles on politics, economics and literature in various Arabic journals.
Permanent Mission of the Yemen Arab Republic to the United Nations, 211 East 43rd Street, Room 1904, New York, N.Y. 10017, U.S.A.

Gelb, Ignace Jay, PH.D.; American university professor; b. 14 Oct. 1907; ed. Univ. of Rome.
Travelling Fellow, later Instructor, Univ. of Chicago 29-41, Asst. Prof. 41-43, Assoc. Prof. 43, 46-47, Prof. of Assyriology 47-65; Frank P. Hixon Distinguished Service Prof. 65-; U.S. Army 43-45; Guggenheim Fellow 60-61; Colvin Research Prof. 62-63; Editor *Chicago Assyrian Dictionary* 47-; Hon. mem. Société Asiatique, Paris, Societas Orientalis Fennica, Helsinki, Indian Oriental Soc., Hyderabad; Foreign mem. Accad. Nazionale dei Lincei, Rome; Fellow of the American Academy of Arts and Sciences; Pres. American Name Soc. 63-; Pres. American Oriental Soc. 65-.
Publs. *Hittite Hieroglyphs I-III* 31-42, *Inscriptions from Alishar* 35, *Hittite Hieroglyphic Monuments* 39, *Hurrians and Subarians* 44, *A Study of Writing* 52, *Sargonic Texts from the Diyala Region* 52, *Old Akkadian Writing and Grammar* 52, *Glossary of Old Akkadian* 57, *Sequential Reconstruction of Proto-Akkadian* 69.
Oriental Institute, University of Chicago, Chicago, Ill. 60637; and 5454 Woodlawn Avenue, Chicago, Ill., U.S.A.

Gemayel, Sheikh Pierre; Lebanese politician; b. 1905; ed. Univ. St. Joseph, Beirut and Cochin Hospital, Paris.
Trained as a pharmacist; founded Parti Démocrate Social Libanais (Les Phalanges) 36, leader 37-; imprisoned 37, 43; organized general strike 43; established the first Labour Code 44; Minister of Public Works 60, of Finance 60-61, of Communications 60, of Public Health 60, 61; Minister of Public Works May 61-Feb. 64; Minister of the Interior 66-67; Deputy for Beirut 60-; Lebanese, Polish and Egyptian decorations; Pres. Kataeb Party.
Rue de l'Université St. Joseph, Beirut, Lebanon.

Georgy, Guy-Noël; French diplomatist; b. 17 Nov. 1918, Paris; ed. Faculty of Law, Bordeaux and Paris.
Chief of Cabinet and Head of Information Dept., Cameroun 45-49; Attaché, Ministry for French Overseas Territories 50; Head of North-Cameroun District, Maroua 51-55; Chief of Cabinet, Ministry for French Overseas Territories 55; Gen. Sec. to Gabon 56; Gen. Man. of Econ. Affairs and Plan, Equatorial Africa 57, West Africa 58; High Commr. in Congo 59; High Commr. Congo (Brazzaville) 60; Amb. to Bolivia 61-64, to Dahomey 64-69, to Libya 69-.
French Embassy, Sharia Huper, Tripoli, Libya; 9 avenue Franco-Russe, Paris 7e, France.

Germanus Gyula, Julius, PH.D., D.LITT.; Hungarian orientalist and linguist; b. 1884; ed. Univs. of Budapest, Istanbul, Vienna and Leipzig.
Lecturer at Eastern Acad. of Commerce 12, Univ. of Political Economy, Dept. of Oriental Sciences 29, Univ. of Santineketan, Bengal 29-32; Prof. of Arab Language, Budapest Univ. 48-65; numerous journeys in Near East;

pilgrimage to Mecca 35; Visiting Lecturer, Turkish, Egyptian and Indian Univs.; Independent mem. Hungarian Parl. 58-67; Corresp. mem. Arab Acad. of Cairo, Arab Acad. of Damascus, Acad. of Baghdad; mem. Accad. del Mediterráneo.
Publs. *Allah Akhbar* 36, *A félhold fakó fényében* (The Half-Moon's Dim Light) 58, and numerous articles on Arab literature including *History of Arab Literature, Anthology of Arab Poetry, Modern Poetry of South Arabia*.
Petőfitér 3, Budapest V, Hungary.

Ghaffari, Abolghassem, DR. SC. MATH., PH.D.; Iranian mathematician; b. 1909; ed. Darolfonoun School and Univs. of Nancy, Paris, London and Oxford.
Associate Prof., Teheran Univ. 37-42, Prof. of Mathematics 42-; Mathematics Research Asst. King's Coll., London 47-48; Research Fellow, Harvard 50-51, Research Assoc., Princeton 51-52; mem. Inst. for Advanced Study, Princeton 51-52; Senior Mathematician, Nat. Bureau of Standards, Washington, D.C. 56-57; aeronautical research scientist 57-64; Professorial Lecturer, American Univ., Washington 58-62; aerospace scientist, Goddard Space Flight Center, Greenbelt, Md. 64-; has lectured at Univs. of Harvard, Maryland, Princeton and Columbia and at Massachusetts Inst. of Technology; mem. American, French and British Mathematical Societies; Fellow Washington Acad. of Sciences, New York Acad. of Sciences, American Asscn. for the Advancement of Science; mem. Iranian Higher Council of Education 54-58; Iranian Del. to 5th Pakistan Science Conf. Lahore 53, to Int. Congresses of Mathematicians, Amsterdam 54, Edinburgh 58, Stockholm 62; mem. Iranian Comm. for UNESCO 54; mem. American Astronomical Soc.; Orders of Homayoun and of Danesh (first class) and of Sepass (first class); U.S. Special Apollo Achievement Award.
Publs. *Sur l'Equation Fonctionelle de Chapman-Kolmogoroff* 36, *The Hodograph Method in Gas Dynamics* 50.
7109 Connecticut Avenue, Washington, D.C. 20015, U.S.A.; and Shah Reza Avenue, 31 Ladan Street, Teheran, Iran.

Ghaidan, Gen. Saadoun; Iraqi army officer and politician; b. 1930; ed. secondary educ. in Ramadi and Military Coll.
Commissioned 2nd Lieut. 53; Commdr. Repub. Body-Guard Forces 68; mem. Revolutionary Command Council 68; Minister of the Interior April 70-.
Ministry of the Interior, Baghdad, Iraq.

Ghaleb, Mohamed Murad; Egyptian diplomatist; b. 1 April 1922, Cairo.
Under-Sec. for Foreign Affairs 59-60; Amb. to Congo Republic (Léopoldville) 60, to U.S.S.R. 61-71; Minister of Foreign Affairs 71-72, of Information 73-.
Ministry of Information, Cairo; and 78 El Nil Street, Gueza, Cairo, Egypt.

Ghalib, Qasim; Yemeni educationalist.
Minister of Education and Information 65-66; Minister of Educ. 66-67; Pres. Islamic Univ. of Taiz 66-.
Islamic University of Taiz, Taiz, Yemen Arab Republic.

Ghanem, Gen. Iskander A.; Lebanese army officer; b. 1 Jan. 1913; ed. Coll. du Sacré Coeur, Mil. Acad., Homs, and Gen. Staff Coll., Leavenworth, Kan., U.S.A.
Promoted to rank of Capt. in Lebanese Army 45; Artillery Battalion Commdr., Artillery Insp. 47-58; Lieut.-Col. 53, Col. 59; Deputy Chief of Staff 59-66; Brig. 64; Commdr. Northern Region 66, 68; Armed Forces Attaché, Washington, D.C. 66-67; Head Mil. Court 67; Commdr. Beirut Region 67-68, 68-69; Commdr. Lebanese Army 71-; Gen. 71; has attended various mil. tours in Lebanon and abroad; War Medal, Lebanese Merit Medal, Cedars Medal of High Ranking Officers, The Highest Mil. Cedars Medal, French Proficiency Medal, Portuguese Proficiency Medal, and several other decorations.
Ministry of Defence, Lebanese Army Headquarters, Yarzi, Lebanon.

Ghanem, Ismail, D. EN D.; Egyptian lawyer; b. 24 May, Alexandria; ed. Alexandria Univ., Faculté de Droit, Paris and Inst. of Comparative Law, New York Univ.
Member Staff, Faculty of Law, Alexandria Univ. and Ain-Shams Univ. 51-; Dean Faculty of Law, Arab Univ. of Beirut, Lebanon 62-63; Dean, Faculty of Law, Ain-Shams Univ. 66-68, Vice-Rector 68-70, Rector Sept. 71-; Amb. and Perm. Del. to UNESCO, Paris 70-71; Minister of Culture May-Sept. 71; mem. Exec. Board, Cairo Governorate; mem. Board, Acad. for Scientific Research; Chair. Council for the Social Sciences 71.
Publs. *Le Droit du Travail* 62, *La Vente* 63, *Le Droit Subjectif* 63, all in Arabic; *Les Droits réels principaux*, 2 vols., 62, *La Théorie générale des Obligations* 66-67.
Ain-Shams University, Cairo, Egypt.

Ghanem, Mohamed Hafez, PH.D.; Egyptian lawyer and government official; b. 28 Sept. 1925; ed. Cairo Univ. and Univ. de Paris.
Lecturer, Faculty of Law, Alexandria Univ. 49; Prof. of Public Int. Law and Vice-Dean, Faculty of Law, Ain Shams Univ. 60-68; Minister of Tourism 68-71, of Educ. 71; Sec.-Gen. Arab Socialist Union 73-; Hon. Sec. Egyptian Soc. of Int. Law; mem. Arbitration, Conciliation and Mediation Comm. of Org. of African Unity (OAU) 66-71; mem. Legal Consultative Comm. for Afro-Asian Countries 58-65; State Prize for best publ. in field of Int. Law and Political Science 60.
Publs. *Public International Law* (Arabic) 64, *International Organization* 67.
Arab Socialist Union, Cairo; and 3 Sharia El Bergass, Garden City, Cairo, Egypt.

Gherab, Mohamed Habib; Tunisian UN official.
Former Amb. to Spain; Special Adviser to Tunisian Sec. of State for Foreign Affairs 67-69; mem. del. to XXIII session of UN Gen. Assembly; Asst. Sec.-Gen. of UN and Dir. of Personnel March 69-.
Office of Personnel, UN Secretariat, New York, N.Y., U.S.A.

Ghirshman, Roman; French archaeologist; b. 3 Oct. 1895; ed. Sorbonne and Ecole du Louvre.
Mem. French Archæological Mission in Iraq 30; Dir. similar mission in Iran 31; exploration of Seistan desert, Afghanistan 36; Head of French Archæological Dept. in Afghanistan 41-43; mem. Inst. Français d'Archéologie Orientale, Cairo 44-45; Dir. Susa Mission, Iran 46-67; Dir. French Archæological Missions in Iran; Prof. Univ. of Aix-en-Provence; mem. Acad. des Inscriptions et Belles Lettres (three times prizeman); Officier Légion d'Honneur, Grand Officer of two Iranian Orders, hon. degrees (Sorbonne and Univ. of Teheran); hon. Dir.-Gen. Archaeological Delegation in Iran.
Publs. *Fouilles de Tepe Giyan* 36, *Fouilles de Sialk* (2 vols.) 38, 39, *Bégram-Histoire des Kouchans* 46, *Les Chionites-Hephtalites* 48, *Iran, des origines à l'Islam* 50, *Iran: Parthes et Sassanides* 63, *Iran: La Perse ancienne* 2 vols. 62-64, and other works.
96 rue La Fontaine, Paris 16e, France.

Ghorab, Amin Youssef; Egyptian writer; b. 31 March 1913.
Began writing short stories 39; Head of Public Relations, High Council of Arts, Literature and Social Sciences; mem. Admin. Council Quisse Club; mem. Egyptian Asscn. of Writers, P.E.N. Int. Club; Order of Arts and Sciences 65.
Publs. Novels: *Shabab Imraah, Sanawat El Hob, Sit El-*

Banat, El Abwab, El Moghlakah; Scenarios for Films: *Nissa Moharramat, El-Layali El Tawilah, Rannet El-Kholkhal, Nissa-Wa-Theab, El Thalathah Yohebbounaha, Garimet Hob, Shabab Imraah, El-Saphirah Aziza*.
8 Rafei Street, Heliopolis, Cairo, Egypt.

Ghorra, Edward A., L. EN D.; Lebanese diplomatist; b. 1913; ed. Patriarchal Coll., Beirut, American Univ. of Beirut, French Law School (Univ. St. Joseph), Beirut and Univ. of Pittsburgh, U.S.A.
Mem. of staff, American Univ. of Beirut 39-41; barrister 41-45; Consul-Gen. for Lebanon, New York 45-50, Sydney 50-55; attached Ministry of Foreign Affairs as Head Occidental Section 56-57; mem. Lebanese Del. to Economic and Social Council and UN Gen. Assembly 47-49; Dir. of Political Affairs and Int. Relations Dept. 57-58; del. to UN Gen. Assembly 58, 63; Ambassador to U.S.S.R. 59-63; Dir. Dept. for Lebanese Overseas, Ministry of Foreign Affairs 63-65; Amb. to Czechoslovakia and Poland 65-68; Perm. Rep. to UN 68-; Rep. to Human Rights Comm. 69-, Social Comm. 69-, Econ. and Social Council 71-; Vice-Pres. UN Gen. Assembly 68; foreign decorations.
Permanent Mission of Lebanon to the United Nations, 866 United Nations Plaza, Room 533-535, New York, N.Y. 10017, U.S.A.

Ghosheh, Abdallah Shehadeh; Jordanian judge; b. 21 Oct. 1905; ed. Rawdah Coll., Jerusalem, Jerusalem Law Inst.
Teacher 29-34; Chief Clerk, Shariya Hebron Court 34-38; Judge in Vaffa, Nazareth, Hebron and Nablus 38-46; mem. Shariya Court of Appeal 46-48; mem. Cttee. for Unification of Laws in Amman 50; Chief Justice 50; Chief Justice and Minister of Justice 50-51; Acting Minister of Educ. 51; Chief Islamic Higher Cttee. 51; mem. Supreme Council for Educ. in Jordan 53; mem. Devt. Cttee. for Al Aksa Mosque 54; Chief Justice and Head of Al Awkaj Council and Islamic Affairs March 64; mem. Royal Consultative Body Aug. 67; Minister of Awkaj and Islamic Affairs and Holy Places Dec. 68; Kadi Kuda Nov. 69; Chief of Cttee. for collecting of money for rebuilding of Holy Mosque of the Rock 54, 62; Al Kawkab Medal Grade I, Al Nahda Medal Grade I.
Office of the Chief Justice of the Muslim Religious Courts, Amman, Jordan.

Ghoussein, Talat al-; Kuwaiti diplomatist; b. 1924; ed. American Univ. of Cairo.
Foreign News Editor *As-Shaab* (Jaffa, Palestine) 46-47; Controller, Arab Bank Ltd., Jaffa, Palestine 47-48; Editor Foreign News and Dir. of English Section, Broadcasting Station of Jordan 48-49; Dir. Press and Public Information Ministry of Foreign Affairs, Yemen 49-53; Sec. Gen., Development Board, Kuwait 53-60; Dep. Private Sec. to Amir of Kuwait 60-61; Minister-Counsellor, Kuwait Embassy, Washington 62-63; Amb. to U.S.A. 63-70, concurrently to Canada 65-70; Amb. to Morocco 70-71, to Japan 71-.
Embassy of Kuwait, 13-12, Mita 4-chome, Minate-ku, Tokyo, Japan.

Ghozali, Sid Ahmed; Algerian industrialist; b. 31 March 1937.
Président Dir.-Gén. Société nationale de transports et de commercialisation des hydrocarbures (SONATRACH) 66-.
SONATRACH, Immeuble le Maurétanie, Algiers, Algeria.

Ghunaim, Khalifa Khalid al; Kuwaiti diplomatist and politician; b. 1921; ed. American Univ. of Beirut.
Deputy Chair Nat. Bank of Kuwait; mem. Kuwait Tanker Co., Kuwait Currency Board, Kuwait Development Board, Kuwait Chamber of Commerce; Ambassador to U.K. 61-62; Minister of Commerce 63-65.
c/o Ministry of Commerce, Kuwait.

Givton, Hanoch, M.A.; Israeli broadcasting official; b. 16 April 1917; ed. Hebrew Univ. Law School.
General Sec. Palestine Students' Union 40-41; Senior Programme Asst., Hebrew Section, Palestine Broadcasting Service 45; Head, News Dept., Kol Israel 50; mem. Israel Del. to 10th UN Gen. Assembly 55; Dep. Dir. Kol Israel 59-60, Dir. 60; Dir.-Gen. Israel Broadcasting Authority 65-68; Minister Plenipotentiary, Israel Perm. Mission to the UN 68-69; Dir.-Gen. Ministry of Tourism 70-.
Ministry of Tourism, Hakirya, P.O. Box 1018, Jerusalem; and 4 Shlein Street, Beit Hakerem, Jerusalem, Israel.

Glubb, Lieut.-Gen. Sir John Bagot, K.C.B., C.M.G., D.S.O., O.B.E., M.C.; British officer; b. 16 April 1897; ed. Cheltenham and Royal Military Acad. Woolwich.
2nd Lieut. Royal Engineers 15, served France; served Iraq 20; Admin. Inspector Iraq Govt. 26; Officer Commdg. Desert Area (Transjordan) 30; Officer Commdg. Arab Legion, Transjordan (now Jordan) 38-56.
Publs. *Story of the Arab Legion* 48, *A Soldier with the Arabs* 57, *Britain and the Arabs* 59, *War in the Desert* 60, *The Great Arab Conquests* 63, *The Empire of the Arabs* 65, *The Course of Empire* 65, *The Lost Centuries* 67, *Syria, Lebanon, Jordan* 67, *A Short History of the Arab Peoples* 69, *The Life and Times of Muhammad* 70, *Peace in the Holy Land* 71, *Soldiers of Fortune* 73.
West Wood St. Dunstan, Mayfield, Sussex, England.

Glykys, Michael; Cypriot lawyer and politician; b. 25 June 1912, Nicosia; ed. Pancyprian Gymnasium and Middle Temple, London.
Called to Bar; advocate 35-40; later joined Hellenic Chemical Products and Fertilizers Co. 40-55; Sec. to Hellenic Mining Co. 45-55; Man. Dir. Cyprus Textiles Co. Ltd., Model Famagusta Bakeries Ltd., Tricomo Agricultural Co. Ltd.; Cyprus Products Co. Ltd.; Glyks Estates Ltd., Glykys Bros. Ltd.; mem. Electricity Authority of Cyprus 60-70, Chair. 63-70; mem. Board of Dirs. Central Bank of Cyprus 63-70; Minister of Health 70-72.
c/o Ministry of Health, Nicosia, Cyprus.

Godik, Giora; Israeli theatre producer; b. 5 May 1921; ed. Magnus Krynski, Warsaw and Stefan Batory Univ., Wilna.
Fought with Polish Army during Second World War; settled in Israel 48; with Israeli Army 48-55; opened artists' agency Giora Godik Productions Ltd. 55; opened Giora Godik Theatre, Alhambra Theatre, Tel-Aviv 65; productions include *Barefoot in the Park*, *Fiddler on the Roof*, *The King and I*, *Kazablan*, *Hello Dolly*, *I Like Mike*, *Long Live the Horses*, *The Witch*.
Office: 10 Glikson Street, Tel-Aviv; Home: 53 King David Blvd., Tel-Aviv, Israel.

Gökay, Dr. Fahreddin Kerim; Turkish physician, diplomatist and politician; b. 1922; ed. Faculty of Medicine, Univ. of Istanbul.
Specialist in mental health; fmr. Prof. of Mental Health and Neurology, Univ. of Istanbul; fmr. Gov. and Mayor of Istanbul; Ambassador to Switzerland 58-60; Minister of Reconstruction and Redevelopment 62-63; Minister of Health and Social Welfare 63; Deputy for Istanbul; fmr. Pres. Republican People's Party, Istanbul; Pres. Turkish Asscn. for Social Psychiatry and Research; Editor, *Medical World;* Counsellor at Council of Europe 64-; Past Gov. Turkish Lions Int. Club.
Republican People's Party, Istanbul, Turkey.

Gökmen, Oğuz; Turkish diplomatist; b. 4 May 1916; ed. Ankara Universitesi and Univ. de Paris à la Sorbonne.
Entered Ministry of Foreign Affairs, Ankara 40; Second Sec. Turkish Embassy, Paris 44-47, First Sec. 47-49; Chief of Section, Dept. of Trade, Ministry of Foreign Affairs 49-50; Chargé d'Affaires, Buenos Aires 50-53; Counsellor,

Sofia 53-54; Asst. Chief, Dept. of Trade and Trade Agreements 55; Dir.-Gen. Dept. of Commerce and Commercial Agreements 56; Dir.-Gen. Econ. Dept. at the Ministry 58; Amb. to Argentina, also accred. to Uruguay and Paraguay 62-64; Perm. Rep. to European Econ. Community (EEC) 64-66; Amb. to German Fed. Repub. Dec. 66-72.
c/o Ministry of Foreign Affairs, Ankara, Turkey.

Goldmann, Nahum; Polish-born Zionist leader; b. 10 July 1895; ed. Heidelberg, Berlin and Marburg Univs.
Editor and Publisher German Encyclopaedia Judaica 22-34; mem. Zionist Political Comm. 27; Act. Chair. Zionist Editor and Publisher German Hebrew Encyclopedia 22-34; mem. Zionist Political Comm. 27; Act. Chair. Zionist Action Cttee. 33; escaped from Germany 34; Rep. of Jewish Agency to L. of N.; in U.S. 41; Rep. Jewish Agency for Palestine in U.S.A. during Second World War; Pres. World Jewish Congress 51-, World Zionist Org. 56-68, Conf. on Jewish Claims against Germany, Memorial Foundation for Jewish Culture; Chair. Cttee. on Jewish Claims against Austria 50-.
Ahad Haam 18, Jerusalem, Israel; 12 avenue Montaigne, Paris, France.

Goldstein, Rabbi Israel, M.A., D.D., D.H.L., LITT.H.D., LL.D., PH.D.; American Rabbi; b. 18 June 1896; ed. Univ. of Pennsylvania, Jewish Theological Seminary of America and Columbia Univ.
Rabbi Congregation B'nai Jeshurun N.Y.C. 18-60, Rabbi Emeritus 61-; Pres. Jewish Conciliation Board of America 29-68 (now Hon. Pres.), Jewish Nat. Fund of America 33-43 (now Hon. Pres.); Pres. Synagogue Council of America 42-44, Zionist Organization of America 44-46; Chair. World Confed. of Gen. Zionists 46-72 (now Hon. Pres.); United Palestine Appeal 47-49; Co-Chair. United Jewish Appeal 47-49; Treas. Jewish Agency 47-49; Pres. Amidar Israel Nat. Housing Co. for Immigrants 48-49; mem. World Jewish Congress Exec. 48-, and Chair. of its Western Hemisphere Exec. 50-60, Hon. Vice-Pres. 59-; Pres. American Jewish Congress 51-58; now Hon. Pres.; Pres. World Hebrew Union; mem. Jewish Agency for Palestine Exec. 48-72; World Chair. Keren Hayesod-United Israel Appeal 61-71; mem. Board of Govs. Hebrew Univ. of Jerusalem, Weizmann Inst. of Science; Univ. of Haifa; Founder Brandeis Univ. 46; Chair. Jerusalem Artists' House 65-70; founded Israel Goldstein Jerusalem Youth Village; Chair. in Zionism at Hebrew Univ. of Jerusalem, Synagogue of Hebrew Univ. of Jerusalem; Chair. in Practical Theology, Jewish Theological Seminary of America; Chair. Jerusalem Council of Israel-America Friendship League; Hon. Chair. Asscn. of Americans and Canadians in Israel.
Publs. *A Century of Judaism in New York* 30, *Towards a Solution* 40, *Mourner's Devotions* 41, *Brandeis University* 51, *American Jewry Comes of Age* 55, *Transition Years* 62, *Israel at Home and Abroad* 73.
12 Pinsker Street, Jerusalem, Israel.

Golesorkhy, Nassir, M.SC.; Iranian agriculturalist and politician; b. 1923, Teheran; ed. Univ. of Teheran and in U.S.A.
Director, Gen. Dept. of Econs. of Agriculture; Supervisor, Gen. Org. of Animal Husbandry; Technical and Parliamentary Asst., Ministry of Agriculture; Minister of Natural Resources 71.
Teheran, Iran.

Gomaa, Mohamed Sharawy; Egyptian politician; b. 25 July 1920; ed. Military Coll.
Governor of Suez 61-64; Minister and mem. U.A.R.-Iraq Joint Presidency Council 64; Cabinet State Minister 65-66; Minister of the Interior 66-71; Deputy Prime Minister 70-71; charged with high treason July 71, sentenced to imprisonment Dec. 71.
c/o Ministry of the Interior, Cairo, Egypt.

Goodarzi, Dr. Manouchehr; Iranian administrator; b. 1925; ed. Princeton Univ. and Univ. of S. Calif., U.S.A.
Lecturer, Princeton Univ.; Lecturer in Public Admin., Teheran Univ.; Founding Dir. Org. and Management Bureau 56-57, Dir. Dept. of Social and Municipal Devt. 57-60, Deputy Man. Dir. 60-62, Plan Org.; Deputy Prime Minister, Sec.-Gen. High Admin. Council 62-64; Minister of Agricultural Products and Consumer Goods 69-70; Minister in charge of Nat. Transport Co-ordination 70-71; Special Adviser to the Prime Minister 71-73; Pres. Arj Mfg. Corpn. 73-; mem. Board of Dirs. Nat. Iranian Airline, State Corpn. for Foreign Trade, Board of Trustees of Univs. of Teheran, Mashad, Esphahan, Tabriz, Joundishahpoor; Chair. Exec. Council Eastern Regional Org. for Public Admin., Manila; decorations from Iran, Repub. of Korea and Philippines.
Arj Corporation, P.O. Box 3427, Teheran, Iran.

Goren, Brig.-Gen. Shlomo; Israeli Rabbi; b. 1917, Poland; ed. Hebrew Univ.
In Israel 25-; co-founder Kfar Hassidim; Chief Chaplain, Israeli Army; Chief Rabbi of Tel-Aviv (elected June 68); Ashkenazi Chief Rabbi of Israel Oct. 72-; Rabbi Kook Prize.
Publs. *Nezer Hakodesh* (on Maimonides), *Shaarei Tahara*, *Talmud Yerushalmi Meforash, Torath Ha Moadim*; works on religion in military life, prayers for soldiers, etc.
Chief Rabbinate, 51 Hamelech David Boulevard, Tel-Aviv, Israel.

Goulli, Slaheddine el, LL.D.; Tunisian diplomatist; b. 22 June 1919, Sousse; ed. Collège de Sousse and Université de Paris.
Tunisian Bar 47; in private industry 49-56; active in Tunisian Nat. Liberation Movement, Europe 47-56; Gen. Consul, Marseilles 56-57; Counsellor, Washington 58, Minister, Washington 59-61; Alt. Exec. Dir. World Bank 61; Amb. to Belgium, also accred. to Netherlands and Luxembourg 62, concurrently Perm. Rep. to EEC; Perm. Rep. to UN 69; Amb. to U.S.A. Dec. 69-, concurrently to Mexico 70-, to Venezuela 72-; Grand Cordon de l'Ordre de la République Tunisienne 66, also decorations from Belgium, Netherlands and Luxembourg.
Embassy of Tunisia, 2408 Massachusetts Avenue, N.W., Washington, D.C., U.S.A.

Grivas, Lieut.-Gen. George; Greek (b. Cypriot) officer; b. 1898.
Adopted Greek nationality; Military School for Officers 16-19; Officer, Infantry Corps., Asia Minor 19-22, School for Captains, Athens; Staff Officer 28; Infantry School, Versailles; Firing School, Châlons-sur-Marne; War Coll., Paris; lecturer in Tactics, Salonika Training School; Chief of Staff, II Division 40; founded and led "X" underground organization in Athens during German occupation in Second World War; returned to Cyprus 51; organised and led, under the name "Dighenis", EOKA movement 55-58; returned to Greece after Cyprus settlement 59; returned to Cyprus 64, and again 71-; Commdr. of Armed Forces, Cyprus Aug. 64-67; Freedom and Gold Medal, City of Athens; Gold Medal, Athens Acad.; Grand Cross, Order of George I; Commdr., Order of Military Merit.
Publs. *Military Essay on the Infantry Fire Plan, Memoirs* 64, (2nd vol.) 70, *Guerilla Warfare* 64, *The Chronicle of EOKA Struggle* 70.
Aristidou 3, Halandri, Athens, Greece.

Guiga, Driss, L. EN D.; Tunisian politician; b. 21 Aug. 1924, Testour; ed. Sadiki Coll., Tunis.
Tunisian Bar; Chef de Cabinet, Ministry of Public Health 52; Dir. Nat. Security until 63; Dir.-Gen. of Tourism and Thermal Affairs 63; Sec. of State for Public Health Sept.-Nov. 69; Minister of Public Health 69-73, of Nat. Educ. 73-; mem. Destour Socialist Party 43-, has held several party posts, currently mem. Cen. Cttee.
Ministère de l'Education Nationale, Tunis, Tunisia.

Guillaumat, Pierre L. J.; French civil servant; b. 5 Aug. 1909; ed. Prytanée Militaire, La Flèche and Ecole Polytechnique.
Chef du Service des Mines, Indochina 34-39, Tunisia 39-43; Dir. of Carburants 44-51; Admin.-Gen. Atomic Energy Comm. 51-58; Pres. Petroleum Research Bureau 45-58; Minister of the Armies, de Gaulle Cabinet, June 58-Jan. 59, Debré Cabinet Jan. 59-Feb. 60; Minister attached to Prime Minister's Office Feb. 60-April 62; Minister of Education (*a.i.*) Nov. 60-Feb. 61; Pres. Union Générales des Pétroles 62-65, Electricité de France 64-66, Entreprise de Recherches et d'Activités Pétrolières 65-, Soc. Nat. des Pétroles d'Aquitaine 65-; Pres. Conseil d'Admin., l'Ecole Polytechnique 71-; Grand Officier de la Légion d'Honneur, Croix de Guerre.
7 rue Nélaton, Paris 15e, France.

Gülek, Dr. Kasim, B.SC.(COM.), PH.D., LL.D.; Turkish politician economist and farmer; b. 1910; ed. Robert Coll., Ecole des Sciences Politiques, Paris, Columbia, Cambridge, London, Berlin and Hamburg Univs.
Member of Parl. 40-; mem. Central Exec. Council of People's Republican Party 42; Chair. Cttee. on Commerce 43; del. to Int. Labour Conf. 44; Minister of Public Works 47; Minister of Communications 48, of State 49; Vice-Pres. Council of Europe 62; Chair. UN Comm. on Korea; Sec.-Gen. Republican People's Party 50-59, resigned from Republican People's Party 67; mem. Constituent Assembly 60-61; Pres. North Atlantic Assembly 69; Gov. Atlantic Inst. 69-; Senator 69-.
Publs. *Development of Economically Backward Countries* 32, *Development of Banking in Turkey* 33, *Democracy Takes Root in Turkey* 51.
B. Evler, 50 Sokak no. 3, Ankara, Turkey.

Gunter, John Wadsworth, M.A., PH.D.; American economist; b. 17 Feb. 1914; ed. Univ. of North Carolina.
Worked in U.S. Treasury Dept. 40-48, Treasury Rep. in Middle East 43-44, in London 46-48, Deputy Dir. Office of Int. Finance 48; Assoc. Prof. of Int. Trade, Univ. of Texas 48-49; U.S. mem. Greek Currency Cttee., Bank of Greece 49-51; Alt. mem. Comm. on German Debts, London 51-53; Asst. Dir. Middle Eastern Dept., Int. Monetary Fund 53, Deputy Dir., Acting Dir. 58-.
International Monetary Fund, Washington, D.C. 20431, U.S.A.

Gürler, Gen. Faruk; Turkish army officer; b. 1913, Üsküdar, Istanbul; ed. War School, War Acad. for Land Forces.
Commander, Artillery and Infantry Units; Staff Officer, High Defence Council; Instructor War School and War Acad., later Acting Commdr.; Intelligence Officer, NATO; Deputy Chief of Staff of Army Corps, Deputy Artillery Commdr. of Div. and Army Corps, later Army Corps Commdr.; Chief of Staff of Land Forces Command; Acting Under-Sec. of State, then Under-Sec. of State, Ministry of Nat. Defence; promoted to rank of Gen. 68; Deputy Chief of Gen. Staff, Commdr. of Land Forces 68-72; Chief of Staff 72-73.
c/o Ministry of National Defence, Ankara, Turkey.

Gurney, Oliver Robert, M.A., D.PHIL.; British assyriologist; b. 28 Jan. 1911; ed. Eton Coll. and New Coll. Oxford.
Army Service 39-45; Shillito Reader in Assyriology, Oxford Univ. 45-, Prof. 65-; Fellow of British Acad. 59-, Magdalen Coll. Oxford 63-; Editor *Anatolian Studies* 59-.
Publs. *The Geography of the Hittite Empire* (with J. Garstang) 59, *The Hittites* 52, 72, *The Sultantepe Tablets I and II* (with J. J. Finkelstein and P. Hulin) 57, 64, *Ur Excavations—Texts VII* 73.
Bayworth Corner, Boars Hill, Oxford, England.

Gürün, Kâmuran; Turkish diplomatist; b. 1924, Çengelköy (Istanbul); ed. studied political science.

Entered diplomatic service 48; posted to Turkish Embassy, Bonn 51; subsequently held various posts at Ministry of Foreign Affairs and diplomatic missions abroad; Dir.-Gen. Dept. for Admin. Affairs 61, subsequently Perm. Sec. to the Inter-Ministerial Cttee. on External Econ. Relations, Dir.-Gen. Dept. for Econ. and Commercial Affairs, Deputy Sec.-Gen. for Econ. Affairs and Sec.-Gen. Inter-Ministerial Econ. Council; Amb. to Romania 67-70; Perm. Rep. of Turkey at OECD Oct. 70-.
Permanent Representative of Turkey at OECD, 2 rue André Pascal, Paris 16e, France.

Gvati, Chaim; Israeli farmer and politician; b. 29 Jan. 1901; ed. Vilna, Poland, and Russian Univ.
Migrated to Palestine 24; mem. Kibbutz 24-, mem. Kibbutz Meuchad Central Cttee. 42-45; Chair. Security and Econ. Cttees. of The Agriculture Centre 46-49; Dir.-Gen. Ministry of Agriculture 50-57; Sec. Ichud Hakvutzot Veakibutzim 59-62; Sec. Federation of Kibbutz Movement 63-64; Minister of Agriculture Nov. 64-; Mapai.
Kibbutz Yifat; and Ministry of Agriculture, 13 Helena Hamalca Street, Jerusalem, Israel.

H

Habash, George, M.D.; Palestinian resistance leader; b. 1926; ed. American University of Beirut.
Founder Youth of Avengeance 48 and Arab Nationalists' Movement early 50s; practised as doctor 50s and 60s; leader of Popular Front for the Liberation of Palestine June 67-.
c/o Palestine Liberation Organization, Colombani Street, Off Sadat Street, Dr. Raji Nasr Building, Ras Beirut, Lebanon.

Habashi, Wadi; Sudanese agricultural economist and politician; b. 14 Aug. 1917, Merwi; ed. Univ. of Khartoum and Oxford Univ.
Worked on the Al Aalyab, Burgaeg and White Nile devt. schemes; Agricultural Insp. for Khartoum Province and later for Merwi, Dongla and Halfa; Technical Adviser to the Minister of Agriculture; Asst. Dir. for Planning and Devt., Dept. of Agriculture, Dir. 55-66; Rep. of Sudan to FAO Conf. 56, to Int. Tobacco Conf., Rhodesia 63; Chair. Admin. Council of El Gash Scheme Comm.; Dir. Production Section, Equatoria Schemes Comm.; Head, Advisory Comm. for Agricultural Research; mem. Gezira Scheme Admin. Council; mem. Studies Comm., Faculty of Agriculture, Univ. of Khartoum; with FAO 60-71, Dir. Joint Econ. Comm. of Africa and the UN, Addis Ababa; joined Int. Bank and Kuwait Fund of Arab Devt. Oct. 71, Minister of Agriculture Oct. 71-.
c/o Ministry of Agriculture, Khartoum, Sudan.

Haddad, Amin Farid, PH.C., M.SC.; Lebanese university professor; b. 1911; ed. Nat. Coll. of Shwayfat, American Univ. of Beirut, Philadelphia Coll. of Pharmacy and Science.
Chief Pharmacist, The English Pharmacy, Khartoum, Sudan 33-36; Univ. Pharmacist and Instructor in Pharmacy, American Univ. of Beirut 36-42, Adjunct Prof. of Pharmacy 42-49, Assoc. Prof. of Pharmacy and Acting Dir. School of Pharmacy 49-52, Assoc. Prof. School of Pharmacy 52-, Prof. and Dir. 55-; also Dir. Pharmaceutical Service of Univ. Hospital 49-67; mem. American Pharmaceutical Assen., American Soc. of Hospital Pharmacists, Int. Pharmaceutical Fed., Scientific Section; mem. Expert Advisory Panel on the Int. Pharmacopoeia and Pharmaceutical Preparation (WHO); Sec. High Comm. on Drugs, Lebanon 64-68; Chair. Scientific Cttee, Lebanese Order of Pharmacists 52-67; Temp. Adviser to WHO (Eastern Mediterranean Region) on pharmaceutical educ. 68-70,

71-73; Editor Lebanese Pharmaceutical Journal 53-; Hon. Fellow, Univ. of Wisconsin, Madison, U.S.A. 58-July 59.
American University of Beirut, Beirut, Lebanon.

Haddad, Dr. Ghassan, D.ECON.SC.; Syrian educationist and politician; b. 26 Jan. 1926, Lattakia; ed. secondary schools, Lattakia and Damascus, Mil. Acad., and U.S.S.R. Served in various mil. posts 48-61; promoted to rank of Gen. 63; mem. Higher Nat. Council of the Revolution, mem. of Gen. Leadership of the Army and Armed Forces 63; Minister of Planning 63-65, later Pres. Parl. Planning Cttee.; carried out scientific research 66-68; Conf. Prof. Univ. of Damascus, Planning Inst. for Social and Econ. Devt. 69-; mem. Union of Arab Writers, Union of the Arab Economists; several decorations including Médaille de Mérite de Hors Classe, Médaille de la Loyauté de Premier Classe.
Publs. many articles and works.
Planning Institute for Social and Economic Development, University of Damascus, Damascus, Syria.

Haddad, Mustapha H., PH.D.; Syrian university professor; b. 1930; ed. Damascus Univ. and Univ. of Paris at the Sorbonne.
Instructor, High Schools of Aleppo 54; postgraduate studies in France 59; Instructor, Faculty of Science, Damascus Univ. 60; Minister of Educ. 63-66; Asst. Prof. Faculty of Science, Damascus Univ. 64-; later Minister of Higher Educ.; Rep. of Syria to 14th Session of UNESCO 66; Vice-Chair. Syrian Del. to Conf. of Arab Ministers of Educ., Kuwait 68.
Faculty of Science, Damascus University, Damascus, Syria.

Haddad, Sulaiman Ahmed el; Kuwaiti banker and politician; b. 1930; ed. Kuwait Aazamieh Secondary School, and Cairo Univ.
Secretary of Educ. Council of Kuwait; fmr. Financial Asst., Ministry of Educ. and mem. Constituent Assembly for formation of Kuwaiti Constitution; mem. National Assembly 63-; Chair. Arab African Bank.
Arab African Bank, 44 Abdel Khalek Sarwat Street, Cairo, Egypt.

Hadid, Mohammed Haj Hussein, B.SC. (ECON.); Iraqi economist; b. 1906; ed. American Univ. of Beirut, and London School of Economics.
Finance Inspector 31; in charge of Statistics Section, Min. of Finance 32, of Commerce Section 34, Acting Dir. of Commerce 35, Acting Dir.-Gen. of Revenue 36; elected deputy for Mosul 37, 48, 54; Vice-Pres. Nat. Democratic Party 46-54; Minister of Supply 46; Minister of Finance 58-60; Founder of Nat. Progressive Party 60; now Man. Dir. Consolidated Modern Enterprises Co.
Saadun, Baghdad, Iraq.

Hadithi, Murtada al-; Iraqi politician; b. 1939, Ramadi; ed. Higher Teachers' Training Inst. and Univ. of Baghdad. School Teacher, Fallouja 66-67; mem. Revolutionary Command Council 67; Chair. Kurdish Affairs Bureau and Peace Cttee. 67; mem. World Peace Cttee.; Minister of Labour March 70-Oct. 71; Minister of Foreign Affairs Oct. 71-.
Ministry of Foreign Affairs, Baghdad, Iraq.

Hadj, Messali Ahmed bin; Algerian politician; b. 1898. Service in French Army, First World War; f. independence movement L'Etoile Nord-Africaine 25, banned and imprisoned 29, 34, 35; f. *Al Oumma* (The Nation) 29; f. Algerian People's Party, imprisoned during subsequent disturbances 36, 39-41, sentenced to sixteen years' hard labour 41, pardoned, placed in enforced residence 43-45; restored as nationalist leader but then sent to Brazzaville 45-47; f. Movement for the Triumph of Democratic Liberties (M.T.L.D.) (later split into M.N.A. and F.L.N.) 47; in enforced residence, France 52-62; fmr. Pres. M.N.A.
Algiers, Algeria.

Hadjioannou, Kyriacos, F.R.A.I., PH.D.; Cypriot teacher and diplomatist; b. 1909; ed. Famagusta Gymnasium, Athens Univ. and Oxford Univ.
Greek Master, Kyrenia Gymnasium 32-35, Famagusta 36-45; Principal, Famagusta Gymnasium 46-48, 57-60; 63-69; Amb. to U.A.R. 60-63; Lecturer, Teachers' Training Coll., Morphou 48-53; Principal, Morphou Gymnasium 53-57; Pres. United Nat. Solid Front 57-59; Founder and Pres. Philological and Scientific Soc. of Famagusta 60-61, 64-; Fellow, Royal Anthropological Inst. of Great Britain and Ireland 46-; Grand Cordon of the Repub. (Egypt).
Publs. *The Loan-words of Medieval and Modern Greek Cypriot Dialect* 36, *Cypriot Fables* 48, *Literary Texts of the Medieval and Modern Greek Cypriot Dialect with Introductions and Commentaries* 61, *Ta en Diaspora* 69, *Diplomacy and mechinations in the Courts of the Lusignan Kings of Cyprus* 70, *Ancient Cyprus in Greek Sources Vol. I, Legendary Traditions, History and Ethnology from Prehistoric Times to the Year 395 A.D.* 71, and articles in Greek, German, English, French and Belgian journals.
Ay. Spyridon 8, Famagusta 58, Cyprus.

Hafez, Maj.-Gen. Amin el; Syrian army officer and politician; b. 1911.
Former Military Attaché in Argentina; took part in the revolution of March 1963; Dep. Prime Minister, Mil. Gov. of Syria and Minister of Interior March-Aug. 63; Minister of Defence and Army Chief of Staff July-Aug. 63; C.-in-C. of Armed Forces July 63-64; Pres. of Revolutionary Council July 63-May 64; Pres. Presidency Council May 64-Feb. 66; Prime Minister Nov. 63-May 64, Oct. 64-Sept. 65; imprisoned 71.
Damascus, Syria.

Hagri, Al-qadi Abdullah Admed Al-; Yemeni politician; b. 1917.
Minister of Communications and Culture before revolution (Sept. 62); Amb. to Kuwait 62-72; mem. Pres. Council 72-Jan. 73; Prime Minister Jan. 73-.
Office of the Prime Minister, Sana'a, Yemen Arab Republic.

Haidar, Mohamed Haider, LL.B.; Syrian politician; b. 1931; ed. secondary schools, Lattakia, Univ. of Damascus.
Teacher, Lattakia, Hama, Damascus 51-60; with Ministry of Agrarian Reform 60-63; Dir. Agrarian Reform Inst., Hama 63; Dir. Agrarian Reform, Damascus, Daraa, Al-Suaida 64; Dir. Legal and Admin. Affairs, Ministry of Agriculture and Agrarian Reform 65; Gov. Al-Hasakeh 66; mem. Command, Damascus Branch of Arab Socialist Baath Party 67, Temporal Regional Command 70, now Regional and Nat. Commands, mem. Cen. Command Progressive Nat. Front of Syria; now Deputy Prime Minister, Minister of Agriculture and Agrarian Reform.
Ministry of Agriculture and Agrarian Reform, Damascus, Syria.

Haikal, Yousef, PH.D., D. EN DROIT; Jordanian diplomatist; b. 15 Aug. 1912; ed. Arab Coll. Jerusalem and Univs. of London and Paris.
Gen. Inspector of Awqaf (Moslem Public Properties in Palestine); District Judge (Palestine) 43-45; Mayor of Jaffa 45-48; Minister to U.S.A. 49-53; Chief Jordan Del. with Mixed Armistice Comm., Jerusalem 53-54; Ambassador to Great Britain 54-56, to France 56-57, 62-64, to U.S.A. 57-58, 59-62, to Republic of China 64-65; Istiqlal Medal (1st Class).
Publs. include (in French) *The Prime Minister and the Evolution of the Parliamentary System, The Dissolution of Parliament*; (in Arabic) *The Palestine Problem, Towards Arab Unity, Palestine Before and After* 71.
c/o Byblos Hotel, Georges Picot Street, Beirut, Lebanon.

Haithem, Muhammad Ali; Yemeni politician; b. 1940, Dathina, Southern Arabia.
Formerly school teacher; Minister of Interior 67; mem.

Presidential Council of S. Yemen 69-71; Chair. Council of Ministers 69-70; mem. Nat. Front Gen. Command.
c/o Council of Ministers, Aden, People's Democratic Republic of Yemen.

Hakim, Abdul Karim; Afghan politician; b. 25 June 1924, Mazar-i-Sharif; ed. Habibia, Kabul Coll. of Letters, Columbia and Texas Univs.
Vice-Pres. Afghan Air Authority 56-63; Deputy Minister of Finance 57-60; fmr. Gov. Herat, Helmand; Minister of Communications 67, of Finance 67-70, of Agric. and Irrigation 70; mem. Econ. Council 69-70; Afghan Del. to Econ. Cttee. UN 55, 56, 69, IBRD and IMF 55, 56, 57, 67, Colombo Plan 61, ECAFE 56, ECAFE Ministerial Meeting 70.
Publs. *Our Economic Problems* (Persian) 56, *Economic Report of Afghanistan* (English) 55, *Facts About Transit Difficulties* (English) 56, *Govt. Acct. System of Afghanistan* (Persian) 64.
c/o Ministry of Finance, Kabul, Afghanistan.

Hakim, George: (*see* Maximos V Hakim).

Hakim, Georges, M.A., L. en D.; Lebanese diplomatist; b. 1913; ed. American Univ., Beirut, and Univ. St. Joseph.
Appointed Adjunct Prof. of Economics, American Univ., Beirut 43; mem. of several advisory govt. cttees. on economic and financial questions 42-46; appointed alternate del. of Lebanon to Economic and Social Council of UN 46; Chief Del. 49; Counsellor Lebanese Legation Washington, D.C. 46-52, Chargé d'Affaires 48 and 51; Minister of Finance, Nat. Economy and Agriculture 52-53; represented Lebanon at numerous int. confs. including Int. Health Conf. N.Y. 46, UN Conf. on Trade and Employment, London 46, Geneva 47, Havana 47-48, etc.; Board of Govs. of the Int. Bank for Reconstruction and Development and the Int. Monetary Fund 47-50; Vice-Chair. Economic and Financial Cttee. UN 49; Chair. Group of Experts on economic development of underdeveloped countries, apptd. by Sec.-Gen. of UN Feb.-May 51; Minister of Foreign Affairs and of Economy 53; Deputy Sec.-Gen. Ministry of Foreign Affairs Mar.-July 55; Minister to German Fed. Republic July 55-57, Ambassador 57-58; Minister of Nat. Economy Mar.-June 56; Perm. Rep. to UN 59-65, 66; Chair. UN Comm. on Human Rights 62; Deputy Prime Minister and Minister of Foreign Affairs July 65-Feb. 66, Dec. 66-67; Vice-Pres. American Univ. of Beirut 68-.
American University of Beirut, Beirut, Lebanon.

Hakim, Tewfik al-; Egyptian writer; b. 1902.
Leading playwright; mem. Acad. of the Arabic Language, Higher Council of the Arts, etc.
Publs. *The Confused Sultan* 59, *Scheherezade, Pygmalion, The Cave-Dweller, You Who are Climbing the Tree* 63, *A Magistrate's Diary, Solomon the Wise, Bird of Lebanon, Fate of a Cockroach* 72.
Higher Council of the Arts, 4 Brazil Street, Zamalek, Cairo, Egypt.

Halefoğlu, Vahit M., M.A.; Turkish diplomatist; b. 1919; ed. Antakya Coll. and Univ. of Ankara.
Turkish Foreign Service 43-, served Vienna, Moscow, Ministry of Foreign Affairs, London 46-59; Dir.-Gen. First Political Dept., Ministry of Foreign Affairs 59-62; Ambassador to Lebanon 62-65, concurrently accred. to Kuwait 64-65; Ambassador to U.S.S.R. 65-66; Ambassador to the Netherlands 66-70; Deputy Sec.-Gen. for Political Affairs, Ministry of Foreign Affairs Dec. 70-Feb. 72; Amb. to Fed. Repub. of Germany 72-; Lebanese, Finnish, British, Greek, Italian, German and Spanish decorations.
Embassy of Turkey, Utestrasse 47, Bonn-Bad Godesberg, Federal Republic of Germany.

Halim, Brig. Mohammed Abdel; Sudanese politician; b. May 1927, Cairo, Egypt; ed. secondary school in Cairo and Mil. Coll.
Commissioned 48 and served with Egyptian Armed Forces until 58; Editor *Sot El Shabab* 55; transferred to Sudan Armed Forces 58, Deputy Legal Adviser 61; Registrar of societies and trade unions and Dir. Labour Dept. 64; Man. Bank Misr (Bank of Egypt) until 69; Minister of State Oct. 69; Minister of the Treasury July 70-72; decorations from Egypt and Sudan.
c/o Ministry of the Treasury, Khartoum, Sudan.

Halkin, Simon, B.A., M.A., D.H.L.; American Hebrew scholar and author; b. 30 Oct. 1899, Dovsk, Russia; ed. N.Y. City Coll., Chicago, New York and Columbia Univs.
Instructor in Hebrew, Hebrew Union School for Teachers, New York City 24-32; Teacher, Geulah High School, Tel-Aviv 32-39; Lecturer in Bible, Jewish History and Sociology and Modern Jewish History, Chicago Coll. of Jewish Studies 40-43; Prof. of Hebrew and Hebrew Literature, Jew Inst. of Religion, New York City 43-49; Assoc. Prof. of Hebrew Literature, Hebrew Univ. of Jerusalem 49-56, Prof. and Head of Dept. 56-67; Visiting Prof., Univ. of Calif. 54-55, Jewish Theological Seminary, N.Y. 65-66; Emer., Hebrew Univ. of Jerusalem 69; mem. Acad. of Hebrew Language; Pres. Israel PEN Club; Tchernichovsky Prize for translation (of Whitman) 53; Bialik Prize for Literature 68.
Publs. *Yehiel Ha-Hagri* (novel) 28, *Arai va-Keva* 43, *Ad Mashber* 45, *Al Haiy* (collected poems) 46, *Ma'avar Yabok* (collected poems), *Modern Hebrew Literature: Trends and Values* 51, *Literatura Hebrea Moderna* 68, *Collected Literary Essays and Studies* (3 vols., Hebrew) 70, and numerous others; translations of Shakespeare, Maeterlinck, Whitman, Shelley, Jack London, etc.
5 Radak Street, Jerusalem, Israel.

Hall, Harvey Porter, M.A.; American executive; b. 16 Nov. 1909; ed. Union Coll. and Harvard Univ.
Instructor, American Univ. of Beirut 30-33, Robert Coll., Istanbul 36-41; Dept. of State, Washington, D.C. 45-46; Dir. of Publs., The Middle East Inst. and Editor *The Middle East Journal* 46-56; Ford Foundation Fellowship 52-53, Programme Assoc. Ford Foundation 56-64, 71-, Assoc. Dir. Middle East-Africa Programme 64-67, Assoc. Rep., Beirut 67-71.
Publ. *American Interests in the Middle East* (Foreign Policy Asscn. Headline Series) 48.
Ford Foundation, P.O. Box 2379, Beirut, Lebanon.

Hamad, Abdlatif Yousef al-; Kuwaiti economist.
Director-General Kuwait Fund for Arab Econ. Devt. 63-; Man. Dir. Kuwait Investment Co.; Chair. Prefabricated Buildings Co. of Kuwait, United Bank of Kuwait Ltd., London, Middle East Int. Fund; Dir. American Express Int. Fund; Exec. Dir. Arab Fund for Econ. and Social Devt.; Trustee Kuwait Inst. of Econ. and Social Planning in the Middle East; mem. Perm. Cttee. for Aid to the Arabian Gulf and Yemen.
Kuwait Fund for Arab Economic Development, P.O.B. 2921, Kuwait City, Kuwait.

Hamada, Sabri; Lebanese politician; b. 1902.
Former Speaker, Chamber of Deputies; Deputy Prime Minister, Minister of the Interior 47; Minister of Public Works and Transport May 72-73, of Agriculture July 73-.
Ministry of Agriculture, Beirut, Lebanon.

Hamed, Abdul Samad, PH.D.; Afghan politician; b. 8 Jan. 1930, Khoguiany (Djelalabad); ed. Nedjat High School and in Switzerland.
Director-General, Training Dept., Univ. of Kabul 57; Legal Adviser to Parl. 57-63; Pres. Secondary Educ. Dept., Ministry of Educ. 62; mem. Drafting Cttee. of the

Constitution 63, Constituent Assembly 63; Gov. Parwan Province 64; Pres. Univ. of Kabul 65; Minister of Planning 66, 67; Sec.-Gen. Afghan Red Crescent Soc. 67; Deputy Prime Minister and Pres. of Tribal Affairs 71-72.
c/o Office of the Deputy Prime Minister, Kabul, Afghanistan.

Hammad, Salama Ibrahim, B.A., M.A., PH.D.; Egyptian university president; b. 22 April 1909; ed. Cairo Univ., Inst of Education, Cairo, Exeter Univ. and Univ. of London.
Teacher in Govt. Secondary Schools for five years; fmr. Prof. of Comparative Educ., Ain Shams Univ.; attached to Ministry of Foreign Affairs 56-, Cultural Counsellor Beirut and Washington 60; Dir.-Gen. Foreign Cultural Relations 60-63; Under-Sec. of State for Foreign Cultural Relations 63-65; Pres. Beirut Arab Univ. 65-; mem. Del. to UNESCO 60, 62, 64, 66, Suppliant at Exec. Council 67.
Publs. Series of books for English reading, a book on Shakespeare, various translations.
Beirut Arab University, El Tareek Elguidida, Beirut, Lebanon.

Hammadi, Sadoon; Iraqi economist and politician; b. 22 June 1930, Karbala; ed. in Beirut, Lebanon and U.S.A.
Professor of Econs., Univ. of Baghdad 57; Deputy Head of Econ. Research, Nat. Bank of Libya, Tripoli 61-62; Minister of Agrarian Reform 63; Econ. Adviser to Presidential Council, Govt. of Syria 64; Econ. Expert, UN Planning Inst., Syria 65-68; Pres. Iraq Nat. Oil Co. (INOC) 68-69; Minister of Oil and Minerals 68-.
Publs. *Towards a Socialistic Agrarian Reform in Iraq* 64, *Views About Arab Revolution* 69.
Ministry of Oil and Minerals, Baghdad, Iraq.

Hamzah, Mohammed al Nasri-; Sudanese politician; b. 1925, El Dueim; ed. Cairo, London and Cambridge Univs.
Worked at Veterinary Research Lab., Khartoum 52-57, Malakal 58-60; Lecturer in Bacteriology, Faculty of Veterinary Medicine, Univ. of Khartoum 60, Head, Section of Preventive Medicine and Public Health 65, Dean, Faculty of Veterinary Medicine and mem. Univ. Council 68, Prof. 69; Minister of Animal Production 71; mem. Nat. Council for Research; mem. OAU and FAO Technical Cttees. for Cattle Diseases.
Ministry of Animal Production, Khartoum, Sudan.

Handley, William J., B.A.; American diplomatist; b. 17 Dec. 1918; ed. Univs. of London and Maryland, American Univ.
With War Production Board 42-44, Foreign Econ. Admin. 44; joined Foreign Service 44, served on numerous posts in Middle East; Labor Admin., Bureau of Near Eastern, South Asian and African Affairs 49; New Delhi 51-52; transferred to U.S. Information Agency 53; Chief, Near Eastern Policy Staff 55; Dep. Asst. Dir. Near East, South Asia and Africa 56, Asst. Dir. 57; Dir. Information Center Service 60; Ambassador to Mali 61-64; Deputy Asst. Sec. of State for Near Eastern and S. Asian Affairs 64-69; Amb. to Turkey 69-73.
c/o Department of State, Washington, D.C., U.S.A.

Hare, Raymond Arthur, A.B.; American diplomatist; b. 3 April 1901; ed. Grinnell Coll.
Instructor, Robert Coll., Constantinople 24-27; Exec. Sec. American Chamber of Commerce for Levant 26-27; Clerk, later Vice-Consul, U.S. Consulate-Gen., Constantinople 27-28; Language Officer, Paris 29, also Vice-Consul 31; Sec. in Diplomatic Service and Vice-Consul, Cairo 31; Beirut 32; Third Sec. and Vice-Consul, Teheran 33, Consul 35; Second Sec. Cairo 39, also at Jeddah 40-44, also Consul, Cairo 40; Second Sec., later First Sec. and Consul, London 44; Dept. of State 46; Nat. War Coll. 46-47; Chief, Div. of S. Asian Affairs 47; Deputy Dir. Office of Near East and African Affairs 48; Deputy Asst. Sec. State for Near East, S. Asian and African Affairs Oct. 49; Ambassador to Saudi Arabia and Minister to Yemen 50-53; Ambassador to Lebanon 53-54; Dir.-Gen. U.S. Foreign Service 54-56; Ambassador to Egypt 56-58, to United Arab Republic 58-59, also Minister to Yemen 59; Dep. Under-Sec. of State for Political Affairs 60-61; Ambassador to Turkey 61-65; Asst. Sec. of State for Near Eastern and South Asian Affairs 65-66; Pres. Middle East Inst. 66-69, Nat. Chair. 69-.
Middle East Institute, 1761 N. Street, N.W., Washington, D.C. 20036; 3214 39th Street, N.W., Washington, D.C. 20016, U.S.A.

Harkavy, Rabbi Zvi, B.A., M.A., TH.D.; Israeli (b. Russian) author and bibliographer; b. 1 Feb. 1908; ed. Inst. in U.S.S.R., Jerusalem Teachers' Seminary, Haifa Technion, Hebrew Univ. of Jerusalem, Petach Tikva Yeshiva, Rabbinical Seminary, C.S.R.A.
Leader in Zion underground in U.S.S.R.; immigrated to Palestine 26; schoolmaster and lecturer Jerusalem Teachers' Seminaries 30-; Dir. Eretz Yisrael Publishing House 35-; Chaplain in Israeli Army 48-49; Dir. Dept. of Refugees in Ministry of War Casualties and later Editor of Ministry of Religious Affairs *Monthly* 49-53; Dir. Central Rabbinical Library of Israel 53-68; Editor *Hasefer* 54-; participated in world congresses; Visiting Prof., Yeshiva Univ., N.Y. 59; lectured at U.S.S.R. Acad. of Sciences, Leningrad 62; one of the founders of the Religious Academics and Authors Orgs. and fmr. Chair.; Leader, Hapoel Hamizrachi, "Great Israel" Movement; an Editor of the *General Encyclopaedia* and of numerous periodicals and 100 books; Komemiut, Hamishmar, Haganah, Ale, Hagana-Yerushalayim and Etziony Medals.
Publs. Biographies: *Rambam, Rabbi Shmuel Strashun, Rabbi Mates Strashun, Rabbi I. M. Pines, Professor Simcha Assaf, A. E. Harkavy, Rabbi Reuven Katz—Chief Rabbi of Petach Tikva, The Family Maskil L'eytan, The Family Harkavy*; Essays: *Jews of Salonica, The Jewish Community of Ekaterinoslav; Scepticism of Pascal; The Man, The Plant, The Animal, Inorganic Nature; The Secret of Happy Marriage, Sexual Hygiene from the Religious and Scientific Viewpoint; Shomrei Hagachelet—Responsa of Soviet Rabbis* 66, *My Father's Home* 68, *Autobibliography* 71, *Ein Roe* 72; also 1,100 articles and papers on Rabbinics, bibliography, theology, philosophy, archaeology, philology, history and the Dead Sea Scrolls.
P.O. Box 7031, 7 Haran Street, Jerusalem 91070, Israel.

Harman, Avraham, B.A.; Israeli diplomatist; b. 1914; ed. Oxford Univ.
Moved to Palestine 38; held posts in Jewish Agency 38-48; Deputy Dir. Govt. Information Bureau 48-49; Consul-Gen. Montreal 49-50; Dir. Israel Information Office, N.Y. 50-53; Consul-Gen. Washington 53-55; Ministry of Foreign Affairs 55-56; Exec. Jewish Agency 56-59; Ambassador to the U.S.A. 59-68; Pres. Hebrew Univ. 68-.
The Hebrew University, Jerusalem, Israel.

Hart, Parke T.; American business executive; b. 28 Sept. 1910; ed. Dartmouth Coll., Harvard and Georgetown Univs., Institut Universitaire de Hautes Etudes Internationales, Geneva, and School of Foreign Service.
Translator, Dept. of State 37-38; Foreign Service Officer 38-69, served Vienna, Pará (Brazil), Cairo, Jeddah, Dhahran 38-47; Dept. of State 47-49; Consul-Gen. Dhahran 49-51; Nat. War Coll. 51-52; Dir. Office of Near Eastern Affairs, Dept. of State 52-55; Dep. Chief of Mission and Counsellor, Cairo 55-58; Consul-Gen., Damascus 58; Dep. Asst. Sec. of State, Near East and South Asia Affairs 58-61; Ambassador to Saudi Arabia 61-65, concurrently Minister to Kingdom of Yemen 61-62 and Amb. to Kuwait 62-63; Amb. to Turkey 65-68; Asst. Sec. of State for Near Eastern and South Asian Affairs 68-69; Dir. Foreign Service Inst. 69; Pres. Middle East Inst., Washington, D.C. 69-73; Special

Rep. for Middle East and North Africa, Bechtel Corpn. 73-; Co-Pres. American-Turkish Soc., N.Y.; mem. Board of Trustees, American Univ. of Beirut, Board of Advisers, Industrial Coll. of the Armed Forces; mem. Visiting Cttee. on Middle East Civilizations, Harvard Univ.; Royal Central Asian Soc.
4705 Berkeley Terrace, N.W., Washington, D.C. 20007, U.S.A.

Harvey, John F(rederick), PH.D.; American librarian and university professor; b. 24 Aug. 1921; ed. Dartmouth Coll., Univ. of Illinois, Univ. of Chicago.
Dean and Prof. Graduate School of Library Science, Drexel Inst. of Technology, Philadelphia 58-67; Chair. Dept. of Library Science, Coll. of Educ., Univ. of Teheran 67-68, Prof. 67-71; Technical Dir. Iranian Documentation Centre and Teheran Book Processing Centre 68-71; Library Consultant, Iran, Pakistan, Lebanon 68-71; mem. Eisenhower Fellowship Cttee., U.S. Embassy, Teheran 70; Founder, Hon. Life, and mem. of numerous asscns. and learned socs.
Publs. *Data Processing in Public and University Libraries* 66, *Comparative and International Library Science* 72, and various articles in specialist journals.
P.O. Box 1286, Teheran, Iran.

Hasani, Baqir Husain, B.SC., LL.B.; Iraqi diplomatist; b. 15; ed. Columbia Univ., New York and Baghdad Law Coll. Dir. of Commerce and Registrar of Companies, Iraq Ministry of Econs. 47-51; Dir.-Gen. of Contracts and Econ. Affairs, Development Board 51-54; Dir.-Gen. of Income Tax, Ministry of Finance 56-57; Dir.-Gen. and Chair. of Board of Dirs., Tobacco Monopoly Admin. 57-59; Minister to Austria 59-62, Ambassador 62-63; Chair. Board of Govs. Int. Atomic Energy Agency (IAEA) 61-62, Special Adviser to Dir.-Gen. 63-.
c/o International Atomic Energy Agency, Vienna 1010, Kaerntnerring 11, Austria; and Masbah, Karradah, Baghdad, Iraq.

Haseeb, Dr. Khair El-Din, M.SC., PH.D.; Iraqi economist and statistician; b. 1 Aug. 1929, Mosul; ed. Baghdad Univ. London School of Econs., Cambridge Univ.
Civil Service 47-54; Head of Research and Statistics Dept., Iraq Petroleum Co. 59-60; Lecturer, Baghdad Univ. 60-61, part-time lecturer 61-63; Dir.-Gen. Iraqi Fed. of Industries 60-63; Gov. Central Bank of Iraq 63-65; Actg. Pres. Econ. Org. 64-65; Pres. Gen. Org. for Banks 64-65; Reader, Coll. of Admin. and Econs. 65-71, Prof. of Econs. Oct. 71-; Gov. of Iraq, IMF 63-65; Alt. Gov. of Iraq, IBRD 63-65; Chair. of Board, Centre for Development of Industrial Management 63, Social Security Org. 63-65, Central Bank of Iraq 63-65; Dir. Iraq Nat. Oil Co. 67-68; fmr. mem. of Board of several orgs.
Publs. *The National Income of Iraq, 1953-1961* 64, *Sources of Arab Thought in Economics in Iraq* 71, *Workers' Participation in Management in Arab Countries* 71, and several articles in English and Arabic on economic and development planning problems.
15/18/4, Al-Mansoor, Baghdad, Iraq.

Hashim, Maj. Abu al Qassim; Sudanese army officer and politician; b. 22 Nov. 1935; ed. Military Coll.
Commissioned 57; mem. Revolutionary Command Council May 69; Minister of Youth July 70-Oct. 71; Minister of State for the Presidency of the Repub. 71-72; Minister of Planning 72-73.
c/o Ministry of Planning, Khartoum, Sudan.

Hashim, Jawad M., PH.D.; Iraqi politician; b. 10 Feb. 1938; ed. London School of Econs. and Political Science, Univ. of London.
Professor of Statistics, Univ. of Baghdad 67; Dir.-Gen. Cen. Statistical Org. 68; Minister of Planning 68-71, May 72-; mem. Econ. Office, Revolutionary Command Council.
Publs. *Capital Formation in Iraq 1957-1970*, *National Income—Its Methods of Estimation*, *The Evaluation of Economic Growth in Iraq 1950-1970*, and eighteen articles.
Ministry of Planning, Baghdad, Iraq.

Hassan II, King of Morocco; 17th Sovereign of the Alouite dynasty; b. 9 July 1929; ed. Bordeaux Univ.
Son of Mohammed V; invested as Crown Prince Moulay Hassan 57; C.-in-C. and Chief of Staff of Royal Moroccan Army 57; personally directed rescue operations at Agadir earthquake disaster 60; Minister of Defence May 60-June 61; Vice-Premier May 60-Feb. 61; Prime Minister Feb. 61-Nov. 63, June 65-67; succeeded to throne on death of his father, 26 Feb. 1961; Minister of Defence, Commdr.-in-Chief of the Army Aug. 71-; Chair. Org. of African Unity 72-73.
Royal Palace, Rabat, Morocco.

Hassan, Ahmed Mohammed al-, D.PATH.; Sudanese pathologist and politician; b. 1930; ed. Univs. of Khartoum, Edinburgh and London.
Doctor 55-57; Research Asst., Univ. of Khartoum 58-60, Lecturer in Pathology 62-63, Senior Lecturer and Head of Dept. 65-66, Prof. 66-, Dean, Faculty of Medicine 69-71, Deputy Vice-Chancellor 71; Minister of Higher Educ. and Scientific Research 71-72.
Faculty of Medicine, University of Khartoum, Khartoum, Sudan.

Hassan, Mahmoud Ali, PH.D.; Egyptian engineer; b. 17 July 1915; ed. Cairo and Zürich Univs.
Director-General Industrial Control Dept. 56-59; Under-Sec. of State for Industry 59-61; Chair. Org. for Engineering Industries 61-66; Pres. Fed. of Egyptian Industries, Org. for Metallurgical Industries; Order of Trade and Industry (1st Class).
Publs. *Druckverlüste in Abzweigen von quadratischen Kanälen*, *Anwendungen der elektrolytischen Methode auf die Betzsche Theorie der Spaltverlüste an Schaufelgittern*.
45 Road 15 Maadi, Cairo, Egypt.

Hassouna, Mohammed Abdel-Khalek; Egyptian diplomatist; b. 28 Oct. 1898; ed. Cairo Univ. and Cambridge Univ.
Began as lawyer 21; then joined Diplomatic Corps, served in Berlin 26, Prague 28, Brussels 28, Rome 30, Ministry for Foreign Affairs Cairo 32-39; Under-Sec. of State, Ministry of Social Affairs 39; served in Diplomatic Service in Belgium, Italy, Germany, Czechoslovakia; Gov. of Alexandria 42; Under-Sec. of State for Foreign Affairs 48; Minister of Social Affairs, Sirry Cabinet Nov. 49-Jan. 50; Minister of Education, Maher Cabinet Jan.-March 52; Minister of Foreign Affairs, Hilaly Cabinet March-June, July 52; Sec.-Gen. League of Arab States 52-72; Grand Cordon Order of the Nile (Egypt); Nile Collar (Egypt) 72; Legion of Honour (France); decorations conferred by Belgium, China, Italy and Ethiopia.
3 Sharia Rifaa, Manchiet El-Bakry, Cairo, Egypt.

Hatem, Mohammed Abdel Kader, M.SC., PH.D.; Egyptian politician; b. 1917, Alexandria; ed. Military Acad., Univs. of London and Cairo.
Member, Nat. Assembly 57; Adviser to the Presidency, subsequently Deputy Minister for Presidential Affairs 57; Minister of State responsible for broadcasting and television 59; Minister for Culture, Nat. Guidance and Tourism 62; Deputy Prime Minister for Cultural Affairs and Nat. Guidance 65; Deputy Prime Minister and Minister for Culture and Information 71-; mem. Gen. Secr. Arab Socialist Union; two hon. doctorates from French Univs. Office of the Deputy Prime Minister for Culture and Information, Cairo, Egypt.

Hawari Ahmed, Mahmoud el-; Egyptian journalist; b. 12 April 1921; ed. Polytechnic School, Cairo.
Director, Arab Information Center Press Office, New York 55-58; Man. Editor Middle East News Agency, Cairo 58-65,

now Chair. of Board; Dir. Magazine Dept., Nat. Publishing House 65-67; Chair. Nat. Distributing Co. 67; Publishing Man. Al-Katib Al-Arabi Publishing House 67-69; Adviser, Editing and Publishing Org. 69-71; Dir.-Gen. Egyptian Book Org. 71-72; Gold Cross, Order of King George I of Greece 60.
Middle East News Agency, 4 Sherifeen Street, Cairo; Home: Isis Building, Garden City, Cairo, Egypt.

Hawley, Donald Frederick, C.M.G., M.B.E.; British diplomatist; b. 22 May 1921; ed. Radley and New Coll. Oxford.
H.M. Forces 41; Sudan Political Service 44; joined Sudan Judiciary 47; called to Bar, Inner Temple 51; Chief Registrar, Sudan Judiciary, and Registrar-Gen. of Marriages 51; resigned from Sudan Service 55; joined British Foreign Service 55, Foreign Office 56; Political Agent, Trucial States in Dubai 58, Head of Chancery, British Embassy, Cairo 62, Counsellor and Head of Chancery, Lagos 65; Visiting Fellow, Dept. of Geography, Durham Univ. 67; Counsellor (Commercial), Baghdad 68-71, Chargé d'Affaires in Iraq 69, 70; Consul-Gen., Muscat 71, Amb. to Oman 71-.
Publ. *The Trucial States* 71.
British Embassy, Muscat, Oman.

Hayek, His Beatitude Ignace Antoine, D.PHIL., D. ÈS SC., Syrian ecclesiastic; b. 14 Sept. 1910: ed. Seminaire Patriarcal, Charfé, Lebanon, Pontifical Coll. of Propaganda Fide, Rome, and Oriental Pontifical Inst., Rome.
Ordained priest 33; successively or concurrently Dir. of School, Curate and Vicar-Gen., Aleppo; Archbishop of Aleppo 59-68; Syrian Patriarch March 68-.
Patriarcat Syrien Catholique d'Antioche, Beirut, Lebanon.

Hazani, Michael Yaakov; Israeli economist and politician; b. 1913, Bendin, Poland; ed. Torat Chaim Yeshiva, Warsaw, Hebrew Univ., Jerusalem, and London.
Entered Palestine illegally 32; pioneer in Kfar Yavitz, a border settlement, became agricultural co-ordinator of the Poel Hamizrachi, established many religious settlements before and after 48, leader of Choma Umigdal settlements, Hagana; mem. 2nd Knesset (Parl.); Vice-Chair Advisory Cttee., Bank of Israel; fmr. mem. Finance Cttee., Knesset; fmr. Econ. Adviser, Ministers' Council for Econ. Affairs; Deputy Minister of Educ. and Culture 69-70; Minister of Social Welfare 70-.
Ministry of Social Welfare, Jerusalem, Israel.

Hedayati, Hadi; Iranian educationalist and politician; b. 1923; ed. Teheran Univ., Faculté de Droit, Paris Univ., and Sorbonne, Paris.
Assistant Prof. Teheran Univ. 52-62, Prof. 62-; Legal Counsellor, Iran Insurance Co. 52-57; Counsellor, High Council of Econs. 57-60; High Counsellor, Ministry of Commerce 60; Exec. Man. Bimeh (Insurance) Bank 60-62; Deputy to Majlis 63-; Advisory Minister 63; Minister of Educ. 64-68; Advisory Minister 68-; Homayoun Medal, Palme Académique (France); Imperial Award for best book of the year 58, 59.
Publs. *History of the Zand Dynasty in Iran, A Study of Iranian Handwritten Works in the 13th Hegyra Century, Cyrus the Great*; translations into Persian: *History of Herodotus, The Principles of Administrative Management.*
Iranshahr Avenue, Kamyar Street, Teheran, Iran.

Hedayati, Mohammad Ali; Iranian lawyer and politician; b. 1912; ed. Teheran and Geneva Univs., Geneva Inst. of Int. Studies and Inst. of Criminology of Faculty of Law, Univ. of Paris.
Military service 35; joined Iranian Judicial Service 36, mem. Dept. of Legislative Revisions 37, Dep. Public Prosecutor of Teheran 37-38, Interrogator for Teheran 38-40, Judge of the Court of Appeal (Teheran) 40, Advocate in Courts of Justice 40; transferred to Ministry of Education 40, Assoc. Prof., Faculty of Law, Teheran Univ. 40-45, Prof. of Law of Criminal Procedure 45-; Minister of Justice 58-61; mem. 16th and 19th Sessions of Majlis; Order of Homayoun (First Class) 60.
Publs. *Les Mesures de Sûreté* (French), *The Law of Criminal Procedure* (Persian), *Economics* (Persian).
Teheran University, Teheran, Iran.

Hegazy, Abdel Aziz, D.PHIL.; Egyptian economist and politician; b. 3 Jan. 1923; ed. Fuad Univ., Cairo, Birmingham Univ., England.
Dean, Faculty of Commerce, Ain Shams Univ. 66-68; mem. Nat. Assembly 69-; Minister of the Treasury 68-73; Deputy Prime Minister, Minister of Finance, Econ. and Foreign Trade 73-.
Ministry of Finance, Cairo, Egypt.

Heikal, Mohammed Hasanein; Egyptian journalist; b. 1923.
Reporter Akher Saa Magazine 44; Editor *Al-Akhbar* 56-57; Editor-in-Chief *Al-Ahram* daily newspaper 57-, Editor and Chair. Establishment Board 60-; mem. Central Cttee. Arab Socialist Union 68-; Minister of Nat. Guidance April 70-Oct. 70.
Publs. *Nahnou wa America* 67 and 8 others.
Al Ahram Building, Galaa Street, Cairo, Egypt.

Hejazi, Mohammed; Iranian writer and politician; b. 1899; ed. French School, Teheran and Ecole Libre des Sciences Politiques, Paris.
Joined Ministry of Posts; served Dept. of Customs, Ministries of Finance and Educ., Office of Press Censor, Dept. of Publs. and Propaganda; twice Asst. to Prime Minister; Senator 54-; mem. Iranian Academy, Royal Cultural Council of Iran; Chair. Iran-Pakistan Cultural Soc.; two Royal Literary Prizes.
Publs. thirty literary works, including *Ahang, Andisheh, Homa, Parichehr, Reza Penhan, Zaghar, Ziba;* also several translations.
34 rue Fardis, Teheran, Iran.

Helaissi, Sheikh Abdulrahman al-; Saudi Arabian diplomatist; b. 24 July 1922; ed. Cairo Univ. and Univ. of London.
Official at Ministry of Foreign Affairs; Secretary Embassy London 47-54; Under-Sec. Ministry of Agriculture 54-57; Rep. to UN 47, and at conferences on Health, Agriculture, Wheat, Sugar and Locusts; Head of Del. to FAO 55, 61-Ambassador to Sudan 57-60; Del. to Conference of Non-Aligned Nations, Belgrade 61; Amb. to Italy 61-66, concurrently to Austria; Amb. to U.K. 66-, concurrently to Denmark 66-69.
Publ. *The Rehabilitation of the Bedouins* 59.
Embassy of Saudi Arabia, 27 Eaton Place, London, S.W.1, England.

Helms, Richard M.; American government official; b. 30 March 1913; ed. high schools in France and Germany, and Williams Coll.
Worked for United Press and *The Indianapolis Times* 35-42; joined U.S. Navy 42, in Office of Strategic Services, Second World War; Central Intelligence Group 47-49, Central Intelligence Agency 49-73, Deputy Dir. for Plans 62, Deputy Dir. 65, Dir. 66-73; Amb. to Iran 73-.
United States Embassy, Takhte Jamshid Avenue, Roosevelt Avenue, Teheran, Iran.

Helou, Charles; Lebanese lawyer and journalist; b. 1911; ed. St. Joseph (Jesuit) Univ. and Ecole Française de Droit, Beirut.
Barrister at Court of Appeal and Cassation Beirut 36; founded newspaper *L'Eclair du Nord* at Aleppo Syria 32; founded *Le Jour* Beirut 34; was Political Dir. of the latter until apptd. Lebanese Minister to the Vatican 47; fmr. Pres. Cercle de la Jeunesse Catholique Beirut; fmr. Sec.-Gen. Catholic Action of Lebanon; Minister of Justice and Health Sept. 54-May 55; Minister of Education Feb.-Sept.

64; President of Lebanon 64-70; Pres. Asscn. des Parlementaires de Langue Française 73-.
Beirut, Lebanon.

Henein, Georges; Egyptian writer.
Founded surrealist weekly review *Al Tatawwor* (Evolution) 43; now lives in Paris.
Publs. include *Deux Effigies*, *Seuil Interdit* (fantasy stories) 57.
11B rue Vézelay, Paris 8e, France.

Henshaw, Kenneth Ralph, M.A.; British oil company executive; b. 1 Nov. 1918; ed. King's School, Canterbury and Trinity Coll., Oxford.
Senior Vice-Pres. Sinclair and BP Explorations Inc. 59-63; Regional Man. Exploration Dept., British Petroleum Co. Ltd. 63-65; Man. Dir. Kuwait Oil Co. Ltd. 65-; Dir. Middle East Navigation Aids Service 65-.
Burgan House, 105 Wigmore Street, London W.1, England.

Heppling, Sixten K.D.; Swedish United Nations official.
Executive Sec. Swedish Govt. Cttee. for the exchange of foreign students 46; joined Swedish Inst., Stockholm, Asst. Dir., Head, Technical Assistance Div. 57-62; Resident Rep. UN Devt. Programme (UNDP), Afghanistan 62-66; Dir. Dept. of Multilateral Aid, Swedish Int. Devt. Authority 66-70; Resident Rep. UNDP, Turkey 70-.
United Nations Development Programme, P.K. 407, Ankara, Turkey.

Hewedy, Amin; Egyptian diplomatist; b. 1921; ed. Military and Staff Colls., Egypt, and General Staff Coll., Fort Leavenworth, U.S.A., and Press Coll., Egypt.
Former Army Officer; fmr. Ambassador of United Arab Republic to Morocco; Ambassador to Iraq 58, 63-66; Minister of State 66-67, of War 67-68, of State 69-70.
Publs. *Speeches in Strategy* 55, *Sun-Tso* 57.
Cairo, Egypt.

Hillel, Shlomo; Israeli politician; b. 23 April 1923, Baghdad, Iraq; ed. Herzliah School, Tel-Aviv, Hebrew Univ., Jerusalem.
Settled in Palestine 30s; mem. 2nd, 3rd Knessets (Parl.) 53-59; Amb. to Guinea 59-61, to Ivory Coast 61-63, concurrently to Dahomey, Upper Volta and Niger; mem. Perm. Mission to UN 64-67; Asst. Dir.-Gen. Ministry of Foreign Affairs, in charge of Middle East Affairs 67-69; Minister of Police 69-; Commdr. Nat. Order of the Repubs. of the Ivory Coast, Upper Volta, Dahomey.
Ministry of Police, Jerusalem, Israel.

Himadeh, Sa'id B., B.COMM., M.A.; Lebanese university professor; b. 3 April 1894; ed. American Univ. of Beirut and Columbia Univ., U.S.A.
Lecturer in Applied Economics, American Univ. of Beirut 20, Assoc. Prof. 23, Prof. of Applied Economics 39-, Head, Dept. of Economics 35-48, of Dept. of Commerce 35-59, Emer. Prof. of Applied Economics 59-; Section Dir., Social Science Research 47-50; part-time Economic Adviser to Lebanese Ministry of Nat. Economy 47; Gen. Sec. Higher Economic Advisory Council of Lebanese Govt. 46-48; Alternate Del. to UNESCO Gen. Conf. 48; Lebanese Govt. Del. First U.N. Social Welfare Seminar for Arab States of the Middle East 49, U.N. Economic Expert, U.N. Social Welfare Seminars 50 and 52; Chief Editor *Social Studies Series* (in Arabic) 45-47 and of its successor, *Al-Abhath* (quarterly journal of American Univ. of Beirut) 48-59, mem. Economic Development Board of Lebanon 53-; FAO Consultant and Discussion Leader, Centre on Land Problems in the Near East 55; mem. UNESCO Nat. Cttee. of Lebanon 55-59; Minister of Economy and Agriculture 66-68; mem. Editorial Advisory Board, Int. Encyclopaedia of Social Sciences 61-63; mem. Board of Dirs., Industry Inst. 62-67, Lebanese Govt. Housing Board 63-; mem. Board of Trustees, Inst. for Palestine Studies; Chair. Advisory Cttee. Bank of Lebanon 66-; Order of the Cedar and other decorations.
Publs. *Monetary and Banking System of Syria (including Lebanon)* 35, *Economic Organisation of Iraq* 38; editor and co-author: *Economic Organisation of Syria (including Lebanon)* 36, *Economic Organisation of Palestine* 38; many articles on Middle East economy.
Home: Manara (Ras Beirut), Beirut; Office: American University of Beirut, Beirut, Lebanon.

Hitti, Philip Khuri, B.A., PH.D.; American orientalist; b. 24 June 1886; ed. American Univ. of Beirut, Columbia Univ.
Lecturer, Oriental Dept., Columbia Univ. 15-19; Prof., American Univ. of Beirut 19-26; Asst. Prof. Semitic Literature, Princeton 26-29, Assoc. Prof. 29-36; Chair. Dept. of Oriental Languages 44; Dir. Programme in Near-Eastern Studies 47-54; mem. American Oriental Society, American Historical Asscn., etc.; Hon. Litt.D. (Princeton) 66, Hon. L.H.D. (Amer. Univ. Beirut) 69.
Publs. *The Origins of the Islamic State* 16, *The Semitic Languages Spoken in Syria and Lebanon* 22, *The Syrians in America* 24, *Characteristics of Moslem Sects* 24, *Syria and the Syrians* 26, *An Arab-Syrian Gentleman and Warrior in the Period of the Crusaders* 29, *The Origins of the Druze People and Religion* 29 (new edn. 64), *Kitab al I'tibar li-Usamah* 30, 64, *History of the Arabs* 37 (revised edn. 70), *The Arabs* 43-44 (revised edn. 67), *History of Syria, including Lebanon and Palestine* 51, 57, *Lebanon in History* 57 (revised 67), *Syria: A Short History* 59, *The Near East in History* 61, *Islam and the West* 62, *Short History of Lebanon* 65 (revised 68), *Short History of the Near East* 66, *A Short History of Syria* 67, *Makers of Arab History* 68, *Islam: A Way of Life* 70, *Capital Cities of Arab Islam* 73.
144 Prospect Avenue, Princeton, N.J., U.S.A.

Horowitz, David; Israeli banker; b. Feb. 1899; ed. Vienna and Lwów.
Member Exec. Cttee. Gen. Fed. of Jewish Labour 23; journalist and writer; Econ. Adviser and Sec. American Econ. Cttee. for Palestine 32-35; Dir. Econ. Dept. of Jewish Agency for Palestine 35-48; mem. various Govt. Cttees. under Mandatory Regime, and dir. various enterprises 35-48; Liaison Officer to UN Special Cttee. on Palestine 46; mem. Jewish Del. to Lake Success 47; Head of Israel Del. to Econ. Survey Comm. of UN 48; Head of Israel Del. Financial Talks on Sterling Releases between Israel and Great Britain, London 49, and in negotiations between Israel and Great Britain on econ. and financial affairs in connection with termination of the Mandate; Dir.-Gen. Ministry of Finance 48-52; Gov. Designate, Bank of Israel 52-54, Gov. 54-71, Chair. Advisory Cttee. and Council 71-; Gov. (for Israel) Int. Bank for Reconstruction and Devt., Int. Devt. Asscn. and Int. Finance Corpn.; Chair. Board of Dirs., the Eliezer Kaplan School of Econs. and Social Sciences, Hebrew Univ.; mem. State Council for Higher Educ., Board of Govs. Hebrew Univ., Exec. Council Weizmann Inst. of Science, Board of Trustees of the Truman Center for the Advancement of Peace; Head, Israel Del. to UN Conf. on Trade and Devt., Geneva 64; Hon. Pres. Istituto per le Relazioni Internazionali (Rome); Dr. h.c. (Hebrew Univ. and Tel-Aviv Univ.); Israel Prize for Social Sciences 68.
Publs. *Aspects of Economic Policy in Palestine* 36, *Jewish Colonisation in Palestine* 37, *Economic Survey of Palestine* 38, *Jewry's Economic War Effort* 42, *Postwar Reconstruction* 42, *Palestine and the Middle East, An Essay in Regional Economy* 43, *Prediction and Reality in Palestine* 45, *State in the Making* 53, *Anatomie unserer Zeit* 64, *Hemispheres North and South* 66, *The Economics of Israel* 67, *The Abolition of Poverty* 69, *Anatomia de Nuestro Tiempo* 69, *The Enigma of Economic Growth—The Case Study of Israel* 72, and several publs. in Hebrew.
4 Halamed Hé Street, Jerusalem; and Bank of Israel, Jerusalem, Israel.

Hoveida, Amir Abbas, M.A., PH.D.; Iranian diplomatist, business executive and politician; b. Feb. 1919; ed. Univs. of Brussels and Paris.
Ministry of Foreign Affairs 42-58, served Federal Germany, Teheran, United Nations, New York, Ankara; mem. Board of Dirs. and Head of Admin., Nat. Iranian Oil Co. 58-64; founder mem. New Iran Party 63-; Minister of Finance 64-65; Prime Minister Jan. 65-.
Office of the Prime Minister, Teheran; Home: No. 5 Kh. Cyrus Ehteshamieh, Darrous, Teheran, Iran.

Hoveyda, Fereydoun, LL.D.; Iranian diplomatist; b. 21 Sept. 1924, Damascus; ed. Univ. of Paris.
Various positions, Imperial Iranian Embassy, Paris 46-51; Programme Specialist, Mass Communications Dept., UNESCO 52-64; Under-Sec. of State for Int. and Econ. Affairs, Ministry of Foreign Affairs 65-71; Perm. Rep. to UN Aug. 71-; del. to various int. confs. including UN Gen. Assembly 48, 51, 65, UNESCO Confs. 66, 68, 70 and ECOSOC sessions 66-69.
Permanent Mission of Iran at United Nations, 777 Third Avenue, 26th Floor, New York, N.Y. 10017, U.S.A.

Howard, Harry Nicholas, A.B., M.A., PH.D.; American historian; b. 19 Feb. 1902; ed. Univs. of Missouri and California.
Gregory Fellow in History Univ. of Missouri 26-27; Research Asst. in Modern European History Univ. of California 28-29; Asst. Prof. History Univ. of Oklahoma 29-30; Associate Prof. History, Miami Univ. 30-37, Prof. 40-42; Lecturer Contemporary Problems, Univ. of Cincinnati 37-42; served Dept. of State as Head, East European Unit 42-44, mem. U.S. Del. UN Conf. on Int. Orgs. 45, Chief, Near East Branch Research Div. 45-47, Adviser Div. of Greek, Turkish and Iranian Affairs 47-49, UN Adviser, Dept. of State, Bureau of Near East, S. Asian and African Affairs 49-56; Acting U.S. Rep. Advisory Comm. UNRWA, Beirut 56-61; Special Asst. to Dir. of UNRWA 62-63; Adviser U.S. Del. UN Balkan Comm. 47-50; Prof. of Middle East Studies, School of Int. Service, American Univ., Washington, D.C. 63-68, Adjunct Prof. 68-; Chair. Middle East Program, Foreign Service Inst., Dept. of State 66, 71-72; Faculty Adviser FSI 66-67; Reserve Consultant, Dept. of State 67-; Assoc. Editor *Middle East Journal* 63-; mem. Board of Govs. Middle East Inst. 63-; Consultant, Middle East, Cincinatti Council on World Affairs 68-69; mem. Board of Dirs. ANERA 68-; Lecturer, Middle East, U.S. Army War Coll., Pa. 70-72; Visiting Prof. Missouri, Indiana, Calif. (Berkeley), Columbia and Colorado Univs.; Order of the Phoenix (Greece).
Publs. *The Partition of Turkey, A Diplomatic History 1913-1923* 31, *Military Government in the Panama Canal Zone* 31 (with Prof. R. Kerner), *The Balkan Conferences and the Balkan Entente* 30-35, *A Study in the Recent History of the Balkan and Near Eastern People* 36, *The Problem of the Turkish Straits* 47, *The United Nations and the Problem of Greece* 47, *The General Assembly and the Problem of Greece* 48, *Yugoslavia* (co-author) 49, *Soviet Power and Policy* (co-author) 55, *The King-Crane Commission* 63.
6508 Greentree Road, Bradley Hills Grove, Bethesda, Md. 20034, U.S.A.; and American University, Washington, D.C., U.S.A.

Humaida, Ahmed el Amin; Sudanese mechanical engineer and politician; b. 6 March 1922, Omdurman; ed. Univ. of Khartoum.
Director-General Sudan Railways (introduced diesel engines); Chair. Admin. Council, Sudan Airways Corpn.; Head Govt. Stores Methods Revising Comm.; Head Cen. Provisions Unit; Minister of Transport Oct. 72; Fellow, Sudanese Engineering Soc., British Mechanical Engineering Soc.; est. Sudanese Benefactory Soc., Attbara; responsible for construction of schools at Attbara.
c/o Ministry of Transport, Khartoum, Sudan.

Humaidan, Dr. Ali; diplomatist; b. 20 Sept. 1931, Bahrain; ed. Univs. of Baghdad and Paris.
Deputy Rep. of Kuwait to UNESCO 67-69; Prof. of Political Science, Univ. of Kuwait 69-70; Legal Adviser to the Abu Dhabi Govt. 71-72; Perm. Rep. of the United Arab Emirates to UN 72-.
Permanent Mission of the United Arab Emirates to the United Nations, 866 Second Avenue, New York, N.Y. 10017, U.S.A.

Hussain, Abdul Aziz; Kuwaiti politician; b. 1921; ed. Teachers' Higher Inst., Cairo and Univ. of London.
Head, Kuwait Cultural Bureau, Cairo 45-50; Gen. Dir. of Education, Kuwait 52-61; Ambassador to Egypt 61-62; Minister of State for Cabinet Affairs 63-65, 71-.
Publ. *Arab Community in Kuwait* 60.
Ministry of State for Cabinet Affairs, Kuwait.

Hussein, Aly Hamdy, M.COM.; Egyptian diplomatist; b. 20 Dec. 1915; ed. Univ. of Cairo and Univ. of Madrid.
Commercial Counsellor 48-57; Counsellor to Foreign Office 58; Consul-Gen. in São Paulo 60-64; Amb. to Bolivia 64-65; Dir. of Econ. Dept. of Foreign Office, Cairo 66-68; Amb. to Belgium and Luxembourg 68-.
Embassy of Egypt, 2 avenue Victoria, 1050 Brussels, Belgium.

Hussein, Taha, DR. LITT.; Egyptian writer; b. 1889; ed. Cairo and Paris Univs.
Prof. of Arabic Literature, Fouad I Univ. Cairo 20-32; fmr. Dean of the Faculty of Arts, Fouad I Univ., Under-Sec. of State at Ministry of Education, Rector Farouk I Univ. Alexandria; Minister of Education 50-52; fmr. Senator, Vice-Pres. Acad. for the Arabic Language; Pres. Inst. d'Egypte; corresp. mem. Acad. des Inscriptions et Belles Lettres Paris, Accad. dei Lincei Rome, Acads. of Mainz, Teheran, Damascus and Baghdad, and Royal Acad. of History, Madrid; Grande Médaille de l'Univ. de Paris, Grand Officier de la Légion d'Honneur (France), Commdr. Order of the Nile (Egypt), Grand Cross Order of the Phoenix (Greece), Dr. h.c. (Univs. of Lyons, Montpellier, Rome, Oxford, Athens and Madrid).
Publs. Over 40 works: novels, translations from French and Ancient Greek into Arabic, studies on Arabic literature, on educational problems of modern Egypt, etc., and including *The Stream of Days* (2 vols.).
Ramatane, avenue des Pyramides, Guizeh, Egypt.

Hussein ibn Talal, King of Jordan; b. 14 Nov. 1935; ed. Victoria Coll., Alexandria, Egypt, Harrow School and R.M.A. Sandhurst (both in England).
Succeeded his father August 11th, 1952; came to power May 2nd, 1953; married 55, Princess Dina, daughter of Abdel-Hamid Aoun of Saudi Arabia; daughter Princess Alia' b. 56 (marriage dissolved); married 61, Antoinette Gardiner (assumed name of Muna el Hussein); sons, Prince Abdullah, b. 62, Prince Feisal, b. 63; twin daughters, Princess Zein, Princess Aisha' b. 68 (marriage dissolved); married 72, Alia Toukan.
Publ. *Uneasy Lies the Head* 62.
Royal Palace, Amman, Jordan.

Husseini, H.E. Haj Amin; Grand Mufti of Palestine; b. 1897; ed. Jerusalem and Al-Azhar Univ. Cairo.
Officer in Ottoman Army during First World War 14-18; became Mufti 21; elected Pres. of Supreme Muslim Council for life 22; elected Pres. World Muslim Conf. Jerusalem 31 and Pres. Arab Higher Cttee. for Palestine 36; left Palestine after disagreement with Mandate Govt. over policy of establishing Jewish Nat. Home in Palestine 37; in Lebanon 37-39, Iraq 39-41, in Persia and Europe 41-45, France 45-46; on return from Europe 46, re-elected Pres. Arab Higher Cttee. for Palestine; in Egypt as guest of King Farouk 46; elected Pres. Assembly and Supreme Council All-Palestine Govt. 48; Pres. World Muslim Conf., Karachi 51, Muslim

Ulama Conf., Karachi 52, Exec. Cttee. World Muslim Conf., Karachi 52; Chair. Palestine Arab Del. to Asiatic-African Conf., Bandung 55; mem. Constituent Assembly, Rabitat al-A'lam al-Islami, Mecca 62; Pres. World Moslem Congresses, Baghdad 62, Mogadishu 65.
Blvd. Hadeth, Beirut, Lebanon.

Huzayin, Soliman Ahmed, M.A., PH.D., LL.L.; Egyptian university professor; b. 1909; ed. Cairo, Liverpool and Manchester Univs.
Lecturer, Cairo Univ. 35; Dir.-Gen. Cultural Relations, Ministry of Educ., Cairo 50; Under-Sec. of State for Educ., Cairo 54; Rector, Univ. of Assiut 55-65; Minister of Culture Oct. 65-66; mem. Institut d'Egypte 47-, Pres. Institut d'Egypte 54, Int. Council for the Study of the Geography of Africa and Asia 56-, Perm. Cttee. for Social Affairs, League of Arab States.
Publs. *Some Contributions of the Arabs to Geography* 32, *Some New Light on the Beginnings of Egyptian Civilization* 37, *The Place of Egypt in Prehistory* 41, *Arabia and the Far East* 42, numerous articles.
c/o Institut d'Egypte, 13 Sh. Sheikh Rihane, Cairo, Egypt.

I

Ibrahim, Abdel Aziz el Sayed, PH.D.; Egyptian educationist; b. 30 April 1907; ed. Teachers' Coll. and Higher Inst. of Educ., Cairo and Ohio State Univ., U.S.A.
Formerly Lecturer in Mathematics, Mil. Coll., Cairo; Prof. of Educ., Head of Dept., Ain Shams Univ.; Vice-Rector Cairo Univ., Rector Khartoum Branch, Cairo Univ.; Rector Alexandria Univ.; Minister of Higher Educ., later of Educ.; Visiting Prof. Columbia Univ., U.S.A.; now Dir.-Gen. Arab Educational, Cultural and Scientific Org., Arab League; mem. Arabic Language Acad. (Egypt), Scientific Acad. (Iraq); decorations from Egypt, Lebanon, Morocco, Tunisia, Jordan, German Democratic Repub.
Publs. *The Slide Rule for Military Cadets* 39, *The Preparation of Teachers in Arab States* 54, *The University and Culture* 60.
Arab Educational, Cultural and Scientific Organization, Arab League, Cairo; Home: 52 Merghani Street, Heliopolis, Cairo, Egypt.

Ibrahim, Major Abu al-Qassim Mohammed; Sudanese army officer and politician; b. 1937, Omdurman; ed. Khartoum Secondary School and Military Coll.
Commissioned 61; mem. Revolutionary Council 69; Minister of Local Govt. 69; Asst. Prime Minister for Services July 70; Minister of Interior Nov. 70; Minister of Health Oct. 71-.
Ministry of Health, Khartoum, Sudan.

Ibrahim, Wing Commdr. Hassan; Egyptian businessman and former air force officer and politician; b. 1917; ed. Egyptian Mil. Coll. and Egyptian Air Force Coll.
Served Egyptian Air Force 39-52; mem. Revolutionary Council 52-56; Minister for Presidency and for Production 54-56; Chair. Economic Development Organization 57-59; Pres. El Nasr Company (pencil and graphite production) 58-61, Paints and Chemicals Industries 59-61; mem. Presidential Council 62-64; Vice-Pres. of U.A.R. 64-65; business exec. 66-; Nile Collar of Egypt; various orders and decorations from Syria, Yugoslavia, Cameroon, Niger, Yemen, Bulgaria, Poland, Lebanon, G.D.R., Morocco, Malaysia, Libya.
6 Khartoum Street, Heliopolis, Cairo, Egypt.

Ibrahim, Sid Moulay Abdullah; Moroccan politician; b. 1918; ed. Ben Youssef Univ., Marrakesh and the Sorbonne, Paris.
Mem. Istiqlal (Independence) Party 44-59; mem. Editorial Cttee. *Al Alam* (Istiqlal organ) 50-52; imprisoned for political reasons 52-54; Sec. of State for Information and Tourism, First Moroccan Nat. Govt. 55-56; Minister of Labour and Social Affairs 56-57; Prime Minister and Minister of Foreign Affairs Dec. 58-May 60; leader Union National des Forces Populaires 59-, suspended from party 72.
c/o Union National des Forces Populaires, B.P. 747, Casablanca, Morocco.

Idelson, Beba; Israeli statistician; b. 14 Oct. 1895; ed. Kharkov.
Teacher 12-15; Statistician in Russian Govt. depts. 16-22; Berlin 24-25; manual work as pioneer in Palestine 26-29; Statistician, Jewish Agency, Jerusalem 29-30; Gen. Sec. of Moetzet Hapoalot (Council of Women Workers in Israel) 30-72; mem. Council of State 48-; mem. and Deputy Speaker of Knesset (Israel Parl.) 48-65; mem. of the Exec. of the Labour Party 35-, of Fed. of Labour.
22 Rembrandt Street, Tel-Aviv, Israel.

Idris I (Sayyid Muhammad Idris as-Sanusi); former King of Libya; b. 1889.
Son of Sayyid Muhammad al-Mahdi; succeeded his uncle, Sayyid Ahmed Sherif as-Sanusi, in charge of affairs of the Senusiya Order 16; became Amir of Cyrenaica; proclaimed King of Libya Dec. 2nd 50; ascended the throne 24 December 51; deposed by military coup Sept. 69; sentenced to death *in absentia* 71.
Now living in Egypt.

Idris, Yusef, M.D.; Egyptian physician and writer; b. 1927; ed. Qasr al-Aini.
Qualified as psychiatrist; politically active 51-, several times imprisoned; first publication 53; awarded Hiwar literary prize 65 but refused award; Medal of Republic 66.
Publs. include drama: *The Republic of Farhat*, *The Cotton King*, *The Critical Moment*, *Al Farafir* 64; fiction: *Love Story* 56, *The Hero* 56, *The Sin* 59, *A Matter of Honour* 59, *The Vice* 62.
c/o *Al-Gomhouriya*, Galal Street, Cairo, Egypt.

Inönü, Gen. Ismet; Turkish politician; b. 24 Sept. 1884; ed. Military and Staff Colls.
Attached 2nd Army Edirne 06; organised local patriotic society Party of Union and Progress; Gen. Staff 4th Army Edirne 08; mem. expeditionary force against insurgents, Arabia 10; Major, Chief of Gen. Staff Yemen Army 12; Dir. 1st section Gen. Staff Istanbul April 13; military adviser Turkish Del. Turco-Bulgarian peace negotiations Aug. 13; Lieut.-Col. 14; Col., Chief of Gen. Staff 2nd Army Eastern Thrace 15; Comm. 4th Army Corps, Russian front 16, 20th Army Corps 17, 3rd Army Corps, Syria 17; Under-Sec. for War 18; joined Mustafa Kemal 20; Deputy for Edirne Nat. Assembly, Minister and Chief of Gen. Staff 20; commd. Western Front and victor Battles of Inönü 21; promoted Brig.-Gen. 21, Lieut.-Gen. 22, Gen. 26-27, retd.; Minister of Foreign Affairs 22; signed Treaty of Lausanne 23; fmr. Vice-Pres. Republican People's Party, Leader 38-72; Prime Minister 23-24 and 25-37; Pres. of Turkish Republic 38-50; Opposition Leader 50-60, 65-72; Prime Minister 61-65.
c/o The Republican People's Party, Ankara, Turkey.

Ioannides, George X.; Cypriot lawyer and politician; b. 1924, Ktima, Paphos; ed. Greek Gymnasium, Paphos.
Clerk, Civil Service 41-45; did correspondence course in commerce and accountancy; studied law, Middle Temple, London, and called to Bar 47; lawyer, Paphos 48-70; mem. House of Reps. (Patriotic Front Group) 60-70; Minister of Justice 70-June 72, of the Interior and Defence June 72-Ministry of the Interior, Nicosia, Cyprus.

Iran (Persia, Shah of; *see* Pahlavi, Mohammad-Reza).

Iryani, Sheikh Qadi Abd al Rahman al-; Yemeni religious and political leader.
Member of Revolutionary Council 62-; Minister of Justice 62-63; Vice-Pres. Exec. Council Oct. 63-Feb. 64; mem.

Political Bureau Jan. 64-; mem. Presidency Council April 65-, Chair. 69-; Chair. Peace Cttee. set up after Khamer Peace Talks May 65; leader of Zaidi (Shi'a) sect.
Presidency Council, Sana'a, Yemen Arab Republic.

Işik, Hasan Esat; Turkish diplomatist and politician; b. 1916, Istanbul; ed. Lycée of Galatasaray, Faculty of Law, Univ. of Ankara.
Ministry of Foreign Affairs 40-; Consulate-Gen., Paris 45-49; Head of Section, Dept. of Commerce and Econ. Affairs, and Dept. of Int. Econ. Relations 49-52; staff of Perm. Turkish Del. to European Office of UN, Geneva 52-54; Dir.-Gen. of Dept. of Commerce and Commercial Agreements, Ministry of Foreign Affairs 54-57; Asst. for Econ. Affairs to Sec.-Gen. of Ministry of Foreign Affairs, Sec.-Gen. Econ. Co-operation Int. Org. 57-62; Ambassador to Belgium, led negotiations for Turkey's entry to EEC 62-64, to U.S.S.R. 64-65, 66-68; Minister of Foreign Affairs 65; Amb. to France 68-.
Turkish Embassy, rue d'Ankara, Paris 16e, France.

Ismail, Abdul Fattah; Yemeni politician.
Member Exec. Cttee., Nat. Liberation Front (NLF), Sec.-Gen. 71-; mem. of dels. of NLF and FLOSY (Front for the Liberation of Occupied South Yemen) 67; Sec.-Gen. Afro-Asian Solidarity Org. Feb. 73-.
Presidential Council, Aden, People's Democratic Republic of Yemen.

Ismail, Abdul Malek; Yemeni diplomatist; b. 26 Nov. 1937, Aden; ed. Tawahi and Crater, Aden, Tech. School, Maalla, Khediwi High School, Cairo and Cairo Univ. Faculty of Commerce.
Member, United Nat. Front; Editor *A-Nour* and *Hakikah* (newspapers) 61-63; Vice-Chair. Gen. Union of Petroleum Workers 61-62, Chair. Petroleum Workers Union 62-64; Vice-Pres. Arab Fed. of Petroleum Workers 62-65; leading mem. Arab Nationalist Movement 56-63; leading mem. Nat. Liberation Front for Southern Yemen (NLF) 63-65; Dir. Nat. Front Office, Cairo 65-66; mem. Gen. Command of Nat. Liberation Front 66-68; Minister of Labour and Social Affairs 67-68; Minister of Econs., Commerce and Planning 68-70; Perm. Rep. to UN Aug. 70-.
Permanent Mission of the People's Democratic Republic of Yemen at United Nations, 211 East 43rd Street, Room 605, New York, N.Y. 10017, U.S.A.

Ismail, Gen. Mohamed Hafez; Egyptian soldier and diplomatist.
Assistant Under-Sec. of Foreign Affairs 60-64; Ambassador to United Kingdom 64-65; Amb. to Italy 67-69; Adviser to the Pres. on Nat. Security Sept. 71-, Head of Pres. Cabinet 73-.
Office of the President, Cairo, Egypt.

Issawi, Charles Philip, M.A.; American economist; b. 1916; ed. Victoria Coll. Alexandria and Magdalen Coll. Oxford.
Sec. to Under-Sec. of State, Ministry of Finance, Cairo 37-38; Head of Research Section, Nat. Bank of Egypt, Cairo 38-43; Adjunct Prof. American Univ. of Beirut 43-47; UN Secretariat Economic Affairs Officer 48-55; Visiting Lecturer, Harvard Univ. 50, Johns Hopkins 67; Prof. Columbia Univ. 51-.
Publs. *Egypt: an Economic and Social Analysis* 47, *An Arab Philosophy of History* 50, *Egypt at Mid-Century* 54, *Mushkilat Qaumia* 59, *The Economics of Middle East Oil* (co-author) 62, *Egypt in Revolution* 63, *The Economic History of the Middle East 1800–1914* 66, *The Economic History of Iran 1800-1914* 71, *Oil, the Middle East and the World* 72, *Issawi's Laws of Social Motion* 73.
Columbia University, New York, N.Y., U.S.A.

İzmen, Mehmet; Turkish politician; b. 1909, Giresun; ed. Univ. of Istanbul.
Worked in several depts., Ministry of Finance; Under Sec. of State, Ministry of Finance -61; Senator for Giresun (New Turkey Party—NTP) 61; Minister of Agriculture 62-69; Minister of Communications 69; Senator appointed by the Pres. 68-73; Minister of Nat. Defence 72-73.
Ministry of National Defence, Ankara, Turkey.

J

Jabbur, Jibrail S., M.A., PH.D.; Lebanese university professor; b. 1904; ed. American Univ. of Beirut, Egyptian Univ. and Princeton Univ.
Vice-Principal, Homs Nat. Coll. 25-26; Instructor in Arabic, American Univ. of Beirut 26-29, 30-35, Asst. Prof. 35-42, Assoc. Prof. 42-46, 47-48, Prof. 48-; Chair. of Arabic Dept. (Margaret Weyerhauser Jewett Prof. of Arabic) 49-; Gold Medal (Merit) of Nat. Education and Public Instruction 51, Officer, Nat. Order of Cedars (Lebanon).
Publs. *Ibn Abd Rabbihi and his 'Iqd.* 33, *Al-Hayah al-'Arabiyyah fi al mi'at sanah al-'Ula ba'd wafat al-Nabi al 'Arabi* 34, *Umar Ibn Abi Rabiah*, Vol. I 35, Vol. II 39, Vol. III 70, *Fi al-Adab al-Andalusi* 49; Editor *Al-Kawakib al-Sa'irah*, Vol. I 45, Vol. II 49, Vol. III 59, *Kitab al 'Id* 67; translated and wrote with Philip Hitti and Edward Jurji, *Tarikh al-'Arab (al Mutawwal)* 3 vols. 49-51.
American University of Beirut, Beirut, Lebanon.

Jabre, Jamil Louis; Lebanese writer; b. 1924; ed. Univ. Saint-Joseph, Beirut.
Director of *Al-Hikmal* Revue; Cultural Counsellor for dailies *Al Jaryda* and *L'Orient* and United Unions for Employees and Workers; Founder-mem. Lebanese P.E.N. Club, Amis du Livre, Club du Roman, Club de la Jeunesse Vivante.
Publs. include: *Fever, After the Storm, Agony* (3 vols.), *May Ziadé, Amine Rihani, Gébrane Khalil Gébrane, Tagore, May: Authoress, Jahiz and the Society of His Times, Views on Contemporary American Literature* (essays), *Dream of Nemrod*.
Beit-Chabab, Lebanon.

Jabre, Kamal Rachid; Lebanese commercial official; b. 1898.
Member Chamber of Deputies 37-39; Vice-Pres. Asscn. des Industriels Libanais; Pres. Beirut Chamber of Commerce and Industry 64-; Vice-Pres. Banque de Crédit Agricole, Industriel et Foncier; Founder Dir. Soc. de Filature et de Tissage; also founder of several industrial socs. and banks; Commdr. Ordre National du Cèdre.
Beirut Chamber of Commerce and Industry, P.O.B. 1801, Beirut, Lebanon.

Jaffar, Khalid Mohammed; Kuwaiti diplomatist; b. 12 June 1922; ed. Mubarakia School, Kuwait.
Teacher, Kuwait 40-42; Chief Cashier, Kuwait Municipality 43-45; Kuwait Oil Co., rose to Supt. of Public Relations 45-61; Lord Chamberlain to His Highness The Amir of Kuwait 61-62; Ambassador, Foreign Affairs, Kuwait May-Dec. 62, concurrently Head of Press and Culture Div., Ministry of Foreign Affairs; mem. Delegation to UN before admission of Kuwait as a mem. Sept.-Oct. 62; deputized for Under-Sec. of State at the Ministry of Foreign Affairs 62-63; Amb. to U.K. 63-65, to France 65-67, concurrently to Lebanon 65-70, to Turkey 68-73, concurrently to Bulgaria, Greece 71-73.
c/o Ministry of Foreign Affairs, Kuwait City, Kuwait.

Jahanshahi, Abdol Ali, PH.D.; Iranian economist; b. 1924; ed. Univ. de Paris.
Ministry of Justice 46-57; Univ. of Teheran 57; Bank Melli Iran 57-60; Vice-Gov. Bank Markazi Iran 62-63; Minister of Educ. 64; Minister of State 64-65; Chancellor, Nat. Univ. of Iran 65-66; Alt. Exec. Dir. World Bank 66-71; Gov. Bank Markazi Iran (Central Bank of Iran) 71-.
Bank Markazi Iran, Ferdowsi Avenue, Teheran, Iran.

Jaifi, Gen. Hammud; Yemeni politician.
Prime Minister April 64-Jan. 65; Minister of Economy Jan.-April 65; Vice-Premier for Military Affairs and mem. Presidency Council July 65-July 66; Minister of War 66; Deputy C.-in-C. 68-.
c/o Council of Ministers, Sana'a, Yemen Arab Republic.

Jalloud, Abdul Salam Ahmed; Libyan politician; b. 15 Dec. 1944; ed. Secondary School, Sebha, Mil. Acad., Benghazi.
Member Revolutionary Command Council (RCC); Minister of Industry and the Econ., Acting Minister of the Treasury until 72; Prime Minister July 72-.
Office of the Prime Minister, Tripoli, Libyan Arab Republic.

Jamal, Jasim Yousif; Qatar diplomatist; b. 17 Sept. 1940; ed. Northeast Mo. State Coll., Kirksville, Mo., U.S.A.
Ministry of Educ., Dir. Admin. Affairs 58-63, Cultural Adviser, U.S.A. 63-68; Dir. of Cultural Affairs 68-72; Perm. Rep. to UN 72-.
Permanent Mission of Qatar to the United Nations, 845 Third Avenue, 20th Floor, New York, N.Y. 10022, U.S.A.

Jamil, Sharif Husain ben; Jordanian politician.
Former Minister of Royal Court; Prime Minister April 63-July 64; Chief of the Royal Cabinet 67; mem. Consultative Council 67; C.-in-C. Armed Forces 69-70; Great Uncle of King Hussein.
The Royal Palace, Amman, Jordan.

Jamil, Talib; Iraqi lawyer and businessman; b. 1919; ed. Baghdad Coll. of Law.
In private law practice 41-53, becoming Sec.-Gen. of Iraqi Bar; Dir.-Gen. of Legal and Economic Affairs, Ministry of Planning, then Dir.-Gen. of Commerce and Economics, Ministry of Economy 53-59; returned to private practice 59-64; Under-Sec. Ministry of Economics Jan.-July 64; Pres. State Organization of Insurance July-Dec. 64; Perm. Del. to Arab Economic Unity Council, Cairo, with rank of Amb. Dec. 64-Aug. 68; Chair. Al Karamak Agencies and Export Co., Baghdad; Chair. Asia Printing and Publishing Co., Baghdad.
Apt. 11, Gawhart el-Nil Building, 92 Sharia el-Nil, near el-Galaa Bridge, Cairo, Egypt.

Jamjoom, Ahmed Salah, B.COM.; Saudi Arabian businessman and politician; b. 1925; ed. Fouad Univ. Cairo and Harvard Law School.
Joined Arab Bank, Jeddah 50; Minister of State and mem. Council of Ministers 58-59; Supervisor of Economic Dept. 59-Dec. 60; Minister of Commerce July-Dec. 60; Minister of Trade and Industry 61-62; Dir. and Partner, Mohd. Nour Salah Jamjoom & Bros. 62-; Dir. Jamjoom Vehicles and Equipment and Jamjoom Construction.
Publs. *An Approach to an Integrated Economic Development* 60, *Economics of Mecca* 67.
Mohamed Nour Salah Jamjoom and Brothers, Riyadh, and P.O. Box 1247, Jeddah, Saudi Arabia.

Jaq, Dr. Said Ahmed el-, M.A., PH.D.; Sudanese politician; b. 1930, Khartoum; ed. Univ. of Khartoum and in U.S.A.
Worked in Ministry of Works 54-56, later in consultative and design engineering; lecturer in Civil Eng., Univ. of Khartoum; worked on water and electricity projects for Shendi and Berber towns; founder and board mem. Sudanese Engineers Trade Union; helped to found Sudanese Teachers Asscn., Univ. of Khartoum; Minister of Works May 69-June 70; Minister of Transport and Communications 70-71; mem. American Eng. Soc., Sudanese Engineers Soc.
c/o Ministry of Transport and Communications, Khartoum, Sudan.

Jarring, Gunnar, PH.D.; Swedish diplomatist; b. 12 Oct. 1907; ed. Lund Univ.
Associate Prof. Turkic Languages Lund Univ. 33-40; Attaché Ankara 40-41; Chief Section B Teheran 41; Chargé d'Affaires a.i. Teheran and Baghdad 45, Addis Ababa 46-48; Minister to India 48-51, concurrently to Ceylon 50-51, to Persia, Iraq and Pakistan 51-52; Dir. Political Div. Ministry of Foreign Affairs 53-56; Perm. Rep. to UN 56-58; rep. on Security Council 57-58; Amb. to U.S.A. 58-64, to U.S.S.R. 64-, and to Mongolia 65-; Special Rep. of Sec.-Gen. of UN on Middle East situation Nov. 67-; Grand Cross, Order of the North Star.
Publs. *Studien zu einer osttürkischen Lautlehre* 33, *The Contest of the Fruits—An Eastern Turki Allegory* 36, *The Uzbek Dialect of Qilich, Russian Turkestan* 37, *Uzbek Texts from Afghan Turkestan* 38, *The Distribution of Turk Tribes in Afghanistan* 39, *Materials for the Knowledge of Eastern Turkestan* (Vols. I-IV) 47-51, *An Eastern Turki-English Dialect Dictionary* 64.
Swedish Embassy, Ul. Mosfilmovskaya 60, Moscow, U.S.S.R.

Jezrawi, Taha al; Iraqi politician; b. 1938, Mosul; ed. schools in Mosul and Military Coll.
Former army officer; mem. Regional Leadership, Arab Baath Socialist Party; Head, Arab Affairs Office, Revolutionary Command Council Nov. 69; Minister of Industry March 70-.
Ministry of Industry, Baghdad, Iraq.

Jordan, King of (see Hussein ibn Talal).

Joukhdar, H.E. Mohammed Salen, B.A., M.A.; Saudi Arabian economist; b. 1932; ed. Univs. of California and Southern California.
Economic Consultant to Directorate-Gen. of Petroleum and Minerals, Saudi Arabia 58; Govt. Rep. Supervisory Cttee. for Expenditure and Purchasing, Arabian Oil Co. 61, Dir. 61-66; Sec.-Gen. Org. of Petroleum Exporting Countries (OPEC) 67-68; Deputy Minister of Petroleum and Mineral Resources 69-; mem. American Soc. of Economists.
Ministry of Petroleum and Mineral Resources, P.O. Box 247, Riyadh, Saudi Arabia.

Joumblatt, Kamal; Lebanese politician and hereditary Druse chieftain; b. 1919.
Fmr. Minister of Nat. Economy; Pres. Social Progress Party of Lebanon; Minister of Education and Fine Arts 60-61; Minister of State for the Interior and Planning Services 61-64; Minister of Public Works and P.T.T. 66-67; Minister of the Interior April-June 70; Pres. Parti Socialiste Progressive; Lenin Peace Prize 71.
Publ. *The Truth about the Lebanese Revolution* 59.
Chamber of Deputies, Beirut; and Zodak el Blat, Beirut, Lebanon.

Juffali, Ahmad; Saudi Arabian businessman; b. 15 Oct. 1924; ed. Saudi Arabia and United Kingdom.
Managing Dir., E. A. Juffali & Bros. 45-; mem. Board of Dirs. Saudi Electric Co. 52-; Man. Dir. Saudi Cement Co. 58, Medina Electric Co. 58-; Hon. Danish Consul 59-.
E. A. Juffali & Bros., King Abdul Aziz Street, P.O.B. 1049, Jeddah, Saudi Arabia.

Juma, Midhet (brother of Saad Juma, q.v.); Jordanian diplomatist; b. 19 Aug. 1920; ed. Cairo Univ.
Attaché to Arab League, Cairo 45-47; First Sec. and Counsellor, Cairo 47-52; Counsellor and Chargé d'Affaires, London 52-53; Minister to Pakistan 53-55; Chief of Protocol, Royal Palace Amman 56; Under-Sec. for Press and Broadcasting 56-58; Ambassador to the U.S.A. 58-59, to Morocco 59-62, to Federal Repub. of Germany 62-65, to Lebanon 65-67, to U.K. 67-69, to Tunisia 69-70, to Spain Sept. 71-; numerous decorations.
Embassy of Jordan, Avenida Generalísimo, Madrid, Spain.

WHO'S WHO IN THE MIDDLE EAST AND NORTH AFRICA

Juma, Saad (brother of Midhet Juma, *q.v.*); Jordanian diplomatist; b. 1916; ed. Syrian Univ., Damascus.
Civil Service for twenty-six years; Dir. Press and Publicity; Chief Censor; Sec. to Prime Minister; Perm. Under-Sec., Gov. of Amman; Under-Sec. for Foreign Affairs; Ambassador to Syrian Arab Republic 62, to U.S.A. 62-65; Minister of the Royal Court 65-67; Prime Minister and Minister of Nat. Defence April-Oct. 67; mem. Consultative Council 67; Amb. to U.K. 69-70; Personal Rep. to H.M. King Hussein; honours from Jordan, Iran, Syria, Italy and China (Taiwan).
Royal Palace, Amman, Jordan.

Jumeia'an, Mikhael; Jordanian administrator; b. 1915; ed. American Univ., Cairo.
Interpreter 40-43; Teacher 43-45; Govt. Agency Sec. 45-47; Asst. Chief Accountant 47-50; Registrar of Patents, Trademarks and Cos. 50-55; Asst. Div. Head, Civil Service 55-57, Div. Head 57-62, Asst. Under-Sec. 62-65, Under-Sec. 65-68; Dir. of Antiquities 68-70; Dir. Inst. of Public Admin. 70-; del. to many Arab and int. confs.
Publs. *International Laws of Chess* (transl. into Arabic), *Fundamentals of Supervision* (in Arabic) 64, *Fundamentals of Public Administration* 69, and many papers on public administration.
Institute of Public Administration, P.O. Box 13055, Amman, Jordan.

K

Kaddori, Fakhri Yassin, DR.RER.POL.; Iraqi economist; b. 28 Aug. 1932; ed. Adhamiya Intermediate School and Central Secondary School, Baghdad, Coll. of Commerce and Econs. (Univ. of Baghdad), State Univ. of Iowa, Cologne Univ., Int. Marketing Inst. (Harvard Univ.).
Director of Internal Trade, Ministry of the Economy 64-68; Minister of the Economy 68-71, now Chair. Bureau of Econ. Affairs, Revolutionary Command Council; Pres. Iraqi Economist Asscn.
Bureau of Economic Affairs, Revolutionary Command Council, National Building, Baghdad, Iraq.

Kader, Yehia Abdel; Egyptian diplomatist; b. 1920, Alexandria; ed. Univ. of Cairo.
Secretary, Counsellor Egyptian Embassies in Belgrade, Khartoum, Milan; Amb. to Saudi Arabia 64-68, to Yugoslavia 68-71; Chair. Egyptian Radio and Television 71; Amb. to U.S.S.R. 71-.
Embassy of Egypt, 56 Ulitsa Gertsena, Moscow, U.S.S.R.

Kafai, Djafar; Iranian diplomatist; b. 1909; ed. Univ. of Paris.
Former Secretary, Supreme Court; Ministry of Foreign Affairs; Attaché, Iranian Embassy, France; Second Sec. Cairo; mem. Parl; mem. Constituent Assembly; Consul-Gen., Geneva; Dir. of Information and Publication, Ministry of Foreign Affairs; Perm. Rep. to European Office of UN 54; Under-Sec. Ministry of Foreign Affairs 58; Amb. to Greece, to Pakistan and Ceylon 63-65, to Turkey 65-68, retd.; Man. Dir. South Shipping Lines-Iran Line; Dir. Sté. Foriran; Homayoun Award Class II, Grand Award of St. George (Greece), Grand Award of Istiklal (Jordan).
South Shipping Lines-Iran Line, 130 Avenue Sorya, Teheran, Iran.

Kahale, Noureddin, B.S., M.S.; Syrian engineer; b. 1911, ed. Robert Coll., Istanbul, and Purdue and Illinois Univs., U.S.A.
With Ministry of Public Works and Communications 41-51, Head Irrigation Section 41-43, Acting Dir. of Irrigation 43-46, Dir.-Gen. 47, Sec.-Gen. 48-51; Chair. Board and Dir. Latakia Port Co. 51-58; Minister of Public Works, Syrian Region, United Arab Republic 58-60, concurrently Pres. Syrian Exec. Council, Acting Minister of Planning, and Minister of State, Central Govt.; Vice-President U.A.R. and Minister of Planning, Central Govt. 60-61; Vice-President U.A.R. in charge of Production Sector 61; Chair. and Dir.-Gen. Euphrates Project Authority 61-; Sec. Asscn. of Syrian Engineers 43-49; Pres. Damascus Asscn. of Chartered Engineers 61-62; Pres. Supreme Council of Engineering Asscns. of U.A.R. 61; Syrian Rep. to various Int. Confs.; decorations from Govts. of Syria, Khmer Repub., Denmark, Ethiopia, Greece, Morocco, Spain, Sudan and Yugoslavia.
Principal works: design and execution, Hama Irrigation Scheme 45-46; planning and execution, Latakia Harbour 51-58; planning Tartousse Harbour 58-60, Euphrates Dam, Power Plant and Irrigation Project, Habur Dam and Irrigation Project 62-.
Publs. *The Solution of the Water Supply Shortage in Aleppo* 47, *The Latakia Harbour Project* 55 (Papers presented to Pan-Arab Engineers Confs.).
West Adnan Malki, Mohammed Kurd-Ali Street, Damascus, Syria.

Kaid, Ahmed (Commandant Slimane); Algerian politician; b. 1924.
Joined Nat. Liberation Army (ALN) 56; mem. of Ghardimaou Gen. Staff, and ALN Rep. to Evian talks 62; Deputy for Tiaret 62-; Minister of Tourism 63-64; Minister of Finance 65-68; Sec.-Gen. FLN Dec. 67-72; mem. Revolutionary Council 65-72.
c/o Council of the Revolution, Algiers, Algeria.

Kaissouni, Abdel Moneim, B.COM., B.SC., PH.D.; Egyptian financial administrator and politician; b. 1916; ed. Univ. of Cairo and London School of Economics.
With Barclays Bank, England 42-43; Lecturer and Asst. Prof. of Econs., Univ. of Cairo 44-50; Dir. Middle East Dept. Int. Monetary Fund, Washington, and later Chief Technical Rep. in Middle East 46-50; with Nat. Bank of Egypt 50-54; Minister of Finance, Economy and Deputy Prime Minister 54-66, 68; Chair. Arab Int. Bank 71-; Pres. Cairo Conf. on Devt. 61; Pres. UN Conf. on Trade and Devt. 64; Grand Cordon of the Repub. (Egypt) Order of Merit (Syria), St. Mark 2nd Grade (Greece), El Kawkab 1st Grade (Jordan), Grand Cordon (Lebanon), Zaskave (Yugoslavia).
23 Sesostris Street, Heliopolis, Cairo, Egypt.

Kalali, Manouchehr, D.ECON.; Iranian politician; b. 1925; ed. Teheran Univ. and Paris, France.
Joined Ministry of Labour and Social Services, later Perm. Under-Sec.; mem. Parl for Mashad 65-; founder mem. "Kanoon Motara Ghi" (now Iran Novin Party), Sec.; mem. Exec. Board, Iran Novin Party; Asst. to Sec.-Gen. Iran Novin Party, Deputy Sec.-Gen., Sec.-Gen. 69-; Minister of State 71.
Iran Novin Party, Sepand Avenue, Teheran, Iran.

Kamel, Hassan, PH.D.; Egyptian diplomatist and administrator; b. 6 Sept. 1907; ed. Univs. of Montpellier, Cairo and Paris.
Member Mixed Bar 30-36; Lecturer, Admin. Law, High Coll. of Police and Admin. 36-37; Ministry of Foreign Affairs 37, served in several countries including France, Italy, Iran, Syria, Portugal, Switzerland, Libya, Argentina, Turkey and Hungary until 59; Legal Adviser, Govt. of Qatar 60, Dir.-Gen. 61-67, Adviser 67-; Perm. Rep. of Qatar to UN 71-72; Adviser of several dels. to UN and Rep. on numerous Int. Confs.; mem. several Law Asscns.; mem. Board of Dirs. Shell (Qatar) Ltd., Qatar Petroleum Ltd.; Officier, Légion d'Honneur, Commdr., Ordre Nat. du Mérite.
Publs. numerous legal articles.
P.O. Box 636, Doha, Qatar.

Kamel, Mustafa, LL.B.; Egyptian diplomatist; b. 27 Oct. 1908; ed. Univs. of Cairo and the Sorbonne.
Professor of Constitutional Law, Univ. of Cairo; Govt. Observer, Summit Conf., Geneva 55; mem. Egyptian Del. to first Asian-African Conf., Bandung 55; Ambassador of Egypt to India 55-58; Amb. of U.A.R. to U.S.A. 58-67, to Belgium and Luxembourg 67-68.
Publs. Textbooks on constitutional, administrative and penal law.
c/o Ministry of Foreign Affairs, Cairo, Egypt.

Karageorghis, Vassos, PH.D., F.S.A.; Cypriot archaeologist; b. 1929; ed. Pancyprian Gymnasium, Nicosia, Univ. Coll., and Inst. of Archaeology, London Univ.
Assistant Curator, Cyprus Museum 52-60, Curator 60-63, Acting Dir., Dept. of Antiquities, Cyprus 63-64, Dir. 64-; Vice-Pres. Council of Soc. for Cypriot Studies, mem. Governing Body, Cyprus Research Centre; Fellow Soc. of Antiquaries, London, Corresp. mem. Archæological Soc., Athens, Acad. of Athens; mem. German Archaeological Inst., Berlin, Royal Soc. for Humanistic Studies, Lund; Dr. h.c. (Univs. of Lyon, Göteborg, Athens); Chevalier de l'Ordre de la Légion d'Honneur.
Publs. *Treasures in the Cyprus Museum* 62, *Nouveaux Documents pour l'Etude du Bronze Récent à Chypre* 64, *Corpus Vasorum Antiquorum I* 63, and *II* 65, *Sculptures from Salamis I* 64, *II* 66, *Excavations in the Necropolis of Salamis I* 67, *II* 70, *Cyprus* (Archaeologia Mundi) 68, *Salamis-New Aspects of Antiquity* 69, *Altägäis und Altkypros* (with H.-G. Buchholz) 71, and articles in German, American, English and French journals.
c/o Cyprus Museum, Nicosia, Cyprus.

Karami, Rashid; Lebanese politician; b. 1921; ed. Fuad I Univ., Cairo.
Minister of Nat. Economy and Social Affairs 54-55; Prime Minister and Minister of the Interior Sept. 55-March 56; Prime Minister Sept. 58-May 60; Minister of Finance, Economy, Defence and Information Oct. 58-Oct. 59, of Finance and Defence Oct. 59-May 60; Prime Minister and Min. of Finance Oct. 61-April 64; Prime Minister July 65-66, Dec. 66-67, 67-68, 69-70.
Rue Karm Ellé, Beirut, Lebanon.

Karim, Amin Abdul; Iraqi politician; b. 1921, Baghdad; ed. Coll. of Law.
Entered Govt. service March 43; has held various govt. posts including Dir. Gen. of Finance and Revenues, and Pres. State Org. of Banks (until 68); Minister of Finance July 68-.
Ministry of Finance, Baghdad, Iraq.

Karlin, Dr. Samuel, PH.D.; American mathematician; b. 8 June 1924, Poland; ed. Ill. Inst. of Technology and Princeton Univ.
California Inst. of Technology, Bateman Research Fellow 47-48, Asst. Prof. 49-51, Assoc. Prof. 51-55, Prof. 55-56; Visiting Asst. Prof., Princeton Univ. 50; Prof., Stanford Univ. 56-70; Guggenheim Fellow to Israel and France 60-61; Guest Mathematical Soc. of Japan 64; Head, Dept. of Pure Mathematics, Weizmann Inst. of Science, Rehovot, Israel 70-; Consultant Rand Corpn., Santa Monica; Chief Editor, *Theoretical Population Biology;* Editor or Assoc. Editor of *Journal of Mathematical Analysis, Logistics Journal, Journal of Applied Probability, Journal d'Analyse, Journal of Mathematics and Mechanics, Journal of Mathematical Biosciences, Journal of Approximation Theory and Advances in Mathematics;* Fellow, Inst. of Mathematical Statistics 56; fmr. mem. Int. Statistics Inst., American Acad. of Arts and Sciences and Council of American Mathematical Soc.; mem. of American Mathematical Soc., Inst. of Mathematical Statistics, Applied Mathematics panel, Nat. Research Council, U.S. Acad. of Sciences; Procter Fellow, Princeton Univ. 46; Wald Memorial Lecturer 57; Henry and Bertha Benson Chair. of Mathematics 71.
Publs. over 150 articles in various journals on topics of pure and applied probability theory, game theory, decision theory and statistical methodology, mathematical analysis and mathematical biology.
Meonot Shine 13, Rehovot, Israel.

Kassab, Adnan Ali; Iraqi civil servant; b. 1934; ed. Higher Inst. of Industrial Engineering.
Resident Engineer to Army Canal Project 61-63; Dir. of Admin. in Industrial Govt. Projects 63-64; later arrested and underwent political imprisonment; Dir.-Gen. of Iraqi Ports Admin. 68-.
Iraqi Ports Administration, Basra, Iraq.

Katz, Katriel; Israeli diplomatist; b. Poland 16 Oct. 1908; ed. Herzliya Gymnasium and Warsaw Univ.
Head, Dept. of Propaganda and Education, Haganah 42-43; spokesman of the Haganah 48; spokesman, Public Relations Office, Israel Defence Army 49; on staff of Ministry for Foreign Affairs 49-53; fmr. Head, Div. of Political Research; Chargé d'Affaires, Budapest 53-56; Minister to Poland 56-58; Sec. to the Government 58-62; Consul-Gen. of Israel, New York 62-65; Ambassador to U.S.S.R. 65-67; Chair. Yad Vashem (Martyrs and Heroes' Remembrance Authority) Jerusalem 67-72; Amb. to Finland 72-.
Publ. *Israel's Foreign Policy—First Five Years* (in Hebrew).
c/o Ministry of Foreign Affairs, Jerusalem, Israel.

Katz, Mindru; Israeli (b. Rumanian) pianist; b. 3 June 1925; ed. Bucharest Acad. of Music.
First public recital 31; first public concert with Bucharest Philharmonic Orchestra 47; extensive tours of E. Europe 47-, U.K. 58-, South and East Africa 60, 62, Far East, Australia, New Zealand and S. America 61; has also played in France, Germany, Portugal, Denmark, Sweden and Turkey; settled in Israel 59; Prizewinner, Berlin, Prague, Bucharest Int. Piano Competitions 51, 53, Rumanian State Prize.
45 Hanassi Street, Herzliya, Nof-Yam, Israel.

Katzir, Lt.-Col. Ephraim Katchalski, M.SC., PH.D.; Israeli army officer and professor of biophysics; b. 16 May 1916, Russia; ed. Hebrew Univ., Jerusalem.
Professor, Dept. of Biophysics, Weizmann Inst. of Science 51-; Chief Scientist, Ministry of Defence 66-68; Pres. of Israel 73-; mem. Israel Acad. of Sciences and Humanities, Nat. Council for Research and Devt., Council for Higher Educ., Biochemical Soc. of Israel, Israel Chemical Soc., Nat. Acad. of Sciences, U.S.A., American Acad. of Arts and Sciences (Foreign Hon. mem.), Leopoldina Acad. of Science, German Democratic Repub., American Soc. of Biological Chemists (Hon.), Ciba Foundation, Int. Union of Biochemistry and many other orgs.; mem. Board, *Analytical Biochemistry, Archives of Biochemistry and Biophysics, Biopolymers, Excerpta Medica* and Amino Acids and Proteins Section of *European Journal of Biochemistry;* Tchernikhovski Prize 48, Weizmann Prize 50, Israel Prize Natural Sciences 59, Rothschild Prize Natural Sciences 61; Linderstrom-Lang Gold Medal 69.
Publs. numerous papers and articles on proteins and polyamino acids.
Office of the President, Jerusalem, Israel.

Kayla, Ziya; Turkish economist; b. 28 Dec. 1912; ed. School of Political Sciences, Istanbul.
Ministry of Finance 34-63, Asst. Inspector, Inspector and Chief Inspector of Finance 34-60; Deputy Minister of Finance 60-63; Chair. Board of Dirs. and Dir.-Gen. Central Bank of Turkey 63-66; Alternate Gov. for Turkey of Int. Bank for Reconstruction and Development 61-66; **Pres.** Banks' Assen. of Turkey 63-66; Sec.-Gen. Comm. of

Regulation of Bank Credits 63-66, Head of Foreign Investment Encouragement Cttee. 63-66; mem. Board of Controllers of the Prime Ministry 66-70; Pres. Council of Administrators, Türkiye Vakıflar Bankası 71-.
Publs. *Emission Movements in Turkey* 67, *Treasury and Central Banks Relations* 70.
Mesneri sokak 8/8, Ankara, Turkey.

Kayra, Cahit; Turkish civil servant and diplomatist; b. 13 March 1917; ed. Univ. of Ankara.
Inspector of Finance 42-50; Counsellor, Gen. Dir. of Finance 50-55; private financial adviser 55-59; Head of Foreign Trade Dept., Ministry of Trade 59-60; Head of Turkish Perm. Del. to Gen. Agreement on Tariffs and Trade (GATT) 60-63; Deputy Under-Sec. of State to Min. of Finance 63-64; Head of Turkish Del. to OECD 64-67; Head of Research Dept., Ministry of Finance 67-.
Publs. *Middle Eastern Oil* 53, *A Guide to the Turkish System of Taxation* 57, *Import Policy in Turkey* 63.
Research Department, Ministry of Finance, Ankara, Turkey.

Kazemzadeh, Hossein, LL.B.; Iranian lawyer and politician; b. 1923, Shiraz; ed. Univ. of Teheran and Princeton Univ., U.S.A.
Assistant Lecturer, Inst. of Business and Admin., Teheran Univ.; Deputy Man. Dir. Planning Org.; Deputy Prime Minister; Dir. Budget Dept.; Consulting Minister and Sec.-Gen. Org. for Admin. Affairs and Employment; now Minister of Science and Higher Educ.
Ministry of Science and Higher Education, Teheran, Iran.

Keating, Kenneth B., A.B., LL.B.; American lawyer and politician; b. 18 May 1900; ed. Rochester and Harvard Univs.
Law practice in Rochester, N.Y. 23-; mem. law firm of Harris, Beach, Keating, Wilcox, Dale and Linowitz; mem. U.S. House of Reps., New York 38th District 46-58; mem. U.S. del. to Consultative Assembly of Council of Europe 51; mem. U.S. del. Interparliamentary Union Confs., Washington 53, Vienna 54, Helsinki 55, Bangkok 56, London 57, Rio de Janeiro 58, Senate Observer at Commonwealth Parl. Asscn. Conf., Canberra 59, Lagos 61; mem. U.S. del. ICEM Confs. 56, 57 and 59; Senator from New York 58-64; Assoc. Judge, New York Court of Appeals 66-69; Amb. to India 69-72, to Israel 73-; Service with U.S. Army (Sergeant) in First World War; Col. and Exec. Asst. to Deputy Supreme Commdr., S.E. Asia Command in Second World War, later Brig.-Gen.; mem. Rochester, City of New York, New York County, New York State and American Bar Asscns.; Legion of Merit with Oak Leaf Cluster; Hon. O.B.E., Cross of Greater Officer in the Order of Merit (Italy); Hon. LL.D. (Rochester, LeMoyne, Hobart, Long Island, Hamilton, Union, Iona, Adelphi, Rhode Island, Franklin Pierce, Brooklyn Law), Hon. L.H.D. (Yeshiva, Elmira, Alfred, N.Y. Medical, Clarkson, Dowling), Hon. D.C.L. (Pace); Republican.
American Embassy, 71 Hayarkon Street, Tel-Aviv, Israel.

Kedourie, Elie, B.SC.(ECON.); British university teacher.
Assistant Lecturer, then Lecturer in Politics and Public Admin., London School of Economics 53-60; Reader in Political Studies with special reference to the Middle East, London Univ. 61-65; Prof. of Politics, London Univ. 65-; Editor *Middle Eastern Studies* 64-.
Publs. *England and the Middle East: the Destruction of the Ottoman Empire* 56, *Nationalism* 60, *Afghani and Abduh* 66, *The Chatham House Version* 70, *Nationalism in Asia and Africa* 71.
London School of Economics, Houghton Street, Aldwych, London, W.C.1, England.

Kelani, Haissam; Syrian diplomatist; b. 6 Aug. 1926, Hamah; ed. Mil. Coll., Air Gen. Staff Coll., Paris and High Mil. Air Acad., Paris.

General Pilot 61-62; Amb. to Algeria 62-65, to Morocco 65-67; Sec.-Gen. Ministry of Foreign Affairs 67-69; Amb. to the German Democratic Repub. 69-72; Perm. Rep. to UN 72-.
Publs. eight books, many articles in Arab reviews.
Permanent Mission of Syria to the United Nations, 150 East 58th Street, Room 1500, New York, N.Y. 10022, U.S.A.

Kellou, Mohamed; Algerian lawyer and diplomatist; b. 27 March 1931; ed. Univs. of Algiers and Montpellier.
Lawyer, Algiers; fmr. Vice-Pres. Union Générale des Etudiants Musulmans Algériens (U.G.E.M.A.) (in charge of Foreign Affairs); Front de Libération Nationale (F.L.N.) Rep. in U.K. 57-61; Chief of Provisional Govt. of Algeria Diplomatic Mission to Pakistan 61-62; Chief of Africa-Asia-America Div., Ministry of Foreign Affairs, Republic of Algeria 62-63; Amb. to U.K. 63-64, to Czechoslovakia 64-70, concurrently to Hungary 65-70, to Poland 66-70, to Argentina 70-, concurrently to Chile, Uruguay and Peru.
Embassy of Algeria, Montevideo 1889, Buenos Aires, Argentina; Home: 40 boulevard des Martyrs, Algiers, Algeria.

Kemal, Yaşar; Turkish writer and journalist; b. 1922; self-educated.
Publs. *Memed, My Hawk* 61, *The Wind from the Plain* 63, *Anatolian Tales, They Burn the Thistles* 73; novels, short stories and essays in Turkish.
P.K. 14, Basinköy, Istanbul, Turkey.

Kenter, Ayşe Yıldız; Turkish actress and producer; b. 1928; ed. State Conservatoire.
Worked in State Theatre for eleven years, playing about forty parts; Rockefeller Fellowship in Dramatic Art; teacher of Dramatic Art, State Conservatoire; now acting and producing independently; twice awarded Iskender Prize for best performance of the year.
Ihlamur Cad. Kuyulu bostan Sokak No. 31/5 Nişantaş, Istanbul, Turkey.

Kenyon, Kathleen Mary, D.B.E., D.LITT., D.LIT., L.H.D., F.B.A., F.S.A.; British archaeologist; b. 5 Jan. 1906; ed. St. Paul's Girls' School and Somerville Coll., Oxford.
Sec. Inst. of Archaeology 35-48, Council for British Archaeology 44-49; Lecturer Univ. of London Inst. of Archaeology 48-62; Principal St. Hugh's Coll. Oxford 62-73; Dir. British School of Archaeology in Jerusalem 51-66; Dir. Joint U.K.-Canadian Expedition in Jerusalem; has participated in and directed numerous excavations in U.K. and Middle East.
Publs. *Excavations at the Jewry Wall, Leicester* 48, *Samaria-Sebaste I* 42, *III* 57 (joint author), *Beginning in Archaeology* 54, *Digging up Jericho* 57, *Excavations at Jericho I* 60, *II* 66, *Archaeology in the Holy Land* 60, *Amorites and Canaanites* 66, *Jerusalem* 68, *Royal Cities of the Old Testament* 71.
Old Brands Lodge, Terriers, High Wycombe, Bucks., England.

Khaddam, Abdel Halim; Syrian politician.
Deputy Prime Minister and Minister of Foreign Affairs April 71-; mem. Regional Command, Baath Party May 71-.
Ministry of Foreign Affairs, Damascus, Syria.

Khadduri, Majid, B.A., PH.D.; Iraqi educationist and writer; b. 27 Sept. 1909; ed. American Univ. of Beirut and Univ. of Chicago.
Sec.-Treas. Baghdad P.E.N. Club; mem. American Society of Int. Law; Iraqi Del. to the 14th Conf. of the P.E.N. Clubs in Buenos Aires 36; adviser to the Iraq Delegation at the San Francisco Conf. 45; Visiting Lecturer in Near Eastern History at Indiana Univ. 47-48; fmr. Prof. Modern Middle Eastern History at the Higher Teachers' Coll.,

Baghdad, Iraq 48-49; taught Middle East politics at Chicago and Harvard Univs. 49-50; Prof. Middle East Studies, Johns Hopkins Univ. 50-, Distinguished Research Prof. 70-; Dir. of Research and Education, Middle East Inst. 50-; Visiting Middle East Prof., Columbia Univ.; mem. American Pol. Science Asscn.; Pres. Shaybani Soc. of Int. Law Washington D.C.
Publs. *The Liberation of Iraq from the Mandate* (in Arabic) 35, *The Law of War and Peace in Islam* 41, *The Government of Iraq* 44, *The System of Government in Iraq* (in Arabic) 46, *Independent Iraq* 51, *War and Peace in the Law of Islam* 55, *Islamic Jurisprudence* 61, *Modern Libya* 63, *The Islamic Law of Nations* 66, *Republican Iraq* 69, *Political Trends in the Arab World* 70.
Office: 4454 Tindall Street, N.W., Washington 16, D.C., U.S.A.

Khal, Yusuf A. al-, B.A.; Lebanese writer and publisher b. 25 Dec. 1917; ed. American Univ. of Beirut.
Teacher of Arabic Literature, American Univ. of Beirut 45-47, 55-58; Editor *Sawt al Mar'at* women's monthly 46-48; Editor-Writer, Dept. of Public Information, UN Secretariat 48-50; Information Officer Libyan Mission to UN 50-52; Editor *Al Hoda* daily, New York 52-55; Founder and Editor *Shir* poetry magazine, *Adab* literary quarterly 57-; owner Gallery One, Beirut; Editorial Dir. Dar An-Nahar Publishing Co., Beirut 67-70.
Publs. *Al Hurriyat* (poetry) 44, *Herodiat* (poetical play) 54, *Al Bi'r al Mahjourat* (poetry) 58, *Quasa'id fil Arba'yn* (poetry) 60; translations works by T. S. Eliot, Auden, Pound, Sandberg, Frost and others; numerous essays and articles of literary criticism.
Rue Patriarcat, Beirut, Lebanon.

Khalaf, Kadhim M.; Iraqi diplomatist; b. 1922; ed. American Univ. of Beirut and Inst. des Hautes Etudes Internationales, Paris.
Member staff Perm. Mission of Iraq to UN 48; Del. to numerous confs.; Dir.-Gen. UN Dept., Ministry of Foreign Affairs, Iraq 62-64; Under-Sec. of Ministry of Foreign Affairs 64-66, 67-68; Perm. Rep. to UN 66-67; Head of Iraqi Del. to Int. Conf. on Human Rights 68; Amb. to U.K. 68-71.
c/o Ministry of Foreign Affairs, Baghdad, Iraq.

Khalatbary, Abbas Ali, PH.D.; Iranian diplomatist; b. 1912; ed. Univ. of Paris.
With Ministry of Foreign Affairs 42-; Dept. of Protocol and Third Political Div. 42; Second Sec., Berne 45, First Sec., Warsaw 47; Acting Head, Dept. of Int. Orgs. 50, Dir. 51; Counsellor, Iranian Embassy, Paris 53; Dir. Third Political Div. 57, Protocol Dept. 58; Amb. to Poland 59, concurrently Minister, Bucharest; Sec.-Gen. Central Treaty Org. (CENTO) 62-68; Deputy Minister of Foreign Affairs, Under-Sec. for Political Affairs 68-70, Vice-Minister 70-71, Minister 71-; del. to various int. confs. including several sessions of UN Gen. Assembly (Head of Iranian Del. 71).
Imperial Iranian Ministry of Foreign Affairs, Teheran, Iran.

Khalid ibn Abdulaziz, Crown Prince; Saudi Arabian Amir; b. 1913; ed. religious schools.
Appointed Asst. to his brother, Prince Faisal 34; Rep. of Saudi Arabia to various Int. Confs.; Vice-Pres. Council of Ministers Oct. 62-; nominated Crown Prince 65.
Vice-President's Office, Council of Ministers, Riyadh, Saudi Arabia.

Khalid, Mansour, LL.D.; Sudanese diplomatist and lawyer; b. 17 Jan. 1931, Sudan; ed. Univs. of Khartoum, Pennsylvania and Paris.
Began his career as an attorney, Khartoum 57-59; Legal officer, UN, N.Y. 62-63; Deputy UN resident rep., Algeria 64-65; Bureau of Relations with Member States, UNESCO, Paris 65-69; Visiting Prof. of Int. Law, Univ. of Colorado 68; Minister of Youth and Social Affairs, Sudan 69-71; Chair. of Del. of Sudan to UN Gen. Assembly, Special Consultant and Personal Rep. of UNESCO Dir.-Gen. for UNWRA fund-raising mission 70; Perm. Rep. to UN for Sudan 71; Minister of Foreign Affairs 71-.
Ministry of Foreign Affairs, Khartoum, Sudan.

Khalidi, Ismail Raghib, B.A., M.A., PH.D.; Saudi Arabian United Nations official; b. 13 Nov. 1916; ed. St. George's School and Govt. Arab Coll., Jerusalem, American Univ. of Beirut, Michigan Univ. and Columbia Univ., U.S.A.
Assistant Script Editor, Radio Arabic Desk, U.S. Office of War Information, New York 42-44; Sec.-Gen., Inst. of Arab-American Affairs, New York 44-47; New York Corresp. for *Al Misri* (Cairo daily) 46-47; Assoc. Dir. Asia Inst. for Arabic Studies, New York 47-48; Adviser to Saudi Arabian Del. UN 49; mem. UN Secretariat 49-, UN Mission to Libya 50-52, UN Observer, British N. Cameroons 60-61, Political Affairs Officer, UN Security Council Affairs Div. 55-; Principal Sec. UN Comm. for Unification and Rehabilitation of Korea (UNCURK) 62-65.
Publ. *Constitutional Development in Libya* 56.
121 Lorraine Avenue, Mount Vernon, N.Y. 10553, U.S.A.

Khalifa, Sirr el Khatim, G.C.M.G.; Sudanese educationalist and politician; b. 1 Jan. 1919; ed. Gordon Coll., Khartoum.
Former teacher, Gordon Coll., Khartoum, and Bakht-er-Ruda Inst.; Head, Khartoum Technical Inst. 60-64; Deputy Under-Sec. Ministry of Educ. 64; Prime Minister 64-65; Amb. to Italy 65-68, to United Kingdom 68-69; Minister of Higher Educ. and Scientific Research 72-.
Ministry of Higher Education and Scientific Research, P.O. Box 2081, Khartoum, Sudan.

Khalifa Abbas, El Obeid; Sudanese diplomatist; b. 1915; ed. Gordon Memorial Coll., Khartoum.
Sudan Railway Service 33-44, 48-54; Dep. Under-Sec. for Special Functions 55; Dep. Perm. Under-Sec. Ministry of Foreign Affairs 56-57; Ambassador to Ethiopia 57-59; Ambassador to Iraq, Lebanon, Jordan and Turkey 59-61, to U.S.A. 65-Jan. 66; Permanent Under-Sec. for Foreign Affairs March 66-69; Chair. Board of Dirs., Omdurman Nat. Bank 69-70; Diplomatic Adviser, Embassy of Qatar, London 72-.
Ministry of Foreign Affairs, Khartoum, Sudan; Suite No. 1027, Royal Lancaster Hotel, London, W.2., England.

Khalifa bin Hamad al-Thani, Sheikh; Amir of Qatar; b. 1934.
Deputy Ruler of Qatar, Prime Minister and Minister of Finance and Petroleum Affairs Sept. 71-Feb. 72; deposed his cousin Sheikh Ahmad and took office as Amir of Qatar Feb. 72.
The Royal Palace, Doha, Qatar.

Khalifah, H. H. Shaikh Isa bin Sulman al-; Ruler of the State of Bahrain; b. 1933.
Appointed heir-apparent by his father, H.H. Sheikh Sulman bin Hamad al-Khalifah 58; succeeded as Sheikh on the death of his father Nov. 61.
The Palace, Manama, Bahrain.

Khalifah, Khalifah bin Sulman al-; Bahrain politician; b. 1935.
Son of the late Sheikh Sulman and brother of the ruler, Sheikh Isa; Dir. of Finance and Pres. of Electricity Board 61; Pres. Council of Admin. 66-70; Pres. State Council 70-.
The State Council, P.O. Box 78, Bahrain.

Khalil, Abdullah, O.B.E.; Sudanese politician; b. 1892; ed. Khartoum.
Served Egyptian Army 10-24 and Sudan Defence Force 25-44, reaching rank of Brig.; founder-mem. Umma Party, Sec.-Gen. 45; mem. and leader Legislative Assembly 48; mem. Executive Council and fmr. Minister of Agriculture; mem. Constitution Amendment Comm.; Minister of

Defence and Public Works 56; Prime Minister and Minister of Defence 56-58.
Khartoum, Sudan.

Khalil, Mohamed Kamal El-Din; Egyptian diplomatist. Lecturer in Int. and Public Law 41-56; Dir. of Research Dept., U.A.R. Ministry of Foreign Affairs 56-60; Minister Plenipotentiary, London 60-61; Dir. North American Dept., U.A.R. Ministry of Foreign Affairs 61-64; Ambassador to Jordan 64-66; Ambassador to Sudan 66-71; Under-Sec. of State for Foreign Affairs Sept. 71-.
Publ. *The Arab States and the Arab League* (2 vols.) 62.
Ministry of Foreign Affairs, Cairo; and 1103 Sh. El-Nil, Garden City, Cairo, Egypt.

Khamri, Abdulla Ahmed al; Yemeni diplomatist; b. 2 June 1936.
Director, Nat. Liberation Front, Cairo; mem. NLF Exec. Cttee. until 68; Minister of Information and Culture; now Minister of State for Council Affairs, Personal Rep. of the Pres.
Council of Ministers, Aden, People's Democratic Republic of Yemen.

Khanlari, Parviz, PH.D.; Iranian historian and politician; b. 1913; ed. Teheran Univ. and Univ. of Paris.
Professor of Iranian Linguistics, Teheran Univ. 48-; Ed. *Sokhan* (literary monthly) 44-64, and of its *Scientific Supplement* 61-64; Dep. Minister of Interior 55; Senator 57; Minister of Education 62-64; Co-Founder *Mardom* Party 57; Gen. Sec. Imperial Foundation for Iranian Cultural Studies.
P.O. Box 984, Teheran, Iran.

Khatib, Ahmed al-; Syrian school teacher; b. 1931, Salkhad, Jabal al-Arab region.
Formerly Head, Syrian Teachers Asscn.; mem. Presidential Council Sept. 65-Feb. 66; Pres. of Syria Nov. 70-Feb. 71; Chair. People's Council Feb.-Dec. 71; Premier Fed. of Arab Repubs. Dec. 71-; mem. Baath Party, elected to Leadership Cttee. May 71.
People's Council, Damascus, Syria.

Khatib, Mohammed Fathalla el-, B.COMM., PH.D.; Egyptian politician; b. 1 Jan. 1927, Gharbiyah; ed. Univs. of Cairo and Edinburgh.
Director of Research and UN sections, Arab States Delegations Office, New York 58-61; Prof. of Comparative Govt., Univ. of Cairo 67-71, Dean of Faculty of Econs. and Political Science 68-71; Minister of Social Affairs May-Sept. 71; Adviser to the Pres. on Home, Econ. and Social Affairs Sept. 71-72; Sec.-Gen. Arab Socialist Union Governorate of Cairo 71-72; Minister of Foreign Affairs, Fed. of Arab Repubs. Dec. 71-.
Publs. include *Power Politics in the UN* 62, *Local Government in U.A.R.* 64, *Studies in the Government of China* 65, *Studies in Comparative Government* 67, *Introduction to Political Science* 69.
11 Sh. Ibn Zinki-Zamalek, Cairo, Egypt.

Khayyal, Abdullah al; Saudi Arabian diplomatist; b. 1913; ed. Fuad I Univ., Cairo.
Private Sec. to Minister of Foreign Affairs, H.R.H. Prince Faisal 32; Dir.-Gen. of Schools, Eastern Saudi Arabia and Dir. A.H.S.A. Central School 41; Second Sec. Saudi Arabian Legation, Baghdad 43, First Sec. and Chargé d'Affaires 45; Minister to Iraq 47-55; Perm. Del. to UN 55-57; Ambassador to U.S.A. 55-63, concurrently Minister to Mexico 56-60, Ambassador 60-63; Pres. Islamic Center, Washington, D.C. 56-58; Dir. of Public Works 64-.
Department of Public Works, Jeddah, Saudi Arabia.

Khefacha, Mohamed El Hédi, L. ès L.; Tunisian politician; b. 11 Oct. 1916; ed. Coll. Sadiki, Lycée Carnot, Tunis and Faculté de Droit, Algiers.
Called to Bar, Tunis 42; Pres. Union of Young Lawyers of Tunisia 50-56; Gen. Inspector of Customs 56-58; Deputy 59; Sec. of State for Justice 58-66, concurrently Sec. of State for Finance 60-61; Sec. of State for Public Health 66-69, of the Interior 69-70, 71-73, of Public Works and Housing June 73-; mem. Political Office, Destour Socialist Party 69-; Grand Cordon, Order of the Repub. 64, Grand Cordon, Order of Independence 66.
Ministry of Public Works and Housing, Tunis, Tunisia.

Kheir, Ahmed Mohamed; Sudanese politician; ed. Gordon Memorial Coll., and Khartoum School of Law.
Advocate 44; mem. Sudan del. which negotiated Sudan's future 46; fmr. Vice-Pres. and Pres. of Nat. Cttee. for the Constitution; Minister of Foreign Affairs 58-64, of Mineral Resources 62-64.
Publs. (Arabic) *The Struggle of a Generation, Calamities of the British in the Sudan* (English), *Sudan Appeals to U.N.O.*
Khartoum, Sudan.

Khene, Abderrahman, M.D.; Algerian doctor, politician and administrator; b. 6 March 1931; ed. Univ. of Algiers.
Secretary of State, Provisional Govt. of Algeria (G.P.R.A.) 58-60; Dir. of Political Affairs, Ministry of Interior, G.P.R.A. 60-61; Dir. of Cabinet, Ministry of Finances G.P.R.A. 61-62; Pres. of Technical Org. for Exploiting Wealth of Saharan Sub-Soil (l'Organisme Saharien) Sept. 62-Dec. 65; Pres. Electricité et Gaz d'Algérie (E.G.A.) July-Oct. 64; Pres. Industrial Co-operation Org. (O.C.I.) Jan. 66-Aug. 71; Minister of Public Works and Construction 66-70; Sec.-Gen. Org. of the Petroleum Exporting Countries 73-.
Organization of the Petroleum Exporting Countries, Dr. Karl Lueger-Ring 10, Vienna, Austria.

Khiary, Mahmoud; Tunisian politician and trades union official; b. 1911; ed. Ecole Normale, Tunis.
Teacher 31-55; Sec.-Gen. Tunisian Union of Teachers 41-52; Pres. Gen. Fed. of Tunisian Officials 47-58; fmr. Sec.-Gen., Gen. Union of Tunisian Workers; fmr. Minister of Posts and Telegraphs; fmr. Minister of Agriculture; mem. Nat. Constituent Ass.; Chief, UN Civil Operations in the Congo 61-62; Pres. Dir.-Gen. Soc. Nat. Tunisienne de Cellulose, Soc. Nat. Tunisienne de Papier Alfa 63-72; Pres. Dir.-Gen. Société Nationale de Mise en Valeur du Sud (SONMIVAS) 72-.
SONMAVIS, 23 avenue des Etats Unis d'Amérique, Tunis, Tunisia.

Khlefawi, Gen. Abdel Rahman; Syrian army officer and politician; b. 1927, Damascus; ed. schools in Damascus, Military School, Homs.
Representative of Syria, Joint Arab Command, Cairo 64-67; Head, Armoured Forces Admin., Damascus 67-68; Head, Officers' Board, Ministry of Defence 68-70; Minister of the Interior Nov. 70-April 71; Prime Minister 71-72; mem. Regional Command, Baath Party.
c/o Office of the Prime Minister, Damascus, Syria.

Kholi, Hassan Sabri el-; Egyptian diplomatist; b. 25 Feb. 1922; ed. Univ. of Cairo, Mil. and Staff Colls.
Fought in Palestine War 48; Prof., Senior Officer Studies Inst.; opened Infantry School, Syria 57; Dir. Office for Palestine at the Presidency, Office for Public Affairs; Personal Rep. of the Pres. 64-; has represented Egypt at UN, Arab League and Arab Summit Confs., numerous foreign decorations.
Publs. *The Palestine Case, Sinai, The Policy of the Imperialism and Zionism towards Palestine during the First Half of the Twentieth Century*, and several research papers on Palestine.
The Presidency, Cairo, Egypt.

Khoshkish, Youssof; Iranian banker; b. 1906; ed. Teheran Secondary School and Sorbonne, Paris.
Bank Melli Iran 34-36; Chair. Foreign Trade Bank of Iran; Iranian del. Ministry of Finance, Europe 39-40,

India 40-44; Vice-Pres. Bank Sepah 45-61; Pres. Bank Melli Iran 61-.
Bank Melli Iran, P.O. Box 40, Khiaban Ferdowsi, Teheran, Iran.

Khosrovani, Attaollah; Iranian politician; b. 1919; ed. Univ. of Teheran and Univ. of Paris.
Former Labour Attaché, France; Govt. Supervisor to Workers Social Insurance Organisation, later Head 54-58; Under-Sec. (Admin.) Ministry of Labour and Under-Sec. (Parl.) Ministry of Labour 58; Minister of Labour and Social Services 61-64; Minister of Labour 64-68 and of Social Affairs 65-68; Sec.-Gen. Iran Novin Party 65; Order of Homayoun, Second Class, Order of Sepasse, Order of Homayoun, First Class.
c/o Ministry of Foreign Affairs, Teheran, Iran.

Khosrovani, Khosro, D.SC.; Iranian diplomatist; b. 16 June 1914; ed. Iran and England.
Foreign Service, served Ministry of Foreign Affairs, UN, Washington; later Deputy Minister of Nat. Economy; Chair. Board of Inspectorate N.I.O.C. 63; Ambassador to Turkey 63-65, to U.S.A. 65-67; High Insp. Ministry of Foreign Affairs 67; Pres. Council of Political Planning and Programmes 70; Amb. to Egypt 71-; Order of Homayoun, First Class.
11 Okbah Street, Dokki, Cairo, Egypt.

Khoury, Sheikh Maître Michel, LL.B.; Lebanese businessman and politician; b. 24 Nov. 1926; ed. Univ. St. Joseph, Beirut, Paris Univ. Faculté de Droit, Inst. d'Etudes Politiques and Coll. de France.
Political section, Ministry of Foreign Affairs 46-49; Contributor to *Le Jour* daily 44-; Dir.-Gen. Ets. Derwiche Youssef Haddad 53-; mem. Board Nat. Council of Tourism 62-66, Pres. 64-66; Minister of Defence and of Guidance, Information and Tourism Dec. 65-April 66; Minister of Planning and Tourism 66-68; Middle East Regional Editor *Columbia Journal of World Business*.
Ets. Derwiche Youssef Haddad, Beirut, Lebanon.

Kikhia, Mansur Rashid; Libyan diplomatist; b. 1 Dec. 1931, Benghazi; ed. Faculty of Law, Univ. of Cairo and Paris.
Joined Diplomatic Service 57; Asst. in Nationality and Consular Affairs Section, Ministry of Foreign Affairs 57, Head, Treaties and Int. Confs. Section 58-60, 62-65; Second Sec. for Consular and Cultural Affairs, Libyan Embassy to France 60-62; Chargé d'Affaires, France Jan.-Aug. 62, Algeria Feb.-Aug. 63; Consul-Gen., Geneva 65-67; mem. Perm. Mission of Libya to UN 67-69; Under-Sec. Ministry of Unity and Foreign Affairs 69-72; Perm. Rep. to UN Feb.-July 72; Minister of Foreign Affairs July 72-73; has attended numerous int. confs., has represented Libyan Govt. at six sessions of UN Gen. Assembly, mem. Perm. Mission to UNESCO.
c/o Ministry of Foreign Affairs, Tripoli, Libya.

Kirk, George Eden, M.A.; American (b. British) author; b. 1911; ed. Cambridge, and Schools of Archaeology Athens and Jerusalem.
Epigraphist with Colt expedition, Palestine 35-38; Staff Officer (Int.) at G.H.Q Middle East Forces 40-45; Instructor Middle East Centre for Arab studies 45-47; M.E. specialist Royal Inst. of International Affairs 47-52; Assoc. Prof. Int. Relations, American Univ. of Beirut 53-57; Lecturer, Harvard Univ. Center for Middle Eastern Studies 57-66; Prof. of History, Univ. of Mass. 66-, Dir. of Graduate Studies in History 70-73.
Publs. *A Short History of the Middle East* 48 (definitive edn. 64), *The Middle East in the War* 52, *The Middle East, 1945-50* 55, *Contemporary Arab Politics* 61; contributed to: *The Military in the Middle East* (ed. Sydney N. Fisher) 63, *Forces of Change in the Middle East* (ed. Maurice M. Roumani) 71.
32 Cosby Ave., Amherst, Mass. 01002, U.S.A.

Kittani, Ismat T.; Iraqi United Nations official; b. 5 April 1929, Amadiya; ed. Knox Coll, Galesburg, Ill.
High School teacher, Iraq; joined Foreign Ministry 52; Attaché, Cairo 54-57; mem. Iraqi mission to UN 57, Acting Perm. Rep. 58-59; Perm. Rep. to European Office of UN 61-64; Chief, Specialized Agencies and Admin. Cttee. of Co-ordination Affairs, Dept. of Econ. and Social Affairs, UN Secr. 64; Sec. Econ. and Social Council 65-67; Principal Officer, later Dir. Exec. Office of Sec.-Gen. of UN 67-69; Deputy to Asst. Sec.-Gen. for Inter-Agency Affairs Nov. 69-70; Asst. Sec.-Gen. for Inter-Agency Affairs 71-; fmr. del. of Iraq to various int. comms. and confs.; mem. Gov. Board ILO 59; alt. mem. Exec. Board WHO 61.
United Nations, New York, N.Y., U.S.A.

Kizilkaya, Metin; Turkish civil servant and diplomatist; b. 1918; ed. Ankara Univ.
Inspector of Finance 45-55; Deputy Dir.-Gen. of Revenue Dept., Ministry of Finance 56-60; Financial Commr. of Istanbul 60-61; mem. Turkish Del. to Org. for Econ. Co-operation and Devt. (OECD) 61-64; Dir.- Gen.of Treasury, later Counsellor, Ministry of Finance 64-65; Dir.-Gen. Army Savings Bank 65-66; Deputy Under-Sec. of State, Min. of Finance 66-68; Rep. of Turkey at OECD 68-70.
184 boulevard Malesherbes, Paris 17e, France.

Klibi, Chadli; Tunisian politician.
Secretary of State for Information and Cultural Affairs 61, 64, for Cultural Affairs Nov. 64, also for Information and Guidance 66-69; Minister of Cultural Affairs and Information 69-70.
c/o Ministry of Cultural Affairs, Government Place, Tunis, Tunisia.

Koç, Vehbi; Turkish businessman; b. 1901.
Opened first grocery shop in Ankara 16; formed Koç Trading Corpn. 37, General Elektrik Türk 49, and many other companies; Chair. Koç Holding Corpn. 64-; manufactured Turkey's first passenger car 66; Founded Vehbi Koç Foundation 69.
Koç Holding Corporation, Ankara, Turkey.

Kol, Moshe; Israeli educator and politician; b. 1911, Russia; ed. Hebrew Secondary School, Pinsk and Hebrew Univ. Jerusalem.
Co-Founder Hanoar Hazioni (Zionist Youth) movement in Poland and its Rep. on Cen. Cttee. of Zionist Org. in Poland; came to Israel and joined Hamefales pioneer group in Kfar Saba 32; Del. to all Zionist Congresses 33-; mem. Histadrut Exec. 41-46; mem. Jewish Agency Exec. and Head of its Youth Aliya Dept. 46-66; mem. Provisional State Council 48, and Chair. of its Foreign Affairs Cttee.; mem. Knesset (Parl.) 49-66; Minister of Devt. and of Tourism 66-69, of Tourism 69-; Chair. Independent Liberal Party; Vice-Pres. Liberal Int. 69-; Co-Founder (in Israel), Oved Hazioni (Zionist Workers) Movement, World Confed. of Gen. Zionists; many Jewish Agency and govt. missions abroad; Hon. Treas. Israel Exploration Soc.
Publs. in Hebrew. *Arichim, Misholim Bezionout, Netivot Bechinouch Uveshikum, Morim Vechaverim, Youth Aliya* (also in English and French).
Ministry of Tourism, 24 King George Street, Jerusalem, Israel.

Kollek, Theodore (Teddy); Israeli politician; b. 1911; ed. Vienna.
Went to Palestine 34; mem. Kibbutz Ein-Gev. 37; with Zionist Youth groups in Europe and U.K. 38-40; Political Dept., Jewish Agency 42-47; Liaison with Jewish Underground in Europe 42-45; mem. Haganah mission to U.S.A. 47-48; Minister Plenipotentiary, Washington 51-52; Dir.-Gen. Prime Minister's Office, including Dept. for Applied Civilian Scientific Research, Bureau of Statistics, Govt. Press and Information Office, the devt. of broadcasting services, est. Israel Govt. Tourist Office, 52-64; Chair. Govt. Tourist Corpn. 56-65; Chair. Israel 10th

Anniversary Celebrations; Mayor of Jerusalem 65-; Head of Nuclear Desalination of Water Project 64-66; Chair. Board of Governors, Israel Museum 65-.
Publs. (with Moshe Pearlman) *Jerusalem: Sacred City of Mankind* 68, *Pilgrims to the Holy Land* 70.
Municipality of Jerusalem, Jerusalem; Home: 6 Rashba Street, Jerusalem, Israel.

Komodromos, Epaminondas M.; Cypriot politician; b. May 1912, Drousha Village, Paphos District; ed. Ambetios School, Cairo and Athens Univ.
Lawyer 36-68; mem. Paphos School Cttee. 50-53; Minister of Interior and Defence 68-72.
c/o Ministry of Interior, Nicosia, Cyprus.

Kony, Mohammed Awad el; Egyptian diplomatist; b. 1906.
Consulate, Rome 29-32; Attaché, Washington 37-39; Ministry of Foreign Affairs 39-41; Consul, Bombay 41-43; Second Sec. Moscow 44-46; Ministry of Foreign Affairs 46-49; Counsellor, Washington 49-52; Dir. Political Dept., Ministry of Foreign Affairs 52-55; Ambassador to U.S.S.R. 55-61; Amb. to U.K. 61-64; Perm. Rep. of U.A.R. to UN 64-69; Minister of Tourism 69-70.
c/o Ministry of Tourism, Cairo, Egypt.

Koper, Daniş; Turkish politician and businessman; b. 19 Dec. 1908 Diyadin; ed. Ankara Lisesi and Munich Coll. of Technology.
Engineer Water Works Dept. 36-48; Dir. Provincial Bank 51; Gen. Man. Highways Admin. 51-56; Under-Sec. Ministry of Public Works 56-57; Minister of Public Works 60; Chair. Asscn. of Chamber of Engineering and Architecture 58-60; Chair. Turkish Airlines 59-60; Trustee Middle East Technical Univ., Ankara 59-60; mem. Constitutional Assembly 61; Partner Kuyaş Construction Co., and Bormak Ltd. 60-; Chair. Board and Exec. Cttee. Ereğli Iron and Steel Co. 61-68; Gen. Sec. Turkish Atomic Energy Comm. 70-71; Chair. Board of Trustees, Middle East Technical Univ. 63-66; Chair. Board of Trustees, Ankara Koleji (High School) 63-68; Trustee, Hacettepe Univ. 70-71; Chevalier, Légion d'Honneur.
Office: 16/4 Gazi Mustafa Kemal Blv., Yenişehir, Ankara; Home: 6 Sokak Nr. 37, Bahçelievler, Ankara, Turkey.

Korutürk, Admiral Fahri S.; Turkish naval officer and diplomatist; b. 1903, Istanbul; ed. Naval Acad. and Naval War Coll.
Joined Navy 20; Naval Attaché, Rome 35-36, Berlin 37-38, Berlin and Stockholm 42-43; Commdr. of Submarine Fleet 47-50; Commdr. of Sea-Going Fleet 53-54; Chief of Intelligence, Armed Forces 54; Commdr. of the Fleet 55; Commdr.-in-Chief, Straits Area 56; Commdr.-in-Chief of Navy and Commdr. of Allied Forces, Black Sea 57-60; Amb. to U.S.S.R. 60-64, to Spain 64-65; Senator apptd. by Pres. 68; Head Presidential Senate Group 71-73; Pres. of the Repub. 73-.
Office of the President, Ankara, Turkey.

Kotaite, Assad, LL.D.; Lebanese lawyer and aviation official; b 6 Nov. 1924; ed. French Univ. of Beirut, Univ. of Paris, Inst. des Hautes Etudes Internationales, Paris and Acad. of Int. Law, The Hague.
Practising barrister 48-49; Head, Legal Services, Int. Agreements and External Relations, Dir. of Civil Aviation, Ministry of Public Works and Transport 53-56; Rep. to Int. Civil Aviation Org. (ICAO) 56-70, Sec.-Gen. 70-; mem. UN Transport and Communications Comm. 57-59, Chair. 59; Chair. Air Transport Cttee., ICAO 59-62, 65-68.
International Civil Aviation Organization, 1080 University Street, Montreal 101, Quebec, Canada.

Kouros, Andreas Kyriakou, M.A., PH.D.; Cypriot educationist; b. 6 Nov. 1918; ed. London and Oxford Univs., Int. Inst. of Educ. Planning, Paris.
Teacher 44-53; Insp. of Schools, Ministry of Educ. 53-59, Senior Insp. 59-61; Head Dept. of Primary Educ. 61-68; Head of Educ. Planning 68-70; Dir. of Educ. 70-72, Minister 72-.
Publs. *The Construction and Validation of a Group Test of Intelligence for Greek Cypriot Children* 56, *Education in Cyprus under the British Administration* 59, *Electra* 68.
Ministry of Education, Nicosia; Home: 1 Souliou Street, Ayios Dhometios, Nicosia, Cyprus.

Kranidiotis, Nicos; Greek-Cypriot scholar and diplomatist; b. 25 Nov. 1911; ed. Pan Cyprian Gymnasium, Cyprus, Athens Univ., and Harvard Univ. Center for Int. Affairs.
Worked as schoolmaster in Cyprus; Dir. of *Hellenic Cyprus* (official political organ of Cyprus Ethnarchy) 49; Gen. Sec. Cyprus Ethnarchy 53-57, Councillor 57-60; Ambassador to Greece 60-63, to Yugoslavia 63-64, to Italy 64-70, to Bulgaria and Romania 70-; Sec. of 2nd and 3rd Cyprus Nat. Assemblies 54, 55; Founder, Dir. and Editor (with others) of *Kypriaka Grammata* (Cyprus Literature), a literary magazine.
Publs. *Chronicles* (short stories) 45, *The Neohellenic Theatre* (essay) 50, *Studies* (poems) 51, *Forms of Myth* (short stories) 54, *The Poet G. Seferis* (essay) 55, *The National Character of the Cyprus Literature* 58, *Cyprus in her Struggle for Freedom* (history) 58, *An Introduction to the Poetry of George Seferis* 64, *Cyprus-Greece* 66, *Cyprus Poetry* 69.
16 Prometheus Street, Nicosia, Cyprus.

Kubar, Abd al-Majid (see Coobar, Abdulmegid).

Kubat, Ferit; Turkish politician; b. 1919, Diyarbakır; ed. American Coll. of Tarsus, Faculty of Law, Istanbul Univ.
Held various posts in local admin. until 64; Gov. of Edirne, Hatay and Muş successively; Under-Sec., Ministry of Foreign Affairs; Minister of the Interior 71-73.
National Assembly, Ankara, Turkey.

Kubbah, Salih; Iraqi politician and economist.
Chairman Iraq Nat. Oil Co. (INOC) 64-67; Gov. Central Bank of Iraq 67-69; Minister of Finance July 68.
c/o Central Bank of Iraq, Banks Street, Baghdad, Iraq.

Küçük, Fazil, M.D.; Cypriot politician; b. 1906; ed. Istanbul and Lausanne Univs.
Owner and Editor *Halkın Sesi* (daily) 41-; Leader, Cyprus Turkish Party (now Cyprus Turkish National Union) 43-; Chair. Evcaf High Council 56-; Vice-Pres. Cyprus 60-73.
P.O. Box 339, Nicosia, Cyprus.

Kudsi, Nazem el, PH.D.; Syrian politician; b. 1906; ed. American Coll., Beirut, Damascus Univ. and Univ. of Geneva.
Barrister in Aleppo 30; Dep. for Aleppo 36, 47, 55; Minister Plenipotentiary, Washington 44-45; Prime Minister and Minister for Foreign Affairs 50; Pres. Council of Ministers 54-57; Leader, Populist Party; held no political office during United Arab Republic régime 58-61; Pres. of the Syrian Arab Republic 61-63, retired 63.
Aleppo, Syria.

Kuneralp, Zeki, DR.IUR.; Turkish diplomatist; b. 5 Oct. 1914, Istanbul; ed. Univ. of Berne.
Entered Diplomatic Service 40; Official, Ministry of Foreign Affairs, Turkey 41-42, 47-49; Attaché to Embassy Bucharest 43-47, Prague 49-52; Del. to NATO (Paris) 52-57; Asst. Sec.-Gen. Diplomatic Service 57-60, Sec.-Gen. 60; Ambassador to Switzerland Sept. 60-64, to U.K. Feb. 64-66; Sec.-Gen. Ministry of Foreign Affairs Aug. 66-69; Amb. to U.K. 69-72; Hon. G.C.V.O. 71.
c/o Ministry of Foreign Affairs, Ankara, Turkey.

Kurtbek, Col. Seyfi; Turkish army officer; b. 1906; ed. War Academy.
Commissioned Lieut. 23; Mil. expert, Disarmament Confs.,

Geneva 33; Mil. Attaché, Paris 33; Mil. Expert, Montreux Conf. (Straits) 36; Major, Chief of Operations Army Corps 39; Mil. Attaché, Athens 40; Lt.-Col., Dir. of the Mobilization Section of Gen. Staff, Ankara 44; Col. 48; resgnd. from the Army and elected Democratic Party Deputy for Ankara 50, re-elected 54; Minister of Communications 51-52; Minister of Defence 52-53; arrested 60, released 61; Vice-Pres. Justice Party 61-; Deputy for Sivas 65-; Chair. Parl. Foreign Affairs Comm. 65-; Medal of Independence. Publs. (in Turkish) *War and Economy, Preparation of the Nation for Defence, Mobilization of Germany, To Arms, Women in National Defence.*
T.B.M.M., Ankara, Turkey.

Kuwait, H.H. The Ruler of (*see* Sabah, Amir Sabah al Salem al).

Kyprianou, Spyros; Cypriot politician; b. 28 Oct. 1932; ed. City of London Coll. and Gray's Inn.
Qualified as barrister; mem. Cyprus Ethnarchy Secretariat, London 54-59; Cyprus observer at UN 57; headed del. to UN General Assembly 19, 20, 21 sessions; rep. Greek-Cypriot side in negotiations for tri-partite pact between Greece, Turkey and Cyprus 59; Minister of Justice Aug. 60; Minister of Foreign Affairs 60-72; several decorations.
3 Georghiou Tyrimou Street, Nicosia, Cyprus.

L

Labidi, Abdelwahab; Tunisian financier; b. 1929.
Former Gen. Man. Banque de Tunisie; Insp.-Gen. Banque Nat. Agricole de Tunisie; Man. Soc. Tunisienne de Banque; Man. Dir. Nat. Devt. Bank of Niger; Vice-Pres. African Devt. Bank June 69-Sept. 70, Pres. Sept. 70-.
African Development Bank, B.P. 1387 Abidjan, Ivory Coast.

Ladgham, Bahi; Tunisian politician; b. 10 Jan. 1913, Tunis.
Joined Dept. of Interior 33, subsequently moved to Finance Dept.; Sec. of State for the Presidency and Sec. of State for Defence 56-Sept. 69; Prime Minister of Tunisia Nov. 69-Nov. 70; Chair. Arab Cttee. supervising the cease-fire between Jordanian Govt. and the Palestinian guerrillas in Jordan Sept. 70-April 71; now personal rep. of Pres. Bourguiba; fmr. Sec.-Gen. Destour Socialist Party (fmrly. Néo-Destour Party).
c/o Destour Socialist Party, 10 rue de Rome, Tunis, Tunisia.

Laghzaoui, Mohamed; Moroccan politician.
Former Minister of Economics; fmr. Director of National Security; Rep. of King Hassan to Algerian leaders Conf. held by French Govt. Dec. 61-March 62; Dir.-Gen. Office Chérifien des Phosphates and Chief Co-ordinator of State Econ. Enterprises Jan. 63-July 65; Minister of Tourism, Industry and Mines June-July 65; Pres. Afro-Asian Org. for Economic Co-operation 66; Treas. Democratic Socialist Party (P.S.D.) May 64-; Amb. to U.K. 69-71, to France 71-72.
Ministère des Affaires Etrangères, Rabat, Morocco.

Lagu, Joseph; Sudanese army officer; b. 21 Nov. 1931; ed. Rumbek Secondary School, Mil. Acad., Omdurman.
Served in Sudanese Army 60-63; joined South Sudan Liberation Movt. 63, Leader SSLM 69; signed peace agreement with Govt. of Sudan March 72; Order of the Two Niles 72.
Publ. *The Anya-Nya—what we fight for.* 72.
People's Armed Forces General Headquarters, Khartoum, Sudan.

Lahoud, Gen. Jamil Georges; Lebanese army officer and politician; b. 1903; ed. Coll. de la Sagesse, Beirut, and Ecole Militaire, Damascus and Staff Coll. in Turkey and England.
Army career 23-60, General 59; Dir.-Gen. Military Office, Presidency of the Republic 59-60; mem. Chamber of Deputies 60-; Minister of Social Affairs and Works 66-67; numerous national and international decorations including Ordre Nat. du Cèdre (Lebanon), Officier Légion d'Honneur (France), Grand Officier Ordre Chéhani (Iran), and Grand Officier Ordre Royal (Morocco).
c/o Ministry of Social Affairs and Works, Beirut, Lebanon.

Lalla Aicha, H.R.H. Princess; Moroccan diplomatist; b. 1930.
Eldest daughter of late King Mohammed V; Ambassador to United Kingdom 65-69, to Italy 69-71; Pres. Moroccan Red Crescent; Grand Cordon of Order of the Throne.
c/o Ministry of Foreign Affairs, Rabat, Morocco.

Lamrani, Muhammad Karim; Moroccan politician; b. 1919, Fez.
Appointed to Ministry of Nat. Economy 59; in private business 60; mem. boards of several banks and Royal Air Maroc; Vice-Chair. Casablanca Chamber of Commerce 61, later Pres.; Dir.-Gen. Office Chérifien des Phosphates 67-; mem. Royal Cabinet 67; Acting Dir.-Gen. Bureau de Recherche et de Participation Minière (BRPM) (state mining org.) April 71; Minister of Finance April-Aug. 71; Prime Minister 71-72.
Office Chérifien des Phosphates, Rabat, Morocco.

Landau, Moshe, LL.B.; Israeli judge; b. Danzig 1912; ed. London Univ.
Immigrated 33; called to Palestine Bar 37, Magistrate of Haifa 40, District Court Judge, Haifa 48, Justice Supreme Court, Jerusalem 53-.
The Supreme Court, Jerusalem, Israel.

Landau, Rom; British writer and educationalist.
Sculptor and art critic; visited King Ibn Saud and other religious leaders, Near East 37; mem. Exec. Cttee. World Congress of Faiths, London 35-44; R.A.F. Liaison Officer 39, later Air Gunner and Flight-Lieut.; Senior Specialist Middle East Section Ministry of Information 41; mem. Arab Cttee. Political Intelligence Dept., Foreign Office 41-44; lectured on Morocco at Columbia, Princeton, Yale and other U.S. Univs. 52 and 53-54; Prof. Islamic and North African Studies, American Acad. of Asian Studies, San Francisco 52-58; and Univ. of the Pacific 56-67; Peace Corps, Dir. Area Studies, Morocco Project I 62-63; Commdr. Ouissam Alaouite Order of Morocco 56; D.Hum. Litt. (Univ. of the Pacific) 67.
Publs. *Minos the Incorruptible* 25, *Pilsudski: Hero of Poland* 29, *Paderewski* 34, *God is my Adventure* 35, 64, *Seven* 36, *Thy Kingdom Come* 37, *Search for Tomorrow* 38, *Arm the Apostles* 39, *Love for a Country* 39, *Of No Importance* 40, *We Have Seen Evil* 41, *Hitler's Paradise* 41, *The Fool's Progress* 42, *Letter to Andrew* 43, *Islam To-day* (with Prof. A. J. Arberry) 43, *The Brother Vane* 44, *The Wing* 45, *Sex, Life and Faith* 46, *The Merry Oasis* 47, *Odysseus* 48, *Human Relations* 49, *Personalia* 49, *Invitation to Morocco* 50, *The Sultan of Morocco* 51, *The Beauty of Morocco* 51, *Moroccan Journal* 52, *Morocco* (survey for Carnegie Endowment for Int. Peace) 52, *Portrait of Tangier* 52, *France and the Arabs* 53, *Among the Americans* 54, *The Arabesque* 55, *Moroccan Drama, 1900-55* 56, *Mohammed V; King of Morocco* 57, *An Outline of Moroccan Culture* 57, *Islam and the Arabs* 58, *The Philosophy of Ibn Arabi* 59, *Morocco Independent* 61, *The Arab Heritage of Western Civilisation* 62, *King Hassan II* 62, *The Moroccans—Yesterday and Today* 63, *History of Morocco in the Twentieth Century* (in Arabic) 63, *Morocco: Fez, Rabat and Marrakesh* 67, *The Kasbas of Southern Morocco* 69, *Al Hassan al Thani Malik al Maghrib* (in Arabic) 69, *The Alaouites-King Hassan's Cultural Contribution* 70.
Echchouhada, Marrakesh, Morocco; Faber & Faber, 3 Queen's Square, London, W.C.1, England.

Laraki, Moulay Ahmed; Moroccan diplomatist; b. 1931; ed. Univ. of Paris.
With Ministry of Foreign Affairs 56-57; Perm. Rep. to UN 57-58; medical affairs 59-61; Ambassador to Spain 61-65, to U.S.A., concurrently accred. to Mexico, Canada and Venezuela 65-67; Minister of Foreign Affairs 67-69; Prime Minister 69-Aug. 71.
c/o Presidence du Conseil, Palais Royal, Rabat, Morocco.

Laskov, Haim; Israeli army officer; b. 4 April 1919; ed. Reali High School Haifa and St. Anthony's Coll. Oxford.
Guide to British Army units in Palestine 36-39; served with British Army (major) 41-46; Commdr. of Israel forces in capture of Nazareth and Upper Gallilee 48; G.O.C. Training Command and Dir. Mil. Training 48-51; Air Officer Commanding, Israel Air Force 51-53; Dep. Chief of Staff and Dir. of Operations 55; Commdr. Armoured Forces, Sinai Campaign 56; G.O.C. Southern Command 57-58; Chief of Staff, Israel Defence Force 58-60; Dir.-Gen. Israel Ports Authority 61-70; Ombudsman to IDF 72-.
75 Einstein St., Tel-Aviv, Israel.

Lasky, Ahmed; Moroccan civil engineer and politician; b. 30 April 1932; ed. Casablanca High School, Ecole spéciale des travaux publics and Ecole nationale des ponts et chaussées, Paris.
Public Works Engineer, Casablanca 56; Chief Engineer Agadir Region 59; Chief Engineer Casablanca Region 60-62; Dir. Casablanca Harbour 62-65; Minister of Public Works and Communications 65-67; Dir.-Gen. Royal Air Maroc 67-; Minister of Higher, Secondary and Technical Educ. 71-72; Officier, Ordre du Trône (Morocco), Ordre de George I (Greece), Commdr. Ordre de l'Istiqlal (Tunisia), Ordre Egyptien, Ordre Iranien.
Publs. numerous technical pamphlets about bridges and harbours in French and foreign magazines.
c/o Royal Air Maroc, Aéroport International Casablanca, Nouassenr; and 6 Rue de Liège, Casablanca, Morocco.

Lavon, Pinchas; Israeli politician; b. Poland 1904; ed. Lwów Univ.
Co-founder Gordonia (Zionist Youth Organization in Poland) 24; settled in Palestine 29; Sec. Mapai 35-37; Exec. Cttee. Mapai and Histadrut 42-; mem. Knesset 49-; Minister of Agriculture 50-51; Minister of Defence 51-54; Minister without portfolio 54-55; Chair. Solel Boneh Ltd.; mem. Zionist Actions Cttee.; Sec.-Gen. Histadrut (Gen. Fed. of Labour in Israel) 56-61; Editor *Min Hayesod* 62-.
Publ. *Yesodot* (Foundation).
85 Gordon Street, Tel-Aviv, Israel.

Lawzi, Ahmed Abdel Kareem al-; Jordanian politician; b. 1925, Jubeiha, nr. Amman; ed. Teachers' Training Coll., Baghdad, Iraq.
Teacher, 50-53; Asst. to Chief of Royal Protocol 53-56; Head of Ceremonies, Ministry of Foreign Affairs 57; mem. Parl. 61-62, 62-63; Asst. to Chief of Royal Court 63-64; Minister of State, Prime Minister's Office 64-65; mem. Senate 65; Minister of the Interior for Municipal and Rural Affairs April-Oct. 67; mem. Senate 67; Minister of Finance Oct. 70-Nov. 71; Prime Minister 71-73; various Jordanian and foreign decorations.
The Senate, Amman, Jordan.

Leclant, Jean, D. ès L.; French archaeologist and epigrapher; b. 8 Aug. 1920; ed. Lycées Voltaire and Henri IV, Ecole normale supérieure and Univ. de Paris.
Studied at Institut français d'archéologie orientale, Cairo 48-52; Dir. of excavations for Ethiopian Govt. 52-55; Prof. of Egyptology, Univ. de Strasbourg 54-64; developed a special interest in Meroitic script; Prof. of Egyptology, Univ. of Paris and Dir. of Studies, Ecole pratique des hautes études 64-; excavations at Karnak, Tanis, Sakkarah, Soleb, Axum; Prés. Soc. française d'égyptologie; mem. Deutsches Archäol. Inst., Berlin, Inst. d'Egypte, Cairo.
Publs. *Enquêtes sur les sacerdoces de la XXVe dynastie* 54, *Dans les pas des pharaons* 58, *Montouemhat, prince de la ville* 61, *Recherches sur les monuments thébains de la XXVe dynastie dite éthiopienne* 65; co-Editor *Annales d'Ethiopie* and *Meroitic Newsletter*.
77 rue Georges-Lardennois, Paris 19e, France.

Ledwidge, William Bernard John, M.A., A.M., C.M.G.; British diplomat; b. 9 Nov. 1915, London; ed. King's Coll., Cambridge Univ. and Princeton Univ.
Commonwealth Fund Fellow, Princeton Univ. 37-39; Mil. Service, H.M. Forces 40-46; First Sec., Foreign Office 48-49; British Consul, St. Louis, U.S.A. 49-52; First Sec., Kabul 52-56; Political Adviser, British Mil. Govt., Berlin 56-61; Counsellor, Foreign Office 61-65; Minister, U.K. Embassy, Paris 65-69; Amb. to Finland 69-72, to Israel 72-; C.M.G. 60.
54 rue de Bourgogne, Paris 7e, France; British Embassy, Tel-Aviv, Israel.
Telephone: 705-8026 (Home).

Lee, James E., B.S.; American oil executive; b. 1921; ed. Louisiana Polytechnic Inst.
With Gulf Oil Corpn. 42-66; Man. Dir. Kuwait Operations, Kuwait Oil Co. Ltd. Aug. 66-June 69; Pres. Gulf Oil Co.
Gulf House, 2 Portman Street, London, W.1, England.

Léger, Jacques; Haitian international official; b. Port-au-Prince; ed. Faculty of Law, Univ. of Haiti.
Attached to Protocol Sec., Dept. of State 34-35; Sec. to Sec. of State for Foreign Affairs 35-36; service with legation in Venezuela; Dir. Haiti Service of Inter-American Affairs; Chargé d'Affaires, Venezuela 44-47; Amb. to Cuba 47-48, to Argentina and Brazil 48-50; Sec. of State for Foreign Affairs 50-51; Amb. to U.S.A. and Canada 52-56; Perm. Rep. to UN 56-57; research activities, N.Y. Public Library and Library of Congress 57-59; translator 59-63; UNDP Regional Rep., Ivory Coast 64-67; Democratic Repub. of Congo (now Zaire) 67-69, N.W. Africa 69-72, Kuwait 72-; Grand Officer, Légion d'Honneur, and other decorations.
United Nations Development Programme, P.O. Box 2193, Kuwait City, Kuwait.

Lehmann, Ernst, DR.RER.POL.; Israeli banker; b. 29 April 1902; ed. Berlin and Munich Univs.
Worked for several banks in Germany 24-35; emigrated to Palestine, apptd. Man. The Gen. Mortgage Bank of Palestine Ltd. 35; Man. Issue Dept., Anglo-Israel Bank Ltd. (now Bank Leumi le-Israel) dealt with issue of currency of Israel and admin. of Govt. Loans 48; Chair. Board of Dirs., Bank Leumi le-Israel B.M. 70-, Migdal-Binyan Insurance Co. Ltd., Africa-Israel Investment Ltd., Tel-Aviv Stock Exchange Ltd., Ihud Insurance Agencies Ltd.; Pres. Asscn. of Banks in Israel 70-; mem. Advisory Council, Advisory Cttee. Bank of Israel.
Publs. various articles on financial and currency problems.
Bank Leumi le-Israel B.M., 24-32 Yehuda Halevy Street, Tel-Aviv; Home: 23 Benjamin Street, 52 512 Ramat-Gan, Israel.

Levanon, Chaim; Israeli politician; b. 25 March 1899; ed. Cracow Univ.
Went to Palestine 27; mem. Jewish Agency Exec.; Mayor Tel-Aviv-Jaffa 53-59; Chair. Exec. Council, Gen. Zionist Party (now Liberal Party) 53-; Founder Tel-Aviv Univ.; Initiator, Freddy Mann Auditorium; Founder Havazelet Hasharon Settlement, Sharon.
18 Dubnov Street, Tel-Aviv, Israel.

Lewis, Bernard, B.A., PH.D., F.B.A., F.R.HIST.S.; British university professor; b. 31 May 1916; ed. Univs. of London and Paris.
Lecturer in Islamic History, School of Oriental Studies, Univ. of London 38; served R.A.C. and Intelligence Corps 40-41; attached to Foreign Office 41-45; Prof. of History of the Near and Middle East, Univ. of London 49-; Visiting

Prof. of History, Univ. of California at Los Angeles 55-56, Columbia Univ. 60; Indiana Univ. 63, Princeton Univ. 64, Inst. for Advanced Study 69; Corresp. Fellow Inst. d'Egypte, Cairo; hon. mem. Turkish Historical Soc.
Publs. *The Origins of Isma'ilism* 40, *Turkey Today* 40, *British Contributions to Arabic Studies* 41, *Handbook of Diplomatic and Political Arabic* 47, *Land of Enchanters* (Editor) 48, *The Arabs in History* 50 (revised edns. 58, 64, 66, 70), *Notes and Documents from the Turkish Archives* 52, *The Kingly Crown* 61, *The Emergence of Modern Turkey* 61 (revised edn. 68), *Historians of the Middle East* (ed. with P. M. Holt) 62, 64, *Istanbul and the Civilization of the Ottoman Empire* 63, 68, *The Middle East and the West* 64, 68, *The Assassins* 67, *Race and Colour in Islam* 71, Coeditor *Encyclopaedia of Islam* 56-, *Cambridge History of Islam* 70, *Islam in History: Ideas, Men and Events in the Middle East* 73.
School of Oriental and African Studies, University of London, London, W.C.1, England.

Lifson, Shneior, PH.D.; Israeli scientist; b. 18 March 1914, Tel-Aviv; ed. Hebrew Univ.
Member of kibbutz 32-43; served in Science Unit, Israel Defence Forces 48-49; Weizmann Inst. of Science, attached to Polymer Dept. 49, Chair. Scientific Council 61-63, Head Chemical Physics Dept. 63-, Science Dir. 63-67; mem. Council for Higher Educ., Israel Science Teaching Center, Comm. of Molecular Biophysics of Int. Union of Pure and Applied Biophysics, European Molecular Biology Org., Advisory Board *Biopolymers* and Editorial Board *Journal of Statistical Physics* (U.S.A.); Weizmann Prize 58, Israel Prize 69.
Publs. numerous scientific papers.
15 Neve Weizmann, Rehovot, Israel.
Telephone: 951721/589.

Likhachev, Veniamin Andreevich; Soviet diplomatist; b. 29 Oct. 1921, Belinsky, Pensa Region; ed. Moscow Aviation Inst. and High Diplomatic School.
Second, First Sec., Soviet Embassy, Turkey 47-55; ranking official, Ministry of Foreign Affairs, 55-58; Counsellor, Soviet Embassy, Turkey 58-62; ranking official, Ministry of Foreign Affairs 62-70; Amb. to Iraq 70-.
U.S.S.R. Embassy, Baghdad, Iraq.

Lloyd, Seton, C.B.E., M.A., F.B.A., F.S.A., A.R.I.B.A.; British archaeologist; b. 30 May 1902; ed. Uppingham and Architectural Assen.
Asst. to Sir Edwin Lutyens, P.R.A. 27-28; excavated for Egypt Exploration Society, Egypt 29-30, for Oriental Inst., Univ. of Chicago in Iraq 30-37, for Univ. of Liverpool in Turkey 37-39; Technical Adviser, Govt. of Iraq, Directorate-Gen. of Antiquities 39-49; Dir. British Inst. of Archæology in Ankara 49-61, Hon. Sec. 64-; Prof. of Western Asiatic Archaeology, Univ. of London 62-69; Hon. M.A. (Edinburgh).
Publs. *Mesopotamia* 34, *Sennacherib's Aqueduct at Jerwan* 35, *The Gimilsin Temple* 40, *Presargonid Temples* 42, *Ruined Cities of Iraq* 42, *Twin Rivers* 43, *Foundations in the Dust* 48, *Early Anatolia* 56, *Alanya-Ala'iyya* 58, *Art of the Ancient Near East, Beycesultan* 62, *Mounds of the Near East* 63, *Highland Peoples of Early Anatolia* 67.
Woolstone Lodge, Faringdon, Berkshire, England.

Logali, Hilary Nyigilo Paul; Sudanese politician; b. 1931, Juba, Equatoria Province; ed. Khartoum Univ., Yale Univ.
Official with Ministry of Finance; Sec.-Gen. Southern Front 64-; Minister of Public Works, then of Communications 65; Minister of Labour and Co-operatives 67-69; fmr. Man. Dir. Bata Nationalized Corpn.; apptd. to rank of Minister 71-; mem. for Finance, Econ. Planning and Agriculture, High Exec. Council for the Southern Region April 72-.
High Executive Council for the Southern Region, Juba, Sudan.

Loizides, Andreas M.; Cypriot accountant and politician; b. 1932, Limassol; ed. Limassol Greek Gymnasium, and studied as a chartered accountant, Scotland.
Qualified as chartered accountant, Scotland 57; later partner in firms Metaxas, Christofides, Loizides and Scottis, and Touche Ross & Co.; founder mem. Inst. of Certified Public Accountants of Cyprus, later Pres.; mem. Council of Cyprus Employers' Consultative Assen. 65-69; mem. Board Central Bank of Cyprus 68-70; Minister of Commerce and Industry July 70-72.
c/o Ministry of Commerce and Industry, Nicosia, Cyprus.

Loombe, Claude Evan, C.M.G.; British banker; b. 9 Aug. 1905.
Banking posts in Ceylon, India and China 32-41; Ministry of Finance, Iraq Govt. 41-45; with Bank of England 45-65, latterly as Adviser to Govs.; Chair. British Bank of the Middle East 67-; mem. Currency Boards Jordan 48-65, Sudan 56-60, Kuwait 60-69, Libyan Currency Comm. 52-56; Order of Al-Rafidain, 4th Class (Iraq) 46, Order of Independence, 2nd Class 61, and Order of Jordanian Star, 1st Class 65.
Flowermead, Maori Road, Guildford, Surrey, England.

Lourie, Arthur, M.A., LL.B.; Israeli diplomatist; b. South Africa 10 March 1903; ed. Univs. of Cambridge and Cape Town, and Harvard Univ.
In legal practice, also lecturer in Law, Witwatersrand Univ. 27-32; Political Sec. to Jewish Agency for Palestine, London 33; fmr. Dir. UN Office of the Jewish Agency, New York; liaison officer with Anglo-American Cttee. of Enquiry, Palestine 46; promoted to Minister Plenipotentiary and Envoy Extraordinary 50; fmr. Consul-Gen. of Israel in New York and Deputy Rep. of Israel to UN; Asst. Dir.-Gen. Ministry of Foreign Affairs, Jerusalem 54-57; Ambassador to Canada 57-59, to Great Britain 60-65; Chair. Israeli Del. to XIV Session UN; Deputy Dir.-Gen. Ministry of Foreign Affairs 65-.
Ministry of Foreign Affairs, Jerusalem, Israel.

Luce, Sir William Henry Tucker, G.B.E., K.C.M.G.; British overseas administrator; b. 25 Aug. 1907; ed. Clifton Coll. and Christ's Coll. Cambridge.
Joined Sudan Political Service 30; Private Sec. to Gov.-Gen. 41-47, Deputy Gov. Equatoria Province 50-51, Gov. of Blue Nile Province and Dir. Sudan Gezira Board 51-53, Adviser to Gov.-Gen. on Constitutional and External Affairs 53-56; Gov. and C.-in-C. Aden 56-60, Political Resident, Persian Gulf 61-66; Dir. Eastern Bank 66-70, Tilbury Overseas Contractors and Gray, Mackenzie 67-70; Special Rep. of U.K. to Persian Gulf States 70-72; Dir. Chartered Bank and Gray, Mackenzie 72-.
Brook House, Fovant, Salisbury, Wiltshire, England.

Luqman, Ali Muhammad Ali, B.A.; Yemeni journalist, poet and politician; b. 6 Aug. 1918; ed. Univ. of Aligarh, India, and American Univ., Cairo.
Editor *Fatat-ul-Jezirah* (Arabic daily) 47-62, *Al Qalam al Adani* (Arabic weekly) 53-63, *Al Akhbar* (Arabic daily) 63-67; mem. Legislative Council, Aden 58-65; Trustee, Aden Port Trust, Aden 59-64; Sec. Aden Assen. 49-58; Sec., Aden People's Congress, Aden 60-65; Aden Rep., Commonwealth Parl. Conf., London 61, Jamaica 64; Minister for Civil Aviation, Fed. of S. Arabia 64-65; Chair. Aden Electricity Corpn. 66-; Dir. Aden Press Agency 65-.
Publs. Poetry: *Alwatr Almaghmoor* 44, *Ashjan Fil Lail* 45, *Ala Rimal Sirah, Annat Shaab, Layali Ghareeb, Hadeer al Qafilah*; Poetical Drama: *Pygmalion, Ad Dhil Almanshood, Qais Laila, Al Adl al Mafqood, Samraa al Arab; Fatat-ul-Jezirah* (English) 48; Political: *Self Government* 49.
News House, Holkat Road, P.O. Box 435, Crater, Aden, People's Democratic Republic of Yemen.

Luqman, Muhammad Ali Ibrahim; Yemeni lawyer and journalist; b. 1898; ed. Aden and India.
Man. Clayton Ghaleb and Co. Ltd. 18-19; Man. English

Pharmacy 21-22; Headmaster Govt. School Aden 24-28; Founder Arab Literary Club 24-30; Man. A. Besse (British Somaliland Branches) 32-34; Pres. Arab Reform Club 30-35, etc.; Pres. Poor Boys' Asscn.; Pleader of the Supreme Court Aden Colony; Ed. *Fatat-ul-Jezirah Newspaper* 40-, and *The Aden Chronicle*; Minister of Civil Aviation Nov. 64-May 65; Sec.-Gen. People's Congress Party; Adviser to Aden Cultural Council; mem. Township Authority Exec. Cttee.
Publs. *Springs of European Progress* 33, *The British Nation* 40, *Saeed* 40, *Ardh Adhhaher* 45, *Kamla Devi* 47, *The French Revolution* 48, *Lahej Constitution* 52, *Aden Needs Self-Government* 53, *The Story of the Yemen Revolution* (joint editor) 62.
Esplanade Road, Crater, Aden, People's Democratic Republic of Yemen.

Lutfi, Ashraf Taufiq, B.A.; Kuwaiti petroleum consultant; b. 1 Jan. 1919; ed. Scots Coll., Safad, Palestine.
Teacher in elementary and secondary schools 38-46; Welfare Officer 46-48; Sec. to State Sec. in Govt. Secr. 48-55, Asst. Sec. of State 55-61; Dir. of Office of Amir of Kuwait 61-64; Adviser on Oil Affairs, Ministry of Finance and Industry 64-; Sec.-Gen. Org. of Petroleum Exporting Countries (OPEC) 65-Jan. 67; Adviser on Oil Affairs to Ministry of Finance and Oil 67-69; mem. Board Kuwait Nat. Petroleum Co. 61-71; Chair. Board Kuwait Aviation Fuelling Co. 62-71; Assoc. Dir. Petrolo Int., Beirut.
Publs. *Arab Oil: A Plan for the Future* 60, *OPEC Oil: A Review of its Problems* 66.
Box 7030, Beirut, Lebanon.

M

Ma'ayani, Ami; Israeli composer; b. 1936, Tel-Aviv; ed. Tel-Aviv Univ., Haifa Technion and Columbia Univ., New York.
Studied music with Paul Ben-Haim and Prof. Vladimir Ussachevsky; Chair. League of Composers of Israel; Musical Dir. and Conductor of Nat. Youth Orchestra.
Works include: *Toccata for Harp* 59-60, *Concerto for Harp and Orchestra No. 1* 60, *Maquamat for Harp* 60, *Music for Strings* 62, *Teamin* 64, *Electronic Music* 64-65, *Concerto for Percussion and Eight Wind Instruments* 66, *Symphonic Concerto for Harp and Orchestra* 66, *Regalim* 66, *Concerto for Violin and Orchestra* 67, *Concerto for Violoncello and Orchestra* 67, *Concerto for Two Pianos and Orchestra* 69, *Qumran-Symphonic Metaphor* 70, *The War of the Sons of Light* (opera-oratorio in one act for solos, chorus, dancers and orchestra), chamber music, songs, etc.
8 Nahum Street, Tel-Aviv, Israel.

Mabrouk, Ezzidin Ali, LL.B., LL.M.; Libyan politician; b. 28 May 1932; ed. Cairo Univ. and Univ. Coll., London.
Public Prosecutor, Tripoli 56; subsequently Judge, Summary Court, Tripoli, Pres. Tripoli Court and Counsellor of Supreme Appeal Court; Senior Legal Adviser, Org. of Petroleum Exporting Countries (OPEC); Minister of Petroleum, Libya 70-.
Ministry of Petroleum, P.O. Box 256, Tripoli, Libya.

McDougall, James Forsyth; New Zealand international civil servant; b. 3 Oct. 1918; ed. Otago Univ.
Member of staff, Auckland Univ. 46-50, Educ. Dept., UNESCO, Paris 51-68; Assoc. Sec. Nat. Educ. Comm., Pakistan 59, Educ. Comm., India 64-66; Regional Dir. UNICEF, Eastern Mediterranean 68-.
Publs. various UNESCO publs. on education 53-64.
UNICEF, P.O. Box 5902, Beirut, Lebanon.

Mackenzie, Alfred H.; Canadian United Nations official; ed. Cambridge and Toronto Univs.
War Service 40-46, Officer in Canadian Army; Prof. of Languages, Khaki Univ. 46; Asst. Sales Man. De La Rue Insulation 46-47; Co-Dir. United Plastics and Chemicals 47-48; Textile Firm Rep. for Cen. and S. America 48-50; joined UN, Head of UNESCO Latin America Desk 50-57; Regional Rep. for Cen. America, UN Technical Assistance Board 58-62, Resident Rep., Philippines 62-65; Resident Rep. UN Devt. Programme (UNDP), Morocco 65-69, Cyprus 69-.
United Nations Development Programme, P.O. Box 3521, Nicosia, Cyprus.

Macki, Ahmed al-Nabi; Omani diplomatist; b. 17 Dec. 1939, Muscat; ed. Cairo and Paris.
Member, Oman Del. to UNESCO 69-70; Dir. of Offices of Prime Minister and Minister of Foreign Affairs 70-71; First Perm. Rep. of Oman to UN 71-72.
P.O. Box 472, Muscat, Oman.

Maghrabi, Mahmoud Soliman; Libyan politician; b. 1935; ed. George Washington Univ., U.S.A.
Helped to organize strikes of port workers June 67, for which he was sentenced to four years imprisonment and deprived of Libyan nationality; released Aug. 69; following the coup of Sept. 69 became Prime Minister, Minister of Finance and Agriculture, and of Agricultural Reform; dismissed from the Govt. 70; Perm. Rep. to UN 71-72; Amb. to U.K. 73-.
Embassy of Libyan Arab Republic, 58 Prince's Gate, London, SW7 2PW, England

Maghur, Kamel Hassan; Libyan diplomatist; b. 1 Jan. 1935, Tripoli; ed. univs. of Cairo, Paris and Grenoble.
Assistant Counsellor, Admin. of Legislation, Tripoli 59-60; Counsellor, Court of Cassation and Deputy, Dept. of Casuistry and Legislation 60-69; Counsellor, Supreme Court 69-71; Perm. Rep. to UN 72-.
Permanent Mission of Libya to the United Nations, 866 United Nations Plaza, New York, N.Y. 10017, U.S.A.

Maguid, Yahya Abdel, C.ENG., A.M.I.C.E.; Sudanese politician; b. 7 Oct. 1925, Omdurman; ed. Gordon Memorial Coll. and Imperial Coll., London.
Received practical training in construction of irrigation projects with British companies specializing in this field; held various posts in Ministry of Irrigation, rising to Under-Sec. Sept. 69; part-time lecturer, Univ. of Khartoum; Minister of Irrigation and Hydro-electric Power Aug. 71-; mem. Int. Comm. for Hydraulic Law.
Ministry of Irrigation and Electric Power, Khartoum, Sudan.

Mahdi, Saadik El (Great grandson of Imam Abdul-Rahman El-Madhi); Sudanese politician; b. 1936; ed. Comboni Coll., Khartoum and St. John's Coll., Oxford.
Son of the late Siddik El Mahdi; Leader, Umma Mahdist Party 61; Prime Minister 66-67; arrested on a charge of high treason 69; exiled April 70; returned to Sudan and arrested Feb. 72; released May 73.
Publ. *Problems of the South Sudan*.
Khartoum, Sudan.

Mahdi al Tajir, Mohamed; Dubai administrator; b. 26 Dec. 1931; ed. Bahrain Govt. School and Preston Grammar School, Lancs., England.
Department of Port and Customs, Govt. of Bahrain, Dir. 55-63; Dir. Dept. of His Highness the Ruler's Affairs and Petroleum Affairs March 63-; Dir. Nat. Bank of Dubai Ltd. 63-; Dir. Dubai Petroleum Co. April 63-; Chair. Dubai Nat. Air Travel Agency Jan. 66-; Dir. Qatar-Dubai Currency Board Oct. 66-; Chair. South Eastern Dubai Drilling Co. April 68-; Amb. of the United Arab Emirates to U.K. 72-; Dir. Dubai Dry Dock Co. 73-; Hon. Citizen of State of Texas, U.S.A. 63.
Department of H.H. The Ruler's Affairs and Petroleum Affairs, P.O. Box 207, Dubai; and Embassy of the United Arab Emirates, 30 Prince's Gate, London, S.W.7, England.

Mahfouz, Naguib; Egyptian author; b. 11 Dec. 1911; ed. University of Cairo.
Civil servant 34-, successively with Univ. of Cairo, Ministry of Waqfs, Dept. of Arts and Censorship Board; fmr. Dir.-Gen., now Adviser, Cinema Org. of Egypt; State Prize for 1st volume of *Bein el Kasrein* 57.
Publs. *Whisper of Madness* 38, *Play of Destiny* 39, *Radobis* 43, *Struggle of Tayiba* 44, *New Cairo* 45, *Khan el Khalil* 46, *Zuqaq el Madaq* 47, *The Mirage* 48, *Beginning and End* 49, *Bein el Kasrein* (trilogy) 52, *Children of our Quarter* 59, *Quails and Autumn* 62, *The Road* 64, *The Beggar* 65, *Small-talk on the Nile* 66, *Thief and Dogs*, *God's World*.
c/o Cinema Organisation, TV Building, Maspero Street, Cairo, Egypt.

Mahgoub, Mansour; Sudanese accountant and politician; b. 1912, El Kowa; ed. Gordon Memorial Coll.
Joined Dept. of Finance 35; trained with various companies in England 50-51; Inspector, Auditory Dept., Sudan Dec. 51-Jan. 54; Asst. Dir. of Accounts, Ministry of Finance Jan. 54-March 55; Under-Sec. for Internal and Monetary Affairs March 55-58; Under-Sec. Ministry of Commerce, Industry and Supply 58, retd. 64; joined Sudan Commercial Bank as Asst. Dir. 64; Minister of the Treasury May 69-June 70; Minister of Economy, Trade and Supplies June 70-72.
c/o Ministry of Economy, Trade and Supplies, Khartoum, Sudan.

Mahgoub, Mohammed Ahmed; Sudanese lawyer and politician; b. 1908; ed. Gordon Coll. and Khartoum School of Law.
Qualified as an architect and lawyer; practising lawyer; mem. Legislative Assembly 48-54; accompanied Umma Party Del. to Lake Success 47; mem. Constitution Amendment Comm.; non-party candidate in Gen. Election 54; Leader of the Opposition 54-56; Minister of Foreign Affairs 56-58; practising solicitor 58-64; Minister of Foreign Affairs Oct. 64-Feb. 65; Prime Minister June 65-July 66; Prime Minister and Minister of Foreign Affairs May 67-June 68; Prime Minister and Minister of Defence June 68-69.
Publ. several vols. of poetry (in Arabic).
Khartoum, Sudan.

Mahmassani, Sobhi Mohamed Ragab el; Lebanese politician; b. 1909; ed. American Univ. of Beirut, Univ. of Lyon, France, and Univ. of London, England.
President of Court of Appeal, Beirut 44-46, now Hon. Pres.; Legal Counsellor Lebanese Del. to UN at San Francisco 45; Prof. of Muslim Law, Univ. Libanaise; mem. Chamber of Deputies 64-; Minister of Nat. Econ. 66-67; Attorney-at-Law 67-.
Publs. several legal works in French, English and Arabic.
Azaria Building, Beirut, Lebanon.

Mahroug, Smail; Algerian economist.
Economic Counsellor to the Presidency and Dir.-Gen. Caisse Algérienne de Développement 63-65; Dir.-Gen. of Finance 65-66; Econ. Counsellor to the Presidency 67-.
Ministry of Finance, Algiers, Algeria.

Maiwandwal, Mohamed Hashim; Afghan diplomatist, scholar and writer; b. 23 March 1921; ed. privately in Habibia, Kabul.
Editor of *Ittifâq-i Islam* 42; Dir. Afghan Encyclopaedia 44; Editor of *Anis* 45; Acting Pres. of Press Dept. of the Royal Afghan Govt. 49; Press Adviser of His Afghan Majesty 50; Pres. Press Dept. of Afghan Govt. 51; Counsellor Afghan Embassy in Washington 53; Pres. Press Dept. Afghan Govt. 54; Deputy Foreign Minister 55; Amb. to United Kingdom 57, to Pakistan 57-58, 63-65, to the U.S.A. 58-63; First Class Star 58; Minister of Press and Information 64; Prime Minister Nov. 65-Oct.67; leader of nat. political movement "Progressive Democracy".
Kabul, Afghanistan.

Majdalani, Nassim Mikail; Lebanese banker and politician; b. 1912, Beirut; ed. American Univ. of Beirut and Université de Lyon.
Barrister 37-44; Deputy for Beirut 57, 60, 64; Vice-Pres. of Council of Ministers and Minister of Justice 60-61, 64-65; mem. of Admin. Council of Bank N. Majdalani, Beirut; Minister of Economy 68-69; Minister of Foreign Affairs 69-71; Deputy Speaker, Chamber of Deputies Oct. 71-; Grand Cordon of Order of Tunisia; Medal of Order of St. Vladimir.
Chamber of Deputies, Beirut; Home: Rue Omar Ben Khattab, Beirut, Lebanon.

Majid, Abdul, PH.D.; Afghan diplomatist; b. 14 July 1914; ed. Cornell Univ. and Univ. of California (Berkeley).
Member Afghan Inst. of Bacteriology 41, Dir. 41-42; Prof. of Biology and Physiology, Kabul Univ. 40-46, Pres. of Univ. 46-48; Minister of Public Health 48-50; Minister of Education 50-56; Amb. to Japan 56-63, to U.S.A. 63-67, to U.K. 67-70; Minister of Justice 73-; Leader of Afghan del. to UN 66; Order of Educ. First Class 56, Sardar-i Ali 59, A. Haas Award (Univ. of Calif.) 66.
c/o Ministry of Justice, Kabul, Afghanistan.

Majidi, Abdol-Majid, PH.D.; Iranian politician and lawyer; ed. Teheran, Paris, Harvard and Illinois Univs.
Held posts in Export Devt. Bank and in Plan Org.; Head of Budget Bureau of Plan Org. 59-60; Financial and Admin. Asst. Man. Dir. of Plan Org. 62-64; Head of Budget Bureau formed in 1964; Deputy Prime Minister, Head of Cen. Budget Bureau, Plan Org. 66; Minister of Agricultural Products and Consumer Goods 67-68, of Labour and Social Affairs 68-73, of State in charge of Plan and Budget Org. 73-; mem. Arts and Culture High Council 68; Sec.-Gen. Red Lion and Sun Soc.
Plan and Budget Organization, Avenue Daneshkhadeh, Teheran, Iran.

Makarios III, Archbishop; Cypriot ecclesiastic and statesman; b. 13 Aug. 1913, Panayia, Paphos District; ed. Pancyprian Gymnasium, Nicosia, Theological Coll. of Athens Univ. and School of Theology, Boston Univ.
Ordained Deacon and Priest, Greek Orthodox Church 38; studied in Greece 38-43; mem. teaching staff Kykkos Abbey 43-46; ordained Archimandrite 46; studied in U.S.A. supported by World Council of Churches Fellowship 46-48; Bishop of Kitium 48-50; Archbishop of Cyprus and Ethnarch 50-; Cypriot national leader identified with *Enosis* (Union with Greece) movement; has travelled abroad to promote interest and support for *Enosis*; led negotiations with Sir John Harding, Gov. of Cyprus 55-56; deported to the Seychelles 56, released Mar. 57; in Athens until return to Cyprus March 59; President-elect 59-60; President of Cyrpus 60- (re-elected 63, 68, 73); Hon. D.D. (Boston, Athens Univs.), Hon. LL.D. (Kerala, Salonica Univs., Jorge Tadeo Lozano Univ. of Bogota); many foreign decorations.
Presidential Palace, Nicosia, Cyprus.

Makhebar, Albert; Lebanese politician; b. 1915.
Minister of Health 58; fmr. Minister of Foreign Affairs; Deputy Premier, Minister of State for Co-operatives and Housing Affairs May 72-73; Minister of State 73-.
Office of the Minister of State, Beirut, Lebanon.

Makhous, Dr. Ibrahim; Syrian politician.
Member of Baath Party's Supreme Command 65; Deputy Prime Minister and Minister of Foreign Affairs Sept. 65-Dec. 65, March 66-68.
c/o Ministry of Foreign Affairs, Damascus, Syrian Arab Republic.

Makki, Dr. Hassan; Yemeni politician.
Minister of Economy April 63-64; Minister of Foreign Affairs April-Sept. 66; Deputy Prime Minister for Internal

Affairs Nov.-Dec. 67; Minister of Foreign Affairs Dec. 67-69; Deputy Prime Minister for Econ. Affairs July 72-.
Ministry of the Economy, Sana'a, Yemen Arab Republic.

Maktum, H.H. Sheikh Rashid bin Said Al-; Ruler of Dubai; b. 1914; ed. privately.
Succeeded his father, Said bin Maktum, as 4th Sheikh 58; Vice-Pres. United Arab Emirates (UAE) Dec. 71-.
Royal Palace, Dubai.

Malek, Reda; Algerian diplomatist; b. 1931; ed. Univs. of Algiers and Paris.
Director of weekly *El Moudjahid*, Tunis 57-61; mem. F.L.N. Del. to Evian talks 61; Amb. to Yugoslavia 63-65, to France 65-70, to U.S.S.R. 70-.
Embassy of Algeria, Krapivinsky per. 1-A, Moscow, U.S.S.R.

Malik, Charles Habib, M.A., PH.D.; Lebanese philosopher, educationist and diplomatist; b. 1906, Btirram, Al-Koura; ed. American Univ. of Beirut, and Harvard and Freiburg Univs.
Instructor Maths. and Physics American Univ. Beirut 27-29; with *Al Hilal* Publ. House, Cairo 29-30; with Rockefeller Found. Exped., Cairo 30-32; Asst. in Philosophy Harvard 36-37; Instructor in Philosophy American Univ. Beirut 37-39; Adjunct-Prof. 39-43; Assoc. Prof. 43-45; Head of Dept. 39-45; on leave 45-55; Dean of Graduate Studies and Prof. of Philosophy 55-60; E. K. Hall Visiting Prof., Dartmouth Coll. 60; Visiting Prof. Harvard Summer School 60; Minister of Lebanon to U.S.A. 45-53, to Cuba 46-55; Minister designate to Venezuela 47-48; Amb. to U.S.A. 53-55; Lebanese del. UN Conf. and Signatory UN Charter 45; mem. and Chair. Lebanese del. to UN 45-54; Pres. 13th Gen. Assembly UN 58-59; del. to Bandung Conf. 55; Minister for Foreign Affairs 56-58, for Nat. Education and Fine Arts 56-57; mem. of Parl. 57-60; Pres. Security Council 53, 54; Pres. Economic and Social Council 45; Chair. Human Rights Cttee. 51, 52; Chair. Lebanese del. for Peace Treaty with Japan 51; Grand First Magistrate of the Holy Orthodox Church; Pres. World Council of Christian Educ. 67-71; Vice-Pres. United Bible Societies 66-72; Fellow Inst. for Advanced Religious Studies at the Univ. of Notre Dame, Indiana 69; Hon. life mem. American Bible Soc.; mem. Société européenne de Culture; Fellow American Asscn. for Advancement of Science, American Geog. Soc.; mem. American Philos. Asscn., American Philos. Soc., American Acad. of Arts and Sciences, Acad. of Human Rights, etc.; founding mem. Lebanese Acad.; Gold Medal, Nat. Institute of Social Sciences, N.Y.; Hon. Litt.D. (Princeton, James Millikin Univs.), Hon. LL.D. (Notre Dame, Brown, Denison, Fairfield, Syracuse, Harvard, Boston, Lehigh, Yale, Georgetown, Wash., Columbia, Ohio, Calif., Dartmouth, St. Mary's Halifax, Wesleyan Univs., Colby, Williams and Albright Colls.); Hon. Rector, Univ. Dubuque 51; decorated by governments of Lebanon, Italy, Jordan, Syria, Iraq, Cuba, Iran, Brazil, Dominican Repub., Austria, Greece, Rep. of China.
Leisure interests: hiking, walking, spiritual exercises, discussion with friends.
Publs. *War and Peace* 50, *Problems of Asia* 51, *Problem of Coexistence* 55, *Christ and Crisis* 62, *Man in the Struggle for Peace* 63, *God and Man in Contemporary Christian Thought* 70, *God and Man in Contemporary Islamic Thought* 72; numerous other published works and articles.
American University, Beirut, Lebanon; and Harvard Club, 27 West 44th Street, New York, U.S.A.

Malikyar, Abdullah; Afghan diplomatist; b. 1909; ed. Isteklal Coll., Kabul, and Franco-Persian Coll., Teheran.
Secretary and Gen. Dir. Prime Minister's Office 31-35; Head, Govt. Purchasing Office, Europe 36-40; Vice-Pres. Central Bank and Deputy Minister of Commerce 41-42; Gov. of Herat 42-47, 51-52; Minister of Communications 48-50; Pres. Hillmand Valley Authority Projects 53-62; Minister of Commerce 55-57, of Finance 57-June 64, Deputy Prime Minister 63-Feb. 64; Acting Prime Minister Feb.-June 64; Amb. to U.K. 64-67, to U.S.A. 67-; Sardar Ali Reshteen Decoration.
Afghan Embassy, 2001 24th Street, N.W., Washington, D.C., U.S.A.

Mallowan, Sir Max Edgar Lucien, Kt., C.B.E., M.A., D.LIT., F.B.A., F.S.A.; British archaeologist; b. 6 May 1904; ed. Lancing and New Coll. Oxford.
Expeditions Ur of the Chaldees 25-30, Nineveh 31-32, Arpachiyah 33, Chagar Bazar and Brak 34-38, Balikh Valley 38, Nimrud 49-57; Wing Commdr. R.A.F.V.R.; Adviser Arab Affairs, Tripolitania; Pres. British School of Archaeology, Iraq, and Editor of the journal *Iraq* 47-71; Pres. British Inst. of Persian Studies 62-; Prof. Western Asiatic Archaeology, Univ. of London 47-62, Prof. Emeritus 62-; Fellow of All Souls Coll., Oxford 62-71; corresp. mem. Arab Acad., Baghdad 54; Schweich Lecturer, British Acad. 55; Lucy Wharton Drexel Medal for Archaeological Research 57; Lawrence of Arabia Memorial Medal, Royal Central Asian Soc. 69; fmr. Editor of Near-Eastern and Western Asiatic Series of Penguin Books; foreign mem. Acad. des Inscriptions et Belles-Lettres 64; Hon. Fellow, New Coll., Oxford 73.
Publs. *Prehistoric Assyria, Excavations at Chagar Bazar, Excavations in the Balikh Valley, Excavations at Brak, Excavations at Nimrud, Twenty-Five Years of Mesopotamian Discovery, Early Mesopotamia and Iran, Nimrud and Its Remains, Ivories in Assyrian Style.*
Winterbrook House, Wallingford, Berkshire, England.

Mammeri, Mouloud; Algerian writer; b. 28 Dec.1917; ed. Rabat, Algiers and Paris.
Director Inst. of Ethnology, Univ. of Algiers; mem. Algerian Writers' Union.
Publs. Novels: in French *La colline oubliée* 52, *Le Sommeil du juste* 55, *L'opium et le bâton* 65; Play: *Le Foehn* 67; *Les isefra de Si Mohand* (collection of oral poems in Berber).
Institut d'Ethnologie, Faculté des Lettres, Université d'Alger, Algiers, Algeria.

Mansour, Ali Ali, LL.B., LL.M.; Egyptian judge; b. 25 Nov. 1902; ed. Cairo Univ.
Member of Parl. for Cairo 44-45; Dir. of Litigation Dept. Ministry of Awqaf, Cairo 46-48; Counsellor of the Egyptian Council of State 49-55; Pres. Court of Appeal, Tanta 55-60, Cairo 60-64; mem. Supreme Council for Islamic Affairs 60-69, Chair. Cttee. of Scientific Experts and Cttee. of Islamic Heritage 60-69; Chief Justice, Supreme Court of Libya 69; Bikawiyya Order, First Class 46.
Publs. *Islamic Law and International Law: A comparative analysis* 62, *Constitutional and Administrative Systems in Islamic Law and Positive Laws: A comparative analysis* 64, *Introduction to Legal Sciences and Islamic Jurisprudence* 67, *Religions and Personal Status Laws* 68, *Comparison Between Islamic Law and Positive Laws* 70; several legal treatises and dissertations in magazines and periodicals.
15 Share' An-Nabatat, Garden City, Cairo, Egypt.

Mansour, Ibrahim Moneim; Sudanese politician; b. 1933, Nuhud; ed. Alexandria Univ.
Formerly with Ministry of Commerce and The Agricultural Bank; Deputy Dir. Khartoum Textile Co. 64; Dir. Sudan Textile Factory; Gen. Man. Gulf Int. Corpn.; Minister of Economy and Trade Oct. 71-73, of Nat. Economy and the Treasury 73-.
Ministry of the National Economy, Khartoum, Sudan.

Marei, Sayed; Egyptian agriculturalist and politician; b. 26 Aug. 1913; ed. Faculty of Agriculture, Cairo Univ.
Worked on his father's farm after graduation; subsequently with import-export, pharmaceutical, seed, and fertilizer

companies; mem. Egyptian House of Commons 44; Del. mem. Higher Cttee. for Agrarian Reform 52-; Chair. of Board, Agricultural Co-operative Credit Bank 55-; initiated "Supervised Credit System"; Minister of State for Agrarian Reform 56-57; Minister of Agriculture and Agrarian Reform 57-58; Central Minister for Agricultural and Agrarian Reform in the U.A.R. 58-61; Dep. Speaker, Nat. Assembly and Man. Dir. Bank Misr, Cairo 62-67; Minister of Agriculture and Agrarian Reform 67-70; Deputy Premier for Agriculture and Irrigation 72-73; Personal Asst. to Pres. Sadat 73-; First Sec. Arab Socialist Union (ASU) 72-73.
Publs. *Agrarian Reform in Egypt* 57, *U.A.R. Agriculture Enters a New Age* 60, *Food Production in Developing Countries* 68.
Office of the President, Cairo; and 9 Sh. Shagaret El Dorr, Zamalek, Cairo, Egypt.

Martin, Jean-Pierre, PH.D.; French United Nations official; b. 2 Jan. 1926; ed. Univs. of Montpellier and Paris.
Economist, UN Dept. of Econ. and Social Affairs 49-60; Special Asst. to the Special Rep. of Sec.-Gen. of UN in Congo 60-61; Chief, Financial Policies and Institutions Section. UN Dept. of Econ. and Social Affairs 61-62; Chef de Cabinet of Under-Sec.-Gen. of UN for Econ. and Social Affairs 62-66; Dir. UN Econ. and Social Office, Beirut 66-.
Publs. *Les Finances de Guerre du Canada* 51, *Les Finances publiques britanniques 1939-1955* 56; articles on financial and econ. subjects.
United Nations, B.P. 4656, Beirut, Lebanon.

Mashayekh Faridani, Mohammed Hossein, M.A., PH.D.; Iranian diplomatist and educationist; b. 1914; ed. Pahlavi Coll., Darolfonoon Coll. and Teheran Univ.
Lecturer in Literature and Philosophy, Teheran 40-44; Technical Inspector, Teheran Secondary Schools 44-46; Dir. of Cultural Dept., Ministry of Education 46; Editor, Education and Instruction Magazine 46; Cultural Counsellor, Karachi 48-52, New Delhi 52-55; Cultural Adviser, Ministry of Foreign Affairs 55-56; Dir. of Cultural Relations, Ministry of Foreign Affairs 57, Dir. of Public Relations and Editor of Magazine 57, Dir. Asian Countries Dept. 58; Minister-Counsellor, Baghdad 59-63; Ambassador to Iraq 63-64; Political Dir.-Gen., Ministry of Foreign Affairs 64; Amb. to Saudi Arabia 64-68, to Pakistan 69-; several decorations from Iran, Pakistan, Holland and Jordan.
Imperial Embassy of Iran, 37 Sixth Avenue, Ramna 6, Islamabad, Pakistan.

Mashour, Ahmed Mashour; Egyptian engineer; b. April 1918; ed. Cairo Univ., Staff Officers Coll. U.K., and Fort Belvoir, U.S.A.
With Ministry of Transport 41; Army Engineer 42; Lecturer at Egyptian Acad. of War 48-52; Staff Officer Egyptian Corps of Engineers; Dir. of Transit, Suez Canal Authority 56; mem. Board of Dirs. Timsah Shipbuilding Co., Ismailia; Chair. and Man. Dir. Suez Canal Authority 65-; various decorations.
Suez Canal Authority, Ismailia, Egypt.

Masmoudi, Mohamed, LL.B.; Tunisian politician; b. 29 May 1925; ed. Tunis and Univ. of Paris.
Member of Tunisian Nationalist Movement 34-; Minister of State in Govt. negotiating Tunisian independence 53-55; Minister of the Economy 55-56; Amb. to France 56-58, 61-70; Minister of Information 58-61; Sec.-Gen. Destour Socialist Party 69-; Minister of Foreign Affairs 70-; assoc. with *Action*, later renamed *Afrique Action*.
Ministry of Foreign Affairs, Tunis; and La Manouba, Tunis, Tunisia.

Massoudi, Abbas; Iranian publisher; b. 1901.
Founded daily *Ettela'at* 25; Propr. and Pres. of *Ettela'at* and its other publications; Vice-Pres. Iranian Senate; numerous articles.
Ettela'at, Kh. Kayyam, Teheran, Iran.

Mavrommatis, Andreas; Cypriot lawyer and politician; b. 1932, Larnaca; ed. Greek Gymnasium, Limassol, and Lincoln's Inn, London.
Called to Bar 54; practised law, Cyprus 54-58; Magistrate, Paphos 58-60; District Judge 60; District Judge, Nicosia 64-70; Minister of Labour and Social Insurance 70-72.
c/o Ministry of Labour and Social Insurance, Nicosia, Cyprus.

Maximos V Hakim, (fmrly. **Archbishop George S. Hakim**), D.D.; Lebanese ecclesiastic; b. 18 May 1908; ed. St. Louis School, Tanta, Holy Family Jesuit School, Cairo and St. Anne Seminary, Jerusalem.
Teacher Patriarchal School, Beirut 30-31; Rector and Principal Patriarchal School, Cairo 31-43; Archbishop of Acre, Haifa, Nazareth and all Galilee 43-67; elected Patriarch of Antioch and all the East, Alexandria and Jerusalem Nov. 67; founded *Le Lien*, (French) Cairo 36, *Ar-Rabita* (Arabic) Haifa 43; Commdr. Légion d'Honneur; Dr. h.c. (Laval Univ. Canada and many U.S. univs.)
Publ. *Pages d'Evangile lues en Galilée* (transl. into English Dutch and Spanish) 54.
Greek Catholic Patriarchate, P.O. Box 50076, Beirut, Lebanon.

Mazar, Benjamin, D.PHIL.; Russian-born Israeli archaeologist; b. 28 June 1906; ed. Berlin and Giessen Univs.
Settled in Palestine 29; joined staff of Hebrew Univ. Jerusalem 43, Prof. of Biblical History and Historical Geography of Palestine 51-, Rector 52-61, Pres. 53-61, Pro-Rector 61-; Chair. Israel Exploration Soc.; Dir. excavations Ramat Rahel 32, Beth Shearim 36-40, Beth Yerah 42-43, Tell Qasile 48-50, 59, Ein Ged 60, 62, 64, 65, Old City of Jerusalem 68-73; Hon. mem. British Soc. for Old Testament Study, American Soc. of Biblical Literature and Exegesis; Hon. D.H.L. Hebrew Union Coll. (Jewish Inst. of Religion, U.S.A.), Jewish Theological Seminary of America.
Publs. *Untersuchungen zur alten Geschichte Syriens und Palästinas* 30, *History of Archaeological Research in Palestine* 36, *History of Palestine from the early days to the Israelite Kingdom* 38, *Beth Shearim Excavations 1936-40* 40 (2nd edn. 58), *Historical Atlas of Palestine: Israel in Biblical Times* 41, *Excavations at Tell Qasile* 51; Chair. Editorial Board *Encyclopaedia Biblica* 50, *Ein Gedi* 64, *The World History of the Jewish People Vol. II* 67.
Hebrew University of Jerusalem, Jerusalem; and 9 Abarbanel Street, Jerusalem, Israel.

Mazidi, Feisal, B.ECON.; Kuwaiti economist; b. 1933; ed. Kuwait and Univ. Coll. of N. Staffordshire, Keele, England.
Appointed to Dept. of Finance and Economy 59; Dir. State Chlorine and Salt Board; Dir. Kuwait Oil Co. Ltd. 60; Econ. Asst. to Minister of Finance and Economy 60; Chair. Econ. and Industrial Cttee. 61; Dir. Kuwait Fund for Econ. Development of Arab Countries 62; mem. Kuwait Univ. Higher Council 62-64; Chair. and Man. Dir. Kuwait Chemical Fertilizer Co. 64-71; Chair. Govt. Oil Concession Cttee. 63-, Govt. Refinery Cttee. 64-, Kuwait Maritime Mercantile Co. 65-; Dir. Petrochemical Industries Co. 63-71, Kuwait United Fisheries 71-; Pres. Kuwait Associated Consultants 71-.
KASCON, P.O. Box 5443, Kuwait.

Mboro, Clement; Sudanese politician; b. *c.* 1920.
Joined Govt. Service 40, rose to Deputy Gov. Darfur Province 64; Minister of Interior 64-65; Minister of Industry and Mining 68-69; mem. and fmr. Pres. Southern Front 64; mem. for Repatriation and Resettlement, High Exec. Council for the Southern Region 72-.
High Executive Council for the Southern Region, Juba, Sudan.

Medeghri, Ahmed; Algerian politician; b. 1935. Former mem. A.L.N. in Tunisia; Prefect, Tlemcen 62; Minister of Interior 62-64, 65-; mem. F.L.N. Political Bureau 64-; mem. Revolutionary Council June 65-.
Ministry of the Interior, Algiers, Algeria.

Mehedebi Bashir; Tunisian politician; b. 1912. Ambassador to Lebanon, Kuwait, Libya 65-70; Sec.-Gen. Ministry of Foreign Affairs 70-71; Minister of Defence 71-72; Amb. to U.K. 72-; mem. Political Bureau, Destour Socialist Party Oct. 71-.
Embassy of Tunisia, 29 Prince's Gate, London SW7 1QG, England.

Meir, Golda; Israeli politician; b. Kiev 3 May 1898; ed. Teachers' Seminary, Milwaukee, U.S.A.
Teacher and leading mem. Zionist Labour Party, Milwaukee; del. U.S. Section, World Jewish Congress until 21; emigrated to Palestine 21; joined Merhavia collective farm village; with Solel Boneh, Histadrut Contracting and Public Works Enterprise 24-26; Sec. Women's Labour Council of Histadrut 28; mem. Exec. and Secretariat, Fed. of Labour 29-34; Chair. Board of Dirs., Workers' Sick Fund 36; Head, Political Dept., Fed. of Labour; Mapai Del., Action Cttee., World Zionist Organization; mem. War Economic Advisory Council of Palestine Govt. 39; Head, Political Dept., Jewish Agency for Palestine, Jerusalem 46-48; Israel Minister to U.S.S.R. Aug. 48-April 49; Minister of Labour and Social Insurance 49-52, of Labour 52-56; Minister for Foreign Affairs June 56-66; Sec.-Gen. Mapai Feb. 66-68; Prime Minister 69-, Acting Minister of Justice June-Sept. 72; Hon. LL.D. (Brandeis Univ.) 73.
Office of the Prime Minister, Jerusalem, Israel.

Melen, Ferit; Turkish politician; b. 1906, Van; ed. School of Political Science, Univ. of Ankara.
District Officer, Local Admin. 31-33; Auditor, Ministry of Finance 33-43, Dir.-Gen. of Incomes 43-50; Deputy for Van (Repub. People's Party) 50-64; Minister of Finance 62-65; Senator for Van 64-67; mem. Council of Europe 66-67; participated in formation of Nat. Reliance Party 67, now Deputy Leader; Minister of Nat. Defence 71-72; Prime Minister May 72-73.
Republican Reliance Party, Ankara, Turkey.

Melikishvili, Georgy Alexandrovich; Soviet (Georgian) historian; b. 30 Dec. 1918; ed. Tbilisi Univ.
Works deal with the ancient history of the Near East and Transcaucasia; Prof. Tbilisi Univ.; Dir. Dept. of Ancient History, Historical Inst. of Georgian Acad. of Sciences; mem. Acad. of Sciences of Georgian S.S.R. 60-; Lenin Prize 57.
Publs. *Nairi-Urartu* 54, *Urartian Inscriptions in Cuneiform Characters* 60, *History of Ancient Georgia* 59.
Academy of Sciences, Tbilisi, Georgian S.S.R., U.S.S.R.

Mellink, Machteld Johanna, PH.D.; Netherlands archaeologist; b. 26 Oct. 1917; ed. Amsterdam and Utrecht Univs.
Field Asst. Tarsus excavations 47-49; Asst. Prof. of Classical Archæology Bryn Mawr Coll. 49-53, Assoc. Prof., Chair. Dept. of Classical and Near Eastern Archæology 53-62, Prof. 62-; staff mem. Gordion excavations organised by Pennsylvania Univ. Museum 50-, during which the putative tomb of King Midas was discovered 57; field dir. excavations at Karataş-Semayük in Lycia 63-, excavations of painted tombs in Elmali district 70-.
Publs. *Hyakinthos* 43, *A Hittite Cemetery at Gordion* 56; *Archaeology in Asia Minor* (reports in *American Journal of Archaeology*) 55-, editor *Dark Ages and Nomads c. 1000 B.C.*
Department of Classical and Near Eastern Archaeology, Bryn Mawr College, Bryn Mawr, Pa. 19010, U.S.A.

Memmi, Albert; Tunisian writer; b. 15 Dec. 1920; ed. Lycée Carnot, Tunis, Univ. of Algiers and Univ. de Paris.
Teacher of Philosophy in Tunis 55; Dir. Psychological Centre, Tunis 56; Researcher, Centre national de la recherche scientifique, Paris 59-; Asst. Prof. Ecole pratique des hautes études 59-66, Prof. 66-70; Prof. Univ. of Paris 70-; Commdr. Ordre de Nichan Iftikhar; Palmes Académiques.
Publs. include: *The Pillar of Salt* 53, *Strangers* 55, *Anthologie des écrivains nord-africains* 55, *Colonizer, Colonized* 57, *Portrait of a Jew* 62, *Le français et le racisme* 65, *The Liberation of the Jew* 66, *The Dominated Man* 68, *Le Scorpion* 69.
5 rue Saint Merri, Paris 4e, France.

Menemencioğlu, Turgut; Turkish diplomatist; b. 1914; ed. Robert Coll., Istanbul, and Geneva Univ.
Turkish Ministry of Foreign Affairs 39-; Perm. Del., European Office UN, Geneva 50-52; Counsellor, Turkish Embassy, Washington 52; Dir. Gen. Econ. Affairs, Ministry of Foreign Affairs 52-54; Dep. Perm. Rep. to UN 54-60; Ambassador to Canada 60; Perm. Rep. to UN 60-62; Amb. to U.S.A. 62-66; High Political Adviser Ministry of Foreign Affairs 67; Sec.-Gen. Central Treaty Org. 68-71; Adviser, Ministry of Foreign Affairs 71-72; Amb. to U.K. Nov. 72-.
Turkish Embassy, 43 Belgrave Square, London SW1X 8PA; and 69 Portland Place, London, W.1, England.

Méouchi, Badri Selim, L. en D.; Lebanese judge; b. 1 Dec. 1902, Beirut; ed. Univ. of St. Joseph, Beirut.
Magistrate 27; Pres. of Court of First Instance 29-39; Judge, Court of Appeal, Beirut 39-46; Pres. Court of First Instance, Beirut 46; Pres. Court of Appeal, Beirut 46-50; First Pres. Court of Cassation 50-66; Pres. Conseil Supérieur de la Magistrature; Minister of the Interior and of Nat. Defence 66-68; Advocat à la Cour 68; Grand Officier, Ordre National de Cèdre; Grand Officier de Jordani, de Haïti.
Court of Cassation, Palais de Justice, Beirut, Lebanon.

Meouchi, H.E. Cardinal Paul Pierre; Lebanese ecclesiastic; b. 1894.
Ordained priest 17; fmr. pastor in New Bedford, Mass. and Los Angeles; Bishop of Tyre 34-55; Patriarch of the Maronites 55-; Asst. at the Papal Throne; created Cardinal 65.
Winter: Patriarcat Maronite, Bkerké, Lebanon; Summer: Patriarcat Maronite, El-Diman, Lebanon.

Merlin, Samuel; Israeli author and director of political studies; b. 17 Jan. 1910; ed. Lycée, Kishineff, Univ. of Paris.
Secretary-General World Exec., Zionist Revisionist and New Zionist Org. 34-38; Editor-in-Chief Yiddish daily *Di Tat*, Warsaw, Poland 38-39; Sec.-Gen. Hebrew Cttee. for Nat. Liberation 40-48; mem. First Knesset 48-51; Pres. Israel Press Ltd. 50-57; Dir. of Political Studies, Inst. for Mediterranean Affairs, N.Y. 57-; Lecturer, Middle East Studies, Fairleigh Dickinson Univ., N.J. 71-; Hon. mem. of Abu Gosh village near Jerusalem.
Publs. *The Palestine Refugee Problem* 58, *United States Policy in the Middle East* 60, *The Ascent of Man* (Co-Author) 63, *The Cyprus Dilemma* (Editor) 67, *The Big Powers and the Present Crisis in the Middle East* 68, *The Search for Peace in the Middle East* 69, *Guerre et Paix au Moyen Orient* 70.
Institute for Mediterranean Affairs, 1078 Madison Avenue, New York, N.Y. 10028, U.S.A.

Merzban, Mohammed Abdullah, M.A.; Egyptian politician; b. 20 Jan. 1918, Fayoum; ed. Fuad Univ. and Harvard Univ.
Lecturer, Faculty of Commerce, Cairo Univ. until 56; Sec.-Gen. Ministry of Industry 56-58; Gen. Man. Industrialization Authority 58-60; Chair. Al-Nasr. Org. 60-61; Chair. Spinning & Weaving Org. 61-66; Chair. Bank of Cairo 66-68; Minister of Supply and Home Trade 68-70; Minister of Economy and Foreign Trade 70-73, also acting Minister of Supply and Home Trade 71-73.

Publs. *Financial Management, Sales Management, Mathematics of Marketing.*
c/o People's Assembly, Cairo, Egypt.

Mesnil du Buisson, Robert du, Count, D. ès L., D. en D.; French archaeologist; b. 19 April 1895.
Dir. French Archaeological Missions in Syria, Egypt and France; Lecturer Ecole des Hautes Etudes 38-; Head Archaeological Mission, Centre Nat. de la Recherche Scientifique, Palmyra 65-; Pres. Société Nat. des Antiquaires de France 46-47; Pres. Société Historique et Archéologique de l'Orne 47-55, Hon. Pres. 56-; Pres. Soc. du Manoir d'Argentelles 57-; Dir. Centre Culturel et Touristique de l'Orne 67-; Vice-Pres. Fédération des Sociétés normandes 47-55, Soc. d'Ethnographie de Paris 60-69, Pres. 69-; Commdr. of Legion of Honour 46; Lauréat Acad. des Inscriptions et Belles-Lettres 40, 63, Acad. des Beaux-Arts 58.
Publs. *Les Ruines d'El-Mishrifé au Nord-Est de Homs* 27, *La Technique des fouilles archéologiques* 33, *Le Site Archéologique de Mishrifé-Qatna* 35, *Les noms et signes égyptiens désignant des vases* 35, *Souran et Tell Masin* 35, *Le Site de Qadesh* 36, *Inscriptions juives de Doura-Europos* 37, *Inventaire des inscriptions palmyréniennes de Doura-Europos* 39, *Les peintures de la Synagogue de Doura 245-256 ap. J.-C.* 39, *Tessères et monnaies de Palmyre* 44, *Les ouvrages du siège a Doura-Europos* 45, *Le site archéologique d'Exmes (Uxoma)* 46, *Le sautoir d'Atargatis et la chaîne d'amulettes* 47, *Baghouz, l'ancienne Corsôté* 48, *Une voie commerciale de haute antiquité dans l'Orne* 51, *Les dieux et les déesses en forme de vase dans L'Antiquité Orientale, La palissade gauloise d'Alençon* 52, *L'alcôve royale dite "Lit de Justice d'Argentelles"* 53, *Un constructeur du Château de la Celle-Saint-Cloud, Jacques Jérémie Roussel* 54, *Les barques de la Grande Pyramide et le voyage au Paradis* 56, *Les enceintes gauloises d'Alençon* 58, *Inscriptions sur jarres de Doura-Europos* 59, *Une famille de Chevaliers de Malte, Les Costart* 60, *Le vrai nom de Bôl, prédécesseur de Bêl, à Palmyre* 61, *Les Tessères et les monnaies de Palmyre de la Bibliothèque Nationale* 62, *Origine et évolution du Panthéon de Tyr, Les Chaussons de la Salle* 63, *Les origines du Panthéon Palmyrénien* 64, *Le dieu-Griffon à Palmyre et chez les Hittites* 65, *Le dieu Ousô sur des monnaies de Tyr* 65, *Le drame des deux étoiles du matin et du soir dans l'antiquité orientale* 67, *Les origines du mythe animalier de la planète Vénus, Une ancienne famille de Normandie les du Mesnil du Buisson* 68, *Etudes sur les dieux phéniciens* 70, *Nouvelles études sur les dieux et les mythes de Canaan* 73.
63 rue de Varenne, Paris 7e; and Château de Champobert, par Exmes (Orne), France.

Messadi, Mahmoud; Tunisian politician and writer; b. 28 Jan. 1911; ed. Univ. of Paris.
Secretary of State for Educ. 58-68; mem. Nat. Assembly 59-; mem. Political Bureau Destour Socialist Party 64-70; Minister of State 69-70.
Publ. *Le Barrage* (play).
Destour Socialist Party, 10 rue de Rome, Tunis, Tunisia.

Mestiri, Ahmed; Tunisian politician; b. 1925, Marsa.
Member of Central Cttee. of Néo-Destour Party 52-64, of Destour Socialist Party 64-68, 70; expelled from the Party 68, 71, Jan. 72; Ministerial Sec. 54-55; Sec. of State for Justice 56-58; Sec. of State for Finance and Commerce 58-60; Amb. to U.S.S.R., U.A.R., Algeria 60-66; Sec. of State for Defence 66-68; Minister of the Interior 70-71.
c/o Ministry of the Interior, Tunis, Tunisia.

Mestiri, Mahmoud; Tunisian diplomatist; b. 25 Dec. 1929; ed. Inst. d'Etudes Politiques, Univ. de Lyons.
Served in several Tunisian Dels. to UN; Alt. Rep. to UN 58, 59; Head of Tunisian special Diplomatic Mission to Congo (Léopoldville) 60; Asst. to Personal Rep. of UN Sec.-Gen. to Govt. of Belgium 61; Deputy Perm. Rep. of Tunisia to UN 62-65; Sec.-Gen. for Foreign Affairs, Tunis 65-67; Perm. Rep. to UN 67-69; Chair. UN Special Cttee. on the Situation with Regard to Implementation of Declaration on the Granting of Independence to Colonial Countries and Peoples 68; Amb. to Belgium Sept. 69, to Luxembourg Oct. 69, to EEC Nov. 69, to Germany Jan. 71-.
Embassy of Tunisia, Kölnerstr. 103, Bonn-Bad Godesberg, Germany.

Meulen, Daniel van der; Netherlands author and explorer; b. 1894; ed. Arnhem, and Univ. of Leyden.
Dutch East India Civil Service 15-23, 32-41, 45-48; Neths. Consul, Jeddah 26-31; Minister to Saudi Arabia 41-45; Adviser to Lieut. Gov.-Gen. van Mook, Java 45-48; organiser and leader Arabic broadcasts, Neths. Radio, Hilversum 48-50; exploration of S.W. Arabia 31, 39, 43, 52, 58-59, 62-63, 64, 67, 71, 72; hon. mem. Netherlands Royal Geographical Soc.; Patron's Medal, Royal Geographical Soc., London 47; Order Orange Nassau (Neths.).
Publs. *Hadhramaut, Some of its Mysteries Unveiled* 32, *Aden to The Hadhramaut* in English 47, Swedish and German, *Onbekend Arabië* 51, *Ontwakend Arabië* 53, *The Life Story of King Ibn Saud of Saudi Arabia* (in Indonesian, Dutch and English) 52, revised edn. 57, re-titled *The Wells of Ibn Saud, Faces in Shem* 61, *Ik Stond Erbij* (Dutch) 64, *Verdwynend Arabië, Myn Weg Naar Arabië en de Islam.*
9 Flierderweg, Gorssel, Netherlands.

Mhaidi, Kadhim Abdul Hamid al-; Iraqi businessman; b. 12 Feb. 1922; ed. College of Law, Baghdad, England and U.S.A.
Director-General Baghdad Chamber of Commerce, until 63; Gen.-Man. Exhibitions Org. 63; Gen.-Man. Bank of Baghdad 64-65; Minister of Econ. July-Sept. 65; Chair. of Board and the Gen. Trade Establishment 66; Minister of Economy 66-67; Econ. Adviser of the Baghdad Chamber of Commerce 68; Sec.-Gen. Fed. of Iraqi Chambers of Commerce April 69-.
Federation of Iraqi Chambers of Commerce, Munstansir Street, Baghdad, Iraq.

Michałowski, Kazimierz; Polish archaeologist; b. 14 Dec. 1901.
Prof. of Mediterranean Archæology, Warsaw Univ.; mem. Presidium, Polish Acad. of Sciences; mem. numerous foreign acads. and scientific socs.; Vice-Dir. Warsaw Nat. Museum; in charge of Franco-Polish excavations, Egypt 37-39, Polish excavations, Crimea 56-58, Egypt 57-, Syria 59-, Sudan 62-, Cyprus 65-; Chair. Int. Working Group of Archaeologists and Landscape Architects, Abu Simbel; Pres. Soc. for Nubian Studies; Dir. of Polish Centre of Archaeology, Cairo; Prix de l'Acad. des Inscriptions et Belles Lettres 33; State Prize 55, 66; Dr. h.c. (Strasbourg and Cambridge), etc.
Publs. *Les portraits hellénistiques et romains* 32, *Fouilles Franco-Polonaises à Tell Edfou* 37-50, *Mirmeki* 56, *Fouilles Polonaises à Palmyre* 60-64, *Fouilles Polonaises à Faras* 62-65, *Die Kathedrale aus dem Wüstensand* 67, *L'Art de l'Egypte Ancienne* 68 (English edn. 69).
Sewerynów 6, Warsaw, Poland.

Mili, Mohamed; Tunisian civil servant; b. 4 Dec. 1917; ed. Ecole Normale Supérieure de Saint-Cloud and Ecole Nationale Supérieure des Télécommunications, Paris.
Telecommunications Engineer, Ministry of Posts 47-56; Dir.-Gen. of Telecommunications 57-65; Vice-Pres. Plan for Africa, Union Int. des Télécommunications (UIT) 60-64; Pres. Admin. Council 64, Pres. Plan for Africa UIT 64-65, Vice-Sec.-Gen. UIT 65-66, Sec.-Gen. 66-; Commdr. Ordre de la République (Tunisia), Commdr. Order of Vasa (Sweden), Officier Ordre de l'Indépendance (Tunisia),

Gran Cruz del Orden de Duarte, Sánchez y Mella con Placa de Platá (Dominican Repub.).
Union Internationale des Télécommunications, Place des Nations, 1211 Geneva 20, Switzerland.

Mirfenderesky, Ahmad, L.L.B.; Iranian diplomatist; b. 1918; ed. French Univ., Beirut.
Career with Ministry of Foreign Affairs 42-, served U.S.S.R., Netherlands, India, Turkey; Dir. Dept. of Econ. Affairs, Second Political Dept., Political Dir.-Gen. 62-64; Deputy Minister, Political and Parl. Depts. 64-65; Ambassador to U.S.S.R. Oct. 65-71; now Deputy Minister for Foreign Affairs.
Ministry of Foreign Affairs, Teheran, Iran.

Mirghani, Abdel Karim, B.A.; Sudanese politician: b. 1 Jan. 1924; ed. Omdurman Intermediate School, Gordon Memorial Coll., Univ. of Bristol.
Sub-mamour 46-48; teacher in nat. schools 48-53; joined Ministry of Foreign Affairs 56 as Chargé d'Affairs in London, later Head, Political Section, Khartoum; mem. Sudan del. to the Admission of Sudan to the UN 56; Deputy Perm. Rep. of Sudan to UN, N.Y. 58-60; Amb. of Sudan to India, Japan, Ceylon 60-64; Minister of Commerce, Industry, Supply and Co-operation 64; Amb. to Italy 65, to Greece 66, to U.A.R. 68; Minister of Econs. and Foreign Trade May-Oct. 69; Minister of Planning Oct. 69-Nov. 70.
c/o Ministry of Planning, Khartoum, Sudan.

Mirghani, Mohamed; Sudanese journalist; b. 1932; ed. Univ. of Besançon and London School of Journalism.
Foreign News Editor, Al Ayam Press House 49-58; Man Regional News Services and Reuters, Khartoum 58-; Sudan Corresp. for Reuters and *Daily* and *Sunday Telegraph*, contributor to B.B.C. programmes.
Regional News Services, P.O. Box 972, Khartoum, Sudan.

Moalla, Mansour, L. EN D., L. ÈS L., LL.D.; Tunisian economist; b. 1 May 1930, Sfax; ed. Inst. des Etudes Politiques, Ecole Nat. d'Administration, Paris.
Inspecteur des Finances 56; Technical Adviser, Ministry of Finance 57-58; Dir.-Gen. Banque Centrale de Tunisie 58-61; Dir. of Admin., Office of the Pres. 61-63, 68-69; Dir. Ecole Nat. d'Administration (ENA) 63-67; Under-Sec. of State, Ministry of Commerce and Industry 67-68; Sec. of State (then Minister) for Posts, Telegraphs and Telecommunications (PTT) 69-70; Deputy Minister in charge of the Nat. Plan 70-71, Minister Oct. 71-; mem. Cen. Cttee., Political Bureau, Destour Socialist Party 71-; Grand Cordon, Order of the Repub.; Officer, Order of Independence.
Ministère du Plan, 1 rue de Béja, Tunis; Home: 32 avenue de la République, Carthage, Tunisia.

Mohammed Zahir Shah; King of Afghanistan; b. 15 Oct. 1914; ed. Habibia High School, Istiqlal Coll. (both in Kabul), Lycée Janson-de-Sailly and Univ. of Montpellier, France.
Graduated with highest honours; attended Infantry Officers' School, Kabul 32; married Lady Homira, Nov. 4th 1931; children, Princess Bilqis, Prince Ahmad Shah Khan, Princess Maryam, Prince Mohammed Nadir Khan, Prince Shah Mahmoud Khan, Prince Mohammed Daoud Jan, Prince Mirvis Jan; Asst. Min. in Ministry of Nat. Defence 32-33; acting Minister of Educ. 33; crowned King Nov. 8th, 33, deposed July 73.
c/o Dilkusha, Royal Palace, Kabul, Afghanistan.

Mohieddin, Zakaria; Egyptian army officer and politician; b. May 1918; ed. Mil. Coll. and Staff Officers' Coll., Cairo.
Former lecturer Mil. Coll. and Staff Officers' Coll. and Dir.-Gen. Intelligence; Minister of the Interior 53-58; Minister of the Interior U.A.R. 58-62, Vice-Pres. U.A.R. and Chair. Aswan Dam Cttee. 61-62; mem. Nat. Defence Cttee. 62-, Presidency Council 62-64; mem. Exec. Cttee. Arab Socialist Union 64-; Deputy Prime Minister 64-65, June 67-68; Prime Minister and Minister of the Interior 65-66.
c/o Arab Socialist Union, Cairo, Egypt.

Moini, Amir-Ghassem; Iranian mechanical engineer and politician; b. June 1925; ed. Teheran Univ.
Ministry of Labour and Social Affairs 47-; Teheran Labour Dept.; Deputy Head Inspection Office; Acting Head of Fars Prov. Labour Dept., later Head; Deputy Head Teheran Branch of Workers' Social Insurance Org.; Deputy Dir.-Gen. Employment Services, later Dir.-Gen.; Sec.-Gen. Graduate Guidance Org.; Technical Under-Sec., Ministry of Labour and Social Affairs; mem. Board of Dirs. Social Insurance Org.; mem. Parl.; Acting Sec.-Gen. Iran Novin Party 71-; Minister of Labour and Social Affairs 73-; Homayoun Medal of Third Order.
Ministry of Labour and Social Affairs, 457 Avenue Eisenhower, Teheran, Iraq.

Mokaddem, Sadok; Tunisian diplomatist; b. 1914; ed. Lycée Carnot, Tunis, Faculty of Sciences, Montpellier and Faculty of Medicine, Paris.
Physician, Tunis; mem. Néo-Destour 34-, mem. Political Bureau 52-; Sec. of State for Justice 54-55, for Public Health 55-56; mem. to Constituent Ass. 56-59, mem. Nat. Assembly 59-; Ambassador to Egypt 56-57; Sec. of State for Foreign Affairs 57-62; Ambassador to France 62-64; Pres. Nat. Assembly Nov. 64; Chair. Destour Socialist Party 70-; Grand Cordon of Nat. Order of Independence, Grand Cordon, Nat. Order of the Repub.; several foreign decorations.
National Assembly, Palais du Bardo, Tunis, Tunisia.

Mokady, Moshe; Israeli artist; b. 1902; ed. Vienna, Zürich and Paris.
Went to Palestine 20; taught music, painting, Vienna 24-25, Paris 27-33, France, Belgium and Sweden 46-47, U.S.A. 48; Dir. of Arts, Ministry of Education and Culture, Govt. of Israel 51-52; paintings in several museums in Europe, U.S.A., Egypt and Israel and in many private collections.
4 Liebermann Street, Tel-Aviv, Israel.

Moses, Siegfried, DR. JUR.; Israeli (b. German) lawyer and administrator; b. 3 May 1887; ed. Univ. of Berlin.
Began law practice 12; organised food control, Danzig, during First World War; later Man. Dir. Deutscher Städtetag (organization of German towns); Chair. Reichstelle für Schuh-Versorgung (Controller of Footwear Supply); law practice 20-36; Dir .Schocken concern (chain stores) 23-29, mem. Board 30, Chair. 35; emigrated 36; Man. Dir. Haavara (organization for transfer of Jewish property from Germany to Palestine) 37; expert on tax problems 41-49; Public Auditor, Tel-Aviv 38-49; State Comptroller of Israel 49-61; Pres. Zionist Organization for Germany 33-37, Council of Jews from Germany 57-, Leo Baeck Inst. of Jews from Germany 55-; mem. Board of Van Leer Jerusalem Foundation, Bank Leumi le-Israel 62-, ATA Co. 62-; Dr. phil. h.c.
Publs. *Deutsches Kohlen-Wirtschaftsgesetz* 20, *Reform des Obligationen-Wesens* 33, *The Income Tax Ordinance of Palestine* 42 (2nd edn. 46), *Jewish Post-War Claims* 44, etc.
Shlomo Molchostr. 9, Jerusalem, Israel.

Mosevics, Mark; Israeli industrialist; b. 22 Aug. 1920; ed. Dulwich Coll., London, Jesus Coll., Cambridge, England, Hebrew Univ. Jerusalem.
Chairman Board of Dirs., Israel Export Inst. 66-68; Chair. Board of Dirs., Israel Industrial Bank 68-72, mem. Board of Dirs. 72-; Chair. Board of Dirs., Elite Chocolate and Sweets Mfg. Co. Ltd., Co-ordinating Bureau of Econ. Orgs. 68-; Pres. Mfrs. Asscn. of Israel 69-; mem. Board of Dirs. Israel Corpn. Ltd. 70-; Chair. Board, First Int. Bank of Israel 73-; mem. Presidium, Prime Minister's 3rd Econ.

Conf.; Hon. Pres. A'KIM (Appeal for Retarded Children) 72-.
Elite Chocolate and Sweets Manufacturing Co. Ltd., P.O. Box 19, Tel-Aviv; and 7 Wisotsky Street, Tel-Aviv, Israel.

Mostofi, Khosrow, M.A., PH.D.; Iranian professor; b. 8 July 1921; ed. Univs. of Teheran and Utah.
Assistant Prof. Political Science, Portland State Univ. 58-60, Univ. of Utah 60-65; Acting Dir. Inst. of Int. Studies, Univ. of Utah 62-63; Assoc. Prof., Univ. of Utah. 65-70, Prof. 70-; Acting Chair. Dept. of Political Science 67; Dir. Middle East Center, Univ. of Utah 67-; Fulbright-Hays Fellow, Turkey and Iran 65-66; Research Fellow, Univ. of Utah 66-68; Board mem. American Inst. of Iranian Studies 68-, Exec. Cttee. 71-; Co-Dir. American Center for Iranian Studies in Teheran 70; mem. N.D.F.L. Panel of Consultants, U.S.O.E. 68-70, American Asscn. of Univ. Profs., American Acad. of Political Sciences, Western Political Science Asscn.
Publs. *Suez Dispute: A Case Study of a Treaty* 57, *Aspects of Nationalism: The Sociology of Colonial Revolt* 64, *Parsee Nameh: A Persian Reader in 8 Vols.* Vol. I, II 63, 4th edn. Vol. I 69.
Room 19, Middle East Center, University of Utah, Salt Lake City, Utah 84112; Home: 2481 East 13th South Street, Salt Lake City, Utah 84108, U.S.A.

Moulay Hassan Ben El Mehdi, H.R.H. Prince, (Uncle of King Hassan II); Moroccan diplomatist; b. 1911.
Caliph Northern Zone of Morocco 25; Amb. to Great Britain 57-64, to Italy 64-67; now Gov. Banque du Maroc; decorations include, Ouissam Alaoui, Charles I Medal, Great Military Ouissam, Great Medal of Portugal, Great Dominican Medal, Great Naval Medal, Great Mahdaoui Medal, Great Houssni Medal.
Banque du Maroc, 277 avenue Mohammed V, Rabat, Morocco.

Mounayer, H.E. Eustache Joseph, D. CN. L.; Syrian ecclesiastic; b. 6 June 1925; ed. Seminary of Benedictine Fathers, Jerusalem, Patriarchal Seminary, Charfé, Lebanon and Pontifical Univ. of Latran, Rome.
Ordained priest 49; Sec. of Archbishop of Damascus 54-59, concurrently Sec. of Apostolic Nunzio, Pres. ecclesiastic court; Sec. of Cardinal Tappouni 59-71; consecrated bishop 71; Patriarchal Auxiliary Bishop 71-.
Publs. *Les Synodes Syriens Jacobites* (in French), *Le Schihim* (in Arabic).
Patriarcat Syrien Catholique d'Antioche, Beirut, Lebanon.

Mousa, Omer al-Hajj; Sudanese politician; b. 1924, El Kowa; ed. Gordon Memorial Coll. and Mil. Coll.
Former army officer, Dir. of Gen. Staff until 69; Minister of Nat. Guidance 69-71, of Information and Culture Oct. 71-73.
c/o Ministry of Information and Culture, Khartoum, Sudan.

Moussalli, Paul Michel Négib, LIC. en D.; Lebanese lawyer and United Nations official; b. 9 April 1932; ed. Lycée français de garçons, Beirut, Faculty of Law, Beirut, Univ. of Lyons, France, Max Planck Inst. für Ausländisches Öffentliches Recht und Völkerrecht, Heidelberg, Germany, and Graduate Inst. of Int. Studies, Geneva, Switzerland.
Legal Adviser, Office of UN High Commr. for Refugees (UNHCR), Geneva 61-62; UNHCR Rep. for Tunisia 62; UNHCR Rep. at Tripartite Repatriation Comm. (Algerian refugees) 62; UNHCR Rep. for Algeria 62-63; UNHCR Legal Adviser, Geneva (questions relating to refugees in Africa and Asia) 63-66; UNHCR Regional Rep. for Africa 66-70; Acting Dir. of Admin. and Management, UNHCR, Geneva 71-.
Office of United Nations High Commissioner for Refugees, Palais des Nations, Geneva, Switzerland.

Mubarak, Mousa al-, M.A.; Sudanese politician; b. Abu Si'id, Omdurman; ed. Univs. of London and Khartoum.
Former schoolteacher; Lecturer in History, Univ. of Khartoum; mem. Parl. (Nat. Unionist Party) 65-68, (Democratic Unionist Party) 68-69; Minister of Industry and Mineral Resources May 69-Aug. 71; Minister of Labour Aug.-Oct. 71; Minister of State for Premiership Affairs 71-72; Minister of the Treasury 72.
c/o Council of Ministers, Khartoum, Sudan.

Mudhaf, Muhalhel Mohamed al-; Kuwaiti diplomatist; ed. in schools in Kuwait, Egypt and U.K.
Member staff Ministry of Education 53-61; Chargé d'Affaires, Lebanon 62-64, Syria 64-65; Amb. to Pakistan 65-67; Perm. Rep. to UN 67-71.
c/o Ministry of Foreign Affairs, Kuwait City, Kuwait.

Müezzinoğlu, Ziya; Turkish civil servant and diplomatist; b. 5 May 1919; ed. Ankara Univ.
Inspector of Finance, Turkish Ministry of Finance 42-53; Adviser to Treasury, Ministry of Finance 53-59; Dir.-Gen. of Treasury 59-60; Dir.-Gen. of Treasury and Sec.-Gen. Org. for Int. Econ. Co-operation in Turkey 60; mem. Constituent Assembly 60; Chair. Interministerial Cttee. for Foreign Econ. Relations 62; Sec. of State of State Planning Org. 62-64; Amb. to Fed. Repub. of Germany 64-67; Amb., Perm. Del. to EEC 67; Minister of Finance May 72-73; mem. Nat. Security Council.
Ministry of Finance, Ankara, Turkey.

Mufti, Ebrahim el; Sudanese politician.
Minister of Finance and Econ. May-July 65; Deputy Prime Minister and Minister of Foreign Affairs 66-67; Minister of Irrigation and Hydro-Electric Power 68-71.
c/o Ministry of Irrigation, Khartoum, Sudan.

Mufti, Said el-; Jordanian politician; b. 1898; ed. Turkish School, Damascus.
Governor of Amman 25, 39; Mayor of Amman 27, 38; mem. First Legislative Council 29, 31; Head of Treasury 39; Minister of Communications 44; Minister of Interior 44, 48; Minister of Finance and Communications 45; Deputy 47, 51 and 54; Minister of Commerce and Agriculture 47; Prime Minister and Minister of Foreign Affairs 55; Prime Minister 56; Deputy Prime Minister and Minister of Interior and Agriculture 57; Pres. of Senate 58; Deputy Prime Minister 63; Pres. of Senate 63-; mem. Consultative Council 67-; Jordan Medal of Independence First Class, Jordan Star First Class, and many others.
The Senate, Amman, Jordan.

Müftüoğlu, Sadık Tekin; Turkish politician; b. 1927, Çaycuma, Zonguldak.
Member of Parl. for Zonguldak 65-; Minister of Commerce 66-67, of State 67-69, of Finance 73-; Justice Party.
Ministry of Finance, Ankara, Turkey.

Muhammad, Ali Nasser; Yemeni politician; b. 1944, Dafia rural district.
Active mem. of Nat. Liberation Front (NLF) 63-67; Gov. Second Province 67-69; Minister of Local Govt. and Agriculture April 69; Minister of Defence Dec. 69-; mem. Exec. Council, Nat. Liberation Front Gen. Command Aug. 70; Prime Minister Aug. 71-.
Office of the Prime Minister, Aden, People's Democratic Republic of Yemen.

Mumcuoğlu, Hayri; Turkish lawyer; b. 1914, Istanbul; ed. secondary schools, Istanbul.
Assistant Judge, Bartın 37; Judge for Penal Affairs, Akçaabat, Saframbolu; Asst. Prosecutor, Ankara; Judge, Chief Prosecutor of the Repub.; Chief Prosecutor, Ministry of Justice; mem. Court of Cassation; mem. Parl. for Tekirdağ (New Turkey Party) 61; Minister of Housing and

Reconstruction 63; joined Repub. People's Party 67, resigned 72; Minister of Justice 73-; Independent.
Ministry of Justice, Ankara, Turkey.

Muntasser, Dr. Omar Mahmud; Libyan politician and diplomatist; b. 28 July 1930; ed. Univs. of Florence and Oxford.
Minister, Libyan Embassy, Washington 60-61, London 61-62; Minister of Justice, Libya 62-63, 63-64, of Foreign Affairs 63; Ambassador to U.K., concurrently to the Netherlands 64-69, and Malta 66-69; now Under-Sec. for Petroleum.
Ministry of Petroleum, P.O. Box 256, Tripoli, Libya.

Muntasser, Saddiqh al; Libyan diplomatist; b. 17 Dec. 1913; ed. High School in Libya, and Oriental Univ., Naples, Italy.
Posts held include: District Officer of S. Desert Area, District Commr. of Misurata District, Provincial Commr. of E. Provinces, Under-Sec. of Communications of Govt. of Tripolitania, Governor-Gen., Rep. of King Idris I, Tripolitania; Amb. to U.S.A., Chief of Libyan Del. to UN, Amb. to U.A.R. and to Saudi Arabia, Chief of Libyan Del. to Arab League, Minister of Defence; business positions held include: Chair. Commercial Bank S.A.L., Tripoli, Libya Texas and Oil & Refining Co. Ltd., Gordon Woodroffe Co. Libya Ltd., Latco (Libyan Agency and Trading Co.), Lavco (Libyan Aviation Co.); Rep. of Richard Costain Civil Engineering Ltd., Costain and Press, Tripe and Wakeham; Amb. to German Fed. Repub. 67-71, to Switzerland 68-71; decorations from Libya and Egypt.
c/o Ministry of Foreign Affairs, Tripoli, Libya.

N

Nabi, Belkacem; Algerian oil executive.
Director of Energy and Oils, Ministry of Industry and Energy, Algeria until 66; Président-Directeur Général Soc. Nat. de Recherche et d'Exploitation des Pétroles en Algérie (S.N. REPAL) 66-; Adviser to Minister of Finance 66-70; Wali de Tlemcen 70.
S.N. REPAL, Algiers, Algeria.

Nabulsi, Omar, L. EN D., M.A.; Jordanian politician; b. 1 April 1936, Nablus; ed. Cairo and Ain Shams Univs.
Legal Adviser, Masco Petroleum Co., Libya 59-61; Political Attaché, Arab League 61-70; Asst. Head, Admin. Section, Royal Hashemite Court Jan.-Sept. 70; Minister of Nat. Economy 70-72; Amb., Ministry of Foreign Affairs 72; Amb. to U.K. 72-73; Minister of Agriculture 73-; Order of Al-Kawkab (First Class).
Ministry of Agriculture, Amman, Jordan.

Nabulsi, Suleiman; Jordanian diplomatist and politician; b. 1910; ed. American Univ. Beirut.
Bank official and Man. till 46; Minister of Finance and Economics 46-47 and 50-51; Ambassador to London 53-54 (resigned); leader Nat. Socialist Party; Prime Minister and Foreign Minister Oct. 56-April 57; mem. Consultative Council 67; Chair. Jordanian Cttee. for Afro-Asian Solidarity; mem. World Peace Council; Orders of Nahda and of Istiqlal, Jordan Star.
c/o Ministry of Foreign Affairs, Amman, Jordan.

Naffah, Fouad Georges, LIC. EN DROIT; Lebanese lawyer; b. 1 March 1925, Zouk Mikhaël; ed. Coll. des Frères Maristes, Coll. d'Antoura, Univ. St. Joseph, Beirut.
Elected Deputy for Kesrouan 60, 72; Lecturer in Constitutional Law and Lebanese Constitution, Coll. de la Sagesse and Univ. Libanaise; Minister of Agriculture March-May 72, of Finance May-July 72, of Foreign Affairs July 72-.
Ministère des Affaires Etrangères, Beirut; Home: Raouché, Beirut, Lebanon.
Telephone: 233561 (Office); 314333 (Home).

Naficy, Said; Iranian writer; b. 1896; ed. France and Persia.
Professor, Faculty of Arts, Teheran Univ. 36; mem. Iranian Acad.; Visiting Prof. Univs. in America, Lebanon, Germany, India, etc.; Hon. Prof. Univ. of Kabul.
Publs. 220 including *History of Persian Literature, Social History of Iran.*
Rue Naficy, Avenue Hedayat, Teheran; and University of Teheran, Iran.

Naggar, Abd el Moneim el; Egyptian army officer and diplomatist; b. 1920; ed. Cairo Military Academy, Cairo Staff Academy, Cairo Univ. and Inst. de Hautes Etudes, Univ. of Paris.
Egyptian Army 39-57; Military Attaché, Paris 53-54, Madrid 55-57; Head of East European Dept., Ministry of Foreign Affairs, Cairo 58; U.A.R. Consul-General, Bombay 59-62, Hong Kong 62-63; Ambassador to Greece 63-64, to France 64-68; Minister of Foreign Affairs 69-71; Amb. to Iraq 72; numerous decorations.
Embassy of Egypt, Baghdad, Iraq.

Nahavandi, Houshang, L. EN D., DR. ECON. SC.; Iranian economist, educationist and politician; b. 1930; ed. Univ. of Paris.
Adviser to High Council of Econs. 58-61, to Ministry of Labour 59-61; Econ. Attaché, Iranian Embassy, Brussels 61-63; Deputy Head, Del. to European Econ. Community 62-63; Man. Dir. Foreign Trade Co. 63-64; Minister of Housing and Devt. 64-68; Chancellor Pahlavi Univ. 68-71, Univ. of Teheran 71-; Civil Aide-de-Camp to H.I.M. The Shahanshah Aryamehr; mem. Board of Trustees, Mashad Univ., Charity Foundation of H.I.H. Princess Shams, High Council of Nat. Soc. for the Protection of Animals, High Council for Nat. Educ.; Chevalier Légion d'Honneur (France); Commdr. Ordre de la Couronne (Belgium); Homayoun Decoration 1st Class, 4th Class; Sepasse Decoration and several other awards.
Publs. numerous books and articles.
University of Teheran, Teheran, Iran.

Najar, Amiel Emile, LIC. en DR.; Israeli diplomatist; b. 6 Sept. 1912; ed. Univ. of Paris.
President of Exec., Zionist Fed. of Egypt 43-47; Dir. Western European Div., Ministry of Foreign Affairs 52-57, Asst. Dir.-Gen. Ministry of Foreign Affairs 57-58; Minister to Japan 58-60; Ambassador to Belgium and Luxembourg, Chief of Mission to the European Communities 61-68; mem. Israeli Del. to UN 48, 51-53, 55-57, 61, 64, 67, 70; Observer, Suez Conf., London 56; Amb. to Italy 68-, concurrently to Malta 68-71.
Embassy of Israel, Via M. Mercati 12, Rome, Italy.

Najjar, Joseph; Lebanese engineer and politician; b. 1908; ed. Univ. St. Joseph, Beirut, Ecole Nat. des Ponts et Chaussées, Paris.
Consultant to Ministry of Interior 33-38; Dir. Hydraulic Service 38-40; Sec. of State to Ministry of Finance 40-41; mem. Planning Council 52-64; mem. Admin. Council, Office of Electricity 59-64; Prof. of Higher Engineering School, Beirut 41-; Pres. Nat. Scientific Research Council 63-; Minister of Planning, Agriculture, Posts and Telegraphs July 65-66; Perm. Rep. to UNESCO 66-67; Minister of Posts and Telegraphs 67-68; Ordre du Mérite Libanais, 1er classe; Officier Légion d'Honneur, etc.
c/o Ministry of Posts and Telegraphs, Beirut, Lebanon.

Nakhai, Hossein Ghods, G.C.V.O.; Iranian diplomatist; ed. Coll. of Political Sciences, Teheran.
Counsellor, Iranian Embassy, Washington 34, London 42; Dir.-Gen. Ministry of Foreign Affairs 50; Deputy Minister and Acting Minister of Foreign Affairs 50; Iranian Ambassador to Iraq 51 and 53, to Japan 56-58, to Great Britain 58-61; Minister of Foreign Affairs 61-62; Amb. to U.S.A. 62-63; Minister of the Imperial Court 63-67; Amb. to Vatican 67-70; Homayoun Order (1st Class).

Publs. *Rubaiyat* (in Persian and English), *God and Man, The Development of Personality, The Shahsavan's Daughter, Paradise, Lady of the Isles* (in English).
c/o Ministry of Foreign Affairs, Teheran, Iran.

Nashashibi, Nasser Eddin; Egyptian (b. Palestine) editor and diplomatist; b. 1924; ed. Arab Coll., Jerusalem and American Univ. Beirut.
Arab Office, Jerusalem 45-47; Chief Chamberlain, Amman 51; Dir.-Gen. Hashemite Broadcasting 52; Roving Editor *Akhbar El Yom*, Cairo; Chief Editor *Al Gomhouria*, Cairo 59-65; Roving Rep. of the Arab League June 65-67; Roving Dip. Editor *Al-Ahram*, Cairo; Jordanian Independence Star, 1st degree.
Publs. *Steps in Britain* (Arabic) 48, *What Happened in the Middle East* 58, *Short Political Stories* 59, *Return Ticket to Palestine* 60, *Some Sand* (Arabic) 62, *An Arab in China* (Arabic and English) 64.
38 Rue Athenée, Geneva, Switzerland.

Nasir, Mohammed, B.SC., M.A., ED.D.; Iraqi educator and diplomatist; b. 1911; ed. Teacher Training Coll., Baghdad, American Univ., Beirut and Columbia Univ., New York.
Schoolteacher 31-32; Prof. of Educ. and Dean of Coll. of Educ., Baghdad Univ. 41-45, 55-63; Cultural Attaché and Perm. Rep. of Iraq to Arab League Cultural Comm. 45-48; Cultural Attaché, Washington 48-54; Alternate Del. to UN 5th Gen. Assembly; Pres. Teachers Union of Iraq 63-64; mem. Council, Univ. of Baghdad 63-64; Minister of Educ. 64; Ambassador to U.S.S.R. Nov. 64-66; Minister of Culture and Nat. Orientation 66; Prof. of Educational Admin., Kuwait Univ. 67-.
Publs. include many school books in Arabic, *Arabic Readings* (2 vols., joint author) 40, *Civic Education* (joint author) 40, *Guide to Higher Education in the U.S.A.* 58.
c/o Kuwait University, P.O. Box 5969, Kuwait.

Nassiri, Gen. Ne'matollah; Iranian army officer; b. 1910; ed. Teheran Military Acad.
Early career in army posts including Chief, Mil. Police HQ 49, Commdr. Pahlavi Infantry Regiment 50, Imperial Guards 51; arrested Mossadegh under Shahanshah's orders 53; promoted to rank of Maj.-Gen. 58, Lt.-Gen. 62, Gen. 71; Deputy Mil ADC to Shahanshah Aryamehr 60; Chief of Police 61-65; Mil. Gov., Teheran 63; Head, State Security and Intelligence Org. (SAVAK) and Asst. to Prime Minister 65-.
SAVAK, Teheran, Iran.

Nassif, Albert; Lebanese lawyer and diplomatist; b. 1915; ed. Univs. of Cairo and Paris.
Studied Law and Political Economy, Paris, also journalist, Egypt, Lebanon, and French Equatorial Africa 36-44; ed. journal *Le Jour* 44-47; Lecturer, Faculty of Law, Beirut 45-47; 2nd Sec., Lebanese Legation, Vatican 47-50; 1st Sec., Lebanese Legation, Switzerland 50-53; Counsellor, Lebanese Embassy, France 53-55; Head of Social and Cultural Dept., Lebanese Ministry of Foreign Affairs 56; Counsellor, London 57-59; Ambassador to Liberia 59-61, to India 61-63, to Turkey 63-65; Dir. Int. Dept., Ministry of Foreign Affairs 66-69; Amb. to Tunisia 69-71, to Switzerland Nov. 71-; Commdr. Order of St. Grégoire; Chevalier Légion d'Honneur; Officer Order of the Cedar (Lebanon), Ordine al Merito della Repubblica Italiana, Chevalier, Ordre Humain de la Libération Africaine.
Publs. political, economic and legal studies.
18 Marienstrasse, Berne, Switzerland.

Natra, Sergiu; Israeli composer; b. 1924, Romania; ed. National Conservatoire, Bucharest.
Settled in Israel 61; G. Enesco Prize 45, State Prize 51, Engel Prize 69.
Works include: *March and Chorale* 44, *Suite for Orchestra* 48, *Sinfonia* 60, *Music for Violin and Harp* 60, *Toccata for Orchestra* 63, *Music for Harpsichord and Six Instruments* 64, *Sonatina for Harp* 65, *Voices of Fire* (ballet music), *Music for Oboe and Strings* 65, *Prelude for Narrator and Orchestra*, *Commentary on Nehemia*, *Song of Deborah for Mezzo-Soprano and Chamber Orchestra* 67, *Prayer for Harp* 70, *Trio in One Movement for Violin, Violincello and Piano* 71, *Dedication: Two Poems for Mezzo-Soprano and Orchestra* 72.
10 Barth Street, Ramat Aviv, Tel-Aviv, Israel.

Nawwar, Maj.-Gen. Ali Abu; Jordanian army officer and diplomatist.
Chief of Staff, Jordanian army 56; in exile in Egypt 57-64; Personal Rep. of King Hussein Oct. 70-Feb. 71; Amb. at Ministry of Foreign Affairs May 70; Amb. to France 71-, also accred. to Belgium.
Jordanian Embassy, 80 boulevard Maurice Barrès, 92 Neuilly sur Seine, France.

Nebenzahl, Itzhak Ernst, DR.IUR.; Israeli administrator; b. 24 Oct. 1907; ed. Univs. of Frankfurt and Freiburg.
Settled in Palestine 33; Dir. Jerusalem Econ. Corpn. 47-61, Jerusalem Devt. Dept., Jewish Agency 48-50, Bank Leumi le-Israel Ltd. 56-61; Hon. Consul-Gen. of Sweden 52-62; Chair. Post Office Bank 54-61, of Advisory Cttee. and Council, Bank of Israel 57-62; State Comptroller of Israel 61, re-elected 66, 71-; Pres. Fifth Int. Congress of Int. Org. of Supreme Audit Insts. (INTOSAI) 65, Chair. 65-68, now mem. Gov. Board; Public Complaints Commr. (Ombudsman) 71-; fmr. mem. Petroleum Board, Anti-Trust Council, and several govt. inquiry cttees.; Partner, Hollander Concern (Stockholm, New York, London, Buenos Aires, Paris, Tokyo, etc.), Chair. Board of Dirs. 47-61; Chevalier (First Class), Royal Swedish Order of Vasa 57.
Office of the State Comptroller, P.O. Box 1081, Jerusalem; Home: 9 Batei Mahse Street, Old City, Jerusalem, Israel.

Ne'eman, Yuval, B.SC., DIP. ING., D.E.M., D.I.C., PH.D.; Israeli soldier and scientist; b. 14 May 1925; ed. Herzlia High School, Tel-Aviv, Israel Inst. of Technology, Haifa, Ecole Supérieure de Guerre, Paris, and London Univ.
Hydrodynamics Design Engineer 45; in Hagana 46; Captain, Israeli Defence Forces (Infantry) 48, Major 49, Lieut.-Col. 50, Col. 55; Defence Attaché, London 58-60; joined Israel Atomic Energy Establishments 60, Scientific Dir., Soreq Research Establishment 61-63; Head, Physics Dept., Tel-Aviv Univ. 62-, Prof. of Physics 64-; Research Fellow, Calif. Inst. of Technology 63, Visiting Prof. of Physics 64-65; Vice-Rector and Vice-Pres., Tel-Aviv Univ. 65-66, Pres. 71-; mem. Israel Atomic Energy Comm. 66-, Israel Nat. Acad. of Sciences 66-; known mainly for his co-discovery of Unitary Symmetry (The Eightfold Way) 61; Foreign Hon. mem., American Acad. of Arts and Sciences 70; Foreign Assoc., Nat. Acad. of Sciences, U.S.A. 72; Hon. D.Sc.; Weizmann Prize for the Sciences 66, Rothschild Prize 68, Israel Prize for Exact Sciences 69; Albert Einstein Medal and Prize (U.S.A.) 70.
Publs. *The Eightfold Way* (with M. Gell-Mann) 64, *Algebraic Theory of Particle Physics* 67.
Department of Physics and Astronomy, Tel-Aviv University, Tel-Aviv, Israel.

Negahban, Ezatollah, B.A., M.A., PH.D.; Iranian archaeologist; b. 1 March 1925; ed. Teheran and Chicago Univs.
Assoc. Prof. Univ. of Teheran 56-62, Prof. 62-, Dir. Univ. Inst. of Archaeology 58-; Technical Dir. Iranian Archaeological Service 60-65; Technical Adviser to Ministry of Culture 65-; Hon. mem. German Archaeological Inst.; mem. Perm. Council, Congress of Pre- and Protohistoric Archaeology; excavated at Marlik 61-62, Haft Tepe; Dir. Iranian Archaeological (Iran Bastan) Museum 66-.
Publs. *The Gold Treasures of Marlik* 62, *Preliminary Report on Marlik Excavation* 64.
Darband, Teheran, Iran.

Neguib, Gen. Mohamed; Egyptian army officer; b. Khartoum 1901; ed. Sudan Schools, Gordon Coll., Khartoum, Royal Mil. Acad. and Egyptian Univ., Cairo.
Commissioned in infantry 17; served in Gen. Staff, Adjutant-Gen. and Q.M.-Gens'. departments during Second World War; Sub-Governor of Sinai and Governor of Red Sea Provinces in Frontier Corps; Col. Commdg. 2nd Machine Gun Bn.; Brig., 2nd in commd. of Egyptian troops in Palestine and commdg. successively 1st, 2nd, 3rd, 4th and 10th Inf. Bdes. during hostilities with Israel 48; Dir.-Gen. Frontier Corps 50, Dir.-Gen. Infantry 51, C.-in-C. Egyptian Army July 52; Prime Minister, Minister for War and Marine, C.-in-C. of the Army and Military Gov. of Egypt Sept. 52-53; President of the Republic of Egypt June 53-December 54.
Cairo, Egypt.

Nekrouf, Younès, L. ès L.; Moroccan diplomatist; b. 1916; ed. Inst. des Hautes Etudes Marocaines, Rabat and Univs. of Bordeaux and Algiers.
Government Interpreter 35-39; School Teacher and Inspector of Schools 39-55; Dir. de Cabinet to Minister of Education 55-57; Cultural Counsellor, Moroccan Embassy, Paris, and Perm. Del. to UNESCO 57-59; Dir. Cultural Affairs and Technical Assistance, Ministry of Foreign Affairs 59-61; Counsellor, then Minister Plenipotentiary, Paris 61-64; Ambassador to Senegal 65-67, concurrently to the Gambia, Guinea and Liberia; Ambassador to Yugoslavia 67-68; Dir. Political Affairs, Ministry of Foreign Affairs 68-71; Amb. to India Jan. 71-; del. to UN Gen. Assembly 65, 68-71; Moroccan Rep. to several int. confs.; Officier, Légion d'Honneur; Palmes Académiques, France; Ouissame Alaouite, Morocco; Officier, Ordre du Trône, Morocco; Grand Officer, Nat. Order of Yugoslavia, Order of Tudor Vladimirescu of Romania; Knight of Grand Cross, Order of Merit of the Repub. of Italy.
Publ. *Méthode Active d'Arabe* (2 vols.) 58, various essays and articles on Portuguese colonization.
Embassy of Morocco, New Delhi, India.

Nemery, Maj.-Gen. Jaafar Mohammed al-; Sudanese army officer and political leader; b. 1 Jan. 1930, Omdurman; ed. Sudan Military Coll.
Former Commdr. Khartoum garrison; campaigns against rebels in Southern Sudan; placed under arrest on suspicion of plotting to overthrow the government; Chair. Revolutionary Command Council (R.C.C.) and C.-in-C. of Armed Forces May 69-; Prime Minister Oct. 69-, Minister of Foreign Affairs July 70-71, of Planning Oct. 71-72, of Defence; Pres. Political Bureau, Sudanese Socialist Union 71-; Pres. of Sudan Oct. 71-.
Office of the President, Khartoum, Sudan.

Newsom, David Dunlop, A.B., M.S.; American diplomatist; b. 6 Jan 1918; ed. Richmond Union High School and Calif. and Columbia Univs.
Reporter, *San Francisco Chronicle* 40-41; U.S. Navy 41-45; Newspaper publisher 45-47; Information Officer, U.S. Embassy, Karachi 47-50; Consul, Oslo 50-51; Public Affairs Officer, U.S. Embassy, Baghdad 51-55; Dept. of State 55-59; U.S. Nat. War Coll. 59-60; First Sec., U.S. Embassy, London 60-62; Dir. Office of Northern African Affairs, State Dept. 62-65; Amb. to Libya 65-69; Asst. Sec. of State for African Affairs 69-; Dept. of State Meritorious Service Award 58, Nat. Civil Service League Career Service Award 71.
Department of State, Washington, D.C., U.S.A.

Niamir, Kazem; Iranian diplomatist; b. 1914; ed. Sarvat Coll., Teheran, and Teheran and London Univs.
Court of Justice Teheran 34-37; Ministry of Foreign Affairs 38-; served London 40-46; Political Adviser to Iranian UN Mission 46; Ministry of Foreign Affairs 46-48; Counsellor New Delhi 49-52; Chief of Cultural Dept., Ministry of Foreign Affairs 52-54; Minister-Counsellor to Japan 54-58; Chief Third Political Dept. of Ministry of Foreign Affairs 59-63; Amb. to Jordan 63-65; mem. Ministry of Foreign Affairs High Political Council 66; Sec.-Gen. of the Iranian Asscn. for the UN 66-70; Amb. to Ethiopia 71-; numerous Iranian and foreign decorations.
Publs. *Treaty of Versailles and after* 37, *Demography* 37, *Political Organisation of Japan* 55.
Imperial Embassy of Iran, Ras Desta Damten Avenue, Addis Ababa, Ethiopia.

Nissim, Isaac; Israeli Rabbi; b. 1896 Baghdad.
In Israel since 25; advocates consolidation of the various Jewish tribes into one single community; elected Rishon le Zion and Chief Rabbi (Sephardi) of Israel Feb. 55, installed March 55 until 72; Pres. Rabbinical High Court 55-72; Pres. Beth Hamidrash le Rabbanim Ule-Dayanim, Jerusalem.
Publs. *Yen Hatov, Canogah Zidkah Umishpat*.
Office of the Rishon Le-Zion, The Chief Rabbi of Israel, Jerusalem, Israel.

Nofal, Sayed, DR. ARTS; Egyptian international civil servant; b. 1910; ed. Cairo Univ.
Head of Literary Dept. *Al Siyassa* 35-38; Teacher, Cairo Univ. 38; later Dir. of Technical Secr., Ministry of Educ. and Ministry of Social Affairs; later Dir. of Legislative Dept., Upper House of Egyptian Parl.; later Dir. Political Dept., League of Arab States, Asst. Sec.-Gen. 60-.
Publs. include *Poetry of Nature in Arabic and Western Literature* 44, *Egypt in the United Nations* 47, *The Egyptian Parliament in a Quarter of a Century* 51, *The Political Status of the Emirates of the Arab Gulf and Southern Arabia* 59, *The Arab-Israeli Conflict* 62, *Arab Unity* 64, *Arab Nationalism* 65, *Arab Socialism* 66, *The Record of Israel* 66, *Joint Arab Action Book I* 68, *Book II* 71, *The Arab Gulf or The Eastern Borders of the Arab Homeland* 69, *An Introduction to Israeli Foreign Policy* 72.
League of Arab States, Midan Al Tahrir, Cairo; and 9 Khan Younis Street, Madinet al Mohandesseen, Dokki, Cairo, Egypt.

Noman, Ismail Said; Yemeni diplomatist; b. 1941, Aden; ed. Boston, Mass., U.S.A.
Instructor, Aden Coll. 67; Asst. Sec. Aden Electricity Corpn. 67-68; Amb. and Perm. Rep. to UN 68-70; Sales Man., Nat. Co. for Home Trade 70-72, Technical Man. June 72-.
Khalifa Street Block 31/72, Al-Mansorah, Aden, People's Democratic Republic of Yemen.

Noman, Muhammad Ahmed; Yemeni politician; b. 1933; ed. Taiz, Aden, Sana'a.
Leader of Shaf'i (Sunni) sect; fmr. leader Free Yemen Movement; Rep. to Arab League 64-65; mem. Political Bureau Jan.-April 64-; Vice-Pres. Exec. Council Feb.-April 64; Amb.-at-Large May 65-; Political Adviser to the Republican Council 70-; Prime Minister, Minister of Foreign Affairs May-July 71; Amb. to France 71-72; Deputy Prime Minister, Minister of Foreign Affairs Dec. 72-.
Ministry of Foreign Affairs, Sana'a, Yemen Arab Republic.

Nouira, Hedi; Tunisian politician; b. 1911, Monastir.
Secretary of Gen. Confed. of Tunisian Workers 38; in detention 38-42; Sec.-Gen. of Néo-Destour Party 42-54; Minister of Commerce 54-55; Minister of Finance 55-56; Dir. of Central Bank of Tunisia 58-70; Minister of the Economy 70; Prime Minister Nov. 70-.
Office of the Prime Minister, Tunis, Tunisia.

Noujaim, Gen. Jean; Lebanese army officer; b. 1915, Kesrwan; ed. Saida, Beirut, and Homs Military Acad., Syria.
Instructor, Homs Mil. Acad. 38-40; Chief of Fourth Bureau 42-43; Capt. and Commdr. of Mil. Acad. 45;

Commdr. intercommunications branch 46-51; Lt.-Col. 51; Col. 58; Commdr. Bekka Sector 62; Brig. 64; Commdr. Southern Lebanon and Western Sector of Israel front 66-68; Commdr. Bekka Sector and section of Israeli front 68-70; C.-in-C. of Army Jan. 70-; many Lebanese and foreign decorations.
c/o Ministry of Defence, Beirut, Lebanon.

Nowar, Ma'an Abu; Jordanian diplomat; b. 26 July 1928, Salt; ed. London Univ.
Joined Jordanian Arab Army 43, Commdr. Infantry Brigade 57-63; Counsellor, Jordanian Embassy, London 63; Dir. Jordan Civil Defence 64-67, Jordan Public Security 67-69; Asst. Chief of Staff for Gen. Affairs 69-72; Minister of Culture and Information 72; Amb. to U.K. 73-; Jordanian Star 1st Class.
Royal Jordan Embassy, 6 Upper Phillimore Gardens, London, W8 7HB, England.

Nur, Abdul Mohsen Abu al-; Egyptian politician; b. 4 Aug. 1918; ed. Egyptian Military Acad.
Fought in Palestine war 48-49; took part in revolution 52; subsequently served as Mil. Attaché, Egyptian embassies in Sudan, Syria, Lebanon; Deputy Commdr. of the First Army 58; Gov. of Suez (town); Minister of State for Land Reform 62, for Agrarian Reform and Land Reclamation 63; Deputy Prime Minister for Agriculture and Irrigation 64-68; Minister for Local Admin. 68; Deputy Sec.-Gen. Arab Socialist Union 67-70, Sec.-Gen. 70-May 71; sentenced to imprisonment for treason Dec. 71.
Cairo, Egypt.

Nurock, Mordekhai, O.B.E., M.A., LL.D. (HON.); Israeli diplomat; b. 1893; ed. Dublin Univ.
With British Colonial Admin. Service, Palestine 20-36, Uganda 37-45; with British Control Comm., Germany and Austria 45-49; Adviser on Personnel to Israel Govt. 49-51; Financial Sec. Hebrew Univ. 51-52; Israel Minister to Australia and New Zealand 53-58; Israel Chargé d'Affaires, South Africa 59; mem. Board of Govs. Hebrew Univ. 63-; Editor Govt. Year Book 63-; ranking Ambassador 64-; Adviser on Publications, Foreign Ministry.
Publs. *Fruits of the Holy Land* (co-author), *Words of the Wise* (co-author).
201 Elm Tree Court, St. John's Wood, London, N.W.8, England; and Ministry for Foreign Affairs, Jerusalem, Israel.

Nuseibeh, Anwar Zaki, M.A.; Jordanian diplomat and lawyer; b. 20 Jan. 1913; ed. Govt. Arab Coll., Jerusalem, and Queens Coll., Cambridge.
Land Officer, Palestine 36, Magistrate 37-42; Lecturer in Constitutional Law, Jerusalem Law Classes 36-48; fmr. mem. Jordan Parl. and Senator; Chief Arab Del., Jordan and Israel Mixed Armistice Comm. 51; Minister of Defence 53, of Educ. 54-55, of Reconstruction and Devt. 54-55; Gov. of Jerusalem, Jordan 61-62; Ambassador to U.K. 65-66; private business in Jordan 66-; Order of El Kawkab (1st Class); Assoc. Knight Order of St. John of Jerusalem; Knight of Order of Holy Sepulchre.
c/o Ministry of Foreign Affairs, Amman, Jordan.

Nuseibeh, Hazem, M.A., PH.D.; Jordanian politician; ed. Rawda Coll., Jerusalem, Victoria Coll., Alexandria, American Univ. of Beirut, Law School, Jerusalem, Woodrow Wilson School of Public and Int. Affairs and Princeton Univ.
Under-Secretary, Ministry of Nat. Econ. 57-59; Pres. Jordan Devt. Board 59-61; Minister of Foreign Affairs 62-63, 65-66; Minister of Royal Court 63-65; Prof. of Int. Affairs, Jordan Univ. 66-67; Minister of Reconstruction and Devt. 67-69; Amb. to Egypt 69-71, to Turkey 71-.
Publ. *Ideas of Arab Nationalism* 56.
Embassy of Jordan, Vali Dr. Resit, Dedekorkut 18, Cankaya-Ankara, Turkey.

Nutting, Rt. Hon. Sir (Harold) Anthony, Bt., P.C.; British politician and writer; b. 11 Jan. 1920; ed. Eton and Trinity Coll., Cambridge.
In British Foreign Service 40-45; mem. Parl. 45-56; Chair. Young Conservative and Unionist Movement 46, Nat. Union of Conservative and Unionist Asscns. 50, Conservative Nat. Exec. Cttee. 51; Parl. Under-Sec. of State for Foreign Affairs 51-54; Minister of State for Foreign Affairs 54-56 (resigned over British Suez policy); Leader, Brit. Del. to UN Gen. Assembly and UN Disarmament Comm. 54-56.
Publs. *I Saw for Myself* 58, *Disarmament* 59, *Europe Will Not Wait* 60, *Lawrence of Arabia* 61, *The Arabs* 64, *Gordon, Martyr and Misfit* 66, *No End of a Lesson* 67, *Scramble for Africa* 70, *Nasser* 72.
47 Addison Road, London, W.14, England.

O

Okasha, Sarwat Mahmoud Fahmy, D. ÈS L.; Egyptian diplomat, politician and banker; b. 1921; ed. Military Coll. and Cairo Univ.
Cavalry officer 39; took part in Palestine war 48-49; Mil. Attaché, Berne 53-54, Paris and Madrid 54-56; Attaché in Presidency of Republic 56-67; U.A.R. Ambassador to Italy 57-58; Minister of Culture and Nat. Guidance and Pres. of Supreme Council for Literature, Art and Social Sciences 58-62; Chair. Board of Dirs. of Nat. Bank of Egypt 62-; mem. UNESCO Exec. Board 62; mem. Nat. Assembly and Pres. Foreign Affairs Comm. 64-66; Deputy Prime Minister, Minister of Culture 66-68; Minister of Culture 68-71; Asst. to the Pres. 71-June 72; Pres. of Supreme Council for Literature, Art and Social Sciences; Pres. Egypt-France Asscn. 65-; numerous awards.
Publs. Nineteen works (incl. translations) since 42.
Villa 34, St. 14, Maadi, Cairo, Egypt.

Olcay, Osman; Turkish diplomat; b. 17 Jan. 1924; ed. St. Joseph French Coll., Istanbul, and Faculty of Political Science, Univ. of Ankara.
Joined Ministry of Foreign Affairs, Turkey 45; Lieut., Turkish Army 46; Foreign Ministry 47; Vice-Consul, London 48-50, Second Sec., London 50-52; Chief of Section, Dept. of Econ. Affairs, Ministry of Foreign Affairs 52-54; First Sec. NATO, Paris 54, Councellor and Deputy Perm. Rep. 58-59; Asst. Dir.-Gen. NATO Dept., Min. of Foreign Affairs, Ankara 59-60, Dir.-Gen. 60-63, Asst. Sec.-Gen. 63-64; Amb. to Finland 64-66, to India and Ceylon 66-68; Deputy Sec.-Gen. of NATO, Brussels 69-71; Minister of Foreign Affairs March-Oct. 71.
c/o Ministry of Foreign Affairs, Ankara, Turkey.

Ollendorff, Franz, DR. ING.; Israeli electrical engineer; b. 1900; ed. Technische Hochschule, Berlin, and Danzig.
Asst. Technische Hochschule, Danzig 22-24; Asst. to Chief Engineer, Siemens-Schuckert Werke A. G., Berlin 24-28; Lecturer, Technische Hochschule, Berlin-Charlottenberg 28-33; teacher in several high schools in Germany and Palestine 33-37; Prof. of Electrical Engineering, Haifa 37-, and former Dean of the Faculty; mem. Research Council of Israel; mem. Israel Acad. of Sciences and Humanities; Weizmann Prize 48; Israel State Prize 50.
Publs. *Die Grundlagen der Hochfrequenztechnik* 26, *Erdströme* 28, *Potentialfelder der Elektrotechnik* 32, *Die Welt der Vectoren* 50, *Technische Elektrodynamik I—Berechnung magnetischer Felder* 52, *II—Innere Elektronik des Feinzelelektrons* 52, *Gasentladungs-tabellen* (with Knoll and Rompe) 3 vols. 35.
15 Hillel Street, Haifa, Israel.

Osen, Bjørn; Danish United Nations official; b. 19 March 1930, Copenhagen; ed. Frederiksberg Gymnasium, Univ. of Copenhagen.
Worked for Asscn. for the Promotion of Int. Co-operation

54; joined Ministry of Foreign Affairs 55, served no. of posts including Principal Private Sec. to Minister of Foreign Affairs; Econ. Counsellor, Perm. Mission of Denmark to UN; Econ. Counsellor, Embassy of Denmark to U.S.A. -71; Resident Rep. UN Devt. Programme (UNDP) Afghanistan 71-.
United Nations Development Programme, P.O. Box 5, Kabul, Afghanistan.

Örek, Osman Nuri; Cypriot lawyer and politician; b. 1925; ed. Turkish Lycée, Nicosia, Univ. of Istanbul and Middle Temple, London.
Founder-mem. Cyprus-is-Turkish Asscn., London, Chair. 51-52; Sec. Nicosia Branch, Cyprus Turkish Nat. Union Party 53-55, Sec.-Gen. 55-July 60, Dep. Chair. July 60-; Dep. Chair. High Council of Evcaf 56-60; rep. Turkish Cypriot Community at London Conf. 59 and subsequent Joint Cttee.; Minister of Defence 59; mem. Exec. Council of Turkish Cypriot Provisional Admin. for Defence 67-, concurrently for Internal Affairs 67-70, and External Affairs 67-73.
Office of the Minister of Defence, 9 Server Somuncuoglu Street, Nicosia; Home: 10 Ismail Beyoglu Street, Nicosia, Cyprus.

Orgad, Ben Zion; Israeli composer; b. 1926, Germany; ed. Acad. of Music in Jerusalem and Brandeis Univ., U.S.A.
Studied violin with Kinory and Bergman and composition with Paul Ben-Haim and Josef Tal; studied in U.S.A. under Aaron Copland and Irving Fine; now Supervisor of Musical Educ., Israel Ministry of Educ. and Culture; recipient of several awards for compositions.
Compositions include: cantatas: *The Story of the Spies* (UNESCO Koussevitsky Prize 52), *Isiah's Vision*; works for orchestra, *Building a King's Stage, Choreographic Sketches, Movements on "A", Kaleidoscope, Music for Horn and Orchestra*; *Hatsvi Israel* (Symphony for baritone and orch.); *Out of the Dust* (for solo and instruments); *Ballada* (for violin), *Taksim* (for harp), *Monologue* (for viola); works for soloists and orchestra, songs, piano pieces, etc.
Ministry of Education and Culture, Hadar-Daphna Building, Tel-Aviv; Home: 14 Bloch Street, Tel-Aviv, Israel.

Osma, Şinasi; Turkish army officer and politician; b. 1913; ed. Military War Coll. and Gen. Staff Coll.
In various units and branches of the Armed Forces 42-50; Mil. Attaché at Amman and Baghdad 55-58; retd. from Army 60; co-founder, Justice Party 61, then Gen. Sec. for three years, now Pres. of its Central Cttee. of Arbitration and mem. of Central Exec. Cttee.; mem. for Izmir, Nat. Assembly 61-, also mem. Foreign Affairs and Defence Cttees., Nat. Assembly.
Yenşiehir Ferzi, Çakmak, Sokak 10/12, Ankara, Turkey.

Osman, Ahmed, LL.D.; Moroccan diplomatist and politician; b. 3 Jan. 1930; m. Princess Lallah Nezh; ed. Royal High School, Rabat, Univ. of Rabat and Univ. of Bordeaux, France.
Member of Royal Cabinet (judicial matters) 56; joined Ministry of Foreign Affairs 57; Sec.-Gen. Ministry of Nat. Defence 59-61; Amb. to Fed. Repub. of Germany 61-62; Under Sec.-of-State for Industry and Mines 63-64; Pres. and Gen. Man. Moroccan Navigation Co. 64-67; Ambassador to U.S.A., Canada and Mexico 67-70; Minister of Admin. Affairs 70-71; Dir. of Royal Cabinet 71-72; Prime Minister 72-; participated in UN sessions 57, 58, 60, 61, Conf. on Maritime Law 58, Conf. of the League of Arab States 61.
Office of the Prime Minister, Rabat, Morocco.
Telephone: 245 54-33804.

Osman, Hassan Mutwakil Mohamed; Sudanese cotton executive; b. Jan. 1918; ed. Coll. of Agriculture, Sudan.
Agriculturalist with Sudanese Dept. of Agriculture 42-48; Senior Officer Atbara Dairy 48-50; Insp. of Mechanized Crop Production 50-51; Insp. of Agriculture, Sennor and Fung Districts 51-54; Govt. Soil Conservation Officer 54-57; Asst. Dir. of Agriculture, Dept. of Agriculture 59-62, Deputy Dir. 63-65, Dir. Ministry of Agriculture 65-66; Dir. Sudan Gezira Board 64-66; mem. Council, Univ. of Khartoum and Board of Faculty of Agriculture 64-69; Man. Dir. and Chair. Sudan Gezira Board 66-70; Chair. Board of El Nilein Bank May 70-.
El Nilein Bank, P.O. Box 466, Khartoum, Sudan.

Osman, Osman Ahmed, B.SC.; Egyptian civil engineer; b. 1917; ed. Cairo Univ.
Chairman The Arab Contractors (Osman Ahmed Osman & Co.) 52-, and of its assoc. companies, Saudi Enterprises, Kuwaiti Engineering Co., The Libyan Co. for Contracting and Devt.; Medal (First Class), Egypt, Russian Hero of Labour Medal.
Chief works undertaken include: (in Egypt) Aswan High Dam, Suez Canal deepening and widening, Port Said Shipyard, Cairo Int. Airport, Salehaieh reclamation project, High Dam Electric Power Transmission Lines, Guiza Bridge, Ramses Bridge over the Nile; (in Saudi Arabia) Dhahran Airport, Riyadh Mil. Coll., Dammam Mil. Barracks; (in Kuwait) Municipality Centre, Kuwait drainage system; (in Libya) Benghazi drainage system, Benghazi Stadium; (in Iraq) Kirkuk Feeder Canal No. 2 and 3; (in Jordan) Khaled Ibn El-Walid Dam and Tunnels; (in Sudan) 200 bedroom First Class Hotel.
The Arab Contractors, 34 Adly Street, Cairo, Egypt.

Osman, Yacoub, LL.B.; Sudanese diplomatist; b. 1912; ed. Gordon Coll., Khartoum, Secondary School, Cairo and Leeds Univ.
Worked in aircraft factory in London in Second World War, also Arabic translator in British Broadcasting Corporation; returned to Sudan 45; joined independence movement, became Editor of *El-Nil* (daily of independence movement) and Asst. Gen. Sec. of Umma (Independence) Party; rep. independence movement in London; resigned from Umma Party 55; Perm. Rep. to UN 56-59; Ambassador to U.S.S.R. 59-64, also accred. to Czechoslovakia 64, to Ethiopia 64-.
c/o Ministry of Foreign Affairs, Khartoum, Sudan.

Osorio-Tafall, Bibiano F.; Mexican United Nations official; b. 1903, Spain; ed. Universities of Santiago and Madrid and Biologische Anstalt, Dahlen.
Government posts in Spain and prof. of several academic insts. in Spain and Mexico until 49; Fisheries Regional Officer for Latin America, Food and Agriculture Org. (FAO) 49-51, Dir. Regional Office for Western Latin America, Santiago, Chile 51-55, Chief, Technical Assistance Mission in Chile 55-56; Resident Rep. in Chile, UN Technical Assistance Board (now UN Devt. Programme UNDP) 56-59, in Indonesia 59-61, in U.A.R. 61-64; Resident Rep. UNDP, Dem. Repub. of Congo 64-66; Special Rep. of the Sec.-Gen. of UN in Cyprus Feb. 67-.
Office of UN Special Representative in Cyprus, P.O. Box 1642, Nicosia, Cyprus.

Osseyran, Adel; Lebanese politician; b. 1905, Saida; ed. American Univ. of Beirut.
Deputy for Southern Lebanon 43; Minister of Supplies in first Cabinet after Independence 43; mem. of Lebanese Del. to UN 47, 48; Deputy for Zahrani 53, 57, 60; Pres. Chamber of Deputies 53, 57, 58; Minister of the Interior 68-69; Grand Cordon of the Order of the Cedar; several foreign decorations.
Ministry of the Interior, Beirut, Lebanon.

Othman as-Said, Muhammad; Libyan politician; b. Oct. 1922; ed. Sanusi religious institutions, Fezzan.
Head of Religious Court for Admin. Region of Brak 45; organized Libyan Nationalist Activity in Fezzan 47; imprisoned by French 48-50; Leader Fezzan Del. to Libyan

Independence Comm. 50; mem. Constituent Assembly 50; mem. Advisory Comm. to UN in Libya 50; Minister of Health, Libya 51, later Minister of Public Health until 58; Deputy to Constituent Assembly 58; Minister for Econ. Affairs 60; Prime Minister 60-March 63; Deputy 64; private business 64-; numerous decorations.
Geraba Street 6, Tripoli, Libya.

Otten, Heinrich; German orientalist; b. 27 Dec. 1913. Professor and Dir. Oriental Seminar, Marburg Univ. 59-; mem. Acad. of Sciences and Literature, Mainz 59-; Exec. mem. Deutsche Orientgesellschaft 64-; mem. German Archaeological Inst., Berlin 69-; corresp. mem. Vienna Acad. of Sciences 72.
Publs. several works on Hittitology and history of the Ancient Near East.
355 Marburg/Lahn, Sudetenstrasse 4, Federal Republic of Germany.

Ötüken, Adnan; Turkish librarian; b. 1911; ed. Lycée and Univ. of Istanbul, and Germany.
Asst. Turkish Language and Literature Dept., Univ. of Istanbul 40; Dir. of Publs., Asst. Dir.-Gen. of Fine Arts, Ministry of Education 52-54; Lecturer of Library Science, Univ. of Ankara; mem. Exec. Cttee. Turkish Nat. Comm. of UNESCO and Exec. Board Turkish Librarians' Asscn.; Dir. Turkish Nat. Library 60-65; Under-Sec. for Culture, Ministry of Educ. 65-67; Lecturer in Turkish Language and Literature, Lycée Teachers' Training Coll., Ankara 67-; Gen. Sec. Turkish-Iraqi Standing Cttee. of Cultural Agreement; fmrly. Turkish Cultural Attaché in Germany.
Publs. *Bibliyotek bilgisi ve bibliyografi* (Library Science and Bibliography) 40, *Istanbul Üniversitesi Yayımları Bibliyografyası* (Bibliography of the Publs. of the Univ. of Istanbul) 41, *Seçme eserler bibliyografyası. 1. cilt* (Selected Bibliography, Vol. 1) 46, *Milli Kütüphane kurulurken* (Establishing the National Library) 46, *Istanbul Universities Yayimlari Bibliyografyası, 1933-45* (Bibliography of the Publs. of the Univ. of Istanbul, 1933-45, with Acaroğlu) 47, *Dünya edebiyatından tercemeler. Klâsikler Bibliyografyası, 1940-48* (Bibliography of classical and modern works translated and published by Turkish Ministry of Education, 1940-48) 47, (2nd edn.) *1940-50* 52, *Bibliyotekçinin el kitabi, 2 cilt* (Manual of the Librarian, 2 vols.) 47-48, *Milli Kütüphane Nasıl Kuruldu* (How the Turkish National Library was founded) 55, *Türk dilinin Başina gelenler* (The Things that Happened to Turkish language, 2 vols.) 68, *Iki yılda 600 den fazla yazi* (bibliography) 69.
Lycée Teachers' Training College, Ankara, Turkey.

Ouazzani, Thami; Moroccan diplomatist; b. 27 Dec. 1927, Fez; ed. Collège Moulay Idriss, Fez, Faculté de Droit, Paris and the Sorbonne.
Called to the Bar, Casablanca 51; Minister of Industry and Mines 55-56; mem. Conseil de l'Ordre des Avocats de Casablanca 59; Amb. to Yugoslavia and Greece 61; Sec. Gen. Charte de Casablanca 62; Minister of Labour and Social Affairs 63-64, of Public Works and Admin. Reform 65; Amb. to Algeria 65-67; Minister of Tourism 68; Minister in Royal Cabinet 68-69; Amb. to Tunisia 69-71; Amb. to U.K. 71-; Grand Cordon Alaouite and decorations from Yugoslavia and Tunisia.
Embassy of Morocco, 49 Queen's Gate Gardens, London, S.W.7; Home: Kent Holme, 44 The Bishop's Avenue, London, N.2, England.

Oussedik, Omar; Algerian diplomatist; b. 2 Jan. 1922.
Member Algerian People's Party 45-; Major, Armée de Libération Nationale 54-58; Sec. of State 58-60; FLN Rep. in Guinea 60-61; Ambassador to Bulgaria 63-65, to U.S.S.R. 65-70.
c/o Ministry of Foreign Affairs, Algiers, Algeria.

Özbek, Dr. Sabahattin; Turkish agronomist; b. 1915, Erzincan; ed. Secondary School, Istanbul, Faculty of Agriculture, Univ. of Ankara.
Lecturer, Faculty of Agriculture, Univ. of Ankara 38, Asst. Prof. 41, Prof. 53, Dean 55-57, 65-68; Visiting Prof. Univs. of Michigan and Calif. 50-51, 57-58; Minister of Nat. Educ. 72-73, of Communications 73-; founded Atatürk Üniv., Erzurum, later Co-Founder Faculty of Agriculture, Adana; Chair. Agricultural Cttee. for the preparation of First Five-Year Devt. Plan; mem. Turkish Atomic Energy Comm.; Prize of Professional Honour, Union of Agricultural Engineers; Independent.
Publs. 35 books in Turkish and foreign languages.
Ministry of Communications, Ankara, Turkey.

Özel, Ahmet; Turkish engineer, educationist and politician; b. 1910; ed. Technical Univ. of Istanbul, and Paris Ecole Nat. Supérieure de Télécommunications.
Docent Technical Univ. of Istanbul and Factory Engineer 39, Prof. 49, Dir. Civil Aeronautical Inst. and Dean Electrical Faculty 52, Pres. 53-54; Dep. from Sivas to Grand Nat. Assembly 54-57; Minister of Education 55-57; Pres. Atatürk Üniv. 57-58, Prof. of Mathematics and Physics, Atatürk Üniv. 58-67; Pres. Black Sea Technical Univ. 67-; mem. Democratic Party.
Publs. *Courses on Radio-Electricity, The Role of the Atmosphere on the Propagation of Electro-Magnetic Waves, The Application of Heaviside's Symbolic Computations of Electrotechnics, Electro-Magnetic Theory and Radiation, General Mathematics Courses.*
Black Sea University, Trabzon, Turkey.

Öztekin, Mukadder; Turkish politician; b. 1919, Bor, Niğde Prov.; ed. Galatasaray Lycée, Istanbul, Ankara Univ.
Joined Ministry of Interior 44; County Chief Officer in various districts, Insp.; Gov. of Adana 60; Senator for Adana 66-; Minister of Public Works 71-73, of the Interior 73-; Independent.
Ministry of the Interior, Ankara, Turkey.

Öztrak, Ilhan, PH.D.; Turkish lawyer and politician; b. 1925, Ankara; ed. Faculty of Law, Ankara Univ. and Univ. of Neuchâtel, Switzerland.
Lecturer in Civil Law, Faculty of Political Sciences, Ankara Univ. 57, Asst. Prof. 61, Prof. 71; Dir. School of Journalism, Ankara 71; Minister of State 72-.
Publs. several works on civil law.
Ministry of State, Ankara, Turkey.

P

Pachachi, Adnan al, PH.D.; Iraqi diplomatist; b. 14 May 1923; ed. American Univ. of Beirut.
Joined Foreign Service 44, served Washington, Alexandria; Dir.-Gen. of Political Affairs, Council of Ministers 57-58; Dir.-Gen. Ministry of Foreign Affairs 58-59; Perm. Rep. of Iraq to UN 59-65; Minister of State Dec. 65-66; Minister of Foreign Affairs 66-67; Perm. Rep. to UN 67-69.
c/o Ministry of Foreign Affairs, Baghdad, Iraq.

Pachachi, Nadim, A.R.S.M., PH.D.; Iraqi oil expert; b. 18 March 1914, Baghdad; ed. Imperial Coll., London.
Minister of Econs. 53-57; Minister of Finance 57-58; mem. of Parl. 52-58; Oil Adviser to the Libyan Govt. 60-64, to the Kuwaiti Govt. 66-68, to His Highness The Ruler of Abu Dhabi and the Govt. of Abu Dhabi 66-; Sec.-Gen. Org. of Petroleum Exporting Countries 70-72; Order of Rafidain, Hashemite Order.
c/o Organization of Petroleum Exporting Countries, Dr. Karl Lueger Ring 10, 1010 Vienna, Austria.

Pahlavi, Mohammad-Reza; His Imperial Majesty the Shahanshah Aryamehr, Emperor of Iran; b. 26 Oct. 1919. Succeeded to throne on the abdication of his father, Reza Shah the Great, Sept. 16th, 41; married (1) Princess Fawzia, sister of King Farouk of Egypt; divorced Nov. 48; daughter, Princess Shahnaz Pahlavi; (2) Soraya Esfandiari, Feb. 12th, 51; divorced March 58; (3) Farah Diba, Dec. 21st, 59; sons: Prince Reza Pahlavi and Prince Ali Reza Pahlavi; daughters Princess Farahnaz and Princess Leyla; Dr. h.c. Columbia, Michigan, Pennsylvania, California (U.C.L.A.), Harvard, New York, Washington Univs., U.S.A. and Univs of Teheran, Punjab, Agra, Istanbul, Beirut, Rio de Janeiro, Bucharest, Sofia, Malaya, Bangkok, Madras, Nat. Univ. of Iran.
Publs. *Mission for My Country* 61, *The White Revolution* 61.
The Imperial Palace, Teheran, Iran.

Pahlbod, Mehrdad, B.SC.; Iranian politician; b. Teheran; ed. Univ. of Teheran and in France.
Official, Ministry of Educ.; Supervisor, Org. of Fine Arts; Deputy Prime Minister; now Minister of Culture and Art.
Ministry of Culture and Art, Teheran, Iran.

Pakravan, Gen. Hassan; Iranian army officer and diplomatist; b. 1911; ed. French Military Acad.
Assistant Mil. Attaché, Paris; Mil. Attaché, Pakistan 49-50; Head of Army Intelligence 50-53; Mil. Attaché, New Delhi 54-56; Deputy Chief, State Security and Intelligence Org. (SAVAK) 56-61; Asst. to Prime Minister and Head of SAVAK 61-65; Minister of Information Feb. 65-July 66; Amb. to Pakistan 66-69, to France 70-.
Embassy of Iran, Paris, France.

Palmer, Joseph, II, B.S.; American diplomatist; b. 16 June 1914; ed. Cambridge High School, Mass., Harvard and Georgetown Univs., and Dept. of State Foreign Service School.
Federal Bureau of Investigation 38-39; Officer Foreign Service 39; Vice-Consul Mexico City 40-41, Nairobi 41-45; Asst. Chief Div. of African Affairs, Dept. of State 45-49, Acting Chief 48; Second Sec. London 49-50, First Sec. 50-53; Deputy Dir. Office European Regional Affairs. Dept. of State 53-56, Acting Dir. 55; Deputy Asst. Sec, of State for African Affairs 56-58; Consul-Gen. Salisbury, Rhodesia and Nyasaland 58-60; Ambassador to Nigeria 60-64; responsible for co-ordination of U.S. organizations involved in Congo crisis 64; Dir.-Gen. of Foreign Service, Dept. of State Feb. 64-March 66; Asst. Sec. of State for African Affairs March 66-July 69; Amb. to Libya 69-73.
5414 Kirkwood Drive, Washington, D.C. 20016, U.S.A.

Papadopoulos, Tassos; Cypriot lawyer and politician; b. 1934; ed. Pancyprian Gymnasium, Nicosia, King's Coll., London, and Gray's Inn, London.
Law practice, Nicosia 55-59; fmr. mem. EOKA; mem. Constitutional Comm. drafting Cyprus Constitution 59-60; Minister of Interior *a.i.* 59-60; Minister of Labour and Social Insurance 60-70; Acting Minister of Agriculture 64-66, Minister of Health 60-70; M.P., Deputy Pres. House of Reps. July 70-.
House of Representatives, Nicosia, Cyprus.

Papaioannou, Ezekias; Cypriot journalist; b. 8 Oct. 1908; ed. American Acad., Larnaca, Cyprus.
Secretary-General, Progressive Party of the Working People (Anorthotikon Komma Ergazomenou Laou— AKEL) 49-; Deputy of AKEL, House of Reps. 60-; mem. Foreign Affairs Cttee., House of Reps. 60-, Chair. Communications and Works Cttee. 70-.
c/o AKEL, 2 Spyrou Lambrou Street, Nicosia; and 8 Doiranis Street, Nicosia, Cyprus.

Parrot, André; French archaeologist; b. 15 Feb. 1901; ed. Univ. de Paris à la Sorbonne, Faculté de Theologie Protestante, Ecole du Louvre and Ecole Archéologique Française de Jerusalem.
Professor, Faculty of Protestant Theology, Univ. of Paris 37-55, Ecole du Louvre 37-; Head Keeper of Nat. Museums 46-65, Insp.-Gen. 65-; Dir. of Louvre Museum 68-72; Dir. of French archaeological expeditions to Mari (Syrian Arab Republic) and Larsa (Iraq); mem. Institut Français (Académie des Inscriptions et Belles-Lettres); mem. British Acad., Belgian Acad.; Commandeur Légion d'Honneur; Commandeur des Arts et des Lettres; Croix de Guerre 39-45; Grand Officer, Ordre Nat. du Mérite.
Publs. *Mari, une ville perdue* 36, *Archéologie mésopotamienne* 46-53; *Tello-vingt campagnes de fouilles* 48, *Ziggurats et Tour de Babel* 48, *Découverte des Mondes ensevelis* 52, *Mari—le temple d'Ishtar* 56, *Mari—le Palais* (3 vols.) 58-59, *Les temples d'Ishtarat et Ninni—zaza* 67, *Le trésor d'Ur* 68, *Sumer* 60, *Assur* 61, *Abraham et son temps* 62, *Terre du Christ* 65, *Clés pour l'archéologie* 67.
11 rue du Val Groce, Paris 75005, France.

Parsay, (Mrs.) Farrokhrou, M.D.; Iranian politician; b. March 1922; ed. Homa Primary School, Teheran, High Normal School, Teheran Univ.
Teacher 42-57; Principal of Secondary School, Teheran 57; mem. Parl. 63-; Under-Sec. Ministry of Educ. 65-68; Minister of Educ. 68-; established Soc. of Woman Educators; Pres. Org. of Co-operation between Women's Socs., Soc. of Univ. Women; mem. Women's Sport Council; Chief, Educ. Cttee. of High Council of Iranian Women's Socs.
Publs. *Women in Ancient Iran* (in Persian), books on education, hygiene, nursing and motherhood.
Ministry of Education, Ekbatan Avenue, Teheran, Iran.

Partos, Oedeon; Israeli composer; b. 1907, Budapest; ed. in Budapest under Hubay (violin) and Kodaly (composition).
Founding mem. Int. Soc. for Contemporary Music; Leader of viola section, Israel Philharmonic Orchestra 38-56; Dir. Israel Acad. of Music, Tel-Aviv 51-; Prof. Tel-Aviv Univ. 61-; now devotes time to musical educ., composition and solo appearances.
Compositions include *Concerto* (for violin and orchestra), *Sinfonia Concertante* (for viola and orchestra), *Yiskor* (for strings), *Visions* (for flute, piano and strings), *Makamat* (for flute and string quartet), *Ein Gev* (symphonic fantasy, UNESCO Prize 52, Israel State Prize 54), *Images* (for orchestra), *Symphonic Movements*, *Five Israeli Songs*, *Tehilim* (for string quartet), *Agada* (for viola, piano and percussion), *Nebulae* (for woodwind quintet), *Iltur* (for 12 harps); piano pieces, etc.
The Israel Academy of Music, Tel-Aviv; 25 Tsimchei Hayehudim Street, Ramat Aviv, Tel-Aviv, Israel.

Partou, Manouchehr, LL.B.; Iranian lawyer and politician; b. 1921, Teheran; ed. Univ. of Teheran.
Former Public Prosecutor of Teheran; Public Prosecutor of the Civil Service Tribunal; Counsel to the Supreme Court; Minister of Justice 69-71.
c/o Ministry of Justice, Teheran, Iran.

Patinkin, Don, PH.D.; Israeli economist; b. 8 Jan. 1922; ed. Univ. of Chicago.
Asst. Prof. of Economics, Univ. of Chicago 47-48; Research Assoc., Cowles Comm. for Economic Research 47-48; Assoc. Prof. of Economics, Univ. of Ill. 48-49; Lecturer, The Eliezer Kaplan School of Economics and Social Sciences, Hebrew Univ. 49, later Prof. of Economics; Dir. of Research, Maurice Falk Inst. for Economic Research in Israel 56-72; mem. Israel Acad. of Sciences and Humanities; Foreign Hon. mem. American Acad. of Arts and Sciences.
Publs. *Money, Interest and Prices: An Integration of Monetary and Value Theory* 56 (2nd edn. 65), *The Israel Economy: The First Decade* 59, *Studies in Monetary Economics* 72.
Chovevei Zion 5, Talbieh, Jerusalem, Israel.

Patsalides, Andreas, B.SC.ECONS.; Cypriot politician; b. 1922; ed. Greek Gymnasium, Limassol, School of Econs. and Political Science, London, and Harvard Univ., Mass.
Various posts in Public Service; Gen. Dir., Planning Bureau 59-68; Minister of Finance 68-.
Ministry of Finance, Nicosia, Cyprus.

Pazhwak, Abdurrahman; Afghan civil servant; b. 7 March 1919.
Has been successively mem. Historical Section of Afghan Acad.; Dir. Foreign Publications Section of Afghan Press Dept.; Editor daily *Islah* and acting Dir.-Gen. of Bakhtar News Agency; Pres. Pashto-Tolana; Dir.-Gen. Publs. Section, Afghan Press Dept.; Press and Cultural Attaché, Afghan Embassy, London; mem. of Section of Information Dept. of ILO; Press and Cultural Attaché, Afghan Embassy, Washington; Dir. Section for East Asia and Dir. a.i., Section for UN, and Int. Confs., Afghan Ministry for Foreign Affairs; Dir.-Gen. Political Affairs in Ministry of Foreign Affairs 56; Perm. Rep. to UN 58-; Pres. UN Human Rights Comm. 63, 21st Session of UN Gen. Assembly 66, 5th Special Session 66 and of Emergency Session of Gen. Assembly on Middle East 66.
Publs. *Aryana or Ancient Afghanistan, Pakhtunistan* (both in English), *Tales of the People* 58 (in Persian), and many other works.
Afghan Mission to the United Nations, 866 UN Plaza, New York City, N.Y., U.S.A.

Pazhwak, Niamatullah, PH.D.; Afghan educationist; b. 17 Aug. 1928; ed. Habibia High School, Kabul, Kabul Univ., Columbia Univ., U.S.A.
Director Teacher's Training School, Kabul 56, Habibia High School 58; Pres. Secondary Schools in Afghanistan 65; Cultural Counsellor, Royal Afghan Embassy to U.S.S.R. 68; Pres. of Compilation and Translation, Ministry of Educ. 70; Gov. Bamiyan Prov. March-Sept. 71, Kabul Prov. 71-72; Minister of the Interior 72-73, of Education 73-.
Publs. articles on education in professional journals.
Ministry of Education, Kabul, Afghanistan.

Peled, Natan; Israeli politician; b. 3 June 1913, Odessa; ed. secondary education.
Immigrated to Palestine 32; agricultural labourer in Kibbutz; Sec. Gen. of Kibbutz Fed. 'Hashomer Hatzair' 50-55; Political Sec., Mapam Party 56-58; Minister of Israel to Bulgaria 58-60; Amb. to Austria 60-63; mem. Knesset 65-69; Minister of Immigrant Absorption 70-.
Kibbutz Sarid, Israel.

Peres, Shimon; Israeli politician; b. 1923; ed. Harvard Univ.
Went to Israel 34; fmr. Sec. Hano'ar Ha'oved Movt.; mem. Mapai Secr.; Dir. Gen. Ministry of Defence 53-59; Deputy Minister of Defence 59-65; Minister without Portfolio 69-70; Minister of Posts and Transport 70-.
Publs. *The Next Step* and articles on political themes.
Ministry of Posts and Transport, Jerusalem; 186 Arlosoroff Street, Tel-Aviv, Israel.

Perowne, Stewart Henry, O.B.E., K.ST.J., M.A., F.S.A.; British orientalist and historian; b. 17 June 1901; ed. Haileybury Coll., Corpus Christi Coll. Cambridge, and Harvard Univ.
English Lecturer, Govt. Arab Coll. Jerusalem 27-30; Asst. Sec. Palestine Govt. 30-32, Asst. District Commr. 32-34; Asst. Sec. Malta 34-37; Political Officer, Aden 37; Arabic Programme Organizer, B.B.C. 38; Information Officer, Aden 39-41; Public Relations Attaché, British Embassy, Baghdad 41-44, Oriental Counsellor 44-47; Colonial Sec. Barbados 47-50; Acting Gov. March-Oct. 49; Adviser, Ministry of Interior, Cyrenaica 50-51; Adviser on Arab Affairs, U.K. Del. UN Gen. Assembly 51; discovered ancient Aziris 51; Hon. Asst. Jerusalem Diocesan Refugee Organization 52; designed and supervised seven Arab refugee villages 52-56; Faculty mem. "College Year in Athens" 65-66.
Publs. *The One Remains* 54, *Herod the Great* 56, *The Later Herods* 58, *Hadrian* 60, *Caesars and Saints* 62, *The Pilgrim's Companion in Jerusalem and Bethlehem* 63, *The Pilgrim's Companion in Roman Rome* 63, *The Pilgrim's Companion in Athens* 65, *Jerusalem* 65, *The End of the Roman World* 66, *Death of the Roman Republic* 68, *Roman Mythology* 69, *The Siege within the Walls* 70, *Rome* 71, *The Journeys of Saint Paul* 73.
44 Arminger Road, London, W.12, England.

Perrin, René Jean Louis; French marine engineer and business executive; b. 22 Aug. 1897; ed. Ecole Polytechnique.
Former Marine Engineer and Chief Marine Engineer; Prés. d'Hon. Compagnie Française de Raffinage; Administrateur, Soc. Nat. d'Investissement, Lille-Bonnières et Colombes, Compagnie Auxiliaire de Navigation; Commandeur, Légion d'Honneur.
86 avenue Raymond-Poincaré, 75116 Paris, France.

Persia, Shah of (see Pahlavi, Mohammad-Reza).

Petrides, Frixos L.; Cypriot teacher and politician; b. 1915, Nicosia; ed. Pancyprian Gymnasium and Univ. of Athens.
In Athens during Second World War; teacher, Pancyprian Gymnasium after Second World War; Chair. Pancyprian Asscn. 47-60; Headmaster, Pancyprian Gymnasium 60; Chair. of Board, Cyprus Broadcasting Corpn. 60-70; Minister of Educ. 70-72; Chair. Cyprus Tourism Org. 72-.
Cyprus Tourism Organization, P.O. Box 4535, Nicosia, Cyprus.

Phanos, Titos; Cypriot politician; b. 23 Jan. 1929; ed. Pancyprian Gymnasium, Nicosia, Middle Temple, London.
Called to Bar 51; mem. EOKA fighters union; mem. of Cttee. of Human Rights of the Nicosia Bar Asscn.; arrested by British administration and served 16 months as political detainee 56-58; mem. Consultative Body to Archbishop Makarios 59-60; mem. House of Representatives for Nicosia 60-66; Parl. Spokesman (Floor Leader) of pro-government Patriotic Front 63-66; mem. Consultative Assembly of Council of Europe 63-65; Minister of Communications and Works 66-70; Amb. to Belgium, Head of Mission to EEC 71-.
Embassy of Cyprus, 83-85 rue de la Loi, Brussels, Belgium.

Phillips, Sir Horace, K.C.M.G.; British diplomatist; b. 31 May 1917, Glasgow, Scotland; ed. Hillhead High School, Glasgow.
Inland Revenue Dept., London 35-39; Indian Army 40-47; Consul, Persia and Afghanistan 47-50; Foreign Office 51-53; Chargé d'Affaires, Saudi Arabia 53-56; Aden Protectorate Sec. 56-60; Counsellor, Teheran 60-64; Deputy Political Resident, Persian Gulf 64-66; Amb. to Indonesia 66-68; British High Commr. in Tanzania 68-72; Amb. to Turkey 73-.
Embassy of United Kingdom, Çankaya, Şehit Ersan Cad. 46/A, Ankara, Turkey.

Phillips, John Fleetwood Stewart, C.M.G., M.A.; British diplomatist; b. 16 Dec. 1917; ed. Worcester Coll., Oxford.
H.M. Forces 39-45; Sudan political service 45-54; First Sec., Foreign Office 55-56; Oriental Sec., Libya 57-60; H.M. Consul-Gen., Muscat 60-63; Counsellor, Amman 63-66; Imperial Defence Coll. 67; Deputy High Commr., Cyprus 68; Amb. to People's Democratic Republic of Yemen Feb. 69-70, to Jordan 70-72, to Sudan 73-; Fellow, Royal Commonwealth Soc., British Museum rep. on Board of Trustees, Palestine Archaeological Museum, Jerusalem 66.
c/o British Embassy, P.O. Box 801, Khartoum, Sudan; and Records Section, Foreign and Commonwealth Office, London, S.W.1, England.

Phillips, Wendell, A.B., PH.D., F.R.G.S., F.R.A.I., F.A.G.S., F.R.C.A.S., F.R.A.S.; American explorer and archaeologist; b. 25 Sept. 1921, Oakland, Calif.; ed. Univ. of Calif., Berkeley.
President and Dir. Philpryor Corpn. 51-58; Pres. Middle East American Oil Co. 55-56; Chair. P.T.P. Corpn., Reno, Nev. 62-, Phillips Pacific, Sacramento, Calif. 60-; Pres. American Foundation for Study of Man, Washington 49-; Dir.-Gen. Antiquities, Oman 53; Econ. Adviser and Rep. of H.M. Sultan of Oman 56-; mem. many scientific expeditions; Dir. African expedition 47-49, Sinai Expedition 50, Oman Geographical Expedition 61; excavations in Yemen 51-52, Sumhuram, Dhofar 52-53, Sohar, Oman 58; Prof. of Archaeology, Univ. of Wyoming 68; Pres. Wendell Phillips Oil Co., Wendell Phillips Oil Co. (Korea) Ltd.; Trustee, Hawaii Loa Coll 68, San Francisco Theological Seminary 70; mem. several learned socs.; Hon. Dr. Univs. of Redlands, Colorado, Trinity, Pacific, and Kyungpook Nat. Univ., Calvin Coolidge, Emporia, Sterling, and Whitworth Colls Idaho Coll., Grand Canyon Coll., Miami, Calif. Baptist Coll., Emmanuel Coll., Florida Southern Coll., John Brown Univ., Eastern Coll., Union Coll., Utah, Fort Lauderdale Univ., Davis and Elkins Coll.; Hon. Sheikh of Bal-Harith tribe; Brussels Univ. Commemorative Medal 69, Gold Plate Award of American Soc. of Achievement 72.
Publs. *Qataban and Sheba* 55, *Unknown Oman* 66, *Oman, a History* 67.
Suite 1409, Bank of Hawaii, 2222 Kalakaua Avenue, Honolulu, Hawaii 96815, U.S.A.

Picard, Leo Yehuda, PH.D., D.SC.; Israeli geologist; b. 3 June 1900; ed. Freiburg, Bonn, Berlin, Zürich and London Univs.
Assistant, Univ. of Florence 24; emigrated to Palestine 24; Asst. Hebrew Univ. of Jerusalem Geology Dept. 25-33, Lecturer 34-63, Head of Dept. 36-37, Assoc. Prof. 37-39, Prof. 39-, now Emer; Research in Paris 26, London 29-30; Consultant to Argentine Govt. 45; Dir. Geol. Survey of Israel 50-54; Adviser to Israel Govt. 55-; Chair. Cttee of Experts on Arid Regions, UNESCO 54; Adviser to Greek Govt. on groundwater 56-57; Chief Geological Cons. TAHAL Water Planning Israel 57-; Chair. Nat. Cttee., 6th World Petroleum Congress 62; Special Adviser to UN on groundwater exploration in Cyprus 63, Iran 64, and Bolivia 65; Dir. Groundwater Research Centre, Hebrew Univ. Jerusalem; Cons. in Oil Exploration to Finance Ministry 68; mem. Cttee. for Neotectonics and Pleistocene Stratigraphy (INQUA Congress, Paris) 69; member Israel Acad. of Sciences and Humanities; Foreign Corresp. Soc. Géol., France; Israel Prize for Natural Sciences 58.
Publs. numerous works on geology, palaeontology, hydrogeology, petroleum, and pure geological research.
Groundwater Research Centre, the Hebrew University, Jeruslaem, Israel.

Pirasteh, Said Mehdi, PH.D.; Iranian lawyer and politician; b. 1919; ed. Teheran Univ.
Successively clerk, Ministry of Justice, Public Prosecutor, Rep. of Public Prosecutor at Judicial Court, Asst. to Public Prosecutor of Supreme Court, Parl. Deputy, Under-Sec. Ministry of Interior, Gov.-Gen. of Fars and Southern Ports, Gov.-Gen. of Khuzistan; Minister of Interior 63-64; Amb. to Iraq 64-67, to Belgium 68-71.
c/o Ministry of Foreign Affairs, Teheran, Iran.

Pirenne, Jacques, Comte, LL.D., PH.D.; Belgian historian; b. 26 June 1891; ed. Ghent Univ.
Tutor to Prince Leopold (later King Leopold III) 20-24; Chargé de Cours Univ. of Brussels 21, Prof. 24-, Sec. Oriental Inst. 30-; scientific mem. Oriental Inst. of Prague 33; Michonis Prof. Coll. de France 35; awarded Quinquennial Prize for Historical Sciences for work 30-35; Lecturer Univ. of Cairo 39; Prof. Univ. of Grenoble 40, Univ. of Geneva 41-44; Head King Leopold's Secretariat with title "Secretary to the King" Aug. 45; Editor *Archives d'Histoire du Droit Oriental* 35-; mem. Académie Royale de Belgique 45-, Acad. Septentrional (Paris) 59-; Grand Croix Ordre de la Couronne; Grand Officier Ordre de Léopold; Officier Légion d'Honneur.
Publs. *Histoire des Institutions et du Droit Privé de l'Ancienne Egypte* (3 vols.) 32-35, *La civilisation sumérienne* 44, *La civilisation babylonienne* 45, *Les Grands Courants de l'Histoire Universelle* (7 vols.) 44-56 (German, Italian, Spanish, Portuguese, English), *La Belgique devant le nouvel équilibre du monde* 45, *Civilisations Antiques* 50, *Histoire de la Civilisation de l'Egypte Ancienne* (3 vols.) 61-63 (Italian, Spanish), *Histoire de l'Europe de 1500 à 1955* (3 vols.) 60-62, *La Religion et la Morale dans l'Egypte Antique* 65, *La Société hebraïque d'apres la Bible* 65, *Le Dossier du Roi Leopold III* 69, *Les Hommes d'Etat célèbres de l'Antiquité* 70.
49 Rue des Echevins, Brussels, Belgium; and Château de Hierges, par Aubrîves, 08 Ardennes, France.

Popal, Ali Ahmad, PH.D.; Afghan educationist; b. 22 Feb. 1916; ed. Nedjat Secondary School, Kabul, and Univ. of Jena.
Teacher and Dir., Nedjat School, Kabul 42-46; Dir. of Teachers Training Coll. 46-47; Head of Primary Educ. Dept., Ministry of Educ. 47-49, also Teacher and Dean in Faculty of Women, Kabul Univ. 47-49; Head of Gen. Educ. Dept., Ministry of Educ. 49-51, Deputy Minister of Educ. 52-56, Minister of Educ. 56-64, Second Vice-Premier 62-64; Amb. to German Fed. Repub., also accred. to Sweden and Switzerland 64-66; Amb. to Turkey 66-67; First Deputy Prime Minister 67-69; Minister of Educ. 67; Amb. to Pakistan, also accred. Sri Lanka and Thailand 69-; Order of Maaref, 3rd Class 46, 1st Class 64, Order of Sardarie-Ahlie 58, and orders from Egypt, Yugoslavia and Federal Republic of Germany.
Publs. *Education in Afghanistan, A Comparison of Education in Europe (Germany) and America, The Republic of Turkey.*
Afghan Embassy, 176 F-7-3, Islamabad, Pakistan.

Pourhomayoun, Ali-Asghar, D. en D.; Iranian economist; b. 1912; ed. legal studies in Europe.
Assistant Prosecutor and Counsellor, Court of Appeal 37; Prof. of Econs., Law Faculty, Univ. of Teheran 43-; Under-Sec. Ministry of Nat. Economy 50-53, Minister of Nat. Economy 53; Pres. Bd. of Dirs., Iran Insurance Co. 53, Pres. and Man. Dir. 53-55; Dir. Inst. for Public Admin., Faculty of Law 56-60; Minister of Commerce 60; Minister without Portfolio 61; Gov. Central Bank of Iran 61-65; Pres. Currency and Credit Council 61-63; mem. High Econ. Council 61-63; Grand Cross of Merit with Star (Germany); Grand Cross Order of Leopold II (Belgium).
Publs. *La Banque Nationale de l'Iran et son rôle dans le développement, Principles of Economics, Planning and Business Cycles.*
Shahreza Avenue, 21st Azar Street, Prof. Edward Brown Road, No. 10, Teheran, Iran.

Prem Chand, Maj.-Gen. D.; Indian army officer (retd.) and United Nations official; b. 1916, Muzaffargarh, now West Pakistan; ed. Govt. Coll., Lahore and Staff Coll., Quetta.
Commissioned Indian Army 37; served in Gen. Staff, Army HQ, New Delhi 47, later apptd. Mil. Asst. to Chief of Army Staff; commanded Regimental Centre of First Gurkha Rifles; Instructor, Defence Services Staff Coll., Wellington; subsequently apptd. Deputy Dir. of Mil. Training, Dir. of Personnel Services, Dir. of Mil. Intelligence, New Delhi; Chief of Staff, HQ Western Command, Simla 61, Commanded Div. in Western Command; Gen. Officer, Katanga Area, UN Operation in the Congo 62-63; Commanded Div. in Eastern Command, Chief of Staff,

HQ Eastern Command, Calcutta; retd. 67 then held admin. post in industrial concern; Commdr. UN Force in Cyprus (UNFICYP) 69-.
UNFICYP, P.O. Box 1642, Nicosia, Cyprus.

Pritchard, James Bennett, A.B., B.D., PH.D., S.T.D., D.D.; American orientalist; b. 4 Oct. 1909; ed. Asbury Coll., Drew Univ., Univ. of Pa. and Philadelphia Divinity School.
Professor of Old Testament Literature, Crozer Theological Seminary 42-54; Annual Prof. American School of Oriental Research, Jerusalem 50-51, Archaeological Dir. 51, Visiting Prof. 56-57, 61-62; Prof. Old Testament Literature Church Divinity School of the Pacific 54-62; Prof. Religious Thought, Univ. of Pa. and Curator of Biblical Archaeology Univ. Museum 62-, Dir. 67-; Visiting Prof. of Archaeology, American Univ. of Beirut 67; mem. American Oriental Soc., Archaeological Inst. of America, Soc. for Biblical Literature; Editor *Journal of the American Oriental Soc.* 52-54.
Publs. *Palestinian Figures* 43, *Ancient Near Eastern Texts* 50, *The Ancient Near East in Pictures* 54, *Archaeology and the Old Testament* 58, *Gibeon, Where the Sun Stood Still* 62.
University Museum, 33rd and Spruce Streets, Philadelphia 4, Pa., U.S.A.

Q

Qaboos bin Said; Sultan of Oman; b. 1942; ed. by British tutors and at Royal Military Coll., Sandhurst.
In Britain 58-66; served in British Army and studied local government; returned to Salalah 66; deposed his father Said bin Taimur (*q.v.*) 70; Sultan July 70-.
The Palace, Muscat, Sultanate of Oman.

Qadir, Maj. Zain al-Abdin Mohammed Ahmed Abdel; Sudanese politician; b. 7 May 1940, Tuti; ed. Military Coll.
Commissioned 62; mem. Revolutionary Command Council May 69; Ombudsman 70; Minister of Animal Production Nov. 70; Asst. Prime Minister for Agricultural Sector Feb. 71; Minister of Communications and Transport Aug. 71; Minister of Transport 71-72.
c/o Ministry of Transport, Khartoum, Sudan.
Ministry of Transport, Khartoum, Sudan.

Qalhud, Abdul Rahman; Libyan politician and religious leader.
Minister of Justice until Oct. 64; Grand Mufti of Libya 64-.
Office of the Grand Mufti, Tripoli, Libya.

Qassim, Awn al-Sharif, M.A., PH.D.; Sudanese politician; b. 15 Oct. 1933, Halfaiat al Molook; ed. Univs. of Khartoum, London and Edinburgh.
Lecturer, School of Oriental and African Studies, London Univ. 59-61; Lecturer, Dept. of Arabic, Univ. of Khartoum 61-64, Senior Lecturer 69, Dir. Translation Section 69-70; Minister of Waqfs and Religious Affairs Oct. 71-73.
c/o Ministry of Waqfs and Religious Affairs, Khartoum, Sudan.

Qassim, Osman Abu al-, D.SC.; Sudanese politician; b. 1930, Omdurman; ed. Faculty of Agriculture, Univ. of Khartoum and in U.K. and U.S.A.
Teacher, Shambat Agricultural Inst. 59-63, later Dean; Asst. Under-Sec., Ministry of Agriculture 65-67; Man. at UN 67; later mem. staff, Univ. of Baghdad; Minister of Co-operatives and Rural Devt. 69-73; del. to several int. confs.
c/o Ministry of Co-operatives and Rural Development, Khartoum, Sudan.

Quddus, Ihsan Abdul (son of the late Rose al-Yussuf, famous actress and writer); Egyptian writer; b. 1 Jan. 1919; ed. Univ. of Cairo.
Practised in law 42; joined magazine *Rose al-Yussuf* 42, imprisoned for attack on govt. 45, released and became Chief Editor, again imprisoned 50, 51; first novel publ. 54; Editor *Akhbar al-Yom*.
Publs. include *I am Free* 54, *Do not Turn out the Sun* (two vols.) 60, *Nothing Matters* 63.
Cairo, Egypt.

Qusus, Jiryis; Jordanian educationalist and writer; b. 1913; ed. American Univ. of Beirut.
Teacher in various schools 36-51; Headmaster of Es-Salt Govt. Secondary School 51-53; Insp. of English, Ministry of Educ. 53-57; Asst. Under-Sec. and Senior Chief Insp. Ministry of Educ. 57-61; Asst. Under-Sec. Ministry of Communications 61; Ambassador in the Ministry of Foreign Affairs and Head of the Research and Studies Dept. 62, Consular Dept. 63-65, Under-Sec. 65, Ambassador and Head of Research Dept. 66-; Order of Istiklal.
Publs. *Selected Poems* 53, *Selected English Prose* 56, *Applied Translation* (3 vols.) (co-author) 57, *Selected Verses* 58, *Fables from the Middle East* 60, *Education and Art* (co-translator), *The Genius of Shakespeare* (Arabic) 60.
Ministry for Foreign Affairs, Amman, Jordan.

R

Rabin, Maj.-Gen. Yitzhak; Israeli army officer; b. 1922, ed. Agricultural School, Kfar Tabor, and Staff Coll., England.
Palmach commands 43-48, including War of Independence; represented Israel Defence Forces (I.D.F.) at Rhodes armistice negotiations; fmr. Head of Training Dept., I.D.F.; C.-in-C. Northern Command 56-59; Head, Manpower Branch 59-60; Deputy Chief of Staff and Head, Gen. Staff Branch 60-64, Chief of Staff I.D.F. 64-68; Amb- to U.S.A. 68-72; Hon. Doctorates, Jerusalem Univ. 67, Dropsie Coll. 68, Brandeis Univ. 68, Yeshiva Univ. 68, Coll. of Jewish Studies, Chicago 69, Univ. of Miami 70, Hebrew Union Coll., Boston 71.
c/o Ministry of Foreign Affairs, Jerusalem, Israel.

Rachmilewitz, Moshe, M.D.; Israeli physician; b. Russia 2 Sept. 1899; ed. Univs. of Königsberg and Berlin.
Post-graduate studies as E. Libman Fellow, New York, Hamburg, Vienna, Amsterdam and Paris 27-31; came to Palestine 31; research in haematology and cardiology; Head Dept. Rothschild Hadassah Univ. Hospital "B", Jerusalem; Prof. School of Medicine, Hebrew Univ.
11 Ussishkin Street, Jerusalem, Israel.

Rafael, Gideon; Israeli diplomatist; b. Germany 5 March 1913; ed. Univ. of Berlin.
Emigrated 34; mem. Kibbutz 34-43; active in Haganah and war services 39-42; Jewish Agency, Political Dept. 43; in charge of preparation of Jewish case for Jewish Agency, Political Dept., Nuremberg War Crimes Trial 45-46; mem. of Jewish Agency Comm. to Anglo-American Comm. of Enquiry 46, and of Jewish Agency mission to UN Special Comm. for Palestine 47; mem. Israel Permanent Del. to UN 51-52; alternate rep. to UN 53; rep. at UN Gen. Assemblies 47-66; Counsellor in charge of Middle East and UN Affairs, Ministry for Foreign Affairs 53-57; Ambassador to Belgium and Luxembourg 57-60, to the European Econ. Community 59; Dep. Dir.-Gen. Ministry of Foreign Affairs 60; Head of Israel Del. Int. Conf. Law of the Sea, Geneva 60; Deputy Dir.-Gen. Ministry for Foreign Affairs 60-65; Perm. Rep. to UN, Geneva 65-66; Special Ambassador and Adviser to Foreign Minister May 66-67; Perm. Rep. of Israel to UN 67; Dir.-Gen. Ministry of Foreign Affairs 67-71; Senior Political Adviser to Minister of Foreign

Affairs 72-73; Amb. to U.K. Oct. 73-; Head of Del. to UNCTAD III 72.
Embassy of Israel, 2 Palace Green, Kensington, London, W8 4QB, England; and Kiryath Yovel, Jerusalem, Israel.

Rahal, Abdul Latif; Algerian diplomatist; b. 1923.
Ambassador to France 63; then posts in Ministry of Foreign Affairs; Sec.-Gen. Ministry of Foreign Affairs until 70; Perm. Rep. to UN 70-.
Permanent Mission of Algeria at United Nations, 750 Third Avenue, 14th Floor, New York, N.Y. 10017, U.S.A.

Rannat, Mohamed Ahmed Abu; Sudanese judge; b. 1905; ed. Gordon Coll., Khartoum and School of Law, Khartoum.
Translator 25-33; Clerk 33-36; went to School of Law 36-38; District Judge (2nd Grade) 38-44; District Judge (1st Grade) and Dep. Asst. Legal Sec. and Inspector of Native Courts 44-49; Studied in England 49-50; Judge of High Court attached to Court of Appeal 50-55; Chief Justice of Sudan 55-64; mem. UN Sub-Comm. on Prevention of Discrimination and Protection of Minorities 64-; mem. Constitutional Comm. for South Arabia May-July 65.
United Nations Sub-Commission on Prevention of Discrimination, Geneva, Switzerland.

Raphael, Yitzchak, M.A., PH.D.; Israeli politician; b. 5 July 1914; ed. Hebrew Univ.
Settled in Palestine 35; mem. Exec. Jewish Agency and Head, Emigration Dept. 48-54; mem. of 2nd, 3rd, 4th, 5th, 6th and 7th Knesset; Chair. Exec. Hapoel Hamizrachi (Nat. Religious Party); mem. World Exec. Nat. Religious Party Mizrachi; Chair. Legislative Cttee. Knesset; Chair. Mossad Harav Kook (Publishers); Deputy Minister of Health 62-; Chair. Yad Harow Maimon Judaic Studies Centre.
Publs. *Sefer Hachasidith, Rishonim v'achronim, Hachasidut v'Eretz Israel*; Ed. *Encyclopaedia of Religious Zionism* 59, 60.
P.O.B. 642, Jerusalem, Israel.

Rashid, Rashid A. al-, M.A.; Kuwaiti civil servant and diplomatist; b. 23 Dec. 1934; ed. Claremont Men's Coll., California, U.S.A., and Claremont Graduate School.
Assistant Technical Dir., Public Works Dept., Kuwait 59-61; Asst. Sec. for Kuwait Govt. Secretariat 61; Dir. of Political Dept., Ministry of Foreign Affairs, Kuwait until 63; Perm. Rep. of Kuwait to UN Sept. 63-67; Under-Sec. Ministry of Foreign Affairs, Kuwait March 67-.
Ministry of Foreign Affairs, Kuwait.

Rateb, Aisha, PH.D.; Egyptian politician; ed. Faculty of Law, Cairo Univ.
Junior Lecturer, Faculty of Law, Cairo Univ., Prof. of Int. Law; Minister of Social Affairs 71-.
Ministry of Social Affairs, Cairo, Egypt.

Raya, His Grace Archbishop Joseph Marie; Israeli ecclesiastic; b. 15 Aug. 1917; ed. Lebanon and St. Anne Seminary, Jerusalem.
Parish Priest, Zahlé, Lebanon 41-45, Paterson, New Jersey 49-51, Birmingham, Alabama 51-68; Archbishop of St. Jean d'Acre, Haifa, Nazareth and all Galilee 68-.
Greek Catholic Archbishopric, P.O. Box 279, Haifa, Israel.

Razzaz, Ahmed Munif, M.B., B.CH.; Jordanian physician and politician; b. 1919; ed. Amman Secondary School, American Univ. of Beirut and Cairo.
Teacher 39-41; mem. Baath Party 49-, Jordan Regional Leadership 56-66, Sec. 60-66, Sec.-Gen. Baath Party 65-66; exiled to Syria 52-53; imprisoned 57-59, 61, 63-64; arrested Feb. 66; Arab League Prize 63.
Publs. *Features of New Arab Life* (in Arabic) 53, *Evolution of the Meaning of Nationalism* (in Arabic) 60, (English trans.) 63, *Freedom and its Problems in Underdeveloped Countries* 65.
Baath Party, rue Abdul Aziz 66, Damascus, Syria.

Razzek, Brig. Aref Abdel; Iraqi politician; b. 1914; ed. Military Acad.
Entered Air Force 36; became Commdr. Habbaniya base; Minister of Agriculture Nov. 63-Dec. 63; Commdr. of Air Forces Dec. 63-July 65; Prime Minister and Acting Minister of Defence Sept. 65; Abortive *coup d'état* Sept. 65, June 66; imprisoned June 66.
c/o Ministry of Justice, Baghdad, Iraq.

Rechter, Zvi; Israeli business executive; b. 16 Nov. 1920, Vienna; ed. High School.
Emigrated to Palestine 40; mem. Kibbutz Ma'aleh Ha-Hamisha until 68; Man. Co-operative Centre for Bldg. 58-66; Treas. Solel Boneh Bldg. and Public Works Co. Ltd. 66-70, Man. Dir. 71-.
Solel Boneh Ltd., P.O. Box 1678, Tel-Aviv, Israel. Telephone: (03) 62-53-11 (Office).

Reiner, Markus, D.TECH.; Israeli university professor; b. 5 Jan. 1886; ed. Technische Hochschule, Vienna.
Engineer, Austrian State Railways 11-18, Romanian State Railways 18-22; Civil and Structural Engineer, Govt. of Palestine 22-45; Research Prof., Lafayette Coll., Easton, Pa., U.S.A. 31-33; Scientific Adviser, Standards Inst. of Palestine 45-47; Head of Rheological Laboratory, Technion, Haifa 48-60; Prof. of Mechanics, Technion, Haifa 48-60; Research Prof., Israel Inst. of Technology 60-; mem. Israel Acad. of Sciences and Humanities; Hon. mem. Groupe Français de Rhéologie; Weizmann Prize for Township of Tel-Aviv 56; Israel Prize, Govt. of Israel 58; Rothschild Prize 63; Gold Medal, British Soc. of Rheology 66.
Publs. *Lectures on Theoretical Rheology* 60, *Deformation Strain and Flow* 60, *Advanced Rheology* 71.
Technion City, Haifa, Israel.

Remez, Brig.-Gen. Aharon; Israeli air force officer and diplomatist; b. 8 May 1919; ed. Herzliah Grammar School, Tel-Aviv, Harvard School of Business Administration, U.S.A., and Woodrow Wilson School of Public and International Affairs, Princeton, U.S.A.
Agricultural training in Kibbutz, Givat Haim 37-39; Emissary to Zionist Youth Movement, U.S.A. 39-41; Royal Air Force 42-47; mem. Kibbutz Kfar Blum 47-; Dir. of Planning and Operations, later Chief of Staff, Israel Air Force 48; Commdr.-in-Chief Israel Air Force 48-51; Head, Ministry of Defence Purchasing Mission, U.S.A. 51-53; Aviation Adviser to Minister of Defence 53-54; mem. Board of Dirs. Solel Boneh Ltd., Exec. Dir. Koor Industries Ltd. 54-59; mem. Knesset 56-57; Admin. Dir. Weizmann Inst. of Science, Rehovot 59-60; Dir. Int. Co-operation Dept., Ministry for Foreign Affairs 60-64, Adviser on Int. Co-operation to Minister for Foreign Affairs 64-65; Consultant to OECD 64-65; Chair. Nat. Aviation Council 63-65; Amb. to U.K. 65-70; Dir.-Gen. Israel Ports Authority 70-.
P.O. Box 20211, Tel-Aviv, Israel.

Rennie, Sir John Shaw, G.C.M.G., O.B.E.; British UN official; b. 12 Jan. 1917; ed. Glasgow Univ., Balliol Coll., Oxford.
Assistant District Officer, Tanganyika 40-49; District Officer 49-51; Deputy Colonial Sec., Mauritius 51-55; British Resident Commr., New Hebrides 55-62; Gov. and C.-in-C. of Mauritius 62-68, Gov.-Gen. and C.-in-C. 68; Deputy Commr.-Gen. UNRWA 68-71; Commr.-Gen. UNRWA 71-; Hon. LL.D. (Glasgow Univ.) 72.
UNRWA Headquarters, Museitbeh Quarter, Beirut, Lebanon.

Riad, Mahmoud; Egyptian diplomatist; b. 8 Jan. 1917; de. Military Acad. and General Staff Coll.
Egyptian Rep. to Mixed Armistice Comm. 49-52; Dir. Dept. of Arab Affairs, Ministry of Foreign Affairs 54-55; Ambassador to Syria 55-58; President's Counsellor on Foreign Affairs 58-62; Chair. Del. to UN Econ. Comm. for

WHO'S WHO IN THE MIDDLE EAST AND NORTH AFRICA

Africa 61; Ambassador and Perm. Rep. to UN 62-64; Minister of Foreign Affairs 64-72, Deputy Premier 71-72; Pres. Adviser Jan.-June 72; Sec.-Gen. League of Arab States June 72-.
League of Arab States, Midan al Tahrir, Cairo, Egypt.

Riahi, Lt.-Gen. Esmail; Iranian army officer and politician; ed. Imperial Iranian Staff Coll.
Instructor, Imperial Army Staff Coll., fmr. Corps Commdr. Fars Province, mem. Supreme Commdr.'s Staff, fmr. Deputy Chief of Staff for Operations Supreme Commdr.'s Staff; Minister of Agriculture March 63-67; Amb. to Netherlands 67-71; several decorations.
Publ. several papers on military subjects.
103 Rudsor Street, Takht-i-Jamshid Avenue, Teheran, Iran.

Riazi, Abdollah; Iranian politician; b. 1906; ed. Univ. de Paris à la Sorbonne.
Assistant Dean, Technical Coll. 36-45, Dean 56-; Pres. of Majlis 64-.
The Majlis, Teheran, Iran.

Richmond, Sir John Christopher Blake, K.C.M.G.; British diplomatist; b. 7 Sept. 1909; ed. Lancing Coll., Hertford Coll., Oxford, and Univ. Coll., London.
On archaeological expeditions, Beisan, Jericho, Tel El Duweir, Ithaca 31-36; H.M. Office of Works 37-39; served in Middle East in Second World War 39-46; Dept. of Antiquities, Palestine Govt. 46-47; British Foreign Service, Oriental Sec., Baghdad 47-51; Foreign Office 51-53; Counsellor, Amman 53-55; Consul-Gen. Houston, Texas 55-58; British Property Comm. Cairo 59; Political Agent, Kuwait Oct. 59-61, British Ambassador 61-63; Supernumerary Fellow, St. Antony's Coll., Oxford 63-64; Ambassador to Sudan 65-66; Lecturer in Modern Near East History, Durham Univ. 66-.
20 The Avenue, Durham City, Durham, England.

Rifaat, Kamal Eldin Mahmoud; Egyptian diplomatist and politician; b. 1921; ed. Military Academy.
Served in Armed Forces 42-55; mem. Nat. Ass. 57; Deputy Minister for Presidential Affairs 58; Minister of Labour 61, 67; mem. Presidential Council; Deputy Prime Minister for Scientific Affairs 64; mem. Gen. Secr. Arab Socialist Union 64; Amb. at Ministry of Foreign Affairs Nov. 70; Amb. to U.K. Aug. 71-; Order of the Repub., Mil. Star, and decorations from Cameroon, Morocco, Tunisia, Yugoslavia.
Publs. *Strategy, The Social Experiment, The Third World and the Socialist Solution, National Liberation.*
Embassy of the Arab Republic of Egypt, 75 South Audley Street, London, W.1, England.

Rifa'i, Abdul Munem; Jordanian diplomatist; b. 1917; ed. American Univ. of Beirut.
In Service of King Abdullah 38; Chief Sec. of Govt. 40; Asst. Chief of Royal Court 41-42; Consul-Gen. in Cairo, Lebanon and Syria 43-44; Del. to Treaty Conf. with Great Britain 46; Under-Sec. of Foreign Affairs 47; Minister to Iran and Pakistan 49; Amb. to United States and Perm. Rep. to UN 53-57, to Lebanon 57, to Great Britain 58; Chief of Nat. Guidance 59; Perm. Rep. to UN 59-66; Amb. to U.A.R. 66, 67-68; Minister of Foreign Affairs 68-69; Prime Minister March-Aug. 69; Deputy Prime Minister, Minister of Foreign Affairs and Senator 69-70; Prime Minister June 70-71; Personal Rep. to H.M. King Hussein 72-; Perm. Rep. to Arab League 73-; numerous decorations.
League of Arab States, Midan al Tahrir, Cairo, Egypt.

Rifa'i, Abdul Wahab, B.A.; Lebanese businessman; b. 1909; ed. American Univ. of Beirut.
Teacher, Tripoli Tarbia Coll. 32-33, American Univ. of Beirut 34-42; Chief of O.C.P. Centre, Tyre, Lebanon 42-43; Sales Man. 43-50; Man. Middle East Airlines, Beirut 50-51; Dir.-Gen. Chamber of Commerce and Industry, Beirut 51-.
Chamber of Commerce and Industry of Beirut, P.O.B. 1801, Allenby Street, Beirut, Lebanon.

Rifai, Yousuf Hashim Ahmed al-; Kuwaiti politician; b. 1932; ed. Shuwaikh Secondary School, Kuwait.
Director, Travel and Residence Dept. 61-63; mem. Nat. Assembly 63-, Sec. 63; Minister of Posts, Telegraphs and Telephones 64; Minister of State for Cabinet Affairs Nov. 64-, also Chair. of Municipal Council 66-.
P.O.B. 420, Kuwait.

Rifa'i, Zaid al-, M.A.; Jordanian diplomatist; b. 27 Nov. 1936, Amman (nephew of Abdul Munem Rifa'i, *q.v.*); ed. Victoria Coll., Cairo, and Harvard and Columbia Univs. Joined diplomatic service 57; served at embassies in Cairo, Beirut and London and at the Perm. Mission of Jordan at UN; Chief of Royal Protocol 65; Sec.-Gen. of Royal Court and Private Sec. to H.M. King Hussein 67; Chief of Royal Court 69-70; Amb. to U.K. 70-72; Political Adviser to H.M. King Hussein 72-73; Prime Minister May 73-; Minister of Foreign Affairs and Defence 73-.
Office of the Prime Minister, Amman, Jordan.

Rimalt, Elimelech, PH.D.; Israeli politician; b. 1 Nov. 1907, Poland; ed. Hebrew High School, Cracow, Poland, Univ. of Vienna and Rabbinical Seminary, Vienna, Austria.
Emigrated to Palestine from Austria 39, and served as Head of Schools in Ramat Gan, Israel and Dir. of Educ. Dept. of Ramat Gan Municipality; Mayor of Ramat Gan 55-59; Minister of Posts, Israel Govt. 69-; Founder, Union of Gen. Zionist (now Liberal) Workers; mem. Knesset; Chair. Liberal Party in fifth Knesset; Co-Chair. Herut-Liberal bloc (Gahal), Knesset 65-68; Past Chair. and mem. of numerous Parl. Cttees; now Chair. Liberal Party of Israel.
Publs. Scientific work in the field of Semitic languages.
68 Ibn Gvirol Street, Tel-Aviv, Israel.

Rishtya, Kassim; Afghan writer and diplomatist; b. 1913; ed. Istiklal High School, Kabul, Banking Inst., Kabul.
Clerk in Press Section, Ministry of Foreign Affairs 31; Chief Clerk Foreign Relations Section, Ministry of Communications 32; mem. Kabul Literary Circle 33; Dir. Publs. Div. 36, Vice-Pres. 38; Editor *Kabul Almanach* and *Kabul Magazine* 36-38; Dir.-Gen. of Publs. Press Dept. 40-44, Vice-Pres. 44-47, Pres. 47-48; Pres. Govt. Econ. Planning Board 49, Govt. Co-operative Org. 49-52, Bakhtar News Agency 52-55; Minister of Information 56-59; Amb. to Czechoslovakia, Poland and Hungary 60-62, to Egypt, Greece, Sudan, Ghana 62-63; Minister of Information 63; Vice-Chair. Cttee. for Revision of Constitution 63; Minister of Finance 64-65; Rep. for Afghanistan at Second Conf. for the Support of the Arab People 69; Del. to UN Gen. Assembly 69; Amb. to Japan and Philippines 70-.
Publs. *Afghanistan in the 19th Century, Jawani Afghan,* short stories, translations and several novels.
Afghan Embassy, 31-21 Jingumae 6-chome, Shibuya-ku, Tokyo, Japan; and c/o Ministry of Foreign Affairs, Kabul, Afghanistan.

Rivlin, Moshe; Israeli administrator; b. 1925, Jerusalem; ed. Teacher's Seminary, Graduate Aluma Inst. for Jewish Studies, Mizrachi Teachers' Coll. and Hebrew Univ., Jerusalem.
Joined Haganah 40; Head, Council of Youth Movts., Jerusalem 44-46; Consul, New York 52-58; Former Head of Admin. and Public Relations Dept., The Jewish Agency, Dir. Information Dept. 58-60; Sec.-Gen. The Jewish Agency 60-68, Dir.-Gen. 66-; Assoc. mem. of Exec. World Zionist Org. 71-.
The Jewish Agency, P.O. Box 92, Jerusalem, Israel.

Robert, Louis; French archaeologist; b. 15 Feb. 1904; ed. Paris Univ., Ecole Normale Supérieure.
Member French School, Athens 27-32; Dir. of Studies Ecole des Hautes Etudes 32-; Prof. of Greek Epigraphy and Antiquities Coll. de France 39-; dir. excavations at Amyzon 49 and Claros (Temple of Apollo) 50-61; Officier Légion d'Honneur.
Publs. *Villes d'Asie Mineure, Etudes Anatoliennes, Les Gladiateurs dans l'Orient Grec, Etudes de Numismatique Grecque, Hellenica* (13 vols.), *Noms Indigènes dans l'Asie Mineure, La Carie* (with his wife, Jeanne Robert), *Monnaies antiques en Troade, Documents de l'Asie Mineure méridionale, La déesse de Hiérapolis Castabala, Monnaies Grecques, Opera Minora Selecta* (4 vols.).
31 avenue René Coty, Paris 14e, France.

Rosen, Pinhas Felix; Israeli lawyer and politician; b. 1 May 1887; ed. Univs. of Freiburg and Berlin.
Called to Bar, Germany 14; served in German Army First World War 14-18; Chair. Zionist Fed. in Germany 20-23; mem. Zionist Exec. London 26-31; went to Palestine 31; called to Palestine Bar 32; Municipal Councillor Tel-Aviv 35-46; Minister of Justice, Govt. of Israel 48-51, and Dec. 52-61; mem. Knesset (Israel Parl.) 48-68.
10 Ramban Street, Jerusalem, Israel.

Rosenne, Shabtai, LL.B., PH.D.; Israeli lawyer and diplomatist; b. 24 Nov. 1917; ed. London Univ. and Hebrew Univ. of Jerusalem.
Advocate (Israel), Political Dept., Jewish Agency for Palestine 46-48; Legal Adviser, Ministry of Foreign Affairs 48-66; Deputy Perm. Rep. to UN 67-71; Perm. Rep. to UN (Geneva) 71-; mem. Israeli Del. to UN Gen. Assemblies 48-71, Vice-Chair. Legal Cttee. Gen. Assembly 60; mem. Israeli Del. to Armistice Negotiations with Egypt, Jordan, Lebanon and Syria 49; Vice-Chair. Israel Del. to UN Conf. on Law of the Sea 58, 60, Chair. Israel Del. to UN Conf. on Law of Treaties 68, 69, mem. other UN confs.; Govt. Rep. before Int. Court of Justice in several cases; mem. Int. Law Comm. 62-71, UN Comm. on Human Rights 68-70; Assoc. Inst. of Int. Law 63-, Rapporteur, Termination and Modification of Treaties 65; Israel Prize 60, Certificate of Merit, American Soc. of Int. Law 68.
Publs. *International Court of Justice* 57, *The Time Factor in Jurisdiction of the International Court of Justice* 60, *The Law and Practice of the International Court* (2 vols.) 65, *The Law of Treaties: Guide to the Vienna Convention* 70; *The World Court: What it is and how it works* 73; and numerous articles, mainly on law.
Israel Mission to the United Nations, 9 chemin Bonvent, CH 1216 Cointrin, Switzerland.

Ross, John-Paul Beverley; British former United Nations official; b. 21 Nov. 1908; ed. Dragon School, Oxford, Repton School and Cambridge Univ.
Worked for Ministry of Econ. Warfare, London 39-43, Combined Econ. Warfare Agency, Cairo and Caserta 43-45, later with Supreme Headquarters Allied Expeditionary Force (SHAEF), Versailles; mem. British del. to Council of Foreign Ministers, London, Paris, New York, Moscow 45-47, to Peace Conf., Paris 46; mem. Int. Secr., Preparatory Comm. for the OEEC 47; Deputy Dir. (later Dir.) German External Assets Div., Inter-Allied Reparations Agency, Brussels 47-52; Acting Resident Rep. UN Technical Assistance Board, Burma 52-53, Philippines 53-54, Pakistan 54-55, Deputy Resident Rep., Indonesia 55-59, Iran 59-64; Resident Rep. UN Devt. Programme (UNDP), Israel 64-73, retd.; mem. Law Soc., Royal Inst. of Int. Affairs.
14 Agron Street, Jerusalem, Israel; and Thieux par Dammartin-en-Goële, Seine et Marne, France.

Rossides, Zenon; Cypriot diplomatist; b. 8 Feb. 1895; ed. Limassol Coll. and Middle Temple, London.
Called to Bar 23; law practice in Cyprus 25-54; mem. Nat. Del. to London 29-31; mem. Ethnarchy Council 46-48 and 58-59; mem. Exec. 50-59; Greek Cypriot Rep. on Joint Cttee. in London, leading to Independence of Cyprus 59-60; Ambassador to U.S.A. and Perm. Rep. of Cyprus to UN 60-; Vice-Pres. UN Gen. Assembly 61-62, 63-64; Chair. UN Cttee. on Portuguese Colonies 62.
Publs. *The Island of Cyprus and Union with Greece* 51, *The Problem of Cyprus* 58.
Embassy of Cyprus, 2211 R Street N.W., Washington, D.C.; and 820 Second Ave., New York, N.Y. 10017, U.S.A.

Rouhani, Fuad, LL.M.; Iranian lawyer and executive; b. 23 Oct. 1907; ed. Teheran and London Univ.
Anglo-Iranian Oil Co., Legal and Administrative Branches 26-51; Chief Legal Adviser, Nat. Iranian Oil Co. 51-54, Dir. 54-, Deputy Chair. 56; Sec.-Gen. and Chair. Board of Govs., Organization of Petroleum Exporting Countries (OPEC) 61-64; Adviser to the Prime Minister 64; Sec.-Gen. Regional Co-operation for Devt. 64-68.
Teheran, Iran.

Rouhani, Mansour, M.SC.; Iranian politician; b. 1921, Teheran; ed. Univs. of Teheran and London.
Chairman and Gen. Dir. Technical Dept., Teheran Water Supply Org.; Minister of Water and Power 65-71, of Agriculture and Natural Resources 71-.
Ministry of Agriculture and Natural Resources, Teheran, Iran.

Roussos, Nicolaos S.; Cypriot civil engineer and politician; b. 1906, Lania Village, Limassol District, ed. Greek Gymnasium, Limassol, and Athens Technical Univ.
Practised civil engineering in Greece, mainly road construction work 29-33; Municipal Engineer, Limassol 33-47; Senior Partner, N. S. Roussos & J. Pericleous (civil engineers and architects) 38-70; Minister of Communications and Works 70-72; mem. of Board, Cyprus Telecommunications Authority 60-68, Vice-Chair. 68-70, Chair. June 72-; Pres. Cyprus Civil Engineers and Architects Asscn. 46-62; Pres. UN Asscn. of Cyprus 70, Limassol Rotary 61-62, Limassol Wine Festival 64, 65.
Cyprus Telecommunications Authority, Nicosia; and P.O. Box 270, Limassol, Cyprus.

Rubayyi, Salem (see Ali, Salem Rubia).

Rubin, Reuben; Israeli artist; b. 13 Nov. 1893; ed. Ecole des Beaux Arts, Paris, and Acad. Collarossi.
Israeli Minister to Rumania 48-50; first one-man exhibition, Anderson Galleries, N.Y. 20; since 20 numerous one-man exhbns. in Jerusalem, Tel-Aviv, Paris, London, New York, Los Angeles, San Francisco, Geneva; exhibited Venice Biennale 48, 50, 52; exhibition at Metropolitan Museum, N.Y. (with six other Israel artists) 53, etc.; works in Museum of Modern Art, N.Y., San Antonio Museum, Texas, Norton Gallery, Palm Beach, Brooklyn Museum, Princeton Univ. Museum, and other U.S. museums, Musée d'Art Moderne, Paris, Manchester (England), Melbourne, Tel-Aviv and Jerusalem Museums and in private collections in Europe and America; décor for Habimah and Ohel Theatres, Israel; murals for Jerusalem Religious Centre 59, Knesset 66; stained glass windows, President's Residence, Jerusalem; mem. The Hebrew Inst. of Religion, N.Y. 45-; mem. Provisional Council for UNESCO in Israel, Fellow of Int. Inst. of Arts and Letters 58-; Prize of Honour, City of Tel-Aviv 64; commissioned for mural in Jerusalem Parl. 66; Israel Prize for life-work's achievement on 25th Anniversary of the State 73.
Publs. *Rubin* 58, *Visages d'Israël* 61, *Godseekers* 67, *My Life, My Art* 69, *The Story of King David* 71, *Visions of the Bible* 72, *The Prophets* 73.
14 Bialik Street, Tel-Aviv; and Caesarea-by-the-Sea, Israel.

Runciman, The Hon. Sir Steven (James Cochran Stevenson), Kt., M.A., F.B.A.; British historian; b. 7 July 1903; ed. Eton Coll. and Trinity Coll., Cambridge.
Fellow Trinity Coll., Cambridge 27-38; Lecturer Cambridge Univ. 31-38; Pres Attaché, British Legation, Sofia 40-41; Prof. of Byzantine Studies, Istanbul Univ. 42-45; Rep. of British Council, Greece 45-47; Chair. Anglo-Hellenic League 51-67; Trustee, British Museum 60-67; Pres. British Inst. of Archaeology at Ankara 62-; Fellow British Acad. 57; Hon. Fellow Trinity Coll., Cambridge 65; Hon. Litt.D. (Cambridge, London, Chicago, Durham, St. Andrews, Oxford, Birmingham), Hon. LL.D. (Glasgow), Hon. D.Phil. (Thessalonika), Hon. D.D. (Wabash, U.S.A.).
Publs. *The Emperor Romanus Lecapenus* 29, *The First Bulgarian Empire* 30, *Byzantine Civilization* 33, *The Medieval Manichee* 47, *History of the Crusades* (3 vols.) 51-54, *The Eastern Schism* 55, *The Sicilian Vespers* 58, *The White Rajahs* 60, *The Fall of Constantinople 1453* 65, *The Great Church in Captivity* 68, *The Last Byzantine Renaissance* 70, *The Orthodox Churches and the Secular State* 71.
Elshieshields, Lockerbie, Dumfriesshire, Scotland.

S

Saam, Mohammad, M.A., PH.D.; Iranian educationalist and politician; b. 1924, Kerman, Iran; ed. Univs. of Teheran, Nebraska and S. Calif., U.S.A.
Former teacher; Dir. Dept. of Educ.; Del. of Dept. of Educ. to Near East Inst.; Admin. Consultant to Cen. Bank of Iran; mem. Parl.; Gov. Gen. of Gilan and Isfahan; now Minister of Information.
Ministry of Information, Teheran, Iran.

Saba, Elias, B.LITT.; Lebanese economist and politician; b. 1932, Lebanon; ed. American Univ. of Beirut and Univ. of Oxford.
Economic Adviser to Ministry of Finance and Petroleum, Kuwait and Kuwait Fund for Arab Econ. Devt. 61-62; Chair. Dept. of Econs., American Univ. of Beirut 63-67; Assoc. Prof. of Econs., American Univ. of Beirut 67-69; Deputy Prime Minister of the Lebanon, Minister of Finance and Minister of Defence Oct. 70-May 72.
Publ. *Postwar Developments in the Foreign Exchange Systems of Lebanon and Syria* 62.
Biarritz Building, P.O. Box 9500, Beirut, Lebanon.

Saba, Hanna, D. en D.; Egyptian jurist and diplomatist; b. 23 July 1909; ed. Coll. of Jesuit Fathers, Cairo, Faculté de Droit, Paris, and Ecole Libre des Sciences Politiques, Paris.
Ministry of Foreign Affairs, Cairo 42, Counsellor 46, Minister 52; Dir. of Treaties Div., UN Secr. 46-50; Juridical Adviser, UNESCO 50-67; Asst. Dir.-Gen. of UNESCO 67-71; Alt. Chair. UNESCO Appeal Board 73-; Grand Officer of Merit, Egypt; Officer of the Nile.
Publs. *L'Islam et la nationalité* 32, *L'évolution dans la technique des traités*, *Les droits économiques et sociaux dans le projet de pacte des droits de l'homme*, *Les ententes et accords régionaux dans la Charte des Nations Unies* (Course at Acad. of Int. Law, The Hague 52), *L'Activité quasi-législative des institutions spécialisées des Nations Unies* (Course at Acad. of Int. Law, The Hague 64).
UNESCO, Place de Fontenoy, Paris 7e; Home: 3 boulevard de la Sassaye, Neuilly (Hauts de Seine), France.

Sabah, His Highness Sheikh Jabir al-Ahmed al-Jabir al-; Kuwaiti politician; b. 1928; ed. Almubarakiyyah School and privately.
Governor, Ahmedi and Oil Areas 49-59; Pres. Dept. of Finance and Economy 59; Minister of Finance, Industry and Commerce 63; Prime Minister 65-; appointed Crown Prince 66.
Office of the Prime Minister, Council of Ministers, Kuwait.

Sabah, Sheikh Saad al-Abdullah al-Salem al-; Kuwaiti politician.
Deputy Pres., Police and Public Security Dept. until 61; Minister of the Interior 61-65; Minister of the Interior and Defence Nov. 65-.
Ministry of the Interior, Kuwait.

Sabah, Sheikh Sabah al-Ahmed al-Jabir al-; Kuwaiti politician; b. 1929; ed. Mubarakiyyah National School, Kuwait and privately.
Member Supreme Cttee. 56-61; Head of Dept. of Social Affairs and Dept. of Printing, Press and Publications 61; Minister of Guidance of News 63; Minister of Foreign Affairs 63-, acting Minister of Oil 65-67; Minister of Oil Affairs 67.
Ministry of Foreign Affairs, Kuwait.

Sabah, Sheikh Sabah al-Salem al-; Amir of Kuwait, twelfth ruler of the Sabah dynasty; b. 1913; ed. privately.
Head of Police Dept. 38-59; mem. Supreme Exec. Cttee. 55-61; Deputy Prime Minister and Minister of Foreign Affairs 61-63; Prime Minister 63-65; succeeded his brother Sheikh Abdullah al-Salem al-Sabah as Amir of Kuwait Nov. 65.
Sief Palace, Amiry Diwan, Kuwait.

Sabah, Sheikh Salem al-Sabah al- (son of Sheikh Sabah al-Salem al-Sabah, Amir of Kuwait *q.v.*); Kuwaiti diplomatist; b. 18 June 1937; ed. Secondary School, Kuwait, Gray's Inn, London, and Christ Church, Oxford.
Joined Foreign Service 62; Head of Legal (later Political) Dept. Ministry of Foreign Affairs; Amb. to the U.K. 65-70, to U.S.A. 70-; rep of Kuwait to confs. in Middle East and Africa, including Arab Summit Conf., Casablanca Oct. 65.
Embassy of Kuwait, 2940 Tilden Street, N.W., Washington, D.C., U.S.A.

Sabbagh, Basheer, B.A.; Jordanian politician; b. 1918; ed. American Univ. of Beirut.
Teacher, Irbid 43; Headmaster, Irbid 44, Salt 46; Acting Islamic Chief Justice and Minister of Social Affairs 61; Minister of Educ. and Social Affairs 61, of Educ. July 64-65, 68-Aug. 69; Acting Islamic Chief Justice and Minister of Educ. 62-64; Vice-Chair. Royal Cttee. for Educ. Affairs 62, Board of Dirs. of Shereiah Coll. 64-; Dir. Moslem Educational Coll. 47-; Al Kawkab Medal (1st and 3rd Grades), Egyptian Repub. Medal (4th Grade), Syrian Istiqlal Medal (2nd Grade).
c/o Ministry of Education, Amman, Jordan.

Sabin, Albert B(ruce), B.S., M.D.; American virologist; b. 26 Aug. 1906, Bialystok, Russia; ed. New York Univ.
Research Assoc. in bacteriology, New York Univ. Coll. of Medicine 26-31; House Physician, Bellevue Hospital, New York City 32-33; Fellow in Medicine, Nat. Research Council, Lister Inst. (England) 34; Asst. Rockefeller Inst., N.Y.C. 35-37, Assoc. 37-39; Assoc. Prof. of Research Pediatrics, Univ. of Cincinnati Coll. of Medicine 39-46, Prof. 46-60, Distinguished Service Prof. 60-70; Pres. Weizmann Inst. of Science 70-72; developer of oral polio vaccine; Medical Corps U.S. Army, Second World War; mem. Nat. Acad. of Sciences (U.S.A.), American Acad. of Arts and Sciences (Fellow), A.A.A.S.; hon. mem. numerous acads. and socs.; numerous honorary degrees; hon. fellow, Royal Soc. of Health, London; Int. Antonio Feltrinelli Prize 64, Lasker Award 65, Royal Soc. of Health Gold Medal 69, Nat. Medal of Science (U.S.A.) 71, and numerous awards and honours for work in medical research.
c/o The Weizmann Institute of Science, Rehovot, Israel.

Sabir, Mohieddin, PH.D.; Sudanese politician; b. 1919, Dalgo; ed. Univ. of Cairo, Bordeaux Univ. and the Sorbonne, France.
Director, Ministry of Social Affairs 54; Editor-in-Chief *El Estglal* and *Sot El Sudan* (daily papers); Man. *El Zaman* (daily paper); UNESCO Expert and Head,

Social Sciences Dept., Regional Centre for Social Devt., Sirra Llyan; mem. Constituent Assembly 68; Minister of Educ. 69-72.
c/o Ministry of Education, Khartoum, Sudan.

Sabri, Aly; Egyptian politician; b. 30 Aug. 1920; ed. Military Acad. and Air Force Acad.
Fought in Palestine War 48; Minister for Presidential Affairs, Egypt 57-58, U.A.R. 58-62; Pres. Exec. Council 62-64, Prime Minister 64-65; Vice-Pres. of Repub. Oct. 65-67; Sec.-Gen. Arab Socialist Union Oct. 65-67, 68-Sept. 69; Deputy Prime Minister 67 and Minister of Local Govt. 67-Oct. 67; Resident Minister for Suez Canal Zone Oct. 67-68; Vice-Pres. of Repub. 70-71; on trial for treason Aug. 71, sentenced to life imprisonment Dec. 71.
Cairo, Egypt.

Sa'd, Farid Ali, B.SC.; Jordanian economist; b. 1908; ed. American Univ. of Beirut, Lebanon.
Science Teacher, Principal, Insp. of Educ. in Transjordan and Palestine 28-35; District Officer, Palestine Govt. 35-43; Man. Arab Bank Ltd., Haifa 43-48; mem. War Econ. Advisory Council of Palestine Govt. 43-46; Senator 51-55; mem. Royal Fiscal Comm., Cttee. of Educ. Moslem Coll.; Minister of Finance; Chair., Man. Dir. Jordan Tobacco and Cigarette Co. Ltd., Jordan Bata Co.; Dir. Jordan Petroleum Refinery Co. Ltd.; Chair. Advisory Board, Nat. and Grindlays Bank Ltd.; mem. Arab Orphans Cttee., Board of Royal Jordanian Airlines; Vice-Mayor Amman Municipality; Trustee, Jordan Univ., American Univ. of Beirut.
P.O. Box 59, Amman, Jordan.

Sadaghiani, Reza; Iranian agriculturalist; ed. Karaj Agricultural Faculty, near Teheran, and Syracuse Univ., U.S.A.
Iranian Ministry of Agriculture 39, served as Technical Under-Sec. to Dept. of Forestry, Head of Karkheh Devt. Org. of the Plan Org., Head of Agriculture Div. of Plan Org., Dir. of Rural Devt., Under-Sec. for Research and Planning to Ministry of Agriculture, Deputy Chief of Central Bureau of Planning, Under-Sec. for Technical Affairs to Minister of Agriculture; now Pres. Agricultural Bank of Iran.
Bank Keshavarzi Iran (Agricultural Bank of Iran), Teheran, Iran.

Sadaka, Nagib, B.A., L. ès L., D. en D.; Lebanese diplomatist; b. 1915; ed. American Univ. of Beirut, French Faculty of Law, Beirut, and the Sorbonne.
Lecturer, Inst. of Political Science, French Faculty of Law, Beirut 46; Head of Western Political Section, Ministry of Foreign Affairs 47, Head of UN Service 49; Counsellor, Paris 52; Dir.-Gen. Ministry of Educ. 52-55; Amb. to Switzerland and U.A.R. 58-60; Amb. to Belgium and Perm. Rep. to EEC 60-66; Sec.-Gen. Ministry of Foreign Affairs 66-.
Publs. *Paternal power in Moslem law* (in Arabic) 39, *La question syrienne pendant la guerre de 1914-1918* 40, *The Palestinian Question* (in Arabic) 46.
Ministry of Foreign Affairs, Beirut, Lebanon.

Sadat, Col. Anwar es-; Egyptian officer and politician; b. 1918; ed. Military Coll.
Commissioned 33; fmr. Gen. Sec. Islamic Congress; one of Free Officers who overthrew monarchy 52; Editor *Al Jumhuriya* and *Al Tahrir* 55-56; Pres. Egyptian Nat. Union 57-61; Pres. Afro-Asian Conf., Cairo 58; Speaker U.A.R. Nat. Assembly 61-Jan. 69; mem. Presidency Council 62-64, Vice-Pres. of U.A.R. 64-67, 69-70; interim Pres. Sept.-Oct. 70, Pres. Oct. 70-; Chair. Pres. Council, Fed. of Arab Republics 71-; Chair. Arab Socialist Union (ASU); Prime Minister 73-; Mil. Gov.-Gen. 73-.
The Presidency, Cairo, Egypt.

Sadawi, A. M. Suhail; Libyan oil executive; b. 1928, Beirut; ed. American Univ. of Beirut.
With Gulf Oil Corpn., Libya 58-61; Int. Labour Office, Geneva 62-63; Head, Gen. Econ. Section, Org. of Petroleum Exporting Countries (OPEC) 63; participated in negotiations for amendment of Libyan Petroleum Law 65; mem. Pricing Comm., Libya 67, Chair. 68; Asst. Under Sec., Libyan Ministry of Petroleum 68; Deputy Dir. Gen. Libyan Nat. Petroleum Corpn. 68; Sec.-Gen. Org. of Arab Petroleum Exporting Countries 70-73.
c/o Organization of Arab Petroleum Exporting Countries, P.O. Box 20501, Kuwait.

Sadek, Gen. Mohammed Ahmed; Egyptian army officer; ed. Frunze Mil. Acad., U.S.S.R.
Served in Egyptian army, World War II, Palestine War 48, Suez Campaign 56; Mil. Attaché, Egyptian Embassy to Fed. Repub. of Germany 64; Dir. of Studies, Mil. Acad., Cairo 65-67; Dir. of Information, Army Intelligence Dept. 67; Chief of Staff of the Army 69; Minister of War and Mil. Production 71-72; Deputy Premier for Nat. Defence Jan.-Oct. 72; mem. Supreme Council of the Armed Forces.
c/o Ministry of War, Cairo, Egypt.

Sadiq, Issa, PH.D.; Iranian educationist; b. 1894; ed. Univs. of Paris, Cambridge (England), and Columbia (N.Y.).
Directed various depts. Ministry of Education 19-30; mem. Nat. Constituent Assembly 25-49, 67; Pres. and Prof. Nat. Teachers' Coll.; Dean of Faculties of Arts and Science Teheran Univ. 32-41; Chancellor of Univ. 41; Minister of Education 41, 43, 45, 47 and 60-61; Senator for Teheran 49-52, 54-60, 63-67, 67-71; Vice-Pres. Iranian Acad. 37-70; mem. Board of Govs., Nat. Bank of Iran 37-52; Prof. of History of Educ., Univ. of Teheran 32-; Pres. Persia-America Relations Soc. 49-53; mem. Royal Cultural Council 62-; Founder mem. Nat. Soc. for Physical Educ. 33-54; Founder mem. Soc. for Preservation of Nat. Monuments 44-; Founder mem. of Nat. Soc. for Protection of Children 53-; mem. High Educational Council 34-41, 51-58, 72-, Iranian Acad. of Language 70-, High Council for Culture and Art 72-.
Publs. *Principles of Education, New Methods in Education, History of Education, Modern Persia and her Educational System* (in English), *A Year in America, The March of Education in Iran and the West, A Brief Course in the History of Education in Iran, History of Education in Persia from the Earliest Times to the Present Day, History of Education in Europe, Memoirs*, etc.
316 Avenue Hedayat, Valiabad, Teheran; and The University, Avenue Shah Reza, Teheran, Iran.

Sadr Javad, PH.D.; Iranian diplomatist and politician; b. 1912; ed. Univ. de Paris à la Sorbonne.
Ministry of Interior 39, Ministry of Foreign Affairs 41; fmr. mem. Information and Legal Affairs Div., Ministry of Foreign Affairs, later First Sec. and Consul, Palestine; fmr. Chief of Secr. to Prime Minister; fmr. Minister in Yugoslavia; fmr. Deputy Minister of Interior and of Foreign Affairs; fmr. Ambassador to Japan; Minister of Interior 64-66; Minister of Justice 66-68; Foreign Office Adviser 68; Grand Officer Homayoun, Officer Tadj Order, Order of Merit for Justice, 8 foreign decorations.
Ministry of Foreign Affairs, Teheran, Iran.

Saffar, Salman Mohamed, PH.D.; Bahrain diplomatist; b. 1931, Bahrain; ed. Baghdad Univ., Iraq and Sorbonne, Paris.
Primary school teacher, Bahrain 49-54, Secondary school teacher 59-60; Perm. Rep. to UN Sept. 73-.
Permanent Mission of Bahrain to United Nations, 747 Third Avenue, 19th Floor, New York, N.Y. 10017, U.S.A.

Safieddine, Mohammed Hussein; Lebanese politician; b. 1911, Tyre; ed. Arab Univ. of Law, Damascus.
Barrister -42; Judge 42-47; Deputy for Tyre 47, 53, 60, 64; Minister of Information 51-52; Minister of Educ. Sept.-Oct. 58; Minister of Agriculture 60-61; Minister of Educ., Work, and Social Affairs May-Oct. 61; mem. of Parl. Comm. on the Admin. of Justice; Minister of Planning 68-69.
Ras El Nab'e, Imm. Chaar, Beirut, Lebanon.

Sagar, Abdul Aziz al-Hamad al; Kuwaiti businessman and politician; b. 1913; ed. Secondary School, Bombay.
Member Municipality Board 52-55, Devt. Board 52-55; Chair. Kuwait Chamber of Commerce 59-, Nat. Bank of Kuwait 59-65; Jt. Council 61-62; Chair. Kuwait Oil Tanker Co. 61-64, 65-; mem. Constituent Assembly 63-, Speaker 63-65; Minister of Health 63; Chair. Red Crescent Soc. 66-.
P.O. Box 244, Kuwait City, Kuwait.

Sahnoun, Hadj Mohamed, M.A.; Algerian diplomatist; b. 8 April 1931; ed. Lycée of Constantine, Univ. de Paris à la Sorbonne and New York Univ.
Director of African, Asian and Latin American Affairs Ministry of Foriegn Affairs 62-63, of Political Affairs 64; Del. to UN Gen. Assembly 62-63, 64-65; Asst. Sec.-Gen. Org. of African Unity (OAU) 64-.
Publ. *Economic and Social Aspects of the Algerian Revolution* 62.
OAU, P.O. Box 3243, Addis Ababa, Ethiopia.

Said, Faisal al-; Omani diplomatist; b. 1927, Muscat.
Attached to Ministry of Foreign Affairs, Muscat 53-57; lived abroad 57-70; Perm. Under-Sec. Ministry of Educ. 70-72; Minister of Econ. Affairs 72; Perm. Rep. to UN 72-.
Permanent Mission of Oman to United Nations, United Nations, New York, N.Y. 10017, U.S.A.

Said, Mostafa Tewfik el-, LL.B., LL.D., Egyptian lawyer and professor; b. 1908; ed. Mansourah Secondary School and Cairo Univ.
Public Prosecutor 29-38; Lecturer and Asst. Prof. of Criminal Law, Cairo Univ. 38-42; Prof. of Criminal Law, Alexandria Univ. 42; Dean of Faculty of Law, Alexandria Univ. 46; Attorney-Gen., Alexandria Court of Appeal 49, Prof. of Criminal Law, Cairo Univ. 50; Dean of Faculty of Law, Cairo Univ. 52; Rector of Alexandria Univ. 54-58; Rector of Cairo Univ. 58-61; Chair. of Supreme Council of the Univs.; Ambassador to Portugal 62-64, to Somalia 64-68, to German Democratic Repub. Feb. 72-.
Publs. *On the Scope and Exercise of Marital Rights* 36, *The Egyptian Penal Code Annotated*, 3rd edition 37, *Crimes of Forgery Under the Egyptian Law*, 4th edition 53, *Principles of Criminal Law*, 3rd edition 47, *The Expansion of Higher Education in the United Arab Republic* 60.
Egyptian Embassy, Warmbader Strasse 50/52, Berlin-Karlshorst, Germany.

Said Ansary, Alinaghi, M.RER.POL.; Iranian diplomatist; b. 18 Jan. 1920, Teheran; ed. Teheran Univ. and Faculty of Int. Relations, George Washington Univ., U.S.A.
Served in various political and admin. depts., Ministry of Foreign Affairs 47-49; First Sec., Iranian Embassy to U.S.A. 49-54; Asst. Head of Protocol, Ministry of Foreign Affairs 54-58; First Sec., Iranian Embassy to Italy 58-61; Consul-Gen., Milan 61-62; apptd. Sec.-Gen. Household of H.I.H. Princess Shams Pahlavi 62-66, concurrently Aide-de-Camp to H.I.M. the Shahanshah Aryamehr; Head of Protocol of the Imperial Court 66; apptd. Amb. 70; Amb. to Italy May 72-, concurrently to Albania.
Imperial Embassy of Iran, Via Nomentana 363, 00162 Rome, Italy.

Saif al-Islam, Abdullah ben Hassan; Yemeni politician.
Minister of the Interior April 67-69; mem. Mil. Council 67; Prime Minister *ad interim* June 68; in exile 68-.

Saif al-Islam, al-Hassan ben Yahya, H.H.; Yemeni politician.
Crown Prince of the Yemen 62-; Prime Minister 62-67; Head of Mil. Council 67; in exile 68-.

Saif al-Islam, Mohamed al-Badr, H.R.H.; Prince of the Yemen; b. 1927; ed. Coll. for Higher Education, Sana'a.
Son of King of the Yemen; Minister for Foreign Affairs 55-61, and Minister of Defence and C.-in-C. 55-62; succeeded to Imamate on the death of his father, Imam Ahmed Sept. 62; left Taiz following Republican *coup d'état* Sept. 62, leading Royalist resistance 62-68; replaced by Imamate Council May 68; in exile 68-.

Saif al-Islam, Mohammed ben Hussein; Yemeni politician; b. 1938.
Former diplomatic rep. to Fed. Germany; Vice-Pres. Imamate Council 67-May 68, Pres. of Council May 68; Commdr. of Royalist Armed Forces 67-68; in exile 68-.

Salah, Abdullah A.; Jordanian diplomatist; b. 31 Dec. 1922; ed. Bishop Gobat's School, Jerusalem, and American Univ. of Beirut.
Field Educ. Officer, United Nations Relief and Works Agency (UNRWA), Jordan 52-62; Ambassador to Kuwait 62-63, to India 63-64, to France 64-66, 67-70; Minister of Foreign Affairs 66-67, 70-72; several decorations.
c/o Ministry of Foreign Affairs, Amman, Jordan.

Salam, Saeb; Lebanese politician; b. 1905; ed. American Univ. of Beirut.
Elected Provisional Head Lebanese Govt. 43; deputy 43-47, 51; Minister of Interior 46, 60-61; Minister Foreign Affairs 46; Prime Minister 52, 53, 60-61; concurrently Minister of Defence 61; pioneer Lebanese civil aviation 45; Pres. Middle East Airlines Co., Beirut 45-56; Pres. Nat. Fats & Oil Co. Ltd., Beirut; Prime Minister 70-73.
Chamber of Deputies, Beirut, Lebanon.

Saleh, Jehanshah, M.D., F.I.C.S., F.R.C.O.G.; Iranian surgeon, gynaecologist and politician; b. 1905; ed. Syracuse Univ., N.Y.
Intern, St. Joseph's Hospital, Syracuse, N.Y. 33, Orange Memorial Hospital, N.J. 34, Resident Surgeon 35; Prof. of Anatomy, Teheran Univ. Faculty of Medicine 36-41, Prof. of Gynaecology 40-, Dean 47-54; Dir. and Chief of Gynaecological and Obstetrical Service, Vaziri Hospital, Teheran 36-37; Dir. and Chief Surgeon, Women's Hospital, Teheran 37; Minister of Public Health 50, 53, 54, 55, 60-61; Minister of Educ. 61-63; mem. Board of Dirs. and Chief of Public Health Section, Red Lion and Sun (analogous to the Red Cross) 38-; Fellow, Int. Coll. of Surgeons; Pres. Iranian Asscn. of Obstetricians and Gynaecologists, and of Iran-America Medical Society; mem. American Medical Asscn., Iranian Central Council of Sanitation, Central Council for Education; Chancellor Teheran Univ.; WHO adviser in medical education and auxiliary branches 52-; Senator 69-; Hon. LL.D. (Syracuse Univ.), Hon. Sc.D. (Univ. of Bordeaux), Hon. F.R.C.O.G. (England), Hon. M.D. (Univ. of Vienna).
Publs. *The Relation of Diet to the Preservation of Teeth* 31, *Morphine Addiction and its Treatment* 32, *Diseases of Women* 41, *Normal and Abnormal Obstetrics* 42, *Recent Advances in Gynæcology* 60, *Text Book of Gynæcology* 64.
Home: 10 W.Takht-i-Jamshid Avenue, Teheran; Office: University of Teheran, Avenue Shahreza, Teheran, Iran.

Salem, Mamdouh Mohamed; Egyptian civil servant and politician; b. 1918, Alexandria; ed. Police Acad.
Police Commdr., Alexandria 64-68; Gov. of Assiyut 68-70, of Alexandria 70-; Deputy Premier, Minister of the Interior 71-.
Ministry of the Interior, Cairo, Egypt.

Salih, Salih Mohammed; Sudanese banker; b. 1918; ed. Sudan Higher School.
Municipal Engineer, Govt. Survey Dept. 42, Agricultural

Engineer 43-45, Chief Surveyor 45-51; Field Insp. Sudan Gezira Board 51-55, Group Insp. 55-56, Asst. Gen. Man. 56-62, Gen. Man. 62-64, Acting Man. Dir. 65-66; Chair. Board of Dirs., Gen. Man. Agricultural Bank of Sudan 67-; mem. People's Council 72-, Head Finance and Audit Cttee. Agricultural Bank of Sudan, P.O. Box 1363, Khartoum, Sudan.

Salim, Khalil, B.A., DIP.ED., ED.D.; Jordanian educator, politician and banker; b. 1921; ed. American Univ. of Beirut, Inst. of Education, London and Columbia Univ. Teacher in Secondary Schools 41-49; Lecturer Teachers Coll. 50; Dir. Cultural Affairs 52; Sec. Jordan Nat. Comm. for UNESCO 50-58; Asst. Under-Sec. of Educ. 55-62; Minister of Social Affairs 62; Minister of State, Prime Minister's Office 62-63; Chair. Authority for Tourism and Antiquities 62-63; Minister of Nat. Economy 62-63; Gov. Central Bank of Jordan 63-; Chair. Board of Jordan Co-operation Union 65-68; mem. Jordan Devt. Board, lecturer, and mem. Board of Trustees, Univ. of Jordan; mem. Jordan Scientific Board; Sec.-Gen. Royal Scientific Soc. 70; Deputy Chair. Alia Airline 70.
Publs. *Re-organization of Educational Administration in Jordan* 60, 15 textbooks on mathematics and numerous articles on mathematics, popular science, education, economics and banking.
Central Bank of Jordan, P.O.B. 37, Amman, Jordan.

Sallal, Marshal Abdullah; Yemeni army officer and politician; b. 1917; ed. in Iraq.
Returned to Yemen from Iraq 39; imprisoned 39; army service 40-48, 55-; imprisoned 48-55; Gov. of Hodeida 59-62; Chief of Staff to Imam Mohammed 62; Pres. of the Revolutionary Council and C.-in-C. 62-67; Prime Minister Sept. 62-Feb. 64, Sept. 66-67, concurrently Minister of Foreign Affairs Feb. 63-Feb. 64.
Cairo, Egypt.

Salzman, Pnina; Israeli pianist; b. 1923; ed. Ecole Normale de Musique and Conservatoire National de Musique, Paris.
Gave first concert in Paris at age of twelve; since then has given concerts in five continents; travels all over the world every year, playing with most of the major orchestras; over 300 concerts with Israeli orchestras.
20 Dubnov St., Tel-Aviv, Israel.

Sambursky, Shmuel, PH.D.; Israeli physicist; b. 28 Oct. 1900; ed. Univs. of Königsberg, Berlin and Utrecht.
Staff, Dept. of Physics, Hebrew Univ. Jerusalem 28-, Lecturer 34, Assoc. Prof. of Experimental Physics 49-60, Prof. and Head of Dept. of History and Philosophy of Science 60-; Exec. Sec. Palestine Board for Scientific and Industrial Research 45-48; Dir. Research Council of Israel 49-56, Vice-Chair. 56-59; mem. Exec. Cttee. of Nat. Comm. for UNESCO; Israeli del. UNESCO Gen. Confs. 49, 50, 51, 52, 54, 56, 58, 62; mem. Int. Advisory Cttee. on Scientific Research of UNESCO 54-57; Dean, Faculty of Science, Hebrew Univ. 57-59; Visiting Fellow, St. Catherine's Coll. Oxford 64-65; mem. Israel Acad. of Sciences and Humanities.
Publs. *The Physical World of the Greeks* 56, *Physics of the Stoics* 59, *The Physical World of Late Antiquity* 62.
c/o Hebrew University, Jerusalem, Israel.

Samii, Mohammad Mehdi; Iranian banker; b. 1918; ed. Inst. of Chartered Accountants in England and Wales.
Bank Melli Iran 45-51; National Iranian Oil Co. 51-53; Bank Melli Iran 53-59; Industrial and Mining Development Bank of Iran 59-63; Gov. Bank Markazi Iran (Central Bank of Iran) 63-68, 70-71; Man. Dir. Plan Org. 68-70; Adviser to the Prime Minister 71-.
Office of the Prime Minister, Teheran, Iran.

Samuel, 2nd Viscount, cr. 37, of Mount Carmel and of Toxteth, Liverpool, **Edwin Herbert Samuel,** C.M.G.; British lecturer and author; b. 1898; ed. Westminster School, Balliol Coll. Oxford, and Columbia Univ.
Served First World War; Palestine Civil Service 20-48; Visiting Prof. Dropsie Coll., Philadelphia 48-49, Graduate School of Public Affairs, Albany, New York 63, Univ. of Pittsburgh 70; Visiting Lecturer, Witwatersrand Univ., Johannesburg 53; European Dir. *The Conquest of the Desert* Exhibition, Jerusalem 51-53; Principal of the Inst. of Public Admin. in Israel; Dir. *Jewish Chronicle*, London, 51-70, Vallentine Mitchell (Publishers) Ltd., (London) 65-, Ellern Investment Corpn., Tel-Aviv 64-, Moller Textile Co., Nahariya 65-; Senior Lecturer in British Institutions, The Hebrew Univ., Jerusalem 54-69; Adviser, Magen David Adom (Israeli Red Cross) 57-.
Publs. *A Primer on Palestine* 32, *The Jewish Communal Villages of Palestine* 38, *The Theory of Administration* 46, *Problems of Government in the State of Israel* 56, *British Traditions in the Administration of Israel* 57, *The Structure of Society in Israel* 69, *Anglo-Israel Relations 1948-1968: A Catalogue* 69, *A Lifetime in Jerusalem: Memoirs* 69; Short Stories: *A Cottage in Galilee* 57, *A Coat of Many Colours* 60, *My Friend Musa* 63, *The Cucumber King* 65, *His Celestial Highness* 68, *Roots* (with Mordechai Kamrat) 69, *The Man Who Liked Cats* 73.
House of Lords, London S.W.1, England; and 15 Rashba Road, Jerusalem, Israel.

Sanbar, Moshe, M.A.(ECON.); Israeli banker and economist; b. 29 March 1926, Kecskemét, Hungary; ed. Univ. of Budapest and Hebrew Univ., Jerusalem.
Emigrated to Israel 48; Project Dir., Israel Inst. of Applied Social Research and later Deputy Dir. 51-58; Lecturer in Statistics, Hebrew Univ., Jerusalem 57-61; Dir. Research Dept., Deputy Dir. Internal State Revenue Div., Ministry of Finance 58-63, Dir. of Budgets 63-68; Econ. Adviser to Ministry of Finance 63-68; Deputy Chair., and later Chair., Industrial Devt. Bank of Israel 68-71; Chief Econ. Adviser to Minister of Finance 69-71; Acting Deputy Minister of Commerce and Industry 70-71; Gov. Bank of Israel Nov. 71-; Gov. for Israel, IBRD, IFC, IDA; Chair. Econ. Devt. and Refugee Rehabilitation Trust, Board of Dirs. Habimah Nat. Theatre.
Publs. *My Longest Year* (Yad Vashem Prize) 66; many articles and research studies on economic subjects.
Bank of Israel, Mizpan Building, Jerusalem; Home: 44 Pincas Street, Tel-Aviv, Israel.

Sançar, Ilhami, B.A.; Turkish lawyer; b. 1909, Gördes; ed. secondary school, Izmir, Univ. of Ankara.
Appointed bailiff 36; Attorney-Gen. for Menemen 36, for Urgüp 39; worked as lawyer in local govt. 39; practised as barrister 40; mem. Constitutional Assembly 61; Deputy for Istanbul 61, 65-; Minister of Defence 61-65, 73-.
Tunalı Hilmi Caddesi No. 90/7 Kavaklıdere, Ankara, Turkey.

Sancar, Gen. Semih; Turkish army officer; b. 1911, Erzurum; ed. Artillery School, War Acad.
Served in Turkish Army as Commdr. of Artillery Battery and Battalion, Asst. Commdr. Army Corps Artillery, Dept. Chief, Branch Section Dir. in Land Forces and Gen. Staff H.Q.; then Instructor War Acad.; Dir. of Personnel, Dir. of Operations Turkish Gen. Staff; promoted to rank of Gen. 69; Commdr. of Gendarmerie 69; Commdr. 2nd Army; Commdr. Turkish Land Forces 72-73; Chief of Gen. Staff 73-.
General Staff Headquarters, Ankara, Turkey.

Sani'i, Gen. Asadollah; Iranian army officer and politician; b. 1904; ed. Officers' Training Coll.
Special Adjutant to Shahanshah; Deputy Minister of War 61, 62, Minister of War 63-70; Minister of Agricultural Products and Consumer Goods 70-71; Third, Second and First Order of Merit; Third, Second and First Order of

Honour; Second and First Order of Homayoun; First Order of Service and several other decorations.
Teheran, Iran.

Sanusi, H.R.H. Prince Hassan Rida; Former Crown Prince of Libya; b. 1934.
Son of H.M. King Idris I; became Crown Prince on death of his Great Uncle, Ahmed Sherif as-Sanusi, Dec. 50; in exile 69-.

Sapir, Pinhas; Israeli politician; b. Lithuania 1909.
Emigrated to Palestine 29; employed as agricultural labourer; Asst. Dir. Mekorot (Israel's major water development Co.) 37-47; after establishment of State of Israel, became Dir.-Gen. Ministry of Defence and subsequently Dir.-Gen. of Treasury; Minister of Commerce and Industry 55-65, concurrently of Finance 63-68; Sec.-Gen. Israel Labour Party 68-69; Minister of Finance 69-, concurrently of Commerce and Industry 69-72.
Ministry of Finance, Jerusalem, Israel.

Saqqaf, Sheikh Omar; Saudi Arabian politician; b. 1923.
Former Amb. to Ethiopia; Perm. Under-Sec. Ministry of Foreign Affairs -67, Deputy Minister 67-April 68; Minister of State for Foreign Affairs April 68-, and Personal Rep. of H.M. King Faisal on diplomatic missions.
Ministry of Foreign Affairs, Riyadh, Saudi Arabia.

Sarc, Omer Celâl, DR.RER.POL.; Turkish professor and administrator; b. 1901; ed. Robert Coll., Istanbul, Handelshochschule, Berlin, and Univ. of Berlin.
Asst. Prof. of Econs., Univ. of Istanbul 26, Assoc. Prof. of Applied Econs. and Statistics 33, Prof. of Applied Econs. and Statistics 38-55, 57-, Dean of Faculty of Econs. 36-48, Rector of the Univ. 49-51, 63-65, Pro-Rector 51-53, 63-; Visiting Prof. Columbia Univ., School of Int. Affairs 54-55, 67-68; Chief, Middle East Unit, Dept. of Econ. Affairs, UN, New York 55-56; Dir. Econ. and Social Affairs, Council of Europe 59-61; Hon. Dr. Jur (Fuad I Univ., Cairo); Officer, Legion of Honour, Great Cross of Merit (Fed. Germany).
Publs. *Agricultural and Industrial Policy* 34, *Theory of Statistics* 35, *The Foundations of Turkish Economy* 50.
c/o University of Istanbul, Beyazit, Istanbul; Home: Kalipci Sok. 156-I, Divan AP, Tesvikiye, Istanbul, Turkey.

Sarrûf, Fûad, B.A., LL.D.; Lebanese author and university official; b. 1900; ed. Shwaifat Nat. Coll., and American Univ. of Beirut.
Teacher and Headmaster, Lebanon 19-22; Asst. Editor *Al-Muqtataf* (monthly), Cairo 22-27, Editor 27-44; Editor *Al-Mukhtar* (Arabic edition of *Reader's Digest*), Cairo 43-47; Columnist, *Al-Ahram* (daily), Cairo 48-51; Vice-Pres. in charge of Univ. Relations, American Univ., Beirut 52-68; started Dept. of Journalism, American Univ., Cairo 35-43; Pres. Lebanese Nat. Comm. for UNESCO; mem. Exec. Board of UNESCO 66-70, Vice-Pres. 70-73, Pres. Jan. 73-; mem. Lebanese Nat. Research Council, Baalbek Int. Festival Cttee.; several decorations.
Publs. *Pillars of Modern Science* 35, *Horizons of Modern Science* 39, *The Conquest Goes On* 44, *Horizons Without End* 58, *Man and the Universe* 61, *Modern Science in Modern Society* 66, *Scientific Papers* 72, numerous other books.
55 rue du Caire, Ras, Beirut, Lebanon.

Sasson, Eliahu (Elias); Israeli diplomatist and politician; b. 2 Feb. 1902, Damascus; ed. St. Joseph Coll., Beirut.
Owner and Editor of Arab newspaper *Al Hayyat*, Damascus 19-21; corresp. and editor of various Hebrew and Arab newspapers, Jerusalem, Damascus, Beirut, Baghdad, Cairo and Tel-Aviv 24-31; Head of Div. for Arab Affairs, Political Dept., Jewish Agency 32-47; Head of Middle Eastern Dept. Israeli Ministry of Foreign Affairs 47-50; Minister to Turkey 50-53, to Italy 53-57, Ambassador 57-60, to Switzerland 60-61; Minister of Posts 61-67, of Police 67-69; mem. Knesset (Parl.) 69-; mem. Israeli del. at Israeli-Egyptian Armistice negotiations, Rhodes, and signatory of the Armistice Treaty 48-49; joint head of Israeli del. at Lausanne Conf. of Palestine Conciliation Comm. 49; mem. Israeli del. at UN 47-48; numerous foreign awards and honours.
24 Lincoln Street, Jerusalem, Israel.

Satir, Kemal; Turkish physician and politician; b. 1911, Adana; ed. Adana.
Practised as X-ray specialist; mem. Parl. for Adana (Republican People's Party) 43-60, 69-, for Elazig 61-69; Minister of Communications 48-50; private practice, Adana 50-57; Deputy Sec.-Gen. RPP, Sec.-Gen. 61-66; mem. Constituent Assembly; Deputy Prime Minister 63-65; resigned RPP 72; formed Republican Party which joined Nat. Reliance Party to become Republican Reliance Party, Pres. Council of RRP; Minister of State and Deputy Prime Minister 73-.
Ministry of State, Ankara, Turkey.

Saudi Arabia, Royal Family of (*see* under first names, as Faisal (King)).

Sayah, Mohamed; Tunisian politician; b. 31 Dec. 1933; ed. Sadikia, Sfax, and Training School for Higher Education, Tunis.
Joined Néo-Destour Party 49; mem. Gen. Union of Tunisian Students 52-62, mem. Exec. Bureau 57-62, Sec.-Gen. 60-62; Asst. Dir. Néo-Destour Party and Chief Editor *L'Action* 62-64, Gen. Sec. of Destourian Youth, Gen. Sec. of Tunisian Youth 63-64; mem. High Comm. SDP 70-; Deputy Nat. Assembly 64-; Minister of Information 69-70, of Public Works and Housing Oct. 71-; Perm. Rep. to UN, Geneva 70; mem. Central Cttee., then mem. Political Bureau and Dir. Destour Socialist Party 64-.
Publs. Several books on the history of the National Tunisian Movement.
Ministère des Travaux Publics et de l'Habitat, Cité-Jardins, Tunis, Tunisia.

Sayegh, Yusef A., M.A., PH.D.; Syrian economist; b. 26 March 1916; ed. American Univ. of Beirut and Johns Hopkins Univ.
At American Univ. of Beirut, Asst. Prof. of Econ. 53-54, 56-57, Assoc. Prof. 57-58, 62-63, Prof. 63-; Dir. Econ. Research Inst. 57-59, 62-64; Econ. Adviser, Planning Board of Kuwait 64-65; Econ. Consultant, Jordan East Ghor Study 66-67; Chair. Planning Board, Nat. Fund of Palestine Liberation Org. (PLO); Grand Prix twice from Lebanese "Friends of the Book" Soc.
Publs. *Bread with Dignity: Socio-economic Content of Arab Nationalism* (Arabic) 61, *Enterpreneurs of Lebanon* 62, *Economics and Economists in the Arab World* 64, *Second Look at Lebanese Economy* (Co-Author) (Arabic) 66, *The Israeli Economy* (Arabic) 66, *The Strategy of Action for the Liberation of Palestine* (Arabic) 68, *Jordan: Country Study* (Mediterranean Development Project) (Co-Author).
Economics Department, American University of Beirut, Beirut, Lebanon.

Sbihi, Abdelhadi; Moroccan diplomatist; b. 18 Nov. 1925; ed. Lycée Meknes, Rabat, and Ecole Supérieure Agronomique, Grignon, France.
Graduated as engineer-agronomist; later Insp.-Del., Ministry of Agriculture; Gov. of Casablanca Province 61; Perm. Rep. of Morocco at UN Food and Agricultural Org. (FAO) 61-65; Pres. Intergovernmental Cttee. of World Food Programme 63; Ambassador to West African countries, Abidjan, Ivory Coast 65-67; Amb. to U.S.S.R. 67-70; Minister of Agriculture and Agrarian Reforms April-Aug. 71; Officier du Mérite du Trône Marocain, du Mérite de la République Italienne.
c/o Ministry of Agriculture, Rabat, Morocco.

Schaeffer, Claude Frédéric Armand, M.A.; French archaeologist; b. 6 March 1898; ed. Strasbourg and Paris Univs.
Curator Prehistoric, Roman and Early Medieval Museum, Palais Rohan, Strasbourg 21-32; Curator Coins and Medals Dept. Strasbourg Univ. 26-32; Curator French Nat. Museums 33-54; Dir. of Research at Nat. Centre of Scientific Research, Paris 46-54; Vice-Pres. Comm. des Fouilles, Direction Générale des Relations Culturelles, Ministry of Foreign Affairs; mem. French Inst. 53; Hon. Prof. Collège de France 54; Dir. expedition Ras Shamra, Syria 29- (discovered Canaanite alphabetic cuneiform records); Cyprus 32, 34, 35, 46, 47, 49-, Malatya, Turkey 46, 47, 48, 50; mem. Archaeological Cttee. Ministry of Education; Hon. Fellow St. John's Coll. Oxford; mem. Nat. Society of Antiquaries, France; corresp. mem. Belgian Royal Acad., Danish Royal Acad.; corresp. Fellow of British Acad.; Hon. Fellow Royal Anthropological Inst. of Great Britain and Ireland, etc.; hon. mem. Deutsche Morgenländische Gesellschaft; served as Capt. Corvette with Fighting French Naval Forces 40-45; D.Litt. h.c. (Oxon.), D.C.L. h.c. (Glasgow), Hon. F.S.A.; Gold Medal, Soc. of Antiquaries 58, Scientific and Philological Soc., Famagusta, Cyprus 65, Hon. Citizen of Latakia (Syria), Famagusta (Cyprus).
Publs. *Haches néolithiques* 24, *Tertres funéraires préhistoriques dans la forêt de Haguenau* (2 vols.) 26, 30, *Missions en Chypre* 36, *Ugaritica I* 39, *Cuneiform Texts of Ras Shamra-Ugarit* 39, *Stratigraphie comparée et Chronologie de l'Asie occidentale* 48, *Ugaritica II* 49, *Enkomi-Alasia* 52, *Ugaritica III* 56, *Ugaritica IV* 62, *Ugaritica V* 65, *Ugaritica VI* 69, *Alasia I* 72.
Le Castel Blanc, 16 rue Turgot, St. Germain-en-Laye; and l'Escale, B.P. 16, La Croix-Valmer (83), France.

Schlumberger, Daniel Théodore, D. ès L.; French archaeologist; b. 19 Dec. 1904; ed. Lycée de Mulhouse, Univs. of Strasbourg and Paris.
Dep. Insp. later Insp. Antiquities Services, French High Comm. in the Levant 29-40; explorations and excavations in N.W. Palmyra 33-35, excavations at Qasr el-Heir el-Gharbi 36-39; Dir. Délégation Archéologique Française, Afghanistan 45-65, excavations in Bactria 47, Kama Dacca and Mir Zakah 48, Lashkari Bazar 49-51, Surkh Kotal 52-64, Ai Khanum 64; Prof. Strasbourg Univ. 55-; mem. Inst. de France 58-.
Publs. Numerous papers and reports in learned journals, notably *Les Formes anciennes du chapiteau corinthien en Syrie, en Palestine et en Arabie* (Syria XIV), *Réflexions sur la Loi fiscale de Palmyre* (Syria XVIII), *Les Fouilles de Qasr el-Heir el-Gharbi* (Syria XX), *L'Inscription d'Hérodien and Les Gentilices romains des Palmyréniens* (Bulletin d'Etudes Orientales de l'Inst. Français de Damas IX), *Deux Fresques omeyyades* (Syria XXV), *La Palmyrène du Nord-Ouest* (Bibl. Arch. Hist. XLIX), *Le Palais ghaznévide de Lashkari Bazar* (Syria XXIX), *L'Argent grec dans l'Empire achéménide* (Mémoires de la Délégation Archéologique Française en Afghanistan XIV), *Le temple de Surkh en Bactriane I-IV* (Journal Asiatique) 52, 54, 55, 64, *Descendants non-méditerranéens de l'art grec* (Syria XXXVII), *Observations sur les remparts de Bactres*; (with M. Leberre, *Mémoires de la Délégation Archéologique Française en Afghanistan* XIX), *Le Prétendu camp de Dioclétien à Palmyre, Une nouvelle inscription grecque d'Acoka, Al Khanoum* 65, *La représentation frontale dans l'art des Sassamdes* (La Persia e il mondo greco-romano) 66.
10 rue Richard-Brunck, Strasbourg, France.

Schnitzer, Moshe, M.A.; Israeli diamond exporter; b. 21 Jan. 1921; ed. Balfour High School, Tel-Aviv, Hebrew Univ. of Jerusalem.
Chairman, Asscn. of Diamond Instructors 43-46; Vice-Pres. Israel Diamond Exchange 51-66, Pres. 66-; Pres. Israel Exporters' Asscn. of Diamonds 62-; World Pres. Int. Fed. of Diamond Exchanges 68-72; partner, Diamond Export Enterprise 53-; mem. Consulting Cttee. to Minister of Commerce and Industry 68-; Editor *The Diamond;* Most Distinguished Exporter of Israel 64.
Publ. *Diamond Book* (in Hebrew) 46.
Israel Diamond Exchange, 3 Jabotinsky Road, Ramat Gan; and 78 Sharet Street, Tel-Aviv, Israel.

Schocken, Gershom; Israeli editor and publisher; b. Sept. 1912; ed. Univ. of Heidelberg and London School of Economics.
Joined staff of *Haaretz* (daily newspaper) 37, publisher and editor 39-; Dir. Schocken Publishing House Ltd.; mem. Knesset (Parl.) 55-59.
Haaretz Building, 56 Mazeh Street, Tel-Aviv, Israel.

Scholem, Gershom, PH.D.; Israeli professor; b. 5 Dec. 1897, Berlin, Germany; ed. Berlin, Jena, Berne and Munich Univs.
Lecturer, Hebrew Univ. Jerusalem 25, Prof. of Jewish Mysticism 33-65; Dean, Hebrew Univ. 41-43, now Prof. Emer. Inst. of Jewish Studies; Visiting Prof., Jewish Inst. of Religion, New York 38, 49, Brown Univ., Providence, R.I. 56-57, Hebrew Union Coll., Cincinnati 66; Pres. Israel Acad. of Sciences and Humanities 68-; Israel State Prize 55, Rothschild Prize 62, Reuchlin Prize 69.
Publs. several books on Judaism and Jewish Mysticism (in Hebrew, German and English).
The Israel Academy of Sciences and Humanities, P.O. Box 4040, Jerusalem; Home: 28 Abarbanel Street, Jerusalem, Israel.

Sebai, Youssef Mohamed; Egyptian writer; b. 1917; ed. Military Acad. and Cairo Univ.
Began writing while at school; teacher of military history 43-52, Dir. Military Museum 52-53; Editor-in-Chief *Arissala al Gadida* 53-56; Sec.-Gen. High Council of Arts, Letters and Social Sciences 56, Afro-Asian People's Solidarity Org. 57-73; Minister of Culture 73-; Italian and Egyptian decorations; Ministry of Culture Prize for best film story (for *Rodda Qalbi* and *Gamila*) (*Rodda Qalbi* also won a prize for the best dialogue).
Publs. Novels: *Na'eb Azra'il, Ard el Nifaq* (Land of Hypocrisy), *Inny Rahila* (I am Going Away), *Bein el Atlal* (Among the Ruins), *El Sakka Mat* (Death of a Water Carrier), *Rodda Qalbi, Tarik el Awda* (The Return), *Nadia;* Short Stories: *Ya Ommatun Dahikat* (A Nation that Laughed), *A Night of Wine, Sheikh Zo'orob;* Plays: *Om Ratiba, Behind the Curtain, Stronger than Time.*
Ministry of Culture, Cairo; Home: Villa Sebai, Mokatam City, Cairo, Egypt.

Seelye, Talcott Williams; American diplomatist; b. 6 March 1922, Beirut; ed. Deerfield Acad., Amherst Coll. and George Washington Univ.
Army service 43-46; teacher, Deerfield Acad., Deerfield, Mass. 47-48; speech writer, Washington 48-49; joined State Dept. 49; served in Germany, Jordan, and Lebanon; Consul, Kuwait 56-60; Chargé d'Affaires, Saudi Arabia 65-66, Deputy Chief of Mission 66-68; Amb. to Tunisia 72-; White House Commendation.
Publs. articles in various journals.
American Embassy, Tunis, Tunisia.
Telephone: 282-566.

Sela, Michael (Salomonowicz), M.SC., PH.D.; Israeli chemist; b. 6 March 1924, Tomaszow, Poland; ed. Hebrew Univ., Jerusalem and Geneva Univ.
Prof. and Head Dept. of Chemical Immunology, Weizmann Inst. of Science; Hon. mem. American Soc. of Biological Chemists; Foreign Hon. mem. American Acad. of Arts and Sciences; Israel Prize Natural Sciences 59, Rothschild Prize Chemistry 68; Otto Warburg Medal 68.
Weizmann Institute of Science, Rehovot, Israel.

Senoussi, Badreddine, LL.M., M.H.; Moroccan politician; b. 30 March 1933, Fez; ed. Univ. of Bordeaux, Chamber of Commerce, Paris.

Adviser, "Haut Tribunal Chérifien", Rabat 56; Civil Service Admin., Ministry of State 57; Sec.-Gen. Nat. Tobacco Co. 58; Head, Royal Cabinet 63; Under-Sec. of State for Admin. Affairs 65; Minister of Post Office and Telecommunications 66, of Youth, Sports and Social Affairs 70-71; Amb. to U.S.A. Oct. 71-, also accred. to Canada and Mexico; awarded many foreign decorations.
Embassy of Morocco, 1601 21st Street, N.W., Washington, D.C. 20009, U.S.A.

Seter, Mordecai; Israeli composer; b. 1916, Russia.
Studied Paris with Paul Dukas and Nadia Boulanger 32-37; Prof. Israel Acad. of Music, Tel-Aviv; Prix Italia 62; Israel State Prize 65.
Works include: *Sabbath Cantata* 40, *Three Motets* 51, *Dithyramb* 66, etc. (choral music); *Ricercar* 56, *Variations* 59-67, *Jephthah's Daughter* 65, *Chamber Music* 70, etc. (chamber music); *The Legend of Judith* 62 (ballet); *Partita* for violin and piano 51, *Jerusalem* symphony for choir and orchestra 66, *Meditation* for orchestra 67, *Rounds* for orchestra 68; violin sonatas, etc.
The Israel Academy of Music, Tel-Aviv; Home: 1 Karny Street, Ramat Aviv, Tel-Aviv, Israel.

Shaabi, Qahtan Muhammed as-; Yemeni politician; b. 1920; ed. school in Aden, and studied agricultural engineering, Khartoum Univ.
Director of Agriculture, Lahej State 55-58; joined South Arabian League 58, Public Relations Officer 59-60; Adviser to Ministry of South Yemen Affairs, Govt. of Yemen People's Repub. 63; founder-mem. Nat. Liberation Front (N.L.F.) 63, later Sec.-Gen.; mem. N.L.F. Del. to Geneva talks on independence of S. Arabia Nov. 67; Pres. of People's Repub. of Southern Yemen, also Prime Minister and Supreme Commdr. of Armed Forces Nov. 67, resigned June 69.
c/o National Liberation Front, Aden, People's Democratic Republic of Yemen.

Shabib, Talib al-; Iraqi diplomatist; b. 22 March 1934, Hilla; ed. in Baghdad and Univ. of London.
Former journalist; Minister of Foreign Affairs 63; Rep. of League of Arab States 66-68; Amb. in Foreign Ministry 68-69; Amb. to Turkey 69-70; Perm. Rep. to UN 70-71.
c/o Ministry of Foreign Affairs, Baghdad, Iraq.

Shafei, Col. Hussein; Egyptian army officer and politician; b. 1918; ed. Mil. Coll., Cairo.
Commissioned as 2nd Lieut. 38; took part in Palestine hostilities 48; graduated from Staff Officers' Coll. 53 and apptd. Officer-in-Charge Cavalry Corps; Minister of War and Marine April-Sept. 54, of Social Affairs Sept. 54-58; Minister of Labour and Social Affairs, U.A.R. 58-61; Vice-Pres. and Minister of Social Affairs and Waqfs 61-62; mem. Presidency Council 62-64; Vice-Pres. of U.A.R. (Egypt) 64-67, 70-; Deputy Prime Minister and Minister of Waqfs 67-71.
Office of the Vice-President, Cairo, Egypt.

Shafik, Doria (Ahmad); Egyptian journalist and feminist; b. 1919; ed. Univ. of Paris.
Studied abroad; on return became Editor *La Femme Nouvelle* 45, *Bent el Nil* (in Arabic) 46-, *Katkout* and *Doria Shafik Magazine*; organised Bent el Nil Union (feminist movement) 48.
Publs. *La Bonne Aventure, l'Esclave Sultane, L'Amour Perdu, L'Art pour l'Art dans L'Egypte Antique, La Femme et l'Islam, La Femme Egyptienne, Voyage autour du Monde*.
6 Salah el Din, Zamalek, Cairo, Egypt.

Shafiq, Mohammad Moussa, LL.M., M.C.L., M.A.; Afghan scholar and politician; b. 30 May 1932, Kabul; ed. Ghazi High School, Al Azhar Univ., Cairo, and Columbia Univ., U.S.A.
Joined Ministry of Justice 57, Dir. Nat. Office for Legislation 57-62; Prof. of Int. Law, Kabul Univ., 57-68; Deputy Minister of Justice 63-64; Adviser, Ministry of Foreign Affairs 66-68; Amb. to Egypt, concurrently to Lebanon, Sudan and Ghana 68-71; Minister of Foreign Affairs 71, Prime Minister 72-73.
Kabul, Afghanistan.

Shah, Idries; author; b. 16 June 1924; ed. private and traditional Middle Eastern schools.
Studied in Middle East, Europe and S. America; Dir. of Studies, Inst. for Cultural Research 66-; Visiting Prof. Univ. of Geneva 72-73; author of numerous works on philosophy.
Publs. *Oriental Magic* 56, *Secret Lore of Magic* 57, *Destination Mecca* 57, *The Sufis* 64, *Special Problems* 66, *Exploits of Nasruddin* 66, *Tales of the Dervishes* 67, *The Pleasantries* 68, *The Way of the Sufi* 68, *Reflections* 68, *Caravan of Dreams* 68, *Wisdom of the Idiots* 69, *The Dermis Probe* 69, *The Book of the Book* 69, *Thinkers of the East* 70, *The Magic Monastery* 72, *The Subtleties of the Inimitable Mulla Nasrudin* 73.
c/o Jonathan Cape Ltd., 30 Bedford Square, London, WC1B 3EL, England.

Shahbaz, Arsene; United Nations official; b. 1917, Istanbul, Turkey; ed. Geneva, London.
Joined UN 46; Political Affairs Officer, Korea 49; has held numerous senior posts in admin. and personnel services of UN and UNESCO; Chief of Admin., Econ. Comm. for Asia and the Far East 51-55; Chief of Personnel, UNESCO 55; Deputy Resident Rep., UN Technical Assistance Board, Deputy Dir. Special Fund Programme, New Delhi 59-66; Resident Rep. UN Devt. Programme (UNDP), Afghanistan 66; now Resident Rep. UNDP, Iraq.
United Nations Development Programme, P.O. Box 2048, Baghdad, Iraq.

Shahgholi, Manouchehr, M.D.; Iranian physician and politician; ed. Univ. of Teheran and in New York.
Minister of Health 65-.
Ministry of Health, Teheran, Iran.

Shakhbut bin Sultan bin Zaid, H.H. Sheikh; former Ruler of Abu Dhabi; b. 1905.
Succeeded to Sheikdom 28, deposed Aug. 66; sons Zaid b. 30, Sultan b. 36.
Manama, Bahrain.

Shakir, Bahjat; Iraqi politician; b. 1928; ed. Coll. of Arts.
Former teacher; detained several times for political activities; Editing Sec. *Al-Jamahir* newspaper (organ of Nat. Council) 63; political arrest 64; Dir.-Gen. of Information, Ministry of Culture and Information 68; Dir.-Gen. of Iraqi News Agency 69-72.
c/o Iraqi News Agency, Baghdad, Iraq.

Shalchian, Hassan; Iranian civil engineer and politician; b. 1913; ed. State Univ. of Belgium.
Ministry of Roads 39-, successively Dir. of Technical Dept., Dir. Chalus Road Dept., Dir. Dept. of Technical Inspectorate Dir.-Gen. of Roads, mem. Supervisory Board of Ministry of Roads; fmr. Head of Construction Dept. Ministry of Roads; fmr. Exec. for Implementation of Third Plan Projects; Perm. Under-Sec. Ministry of Roads 62; Technical Deputy Minister of Roads 63; Minister of Roads and Communications 63, Dec. 64-; Chair. Technical Cttee. Training Centre; Man. Dir. Water and Power Authority, Azarbaijan Province 64; Univ. Lecturer 64-; mem. Exec. Board Queen Pahlavi Foundation 68; mem. High Council Ports and Shipping Org. 69-.
Ministry of Roads and Communications, Teheran, Iran.

Shallon, Nessim, L. EN D.; American United Nations official; ed. Ecole Supérieure, Paris, Faculty of Law, Paris, Ecole Française de Droit.

First Sec. Fed. of Egyptian Industry; Export Consultant General Overseas Corpn., New York 45-46; served in U.S. Army 46; Liaison Officer UN 46, Officer for Econ. Affairs 48, Asst. to Dir. of Co-ordination for Specialized Agencies, Econ. and Social Affairs, Exec. Office of Sec.-Gen. 49-50; Technical Assistance Officer, UN Technical Assistance Board, New York 50-53, Asst. Dir. Field Co-ordination 53-; Deputy Resident Rep. UN Devt. Programme (UNDP) India 64-69, Iran 69-; Pres. Tanglewood Manor Inc. 56-64.
United Nations Development Programme, P.O. Box 1555, Teheran, Iran.

Shamgar, Meir; Israeli lawyer; b. 1925, Danzig; ed. Hebrew Univ., Jerusalem, and London Univ.
Settled in Palestine 39; detained by British Admin. for underground activities, deported to East Africa 44-48; Col. in Israeli Army 48-68; Mil. Advocate-Gen. 61-68; Attorney-Gen. 68-; Chair. Advisory Council, Inst. of Criminology, Tel-Aviv Univ., Inter-dept. Cttee. on Drugs; fmr. Law Lecturer, Hebrew Univ., Jerusalem, Tel-Aviv; mem. Israel Bar Council 61-68; mem. of Council, Int. Soc. of Mil. Law and Law of War.
Publs. various legal essays in Israeli and foreign journals.
Ministry of Justice, Jerusalem, Israel.

Shamir, Moshe; Israeli writer; b. 15 Sept. 1921; ed. Tel-Aviv Herzliya Gymnasium.
Former mem. Kibbutz Mishmar Haemek; in Haganah underground units 47-48; Capt. in Israel Army 48; mem. Hebrew Acad.; Ussiskin Prize 48, Brenner Prize 53, Bialik Prize 55.
Publs. (novels) *He Walked in the Fields under the Sun, With his own Hands, King of Flesh and Blood, David's Stranger, Naked You Are, The Border*; (plays) *He Walked in the Fields, The War of the Sons of Light, The Heir*, and ten others.
3 Rosanis Street, Tel Baruch, Tel-Aviv, Israel.

Shammas, Saeed Yacoob; Kuwaiti administrator and diplomatist; b. 1927; ed. Mubarakiyya School, Kuwait, Bristol Coll. of Commerce, U.K., London School of Economics and Oxford Univ.
Manager, Municipality Dept., Kuwait 54-55; Admin. Asst., Civil Service Comm., Kuwait 55-57, Dep. Dir.-Gen. 58-60; Consul-Gen. and Chargé d'Affaires; Kuwait Mission to UN 62-63; Ambassador of Kuwait to U.S.S.R. 64-67, concurrently to Poland, Czechoslovakia, Hungary and Romania 65-67, Ambassador to France 67-71.
P.O. Box 547, Kuwait.

Shankiti, Sheikh Mohammed Amin; Jordanian politician and diplomatist.
Chief Justice, Muslim Religious Courts -59; Minister of Education 59-61; Ambassador to Saudi Arabia 63-, concurrently to the Sudan, to the Yemen Arab Repub. 71-; mem. Joint Comm. for Border Disputes 66-.
Embassy of the Hashemite Kingdom of Jordan, Jeddah, Saudi Arabia.

Shapiro, Jacob Shimshon, LL.B.; Israeli lawyer and politician; b. 1902; ed. Kharkov Univ. and Law School, Jerusalem.
Settled in Palestine (now Israel) 24; co-founder Kibbutz Givat Hashlosha; Attorney-Gen., Govt. of Israel 48-49; Minister of Justice 66-; Chair. Cabinet Policy Cttee., East Jerusalem; mem. Labour Party.
c/o Ministry of Justice, Jerusalem, Israel.

Sharabi, Nizam B. al-, B.A., M.A.; Jordanian politician; b. 1 March 1916; ed. Birmingham Univ.
Lecturer, American Univ. at Beirut 38-41; Dir. of Social Affairs Dept., Gaza and Jaffa 42-47; Asst. Dir. Jordan Red Cross 48-49; Controller of Trade 49-51; Under-Sec. Ministry of Social Affairs 51-54; Snr. Man. Arab Bank 54-63; Asst. Dir.-Gen. 65-68, March 69-; Minister of Finance Dec. 63, of Nat. Econ. and Finance 64, of Communications and Defence July 64-Feb. 65, of Nat. Economy Dec. 68-March 69; El-Kawkab El-Urdouii First Class.
c/o Head Office, Arab Bank, Amman, Jordan.

Sharaf, Abdul Hamid; Jordanian diplomatist.
Former Head, Arab and Palestine Affairs, Ministry of Foreign Affairs; Dir. Broadcasting Service 63-64; Dir. Political Dept., Ministry of Foreign Affairs; Asst. Chief of Royal Cabinet 64-65; Minister of Information 65-67; Amb. to U.S.A. 67-72, to Canada 69-72; Perm. Rep. to UN March 72-.
Permanent Mission of Jordan to the United Nations, 866 United Nations Plaza, Room 550-552, New York, N.Y. 10017, U.S.A.

Sharef, Ze'ev; Israeli politician; b. 1906, Bukovina, Romania.
Went to Palestine 25, worked as labourer; joined Kibbutz Givat Brenner 29; Sec. Israel Sports Org. of Gen. Fed. of Labour in Israel (Histadrut); active in Haganah 40; Sec. of Political Dept. of Jewish Agency 43-47; worked on admin. blueprint of Jewish State 47-48; Sec. of Israel Govt. 48-57; Dir.-Gen. of Prime Minister's Office 48-49; Civil Service Commr. 51-52; Dir. of State Revenue, Ministry of Finance 54-61; Special Adviser to Prime Minister 64-65; mem. Knesset 65-; Chair. of Ports Authority 62-66; Minister of Commerce and Industry 66-69, Minister of Finance Aug. 68-Dec. 69; Minister of Housing Dec. 69-; Mapai.
Publ. *Shlosha Yamim* (Three Days).
Ministry of Housing, Jerusalem, Israel.

Sharif, Omar (Michel Shalhoub); Egyptian actor; ed. Victoria Coll. Cairo.
Salesman, lumber-import firm; made first film *The Blazing Sun* 53; starred in 24 Egyptian films and two French coproduction films during following five years; commenced int. film career with *Lawrence of Arabia*.
Films include: *Lawrence of Arabia, The Fall of the Roman Empire, Behold a Pale Horse, Ghengis Khan, The Yellow Rolls Royce, Doctor Zhivago, Night of the Generals, Mackenna's Gold, Funny Girl, Cinderella—Italian Style, Mayerling, The Appointment, Che, The Last Valley, The Horsemen, The Burglars, The Mysterious Island, The Tamarind Seed.*
c/o Carolyn Pfeiffer Ltd., Flat 2, 10 Connaught Place, London, W.2, England.

Sharif Emami, Jafar; Iranian engineer and politician; b. 8 Sept. 1910, Teheran; ed. primary and secondary studies in Teheran; Railway Central Coll., Brandenburg, Germany, and Government Technical High School, Boras, Sweden.
Joined Iranian State Railways 31; Technical Deputy Dir.-Gen. of Iranian Govt. Railways 42; Chair. and Man. Dir. of Irrigation Corpn. 46-50; Under-Sec. to Minister of Roads and Communications, Dir.-Gen. Iranian Govt. Railways and then Minister of Roads and Communications 50-51; mem. High Council of the Plan Org. 51-52; Man. Dir. of Plan Org. and Chair. High Council of Plan Org. 53-54; Senator from Teheran 55-57, 63-; Pres. of Senate 63-; Minister of Industries and Mines 57-60; Prime Minister 60-61; Deputy Custodian of Pahlavi Foundation 62-; mem. Board of Dirs. Royal Org. of Social Services 62-; Chair. Board of Dirs. Industrial and Mining Devt. Bank 63-; Pres. Iranian Asscn. of World Federalists 63-; mem. Board of Red Lion and Sun of Iran 63, Deputy Chair. 66-; Pres. Iranian Engineers Asscn. 66-; Pres. Third Constituent Assembly 67; mem. American Soc. of Civil Engineers 46-, Board of Trustees, Pahlavi Univ. Shiraz, Nat. Univ. Teheran 62, and Aria Mehr Tech. Univ. 65, Queen Pahlavi's Foundation 66; mem. Founding Board, Soc. for Preservation of Nat. Monuments 66; decorations from Iran, Italy, Fed. Repub. of Germany, France,

Sweden, Belgium, Austria, U.K., Japan, Romania, Thailand, Tunisia, Norway, Denmark, Morocco, Yugoslavia, Poland, Hungary, Pakistan, Ethiopia, Malaysia.
Darrooss Ehteshamieh 48, Teheran, Iran.

Sharqawy, Abdel Rahman, LL.B.; Egyptian writer; b. 1920; ed. Cairo Univ.
In legal practice 43-45; solicitor with Ministry of Education 45-56; Literary Editor *Ash-Sha'b* and *Al Goumhouriya*, then Editor *At-Tah'a* and *Tomorrow* magazines; Counsellor, Ministry of Culture and Guidance 64-.
Publs. *An Open Letter from an Egyptian Father to President Truman* (long poem) 52, *The Earth* (novel) 54, *Empty Hearts* (novel) 55, *Little Dreams* (short stories) 56, *Back Streets* (novel) 58, *Muhammad, a Prophet of Freedom* 62, *An Algerian Tragedy* (poetic drama) 62, *Mahran the Cavalier* (poetic drama) 65.
17 Sharia Al Mathaf Alzna'i, Doqqi, Cairo, Egypt.

Shawi, Dr. Khalid al-; Iraqi politician; b. 1930; ed. Michigan Univ.
Former commercial attaché, London; Dir.-Gen. Iraq Nat. Bank 62; Deputy Chair. Board of Nat. Oil Co., Chair. Trade Org., Under-Sec. of Economy, Acting Minister of Finance; Minister of Industry 66-67; Dean of Faculty of Law and Political Science, Univ. of Mustanseria, Baghdad 67-.
Publs. *The Role of the Corporate Entity in International Law* and numerous articles in Arabic.
17/18/4 Mansour, Baghdad, Iraq.

Shazar, Zalman (Schneor Zalman Rubashov); Israeli (b. Russian) Jewish historian and head of state; b. 6 Oct. 1889; ed. St. Petersburg Acad. of Jewish Studies and Univs. of Freiburg, Strasbourg and Berlin.
Delegate to Labour Zionist Conf., Minsk, Russia 06; settled in Palestine 24; Editorial staff *Davar* (Histadrut daily), later Ed. 25-49; Minister of Education, Israel 49-50; mem. Exec. Jewish Agency (in charge of Information Dept.) 52, Acting Chair. 56; Head, Zionist Organisation Dept. for Education and Culture in the Dispersion 54-63; President of Israel 63-73; Mapai.
Publs. *Kochvei Boker* (autobiographical sketches) 50 (English trans. 67), *Or Ishim* (biographical and historical studies) 55, *Zion ve-Zedek* 71, *Orei Dorot* 71.
The President's House, Jerusalem, Israel.

Sheikhly, Abdul Kareem Abdul Sattar al-; Iraqi politician; b. 1937, Baghdad.
Political emigré in Cairo 60-63; Asst. Attaché Iraqi Embassy, Beirut 63-68; mem. Revolutionary Command Council; Minister of Foreign Affairs 68-72; Perm. Rep. to UN Sept. 72-; Head of del. to UN Gen. Assembly 68-.
Permanent Mission of Iraq to the United Nations, 14 East 79th Street, New York, N.Y. 10021, U.S.A.

Shendouna III; Egyptian ecclesiastic; b. 1923.
Former Prof. of Theology, Orthodox Clerical Coll., Cairo; Pope of Alexandria and Patriarch of The See of St. Mark in all Africa and the Near East 71-.
St. Mark's Patriarchate Cathedral, Azbakiya, Cairo, Egypt.

Sheriff, Noam; Israeli composer; b. 1935, Tel-Aviv; ed. Hebrew Univ., Jerusalem.
Arranger of folk and light music for Israeli Broadcasting Authority; Prof. of Orchestration, Israel Acad. of Music, Tel-Aviv; First Prize of Israel Philharmonic Orchestra 57, 60.
Works include: *Ashrei* 61, *Destination 5* 61, *Sonata for Piano* 62, *Heptaprisms* 65, *Confession* 66, *Piece for Ray* 66, *Arabesque* 66, *Invention for Flute* 67, *Invention for Harp* 68, *Invention for Horn* 68, *Metamorphosis on a Galliard* 67, *Chaconne* 68, *Two Epigrams* 68, etc.
22 Maoz Aviv, Tel-Aviv, Israel.

Shiebani, Dr. Omar, M.A., PH.D.; Libyan educationist; b. 1930; ed. Cairo, Ain-Shams Univs. and Boston, George Washington Univs., U.S.A.
Assistant Dir. Teachers' Coll., Univ. of Libya 65, Dir. of Youth Dept. 68, Asst. Prof., Pres. 70-.
General Administration, University of Libya, Benghazi, Libya.

Shlonsky, Avraham; Israeli poet; b. March 1900; ed. High School and Sorbonne.
Went to Palestine 21; mem. Editorial Board *Davar*; founder and Editor *Groovim, Toopim, Itim, Orlogin*; Literary Editor *Sifriat Hapoalim*; mem. Board, Mosad Bialik; mem. Hebrew Acad.
Publs. *Davai* (poems) 24, *Le-Aba Ima* 25, *Bagalgal* 26, *Be-Ele Hayamim* 29, *Avne Bohu* 34, *Yalkut Shirat Haamim, Al Milet, Shirei Hamapolet Vehapius, Avnei Gvil, Mishivei Hapkosdok Haarooch*; trans. several foreign works into Hebrew, including Shakespeare, Pushkin, Gogol, Brecht, Chekhov and Gorki.
50 Gordon Street, Tel-Aviv, Israel.

Shoman, Abdul Hameed; Palestinian-Arab banker; b. 88; ed. privately.
Migrated to the U.S.A. 11; commenced business as a manufacturer 17; estab. Arab Bank Ltd., Jerusalem 30; Gen. Man. Arab Bank Ltd. 30-43, Chair. Board and Gen. Man. 43-.
c/o Arab Bank Ltd., P.O. Box 68, Amman, Jordan.

Shoukry, Mohammed Anwar; Egyptian egyptologist; b. 05; ed. Cairo Univ. Inst. of Egyptology and Univ. of Göttingen.
Asst. Prof. of Egyptology, Cairo Univ. 48-52, fmr. Prof.; Chief Archæologist Cen. of Documentation of Egyptian Art and Civilization 56-59; Dir.-Gen. Dept. of Egyptian Antiquities 59-; Asst. Under-Sec. of State, Ministry of Culture and National Guidance 61-64; Resident Archaeologist in Nubia 64-.
Publs. *Die Grabstatue im Alten Reich, Egyptian Art from the Beginning till the End of the Ancient Kingdom* (in Arabic).
Resident Archaeologist, Abu Simbel, Egypt.

Shragai, Shlomo Zalman; Israeli journalist; b. 31 Dec. 1899; ed. Jeshivoth-Talmudical Colls. in Poland.
Founder of Young Mizrachi Movement in Poland 17; founder of organisation for training religious youth for Eretz Israel 19; elected mem. Jewish Nat. Council of Poland 20; Editor religious Zionist-Hebrew newspaper, *Hatechia* 20; migrated to Palestine and employed as builder in Jerusalem 24; elected mem. Hapoel Hamizrachi Party 24-; exec. mem. Va'ad Leumi (Jewish Nat. Council) of Eretz Israel 29, Zionist Actions Cttee. 23; Chair. Broadcasting Services of Palestine 38; elected exec. mem. Jewish Agency, London 46; first Mayor of Jerusalem 50-52; Head of Immigration Dept. of Jewish Agency 53-; Contrib. to Israeli daily *Hatzofe* and *Sinai-Monthly for Thora and Jewish History Research*.
Publs. *Vision and Fulfilment* (Hebrew) 25, *Tehumin, Beit Ushbitza, Tahalichey Hageula Vhatmura, Shaa Vanezach, Peame Geula*.
Rosh Rechavia, Jerusalem, Israel.

Shubeilat, Farhan; Jordanian diplomatist.
Former Minister to Iraq; Amb. to Libya 59, to Tunisia 59-66, to U.S.A. 66-67, to Federal Repub. of Germany 67-70.
c/o Ministry of Foreign Affairs, Amman, Jordan.

Shukair, Dr. Muhammad Habib; Egyptian politician.
Minister of State for Planning March-Aug. 64; Minister of Economy and Foreign Trade Aug. 64-66, of Planning 66-67, of Higher Educ. 67-68; Pres. Econ. Comm. Org. for African Unity, Cairo 65.
c/o Ministry of Higher Education, Cairo, Egypt.

Shukairy, Ahmed, M.A., LL.D.; Jordanian lawyer and politician; b. 1908; ed. American Univ., Beirut.
Former Minister of State for UN Affairs; Perm. Rep. to the UN until 63; Chair. Palestine Liberation Org. 63-67.
19 Gabalaya Street, Zamalek, Cairo, Egypt.

Siassi, Ali-Akbar, PH.D.; Iranian psychologist and politician; b. 96; ed. Persia and France.
Professor Univ. of Teheran 27-; Head Dept. of Advanced Studies of the Ministry of Educ. 32; Chancellor of the Univ. of Teheran 42; Minister of Educ. 43; drafted bill and law for national compulsory free education, and took necessary measures for its enforcement 43; Minister of State without portfolio 45, of Education 48-50, of Foreign Affairs 50; del. III Int. Congress of Persian Art and Archæology 35, UN Conf. San Francisco 45; Pres. Iranian del. UNESCO Conf. Paris 49, Int. Conf. of Univs. 50, UNESCO Conf. Paris 51, Int. Conf. of Univs., Mexico City 60, Royal Soc. Tricentenary Celebrations, London 60; Perm. mem. Iranian Acad.; Hon. Pres. Univ. of Teheran; Dr. h.c. Univ. of Charles 1st, Prague 47, Univ. of Strasbourg 65, etc.; mem. Int. Cttee. Scientific and Cultural History of Humanity; Pres. Iranian Council of Philosophy and Human Sciences, Iranian Psychological Assen. of Iran; mem. Royal Cultural Council, etc.; Commdr. Légion d'Honneur; Commdr. Palmes Académiques, etc.
Publs. In French: *L'Education en Perse* 21, *La Perse au Contact de l'Occident* 31, *La Méthode des Tests* 31, *Le Génie et l'Art iraniens aux prises avec l'Islam* 35, *De l'Unesco à la Sorbonne* 53, *L'Iran au XIXe siècle* 55; In Persian: *Psychology* 38, *Educational Psychology for Teachers' Colleges* 41, *Introduction to Philosophy* 47, *Mind and Body* 53, *The Psychology of Avicenna and its similarities with the Modern Psychology* 54, *Logic* 56, *Ethics* 57, *Logic and Philosophy* 58, *Intelligence and Reason* 62, *Criminal Psychology* 64, *Psychology of Personality* 70.
President Roosevelt Avenue, Namdjou Street, Teheran, Iran.

Sibsi, Baji Qaid; Tunisian lawyer, politician and diplomatist; b. 1926; ed. in Paris.
Chef de cabinet to Pres. Bourguiba 56; Dir. of Tourist Office and Chief of Security until July 65; Minister of Interior 65-69, of Defence 69-70; Amb. to France 70-71.
c/o Ministry of Foreign Affairs, Tunis, Tunisia.

Sidarouss, H.E. Cardinal Stephanos I; Egyptian ecclesiastic; b. 1904; ed. Jesuits' Coll. Cairo, Univ. de Paris, Faculté de Droit, and Ecole Libre des Sciences Politiques.
Barrister, Egypt 26-32; Vincentian Priest 39-; Prof. Seminaries at Evreux, Dax and Beauvais (France); Rector Coptic Catholic Seminary, Tahta 46, Tanta 47-53, Maadi 53-58; Auxiliary Bishop to the Patriarch of Alexandria 47-58, Patriarch 58-; created Cardinal 65.
34 Ibn Sandar Street, Koubbeh Bridge, Cairo, Egypt.

Sidi Baba, Dey Ould; Moroccan diplomatist; b. 1921, Mauritania.
Counsellor, Ministry of Foreign Affairs, Morocco 58, Head of African Div. 59; mem. Moroccan Dels. to UN Gen. Assembly 59-64; Acting Perm. Rep. of Morocco to UN 63-65, Perm. Rep. 65-67; Minister of Royal Cabinet 67-; Amb. to Saudi Arabia 71-72; Dir. Royal Cabinet 72-73; Minister of Educ. 73-; Commandeur du Trône Alaouite; Niger Grand Order of Merit; Officer of Libyan Order of Independence; Commdr. of Syrian Order of Merit.
Ministère de l'Education Nationale, Rabat, Morocco.

Sidky, Aziz, B.ENG., M.A., PH.D.; Egyptian politician; b. 1 July 1920; ed. Cairo Univ., Univ. of Oregon and Harvard Univ.
Minister of Industry 56-63; Deputy Prime Minister for Industry and Mineral Wealth 64-65; Adviser for Production Affairs to Pres. of U.A.R. 66-67; Minister of Industry, Petroleum and Mineral Wealth 68-71; Deputy Prime Minister 71-72, Prime Minister 72-73; Personal Asst. to Pres. Sadat 73-.
c/o The Presidency, Cairo, Egypt.

Siemienski, Zbigniew; Polish banker; b. 1 June 1909; ed. Univ. of Warsaw.
With Bank of Poland 34-39, 42-45; Lecturer in Polish, Univ. Coll., London 46-51; Econ. Adviser, Devel. Bank of Ethiopia 52-53, Deputy Managing Dir. 54; Currency and Banking Adviser to Govt. of Yemen on behalf of UN T.A.B. 55; Currency Controller, Sudan Currency Board 56-59; Gen. Man. Bank of Sudan 60-66; Adviser Central Bank of Cyprus 66-67, of Kenya 67-70; Banque du Maroc 71-; Technical Dir. Qatar and Dubai Currency Board 66-.
Publs. *Fixed Interest Bond* (in Polish) 35, and articles in Polish *Economist* 44-46, *Middle East Journal (Impact of Coffee Boom on Ethiopia)* 55.
c/o Banque du Maroc, Rabat, Morocco; and 12 Mount Park Crescent, London, W.5, England.

Siilasvuo, Maj. Gen. Ensio; Finnish army officer; b. 1 Jan. 1922, Helsinki; ed. Lycée of Oulu, Finnish Mil. Acad., Finnish Command and Staff Coll.
Platoon Commdr., Infantry Co. Commdr. and Chief of Staff, Infantry Regiment 11 41-44; Company Commdr., Infantry Regiment 1 45-50; attended Command and Staff Coll. 51-52; various staff appointments in mil. districts of N. Finland 53-57; Commdr. Finnish Contingent, UN Emergency Force 57; Mil. Observer, UN Observation Group in Lebanon 58; Finnish Defence Attaché in Warsaw 59-61; Staff Officer Third Div. 62-64; Commdr. Finnish Contingent, UN Force in Cyprus 64-65; Instructor, Nat. Defence Coll. 65-67; Chief, Foreign Dept. GHQ 67; Senior Staff Officer, UN Truce Supervision Org. in Palestine 67-70; Chief of Staff, UN Truce Supervision Org. in Palestine 70-; Commdr. Order of the Lion of Finland 1st Class; Finnish Cross of Freedom 3rd and 4th Class; Knight of the Order of the White Rose of Finland 1st Class.
UNTSO, P.O. Box 490, Jerusalem, Israel.

Simavî, Haldûn; Turkish journalist; b. 1925; ed. Kabataş Lisesi, Istanbul.
Publisher and Gen. Man. of Istanbul daily newspaper *Hürriyet* 53-.
Hürriyet, Istanbul-Cağaloğlu, Turkey.

Simon, Ernst, PH.D., DR. THEOL. (h.c.); Israeli educationist; b. 15 March 1899; ed. Univs. of Berlin and Heidelberg.
Editor (with Martin Buber) *Der Jude* 23-24; Lecturer in Jewish subjects, Frankfurt-am-Main 22-28; taught at various schools in Germany and Palestine 28; Assoc. Dir. of Jewish Adult Education Centre of Germany 33-34; Lecturer Hebrew Univ. of Jerusalem 38-50, Assoc. Prof. of Educ. 55-67, Prof. Emer. 68-; Visiting Prof. of Educ. Jewish Theological Seminary of America, N.Y. 47-48, 62; Visiting Prof. of Educ. at Univ. of Judaism, L.A., Calif. 56-57; mem. Research Board Leo Baeck Inst. of Jews from Germany; mem. Board Ihud Organization for Jewish-Arab co-operation; mem. Board Religious Youth Village; co-Editor Pedagogical Encyclopaedia (Hebrew), Israeli State Prize for Educ. 67; Buber-Rosenzweig Medal 69.
Publs. *Ranke und Hegel* 29, *Das Werturteil im Geschichtsunterricht* 31, *Bialik* 35, *Educational Meaning of Socratic Irony* (Hebrew) 49, *Pioneers of Social Education—Pestalozzi and Korczak* (Hebrew), *The Teaching of Pestalozzi* 53 (Hebrew), *Jewish Adult Education in Nazi Germany as Spiritual Resistance, Franz Rosenzweig's Position in the History of Jewish Education* (Hebrew), *Freud the Jew* (Hebrew, German and English), *Martin Buber and the Faith of Judaism* (Hebrew), *Martin Buber and German Jewry* (English) 58, *Aims of Secondary Education in Israel* (Hebrew) 61,

Brücken (Collected Essays—German) 65, *M. Buber's Correspondence* 3 vols. (German, with G. Schaeder), 72.
35 Ben Maimon Avenue, Jerusalem, Israel.

Sinadah, Mubarek Osman; Sudanese politician; b. 1919, Omdurman; ed. El Higra School, Omdurman, Omdurman Intermediate School and Gordon Coll.
Former civil servant; Sec.-Gen. Town Planning Board 62-64; Commr. of Lands 64-69; Minister of Housing 69-71, of Housing and Public Utilities 71-73, of Construction and Public Works May 73-.
Ministry of Construction and Public Works, P.O. Box 300, Khartoum, Sudan.

Slaoui, Driss; Moroccan politician and banker.
Minister of Commerce and Industry 59-61; Dir. of Royal Cabinet March 62; Minister of Public Works 62-63, of Finance 63-64, of Nat. Economy and Agriculture Nov. 63-Aug. 64; Gov. Banque du Maroc (Central Bank) 64-68; Minister of Justice 68-69; Dir.-Gen. Royal Cabinet 69-71.
Rabat, Morocco.

Slim, Taieb; Tunisian politician and diplomatist; b. 1914; ed. Tunis Lycée and Univ. of Paris.
Member Néo-Destour Party, detained 41-43; Arab Maghreb Bureau, Cairo 46-49; Head, Tunisian Office, Cairo 49, established Tunisian offices, New Delhi, Djakarta, Karachi; Head, Foreign Affairs, Presidency of Council of Ministers 55-56; Ambassador to U.K. 56-62, also accredited to Denmark, Norway and Sweden 60-62; Perm. Rep. to UN 62-67, concurrently Amb. to Canada; Minister, Personal Rep. of the Pres. 67-70; mem. Nat. Assembly 69-; Amb. to Morocco 70-71; Minister of State 71-72; Amb., Perm. Rep. to UN, Geneva 73-; mem. Political Bureau Destour Socialist Party 71-.
Mission Permanente de Tunisie, Geneva, Switzerland.

Slimane, Commandant (*see* Kaid, Ahmed).

Smilanski, Izhar; Israeli writer; b. 1916; ed. Teachers' Seminary and Hebrew Univ.
Former teacher; mem. Knesset 48-; Brenner Prize for *Midnight Caravan*.
Publs. include: *Midnight Caravan, Hirbeth Hiza'a, The House on the Hill, Days of Ziklag* (2 vols.).
14 Moskowitz Street, Rehovot, Israel.

Smith, Wilfred Cantwell, M.A., PH.D., D.D.; Canadian university professor; b. 21 July 1916; ed. Upper Canada Coll., Univ. of Grenoble, Univ. of Madrid, American Univ. Cairo, Univ. of Toronto, Cambridge and Princeton Univs.
Served as rep. among Muslims of the Canadian Overseas Missions Council, chiefly in Lahore 40-49; Lecturer in Indian and Islamic History, Univ. of the Punjab, Lahore 41-45; Prof. of Comparative Religion 49-63, and Dir. Inst. of Islamic Studies, McGill Univ. 51-63; Pres. American Soc. for the Study of Religion 66-69; Prof. of World Religions and Dir. Center for the Study of World Religions, Harvard Univ. 64-73; McCulloch Prof. of Religion, Dalhousie Univ. 73-; Fellow, Royal Soc. of Canada, American Acad. of Arts and Sciences.
Publs. *Modern Islam in India* 43 (revised edns. 47, 65), *Islam in Modern History* 57, *Meaning and End of Religion* 63, *Faith of Other Men* 63, *Modernisation of a Traditional Society* 66, *Questions of Religious Truth* 67.
42 Francis Avenue, Cambridge, Mass. 02138, U.S.A.

Snoussi, Ahmed, LL.D.; Moroccan diplomatist; b. 22 April 1929; ed. Lycées at Meknes and Casablanca, Schools of Law and Political Sciences, Paris.
In Nationalist Movement; cabinet attaché to Minister of State in negotiations with France 56; Head, Press Div. Ministry of External Affairs 56; Sec.-Gen. Conf. on status of Tangiers; Moroccan Del. to UNESCO Conf. and UN; Dir.-Gen. Information; mem. Tech. Co-op. Mission to Congo and King's special envoy to Congo 58-59; UN Conciliation Mission to Congo 61; Sec.-Gen. Ministry of Information, Tourism Handicrafts and Fine Arts 61-65; Ambassador to Nigeria and Cameroon 65-67; Minister of Information 67-71; Amb. to Tunisia Sept. 71-; Editor numerous magazines, including *Maroc* (Ministry of External Affairs) and *Maroc Documents* (Ministry of Information); Officer Order of the Throne of Morocco, Cross of Courage and Endurance (Mission to Congo), decorations from Jordan and Yugoslavia.
Embassy of Morocco, 5 rue Didon Notre Dame, Tunis, Tunisia.

Solh, Takieddine; Lebanese politician and diplomatist; b. 1909; ed. American Univ. of Beirut, and Univ. Saint Joseph, Beirut.
Former Civil Servant; fmr. Counsellor, Embassy to United Arab Republic, and to the Arab League; mem. of Parl. 57, 64-; Pres. Foreign Affairs Comm. 64-; Minister of the Interior 65; Prime Minister, Minister of Finance 73-; Pres. L'Appel Nat. Party (*Al Nida'a El Quaoumi*).
Office of the Prime Minister, Beirut; and rue de Damas, Beirut, Lebanon.

Soliman, Mohammed Sidki; Egyptian army officer and politician; b. 1919; ed. Fuad I Univ., Cairo.
Colonel in U.A.R. Army -62; Minister for the High Dam Sept. 62-Sept. 66; Prime Minister 66-67; Deputy Prime Minister, Minister of Industry and Power June 67-; Pres. Soviet-Egyptian Friendship Soc.; Order of Lenin.
Ministry of Industry, Cairo, Egypt.

Solomides, Renos; Cypriot business executive and politician; b. 1928; ed. Univ. of Paris.
Former Asst. Gen. Sec. Hellenic Mining Co., Commercial Man. Cyprus Textiles Ltd., Gen. Man. KEO Ltd. (wine firm and brewery); Minister of Finance 62-68; Financial Adviser, Research and Investments Bureau.
Research and Investments Bureau, P.O.B. 2444, Nicosia, Cyprus.

Soteriades, Antis; Cypriot lawyer and diplomatist; b. 10 Sept. 1924; ed. London Univ. and Gray's Inn, London.
In legal practice, Nicosia 51-56; detained on suspicion of assisting EOKA 56; escaped and became EOKA leader for Kyrenia district; mem. Exec., Edma Party May 59; High Commr. to U.K. Oct. 60-66; Ambassador to United Arab Republic 66-, concurrently to Lebanon, Syria 67-, to Iraq 73-; Knight of Order of St. Gregory the Great (Vatican) 63.
Embassy of Cyprus, Cairo, Egypt.

Sotoodeh, Fatholah, B.S., M.A.; Iranian engineer and politician; b. 1924; ed. Polytechnic Inst. of Teheran and New York Univ.
Engineer with Vanak Metalworks 45-46; studies in U.S.A., then Senior Engineer and Asst. to Prof. of Industrial Engineering, New York Univ., and consulting engineer 46-58; Consulting Engineer, Plan Org. of Iran 58; Man. Dir. Vanak Metalworks and Rubber Factory 59-64, Iran Fisheries 64-65; Minister of P.T.T. 65-; Prof. of Industrial Management, Teheran Polytechnic Inst.; Iran Novin Party.
Publs. research into the use of sunlight in water heaters, water distillators and sun-stoves.
Ministry of Posts, Telegraphs and Telephones, Old Shimran Road, Teheran, Iran.

Soulioti, (Mrs.) Stella; Cypriot lawyer and politician; b. 1920; ed. Limassol, Victoria Girls' Coll., Alexandria, St. James' Secretarial Coll., London and Gray's Inn, London.
Worked in Cyprus Govt. Public Information Office; in W.A.A.F. Middle East in Second World War; qualified as barrister after war; joined family practice; Minister of Justice Aug. 60-70, concurrently Minister of Health 64-66; Law Commr. 71-; Pres. Cyprus Red Cross Soc.; Chair. Scholarship Board; Vice-Pres. Cyprus Anti-Cancer Soc.; Hon. LL.D. (Nottingham Univ.) 72.
8 Charalambous Mouskou, Nicosia 116, Cyprus.

Sowayel, Ibrahim 'Abd Allah al-; Saudi Arabian diplomatist; b. 31 Aug. 1916; ed. Saudi Inst., Mecca, and Cairo Univ.
Taught Arabic literature for a year in school for Preparation of (Student) Missions Abroad, Mecca; First Sec. Saudi Legation, Cairo 45; later Chargé d'Affaires, Beirut; Counsellor, Ministry of Foreign Affairs, Jeddah 54-56, Minister and Deputy Foreign Minister 56; Amb. to Iraq 57-60; Minister of Foreign Affairs 60-62; Head of Political Branch of Royal Diwan and Special Adviser to King with rank of Minister April-Sept. 62; Minister of Agriculture Oct. 62-Aug. 64; Amb. to U.S.A. 64-, concurrently to Mexico 65-.
Royal Embassy of Saudi Arabia, 2800 Woodland Drive, N.W., Washington, D.C., 20008, U.S.A.

Spanos, Marcos; Cypriot politician; b. 6 Aug. 1932, Lefkonico; ed. Famagusta Greek Gymnasium and American Acad., Larnaca, Gray's Inn, London.
Called to the Bar 56; practised law in Nicosia 57; Dir.-Gen. Office of the Pancyprian Cttee. of Human Rights 58, resident corresp. Int. League for the rights of Man 59; Rapporteur, Supreme Constitutional Court 62-64, Counsel of the Repub., Legal Dept. 64-67; seconded to Ministry of Labour to establish Arbitration Tribunal 67, Chair. Arbitration Tribunal 68; Minister of Labour and Social Insurance 72-; founder mem. UN Asscn. of Cyprus; Chair. Consultative Cttee. to Cyprus Athletic Org. 69; mem. Cttee. School for Deaf Children.
Ministry of Labour and Social Insurance, Nicosia, Cyprus.

Spuler, Bertold, DR. PHIL.; German university professor; b. 5 Dec. 1911; ed. Univs. of Heidelberg, Munich, Hamburg and Breslau.
Collaborator, Soc. for Silesian History 34-35; Asst. Dept. of East European History, Univ. of Berlin and Co-editor *Jahrbücher für Geschichte Osteuropas* 35-37; Asst. Dept. of Near Eastern Studies, Univ. of Göttingen 37-38; Dozent, Univ. of Göttingen 38-42; Full Prof. Univ. of Munich 42, Göttingen 45, Hamburg 48-; Hon. Dr. Theol. (Berne); Hon. Dr. ès Lettres (Bordeaux).
Publs. include *Die europäische Diplomatie in Konstantinopel bis 1739* 35, *Die Minderheitenschulen der europäischen Türkei von der Reformzeit bis zum Weltkriege* 36, *Die Mongolen in Iran: Politik, Verwaltung und Kultur der Ilchanzeit 1220-1350* 39, 3rd edn., 68, *Die Goldene Horde, Die Mongolen in Russland, 1223-1302* 43, 2nd edn. 65, *Die Gegenwartslage der Ostkirchen in ihrer staatlichen und volklichen Umwelt* 48, 2nd edn. 69, *Geschichte der islamischen Länder im Überblick I: Chalifenzeit II: Mongolenzeit* 52-53, *Iran in frühislamischer Zeit: Politik, Kultur, Verwaltung und öffentliches Leben 633-1055* 52, *Regenten und Regierungen der Welt* 53, 2nd edn. 62-64 (with additions) 66, 72, *Wissenshaftl. Forschungsbericht: Der Vordere Orient in islamischer Zeit* 54, *The Age of the Caliphs* 60, 2nd edn. 68, *The Age o, the Mongols* 60, 2nd edn. 68, *Geschichte der morgenländischen Kirchen* 61, *Les Mongols et l'Europe* (English edn. 71) 61, *Wüstenfeld-Mahlersche Vergleichungstabellen zur muslimischen, iranischen und orient-christlichen Zeitrechnung*, 3rd edn. 61, *Innerasien seit dem Aufkommen der Türken* 65, *Geschichte des Mongolen nach Zeugnissen des 13 u. 14 Jahrhunderts* (English edn. 71) 68, *Die historische und geographische Literatur Irans* 68, *Der Islam: Saeculum-Weltgeschichte III-VII* 66-72, *Kulturgeschichte des Islams (Östlicher Teil)* 71.
Mittelweg 90, Hamburg 13, German Federal Republic.

Spyridakis, Constantinos, PH.D.; Cypriot educationist and politician; b. 1903; ed. Pancyprian Gymnasium, Nicosia and Univs. of Athens and Berlin.
Teacher, Pancyprian Gymnasium, Nicosia 23-31, 34-35, Asst. Headmaster 35-36, Principal 36-60; Chair. Greek Board of Education 59-60; Pres. Greek Communal Chamber 60-65; Minister of Educ. 65-70; Corresp. mem. Acad. of Athens; Pres., mem. and official of numerous Academic and Scientific orgs.; Dr. h.c. (Univ. of Salonika); Grand Cross of Royal Order of Phoenix (Greece); Gold Medal of Goethe Inst., Munich, Gold Medal of the Church of Cyprus, etc.
Publs. *Evagoras the First, King of Salamis* (German 35, Greek 45), *An Outline of the History of Cyprus* 58, *The Kings of Cyprus* (Greek) 63, *A Brief History of Cyprus* 63, (Greek 64, new edn. 72), etc.
Ministry of Education, St. Helen Street 8B, Nicosia, Cyprus.

Stark, Dame Freya Madeline, D.B.E.; British explorer and writer; b. 31 Jan. 1893; ed. School of Oriental Studies and privately.
Travelled in Middle East and Iran 27-39 and in South Arabia 34-35, 37-38; joined Ministry of Information Sept. 39, sent to Aden 39, Cairo 40, Baghdad as attaché to Embassy 41, U.S.A. and Canada 44; Hon. LL.D. (Glasgow Univ.) 52, Hon. D.Litt. (Durham) 70; C.B.E. 53; recipient of the Founders' Medal (Royal Geographical Soc.), of Mungo Park Medal (Royal Scottish Geographical Soc.), Richard Burton Memorial Medal (Royal Asiatic Soc.), and of Sir Percy Sykes Medal (Royal Central Asian Soc.).
Publs. *The Valley of the Assassins* 34, *The Southern Gates of Arabia* 36, *Baghdad Sketches* 37, *Seen in the Hadhramaut* 38, *A Winter in Arabia* 40, *Letters from Syria,* 42, *East is West* 45, *Perseus in the Wind* 48, *Traveller's Prelude* 50, *Beyond Euphrates* 51, *Winter in Arabia* 52, *Ionia* 54, *The Lycian Shore* 56, *Alexander's Path* 58, *Riding to the Tigris* 59, *Dust in the Lion's Paw* 61, *The Journey's Echo* (an anthology) 63, *Rome on the Euphrates* 66, *The Zodiac Arch, Time, Movement and Space in Landscape* 69, *The Minaret of Djam* 70, *Turkey, Sketch of Turkish History* 71.
Asolo, Treviso, Italy; and c/o John Murray, 50 Albermarle Street, London, W.1, England.

Steel, David Edward Charles, B.A.; British company director; b. 29 Nov. 1916; ed. Rugby School and Univ. Coll., Oxford.
Officer, Q.R. Lancers, in France, the Middle East, N. Africa and Italy 40-45; Admitted as solicitor 48, worked for Linklaters and Paines 48-50; Legal Dept., British Petroleum Co. Ltd. 50-56, N.Y. 58, Pres. B.P. (N. America) Ltd. 59-61, Regional Co-ordinator, Western Hemisphere, B.P. Co. Ltd. 61-62; Man. Dir. Kuwait Oil Co. Ltd. 62-65, Dir. 65; Man. Dir. B.P. Co. Ltd. 65-, Deputy Chair. 72-; D.S.O. 40, M.C. 45.
37 Ormonde Gate, London, S.W.3, England.

Stephani, Christakis, B.COMM., F.C.A.; Cypriot banker; b. 28 Sept. 1926, Cyprus; ed. London School of Econs. and Political Science.
Accountant-General of the Repub. of Cyprus 60-65; Gov. Cen. Bank of Cyprus 65-.
Central Bank of Cyprus, P.O. Box 1087, Nicosia, Cyprus.

Stino, Kamal Ramzy; Egyptian politician.
Minister of Supplies 59, 62-63; Dep. Prime Minister for Supply and Home Trade 64-66; mem. Gen. Secretariat Arab Socialist Union 66-.
Arab Socialist Union, Cairo, Egypt.

Stylianou, Petros Savva; Cypriot politician; b. 8 June 1933; ed. Pancyprian Gymnasium and Univ. of Athens.
Served with Panhellenic Cttee. of the Cyprus Struggle (PEKA) and Nat. Union of Cypriot Univ. Students (EFEK), Pres. EFEK 53-54; Co-founder Dauntless Leaders of the Cypriot Fighters Org. (KARI); joined liberation movement of Cyprus May 55, arrested and imprisoned in Kyrenia Castle Sept. 55, but escaped; leader Nat. Striking Group; arrested Jan. 56 and sentenced to 15 years imprisonment; transferred to English prison, repatriated March 59; mem. Central Cttee. United Democratic Re-creation Front (EDMA) April 59; Deputy Sec.-Gen. Cyprus Labour Confederation (SEK) June 59, Sec.-Gen. Nov. 60-Jan. 62; founded Cyprus Democratic Labour Federation (DEOK)

Jan. 62, Sec.-Gen. 62-; mem. House of Reps. July 60, Sec. of House Aug. 60-Feb. 62; Man. Editor *Ergatiki Foni* (Voice of the Working Class) newspaper Nov. 60-Jan. 62; Man. Ed. DEOK newspaper *Ergalikos* (The Workers' Struggle) Feb. 62-Feb. 63; Man. Editor political newspaper *Allagi* (Change) March-June 63; mem. Co-ordination Cttee. of 28 associated vocational and scientific orgs. 64-66; Pres. Pancyprian Org. for the Disabled; founder Pancyprian Olive Produce Org. 67; Man. Dir. *Kypriakos Logos* (Scientific Cypriot) 69-; mem. numerous cttees.
Publs. *The Kyrenia Castle* 66, *The Epic of Central Prisons* 67, *Hours of Resurrection* 67, *Problems on Education* 68, *Sean Macstiofain, Leader of the IRA and Adorer of Hellenism* 73, *Saint Demetrianos—Bishop of Chytri-Cyprus* 73.
10 Kimon Street, Engomi, Nicosia, Cyprus.

Succar, Abdullatif Zeki; Syrian United Nations official; b. 27 Dec. 1924; ed. Coll. des Frères Maristes, Jounieh, Lebanon, American Univ. of Beirut and New York Univ. With UN, New York 48-56; Consultant on Palestine Affairs, Syrian Ministry of Foreign Affairs 56-61; Deputy Civilian Officer, Katanga, UN Operation in the Congo, Senior Programme Officer 61-64; Deputy Resident Rep., UN Devt. Programme, Somalia 65-68; Resident Rep. UNDP, People's Democratic Repub. of Yemen 68-71; Regional Rep. UNDP, Saudi Arabia, Bahrain, Qatar, U.A.E. and Oman 71-.
United Nations Development Programme, P.O. Box 558, Riyadh, Saudi Arabia; and c/o United Nations Development Programme, New York, N.Y., U.S.A.

Sultan ibn Abdulaziz, H.R.H. Prince; Saudi Arabian politician; b. 1924.
Brother of H.M. King Faisal; fmr. Minister of Communications; Minister of Defence and Aviation 62-.
Ministry of Defence, Jeddah, Saudi Arabia.

Sunay, Cevdet; Turkish army officer and politician; b. 10 Feb. 1900; ed. Kuleli Military Lyceum, Istanbul and Military Acad.
With Turkish Army 16-66; served in Palestine 17, later under Atatürk; Capt. 30; Officer Operations Dept. Gen. Staff 33; Teacher Mil. Acad. 42-47; Commdr. Artillery Regt. 47; Chief Operations Dept. Gen. Staff; Gen. 59; Deputy Chief Gen. Staff Aug. 58-May 60; C.-in-C. Land Forces 60, Chief of Staff Aug. 60-66; Senator 66; Pres. of Turkey 66-73; Hon. K.C.B. 67.
Office of the President, Ankara, Turkey.

Sussmann, Joel, LL.B., DR.JUR.; Israeli judge; b. Poland 24 Oct. 1910; ed. Univs. of Frankfurt, Heidelberg, Berlin, and Cambridge.
In private legal practice 38-49; Mil. Prosecutor, Israel Defence Army 49; Judge, Supreme Court of Israel 53-, Deputy Pres. 70-.
Publs. *Wechsel- und Scheckrecht Palästinas, Bills of Exchange, Dine'i Staroth, Dine'i Borerut, Sidrei Hadin Haesrachi* (Law of Civil Procedure).
13 Balfour Street, Jerusalem; and The Supreme Court, Jerusalem, Israel.

T

Taba, Abdol Hossein, M.D.; Iranian physician; b. 1912; ed. Birmingham and London Univs.
Former Dir.-Gen. of Health, Teheran; Vice-Pres. World Health Assembly 51; Deputy Regional Dir. WHO Eastern Mediterranean Regional Office 52-57, Regional Dir. 57-.
World Health Organization Eastern Mediterranean Regional Office, P.O.B. 1517, Alexandria, Egypt.

Tabibi, Abdul Hakim, M.A., PH.D.; Afghan diplomat; b. 7 Oct. 1924, Kabul; ed. Habibia High School, Kabul Univ., and George Washington and American Univs., U.S.A.

Entered Ministry of Foreign Affairs 54; First Sec. Perm. Mission to UN 56-58, Counsellor 59-61, Minister Counsellor 61-64; Amb. to Yugoslavia and Bulgaria 64-65; Minister of Justice and Attorney-Gen. 65-66; Amb. to Japan and the Philippines 67-70, to India, Nepal and Burma 70-; Gov. Asian Devt. Bank 67; mem. UN Int. Law Comm. 71-; del to various UN and other int. confs.; decorations from Afghanistan, Yugoslavia and Japan.
Publs. *Law of the Sea and its Relation to the Countries without Sea Coast* 59, *Free Access to the Sea for Land-locked Countries* 58, *The Right of Transit* 70, and various articles.
Embassy of Afghanistan, 9A Ring Road, Layapatnabar III, New Delhi, India.

Tağmaç, Gen. Memduh; Turkish army officer; b. 1904, Erzurum; ed. Army War Coll., Artillery Coll., War Acad.
Commander of Artillery Maintenance battery, batallion, then Chief Gen. Staff Depts. Div. and Corps, instructor in War Acad.; Commdr. Gendarmery School, Gendarmery Brigade C.-in-C. Army; C.-in-C. Land Forces; Chief of Turkish Gen. Staff until 72.
c/o Genelkurmay Baskani, Ankara, Turkey.

Taha, Mohammed Fathi; Egyptian meteorologist; ed. Cairo Univ. and Imperial Coll. of Science and Technology, London.
Under-Sec. of State and Dir.-Gen. Meteorological Dept., Egypt 53-; mem. WMO Exec. Cttee. 55, Second Vice-Pres. 59-63, Pres. 71-(75); fmr. Chair. Nat. Cttee. on Geodesy and Geophysics; fmr. mem. High Comm. on Outer Space Research and many other cttees. dealing with scientific research in Egypt.
World Meteorological Organisation, 41 avenue Giuseppe Motta, Geneva, Switzerland.

Taher, Abdulhady H., PH.D.; Saudi Arabian government official; b. 1930; ed. Ain Shams Univ. Cairo and California Univ.
Entered Saudi Arabian Govt. service 55; Dir.-Gen. Ministry of Petroleum and Mineral Resources 60; Gov.-Gen. Petroleum and Mineral Org. (PETROMIN) 62-; Man. Dir. Saudi Arabian Fertilizers Co. (SAFCO); Dir. Coll. of Petroleum and Minerals, Saudi Arabian Railroads, Arabian Oil Co. (ARAMCO); Hon. mem. American Petroleum Engineers' Asscn.
Publ. *Income Determination in the International Petroleum Industry* 66.
PETROMIN, P.O.B. 757, Riyadh, Saudi Arabia.

Taher, Ali Nassouh al-; Jordanian politician; b. 1906; ed. El Hamiya Secondary School, Cairo, American Univ., Cairo, Univs. of Nancy and Paris.
Under-Secretary for Agriculture 46-60; Minister of Agriculture and Construction and Devt. 60-62, 63; Senator 62; Pres. of East Ghor Authority, Amman 62; Vice-Pres. Devt. Board 63-; Ambassador to Iran and Afghanistan 66-; several decorations.
Publs. *The Olive Tree* 47, *Phylloxera* 47, *Local and Foreign Varieties of Apricots*, *The Alphabetical Openings of Chapters in the Koran* 54, *The Eternal Soul* 60, *History of the Arab Tribes in Jordan* 67, *Genealogy of the Arab Tribes in the Arab World* 68.
Embassy of Jordan, P.O. Box 1573, Teheran, Iran.

Taimur al-Said, Tarikbin; Omani diplomatist; b. 2 July 1923; ed. English High for Boys, Istanbul, Robert Coll., Istanbul, and Germany.
Commissioned in Muscat Army 41-44; Chair., Administrator, Muscat Mutrah Municipality 45-57; in charge of Operational Area in Jabal War 58-59; self-exile 62-70; Prime Minister 70-71; Personal Adviser for Diplomatic Affairs to Sultan of Oman, Senior Amb. Extraordinary and Plenipotentiary 72-; Order of Oman 1st Class.
P.O. Box 202, Muscat, Oman; and Leuchtturmweg 21, 2000 Hamburg 56, Federal Republic of Germany.

Tajaddod, Mostafa; Iranian banker and politician; b. 1909; ed. secondary school, Teheran, and in Europe.
In Europe 33-45; Deputy Gov. Industrial Bank of Iran 45-50; Chair. Board of Dirs. Bank Bazargani Iran (Commercial Bank of Iran) 50-; fmr. mem. of Majlis, now mem. Senate; fmr. Minister of Commerce.
Bank Bazargani Iran, Maiden Sepah, Teheran, Iran.

Takieddine, Bahiqe Mahmoud; Lebanese politician; b. 1909, Baakline; ed. Université St. Joseph, Beirut.
Barrister 31-47; Deputy for Mont Liban 47; Minister of Agriculture 49; Deputy for Chouf 51, 53, 60, 64; Minister of Social Affairs and Health 53-60; fmr. Pres. Parl. Comm. on the Admin. of Justice; Minister of Economy 64-65; Minister of Information 68-69, of the Interior 73-.
Ministère de l'Intérieur, Beirut; Home: Rue Verdun, Beirut, Lebanon.

Takla, Philippe; Lebanese politician; b. 1915; ed. Univ. Law School, Beirut.
Law practice, Beirut 35-45; M.P. 45, 47; Minister of Nat. Economy and Communication 45-46, 48-49; Minister of Foreign Affairs 49, 61-64, 64-65; Gov. Bank of Lebanon 64-66, 66-67; Minister of Foreign Affairs and of Justice 66; Perm. Rep. to UN 67-68; Amb. to France 68-71.
c/o Ministry of Foreign Affairs, Beirut, Lebanon.

Tal, Josef; Israeli composer; b. 1910, Poland; ed. Berlin State Acad. of Music.
Went to Israel 34; taught piano and composition at Jerusalem Acad. of Music 37, Dir. 48-52; now Head, Dept. of Musicology, Hebrew Univ., Jerusalem; Dir. Israel Centre for Electronic Music 61-; has appeared with Israel Philharmonic Orchestra and others as pianist and conductor; concert tours of Europe, U.S.A., Far East; UNESCO Scholarship for research in electronic music.
Works include: *Saul at Ein Dor* 57, *Amnon and Tamar* 61, *Ashmedai* 69 (operas), Symphony No. 1 53, No. 2 60, *Concerto for Harpsichord and Electronics* 64, *Double Concerto* (for violin and violoncello) 70, other cantatas, quintets, music for ballet and several books on the theory of music.
Department of Musicology, Hebrew University, Jerusalem; Home: 3 Dvora Haneviyah Street, Jerusalem, Israel.

Talal ibn Abdulaziz, Amir; Saudi Arabian Prince; b. 1930; ed. secondary school.
Son of the late King Abdul ibn Saud; half brother of former King Saud; Minister of Communications 53-54; Ambassador to France 55-56; Minister of Finance 61.
Cairo, Egypt.

Taleb-Ibrahimi, Ahmed, M.D.; Algerian doctor and politician; b. 5 Jan. 1932; ed. Univ. of Paris.
Son of Sheikh Bachir Brahimi, spiritual leader of Islam in Algeria; Dir. Jeune Musulman 52-54, Union Générale des Etudiants Musulmans Algériens 55-56, French Fed. of the FLN 56-57; imprisoned in France 57-62, in Algeria 64-65; Doctor, Hôpital Mustapha, Algiers 62-64; Minister of Nat. Educ. 65-70; mem. UNESCO Exec. Board; Minister of Information and Culture 70-.
Publs. *Contribution à l'histoire de la médecine arabe au Maghreb* 63, *Lettres de Prison* 66, *De la décolonisation à la révolution culturelle* 73.
Ministry of Information and Culture, 119 rue Didouche Mourad, Algiers, Algeria.

Taleghani, Khalil, B.SC.; Iranian civil engineer and politician; b. 13 Sept. 1913; ed. American Coll. of Teheran and Univ. of Birmingham.
Junior engineer, England 37-39; Engineer, Persian Army 39-41; Chief Engineer, Technical Dir., Dir. of Ebtekar and other construction companies and Golpayegan Water Co. 41-51; Minister of Agriculture Dec. 51-June 52, July 52-March 53 and 55-56; Minister of State June 56-59; Dir. Taelghani-Tashakori Co. (consulting engineers); Man. Karaj Dam Authority 54-59; Chair. Industrial and Mining Development Bank of Iran 60-62; Dir. Taleghani-Daftari (Consulting Engineers) 60-; Chair. B. F. Goodrich Tyre Manufacturing Co. 60-; Chair. Pars Paper Co. 67-, Iran-California Co. 70-, Manem Consultants 70-; mem. Iranian Asscn. of Consulting Engineers; Fellow A.S.C.E.; Tadj and Homayoun Medals.
Baghe-Bank Street Golhak, Tehran, Iran.

Talhouni, Bahjat al-; Jordanian politician; b. 1913; ed. Damascus Univ.
Former Judge, Kerak; fmr. Minister of Interior; Chief of Royal Court 55-60; Prime Minister Aug. 60-61, 64-65, 67-March 69, Aug. 69-June 70; Minister of Foreign Affairs 61-62; Chief of Royal Cabinet 63-64; mem. House of Notables 65-; Personal Rep. of the King; mem. Consultative Council 67-.
c/o Royal Palace, Amman, Jordan.

Talib, Maj.-Gen. Naji; Iraqi soldier and politician; b. 1917; ed. Iraqi Staff Coll. and Sandhurst, England.
Military Attaché, London 54-55; Commdr. Basra Garrison 57-58; Minister of Social Affairs 58-59; lived abroad 59-62; Minister of Industry March 63-Nov. 64; mem. U.A.R.-Iraq Joint Presidency Council May 64-65; Minister of Foreign Affairs Nov. 64-Sept. 65; Prime Minister and Minister of Petroleum Affairs 66-May 67.
Baghdad, Iraq.

Talû, Naim; Turkish banker and politician; b. 22 July 1919; ed. Faculty of Economics, Istanbul Univ.
Joined Türkiye Cumhuriyet Merkez Bankası (Central Bank of Repub. of Turkey) 46, Chief 52, Asst. Dir. of Ankara Branch 55-58, Dir. of Exchange Dept. 58-62, Asst. Gen. Dir. 62-66, Acting Pres. and Gen. Dir. 66-67, Pres. and Gen. Dir. 67-70, Gov. 70-71; Chair. Foreign Investment Encouragement Cttee. 67-68; Chair. Banks' Asscn. of Turkey 67-71; Sec.-Gen. Cttee. for Regulations of Bank Credits 67-70; Minister of Commerce 71-73; Prime Minister 73-; mem. of Board Turkish Air Force Reinforcement Foundation; mem. Ankara Educ. Foundation, Soc. for Protection of Children in Turkey.
Office of the Prime Minister, Ankara; and Ticaret Bakani, Ankara, Turkey.

Tarazi, Salah el Dine, L. EN D., D. EN D.; Syrian diplomatist; b. 1919; ed. Coll. des. Frères, Damascus and Faculté Française de Droit, Beirut.
Lawyer 40-47; Lecturer and Asst. Prof. of Law, Damascus Univ. 46-48; Ministry of Foreign Affairs 49-50; Chargé d'Affaires, Brussels 51-53; Alternate Perm. Rep. to UN 53-56; Sec.-Gen. Ministry of Foreign Affairs 56-57; Ambassador to U.S.S.R. 57-58; Ambassador of United Arab Republic to Czechoslovakia 58-59, to People's Republic of China 59-61; Syrian Ambassador to People's Republic of China 61-62; Perm. Rep. of Syria to UN 62-65; Ambassador to U.S.S.R., also accredited to Poland 64; now Amb. to Turkey; Syrian, Belgian and Czech awards.
Publs. *Les Services Publics Libano-Syriens* 46; articles concerning law and political science in Arabic and French.
Syrian Embassy, Çankaya, Abdullah Cevdat Sok 7, Ankara, Turkey.

Tariki, Abdallah; Saudi Arabian oil executive; b. 1919; ed. Univs. of Cairo and Texas.
Studied at Univ. of Texas and worked as trainee with Texaco Inc. in W. Texas and California 45-49; Dir. Oil Supervision Office, Eastern Province, Saudi Arabia (under Ministry of Finance) 49-55; Dir.-Gen. of Oil and Mineral Affairs (Saudi Arabia) 55-60; Minister of Oil and Mineral Resources 60-62; Dir. Arabian American Oil Co. 59-62; Leader Saudi Arabian Del. at Arab Oil Congresses 59, 60; Independent Consultant 62-; adviser to Egyptian, Algerian and Kuwaiti Govts. on oil matters.
c/o Ministry of Economy, Damascus, Syrian Arab Republic.

Tartakower, Arie, DR. IUR., D.RER.POL.; Israeli (b. Polish) university professor; b. 24 Sept. 1897; ed. Univ. of Vienna.
Co-founder Zionist Labour Movement and Chair. Zionist Labour Party, Poland 22-39; Lecturer, Inst. of Jewish Sciences, Warsaw 32-39; Dir. Dept. of Relief and Rehabilitation of World Jewish Congress (U.S.A.) 39-46; fmr. Prof., Lecturer and Head, Dept. of Sociology of the Jews, Hebrew Univ., Jerusalem; Chair. Israel Exec., World Jewish Congress; mem. Gen. Council World Zionist Org.; mem. World Secr. Zionist Labour Movement; Co-founder and fmr. Pres. Israel Asscn. for UN; Chair. World Asscn. for Hebrew Language and Culture.
Publs. include: *History of the Jewish Labour Movement, Jewish Emigration and Jewish Policy of Migration, The Jewish Refugee, Jewish Wanderings in the World, The Wandering Man, The Jewish Society, History of Jewish Colonization* (2 vols.), *The Tribes of Israel* (3 vols.).
1 Ben Yehuda Road, Jerusalem, Israel.

Taşkent, Arıf Kâzim; Turkish businessman.
Founder and Pres. of Board of Dirs. Yapı ve Kredi Bankası (Construction and Credit Bank); former Dir.-Gen. Sugar Industries Administration.
Yapı ve Kredi Bankası, Genel Müdürlüğü, Istanbul, Turkey.

Tawfiq, Mohammad 'Omar; Saudi Arabian politician; b. 1917; ed. Shari'a Coll. of Literature and Islamics, Medina.
Former teacher; fmr. clerk, Post and Telegraph Dept. 41-58, rose to Chief Sec. Council of Ministers; retd. 58; business and press activities 58-62; Minister of Communications 62-, of Pilgrimage and Religious Endowment Affairs 63-70.
Ministry of Communications, Riyadh, Saudi Arabia.

Tazi, Abderrahman; Moroccan industrial engineer and international banking official; b. 1929; ed. Univ. of Lille.
Industrial Engineer 49-53; Dir. of Industrial Production, Ministry of Commerce and Industry 56; Econ. Counsellor, Moroccan Embassy, Bonn 57-58; First Counsellor, Perm. Moroccan Mission to UN 61, Moroccan Rep. to Econ. Comm. to UN 61; Dir.-Gen. of Econ. Affairs, Ministry of Foreign Affairs, Rabat 62-; Exec. Dir. for Afghanistan, Algeria, Ghana, Indonesia, Khmer Repub., Libya, Greece, Tunisia, Morocco, Int. Bank for Reconstruction and Devt. 62-.
16 rue Pilote Masset, Casablanca, Morocco.

Tekinel, Ismail Hakki; Turkish lawyer; b. 1925, Babaeski, Edirne.
Served as judge in many provs.; private practice as solicitor; mem. Parl. for Istanbul 61; Deputy Chair. Justice Party; Chair. Justice Cttee. of Nat. Assembly; Minister of State 73-; Justice Party.
Ministry of State, Ankara, Turkey.

Tekoah, Yosef; Israeli diplomatist; b. 4 March 1925; ed. Université L'Aurore, China, and Harvard Univ.
Instructor in Int. Relations, Harvard Univ. 47-48; Dep. Legal Adviser, Ministry of Foreign Affairs 49-53; Dir. Armistice Affairs, and Head Israel Dels. to Armistice Comms. with Egypt, Jordan, Syria and Lebanon 53-58; Dep. Perm. Rep. to UN 58, Act. Perm. Rep. 59-60; Ambassador to Brazil 60-62, to U.S.S.R. 62-65; Asst. Dir.-Gen. Ministry of Foreign Affairs 66-68; Perm. Rep. to UN 68-.
Permanent Mission of Israel to the United Nations, 15 East 70th Street, New York, N.Y. 10021, U.S.A.

Tevetoğlu, C. Fethi, M.D.; Turkish politician and author; b. 31 Jan. 1916; ed. Faculty of Medicine, Univ. of Istanbul, Texas and Baylor Univs.
Served in Turkish army for twenty years; active in politics since 57; Chief. Del. Asian Peoples Anti-Communist Leagues and World Anti-Communist Leagues Corp. 63-; mem. APACL Exec. Cttee.; Pres. Cttee. for Foreign Affairs in the Senate; Pres. Turkish Parl. group in the Common Market 65-; mem. Directing Cttee. Justice Party 62-; Editor-in-Chief Turkish Encyclopaedia.
Publs. *Rabindranath Tagore* 38, *Muftuoğlu Ahmed Hikmet* 51, *Enis Behiç Koryürek* 52, *No Fascist, but Communist* 62, *Our Views on Foreign Policy* (4 languages) 63, *Two Declarations* 63, *The Shamewall* (Berlin) 64, *I am disclosing* 65, *The Holy Lands* 65, *Cyprus and Communism* 66, *The Socialist and Communist Activities in Turkey* (1910-1960) 67, *The Russia I saw of Today* 68.
Bakanlikar, P.K. 250, Ankara, Turkey.

Tewfik, Hammad; Sudanese politician; b. 1904; ed. Gordon Coll. Khartoum.
Joined Finance Dept. 24 and became Inspector of Accounts, Dept. of Agriculture; founder mem. Graduates Congress; Sec. Nat. Front Party until formation of Nat. Unionist Party of which he became exec. mem. 52; mem. House of Reps. for Messellemiya 54-; Minister of Finance and Economics 54-56, of Communications Feb.-July 56, of Commerce, Industry, and Supply July 56-58; mem. of Senate March-July 58; Man. Dir. Agricultural Bank of Sudan, Aug. 58-64, Chair. 65-.
Agricultural Bank of Sudan, P.O.B. 1363, Khartoum, Sudan.

Tewfik, Zakaria; Egyptian cotton executive; b. 1920; ed. Cairo Univ.
With Bank Misr; then Commercial Attaché, Belgium, Spain; Dir.-Gen. Exchange Control Office 61; Under-Sec. for Cotton Affairs, Ministry of Economy 61-; Dir.-Gen. Cotton Org. 61-; Egyptian Del. to many int. cotton confs.
General Organization for Cotton, 19 El-Gomhouriya Street, Cairo, Egypt.

Teymour, Mahmoud; Egyptian writer and playwright; b. 1894; ed. Egyptian schools.
Member Acad. for the Arabic Language, Cairo; Decoration of Merit 63, of Arts and Sciences 64; State Prize for Literature 50, 64.
Publs. in Arabic: Some sixty works, including collections of short stories, novels, plays, memoirs, essays, etc.: in French: *La Fille du Diable* 42, *Le Courtier de la Mort* 51, *La Belle aux lèvres charnues* 52, *La Fleur du Cabaret* 53, *Bonne Fête* 54, *L'Amour par-delà l'Inconnu* 55; in English: *Tales from Egyptian Life* 48, *The Call of the Unknown* 65; Collections of short stories in German, Yugoslav, Hungarian, Russian and Chinese.
6 Yahia Ibrahim Street, Zamalek, Cairo, Egypt.

Thacher, Nicholas Gilman; American diplomatist; b. 20 Aug. 1915, Kansas City, Mo.; ed. Princeton and Fordham Univs. and Univ. of Pennsylvania.
Banker, New York City 37-42; entered foreign service 47; Third Sec., Karachi 47-49; Vice-Consul, Calcutta 50-51, Consul 52; Indian Affairs Officer, Dept. of State 53-54; Officer in charge of Afghanistan-Pakistan Affairs 54-56; First Sec., Baghdad 56-58; Nat. War Coll. 58-59; Deputy Dir. Office of Near Eastern Affairs, Dept. of State 59-62; Counsellor, Jeddah 62-65; Minister-Counsellor, Teheran 65-70; Amb. to Saudi Arabia 70-.
American Embassy, Jeddah, Saudi Arabia; Home: 2565 Larkin Street, San Francisco, Calif., U.S.A.

Thacker, Thomas William, M.A.; British university professor; b. 6 Nov. 1911; ed. City of Oxford School, Univs. of Oxford and Berlin.
Goldsmiths' Research Scholar, Oxford and Berlin 33-35; Senior Research Student, Oxford 35-37; Lecturer in Semitic Languages, Univ. Coll. of Bangor, North Wales 37-38; Reader in Hebrew, Univ. of Durham 38-40; Foreign Office 40-45; Prof. of Hebrew and Oriental Languages, Univ. of Durham 45-51, Prof. of Semitic Philology and Dir. School of Oriental Studies, Univ. of Durham 51-; Foreign mem. Royal Belgian Acad.
28 Church Street, Durham, England.

Theocharis, Reghinos D., D.PHIL. (London); Cypriot economist and banker; b. 10 Feb. 1929; ed. Highest School of Economics, Athens, Univ. of Aberdeen and London School of Economics.
Inspector of Commercial Education, Cyprus 53-56; at London School of Economics 56-58; Chief, Economic Development Unit, Bank of Greece, Athens 58-59; Minister of Finance in Cyprus Provisional Govt. March 59-Aug. 60; Minister of Finance Aug. 60-62; Governor, Bank of Cyprus Ltd. 62-; Hon. Fellow, London School of Econs. and Political Sciences 71.
Publ. *Early Developments in Mathematical Economics* 61.
Bank of Cyprus Ltd., Nicosia, Cyprus.

Theodosios VI; Greek ecclesiastic; born in Lebanon; ed. theological schools of Halki, Istanbul and Univ. of Athens.
Greek Orthodox Patriarch of Antioch (Antyarka) and of All the East 59-.
The Patriarchate, P.O. Box 19, Damascus, Syria.

Thesiger, Wilfred, C.B.E., D.S.O., M.A.; British traveller; b. 3 Jan. 1910; ed. Eton and Magdalen Coll., Oxford.
Explored Danakil country of Abyssinia 33-34; Sudan Political Service, Darfur and Upper Nile Provinces 35-39; served in Ethiopia, Syria and Western Desert with Sudan Defence Force and Special Air Service, Second World War; explored the Empty Quarter of Arabia 45-50; lived with the Madan in the Marshes of Southern Iraq 50-58; awarded Back Grant, Royal Geographical Soc. 36, Founders Medal 48; Lawrence of Arabia Medal, Royal Central Asian Soc. 55; David Livingstone Medal, Royal Scottish Geographical Soc. 61, Royal Soc. of Literature Award 64, Burton Memorial Medal, Royal Asiatic Soc. 66; Hon. D.Litt. (Leicester) 68.
Publs. *Arabian Sands* 58, *The Marsh Arabs* 64.
15 Shelley Court, Tite Street, London, S.W.3, England.

Tixier, Claude, L. ès L., D. ès D.; French economist; b. 22 Nov. 1913; ed. Arts and Law Faculties and Ecole des Sciences Politiques, Univ. of Paris.
Deputy Inspector of Finances 39, Inspector of Finances 42; Deputy Dir. to Ministry of Nat. Economy 45; Chief, Service of Economic Survey 46; Dir. Cabinet of Sec. of State for the Budget 47; Deputy Dir. Cabinet of Minister of Finances 48; Dir. Cabinet of Prime Minister (Finances) 48; Dir. Cabinet of Minister of Finances 49; Dir.-Gen. of Finances to the Algerian Ministry, Algiers 49-58; Vice-Pres. European Investment Bank July 58-62; Pres. Banque Industrielle de Financement et de Crédit 62-67; admin. Worms et Cie. (Maroc), Union Bancaire pour le Commerce et l'Industrie; Vice-Pres. Banque Worms 67-; Chevalier de la Légion d'Honneur.
45 Boulevard Haussmann, Paris 9e; and 5 square des Ecrivains Combattants, Paris 16e, France.

Tlass, Gen. Mustapha el-; Syrian army officer and politician; ed. Military and Law Colls.
President of Damascus Mil. Tribunal 64, of Homs Mil. Tribunal; Chief of Staff of the Syrian Army 68; Deputy Minister of Defence 68, Minister 71-; mem. Regional Bureau of Baath Party; Nat. Order of Cedar (Lebanon) 71.
Ministry of Defence, Damascus, Syria.

Tombazos, George; Cypriot politician; b. 2 Feb. 1919; ed. Pancyprian Gymnasium, Cyprus Coll., Dentists' School of Athens.
Worked as dentist at Morphou 50-66; M.P. for Nicosia 60-66; Chair. Board of Greek Education 59-60; Pres. Greek Communal Chamber of Cyprus 60-65; Minister of Education 65-66; Minister of Agricultural and Natural Resources 66-70; Gold Medal of Patriarchate of Jerusalem; Gold Medal of Goethe Inst. Munich; Grand Cross of Royal Order of Phoenix 66.
Ministry of Agriculture, Nicosia, Cyprus.

Tomeh, Georges J., M.A., PH.D.; Syrian university professor and diplomatist; b. 1922; ed. American Univ. of Beirut and Georgetown Univ.
Attaché, London, and Alt. Del. to UNESCO 45-46; Syrian Embassy, Washington 47-52; Alt. Gov. Int. Monetary Fund 50; Dir. UN and Treaties Dept., Ministry of Foreign Affairs, Damascus 53-54; Asst. Prof. of Philosophy and Asst. to Dean of Arts and Sciences, American Univ. of Beirut 54-56; Dir. Research Dept., Ministry of Foreign Affairs, Damascus 56-57; Consul-Gen., New York 57-58; Minister Consul-Gen. of United Arab Republic in New York 58, Minister, New York 61; Consul-Gen. and Deputy Perm. Rep. of Syria to UN 61-63; Minister of Economy, Syrian Arab Repub. 63-64; Prof. of Philosophy, Syrian Univ. 64-65, Perm. Rep. to UN 65-72; Order of Syrian Merit, Commdr. Order of St. Paul and St. Peter.
Publs. (in Arabic) *The Idea of Nationalism* 54, *Philosophy of Leibnitz* 54, 65, *Making of the Modern Mind* (2 vols.) (trans. from English) 55-57, 65, *Arab Emigrants to the United States* 65; (in English) *Islam, Year Book of Education and Philosophy* 57, *Neutralism in Syria* 64, *Challenge and Response: A Judgement of History* 69.
c/o Ministry of Foreign Affairs, Damascus, Syria.

Toukan, Baha'ud-din, B.A.; Jordanian diplomatist; b. 1910; ed. American Univ. of Beirut.
Joined Arab Legion and Sec. to Officer Commdg. 32; transferred to Court of H.R.H. the Amir of Transjordan 37; joined staff of B.B.C., London 42; Income Tax Assessor, Transjordan Govt. April 45-46; Gov. of Belqa District July 46-47; Sec. to Transjordan Del. to negotiate Independence Treaty, London Feb. 46; Transjordan Consul-Gen. in Jerusalem 47-48; Jordan Minister to Egypt 48-51, to Turkey 51-54; Under-Secretary, Ministry of Foreign Affairs 54-56; Ambassador to U.K. 56-58; Permanent Rep. to UN 58, Feb. 71-72; Under-Sec. Ministry of Foreign Affairs 62-71; Amb. to Italy 72-; decorations include: First Order of Istiqlal, Grand Officer Lebanese Republic.
Publ. *Short History of Transjordan* (in English) 45.
Embassy of Jordan, Rome, Italy.

Toukan, Mohammed Ahmed, M.A.; Jordanian politician and banker; b. 15 Aug. 1903; ed. Oxford Univ.
Various teaching posts 30-48; Minister of Public Works, Devt. and Reconstruction 50, of Education 50-53; former Man. Nat. Bank of Jordan; Minister of State for Prime Ministry Affairs and Minister of Tourism Feb.-July 66; Minister of Communications 66; Minister of Foreign Affairs April 67-July 67; Deputy Prime Minister July 67-69; Minister of Defence Dec. 68-69; Al Istiqlal Medal, Al Kawkab Medal.
Amman, Jordan.

Toumazis, Panayiotis; Cypriot civil engineer; b. 1912, Famagusta; ed. Greek Gymnasium, Famagusta, and Metsovian Polytechnic, Athens.
Municipal engineer, Famagusta; later served as Pres. Famagusta Devt. Corpn., Famagusta Fed. of Trade and Industry, and Architects and Civil Engineers Council of Registration; mem. House of Reps. 60-70; Minister of Agriculture and Natural Resources 70-72; mem. Cyprus Civil Engineers' and Architects' Asscn.
5 Edisson Street, Famagusta, Cyprus.

Tourky, Ahmad Riad, PH.D.; Egyptian scientist.
Former Prof. of Chemistry, Cairo Univ., Dean of Science 53-59; Pres. Nat. Research Centre 56-; mem. Inst. d'Egypte, Section III 55-, Pres. 62-64, Vice-Pres. 64-; Minister of Scientific Research 64-66.
c/o Ministry of Scientific Research, Cairo, Egypt.

Tritton, Arthur Stanley, M.A., D.LITT.; British orientalist; b. 1881; ed. Mansfield Coll. and St. Catherine's Soc., Oxford, and Univ. of Göttingen.
Assistant, Edinburgh Univ. 11, Glasgow Univ. 19; Prof. of

Arabic, Univ. of Aligarh, India 21; School of Oriental Studies, London 31, Prof. of Arabic 38-47.
Publs. *Rise of the Imams of Sanaa* 25, *Caliphs and their non-Muslim Subjects* 30 (revised edn. 66), *Teach Yourself Arabic* 43, *Muslim Theology* 47, *Islam, Belief and Practices* 50, *Materials on Muslim Education* 57.
11 Rusthall Road, Tunbridge Wells, Kent, England.

Tsur, Yaakov; Israeli diplomatist; b. 18 Oct. 1906; ed. Hebrew Coll. Jerusalem, Univ. of Florence and Sorbonne.
Mem. staff daily newspaper *Haaretz*, Tel-Aviv 29; Dir. French Dept. and later Co-Dir. Propaganda Dept. Jewish Nat. Fund, Jerusalem 30; special Zionist missions, Belgium, Greece, France 34-35, Bulgaria and Greece 40; Dir. Publicity Dept. Jewish Agency Recruiting Council 42; Liaison officer with G.H.Q. British Troops in Egypt 43-45; Head del. to Greece 45; Pres. Israeli Army Recruiting Cttee. Jerusalem 48; Minister to Argentina 49-53, Uruguay 49-53, Chile 50-53 and Paraguay 50-53; Ambassador to France 53-59; Dir.-Gen. Foreign Office 59; Chair. Zionist Gen. Council 61-68; Chair. Jewish Nat. Fund.
Publs. *Juifs en Guerre* 47, *The Birth of Israel* 49, *Preludio a Israel* 56, *Shaharit shel Etmol* (autobiography) 66, French trans.—*Prière du Matin* 67 (English ed. *Sunrise in Zion*) *An Ambassador's Diary in Paris* 68, *La Révolte Juive* (Italian, Spanish trans.) 70.
P.O. Box 283, Jerusalem, Israel.

Tueni, Ghassan, M.A.; Lebanese newspaper editor; b. 1926; ed. Harvard Univ.
Publisher and Editor-in-Chief, *An-Nahar* (daily newspaper); Deputy Prime Minister, Minister of Educ. and Information 70-71; fmr. Parl. Deputy.
An-Nahar, rue Banque Centrale du Liban, Hamra, Lebanon.

Tuhami, Hassan Muhammed el-; Egyptian politician; b. 1924; ed. Military Coll., Cairo.
Ambassador, Ministry of Foreign Affairs 61; Amb. to Austria 62; Sec.-Gen. of the Presidency 69; Minister of State 70-71; Adviser to the Pres. Sept. 71-.
The Presidency, Cairo, Egypt.

Tuna, Ahmet Nusret; Turkish politician; b. 1916, Mucur, Kireşehir.
Has worked as a teacher, lawyer and journalist; Senator for Kastamonu 61; Deputy Chair. of Justice Party, in Senate until 73; Minister of Agriculture 73-; Justice Party.
Ministry of Agriculture, Ankara, Turkey.

Tural, Gen. Cemal; Turkish soldier.
Commander 2nd Army until Aug. 64; C.-in-C. Land Forces 64-66; Chief of Staff Feb. 66-Mar. 69; mem. Supreme Military Council 69-.
Ministry of Defence, Ankara, Turkey.

Turgut, Mehmet; Turkish politician; b. 1929; ed. Istanbul Technical Univ.
Deputy for Afyon 61-65, Bursa 65-; fmr. Minister of Power; Minister of Industry Nov. 65-70; Justice Party.
Ministry of Industry, Ankara, Turkey.

Tutunji, Djamil, M.D.; Jordanian doctor and diplomatist; b. 1896; ed. Syrian Protestant Coll., Homs, American Univ. of Beirut and Medical Univ., Constantinople.
Medical Officer, Ottoman Army 18, Madeba District 19-22, Arab Legion 23; Royal Physician 23-40; Dir. of Health 40-50; Dep. Minister of Health 50-51, Minister 51-62; mem. Senate 62-63; Amb. to U.S.S.R. 64-65; Senator 67-71; Star of Jordan, Knight of St. John of Jerusalem, Knight of the Holy Sepulchre, Decoration of Revolution and of Independence.
P.O. Box 643, Amman, Jordan.

Tzur, Michael; Israeli shipping executive; b. 1 May 1923; ed. Tel-Aviv Univ.
Service with Ministry of Commerce and Industry and the Treasury 51-66; Dir.-Gen. Ministry of Commerce and Industry 58-66; Chair. of Board of Dirs. Zim Israel Navigation Co. 66-.
Zim Israel Navigation Co. Ltd., 209 Hameginim Avenue, Haifa, Israel.

Tzounis, John Alexander; Greek diplomatist; b. 13 Oct. 1920, Bucharest, Romania; ed. Univ. of Athens and French Inst., Athens.
Joined diplomatic service 47; posts at Ministry of Foreign Affairs, Athens, 47-50, 59-62, 67-69; Vice-Consul, San Francisco 51, Acting Consul-Gen. 54; Chief Information Officer, Greek Embassy, Washington, D.C. 55; Counsellor, Moscow 62, Chargé d'Affaires 63-65; Counsellor, London 65-67; Amb. to Turkey 69-; mem. Greek del. to UN Gen. Assembly 51, 54; Commdr., Royal Order of Phoenix, Royal Order of George I.
Greek Embassy, 285 Ataturk Bulvari, Ankara, Turkey.

U

Ulay, Sitki; Turkish army officer; b. 1907; ed. War Acad. Ankara.
Has served as Military Attaché in Egypt and Afghanistan; Commandant, War School; Minister of Communications 60-Jan. 61; Minister of State 61-62; founder Social Democratic Party later incorporated with Republican People's Party; elected to Supreme Consultative Assembly of R.P.P.; mem. Senate.
Publ. *War School Called to Arms*.
Evkaf Apt. 1/3-3, Ankara, Turkey.

Ulfat, Gul Pacha; Afghan poet and writer; b. 1909; ed. private studies.
Staff writer *Anis* (daily) 35-36; Writers' Soc. 36; later mem. staff *Islah* (daily); Editor *Kabul Magazine* 46; Editor *Nangrahar* (weekly) 48; Chief of Tribal Affairs in Nangrahar Province; mem. House of Reps. from Jalalabad (Nangrahar), and Second Deputy to Pres. of House 49, mem. from Karghaie 52; Pres. of Afghan Acad. 56, Afghan-U.S.S.R. Friendship Soc. 59-63, Tribal Affairs (mem. Central Cabinet) 63-65; Rep. in Wolise Jerga (formerly House of Reps.) from Jalalabad 65-69.
Publs. Twenty-five books on literary, social and political subjects, and numerous essays.
Sher Shah Maina, Kabul, Afghanistan.

Umri, Gen. Hassan (*see* Amri, Gen. H.).

Unterman, Rabbi Iser Jehudah; Israeli Rabbi; b. 1886; ed. Rabbinical Colls. in Poland and Lithuania.
Rabbinical posts in Poland 13-23; Rabbi of Liverpool and District 23; Pres. Mizrachi Fed. of Great Britain and Ireland 43-46; Chief Rabbi, Tel-Aviv and District 46-72; Pres. Rabbinical Courts, Tel-Aviv; Pres. Union of Rabbinical Colls.; mem. Exec. Cttee., Chief Rabbinate of the Holy Land.
Publ. *Shevet Myehuda* 55; contrib. rabbinical publs. in Israel, Great Britain and the U.S.A.
6 Engel Street, Tel-Aviv, Israel.

Uqaili, Maj.-Gen. Abdul Aziz al-; Iraqi army officer and politician; b. 1920; ed. Military Coll., Artillery School, Staff Coll., Baghdad, Staff Coll., Camberley, England, and Law Acad., Baghdad.
Army service 38-; Instructor, later Senior Instructor, Staff Coll., Baghdad; Ambassador to Iran Feb. 59; arrested in Mosul Revolt March 59, acquitted Sept. 59; Dir.-Gen. Iraqi Ports Admin. Feb.-April 63; rejected appt. of Ambassador to Japan July 63; Dir.-Gen. Iraqi Ports Admin. Nov. 63-; Minister of Defence Sept. 65-66; under detention 69.
Publs. *History of the First Barzan Insurrection 1931* and articles in various journals.
Directorate-General of Navigation, Basra; and Nassah No. 24/9/1, Adhamiah, Baghdad, Iraq.

Ürgüplü, Suat Hayri; Turkish diplomatist and politician; b. 1903; ed. Lycée and Univ. of Istanbul.
Lawyer; mem. Parl. 39-46; Minister of Customs and Monopolies in Sarajoğlu Govt. 43-46, resigned and left People's Party; re-elected to Grand Nat. Assembly 50 with support of Democratic Party which he subsequently joined; mem. and Vice-Chair. Council of Europe 50-52; Ambassador to Fed. Republic of Germany 52-55, to United Kingdom 55-57, to U.S.A. 57-60, to Spain 60; Independent Senator and Speaker of Senate 60-63; Prime Minister Jan.-Oct. 65, 72.
The Senate, Ankara, Turkey.

Ussoskin, Moshe; Israeli social worker; b. 8 March 1899, Moghileiv-Podolsk, Russia; ed. Cernauti Univ.
Zionist work in Bessarabia 17; Controller Bank Moldova Bucharest and Co-Dir. Branche Reni 18-28; Dir. American Joint Distribution Cttee. and Foundation for Hungary, Turkey and Balkan countries 28-41; Dir. Cen. Bank for Jewish Co-operatives in Romania 33-41; in Israel 41-; Senior Officer Migdal Ins. Co. Jerusalem 41-48; exec. comm. Union Credit Co-operatives 42-47; Dir.-Gen. and Treas. *Keren Hayessod* United Israel Appeal 49-68; Vice-Chair. Tel-Aviv Devt. Co.; mem. Board Israel Land Devt. Co., Jerusalem Econ. Corpn., Binjaneh Haumah Ltd., and others; mem. Presidium of Credit Co-operatives in Palestine 42-47, of World Fed. of Bessarabian Jews; Board of Govs. Hebrew Univ. Jerusalem; has organized much relief work for refugees.
Publs. Co-Editor of co-operative monthly *Die Genossenschaft Czernowitz-Bukovina; Social Welfare among Jews in Bessarabia, Social Welfare among Jews in Saloniki (Greece)*, and many articles on co-operative, economic, zionist, and Jewish matters in many languages.
16 Arlosoroff Street, Jerusalem 92181, Israel.

Uzuner, Ali Riza; Turkish politician; b. 1926, Of, Trabzon; ed. secondary school, Erzurum, and Faculty of Forestry.
Carried out research in various branches of forestry in Sweden for three years; Dir. Forestry Research Inst. until 61; mem. Parl. (Republican People's Party) 61-; Minister of Labour 71-73; mem. Nat. Security Council.
Republican People's Party, Ankara, Turkey.

V

Vahidi, Iraj, M.SC., PH.D.; Iranian politician; b. 1927, Khorramshahr; ed. Univs. of Teheran and London.
Engineer, Ministry of Roads; mem. Board of Dirs., Independent Irrigation Inst., subsequently Man. Dir.; Technical Asst. to Ministry of Water and Power; Supervisor of Nat. Water Supply; Minister of Agriculture 71, of Water and Power Sept. 71-.
Ministry of Water and Power, Teheran, Iran.

Vajda, Georges; French professor; b. 18 Nov. 1908; ed. Séminaire Rabbinique, Budapest, and Paris, Ecole des Langues Orientales and Sorbonne.
Prof., Séminaire Israélite de France 36-; Lecturer, Ecole Pratique des Hautes Etudes, Sorbonne 37, Dir. 54-; Head of Oriental Section, Inst. de Recherche et d'Histoire des Textes 40; Prof. 70.
Publs. *Introduction à la Pensée Juive du Moyen Age* 47, *La Théologie ascétique de Bahya ibn Paquda* 47, *Répertoire des Catalogues et Inventaires de Manuscrits Arabes* 49, *Un Recueil de Textes Historiques Judéo-Marocains* 51, *Inventaire des Manuscrits Arabes Musulmans de la Bibliothèque Nationale* 53, *Juda ben Nissim Ibn Malka, philosophe juif marocain* 54, *Les certificats de lecture dans les manuscrits arabes de la Bibliothèque Nationale* 57, *L'amour de Dieu dans la théologie juive du moyen âge* 57, *Isaac Albalag* 60, *Recherches sur les relations entre la Philosophie et la Kabbale* 62, *Le Dictionnaire des Autorités de 'Abd al-Mu'min ad-Dimyati* 62, *Le commentaire d'Ezra de Gérone sur le Cantique* 69, *Deux commentaires Karaïtes sur l'Ecclésiaste* 71.
Institut de Recherche et d'Histoire des Textes, 40 avenue d'Iéna, Paris 16e, France.

Valian, Abdol-Azim, B.A., PH.D.; Iranian politician; b. 1925, Teheran; ed. Univ. of Teheran and Military Faculty of Teheran.
Commissioned army officer; Dir. Org. of Land Reform; official, Ministry of Agriculture; Minister of Land Reform and Rural Co-operatives 71-.
Ministry of Land Reform and Co-operatives, Teheran, Iran.

Vanden Berghe, Louis, PH.D.; Belgian oriental archaeologist; b. 24 Dec. 1923; ed. Univs. of Ghent, Brussels, Amsterdam and Leyden.
At Univ. of Ghent, Assoc. Prof. 53-57, Prof. of Western Asiatic Archaeology and Civilizations 57-; Prof. of History and Archaeology of Ancient Iran, Univ. of Brussels 58-; Curator of the Iran Dept. of Musées Royaux d'Art et d'Histoire, Brussels 66-; Visiting Prof., Rome Univ. 65; Dir. Belgian Archaeological Expedition in Iran 65-; explorations and excavations in S. Iran 51-64; discoveries include several new prehistoric cultures, unknown Elamite, Parthian and Sassanid Rock-Reliefs, the great Kunar Siah complex and other Sassanid Fire Temples; mem. Royal Acad. of Sciences, Letters and Arts, Belgium; Corresp. mem. German Archaeological Inst., Berlin; Hon. Dr. Teheran Univ.; Iranian Orders of Homayoun and of Sepass; Officer of the Order of Leopold.
Publs. Co-Editor of *Iranica Antiqua*, Author of *Archéologie de l'Iran Ancien* 59, 66, *La nécropole de Khurvin* 64, *Art Iranian Ancien, préhistoire, protohistoire* 66, *Opgravingen in Pusht-i Kuh, I Kalwali en War Kabud* 68, *On the Track of the Civilizations of Ancient Iran* 68.
Department of Western Asiatic Archaeology and Civilizations, University of Ghent, Blandijnberg, 2 Ghent; Home: Oost-Nieuwkerke, Belgium.

Vinogradov, Sergei Alexandrovich; Soviet historian and diplomatist; b. 1907; ed. Leningrad Univ.
Former Prof. of History; Diplomatic Service 39-; Counsellor, Turkey 40, Ambassador 40-48; Head, Dept. of UN Affairs, Ministry of Foreign Affairs 48-50; Chair. U.S.S.R. Council of Ministers Radio Cttee. 50-53; Ambassador to France 53-65; on staff of Ministry of Foreign Affairs 65-67; Amb. to Egypt (fmrly. United Arab Repub.) 67-; mem. Central Auditing Comm. of C.P.S.U. 62-66; Grand Croix Légion d'Honneur.
Embassy of the U.S.S.R., 95 Sh. El Giza (Giza), Cairo, Egypt.

Vishkai, Mohammed Razi; Iranian politician and banker b. 1918; ed. Teheran Univ.
Joined Ministry of Finance 40, rose to Perm. Under-Sec.; studied Budget Affairs in United States 56; Minister of Customs and Monopolies 60-61; Pres. Bank Rahni Iran 61-.
Bank Rahni Iran, Ferdowsi Street, Teheran, Iran.

W

Waely, Faisal el-, PH.D.; Iraqi professor and government official; b. 1922; ed. Teacher-Training Coll., Baghdad and Oriental Inst. of Chicago.
Professor, Baghdad Univ. (Coll. of Literature) 53-56; Dir.-Gen. of Technical Affairs, Ministry of Education, Baghdad 58-59; Prof. Cairo Univ. 59-63; Dir.-Gen. of Antiquities, Baghdad 63-.
Publs. Various articles in journal *Sumer*.
Directorate-General of Antiquities, Baghdad West, Iraq.

Wahrhaftig, Zorach, D. JUR.; Israeli lawyer and politician; b. Warsaw 2 Feb. 1906; ed. Univ. of Warsaw.
Private law practice, Warsaw 32-39; Vice-Pres. Mizrachi, Poland 26-39; mem. of exec., Keren Hayesod, Hechalutz Hamizrachi, World Jewish Congress; Deputy Dir. Inst. of Jewish Affairs, New York 43-47; Vice-Pres. Hapoel Hamizrachi, U.S.A. 43-47; Dir. Vaad Leumi Law Dept. 47; mem. Provisional Council, Govt. of Israel 49; mem. of Knesset; Dep. Minister for Religious Affairs 56-59, Minister of Religious Affairs 61-; mem. Jewish Law Research Inst., Ministry of Justice 48; Lecturer on Talmudic Law, Hebrew Univ.; mem. American Soc. for Int. Law, Board of Trustees, Bar-Ilan Univ.
Publs. *Starvation over Europe* 43, *Relief and Rehabilitation* 44, *Where Shall They Go?* 46, *Uprooted* 46, *Hazaka in Jewish Law* 64, and many publs. in Hebrew on Israel Law and Religion.
Ministry of Religious Affairs, Jerusalem, Israel.

Weisgal, Meyer Wolf; American journalist and executive; b. 11 Oct. 1894; ed. Columbia Univ.
National Secretary Zionist Org. of America 21-30; Dir.-Gen. Palestine Pavilion, World's Fair, New York 39-40; Personal Political Rep. Dr. Weizmann in U.S.A. 40-48; Organiser, American Section Jewish Agency for Palestine, Sec.-Gen. 43-46; Organiser and Exec. Vice-Chair. American Cttee. Weizmann Inst. 46-59; Chair. Exec. Council Weizmann Inst. of Science, Israel 49-66, Pres. of Inst. 66-69, Chancellor 70-; del. World Zionist Congress 24-; fmr. Editor *The New Palestine* (New York) 21-30, *Jewish Standard* (Toronto) 30-32.
Publs. *Chaim Weizmann: Statesman, Scientist, Builder of the Jewish Commonwealth* 44, *Chaim Weizmann, a Biography by Several Hands* 62, *Meyer Weisgal ... So Far: An Autobiography*, and numerous Jewish and Zionist pamphlets, etc.
14 Neveh Weizmann, Rehovot, Israel; and 240 Central Park South, New York 19, N.Y., U.S.A.

Weitz, Raanan, PH.D.; Israeli rural development planner; b. 27 July 1913; ed. Hebrew Gymnasia, Jerusalem, Hebrew Univ. and Univ. of Florence.
Agricultural Settlement Dept., Jewish Agency 37-, fmr. Village Instructor, now Head of Dept.; service with Intelligence Corps, British 8th Army, Second World War; fmr. mem. Haganah; mem. Exec., Zionist Org. 63-; Chair. Nat. and Univ. Inst. of Agriculture 60-66; Head, Settlement Study Centre 63-; Prof. of Rural Devt. Planning, Univ. of Haifa 73-.
Publs. *Agriculture and Rural Development in Israel: Projection and Planning* 63, *Rural Planning in Developing Countries* (Editor) 65, *Agricultural Development—Planning and Implementation* 68, *From Peasant to Farmer: A Revolutionary Strategy for Development* 71, *Rural Development in a Changing World* (Editor) 71.
Zionist Organization, P.O. Box 92, Jerusalem, Israel.

Weizman, Ezer; Israeli politician and air force officer (retd.); b. 15 June 1924; ed. Hareali School, Haifa and R.A.F. Staff Coll.
Served in first Israeli fighting squadron, War of Independence 48; founded Israeli Air Force Air Staff 52-53; commanded fighter wing 53-56, in Sinai Campaign 56-57; Head of Air Div., Israeli Air Force 57-58; Commdr. I.A.F. 58-66; Head of Gen. Staff Div., Israeli Defence Force 66-69; Minister of Transportation 69-70, resigned with other Gahal Ministers; Dir. Maritime Fruit Carriers Ltd. 70-; Chair. Exec. Cttee., Herut Party 71-.
Maritime Fruit Carriers Ltd., 32 Ben Yehuda Street, Tel-Aviv, Israel.

Wise, George S.; American university professor; b. Poland 1906; ed. Columbia Univ.
Former lecturer in Sociology at Columbia Univ. and Univ. of Mexico; business interests in U.S.A., Mexico and Israel; Pres. Tel-Aviv Univ. 63-71, Chancellor 71-.
Tel-Aviv University, Ramat-Aviv, Tel-Aviv, Israel.

Witkon, Alfred, DR.JUR.; Israeli judge; b. 23 Feb. 1910; ed. Univs. of Bonn, Berlin and Freiburg, and Middle Temple, London.
Called to Middle Temple Bar 36, to Palestine Bar 37; practised law, Palestine 37-48; Pres. District Court, Jerusalem 48; Justice, Supreme Court of Israel 54-.
Publs. *Law and Society* 55, *The Law of Taxation* 69, *Law and Politics* 65.
17 Shmaryahu Lewin Street, Jerusalem, Israel.

Wright, Edwin Milton, M.A., L.H.D.; American education and government officer (Retd.); b. 12 Jan. 1897; ed. Wooster Coll. and Columbia Univ.
Refugee resettlement, Iraq 21-24; educational work in American Secondary Schools, Persia 24-37; Lecturer in History, Columbia Univ. 38-41; Fellow, American Council of Learned Societies 39-40; U.S. Army Mil. Intelligence in Middle East (H.Q. in Teheran and Cairo) with final rank of Lieut.-Col. 41-46; U.S. Dept. of State, Office of Near Eastern, South Asian and African Affairs, Washington, D.C. 46-53; Lecturer in the History of the Contemporary Middle East, Graduate School of Int. Relations of Johns Hopkins Univ. 46-70; Foreign Service Inst., Dept. of State 55-56; Visiting Prof. Mills Coll. 67; mem. Board of Govs., Middle East Inst. 56-70, Advisory Council, Oriental Dept., Princeton Univ.; Superior Merit Medal, Dept. of State 64, Dist. Alumni Award, Wooster Coll. 67, also Visiting Prof. 67-68; Dist. Scholar, Univ. of S. Carolina 68-70.
626E Wayne Avenue, Wooster, Ohio 44691, U.S.A.

Wright, Rev. Dr. G(eorge) Ernest; American museum curator; b. 5 Sept. 1905; ed. Wooster Coll., McCormick Theological Seminary and Johns Hopkins Univ.
Ordained Presbyterian Minister 34; Field Sec. American Schools of Oriental Research 38; Asst. Prof. McCormick Theological Seminary 39-45, Prof. Old Testament History and Theology 45-58; Parkman Prof. of Divinity, Harvard Univ. 58-; Dir. Drew-McCormick Archaeological Expedition to Palestine 56-; Curator Harvard Semitic Museum; Pres. American Schools of Oriental Research 66-; mem. numerous learned socs.; founder and mem. Editorial Board *Biblical Archaeologist*.
Publs. *Pottery of Palestine from Earliest Times to the End of the Early Bronze Age*, *The Old Testament against its Environment* 50, *Biblical Archaeology*, *The Biblical Doctrine of Man in Society* 54, *The Book of the Acts of God* 57, *Isaiah in Laymen's Bible Commentaries* 64, *Shechem: Biography of a Biblical City* 65, *The Old Testament and Theology* 69; co-author *Ain Shems Excavations*, *Westminster Historical Atlas to the Bible*; Editor *The Bible and the Ancient Near East* 61.
6 Divinity Ave., Cambridge, Mass. 02138; and 7 Alcott Road, Lexington, Mass. 02173, U.S.A.

Y

Yaari, Meir; Israeli politician; b. 25 April 1897; ed. Vienna Univ. and Agricultural Inst., Vienna (pupil of Freud).
Served in Austrian Army 14-18; founded Hashomer Hatzair, Vienna; went to Palestine 20; worked with Jewish Nat. Fund and Zionist Org.; mem. Hashomer Hatzair World Exec., Zionist Gen. Council, Gen. Fed. of Jewish Labour; mem. Knesset 49-; Sec.-Gen. Mapam 64-.
Mapam Offices, P.O.B. 1777, Tel-Aviv, Israel.

Yadin (formerly Sukenik), **Lt.-Gen. Yigael,** M.A., PH.D.; Israeli soldier and archaeologist; b. 21 March 1917; ed. Hebrew Univ., Jerusalem.

Chief of Gen. Staff Branch, Haganah H.Q. 47; Chief of Operations, Gen. Staff, Israel Defence Forces 48; Chief of Gen. Staff Branch 49, Chief of Staff 49-52; Archæological Research Fellow, Hebrew Univ. 53-54; Lecturer in Archæology, Hebrew Univ. 55-59, Assoc. Prof. 59-63, Prof. 63-; Dir. Hazor Excavations 55-58, 69, Bar Kochba Excavations 60-61, Megiddo Excavations 60, 66-67, 70-71, Masada Excavations 63-65; mem. Israel Acad. of Sciences and Humanities; corresp. mem. British and French Acads. Publs. *The Scroll of the War of the Sons of Light against the Sons of Darkness* 55, *The Message of the Scrolls* 57, *Hazor I: The First Season of Excavations*, *Hazor II: Second Season*, *Hazor III-IV: Third Season*, *A Genesis Apocryphon* (with N. Avigad) 56, *Warfare in Biblical Lands* 63, *Finds in a cave in the Judaean Desert* 63, *Masada: First Season of Excavations* 65, *The Ben-Sirah Scroll from Masada* 65, *Masada: Herod's Fort and the Zealots' Last Stand* 66, *Philacteries from Quuraw* 69, *Bar-Kochba* 71, *Hazor* 72.
47 Ramban Road, Jerusalem, Israel.

Yafi, Abdullah al-; Lebanese lawyer and politician; b. 1901; ed. Univ. of Paris.
Admitted to Beirut Bar 26; Prime Minister and Minister of Justice 38-39; Minister of Justice and Finance 47; mem. Lebanese del. to Preparatory Conf. for founding League of Arab States 44, to UN San Francisco Conf. 45; Prime Minister 54 and 56; in private practice 56-66; Prime Minister 66, also Minister of Finance and Information 66; Prime Minister 68-69.
Beirut, Lebanon.

Yahia, General Tahir; Iraqi army officer and politician; b. 1915; ed. primary school, Tikrit, secondary school, Baghdad, Teachers' Training Coll. and Military Coll.
Former teacher, Mamounia School, Baghdad; mem. Nat. Movement 41; Commdr., Armoured Cars' Battalion, Palestine War 48; mem. Military Court, Habaniya 48; mem. Free Officers' Group 58, later Dir.-Gen. of Police; Chief-of-Staff, Iraqi Army Feb. 63-Nov. 63; Prime Minister of Iraq Nov. 63-Sept. 65; Deputy Prime Minister 67; Prime Minister and acting Minister of the Interior 67-68; Al-Khidma Medal, Al-Chaja Medal, Al-Rafidain Medal.
Baghdad, Iraq.

Yamani, Ahmed Zaki; Saudi Arabian politician; b. 1930; ed. Cairo Univ., New York Univ. and Harvard Univ.
Saudi Arabian Govt. service; private law practice; Legal Adviser to Council of Ministers 58-60; Minister of State 60-62; mem. Council of Ministers 60-; Minister of Petroleum and Mineral Resources 62-; Dir. Arabian American Oil Co. 62-; Chair. Board of Dirs. Gen. Petroleum and Mineral Org. (PETROMIN) 63-, Coll. of Petroleum and Minerals, Dhahran 63-; Chair., Board of Dirs. Saudi Arabian Fertilizer Co. (SAFCO) 66-; Sec. Gen. Org. of Arab Petroleum Exporting Countries (OAPEC) 68-69; mem. several int. law asscns.
Publ. *Islamic Law and Contemporary Issues*.
Ministry of Petroleum and Mineral Resources, Riyadh, Saudi Arabia.

Yariv, Brig.-Gen. Aharon; Israeli army officer; b. 1920, Latvia; ed. French Staff Coll.
Emigrated to Palestine 35; Capt. British Army 41-46; Haganah 46-47; various posts with Northern Command, Israel Defence Forces 48-50, Operations Div., H.Q. 51; IDF Officers' Staff Coll. 52-56; Mil. Attaché, Washington and Ottawa 57-60; joined Mil. Intelligence 61, Dir. until 72; Special Adviser to the Prime Minister Oct. 72-73.
Office of the Prime Minister, Jerusalem, Israel.

Yasin, Abdul-Hamid; Jordanian educationist and administrator; b. 1908; ed. Teachers' Coll. Jerusalem and American Univ. Cairo.
Teacher 24-36; Broadcaster and translator, Jerusalem 36-42; Labour and Co-operatives Inspector, Jerusalem 42-46; mem. Arab Information Office, Jerusalem 46-47; Town Clerk, Jaffa 47-48; Registrar and instructor, American Univ. Cairo 48-52, Dean of Educ. Faculty 52-53; Principal, Teachers' Coll., Amman 53-60; UNESCO Adviser on Educ., Libya 60-62; Sec.-Gen. Jordan Univ. 62-64; Head of UNRWA Educ. Dept., Jerusalem 64-65; mem. Exec. Cttee. and Del. to Arab League, Palestine Liberation Org., Jerusalem and Cairo 65-66; Dir.-Gen. Housing Corpn., Amman 66-67; Dir.-Gen. Broadcasting 67-68; Counsellor, Ministry of Educ. 68-, Dir. Public Admin. Inst. Amman 68-70; Editor *Journal of Modern Education*, Cairo 52-53, *Teacher's Message*, Amman 56-60.
Publs. *Short Stories* (Arabic) 46, *10 Short Stories* (Arabic) 59; Translations: Overstreet, *The Mind Goes Forth* 60, and contributions on education to magazines, papers and broadcasts.
c/o Institute of Public Administration, Amman, Jordan.

Yasseen, Mustafa Kamil, D. EN D.; Iraqi international lawyer; b. 1920, Iraq; ed. Univs. of Baghdad, Cairo and Paris.
Member, Baghdad Bar 42; Lecturer in Private Int. and Penal Law 50, Asst. Prof. 54; Prof. and Head, Dept. of Int. Law, Univ. of Baghdad 59; Gen. Dir. Political Dept., Ministry of Foreign Affairs 59, Dept. of Int. Orgs. 64; Amb. and Perm. Rep. to Office of UN, Geneva 66; Gen. Dir. Dept. of Int. Orgs., Ministry of Foreign Affairs 71-; mem. UN Int. Law Comm. 60-, Pres. 66; Assoc. Inst. of Int. Law 61, mem. 71; mem. Curatorium, Hague Acad. of Int. Law; Iraqi rep. to several int. confs., to Vienna Conf. on the Law of Treaties 68, 69, Chair. of Drafting Cttee., to Council of UNCTAD 66-69, to Gov. Body, ILO 66-69, to UN Gen. Assembly 58-, to various UN, ILO confs., etc.; Dr. h.c. (Nice) 70; Grand Cross of Civil Merit (Spain); Grand Officer, Nat. Order of Merit (France).
Publs. various books and articles on int. law.
Ministry of Foreign Affairs, Baghdad, Iraq.

Yassein, Mohammed Osman, B.SC.; Sudanese civil servant; b. 1915; ed. Gordon Coll. and London School of Economics.
Joined Sudanese Political Service 45; Liaison Officer in Ethiopia 52-53; Gov. Upper Nile Province 54-55; Perm. Under-Sec. of Foreign Affairs 56-65; mem. Sudanese del. to UN 56; Del. to Independent African States Conf., Monrovia 59, to Accra Conf. on Positive Action for Peace and Security in Africa 60, to Independent African States Conf., Léopoldville 60; Special Adviser to UN on training of diplomatists 61-62; Special Envoy to Ethiopia and Somalia on border dispute; mem. African Unity Org. Comm. for Conciliation and Arbitration between Algeria and Morocco; Organizer, African Finance Ministers first Conf., Khartoum 63, Grading Structure and Salaries Comm. of Zambia 66; joined UN Office of Technical Co-operation 66; Resident Rep. UN Devt. Programme (UNDP), Jordan 70-; Hon. mem. Inst. of Differing Civilizations, Brussels; Kt. Great Band of Humane Order of African Redemption, Liberia, Grand Officer, Order of Menelik II, Republican Order, Egypt, Star of Yugoslavia.
Publs. *The Sudan Civil Service* 54, *Analysis of the Economic Situation in the Sudan* 58, *Problems of Transfer of Power—the Administration Aspect* 61, *Germany and Africa* 62.
United Nations Development Programme, P.O. Box 565, Amman, Jordan.

Yassin, Aziz Ahmed, PH.D., D.I.C., B.SC.; Egyptian consulting engineer; b. 13 Aug. 1918; ed. Abbassia Secondary School, Cairo Univ., and Imperial Coll., London.
Ministry of Housing and Public Utilities, rising to Under-Sec. of State 39-59; Dir.-Gen., Vice-Chair. Building Research Centre 54-59, Chair., Pres. Tourah Portland Cement Co., Alexandria Portland Cement Co. 59-63; mem. Board of Dirs. Helwan Portland Cement Co., Sudan Portland Cement Co. 59-63; Chair. Egyptian Cement Cos. Marketing

Board 59-63; Chair., Pres. Egyptian Gen. Org. for Housing and Public Building Contracting Cos. 63-65; Minister of Tourism and Antiquities 65-67, of Housing and Construction 66-68; mem. Board of Aswan High Dam Authority 66-68; External Prof. of Soil Mechanics, Cairo Univ. 51-, of Civil Engineering, Ain Shams Univ.; mem. Building Research and Technology Council, Egyptian Acad. of Science and Technology 72-; mem. several other scientific, civil engineering and building orgs.; Order of the Repub. 1st Class, Order of the Banner (Hungary), Commdr.'s Cross with Star of Order of Resurrection of Poland.
Publs. *Model Studies on the Bearing Capacity of Piles* 51, *Bearing Capacity of Deep Foundations in Clay Soils*, *Testing Sand Dry Samples with the Tri-axial Apparatus* 53, *Bearing Capacity of Piles* 53, *The Industry of Building Materials in Egypt* 57.
4 Waheeb Doas Street, Maadi, Cairo, Egypt.
Telephone: Cairo 34519.

Yassin, Mohammed Hussain al-, M.SC.; Iraqi diplomatist; b. 1913; ed. American Univ. of Beirut and Columbia Univ., New York, U.S.A.
Director of Primary Teachers Coll., Baghdad 41-43; Asst. Dean of Coll. of Educ. and Prof. of Educ. and Philosophy, Baghdad 43; Cultural Counsellor, Iraq Embassies, Beirut and Damascus 49-51; Prof., Univ. of Baghdad 51; Dir.-Gen. of Cultural Affairs, Ministry of Educ., Baghdad 51-54; Perm. Del. to UNESCO and Cultural Counsellor, Paris 55-56; Inspector-Gen. of Ministry of Labour and Social Affairs, Baghdad 57; mem. Public Service Board of Iraq 57-61; Pres. of Public Service Board of Iraq and mem. Board of Trustees, Univ. of Baghdad 61-67; Amb. to Iran 68-71.
c/o Ministry of Foreign Affairs, Baghdad, Iraq.

Yazıcı, Bedi, M.SC.; Turkish business executive; b. 1917; ed. Robert Coll., Columbia Univ.
Fire and Marine Man. Nat. Reinsurance Co. 43-48; Prof. of Insurance, Business School of Istanbul 45-50; Man. Dir. The Credit Bank of Turkey 62-63, Porcelain Industries Inc. of Istanbul 62-63; Pres. The Gen. Insurance Co. of Turkey 48-63, Istanbul Chamber of Commerce 60-63; mem. Insurance Board, Ministry of Commerce 44-64; Chair. and Managing Dir., TAM Insurance Co. 64-, TAM Life Insurance Co. 66-; Trustee, Robert Coll. 64-.
15 Büyükdere Caddesi, Tamhan, Istanbul, Turkey.

Yazıcı, Bülent, M.S.; Turkish banker; b. 3 Feb. 1911; ed. Robert Coll., Istanbul, and Columbia Univ.
Ministry of Finance 34-38; Insp. 38-45; Financial Counsellor, Turkish Embassy, Washington 45-49; Dep. Gen. Dir. Dept. of the Treasury 49-50; Dep. Gen. Man. Industrial Development Bank of Turkey 50-60; Dir. and Gen. Man. Türkiye Is Bankası A.S. 60-67; Chair. American-Turkish Foreign Trade Bank 64-67, Union of Chambers of Commerce, Industry and Exchanges of Turkey 60-62; Vice-Chair. Asscn. of Banks of Turkey 60-67; Chair. Industrial Devt. Bank of Turkey 60-69, Man. Dir. 69-; Dir. Mensucat Santral T.A.S. 67-; Dir. Tam Hayat Sigorta A.S. 67-; Advisory Dir. Unilever-İş Ticerat ve Sanayi, Sti 68-; Trustee, Robert Coll., Istanbul; Commodore, Deniz Klubu.
36 Devriye Sok., Moda, Kadıköy, Istanbul, Turkey.

Yemen, Former King of the (see Saif Al-Islam Mohamed Al-Badr, H.M. The Imam).

Yeshayahu, Yisrael; Israeli politician; b. 14 April 1910, Yemen.
Settled in Israel 29; Head, Dept. for Yemenites and Eastern Communities, Histadrut 34-38; delegated by Histadrut and Israeli Govt. to organize operation "Magic Carpet" (mass airlift of Yemenite Jews to Israel) 48; mem. Labour Party 49-; founder of 45 co-operative settlements for Yemenite Jews; del. to Zionist congresses, to Assefat Hanivharim; perm. collaborator on Hapoel Hazair, Davar, etc.; Deputy Speaker of Knesset 55-66, Speaker 72-; Minister of Posts 66-69; mem. Cen. Cttee., Histadrut; mem. leading bodies of Labour Party, Sec.-Gen. Labour Party 71-72.
Publs. research in Yemenite folklore; *Miteiman le-Zion*, *Shvut Teiman*, *Shevatim ve-Edot be Kur Ha-Histadrut*; Editor: *Maslul*, *Shluhot* (periodicals).
The Knesset Building, Jerusalem; and 49, Homa u-Migdal Street, Holon, Israel.

Yetkin, Suut Kemal; Turkish scholar; b. 1903; ed. Univs. of Paris and Rennes.
Asst. Prof. of History of Art and Aesthetics, Univ. of Istanbul 33-36; Dir.-Gen. of Fine Arts, Ministry of Education 39-41; Prof. of History of Art and Aesthetics, Ankara Univ. 41-50, of History of Turkish and Islamic Arts 50-59; Rector Ankara Univ. 59-63; Officier Légion d'Honneur; Republican Party.
Publs. (in Turkish) *Philosophy of Art* 34, *Courses in Aesthetics* 42, *Literary Doctrines* 43, *Speeches on Literature* 44, *The Art of Leonardo da Vinci* 45, *Art Problems* 45, *On Literature* 53, *Famous Painters* 55, *A. Gide: A Selection of his Critical Writings* 55, *History of Islamic Architecture* 59 (3rd edn. 65), *Problems in Art* 62, *Turkish Architecture* 65, *Currents in Literature* 67, *Essays* 72, *Baroque Art* 74; (in French) *L'Architecture turque en Turquie* 62, *Ancienne Peinture Turque* 70.
Kavaklidere Sok., Güney Apartman 23/5, Ankara, Turkey.

Yoseph, Ovadya; Israeli Rabbi; b. Baghdad, Iraq.
Member, Sephard Rabbinical Court 45; Chief of Rabbinical Court of Appeals and Deputy Chief Rabbi of Egypt (Cairo) 47; mem. regional Rabbinical Court of Petach Tiqva 51, Jerusalem 58; mem. Grand Court of Appeals, Jerusalem 65; Pres. of Great Metivta, Jerusalem; Pres. "Yeshivat Thora Ve-horaa", Tel-Aviv; mem. Management "Yeshivat Porath" Jerusalem; Pres. Cttee. of Building Fund for Yeshivat "Porath Yoseph" in the Old City; Chief Rabbi and Chief of Rabbinical Court of Tel-Aviv May 68-; Sephardi Chief Rabbi of Israel Oct. 72-; Rabbi Kook Prize, Rabbi Uziel Prize.
Publs. *Yobia Omer*, several vols. of Responsa, *Hazon Ovadia*.
Chief Rabbinate, 51 Hamelech David Boulevard, Tel-Aviv, Israel.

Younes, Mahmoud; Egyptian engineer; b. 3 April 1912; ed. Royal Coll. of Engineers, Cairo Univ. and Staff Officers' Coll.
Engineer 37; M.Sc. 42; with Mil. Operations Directorate 43; Lecturer, Staff Officers' Coll. 44 and 47; Dir. Technical Affairs Office, G.H.Q. 52; Man. Dir. and Chair. Gen. Petroleum Authority 54; Counsellor, Ministry of Commerce and Industry for Mineral Wealth; Man. Dir. and Chair. Suez Canal Authority 56; Chair. 57-65; Pres. Engineers' Syndicate 54-65; Dir. and Chair. Cie. Orientale des Pétroles d'Egypte et Soc. Coopérative des Pétroles 58-65; mem. Nat. Assembly 64-; Deputy Prime Minister for Transport and Communications Sept. 65-66; for Electric Power, Oil and Mining 66-67, for Petroleum and Transport 67-68; Cons. ENI. GP 68; Order of Merit (Class I), Order of the Nile (Class III), Military Star, Liberation Medal, Palestine Medal, Grand Cordon of the Order of the Yugoslav Standard, Grand Officer Order of Vasco Núñez de Balboa (Panama), Republic Medal (Class III), Military Service Medal (Class I), Order of the Republic (Class I).
P.O.B. 7272, Beirut, Lebanon.

Yussof, Dr. Mohammed; Afghan politician.
Former Minister of Mines and Industries; Prime Minister and Minister of Foreign Affairs March 63-Nov. 65; Amb. to Fed. Repub. of Germany, Switzerland, Sweden, Denmark 66-.
Embassy of Afghanistan, Röttgen, Liebfrauenweg 1a, Federal Republic of Germany.

WHO'S WHO IN THE MIDDLE EAST AND NORTH AFRICA

Z

Zabarsky, Abraham; Israeli banker; b. 29 March 1897; ed. Kharkov Univ.
Town Councillor, Tel-Aviv 25-50; Treas. Israeli Defence Forces 47-49, mission to U.S.A. 48-49; Chair. and Man. Dir. Bank Hapoalim B.M.; Gen. Man. Israel-American Industrial Devt. Bank Ltd.; Chair. Housing Mortgage Bank Ltd.; mem. Advisory Cttee. Bank of Israel; mem. Gen. Council of Histadrut; mem. Editorial Board *Economic Quarterly*; Dir. of several companies and del. to numerous Zionist congresses.
Publs. *Jewish Cooperative Movement in Palestine and Abroad*, *Labour Economy in Israel*, and numerous articles.
Bank Hapoalim B.M., 50 Rothschild Boulevard, Tel-Aviv; and 11 Keren Kayemeth Boulevard, Tel-Aviv, Israel.

Zadok, Chaim; Israeli lawyer and politician; b. 2 Oct. 1913; ed. Ukraine and Warsaw Univ.
Immigrated 35; took up private practice as lawyer 45; Deputy Attorney-Gen. 49-52; Lecturer Tel-Aviv Univ. 53-61; mem. Knesset 59-; mem. Advisory Cttee. Bank of Israel; Chair. Income Tax Reform Cttee.; Israel Del. to Council of Europe 61-65; Minister of Commerce and Industry May 65-67, concurrently Minister of Devt. May 65-66; Mapai.
Knesset Building, Jerusalem; and 31 Hamitnader Street, Afeka, Tel-Aviv, Israel.

Zahedi, Ardeshir, B.SC.; Iranian diplomat; b. 17 Oct. 1928; ed. in Teheran, American Univ. of Beirut and Univ. of Utah (U.S.A.).
Treasurer, Iran-American Comm. 50-52; Civil Adjutant to His Imperial Majesty the Shah of Iran 54-; Iranian Ambassador to U.S.A. 60-62, 73-, to U.K. 62-67; Minister of Foreign Affairs 67-71; Hon. LL.D., Utah State Univ., Chungang Univ., Seoul; numerous decorations.
Imperial Iranian Embassy, 3005 Massachusetts Avenue, N.W., Washington, D.C. 20008, U.S.A.

Zahedi, Hassan; Iranian politician; b. 1913; ed. Teheran Univ. and Columbia Univ., U.S.A.
Entered Government Service 36, in Agricultural Bank until 45; in U.S. and posts with UN 45-58; in Ministry of Finance 58-61; Pres. Agricultural Bank, Teheran 61-68; Minister of Agriculture 68-70; Minister of the Interior 70-71; Gov.-Gen. of Khorassan 71-.
Alam Avenue-Alam Street, Tajrich, Teheran, Iran.

Zahir, Abdul; Afghan politician; b. 1909, Lagham; ed. Habibia High School, Kabul and Columbia and Johns Hopkins Univs., U.S.A.
Practised medicine in U.S.A. before returning to Kabul 43; Chief Doctor, Municipal Hospital, Kabul 43-50; Deputy Minister of Health 50-55, Minister 55-58; Amb. to Pakistan 58-61; Chair. House of the People 61-64, 65-69; Deputy Prime Minister and Minister of Health 64-65; Amb. to Italy 69-71; Prime Minister 71-72.
c/o Office of the Prime Minister, Kabul, Afghanistan.

Zaid bin Sultan Al-Nihyan, H.H. Sheikh; President of the United Arab Emirates and Ruler of Abu Dhabi; b. 1918.
Governor of Eastern Province 46-66; deposed his brother Sheikh Shakhbut and succeeded to Sheikhdom 66; Pres. Fed. of Arabian Emirates 69-71; Pres. United Arab Emirates (U.A.E.) 71-.
Amiri Palace, Abu Dhabi, Arabian Gulf.

Zaki, Hassan Abbas; Egyptian politician; b. 2 Jan. 1917; ed. primary and secondary schools and Cairo Univ.
Commercial Sec. U.A.R. Embassy, Wash. 52; Govt. Rep. in Stock Exchange Mina El Bassal 55; Dir.-Gen. Exchange Control Dept. Ministry of Econs.; mem. Nat. Assembly; Minister of the Treasury 58, of Economy and Supply 61; Head of Board of Dirs. Egyptian Org. for Insurance 65; Minister of Economy and Foreign Trade 66-70; Order of Merit (Fourth Class) and awards from Yugoslavia, Greece, Somalia and Romania.
Publs. Various articles on monetary, international trade and cotton policies.
23 Gabalia Street, Zamalek, Egypt.

Zalzalah, Abdul Hassan, M.SC., PH.D.; Iraqi banker and politician; b. 1926; ed. Coll. of Law, Univ. of Baghdad and Indiana Univ., U.S.A.
Director Loans and Investments Dept., Central Bank of Iraq 57, Foreign Exchange Dept. 57, Econ. Research Dept. 59-62; Deputy Gov. Central Bank of Iraq 62-63, Acting Gov. 62-63, Chair. of Board of Admin. 62-63; Amb. to Iran 63-64; Minister of Industry 64-65, of Planning 64-65; Acting Minister of Finance Aug. 65; Amb. to Austria 66, to Egypt (also accred. to Somalia) 66-68; Gov. Cen. Bank of Iraq 69-73.
Publs. Economic, political, literary and poetic works in Arabic and English in local and foreign newspapers and magazines.
Central Bank of Iraq, Banks Street, Baghdad, Iraq.

Zayyat, Mohamed Hassan el-, M.A., D.PHIL.; Egyptian diplomatist; b. 14 Feb. 1915; ed. Cairo and Oxford Univs.
Lecturer and Asst. Prof. Alexandria Univ. 42-50; Cultural Attaché, Egyptian Embassy, Washington, D.C. 50-54, First Sec. and Counsellor 54; Counsellor, Egyptian Embassy, Teheran 55-57, Minister 57; Del. of Egypt on UN Advisory Council for Somaliland 57-60, Special Envoy and Ambassador of U.A.R. in Somaliland 60; Head of Dept. of Arab Affairs and Perm. Del. of U.A.R. to Arab League 60-62; Alt. Perm. Rep. of U.A.R. to UN 62-64; Ambassador to India, concurrently accred. to Nepal 64-66; Under-Sec. of State for Foreign Affairs 65-67; Deputy Minister, Chair. U.A.R. State Information Services and Govt. Spokesman 67-69; Perm. Rep. to UN 69-72; Minister of State for Information 72, of Foreign Affairs 72-.
Ministry of Foreign Affairs, Cairo; Home: 1 Midan al Nasr, Almaadi, Cairo, Egypt.

Zayyen, Dr. Yousef; Syrian politician; b. 1931; ed. Damascus Univ. and osteopathy study in the U.K.
Minister of Agrarian Reform Nov. 63-May 64; Ambassador-designate to U.K. Aug. 64; mem. Syrian Presidential Council 64; mem. Nat. Revolutionary Council 65; Prime Minister Sept. 65-Dec. 65, March 66-68; Baath Party.
c/o The Baath Party, Damascus, Syrian Arab Republic.

Zein, Youssef el-; Lebanese politician; b. 1939, Kafaremane; ed. Collège de la Sagesse, Beirut.
Deputy 62-; Minister of Educ., Labour, and Social Affairs 67-68; Minister of Agriculture 68-70.
c/o Ministry of Agriculture, Beirut, Lebanon.

Zekia, Mehmed; Cypriot judge; b. 1903; ed. Univ. of Istanbul and Middle Temple, London.
Member, Legislative Council of Cyprus 30; mem. Advisory Council of Cyprus 33; Chair. Cttee. on Turkish Affairs 48; Advocate 31-40; District Judge 40; Pres. District Court 47; Judge, Supreme Court 52; Judge, High Court of Justice 60; Judge, European Court of Human Rights 61-; Chief Justice of Cyprus 64-66.
The Supreme Court, Nicosia, Cyprus.

Zentar Mrani, Mehdi, L. en D.; Moroccan diplomatist; b. 6 Sept. 1929; ed. Coll. Moulay Idriss de Fez, Lycée de Meknes, and Faculté de Droit, Paris.
Called to Bar, Casablanca 55; Head of Office of Minister of State in Charge of Moroccan Independence Negotiations 56; Dir. African Affairs, Ministry of Foreign Affairs 57; Dir. of Tourism 58; Consul-Gen. Paris 59; Legal Adviser, Ministry of Foreign Affairs, Rabat 60-61, Dir. of Political Affairs 61-63; Ambassador to Algeria 63-64, to Yugoslavia 64-67, to U.A.R. May 67-71; Perm. Rep. to UN 71-; Vice-Pres. Moroccan Del. to Constitutional Conf. of Org. of

African Unity (OAU) and signed Charter for Morocco; Commissaire at Conciliation Comm. of OAU; Pres. 48th Session of Arab League 67-68; Officer Order of the Throne, Morocco, Grand Cordon, Order of the Flag, Yugoslavia, Greek decoration.
Permanent Mission of Morocco to the United Nations, 757 Third Avenue, 23rd Floor, New York, N.Y. 10017, U.S.A.

Zhiri, Kacem; Moroccan diplomatist; b. 25 March 1920; ed. Inst. of Higher Studies, Rabat.
Detained for activities in independence movement of Morocco 36, 44, exiled and detained 52; fmr. Man. daily newspapers *Al-Maghrib* and *Al Alam*; Gen. Dir. Broadcasting Station of Morocco 56-59; Ambassador to Senegal 60-61, to Yugoslavia 62-64, to Algeria 64-65; Dir. of Information, Ministry of Foreign Affairs 66; Perm. Del. of League of Arab States to UN, Geneva 66-68; Minister of Secondary and Technical Educ. 68-69; Amb. to Mauritania 70-72, to People's Repub. of China June 72-; Founder, Free School in Al-Jadida; Moroccan and Yugoslav decorations. Publs. *Biography of Mohammed V* 56, *The Gold of Sous* (novel) 55, Political commentaries 56-58, Social and historical studies.
Embassy of Morocco, Peking, People's Republic of China; Home: 61 rue de la Marne, Rabat, Morocco.

Ziai, Taher, B.SC., PH.D.; Iranian professor and politician; b. 1917; ed. American Coll. of Teheran, Technische Hochschule, Berlin and Univ. of Vienna.
Professor (Geology and Mining) Teheran Univ. 46-; Dir. Nat. Iranian Oil Co. 47; Under-Sec. Ministry of Nat. Econs. 55; Ministry of Industry and Mines 56; Minister of Industry and Mines 60-61, 62-63; mem. of the Senate 67-; Pres. Iran Chamber of Industries and Mines 67-; Homayoun Decoration of Iran; Grand Cross of Merit of Fed. German Repub.
Technical Faculty, University of Teheran, Teheran, Iran.

Ziaie, Abdul Hakim, PH.D.; Afghan judge; b. 15 Sept. 1915; ed. Esteqlal High School, Kabul, Tokyo Univ. and the Sorbonne.
Director higher and vocational educ. 43-45; Dean, Faculty of Law and Political Science 45-47; Pres. Dept. for Secondary Educ. 47-49; Educational Adviser, Ministry of Educ. 55-57, Pres. of its Planning Board 56-63; Deputy Pres. Kabul Univ. 57-58; Dean, Faculty of Econs. 57-60; Dean, Faculty of Law and Political Science 60-63; Acting Deputy Minister of Educ. 61, Deputy Minister 63-65; Minister of Planning 65-67; Chief Justice of Afghanistan 67-; has participated in over 25 int. confs. throughout the world; Kabul Acad. Prize for Literature 35; Medal of Educ. 58; Medal of Stoor 62.
Publs. all 17 of which have been published in Afghanistan, France and Japan, include: *Educational Development in Afghanistan* 51, *Afghanistan's General Progress* 56, *The Rule of Education in securing Human Rights* 64.
Supreme Court, Kabul, Afghanistan.

Ziartides, Andreas; Cypriot trade unionist; b. 1919; ed. Pancyprian Gymnasium, Nicosia.
Trade unionist 37-; mem. Pancyprian Trade Union Cttee. 41, Gen. Sec. 43-47; Gen. Sec. Pancyprian Fed. of Labour 47-; mem. Central Cttee. Cyprus Working People's Progressive Party (AKEL); mem. House of Reps. Cyprus 60-; mem. Exec. Cttee. World Fed. of Trade Unions (WFTU).
Pancyprian Federation of Labour, 31-35 Archemos Street, Nicosia, Cyprus.

Zinder, Zvi, B.SC.; Israeli journalist and government official; b. 26 Aug. 1909; ed. Northwestern Univ.
On editorial staff *The Palestine Post* 34-37; Associated Press Correspondent in Middle East 37-40; Foreign and War Correspondent, Time-Life Publications 40-48; Public Relations Adviser to Israeli Govt., Washington and New York 48-54; Dir. Israel Broadcasting Service 54-60; Dir. Israel Central Office of Information, Aug. 60-April 63; Dir. of Admin., Instructional Television Trust 63-65; Deputy Commr.-Gen. Israel Pavilion, Expo 67, Montreal 65-; Dir. Harry S. Truman Centre for Advancement of Peace, Hebrew Univ.; Man. Dir. Zinkoe Productions Ltd. 71-.
31 Ben Maimon Road, Jerusalem, Israel.

Ziv-Av, Itzhak; Israeli administrative official; b. 4 June 1907; ed. Inst. of Pedagogy, Smolensk.
In Palestine 26; Man. Editor *Haboker* 35-48; Dir. Public Relations Div., Ministry of Defence and Gen. H.Q., Israel Defence Forces 48-52; Dir.-Gen. Israel Farmers' Federation 52-; Chair. Exec. Cttee., Co-ordinating Bureau, Israeli Econ. Orgs. 67-; Editor *Farmers of Israel* (monthly) 62-; mem. Board of Dirs. Jewish Nat. Fund; mem. Council, State Land Authority.
Publs. *The Unknown Land, I seek my Brethren, The Price of Freedom, Forever Ours, From Frontier to Frontier, A World to Live In, Another World.*
Israel Farmers' Federation, P.O. Box 209, Tel-Aviv, Israel.

Zobu, Fazil, M.S.; Turkish business executive; b. 1915; ed. Robert Coll., Istanbul, and Purdue Univ., U.S.A.
Manager Turkish State Monopolies Cigarette Factories 43-48; Vice-Pres. (Production), State Monopolies 48-54; Gen. Man. Türkay Endüstri ve Ticaret A.Ş. 54-64, Dir. 64-; Pres. Chamber of Industry of Istanbul 63; Man. Dir. EVAL A.S. 68-; Dir. Industrial Devt. Bank of Turkey.
Çatalkaya Apt. 12, Topağaci-Nişantas, Istanbul, Turkey.

Zondek, Herman, M.D.; Israeli physician; b. 4 Sept. 1887; ed. Gymnasium, Rogasen, Prussia, and Univs. of Göttingen and Berlin.
Lecturer Friedrich Wilhelm Univ., Berlin 18-21; Dir. Municipal Hospital am Urban, Berlin 26; Prof. of Medicine, Berlin Univ. 34; Dir. Medical Div. Bikur Holim Hospital, 34; Visiting Prof. Hebrew Univ. Medical School, Jerusalem 40; Hon. Pres. Scientific Council of Israel Medical Asscn., Israel Soc. of Internal Medicine, Jerusalem Acad. of Medicine; mem. Israel Acad. of Sciences and Humanities; affiliated to Royal Soc. of Medicine, London, World Acad., of Art and Science; Hon. mem. Foreign Endocrine Socs.; Worthy of Jerusalem.
Publs. *Das Hungerödem* (Hunger Oedema) 20, *The Diseases of the Endocrine Glands* (German) 23, later revised and enlarged editions in German, English, French, Polish, Russian and Italian 26-58; about 250 papers on endocrine physio-pathology and diseases.
8 Ben Maimon Avenue, Jerusalem, Israel.

Zuayter, Akram; Jordanian educationist and diplomatist; b. 1909; ed. Al-Najah Coll., Nablus, American Univ. of Beirut, and School of Law, Jerusalem.
Teacher, secondary schools, Nablus and Acre 27-30; Chief Ed. *Mira'at-al-Shark* and *Al-Hayat*, Jerusalem 30-31; Prof. of History, Training Coll., Baghdad 34-35; Sec. Palestinian Nat. Cttee. 36; exiled 37-50; Insp. of Education, Iraq 40-41; Pres. Arab Del. to Latin America for Palestine Cause 47-48; Minister of Education, All-Palestine Govt. 49; Counsellor, Syrian Del. to Arab League, mem. Perm. Palestine Cttee. 50; Jordan Del. to UN 61; Gen. Sec. Moslem Confs., Jerusalem 60-62; Ambassador of Jordan to Syria 62-63, to Iran 63-66, also accred. to Afghanistan 64-66; Minister of Foreign Affairs 66; Senator 66; Minister of the Royal Court 67-; mem. Consultative Council 67-; Amb. to Lebanon March 71-; Al Kawkab Medal and Al Istiqlal Medal (Jordan), Hon. G.C.M.G., and orders from Iran, Libya, and Repub. of Korea.
Publs. *Our History* 35, *Arabic Readings* 39, *Recent History* 41, *Mission to a Continent* 50, *The Palestine Cause* 54, *An Essay in Federation* 55.
Jordanian Embassy, Beirut, Lebanon.

Zurayk, Constantine Kaysar, M.A., PH.D.; Lebanese educationist; b. 18 April 1909; ed. American Univ. of Beirut, Univ. of Chicago and Princeton Univ.

Assistant Prof. of History, American Univ. of Beirut 30-42, Assoc. Prof. 42-45; First Counsellor, Syrian Legation, Washington 45-46; Syrian Minister to U.S.A. 46-47; Vice-Pres. and Prof. of History, American Univ. of Beirut 47-49; Rector, Syrian Univ. Damascus 49-52; Vice-Pres. American Univ. of Beirut 52-54, Acting Pres. 54-57; Distinguished Prof. of History, American Univ. of Beirut 56-; mem. Syrian Del. to UN Gen. Assembly and Alternate Rep. of Syria on Security Council 46-47; mem. Exec. Board UNESCO 50-54; Pres. Int. Asscn. of Univs. 65-70, Hon. Pres. 70-; mem. Int. Comm. for Scientific and Cultural History of Mankind; Corresp. mem. Iraq Acad., Arab Acad., Damascus; Hon. mem. American Historical Asscn.; Chair. Inst. for Palestine Studies 65-; Order of Merit, Distinguished Class, Syria, Educ. Medal, First Class (Lebanon); Commdr. Order of the Cedar (Lebanon).

Publs. *Al-Wa'y al Qawmi* (National Consciousness); *Ma'na al-Nakbah* (The Meaning of the Disaster); *Ayyu Ghadin* (Whither Tomorrow); *Nahnu wa-al-Tarikh* (Facing History); *Hadha al-'Asr al-Mutafajjir* (This Explosive Age); *Fi Ma'rakat al-Hadarah* (In the Battle for Culture); *Ma'na al-Nakbah Mujaddadan* (The Meaning of the Disaster Again), *More than Conquerors*; Editor, Ismai'l Beg Chol's *Al-Yazidiyyah qadiman wa hadithan* (Yazidis past and present), *Ibn al-Furat's History* Vols. VII-IX (partly with Najla Izzeddin); Editor and translator Miskawayh's *Tahdhib al-Akhlaq* (The Refinement of Character).

American University of Beirut, Beirut, Lebanon.

Calendars, Time Reckoning and Weights and Measures

Muslim Calendar

The Muslim era dates from July 16th, A.D. 622, which was the beginning of the Arab year in which the *Hijra*, Muhammad's flight from Mecca to Medina, took place. The Muslim or Hijra Calendar is lunar, each year having 354 or 355 days, the extra day being intercalated eleven times every thirty years. Accordingly the beginning of the Hijra year occurs earlier in the Gregorian Calendar by a few days each year. The Muslim year 1394 A.H. begins on January 25th, 1974.

The year is divided into the following months:

1. Muharram	30 days	7. Rajab	30 days
2. Saphar	29 ,,	8. Shaaban	29 ,,
3. Rabia I	30 ,,	9. Ramadan	30 ,,
4. Rabia II	29 ,,	10. Shawwal	29 ,,
5. Jamada I	30 ,,	11. Dulkaada	30 ,,
6. Jamada II	29 ,,	12. Dulheggia	29 or 30 days

The Hijra Calendar is used for religious purposes throughout the Islamic world and is the official calendar in Saudi Arabia and the Yemen. In most Arab countries it is used side by side with the Gregorian Calendar for official purposes, but in Turkey and Egypt the Gregorian Calendar has replaced it.

PRINCIPAL MUSLIM FESTIVALS

New Year: 1st Muharram. The first ten days of the year are regarded as holy, especially the tenth.

Ashoura: 10th Muharram. Celebrates the first meeting of Adam and Eve after leaving Paradise, also the ending of the Flood and the death of Husain, grandson of Muhammad. The feast is celebrated with fairs and processions.

Mouloud (*Birth of Muhammad*): 12th Rabia I.

Leilat al Meiraj (*Ascension of Muhammad*): 27th Rajab.

Ramadan (*Month of Fasting*).

Id ul Fitr or **Id ul Saghir** or **Küçük Bayram** (*The Small Feast*): Three days beginning 1st Shawwal. This celebration follows the constraint of the Ramadan fast.

Id ul Adha or **Id al Kabir** or **Büyük Bayram** (*The Great Feast, Feast of the Sacrifice*): Four days beginning on 10th Dulheggia. The principal Muslim festival, commemorating Abraham's sacrifice and coinciding with the pilgrimage to Mecca. Celebrated by the sacrifice of a sheep, by feasting and by donations to the poor.

Hijra Year	1392	1393	1394
New Year	Feb. 16th, 1972	Feb. 4th, 1973	Jan. 25th, 1974
Ashoura	Feb. 26th, ,,	Feb. 14th, ,,	Feb. 3rd, ,,
Mouloud	April 26th, ,,	April 16th, ,,	April 6th, ,,
Leilat al Meiraj	Sept. 8th, ,,	Aug. 28th, ,,	Aug. 5th, ,,
Ramadan begins	Oct. 9th, ,,	Sept. 29th, ,,	Sept. 19th, ,,
Id ul Fitr	Nov. 8th, ,,	Oct. 29th, ,,	Oct. 18th, ,,
Id ul Adha	Jan. 18th, 1973	Jan. 5th, 1974	Dec. 26th, ,,

Note: Local determinations may vary by one day from those given here.

Iranian Calendar

The Iranian Calendar, introduced in 1925, is based on the Hijra Calendar, adapted to the solar year. Iranian New Year (*Nowruz*) occurs at the vernal equinox, which usually falls on March 21st Gregorian. The year 1352 began on March 21st, 1973.

The Iranian year is divided into the following months:

1. Favardine	31 days	7. Mehr	30 days
2. Ordibehecth	31 ,,	8. Aban	30 ,,
3. Khordad	31 ,,	9. Azar	30 ,,
4. Tir	31 ,,	10. Dey	30 ,,
5. Mordad	31 ,,	11. Bahman	30 ,,
6. Chariver	31 ,,	12. Esfand	29 or 30 days

The Iranian Calendar is used for all purposes in Iran and Afghanistan, except the determining of Islamic religious festivals, for which the lunar Hijra Calendar is used.

Hebrew Calendar

The Hebrew Calendar is solar with respect to the year, but lunar with respect to the months. The normal year has 353–355 days in twelve lunar months, but seven times in each nineteen years an extra month of 30 days (*Adar II*) is intercalated after the normal month of Adar to adjust the calendar to the solar year. New Year (*Rosh Hashanah*) usually falls in September of the Gregorian Calendar, but the day varies considerably. The year 5733 began on September 9th, and 5734 began on September 27th, 1973.

The months are as follows:

1. Tishri	30 days	7. Nisan	30 days
2. Marcheshvan	29 or 30 days	8. Iyyar	29 ,,
3. Kislev	29 or 30 ,,	9. Sivan	30 ,,
4. Tebeth	29 days	10. Tammuz	29 ,,
5. Shebat	30 ,,	11. Ab	30 ,,
6. Adar	29 ,,	12. Ellul	29 ,,
(Adar II)	30 ,,		

The Hebrew Calendar is used to determine the dates of Jewish religious festivals only.

CALENDARS, TIME RECKONING AND WEIGHTS AND MEASURES

Standard Time

The table shows zones of standard time, relative to Greenwich Mean Time (G.M.T.). Many of the individual countries adopt daylight saving time at certain times of year.

Traditional Arabic time is still widely used by the local population in Saudi Arabia except in most of the Eastern Province. This system is based upon the local time of sunset when timepieces are all set to 12.

G.M.T.	1 Hour Ahead	2 Hours Ahead	3 Hours Ahead	3½ Hours Ahead	4 Hours Ahead	4½ Hours Ahead
Algeria Morocco Spanish Sahara	Tunisia	Cyprus Egypt Israel Jordan Lebanon Libya Sudan Syria Turkey	Bahrain Iraq Kuwait Yemen P.D.R.	Iran	Oman Qatar	Afghanistan

Note: Saudi Arabia and the Yemen Arab Republic use solar time.

Weights and Measures

Principal weights and units of measurement in common use as alternatives to the Metric and Imperial systems.

WEIGHT

Unit	Country	Metric Equivalent	Imperial Equivalent
Charak	Afghanistan	1·764 kilos.	3·89 lb.
Hogga	Iraq	1·27 kilos.	2·8 lb.
Kantar, or Cantaro	{ Cyprus { Egypt	228·614 kilos. 44·928 kilos.	504 lb. 99·05 lb.
Kharwar	Afghanistan	564·528 kilos.	1,246·2 lb.
Khord	Afghanistan	110·28 grammes	3·89 oz.
Maund	{ Yemen P.D.R. { Saudi Arabia	37·29 kilos.	82·28 lb.
Oke or Okka	{ Cyprus { Egypt	1·27 kilos. 1·245 kilos.	2·8 lb. 2·751 lb.
Ratel or Rotl	{ Saudi Arabia { Egypt	0·449 kilo.	0·99 lb.
Seer	Afghanistan	7·058 kilos.	15·58 lb.
Yeni Okka	Turkey	1 kilo.	2·205 lb.

LENGTH

Unit	Country	Metric Equivalent	Imperial Equivalent
Busa	{ Saudi Arabia { Sudan	2·540 cm.	1 in.
Dirraa, Dra or Pic	Cyprus	60·96 cm.	2 ft.
Gereh-gaz-sha	Afghanistan	6·6 cm.	2·6 in.
Kadam or Qadam	Sudan	30·48 cm.	1 ft.

CALENDARS, TIME RECKONING AND WEIGHTS AND MEASURES

CAPACITY

Unit	Country	Metric Equivalent	Imperial Equivalent
Ardeb	Saudi Arabia, Sudan, Egypt	198·024 litres	43·56 gallons
Kadah	Sudan, Egypt	2·063 litres	3·63 pints
Keila	Cyprus	36·368 litres	8 gallons
	Sudan, Egypt	16·502	3·63 gallons
Ratel	Sudan	0·568 litre	1 pint

AREA

Unit	Country	Metric Equivalent	Imperial Equivalent
Donum or Dunum	Cyprus	1,335·8 sq. metres	0·33 acre
	Iraq	2,500 sq. metres	0·62 acre
	Israel, Jordan	1,000 sq. metres	0·2471 acre
	Syria, Turkey	919·04 sq. metres	0·2272 acre
Feddan	Saudi Arabia, Sudan, Egypt	4,201 sq. metres	1·038 acres
Yeni Donum	Turkey	10,000 sq. metres (1 hectare)	2·471 acres

METRIC TO IMPERIAL CONVERSIONS

Metric Units	Imperial Units	To Convert Metric into Imperial Units Multiply by:	To Convert Imperial into Metric Units Multiply by:
Weight			
Gramme	Ounce (Avoirdupois)	0·035274	28·3495
Kilogramme (Kilo.)	Pound (lb.)	2·204622	0·453592
Metric ton	Short ton (2,000 lb.)	1·102311	0·907185
	Long ton (2,240 lb.)	0·984207	0·01605

(The short ton is in general use in the U.S.A., while the long ton is normally used in Britain and the Commonwealth.)

Length			
Centimetre	Inch	0·3937008	2·54
Metre	Yard (=3 feet)	1·09361	0·9144
Kilometre	Mile	0·62137	1·609344
Volume			
Cubic metre	Cubic foot	35·315	0·0283
	Cubic yard	1·30795	0·764555
Capacity			
Litre	Gallon (=8 pints)	0·219976	4·54596
	Gallon (U.S.)	0·264178	3·78533
Area			
Square metre	Square yard	1·19599	0·836127
Hectare	Acre	2·47105	0·404686
Square kilometre	Square mile	0·386102	2·589988

SELECT BIBLIOGRAPHIES

BOOKS ON THE MIDDLE EAST

(See also Bibliographies at end of Chapters in Part II)

ABDEL MALEK, A. Anthologie de la Littérature Arabe Contemporaine—les Essais (Editions du Seuil, Paris, 1966).
La Pensée Politique Arab Contemporaine (Editions du Seuil, Paris, 1970).

ABU JABER, KAMEL S. The Arab Baath Socialist Party (Syracuse University Press, New York, 1966).

ABU-LUGHOD, IBRAHIM (ed.). The Transformation of Palestine: Essays on the Development of the Arab-Israeli Conflict (Northwestern University Press, Evanston, Ill., 1971).

ADAMS, MICHAEL (ed.). The Middle East: A Handbook (Anthony Blond, London, 1971).

AFIFI, MUHAMMAD. The Arabs and the United Nations (Longmans, London, 1964).

ALDERSON, A. D, The Structure of the Ottoman Dynasty (New York, Oxford University Press, 1956).

AMERICAN ENTERPRISE INSTITUTE. United States Interests in the Middle East (Washington, D.C., 1968).

ANTONIUS, GEORGE. The Arab Awakening. 4th edition (Beirut, 1961).

ARBERRY, A. J. (ed.). Religion in the Middle East—Volume I Judaism and Christianity, Volume II Islam and General Summary (Cambridge University Press, 1969).

ATIYAH, EDWARD. The Arabs (Baltimore, 1955).

ATLAS OF THE ARAB WORLD AND THE MIDDLE EAST (Macmillan, London, 1960).

BASTER, JAMES. The Introduction of Western Economic Institutions into the Middle East (Royal Inst. of Int. Affairs and O.U.P., 1960).

BAER, GABRIEL. Population and Society in the Arab East (Routledge, London, 1964).

BE'ERI, ELIEZER. Army Officers in Arab Politics and Society (Pall Mall Press, London, 1969).

BELL, J. BOWYER. The Long War, Israel and the Arabs since 1946 (Englewood Cliffs, 1969).

BELYAEV, J. C. (ed.). Arabs, Islam and the Arab Caliphate in the early Middle Ages (Pall Mall Press, London, 1969).

BERGER, MORROE. The Arab World Today (Doubleday New York, 1962).

BERQUE, JACQUES and CHARNAY, J.-P. Normes et Valeurs dans l'Islam Contemporaine (Payot, Paris, 1966).

BETHMANN, ERICH W. A Selected Basic Bibliography on the Middle East (American Friends of the Middle East, Washington, 1964).

BINDER, LEONARD. The Ideological Revolution in the Middle East (New York, 1964).

BIROT, P. & DRESCH, J. La Méditerranée et le Moyen Orient, Vol. II (Paris 1955).

BLACHÈRE, M. Histoire de la Littérature Arabe (Paris, 1966).

BROCKELMANN, C. History of the Islamic Peoples (New York and London, 1947-48).
Geschichte der Arabischen Litteratur (Leyden, 1938).

BULLARD, Sir R. Britain and the Middle East from the earliest times to 1952 (London, 1952).

CAMPBELL, J. C. Defense of the Middle East (New York, 1950, 2nd edition 1961).

CATTAN, J. Evolution of Oil Concessions in the Middle East and North Africa (Oceana, Dobbs Ferry, New York, 1967).

COOK, M. A. (ed.). Studies in the Economic History of the Middle East (Oxford University Press, 1970).

COON, C. S. Caravan: the Story of the Middle East (New York, 1951, and London, 1952).
The Impact of the West on Social Institutions (New York, 1952).

COPELAND, MILES. The Game of Nations (Weidenfeld and Nicholson, London, 1969).

CRAGG, K. A. Counsels in Contemporary Islam (Edinburgh, 1964).

CREMEANS, CHARLES D. The Arabs and the World (London, Pall Mall Press, 1963).

DANIEL, NORMAN. Islam and the West (Edinburgh University Press, revised edition 1963).
Islam, Europe and Empire (Edinburgh University Press, 1964).

DISHON, DANIEL (ed.). Middle East Record Vol. III, 1967 (Israel Universities Press, Jerusalem, 1972).

DODD, S. C. Social Relations in the Near East. 2nd revised and enlarged edition (London, New York, and Toronto, Oxford University Press, 1940).

EL-GHONEMY, MOHAMMED RIAD (ed.). Land Policy in the Near East (Rome, 1967).

ENCYCLOPAEDIA OF ISLAM, THE. 4 vols. and supplement (Leiden, 1913-38).

EL-ERIAN, TAHANY. References dealing with the Arab World: A selected and annotated list (Organization of Arab Students in the U.S.A. and Canada, New York, 1966).

ETTINGHAUSEN, RICHARD. Books and Periodicals in Western Languages dealing with the Near and Middle East (Washington, Middle East Institute, 1952).

FARIS, N. A. (ed.). The Arab Heritage (Princeton, N.J., Princeton University Press, 1944).

FIELD, HENRY. Bibliography on Southwestern Asia: VII, A Seventh Compilation (University of Miami, 1962).

FINNIE, D. H. Desert Enterprise: The Middle East Oil Industry and its Local Environment (Cambridge, Mass., 1958).

FISHER, S. N. Social Forces in the Middle East (Cornell University Press, Ithaca, N.Y., 1955).
The Middle East: A History (Alfred Knopf, New York, 6th edition, 1971).

FISHER, W. B. The Middle East—a Physical, Social and Regional Geography (London, 3rd edition, 1954).

FRYE, R. N. (ed.). The Near East and the Great Powers (Harvard University Press, Cambridge, Mass., 1951, and Oxford University Press, London, New York, and Toronto, 1952).

GIBB, H. A. R. Mohammedanism (London, 1949).
Modern Trends in Islam (Chicago, 1947).
Studies on the Civilisation of Islam (London, 1962).

THE MIDDLE EAST AND NORTH AFRICA—(Select Bibliographies)

Gibb, H. A. R., and Bowen, Harold. Islamic Society and the West (2 vols., London, 1950, 1957).
Glubb, Lt.-Gen. Sir John. A Short History of the Arab Peoples (Hodder and Stoughton, London, 1969).
Grant, D. (ed.). The Islamic Near East (University of Toronto Press, 1960).
Grundwald, K., and Ronall, J. O. Industrialisation in the Middle East (Council for Middle East Affairs, New York, 1960).
Grunebaum, Gustave E. von (ed.). Unity and Variety in Muslim Civilisation (Chicago, 1955).
Islam: Essays in the Nature and Growth of a Cultural Tradition (London, Routledge and Kegan Paul, 1961).
Modern Islam: the Search for Cultural Identity (London, 1962).
Haim, Sylvia G. Arab Nationalism: An Anthology (Berkeley, Calif., 1962).
Hall, Hervey P. (ed.) The Evolution of Public Responsibility in the Middle East (Washington, 1955).
Halpern, Manfred. The Politics of Social Change in the Middle East and North Africa (Princeton University Press, N.Y., 1963).
Hartshorn, J. E. Oil Companies and Governments (Faber, London, 1962).
Hazard. Atlas of Islamic History (Oxford University Press, 1951).
Hershlag, Z. Y. Introduction to the Modern Economic History of the Middle East (E. J. Brill, Leiden, 1964).
Higgins, Rosalyn. United Nations Peacekeeping 1946-67: Documents and Commentary, Volume I The Middle East (Oxford University Press, 1969).
Hirst, David. Oil and Public Opinion in the Middle East (Praeger, New York, 1966).
Hirszowicz, Lukasz. The Third Reich and the Arab East (Routledge and Kegan Paul, London, 1966).
Hitti, Philip K. History of the Arabs (London, 1940, 10th edn., 1970).
A Short History of the Near East (New York, 1966).
Makers of Arab History (Macmillan, London, 1968).
Islam. A Way of Life (Oxford University Press, London, 1971).
Hoare, Ian, and Tayar, Graham (eds.). The Arabs. A handbook on the politics and economics of the contemporary Arab world (B.B.C. Publications, London, 1971).
Hodgkin, E. C. The Arabs (Modern World Series, Oxford University Press, 1966).
Hollingworth, Claire. The Arabs and the West (London, 1952).
Holt, P. M. Studies in the History of the Near East (Cass, London, 1973).
Holt, P. M., Lambton, A. K. S., Lewis, B. (eds.). The Cambridge History of Islam. Vol. I The Central Islamic Lands (Cambridge University Press, 1970); Vol. II The Further Islamic Lands, Islamic Society and Civilization (Cambridge University Press, 1971).
Hoskins, H. A. Middle East: Problem Area (New York, 1954).
Hourani, A. H. Minorities in the Arab World (London, 1947).
A Vision of History (Beirut, 1961).
Arabic Thought in the Liberal Age 1798-1939 (Oxford Univ. Press, 1962).
Hurewitz, J. C. Unity and Disunity in the Middle East (New York, Carnegie Endowment for International Peace, 1952).
Middle East Dilemmas (New York, 1953).
Diplomacy in the Near and Middle East (Vol. I, 1535-1914; Vol. II, 1914-56; Van Nostrand, 1956).
Soviet-American Rivalry in the Middle East (ed.) (Pall Mall Press, London, and Praeger, New York, 1969).
Al-Husay, Khaldun S. Three Reformers; A Study in Modern Arab Political Thought (Khayats, Beirut, 1966).
Huxley, J. From an Antique Land: Ancient and Modern in the Middle East (London, 1954).
Ionides, Michael. Divide and Lose: the Arab Revolt 1955-58 (Bles, London, 1960).
Institute for Strategic Studies. Sources of Conflict in the Middle East (Adelphi Papers, Institute for Strategic Studies, London, 1966).
Ireland, P. W. (ed.). The Near East, Problems and Prospects (Chicago, 1942).
Irwin, I. J. Islam in the Modern National State (Cambridge University Press, Cambridge, 1965).
Issawi, Charles (ed.). The Economic History of the Middle East, 1800–1914 (University of Chicago Press, 1966).
Issawi, Charles and Yeganeh, Mohammed, The Economics of Middle Eastern Oil (Faber, London, 1963).
Izzeddin, N. The Arab World (Chicago, 1953).
Janin, R. Les Eglises orientales et les Rites orientaux (Paris, 1926).
Jansen, G. H. Non-Alignment and the Afro-Asian States (Praeger, New York, 1966).
Johnson-Davies, Denys. Modern Arabic Short Stories (Oxford University Press, 1967).
Jones, David. The Arab World (Hilary House, New York, 1967).
Karpat, Kemal H. Political and Social Thought in the Contemporary Middle East (Pall Mall Press, London, 1968).
Kedourie, Elie. England and the Middle East (London, 1956).
The Chatham House Version and other Middle-Eastern Studies (Weidenfeld and Nicholson, London, 1970).
Keen, B. A. The Agricultural Development of the Middle East (London, H.M.S.O., 1946).
Kelly, J. B. Eastern Arabian Frontiers (Faber, London, 1963).
Kerr, Malcolm. The Arab Cold War 1958–1964 (Oxford University Press, 1965).
Khadouri, M. & Lievesny, H. J. (ed.). Law in the Middle East, Vol. I (Washington, 1955).
Khalil, Muhammad. The Arab States and the Arab League (historical documents) (Khayat's, Beirut).
Khayat, M. K. and Keatinge, M. C. Food from the Arab World (Beirut, 1959).
Khouri, Fred J. The Arab-Israeli Dilemma (Syracuse/New York, 1968).
Kingsbury, R. C. and Pounds, N. J. G. An Atlas of Middle Eastern Affairs (New York, 1963).
Kirk, George E. The Middle East in the War (London, 1953).
A Short History of the Middle East: from the Rise of Islam to Modern Times (New York, 1955).
Contemporary Arab Politics (Methuen, London, 1961).
Kumar, Ravinder. India and the Persian Gulf Region (London, 1965).
Lahbabi, Mohamed Aziz. Le Personnalisme Musulmane (Presses Universitaires de France, Paris, 1964).
Lall, Arthur. The UN and the Middle East Crisis (New York/London, 1968).

THE MIDDLE EAST AND NORTH AFRICA—(Select Bibliographies)

Landen, R. G. (ed.). The Emergence of the Modern Middle East: Selected Readings (Van Nostrand Reinhold, New York, 1970).

Laqueur, W. Z. Communism and Nationalism in the Middle East (London and New York, 1957).
A History of Zionism (Weidenfeld and Nicholson, London, 1972).
(ed.) The Middle East in Transition (Routledge and Kegan Paul, London, 1958).
(ed.) The Israel-Arab Reader (New York/Toronto/London, 1969).

Lawrence, T. E. The Seven Pillars of Wisdom (London, 1935).

Leiden, Carl (ed.). The conflict of traditionalism and modernism in the Muslim Middle East (Austin, Texas, 1969).

Lenczowski, George. The Middle East in World Affairs (Ithaca, N.Y., Cornell University Press, 1956).
Oil and State in the Middle East (Cornell Univ. Press, 1960).

Lengyel, Emil. The Changing Middle East (New York, 1962).

Lerner, D. The Passing of Traditional Society: Modernising the Middle East (Glencoe, Illinois, 1958).

Lewis, B. The Arabs in History (London, 1950 and 1954).
The Middle East and the West (London, 1963).
Islam in History (London, 1973).

Ljunggren and Geddes (Editors). International Directory of Institutes and Societies Interested in the Middle East (Amsterdam, 1962).

Longrigg, S. H. Oil in the Middle East (London, 1954, 3rd edn., London, 1968).
The Middle East: a Social Geography (London, 1963).

Macdonald, Robert W. The League of Arab States (Princeton University Press, Princeton, 1965).

Makarius, Raoul. Anthologie de la Littérature Arabe Contemporaine (Seuil, Paris, 1964).

Mannin, Ethel. A Lance for the Arabs (London, 1963).

Mansfield, Peter (ed.). The Middle East: A Political and Economic Survey, 4th edition (Oxford U.P., London, 1972).

Mason, Herbert (ed.). Reflections on the Middle East Crisis (Paris/The Hague, 1970).

Michaelis, Alfred. Wirtschaftliche Entwicklungsprobleme des Mittleren Ostens (Kiel, 1960).

Middle East in the War (London, Royal Institute of International Affairs).

Middle East: Tricontinental Hub—A Strategic Survey. Headquarters Dept. U.S. Army (U.S. Government Printing Office, Washington, 1965).

Mikdashi, Zuhayr. The Community of Oil Exporting Countries (George Allen and Unwin, London, 1972).

Miquel, André. Islam et sa civilisation (Paris, 1968).

Monroe, Elizabeth. Britain's Moment in the Middle East (Chatto and Windus, London, 1963).

Musrey, Alfred A. An Arab Common Market: A Study in Inter-Arab Trade Relations 1920–67 (Praeger, New York, 1969).

Nasr, Seyyed Hossein. Science and Civilization in Islam (Harvard, 1968).

Nevakivi, Jukka. Britain, France and the Arab Middle East 1914–20 (Athlone Press, University of London, 1969).

Nicholson, Reynold A. A Literary History of the Arabs (Cambridge University Press, 1969).

Norin, Luc and Taraby, Edouard. Anthologie de la Littérature Arabe Contemporaine—les Poésies (Editions du Seuil, Paris, 1967).

Nutting, Anthony. The Arabs (Hollis and Carter, London, 1965).
No End of a Lesson, The Story of Suez (Constable, London, 1967).

Oron, Yitzhak (ed.). Middle East Record Vol. I 1960 (Weidenfeld and Nicholson, 1962); Vol. II 1961 (Jerusalem, 1966).

Oxford Regional Economic Atlas. The Middle East and North Africa (Oxford University Press, 1960).

Pannikkar, K. M. The Afro-Asian States and their Problems (Allen and Unwin, London, 1960).

Partner, Peter. The Arab World (Pall Mall, London, 1962).

Patai, R. Golden River to Golden Road (Philadelphia, 1962).

Pearson, J. D. (ed.). Index Islamicus (Cambridge, 1967).

Playfair, Ian S. O. The Mediterranean and the Middle East (History of the Second World War, H.M.S.O., London, 1966).

Poliak, A. N. Feudalism in Egypt, Syria, Palestine, and the Lebanon, 1250–1900 (London, Luzac, for the Royal Asiatic Society, 1939).

Polk, W. R. The United States and the Arab World (Harvard University Press, 1965).
(ed. with Chambers, R. L.) Beginnings of Modernization in the Middle East: the Nineteenth Century (University of Chicago Press, 1969).

Proctor, J. Harris (ed.). Islam and International Relations (Pall Mall Press, London, 1965).

Puryear, V. J. France and the Levant from the Bourbon restoration to the Peace of Kutiah. (California, University of California Press, 1941).

Qubain, Fahim I. Education and Science in the Arab World (Johns Hopkins Press, Baltimore, 1967).

Rivlin, B., and Szyliowicz, J. S. (eds.). The Contemporary Middle East—Tradition and Innovation (Random House, New York, 1965).

Ronart, Stephan and Nandy. Concise Encyclopaedia of Arabic Civilization (Amsterdam, 1966).

Rondot, Pierre. The Destiny of the Middle East (Chatto & Windus, London, 1960).
L'Islam (Prismes, Paris, 1965).

Rouhani, Fuad. A History of OPEC (Pall Mall Press, London, 1972).

Sauvaget, J. Introduction à l'histoire de l'orient musulman (Paris, 1943) (2nd edn. re-cast by C. Cahen, Univ. of Calif. Press, 1965).

Searight, Sarah. The British in the Middle East (Weidenfeld and Nicholson, London, 1969).

Segesvary, Victor. Le Réalisme Khrouchtchévien: La politique sovietique au Proche-Orient (Editions de la Baconnière, Neuchâtel, Switzerland, 1968).

Shaban, M. A. The Abbasid Revolution (Cambridge University Press, 1970).
Islamic History A.D. 600–750 (A.H. 132) A New Interpretation (Cambridge University Press, 1971).

Sharabi, H. B. Governments and Politics of the Middle East in the Twentieth Century (Van Nostrand, New York, 1962).
Nationalism and Revolution in the Arab World (Van Nostrand, New York, 1966).
Palestine and Israel: The Lethal Dilemma (Pegasus Press, N.Y., 1969).

THE MIDDLE EAST AND NORTH AFRICA—(Select Bibliographies)

Simmons, J. S. & Others. Global Epidemiology, Vol. 3: The Near and Middle East (Philadelphia, 1954).

Simon, Jan. Men and Medicine in the Middle East (World Health Organization, Alexandria, 1967).

Smith, W. Cantwell. Islam and Modern History (Toronto, 1957).

Southern, R. W. Western Views of Islam in the Middle Ages (Oxford, 1957).

Spencer, W. Political Evolution in the Middle East (Philadelphia, 1962).

Spector, Ivar. The Soviet Union and the Muslim World (Seattle, University of Washington Press, 1956).

Stark, Freya. Dust in the Lion's Paw (London and New York, 1961).

Stevens, Georgina G. (ed.). The United States and the Middle East (Prentice Hall, N.J., 1964).

Stewart, Desmond. The Middle East: Temple of Janus (Hamish Hamilton, London, 1972).

Stocking, G. W. Middle East Oil. A Study in Political and Economic Controversy (Vanderbilt University Press, Nashville, 1970).

Sumner, B. H. Tsardom and Imperialism in the Far East and Middle East (London, Oxford University Press, 1940).

Swadran, Benjamin. The Middle East, Oil and the Great Powers (London, 1956).

Thayer, P. W. (ed.). Tensions in the Middle East (Baltimore, 1958).

Thomas, D. Winton (ed.). Archaeology and Old Testament Study (Oxford University Press, 1967).

Thomas, L. V. and Frye, R. N. The United States and Turkey and Iran (Cambridge, Mass., 1951).

Trevelyan, Humphrey (Lord). The Middle East in Revolution (Macmillan, London, 1970).

Trimingham, J. Spencer. The Sufi Orders in Islam (Clarendon Press, Oxford, 1971).

Tugendhat, C. Oil: The Biggest Business (Eyre and Spottiswoode, London, 1968).

Vatikiotis, P. J. Conflict in the Middle East (George Allen and Unwin, London, 1971).

Wadsman, P., and Teissedre, R.-F. Nos Politiciens face au Conflict Israélo Arabe (Paris, 1969).

Waines, David. The Unholy War (Medina Press, Wilmette, 1971).

Warriner, Doreen. Land and Poverty in the Middle East (London, 1948).
Land Reform and Development in the Middle East: Study of Egypt, Syria and Iraq (London, 1962).

Watt, W. Montgomery. Muhammad at Mecca (Clarendon Press, Oxford, 1953).
Muhammad at Medina (Clarendon Press, Oxford, 1956).
Muhammad, Prophet and Statesman (Oxford University Press, 1961).
Muslim Intellectual—Al Ghazari (Edinburgh University Press, 1962).
Islamic Philosophy and Theology (Edinburgh University Press, 1963).

Wiet, G. P. Introduction à la Littérature Arabe (Maisonneuve, Paris, 1966).

Yale, William. The Near East (University of Michigan Press, Ann Arbor, 1968).

Young, T. C. (ed). Near Eastern Culture and Society (Princeton, N.J., Princeton University Press, 1951).

Zeine, Z. N. The Struggle for Arab Independence (Beirut, 1960).

BOOKS ON NORTH AFRICA
(See also Bibliographies at end of Chapters in Part III)

Allal El-Fassi. The Independence Movements in Arab North Africa, trans. H. Z. Nuseibeh (Washington, 1954).

Amin, Samir. L'Economie du Maghreb (2 vols., Editions du Minuit, Paris, 1966).
The Maghreb in the Modern World (Penguin Books, London, 1971).

Barbour, Neville, Editor. A Survey of North West Africa (The Maghreb) (Royal Institute of International Affairs, Oxford University Press, 1959).

Berque, Jaques. Le Maghreb entre Deux Guerres (2nd edn., Editions du Seuil, Paris, 1967).

Brace, R. M. Morocco, Algeria, Tunisia (Prentice-Hall, Englewood Cliffs, N.J., 1964).

Brown, Leon Carl (ed.). State and Society in Independent North Africa (Middle East Institute, Washington, 1966).

Capot-Rey, R. Le Sahara Français (Paris, 1953).

Centre d'Etudes des Relations Internationales. Le Maghreb et la Communauté Economique Européenne (Editions F.N.S.P., Paris, 1965).

Centre de Recherches sur l'Afrique Méditerranéene d'Aix en Provence. L'Annuaire de l'Afrique du Nord (Centre Nationale de la recherche scientifique, Paris, annually).

Charbonneau, J. Editor. Le Sahara Français (Cahiers Charles de Foucauld, No. 38, Paris, 1955).

Duclos, J., Leca, J., and Duvignaud, J. Les Nationalismes Maghrébins (Centre d'Etudes des Relations Internationales, Paris, 1966).

Economic Commission for Africa. Main Problems of Economic Co-operation in North Africa (Tangier, 1966).

Food and Agriculture Organisation. Mediterranean Development Project (Rome, 1959).

Furlonge, Sir Geoffrey. The Lands of Barbary (Murray, London, 1966).

Gallagher, C. F. The U.S. and North Africa (Cambridge, Mass., 1964).

Gardi, René. Sahara, Monographie einer grossen Wüste (Kummerley and Frey, Berne, 1967).

Gautier, E. F. Le Passé de l'Afrique du Nord (Paris, 1937).

Gordon, D. C. North Africa's French Legacy 1954-62 (Harvard, 1962).

Hahn, Lorna. North Africa: from Nationalism to Nationhood (Washington, 1960).

Heseltine, N. From Libyan Sands to Chad (Leiden, 1960).

Julien, Ch.-A. Histoire de l'Afrique du Nord (2nd Edition, 2 Vols., Paris 1951-52).
L'Afrique du Nord en Marche (Paris, 1953).
History of North Africa: From the Arab Conquest to 1830. Revised by R. Le Tourneau. Ed. C. C. Stewart (Routledge and Kegan Paul, London, 1970).

THE MIDDLE EAST AND NORTH AFRICA—(Select Bibliographies)

KHALDOUN, IBN. History of the Berbers. Translated into French by Slane (4 vols., Algiers, 1852-56).

LE TOURNEAU, ROGER. Evolution Politique de l'Afrique du Nord Musulmane (Paris, 1962).

LEVI-PROVENÇAL, E. Islam d'Occident (Etudes d'Histoire Médiévale, Paris, 1948).

LISKA, G. The Greater Maghreb: From Independence to Unity? (Center of Foreign Policy Research, Washington, 1963).

MARÇAIS, G. La Berberie Musulmane et l'Orient au Moyen Age (Paris, 1946).

MOORE, C. H. Politics in North Africa (Little, Brown, Boston, 1970).

MORTIMER, EDWARD. France and the Africans, 1944-1960 (Faber, London, 1969).

MUZIKÁR, JOSEPH. Les perspectives de l'intégration des pays maghrébins et leur attitude vis-à-vis du Marché Commun (Nancy, 1968).

NICKERSON, JANE S. Short History of North Africa (New York, 1961).

PARRINDER, GEOFFREY. Religion in Africa (Pall Mall Press, London, 1970).

POLK, WILLIAM R. (ed.). Developmental Revolution: North Africa, Middle East, South Asia (Middle East Institute, Washington, 1963).

RAVEN, SUSAN. Rome in Africa (Evans Brothers, London, 1970).

SAHLI, MOHAMED CHERIF. Décoloniser l'Histoire; introduction à l'histoire du Maghreb (Maspero, Paris, 1965).

SCHRAMM, JOSEF. Die Westsahara (Paunonia-Verlag, Freilassing, 1969).

STEEL, R. (ed.). North Africa (Wilson, New York, 1967).

TOYNBEE, Sir ARNOLD. Between Niger and Nile (Oxford University Press, 1965).

TRIMINGHAM, J. S., The Influence of Islam upon Africa (Longmans, London, and Librairie du Liban, Beirut, 1968).

TUTSCH, HANS E. Nordafrika in Gärung (Frankfurt, 1961). From Ankara to Marrakesh (New York, 1962).

UNESCO. Arid Zone Research, Vol. XIX: Nomades et Nomadisme au Sahara (UNESCO, 1963).

UNIONS, LABOUR AND INDUSTRIAL RELATIONS IN AFRICA; AN ANNOTATED BIBLIOGRAPHY. Cornell Research Papers in International Relations, 4 (Cornell University Press, New York, 1965).

WARREN, CLINE and SANTMYER, C. Agriculture of Northern Africa (U.S. Dept. of Agriculture, Washington, 1965).

ZARTMAN, I. W. Government and Politics in North Africa (New York, 1964).

SELECT BIBLIOGRAPHY (PERIODICALS)

ACTA ORIENTALIA ACADEMIAE SCIENTIARUM HUNGARICAE. H-1363 Budapest, P.O.B. 502, Hungary; 1950; three times a year; text in English, French, German or Russian; Editor L. LIGETI.

ACTA ORIENTALIA. Publ. Munksgaard, Norre Sogade 35, DK 1370 Copenhagen K, Denmark, by the Oriental Societies of Denmark, Norway, and Sweden; history and language of the Near and Far East; once or twice yearly; Editor Prof. SØREN EGEROD.

AFRICA. Dirección General de Promoción de Sahara, Sección de Archivo, Castellana 5, Madrid 1, Spain.

AFRICA RESEARCH BULLETINS. Africa Research Ltd., 1 Parliament St., Exeter, EX4 3DZ, Devon, England; f. 1964; monthly bulletins on (a) political and (b) economic subjects.

AFRICA CONTEMPORARY RECORD. Rex Collings Ltd., 6 Paddington St., London, W1M 3LA; annual documented survey.

AFRICAN QUARTERLY. Indian Council for Africa, 5 Curzon Lane, New Delhi, India.

L'AFRIQUE ET L'ASIE. 8 rue de Furstenberg, Paris 6e, France; f. 1948; quarterly.

AL-ABHATH. Publ. American University of Beirut, Beirut, Lebanon; f. 1948; Editor MAHMUD A. GHUL; quarterly on Arab affairs.

AL-TIJARA AL-ARABIYA AL-INKLEEZYA (Anglo-Arab Trade). British Industrial Publicity Overseas Ltd., London W.C.2; Arabic; bi-monthly.

ANATOLIAN STUDIES. 140 Cromwell Rd., London, S.W.7, England; f. 1949; annual of the British Inst. of Archaeology at Ankara; Editor Prof. O. R. GURNEY.

ANATOLICA. Netherlands Historical and Archaeological Institute at Istanbul, Istiklâl Caddesi 393, Istanbul-Beyoğlu, Turkey; f. 1967; annual; Editors: Prof. Dr. A. A. KAMPMAN, HANDAN ALKIM, Dr. SEMRA ÖGEL.

ANNALES ARCHÉOLOGIQUES ARABES SYRIENNES. Direction Générale des Antiquités et des Musées, University St., Damascus, Syria; semi-annually.

ANNALES DE L'INSTITUT D'ÉTUDES ORIENTALES DE LA FACULTÉ DES LETTRES D'ALGER. Institut d'Études Orientales, Faculté des Lettres, Algiers, Algeria.

ANNUAIRE DE L'AFRIQUE DU NORD—ALGÉRIE, MAROC, TUNISIE, LIBYE. Editions C.N.R.S., 15 quai Anatole-France, Paris 7e, France; f. 1962; contains special studies, chronologies, documentation and bibliographies.

THE ARAB ECONOMIST. Centre for Economic, Financial and Social Research and Documentation SAL, Gefinor Tower, Clemenceau Street, Bloc B—room 501, P.O.B. 6068, Beirut, Lebanon; f. 1969; Chair. Dr. CHAFIC AKHRAS; monthly; circ. 5,000.

ARAB REPORT AND RECORD. 84 Chancery Lane, London, W.C.2, England; f. 1966; digest of Arab political, economic and social affairs; twice monthly; Editor PETER KILNER.

THE ARAB WORLD. 84 rue Kantari, Beirut; daily and weekly editions of newsletter on current affairs; Editor I. A. HIJAZI.

ARABICA. Centre Universitaire Censier, 13 rue de Santeuil, Paris 5e, France; Editor G. LECOMTE; three issues annually.

THE MIDDLE EAST AND NORTH AFRICA—(Select Bibliographies)

Archiv für Orientforschung. Graz, Austria; f. 1923; annual; Editor and Publisher Dr. Ernst Weidner.

Armenian Review. Hairenik Association, Inc., 212 Stuart St., Boston, Mass. 02216, U.S.A.

Asian Affairs. Royal Central Asian Society, 42 Devonshire St., London, W.1, England; f. 1901; three times per year.

Asian and African Studies. Israel Oriental Society, The Hebrew University, Jerusalem, Israel; f. 1965; Editor Gabriel Baer; annual.

L'Asie Nouvelle. 97 rue St. Lazare, Paris 9e, France; weekly and special issues; Dir. André Roux.

Asien-Bibliographie. Asien Bucherei, D-359 Bad Wildungen, German Federal Republic; quarterly.

Belleten. Türk Tarih Kurumu, Kizilay Sokak no. 1, Ankara, Turkey; f. 1931; history and archaeology; quarterly.

Bibliography of the Middle East. P.O.B. 2712, Damascus, Syria; f. 1968; annual.

Biblioteca Orientalis. Prof. Dr. A. A. Kampman (ed.), Noordeindsplein 4-6, Leiden, Netherlands; f. 1943; bi-monthly.

Bulletin of the School of Oriental and African Studies. School of Oriental and African Studies, University of London, London, W.C.1, England; three issues annually.

Bulletin of Sudanese Studies. P.O.B. 321, Khartoum; Arabic; published by Sudan Research Unit, University of Khartoum; f. 1968; bi-annual; Editor Awn al-Sharif Qasim.

Cahiers de L'Orient Contemporain. La Documentation française, 29–31 quai Voltaire, Paris 7e, France; f. 1945; detailed coverage of current affairs in the Near East countries since the close of World War II; five issues annually; Dir. Mme. N. Tomiche.

Les Cahiers de Tunisie. 55 rue Djemaâ Ez-Zitouna, Tunis; f. 1953; quarterly; Dir. Mohamed Talbi, Editor-in-Chief Azzedine Guellouz.

Le Commerce du Levant. Kantari St., SFAH Building, Beirut, Lebanon; two editions (bi-weekly and monthly).

Comunitá Mediterranea. Lungotevere Flaminio 34, Rome; law and political science relating to Mediterranean countries; Pres. E. Bussi.

Cultura Turcica. T. K. Araştırma Enstitüsü, P.K. 14, Çankaya, Ankara, Turkey; f. 1964; articles in English, French and German; semi-annual; editor Prof. Dr. Ahmet Temir.

Deutsche Morgenländische Gesellschaft; Zeitschrift. Deutsche Morgenländische Gesellschaft, 355 Marburg/Lahn, Postfach 642, Federal Republic of Germany; f. 1948; covers the history, languages and literature of the Orient; bi-annual.

L'Economie et les Finances des Pays Arabes. Centre d'Etudes et de Documentation Economiques, Financières et Sociales, S.A.L., B.P. 6068, Beirut, Lebanon; monthly.

Egypte Contemporaine. Société Egyptienne d'Economie Politique, de Statistique et de Législation, B.P. 732, Cairo, Egypt; . 1909; quarterly in Arabic, French and English.

Europe France Outremer. 6 rue de Bassano, Paris 16e, France; f. 1923; economic and political material on French-speaking states of Africa; monthly.

Free Palestine. P.O.B. 492, London, S.W.1; f. 1968; monthly; Editor Aziz Yafi.

Hamizrah Hehadash. Israel Oriental Society. The Hebrew University, Jerusalem, Israel; f. 1949; Hebrew with English summary; Middle Eastern, Asian and African affairs; quarterly; Editor Yehoshua Porath.

Hesperis-Tamuda. Faculté des Lettres, Université Mohammed V, Rabat, Morocco; f. 1921; history, archaeology, special reference to bibliography; irregular.

Huna London (BBC Arabic Radio Times). BBC Arabic Service, Bush House, Strand, London, WC2B 4PH.

Ibla. Institut des Belles Lettres Arabes, 12 rue Jamâa el Haoua, Tunis, Tunisia; f. 1937; twice a year.

Indo-Iranian Journal. N.V. Uitgeverij Mouton & Co., Herderstraat 5, The Hague, Netherlands; f. 1957; quarterly.

Industrial Egypt. Federation of Industries in the U.A.R., 26A Sherif Street, P.O.B. 251, Cairo, Egypt; f. 1924; Arabic and English; quarterly.

International Journal of Middle East Studies. Cambridge University Press, 200 Euston Rd., P.O.B. 92, London, NW1 2DB; Journal of the Middle East Studies Association of North America; first issue Jan. 1970; quarterly.

Internationales Afrika Forum. Weltforum Verlags G.m.b.H., 8000 Munich 19, Hubertusstrasse 22/I, German Federal Republic; f. 1965; monthly.

Iranistische Mitteilungen. Antigone-Verlag, 3559 Allendorf an der Eder, German Federal Republic; f. 1967; Editor Helmhart Kanus-Crede.

Iraq. British School of Archaeology in Iraq, 31–34 Gordon Square, London, W.C.1, England; f. 1932; semi-annually.

Der Islam. 4D2 Hamburg 13, Rothenbaumchaussee 36, German Federal Republic; two issues annually.

Islamic Culture. Islamic Culture Board, Post Box 171, opp. Osmania University Post Office, Hyderabad 7, India; f. 1927; quarterly.

Islamic Quarterly. The Islamic Cultural Centre, Regent's Lodge, 146 Park Rd., London, N.W.8, England; f. 1954; quarterly.

Islamic Review. Woking Muslim Mission and Literary Trust, 18 Eccleston Sq., London, S.W.1, England.

Izvestia Akademii Nauk-Otedelenie Literatury i Yazyka. Soviet Academy of Sciences, Moscow, U.S.S.R.; bi-monthly.

Jeune Afrique. Presse Africaine Associée, 51 av. des Ternes, Paris 17e, France; f. 1960; weekl

Jewish Observer and Middle East Review. 36 Whitefriars St., London, E.C.4, England; weekly; Editor Maurice Samuelson.

Journal of the American Oriental Society. American Oriental Society, 329 Sterling Memorial Library, New Haven, Conn., U.S.A.; f. 1842; Biblical studies, Ancient Near East and Far East; quarterly.

Journal Asiatique. Journal de la Société Asiatique, 3 rue Mazarine, Paris 6e, France; f. 1822; Dir. J. Février; covers all phases of Oriental research; quarterly.

Journal of Near Eastern Studies. Oriental Institute, University of Chicago, 1155 East 58th St., Chicago, Ill. 60637, U.S.A.; devoted to the Ancient and Medieval Near and Middle East, archaeology, languages, history, Islam.

Journal of Palestine Studies. P.O.B. 7164, Beirut, Lebanon; f. 1971; Palestinian affairs and the Arab-Israeli conflict; Editor Hisham Sharabi; circ. 4,000.

THE MIDDLE EAST AND NORTH AFRICA—(Select Bibliographies)

MAGHREB. Fondation Nationale des Sciences Politiques, La Documentation Française, 29–31 quai Voltaire, Paris 7e, France; f. 1964; bi-monthly.

M.E.N. WEEKLY. Middle East News Agency, 4 Sharia Sheruffin, Cairo, Egypt; f. 1956; weekly news bulletin.

MIDDLE EAST ECONOMIC DIGEST—MEED. Economic Features Ltd., 84-86 Chancery Lane, London, W.C.2, England; f. 1957; weekly report on economic developments; Chair. and Editorial Dir. ELIZABETH COLLARD, Editor RICHARD PURDY.

MIDDLE EAST ECONOMIC SURVEY. P.O.B. 1224, Beirut, Lebanon; f. 1957; weekly review of news and views on Middle East/North African oil.

MIDDLE EAST FORUM. Alumni Office, American University of Beirut, P.O.B. 19, Beirut, Lebanon.

MIDDLE EASTERN STUDIES. Frank Cass & Co. Ltd., 67 Great Russell St., London, WC1B 3BT, England; f. 1964; Editor ELIE KEDOURIE; three times yearly.

MIDDLE EAST INTERNATIONAL. Room 105, Grand Buildings, Trafalgar Square, London WC2N 5EP; f. 1971; monthly; politics, economics and culture.

THE MIDDLE EAST JOURNAL. Middle East Institute, 1761 N St., N.W., Washington, D.C. 20036, U.S.A.; journal in English devoted to the study of the modern Near East; f. 1947; quarterly; Editor WILLIAM SANDS.

MIZAN. Central Asian Research Centre, 1B Parkfield St., London N1, England; analyses Soviet and Chinese policies in the Middle East; six issues per year.

MUSLIM CHRONICLE. P.O.B. 700, London, W.2; f. 1970; weekly; Editor FAREED S. JAFRI.

THE MUSLIM WORLD. 55 Elizabeth St., Hartford, Conn. 06105, U.S.A.; f. 1911; Islamic studies, with special attention to current affairs and Muslim-Christian relations; quarterly; Editor WILLEM A. BIJLEFELD.

NARODY ASII I AFRIKI (Istoriya, Ekonomika, Kultura). Akad. Nauk S.S.S.R., Khokhlovsky per., 13, Moscow, U.S.S.R.; f. 1955; bi-monthly.

NATIONS NOUVELLES, OCAM, B.P. 437, Yaoundé, Cameroon; f. 1964; articles on French-speaking Africa; every two months; Editor KANE FALILOU.

NEAR EAST REPORT. 1341 G St., N.W., Washington, D.C. 20005, U.S.A.; f. 1957; analyses U.S. policy in the Near East; circ. 34,000; weekly; Editor I. L. KENEN.

THE NEW MIDDLE EAST. 68 Fleet St., London, E.C.4; f. 1968; general review of Middle East current affairs; monthly.

OEL (Zeitschrift für die Mineralölwirtschaft). 2 Hamburg 13, Alsterkamp 20, Federal Republic of Germany; f. 1963; monthly.

OIL AND GAS JOURNAL. Petroleum Publishing Co., 211 S. Cheyenne Ave., Tulsa, Okla. 74101, U.S.A.; f. 1902; weekly.

ORIENS. International Society for Oriental Research, Frankfurt/Main, Federal Republic of Germany; f. 1948; articles in German, French and English, on the history and archaeology of the Near and Far East; annual; Editor Prof. Dr. R. SELLHEIM.

ORIENT. German Near and Middle East Association, 2 Hamburg 13, Mittelweg 150, German Federal Republic; f. 1960; current affairs articles in German, French and English; quarterly.

ORIENT. 11 rue Saint-Sulpice, Paris 6e, France; f. 1959; quarterly.

ORIENTE MODERNO. Istituto per l'Oriente, via A. Caroncini 19, Rome, Italy; f. 1921; chronicle of events, extremely useful for students of the modern Near East; monthly.

PALESTINE AFFAIRS. P.O.B. 1691, Beirut, Lebanon; studies of Palestine problem; quarterly in English, twice monthly in Arabic; Editor Dr. ANIS SAYEGH.

PALESTINE EXPLORATION QUARTERLY. Palestine Exploration Fund, 2 Hinde Mews, London, W.1, England; f. 1865.

PALESTINE EXPLORATION QUARTERLY. Palestine Exploration Fund, 2 Hinde Mews, London, W.1, England.

PERSICA. Netherlands-Iranian Society; Noordeindsplein 4-6, Leiden, Netherlands; f. 1963; annual; Editors Prof. Dr. A. A. KAMPMAN and Dr. C. NIJLAND.

PETROLEUM PRESS SERVICE. 24 Ludgate Hill, London, EC4M 7DS, England; f. 1934; monthly; in English, French, Spanish, German, Arabic and Japanese editions.

PETROLEUM TIMES. IPC Industrial Press Ltd., 33/40 Bowling Green Lane, London, EC1R 0NE, England; f. 1899; fortnightly.

RECORD OF THE ARAB WORLD. English Language Edition, Euromark Ltd., Walter House, 418-422 Strand, London WC2; Editor JEBRAN CHAMIEH.

REVUE D'ASSYRIOLOGIE. Presses Universitaires de France, 12 rue Jean-de-Beauvais, Paris 5e, France; f. 1923; bi-annual; Editor JEAN NOUGAYROL.

LA REVUE BIBLIOGRAPHIQUE DU MOYEN ORIENTAL. Publisher L. FARÈS, B.P. 2712, Damascus, Syria.

REVUE DES ETUDES ISLAMIQUES. Librarie Orientaliste Paul Geuthner, 12 rue Vavin, Paris 6e, France; f. 1927; ed. H. LAOUST.

RIVISTA DEGLI STUDII ORIENTALI. Scuola di Studi Orientali, University of Rome, Rome, Italy; quarterly; Editor GIOVANNI BARDI.

ROCZNIK ORIENTALISTYCZNY. Grójecka 17, Warsaw, Poland; f. 1915; Editor-in-Chief JAN REYCHAM; semi-annual.

ROYAL ASIATIC SOCIETY OF GREAT BRITAIN AND IRELAND JOURNAL. 42 Devonshire Street, London, W.1., England; f. 1834; covers all phases of Oriental research.

AL SINAI (The Industrialist). Iraqi Federation of Industry, P.O.B. 11,120, Baghdad, Iraq; f. 1960; articles in Arabic, and English; quarterly.

STUDIA ISLAMICA, G. P. Maisonneuve et Larose, 11 rue Victor-Cousin, Paris 5e, France; bi-annual.

STUDIES IN ISLAM. Indian Institute of Islamic Studies, Panchkuin Rd., New Delhi, India; quarterly.

SUMER. Directorate-General of Antiquities, Baghdad, Iraq; archaeological; bi-annual.

TÜRK KÜLTÜRÜ. T. K. Araştırma Enstitüsü, P.K. 14, Çankaya, Ankara, Turkey; f. 1962; Turkish language articles on current affairs and history; Editor Dr. AHMET TEMIR; monthly.

TÜRK KÜLTÜRÜ ARAŞTIRMALARI. T. K. Araştırma Enstitüsü, P.K. 14, Çankaya, Ankara, Turkey; f. 1964; scholarly articles in Turkish; bi-annual.

DIE WELT DES ISLAMS. Publ. E. J. Brill, Oude Rijn 33a, Leiden, Netherlands; f. 1913; contains articles in German, English and French; Editor Prof. Dr. O. SPIES.

WIENER ZEITSCHRIFT FÜR DIE KUNDE DES MORGENLANDES. Oriental Institute of the University of Vienna, A-1010 Wien I, Universitätstrasse 7/V, Austria; irregular.

WORLD PETROLEUM. 25 West 45th St., New York, N.Y. 10036, U.S.A.; f. 1930; monthly.

Research Institutes
Associations and Institutes Studying the Middle East and North Africa.
(*See also* Regional Organizations—Education in Part I)

AFGHANISTAN
The Asia Foundation: P.O.B. 257, Kabul.

ALGERIA
Centre de Recherches Africaines: Faculté des Lettres, Université d'Alger, 2 rue Didouche Mourad, Algiers.

Institut d'Etudes Arabes: Université d'Alger, 2 rue Didouche Mourad, Algiers.

Institut d'Etudes Orientales: Université d'Alger, 2 rue Didouche Mourad, Algiers; publ. *Annales*.

AUSTRIA
Afro-Asiatisches Institut in Wien: A-1090 Vienna, Türkenstrasse 3; f. 1959; seminars and language courses and other cultural exchange between African and Asian students in Vienna; library of 1,000 vols.; Gen. Sec. A. GRÜNFELDER.

Orientalisches Institut der Universität Wien: A-1010 Vienna, Universitätstrasse 7/V; f. 1886; 50 mems.; library of 25,000 vols.; Pres. Prof. Dr. HANS L. GOTTSCHALK, Prof. Dr. HANS HIRSCH; publ. *Wiener Zeitschrift für die Kunde des Morgenlandes* (irregular).

BELGIUM
Centre pour l'Etude des Problèmes du Monde Musulman Contemporain: 44 ave. Jeanne, 1050 Brussels; f. 1957; Scientific Dir. Prof. A. ABEL; publs. *Correspondance d'Orient-Etudes* (half-yearly) and collections *Correspondance d'Orient* and *Le monde musulman contemporain—Initiations*.

Departement Oriëntalistiek: Faculteit van de Wijsbegeerte en Letteren, Katholieke Universiteit te Leuven, Mgr. Ladeuzeplein 18, B3000 Leuven; f. 1936; Pres. Prof. P. NASTER; 25 mems.; publs. *Orientalia Lovaniensia Analecta, Orientalia Lovaniensia Periodica, Bibliothèque du Muséon* (1929–68), *Orientalia et Biblica Lovaniensia* (1957–68).

Fondation Egyptologique Reine Elisabeth: Parc du Cinquantenaire, Brussels B1040; f. 1923 to encourage Egyptian studies; 750 mems.; library of 80,000 vols.; Pres. M. E. BONVOISIN; Dir. M. J. BINGEN; publs. *Chronique d'Egypte, Bibliotheca Aegyptiaca, Papyrologica Bruxellensia, Bibliographie Papyrologique sur fiches*.

Private Information Center on Eastern Arabia: Heldenplein 12, 1800 Vilvoorde; f. 1970; documents on Bahrain, Qatar, U.A.E., Oman and the Arabian Peninsular; Dir. M. VAN DAELE; publs. (monthly list of new acquisitions, fact sheets on Eastern Arabia).

CZECHOSLOVAKIA
Department of Oriental Studies of the Slovak Academy of Sciences: Slovak Academy of Sciences, Klemensova 27, Bratislava; f. 1960; 10 mems.; Pres. Dr. I. DOLEŽAL; Vice-Dir. Dr. M. GÁLIK; publ. *Asian and African Studies* (annual).

Oriental Institute: Prague I, Lázeňská 4; f. 1922; Head of library Mrs. VLASTA RUZKOVÁ; publs. *Archiv Orientální* (quarterly), *Nový Orient* (monthly).

DENMARK
Orientalsk Samfund (*Orientalist Association*): Scandinavian Inst. of Asian Studies, Kejsergade 2, Copenhagen K; f. 1915 to undertake the study and further the understanding of Oriental cultures and civilizations; 75 mems.; Pres. Prof. SØREN EGERØD; Sec. Prof. J. P. ASMUSSEN; publ. *Acta Orientalia* (annually).

EGYPT
Academy of the Arabic Language: 26 Sharia Mourad, Giza, Cairo; f. 1932; Pres. Dr. AHMED LOUTFI EL SAYED; Sec.-Gen. Dr. IBRAHIM MAKDOUR; publ. *Review*, collections of scientific and Koranic terms.

American Research Center in Egypt Inc.: 2 Midan Kasr el Doubara, Cairo, and 20 Nassau St., Princeton, N.J. 08540; f. 1948 by American universities to promote research by U.S. scholars in all phases of Egyptian civilization, including archaeology; 19 institutional mems. and 235 individual mems.; Pres. Prof. JOHN A. WILSON; Vice-Pres. Prof. MORROE BERGER; American Dir. LILY M. BROWN; Cairo Dir. JOHN DORMAN.

Deutsches Archäologisches Institut (*German Archaeological Institute*): 22 Sharia Gezira al Wusta, Zamalek, Cairo; Dir. Prof. Dr. WERNER KAISER.

Institut Dominicain d'Etudes Orientales: Priory of the Dominican Fathers, 1 Sharia Masma al-Tarabish, Abbasiyah, Cairo; f. 1952; Dir. Père G. C. ANAWATI; publ. *Mélanges* (yearly).

Institut d'Egypte: 13 Sharia Sheikh Rihane, Cairo; f. 1798; studies literary, artistic and scientific questions relating to Egypt and neighbouring countries; Pres. MUHAMMAD REDA MADWAR; Sec.-Gen. P. GHALIOUNGUI; publs. *Bulletin* (annual), *Mémoires* (irregular).

Institut Français d'Archéologie Orientale: 37 Sharia Sheikh Ali Youssef, Cairo; f. 1898; Dir. S. SAUNERON.

Société Archéologique d'Alexandrie: 6 Sharia Mahmoud Moukhtar, Alexandria; f. 1893; 100 mems.; Pres. MOHIE EL-DIN EL-SHAZILI; Sec.-Gen. D. A. DAOUD; Treas. A. SADEK; Editor MAX DEBBANE; publs. *Bulletins, Mémoires, Monuments de l'Egypte Gréco-Romaine, Cahiers, Publications Spéciales*.

Société Egyptienne d'Economie Politique, de Statistique et de Législation: B.P. 732, Cairo; f. 1909; 900 mems.; Pres. Dr. ABDEL HAKIM RIFAI; Sec.-Gen. Dr. GAMAL EL OTEIFI; publ. *Revue* (quarterly in Arabic, French and English).

Society for Coptic Archaeology: 222 Avenue Ramses, Cairo; f. 1934; 360 mems.; library of 8,500 vols.; Pres. MIRRIT BOUTROS GHALI; Sec. Dr. ANTOINE KHATER; Treas. Dr. BOUTROS BOUTROS GHALI; Librarian Dr. O. H. E. KHS-BURMESTER; publs. *Bulletin* (annual), *Fouilles, Bibliothèque d'Art et d'Archéologie, Textes et Documents et Divers*.

FINLAND
Suomen Itämainen Seura (*Finnish Oriental Society*): Helsinki, Snellmaninkatu 9-11; f. 1917; 200 mems.; Pres. Dr. E. SALONEN; Sec. Dr. I. KÄRKI; publ. *Studia Orientalia*.

THE MIDDLE EAST AND NORTH AFRICA—(RESEARCH INSTITUTES)

FRANCE

Centre d'Etudes de l'Orient Contemporain: 13 rue du Four, Paris 6e; f. 1943; Dir. Prof. CH. PELLAT; publ. *Cahiers de l'Orient Contemporain* (five times a year).

Centre d'Information du Proche-Orient: 62 rue Lhomonde, Paris 5e.

Centre de Hautes Etudes Administratives sur l'Afrique et l'Asie Modernes: 13 rue du Four, Paris 6e; Dir. *ad interim* G. MALECOT; publs. *L'Afrique et L'Asie* (quarterly), *Cahiers de l'Afrique et l'Asie* (irregular), *Langues et Dialects d'Outre-Mer* (irregular), *Recherches et Documents du CHEAM* (irregular).

Centre de Recherches Africaines: 17 rue de la Sorbonne, Paris 5e.

Centre de Recherches et d'Etudes sur les Sociétés Méditerranéennes: Faculté de Droit, 3 ave. Robert Schuman, Aix-en-Provence; Dirs. MM. LE TOURNEAU, MANTRAN, DEBBASCH; publ. *Annuaire de l'Afrique du Nord*.

Centre Universitaire Censier: 13 rue de Santeuil, Paris 5e; publ. *Arabica* (three times a year).

Fondation Nationale des Sciences Politiques: 27 rue Saint-Guillaume, Paris 7e; f. 1945; Administrator J. CHAPSAL; Centre d'Etudes des Relations Internationales, Dir. J. MEYRIAT; Arab World section has research team of 9 mems.; publs. include *Maghreb-Machrek* (bi-monthly).

Institut d'Etudes Iraniennes de l'Université de Paris: 22 ave. du Président Wilson, Paris 16e; f. 1947; Dir. EMILE BENVENISTE; publ. *Travaux*.

Institut d'Etudes Islamiques de l'Université de Paris: 13 rue de Santeuil, Paris 5e; f. 1929; Dir. Prof. CH. PELLAT.

Institut d'Etudes Sémitiques: 16 rue de la Sorbonne, Paris 5e; f. 1930; publ. *Semitica*.

Institut d'Etudes Turques de l'Université de Paris: 13 rue du Four, Paris 6e; Dir. L. BAZIN.

Institut National des Langues et Civilisations Orientales: 2 rue de Lille, Paris 7e; attached to Univ. de la Sorbonne Nouvelle Paris III; f. 1795; faculties of languages and civilizations of West Asia and Africa; the Far East, India and Oceania; Eastern Europe; library of 600,000 vols. and 2,000 MSS.; over 5,500 students, 83 teachers, 107 lecturers; Pres. R. SIEFFERT; Sec. Mme J. FIATTE; publs. various Oriental studies.

Institut de Papyrologie: Université de Paris-Sorbonne, 1 rue Victor-Cousin, Paris 5e; Dir. JEAN SCHERER.

Société Asiatique: 3 rue Mazarine, Paris 6e; f. 1822; 500 mems.; library of 80,000 vols.; Pres. R. LABAT; Secs. J. FILLIOZAT, M. SOYMIE, L. BAZIN; Dir. J. FÉVRIER; publs. *Journal Asiatique* (quarterly), *Cahiers de la Société Asiatique*.

FEDERAL REPUBLIC OF GERMANY

Altorientalisches Seminar der Freien Universität Berlin: 1 Berlin 45, Unter den Eichen 78/79; f. 1950.

Deutsche Afrika Gesellschaft: Bonn, Markt 10-12; publ. *Afrika Heute* (monthly).

Deutsche Morgenländische Gesellschaft: 355 Marburg/Lahn, Postfach 642; Sec. Dr. WOLFGANG VOIGT; publs. *Zeitschrift* (semi-annual), *Abhandlungen für die Kunde des Morgenländes*, *Bibliotheca Islamica*, *Wörterbuch der Klassischen Arabischen Sprache*, *Beiruter Texte und Studien*, *Verzeichnis der orientalischen Handschriften in Deutschland*.

Deutsche Orient-Gesellschaft: 33 Takustrasse 40, Berlin; f. 1898; 450 mems.; Pres. Prof. Dr. KLAUS BRISCH; Sec. Prof. PETER G. AHRENS; publs. *Mitteilungen*, *Wissenschaftliche Veröffentlichungen*, *Abhandlungen*.

Internationale Gesellschaft fuer Orientforschung: 17/25 Mertonstrasse, Frankfurt; f. 1948; 400 mems.; Pres. Prof. R. SELLHEIM; publ. *Oriens* (bi-annual).

Nah- und Mittelost Verein: Hamburg 13, Mittelweg 151; f. 1934; 600 mems.; Chair. HANS-OTTO THIERBACH; Gen. Sec. R.-E. FRHR. V. LÜTTWITZ; publ. *Orient* (three-monthly).

Orient-Institut Frankfurt am Main: Frankfurt I, Savignystrasse 65; Dir. Prof. Dr. F. NEUMARK.

Seminar für Orientalische Sprachen: Adenauerallee 102, Bonn 53; institute attached to the University of Bonn; Dir. Prof. Dr. W. HOENERBACH.

HUNGARY

Magyar Tudományos Akadémia, Orientalisztikai Bizottsága (*Oriental Committee of the Hungarian Academy of Sciences*): Budapest V, Roosevelt tér. 9; publ. *Acta Orientalia Hung.* (three times a year).

INDIA

Asiatic Society of Bombay: Town Hall, Bombay; f. 1804; 1,380 mems.; Pres. Hon. Mr. Justice Y. V. CHANDRACHUD, B.A., LL.B.

Indian Institute of Islamic Studies: Panchkuin Rd., New Delhi 1 and Tughlaqabad, New Delhi 62; f. 1963; library of 25,000 vols. and 1,000 MSS; Pres. HAKEEM ABDUL HAMEED; Dir. S. A. ALI; publ. *Studies in Islam* (quarterly).

International Council for Africa: 5 Curzon Lane, New Delhi; publ. *Africa Quarterly*.

Iran League: Navsari Bldg. (2nd floor), Dr. Dadabhai Navroji Rd., Fort, Bombay I; f. 1922; 500 mems.; Pres. J. C. TARAPORE; Sec. J. E. RANDERIA; publs. *Iran League Journal* and translations and commentaries in modern Persian of Avesta texts.

Iran Society: 12 Kyd St., Calcutta; f. 1944; 171 mems.; Pres. S. N. KODAK; Sec. Dr. M. ISHAQUE; publ. *Indo-Iranica*.

Ismali Society: P.O.B. 6052, Bombay 5; 1946; Pres. G. H. BUNDALLY; Hon. Editor W. IVANOW; publ. translations and texts of Ismaili works, monographs on Ismailism.

IRAN

The Asia Institute: Pahlavi University, Shiraz; Dir. Dr. RICHARD N. FRYE; publs. *Bulletin of the Asia Institute*, *Monographs of the Asia Institute*.

British Institute of Persian Studies: 238 ave. Takhte Jamshid, P.O.B. 2617, Teheran; f. 1961; cultural institute, with emphasis on history and archaeology; 318 mems.; Pres. Sir MAX MALLOWAN, C.B.E., D.LIT., F.B.A., F.S.A.; Hon. Sec. J. E. F. GUERITZ; Dir. DAVID STRONACH, M.A., F.S.A.; *Iran* (annual).

Regional Cultural Institute: 5 Los Angeles Ave., Teheran; f. 1966; Dir. Dr. SALIM NEYSARI; publs. *Journal* (quarterly), also publications on the history and culture of Iran, Turkey and Pakistan.

IRAQ

American School of Oriental Research: Baghdad; f. 1923; undertakes archaeological surveys and excavations; Dir. (vacant); publ. *Bulletin*, quarterlies and monographs.

THE MIDDLE EAST AND NORTH AFRICA—(RESEARCH INSTITUTES)

British School of Archaeology in Iraq (Gertrude Bell Memorial): Karradet Mariam, Baghdad; f. 1932; Pres. Prof. Sir MAX MALLOWAN, C.B.E., M.A., D.LIT., F.B.A., F.S.A.; Dir. in Iraq Mrs. DIANNA HELBAEK; publ. *Iraq* (twice annually).

Deutsches Archäologisches Institut: 71B/11 Hurriya Square, Karrada, Baghdad.

Instituto Hispano-Arabe de Cultura: Park Sa'adun, P.O.B. 256, Baghdad.

Iraq Academy: Waziriyah, Baghdad; f. 1947 to maintain the Arabic language, to undertake research into Arabic history and the history of Iraq, and to encourage research in the modern arts and sciences; Pres. ABDUL RAZZAQ MUHIDDIN; Sec. Dr. Y. IZZIDIEN; publ. *Literary Criticism in Iraq, Bulletin*.

ISRAEL

Academy of the Hebrew Language: P.O.B. 3449, Jerusalem; f. 1953; study of the Hebrew language and compilation of an historical dictionary; Pres. Prof. N. H. TUR-SINAI; publ. *Zikhronot, Leshonenu, Leshonenu La'am*, monographs and dictionaries.

American Institute of Holy Land Studies: P.O.B. 1276, Jerusalem; f. 1959; Christian study centre; Pres. Dr. G. DOUGLAS YOUNG.

American School of Oriental Research: Herod's Gate, Jerusalem; f. 1900; research in Semitic languages, literature and history, archaeological research and excavations; Pres. G. ERNEST WRIGHT; Dir. J. H. MARKS; publ. *Bulletin*.

The Ben-Zvi Institute: Yad Izhak Ben-Zvi and the Hebrew University of Jerusalem; f. 1948; sponsors research in the history and culture of Jewish communities in the East; Chair. Prof. SHELOMO MORAG; Research Dir. Prof. JACOB M. LANDAU.

British School of Archaeology in Jerusalem: P.O.B. 19/283, Jerusalem; f. 1920; archaeological research and excavation; hostel and library; Chair. Miss K. M. KENYON, C.B.E.; Dir. Mrs. C. M. BENNETT, F.S.A.; publ. *Levant*.

Couvent Saint Etienne des Pères Dominicains, Ecole Biblique et Archéologique Française: P.O.B. 178, Jerusalem; f. 1890; research, Biblical and Oriental studies, exploration and excavation in Palestine; Dir. R. P. TOURNAY; library of 50,000 vols.; publs. *Revue Biblique, Etudes Bibliques, Etudes Palestiniennes et Orientales, Cahiers de la Revue Biblique, Bible de Jérusalem*.

Historical Society of Israel: P.O.B. 1062, Jerusalem; f. 1925 to promote the study of Jewish history and general history; 850 mems.; Pres. Prof. B. DINUR; publ. *Zion* (quarterly).

Institute of Asian and African Studies: Hebrew University of Jerusalem, Jerusalem; f. 1926; studies of medieval and modern languages, culture and history of Middle East, Asia and Africa; Dir. Prof. GABRIEL BAER; irregular publications.

Israel Exploration Society: 3 Shemuel ha-Nagid St., P.O.B. 7041, Jerusalem; f. 1913; excavations and historical research, congresses and lectures; 2,500 mems.; Chair. Prof. Y. YADIN; Pres. Prof. B. MAZAR; Hon. Sec. J. AVIRAM; publ. *Eretz Yisrael* (Hebrew annual), *Qadmoniot* (Hebrew quarterly), *Israel Exploration Journal* (English quarterly).

Israel Oriental Society: The Hebrew University, Jerusalem; f. 1949; lectures and symposia to study all aspects of contemporary Middle Eastern, Asian and African affairs; Pres. E. ELATH; publ. *Hamizrah Hehadash* (Hebrew quarterly), *Oriental Notes and Studies* (irregular), *Asian and African Studies* (annual).

Near East School of Archaeology: Jerusalem; Dir. J. P. FREE.

Orientalisches Institut der Görres-Gesellschaft: Jerusalem; historical and archaeological studies.

Pontifical Biblical Institute: King David and Botta Streets, P.O.B. 497, Jerusalem; f. 1927; study of Biblical geography and archaeology, student tours, excavations; Dir. Rev. SAMUEL PITTS, S.J.; publ. *Biblica, Orientalia*.

Wilfred Israel House for Oriental Art and Studies: Kibbutz Hazorea, Post Hazorea, near Haifa; f. 1947; opened 1951 in memory of late Wilfred Israel; a cultural centre for reading, study and art exhbns.; houses Wilfred Israel collection of Near and Far Eastern art and cultural materials; local archaeological exhibits from neolithic to Byzantine times; science and art library; Dir. Dr. U. R. BAER; Curator E. MEIRHOF.

ITALY

Istituto Italiano per il Medio ed Estremo Oriente (ISMEO): Palazzo Brancaccio, via Merulana 248, Rome; f. 1933; Pres. Prof. GIUSEPPE TUCCI; Gen. Sec. Rear-Admiral I. N. R. MARIANO IMPERIALI; Cultural Dir. Prof. ANTONIO GARGANO; publs. *East and West* (quarterly), *Rome Oriental Series, Nuovo Ramusio*, Archaeological Reports and Memoirs.

Istituto Italo-Africano: via Ulisse Aldrovandi 16, Rome; Govt. Commissary Prof. R. RUSSO.

Istituto per l'Oriente: via Alberto Caroncini 19, Rome; f. 1921; Pres. Prof. F. GABRIELI; publ. *Oriente Moderno* (monthly).

Istituto Universitario Orientale: Piazza San Giovanni Maggiore 30, Naples; f. 1888; library of 63,646 vols.; Dir. Prof. A. BOMBACI.

Istituto di Studi del Vicino Oriente: Universita degli Studi, Città Universitarià, Rome; Dir. Prof. P. MATTHIAE.

JAPAN

Ajia Keizai Kenkyusho (*Institute of Developing Economies*, formerly *Institute of Asian Economic Affairs*): 42 Ichigaya-Hommura-cho, Shinjuku-ku, Tokyo 162; f. 1958; 260 mems.; Chair. TAKEKAZU OGURA; Pres. NOBORU KANOKOGI; library of 104,000 vols.; publs. *Ajia Keizai* (Japanese, monthly), *The Developing Economies* (English, quarterly), occasional papers in English.

Ajia Seikai Gakkai (*Society for Asian Political and Economic Studies*): Hitotsubashi University, Kunitachi, Tokyo; f. 1953; 353 mems.; Pres. T. ITAGAKI; publ. *Asiatic Studies* (quarterly).

Nippon Orient Gakkai (*Society for Near Eastern Studies in Japan*): Tokyo Tenrikyokan, 9, 1-chome, Kanda Nishiki-cho, Chiyoda-ku, Tokyo; f. 1954; 438 mems.; Pres. H.I.H. Prince TAKAHITO MIKASA; publs. *Orient* (Japanese, twice-yearly), *Orient* (European languages annual).

LEBANON

Centre for Economic, Financial and Social Research and Documentation S.A.L.: Gefinor Centre, Bloc B, 500-502 Clemenceau St., P.O.B. 6068, Beirut; f. 1958; Chair. Dr. CHAFIC AKHRAS.

Institut de Géographie du Proche et Moyen Orient: ave. de Damas, B.P. 2691, Beirut; f. 1946; Dir. M. LE LANNOU.

THE MIDDLE EAST AND NORTH AFRICA—(RESEARCH INSTITUTES)

Institut de Recherches d'Economie Appliquée: Faculté de Droit et des Sciences Economiques, Université Saint Joseph, B.P. 293, Beirut; f. 1963; economic studies of the Lebanon and other countries of the Middle East; Dir. Prof. ELIAS GANNAGE; publ. *Proche-Orient, études économiques* (quarterly).

Institut Français d'Archéologie: rue Georges Picot, B.P. 1424, Beirut; f. 1946; library of 24,000 vols.; Dir. DANIEL SCHLUMBERGER; publ. *Syria, Revue d'Art et d'Archéologie* (annual), *Bibliothèque Archéologique et Historique*.

MOROCCO

Faculté des Lettres et des Sciences Humaines: Université Mohammed V, Rabat; f. 1959; publs. *Hespéris-Tamucla La Revue de Géographie du Maroc, La Revue des Etudes Littéraires et Philosophiques*.

THE NETHERLANDS

Assyriologisch Instituut der Rijksuniversiteit: Rijksuniversiteit te Leiden, Noordeindsplein 4A, Leiden; Dir. F. R. KRAUS.

Netherlands Institute for the Middle East (*Midden Oosten Instituut*): 7 Prinses Beatrixlaan, P.O.B. 2085, The Hague; f. 1949; Dir. C. HILLEN, PH.D.; publ. *Barid Hollanda*.

Netherlands Institute for the Near East (*Nederlands Instituut voor het Nabije Oosten*): Noordeindsplein 4-6, Leiden; Dir. Prof. Dr. A. A. KAMPMAN.

NORWAY

Indo-Iransk Institutt: Nils Treschows Hus, Blindern, Oslo; f. 1920; studies Indian and Iranian languages, culture and history; library of 20,000 vols.; Pres. Prof. NILS SIMONSSON.

PAKISTAN

Institute of Islamic Culture: Club Rd., Lahore; f. 1950; Dir. Prof. M. SAEED SHEIKH; Admin. Officer and Sec. M. ASHRAF DARR; publs. *al-Maarif* (monthly), and about 135 publications on Islamic subjects in English and Urdu.

Institute of Islamic Research: P.O.B. 1035, Islamabad; f. 1960; Dir. Dr. M. S. H. MASUMI.

POLAND

Polskie Towarzystwo Orientalistyczne (*Polish Oriental Society*): ul. Grojecka 17, Warsaw; f. 1922; mems. 260; Pres. TADEUSZ LEWICKI, EDWARD SZYMANSKI, TADEUSZ POBOŻNIAK; Sec. LESZEK CYRZYK; publ. *Przeglad Orientalistyczny* (quarterly).

Research Centre for Mediterranean Archaeology: Palac Kultury i Nauki, Room 1909, Warsaw; f. 1956; documentation and publication of Polish excavations in the Middle East; Dir. Prof. Dr. KAZIMIERZ MICHAŁOWSKI; publs. *Travaux du Centre d'Archéologie Méditerranéenne, Palmyre-Fouilles Polonaises* 1959–, *Faras-Fouilles Polonaises* 1961–, *Etudes et Travaux I-VI, Deir el Bahari, Corpus Vasorum Antiquorum, Corpus Signorum Imperii Romani*.

Zaklad Orientalistyki P.A.N. (*Research Centre for Oriental Studies*): Freta 16, Warsaw; f. 1953; Dir. Prof. Dr. ANANIASZ ZAJĄCZKOWSKI.

PORTUGAL

Instituto de Linguas Africanas e Orientais: Rua da Junqueira 86, Lisbon 3; f. 1946; library; 10 teachers; specializes in African and Oriental studies.

SENEGAL

Institut d'Etudes Islamiques: Université de Dakar, Fann Parc, Dakar; Dir. Prof. V. MONTEIL.

SPAIN

Asociacion Española de Orientalistas: Límite 5, Madrid 3; publ. *Boletin* (annual).

Instituto "Benito Arias Montano" de Estudios Hebraicos Sefardies y Oriente Próximo (*Institute of Hebrew and Near East Studies*): Duque de Medinaceli 4, Madrid 14; f. 1940; branch in Barcelona; 18 mems.; Dir. FEDERICO PEREZ CASTRO; Sec. JOSÉ LUIS LACAVE RIAÑO; publ. *Sefarad* (quarterly).

Instituto de Estudios Islamicos: Francisco de Asis Mendez Casariego 10, Madrid 2; affiliated to Ministry of Higher Education, Cairo; f. 1950; Dir. Dr. AHMED MUKHTAR EL ABBADY; publ. *Revista del Instituto de Estudios Islámicos*.

SWEDEN

Scandinavian Institute of African Studies: P.O.B. 2126, S-75002, Uppsala; information and documentation centre, organizes seminars and publishes wide range of books and pamphlets, also newsletters in Swedish, English and French; library of 16,000 vols.

Swedish Oriental Society: Stockholm; publ. *Acta Orientalia* (bi-annual), *Orientalia Suecana*.

SWITZERLAND

Centre d'Etudes Orientales: Université de Genève, rue de Candolle 3, Geneva; Dir. Prof. C. MAYSTRE.

Schweizerische Gesellschaft für Asienkunde: Zurich; publ. *Asiatische Studien* (bi-annual).

SYRIA

Institut Français d'Etudes Arabes: B.P. 344, Damascus, f. 1922; library of 30,000 vols.; Dir. ANDRÉ RAYMOND; publs. *Bulletin d'Etudes Orientales* (annually, 25 vols. published), monographs, translations and Arabic texts (90 vols. published), Islamic archaeology.

Near East Foundation: B.P. 427, Damascus.

TUNISIA

Institut des Belles Lettres Arabes: 12 rue Jamâa el Haoua, Tunis; f. 1930; cultural centre; Dir. A. DEMEERSEMAN; publ. *IBLA* (twice yearly) and special studies.

Mission Archéologique Française en Tunisie: 8 rue M'hamed Ali, Tunis; Dir. PIERRE CINTAS; Publications Dir. CL. POINSSOT; publ. *Karthago* (quarterly).

TURKEY

British Institute of Archaeology at Ankara: Tahran Caddesi 21, Kavaklıdere, Ankara; f. 1948; archaeological research and excavation; Pres. Sir STEVEN RUNCIMAN; Dir. D. H. FRENCH; publs. *Anatolian Studies* (annual), *Occasional Publications*.

Centri di Studi Italiani in Turchia: Menekse Sokak 8, Yenişehir, Ankara; Dir. Prof. GIUSEPPE GARINO; Mesrutiyet Caddesi 161, Istanbul; Dir. Prof. LUCIANO PERSELLI.

Deutsches Archäologisches Institut: Siraselvi 123, Taksim, Istanbul; Dir. Prof. Dr.-Ing. R. NAUMANN; publ. *Istanbuler Mitteilungen* (annual), *Istanbuler Forschungen, Beihefte zu Istanbuler Mitteilungen*.

Institut Français d'Archéologie: Istanbul; f. 1930; Dir. EMMANUEL LAROCHE.

THE MIDDLE EAST AND NORTH AFRICA—(RESEARCH INSTITUTES)

Netherlands Historical and Archaeological Institute: Istiklâl Caddesi 393, Beyoğlu, Istanbul; f. 1958; library of 12,000 vols.; Dir. Prof. Dr. A. A. KAMPMAN; publs. *Publications de l'Institut Historique et Archeologique Néerlandais de Stamboul, Revue Anatolica.*

Österreichisches Generalkonsulat Kulturinstitut Istanbul: Belvedere Apt. 101/2, Tesvikiye, Istanbul; Dir. Prof. Dr. J. E. KASPER.

Türk Dil Kurumu (*Turkish Linguistic Society*): Ankara; f. 1932; 542 mems.; library of 17,300 vols.; Pres. Prof. MACIT GÖKBERK; Sec.-Gen. OMER ASIM AKSOY; publs. *Türk Dili* (monthly), *Türk Dili Arastırmaları-Belleten* (annual).

Türk Kültürünü Araştırma Enstitüsü (*Institute for the Study of Turkish Culture*): P.K. 14, Çankaya, Ankara; f. 1961; scholarly research into all aspects of Turkish culture; Dir. Prof. Dr. AHMET TEMIR; publs. *Türk Kültürü* (monthly), *Cultura Turcica* (semi-annual), *Türk Kültürü Araştırmaları* (semi-annual).

Türk Tarih Kurumu (*Turkish Historical Society*): Ankara; f. 1931; 41 mems.; library of 100,000 vols.; Pres. Ord. Prof. Dr. ŞEVKET AZIZ KANSU; Gen. Dir. ULUĞ İĞDEMİR; publs. *T.T.K. Belleten* (quarterly), *Belgeler* (twice a year).

Türkiyat Enstitüsü (*Institute of Turcology*): University of Istanbul, Bayezit, Istanbul; f. 1924; research into Turkish language, literature, history and culture; library of 20,000 vols.; Dir. Dr. M. CAVID BAYSUN.

U.S.S.R.

Commission on Oriental Literature of the Department of Literature and Language, U.S.S.R. Academy of Sciences: Volkhonka 18/2, Moscow; Chair. Acad. N. I. KONRAD.

Institute of Asian Peoples of the Department of History, U.S.S.R. Academy of Sciences: Armyansky per. 2, Moscow, Dir. Acad. B. GAFUROV.

Institute of Oriental Studies of the Academy of Sciences of the Georgian S.S.R.: Tbilisi, Georgian S.S.R.

Institute of Oriental Studies, U.S.S.R. Academy of Sciences: Armyansky per. 2, Moscow; Chair. B. G. GAFUROV.

Research Institute of Oriental Studies of the Academy of Sciences of the Azerbaijanian S.S.R.: Baku, Azerbaijanian S.S.R.

Section of Oriental Studies of the Academy of Sciences of the Armenian S.S.R.: Erevan, Armenian S.S.R.

Section of Orientology and Calligraphy of the Academy of Sciences of the Tajik S.S.R.: Dushanbe, Tajik S.S.R.

UNITED KINGDOM

Anglo-Arab Association, The: West End House, 11 Hills Place, London, W1R 1AG.

Council for the Advancement of Arab-British Understanding (CAABU): Room 106, Grand Buildings, Trafalgar Square, London, WC2N 5EP; f. 1967; 911 mems.

Egypt Exploration Society: 3 Doughty Mews, London, WC1 2PG; f. 1882; library of 4,000 vols.; Sec. MARY D. ST. B. CRAWFORD; publs. *Excavation Memoirs, Archaeological Survey, Graeco-Roman Memoirs, Journal of Egyptian Archaeology*, etc.

Islamic Cultural Centre (and London Central Mosque): Regent's Lodge, 146 Park Rd., London, N.W.8; f. 1944 to spread Islamic culture in Great Britain; library of 3,000 vols., mostly Arabic; Dir. H.E. RAJA OF MAHMUDABAD; publ. *Islamic Quarterly.*

Middle East Association: Bury House, 33 Bury St., London, SW1; trade asscn. for Middle East and North Africa; Dir.-Gen. Sir RICHARD BEAUMONT, K.C.M.G., O.B.E.; Dep. Dir.-Gen. and Sec. R. GODDARD-WILSON.

Middle East Centre: Faculty of Oriental Studies, Sidgwick Ave., Cambridge CB3 9DA; Dir. Prof. R. B. SERJEANT, PH.D.; Sec. R. L. BIDWELL, PH.D.

Middle East Centre: St. Antony's College, Oxford OX2 6JF; Dir. Dr. E. R. J. OWEN; library of 20,000 vols.

Palestine Exploration Fund: 2 Hinde Mews, London, W.1; f. 1865; 900 subscribers; Pres. The Archbishop of Canterbury; Hon. Sec. M. A. KNIBB, B.D., S.T.M.; publ. *Palestine Exploration Quarterly.*

Royal Asiatic Society of Great Britain and Ireland: 56 Queen Anne St., London, W.1; f. 1823 for the study of the history, sociology, institutions, customs, languages and art of Asia; approx. 800 mems.; library of 100,000 vols. and 1,500 MSS.; branches in various Asian cities; Pres. B. W. ROBINSON, M.A., B.LIT.; Sec. Miss D. CRAWFORD; publs. *Journal* and monographs.

Royal Central Asian Society: 42 Devonshire St., London, W.1; f. 1901; 2,000 mems. with past or present knowledge of the Middle East, Central Asia or the Far East; library of about 5,000 vols.; Pres. Lord SELKIRK; Chair. Sir NORMAN BRAIN, K.B.E., C.M.G.; Sec. Miss M. FITZSIMONS; publ. *Journal* (three times a year).

School of African and Asian Studies: University of Sussex, Falmer, Brighton, Sussex BN1 9QN; Dean DAVID F. POCOCK, M.A., B.LITT., D.PHIL.

School of Oriental and African Studies, University of London: Malet St., London, WC1E 7HP; f. 1916; library of over 350,000 vols. and 2,000 MSS.; Dir. Prof. C. H. PHILIPS.

UNITED STATES OF AMERICA

Academy of Asian Studies: 431 Duboce Ave., San Francisco, Calif., 94117; Pres. Dr. EDSZEN N. LANDRUM.

American Friends of the Middle East, Inc.: 1717 Massachusetts Ave., N.W., Washington, D.C. 20036; f. 1951; a private, non-profit organization for furthering communication and understanding between the peoples of the Middle East and N. Africa and the people of the U.S.A. through educational and international programmes; offices in Washington D.C. and Egypt, Iran, Jordan, Lebanon, Tunisia.

American Oriental Society: 329 Sterling Memorial Library, Yale Station, New Haven, Conn. 06520; f. 1842; 1,850 mems.; Sec. HUGH M. STIMSON; publ. *Journal.*

American Schools of Oriental Research: 126 Inman Street, Cambridge, Mass. 02138; f. 1900; approx. 1,200 mems.; Pres. G. ERNEST WRIGHT; Sec. JAMES B. PRITCHARD, Univ. of Pennsylvania; Schools in Jerusalem and Baghdad; publs. *Biblical Archaeologist* (quarterly), *Bulletin* (quarterly), *Journal of Cuneiform Studies* (quarterly), *Annual.*

Center for Middle Eastern Studies: University of Chicago, 1130 E. 59th St., Chicago, Ill. 60637; f. 1966; research into medieval and modern cultures of the Middle East from Morocco to Pakistan; Dir. MARVIN ZONIS.

Center for Middle Eastern Studies: Harvard University, 1737 Cambridge St., Cambridge, Mass. 02138; research in social sciences and humanities.

Center for Middle Eastern Studies: The University of Texas at Austin, Social Work Bldg., 2609 University Ave., Austin, Tex. 78712; f. 1960; linguistic and social studies of Middle East languages and cultures; Dir. Dr. PAUL W. ENGLISH.

THE MIDDLE EAST AND NORTH AFRICA—(RESEARCH INSTITUTES)

Center for Near East and North African Studies: University of Michigan, 144 Lane Hall, Ann Arbor, Mich. 48104; f. 1961; research into the ancient, medieval and modern cultures of the Near East and North Africa, Near Eastern languages and literature; Dir. Dr. KENNETH A. LUTHER.

The Dropsie University: Broad and York Streets, Philadelphia, Pa. 19132; f. 1907; Pres. A. I. KATSH.

Hairenik Association, Inc.: 212 Stuart St., Boston, Mass. 02216; publ. *Armenian Review*.

Hoover Institution on War, Revolution and Peace: Stanford University, Stanford, Calif. 94305; f. 1919; contains important collection of documents on Middle East and North Africa; Dir. W. G. CAMPBELL; publs. about twenty books published each year, plus six-volume survey of the holdings of the Institute library.

The Iran Foundation, Inc.: Empire State Bldg., New York, N.Y. 10001; intermediary for U.S. welfare assistance to Iran.

Institute for Mediterranean Affairs: 1078 Madison Ave., New York, N.Y. 10018; established under charter of the University of the State of New York to evolve a better understanding of the historical background and contemporary political and socio-economic problems of the nations and regions that border on the Mediterranean Sea, with special reference to the Middle East and North Africa; 350 mems.; Pres. Ambassador SEYMOUR M. FINGER; Chair. Prof. N. S. FATEMI; Vice-Chair. Prof. A. P. LERNER; Dir. SAMUEL MERLIN.

Israel Institute: Yeshiva University, Amsterdam Ave. and 185th St., New York, N.Y. 10033; f. 1954; research into modern Israel and her cultural and political problems, Jewish history and culture; Dir. Dr. SAMUEL K. MIRSKY; publ. *Sura, Talpioth*.

Joint Committee on the Near and Middle East: c/o Social Science Research Council, 230 Park Ave., New York, N.Y. 10017; the Committee is co-sponsored by the American Council of Learned Societies and administers a programme of grants for research by individual scholars in the social sciences and humanities, and a programme of joint research grants for scholars in the area who wish to collaborate with scholars in the United States or Canada.

Middle East Center: University of Utah, Salt Lake City, Utah 84112; f. 1960; graduate courses in Middle Eastern studies (Arabic, Hebrew, Persian or Turkish); library of over 80,000 vols.; Dir. Dr. KHOSROW MOSTOFI.

Middle East Institute: 1761 N. St., N.W., Washington, D.C. 20036; f. 1946; exists to develop and maintain facilities for research, publication and dissemination of information, with a view to developing in the United States a more thorough understanding of the countries of the Middle East; the Institute holds an annual conference on Middle East affairs; 1,275 mems.; National Chair. Hon. RAYMOND A. HARE; Pres. Hon. LUCIUS D. BATTLE; Sec. MALCOLM C. PECK; Dir. of Publs. WILLIAM SANDS; publs. *Middle East Journal* (quarterly), *Middle East Monitor* (two per month), and occasional books.

Middle East Institute: Columbia University, 113 International Affairs Bldg, New York, N.Y. 10027; f. 1954; research into current problems of economics, government and international relations of the Middle East countries, and their languages and history; library of 100,000 vols.; Dir. Prof. J. C. HUREWITZ; publs. *Publications in Near and Middle East Studies* (irregular), *Modern Middle East Series* (irregular).

Middle East Studies Association: New York University, Washington Square, New York, N.Y. 10003; f. 1967 to promote high standards of scholarship and instruction and to facilitate communication on the area; membership open to all persons of scholarly attainment in the field of Middle Eastern studies; 1,500 mems.; Pres. (1973) Prof. CHARLES ISSAWI; Vice-Pres. Prof. ROGER SAVORY; Sec. Prof. I. W. ZARTMAN; publs. *Bulletin* (quarterly), *International Journal of Middle East Studies* (quarterly).

Middle East Studies Centre: Portland State Univ., Portland, Ore. 97207; language and area studies in Arabic, Persian, Turkish and Hebrew; Dir. Prof. FREDERICK J. COX.

Near East College Association, Inc.: 40 Worth St., New York, N.Y. 10013; and 548 Fifth Ave., New York, N.Y. 10036.

Near East Foundation: 54 East 64th St., New York, N.Y. 10021, U.S.A.; f. 1930. Aims: to conduct educational programmes and agricultural projects in order to improve standards of living in underdeveloped areas of the world, primarily the Near East; Hon. Chair. CLEVELAND E. DODGE; Vice-Chair. J. B. SUNDERLAND; Pres. HERRICK B. YOUNG; Exec. Dir. DELMER J. DOOLEY.

Near Eastern Center: University of California, Los Angeles, 405 Hilgard Ave., Los Angeles, Calif. 90024; f. 1957; social sciences and language studies of the Near East since the rise of Islam; library of over 100,000 vols. and outstanding MSS. collection in Arabic, Armenian, Persian and Turkish; Dir. G. E. VON GRUNEBAUM.

Near Eastern Studies: Indiana University, Bloomington, Indiana 47401; courses in Arabic, Hebrew and Turkish languages and literature both modern and classical, and political science and religions of the area; Chair. WADIE JWAIDEH.

Oriental Institute: 1155 E. 58th St., Chicago, Ill. 60637; f. 1919; principally concerned with cultures and languages of the ancient Near East; extensive museum; affiliated to the University of Chicago; Dir. JOHN A. BRINKMAN.

Program in Near Eastern Studies: Princeton University, Jones Hall, Princeton, N.J. 08540; f. 1947; research in all aspects of the modern Near East; library of 100.000 vols.; Dir. MORROE BERGER; publs. *Proceedings of Annual Near East Conference* (annual), *Princeton Studies in the Modern Near East* (irregular), *Princeton Near East Papers* (irregular).

Semitic Museum: Harvard University, 6 Divinity Ave., Cambridge, Mass. 02138; f. 1889; sponsors exploration and research in Western Asia; contains collection of exhibits from ancient Near East; Curator Dr. G. ERNEST WRIGHT.

Society of Oriental Studies: Claremont University College, Harper Hall, Claremont, Calif.; f. 1936; literary, social and economic studies in Asian areas; library of 50,000 vols.; Head Dr. MERRILL R. GOODALL; publ. *Claremont Asian Studies*.

VATICAN

Pontificium Institutum Orientalium Studiorum (*Pontifical Institute of Oriental Studies*): 7 Piazza Santa Maria Maggiore, 00185-Rome; f. 1917; library of 100,000 vols.; Rector Rev. IVAN ŽUŽEK, S.J.; Sec. Rev. J. ŘEZÁČ, S.J.; publs. *Orientalia Christiana Periodica*, *Orientalia Christiana Analecta, Concilium Florentinum* (*Documenta et Scriptores*), *Anaphorae Syriacae*.

Middle East & North Africa